Holy Bible

Easy-to-Read Version™

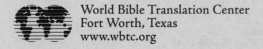

World Bible Translation Center
Fort Worth, Texas
www.wbtc.org

Holy Bible: Easy-to-Read Version™

Permissions
This copyrighted material may be quoted up to 1000 verses without written permission. However, the extent of quotation must not comprise a complete book nor should it amount to more than 50% of the work in which it is quoted. This copyright notice must appear on the title or copyright page:

> Holy Bible: Easy-to-Read Version™
> Taken from the HOLY BIBLE: EASY-TO-READ VERSION™
> © 2006 by World Bible Translation Center, Inc. and used by permission.

When quotations from the ERV are used in non-saleable media, such as church bulletins, orders of service, posters, transparencies or similar media, a complete copyright notice is not required, but the initials (ERV) must appear at the end of each quotation.

Requests for permission to use quotations or reprints in excess of 1000 verses or more than 50% of the work in which they are quoted, or other permission requests, must be directed to and approved in writing by World Bible Translation Center, Inc.

Address
World Bible Translation Center, Inc.
P.O. Box 820648
Fort Worth, Texas 76182-0648

Email: bibles@wbtc.org
Web: www.wbtc.org

Free Downloads
Download free electronic copies of
World Bible Translation Center's Bibles and New Testaments at:
www.wbtc.org

ISBN Number
ISBN-13: 978-1-932438-15-4
ISBN-10: 1-932438-15-7

Contents

Contents
In alphabetical order with abbreviations

New Testament book names are *in italics*.

Preface

This version of the Bible has been prepared especially for people who want an English translation that accurately expresses the full meaning of the original text in a style that is clear and easy to understand. It is especially helpful for those who have limited experience with English, including children and people who are just learning English. It is designed to help such people overcome or avoid the most common difficulties to reading with understanding.

The writers of Scripture, especially those who produced the New Testament writings, showed by the language style they used that they were interested in good communication. The translators of this English version considered this an important example to follow. So they worked to express the meaning of the Biblical text in a form that would be simple and natural. They used language that, instead of working as a barrier to understanding, would provide a key to unlock the truths of the Scriptures for a large segment of the English-speaking world.

The translation is based directly on the original languages of Scripture. In the case of the Old Testament, the translators followed the Hebrew Masoretic Text as it is found in the latest printed edition of *Biblia Hebraica Stuttgartensia* (1984), while referring occasionally to some earlier readings in the Dead Sea Scrolls. In some cases, they also followed the *Septuagint* (LXX), the Greek translation of the Old Testament, where it has readings that are actually earlier than any known Hebrew manuscript. For the New Testament, the source text was that which is found in both the United Bible Societies' *Greek New Testament* (fourth revised edition, 1993) and the Nestle-Aland *Novum Testamentum Graece* (twenty-seventh edition, 1993). The occasional variation from these printed editions was guided by reference to the findings of more recent scholarship.

Several special features are used to aid understanding. Brief explanations or synonyms (italicized within parentheses) sometimes follow difficult or unusual words in the text. If a word or phrase needs fuller explanation, it is specially marked in one of two ways: *(1)* If its usage is unique or unusual, it is marked by a letter of the alphabet (*a*) linking it to a footnote that provides an explanation or important information. Included in such footnotes are references to Scripture quotations and information about alternate readings when significant differences occur in the ancient manuscripts. *(2)* If it is a word that occurs frequently with the same meaning, its first occurrence in a section is marked with an asterisk (*) indicating that an explanation can be found in a Word List at the end of the Bible.

As in all translations, words that are implied by the context are often supplied in the text to make the meaning clear. For example, the phrase that in Greek is simply "David of Jesse" is always translated into English as "David the son of Jesse." If such explanatory words or phrases are extensive or unusual, they may be marked by half brackets. For example, in the translation, "The Lord gave this command to Moses ⌊for the people⌋," the phrase in half brackets is added to avoid any misunderstanding that the Lord's command was intended only for Moses and not for all the people.

In the Old Testament two different words are translated "Lord." When "Lord" is printed with small capital letters (Lord), it represents the Hebrew *YHWH*, which in some versions has been transliterated into English as "Jehovah" or "Yahweh." In a few cases, where *YHWH* is obviously used as the name of God or in place names, it is translated "Yahweh." When the word "Lord" contains lower case letters, it represents the Hebrew word *adonai* or a pronoun that refers to either *adonai* or *YHWH*. When *adonai* occurs together with *YHWH*, it is translated "Lord" and *YHWH* is translated God, as in "the Lord God." In cases where the speaker does not recognize that the one being addressed is God, *adonai* may be translated "Sir." The same is true in the New Testament for the Greek word *kurios*, which may be translated either "Lord" or "Sir," depending on the context.

Finally, in the Gospels, the first four books of the New Testament, the section headings are often followed by cross references. These identify where the same or similar material is found in one or more of the other Gospels.

Introduction

The word Bible comes from a Greek word meaning "books." The Bible is actually two collections of books, often referred to as the "Old Testament" and the "New Testament." The word translated "testament" was used to mean a covenant or agreement. It refers to God's promise to bless his people. The Old Testament is the collection of writings that relate to the agreement that God made with the descendants of Jacob (Israel) in the time of Moses. The New Testament is the collection of writings that relate to the agreement God made with all people who believe in Jesus Christ.

The Old Testament writings tell about the great things God did for the people of Israel and his plan for them as his chosen people to bring his blessings to the whole world. These writings look forward to the coming of a savior or "Messiah" (see "Christ" in the Word List). The New Testament writings continue the Old Testament story. They describe the coming of that savior (Jesus Christ) and the meaning of his coming for all people. The Old Testament is important for understanding the New Testament, because it provides the necessary background. And the New Testament completes the story of salvation that began in the Old Testament.

THE OLD TESTAMENT

The Old Testament writings are a collection of thirty-nine different books produced by many different authors. They were written mainly in Hebrew, the language of ancient Israel. There are a few sections in Aramaic, an international language in Bible times. Portions of the Old Testament were written over 3500 years ago, and more than 1000 years passed between the writing of the first book and the last. In this collection there are books of law, history, prose, songs, poetry, and wise sayings.

The Old Testament is often divided into three main sections: the Law, the Prophets, and the Holy Writings. The Law contains five books called "The Five Books of Moses." The first book is Genesis. It tells about the beginning of the world as we know it, the first man and woman, and their first sin against God. It tells about the Great Flood and the family God saved through that flood, and it tells about the beginnings of the nation of Israel, the people God chose to use for a special purpose.

THE STORY OF ABRAHAM

God made an agreement with Abraham, a great man of faith. In that agreement God promised to make Abraham the father of a great nation and to give him and his descendants the land of Canaan. Abraham was circumcised to show that he had accepted the agreement, and circumcision became the proof of the agreement between God and his people. Abraham did not know how God would do what he had promised but trusted him to make it happen. This pleased God very much.

God told Abraham to leave his home in Mesopotamia and led him to Canaan (later called the land of Israel, which was approximately the same geographical area known today as Palestine). In his old age Abraham had a son named Isaac, who had a son named Jacob. Jacob (also called Israel) had twelve sons and a daughter. This family became the nation of Israel, but it never forgot its tribal origin. It continued to refer to itself as the twelve tribes of Israel—descendants of the twelve sons of Jacob: Reuben, Simeon, Levi, Judah, Dan, Naphtali, Gad, Asher, Issachar, Zebulun, Joseph, and Benjamin. The three main ancestors—Abraham, Isaac, and Jacob (Israel)—are known as the "fathers" or "patriarchs" of Israel.

Abraham was also a "father" of another kind. Many times in ancient Israel, God called certain people to speak for him. These special people, or prophets, were God's representatives to the rest of his people. Through the prophets God gave the people of Israel promises, warnings, laws, teachings, lessons drawn from past experiences, and lessons based on future events. Abraham "the Hebrew" is the first prophet mentioned in the Scriptures.

ISRAEL SET FREE FROM SLAVERY

The family of Jacob (Israel) grew to include about 70 of his direct descendants. One of his sons, Joseph, became a high official in Egypt. Times were hard, so Jacob and his family moved to Egypt, where there was plenty of food and life was easier. This tribe of Hebrews grew to be a small nation, and the Pharaoh (the title or name of the king of Egypt) made them serve as slaves. The book of Exodus tells about how finally, after 400 years, God used the prophet Moses to free the people of Israel from slavery and lead them eventually to settle again in Palestine. The price for freedom was high, but the Egyptians were the ones who had to pay. God punished them with a series of ten plagues, demanding with each one that his chosen people be set free. But following each disaster, the king stubbornly refused to free them. The final plague, however, brought about the death of the firstborn sons of all the families of Egypt, including the Pharaoh's son. This caused the king finally to agree to let the Israelites go free.

The people of Israel had been given special preparations to make for their trip to freedom. Dressed and ready for the escape, each family killed and roasted a lamb. They put the blood from the lamb on their doorposts as a special sign to God. They hurriedly baked bread without yeast and ate their meal. That night the Lord went through the land. If the blood of the lamb was not on the doorposts, the firstborn of that family died. This is why the firstborn sons of the Egyptians were put to death, while the Lord "passed over" the homes of his people. This night and the events surrounding it were later remembered in many ways in the worship and sacrifices of the people of Israel.

After the Israelite slaves were set free and were leaving Egypt, the Pharaoh changed his mind again. He sent his army to catch them and bring them back, but God saved his people. He divided the Red Sea, making a path through it to lead them to freedom on the other side. Then he released the waters to destroy the army of Egyptians that was following them. After Moses led the people in a song of praise to God for his protection and kindness, he led them on a long and difficult journey. Finally, they came to a mountain in the desert of Sinai on the Arabian Peninsula, where God made a special agreement with his people.

THE LAW OF MOSES

God's rescue of the people of Israel and his agreement with them at Mount Sinai set this nation apart from all others. This agreement contained promises and laws for the people of Israel. A part of this agreement, known as the Ten Commandments, was written by God on two stone tablets and given to the people. These commands contain the basic principles for the kind of life God wanted the people of Israel to live, including their duty to God, family, and others.

The Ten Commandments and the rest of the rules and teachings given at Mount Sinai became known as "the Law of Moses" or simply "the law." Many times these terms are used to refer to the first five books of the Scriptures and often to the entire Old Testament.

Besides the Ten Commandments and other rules of conduct, the Law of Moses contains rules about priests, sacrifices, worship, and holy days. These rules are found in the book of Leviticus. According to the Law of Moses, all priests and their helpers came from the tribe of Levi. These helpers were called "Levites." The most important priest was called the high priest.

The Law of Moses included instructions for building the Holy Tent ("Tabernacle"), or Meeting Tent, the place where the people of Israel went to worship God. It also has instructions for making all the things to be used in their worship. This prepared the Israelites for the building of the Temple, the holy building in Jerusalem on Mount Zion, where the people would later go to worship God. The rules about sacrifices and worship forced the people to see that they sinned against each other and against God. But they also gave the people a way to be forgiven and to be reunited with one another and with God. These sacrifices prepared the way for a better understanding of the sacrifice God was preparing to give for all the people of the world.

The Law of Moses also contained instructions for celebrating a number of holy days or festivals. Each festival had its own special meaning. Some festivals were happy occasions to celebrate special times of the year, especially harvest times. These included the Festival of Weeks in the spring and the Festival of Shelters in the fall. (See these terms in the Word List.)

Other festivals were for remembering the wonderful things God had done for his people. Passover was this kind of holy day. Each family relived the escape from Egypt, gathering in their homes to remember this part of Israel's history and to sing songs of praise to God. A lamb was slaughtered and the meal prepared. Each cup of wine and piece of food reminded the people of the things God had done to save them from a life of pain and sadness.

One holy day, in particular, was very serious. Every year, on the Day of Atonement, the people had to remember the many wrong things they had done to others and to God. This was a day of sadness, and the people did not eat. But on that day the high priest offered special sacrifices to "cover over" or atone for their sins.

The agreement between God and Israel was very important to the writers of the Old Testament. Almost all the books of the Prophets and Holy Writings are based on the fact that the nation of Israel, and every citizen of Israel, had made a very special agreement with their God. They called it the "agreement of the LORD" or simply "the agreement." Their books of history interpret events in light of the agreement: If the individual or nation was faithful to God and the agreement, then God rewarded them. If the people abandoned the agreement, then God punished them. God sent his prophets to remind the people of their agreement with him. The poets of Israel sang of the wonderful things God did for his obedient people, and they mourned the pain and punishments that came to those who disobeyed. These writers based their concepts of right and wrong on the teaching of the agreement. And when innocent people suffered, the poets struggled to understand why.

THE KINGDOM OF ISRAEL

The story of ancient Israel is the story of people who were always leaving God, God rescuing the people, the people turning back to God and eventually leaving him again. This cycle began almost as soon as the people had accepted God's agreement, and it was repeated again and again. At Mount Sinai the people of Israel agreed to follow God, and then they rebelled and were forced to wander 40 years in the desert. Finally, Moses' helper, Joshua, led the people into the promised land. Then came the battles to gain control of the different areas and settle the first parts of what later came to be known as the land of Israel. For the first few centuries after this settlement, the people were governed by local leaders called judges.

Eventually, the people wanted a king. The first king God appointed for them was Saul. But Saul did not obey God, so God chose a shepherd boy named David to be the new king. The prophet Samuel came and poured oil on his head, anointing him king of Israel. God promised David that the future kings of Israel would be his descendants from the tribe of Judah. David conquered the city of Jerusalem and made it his capital and the future site of the Temple. He organized the priests, prophets, songwriters, musicians, and singers for the Temple worship. David even wrote many of the songs (or psalms) himself, but God did not let him build the Temple.

When David was old and about to die, with God's blessing he made his son Solomon king of Israel. David warned his son to always follow God and obey the agreement. As king, Solomon built the Temple in Jerusalem that David had planned, and he expanded Israel's borders. At this time Israel was at the high point of its power. Solomon became famous, and Israel became strong.

JUDAH AND ISRAEL—THE DIVIDED KINGDOM

At Solomon's death there was disagreement and a struggle among the people, and the nation was divided. The northern ten tribes called themselves Israel. The southern tribes called themselves Judah. (The modern term "Jew" comes from this name.) Judah remained loyal to the agreement, and David's dynasty (family of kings) continued ruling in Jerusalem for several hundred years.

In the northern kingdom (Israel) numerous kings and dynasties came and went, because the people did not follow the agreement. The kings of Israel had several capital cities at various times, the last of which was Samaria. In order to strengthen their hold on the people, the kings of Israel changed the way to worship God. They chose new priests and built two new temples—one at Dan (on the northern border of Israel) and the other at Bethel (along Israel's border with Judah). There were many wars between Israel and Judah.

During this time of civil war and troubles, God sent many prophets to Judah and Israel. Some of the prophets were priests; others were farmers. Some were advisors to kings; others lived a much simpler life. Some of the prophets wrote their teachings or prophecies; many others did not. But all the prophets spoke for justice, fairness, and the need to depend on God for help.

Many prophets warned that the people would be defeated and scattered if they did not turn back to God. Some prophets saw visions of future glories as well as future punishments. Many of them looked forward to the time when a new king would come to rule the kingdom. Some saw this king as a descendant of David who would lead the people of God into a new Golden Age. Some spoke of this king as ruling forever over an eternal kingdom. Others saw him as a servant who would suffer many things in order to bring his people back to God. But all of them saw him as the Messiah, the one anointed (chosen) by God to bring in a new age.

THE DESTRUCTION OF ISRAEL AND JUDAH

The people of Israel did not listen to God's warnings. So in 722/721 B.C. Samaria fell to the invading Assyrians. The people of Israel were taken from their homes and scattered throughout the Assyrian Empire, lost forever to their brothers and sisters in Judah. Then the Assyrians brought in foreigners to resettle the land of Israel. These people were taught about the religion of Judah and Israel, and many of them tried to follow the agreement. These people came to be known as the Samaritans. The Assyrians tried to invade Judah. Many cities fell to the invaders, but God saved Jerusalem. The defeated king of Assyria returned to his homeland, and there he was murdered by two of his sons. So Judah was saved.

For a while the people of Judah changed. They began to obey God, but only for a short time. They, too, were finally defeated and scattered. The nation of Babylon rose to power and invaded Judah. At first they took only a few important people away as captives. But a few years later, in 587/586 B.C., they returned to destroy Jerusalem and the Temple. Some of the people escaped to Egypt, but most of them were taken as slaves to Babylon. Again God sent prophets to the people, and they began to listen. It seems that the destruction of the Temple and Jerusalem and the exile in Babylon brought about a real change in the people. The prophets spoke more and more about the new king and his kingdom. One of the prophets, Jeremiah, even spoke of a new agreement—an agreement that would not be written on tablets of stone, but would be in the hearts of God's people.

THE RETURN TO PALESTINE

Meanwhile, Cyrus came to power over the Persian Empire and conquered Babylon. Cyrus allowed people to return to their homelands. So after 70 years of exile, many of the people of Judah went back home. The people tried to rebuild their nation, but Judah remained small and weak. The people rebuilt the Temple, although it was not as beautiful as the one Solomon had built. Many of the people truly turned to God and began studying the Law, the writings of the prophets, and the other holy writings. Many men became scribes (special scholars), who made copies of the Scriptures. Eventually, these men organized schools for studying the Scriptures. The people began meeting together on the Sabbath (Saturday) to study, pray, and worship God together. In their synagogues (meetings) they studied the Scriptures, and many people began looking for the Messiah to come.

In the West, Alexander the Great gained control of Greece and soon conquered the world. He spread the Greek language as well as the customs and culture of Greece to many parts of the world. When he died, his kingdom was divided. Soon another empire grew and gained control of a large part of the known world, including Palestine, where the people of Judah lived.

The new rulers, the Romans, were often cruel and harsh, and the Jewish people were proud and not willing to submit to Roman rule. In these troubled times there were many Jews who were looking for the Messiah to come in their own lifetime. They wanted to be ruled only by God and the Messiah who God had promised to send them. They did not understand that God planned to save the world through the Messiah. They thought that God's plan was to save the Jews from the world! Some were content to wait for God to send his Messiah. Others thought that they should "help" God establish his new kingdom by making sure that the Law of Moses was observed and that the Temple, the land, and the Jewish people were kept pure. In order to make this happen, they were willing to suffer, to die, or to kill anyone, foreigners or other Jews, who threatened these goals. Such Jews eventually came to be known as "Zealots."

THE JEWISH RELIGIOUS GROUPS

By the first century B.C., the Law of Moses had become extremely important to the Jews. They had studied and argued over it for centuries. The people understood the law in different ways, but many Jews were ready to die for that law. There were three major religious groups among the Jews, and there were scribes (scholars or experts in the law) in each group.

The Sadducees

One of the groups was called the Sadducees. This name probably comes from the name Zadok, the high priest in King David's time. Many of the priests and the people in authority were Sadducees. These men accepted only the law (the five books of Moses) as their authority in religious matters. The Law of Moses taught many things about the priests and sacrifices, but it did not teach about life after death. So the Sadducees did not believe that people would ever be raised from death.

The Pharisees

Another group was called the Pharisees. This name comes from a Hebrew word meaning "to interpret (explain)" or "to separate." These men tried to teach or interpret the Law of Moses to the common people. The Pharisees believed that there was an oral tradition going back to Moses' time. They believed that people of each generation could interpret the law in a way that would allow it to meet the needs of that generation. This meant that the Pharisees could accept not only the Law of Moses as their authority, but also the Prophets, the Holy Writings, and even their own traditions. These men tried very hard to follow the law and their traditions. So they were very careful about what they ate and what they touched. They were careful about washing their hands and bathing. They also believed that people would be raised from death, because they understood many of the prophets to say that would happen.

The Essenes

The third major group was the Essenes. Many of the priests in Jerusalem did not live the way God wanted them to. Also, the Romans had appointed many of the high priests, and some of these men were not qualified according to the Law of Moses. Because of this, the Essenes did not think that the worship and sacrifices in the Jerusalem Temple were being done properly. So they moved out into the Judean desert to live. They formed their own community, where only other Essenes could come and live. They fasted, prayed, and waited for God to send the Messiah to purify the temple and the priesthood. Many scholars believe that the Essenes were connected in some way with the Qumran Community and the many ancient writings (including the Dead Sea Scrolls) found at Qumran and other places in that area of the Judean desert.

THE NEW TESTAMENT

God had begun his plan. He had chosen a special nation. He had made an agreement with those people that would prepare them to understand his justice and his goodness. Through prophets and poets he had revealed his plan to bless the world by establishing a perfect spiritual "kingdom" based on a new and better agreement. This plan would begin with the coming of the promised Messiah. The prophets had spoken of his coming in great detail. They had told where the Messiah would be born, the kind of person he would be, and the work he would have to do. It was now time for the Messiah to come and begin the new agreement.

The part of the Bible that is now called the New Testament (which means "new agreement") describes how God's new agreement was revealed and put into effect by Jesus, who was the Christ (meaning "the Anointed One," the Messiah). This collection of writings teaches that this agreement was to be for all people. And it tells how people in the first century responded to God's kind offer of love and became a part of the new agreement. The New Testament writings explain how many things that were part of the first agreement are given new meaning under the new agreement, especially ideas related to Israelite worship, such as temple, priesthood, and sacrifice. These writings give instructions to God's people about how to live in this world. They also describe the blessings that God promises his people for a full and meaningful life here and for life with him after death.

The New Testament writings include twenty-seven different "books" by at least eight different writers. All of them wrote in Greek, which was widely spoken in the first-century world. More than half of the total writing was done by four "apostles," men chosen by Jesus to be his special representatives or helpers. Three of these, Matthew, John, and Peter, were among the twelve closest followers of Jesus during his life on earth. The fourth, Paul, was chosen as an apostle later by Jesus through a miraculous appearance.

The first four books, called "Gospels," are separate accounts of the life and death of Jesus Christ. Generally, these books emphasize Jesus' teaching, the purpose of his appearance on earth, and the special significance of his death, rather than just the historical facts of his life. This is especially true of the fourth book, the Gospel of John. The first three Gospels are very similar in content. In fact, much of the material in one is found in one or both of the others. There are differing points of emphasis in each one, however, and each writer seems to have been addressing a different audience, with perhaps a different goal or goals in view.

The four Gospels are followed by Acts, a history of the events following the death of Jesus. It describes how God's offer of love to all people was announced throughout the world by Jesus' followers. It tells how the proclaiming of this "gospel" or "Good News" resulted in the conversion of thousands of people throughout Palestine and the Roman world to faith in Jesus Christ. The book of Acts was written by a medical doctor named Luke, an eyewitness of much that he recorded. Luke was also the author of the third Gospel. His two books make a logical unit with Acts being the natural sequel to his account of the life of Jesus.

Following Acts, there is a collection of letters written to individuals or groups of believers in Christ. These letters were sent from leaders in the faith, such as Paul and Peter, two of Jesus' apostles. These letters were written to help the people of that time deal with problems they were facing. They serve to inform, correct, teach, and encourage not only those people but all who become followers of Jesus in regard to their faith, their life together, and their life in the world.

The final book of the New Testament, Revelation, is very different from all the others, although its purpose is similar to that of other letters to churches. It begins with words of criticism, encouragement, and instruction addressed to groups of believers in seven different cities of Asia Minor (modern Turkey). But it continues with a picture of spiritual warfare that is of interest to all followers of Christ. It uses highly figurative language and tells of visions seen by the author, the apostle John. Many of the figures and images are from the Old Testament and can best be understood by comparing them to the Old Testament writings. This last book of the New Testament is a message of hope given to God's people through the Holy Spirit. This message assures believers in Jesus Christ of ultimate victory over the forces of evil.

THE BIBLE AND TODAY'S READER

Today's reader of the Bible should keep in mind that these books were written thousands of years ago for people who lived in cultures very different from ours today. Many of the historical accounts, illustrations, and references they contain can only be understood with some knowledge of the time and culture in which the writers lived. Generally, however, the writings focus on principles that are universally true. For example, Jesus told a story about a man sowing grain in a field that had different types of soil conditions. Those exact conditions may be unfamiliar to a person today, but the lesson Jesus draws from the example is appropriate for people in any time or place.

The modern reader may find the world of the Bible somewhat strange. The customs, the attitudes, and the way people talk may be quite unfamiliar. It is only reasonable to judge these things by their experience and ideals, not by today's standards. It is also important to note that the Bible was not written as a book of science. It was written mainly to describe historical events and present the significance of those events in ways that relate to all people. Its teachings present universal truths that are beyond the realm of science. It remains relevant even in our own time, because it deals with people's basic spiritual needs, which never change.

If you read the Bible with an open mind, you can expect to receive many benefits. You will gain knowledge about the history and culture of the ancient world. You will learn about the life and teachings of Jesus Christ and what it means to be his follower. You will gain basic spiritual insights and learn practical lessons for living a dynamic and joy-filled life. You will find answers to life's most difficult questions. There are, therefore, many good reasons for reading this book, and if you read it with a sincere and receptive spirit, you may well discover God's purpose for your life.

The
Old
Testament

Genesis

THE BEGINNING OF THE WORLD

The First Day—Light

1 ¹God created the sky and the earth. At first, ²the earth was completely empty. There was nothing on the earth. Darkness covered the ocean, and God's Spirit moved over*ᵃ* the water. ³Then God said, "Let there be light!" And light began to shine.*ᵇ* ⁴He saw the light, and he knew that it was good. Then he separated the light from the darkness. ⁵God named the light "day," and he named the darkness "night."

There was evening, and then there was morning. This was the first day.

The Second Day—Sky

⁶Then God said, "Let there be a space*ᶜ* to separate the water into two parts!" ⁷So God made the space and separated the water. Some of the water was above it, and some of the water was below it. ⁸God named that space "sky." There was evening, and then there was morning. This was the second day.

The Third Day—Dry Land and Plants

⁹Then God said, "Let the water under the sky be gathered together so that the dry land will appear." And it happened. ¹⁰God named the dry land "earth," and he named the water that was gathered together "seas." And God saw that this was good.

¹¹Then God said, "Let the earth grow grass, plants that make grain, and fruit trees. The fruit trees will make fruit with seeds in it. And each plant will make its own kind of seed. Let these plants grow on the earth." And it happened. ¹²The earth grew grass and plants that made grain. And it grew trees that made fruit with seeds in it. Every plant made its own kind of seeds. And God saw that this was good.

¹³There was evening, and then there was morning. This was the third day.

The Fourth Day—Sun, Moon, and Stars

¹⁴Then God said, "Let there be lights in the sky. These lights will separate the days from the nights. They will be used for signs to show when special meetings*ᵈ* begin and to show the days and years. ¹⁵They will be in the sky to shine light on the earth." And it happened.

¹⁶So God made the two large lights. He made the larger light to rule during the day and the smaller light to rule during the night. He also made the stars. ¹⁷God put these lights in the sky to shine on the earth. ¹⁸He put them in the sky to rule over the day and over the night. They separated the light from the darkness. And God saw that this was good.

¹⁹There was evening, and then there was morning. This was the fourth day.

The Fifth Day—Fish and Birds

²⁰Then God said, "Let the water be filled with many living things, and let there be birds to fly in the air over the earth." ²¹So God created the large sea animals.*ᵉ* He created all the many living things in the sea and every kind of bird that flies in the air. And God saw that this was good.

²²God blessed all the living things in the sea and told them to have many babies and fill the seas. And he blessed the birds on land and told them to have many more babies.

²³There was evening, and then there was morning. This was the fifth day.

The Sixth Day—Land Animals and People

²⁴Then God said, "Let the earth produce many kinds of living things. Let there be many different kinds of animals. Let there be large animals and small crawling animals of every kind. And let all these animals produce more animals." And all these things happened.

²⁵So God made every kind of animal. He made the wild animals, the tame animals, and all the small crawling things. And God saw

---

*ᵃ***1:2** *moved over* The Hebrew word means "to fly over" or "to swoop down," like a bird flying over its nest to protect its babies.

*ᵇ***1:1–3** Or "In the beginning, God created the heavens and the earth. While ²the earth had no special shape, and darkness covered the ocean, and God's Spirit hovered over the water, ³God said, 'Let there be light,' and there was light." Or "When God began to create the sky and the earth, ²while the earth was completely empty, and darkness covered the ocean, and a powerful wind blew over the water, ³God said, 'Let there be light,' and there was light."

*ᶜ***1:6** *space* Or "firmament." The Hebrew word can refer to a piece of metal that has been hammered into the shape of a bowl.

*ᵈ***1:14** *special meetings* The Israelites used the sun and moon to decide when the months and years began. Many Israelite festivals and special meetings began at the time of the new moon or full moon.

*ᵉ***1:21** *large sea animals* Or "sea monsters."

that this was good.

26Then God said, "Now let's make humans*a* who will be like us.*b* They will rule over all the fish in the sea and the birds in the air. They will rule over all the large animals and all the little things that crawl on the earth."

27So God created humans in his own image. He created them to be like himself.*c* He created them male and female. 28God blessed them and said to them, "Have many children. Fill the earth and take control of it. Rule over the fish in the sea and the birds in the air. Rule over every living thing that moves on the earth."

29God said, "I am giving you all the grain bearing plants and all the fruit trees. These trees make fruit with seeds in it. This grain and fruit will be your food. 30And I am giving all the green plants to the animals. These green plants will be their food. Every animal on earth, every bird in the air, and all the little things that crawl on the earth will eat that food." And all these things happened.

31God looked at everything he had made. And he saw that everything was very good.

There was evening, and then there was morning. This was the sixth day.

The Seventh Day—Rest

2 1So the earth, the sky, and everything in them were finished. 2God finished the work he was doing, so on the seventh day he rested from his work. 3God blessed the seventh day and made it a holy* day. He made it special because on that day he rested from all the work he did while creating the world.

THE BEGINNING OF HUMANITY

4This is the story about the creation of the sky and the earth. This is what happened when the LORD God made the earth and the sky. 5This was before there were plants on the earth. Nothing was growing in the fields because the LORD God had not yet made it rain on the earth, and there was no one to care for the plants.

6So water*d* came up from the earth and spread over the ground. 7Then the LORD God took dust from the ground and made a man.*e* He breathed the breath of life into the man's nose, and the man became a living thing. 8Then the LORD God planted a garden in the East,*f* in a place named Eden. He put

the man he made in that garden. 9Then the LORD God caused all the beautiful trees that were good for food to grow in the garden. In the middle of the garden, he put the tree of life and the tree that gives knowledge about good and evil.

10A river flowed from Eden and watered the garden. The river then separated and became four smaller rivers. 11The name of the first river was Pishon. This river flowed around the entire country of Havilah.*g* 12(There is gold in that country, and that gold is pure. A kind of expensive perfume and onyx* are also found there.) 13The name of the second river was Gihon. This river flowed around the whole land of Cush.*h* 14The name of the third river was Tigris.* This river flowed east of Assyria. The fourth river was the Euphrates.*

15The LORD God put the man in the Garden of Eden to work the soil and take care of the garden. 16The LORD God gave him this command: "You may eat from any tree in the garden. 17But you must not eat from the tree that gives knowledge about good and evil. If you eat fruit from that tree, on that day you will certainly die!"

A Companion for Adam

18Then the LORD God said, "I see that it is not good for the man to be alone. I will make the companion he needs, one just right for him."

19The LORD God used dust from the ground and made every animal in the fields and every bird in the air. He brought all these animals to the man, and the man gave them all a name. 20The man gave names to all the tame animals, to all the birds in the air, and to all the wild animals. He saw many animals and birds, but he could not find a companion that was right for him. 21So the LORD God caused the man to sleep very deeply. While he was asleep, God took one of the ribs from the man's body. Then he closed the man's skin where the rib had been. 22The LORD God used the rib from the man to make a woman. Then he brought the woman to the man. 23And the man said,

"Finally! One like me,
  with bones from my bones
  and a body from my body.
She was taken out of a man,
  so I will call her 'woman.'"

24That is why a man leaves his father and mother and is joined to his wife. In this way

---

*a***1:26** *humans* The Hebrew word means "man," "people," or the name "Adam." It is like the word meaning "earth" or "red clay."

*b***1:26** *Now let's make ... like us* Or "Now let's make humans in our image and in our likeness."

*c***1:27** *So God created humans ... himself* Or "So God created them in his image. In the image of God he created them." Compare Gen. 5:1, 3.

*d***2:6** *water* Or "a mist."

*e***2:7** *man* The Hebrew word means "man," "people," or the name "Adam." It is like the word meaning "earth" or "red clay."

*f***2:8** *East* This usually means the area between the

Tigris and Euphrates rivers as far east as the Persian Gulf.

*g***2:11** *Havilah* The land along the west coast of the Arabian peninsula and possibly, the part of Africa south of Ethiopia.

*h***2:13** *Cush* Usually this means Ethiopia, but here, it probably refers to the area north and east of the Tigris River.

two people become one.

25The man and his wife were naked, but they were not ashamed.

The Beginning of Sin

3 1The snake was the most clever of all the wild animals that the LORD God had made. The snake spoke to the woman and said, "Woman, did God really tell you that you must not eat from any tree in the garden?"

2The woman answered the snake, "No, we can eat fruit from the trees in the garden. 3But there is one tree we must not eat from. God told us, 'You must not eat fruit from the tree that is in the middle of the garden. You must not even touch that tree, or you will die.'"

4But the snake said to the woman, "You will not die. 5God knows that if you eat the fruit from that tree you will learn about good and evil, and then you will be like God!"

6The woman could see that the tree was beautiful and the fruit looked so good to eat. She also liked the idea that it would make her wise. So she took some of the fruit from the tree and ate it. Her husband was there with her, so she gave him some of the fruit, and he ate it.

7Then it was as if their eyes opened, and they saw things differently. They saw that they were naked. So they got some fig leaves, sewed them together, and wore them for clothes.

8During the cool part of the day, the LORD God was walking in the garden. The man and the woman heard him, and they hid among the trees in the garden. 9The LORD God called to the man and said, "Where are you?"

10The man said, "I heard you walking in the garden, and I was afraid. I was naked, so I hid."

11The LORD God said to the man, "Who told you that you were naked? Did you eat fruit from that special tree? I told you not to eat from that tree!"

12The man said, "The woman you put here with me gave me fruit from that tree. So I ate it."

13Then the LORD God said to the woman, "What have you done?"

She said, "The snake tricked me, so I ate the fruit."

14So the LORD God said to the snake,

"You did this very bad thing,
    so bad things will happen to you.
It will be worse for you
    than for any other animal.
You must crawl on your belly
    and eat dust all the days of your life.
15 I will make you and the woman
    enemies to each other.
Your children and her children
    will be enemies.
You will bite her child's foot,
    but he will crush your head."

16Then the LORD God said to the woman,

"I will cause you to have much trouble
    when you are pregnant.
And when you give birth to children,
    you will have much pain.
You will want your husband very much,
    but he will rule over you."a

17Then the LORD God said to the man,

"I commanded you not to eat from that
    tree.
    But you listened to your wife and ate
        from it.
So I will curse* the ground because of
        you.
    You will have to work hard all your life
        for the food the ground produces.
18 The ground will grow thorns and weeds
        for you.
    And you will have to eat the plants that
        grow wild in the fields.b
19 You will work hard for your food,
    until your face is covered with sweat.
You will work hard until the day you die,
    and then you will become dust again.
I used dust to make you,
    and when you die, you will become dust
        again."

20Adamc named his wife Eve.d He gave her this name because Eve would be the mother of everyone who ever lived.

21The LORD God used animal skins and made some clothes for the man and his wife. Then he put the clothes on them.

22The LORD God said, "Look, the man has become like us—he knows about good and evil. And now the man might take the fruit from the tree of life. If the man eats that fruit, he will live forever."

23So the LORD God forced the man out of the Garden of Eden to work the ground he was made from. 24The LORD God forced the man to leave the garden. Then he put Cherub angels* and a sword of fire at the entrance to the garden to protect it. The sword flashed around and around, guarding the way to the tree of life.

The First Family

4 1Adam had sexual relations with his wife Eve. She became pregnant and gave birth to a son. She named him Cain.e Eve said,

---

a3:16 *You will ... over you* Or "You will want to rule your husband, but he will rule over you." In Hebrew this is like the last part of Gen. 4:7.
b3:18 See Gen. 1:28–29.
c3:20 *Adam* This name means "man" or "people." It is like the word meaning "earth" or "red clay."
d3:20 *Eve* This name is like the Hebrew word meaning "life."
e4:1 *Cain* This name is like the Hebrew word meaning "make" or "get."

"With the LORD's help, I have made a man!"

²Eve gave birth again to Cain's brother Abel. Abel became a shepherd, and Cain became a farmer.

The First Murder

³⁻⁴At harvest time,ᵃ Cain brought a gift to the LORD. He brought some of the food that he grew from the ground, but Abel brought some animals from his flock. He chose some of his best sheep and brought the best parts from them.ᵇ

The LORD accepted Abel and his gift. ⁵But he did not accept Cain and his offering. Cain was sad because of this, and he became very angry. ⁶The LORD asked Cain, "Why are you angry? Why does your face look sad? ⁷You know that if you do what is right, I will accept you. But if you don't, sin is ready to attack you. That sin will want to control you, but you must control it."ᶜ

⁸Cain said to his brother Abel, "Let's go out to the field."ᵈ So they went to the field. Then Cain attacked his brother Abel and killed him.

⁹Later, the LORD said to Cain, "Where is your brother Abel?"

Cain answered, "I don't know. Is it my job to watch over my brother?"

¹⁰⁻¹¹Then the LORD said, "What have you done? You killed your brother and the ground opened up to take his blood from your hands. Now his blood is shouting to me from the ground. So you will be cursed from this ground. ¹²Now when you work the soil, the ground will not help your plants grow. You will not have a home in this land. You will wander from place to place."

¹³Then Cain said, "This punishment is more than I can bear! ¹⁴You are forcing me to leave the land, and I will not be able to be near you or have a home! Now I must wander from place to place, and anyone I meet could kill me."

¹⁵Then the LORD said to Cain, "No, if anyone kills you, I will punish that person much, much more." Then the LORD put a mark on Cain to show that no one should kill him.

Cain's Family

¹⁶Cain went away from the LORD and lived in the land of Nod.ᵉ

¹⁷Cain had sexual relations with his wife. She became pregnant and gave birth to a son named Enoch. Cain built a city and gave the city the same name as his son Enoch.

¹⁸Enoch had a son named Irad. Irad had a son named Mehujael. Mehujael had a son named Methushael. And Methushael had a son named Lamech.

¹⁹Lamech married two women. One wife was named Adah, and the other was named Zillah. ²⁰Adah gave birth to Jabal. Jabal was the fatherᶠ of people who live in tents and earn their living by keeping cattle. ²¹Jabal was Jubal's brother. Jubal was the father of people who play the harp and flute. ²²Zillah gave birth to Tubal-Cain. Tubal-Cain was the father of people who work with bronze and iron. The sister of Tubal-Cain was named Naamah.

²³Lamech said to his wives:

"Adah and Zillah, hear my voice!
  You wives of Lamech, listen to me.
A man hurt me, so I killed him.
  I even killed a child for hitting me.
²⁴ The punishment for killing Cain was very bad.
  But the punishment for killing me will be many times worse!"

Adam and Eve Have a New Son

²⁵Adam again had sexual relations with his wife, and she gave birth to another son. She named him Seth.ᵍ Eve said, "God has given me another son. Cain killed Abel, but now I have Seth." ²⁶Seth also had a son. He named him Enosh. At that time people began to pray to the LORD.ʰ

The History of Adam's Family

5 ¹This is the history of Adam'sⁱ family. When God created people, he made them like himself.ʲ ²He created them male and female. And on the same day he made them, he blessed them and called them "humans."ᵏ

³After Adam was 130 years old, he had another son. This son looked just like Adam.ˡ Adam named his son Seth. ⁴After Seth was born, Adam lived 800 years and had other sons and daughters. ⁵So Adam lived a total of 930 years; then he died.

⁶After Seth was 105 years old, he had a son named Enosh. ⁷After Enosh was born,

---

ᶠ**4:20** *father* This probably means that this man invented these things or was the first one to use them.
ᵍ**4:25** *Seth* This is like a Hebrew word meaning "to give."
ʰ**4:26** *people ... the LORD* Literally, "people began calling on the name YAHWEH."
ⁱ**5:1** *Adam* This name means "man" or "people." It is like the word meaning "earth" or "red clay."
ʲ**5:1** *When God ... like himself* Literally, "He made him in the image of God." See Gen. 1:27; 5:3.
ᵏ**5:2** *humans* The Hebrew word means "Adam," "man," or "people."
ˡ**5:3** *he had ... like Adam* Or "he fathered a son in his image and likeness." In Hebrew this is like Gen. 1:27; 5:1.

ᵃ**4:3–4** *At harvest time* Literally, "at the end of days."
ᵇ**4:3–4** *He chose ... from them* Literally, "He brought some of his firstborn sheep, especially their fat."
ᶜ**4:7** *But if you ... control it* Or "But if you don't do right, sin is crouching at your door. It wants you, but you must rule over it."
ᵈ**4:8** *Let's go ... field* This sentence is found in the ancient versions but not in the standard Hebrew text.
ᵉ**4:16** *Nod* This name means "wandering."

Seth lived 807 years and had other sons and daughters. [8]So Seth lived a total of 912 years; then he died.

[9]After Enosh was 90 years old, he had a son named Kenan. [10]After Kenan was born, Enosh lived 815 years and had other sons and daughters. [11]So Enosh lived a total of 905 years; then he died.

[12]After Kenan was 70 years old, he had a son named Mahalalel. [13]After Mahalalel was born, Kenan lived 840 years and had other sons and daughters. [14]So Kenan lived a total of 910 years; then he died.

[15]When Mahalalel was 65 years old, he had a son named Jared. [16]After Jared was born, Mahalalel lived 830 years and had other sons and daughters. [17]So Mahalalel lived a total of 895 years; then he died.

[18]After Jared was 162 years old, he had a son named Enoch. [19]After Enoch was born, Jared lived 800 years and had other sons and daughters. [20]So Jared lived a total of 962 years; then he died.

[21]After Enoch was 65 years old, he had a son named Methuselah. [22]After Methuselah was born, Enoch walked with God for 300 years and had other sons and daughters. [23]So Enoch lived a total of 365 years. [24]One day Enoch was walking with God, and he disappeared. God took him.[a]

[25]After Methuselah was 187 years old, he had a son named Lamech. [26]After Lamech was born, Methuselah lived 782 years and had other sons and daughters. [27]So Methuselah lived a total of 969 years; then he died.

[28]When Lamech was 182 years old, he had a son. [29]Lamech named his son Noah.[b] Lamech said, "We work very hard as farmers because God cursed the ground. But Noah will bring us rest."

[30]After Noah was born, Lamech lived 595 years and had other sons and daughters. [31]So Lamech lived a total of 777 years; then he died.

[32]After Noah was 500 years old, he had sons named Shem, Ham, and Japheth.

People Become Evil

6 [1-4]The number of people on earth continued to increase. When these people had daughters, the sons of God saw how beautiful they were. So they chose the women they wanted. They married them, and the women had their children.

Then the LORD said, "People are only human. I will not let my Spirit be troubled by them forever. I will let them live only 120 years."[c]

During this time and also later, the Nephilim* people lived in the land. They have been famous as powerful soldiers since ancient times.

[5]The LORD saw that the people on the earth were very evil. He saw that they thought only about evil things all the time. [6]He was sorry that he had made people on the earth. It made him very sad in his heart. [7]So the LORD said, "I will destroy all the people I created on the earth. I will destroy every person and every animal and everything that crawls on the earth. And I will destroy all the birds in the air, because I am sorry that I have made them."

[8]But Noah pleased the LORD.

Noah and the Great Flood

[9]This is the history of Noah's family. He was a good man all his life, and he always followed God. [10]Noah had three sons: Shem, Ham, and Japheth.

[11-12]When God looked at the earth, he saw that people had ruined it. Violence was everywhere, and it had ruined their life on earth.

[13]So God said to Noah, "Everyone has filled the earth with anger and violence. So I will destroy all living things. I will remove them from the earth. [14]Use cypress wood[d] and build a boat for yourself. Make rooms in the boat[e] and cover it with tar inside and out.*

[15]"This is the size I want you to make the boat: 300 cubits[f] long, 50 cubits[g] wide, and 30 cubits[h] high. [16]Make a window for the boat about 1 cubit[i] below the roof.[j] Put a door in the side of the boat. Make three floors in the boat: a top deck, a middle deck, and a lower deck.

[17]"Understand what I am telling you. I will bring a great flood of water on the earth. I will destroy all living things that live under heaven. Everything on the earth will die. [18]I will make a special agreement with you. You, your wife, your sons, and their wives will all go into the boat. [19]Also, you will take two of every living thing on the earth with you into

[a]5:24 Or "Enoch pleased God. Enoch disappeared. God took him."
[b]5:29 *Noah* This name is like the Hebrew word meaning "to rest," "to be sorry," or "comfort."
[c]6:1–4 *People ... 120 years* Or "The spirit from me will not live in people forever, because they are flesh. They will live only 120 years." Or "My Spirit will

not judge people forever, because they will all die in 120 years."
[d]6:14 *cypress wood* Hebrew, "gopher timbers." It is uncertain what kind of wood this is. It might be a kind of tree or squared timbers.
[e]6:14 *Make rooms in the boat* Or "Make caulking for the boat." This could be small plants that were stuffed into the cracks and covered with tar.
[f]6:15 *300 cubits* 437' 1/8" (133 m) if this was the short cubit or 510' 1 13/16" (155.5 m) if it was the long cubit.
[g]6:15 *50 cubits* 72' 10" (22.2 m) if this was the short cubit or 85' 5/16" (25.92 m) if it was the long cubit.
[h]6:15 *30 cubits* 43' 8 7/16" (13.3 m) if this was the short cubit or 51' 3/16" (15.55 m) if it was the long cubit.
[i]6:16 *1 cubit* 17 1/2" (44.4 cm) if this was the short cubit or 20 5/8" (51.83 cm) if it was the long cubit.
[j]6:16 *Make a window ... below the roof* Or "Make an opening for the boat about 18 inches tall."

the boat. Take a male and female of every kind of animal so that they might survive with you. ²⁰Two of every kind of bird, animal, and creeping thing will come to you so that you might keep them alive. ²¹Also bring every kind of food into the boat, for you and for the animals."

²²Noah did everything the LORD commanded him.

The Flood Begins

7 ¹Then the LORD said to Noah, "I have seen that you are a good man, even among the evil people of this time. So gather your family, and all of you go into the boat. ²Get seven pairs (seven males and seven females) of every kind of clean* animal. And get one pair (one male and one female) of every other animal on the earth. ³Get seven pairs (seven males and seven females) of all the birds. This will allow all these animals to continue living on the earth after the other animals are destroyed. ⁴Seven days from now, I will send much rain on the earth. It will rain for 40 days and 40 nights, and I will wipe everything off the face of the earth. I will destroy everything I made." ⁵Noah did everything the LORD told him to do.

⁶Noah was 600 years old at the time the rains came. ⁷He and his family went into the boat to be saved from the flood. His wife and his sons and their wives were on the boat with him. ⁸All the clean animals, all the other animals on the earth, the birds, and everything that crawls on the earth ⁹went into the boat with Noah. These animals went into the boat in groups of two, male and female, just as God commanded. ¹⁰Seven days later the flood started. The rain began to fall on the earth.

¹¹⁻¹³On the 17th day of the second month, when Noah was 600 years old, the springs under the earth broke through the ground, and water flowed out everywhere. The sky also opened like windows and rain poured down. The rain fell on the earth for 40 days and 40 nights. That same day Noah went into the boat with his wife, his sons Shem, Ham, and Japheth, and their wives. ¹⁴They and every kind of animal on the earth were in the boat. Every kind of cattle, every kind of animal that crawls on the earth, and every kind of bird were in the boat. ¹⁵All these animals went into the boat with Noah. They came in groups of two from every kind of animal that had the breath of life. ¹⁶All these animals went into the boat in groups of two, just as God had commanded Noah. Then the LORD closed the door behind Noah.

¹⁷Water flooded the earth for 40 days. The water began rising and lifted the boat off the ground. ¹⁸The water continued to rise, and the boat floated on the water high above the earth. ¹⁹The water rose so much that even the highest mountains were covered by the water. ²⁰The water continued to rise above the mountains. The water was more than 20 feet*ᵃ above the highest mountain.

²¹⁻²²Every living thing on earth died— every man and woman, every bird, and every kind of animal. All the many kinds of animals and all the things that crawl on the ground died. Every living, breathing thing on dry land died. ²³In this way God wiped the earth clean—he destroyed every living thing on the earth—every human, every animal, everything that crawls, and every bird. All that was left was Noah and his family and the animals that were with him in the boat. ²⁴The water continued to cover the earth for 150 days.

The Flood Ends

8 ¹But God did not forget about Noah. God remembered him and all the animals that were with him in the boat. God made a wind blow over the earth, and all the water began to disappear.

²Rain stopped falling from the sky, and water stopped flowing from under the earth. ³⁻⁴The water that covered the earth began to go down. After 150 days the water was low enough that the boat touched land again. The boat stopped on one of the mountains of Ararat.* This was the 17th day of the seventh month. ⁵The water continued to go down, and by the first day of the tenth month, the tops of the mountains were above the water.

⁶Forty days later Noah opened the window he had made in the boat. ⁷Then he sent out a raven. The raven flew from place to place until the ground was dry and the water was gone. ⁸Noah also sent out a dove. He wanted it to find dry ground. He wanted to know if water still covered the earth.

⁹The dove could not find a place to rest because water still covered the earth, so the dove came back to the boat. Noah reached out his hand and caught the dove and brought it back into the boat.

¹⁰After seven days Noah again sent out the dove. ¹¹And that afternoon the dove came back to Noah. The dove had a fresh olive leaf in its mouth. This was a sign to show Noah that there was dry ground on the earth. ¹²Seven days later Noah sent the dove out again. But this time the dove didn't come back.

¹³After that Noah opened the doorᵇ of the boat. He looked and saw that the ground was dry. This was the first day of the first month of the year. He was 601 years old. ¹⁴By the 27th day of the second month, the ground was completely dry.

¹⁵Then God said to Noah, ¹⁶"Leave the boat. You, your wife, your sons, and your sons' wives should go out now. ¹⁷Bring every living

ᵃ7:20 20 feet Literally, "15 cubits" which would be 21' 10 3/16" (6.66 m) if this was the short cubit or 25' 6 1/16" (7.77 m) if it was the long cubit.
ᵇ8:13 opened the door Literally, "removed the covering."

animal out of the boat with you—all the birds, animals, and everything that crawls on the earth. These animals will make many more animals, and they will fill the earth again."

¹⁸So Noah went out with his sons, his wife, and his sons' wives. ¹⁹All the animals, everything that crawls, and every bird left the boat. All the animals came out of the boat in family groups.

²⁰Then Noah built an altar* to honor the Lord. Noah took some of all the clean* birds and some of all the clean animals and burned them on the altar as a gift to God.

²¹The Lord smelled these sacrifices, and it pleased him. He said to himself, "I will never again curse the earth as a way to punish people. People are evil from the time they are young, but I will never again destroy every living thing on the earth like I have just done. ²²As long as the earth continues, there will always be a time for planting and a time for harvest. There will always be cold and hot, summer and winter, day and night on earth."

The New Beginning

9 ¹God blessed Noah and his sons and said to them, "Have many children. Fill the earth with your people. ²Every animal on earth, every bird in the air, every animal that crawls on the ground, and every fish in the sea will be afraid of you. All of them will be under your control. ³In the past, I gave you the green plants to eat. Now every animal will also be food for you. I give you everything on earth—it is yours. ⁴But I give you one command. You must not eat meat that still has its life (blood) in it. ⁵Also, I will demand your blood for your lives. That is, I will demand the life of any person or animal that takes a human life.

⁶"God made humans to be like himself.
   So whoever kills a person must be killed
      by another person.

⁷"Have many children and fill the earth with your people."

⁸Then God said to Noah and his sons, ⁹"I now make my promise to you and to your people who will live after you. ¹⁰I make my promise to all the birds, and to all the cattle, and to all the animals that came out of the boat with you. I make my promise to every living thing on earth. ¹¹This is my promise to you: All life on the earth was destroyed by the flood. But that will never happen again. A flood will never again destroy all life on the earth."

¹²And God said, "I will give you something to prove that I made this promise to you. It will continue forever to show that I have made an agreement with you and every living thing on earth. ¹³I am putting a rainbow in the clouds as proof of the agreement between me and the earth. ¹⁴When I bring clouds over the earth, you will see the rainbow in the clouds. ¹⁵When I see this rainbow, I will remember the agreement between me and you and every living thing on the earth. This agreement says that a flood will never again destroy all life on the earth. ¹⁶When I look and see the rainbow in the clouds, I will remember the agreement that continues forever. I will remember the agreement between me and every living thing on the earth."

¹⁷So God said to Noah, "This rainbow is proof of the agreement that I made with all living things on earth."

Problems Begin Again

¹⁸Noah's sons came out of the boat with him. Their names were Shem, Ham, and Japheth. (Ham was the father of Canaan.) ¹⁹These three men were Noah's sons. And all the people on earth came from these three sons.

²⁰Noah became a farmer and planted a vineyard.* ²¹One day Noah made some wine. He got drunk, went into his tent, and took off all his clothes. ²²Ham, the father of Canaan, saw that his father was naked and told his brothers who were outside the tent. ²³Shem and Japheth took a robe, put it across their shoulders, and walked backward into the tent. Then they covered their father without looking at him.

²⁴Later, Noah woke up. (He was sleeping because of the wine.) When he learned what his youngest son Ham had done to him, ²⁵he said,

"May there be a curse on Canaanᵃ!
   May he be a slave to his brothers."

²⁶Noah also said,

"May the Lord, the God of Shem, be
      praised!
   May Canaan be Shem's slave.
²⁷ May God give more land to Japheth.
   May God live in Shem's tents,
      and may Canaan be their slave."

²⁸After the flood Noah lived 350 years. ²⁹He lived a total of 950 years; then he died.

Nations Grow and Spread

10 ¹This is the history of the families of Shem, Ham, and Japheth. They are Noah's sons. These men had children after the flood.

Japheth's Descendants

²Japheth's sons were Gomer, Magog, Madai, Javan, Tubal, Meshech, and Tiras.

ᵃ**9:25** *Canaan* Ham's son. The people of Canaan lived along the coast of Palestine, Lebanon, and Syria. Later, God gave this land to the Israelites.

³Gomer's sons were Ashkenaz, Riphath, and Togarmah.

⁴Javan's sons were Elishah, Tarshish, Kittim, and Dodanim.*a*

⁵All the people who lived in the area around the Mediterranean Sea came from these sons of Japheth. The people separated and went to different countries according to languages, families, and nations.

Ham's Descendants

⁶Ham's sons were Cush,*b* Mizraim,*c* Put, and Canaan.

⁷Cush's sons were Seba, Havilah, Sabtah, Raamah, and Sabtecah.

Raamah's sons were Sheba and Dedan.

⁸Cush also had a son named Nimrod who became a very powerful man on earth. ⁹He was a great hunter before the Lord. That is why people compare other men to him and say, "That man is like Nimrod, a great hunter before the Lord."

¹⁰Nimrod's kingdom spread from Babylon to Erech, to Akkad, and then to Calneh in the land of Shinar. ¹¹Nimrod also went into Assyria. In Assyria, Nimrod built the cities of Nineveh, Rehoboth Ir, Calah, and ¹²Resen. (Resen is the city between Nineveh and Calah, the big city.)

¹³Mizraim was the father of the people of Lud, Anam, Lehab, Naphtuh, ¹⁴Pathrus, Casluh, and Caphtor. (The Philistine people came from Casluh.)

¹⁵Canaan was the father of Sidon. Sidon was Canaan's first son. Canaan was also the father of the Hittites, ¹⁶Jebusites, Amorites, Girgashites, ¹⁷Hivites, Arkites, the Sinites, ¹⁸Arvadites, Zemarites, and Hamathites. The families of Canaan spread to different parts of the world.

¹⁹The land where the Canaanites lived went from Sidon down along the coast to Gerar and from Gaza as far east as Sodom and Gomorrah and from Admah and Zeboiim as far north as Laish.

²⁰All these people were descendants of Ham. They are arranged by families, languages, countries, and nations.

Shem's Descendants

²¹Shem was Japheth's older brother. One of Shem's descendants was Eber, the father of all the Hebrew people.*d*

²²Shem's sons were Elam, Asshur, Arphaxad, Lud, and Aram.

²³Aram's sons were Uz, Hul, Gether, and Mash.

²⁴Arphaxad was the father of Shelah. Shelah was the father of Eber. ²⁵Eber was the father of two sons. One son was named Peleg.*e* He was given this name because the earth was divided during his life. The other son was named Joktan.

²⁶Joktan was the father of Almodad, Sheleph, Hazarmaveth, Jerah, ²⁷Hadoram, Uzal, Diklah, ²⁸Obal, Abimael, Sheba, ²⁹Ophir, Havilah, and Jobab. All these people were Joktan's sons. ³⁰They lived in the area between Mesha and the hill country in the East.*f* Mesha was toward the country of Sephar.

³¹These are the people from the family of Shem. They are arranged by families, languages, countries, and nations.

³²This is the list of the families from Noah's sons. They are arranged according to their nations. From these families came all the people who spread across the earth after the flood.

The Tower of Babel

11 ¹There was a time when the whole world spoke one language. Everyone used the same words. ²The people moved from the East and found a plain in the country of Shinar and stayed there to live. ³Then they said to each other, "Let's make some bricks of clay and bake them in the fire." Then they used these bricks as stones, and they used tar* as mortar.

⁴Then the people said, "Let's build ourselves a city and a tower that will reach to the sky. Then we will be famous. This will keep us together so that we will not be scattered all over the earth."

⁵Then the Lord came down to see the city and the tower. ⁶The Lord said, "These people all speak the same language. And I see that they are joined together to do this work. This is only the beginning of what they can do. Soon they will be able to do anything they want. ⁷Let's go down and confuse their language. Then they will not understand each other."

⁸So people stopped building the city, and the Lord scattered them all over the earth. ⁹That is the place where the Lord confused the language of the whole world. That is why it is called Babel.*g* And it was from there that the Lord caused the people to spread out to all the other places on earth.

The History of Shem's Family

¹⁰This is the history of Shem's family. Two years after the flood, when Shem was 100 years old, his son Arphaxad was born. ¹¹After that Shem lived 500 years. He had other sons and daughters.

---

*a***10:4** *Dodanim* Or "Rodanim, the people of Rhodes."
*b***10:6** *Cush* Another name for Ethiopia.
*c***10:6** *Mizraim* Another name for Egypt. Also in verse 13.
*d***10:21** *One ... Hebrew people* Literally, "To Shem was born the father of Eber's sons."

*e***10:25** *Peleg* This name means "division."
*f***10:30** *East* This usually means the area between the Tigris and Euphrates rivers as far east as the Persian Gulf. Also in 11:2.
*g***11:9** *Babel* Or "Babylon." This is like a word meaning "confuse."

¹²When Arphaxad was 35 years old, his son Shelah was born. ¹³After Shelah was born, Arphaxad lived 403 years. During that time he had other sons and daughters.

¹⁴After Shelah was 30 years old, his son Eber was born. ¹⁵After Eber was born, Shelah lived 403 years. During that time he had other sons and daughters.

¹⁶After Eber was 34 years old, his son Peleg was born. ¹⁷After Peleg was born, Eber lived another 430 years. During that time he had other sons and daughters.

¹⁸After Peleg was 30 years old, his son Reu was born. ¹⁹After Reu was born, Peleg lived another 209 years. During that time he had other sons and daughters.

²⁰After Reu was 32 years old, his son Serug was born. ²¹After Serug was born, Reu lived another 207 years. During that time he had other sons and daughters.

²²After Serug was 30 years old, his son Nahor was born. ²³After Nahor was born, Serug lived another 200 years. During that time he had other sons and daughters.

²⁴After Nahor was 29 years old, his son Terah was born. ²⁵After Terah was born, Nahor lived another 119 years. During that time he had other sons and daughters.

²⁶After Terah was 70 years old, his sons Abram, Nahor, and Haran were born.

The History of Terah's Family

²⁷This is the history of Terah's family. Terah was the father of Abram, Nahor, and Haran. Haran was the father of Lot. ²⁸Haran died in his hometown, Ur of Babylonia,ᵃ while his father Terah was still alive. ²⁹Abram and Nahor both married. Abram's wife was named Sarai. Nahor's wife was named Milcah. Milcah was the daughter of Haran. Haran was the father of Milcah and Iscah. ³⁰Sarai did not have any children because she was not able to have children.

³¹Terah took his family and left Ur of Babylonia. They planned to travel to Canaan.* Terah took his son Abram, his grandson Lot (Haran's son), and his daughter-in-law Sarai (Abram's wife). They traveled to the city of Haran and decided to stay there. ³²Terah lived to be 205 years old. He died in Haran.

God Calls Abram

12 ¹The LORD said to Abram,
"Leave your country and your people.
Leave your father's family
    and go to the country that I will show
    you.
² I will build a great nation from you.
I will bless you
    and make your name famous.
People will use your name
    to bless other people.

³ I will bless those who bless you,
    and I will curse* those who curse you.
I will use you to bless
    all the people on earth."

Abram Goes to Canaan

⁴So Abram left Haran just like the LORD said, and Lot went with him. Abram was 75 years old when he left Haran. ⁵He took his wife Sarai, his nephew Lot, all the slaves, and all the other things he had gotten in Haran. Then he and his group moved to the land of Canaan.* ⁶Abram traveled through the land as far as the town of Shechem and then to the big tree at Moreh. The Canaanites were living in the land at that time.

⁷The LORD appearedᵇ to Abram and said, "I will give this land to your descendants."

Abram built an altar* to honor the LORD who appeared to him there. ⁸Then he left that place and traveled to the mountains east of Bethel. He set up his tent there. Bethel was to the west, and Aiᶜ was to the east. Abram built another altar at that place to honor the LORD, and he worshiped the LORD there. ⁹Then he moved on toward the Negev,* stopping for a time at several places on the way.

Abram in Egypt

¹⁰During this time there was not enough food in the land, so Abram went down to Egypt to live. ¹¹Just before they arrived in Egypt, Abram told Sarai, "Look, I know that you are a very beautiful woman. ¹²When the Egyptian men see you, they will say, 'This woman is his wife.' Then they will kill me and keep you alive because they want you. ¹³So tell them that you are my sister. Then they will be good to me because of you. In this way you will save my life."

¹⁴So when Abram went into Egypt, the Egyptian men saw that Sarai was a very beautiful woman. ¹⁵Even some of Pharaoh's officials noticed her and told Pharaoh how beautiful she was. So they took her to Pharaoh's house. ¹⁶Pharaoh was kind to Abram because he thought Abram was Sarai's brother. He gave Abram sheep, cattle, donkeys, camels, and men and women servants.

¹⁷Pharaoh took Abram's wife, so the LORD caused Pharaoh and all the people in his house to have very bad diseases. ¹⁸Pharaoh called Abram and said to him, "You have done a very bad thing to me! Why didn't you tell me Sarai was your wife? ¹⁹You said, 'She is my sister.' Why did you say that? I took her so that she could be my wife, but now I give your wife back to you. Take her and go!" ²⁰Then Pharaoh commanded his men to lead Abram out of Egypt. So Abram and his wife left that place and took everything they had with them.

ᵇ**12:7** *The LORD appeared* God often used special shapes so that people could see him. Sometimes he was like a man, an angel, a fire, or a bright light.
ᶜ**12:8** *Ai* The name of this town means "the ruins."

ᵃ**11:28** *Ur of Babylonia* Literally, "Ur of the Chaldeans." A city in southern Babylonia. Also in verse 31.

Abram Returns to Canaan

13 ¹So Abram left Egypt. He traveled through the Negev* with his wife and everything he owned. Lot was also with them. ²At this time Abram was very rich. He had many animals and much silver and gold.

³Abram continued traveling around. He left the Negev and went back to Bethel. He went to the place between the city of Bethel and Ai,ᵃ where he and his family had camped before. ⁴This was where Abram had built an altar* earlier. So he worshiped the Lord there.

Abram and Lot Separate

⁵During this time Lot was also traveling with Abram. Lot had many animals and tents. ⁶Abram and Lot had so many animals that the land could not support both of them together. ⁷(The Canaanites and the Perizzites were also living in this land at the same time.) The shepherds of Abram and Lot began to argue.

⁸So Abram said to Lot, "There should be no arguing between you and me or between your people and my people. We are all brothers. ⁹We should separate. You can choose any place you want. If you go to the left, I will go to the right. If you go to the right, I will go to the left."

¹⁰Lot looked and saw the whole Jordan Valley. He saw that there was much water there. (This was before the Lord destroyed Sodom and Gomorrah. At that time the Jordan Valley all the way to Zoar was like the Lord's Garden. This was good land, like the land of Egypt.) ¹¹So Lot chose to live in the Jordan Valley. The two men separated, and Lot began traveling east. ¹²Abram stayed in the land of Canaan,* and Lot lived among the cities in the valley. Lot moved as far as Sodom and made his camp there. ¹³The Lord knew that the people of Sodom were very evil sinners.

¹⁴After Lot left, the Lord said to Abram, "Look around you. Look north and south and east and west. ¹⁵All this land that you see I will give to you and your people who live after you. This will be your land forever. ¹⁶I will make your people so many that they will be like the dust of the earth. If people could count all the particles of dust on earth, they could count your people. ¹⁷So go. Walk through your land. I now give it to you."

¹⁸So Abram moved his tents. He went to live near the big trees of Mamre. This was near the city of Hebron. There he built an altar* to honor the Lord.

Lot Is Captured

14 ¹Amraphel was the king of Shinar, Arioch was the king of Ellasar, Kedorlaomer was the king of Elam, and Tidal was the king of Goiim. ²All these kings fought a war against King Bera of Sodom: King Birsha

of Gomorrah, King Shinab of Admah, King Shemeber of Zeboiim, and the king of Bela. (Bela is also called Zoar.)

³All these kings joined their armies in the Valley of Siddim. (The Valley of Siddim is now the Salt Sea.) ⁴These kings had served Kedorlaomer for twelve years. But in the 13th year, they all rebelled against him. ⁵So in the 14th year, King Kedorlaomer and the kings with him came to fight against them. Kedorlaomer and the kings with him defeated the Rephaites in Ashteroth Karnaim. They also defeated the Zuzites in Ham. They defeated the Emites in Shaveh Kiriathaim. ⁶And they defeated the Horites who lived in the area from the hill country of Seirᵇ to El Paran.ᶜ (El Paran is near the desert.) ⁷Then King Kedorlaomer turned back and went to En Mishpat (that is, Kadesh) and defeated the Amalekites. He also defeated the Amorites living in Hazezon Tamar.

⁸At that time the kings of Sodom, Gomorrah, Admah, Zeboiim, and Bela (Zoar) joined together to fight against their enemies in the Valley of Siddim.ᵈ ⁹They fought against King Kedorlaomer of Elam, King Tidal of Goiim, King Amraphel of Shinar, and King Arioch of Ellasar. So there were four kings fighting against five.

¹⁰There were many holes filled with tar* in the Valley of Siddim. When the kings of Sodom and Gomorrah and their armies ran away, some of the soldiers fell into these holes, but the others ran away to the mountains.

¹¹So Kedorlaomer and his armies took everything that the people of Sodom and Gomorrah owned. They took all their food and clothing and left. ¹²Lot, the son of Abram's brother, was living in Sodom, and they captured him. They also took everything he owned and left. ¹³One of the men who had escaped went to Abram the Hebrew and told him what happened. Abram was camped near the trees of Mamre the Amorite. Mamre, Eshcol, and Anerᵉ had made an agreement to help each other, and they had also signed an agreement to help Abram.

Abram Rescues Lot

¹⁴When Abram learned that Lot was captured, he called all of his family together. There were 318 trained soldiers. He led the men and chased the enemy all the way to the town of Dan. ¹⁵That night he and his men made a surprise attack against the enemy. They defeated them and chased them to Hobah, north of Damascus. ¹⁶Then Abram brought back everything the enemy had stolen, as well as the women and servants, his

ᵃ**13:3** *Ai* The name of this town means "the ruins."

ᵇ**14:6** *Seir* Or "Edom."

ᶜ**14:6** *El Paran* Probably the town Elath, at the southern tip of Israel near the Red Sea.

ᵈ**14:8** *Valley of Siddim* The valley or plain along the eastern or southeastern side of the Dead Sea.

ᵉ**14:13** *Mamre ... Aner* Literally, "Mamre ... was a brother of Eshcol and a brother of Aner."

nephew Lot, and everything Lot owned.

¹⁷Then Abram went home after he defeated Kedorlaomer and the kings with him. On his way home, the king of Sodom went out to meet him in the Valley of Shaveh. (This is now called King's Valley.)

. Melchizedek

¹⁸Melchizedek, the king of Salem and a priest of God Most High, also went to meet Abram. He brought bread and wine. ¹⁹He blessed Abram and said,

"Abram, may you be blessed by God Most
    High,
  the one who made heaven and earth.
²⁰ And we praise God Most High,
  who helped you defeat your enemies."

Abram gave Melchizedek one-tenth of everything he had taken during the battle. ²¹Then the king of Sodom told Abram, "Give me my people who were captured. But you can keep everything else."

²²But Abram said to the king of Sodom, "I promise to the LORD, the God Most High, the one who made heaven and earth. ²³I promise that I will not keep anything that is yours—not even a thread or a sandal strap! I don't want you to say, 'I made Abram rich.' ²⁴The only thing I will accept is the food that my young men have eaten, but you should give the other men their share. Take what we won in battle and give some to Aner, Eshcol, and Mamre. These men helped me in the battle."

God's Agreement With Abram

15 ¹After all these things happened, the word of the LORD came to Abram in a vision.* God said, "Abram, don't be afraid. I will defend you and give you a great reward."

²But Abram said, "LORD God, there is nothing you can give me that will make me happy, because I have no son. My slave Eliezer from Damascus will get everything I own after I die." ³Abram said, "You have given me no son, so a slave born in my house will get everything I have."

⁴Then the LORD spoke to Abram and said, "That slave will not be the one to get what you have. You will have a son who will get everything you own."

⁵Then God led Abram outside and said, "Look at the sky. See the many stars. There are so many you cannot count them. Your family will be like that."

⁶Abram believed the LORD, and because of this faith the Lord accepted him as one who has done what is right. ⁷He said to Abram, "I am the LORD who led you from Ur of Babylonia.ᵃ I did this so that I could give you this land. You will own this land."

⁸But Abram said, "Lord GOD, how can I be sure that I will get this land?"

⁹God said to Abram, "We will make an agreement. Bring me a three-year-old cow, a three-year-old goat, a three-year-old ram, a dove, and a young pigeon."

¹⁰Abram brought all these to God. Abram killed these animals and cut each of them into two pieces. Then he laid each half across from the other half. He did not cut the birds into two pieces. ¹¹Later, large birds flew down to eat the animals, but Abram chased them away.

¹²The sun began to go down and Abram got very sleepy. While he was asleep, a very terrible darkness came over him. ¹³Then the LORD said to Abram, "You should know this: Your descendants will live in a country that is not their own. They will be strangers there. The people there will make them slaves and be cruel to them for 400 years. ¹⁴But then I will punish the nation that made them slaves. Your people will leave that land, and they will take many good things with them.

¹⁵"You yourself will live to be very old. You will die in peace and be buried with your family. ¹⁶After four generations your people will come to this land again and defeat the Amorites. That will happen in the future because the Amorites are not yet guilty enough to lose their land."

¹⁷After the sun went down, it got very dark. The dead animals were still on the ground, each animal cut into two pieces. Then a smoking firepotᵇ and a flaming torch passed between the halves of the dead animals.ᶜ

¹⁸So on that day the LORD made a promise and an agreement with Abram. He said, "I will give this land to your descendants. I will give them the land between the River of Egyptᵈ and the great river Euphrates. ¹⁹This is the land of the Kenites, Kenizzites, Kadmonites, ²⁰Hittites, Perizzites, Rephaites, ²¹Amorites, Canaanites, Girgashites, and Jebusites."

Hagar the Servant Girl

16 ¹Sarai was Abram's wife, but she did not have any children. She had an Egyptian slave named Hagar. ²Sarai told Abram, "The LORD has not allowed me to have children, so sleep with my slave. Maybe she can have a son, and I will accept him as my own." Abram did what Sarai said.

ᵇ**15:17** *firepot* A clay pot in which burning coals were placed to be used for starting new fires.
ᶜ**15:17** *passed between ... animals* This showed that God "signed" or "sealed" the agreement he made with Abram. People showed that they were sincere in making an agreement by walking between the parts of animals that had been cut into pieces and saying something like, "May this same thing happen to me if I don't keep the agreement."
ᵈ**15:18** *River of Egypt* That is, the stream called "Wadi El-Arish."

ᵃ**15:7** *Ur of Babylonia* Literally, "Ur of the Chaldeans." A city in southern Babylonia.

³So after living ten years in the land of Canaan,* Sarai gave her Egyptian slave to Abram as a second wife. ⁴Abram slept with Hagar, and she became pregnant. When Hagar realized this, she became very proud and began to feel that she was better than Sarai her owner. ⁵Then Sarai said to Abram, "My slave girl now hates me, and I blame you for this. I gave her to you, and she became pregnant. Then she began to feel that she is better than I am. I want the Lord to judge which of us is right."

⁶But Abram said to Sarai, "She is your slave. You can do anything you want to her." So Sarai was cruel to Hagar, and Hagar ran away.

Hagar's Son Ishmael

⁷The angel of the Lord found Hagar near a spring of water in the desert. The spring was by the road to Shur. ⁸The angel said, "Hagar, Sarai's slave girl, why are you here? Where are you going?"

Hagar said, "I am running away from Sarai."

⁹The angel of the Lord said to her, "Sarai is your owner. Go home to her and obey her." ¹⁰The angel of the Lord also said, "From you will come many people—too many people to count."

¹¹Then the angel of the Lord said,

"Hagar, you are now pregnant,
    and you will have a son.
You will name him Ishmael,ᵃ
    because the Lord has heard that you
       were treated badly.
¹² Ishmael will be wild and free
    like a wild donkey.
He will be against everyone,
    and everyone will be against him.
He will move from place to place
    and camp near his brothers."

¹³The Lord talked to Hagar. She began to use a new name for God. She said to him, "You are 'God Who Sees Me.'" She said this because she thought, "I see that even in this place God sees me and cares for me!" ¹⁴So the well there was called Beer Lahai Roi.ᵇ It is between Kadesh and Bered.

¹⁵Hagar gave birth to Abram's son, and Abram named the son Ishmael. ¹⁶Abram was 86 years old when Ishmael was born from Hagar.

Circumcision—Proof of the Agreement

17 ¹When Abram was 99 years old, the Lord appeared to him. He said, "I am God All-Powerful.ᶜ Obey me and live the right way. ²If you do this, I will prepare an agreement between us. I will promise to make your people a great nation."

³Then Abram bowed down before God. God said to him, ⁴"This is my part of our agreement: I will make you the father of many nations. ⁵I will change your name from Abramᵈ to Abraham,ᵉ because I am making you the father of many nations. ⁶I will give you many descendants. New nations and kings will come from you. ⁷And I will prepare an agreement between me and you. This agreement will also be for all your descendants. It will continue forever. I will be your God and the God of all your descendants. ⁸And I will give this land to you and to all your descendants. I will give you the land you are traveling through—the land of Canaan.* I will give you this land forever, and I will be your God."

⁹Then God said to Abraham, "Now, this is your part of the agreement: You and all your descendants will obey my agreement. ¹⁰This is my agreement that all of you must obey. This is the agreement between me and you and all your descendants. Every male must be circumcised.* ¹¹You will cut the skin to show that you follow the agreement between me and you. ¹²When the baby boy is eight days old, you will circumcise him. Every boy born among your people and every boy who is a slave of your people must be circumcised. ¹³So every baby boy in your nation will be circumcised. Every boy who is born from your family or bought as a slave will be circumcised. ¹⁴Abraham, this is the agreement between you and me: Any male who is not circumcised will be cut off from his peopleᶠ because he has broken my agreement."

Isaac—the Promised Son

¹⁵God said to Abraham, "I will give Sarai,ᵍ your wife, a new name. Her new name will be Sarah.ʰ ¹⁶I will bless her. I will give her a son, and you will be the father. She will be the mother of many new nations. Kings of nations will come from her."

¹⁷Abraham bowed his face to the ground to show he respected God. But he laughed and said to himself, "I am 100 years old. I cannot have a son, and Sarah is 90 years old. She cannot have a child."

¹⁸Then Abraham said to God, "I hope Ishmael will live and serve you."

¹⁹God said, "No, I said that your wife Sarah

ᵃ**16:11 Ishmael** This name means "God hears."
ᵇ**16:14 Beer Lahai Roi** This means "The well of the Living One who sees me."
ᶜ**17:1 God All-Powerful** Literally, "El Shaddai."

ᵈ**17:5 Abram** This name means "honored father."
ᵉ**17:5 Abraham** This name means "great father" or "father of many."
ᶠ**17:14 cut off from his people** This means he must be separated from his family and lose his share of the inheritance.
ᵍ**17:15 Sarai** A name, probably Aramaic, meaning "princess."
ʰ**17:15 Sarah** A Hebrew name meaning "princess."

will have a son. You will name him Isaac.*a* I will make my agreement with him that will continue forever with all his descendants. 20"You mentioned Ishmael, and I heard you. I will bless him, and he will have many children. He will be the father of twelve great leaders. His family will become a great nation. 21But I will make my agreement with Isaac, the son who Sarah will have. He will be born at this same time next year."

22After God finished talking with Abraham, God went up into heaven. 23Then Abraham gathered together Ishmael and all the slaves born in his house. He also gathered all the slaves he had bought. Every man and boy in Abraham's house was gathered together, and they were all circumcised.* Abraham circumcised them that day, just as God had told him to do.

24Abraham was 99 years old when he was circumcised. 25And Ishmael, his son, was 13 years old when he was circumcised. 26Abraham and his son were circumcised on the same day. 27Also, on that day all the men in Abraham's house were circumcised. All the slaves born in his house and all the slaves he had bought were circumcised.

The Three Visitors

18 1Later, the Lord again appeared to Abraham near the oak trees of Mamre. It was the hottest part of the day, and Abraham was sitting at the door of his tent. 2He looked up and saw three men standing in front of him. When he saw the men, he ran to them and bowed before them. 3Abraham said, "Sirs,*b* please stay a while with me, your servant. 4I will bring some water to wash your feet. You can rest under the trees. 5I will get some food for you, and you can eat as much as you want. Then you can continue your journey."

The three men said, "Do as you wish."

6Abraham hurried to the tent. He said to Sarah, "Quickly, prepare enough flour for three loaves of bread." 7Then Abraham ran to his cattle. He took his best young calf and gave it to the servant there. He told the servant to quickly kill the calf and prepare it for food. 8Abraham brought the meat and some milk and cheese and set them down in front of the three men. Then he stood near the men, ready to serve them while they sat under the tree and ate.

9Then the men said to Abraham, "Where is your wife Sarah?"

Abraham said, "She is there, in the tent."

10Then one of them said, "I will come again in the spring. At that time your wife Sarah will have a son."

Sarah was listening in the tent and heard these things. 11Abraham and Sarah were very old. Sarah was past the right age for women to have children. 12So she laughed to herself and said, "I am old, and my husband is old. I am too old to have a baby."

13Then the Lord said to Abraham, "Sarah laughed and said she was too old to have a baby. 14But is anything too hard for the Lord? I will come again in the spring, just as I said I would, and your wife Sarah will have a son."

15Sarah said, "I didn't laugh!" (She said this because she was afraid.)

Then the Lord said, "No, I know that is not true. You did laugh!"

16Then the men got up to leave. They looked toward Sodom and began walking in that direction. Abraham walked with them to send them on their way.

Abraham's Bargain With God

17The Lord said to himself, "Should I tell Abraham what I am going to do now? 18Abraham will become a great and powerful nation, and all the nations on earth will be blessed because of him. 19I have made a special agreement with him. I did this so that he would command his children and his descendants to live the way the Lord wants them to. I did this so that they would live right and be fair. Then I, the Lord, can give him what I promised."

20Then the Lord said, "I have heard many times that the people of Sodom and Gomorrah are very evil. 21I will go and see if they are as bad as I have heard. Then I will know for sure."

22So the men turned and started walking toward Sodom while Abraham stood there before the Lord. 23Then Abraham approached him and asked, "Will you destroy the good people while you are destroying those who are evil? 24What if there are fifty good people in that city? Will you still destroy it? Surely you will save the city for the fifty good people living there. 25Surely you would not destroy the city. You would not destroy fifty good people to kill those who are evil. If that happened, those who are good would be the same as those who are evil—both would be punished. As the judge of the whole world, surely you would do the right thing!"

26Then the Lord said, "If I find fifty good people in the city of Sodom, I will save the whole city."

27Then Abraham said, "Compared to you, Lord, I am only dust and ashes. But let me bother you again and ask you this question. 28What if there are five less than fifty? Will you destroy a whole city because of just five people?"

The Lord said, "If I find forty-five good people there, I will not destroy the city."

29Abraham spoke again. He said, "And if you find only forty good people there, will you destroy the city?"

a17:19 Isaac This name means "he laughs" or "he is happy."

b18:3 Sirs This Hebrew word can mean "sirs" or "Lord." This might show that these were not ordinary men.

The LORD said, "If I find forty good people, I will not destroy the city."

30Then Abraham said, "Lord, please don't be angry with me, but let me ask you this. If only thirty good people are in the city, will you destroy it?"

The LORD said, "If I find thirty good people there, I will not destroy the city."

31Then Abraham said, "Lord, may I bother you again and ask, what if there are twenty good people?"

The LORD answered, "If I find twenty good people, I will not destroy the city."

32Then Abraham said, "Lord, please don't be angry with me, but let me bother you this one last time. If you find ten good people there, what will you do?"

The LORD said, "If I find ten good people in the city, I will not destroy it."

33The LORD finished speaking to Abraham and left. Then Abraham went back home.

Lot's Visitors

19 1-2That evening the two angels came to the city of Sodom. Lot was sitting near the city gates and saw them. He got up and went to them. He bowed to show respect and said, "Sirs, please come to my house, and I will serve you. There you can wash your feet and stay the night. Then tomorrow you can continue your journey."

The angels answered, "No, we will stay the night in the city square."

3But Lot continued to ask them to come to his house, so they agreed and went with him. Lot gave them something to drink. He baked some bread for them, and they ate it.

4That evening, just before bedtime, men from every part of town came to Lot's house. They stood around the house and called to Lot. They said, 5"Where are the two men who came to you tonight? Bring them out to us. We want to have sex with them."

6Lot went outside and closed the door behind him. 7He said to the men, "No, my friends, I beg you, please don't do this evil thing! 8Look, I have two daughters who have never slept with a man before. I will give my daughters to you. You can do anything you want with them. But please don't do anything to these men. They have come to my house, and I must protect them."a

9The men surrounding the house answered, "Get out of our way!" They said to themselves, "This man Lot came to our city as a visitor. Now he wants to tell us how we should live!" Then the men said to Lot, "We will do worse things to you than to them." So the men started moving closer and closer to Lot. They were about to break down the door.

10But the two men staying with Lot opened the door, pulled him back inside the house, and closed the door. 11Then they did something to the men outside the door—they caused all these evil men, young and old, to become blind. So the men trying to get in the house could not find the door.

The Escape From Sodom

12The two men said to Lot, "Are there any other people from your family living in this city? Do you have any sons-in-law, sons, daughters, or any other people from your family here? If so, you should tell them to leave now. 13We are going to destroy this city. The LORD heard how evil this city is, so he sent us to destroy it."

14So Lot went out and spoke to his sons-in-law, the men who had married his other daughters. He said, "Hurry and leave this city! The LORD will soon destroy it!" But they thought he was joking.

15The next morning at dawn, the angels were trying to make Lot hurry. They said, "This city will be punished, so take your wife and your two daughters who are still with you and leave this place. Then you will not be destroyed with the city."

16When Lot did not move fast enough, the two men grabbed his hand. They also took the hands of his wife and his two daughters. The two men led Lot and his family safely out of the city. The LORD was kind to Lot and his family. 17So after the two men brought Lot and his family out of the city, one of the men said, "Now run to save your life! Don't look back at the city, and don't stop anywhere in the valley. Run until you are in the mountains. If you stop, you will be destroyed with the city!"

18But Lot said to the two men, "Sirs, please don't force me to run so far! 19You have been very kind to me, your servant. You have been very kind to save me, but I cannot run all the way to the mountains. What if I am too slow and something happens? I will be killed! 20Look, there is a very small town near here. Let me run to that town. I can run there and be safe."

21The angel said to Lot, "Very well, I'll let you do that. I will not destroy that town. 22But run there quickly. I cannot destroy Sodom until you are safely in that town." (That town is named Zoar,b because it is a small town.)

Sodom and Gomorrah Destroyed

23Lot was entering the town as the sun came up, 24and the LORD began to destroy Sodom and Gomorrah. He caused fire and burning sulfur to fall from the sky. 25He destroyed the whole valley—all the cities, the people living in the cities, and all the plants in the valley.

26Lot's wife was following behind him and looked back at the city. When she did, she

---

a**19:8 I must protect them** Whoever invited a traveler in as a guest was also promising to protect the traveler.

b**19:22 Zoar** This name means "small."

became a block of salt.

27Early the next morning, Abraham got up and went to the place where he stood before the Lord. 28Abraham looked down into the valley toward the cities of Sodom and Gomorrah. He saw clouds of smoke rising from the land, like smoke from a furnace.*

29God destroyed the cities in the valley, but he remembered what Abraham had said. So God sent Lot away from those cities before destroying them.

Lot and His Daughters

30Lot was afraid to stay in Zoar, so he and his two daughters went to live in the mountains in a cave. 31One day the older daughter said to the younger, "Everywhere on the earth, men and women marry and have a family. But our father is old, and there are no men around here to give us children. 32So let's get our father drunk with wine. Then we can have sex with him. That way we can use our father to keep our family alive!"

33That night the two girls went to their father and got him drunk with wine. Then the older daughter went and had sexual relations with him. He did not even know when she came to bed or when she got up.

34The next day the older daughter said to the younger daughter, "Last night I went to bed with my father. Let's get him drunk with wine again tonight. Then you can go and have sex with him. In this way we can use our father to have children, and our family will not come to an end." 35So that night the two girls got their father drunk with wine. Then the younger daughter went and had sexual relations with him. Again, Lot did not know when she came to bed or when she got up.

36Both of Lot's daughters became pregnant. Their father was the father of their babies. 37The older daughter gave birth to a son. She named him Moab.a Moab is the ancestor* of all the Moabites living today. 38The younger daughter also gave birth to a son. She named him Ben-Ammi.b Ben-Ammi is the ancestor of all the Ammonites living today.

Abraham Goes to Gerar

20 1Abraham left that place and traveled to the Negev.* He settled in the city of Gerar, between Kadesh and Shur. While in Gerar, 2Abraham told people that Sarah was his sister. King Abimelech of Gerar heard this. Abimelech wanted Sarah, so he sent some servants to take her. 3But one night God spoke to Abimelech in a dream and said, "You will die. The woman you took is married."

4But Abimelech had not yet slept with Sarah, so he said, "Lord, I am not guilty. Would you kill an innocent man? 5Abraham

himself told me, 'This woman is my sister,' and she also said, 'This man is my brother.' I am innocent. I did not know what I was doing."

6Then God said to Abimelech in a dream, "Yes, I know that you are innocent and that you did not know what you were doing. I saved you. I did not allow you to sin against me. I was the one who did not allow you to sleep with her. 7So give Abraham his wife again. He is a prophet.* He will pray for you, and you will live. But if you don't give Sarah back to him, I promise that you will die. And all your family will die with you."

8So very early the next morning, Abimelech called all his servants and told them about the dream. The servants were very afraid. 9Then Abimelech called Abraham and said to him, "Why have you done this to us? What wrong did I do to you? Why did you lie and say that she was your sister? You brought great trouble to my kingdom. You should not have done this to me. 10What were you afraid of? Why did you do this to me?"

11Then Abraham said, "I thought no one in this place respected God. I thought someone would kill me to get Sarah. 12She is my wife, but she is also my sister. She is the daughter of my father but not the daughter of my mother. 13God led me away from my father's house. He led me to wander to many different places. When that happened, I told Sarah, 'Do something for me. Wherever we go, tell people you are my sister.'"

14So Abimelech gave Sarah back to Abraham. Abimelech also gave Abraham some sheep, cattle, and slaves. 15And Abimelech said, "Look all around you. This is my land. You may live any place you want."

16Abimelech said to Sarah, "I gave your brother Abraham 1000 pieces of silver. I did this to show that I am very sorry. I want everyone to see that I did the right thing."

17-18The Lord made all the women in Abimelech's family not able to have children. God did this because Abimelech had taken Sarah, Abraham's wife. But Abraham prayed to God, and God healed Abimelech, his wife, and his servant girls.

Finally, a Baby for Sarah

21 1The Lord came back to visit Sarah as he said he would, and he kept his promise to her. 2At exactly the time God said it would happen, Sarah became pregnant and gave birth to a son for Abraham in his old age. 3Abraham named his son Isaac.c 4Abraham did what God commanded and circumcised* Isaac when he was eight days old.

5Abraham was 100 years old when his son Isaac was born. 6Sarah said, "God has made me happy, and everyone who hears about this

---

a19:37 Moab In Hebrew this name sounds like "from father."

b19:38 Ben-Ammi In Hebrew this name sounds like "son of my father" or "son of my people."

c21:3 Isaac This name means "he laughs" or "he is happy."

will be happy with me. 7No one thought that I, Sarah, would be able to have Abraham's child. But I have given Abraham a son, even though he is old."

Trouble at Home

8Isaac continued to grow, and soon he was old enough to begin eating solid food. So Abraham gave a big party. 9Sarah saw Hagar's son playing. (Hagar was the Egyptian slave woman who gave birth to Abraham's first son.) 10Sarah said to Abraham, "Get rid of that slave woman and her son. Send them away! When we die, our son Isaac will get everything we have. I don't want that slave woman's son sharing these things with my son Isaac!"

11This upset Abraham very much. He was worried about his son Ishmael. 12But God said to Abraham, "Don't worry about the boy and the slave woman. Do what Sarah wants. Your descendants will be those who come through Isaac. 13But I will also bless the son of your slave woman. He is your son, so I will make a great nation from his family also."

14Early the next morning Abraham took some food and water and gave them to Hagar. She carried them and left with her boy. She left that place and wandered in the desert of Beersheba.

15After some time, when all their drinking water was gone, Hagar put her son under a bush. 16Then she walked a short distance away and sat down. She thought her son would die because there was no water. She did not want to watch him die. She sat there and began to cry.

17God heard the boy crying, and God's angel called to Hagar from heaven. He said, "What is wrong, Hagar? Don't be afraid! The Lord has heard the boy crying there. 18Go help the boy. Hold his hand and lead him. I will make him the father of many people."

19Then God allowed Hagar to see a well of water. So she went to the well and filled her bag with water. Then she gave water to the boy to drink.

20God continued to be with the boy while he grew up. Ishmael lived in the desert and became a hunter. He learned to shoot a bow very well. 21His mother found a wife for him in Egypt. They continued to live in the Paran desert.

Abraham's Bargain With Abimelech

22Then Abimelech and Phicol spoke with Abraham. Phicol was the commander of Abimelech's army. They said to Abraham, "God is with you in everything you do. 23So make a promise to me here before God. Promise that you will be fair with me and with my children. Promise that you will be kind to me and this country where you have lived. Promise that you will be as kind to me as I have been to you."

24And Abraham said, "I promise to treat you the same way you have treated me." 25Then Abraham complained to Abimelech because Abimelech's servants had captured a well of water.

26But Abimelech said, "I don't know who did this. You never told me about this before today!"

27So Abraham and Abimelech made an agreement. Abraham gave Abimelech some sheep and cattle as proof of the agreement. 28Abraham also put seven*a* female lambs in front of Abimelech.

29Abimelech asked Abraham, "Why did you put these seven female lambs by themselves?"

30Abraham answered, "When you accept these lambs from me, it will be proof that I dug this well."

31So after that, the well was called Beersheba.*b* Abraham gave the well this name because it was the place where they made a promise to each other.

32So Abraham and Abimelech made an agreement at Beersheba. Then Abimelech and Phicol, his military commander, went back to the country of the Philistines.

33Abraham planted a special tree at Beersheba and prayed to the Lord, the God who lives forever. 34And Abraham lived as a stranger for a long time in the country of the Philistines.

Abraham, Kill Your Son

22 1After these things God decided to test Abraham's faith. God said to him, "Abraham!"

And he said, "Yes!"

2Then God said, "Take your son to the land of Moriah and kill your son there as a sacrifice* for me. This must be Isaac, your only son, the one you love. Use him as a burnt offering* on one of the mountains there. I will tell you which mountain."

3In the morning Abraham got up and saddled his donkey. He took Isaac and two servants with him. He cut the wood for the sacrifice. Then they went to the place where God told them to go. 4After they traveled three days, Abraham looked up, and in the distance he saw the place where they were going. 5Then he said to his servants, "Stay here with the donkey. The boy and I will go to that place and worship. Then we will come back to you later."

6Abraham took the wood for the sacrifice and put it on his son's shoulder. Abraham took the special knife and fire. Then both he

a21:28 seven The Hebrew word for "seven" is like the Hebrew word for "oath" or "promise," and it is like the last part of the name Beersheba. The seven animals were proof of this promise.
b21:31 Beersheba This name means "well of the oath."

and his son went together to the place for worship.

⁷Isaac said to his father Abraham, "Father!"

Abraham answered, "Yes, son?"

Isaac said, "I see the wood and the fire. But where is the lamb we will burn as a sacrifice?"

⁸Abraham answered, "God himself is providing the lamb for the sacrifice, my son."

So both Abraham and his son went together to that place. ⁹When they came to the place where God told them to go, Abraham built an altar.* He carefully laid the wood on the altar. Then he tied up his son Isaac and laid him on the altar on top of the wood. ¹⁰Then Abraham reached for his knife to kill his son.

¹¹But the angel of the LORD stopped him. The angel called from heaven and said, "Abraham, Abraham!"

Abraham answered, "Yes?"

¹²The angel said, "Don't kill your son or hurt him in any way. Now I can see that you do respect and obey God. I see that you are ready to kill your son, your only son, for me."

¹³Then Abraham noticed a ram whose horns were caught in a bush. So Abraham went and took the ram. He offered it, instead of his son, as a sacrifice to God. ¹⁴So Abraham gave that place a name, "The LORD Provides."ᵃ Even today people say, "On the mountain of the LORD, he will give us what we need."ᵇ

¹⁵The angel of the LORD called to Abraham from heaven a second time. ¹⁶The angel said, "You were ready to kill your only son for me. Since you did this for me, I make you this promise: I, the LORD, promise that ¹⁷I will surely bless you and give you as many descendants as the stars in the sky. There will be as many people as sand on the seashore. And your people will live in cities that they will take from their enemies. ¹⁸Every nation on the earth will be blessed through your descendants. I will do this because you obeyed me."

¹⁹Then Abraham went back to his servants. They all traveled back to Beersheba, and Abraham stayed there.

²⁰After all these things happened, a message was sent to Abraham. It said, "Your brother Nahor and his wife Milcah have children now. ²¹The first son is Uz. The second son is Buz. The third son is Kemuel, the father of Aram. ²²Then there are Kesed, Hazo, Pildash, Jidlaph, and Bethuel." ²³Bethuel was the father of Rebekah. Milcah was the mother of these eight sons, and Nahor was the father. Nahor was Abraham's brother. ²⁴Also Nahor had four other sons from his slave woman* Reumah. The sons were Tebah, Gaham, Tahash, and Maacah.

Sarah Dies

23 ¹Sarah lived to be 127 years old. ²She died in the city of Kiriath Arba (Hebron) in the land of Canaan.* Abraham was very sad and cried for her there. ³Then he left his dead wife and went to talk to the Hittites. He said, ⁴"I am only a foreigner staying in your country. I have no place to bury my wife. Please give me some land so that I can bury her."

⁵The Hittites answered Abraham, ⁶"Sir, you are a great leaderᶜ among us. You can have the best place we have to bury your dead. You can have any of our burying places that you want. None of us will stop you from burying your wife there."

⁷Abraham got up and bowed to the people. ⁸He said to them, "If you really want to help me bury my dead wife, speak to Ephron the son of Zohar for me. ⁹I would like to buy the cave of Machpelah, which belongs to Ephron. It is at the end of his field. I will pay him the full price. I want all of you to be witnesses that I am buying it as a burial place."

¹⁰Ephron was sitting there among the people. He answered Abraham, ¹¹"No, sir. Here in front of my people, I give you that land and the cave on it so that you can bury your wife."

¹²Abraham bowed before the Hittites. ¹³He said to Ephron before all the people, "But I want to give you the full price for the field. Accept my money, and I will bury my dead."

¹⁴Ephron answered Abraham, ¹⁵"Sir, listen to me. Ten poundsᵈ of silver mean nothing to you or me. Take the land and bury your dead wife."

¹⁶Abraham understood that Ephron was telling him the price of the land.ᵉ So Abraham paid him for the land. He weighed out ten pounds of silver for Ephron and gave it to the merchant.ᶠ

¹⁷⁻¹⁸So the field of Ephron changed owners. This field was in Machpelah, near Mamre. Abraham became the owner of the field, the cave in it, and all the trees in the field. Everyone in the city saw the agreement between Ephron and Abraham. ¹⁹After this, Abraham buried his wife Sarah in the cave of that field near Mamre (Hebron) in the land of Canaan. ²⁰Abraham bought the field and the cave in it from the Hittites. So this became his property to be used as a burial place.

ᵃ**22:14 The LORD Provides** Hebrew, "Yahweh Yireh," which can mean "the LORD sees" or "the LORD gives."
ᵇ**22:14 On the mountain … need** Or "On this mountain the LORD can be seen."
ᶜ**23:6 great leader** Literally, "God's prince."
ᵈ**23:15 Ten pounds** Literally, "400 shekels" (4.6 kg). Also in verse 16.
ᵉ**23:16 Abraham understood … the land** Literally, "Abraham heard."
ᶠ**23:16 merchant** Someone who earns their living by buying and selling things. Here, this is probably a person who was helping Abraham and Ephron write the contract in verses 17 and 18.

A Wife for Isaac

24 ¹Abraham lived to be a very old man. The LORD blessed him and everything he did. ²Abraham's oldest servant was in charge of everything he owned. Abraham called that servant to him and said, "Put your hand under my leg.ᵃ ³Now I want you to make a promise to me. Promise to me before the LORD, the God of heaven and earth, that you will not allow my son to marry a girl from Canaan.* We live among these people, but don't let him marry a Canaanite girl. ⁴Go back to my country, to my own people, to find a wife for my son Isaac. Bring her here to him."

⁵The servant said to him, "Maybe this woman will not want to come back with me to this land. If that happens, should I take your son with me to your homeland?"

⁶Abraham said to him, "No, don't take my son to that place. ⁷The LORD, the God of heaven, brought me from my homeland to this place. That place was the home of my father and the home of my family, but he promised that this new land would belong to my family. May the LORD send his angel before you so that you can choose a wife for my son. ⁸If the girl refuses to come with you, you will be free from this promise. But you must not take my son back to that place."

⁹So the servant put his hand under his master's leg and made the promise.

The Search Begins

¹⁰The servant took ten of Abraham's camels and left that place. The servant carried with him many different kinds of beautiful gifts. He went to Mesopotamia, to Nahor's city. ¹¹In the evening, when the women come out to get water, he went to the water well outside the city. He made the camels kneel down at the well.

¹²The servant said, "LORD, you are the God of my master Abraham. Allow me to find a wife for his son today. Please show this kindness to my master Abraham. ¹³Here I am, standing by this well of water, and the young women from the city are coming out to get water. ¹⁴I am waiting for a special sign to know which is the right one for Isaac. This is the special sign: I will say to the girl, 'Please put your jar down so that I can drink.' I will know that she is the right one if she says, 'Drink, and I will also give water to your camels.' If that happens, it will be proof that she is the right one for Isaac and that you have shown kindness to my master."

A Wife Is Found

¹⁵Before the servant finished praying, a young woman named Rebekah came to

the well. She was the daughter of Bethuel. (Bethuel was the son of Milcah and Nahor, Abraham's brother.) Rebekah came to the well with her water jar on her shoulder. ¹⁶She was very pretty. She was a virgin; no man had ever had sexual relations with her. She went down to the well and filled her jar. ¹⁷Then the servant ran to her and said, "Please give me a little water to drink from your jar."

¹⁸Rebekah quickly lowered the jar from her shoulder and gave him a drink. She said, "Drink this, sir." ¹⁹As soon as she finished giving him something to drink, Rebekah said, "I will also pour some water for your camels." ²⁰So Rebekah quickly poured all the water from her jar into the drinking trough for the camels. Then she ran to the well to get more water, and she gave water to all the camels.

²¹The servant quietly watched her. He wanted to be sure that the LORD had given him an answer and had made his trip successful. ²²After the camels finished drinking, he gave Rebekah a gold ring that weighed ¼ ounce.ᵇ He also gave her two gold arm bracelets that weighed 2 ouncesᶜ each. ²³The servant asked, "Who is your father? And is there a place in your father's house for me and my men to sleep?"

²⁴Rebekah answered, "My father is Bethuel, the son of Milcah and Nahor." ²⁵Then she said, "Yes, we have straw and other food for your camels and a place for you to sleep."

²⁶The servant bowed and worshiped the LORD. ²⁷He said, "Praise be to the LORD, the God of my master Abraham. The LORD has been kind and loyal to him by leading me to his own people."

²⁸Then Rebekah ran and told her family about all these things. ²⁹⁻³⁰She had a brother named Laban. She told him what the man had said to her. Laban was listening to her. And when he saw the ring and the bracelets on his sister's arms, he ran out to the well. There the man was, standing by the camels at the well. ³¹Laban said, "Sir, you are welcome to come in!ᵈ You don't have to stand outside here. I have prepared a room for you to sleep in and a place for your camels."

³²So Abraham's servant went into the house. Laban unloaded his camels and gave them straw and feed. Then he gave Abraham's servant water so that he and the men with him could wash their feet. ³³Laban then gave him food to eat, but the servant refused to eat. He said, "I will not eat until I have told you why I came."

So Laban said, "Then tell us."

Bargaining for Rebekah

³⁴The servant said, "I am Abraham's servant. ³⁵The LORD has greatly blessed my master in

---

ᵃ**24:2** *Put your hand under my leg* This was a sign of a very important promise that Abraham trusted his servant to keep.
ᵇ**24:22** *1/4 ounce* Literally, "1 *beka*" (5.75 g).
ᶜ**24:22** *2 ounces* Literally, "5 measures" (57.5 g).
ᵈ**24:31** *Sir, you are welcome to come in* Literally, "Come in, blessed of the LORD!"

everything. My master has become a great man. The Lord has given him many flocks of sheep and herds of cattle. He has much silver and gold and many servants. He has many camels and donkeys. ³⁶Sarah was my master's wife. When she was very old, she gave birth to a son, and my master has given everything he owns to that son. ³⁷My master forced me to make a promise to him. He said to me, 'You must not allow my son to marry a girl from Canaan.* We live among these people, but I don't want him to marry one of the Canaanite girls. ³⁸So you must promise to go to my father's country. Go to my family and choose a wife for my son.' ³⁹I said to my master, 'Maybe the woman will not come back to this place with me.' ⁴⁰But my master said to me, 'I serve the Lord, and he will send his angel with you and help you. You will find a wife for my son among my people there. ⁴¹But if you go to my father's country, and they refuse to give you a wife for my son, you will be free from this promise.'

⁴²"Today I came to this well and said, 'Lord, God of my master Abraham, please make my trip successful. ⁴³I will stand by this well and wait for a young woman to come to get water. Then I will say, "Please give me water from your jar to drink." ⁴⁴The right woman will answer in a special way. She will say, "Drink this water, and I will also get water for your camels." That way I will know that she is the one the Lord has chosen for my master's son.'

⁴⁵"Before I finished praying, Rebekah came out to the well to get water. She had her water jar on her shoulder as she went to get water from the well. I asked her to give me some water. ⁴⁶She quickly lowered the jar from her shoulder and poured me some water. Then she said, 'Drink this, and I'll get some water for your camels.' So I drank the water, and she gave water to my camels. ⁴⁷Then I asked her, 'Who is your father?' She answered, 'My father is Bethuel the son of Milcah and Nahor.' Then I gave her the ring and bracelets for her arms. ⁴⁸I bowed my head and worshiped the Lord. I praised the Lord, the God of my master Abraham. I thanked him for leading me straight to the granddaughter of my master's brother. ⁴⁹Now, tell me, will you be kind and loyal to my master and give him your daughter? Or will you refuse to give her to him? Tell me so that I will know what I should do."

⁵⁰Then Laban and Bethuel answered, "We see that this is from the Lord, so there is nothing we can say to change it. ⁵¹Here is Rebekah. Take her and go. Let her marry your master's son. This is what the Lord wants."

⁵²When Abraham's servant heard this, he bowed to the ground before the Lord. ⁵³Then he gave Rebekah the gifts he brought. He gave her beautiful clothes and gold and silver jewelry. He also gave expensive gifts to her mother and brother. ⁵⁴Then he and his men had something to eat and drink, and they spent the night there. Early the next morning they got up and the servant said, "Now we must go back to my master."

⁵⁵Rebekah's mother and her brother said, "Let Rebekah stay with us for a short time. Let her stay with us ten days. After that she can go."

⁵⁶But the servant said to them, "Don't make me wait. The Lord has made my trip successful. Now let me go back to my master."

⁵⁷Rebekah's brother and mother said, "We will call Rebekah and ask her what she wants to do." ⁵⁸They called her and asked her, "Do you want to go with this man now?"

Rebekah said, "Yes, I will go."

⁵⁹So they allowed Rebekah to go with Abraham's servant and his men. Her nurse also went with them. ⁶⁰While Rebekah was leaving they said to her,

"Our sister, may you be the mother of
     millions of people,
   and may your descendants defeat their
     enemies and take their cities."

⁶¹Then Rebekah and her nurse got on the camels and followed the servant and his men. So the servant took Rebekah and left.

⁶²Isaac had left Beer Lahai Roi and was now living in the Negev.* ⁶³One evening he went out to the field to think.ᵃ He looked up and saw the camels coming from far away. ⁶⁴Rebekah also looked and saw Isaac. Then she jumped down from the camel. ⁶⁵She said to the servant, "Who is that young man walking in the field to meet us?"

The servant said, "That is my master's son." So Rebekah covered her face with her veil.

⁶⁶The servant told Isaac everything that had happened. ⁶⁷Then Isaac brought the girl into his mother's tent. Rebekah became his wife that day. Isaac loved her very much. So he was comforted after his mother's death.

Abraham's Family

25 ¹Abraham married again. His new wife was named Keturah. ²She gave birth to Zimran, Jokshan, Medan, Midian, Ishbak, and Shuah. ³Jokshan was the father of Sheba and Dedan. The people of Asshur,ᵇ Leum, and Letush were descendants of Dedan. ⁴The sons of Midian were Ephah, Epher, Hanoch, Abida, and Eldaah. All these sons came from the marriage of Abraham and Keturah. ⁵⁻⁶Before Abraham died, he gave some gifts to his sons who were from his slave women.* He sent them to the East,ᶜ away from Isaac. Then Abraham gave everything he owned to Isaac.

⁷Abraham lived to be 175 years old. ⁸Then

ᵃ**24:63** *think* Or "to go for a walk."
ᵇ**25:3** *Asshur* Or "Assyria."
ᶜ**25:5** *East* This usually means the area between the Tigris and Euphrates rivers as far east as the Persian Gulf.

he grew weak and died. He had lived a long and satisfying life. He died and went to be with his people. ⁹His sons Isaac and Ishmael buried him in the cave of Machpelah. This cave is in the field of Ephron, the son of Zohar. It was east of Mamre. ¹⁰This is the same cave that Abraham bought from the Hittites. He was buried there with his wife Sarah. ¹¹After Abraham died, God blessed Isaac. Isaac was living at Beer Lahai Roi.

¹²This is the list of Ishmael's family. Ishmael was Abraham and Hagar's son. (Hagar was Sarah's Egyptian maid.) ¹³These are the names of Ishmael's sons: The first son was Nebaioth; then Kedar was born, then Adbeel, Mibsam, ¹⁴Mishma, Dumah, Massa, ¹⁵Hadad, Tema, Jetur, Naphish, and Kedemah. ¹⁶These were the names of Ishmael's sons. Each son had his own camp that became a small town. The twelve sons were leaders over their own people. ¹⁷Ishmael lived to be 137 years old. Then he died and went to be with his people. ¹⁸His descendants camped throughout the desert area from Havilah to Shur, near Egypt, all the way to Assyria. And they often attacked his brothers' people.ᵃ

Isaac's Family

¹⁹This is the story of Isaac. Abraham had a son named Isaac. ²⁰When Isaac was 40 years old, he married Rebekah. Rebekah was from Paddan Aram. She was Bethuel's daughter and the sister of Laban the Aramean. ²¹Isaac's wife could not have children. So Isaac prayed to the Lord for her. The Lord heard Isaac's prayer, and he allowed Rebekah to become pregnant.

²²While Rebekah was pregnant, the babies inside her struggled with one another. She prayed to the Lord and said, "What is happening to me?" ²³The Lord said to her,

"The leaders of two nations
   are in your body.
Two nations will come from you,
   and they will be divided.
One of them will be stronger,
   and the older will serve the younger."

²⁴When the right time came, Rebekah gave birth to twins. ²⁵The first baby was red. His skin was like a hairy robe. So he was named Esau.ᵇ ²⁶When the second baby was born, he was holding tightly to Esau's heel. So that baby was named Jacob.ᶜ Isaac was 60 years old when Jacob and Esau were born.

²⁷The boys grew up. Esau became a skilled hunter, who loved to be out in the fields. But Jacob was a quiet man, who stayed at home. ²⁸Isaac loved Esau. He liked to eat the animals Esau killed. But Rebekah loved Jacob.

²⁹One day Esau came back from hunting. He was tired and weak from hunger. Jacob was boiling a pot of beans. ³⁰So Esau said to Jacob, "I am weak with hunger. Let me have some of that red soup." (That is why people call him "Red."ᵈ)

³¹But Jacob said, "You must sell me your rights as the firstborn son.ᵉ"

³²Esau said, "I am almost dead with hunger, so what good are these rights to me now?"

³³But Jacob said, "First, promise me that you will give them to me." So Esau made an oath* to him and sold his rights as the firstborn son to Jacob. ³⁴Then Jacob gave Esau bread and lentilᶠ soup. Esau ate the food, had something to drink, and then left. So Esau showed that he did not care about his rights as the firstborn son.

Isaac Lies to Abimelech

26 ¹Now there was a famine.* This was like the famine that happened during Abraham's life. So Isaac went to the town of Gerar, to King Abimelech of the Philistines. ²The Lord spoke to Isaac and said, "Don't go down to Egypt. Live in the land that I commanded you to live in. ³Stay in this land, and I will be with you. I will bless you. I will give you and your family all these lands. I will do what I promised to Abraham your father. ⁴I will make your family as many as the stars of heaven, and I will give all these lands to your family. Through your descendantsᵍ every nation on earth will be blessed. ⁵I will do this because your father Abraham obeyed my words and did what I said. He obeyed my commands, my laws, and my rules."

⁶So Isaac settled in Gerar. ⁷His wife Rebekah was very beautiful. The men of that place asked Isaac about Rebekah. He said, "She is my sister." He was afraid to tell them Rebekah was his wife. He was afraid the men would kill him so that they could have her.

⁸After Isaac had lived there a long time, Abimelech looked out of his window and saw Isaac and his wife enjoying one another. ⁹Abimelech called for Isaac and said, "This woman is your wife. Why did you tell us that she was your sister?"

Isaac said to him, "I was afraid that you would kill me so that you could have her."

¹⁰Abimelech said, "You have done a bad thing to us. One of our men might have had

---

ᵃ**25:18** *attacked his brothers' people* See Gen. 16:12. This could also mean "He fell *(settled)* alongside all his brothers."

ᵇ**25:25** *Esau* This name is like the word meaning "hairy."

ᶜ**25:26** *Jacob* This name is like the Hebrew word meaning "heel." It also means "the one who follows" or "tricky."

ᵈ**25:30** *Red* Literally, "Edom," a name that means "red."

ᵉ**25:31** *rights as the firstborn son* Usually, after the father died, the firstborn son got half of the father's property and became the new head of the family. Also in verse 34.

ᶠ**25:34** *lentil* A type of bean.

ᵍ**26:4** *descendants* Or "Descendant." See Gal. 3:16.

sex with your wife. Then he would be guilty of a great sin."

¹¹So Abimelech gave a warning to all the people. He said, "No one must hurt this man or this woman. If anyone hurts them, they will be killed."

Isaac Becomes Rich

¹²Isaac planted fields in that place, and that year he gathered a great harvest. The Lord blessed him very much. ¹³Isaac became rich. He gathered more and more wealth until he became a very rich man. ¹⁴He had many flocks and herds of animals. He also had many slaves. All the Philistines were jealous of him. ¹⁵So they destroyed all the wells that Isaac's father Abraham and his servants had dug many years before. They filled them with sand. ¹⁶Abimelech said to Isaac, "Leave our country. You have become much more powerful than we are."

¹⁷So Isaac left that place and camped near the little river of Gerar. He stayed there and lived. ¹⁸Long before this time, Abraham had dug many wells. After he died, the Philistines filled the wells with sand. So Isaac went back and dug those wells again. He gave them the same names his father had given them. ¹⁹Isaac's servants also dug a well near the little river and found fresh water.ᵃ ²⁰But the men who herded sheep in the Valley of Gerar argued with Isaac's servants. They said, "This water is ours." So Isaac named that well Esek.ᵇ He gave it that name because it was the place where they had argued with him.

²¹Then Isaac's servants dug another well. But there was an argument over this well too. So Isaac named that well Sitnah.ᶜ

²²Isaac moved from there and dug another well. No one came to argue about this well. So Isaac named it Rehoboth.ᵈ He said, "Now the Lord has found a place for us. We will grow and be successful in this place."

²³From there Isaac went to Beersheba. ²⁴The Lord spoke to him that night and said, "I am the God of your father Abraham. Don't be afraid. I am with you, and I will bless you. I will make your family great. I will do this because of my servant Abraham." ²⁵So Isaac built an altar and worshiped the Lord in that place. He set up camp there, and his servants dug a well.

²⁶Abimelech came from Gerar to see Isaac. He brought with him Ahuzzath, his advisor, and Phicol, the commander of his army. ²⁷Isaac asked, "Why have you come to see me? You were not friendly to me before. You even forced me to leave your country."

²⁸They answered, "Now we know that the Lord is with you. We think that we should make an agreement. We want you to make a promise to us. ²⁹We did not hurt you; now you should promise not to hurt us. We sent you away, but we sent you away in peace. Now it is clear that the Lord has blessed you."

³⁰So Isaac gave a party for them. They all ate and drank. ³¹Early the next morning each man made a promise and a vow.* Then the men left in peace.

³²On that day Isaac's servants came and told him about the well they had dug. The servants said, "We found water in that well." ³³So Isaac named it Shibah.ᵉ And that city is still called Beersheba.ᶠ

Esau's Wives

³⁴When Esau was 40 years old, he married two Hittite women. One was Judith the daughter of Beeri. The other was Basemath the daughter of Elon. ³⁵These marriages made Isaac and Rebekah very unhappy.

Jacob Tricks Isaac

27 ¹Isaac grew old, and his eyes became so weak that he could not see clearly. One day he called his older son Esau to him and said, "Son!"

Esau answered, "Here I am."

²Isaac said, "I am old. Maybe I will die soon. ³So take your bow and arrows and go hunting. Kill an animal for me to eat. ⁴Prepare the food that I love. Bring it to me, and I will eat it. Then I will bless you before I die." ⁵So Esau went hunting.

Rebekah was listening when Isaac told this to his son Esau. ⁶Rebekah said to her son Jacob, "Listen, I heard your father talking to your brother Esau. ⁷Your father said, 'Kill an animal for me to eat. Prepare the food for me, and I will eat it. Then I will bless you before I die.' ⁸So listen, son, and do what I tell you. ⁹Go out to our goats and bring me two young ones. I will prepare them the way your father loves them. ¹⁰Then you will carry the food to your father, and he will bless you before he dies."

¹¹But Jacob told his mother Rebekah, "My brother Esau is a hairy man. I am not hairy like him. ¹²If my father touches me, he will know that I am not Esau. Then he will not bless me—he will curse* me because I tried to trick him."

¹³So Rebekah said to him, "I will accept the blame if there is trouble. Do what I said. Go get the goats for me."

¹⁴So Jacob went out and got two goats and brought them to his mother. His mother cooked the goats in the special way that Isaac loved. ¹⁵Then Rebekah took the clothes that

---

ᵃ**26:19** *fresh water* Or "an underground stream." Literally, "living water."

ᵇ**26:20** *Esek* This means "argument" or "fight."

ᶜ**26:21** *Sitnah* This means "hatred" or "being an enemy."

ᵈ**26:22** *Rehoboth* This means "open place" or "crossroads."

ᵉ**26:33** *Shibah* A Hebrew word meaning "seven" or "oath."

ᶠ**26:33** *Beersheba* This name means "well of the oath."

her older son Esau loved to wear. She put these clothes on the younger son Jacob. ¹⁶She took the skins of the goats and put them on Jacob's hands and on his neck. ¹⁷Then she got the food she had cooked and gave it to Jacob.

¹⁸Jacob went to his father and said, "Father."

His father answered, "Yes, son. Who are you?"

¹⁹Jacob said to his father, "I am Esau, your first son. I have done what you told me. Now sit up and eat the meat from the animals that I hunted for you. Then you can bless me."

²⁰But Isaac said to his son, "How have you hunted and killed the animals so quickly?"

Jacob answered, "Because the LORD your God allowed me to find the animals quickly."

²¹Then Isaac said to Jacob, "Come near to me so that I can feel you, my son. If I can feel you, I will know if you are really my son Esau."

²²So Jacob went to Isaac his father. Isaac felt him and said, "Your voice sounds like Jacob's voice, but your arms are hairy like the arms of Esau." ²³Isaac did not know it was Jacob, because his arms were hairy like Esau's. So Isaac blessed Jacob.

²⁴Isaac said, "Are you really my son Esau?"
Jacob answered, "Yes, I am."

The Blessing for Jacob

²⁵Then Isaac said, "Bring me the food. I will eat it and bless you." So Jacob gave him the food, and he ate it. Then Jacob gave him some wine, and he drank it.

²⁶Then Isaac said to him. "Son, come near and kiss me." ²⁷So Jacob went to his father and kissed him. When Isaac smelled Esau's clothes, he blessed him and said,

"My son smells like the fields the LORD has
     blessed.
²⁸ May the LORD give you plenty of rain,
     good crops, and wine.
²⁹ May the nations serve you
     and many people bow down to you.
   You will rule over your brothers.
   Your mother's sons will bow down to you
     and obey you.

"Whoever curses* you will be cursed.
   Whoever blesses you will be blessed."

Esau's "Blessing"

³⁰Isaac finished blessing Jacob. Then, just as Jacob left his father Isaac, Esau came in from hunting. ³¹Esau prepared the food in the special way his father loved. He brought it to his father and said, "Father, I am your son. Get up and eat the meat from the animals that I killed for you. Then you can bless me."

³²But Isaac said to him, "Who are you?"
He answered, "I am your son—your first son—Esau."

³³Then Isaac became so upset that he began to shake. He said, "Then who was it that cooked and brought me food before you came? I ate it all, and I blessed him. Now it is too late to take back my blessing."

³⁴When Esau heard his father's words, he became very angry and bitter. He cried out and said to his father, "Then bless me also, father!"

³⁵Isaac said, "Your brother tricked me! He came and took your blessing!"

³⁶Esau said, "His name is Jacob.ᵃ That is the right name for him. He has tricked me twice. He took away my rights as the firstborn son.ᵇ And now he has taken away my blessing." Then Esau said, "Have you saved any blessing for me?"

³⁷Isaac answered, "I have already given Jacob the power to rule over you. And I said all his brothers would be his servants. I have given him the blessing for much grain and wine. There is nothing left to give you, my son."

³⁸But Esau continued to beg his father. "Do you have only one blessing, father? Bless me also, father!" Esau began to cry.

³⁹Then Isaac said to him,

"You will not live on good land.
     You will not have much rain.
⁴⁰ You will have to fight to live,
     and you will be a slave to your brother.
   But when you fight to be free,
     you will break away from his control."

Jacob Leaves the Country

⁴¹After that Esau hated Jacob because of this blessing. Esau said to himself, "My father will soon die, and after we are finished with that, I will kill Jacob."

⁴²Rebekah heard about Esau's plan to kill Jacob. She sent for Jacob and said to him, "Listen, your brother Esau is planning to kill you. ⁴³So, son, do what I say. My brother Laban is living in Haran. Go to him and hide. ⁴⁴Stay with him for a short time until your brother stops being angry. ⁴⁵When your brother forgets what you did to him, I will send a servant to bring you back. I don't want to lose both of my sons the same day."

⁴⁶Then Rebekah said to Isaac, "Your son Esau married Hittite women. I am very upset about this, because they are not our people. I'll have nothing to live for if Jacob marries one of these women!"

28

¹Isaac called Jacob and blessed him. Then Isaac gave him a command and said, "You must not marry a Canaanite woman. ²So leave this place and go to Paddan Aram. Go to the house of Bethuel, your

---

ᵃ**27:36 Jacob** This name is like the Hebrew word meaning "heel." It also means "the one who follows" or "tricky."

ᵇ**27:36 rights as the firstborn son** Usually, after the father died, the firstborn son got half of the father's property and became the new head of the family.

mother's father. Laban, your mother's brother, lives there. Marry one of his daughters. ³I pray that God All-Powerful*ᵃ* will bless you and give you many children. I pray that you will become the father of a great nation ⁴and that God will bless you and your children the same way he blessed Abraham. And I pray that you will own the land where you live. This is the land God gave to Abraham."

⁵So Isaac sent Jacob to Rebekah's brother in Paddan Aram. Jacob went to Laban, son of Bethuel the Aramean. Laban was the brother of Rebekah, the mother of Jacob and Esau.

⁶Esau learned that his father Isaac blessed Jacob and sent him away to Paddan Aram to find a wife here. He also learned that Isaac commanded Jacob not to marry a Canaanite woman. ⁷Esau learned that Jacob obeyed his father and his mother and went to Paddan Aram. ⁸Esau saw from this that his father did not want his sons to marry Canaanite women. ⁹Esau already had two wives, but he went to Abraham's son Ishmael and married another woman, Mahalath, the daughter of Ishmael. Mahalath was Nebaioth's sister.

Jacob's Dream at Bethel

¹⁰Jacob left Beersheba and went to Haran. ¹¹The sun had already set when he came to a good place to spend the night. He took a rock there and laid his head on it to sleep. ¹²Jacob had a dream. He dreamed there was a ladder that was on the ground and reached up into heaven. He saw the angels of God going up and down the ladder. ¹³And then Jacob saw the Lord standing by the ladder. He said, "I am the Lord, the God of your grandfather Abraham. I am the God of Isaac. I will give you the land that you are lying on now. I will give this land to you and to your children. ¹⁴You will have as many descendants as there are particles of dust on the earth. They will spread east and west, north and south. All the families on earth will be blessed because of you and your descendants.

¹⁵"I am with you, and I will protect you everywhere you go. I will bring you back to this land. I will not leave you until I have done what I have promised."

¹⁶Then Jacob woke up and said, "I know that the Lord is in this place, but I did not know he was here until I slept."

¹⁷Jacob was afraid and said, "This is a very great place. This is the house of God. This is the gate to heaven."

¹⁸Jacob got up very early in the morning. He took the rock he had slept on and set it up on its edge. Then he poured oil on the rock. In this way he made it a memorial to God. ¹⁹The name of that place was Luz, but Jacob named it Bethel.*ᵇ*

²⁰Then Jacob made a promise. He said, "If God will be with me, and if he will protect me on this trip, and if he gives me food to eat and clothes to wear, ²¹and if I return in peace to my father's house—if he does all these things—then the Lord will be my God. ²²I am setting this stone up as a memorial stone. It will show that this is a holy* place for God, and I will give God one-tenth of all he gives me."

Jacob Meets Rachel

29¹Then Jacob continued his trip. He went to the country in the East. ²He looked and saw a well in the field. There were three flocks of sheep lying near the well, where the sheep drank water. There was a large rock covering the mouth of the well. ³When all the flocks were gathered there, the shepherds would roll the rock away from the well. Then all the sheep could drink from the water. After the sheep were full, the shepherds would put the rock back in its place.

⁴Jacob said to the shepherds there, "Brothers, where are you from?"

They answered, "We are from Haran."

⁵Then Jacob said, "Do you know Laban, the son of Nahor?"

The shepherds answered, "We know him."

⁶Then Jacob said, "How is he?"

They answered, "He is well. Look, that is his daughter Rachel coming now with his sheep."

⁷Jacob said, "Look, it is still day and long before the sun sets. It is not yet time for the animals to be gathered together for the night. So give them water and let them go back into the field."

⁸But they said, "We cannot do that until all the flocks are gathered together. Then we will move the rock from the well, and all the sheep will drink."

⁹While Jacob was talking with the shepherds, Rachel came with her father's sheep. (It was her job to take care of the sheep.) ¹⁰Rachel was Laban's daughter. Laban was the brother of Rebekah, Jacob's mother. When Jacob saw Rachel, he went and moved the rock and gave water to the sheep. ¹¹Then Jacob kissed Rachel and cried. ¹²He told her that he was from her father's family. He told her that he was the son of Rebekah. So Rachel ran home and told her father.

¹³When Laban heard the news about his sister's son Jacob, he ran to meet him. Laban hugged him and kissed him and brought him to his house. Jacob told Laban everything that had happened. ¹⁴Then Laban said, "This is wonderful! You are from my own family." So Jacob stayed with Laban for a month.

Laban Tricks Jacob

¹⁵One day Laban said to Jacob, "You are a relative of mine. It is not right for you to

---

*ᵃ***28:3 God All-Powerful** Literally, "El Shaddai."
*ᵇ***28:19 Bethel** A town in Israel. This name means "God's house."

continue working for me without pay. What should I pay you?"

16Now Laban had two daughters. The older was Leah and the younger was Rachel. 17Leah's eyes were gentle,*a* but Rachel was beautiful. 18Jacob loved Rachel, so he said to Laban, "I will work seven years for you if you will allow me to marry your daughter Rachel."

19Laban said, "It would be better for her to marry you than someone else. So stay with me."

20So Jacob stayed and worked for Laban for seven years. But it seemed like a very short time because he loved Rachel very much.

21After seven years Jacob said to Laban, "Give me Rachel so that I can marry her. My time of work for you is finished."

22So Laban gave a party for all the people in that place. 23That night Laban brought his daughter Leah to Jacob. Jacob and Leah had sexual relations together. 24(Laban gave his maid Zilpah to his daughter to be her maid.) 25In the morning Jacob saw that it was Leah he had slept with, and he said to Laban, "You have tricked me. I worked hard for you so that I could marry Rachel. Why did you trick me?"

26Laban said, "In our country we don't allow the younger daughter to marry before the older daughter. 27Continue for the full week of the marriage ceremony, and I will also give you Rachel to marry. But you must serve me another seven years."

28So Jacob did this and finished the week. Then Laban gave him his daughter Rachel as a wife. 29(Laban gave his maid Bilhah to his daughter Rachel to be her maid.) 30So Jacob had sexual relations with Rachel also. And Jacob loved Rachel more than Leah. Jacob worked for Laban for another seven years.

Jacob's Family Grows

31The LORD saw that Jacob loved Rachel more than Leah, so he made it possible for Leah to have children. But Rachel did not have any children.

32Leah gave birth to a son, and she named him Reuben.*b* She named him this because she said, "The LORD has seen my troubles. My husband does not love me. So now maybe my husband will love me."

33Leah became pregnant again and had another son. She named this son Simeon.*c* She said, "The LORD has heard that I am not loved, so he gave me this son."

34Leah became pregnant again and had another son. She named this son Levi.*d* She

said, "Now, surely my husband will love me. I have given him three sons."

35Then Leah gave birth to another son. She named this son Judah.*e* Leah named him this because she said, "Now I will praise the LORD." Then Leah stopped having children.

30 1Rachel saw that she was not giving Jacob any children. She became jealous of her sister Leah. So Rachel said to Jacob, "Give me children, or I will die!"

2Jacob became angry with Rachel and said, "I am not God. He is the one who has caused you to not have children."

3Then Rachel said, "You can have my maid Bilhah. Sleep with her, and she will have a child for me.*f* Then I can be a mother through her."

4So Rachel gave Bilhah to her husband Jacob. He had sexual relations with Bilhah. 5She became pregnant and gave birth to a son for Jacob.

6Rachel said, "God has listened to my prayer. He decided to give me a son." So she named this son Dan.*g*

7Bilhah became pregnant again and gave Jacob a second son. 8Rachel said, "I have fought hard to compete with my sister, and I have won." So she named that son Naphtali.*h*

9Leah saw that she could have no more children. So she gave her slave girl Zilpah to Jacob. 10Then Zilpah had a son. 11Leah said, "I am lucky." So she named the son Gad.*i* 12Zilpah gave birth to another son. 13Leah said, "I am very happy! Now women will call me happy." So she named that son Asher.*j*

14During the wheat harvest Reuben went into the fields and found some special flowers.*k* He brought them to his mother Leah. But Rachel said to Leah, "Please give me some of your son's flowers."

15Leah answered, "You have already taken away my husband. Now you are trying to take away my son's flowers."

But Rachel answered, "If you will give me your son's flowers, you can sleep with Jacob tonight."

16Jacob came in from the fields that night. Leah saw him and went out to meet him. She said, "You will sleep with me tonight. I have

---

*e*29:35 Judah This name is like the word meaning "He is praised."

*f*30:3 she will have a child for me Literally, "she will give birth on my knees, and I, too, will have a son through her."

*g*30:6 Dan This is like the Hebrew word meaning "to decide" or "to judge."

*h*30:8 Naphtali This is like the Hebrew word meaning "my struggle."

*i*30:11 Gad This is like the Hebrew word meaning "lucky" or "fortunate."

*j*30:13 Asher This is like the Hebrew word meaning "blessed" or "happy."

*k*30:14 special flowers Or "mandrakes." The Hebrew word means "love plant." People thought these plants could help women have babies.

---

*a*29:17 Leah's eyes were gentle This might be a polite way of saying Leah was not very pretty.

*b*29:32 Reuben This is like the Hebrew word meaning "Look, a son."

*c*29:33 Simeon This is like the Hebrew word meaning "He hears."

*d*29:34 Levi This is like the Hebrew word meaning "accompany," "be joined together," or "become close."

paid for you with my son's flowers." So Jacob slept with Leah that night.

[17]Then God allowed Leah to become pregnant again. She gave birth to a fifth son. [18]She said, "God has given me a reward because I gave my slave to my husband." So she named her son Issachar.[a]

[19]Leah became pregnant again and gave birth to a sixth son. [20]She said, "God has given me a fine gift. Now surely Jacob will accept me, because I have given him six sons." So she named this son Zebulun.[b]

[21]Later, Leah gave birth to a daughter. She named her Dinah.

[22]Then God heard Rachel's prayer and made it possible for Rachel to have children. [23]She became pregnant and gave birth to a son. She said, "God has taken away my shame." [24]Rachel named the son Joseph,[c] saying, "May the Lord give me another son."

Jacob Tricks Laban

[25]After the birth of Joseph, Jacob said to Laban, "Now let me go back to my own homeland. [26]Give me my wives and my children. I have earned them by working for you. You know that I served you well."

[27]Laban said to him, "Please, let me say something. I know[d] that the Lord has blessed me because of you. [28]Tell me what I should pay you, and I will give it to you."

[29]Jacob answered, "You know that I have worked hard for you. Your flocks have grown and been well while I cared for them. [30]When I came, you had little. Now you have much, much more. Every time I did something for you, the Lord blessed you. Now it is time for me to work for myself—it is time to do things for my family."

[31]Laban asked, "Then what should I give you?"

Jacob answered, "I don't want you to give me anything! I only want you to let me do this one thing: I will go back and take care of your sheep. [32]But let me go through all your flocks today and take every lamb with spots or stripes. Let me take every black young goat and every female goat with stripes or spots. That will be my pay. [33]In the future you can easily see if I am honest. You can come to look at my flocks. If I have any goat that isn't spotted or any sheep that isn't black, you will know that I stole it."

[34]Laban answered, "I agree to that. We will do what you ask." [35]But that day Laban hid all the male goats that had spots. And he hid all the female goats that had spots on them. He also hid all the black sheep. Laban told his sons to watch these sheep. [36]So the sons took all the spotted animals and led them to another place. They traveled for three days. Jacob stayed and took care of all the animals that were left.

[37]Then Jacob cut green branches from poplar and almond trees. He stripped off some of the bark so that the branches had white stripes on them. [38]He put the branches in front of the flocks at the watering places. When the animals came to drink, they also mated in that place. [39]Then when the goats mated in front of the branches, the young that were born were spotted, striped, or black.

[40]Jacob separated the spotted and the black animals from the other animals in the flock. He kept his animals separate from Laban's. [41]Any time the stronger animals in the flock were mating, Jacob put the branches before their eyes. The animals mated near those branches. [42]But when the weaker animals mated, Jacob did not put the branches there. So the young animals born from the weak animals were Laban's. And the young animals born from the stronger animals were Jacob's. [43]In this way Jacob became very rich. He had large flocks, many servants, camels, and donkeys.

Time to Leave—Jacob Runs Away

31 [1]One day Jacob heard Laban's sons talking. They said, "Jacob has taken everything that our father owned. He has become rich—and he has taken all this wealth from our father." [2]Then Jacob noticed that Laban was not as friendly as he had been in the past. [3]The Lord said to Jacob, "Go back to your own land where your ancestors* lived. I will be with you."

[4]So Jacob told Rachel and Leah to meet him in the field where he kept his flocks of sheep and goats. [5]He said to them, "I have seen that your father is angry with me. He was always friendly with me in the past, but now he is not. [6]You both know that I have worked as hard as I could for your father. [7]But he cheated me. He has changed my pay ten times. But during all this time, God protected me from all of Laban's tricks.

[8]"At one time Laban said, 'You can keep all the goats with spots. This will be your pay.' After he said this, all the animals gave birth to spotted goats, so they were all mine. But then Laban said, 'I will keep the spotted goats. You can have all the striped goats. That will be your pay.' After he said this, all the animals gave birth to striped goats. [9]So God has taken the animals away from your father and has given them to me.

[10]"I had a dream during the time when the animals were mating. I saw that the only male goats that were mating were the ones with stripes and spots. [11]The angel of God spoke to me in that dream. The angel said, 'Jacob!'

"I answered, 'Yes!'

---

[a]**30:18 Issachar** This is like the Hebrew word meaning "reward" or "salary."

[b]**30:20 Zebulun** This is like the Hebrew word meaning "praise" or "honor."

[c]**30:23–24 Joseph** This is like the Hebrew word meaning "to add."

[d]**30:27 know** Or "guessed," "divined," or "concluded."

¹²"The angel said, 'Look, only the striped and spotted goats are mating. I am causing this to happen. I have seen all the wrong things Laban has been doing to you. I am doing this so that you can have all the new baby goats. ¹³I am the God who came to you at Bethel, and there you made an altar, poured olive oil on it, and made a promise to me. Now I want you to be ready to go back to the country where you were born.'"

¹⁴Rachel and Leah answered Jacob, "Our father has nothing to give us when he dies. ¹⁵He treated us like strangers. He sold us to you, and then he spent all the money that should have been ours. ¹⁶God took all this wealth from our father, and now it belongs to us and our children. So you should do whatever God told you to do."

¹⁷So Jacob prepared for the trip. He put his children and his wives on camels. ¹⁸Then they began traveling back to the land of Canaan,* where his father lived. All the flocks of animals that Jacob owned walked ahead of them. He carried everything with him that he had gotten while he lived in Paddan Aram.

¹⁹While Laban was gone to cut the wool from his sheep, Rachel went into his house and stole the false gods that belonged to her father.

²⁰Jacob tricked Laban the Aramean. He did not tell Laban he was leaving. ²¹Jacob took his family and everything he owned and left quickly. They crossed the Euphrates River and traveled toward the hill country of Gilead.

²²Three days later Laban learned that Jacob had run away. ²³So he gathered his men together and began to chase Jacob. After seven days Laban found Jacob near the hill country of Gilead. ²⁴That night God came to Laban in a dream and said, "Be careful! Be careful of every word you say to Jacob."

The Search for the Stolen Gods

²⁵The next morning Laban caught up with Jacob. Jacob had set up his camp on the mountain, so Laban and all his men set up their camp in the hill country of Gilead. ²⁶Laban said to Jacob, "Why did you trick me? Why did you take my daughters like they were women you captured during war? ²⁷Why did you run away without telling me? If you had told me, I would have given you a party. There would have been singing and dancing with music. ²⁸You didn't even let me kiss my grandchildren and my daughters goodbye. You were very foolish to do this! ²⁹I have the power to really hurt you. But last night the God of your father came to me in a dream. He warned me not to hurt you in any way. ³⁰I know that you want to go back to your home. That is why you left. But why did you steal the gods from my house?"

³¹Jacob answered, "I left without telling you, because I was afraid. I thought you would take your daughters away from me. ³²But I did

not steal your gods. If you find anyone here with me who has taken your gods, they will be killed. Your men will be my witnesses. You can look for anything that belongs to you. Take anything that is yours." (Jacob did not know that Rachel had stolen Laban's gods.)

³³So Laban went and looked through Jacob's camp. He looked in Jacob's tent and then in Leah's tent. Then he looked in the tent where the two slave women stayed, but he did not find the gods from his house. Then he went into Rachel's tent. ³⁴Rachel had hidden the gods inside her camel's saddle, and she was sitting on them. Laban looked through the whole tent, but he did not find the gods.

³⁵And Rachel said to her father, "Father, don't be angry with me. I am not able to stand up before you. I am having my monthly time of bleeding." So Laban looked through the camp, but he did not find the gods from his house.

³⁶Then Jacob became very angry and said, "What wrong have I done? What law have I broken? What right do you have to chase me and stop me? ³⁷You looked through everything I own and found nothing that belongs to you. If you found something, show it to me. Put it here where our men can see it. Let our men decide which one of us is right. ³⁸I have worked 20 years for you. During all that time none of the baby sheep and goats died during birth. And I have not eaten any of the rams from your flocks. ³⁹Any time a sheep was killed by wild animals, I always paid for the loss myself. I did not take the dead animal to you and say that it was not my fault. But I was robbed day and night. ⁴⁰In the daytime the sun took away my strength, and at night sleep was taken from my eyes by the cold. ⁴¹I worked 20 years like a slave for you. For the first 14 years I worked to win your two daughters. The last six years I worked to earn your animals. And during that time you changed your pay ten times. ⁴²But the God of my ancestors,* the God of Abraham and the Fear of Isaac,ᵃ was with me. If God had not been with me, you would have sent me away with nothing. But he saw the trouble that I had and the work that I did, and last night God proved that I am right."

Jacob and Laban's Treaty

⁴³Laban said to Jacob, "These women are my daughters. These children belong to me, and these animals are mine. Everything you see here belongs to me, but I can do nothing to keep my daughters and their children. ⁴⁴So I am ready to make an agreement with you. We will set up a pile of stones to show that we have an agreement."

⁴⁵So Jacob found a large rock and put it there to show that he had made an agreement. ⁴⁶He told his men to find some more rocks

ᵃ**31:42** *Fear of Isaac* A name for God.

and to make a pile of rocks. Then they ate beside the pile of rocks. ⁴⁷Laban named that place Yegar Sahadutha.ᵃ But Jacob named that place Galeed.ᵇ

⁴⁸Laban said to Jacob, "This pile of rocks will help us both remember our agreement." That is why Jacob called the place Galeed.

⁴⁹Then Laban said, "Let the LORD watch over us while we are separated from each other." So that place was also named Mizpah.ᶜ

⁵⁰Then Laban said, "If you hurt my daughters, remember that God will punish you. If you marry other women, remember that God is watching. ⁵¹Here are the rocks that I have put between us, and here is the special rock to show that we made an agreement. ⁵²This pile of rocks and this one special rock both help us to remember our agreement. I will never go past these rocks to fight against you, and you must never go on my side of these rocks to fight against me. ⁵³May the God of Abraham, the God of Nahor, and the God of their ancestors* judge us guilty if we break this agreement."

Jacob's father, Isaac, called God "Fear." So Jacob used that name to make the promise. ⁵⁴Then Jacob killed an animal and offered it as a sacrifice* on the mountain. And he invited his men to come and share a meal. After they finished eating, they spent the night on the mountain. ⁵⁵Early the next morning Laban kissed his grandchildren and his daughters goodbye. He blessed them and went back home.

Jacob Prepares to Meet Esau

32 ¹Jacob also left that place. While he was traveling, he saw God's angels. ²When he saw them, he said, "This is God's camp!" So Jacob named that place Mahanaim.ᵈ

³Jacob's brother Esau was living in the area called Seir in the hill country of Edom.* Jacob sent messengers to Esau. ⁴He told them, "Tell this to my master Esau: 'Your servant Jacob says, I have lived with Laban all these years. ⁵I have many cattle, donkeys, flocks, and servants. Sir, I am sending you this message to ask you to accept us.'"

⁶The messengers came back to Jacob and said, "We went to your brother Esau. He is coming to meet you. He has 400 men with him."

⁷Jacob was very frightened and worried. He divided the people who were with him and all the flocks, herds, and camels into two groups. ⁸Jacob thought, "If Esau comes and destroys one group, the other group can run away and be saved."

⁹Then Jacob said, "God of my father Abraham! God of my father Isaac! LORD, you told me to come back to my country and to my family. You said that you would do good to me. ¹⁰You have been very kind to me. You did many good things for me. The first time I traveled across the Jordan River, I owned nothing—only my walking stick. But now I own enough things to have two full groups. ¹¹I ask you to please save me from my brother Esau. I am afraid that he will come and kill us all, even the mothers with the children. ¹²Lord, you said to me, 'I will be good to you. I will increase your family and make your children as many as the sands of the sea. There will be too many to count.'"

¹³Jacob stayed in that place for the night. He prepared some things to give to Esau as a gift. ¹⁴He took 200 female goats and 20 male goats, 200 female sheep and 20 male sheep. ¹⁵He took 30 camels and their colts, 40 cows and 10 bulls, 20 female donkeys and 10 male donkeys. ¹⁶He gave each flock of animals to his servants. Then he said to them, "Separate each group of animals. Go ahead of me and keep some space between each herd." ¹⁷Jacob gave them their orders. To the servant with the first group of animals he said, "When Esau my brother comes to you and asks you, 'Whose animals are these? Where are you going? Whose servant are you?' ¹⁸then you should answer, 'These animals belong to your servant Jacob. He sent them as a gift to you, my master Esau. And he also is coming behind us.'"

¹⁹Jacob also ordered the second servant, the third servant, and all the other servants to do the same thing. He said, "You will say the same thing to Esau when you meet him. ²⁰You will say, 'This is a gift to you, and your servant Jacob is behind us.'"

Jacob thought, "If I send these men ahead with gifts, maybe Esau will forgive me and accept me." ²¹So Jacob sent the gifts to Esau, but he stayed that night in the camp.

²²During the night, Jacob got up and began moving his two wives, his two maids, and his eleven sons across the Jabbok River at the crossing. ²³After he sent his family across the river, he sent across everything he had.

The Fight With God

²⁴Jacob was left alone, and a man came and wrestled with him. The man fought with him until the sun came up. ²⁵When the man saw that he could not defeat Jacob, he touched Jacob's leg and put it out of joint.

²⁶Then the man said to Jacob, "Let me go. The sun is coming up."

But Jacob said, "I will not let you go. You must bless me."

²⁷And the man said to him, "What is your name?"

And Jacob said, "My name is Jacob."

²⁸Then the man said, "Your name will not

ᵃ**31:47** *Yegar Sahadutha* Aramaic words meaning "rock pile of the agreement."
ᵇ**31:47** *Galeed* Another name for Gilead. This Hebrew name means "rock pile of the agreement."
ᶜ**31:49** *Mizpah* This means "a place to watch from."
ᵈ**32:2** *Mahanaim* This name means "two camps."

be Jacob. Your name will now be Israel.*a* I give you this name because you have fought with God and with men, and you have won."

²⁹Then Jacob asked him, "Please tell me your name."

But the man said, "Why do you ask my name?" Then the man blessed Jacob at that place.

³⁰So Jacob named that place Peniel.*b* He said, "At this place, I saw God face to face, but my life was spared." ³¹Then the sun came up as Jacob left Peniel. He was limping because of his leg. ³²So even today, the people of Israel don't eat the muscle that is on the hip joint, because this is the muscle where Jacob was hurt.

Jacob Meets Esau

33 ¹Jacob looked and saw Esau coming with 400 men. Jacob divided his family into four groups. Leah and her children were in one group, Rachel and Joseph were in one group, and the two maids and their children were in two groups. ²Jacob put the maids with their children first. Then he put Leah and her children behind them, and he put Rachel and Joseph in the last place.

³Jacob himself went out before them. While he was walking toward his brother Esau, he bowed down to the ground seven times.

⁴When Esau saw Jacob, he ran to meet him. He put his arms around Jacob, hugged his neck, and kissed him. Then they both cried. ⁵Esau looked up and saw the women and children. He said, "Who are all these people with you?"

Jacob answered, "These are the children that God gave me. God has been good to me."

⁶Then the two maids and the children with them went to Esau. They bowed down before him. ⁷Then Leah and the children with her went to Esau and bowed down. And then Rachel and Joseph went to him and bowed down.

⁸Esau said, "Who were all those people I saw while I was coming here? And what were all those animals for?"

Jacob answered, "These are my gifts to you so that you might accept me."

⁹But Esau said, "You don't have to give me gifts, brother. I have enough for myself."

¹⁰Jacob said, "No, I beg you! If you really accept me, please accept the gifts I give you. I am very happy to see your face again. It is like seeing the face of God. I am very happy to see that you accept me. ¹¹So I beg you to also accept the gifts I give you. God has been very good to me. I have more than I need." Because Jacob begged Esau to take the gifts, he accepted them.

¹²Then Esau said, "Now you can continue your journey. I will go with you."

¹³But Jacob said to him, "You know that my children are weak. And I must be careful with my flocks and their young animals. If I force them to walk too far in one day, all the animals will die. ¹⁴So you go on ahead. I will follow you slowly. I will go slowly enough for the cattle and other animals to be safe and so that my children will not get too tired. I will meet you in Seir."

¹⁵So Esau said, "Then I will leave some of my men to help you."

But Jacob said, "That is very kind of you, but there is no need to do that." ¹⁶So that day Esau started on his trip back to Seir. ¹⁷But Jacob went to Succoth.*c* There he built a house for himself and small barns for his cattle. That is why the place was named Succoth.

¹⁸Jacob safely ended his trip from Paddan Aram when he came to the town of Shechem in Canaan.* He made his camp in a field near the city. ¹⁹He bought the field where he camped from the family of Hamor, father of Shechem. He paid 100 pieces of silver for it. ²⁰He built an altar there to honor God. He named the place "El,*d* the God of Israel."

The Rape of Dinah

34 ¹One day, Dinah, the daughter of Leah and Jacob, went out to see the women of that place. ²She was seen by Shechem, the son of Hamor the Hivite, who ruled that area. Shechem took Dinah and raped her. ³But he was so attracted to her that he fell in love and began expressing his feelings to her. ⁴He told his father, "Please get this girl for me so that I can marry her."

⁵Jacob learned that Shechem had done this very bad thing to his daughter. But all his sons were out in the fields with the cattle. So he did nothing until they came home. ⁶Then Shechem's father, Hamor, came out to talk with Jacob.

⁷In the fields Jacob's sons heard the news about what had happened. They were very angry because Shechem had brought shame to Israel by raping Jacob's daughter. They came in from the fields as soon as they heard about the terrible thing Shechem had done.

⁸But Hamor talked to Dinah's brothers and said, "My son Shechem wants Dinah very much. Please let him marry her. ⁹This marriage will show we have a special agreement. Then our men can marry your women, and your men can marry our women. ¹⁰You can live in the same land with us. You will be free to own the land and to trade here."

¹¹Shechem also talked to Jacob and to Dinah's brothers and said, "Please accept me. I will do anything you ask me to do. ¹²I will

---

*a***32:28** *Israel* This name might mean "he fights for God," "he fights with God," or "God fights."
*b***32:30** *Peniel* A name that means "the face of God."

*c***33:17** *Succoth* A town east of the Jordan River. This name means "temporary shelters."
*d***33:20** *El* A Hebrew name for God.

give you any gift^a you want if you will only allow me to marry Dinah. I will give you anything you ask, but let me marry her."

¹³Jacob's sons decided to lie to Shechem and his father because Shechem had done such a bad thing to their sister Dinah. ¹⁴The brothers said to them, "We cannot allow our sister to marry you because you are not yet circumcised.* That would bring us shame. ¹⁵But we will allow you to marry her if you do this one thing: Every man in your town must be circumcised like us. ¹⁶Then your men can marry our women, and our men can marry your women. Then we will become one people. ¹⁷If you refuse to be circumcised, we will take Dinah away."

¹⁸This agreement made Hamor and Shechem very happy. ¹⁹Shechem was very happy to do what Dinah's brothers asked.

Shechem was the most honored man in his family. ²⁰Hamor and Shechem went to the meeting place of their city. They spoke to the men of the city and said, ²¹"These people want to be friends with us. We want to let them live in our land and be at peace with us. We have enough land for all of us. We are free to marry their women, and we are happy to give them our women to marry. ²²But there is one thing that all our men must agree to do. All our men must agree to be circumcised like they are. ²³If we do this, we will become rich from all their cattle and other animals. We should make this agreement with them so that they will stay here with us." ²⁴All the men who heard this in the meeting place agreed with Hamor and Shechem. And every man was circumcised at that time.

²⁵Three days later the men who were circumcised were still sore. Two of Jacob's sons, Simeon and Levi, knew that the men would be weak at this time. So they went to the city and killed all the men there. ²⁶Dinah's brothers, Simeon and Levi, killed Hamor and his son Shechem. Then they took Dinah out of Shechem's house and left. ²⁷Jacob's sons went to the city and stole everything that was there because of what Shechem had done to their sister. ²⁸So the brothers took all their animals, all their donkeys, and everything else in the city and in the fields. ²⁹The brothers took everything those people owned. They even took their wives and children.

³⁰But Jacob said to Simeon and Levi, "You have caused me a lot of trouble. All the people in this place will hate me. All the Canaanites and the Perizzites will turn against me. There are only a few of us. If the people in this place gather together to fight against us, I will be destroyed. And all our people will be destroyed with me."

³¹But the brothers said, "Should we let these people treat our sister like a prostitute? They were wrong to do that to our sister!"

Jacob in Bethel

35 ¹God said to Jacob, "Go to the town of Bethel.^b That is where I appeared to you when you were running away from your brother Esau. Live there and make an altar* to honor me as El,^c the God who appeared to you."

²So Jacob told his family and all the other people with him, "Destroy all these foreign gods that you have. Make yourselves pure. Put on clean clothes. ³We will leave here and go to Bethel. There I will build an altar to the God who has always helped me during times of trouble. He has been with me wherever I have gone."

⁴So the people gave Jacob all the foreign gods they had, and they gave him all the rings they were wearing in their ears. He buried everything under an oak tree near the town called Shechem.

⁵Then Jacob and his sons left that place. The people in the surrounding cities wanted to follow and kill them, but God filled them with such great fear that they did not go after them. ⁶So Jacob and his people went to Luz, which is now called Bethel. It is in the land of Canaan.* ⁷Jacob built an altar there. He named the place "El Bethel."^d Jacob chose this name because that is the place where God first appeared to him when he was running from his brother.

⁸Deborah, Rebekah's nurse, died there. They buried her under the oak tree at Bethel. They named that place Allon Bacuth.^e

Jacob's New Name

⁹When Jacob came back from Paddan Aram, God appeared to him again. God blessed Jacob ¹⁰and said to him, "Your name is Jacob, but I will change that name. You will no longer be called Jacob. Your new name will be Israel.^f" So God named him Israel.

¹¹God said to him, "I am God All-Powerful,^g and I give you this blessing: Have many children and grow into a great nation. Other nations and other kings will come out of you. ¹²I gave Abraham and Isaac some special land. Now I give the land to you and to all your people who will live after you." ¹³Then God left that place. ¹⁴⁻¹⁵Jacob set up a memorial stone* there. He made the rock holy* by pouring wine and oil on it. This was a special place

^b**35:1** *Bethel* A town in Israel. This name means "God's house."
^c**35:1** *El* A Hebrew name for God.
^d**35:7** *El Bethel* A name that means "the God of Bethel."
^e**35:8** *Allon Bacuth* This name means "the oak tree of sadness."
^f**35:10** *Israel* This name might mean "he fights for God," "he fights with God," or "God fights."
^g**35:11** *God All-Powerful* Literally, "El Shaddai."

because God spoke to Jacob there, and Jacob named the place Bethel.

Rachel Dies Giving Birth

[16]Jacob and his group left Bethel. Before they came to Ephrath, Rachel began giving birth to her baby. [17]She was having a lot of trouble with this birth. She was in great pain. When her nurse saw this, she said, "Don't be afraid, Rachel. You are giving birth to another son."

[18]Rachel died while giving birth to the son. Before dying, she named the boy Benoni.[a] But Jacob called him Benjamin.[b]

[19]Rachel was buried on the road to Ephrath (that is, Bethlehem). [20]Jacob put a special rock on Rachel's grave to honor her. That special rock is still there today. [21]Then Israel* continued his journey. He camped just south of Eder tower.[c]

[22]Israel stayed there for a short time. While he was there, Reuben slept with Israel's slave woman* Bilhah, and Israel heard about it.

The Family of Israel

Jacob had twelve sons.

[23]Jacob and Leah's sons were his firstborn* son Reuben, Simeon, Levi, Judah, Issachar, and Zebulun.

[24]Jacob and Rachel's sons were Joseph and Benjamin.

[25]Bilhah was Rachel's maid. Jacob and Bilhah's sons were Dan and Naphtali.

[26]Zilpah was Leah's maid. Jacob and Zilpah's sons were Gad and Asher.

These are Jacob's sons who were born in Paddan Aram.

[27]Jacob went to his father Isaac at Mamre in Kiriath Arba (Hebron). This is where Abraham and Isaac had lived. [28]Isaac lived 180 years. [29]Then Isaac became weak and died and went to be with his people. He had lived a long and full life. His sons Esau and Jacob buried him.

Esau's Family

36 [1]This is the history of the family of Esau (Edom). [2]Esau married women from the land of Canaan.* His wives were Adah, the daughter of Elon the Hittite, Oholibamah, the daughter of Anah, the son of Zibeon the Hivite, and [3]Basemath, Ishmael's daughter, the sister of Nebaioth. [4]Esau and Adah had a son named Eliphaz. Basemath had a son named Reuel. [5]Oholibamah had three sons: Jeush, Jalam, and Korah. These were Esau's sons who were born in the land of Canaan.

[6-8]Jacob and Esau's families became too big for the land in Canaan to support them all, so Esau moved away from his brother Jacob. He took his wives, sons, daughters, all his slaves, cattle and other animals, and everything else that he had gotten in Canaan and moved to the hill country of Seir.[d] (Esau is also named Edom.)

[9]Esau is the father of the people of Edom.* These are the names of Esau's family living in the hill country of Seir:

[10]Esau and Adah's son was Eliphaz. Esau and Basemath's son was Reuel.

[11]Eliphaz had five sons: Teman, Omar, Zepho, Gatam, and Kenaz. [12]Eliphaz also had a slave woman* named Timna. Timna and Eliphaz had a son named Amalek.

[13]Reuel had four sons: Nahath, Zerah, Shammah, and Mizzah.

These were Esau's grandsons from his wife Basemath.

[14]Esau's third wife was Oholibamah, the daughter of Anah. (Anah was the son of Zibeon.) Esau and Oholibamah's children were Jeush, Jalam, and Korah.

[15]These are the family groups that came from Esau:

Esau's first son was Eliphaz. From Eliphaz came Teman, Omar, Zepho, Kenaz, [16]Korah, Gatam, and Amalek.

All these family groups came from Esau's wife Adah.

[17]Esau's son Reuel was the father of these families: Nahath, Zerah, Shammah, and Mizzah.

All these families came from Esau's wife Basemath.

[18]Esau's wife Oholibamah, daughter of Anah, gave birth to Jeush, Jalam, and Korah. These three men were the leaders of their families. [19]They were all sons of Esau and leaders of the family groups of Edom.[e]

[20]Seir, a Horite man, lived in Edom before Esau. These are the sons of Seir: Lotan, Shobal, Zibeon, Anah, [21]Dishon, Ezer, and Dishan. These sons were all Horite family leaders from Seir in Edom.

[22]Lotan was the father of Hori and Heman.[f] (Timna was Lotan's sister.)

[23]Shobal was the father of Alvan, Manahath, Ebal, Shepho, and Onam.

[24]Zibeon had two sons, Aiah and Anah. Anah is the man who found the springs in the desert while he was caring for his father's donkeys.

[25]Anah was the father of Dishon and Oholibamah.

[26]Dishon had four sons. They were Hemdan, Eshban, Ithran, and Keran.

[27]Ezer had three sons. They were Bilhan, Zaavan, and Akan.

[28]Dishan had two sons. They were Uz and Aran.

---

[a]**35:18 Benoni** This name means "son of my suffering."

[b]**35:18 Benjamin** This name means "right-hand" or "favorite son."

[c]**35:21 Eder tower** Or "Migdal Eder."

[d]**36:6–8 Seir** A mountain range in Edom.

[e]**36:19 Esau … Edom** Two names for the man Esau and the country Edom.

[f]**36:22 Heman** Or "Homam."

29These are the names of the leaders of the Horite families: Lotan, Shobal, Zibeon, Anah, 30Dishon, Ezer, and Dishan. These men were the leaders of the families that lived in the country of Seir. 31At that time there were kings in Edom. Edom had kings a long time before Israel did.

32Bela son of Beor was a king who ruled in Edom. He ruled over the city of Dinhabah. 33When Bela died, Jobab became king. Jobab was the son of Zerah from Bozrah. 34When Jobab died, Husham ruled. Husham was from the land of the Temanite. 35When Husham died, Hadad ruled that area. Hadad was the son of Bedad. (He was the man who defeated Midian in the country of Moab.) Hadad was from the city of Avith. 36When Hadad died, Samlah ruled that country. Samlah was from Masrekah. 37When Samlah died, Shaul ruled that area. Shaul was from Rehoboth by the River. 38When Shaul died, Baal Hanan ruled that country. Baal Hanan was the son of Acbor. 39When Baal Hanan died, Hadad*a* ruled that country. Hadad was from the city of Pau. His wife's name was Mehetabel, the daughter of Matred. (Mezahab was Matred's father.)

40–43Esau was the father of the Edomite families: Timna, Alvah, Jetheth, Oholibamah, Elah, Pinon, Kenaz, Teman, Mibzar, Magdiel, and Iram. Each of these families lived in an area that was called by the same name as their family.

Joseph the Dreamer

37 1Jacob stayed and lived in the land of Canaan.* This is the same land where his father had lived. 2This is the story of Jacob's family.

Joseph was a young man, 17 years old. His job was to take care of the sheep and the goats. Joseph did this work with his brothers, the sons of Bilhah and Zilpah. (Bilhah and Zilpah were his father's wives.) Joseph told his father about the bad things that his brothers did. 3Joseph was born at a time when his father Israel* was very old, so Israel loved him more than he loved his other sons. Jacob gave him a special coat, which was long and very beautiful.*b* 4When Joseph's brothers saw that their father loved Joseph more than he loved them, they hated their brother because of this. They refused to say nice things to him.

5One time Joseph had a special dream. Later, he told his brothers about this dream, and after that his brothers hated him even more.

6Joseph said, "I had a dream. 7We were all working in the field, tying stacks of wheat together. Then my stack got up. It stood there while all of your stacks of wheat made a circle around mine and bowed down to it."

8His brothers said, "Do you think this means that you will be a king and rule over us?" His brothers hated Joseph more now because of the dreams he had about them.

9Then Joseph had another dream, and he told his brothers about it. He said, "I had another dream. I saw the sun, the moon, and eleven stars bowing down to me."

10Joseph also told his father about this dream, but his father criticized him. His father said, "What kind of dream is this? Do you believe that your mother, your brothers, and I will bow down to you?" 11Joseph's brothers continued to be jealous of him, but his father thought about all these things and wondered what they could mean.

12One day Joseph's brothers went to Shechem to care for their father's sheep. 13Jacob said to Joseph, "Go to Shechem. Your brothers are there with my sheep."

Joseph answered, "I will go."

14His father said, "Go and see if your brothers are safe. Come back and tell me if my sheep are all fine." So Joseph's father sent him from the Valley of Hebron to Shechem.

15At Shechem, Joseph got lost. A man found him wandering in the fields. The man said, "What are you looking for?"

16Joseph answered, "I am looking for my brothers. Can you tell me where they are with their sheep?"

17The man said, "They have already gone away. I heard them say that they were going to Dothan." So Joseph followed his brothers and found them in Dothan.

Joseph Sold Into Slavery

18Joseph's brothers saw him coming from far away. They decided to make a plan to kill him. 19They said to each other, "Here comes Joseph the dreamer. 20We should kill him now while we can. We could throw his body into one of the empty wells and tell our father that a wild animal killed him. Then we will show him that his dreams are useless."

21But Reuben wanted to save Joseph. He said, "Let's not kill him. 22We can put him into a well without hurting him." Reuben planned to save Joseph and send him back to his father. 23When Joseph came to his brothers, they attacked him and tore off his long and beautiful coat. 24Then they threw him into an empty well that was dry.

25While Joseph was in the well, the brothers sat down to eat. They looked up and saw a group of traders*c* traveling from Gilead to Egypt. Their camels were carrying many different spices and riches. 26So Judah said to his brothers, "What profit will we get if we kill our brother and hide his death? 27We will profit more if we sell him to these traders. Then we will not be guilty of killing our own brother." The other brothers agreed. 28When

---

*a***36:39** *Hadad* Or "Hadar."
*b***37:3** *beautiful* The Hebrew means "striped," or possibly, "many colored."

*c***37:25** *traders* Literally, "Ishmaelites."

the Midianite traders came by, the brothers took Joseph out of the well and sold him to the traders for 20 pieces of silver. The traders took him to Egypt.

²⁹Reuben had been gone, but when he came back to the well, he saw that Joseph was not there. He tore his clothes to show that he was upset. ³⁰Reuben went to the brothers and said, "The boy is not in the well! What will I do?" ³¹The brothers killed a goat and put the goat's blood on Joseph's beautiful coat. ³²Then the brothers showed the coat to their father. And the brothers said, "We found this coat. Is this Joseph's coat?"

³³His father saw the coat and knew that it was Joseph's. He said, "Yes, that is his! Maybe some wild animal has killed him. My son Joseph has been eaten by a wild animal!" ³⁴Jacob was so sorry about his son that he tore his clothes. Then Jacob put on special clothes to show that he was sad. He continued to be sad about his son for a long time. ³⁵All of Jacob's sons and daughters tried to comfort him, but Jacob was never comforted. He said, "I will be sorry for my son until the day I die."ᵃ So Jacob continued to be sad for his son Joseph.

³⁶The Midianite traders later sold Joseph in Egypt. They sold him to Potiphar, the captain of the Pharaoh's guards.

Judah and Tamar

38 ¹About that time, Judah left his brothers and went to stay with a man named Hirah from the town of Adullam. ²Judah met a Canaanite girl there and married her. The girl's father was named Shua. ³The Canaanite girl gave birth to a son and named him Er. ⁴Later, she gave birth to another son and named him Onan. ⁵Then she had another son named Shelah. Judah lived in Kezib when his third son was born.

⁶Judah chose a woman named Tamar to be the wife of his first son Er. ⁷But Er did many bad things. The Lᴏʀᴅ was not happy with him, so the Lᴏʀᴅ killed him. ⁸Then Judah said to Er's brother Onan, "Go and sleep with your dead brother's wife.ᵇ Become like a husband to her. If children are born, they will belong to your brother Er."

⁹Onan knew that the children from this union would not belong to him. He had sexual relations with Tamar, but he did not allow himself to stay inside her. ¹⁰This made the Lᴏʀᴅ angry. So he killed Onan also. ¹¹Then Judah said to his daughter-in-law Tamar, "Go back to your father's house. Stay there and don't marry until my young son Shelah grows up." Judah was afraid that Shelah would also

be killed like his brothers. So Tamar went back to her father's home.

¹²Later, Judah's wife, the daughter of Shua, died. After Judah's time of sadness, he went to Timnah with his friend Hirah from Adullam. Judah went to Timnah to have the wool cut from his sheep. ¹³Tamar learned that Judah, her father-in-law, was going to Timnah to cut the wool from his sheep. ¹⁴Tamar always wore clothes that showed that she was a widow. So she put on some different clothes and covered her face with a veil. Then she sat down near the road going to Enaim, a town near Timnah. Tamar knew that Judah's younger son Shelah was now grown up, but Judah would not make plans for her to marry him.

¹⁵Judah traveled on that road and saw her, but he thought that she was a prostitute. (Her face was covered with a veil like a prostitute.) ¹⁶So he went to her and said, "Let me have sex with you." (Judah did not know that she was Tamar, his daughter-in-law.)

She said, "How much will you give me?"

¹⁷Judah answered, "I will send you a young goat from my flock."

She answered, "I agree to that. But first you must give me something to keep until you send me the goat."

¹⁸Judah asked, "What do you want me to give you as proof that I will send you the goat?"

Tamar answered, "Give me your seal and its stringᶜ and your walking stick." Judah gave these things to her. Then Judah and Tamar had sexual relations, and she became pregnant. ¹⁹Then Tamar went home, took off her veil that covered her face, and again put on the special clothes that showed she was a widow.

²⁰Later, Judah sent his friend Hirah to Enaim to give the prostitute the goat he promised. Judah also told Hirah to get the special seal and the walking stick from her, but Hirah could not find her. ²¹He asked some of the men at the town of Enaim, "Where is the prostitute who was here by the road?"

The men answered, "There has never been a prostitute here."

²²So Judah's friend went back to Judah and said, "I could not find the woman. The men who live in that place said that there was never a prostitute there."

²³So Judah said, "Let her keep the things. I don't want people to laugh at us. I tried to give her the goat, but we could not find her. That is enough."

Tamar Is Pregnant

²⁴About three months later, someone told Judah, "Your daughter-in-law Tamar sinned like a prostitute, and now she is pregnant."

ᵃ**37:35 I will be sorry ... die** Literally, "I will go down to my son in Sheol (the place of death) in sadness."
ᵇ**38:8 Go and sleep ... wife** In Israel if a man died without children, one of his brothers would take the widow. If a child was born, it would be considered the dead man's child.

ᶜ**38:18 seal ... string** People wrote a contract, folded it, tied it with string, put wax or clay on the string, and pressed the seal onto it to seal it. This was like signing the agreement. Also in verse 25.

Then Judah said, "Take her out and burn her."

25The men went to Tamar to kill her, but she sent a message to her father-in-law that said, "The man who made me pregnant is the man who owns these things. Look at them. Whose are they? Whose special seal and string is this? Whose walking stick is this?"

26Judah recognized these things and said, "She is right. I was wrong. I did not give her my son Shelah like I promised." And Judah did not sleep with her again.

27The time came for Tamar to give birth. She was going to have twins. 28While she was giving birth, one baby put his hand out. The nurse tied a red string on the hand and said, "This baby was born first." 29But that baby pulled his hand back in, so the other baby was born first. So the nurse said, "You were able to break out first!" So they named him Perez.a 30After this, the other baby was born. This was the baby with the red string on his hand. They named him Zerah.b

Joseph Is Sold to Potiphar in Egypt

39 1The tradersc who bought Joseph took him down to Egypt. They sold him to the captain of Pharaoh's guard, Potiphar. 2The Lord helped Joseph become a successful man. Joseph lived in the house of his master, Potiphar the Egyptian.

3Potiphar saw that the Lord was with Joseph and that the Lord helped Joseph be successful in everything he did. 4So Potiphar was very happy with Joseph. He allowed Joseph to work for him and to help him rule the house. Joseph was the ruler over everything Potiphar owned. 5After Joseph was made the ruler over the house, the Lord blessed the house and everything that Potiphar owned. The Lord also blessed everything that grew in Potiphar's fields. The Lord did this because of Joseph. 6So Potiphar allowed Joseph to take responsibility for everything in the house. Potiphar didn't have to worry about anything except deciding what to eat.

Joseph Refuses Potiphar's Wife

Joseph was a very handsome, good-looking man. 7After some time, the wife of Joseph's master began to pay special attention to him. One day she said to him, "Sleep with me."

8But Joseph refused. He said, "My master trusts me with everything in his house. He has given me responsibility for everything here. 9My master has made me almost equal to him in his house. I cannot sleep with his wife! That is wrong! It is a sin against God."

10The woman talked with Joseph every day,

but he refused to sleep with her. 11One day Joseph went into the house to do his work. He was the only man in the house at the time. 12His master's wife grabbed his coat and said to him, "Come to bed with me." But Joseph ran out of the house so fast that he left his coat in her hand.

13The woman saw that Joseph had left his coat in her hand and had run out of the house. 14She called to the men outside and said, "Look! This Hebrew slave was brought here to make fun of us. He came in and tried to attack me, but I screamed. 15My scream scared him and he ran away, but he left his coat with me." 16Then she kept his coat until her husband, Joseph's master, came home. 17She told her husband the same story. She said, "This Hebrew slave you brought here tried to attack me! 18But when he came near me, I screamed. He ran away, but he left his coat."

19Joseph's master listened to what his wife said, and he became very angry. 20So Potiphar put Joseph into the prison where the king's enemies were held, and that is where Joseph remained.

Joseph in Prison

21The Lord was with Joseph and continued to show his kindness to him, so the commander of the prison guards began to like Joseph. 22The commander of the guards put Joseph in charge of all the prisoners. Joseph was their leader, but he still did the same work they did. 23The commander of the guards trusted Joseph with everything that was in the prison. This happened because the Lord was with Joseph. He helped Joseph be successful in everything he did. ·

Joseph Explains Two Dreams

40 1Later, two of Pharaoh's servants did something wrong to Pharaoh. These servants were the baker and the man who served wine to Pharaoh. 2Pharaoh became angry with his baker and wine server, 3so he put them in the same prison as Joseph. Potiphar, the commander of Pharaoh's guards, was in charge of this prison. 4The commander put the two prisoners under Joseph's care. The two men continued to stay in prison for some time. 5One night both of the prisoners had a dream. The baker and the wine server each had his own dream, and each dream had its own meaning. 6Joseph went to them the next morning and saw that the two men were worried. 7He asked them, "Why do you look so worried today?"

8The two men answered, "We both had dreams last night, but we don't understand what we dreamed. There is no one to explain the dreams to us."

Joseph said to them, "God is the only one who can understand and explain dreams. So I beg you, tell me your dreams."

---

a38:29 *Perez* This name is like the word meaning "to break out."
b38:30 *Zerah* This name is like the word meaning "bright."
c39:1 *traders* Literally, "Ishmaelites."

The Wine Server's Dream

9So the wine server told Joseph his dream. The server said, "I dreamed I saw a vine. 10On the vine there were three branches. I watched the branches grow flowers and then become grapes. 11I was holding Pharaoh's cup, so I took the grapes and squeezed the juice into the cup. Then I gave the cup to Pharaoh."

12Then Joseph said, "I will explain the dream to you. The three branches mean three days. 13Before the end of three days, Pharaoh will forgive you and allow you to go back to your work. You will do the same work for Pharaoh as you did before. 14But when you are free, remember me. Be good to me and help me. Tell Pharaoh about me so that I can get out of this prison. 15I was kidnapped and taken from the land of my people, the Hebrews. I have done nothing wrong! I should not be in prison."

The Baker's Dream

16The baker saw that the other servant's dream was good, so he said to Joseph, "I also had a dream. I dreamed there were three baskets of bread on my head. 17In the top basket there were all kinds of baked food for the king, but birds were eating this food."

18Joseph answered, "I will tell you what the dream means. The three baskets mean three days. 19Before the end of three days, the king will take you out of this prison and cut off your head! He will hang your body on a pole, and the birds will eat it."

Joseph Is Forgotten

20Three days later it was Pharaoh's birthday. He gave a party for all his servants. At the party Pharaoh allowed the wine server and the baker to leave the prison. 21He freed the wine server and gave him his job back, and once again the wine server put a cup of wine in Pharaoh's hand. 22But Pharaoh hanged the baker, and everything happened the way Joseph said it would. 23But the wine server did not remember to help Joseph. He said nothing about him to Pharaoh. The wine server forgot about Joseph.

Pharaoh's Dreams

41 1Two years later Pharaoh dreamed that he was standing by the Nile River. 2In the dream, seven cows came out of the river and stood there eating grass. They were healthy, good-looking cows. 3Then seven more cows came out of the river and stood on the bank of the river by the healthy cows. But these cows were thin and looked sick. 4The seven sick cows ate the seven healthy cows. Then Pharaoh woke up.

5Pharaoh went back to sleep and began dreaming again. This time he dreamed that he saw seven heads of grain growing on one plant. They were healthy and full of grain. 6Then he saw seven more heads of grain sprouting, but they were thin and scorched by the hot wind. 7The thin heads of grain ate the seven good heads of grain. Then Pharaoh woke up again and realized it was only a dream. 8The next morning Pharaoh was worried about these dreams, so he sent for all the magicians and wise men of Egypt. Pharaoh told these men the dreams, but none of them could explain the dreams.

The Servant Tells Pharaoh About Joseph

9Then the wine servant remembered Joseph and said to Pharaoh, "I remember something that happened to me. 10You were angry with the baker and me, and you put us in prison. 11Then one night he and I had a dream. Each dream had a different meaning. 12There was a young Hebrew man in prison with us. He was a servant of the commander of the guards. We told him our dreams, and he explained them to us. He told us the meaning of each dream, 13and what he said came true. He said I would be free and have my old job back, and it happened. He also said the baker would die, and it happened!"

Joseph Is Called to Explain the Dreams

14So Pharaoh called Joseph from the prison. The guards quickly got Joseph out of prison. Joseph shaved, put on some clean clothes, and went to see Pharaoh. 15Pharaoh said to Joseph, "I had a dream, and no one can explain it for me. I heard that you can explain dreams when someone tells you about them."

16Joseph answered, "I cannot! But God can explain the dream for you, Pharaoh."

17Then Pharaoh said to Joseph, "In my dream I was standing by the Nile River. 18Seven cows came up out of the river and stood there eating the grass. They were healthy, good-looking cows. 19Then I saw seven more cows come up out of the river after them, but these cows were thin and looked sick. They were the worst cows I had ever seen anywhere in Egypt! 20The thin, sick cows ate the first healthy cows, 21but they still looked thin and sick. You couldn't even tell they had eaten the healthy cows. They looked as thin and sick as they did in the beginning. Then I woke up.

22"In my next dream I saw seven heads of grain growing on one plant. They were healthy and full of grain. 23And then seven more heads of grain grew after them, but they were thin and scorched by the hot wind. 24Then the thin heads of grain ate the seven good heads of grain.

"I told these dreams to my magicians. But no one could explain the dreams to me. What do they mean?"

Joseph Explains the Dream

25Then Joseph said to Pharaoh, "Both of these dreams have the same meaning. God is telling you what will happen soon. 26The seven good cows and the seven good heads of grain are seven good years. ²⁷And the seven thin, sick-looking cows and the seven thin heads of grain mean that there will be seven years of hunger in this area. These seven bad years will come after the seven good years. ²⁸God has shown you what will happen soon. He will make these things happen just as I told you. ²⁹For seven years there will be plenty of food in Egypt. ³⁰But then there will be seven years of hunger. The people will forget how much food there had been in Egypt before. This famine* will ruin the country. ³¹It will be so bad that people will forget what it was like to have plenty of food.

³²"Pharaoh, you had two dreams about the same thing. That means God wanted to show you that he really will make this happen, and he will make it happen soon! ³³So, Pharaoh, you should choose a wise, intelligent man and put him in charge of Egypt. ³⁴Then you should choose other men to collect food from the people. During the seven good years, the people must give them one-fifth of all the food they grow. ³⁵In this way these men will collect all the food during the seven good years and store it in the cities until it is needed. Pharaoh, this food will be under your control. ³⁶Then during the seven years of hunger, there will be food for the country of Egypt. And Egypt will not be destroyed by the famine."

³⁷This seemed like a very good idea to Pharaoh, and all his officials agreed. ³⁸Then Pharaoh told them, "I don't think we can find anyone better than Joseph to take this job! God's Spirit is in him, making him very wise!"

³⁹So Pharaoh said to Joseph, "God showed these things to you, so you must be the wisest man. ⁴⁰I will put you in charge of my country, and the people will obey all your commands. I will be the only one more powerful than you."

⁴¹Pharaoh said to Joseph, "I now make you governor over all of Egypt." ⁴²Then Pharaoh gave his special ring to Joseph. The royal seal was on this ring. Pharaoh also gave Joseph a fine linen robe and put a gold chain around his neck. ⁴³Then he told Joseph to ride in his second chariot. Pharaoh's officials said, "Let him be the governor over the whole land of Egypt!"ᵃ

⁴⁴Then Pharaoh said to him, "I am Pharaoh, the king over everyone in Egypt, but no one else in Egypt can lift a hand or move a foot unless you say he can." ⁴⁵Then Pharaoh gave Joseph another name, Zaphenath Paneah.ᵇ He

also gave Joseph a wife named Asenath. She was the daughter of Potiphera, a priest in the city of On. So Joseph became the governor over the whole country of Egypt.

⁴⁶Joseph was 30 years old when he began serving the king of Egypt. He traveled throughout the country of Egypt. ⁴⁷During the seven good years, the crops in Egypt grew very well. ⁴⁸Joseph saved the food in Egypt during those seven years and stored the food in the cities. In every city he stored grain that grew in the fields around the city. ⁴⁹Joseph stored so much grain that it was like the sands of the sea. He stored so much grain that it could not be measured.

⁵⁰Joseph's wife, Asenath, was the daughter of Potiphera, the priest in the city of On. Before the first year of hunger came, Joseph and Asenath had two sons. ⁵¹Joseph named the first son Manasseh.ᶜ He was given this name because Joseph said, "God made me forget all my hard work and everything back home in my father's house." ⁵²Joseph named the second son Ephraim.ᵈ Joseph gave him this name because he said, "I had great troubles, but God has made me successful in everything."

The Famine Begins

⁵³For seven years people had all the food they needed, but those years ended. ⁵⁴Then the seven years of hunger began, just as Joseph had said. No food grew anywhere in any of the countries in that area. But in Egypt people had plenty to eat because Joseph had stored the grain. ⁵⁵The famine* began, and the people cried to Pharaoh for food. Pharaoh said to the Egyptian people, "Go ask Joseph what to do."

⁵⁶There was famine everywhere, so Joseph gave the people grain from the warehouses. He sold the stored grain to the people of Egypt. The famine was bad in Egypt, ⁵⁷but the famine was bad everywhere. So people from the countries around Egypt had to come to Joseph in Egypt to buy grain.

The Dreams Come True

42 ¹During the famine* in Canaan,* Jacob learned that there was grain in Egypt. So he said to his sons, "Why are you sitting here doing nothing? ²I have heard that there is grain for sale in Egypt. Go there and buy grain for us so that we will live and not die!"

³So ten of Joseph's brothers went to Egypt to buy grain. ⁴Jacob did not send Benjamin. (Benjamin was Joseph's only full brother.ᵉ)

Hebrew words meaning "a person who explains secret things."
ᶜ**41:51 Manasseh** This is like the Hebrew word meaning "to forget."
ᵈ**41:52 Ephraim** This name is like the Hebrew word meaning "twice fruitful."
ᵉ**42:4 full brother** Literally, "brother." Joseph and Benjamin had the same mother.

ᵃ**41:43** Or "Then Pharaoh had Joseph ride in the chariot of his second-in-command, and they said, 'Bow before Joseph.' In this way Joseph became the governor over all of Egypt."
ᵇ**41:45 Zaphenath Paneah** This Egyptian name probably means "sustainer of life," but it is like

Jacob was afraid that something bad might happen to Benjamin.

⁵The famine was very bad in Canaan, so there were many people from Canaan who went to Egypt to buy grain. Among them were the sons of Israel.*

⁶Joseph was the governor of Egypt at the time. He was the one who checked the sale of grain to people who came to Egypt to buy it. Joseph's brothers came to him and bowed before him. ⁷Joseph saw his brothers and recognized them, but he acted like he didn't know them. He was rude when he spoke to them. He said, "Where do you come from?"

The brothers answered, "We have come from the land of Canaan to buy food."

⁸Joseph recognized his brothers, but they did not know who he was. ⁹Then Joseph remembered the dreams that he had dreamed about his brothers.

Joseph said to his brothers, "You have not come to buy food! You are spies. You came to learn where we are weak."

¹⁰But the brothers said to him, "No, sir, we come as your servants. We have come only to buy food. ¹¹We are all brothers—we all have the same father. We are honest men. We have come only to buy food."

¹²Then Joseph said to them, "No, you have come to spy on us!"

¹³And the brothers said, "No, sir, we come as servants from Canaan. We are all brothers, sons of the same father. There were twelve brothers in our family. Our youngest brother is still at home with our father, and the other brother died a long time ago."

¹⁴But Joseph said to them, "No! I can see that I am right. You are spies. ¹⁵But I will let you prove that you are telling the truth. In the name of Pharaoh, I swear that I will not let you go until your youngest brother comes here. ¹⁶One of you must go back to get your youngest brother while the rest of you stay here in prison. Then we can prove whether you are telling the truth or not. If you are not telling the truth, then by Pharaoh, I swear that you are spies!" ¹⁷Then Joseph put them all in prison for three days.

The Troubles Begin

¹⁸After three days Joseph said to them, "I am a God-fearing man. Do this, and I will let you live. ¹⁹If you are honest men, one of your brothers can stay here in prison, and the others can go and carry grain back to your people. ²⁰But then you must bring your youngest brother back here to me. Then I will know that you are telling the truth, and you will not have to die."

The brothers agreed to this. ²¹They said to each other, "We are being punished for the bad thing we did to our younger brother Joseph. We saw the trouble he was in. He begged us to save him, but we refused to listen. So now we are in trouble."

²²Then Reuben said to them, "I told you not to do anything bad to that boy, but you refused to listen to me. Now we are being punished for his death."

²³⁻²⁴Joseph was using an interpreter to talk to his brothers, so the brothers did not know that he understood their language. He heard and understood everything they said, and that made him want to cry. So he turned away and left the room. When he came back, he took one of the brothers, Simeon, and tied him up while the others watched. ²⁵Joseph told the servants to fill the bags with grain. The brothers had given Joseph the money for the grain, but he didn't keep the money. He put the money in their bags of grain. Then he gave them what they would need for their trip back home.

²⁶So the brothers put the grain on their donkeys and left. ²⁷That night the brothers stopped at a place to spend the night. One of the brothers opened his sack to get some grain for his donkey. And there in the sack, he saw his money! ²⁸He said to the other brothers, "Look! Here is the money I paid for the grain. Someone put the money back in my sack." The brothers were very afraid. They said to one another, "What is God doing to us?"

The Brothers Report to Jacob

²⁹The brothers went back to their father Jacob in the land of Canaan.* They told him about everything that had happened. ³⁰They said, "The governor of that country spoke rudely to us. He thought that we were spies! ³¹We told him, 'We are honest men, not spies. ³²There are twelve of us brothers, all from the same father. But one of our brothers is no longer living, and the youngest is still at home with our father in Canaan.'

³³"Then the governor of that country said to us, 'Here is a way to prove that you are honest men: Leave one of your brothers here with me. Take your grain back to your families. ³⁴Bring your youngest brother to me. Then I will know if you are honest men or if you were sent from an army to destroy us. If you are telling the truth, I will give your brother back to you. I will give him to you, and you will be free to buy grain in our country.'"

³⁵Then the brothers started taking the grain out of their sacks, and every brother found his bag of money in his sack of grain. When the brothers and their father saw the money, they were afraid.

³⁶Jacob said to them, "Do you want me to lose all of my children? Joseph is gone. Simeon is gone, and now you want to take Benjamin away too!"

³⁷But Reuben said to his father, "Father, you may kill my two sons if I don't bring Benjamin back to you. Trust me. I will bring him back to you."

³⁸But Jacob said, "I will not let Benjamin go with you. His brother is dead, and he is the

only son left from my wife Rachel. It would kill me if anything happened to him during the trip to Egypt. You would send me to the grave[a] a very sad, old man."

Jacob Lets Benjamin Go to Egypt

43 [1]The famine* was very bad in that country. [2]The people ate all the grain they had brought from Egypt. When that grain was gone, Jacob said to his sons, "Go to Egypt and buy some more grain for us to eat."

[3]But Judah said to Jacob, "But the governor of that country warned us. He said, 'If you don't bring your brother back to me, I will refuse to talk to you.' [4]If you send Benjamin with us, we will go down and buy grain. [5]But if you refuse to send Benjamin, we will not go. The man warned us to not come back without him."

[6]Israel* said, "Why did you tell him you had another brother? Why did you do such a bad thing to me?"

[7]The brothers answered, "He asked lots of questions. He wanted to know all about us and about our family. He asked us, 'Is your father still alive? Do you have another brother at home?' We only answered his questions. We didn't know he would ask us to bring our brother to him!"

[8]Then Judah said to his father Israel, "Let Benjamin go with me. I will take care of him. We have to go to Egypt to get food. If we don't go, we will all die—including our children. [9]I will make sure he is safe. I will be responsible for him. If I don't bring him back to you, you can blame me forever. [10]If you had let us go before, we could have already made two trips for food."

[11]Then their father Israel said, "If it is really true, take Benjamin with you. But take some gifts to the governor. Take some of the things we have been able to gather in our land. Take him some honey, pistachio nuts, almonds, spices, and myrrh.* [12]Take twice as much money with you this time. Take the money that was given back to you after you paid last time. Maybe the governor made a mistake. [13]Take Benjamin, and go back to the man. [14]I pray that God All-Powerful will help you when you stand before the governor. I pray that he will let Benjamin, and also Simeon, come back safely. If not, I will again be sad from losing my children."

[15]So the brothers took the gifts to give to the governor. And the brothers took twice as much money with them as they took the first time. This time Benjamin went with the brothers to Egypt.

The Brothers at Joseph's House

[16]When Joseph saw Benjamin with them, he said to his servant, "Bring these men into my house. Kill an animal and cook it. They will eat with me at noon today." [17]The servant did as he was told. He brought the men into Joseph's house.

[18]The brothers were afraid when they were taken to Joseph's house and said, "We have been brought here because of the money that was put back in our sacks the last time. They will use this as proof against us and steal our donkeys and make us slaves."

[19]So the brothers went to the servant in charge of Joseph's house. [20]They said, "Sir, I promise this is the truth. The last time we came, we came to buy food. [21-22]On the way home we opened our sacks and found our money in every sack. We don't know how it got there, but we brought that money with us to give it back to you. And we have brought more money to pay for the food that we want to buy this time."

[23]But the servant answered, "Don't be afraid; believe me. Your God, the God of your father, must have put the money in your sack as a gift. I remember that you paid me for the grain the last time."

Then the servant brought Simeon out of the prison. [24]The servant led the men into Joseph's house. He gave them water, and they washed their feet. Then he fed their donkeys.

[25]The brothers heard that they were going to eat with Joseph, so they worked until noon preparing their gifts for him.

[26]When Joseph came home, the brothers gave him the gifts they had brought with them. Then they bowed down to the ground in front of him.

[27]Joseph asked them how they were doing. He said, "How is your elderly father you told me about. Is he still alive and well?"

[28]The brothers answered, "Yes, sir, our father is still alive." And they again bowed before Joseph.

[29]Then Joseph saw his brother Benjamin. (Benjamin and Joseph had the same mother.) Joseph said, "Is this your youngest brother that you told me about?" Then Joseph said to Benjamin, "God bless you, my son!"

[30]Joseph felt a strong desire to show his brother Benjamin that he loved him. He was about to cry and didn't want his brothers to see him, so he ran into his private room and cried there. [31]Then Joseph washed his face and came out. He regained control of himself and said, "Now it is time to eat."

[32]The servants seated Joseph at a table by himself. His brothers were at another table by themselves, and the Egyptians were at a table by themselves. The Egyptians believed that it was wrong for them to eat with Hebrews.[b] [33]Joseph's brothers were seated at a table

---

[b]**43:32** *The Egyptians ... Hebrews* The Egyptians would not eat with them because they were shepherds and ate meat from cattle, sheep, and goats. To the Egyptians, these animals represented some of their gods. See Gen. 46:34.

[a]**42:38** *grave* Or "Sheol," the place of death.

facing him. The brothers were looking at each other because, to their surprise, they had been seated in order, from the oldest to the youngest. ³⁴Servants were taking food from Joseph's table and bringing it to them. But the servants gave Benjamin five times more than the others. The brothers continued to eat and drink with Joseph until they were drunk.

Joseph Sets a Trap

44 ¹Then Joseph gave a command to his servant. He said, "Fill the men's sacks with as much grain as they can carry. Then put each man's money into his sack with the grain. ²Put the youngest brother's money in his sack too. But also put my special silver cup in his sack." So the servant obeyed Joseph.

³Early the next morning the brothers and their donkeys were sent back to their country. ⁴After they had left the city, Joseph said to his servant, "Go and follow the men. Stop them and say to them, 'We were good to you! So why have you been bad to us? Why did you steal my master's silver cup? ⁵My master drinks from that cup, and he uses it to learn secret things. What you did was wrong!'"

⁶So the servant obeyed. He rode out to the brothers and stopped them. The servant said to them what Joseph had told him to say.

⁷But the brothers said to the servant, "Why does the governor say these things? We wouldn't do anything like that! ⁸We brought back the money that we found in our sacks before. So surely we wouldn't steal silver or gold from your master's house. ⁹If you find the silver cup in any of our sacks, let that man die. You can kill him, and we will be your slaves."

¹⁰The servant said, "I agree, except that only the man who is found to have the cup will be my slave. The others will be free."

The Trap Is Sprung; Benjamin Is Caught

¹¹Then every brother quickly opened his sack on the ground. ¹²The servant started looking in the sacks. He started with the oldest brother and ended with the youngest. He found the cup in Benjamin's sack. ¹³The brothers were very sad. They tore their clothes to show their sadness. They put their sacks back on the donkeys and went back to the city.

¹⁴When Judah and his brothers went back to Joseph's house, Joseph was still there. The brothers fell to the ground and bowed down before him. ¹⁵Joseph said to them, "Why have you done this? Didn't you know that I have a special way of learning secrets? No one is better at this than I am!"

¹⁶Judah said, "Sir, there is nothing we can say. There is no way to explain. There is no way to show that we are not guilty. God has judged us guilty for something else we have done. So all of us, even Benjamin, will be your slaves."

¹⁷But Joseph said, "I will not make you all slaves! Only the man who stole the cup will be my slave. You others can go in peace to your father."

Judah Pleads for Benjamin

¹⁸Then Judah went to Joseph and said, "Sir, please let me speak plainly with you. Please don't be angry with me. I know that you are like Pharaoh himself. ¹⁹When we were here before, you asked us, 'Do you have a father or a brother?' ²⁰And we answered you, 'We have a father—he is an old man. And we have a younger brother. Our father loves him because he was born while our father was old. This youngest son's brother is dead, so he is the only son who is left from that mother. Our father loves him very much.' ²¹Then you said to us, 'Bring that brother to me. I want to see him.' ²²And we said to you, 'That young boy cannot come. He cannot leave his father. If his father loses him, his father will be so sad that he will die.' ²³But you said to us, 'You must bring your youngest brother, or I will not sell you grain again.' ²⁴So we went back to our father and told him what you said.

²⁵"Later, our father said, 'Go back and buy us some more food.' ²⁶We said to our father, 'We cannot go without our youngest brother. The governor said he will not sell us grain again until he sees our youngest brother.' ²⁷Then my father said to us, 'You know that my wife Rachel gave me two sons. ²⁸I let one son go away, and he was killed by a wild animal. And I haven't seen him since. ²⁹If you take my other son away from me, and something happens to him, I will be sad enough to die.' ³⁰Now, imagine what will happen when we go home without our youngest brother—he is the most important thing in our father's life! ³¹Our father will die if he sees that the boy isn't with us—and it will be our fault. We will send our father to his grave a very sad man.

³²"I took responsibility for the young boy. I told my father, 'If I don't bring him back to you, you can blame me for the rest of my life.' ³³So now I beg you, please let the boy go back with his brothers, and I will stay and be your slave. ³⁴I cannot go back to my father if the boy is not with me. I am very afraid of what would happen to my father."

Joseph Tells Who He Is

45 ¹Joseph could not control himself any longer. He cried in front of all the people who were there. Joseph said, "Tell everyone to leave here." So all the people left. Only the brothers were left with Joseph. Then he told them who he was. ²Joseph continued to cry, and all the Egyptian people in Pharaoh's house heard it. ³He said to his brothers, "I am your brother Joseph. Is my father doing well?" But the brothers did not answer him because they were confused and afraid.

⁴So Joseph said to his brothers again, "Come

here to me. I beg you, come here." When the brothers went to him, he said to them, "I am your brother Joseph. I am the one you sold as a slave to Egypt. ⁵Now don't be worried. Don't be angry with yourselves for what you did. It was God's plan for me to come here. I am here to save people's lives. ⁶This terrible famine* has continued for two years now, and there will be five more years without planting or harvest. ⁷So God sent me here ahead of you so that I can save my people in this country. ⁸It wasn't your fault that I was sent here. It was God's plan. God made me like a father to Pharaoh. I am the governor over all his house and over all of Egypt."

Israel Invited to Egypt

⁹Joseph said, "Hurry up and go to my father. Tell him his son Joseph sent this message:

'God made me the governor of Egypt. So come here to me quickly. Don't wait. ¹⁰You can live near me in the land of Goshen. You, your children, your grand-children, and all of your animals are wel-come here. ¹¹I will take care of you dur-ing the next five years of hunger. So you and your family will not lose everything you own.'

¹²"Surely you can see that I really am Joseph. Even my brother Benjamin knows it is me, your brother, talking to you. ¹³So tell my father about the honor I have received here in Egypt. Tell him about everything you have seen here. Now hurry, go bring my father back to me." ¹⁴Then Joseph hugged his brother Benjamin, and they both began cry-ing. ¹⁵Then Joseph cried as he kissed all his brothers. After this, the brothers began talk-ing with him.

¹⁶Pharaoh learned that Joseph's brothers had come to him. This news spread through-out Pharaoh's house. Pharaoh and his ser-vants were very excited! ¹⁷So Pharaoh told Joseph, "Tell your brothers to take all the food they need and go back to the land of Canaan.* ¹⁸Tell them to bring your father and their fam-ilies back here to me. I will give you the best land in Egypt to live on. And your family can eat the best food we have here. ¹⁹Also give your brothers some of our best wagons. Tell them to go to Canaan and bring your father and all the women and children back in the wagons. ²⁰Don't worry about bringing all of their belongings. We can give them the best of Egypt."

²¹So the sons of Israel did this. Joseph gave them good wagons just as Pharaoh had promised. And Joseph gave them enough food for their trip. ²²He gave each brother a suit of beautiful clothes. But to Benjamin he gave five suits of beautiful clothes and 300 pieces of silver. ²³Joseph also sent gifts to his father. He sent ten donkeys with bags full of many good things from Egypt. And he sent ten female donkeys loaded with grain, bread, and other food for his father on his trip back. ²⁴Then Joseph told his brothers to go. While they were leaving, he said to them, "Go straight home, and don't fight on the way."

²⁵So the brothers left Egypt and went to their father in the land of Canaan. ²⁶They told him, "Father, Joseph is still alive! And he is the governor over the whole country of Egypt."

Their father did not know what to think. At first he didn't believe them. ²⁷But then they told him everything Joseph had said. Then their father saw the wagons that Joseph had sent to bring him back to Egypt, and he became excited and very happy. ²⁸Israel said, "Now I believe you. My son Joseph is still alive! I am going to see him before I die!"

God Assures Israel

46 ¹So Israel* began his trip to Egypt. First he went to Beersheba. There he worshiped God, the God of his father Isaac. He offered sacrifices.* ²During the night God spoke to Israel in a dream and said, "Jacob, Jacob."

Israel answered, "Here I am."

³Then God said, "I am God, the God of your father. Don't be afraid to go to Egypt. In Egypt I will make you a great nation. ⁴I will go to Egypt with you, and I will bring you out of Egypt again. You will die there, but Joseph will be with you. His own hands will close your eyes when you die."

Israel Goes to Egypt

⁵Then Jacob left Beersheba and traveled to Egypt. His sons, the sons of Israel, brought their father, their wives, and all their chil-dren to Egypt. They traveled in the wagons the Pharaoh had sent. ⁶They also had their cattle and everything they owned in the land of Canaan.* So Israel went to Egypt with all his children and his family. ⁷With him were his sons and his grandsons, his daughters and his granddaughters. All of his family went with him.

Jacob's Family

⁸Here are the names of Israel's sons and family that went to Egypt with him:

Reuben was Jacob's first son. ⁹Reuben's sons were Hanoch, Pallu, Hezron, and Carmi.

¹⁰Simeon's sons were Jemuel, Jamin, Ohad, Jakin, and Zohar. There was also Shaul. (Shaul was born from a Canaanite woman.)

¹¹Levi's sons were Gershon, Kohath, and Merari.

¹²Judah's sons were Er, Onan, Shelah, Perez, and Zerah. (Er and Onan died while still in Canaan.) Perez's sons were Hezron and Hamul.

¹³Issachar's sons were Tola, Puah, Job, and Shimron.

¹⁴Zebulun's sons were Sered, Elon, and Jahleel.

¹⁵Reuben, Simeon, Levi, Judah, Issachar, and Zebulun were Jacob's sons from his wife Leah. Leah had these sons in Paddan Aram. She also had a daughter named Dinah. There were 33 people in this family.

¹⁶Gad's sons were Zephon, Haggi, Shuni, Ezbon, Eri, Arodi, and Areli.

¹⁷Asher's sons were Imnah, Ishvah, Ishvi, Beriah, and their sister Serah. Also there were Beriah's sons, Heber and Malkiel.

¹⁸All these were Jacob's sons from his wife's servant, Zilpah. (Zilpah was the maid that Laban had given to his daughter Leah.) There were 16 people in this family.

¹⁹Benjamin was also with Jacob. Benjamin was Jacob and Rachel's son. (Joseph was also Rachel's son, but he was already in Egypt.)

²⁰In Egypt, Joseph had two sons, Manasseh and Ephraim. (Joseph's wife was Asenath, the daughter of Potiphera, the priest in the city of On.)

²¹Benjamin's sons were Bela, Beker, Ashbel, Gera, Naaman, Ehi, Rosh, Muppim, Huppim, and Ard.

²²These were the sons of Jacob from his wife Rachel. There were 14 people in this family.

²³Dan's son was Hushim.

²⁴Naphtali's sons were Jahziel, Guni, Jezer, and Shillem.

²⁵These were the sons of Jacob and Bilhah. (Bilhah was the maid that Laban had given to his daughter Rachel.) There were seven people in this family.

²⁶The total number of Jacob's direct descendants who went with him to Egypt was 66 people. (The wives of Jacob's sons were not counted in this number.) ²⁷Also, there were the two sons of Joseph. They had been born in Egypt. So there was a total of 70 people in Jacob's family in Egypt.

Israel Arrives in Egypt

²⁸Jacob sent Judah ahead to speak to Joseph. Judah went to Joseph in the land of Goshen. Then Jacob and his people followed into the land. ²⁹Joseph learned that his father was coming. So he prepared his chariot and went out to meet his father, Israel, in Goshen. When Joseph saw his father, he hugged his neck and cried for a long time.

³⁰Then Israel said to Joseph, "Now I can die in peace. I have seen your face, and I know that you are still alive."

³¹Joseph said to his brothers and to the rest of his father's family, "I will go and tell Pharaoh that you are here. I will say to Pharaoh, 'My brothers and the rest of my father's family have left the land of Canaan* and have come here to me. ³²They are a family of shepherds. They have always kept sheep and cattle. They have brought all their animals and everything they own with them.' ³³When Pharaoh

calls you, he will ask, 'What work do you do?' ³⁴You tell him, 'We are shepherds. All our lives we have been shepherds, and our ancestors* were shepherds before us.' Then Pharaoh will allow you to live in the land of Goshen. Egyptians don't like shepherds, so it is better that you stay in Goshen."

Israel Settles in Goshen

47 ¹Joseph went in to Pharaoh and said, "My father and my brothers and all their families are here. They have all their animals and everything they own from the land of Canaan* with them. They are now in the land of Goshen." ²Joseph chose five of his brothers to be with him before the Pharaoh.

³Pharaoh said to the brothers, "What work do you do?"

The brothers said to Pharaoh, "Sir, we are shepherds, just as our ancestors* were shepherds before us." ⁴They said to Pharaoh, "The famine* is very bad in Canaan. There are no fields left with grass for our animals, so we have come to live in this land. We ask you to please let us live in Goshen."

⁵Then Pharaoh said to Joseph, "Your father and your brothers have come to you. ⁶You can choose any place in Egypt for them to live. Give your father and your brothers the best land. Let them live in the land of Goshen. And if they are skilled shepherds, they can also care for my cattle."

⁷Then Joseph called his father Jacob to come in to meet Pharaoh. Jacob blessed Pharaoh.

⁸Then Pharaoh said to him, "How old are you?"

⁹Jacob said to Pharaoh, "I have had a short life with many troubles. I am only 130 years old. My father and his ancestors lived to be much older than I am."

¹⁰Then Jacob blessed Pharaoh and left from his meeting with him.

¹¹Joseph did what Pharaoh said and gave his father and brothers land in Egypt. It was the best land in Egypt, in the eastern part of the country, around Rameses. ¹²Joseph also gave his father, his brothers, and all their people the food they needed.

Joseph Buys Land for Pharaoh

¹³The famine* got worse; there was no food anywhere in the land. Egypt and Canaan* became very poor because of this bad time. ¹⁴People in the land bought more and more grain. Joseph saved the money and brought it to Pharaoh's house. ¹⁵After some time the people in Egypt and Canaan had no money left. They had spent all their money to buy grain. So the people of Egypt went to Joseph and said, "Please give us food. Our money is gone. If we don't eat, we will die while you are watching."

¹⁶But Joseph answered, "Give me your cattle, and I will give you food." ¹⁷So the people used their cattle and horses and all their other

animals to buy food. And that year, Joseph gave them food and took their animals.

18But the next year the people had no animals and nothing to buy food with. So they went to Joseph and said, "You know that we have no money left, and all our animals belong to you. So we have nothing left—only what you see—our bodies and our land. 19Surely we will die while you are watching. But if you give us food, we will give Pharaoh our land, and we will be his slaves. Give us seed so that we can plant. Then we will live and not die, and the land will grow food for us again."

20So Joseph bought all the land in Egypt for Pharaoh. All the people in Egypt sold Joseph their fields. They did this because they were very hungry. 21And everywhere in Egypt all the people became Pharaoh's slaves. 22The only land Joseph didn't buy was the land that the priests owned. The priests didn't need to sell their land because Pharaoh paid them for their work. So they used this money to buy food to eat.

23Joseph said to the people, "Now I have bought you and your land for Pharaoh. So I will give you seed, and you can plant your fields. 24At harvest time, you must give one-fifth of your crops to Pharaoh. You can keep four-fifths for yourselves. You can use the seed you keep for food and planting the next year. Now you can feed your families and your children."

25The people said, "You have saved our lives. We are happy to be slaves to Pharaoh."

26So Joseph made a law at that time in the land, and that law still continues today. The law says that one-fifth of everything from the land belongs to the Pharaoh who owns all the land. The only land he does not own is the land of the priests.

Don't Bury Me in Egypt

27Israel* stayed in Egypt. He lived in the land of Goshen. His family grew and became very large. They became landowners there and did very well.

28Jacob lived in Egypt 17 years, so he was 147 years old. 29The time came when Israel knew he would soon die, so he called his son Joseph to him. He said, "If you love me, put your hand under my leg and make a promise.a Promise that you will do what I say and that you will be truthful with me. When I die, don't bury me in Egypt. 30Bury me in the place where my ancestors* are buried. Carry me out of Egypt and bury me in our family grave."

Joseph answered, "I promise that I will do what you say."

31Then Jacob said, "Make a vow to me." And Joseph vowed to him that he would do this. Then Israel laid his head back down on the bed.b

Blessings for Manasseh and Ephraim

48 1Some time later, Joseph learned that his father was very sick. So he took his two sons, Manasseh and Ephraim, and went to his father. 2When Joseph arrived, someone told Israel, "Your son Joseph has come to see you." Israel was very weak, but he tried hard and sat up in his bed.

3Then Israel said to Joseph, "God All-Powerful appeared to me at Luz in the land of Canaan.* God blessed me there. 4He said to me, 'I will make you a great family. I will give you many children and you will be a great people. Your family will own this land forever.' 5Now you have two sons. These two sons were born here in the country of Egypt before I came. Your two sons, Ephraim and Manasseh, will be like my own sons. They will be like Reuben and Simeon to me. 6So these two boys will be my sons. They will share in everything I own. But if you have other sons, they will be your sons. But they will also be like sons to Ephraim and Manasseh—that is, in the future, they will share in everything that Ephraim and Manasseh own. 7On the trip from Paddan Aram, Rachel died in the land of Canaan. This made me very sad. We were still traveling toward Ephrath. I buried her there on the road to Ephrath. (Ephrath is Bethlehem.)

8Then Israel saw Joseph's sons. Israel said, "Who are these boys?"

9Joseph said to his father, "These are my sons. These are the boys God gave me."

Israel said, "Bring your sons to me. I will bless them."

10Israel was old and his eyes were not good. So Joseph brought the boys close to his father. Israel kissed and hugged the boys. 11Then Israel said to Joseph, "I never thought I would see your face again. But look! God has let me see you and your children."

12Then Joseph took the boys off Israel's lap, and they bowed down in front of his father. 13Joseph put Ephraim on his right side and Manasseh on his left side. (So Ephraim was on Israel's left side, and Manasseh was on Israel's right side.) 14But Israel crossed his hands and put his right hand on the head of the younger boy Ephraim. Then he put his left hand on Manasseh, even though Manasseh was the firstborn.* 15And Israel blessed Joseph and said,

> "My ancestors,* Abraham and Isaac,
>   worshiped our God,
>   and that God has led me all my life.
> 16 He was the Angel who saved me from all
>   my troubles.

---

a47:29 put your hand ... make a promise This was a sign of a very important promise that Jacob trusted Joseph to keep.

b47:31 Then Israel ... on the bed Or "Then Israel bowed down at the head of his bed" or "Then Israel worshiped on the head of the staff."

And I pray that he will bless these boys.
Now they will have my name and the
    name of our ancestors, Abraham and
    Isaac.
I pray that they will grow to become
    great families and nations on earth."

¹⁷Joseph saw that his father put his right hand on Ephraim's head. This didn't make Joseph happy. Joseph took his father's hand because he wanted to move it from Ephraim's head and put it on Manasseh's head. ¹⁸Joseph said to his father, "You have your right hand on the wrong boy. Manasseh is the firstborn. Put your right hand on him."

¹⁹But his father refused and said, "I know, son. I know. Manasseh is the firstborn. He will be great and will be the father of many people. But his younger brother will be greater than he is. And the younger brother's family will be much larger."

²⁰So Israel blessed them that day. He said,

"The Israelites will use your names
    whenever they bless someone.
They will say, 'May God make you
    like Ephraim and Manasseh.'"

In this way Israel made Ephraim greater than Manasseh.

²¹Then Israel said to Joseph, "Look, my time to die is almost here, but God will still be with you. He will lead you back to the land of your ancestors. ²²I have given you one portion more than I gave to your brothers. I gave you the land that I won from the Amorites. I used my sword and bow to take that land."

Jacob Blesses His Sons

49 ¹Then Jacob called all his sons to him. He said, "My sons, come here to me. I will tell you what will happen in the future.

²"Children of Jacob, gather around.
Come listen to Israel, your father.

Reuben

³"Reuben, my first son, you are my
    strength,
    the first proof of my manhood.
You were the most honored
    and powerful of all my sons.
⁴ But your passion was like a flood
    you couldn't control.
So you will not remain
    my most honored son.
You climbed into your father's bed
    and slept with one of his wives.
You brought shame to my bed,
    to the bed you lay on.

Simeon and Levi

⁵"Simeon and Levi are brothers.
    They are violent with their swords.

⁶ I will not join their secret meetings.
    I will not take part in their evil plans.
They have killed people out of anger
    and crippled animals for fun.
⁷ Their anger is so strong that it is a curse.
    They are too cruel when they are angry.
They will not get their own land in the
    land of Jacob.
They will be spread throughout Israel.

Judah

⁸"Judah, your brothers will praise you.
    You will defeat your enemies.
    Your brothers will bow down to you.
⁹ Judah is like a young lion.
    My son, you are like a lion standing
        over the animal it killed.
Like a lion, Judah lies down to rest,
    and no one is brave enough to disturb
        him.
¹⁰ Men from Judah's family will be kings.
    The sign that his family rules
        will not leave his family before the real
            king comes.ᵃ
    Then many people will obey and serve
        him.
¹¹ He ties his donkeys to the best
        grapevines.
    He washes his clothes in the best wine.
¹² His eyes are red from drinking wine.
    His teeth are white from drinking milk.ᵇ

Zebulun

¹³"Zebulun will live near the sea.
    His seacoast will be a safe place for
        ships.
    His land will continue as far as the city
        of Sidon.

Issachar

¹⁴"Issachar is like a donkey that has worked
        too hard.
    He will lie down under his heavy load.
¹⁵ He will see his land is pleasant
    and that his resting place is good.
But he will agree to carry heavy loads;
    he will agree to work as a slave.

Dan

¹⁶"Danᶜ will rule his people
    as one of the tribes of Israel.
¹⁷ Dan will be like a snake
    at the side of the road.

ᵃ**49:10** *before the real king comes* Or "until Shiloh comes," "until the man it belongs to comes," or "until his tribute comes."
ᵇ**49:10-12** Or "¹⁰The ruler's scepter will not pass from between Judah's feet before he gets what is his, that is, the people's obedience. ¹¹His young donkey will be tied to the very best grapevines. He will wash his finest clothes in wine, the blood of grapes. ¹²His eyes will be redder than wine, his teeth whiter than milk."
ᶜ**49:16** *Dan* This name means "judge" and is a wordplay with "rule."

He will be like a dangerous snake
  lying near the path.
That snake bites a horse's foot,
  and the rider falls to the ground.

[18]"LORD, I am waiting for your salvation.

Gad

[19]"A group of robbers will attack[a] Gad,
  but Gad will chase them away.

Asher

[20]"Asher's land will grow much good food.
  He will have food fit for a king!

Naphtali

[21]"Naphtali is like a deer running free,
  and his words are beautiful.

Joseph

[22]"Joseph is like a wild donkey,
  like a young donkey by a spring,
  like colts grazing in a pasture.[b]
[23] People attacked him
  and made life hard for him.
  Men with arrows became his enemies.
[24] But he won the fight with his mighty bow
  and his skillful arms.
  He gets power from the Mighty One of
    Jacob, from the Shepherd, the Rock of
    Israel,
[25] the God of your father who helps you.

"May God All-Powerful bless you
  and give you blessings from the sky
    above and from the deep below.
May he give you blessings from breast and
  womb.
[26] My parents had many good things happen
  to them.
And I, your father, was blessed even
  more.
Your brothers left you with nothing.
But now I pile all my blessings on you,
  as high as a mountain.

Benjamin

[27]"Benjamin is like a hungry wolf.
  In the morning he kills and eats.
  In the evening he shares what is left."

[28]These are the twelve families of Israel.
And this is what their father said to them.
He gave each son a blessing that was right for
him. [29]Then Israel gave them a command. He
said, "When I die, I want to be with my people. I want to be buried with my ancestors*

in the cave in the field of Ephron the Hittite. [30]That cave is in the field of Machpelah
near Mamre in the land of Canaan.* Abraham
bought that field from Ephron so that he could
have a burying place. [31]Abraham and his wife
Sarah are buried in that cave. Isaac and his
wife Rebekah are buried in that cave. I buried
my wife Leah in that cave. [32]That cave is in
the field that was bought from the Hittites."
[33]After Jacob finished talking to his sons, he
lay down, put his feet back on the bed, and
died.

Jacob's Funeral

50 [1]When Israel died, Joseph was very
sad. He hugged his father and cried
over him and kissed him. [2]Joseph commanded his servants to prepare his father's
body. (These servants were doctors.) The doctors prepared Jacob's body to be buried. They
prepared the body in the special way of the
Egyptians. [3]When the Egyptians prepared the
body in this special way, they waited 40 days
before they buried the body. Then the Egyptians had a special time of sadness for Jacob.
This time was 70 days.

[4]After the time of sadness was finished,
Joseph spoke to Pharaoh's officers and said,
"Please tell this to Pharaoh: [5]'When my father
was near death, I made a promise to him. I
promised that I would bury him in a cave in
the land of Canaan.* This is the cave that he
prepared for himself. So please let me go and
bury my father. Then I will come back here
to you.'"

[6]Pharaoh answered, "Keep your promise.
Go and bury your father."

[7]So Joseph went to bury his father. All of
Pharaoh's officials, personal advisors, and all
the older leaders of Egypt went with Joseph.
[8]All the people in Joseph's family, his brothers, and all the people in his father's family
went with him. Only the children and the
animals stayed in the land of Goshen. [9]So
there was a large crowd of people with him.
There was even a group of soldiers riding in
chariots and some on horses.

[10]They went to Goren Atad,[c] east of the
Jordan River. There they had a long funeral
service for Israel, which continued for seven
days. [11]When the people who lived in Canaan
saw the funeral service at Goren Atad, they
said, "This is a time of great sorrow for those
Egyptians." So now that place across the Jordan River is named Abel Mizraim.[d]

[12]So Jacob's sons did what their father told
them. [13]They carried his body to Canaan
and buried it in the cave at Machpelah. This
was the cave near Mamre in the field that
Abraham bought from Ephron the Hittite.
Abraham bought that cave to use as a burial

---

[a]49:19 *A group of robbers will attack* The Hebrew
words for "group of robbers" and "attack" sound like
the name Gad.
[b]49:22 Or "Joseph is very successful. Joseph is like
a vine covered with fruit, like a vine growing by a
spring, like a vine growing along a fence."

[c]50:10 *Goren Atad* Or "Atad's threshing floor."
[d]50:11 *Abel Mizraim* This means "Egyptian time of
sadness."

place. ¹⁴After Joseph buried his father, he and everyone in the group with him went back to Egypt.

The Brothers Are Still Afraid of Joseph

¹⁵After Jacob died, Joseph's brothers were worried. They were afraid that Joseph would still be mad at them for what they had done years before. They said, "Maybe Joseph still hates us for what we did." ¹⁶So the brothers sent this message to Joseph:

"Before your father died, he told us to give you a message. ¹⁷He said, 'Tell Joseph that I beg him to please forgive his brothers for the bad things they did to him.' So now Joseph, we beg you, please forgive us for the bad things we did to you. We are the servants of God, the God of your father."

That message made Joseph very sad, and he cried. ¹⁸His brothers went to him and bowed down in front of him. They said, "We will be your servants."

¹⁹Then Joseph said to them, "Don't be afraid. I am not God! I have no right to punish you. ²⁰It is true that you planned to do something bad to me. But really, God was planning good things. God's plan was to use me to save the lives of many people. And that is what happened. ²¹So don't be afraid. I will take care of you and your children." And so Joseph said kind things to his brothers, and this made them feel better.

²²Joseph continued to live in Egypt with his father's family. He died when he was 110 years old. ²³During Joseph's life Ephraim had children and grandchildren. And his son Manasseh had a son named Makir. Joseph lived to see Makir's children.

The Death of Joseph

²⁴When Joseph was near death, he said to his brothers, "My time to die is almost here. But I know that God will take care of you and lead you out of this country. God will lead you to the land he promised to give Abraham, Isaac, and Jacob."

²⁵Then Joseph asked his people to make a promise. Joseph said, "Promise me that you will carry my bones with you when God leads you out of Egypt."

²⁶Joseph died in Egypt when he was 110 years old. Doctors prepared his body for burial and put the body in a coffin in Egypt.

Exodus

Jacob's Family in Egypt

1 ¹Jacob traveled to Egypt with his sons. Each son had his own family with him. These are the sons of Israel: ²Reuben, Simeon, Levi, Judah, ³Issachar, Zebulun, Benjamin, ⁴Dan, Naphtali, Gad, and Asher. ⁵There was a total of 70 people who were direct descendants of Jacob. (Joseph was one of the twelve sons, but he was already in Egypt.)

⁶Later, Joseph, his brothers, and all the people of that generation died. ⁷But the Israelites had many children, and their number grew and grew and the country of Egypt was filled with them.

Trouble for the Israelites

⁸Then a new king began to rule Egypt. He did not know Joseph. ⁹This king said to his people, "Look at the Israelites. There are too many of them, and they are stronger than we are! ¹⁰We must make plans to stop them from growing stronger. If there is a war, they might join our enemies, defeat us, and escape from the land!"

¹¹The Egyptians decided to make life hard for the Israelites, so they put slave masters over the people. These masters forced the Israelites to build the cities of Pithom and Rameses for the king. The king used these cities to store grain and other things.

¹²The Egyptians forced the Israelites to work harder and harder. But the harder they worked, the more they grew and spread, and the more the Egyptians became afraid of them. ¹³So the Egyptians made them work even harder.

¹⁴They made life hard for the Israelites. They forced the Israelites to work hard at making bricks and mortar and to work hard in the fields. The Egyptians showed no mercy in all the hard work they made the Israelites do!

The Nurses Who Followed God

¹⁵There were two Hebrewᵃ nurses who helped the Israelite women give birth. They were named Shiphrah and Puah. The king of

---

ᵃ1:15 *Hebrew* Or "Israelite." This name might also mean "descendants of Eber" (read Gen.10:25–31) or "people from beyond the Euphrates River." Also in verse 19.

Egypt said to the nurses, 16"You will continue to help the Hebrew women give birth to their children. If a girl baby is born, let the baby live. But if the baby is a boy, you must kill him!"

17But the nurses trusted*a* God, so they did not obey the king's command. They let all the baby boys live.

18The king of Egypt called for the nurses and asked them, "Why did you do this? Why did you let the baby boys live?"

19The nurses said to the king, "The Hebrew women are much stronger than the Egyptian women. They give birth to their babies before we can go to help them." 20–21The nurses trusted God, so he was good to them and allowed them to have their own families.

The Hebrews continued to have more children, and they became very strong. 22So Pharaoh* gave this command to his own people: "If the Hebrew women give birth to a baby girl, let it live. But if they have a baby boy, you must throw it into the Nile River."

Baby Moses

2 1There was a man from the family of Levi who decided to marry a woman from the tribe of Levi.*b* 2She became pregnant and gave birth to a baby boy. The mother saw how beautiful the baby was and hid him for three months. 3She hid him for as long as she could. After three months she made a basket and covered it with tar* so that it would float. Then she put the baby in the basket and put the basket in the river in the tall grass. 4The baby's sister stayed and watched to see what would happen to the baby.

5Just then, Pharaoh's daughter went to the river to bathe. She saw the basket in the tall grass, so she told one of them to go get the basket. 6The king's daughter opened the basket and saw a baby boy. The baby was crying and she felt sorry for it. Then she noticed that it was one of the Hebrew*c* babies.

7The baby's sister was still hiding. She stood and asked the king's daughter, "Do you want me to go find a Hebrew woman who can nurse the baby and help you care for it?"

8The king's daughter said, "Yes, please."

So the girl went and brought the baby's own mother.

9The king's daughter said to the mother, "Take this baby and feed him for me. I'll pay you to take care of him."

So the woman took her baby and cared for him. 10The baby grew, and after some time, the woman gave the baby to the king's daughter. The king's daughter accepted the baby as

her own son. She named him Moses*d* because she had pulled him from the water.

Moses Helps His People

11Moses grew and became a man. He saw that his own people, the Hebrews, were forced to work very hard. One day he saw an Egyptian man beating a Hebrew man. 12Moses looked around and saw that no one was watching, so he killed the Egyptian and buried him in the sand.

13The next day Moses saw two Hebrew men fighting each other. He saw that one man was wrong and said to him, "Why are you hurting your neighbor?"

14The man answered, "Did anyone say you could be our ruler and judge? Tell me, will you kill me as you killed the Egyptian yesterday*e*?"

Then Moses was afraid. He thought to himself, "Now everyone knows what I did."

15Pharaoh heard about what Moses did, so he decided to kill him. But Moses ran away from Pharaoh and went to the land of Midian.

Moses in Midian

Moses stopped near a well in Midian. 16There was a priest there who had seven daughters. These girls came to that well to get water for their father's sheep. They were trying to fill the water trough with water. 17But there were some shepherds there who chased the girls away and would not let them get water. So Moses helped the girls and gave water to their animals.

18Then they went back to their father, Reuel.*f* He asked them, "Why have you come home early today?"

19The girls answered, "The shepherds chased us away, but an Egyptian rescued us. He got water for us and gave it to our animals."

20So Reuel said to his daughters, "Where is this man? Why did you leave him? Go invite him to eat with us."

21Moses was happy to stay with that man. Reuel let Moses marry his daughter, Zipporah. 22Zipporah became pregnant and had a son. Moses named him Gershom*g* because Moses was a stranger in a land that was not his own.

God Decides to Help Israel

23A long time passed and that king of Egypt died. But the Israelites were still forced to

*a*1:17 *trusted* Literally, "feared" or "respected." Also in verses 20–21.
*b*2:1 *woman ... Levi* Literally, "the daughter of Levi." See Ex. 6:20; Num. 26:59.
*c*2:6 *Hebrew* Or "Israelite." Also in verses 7, 11, 13.
*d*2:10 *Moses* This name is like a Hebrew word meaning "to pull or draw out."
*e*2:14 *yesterday* This word is from the ancient Greek version.
*f*2:18 *Reuel* He is also called Jethro.
*g*2:22 *Gershom* This name is like the Hebrew words meaning "a stranger there."

work very hard. They cried for help, and God heard them. ²⁴God heard their painful cries and remembered the agreement he made with Abraham, Isaac, and Jacob. ²⁵God saw the troubles of the Israelites, and he knew that he would soon help them.

The Burning Bush

3 ¹Moses' father-in-law was named Jethro.ᵃ Jethro was a priest of Midian. Moses took care of Jethro's sheep. One day, Moses led the sheep to the west side of the desert. He went to a mountain called Horeb,ᵇ the mountain of God. ²On that mountain, Moses saw the angel of the Lord in a burning bush.

Moses saw a bush that was burning without being destroyed. ³So he decided to go closer to the bush and see how a bush could continue burning without being burned up.

⁴The Lord saw Moses was coming to look at the bush. So he called to him from the bush. He said, "Moses, Moses!"

Moses said, "Yes, Lord."

⁵Then God said, "Don't come any closer. Take off your sandals. You are standing on holy* ground. ⁶I am the God of your ancestors.* I am the God of Abraham, the God of Isaac, and the God of Jacob."

Moses covered his face because he was afraid to look at God.

⁷Then the Lord said, "I have seen the troubles my people have suffered in Egypt, and I have heard their cries when the Egyptians hurt them. I know about their pain. ⁸Now I will go down and save my people from the Egyptians. I will take them from that land and lead them to a good land where they can be free from these troubles.ᶜ It is a land filled with many good things.ᵈ Many different people live in that land: the Canaanites, Hittites, Amorites, Perizzites, Hivites, and Jebusites. ⁹I have heard the cries of the Israelites, and I have seen the way the Egyptians have made life hard for them. ¹⁰So now I am sending you to Pharaoh. Go! Lead my people, the Israelites, out of Egypt."

¹¹But Moses said to God, "I am not a great man! How can I be the one to go to Pharaoh and lead the Israelites out of Egypt?"

¹²God said, "You can do it because I will be with you. This will be the proof that I am sending you: After you lead the people out of Egypt, you will come and worship me on this mountain."

¹³Then Moses said to God, "But if I go to the Israelites and say to them, 'The God of your ancestors sent me,' then the people will ask, 'What is his name?' What should I tell them?"

¹⁴Then God said to Moses, "Tell them, 'I AM WHO I AM.'ᵉ When you go to the Israelites, tell them, 'I AM' sent me to you."

¹⁵God also said to Moses, "This is what you should tell the people: 'Yahweh* is the God of your ancestors, the God of Abraham, the God of Isaac, and the God of Jacob. My name will always be Yahweh.' That is how the people will know me for generations and generations to come. Tell the people, 'Yahweh has sent me to you!'"

¹⁶The Lord also said, "Go and gather together the elders* of the people and tell them, 'Yahweh, the God of your ancestors, has appeared to me. The God of Abraham, Isaac, and Jacob spoke to me. The Lord says, I have been watching over you and I have seen what people did to you in Egypt. ¹⁷And I have decided that I will take you from the troubles you are suffering in Egypt. I will lead you to the land that now belongs to many different people: the Canaanites, Hittites, Amorites, Perizzites, Hivites, and Jebusites. I will lead you to a land filled with many good things.'

¹⁸"The elders will listen to you. And then you and the elders will go to the Pharaoh. You will tell him, 'Yahweh is the God of the Hebrews.ᶠ He came to us and told us to travel three days into the desert. There we must offer sacrifices* to Yahweh our God.'

¹⁹"But I know that the Pharaoh will not let you go. Only a great power will force him to let you go, ²⁰so I will use my great power against Egypt. I will cause amazing things to happen in that land. After I do this, he will let you go. ²¹And I will cause the Egyptians to be kind to the Israelites. They will give many gifts to your people when they leave Egypt.

²²"All the Hebrew women will ask their Egyptian neighbors and the Egyptian women living in their houses for gifts. And those Egyptian women will give them gifts of silver, gold, and fine clothing. Then you will put those gifts on your children. In this way you will take away the wealth of the Egyptians."

Proof for Moses

4 ¹Then Moses said to God, "But the Israelites will not believe me when I tell them that you sent me. They will say, 'The Lordᵍ did not appear to you.'"

²But God said to Moses, "What is that you have in your hand?"

Moses answered, "It is my walking stick."

³Then God said, "Throw your walking stick on the ground."

So Moses threw his walking stick on the ground, and it became a snake. Moses ran from it, ⁴but the Lord said to him, "Reach out and grab the snake by its tail."

ᵃ3:1 *Jethro* He is also called Reuel.
ᵇ3:1 *a mountain called Horeb* That is, "Mount Sinai."
ᶜ3:8 *land ... troubles* Or "a spacious land."
ᵈ3:8 *land ... things* Literally, "land flowing with milk and honey." Also in verse 17.

ᵉ3:14 *I AM WHO I AM* The Hebrew words are like the name Yahweh. See "Yahweh" in the Word List.
ᶠ3:18 *Hebrew* Or "Israelite." Also in verse 22.
ᵍ4:1 *The Lord* Or "Yahweh." See "Yahweh" in the Word List.

When Moses reached out and caught the snake's tail, the snake became a walking stick again. ⁵Then God said, "Use your stick in this way, and the people will believe that you saw the LORD, the God of your ancestors,* the God of Abraham, the God of Isaac, and the God of Jacob."

⁶Then the LORD said to Moses, "I will give you another proof. Put your hand under your robe."

So Moses opened his robe and put his hand inside. Then he brought his hand out of the robe and it was changed. His hand was covered with spots that were white like snow.

⁷Then God said, "Now put your hand into your robe again." So Moses put his hand into his robe again. Then he brought his hand out, and his hand was changed. Now his hand was good again, as it was before.

⁸Then God said, "If the people don't believe you when you use your walking stick, then they will believe you when you show them this sign. ⁹If they still refuse to believe after you show them both of these signs, then take some water from the Nile River. Pour the water on the ground, and as soon as it touches the ground, it will become blood."

¹⁰Then Moses said to the LORD, "But, Lord, I am telling you, I am not a good speaker. I have never been able to speak well. And that hasn't changed since you started talking to me. I am still not a good speaker. You know that I speak slowly and don't use the best words."ᵃ

¹¹Then the LORD said to him, "Who made a person's mouth? And who can make someone deaf or not able to speak? Who can make a person blind? Who can make a person able to see? I am the one. I am the LORD. ¹²So go. I will be with you when you speak. I will give you the words to say."

¹³But Moses said, "My Lord, I beg you to send someone else, not me."

¹⁴Then the LORD became angry with Moses and said, "All right! I'll give you someone to help you. Aaron the Levite* is your brother, isn't he? He is a good speaker. In fact, Aaron is already coming to meet you, and he will be happy to see you. ¹⁵I will tell you what to say. Then you will tell Aaron, and I will help him say it well. I will tell both of you what to do. ¹⁶So Aaron will speak to the people for you. You will be like a great king, and he will be your official speaker.ᵇ ¹⁷So go and carry your walking stick with you. Use it and the other miracles to show the people that I am with you."

Moses Leaves Midian

¹⁸Then Moses went back to Jethro, his father-in-law. Moses said to him, "Please let me go back to Egypt. I want to see if my people are still alive."

Jethro said to Moses, "Go in peace."

¹⁹Then, while Moses was still in Midian, God said to him, "It is safe for you to go back to Egypt now. The men who wanted to kill you are now dead."

²⁰So Moses put his wife and children on the donkey and returned to Egypt. He carried his walking stick with him—the walking stick with the power of God.

²¹While Moses was traveling back to Egypt, the LORD spoke to him, "When you talk to Pharaoh remember to show him all the miracles that I have given you the power to do. But I will cause Pharaoh to be very stubborn. He will not let the people go. ²²Then you should say to Pharaoh, 'This is what the LORD says: ²³Israel is my firstborn* son. And I am telling you to let my son go and worship me. If you refuse to let Israel go, then I will kill your firstborn son.'"

Moses' Son Circumcised

²⁴On the way to Egypt, Moses stopped at a place to spend the night. The LORD met Moses at that place and tried to kill him.ᶜ ²⁵But Zipporah took a flint knifeᵈ and circumcised* her son. She took the skin and touched his feet. Then she said to Moses, "You are a bridegroom of blood to me." ²⁶Zipporah said this because she had to circumcise her son. So God let Moses live.ᵉ

Moses Arrives in Egypt

²⁷The LORD had spoken to Aaron and told him, "Go out into the desert and meet Moses." So Aaron went and met Moses at the Mountain of God.ᶠ He saw Moses and kissed him. ²⁸Moses told Aaron why the LORD had sent him. And he told Aaron about all the miracles and things he must do to prove that God had sent him. Moses told him everything the LORD had said.

²⁹So Moses and Aaron went and gathered together all the elders* of the Israelites. ³⁰Then Aaron spoke to the people and told them everything the LORD had told Moses. Then Moses did the miracles for all the people to see. ³¹The people believed that God had sent Moses. The Israelites knew that God had seen their troubles, and that he had come to help them. So they bowed down and worshiped God.

Moses and Aaron Before Pharaoh

5 ¹After Moses and Aaron talked to the people, they went to Pharaoh and said, "The LORD,ᵍ the God of Israel, says, 'Let my people

ᵃ4:10 *I talk ... words* Or "I stutter and don't speak clearly."
ᵇ4:16 *You will be ... speaker* Literally, "He will be your mouth, and you will be his God."
ᶜ4:24 *tried to kill him* Or possibly, "wanted to circumcise him."
ᵈ4:25 *flint knife* A sharp knife made from flint rock.
ᵉ4:26 Or "And he was healed. She said, 'You are a bridegroom of blood' because of the circumcision."
ᶠ4:27 *Mountain of God* That is, Mount Horeb (Sinai).
ᵍ5:1 *LORD* Or "YAHWEH." See "YAHWEH" in the Word List.

go into the desert so that they can have a festival to honor me.'"

²But Pharaoh said, "Who is the LORD? Why should I obey him? Why should I let Israel go? I don't even know who this LORD is, so I refuse to let Israel go."

³Then Aaron and Moses said, "The God of the Hebrews[a] has talked with us. So we beg you to let us travel three days into the desert. There we will offer a sacrifice* to the LORD our God. If we don't do this, he might become angry and destroy us. He might make us die from sickness or war."

⁴But Pharaoh said to them, "Moses and Aaron, you are bothering the workers. Let them do their work. Go back to your own work! ⁵There are very many workers, and you are keeping them from doing their jobs."

Pharaoh Punishes the People

⁶That same day, Pharaoh gave a command to the slave masters and Hebrew foremen. ⁷He said, "You have always given the people straw to use to make bricks. But now, tell them they have to go and find their own straw to make bricks. ⁸But they must still make the same number of bricks as they did before. They have gotten lazy. That is why they are asking me to let them go. They don't have enough work to do. That is why they asked me to let them make sacrifices* to their God. ⁹So make these people work harder. Keep them busy. Then they will not have enough time to listen to the lies of Moses."

¹⁰So the Egyptian slave masters and the Hebrew foremen went to the Israelites and said, "Pharaoh has decided that he will not give you straw for your bricks. ¹¹You must go and get the straw for yourselves. So go and find straw, but you must still make as many bricks as you made before."

¹²So the people went everywhere in Egypt looking for straw. ¹³The slave masters forced the people to work even harder. They forced the people to make as many bricks as before. ¹⁴The Egyptian slave masters had chosen the Hebrew foremen and had made them responsible for the work the people did. The Egyptian slave masters beat these foremen and said to them, "Why aren't you making as many bricks as you made in the past? If you could do it then, you can do it now!"

¹⁵Then the Hebrew foremen went to Pharaoh. They complained and said, "We are your servants. Why are you treating us like this? ¹⁶You give us no straw, but you tell us to make as many bricks as before. And now our masters are beating us. Your people are wrong for doing this."

¹⁷Pharaoh answered, "You are lazy, and you don't want to work! That is why you ask me to let you go. And that is why you want to leave here and make sacrifices to the LORD. ¹⁸Now, go back to work! We will not give you any straw. And you must still make as many bricks as you did before."

¹⁹The Hebrew foremen knew they were in trouble, because the Pharaoh had told them, "You must still make as many bricks as you made before."

²⁰When they were leaving the meeting with Pharaoh, they passed Moses and Aaron. Moses and Aaron were waiting for them. ²¹So they said to Moses and Aaron, "May the LORD take care of you. May the LORD judge you for what you did! You made Pharaoh and his rulers hate us. You have given them an excuse to kill us."

Moses Complains to God

²²Then Moses prayed to the LORD and said, "Lord, why have you done this terrible thing to your people? Why did you send me here? ²³I went to Pharaoh and said what you told me to say. But since that time he has made the people suffer, and you have done nothing to help them!"

6 ¹Then the LORD said to Moses, "Now you will see what I will do to Pharaoh. I will use my great power against him, and he will let my people go. He will be so ready for them to leave that he will force them to go."

²Then God said to Moses, ³"I am the LORD. I appeared to Abraham, Isaac, and Jacob. They called me God All-Powerful. They did not know my name, the LORD. ⁴I made an agreement with them. I promised to give them the land of Canaan.* They lived in that land, but it was not their own. ⁵Now, I have heard their painful cries. I know that they are slaves in Egypt. And I remember my agreement. ⁶So tell the Israelites that I say to them, 'I am the LORD. I will save you. You will no longer be slaves of the Egyptians. I will use my great power to make you free, and I will bring terrible punishment to the Egyptians. ⁷You will be my people and I will be your God. I am the LORD your God, and you will know that I made you free from Egypt. ⁸I made a great promise to Abraham, Isaac, and Jacob. I promised to give them a special land. So I will lead you to that land. I will give you that land. It will be yours. I am the LORD.'"

⁹So Moses told this to the Israelites, but the people would not listen to him. They were working so hard that they were not patient with Moses.

¹⁰Then the LORD said to Moses, ¹¹"Go tell Pharaoh that he must let the Israelites leave his land."

¹²But Moses answered, "The Israelites refuse to listen to me. So surely Pharaoh will also refuse to listen. I am a very bad speaker."[b]

---

[a]**5:3** *Hebrews* Or "Israelites." Also in verses 10, 14, 15, 19.

[b]**6:12** *I am a very bad speaker* Or "I sound like a foreigner." Literally, "I have uncircumcised lips."

¹³But the LORD talked with Moses and Aaron and commanded them to go and talk to the Israelites and to Pharaoh, the king of Egypt. God commanded them to lead the Israelites out of the land of Egypt.

Some of the Families of Israel

¹⁴Here are the names of the leaders of the families of Israel: Israel's first son, Reuben, had four sons. They were Hanoch, Pallu, Hezron, and Carmi. ¹⁵Simeon's sons were Jemuel, Jamin, Ohad, Jakin, Zohar, and Shaul. (Shaul was the son from a Canaanite woman). ¹⁶Levi lived 137 years. His sons were Gershon, Kohath, and Merari. ¹⁷Gershon had two sons, Libni and Shimei. ¹⁸Kohath lived 133 years. His sons were Amram, Izhar, Hebron, and Uzziel. ¹⁹Merari's sons were Mahli and Mushi. All these families were from Israel's son Levi.

²⁰Amram lived 137 years. He married his father's sister, Jochebed. Amram and Jochebed gave birth to Aaron and Moses. ²¹Izhar's sons were Korah, Nepheg, and Zicri. ²²Uzziel's sons were Mishael, Elzaphan, and Sithri.

²³Aaron married Elisheba. (Elisheba was the daughter of Amminadab, and the sister of Nahshon.) Aaron and Elisheba gave birth to Nadab, Abihu, Eleazar, and Ithamar. ²⁴The sons of Korah (that is, the ancestors of the Korahites) were Assir, Elkanah, and Abiasaph. ²⁵Aaron's son, Eleazar, married a daughter of Putiel. She gave birth to Phinehas. All these people were from Israel's son, Levi.

²⁶Aaron and Moses were from this tribe. And they are the men who God spoke to and said, "Lead my people out of Israel in groups.ᵃ" ²⁷Aaron and Moses are the men who talked to Pharaoh, the king of Egypt, and told him to let the Israelites leave Egypt.

. God Repeats His Call to Moses

²⁸In the land of Egypt God spoke to Moses. ²⁹He said, "I am the LORD. Tell the king of Egypt everything that I tell you."

³⁰But Moses answered, "I am a very bad speaker. The king will not listen to me."

7 ¹The LORD said to Moses, "I will be with you. You will be like a great king to Pharaoh, and your brother will be your official speaker.ᵇ ²You will tell Aaron everything that I command you. Then he will tell the king what I say. And Pharaoh will let the Israelites leave this country. ³But I will make Pharaoh stubborn so that he will not do what you tell him. Then I will do many miracles in Egypt to prove who I am. ⁴But he will still refuse to listen. So then I will punish Egypt very much. And I will lead my army, my people, out of that land. ⁵I will punish the people of Egypt,

ᵃ6:26 *groups* Or "divisions." This is a military term. It shows that Israel was organized like an army.

ᵇ7:1 *You will be ... official speaker* Literally, "You will be a god to Pharaoh and your brother Aaron will be your prophet."

and they will learn that I am the LORD. Then I will lead my people out of their country."

⁶Moses and Aaron did what the LORD told them. ⁷Moses was 80 years old at the time, and Aaron was 83.

Moses' Walking Stick Becomes a Snake

⁸The LORD said to Moses and Aaron, ⁹"Pharaoh will ask you to prove your power. He will ask you to do a miracle. Tell Aaron to throw his walking stick on the ground. While Pharaoh is watching, the stick will become a snake."

¹⁰So Moses and Aaron went to Pharaoh and obeyed the LORD. Aaron threw his walking stick down. While Pharaoh and his officers watched, the stick became a snake. ¹¹So Pharaoh called for his wise men and magicians. These men used their magic, and they were able to do the same thing as Aaron. ¹²They threw their walking sticks on the ground, and their sticks became snakes. But then Aaron's walking stick ate theirs. ¹³Pharaoh still refused to let the people go, just as the LORD had said. Pharaoh refused to listen to Moses and Aaron.

The Water Becomes Blood

¹⁴Then the LORD said to Moses, "Pharaoh is being stubborn. He refuses to let the people go. ¹⁵In the morning, Pharaoh will go out to the river. Go to him by the edge of the Nile River. Take the walking stick that became a snake. ¹⁶Tell him this: 'The LORD, the God of the Hebrews, sent me to you. He told me to tell you to let his people go worship him in the desert. Until now you have not listened to the Lord. ¹⁷So the LORD says that he will do something to show you that he is the LORD. I will hit the water of the Nile River with this walking stick in my hand, and the river will turn into blood. ¹⁸The fish in the river will die, and the river will begin to stink. Then the Egyptians will not be able to drink the water from the river.'"

¹⁹The LORD said to Moses: "Tell Aaron to hold the walking stick in his hand over the rivers, canals, lakes, and every place where they store water. When he does this, all the water will turn into blood. All of the water, even the water stored in wood and stone jars, will turn into blood."

²⁰So Moses and Aaron did what the LORD commanded. Aaron raised the walking stick and hit the water in the Nile River. He did this in front of Pharaoh and his officials. So all the water in the river changed into blood. ²¹The fish in the river died, and the river began to stink. So the Egyptians could not drink water from the river. The blood was everywhere in Egypt.

²²The magicians used their magic to do the same thing. So Pharaoh refused to listen to Moses and Aaron. This happened just as the LORD said. ²³Pharaoh ignored what Moses and

Aaron had done. He turned and went into his house.

²⁴The Egyptians could not drink the water from the river, so they dug wells around the river for water to drink.

The Frogs

²⁵Seven days passed after the LORD changed the Nile River.

8 ¹Then the LORD told Moses, "Go to Pharaoh and tell him that the LORD says, 'Let my people go to worship me! ²If you refuse to let my people go, then I will fill Egypt with frogs. ³The Nile River will be filled with frogs. They will come from the river and enter your houses. They will be in your bedrooms and in your beds. They will be in the houses of your officials and in your ovens and in your jars of water. ⁴The frogs will be all over you, your people, and your officials.'"

⁵Then the LORD said to Moses, "Tell Aaron to hold the walking stick in his hand over the canals, rivers, and lakes. Then the frogs will come out onto the land of Egypt."

⁶So Aaron raised his hand over the waters of Egypt, and the frogs began coming out of the water and covered the land of Egypt.

⁷The magicians used their magic to do the same thing—so even more frogs came out onto the land in Egypt!

⁸Pharaoh called for Moses and Aaron and said, "Ask the LORD to remove the frogs from me and my people. I will let the people go to offer sacrifices* to the LORD."

⁹Moses said to Pharaoh, "I will pray for you, your people, and your officials. Then the frogs will leave you and your houses. They will remain only in the river. When do you want the frogs to go away?"

¹⁰Pharaoh said, "Tomorrow."

Moses said, "It will happen as you say. In this way you will know that there is no god like the LORD our God. ¹¹The frogs will leave you, your house, your officials, and your people. They will remain only in the river."

¹²Moses and Aaron left Pharaoh. Moses prayed to the LORD about the frogs he had sent against Pharaoh. ¹³And the LORD did what Moses asked. The frogs died in the houses, in the yards, and in the fields. ¹⁴They began to rot, and the whole country began to stink. ¹⁵But when Pharaoh saw that they were free of the frogs, he again became stubborn. Pharaoh did not do what Moses and Aaron had asked him to do. This happened just as the LORD had said.

The Lice

¹⁶Then the LORD said to Moses, "Tell Aaron to raise his stick and hit the dust on the ground, and everywhere in Egypt dust will become lice."

¹⁷They did this. Aaron raised the stick in his hand and hit the dust on the ground, and everywhere in Egypt the dust became lice.

The lice got on the animals and the people.

¹⁸The magicians used their magic and tried to do the same thing. But the magicians could not make lice come from the dust. The lice remained on the animals and the people. ¹⁹So the magicians told Pharaoh that the power of God did this. But Pharaoh refused to listen to them. This happened just as the LORD had said.

The Flies

²⁰The LORD said to Moses, "Get up in the morning and go to Pharaoh. He will go out to the river. Tell him that the LORD says, 'Let my people go and worship me! ²¹If you don't let my people go, then flies will come into your houses. The flies will be on you and your officials. The houses of Egypt will be full of flies. They will be all over the ground too! ²²But I will not treat the Israelites the same as the Egyptians. There will not be any flies in Goshen, where my people live. In this way you will know that I, the LORD, am in this land. ²³So tomorrow I will treat my people differently from your people. This will be my proof.'"

²⁴So the LORD did just what he said. Millions of flies came into Egypt. The flies were in Pharaoh's house, and they were in all his officials' houses. They were all over Egypt. The flies were ruining the country. ²⁵So Pharaoh called for Moses and Aaron and told them, "Offer sacrifices* to your God here in this country."

²⁶But Moses said, "It would not be right to do that. The Egyptians think it is terrible to kill animals as sacrifices for the LORD our God. If we do this here, the Egyptians will see us and throw stones at us and kill us. ²⁷Let us go three days into the desert and offer sacrifices to the LORD our God. This is what the LORD told us to do."

²⁸So Pharaoh said, "I will let you go and offer sacrifices to the LORD your God in the desert, but you must not go very far. Now, go and pray for me."

²⁹Moses said, "Look, I will leave and ask the LORD to remove the flies from you, your people, and your officials tomorrow. But you must not stop the people from offering sacrifices to the LORD."

³⁰So Moses left Pharaoh and prayed to the LORD. ³¹And the LORD did what Moses asked. He removed the flies from Pharaoh, his officials, and his people. None of the flies remained. ³²But Pharaoh again became stubborn and did not let the people go.

The Disease of the Farm Animals

9 ¹Then the LORD told Moses to go to Pharaoh and tell him: "The LORD, the God of the Hebrews, says, 'Let my people go to worship me!' ²If you continue to hold them and refuse to let them go, ³then the LORD will use his power against your animals in the fields.

He will cause all of your horses, donkeys, camels, cattle, and sheep to get sick with a terrible disease. ⁴But the LORD will treat Israel's animals differently from the animals of Egypt. None of the animals that belong to the Israelites will die. ⁵The LORD has set the time for this to happen. Tomorrow he will make this happen in this country."

⁶The next morning all the farm animals in Egypt died, but none of the animals that belonged to the Israelites died. ⁷Pharaoh sent people to see if any of the animals of Israel died. Not one of them died. But Pharaoh remained stubborn and did not let the people go.

The Boils

⁸The LORD said to Moses and Aaron, "Fill your hands with the ashes from a furnace.* Moses, you throw the ashes into the air in front of Pharaoh. ⁹This will become dust that will go throughout the land of Egypt. Whenever the dust touches a person or an animal in Egypt, sores will break out on the skin."

¹⁰So Moses and Aaron took ashes from a furnace and went and stood before Pharaoh. Moses threw the ashes into the air, and sores began breaking out on people and animals. ¹¹The magicians could not stop Moses from doing this, because even the magicians had the sores. This happened everywhere in Egypt. ¹²But the LORD made Pharaoh stubborn, so he refused to listen to Moses and Aaron, just as the LORD had said.

The Hail

¹³Then the LORD said to Moses, "Get up in the morning and go to Pharaoh. Tell him that the LORD, the God of the Hebrews, says, 'Let my people go to worship me! ¹⁴This time, I will use my full power against you, your officials, and your people. Then you will know that there is no god in the world like me. ¹⁵I could use my power and cause a disease that would wipe you and your people off the earth. ¹⁶But I have put you here for a reason. I have put you here so that I could show you my power. Then people all over the world will learn about me! ¹⁷You are still against my people. You are not letting them go free. ¹⁸So at this time tomorrow, I will cause a very bad hailstorm. There has never been a hailstorm like this in Egypt, not since Egypt became a nation. ¹⁹Now, you must put your animals in a safe place. Everything you own that is now in the fields must be put in a safe place. Any person or animal that remains in the fields will be killed. The hail will fall on everything that is not gathered into your houses.'"

²⁰Some of Pharaoh's officials paid attention to the LORD's message. They quickly put all of their animals and slaves into houses. ²¹But other people ignored the LORD's message and lost all their slaves and animals that were in the fields.

²²The LORD told Moses, "Raise your hand into the air and the hail will start falling all over Egypt. The hail will fall on all the people, animals, and plants in all the fields of Egypt."

²³So Moses raised his walking stick into the air, and the LORD caused thunder, lightning, and hail. The hail fell all over Egypt. ²⁴The hail was falling, and lightning was flashing all through it. It was the worst hailstorm that had ever hit Egypt since it had become a nation. ²⁵The storm destroyed everything in the fields in Egypt. The hail destroyed people, animals, and plants. The hail also broke all the trees in the fields. ²⁶The only place that did not get hail was the land of Goshen, where the Israelites lived.

²⁷Pharaoh sent for Moses and Aaron and told them, "This time I have sinned. The LORD is right, and I and my people are wrong. ²⁸The hail and thunder from God are too much! Ask God to stop the storm and I will let you go. You don't have to stay here."

²⁹Moses told Pharaoh, "When I leave the city, I will lift my hands in prayer to the LORD, and the thunder and hail will stop. Then you will know that the LORD is in this land. ³⁰But I know that you and your officials don't really fear and respect the LORD yet."

³¹The flax had already developed its seeds, and the barley was already blooming. So these plants were destroyed. ³²But wheat and spelt* ripen later than the other grains, so these plants were not destroyed.

³³Moses left Pharaoh and went outside the city. He lifted his hands in prayer to the LORD. And the thunder and hail stopped, and then even the rain stopped. ³⁴When Pharaoh saw that the rain, hail, and thunder had stopped, he again did wrong. He and his officials became stubborn again. ³⁵Pharaoh refused to let the Israelites go free, just as the LORD had said through Moses.

The Locusts

10 ¹The LORD said to Moses, "Go to Pharaoh. I have made him and his officials stubborn. I did this so that I could show them my powerful miracles. ²I also did this so that you could tell your children and your grandchildren about the miracles and other wonderful things that I have done in Egypt. Then all of you will know that I am the LORD."

³So Moses and Aaron went to Pharaoh. They told him, "The LORD, the God of the Hebrews,ᵃ says, 'How long will you refuse to obey me? Let my people go to worship me! ⁴If you refuse to let my people go, then tomorrow I will bring locusts into your country. ⁵The locusts will cover the land. There will be so many locusts that you will not be able

---

ᵃ10:3 *Hebrews* Or "Israelites." This name might also mean "descendants of Eber" (read Gen. 10:25–31) or "people from beyond the Euphrates River."

to see the ground. Anything that was left from the hailstorm will be eaten by the locusts. The locusts will eat all the leaves from every tree in the field. 6They will fill all your houses, and all your officials' houses, and all the houses in Egypt. There will be more locusts than your fathers or your grandfathers ever saw. There will be more locusts than there have ever been since people began living in Egypt.'" Then Moses turned and left Pharaoh.

7Then the officials asked Pharaoh, "How long will we be trapped by these people? Let the men go to worship the LORD their God. If you don't let them go, before you know it, Egypt will be destroyed!"

8So Pharaoh told his officials to bring Moses and Aaron back to him. Pharaoh said to them, "Go and worship the LORD your God. But tell me, just who is going?"

9Moses answered, "All of our people, young and old, will go. And we will take our sons and daughters, and our sheep and cattle with us. We will all go because the LORD's festival is for all of us."

10Pharaoh said to them, "The LORD really will have to be with you before I let you and all of your children leave Egypt. Look, you are planning something evil. 11The men can go worship the LORD. That is what you asked for in the beginning. But all of your people cannot go." Then Pharaoh sent Moses and Aaron away.

12The LORD told Moses, "Raise your hand over the land of Egypt and the locusts will come! They will spread all over the land of Egypt and will eat all the plants that the hail did not destroy."

13So Moses raised his walking stick over the land of Egypt, and the LORD caused a strong wind to blow from the east. The wind blew all that day and night. When morning came, the wind had brought the locusts to the land of Egypt. 14The locusts flew into the country of Egypt and landed on the ground. There were more locusts than there had ever been in Egypt. And there will never again be that many locusts there. 15They covered the ground, and the whole country became dark. The locusts ate every plant on the ground and all the fruit in the trees that the hail had not destroyed. There were no leaves left on any of the trees or plants anywhere in Egypt.

16Pharaoh quickly called for Moses and Aaron. Pharaoh said, "I have sinned against the LORD your God and against you. 17Now, forgive me for my sins this time. Ask the LORD to remove this 'death' from me."

18Moses left Pharaoh and prayed to the LORD. 19So the LORD changed the wind. He made a very strong wind blow from the west, and it blew the locusts out of Egypt and into the Red Sea. Not one locust was left in Egypt! 20But the LORD caused Pharaoh to be stubborn again, and Pharaoh did not let the Israelites go.

The Darkness

21Then the LORD told Moses, "Raise your hand into the air and darkness will cover Egypt. It will be so dark you can feel it!"

22So Moses raised his hand into the air and a cloud of darkness covered Egypt. The darkness stayed in Egypt for three days. 23None of the people could see each other, and no one got up to go any place for three days. But there was light in all the places where the Israelites lived.

24Again Pharaoh called for Moses. He said, "Go and worship the LORD! You can take your children with you. But you must leave your sheep and cattle here."

25Moses said, "No, we will take them all. In fact, you will give us offerings and sacrifices* for us to use in worshiping the LORD our God. 26Yes, we will take our animals with us to worship the LORD our God. Not one hoof will be left behind. We don't know yet exactly what we will need to worship the LORD. We will learn that only when we get there."

27The LORD made Pharaoh stubborn again, so he refused to let them go. 28Then Pharaoh told Moses, "Get out of here. I don't want you to come here again. The next time you come to see me, you will die!"

29Then Moses told Pharaoh, "You are right about one thing. I will not come to see you again."

The Death of the Firstborn

11 1Then the LORD told Moses, "I have one more disaster to bring against Pharaoh and Egypt. After this, he will ask you to leave Egypt. In fact, he will force you to leave this country. 2You must give this message to the Israelites: 'Men and women, you must ask your neighbors to give you things made of silver and gold.'" 3The LORD caused the Egyptians to be kind to the Israelites. The Egyptians, even Pharaoh's own officials, already considered Moses to be a great man.

4Moses said to the king, "The LORD says, 'At midnight tonight, I will go through Egypt, 5and every firstborn* son in Egypt will die, from the firstborn son of Pharaoh, the ruler of Egypt, to the firstborn son of the slave girl grinding grain. Even the firstborn animals will die. 6The crying in Egypt will be worse than at any time in the past or any time in the future. 7But none of the Israelites or their animals will be hurt—not even a dog will bark at them.' Then you will know that the LORD has treated Israel differently from Egypt. 8All these officials of yours will come down and bow to me. They will say, 'Leave and take all your people with you.' Only then will I leave!" Then in anger, Moses left the meeting with Pharaoh.

9Then the LORD told Moses, "The reason Pharaoh did not listen to you is so that I could show my great power in Egypt." 10That is why Moses and Aaron did all these great miracles in front of Pharaoh. And that is why the LORD made Pharaoh so stubborn that he would not let the Israelites leave his country.

Passover

12 [1]While Moses and Aaron were still in Egypt, the LORD spoke to them. He said, [2]"This month[a] will be the first month of the year for you. [3]This command is for the whole community of Israel: On the tenth day of this month each man must get one lamb for the people in his house. [4]If there are not enough people in his house to eat a whole lamb, then he should invite some of his neighbors to share the meal. There must be enough lamb for everyone to eat. [5]The lamb must be a one-year-old male, and it must be completely healthy. This animal can be either a young sheep or a young goat. [6]You should watch over the animal until the 14th day of the month. On that day, all the people of the community of Israel must kill these animals just before dark. [7]You must collect the blood from these animals and put it on the top and sides of the doorframe of every house where the people eat this meal.

[8]"On this night you must roast the lamb and eat all the meat. You must also eat bitter herbs and bread made without yeast. [9]You must not eat the lamb raw or boiled in water. You must roast the whole lamb over a fire. The lamb must still have its head, legs, and inner parts. [10]You must eat all the meat that night. If any of the meat is left until morning, you must burn it in the fire.

[11]"When you eat the meal, you must be fully dressed and ready to travel. You must have your sandals on your feet and your walking stick in your hand. You must eat in a hurry, because this is the LORD's Passover.*

[12]"Tonight I will go through Egypt and kill every firstborn* man and animal in Egypt. In this way I will judge all the gods of Egypt and show that I am the LORD. [13]But the blood on your houses will be a special sign. When I see the blood, I will pass over[b] your house. I will cause bad things to happen to the people of Egypt. But none of these bad diseases will hurt you.

[14]"You will always remember tonight—it will be a special festival for you. Your descendants will honor the LORD with this festival forever. [15]For this festival you will eat bread made without yeast for seven days. On the first day, you will remove all the yeast from your houses. No one should eat any yeast for the full seven days of this festival. Anyone who eats yeast must be separated from the rest of Israel. [16]There will be holy assemblies on the first day and the last day of the festival. You must not do any work on these days. The

only work you can do is preparing the food for your meals. [17]You must remember the Festival of Unleavened Bread,* because on this day I took all of your people out of Egypt in groups.[c] All of your descendants must remember this day. This is a law that will last forever. [18]So on the evening of the 14th day of the first month, you will begin eating bread without yeast. You will eat this bread until the evening of the 21st day of the same month. [19]For seven days there must not be any yeast in your houses. Anyone, either a citizen of Israel or a foreigner living among you,[d] who eats yeast at this time must be separated from the rest of Israel. [20]During this festival you must not eat any yeast. You must eat bread without yeast wherever you live."

[21]So Moses called all the elders* together and told them, "Get the lambs for your families. Kill the lambs for the Passover. [22]Take bunches of hyssop* and dip them in the bowls filled with blood. Paint the blood on the sides and top of each doorframe. No one must leave their house until morning. [23]At the time the LORD goes through Egypt to kill the firstborn, he will see the blood on the sides and top of each doorframe. Then he will protect[e] that house and not let the Destroyer come into any of your houses and hurt you. [24]You must remember this command. This law is for you and your descendants forever. [25]You must remember to do this even when you go to the land the LORD is giving you. [26]When your children ask you, 'Why are we doing this ceremony?' [27]you will say, 'This Passover is to honor the LORD, because when we were in Egypt, the LORD passed over the houses of Israel. He killed the Egyptians, but he saved the people in our houses.'"

Then the people bowed down and worshiped the LORD. [28]The LORD had given this command to Moses and Aaron, so the Israelites did what the Lord commanded.

[29]At midnight the LORD killed all the firstborn sons in Egypt, from the firstborn son of Pharaoh (who ruled Egypt) to the firstborn son of the prisoner sitting in jail. Also all the firstborn animals died. [30]That night someone died in every house in Egypt. Pharaoh, his officials, and all the people of Egypt began to cry loudly.

Israel Leaves Egypt

[31]So that night Pharaoh called for Moses and Aaron and said to them, "Get up and leave my people. You and your people can do as you say. Go and worship the LORD. [32]Take all of your sheep and cattle with you, just as

---

[a]**12:2** *month* Abib (or Nisan). See "Abib" in the Word List.
[b]**12:13** *pass over* Or "protect." Also in verse 27.

[c]**12:17** *groups* Or "divisions." This is a military term. It shows that Israel was organized like an army. Also in verse 51.
[d]**12:19** *foreigner living among you* That is, someone who has chosen to live among the Israelites and obey their laws and customs. Also in verse 48.
[e]**12:23** *protect* Or "pass over."

you said you would. Go! And say a blessing for me too." ³³The people of Egypt also asked them to hurry and leave. They said, "If you don't leave, we will all die!"

³⁴The Israelites did not have time to put the yeast in their bread. They just wrapped the bowls of dough with cloth and carried them on their shoulders. ³⁵Then the Israelites did what Moses asked them to do. They went to their Egyptian neighbors and asked for clothing and things made from silver and gold. ³⁶The LORD caused the Egyptians to be kind to the Israelites, so the Egyptians gave their riches to the Israelites.

³⁷The Israelites traveled from Rameses to Succoth. There were about 600,000 men, not counting the small boys. ³⁸A great number of people who were not Israelites went with them, along with many sheep, cattle, and other livestock. ³⁹The people did not have time to put yeast in their bread or make any special food for their journey. So they had to bake their bread without yeast.

⁴⁰The Israelites had lived in Egypt^a for 430 years. ⁴¹After 430 years, to the very day, all the armies of the LORD^b left Egypt. ⁴²So that is a very special night when the people remember what the LORD did. All the Israelites will remember that night forever.

⁴³The LORD told Moses and Aaron, "Here are the rules for Passover: No foreigner^c is allowed to eat the Passover. ⁴⁴⁻⁴⁵A foreigner who is only a hired worker or is only staying in your country is not allowed to eat the Passover. But if someone buys a slave and circumcises* him, then the slave can eat the Passover.

⁴⁶"Each family must eat the meal in one house. None of the food is to be taken outside the house. Don't break any of the lamb's bones. ⁴⁷The whole community of Israel must do this ceremony. ⁴⁸If a foreigner living among you wants to share in the LORD's Passover, he must be circumcised. Then he can share in the meal like any other citizen of Israel. But a man who is not circumcised cannot eat the Passover meal. ⁴⁹The same rules are for everyone. It doesn't matter if they are citizens or foreigners living among you."

⁵⁰So all the Israelites obeyed the commands that the LORD gave to Moses and Aaron. ⁵¹On that same day the LORD led all the Israelites out of the country of Egypt. The people left in groups.

13 ¹Then the LORD said to Moses, ²"You must give me every male in Israel who is his mother's first child. That means that every firstborn baby boy and every firstborn male animal will be mine."

³Moses said to the people, "Remember this day. You were slaves in Egypt, but on this day the LORD used his great power and made you free. You must not eat bread with yeast. ⁴Today, in the month of Abib,* you are leaving Egypt. ⁵The LORD made a special promise to your ancestors.* He promised to give you the land of the Canaanites, Hittites, Amorites, Hivites, and Jebusites. After the Lord leads you to the land filled with many good things,^d then you must remember this day. You must have a special day of worship on this day during the first month of every year.

⁶"For seven days you must eat only bread without yeast. On the seventh day there will be a great festival to show honor to the LORD. ⁷So for seven days you must not eat any bread made with yeast. There must be no bread with yeast any place in your land. ⁸On this day you should tell your children, 'We are having this festival because the LORD took me out of Egypt.'

⁹"This festival will help you remember; it will be like a string tied on your hand. It will be like a sign before your eyes.^e This festival will help you remember the LORD's teachings. It will help you remember that the LORD used his great power to take you out of Egypt. ¹⁰So remember this festival every year at the right time.

¹¹"The LORD will lead you into the land he promised to give you. The Canaanites live there now. But God promised your ancestors that he would give you this land. After God gives you this land, ¹²you must remember to give him every firstborn boy. Every male animal that is the firstborn must also be given to the LORD. ¹³Every firstborn donkey can be bought back. You can offer a lamb and keep the donkey. If you don't want to buy back the donkey like this, then you must break its neck to kill it. But every firstborn baby boy^f must be bought back from the LORD.

¹⁴"In the future, your children will ask why you do this. They will say, 'What does all this mean?' And you will answer, 'The LORD used his great power to save us from Egypt. We were slaves in that place, but he led us out and brought us here. ¹⁵In Egypt, Pharaoh was stubborn and refused to let us leave. So the LORD killed every firstborn* in all the land. (The Lord killed the firstborn males—animal and human.) That is why I give every firstborn male animal to the LORD, and that is why I buy back each of my firstborn sons from

---

^a**12:40** *Egypt* The ancient Greek and Samaritan versions say, "Egypt and Canaan." This would mean they counted the years from about Abraham's time, not from Joseph's. See Gen. 15:12–16 and Gal. 3:17.
^b**12:41** *armies of the LORD* The Israelites.
^c**12:43** *foreigner* Here, this means someone who has not agreed to follow the laws and customs of Israel.

^d**13:5** *land … things* Literally, "land flowing with milk and honey."
^e**13:9** *string … eyes* Literally, "a mark on your hands and a reminder between your eyes." This might refer to the special things an Israelite ties to his arm and forehead to help him remember God's laws for him. Also in verse 16.
^f**13:13** *baby boy* Or "baby."

the Lord.' ¹⁶This is like a string tied on your hand, like a sign in front of your eyes. It helps you remember that the Lord brought us out of Egypt with his great power."

The Trip Out of Egypt

¹⁷Pharaoh made the people leave Egypt. God did not let the people take the road leading to the land of the Philistines. That road by the Mediterranean Sea is the shortest way, but God said, "If the people go that way they will have to fight. Then they might change their minds and go back to Egypt." ¹⁸So God led them another way through the desert by the Red Sea.ᵃ The Israelites were dressed for war when they left Egypt.

Joseph Goes Home

¹⁹Moses carried the bones of Joseph with him. Before Joseph died, he made the Israelites promise to do this for him. He said, "When God saves you, remember to carry my bones with you out of Egypt."

The Lord Leads His People

²⁰The Israelites left Succoth and camped at Etham. Etham was near the desert. ²¹The Lord led the way. During the day, he used a tall cloud to lead the people. And during the night, he used a tall column of fire to lead the way. This fire gave them light so that they could also travel at night. ²²The cloud was always with them during the day, and the column of fire was always with them at night.

14 ¹Then the Lord said to Moses, ²"Tell the people to go back to Pi Hahiroth. Tell them to spend the night between Migdol and the Red Sea, near Baal Zephon. ³Pharaoh will think that the Israelites are lost in the desert and that the people will have no place to go. ⁴I will make Pharaoh brave, and he will chase you. But I will defeat Pharaoh and his army. This will bring honor to me. Then the people of Egypt will know that I am the Lord." So the Israelites did what he told them.

Pharaoh Chases the Israelites

⁵Pharaoh received a report that the Israelites had escaped. When he heard this, he and his officials changed their minds about what they had done. Pharaoh said, "Why did we let the Israelites leave? Why did we let them run away? Now we have lost our slaves!"

⁶So Pharaoh prepared his chariot* and took his men with him. ⁷He took 600 of his best men and all of his chariots. There was an officer in each chariot.ᵇ ⁸The Israelites were leaving with their arms raised in victory. But the Lord caused Pharaoh, the king of Egypt, to become brave. And Pharaoh chased the Israelites.

ᵃ**13:18 Red Sea** Or "Reed Sea." Also in 14:9, 16, 21, 30. See 1 Kings 9:26.
ᵇ**14:7 There was ... chariot** Or "There were three soldiers in each chariot."

⁹The Egyptian army had many horse soldiers and chariots. They chased the Israelites and caught up with them while they were camped near the Red Sea at Pi Hahiroth, east of Baal Zephon.

¹⁰When the Israelites saw Pharaoh and his army coming toward them, they were very frightened and cried to the Lord for help. ¹¹They said to Moses, "Why did you bring us out of Egypt? Did you bring us out here in the desert to die? We could have died peacefully in Egypt; there were plenty of graves in Egypt. ¹²We told you this would happen! In Egypt we said, 'Please don't bother us. Let us stay and serve the Egyptians.' It would have been better for us to stay and be slaves than to come out here and die in the desert."

¹³But Moses answered, "Don't be afraid! Don't run away! Stand where you are and watch the Lord save you today. You will never see these Egyptians again. ¹⁴You will not have to do anything but stay calm. The Lord will do the fighting for you."

¹⁵Then the Lord said to Moses, "Why are you still crying to me? Tell the Israelites to start moving. ¹⁶Raise the walking stick in your hand over the Red Sea, and the sea will split. Then the people can go across on dry land. ¹⁷I have made the Egyptians brave, so they will chase you. But I will show you that I am more powerful than Pharaoh and all of his horses and chariots. ¹⁸Then Egypt will know that I am the Lord. They will honor me when I defeat Pharaoh and his horse soldiers and chariots."

The Lord Defeats the Egyptian Army

¹⁹Then the angel of God moved to the back of the people. (The angel was usually in front of the people, leading them.) So the tall cloud moved from in front of the people and went to the back of the people. ²⁰In this way the cloud stood between the Egyptians and the Israelites. There was light for the Israelites. But there was darkness for the Egyptians. So the Egyptians did not come any closer to the Israelites that night.

²¹Moses raised his hand over the Red Sea, and the Lord caused a strong wind to blow from the east. The wind blew all night long. The sea split, and the wind made the ground dry. ²²The Israelites went through the sea on dry land. The water was like a wall on their right and on their left. ²³Then all of Pharaoh's chariots* and horse soldiers followed them into the sea. ²⁴Early that morning the Lord looked down from the tall cloud and column of fire at the Egyptian army. Then he made them panic. ²⁵The wheels of the chariots became stuck. It was very hard to control the chariots. The Egyptians shouted, "Let's get out of here! The Lord is fighting against us. He is fighting for the Israelites."

²⁶Then the Lord told Moses, "Raise your hand over the sea to make the water fall

and cover the Egyptian chariots and horse soldiers."

27So just before daylight, Moses raised his hand over the sea. And the water rushed back to its proper level. The Egyptians were running as fast as they could from the water, but the LORD swept them away with the sea. 28The water returned to its normal level and covered the chariots and horse soldiers. Pharaoh's army had been chasing the Israelites, but that army was destroyed. None of them survived!

29But the Israelites crossed the sea on dry land. The water was like a wall on their right and on their left. 30So that day the LORD saved the Israelites from the Egyptians. Later, the Israelites saw the dead bodies of the Egyptians on the shore of the Red Sea. 31The Israelites saw the great power of the LORD when he defeated the Egyptians. So the people feared and respected the LORD, and they began to trust him and his servant Moses.

The Song of Moses

15 ¹Then Moses and the Israelites began singing this song to the LORD:

"I will sing to the LORD!
  He has done great things.
  He threw horse and rider into the sea.
2 The LORD is my strength.
  He saves me,
    and I sing songs of praise to him.ᵃ
  He is my God,
    and I praise him.
  He is the God of my ancestors,*
    and I honor him.
3 The LORD is a great soldier.
  The LORD is his name.
4 He threw Pharaoh's chariots*
    and soldiers into the sea.
  Pharaoh's very best soldiers
    drowned in the Red Sea.ᵇ
5 The deep water covered them,
    and they sank to the bottom like rocks.

6"LORD, your right hand is amazingly strong.
  With your right hand, LORD, you broke
    the enemy to pieces.
7 In your great majesty you destroyed
    those who stood against you.
  Your anger destroyed them,
    like fire burning straw.
8 The wind you sent in anger
    piled the water high.
  The flowing water became a wall,
    solid to its deepest parts.

9"The enemy said,
  'I'll chase them and catch them.

I'll take all their riches.
  I'll take it all with my sword.
  I'll take everything for myself.'
10 But you blew on them
    and covered them with the sea.
  They sank like lead into the deep sea.

11"Are there any gods like the LORD?
  No, there are no gods like you—
    you are wonderfully holy*!
  You are amazingly powerful!
  You do great miracles!
12 You raised your right hand to punish the
    enemy,
    and the ground opened up to swallow
    them.
13 But with your kindness
    you led the people you saved.
  And with your strength
    you led them to your holy land.ᶜ

14"The other nations will hear this story,
    and they will be frightened.
  The Philistines will shake with fear.
15 The commanders of Edom will tremble.
  The leaders of Moab will be afraid.
  The people of Canaan* will lose courage.
16 They will be filled with fear
    when they see your strength.
  They will be as still as a rock, LORD,
    while your people, the ones you made,
    pass by.
17 You will lead your people to your
    mountain.
  You will let them live near the place
    that you, LORD, prepared for your
    throne.
  You will build your temple.

18"The LORD will rule forever and ever!"

19Yes, it really happened! Pharaoh's horses and riders, and chariots went into the sea. And the LORD brought all the water of the sea down on top of them. But the Israelites walked through that sea on dry land. 20Then Aaron's sister, the woman prophet Miriam, took a tambourine. She and the women began singing and dancing. 21Miriam repeated the words,

"Sing to the LORD!
  He has done great things.
  He threw horse and rider into the sea ...."

Israel Goes Into the Desert

22Moses led the Israelites away from the Red Sea and into the Shur desert. They traveled for three days in the desert. They could not find any water. 23Then they came to Marah.ᵈ There was water at Marah, but it was

---

ᵃ15:2 *The LORD ... him* Literally, "Yᴀʜ is my strength and praise. He became my salvation."
ᵇ15:4 *Red Sea* Or "Reed Sea." Also in verse 22. See 1 Kings 9:26.

ᶜ15:13 *holy land* Israel, the special land God set apart for the Israelites.
ᵈ15:23 *Marah* This name means "Bitter" or "Sad."

too bitter to drink. (That is why the place was named Marah.)

²⁴The people began complaining to Moses. They said, "Now what will we drink?"

²⁵So Moses called to the Lord, and the Lord showed him a large piece of wood. When Moses put the wood in the water, the water became good to drink.

There the Lord put in place a law and a command for him and tested him to see if he would obey.ᵃ ²⁶The Lord said to him, "I am the Lord your God. If you listen to me and do what I say is right, and if you obey all my commands and laws, then I will not give you any of the sicknesses that I gave the Egyptians. I am the Lord who heals you."

²⁷Then the people traveled to Elim. At Elim there were twelve springs of water and 70 palm trees. So the people made their camp there near that water.

Israel Complains, So God Sends Food

16 ¹Then the people left Elim and came to the Desert of Zin, between Elim and Sinai. They arrived at that place on the 15th day of the second monthᵇ after leaving Egypt. ²Then the whole community of Israelites began complaining again. They complained to Moses and Aaron in the desert. ³They said, "It would have been better if the Lord had just killed us in the land of Egypt. At least there we had plenty to eat. We had all the food we needed. But now you have brought us out here into this desert to make us all die from hunger."

⁴Then the Lord said to Moses, "I will cause food to fall from the sky. This food will be for you to eat. Every day the people should go out and gather the food they need that day. I will do this to see if they will do what I tell them. ⁵Every day the people will gather only enough food for one day. But on Friday, when the people prepare their food, they will see that they have enough food for two days."ᶜ

⁶So Moses and Aaron said to the Israelites, "Tonight you will see the power of the Lord. You will know that he is the one who brought you out of Egypt. ⁷You have been complaining about the Lord, and he heard you. So tomorrow morning you will see the Glory of the Lord.* You have been complaining and complaining about us. Maybe now we can have a little rest."ᵈ

⁸Then Moses said, "You have been complaining, and the Lord has heard your complaints. So tonight he will give you meat, and in the morning you will have all the bread you need. You have been complaining to Aaron and me. But now, maybe we will have a little rest. Remember, you are not complaining against Aaron and me. You are complaining against the Lord."

⁹Then Moses said to Aaron, "Tell the whole community of Israelites to come together before the Lord, because he has heard their complaints."

¹⁰So Aaron spoke to all the Israelites. While he was talking, the people turned and looked into the desert. And they saw the Glory of the Lord appear in a cloud.

¹¹The Lord said to Moses, ¹²"I have heard the complaints of the Israelites. So tell them, 'Tonight you will eat meat. And in the morning you will have all the bread you want. Then you will know you can trust the Lord, your God.'"

¹³That night, quails *(birds)* came all around the camp, and in the morning dew lay on the ground near the camp. ¹⁴After the dew was gone, something like thin flakes of frost was on the ground. ¹⁵When the Israelites saw it, they asked each other, "What is that?" because they did not know what it was. So Moses told them, "This is the food the Lord is giving you to eat. ¹⁶The Lord says, 'Each of you should gather what you need, a basketᵉ of manna for everyone in your family.'"

¹⁷So that is what the Israelites did. Some people gathered a large amount, some people gathered a little. ¹⁸But when they measured what they had gathered, there was no shortage and there was none left over. Everyone gathered just what they needed.

¹⁹Moses told them, "Don't save that food to eat the next day." ²⁰But some of the people did not obey Moses. They saved their food for the next day. But worms got into the food and it began to stink. Moses was angry with the people who did this.

²¹Every morning the people gathered as much food as they could eat, but by noonᶠ the food melted and was gone.

²²On Friday the people gathered twice as much food—two basketsᵍ for every person. So all the leaders of the people came and told this to Moses.

²³Moses told them, "This is what the Lord said would happen. It happened because tomorrow is the Sabbath, the special day of rest to honor the Lord. You can cook all the food you need to cook for today, but save the rest of this food for tomorrow morning."

²⁴So the people saved the rest of the food for the next day, as Moses had commanded,

---

ᵃ**15:25 There ... he would obey** Or "There the Lord put in place a law and a command for them and tested them to see if they would obey."

ᵇ**16:1 15th day of the second month** That is, the 15th of Iyyar. The Israelites had been traveling for a month.

ᶜ**16:5 Friday, ... two days** This happened so that the people would not have to work on the Sabbath (Saturday), the day of rest.

ᵈ**16:7 You ... rest** Or "Who are we that you should be complaining about us?"

ᵉ**16:16 basket** Literally, "1 omer" (2.2 l). Also in verses 32, 33.

ᶠ**16:21 noon** Literally, "the heat of the day."

ᵍ**16:22 two baskets** Literally, "2 omers" (4.4 l).

and none of the food spoiled or had worms in it.

25On Saturday, Moses told the people, "Today is the Sabbath, the special day of rest to honor the LORD. So none of you should be out in the fields. Eat the food you gathered yesterday. 26You should gather the food for six days. But the seventh day of the week is a day of rest—so there will not be any of the special food on the ground."

27On Saturday, some of the people went out to gather some of the food, but they could not find any. 28Then the LORD said to Moses, "How long will you people refuse to obey my commands and teachings? 29Look, the LORD has made the Sabbath a day of rest for you. So on Friday he will give you enough food for two days. Then, on the Sabbath, each of you should sit down and relax. Stay where you are." 30So the people rested on the Sabbath.

31The people called the special food "manna.a" It was like small white coriander seeds and tasted like thin cakes made with honey. 32Moses told the people what the LORD said: "Save a basket of this food for your descendants. Then they can see the food that I gave to you in the desert when I took you out of Egypt."

33So Moses told Aaron, "Take a jar and fill it with a full basket of manna. Save this manna to put before the LORD. Save it for our descendants." 34(Aaron did what the LORD had commanded Moses. Aaron put the jar of manna in front of the Box of the Agreement.*) 35The people ate the manna for 40 years, until they came to the land of rest, that is, until they came to the edge of the land of Canaan.* 36(The measure they used for the manna was an omer. An omer was about 8 cups.b)

Water From the Rock

17 1All the Israelites traveled together from the Desert of Zin. They traveled from place to place as the LORD commanded. The people traveled to Rephidim and camped there. There was no water there for the people to drink. 2So they turned against Moses and started arguing with him. They said, "Give us water to drink."

Moses said to them, "Why have you turned against me? Why are you testing the LORD?"

3But the people were very thirsty, so they continued complaining to Moses. They said, "Why did you bring us out of Egypt? Did you bring us out here so that we, our children, and our cattle will all die without water?"

4So Moses cried to the LORD, "What can I do with these people? They are ready to kill me."

5The LORD said to Moses, "Go before the Israelites. Take some of the elders* of the people with you. Carry your walking stick with you. This is the stick that you used when you hit the Nile River. 6I will stand before you on a rock at Horeb.c Hit that rock with the walking stick and water will come out of it. Then the people can drink."

Moses did these things and the elders of Israel saw it. 7Moses named that place Meribahd and Massah,e because this was the place that the Israelites turned against him and tested the LORD. The people wanted to know if the LORD was with them or not.

War With the Amalekites

8At Rephidim the Amalekites came and fought against the Israelites. 9So Moses said to Joshua, "Choose some men and go and fight the Amalekites tomorrow. I will stand on the top of the hill and watch you. I will be holding the walking stick God gave me."

10Joshua obeyed Moses and went to fight the Amalekites the next day. At the same time Moses, Aaron, and Hur went to the top of the hill. 11Any time Moses held his hands in the air, the men of Israel would start winning the fight. But when Moses put his hands down, the men of Israel began to lose the fight.

12After some time, Moses' arms became tired. So they put a large rock under Moses for him to sit on. Then Aaron and Hur held Moses' hands in the air. Aaron was on one side of Moses and Hur was on the other side. They held his hands up like this until the sun went down. 13So Joshua and his men defeated the Amalekites in this battle.

14Then the LORD said to Moses, "Write about this battle. Write these things in a book so that people will remember what happened here. And be sure to tell Joshua that I will completely destroy the Amalekites from the earth."

15Then Moses built an altar* and named it, "The LORD is My Flag." 16Moses said, "I lifted my hands toward the LORD's throne. So the LORD fought against the Amalekites, as he always has."

Advice From Moses' Father-in-Law

18 1Jethro, Moses' father-in-law, was a priest in Midian. He heard about the many ways that God helped Moses and the Israelites. He heard about the LORD leading the Israelites out of Egypt. 2So Jethro went to Moses while Moses was camped near the mountain of God.f Jethro brought Moses' wife, Zipporah, with him. (Zipporah was not with Moses, because Moses had sent her home.) 3Jethro also brought Moses' two sons with him. The first son

---

a16:31 *manna* This name is like the Hebrew phrase in verse 15 meaning "What is that?"

b16:36 *about 8 cups* Literally, "1/10 of an ephah" (2.2 l).

c17:6 *Horeb* Another name for Mount Sinai.

d17:7 *Meribah* This name means "argument" or "rebellion."

e17:7 *Massah* This name means "trial," "temptation," or "test."

f18:2 *mountain of God* That is, Mount Horeb (Sinai).

was named Gershom,[a] because when he was born, Moses said, "I am a stranger in a foreign country." [4]The other son was named Eliezer,[b] because when he was born, Moses said, "The God of my father helped me and saved me from the king of Egypt."

[5]So Jethro went to Moses while Moses was camped in the desert near the mountain of God. Moses' wife and his two sons were with Jethro.

[6]Jethro sent a message to Moses that said, "This is your father-in-law Jethro. I am bringing your wife and her two sons to you."

[7]So Moses went out to meet his father-in-law. Moses bowed down before him and kissed him. The two men asked about each other's health. Then they went into Moses' tent to talk more. [8]Moses told Jethro everything the LORD had done for the Israelites. He told what the Lord did to Pharaoh and the people of Egypt. He told about all the problems they had along the way. And he told his father-in-law how the LORD saved the Israelites every time there was trouble.

[9]Jethro was happy when he heard all the good things the LORD had done for Israel. He was glad that the Lord had freed the Israelites from the Egyptians. [10]He said,

"Praise the LORD!
    He freed you from the power of Egypt.
    He saved you from Pharaoh.
[11] Now I know the LORD is greater than all
        the gods.
    They thought they were in control, but
        look what God did!"

[12]Jethro got some sacrifices* and offerings to honor God. Then Aaron and all the elders* of Israel came to eat with Moses' father-in-law Jethro. They all ate together there with God.

[13]The next day, Moses had the special job of judging the people. There were so many people that they had to stand before him all day.

[14]Jethro saw Moses judging the people. He asked, "Why are you doing this? Why are you the only judge? And why do people come to you all day?"

[15]Then Moses said to his father-in-law, "The people come to me and ask me to ask for God's decision for their problem. [16]If people have an argument, they come to me, and I decide which person is right. In this way I teach the people God's laws and teachings."

[17]But Moses' father-in-law said to him, "This isn't the right way to do this. [18]It is too much work for you to do alone. You cannot do this job by yourself. It wears you out. And it makes the people tired too. [19]Now, listen to me. Let me give you some advice. And I pray God will be with you. You should continue listening to the problems of the people. And you should continue to speak to God about these things. [20]You should explain God's laws and teachings to the people. Warn them not to break the laws. Tell them the right way to live and what they should do. [21]But you should also choose some of the people to be judges and leaders.

"Choose good men you can trust—men who respect God. Choose men who will not change their decisions for money. Make these men rulers over the people. There should be rulers over 1000 people, 100 people, 50 people, and even over ten people. [22]Let these rulers judge the people. If there is a very important case, then they can come to you and let you decide what to do. But they can decide the other cases themselves. In this way these men will share your work with you, and it will be easier for you to lead the people. [23]If you do this as God directs you, then you will be able to do your job without tiring yourself out. And the people can still have all their problems solved before they return home."

[24]So Moses did what Jethro told him. [25]Moses chose good men from among the Israelites. He made them leaders over the people. There were rulers over 1000 people, 100 people, 50 people, and ten people. [26]These rulers were judges for the people. The people could always bring their arguments to these rulers, and Moses had to decide only the most important cases.

[27]After a short time, Moses said goodbye to his father-in-law Jethro, and Jethro went back to his own home.

God's Agreement With Israel

19 [1]The Israelites reached the Sinai desert in the third month of their trip from Egypt. [2]They had traveled from Rephidim to the Sinai desert. The Israelites camped in the desert near Mount Sinai. [3]Then Moses climbed up the mountain to meet with God. God spoke to him on the mountain and said, "Tell this to the Israelites, the great family of Jacob: [4]'You people saw what I did to the people of Egypt. You saw that I carried you out of Egypt like an eagle and brought you here to me. [5]So now I tell you to obey my commands and keep my agreement.* So if you do this, you will be my own special people. The whole world belongs to me, but I am choosing you to be my own special people. [6]You will be a special nation—a kingdom of priests.' Moses, you must tell the Israelites what I have said."

[7]So Moses climbed down the mountain and called the elders* of the people together. Moses told the elders everything the LORD had commanded him to tell them. [8]All the people spoke at the same time and said, "We will obey everything the LORD says."

---

[a]**18:3 Gershom** This name is like the Hebrew words meaning "a stranger there."
[b]**18:4 Eliezer** This name means "My God helps."

Then Moses went back up the mountain and told the Lord that the people would obey him. 9Then the LORD said to Moses, "I will come to you in the thick cloud. I will speak to you. All the people will hear me talking to you. I will do this so that they will always believe what you tell them."

Then Moses told God everything the people had said.

10And the LORD said to Moses, "Today and tomorrow you must prepare the people for a special meeting. They must wash their clothes 11and be ready for me on the third day. On the third day, the LORD will come down to Mount Sinai. And all the people will see me. 12-13But you must tell the people to stay away from the mountain. Make a line and don't let them cross it. Any person or animal that touches the mountain must be killed with stones or shot with arrows. But don't let anyone touch them. The people must wait until the trumpet blows. Only then can they go up the mountain."

14So Moses climbed down the mountain and went to the people. He got them ready for the special meeting and they washed their clothes.

15Then Moses said to the people, "Be ready for the meeting with God in three days. Until that time do not have sexual relations."

16On the morning of the third day, a thick cloud came down onto the mountain. There was thunder and lightning and a very loud sound from a trumpet. All the people in the camp were frightened. 17Then Moses led the people out of the camp to a place near the mountain to meet God. 18Mount Sinai was covered with smoke. Smoke rose off the mountain like smoke from a furnace.* This happened because the LORD came down to the mountain in fire. Also the whole mountain began to shake. 19The noise from the trumpet became louder and louder. Every time Moses spoke to God, God answered him with a voice like thunder.

20So the LORD came down to Mount Sinai. He came from heaven to the top of the mountain. Then he called Moses to come up to the top of the mountain with him. So Moses went up the mountain.

21The LORD said to Moses, "Go down and warn the people not to come near me and look at me. If they do, many will die. 22Also tell the priests who will come near me that they must prepare themselves for this special meeting. If they don't, I, the LORD, will punish them."

23Moses told the LORD, "But the people cannot come up the mountain. You yourself told us to make a line and not allow the people to cross the line to holy* ground."

24The LORD said to him, "Go down to the people. Get Aaron and bring him back with you. But don't let the priests or the people come near me. I will punish them if they come too close."

25So Moses went down to the people and told them these things.

The Ten Commandments

20 1Then God said, 2"I am the LORD*a* your God. I led you out of the land of Egypt where you were slaves. These are the commands I give you:

3"You must not worship any other gods except me.

4"You must not make any idols.* Don't make any statues or pictures of anything up in the sky or of anything on the earth or of anything down in the water. 5Don't worship or serve idols of any kind, because I, the LORD, am your God. I hate my people worshiping other gods.*b* People who sin against me become my enemies, and I will punish them. And I will punish their children, their grandchildren, and even their great-grandchildren. 6But I will be very kind to people who love me and obey my commands. I will be kind to their families for thousands of generations.*c*

7"You must not use the name of the LORD your God to make empty promises. If you do, the LORD will not let you go unpunished.

8"You must remember to keep the Sabbath* a special day. 9You may work six days a week to do your job. 10But the seventh day is a day of rest in honor of the LORD your God. So on that day no one should work—not you, your sons and daughters, or your men and women slaves. Even your animals and the foreigners living in your cities must not work! 11That is because the LORD worked six days and made the sky, the earth, the sea, and everything in them. And on the seventh day, he rested. In this way the LORD blessed the Sabbath—the day of rest. He made that a very special day.

12"You must honor and respect your father and your mother. Do this so that you will have a full life in the land that the LORD your God gives you.

13"You must not murder anyone.

14"You must not commit adultery.*

15"You must not steal anything.

16"You must not tell lies about other people.*d*

17"You must not want to take your neighbor's house. You must not want his wife. And you must not want his men

*a20:2 LORD Or "YAHWEH." See "YAHWEH" in the Word List.
*b20:5 I hate ... gods Or "I am El Kanah—the Jealous God."
*c20:6 Or "But I will show mercy to thousands of people who love me and obey my commands."
*d20:16 Or "You must not be a false witness against your neighbor."

and women servants or his cattle or his donkeys. You must not want to take anything that belongs to another person."

The People Are Afraid of God

¹⁸During all this time, the people in the valley heard the thundering and saw the lightning on the mountain. They saw smoke rising from the mountain and heard the sound of the trumpet. They were afraid and shook with fear. They stood away from the mountain and watched. ¹⁹Then the people said to Moses, "If you want to speak to us, then we will listen. But please don't let God speak to us. If this happens, we will die."

²⁰Then Moses said to them, "Don't be afraid! God has come to test you. He wants you to respect him so that you will not sin."

²¹The people stood far away from the mountain while Moses went to the dark cloud where God was. ²²Then the Lord told Moses to say this to the Israelites: "You people have seen that I talked with you from heaven. ²³So you must not make idols using gold or silver to compete with me. You must not make these false gods.

²⁴"Make a special altar* for me. You should use dirt to make this altar. Offer sheep and cattle as burnt offerings* and fellowship offerings* on this altar. Do this in every place where I tell you to remember me. Then I will come and bless you. ²⁵But if you use stones to make an altar, then don't use stones that were cut with an iron tool.ᵃ If you do that, it will make the altar unacceptable. ²⁶And you must not make steps leading up to the altar. If there are steps, when people look up to the altar, they will be able to see under your clothes."

Other Laws and Commands

21 ¹Then God said to Moses, "These are the other laws that you will give to the people:

²"If you buy a Hebrewᵇ slave, then that slave will serve for only six years. After six years, he will be free, and he will have to pay nothing. ³If he is not married when he becomes your slave, when he becomes free, he will leave without a wife. But if the man is married when he becomes your slave, then he will keep his wife at the time he is made free. ⁴If the slave is not married, the master can give him a wife. If that wife gives birth to sons or daughters, she and her children will belong to the master. After the slave is finished with his years of service, he will be made free.

⁵"But if the slave decides that he wants to stay with the master, he must say, 'I love my master. I love my wife and my children. I will not become free—I will stay.' ⁶If this happens,

the master will bring the slave before God.ᶜ The master will take the slave to a door or the wooden frame around the door and pierce the slave's ear using a sharp tool to show that the slave will serve that master for all his life.

⁷"A man might decide to sell his daughter as a slave. If this happens, the rules for making her free are not the same as the rules for making the men slaves free. ⁸If the master who chose her for himself is not pleased with her, then he can sell the woman back to her father. If the master broke his promise to marry her, he loses the right to sell her to other people. ⁹If the master promised to let the slave woman marry his son, he must treat her like a daughter, not like a slave.

¹⁰"If the master marries another woman, he must not give less food or clothing to the first wife. And he must continue to give her what she has a right to have in marriage. ¹¹The man must do these three things for her. If he does not, the woman is made free, and it will cost her nothing. She owes no money to the man.

¹²"Whoever hits and kills someone must be killed too. ¹³But if an accident happens, and a person kills someone without planning it, then God allowed that thing to happen. I will choose some special places where people can run to for safety. So that person can run to one of those places. ¹⁴But whoever plans to kill someone out of anger or hatred must be punished. Take them away from my altarᵈ and kill them.

¹⁵"Whoever hits their father or their mother must be killed.

¹⁶"Whoever steals someone to sell them as a slave or to keep them for their own slave must be killed.

¹⁷"Whoever curses* their father or mother must be killed.

¹⁸"Two men might argue and one might hit the other with a rock or with his fist. If the man who was hurt is not killed, the man who hurt him should not be killed. ¹⁹If the man was hurt and must stay in bed for some time, the man who hurt him must support him. The man who hurt him must pay for the loss of his time. He must support him until he is completely healed.

²⁰"Sometimes people beat their slaves. If the slave dies after being beaten, the killer must be punished. ²¹But if the slave gets up after a few days, then the master will not be punished.ᵉ That is because someone paid their money for the slave, and the slave belongs to them.

²²"Two men might be fighting and hurt a pregnant woman. This might make the

---

ᵃ**20:25** *iron tool* Literally, "sword."
ᵇ**21:2** *Hebrew* Or "Israelite."
ᶜ**21:6** *before God* Or "before the judges."
ᵈ**21:14** *altar* It was one of the special places an innocent person could run to for safety. See "altar" in the Word List.
ᵉ**21:21** *punished* Or "punished for murder."

woman give birth to her baby before its time. If the woman was not hurt badly,[a] then the man who hurt her must pay a fine. The woman's husband will decide how much the man must pay. The judges will help the man decide how much the fine will be. ²³But if the woman was hurt badly, then the man who hurt her must be punished. The punishment must fit the crime. You must trade one life for another life. ²⁴You must trade an eye for an eye, a tooth for a tooth, a hand for a hand, a foot for a foot, ²⁵a burn for a burn, a bruise for a bruise, a cut for a cut.

²⁶"If a man hits a slave in the eye, and the slave is blinded in that eye, then the slave will be allowed to go free. His eye is the payment for his freedom. This is the same for a man or a woman slave. ²⁷If a master hits his slave in the mouth, and the slave loses a tooth, then the slave will be allowed to go free. The slave's tooth is payment for the slave's freedom. This is the same for a man or a woman slave.

²⁸"If a man's bull kills a man or woman, then you should use stones and kill that bull. You should not eat the bull. The owner of the bull is not guilty. ²⁹But if the bull had hurt people in the past, and if the owner was warned, then the owner is guilty. That is because he did not keep the bull tied or locked in its place. So if the bull is allowed to be free and kills someone, the owner is guilty. You should kill the bull with stones and also kill the owner. ³⁰But the family of the dead man may accept money. If they accept money, the man who owned the bull should not be killed. But he must pay as much money as the judge decides.

◦ ³¹"This same law must be followed if the bull kills someone's son or daughter. ³²But if the bull kills a slave, the owner of the animal must pay the master 30 pieces of silver.[b] And the bull must also be killed with stones. This law will be the same for men and women slaves.

³³"A man might take a cover off a well or dig a hole and not cover it. If another man's animal comes and falls into that hole, the man who owns the hole is guilty. ³⁴The man who owns the hole must pay for the animal. But after he pays for the animal, he will be allowed to keep the body of that animal.

³⁵"If one man's bull kills another man's bull, they should sell the bull that is alive. Both men will get half of the money that comes from selling the bull, and both men will also get half of the bull that was killed. ³⁶But if a man's bull has hurt other animals in the past, that owner is responsible for his bull. If his bull kills another bull, he is guilty because he allowed the bull to be free. That man must pay bull for bull. He must trade his bull for the bull that was killed.

22 ¹"How should you punish a man who steals a bull or a sheep? If the man kills the animal or sells it, then he cannot give it back. So he must pay five bulls for the one he stole. Or he must pay four sheep for the one he stole. He must pay for stealing. ²⁻⁴If he owns nothing, then he will be sold as a slave. But if the man still has the animal and you find it, that man must give the owner two animals for every animal he stole. It doesn't matter if the animal was a bull, a donkey, or a sheep.

"If a thief is killed while trying to break into a house at night, then no one will be guilty for killing him. But if this happens during the day, the one who killed him will be guilty of murder.

⁵"A man might let his animal loose to graze in his field or vineyard.* If the animal wanders into another person's field or vineyard, then the owner must pay. The payment must come from the best of his crop.[c]

⁶"A man might start a fire to burn thornbushes on his field. But if the fire grows and burns his neighbor's crops or the grain growing on the neighbor's field, the man who started the fire must pay for what he burned.

⁷"Someone might give some money or tools to a neighbor for safekeeping. What should you do if someone steals those things from the neighbor's house? If you find the one who stole them, then that thief must pay twice as much as the things are worth. ⁸If you don't find the thief, then the owner of the house must go before the judges[d] who will decide if that person is guilty.

⁹"What should you do if two men disagree about a bull or a donkey or sheep or clothing or something that is lost? One man says, 'This is mine,' and the other says, 'No, it is mine.' Both men should go before the judges who will decide who is guilty. The one who was wrong must pay the other man twice as much as the thing is worth.

¹⁰"A man might ask his neighbor to take care of an animal for a short time. It might be a donkey, a bull, or a sheep. But what should you do if that animal is hurt or dies or someone takes the animal while no one is looking? ¹¹That neighbor must explain that he did not steal the animal. If this is true, the neighbor will promise to the Lord that he did not steal it. The owner of the animal must accept this promise. The neighbor does not have to pay the owner for the animal. ¹²But if the neighbor stole the animal, then he must pay the owner for the animal. ¹³If wild animals killed the animal, then the neighbor should bring the body as proof. The neighbor will not have

---

[c]**22:5** Or "A man might start a fire in his field or vineyard. If he lets the fire spread and it burns his neighbor's field or vineyard, he must use his best crops to pay his neighbor for his loss."
[d]**22:8** *judges* Or "God." Also in verse 9.

---

[a]**21:22** *hurt badly* Or "killed."
[b]**21:32** *30 pieces of silver* The price for a new slave.

to pay the owner for the animal that was killed.

¹⁴"If a man borrows an animal from his neighbor, and the animal is hurt or dies, then the neighbor must pay the owner for the animal. The neighbor is responsible, because the owner was not there himself. ¹⁵But if the owner was there, then the neighbor does not have to pay. Or if the neighbor was paying money to use the animal for work, he will not have to pay if the animal dies or is hurt. The money he paid to use the animal will be enough payment.

¹⁶"If a man has sexual relations with a virgin who he is not engaged to,ᵃ then he must pay her father the full amount necessary to marry her. ¹⁷If the father refuses to allow his daughter to marry him, then the man must still pay the full amount for her.

¹⁸"You must not allow any woman to do evil magic. If she does magic, you must not let her live.

¹⁹"You must not allow anyone to have sexual relations with an animal. If this happens, that person must be killed.

²⁰"Whoever makes a sacrifice* to a false god should be destroyed. The Lord is the only one you should make sacrifices to.

²¹"Remember, in the past you were foreigners in the land of Egypt. So you should not cheat or hurt anyone who is a foreigner in your land.

²²"You must never do anything bad to women whose husbands are dead or to orphans. ²³If you do anything wrong to these widows or orphans, I will know it. I will hear about their suffering. ²⁴And I will be very angry. I will kill you with a sword. Then your wives will become widows, and your children will become orphans.

²⁵"If you loan money to any of my people, that is, the poor among you, don't be like a moneylender and charge them interest. ²⁶You might take their cloak to make sure they pay the money back, but you must give that cloak back to them before sunset. ²⁷That cloak might be their only protection against the cold when they lie down to sleep. If they call to me for help, I will listen because I am kind.

²⁸"You must not curse God or the leaders of your people.

²⁹"At harvest time you should give me the first grain and the first juice from your fruit. Don't wait until late in the year.

"Give me your firstborn* sons. ³⁰Also, give me your firstborn cattle and sheep. Let the firstborn stay with its mother for seven days. Then on the eighth day, give him to me.

³¹"You are my special people. So don't eat the meat from something that was killed by wild animals. Let the dogs eat that dead animal.

23 ¹"Don't tell lies against other people. If you are a witness in court, don't agree to help a bad person tell lies.

²"Don't do something just because everyone else is doing it. If a group of people are doing wrong, don't join them. You must not let them persuade you to do wrong things— you must do what is right and fair.

³"In court, don't treat a person in a special way simply because that person is poor.

⁴"If you see a lost bull or donkey, then you must return it to its owner—even if the owner is your enemy.

⁵"If you see an animal that cannot walk because it has too much to carry, you must stop and help that animal. You must help that animal even if it belongs to one of your enemies.

⁶"In court, don't let anyone take advantage of a person simply because that person is poor.

⁷"Be very careful if you say that someone is guilty of something. Don't make false charges against a person. Never allow innocent people to be killed as punishment for something they did not do. Whoever kills an innocent person is evil, and I will not treat a guilty person as innocent.

⁸"If someone tries to pay you to agree with them when they are wrong, don't accept that payment. A payment like that can blind judges so that they cannot see the truth. It can make good people tell lies.

⁹"You must never do wrong things to a foreigner. Remember, you know what it is like to be a foreigner because at one time you were foreigners in the land of Egypt.

The Special Festivals

¹⁰"Plant seeds, harvest your crops, and work the ground for six years. ¹¹But the seventh year must be a special time of rest for the land. Don't plant anything in your fields. If any crops grow there, allow the poor to have it. And allow the wild animals to eat the food that is left. You should do the same with your vineyards* and with your fields of olive trees.

¹²"Work for six days, but on the seventh day, rest! This will allow your slaves and other workers a time to rest and relax. And your bulls and donkeys will also have a time of rest.

¹³"Be sure that you obey all these laws. Don't worship false gods. You should not even speak their names!

¹⁴"You will have three special festivals each year. You must come to my special place to worship me during these festivals. ¹⁵The first festival is the Festival of Unleavened Bread.* This is as I commanded you. During this time you will eat bread that is made without yeast. This will continue for seven days. You will do this during the month of Abib,* because this is the time when you came out of Egypt. Everyone must bring a sacrifice to me at that time.

ᵃ**22:16** *a virgin … engaged to* Literally, "a virgin who is not engaged."

¹⁶"The second festival will be the Festival of Harvest.* This festival will be during the early summer when you begin harvesting the first crops that you planted in your fields.

"The third festival will be the Festival of Shelters.* This will be in the fall, when you finish gathering the rest of the crops from your fields.

¹⁷"So three times each year all the men will come to the special place to be with the Lord God.

¹⁸"When you kill an animal and offer its blood as a sacrifice,* you must not include anything that has yeast in it. And when you burn the fat from my sacrifice, don't let any of it remain until morning.

¹⁹"When you gather your crops at harvest time, you should bring the first of everything you harvest to the house*ᵃ of the Lord your God.

"You must not eat the meat from a young goat that is boiled in its mother's milk."

God Will Help Israel Take Their Land

²⁰"I am sending an angel before you to protect you along the way and to lead you to the place that I have prepared for you. ²¹Obey the angel and follow him. Be careful in his presence, and don't rebel against him. The angel will not forgive the wrong things you do to him. He has my power*ᵇ in him. ²²If you listen to what he says and do everything I tell you, then I will be an enemy to all of your enemies. I will be against everyone who is against you.

²³"My angel will lead you through the land. He will lead you against many different people—the Amorites, Hittites, Perizzites, Canaanites, Hivites, and Jebusites. But I will defeat all of them.

²⁴"Don't worship their gods. Don't ever bow down to those gods. You must never live the way those people live. You must destroy their idols.* And you must break the stones that help them remember their gods.*ᶜ ²⁵You must serve the Lord your God. If you do this, I will bless you with plenty of bread and water. I will take away all sickness from you. ²⁶Your women will all be able to have babies. None of their babies will die at birth. And I will allow you to live long lives.

²⁷"When you fight against your enemies, I will send my great power before you.*ᵈ I will help you defeat all your enemies. The people who are against you will become confused in battle and run away. ²⁸I will send the hornet*ᵉ in front of you. He will force your enemies to leave. The Hivites, Canaanites, and Hittites will leave your country. ²⁹But I will not force all of them out of your land quickly. I will not do this in only one year. The land will be empty if I force the people out too fast. Then all the wild animals would increase and control the land. And they would be much trouble for you. ³⁰So I will force them out of your land very slowly. I will do this as you grow and eventually take the land to be your own.

³¹"I will give you all the land from the Red Sea to the Euphrates River. The western border will be the Philistine Sea,*ᶠ and the eastern border will be the Arabian Desert. I will let you defeat the people living there and force them all to leave.

³²"You must not make any agreements with any of those people or their gods. ³³Don't let them stay in your country. If you let them stay, they will be like a trap to you—they will cause you to sin against me. And you will begin worshiping their gods."

God and Israel Make Their Agreement

24 ¹God told Moses, "You, Aaron, Nadab, Abihu, and the 70 elders* of Israel must come up the mountain and worship me from a distance. ²Then Moses will come close to the Lord by himself. The other men must not come close to the Lord, and the rest of the people must not even come up the mountain."

³Moses told the people all the rules and commands from the Lord. Then all the people said, "We will obey all the commands that the Lord has spoken."

⁴So Moses wrote down all the commands of the Lord. The next morning he got up and built an altar* near the bottom of the mountain. And he set up twelve stones—one for each of the twelve tribes of Israel. ⁵Then Moses sent young men of Israel to offer sacrifices.* These men offered bulls to the Lord as burnt offerings* and fellowship offerings.*

⁶Moses saved the blood from these animals. He put half of the blood in bowls, and he poured the other half of the blood on the altar.*ᵍ

⁷Moses read the scroll with the special agreement* written on it. He read the agreement so that all the people could hear him. And the people said, "We have heard the laws that the Lord has given us. And we agree to obey them."

⁸Then Moses held the bowls full of the

*ᵃ23:19 house The "Holy Tent" where the people went to meet with God. See Ex. 25:8, 9.
*ᵇ23:21 my power Literally, "my name."
*ᶜ23:24 stones … gods Or "memorials." Here, these were stone markers that people used in worshiping their gods.
*ᵈ23:27 When you fight … you Or "News of my power will go before you, and your enemies will be frightened."

*ᵉ23:28 hornet A stinging insect like a large wasp or bee. Here, it might mean "God's angel" or "his great power."
*ᶠ23:31 Philistine Sea That is, the Mediterranean Sea.
*ᵍ24:6 The blood was used to seal the agreement between God and the people. It was poured on the altar to show that God shared in the agreement.

blood from the sacrifices. He threw that blood on the people. He said, "This blood shows that the LORD has made a special agreement with you. The laws God gave you explain the agreement."

⁹Then Moses, Aaron, Nadab, Abihu, and the 70 elders of Israel went up the mountain. ¹⁰On the mountain, these men saw the God of Israel. He was standing on something that looked like blue sapphires, as clear as the sky! ¹¹All the leaders of Israel saw God, but God did not destroy them.ᵃ They all ate and drank together.

Moses Goes to Get God's Law

¹²The LORD said to Moses, "Come to me on the mountain. I have written my teachings and laws on two stone tablets. These teachings and laws are for the people. I will give these stone tablets to you."

¹³So Moses and his helper, Joshua, went up the mountain of God. ¹⁴Moses said to the elders,* "Wait here for us until we come back to you. While I am gone, Aaron and Hur will rule over you. Go to them if anyone has a problem."

Moses Meets With God

¹⁵Then Moses went up the mountain, and the cloud covered the mountain. ¹⁶The Glory of the LORD* came down on Mount Sinai. The cloud covered the mountain for six days. On the seventh day, the LORD spoke to Moses from the cloud. ¹⁷The Israelites could see the Glory of the LORD. It was like a fire burning on top of the mountain.

¹⁸Then Moses went higher up the mountain into the cloud. He was on the mountain for 40 days and 40 nights.

Gifts for the Holy Things

25 ¹The LORD said to Moses, ²"Tell the Israelites to bring me gifts. You will accept gifts for me from everyone who is willing to give. ³Here is the list of the things that you should accept from the people: gold, silver, and bronze*; ⁴blue, purple, and red yarn and fine linen; goat hair, ⁵ram skins dyed red, and fine leather; acacia wood; ⁶oil for the lamps; spices for the anointing* oil and spices for the sweet-smelling incense.* ⁷Also accept onyx* stones and other jewels to be put on the ephod* and the judgment pouch.*

The Holy Tent

⁸"The people will build a holy* place for me. Then I can live among them. ⁹I will show you what the Holy Tent* and everything in it should look like. Build everything exactly as I show you.

The Box of the Agreement

¹⁰"Use acacia wood and build a special box. This Holy Box* must be 2½ cubitsᵇ long, 1½ cubitsᶜ wide, and 1½ cubits high. ¹¹Use pure gold to cover the Box inside and out. Put gold trim around the edges of the Box. ¹²Make four gold rings for carrying the Box. Put the gold rings on the four corners, two rings on each side. ¹³Then make poles for carrying the Box. These poles should be made from acacia wood and covered with gold. ¹⁴Put the poles through the rings on the corners of the Box. Use these poles to carry the Box. ¹⁵These poles should always stay in the rings of the Box. Don't take the poles out.

¹⁶"I will give you the Agreement.* Put it into this Box. ¹⁷Then make a lid, the mercy-cover.* Make it from pure gold. Make it 2½ cubits long and 1½ cubits wide. ¹⁸"Then make two Cherub angels* and put them on each end of the mercy-cover. Hammer gold to make these angels. ¹⁹Put one angel on one end of the mercy-cover, and put the other angel on the other end. Join the angels together with the mercy-cover to make one piece. ²⁰The wings of these angels should spread up toward the sky. The angels should cover the Box with their wings and should face each other, looking toward the mercy-cover.

²¹"I will give you the Agreement.* Put it in the Box, and put the mercy-cover on the Box. ²²When I meet with you, I will speak from between the Cherub angels on the mercy-cover that is on the Box of the Agreement.* From that place, I will give all my commands to the Israelites.

The Table

²³"Make a table from acacia wood. The table must be 2 cubitsᵈ long, 1 cubitᵉ wide, and 1½ cubits high. ²⁴Cover the table with pure gold and put gold trim around it. ²⁵Then make a frame 1 handbreadthᶠ wide around the table. And put gold trim on the frame. ²⁶Then make four gold rings and put them on the four corners of the table, where the four legs are. ²⁷Put the rings close to the frame around the top of the table. These rings will hold the poles used to carry the table. ²⁸Use acacia wood to make the poles, and cover them with gold. The poles are for carrying the table. ²⁹Make the plates, the spoons, the pitchers, and the bowls from pure gold. The pitchers and bowls will be used for pouring the drink offerings. ³⁰Put the special breadᵍ

ᵇ**25:10** *2 1/2 cubits* 4' 3" (1.3 m). Also in verse 17.
ᶜ**25:10** *1 1/2 cubits* 30 5/8" (77.75 cm). Also in verses 17, 23.
ᵈ**25:23** *2 cubits* 3' 4 13/16" (104 cm).
ᵉ**25:23** *cubit* 20 5/8" (51.83 cm).
ᶠ**25:25** *handbreadth* The width of 4 fingers, about 3" (7.4 cm).
ᵍ**25:30** *special bread* Also called "bread of the Presence." Every day this bread was put before God on the special table in the Holy Place.

ᵃ**24:11** *saw God … destroy them* In other places, the Bible says that people cannot see God. But God wanted these leaders to know what he was like, so he allowed them to see him in some special way.

before me on the table. It must always be there in front of me.

The Lampstand

31"Then you must make a lampstand. Use pure gold and hammer it to make the base and the shaft.*a* Make flowers, buds, and petals from pure gold. Join all these things together into one piece.

32"The lampstand must have six branches— three branches on one side, and three branches on the other. 33Each branch must have three flowers. Make these flowers like almond flowers with buds and petals. 34Make four more flowers for the lampstand. These flowers must be made like almond flowers with buds and petals. 35There will be six branches on the lampstand—three branches coming out from each side of the shaft. Make a flower with buds and petals below each of the three places where the branches join the shaft. 36The whole lampstand with the flowers and branches must be made from pure gold. All this gold must be hammered and joined together into one piece. 37Then make seven lamps*b* to go on the lampstand. These lamps will give light to the area in front of the lampstand. 38Use pure gold to make the lamp snuffers* and trays. 39Use 75 pounds*c* of pure gold to make the lampstand and the things to be used with it. 40Be very careful to make everything exactly the way I showed you on the mountain.

The Holy Tent

26 1"The Holy Tent* should be made from ten curtains. These curtains must be made from fine linen* and blue, purple, and red yarn. A skilled worker should sew pictures of Cherub angels* with wings into the curtains. 2Make each curtain the same size. Each curtain should be 28 cubits*d* long and 4 cubits*e* wide. 3Join the curtains together into two groups. Join five curtains together to make one group and join five curtains together to make the other group. 4Use blue cloth to make loops along the edge of the end curtain in one group. Do the same on the end curtain in the other group. 5There must be 50 loops on the end curtain of the first group. And there must be 50 loops on the end curtain of the other group. These loops must be opposite each other. 6Then make 50 gold rings to join the curtains together. This will join the Holy Tent together into one piece.

7"Make another tent that will cover the Holy Tent. Use eleven curtains to make this tent. Make these curtains from goat hair. 8All these curtains must be the same size.

They must be 30 cubits*f* long and 4 cubits wide. 9Join five of the curtains together into one group. Then join the other six curtains together into another group. Fold back half of the sixth curtain at the front of the Tent. 10Make 50 loops down the edge of the end curtain of one group. Do the same for the end curtain of the other group. 11Then make 50 bronze* rings to join the curtains together. This will join the tent together into one piece. 12Half of the end curtain of this tent will hang down below the back edge of the Holy Tent. 13On the sides, the curtains of this tent will hang down 1 cubit*g* below the bottom edges of the Holy Tent. So this tent will completely cover the Holy Tent. 14Make two coverings to go over the outer tent. One covering should be made from ram skins dyed red. The other covering should be made from fine leather.

15"Use acacia wood to make frames to support the Holy Tent. 16The frames should be 10 cubits*h* high and 1½ cubits*i* wide. 17Two side poles should be joined together with cross pieces to make each frame. All the frames for the Holy Tent must be the same. 18Make 20 frames for the south side of the Holy Tent. 19And make 40 silver bases for the frames. Each frame should have two silver bases to go under it—one base for each side pole. 20Make 20 more frames for the other side (the north side) of the Holy Tent. 21And make 40 silver bases for these frames—two bases under each frame. 22Make six more frames for the back (the west side) of the Holy Tent. 23Make two frames for the corners at the back of the Holy Tent. 24The frames at the corners should be joined together at the bottom. At the top a ring will hold the frames together. Do the same for both corners. 25There will be a total of eight frames for the west end of the Tent. There will be 16 silver bases—two bases under each frame.

26"Use acacia wood and make braces for the frames of the Holy Tent. There should be five braces for the first side of the Holy Tent. 27And there should be five braces for the frames on the other side of the Holy Tent. And there should be five braces for the frames at the back (the west side) of the Holy Tent. 28The middle brace should pass through the frames from one end to the other. 29"Cover the frames with gold. And make rings for the frames to hold the braces. Make these rings from gold. Also cover the braces with gold. 30Build the Holy Tent the way I showed you on the mountain.

Inside the Holy Tent

31"Use fine linen* and make a special curtain for the inside of the Holy Tent. Use blue, purple, and red yarn and sew pictures

---

*a*25:31 *base and the shaft* Or "flared base."
*b*25:37 *lamps* Small bowls filled with oil. A wick was put in the bowl and lit to produce light.
*c*25:39 *75 pounds* Literally, "1 talent" (34.5 kg).
*d*26:2 *28 cubits* 47' 7 3/8" (14.5 m).
*e*26:2 *4 cubits* 6' 9 5/8" (2.1 m). Also in verse 8.

*f*26:8 *30 cubits* 51' 3/16" (15.55 m).
*g*26:13 *1 cubit* 20 5/8" (51.83 cm).
*h*26:16 *10 cubits* 17' 1/16" (5.18 m).
*i*26:16 *1 1/2 cubits* 30 5/8" (77.75 cm).

of Cherub angels* into the curtain. 32Make four posts from acacia wood, and cover the posts with gold. Put hooks made from gold on the four posts. Put four silver bases under the posts. Then hang the curtain on the gold hooks. 33Put the curtain under the gold rings.ᵃ Then put the Box of the Agreement* behind the curtain. This curtain will separate the Holy Place from the Most Holy Place. 34Put the mercy-cover* on the Box of the Agreement in the Most Holy Place.

35"Put the special table you made outside of the curtain. The table should be on the north side of the Holy Tent.* Then put the lampstand on the south side, across from the table.

The Door of the Holy Tent

36"Then make a curtain to cover the entrance to the Holy Tent.* Use blue, purple, and red yarn and fine linen to make this curtain. Weave pictures into it. 37Make gold hooks for this curtain. Make five posts using acacia wood covered with gold and make five bronze* bases for the five posts.

The Altar for Burning Offerings

27 1"Use acacia wood and build an altar.* The altar should be square. It must be 5 cubitsᵇ long, 5 cubits wide, and 3 cubitsᶜ high. 2Make a horn for each of the four corners of the altar. Join each horn to its corner so that everything is one piece. Then cover the altar with bronze.*

3"Use bronze to make all the tools and dishes that will be used on the altar. Make pots, shovels, bowls, forks, and pans. These will be used for cleaning ashes from the altar. 4Make a grating for the altar. This grating will be shaped like a net. And make a bronze ring at each of the four corners of the grating. 5Put the grating under the ledge at the bottom of the altar. The grating will go halfway up into the altar from below.

6"Use acacia wood to make poles for the altar, and cover them with bronze. 7Put the poles through the rings on both sides of the altar. Use these poles for carrying the altar. 8Make the altar like an empty box with the sides made from boards. Make the altar just as I showed you on the mountain.

The Courtyard Around the Holy Tent

9"Make a courtyard for the Holy Tent.* The south side should have a wall of curtains 100 cubitsᵈ long. These curtains must be made from fine linen.* 10Use 20 posts and 20 bronze* bases under the posts. The hooks

for the posts and the curtain rodsᵉ should be made from silver. 11The north side must also have a wall of curtains 100 cubits long. It must have 20 posts and 20 bronze bases. The hooks for the posts and the curtain rods must be made from silver.

12"On the west side of the courtyard there must be a wall of curtains 50 cubitsᶠ long. There must be ten posts and ten bases. 13The east side of the courtyard must also be 50 cubits long. 14Here at the entrance to the courtyard, one side must have curtains 15 cubitsᵍ long. There must be three posts and three bases on this side. 15The other side of the entrance must also have curtains 15 cubits long. There must be three posts and three bases on that side.

16"Make a curtain 20 cubitsʰ long to cover the entrance to the courtyard. Make that curtain from fine linen and blue, purple, and red yarn. Weave designs into that curtain. There must be four posts and four bases for that curtain. 17All the posts around the courtyard must be joined with silver curtain rods. The hooks on the posts must be made from silver, and the bases for the posts must be bronze. 18The courtyard should be 100 cubits long and 50 cubits wide. The wall of curtains around the courtyard should be 5 cubits high. The curtains must be made from fine linen. The bases under the posts must be bronze. 19All the tools, tent pegs, and other things used in the Holy Tent must be made from bronze. And all the pegs for the curtains around the courtyard must be made from bronze.

Oil for the Lamp

20"Command the Israelites to bring their best olive oil for the lamp that must be lit each evening. 21This lamp is in the first room of the Meeting Tent,* outside the curtain for the room where the Agreement* is. Aaron and his sons will make sure this lamp is burning before the LORD every day from evening until morning. The Israelites and their descendants must obey this law forever.

Clothes for the Priests

28 1"Tell your brother Aaron and his sons, Nadab, Abihu, Eleazar, and Ithamar, to come to you from the Israelites. These men will serve me as priests.

2"Make special clothes for your brother Aaron. These clothes will give him honor and respect. 3I have given special wisdom to some of the skilled men. Tell them to make the clothes for Aaron. These clothes will show that he serves me in a special way. Then he can serve me as a priest. 4These

---

ᵃ**26:33** *under the gold rings* The 50 gold rings that joined together the two parts of the Holy Tent. See Ex. 26:6.
ᵇ**27:1** *5 cubits* 8' 6" (2.6 m). Also in verse 18.
ᶜ**27:1** *3 cubits* 5' 1 3/16" (1.55 m).
ᵈ**27:9** *100 cubits* 170' 5/8" (51.83 m). Also in verse 18.

ᵉ**27:10** *curtain rods* These were either rods that joined the posts together or grommets (rings) sewn into the curtains.
ᶠ**27:12** *50 cubits* 85' 5/16" (25.92 m). Also in verse 18.
ᵍ**27:14** *15 cubits* 25' 6 1/16" (7.77 m).
ʰ**27:16** *20 cubits* 34' 1/8" (10.37 m).

are the clothes the men should make: the judgment pouch,* the ephod,* a blue robe, a white woven robe, a turban,* and a cloth belt. They must make these special clothes for your brother Aaron and his sons. Then Aaron and his sons can serve me as priests. ⁵Tell the men to use gold thread, fine linen,* and blue, purple, and red yarn.

The Ephod and the Cloth Belt

⁶"Use gold thread, fine linen,* and blue, purple, and red yarn to make the ephod.* This must be the work of a very skilled person. ⁷At each shoulder of the ephod, there should be a shoulder piece. These shoulder pieces should be tied to the two corners of the ephod.

⁸"The men will very carefully weave a cloth belt for the ephod. This belt must be made the same way as the ephod—use gold threads, fine linen, and blue, purple, and red yarn.

⁹"Take two onyx* stones. Write the names of the twelve sons of Israel* on these jewels. ¹⁰Write six names on one jewel and six names on the other jewel. Write the names in order, from the oldest son to the youngest. ¹¹Cut the names of the sons of Israel into these stones. Do this the way a worker makes a seal.* Put the jewels in gold settings. ¹²Then put these two jewels on the shoulder pieces of the ephod. Aaron will wear this special coat when he stands before the LORD. And the two stones with the names of the sons of Israel will be on the ephod. These jewels will cause the Lord to remember the Israelites. ¹³Use fine gold to hold the stones on the ephod. ¹⁴Twist chains of pure gold together like a rope. Make two of these gold chains and fasten them to the gold settings.

The Judgment Pouch

¹⁵"Make the judgment pouch* for the high priest. Skilled workers should make this pouch just as they made the ephod.* They must use gold threads, fine linen,* and blue, purple, and red yarn. ¹⁶The judgment pouch should be folded double to make a square pocket. It should be 1 spanᵃ long and 1 span wide. ¹⁷Put four rows of beautiful jewels on the judgment pouch. The first row of jewels should have a ruby, a topaz, and a beryl. ¹⁸The second row should have a turquoise, a sapphire, and an emerald. ¹⁹The third row should have a jacinth, an agate, and an amethyst. ²⁰The fourth row should have a chrysolite, an onyx, and a jasper. Set all these jewels in gold. ²¹There will be twelve jewels on the judgment pouch—one jewel for each of the sons of Israel.* Write the name of one of the sons of Israel on each of the stones. Cut these names into each stone like a worker makes a seal.*

²²"Make chains of pure gold for the judgment pouch. These chains must be braided like a rope. ²³Make two gold rings and put them on two corners of the judgment pouch. ²⁴Put the two golden chains through the two rings at the corners of the judgment pouch. ²⁵Fasten the other ends of the gold chains to the two settings. This will fasten them to the two shoulder pieces of the ephod on the front. ²⁶Make two more gold rings and put them on the other two corners of the judgment pouch. This will be on the inside edge of the judgment pouch next to the ephod. ²⁷Make two more gold rings and put them on the bottom of the shoulder pieces on the front of the ephod. Put the gold rings above the cloth belt of the ephod. ²⁸Use blue ribbon to tie the rings of the judgment pouch to the rings of the ephod. In this way the judgment pouch will rest close to the cloth belt and will be held against the ephod.

²⁹"When Aaron enters the Holy Place,* he must wear the judgment pouch. In this way he will wear the names of the twelve sons of Israel over his heart. And the LORD will always be reminded of them. ³⁰Put the Urim* and Thummim* inside the judgment pouch. They will be over Aaron's heart when he goes before the LORD. So Aaron will always carry with him a way of judging for the Israelites when he is before the LORD.

Other Clothes for the Priests

³¹"Make a blue robe for the ephod.* ³²Make a hole in the center for the head. And sew a piece of cloth around the edge of this hole. This cloth will be like a collar that keeps the hole from tearing. ³³Use blue, purple, and red yarn to make cloth pomegranates.* Hang these pomegranates around the bottom edge of the robe, and hang gold bells between the pomegranates. ³⁴So around the bottom edge of the robe there should be bells and pomegranates. There should be a bell following each pomegranate. ³⁵Aaron will wear this robe when he serves as a priest. The bells will ring as Aaron goes into the Holy Place* to stand before the LORD, and the bells will ring as he leaves the Holy Place. This way Aaron will not die.

³⁶"Make a strip of pure gold and carve these words into the gold like the writing on a seal*: HOLY TO THE LORD.ᵇ ³⁷Fasten the gold strip to a blue ribbon. Tie the blue ribbon around the turban.* The gold strip should be on the front of the turban. ³⁸Aaron will wear this on his head. In this way he will remove the guilt if anything is wrong with the gifts

---

ᵃ**28:16** *1 span* The distance from the tip of the thumb to the tip of the little finger, about 9" (23 cm).

ᵇ**28:36** HOLY TO THE LORD These words were written on everything that was used in the Temple. This showed that these things belonged to the Lord and that they could be used only for special purposes. Dishes with this label could be used only by the priests in a holy place.

that the Israelites[a] give to God. Aaron will always wear this on his head so that the LORD will accept the gifts of the people.

39"Use fine linen to make the white woven robe and the turban. The cloth belt should have designs sewn into it. 40Also make coats, belts, and cloth caps for Aaron's sons. This will give them honor and respect. 41Put the clothes on your brother Aaron and his sons. Then pour the special oil on them to make them priests. This will make them holy,* and they will serve me as priests.

42"Use linen* to make underclothes for the priests. These underclothes will cover them from the waist to the thighs. 43Aaron and his sons must wear these clothes whenever they enter the Meeting Tent.* They must wear these clothes when they come near to the altar* to serve as priests in the Holy Place. If they don't wear these clothes, they will be guilty of wrong and will have to die. All this should be a law that continues forever for Aaron and all his family after him.

The Ceremony for Appointing the Priests

29 1"Now I will tell you what you must do to show that Aaron and his sons serve me in a special way as priests. Find one young bull and two rams that have nothing wrong with them. 2Then use fine wheat flour without yeast to make bread. And use the same things to make cakes mixed with olive oil. Make small thin cakes spread with oil. 3Put this bread and the cakes in a basket. Then give the basket to Aaron and his sons. At the same time, give them the bull and the two rams.

4"Then bring Aaron and his sons to the entrance of the Meeting Tent.* Wash them with water. 5Put the special clothes on Aaron. Put on him the white woven robe and the blue robe that is worn with the ephod.* Put the ephod and the judgment pouch* on him. Then tie the beautiful cloth belt on him. 6Put the turban* on his head and the special crown around the turban. 7Take the anointing* oil and pour it on Aaron's head. This will show that he is chosen for this work.

8"Then bring Aaron's sons to that place. Put the white woven robes on them. 9Then tie cloth belts around their waists, and give them cloth caps to wear. At that time they will begin to be priests. They will be priests because of the special law that will continue forever. This is the way you will make Aaron and his sons priests.

10"Then bring the bull to that place at the front of the Meeting Tent. Aaron and his sons must put their hands on the bull's head. 11Then kill the bull there in the LORD's presence at the entrance to the Meeting Tent.

12Then take some of the bull's blood and go to the altar.* Use your finger to put some blood on the horns of the altar.* Pour out all the blood that is left at the bottom of the altar. 13Then take all the fat from inside the bull, the fatty part of the liver, both kidneys, and the fat around them. Burn this fat on the altar. 14Then take the bull's meat, his skin, and his other parts and go outside your camp and burn them. This bull is an offering to take away the sins of the priests.

15"Then tell Aaron and his sons to put their hands on the head of one of the rams. 16Kill that ram and save the blood. Throw the blood against the altar on all four sides. 17Then cut the ram into several pieces. Wash all the parts from inside the ram and the legs. Put these things with the head and the other pieces of the ram. 18Then burn everything on the altar. It is a burnt offering* to the LORD. It is a sweet-smelling gift to the LORD.

19"Tell Aaron and his sons to put their hands on the other ram. 20Kill that ram and save some of its blood. Put that blood on the right ear lobes of Aaron and his sons. Also put some of the blood on the thumbs of their right hands and on the big toes of their right feet. Then throw blood against all four sides of the altar. 21Then take some of the blood from the altar. Mix it with the special oil and sprinkle it on Aaron and his clothes. And sprinkle it on his sons and their clothes. This will show that Aaron and his sons serve me in a special way. And it will show that their clothes are used only at special times.

22"Then take the fat from the ram. (This is the ram that will be used in the ceremony to make Aaron the high priest.) Take the fat from around the tail and the fat that covers the organs inside the body. Then take the fat that covers the liver, both kidneys and the fat on them, and the right leg. 23Then take the basket of bread that you made without yeast. This is the basket you put before the LORD. Take these things out of the basket: one loaf of bread, one cake made with oil, and one small thin cake. 24Give them to Aaron and his sons. Tell them to hold these things in their hands before the Lord. This will be a special offering to the LORD. 25Then take them from Aaron and his sons and put them on the altar with the ram. Then burn everything on the altar. It is a burnt offering to the LORD. It is a sweet-smelling gift to the LORD.

26"Then take the breast from the ram. (This is the ram that will be used in the ceremony to make Aaron the high priest.) Hold the breast of the ram before the LORD as a special offering. Then take it back and keep it. This part of the animal will be for you. 27Take the breast and the leg of the ram that was used to make Aaron the high priest and make these parts holy.* Then give these special parts to Aaron and his sons. 28The Israelites will always give Aaron and his sons these parts. These parts

---

[a]**28:38 In this way … Israelites** Literally, "It will keep him holy when he bears the guilt from the gifts of the Israelites."

will always belong to the priests when the Israelites make an offering to the LORD. When they give these parts to the priest, it will be the same as giving them to the Lord.

29"Save these special clothes that were made for Aaron and his descendants. They will wear these clothes when they are chosen to be priests. 30Aaron's son will become the next high priest after him. That son will wear these clothes seven days when he comes to the Meeting Tent to serve in the Holy Place.*

31"Cook the meat from the ram that was used to make Aaron the high priest. Cook that meat in a holy place. 32Then Aaron and his sons must eat the meat at the front door of the Meeting Tent. And they must also eat the bread that is in the basket. 33These offerings were used to take away their sins when they were made priests. Now they should eat these offerings. 34If any of the meat from that ram or any of the bread is left the next morning, then it must be burned. You must not eat that bread or the meat because it should be eaten only in a special way at a special time.

35"You must do all these things for Aaron and his sons. You must do them exactly as I told you. The ceremony for appointing them to be priests must continue for seven days. 36You must kill one bull every day for seven days. This will be an offering for the sins of Aaron and his sons. You will use these sacrifices* to make the altar pure, and pour olive oil on the altar to make it holy. 37You will make the altar pure and holy for seven days. At that time the altar will be most holy. Anything that touches the altar will also be holy.

38"Every day you must make an offering on the altar. You must kill two lambs that are one year old. 39Offer one lamb in the morning and the other in the evening. 40-41When you kill the first lamb, also offer 8 cups*a* of fine wheat flour. Mix that flour with 1 quart*b* of the best oil. Also offer 1 quart of wine as an offering. When you kill the second lamb in the evening, also offer the 8 cups of fine flour mixed with 1 quart of the best oil and offer 1 quart of wine. This is the same as you did in the morning. This will be a sweet-smelling gift to the LORD. When you burn this offering, he will smell it, and it will please him.

42"You must burn these things as an offering to the LORD every day. Do this at the entrance of the Meeting Tent before the LORD. Continue to do this for all time. When you make the offering, I, the LORD, will meet you there and speak to you. 43I will meet with the Israelites at that place, and my Glory* will make that place holy.

44"So I will make the Meeting Tent and the altar holy. I will also make Aaron and his sons holy so that they can serve me as priests. 45I will live with the Israelites. I will be their God. 46The people will know that I am the LORD their God. They will know that I am the one who led them out of Egypt so that I could live with them. I am the LORD their God.

The Altar for Burning Incense

30 1"Make an altar* from acacia wood. You will use this altar for burning incense.* 2You must make the altar square—1 cubit*c* long and 1 cubit wide. It must be 2 cubits*d* high. There will be horns at the four corners. These horns must be made as one piece with the altar. 3Cover the top, the horns, and all four sides of the altar with pure gold. Then put gold trim all around the altar. 4Below this trim there should be two gold rings. There should be two gold rings on opposite sides of the altar. These gold rings will be used with poles to carry the altar. 5Make the poles from acacia wood and cover them with gold. 6Put the altar just outside the special curtain that hangs in front of the Box of the Agreement.* So the altar will be in front of the mercy-cover* that is above the Agreement.* This is the place where I will meet with you.

7"Aaron must burn sweet-smelling incense on the altar every morning. He will do this when he comes to care for the lamps. 8He must burn incense again when he checks the lamps in the evening so that incense will be burned before the LORD every day forever. 9Don't use this altar for offering any other kind of incense or burnt offering* or for any kind of grain offering or drink offering.

10"Once a year Aaron must make a special sacrifice.* He will use the blood of the sin offering* to erase the sins of the people. He will do this at the horns of this altar. This day will be called the Day of Atonement, and it will be a very special day for the LORD."

The Temple Tax

11The LORD said to Moses, 12"Count the Israelites so that you will know how many people there are. Every time this is done, each man must make a payment for himself to the LORD so that nothing terrible will happen to the people. 13Each man who is counted must pay ½ shekel of silver. (That is ½ shekel by the official measure.* This shekel weighs 20 gerahs.*e*) This half shekel is an offering to the LORD. 14Every man who is at least 20 years old must be counted. And every man who is counted must give the LORD this offering. 15The rich must not give more than ½ shekel, and the poor must not give less than ½ shekel. All people will make the same offering to the LORD. This will be a payment for your life. 16Gather this money from the Israelites. Use the money for the service

---

*a***29:40–41** *8 cups* Literally, "1/10 of a measure" (2.2 l).
*b***29:40–41** *1 quart* Literally, "1/4 hin" (.8 l).
*c***30:2** *cubit* 20 5/8" (51.83 cm).
*d***30:2** *2 cubits* 3' 4 13/16" (104 cm).
*e***30:13** *gerahs* 1/50 of an ounce (.6 g).

in the Meeting Tent.* This payment will be a way for the LORD to remember his people. They will be paying for their own lives."

The Washing Bowl

[17]The LORD said to Moses, [18]"Make a bronze* bowl and put it on a bronze base. You will use this for washing. Put the bowl between the Meeting Tent* and the altar.* Fill the bowl with water. [19]Aaron and his sons must wash their hands and feet with the water from this bowl. [20]Every time they enter the Meeting Tent, they must wash with that water so that they will not die. They must also wash every time they come near the altar to burn incense or to offer gifts to the LORD. [21]They must wash their hands and their feet so that they will not die. This will be a law that continues forever for Aaron and his people who will live in the future."

The Anointing Oil

[22]Then the LORD said to Moses, [23]"Find the finest spices. Get 12 pounds[a] of liquid myrrh,* half that amount (that is, 6 pounds[b]) of sweet-smelling cinnamon, and 12 pounds of sweet-smelling cane, [24]and 12 pounds of cassia.* Use the official measure* to measure all these things. Also get 1 gallon[c] of olive oil.

[25]"Mix all these things to make a special sweet-smelling anointing* oil. [26]Pour this oil on the Meeting Tent* and on the Box of the Agreement.* This will show that these things have a special purpose. [27]Pour the oil on the table and on all the dishes on the table. And pour this oil on the lamp and on all its tools. Pour the oil on the incense* altar. [28]Also, pour the oil on the altar for burning offerings to God. Pour this oil on everything on that altar. Pour this oil on the bowl and on the base under the bowl. [29]You will make all these things holy.* They will be very special to the Lord. Anything that touches these things will also become holy.

[30]"Pour the oil on Aaron and his sons to show that they are separated from the rest of the people to serve as priests. [31]Tell the Israelites that the anointing oil is holy—it must always be used only for me. [32]This oil is holy and you must treat it as something special. Don't use the same formula for making perfume, and don't let people use this oil like an ordinary perfume. [33]Whoever makes a perfume like that and puts it on anyone except a priest[d] must be separated from the people."

The Incense

[34]Then the LORD said to Moses, "Get these sweet-smelling spices: resin, onycha, galbanum, and pure frankincense. Be sure that you have equal amounts of these spices. [35]Mix the spices together to make a sweet-smelling incense.* Do this the same as a perfume maker would do it. Also mix salt with this incense. This will make it pure and special. [36]Grind some of the incense until it becomes a fine powder. Put the powder in front of the Holy Box that holds the Agreement[e] in the Meeting Tent.* This is the place where I meet with you. You must use this incense powder only for its very special purpose. [37]You must use it only in this special way for the LORD. You must also make it in a special way. Don't make any other incense in this way. [38]There may be people who will want to make some of this incense for themselves so that they can enjoy the smell. But whoever does this must be separated from their people."

Bezalel and Oholiab

31 [1]Then the LORD said to Moses, [2]"I have chosen a man from the tribe of Judah to do some special work for me. His name is Bezalel son of Uri son of Hur. [3]I have filled Bezalel with the Spirit of God—I have given him the skill and knowledge to do all kinds of things. [4]He is a very good designer. And he can make things from gold, silver, and bronze.* [5]He can cut and set beautiful jewels. And he can work with wood. He can do all kinds of work. [6]I have also chosen Oholiab to work with him. Oholiab is the son of Ahisamach from the tribe of Dan. And I have given skills to all the other workers so that they can make everything that I have commanded you:

[7] the Meeting Tent;*
the Box of the Agreement;*
the mercy-cover* that is on it;
[8] the table and everything on it;
the pure gold lampstand and everything used with it;
the altar* for burning incense;*
[9] the altar for burning offerings and the things used at the altar;
the bowl and the base under it;
[10] the special clothes for Aaron the priest;
the special clothes for Aaron's sons when they serve as priests;
[11] the sweet-smelling anointing* oil;
the sweet-smelling incense for the Holy Place.*

These workers must make everything the way that I have commanded you."

The Sabbath

[12]Then the LORD said to Moses, [13]"Tell the Israelites this: 'You must follow the rules about my special days of rest. You must do this because they will be a sign between you and me for all generations. This will show you

---

[a]**30:23** *12 pounds* Literally, "500 measures" (5.75 kg).
[b]**30:23** *6 pounds* Literally, "250 measures" (2.9 kg).
[c]**30:24** *gallon* Literally, "a hin" (3.2 l).
[d]**30:33** *priest* Literally, "stranger."

[e]**30:36** *Holy Box that holds the Agreement* Literally, "Testimony." See "Agreement" in the Word List.

that I, the LORD, have made you my special people.

14"'Make the Sabbath* a special day. If someone treats the Sabbath like any other day, that person must be killed. Whoever works on the Sabbath day must be separated from their people. 15There are six other days in the week for working. But the seventh day is a very special day of rest. That is the special day to honor the LORD. Anyone who works during the Sabbath must be killed. 16The Israelites must remember the Sabbath and make it a special day. They must continue to do this forever. It is an agreement between them and me that will continue forever. 17The Sabbath will be a sign between me and the Israelites forever.'" (The LORD worked six days and made the sky and the earth, and on the seventh day he rested and relaxed.)

18When God finished speaking to Moses on Mount Sinai, he gave him the two stone tablets of the Agreement.* God had written on the stones with his finger.

The Golden Calf

32 1The people saw that a long time had passed and Moses had not come down from the mountain. So they gathered around Aaron. They said to him, "Look, Moses led us out of the land of Egypt, but we don't know what has happened to him. So make us some gods to go before us and lead us."

2Aaron said to the people, "Bring me the gold earrings that belong to your wives, sons, and daughters."

3So the people collected all their gold earrings and brought them to Aaron. 4He took the gold from the people and used it to make an idol. Using a special tool, he shaped the gold into a statue of a calf.

Then the people said, "Israel, here are your gods! These are the gods that brought you out of the land of Egypt!"a

5Aaron saw all these things, so he built an altar* in front of the calf. Then Aaron made an announcement. He said, "Tomorrow will be a special festival to honor the LORD."

6The people woke up very early the next morning. They killed animals and offered them as burnt offerings* and fellowship offerings.* They sat down to eat and drink. Then they got up and had a wild party.

7At the same time, the LORD said to Moses, "Go down from this mountain. Your people, the people you brought out of the land of Egypt, have committed a terrible sin. 8They have very quickly turned away from what I commanded them to do. They made a calf from melted gold for themselves. They are worshiping that calf and making sacrifices* to it. The people have said, 'Israel, these are the

gods that led you out of Egypt.'"

9The LORD said to Moses, "I have seen these people, and I know that they are very stubborn. They will always turn against me. 10So now let me destroy them in anger. Then I will make a great nation from you."

11But Moses begged the LORD his God, "LORD, don't let your anger destroy your people. You brought them out of Egypt with your great power and strength. 12But if you destroy your people, the Egyptians will say, 'The LORD planned to do bad things to his people. That is why he led them out of Egypt. He wanted to kill them in the mountains. He wanted to wipe them off the earth.' So don't be angry with your people. Please change your mind! Don't destroy them. 13Remember Abraham, Isaac, and Israel. These men served you, and you used your name to make a promise to them. You said, 'I will make your people as many as the stars in the sky. I will give your people all this land as I promised. This land will be theirs forever.'"

14So the LORD felt sorry for the people. He did not do what he said he might do—he did not destroy them.

15Then Moses went down the mountain. He had the two stone tablets with the agreement* on them. The commandments were written on both sides of the stone, front and back. 16God himself made the stones, and God himself wrote the commandments on them.

17Joshua heard the noise from the party in camp. He said to Moses, "It sounds like war down in the camp!"

18Moses answered, "It is not the noise of an army shouting for victory. And it is not the noise of an army crying from defeat. The noise I hear is the sound of music.b"

19When Moses came near the camp, he saw the golden calf and the people dancing. He became very angry, and he threw the stone tablets on the ground. The stones broke into several pieces at the bottom of the mountain. 20Then Moses destroyed the calf that the people had made. He melted it in the fire. Then he ground the gold until it became dust and threw it into the water. Then he forced the Israelites to drink that water.

21Moses said to Aaron, "What did these people do to you that would make you do this? Why did you lead them to do such a terrible sin?"

22Aaron answered, "Don't be angry, sir. You know that these people are always ready to do wrong. 23The people said to me, 'Moses led us out of Egypt, but we don't know what has happened to him. So make us some gods to lead us.' 24So I told the people, 'If you have any gold rings, then give them to me.' The people gave me their gold. I threw the gold into the fire, and out of the fire came this calf!"

---

a32:4 *Israel ... Egypt* This shows that the people worshiped the calf as a special symbol for the Lord, and even this was forbidden. See 1 Kings. 12:26–30.

b32:18 *music* Or "singing."

²⁵Moses saw that Aaron had let the people get out of control. They were being wild, and all their enemies could see them acting like fools. ²⁶So Moses stood at the entrance to the camp and said, "Anyone who wants to follow the Lord should come to me." Everyone from the tribe of Levi ran to Moses.

²⁷Then Moses said to them, "I will tell you what the Lord, the God of Israel, says: 'Every man must get his sword and go from one end of the camp to the other. You men must kill ⌊those who are against the Lord⌋, even if they are your brothers, friends, or neighbors.'"

²⁸The people from the tribe of Levi obeyed Moses. That day about 3000 of the people died. ²⁹Then Moses said, "Take your role today as special servants of the Lord because you were willing to fight against even your own sons and brothers. You will receive a blessing for this."^a

³⁰The next morning Moses told the people, "You have committed a terrible sin! But now I will go up to the Lord, and maybe I can do something so that he will forgive you for your sin." ³¹So Moses went back to the Lord and said, "Please listen! These people committed a terrible sin and made a god from gold. ³²Now, forgive them of this sin. If you will not forgive them, then erase my name from your book.^b"

³³But the Lord said to Moses, "The only people I erase from my book are those who sin against me. ³⁴So now, go down and lead the people where I tell you to go. My angel will go before you and lead you. When the time comes to punish those who sinned, they will be punished." ³⁵So the Lord caused a terrible sickness to come to the people. He did this because they told Aaron to make the golden calf.

I Will Not Go With You

33 ¹Then the Lord said to Moses, "You and the people you brought out of Egypt must leave this place. Go to the land that I promised to give to Abraham, Isaac, and Jacob. I promised them that I would give that land to their descendants. ²So I will send an angel to go before you, and I will defeat the Canaanites, Amorites, Hittites, Perizzites, Hivites, and Jebusites. I will force them to leave your land. ³So go to the land filled with many good things,^c but I will not go with you. You people are very stubborn. If I go with you, I might destroy you along the way."

⁴The people heard this bad news and became very sad, so they stopped wearing jewelry. ⁵This was because the Lord said to Moses, "Tell the Israelites, 'You are a stubborn people. I might destroy you even if I travel with you only a short time. So take off all your jewelry while I decide^d what to do with you.'" ⁶So the Israelites stopped wearing their jewelry at Mount Horeb.*

The Temporary Meeting Tent

⁷Moses used to take a tent a short way outside the camp. He called it "the meeting tent.^e" Anyone who wanted to ask something from the Lord would go to the meeting tent outside the camp. ⁸Any time Moses went out to the tent, all the people watched him. They stood at the entrance of their tents and watched Moses until he entered the meeting tent. ⁹Whenever Moses went into the tent, the tall cloud would come down and stay at the entrance to the tent. And the Lord would speak with Moses. ¹⁰So when the people saw the cloud at the entrance of the tent, they would go to the entrance of their own tents and bow down to worship God.

¹¹In this way the Lord spoke to Moses face to face like a man speaks with his friend. Then Moses would go back to the camp, but his helper, Joshua son of Nun, always stayed in the tent.

Moses Sees the Glory of the Lord

¹²Moses said to the Lord, "You told me to lead these people, but you did not say who you would send with me. You said to me, 'I know you very well, and I am pleased with you.' ¹³If I have really pleased you, then teach me your ways. I want to know you. Then I can continue to please you. Remember that these people are your nation."

¹⁴The Lord answered, "I myself will go with you. I will lead you."^f

¹⁵Then Moses said to him, "If you don't go with us, then don't make us leave this place. ¹⁶Also, how will we know if you are pleased with me and these people? If you go with us, we will know for sure. If you don't go with us, these people and I will be no different from any other people on the earth."

¹⁷Then the Lord said to Moses, "I will do what you ask. I will do this because I am pleased with you and because I know you very well."^g

¹⁸Then Moses said, "Now, please show me your Glory.*"

---

^a**32:29 Take your role … blessing for this** This seems to be the point when the priesthood changed. Before this time, the priests came from the firstborn sons; after this time, they came from the sons of Aaron of the tribe of Levi.

^b**32:32 your book** The book of life, in which God has written the names of his chosen people. See Rev. 3:5; 21:27.

^c**33:3 land … things** Literally, "land flowing with milk and honey."

^d**33:5 jewelry … decide** This is a wordplay in Hebrew, but people often wore jewelry to remind them of their false gods.

^e**33:7 meeting tent** This is probably a tent that Moses used only until the real Meeting Tent was built.

^f**33:14 lead you** Or "give you rest."

^g**33:17 I know you very well** Literally, "I know you by name."

¹⁹Then the Lord answered, "I will show my love and mercy to anyone I want to. So I will cause my perfect goodness to pass by in front of you, and I will speak my name, the Lord, so that you can hear it. ²⁰But you cannot see my face. No one can see me and continue to live.

²¹"Here is a place for you to stand by me on this large rock. ²²I will put you in a large crack in that rock. Then I will cover you with my hand, and my Glory will pass by. ²³Then I will take away my hand, and you will see my back. But you will not see my face."

The New Stone Tablets

34 ¹Then the Lord said to Moses, "Make two more stone tablets like the first two that were broken. I will write the same words on these stones that were written on the first two stones. ²Be ready tomorrow morning and come up on Mount Sinai. Stand before me there on the top of the mountain. ³No one will be allowed to come with you. No one should even be seen anywhere on the mountain. Even your herds of animals or flocks of sheep will not be allowed to eat grass at the bottom of the mountain."

⁴So Moses made two more stone tablets like the first ones. Early the next morning Moses went up Mount Sinai, just as the Lord had commanded. Moses carried the two stone tablets with him. ⁵Then the Lord came down to him in a cloud, stood there with Moses, and spoke his own name. ⁶That is, the Lord passed in front of Moses and said, "Yahweh,* the Lord, is a kind and merciful God. He is slow to become angry. He is full of great love. He can be trusted. ⁷He shows his faithful love for thousands of generations.ᵃ The Lord forgivesᵇ people for the wrong things they do, but he does not forget to punish guilty people. Not only will he punish the guilty people, but their children, their grandchildren, and their great-grandchildren will also suffer for the bad things these people do."ᶜ

⁸Then Moses quickly bowed to the ground and worshiped the Lord. Moses said, ⁹"Lord, if you are pleased with me, please go with us. I know that these are stubborn people, but forgive us for the bad things we did. Accept us as your people."

¹⁰Then the Lord said, "I am making this agreement with all of your people. I will do amazing things that have never before been done for any other nation on earth. The people with you will see that I, the Lord, am very great. They will see the wonderful things that I will do for you. ¹¹Obey what I command you today, and I will force your enemies to leave your land. I will force out the Amorites, Canaanites, Hittites, Perizzites, Hivites, and Jebusites. ¹²Be careful! Don't make any agreement with the people who live in the land where you are going. If you make an agreement with them, it will bring you trouble. ¹³So destroy their altars,* break the stones they worship, and cut down their idols.ᵈ ¹⁴Don't worship any other god. I am Yahweh Kanah—the jealous Lord. That is my name. I hate for my people to worship other gods.ᵉ

¹⁵"Be careful not to make any agreements with the people who live in that land. If you do this, you might join them when they worship their gods. They will invite you to join them, and you will eat their sacrifices.* ¹⁶You might choose some of their daughters as wives for your sons. Those daughters serve false gods. They might lead your sons to do the same thing.

¹⁷"Don't make idols.*

¹⁸"Celebrate the Festival of Unleavened Bread.* For seven days eat the bread made without yeast as I commanded you before. Do this during the month I have chosen, the month of Abib,* because that is the month you came out of Egypt.

¹⁹"A woman's first baby always belongs to me. Even the first animals that are born from your cattle or sheep belong to me. ²⁰If you want to keep a donkey that is the first born, then you can buy it with a lamb. But if you don't buy that donkey with a lamb, you must break the donkey's neck. You must buy back all of your firstborn* sons from me. No one should come before me without a gift.

²¹"You will work for six days, but on the seventh day you must rest. You must rest even during the times of planting and harvesting.

²²"Celebrate the Festival of Harvest.* Use the first grain from the wheat harvest for this festival. And in the fallᶠ celebrate the Festival of Shelters.*

²³"Three times each year all your men must go to be with the Lord God, the God of Israel.

²⁴"When you go into your land, I will force your enemies out of that land. I will expand your borders—you will get more and more land. You will go before the Lord your God three times each year. At that time no one will try to take your land from you.

²⁵"When you kill an animal and offer its blood as a sacrifice, you must not include anything that has yeast in it.

"Don't let any of the meat from the Passover* meal remain until morning.

ᵃ**34:7 He ... generations** Or "He shows his faithful love for thousands of people" or "He shows his faithful love to the tribes."
ᵇ**34:7 forgives** Or "spares."
ᶜ**34:7 The Lord ... people do** Or "The Lord credits the guilt of the fathers to their children and grandchildren, to the third and fourth generation."
ᵈ**34:13 stones ... idols** Literally, "memorials ... Asherah poles." These were stone markers and wood poles that the people set up to help them remember and honor false gods.
ᵉ**34:14 I hate ... gods** Or "I am El Kanah—the Jealous God."
ᶠ**34:22 fall** Literally, "at the changing of the year."

26"Give the Lord the very first crops that you harvest. Bring them to the house*a* of the LORD your God.

"Never cook a young goat in its mother's milk."

27Then the LORD said to Moses, "Write everything that I have told you. This is the agreement* that I made with you and the Israelites."

28Moses stayed there with the LORD for 40 days and 40 nights. Moses did not eat any food or drink any water. And he wrote the words of the agreement (the Ten Commandments) on the two stone tablets.

Moses' Shining Face

29When Moses came down from Mount Sinai, he carried the two stone tablets of the Agreement.* Because he had talked with the LORD, his face was shining, but he did not know it. 30Aaron and all the people of Israel saw that Moses' face was shining bright. So they were afraid to go near him. 31But Moses called to them. So Aaron and all the leaders of the people went to him. Moses talked with them. 32After that, all the Israelites came near Moses, and he gave them the commands that the LORD had given him on Mount Sinai.

33When Moses finished speaking to the people, he put a covering over his face. 34Any time Moses went before the LORD to speak with him, Moses took off the covering. Then Moses would come out and tell the Israelites what the LORD commanded. 35The people would see that Moses' face was shining bright, so he would cover his face again. He kept his face covered until the next time he went in to speak with the LORD.

Rules About the Sabbath

35 1Moses gathered all the Israelites together and said to them, "I will tell you what the LORD has commanded you to do:

2"There are six days for working, but the seventh day will be a very special day of rest for you. You will honor the LORD by resting on that special day. Anyone who works on the seventh day must be killed. 3On the Sabbath* you should not even light a fire in any of the places where you live."

Things for the Holy Tent

4Moses said to all the Israelites, "This is what the LORD commanded: 5Gather special gifts for the LORD. Each of you should decide in your heart what you will give. And then you should bring that gift to the LORD. Bring gold, silver, and bronze*; 6blue, purple, and red yarn and fine linen*; goat hair; 7ram skins dyed red and fine leather; acacia wood; 8oil for the lamps; spices for the anointing* oil and

spices for the sweet-smelling incense.* 9Also, bring onyx* stones and other jewels to be put on the ephod* and the judgment pouch.*

10"All of you who are skilled workers should make all the things the LORD commanded: 11the Holy Tent,* its outer tent, and its covering; the hooks, boards, braces, posts, and bases; 12the Holy Box,* its poles, the mercy-cover,* and the curtain that covers the area where the Box stays; 13the table and its poles, all the things on the table, and the special bread on the table; 14the lampstand that is used for light and the things used with the lampstand, the lamps, and oil for the light; 15the altar* for burning incense and its poles; the anointing oil and the sweet-smelling incense; the curtain that covers the door at the entrance to the Holy Tent; 16the altar for burning offerings and its bronze grating, the poles, and all the things used at the altar; the bronze bowl and its base; 17the curtains around the yard, their posts and bases, and the curtain that covers the entrance to the yard; 18the pegs used to support the Tent and the wall of curtains around the courtyard, and the ropes that tie to the pegs; 19and the special woven clothes for the priest to wear in the Holy Place.* These are the special clothes for Aaron the priest and his sons to wear when they serve as priests."

The Great Offering From the People

20Then all the Israelites went away from Moses. 21All the people who wanted to give came and brought a gift to the LORD. These gifts were used for making the Meeting Tent,* everything in the Tent, and the special clothes. 22All the men and women who wanted to give brought gold jewelry of all kinds. They brought pins,*b* earrings, rings, and other jewelry. They all gave their jewelry as a special offering to the LORD.

23Everyone who had fine linen* and blue, purple, and red yarn brought it to the Lord. Anyone who had goat hair or ram skins dyed red or fine leather brought it to the Lord. 24Everyone who wanted to give silver or bronze* brought that as a gift to the LORD. Everyone who had acacia wood came and gave it to the Lord. 25Every skilled woman made fine linen and blue, purple, and red yarn. 26And all the women who were skilled and wanted to help made cloth from the goat hair.

27The leaders brought onyx stones and other jewels. These stones and jewels were put on the ephod* and judgment pouch* of the priest. 28The people also brought spices and olive oil. These things were used for the sweet-smelling incense,* the anointing* oil, and the oil for the lamps.

29All the Israelites who wanted to help brought gifts to the LORD. They gave these gifts

---

*a*34:26 *house* The "Holy Tent" where the people went to meet with God. See Ex. 25:8, 9.

*b*35:22 *pins* Or "hooks." These were like safety pins and were used like buttons to fasten their robes.

freely, because they wanted to. These gifts were used to make everything the LORD had commanded Moses and the people to make.

Bezalel and Oholiab

³⁰Then Moses said to the Israelites, "Look, the LORD has chosen Bezalel son of Uri, from the tribe of Judah. (Uri was the son of Hur.) ³¹The LORD filled Bezalel with the Spirit of God—he gave Bezalel special skill and knowledge to do all kinds of things. ³²He can design and make things with gold, silver, and bronze.* ³³He can cut and set stones and jewels. He can work with wood and make all kinds of things. ³⁴The LORD has given Bezalel and Oholiab special skills to teach other people. (Oholiab was the son of Ahisamach from the tribe of Dan.) ³⁵The LORD has given both of these men special skills to do all kinds of work. They are able to do the work of carpenters and metalworkers. They can weave cloth with designs in it from the blue, purple, and red yarn and fine linen.* And they are able to weave things with wool.

36 ¹"So Bezalel, Oholiab, and all the other skilled men must do the work the LORD has commanded. The Lord has given these men the wisdom and understanding to do all the skilled work needed to build this holy* place."

²Then Moses called Bezalel, Oholiab, and all the other skilled men who the LORD had given special skills to. And they came because they wanted to help with the work. ³Moses gave them everything the Israelites had brought as gifts, and they used these things to build the holy place. The people continued to bring gifts each morning. ⁴Finally, all the skilled workers left the work they were doing on the holy place, and they went to speak to Moses. They said, ⁵"The people have brought too much. We have more than we need to finish the work the LORD told us to do."

⁶Then Moses sent this message throughout the camp: "No man or woman should make anything else as a gift for the holy place." So the people were forced to stop giving more. ⁷The people had brought more than enough things to finish the work of building God's holy place.

The Holy Tent

⁸Then the skilled workers began making the Holy Tent.* They made the ten curtains from fine linen and blue, purple, and red yarn. And they sewed pictures of Cherub angels* with wings into the curtains. ⁹Each curtain was the same size—28 cubits^a long and 4 cubits^b wide. ¹⁰The workers joined the curtains together into two groups of curtains. They joined five curtains together to make one group and five curtains together to make

the other group. ¹¹Then they used blue cloth to make loops along the edge of the end curtain of one group. And they did the same on the end curtain in the other group. ¹²There were 50 loops on the end curtain in one group and 50 loops on the end curtain in the other group. The loops were opposite each other. ¹³Then they made 50 gold rings to join the two curtains together. So the Holy Tent was joined together into one piece.

¹⁴Then the workers made another tent to cover the Holy Tent. They used goat hair to make eleven curtains. ¹⁵All the curtains were the same size—30 cubits^c long and 4 cubits wide. ¹⁶The workers joined five curtains together into one group and six curtains together into another group. ¹⁷They put 50 loops along the edge of the end curtain of one group. And they did the same on the end curtain of the other group. ¹⁸The workers made 50 bronze* rings to join the two groups of curtains together to form one tent. ¹⁹Then they made two more coverings for the Holy Tent. One covering was made from ram skins dyed red. The other covering was made from fine leather.

²⁰Then the workers made frames from acacia wood to support the Holy Tent. ²¹Each frame was 10 cubits^d long and 1½ cubits^e wide. ²²There were two side poles joined together with cross pieces to make each frame. Every frame for the Holy Tent was made the same. ²³They made 20 frames for the south side of the Holy Tent. ²⁴Then they made 40 silver bases for the frames. There were two bases for each frame—one base for each side pole. ²⁵They also made 20 frames for the other side (the north side) of the Holy Tent. ²⁶They made 40 silver bases for the frames—two bases for each frame. ²⁷They made six more frames for the back (the west side) of the Holy Tent. ²⁸They also made two frames for the corners at the back of the Holy Tent. ²⁹These frames were joined together at the bottom. And at the top a ring held the corner frames together. They did the same for both corners. ³⁰There was a total of eight frames for the west side of the Holy Tent. And there were 16 silver bases—two bases for each frame.

³¹Then the workers used acacia wood to make the braces for the frames—five braces for the first side of the Holy Tent, ³²five braces for the other side, and five braces for the back of the Holy Tent (that is, the west side). ³³They made the middle brace so that it passed through the frames from one end to the other. ³⁴They covered these frames with gold. Then they used gold to make the rings to hold the braces, and they covered the braces with gold.

---

^{a}**36:9** *28 cubits* 47' 7 3/8" (14.5 m).
^{b}**36:9** *4 cubits* 6' 9 5/8" (2.1 m). Also in verse 15.

^{c}**36:15** *30 cubits* 51' 3/16" (15.55 m).
^{d}**36:21** *10 cubits* 17' 1/16" (5.18 m).
^{e}**36:21** *1 1/2 cubits* 30 5/8" (77.75 cm). Also in 37:1.

35They used fine linen* and blue, purple, and red yarn to make the special curtain for the entrance to the Most Holy Place. And they sewed pictures of Cherub angels into the curtain. 36They made four posts using acacia wood, and they covered the posts with gold. Then they made gold hooks for the posts and four silver bases for the posts. 37Then they made the curtain to cover the entrance to the Tent. They used blue, purple, and red yarn and fine linen to make this curtain. And they wove pictures into it. 38Then they made the five posts and the hooks for this curtain over the entrance. They covered the tops of the posts and the curtain rods*a* with gold. And they made the five bronze bases for the posts.

The Box of the Agreement

37 1Bezalel made the Holy Box* from acacia wood. The Box was 2½ cubits*b* long, 1½ cubits wide,*c* and 1½ cubits high. 2He covered the inside and outside of the Box with pure gold. Then he put gold trim around the Box. 3He made four rings of gold and put them on the four corners. These rings were used for carrying the Box. There were two rings on each side. 4Then he made the poles for carrying the Box. He used acacia wood and covered the poles with pure gold. 5He put the poles through the rings on each side of the Box. 6Then he made the mercy-cover* from pure gold. It was 2½ cubits long and 1½ cubits wide. 7Then Bezalel hammered gold to make two Cherub angels.* He put the Cherub angels on each end of the mercy-cover. 8He put one angel on one end and the other angel on the other end. The angels were joined together with the mercy-cover to make one piece. 9The wings of the angels were spread up toward the sky. The angels covered the Box with their wings and faced each other, looking toward the mercy-cover.

The Special Table

10Then he made the table from acacia wood. The table was 2 cubits*d* long, 1 cubit*e* wide, and 1½ cubits high. 11He covered it with pure gold and put gold trim around it. 12Then he made a frame 1 handbreadth*f* wide around the table. He put gold trim on the frame. 13Then he made four gold rings and put them at the four corners of the table, where the four legs were. 14He put the rings close to the frame. The rings were to hold the poles used to carry the table. 15Then he used acacia wood to make the poles for carrying the

table. He covered the poles with pure gold. 16Then he made everything that was used on the table. He made the plates, the spoons, the bowls, and the pitchers from pure gold. The bowls and pitchers are used for pouring the drink offerings.

The Lampstand

17Then he made the lampstand. He used pure gold and hammered it to make the base and the shaft.*g* Then he made flowers, buds, and petals and joined everything together into one piece. 18The lampstand had six branches—three branches on one side and three branches on the other side. 19Each branch had three flowers on it. These flowers were made like almond flowers with buds and petals. 20The shaft of the lampstand had four more flowers. They were also made like almond flowers with buds and petals. 21There were six branches—three branches coming out from each side of the shaft. And there was a flower with buds and petals below each of the three places where the branches joined the shaft. 22The whole lampstand, with the flowers and branches, was made from pure gold. All this gold was hammered and joined together into one piece. 23He made seven lamps for this lampstand. Then he made lamp snuffers* and trays from pure gold. 24He used 75 pounds*h* of pure gold to make the lampstand and the things used with it.

The Altar for Burning Incense

25He made the altar* for burning incense* from acacia wood. The altar was square. It was 1 cubit long, 1 cubit wide, and 2 cubits high. There were four horns on the altar. There was one horn on each corner. These horns were joined together with the altar to make one piece. 26He covered the top, all the sides, and the horns with pure gold. Then he put gold trim around the altar. 27He made two gold rings for the altar. He put the gold rings below the trim on each side of the altar. These gold rings held the poles for carrying the altar. 28He made the poles from acacia wood and covered them with gold. 29Then he made the holy anointing* oil. He also made the pure, sweet-smelling incense. These things were made the same way that a perfume maker would make them.

The Altar for Burning Offerings

38 1Then Bezalel used acacia wood to build the altar. This was the altar used for burning offerings. The altar was square. It was 5 cubits*i* long, 5 cubits wide, and 3 cubits*j* high. 2He made a horn for each of the four corners of the altar. He joined each

---

*a***36:38** *curtain rods* Or "fasteners."
*b***37:1** *2 1/2 cubits* 4' 3" (1.3 m).
*c***37:1** *1 1/2 cubits* 30 5/8" (77.75 cm). Also in verse 10.
*d***37:10** *2 cubits* 3' 4 13/16" (104 cm). See also in verse 25.
*e***37:10** *cubit* 20 5/8" (51.83 cm). Also in verse 25.
*f***37:12** *handbreadth* The width of 4 fingers, about 3" (7.4 cm).

*g***37:17** *base and the shaft* Or "flared base."
*h***37:24** *75 pounds* Literally, "1 talent" (34.5 kg).
*i***38:1** *5 cubits* 8' 6" (2.6 m). Also in verse 18.
*j***38:1** *3 cubits* 5' 1 3/16" (1.55 m).

horn to its corner so that everything was one piece. He covered the altar with bronze.* ³Then he used bronze to make all the tools to be used on the altar. He made the pots, shovels, bowls, forks, and pans. ⁴Then he made a bronze grating for the altar. This grating was shaped like a net. The grating was put under the ledge at the bottom of the altar. It went halfway up into the altar from below. ⁵Then he made bronze rings to hold the poles for carrying the altar. He put the rings at the four corners of the grating. ⁶Then he used acacia wood to make the poles and covered them with bronze. ⁷He put the poles through the rings on the sides of the altar to carry it. He used boards to make the sides of the altar. It was hollow, like an empty box.

⁸He made the bowl and its base with bronze. He used the bronze mirrors that the women gave. These were the women who served at the entrance to the Meeting Tent.*

The Courtyard Around the Holy Tent

⁹Then he made a wall of curtains around the courtyard. On the south side, he made a wall of curtains 100 cubits*ᵃ* long. The curtains were made from fine linen.* ¹⁰The curtains on the south side were supported by 20 posts. The posts were on 20 bronze* bases. The hooks for the posts and the curtain rods*ᵇ* were made from silver. ¹¹The north side of the courtyard also had a wall of curtains 100 cubits long. There were 20 posts with 20 bronze bases. The hooks for the posts and the curtain rods were made from silver.

¹²On the west side of the courtyard the wall of curtains was 50 cubits*ᶜ* long. There were 10 posts and 10 bases. The hooks for the posts and the curtain rods were made from silver.

¹³The east side of the courtyard was 50 cubits wide. The entrance to the courtyard was on this side. ¹⁴On one side of the entrance the wall of curtains was 15 cubits*ᵈ* long. There were three posts and three bases on this side. ¹⁵The wall of curtains on the other side of the entrance was also 15 cubits long. There were three posts and three bases on that side. ¹⁶All the curtains around the courtyard were made from fine linen. ¹⁷The bases for the posts were made from bronze. The hooks and the curtain rods were made from silver. The tops of the posts were covered with silver also. All the posts in the courtyard had silver curtain rods.

¹⁸The curtain for the entrance of the courtyard was made from fine linen and blue, purple, and red yarn. Designs were woven into that curtain. The curtain was 20 cubits*ᵉ* long and 5 cubits high. It was the same height as the curtains around the courtyard. ¹⁹The

curtain was supported by four posts and four bronze bases. The hooks on the posts were made from silver. The tops on the posts were covered with silver, and the curtain rods were also made from silver. ²⁰All the tent pegs for the Holy Tent* and for the curtains around the courtyard were made from bronze.

²¹Moses commanded the Levites to write down everything that was used to make the Holy Tent, that is, the Tent of the Agreement.* Ithamar son of Aaron was in charge of keeping the list.

²²Bezalel son of Uri, the son of Hur, from the tribe of Judah, made everything the LORD commanded Moses. ²³Also Oholiab son of Ahisamach, from the tribe of Dan, helped him. Oholiab was a skilled worker and designer. He was skilled at weaving fine linen and blue, purple, and red yarn.

²⁴The people gave over a ton*ᶠ* of gold as an offering to the LORD for his holy* place. (This was weighed using the official measure.*)

²⁵⁻²⁶All the men 20 years old or older were counted. Each man had to pay a tax of 1 beka*ᵍ* of silver. (Using the official measure, 1 beka is ½ shekel.*ʰ*) There were 603,550 men. So they collected about 7550 pounds of silver. ²⁷They used 7550 pounds of that silver to make 100 bases for the holy place and its curtains. They used 75 pounds*ⁱ* of silver for each base. ²⁸They used the remaining 44 pounds*ʲ* of silver to make the hooks, the curtain rods, and the silver covers for the posts.

²⁹They gave more than 2½ tons*ᵏ* of bronze to the LORD. ³⁰That bronze was used to make the bases at the entrance of the Meeting Tent.* They also used the bronze to make the altar* and the bronze grating. And the bronze was used to make all the tools and dishes for the altar. ³¹It was also used to make the bases for the curtains around the courtyard and the bases for the curtains at the entrance. And the bronze was used to make the tent pegs for the Holy Tent and for the curtains around the courtyard.

The Priests' Special Clothes

39 ¹The workers used the blue, purple, and red yarn to make special clothes for the priests to wear when they served in the holy* place. They also made the special clothes for Aaron as the LORD had commanded Moses.

The Ephod

²They made the ephod* from gold thread, fine linen,* and blue, purple, and red yarn. ³(They hammered the gold into thin strips

---

*ᵃ*38:9 *100 cubits* 170' 5/8" (51.83 m).
*ᵇ*38:10 *curtain rods* Or "fasteners." Also in verses 12, 17, 19, 28.
*ᶜ*38:12 *50 cubits* 85' 5/16" (25.92 m).
*ᵈ*38:14 *15 cubits* 25' 6 1/16" (7.77 m).
*ᵉ*38:18 *20 cubits* 34' 1/8" (10.37 m).

*ᶠ*38:24 *ton* Literally, "29 talents and 730 shekels."
*ᵍ*38:25–26 *beka* About 1/5 of an ounce (6 g).
*ʰ*38:25–26 *shekel* Two-fifths of an ounce (11.5 g).
*ⁱ*38:27 *75 pounds* Literally, "1 talent" (34.5 kg).
*ʲ*38:28 *44 pounds* Literally, "1775 shekels" (20.4 kg).
*ᵏ*38:29 *2 1/2 tons* Literally, "70 talents and 2400 shekels" (2447 kg).

and cut the gold into long threads. They wove the gold into the blue, purple, and red yarn and fine linen. This was the work of a very skilled person.) 4They made the shoulder pieces for the ephod. They tied these shoulder pieces to the two corners of the ephod. 5They wove the cloth belt and fastened it to the ephod. It was made the same way as the ephod—they used gold thread, fine linen, and blue, purple, and red yarn, just as the Lord commanded Moses.

6The workers put the onyx* stones for the ephod in gold settings. They wrote the names of the sons of Israel on these stones. 7Then they put these jewels on the shoulder pieces of the ephod. These jewels were to help God to remember the Israelites. This was done as the Lord commanded Moses.

The Judgment Pouch

8Then they made the judgment pouch.* It was the work of a skilled person, just like the ephod.* It was made from gold threads, fine linen,* and blue, purple, and red yarn. 9The judgment pouch was folded in half to make a square pocket. It was 1 span*a* long and 1 span wide. 10Then the workers put four rows of beautiful jewels on the judgment pouch. The first row had a ruby, a topaz, and a beryl. 11The second row had a turquoise, a sapphire, and an emerald. 12The third row had a jacinth, an agate, and an amethyst. 13The fourth row had a chrysolite, an onyx, and a jasper. All these jewels were set in gold. 14There were twelve jewels on the judgment pouch—one jewel for each of the sons of Israel.* Each stone had the name of one of the sons of Israel carved onto it, like a seal.*

15The workers made two chains from pure gold for the judgment pouch. The chains were braided like a rope. 16The workers made two gold rings and fastened them to two corners of the judgment pouch. Then they made two gold settings for the shoulder pieces. 17They fastened the gold chains to the rings at the corners of the judgment pouch. 18They fastened the other ends of the gold chains to the settings on the shoulder pieces. They fastened these to the front of the ephod. 19Then they made two more gold rings and put them on the other two corners of the judgment pouch. This was on the inside edge of the judgment pouch next to the ephod. 20They also put two gold rings on the bottom of the shoulder pieces on the front of the ephod. These rings were near the fastener, just above the cloth belt. 21Then they used a blue ribbon and tied the rings of the judgment pouch to the rings of the ephod. In this way the judgment pouch would rest close to the cloth belt and would be held tight against the ephod. They did everything just as the Lord commanded.

Other Clothes for the Priests

22Then they made the robe for the ephod* from blue cloth. It was woven by a skilled worker. 23They made a hole in the center of the robe and sewed a piece of cloth around the edge of this hole. This cloth kept the hole from tearing.

24Then they used fine linen* and blue, purple, and red yarn to make the cloth pomegranates.* They hung these pomegranates around the bottom edge of the robe. 25Then they made bells from pure gold. They hung these bells around the bottom edge of the robe between the pomegranates. 26Around the bottom edge of the robe there were bells and pomegranates. There was a bell following each pomegranate. This robe was for the priest to wear when he served the Lord. It was made just as the Lord commanded Moses.

27Skilled workers wove shirts for Aaron and his sons. These shirts were made from fine linen. 28And the workers made a turban* from fine linen. They also used fine linen to make cloth caps and underclothes. 29Then they made the cloth belt from fine linen and blue, purple, and red yarn. Designs were sewn into the cloth. These things were made as the Lord had commanded Moses.

30Then they made a strip of pure gold for the holy crown. They carved these words into the gold like the writing on a seal: HOLY TO THE LORD.*b* 31They fastened the gold strip to a blue ribbon. Then they tied the blue ribbon around the turban like the Lord had commanded Moses.

Moses Inspects the Holy Tent

32So all the work on the Holy Tent,* that is, the Meeting Tent, was finished. The Israelites did everything exactly like the Lord had commanded Moses. 33Then they showed the Holy Tent and everything in it to Moses. They showed him the rings, the frames, the braces, the posts, and the bases. 34They showed him the covering of the Tent that was made from ram skins dyed red and the covering that was made from fine leather. And they showed him the curtain that covered the entrance to the Most Holy Place.

35They showed Moses the Box of the Agreement,* the poles used for carrying it, and the mercy-cover.* 36They showed him the table with everything on it and the special bread.*c* 37They showed him the pure gold lampstand and the lamps on it, the oil, and all the other things that were used with the lamps. 38They

a39:9 1 span The distance from the tip of the thumb to the tip of the little finger, about 9" (23 cm).

b39:30 HOLY TO THE LORD These words were written on everything that was used in the Temple. This showed that these things belonged to the Lord, and that they could be used only for special purposes. Dishes with this label could be used only by the priests in a holy place.

c39:36 special bread Also called "bread of the Presence." Every day this bread was put before God on the special table in the Holy Place.

showed Moses the golden altar,* the anointing* oil, the sweet-smelling incense,* and
the curtain that covered the entrance to the
Tent. 39They showed him the bronze* altar,
the bronze screen, the poles used for carrying
the altar, and everything that was used on the
altar. They showed him the bowl and the base
under the bowl.

40They showed Moses the wall of curtains
around the courtyard with the posts and
bases. They showed him the curtain that
covered the entrance to the courtyard. They
showed him the ropes and the tent pegs. They
showed him everything in the Holy Tent, that
is, the Meeting Tent.

41Then they showed Moses the clothes that
were made for the priests serving in the holy
area.*a They showed him the special clothes
for Aaron the priest and his sons to wear
when they served as priests.

42The Israelites did all this work exactly as
the LORD had commanded Moses. 43Moses
looked closely at all the work and saw that
it was done exactly as the LORD had commanded. So Moses blessed them.

Moses Sets Up the Holy Tent

40 1Then the LORD said to Moses, 2"On
the first day of the first month, set
up the Holy Tent,* that is, the Meeting Tent.
3Put the Box of the Agreement* in the Holy
Tent. Cover the Box with the curtain. 4Then
bring in the table. Put the things on the table
that should be there. Then put the lampstand
in the Tent. Put the lamps on the lampstand
in the right places. 5Put the golden altar* for
offering incense* in the Tent in front of the
Box of the Agreement. Then put the curtain
at the entrance to the Holy Tent.

6"Put the altar* for burning offerings in
front of the entrance of the Holy Tent, that
is, the Meeting Tent. 7Put the bowl between
the Meeting Tent and the altar. Put water in
the bowl. 8Set up the wall of curtains around
the courtyard. Then put the curtain at the
entrance to the courtyard.

9"Use the anointing oil and anoint* the
Holy Tent and everything in it. When you put
the oil on these things, you will make them
holy.* 10Anoint the altar for burning offerings.
Anoint everything on the altar. You will make
the altar holy. It will be very holy. 11Then
anoint the bowl and the base under it to make
these things holy.

12"Bring Aaron and his sons to the entrance
of the Meeting Tent.* Wash them with water.
13Then put the special clothes on Aaron.
Anoint him with the oil and make him holy.
Then he can serve me as a priest. 14Then put
the clothes on his sons. 15Anoint the sons in
the same way you anointed their father. Then

they can also serve me as priests. When you
anoint them, they will become priests. That
family will continue to be priests for all time
to come." 16Moses obeyed the Lord. He did
everything that the LORD commanded him.

17So the Holy Tent was set up at the right
time. It was the first day of the first month
during the second year from the time they
left Egypt. 18Moses set up the Holy Tent just
as the Lord had said. He put the bases down
first. Then he put the frames on the bases.
Then he put the braces on and set up the
posts. 19After that, Moses put the outer tent
over the Holy Tent. Then he put the covering
over the outer tent. He did these things just
as the LORD had commanded.

20Moses took the Agreement* and put it in
the Holy Box. He put the poles on the Box
and put the mercy-cover* on it. 21Then Moses
put the Holy Box into the Holy Tent. He hung
the curtain in the right place to protect it. In
this way he protected the Box of the Agreement* behind the curtain just as the LORD had
commanded him. 22Then Moses put the table
in the Meeting Tent on the north side of the
Holy Tent. He put it in the Holy Place, in front
of the curtain. 23Then he put the bread on
the table before the LORD. He did this just as
the LORD had commanded him. 24Then Moses
put the lampstand in the Meeting Tent on the
south side of the Tent, across from the table.
25Then Moses put the lamps on the lampstand
before the LORD. He did this just as the LORD
had commanded him.

26Then Moses put the golden altar in the
Meeting Tent, in front of the curtain. 27Then
he burned sweet-smelling incense on the
altar. He did this as the LORD had commanded
him. 28Then Moses put the curtain at the
entrance to the Holy Tent.

29Moses put the altar for burning offerings
at the entrance to the Holy Tent, that is, the
Meeting Tent. Then Moses offered a burnt
offering* on that altar. He also offered grain
offerings to the Lord. He did these things just
as the LORD had commanded him.

30Then Moses put the bowl between the
Meeting Tent and the altar. He put water in
the bowl for washing. 31Moses, Aaron, and
Aaron's sons used this bowl to wash their
hands and feet. 32They washed themselves
every time they entered the Meeting Tent.
They also washed themselves every time they
went near the altar. They did these things just
as the LORD commanded Moses.

33Then Moses set up the curtains around
the courtyard of the Holy Tent. He put the
altar in the courtyard. Then he put the curtain at the entrance to the courtyard. So he
finished all the work.

The Glory of the Lord

34Then the cloud covered the Meeting
Tent* and the Glory of the LORD* filled the
Holy Tent.* 35Moses could not go into the

---

a39:41 holy area A restricted area that was considered sacred (special) because of God's presence.

Meeting Tent because the cloud had settled on it, and the Glory of the LORD had filled the Holy Tent.

³⁶When the cloud rose from the Holy Tent, the Israelites would begin to travel. ³⁷But when the cloud stayed on the Holy Tent, the people did not try to move. They stayed in that place until the cloud rose. ³⁸So the cloud of the LORD was over the Holy Tent during the day, and at night there was a fire in the cloud. So all the Israelites could see the cloud while they traveled.

Leviticus

Voluntary Sacrifices and Offerings

1 ¹^a So the LORD called out to Moses from inside the Meeting Tent* and said, ²"Tell the Israelites: When you bring an offering to the LORD, the offering must be one of your tame animals—it can be a sheep, a goat, or one of your cattle.

³"If you offer one of your cattle as a burnt offering,* it must be a bull that has nothing wrong with it. You must take the animal to the entrance of the Meeting Tent where the LORD will accept the offering. ⁴You must put your hand on the animal's head while it is being killed. So the LORD will accept it as your burnt offering to make you pure.*

⁵"You^b must kill the young bull in front of the LORD. Then Aaron's sons, the priests, will bring the blood to the altar* that is near the entrance of the Meeting Tent. He will splash the blood on all four sides of the altar. ⁶You must remove the skin from that animal and then cut the animal into pieces. ⁷Aaron's sons, the priests, will put the fire on the altar and arrange the wood on the fire. ⁸They will lay the pieces of the animal, including the head and fat, on top of the burning wood. ⁹You must wash the legs and inner parts of the animal with water. Then the priest will bring all these parts to the altar to be offered as a burnt offering, a sweet-smelling gift to the LORD.

¹⁰"If you offer a sheep or a goat as a burnt offering, it must be a male that has nothing wrong with it. ¹¹You must kill the animal on the north side of the altar in front of the LORD. Then Aaron's sons, the priests, will splash the animal's blood on all four sides of the altar. ¹²You must cut the animal into pieces and remove the head and the fat. The priest will then lay them on the wood that is on the fire of the altar. ¹³You must wash the legs and inner parts of the animal with water. Then the priest will bring all these parts to the altar to be offered as a burnt offering, a sweet-smelling gift to the LORD.

¹⁴"If you offer a bird as a burnt offering to the LORD, that bird must be a dove or a young pigeon. ¹⁵The priest will bring the offering to the altar. There the priest will remove the bird's head, drain out the blood on the side of the altar, and burn the bird on the altar. ¹⁶He will remove the bird's tail and inner parts^c and throw them onto the pile of ashes east of the altar. ¹⁷Then the priest will tear the bird open by its wings, but he must not divide it completely into two parts. So he will bring the bird to the altar to be offered as a burnt offering, a sweet-smelling gift to the LORD.

Grain Offerings

2 ¹"When you give a grain offering to the LORD, your offering must be made from fine flour. You must pour oil on this flour and put frankincense* on it. ²Then you must bring it to Aaron's sons, the priests. One of them will take a handful of the fine flour with oil and frankincense in it. He will bring this part, which represents the whole grain offering, to the altar.* There it will be burned up as a sweet-smelling gift to the LORD. ³The rest of that grain offering will belong to Aaron and his sons. This gift to the LORD is very holy.*

Baked Grain Offerings

⁴"If you give a grain offering that was baked in the oven, it must be unleavened* bread made from fine flour mixed with oil, or it must be wafers* with oil poured over them. ⁵If you bring a grain offering cooked in a baking pan, it must be made from fine flour without yeast and mixed with oil. ⁶You must break it into pieces and pour oil over it. It is a grain offering. ⁷If you bring a grain offering cooked in a frying pan, it must be made from fine flour mixed with oil.

⁸"When you bring grain offerings made from these things to the LORD, you must give them to the priest, and he will take them to the altar.* ⁹Then the priest will take part of the grain offering and lift it up as a memorial

---

^a**1:1** This continues the story in Ex. 40:34–35 where the Glory of the Lord filled the Meeting Tent and Moses was unable to enter.

^b**1:5** *You* Or "They (the priests)." Also in verse 11.

^c**1:16** *tail … inner parts* Or "crop and its feathers."

offering. He will bring it to the altar to be burned up as a sweet-smelling gift to the LORD. ¹⁰The rest of that grain offering will belong to Aaron and his sons. This gift to the LORD is very holy.*

¹¹"You must not give any grain offering to the LORD that has yeast in it. You must not burn yeast or honey as a gift to the LORD. ¹²You may bring yeast and honey to the LORD as an offering from the first harvest, but they must not be put on the altar to be burned as a sweet smell. ¹³Also, you must put salt on every grain offering you bring. You must not forget to add salt, because it represents God's agreement* with you. Always put salt on these offerings.

Grain Offerings From the First Harvest

¹⁴"If you bring a grain offering from the first harvest to the LORD, you must bring roasted heads of grain. They must be crushed heads of fresh grain. This will be your grain offering from the first harvest. ¹⁵You must put oil and frankincense* on it. It is a grain offering. ¹⁶The priest must burn part of the crushed grain, the oil, and all the frankincense on it as a memorial offering. It is a gift to the LORD.

Fellowship Offerings

3 ¹"If you offer one of your cattle as a fellowship offering,* whether it is a bull or a cow, it must have nothing wrong with it. ²You must put your hand on the animal's head and kill the animal at the entrance of the Meeting Tent.* Then Aaron's sons, the priests, will splash the blood on all four sides of the altar.* ³The priest will take a part of that fellowship offering as a gift to the LORD. He will take the fat that is over and around the inner parts. ⁴He will take the two kidneys and the fat covering them near the lower back muscle. He will also remove the fat part of the liver that is near the kidneys. ⁵Then Aaron's sons will bring the fat to the altar and put it on the burnt offering* that is on the wood on the fire. It is a sweet-smelling gift to the LORD.

⁶"If you offer a sheep or a goat as a fellowship offering to the LORD, whether it is a male or a female, it must have nothing wrong with it. ⁷If you bring a lamb as an offering to the LORD, ⁸you must put your hand on the animal's head and kill it in front of the Meeting Tent. Then Aaron's sons will splash the animal's blood on all four sides of the altar. ⁹The priest will take part of the fellowship offering to the altar as a gift to the LORD. The priest must cut off the tail close to the backbone. Then he will offer the whole fat tail and the fat that is over and around the animal's inner parts. ¹⁰He will also offer the two kidneys and the fat covering them near the lower back muscles. He will also offer the fat part of the liver. He must remove it with the kidneys. ¹¹Then the priest will take that part to the altar to be burned up as food, a gift to the LORD.

¹²"If the offering is a goat, you must bring it before the LORD. ¹³You must put your hand on the goat's head and kill it in front of the Meeting Tent. Then Aaron's sons, the priests, must splash the goat's blood on all four sides of the altar. ¹⁴The priest will give part of the fellowship offering as a gift to the LORD. He will offer the fat that is over and around the animal's inner parts. ¹⁵He will offer the two kidneys and the fat covering them near the lower back muscle. He will also offer the fat part of the liver. He will remove it with the kidneys. ¹⁶Then the priest will bring that food as a sweet-smelling gift to the LORD. The fat belongs to the LORD. ¹⁷This rule will continue forever through all your generations. Wherever you live, you must never eat fat or blood."

Offerings for Accidental Sins

4 ¹The LORD spoke to Moses and said, ²"Tell the Israelites this: A person might sin without meaning to and do something that the LORD commanded should not be done. For example:

³"If the anointed priest*ᵃ* makes a mistake that leaves the people guilty for their sin, he must offer a young bull to the LORD as a sin offering.* The bull must have nothing wrong with it. ⁴The anointed priest must bring the bull to the entrance of the Meeting Tent* in front of the LORD. He must put his hand on the bull's head and kill the bull in front of the LORD. ⁵Then the anointed priest must get some of the blood from the bull and take it into the Meeting Tent. ⁶He must put his finger in the blood and sprinkle the blood seven times before the LORD in front of the curtain of the Most Holy Place.* ⁷The priest must put some of the blood on the corners of the incense* altar.* (This altar is in the Meeting Tent, in front of the LORD.) He must pour out the rest of the bull's blood at the base of the altar of burnt offering.* (This altar is at the entrance of the Meeting Tent.) ⁸Then the priest must take all the fat from the bull of the sin offering. He must take the fat that is on and around the inner parts. ⁹He must take the two kidneys and the fat covering them near the lower back muscle. He must also take the fat part of the liver. He must remove it with the kidneys. ¹⁰The priest must lift up these things and burn them on the altar for burnt offerings, just as he does for the fellowship offering.*ᵇ* ¹¹⁻¹²But the priest must carry out the bull's skin, inner parts and body waste, and all the meat, including the head and legs. He must carry those parts outside the camp to the special place where the ashes are poured out. He must put those parts on the wood and burn them there on the ash pile.

ᵃ4:3 anointed priest Special oil was poured on the priest's head to show that God chose him to serve. Here, this refers to the high priest. Also in verse 16.
ᵇ4:10 just as … fellowship offering See Lev. 3:1–5.

13"The whole nation of Israel might sin without knowing it. They might break one of the commands of the Lord and become guilty of doing something he said must not be done. 14When they learn about that sin, the community of Israel must offer a young bull as a sin offering for the whole nation. They must bring the bull to the Meeting Tent. 15The elders* of the people must put their hands on the bull's head in front of the Lord. Then they must kill the bull in front of the Lord. 16The anointed priest must get some of the bull's blood and take it into the Meeting Tent. 17He must put his finger in the blood and sprinkle it seven times in front of the curtain before the Lord. 18He must put some of the blood on the corners of the altar. (This altar is inside the Meeting Tent, in front of the Lord.) He must then pour out all the blood at the base of the altar of burnt offering. (This altar is at the entrance of the Meeting Tent.) 19Then he must take all the fat from the animal and bring it to the altar. 20He must offer these parts, just as he offered the bull of the sin offering. In this way the priest will make the people pure,* and God will forgive them. 21The priest must carry this bull outside the camp and burn it, just as he burned the other bull. This is the sin offering for the whole community.

22"A ruler might sin without meaning to and break one of the commands of the Lord. He might do something that his God said must not be done. 23If he learns about his sin, he must bring a male goat that has nothing wrong with it as his offering. 24The ruler must put his hand on the goat's head and kill the goat at the place where they kill the burnt offering before the Lord. The goat is a sin offering. 25The priest will take some of the blood of the sin offering on his finger and put it on the corners of the altar of burnt offering. He will pour out the rest of the blood at the base of the altar. 26The priest will burn all the goat's fat on the altar, just as he does for the fellowship offerings.* In this way the priest will make the ruler pure, and God will forgive him.

27"Finally, one of you common people might sin without meaning to. You might break one of the commands of the Lord and become guilty of doing something he said must not be done. 28If you learn about that sin, you must bring a female goat that has nothing wrong with it as your sin offering. 29You must put your hand on the animal's head and kill it at the place for the burnt offering. 30Then the priest will take some of the goat's blood on his finger and put it on the corners of the altar of burnt offering. He will pour out the rest of its blood at the base of the altar. 31The priest will then remove all of its fat, just as he does for the fellowship offerings. Then he will bring it to the altar as a sweet smell to the Lord. The priest will do this to make you pure, and God will forgive you.

32"If you bring a lamb as your sin offering, then you must bring a female lamb that has nothing wrong with it. 33You must put your hand on the animal's head and kill it as a sin offering in the place where people kill the burnt offering. 34The priest will take some of the blood from the sin offering on his finger and put it on the corners of the altar of burnt offering. He will pour out the rest of the lamb's blood at the base of the altar. 35He will then remove all the lamb's fat, just as he does for the fellowship offerings. Then he will bring it to the altar as a gift to the Lord. The priest will do this to make you pure, and God will forgive you.

Different Accidental Sins

5 1"You might be called as a witness and take an oath* to tell the truth. If you saw something or knew something but did not tell it, you are guilty of doing wrong and must bear the responsibility for your guilt.

2"You might touch something unclean.* It might be the dead body of any kind of animal. You might not know that you touched these things, but you will still become unclean and must pay a fine.

3"You might touch any of the many things that can make a person unclean. You might touch something unclean, but not know about it. When you learn that you have touched something unclean, you must pay a fine.

4"You might make a quick promise to do something—it makes no difference if it is bad or good. People make many kinds of quick promises. You might make such a promise and forget it.a When you rememberb your promise, you must pay a fine because you did not keep it. 5If you are guilty of any of these things, you must confess whatever you did wrong. 6Then you must bring your guilt offering to the Lord for the sin you did. You must bring a female lamb or a female goat as a sin offering.* The priest will do this to make you pure* from your sin.

7"If you cannot afford a lamb, you must bring two doves or two young pigeons to the Lord. These will be the guilt offering for your sin. One bird must be for a sin offering, and the other must be for a burnt offering.* 8Take them to the priest. First, the priest will offer one bird for the sin offering. The priest will pull the bird's head from its neck but he will not pull it off completely. 9The priest will sprinkle the blood from the sin offering on the side of the altar.* Then he will pour out the rest of the blood at the base of the altar. It is a sin offering. 10Then he will offer the second bird according to the rules for a burnt offering. The priest will do this to make you pure from the sin you did, and God will forgive you.

a5:4 forget it Literally, "it is hid from him."
b5:4 remember Literally, "know of."

[11]"If you cannot afford two doves or two pigeons, you must bring 8 cups[a] of fine flour as your sin offering. You must not put oil or frankincense* on the flour because it is a sin offering. [12]You must bring the flour to the priest. The priest will take a handful of the flour as the memorial offering and bring it to the altar as a gift to the LORD. It is a sin offering. [13]The priest will do this to make you pure, and God will forgive you. The part that is left will belong to the priest, just as the regular grain offering."

[14]The LORD gave this command to Moses for the people: [15]"You might promise to give something to the LORD. You might sin against me without meaning to by not giving what you promised. If you do that, you must bring a ram that has nothing wrong with it (or the same amount in silver using the official measure*) as a guilt offering. [16]You must give what you promised and add one-fifth of that amount as a fine. Give it to the priest and he will use the ram to make you pure, and God will forgive you.

[17]"If you sin and break any of the commands that the LORD said must not be done, you are guilty. Even if you did not know about it, you are still responsible for your sin. [18]You must bring a ram that has nothing wrong with it (or the same amount in silver) to the priest. The priest will offer the ram, and God will forgive you for the sin you did without knowing it. [19]You are guilty, and you must pay the guilt offering to the LORD."

Guilt Offerings for Other Sins

6 [1]The LORD gave this command to Moses for the people: [2]"You might sin against the LORD by doing one of these sins: You might lie about what happened to something you were taking care of for someone else; you might lie about a deposit[b] you received; you might steal something; you might cheat someone; [3]you might find something that was lost and then lie about it; you might promise to do something and then not do what you promised, or you might do some other bad thing like these. [4]If you do any of these things, you are guilty of doing wrong. You must give back whatever you stole, or whatever you took by cheating, or whatever you took that another person asked you to hold, or whatever you found and lied about, or [5]whatever you made a false promise about. You must pay the full price and then add one-fifth of that amount as a fine and give it all to the true owner. [6]You must also bring a ram to the LORD that has nothing wrong with it (or the same amount in silver) to the priest. [7]Then the priest will go to the LORD to make you pure,* and God will

forgive you for whichever of these things you did that made you guilty."

Burnt Offerings

[8]The LORD said to Moses, [9]"Give this command to Aaron and his sons: This is the law of the burnt offering.* The burnt offering must stay on the hearth[c] of the altar* all night until morning. The altar's fire must be kept burning. [10]The priest must change clothes and put on the special linen underwear and linen robe. Then he must gather up the ashes from the fire and burnt offerings and set them down by the altar. [11]Then he must take off the special clothes and put on the other clothes and carry the ashes outside the camp to a special place that is pure. [12]The fire that was started on the altar must never be allowed to stop burning. Every morning the priests must put wood on the altar. They must arrange the burnt offerings on the wood, and they must burn the fat of the fellowship offerings* on it. [13]That fire must always be kept burning on the altar. It must never be allowed to stop burning.

Grain Offerings

[14]"This is the law for the grain offering: The sons of Aaron will bring it to the front of the altar* as an offering to the LORD. [15]There must be some oil and frankincense* on the grain offering. The priest will take a handful of fine flour from the grain offering and burn it on the altar as a sweet-smelling memorial offering to the LORD.

[16]"Aaron and his sons will use the rest of that grain to make bread without yeast. This must be eaten in a holy* place—in the courtyard around the Meeting Tent.* [17]I have given this part of the grain offering as the priests' share of the gifts offered to me. Like the sin offering* and the guilt offering, it is most holy. It must not be baked with yeast. [18]Any male descendant of Aaron may eat from these gifts to the LORD. This is their share forever throughout your generations. Whatever touches these offerings will be made holy.[d]"

The Priests' Grain Offering

[19]The LORD said to Moses, [20]"This is the offering that Aaron and his sons must bring to the LORD when Aaron is anointed* to be the high priest. They must bring 8 cups[e] of fine flour for a grain offering. This will be offered at the times of the daily offering—half of it in the morning and half of it in the evening. [21]The fine flour must be mixed with oil and baked on a pan. After it is cooked, you must

---

[a]**5:11** *8 cups* Literally, "1/10 of an ephah" (2.2 l).
[b]**6:2** *deposit* Literally, "pledge" or "security." This is something like a down payment given as proof that something more important will be done.

[c]**6:9** *hearth* The place on an altar or in a fireplace where a fire is burned.
[d]**6:18** *Whatever ... holy* Or "Whoever touches these offerings will become holy." This might mean that anyone but the priests must die for touching the sacred food.
[e]**6:20** *8 cups* Literally, "1/10 of an ephah" (2.2 l).

bring it in, break it into pieces, and offer it as a sweet-smelling gift to Lord.

²²"In the future, when Aaron's descendants take their place as the anointed priests,ᵃ they will continue to make this grain offering to the Lord. This rule will continue forever. The grain offering must be completely burned for the Lord. ²³Every grain offering that a priest gives must be completely burned. It must not be eaten."

The Law of the Sin Offering

²⁴The Lord said to Moses, ²⁵"Tell Aaron and his sons: This is the law of the sin offering.* The sin offering must be killed in the place where the burnt offering* is killed before the Lord. It is most holy.* ²⁶The priest who offers the sin offering must eat it. But he must eat it in a holy place, in the courtyard around the Meeting Tent.* ²⁷Touching the meat of the sin offering makes a person or a thing holy.

"If any of the sprinkled blood falls on a person's clothes, you must wash the clothes in a holy place. ²⁸If the sin offering was boiled in a clay pot, the pot must be broken. If the sin offering was boiled in a bronze* pot, the pot must be washed and rinsed in water.

²⁹"Any male in a priest's family may eat the sin offering. It is very holy. ³⁰But if the blood of the sin offering was taken into the Meeting Tent and used in the Holy Place to make people pure,* that sin offering must not be eaten. It must be completely burned in the fire.

Guilt Offerings

7 ¹"These are the rules for the guilt offering, which is very holy*: ²A priest must kill the guilt offering in the same place where they kill the burnt offerings.* Then he must sprinkle the blood from the guilt offering around the altar.*

³"The priest must offer all the fat from the guilt offering. He must offer the fat tail and the fat that covers the inner parts. ⁴He must offer the two kidneys and the fat covering them at the lower back muscle. He must also offer the fat part of the liver. He must remove it with the kidneys. ⁵He must bring these things to the altar as a gift to the Lord. It is a guilt offering.

⁶"Any male in a priest's family may eat the guilt offering. It is very holy, so it must be eaten in a holy place. ⁷The guilt offering is like the sin offering.* The same rules are for both offerings. The priest who does the sacrificing will get the meat for food. ⁸He will also get the skinᵇ from the burnt offering. ⁹Every grain offering belongs to the priest who offers it. That priest will get the grain offerings that were baked in an oven, or cooked on a frying pan, or in a baking dish. ¹⁰The grain offerings

ᵃ**6:22** *anointed priests* Special oil was poured on the priest's head to show that God chose him to serve. Here, this refers to the high priest.
ᵇ**7:8** *skin* This was used for making leather.

will belong to Aaron's sons. It doesn't make any difference if the grain offerings are dry or mixed with oil. The sons of Aaron will all share this food.

Fellowship Offerings

¹¹"This is the law of the sacrifice* of fellowship offerings* that you bring to the Lord: ¹²People can bring fellowship offerings to show their thanks to God. If you bring your sacrifice to give thanks, you should also bring unleavened* bread mixed with oil, wafers* with oil poured over them, and loaves of fine flour mixed with oil. ¹³You must also bring loaves of bread made with yeast to go with your fellowship offering. ¹⁴One of these loaves of bread will belong to the priest who sprinkles the blood of the fellowship offerings. ¹⁵The meat of the fellowship offering must be eaten on the same day it is offered as a way of showing thanks to God. None of the meat should remain until the next morning.

¹⁶"If you bring a fellowship offering simply because you want to give a gift to God or because it is part of a special promise you made to him, the sacrifice should be eaten the same day you offer it. But if there is any left, it must be eaten the next day. ¹⁷If any meat from this sacrifice is still left over on the third day, it must be burned in the fire. ¹⁸The Lord will not accept the offering from anyone who eats any of that meat on the third day. The Lord will not count the sacrifice for you—he will treat it like rotten meat! Whoever eats that meat will be responsible for their own sin.

¹⁹"People must not eat any of the meat that touches anything unclean.* They must burn this meat in the fire. Whoever is clean* may eat the meat from the fellowship offering. ²⁰But anyone who is unclean and eats the meat from the fellowship offerings that was offered to the Lord must be separated from their people. ²¹If you touch something that is unclean, it doesn't matter if it was made unclean by a person, an animal, or some disgusting thing, you will become unclean. And if you eat any of the meat from the fellowship offerings that was given to the Lord, you must be separated from your people."

²²The Lord said to Moses, ²³"Tell the Israelites: You must not eat any fat from your cattle, sheep, or goats. ²⁴You may use the fat from any animal that has died by itself or was torn by other animals, but you must never eat it. ²⁵Whoever eats the fat from an animal that was offered as a gift to the Lord must be separated from their people.

²⁶"No matter where you live, you must never eat blood from any bird or any animal. ²⁷Anyone who eats blood must be separated from their people."

Rules for the Offerings Presented to God

²⁸The Lord said to Moses, ²⁹"Tell the Israelites: If you bring a fellowship offering* to

the Lord, you must present that gift to the Lord yourself. ³⁰You must bring the fat and the breast of the animal to the priest. Then he will lift up the breast in front of the Lord to show it was presented to God. ³¹The priest will burn the fat on the altar,* but the breast of the animal will belong to Aaron and his sons. ³²You must also give the right thigh from the fellowship offering as a gift to the priest. ³³That part of the fellowship offering will belong to the priest*a* who carries the blood and fat to the altar. ³⁴I will accept the breast that was lifted up and the gift of the right thigh from the Israelites. Then I will give these things to Aaron and his sons. This is their share from the fellowship offerings of the Israelites forever."

³⁵Those parts from the gifts offered to the Lord were given to Aaron and his sons. Whenever Aaron and his sons serve as the Lord's priests, they get that share of the sacrifices.* ³⁶The Lord commanded the Israelites to give those parts to the priests once they have been anointed.* That will be their share from the Israelites forever.

³⁷These are the laws about burnt offerings,* grain offerings, sin offerings, guilt offerings, fellowship offerings, and offerings for when the priests are appointed. ³⁸The Lord gave these laws to Moses on Mount Sinai when he commanded the Israelites to bring their offerings to the Lord in the Sinai desert.

Moses Appoints the Priests

8 ¹The Lord said to Moses, ²"Take Aaron and his sons with him and the clothes, the anointing* oil, the bull of the sin offering, the two rams, and the basket of unleavened* bread. ³Then gather the people together at the entrance of the Meeting Tent.*"

⁴Moses did what the Lord commanded him. The people met together at the entrance of the Meeting Tent. ⁵Then Moses said to them, "This is what the Lord has commanded must be done."

⁶Moses brought Aaron and his sons forward and washed them with water. ⁷Moses put the woven shirt on Aaron and tied the cloth belt around him. Then Moses put the robe and the ephod* on Aaron and tied the beautiful cloth belt around him. ⁸Moses put the judgment pouch* on Aaron and put the Urim* and Thummim* inside its pocket. ⁹He also put the turban* on Aaron's head. He put the strip of gold on the front of the turban. This strip of gold is the holy* crown. Moses did this just as the Lord had commanded.

¹⁰Then Moses took the anointing oil and sprinkled it on the Holy Tent* and on everything in it. In this way he made them holy. ¹¹He sprinkled some of the anointing oil on the altar* seven times. He sprinkled the oil on the altar, on all its tools and dishes, and

on the bowl and its base. In this way he made them holy. ¹²He poured some of the anointing oil on Aaron's head to make him holy. ¹³Then Moses brought Aaron's sons forward. He put their woven shirts on them, tied belts around them, and put cloth caps on their heads. He did everything just as the Lord had commanded.

¹⁴Then Moses brought out the bull of the sin offering.* Aaron and his sons put their hands on the bull's head. ¹⁵Then Moses killed the bull and collected its blood. He used his finger to put some of the blood on all the corners of the altar. In this way he made the altar ready for sacrifices.* Then he poured out the blood at the base of the altar to make the altar ready for sacrifices to make the people pure.* ¹⁶Moses took all the fat from the inner parts of the bull. He took the fat part of the liver with the two kidneys and the fat on them. Then he burned them on the altar. ¹⁷Moses took the bull's skin, its meat, and its body waste outside the camp. He burned these things in a fire outside the camp. He did everything just as the Lord commanded him.

¹⁸Then Moses brought the ram of the burnt offering.* Aaron and his sons put their hands on the ram's head. ¹⁹Then Moses killed the ram. He sprinkled the blood around on the altar. ²⁰⁻²¹He cut the ram into pieces. He washed the inner parts and legs with water. Then he burned the whole ram on the altar. He burned the head, the pieces, and the fat as a burnt offering. It was a sweet-smelling gift to the Lord. Moses did everything just as the Lord commanded.

²²Then Moses brought the other ram. This ram was used for appointing Aaron and his sons to become priests. Aaron and his sons put their hands on the ram's head. ²³Then Moses killed the ram. He put some of its blood on the tip of Aaron's ear, on the thumb of his right hand, and on the big toe of his right foot. ²⁴Then Moses brought Aaron's sons close to the altar. He put some of the blood on the tip of their right ears, on the thumb of their right hands, and on the big toe of their right feet. Then he sprinkled the blood around on the altar. ²⁵He took the fat, the fat tail, all the fat on the inner parts, the fat covering of the liver, the two kidneys and their fat, and the right thigh. ²⁶A basket of unleavened bread is put before the Lord each day. Moses took one of those loaves of bread, one loaf of bread mixed with oil, and one unleavened wafer.* He put these pieces of bread on the fat and on the right thigh of the ram. ²⁷Then he put all of it in the hands of Aaron and his sons. Moses lifted these pieces to show he was offering them before the Lord. ²⁸Then Moses took these things from the hands of Aaron and his sons and burned them on the altar on top of the burnt offering. So this was the offering for appointing Aaron and his sons as priests. It was a sweet-smelling gift to the Lord. ²⁹Moses

---

*a***7:33 the priest** Literally, "him of the sons of Aaron."

took the breast and lifted it to show he had presented it to the LORD. It was Moses' share of the ram for appointing the priests. This was just as the LORD had commanded him.

30Moses took some of the anointing oil and some of the blood that was on the altar. He sprinkled some on Aaron and on Aaron's clothes. He sprinkled some on Aaron's sons who were with Aaron and on their clothes. In this way Moses made Aaron, his clothes, his sons, and his sons' clothes holy.

31Then Moses said to Aaron and his sons, "I told you, 'Aaron and his sons must eat these things.' So take the basket of bread and meat from the ceremony for appointing the priests. Boil that meat at the entrance of the Meeting Tent. Eat the meat and bread at that place. Do this as I told you. 32If any of the meat or bread is left, burn it. 33The ceremony for appointing the priests will last for seven days. You must not leave the entrance of the Meeting Tent until that time is finished. 34Everything we did today was what the LORD commanded us to do in order to make you pure. 35You must stay at the entrance of the Meeting Tent day and night for seven days. If you don't obey the LORD's commands, you will die! The LORD gave me these commands."

36So Aaron and his sons did everything that the LORD had commanded Moses.

God Accepts the Priests

9 1On the eighth day, Moses called for Aaron and his sons and the elders* of Israel. 2He said to Aaron, "Take a bull and a ram. There must be nothing wrong with them. The bull will be a sin offering,* and the ram will be a burnt offering.* Offer these animals to the LORD. 3Tell the Israelites, 'Take a male goat for a sin offering, and take a calf and a lamb for a burnt offering. The calf and the lamb must each be one year old. There must be nothing wrong with them. 4Take a bull and a ram for fellowship offerings.* Take these animals and a grain offering mixed with oil for an offering to the LORD. Do this because the LORD will appear to you today.'"

5So all the people came to the Meeting Tent.* They all brought the things that Moses had commanded. All the people stood before the LORD. 6Moses said, "You must do what the LORD commanded. Then the Glory of the LORD* will appear to you."

7Then Moses told Aaron: "Go do what the LORD commanded. Go to the altar* and offer sin offerings and burnt offerings. Do what will make you and the people pure.* Take the people's sacrifices* and make them pure."

8So Aaron went to the altar. He killed the bull for the sin offering. This sin offering was for himself. 9Then the sons of Aaron brought the blood to Aaron. Aaron put his finger in the blood and put it on the corners of the altar. Then he poured out the blood at the base of the altar. 10He took the fat, the kidneys, and

the fat part of the liver from the sin offering. He burned them on the altar just as the LORD had commanded Moses. 11Then Aaron burned the meat and skin on a fire outside the camp.

12Next, Aaron killed the animal for the burnt offering. His sons brought the blood to him, and he sprinkled the blood around on the altar. 13Aaron's sons gave the pieces and head of the burnt offering to Aaron, and he burned them on the altar. 14He also washed the inner parts and the legs of the burnt offering and burned them on the altar.

15Then Aaron brought the people's offering. He killed the goat of the sin offering that was for the people. He offered the goat for sin, like the earlier sin offering. 16He brought the burnt offering and offered it, just as the LORD had commanded. 17He brought the grain offering to the altar. He took a handful of the grain and put it on the altar beside that morning's daily sacrifice.

18Aaron also killed the bull and the ram that were the fellowship offerings from the people. His sons brought the blood to him, and he sprinkled this blood around on the altar. 19Aaron's sons also brought him the fat of the bull and the ram. They brought the fat tail, the fat covering the inner parts, the kidneys, and the fat part of the liver. 20Aaron's sons put these fat parts on the breasts of the bull and the ram. Aaron burned them on the altar. 21He lifted the breasts and the gift of the right thigh to show he was offering them before the LORD, just as Moses had commanded.

22Then Aaron lifted up his hands toward the people and blessed them. After he finished offering the sin offering, the burnt offering, and the fellowship offerings, he came down from the altar.

23Moses and Aaron went into the Meeting Tent. They came out and blessed the people. Then the Glory of the LORD appeared to all the people. 24Fire came out from the LORD and burned the burnt offering and fat on the altar. When all the people saw this, they shouted with joy and then bowed to the ground to show their respect.

God Destroys Nadab and Abihu

10 1Then Aaron's sons Nadab and Abihu made a mistake. They took their incense* dishes and put some fire and incense in them. But they did not use the fire that was on the altar—they took fire from some other place and brought it to the LORD. This was not what he had commanded. 2So fire came from the LORD and destroyed Nadab and Abihu, and they died there in front of the LORD.

3Then Moses said to Aaron, "The LORD says, 'The priests who come near me must respect me. I must be holy* to them and to all the people.'" So Aaron did not say anything about his sons dying.

4Aaron's uncle Uzziel had two sons. They were Mishael and Elzaphan. Moses said to these sons, "Come here and get your cousins' bodies and carry them away from this holy place and take them outside the camp."

⁵So Mishael and Elzaphan obeyed Moses. They carried the bodies of Nadab and Abihu outside the camp. Nadab and Abihu were still wearing their special woven shirts.

⁶Then Moses spoke to Aaron and his other sons Eleazar and Ithamar. Moses told them, "Don't show any sadness! Don't tear your clothes or mess up your hair!ᵃ Don't show your sadness and you will not be killed, and the LORD will not be angry against all the people. All the Israelites are your relatives—they can cry about the LORD burning Nadab and Abihu. ⁷But you must not even leave the entrance of the Meeting Tent.* If you leave, you will die because the LORD's anointing* oil is on you." So Aaron, Eleazar, and Ithamar obeyed Moses.

⁸Then the LORD said to Aaron, ⁹"You and your sons must not drink wine or beer when you come into the Meeting Tent. If you do, you will die. This law continues forever through your generations. ¹⁰You must be able to clearly tell the difference between what is holy and what is not holy, between what is clean* and what is unclean.* ¹¹And you must teach the people about all the laws that the LORD gave them through Moses."

¹²Aaron had two sons who were still alive, Eleazar and Ithamar. Moses said to Aaron and his two sons, "When people give sacrifices* as a gift to the LORD, some of the grain offering is not burned. Use that grain to make bread without yeast. You priests must eat that bread near the altar* because that grain is very holy. ¹³The portion of food for you and your sons will come from the special gifts to the LORD, so you must eat that food in a holy place. ¹⁴"Also you, your sons, and your daughters will be able to eat the breast and thigh from the offerings you presented to the LORD. You don't have to eat these in a holy place, but you must eat them in a clean place because they come from the fellowship offerings.* The Israelites give these gifts to God. The people eat part of these animals, but the breast is your share. ¹⁵The people must bring the gifts of fat from their animals as part of the sacrifice. They must also bring the thigh of the fellowship offering and the breast that is lifted up to show it is offered in front of the LORD. Then it will be your share of the offering. It will belong to you and your children. That part of the sacrifices will be your share forever, just as the LORD said."

¹⁶Moses looked for the goat of the sin offering,* but it was already burned up. Moses became very angry with Aaron's other sons Eleazar and Ithamar. Moses said, ¹⁷"You were supposed to eat that goat in the holy area! It is very holy! Why did you not eat it in front of the LORD? The LORD gave it to you to carry away the guilt of the people—to make the people pure.* ¹⁸That goat's blood was not brought into the Holy Place.* So you should have eaten the meat in the holy area, just as I commanded!"

¹⁹But Aaron said to Moses, "Look, today they brought their sin offering and burnt offering* before the LORD. But you know what happened to me today! Do you think the LORD would be happy if I ate the sin offering today?"

²⁰When Moses heard this, he agreed.

Rules About Eating Meat

11 ¹The LORD said to Moses and Aaron, ²"Tell the Israelites: These are the animals you can eat: ³If an animal has hooves that are split into two parts, and if that animal also chews the cud,* then you may eat the meat from that animal.

⁴⁻⁶"Some animals chew the cud, but they don't have split hooves. Don't eat these animals. Camels, rock badgers, and rabbits are like that, so they are unclean* for you. ⁷Other animals have hooves that are split into two parts, but they don't chew the cud. Don't eat these animals. Pigs are like that, so they are unclean for you. ⁸Don't eat the meat from these animals. Don't even touch their dead bodies! They are unclean for you.

Rules About Sea Food

⁹"If an animal lives in the sea or in a river and it has fins and scales, you may eat that animal. ¹⁰⁻¹¹But if an animal lives in the sea or in a river and does not have fins and scales, you must not eat that animal. It is one of the animals the LORD says is bad to eat. Don't eat the meat from that animal. Don't even touch its dead body! ¹²You must treat any animal in the water that does not have fins and scales as one of the animals that God says is wrong to eat.

Birds That Must Not Be Eaten

¹³"You must also treat these birds as animals that God says are wrong to eat. Don't eat any of these birds: eagles, vultures, buzzards, ¹⁴kites, all kinds of falcons, ¹⁵all kinds of black birds, ¹⁶ostriches,* nighthawks, sea gulls, all kinds of hawks, ¹⁷owls, cormorants, great owls, ¹⁸water hens, pelicans, carrion vultures, ¹⁹storks, all kinds of herons, hoopoes, and bats.

Rules About Eating Insects

²⁰"If insects have wings and crawl,ᵇ then you should treat them as those the LORD says you must not eat. Don't eat these insects!

ᵃ10:6 *tear ... hair* Torn clothes and messed up hair showed that a person was mourning (showing sadness) for a dead person.

ᵇ11:20 *crawl* Literally, "walk on four feet." Also in verse 23.

²¹But you may eat insects if they have legs with joints above their feet so that they can jump. ²²You may also eat all kinds of locusts, all kinds of winged locusts, all kinds of crickets, and all kinds of grasshoppers.

²³"But all the other insects that have wings and crawl are those the Lord says you must not eat. ²⁴They will make you unclean.* If you touch the dead bodies of these insects you will become unclean until evening. ²⁵If you pick up one of these dead insects, you must wash your clothes. You will be unclean until evening.

More Rules About Animals

²⁶⁻²⁷"Some animals have split hooves, but the hooves don't make exactly two parts. Some animals don't chew the cud.* Some animals don't have hooves—they walk on their paws.ᵃ All these animals are unclean* for you. If you touch them, you will become unclean until evening. ²⁸If you pick up the dead bodies of these unclean animals, you must wash your clothes. You will be unclean until evening. These animals are unclean for you.

Rules About Crawling Animals

²⁹"These small animals are unclean* for you: moles, mice, all kinds of great lizards, ³⁰geckos, crocodiles, lizards, sand reptiles, and chameleons. ³¹Whoever touches their dead bodies will be unclean until evening.

Rules About Unclean Animals

³²"If any of these unclean* animals dies and falls on something, that thing will become unclean. It might be something made from wood, cloth, leather, or sackcloth.* Whatever it is or is used for, it must be washed with water. It will be unclean until evening. Then it will become clean* again. ³³If any of these unclean animals dies and falls into a clay dish, anything in the dish will become unclean. And you must break the dish. ³⁴If water from the unclean clay dish touches any food, that food will become unclean. Any drink in the unclean dish will become unclean. ³⁵If any part of a dead, unclean animal falls on something, that thing is unclean. It may be a clay oven or a clay baking pan. It must be broken into pieces. These things will remain unclean. They will always be unclean for you. ³⁶"A spring or a well that collects water will remain clean, but anyone who touches the dead bodies of any unclean animal ⌊in that water⌋ will become unclean. ³⁷If any part of a dead, unclean animal falls on seed that is to be planted, that seed is still clean. ³⁸But if you put water on some seed and if any part of a dead, unclean animal falls on those seeds, they are unclean for you.

³⁹"Also, if an animal which you use for food dies, whoever touches its dead body will be unclean until evening. ⁴⁰If you eat meat from this animal's body, you must wash your clothes. You will be unclean until evening. If you pick up the dead body of the animal, you must wash your clothes. You will be unclean until evening.

⁴¹"You must treat all the crawling animals that live on the dirt as disgusting things that you must not eat. ⁴²You must not eat any of the reptiles that crawl on their bellies or that walk on all four feet, or that have many feet. Don't eat these animals! ⁴³Don't let them make you filthy.ᵇ You must not become unclean, ⁴⁴because I am the Lord your God. I am holy, so you should keep yourselves holy. Don't make yourselves unclean with these crawling things. ⁴⁵I brought you out of Egypt so that you could be my special people and I could be your God. I am holy, so you must be holy too."

⁴⁶These are the rules about all the tame animals, birds, all the animals in the sea, and all the animals that crawl on the ground. ⁴⁷These rules will help the people know which animals are unclean and which animals they are allowed to eat and which ones they cannot eat.

Rules for New Mothers

12 ¹The Lord said to Moses, ²"Tell the Israelites:

"When a woman gives birth, she will be unclean,* just as she is during her monthly time of bleeding. If the baby is a boy, the mother will be unclean for seven days. ³The baby boy must be circumcised* on the eighth day. ⁴Because of the blood from childbirth, another 33 days must pass before she can touch anything that is holy.* She must not enter the Holy Place until the time of her purificationᶜ is finished. ⁵But if she gives birth to a girl, the mother will be unclean for 14 days, just as she is during her monthly time of bleeding. Because of the blood from childbirth, another 66 days must pass before she becomes clean.*

⁶"After the time of her purification is finished, the new mother of a baby girl or boy must bring special sacrifices* to the Meeting Tent.* She must give her sacrifices to the priest at the entrance of the Meeting Tent. She must bring a one-year-old lamb for a burnt offering* and a dove or young pigeon for a sin offering.* ⁷⁻⁸If the woman cannot afford a lamb, she may bring two doves or two young pigeons. One bird will be for a burnt offering and one for a sin offering. The priest will offer them before the Lord. In this way the priest will make her pure,* and she will be clean from the blood of childbirth. These

---

ᵃ**11:26–27 paws** The soft feet with claws on certain animals.

ᵇ**11:43 filthy** Or "hated." Not pure or not acceptable to God for worship.

ᶜ**12:4 purification** Being made clean or acceptable to God for worship.

are the rules for a woman who gives birth to a baby boy or a baby girl."

Rules About Skin Diseases

13 ¹The Lord said to Moses and Aaron, ²"Someone might have a swelling on their skin, or it may be a rash or a bright spot. If the sore looks like the disease of leprosy,* the person must be brought to Aaron the priest or to one of his sons, the priests. ³The priest must look at the sore on the person's skin. If the hair in the sore has become white, and if the sore seems deeper than the person's skin, it is leprosy. When the priest has finished looking at the person, he must announce that the person is unclean.*

⁴"Sometimes there is a white spot on a person's skin that does not seem deeper than the skin. If that is true, the priest must separate that person from other people for seven days. ⁵On the seventh day the priest must look at the person again. If the priest sees that the sore has not changed and has not spread on the skin, he must separate the person for seven more days. ⁶Seven days later the priest must look at the person again. If the sore has faded and has not spread on the skin, the priest must announce that the person is clean.* The sore is only a rash. After washing the clothes, that person will be clean again.

⁷"But if the rash spreads over the skin after the person has shown himself to the priest to be made clean again, that person must come again to the priest. ⁸The priest must look, and if the rash has spread, he must announce that the person is unclean. The disease is leprosy.

⁹"Whoever has leprosy must be brought to the priest. ¹⁰He must look at that person. If there is a white swelling on the skin, if the hair has become white, and if the skin looks raw in the swelling, ¹¹it is leprosy that has been there for a long time. The priest must announce that the person is unclean. He does not have to wait until after a period of separation, because he already knows that the person is unclean.

¹²"Sometimes a skin disease* will spread all over a person's body, covering the skin from head to foot. The priest must look at that person's whole body. ¹³If the priest sees that the skin disease covers the whole body and that it has turned all the skin white, the priest must announce that the person is clean. ¹⁴But if the skin is raw, that person is not clean. ¹⁵When the priest sees the raw skin, he must announce that the person is unclean. The raw skin is not clean. It is leprosy.

¹⁶"If the raw skin changes and becomes white, the person must come to the priest. ¹⁷The priest must look at the person. If the skin has become white, the person who had the infection is clean, and the priest must announce this.

¹⁸"Someone might get a boil on their skin that heals over. ¹⁹Then that boil might become a white swelling or a bright, white spot with red streaks in it. If this happens, the person must show that spot to the priest. ²⁰The priest must look at it. If the swelling is deeper than the skin, and the hair on it has become white, the priest must announce that the person is unclean. The spot is leprosy that has broken out from inside the boil. ²¹But if the priest looks at the spot, and there are no white hairs in it, and the spot is not deeper than the skin but is faded, the priest must separate the person for seven days. ²²If the spot spreads on the skin, the priest must announce that the person is unclean; it is an infection. ²³But if the bright spot stays in its place and does not spread, it is only the scar from the old boil. The priest must announce that the person is clean.

²⁴⁻²⁵"Someone might get a burn on the skin. If the raw skin becomes a white spot or a white spot with red streaks in it, the priest must look at it. If that white spot seems to be deeper than the skin, and the hair at that spot has become white, it is leprosy that has broken out in the burn. The priest must announce that the person is unclean. ²⁶But if the priest looks at the spot, and there is no white hair in the bright spot, and the spot is not deeper than the skin but is faded, the priest must separate the person for seven days. ²⁷On the seventh day, the priest must look at the person again. If the spot has spread on the skin, the priest must announce that the person is unclean. It is leprosy. ²⁸But if the bright spot has not spread on the skin but has faded, it is only a scar from the burn. The priest must announce that the person is clean.

²⁹"Someone might get an infection on the scalp*a* or beard. ³⁰A priest must look at the infection. If the infection seems to be deeper than the skin, and if the hair around it is thin and yellow, the priest must announce that the person is unclean. It is a serious skin disease.*b* ³¹If the disease does not seem deeper than the skin, but there is no dark hair in it, the priest must separate that person for seven days. ³²On the seventh day, the priest must look at it again. If the disease has not spread, and there are no yellow hairs growing in it, and the disease does not seem deeper than the skin, ³³the person must shave. But the diseased area should not be shaved. The priest must separate that person for seven more days. ³⁴On the seventh day, the priest must look at it again. If the disease has not spread, and it does not seem deeper than the skin, the priest must announce that the person is clean. After washing those clothes, that person will be clean. ³⁵But if the disease spreads on the skin after the person has

*a***13:29** *scalp* The skin on a person's head. Also in verse 42.

*b***13:30** *serious skin disease* This could be leprosy, or it could be another kind of contagious skin disease.

become clean, ³⁶then the priest must look at the person again. If the disease has spread, the priest does not need to look for yellow hair. The person is unclean. ³⁷But if the priest thinks that the disease has stopped, and black hair is growing in it, the disease has healed. The person is clean, and the priest must announce this.

³⁸"If anyone has white spots on the skin, ³⁹a priest must look at them. If the spots on that person's skin are dull white, the disease is only a harmless rash. That person is clean.

⁴⁰"A man might begin to lose the hair on his head. It is only baldness, so he is clean. ⁴¹A man might lose hair from the sides of his head. He is clean. It is only another kind of baldness. ⁴²But if there is a red and white infection on his scalp, it is a skin disease. ⁴³A priest must look at him. If the swelling of the infection is red and white and looks like the leprosy on other parts of his body, ⁴⁴then he has leprosy on his scalp. The person is unclean. The priest must announce that he is unclean.

⁴⁵"People with leprosy must warn other people. They must shout, 'Unclean, unclean!' They must tear their clothes at the seams. They must let their hair grow wild,^a and they must cover their mouth. ⁴⁶They are unclean the whole time that they have the infection. They are unclean and must live outside the camp.

⁴⁷⁻⁴⁸"Some clothing might have mildew* on it. The cloth could be linen* or wool, woven or knitted. Or the mildew might be on a piece of leather or on something made from leather. ⁴⁹If the mildew is green or red, it must be shown to the priest. ⁵⁰The priest must look at it and put it in a separate place for seven days. ⁵¹⁻⁵²On the seventh day, he must look at it again. It doesn't matter if the mildew is on leather or cloth or if the cloth is woven or knitted. And it doesn't matter what the leather was used for. If the mildew has spread, the object is unclean because of the infection. The priest must burn it.

⁵³"If the priest sees that the mildew did not spread on the object, it must be washed. It doesn't matter if it is leather or cloth, or if the cloth is knitted or woven, it must be washed. ⁵⁴He must order the people to wash it. Then he must separate the clothing for seven more days. ⁵⁵After that time, the priest must look at it again. If the mildew still looks the same, the object is unclean. It doesn't matter if the infection has not spread; you must burn that cloth or piece of leather.

⁵⁶"But if the priest looks at that piece of leather or cloth, and the mildew has faded, he must tear the infected spot out of the piece of leather or cloth. It doesn't matter if the cloth is woven or knitted. ⁵⁷But the mildew might come back to that piece of leather or cloth. If that happens, the mildew is spreading, and the object must be burned. ⁵⁸But if the mildew did not come back after washing, that piece of leather or cloth is clean, whether the cloth was woven or knitted."

⁵⁹These are the rules for mildew on pieces of leather or cloth, whether the cloth is woven or knitted.

Rules for Those With Skin Diseases

14 ¹The Lord said to Moses, ²"These are the rules for people who have had a skin disease* and have been made well. These rules are for making them clean.*

"A priest must look at those who had the skin disease. ³The priest must go to them outside the camp and look to see if the skin disease is healed. ⁴If they are healthy, the priest will tell them to do these things: They must bring two clean birds that are still alive, a piece of cedar wood, a piece of red cloth, and a hyssop* plant. ⁵Then the priest must order one bird to be killed in a clay bowl over running water. ⁶He must take the other bird that is still alive and the piece of cedar wood, the piece of red cloth, and the hyssop plant and dip them in the blood of the bird that was killed over the running water. ⁷He must sprinkle the blood seven times on those who had the skin disease. Then he must announce that they are clean. After that the priest must go to an open field and let the living bird go free.

⁸"The people going through this purification ceremony must wash their clothes, shave off all their hair, and wash with water. Then they will be clean. They may then go into the camp, but they must stay outside their tent for seven days. ⁹On the seventh day, they must shave off all their hair. They must shave their head, their beard, and their eyebrows—yes, all their hair. Then they must wash their clothes and bathe their bodies in water. Then they will be clean.

¹⁰"On the eighth day, anyone who had a skin disease must take two male lambs that have nothing wrong with them and a one-year-old female lamb that has nothing wrong with it. They must also take 24 cups^b of fine flour mixed with oil for a grain offering and ⅔ of a pint^c of olive oil. ¹¹The priest must bring that person and those sacrifices* before the Lord at the entrance of the Meeting Tent.* (This must be the same priest who announced that the person is clean.) ¹²The priest will take one of the lambs and the oil as a guilt offering. He will lift them in front of the Lord to show they were presented to God. ¹³Then the priest will kill the male lamb in the holy* place where they kill the sin offering* and the burnt offering.* Like the

---

^a**13:45 They must tear ... wild** This also showed that a person was very sad about something.

^b**14:10 24 cups** Literally, "3/10," probably meaning 3/10 of an ephah (6.6 l).

^c**14:10 2/3 of a pint** Literally, "1 *log*" (.3 l). Also in verse 21.

sin offering, the guilt offering belongs to the priest. It is very holy.

14"The priest will take some of the blood of the guilt offering. He will put some of this blood on the tip of the right ear of the person to be made clean. The priest will put some of this blood on the thumb of the right hand and on the big toe of the right foot of that person. 15The priest will also take some of the oil and pour it into his own left palm. 16Then the priest will dip the finger of his right hand into the oil that is in his left palm. He will use his finger to sprinkle some of the oil seven times before the LORD. 17Then he will put some of the oil that is in his palm on the person to be made clean. He will put that oil on the same places he put the blood of the guilt offering. The priest will put some of the oil on the tip of the person's right ear, on the thumb of the right hand, and on the big toe of the person's right foot. 18He will put the oil that is left in his palm on the head of the person to be made clean. In this way he will make that person pure* before the LORD.

19"Then the priest must offer the sin offering to make that person pure. After that he will kill the animal for the burnt offering. 20He will then offer up the burnt offering and the grain offering on the altar.* In this way the priest will make that person pure, and that person will become clean.

21"A poor person might not be able to afford all these offerings. So that poor person can use one male lamb as a guilt offering. It will be presented to God so that the priest can make that person pure. The poor person must take 8 cups*a* of fine flour mixed with oil. This flour will be used for a grain offering. The poor person must also take ⅔ of a pint of olive oil 22and two doves or two young pigeons. Even poor people can afford these things. One bird will be a sin offering, and the other will be a burnt offering.

23"On the eighth day, that person will bring these things to the priest at the entrance of the Meeting Tent. These things will be offered before the LORD so that the person can become clean. 24The priest will take the lamb for the guilt offering and the oil, and he will lift them up to show they were offered before the LORD. 25Then he will kill the lamb of the guilt offering, take some of its blood, and put it on the tip of the right ear of the person to be made clean. The priest will put some of this blood on the thumb of the right hand and on the big toe of the right foot of this person. 26He will also pour some of this oil into his own left palm. 27He will use the finger of his right hand to sprinkle some of the oil that is in his left palm seven times before the LORD. 28Then he will put some of the oil that is in his palm on the same places he put the blood from the guilt offering. He will put some of

the oil on the tip of the right ear of the person to be made clean. The priest will put some of the oil on the thumb of the right hand and on the big toe of the person's right foot. 29He will put the oil that is left in his palm on the head of the person to be made clean. In this way he will make that person pure before the LORD.

30"Then the priest must offer one of the doves or young pigeons. (He must offer whichever the person can afford.) 31He must offer one of these birds as a sin offering and the other bird as a burnt offering. He must offer the birds with the grain offering. In this way the priest will make that person pure before the LORD, and that person will become clean."

32These are the rules for making people clean after they become well from a skin disease. These are the rules for those who cannot afford the regular sacrifices for becoming clean.

Rules for Mildew in a House

33The LORD also said to Moses and Aaron, 34"I am giving the land of Canaan* to your people. Your people will enter that land. At that time I might cause mildew* to grow in someone's house. 35The person who owns that house must come and tell the priest, 'I see something like mildew in my house.'

36"Then the priest must order the people to take everything out of the house before he goes in to look at the mildew. Then the priest will not have to say everything in the house is unclean.* After the people have taken everything out of the house, the priest will go in to look at the house. 37He will look at the mildew. If the mildew on the walls of the house has holes that are a green or red color, and if the mildew goes into the wall's surface, 38he must go out of the house and lock the house for seven days.

39"On the seventh day the priest must come back and check the house. If the mildew has spread on the walls of the house, 40then he must order the people to tear out the stones with the mildew on them and throw them away. They must put these stones at a special unclean place outside the city. 41Then the priest must have the entire house scraped inside. The people must throw away the plaster that was scraped off the walls. They must put that plaster at a special unclean place outside the city. 42Then new stones must be put in the walls, and the walls must be covered with new plaster.

43"Maybe someone took away the old stones and plaster and put in new stones and plaster. And maybe mildew again appears in that house. 44Then the priest must come in and check the house. If the infection has spread in the house, it is a disease that spreads quickly to other places. So the house is unclean. 45The house must be torn down. All the stones, plaster, and pieces of wood

---

*a*14:21 *8 cups* Literally, "1/10 of an ephah" (2.2 l).

must be taken to the special unclean place outside the city. 46Anyone who goes into that house will be unclean until evening. 47Anyone who eats in that house or lies down in there must wash their clothes.

48"After new stones and plaster are put in a house, the priest must check the house. If the mildew has not spread through the house, the priest will announce that the house is clean,* because the mildew is gone.

49"Then, to make the house clean, the priest must take two birds, a piece of cedar wood, a piece of red cloth, and a hyssop* plant. 50He will kill one bird in a clay bowl over running water. 51Then he will take the cedar wood, the hyssop, the piece of red cloth, and the living bird and dip them in the blood of the bird that was killed over running water. Then he will sprinkle that blood on the house seven times. 52In this way he will use these things to make the house clean. 53He will go to an open field outside the city and let the living bird go free. In this way the priest will make the house pure.* The house will be clean."

54These are the rules for any infection of leprosy,* 55for mildew on pieces of cloth or in a house. 56These are the rules for swellings, rashes, or bright spots on the skin. 57These rules teach when something is clean and when something is unclean. These are the rules about these kinds of disease.

Rules for Discharges From the Body

15 1The Lord also said to Moses and Aaron, 2"Say to the Israelites: Whoever has a genital discharge* is unclean.* 3The person is unclean whether the discharge continues to flow or whether it stops.

4"If a man with a discharge lies on a bed, that bed becomes unclean. Everything he sits on will become unclean. 5If you touch that bed, you must wash your clothes and bathe in water. You will be unclean until evening. 6If you sit on anything that he sat on, you must wash your clothes and bathe in water. You will be unclean until evening. 7If you touch him, you must wash your clothes and bathe in water. You will be unclean until evening. 8If he spits on you, you must wash your clothes and bathe in water. You will be unclean until evening. 9If that man sits on a saddle, it will become unclean. 10If you touch or carry anything that was under him, you will be unclean until evening. 11If he touches you, you must wash your clothes and bathe in water. You will be unclean until evening.

12"If a man with a discharge touches a clay bowl, that bowl must be broken. If he touches a wooden bowl, that bowl must be washed in water.

13"When it comes time for a man with a discharge to be made clean, he must wait seven days. Then he must wash his clothes and bathe his body in running water. Then he will become clean.* 14On the eighth day

he must take for himself two doves or two young pigeons and come before the Lord at the entrance of the Meeting Tent.* He will give the two birds to the priest. 15The priest will offer the birds, one for a sin offering,* and the other for a burnt offering.* In this way the priest will make that man pure* before the Lord.

16"If a man has a flow of semen, he must bathe his whole body in water. He will be unclean until evening. 17If the semen is on any clothing or leather, that clothing or leather must be washed with water. It will be unclean until evening. 18If a woman has sexual relations with a man, and he has a flow of semen, both the man and the woman must bathe in water. They will be unclean until evening.

19"If a woman has a discharge from her monthly time of bleeding, she will be unclean for seven days. Anyone who touches her will be unclean until evening. 20Everything she lies on during her monthly time of bleeding will be unclean. And everything she sits on during that time will be unclean. 21Whoever touches her bed must wash their clothes and bathe in water. They will be unclean until evening. 22Whoever touches anything she has sat on must wash their clothes and bathe in water. They will be unclean until evening. 23It doesn't matter if they touched the woman's bed or if they touched something she sat on, they will be unclean until evening.

24"If a man has sexual relations with a woman during her monthly time of bleeding, he will be unclean for seven days. Every bed he lies on will be unclean.

25"If a woman has a discharge of blood for many days, not during her time of monthly bleeding, or if she has a discharge after that time, she will be unclean, just as during the time of her monthly bleeding. She will be unclean for as long as she has a discharge. 26Any bed she lies on during the time of her discharge will be like her bed during the time of her monthly bleeding. Everything she sits on will be unclean, just as it is during the time she is unclean from her monthly bleeding. 27Whoever touches these things will be unclean until evening. They must wash their own clothes and bathe in water. 28After the woman's discharge stops, she must wait seven days. After that she will be clean. 29Then on the eighth day she must bring two doves or two young pigeons to the priest at the entrance of the Meeting Tent. 30Then the priest must offer one bird for a sin offering and the other bird for a burnt offering. In this way the priest will make her pure before the Lord.

31"So you must warn the Israelites about being unclean. If you don't warn the people, they might make my Holy Tent* unclean. And then they would have to die!"

32These are the rules for anyone with a discharge from the body. These rules are for men who become unclean from a flow of semen. ³³And these rules are for women who become unclean from their monthly time of bleeding. And these are the rules for anyone who becomes unclean by sleeping with another person who is unclean.

The Day of Atonement

16 ¹Two of Aaron's sons died while offering incense* to the LORD.ᵈ After that time, the LORD spoke to Moses. ²The LORD said, "Talk to your brother Aaron. Tell him that he cannot go behind the curtain into the Most Holy Place* anytime he wants to. The mercy-cover* is in the room behind that curtain on top of the Holy Box,* and I appear in a cloud over that mercy-cover. If Aaron goes into that room, he will die!

³"Before Aaron enters the Most Holy Place, he will offer a bull for a sin offering* and a ram for a burnt offering.* ⁴Aaron will wash his whole body with water and put on the special clothes. He will put on the linen underwear next to his body, the linen robe, the linen belt, and then he will put the linen turban* on his head.

⁵"From the whole community of Israel, Aaron will accept two male goats for a sin offering and one ram for a burnt offering. ⁶Then he will offer the bull for the sin offering. This sin offering is for himself. He will do this to purifyᵇ himself and his family.

⁷"Then Aaron will take the two goats and bring them before the LORD at the doorway of the Meeting Tent.* ⁸Aaron will throw lots* for the two goats. One lot will be for the LORD. The other lot will be for Azazel.ᶜ ⁹"Then Aaron will offer the goat chosen by the lot for the LORD. Aaron will make this goat a sin offering. ¹⁰But the goat chosen by the lot for Azazel will be brought alive before the LORD. Then this goat will be sent out to Azazel in the desert. This is to make the people pure.*

¹¹"Then Aaron will offer the bull as a sin offering for himself. He will purify himself and his family. He will kill the bull for the sin offering for himself. ¹²Then he will take a firepan* full of coals of fire from the altar* before the LORD. Aaron will take two handfuls of sweet incense that has been ground into powder and take it into the room behind the curtain. ¹³He will put the incense on the fire before the LORD. Then the cloud of incense will hide the mercy-cover that is over

the Box that holds the Agreement.ᵈ This way Aaron will not die. ¹⁴Aaron will dip his finger into the bull's blood and sprinkle it on the front of the Holy Box. Then he will sprinkle the blood seven times onto the front of the mercy-cover.

¹⁵"Then Aaron will kill the goat of the sin offering for the people. He will bring this goat's blood into the room behind the curtain. He will do with the goat's blood as he did with the bull's blood. He will sprinkle the goat's blood on the mercy-cover and in front of it. ¹⁶In this way Aaron will purify the Most Holy Place from all the uncleanness and sins of the Israelites. He will also purify the Meeting Tent, because it stands in the middle of people whose sins have made them unclean.

¹⁷"No one must be in the Meeting Tent when Aaron goes in to purify the Most Holy Place. No one is to go in there until Aaron comes out after purifying himself, his family, and all the Israelites. ¹⁸Then Aaron will go out to the altar that is before the LORD. Aaron will make the altar pure. He will take some of the blood from the bull and from the goat and put it on the corners of the altar on all four sides. ¹⁹Then he will dip his finger in the blood and sprinkle it on the altar seven times. In this way Aaron will make the altar holy* and clean* from all the sins of the Israelites.

²⁰"So Aaron will make the Most Holy Place, the Meeting Tent, and the altar pure. Then he will bring the living goat to the LORD. ²¹He will put both his hands on the head of the living goat. Then he will confess the sins and crimes of the Israelites over the goat. In this way Aaron will lay the people's sins on the goat's head. Then he will send the goat away into the desert. A man will be standing by, ready to lead this goat away. ²²So the goat will carry all the people's sins on itself into the empty desert. The man who leads the goat will let it loose in the desert.

²³"Then Aaron will enter the Meeting Tent. He will take off the linen clothes that he put on when he went into the Holy Place. He will leave these clothes there. ²⁴He will wash his whole body with water in a holy place. Then he will put on his clothes. He will come out and offer his burnt offering and the people's burnt offering. He will make himself and the people pure. ²⁵Then he will burn the fat of the sin offering on the altar.

²⁶"The man who led the goat to Azazel must wash his clothes and his whole body with water. After that he may come into the camp.

²⁷"The bull and the goat for the sin offerings will be taken outside the camp. (The blood from these animals was brought into the Holy Place to make ⌊the holy things⌋ pure.) The skins, bodies, and body waste of those

ᵃ16:1 *Two of Aaron's sons … LORD* See Lev. 10:1–2.
ᵇ16:6 *purify* Or "make atonement." The Hebrew word means "to cover," or "to erase" a person's sins. Also in verses 11, 16, 17, 34.
ᶜ16:8 *Azazel* This name means "scapegoat," "the goat for God," or "the goat demon." This might be the name of a particular place in the desert where the goat was released. Also in verse 10, 26.

ᵈ16:13 *Box that holds the Agreement* Literally, "Testimony." See "Agreement" in the Word List.

animals will be burned in the fire. ²⁸Then the man who burns them must wash his clothes and bathe his whole body with water. After that he may come into the camp.

²⁹"This law will always continue for you: On the tenth day of the seventh month, you must not eat food.ᵃ You must not do any work. None of the travelers or foreigners living in your land can do any work either. ³⁰Because on this day, the priest will do this to make you pure and wash away your sins. Then you will be clean to the LORD. ³¹You must humble yourselvesᵇ because this day is a very important day of rest for you. This law will continue forever.

³²"In the future, this ceremony will be done by the priest who will be anointed and appointed to serve after his father. That priest will put on the holy linen clothes ³³and make the Most Holy Place, the Meeting Tent, and the altar pure. He will also make the priests and all the people pure. ³⁴That law will continue forever. Once every year you will purify the Israelites from all their sins."

So they did everything that the LORD had commanded Moses.

Rules About Killing and Eating Animals

17 ¹The LORD said to Moses, ²"Speak to Aaron and to his sons, and to all the Israelites. Tell them this is what the LORD has commanded: ³Any one of you Israelites might kill a bull, a lamb, or a goat. You might be in the camp or outside the camp. ⁴It doesn't matter; you must bring that animal to the entrance of the Meeting Tent.* You must give a part of that animal as a gift to the LORD. You spilled blood, so you must take a gift to the LORD's Holy Tent.* If you don't take part of the animal as a gift to the LORD, you must be separated from your people! ⁵This rule is so that you will bring your fellowship offering* to the LORD. You must bring any animal that you kill in the field to the LORD at the entrance of the Meeting Tent. Bring those animals to the priest. ⁶Then the priest will throw their blood onto the LORD's altar* near the entrance of the Meeting Tent. And the priest will burn the fat from those animals on the altar as a sweet-smelling gift to the LORD. ⁷In this way you will stop being unfaithful to me by offering sacrifices* to your 'goat gods.' This law will continue forever.

⁸"Tell the people: Any citizen of Israel, traveler, or foreigner living among you might want to offer a burnt offering* or some other sacrifice. ⁹They must take the sacrifice to the entrance of the Meeting Tent and offer it to the LORD. Whoever does not do this will be separated from their people.

¹⁰"I will turn against those who eat blood

whether they are citizens of Israel or foreigners living among you, I will separate them from their people. ¹¹This is because the life of the body is in the blood. I have told you that you must pour the blood on the altar to purify yourselves. It is the blood that makes a person pure.* ¹²That is why I am telling you Israelites and the foreigners living among you that you must not eat blood.

¹³"If any of you, whether Israelite or foreigner living among you, goes hunting and kills a wild animal or bird that you are allowed to eat, you must pour the blood of that animal on the ground and cover it with dirt. ¹⁴This is because the life of every kind of animal is in its blood. So I give this command to the Israelites: Don't eat meat that still has blood in it! Whoever eats blood must be separated from their people.

¹⁵"If any of you, whether Israelite or foreigner living among you, eats an animal that died by itself or was killed by some other animal, you will be unclean* until evening. You must wash your clothes and bathe your whole body with water. ¹⁶If you don't wash your clothes and bathe your whole body, you will be responsible for your guilt."

Rules About Sexual Relations

18 ¹The LORD said to Moses, ²"Tell the Israelites: I am the LORD your God. ³You must not follow the customs of Egypt where you lived, and you must not follow the customs of the Canaanites where I am leading you. You must not live like they do. ⁴You must obey my rules and follow my laws. Be sure to follow my rules because I am the LORD your God. ⁵You must obey my rules and my laws, because whoever obeys them will live. I am the LORD.

⁶"You must never have sexual relations withᶜ your close relatives. I am the LORD.

⁷"You must never have sexual relations with your father or mother. She is your mother, so you must not have sexual relations with her. ⁸You must not have sexual relations with your father's wife, even if she is not your mother, because that is like having sexual relations with your father.ᵈ

⁹"You must not have sexual relations with your sister. It doesn't matter if she is the daughter of your father or your mother. And it doesn't matter if your sister was born in your houseᵉ or at some other place.

ᵃ**16:29 not eat food** Literally, "humble yourselves."
ᵇ**16:31 humble yourselves** This also means that the people were not supposed to eat any food on this day.

ᶜ**18:6 have sexual relations with** Literally, "uncover the nakedness of." Also in verses 7, 9–12, 15–19.
ᵈ**18:8 sexual relations ... father** Literally, "She is the nakedness of your father." Husband and wife are like one person. See Gen. 2:24.
ᵉ**18:9 sister was born in your house** Or "household." If a man had many wives, each wife and her children had their own tent or part of the house. So this probably means a man was not supposed to have sexual relations with any of his father's daughters, whether sister or half-sister.

¹⁰"You must not have sexual relations with your granddaughter. It doesn't matter whether she is the daughter of your son or the daughter of your daughter—they are all a part of you!

¹¹"If your father and his wife*a* have a daughter, she is your sister. You must not have sexual relations with her.

¹²"You must not have sexual relations with your father's sister. She is your father's close relative. ¹³You must not have sexual relations with your mother's sister. She is your mother's close relative. ¹⁴You must not have sexual relations with the wife of your father's brother. You must not go near your uncle's wife for sexual relations. She is your aunt.

¹⁵"You must not have sexual relations with your daughter-in-law. She is your son's wife, so you must not have sexual relations with her.

¹⁶"You must not have sexual relations with your brother's wife. That would be like having sexual relations with your brother.*b*

¹⁷"You must not have sexual relations with a mother and her daughter or her granddaughter. It doesn't matter if this granddaughter is the daughter of this woman's son or daughter. Her granddaughters are her close relatives. It is wrong to do this.

¹⁸"While your wife is still living, you must not take her sister as another wife. This will make the sisters become enemies. You must not have sexual relations with your wife's sister.

¹⁹"You must not go near a woman to have sexual relations with her during her monthly time of bleeding. She is unclean* during this time.

²⁰"You must not have sexual relations with your neighbor's wife. This will only make you filthy.*c*

²¹"You must not give any of your children through the fire to Molech.* If you do this, you will show that you don't respect the name of your God. I am the LORD.

²²"Men, you must not have sexual relations with another man as with a woman. That is a terrible sin!

²³"Men, you must not have sexual relations with any animal. This will make you filthy. And women, you must not have sexual relations with any animal. It is against nature!

²⁴"Don't make yourself unclean by doing any of these wrong things! I am throwing nations off their land and giving it to you because they did those terrible sins. ²⁵They made the land filthy. Now the land is sick of those things, and it will vomit out the people who live there.

²⁶"So you must obey my laws and rules. You must not do any of these terrible sins. These rules are for the citizens of Israel and the people living among you. ²⁷Those who lived in the land before you have done all these terrible things. So the land became filthy. ²⁸If you do these things, you will make the land filthy. And it will vomit you out as it vomited out the nations that were there before you. ²⁹Whoever does any of these terrible sins must be separated from their people! ³⁰Other people have done these terrible sins, but you must obey my laws. You must not do any of these terrible sins. Do not make yourself filthy with these terrible sins. I am the LORD your God."

Israel Belongs to God

19 ¹The LORD said to Moses, ²"Tell all the Israelites: I am the LORD your God. I am holy, so you must be holy.

³"Each of you must honor your mother and father and keep my special days of rest.*d* I am the LORD your God!

⁴"Do not worship idols.* Do not make statues of gods for yourselves. I am the LORD your God.

⁵"When you offer a sacrifice* of fellowship offerings* to the LORD, you must offer it in the right way so that you will be accepted. ⁶You may eat it the same day you offer it and on the next day. But if any of that sacrifice is left on the third day, you must burn it in the fire. ⁷You must not eat any of that sacrifice on the third day. It will be unclean,*e* and it will not be accepted. ⁸You will be guilty of sin if you do that because you did not respect the holy* things that belong to the LORD. If you do that you will be separated from your people.

⁹"When you cut your crops at harvest time, don't cut all the way to the corners of your fields. And if grain falls on the ground, you must not gather up that grain. ¹⁰Don't pick all the grapes in your vineyards* or pick up the grapes that fall to the ground. You must leave those things for your poor people and for people traveling through your country. I am the LORD your God.

¹¹"You must not steal. You must not cheat people. You must not lie to each other. ¹²You must not use my name to make false promises. If you do that, you will show that you don't respect the name of your God. I am the LORD!

¹³"You must not cheat or rob your neighbor. You must not hold a hired worker's salary overnight until morning.*f*

---

*a*18:11 *his wife* This probably means "your stepmother."
*b*18:16 *sexual relations … brother* Literally, "She is the nakedness of your brother."
*c*18:20 *filthy* Or "polluted" or "unclean." Also in verses 23, 25, 27.
*d*19:3 *special days of rest* Or "Sabbaths." This might mean Saturday, or it might mean all the special days when the people were not supposed to work. Also in verse 30.
*e*19:7 *unclean* Or "offensive," "bad," or "rotten." This means the meat is not good to eat as part of a sacrifice.
*f*19:13 Workers were paid at the end of each day for the work they did that day. See Mt. 20:1–16.

14"You must not curse anyone who is deaf. You must not do anything to make a blind person fall. But you must respect your God. I am the Lord.

15"You must be fair in judgment. You must not show special favor to the poor. And you must not show special favor to important people. You must be fair when you judge your neighbor. **16**You must not go around spreading false stories against other people. Don't do anything that would put your neighbor's life in danger. I am the Lord.

17"Don't secretly hate any of your neighbors. But tell them openly what they have done wrong so that you will not be just as guilty of sin as they are. **18**Forget about the wrong things people do to you. Don't try to get even. Love your neighbor as yourself. I am the Lord.

19"You must obey my laws. You must not let your animals mate with animals of a different kind. You must not sow your field with two kinds of seed. You must not wear clothing made from two kinds of material mixed together.

20"It may happen that a man has sexual relations with a woman who is the slave of another man. But this slave woman has not been bought or given her freedom. If this happens, there must be punishment. But they will not be put to death because the woman was not free. **21**The man must bring his guilt offering to the Lord at the entrance of the Meeting Tent.* He must bring a ram for a guilt offering. **22**The priest will make him pure* by offering the ram as a guilt offering before the Lord. The offering is for the man's sins, which will then be forgiven.

23"In the future, when you enter your country, you will plant many kinds of trees for food. After planting a tree, you must wait three years before you can use any of the fruit from that tree. You must not use that fruit. **24**In the fourth year, the fruit from that tree will be the Lord's. It will be a holy offering of praise to the Lord. **25**Then, in the fifth year, you can eat the fruit from that tree. And the tree will produce more and more fruit for you. I am the Lord your God.

26"You must not eat any meat with blood still in it.

"You must not try to use different kinds of magic to tell the future.

27"You must not round off the hair that grows on the side of your face. You must not cut your beard that grows on the side of your face. **28**You must not cut your body as a way to remember the dead. You must not make any tattoo marks on yourselves. I am the Lord.

29"Do not dishonor your daughters by making them become prostitutes. If you do that, your whole country will turn away from God and be filled with all kinds of sinful things.

30"You must not work on my special days of rest. You must honor my holy place.

I am the Lord.

31"Do not go to mediums* or wizards* for advice—they will only make you unclean.* I am the Lord your God.

32"Show honor to old people. Stand up when they come into the room. And show respect to your leaders.*ᵃ* I am the Lord.

33"Do not do bad things to foreigners living in your country. **34**You must treat them the same as you treat your own citizens. Love them as you love yourselves. Remember, you were foreigners in Egypt. I am the Lord your God!

35"You must be fair when you judge people, and you must be fair when you measure and weigh things. **36**Your baskets should be the right size. Your jars should hold the right amount of liquids. Your weights and balances should weigh things correctly. I am the Lord your God. I brought you out of the land of Egypt.

37"You must remember all my laws and rules. And you must obey them. I am the Lord."

Warning Against Worshiping Idols

20 ¹The Lord said to Moses, ²"You must also tell the Israelites these things: Anyone living in Israel who gives one of their children to the false god Molech* must be killed! It doesn't matter if they are a citizen of Israel or a foreigner, you must throw stones at them and kill them. ³I will be against them and separate them from their people, because they gave their children to Molech. They showed that they did not respect my holy name. And they made my holy* place unclean.* ⁴Maybe the common people will ignore them. Maybe they will not kill those who gave their children to Molech. ⁵But I will be against these people and their families. I will separate them from their people. I will separate anyone who is unfaithful to me and chases after Molech.

⁶"I will be against anyone who goes to mediums* and wizards* for advice. Whoever does this is being unfaithful to me. So I will separate them from their people.

⁷"Be special. Make yourselves holy, because I am the Lord your God. ⁸Remember and obey my laws. I am the Lord. And I have made you my special people.

⁹"Whoever curses* their father or mother must be put to death. They cursed their father or mother, so they are responsible for their own death!ᵇ

Punishments for Sexual Sins

10"If a man has sexual relations with his neighbor's wife, both the man and the woman are guilty of adultery and must be put to death! **11**If a man has sexual relations with his

<hr>

*ᵃ***19:32** *leaders* Or "God."
*ᵇ***20:9** *they ... death* Literally, "his blood is on him."

father's wife, both the man and the woman must be put to death. They are responsible for their own death.[a] It is as if that man had sexual relations with his father![b]

12"If a man has sexual relations with his daughter-in-law, both of them must be put to death. They have committed a terrible sexual sin! They are responsible for their own death.

13"If a man has sexual relations with another man as with a woman, they have committed a terrible sin. They must be put to death. They are responsible for their own death.

14"It is a sexual sin if a man has sexual relations with a woman and her mother. The people must burn that man and the two women in fire! Don't let this sexual sin happen among your people.

15"If a man has sexual relations with an animal, both the man and the animal must be put to death. 16If a woman has sexual relations with an animal, you must kill the woman and the animal. They must be put to death. They are responsible for their own death.

17"It is a shameful thing for a brother and his sister or half-sister to marry each other and have sexual relations with each other.[c] They must be punished in public. They must be separated from their people. The man who has sexual relations with his sister must be punished for his sin.[d]

18"If a man has sexual relations with a woman during her monthly time of bleeding, both the woman and the man must be separated from their people. They sinned because they exposed her source of blood.

19"You must not have sexual relations with[e] your mother's sister or your father's sister. That is a sin of incest.[f] You must be punished for your sins.[g]

20"A man must not have sexual relations with his uncle's wife. It would be like having sexual relations with his uncle. That man and his uncle's wife will be punished for their sins. They will die without children.[h]

21"It is wrong for a man to take his brother's wife. It would be like having sexual relations with his brother! They will have no children.

22"You must remember all my laws and rules. And you must obey them. I am leading you to your land. You will live in that country.

If you obey my laws and rules, that land will not vomit you out. 23I am forcing other people to leave that country because they committed all those sins. I hate those sins! So don't live the way those people lived. 24But I have told you that you will get their land. I will give their land to you. It will be your land! It is a land filled with many good things.[i] I am the LORD your God.

"I have treated you differently from other people. 25So you must treat clean* animals differently from unclean* animals. You must also treat clean birds differently from unclean birds. Don't eat any of these unclean birds or animals or things that crawl on the ground. I have made these things unclean. 26I have separated you from other nations to be my own special people. So you must be holy* because I am the LORD, and I am holy.

27"A man or a woman who is a medium* or a wizard* must be put to death. The people must kill them with stones. They are responsible for their own death."

Rules for Priests

21 1The LORD said to Moses, "Tell these things to Aaron's sons, the priests: A priest must not make himself unclean* by touching a dead person. 2But if the dead person was one of his close relatives, he can touch the dead body. The priest can make himself unclean if the dead person is his mother or father, his son or daughter, his brother or 3his unmarried[j] sister. (This sister is close to him because she has no husband. So the priest may make himself unclean for her if she dies.) 4But a priest must not make himself unclean if the dead person was only one of his slaves.[k]

5"Priests must not shave their heads bald. They must not shave off the edges of their beards. They must not make any cuts in their bodies. 6Priests must be holy* for their God. They must show respect for God's name. They offer the bread and special gifts to the LORD, so they must be holy.

7"A priest serves God in a special way, so he must not marry a woman who has had sexual relations with any other man. He must not marry a prostitute or a divorced woman. 8A priest serves God in a special way. So you must treat him in a special way, because he carries holy things. He brings the holy bread* to me, and I am holy. I am the LORD, and I make you holy.

9"If a priest's daughter becomes a prostitute, she ruins her reputation and brings shame to her father. She must be burned to death in the fire!

---

[a]20:11 They ... death Literally, "Their blood is on them." Also in verses 12, 13, 16, 27.

[b]20:11 man ... father Literally, "he uncovered his father's nakedness."

[c]20:17 sexual relations with each other Literally, "he sees her nakedness, and she sees his nakedness."

[d]20:17 The man ... sin Literally, "He will carry his guilt."

[e]20:19 have sexual relations with Literally, "uncover the nakedness of." Also in verse 21.

[f]20:19 incest Having sexual relations with a close relative.

[g]20:19 You ... sins Literally, "You will carry your guilt."

[h]20:20 That man ... children Literally, "They must bear their childlessness. They will die."

[i]20:24 land ... things Literally, "land flowing with milk and honey."

[j]21:3 unmarried Literally, "virgin," a girl who was never married and never had sexual relations.

[k]21:4 Or "A master must not become unclean for his people."

¹⁰"The high priest was chosen from among his brothers. The anointing* oil was poured on his head. In this way he was chosen for the special job of being high priest. He was chosen to wear the special clothes, so he must not do things to show his sadness in public. He must not let his hair grow wild. He must not tear his clothes. ¹¹He must not make himself unclean by touching a dead body. He must not go near a dead body, even if it is his own father or mother. ¹²The high priest must not leave God's holy place, because he might become unclean and then make God's holy place unclean. The anointing oil was poured on the high priest's head. This separated him from the rest of the people. I am the LORD.

¹³"The high priest must marry a woman who is a virgin.* ¹⁴He must not marry a woman who has had sexual relations with any man. He must not marry a prostitute, a divorced woman, or a widow. The high priest must marry a virgin from his own people. ¹⁵In this way people will show respect for his children.ᵃ I, the LORD, have separated the high priest for his special work."

¹⁶The LORD said to Moses, ¹⁷"Tell Aaron: If any of your descendants have anything wrong with them, they must not carry the special bread to God. ¹⁸Any man who has something wrong with him must not serve as priest and bring sacrifices* to me. These men cannot serve as priests: blind men, crippled men, men with bad scars on their faces, men with arms or legs that are too long, ¹⁹men with broken feet or hands, ²⁰men with bent backs, men who are dwarfs,ᵇ men who are cross-eyed, men with rashes or bad skin diseases, and men with crushed testicles.

²¹"If one of Aaron's descendants has something wrong with him, he cannot approach the altar to bring gifts to the LORD. And he cannot carry the special bread to God. ²²He is from the family of priests, so he can eat the holy bread. He can also eat the very holy bread. ²³But he cannot go through the curtain into the Most Holy Place and he cannot go near the altar.* This is because he has something wrong with him. He must not make my holy places unholy. I am the LORD, and I make these places holy."

²⁴So Moses told these things to Aaron, Aaron's sons, and all the Israelites.

22 ¹The LORD God said to Moses, ²"Tell Aaron and his sons: The gifts that the Israelites bring to me become holy. They belong to me, so you priests must show respect for these things. If you don't, you will show that you don't respect my holy name. I am the LORD. ³If any one of your descendants touches these things, that person will become unclean. That person must be separated from me. The Israelites gave these things to me. I am the LORD.

⁴"If any of Aaron's descendants has a serious skin diseaseᶜ or a discharge,* he cannot eat the holy food until he becomes clean.* This rule is for any priest who becomes unclean. That priest can become unclean from a dead body or from his own semen. ⁵He can also become unclean if he touches any unclean crawling animal. And he can become unclean if he touches an unclean person. It doesn't matter what made that person unclean. ⁶If he touches any of these things, he will become unclean until evening. He must not eat any of the holy food. Even if he washes with water, he cannot eat the holy food. ⁷He will be clean only after the sun goes down. Then he can eat the holy food because it is his share.

⁸"A priest must not eat any animal that died by itself or that was killed by wild animals. If he eats that animal, he will be unclean. I am the LORD.

⁹"The priests must be very careful when it comes time to serve me. They must be careful not to dishonor the holy things. If they are careful, they will not die. I, the LORD, have separated them from the rest of the people for this special job. ¹⁰Only a priest's family can eat the holy food. A visitor staying with the priest or a hired worker must not eat any of the holy food. ¹¹But if the priest buys a person as a slave with his own money, that person may eat some of the holy things. Slaves who were born in the priest's house may also eat some of the priest's food. ¹²A priest's daughter might marry a man who is not a priest. If she does that, she cannot eat any of the holy offerings. ¹³A priest's daughter might become a widow, or she might be divorced. If she does not have any children to support her, and she goes back to her father's house where she lived as a child, she can eat some of her father's food. But only people from a priest's family can eat this food.

¹⁴"Whoever eats some of the holy food by mistake must give the priest the price of that food and add another one-fifth of the price as a fine.

¹⁵"The Israelites will give gifts to the LORD. These gifts become holy, so the priests must not treat them like they are not important. ¹⁶If they do, they are guilty of doing wrong, and they must bear the responsibility for their guilt. I am the LORD, and I make them holy."

¹⁷The LORD God said to Moses, ¹⁸"Tell Aaron and his sons and all the Israelites: A citizen of Israel or a foreigner might want to bring an offering. It might be because of a promise that person made, or it might just be a special sacrifice that person wanted to

---

ᵃ21:15 people ... children Or "his children will not become unclean from the people."
ᵇ21:20 dwarfs A small person whose body stopped growing properly.

ᶜ22:4 serious skin disease This could be leprosy, or it could be another kind of contagious skin disease. Also in verse 22.

bring. ¹⁹⁻²⁰These are gifts that the people bring because they really want to give a gift to God. If the gift is a bull, or a sheep, or a goat, the animal must be a male. And it must not have anything wrong with it. You must not accept any offering that has anything wrong with it. I will not accept that gift.

²¹"You might bring a fellowship offering* to the Lord. That fellowship offering might be payment for a special promise that you made. Or maybe it is a special gift that you wanted to give to the Lord. It can be a bull or a sheep, but it must be healthy. There must be nothing wrong with that animal. ²²You must not offer to the Lord any animal that is blind, that has broken bones or is crippled, that has a discharge or a serious skin disease. You must not offer sick animals as a gift to the Lord. You must not put anything like that on his altar.

²³"Sometimes a bull or lamb will have a leg that is too long, or a foot that did not grow right. If you want to give that animal as a special gift to the Lord, it will be accepted. But it will not be accepted as payment for a special promise that you made.

²⁴"If an animal has bruised, crushed, or torn testicles, you must not offer that animal to the Lord. You must not do this anywhere in your land.

²⁵"You must not take animals from foreigners as sacrifices to the Lord. The animals might have been hurt in some way. They might have something wrong with them, so they will not be accepted."

²⁶The Lord said to Moses, ²⁷"When a calf, or a sheep, or a goat is born, it must stay seven days with its mother. Then from the eighth day on, this animal will be accepted as a sacrifice offered as a gift to the Lord. ²⁸But you must not kill the animal and its mother on the same day. This rule is the same for cattle and sheep.

²⁹"If you want to offer some special offering of thanks to the Lord, you are free to offer that gift. But you must do it in a way that pleases God. ³⁰You must eat the whole animal that day. You must not leave any of the meat for the next morning. I am the Lord.

³¹"Remember my commands, and obey them. I am the Lord. ³²Show respect for my holy name. I must be very special to the Israelites. I, the Lord, have made you my special people. ³³I brought you out of Egypt in order to be your God. I am the Lord."

The Special Festivals

23 ¹The Lord said to Moses, ²"Tell the Israelites: You will announce the Lord's chosen festivals as holy* meetings. These are my special festivals.

Sabbath

³"Work for six days, but the seventh day, the Sabbath, will be a special day of rest, a holy* meeting. You must not do any work. It is a day of rest to honor the Lord in all your homes.

Passover

⁴"These are the Lord's chosen festivals. You will announce the holy* meetings at the times chosen for them. ⁵The Lord's Passover is on the 14th day of the first month*ᵃ* just before dark.

Festival of Unleavened Bread

⁶"The Festival of Unleavened Bread* is on the 15th day of the same month. You will eat unleavened* bread for seven days. ⁷On the first day of this festival, you will have a special meeting. You must not do any work on that day. ⁸For seven days, you will bring sacrifices* offered as gifts to the Lord. Then there will be another special meeting on the seventh day. You must not do any work on that day."

Festival of the First Harvests

⁹The Lord said to Moses, ¹⁰"Tell the Israelites: You will enter the land that I will give you and reap its harvest. At that time you must bring in the first sheafᵇ of your harvest to the priest. ¹¹The priest will lift the sheaf to show it was offered before the Lord. Then you will be accepted. The priest will present the sheaf on Sunday morning.ᶜ

¹²"On the day when you present the sheaf, you will offer a one-year-old male lamb. There must be nothing wrong with that lamb. That lamb will be a burnt offering* to the Lord. ¹³You must also offer a grain offering of 16 cupsᵈ of fine flour mixed with olive oil. You must also offer 1 quartᵉ of wine. The smell of that offering will please the Lord. ¹⁴You must not eat any of the new grain, or fruit, or bread made from the new grain until you bring that offering to your God. This law will always continue through your generations, wherever you live.

Festival of Harvest

¹⁵"From that Sunday morning (the day you bring the sheaf to be presented to God), count seven weeks. ¹⁶On the Sunday following the seventh week (that is, 50 days later), you will bring a new grain offering to the Lord. ¹⁷On that day, bring two loaves of bread from your homes. That bread will be lifted up to show it was offered to God. Use yeast and 16 cups of flour to make those loaves of bread. That will be your gift to the Lord from your first harvest.

---

*ᵃ***23:5** *first month* Abib (or Nisan). See "Abib" in the Word List.
*ᵇ***23:10** *sheaf* A stack of grain. Also in verses 12, 15.
*ᶜ***23:11** *Sunday morning* Literally, "the morning after the Sabbath." Also in verse 15.
*ᵈ***23:13** *16 cups* Literally, "2/10 of an ephah" (4.4 l). Also in verse 17.
*ᵉ***23:13** *1 quart* Literally, "1/4 hin" (.8 l).

18"One bull, one ram, and seven one-year-old male lambs will be offered with the grain offerings from the people. There must be nothing wrong with these animals. They will be a burnt offering* offered as a sweet-smelling gift to the LORD. 19You will also offer one male goat for a sin offering* and two one-year-old male lambs as a fellowship offering.*

20"The priest will lift them up with the bread from the first harvest to show they were offered with the two lambs before the LORD. They are holy* to the LORD. They will belong to the priest. 21On that same day, you will call a holy meeting. You must not do any work. This law continues forever in all your homes.

22"Also, when you harvest the crops on your land, don't cut all the way to the corners of your field. Don't pick up the grain that falls on the ground. Leave it for poor people and for foreigners traveling through your country. I am the LORD your God."

Festival of Trumpets

23Again the LORD said to Moses, 24"Tell the Israelites: On the first day of the seventh month, you must have a special day of rest. Blow the trumpet to remind the people that this is a holy* meeting. 25You must not do any work. You must bring an offering as a gift to the LORD."

Day of Atonement

26The LORD said to Moses, 27"The Day of Atonement* will be on the tenth day of the seventh month. There will be a holy meeting. You must not eat food,a and you must bring an offering as a gift to the LORD. 28You must not do any work on that day, because it is the Day of Atonement. On that day the priests will go before the LORD and perform the ceremony that makes you pure.*

29"Anyone who refuses to fast* on this day must be separated from their people. 30If anyone does any work on this day, I will destroy that person from among the people. 31You must not do any work at all. This is a law that continues forever for you, wherever you live. 32It will be a special day of rest for you. You must not eat food. You will start this special day of rest on the evening following the ninth day of the month.b This special day of rest continues from that evening until the next evening."

Festival of Shelters

33Again the LORD said to Moses, 34"Tell the Israelites: On the 15th day of the seventh month is the Festival of Shelters.* This festival to the LORD will continue for seven days. 35There will be a holy* meeting on the first day. You must not do any work. 36You will bring offerings as gifts to the LORD for seven days. On the eighth day you will have another holy meeting. You must not do any work. You will bring an offering as a gift to the LORD.

37"These are the LORD's special festivals. There will be holy meetings during these festivals. You will bring offerings as gifts to the LORD—burnt offerings, grain offerings, sacrifices,* and drink offerings. You will bring these gifts at the right time. 38You will celebrate these festivals in addition to remembering the LORD's Sabbath* days. You will offer these gifts in addition to your other gifts to the LORD. You will offer these things in addition to any offerings you give as payment for your special promises. They will be in addition to any special offerings you want to give to the LORD.

39"On the 15th day of the seventh month, when you have gathered in the crops of the land, you will celebrate the LORD's festival for seven days. The first day will be a special day of rest, and then the eighth day will also be a special day of rest. 40On the first day you will take good fruit from fruit trees. And you will take branches from palm trees, poplar trees, and willow trees by the brook. You will celebrate before the LORD your God for seven days. 41You will celebrate this festival to the LORD for seven days each year. This law will continue forever. You will celebrate this festival in the seventh month. 42You will live in temporary shelters for seven days. All the people born in Israel will live in them. 43Why? So all your descendants will know that I made the Israelites live in temporary shelters during the time I brought them out of Egypt. I am the LORD your God."

44So Moses told the Israelites about all the special meetings to honor the LORD.

The Lampstand and the Holy Bread

24 1The LORD said to Moses, 2"Command the Israelites to bring to you pure oil from crushed olives. That oil is for the lamps that must burn without stopping. 3Aaron will keep the light burning in the Meeting Tent* before the LORD from evening until morning. This light will be outside the curtain that hangs in front of the Box that holds the Agreement.c This law will continue forever. 4Aaron must always keep the lamps burning on the lampstand of pure gold before the LORD.

5"Take fine flour and bake twelve loaves with it. Use 16 cupsd of flour for each loaf. 6Put them in two rows on the golden table before the LORD. Six loaves will be in each row. 7Put pure frankincense* on each row. This will help the LORD remember the gift.

---

a23:27 You must not eat food Literally, "You must humble yourselves." Also in verse 32.
b23:32 evening following ... month A day starts at sunset.

c24:3 Box that holds the Agreement Literally, "Testimony." See "Agreement" in the Word List.
d24:5 16 cups Literally, "2/10 of an ephah" (4.4 l).

[8]Every Sabbath* day Aaron will put the bread in order before the LORD. This must be done forever. This agreement with the Israelites will continue forever. [9]That bread will belong to Aaron and his sons. They will eat the bread in a holy* place, because that bread is one of the special gifts to the LORD. It is Aaron's share forever."

The Man Who Cursed God

[10]There was a son of an Israelite woman and an Egyptian father. He was walking among the Israelites, and he started fighting in camp. [11]The Israelite woman's son began cursing* and saying bad things about the LORD's name, so the people brought him to Moses. (The name of the man's mother was Shelomith, the daughter of Dibri, from the tribe of Dan.) [12]The people held him as a prisoner and waited for the LORD's command to be made clear to them.

[13]Then the LORD said to Moses, [14]"Bring the man who cursed to a place outside the camp. Then bring together everyone who heard him curse. They will put their hands on his head.[a] And then all the people must throw stones at him and kill him. [15]You must tell the Israelites: Anyone who curses their God must be punished. [16]Anyone who speaks against the name of the LORD must be put to death. All the people must stone him. Foreigners must be punished just as the person who was born in Israel. Anyone who curses the LORD's name must be put to death.

[17]"And whoever kills another person must be put to death. [18]Whoever kills an animal that belongs to another person must give another animal to take its place.[b]

[19]"And whoever causes an injury to their neighbor must be given the same kind of injury: [20]a broken bone for a broken bone, an eye for an eye, and a tooth for a tooth. The same kind of injury a person gives another person must be given that person. [21]Whoever kills an animal must pay for the animal. But whoever kills another person must be put to death.

[22]"The law will be the same for foreigners and for people from your own country. This is because I am the LORD your God."

[23]Then Moses spoke to the Israelites, and they took the man who cursed to a place outside the camp. Then they killed him with stones. So the Israelites did just what the LORD had commanded Moses.

A Time of Rest for the Land

25 [1]The LORD spoke to Moses at Mount Sinai. He said, [2]"Tell the Israelites: When you enter the land that I am giving to you, you must let the land have a special time of rest. This will be a special time of rest to honor the LORD. [3]You will plant seed in your field for six years. You will trim your vineyards* for six years and bring in its fruits. [4]But during the seventh year, you will let the land rest. This will be a special time of rest to honor the LORD. You must not plant seed in your field or trim your vineyards. [5]You must not cut the crops that grow by themselves after your harvest. You must not gather the grapes from your vines that are not trimmed. The land will have a year of rest.

[6]"The land will have a year of rest, but you will still have enough food. There will be enough food for your men and women servants. There will be food for your hired workers and for the foreigners living in your country. [7]And there will be enough food for your cattle and other animals to eat.

Jubilee—the Year of Release

[8]"You will also count seven groups of seven years. This will be 49 years. During that time there will be seven years of rest for the land. [9]On the Day of Atonement,* you must blow a ram's horn. That will be on the tenth day of the seventh month. You must blow the ram's horn through the whole country. [10]You will make the 50th year a special year. You will announce freedom for everyone living in your country. This time will be called 'Jubilee.'* Each of you will go back to your own property.[c] And each of you will go back to your own family. [11]The 50th year will be a special celebration[d] for you. Don't plant seeds, don't harvest the crops that grow by themselves, and don't gather grapes from the vines that are not trimmed. [12]That year is Jubilee. It will be a holy* time for you. You will eat the crops that come from the field. [13]In the year of Jubilee, you will go back to your own property.

[14]"Don't cheat your neighbors when you sell your land to them. Don't cheat one another when you buy or sell land. [15]If you want to buy your neighbor's land, count the number of years since the last Jubilee, and use that number to decide the right price. You are only buying the rights for harvesting crops ⌊until the next Jubilee⌋. [16]If there are many years ⌊before the next Jubilee⌋, the price will be high. If the years are few, the price will be lower. So your neighbor is really only selling a number of crops to you. ⌊At the next Jubilee the land will again belong to that family.⌋ [17]You must not cheat each other. You must honor your God. I am the LORD your God.

[18]"Remember my laws and rules. Obey them and you will live safely in your country. [19]And the land will produce good crops for

[a]**24:14** *put their hands on his head* To show that all these people were sharing in punishing the man.
[b]**24:18** *give … its place* Literally, "pay for it, life for life."
[c]**25:10** *own property* In Israel, the land belonged to the family or tribe. A person might sell his land, but at Jubilee that land again belonged to the family and tribe that it was originally given to.
[d]**25:11** *special celebration* Literally, "Jubilee." See "Jubilee" in the Word List.

you. Then you will have plenty of food, and you will live safely on the land.

²⁰"But maybe you will say, 'If we don't plant seeds or gather our crops, we will not have anything to eat during the seventh year.' ²¹I will order my blessing to come to you during the sixth year. The land will continue growing crops for three years. ²²When you plant in the eighth year, you will still be eating from the old crop. You will eat the old crop until the ninth year, when the crop ₍you planted in the eighth year₎ comes in.

Property Laws

²³"The land really belongs to me, so you cannot sell it permanently. You are only foreigners and travelers living on my land with me. ²⁴People might sell their land, but the family will always get their land back. ²⁵If someone in your country becomes very poor and must sell their property, a close relative must come and buy it back. ²⁶If there is not a close relative to buy back the land, the person might get enough money to buy it back. ²⁷Then the years must be counted since the land was sold. That number must be used to decide how much to pay for the land. The person must then buy back the land, and it will be their property again. ²⁸But if this first owner cannot find enough money to buy the land back, it will stay in the hands of the one who bought it until the year of Jubilee.* Then during that special celebration, the land will go back ₍to the first owner's family₎. So the property will again belong to the right family.

²⁹"Anyone who sells a home in a walled city still has the right to get it back until a full year after it was sold. Their right to get the house back will continue one year. ³⁰But if the owner does not buy back the house before a full year is finished, the house that is in the walled city will belong to the one who bought it and to their descendants. The house will not go back to the first owner at the time of Jubilee. ³¹Towns without walls around them will be treated like open fields. So houses built in these small towns will go back to the first owners at the time of Jubilee.

³²"But about the cities of the Levites: The Levites can buy back at any time their houses in the cities that belong to them. ³³If someone buys a house from a Levite, that house in the Levites' city will again belong to the Levites at the time of Jubilee. This is because houses in Levite cities belong to those from the tribe of Levi. The Israelites gave these cities to the Levites. ³⁴Also, the fields and pastures around the Levite cities cannot be sold. They belong to the Levites forever.

Rules for Slave Owners

³⁵"If anyone from your own country becomes too poor to support themselves, you must let them live with you like a visitor. ³⁶Don't charge them any interest on money

you might loan to them. Respect your God and let those from your own country live with you. ³⁷Don't charge them interest on any money you lend them. And don't try to make a profit from the food you sell them. ³⁸I am the LORD your God. I brought you out of the land of Egypt to give the land of Canaan* to you and to become your God.

³⁹"If anyone from your own country becomes so poor that they must sell themselves to you, don't make them work like slaves. ⁴⁰They will be like hired workers and visitors with you until the year of Jubilee.* ⁴¹Then they can leave you, take their children, and go back to their family. They can go back to the property of their ancestors,* ⁴²because they are my servants. I brought them out of slavery in Egypt. They must not become slaves again. ⁴³You must not be a cruel master to them. You must respect your God.

⁴⁴"About your men and women slaves: You may get men and women slaves from the other nations around you. ⁴⁵Also, you may get children as slaves if they come from the families of the foreigners living in your land. These child slaves will belong to you. ⁴⁶You may even pass these foreign slaves on to your children after you die so that they will belong to them. They will be your slaves forever. You may make slaves of these foreigners. But you must not be a cruel master over your own brothers, the Israelites.

⁴⁷"Maybe a foreigner or visitor among you becomes rich. Or maybe someone from your own country becomes so poor that they sell themselves as slaves to a foreigner living among you or to a member of a foreigner's family. ⁴⁸These people have the right to be bought back and become free. Someone from their own country can buy them back. ⁴⁹Or their uncle, their cousin, or one of their close relatives from their family can buy him back. Or if they get enough money, they can pay the money themselves and become free again.

⁵⁰"You must count the years from the time they sold themselves to the foreigner up to the next year of Jubilee. Use that number to decide the price, because really the person only 'hired' them for a few years. ⁵¹If there are still many years before the year of Jubilee, the one sold must give back a large part of the price. It all depends on the number of years. ⁵²If only a few years are left until the year of Jubilee, the one who was sold must pay a small part of the original price. ⁵³But that person will live like a hired worker with the foreigner every year. Don't let the foreigner be a cruel master over that person.

⁵⁴"Those who sold themselves will become free, even if no one buys them back. At the year of Jubilee they and their children will become free. ⁵⁵This is because the Israelites are my servants. They are the servants who I brought out of slavery in Egypt. I am the LORD your God!

Rewards for Obeying God

26 ¹"Don't make idols for yourselves. Don't set up statues or memorial stones* in your land to bow down to, because I am the Lord your God!

²"Remember my special days of rest*ᵃ* and honor my holy* place. I am the Lord.

³"Remember my laws and commands, and obey them. ⁴If you do these things, I will give you rains at the time they should come. The land will grow crops and the trees of the field will grow their fruit. ⁵Your threshing* will continue until it is time to gather grapes. And your grape gathering will continue until it is time to plant. Then you will have plenty to eat. And you will live safely in your land. ⁶I will give peace to your country. You will lie down in peace. No one will come to make you afraid. I will keep harmful animals out of your country. And armies will not come through your country.

⁷"You will chase your enemies and defeat them. You will kill them with your sword. ⁸Five of you will chase 100 men, and 100 of you will chase 10,000 men. You will defeat your enemies and kill them with your sword.

⁹"Then I will turn to you. I will let you have many children. I will keep my agreement* with you. ¹⁰You will have enough crops to last for more than a year. You will harvest the new crops. But then you will have to throw out the old crops to make room for the new crops. ¹¹Also, I will place my Holy Tent* among you. I will not turn away from you. ¹²I will walk with you and be your God. And you will be my people. ¹³I am the Lord your God. You were slaves in Egypt, but I brought you out of Egypt. You were bent low from the heavy weights you carried as slaves, but I broke the poles that were on your shoulders. I let you walk proudly again.

Punishment for Not Obeying God

¹⁴"But if you don't obey me and all my commands, bad things will happen to you. ¹⁵If you refuse to obey my laws and commands, you have broken my agreement.* ¹⁶If you do that, I will cause terrible things to happen to you. I will cause you to have disease and fever. They will destroy your eyes and take away your life. You will not have success when you plant your seed. And your enemies will eat your crops. ¹⁷I will be against you, so your enemies will defeat you. These enemies will hate you and rule over you. You will run away even when no one is chasing you.

¹⁸"After these things, if you still don't obey me, I will punish you seven times more for your sins. ¹⁹And I will also destroy the great cities that make you proud. The skies will not give rain, and the earth will not produce crops.*ᵇ* ²⁰You will work hard, but it will not help. Your land will not give any crops, and your trees will not grow their fruit.

²¹"If you still turn against me and refuse to obey me, I will beat you seven times harder! The more you sin, the more you will be punished. ²²I will send wild animals against you. They will take your children away from you. They will destroy your animals. They will kill many of your people. The roads will all be empty.

²³"If you don't learn your lesson after all this, and if you still turn against me, ²⁴then I will also turn against you. I—yes, I myself—will punish you seven times for your sins. ²⁵You will have broken my agreement, so I will punish you. I will bring armies against you. You will go into your cities for safety, but I will cause diseases to spread among you. And your enemies will defeat you. ²⁶I will give you a share of the grain left in that city. But there will be very little food to eat. Ten women will be able to cook all their bread in one oven. They will measure each piece of bread. You will eat, but you will still be hungry.

²⁷"If you still refuse to listen to me, and if you still turn against me, ²⁸then I will really show my anger! I—yes, I myself—will punish you seven times for your sins. ²⁹₍You will become so hungry that₎ you will eat the bodies of your sons and daughters. ³⁰I will destroy your high places.* I will cut down your incense* altars.* I will put your dead bodies on the dead bodies of your idols.* You will be disgusting to me. ³¹I will destroy your cities. I will make your holy* places empty. I will stop smelling your offerings. ³²I will make your land empty. And your enemies who come to live there will be shocked at it. ³³I will scatter you among the nations. I will pull out my sword and destroy you. Your land will become empty, and your cities will be destroyed.

³⁴"You will be taken to your enemy's country. Your country will be empty. So your land will finally get its rest. The land will enjoy its time of rest. ³⁵During the time that the land is empty, it will get the time of rest that you did not give it while you lived there. ³⁶The survivors* will lose their courage in the land of their enemies. They will be afraid of everything. They will run around like a leaf blown by the wind. They will run as if someone is chasing them with a sword. They will fall even when no one is chasing them. ³⁷They will run as if someone is chasing them with a sword. They will fall over each other—even when no one is chasing them.

"You will not be strong enough to stand up against your enemies. ³⁸You will be lost in other nations. You will disappear in the land

---

*ᵃ***26:2** *special days of rest* Or "Sabbaths." This might mean Saturday, or it might mean all the special days when the people were not supposed to work.

*ᵇ***26:19** *The skies ... crops* Literally, "Your skies will be like iron, your land like bronze."

of your enemies. ³⁹So the survivors will rot away in their sin in their enemies' countries. They will rot away in their sins just as their ancestors* did.

There Is Always Hope

⁴⁰"But maybe the people will confess their sins. And maybe they will confess the sins of their ancestors.* Maybe they will admit that they turned against me. Maybe they will admit that they sinned against me. ⁴¹Maybe they will admit that I turned against them and brought them into the land of their enemies. These people will be like strangers to me. But maybe they will become humble*ᵃ* and accept the punishment for their sin. ⁴²If they do, I will remember my agreement* with Jacob. I will remember my agreement with Isaac. I will remember my agreement with Abraham, and I will remember the land.

⁴³"The land will be empty. The land will enjoy its time of rest. Then the survivors will accept the punishment for their sins. They will learn that they were punished because they hated my laws and refused to obey my rules. ⁴⁴They have sinned. ₁But if they come to me for help,₁ I will not turn away from them. I will listen to them, even if they are in the land of their enemies. I will not completely destroy them. I will not break my agreement with them, because I am the Lord their God. ⁴⁵For them, I will remember the agreement with their ancestors. I brought their ancestors out of the land of Egypt so that I could become their God. The other nations saw these things. I am the Lord."

⁴⁶These are the laws, rules, and teachings that the Lord gave to the Israelites. These laws are the agreement between the Lord and the Israelites. The Lord gave these laws to Moses at Mount Sinai.

Promises Are Important

27 ¹The Lord said to Moses, ²"Tell the Israelites: You might promise to give someone to the Lord as a servant. The priest must set a price for that person. ³The price for a man from 20 to 60 years old is 50 shekels*ᵇ* of silver. (You must use the official measure* for the silver.) ⁴The price for a woman who is 20 to 60 years old is 30 shekels. ⁵The price for a man from 5 to 20 years old is 20 shekels. For a woman the price is 10 shekels. ⁶The price for a boy from one month to five years old is 5 shekels. For a girl, the price is 3 shekels. ⁷The price for a man who is 60 years old or older is 15 shekels. The price for a woman is 10 shekels.

⁸"If anyone is too poor to pay the price, bring that person to the priest. The priest will decide how much money the person can afford to pay.

Gifts to the Lord

⁹"Some animals can be used as sacrifices* to the Lord. If you bring one of these animals, the animal will become holy.* ¹⁰You must not try to put another animal in its place. You must not try to change it for something else. You must not try to change a good animal for a bad animal. You must not change a bad animal for a good animal. If you do try to change animals, both animals will become holy—both animals will belong to the Lord.

¹¹"Some animals cannot be offered as sacrifices to the Lord. If you bring one of these unclean* animals to the Lord, that animal must be brought to the priest. ¹²The priest will decide a price for that animal. It doesn't make any difference if the animal is good or bad. If the priest decides on a price, that is the price for the animal. ¹³If you want to buy back the animal,*ᶜ* then you must add one-fifth to the price.

The Value of a House

¹⁴"If you dedicate* your house as holy* to the Lord, the priest must decide its price. It doesn't make any difference if the house is good or bad. If the priest decides on a price, that is the price for the house. ¹⁵But if you want to get the house back, you must add one-fifth to the price. Then you will get the house back.

Value of Property

¹⁶"You might dedicate* a field to God. The value of this field will depend on how much seed is needed to plant it. It will be 50 shekels of silver for each homer*ᵈ* of barley seed. ¹⁷If you give your field to God during the year of Jubilee,* then its value will be whatever the priest decides. ¹⁸But if you give your field after the Jubilee, the priest must decide its exact price. He must count the number of years to the next year of Jubilee and use that number to decide the price. ¹⁹If you want to buy the field back, you must add one-fifth to that price. Then you will get the field back. ²⁰If you don't buy the field back and the land is sold to someone else, you cannot get the land back. ²¹If you don't buy the land back by the year of Jubilee, the field will remain holy* to the Lord—it will belong to the priest forever. It will be treated like any other thing that was given completely to the Lord.

²²"If you dedicate a field to the Lord that you had bought, and it is not a part of your

---

*ᵃ***26:41** *These people ... humble* Literally, "If they humble their uncircumcised heart."
*ᵇ***27:3** *shekel* 2/5 of an ounce (11.5 g).

*ᶜ***27:13** *buy back the animal* See Ex. 13:1–16 for the laws about giving to God or "buying back" firstborn children or animals.
*ᵈ***27:16** *homer* A measure equal to about 7 bushels or about 60 gallons (220 l).

family's property,*a* ²³then the priest must count the years to the year of Jubilee and decide the price for the land. Then that land will belong to the LORD. ²⁴At the year of Jubilee, the land will go to the family that originally owned the land.

²⁵"You must use the official measure* in paying these prices. The shekel by that measure weighs 20 gerahs.*b*

Value of Animals

²⁶"You can give cattle and sheep as special gifts to the LORD. But if the animal is the firstborn, it already belongs to the LORD. So you cannot give these animals as special gifts. ²⁷If the firstborn animal is an unclean* animal, you must buy back that animal. The priest will decide the price of the animal, and you must add one-fifth to that price. If you don't buy that animal back, the priest will sell the animal for whatever price he decides.

Special Gifts

²⁸"There is a special kind of gift*c* that people give to the LORD. It belongs only to him, and it cannot be bought back or sold. This gift belongs to the LORD. This type of gift includes people, animals, and fields from the family property. ²⁹If this gift is a person, that person cannot be bought back. That person must be killed.

³⁰"A tenth of all crops belongs to the LORD. This means the crops from fields and the fruit from trees—a tenth belongs to the LORD. ³¹So if you want to get back your tenth, you must add one-fifth to its price and then buy it back.

³²"The priests will take every tenth animal from a person's cattle or sheep. Every tenth animal will belong to the LORD. ³³The owner should not worry if the chosen animal is good or bad or change the animal for another animal. If this happens, both animals will belong to the LORD. That animal cannot be bought back."

³⁴These are the commands that the LORD gave Moses at Mount Sinai for the Israelites.

---

*a***27:22** *family's property* In ancient Israel, land was given by God to the family, not the individual. Usually it could not be sold, only leased for up to 50 years.
*b***27:25** *gerahs* 1/50 of an ounce (.6 g).

*c***27:28** *special kind of gift* This usually means things taken in war. These things (gifts) belonged only to the Lord, so they could not be used for anything else.

Numbers

Moses Counts the Israelites

1 ¹The LORD spoke to Moses in the Meeting Tent.* This was in the Sinai Desert. It was on the first day of the second month of the second year after the Israelites left Egypt. He said to Moses, ²"Count all the Israelites. List the name of each man with his family and his family group. ³You and Aaron must count the men of Israel who are 20 years old or older. (These are all the men who are able to serve in the army of Israel.) List them by their divisions. ⁴One man from each tribe will help you. This man will be the leader of his tribe. ⁵These are the names of the men who will stand with you and help you:

from the tribe of Reuben—Elizur son of Shedeur;
⁶ from the tribe of Simeon—Shelumiel son of Zurishaddai;
⁷ from the tribe of Judah—Nahshon son of Amminadab;
⁸ from the tribe of Issachar—Nethanel son of Zuar;
⁹ from the tribe of Zebulun—Eliab son of Helon;

¹⁰ from the descendants of Joseph:
from the tribe of Ephraim—Elishama son of Ammihud;
from the tribe of Manasseh—Gamaliel son of Pedahzur;
¹¹ from the tribe of Benjamin—Abidan son of Gideoni;
¹² from the tribe of Dan—Ahiezer son of Ammishaddai;
¹³ from the tribe of Asher—Pagiel son of Ocran;
¹⁴ from the tribe of Gad—Eliasaph son of Deuel*d*;
¹⁵ from the tribe of Naphtali—Ahira son of Enan."

¹⁶All these men were the leaders of their families. The people also chose them to be leaders of their tribes. ¹⁷Moses and Aaron took the men who had been chosen to be leaders ¹⁸and called all the Israelites together on the first day of the second month. Then the people were listed by their families and

---

*d***1:14** *Deuel* Or "Reuel."

their family groups. All the men who were 20 years old or older were listed. [19]Moses did exactly what the Lord commanded—he counted the people while they were in the Sinai desert.

[20]The tribe of Reuben was counted. (Reuben was the firstborn* son of Israel.) The names of all the men who were 20 years old or older and able to serve in the army were listed. They were listed with their families and family groups. [21]The total number of men counted from the tribe of Reuben was 46,500.

[22]The tribe of Simeon was counted. The names of all the men who were 20 years old or older and able to serve in the army were listed. They were listed with their families and family groups. [23]The total number of men counted from the tribe of Simeon was 59,300.

[24]The tribe of Gad was counted. The names of all the men who were 20 years old or older and able to serve in the army were listed. They were listed with their families and family groups. [25]The total number of men counted from the tribe of Gad was 45,650.

[26]The tribe of Judah was counted. The names of all the men who were 20 years old or older and able to serve in the army were listed. They were listed with their families and family groups. [27]The total number of men counted from the tribe of Judah was 74,600.

[28]The tribe of Issachar was counted. The names of all the men who were 20 years old or older and able to serve in the army were listed. They were listed with their families and family groups. [29]The total number of men counted from the tribe of Issachar was 54,400.

[30]The tribe of Zebulun was counted. The names of all the men who were 20 years old or older and able to serve in the army were listed. They were listed with their families and family groups. [31]The total number of men counted from the tribe of Zebulun was 57,400.

[32]The tribe of Ephraim was counted. (Ephraim was Joseph's son.) The names of all the men who were 20 years old or older and able to serve in the army were listed. They were listed with their families and family groups. [33]The total number of men counted from the tribe of Ephraim was 40,500.

[34]The tribe of Manasseh was counted. (Manasseh was also Joseph's son.) The names of all the men who were 20 years old or older and able to serve in the army were listed. They were listed with their families and family groups. [35]The total number of men counted from the tribe of Manasseh was 32,200.

[36]The tribe of Benjamin was counted. The names of all the men who were 20 years old or older and able to serve in the army were listed. They were listed with their families and family groups. [37]The total number of

men counted from the tribe of Benjamin was 35,400.

[38]The tribe of Dan was counted. The names of all the men who were 20 years old or older and able to serve in the army were listed. They were listed with their families and family groups. [39]The total number of men counted from the tribe of Dan was 62,700.

[40]The tribe of Asher was counted. The names of all the men who were 20 years old or older and able to serve in the army were listed. They were listed with their families and family groups. [41]The total number of men counted from the tribe of Asher was 41,500.

[42]The tribe of Naphtali was counted. The names of all the men who were 20 years old or older and able to serve in the army were listed. They were listed by name with their families and family groups. [43]The total number of men counted from the tribe of Naphtali was 53,400.

[44]Moses, Aaron, and the twelve leaders of Israel counted these men. (There was one leader from each tribe.) [45]They counted every man who was 20 years old or older and able to serve in the army. Each man was listed with his family. [46]The total number of men counted was 603,550 men.

[47]The families from the tribe of Levi were not counted with the other Israelites. [48]The Lord had told Moses: [49]"Don't count the men from the tribe of Levi or include them with the other Israelites. [50]Tell the Levites that they are responsible for the Tent of the Agreement.* They must take care of that tent and everything that is with it. They must carry the Holy Tent and everything in it. They must make their camp around it and take care of it. [51]Whenever the Holy Tent is moved, the Levites must do it. Whenever the Holy Tent is set up, the Levites must do it. They are the men who will take care of the Holy Tent. Anyone else who tries to take care of the tent must be killed. [52]The Israelites will make their camps in separate divisions. Everyone must camp near their family flag. [53]The Levites will set up their tents so that they surround the Tent of the Agreement. Then they will serve as guards to keep people from doing anything to the Tent that will make the Lord angry. This will protect their people."

[54]The Lord had given these commandments to Moses. So the Israelites did everything he commanded.

The Camp Arrangement

2 [1]The Lord said to Moses and Aaron: [2]"The Israelites should make their camps around the Meeting Tent.* Each division will have its own special flag, and everyone will camp near their group's flag.

[3]"The flag of the camp of Judah will be on the east side, where the sun rises. The people of Judah will camp near its flag. The leader of the people of Judah is Nahshon son of

Amminadab. [4]There are 74,600 men in his division.

[5]"The tribe of Issachar will camp next to the tribe of Judah. The leader of the tribe of Issachar is Nethanel son of Zuar. [6]There are 54,400 men in his division.

[7]"The tribe of Zebulun will also camp next to the tribe of Judah. The leader of the tribe of Zebulun is Eliab son of Helon. [8]There are 57,400 men in his division.

[9]"There is a total of 186,400 men in Judah's camp. All these men are divided into their different tribes. Judah will be the first group to move when the people travel from one place to another.

[10]"The flag of Reuben's camp will be south of the Holy Tent.* Each group will camp near its flag. The leader of the tribe of Reuben is Elizur son of Shedeur. [11]There are 46,500 men in this division.

[12]"The tribe of Simeon will camp next to the tribe of Reuben. The leader of the tribe of Simeon is Shelumiel son of Zurishaddai. [13]There are 59,300 men in this division.

[14]"The tribe of Gad will also camp next to the tribe of Reuben. The leader of the tribe of Gad is Eliasaph son of Deuel.[a] [15]There are 45,650 men in this division.

[16]"There is a total of 151,450 men in all the divisions in Reuben's camp. His camp will be the second group to move when the people travel from place to place.

[17]"When the people travel, Levi's camp will move next. The Meeting Tent will be with them between the other camps. The people will make their camps in the same order that they move.

[18]"The flag of the camp of Ephraim will be on the west side. The division of Ephraim will camp there. The leader of the tribe of Ephraim is Elishama son of Ammihud. [19]There are 40,500 men in this division.

[20]"The tribe of Manasseh will camp next to Ephraim's family. The leader of the tribe of Manasseh is Gamaliel son of Pedahzur. [21]There are 32,200 men in this division.

[22]"The tribe of Benjamin will also camp next to Ephraim's family. The leader of the tribe of Benjamin is Abidan son of Gideoni. [23]There are 35,400 men in this division.

[24]"There is a total of 108,100 men in Ephraim's camp. They will be the third family to move when the people travel from one place to another.

[25]"The flag of Dan's camp will be on the north side. The tribes of Dan will camp there. The leader of the tribe of Dan is Ahiezer son of Ammishaddai. [26]There are 62,700 men in this division.

[27]"The people from the tribe of Asher will camp next to the tribe of Dan. The leader of the tribe of Asher is Pagiel son of Ocran. [28]There are 41,500 men in this division.

[29]"The tribe of Naphtali will also camp next to the tribe of Dan. The leader of the tribe of Naphtali is Ahira son of Enan. [30]There are 53,400 men in this division.

[31]"There are 157,600 men in Dan's camp. They will be the last to move when the people travel from place to place. Each group will have its own flag."

[32]So these were the Israelites. They were counted by families. The total number of Israelite men in the camps, counted by divisions, is 603,550. [33]Moses obeyed the LORD and did not count the Levites with the other Israelites.

[34]So the Israelites did everything the LORD told Moses. Each group camped under its own flag. And everyone stayed with their own family and family group.

Aaron's Family, the Priests

3 [1]This is the family history of Aaron and Moses at the time the LORD talked to Moses on Mount Sinai.

[2]Aaron had four sons. Nadab was the first-born* son. Then there were Abihu, Eleazar, and Ithamar. [3]These sons were the chosen[b] priests. They were given the special work of serving the LORD as priests. [4]But Nadab and Abihu died while serving the LORD. They used fire that the LORD did not allow when they made an offering to him. So Nadab and Abihu died there, in the Sinai desert. They had no sons, so Eleazar and Ithamar took their place and served the Lord as priests. This happened while their father Aaron was still alive.

Levites—the Priests' Helpers

[5]The LORD said to Moses, [6]"Bring all the men from the tribe of Levi. Bring them to Aaron the priest. These men will be his helpers. [7]The Levites will help him when he serves at the Meeting Tent.* And they will help all the Israelites when they come to worship at the Holy Tent.* [8]The Israelites should protect everything in the Meeting Tent; it is their duty. But the Levites will serve the Israelites by caring for these things. This will be their way of serving at the Holy Tent.

[9]"Give the Levites to Aaron and his sons. The Levites were chosen from all the Israelites to help Aaron and his sons.

[10]"Appoint Aaron and his sons to be priests. They must do their duty and serve as priests. Anyone else who tries to come near the holy things[c] must be killed."

[11]The LORD also said to Moses, [12-13]"I destroyed all the firstborn* in Egypt. At that time I chose all the firstborn from every family in Israel to be mine in a special way. That included all the firstborn men and animals.

[a]2:14 *Deuel* Or "Reuel."

[b]3:3 *chosen* Or "anointed." See "anoint" in the Word List.

[c]3:10 *tries ... holy things* Or "tries to serve as a priest."

But now I am choosing the Levites to take their place. Now they will be my special servants. I, the LORD, give this command!"

[14]The LORD again said to Moses in the Sinai desert, [15]"Count all the families and family groups in the tribe of Levi. Count every man or boy who is one month old or older." [16]So Moses obeyed the LORD. He counted them all.

[17]Levi had three sons. Their names were Gershon, Kohath, and Merari. [18]Each son was the leader of several family groups.

The Gershon family groups were Libni and Shimei.

[19]The Kohath family groups were Amram, Izhar, Hebron, and Uzziel.

[20]The Merari family groups were Mahli and Mushi.

These are the families that belonged to Levi's family group.

[21]The families of Libni and Shimei belonged to the family of Gershon. They were the Gershonite family groups. [22]There were 7500 men and boys over one month old in these two family groups. [23]The Gershonite family groups were told to camp in the west. They made their camp behind the Holy Tent. [24]The leader of the family groups of the Gershonites was Eliasaph son of Lael. [25]In the Meeting Tent, the Gershonites had the job of taking care of the Holy Tent, the outer tent, and the covering. They also took care of the curtain at the entrance of the Meeting Tent. [26]They cared for the curtain in the courtyard. And they cared for the curtain at the entrance of the courtyard. This courtyard was around the Holy Tent and the altar.* And they cared for the ropes and for everything that was used with the curtains.

[27]The families of Amram, Izhar, Hebron, and Uzziel belonged to the family of Kohath. They were the Kohathite family groups. [28]In this family group there were 8300[a] men and boys a month old or over. The Kohathites were given the job of taking care of the things in the Holy Place.* [29]The Kohathite family groups were given the area to the south of the Holy Tent. This was the area where they camped. [30]The leader of the Kohathite family groups was Elizaphan son of Uzziel. [31]Their job was to take care of the Holy Box,* the table, the lampstand, the altars, and the dishes of the Holy Place. They also cared for the curtain and all the things that were used with the curtain.

[32]The leader over the leaders of the Levites was Eleazar son of Aaron the priest. Eleazar was in charge of everyone who took care of the holy* things.

[33-34]The family groups of Mahli and Mushi belonged to the Merari family. There were

6200 men and boys who were one month old or older in the Mahli family group. [35]The leader of the Merari family group was Zuriel son of Abihail. This family group was given the area to the north of the Holy Tent. This is the area where they camped. [36]The people from the Merari family were given the job of caring for the frames of the Holy Tent. They cared for all the braces, posts, bases, and everything that was used with the frames of the Holy Tent. [37]They also cared for all the posts in the courtyard around the Holy Tent. This included all the bases, tent pegs, and ropes.

[38]Moses, Aaron, and his sons camped east of the Holy Tent, in front of the Meeting Tent. They were given the work of caring for the Holy Place. They did this for all the Israelites. Anyone else who came near the Holy Place was to be killed.

[39]The LORD commanded Moses and Aaron to count all the men and boys one month old or older in Levi's family group. The total number was 22,000.

Levites Take the Place of the Firstborn

[40]The LORD said to Moses, "Count all the firstborn* men and boys in Israel who are at least one month old. Write their names on a list. [41]I will take the Levites instead of all the firstborn men and boys of Israel. I will also take the animals from the Levites instead of taking all the firstborn animals from the other people in Israel."

[42]So Moses did what the LORD commanded. He counted all the firstborn children of the Israelites. [43]He listed all the firstborn men and boys who were one month old or older. There were 22,273 names on that list.

[44]The LORD also said to Moses, [45]"I, the LORD, give this command: 'Take the Levites instead of all the firstborn men from the other families of Israel. And I will take the animals of the Levites instead of the animals of the other people. The Levites are mine. [46]There are 22,000 Levites, but there are 22,273 firstborn sons from the other families. This leaves 273 more firstborn sons than Levites. [47]Using the official measure,* collect five shekels[b] of silver for each of the 273 people. (The shekel by the official measure weighs 20 gerahs.[c]) Collect that silver from the Israelites. [48]Give the silver to Aaron and his sons as payment for the 273 Israelites.'"

[49]There were not enough Levites to take the place of all the men from the other family groups, so Moses gathered the money for them. [50]Moses collected the silver from the firstborn men of the Israelites. He collected 1365 shekels[d] of silver, using the official measure. [51]Moses obeyed the LORD's

---

[a]3:28 8300 Some copies of the ancient Greek version have "8300." The Hebrew copies have "8600." See Num. 3:22, 28, 34, 39.

[b]3:47 five shekels 2 ounces (57.5 g).

[c]3:47 gerahs 1/50 of an ounce (.6 g).

[d]3:50 1365 shekels 35 pounds (15.7 kg).

command and gave the silver to Aaron and his sons.

The Jobs of the Kohath Family

4 ¹The LORD said to Moses and Aaron, ²"Count the men in the families of the Kohath family group. (The Kohath family group is a part of Levi's family group.) ³Count all the men from 30 to 50 years old who come to serve. These men will work in the Meeting Tent.* ⁴Their job is to take care of the most holy* things in the Meeting Tent.

⁵"When the Israelites travel to a new place, Aaron and his sons must go into the Meeting Tent and take down the curtain and cover the Box of the Agreement* with it. ⁶Then they must cover all of this with covering made from fine leather. Then they must spread the solid blue cloth over the leather and put the poles in the rings on the Holy Box.

⁷"Then they must spread a blue cloth over the holy table. Then they must put the plates, spoons, bowls, and the jars for drink offerings on the table. Put the special bread on the table. ⁸Then you must put a red cloth over all these things, cover everything with fine leather, and put the poles in the rings of the table.

⁹"Then they must cover the lampstand and its lamps with a blue cloth. They must also cover all the things used to keep the lamps burning and all the jars of oil that are used in the lamps. ¹⁰Then wrap everything in fine leather. Then they must put all these things on poles used for carrying them.

¹¹"They must spread a blue cloth over the golden altar.* They must cover that with fine leather. Then they must put the poles for carrying it in the rings on the altar.

¹²"Then they must gather together all the special things that are used for worship in the Holy Place.* They must gather them together and wrap them in a blue cloth. Then they must cover that with fine leather. They must put these things on a frame for carrying them.

¹³"They must clean the ashes out of the bronze altar and spread a purple cloth over it. ¹⁴Then they must gather together all the things that are used for worship at the altar. These are the firepans, forks, shovels, and the bowls. They must put these things on the bronze altar. Then they must spread a covering of fine leather over the altar and put the poles for carrying it in the rings on the altar.

¹⁵"Aaron and his sons must finish covering all the holy things in the Holy Place. Then the men from the Kohath family can go in and begin carrying these things. In this way they will not touch the holy things and die.

¹⁶"Eleazar son of Aaron the priest will be responsible for the Holy Tent.* He will be responsible for everything in it, including the holy things. He will be responsible for the oil for the lamp, the sweet-smelling incense,* the daily offering,ᵃ and the anointing* oil."

¹⁷The LORD said to Moses and Aaron, ¹⁸"Be careful! Don't let these Kohathite men be destroyed. ¹⁹You must do these things so that the Kohathite men can go near the most holy things and not die. Aaron and his sons must go in and show each Kohathite man what to do and what to carry. ²⁰If you don't do this, the Kohathite men might go in and look at the holy things. If they look at these things, even for a moment, they must die."

The Jobs of the Gershon Family

²¹The LORD said to Moses, ²²"Count all the people of the Gershon family. List them by family and family group. ²³Count all the men who are from 30 to 50 years old who come to serve. These men will have the job of caring for the Meeting Tent.*

²⁴"This is what the Gershonite family must do and the things they must carry: ²⁵They must carry the curtains of the Holy Tent,* the Meeting Tent, its covering, and the covering made from fine leather. They must also carry the curtain at the entrance of the Meeting Tent. ²⁶They must carry the curtains of the courtyard that are around the Holy Tent and the altar.* And they must carry the curtain for the entrance of the courtyard. They must also carry all the ropes and all the things that are used with the curtains. The Gershonite men will be responsible for anything that needs to be done with these things. ²⁷Aaron and his sons will watch all the work that is done. Everything the Gershonites carry and the other work they do will be watched by Aaron and his sons. You must tell them what they are responsible for carrying. ²⁸This is the work that the men of the Gershonite family group must do for the Meeting Tent. Ithamar son of Aaron the priest will be responsible for their work."

The Jobs of the Merari Family

²⁹"Count all the men in the families and family groups in the Merari family group. ³⁰Count all the men who are from 30 to 50 years old and come to serve. These men will do a special work for the Meeting Tent.* ³¹When you travel, it is their job to carry the frames of the Meeting Tent. They must carry the braces, the posts, and the bases. ³²They must also carry the posts that are around the courtyard. They must carry the bases, the tent pegs, the ropes, and everything that is used for the poles around the courtyard. List the names and tell each man exactly what he must carry. ³³This is what the people from the Merari family will do to serve in the work for the Meeting Tent. Ithamar son of Aaron the priest will be responsible for their work."

ᵃ4:16 daily offering Offerings that were made twice each day as a gift to God.

The Levite Families

³⁴Moses, Aaron, and the leaders of the Israelites counted the Kohathites. They counted them by families and family groups. ³⁵They counted all the men from 30 to 50 years old who were able to serve. These men were given special work to do for the Meeting Tent.*

³⁶There were 2750 men in the Kohath family group who were qualified to do this work. ³⁷So these men from the Kohath family group were given their special work to do for the Meeting Tent. Moses and Aaron did this the way the LORD had told Moses to do.

³⁸Also, the Gershonite family group was counted. ³⁹All the men from 30 to 50 years old who qualified to serve were counted. These men were given their special work to do for the Meeting Tent. ⁴⁰There were 2630 men in the families of the Gershon family group who were qualified. ⁴¹So these men from the Gershon family group were given their special work to do for the Meeting Tent. Moses and Aaron did this the way the LORD had told Moses to do.

⁴²Also, the men in the families and family groups of the Merari family were counted. ⁴³All the men from 30 to 50 years old who qualified to serve were counted. These men were given their special work to do for the Meeting Tent. ⁴⁴There were 3200 men in the families of the Merari family group who were qualified. ⁴⁵So these men from the Merari family group were given their special work. Moses and Aaron did this the way the LORD told Moses to do.

⁴⁶So Moses, Aaron, and the leaders of the Israelites counted all the people in Levi's family group. They had counted each family and each family group. ⁴⁷All the men between the ages of 30 and 50 who qualified to serve were counted. These men were given a special work to do for the Meeting Tent. They did the work of carrying the Meeting Tent when they traveled. ⁴⁸The total number was 8580. ⁴⁹Each man was counted just as the LORD commanded Moses. Each man was given his own work and told what he must carry just as the LORD had said.

Rules About Cleanliness

5 ¹The LORD said to Moses, ²"Tell the people to send away from the camp anyone who is unclean,* that is, anyone who has a serious skin diseaseᵃ or discharge* and anyone who has touched a dead body. ³Whether they are a man or a woman, send them away so that the camp where I am living among you will not be made unclean."

⁴So the Israelites obeyed God's command. They sent those people outside the camp. They did what the LORD had told Moses.

Paying for Doing Wrong

⁵The LORD said to Moses, ⁶"Tell this to the Israelites: You might do something wrong to another person. When you do that, you are really sinning against God. So you are guilty of doing wrong. ⁷You must confess that sin. Then you must fully pay for that wrong thing you did. You must add one-fifth to the payment and give it all to the person you had done wrong to. ⁸But maybe the person is dead and does not have any close relatives to accept the payment. In that case, you will give the payment to the LORD. That is, you will give the full payment to the priest. The priest must sacrifice the ram that makes people pure.* This ram will be sacrificed to cover over your sins, but the priest will keep the rest of the payment.

⁹"If any of you Israelites gives a special gift to God, the priest who accepts that gift can keep it. It is his. ¹⁰You don't have to give these special gifts, but if you do, the gifts belong to the priest."

Jealous Husbands

¹¹Then the LORD said to Moses, ¹²"Tell the Israelites this: A man's wife might be unfaithful to him. ¹³She might have sexual relations with another man and hide this from her husband. And there might not be anyone to tell him that his wife committed this sin. Her husband might never know about the wrong thing she did, and she might not tell her husband about her sin. ¹⁴But the husband might begin to think that his wife sinned against him, whether she has or not. He might become jealous. He might begin to believe that she is not pure and true to him. ¹⁵If that happens, he must take his wife to the priest. The husband must also take an offering of 8 cupsᵇ of barley flour. He must not pour oil or incense* on the barley flour. This barley flour is a grain offering to the LORD that is given because the husband is jealous. This offering will show that he thinks his wife has been unfaithful to him.

¹⁶"The priest will take the woman before the LORD and make her stand there. ¹⁷Then he will take some special water and put it in a clay jar. He will put some dirt from the floor of the Holy Tent* into the water. ¹⁸He will force the woman to stand before the LORD. Then he will loosen her hair and put the grain offering in her hand. This is the barley flour that her husband gave because he was jealous. At the same time, he will hold the clay jar of special water. This is the special water that can bring trouble to the woman.

¹⁹"Then the priest will make the woman promise to tell the truth and say to her: 'If you have not slept with another man, and if you have not sinned against your husband

---

ᵃ5:2 serious skin disease This could be leprosy, or it could be another kind of contagious skin disease.

ᵇ5:15 8 cups Literally, "1/10 of an ephah" (2.2 l).

while you were married to him, then this water that causes trouble will not hurt you. [20]But if you have sinned against your husband—if you had sexual relations with a man who is not your husband—then you are not pure. [21]If that is true, you will have much trouble when you drink this special water. You will not be able to have any children. And if you are pregnant now, your baby will die.[a] Then your people will leave you and say bad things about you.'

"Then the priest must tell the woman to make a special promise to the LORD. She must agree that these bad things will happen to her if she lies. [22]The priest must say, 'You must drink this water that causes trouble. If you have sinned, you will not be able to have children. Any baby you have will die before it is born.' And the woman should say, 'I agree to do as you say.'

[23]"The priest should write these warnings on a scroll.* Then he should wash the words off into the water. [24]Then the woman must drink the water that brings trouble. This water will enter her and, if she is guilty, it will cause her much suffering.

[25]"Then the priest will take the grain offering from her (the offering for jealousy) and raise it before the LORD. Then he will carry it to the altar.* [26]The priest will fill his hands with some of the grain and put it on the altar and let it burn there. After that he will tell the woman to drink the water. [27]If the woman has sinned against her husband, the water will bring her trouble. The water will go into her body and cause her much suffering. Any baby that is in her will die before it is born, and she will never be able to have children. All the people will turn against her.[b] [28]But if the woman has not sinned against her husband and she is pure, the priest will say that she is not guilty. Then she will be normal and able to have children.

[29]"So this is the law about jealousy. This is what you should do when a woman sins against her husband while she is married to him. [30]Or if the man becomes jealous and thinks his wife has sinned against him, this is what the man should do. The priest must tell her to stand before the LORD. Then the priest will do all these things. This is the law. [31]The husband will not be guilty of doing anything wrong, but the woman will suffer if she has sinned."

Nazirites

6 [1]The LORD said to Moses, [2]"Tell the Israelites this: If there are people, men or women, who want to make a vow* dedicating*

themselves completely to the Lord for a time, they will be called Nazirites. [3]During this time, they must not drink any wine or other strong drink. They must not drink vinegar that is made from wine or from other strong drink. They must not drink grape juice or eat grapes or raisins. [4]They must not eat anything that comes from grapes during that special time of separation. They must not even eat the seeds or the skins from grapes.

[5]"They must not cut their hair during that special time of dedication. They must be holy until the time that their dedication is ended. They must let their hair grow long. Their hair is a special part of their promise to God, so they must let their hair grow long until this time is ended.

[6]"If you have taken the Nazirite vow, you must not go near someone who is dying[c] during that special time of dedication. You have given yourself fully to the LORD, [7]so you must not let yourself become unclean like this— even for your own father or mother, brother or sister when they die.[d] This is because you have the hair that you dedicated to God on your head! [8]It is holy because you have given yourself fully to the LORD for the full time of that dedication. [9]So if you are with someone when they suddenly die, you will be unclean and you will have to shave the hair from your head. You must do that on the seventh day of your purification ceremony when you are made clean.* [10]Then on the eighth day, you must bring two doves or two young pigeons and give them to the priest at the entrance of the Meeting Tent.* [11]Then the priest will offer one bird as a sin offering* and the other one as a burnt offering.* The burnt offering will be a payment for the sin of touching a dead body during your special time of dedication. Then you must again promise to give the hair on your head as a gift to God. [12]This means you must again give yourself to the LORD for another time of dedication. You must bring a one-year-old male lamb to offer as a guilt offering. You must start over from the beginning with a new time of dedication because you touched a dead body during your first time of dedication.

[13]"After their time of dedication is ended, Nazirites must go to the entrance of the Meeting Tent [14]and give their offering to the LORD. Their offering must be:

> a one-year-old male lamb that has nothing
>   wrong with it for a burnt offering;
> a one-year-old female lamb that has
>   nothing wrong with it for a sin offering;
> one ram that has nothing wrong with it
>   for a fellowship offering*;

---

[a]**5:21** *You will … die* Literally, "Your loins will fall and your belly will swell."
[b]**5:27** *All … against her* Literally, "She will be like a curse among the people."

[c]**6:6** *someone who is dying* Or "a dead person."
[d]**6:7** *when they die* Or "that have died."

15 a basket of bread made without yeast—bread made with fine flour mixed with oil and wafers* with oil spread on top; and the grain offerings and drink offerings that are a part of these gifts.

16"The priest will give these things to the Lord, and then the priest will make the sin offering and the burnt offering. 17He will give the basket of bread without yeast to the Lord. Then he will kill the ram as a fellowship offering to the Lord. He will give it to the Lord with the grain offering and the drink offering.

18"The Nazirites must go to the entrance of the Meeting Tent. There they must shave off their hair that they grew for the Lord. That hair will be put in the fire that is burning under the sacrifice of the fellowship offering.

19"After the Nazirites have cut off their hair, the priest will give them a boiled shoulder from the ram and a large and a small cake from the basket. Both of these cakes are made without yeast. 20Then the priest will lift these things up to show they were presented before the Lord. These things are holy* and belong to the priest. Also, the breast and the thigh from the ram are lifted before the Lord. These things also belong to the priest. After that the Nazirite can drink wine.

21"These are the rules for someone who decides to make the Nazirite vow. They must give all these gifts to the Lord. But they might be able to give much more to the Lord. If they promise to do more, they must keep their promise. But they must give at least all the things listed in these rules for the Nazirite promise."

The Priests' Blessings

22The Lord said to Moses, 23"Tell Aaron and his sons that this is the way they should bless the Israelites. They should say:

24 May the Lord bless you and keep you.
25 May the Lord smile down on youᵃ
    and show you his kindness.
26 May the Lord answer your prayersᵇ
    and give you peace."

27Then the Lord said, "In that way Aaron and his sons will use my name to give a blessing to the Israelites, and I will bless them."

Dedicating the Holy Tent

7 ¹Moses finished setting up the Holy Tent.* On that day he dedicated* it to the Lord. Moses anointed* the Tent and everything in it. He also anointed the altar* and all the things used with it. This showed that these things

should be used only for worshiping the Lord.

2Then the leaders of Israel gave offerings to the Lord. These men were the heads of their families and leaders of their tribes. These were the same men who were in charge of counting the people. 3These leaders brought gifts to the Lord. They brought six covered wagons and twelve oxen for pulling the wagons. (One ox was given by each leader. Each leader joined with another leader to give one wagon.) The leaders gave these things to the Lord at the Holy Tent.

4The Lord said to Moses, 5"Accept these gifts from the leaders. These gifts can be used in the work of the Meeting Tent.* Give them to the Levites to help them do their work."

6So Moses accepted the wagons and the oxen and gave them to the Levites. 7He gave two wagons and four oxen to the men in Gershon's group. They needed the wagons and the oxen for their work. 8Then Moses gave four wagons and eight oxen to the men in Merari's group. They needed the wagons and oxen for their work. Ithamar son of Aaron the priest was responsible for the work of all these men. 9Moses did not give any oxen or wagons to the men in Kohath's group, because their job was to carry the holy things on their shoulders.

10Moses anointed the altar. That same day the leaders brought their offerings for dedicating the altar. They gave their offerings to the Lord at the altar. 11The Lord told Moses, "Each day one leader must bring his gift for dedicating the altar."

12–83ᶜ Each of the twelve leaders brought these gifts:

Each leader brought one silver plate that weighed 3¼ pounds.ᵈ Each leader brought one silver bowl that weighed 1¾ pounds.ᵉ Both of these gifts were weighed by the official measure.* The bowl and the plate were each filled with fine flour mixed with oil. This was to be used as a grain offering. Each leader also brought a large gold spoon that weighed about 4 ounces.ᶠ The spoon was filled with incense.*

Each leader also brought 1 young bull, 1 ram, and 1 male lamb a year old. These animals were for a burnt offering.* Each leader also brought 1 male goat to be used as a sin offering.* Each leader brought 2 cattle, 5 rams, 5 male goats, and 5 male lambs a year old. All of them were sacrificed for a fellowship offering.*

ᵃ6:25 May ... on you Literally, "May the Lord make his face shine on you."
ᵇ6:26 May ... prayers Literally, "May the Lord lift his face to you," that is, "may he accept you into his presence and grant your request."

ᶜ7:12–83 In the Hebrew text each leader's gift is listed separately. But the text is the same for each gift, so these verses have been combined for easier reading.
ᵈ7:12–83 3 1/4 pounds Literally, "130 shekels" (1.5 kg). Also in verse 85.
ᵉ7:12–83 1 3/4 pounds Literally, "70 shekels" (.8 kg). Also in verse 85.
ᶠ7:12–83 4 ounces Literally, "10 shekels" (115 g). Also in verse 86.

On the first day, the leader of the tribe of Judah, Nahshon son of Amminadab brought his gifts.

On the second day, the leader of the tribe of Issachar, Nethanel son of Zuar brought his gifts.

On the third day, the leader of the tribe of Zebulun, Eliab son of Helon brought his gifts.

On the fourth day, the leader of the tribe of Reuben, Elizur son of Shedeur brought his gifts.

On the fifth day, the leader of the tribe of Simeon, Shelumiel son of Zurishaddai brought his gifts.

On the sixth day, the leader of the tribe of Gad, Eliasaph son of Deuel[a] brought his gifts.

On the seventh day, the leader of the tribe of Ephraim, Elishama son of Ammihud brought his gifts.

On the eighth day, the leader of the tribe of Manasseh, Gamaliel son of Pedahzur brought his gifts.

On the ninth day, the leader of the tribe of Benjamin, Abidan son of Gideoni brought his gifts.

On the tenth day, the leader of the tribe of Dan, Ahiezer son of Ammishaddai brought his gifts.

On the eleventh day, the leader of the tribe of Asher, Pagiel son of Ocran brought his gifts.

On the twelfth day, the leader of the tribe of Naphtali, Ahira son of Enan brought his gifts.

84So all these things were the gifts from the leaders of the Israelites. They brought them during the time that Moses dedicated the altar by anointing it. They brought 12 silver plates, 12 silver bowls, and 12 gold spoons. 85Each silver plate weighed about 3¼ pounds. And each bowl weighed about 1¾ pounds. The silver plates and the silver bowls together all weighed about 60 pounds,[b] using the official measure 86The 12 gold spoons filled with incense weighed 4 ounces each, using the official measure. The 12 gold spoons all together weighed about 3 pounds.[c]

87The total number of animals for the burnt offering was 12 bulls, 12 rams, and 12 one-year-old male lambs. There were also the grain offerings that must be given with these offerings. And there were 12 male goats for a sin offering to the LORD. 88The leaders also gave animals to be killed and used as a fellowship offering. The total number of these animals was 24 bulls, 60 rams, 60 male goats, and 60 one-year-old male lambs. In this way they dedicated the altar after Moses anointed it.

89When Moses went into the Meeting Tent to speak to the LORD, he heard the Lord's voice speaking to him. The voice was coming from the area between the two Cherub angels on the mercy-cover* on top of the Box of the Agreement.* In this way the Lord spoke to Moses.

The Lampstand

8 1The LORD said to Moses, 2"Tell Aaron to put the seven lamps in the place I showed you. These lamps will light the area in front of the lampstand."

3Aaron did this. He put the lamps in the right place so that they lighted the area in front of the lampstand. He obeyed the command that the LORD gave Moses. 4This is how the lampstand was made: It was made from hammered gold, all the way from the gold base at the bottom to the gold flowers at the top. It looked just like the pattern that the LORD had shown to Moses.

Dedicating the Levites

5The LORD said to Moses, 6"Separate the Levites from the other Israelites. Make these Levites clean.* 7This is what you should do to make them clean: Sprinkle the special water from the sin offering[d] on them. This water will make them clean. Then they must shave their bodies and wash their clothes. This will make their bodies clean.

8"They must take a young bull and the grain offering that must be offered with it. This grain offering will be flour mixed with oil. Then take another young bull for a sin offering.* 9Bring the Levites to the area in front of the Meeting Tent.* Then bring all the Israelites together at that place. 10Bring the Levites before the LORD. The Israelites will put their hands on them.[e] 11Aaron will give the Levites to the LORD as an offering from the Israelites. Then the Levites will be ready to do their special work for the LORD.

12"Tell the Levites to put their hands on the heads of the bulls. One bull will be a sin offering to the LORD. The other bull will be used as a burnt offering* to the LORD. These offerings will make the Levites pure.* 13Tell the Levites to stand in front of Aaron and his sons. Then give the Levites to the LORD. They will be like an offering. 14This will make the Levites holy. They will be different from the other Israelites. The Levites will belong to me.

15"So make the Levites pure and give them to the LORD as a special offering.[f] After you do this, they can come and do their work at the Meeting Tent. 16The Israelites will give me the Levites. They will belong to me. In the past I told every Israelite family to give me their firstborn* son. But now I am taking the

---

[d]**8:7** *water from the sin offering* In this water were the ashes from the red cow that had been burned on the altar as a sin offering.

[e]**8:10** *put their hands on them* This showed that the people shared in appointing the Levites to their special work.

[f]**8:15** *special offering* Literally, "a lifted offering." Also in verse 21.

---

[a]**7:12–83** *Deuel* Or "Reuel."
[b]**7:85** *60 pounds* Literally, "2400 shekels" (27.6 kg).
[c]**7:86** *3 pounds* Literally, "120 shekels" (1.4 kg).

Levites in place of these firstborn sons from the other families in Israel. [17]Every firstborn in Israel—man or animal—is mine, because I killed all the firstborn children and animals in Egypt. And I chose to take the firstborn sons to belong to me. [18]But now I will take the Levites in their place. I will take the Levites in place of all the firstborn sons from the other families in Israel. [19]I chose the Levites from among the Israelites. And I give them as gifts to Aaron and his sons. I want them to do the work at the Meeting Tent. They will serve for all the Israelites. They will help make the sacrifices that make the Israelites pure. Then no great sickness or trouble will come to the Israelites when they come near the holy place."

[20]So Moses, Aaron, and all the Israelites obeyed the LORD. They did with the Levites everything that the Lord commanded Moses. [21]The Levites washed themselves and their clothes. Then Aaron gave them to the LORD as special offerings. Aaron gave the offerings that covered their sins and made them pure. [22]After that the Levites came to the Meeting Tent to do their work. Aaron and his sons watched them. They were responsible for the work of the Levites. Aaron and his sons did what the LORD commanded Moses.

[23]Then the LORD said to Moses, [24]"This is a special command for the Levites: Every Levite man who is 25 years old or older must come and share in the work at the Meeting Tent. [25]But when a man is 50 years old, he will retire from this hard work. [26]Men who are at least 50 years old will be on duty to help their brothers, but they will not do the work themselves. That is what you must do for the Levites so that they can do their duty."

Passover

9 [1]The LORD spoke to Moses in the Sinai desert. This was during the first month of the second year after the Israelites came out of Egypt. He said to Moses, [2]"Tell the Israelites to celebrate Passover* at the chosen time. [3]They must eat the Passover meal just before dark on the 14th day of this month. They must do this at the chosen time, and they must follow all the rules about Passover."

[4]So Moses told the Israelites to celebrate Passover. [5]The people did this in the Sinai desert just before dark on the 14th day of the first month. The Israelites did everything just as the LORD commanded Moses.

[6]But some of the people could not celebrate Passover that day. They were unclean* because they had touched a dead body. So they went to Moses and Aaron that day [7]and said to Moses, "We touched a dead body and became unclean. But why must we be kept from offering our gifts to the LORD at the chosen time with the rest of the Israelites?"

[8]Moses said to them, "I will ask the LORD what he says about this."

[9]Then the LORD said to Moses, [10]"Tell the Israelites this: This rule will be for you and your descendants. Maybe someone is not able to celebrate Passover at the right time. Maybe they are unclean because they touched a dead body. Or maybe they were away on a trip. [11]They will still be able to celebrate Passover at another time. They must celebrate Passover just before dark on the 14th day of the second month. At that time they must eat the lamb, the bread made without yeast, and the bitter herbs. [12]They must not leave any of that food until the next morning. And they must not break any of the bones of the lamb. They must follow all the rules about Passover. [13]But anyone who is able must celebrate Passover at the right time. If they are clean* and they are not away on a trip, there is no excuse for them not to do it. If they don't celebrate Passover at the right time, they must be separated from their people. They are guilty and must be punished, because they did not give the LORD his gift at the right time.

[14]"A foreigner living among you might want to share in the LORD's Passover with you. This is allowed, but that person must follow all the rules about Passover. The same rules are for everyone."

The Cloud and the Fire

[15]On the day the Holy Tent,* the Tent of the Agreement,* was set up, the LORD's cloud covered it. At night the cloud over the Holy Tent looked like fire. [16]The cloud stayed over the Holy Tent all the time. And at night the cloud looked like fire. [17]When the cloud moved from its place over the Holy Tent, the Israelites followed it. When the cloud stopped, that is the place where the Israelites camped. [18]This was the way the LORD showed the Israelites when to move and when to stop and set up camp. While the cloud stayed over the Holy Tent, the people continued to camp in that same place. [19]Sometimes the cloud would stay over the Holy Tent for a long time. The Israelites obeyed the LORD and did not move. [20]Sometimes the cloud was over the Holy Tent for only a few days. So the people obeyed the LORD's command—they followed the cloud when it moved. [21]Sometimes the cloud stayed only during the night—the next morning the cloud moved. So the people gathered their things and followed it. If the cloud moved, during the day or during the night, they followed it. [22]If the cloud stayed over the Holy Tent for two days, or a month, or a year, the people continued to obey the LORD. They stayed at that place and did not leave until the cloud moved. When the cloud rose from its place and moved, they also moved. [23]So the people obeyed the LORD's commands. They camped when the LORD told them to, and they moved when he told them to. They watched carefully and obeyed the LORD's commands to Moses.

The Silver Trumpets

10 ¹The Lord said to Moses, ²"Make two trumpets. Use silver and hammer it to make the trumpets. These trumpets will be for calling the people together and for telling them when it is time to move the camp. ³If you blow long blasts on both trumpets, all the people must meet together at the entrance of the Meeting Tent.* ⁴But if you blow long blasts on only one trumpet, only the leaders will come to meet with you. (These are the leaders of the twelve tribes of Israel.)

⁵"Short blasts on the trumpets will be the way to tell the people to move the camp. The first time you blow a short blast on the trumpets, the tribes camping on the east side of the Meeting Tent must begin to move. ⁶The second time you blow a short blast on the trumpets, the tribes camping on the south side of the Meeting Tent will begin to move. ⁷But if you want to gather the people together for a special meeting, blow the trumpets in a different way—blow a long steady blast on the trumpets. ⁸Only Aaron's sons, the priests, should blow the trumpets. This is a law for you that will continue forever, for generations to come.

⁹"If you are fighting an enemy in your own land, blow loudly on the trumpets before you go to fight them. The Lord your God will hear you, and he will save you from your enemies. ¹⁰Also blow these trumpets for your special meetings, New Moon* celebrations, and all your happy times together. Blow the trumpets when you give your burnt offerings* and fellowship offerings.* This will be a special way for the Lord your God to remember you. I command you to do this; I am the Lord your God."

The Israelites Move Their Camp

¹¹On the 20th day of the second month of the second year after the Israelites left Egypt, the cloud rose from above the Tent of the Agreement.* ¹²So the Israelites began their journey. They left the Sinai desert and traveled until the cloud stopped in the desert of Paran. ¹³This was the first time the people moved their camp. They moved it the way the Lord commanded Moses.

¹⁴The three divisions from Judah's camp went first. They traveled under their flag. The first group was the tribe of Judah. Nahshon son of Amminadab was the commander of that group. ¹⁵Next came the tribe of Issachar. Nethanel son of Zuar was the commander of that group. ¹⁶And then came the tribe of Zebulun. Eliab son of Helon was the commander of that group.

¹⁷Then the Holy Tent* was taken down. And the men from the Gershon and the Merari families carried the Holy Tent. So the people from these families were next in line. ¹⁸Then came the three divisions from Reuben's camp. They traveled under their flag. The first group was the tribe of Reuben. Elizur son of Shedeur was the commander of that group. ¹⁹Next came the tribe of Simeon. Shelumiel son of Zurishaddai was the commander of that group. ²⁰And then came the tribe of Gad. Eliasaph son of Deuel*a* was the commander of that group. ²¹Then came the Kohath family. They carried the holy things from inside the Holy Tent. These people came at this time so that the other people could set up the Holy Tent and make it ready at the new camp before these people arrived.

²²Next came the three groups from Ephraim's camp. They traveled under their flag. The first group was the tribe of Ephraim. Elishama son of Ammihud was the commander of that group. ²³Next came the tribe of Manasseh. Gamaliel son of Pedahzur was the commander of that group. ²⁴Then came the tribe of Benjamin. Abidan son of Gideoni was the commander of that group.

²⁵The last three tribes in the line were the rear guard for all the other tribes. These were the groups from Dan's camp. They traveled under their flag. The first group was the tribe of Dan. Ahiezer son of Ammishaddai was their commander. ²⁶Next came the tribe of Asher. Pagiel son of Ocran was the commander of that group. ²⁷Then came the tribe of Naphtali. Ahira son of Enan was the commander of that group. ²⁸That was the way the Israelites marched when they moved from place to place.

²⁹Hobab was the son of Reuel, the Midianite. (Reuel was Moses' father-in-law.) Moses said to Hobab, "We are traveling to the land that God promised to give to us. Come with us and we will be good to you. The Lord has promised good things to the Israelites."

³⁰But Hobab answered, "No, I will not go with you. I will go back to my homeland and to my own people."

³¹Then Moses said, "Please don't leave us. You know more about the desert than we do. You can be our guide. ³²If you come with us, we will share with you all the good things that the Lord gives us."

³³So they began traveling from the mountain of the Lord. The priests took the Box of the Lord's Agreement* and walked in front of the people. They carried the Holy Box for three days, looking for a place to camp. ³⁴The Lord's cloud was over them every day. And when they left their camp every morning, the cloud was there to lead them.

³⁵When the people lifted the Holy Box to move the camp, Moses always said,

"Get up, Lord!
    May your enemies be scattered.
    May your enemies run away from you."

*a***10:20** *Deuel* Or "Reuel."

36And when the Holy Box was put in its place, Moses always said,

"Come back, Lord, to the millions of
  Israelites."

The People Complain Again

11 1The people started complaining about their troubles. The Lord heard their complaints. He heard these things and became angry. Fire from the Lord burned among the people. The fire burned some of the areas at the edge of the camp. 2So the people cried to Moses for help. He prayed to the Lord and the fire stopped burning. 3So that place was called Taberah.a The people gave the place that name because the Lord caused a fire to burn in their camp.

The 70 Older Leaders

4The foreigners who had joined the Israelites began wanting other things to eat. Soon all the Israelites began complaining again. The people said, "We want to eat meat! 5We remember the fish we ate in Egypt. That fish cost us nothing. We also had good vegetables like cucumbers, melons, chives, onions, and garlic. 6But now we have lost our strength. We never eat anything—only this manna*!" 7(The manna was like small coriander seeds, and it looked like sap from a tree. 8The people gathered the manna. Then they used rocks to crush it and cooked it in a pot. Or they ground it into flour and made thin cakes with it. The cakes tasted like sweet cakes cooked with olive oil. 9The manna fell on the ground each night when the ground became wet with dew.)

10Moses heard the people complaining. People from every family were sitting by their tents and complaining. The Lord became very angry, and this made Moses very upset. 11He asked the Lord, "Why did you bring this trouble on me? I am your servant. What did I do wrong? What did I do to upset you? Why did you give me responsibility over all these people? 12You know that I am not the father of all these people. You know that I did not give birth to them. But I must take care of them, like a nurse carrying a baby in her arms. Why do you force me to do this? Why do you force me to carry them to the land that you promised to our fathers? 13I don't have enough meat for all these people! And they continue complaining to me. They say, 'Give us meat to eat!' 14I cannot take care of all these people alone. The burden is too heavy for me. 15If you plan to continue giving me their troubles, kill me now. If you accept me as your servant, let me die now. Then I will be finished with all my troubles!"

16The Lord said to Moses, "Bring to me 70 of the elders of Israel. These men are the leaders among the people. Bring them to the Meeting Tent.* Let them stand there with you. 17Then I will come down and speak with you there. The Spiritb is on you now. But I will also give some of that Spirit to them. Then they will help you take care of the people. In this way you will not have to be responsible for these people alone.

18"Tell the people this: Make yourselves ready for tomorrow. Tomorrow you will eat meat. The Lord heard you when you cried. The Lord heard your words when you said, 'We need meat to eat! It was better for us in Egypt!' So now the Lord will give you meat. And you will eat it. 19You will eat it for more than one, or two, or five, or ten, or even twenty days! 20You will eat that meat for a whole month until you are sick of it. This will happen to you because you complained against the Lord. He lives among you and knows what you need, but you cried and complained to him! You said, 'Why did we ever leave Egypt?'"

21Moses said, "Lord, there are 600,000 soldiers here, and you say, 'I will give them enough meat to eat for a whole month!' 22If we were to kill all the sheep and cattle, that would still not be enough to feed this many people for a month. And if we caught all the fish in the sea, it would not be enough for them!"

23But the Lord said to Moses, "Don't limit my power! You will see that I can do what I say I can do."

24So Moses went out to speak with the people. He told them what the Lord said. Then he gathered 70 of the elders* together and told them to stand around the Tent. 25Then the Lord came down in the cloud and spoke to Moses. The Spirit was on Moses. The Lord put that same Spirit on the 70 elders. After the Spirit came down on them, they began to prophesy.c But that was the only time these men ever did this.

26Two of the elders, Eldad and Medad, did not go out to the Tent. Their names were on the list of elders, but they stayed in camp. But the Spirit also came on them, and they began prophesying in camp. 27A young man ran and told Moses. The man said, "Eldad and Medad are prophesying in camp."

28Joshua son of Nun said to Moses, "Moses, sir, you must stop them!" (Joshua had been Moses' helper since Joshua was a boy.)

29But Moses answered, "Are you afraid the people will think that I am not the leader now? I wish that all the Lord's people were able to prophesy. I wish that the Lord would put his Spirit on all of them!" 30Then Moses

---

a11:3 *Taberah* This name means "burning."

b11:17 *Spirit* Or "spirit." Also in verses 25, 29.
c11:25 *prophesy* Usually this means "to speak for God." But here, it might mean that God's Spirit took control of these men in some special way. Also in verse 26.

and the leaders of Israel went back to the camp.

The Quail Come

³¹Then the LORD made a powerful wind to blow in from the sea, and it blew quail into the area all around the camp. There were so many birds that the ground was covered. They were about three feet deep on the ground. There were quail in every direction as far as a man can walk in one day. ³²They went out and gathered quail all that day and all that night. And they gathered quail all the next day too! The smallest amount anyone gathered was 60 bushels. Then the people spread the quail meat all around the camp to dry in the sun.

³³People began to eat the meat, but the LORD became very angry. While the meat was still in their mouths, before the people could finish eating it, the LORD caused the people to become very sick and die. ³⁴So the people named that place Kibroth Hattaavah,ᵃ because there they buried those who had the strong desire for meat.

³⁵From Kibroth Hattaavah the people traveled to Hazeroth and stayed there.

Miriam and Aaron Criticize Moses

12 ¹Miriam and Aaron began to talk against Moses. They criticized him because he married an Ethiopianᵇ woman. ²They said to themselves, "The LORD used Moses to speak to the people, but he is not the only one. The LORD also spoke through us!" The LORD heard this. ³(Moses was a very humble man. He was more humble than any other man on earth.) ⁴So suddenly, the LORD came and spoke to Moses, Aaron, and Miriam. He said, "You three, come to the Meeting Tent,* now!"

So Moses, Aaron, and Miriam went to the Tent. ⁵The LORD came down in the tall cloud and stood at the entrance to the Tent. He called out, "Aaron and Miriam!" They went to him. ⁶God said, "Listen to me! You will have prophets.* I, the LORD, will let them learn about me through visions.* I will speak to them in dreams. ⁷But Moses is not like that. He is my faithful servant—I trust him with everyone in my house. ⁸When I speak to him, I talk face to face with him. I don't use stories with hidden meanings—I show him clearly what I want him to know. And Moses can look at the very image of the LORD. So why were you brave enough to speak against my servant Moses?"

⁹The LORD was very angry with them, and he left them. ¹⁰The cloud rose from the Tent. Aaron turned and looked at Miriam. Her skin was white like snow—she had a terrible skin disease*!

¹¹Then Aaron said to Moses, "Please, sir, forgive us for the foolish sin that we did. ¹²Don't let her lose her skin like a baby who is born dead." (Sometimes a baby will be born like that, with half of its skin eaten away.)

¹³So Moses prayed to the LORD, "God, please heal her from this sickness!"

¹⁴The LORD answered Moses, "If her father spit in her face, she would be shamed for seven days. So put her outside the camp for seven days. After that she can come back into the camp."

¹⁵So they took Miriam outside the camp for seven days. And the people did not move from that place until she was brought in again. ¹⁶After that, the people left Hazeroth and traveled to the desert of Paran where they set up camp.

The Spies Go to Canaan

13 ¹The LORD said to Moses, ²"Send some men to explore the land of Canaan.* I will give this land to the Israelites. Send one leader from each of the twelve tribes."

³So Moses obeyed the LORD's command and sent out the Israelite leaders while the people were camped in the desert of Paran. ⁴These are their names:

from the tribe of Reuben—Shammua son of Zaccur;

⁵ from the tribe of Simeon—Shaphat son of Hori;

⁶ from the tribe of Judah—Caleb son of Jephunneh;

⁷ from the tribe of Issachar—Igal son of Joseph;

⁸ from the tribe of Ephraim—Hosheaᶜ son of Nun;

⁹ from the tribe of Benjamin—Palti son of Raphu;

¹⁰ from the tribe of Zebulun—Gaddiel son of Sodi;

¹¹ from the tribe of Manasseh (a tribe from Joseph)—Gaddi son of Susi;

¹² from the tribe of Dan—Ammiel son of Gemalli;

¹³ from the tribe of Asher—Sethur son of Michael;

¹⁴ from the tribe of Naphtali—Nahbi son of Vophsi;

¹⁵ from the tribe of Gad—Geuel son of Maki.

¹⁶These are the names of the men Moses sent to look at and study the land. (Moses called Hoshea son of Nun by another name. Moses called him Joshua.)

¹⁷When Moses was sending them out to explore Canaan, he said, "Go through the

---

ᵃ**11:34** *Kibroth Hattaavah* This name means "Graves of Strong Desire."

ᵇ**12:1** *Ethiopian* Or "Cushite," a person from Ethiopia, in Africa.

ᶜ**13:8** *Hoshea* Or "Joshua."

Negev* and then into the hill country. [18]See what the land looks like. Learn about the people who live there. Are they strong or are they weak? Are they few or are they many? [19]Learn about the land that they live in. Is it good land or bad land? What kind of towns do they live in? Do the towns have walls protecting them? Are the towns strongly defended? [20]And learn other things about the land. Is the soil good for growing things, or is it poor soil? Are there trees on the land? Try to bring back some of the fruit from that land." (This was during the time when the first grapes should be ripe.)

[21]So they went to explore the country. They explored the area from the Zin desert to Rehob and Lebo Hamath. [22]They entered the country through the Negev and went to Hebron. (The town of Hebron was built seven years before the town of Zoan in Egypt.) Ahiman, Sheshai, and Talmai lived there. These men were descendants of Anak. [23]Then the men went to Eshcol Valley. There they cut off a branch from a grapevine that had a bunch of grapes on it. They put that branch on a pole, and two men carried it between them. They also carried some pomegranates* and figs. [24]That place is called the Eshcol[a] Valley, because there the men of Israel cut off the bunch of grapes.

[25]The men explored that country for 40 days, and then they went back to the camp. [26]The Israelites were camped near Kadesh, in the desert of Paran. The men went to Moses and Aaron and all the Israelites. They told Moses, Aaron, and all the people what they saw and showed them the fruit from the land. [27]The men told Moses, "We went to the land where you sent us. It is a land filled with many good things[b]! Here is some of the fruit that grows there. [28]But the people living there are very powerful. The cities are very large and strongly defended. We even saw some Anakites* there. [29]The Amalekites live in the Negev. The Hittites, Jebusites, and Amorites live in the hill country. The Canaanites live near the sea and by the Jordan River."

[30]Caleb told the people near Moses to be quiet. Then Caleb said, "We should go up and take that land for ourselves. We can easily take that land."

[31]But the men who had gone with him said, "We cannot fight those people! They are much stronger than we are." [32]So those men gave a report that discouraged the people. They said, "The land we saw is full of strong people. They are strong enough to easily defeat anyone who goes there. [33]We saw the giant Nephilim* people there! (The descendants of Anak come from the Nephilim.) We felt like little grasshoppers. Yes, we were like grasshoppers to them!"

The People Complain Again

14 [1]That night all the people in the camp began shouting loudly. [2]The Israelites complained against Moses and Aaron. All the people came together and said to Moses and Aaron, "We should have died in Egypt or in the desert. [3]Did the LORD bring us to this new land to be killed in war? The enemy will kill us and take our wives and children! It would be better for us to go back to Egypt."

[4]Then the people said to each other, "Let's choose another leader and go back to Egypt."

[5]Moses and Aaron bowed low to the ground in front of all the people gathered there. [6]Joshua and Caleb became very upset. (Joshua son of Nun and Caleb son of Jephunneh were two of the men who explored the land.) [7]These two men said to all the Israelites gathered there, "The land that we saw is very good. [8]It is a land filled with many good things. If the LORD is pleased with us, he will lead us into that land. And the LORD will give that land to us. [9]So don't turn against the LORD! Don't be afraid of the people in that land. We can defeat them. They have no protection, nothing to keep them safe. But we have the LORD with us, so don't be afraid!"

[10]All the people began talking about killing Joshua and Caleb with stones. But the Glory of the LORD* appeared over the Meeting Tent* where all the people could see it. [11]The LORD spoke to Moses and said, "How long will these people continue to turn against me? They show that they don't trust me or believe in my power, in spite of the many miracles I have done among them. [12]I will kill them all with a terrible sickness. I will destroy them, and I will use you to make another nation. Your nation will be greater and stronger than these people."

[13]Then Moses said to the LORD, "If you do that, the Egyptians will hear about it! They know that you used your great power to bring your people out of Egypt. [14]The Egyptians have already told the people in Canaan* about it. They already know you are the LORD. They know that you are with your people. They know that the people saw you. Those people know about the special cloud. They know you use the cloud to lead your people during the day. And they know the cloud becomes a fire to lead your people at night. [15]So you must not kill these people now. If you kill them, all the nations who have heard about your power will say, [16]'The LORD was not able to bring them into the land he promised them. So he killed them in the desert.'

[17]"So now, Lord, show your strength! Show it the way you said you would. [18]You said, 'The LORD is slow to become angry. He is full of great love. He forgives[c] those who are guilty and break the law. But the LORD always

---

[a]13:24 *Eshcol* This name is like the Hebrew word meaning "a bunch of grapes."

[b]13:27 *land … things* Literally, "land flowing with milk and honey." Also in 14:8.

[c]14:18 *forgives* Or "spares."

punishes those who are guilty. He punishes them, and he also punishes their children, their grandchildren, and even their great-grandchildren for those bad things.'*a* ¹⁹Now, show your great love to these people. Forgive their sin. Forgive them the same way you have been forgiving them since the time they left Egypt until now."

²⁰The LORD answered, "Yes, I will forgive the people as you asked. ²¹But, I tell you the truth. As surely as I live and as surely as my power fills the whole earth, I make you this promise: ²²None of the people I led out of Egypt will ever see the land of Canaan. They saw my glory and the great signs that I did in Egypt and in the desert. But they disobeyed me and tested me ten times. ²³I promised their ancestors* that I would give them that land. But none of those people who turned against me will ever enter that land! ²⁴But my servant Caleb was different. He follows me completely. So I will bring him into the land that he has already seen, and his people will get that land. ²⁵The Amalekites and the Canaanites are living in the valley. So tomorrow you must leave this place. Go back to the desert on the road to the Red Sea."

The Lord Punishes the People

²⁶The LORD said to Moses and Aaron, ²⁷"How long will these evil people continue to complain against me? I have heard their complaints and their griping. ²⁸So tell them, 'The LORD says that he will surely do all those things to you that you complained about. This is what will happen to you: ²⁹You will die in this desert. Every person who is 20 years old or older and was counted as one of my people will die. You complained against me, the LORD. ³⁰So none of you will ever enter and live in the land that I promised to give you. Only Caleb son of Jephunneh and Joshua son of Nun will enter that land. ³¹You were afraid and complained that your enemies in that new land would take your children away from you. But I tell you that I will bring them into the land. They will enjoy what you refused to accept. ³²As for you people, you will die in this desert.

³³"'Your children will wander around like shepherds here in the desert for 40 years. They will suffer because you were not faithful to me. They must suffer until all of you lie dead in the desert. ³⁴For 40 years you will suffer for your sins. (That is one year for each of the 40 days that the men explored the land.) You will know that it is a terrible thing for me to be against you.'

³⁵"I am the LORD, and I have spoken. And I promise that I will do these things to all these evil people. They have come together against me. So they will all die here in this desert."

³⁶The men Moses sent to explore the new land were the ones who came back complaining about him to all the Israelites. They said that the people were not strong enough to enter that land. ³⁷The men were responsible for spreading the trouble among the Israelites. So the LORD caused a sickness to kill all those men. ³⁸But Joshua son of Nun and Caleb son of Jephunneh were among the men who were sent out to explore the land, and the LORD saved them. They did not get the sickness that caused the other ten men to die.

The People Try to Go Into Canaan

³⁹When Moses told the Israelites this, they were very sad. ⁴⁰Early the next morning the people started to go up to the high hill country. They said, "We have sinned. We are sorry that we did not trust the Lord. We will go to the place that the LORD promised."

⁴¹But Moses said, "Why are you not obeying the LORD's command? You will not be successful! ⁴²Don't go into that land. The LORD is not with you, so your enemies will easily defeat you. ⁴³The Amalekites and Canaanites will fight against you there. You have turned away from the LORD, so he will not be with you when you fight them. And you will all be killed in battle."

⁴⁴But the people did not believe Moses. They went toward the high hill country. But Moses and the Box of the LORD's Agreement* did not go with the people. ⁴⁵The Amalekites and the Canaanites living in the hill country came down and attacked the Israelites and easily defeated them and chased them all the way to Hormah.

Rules About Sacrifices

15 ¹The LORD said to Moses, ²"Speak to the Israelites and say to them: I am giving you a land to be your home. When you enter that land, ³you must give special gifts to the LORD. Their smell will please the LORD. You will use your cattle, sheep, and goats for burnt offerings,* sacrifices, special promises, special gifts, fellowship offerings,* or at your special festivals.

⁴"At the time someone brings their offering, they must also give a grain offering to the LORD. The grain offering will be 8 cups*b* of fine flour mixed with 1 quart*c* of olive oil. ⁵Each time you offer a lamb as a burnt offering or sacrifice, you must also prepare a quart of wine as a drink offering.

⁶"If you are giving a ram, you must also prepare a grain offering. This grain offering should be 16 cups*d* of fine flour mixed with

---

*a***14:18 But the LORD … bad things** Or "The LORD credits the guilt of the fathers to their children and grandchildren, to the third and fourth generation."

*b***15:4 8 cups** Literally, "1/10 of an ephah" (2.2 l).

*c***15:4 1 quart** Literally, "1/4 hin" (.8 l).

*d***15:6 16 cups** Literally, "2/10 of an ephah" (4.4 l).

1¼ quarts*a* of olive oil. ⁷And you must prepare 1¼ quarts of wine as a drink offering. Its smell will please the LORD.

⁸"You might prepare a young bull as a burnt offering, a sacrifice, a fellowship offering, or to keep a special promise to the LORD. ⁹At that time you must also bring a grain offering with the bull. That grain offering should be 24 cups*b* of fine flour mixed with 2 quarts*c* of olive oil. ¹⁰Also bring 2 quarts of wine as a drink offering as a sweet-smelling gift to the LORD. ¹¹Each bull or ram, or lamb or young goat that you give to the LORD must be prepared in this way. ¹²Do this for every one of these animals that you give.

¹³"This is the way every citizen of Israel must give gifts to please the LORD. ¹⁴Foreigners will live among you. If they give gifts to please the LORD, they must offer them the same way you do. ¹⁵The same rules will be for everyone—the Israelites and the foreigners living among you. This law will continue forever. You and the people living among you will be the same before the LORD. ¹⁶This means that you must follow the same laws and the same rules. These laws and rules are for you Israelites and for the other people who are living among you."

¹⁷The LORD said to Moses, ¹⁸"Tell the Israelites this: I am taking you to another land. ¹⁹When you eat the food that grows in that land, you must give part of that food as an offering to the LORD. ²⁰You will gather grain and grind it into flour to make dough for bread. You must give the first of that dough as a gift to the LORD. It will be like the grain offering that comes from the threshing* floor. ²¹This rule will continue forever, you must give the first of that dough as a gift to the LORD.

²²"As you try to obey all the commands that the LORD gave Moses, you might fail and make a mistake. ²³God gave you those commands through Moses, and they have been in effect from the day they were given throughout the generations until today. ²⁴If you made this mistake where everyone could see it, the whole community must offer a young bull as a burnt offering, as a sweet-smelling gift to the LORD. You must also offer the grain offering and the drink offering with the bull. And you must also give a male goat as a sin offering.*

²⁵"So the priest will make the whole community of Israel pure,* and they will be forgiven for the mistake they made. Since they made the mistake, they must bring a gift and a sin offering to the LORD. ²⁶Then the whole community of Israel and any foreigners among them will be forgiven for the mistake.

²⁷"But if only one person makes a mistake and sins, that person must bring a female goat that is one year old. That goat will be the sin

offering. ²⁸The priest will make the one who sinned pure and that person will be forgiven. ²⁹This law is for everyone who makes a mistake and sins. The same law is for the people born in the family of Israel and for the foreigners living among you.

³⁰"If someone sins and knows they are doing wrong, they are rebelling against the LORD. They must be separated from their people. The same law applies to citizens of Israel and to foreigners living among you. ³¹They thought the LORD's word was not important, so they broke his commands. That is why they must be separated from their people—they must bear the responsibility for their guilt."

A Man Works on the Day of Rest

³²While the Israelites were in the desert, some of them saw a man gathering firewood on the Sabbath* day. ³³The people who saw him gathering the wood brought him to Moses, Aaron, and the whole community of Israel. ³⁴They guarded the man carefully because they did not know how they should punish him.

³⁵Then the LORD said to Moses, "The man must die. All the people must throw stones at him outside the camp." ³⁶So the people took him outside the camp and killed him with stones. They did this just as the LORD commanded Moses.

A Way to Remember God's Commands

³⁷The LORD said to Moses, ³⁸"Speak to the Israelites. Tell them this: Tie several pieces of thread together and tie them in the corner of your clothes. Put a piece of blue thread in each one of these tassels. You must wear these things now and forever. ³⁹You will be able to look at these tassels and remember all the commands that the LORD has given you. Then you will obey the commands. You will not do wrong by forgetting about the commands and doing the things that your own bodies and eyes want. ⁴⁰You will remember to obey all my commands. Then you will be God's special people. ⁴¹I am the LORD your God. I am the one who brought you out of Egypt. I did this to be your God. I am the LORD your God."

Some Leaders Turn Against Moses

16 ¹Korah, Dathan, Abiram, and On turned against Moses. (Korah was the son of Izhar. Izhar was the son of Kohath, and Kohath was the son of Levi. Dathan and Abiram were brothers, the sons of Eliab. And On was the son of Peleth. Dathan, Abiram, and On were descendants of Reuben.) ²These four men gathered 250 other men from Israel together and came against Moses. They were leaders who had been chosen by the people. All the people knew them. ³They came as a group to speak against Moses and Aaron and said, "You have gone too far—you are wrong!

---

a **15:6** *1 1/4 quarts* Literally, "1/3 hin" (1 l).
b **15:9** *24 cups* Literally, "3/10 of an ephah" (6.6 l).
c **15:9** *2 quarts* Literally, "1/2 hin" (1.6 l).

All the Israelites are holy—the LORD still lives among them. You are making yourselves more important than the rest of the LORD's people."

⁴When Moses heard this, he bowed his face to the ground to show he was not being proud. ⁵Then Moses said to Korah and all his followers, "Tomorrow morning the LORD will show who belongs to him. He will show who is holy, and he will bring that man near to him. He will choose him and bring that man near to him. ⁶So Korah, you and all your followers should do this: ⁷Tomorrow put fire and incense* in some special pans. Then bring those pans before the LORD. He will choose the man who is holy. You Levites have gone too far—you are wrong!"

⁸Moses also said to Korah, "You Levites, listen to me. ⁹You should be happy that the God of Israel chose you and made you special. You are different from the rest of the Israelites. The LORD brought you near to him to do the special work in the LORD's Holy Tent* to help the Israelites worship him. Isn't that enough? ¹⁰He brought you Levites near to him to help the priests, but now you are trying to become priests also. ¹¹You and your followers have joined together and turned against the LORD! Did Aaron do anything wrong? No, so why are you complaining against Aaron?"

¹²Then Moses called Dathan and Abiram, the sons of Eliab. But the two men said, "We will not come! ¹³You have brought us out of a land filled with many good things.ᵃ You brought us to the desert to kill us. And now you want to show that you have even more power over us. ¹⁴Why should we follow you? You did not bring us into the new land filled with many good things. You did not give us the land God promised. You did not give us the fields or the vineyards.* Will you make these men your slaves? No! We will not come."

¹⁵So Moses became very angry. He said to the LORD, "I never did anything wrong to these people. I never took anything from them—not even a donkey! Don't accept their gifts!"

¹⁶Then Moses said to Korah, "You and all your followers will stand before the LORD tomorrow. Aaron will also be there with you and your followers. ¹⁷Each of you must bring a pan, put incense in it, and present it to the LORD. There will be 250 pans for the leaders and one pan for you and one pan for Aaron."

¹⁸So each man got a pan and put burning incense in it. Then they stood at the entrance of the Meeting Tent.* Moses and Aaron also stood there. ¹⁹Korah also gathered all the people together at the entrance of the Meeting Tent. Then the Glory of the LORD* appeared to everyone there.

²⁰The LORD said to Moses and Aaron, ²¹"Move away from these men! I want to destroy them now!"

²²But Moses and Aaron bowed to the ground and cried out, "God, you know what people are thinking.ᵇ Please don't be angry with all these people. Only one man really sinned."

²³Then the LORD said to Moses, ²⁴"Tell the people to move away from the tents of Korah, Dathan, and Abiram."

²⁵Moses stood and went to Dathan and Abiram. All the elders* of Israel followed him. ²⁶Moses warned the people, "Move away from the tents of these evil men. Don't touch anything that belongs to them! If you do, you will be destroyed because of their sins."

²⁷So the men moved away from the tents of Korah, Dathan, and Abiram. Dathan and Abiram went to their tents. They stood outside of their tents with their wives, children, and little babies.

²⁸Then Moses said, "I will show you proof that the LORD sent me to do all the things I told you. I will show you that all these things were not my own idea. ²⁹These men will die, but if they die in a normal way—the way people always die—then that will show that the LORD did not really send me. ³⁰But if the LORD causes them to die in a different way, then you will know that these men have sinned against the LORD. This is the proof: The earth will open and swallow them. They will go down to their grave still alive. And everything that belongs to these men will go down with them."

³¹When Moses finished saying these things, the ground under the men opened. ³²It was as if the earth opened its mouth and swallowed them. All of Korah's men, their families, and everything they owned went down into the earth. ³³They went down into their grave alive. Everything they owned went with them. Then the earth closed over them. They were finished—gone from the camp!

³⁴The Israelites heard the cries of the men being destroyed. So they all ran in different directions and said, "The earth will swallow us too!"

³⁵Then a fire came from the LORD and destroyed the 250 men who were offering the incense.

³⁶The LORD said to Moses, ³⁷⁻³⁸"Tell Eleazar son of Aaron the priest to get all the incense pans from the fire. Tell him to scatter the coals and ashes. These men sinned against me, and their sin cost them their lives. But the incense pans are still holy.* The pans became holy when people gave them to the LORD. Hammer the pans into flat sheets. Use the metal sheets to cover the altar.* This will be a warning to all the Israelites."

ᵃ16:13 land ... things Literally, "land flowing with milk and honey."

ᵇ16:22 God, ... thinking Literally, "God, the God of the spirits of all people."

³⁹So Eleazar the priest gathered together all the bronze* pans that the men had brought. These men were all burned up, but the pans were still there. Then Eleazar told some men to hammer the pans into flat metal. Then he put the metal sheets on the altar. ⁴⁰He did this the way the LORD commanded him through Moses. This was a sign to help the Israelites remember that only someone from the family of Aaron should burn incense before the LORD. Any other person who burns incense before the Lord will die like Korah and his followers.

Aaron Saves the People

⁴¹The next day all the Israelites complained against Moses and Aaron. They said, "You killed the LORD's people."

⁴²Moses and Aaron were standing at the entrance of the Meeting Tent.* The people gathered together at that place to complain against Moses and Aaron. But when they looked toward the Meeting Tent, the cloud covered it and the Glory of the LORD* appeared there. ⁴³Then Moses and Aaron went to the front of the Meeting Tent.

⁴⁴The LORD said to Moses, ⁴⁵"Move away from these people so that I can destroy them now." So Moses and Aaron bowed with their faces to the ground.

⁴⁶Then Moses said to Aaron, "Get your bronze* pan and some fire from the altar.* Then put incense* in it. Hurry to the people and do the things that will make them pure.* The LORD is angry with them. The trouble has already started."

^{47–48}So Aaron got the incense and the fire, and he ran to the middle of the people. But the sickness had already started among them. So Aaron stood between the dead and those who were still alive. He did what Moses said to remove their sin, and the sickness stopped there. ⁴⁹But 14,700 people died from that sickness—and that is not counting the people who died because of Korah. ⁵⁰So the terrible sickness was stopped, and Aaron went back to Moses at the entrance of the Meeting Tent.

God Proves Aaron Is the High Priest

17 ¹The LORD said to Moses, ²"Speak to the Israelites. Get twelve wooden walking sticks from them. Get one from the leader of each of the twelve tribes. Write the name of each man on his walking stick. ³On the stick from Levi, write Aaron's name. There must be one stick for the head of each of the twelve tribes. ⁴Put these walking sticks in the Meeting Tent* in front of the Box of the Agreement.* This is the place where I meet with you. ⁵I will choose one man to be the true priest. You will know which man I choose because his walking stick will begin to grow new leaves. In this way I will stop the people from always complaining against you and me."

⁶So Moses spoke to the Israelites. Each of the leaders gave him a walking stick. There were twelve walking sticks. There was one stick from each leader of each tribe. One of the walking sticks belonged to Aaron. ⁷Moses put the walking sticks before the LORD in the Tent of the Agreement.*

⁸The next day Moses entered the Tent. He saw that Aaron's walking stick, the stick from the family of Levi, was the one that had grown new leaves. That walking stick had even grown branches and made almonds. ⁹So Moses brought out all the sticks from the LORD's place. He showed the walking sticks to the Israelites. They all looked at the sticks, and each man took his own stick back.

¹⁰Then the LORD said to Moses, "Put Aaron's walking stick back in front of the Box that holds the Agreement.^a This will be a warning for these people who are always turning against me. This will stop their complaining against me so that I will not destroy them." ¹¹So Moses did what the LORD commanded him.

¹²The Israelites said to Moses, "We know that we will die! We are lost! We will all be destroyed! ¹³Anyone who even comes near the LORD's holy place will die. Is it true that we will all die?"

The Work of the Priests and Levites

18 ¹The LORD said to Aaron, "You, your sons, and all the people in your father's family must bear the responsibility for any wrong that is done against the holy place or against the priests. ²To prevent that from happening, you must bring the rest of the men from the tribe of Levi to join you. These Levites will help you and your sons do your work in the Tent of the Agreement.* ³These Levites will be under your control. They will do all the work that needs to be done in the Tent. But they must not go near the things in the Holy Place* or the altar.* If they do, they will die—and you also will die. ⁴They will join you and work with you. They will be responsible for caring for the Meeting Tent.* All the work that must be done in the Tent will be done by them. No one else may come near the place where you are.

⁵"You are responsible for caring for the holy place and the altar. I don't want to become angry with the Israelites again. ⁶I myself chose the Levites from among all the Israelites. They are as a gift to you. I gave them to you to serve the LORD and work in the Meeting Tent. ⁷But, Aaron, only you and your sons may serve as priests. You are the only ones who can go near the altar or behind the curtain into the Most Holy Place. I am giving you a gift—your service as a priest. Anyone else who tries to come too close must be killed."

---

^a**17:10** *Box that holds the Agreement* Literally, "Testimony." See "Agreement" in the Word List.

⁸Then the LORD said to Aaron, "I myself gave you responsibility over all the special gifts people give to me. All the holy* gifts that the Israelites give to me, I give to you. You and your sons can share in these gifts. They will always belong to you. ⁹The people will bring gifts, grain offerings, sin offerings,* and guilt offerings. These offerings are most holy. Your share in the most holy offerings will come from the parts that are not burned. All these things will be for you and your sons. ¹⁰Eat these things only in a very holy place. Every male in your family may eat them, but you must remember that these offerings are holy.

¹¹"The Israelites will bring special gifts that you will lift up to me. I give these gifts to you and your sons and daughters. That is your share. Everyone in your family who is clean* will be able to eat it.

¹²"And I give you all the best olive oil and all the best new wine and grain. These are the things that the Israelites give to me, the LORD. These are the first things that they gather in their harvest. ¹³When the people gather a harvest, they bring all the first things to the LORD. So these things I will give to you. And everyone in your family who is clean may eat it.

¹⁴"Everything in Israel that is given to the LORD*a* is yours.

¹⁵"A woman's first baby and an animal's first baby must be given to the LORD. That baby will belong to you. If the firstborn animal is unclean,* then it must be bought back. If the baby is a child, that child must be bought back. ¹⁶They must make the payment when the baby is one month old. The cost will be 5 shekels*b* of silver. You must use the official measure* to weigh this silver. A shekel by the official measure is 20 gerahs.*c*

¹⁷"But you must not make a payment for the firstborn cow, sheep, or goat. These animals are holy. Sprinkle their blood on the altar and burn their fat as a sweet-smelling gift to the LORD. ¹⁸But the meat from these animals will be yours. And also the breast that was lifted up to the Lord will be yours. And the right thigh from other offerings will be yours. ¹⁹Anything that the people offer as holy gifts, I, the LORD, give to you. This is your share. I give it to you and your sons and daughters. This law will continue forever. It is an agreement with the LORD that cannot be broken.*d* I make this promise to you and to your descendants."

²⁰The LORD also said to Aaron, "You will not get any of the land. And you will not own anything that the other people own. I, the LORD, will be yours. The Israelites will get the land that I promised, but I am my gift to you.

²¹"The Israelites will give one-tenth of everything they have. So I give that one-tenth to the Levites. This is their payment for the work that they do while they serve at the Meeting Tent. ²²But the other Israelites must never go near that Meeting Tent. If they do, they must be put to death! ²³The Levites will do the work of caring for the Meeting Tent. They must bear the responsibility for anything done against it. This is a law that will continue forever. The Levites will not get any of the land that I promised to the other Israelites. ²⁴But the Israelites will give one-tenth of everything they have to me, and I will give that one-tenth to the Levites. That is why I said these words about the Levites: They will not get the land that I promised the Israelites."

²⁵The LORD said to Moses, ²⁶"Speak to the Levites and tell them: The Israelites will give one-tenth of everything they own to the LORD. That one-tenth will belong to the Levites. But you must give one-tenth of that to the Lord as your offering. ²⁷That tenth will be your offering to the LORD and will be treated like the grain from the threshing* floor and the wine from the winepress.* ²⁸In this way you will also give an offering to the LORD just like the other Israelites do. You will get the one-tenth that the Israelites give to the LORD, and then you will give one-tenth of that to Aaron the priest. ²⁹When the Israelites give you one-tenth of everything that they own, then you must give the best and the holiest part of these things as your gift to the LORD.

³⁰"Moses, tell the Levites: The Israelites will give you one-tenth of their harvest and of their wine. Then you will give the best part of that to the LORD. ³¹You and your families can eat all that is left. This is your payment for the work you do in the Meeting Tent. ³²And if you always give the best part of it to the LORD, you will never be guilty. You will always remember that these gifts are the holy offerings from the Israelites. And you will not die."

The Ashes of the Red Cow

19 ¹The LORD spoke to Moses and Aaron. He said, ²"These are the laws from the teachings that the LORD gave to the Israelites. Get a red cow that has nothing wrong with it. That cow must not have any bruises. And it must never have worn a yoke.* ³Give that cow to Eleazar, and he will take it outside the camp and kill it there. ⁴Then Eleazar the priest must put some of its blood on his finger and sprinkle some of the blood toward the Holy Tent.* He must do this seven times. ⁵Then the whole cow must be burned in front of him; the skin, the meat, the blood, and the intestines must all be burned. ⁶Then the priest must take a cedar stick, a hyssop* branch, and some red string. He must throw

---

*a*18:14 *given to the LORD* Things that were given to God and could not be bought back. See Lev. 27:28–29.

*b*18:16 *5 shekels* 2 ounces (57.5 g).

*c*18:16 *20 gerahs* 2/5 of an ounce (11.5 g).

*d*18:19 *It is an agreement … broken* Literally, "It is an eternal, salt agreement before the LORD."

these things into the fire where the cow is burning. 7Then the priest must wash himself and his clothes with water. Then he must come back into the camp. He will be unclean* until evening. 8The man who burns that cow must wash himself and his clothes in water. He will be unclean until evening.

9"Then someone who is clean* will collect the ashes from the cow and put them in a clean place outside the camp. These ashes will be used when someone must keep a special ceremony to become clean. These ashes will also be used to remove a person's sins.

10"The man who collected the cow's ashes must wash his clothes. He will be unclean until evening.

"This rule will continue forever. This rule is for the citizens of Israel and for the foreigners living with you. 11Those who touch a dead body will be unclean for seven days. 12They must wash themselves with the special water on the third day and again on the seventh day. If they don't do this, they will remain unclean. 13Those who touch a dead body are unclean. If they stay unclean and then go to the Holy Tent, the Holy Tent becomes unclean. So they must be separated from the Israelites. If the special water is not thrown on an unclean person, that person will stay unclean.

14"This is the rule about those who die in their tents: If someone dies in the tent, everyone in the tent will be unclean for seven days. 15And every jar or pot without a lid becomes unclean. 16If there is a dead body out in a field, whether the person died in battle or for some other reason, whoever touches that dead body, or its bones, or even its grave will be unclean for seven days.

17"If you have become unclean, someone must use the ashes from the burned cow to make you clean again. They must pour fresh water*a* over the ashes into a jar. 18That clean person must take a hyssop branch and dip it into the water. The clean person must sprinkle it over the tent, the dishes, and any people who were in the tent. That clean person must do this for anyone who touches a dead body, its bones, or even a grave.

19"Then that clean person must sprinkle this water on you on the third day and again on the seventh day. On the seventh day you will become clean. You must wash your clothes in water and you will become clean in the evening.

20"Whoever becomes unclean and does not become clean must be separated from the community. If an unclean person is not sprinkled with that special water and does not become clean, that person might make the Holy Tent unclean. 21This rule will be for you forever. And whoever sprinkled the special water must wash their clothes because they will be unclean until evening. 22And whoever an unclean person touches will be unclean until evening."

Miriam Dies

20 1The Israelites arrived at the Zin desert on the first month. The people stayed at Kadesh. Miriam died and was buried there.

Moses Makes a Mistake

2There was not enough water for the people at that place. So the people met together to complain against Moses and Aaron. 3The people argued with Moses and said, "Maybe we should have died in front of the LORD like our brothers did. 4Why did you bring the LORD's people into this desert? Do you want us and our animals to die here? 5Why did you bring us from Egypt? Why did you bring us to this bad place? There is no grain. There are no figs, grapes, or pomegranates,* and there is no water to drink."

6So Moses and Aaron left the crowd of people and went to the entrance of the Meeting Tent.* They bowed down to the ground, and the Glory of the LORD* appeared to them.

7The LORD spoke to Moses and said, 8"Get the special walking stick. Take your brother Aaron and the crowd of people and go to that rock. Speak to the rock in front of the people. Then water will flow from the rock, and you can give that water to the people and to their animals."

9The walking stick was in the Holy Tent, in front of the LORD. Moses took the walking stick as the Lord said. 10Moses and Aaron told the people to meet together in front of the rock. Then Moses said, "You people are always complaining. Now listen to me. I will cause water to flow from this rock." 11Moses lifted his arm and hit the rock twice. Water began flowing from the rock, and the people and their animals drank that water.

12But the LORD said to Moses and Aaron, "You did not trust me enough to honor me and show the people that I am holy. You did not show the Israelites that the power to make the water came from me. So you will not lead the people into the land that I have given them."

13This place was called the waters of Meribah.*b* This is where the Israelites argued with the LORD and where the LORD showed them that he was holy.*

Edom Will Not Let Israel Pass

14While Moses was at Kadesh, he sent some men with a message to the king of Edom. The message said, "This is what your brothers, the Israelites, say to you: You know about all the troubles we have had. 15Many years ago

---

*a*19:17 *fresh water* Literally, "living water." This means fresh, flowing water.

*b*20:13 *Meribah* This name means "argument" or "rebellion."

our ancestors* went down into Egypt, and we lived there for many years. The people of Egypt were cruel to us. ¹⁶But we asked the Lord for help, and he heard us and sent an angel to help us. The Lord has brought us out of Egypt.

"Now we are here at Kadesh, where your land begins. ¹⁷Please let us travel through your country. We will not travel through any fields or vineyards.* We will not drink water from any of your wells. We will travel only along King's Road. We will not leave that road to the right or to the left. We will stay on the road until we have traveled through your country."

¹⁸But the king of Edom answered, "You may not travel through our land. If you try to travel through our land, we will come and fight you with swords."

¹⁹The Israelites answered, "We will travel along the main road. If our animals drink any of your water, we will pay you for it. We only want to walk through your country. We don't want to take it for ourselves."

²⁰But again the king of Edom answered, "We will not allow you to come through our country."

Then the king of Edom gathered a large and powerful army and went out to fight against the Israelites. ²¹The king of Edom refused to let the Israelites travel through his country, so the Israelites turned around and went another way.

Aaron Dies

²²All the Israelites traveled from Kadesh to Mount Hor. ²³Mount Hor was near the border of Edom. The Lord said to Moses and Aaron, ²⁴"It is time for Aaron to die and go to be with his ancestors.* Aaron will not enter the land that I promised to the Israelites. Moses, I say this to you because both you and Aaron did not fully obey the command I gave you at the waters of Meribah.

²⁵"Now, bring Aaron and his son Eleazar up to Mount Hor. ²⁶Take Aaron's special clothes from him and put these clothes on his son Eleazar. Aaron will die there on the mountain. And he will go to be with his ancestors."

²⁷Moses obeyed the Lord's command. Moses, Aaron, and Eleazar went up on Mount Hor. All the Israelites watched them go. ²⁸Moses removed Aaron's special clothes and put them on Aaron's son Eleazar. Then Aaron died there on top of the mountain. Moses and Eleazar came back down the mountain. ²⁹All the Israelites learned that Aaron was dead. So everyone in Israel mourned* for 30 days.

War With the Canaanites

21 ¹The Canaanite king of Arad lived in the Negev.* He heard that the Israelites were coming on the road to Atharim, so the king went out and attacked the Israelites. Arad captured some of the people and made them prisoners. ²Then the Israelites made a special promise to the Lord: "Please help us defeat these people. If you do this, we will give their cities to you. We will totally destroy them."

³The Lord listened to the Israelites and helped them defeat the Canaanites. They completely destroyed the Canaanites and their cities. So that place was named Hormah.ᵃ

The Bronze Snake

⁴The Israelites left Mount Hor and traveled on the road that goes to the Red Sea. They did this to go around the country of Edom. But the people became impatient. ⁵They began complaining against God and Moses. The people said, "Why did you bring us out of Egypt? We will die here in the desert! There is no bread and no water! And we hate this terrible food!"

⁶So the Lord sent poisonous snakes among the people. The snakes bit the people, and many of the Israelites died. ⁷The people came to Moses and said, "We know that we sinned when we spoke against the Lord and against you. Pray to the Lord. Ask him to take away these snakes." So Moses prayed for them.

⁸The Lord said to Moses, "Make a bronze* snake and put it on a pole. If anyone is bitten by a snake, that person should look at the bronze snake on the pole. Then that person will not die." ⁹So Moses obeyed the Lord. He made a bronze snake and put it on a pole. Then when a snake bit anyone, that person looked at the bronze snake on the pole and lived.

The Trip to Moab

¹⁰The Israelites left that place and camped at Oboth. ¹¹Then they left Oboth and camped at Iye Abarim in the desert east of Moab. ¹²They left that place and camped in Zered Valley. ¹³Then they moved and camped across from the Arnon River in the desert. This river started at the Ammonite border. The valley was the border between Moab and the Amorites. ¹⁴That is why these words are written in the *Book of the Wars of the Lord*:

"... and Waheb in Suphah, and the Valleys of the Arnon, ¹⁵and the hills by the valleys that lead to the town of Ar. These places are at the border of Moab."

¹⁶The Israelites left that place and traveled to Beer.ᵇ This was the place with the well where the Lord said to Moses, "Bring the people together here, and I will give them water." ¹⁷Then the Israelites sang this song:

ᵃ**21:3 Hormah** This name means "completely destroyed" or "a gift given totally to God." See Lev. 27:28-29.
ᵇ**21:16 Beer** This Hebrew name means "well."

"Well, flow with water!
   Sing about it!
18 Great men dug this well.
   Important leaders dug this well.
   They dug this well with their staffs and
      walking sticks.
   It is a gift in the desert."*a*

19The people traveled from Mattanah to
Nahaliel. Then they traveled from Nahaliel to
Bamoth. 20They traveled from Bamoth to the
Valley of Moab. In this place the top of the
Pisgah Mountain looks over the desert.

Sihon and Og

21The Israelites sent some men to King
Sihon of the Amorites. The men said to the
king, 22"Allow us to travel through your country. We will not go through any field or vineyard.* We will not drink water from any of
your wells. We will travel only along King's
Road. We will stay on that road until we have
traveled through your country."

23But King Sihon would not allow the Israelites to travel through his country. He gathered together his army and marched out to the
desert to fight against the Israelites. The king's
army fought against the Israelites at Jahaz.
24But the Israelites defeated the king and
took his land from the Arnon River to the Jabbok River. The Israelites took the land as far
as the Ammonite border. They stopped at that
border because it was strongly defended by the
Ammonites. 25Israel took all the Amorite cities
and began living in them. They even defeated
the city of Heshbon and all the small towns
around it. 26Heshbon was the city where
Sihon, the Amorite king, lived. In the past
Sihon had fought with the king of Moab. Sihon
had taken the land as far as the Arnon River.
27That is why the singers sing this song:

"Go in and rebuild Heshbon!
   Make Sihon's city strong.
28 A fire began in Heshbon.
   That fire began in Sihon's city.
   The fire destroyed Ar in Moab.
   It burned the hills above Arnon River.
29 It is bad for you, Moab.
   You lost Chemosh's* people.
   His sons ran away.
   His daughters were taken prisoners by
      Sihon, king of the Amorites.
30 But we defeated those Amorites.
   We destroyed their towns from Heshbon
      to Dibon, from Nashim to Nophah,
      near Medeba."

31So the Israelites made their camp in the
land of the Amorites.
32Moses sent some men to look at the town
of Jazer. Then the Israelites captured that

town and the small towns that were around
it. They forced the Amorites who were living
there to leave.
33Then the Israelites traveled on the road
toward Bashan. King Og of Bashan got his
army and marched out to meet the Israelites.
He fought against them at Edrei.
34But the LORD said to Moses, "Don't be
afraid of that king. I will allow you to defeat
him. You will take his whole army and all his
land. Do the same to him as you did to Sihon,
the Amorite king who lived in Heshbon."
35So the Israelites defeated Og and his
army. They killed him, his sons, and all his
army. Then the Israelites took all his land.

Balaam and the King of Moab

22 1Then the Israelites traveled to the
Jordan Valley in Moab. They camped
near the Jordan River across from Jericho.

2-3Balak son of Zippor saw everything the
Israelites had done to the Amorites. The king
of Moab was very frightened of the Israelites
because there were so many of them. He was
very afraid.
4The king of Moab said to the leaders of
Midian, "This large group of people will
destroy everything around us, the way an ox
eats all the grass in a field."
Balak son of Zippor was the king of Moab
at this time. 5He sent some men to Balaam
son of Beor. Balaam was at Pethor, near the
Euphrates River. This was where Balaam's
people lived.*b* This was Balak's message: "A
new nation of people has come out of Egypt.
There are so many people that they cover
all the land. They have camped next to me.
6Come and help me. These people are too
powerful for me. I know that you have great
power. If you bless people, good things happen
to them. And if you curse people, bad things
happen to them. So come and curse these
people. Maybe then I will be able to defeat
them and force them to leave my country."
7The leaders of Moab and Midian left. They
went to talk to Balaam. They carried with
them money to pay him for his service.*c* Then
they told him what Balak had said.
8Balaam said to them, "Stay here for the
night. I will talk to the LORD and tell you the
answer he gives me." So the leaders of Moab
stayed there with Balaam that night.
9God came to Balaam and asked, "Who are
these men with you?"
10Balaam said to God, "The king of Moab,
Balak son of Zippor, sent them to give me a
message. 11This is the message: A new nation

---

a21:18 gift in the desert In Hebrew this is the name
"Mattanah."

b22:5 This ... lived Or "This was the land of the
Ammonites."
c22:7 for his service Or "for the things he needed to
make curses." In ancient times, when people asked
bad things to happen to other people, they often
wrote the curses on special bowls and used them in
ceremonies. They did this to try to force these bad
things to happen. See Deut. 18:10.

of people has come out of Egypt. There are so many people that they cover the land. So come and curse these people. Then maybe I will be able to fight them and force them to leave my land."

¹²But God said to Balaam, "Don't go with them. You must not curse those people. They are my people."

¹³The next morning Balaam got up and said to leaders from Balak, "Go back to your own country. The LORD will not let me go with you."

¹⁴So the leaders of Moab went back to Balak and told him this. They said, "Balaam refused to come with us."

¹⁵So Balak sent other leaders to Balaam. This time he sent many more than the first time. And these leaders were much more important than the first ones he sent. ¹⁶They went to Balaam and said, "This is what Balak son of Zippor says to you: Please don't let anything stop you from coming. ¹⁷I will pay you very much,ᵃ and I will do whatever you ask. Come and curse these people for me."

¹⁸Balaam gave Balak's officials his answer. He said, "I must obey the LORD my God. I cannot do anything, great or small, against his command. Even if King Balak gives me his beautiful home filled with silver and gold, I will not do anything against the Lord's command. ¹⁹But you can stay here tonight like the other men did, and during the night I will learn what the LORD wants to tell me."

²⁰That night, God came to Balaam. God said, "These men have come again to ask you to go with them. So you can go with them. But do only what I tell you to do."

Balaam and His Donkey

²¹The next morning, Balaam got up, put a saddle on his donkey, and went with the Moabite leaders. ²²Balaam was riding on his donkey. Two of his servants were with him. While Balaam was traveling, God became angry. So the LORD's angel stood in the road in front of Balaam to stopᵇ him.

²³When Balaam's donkey saw the LORD's angel standing in the road with a sword in his hand, the donkey turned from the road and went into the field. Balaam could not see the angel, so he was very angry at the donkey. He hit the donkey and forced it to go back on the road.

²⁴Later, the LORD's angel stood at a place where the road became narrow. This was between two vineyards.* There were walls on both sides of the road. ²⁵Again the donkey saw the LORD's angel. So the donkey walked very close to one wall. This crushed Balaam's foot against the wall. So Balaam hit his donkey again.

²⁶Later, the LORD's angel stood at another place where the road became narrow. There was no place where the donkey could go around him. It could not turn to the left or to the right. ²⁷The donkey saw the LORD's angel. So the donkey lay down with Balaam sitting on top of it. Balaam was very angry at the donkey. So he hit it with his walking stick.

²⁸Then the LORD caused the donkey to speak. The donkey said to Balaam, "Why are you angry at me? What have I done to you? You have hit me three times!"

²⁹Balaam answered the donkey, "You have made me look foolish. If I had a sword in my hand, I would kill you right now!"

³⁰But the donkey said to Balaam, "Look, I am your donkey. You have ridden me for so many years. And you know that I have never done this to you before!"

"That is true," Balaam said.

³¹Then the LORD allowed Balaam to see the angel. The LORD's angel was standing in the road, holding a sword in his hand. Balaam bowed low to the ground.

³²Then the LORD's angel asked Balaam, "Why did you hit your donkey three times? I am the one who came to stop you. But just in time,ᶜ ³³your donkey saw me and turned away from me. That happened three times. If the donkey had not turned away, I probably would have killed you already. And I would have let your donkey live."

³⁴Then Balaam said to the LORD's angel, "I have sinned. I did not know that you were standing in the road. If I am doing wrong, I will go back home."

³⁵Then the LORD's angel said to Balaam, "No, you can go with these men. But be careful. Speak only the words that I will tell you to say." So Balaam went with the leaders that Balak had sent.

³⁶Balak heard that Balaam was coming. So Balak went out to meet him at the Moabite townᵈ near the Arnon River. This was at the northern border of his country. ³⁷When Balak saw Balaam, he said to him, "I asked you before to come. I told you it was very important. Why didn't you come to me? Did you think I might not be able to pay you?"

³⁸Balaam answered, "Well, I am here now. I came, but I might not be able to do what you asked. I can only say the words that the LORD God tells me to say."

³⁹Then Balaam went with Balak to Kiriath Huzoth. ⁴⁰Balak killed some cattle and some sheep as his sacrifice. He gave some of the meat to Balaam and some to the leaders who were with him.

⁴¹The next morning Balak took Balaam to the town of Bamoth Baal. From there they could see part of the Israelite camp.

ᵃ**22:17** *I will pay you very much* Or "I will honor you very much."

ᵇ**22:22** *stop* Or "oppose" or "accuse." Also in verse 32.

ᶜ**22:32** *But just in time* Or "You should not be going this way," or "You are not doing right." The Hebrew text here is hard to understand.

ᵈ**22:36** *Moabite town* Or possibly, "Ar Moab."

Balaam's First Message

23 ¹Balaam said, "Build seven altars* here. And prepare seven bulls and seven rams for me." ²Balak did what Balaam asked. Then Balak and Balaam killed a ram and a bull on each of the altars.

³Then Balaam said to Balak, "Stay here near this altar. I will go to another place. Then the Lord will come to me, and he will tell me what I must say." Then Balaam went away to a higher place.

⁴God came to Balaam at that place, and Balaam said, "I have prepared seven altars. And I have killed a bull and a ram as a sacrifice on each altar."

⁵Then the Lord told Balaam what he should say. Then the Lord said, "Go back to Balak and say the things that I have given you to say."

⁶So Balaam went back to Balak. Balak was still standing near the altar, and all the leaders of Moab were standing there with them. ⁷Then Balaam said this:

Balak, the king of Moab,
brought me here from the eastern
mountains of Aram.
Balak said to me,
"Come, curse Jacob* for me.
Come, speak against the Israelites."
⁸ But God is not against them,
so I cannot speak against them either!
The Lord has not asked for bad things to
happen to these people.
So I cannot do that either.
⁹ I see these people from the mountain.
I see them from the high hills.
They live alone.
They are not part of another nation.
¹⁰ Who can count Jacob's people?
They are as many as the grains of dust.
No one can count even a fourth of the
Israelites.
Let me die like a good man.
Let my life end as happy as theirs!

¹¹Balak said to Balaam, "What have you done to me? I brought you here to curse my enemies, but you have blessed them!"

¹²But Balaam answered, "I must say the things that the Lord tells me to say."

¹³Then Balak said to him, "So come with me to another place. At that place you can see more of these people. You cannot see all of them—you can only see part of them. Maybe from that place you can curse them for me." ¹⁴So Balak led Balaam to Watchmen Hills.ᵃ This was on top of Mount Pisgah. There Balak built seven altars and killed a bull and a ram on each altar as a sacrifice.

¹⁵Then Balaam said to Balak, "Stay here by this altar while I go meet with God over there."

¹⁶So the Lord came to Balaam and told Balaam what to say. Then he told Balaam to go back to Balak and say these things. ¹⁷So Balaam went to Balak. Balak was still standing near the altar. The leaders of Moab were there with him. Balak saw Balaam coming and said, "What did the Lord say?"

Balaam's Second Message

¹⁸Then Balaam said this:

"Stand up, Balak, and listen to me.
Hear me, Balak son of Zippor.
¹⁹ God is not a man;
he will not lie.
God is not a human being;
his decisions will not change.
If he says he will do something,
then he will do it.
If he makes a promise,
then he will do what he promised.
²⁰ He told me to bless them.
He blessed them, so I cannot change
that.
²¹ God saw no wrong in Jacob's* people.
He saw no sin in the Israelites.
The Lord is their God,
and he is with them.
The Great King is with them!
²² God brought them out of Egypt.
They are as strong as a wild ox.
²³ There is no power that can defeat the
people of Jacob.
There is no magic that can stop the
Israelites.
People will say this about Jacob and the
Israelites:
'Look at the great things God did!'ᵇ
²⁴ The people are as strong as lions,
and they fight like lions.
And a lion will not rest until it eats what
it has caught,
until it drinks the blood of what it has
killed."

²⁵Then Balak said to Balaam, "You didn't ask for good things to happen to these people, but you didn't ask for bad things to happen to them either!"

²⁶Balaam answered, "I told you before that I can only say what the Lord tells me to say."

²⁷Then Balak said to Balaam, "So come with me to another place. Maybe God will be pleased and will allow you to curse them from that place." ²⁸So Balak led Balaam to the top of Mount Peor, which looks out over the desert.

²⁹Balaam said, "Build seven altars* here. Then prepare seven bulls and seven rams for the altars." ³⁰Balak did what Balaam asked. Balak offered the bulls and rams on the altars.

ᵃ**23:14** *Watchmen Hills* Or "the fields of Zophim."

ᵇ**23:23** Or "There is no fortunetelling in Jacob, no magic in Israel. God tells them immediately what he plans to do."

Balaam's Third Message

24 ¹Balaam saw that the LORD wanted to bless Israel, so he did not try to change that by using any kind of magic. But Balaam turned and looked toward the desert. ²He looked out across the desert and saw all the Israelites.* They were camped with the tribes in their different areas. Then the Spirit of God came on him, ³and he gave this message:

"This message is from Balaam son of Beor.
  I am speaking about things I see clearly.
⁴ These are the words I heard from God.
  I saw what God All-Powerful*a* showed
    me.
  I humbly tell what I clearly see.

⁵"People of Jacob, your tents are beautiful!
  Israelites, your homes are beautiful!
⁶ You are like rows of palm trees
    planted by the streams.
  You are like gardens
    growing by the rivers.
  You are like sweet-smelling bushes
    planted by the LORD.
  You are like cedar trees
    growing by the water.
⁷ You will always have enough water,
    enough water for your seeds to grow.
  Your king will be greater than King Agag.
  Your kingdom will be very great.

⁸"God brought them out of Egypt.
  They are as strong as a wild ox.
  They will defeat all their enemies.
    They will break their bones and shatter
      their arrows.
⁹ Israel is like a lion,
    curled up and lying down.
  Yes, they are like a young lion,
    and no one wants to wake him!
  Anyone who blesses you
    will be blessed.
  And anyone who curses you
    will have great troubles."

¹⁰When Balak heard this, he angrily struck his fist against his hand and said to Balaam, "I called you to come and curse my enemies. But you have blessed them. You have blessed them three times. ¹¹Now leave and go home! I told you that I would give you a very good payment, but the LORD has caused you to lose your reward."

¹²Balaam said to Balak, "You sent men to ask me to come. Don't you remember what I told them? I said, ¹³'Even if Balak gives me his most beautiful house filled with silver and gold, I can still say only what the LORD commands me to say. I cannot do anything myself, good or bad. I must say what the LORD

commands.' ¹⁴Now I am going back to my own people. But I will give you this warning. I will tell you what these Israelites will do to you and your people in the future.'"

Balaam's Last Message

¹⁵Then Balaam gave this message:

"This message is from Balaam son of Beor.
  I am speaking about things I see clearly.
¹⁶ I heard this message from God.
  I learned what God Most High taught
    me.
  I saw what God All-Powerful showed
    me.
  I humbly tell what I clearly see.

¹⁷"I see him coming, but not now.
  I see him coming, but not soon.
  A star will come from the family of Jacob.*
  A new ruler will come from the
    Israelites.
  He will smash the heads of the Moabites
    and crush the heads of all the sons of
    Sheth.*b*
¹⁸ Israel will grow strong!
  He will get the land of Edom.
  He will get the land of Seir,*c* his enemy.

¹⁹"A new ruler will come from the family of
    Jacob.
  That ruler will destroy the people left
    alive in that city."

²⁰Then Balaam saw the Amalekites and said this:

"Amalek is the strongest of all nations,
  but even Amalek will be destroyed!"

²¹Then Balaam saw the Kenites and said this:

"You believe that your country is safe,
  like a bird's nest*d* high on a mountain.
²² But you Kenites will be destroyed,
  ⌊just as the Lord destroyed Cain.⌋
  Assyria will make you prisoners."

²³Then Balaam said this:

"No one can live when God does this.
²⁴ Ships will come from Cyprus.*e*

---

*b***24:17** *sons of Sheth* Or "Seth." Seth was Adam's third son. This might be like the phrases "son of Man" (Adam) and "son of Enosh" and mean simply "all these people."
*c***24:18** *Seir* Another name for Edom.
*d***24:21** *nest, Kenite, Cain* A play on words. The names "Cain" and "Kenite" are like the Hebrew word meaning "nest."
*e***24:24** *Cyprus* Literally, "Kittim." This might be Cyprus, Crete, or other places west of Israel in the Mediterranean Sea.

*a***24:4** *God All-Powerful* Literally, "El Shaddai." Also in verse 16.

They will defeat Assyria and Eber,[a]
but those ships will also be destroyed."

25Then Balaam got up and went back home, and Balak went his own way.

Israel at Peor

25 1While the Israelites were camped near Acacia, the men committed sexual sins[b] with Moabite women. 2-3The Moabite women invited the men to come and join in their sacrifices to their false gods. So the Israelites joined in worshiping these false gods—they ate the sacrifices and worshiped these gods. There the Israelites began worshiping the false god, Baal* of Peor. And the LORD became very angry with them.

4The LORD said to Moses, "Get all the leaders of these people. Then kill them so that all the people can see.[c] Lay their bodies before the LORD. Then the LORD will not show his anger against all the Israelites."

5So Moses said to Israel's judges, "Each of you must find the men in your tribe who have led people to worship the false god, Baal of Peor. Then you must kill these men."

6At the time, Moses and all the elders* of Israel were gathered together at the entrance to the Meeting Tent.* An Israelite man brought a Midianite woman home to his brothers.[d] He did this where Moses and all the leaders could see. Moses and the leaders were very sad. 7Phinehas was the son of Eleazar and the grandson of Aaron the priest. Phinehas saw this man bring the woman into camp. So he left the meeting and got his spear. 8He followed the Israelite into the tent. Then he used the spear to kill the Israelite man and the Midianite woman in her tent.[e] He pushed the spear through both of their bodies. At that time there was a great sickness among the Israelites. But when Phinehas killed these two people, the sickness stopped. 9A total of 24,000 people died from that sickness.

10The LORD said to Moses, 11"I have strong feelings for my people—I want them to belong only to me! Phinehas son of Eleazar, and grandson of Aaron the priest, saved the Israelites from my anger. He did this because of his strong feelings for my people. So I will not kill the people like I wanted to. 12Tell

Phinehas that I am making a peace agreement with him. 13This is the agreement: He and all of his family who live after him will always be priests, because he had strong feelings for his God. And he did what was needed to make the Israelites pure.*"

14The Israelite man who was killed with the Midianite woman was named Zimri son of Salu. He was the leader of a family in the tribe of Simeon. 15And the name of the Midianite woman who was killed was Cozbi.[f] She was the daughter of Zur. Zur was the head of a family and leader of a Midianite tribe.

16The LORD said to Moses, 17"The Midianites are your enemies. You must kill them. 18They have already made you their enemies. They tricked you at Peor. And they tricked you with the woman named Cozbi. She was the daughter of a Midianite leader, but she was killed when the sickness came to the Israelites. That sickness was caused because the people were tricked into worshiping the false god Baal of Peor."

The People Are Counted

26 1After the great sickness, the LORD spoke to Moses and Eleazar son of Aaron the priest. 2He said, "Count the Israelites. Count all the men who are 20 years old or older and list them by families. These are the men who are able to serve in the army of Israel."

3At this time the people were camped in the Jordan Valley in Moab. This was near the Jordan River, across from Jericho. So Moses and Eleazar the priest spoke to the people. They said, 4"You must count every man who is 20 years old or older. The LORD gave Moses this command." Here is the list of the Israelites who came out of Egypt:

5These are the people from the tribe of Reuben. (Reuben was the firstborn* son of Israel.) The family groups were

    Hanoch—the Hanochite family group;
    Pallu—the Palluite family group;
  6 Hezron—the Hezronite family group;
    Carmi—the Carmite family group.

7These were the families in the tribe of Reuben. There was a total of 43,730 men.

8Pallu's son was Eliab. 9Eliab had three sons—Nemuel, Dathan, and Abiram. Remember, Dathan and Abiram were the two leaders who turned against Moses and Aaron. They followed Korah when Korah turned against the LORD. 10That was the time when the earth opened and swallowed Korah and all of his followers. And 250 men died! That was a warning to all the Israelites. 11But the other people who were from the family of Korah did not die.

---

[a]24:24 *Eber* This might mean the people living west of the Euphrates River, or it might mean the "Hebrews," the descendants of Eber. See Gen. 10:21.

[b]25:1 *sexual sins* Sexual sin was often connected with temples for false gods. So this can mean that the men were unfaithful to their wives and also that they were unfaithful to God by going to their temples.

[c]25:4 *so that all the people can see* Literally, "before the sun."

[d]25:6 *brothers* Or "family."

[e]25:8 *her tent* This was probably a special tent that showed this woman was a prostitute serving the false god, Baal of Peor.

[f]25:15 *Cozbi* This name is like the Hebrew word meaning "my lie."

¹²These are the family groups from the tribe of Simeon:

Nemuel—the Nemuelite family group;
Jamin—the Jaminite family group;
Jakin—the Jakinite family group;
¹³ Zerah—the Zerahite family group;
Shaul—the Shaulite family group.

¹⁴These were the family groups from the tribe of Simeon. There was a total of 22,200 men.
¹⁵These are the family groups from the tribe of Gad:

Zephon—the Zephonite family group;
Haggi—the Haggite family group;
Shuni—the Shunite family group;
¹⁶ Ozni—the Oznite family group;
Eri—the Erite family group;
¹⁷ Arodi—the Arodite family group;
Areli—the Arelite family group.

¹⁸These were the family groups from the tribe of Gad. There was a total of 40,500 men.
¹⁹⁻²⁰These are the family groups from the tribe of Judah:

Shelah—the Shelanite family group;
Perez—the Perezite family group;
Zerah—the Zerahite family group.
(Two of Judah's sons, Er and Onan, died in Canaan.*)

²¹These are the family groups from Perez:

Hezron—the Hezronite family group;
Hamul—the Hamulite family group.

²²These were the family groups from the tribe of Judah. The total number of men was 76,500.
²³The family groups from the tribe of Issachar were

Tola—the Tolaite family group;
Puah—the Puite family group;
²⁴ Jashub—the Jashubite family group;
Shimron—the Shimronite family group.

²⁵These were the family groups from the tribe of Issachar. The total number of men was 64,300.
²⁶The family groups from the tribe of Zebulun were

Sered—the Seredite family group;
Elon—the Elonite family group;
Jahleel—the Jahleelite family group.

²⁷These were the family groups from the tribe of Zebulun. The total number of men was 60,500.
²⁸Joseph's two sons were Manasseh and Ephraim. Each son became a tribe with its own family groups. ²⁹Manasseh's family groups were

Makir—the Makirite family groups.
(Makir was the father of Gilead.)
Gilead—the Gileadite family groups.

³⁰The family groups from Gilead were

Iezer—the Iezerite family group;
Helek—the Helekite family group;
³¹ Asriel—the Asrielite family group;
Shechem—the Shechemite family group;
³² Shemida—the Shemidaite family group;
Hepher—the Hepherite family group.

³³ Zelophehad was the son of Hepher. But he had no sons—only daughters. His daughters' names were Mahlah, Noah, Hoglah, Milcah, and Tirzah.

³⁴These are all the family groups from the tribe of Manasseh. The total number of men was 52,700.
³⁵The family groups from the tribe of Ephraim were

Shuthelah—the Shuthelahite family group;
Beker—the Bekerite family group;
Tahan—the Tahanite family group.

³⁶ Eran was from Shuthelah's family group;
Eran—the Eranite family group.

³⁷These were the family groups from the tribe of Ephraim. The total number of men was 32,500.
These family groups of Manasseh and Ephraim are all the descendants of Joseph.
³⁸The family groups from the tribe of Benjamin were

Bela—the Belaite family group;
Ashbel—the Ashbelite family group;
Ahiram—the Ahiramite family group;
³⁹ Shupham—the Shuphamite family group;
Hupham—the Huphamite family group;
⁴⁰ The family groups from Bela were
Ard—the Ardite family group;
Naaman—the Naamanite family group.

⁴¹These were all the family groups from the tribe of Benjamin. The total number of men was 45,600.
⁴²The family groups from the tribe of Dan were

Shuham—the Shuhamite family group.

That was the family group from the tribe of Dan. ⁴³There were many family groups from the Shuhamite tribe. The total number of men was 64,400.

⁴⁴The family groups from the tribe of Asher were

Imnah—the Imnite family group;
Ishvi—the Ishvite family group;
Beriah—the Beriite family group.

⁴⁵The family groups from Beriah were

Heber—the Heberite family group;
Malkiel—the Malkielite family group.

⁴⁶(Asher also had a daughter named Serah.) ⁴⁷These were the family groups from the tribe of Asher. The total number of men was 53,400.
⁴⁸The family groups from the tribe of Naphtali were

Jahzeel—the Jahzeelite family group;
Guni—the Gunite family group;
⁴⁹ Jezer—the Jezerite family group;
Shillem—the Shillemite family group.

⁵⁰These were the family groups from the tribe of Naphtali. The total number of men was 45,400.
⁵¹So the total number of men of Israel was 601,730.
⁵²The LORD said to Moses, ⁵³"The land will be divided and given to these people. Each tribe will get enough land for all the people who were counted. ⁵⁴A large tribe will get much land, and a small tribe will get less land. The land that they get will be equal to the number of people who were counted. ⁵⁵But you must use lots* to decide which tribe gets which part of the land. Each tribe will get its share of the land, and that land will be given the name of that tribe. ⁵⁶Land will be given to each tribe—large and small. And you will throw lots to make the decisions."
⁵⁷They also counted the tribe of Levi. These are the family groups from the tribe of Levi:

Gershon—the Gershonite family group;
Kohath—the Kohathite family group;
Merari—the Merarite family group.

⁵⁸These are also family groups from the tribe of Levi:

the Libnite family group;
the Hebronite family group;
the Mahlite family group;
the Mushite family group;
the Korahite family group.

Amram was from the Kohath family group. ⁵⁹Amram's wife was named Jochebed. She was also from the tribe of Levi. She was born in Egypt. Amram and Jochebed had two sons, Aaron and Moses. They also had a daughter, Miriam.
⁶⁰Aaron was the father of Nadab, Abihu,

Eleazar, and Ithamar. ⁶¹But Nadab and Abihu died. They died because they made an offering to the LORD with fire that was not allowed.
⁶²The total number of males one month or older from the tribe of Levi was 23,000. But these men were not counted with the other Israelites. They did not get a share of the land that the LORD gave to the other people.
⁶³Moses and Eleazar the priest counted all these people. They counted the Israelites while they were in the Jordan Valley in Moab. This was near the Jordan River across from Jericho. ⁶⁴Many years before, in the Sinai desert, Moses and Aaron the priest counted the Israelites. But all these people were dead. Not one of them was still alive, ⁶⁵because the LORD told them that they would all die in the desert. The only two men who were left alive were Caleb son of Jephunneh and Joshua son of Nun.

Zelophehad's Daughters

27 ¹Zelophehad was the son of Hepher. Hepher was the son of Gilead. Gilead was the son of Makir. Makir was the son of Manasseh. Manasseh was the son of Joseph. Zelophehad had five daughters. Their names were Mahlah, Noah, Hoglah, Milcah, and Tirzah. ²These five women went to the Meeting Tent* and stood before Moses, Eleazar the priest, the leaders, and all the Israelites.

The five daughters said, ³"Our father died while we were traveling through the desert. He died a natural death. He was not one of the men who joined Korah's group. (Korah was the man who turned against the LORD.) But our father had no sons. ⁴This means that our father's name will not continue. It is not fair that our father's name will not continue. His name will end because he had no sons. So we ask you to give us some of the land that our father's brothers will get."

⁵So Moses asked the LORD what he should do. ⁶The LORD said to him, ⁷"The daughters of Zelophehad are right. They should share the land with their father's brothers. So give them the land that you would have given to their father.

⁸"So tell the Israelites, 'If a man has no son, when he dies everything he owns will be given to his daughter. ⁹If he has no daughter, everything he owns will be given to his brothers. ¹⁰If he has no brothers, everything he owns will be given to his father's brothers. ¹¹If his father had no brothers, everything he owns will be given to the closest relative in his family. This will be a law among the Israelites. The LORD has given this command to Moses.'"

Joshua Is the New Leader

¹²Then the LORD said to Moses, "Go up on one of mountains in the desert east of the Jordan River. There you will see the land that I am giving to the Israelites. ¹³After you have seen this land, you will die like your brother Aaron. ¹⁴Remember when the people became

angry at the water in the Desert of Zin. Both you and Aaron refused to obey my command. You did not honor me and show the people that I am holy.*" (This was at the water of Meribah*a* near Kadesh in the Desert of Zin.)

¹⁵Moses said to the LORD, ¹⁶"LORD, you are the God who knows what people are thinking. I pray that you will choose a leader for these people.*b* ¹⁷I pray that you will choose a leader who will lead them out of this land and bring them into the new land. Then your people will not be like sheep without a shepherd."

¹⁸So the LORD said to Moses, "Joshua son of Nun is very wise.*c* You will place your hand on him and make him the new leader. ¹⁹Tell him to stand before Eleazar the priest and all the people. Then make him the new leader. ²⁰"Show the people that you are making him leader,*d* then all the people will obey him. ²¹If Joshua needs to make a decision, he will go to Eleazar the priest. Eleazar will use the Urim* to learn the LORD's answer. Then Joshua and all the Israelites will do the things God says. If he says, 'go to war,' they will go to war. And if he says, 'go home,' they will go home."

²²Moses obeyed the LORD. Moses told Joshua to stand before Eleazar the priest and all the Israelites. ²³Then Moses put his hands on him to show that he was the new leader. He did this just as the LORD told him to.

Daily Offerings

28 ¹Then the LORD spoke to Moses. He said, ²"Give this command to the Israelites. Tell them to be sure to give the grain offerings and sacrifices to me at the right time as sweet-smelling gifts. ³These are gifts that they must give to the LORD. Every day they must give 2 lambs that are one year old. There must be nothing wrong with them. ⁴Offer one of the lambs in the morning and the other lamb just before dark. ⁵Also give a grain offering of 8 cups*e* of fine flour mixed with 1 quart*f* of olive oil." ⁶(They started giving the daily offerings at Mount Sinai as sweet-smelling gifts to the LORD.) ⁷"The people must also give the drink offerings that go with the gifts. They must give 1 quart of wine with every lamb. Pour that drink offering on the altar in the Holy Place. This is a gift to the LORD. ⁸Offer the second lamb just before dark.

Offer it just as the morning offering. Also give the drink offering that goes with it. This will be a sweet-smelling gift to the LORD.

Sabbath Offerings

⁹"On the Sabbath,* you must give 2 lambs that are one year old. There must be nothing wrong with them. You must also give a grain offering of 16 cups*g* of fine flour mixed with olive oil, and a drink offering. ¹⁰This is a special offering for the day of rest. This offering is in addition to the regular daily offering and drink offering.

Monthly Meetings

¹¹"On the first day of each month you will offer a special burnt offering* to the LORD. This offering will be 2 male bulls, 1 ram, and 7 lambs that are one year old. There must be nothing wrong with them. ¹²With each bull, you must give a grain offering of 24 cups*h* of fine flour mixed with olive oil. And with the ram, you must give a grain offering of 16 cups of fine flour mixed with olive oil. ¹³Also give a grain offering of 8 cups of fine flour mixed with olive oil with each lamb. This will be a sweet-smelling gift to the LORD. ¹⁴The drink offering will be 2 quarts*i* of wine with each bull, 1¼ quarts*j* of wine with the ram, and 1 quart of wine with each lamb. That is the burnt offering that must be offered each month of the year. ¹⁵In addition to the regular daily burnt offering and drink offering, you must also give 1 male goat to the LORD. That goat will be a sin offering.*

Passover

¹⁶"The LORD's Passover will be on the 14th day of the first month. ¹⁷The Festival of Unleavened Bread* begins on the 15th day of that month. This festival lasts for seven days. The only bread you can eat is bread made without yeast. ¹⁸You must have a special meeting on the first day of this festival. You will not do any work on that day. ¹⁹You will give burnt offerings* to the LORD. The burnt offerings will be 2 bulls, 1 ram, and 7 lambs that are one year old. There must be nothing wrong with them. ²⁰⁻²¹You must also give a grain offering of 24 cups of fine flour mixed with olive oil with each bull, and 16 cups of fine flour mixed with oil with the ram, and 8 cups of fine flour mixed with oil for each lamb. ²²You must also give a male goat as a sin offering* to make you pure.* ²³You must give these offerings in addition to the morning burnt offerings that you give every day.

²⁴"In the same way, each day for seven days, you must give the gifts to the LORD and

*a*27:14 *water of Meribah* Or "water of rebellion."
*b*27:16 *LORD, ... these people* Literally, "May the LORD, the God of the spirits of all people, appoint a man for this community."
*c*27:18 *Joshua ... is very wise* Literally, "Take Joshua son of Nun. He is a man with a spirit in him." This might mean that Joshua was very wise, or it might mean that God's Spirit was with him.
*d*27:20 *Show ... leader* Literally, "Give him some of your glory."
*e*28:5 *8 cups* Literally, "1/10 of an ephah" (2.2 l). Also in verses 13, 20–21, 29.
*f*28:5 *1 quart* Literally, "1/4 hin" (.8 l). Also in verse 14.
*g*28:9 *16 cups* Literally, "2/10 of an ephah" (4.4 l). Also in verses 12, 20–21, 28.
*h*28:12 *24 cups* Literally, "3/10 of an ephah" (6.6 l). Also in verses 20–21, 28.
*i*28:14 *2 quarts* Literally, "1/2 hin" (1.6 l).
*j*28:14 *1 1/4 quarts* Literally, "1/3 hin" (1 l).

the drink offerings that go with them. The smell of these offerings will please the LORD. The offerings will be food for the people. You must give these offerings in addition to the burnt offerings that you give every day.

25"Then, on the seventh day of this festival, you will have another special meeting. You will not do any work on that day.

Festival of Harvest

26"The first day of the Festival of Harvest* is the day you bring the first of your new crops and give them as a grain offering to the LORD. At that time you must also call a special meeting. You must not do any work on that day. 27You must offer a burnt offering* as a sweet-smelling gift to the LORD. You must offer 2 bulls, 1 ram, and 7 lambs that are one year old. There must be nothing wrong with them. 28You must also give 24 cups of fine flour mixed with oil with each bull, and 16 cups with each ram, 29and 8 cups with each lamb. 30You must also sacrifice a male goat to make you pure.* 31You must give these offerings in addition to the daily burnt offerings and the grain offering you give with them. Be sure there is nothing wrong with the animals or the drink offerings that you give with them.

Festival of Trumpets

29 1"There will be a special meeting on the first day of the seventh month. You will not do any work on that day. That is the day for blowing the trumpets.*a* 2You will offer burnt offerings.* Their smell will please the LORD. You will offer 1 bull, 1 ram, and 7 lambs that are one year old. There must be nothing wrong with them. 3You will also offer 24 cups*b* of fine flour mixed with oil with the bull, 16 cups*c* with the ram, 4and 8 cups*d* with each of the 7 lambs. 5Also offer a male goat as a sin offering* to make you pure.* 6These offerings are in addition to the New Moon* sacrifice and its grain offering. And they are in addition to the daily sacrifice and its grain offerings and drink offerings. These must be done according to the rules. They will be sweet-smelling gifts to the LORD.

The Day of Atonement

7"There will be a special meeting on the tenth day of the seventh month. During that day you must not eat any food,*e* and you must not do any work. 8You will offer burnt offerings.* Their smell will please the LORD. You

must offer 1 bull, 1 ram, and 7 lambs that are one year old. There must be nothing wrong with them. 9You must also offer 24 cups of fine flour mixed with olive oil with the bull, 16 cups with the ram, 10and 8 cups with each of the 7 lambs. 11You will also offer 1 male goat as a sin offering.* This will be in addition to the sin offering for the Day of Atonement.* This will also be in addition to the daily sacrifice and its grain offerings and drink offerings.

Festival of Shelters

12"There will be a special meeting on the 15th day of the seventh month.*f* You must not do any work on that day. You must celebrate a special festival for the LORD for seven days. 13You will offer burnt offerings* as sweet-smelling gifts to the LORD. You will offer 13 bulls, 2 rams, and 14 lambs that are one year old. There must be nothing wrong with them. 14You must also offer 24 cups of fine flour mixed with oil with each of the 13 bulls, 16 cups with each of the 2 rams, 15and 8 cups with each of the 14 lambs. 16You must also offer 1 male goat. This must be in addition to the daily sacrifice and its grain offerings and drink offerings.

17"On the second day of this festival, you must offer 12 bulls, 2 rams, and 14 lambs that are one year old. There must be nothing wrong with them. 18You must also give the right amount of grain and drink offerings with the bulls, rams, and lambs. 19You must also offer 1 male goat as a sin offering.* This must be in addition to the daily sacrifice and its grain offerings and drink offerings.

20"On the third day of this festival, you must offer 11 bulls, 2 rams, and 14 lambs that are one year old. There must be nothing wrong with them. 21You must also give the right amount of grain and drink offerings with the bulls, rams, and lambs. 22You must also give 1 goat as a sin offering. This must be in addition to the daily sacrifice and its grain offerings and drink offerings.

23"On the fourth day of this festival, you must offer 10 bulls, 2 rams, and 14 lambs that are one year old. There must be nothing wrong with them. 24You must also give the right amount of grain and drink offerings with the bulls, rams, and lambs. 25You must also give 1 male goat as a sin offering. This must be in addition to the daily sacrifice and its grain offerings and drink offerings.

26"On the fifth day of this festival, you must offer 9 bulls, 2 rams, and 14 lambs that are one year old. There must be nothing wrong with them. 27You must also give the right amount of grain and drink offerings with the bulls, rams, and lambs. 28You must also give

---

*a***29:1** *blowing the trumpets* Or "shouting." This might mean this is a day for shouting and being happy.
*b***29:3** *24 cups* Literally, "3/10 of an ephah" (6.6 l). Also in verses 9, 14.
*c***29:3** *16 cups* Literally, "2/10 of an ephah" (4.4 l). Also in verses 9, 14.
*d***29:4** *8 cups* Literally, "1/10 of an ephah" (2.2 l). Also in verses 10, 15.
*e***29:7** *you ... food* Literally, "you will humble your souls."

*f***29:12** *15th day of the seventh month* This is the Festival of Shelters. See "Festival of Shelters" in the Word List.

1 male goat as a sin offering. This must be in addition to the daily sacrifice and its grain offerings and drink offerings.

²⁹"On the sixth day of this festival, you must offer 8 bulls, 2 rams, and 14 lambs that are one year old. There must be nothing wrong with them. ³⁰You must also give the right amount of grain and drink offerings for the bulls, rams, and lambs. ³¹You must also give 1 male goat as a sin offering. This must be in addition to the daily sacrifice and its grain offerings and drink offerings.

³²"On the seventh day of this festival, you must offer 7 bulls, 2 rams, and 14 lambs that are one year old. There must be nothing wrong with them. ³³You must also give the right amount of grain and drink offerings with the bulls, rams, and lambs. ³⁴You must also give 1 male goat as a sin offering. This must be in addition to the daily sacrifice and its grain offerings and drink offerings.

³⁵"The eighth day of this festival is a very special meeting for you. You must not do any work on that day. ³⁶You must offer a burnt offering as a sweet-smelling gift to the Lord. You must offer 1 bull, 1 ram, and 7 lambs that are one year old. There must be nothing wrong with them. ³⁷You must also give the right amount of grain and drink offerings with the bull, ram, and lambs. ³⁸You must also give 1 male goat as a sin offering. This must be in addition to the daily sacrifice and its grain offerings and drink offerings.

³⁹"At the special festivals you must bring your burnt offerings, grain offerings, drink offerings, and fellowship offerings.* You must give these offerings to the Lord. They are in addition to any special gift you might want to give to the Lord and any offering that is part of any special promise you make."

⁴⁰Moses told the Israelites everything the Lord had commanded him.

Special Promises

30 ¹Moses spoke with all the leaders of the Israelite tribes and told them about these commands from the Lord:

²"If a man wants to make a special promise to God, or if he promises to give something special to God, let him do that thing. But he must do exactly what he promises!

³"A young woman might still be living in her father's house. And that young woman might make a special promise to give something to the Lord. ⁴If her father hears about the promise and agrees, the young woman must do what she promised. ⁵But if her father hears about the promise and does not agree, she is free from her promise. She does not have to do what she promised. Her father stopped her, so the Lord will forgive her.

⁶"A woman might make a special promise to give something to the Lord and then get married. ⁷If the husband hears about the promise and does not object, the woman must

do what she promised. ⁸But if the husband hears about the promise and refuses to let her keep her promise, the wife does not have to do what she promised. Her husband broke the promise—he did not let her do what she said. So the Lord will forgive her.

⁹"A widow or a divorced woman might make a special promise. If she does, she must do exactly what she promised.

¹⁰"A married woman might make a promise to give something to the Lord. ¹¹If her husband hears about the promise and lets her keep her promise, she must do exactly what she promised. She must give everything she promised. ¹²But if her husband hears about the promise and refuses to let her keep the promise, she does not have to do what she promised. It doesn't matter what she promised; her husband can break the promise. If her husband breaks the promise, the Lord will forgive her. ¹³A married woman might promise to give something to the Lord, or she might promise to do without something,ᵃ or she might make some other special promise to God. The husband can stop any of these promises, and the husband can let her keep any of these promises. ¹⁴How does the husband let his wife keep her promises? If he hears about the promises and does not stop them, the woman must do exactly what she promised. ¹⁵But if the husband hears about the promises and stops them, he is responsible for breaking her promises."ᵇ

¹⁶These are the commands that the Lord gave to Moses. These are the commands about a man and his wife, and about a father and his daughter who is still young and living at home in her father's house.

Israel Fights Back Against the Midianites

31 ¹The Lord spoke to Moses and said, ²"Moses, tell the Israelites this: 'Go and attack the Midianites, and do to them what they did to you.' After that, Moses, you will die."ᶜ

³So Moses spoke to the people. He said, "Choose some of your men to be soldiers. The Lord will use these men to do to the Midianites what they did to you. ⁴Choose 1000 men from each of the tribes of Israel. ⁵There will be a total of 12,000 soldiers from the tribes of Israel."

⁶Moses sent these 12,000 men to war. He sent Phineas son of Eleazar with them as the priest. Phineas took the holy* things and the horns and trumpets with him. ⁷The Israelites fought the Midianites as the Lord had commanded. They killed all the Midianite men.

ᵃ**30:13 do without something** Literally, "humble her soul." Usually this means to make the body suffer in some way, such as by not eating food.
ᵇ**30:15 he … her promises** Literally, "he carries her guilt."
ᶜ**31:2 you will die** Literally, "you will be gathered to your people."

8Among the people who they killed were Evi, Rekem, Zur, Hur, and Reba—the five kings of Midian. They also killed Balaam son of Beor with a sword.

9The Israelites took the Midianite women and children as prisoners. They also took all their sheep, cattle, and other things. 10Then they burned all their towns and villages. 11They took all the people and animals 12and brought them to Moses, Eleazar the priest, and all the other Israelites. They brought all the things they took in war to the camp of Israel. The Israelites were camped in the Jordan Valley in Moab, on the east side of the Jordan River across from Jericho. 13Then Moses, Eleazar the priest, and the leaders of the people went out of the camp to meet with the soldiers.

14Moses was very angry with the leaders of the army, the commanders of 1000 men, and the commanders of 100 men, who came back from the war. 15Moses said to them, "Why did you let the women live? 16These are the women who listened to Balaam and caused the men of Israel to turn away from the LORD that time at Peor. The disease will come to the LORD's people again. 17Now, kill all the Midianite boys, and kill all the Midianite women who have had sexual relations with a man. 18You can let all the young girls live—but only if they never had sexual relations with any man. 19And then, all you men who killed other people must stay outside the camp for seven days. You must stay outside the camp even if you just touched a dead body. On the third day you and your prisoners must make yourselves pure. You must do the same thing again on the seventh day. 20You must wash all of your clothes. You must wash anything made with leather, wool, or wood. You must purify yourselves."

21Then Eleazar the priest spoke to the soldiers. He said, "These are the rules that the LORD gave to Moses for soldiers coming back from war. 22-23You must put gold, silver, bronze, iron, tin, or lead into the fire and then wash these things with the special water to make them pure. If something can be put in the fire, you must put it in fire to purify it. If things cannot be put in fire, you must still wash them with the special water. 24On the seventh day you must wash all of your clothes. Then you will be pure. After that you can come into camp."

25Then the LORD said to Moses, 26"You, Eleazar the priest, and all the leaders should count all the prisoners, animals, and everything the soldiers took in war. 27Then divide these things between the soldiers who went to war and the rest of the Israelites. 28Take part of these things from the soldiers who went to war. That part will belong to the LORD. His share is one from every 500 items. This includes people, cattle, donkeys, and sheep. 29Take that share from the soldiers'

half of the things they took in war. Then give these things to Eleazar the priest. That part will belong to the LORD. 30And then, from the people's half, take one thing for every 50 items. This includes people, cattle, donkeys, sheep, or any other animal. Give that share to the Levites, because they take care of the LORD's Holy Tent.*"

31So Moses and Eleazar did what the LORD commanded Moses. 32The soldiers had taken 675,000 sheep, 3372,000 cattle, 3461,000 donkeys, 35and 32,000 women. (These are only the women who had not had sexual relations with any man.) 36The soldiers who went to war got 337,500 sheep. 37They gave 675 sheep to the LORD. 38The soldiers got 36,000 cattle. They gave 72 cattle to the LORD. 39The soldiers got 30,500 donkeys. They gave 61 donkeys to the LORD. 40The soldiers got 16,000 women. They gave 32 women to the LORD. 41Moses gave all these gifts for the LORD to Eleazar the priest, as the LORD had commanded him.

42Then Moses counted the people's half. This was their share that Moses had taken from the soldiers who had gone to war. 43The people got 337,500 sheep, 4436,000 cattle, 4530,500 donkeys, 46and 16,000 women. 47For every 50 items, Moses took one thing for the LORD. This included the animals and the people. Then he gave them to the Levites because they took care of the LORD's Holy Tent. Moses did this as the LORD commanded.

48Then the leaders of the army (the leaders over 1000 men and the leaders over 100 men) came to Moses. 49They told Moses, "We, your servants, have counted our soldiers. We have not missed any of them. 50So we are bringing the LORD's gift from every soldier. We are bringing things that are made of gold—armbands, bracelets, rings, earrings, and necklaces. This gift to the LORD is to make us pure.*"

51So Moses and Eleazar the priest accepted all these gold items from them. 52The gold that the commandersa and captainsb gave to the LORD weighed about 424 pounds.c 53The soldiers kept the rest of their share of the things they took in war. 54Moses and Eleazar the priest took the gold from the commanders and captains and then put that gold in the Meeting Tent.* This present was a memoriald before the LORD for the Israelites.

Tribes East of the Jordan River

32 1The tribes of Reuben and Gad had many cattle. These people looked at the land near Jazer and Gilead. They saw that this land was good for their cattle. 2So

a31:52 **commanders** Literally, "leaders of 1000 men."
b31:52 **captains** Literally, "leaders of 100 men."
c31:52 **424 pounds** Literally, "16,750 shekels" (190 kg).
d31:54 **memorial** Something that helps people remember things that happened in the past.

the people from the tribes of Reuben and Gad came to Moses. They spoke to Moses, Eleazar the priest, and the leaders of the people. 3-4They said, "We, your servants, have many cattle. And the land that we have fought against is a good land for cattle. This land includes the area around Ataroth, Dibon, Jazer, Nimrah, Heshbon, Elealeh, Sibmah,ᵃ Nebo, and Beon. 5If it pleases you, we would like this land to be given to us. Don't take us to the other side of the Jordan River."

6Moses told the people from the tribes of Reuben and Gad, "Will you let your brothers go and fight while you settle here? 7Why are you trying to discourage the Israelites? You will make them not want to cross the river and take the land that the LORD has given to them! 8Your fathers did the same thing to me. In Kadesh Barnea I sent spies to look at the land. 9These men went as far as Eshcol Valley. They saw the land, and they discouraged the Israelites. These men made the Israelites not want to go into the land that the LORD had given to them. 10The LORD became very angry with the people. He made this promise: 11'None of the people who came from Egypt and are 20 years old or older will be allowed to see this land. I made a promise to Abraham, Isaac, and Jacob. I promised to give this land to these people, but they did not really follow me. 12Only Caleb son of Jephunneh the Kenizzite and Joshua son of Nun really followed the LORD!'

13"The LORD was very angry with the Israelites. So he made the people stay in the desert for 40 years. He made them stay there until all the people who had sinned against the LORD were dead. 14And now you are doing the same thing that your fathers did. You sinful people, do you want the LORD to be even more angry with his people? 15If you stop following the Lord, he will make Israel stay even longer in the desert. Then you will destroy all these people!"

16But the people from the tribes of Reuben and Gad went to Moses. They said, "We will build cities for our children and barns for our animals here. 17Then our children can be safe from the other people who live in this land. But we will gladly come and help the other Israelites. We will bring them to their land. 18We will not come back home until everyone in Israel has taken his part of the land. 19We will not take any of the land west of the Jordan River. No, our part of the land is east of the Jordan River."

20So Moses told them, "If you do all these things, this land will belong to you. But your soldiers must go before the LORD into battle. 21Your soldiers must cross the Jordan River and force the enemy to leave the country. 22After the LORD helps us all take the land,

you can go back home. Then the LORD and Israel will not think that you are guilty. Then the LORD will let you have this land. 23But if you don't do these things, you will be sinning against the LORD. And know for sure that you will be punished for your sin. 24Build cities for your children and barns for your animals. But then, you must do what you promised."

25Then the people from the tribes of Gad and Reuben said to Moses, "We are your servants. You are our master, so we will do what you say. 26Our wives, children, and all our animals will stay in the cities of Gilead. 27But we, your servants, will cross the Jordan River. We will march before the LORD into battle, as our master says."

28So Moses, Eleazar the priest, Joshua son of Nun, and all the leaders of the tribes of Israel heard them make that promise. 29Moses said to them, "The people of Gad and Reuben will cross the Jordan River. They will march before the LORD into battle. They will help you take the land. And you will give the land of Gilead as their part of the country. 30But if they do not cross the river with you ready to fight, they will not get any land on this side. They will get only a share of the land of Canaan* with the rest of you."

31The people of Gad and Reuben answered, "We promise to do what the LORD commanded. 32We will cross the Jordan River and march before the LORD into the land of Canaan. And our part of the country is the land east of the Jordan River."

33So Moses gave that land to the people of Gad, to the people of Reuben, and to half the tribe of Manasseh. (Manasseh was Joseph's son.) That land included the kingdom of Sihon the Amorite and the kingdom of King Og of Bashan and all the cities around that area.

34The people of Gad built the cities of Dibon, Ataroth, Aroer, 35Atroth Shophan, Jazer, Jogbehah, 36Beth Nimrah, and Beth Haran. They built cities with strong walls, and they built barns for their animals.

37The people of Reuben built Heshbon, Elealeh, Kiriathaim, 38Nebo, Baal Meon, and Sibmah. They used the names of the cities that they rebuilt. But they changed the names of Nebo and Baal Meon.

39People from Makir's family group went to Gilead.ᵇ (Makir was Manasseh's son.) They defeated the city. They defeated the Amorites who lived there. 40So Moses gave Gilead to Makir from the tribe of Manasseh, and his family settled there. 41Jair, from the family of Manasseh, defeated the small towns there. Then he called them Towns of Jair. 42Nobah defeated Kenath and the small towns near it. Then he called that place by his own name.

ᵇ32:39 Gilead Here, this seems to refer to a city, perhaps Ramoth Gilead. But it might refer to the whole area. See Hos. 6:8.

ᵃ32:3–4 Sibmah Or "Sebam."

Israel's Journey From Egypt

33 ¹These are the places the Israelites went when Moses and Aaron led them out of Egypt. ²Moses wrote about the places they went. He wrote what the LORD wanted. Here are the places they went and when they left:

³On the 15th day of the first month, they left Rameses. That morning after Passover, the Israelites marched out of Egypt with their arms raised in victory. All the people of Egypt saw them. ⁴The Egyptians were burying all the people the LORD killed. They were burying all their firstborn* sons. The LORD had shown his judgment against the gods*a* of Egypt.

⁵The Israelites left Rameses and traveled to Succoth. ⁶From Succoth they traveled to Etham. They camped there at the edge of the desert. ⁷They left Etham and went to Pi Hahiroth. This was near Baal Zephon. They camped near Migdol.

⁸They left Pi Hahiroth and walked through the middle of the sea. They went toward the desert. Then they traveled for three days through the Etham desert. The people camped at Marah.

⁹They left Marah and went to Elim and camped there. There were 12 springs of water and 70 palm trees there.

¹⁰They left Elim and camped near the Red Sea.*b*

¹¹They left the Red Sea and camped in the Desert of Zin.

¹²They left the Desert of Zin and camped at Dophkah.

¹³They left Dophkah and camped at Alush.

¹⁴They left Alush and camped at Rephidim. There was no water for the people to drink at that place.

¹⁵They left Rephidim and camped in the Sinai desert.

¹⁶They left the Sinai desert and camped at Kibroth Hattaavah.

¹⁷They left Kibroth Hattaavah and camped at Hazeroth.

¹⁸They left Hazeroth and camped at Rithmah.

¹⁹They left Rithmah and camped at Rimmon Perez.

²⁰They left Rimmon Perez and camped at Libnah.

²¹They left Libnah and camped at Rissah.

²²They left Rissah and camped at Kehelathah.

²³They left Kehelathah and camped at Mount Shepher.

²⁴They left Mount Shepher and camped at Haradah.

²⁵They left Haradah and camped at Makheloth.

²⁶They left Makheloth and camped at Tahath.

²⁷They left Tahath and camped at Terah.

²⁸They left Terah and camped at Mithcah.

²⁹They left Mithcah and camped at Hashmonah.

³⁰They left Hashmonah and camped at Moseroth.

³¹They left Moseroth and camped at Bene Jaakan.

³²They left Bene Jaakan and camped at Hor Haggidgad.

³³They left Hor Haggidgad and camped at Jotbathah.

³⁴They left Jotbathah and camped at Abronah.

³⁵They left Abronah and camped at Ezion Geber.

³⁶They left Ezion Geber and camped at Kadesh, in the Zin desert.

³⁷They left Kadesh and camped at Hor. This was the mountain at the border of the country of Edom. ³⁸Aaron the priest obeyed the LORD and went up Mount Hor. Aaron died at that place on the first day of the fifth month. That was the 40th year after the Israelites had left Egypt. ³⁹Aaron was 123 years old when he died on Mount Hor.

⁴⁰Arad was a town in the Negev,* in the land of Canaan.* The Canaanite king in that place heard that the Israelites were coming. ⁴¹The people left Mount Hor and camped at Zalmonah.

⁴²They left Zalmonah and camped at Punon.

⁴³They left Punon and camped at Oboth.

⁴⁴They left Oboth and camped at Iye Abarim. This was at the border of the country of Moab.

⁴⁵They left Iyim *(Iye Abarim)* and camped at Dibon Gad.

⁴⁶They left Dibon Gad and camped at Almon Diblathaim.

⁴⁷They left Almon Diblathaim and camped on the mountains of Abarim near Nebo.

⁴⁸They left the mountains of Abarim and camped in the Jordan Valley in Moab. This was near the Jordan River across from Jericho. ⁴⁹They camped by the Jordan River in the Jordan Valley in Moab. Their camp went from Beth Jeshimoth to Acacia Field.

⁵⁰There, the LORD spoke to Moses and said, ⁵¹"Speak to the Israelites and tell them this: You will cross the Jordan River. You will go into the land of Canaan. ⁵²You will take the land from the people you find there. You must destroy all of their carved statues and idols.* You must destroy all of their high places.* ⁵³You will take the land and you will settle there, because I am giving this land to you. It will belong to your family groups. ⁵⁴Each of your family groups will get part of the land. You will throw lots* to decide which family group gets each part of the country. Large family groups will get large parts of the land.

---

*a*33:4 *gods* This might be the false gods of Egypt. Or here, it might mean the king and other powerful leaders in Egypt.

*b*33:10 *Red Sea* Or "Reed Sea," but see 1 Kings 9:26.

Small family groups will get small parts of the land. The lots will show which family group gets which part of the land. Each tribe will get its part of the land.

55"You must force these other people to leave the country. If you let them stay in your country, they will bring many troubles to you. They will be like a needle*a* in your eye and a thorn in your side. They will bring many troubles to the country where you will be living. 56I showed you what I would do—and I will do that to you!"

The Borders of Canaan

34 1The LORD spoke to Moses. He said, 2"Speak to the Israelites and tell them this: You will soon enter the land of Canaan.* I am giving you that land to be your very own. These will be its borders: 3On the south, you will get part of the Zin desert near Edom. Your southern border will start at the south end of the Dead Sea. 4It will cross south of Scorpion Pass. It will go through the Zin desert to Kadesh Barnea, and then to Hazar Addar and then it will pass through Azmon. 5From Azmon the border will go to the River of Egypt,*b* and it will end at the Mediterranean Sea. 6Your western border will be the Mediterranean Sea. 7Your northern border will begin at the Mediterranean Sea and go to Mount Hor. 8From Mount Hor it will go to Lebo Hamath, and then to Zedad. 9Then that border will go to Ziphron and it will end at Hazar Enan. So that will be your northern border. 10Your eastern border will begin at Enan and it will go to Shepham. 11From Shepham the border will go east of Ain to Riblah. The border will continue along the hills by Lake Galilee.*c* 12Then the border will continue along the Jordan River. It will end at the Dead Sea. These are the borders around your country."

13So Moses gave this command to the Israelites, "That is the land that you will get. You will throw lots* to divide the land among the nine tribes and half the tribe of Manasseh. 14The tribes of Reuben and Gad, and half the tribe of Manasseh have already taken their land. 15These two and a half tribes took the land near Jericho—they took the land east of the Jordan River."

16Then the LORD spoke to Moses. He said, 17"These are the men who will help you divide the land: Eleazar the priest, Joshua son of Nun, 18and the leaders of all the tribes. There will be one leader from each tribe. These men will divide the land. 19These are the names of the leaders:

from the tribe of Judah—Caleb son of Jephunneh;

20 from the tribe of Simeon—Shemuel son of Ammihud;
21 from the tribe of Benjamin—Elidad son of Kislon;
22 from the tribe of Dan—Bukki son of Jogli;
23 from the descendants of Joseph;
   from the tribe of Manasseh—Hanniel son of Ephod;
24 from the tribe of Ephraim—Kemuel son of Shiphtan;
25 from the tribe of Zebulun—Elizaphan son of Parnach;
26 from the tribe of Issachar—Paltiel son of Azzan;
27 from the tribe of Asher—Ahihud son of Shelomi;
28 from the tribe of Naphtali—Pedahel son of Ammihud."

29The LORD chose these men to divide the land of Canaan among the Israelites.

The Levites' Towns

35 1The LORD spoke to Moses. This was in the Jordan Valley in Moab, near the Jordan River, across from Jericho. He said, 2"Tell the Israelites that they should give some of the cities in their part of the land to the Levites. The Israelites should give these cities and the pastures around them to the Levites. 3The Levites will be able to live in them. And all the cattle and other animals that belong to the Levites will be able to eat from the pastures around these cities. 4How much of your land should you give to the Levites? From the walls of the cities, go out 1500 feet*d*—all of that land will belong to the Levites. 5Measure off an area around the city for the Levites. Start at the northeast corner and measure 3000 feet*e* to the south. Then from this corner, measure 3000 feet to the west. From there measure 3000 feet to the north and from that corner, 3000 feet to the east. The city will be in the center of this area. 6Six of those cities will be cities of safety. If a person accidentally kills someone, that person can run to those towns for safety. In addition to those six cities, you will also give 42 more cities to the Levites. 7So you will give a total of 48 cities to the Levites. You will also give them the land around those cities. 8The large tribes of Israel will get large pieces of land. The small tribes of Israel will get small pieces of land. So the large tribes will give more cities and the small tribes will give fewer cities to the Levites."

9Then the LORD said to Moses, 10"Tell the people this: You will cross the Jordan River

---

*a***33:55** *needle* A thin barb or thorn from a plant.
*b***34:5** *River of Egypt* That is, the stream called "Wadi El-Arish."
*c***34:11** *Lake Galilee* Literally, "Kinnereth Lake."

*d***35:4** *1500 feet* Literally, "1000 cubits" (444 m). The people probably let their sheep and cattle use this land.
*e***35:5** *3000 feet* Literally, "2000 cubits" (1037 m). The Levites probably used this land for gardens and vineyards.

and go into the land of Canaan.* 11You must choose towns to be cities of safety. If someone accidentally kills another person, that person can run to one of those towns for safety. 12That person will be safe from anyone from the dead man's family who wants to punish the killer until that person is judged in court. 13There will be six cities of safety. 14Three of them will be east of the Jordan River and three of them will be in the land of Canaan, west of the Jordan River. 15These cities will be places of safety for citizens of Israel and for foreigners and travelers. Any of these people will be able to run to one of these cities if they accidentally kill someone.

16"If you use an iron weapon*a* to kill someone, you are a murderer, and you must die. 17If you use a rock large enough to kill someone and you kill another person, you are a murderer, and you must die. 18If you use a piece of wood large enough to kill someone and you kill another person, you are a murderer, and you must die. 19A member of the dead person's family*b* can chase you and kill you.

20-21"You might hit someone with your hand or push someone or throw something at them and kill them. If you did that from hate, you are a murderer, and you must be killed. A member of the dead person's family can chase you and kill you.

22"You might accidentally kill someone, maybe by pushing or by accidentally hitting them with a tool or weapon. 23Perhaps you threw a rock that was large enough to kill, but it hit someone you didn't see and killed them. You didn't plan to kill anyone. You didn't hate the person you killed—it was only an accident. 24If that happens, the community must decide what to do. The court must decide if a member of the dead person's family can kill you. 25If the community decides to protect you from the dead person's family, the community must take you back to your city of safety. You must stay there until the official high priest*c* dies.

26-27"You must never go outside the limits of your city of safety. If you do and if a member of the dead person's family catches you and kills you, that family member will not be guilty of murder. 28Whoever accidentally killed someone must stay in their city of safety until the high priest dies. After the high priest dies, that person can go back to their own land. 29These rules will be the law forever in all the towns of your people.

30"A killer should be put to death as a murderer only if there are witnesses. No one can be put to death if there is only one witness.

31"A murderer must be put to death. Don't take money to change the punishment. That murderer must be killed.

32"If a person killed someone and then ran to one of the cities of safety, don't take money to let that person go home. That person must stay in that city until the high priest dies.

33"Don't let your land be polluted with innocent blood. If a person murders someone, the only payment for that crime is that the murderer must be killed! There is no other payment that will free the land from that crime. 34I am the LORD. I will be living in your country with the Israelites, so don't make it unclean* with the blood of innocent people."

The Land of Zelophehad's Daughters

36 1Manasseh was Joseph's son. Makir was Manasseh's son. Gilead was Makir's son. The leaders of Gilead's family went to talk to Moses and the leaders of tribes of Israel. 2They said, "Sir, the LORD commanded us to get our land by throwing lots.* And sir, the LORD commanded that the land of Zelophehad our brother be given to his daughters. 3Maybe a man from one of the other tribes will marry one of Zelophehad's daughters. Will that land leave our family? Will the people of that other tribe get the land? Will we lose the land that we got by throwing lots? 4People might sell their land, but in the Jubilee* year, all the land is returned to the tribe that really owns it. At that time who will get the land that belongs to Zelophehad's daughters? Will our tribe lose that land forever?"

5Moses gave this command from the LORD to the Israelites: "These men from the tribe of Joseph are right. 6This is the LORD's command to Zelophehad's daughters: If you want to marry someone, you must marry someone from your own tribe. 7In this way land will not be passed from tribe to tribe among the Israelites. Each Israelite will keep the land that belonged to their own ancestors.* 8And if a woman gets her father's land, she must marry someone from her own tribe. That way everyone will keep the land that belonged to his ancestors. 9So the land must not be passed from tribe to tribe among the Israelites. Each Israelite will keep the land that belonged to their own ancestors."

10So Zelophehad's daughters obeyed the LORD's command to Moses. 11Zelophehad's daughters—Mahlah, Tirzah, Hoglah, Milcah, and Noah—married their cousins on their father's side of the family. 12Their husbands were from Manasseh's family groups, so their land remained within their father's family group and tribe.

13So these are the laws and commands that the LORD gave to Moses in the Jordan Valley in Moab by the Jordan River, across from Jericho.

---

*a*35:16 *iron weapon* This shows that the murderer chose a weapon he knew could kill the other person.
*b*35:19 *member of the dead person's family* Literally, "the blood avenger." Also in verses 20–21, 24, 26–27.
*c*35:25 *official high priest* Literally, "the high priest who was anointed with the holy oil."

Deuteronomy

Moses Talks to the Israelites

1 ¹These are the commands that Moses gave the Israelites while they were in the Jordan Valley, in the desert east of the Jordan River. This was across from Suph, between the desert of Paran and the cities Tophel, Laban, Hazeroth, and Dizahab.

²The trip from Mount Horeb* through the mountains of Seir to Kadesh Barnea takes only eleven days. ³But it was 40 years from the time the Israelites left Egypt until the time they came to this place. On the first day of the eleventh month of the 40th year, Moses spoke to the people and told them everything the Lord commanded. ⁴This was after he defeated Sihon and Og. (Sihon was the king of the Amorites and lived in Heshbon. Og was the king of Bashan and lived in Ashtaroth and Edrei.) ⁵The Israelites were in Moab on the east side of the Jordan River when Moses began to explain what God had commanded:

⁶"At Mount Horeb the Lord our God spoke to us. He said, 'You have stayed at this mountain long enough. ⁷Go to the hill country where the Amorites live and to all the neighboring areas in the Jordan Valley, the hill country, the western slopes, the Negev,* and the seacoast. Go throughout the land of Canaan* and Lebanon as far as the great river, the Euphrates. ⁸Look, I am giving you this land. Go and take it. I promised to give this land to your ancestors*—Abraham, Isaac, and Jacob. I promised to give this land to them and to their descendants.'

Moses Chooses Leaders

⁹"At that time I told you, 'I can't take care of you by myself. ¹⁰And now, there are even more of you. The Lord your God has added more and more people, so that today you are as many as the stars in the sky. ¹¹May the Lord, the God of your ancestors,* give you 1000 times more people than you are now! May he bless you as he promised. ¹²But I cannot take care of you and solve all your arguments by myself. ¹³So choose some men from each tribe, and I will make them leaders over you. Choose wise men with experience who understand people.'

¹⁴"And you said, 'That is a good thing to do.'

¹⁵"So I took the wise, experienced men you chose from your tribes, and I made them your leaders. In this way I gave you leaders over 1000 people, over 100 people, over 50 people, and over 10 people. I also gave you officers for each of your tribes.

¹⁶"At that time I told these judges, 'Listen to the arguments between your people. Be fair when you judge each case. It doesn't matter if the problem is between two Israelites or between an Israelite and a foreigner. You must judge each case fairly. ¹⁷You must treat everyone the same when you judge. You must listen carefully to everyone—whether they are important or not. Don't be afraid of anyone, because your decision is from God. But if there is a case too hard for you to judge, bring it to me and I will judge it.' ¹⁸At that same time, I also told you everything you must do.

The Spies Go to Canaan

¹⁹"So we obeyed the Lord our God. We left Mount Horeb* and went to the hill country of the Amorites. You remember that big, terrible desert that we walked through. We came as far as Kadesh Barnea. ²⁰Then I said to you, 'You have now come to the hill country of the Amorites. The Lord our God will give us this country. ²¹Look, there it is! Go up and take the land for your own. The Lord, the God of your ancestors,* told you to do this, so don't be afraid or worry about anything.'

²²"But all of you came to me and said, 'Let's send some men to look at the land first. They can spy out the land and come back and tell us the way we should go and which cities we will come to.'

²³"I thought that was a good idea. So I chose twelve men from among you, one man from each tribe. ²⁴Then they left and went up to the hill country. They came to the Valley of Eshcol and explored it. ²⁵They took some of the fruit from that land and brought it back to us. They told us about the land and said, 'The Lord our God is giving us a good land.'

²⁶"But you refused to go into the land. You refused to obey the Lord your God. ²⁷You went to your tents and began to complain. You said, 'The Lord hates us! He brought us out of the land of Egypt just to let the Amorites destroy us. ²⁸Where can we go now? The men we sent have frightened us with their report. They said, "The people there are bigger and taller than we are. The cities are big and have walls as high as the sky. And we

saw giants[a] there!"'

²⁹"So I said to you, 'Don't be upset or afraid of those people. ³⁰The Lord your God is in front, leading you. He will fight for you just as he did in Egypt. ³¹You saw what happened in the desert. You saw how the Lord your God carried you like a man carries his child. He brought you safely all the way to this place.'

³²"But you didn't trust the Lord your God then either. ³³But he was always in front, going ahead to find a place for you to camp. At night, he was in the fire that showed you where to go. And during the day, he was in the cloud.

People Not Allowed to Enter Canaan

³⁴"The Lord heard what you said, and he was angry. He made a vow.* He said, ³⁵'Not one of you evil people who are alive now will go into the good land that I promised to your ancestors.* ³⁶Only Caleb son of Jephunneh will see that land. I will give Caleb the land he walked on, and I will give that land to his descendants, because he did all that I commanded.'

³⁷"The Lord was also angry with me because of you. He said to me, 'Moses, you cannot enter the land, either. ³⁸But your helper, Joshua son of Nun, will go into the land. Encourage Joshua, because he will lead the Israelites to take the land for their own.'

³⁹"And the Lord said to us, 'You said your little children would be taken by your enemies. But those children who are still too young to know right from wrong, they will go into the land. I will give the land to them. Your children will take the land for their own. ⁴⁰But you—you must turn around, take the road to the Red Sea and go back into the desert.'

⁴¹"Then you said, 'Moses, we sinned against the Lord, but now we will do what the Lord our God commanded us before—we will go and fight.'

"Then each of you put on your weapons. You thought it would be easy to go and take the hill country. ⁴²But the Lord said to me, 'Tell the people not to go up there and fight, because I will not be with them. Their enemies will defeat them!'

⁴³"I spoke to you, but you did not listen. You refused to obey the Lord's command. You thought you could use your own power, so you went up into the hill country. ⁴⁴The Amorites who lived there came out like a swarm of bees and chased you all the way from Seir to Hormah. ⁴⁵Then you came back crying to the Lord for help, but the Lord refused to listen to you. ⁴⁶So you stayed at Kadesh for such a long time.

Israel Wanders Through the Desert

2 ¹"Then we did what the Lord told me to do. We went back into the desert on the road that leads to the Red Sea. We traveled for many days to go around the mountains of Seir.[b] ²Then the Lord said to me, ³'You have traveled around these mountains long enough. Turn north. ⁴Tell the people this: You will pass through the land of Seir. This land belongs to your relatives, the descendants of Esau. They will be afraid of you. Be very careful. ⁵Don't fight them. I will not give you any of their land—not even a foot of it, because I gave the hill country of Seir to Esau to keep as his own. ⁶You must pay the people of Esau for any food you eat or water you drink there. ⁷Remember that the Lord your God has blessed you in everything you have done. He knows about everything that happened on the trip through this great desert. The Lord your God has been with you these 40 years. You have always had everything you needed.'

⁸"So we passed by our relatives, the people of Esau living there in Seir. We left the road that leads from the Jordan Valley to the towns of Elath and Ezion Geber. We turned onto the road that goes to the desert in Moab.

Israel at Ar

⁹"The Lord said to me, 'Don't bother the Moabites. Don't start a war against them. I will not give you any of their land. They are the descendants of Lot,[c] and I gave them the city of Ar.'"

¹⁰(In the past, the Emites lived in Ar. They were strong people, and there were many of them. They were very tall, like the Anakites.* ¹¹The Anakites were part of the Rephaites. People thought the Emites were also Rephaites, but the people of Moab called them Emites. ¹²The Horites also lived in Seir in the past. Then Esau's people destroyed the Horites, took their land, and settled there, just as the Israelites did to the people in the land that the Lord gave them.)

¹³"The Lord told me, 'Now, go to the other side of Zered Valley.' So we crossed Zered Valley. ¹⁴It was 38 years from the time we left Kadesh Barnea until the time we crossed Zered Valley. As the Lord had promised, all the fighting men in our camp from that generation had died. ¹⁵The Lord had opposed those men until they were all dead and gone from our camp.

¹⁶"After all the fighting men were dead and gone, ¹⁷the Lord said to me, ¹⁸'Today you must cross the border at Ar and go into Moab. ¹⁹You will be just across from the Ammonites. Don't bother them or fight with them, because I will not give you their land.

---

[a]1:28 giants Literally, "Anakites," descendants of Anak, a family famous for tall and powerful fighting men. See Num. 13:33.

[b]2:1 Seir Another name for Edom.
[c]2:9 descendants of Lot Lot's sons were Moab and Ammon. See Gen. 19:30–38.

They are descendants of Lot, and I have given that land to them.'"

20(That country is also known as the Land of Rephaim. The Rephaites lived there in the past. The people of Ammon called them the Zamzummites. 21There were many Rephaites, and they were very strong and tall like the Anakites. But the LORD helped the Ammonites destroy them. The Ammonites took that land and live there now. 22God did the same thing for Esau's people. In the past the Horites lived in Seir.*a* But Esau's people destroyed the Horites, and Esau's descendants still live there today. 23God did the same thing for some people from Crete. The Avvites lived in the towns around Gaza, but the Cretans destroyed them, took the land, and live there now.)

Fighting the Amorites

24"The LORD told me, 'Get ready to go across Arnon Valley. I will let you defeat Sihon the Amorite, the king of Heshbon. I will let you take his country. So fight against him and take his land. 25Today I will make all people everywhere afraid of you. They will hear the news about you, and they will be afraid and shake with fear.'

26"While we were in the desert of Kedemoth, I sent messengers to King Sihon of Heshbon. The messengers offered peace to Sihon. They said, 27'Let us go through your land. We will stay on the road. We will not turn off the road to the right or to the left. 28We will pay you in silver for any food we eat or any water we drink. We only want to march through your country. 29Let us go through your land until we go across the Jordan River into the land that the LORD our God is giving us. Other people have let us go through their land—the people of Esau living in Seir and the Moabites living in Ar.'

30"But King Sihon of Heshbon would not let us pass through his country. The LORD your God had made him very stubborn. The LORD did this so that he could let you defeat King Sihon. And today we know that really happened.

31"The LORD said to me, 'I am giving King Sihon and his country to you. Now, go take his land!'

32"Then King Sihon and all his people came out to fight against us at Jahaz. 33But the LORD our God gave him to us. We defeated King Sihon, his sons, and all his people. 34We captured all the cities that belonged to King Sihon at that time. We completely destroyed the people in every city—the men, women, and children. We did not leave anyone alive! 35We took only the cattle and the valuable things from those cities. 36We defeated the town of Aroer on the edge of the Arnon Valley and the other town in the middle of that valley. The LORD let us defeat all the cities between

the Arnon Valley and Gilead. No city was too strong for us. 37But you did not go near the land that belongs to the people of Ammon. You did not go near the shores of the Jabbok River or the cities of the hill country. You did not go near any place that the LORD our God would not let us have.

Fighting the People of Bashan

3 1"We turned and went on the road to Bashan. King Og of Bashan and all his men came out to fight against us at Edrei. 2The LORD said to me, 'Don't be afraid of Og. I have decided to give him to you. I will give you all his men and his land. You will defeat him just as you defeated Sihon, the Amorite king who ruled in Heshbon.'

3"So the LORD our God let us defeat King Og of Bashan. We destroyed him and all his men. Not one of them was left. 4Then we took all the cities that belonged to Og at that time. We took all the cities from Og's people—60 cities in the area of Argob, Og's kingdom in Bashan. 5All these cities were very strong. They had high walls, gates, and strong bars on the gates. There were also many towns that did not have walls. 6We destroyed them just as we destroyed the cities of King Sihon of Heshbon. We completely destroyed every city and all the people in them, even the women and the babies. 7But we kept all the cattle and the valuable things from the cities for ourselves.

8"In that way we took the land from the two Amorite kings. We took that land on the east side of the Jordan River, from Arnon Valley to Mount Hermon. 9(The people from Sidon call Mount Hermon, Sirion, but the Amorites called it Senir.) 10We took all the cities in the high plain and all of Gilead. We took all of Bashan, all the way to Salecah and Edrei. Salecah and Edrei were cities of Og's kingdom of Bashan."

11(Og was the king of Bashan. He was one of the few Rephaites still alive. His bed was made from iron, and it was over 13 feet long and 6 feet wide.*b* The bed is still in the city of Rabbah, where the Ammonites live.)

The Land East of the Jordan River

12"So we took that land to be ours. I gave part of this land to the tribes of Reuben and Gad. I gave them the land from Aroer in the Arnon Valley to the hill country of Gilead with the cities in it. They got half of the hill country of Gilead. 13I gave the other half of Gilead and the whole area of Bashan to half the tribe of Manasseh."

(Bashan was Og's kingdom. Part of Bashan was called Argob. It was also called the Land of Rephaim. 14Jair, from the tribe of Manasseh, took the whole area of Argob. That area went

---

*b*3:11 *13 feet long and 6 feet wide* Literally, "9 cubits long and 4 cubits wide, following the measure of a man's cubit."

*a*2:22 *Seir* The hill country of Edom.

all the way to the border of the Geshurites and the Maacathites. It was named for Jair, and even today people call Bashan the Towns of Jair.)

15"I gave Gilead to Makir. 16And to the tribe of Reuben and the tribe of Gad, I gave the land that begins at Gilead and goes from the Arnon Valley to the Jabbok River. The middle of the valley is one border. The Jabbok River is the border for the Ammonites. 17The Jordan River near the desert is their western border. Lake Galilee*a* is north of this area and the Dead Sea*b* is to the south. It is at the bottom of the cliffs of Pisgah, which are to the east.

18"At that time I gave those tribes this command: 'The Lord your God has given you the land on this side of the Jordan River to live in. But now your fighting men must take their weapons and lead the other Israelite tribes across the river. 19Your wives, your little children, and your cattle (I know you have many cattle) will stay here in the cities I have given you. 20But you must help your Israelite relatives until they take the land that the Lord is giving them on the other side of the Jordan River. Help them until the Lord gives them peace there, just as he did for you here. Then you may come back to this land that I have given you.'

21"Then I told Joshua, 'You have seen all that the Lord your God has done to these two kings. The Lord will do the same thing to all the kingdoms you will enter. 22Don't fear the kings of these lands, because the Lord your God will fight for you.'

Moses Not Allowed in Canaan

23"Then I begged the Lord to do something special for me. I said, 24'Lord God, I am your servant. I know that you have shown me only a small part of the wonderful and powerful things you will do. There is no god in heaven or earth that can do the great and powerful things you have done. 25Please let me go across the Jordan River and see the good land on the other side. Let me see the beautiful hill country and Lebanon.'

26"But the Lord was angry with me because of you and refused to listen to me. The Lord said to me, 'That's enough! Don't say another word about this. 27Go up to the top of Mount Pisgah. Look to the west, to the north, to the south, and to the east. You may see these things with your eyes, but you can never go across the Jordan River. 28You must give instructions to Joshua. Encourage him. Make him strong, because Joshua must lead the people across the Jordan River. You can see the land, but Joshua will lead them into that land. He will help them take the land and live in it.'

29"So we stayed in the valley across from Beth Peor.

Moses' Warning to Obey God's Laws

4 1"Now, Israel, listen to the laws and to the commands that I teach you. Obey them and you will live. Then you can go in and take the land that the Lord, the God of your ancestors,* is giving you. 2You must not add to what I command you. And you must not take anything away. You must obey the commands of the Lord your God that I have given you.

3"You have seen what the Lord did at Baal Peor. The Lord your God destroyed all your people who followed the false god Baal* at that place. 4But all of you who stayed with the Lord your God are alive today.

5"I taught you the laws and rules that the Lord my God commanded me. I did this so you could obey them in the land you are ready to enter and take for your own. 6Obey these laws carefully. This will show the people of the other nations that you are wise and sensible. They will hear about these laws and say, 'Truly, the people of this great nation are wise and sensible.'

7"The Lord our God is near when we ask him to help us. No other nation has a god like that! 8And no other nation is great enough to have laws and rules as good as the teachings I give you today. 9But you must be careful! Be sure that as long as you live you never forget what you have seen. You must teach these things to your children and grandchildren. 10Remember the day you stood before the Lord your God at Mount Horeb.* The Lord said to me, 'Gather the people together to listen to what I have to say. Then they will learn to respect me as long as they live on earth. And they will teach these things to their children.' 11You came near and stood at the bottom of the mountain. The mountain burned with fire that reached up to the sky. There were thick black clouds and darkness. 12Then the Lord spoke to you from the fire. You heard the sound of someone speaking, but you did not see any form. There was only a voice. 13The Lord told you about his agreement,* which he commanded you to obey. He told you about the Ten Commandments, which he wrote on two stone tablets. 14At that time the Lord also commanded me to teach you the other laws and rules that you must follow in the land you are going to take and live in.

15"On the day the Lord spoke to you from the fire at Mount Horeb, you did not see him—there was no shape for God. 16So be careful! Don't sin and destroy yourselves by making false gods or statues in the shape of any living thing. Don't make an idol* that looks like a man or a woman, 17or like an animal on the earth, or like a bird that flies in the sky. 18And don't make an idol that looks like anything that crawls on the ground or like a

---

*a*3:17 Lake Galilee Literally, "Kinnereth Lake."
*b*3:17 Dead Sea Literally, "Arabah Sea." Also called the "Salt Sea."

fish in the sea. [19]And be careful when you look up to the sky and see the sun, the moon, and the stars—all the many things in the sky. Be careful that you are not tempted to worship and serve them. The LORD your God lets the other people in the world do this. [20]But the LORD brought you out of Egypt and made you his own special people. It was as if the LORD reached into a hot furnace[a] and pulled you out. And now you are his people.

[21]"The LORD was angry with me because of you. He swore that I could not go across the Jordan River into the good land that the LORD your God is giving you. [22]So I must die here in this land. I cannot go across the Jordan River, but you will soon go across it and take that good land and live there. [23]You must be careful not to forget the agreement that the LORD your God made with you. You must obey the LORD's command. Don't make any idols in any form, [24]because the LORD your God hates for his people to worship other gods. And he can be like a fire that destroys!

[25]"You will live in the country a long time. You will have children and grandchildren there. You will grow old there. And then you will ruin your lives—you will make all kinds of idols! When you do that, you will make God very angry! [26]So I am warning you now. Heaven and earth are my witnesses! If you do this evil thing, you will quickly be destroyed! You are crossing the Jordan River now to take that land. But if you make any idols, you will not live there very long. No, you will be destroyed completely! [27]The LORD will scatter you among the nations. And only a few of you will be left alive to go to the countries where the LORD will send you. [28]There you will serve gods made by men—things made of wood and stone that cannot see or hear or eat or smell! [29]But there in these other lands you will look for the LORD your God. And if you look for him with all your heart and soul, you will find him. [30]When you are in trouble—when all these things happen to you—then you will come back to the LORD your God and obey him. [31]The LORD your God is a merciful God! He will not leave you there or destroy you completely! He will not forget the agreement that he made with your ancestors.

Think About the Great Things God Did

[32]"Has anything this great ever happened before? Never! Look at the past. Think about everything that happened before you were born. Go all the way back to the time when God made people on the earth. Look at everything that has happened anywhere in the world. Has anyone ever heard about anything as great as this? No! [33]You people heard God speaking to you from a fire, and you are still

alive. Has that ever happened to anyone else? No! [34]Has any other god ever tried to go and take a people for himself from inside another nation? No! But you yourselves have seen everything that the LORD your God did for you. He showed you his power and strength. You saw the troubles that tested the people. You saw miracles and wonders. You saw war and the terrible things that happened. [35]The LORD showed you all this so that you would know that he is God. There is no other god like him. [36]The LORD let you hear his voice from heaven so that he could teach you a lesson. On earth he let you see his great fire, and he spoke to you from it.

[37]"The LORD loved your ancestors.* That is why he chose you, their descendants. And that is why the LORD brought you out of Egypt. He was with you and brought you out with his great power. [38]When you moved forward, the LORD forced out nations that were greater and more powerful than you. And the LORD led you into their land. He gave you their land to live in, as he is still doing today.

[39]"So today you must remember and accept that the LORD is God. He is God in heaven above and on the earth below. There is no other god! [40]And you must obey his laws and commands that I give you today. Then everything will go well with you and your children who live after you. And you will live a long time in the land the LORD your God is giving you—it will be yours forever."

Moses Chooses the Cities of Safety

[41]Then Moses chose three cities on the east side of the Jordan River. [42]Any person who killed someone by accident and not out of hate could run away to one of these three cities and not be put to death. [43]The three cities that Moses chose were Bezer in the high plains for the tribe of Reuben, Ramoth in Gilead for the tribe of Gad, and Golan in Bashan for the tribe of Manasseh.

Introduction to the Law of Moses

[44]Moses gave God's law to the Israelites. [45]Moses gave these teachings, laws, and rules to the people after they came out of Egypt. [46]He gave them these laws while they were on the east side of the Jordan River, in the valley across from Beth Peor. They were in the land of Sihon, the Amorite king who lived at Heshbon. Moses and the Israelites had defeated Sihon when they came out of Egypt. [47]They took Sihon's land to keep. They also took the land of King Og of Bashan. These two Amorite kings lived on the east side of the Jordan River. [48]This land goes from Aroer on the edge of the Arnon Valley all the way to Mount Sirion,[b] that is, Mount Hermon. [49]This land also included the whole Jordan Valley on the east side of the Jordan River. To the south,

---

[a]**4:20** *furnace* Literally, "iron furnace." That is, an oven hot enough to soften iron so that it can be hammered into something useful.

[b]**4:48** *Sirion* Or "Siyon."

this land reached to the Dead Sea.[a] To the east, it reached to the foot of Mount Pisgah.

The Ten Commandments

5 [1]Moses called together all the Israelites and said to them, "Israelites, listen to the laws and rules that I tell you today. Learn these laws and be sure to obey them. [2]The LORD our God made an agreement with us at Mount Horeb.* [3]The LORD did not make this agreement with our ancestors,* but with us— yes, with all of us who are alive here today. [4]The LORD spoke with you face to face at that mountain. He spoke to you from the fire. [5]But you were afraid of the fire. And you did not go up the mountain. So I stood between you and the LORD to tell you what the LORD said. He said,

[6]"I am the LORD your God. I led you out of Egypt where you were slaves.

[7]"You must not worship any other gods except me.

[8]"You must not make any idols.* Don't make any statues or pictures of anything up in the sky or of anything on the earth or of anything down in the water. [9]Don't worship or serve idols of any kind, because I am the LORD your God. I hate for my people to worship other gods.[b] People who sin against me become my enemies. And I will punish them, and their children, their grandchildren, and even their great-grandchildren. [10]But I will be very kind to people who love me and obey my commands. I will be kind to their families for thousands of generations![c]

[11]"You must not use the name of the LORD your God to make empty promises. If you do, the LORD will not let you go unpunished.

[12]"You must keep the Sabbath* a special day like the LORD your God commanded. [13]Work six days a week and do your job, [14]but the seventh day is a day of rest in honor of the LORD your God. So on that day no one should work—not you, your sons and daughters, foreigners living in your cities or your men and women slaves. Not even your cattle, donkeys, and other animals should do any work! Your slaves should be able to rest just as you do. [15]Don't forget that you were slaves in the land of Egypt. The LORD your God brought you out of Egypt with his great power and made you free. That is why the LORD your God commands you to always make the Sabbath a special day.

[16]"You must honor your father and your mother. The LORD your God has commanded you to do this. If you follow this command, you will live a long time, and everything will go well for you in the land that the LORD your God gives you.

[17]"You must not murder anyone.

[18]"You must not commit the sin of adultery.*

[19]"You must not steal.

[20]"You must not tell lies about other people.[d]

[21]"You must not want another man's wife. You must not want his house, his fields, his men and women servants, his cattle, or his donkeys. You must not want to take anything that belongs to another person."

The People Were Afraid of God

[22]Moses said, "The LORD gave these commands to all of you when you were together there at the mountain. He spoke in a loud voice that came from the fire, the cloud, and the thick darkness. After he gave us these commands, he didn't say any more. He wrote his words on two stone tablets and gave them to me.

[23]"You heard the voice from the darkness while the mountain was burning with fire. Then all the elders* and the other leaders of your tribes came to me. [24]They said, 'The LORD our God has shown us his Glory* and his greatness! We heard him speak from the fire. We have seen today that it is possible to continue living even after God speaks to us. [25]But if we hear the LORD our God speak to us again, surely we will die! That terrible fire will destroy us. We don't want to die. [26]No one has ever heard the living God speak from the fire like we have and still lived! [27]Moses, you go near and hear everything the LORD our God says. Then tell us everything the LORD tells you. We will listen to you, and we will do everything you say.'

The Lord Speaks to Moses

[28]"The LORD heard what you said and told me, 'I heard what the people said. And that is fine. [29]I only wanted to change their way of thinking—I wanted them to respect me and obey all my commands from the heart. Then everything would be fine with them and with their descendants forever.

[30]"'Go and tell the people to go back to their tents, [31]but you stand here near me. I will tell you all the commands, laws, and rules that you must teach them. They must do these things in the land that I am giving them to live in.'

[32]"So you people must be careful to do everything the LORD commanded you. Do not

---

a4:49 Dead Sea Literally, "Arabah Sea."

b5:9 I hate ... gods Or "I am El Kanah—the Jealous God."

c5:10 Or "But I will show mercy to thousands of people who love me and obey my commands."

d5:20 Or "You must not be a false witness against your neighbor."

stop following God! [33]You must live the way the LORD your God commanded you. Then you will continue to live, and everything will be fine with you. You will live a long life in the land that will belong to you.

Always Love and Obey God

6 [1]"These are the commands, the laws, and the rules that the LORD your God told me to teach you. Obey these laws in the land that you are entering to live in. [2]You and your descendants must respect the LORD your God as long as you live. You must obey all his laws and commands that I give you. If you do this, you will have a long life in that new land. [3]Israelites, listen carefully and obey these laws. Then everything will be fine with you. You will have many children, and you will get the land filled with many good things[a]—just as the LORD, the God of your ancestors,* promised.

[4]"Listen, people of Israel! The LORD is our God. The LORD is one. [5]You must love the LORD your God with all your heart, with all your soul, and with all your strength. [6]Always remember these commands that I give you today. [7]Be sure to teach them to your children. Talk about these commands when you sit in your house and when you walk on the road. Talk about them when you lie down and when you get up. [8]Tie them on your hands and wear them on your foreheads to help you remember my teachings. [9]Write them on the doorposts of your houses and on your gates.

[10]"The LORD your God made a promise to your ancestors, Abraham, Isaac, and Jacob. He promised to give you this land, and he will give it to you. He will give you great and rich cities that you did not build. [11]He will give you houses full of good things that you did not put there. He will give you wells that you did not dig. He will give you vineyards* and olive trees that you did not plant, and you will have plenty to eat.

[12]"But be careful! Don't forget the LORD. You were slaves in Egypt, but he brought you out of the land of Egypt. [13]Respect the LORD your God and serve only him. You must use only his name to make promises. [14]You must not follow other gods. You must not follow the gods of the people who live around you. [15]The LORD your God is always with you, and he hates for his people to worship other gods![b] So if you follow those other gods, the Lord will become very angry with you. He will destroy you from the face of the earth.

[16]"You must not test the LORD your God like you tested him at Massah. [17]You must be sure to obey the commands of the LORD your God. You must follow all the teachings and laws he has given you. [18]You must do what is

right and good—what pleases the LORD. Then everything will go well for you, and you can go in and take the good land that the LORD promised your ancestors. [19]And you will force out all your enemies, just as the LORD said.

Teach Your Children the Things God Did

[20]"In the future, your children might ask you, 'The LORD our God gave you teachings, laws, and rules. What do they mean?' [21]Then you will say to them, 'We were Pharaoh's slaves in Egypt, but the LORD brought us out of Egypt with his great power. [22]The LORD did great and amazing things. We saw him do these things to the Egyptian people, to Pharaoh, and to the people in Pharaoh's house. [23]And the LORD brought us out of Egypt so that he could give us the land that he promised our ancestors.* [24]The LORD commanded us to follow all these teachings. We must respect the LORD our God. Then he will always keep us alive and doing well, as we are today. [25]If we carefully obey the whole law, exactly as the LORD our God told us to, he will say that we have done a very good thing.'[c]

Israel, God's Special People

7 [1]"The LORD your God will lead you into the land that you are entering to take for your own. He will force out many nations for you—the Hittites, Girgashites, Amorites, Canaanites, Perizzites, Hivites, and Jebusites—seven nations greater and more powerful than you. [2]The LORD your God will put these nations under your power. And you will defeat them. You must destroy them completely. Don't make an agreement with them or show them mercy. [3]Don't marry any of them, and don't let your sons or daughters marry any of the people from those other nations. [4]If you do, they will turn your children away from following me. Then your children will serve other gods, and the LORD will be very angry with you. He will quickly destroy you!

Destroy False Gods

[5]"This is what you must do to those nations: You must smash their altars* and break their memorial stones* into pieces. Cut down their Asherah poles* and burn their statues. [6]Do this because you are the LORD's own people. From all the people on earth, the LORD your God chose you to be his special people—people who belong only to him. [7]Why did the LORD love and choose you? It was not because you are such a large nation. You had the fewest of all people! [8]But the LORD brought you out of Egypt with great power and made you free from slavery. He freed you from the control of Pharaoh, the king of Egypt. The LORD did this

---

[a]**6:3 land ... things** Literally, "land flowing with milk and honey."
[b]**6:15 he ... gods** Or "The LORD your God is El Kanah—the Jealous God."

[c]**6:25** Or "The LORD our God will credit us with righteousness (goodness) if we carefully obey the whole law, exactly as he commanded us."

because he loves you and he wanted to keep the promise he made to your ancestors.*

9"So remember that the LORD your God is the only God, and you can trust him! He keeps his agreement.* He shows his love and kindness to all people who love him and obey his commands. He continues to show his love and kindness through a thousand generations, 10but the LORD punishes people who hate him. He will destroy them. He will not be slow to punish those who hate him. 11So you must be careful to obey the commands, laws, and rules that I give you today.

12"If you listen to these laws, and if you are careful to obey them, the LORD your God will keep his agreement of love with you. He promised this to your ancestors. 13He will love you and bless you. He will make your nation grow. He will bless your children. He will bless your fields with good crops and will give you grain, new wine, and oil. He will bless your cows with calves and your sheep with lambs. You will have all these blessings in the land that he promised your ancestors to give you.

14"You will be blessed more than all people. Every husband and wife will be able to have children. Your cows will be able to have calves. 15The LORD will take away all sickness from you and he will not let you catch any of the terrible diseases that you had in Egypt. But he will make your enemies catch those diseases. 16You must destroy all the people the LORD your God helps you defeat. Don't feel sorry for them, and don't worship their gods! They will trap you—they will ruin your life.

The Lord Promises to Help His People

17"Don't say in your heart, 'These nations are stronger than we are. How can we force them out?' 18You must not be afraid of them. You must remember what the LORD your God did to Pharaoh and to all the people of Egypt. 19You saw the great troubles he gave them and the amazing things he did. You saw the LORD use his great power and strength to bring you out of Egypt. The LORD your God will use that same power against all the people you fear. 20"The LORD your God will send the hornet*a* against them. He will do this until he destroys all the people who escaped and tried to hide. 21Don't be afraid of them, because the LORD your God is with you. He is a great and awesome God. 22The LORD your God will force those nations to leave your country little by little. You will not destroy them all at once. If you did, the wild animals would grow to be too many for you. 23But the LORD your God will let you defeat those nations. He will confuse them in battle, until they are destroyed. 24The LORD will help you defeat their kings. You will kill them, and the world will forget

they ever lived. No one will be able to stop you. You will destroy them all!

25"You must throw the statues of their gods into the fire and burn them. You must not want to keep the silver or the gold that is on those statues for yourselves. It will be like a trap to you—it will ruin your life. The LORD your God hates those idols.* 26You must not bring any of those disgusting idols into your homes, or you will be destroyed just as they will be. You must treat them as the disgusting things they are! They are to be destroyed.

Remember the Lord

8 1"You must obey all the commands that I give you today, because then you will live and grow to become a great nation. You will get the land that the LORD promised to your ancestors.* 2And you must remember the entire trip that the LORD your God has led you through these 40 years in the desert. He was testing you. He wanted to make you humble. He wanted to know what is in your heart. He wanted to know if you would obey his commands. 3He humbled you and let you be hungry. Then he fed you with manna*— something you did not know about before. It was something your ancestors had never seen. Why did the Lord do this? Because he wanted you to know that it is not just bread that keeps people alive. People's lives depend on what the LORD says. 4These past 40 years, your clothes did not wear out, and your feet did not swell. 5You must remember that the LORD your God teaches and corrects you as a father teaches and corrects his son.

6"You must obey the commands of the LORD your God. Follow him and respect him. 7The LORD your God is bringing you into a good land—a land with rivers and pools of water. Water flows out of the ground in the valleys and hills. 8It is a land with wheat and barley, grapevines, fig trees, and pomegranates.* It is a land with olive oil and honey. 9There you will have plenty of food and everything you need. It is a land where the rocks are iron. You can dig copper out of the hills. 10You will have all you want to eat. Then you will praise the LORD your God for the good land he has given you.

Don't Forget What the Lord Did

11"Be careful. Don't forget the LORD your God! Be careful to obey the commands, laws, and rules that I give you today. 12Then you will have plenty to eat, and you will build good houses and live in them. 13Your cattle, sheep, and goats will grow large. You will get plenty of gold and silver. You will have plenty of everything. 14When that happens, you must be careful not to become proud. You must not forget the LORD your God. You were slaves in Egypt, but he made you free and brought you out of that land. 15He led you through that great and terrible desert where there were

---

*a***7:20** *hornet* A stinging insect like a large wasp or bee. Here, it might mean God's angel or his great power.

poisonous snakes and scorpions. The ground was dry, and there was no water anywhere. But he gave you water out of a solid rock. 16In the desert he fed you manna*—something your ancestors* had never seen. He tested you to make you humble so that everything would go well for you in the end. 17Don't ever say to yourself, 'I got all this wealth by my own power and ability.' 18Remember the LORD your God is the one who gives you power to do these things. He does this because he wants to keep the agreement* that he made with your ancestors—as he is doing today!

19"Don't ever forget the LORD your God. Don't ever follow other gods or worship and serve them. If you do that, I warn you today: You will surely be destroyed! 20The LORD is destroying other nations for you. But if you stop listening to the LORD your God, you will be destroyed just like them!

The Lord Will Be With Israel

9 1"Listen, you Israelites! You will go across the Jordan River today. You will go into that land to force out nations greater and stronger than you. Their cities are big and have walls as high as the sky! 2The people there are tall and strong. They are the Anakites.* You know about them. You heard our spies say, 'No one can win against the Anakites.' 3But you can be sure that it is the LORD your God who goes across the river before you—and God is like a fire that destroys! He will destroy those nations and make them fall before you. You will force those nations out and quickly destroy them. The LORD has promised you that this will happen.

4"The LORD your God will force those nations out for you. But don't say to yourselves, 'The LORD brought us to live in this land because we are such good people.' No, the LORD forced those nations out because they were evil—not because you were good. 5You are going in to take their land, but not because you are good and live right. You are going in, and the LORD your God is forcing those people out because of the evil way they lived. And the Lord wants to keep the promise he made to your ancestors*—Abraham, Isaac, and Jacob. 6The LORD your God is giving you that good land to live in, but you should know that it is not because you are good. The truth is that you are very stubborn people!

Remember the Lord's Anger

7"Don't forget that you made the LORD your God angry in the desert. You have refused to obey him from the day you left the land of Egypt to the day you came to this place. 8You made the LORD angry at Mount Horeb.* He was angry enough to destroy you! 9I went up the mountain to get the stone tablets. The agreement* that the LORD made with you was written on those stones. I stayed on the mountain 40 days and 40 nights. I did not eat

any food or drink any water. 10The LORD gave me the two stone tablets. He wrote his commands on the stones with his finger. He wrote everything he said to you from the fire when you were gathered together at the mountain.

11"So at the end of 40 days and 40 nights, the LORD gave me two stone tablets—the stones of the agreement. 12Then the LORD said to me, 'Get up and quickly go down from here. The people you brought out of Egypt have ruined themselves. They stopped obeying my commands so quickly. They melted gold and made an idol* for themselves.'

13"The LORD also said to me, 'I have watched these people. They are very stubborn! 14Let me destroy these people completely, so no one will even remember their names. Then I will make another nation from you that is stronger and greater than these people.'

The Golden Calf

15"Then I turned and came down from the mountain. The mountain was burning with fire. And the two stone tablets of the agreement* were in my hands. 16I looked and I saw you had sinned against the LORD your God. I saw the calf you made from melted gold! You stopped obeying the LORD so quickly. 17So I took the two stone tablets and threw them down. There before your eyes I broke the stones into pieces. 18Then I bowed down before the LORD with my face to the ground for 40 days and 40 nights, like I did before. I did not eat any food or drink any water. I did this because you had sinned so badly. You did the thing that is evil to the LORD, and you made him angry. 19I was afraid of the LORD's terrible anger. He was angry enough to destroy you, but the LORD listened to me again. 20The LORD was very angry with Aaron—enough to destroy him! So I also prayed for Aaron at that time. 21I took that terrible thing—the calf you made—and burned it in the fire. I broke it into small pieces. And I crushed the pieces until they were dust. Then I threw the dust into the river that came down from the mountain.

Moses Asks God to Forgive Israel

22"Also, at Taberah, Massah, and Kibroth Hattaavah you made the LORD angry. 23And you did not obey when the LORD told you to leave Kadesh Barnea. He said, 'Go up and take the land I am giving you.' But you refused to obey the LORD your God. You did not trust him. You did not listen to his command. 24All the time that I have known you, you have refused to obey the LORD.

25"So I bowed down before the LORD 40 days and 40 nights, because the LORD said he would destroy you. 26I prayed to the LORD. I said, Lord GOD, don't destroy your people. They belong to you. You freed them and brought them out of Egypt with your great power and strength. 27Remember your promise to your servants

Abraham, Isaac, and Jacob. Forget how stubborn these people are. Don't look at their evil ways or their sins. 28If you punish your people, the Egyptians might say, 'The LORD was not able to take his people into the land he promised them. And he hated them. So he took them into the desert to kill them.' 29But they are your people, LORD. They belong to you. You brought them out of Egypt with your great power and strength.

New Stone Tablets

10 1"At that time the LORD said to me, 'You must cut out two stone tablets like the first two stones. Then you must come up to me on the mountain. Also make a wooden box. 2I will write on the stone tablets the same words that were on the first stones—the stones you broke. Then you must put these new stones in the Box.'

3"So I made a box from acacia wood. I cut two stone tablets like the first two stones. Then I went up on the mountain. I had the two stone tablets in my hand. 4And the LORD wrote on the stones the same words he had written before—the Ten Commandments he spoke to you from the fire, when you were gathered together at the mountain. Then the LORD gave the two stone tablets to me. 5I came back down from the mountain. I put the stones in the Box I had made. The LORD commanded me to put them there. And the stones are still there in that Box."

6(The Israelites traveled from the wells of the people of Jaakan to Moserah. There Aaron died and was buried. Aaron's son Eleazar served in Aaron's place as priest. 7Then the Israelites went from Moserah to Gudgodah. And they went from Gudgodah to Jotbathah, a land of rivers. 8At that time the LORD separated the tribe of Levi from the other tribes for his special work. They had the work of carrying the LORD's Box of the Agreement.* They also served as priests before the LORD. And they had the work of blessing people in the LORD's name. They still do this special work today. 9That is why the people from the tribe of Levi did not get any share of land like the other tribes did. They have the LORD for their share. That is what the LORD your God promised them.)

10"I stayed on the mountain 40 days and 40 nights, like the first time. The LORD also listened to me at that time. He decided not to destroy you. 11The LORD said to me, 'Go and lead the people on their trip. They will go in and live in the land that I promised to give to their ancestors.*'

What the Lord Really Wants

12"Now, Israelites, listen! What does the LORD your God really want from you? The LORD God wants you to respect him and do what he says. He wants you to love him and to serve the LORD your God with all your heart and with all your soul. 13So obey the laws and commands of the LORD that I am giving you today. These laws and commands are for your own good.

14"Everything belongs to the LORD your God. The heavens, even the highest heavens, belong to him. The earth and everything on it belong to him. 15The LORD loved your ancestors* very much. He loved them so much that he chose you, their descendants, to be his people. He chose you instead of any other nation, and you are still his chosen people today.

16"Stop being stubborn. Give your hearts to the LORD. 17The LORD is your God. He is the God of gods and the Lord of lords. He is the great God. He is the amazing and powerful fighter. To him everyone is the same. He does not accept money to change his mind. 18He defends widows and orphans. He loves even the strangers living among us. He gives them food and clothes. 19So you must also love them, because you yourselves were strangers in the land of Egypt.

20"You must respect the LORD your God and worship only him. Never leave him. When you make promises, you must use his name only. 21The LORD is the one you should praise. He is your God. He has done great and amazing things for you. You have seen them with your own eyes. 22When your ancestors went down into Egypt, there were only 70 people. Now the LORD your God has made you as many as the stars in the sky.

Remember the Lord

11 1"So you must love the LORD your God. You must do what he tells you to do and always obey his laws, rules, and commands. 2Remember today all the great things the LORD your God has done to teach you. It was you, not your children, who saw those things happen and lived through them. You saw how great he is. You saw how strong he is, and you saw the powerful things he does. 3You, not your children, saw the miracles he did in Egypt. You saw what he did to Pharaoh, the king of Egypt, and to his whole country. 4You, not your children, saw what he did to the Egyptian army—to their horses and chariots.* They were chasing you, but you saw him cover them with the water from the Red Sea. You saw him completely destroy them. 5It was you, not your children, who saw everything he did for you in the desert until you came to this place. 6You saw what he did to Dathan and Abiram, the sons of Eliab from Reuben's family. All the Israelites watched as the ground opened up like a mouth and swallowed them, their families, their tents, and all of their servants and animals. 7It was you, not your children, who saw all the great things the LORD did.

8"So you must obey every command I tell you today. Then you will be strong. And you will be able to go across the Jordan River and take the land that you are ready to enter. 9Then you will live a long life in that country. The Lord promised to give that land to your ancestors* and all their descendants. It is a land filled with many good things.*ᵃ 10The land that you will get is not like the land of Egypt that you came from. In Egypt you planted your seeds and used your feet to pump water from the canals to water your fields like a vegetable garden. 11But the land that you will soon get is not like that. In Israel there are mountains and valleys, and the land gets its water from the rain that falls from the sky. 12The Lord your God cares for that land. The Lord your God watches over it, from the beginning to the end of the year.

13"The Lord says, 'You must listen carefully to the commands I give you today: You must love the Lord your God, and serve him with all your heart and all your soul. If you do that, 14I will send rain for your land at the right time. I will send the autumn rain and the spring rain. Then you can gather your grain, your new wine, and your oil. 15And I will make grass grow in your fields for your cattle. You will have plenty to eat.'

16"He says, 'Be careful! Don't be fooled. Don't turn away from me to serve other gods and to bow down to them.' 17If you do that, the Lord will become very angry with you. He will shut the skies, and there will be no rain. The land will not make a harvest, and you will soon die in the good land that the Lord is giving you.

18"Remember these commands I give you. Keep them in your hearts. Write them down and tie them on your hands and wear them on your foreheads as a way to remember my laws. 19Teach these laws to your children. Talk about these things when you sit in your houses, when you walk along the road, when you lie down, and when you get up. 20Write these commands on the doorposts of your houses and on your gates. 21Then both you and your children will live a long time in the land that the Lord promised to give to your ancestors. You will live there as long as the skies are above the earth.

22"Be careful to obey every command I have told you to follow: Love the Lord your God, follow all his ways, and be faithful to him. 23Then, when you go into the land, the Lord will force all those other nations out. You will take the land from nations that are larger and more powerful than you. 24All the land you walk on will be yours. Your land will go from the desert in the south all the way to Lebanon in the north. It will go from the Euphrates River in the east all the way to the Mediterranean Sea. 25No one will be able to stand against you. The Lord your God will

make the people fear you wherever you go in that land. That is what he promised you before.

Israel's Choice: Blessings or Curses

26"Today I am giving you a choice. You may choose the blessing or the curse. 27You will get the blessing if you listen and obey the commands of the Lord your God that I have told you today. 28But you will get the curse if you refuse to listen and obey the commands of the Lord your God. So don't stop living the way I command you today, and don't follow other gods that you don't know.

29"The Lord your God will lead you to your land. You will soon go in and take that land. At that time you must go to the top of Mount Gerizim and read the blessings to the people from there. And then you must go to the top of Mount Ebal and read the curses to the people from there. 30These mountains are on the other side of the Jordan River in the land of the Canaanites living in the Jordan Valley. These mountains are toward the west, not far from the oak trees of Moreh near the town of Gilgal. 31You will go across the Jordan River. You will take the land that the Lord your God is giving you. This land will belong to you. When you are living in this land, 32you must carefully obey all the laws and rules I give you today.

The Place for Worshiping God

12 1"These are the laws and rules that you must obey in your new land. You must carefully obey them as long as you live in this land. The Lord is the God of your ancestors,* and he is giving this land to you. 2You will take that land from the nations that live there now. You must completely destroy all the places where the people of these nations worship their gods. These places are on high mountains, on hills, and under green trees. 3You must smash their altars* and break their memorial stones* into pieces. You must burn their Asherah poles* and cut down the statues of their gods. Wipe out everything that would remind you of those gods.

4"You must not worship the Lord your God in the same way these people worship their gods. 5The Lord your God will choose a special place among your tribes. That will be the home for his name. You must go to that place to worship him. 6There you must bring your burnt offerings,* your sacrifices, one-tenth of your crops and animals,*ᵇ your special gifts, any gifts you promised to him, any special gift you want to give, and the first animals born in your herds and flocks. 7You and your families will eat together at that place, and the Lord your God will be there with you. You will enjoy sharing the things you worked for there.

ᵃ11:9 land ... things Literally, "land flowing with milk and honey."

ᵇ12:6 one-tenth ... animals Or "tithes." Also in verse 11.

You will remember that the LORD your God blessed you and gave you these good things.

8"You must not continue to worship the way we have been worshiping. Until now each of us has been worshiping God any way we wanted. 9This is because we have not yet entered the peaceful land that the LORD your God is giving you. 10But you will go across the Jordan River and live in that land. The LORD is giving that land to you. And he will give you rest from all your enemies. You will be safe. 11Then the LORD your God will choose a place that will be the home for his name. You must bring everything I command you to that place. Bring your burnt offerings, your sacrifices, one-tenth of your crops and animals, your special gifts, and any gifts that you promised to give to the LORD. 12Come to that place with all your people—your children, all your servants, and the Levites* living in your towns. (These Levites will not have a share of the land for their own.) Enjoy yourselves together there with the LORD your God. 13Be sure you don't offer your burnt offerings in just any place you see. 14The LORD will choose his special place among your tribes. Offer your burnt offerings and do everything else I told you only in that place.

15"Whenever you want to eat meat, you can enjoy that blessing from the LORD your God wherever you live. You can butcher the animal just as you do gazelles* and deer, and anyone, clean* or unclean,* can eat it. 16But you must not eat the blood. You must pour the blood on the ground like water.

17"There are some things you must not eat in the places where you live. These things are the part of your grain that belongs to God, the part of your new wine and oil that belongs to God, the first animals born in your herd or flock, any gift that you promised to God, any special gifts you want to give, or any other gifts for God. 18You must eat these offerings only in his presence at the special place that the LORD your God will choose. You must go there and eat together with your sons, your daughters, all your servants, and the Levites living in your towns. Enjoy yourselves there with the LORD your God. Enjoy what you have worked for. 19But be sure that you always share these meals with the Levites. Do this as long as you live in your land.

20-21"The LORD your God promised to make your country larger. When he does this, you might live too far from the place the LORD your God chooses to be the home for his name. If it is too far, and you are hungry for meat, you may eat any meat you have. You may kill any animal from the herd or flock that he has given you. Do this the way I have commanded you. You may eat this meat there where you live any time you want. 22You may eat this meat the same as you would eat gazelle or deer meat. Anyone can do this—people who are clean and people who are unclean. 23But be especially careful not to eat the blood, because the life is in the blood. You must not eat meat that still has its life in it. 24Don't eat the blood. Pour it out like water onto the ground. 25So don't eat blood. You must do what the LORD says is right, and good things will happen to you and to your descendants.

26"If you decide to give something special to God, you must go to the special place that the LORD your God will choose. And if you make a special promise, you must go to that place to give that gift to God. 27You must offer your burnt offerings in that place. Offer the meat and the blood of your burnt offerings on the altar of the LORD your God. For your other sacrifices, you must pour the blood on the altar of the LORD your God. Then you may eat the meat. 28Carefully obey all the commands that I give you. When you do what is good and right—what pleases the LORD your God—then everything will go well for you and for your descendants forever.

29"You are going to take your land from other people. The LORD your God will destroy these people for you. You will force them out of that land, and then you will live there. 30But be careful that you don't fall into the same trap they did! Don't go to their false gods for help. Don't say to yourself, 'They worshiped these gods, so I will worship them too.' 31Don't do that to the LORD your God! These people do all kinds of bad things that the LORD hates. They even burn their children as sacrifices to their gods!

32"You must be careful to do everything I command you. Don't add anything to what I tell you, and don't take anything away.

Don't Serve Other Gods

13 1"A prophet or someone who explains dreams might come to you and tell you that they will show you a sign or a miracle. 2And the sign or miracle they told you about might come true. Then they might ask you to follow other gods (gods you don't know) and say to you, 'Let's serve these gods!' 3Don't listen to them, because the LORD your God is testing you. He wants to know if you love him with all your heart and all your soul. 4You must follow the LORD your God. Respect him. Obey his commands and do what he tells you. Serve the LORD your God, and never leave him. 5Also, you must kill that prophet or person who explains dreams, because they told you to turn against the LORD your God. And it was the LORD your God who brought you out of the land of Egypt, where you were slaves. They tried to pull you away from the life he commanded you to live, so you must kill them to remove this evil from your people.

6"Someone close to you might secretly persuade you to worship other gods. It might be your own brother, your son, your daughter, the wife you love, or your closest friend. They might say, 'Let's go and serve other gods.' (These are gods that you and your ancestors* never knew. 7They are the gods of the people who live in the other lands around you, some near and some far away.) 8You must not agree with them. Don't listen to them or feel sorry for them. Don't let them go free or protect them. 9-10No, you must kill them with stones. You be the first one to pick up stones and throw at them. Then everyone must throw stones to kill them, because they tried to pull you away from the LORD your God. And it was the Lord who brought you out of the land of Egypt, where you were slaves. 11Then all the Israelites will hear about it and be afraid. And they will not do those evil things any more.

12"The LORD your God has given you cities to live in. Sometimes you might hear some bad news about one of these cities. You might hear that 13some troublemakers from your own nation are persuading the people of their city to do bad things. They might say to the people of their city, 'Let's go and serve other gods.' (These gods would be gods that you never knew before.) 14If you hear this kind of news, you must do all you can to learn if it is true. If you learn that it is true, if you prove that such a terrible thing really did happen, 15then you must kill all the people of that city and their animals too. You must destroy that city completely. 16You must gather up everything of value and take it to the center of the city. Burn the whole city and everything in it as a burnt offering to the LORD your God. You must turn that city into an empty pile of rocks forever, and that city must never be rebuilt. 17Everything in that city must be given to God to be destroyed. So you must not keep any of the things for yourselves. If you follow this command, the LORD will stop being so angry with you. He will be kind to you. He will feel sorry for you. He will let your nation grow larger, like he promised your ancestors. 18This will happen if you listen to the LORD your God—if you obey all his commands that I give you today. You must do what the LORD your God says is right.

Israel, God's Special People

14 1"You are the children of the LORD your God. When someone dies, you must not cut yourselves or shave your heads[a] to show your sadness. 2This is because you are different from other people. You are the LORD's special people. From all the people in the world, the LORD your God chose you to be his own special people.

Food the Israelites Are Allowed to Eat

3"Don't eat anything that the Lord hates. 4You may eat these animals: cattle, sheep, goats, 5deer, gazelles,* roe deer, wild sheep, wild goats, antelopes, and mountain sheep. 6You may eat any animal that has hooves divided into two parts and that chews the cud.* 7But don't eat camels, rabbits, or rock badgers. These animals chew the cud, but they don't have split hooves. So these animals are not a clean* food for you. 8And you must not eat pigs. Their hooves are divided, but they don't chew the cud. So pigs are not a clean food for you. Don't eat any meat from pigs. Don't even touch a pig's dead body.

9"You may eat any kind of fish that has fins and scales. 10But don't eat anything living in the water that does not have fins and scales. It is not a clean food for you.

11"You may eat any clean bird. 12But don't eat any of these birds: eagles, vultures, buzzards, 13red kites, falcons, any kind of kite, 14any kind of raven, 15horned owls, screech owls, sea gulls, any kind of hawk, 16little owls, great owls, white owls, 17desert owls, ospreys, cormorants, 18storks, any kind of heron, hoopoes or bats.

19"All insects with wings are unclean,* so don't eat them. 20But you may eat any clean bird.

21"Don't eat any animal that has died by itself. You may give the dead animal to the foreigner in your town, and he can eat it. Or you may sell the dead animal to a foreigner. But you yourselves must not eat the dead animal, because you belong to the LORD your God. You are his special people.

"Don't cook a baby goat in its mother's milk.

Giving One-Tenth

22"Every year you must be sure to save one-tenth of all the crops that grow in your fields. 23Then you must go to the place the Lord chooses to be the home for his name. You will go there to be with the LORD your God. At that place you will eat the tenth of your crops—one-tenth of your grain, your new wine, your oil, and the first animals born in your herds and flocks. In this way you will always remember to respect the LORD your God. 24But that place might be too far for you to travel to. Maybe you will not be able to carry one-tenth of all the crops that the LORD has blessed you with. If that happens, 25sell that part of your crops and take the money with you to the special place the LORD has chosen. 26Use the money to buy anything you want—cattle, sheep, wine or beer or any other food. Then you and your family should eat and enjoy yourselves there in that place with the LORD your God. 27But don't forget the Levites* living in your town. Share your food with them because they don't have a share of the land like you have.

28"At the end of every three years, you must gather one-tenth of your harvest for that year. Store this food in your towns. 29Keep this food for the Levites, because they don't have

---

[a]14:1 shave your heads Literally, "shave between your eyes."

any land of their own. Also keep this food for the foreigners, orphans, and widows who live in your towns. This will provide enough for them to come and eat all they want. If you do this, the Lord your God will bless you in everything you do.

The Special Year of Canceling Debts

15 [1]"At the end of every seven years, you must cancel debts. [2]This is the way you must do this: Everyone who has lent money to another Israelite must cancel the debt. He should not ask a fellow Israelite to repay the debt, because the Lord said to cancel debts during that year. [3]You may require a foreigner to repay you, but you must cancel any debt another Israelite owes you. [4]There should not be any poor people in your country, because the Lord your God is giving you this land. And the Lord will greatly bless you. [5]But this will happen only if you obey the Lord your God. You must be careful to obey every command that I have told you today. [6]Then the Lord your God will bless you, as he promised. And you will have enough money to make loans to many nations. But you will not need to borrow from anyone. You will rule over many nations. But none of these nations will rule over you.

[7]"When you are living in the land the Lord your God is giving you, there might be some poor people living among you. You must not be selfish. You must not refuse to give help to them. [8]You must be willing to share with them. You must lend them whatever they need.

[9]"Don't ever refuse to help someone simply because the seventh year, the year for canceling debts, is near. Don't let an evil thought like that enter your mind. You must never have bad thoughts about someone who needs help. You must not refuse to help them. If you don't help the poor, they might complain to the Lord, and he will judge you guilty of sin.

[10]"So be sure to give to the poor. Don't hesitate to give to them, because the Lord your God will bless you for doing this good thing. He will bless you in all your work and in everything you do. [11]There will always be poor people in the land. That is why I command you to be ready to help your brother or sister. Give to the poor in your land who need help.

Letting Slaves Go Free

[12]"You might buy a Hebrew man or woman to serve you as a slave. You may keep that person as a slave for six years. But in the seventh year, you must let that person go free. [13]But when you let your slave go free, don't send him away with nothing. [14]You must give him some of your animals, grain, and wine. The Lord your God blessed you and gave you plenty of good things. In the same way you must give plenty of good things to your slave.

[15]Remember, you were slaves in Egypt. And the Lord your God set you free. So that is why I am giving you this command today.

[16]"But one of your slaves might say to you, 'I will not leave you.' He might say this because he loves you and your family and because he has a good life with you. [17]Make this servant put his ear against your door and use a sharp tool to make a hole in his ear. This will show that he is your slave forever. You must do this even to the women slaves who want to stay with you.

[18]"Don't regret letting your slave go free. Remember, he served you six years for half of what you would have paid a hired worker.[a] The Lord your God will bless you in everything you do.

Rules About Firstborn Animals

[19]"All the first male animals born in your herd and flock are special. You must give them to the Lord. Don't use any of these animals for your work and don't cut wool from any of these sheep. [20]Every year you must take these animals to the place the Lord your God will choose. There with the Lord, you and your family will eat these animals.

[21]"But if an animal has something wrong with it—if it is crippled or blind or has something else wrong with it—then you must not sacrifice that animal to the Lord your God. [22]But you may eat the meat from that animal at home. Anyone may eat it—people who are clean* and people who are unclean.* The rules for eating this meat are the same as the rules for eating gazelles* and deer. [23]But you must not eat the blood from the animal. You must pour the blood out on the ground like water.

Passover

16 [1]"Remember, in the month of Abib* you must celebrate Passover* to honor the Lord your God. It was that night in Abib when the Lord your God brought you out of Egypt. [2]You must go to the place the Lord your God will choose to be the home for his name. There you must offer the Passover sacrifice to honor the Lord. You must offer the cattle and goats. [3]Don't eat bread that has yeast in it with this sacrifice. You must eat unleavened* bread for seven days. This bread is called 'Bread of Trouble.' It will help you remember the troubles you had in Egypt. Remember how quickly you had to leave that country. You must remember that day as long as you live. [4]There must be no yeast in anyone's house anywhere in the country for seven days. And all the meat you sacrifice on the evening of the first day must be eaten before morning.

[a]**15:18** Remember ... hired worker Or "Remember, he served you for six years for the same amount you would have paid a hired worker."

⁵"You must not sacrifice the Passover animal in any of the towns that the LORD your God gives you. ⁶You must sacrifice the Passover animal only at the place that the LORD your God will choose to be the home for his name. There you must sacrifice the Passover animal in the evening when the sun goes down. This is the festival when you remember that God brought you out of Egypt. ⁷You must cook the meal and eat it at the place the LORD your God will choose. The next morning you may go back home. ⁸You must eat unleavened bread six days. On the seventh day you must not do any work. On this day the people will come together for a special meeting to honor the LORD your God.

Festival of Harvest

⁹"You must count seven weeks from the time you begin to harvest the grain. ¹⁰Then celebrate the Festival of Harvest* for the LORD your God. Do this by bringing him some special gift you want to bring. Decide how much to give by thinking about how much the LORD your God has blessed you. ¹¹Go to the place the LORD will choose to be the home for his name. You and your people should enjoy yourselves together there with the LORD your God. Take all your people with you—your sons, your daughters, and all your servants. And take the Levites,* foreigners, orphans, and widows living in your towns. ¹²Remember, you were slaves in Egypt. So be sure to obey these laws.

Festival of Shelters

¹³"Seven days after you have gathered your harvest in from your threshing* floor and from your winepress,* you should celebrate the Festival of Shelters.* ¹⁴Enjoy yourselves at this festival—you, your sons, your daughters, all your servants, and the Levites,* foreigners, orphans, and widows living in your towns. ¹⁵Celebrate this festival for seven days at the special place the LORD will choose. Do this to honor the LORD your God. The LORD your God blessed your harvest and all the work you did, so be very happy!

¹⁶"Three times a year all your men must come to meet with the LORD your God at the special place he will choose. They must come for the Festival of Unleavened Bread,* the Festival of Harvest, and the Festival of Shelters. Everyone who comes to meet with the LORD must bring a gift. ¹⁷Each man should give as much as he can. He should decide how much to give by thinking about how much the LORD has given him.

Judges and Officers for the People

¹⁸"Choose men to be judges and officers in every town that the LORD your God gives you. Every tribe must do this. And these men must be fair in judging the people. ¹⁹You must always be fair. You must not favor some people over other people. You must not take money to change your mind in judgment. Money blinds the eyes of wise people and changes what a good person will say. ²⁰Goodness and Fairness! You must try very hard to be good and fair all the time. Then you will live and keep the land that the LORD your God is giving you.

God Hates Idols

²¹"When you set up an altar* for the LORD your God, you must not place beside the altar any of the wooden poles that honor the goddess Asherah.* ²²You must not set up special stones for worshiping false gods. The LORD your God hates them.

Use Only Good Animals for Sacrifices

17 ¹"You must not sacrifice to the LORD your God an ox or sheep that has anything wrong with it. The LORD your God would hate that.

Punishment for Worshiping Idols

²"You might hear about an evil thing that happens in one of the cities that the LORD your God is giving you. You might hear that a man or woman in your group has sinned against the LORD your God. You might hear that they have broken his agreement* or ³that they have worshiped other gods or maybe the sun, the moon or the stars. I never told you to do that! ⁴If you hear bad news like this, you must check it carefully. You must learn if it is true that this terrible thing has really happened in Israel. If you prove that it is true, ⁵you must punish the person who did this evil thing. You must take that man or woman out to a public place near the city gates and kill them with stones. ⁶But no one should be punished with death if only one witness says that person did that evil thing. But if two or three witnesses say it is true, the person must be killed. ⁷The witnesses must throw the first stones to kill that person. Then the other people should throw stones to finish killing that person. In this way you will remove this evil from your group.

Difficult Court Decisions

⁸"There might be some problems that are too hard for your courts to judge. It might be a murder case or an argument between two people. Or it might be a fight in which someone was hurt. When these cases are argued in your towns, your judges there might not be able to decide what is right. Then you must go to the special place that the LORD your God will choose. ⁹You must go to the priests who are Levites and to the judge on duty at that time. They will decide what to do about that problem. ¹⁰There at the LORD's special place they will tell you their decision. You must do whatever they say. Be sure to do everything they tell you to do. ¹¹You must accept

their decision and follow their instructions exactly—don't change anything! 12"You must punish anyone who refuses to obey the judge or the priest who is there at that time serving the LORD your God. That person must die. You must remove this evil person from Israel. 13All the people will hear about this punishment and be afraid. Then they will not be stubborn anymore.

How to Choose a King

14"You will enter the land that the LORD your God is giving you. You will take that land and live in it. Then you will say, 'We will put a king over us, like all the nations around us.' 15When that happens, you must be sure to choose the king that the LORD chooses. The king over you must be one of your own people. You must not make a foreigner your king. 16The king must not get more and more horses for himself. And he must not send people to Egypt to get more horses, because the LORD has told you, 'You must never go back that way.' 17Also, the king must not have too many wives, because that will make him turn away from the LORD. He must not make himself rich with silver and gold.

18"When the king begins to rule, he must write a copy of the law for himself in a book. He must make that copy from the books that the priests from the tribe of Levi keep. 19He must keep that book with him and read from it all his life, because he must learn to respect the LORD his God. He must learn to completely obey everything the law commands. 20Then the king will not think that he is better than any of his own people. He will not turn away from the law, but he will follow it exactly. Then he and his descendants will rule the kingdom of Israel a long time.

Supporting the Priests and Levites

18 1"The tribe of Levi will not get any share of land in Israel. The priests come from that tribe and they will eat the special sacrifices that are offered as gifts to the LORD. That is the share for the people from the tribe of Levi. 2The tribe of Levi will not get any share of land like the other tribes. Their share is the LORD himself, as he said to them.

3"When you kill one of your sheep or cattle for a sacrifice, you must give the priests these parts: the shoulder, both cheeks, and the stomach. 4You must give the priests the first part of your harvest. You must give them the first part of your grain, your new wine, and your oil. You must give the Levites* the first wool cut from your sheep. 5This is because the LORD your God looked at all your tribes and chose Levi and his descendants to serve him as priests forever.

6"Any Levite living in any town anywhere in Israel may leave his home and come to the LORD's special place. He may do this anytime he wants. 7And this Levite may serve in the name of the LORD his God, the same as all his brother Levites who are on duty before the LORD. 8And that Levite will get an equal share with the other Levites, in addition to the share his family normally gets.*a*

Israel Must Not Live Like Other Nations

9"When you come into the land that the LORD your God is giving you, don't learn to do the terrible things the people of the other nations there do. 10Don't sacrifice your sons or daughters in the fires on your altars.* Don't try to learn what will happen in the future by talking to a fortuneteller or by going to a magician, a witch, or a sorcerer. 11Don't let anyone try to put magic spells on other people. Don't let any of your people become a medium* or a wizard.* And no one should try to talk with someone who has died. 12The LORD your God hates people doing these things. That is why he is forcing these other nations out of this country for you. 13You must be faithful to the LORD your God.

The Lord's Special Prophet

14"You will force the other nations out of your land. They listen to people who use magic and try to tell the future. But the LORD your God will not let you do these things. 15The LORD your God will send to you a prophet.* This prophet will come from among your own people, and he will be like me. You must listen to him. 16God will send you this prophet because that is what you asked him to do. When you were gathered together at Mount Horeb,* you became frightened and said, 'Don't let us hear the voice of the LORD our God again! Don't let us see that great fire or we will die!'

17"The LORD said to me, 'What they ask for is good. 18I will send them a prophet like you. This prophet will be one of their own people. I will tell him what he must say, and he will tell the people everything I command. 19This prophet will speak for me, and I will punish anyone who refuses to listen to my commands.'

How to Know False Prophets

20"But a prophet* might say something that I did not tell him to say. And he might tell people that he is speaking for me. If this happens, that prophet must be killed. Also a prophet might come that speaks for other gods. That prophet must also be killed. 21You might be thinking, 'How can we know if something a prophet says is not from the LORD?' 22If a prophet says he is speaking for the LORD, but what he says does not happen, you will know that the LORD did not say it. You will know that this prophet was speaking his own ideas. You don't need to be afraid of him.

*a*18:8 *in addition ... gets* Or "without regard to gifts from family and friends."

Cities of Safety

19 ¹"The LORD your God is giving you land that belongs to other nations. The LORD your God will destroy those nations. You will live where these people lived. You will take their cities and their houses. When that happens, ²⁻³you must divide the land into three parts. In each part you must choose a city close to everyone in that area, and then you must prepare roads to these cities. Whoever kills another person may run to that city for safety.

⁴"This is the rule for someone who kills another person and runs to one of these three cities for safety: It must be someone who killed another person accidentally, not out of hatred. ⁵Here is an example: A man goes into the forest with another person to cut wood. The man swings his ax to cut down a tree, but the head of the ax separates from the handle. The ax head hits the other person and kills him. The man who swung the ax may then run to one of these three cities and be safe. ⁶But if the city is too far away, he might not be able to run there fast enough. A close relative*a* of the person he killed might run after him and catch him before he reaches the city. The relative might kill the man in anger, even though he did not deserve to die because he did not mean to harm anyone. ⁷That is why I commanded you to choose three special cities.

⁸"The LORD your God promised your fathers that he would make your land larger. He will give you all the land that he promised to give to your ancestors.* ⁹He will do this if you completely obey his commands that I give you today—if you love the LORD your God and always live the way he wants. Then, when the LORD makes your land larger, you should choose three more cities for safety. They should be added to the first three cities. ¹⁰Then innocent people will not be killed in the land that the LORD your God is giving you. And you will not be guilty for any such deaths.

¹¹"But suppose there is a man who hates his neighbor. That man might hide and wait to kill the person he hates. If he kills that person and runs to one of these cities of safety, ¹²the elders* in his hometown must send someone to get him and take him away from the city of safety. These leaders must hand him over to the close relative. He is a murderer and he must die. ¹³Don't feel sorry for him. He is guilty of killing an innocent person, and you must remove that guilt from Israel. Then everything will go well for you.

Property Lines

¹⁴"You must not move the stones that mark your neighbor's property. People put

them there in the past to mark each person's property. These stones mark the land that the LORD your God gave you.

Witnesses

¹⁵"If someone is accused of doing something against the law, one witness is not enough to prove that the person is guilty. There must be two or three witnesses to prove that the person really did wrong.

¹⁶"A witness might try to hurt another person by lying and saying that this person did wrong. ¹⁷If that happens, both of them must go to the LORD's special house and be judged by the priests and judges who are on duty at that time. ¹⁸When the judges carefully ask their questions, they might find that the witness lied against the other person. If the witnesses tell lies, ¹⁹you must punish them with the same punishment the other person would have received. In this way you will remove this evil from your group. ²⁰Other people will hear about this and be afraid, and people will not do evil things like that again.

²¹"Don't feel sorry about punishing someone who does wrong. If a life is taken, a life must be paid for it. The rule is an eye for an eye, a tooth for a tooth, a hand for a hand, a foot for a foot—the punishment must equal the crime.

Rules for War

20 ¹"When you go out to battle against your enemies, and you see horses, chariots,* and many more people than you have, you must not be afraid of them. The LORD your God is with you—and he brought you out of Egypt.

²"When you go to the battle, the priest must go to the soldiers and speak to them. ³The priest will say, 'Men of Israel, listen to me! Today you are going against your enemies in battle. Don't lose your courage. Don't be troubled or upset. Don't be afraid of the enemy. ⁴The LORD your God is going with you to help you fight against your enemies. He will help you win!'

⁵"The Levite officials will say to the soldiers, 'Is there any man here who has built a new house but has not yet dedicated* it? That man should go back home. He might be killed in the battle, and then another person will dedicate that man's house. ⁶Is there any man here who has planted a vineyard* but has not yet gathered any of the grapes? That man should go back home. If that man dies in the battle, someone else will enjoy the fruit from his field. ⁷Is there any man here who is engaged to be married? That man should go back home. If he dies in the battle, another man will marry the woman he is engaged to.'

⁸"These Levite officials must also say to the people, 'Is there any man here who has lost his courage and is afraid? He should go back home. Then he will not cause the other

---

a19:6 close relative Literally, "avenger of blood." When a person was killed, his relative had to be sure the killer was punished. Also in verse 12.

soldiers to lose their courage too.' ⁹Then, after the officers have finished speaking to the army, they must choose captains to lead the soldiers.

¹⁰"When you go to attack a city, you must first offer peace to the people there. ¹¹If they accept your offer and open their gates, all the people in that city will become your slaves and be forced to work for you. ¹²But if the city refuses to make peace with you and fights against you, you should surround the city. ¹³And when the LORD your God lets you take the city, you must kill all the men in it. ¹⁴But you may take for yourselves the women, the children, the cattle, and everything else in the city. You may use all these things. The LORD your God has given these things to you. ¹⁵That is what you must do to all the cities that are very far from you—the cities that are not in the land where you will live.

¹⁶"But when you take cities in the land that the LORD your God is giving you, you must kill everyone. ¹⁷You must completely destroy all the people—the Hittites, Amorites, Canaanites, Perizzites, Hivites, and Jebusites. The LORD your God has commanded you to do this. ¹⁸So then they will not be able teach you to sin against the LORD your God or to do any of the terrible things they do when they worship their gods.

¹⁹"When you are making war against a city, you might surround that city for a long time. You must not cut down the fruit trees around that city. You may eat the fruit from these trees, but you must not cut them down. These trees are not the enemy, so don't make war against them. ²⁰But you may cut down the trees that you know are not fruit trees. You may use these trees to build weapons for making war against that city. You may use them until the city falls.

If Someone Is Found Murdered

21 ¹"In the land that the LORD your God is giving you, you might find a dead body in a field, but no one knows who killed that person. ²Your leaders and judges must come out and measure the distance to the towns around the dead body. ³When you learn which town is nearest to the dead body, the leaders of that town must take a cow from their herds. It must be a cow that never had a calf and that has never been used for work. ⁴The leaders of that town must then bring the cow down to a valley with running water. It must be a valley that has never been plowed or had anything planted in it. Then the leaders must break the cow's neck there in that valley. ⁵The priests, the descendants of Levi, must also go there. (The LORD your God has chosen these priests to serve him and to bless people in his name. The priests will decide who is right in every lawsuit and whenever someone is hurt.) ⁶All the leaders of the town nearest the dead body must wash their hands

over the cow that had its neck broken in the valley. ⁷These leaders must say, 'We did not kill this person, and we did not see it happen. ⁸LORD, you saved your people Israel. Now make us pure.* Don't blame us for killing an innocent person.' In this way these men will not be blamed for killing an innocent person. ⁹In this way you will remove that guilt from your group by doing what the LORD said.

Women Captured in War

¹⁰"You might fight against your enemies, and the LORD your God might let you defeat them and take them as captives. ¹¹You might see a beautiful woman among the captives who you want to be your wife. ¹²You must then bring her into your house where she will shave her head and cut her nails. ¹³She must change her clothes and take off the clothes she was wearing when she was captured in war. She will stay in your house and be sad about losing her father and her mother for a full month. After that you may go to her to be her husband, and she will be your wife. ¹⁴If you are not pleased with her and choose to divorce her, set her free. You cannot sell her. You had sexual relations with her, so you must not treat her like a slave.

The Oldest Son

¹⁵"A man might have two wives. He might love one wife more than the other. Both wives might have children for him, but the firstborn son might be from the wife he does not love. ¹⁶When the man divides his property among his children, he cannot give the rights of the firstborn* to the son of his favorite wife. ¹⁷The man must accept the firstborn son from the wife he does not love. The man must give that son a double share of everything he owns because that son is his first child. The right of the firstborn belongs to that son.

Children Who Refuse to Obey

¹⁸"A man might have a son who is stubborn and refuses to obey. This son does not obey his father or mother. They punish the son, but he still refuses to listen to them. ¹⁹His father and mother must then take him to the leaders of the town at the town meeting place. ²⁰They must say to the leaders of the town: 'Our son is stubborn and refuses to obey. He does not do anything we tell him to do. He eats and he drinks too much.' ²¹Then the men in the town must kill the son with stones. By doing this you will remove this evil from your group. Everyone in Israel will hear about this and be afraid.

Criminals Killed and Hanged on a Tree

²²"A man might be guilty of a sin that must be punished by death. People might kill him and hang his body on a tree. ²³You must not let that body stay on the tree overnight. You must be sure to bury this man on the same

day, because the one who hangs on a tree is cursed by God, and you must not let the land that the LORD your God is giving you become unclean.

Other Laws

22 [1]"If you see that your neighbor's ox or sheep is loose, you must not ignore it. Be sure to take it back to its owner. [2]If the owner does not live near you or if you don't know who it belongs to, take the ox or sheep to your house. Keep it there until the owner comes looking for it; then give it back. [3]You must do the same thing when you find anything that your neighbor might have lost. Don't try selling it to your neighbor—you must give it back.

[4]"If your neighbor's donkey or ox has fallen down on the road, you must not ignore it. You must help your neighbor lift it up again.

[5]"A woman must not wear men's clothes, and a man must not wear women's clothes. That is disgusting to the LORD your God.

[6]"You might be walking along a path and find a bird's nest in a tree or on the ground. If the mother bird is sitting with her baby birds or on the eggs, you must not take the mother bird with the babies. [7]You may take the babies for yourself, but you must let the mother go. If you obey these laws, things will go well for you, and you will live a long time.

[8]"When you build a new house, you must build a wall around your roof.[a] Then you will not be guilty for the death of a person who falls from the house.

Things That Must Not Be Put Together

[9]"You must not plant seeds of grain in the same fields as your grapevines. Why? Because then they become useless[b]—both the grapes and the grain produced by the seeds you planted.

[10]"You must not plow with an ox and a donkey together.

[11]"You must not wear clothes made by weaving together wool and linen.

[12]"Tie several pieces of thread together. Then put these tassels[c] on the four corners of the robes you wear.

Marriage Laws

[13]"A man might marry a woman and have sexual relations with her. Then he might decide that he does not like her. [14]He might accuse her of doing wrong and say, 'I married

this woman, but when we had sexual relations, I found she was not a virgin.' By saying this against her, people might think bad things about her. [15]If this happens, the girl's father and mother must bring the proof that the girl was a virgin to the town elders* at the meeting place of the town. [16]The girl's father must say to the leaders, 'I gave my daughter to this man to be his wife, but now he does not want her. [17]This man accused my daughter of doing wrong and said, "I did not find the proof that your daughter is a virgin." But here is the proof that my daughter was a virgin.' Then they should show the cloth[d] to the town leaders. [18]Then the leaders of that town must take that man and punish him. [19]They must fine him 40 ounces of silver.[e] They will give the money to the girl's father because her husband brought shame to an Israelite girl. And the girl will continue to be the man's wife. He cannot divorce her for the rest of his life.

[20]"But what the husband said about his wife might be true. The wife's parents might not have the proof that she was a virgin. If this happens, [21]the town leaders must bring the girl to the door of her father's house. Then the men of the town must kill her with stones, because she has done a shameful thing in Israel. She has acted like a prostitute in her father's house. You must remove this evil from your group.

Sexual Sins

[22]"If a man is found having sexual relations with another man's wife, both of them must die—the woman and the man who had sexual relations with her. You must remove this evil from Israel.

[23]"A man might meet a virgin* girl engaged to another man. He might have sexual relations with her. If this happens in the city, [24]you must bring them both out to the public place near the gate of that city, and you must kill them with stones. You must kill the man, because he used another man's wife for sexual sin. And you must kill the girl, because she was in the city but did not call for help. You must remove this evil from your people.

[25]"But if a man finds an engaged girl out in the field and forces her to have sexual relations with him, only the man must die. [26]You must do nothing to the girl. She did nothing that deserves the punishment of death. This is like someone attacking their neighbor and killing them. [27]The man found the engaged girl out in the field and attacked her. Maybe she called for help, but there was no one to help her.

---

[a]**22:8 wall around your roof** In ancient Israel, houses had flat roofs that were used as an extra room. This law made the roof a safer place.
[b]**22:9 they become useless** Literally, "they become holy." This means these things belonged only to God, so they couldn't be used by the people.
[c]**22:12 tassels** These pieces of string were made from different materials, so they became holy. This helped the people remember God and his commands.

[d]**22:17 cloth** The bloodstained bed cover that the bride kept from her wedding night to prove she was a virgin when she married.
[e]**22:19 40 ounces of silver** This is probably twice the amount of money that a man usually paid the father of the bride to seal the marriage agreement. See Deut. 22:29.

28"A man might find a virgin girl who is not engaged and force her to have sexual relations with him. If other people see this happen, 29he must pay the girl's father 20 ounces of silver.a And the girl will become the man's wife, because he used her for sexual sin. He cannot divorce her all his life.

30"A man must not bring shame to his father by marrying his father's wife.

People Who Cannot Join in Worship

23 1"A man with a crushed testicle or part of his sex organ cut off may not join with the men of Israel to worship the LORD. 2If a man's parents were not legally married, that man may not join with the men of Israel to worship the LORD. And none of his descendants to the tenth generation—may join in that group.

3"An Ammonite or Moabite may not join with the men of Israel to worship the LORD. And none of their descendants—to the tenth generation—may join in that group. 4The Ammonites and Moabites refused to give you bread and water on your trip at the time you came from Egypt. They also tried to hire Balaam to curse you. (Balaam was the son of Beor from the city of Pethor in Mesopotamia.) 5But the LORD your God refused to listen to Balaam. The Lord changed the curse into a blessing for you, because the LORD your God loves you. 6You must never try to make peace with the Ammonites or Moabites. As long as you live, don't be friendly to them.

People the Israelites Must Accept

7"You must not hate Edomites, because they are your relatives. You must not hate Egyptians, because you were a stranger in their land. 8The children of the third generation born to the Edomites and Egyptians may join with the people of Israel to worship the LORD.

Keeping the Army Camp Clean

9"When your army goes to fight against your enemies, stay away from everything that would make you unclean.* 10If there is any man who is unclean because he had a flow of semen during the night, he must go out of the camp. He must stay away from the camp. 11Then, when evening comes, the man must bathe himself in water. And when the sun goes down, he may come into the camp again.

12"You also must have a place outside the camp where people can go to relieve themselves. 13Among your weapons, you must also carry a stick to dig with. Then, when

you relieve yourself, you must dig a hole and cover it up. 14This is because the LORD your God is there with you in your camp to save you and to help you defeat your enemies. So the camp must be holy. Then he will not see something disgusting and leave you.

Other Laws

15"If slaves run away and come to you, don't force them to go back to their masters. 16Runaway slaves may live with you wherever they like in whatever city they choose. You must not trouble them.

17"An Israelite man or woman must never become a temple prostitute. 18The money earned by a prostitute, either a male or female, must not be brought to the special house of the LORD your God. That money cannot be used to pay for a gift that was promised to the LORD your God, because that kind of sin is disgusting to him.

19"When you loan something to another Israelite, you must not charge interest. Don't charge interest on money, on food or on anything that may earn interest. 20You may charge interest to a foreigner. But you must not charge interest to another Israelite. If you follow these rules, the LORD your God will bless you in everything you do in the land where you are going to live.

21"When you make a promise to the LORD your God, don't be slow to pay everything you promised. The LORD your God will demand that you pay it. You will sin if you don't pay what you promised. 22If you don't make a promise, you are not sinning. 23But you must do what you say you will do. If you make a special promise to God, you chose to make that promise. God did not force you to make that promise. So you must do what you promised!

24"When you go through another person's vineyard,* you may eat as many grapes as you want. But you cannot put any of the grapes in your basket. 25When you go through another person's field of grain, you may eat all the grain you can pick with your hands. But you cannot use a sickle* to cut that person's grain and take it with you.

24 1"A man might marry a woman, and then find some secret thing about her that he does not like. If that man is not pleased with her, he must write the divorce papers and give them to her. Then he must send her from his house. 2When she has left his house, she may go and become another man's wife. 3-4But suppose the new husband also does not like her and sends her away. If that man divorces her, the first husband may not take her again to be his wife. Or if the new husband dies, her first husband may not take her again to be his wife. She has become unclean to him. If he married her again, he would be doing something the LORD hates. You must not sin like this in the land that the LORD your God is giving you.

a22:29 20 ounces of silver This money became the dowry, the money a man paid to a woman's father to seal the marriage agreement. Often the father saved this money to take care of the woman if something happened to her husband.

⁵"When a man is newly married, he must not be sent into the army. And he must not be given any other special work. For one year he must be free to stay home and make his new wife happy.

⁶"When you lend someone something, you must not take as security*a* any part of the stones used to grind flour. That would be the same as taking away their food.

⁷"Someone might kidnap another Israelite—one of their own people. And that kidnapper might sell that person as a slave. If that happens, that kidnapper must be killed. You must remove this evil from your group.

⁸"When you have a very bad skin disease,* be very careful to follow everything the Levite priests teach you. You must follow carefully what I told the priests to do. ⁹Remember what the LORD your God did to Miriam*b* on your trip out of Egypt.

¹⁰"When you give someone any kind of loan, you must not go into their house to get security. ¹¹You must stand outside. Then the person who you gave the loan to will bring out the security to you. ¹²If he is a poor man, ₍then he might give the clothes that keep him warm₎. You must not keep that security overnight. ¹³You must give his security back to him every evening. Then he will have clothes to sleep in. He will bless you, and the LORD your God will accept this as living right and doing good.

¹⁴"You must not cheat a hired servant who is poor and needy. It does not matter if he is an Israelite or if he is a foreigner living in one of your cities. ¹⁵Give him his pay every day before sunset, because he is poor and depends on the money. If you don't pay him, he will complain against you to the LORD, and you will be guilty of sin.

¹⁶"Parents must not be put to death for something their children did. And children must not be put to death for something their parents did. People should be put to death only for a bad thing that they themselves did.

¹⁷"You must make sure that foreigners and orphans are treated fairly. And you must never take clothes from a widow as security. ¹⁸Remember, you were poor slaves in Egypt. And the LORD your God took you from that place and set you free. That is why I tell you to do these things for the poor.

¹⁹"You might be gathering your harvest in the field, and you might forget and leave some grain there. You must not go back to get it. It will be for the foreigners, the orphans, and the widows. If you leave some grain for them, the LORD your God will bless you in everything you do. ²⁰When you beat your olive trees, you must not go back to check the branches. The olives you leave will be for the foreigners, the

orphans, and the widows. ²¹When you gather the grapes from your vineyard, you must not go back to gather the grapes you left. They will be for the foreigners, the orphans, and the widows. ²²Remember you were poor slaves in Egypt. That is why I tell you to do these things for the poor.

25 ¹"When two people have an argument, they should go to the court. The judges will decide which person is right and which is wrong. ²If the judge decides a person must be beaten with a whip, the judge must make that person lie face down. Someone will beat the guilty person while the judge watches. The number of times he must be hit depends on the crime. ³Don't hit anyone more than 40 times during punishment, because more than that means that their life is not important to you.

⁴"When an animal is being used to separate grain, you must not cover its mouth to stop it from eating.

⁵"If two brothers live together, and one of them dies without a son, the wife of the dead man must not marry a stranger outside the family. Her husband's brother must take her as his wife and have sexual relations with her. He must do the duty of a husband's brother for her. ⁶Then the first son she has will be considered the dead man's son in order to keep the dead man's name alive in Israel. ⁷If the man does not want to take his brother's wife, she must go to the town meeting place and tell the leaders, 'My husband's brother refuses to keep his brother's name alive in Israel. He will not do the duty of a husband's brother to me.' ⁸Then the leaders of the city must call the man and talk to him. If the man is stubborn and says, 'I don't want to take her,' ⁹then his brother's wife must come to him in front of the leaders. She must take his sandal off his foot and spit in his face. She must say, 'This is being done to the man who will not give his brother a son!' ¹⁰From then on, the brother's family will be known in Israel as, 'the family of the man whose sandal was removed.'

¹¹"Two men might be fighting against each other. One man's wife might come to help her husband, but she must not grab the other man's private parts. ¹²If she does that, cut off her hand. Don't feel sorry for her.

¹³"Don't use weights that are too heavy or too light. ¹⁴Don't keep measures in your house that are too large or too small. ¹⁵You must use weights and measures that are correct and accurate. Then you will live a long time in the land that the LORD your God is giving you. ¹⁶The LORD your God hates people who cheat with false weights and measures. Yes, he hates all people who do wrong.

The Amalekites Must Be Destroyed

¹⁷"Remember what the Amalekites did to you when you were coming from Egypt.

---

*a***24:6** *security* Anything someone gives as a promise to repay a loan. If the loan is not repaid, the lender keeps whatever was given. Also in verses 10, 17.
*b***24:9** *Miriam* See Num. 12:1-15.

[18]The Amalekites did not respect God. They attacked you when you were weak and tired. They killed all your people who were slow and walking behind everyone else. [19]That is why you must destroy the memory of the Amalekites from the world. You will do this when you enter the land that the LORD your God is giving you. There he will give you rest from all the enemies around you. But do not forget to destroy the Amalekites!

The First Harvest

26 [1]"You will soon enter the land that the LORD your God is giving you. You will take that land and live there. [2]You will gather the crops that grow in the land the LORD your God is giving you. You must take some of the first crops you gather and put them in baskets. Then take that part of your harvest to the place that the LORD your God chooses to be the home for his name. [3]Go to the priest who is serving at that time. Tell him, 'The LORD promised our ancestors* that he would give us some land. Today I come to announce to the LORD your God that I have come to that land.'

[4]"Then the priest will take the basket from you. He will put it down in front of the altar* of the LORD your God. [5]Then there before the LORD your God you will say: 'My ancestor was a wandering Aramean.[a] He went down into Egypt and stayed there. When he went there, he had only a few people in his family. But in Egypt he became a great nation—a powerful nation with many people. [6]The Egyptians treated us badly. They made us slaves. They hurt us and forced us to work very hard. [7]Then we prayed to the LORD, the God of our ancestors, and complained about them. And the LORD heard us. He saw our trouble, our hard work, and our suffering. [8]Then the LORD brought us out of Egypt with his great power and strength. He used great miracles and wonders and did amazing things. [9]So he brought us to this place. He gave us this land—a land filled with many good things.[b] [10]Now, LORD, I bring you the first harvest from the land that you gave me.'

"Then you must put the harvest down before the LORD your God and bow down to worship him. [11]Then you must have a meal together and enjoy all the good things that the LORD your God has given to you and your family. You must share them with the Levites* and the foreigners living among you.

[12]"Every third year is the Year of Tithes. In that year, you must give one-tenth of your harvest to the Levites, to the foreigners living in your country, and to the widows and orphans. Then they will have plenty to eat in every city. [13]You must say to the LORD your God, 'I have taken out of my house the holy part of my harvest. I have given it to the Levites, to the foreigners, and to the orphans and widows. I have followed all the commands you gave me. I have not refused to obey any of your commands. I have not forgotten them. [14]I have not eaten this food when I was sad.[c] I was not unclean when I collected this food.[d] I have not offered any of this food for dead people. I have obeyed you, LORD my God. I have done everything you commanded me. [15]Look down from your holy home, from heaven, and bless your people Israel. And bless the land that you gave us. You promised our ancestors to give us this land—a land filled with many good things.'

Obey the Lord's Commands

[16]"Today the LORD your God commands you to obey all these laws and rules. Be careful to follow them with all your heart and soul. [17]Today you have said that the LORD is your God. You have promised to live the way he wants. You promised to follow his teachings, and to obey his laws and commands. You said you will do everything he tells you to do. [18]And today the LORD has accepted you to be his own people. He has promised you this. The LORD also said that you must obey all his commands. [19]The LORD will make you greater than all the nations he made. He will give you praise, fame, and honor. And you will be his own special people, as he promised."

Stone Memorials for the People

27 [1]Moses and the elders* of Israel spoke to the people. Moses said, "Obey all the commands that I give you today. [2]You will soon go across the Jordan River into the land that the LORD your God is giving you. On that day you must put up large stones. Cover them with plaster. [3]Then write on the stones all these commands and teachings. You must do this when you go across the Jordan River. Then you may go into the land that the LORD your God is giving you—a land filled with many good things.[e] The LORD, the God of your ancestors,* promised to give you this land.

[4]"After you go across the Jordan River, you must do what I command you today. You must set up the stones on Mount Ebal. You must cover these stones with plaster. [5]Also, use some stones there to build an altar* to the LORD your God. Don't use iron tools to cut the stones. [6]You must not use cut stones to build the altar for the LORD your God. Offer burnt

---

[c]**26:14 I have ... sad** People ate this food to be happy about the many things God gave them, so it could not be from food used during a time of sadness.

[d]**26:14 I was ... food** This would mean other people could not eat this food during the celebration to honor the Lord.

[e]**27:3 land ... things** Literally, "land flowing with milk and honey."

---

[a]**26:5 Aramean** A person from ancient Syria. Here, this might be Abraham, Isaac, or probably Jacob (Israel).

[b]**26:9 land ... things** Literally, "land flowing with milk and honey." Also in verse 15.

offerings* on this altar to the LORD your God. 7And you must sacrifice and eat fellowship offerings* there. Eat and enjoy yourselves there together with the LORD your God. 8You must write all these teachings on the stones that you set up. Write clearly so that they are easy to read."

The People Must Agree to God's Rules

9Moses and the Levite priests spoke to all the Israelites. Moses said, "Be quiet and listen, Israel! Today you have become the people of the LORD your God. 10So you must do everything that the LORD your God tells you. You must obey his commands and his laws that I am giving you today."

11That day Moses also told the people, 12"After you have gone across the Jordan River, these tribes will stand on Mount Gerizim to read the blessings to the people: Simeon, Levi, Judah, Issachar, Joseph, and Benjamin. 13And these tribes will stand on Mount Ebal to read the curses: Reuben, Gad, Asher, Zebulun, Dan, and Naphtali.

14"And the Levites* will say to all the Israelites in a loud voice: 15'Cursed is the one who makes a false god and puts it in its secret place. These false gods are only statues that some worker makes from wood, stone or metal. The LORD hates these things!'

"Then all the people will answer, 'Amen*!'

16"The Levites will say, 'Cursed is the one who does not show respect to their father or their mother!'

"Then all the people will answer, 'Amen!'

17"The Levites will say, 'Cursed is the one who moves a neighbor's landmark*a!'

"Then all the people will say, 'Amen!'

18"The Levites will say, 'Cursed is the one who tricks a blind man into going the wrong way!'

"Then all the people will say, 'Amen!'

19"The Levites will say, 'Cursed is the one who does not give fair judgment for the foreigners, orphans, and widows!'

"Then all the people will say, 'Amen!'

20"The Levites will say, 'Cursed is the one who shames his father by marrying his father's wife.'

"Then all the people will say, 'Amen!'

21"The Levites will say, 'Cursed is the one who has sexual relations with any kind of animal!'

"Then all the people will say, 'Amen!'

22"The Levites will say, 'Cursed is the one who has sexual relations with his sister or half sister!'

"Then all the people will say, 'Amen!'

23"The Levites will say, 'Cursed is the one who has sexual relations with his mother-in-law!'

"Then all the people will say, 'Amen!'

24"The Levites will say, 'Cursed is the one who kills anyone, even if he is not caught!'

"Then all the people will say, 'Amen!'

25"The Levites will say, 'Cursed is the one who takes money to kill an innocent person!'

"Then all the people will say, 'Amen!'

26"The Levites will say, 'Cursed is the one who does not support this law and agree to obey it.'

"Then all the people will say, 'Amen!'

Blessings for Obeying the Law

28 1"Now, if you will be careful to obey the LORD your God and follow all his commands that I tell you today, the LORD your God will put you high above all the nations on earth. 2If you will obey the LORD your God, all these blessings will come to you and be yours:

3"He will bless you
  in the city and in the field.
4 He will bless you
  and give you many children.
  He will bless your land
  and give you good crops.
  He will bless your animals
  and let them have many babies.
  He will bless you with calves and lambs.
5 He will bless your baskets and pans
  and fill them with food.
6 He will bless you at all times in
  everything you do.

7"The LORD will help you defeat your enemies who come to fight against you. Your enemies will come against you one way, but they will run away from you seven different ways!

8"The LORD will bless you and fill your barns. He will bless everything you do. The LORD your God will bless you in the land that he is giving you. 9The LORD will make you his own special people, as he promised. The Lord will do this if you follow the LORD your God and obey his commands. 10Then all the people in that land will see that you are called to be the LORD's people, and they will be afraid of you.

11"And the LORD will give you many good things. He will give you many children. He will give your cows many calves. He will give you a good harvest in the land that the LORD promised your ancestors* to give you. 12The LORD will open his storehouse where he keeps his rich blessings. He will send rain at the right time for your land. He will bless everything you do. You will have money to lend to many nations. And you will not need to borrow anything from them. 13The LORD will make you be like the head, not the tail. You will be on top, not on the bottom. This will happen if you listen to the commands of the LORD your God that I tell you today. You must carefully obey these commands. 14You

---

*a*27:17 **landmark** A stone or sign that showed where the limits of a person's property were.

must not turn away from any of the teachings that I give you today. You must not turn away to the right or to the left. You must not follow other gods to serve them.

Curses for Not Obeying the Law

15"But if you don't listen to what the LORD your God tells you—if you don't obey all his commands and laws that I tell you today—then all these bad things will happen to you:

16"The Lord will curse you
    in the city and in the field.
17 He will curse you with empty baskets and
    pans.
18 He will curse you,
    and you will not have many children.
    He will curse your land,
    and you will not have good crops.
    He will curse your animals,
    and they will not have many babies.
    He will curse your calves and lambs.
19 He will curse you at all times in
    everything you do.

20"If you do evil and turn away from the LORD, he will make bad things happen to you. You will have frustration and trouble in everything you do. He will continue to do this until you are quickly and completely destroyed. He will do this because you turned away from him and left him. 21The LORD will send you terrible diseases until you no longer exist, until you are completely gone from the land. 22The LORD will punish you with diseases, fever, and swelling. He will send you terrible heat and you will have no rain. Your crops will die from the heat and disease.*a* All these bad things will happen until you are destroyed! 23There will be no clouds in the sky—the sky will look like polished brass. And the ground under you will be hard like iron. 24The LORD will not send rain—only sand and dust will fall from the sky. It will come down on you until you are destroyed.

25"The LORD will let your enemies defeat you. You will go to fight against your enemies one way, but you will run away from them seven different ways. The bad things that happen to you will make all the people on earth afraid. 26Your dead bodies will be food for the wild birds and animals. There will be no one to scare them away from your dead bodies.

27"The LORD will punish you with boils, like those he sent on the Egyptians. He will punish you with tumors, sores that run, and an itch that cannot be cured. 28The LORD will punish you by making you crazy. He will make you blind and confused. 29In daylight you will have to feel your way like a blind man. You will fail in everything you do. Again and again

people will hurt you and steal from you. And there will be no one to save you.

30"You will be engaged to a woman, but another man will have sexual relations with her. You will build a house, but you will not live in it. You will plant a vineyard,* but you will not gather anything from it. 31People will kill your cattle in front of you, but you will not eat any of the meat. People will take your donkeys, and they will not give them back to you. Your enemies will get your sheep, and there will be no one to help you.

32"Other people will be allowed to take your sons and your daughters. Day after day you will look for your children. You will look for them until your eyes become weak and blind—but you will not find them. And God will not help you.

33"A nation that you don't know will take all your crops and everything you worked for. People will treat you badly and abuse you. 34The things you see will make you go crazy. 35The LORD will punish you with sore boils that cannot be healed. These boils will be on your knees and legs. The boils will be on every part of your body—from the bottom of your feet to the top of your head.

36"The LORD will send you and your king away to a nation you don't know. You and your ancestors* have never seen that nation. There you will serve false gods made of wood and stone. 37In the countries where the LORD will send you, the people will be shocked at the terrible things that happen to you. They will laugh at you and say bad things about you.

The Curse of Failure

38"Your fields will produce plenty of grain. But your harvest will be small, because the locusts* will eat your harvest. 39You will plant vineyards* and work hard in them. But you will not gather the grapes or drink the wine from them, because the worms will eat them. 40You will have olive trees everywhere on your land. But you will not have any of the oil to use, because the olives will drop to the ground and rot. 41You will have sons and daughters. But you will not be able to keep them, because they will be captured and taken away. 42Locusts will destroy all your trees and the crops in your fields. 43The foreigners living among you will get more and more power, and you will lose the power you had. 44The foreigners will have money to loan you, but you will not have any money to loan them. They will control you like the head controls the body. You will be like the tail.

45"All these curses will come on you. They will keep chasing you and catching you, until you are destroyed, because you did not listen to what the LORD your God told you. You did not obey the commands and laws that he gave you. 46These curses will show people that God judged you and your descendants

---

*a*28:22 *disease* This might be mildew, a disease that turns the heads of grain yellow and stops them from growing seeds.

forever. People will be amazed at the terrible things that happen to you.

47"The LORD your God gave you many blessings. But you did not serve him with joy and a glad heart. 48So you will serve the enemies the LORD will send against you. You will be hungry, thirsty, naked, and poor. He will put a load on you that cannot be removed. You will carry that load until he destroys you.[a]

The Curse of an Enemy Nation

49"The LORD will bring a nation from far away to fight you. You will not understand their language. They will come quickly, like an eagle coming down from the sky. 50These people will be cruel. They will not care about old people or show mercy to young children. 51They will take your animals and the food you grow. They will take everything until they destroy you. They will not leave you any grain, wine, oil, cattle, sheep, or goats. They will take everything, until they destroy you.

52"That nation will surround and attack your cities. You think that the tall, strong walls around your cities will protect you. But those walls will fall down. The enemy will surround all your cities everywhere in the land the LORD your God is giving you. 53You will suffer very much. The enemy will surround your cities. They will not let you have any food. You will get very hungry. You will be so hungry that you will eat your own sons and daughters—you will eat the bodies of the children the LORD your God gave you.

54"Even the most kind and gentle man among you will become cruel. He will be cruel to his family, and he will be cruel to his wife he loves so much. And he will be cruel to his children who are still alive. 55He will have nothing left to eat, so he will eat his own children. And he will not share that meat with anyone—not even the other people in his own family. All these bad things will happen when your enemy comes to surround your cities and make you suffer.

56"Even the most kind and gentle woman among you will become cruel. She might be a lady so gentle and delicate that she never put her feet on the ground to walk anywhere. But she will become cruel to her husband she loves so much. And she will be cruel to her own son and daughter. 57She will hide and give birth to a baby. And she will eat the baby and everything that comes out of her body with it. All these bad things will happen when your enemy comes to surround your cities and make you suffer.

58"You must obey all the commands and teachings that are written in this book. And you must respect the wonderful and awesome name of the LORD your God. If you don't obey, 59the LORD will give you and your descendants

many troubles. Your troubles and diseases will be terrible! 60You saw many troubles and diseases in Egypt, and they made you afraid. The LORD will bring all these bad things against you. 61The LORD will even bring troubles and diseases that are not written in this *Book of Teachings*. He will continue to do this until you are destroyed. 62You might have as many people as the stars in the sky. But only a few of you will be left, because you did not listen to the LORD your God.

63"The LORD was happy to be good to you and to make your nation grow. In the same way the LORD will be happy to ruin and destroy you. You are going to take that land to be yours. But people will take you out of that land! 64The LORD will scatter you among all the people in the world. He will scatter you from one end of the earth to the other. There you will serve false gods made of wood and stone. They are false gods that you or your ancestors* never worshiped.

65"You will not have any peace among these nations. You will have no place to rest. The LORD will fill your mind with worry. Your eyes will feel tired. You will be very upset. 66You will live with danger and always be afraid. You will be afraid night and day. You will never feel sure about your life. 67In the morning you will say, 'I wish it were evening!' In the evening you will say, 'I wish it were morning!' This will happen because of the fear in your heart and the terrible things you will see. 68The LORD will send you back to Egypt in ships. I said you would never have to go to that place again, but he will send you there. In Egypt you will try to sell yourselves as slaves to your enemies, but no one will buy you."

The Agreement in Moab

29 1The LORD made an agreement with the Israelites at Mount Horeb.* In addition to that agreement, he also commanded Moses to make another agreement with them while they were in Moab. This is that agreement.

2Moses called together all the Israelites. He said to them, "You saw everything the LORD did in the land of Egypt. You saw what he did to Pharaoh, to Pharaoh's officers, and to his whole country. 3You saw the great troubles he gave them. You saw the miracles and amazing things he did. 4But even today, you still don't understand what happened. The LORD has not let you really understand what you saw and heard. 5The LORD led you through the desert for 40 years, and in all that time your clothes and sandals did not wear out. 6You did not have any food with you. You did not have any wine or anything else to drink. But the Lord took care of you so that you would understand that he is the LORD your God.

7"You came to this place, and King Sihon of Heshbon and King Og of Bashan came out to

---

[a] **28:48** He ... destroys you Literally, "He will put an iron yoke on your neck until he destroys you."

fight against us. But we defeated them. [8]Then we took their land and gave it to the people in the tribes of Reuben and Gad and to half the tribe of Manasseh. [9]If you obey all the commands in this agreement, you will continue to succeed in everything you do.

[10]"Today all of you are standing here before the LORD your God. Your leaders, your officials, your elders,* and all the other men are here. [11]Your wives and children are here and also the foreigners living among you—the people who cut your wood and bring you water. [12]You are all here to enter into an agreement with the LORD your God. The LORD your God is making this agreement with you today. [13]With this agreement, the LORD is making you his own special people, and he himself will become your God. He told you this. He promised this to your ancestors*—Abraham, Isaac, and Jacob. [14]The LORD is making this agreement with its promises not only with you people. [15]He is making this agreement with all of us who stand here today before the LORD our God. But this agreement is also for our descendants who are not here with us today. [16]You remember how we lived in the land of Egypt. And you remember how we traveled through the countries that were on our way here. [17]You saw their hated things—the idols* they had made from wood, stone, silver, and gold. [18]Be sure that there is no man, woman, family or tribe here today who turns away from the LORD our God. No one should go and serve the gods of the other nations. People who do that are like a plant that grows bitter and poisonous fruit.

[19]"Some people might hear these curses and comfort themselves by saying, 'I will continue doing what I want. Nothing bad will happen to me.' But that attitude will bring total disaster. [20-21]The LORD will not forgive them for that. No, the LORD will be angry and upset with them and punish them. The LORD will separate them from the tribes of Israel. He will completely destroy them. All the curses that are written in this book will happen to them. They are a part of the agreement* that is written in this *Book of Teachings*.

[22]"In the future, your descendants and foreigners from faraway countries will see how the land has been ruined. They will see the diseases that the LORD has brought to it. [23]All the land will be useless—destroyed by burning sulfur and covered with salt. The land will have nothing planted in it. Nothing will be growing—not even weeds. The land will be destroyed like Sodom, Gomorrah, Admah, and Zeboiim, the cities the LORD destroyed when he was very angry.

[24]"All the other nations will ask, 'Why did the LORD do this to this land? Why was he so angry?' [25]The answer will be, 'The LORD is angry because the Israelites left the agreement of the LORD, the God of their ancestors. They stopped following the agreement that the LORD made with them when he brought them out of Egypt. [26]The Israelites started serving other gods—gods they never worshiped before. The LORD told his people not to worship those gods. [27]That is why the LORD became very angry with the people of this land. So he brought to them all the curses that are written in this book. [28]The LORD became very angry and upset with them. So he took them out of their land. He put them in another land, where they are today.'

[29]"There are some things that the LORD our God has kept secret. Only he knows these things. But he told us about some things. And these teachings are for us and our descendants forever. And we must obey all the commands in that law.

The Israelites Will Return to Their Land

30 [1]"Everything that I have mentioned will happen to you—both the blessings and the curses. And you will remember these words when the LORD your God sends you away to other nations. [2]Then you and your descendants will turn back to the LORD your God. You will follow him with all your heart and completely obey all his commands that I have given you today. [3]Then the LORD your God will be kind to you. The LORD your God will make you free again! He will bring you back from the nations where he sent you. [4]Even if you were sent to the farthest parts of the earth, the LORD your God will gather you from there and bring you back. [5]The LORD your God will bring you into the land your ancestors* had, and the land will become yours. He will do good to you, and you will have more than your ancestors had. You will have more people in your nation than they ever had. [6]The LORD your God will make you and your descendants want to obey him.[a] Then you will love the LORD your God with all your heart. And you will live!

[7]"Then the LORD your God will make all these bad things happen to your enemies, who hate you and cause you trouble. [8]And you will again obey the LORD. You will obey all his commands that I give you today. [9]The LORD your God will make you successful in everything you do. He will bless you with many children. He will bless your cows—they will have many calves. He will bless your fields—they will grow many good crops. He will be good to you. The LORD will again enjoy doing good for you, the same as he enjoyed doing good for your ancestors. [10]But you must do what the LORD your God tells you to do. You must obey his commands and follow the rules that are written in this *Book of Teachings*. You must obey the LORD your God with all your heart and with all your soul. Then these good things will happen to you.

---

[a]**30:6 make you … obey him** Literally, "circumcise the hearts of you and your seed."

Life or Death

¹¹"This command that I give you today is not too hard for you. It is not a secret hidden in some far away land. ¹²This command is not in heaven so that you should say, 'Who will go up to heaven for us and bring it to us, so that we can hear and do it?' ¹³This command is not on the other side of the sea so that you should say, 'Who will go across the sea for us and bring it to us, so that we can hear it and do it?' ¹⁴No, the word is very near to you. It is in your mouth and in your heart. So you can obey it.

¹⁵"Today I have given you a choice between life and death, success and disaster.ª ¹⁶I command you today to love the LORD your God. I command you to follow him and to obey his commands, laws, and rules. Then you will live, and your nation will grow larger. And the LORD your God will bless you in the land that you are entering to take for your own. ¹⁷But if you turn away from the LORD and refuse to listen—if you are led away to worship and serve other gods, ¹⁸then you will be destroyed. I am warning you today, if you turn away from the LORD, you will not live long in that land across the Jordan River that you are ready to enter and take for your own.

¹⁹"Today I am giving you a choice of two ways. And I ask heaven and earth to be witnesses of your choice. You can choose life or death. The first choice will bring a blessing. The other choice will bring a curse. So choose life! Then you and your children will live. ²⁰You must love the LORD your God and obey him. Never leave him, because the LORD is your life. And the LORD will give you a long life in the land that he promised to give to your ancestors*—Abraham, Isaac, and Jacob."

Joshua Will Be the New Leader

31 ¹Then Moses went and spoke these words to all the Israelites. ²Moses said to them, "I am now 120 years old. I cannot lead you anymore. The LORD said to me, 'You will not go across the Jordan River.' ³But the LORD your God will lead you people into that land. He will destroy these nations for you. You will take their land away from them. The LORD said that Joshua must lead you.

⁴"The LORD destroyed Sihon and Og. He destroyed those Amorite kings and he will do the same thing for you again! ⁵The LORD will help you defeat these nations. But you must do to them everything I told you to do. ⁶Be strong and be brave. Don't be afraid of those people because the LORD your God is with you. He will not fail you or leave you."

⁷Then Moses called Joshua. All the Israelites watched while Moses said to Joshua, "Be strong and brave. You will lead these people into the land that the LORD promised to give to their ancestors.* You will help the Israelites

take that land and divide it among them. ⁸The LORD will lead you. He himself is with you. He will not fail you or leave you. Don't worry. Don't be afraid!"

Moses Writes the Book of Teachings

⁹Then Moses wrote this *Book of Teachings* and gave it to the priests, who are from the tribe of Levi. They have the work of carrying the LORD's Box of the Agreement.* Moses also gave it to all the elders* of Israel. ¹⁰Then Moses spoke to the leaders. He said, "At the end of every seven years, in the Year of Freedom,ᵇ read these teachings at the Festival of Shelters.* ¹¹At that time all the Israelites must come to meet with the LORD your God at the special place he will choose. Then you must read the teachings to the people so that they can hear them. ¹²Bring together all the people—the men, the women, the little children, and the foreigners living in your cities. They will hear the teachings, and they will learn to respect the LORD your God. Then they will be able to do everything in this *Book of Teachings*. ¹³If their descendants don't know the teachings, they will hear them, and they will learn to respect the LORD your God. They will respect him as long as you live in your country. You will soon go across the Jordan River and take that land to be your own."

The Lord Calls Moses and Joshua

¹⁴The LORD said to Moses, "Now the time is near for you to die. Get Joshua and come to the Meeting Tent.* I will tell Joshua what he must do." So Moses and Joshua went to the Meeting Tent.

¹⁵The LORD appeared at the Tent in a tall cloud. The tall cloud stood over the entrance of the Tent. ¹⁶The LORD said to Moses, "You will die soon. And after you have gone to be with your ancestors,* these people will not continue to be faithful to me. They will break the agreement* I made with them. They will leave me and begin worshiping other gods— the false gods of the land where they are going. ¹⁷At that time I will become very angry with them, and I will leave them. I will refuse to help them, and they will be destroyed. Terrible things will happen to them, and they will have many troubles. Then they will say, 'These bad things happened to us because our God is not with us.' ¹⁸And I will refuse to help them, because they have done evil and worshiped other gods.

¹⁹"So write down this song, and teach it to the Israelites. Teach them to sing this song. Then this song will be a witness for me against the Israelites. ²⁰I will take them into the land that I promised to give to their ancestors—a land filled with many good things.ᶜ And they

---

ª**30:15** *success and disaster* Or "good and evil."

ᵇ**31:10** *Year of Freedom* That is, the year for canceling debts.

ᶜ**31:20** *land ... things* Literally, "land flowing with milk and honey."

will have all they want to eat. They will have a rich life. But then they will turn to other gods and serve them. They will turn away from me and break my agreement. ²¹Then many terrible things will happen to them. They will have many troubles. At that time their descendants will still know this song, and it will show them how wrong they are. I have not yet taken them into the land I promised to give them. But I already know what they are planning to do there."

²²So that same day Moses wrote down the song and taught it to the Israelites.

²³Then the LORD spoke to Joshua son of Nun and said, "Be strong and brave. You will lead the Israelites into the land I promised them, and I will be with you."

Moses Warns the Israelites

²⁴Moses carefully wrote all these teachings in a book. When he finished, ²⁵he gave a command to the Levites.* (These men carry the LORD's Box of the Agreement.*) Moses said, ²⁶"Take this *Book of Teachings* and put it by the side of the Box of the Agreement of the LORD your God. Then it will be a witness against you. ²⁷I know you are very stubborn. I know you want to live your own way. Look, you refused to obey the LORD while I was with you. So I know you will refuse to obey him after I die. ²⁸Bring together all the officers and leaders of your tribes. I will tell them these things. And I will call heaven and earth to be witnesses against them. ²⁹I know that after my death you will become evil. You will turn from the way I commanded you to follow. Terrible things will happen to you in the future, because you want to do what the LORD says is wrong. You will make him angry because of the evil things you do."

The Song of Moses

³⁰All the Israelites were gathered together, and Moses sang this whole song for them:

32

¹"Skies, listen and I will speak.
Earth, hear the words of my mouth.
² My teachings will come like the rain,
  like a mist falling to the ground,
  like a gentle rain on the soft grass,
  like rain on the green plants.
³ Praise God*ᵃ* as I speak the LORD's name!

⁴"The Lord is the Rock,*
  and his work is perfect!
  Yes, all his ways are right!
God is true and faithful.
  He is good and honest.
⁵ And you are not really his children.
  You are completely unfaithful to him.
  You are crooked liars.

⁶ Is this the way you repay the LORD for all
  he has done for you?
  You are stupid, foolish people.
He is your Father and your Creator.
  He made you, and he supports you.

⁷"Remember the days of the past.
  Think about what happened so long ago.
Ask your father; he will tell you.
Ask your leaders; they will tell you.
⁸ God Most High separated the people on
    earth
  and gave each nation its land.
He set up borders for all people.
  He made as many nations as there are
    angels.*ᵇ*
⁹ The LORD chose his people to be his own.
  The people of Jacob* belong to him.

¹⁰"The Lord found them in the desert,
  in an empty, windy land.
He surrounded them and watched over
    them.
  He protected them like the pupil of his
    eye,
¹¹ like an eagle when she makes her young
    leave the nest to fly.
  She stays close to them, ready to help.
She spreads her wings to catch them
    when they fall
  and carries them to a safe place.
¹² The LORD alone led his people.
  They had no help from any foreign god.
¹³ The Lord helped them take control of the
    hill country.
  They took the harvest in the fields.
He gave them honey from the cliffs
  and olive oil from the rocky ground.
¹⁴ He gave his people butter from the herd
  and milk from the flock.
He gave them lambs and goats.
  They had the best rams from Bashan and
    the finest wheat.
  They drank the best wine made from
    the juice of red grapes.

¹⁵"But Jeshurun*ᶜ* became fat and kicked like
    a bull.
  (Yes, you people were fed well and
    became full and fat.)
They left the God who made them!
  They ran away from the Rock* who
    saved them.
¹⁶ They made him jealous by worshiping
    other gods.
  They made him angry with those
    disgusting idols.*
¹⁷ They offered sacrifices to demons, to false
    gods.

*ᵇ***32:8** *angels* The ancient Greek version and some Hebrew copies at Qumran have "sons of El *(God)*." The standard Hebrew text has "sons *(people)* of Israel."
*ᶜ***32:15** *Jeshurun* Another name for Israel. It means "good" or "honest."

*ᵃ***32:3** *Praise God* Or "Give honor to God" or "Speak of the greatness of God."

These were new gods they had not
    known before,
gods their ancestors* never knew.
18 You people left the Rock who made you;
    you forgot the God who gave you life.

19"The LORD saw this and became upset.
    His sons and daughters made him angry!
20 So he said,
  'I will turn away from them,
    then let's see what happens!
  They are a rebellious people.
  They are like children who will not learn
    their lessons.
21 They made me jealous with demons that
    aren't gods.
  They made me angry at these worthless
    idols.
  So I will use people who are not a real
    nation to make them jealous.
  I will use a foolish*a* nation to make
    them angry.
22 My anger will burn like a fire,
    burning down to the deepest grave,*
    burning the earth and all it produces,
    burning deep down below the
    mountains.

23"'I will bring troubles to the Israelites.
    I will shoot all my arrows at them.
24 They will become thin from hunger.
    Terrible diseases will destroy them.
  I will send wild animals against them.
    Poisonous snakes and lizards will bite
    them.
25 In the streets, soldiers will kill them.
    In their houses, terrible things will
    happen.
  Soldiers will kill young men and women.
    They will kill babies and old people.

26"'I thought about destroying the Israelites
    so that people would forget them
    completely!
27 But I know what their enemies would say.
    The enemy would not understand.
  They would brag and say,
    "The LORD did not destroy Israel.
    We won by our own power!'

28"They are foolish.
    They don't understand.
29 If they were wise,
    they would understand;
    they would know what would happen to
    them.
30 Can one person chase away 1000 men?
  Can two men cause 10,000 men to run
    away?
  It will happen only if the LORD
    gives them to their enemy.
  This will happen only if their Rock*

*a***32:21** *foolish* This is a wordplay. The Hebrew word
meaning "foolish" is like the word meaning "worthless."

sells them like slaves.
31 The 'rock' of our enemies is not strong
    like our Rock.
  Even our enemies know that.
32 Their vines and fields will be destroyed
    like Sodom* and Gomorrah.*
  Their grapes are like bitter poison.
33   Their wine is like the poison of deadly
    snakes.

34"The Lord says,
  'I am saving that punishment.
    I have it locked up in my storehouse!
35 I will punish them for the bad things they
    did.
  But I am saving that punishment for
    when they slip and do bad things.
  Their time of trouble is near.
    Their punishment will come quickly.'

36"The LORD will judge his people.
    They are his servants, and he will show
    them mercy.
  He will see that their power is gone.
    He will see that they are all helpless—
    the slaves and free people too.
37 Then the Lord will say,
  'Where are the false gods?
    Where is the "rock" that you ran to for
    protection?
38 Those false gods ate the fat of your
    sacrifices.
  And they drank the wine of your
    offerings.
  So let them get up and help you!
    Let them protect you!

39"'Now, see that I, and only I, am God!
    There is no other God!
  I put people to death,
    and I let people live.
  I can hurt people,
    and I can make them well.
  No one can save another person from my
    power!
40 I raise my hand toward heaven and make
    this promise.
  As surely as I live forever,
    these things will happen!
41 I swear,
    I will sharpen my flashing sword.
    I will use it to punish my enemies.
    I will give them the punishment they
    deserve.
42 My enemies will be killed and taken as
    prisoners.
  My arrows will be covered with their
    blood.
  My sword will cut off the heads of their
    soldiers.'

43"The whole world should be happy for
    God's people!
  God punishes people who kill his
    servants.

He gives his enemies the punishment
    they deserve.
And he makes his land and people pure.*"

Moses Teaches the People His Song

⁴⁴Moses and Joshua son of Nun came and
sang all the words of this song for the Israelites to hear. ⁴⁵When Moses finished giving
these teachings to the people, ⁴⁶he said to
them, "You must be sure to pay attention to
all the commands I tell you today. And you
must tell your children to obey completely the
commands in this Law. ⁴⁷Don't think these
teachings are not important. They are your
life! Through these teachings you will live a
long time in the land across the Jordan River
that you are ready to take."

Moses on Mount Nebo

⁴⁸The LORD spoke to Moses that same day.
He said, ⁴⁹"Go to the Abarim Mountains.
Go up on Mount Nebo in the land of Moab
across from the city of Jericho. Then you can
look at the land of Canaan* that I am giving
to the Israelites to live in. ⁵⁰You will die on
that mountain. You will go to be with your
people, the same as your brother Aaron died
on Mount Hor. ⁵¹This is because you both
sinned against me. You were at the waters of
Meribah near Kadesh, in the desert of Zin.
There, in front of the Israelites, you did not
honor me and show that I am holy.* ⁵²So now
you may see the land that I am giving to the
Israelites. But you cannot go into that land."

Moses Blesses the People

33 ¹This is the blessing that Moses, the
man of God, gave the Israelites before
he died:

²"The LORD came from Sinai,
    like a light shining at dawn over Seir,
    like a light shining from Mount Paran.*
He came with 10,000 holy ones.ᵃ
God's mighty soldiers were by his side.ᵇ
³ Yes, the Lord loves his people.
    All his holy people are in his hand.
They sit at his feet and learn his
    teachings!
⁴ Moses gave us the law.
    These teachings are for Jacob's people.
⁵ At that time the Israelites
    and their leaders met together,
    and the LORD became Jeshurun'sᶜ king!

Reuben's Blessing

⁶"Let Reuben live, and not die!
    But let there be only a few people in his
    tribe!"

Judah's Blessing

⁷Moses said this about Judah:

"LORD, listen to the leader from Judah
    when he calls for help.
Bring him to his people.
Make him strong, and help him defeat his
    enemies!"

Levi's Blessing

⁸Moses said this about Levi:

"Levi is your true follower.
    He keeps the Urim* and Thummim.*
At Massah you tested the people of Levi.
At the waters of Meribah,ᵈ you challenged
    them.
⁹ They were more loyal to you, Lord, than
    to their own families.
They ignored their fathers and mothers.
They did not recognize their brothers.
They did not pay attention to their
    children.
But they obeyed your commands.
    They kept your agreement.*
¹⁰ They will teach your rules to Jacob* and
    your Law to Israel.*
They will burn incense* before you.
    They will offer burnt offerings* on your
    altar.*

¹¹"LORD, bless everything Levi has.
    Accept what he does.
Destroy those who attack him!
    Defeat his enemies so that they will
    never attack again."

Benjamin's Blessing

¹²Moses said this about Benjamin:

"The LORD loves Benjamin.
    Benjamin will live safely near him.
He protects him all the time,
    and the Lord will live in his land."ᵉ

Joseph's Blessing

¹³Moses said this about Joseph:

"May the LORD bless Joseph's land
    with rain from the skies above
    and water from the ground below.
¹⁴ Let the sun give them good fruit.
    Let each month bring its best fruit.
¹⁵ Let the hills and ancient mountains
    produce their best fruit.
¹⁶ Let the earth give its best to Joseph.
    He was separated from his brothers.

ᵃ**33:2** *holy one* Here, this probably means an angel.
ᵇ**33:2** *He came ... side* Or "He came from 10,000
holy angels where his troops were by his right side."
ᶜ**33:5** *Jeshurun* Another name for the people of
Israel. It means "good" or "honest." Also in verse 26.

ᵈ**33:8** *Massah ... Meribah* See Num. 20:1–13 for
the story.
ᵉ**33:12** *And the Lord will live in his land* Literally, "And he will dwell between his shoulders."
This probably means the Lord's Temple will be in
Jerusalem, at the border between Benjamin and
Judah's land.

So may the Lord in the burning bush
give his best to Joseph.

17 Joseph is like a powerful bull.
His two sons are like bull's horns.
They will attack other people
and push them to the ends of the earth!
Yes, Manasseh has thousands of people,
and Ephraim has ten thousands."

Zebulun and Issachar's Blessing

18Moses said this about Zebulun:

"Zebulun, be happy when you go out.
Issachar, be happy in your tents at home.

19 They will call the people to their
mountain.
There they will offer good sacrifices.
They will take riches from the sea
and treasures from the shore."

Gad's Blessing

20Moses said this about Gad:

"Praise God who gave Gad more land!
Gad is like a lion, who lies down and
waits.
Then he attacks and tears the animal in
pieces.

21 He chose the best part for himself.
He took the king's share.
The leaders of the people come to him.
He did what the LORD says is good.
He did what is right for the Israelites."

Dan's Blessing

22Moses said this about Dan:

"Dan is a lion's cub that jumps out from
Bashan."

Naphtali's Blessing

23Moses said this about Naphtali:

"Naphtali, you will get all you want.
The LORD will really bless you.
You will get the land by Lake Galilee."

Asher's Blessing

24Moses said this about Asher:

"Asher[a] is the most blessed of the sons.
Let him be the favorite of his brothers.
And let him wash his feet in olive oil.

25 Your gates will have locks made from iron
and bronze.
You will be strong all your life."

Moses Gives Praise to God

26"There is no one like God, Jeshurun!
God rides on the clouds in his glory
through the skies to help you.

27 God lives forever.
He is your place of safety.

His power continues forever!
He is protecting you.
He will force your enemies to leave your
land.
He will say, 'Destroy the enemy!'

28 So Israel will live in safety.
Jacob's well belongs to them.
They will get a land of grain and wine.
And that land will get plenty of rain.

29 Israel, you are blessed.
No other nation is like you.
The LORD saved you.
He is like a strong shield protecting you.
He is like a powerful sword.
Your enemies will be afraid of you,
and you will put your foot on their
backs![b]"

Moses Dies

34 1Moses climbed Mount Nebo. Moses
went from the Jordan Valley in Moab
to the top of Mount Pisgah. This was across
the Jordan River from Jericho. The LORD
showed Moses all the land from Gilead to
Dan. 2The LORD showed him all the land
of Naphtali, Ephraim, and Manasseh. He
showed him all the land of Judah as far as the
Mediterranean Sea. 3The LORD showed Moses
the Negev* and the valley that goes from Zoar
to Jericho, the city of palm trees. 4The LORD
said to Moses, "This is the land I promised
to Abraham, Isaac, and Jacob. I said to them,
'I will give this land to your descendants. I
have let you see the land, but you cannot go
there.'"

5Then Moses, the LORD's servant, died
there in the land of Moab. The LORD had told
Moses this would happen. 6The LORD buried
Moses in Moab. This was in the valley across
from Beth Peor. But even today no one knows
exactly where Moses' grave is. 7Moses was
120 years old when he died. He was as strong
as ever, and his eyes were still good. 8The
Israelites cried for Moses for 30 days. They
stayed in the Jordan Valley in Moab until the
time of sadness was finished.

Joshua Becomes the New Leader

9Moses had put his hands on Joshua and
appointed him to be the new leader. Then
Joshua son of Nun was filled with the spirit
of wisdom. So the Israelites began to obey
Joshua, and they did what the LORD had commanded Moses.

10Israel never had another prophet* like
Moses: The LORD knew Moses face to face.
11The LORD sent Moses to do powerful miracles in the land of Egypt. Pharaoh, all his
officers, and all the people in Egypt saw those
miracles. 12No other prophet ever did as many
powerful and amazing things as Moses did for
the Israelites to see.

a33:24 Asher This name means "blessed" or "happy."

b33:29 and you ... backs Or "You will trample their
holy places."

Joshua

God Chooses Joshua to Lead Israel

1 ¹Moses was the LORD's servant, and Joshua son of Nun was Moses' helper. After Moses died, the LORD spoke to Joshua and said, ²"My servant Moses is dead. Now you and all these people must go across the Jordan River. You must go into the land I am giving to the Israelites. ³I promised Moses that I would give you this land, so I will give you all the land wherever you go. ⁴All the land from the desert to Lebanon all the way to the great river (that is, the Euphrates River) and all the land of the Hittites will be yours. And all the land from here to the Mediterranean Sea in the west (that is, the place where the sun sets) will be within your borders. ⁵Just as I was with Moses, I will be with you. No one will be able to stop you all your life. I will not abandon you. I will never leave you.

⁶"Joshua, you must be strong and brave! You must lead these people so that they can take their land. I promised their fathers that I would give them this land. ⁷But you must be strong and brave about obeying the commands my servant Moses gave you. If you follow his teachings exactly, you will be successful in everything you do. ⁸Always remember what is written in that book of law. Speak about that book and study it day and night. Then you can be sure to obey what is written there. If you do this, you will be wise and successful in everything you do. ⁹Remember, I commanded you to be strong and brave. Don't be afraid, because the LORD your God will be with you wherever you go."

Joshua Takes Command

¹⁰So Joshua gave orders to the leaders of the people: ¹¹"Go through the camp and tell the people, 'Get some food ready. Three days from now we will go across the Jordan River and take the land that the LORD our God is giving us.'"

¹²Then Joshua said to the tribes of Reuben, Gad, and half the tribe of Manasseh, ¹³"Remember what the LORD's servant Moses told you. He said the LORD your God would give you a place to rest. He will give you that land! ¹⁴In fact, the LORD has already given you this land east of the Jordan River. Your wives and children can stay in this land with your animals. But your fighting men must cross the Jordan River with your brothers. You must be ready for war and to help them take their

land. ¹⁵The LORD gave you a place to rest, and he will do the same for your brothers. But you must help them until they get the land the LORD their God is giving them. Then you can come back to your own land, the land east of the Jordan River. The LORD's servant Moses gave you that land."

¹⁶Then the people answered Joshua, "We will do whatever you command us to do. We will go wherever you tell us to go. ¹⁷We will obey whatever you say, just as we obeyed Moses. We only ask that the LORD your God be with you just as he was with Moses. ¹⁸Then anyone who refuses to obey your commands or turns against you will be killed. Just be strong and brave!"

Spies in Jericho

2 ¹Joshua son of Nun and all the people were camped at Acacia.ᵃ Joshua sent out two spies. No one knew that Joshua sent out these men. Joshua said to them, "Go and look at the land, especially the city of Jericho."

So the men went to the city of Jericho and stayed at the house of a prostitute named Rahab.

²But someone told the king of Jericho, "Last night some men from Israel came to look for weaknesses in our country."

³So the king of Jericho sent this message to Rahab: "Do not hide the men who came and stayed in your house. Bring them out. They have come to spy on our country."

⁴Rahab had hidden the two men, but she said, "They did come here, but I didn't know where they came from. ⁵In the evening, when it was time to close the city gate, the men left. I don't know where they went. But if you go quickly, maybe you can catch them." ⁶(Rahab said this, but really she had taken the men up to the roof and had hidden them in the flaxᵇ that she had piled up there.)

⁷So the king's men went out of the city, and the people closed the city gates. The king's men went to look for the two men from Israel. They went to the Jordan River and looked at all the places where people cross the river.

⁸The two men were ready to sleep for the night, but Rahab went to the roof to talk to

---

ᵃ**2:1** *Acacia* Or "Shittim," a town east of the Jordan River. Also in 3:1.
ᵇ**2:6** *flax* A plant used to make linen.

them. 9She said, "I know that the LORD has given this land to your people. You frighten us. Everyone living in this country is afraid of you. 10We are afraid because we have heard about the ways that the LORD helped you. We heard that he dried up the Red Sea when you came out of Egypt. We also heard what you did to the two Amorite kings, Sihon and Og. We heard how you destroyed those kings living east of the Jordan River. 11When we heard about this, we were very afraid. And now, not one of our men is brave enough to fight you, because the LORD your God rules the heavens above and the earth below! 12So now, I want you to make a promise to me. I was kind to you and helped you. So promise me before the LORD that you will be kind to my family. Please tell me that you will do this. 13Tell me that you will allow my family to live—my father, mother, brothers, sisters, and all their families. Promise me that you will save us from death."

14The men agreed and said, "We will trade our lives for yours. Don't tell anyone what we are doing. Then, when the LORD gives us the land, we will be kind to you. You can trust us."

15Rahab's house was built into the city wall, so she used a rope to let the men down through a window. 16Then she said to them, "Go into the hills so that the king's men will not accidentally find you. Hide there for three days. After the king's men come back, you can go on your way."

17The men said to her, "We made a promise to you. But you must do one thing, or we will not be responsible for our promise. 18When we come back to this land, you must tie in your window this red rope you are using to help us escape. You must bring your father, your mother, your brothers, and all your family into your house with you. 19We will protect everyone who stays in this house. If anyone in your house is hurt, we will be responsible. But if they go out of your house and are killed, we will not be responsible. It will be their own fault. 20We are making this agreement with you. But if you tell anyone about what we are doing, we will be free from this agreement."

21Rahab answered, "I will do just what you said." She said goodbye, and the men left her house. Then she tied the red rope in the window.

22The men left her house and went into the hills. They stayed there for three days. The king's men looked all along the road. After three days, they stopped looking and went back to the city. 23Then the two men went back to Joshua. They left the hills and crossed the river. They went to Joshua and told him everything that they had learned. 24They said to him, "The LORD really has given us all the land. All the people in that country are afraid of us."

Miracle at the Jordan River

3 1Early the next morning, Joshua and all the Israelites got up and left Acacia. They traveled to the Jordan River and camped there before they crossed it. 2After three days the leaders went through the camp. 3They gave orders to the people: "When you see the Levite* priests carrying the Box of the Agreement* of the LORD your God, follow them. 4But do not follow too closely. Stay about 1000 yards*a* behind them. You have not been here before, but if you follow them, you will know where to go."

5Then Joshua told the people, "Make yourselves pure. Tomorrow the LORD will do amazing things among us."

6Then Joshua said to the priests, "Take the Box of the Agreement and go across the river in front of the people." So the priests lifted the Box and carried it in front of the people.

7Then the LORD said to Joshua, "Today I will begin to make you a great man for all the Israelites to see. Then the people will know that I am with you just as I was with Moses. 8The priests will carry the Box of the Agreement. Tell them this, 'Walk to the shore of the Jordan River and stop just before you step into the water.'"

9Then Joshua said to the Israelites, "Come and listen to the words of the LORD your God. 10Here is proof that the living God is really with you and that he will surely defeat your enemies. He will defeat the Canaanites, Hittites, Hivites, Perizzites, Girgashites, Amorites, and Jebusites; he will force them to leave their land. 11The Box of the Agreement of the Lord of the whole world will go before you as you cross the Jordan River. 12Now choose twelve men, one from each of the twelve tribes of Israel. 13The priests will carry the Holy Box* of the LORD. He is the Lord of the whole world. They will carry that Box in front of you into the Jordan River. When they enter the water, the water of the Jordan River will stop flowing and fill behind that place like at a dam."

14The priests carried the Box of the Agreement, and the people left the place they had camped. The people started going across the Jordan River. 15(During harvest time the Jordan River overflows its banks, so the river was at its fullest.) The priests who were carrying the Box came to the shore of the river. When they stepped into the water, 16immediately the water stopped flowing and piled up like a wall. The water piled up high a long way up the river—all the way to Adam (a town near Zarethan). And the water flowing down to the sea of Arabah (the Dead Sea) was completely cut off. The people crossed the river near Jericho. 17The ground at that place

*a***3:4** *1000 yards* Literally, "2000 cubits" (888 m).

became dry, and the priests carried the Box of the Agreement of the Lord to the middle of the river and stopped. They waited there while all the Israelites walked across the Jordan River on dry land.

Rocks to Remind the People

4 ¹After all the people had crossed the Jordan River, the Lord said to Joshua, ²"Choose twelve men, one from each tribe. ³Tell them to look in the river where the priests were standing and get twelve rocks from that place.* Carry these rocks with you and put them where you stay tonight."

⁴So Joshua chose one man from each tribe. Then he called the twelve men together. ⁵He said to them, "Go out into the river where the Holy Box* of the Lord your God is. Each of you must find one rock. There will be one rock for each of the twelve tribes of Israel. Carry that rock on your shoulder. ⁶These rocks will be a sign for you. In the future, your children will ask you, 'What do these rocks mean?' ⁷You will tell them that the Lord stopped the water from flowing in the Jordan River. When the Holy Box of the Lord's Agreement crossed the river, the water stopped flowing. These rocks will help the Israelites remember this forever."

⁸So the Israelites obeyed Joshua. They carried twelve rocks from the middle of the Jordan River. There was one rock for each of the twelve tribes of Israel. They did this just as the Lord had commanded Joshua. The men carried the rocks with them. Then they put the rocks at the place where they made their camp. ⁹(Joshua also put twelve rocks in the middle of the Jordan River. He put them at the place where the priests had stood while carrying the Lord's Holy Box. These rocks are still there today.)

¹⁰The Lord had commanded Joshua to tell the people what to do. This is what Moses had said Joshua must do. So the priests carrying the Holy Box stood in the middle of the river until everything was done. Meanwhile, the people hurried across the river. ¹¹After the people finished crossing the river, the priests carried the Lord's Holy Box to the front of the people.

¹²The men from the tribes of Reuben, Gad, and half the tribe of Manasseh obeyed Moses. These men crossed the river in front of the other people. These men were prepared for war. They were going to help the rest of the Israelites take the land God had promised to give them. ¹³About 40,000 soldiers, prepared for war, passed before the Lord. They were marching toward the plains of Jericho.

¹⁴That day the Lord made Joshua a great man to all the Israelites. From that time on, they respected Joshua just as they had Moses.

¹⁵Then the Lord said to Joshua, ¹⁶"Command the priests carrying the Box that holds the Agreement*ᵃ* to come out of the river."

¹⁷So Joshua commanded the priests, "Come out of the Jordan River."

¹⁸The priests obeyed Joshua. They carried the Box with them and came out of the river. When their feet touched the land on the other side of the river, the water in the river began flowing again. The water again overflowed its banks just as it had before the people crossed.

¹⁹The people crossed the Jordan River on the tenth day of the first month and camped at Gilgal, east of Jericho. ²⁰They carried with them the twelve rocks that they had taken from the Jordan River, and Joshua set them up at Gilgal. ²¹Then Joshua told the Israelites, "In the future your children will ask you, 'What do these rocks mean?' ²²Tell them, 'These rocks help us remember the way the people of Israel crossed the Jordan River on dry land.' ²³The Lord your God caused the water in the Jordan River to stop flowing so that you could cross it on dry land—just as the Lord had stopped the water at the Red Sea so that we could cross it on dry land. ²⁴The Lord did this so that all the people in this country would know that he is very powerful. Then they will always be afraid of the Lord your God."

5 ¹So the Lord dried up the Jordan River until the Israelites finished crossing it. The kings of the Amorites living west of the Jordan River and the Canaanites living by the Mediterranean Sea heard about this and became very frightened. After that they were not brave enough to stand and fight against the Israelites.

The Israelites Are Circumcised

²At that time the Lord said to Joshua, "Make knives from flint rocks and circumcise* the men of Israel."

³So Joshua made knives from flint rocks and circumcised the men of Israel at Gibeath Haaraloth.*ᵇ*

⁴⁻⁷This is why Joshua circumcised the men: After the Israelites left Egypt, all the men who were able to serve in the army were circumcised. While in the desert, many of the fighting men did not listen to the Lord. So the Lord promised that they would not see the "land where much food grows." He promised our ancestors* to give us that land, but because of those men, he forced the people to wander in the desert for 40 years. That way all those fighting men would die. So all the fighting men died, and their sons took their place. But none of the boys who were born in the desert on the trip from Egypt had been circumcised. So Joshua circumcised them.

---

*ᵃ***4:16** *Box that holds the Agreement* Literally, "Testimony." See "Agreement" in the Word List.
*ᵇ***5:3** *Gibeath Haaraloth* This name means "Circumcision Hill."

8Joshua finished circumcising all the men. The people camped at that place until all the men were healed.

First Passover in Canaan

9Then the LORD said to Joshua, "You were slaves in Egypt, and this made you ashamed. But today I have taken away that shame." So Joshua named that place Gilgal.a And that place is still named Gilgal today.

10The Israelites celebrated Passover* while they were camped at Gilgal on the plains of Jericho. This was on the evening of the 14th day of the month. 11The day after Passover, the people ate food that grew in that land. They ate bread made without yeast and roasted grain. 12The next morning, the manna* from heaven stopped coming. This happened the first day after the people ate the food that grew in the land of Canaan.* From that time on, the Israelites did not get the manna from heaven.

The Commander of the Lord's Army

13When Joshua was near Jericho, he looked up and saw a man standing in front of him. The man had a sword in his hand. Joshua went to the man and asked, "Are you a friend to our people or are you one of our enemies?"

14The man answered, "I am not an enemy. I am the commander of the LORD's army. I have just now come to you."

Then Joshua bowed his face to the ground to show respect and said, "I am your servant. Does my master have a command for me?"

15The commander of the LORD's army answered, "Take off your sandals. The place where you are standing is holy.*" So Joshua obeyed him.

6 1The gates of the city of Jericho were closed. The people in the city were afraid because the Israelites were near. No one went into the city, and no one came out.

2Then the LORD said to Joshua, "Look, I will let you defeat the city of Jericho. You will defeat the king and all the fighting men in the city. 3March around the city with your army once every day for six days. 4Tell seven of the priests to carry trumpets made from the horns of male sheep and to march in front of the priests who are carrying the Holy Box.* On the seventh day march around the city seven times and tell the priests to blow the trumpets while they march. 5They will make one loud noise from the trumpets. When you hear that noise, tell all the people to begin shouting. When you do this, the walls of the city will fall down and your people will be able to go straight into the city."

The Battle Against Jericho

6So Joshua son of Nun called the priests together and said to them, "Carry the Holy Box* of the LORD. Tell seven priests to carry the trumpets and march in front of it."

7Then Joshua ordered the people, "Now go! March around the city. The soldiers with weapons will march in front of the Holy Box of the LORD."

8After Joshua finished speaking to the people, the seven priests with the trumpets began marching before the LORD, blowing the trumpets as they marched. The priests carrying the LORD's Holy Box followed them. 9The soldiers with weapons marched in front of the priests who were blowing the horns. And the rest of the men walked behind the Holy Box, marching and blowing their trumpets. 10Joshua had told the people not to give a war cry. He said, "Don't shout. Don't say a word until the day I tell you. Then you will shout."

11So Joshua made the priests carry the Holy Box of the LORD around the city one time. Then they went back to the camp and spent the night there.

12Early the next morning Joshua got up, and the priests carried the LORD's Holy Box again. 13The seven priests with the trumpets marched in front of the LORD's Holy Box, blowing their trumpets. The soldiers with weapons marched in front of them. The rest of the people marched behind the LORD's Holy Box. During the whole time they marched, the priests were blowing the trumpets. 14On the second day, they all marched around the city one time. And then they went back to the camp. They continued to do this every day for six days.

15On the seventh day they got up at dawn and marched around the city seven times. They marched in the same way they had marched on the days before, but on that day they marched around the city seven times. 16The seventh time they marched around the city, the priests blew their trumpets. Then Joshua gave the command: "Now, shout! The LORD is giving you this city! 17The city and everything is to be destroyed as an offering to the LORD. Only Rahab the prostitute and everyone in her house will be left alive. These people must not be killed because she helped the two spies. 18Remember, we must destroy everything else. Don't take anything. If you take anything and bring it into our camp, you yourselves will be destroyed, and you will cause trouble for the rest of our people. 19All the things made from silver, gold, bronze, and iron belong to the LORD. They must be put in the LORD's treasury."

20So then the priests blew the trumpets. When the people heard the trumpets, they began shouting. The walls fell down, and the people ran up into the city. So the Israelites defeated that city. 21The people destroyed everything in the city. They destroyed

---

a5:9 *Gilgal* This name is like the Hebrew word meaning "to roll away."

everything that was living there. They killed the young and old men, the young and old women, and the cattle, sheep, and donkeys.

²²Joshua talked to the two spies. He said, "You made a promise to the prostitute. So go to her house and bring her out and all those who are with her."

²³So the two men went into the house and brought out Rahab, her father, mother, brothers, all her family, and all those who were with her. They put all the people in a safe place outside the camp of Israel.

²⁴Then the Israelites burned the whole city and everything in it except for the things made from silver, gold, bronze, and iron. They put these things in the LORD's treasury. ²⁵Joshua saved Rahab the prostitute, her family, and all those who were with her. Joshua let them live because Rahab helped the spies Joshua had sent out to Jericho. Rahab still lives among the Israelites today.

²⁶At that time Joshua made this important promise. He said,

"Whoever rebuilds Jericho
    will be in danger from the LORD.
When he lays the foundation,
    he will lose his oldest son.
When he sets up the gates,
    he will lose his youngest son."ᵃ

²⁷So the LORD was with Joshua, and Joshua became famous throughout the whole country.

Achan's Sin

7 ¹But the Israelites did not obey God. There was a man from the tribe of Judah named Achan son of Carmi, grandson of Zimri, great-grandson of Zerah. Achan kept some of the things that should have been destroyed. So the LORD became very angry with the Israelites.

²After they defeated Jericho, Joshua sent some men to Ai.ᵇ Ai was near Beth Aven, east of Bethel. He told them, "Go to Ai and look for weaknesses in that area." So the men went to spy on that land.

³Later, the men came back to Joshua. They said, "Ai is a weak area. We will not need all of our people to defeat them. Send 2000 or 3000 men to fight there. There is no need to use the whole army. There are only a few men there to fight against us."

⁴⁻⁵So about 3000 men went to Ai, but the people of Ai killed about 36 men of Israel. And the Israelites ran away. The people of Ai chased them from the city gates all the way to the quarries.ᶜ The people of Ai beat them badly.

When the people from Israel saw this, they became very frightened and lost their courage. ⁶When Joshua heard about this, he tore his clothes to show his sadness. He bowed down to the ground before the Holy Box* and stayed there until evening. The leaders of Israel did the same thing. They also threw dirt on their heads to show their sadness.

⁷Joshua said, "Lord GOD, you brought our people across the Jordan River. Why did you bring us this far and then allow the Amorites to destroy us? We should have been satisfied and stayed on the other side of the Jordan River. ⁸I promise by my life, Lord! There is nothing I can say now. Israel has surrendered to the enemy. ⁹The Canaanites and all the other people in this country will hear about what happened. Then they will attack us and kill all of us! Then what will you do to protect your great name?"

¹⁰The LORD said to Joshua, "Why are you down there with your face on the ground? Stand up! ¹¹The Israelites sinned against me. They have broken the agreement* that I commanded them to obey. They took some of the things that I commanded them to destroy. They have stolen from me. They have lied. They have taken those things for themselves. ¹²That is why the army of Israel turned and ran away from the fight. They did that because they have done wrong. They should be destroyed. I will not continue to help you or be with you unless you destroy everything I commanded you to destroy.

¹³"Now go and make the people pure. Tell them, 'Make yourselves pure. Prepare for tomorrow. The LORD, the God of Israel, says that some people are keeping things that he commanded to be destroyed. You will never be able to defeat your enemies until you throw away those things.

¹⁴"'Tomorrow morning you must all stand before the LORD. All the tribes will stand before the LORD, and he will choose one tribe. Only that tribe will stand before him. Then the LORD will choose one family group from that tribe. Only that family group must stand before him. Then he will look at each family in that family group, and the LORD will choose one family. Then he will look at each man in that family. ¹⁵The man who is keeping those things that we should have destroyed will be caught. Then he will be destroyed by fire, and everything that he owns will be destroyed with him. He broke the agreement with the LORD. He has done a very bad thing to the Israelites!'"

¹⁶Early the next morning, Joshua led all the Israelites before the LORD. All the tribes stood before the Lord. He chose the tribe of Judah. ¹⁷So all the family groups of Judah stood before the Lord. He chose the Zerah family group. Then all the families of the Zerah group stood before the LORD. The family of Zimri was chosen. ¹⁸Then Joshua told all the

---

ᵃ6:26 When he ... son See 1 Kings 16:34.
ᵇ7:2 Ai The name of this town means "the ruins."
ᶜ7:4–5 quarries Places where people cut stones from the solid rock.

men in that family to come before the Lord. He chose Achan the son of Carmi. (Carmi was the son of Zimri. And Zimri was the son of Zerah.)

[19]Then Joshua said to Achan, "Son, you must honor the LORD, the God of Israel. Praise him and confess your sins to him. Tell me what you did, and don't try to hide anything from me."

[20]Achan answered, "It is true! I sinned against the LORD, the God of Israel. This is what I did: [21]In Jericho, I saw a beautiful coat from Babylon, about 5 pounds[a] of silver, and about a pound[b] of gold. I wanted these things for myself, so I took them. You will find them buried in the ground under my tent. The silver is under the coat."

[22]So Joshua sent some men to the tent. They ran to the tent and found the things hidden there. The silver was under the coat. [23]The men brought the things out of the tent and took them to Joshua and all the Israelites. They threw them on the ground before the LORD.

[24]Then Joshua and all the people led Achan son of Zerah to the Valley of Achor. They also took the silver, the coat, the gold, Achan's sons and daughters, his cattle, his donkeys, his sheep, his tent, and everything he owned. They took all these things to the Valley of Achor with Achan. [25]Then Joshua said, "You caused much trouble for us, but now the LORD will bring trouble to you." Then all the people threw stones at Achan and his family until they died. Then the people burned them and everything he owned. [26]After they burned Achan, they put many rocks over his body. The rocks are still there today. That is why it is called the Valley of Achor.[c] After this the LORD was not angry with the people.

Ai Destroyed

8 [1]Then the LORD said to Joshua, "Don't be afraid; don't give up. Lead all your fighting men to Ai.[d] I will help you defeat the king of Ai. I am giving you his people, his city, and his land. [2]You will do to Ai and its king the same thing you did to Jericho and its king. Only this time you can take all the wealth and animals and keep it for yourselves. You will share the wealth with your people. Now, tell some of your soldiers to hide behind the city."

[3]So Joshua led his whole army toward Ai. Then Joshua chose 30,000 of his best fighting men and sent them out at night. [4]Joshua gave them this command: "Listen carefully to what I tell you. You must hide in the area behind the city. Wait for the time to attack. Don't go far from the city. Continue to watch and be ready. [5]I will lead the men with me;

we will march toward the city. The men in the city will come out to fight against us. We will turn and run away from them as we did before. [6]These men will chase us away from the city, so we will run away. They will think that we are running away from them as we did before. [7]Then you should come out of your hiding place and take control of the city. The LORD your God will give you the power to win.

[8]"You must do what the LORD says. Watch me and I will give you the command to attack the city. When you have taken control of the city, burn it."

[9]Then Joshua sent them to their hiding place and waited. They went to a place west of Ai, between Bethel and Ai. But Joshua stayed the night with his people.

[10]Early the next morning Joshua gathered the men together. Then Joshua and the leaders of Israel led the men to Ai. [11]All the soldiers who were with Joshua marched to Ai. They stopped in front of the city. The army made its camp north of the city. There was a valley between the army and Ai.

[12]Then Joshua chose about 5000 men. He sent these men to hide in the area west of the city, between Bethel and Ai. [13]So Joshua had prepared his men for the fight. The main camp was north of the city. The other men were hiding to the west. That night Joshua went down into the valley.

[14]Later, the king of Ai saw the army of Israel. The king and his people hurried out to fight the army of Israel. The king of Ai went out the east side of the city toward the Jordan Valley, so he did not see the soldiers hiding behind the city.

[15]Joshua and all the men of Israel let the army of Ai push them back. Joshua and his men began running east toward the desert. [16]The people in the city began to shout and started to chase them. All the people left the city. [17]All the men of Ai and Bethel chased the army of Israel. The city was left open—no one stayed to protect the city.

[18]Then the LORD said to Joshua, "Hold your spear toward the city of Ai, because I will give you that city." So Joshua held his spear toward the city of Ai. [19]When the Israelites who were hiding saw this, they quickly came out from their hiding place and hurried toward the city. They entered the city and took control of it. Then the soldiers started fires to burn the city.

[20]The men from Ai looked back and saw their city burning. When they saw the smoke rising into the sky, they lost their strength and courage. They stopped chasing the men of Israel. The Israelites stopped running away. They turned and went to fight the men from Ai. There was no safe place for the men from Ai to run to. [21]When Joshua and his men saw that his army had taken control of the city and that smoke was rising from it, they stopped

---

[a]**7:21** *5 pounds* Literally, "200 shekels" (2.3 kg).
[b]**7:21** *a pound* Literally, "50 shekels" (575 g).
[c]**7:26** *Achor* This name means "trouble."
[d]**8:1** *Ai* See Josh. 7:2. The name of this town means "the ruins."

running away and turned to fight the men of Ai. 22Then the men who were hiding came out of the city to help with the fight. The army of Israel was on both sides of the men of Ai—the men of Ai were trapped. Israel defeated them. They fought until none of the men from Ai were left alive—none of the enemy escaped. 23But the king of Ai was left alive. Joshua's men brought him to Joshua.

A Review of the Fighting
24During the fighting, the army of Israel chased the men from Ai into the fields and into the desert. So the army of Israel finished killing all the men from Ai in the fields and in the desert. Then the Israelites went back to Ai and killed all the people who were still alive in the city. 25All the people of Ai died that day; there were 12,000 men and women. 26Joshua had held his spear toward Ai as a sign to his people to destroy the city. And he did not stop until all the people of Ai were destroyed. 27The Israelites kept the animals and other things from the city for themselves. This is what the LORD said they could do when he gave Joshua the commands.

28Then Joshua burned the city of Ai. That city became an empty pile of rocks. It is still like that today. 29Joshua hanged the king of Ai on a tree and left him hanging there until evening. At sunset, Joshua told his men to take the king's body down from the tree. They threw his body down at the city gate. Then they covered the body with many rocks. That pile of rocks is still there today.

Reading the Blessings and Curses
30Then Joshua built an altar for the LORD, the God of Israel. He built the altar on Mount Ebal. 31The LORD's servant Moses told the Israelites how to build altars. So Joshua built the altar the way it was explained in the *Book of the Law[a] of Moses*. The altar was made from stones that were not cut. No tool had ever been used on those stones. They offered burnt offerings* to the LORD on that altar. They also gave fellowship offerings.*

32There Joshua copied onto the stones the law Moses had written down. This was for all the people of Israel to see. 33The elders,* officers, judges, and all the Israelites were standing around the Holy Box.* They were standing in front of the priests, the Levites who carried the Holy Box of the LORD's Agreement. The Israelites and the other people with them were all standing there. Half of the people stood in front of Mount Ebal and the other half of the people stood in front of Mount Gerizim. The LORD's servant Moses had told the people to do this. He told them to do this to be blessed.

34Then Joshua read all the words from the law. He read the blessings and the curses. He read everything the way it was written in the *Book of the Law*. 35All the Israelites were gathered together there. All the women and children and all the foreigners who lived with the Israelites were there. And Joshua read every command that Moses had given.

The Gibeonites Trick Joshua
9 1All the kings west of the Jordan River heard about these things. They were the kings of the Hittites, Amorites, Canaanites, Perizzites, Hivites, and Jebusites. They lived in the hill country and in the plains. They also lived along the seacoast of the Mediterranean Sea as far as Lebanon. 2All these kings came together and made plans to fight against Joshua and the Israelites.

3The people from the city of Gibeon heard about the way Joshua had defeated Jericho and Ai. 4So they decided to try to trick the Israelites. This was their plan: They gathered together old wineskins* that were cracked and broken. They put these old wineskins on the backs of their animals. They put old pieces of cloth on their animals to look as if they had traveled from far away. 5The men put old sandals on their feet and wore old clothes. They found some old bread that was dry and moldy. 6Then they went to the camp of the Israelites. This camp was near Gilgal.

The men went to Joshua and said to him, "We have traveled from a faraway country. We want to make a peace agreement with you."

7The men of Israel said to these Hivite men, "Maybe you are trying to trick us. Maybe you live near us. We cannot make a peace agreement with you until we know where you are from."

8The Hivite men said to Joshua, "We are your servants."

But Joshua asked, "Who are you? Where do you come from?"

9The men answered, "We are your servants. We have come from a faraway country. We came because we heard of the great power of the LORD your God. We heard about what he has done and about everything he did in Egypt. 10And we heard that he defeated the two kings of the Amorites east of the Jordan River. This was King Sihon of Heshbon and King Og of Bashan in the land of Ashtaroth. 11So our elders* and our people said to us, 'Take enough food for your journey. Go and meet with the Israelites.' Tell them, 'We are your servants. Make a peace agreement with us.'

12"Look at our bread. When we left home, it was warm and fresh. But now you can see that it is dry and old. 13Look at our wineskins. When we left home they were new and filled with wine. But now you can see that they are cracked and old. Look at our clothes and sandals. You can see that the long journey has almost destroyed the things we wear."

---

[a]8:31 Law Or "Teachings." Also in verses 32, 34.

¹⁴The men of Israel wanted to know if these men were telling the truth. So they tasted the bread—but they did not ask the LORD what they should do. ¹⁵Joshua agreed to make peace with them. He agreed to let them live. The leaders of Israel agreed with this promise of Joshua.

¹⁶Three days later the Israelites learned that these men lived very near their camp. ¹⁷So the Israelites went to the place where they lived. On the third day the Israelites came to the cities of Gibeon, Kephirah, Beeroth, and Kiriath Jearim. ¹⁸But the army of Israel did not try to fight against those cities. They had made a peace agreement with them. They had made a promise to them before the LORD, the God of Israel.

All the people complained against the leaders who made the agreement. ¹⁹But the leaders answered, "We have given our promise. We promised before the LORD, the God of Israel. We cannot fight against them now. ²⁰This is what we must do. We must let them live. We cannot hurt them or God will be angry with us because we broke the promise we made to them. ²¹So let them live, but they will be our servants. They will cut wood for us and carry water for all our people." So the leaders did not break their promise of peace to them.

²²Joshua called the Gibeonites together. He said, "Why did you lie to us? Your land was near our camp. But you told us you were from a faraway country. ²³Now, your people will have many troubles. All of your people will be slaves—they will have to cut wood and carry water for the house of God.ᵃ"

²⁴The Gibeonites answered, "We lied to you because we were afraid you would kill us. We heard that God commanded his servant Moses to give you all this land. And God told you to kill all the people who lived in this land. That is why we lied to you. ²⁵Now we are your servants. You can do whatever you think is right."

²⁶So the Gibeonites became slaves, but Joshua let them live. He did not allow the Israelites to kill them. ²⁷He made them slaves of the Israelites. They cut wood and carried water for the Israelites and for the altar of the LORD—wherever the LORD chose it to be. They are still slaves today.

The Day the Sun Stood Still

10 ¹At this time Adoni Zedek was the king of Jerusalem. He heard that Joshua had defeated Ai and completely destroyed it. The king learned that Joshua had done the same thing to Jericho and its king. He also learned that the Gibeonites had made a peace agreement with Israel and that they lived very near Jerusalem. ²So Adoni Zedek

and his people were very frightened. Gibeon was not a small town like Ai. It was a very big city—as big as any royal city.ᵇ And all the men in that city were good fighters, so the king was afraid. ³King Adoni Zedek of Jerusalem talked with King Hoham of Hebron. He also talked with King Piram of Jarmuth, King Japhia of Lachish, and King Debir of Eglon. The king of Jerusalem begged these men, ⁴"Come with me and help me attack Gibeon. Gibeon has made a peace agreement with Joshua and the Israelites."

⁵So these five Amorite kings joined their armies together. (The five kings were the king of Jerusalem, the king of Hebron, the king of Jarmuth, the king of Lachish, and the king of Eglon.) Their armies went to Gibeon, surrounded the city, and began fighting against it.

⁶The people in the city of Gibeon sent a message to Joshua at his camp at Gilgal: "We are your servants! Don't leave us alone. Come and help us! Hurry! Save us! All the Amorite kings from the hill country have brought their armies together to fight against us."

⁷So Joshua marched out of Gilgal with his whole army. His best fighting men were with him. ⁸The LORD said to Joshua, "Don't be afraid of those armies. I will allow you to defeat them. None of them will be able to defeat you."

⁹Joshua and his army marched all night to Gibeon, so it was a complete surprise when he attacked them.

¹⁰The LORD caused those armies to be very confused when Israel attacked. So Israel defeated them and won a great victory. Israel chased the enemy from Gibeon along the road going up to Beth Horon. The army of Israel killed men all the way to Azekah and Makkedah. ¹¹Then they chased the enemy down the road from Beth Horon to Azekah. While they were chasing the enemy, the LORD caused large hailstones to fall from the sky. Many of the enemy were killed by these large hailstones. More men were killed by the hailstones than by the swords of the soldiers of Israel.

¹²On that day the LORD gave Israel the victory against the Amorites. Joshua stood before all the Israelites and said to the LORD:

"Sun, stop over Gibeon.
    Moon, stand still over the Valley of
        Aijalon."

¹³So the sun did not move, and the moon stopped until the people defeated their enemies. This story is written in the *Book of Jashar*. The sun stopped in the middle of the sky. It did not move for a full day. ¹⁴That had never happened before, and it has never

---

ᵃ9:23 *house of God* This might mean the "family of God" (Israel), "the Holy Tent," or "the Temple."

ᵇ10:2 *royal city* A strong, well-protected city that controlled smaller towns nearby.

happened again. That was the day the LORD obeyed a man. The LORD really was fighting for Israel!

15After this, Joshua and his army went back to the camp at Gilgal. 16But during the fight, the five kings ran away. They hid in a cave near Makkedah, 17but someone found them hiding in that cave. Joshua learned about this. 18He said, "Cover the entrance to the cave with large rocks. Put some men there to guard the cave. 19But don't stay there yourselves. Continue chasing the enemy and attacking them from behind. Don't let the enemy get back to their cities. The LORD your God has given you the victory over them."

20So Joshua and the Israelites killed the enemy. But some of them were able to go to their cities that had tall walls around them and hide. These men were not killed. 21After the fighting, Joshua's men came back to him at Makkedah. Not one of the people in that country was brave enough to say anything against the Israelites.

22Joshua said, "Move the rocks that are covering the entrance to the cave. Bring the five kings to me." 23So Joshua's men brought the five kings out of the cave—the kings of Jerusalem, Hebron, Jarmuth, Lachish, and Eglon. 24When they brought the five kings to Joshua, he called all his men to come to that place. He said to the officers of his army, "Come here! Put your feet on the necks of these kings." So the officers of Joshua's army came close and put their feet on the necks of the kings.

25Then Joshua said to his men, "Be strong and brave! Don't be afraid. I will show you what the LORD will do to all the enemies you will fight in the future."

26Then Joshua killed the five kings and hanged their bodies on five trees. He left them hanging in the trees until evening. 27At sunset Joshua told his men to take the bodies down from the trees. So they threw the bodies into the cave where the kings had been hiding and covered the entrance of the cave with large rocks. Their bodies are still in that cave today.

28That day Joshua defeated Makkedah. He killed the king and the people in that city. No one was left alive. Joshua did the same thing to the king of Makkedah that he had done to the king of Jericho.

Taking the Southern Cities

29Then Joshua and all the Israelites traveled from Makkedah to Libnah and attacked that city. 30The LORD allowed the Israelites to defeat that city and its king. They killed everyone in the city. No one was left alive. And they did the same thing to that king as they had done to the king of Jericho.

31Then Joshua and all the Israelites left Libnah and went to Lachish. Joshua and his army camped around that city and attacked it. 32The LORD allowed them to defeat the city of Lachish. They defeated it on the second day. The Israelites killed everyone in the city, just as they had done in Libnah. 33King Horam of Gezer came to help Lachish, but Joshua also defeated him and his army. No one was left alive.

34Then Joshua and all the Israelites traveled from Lachish to Eglon. They camped around Eglon and attacked it. 35That day they captured the city and killed everyone in the city. This was the same thing they had done to Lachish.

36Then Joshua and all the Israelites traveled from Eglon to Hebron and attacked it. 37They captured the city and all the small towns near Hebron. The Israelites killed everyone in the city, just as they did to Eglon. No one was left alive there. They destroyed the city and killed all the people in it as an offering to the Lord.

38Then Joshua and all the Israelites went back to Debir and attacked it. 39They captured the city, its king, and all the towns near Debir. They killed everyone in the city, just as they had done to Libnah and its king. No one was left alive there. They destroyed the city and killed all the people in it as an offering to the Lord.

40So Joshua defeated all the kings of the cities of the hill country, the Negev,* the western foothills, and the eastern foothills. The LORD, the God of Israel, had told Joshua to kill all the people, so Joshua did not leave anyone alive in those places.

41Joshua captured all the cities from Kadesh Barnea to Gaza. He captured all the cities from Goshen[a] to Gibeon. 42Joshua captured all these cities and their kings in one series of battles. He did this because the LORD, the God of Israel, was fighting for Israel. 43Then Joshua and all the Israelites returned to their camp at Gilgal.

Defeating the Northern Cities

11 1King Jabin of Hazor heard about everything that had happened. So he decided to call together the armies of several kings. He sent a message to King Jobab of Madon to the king of Shimron, to the king of Acshaph, 2and to the kings of the north in the hill country and in the desert. Jabin sent the message to the kings of the Kinnereth,[b] the Negev,* and the western foothills. He also sent the message to the king of Naphoth Dor in the west. 3Jabin sent the message to the kings of the Canaanites in the east and in the west. He sent the message to the Amorites, Hittites, Perizzites, and Jebusites living in the hill country. He also sent the message to the Hivites living below Mount Hermon near Mizpah. 4So the armies of all these kings came together. There were many fighting men and many horses and chariots.* It was a very large

---

a**10:41** *Goshen* The northeastern part of Egypt.
b**11:2** *Kinnereth* The area near the Sea of Galilee.

army—it looked as if there were as many men as grains of sand on the seashore.

5All these kings met together at the small river of Merom. They joined their armies together into one camp and made plans for the battle against Israel.

6Then the LORD said to Joshua, "Don't be afraid of that army, because I will allow you to defeat them. By this time tomorrow, you will have killed them all. You will cut the legs of the horses and burn all their chariots."

7So Joshua and his whole army surprised the enemy and attacked them at the river of Merom. 8The LORD allowed Israel to defeat them. The army of Israel defeated them and chased them to Greater Sidon, Misrephoth Maim, and the Valley of Mizpah in the east. The army of Israel fought until none of the enemy was left alive. 9Joshua did what the LORD said to do; he cut the legs of their horses and burned their chariots.

10Then Joshua went back and captured the city of Hazor and killed its king. (Hazor was the leader of all the kingdoms that fought against Israel.) 11The army of Israel killed everyone in that city and completely destroyed all the people. There was nothing left alive. Then they burned the city.

12Joshua captured all these cities and killed all their kings. He completely destroyed everything in these cities—just as Moses, the LORD's servant, had commanded. 13But the army of Israel did not burn any cities that were built on hills. The only city built on a hill that they burned was Hazor. This is the city Joshua burned. 14The Israelites kept for themselves all the things and all the animals they found in the cities. But they killed all the people there. They left no one alive. 15Long ago the LORD commanded his servant Moses to do this. Then Moses commanded Joshua to do this. So Joshua obeyed God. He did everything that the LORD had commanded Moses.

16So Joshua defeated all the people in that whole area. He had control over the hill country, the Negev, all the area of Goshen, the western foothills, the Jordan Valley, and the mountains of Israel and all the hills near them. 17Joshua had control of all the land from Mount Halak near Seir to Baal Gad in the Valley of Lebanon below Mount Hermon. He captured all the kings in that land and killed them. 18Joshua fought against them for many years. 19Only one city in all the land made a peace agreement with Israel. That was the Hivite city of Gibeon. All the other cities were defeated in war. 20The LORD made those people feel brave enough to fight against Israel. This was so that Israel could destroy them completely without mercy just as the LORD had commanded Moses to do.

21The Anakites* lived in the hill country in the area of Hebron, Debir, Anab, and Judah. Joshua fought them and completely destroyed all the people and their towns. 22There were no Anakites left living in the land of Israel. The only Anakites who were left alive were in Gaza, Gath, and Ashdod. 23Joshua took control of the whole land of Israel as the LORD had told Moses long ago. The Lord gave that land to Israel as he promised. And Joshua divided the land among the tribes of Israel. Finally, the fighting ended and there was peace in the land.

Kings Defeated by Israel

12 1The Israelites had taken control of the land east of the Jordan River. They had all the land from Arnon Ravine to Mount Hermon and all the land along the eastern side of the Jordan Valley. These are all the kings the Israelites defeated to take this land:

2They defeated King Sihon of the Amorites living in the city of Heshbon. He ruled the land from Aroer at the Arnon Ravine to the Jabbok River. His land started in the center of that ravine. This was their border with the Ammonites. Sihon ruled over half of the land of Gilead. 3He also ruled over the eastern side of the Jordan Valley from Lake Galilee to the Dead Sea (Salt Sea). And he ruled from Beth Jeshimoth to the south to the hills of Pisgah.

4They also defeated King Og of Bashan. Og was from the Rephaites. He ruled the land in Ashtaroth and Edrei. 5Og ruled over Mount Hermon, Salecah, and all the area of Bashan. His land ended where the people of Geshur and Maacah lived. Og also ruled half of the land of Gilead. This land ended at the land of King Sihon of Heshbon.

6The LORD's servant Moses and the Israelites defeated all these kings. And Moses gave that land to the tribe of Reuben, the tribe of Gad, and half the tribe of Manasseh. Moses gave them this land to be their own.

7These are the kings of the land west of the Jordan River who were defeated by Joshua and the Israelites. This land was in the area west of Baal Gad in the Lebanon Valley as far as Mount Halak that rises toward Seir. Joshua divided it among the tribes. 8This included the hill country, the western foothills, the Jordan Valley, the eastern mountains, the desert, and the Negev.* This was where the Hittites, Amorites, Canaanites, Perizzites, Hivites, and Jebusites had lived. These are the kings the Israelites defeated: 9the king of Jericho, the king of Ai near Bethel, 10the king of Jerusalem, the king of Hebron, 11the king of Jarmuth, the king of Lachish, 12the king of Eglon, the king of Gezer, 13the king of Debir, the king of Geder, 14the king of Hormah, the king of Arad, 15the king of Libnah, the king of Adullam, 16the king of Makkedah, the king of Bethel, 17the king of Tappuah, the king of Hepher, 18the king of Aphek, the king of Sharon, 19the king of Madon, the king of Hazor, 20the king of Shimron Meron, the king of Acshaph, 21the king of Taanach, the king of Megiddo, 22the king of Kedesh, the king of Jokneam in Carmel, 23the king of Dor at Mount Dor, the king of Goyim in Gilgal, 24and the king of Tirzah.

The total number of kings was 31.

Land Not Yet Taken

13 1When Joshua was very old, the LORD said to him, "Joshua you have grown old, but there is still much land for you to take control of. 2You have not yet taken the land of Geshur or the land of the Philistines. 3You have not yet taken the area from the Shihor River*a* at Egypt to the border of Ekron and the land further north. That land still belongs to the Canaanites. You must still defeat the five Philistine leaders at Gaza, Ashdod, Ashkelon, Gath, and Ekron. You must also defeat the Avvites 4who live south of the Canaanite land. And you must still go north to take Mearah, which the Sidonians control. From there you must still go as far as Aphek on the Amorite border. 5You have not yet defeated the area of the Gebalites. And also there is the area of Lebanon east of Baal Gad below Mount Hermon to Lebo Hamath.

6"The people of Sidon are living in the hill country from Lebanon to Misrephoth Maim. But I will force them out for the Israelites. Be sure to remember this land when you divide the land among the Israelites. Do this as I told you. 7Now divide the land among the nine tribes and half the tribe of Manasseh."

Dividing the Land

8The tribes of Reuben, Gad, and the other half of the tribe of Manasseh had already received all their land. The LORD's servant, Moses, gave them the land east of the Jordan River. 9Their land started at Aroer by the Arnon Ravine and continued to the town in the middle of the ravine. And it included the whole plain from Medeba to Dibon. 10All the towns that King Sihon of the Amorites ruled were in that land. He ruled in the city of Heshbon. The land continued to the area where the Ammonites lived. 11Also the town of Gilead was in that land. And the area where the people of Geshur and Maacah lived was in that land. All of Mount Hermon and all of Bashan as far as Salecah was in that land. 12All the kingdom of King Og was in that land. King Og ruled in Bashan. In the past he ruled in Ashtaroth and Edrei. Og was from the Rephaites. In the past Moses had defeated those people and had taken their land. 13The Israelites did not force out the people of Geshur and Maacah. They still live among the Israelites today.

14The tribe of Levi is the only tribe that did not get any land. Instead, the Levites were given all the animals offered by fire to the

LORD, the God of Israel. That is what the Lord promised them.

15Moses had given each family group from the tribe of Reuben some land. This is the land they received: 16It was the land from Aroer near the Arnon Ravine to the town of Medeba. This included the whole plain and the town in the middle of the ravine. 17The land continued to Heshbon. It included all the towns on the plain. Those towns were Dibon, Bamoth Baal, Beth Baal Meon, 18Jahaz, Kedemoth, Mephaath, 19Kiriathaim, Sibmah, Zereth Shahar on the hill in the valley, 20Beth Peor, the hills of Pisgah, and Beth Jeshimoth. 21So that land included all the towns on the plain and all the area that King Sihon of the Amorites had ruled. He ruled in the town of Heshbon, but Moses had defeated him and the leaders of the Midianites. Those leaders were Evi, Rekem, Zur, Hur, and Reba. (They all fought together with Sihon.) All of them lived in that country. 22The Israelites defeated Balaam son of Beor. (Balaam tried to use magic to tell the future.) The Israelites killed many people during the fighting. 23The land that was given to Reuben stopped at the shore of the Jordan River. So the land that was given to the family groups of Reuben included all these towns and their fields that were listed.

24This is the land Moses gave to the tribe of Gad. He gave this land to each tribe:

25He gave them the land of Jazer, all the towns of Gilead, and half of the land of the Ammonites that went as far as Aroer near Rabbah. 26Their land included the area from Heshbon to Ramath Mizpah and Betonim, from Mahanaim to the land of Debir, 27the valley of Beth Haram, Beth Nimrah, Succoth and Zaphon, including the rest of the kingdom of King Sihon of Heshbon, along the Jordan all the way up to Lake Galilee on the eastern side of the river. 28All this land is the land Moses gave the family groups of Gad. That land included all the towns that were listed. Moses gave that land to each family group.

29This is the land Moses gave to half the tribe of Manasseh. Half of all the families in the tribe of Manasseh got this land: 30The land started at Mahanaim. The land included all of Bashan, all the land ruled by King Og of Bashan, and all the towns of Jair in Bashan. (In all, there were 60 cities.) 31The land also included half of Gilead, Ashtaroth, and Edrei. (Gilead, Ashtaroth, and Edrei were the cities where King Og had lived.) All this land was given to the family of Makir son of Manasseh. Half of all his sons got this land.

32Moses gave all this land to these tribes. He did this while the people were camped on the plains of Moab. This was across the Jordan River, east of Jericho. 33Moses did not give any land to the tribe of Levi. The LORD, God of Israel, promised that he himself would be the gift for the tribe of Levi.

a13:3 Shihor River Probably one of the eastern branches of the Nile River.

14 ¹Eleazar the priest, Joshua son of Nun, and the leaders of all the tribes of Israel decided what land to give to the people. ²The LORD had commanded Moses long ago how he wanted the people to choose their land. The people of the nine and a half tribes threw lots* to decide which land they would get. ³Moses had already given the two and a half tribes their land east of the Jordan River. The tribe of Levi did not receive any land like the other tribes. ⁴The descendants of Joseph had divided into two tribes—Manasseh and Ephraim. Each of these tribes received some land; the tribe of Levi was not given any land. They were given only some towns scattered throughout the other tribes and some fields around those towns for their animals. ⁵The LORD had told Moses how to divide the land among the tribes of Israel. The Israelites divided the land the way the Lord had commanded.

Caleb Gets His Land

⁶One day some people from the tribe of Judah went to Joshua at Gilgal. One of them was Caleb, the son of Jephunneh the Kenizzite. Caleb said to Joshua, "You remember what the LORD said at Kadesh Barnea. The Lord was speaking to Moses, his servant.ª The Lord was talking about you and me. ⁷Moses, the LORD's servant, sent me to look at the land where we were going. I was 40 years old at that time. When I came back, I told Moses what I thought about the land. ⁸The other men who went with me told the people things that made them afraid. But I really believed that the LORD would allow us to take that land. ⁹So that day Moses made a promise to me. He said, 'The land where you went will become your land. Your children will own that land forever. I will give you that land because you really believed in the LORD, my God.'

¹⁰"Now the LORD has kept me alive for 45 more years—as he said he would. During that time we all wandered in the desert. Now, here I am, 85 years old. ¹¹I am still as strong today as I was the day Moses sent me out. I am as ready to fight as I was then. ¹²So give me the hill country that the LORD promised me that day long ago. At that time you heard that the strong Anakites* lived there and the cities were very big and well protected. But now, maybe the LORD will be with me, and I will take that land just as the LORD said."

¹³Joshua blessed Caleb son of Jephunneh. Joshua gave him the city of Hebron as his own. ¹⁴And that city still belongs to the family of Caleb son of Jephunneh the Kenizzite. That land still belongs to his people because he trusted and obeyed the LORD, God of Israel. ¹⁵In the past that city was called Kiriath Arba. It was named for the greatest man among the Anakites—a man named Arba.

After this there was peace in the land.

ª **14:6** *his servant* Literally, "the man of God."

Land for Judah

15 ¹The land that was given to Judah was divided among the families of that tribe. That land went to the border of Edom and south all the way to the desert of Zin at the edge of Teman. ²The southern border of Judah's land started at the south end of the Dead Sea. ³The border went south to Scorpion Pass and continued on to Zin. Then the border continued south to Kadesh Barnea. It continued past Hezron to Addar. From Addar the border turned and continued to Karka. ⁴The border continued to Azmon, the brook of Egypt, and then to the Mediterranean Sea. All that land was on their southern border.

⁵Their eastern border was the shore of the Dead Sea to the area where the Jordan River flowed into the sea.

Their northern border started at the area where the Jordan River flowed into the Dead Sea. ⁶Then the northern border went to Beth Hoglah and continued north of Beth Arabah. The border continued to the stone of Bohan. (Bohan was the son of Reuben). ⁷Then the northern border went through the Valley of Achor to Debir. There the border turned to the north and went to Gilgal. Gilgal is across from the road that goes through the mountain of Adummim. It is on the south side of the brook. The border continued along the waters of En Shemesh. The border stopped at En Rogel. ⁸Then the border went through the Valley of Ben Hinnom beside the southern side of the Jebusite city (that is, Jerusalem). There the border went to the top of the hill on the west side of Hinnom Valley. This was at the northern end of Rephaim Valley. ⁹From there the border went to the spring of water of Nephtoah. Then the border went to the cities near Mount Ephron. There the border turned and went to Baalah. (Baalah is also called Kiriath Jearim.) ¹⁰At Baalah the border turned west and went to the hill country of Seir. The border continued along the north side of Mount Jearim (Kesalon) and continued down to Beth Shemesh. From there the border went past Timnah. ¹¹Then the border went to the hill north of Ekron. From there the border turned to Shikkeron and went past Mount Baalah. The border continued on to Jabneel and ended at the Mediterranean Sea. ¹²The Mediterranean Sea was the western border. So the land of Judah was inside these four borders. The families of Judah lived in this area.

¹³The LORD had commanded Joshua to give Caleb son of Jephunneh part of the land in Judah. So Joshua gave Caleb the land God had commanded. Joshua gave him the town of Kiriath Arba, that is, Hebron. (Arba was the father of Anak.) ¹⁴Caleb forced the three Anakite families living in Hebron to leave there. Those families were Sheshai, Ahiman, and Talmai. They were from the family of Anak. ¹⁵Then Caleb fought against the people

living in Debir. (In the past, Debir was also called Kiriath Sepher.) ¹⁶Caleb said, "I will give my daughter in marriage to the man who attacks and conquers Kiriath Sepher."

¹⁷Othniel was the son of Caleb's brother Kenaz. Othniel defeated that city, so Caleb gave his daughter Acsah to Othniel to be his wife. ¹⁸Acsah went to live with Othniel. Othniel told Acsah*ᵃ* to ask her father Caleb for some more land. Acsah went to her father. When she got off her donkey, Caleb asked her, "What do you want?"

¹⁹Acsah answered, "Give me a blessing.*ᵇ* You gave me dry desert land in the Negev.* Please give me some land with water on it." So Caleb gave her what she wanted. He gave her the upper and lower pools of water in that land.

²⁰The tribe of Judah got the land that God promised them. Each family group got part of the land. ²¹The tribe of Judah got all the towns in the southern part of the Negev. These towns were near the border of Edom. Here is a list of the towns: Kabzeel, Eder, Jagur, ²²Kinah, Dimonah, Adadah, ²³Kedesh, Hazor, Ithnan, ²⁴Ziph, Telem, Bealoth, ²⁵Hazor Hadattah, Kerioth Hezron (Hazor), ²⁶Amam, Shema, Moladah, ²⁷Hazar Gaddah, Heshmon, Beth Pelet, ²⁸Hazar Shual, Beersheba, Biziothiah, ²⁹Baalah, Iim, Ezem, ³⁰Eltolad, Kesil, Hormah, ³¹Ziklag, Madmannah, Sansannah, ³²Lebaoth, Shilhim, Ain, and Rimmon. In all, there were 29 towns and all their fields.

³³The tribe of Judah also got these towns in the western foothills: Eshtaol, Zorah, Ashnah, ³⁴Zanoah, En Gannim, Tappuah, Enam, ³⁵Jarmuth, Adullam, Socoh, Azekah, ³⁶Shaaraim, Adithaim, and Gederah (Gederothaim). In all, there were 14 towns and all their fields.

³⁷The tribe of Judah was also given these towns: Zenan, Hadashah, Migdal Gad, ³⁸Dilean, Mizpah, Joktheel, ³⁹Lachish, Bozkath, Eglon, ⁴⁰Cabbon, Lahmas, Kitlish, ⁴¹Gederoth, Beth Dagon, Naamah, and Makkedah. In all, there were 16 towns and all the fields around them.

⁴²The people of Judah also got these towns: Libnah, Ether, Ashan, ⁴³Iphtah, Ashnah, Nezib, ⁴⁴Keilah, Aczib, and Mareshah. In all, there were nine towns and all the fields around them.

⁴⁵The people of Judah also got the town of Ekron and all the small towns and fields near it. ⁴⁶They also got the area west of Ekron and all the fields and towns near Ashdod. ⁴⁷All the area around Ashdod and the small towns there were part of the land of Judah. The people of Judah also got the area around Gaza and the fields and towns that were near it. Their land continued to the River of Egypt.

And their land continued along the coast of the Mediterranean Sea.

⁴⁸The people of Judah were also given these towns in the hill country: Shamir, Jattir, Socoh, ⁴⁹Dannah, Kiriath Sannah (Debir), ⁵⁰Anab, Eshtemoh, Anim, ⁵¹Goshen, Holon, and Giloh. In all, there were eleven towns and all the fields around them.

⁵²The people of Judah were also given these towns: Arab, Dumah, Eshan, ⁵³Janim, Beth Tappuah, Aphekah, ⁵⁴Humtah, Kiriath Arba (Hebron), and Zior. There were nine towns and all the fields around them.

⁵⁵The people of Judah were also given these towns: Maon, Carmel, Ziph, Juttah, ⁵⁶Jezreel, Jokdeam, Zanoah, ⁵⁷Kain, Gibeah, and Timnah. In all, there were ten towns and all the fields around them.

⁵⁸The people of Judah were also given these towns: Halhul, Beth Zur, Gedor, ⁵⁹Maarath, Beth Anoth, and Eltekon. In all, there were six towns and all the fields around them.

⁶⁰The people of Judah were also given the two towns of Rabbah and Kiriath Baal (Kiriath Jearim).

⁶¹The people of Judah were also given towns in the desert: Beth Arabah, Middin, Secacah, ⁶²Nibshan, Salt City, and En Gedi. In all, there were six towns and all the fields around them.

⁶³The army of Judah was not able to force out the Jebusites living in Jerusalem. So today there are still Jebusites living among the people of Judah in Jerusalem.

Land for Ephraim and Manasseh

16 ¹This is the land that the family of Joseph received. This land started at the Jordan River near Jericho and continued to the waters of Jericho. (This was just east of Jericho.) The border went up from Jericho to the hill country of Bethel. ²Then the border continued from Bethel (Luz) to the Arkite border at Ataroth. ³Then the border went west to the border of the Japhletites. The border continued to Lower Beth Horon. Then the border went to Gezer and continued to the Mediterranean Sea.

⁴So the people of Manasseh and Ephraim got their land. (Manasseh and Ephraim were sons of Joseph.)

⁵This is the land that was given to the people of Ephraim: Their eastern border started at Ataroth Addar near Upper Beth Horon. ⁶And the western border started at Micmethath. The border turned to the east to Taanath Shiloh and continued east to Janoah. ⁷Then it went from Janoah down to Ataroth and to Naarah. The border continued until it touched Jericho and ended at the Jordan River. ⁸The border went from Tappuah west to Kanah Ravine and ended at the sea. This is all the land that was given to the Ephraimites. Each family in that tribe got a part of this land. ⁹Many of the border towns of Ephraim

---

*ᵃ***15:18** *Othniel told Acsah* Or "Acsah told Othniel."
*ᵇ***15:19** *Give me a blessing* Or "Please welcome me" or "Give me a stream of water."

were actually in Manasseh's borders, but the Ephraimites got the towns and the fields around them. ¹⁰But the Ephraimites were not able to force the Canaanites to leave the town of Gezer. So the Canaanites still live among the Ephraimites today, although they did become slaves of the Ephraimites.

17 ¹Then land was given to the tribe of Manasseh. Manasseh was Joseph's first son. Manasseh's first son was Makir, the father of Gilead.ᵃ Makir was a great soldier, so the areas of Gilead and Bashan were given to his family. ²Land was also given to the other families in the tribe of Manasseh. These families were Abiezer, Helek, Asriel, Shechem, Hepher, and Shemida. All these men were the other sons of Manasseh, the son of Joseph. The families of these men got their share of the land.

³Zelophehad was the son of Hepher. Hepher was the son of Gilead. Gilead was the son of Makir, and Makir was the son of Manasseh. Zelophehad did not have any sons, but he had five daughters. The daughters were named Mahlah, Noah, Hoglah, Milcah, and Tirzah. ⁴The daughters went to Eleazar the priest, Joshua son of Nun, and all the leaders. The daughters said, "The LORD told Moses to give us land the same as our male relatives." So Eleazar obeyed the LORD and gave the daughters some land, just like their uncles.

⁵So the tribe of Manasseh had ten areas of land west of the Jordan River and two more areas of land, Gilead and Bashan, on the other side of the Jordan River. ⁶So these women from the tribe of Manasseh got land the same as the men. The land of Gilead was given to the rest of the families of Manasseh.

⁷The lands of Manasseh were in the area between Asher and Micmethath. This is near Shechem. The border went south to the En Tappuah area. ⁸The land around Tappuah belonged to Manasseh, but the town itself did not. The town of Tappuah was at the border of Manasseh's land, and it belonged to the people of Ephraim. ⁹The border of Manasseh continued south to Kanah Ravine. This area belonged to the tribe of Manasseh, but the cities belonged to the people of Ephraim. Manasseh's border was on the north side of the river and it continued west to the Mediterranean Sea. ¹⁰The land to the south belonged to Ephraim. And the land to the north belonged to Manasseh. The Mediterranean Sea was the western border. The border touched Asher's land in the north and Issachar's land in the east.

¹¹The people of Manasseh had towns in the area of Issachar and Asher. Beth Shean, Ibleam, and the small towns around them also belonged to them. The people of Manasseh

also lived in Dor, Endor, Taanach, Megiddo, and the small towns around these cities. They also lived in the three towns of Naphoth. ¹²The people of Manasseh were not able to defeat those cities. So the Canaanites continued to live there. ¹³But the Israelites grew strong. When this happened, they forced the Canaanites to work for them. But they did not force them to leave that land.

¹⁴The tribe of Joseph spoke to Joshua and said, "You gave us only one area of land, but we are many people. Why did you give us only one part of all the land that the LORD gave his people?"

¹⁵Joshua answered them, "If you have too many people, go up to the wooded area in the hill country and clear that land for a place to live. That land now belongs to the Perizzites and the Rephaites. But if the hill country of Ephraim is too small for you, go take that land."

¹⁶The people of Joseph said, "It is true that the hill country of Ephraim is not large enough for us. But the Canaanites living there have powerful weapons—they have iron chariots*! And they control Jezreel Valley, Beth Shean, and all the small towns in that area."

¹⁷Then Joshua said to the people of Joseph, the tribes of Ephraim and Manasseh, "You have many people and you are very strong, so you should get more than one share of the land. ¹⁸You will take these mountains. It is a forest, but you can cut down the trees and make it a good place to live. You can take it from the Canaanites and force them to leave. You can defeat them, even if they are strong and have iron chariots."

Dividing the Rest of the Land

18 ¹All the Israelites gathered together at Shiloh where they set up the Meeting Tent.* The Israelites controlled that country. They had defeated all the enemies in that land. ²But at this time there were still seven tribes of Israel that had not yet received their land.

³So Joshua said to the Israelites, "Why do you wait so long to take your land? The LORD, the God of your ancestors,* has given this land to you. ⁴So each of your tribes should choose three men. I will send them out to study the land. They will describe that land, and then they will come back to me. ⁵They will divide the land into seven parts. The people of Judah will keep their land in the south. The people of Joseph will keep their land in the north. ⁶But you should describe the land and divide it into seven parts. Bring the map to me and we will throw lots* to let the LORD our God decide how to divide the land among the tribes. ⁷The Levites don't get a share of the land. Their share is to serve the LORD as priests. Gad, Reuben, and half the tribe of Manasseh have already received the land that was promised to them. They are on

---

ᵃ**17:1** *father of Gilead* Or "the leader of the area of Gilead."

the east side of the Jordan River. Moses, the LORD's servant, gave them that land."

8So the men who were chosen went to look at the land and write down what they saw. Joshua told them, "Go through the land and describe it in writing. Then come back to me at Shiloh. I will throw the lots and let the LORD decide how you will share the land."

9So the men went into the land. As they walked through it, they wrote down what they saw. They listed all the cities and divided the land into seven parts. Then they went back to Joshua at Shiloh. 10Joshua threw lots for them in front of the LORD at Shiloh. In this way Joshua divided the land and gave each tribe its part of the land.

Land for Benjamin

11The tribe of Benjamin was given the land that was between the areas of Judah and Joseph. Each family in the tribe of Benjamin got its land. This is the land that was chosen for Benjamin: 12The northern border started at the Jordan River. It went along the northern edge of Jericho. Then the border went west into the hill country. It continued until it was just east of Beth Aven. 13Then the border went south to Luz (Bethel), then down to Ataroth Addar. Ataroth Addar is on the hill south of Lower Beth Horon. 14At the hill south of Beth Horon, the border turned south and went along the west side of the hill. The border went to Kiriath Baal (also called Kiriath Jearim). This town belonged to the people of Judah. This was the western border.

15The southern border started near Kiriath Jearim and went to the River of Nephtoah. 16Then the border went down to the bottom of the hill near the valley of Ben Hinnom, north of Rephaim Valley. It continued down Hinnom Valley just south of the Jebusite city. Then the border went on to En Rogel. 17There it turned north, went to En Shemesh, and then continued on to Geliloth. (Geliloth is near the Adummim Pass in the mountains.) The border went down to the Great Stone that was named for Bohan, the son of Reuben. 18It continued to the northern part of Beth Arabah. Then the border went down into the Jordan Valley. 19Then it went to the northern part of Beth Hoglah and ended at the north shore of the Dead Sea. This is where the Jordan River flows into that sea. That was the southern border.

20The Jordan River was the eastern border. So this was the land that was given to the tribe of Benjamin. These were the borders on all sides. 21Each family got its land. These are their cities: Jericho, Beth Hoglah, Emek Keziz, 22Beth Arabah, Zemaraim, Bethel, 23Avvim, Parah, Ophrah, 24Kephar Ammoni, Ophni, and Geba. There were twelve cities and the fields around them.

25The tribe of Benjamin also got Gibeon, Ramah, Beeroth, 26Mizpah, Kephirah, Mozah, 27Rekem, Irpeel, Taralah, 28Zelah, Haeleph, the Jebusite city (that is, Jerusalem), Gibeah, and Kiriath. There were 14 cities and the fields around them. The tribe of Benjamin got all these areas.

Land for Simeon

19 1Then Joshua gave all the families in the tribe of Simeon their share of the land. The land they got was inside the area that belonged to Judah. 2This is the land that was given to that tribe: Beersheba (also called Sheba), Moladah, 3Hazar Shual, Balah, Ezem, 4Eltolad, Bethul, Hormah, 5Ziklag, Beth Marcaboth, Hazar Susah, 6Beth Lebaoth, and Sharuhen. There were 13 towns and all the fields around them.

7They also got the towns of Ain, Rimmon, Ether, and Ashan. There were four towns and all the fields around them. 8They also got all the fields around the cities as far as Baalath Beer (Ramah in the Negev*). So this was the area that was given to the tribe of Simeon. Each family got its land. 9Simeon's share of land was within the area that Judah got. The people of Judah had more land than they needed, so the people of Simeon got part of their land.

Land for Zebulun

10The next tribe to get their land was Zebulun. Each family in Zebulun got the land that was promised to them. The border of Zebulun went as far as Sarid. 11Then the border went west to Maralah and just touched Dabbesheth. Then it went along the ravine near Jokneam. 12Then the border turned to the east. It went from Sarid to Kisloth Tabor. Then it went on to Daberath and to Japhia. 13Then the border continued to the east to Gath Hepher and Eth Kazin. It ended at Rimmon. Then it turned and went to Neah. 14At Neah the border turned again, went north to Hannathon, and then continued to the Valley of Iphtah El. 15Inside this border were the cities of Kattath, Nahalal, Shimron, Idalah, and Bethlehem. In all, there were twelve towns and all the fields around them.

16So these are the towns and fields around them that were given to Zebulun. Each family in Zebulun got its part of the land.

Land for Issachar

17The fourth part of the land was given to the tribe of Issachar. Each family in that tribe got its part of the land. 18This is the land that was given to that tribe: Jezreel, Kesulloth, Shunem, 19Hapharaim, Shion, Anaharath, 20Rabbith, Kishion, Ebez, 21Remeth, En Gannim, En Haddah, and Beth Pazzez. 22The border of their land touched Tabor, Shahazumah, and Beth Shemesh. It ended at the Jordan River. In all, there were 16 towns and the fields around them. 23These cities and towns were part of the land that was given to the tribe of Issachar. Each family got its part of the land.

Land for Asher

²⁴The fifth part of land was given to the tribe of Asher. Each family in that tribe got its part of the land. ²⁵This is the land that was given to that tribe: Helkath, Hali, Beten, Acshaph, ²⁶Allammelech, Amad, and Mishal.

The western border continued to Mount Carmel and Shihor Libnath. ²⁷Then the border turned to the east. It went to Beth Dagon. The border touched Zebulun and the Valley of Iphtah El. Then it went north of Beth Emek and Neiel. It passed north of Cabul. ²⁸Then the border went to Abdon,ᵃ Rehob, Hammon, and Kanah. It continued to the Greater Sidon area. ²⁹Then the border went back south to Ramah. It continued to the strong city of Tyre. Then the border turned and went to Hosah. It ended at the sea, near Aczib, ³⁰Ummah, Aphek, and Rehob.

In all there were 22 towns and the fields around them. ³¹These cities and the fields around them were given to the tribe of Asher. Each family in that tribe got its share of the land.

Land for Naphtali

³²The sixth part of land was given to the tribe of Naphtali. Each family in that tribe got its share of the land. ³³The border of their land started at the large tree near Zaanannim. This is near Heleph. Then the border went through Adami Nekeb and Jabneel. It continued to Lakkum and ended at the Jordan River. ³⁴Then the border went to the west through Aznoth Tabor. It ended at Hukkok. The southern border touched Zebulun and the western border touched Asher. The border went to Judah, at the Jordan River to the east. ³⁵There were some very strong cities inside these borders. They were Ziddim, Zer, Hammath, Rakkath, Kinnereth, ³⁶Adamah, Ramah, Hazor, ³⁷Kedesh, Edrei, En Hazor, ³⁸Iron, Migdal El, Horem, Beth Anath, and Beth Shemesh. In all, there were 19 towns and all the fields around them.

³⁹These cities and the fields around them were given to the tribe of Naphtali. Each family in that tribe got its land.

Land for Dan

⁴⁰Then land was given to the tribe of Dan. Each family in that tribe got its land. ⁴¹This is the land that was given to them: Zorah, Eshtaol, Ir Shemesh, ⁴²Shaalabbin, Aijalon, Ithlah, ⁴³Elon, Timnah, Ekron, ⁴⁴Eltekeh, Gibbethon, Baalath, ⁴⁵Jehud, Bene Berak, Gath Rimmon, ⁴⁶Me Jarkon, Rakkon, and the area near Joppa.

⁴⁷But the people of Dan had trouble taking their land. There were strong enemies there and the people of Dan could not easily defeat them. So the people of Dan went to the northern part of Israel and fought against Laish.ᵇ They defeated Laish and killed the people who lived there. So the people of Dan lived in the town of Laish. They changed the name to Dan because that was the name of the father of their tribe. ⁴⁸All these cities and fields around them were given to the tribe of Dan. Each family got its share of the land.

Land for Joshua

⁴⁹So the leaders finished dividing the land and giving it to the different tribes. After they finished, all the Israelites decided to give Joshua son of Nun some land too. This was land that was promised to him. ⁵⁰The Lord had commanded that he get this land. So they gave Joshua the town of Timnath Serahᶜ in the hill country of Ephraim. This was the town that Joshua told them he wanted. So he built the town stronger and lived there.

⁵¹All these lands were given to the different tribes of Israel. Eleazar the priest, Joshua son of Nun, and the leaders of each tribe met together at Shiloh to divide the land. They met before the Lord at the entrance of the Meeting Tent.* So they finished dividing the land.

Cities of Safety

20 ¹Then the Lord said to Joshua: ²"Through Moses, I told you to choose some cities to be cities of safety. ³Anyone who kills someone accidentally can go to a city of safety to hide from the relatives who want to kill him.

⁴"If you accidentally kill someone and you run away to one of those cities, you must stop at the entrance of the city and tell the leaders of the people what happened. Then the leaders can allow you to enter the city. They will give you a place to live among them. ⁵If someone chases you and follows you to that city, the leaders of the city must not give you up. They must protect you because you came to them for safety after killing someone by accident—you were not angry and did not plan to kill the person. It was something that just happened. ⁶You should stay in that city until the court has judged you and until the high priest dies. Then you may go back to your hometown."

⁷So the Israelites chose some cities to be called cities of safety. These are the cities:

Kedesh in Galilee in the hill country of Naphtali;
Shechem in the hill country of Ephraim;

ᵃ**19:28** *Abdon* Or "Ebron."

ᵇ**19:47** *Laish* Or "Leshem."
ᶜ**19:50** *Timnath Serah* Or "Timnath Heres."

Kiriath Arba (Hebron) in the hill country of Judah;

8 Bezer, east of the Jordan River across from Jericho, in the desert area in the land of Reuben;

Ramoth in Gilead in the land of Gad;
and Golan in Bashan in the land of Manasseh.

9All Israelites or any foreigners living among them who killed someone by accident were allowed to run away to one of these cities of safety. They could be safe there and not be killed by anyone chasing them. The court in that city would judge them.

Towns for Priests and Levites

21 ¹The family rulers of the Levite tribe went to talk to Eleazar the priest, to Joshua son of Nun, and to the rulers of the other tribes of Israel. ²At Shiloh in the land of Canaan,* the Levite rulers said to them, "The LORD gave Moses a command. He commanded that you give us towns to live in and that you give us fields where our animals can eat." ³So the Israelites obeyed this command from the LORD and gave the Levites these towns and the land around them for their animals:

⁴The Kohath family groups were descendants of Aaron the priest from the tribe of Levi. Part of the Kohath family was given 13 towns in the areas that belonged to Judah, Simeon, and Benjamin.

⁵The other Kohath families were given ten towns in the areas that belonged to Ephraim, Dan, and half of Manasseh.

⁶The people from the Gershon family were given 13 towns. These towns were in the areas that belonged to Issachar, Asher, Naphtali, and the half of Manasseh that was in Bashan.

⁷The people from the Merari family were given 12 towns. These towns came from the areas that belonged to Reuben, Gad, and Zebulun.

⁸So the Israelites gave the Levites these towns and the fields around them, just as the LORD had told Moses.

⁹These are the names of the towns that were in the areas that belonged to Judah and Simeon. ¹⁰The first choice of towns was given to the Levites* from the Kohath family group. ¹¹They gave them Kiriath Arba (This is Hebron. It was named for a man named Arba. Arba was the father of Anak.) They also gave them some land near the town for their animals. ¹²But the fields and the small towns around the city of Kiriath Arba belonged to Caleb son of Jephunneh. ¹³So they gave the city of Hebron to Aaron's descendants. (Hebron was a city of safety.) They also gave Aaron's descendants the towns of Libnah, ¹⁴Jattir, Eshtemoa, ¹⁵Holon, Debir, ¹⁶Ain, Juttah, and Beth Shemesh. They also gave them some of the land near these towns for

their animals. These two tribes gave them nine towns.

¹⁷They also gave Aaron's descendants cities that belonged to the tribe of Benjamin. These cities were Gibeon, Geba, ¹⁸Anathoth, and Almon. They gave them these four towns and some of the land near the towns for their animals. ¹⁹In all, they gave 13 towns to the priests. (All priests were descendants of Aaron.) They also gave them some land near each town for their animals.

²⁰The other people from the Kohathite family groups were given towns that were in the areas that belonged to the tribe of Ephraim. They got these towns: ²¹the city of Shechem from the hill country of Ephraim (which was a city of safety), Gezer, ²²Kibzaim, and Beth Horon. In all, Ephraim gave them four towns and some land around each town for their animals.

²³The tribe of Dan gave them Eltekeh, Gibbethon, ²⁴Aijalon, and Gath Rimmon. In all, Dan gave them four towns and some land around each town for their animals.

²⁵Half the tribe of Manasseh gave them Taanach and Gath Rimmon. In all, this half of Manasseh gave them two towns and some land around each town for their animals.

²⁶In all, the rest of the people from the Kohath family groups got ten towns and some land around each town for their animals.

²⁷The Gershon family groups were also from the tribe of Levi. They got these towns:

Half the tribe of Manasseh gave them Golan in Bashan. (Golan was a city of safety.) Manasseh also gave them Be Eshtarah. In all, this half of Manasseh gave them two towns and some land around each town for their animals.

²⁸The tribe of Issachar gave them Kishion, Daberath, ²⁹Jarmuth, and En Gannim. In all, Issachar gave them four towns and some land around each town for their animals.

³⁰The tribe of Asher gave them Mishal, Abdon, ³¹Helkath, and Rehob. In all, Asher gave them four towns and some land around each town for their animals.

³²The tribe of Naphtali gave them Kedesh in Galilee. (Kedesh was a city of safety.) Naphtali also gave them Hammoth Dor and Kartan. In all, Naphtali gave them three towns and some land around each town for their animals.

³³In all, the Gershon family groups got 13 towns and some land around each town for their animals.

³⁴⁻³⁹The other Levite group was the Merari family group. They were given these towns: The tribe of Zebulun gave them Jokneam, Kartah, Dimnah, and Nahalal. In all, Zebulun gave them four towns and some land around each town for their animals. The tribe of Reuben gave them Bezer, Jahaz, Kedemoth, and Mephaath. In all, Reuben gave them four towns and some land around each town for their animals. The tribe of Gad gave them

Ramoth in Gilead. (Ramoth was a city of safety.) They also gave them Mahanaim, Heshbon, and Jazer. In all, Gad gave them four towns and some land around each town for their animals.

⁴⁰In all, the last family of Levites, the Merari family, got 12 towns.

⁴¹So the Levites were given a total of 48 towns and some land around each town for their animals. All these towns were in areas that belonged to the other tribes. ⁴²Each of these towns had some land in it for their animals. That was true for every town.

⁴³So the LORD kept the promise that he had made to the Israelites and gave the people all the land that he had promised. The people took the land and lived there. ⁴⁴And the LORD allowed them to have peace on all sides of their land, just as he had promised their ancestors.* None of their enemies defeated them. The LORD allowed the Israelites to defeat every enemy. ⁴⁵The LORD kept every promise that he made to the Israelites. There were no promises that he failed to keep. Every promise came true.

Three Tribes Go Home

22 ¹Then Joshua called a meeting of all the people from the tribes of Reuben, Gad, and half the tribe of Manasseh. ²Joshua said to them, "Moses was the LORD's servant. You obeyed everything that Moses told you to do. And you also obeyed all of my commands. ³All this time you have supported all the other Israelites. You carefully obeyed all the commands that the LORD your God gave you. ⁴The LORD your God promised to give the Israelites peace. And now, he has kept his promise, so now you can go home. The LORD's servant Moses gave you the land on the east side of the Jordan River. Now you can go home to that land. ⁵But remember—continue to obey the law that Moses gave you. You must love the LORD your God and obey his commands. You must continue to follow him and serve him the very best that you can."

⁶Then Joshua said goodbye to them, and they left and went home. ⁷Moses had given the land of Bashan to half of the Manasseh tribe. Joshua gave land on the west side of the Jordan River to the other half of the Manasseh tribe. Joshua blessed them and sent them home. ⁸He said, "You have become very rich. You have many animals. You have gold, silver, and expensive jewelry. You have many beautiful clothes. You have taken many things from your enemies. Go home and divide these things among yourselves."

⁹So the people from the tribes of Reuben, Gad, and Manasseh left the other Israelites at Shiloh in Canaan.* They went back home to Gilead. This was their own land, the land that Moses gave them, as the LORD had commanded.

¹⁰They went to the place called Geliloth, near the Jordan River in the land of Canaan. There they built a beautiful altar. ¹¹But the other Israelites who were still at Shiloh heard about the altar that these three tribes built. They heard that the altar was at the border of Canaan at the place called Geliloth. It was near the Jordan River on Israel's side. ¹²All the Israelites became very angry with these three tribes. They met together and decided to fight against them.

¹³So the Israelites sent some men to talk to the people of Reuben, Gad, and Manasseh. The leader of these men was Phinehas, son of Eleazar the priest. ¹⁴They also sent ten of the leaders of the tribes there. There was one man from each family group of Israel who was at Shiloh.

¹⁵So these eleven men went to Gilead. They went to talk to the people of Reuben, Gad, and Manasseh. The eleven men said to them, ¹⁶"All the Israelites ask you: 'Why did you do this thing against the God of Israel? Why did you turn against the LORD? Why did you build an altar for yourselves? You know that this is against God's law. ¹⁷Remember what happened at Peor? We are still suffering because of that sin. Because of that great sin, God caused many of the Israelites to become very sick. And we are still suffering because of that sickness today. ¹⁸And now you are doing the same thing. You are turning against the LORD. Will you refuse to follow the LORD? If you don't stop what you are doing, he will be angry with everyone in Israel.

¹⁹"'If your land is not a good enough place to worship, come over into our land. The LORD's Tent is in our land. You can have some of our land and live there. But don't turn against the LORD. Don't build another altar. We already have the altar of the LORD our God at the Meeting Tent.*

²⁰"'Remember how Achan son of Zerah refused to obey the command about things that must be destroyed. That one man broke God's law, but all the Israelites were punished. Achan died because of his sin, but also many other people died.'"

²¹The people from the tribes of Reuben, Gad, and Manasseh answered the eleven men. They said, ²²"The LORD is our God! Again we say that the LORD is our God!ᵃ And God knows why we did this thing. We want you to know also. You can judge what we did. If you believe that we have done something wrong, you can kill us. ²³If we broke God's law, we ask the LORD himself to punish us. ²⁴Do you think we built this altar for burnt offerings,* grain offerings, and fellowship offerings*? No, that is not why we built it. We were afraid that in the future

---

ᵃ**22:22 The LORD is our God** Or "YAHWEH is the true God!" Literally, "El Elohim YAHWEH!"

your descendants would not accept us as part of your nation. Then they would say that we could not worship the LORD, the God of Israel. 25God gave us land on the other side of the Jordan River. This means that the Jordan River separates us. We were afraid that when your children grew up and ruled your land, they would not remember that we were also your people. They would say to us, 'You people of Reuben and Gad are not part of Israel.' Then your children would make our children stop worshiping the LORD.

26"So we decided to build this altar. But we did not plan to use it for burning offerings and sacrifices. 27The real reason we wanted our altar was to show our people that we worship the same God that you do. This altar will be the proof to you and us and to all our future children that we worship the LORD. We give our sacrifices, grain offerings, and fellowship offerings to the LORD. We wanted your children to grow up and know that we are also Israelites like yourselves. 28In the future, if it happens that your children say that we don't belong to Israel, then our children can say, 'Look, our fathers who lived before us made an altar. That altar is exactly like the LORD's altar at the Holy Tent. We don't use this altar for sacrifices—this altar is proof that we are part of Israel.'

29"The truth is, we don't want to be against the LORD. We don't want to stop following him now. We know that the only true altar is the one that is in front of the Holy Tent.* That altar belongs to the LORD our God."

30Phinehas the priest and the leaders with him heard what the people from Reuben, Gad, and Manasseh said. They were satisfied that they were telling the truth. 31So Phinehas the priest said, "Now we know that the LORD is with us and that you did not turn against him. We are happy that the Israelites will not be punished by the LORD."

32Then Phinehas and the leaders left that place and went home. They left the people of Reuben and Gad in the land of Gilead and went back to Canaan. They went back to the Israelites and told them what had happened. 33The Israelites were also satisfied. They were happy and thanked God. They decided not to go and fight against the people of Reuben, Gad, and Manasseh. They decided not to destroy the land where those people live.

34The people of Reuben and Gad named the altar "Proof That We Believe the LORD is God."

Joshua Encourages the People

23 1The LORD gave Israel peace from their enemies around them. The LORD made Israel safe. Many years passed, and Joshua became very old. 2At this time Joshua called a meeting of all the older leaders, heads of families, judges, and officers of the Israelites. Joshua said, "I have grown very old. 3You have seen what the LORD did to our enemies. He did this to help us. The LORD your God fought for you. 4Remember that I told you that your people could have the land between the Jordan River and the Mediterranean Sea in the west. I promised to give you that land, but you don't control it yet. I have taken the land away from those nations, but they are still living there. 5But the LORD your God will force the people living there to leave. You will take that land. The LORD will force them to leave. The LORD your God promised to do this for you.

6"You must be careful to obey everything the LORD has commanded us. Obey everything that is written in the Book of the Law*a of Moses. Don't turn away from that law. 7There are still some people living among us who are not Israelites. They worship their own gods. Don't become friends with them. Don't serve or worship their gods. 8You must continue to follow the LORD your God. You have done this in the past, and you must continue to do it.

9"The LORD helped you defeat many great and powerful nations. He forced them to leave. No nation has been able to defeat you. 10With his help, one man from Israel could defeat 1000 enemy soldiers, because the LORD your God fights for you, as he promised. 11So you must continue to love the LORD your God.

12"Don't stop following the LORD. Don't become friends with these other people who are not part of Israel. Don't marry any of their people. But if you do become friends with these people, 13the LORD your God will not help you defeat your enemies. They will become like a trap for you. They will cause you pain—like smoke and dust in your eyes. And you will be forced to leave this good land. The LORD your God gave you this land. But you can lose it if you don't obey this command.

14"It is almost time for me to die. You know and really believe that the Lord has done many great things for you. You know that the LORD your God has not failed in any of his promises. He has kept every promise that he has made to us. 15Every good promise that the LORD your God made to us has come true. But in the same way, the LORD will make his other promises come true. He promised that if you do wrong, bad things will happen to you. He promised that he will force you to leave this good land that the LORD your God has given to you. 16This will happen if you refuse to keep your agreement with the LORD your God. You will lose this land if you go and serve other gods. You must not worship those other gods. If you do, the LORD will become very angry with you. Then you will quickly

*a23:6 Law Or "Teachings."

be forced to leave this good land that he gave you."

Joshua Says Goodbye

24 ¹Joshua called all the tribes of Israel to meet together at Shechem. Then Joshua called the older leaders, heads of families, judges, and the officers of Israel. These men stood before God.

²Then Joshua spoke to all the people. He said, "I am telling you what the LORD, the God of Israel, says to you:

'A long time ago, your ancestors lived on the other side of the Euphrates River. I am talking about men like Terah, the father of Abraham and Nahor. At that time they worshiped other gods. ³But I, the LORD, took your father Abraham out of the land on the other side of the River. I led him through the land of Canaan* and gave him many children. I gave Abraham his son named Isaac. ⁴And I gave Isaac two sons named Jacob and Esau. To Esau, I gave the land around the mountains of Seir. Jacob and his sons did not live there. They went to live in the land of Egypt.

⁵'Then I sent Moses and Aaron to Egypt. I wanted them to bring my people out of Egypt. I caused many terrible things to happen to the people of Egypt. Then I brought your people out of Egypt. ⁶When I brought your ancestors out of Egypt, they came to the Red Sea, and the men of Egypt were chasing them. There were chariots* and men on horses. ⁷So the people asked me, the LORD, for help. And I caused great trouble to come to the men of Egypt. I, the LORD, caused the sea to cover them. You yourselves saw what I did to the army of Egypt.

'After that you lived in the desert for a long time. ⁸Then I brought you to the land of the Amorites, east of the Jordan River. Those people fought against you, but I allowed you to defeat them. I gave you the power to destroy them, and you took control of that land.

⁹'Then Balak, the son of Zippor, the king of Moab, prepared to fight against the Israelites. The king sent for Balaam the son of Beor to curse* you, ¹⁰but I, the LORD, refused to listen to Balaam. So Balaam asked for good things to happen to you. He blessed you many times. I saved you and brought you out of trouble.

¹¹'Then you went across the Jordan River to the city of Jericho. The people in Jericho fought against you. Also, the Amorites, Perizzites, Canaanites, Hittites, Girgashites, Hivites, and Jebusites fought against you. But I allowed you to defeat them all.

¹²As your army went forward, I sent the Hornet*ᵃ ahead of them and made the people leave the land, as I did to the two Amorite kings.ᵇ It was not your swords and bows that brought you victory!

¹³'I, the LORD, gave that land to you. You didn't work for that land—I gave it to you. You did not build those cities—I gave them to you. And now you live in that land and in those cities. You have vineyards* and olive trees, but you did not have to plant those gardens.'"

¹⁴Then Joshua said to the people, "Now you have heard the Lord's words. So you must respect the LORD and sincerely serve him. Throw away the false gods that your ancestors* worshiped. That was something that happened a long time ago on the other side of the Euphrates River and in Egypt. Now you must serve only the LORD.

¹⁵"But maybe you don't want to serve the LORD. You must choose for yourselves today. Today you must decide who you will serve. Will you serve the gods that your ancestors worshiped when they lived on the other side of the Euphrates River? Or will you serve the gods of the Amorites who lived in this land? You must choose for yourselves. But as for me and my family, we will serve the LORD."

¹⁶Then the people answered, "We will never stop following the LORD. We will never serve other gods! ¹⁷We know that it was the LORD God who brought our people out of Egypt. We were slaves in that land, but he did great things for us there. He brought us out of that land and protected us while we traveled through other lands. ¹⁸The LORD helped us defeat the people living in these lands. He helped us defeat the Amorites who lived in this land where we are now. So we will continue to serve the LORD, because he is our God."

¹⁹Then Joshua said, "You will not be able to continue serving the LORD. God is holy.* And God hates his people worshiping other gods. He will not forgive you if you turn against him like that. ²⁰If you leave the LORD and serve other gods, he will cause terrible things to happen to you. He will destroy you. He has been good to you, but if you turn against him he will destroy you."

²¹Then the people said to Joshua, "No, we will serve the LORD!"

²²Then Joshua said, "Look around at yourselves and the people with you. Do you all know and agree that you have chosen to serve the LORD? Are you all witnesses to this?"

ᵃ**24:12 Hornet** A stinging insect like a large wasp or bee. Here, it probably means God's angel or his great power.
ᵇ**24:12** The Hebrew text here is hard to understand, but it may refer to the events described in Num. 21:21–35 and Deut. 2:24–3:10.

The people answered, "Yes, it is true. We all see that we have chosen to serve the LORD."

23Then Joshua said, "So throw away the false gods that you have among you. Love the LORD, the God of Israel, with all your heart."

24Then the people said to Joshua, "We will serve the LORD our God. We will obey him."

25So that day Joshua made an agreement for the people. He made this agreement at the town called Shechem. It became a law for them to follow. 26Joshua wrote these things in the *Book of the Law of God*. Then he found a large stone to be the proof of this agreement. He put the stone under the oak tree near the LORD's Holy Tent.*

27Then Joshua said to all the people, "This stone will help you remember what we said today. This stone was here when the LORD was speaking to us today. So this stone will be something that helps you remember what happened today. The stone will be a witness against you. It will stop you from turning against your God."

28Then Joshua told the people to go home. So everyone went back to his own land.

Joshua Dies

29After that Joshua son of Nun died. He was 110 years old. 30Joshua was buried on his own land at Timnath Serah, in the hill country of Ephraim, north of Mount Gaash.

31The Israelites served the LORD during the time Joshua was living. After Joshua died, the people continued to serve the Lord while their leaders were alive. These were the leaders who had seen what the LORD had done for Israel.

Joseph Comes Home

32When the Israelites left Egypt, they carried the bones from the body of Joseph with them. They buried the bones of Joseph at Shechem on the land that Jacob had bought from the sons of Hamor, the father of the man named Shechem. Jacob had bought that land for 100 pieces of pure silver. This land belonged to Joseph's children.

33Aaron's son, Eleazar, died and was buried at Gibeah in the hill country of Ephraim. Gibeah had been given to Eleazar's son Phinehas.

Judges

Judah Fights the Canaanites

1 1After Joshua died, the Israelites prayed to the LORD, "Which of our tribes should be the first to go and fight for us against the Canaanites?"

2The LORD said to the Israelites, "The tribe of Judah will go. I will let them take this land."

3The men of Judah asked for help from their brothers from the tribe of Simeon. They said, "Brothers, the LORD promised to give each of us some land. If you will come and help us fight for our land, we will go and help you fight for your land." The men of Simeon agreed to help their brothers from Judah fight.

4The LORD helped the men of Judah defeat the Canaanites and the Perizzites. They killed 10,000 men at the city of Bezek. 5In the city of Bezek, they found the ruler of Bezek*a* and fought him, and they defeated the Canaanites and the Perizzites.

6The ruler of Bezek tried to escape, but the men of Judah chased him and caught him. When they caught him, they cut off his thumbs and big toes. 7Then the ruler of Bezek said, "I cut off the thumbs and big toes of 70 kings. And they had to eat pieces of food that fell from my table. Now God has paid me back for what I did to them." The men of Judah took the ruler of Bezek to Jerusalem, and he died there.

8The men of Judah fought against Jerusalem and captured it. They used their swords to kill the people of Jerusalem. Then they burned the city. 9Later, they went down to fight against some more Canaanites who lived in the hill country, in the Negev,* and in the western foothills.

10Then the men of Judah went to fight against the Canaanites who lived in the city of Hebron. (Hebron used to be called Kiriath Arba.) They defeated the men named Sheshai, Ahiman, and Talmai.*b*

Caleb and His Daughter

11The men of Judah left that place. They went to the city of Debir to fight against the people there. (In the past, Debir was called Kiriath Sepher.) 12Before they started to fight, Caleb made a promise to the men. He said, "I will give my daughter Acsah in marriage to whoever attacks and conquers Kiriath Sepher."

---

*a***1:5** *ruler of Bezek* Or "Adoni Bezek."

*b***1:10** *Sheshai, Ahiman, Talmai* Three sons of a man named Anak. They were giants. See Num. 13:22.

13Caleb had a younger brother named Kenaz. Kenaz had a son named Othniel. Othniel captured the city of Kiriath Sepher. So Caleb gave his daughter Acsah to Othniel to be his wife.

14Acsah went to live with Othniel. Othniel told Acsah*a* to ask her father for some land. She went to her father. When she got off her donkey, Caleb asked her, "What is wrong?"

15Acsah answered him, "Give me a blessing.*b* You gave me dry desert land in the Negev.* Please give me some land with water on it." So Caleb gave her what she wanted. He gave her the upper and lower pools of water in that land.

16The Kenites left the City of Palm Trees*c* and went with the men of Judah. They went to the Desert of Judah to live with the people there. This was in the Negev near the city Arad. (The Kenites were from the family of Moses' father-in-law.)

17Some Canaanites lived in the city of Zephath. The men of Judah and men from the tribe of Simeon attacked them and completely destroyed the city. So they named the city Hormah.*d*

18The men of Judah also captured the cities of Gaza, Ashkelon, and Ekron and all the small towns around them.

19The LORD was on the side of the men of Judah when they fought. They took the land in the hill country, but they failed to take the land in the valleys, because the people living there had iron chariots.*

20Moses had promised to give the land near Hebron to Caleb, so that land was given to Caleb's family. The men of Caleb forced the three sons of Anak*e* to leave that place.

21The tribe of Benjamin could not force the Jebusites to leave Jerusalem. So even today,*f* the Jebusites live with the people of Benjamin in Jerusalem.

Joseph's Descendants Capture Bethel

22The descendants of Joseph went to fight against the city of Bethel, and the LORD was with them. 23They sent some spies to the city of Bethel (which was then called Luz). 24While the spies were watching, they saw a man come out of the city. They said to the man, "Show us a secret way into the city. If you help us, we will not hurt you."

25The man showed the spies the secret way into the city. The men of Joseph used their swords to kill the people of Bethel. But they did not hurt the man who helped them or anyone in his family. The man and his family were allowed to go free. 26He went to the land where the Hittites lived and built a city. He named it Luz, and that city is still called Luz today.

Other Tribes Fight the Canaanites

27There were Canaanites living in the cities of Beth Shean, Taanach, Dor, Ibleam, Megiddo, and the small towns around the cities. The people from the tribe of Manasseh could not force those people to leave their towns. So the Canaanites stayed. They refused to leave their homes. 28Later, the Israelites grew stronger and forced the Canaanites to work as slaves for them. But the Israelites could not force all the Canaanites to leave their land.

29There were Canaanites living in Gezer. And the Ephraimites did not make all the Canaanites leave their land. So they continued to live in Gezer with the Ephraimites.

30Some Canaanites lived in the cities of Kitron and Nahalol. The people of Zebulun did not force those people to leave their land. They stayed and lived with the people of Zebulun. But the people of Zebulun made them work as slaves.

31The people of Asher did not force the other people to leave the cities of Acco, Sidon, Ahlab, Aczib, Helbah, Aphek, and Rehob. 32The people of Asher did not force those Canaanites to leave their land, so the Canaanites continued to live with them.

33The people of Naphtali did not force the people to leave the cities of Beth Shemesh and Beth Anath, so the people of Naphtali continued to live with the people in those cities. Those Canaanites worked as slaves for the people of Naphtali.

34The Amorites forced the tribe of Dan to live in the hill country. They had to stay in the hills because the Amorites would not let them come down to live in the valleys. 35The Amorites decided to stay in Mount Heres, Aijalon, and Shaalbim. Later, when the descendants of Joseph grew stronger, they made the Amorites work as slaves for them. 36The land of the Amorites was from Scorpion Pass to Sela and up into the hill country past Sela.

The Angel of the Lord at Bokim

2 1The angel of the LORD went up to the city of Bokim from the city of Gilgal. The angel spoke this message from the Lord to the Israelites: "I brought you out of Egypt and led you to the land that I promised to give to your ancestors.* I told you I would never break my agreement with you. 2But in return, you must never make any agreement with the people living in that land. You must destroy their altars.* I told you that, but you didn't obey me.

3"Now I will tell you this, 'I will not force

*a*1:14 *Othniel told Acsah* Or "Acsah told Othniel."
*b*1:15 *Give me a blessing* Or "Please welcome me" or "Give me a stream of water."
*c*1:16 *City of Palm Trees* Another name for Jericho.
*d*1:17 *Hormah* This name means "completely destroyed" or "a gift given totally to God." See Lev. 27:28–29.
*e*1:20 *three sons of Anak* Sheshai, Ahiman, and Talmai, mentioned above in verse 10.
*f*1:21 *even today* That is, at the time the book was written.

the other people to leave this land any longer. These people will become a problem for you. They will be like a trap to you. Their false gods will become like a net to trap you.'"

⁴After the angel gave the Israelites this message from the LORD, the people cried loudly. ⁵So they named the place Bokim.ᵃ There they offered sacrifices to the LORD.

Disobedience and Defeat

⁶Then Joshua told the people to go home, so each tribe went to take their area of land. ⁷The Israelites served the LORD as long as Joshua was alive, and they continued serving the Lord during the lifetimes of the elders* who lived after Joshua had died. These old men had seen all the great things the LORD had done for the Israelites. ⁸Joshua son of Nun, the servant of the LORD, died at the age of 110 years. ⁹The Israelites buried Joshua on the land that he had been given. That was at Timnath Heres, in the hill country of Ephraim, north of Mount Gaash.

¹⁰After that whole generation died, the next generation grew up. This new generation did not know about the LORD or what he had done for the Israelites. ¹¹So the Israelites did evil and served the false god Baal.* The LORD saw the people doing this evil thing. ¹²The LORD had brought the Israelites out of Egypt, and their ancestors* had worshiped the Lord. But the Israelites stopped following him. They began to worship the false gods of the people living around them. That made the LORD angry. ¹³The Israelites stopped following the LORD and began worshiping Baal* and Ashtoreth.*

¹⁴The LORD was angry with the Israelites, so he let enemies attack them and take their possessions. He let their enemies who lived around them defeat them. The Israelites could not protect themselves from their enemies. ¹⁵When the Israelites went out to fight, they always lost. They lost because the LORD was not on their side. He had already warned them that they would lose if they served the gods of the people living around them. The Israelites suffered very much.

¹⁶Then the LORD chose leaders called judges. These leaders saved the Israelites from the enemies who took their possessions. ¹⁷But the Israelites did not listen to their judges. The Israelites were not faithful to God—they followed other gods.ᵇ In the past, the ancestors of the Israelites obeyed the LORD's commands. But now the Israelites changed and stopped obeying the Lord.

¹⁸Many times the enemies of Israel did bad things to the people, so the Israelites would cry for help. And each time the LORD felt sorry for the people and sent a judge to save them from their enemies. The LORD was always with those judges. Each time the Israelites were saved from their enemies. ¹⁹But when each judge died, the Israelites again sinned and started worshiping the false gods. They acted worse than their ancestors did. The Israelites were very stubborn and refused to change their evil ways.

²⁰So the LORD became angry with the Israelites, and he said, "This nation has broken the agreement* that I made with their ancestors. They have not listened to me. ²¹So I will no longer defeat the nations and clear the way for the Israelites. Those nations were still in this land when Joshua died, and I will let them stay in this land. ²²I will use them to test the Israelites. I will see if the Israelites can keep the LORD's commands as their ancestors did." ²³The LORD allowed those nations to stay in the land. He did not quickly force them to leave the country. He did not help Joshua's army defeat them.

3 ¹⁻²The LORD did not force all the other nations to leave Israel's land. He wanted to test the Israelites. None of the Israelites living at this time had fought in the wars to take the land of Canaan.* So he let those other nations stay in their country. (He did this to teach the Israelites who had not fought in those wars.) Here are the names of the nations the Lord left in the land: ³the five rulers of the Philistines, all the Canaanites, the people of Sidon, and the Hivites who lived in the Lebanon* mountains from Mount Baal Hermon to Lebo Hamath. ⁴He left those nations in the land to test the Israelites. He wanted to see if the Israelites would obey the LORD's commands that he had given to their ancestors through Moses.

⁵The Israelites lived with the Canaanites, Hittites, the Amorites, Perizzites, Hivites, and Jebusites. ⁶The Israelites began to marry the daughters of those people. They allowed their own daughters to marry the sons of those people. The Israelites also began to worship their gods.

Othniel, the First Judge

⁷The LORD saw that the Israelites did evil things. They forgot about the LORD their God and served the false gods Baal* and Asherah.* ⁸The LORD was angry with the Israelites, so he allowed King Cushan Rishathaim of Aram Naharaimᶜ to defeat the Israelites and to rule over them. The Israelites were under that king's rule for eight years. ⁹But the Israelites cried to the LORD for help, and the LORD sent a man named Othniel to save them. He was the son of Kenaz, who was Caleb's younger brother. Othniel saved the Israelites. ¹⁰The Spirit of the LORD filled Othniel, and he became a judge for the Israelites. He led

---

ᵃ**2:5 Bokim** This name means "people crying."
ᵇ**2:17 were not faithful ... gods** Literally, "acted like a prostitute with other gods."
ᶜ**3:8 Aram Naharaim** The area in northern Syria between the Tigris and Euphrates rivers.

the Israelites to war. The LORD helped Othniel defeat King Cushan Rishathaim of Aram. [11]So the land was at peace for 40 years, until Othniel son of Kenaz died.

Ehud, the Judge

[12]Again the LORD saw the Israelites do evil things. So the LORD gave King Eglon of Moab power to defeat the Israelites. [13]Eglon got help from the Ammonites and the Amalekites. They joined him and attacked the Israelites. Eglon and his army defeated the Israelites and forced them to leave the City of Palm Trees.[a] [14]King Eglon of Moab ruled over the Israelites for 18 years.

[15]The Israelites cried to the LORD for help, so he sent a man named Ehud son of Gera to save them. Ehud was from the tribe of Benjamin and was trained to fight with his left hand. The Israelites sent Ehud with a gift to King Eglon of Moab. [16]Ehud made himself a sword with two sharp edges that was about 12 inches[b] long. He tied the sword to his right thigh and hid it under his uniform.

[17]So Ehud brought the gift to King Eglon of Moab. Eglon was a very fat man. [18]After offering the gift, Ehud left the palace with the men who had carried the gift. [19]When Ehud reached the statues[c] near Gilgal, he turned and went back to King Eglon and said, "King, I have a secret message for you."

The king told him to be quiet and then sent all the servants out of the room. [20]Ehud went to King Eglon. The king was sitting all alone in the upper room of his palace.

Then Ehud said, "I have a message from God for you." The king stood up from his throne. He was very close to Ehud. [21]As the king was getting up from his throne,[d] Ehud reached with his left hand and took out the sword that was tied to his right thigh. Then he pushed the sword into the king's belly. [22]The sword went into Eglon's belly so far that even the handle sank in and the fat closed around it. The point of the blade came out his back. Ehud left the sword inside Eglon.

[23]Then Ehud went out of the private room, closed the doors to the upper room, and locked the king inside. [24]Ehud then left the main room, and the servants went back in. The servants found the doors to the upper room locked, so they said, "The king must be relieving himself in his private toilet." [25]The servants waited for a long time, but the king never opened the doors to the upper room.

Finally the servants got worried. They got the key and unlocked the doors. When the servants entered, they saw their king lying dead on the floor.

[26]While the servants were waiting for the king, Ehud had time to escape. He passed by the statues and went toward the place named Seirah. [27]When Ehud came to Seirah, he blew a trumpet there in the hill country of Ephraim. The Israelites heard the trumpet and went down from the hills with Ehud leading them. [28]He said to the Israelites, "Follow me! The LORD has helped us defeat our enemies, the Moabites."

So the Israelites followed Ehud. They went down with him to take control of the places where people could easily cross the Jordan River into the land of Moab. The Israelites did not allow any one to go across the Jordan River. [29]They killed about 10,000 strong and brave men from Moab. Not one Moabite man escaped. [30]So on that day the Israelites began to rule over the Moabites, and there was peace in the land for 80 years.

Shamgar, the Judge

[31]After Ehud saved the Israelites, another man saved Israel. That man's name was Shamgar son of Anath.[e] Shamgar used an ox goad* to kill 600 Philistine men.

Deborah, the Judge

4 [1]After Ehud died, the people again did what the LORD said was wrong. [2]So the LORD allowed King Jabin of Canaan* to defeat the Israelites. Jabin ruled in a city named Hazor. A man named Sisera was the commander of King Jabin's army. Sisera lived in a town called Harosheth Haggoyim. [3]Sisera had 900 iron chariots,* and he was very cruel to the Israelites for 20 years. So they cried to the LORD for help.

[4]There was a woman prophet named Deborah. She was the wife of a man named Lappidoth. She was judge of Israel at that time. [5]One day Deborah was sitting under the Palm Tree of Deborah, and the Israelites came up to her to ask what to do about Sisera. (The Palm Tree of Deborah is between the cities of Ramah and Bethel in the hill country of Ephraim.) [6]Deborah sent a message to a man named Barak and asked him to come meet with her. Barak was the son of a man named Abinoam. Barak lived in the city of Kedesh, which is in the area of Naphtali. Deborah said to Barak, "The LORD, the God of Israel, commands you: 'Go and gather 10,000 men from the tribes of Naphtali and Zebulun. Lead them to Mount Tabor. [7]I will make Sisera, the commander of King Jabin's army, come to

---

[a]**3:13** *City of Palm Trees* Another name for Jericho.

[b]**3:16** *12 inches* Or 30 cm. Literally, "1 *gomed*," probably equivalent to 2/3 of a cubit.

[c]**3:19** *statues* These were probably statues of gods or animals that "protected" the entrance to the city. Also in verse 26.

[d]**3:20–21** *He was very close ... throne* This section of the text is found in the ancient Greek version but not in the standard Hebrew text.

[e]**3:31** *Anath* The Canaanite goddess of war. Here, this might be Shamgar's father or mother, or it might mean "Shamgar the great soldier" or "Shamgar from the town of Anath."

you. I will make Sisera, his chariots, and his army come to the Kishon River.*a* I will help you defeat Sisera there.'"

[8]Then Barak said to Deborah, "I will go and do this if you will go with me. But if you will not go with me, I will not go."

[9]"Of course I will go with you," Deborah answered. "But because of your attitude, you will not be honored when Sisera is defeated. The LORD will allow a woman to defeat Sisera."

So Deborah went with Barak to the city of Kedesh. [10]At the city of Kedesh, Barak called the tribes of Zebulun and Naphtali together. He gathered 10,000 men to follow him from these tribes, and Deborah also went with him.

[11]There was a man named Heber who was from the Kenites. The Kenites were descendants of Moses' father-in-law,*b* Hobab. Heber had left the other Kenites and had made his home by the oak tree in Zaanannim, near the city of Kedesh.

[12]Someone told Sisera that Barak son of Abinoam was at Mount Tabor. [13]So Sisera gathered his 900 iron chariots and all the men with him, and they marched from the city of Harosheth Haggoyim to the Kishon River.

[14]Then Deborah said to Barak, "Today the LORD will help you defeat Sisera. Surely you know that the LORD has already cleared the way for you." So Barak led the 10,000 men down from Mount Tabor. [15]Barak and his men attacked Sisera. During the battle, the LORD confused Sisera and his army and chariots. They did not know what to do. Barak and his men defeated Sisera's army, but Sisera left his chariot and ran away on foot. [16]Barak continued fighting Sisera's army. He and his men chased Sisera's chariots and army all the way to Harosheth Haggoyim. They used their swords to kill all of Sisera's men. Not one of Sisera's men was left alive.

[17]But Sisera ran away to the tent where a woman named Jael lived. Jael was the wife of Heber the Kenite. His family was at peace with King Jabin of Hazor. That is why Sisera ran to Jael's tent. [18]Jael saw him coming, so she went out to meet him and said, "Sir, come into my tent. Come in. Don't be afraid." So Sisera went into Jael's tent, and she covered him with a blanket.

[19]But first, Sisera asked Jael for a drink of water. Jael had some milk in a bottle made from animal skin. So she gave him a drink of the milk and then covered him up.

[20]Then Sisera said to Jael, "Go stand at the entrance to the tent. If anyone comes by and asks you, 'Is anyone in there?' say, 'No.'"

[21]But Jael found a tent peg and a hammer. She quietly went to Sisera. Sisera was very tired, so he was sleeping. She put the tent peg to the side of Sisera's head and hit it with a hammer. The tent peg went through the side of his head and into the ground. Sisera died.

[22]Just then Barak came by Jael's tent, looking for Sisera. Jael went out to meet Barak and said, "Come in here, and I will show you the man you are looking for." So Barak entered the tent with Jael. There Barak found Sisera lying dead on the ground, with the tent peg through the side of his head.

[23]On that day God defeated King Jabin of Canaan for the Israelites. [24]So the Israelites became stronger and stronger until they defeated King Jabin of Canaan. The Israelites finally destroyed him.

The Song of Deborah

5 [1]*c* On the day that the Israelites defeated Sisera, Deborah and Barak son of Abinoam sang this song:

[2]"The men of Israel prepared for battle.*d*
 They volunteered to go to war.
 Praise the LORD!

[3]"Listen, kings.
 Pay attention, rulers.
 I will sing.
 I myself will sing to the LORD.
 I will make music to the LORD,
 to the God of the Israelites.

[4]"LORD, in the past you came from Seir.*e*
 You marched from the land of Edom.*
You marched and the earth shook.
 The skies rained.
 The clouds dropped water.
[5] The mountains shook before the LORD,
 the God of Mount Sinai,
 before the LORD, the God of Israel!

[6]"In the days of Shamgar son of Anath,*f*
 and in the days of Jael, the main roads
 were empty.
 Caravans* and travelers traveled on the
 back roads.

[7]"There were no soldiers in Israel
 until you came, Deborah,
 until you came to be a mother to Israel.*g*

---

*c***5:1** *Chapter 5* This is a very old song, and many of the lines are hard to understand in the Hebrew text.
*d***5:2** *The men ... battle* This might also mean "When leaders led in Israel" or "When men wore long hair in Israel." Soldiers often dedicated their hair as a special gift to God.
*e***5:4** *Seir* Another name for the land of Edom.
*f***5:6** *Shamgar son of Anath* A judge of Israel. See Judges 3:31.
*g***5:7** *until you ... to Israel* Or "until I came, Deborah, until I came, mother of Israel." Or "until I established you, Deborah, until I established you, mother of Israel."

---

*a***4:7** *Kishon River* A river about ten miles from Mount Tabor.
*b***4:11** *father-in-law* Or possibly, "son-in-law."

8"God chose new leaders
   to fight at the city gates.*a*
No one could find a shield or a spear
   among the 40,000 soldiers of Israel.

9"My heart is with the commanders of
      Israel.
   They volunteered to go to war.
   Praise the LORD!

10"Pay attention you people
      riding on white donkeys,
   sitting on saddle blankets,*b*
   and walking along the road.
11 At the watering holes for the animals,
      we hear the music of cymbals.
   People sing about the victories of the
      LORD,
      the victories of his soldiers in Israel
   when the LORD's people fought at the
      city gates and won!

12"Wake up, wake up, Deborah!
   Wake up, wake up, sing the song!
   Get up, Barak!
      Go capture your enemies, son of
         Abinoam!

13"Now, survivors, go to the leaders.
   People of the LORD, come with me and
      the soldiers.

14"The men of Ephraim came
      from the hill country of Amalek.*c*
   Benjamin, those men followed you
      and your people.
   And there were commanders
      from the family of Makir.*d*
   Leaders from the tribe of Zebulun
      came with their bronze clubs.
15 The leaders of Issachar were with
      Deborah.
   The family of Issachar was true to Barak.
   Those men marched to the valley on
      foot.

   "Reuben, there are many brave soldiers in
      your army groups.
16 So why did you sit there against the walls
      of your sheep pens?*e*
   The brave soldiers of Reuben thought
      hard about war.

But they stayed home listening to the
   music they played for their sheep.
17 The people of Gilead*f* stayed in their
      camps on the other side of the Jordan
      River.
   As for you, people of Dan,
      why did you stay by your ships?
   The people of Asher remained by the sea,
      camped near their safe harbors.

18"But the men of Zebulun and Naphtali
      risked their lives fighting on those
      hills.
19 The kings of Canaan* came to fight,
      but they didn't carry any treasures
      home.
   They fought at the city of Taanach, by the
      waters of Megiddo.
20 The stars fought them from heaven.
      From their paths across the sky, they
      fought against Sisera.
21 The Kishon River, that ancient river,
      swept Sisera's men away.
   My soul, march on with strength!*g*
22 The horses' hooves hammered the
      ground.
   Sisera's mighty horses ran and ran.

23"The angel of the LORD said,
   "Curse the city of Meroz.
      Curse its people!
   They did not come with soldiers to help
      the LORD."
24 Jael was the wife of Heber the Kenite.
   She will be blessed above all women.
25 Sisera asked for water.
   Jael gave him milk.
   In a bowl fit for a ruler,
      she brought him cream.
26 Then Jael reached out and took a tent peg.
   Her right hand reached for a workman's
      hammer.
   She put the peg against the side of Sisera's
      head
      and hit it with the hammer.
27 He sank down between Jael's feet.
   He fell, and there he lay.
   He sank down between her feet.
   He fell there.
   Where Sisera sank, he fell,
      and there he lay, dead!

28"There is Sisera's mother, looking out the
      window,
   looking through the curtains and crying.
   'Why is Sisera's chariot* so late?
   Why can't I hear his wagons?'

29"Her wisest servant girl answers her.
   Yes, the servant gives her an answer:

---

*a*5:8 *God chose ... gates* Or "They chose to follow new gods. So they had to fight at their city gates." The Hebrew text here is hard to understand.
*b*5:10 *saddle blankets* The meaning of this Hebrew word is uncertain.
*c*5:14 *hill country of Amalek* The area settled by the tribe of Ephraim. See Judges 12:15.
*d*5:14 *Makir* This family was part of the tribe of Manasseh that settled in the area east of the Jordan River.
*e*5:16 *walls of your sheep pens* Or "campfires" or "saddlebags."

*f*5:17 *Gilead* This area was east of the Jordan River.
*g*5:21 *My soul ... strength* Or with some changes it could be, "His mighty charging horses marched forward."

³⁰ 'I'm sure they won the war,
    and they are now taking things from the
        people they defeated.
They are dividing those things among
        themselves.
Each soldier is taking a girl or two.
Maybe Sisera found a piece of dyed cloth.
    That's it! Sisera found a piece of fancy
        cloth, or maybe two, to wear around
        his neck in victory.'

³¹"May all your enemies die like this, LORD!
    But may all those who love you be as
        strong as the rising sun!"

And there was peace in the land for 40
years.

The Midianites Fight Israel

6 ¹Again the Israelites did what the LORD
said was wrong. So for seven years the
LORD allowed the Midianites to defeat the
Israelites.

²The Midianites were very powerful and
were cruel to the Israelites. So the Israelites
made many hiding places in the mountains.
They hid their food in caves and places that
were hard to find. ³They did that because
the Midianites and Amalekites from the east
always came and destroyed their crops. ⁴They
camped in the land and destroyed the crops
that the Israelites had planted. They ruined
the crops of the Israelites as far as the land
near the city of Gaza. They did not leave
anything for the Israelites to eat. They did
not even leave them any sheep, cattle, or
donkeys. ⁵The Midianites came with their
families, animals, and tents. They were like
a swarm of locusts*! They and their camels
were too many to count. They came into the
land and ruined it. ⁶The Israelites became
very poor because of the Midianites. So the
Israelites cried to the LORD for help.

^{7 a} The Midianites did all these bad things,
so the Israelites cried to the LORD for help.
⁸The LORD sent a prophet to them. He said,
"This is what the LORD, the God of Israel, says:
'You were slaves in the land of Egypt. I made
you free and brought you out of that land. ⁹I
saved you from the powerful Egyptians. Then
the Canaanites hurt you, so I saved you again.
I made them leave their land. And I gave their
land to you.' ¹⁰Then I said to you, 'I am the
LORD your God. You will live in the land of
the Amorites, but you must not worship their
false gods.' But you did not obey me."

The Angel of the Lord Visits Gideon

¹¹⁻¹²At that time the angel of the LORD
came to a man named Gideon. The angel of

the LORD came and sat down under an oak
tree at a place called Ophrah. This oak tree
belonged to a man named Joash. Joash was
from the Abiezer family. He was the father of
Gideon. Gideon was beating some wheat^b in
a winepress.* He was hiding so that the Midianites could not see the wheat. The angel of
the LORD appeared to Gideon and sat down
next to him. The angel greeted him, saying,
"The LORD be with you, brave soldier."

¹³Then Gideon said, "Pardon me, sir, but
if the LORD is with us, why are we having so
many troubles? We heard that he did wonderful things for our ancestors.* They tell us
the LORD took them out of Egypt. But now it
seems he has left us and is letting the Midianites defeat us."

¹⁴The LORD turned toward Gideon and said,
"Then use your great power and go save the
Israelites from the Midianites. I am sending
you to save them."

¹⁵But Gideon answered and said, "Pardon
me, sir.^c How can I save Israel? My family
group is the weakest in the tribe of Manasseh,
and I am the youngest one in my family."

¹⁶The LORD answered Gideon and said,
"I will be with you, so you can defeat the
Midianites as easily as if they were only one
man."

¹⁷Then Gideon said to him, "If you would,
please give me some proof that you really are
the LORD. ¹⁸Please wait here. Don't go away
until I come back to you. Let me bring my
offering and set it down in front of you."

And the LORD said, "I will wait until you
come back."

¹⁹So Gideon went in and cooked a young
goat in boiling water. He also took about 20
pounds^d of flour and made bread without
yeast. Then he put the meat into a basket
and the broth from the meat into a pot. He
brought out the meat, the broth, and the
bread without yeast and gave them to the
LORD under the oak tree.

²⁰The angel of God said to Gideon, "Put the
meat and the bread on that rock over there.
Then pour the broth on it." Gideon did as he
was told.

²¹The angel of the LORD had a walking
stick in his hand. He touched the meat and
the bread with the end of the stick, and fire
jumped up out of the rock and burned up the
meat and the bread. Then the angel of the
LORD disappeared.

²²Then Gideon realized that he had been
talking to the angel of the LORD. So he shouted,
"Oh, Lord GOD! I have seen the angel of the
LORD face to face!"

---

^a**6:7-10** These verses do not appear in the oldest
Hebrew copy of the book of Judges, the Dead Sea
Scroll fragment, 4QJudgesA.

^b**6:11-12** *beating some wheat* That is, separating
the grains of wheat from the hulls. Usually this is
done near the top of a hill.
^c**6:15** *sir* Or "LORD," a title for God.
^d**6:19** *20 pounds* Literally, "1 ephah" (22 l).

[23]But the Lord said to Gideon, "Calm down![a] Don't be afraid! You will not die!"[b]

[24]So Gideon built an altar* there to worship the Lord and named it "The Lord is Peace." It still stands in the city of Ophrah, where the Abiezer family lives.

Gideon Tears Down the Altar of Baal

[25]That same night the Lord spoke to Gideon and said, "Take the full-grown bull that belongs to your father, the one that is seven years old. Your father has an altar* to the false god Baal.* Also beside the altar a wooden pole was made to honor the false goddess Asherah.* [26]Then build the right kind of altar for the Lord your God. Build it on this high ground. Then kill and burn the full-grown bull on the altar. Use the wood from the Asherah pole to burn your offering."

[27]So Gideon took ten of his servants and did what the Lord had told him to do. But Gideon was afraid that his family and the men of the city might see what he was doing, so he did what the Lord told him to do at night, not in the daytime.

[28]The men of the city got up the next morning and saw that the altar for Baal had been destroyed! They also saw that the Asherah pole* had been cut down. It had been sitting next to the altar for Baal. They also saw the altar* that Gideon had built. And they saw the bull that had been sacrificed on that altar.

[29]The men of the city looked at each other and asked, "Who pulled down our altar? Who cut down our Asherah pole? Who sacrificed this bull on this new altar?" They asked many questions and tried to learn who did this.

Someone told them, "Gideon son of Joash did this."

[30]So the men of the city came to Joash and said, "You must bring your son out. He pulled down the altar for Baal, and he cut down the Asherah pole that was beside it. So your son must die."

[31]Then Joash spoke to the crowd that was standing around him. Joash said, "Are you going to take Baal's side? Are you going to rescue Baal? If anyone takes Baal's side, let him be put to death by morning. If Baal really is a god, let him defend himself when someone pulls down his altar." [32]Joash said, "If Gideon pulled Baal's altar down, let Baal argue with him." On that day Joash gave Gideon a new name. He called him Jerub Baal.[c]

Gideon Defeats the Midianites

[33]The Midianites, Amalekites, and other people from the east joined together to fight against the Israelites. They went across the Jordan River and camped in the Jezreel Valley. [34]The Spirit of the Lord filled Gideon. So Gideon blew a trumpet to call the family of Abiezer to follow him. [35]He sent messengers to all the people of the tribe of Manasseh and told them to get their weapons and prepare for battle. Gideon also sent messengers to the tribes of Asher, Zebulun, and Naphtali. The messengers took the same message to them. So they also went up to meet Gideon and his men.

[36]Then Gideon said to God, "You said that you would help me save the Israelites. Give me proof. [37]I will put a sheepskin on the threshing* floor. If there is dew only on the sheepskin, while all the ground is dry, I will know that you will use me to save Israel, as you said."

[38]And that is exactly what happened. Gideon got up early the next morning and squeezed the sheepskin. He was able to drain a bowl full of water from it.

[39]Then Gideon said to God, "Don't be angry with me. Let me ask just one more thing. Let me test you one more time with the sheepskin. This time let the sheepskin be dry, while the ground around it gets wet with dew."

[40]That night God did that very thing. Just the sheepskin was dry, but the ground around it was wet with dew.

7 [1]Early in the morning Jerub Baal (Gideon) and all his men set up their camp at the spring of Harod. The Midianites were camped in the valley at the bottom of the hill called Moreh, north of Gideon and his men.

[2]Then the Lord said to Gideon, "I am going to help your men defeat the Midianites, but you have too many men. I don't want the Israelites to forget me and brag that they saved themselves. [3]So make an announcement to your men. Tell them, 'Anyone who is afraid may leave Mount Gilead and go back home.'"

At that time 22,000 men left Gideon and went back home, but 10,000 still remained.

[4]Then the Lord said to Gideon, "There are still too many men. Take the men down to the water, and I will test them for you there. If I say, 'This man will go with you,' he will go. But if I say, 'That one will not go with you,' then he will not go."

[5]So Gideon led the men down to the water. There the Lord said to him, "Separate the men like this: Those who drink the water by using their tongue to lap it up like a dog will be in one group. And those who bend down to drink will be in the other group."

[6]There were 300 men who used their hands to bring water to their mouth and lapped it like a dog does. All the other people bent down and drank the water. [7]The Lord said to Gideon, "I will use the 300 men who lapped the water like a dog. I will use them

---

[a]6:23 *Calm down* Literally, "Peace."

[b]6:23 *You will not die* Gideon thought he would die because he had seen the Lord face to face.

[c]6:32 *Jerub Baal* This is like the Hebrew words meaning "Let Baal argue." The same verb is translated "take one's side" and "defend" in verse 31.

to save you, and I will allow you to defeat the Midianites. Let the other men go home."

8So Gideon sent the other men of Israel home. He kept the 300 men with him. Those 300 men kept the supplies and the trumpets of the other men who went home.

The Midianites were camped in the valley below Gideon's camp. 9During the night the LORD spoke to Gideon and said, "Get up. I will let you defeat the Midianite army. Go down to their camp. 10If you are afraid to go alone, take your servant Purah with you. Go into the camp of the Midianites. 11Listen to what they are saying. After that you will not be afraid to attack them."

So Gideon and his servant Purah went down to the edge of the enemy camp. 12The Midianites, the Amalekites, and all the other people from the east were camped in that valley. There were so many people that they seemed like a swarm of locusts.* It seemed like they had as many camels as there are grains of sand on the seashore.

13Gideon came to the enemy camp, and he heard a man talking. That man was telling his friend about a dream that he had. He was saying, "I dreamed that a round loaf of bread came rolling into the camp of the Midianites. That loaf of bread hit the tent so hard that the tent turned over and fell flat."

14The man's friend knew the meaning of the dream. He said, "Your dream can only have one meaning. Your dream is about that man from Israel. It is about Gideon son of Joash. It means that God will let Gideon defeat the whole army of Midian."

15After he heard the men talking about the dream and what it meant, Gideon bowed down to God. Then Gideon went back to the camp of the Israelites and called out to the people, "Get up! The LORD will help us defeat the Midianites." 16Then Gideon divided the 300 men into three groups. He gave each man a trumpet and an empty jar with a burning torch inside it. 17Then Gideon told the men, "Watch me and do what I do. Follow me to the edge of the enemy camp. When I get to the edge of the camp, do exactly what I do. 18You men surround the enemy camp. I and all the men with me will blow our trumpets. When we blow our trumpets, you blow your trumpets too. Then shout these words: 'For the LORD and for Gideon!'"

19So Gideon and the 100 men with him went to the edge of the enemy camp. They came there just after the enemy changed guards. It was during the middle watch of the night. Gideon and his men blew their trumpets and smashed their jars. 20Then all three groups of Gideon's men blew their trumpets and smashed their jars. The men held the torches in their left hands and the trumpets in their right hands. As they blew their trumpets, they shouted, "A sword for the LORD and a sword for Gideon!"

21Gideon's men stayed where they were. But inside the camp, the men of Midian began shouting and running away. 22When Gideon's 300 men blew their trumpets, the LORD caused the men of Midian to kill each other with their swords. The enemy army ran away to the city of Beth Shittah, which is toward the city of Zererah. They ran as far as the border of the city of Abel Meholah, which is near the city of Tabbath.

23Then soldiers from the tribes of Naphtali, Asher, and all of Manasseh were told to chase the Midianites. 24Gideon sent messengers through all the hill country of Ephraim. The messengers said, "Come down and attack the Midianites. Take control of the river as far as Beth Barah and the Jordan River. Do this before the Midianites get there."

So they called all men from the tribe of Ephraim. They took control of the river as far as Beth Barah. 25The men of Ephraim caught two of the Midianite leaders named Oreb and Zeeb. They killed Oreb at a place named the Rock of Oreb and Zeeb at a place named the Winepress of Zeeb. They continued chasing the Midianites, but first they cut off the heads of Oreb and Zeeb and took the heads to Gideon. Gideon was at the place where people cross the Jordan River.

8 1The men of Ephraim were angry with Gideon. When they found him, they asked, "Why did you treat us this way? Why didn't you call us when you went to fight against the Midianites?"

2But Gideon answered the men of Ephraim, "I have not done as well as you. You people of Ephraim have a much better harvest than my family, the Abiezers. At harvest time you leave more grapes in the vineyard* than my family gathers! Isn't that true? 3In the same way you have a better harvest now. God allowed you to capture Oreb and Zeeb, the leaders of Midian. How can I compare my success with what you did?" When the men of Ephraim heard Gideon's answer, they were not as angry as they had been.

Gideon Captures Two Kings of Midian

4Then Gideon and his 300 men came to the Jordan River and went across to the other side, but they were tired and hungry.a 5Gideon said to the men of the city of Succoth, "Give my soldiers something to eat. They are very tired. We are still chasing Zebah and Zalmunna, kings of Midian."

6But the leaders of the city of Succoth said to Gideon, "Why should we give your soldiers something to eat? You haven't caught Zebah and Zalmunna yet."

7Then Gideon said, "The LORD will help me capture Zebah and Zalmunna. And since you

a8:4 *hungry* This is from the ancient Greek version. The standard Hebrew text has "chasing."

would not give us any food, I will come back and beat you with thorns and briers from the desert."

⁸Gideon left the city of Succoth and went to the city of Penuel. He asked the men of Penuel for food, just as he had asked the men of Succoth. But the men of Penuel gave Gideon the same answer that the men of Succoth had given. ⁹So Gideon said to the men of Penuel, "After I win the victory, I will come back here and pull this tower down."

¹⁰Zebah and Zalmunna and their army were in the city of Karkor. Their army had 15,000 soldiers in it. These soldiers were all who were left of the army of the people of the east. 120,000 strong soldiers of that army had already been killed. ¹¹Gideon and his men used Tent Dwellers' Road, which is east of the cities of Nobah and Jogbehah and attacked the enemy at Karkor. The enemy army did not expect the attack. ¹²Zebah and Zalmunna, kings of the Midianites, ran away. But Gideon chased and caught them. Gideon and his men defeated the enemy army.

¹³Then Gideon son of Joash returned from the battle. He and his men returned by going through a mountain pass called the Pass of Heres. ¹⁴Gideon captured a young man from the city of Succoth. He asked the young man some questions. The young man wrote down some names for Gideon. The young man wrote down the names of the leaders and elders of the city of Succoth. He gave Gideon the names of 77 men.

¹⁵When Gideon came to the city of Succoth, he said to the men of that city, "Here are Zebah and Zalmunna. You made fun of me by saying, 'Why should we give food to your tired soldiers? You have not caught Zebah and Zalmunna yet.'" ¹⁶Gideon took the elders of the city of Succoth and beat them with thorns and briers from the desert to punish them. ¹⁷Gideon also pulled down the tower in the city of Penuel and killed the men living in that city.

¹⁸Then Gideon said to Zebah and Zalmunna, "You killed some men on Mount Tabor. What were the men like?"

Zebah and Zalmunna answered, "They were like you. Each one of them seemed like a prince."

¹⁹Gideon said, "Those men were my brothers, my mother's sons! As the LORD lives, if you had not killed them, I would not kill you now."

²⁰Then Gideon turned to Jether, his oldest son, and said, "Kill these kings." But Jether was only a boy and was afraid, so he would not take out his sword.

²¹Then Zebah and Zalmunna said to Gideon, "Come on, kill us yourself. You are a man and strong enough to do the job." So Gideon got up and killed Zebah and Zalmunna. Then Gideon took the decorations shaped like the moon off their camels' necks.

Gideon Makes an Ephod

²²The Israelites said to Gideon, "You saved us from the Midianites. So now rule over us. We want you, your son, and your grandson to rule over us."

²³But Gideon told the Israelites, "The LORD will be your ruler. I will not rule over you, and my son will not rule over you."

²⁴Some of the people who the men of Israel defeated were Ishmaelites. And the Ishmaelite men wore gold earrings. So Gideon said to the Israelites, "I want you to do this one thing for me. I want each of you to give me a gold earring from the things you took in the battle."

²⁵The Israelites said to Gideon, "We will gladly give you what you want." So they put a coat down on the ground, and each man threw an earring onto the coat. ²⁶When the earrings were gathered up, they weighed about 43 pounds.ᵃ This did not include the other gifts the Israelites gave to Gideon. They also gave him jewelry shaped like the moon and jewelry shaped like teardrops. And they gave him purple robes. The kings of the Midianites had worn these things. They also gave him the chains from the camels of the Midianite kings.

²⁷Gideon used the gold to make an ephod,ᵇ which he put in his hometown, the town called Ophrah. All the Israelites worshiped the ephod. In this way the Israelites were not faithful to God—they worshiped the ephod.ᶜ The ephod became a trap that caused Gideon and his family to sin.

The Death of Gideon

²⁸The Midianites were forced to be under the rule of the Israelites. The Midianites did not cause trouble anymore. And the land was at peace for 40 years, as long as Gideon was alive.

²⁹Jerub Baal *(Gideon)* son of Joash went home. ³⁰Gideon had 70 sons of his own. He had so many sons because he had many wives. ³¹He had a slave woman* who lived in the city of Shechem. He had a son by her. He named that son Abimelech.

³²So Gideon son of Joash died at a good old age. He was buried in the tomb that Joash, his father, owned. That tomb is in the city of Ophrah, where the family of Abiezer lives. ³³As soon as Gideon died, the Israelites again were not faithful to God—they followed Baal.ᵈ They made Baal Berithᵉ their god.

ᵃ8:26 *43 pounds* Literally, "1700 shekels" (19.55 kg).
ᵇ8:27 *ephod* This may have been a special vest or coat like that worn by the high priest (see Ex. 28:2–14), or it may have been a kind of idol.
ᶜ8:27 *were not faithful ... ephod* Literally, "acted like a prostitute to it."
ᵈ8:33 *were not faithful ... Baal* Literally, "they acted like a prostitute to Baal."
ᵉ8:33 *Baal Berith* A name that means "Lord of the Agreement." It shows that the people were

34The Israelites did not remember the Lord their God, who had saved them from all their enemies living around them. 35The Israelites were not loyal to the family of Jerub Baal, even though he had done many good things for them.

Abimelech Becomes King

9 1Abimelech was the son of Jerub Baal *(Gideon)*. Abimelech went to his uncles who lived in the city of Shechem. He said to his uncles and all of his mother's family, 2"Ask the leaders of the city of Shechem this question: 'Is it better for you to be ruled by the 70 sons of Jerub Baal or to be ruled by only one man? Remember, I am your relative.'"

3Abimelech's uncles spoke to the leaders of Shechem and asked them that question. The leaders of Shechem decided to follow Abimelech. They said, "After all, he is our brother." 4So the leaders of Shechem gave Abimelech 70 pieces of silver. That silver was from the temple of the god Baal Berith. Abimelech used the silver to hire some men. These men were worthless, reckless men. They followed Abimelech wherever he went.

5Abimelech went to his father's house at Ophrah and murdered his brothers. He killed the 70 sons of his father, Jerub Baal. He killed them all at the same time,*a* but Jerub Baal's youngest son hid from Abimelech and escaped. The youngest son's name was Jotham.

6Then all the leaders in Shechem and the house of Millo*b* came together. Everyone gathered beside the big tree of the pillar in Shechem and made Abimelech their king.

Jotham's Story

7Jotham heard that the leaders of the city of Shechem had made Abimelech king. When he heard this, he went and stood on the top of Mount Gerizim*c* and shouted out this story to the people:

"Listen to me you leaders of the city of Shechem. Then let God listen to you.
8"One day the trees decided to choose a king to rule over them. The trees said to the olive tree, 'You be king over us.'
9"But the olive tree said, 'My oil is used to honor gods and humans. Should I stop making my oil just to go and sway over the other trees?'

10"Then the trees said to the fig tree, 'Come and be our king.'
11"But the fig tree answered, 'Should I stop making my good, sweet fruit just to go and sway over the other trees?'
12"Then the trees said to the vine, 'Come and be our king.'
13"But the vine answered, 'My wine makes men and kings happy. Should I stop making my wine just to go and sway over the trees?'
14"Finally all the trees said to the thornbush, 'Come and be our king.'
15"But the thornbush said to the trees, 'If you really want to make me king over you, come and find shelter in my shade. But if you don't want to do this, let fire come out of the thornbush. Let the fire burn even the cedar trees of Lebanon.'

16"Now if you were completely honest when you made Abimelech king, may you be happy with him. And if you have been fair to Jerub Baal *(Gideon)* and his family, and if you have treated him as you should, this is also good. 17But remember what my father did for you. He fought for you and risked his life when he saved you from the Midianites. 18But now you have turned against my father's family. You have killed 70 of his sons all at the same time. You made Abimelech the new king over the city of Shechem. He is only the son of my father's slave girl. But you made him king because he is your relative. 19So if you have been completely honest to Jerub Baal and his family today, then may you be happy with Abimelech as your king. And may he be happy with you. 20But leaders of Shechem and the house of Millo,*d* if you have not acted right, may Abimelech destroy you. And may Abimelech be destroyed too!"

21After Jotham had said this, he ran away and escaped to the city named Beer. He stayed there because he was afraid of his brother Abimelech.

Abimelech Fights Against Shechem

22Abimelech ruled the Israelites for three years. 23-24Abimelech had killed Jerub Baal's *(Gideon)* 70 sons—and they were his own brothers. The leaders of Shechem had supported him in doing this evil thing. So God caused trouble between Abimelech and the leaders of Shechem. And they began planning ways to hurt Abimelech. 25The leaders of the city of Shechem did not like Abimelech anymore. They put men on the hilltops to attack and rob everyone who went by. Abimelech found out about the attacks.

26A man named Gaal son of Ebed and his brothers moved to the city of Shechem. The leaders of the city of Shechem decided to trust and follow Gaal.

confusing the worship of the true God with the worship of local idols. Also in 9:4.
*a*9:5 *all at the same time* Literally, "on one stone." Also in verse 18.
*b*9:6 *Millo* This was probably a well-protected part of the city, perhaps even the palace area. It might have been in the city itself or somewhere near the city.
*c*9:7 *Mount Gerizim* This mountain is right beside the city of Shechem.

*d*9:20 *house of Millo* Or "Royal Family of Millo."

27One day the people of Shechem went out to the vineyards* to pick grapes. They squeezed the grapes to make wine. And then they had a party at the temple of their god. The people ate and drank and cursed* Abimelech.

28Then Gaal son of Ebed said, "We are the men of Shechem. Why should we obey Abimelech? Who does he think he is? Abimelech is one of Jerub Baal's sons, right? And Abimelech made Zebul his officer, right? We should not obey Abimelech. We should follow our own people, men from Hamor.*ᵃ (Hamor was the father of Shechem.) 29If you make me the commander of these people, I will destroy Abimelech. I will say to him, 'Get your army ready and come out to battle.'"

30Zebul was the governor of the city of Shechem. Zebul heard what Gaal son of Ebed said, and he became very angry. 31Zebul sent messengers to Abimelech in the city of Arumah.ᵇ This is the message:

"Gaal son of Ebed and Gaal's brothers have come to the city of Shechem. They are making trouble for you. Gaal is turning the whole city against you. 32So now you and your men should come tonight and hide in the fields outside the city. 33When the sun comes up in the morning, attack the city. Gaal and his men will come out of the city to fight you. When they come out to fight, do what you can to them."

34So Abimelech and all his soldiers got up during the night and went to the city. The soldiers separated into four groups. They hid near the city of Shechem. 35Gaal son of Ebed went out and was standing at the entrance to the gate of the city of Shechem. While Gaal was standing there, Abimelech and his soldiers came out of their hiding places.

36When Gaal saw the soldiers, he said to Zebul, "Look, there are people coming down from the mountains."

But Zebul said, "You are only seeing the shadows of the mountains. The shadows just look like people."

37But again Gaal said, "Look, there are some people coming down from that place over there by Land's Navel. And there! I saw someone's head over by Magician's Tree.ᶜ"

38Zebul said to Gaal, "Why aren't you bragging now? You said, 'Who is Abimelech? Why should we obey him?' You made fun of these

men. Now go out and fight them."

39So Gaal led the leaders of Shechem out to fight Abimelech. 40Abimelech and his men chased Gaal and his men. Gaal's men ran back toward the gate of the city of Shechem, but many were killed before they could get back to the gate.

41Then Abimelech returned to the city of Arumah. Zebul forced Gaal and his brothers to leave the city of Shechem.

42The next day the people of Shechem went out to the fields to work. Abimelech found out about it. 43So Abimelech separated his men into three groups. He wanted to attack the people of Shechem by surprise. So he hid his men in the fields. When he saw the people coming out of the city, he jumped up and attacked them. 44Abimelech and his group ran to a place near the gate to Shechem. The other two groups ran out to the people in the fields and killed them. 45Abimelech and his men fought against the city of Shechem all that day. They captured the city of Shechem and killed its people. Then Abimelech tore down the city and threw salt over the ruins.

46There were some people who lived at the Tower of Shechem.ᵈ When they heard what had happened to Shechem, they gathered together in the safest roomᵉ of the temple of the god El Berith.ᶠ

47Abimelech heard that all the leaders of the Tower of Shechem had gathered together. 48So Abimelech and all his men went up to Mount Zalmon.ᵍ Abimelech took an ax and cut off some branches and carried them on his shoulders. Then Abimelech said to the men with him, "Hurry! Do the same thing that I have done." 49So all the men cut branches and followed Abimelech. They piled the branches against the safest room of the temple of the god El Berith. Then they set the branches on fire and burned the people in the room. About 1000 men and women living near the Tower of Shechem died.

Abimelech's Death

50Then Abimelech and his men went to the city of Thebez and captured that city. 51But inside the city there was a strong tower, so all the leaders and other men and women of that city ran to the tower. When the people were inside the tower, they locked the door behind them. Then they climbed up to the roof of the tower. 52Abimelech and his men came to the tower to attack it. Abimelech went up to the door of the tower to burn

ᵃ9:28 men from Hamor This refers to native born citizens of Shechem. Hamor was the father of Shechem in a story in Gen. 34. The city of Shechem is said to have been named after Hamor's son.
ᵇ9:31 in the city of Arumah Or "secretly" or "in Tormah," the town where Abimelech lived as king. It was probably about eight miles south of Shechem.
ᶜ9:37 Land's Navel … Magician's Tree Two places in the hills near Shechem.

ᵈ9:46 Tower of Shechem This was probably a place near Shechem but not actually part of the city.
ᵉ9:46 safest room The meaning of this Hebrew word is uncertain. Also in verse 49.
ᶠ9:46 El Berith Another name for the god Baal Berith mentioned in verses 4 and 8:33. The name here means "God of the Agreement." Also in verse 49.
ᵍ9:48 Mount Zalmon This is probably another name for Mount Ebal, a mountain near Shechem.

it. [53]But, while Abimelech was standing at the door of the tower, a woman on the roof dropped a grinding stone on his head. The grinding stone crushed his skull. [54]Abimelech quickly said to the servant who carried his weapons, "Take out your sword and kill me. I want you to kill me so that people will not say, 'A woman killed Abimelech.'" So the servant stabbed Abimelech with his sword, and he died. [55]The Israelites saw that Abimelech was dead, so they all went back home.

[56]In that way God punished Abimelech for all the bad things he had done. Abimelech sinned against his own father by killing his 70 brothers. [57]God also punished the men of the city of Shechem for the bad things they had done. So the things said by Jotham son of Jerub Baal *(Gideon)* came true.

Tola, the Judge

10 [1]After Abimelech died, God sent another judge to save the Israelites. His name was Tola. He was the son of Puah, who was the son of Dodo. Tola was from the tribe of Issachar and lived in the city of Shamir, in the hill country of Ephraim. [2]Tola was a judge for the Israelites for 23 years. Then he died and was buried in the city of Shamir.

Jair, the Judge

[3]After Tola died, God sent another judge. His name was Jair, and he lived in the area of Gilead. He was a judge for the Israelites for 22 years. [4]Jair had 30 sons who rode 30 donkeys.[a] These 30 sons controlled 30 towns in the area of Gilead. These towns are called the Towns of Jair to this very day. [5]Jair died and was buried in the city of Kamon.

The Ammonites Fight Against Israel

[6]Again the Israelites did what the Lord said was wrong. They began worshiping the false gods Baal* and the Ashtoreth.* They also worshiped the gods of the people of Aram, the gods of the people of Sidon, the gods of the Moabites, the gods of the Ammonites, and the gods of the Philistines. The Israelites left the Lord and stopped serving him.

[7]So the Lord became angry with the Israelites and allowed the Philistines and the Ammonites to defeat them. [8]In that same year those people destroyed the Israelites who lived on the east side of the Jordan River, in the area of Gilead. That is the land where the Amorites had lived. The Israelites suffered for 18 years. [9]The Ammonites then went across the Jordan River to fight against the people of Judah, Benjamin, and Ephraim. The Ammonites brought many troubles to the Israelites.

[10]So the Israelites cried to the Lord for help. They said, "God, we have sinned against you. We left our God and worshiped the false god Baal."

[11]The Lord answered the Israelites, "You cried to me when the Egyptians, the Amorites, the Ammonites, and the Philistines hurt you. I saved you from these people. [12]You cried to me when the people of Sidon, the Amalekites, and the Midianites[b] hurt you. I also saved you from those people. [13]But you left me and started worshiping other gods, so I refuse to save you again. [14]You like worshiping those gods, so go call to them for help. Let them save you when you are in trouble."

[15]But the Israelites said to the Lord, "We have sinned. Do whatever you want to do to us, but please save us today." [16]Then the Israelites threw away the foreign gods and began to worship the Lord again. So he felt sorry for them when he saw them suffering.

Jephthah Is Chosen as a Leader

[17]The Ammonites gathered together for war. Their camp was in the area of Gilead. The Israelites gathered together. Their camp was at the city of Mizpah. [18]The leaders of the people living in the area of Gilead said, "Whoever leads us in the attack against the Ammonites will become the head of all the people living in Gilead."

11 [1]Jephthah was from the tribe of Gilead. He was a strong soldier. But Jephthah was the son of a prostitute. His father was a man named Gilead. [2]Gilead's wife had several sons. When they grew up, they did not like Jephthah. They forced Jephthah to leave his hometown. They said to him, "You will not get any of our father's property, because you are the son of another woman." [3]So Jephthah went away because of his brothers and lived in the land of Tob. In the land of Tob, some rough men began to follow Jephthah.

[4]After a time the Ammonites fought with the Israelites. [5]The Ammonites were fighting against Israel, so the elders* in Gilead went to Jephthah. They wanted Jephthah to leave the land of Tob and come back to Gilead. [6]The elders said to Jephthah, "Come and be our leader so that we can fight the Ammonites."

[7]But Jephthah said to the elders of the land of Gilead, "You forced me to leave my father's house. You hate me. So why are you coming to me now that you are having trouble?"

[8]The elders from Gilead said to Jephthah, "That is the reason we have come to you now. Please come with us and fight against the Ammonites. You will be the commander over all the people living in Gilead."

[9]Then Jephthah said to the elders from Gilead, "If you want me to come back to Gilead and fight the Ammonites, I will do it. But if

---

[a] **10:4** *30 sons who rode 30 donkeys* This showed that these men were important leaders, possibly the mayors of the 30 towns in Gilead.

[b] **10:12** *Midianites* This is from the ancient Greek version. The standard Hebrew text has "The Maonites."

the LORD helps me win, I will be your new leader."

¹⁰The elders from Gilead said to Jephthah, "The LORD is listening to everything we are saying. And we promise to do everything you tell us to do."

¹¹So Jephthah went with the elders from Gilead, and the people made him their leader and commander. Jephthah repeated all of his words in front of the LORD at the city of Mizpah.

Jephthah Warns the King of Ammon

¹²Jephthah sent messengers to the king of the Ammonites with this message: "What is the problem between the Ammonites and the Israelites? Why have you come to fight in our land?"

¹³The king of the Ammonites said to the messengers of Jephthah, "We are fighting Israel because the Israelites took our land when they came up from Egypt. They took our land from the Arnon River to the Jabbok River to the Jordan River. Now, tell the Israelites to give our land back to us without fighting for it."

¹⁴So the messengers of Jephthah took this message back to Jephthah.ᵃ Then Jephthah sent the messengers to the king of the Ammonites again. ¹⁵They took this message:

"This is what Jephthah says: Israel did not take the land of the Moabites or the land of the Ammonites. ¹⁶When the Israelites came out of the land of Egypt, they went into the desert. They went to the Red Sea. Then they went to Kadesh. ¹⁷The Israelites sent messengers to the king of Edom. The messengers asked for a favor. They said, 'Let the Israelites cross through your land.' But the king of Edom didn't let us go through his land. We also sent the same message to the king of Moab. But the king of Moab would not let us go through his land either. So the Israelites stayed at Kadesh.

¹⁸"Then the Israelites went through the desert and around the edges of the land of Edom and the land of Moab. They traveled east of the land of Moab. They made their camp on the other side of the Arnon River. They did not cross the border of the land of Moab. (The Arnon River was the border of the land of Moab.)

¹⁹"Then the Israelites sent messengers to King Sihon of the Amorites. Sihon was the king of the city of Heshbon. The messengers asked Sihon, 'Let the Israelites pass through your land. We want to go to our land.' ²⁰But King Sihon of the Amorites would not let the Israelites cross his

borders. So Sihon gathered all of his people and made a camp at Jahaz. Then the Amorites fought with the Israelites. ²¹But the LORD, the God of Israel, helped the Israelites defeat Sihon and his army. So the land of the Amorites became the property of the Israelites. ²²The Israelites got all the land of the Amorites from the Arnon River to the Jabbok River. The land also went from the desert to the Jordan River.

²³"It was the LORD, the God of Israel, who forced the Amorites to leave their land. And he gave the land to the Israelites. Do you think you can make the Israelites leave this land? ²⁴Surely you can live in the land that your god Chemosh* has given to you. So we will live in the land that the LORD our God has given to us. ²⁵Are you any better than Balak son of Zipporᵇ? He was the king of the land of Moab. Did he argue with the Israelites? Did he actually fight with the Israelites? ²⁶The Israelites have lived in the city of Heshbon and the towns around it for 300 years. They have lived in the city of Aroer and the towns around it for 300 years. They have lived in all the cities along the side of the Arnon River for 300 years. Why have you not tried to take these cities in all that time? ²⁷The Israelites have not sinned against you. But you are doing a very bad thing against them. May the LORD, the true Judge, decide whether the Israelites or the Ammonites are right."

²⁸The king of the Ammonites refused to listen to this message from Jephthah.

Jephthah's Promise

²⁹Then the Spirit of the LORD came on Jephthah, and he passed through the area of Gilead and Manasseh. He went through the city of Mizpah in Gilead on his way to the land of the Ammonites.

³⁰Jephthah made a promise to the LORD. He said, "If you will let me defeat the Ammonites, ³¹I will give you the first thing that comes out of my house when I come back from the victory. I will give it to the LORD as a burnt offering.*"

³²Then Jephthah went to the land of the Ammonites. He fought the Ammonites, and the LORD helped him defeat them. ³³He defeated them from the city of Aroer to the city of Minnith. Jephthah captured 20 cities. Then he fought the Ammonites to the city of Abel Keramim. The Israelites defeated them. It was a very great defeat for the Ammonites.

³⁴Jephthah went back to Mizpah. He went to his house, and his daughter came out to

---

ᵃ11:14 *So the messengers ... Jephthah* This is from the ancient Greek version.

ᵇ11:25 *Balak son of Zippor* See Num. 22–24 for his story.

meet him. She was playing a tambourine and dancing. She was his only daughter, and Jephthah loved her very much. He did not have any other sons or daughters. ³⁵When Jephthah saw that his daughter was the first thing to come out of his house, he tore his clothes to show his sadness. Then he said, "Oh, my daughter! You have ruined me! You have made me very sad! I made a promise to the LORD, and I cannot change it!"

³⁶Then his daughter said to Jephthah, "Father, you have made a promise to the LORD, so keep your promise. Do what you said you would do. After all, the LORD did help you defeat your enemies, the Ammonites."

³⁷Then Jephthah's daughter said to her father, "But do this one thing for me first. Let me be alone for two months. Let me go to the mountains. I will not marry and have children, so let me and my friends go and cry together."

³⁸Jephthah said, "Go." He sent her away for two months. Jephthah's daughter and her friends stayed in the mountains. They cried for her because she would not marry and have children.

³⁹At the end of two months, Jephthah's daughter returned to her father, and Jephthah did what he promised to the LORD. His daughter never had sexual relations with anyone. So this became a custom in Israel. ⁴⁰Every year the young women of Israel would go out for four days to remember the daughter of Jephthah from Gilead and to cry for her.

Jephthah and Ephraim

12 ¹The men from the tribe of Ephraim called all their soldiers together. Then they went across the river to the city of Zaphon. They said to Jephthah, "Why didn't you call us to help you fight the Ammonites? We will burn your house down with you in it."

²Jephthah answered them, "The Ammonites have been giving us many problems. So my people and I fought against them. I called you, but you didn't come to help us. ³I saw that you would not help us, so I risked my own life. I went across the river to fight against the Ammonites. The LORD helped me defeat them. Now why have you come to fight against me today?"

⁴Then Jephthah called the men of Gilead together. They fought against the men from the tribe of Ephraim because they had insulted the men of Gilead. They had said, "You men of Gilead are nothing but survivors* of the men of Ephraim. Part of you belongs to Ephraim, and part of you belongs to Manasseh." The men of Gilead defeated the men of Ephraim.

⁵The men of Gilead captured the places where people cross the Jordan River. Those places led to the country of Ephraim. Any time a survivor from Ephraim came to the river and said, "Let me cross," the men of Gilead

would ask him, "Are you from Ephraim?" If he said, "No," ⁶they would say, "Say the word 'Shibboleth.'" The men of Ephraim could not say that word correctly. They pronounced the word "Sibboleth." So if the man said, "Sibboleth," then the men of Gilead knew he was from Ephraim. So they would kill him at the crossing place. They killed 42,000 men from Ephraim.

⁷Jephthah was a judge for the Israelites for six years. Then Jephthah from Gilead died and was buried in his town in Gilead.

Ibzan, the Judge

⁸After Jephthah, a man named Ibzan was a judge for the Israelites. Ibzan was from the city of Bethlehem. ⁹Ibzan had 30 sons and 30 daughters. He told his 30 daughters to marry men who were not his relatives. And he found 30 women who were not his relatives, and his sons married these women. Ibzan was a judge for the Israelites for seven years. ¹⁰Then Ibzan died and was buried in the city of Bethlehem.

Elon, the Judge

¹¹After Ibzan, a man named Elon was a judge for the Israelites. Elon was from the tribe of Zebulun. He was a judge for the Israelites for ten years. ¹²Then Elon from the tribe of Zebulun died and was buried in the city of Aijalon in the land of Zebulun.

Abdon, the Judge

¹³After Elon died, a man named Abdon son of Hillel was a judge for the Israelites. Abdon was from the city of Pirathon. ¹⁴Abdon had 40 sons and 30 grandsons. They rode on 70 donkeys.ᵃ Abdon was a judge for the Israelites for eight years. ¹⁵Then Abdon son of Hillel died and was buried in the city of Pirathon. Pirathon is in the land of Ephraim in the hill country where the Amalekites lived.

The Birth of Samson

13 ¹Again the people started doing what the LORD said was wrong. So the LORD allowed the Philistines to rule over them for 40 years.

²There was a man named Manoah from the city of Zorah. He was from the tribe of Dan. Manoah had a wife, but she was not able to have any children. ³The angel of the LORD appeared to Manoah's wife and said, "You have not been able to have children. But you will become pregnant and have a son. ⁴Don't drink any wine or any other strong drink. Don't eat any food that is unclean,* ⁵because you are pregnant, and you will have a son. He will be dedicated* to God in a special way. He will be a Nazirite.* So you must never cut

---

ᵃ**12:14 They rode on 70 donkeys** This showed that they were important leaders, possibly mayors of their towns.

his hair. He will be God's special person from before he is born. He will save the Israelites from the power of the Philistines.

6Then the woman went to her husband and told him what had happened. She said, "A man of God* came to me. He looked like an angel of God. He frightened me. I didn't ask him where he was from, and he didn't tell me his name. 7But he said to me, 'You are pregnant and will have a son. Don't drink any wine or other strong drink. Don't eat any food that is unclean, because the boy will be dedicated to God in a special way. The boy will be God's special person from before he is born until the day he dies.'"

8Then Manoah prayed to the LORD. He said, "Lord, I beg you to send the man of God to us again. We want him to teach us what we should do for the boy who will soon be born."

9God heard Manoah's prayer. The angel of God came to the woman again. She was sitting in a field and her husband Manoah was not with her. 10So the woman ran to tell her husband, "The man is back! The man who came to me the other day is here."

11Manoah got up and followed his wife. When he came to the man, he said, "Are you the same man who spoke to my wife before?"

The angel said, "I am."

12So Manoah said, "May what you say happen. Tell me, what kind of life will the boy live? What will he do?"

13The angel of the LORD said to Manoah, "Your wife must do everything I told her. 14She must not eat anything that grows on a grapevine. She must not drink any wine or strong drink. She must not eat any food that is unclean. She must do everything that I have commanded her to do."

15Then Manoah said to the angel of the LORD, "We would like for you to stay a while. We want to cook a young goat for you to eat."

16The angel of the LORD said to Manoah, "Even if you keep me from leaving, I will not eat your food. But if you want to prepare something, offer a burnt offering* to the LORD." (Manoah did not understand that the man was really the angel of the LORD.)

17Then Manoah asked the angel of the LORD, "What is your name? We want to know so that we can honor you when what you have said really happens."

18The angel of the LORD said, "Why do you ask my name? It is too amazing for you to believe.a"

19Then Manoah sacrificed a young goat on a rock. He offered the goat and a grain offering as a gift to the LORD and to the One Who Does Amazing Things.b 20Manoah and his wife were watching what happened. As the flames went up to the sky from the altar,* the angel of the LORD went up to heaven in the fire.

When Manoah and his wife saw that, they bowed down with their faces to the ground. 21He finally understood that the man was really the angel of the LORD. The angel of the LORD did not appear to Manoah and his wife again. 22Manoah said to his wife, "We have seen God. Surely we will die because of this."

23But his wife said to him, "The LORD does not want to kill us. If he wanted to kill us, he would not have accepted our burnt offering and grain offering. He would not have shown us all these things or told us this."

24So the woman had a boy. She named him Samson. He grew and the LORD blessed him. 25The Spirit of the LORD began to work in Samson while he was in the city of Mahaneh Dan. That city is between the cities of Zorah and Eshtaol.

Samson's Marriage

14 1Samson went down to the city of Timnah. He saw a young Philistine woman there. 2When he returned home, he said to his father and mother, "I saw a Philistine woman in Timnah. I want you to get her for me. I want to marry her."

3His father and his mother answered, "But surely there is a woman from the Israelites you can marry. Do you have to marry a woman from the Philistines? Their men are not even circumcised.*"

But Samson said, "Get that woman for me! She is the one I want!" 4(Samson's parents did not know that the LORD wanted this to happen. He was looking for a way to do something against the Philistines. They were ruling over the Israelites at that time.)

5Samson went down with his father and mother to the city of Timnah. They went as far as the vineyards* near that city. There a young lion suddenly roared and jumped at Samson! 6The Spirit of the LORD came on Samson with great power. He tore the lion apart with his bare hands. It seemed easy to him. It was as easy as tearing apart a young goat. But Samson did not tell his father or mother what he had done.

7So Samson went down to the city and talked to the Philistine woman. She pleased him. 8Several days later, Samson came back to marry her. On his way, he went over to look at the dead lion. He found a swarm of bees in its body. They had made some honey. 9Samson got some of the honey with his hands.

a13:18 It is … believe Or "It is Pelei." This means "amazing" or "wonderful." This is like the name "Wonderful Counselor" in Isa. 9:6.

b13:19 the LORD … Amazing Things Or "the LORD Who Does Amazing Things." Both of these are names for God, but Manoah didn't know the man was really the angel of the LORD.

He walked along eating the honey. When he came to his parents, he gave them some of the honey, and they ate it too. But Samson did not tell his parents that he had taken the honey from the body of the dead lion.

¹⁰Samson's father went down to see the Philistine woman. The custom was for the bridegroom to give a party. So Samson gave a party. ¹¹When the Philistines saw that he was having a party, they sent 30 men to be with him.

¹²Then Samson said to the 30 men, "I want to tell you a story. This party will last for seven days. Try to find the answer during that time. If you can answer the riddle in that time, I will give you 30 linen shirts and 30 changes of clothes. ¹³But if you cannot find the answer, you must give me 30 linen shirts and 30 changes of clothes." So the 30 men said, "Tell us your riddle, we want to hear it."

¹⁴Samson told them this riddle:

"Out of the eater came something to eat.
Out of the strong came something sweet."

The 30 men tried for three days to find the answer, but they couldn't.

¹⁵On the fourth day,ᵃ the men came to Samson's wife. They said, "Did you invite us here just to make us poor? You must trick your husband into telling us the answer to the riddle. If you don't get the answer for us, we will burn you and everyone in your father's house to death."

¹⁶So Samson's wife went to him and began crying. She said, "You just hate me! You don't really love me! You told my people a riddle, and you will not tell me the answer."

Samson said to her, "Look, I have not even told my father and mother. So why should I tell you?"

¹⁷Samson's wife cried for the rest of the seven days of the party. So he finally gave her the answer to the riddle on the seventh day. He told her because she kept bothering him. Then she went to her people and told them the answer to the riddle.

¹⁸So before the sun went down on the seventh day of the party, the Philistine men had the answer. They came to Samson and said,

"What is sweeter than honey?
What is stronger than a lion?"

Then Samson said to them,

"If you had not plowed with my cow,
you would not have solved my riddle!"

¹⁹Samson was very angry. The Spirit of the Lord came on Samson with great power. He

went down to the city of Ashkelon and killed 30 Philistine men. He took all the clothes and property from the dead bodies and gave them to the men who had answered his riddle. Then he went to his father's house. ²⁰So Samson's wife was given to his best man.

Samson Makes Trouble for the Philistines

15 ¹At the time of the wheat harvest, Samson went to visit his wife. He took a young goat with him as a gift. He said, "I am going to my wife's room."

But her father would not let Samson go in. ²He said, "I thought you hated her, so I let her marry the best man at the wedding. Her younger sister is more beautiful. Take her younger sister."

³But Samson said to him, "Now I have a good reason to hurt you Philistines. No one will blame me now."

⁴So Samson went out and caught 300 foxes. He took two foxes at a time and tied their tails together to make pairs. Then he tied a torch between the tails of each pair of foxes. ⁵He lit the torches that were between the foxes' tails and let them run through the grain fields of the Philistines. In this way he burned up the plants growing in their fields and the stacks of grain they had cut. He also burned up their vineyards* and their olive trees.

⁶The Philistines asked, "Who did this?"

Someone told them, "Samson, the son-in-law of the man from Timnah, did this. He did this because his father-in-law gave Samson's wife to the best man at his wedding." So the Philistines burned Samson's wife and her father to death.

⁷Then Samson said to the Philistines, "You did this bad thing to me, so now I will do bad things to you. Then I will be finished with you!"

⁸Samson attacked the Philistines and killed many of them. Then he went and stayed in a cave in a place named the Rock of Etam.

⁹The Philistines went to the land of Judah and stopped near a place named Lehi. Their army camped there. ¹⁰The men of the tribe of Judah asked them, "Why have you Philistines come here to fight us?"

They answered, "We have come to get Samson. We want to make him our prisoner. We want to punish him for what he has done to our people."

¹¹Then 3000 men from the tribe of Judah went to the cave near the Rock of Etam and said to Samson, "What have you done to us? Don't you know that the Philistines rule over us?"

Samson answered, "I only punished them for what they did to me."

¹²Then they said to Samson, "We have come to tie you up. We will give you to the Philistines."

Samson said to the men from Judah, "Promise me that you yourselves will not hurt me."

ᵃ**14:15 fourth day** This is from the ancient Greek version. The standard Hebrew text has "seventh day."

¹³The men from Judah said, "We agree. We will just tie you up and give you to the Philistines. We promise that we will not kill you." So they tied Samson with two new ropes and led him up from the cave in the rock.

¹⁴When Samson came to the place called Lehi, the Philistines came to meet him. They were shouting with joy. Then the Spirit of the LORD came on Samson with great power. Samson broke the ropes—they were like burned strings falling from his arms and the ropes on his hands seemed to melt away. ¹⁵Samson found a jawbone of a dead donkey and killed 1000 Philistine men with it.

¹⁶Then Samson said,

"With a donkey's jawbone,
　I killed 1000 men!
With a donkey's jawbone,
　I piled*a* them into a tall pile."

¹⁷When Samson finished speaking, he threw the jawbone down. So that place was named Ramath Lehi.*b*

¹⁸Samson was very thirsty. So he cried to the LORD. He said, "I am your servant. You gave me this great victory. Please don't let me die from thirst now. Please don't let me be captured by men who are not even circumcised.*"

¹⁹There is a hole in the ground at Lehi. God made that hole crack open, and water came out. Samson drank the water and felt better. He felt strong again. So he named that water spring En Hakkore.*c* It is still there in the city of Lehi today.

²⁰Samson was a judge for the Israelites for 20 years during the time of the Philistines.

Samson Goes to the City of Gaza

16 ¹One day Samson went to the city of Gaza. He saw a prostitute there and went in to stay the night with her. ²Someone told the people of Gaza, "Samson has come here." They wanted to kill him, so they surrounded the city. They hid near the city gate and waited all night for him. They were very quiet all night long. They had said to each other, "When morning comes, we will kill Samson."

³But Samson only stayed with the prostitute until midnight. Then he got up and grabbed the doors of the city gate and pulled them loose from the wall. He pulled down the doors, the two posts, and the bars that lock the doors shut. He put them on his shoulders and carried them to the top of the hill near the city of Hebron.

Samson and Delilah

⁴Later, Samson fell in love with a woman named Delilah, who was from Sorek Valley.

⁵The rulers of the Philistines went to Delilah and said, "We want to know what makes Samson so strong. Try to trick him into telling you his secret. Then we will know how to capture him and tie him up. Then we will be able to control him. If you do this, each one of us will give you 28 pounds*d* of silver."

⁶So Delilah said to Samson, "Tell me why you are so strong. How could someone tie you up and make you helpless?"

⁷Samson answered, "Someone would have to tie me up with seven fresh, new bowstrings.*e* If someone did that, I would become as weak as any other man."

⁸Then the rulers of the Philistines brought seven fresh, new bowstrings to Delilah, and she tied Samson with the bowstrings. ⁹Some men were hiding in the next room. Delilah said to Samson, "Samson, the Philistine men are going to capture you!" But Samson easily broke the bowstrings. They snapped like a string when it comes too close to a flame. So the Philistines did not find out the secret of Samson's strength.

¹⁰Then Delilah said to Samson, "You lied to me. You made me look foolish. Please tell me the truth. How could someone tie you up?"

¹¹Samson said, "Someone would have to tie me up with new ropes. They would have to tie me with ropes that have not been used before. If someone did that, I would become as weak as any other man."

¹²So Delilah took some new ropes and tied up Samson. Some men were hiding in the next room. Then Delilah called out to him, "Samson, the Philistine men are going to capture you!" But he broke the ropes easily as if they were threads.

¹³Then Delilah said to Samson, "You lied to me again. You made me look foolish. Now, tell me how someone could tie you up."

Samson said, "If you use the loom* to weave the seven braids of hair on my head and tighten it with a pin, I will become as weak as any other man."

¹⁴Later, Samson went to sleep, so Delilah used the loom to weave the seven braids of hair on his head.*f* Then Delilah fastened the loom to the ground with a tent peg. Again she called out to him, "Samson, the Philistine men are going to capture you!" Samson pulled up the tent peg, the loom, and the shuttle.*g*

---

*a***15:16** *piled* In Hebrew, the word "pile" is like the word "donkey."
*b***15:17** *Ramath Lehi* This name means "Jawbone Heights."
*c***15:19** *En Hakkore* This name means "The spring of the one who calls."

*d***16:5** *28 pounds* Literally, "1100 shekels" (12.6 kg).
*e***16:7** *fresh, new bowstrings* Bowstrings were often made from sinew (tendons) which is brittle after it becomes old and dry.
*f***16:14** *so Delilah ... head* This is found in the ancient Greek version but not in the standard Hebrew text.
*g***16:14** *shuttle* The tool used to pull the threads back and forth on a loom to make cloth.

¹⁵Then Delilah said to Samson, "How can you say, 'I love you,' when you don't even trust me? You refuse to tell me your secret. This is the third time you made me look foolish. You haven't told me the secret of your great strength." ¹⁶She kept bothering Samson day after day. He got so tired of her asking him about his secret that he felt like he was going to die. ¹⁷Finally, Samson told Delilah everything. He said, "I have never had my hair cut. I was dedicated* to God before I was born. If someone shaved my head, I would lose my strength. I would become as weak as any other man."

¹⁸Delilah saw that Samson had told her his secret. She sent a message to the rulers of the Philistines. She said, "Come back again. Samson has told me everything." So the rulers of the Philistines came back and brought the money that they had promised to give her.

¹⁹Delilah got Samson to go to sleep with his head lying in her lap. Then she called in a man to shave off the seven braids of Samson's hair. In this way she made Samson weak, and his strength left him. ²⁰Then Delilah called out to him, "Samson, the Philistine men are going to capture you!" He woke up and thought, "I will escape as I did before and free myself." But Samson did not know that the Lord had left him.

²¹The Philistine men captured Samson. They tore out his eyes and took him down to the city of Gaza. Then they put chains on him to keep him from running away. They put him in prison and made him work grinding grain. ²²But his hair began to grow again.

²³The Philistine rulers came together to celebrate. They were going to offer a great sacrifice to their god Dagon.* They said, "Our god helped us defeat Samson our enemy." ²⁴When the Philistines saw Samson, they praised their god. They said,

"This man destroyed our people!
    He killed many of our people!
But our god helped us take our enemy!"

²⁵The people were having a good time at the celebration. So they said, "Bring Samson out. We want to make fun of him." So they brought Samson from the prison and made fun of him. They made him stand between the columns in the temple of the god Dagon. ²⁶A servant was holding his hand. Samson said to him, "Put me where I can feel the columns that hold this temple up. I want to lean against them."

²⁷The temple was crowded with men and women. All the Philistine rulers were there. There were about 3000 men and women on the roof of the temple. They were laughing and making fun of Samson. ²⁸Then Samson said a prayer to the Lord, "Lord All-Powerful, remember me. God, please give me strength one more time. Let me do this one thing to punish these Philistines for tearing out both of my eyes!" ²⁹Then Samson took hold of the two columns in the center of the temple that supported the whole temple. He braced himself between the two columns. One column was at his right side and the other at his left side. ³⁰Samson said, "Let me die with these Philistines!" Then he pushed as hard as he could, and the temple fell on the rulers and everyone in it. In this way Samson killed many more Philistines when he died than when he was alive.

³¹Samson's brothers and all the people in his father's family went down to get his body. They brought him back and buried him in his father's tomb, which is between the cities of Zorah and Eshtaol. Samson was a judge for the Israelites for 20 years.

Micah's Idols

17 ¹There was a man named Micah who lived in the hill country of Ephraim. ²Micah said to his mother, "Do you remember that someone stole 28 pounds*ᵃ* of silver from you? I heard you say a curse about that. Well, I have the silver. I took it."

His mother said, "The Lord bless you, my son."

³Micah gave the 28 pounds of silver back to his mother. Then she said, "I will give this silver as a special gift to the Lord. I will give it to my son so that he can make a statue and cover it with the silver. So now, son, I give the silver back to you."

⁴But Micah gave the silver back to his mother. So she took about 5 pounds*ᵇ* of the silver and gave them to a silversmith.*ᶜ* He used the silver to make a statue covered with silver. The statue was put in Micah's house. ⁵Micah had a temple for worshiping idols.* He made an ephod*ᵈ* and some house idols. Then Micah chose one of his sons to be his priest. ⁶(At that time the Israelites did not have a king, so everyone did what they thought was right.)

⁷There was a young man who was a Levite* from the city of Bethlehem in Judah. He had been living among the tribe of Judah. ⁸He left Bethlehem to look for another place to live. As he was traveling, he came to Micah's house in the hill country of the land of Ephraim. ⁹Micah asked him, "Where have you come from?"

The young man answered, "I am a Levite from the city of Bethlehem in Judah. I am looking for a place to live."

---

*ᵃ***17:2** *28 pounds* Literally, "1100 ₍shekels₎" (12.6 kg). Also in verse 3.
*ᵇ***17:4** *5 pounds* Literally, "200 ₍shekels₎" (2.3 kg).
*ᶜ***17:4** *silversmith* A person who makes things from silver.
*ᵈ***17:5** *ephod* This may have been a special vest or coat like that worn by the high priest (see Ex. 28:2–14), or it may have been a kind of idol. Also in 18:14.

¹⁰Then Micah said to him, "Live with me. Be my father and my priest. I will give you 4 ounces*ᵃ* of silver each year. I will also give you clothes and food."

The Levite did what Micah asked. ¹¹The young Levite agreed to live with Micah. He became like one of Micah's own sons. ¹²Micah chose him to be his priest. So the young man became a priest and lived in Micah's house. ¹³And Micah said, "Now I know that the LORD will be good to me. I know this because I have a man from the tribe of Levi to be my priest."

Dan Captures the City of Laish

18 ¹At that time the Israelites did not have a king. And the tribe of Dan was still looking for a place to live. They did not have their own land yet. The other tribes of Israel already had their land, but the tribe of Dan had not taken their land yet.

²So the tribe of Dan sent five soldiers to look for some land. They went to search for a good place to live. These five men were from the cities of Zorah and Eshtaol. They were chosen because they were from all the families of Dan. They were told, "Go, look for some land."

The five men came to the hill country of Ephraim. They came to Micah's house and spent the night there. ³When the five men came close to Micah's house, they heard the voice of the young Levite.* They recognized his voice, so they stopped at Micah's house. They asked the young man, "Who brought you to this place? What are you doing? Why are you here?"

⁴The young man told them what Micah had done for him. "Micah hired me," he said. "I am his priest."

⁵So they said to him, "Please ask God if our search for a place to live will be successful."

⁶The priest said to the five men, "Yes. Go in peace. The LORD will lead you on your way."

⁷So the five men left. They came to the city of Laish and saw that the people of that city lived in safety. They were ruled by the people of Sidon. Everything was peaceful and quiet. The people had plenty of everything, and they didn't have any enemies nearby to hurt them. Also they lived a long way from the city of Sidon, and they did not have any agreements with the people of Aram.*ᵇ*

⁸The five men went back to the cities of Zorah and Eshtaol. Their relatives asked them, "What did you learn?"

⁹The five men answered, "We have found some land, and it is very good. We should attack them. Don't wait! Let's go and take that land! ¹⁰When you come to that place, you will see that there is plenty of land. There is plenty of everything there. You will also see that the people are not expecting an attack. Surely God has given that land to us."

¹¹So 600 men from the tribe of Dan left the cities of Zorah and Eshtaol. They were ready for war. ¹²On their way to the city of Laish, they stopped near the city of Kiriath Jearim in the land of Judah. They set up a camp there. That is why the place west of Kiriath Jearim is named Mahaneh Dan*ᶜ* to this very day. ¹³From there the 600 men traveled on to the hill country of Ephraim. Then they came to Micah's house.

¹⁴So the five men who had explored the land around Laish spoke. They said to their relatives, "There is an ephod in one of these houses. And there are also household gods, a carved statue, and a silver idol.* You know what to do." ¹⁵So they stopped at Micah's house, where the young Levite lived. They asked the young man how he was. ¹⁶The 600 men from the tribe of Dan stood at the entrance of the gate. They all had their weapons and were ready for war. ¹⁷⁻¹⁸The five spies went into the house. The priest stood just outside by the gate with the 600 men who were ready for war. The men took the carved idol, the ephod, the household idols, and the silver idol. The young Levite priest said, "What are you doing?"

¹⁹The five men answered, "Be quiet! Don't say a word. Come with us. Be our father and our priest. You must choose. Is it better for you to be a priest for just one man or for a whole tribe of Israelites with many family groups?"

²⁰This made the Levite happy. So he took the ephod, the household idols, and the idol. He went with the men from the tribe of Dan.

²¹Then the 600 men from the tribe of Dan and the Levite priest turned and left Micah's house. They put their little children, their animals, and all their things in front of them.

²²The men from the tribe of Dan went a long way from that place. But the people living near Micah met together. Then they began chasing the men of Dan and caught up with them. ²³The men with Micah were shouting at the men of Dan. The men of Dan turned around and said to Micah, "What's the problem? Why are you shouting?"

²⁴Micah answered, "You men from Dan took my idols. I made them for myself. You have also taken my priest. What do I have left now? How can you ask me, 'What's the problem?'"

²⁵The men from the tribe of Dan answered, "You had better not argue with us. Some of our men become angry easily. If you shout at us, they will attack you. You and your families will be killed."

---

*ᵃ*17:10 *4 ounces* Literally, "10 ₁shekels," (115 g).
*ᵇ*18:7 *they did not have ... Aram* Or "they did not have any dealings with people."

*ᶜ*18:12 *Mahaneh Dan* This name means "The Camp of Dan."

26Then the men of Dan turned around and went on their way. Micah knew that these men were too strong for him, so he went back home.

27So the men of Dan took the idols that Micah made. They also took the priest who had been with Micah. Then they came to Laish. They attacked the people living in Laish. Those people were at peace. They were not expecting an attack. The men of Dan killed them with their swords and then burned the city. 28The people living in Laish did not have anyone to rescue them. They lived too far from the city of Sidon for the people there to help. And the people of Laish did not have any agreements with the people of Aram—so they did not help them. The city of Laish was in a valley, which belonged to the town of Beth Rehob. The people from Dan built a new city in that place, and it became their home. 29The people of Dan gave the city a new name. That city had been called Laish, but they changed the name to Dan. They named the city after their ancestor* Dan, one of the sons of Israel.

30The people of the tribe of Dan set up the idol in the city of Dan. They made Jonathan son of Gershom their priest. Gershom was the son of Moses.ᵃ Jonathan and his sons were priests for the tribe of Dan until the time when the Israelites were taken into captivity. 31The people of Dan set up for themselves the idol that Micah had made. That idol was there the whole time that the house of God was in Shiloh.

A Levite and His Woman Servant

19 1At that time the Israelites did not have a king.

There was a Levite* who lived far back in the hill country of Ephraim. He had taken as a wife a slave woman* from the city of Bethlehem in the country of Judah. 2But his slave woman had an argument with him. She left him and went back to her father's house in Bethlehem in Judah. She stayed there for four months. 3Then her husband went after her. He wanted to speak kindly to her so that she would come back to him. He took with him his servant and two donkeys. The Levite came to her father's house. Her father saw the Levite and came out to greet him. The father was very happy. 4The woman's father led the Levite into his house. The Levite's father-in-law invited him to stay. So he stayed for three days. He ate, drank, and slept in his father-in-law's house.

5On the fourth day, they got up early in the morning. The Levite was getting ready to leave. But the young woman's father said to his son-in-law, "Eat something first. After you eat, you can go." 6So the Levite and his father-in-law sat down to eat and drink together.

After that, the young woman's father said to the Levite, "Please stay tonight. Relax and enjoy yourself." So the two men ate together. 7The Levite got up to leave, but his father-in-law persuaded him to stay the night again.

8Then, on the fifth day, the Levite got up early in the morning. He was ready to leave. But the woman's father said to his son-in-law, "Eat something first. Relax and stay until this afternoon." So they both ate together again.

9Then the Levite, his slave woman, and his servant got up to leave. But the young woman's father said, "It is almost dark. The day is almost gone. So stay the night here and enjoy yourself. Tomorrow morning you can get up early and go on your way."

10But the Levite did not want to stay another night. He took his two donkeys and his slave woman. He traveled as far as the city of Jebus (that is, Jerusalem). 11The day was almost over. They were near the city of Jebus. So the servant said to his master, the Levite, "Let's stop at this Jebusite city. Let's stay the night here."

12But his master, the Levite man, said, "No, we will not go inside a strange city. Those people are not Israelites. We will go to the city of Gibeah.ᵇ" 13The Levite said, "Come on. Let's try to make it to Gibeah or Ramah. We can stay the night in one of those cities."

14So the Levite and those with him traveled on. The sun was going down just as they entered the city of Gibeah. Gibeah is in the area that belongs to the tribe of Benjamin. 15They planned to stop there and stay the night. They came to the city square and sat down, but no one invited them home to stay the night.

16That evening an old man came into the city from the fields. His home was in the hill country of Ephraim, but now he was living in the city of Gibeah. (The men of Gibeah were from the tribe of Benjamin.) 17The old man saw the traveler in the public square and asked, "Where are you going? Where did you come from?"

18The Levite answered, "We have come from Bethlehem in Judah, where I went for a visit. Now I am on my way home,ᶜ which is a long way into the hill country of Ephraim. I expected that someone here would invite us in for the night, but no one has. 19We already have straw and food for our donkeys. There is also bread and wine for me, the young woman, and my servant. We don't need anything."

20The old man said, "You are welcome to stay at my house. I will give you anything you need, but don't stay the night in the public square." 21Then the old man took the Levite and the people with him to his house. He fed

---

ᵇ**19:12** *Gibeah* Gibeah was a few miles north of Jebus. Jebus was the old name for Jerusalem.
ᶜ**19:18** *home* This is from the ancient Greek version, which has "to my house." The standard Hebrew text has "to the LORD's house."

ᵃ**18:30** *Moses* Or "Manasseh."

their donkeys. They washed their feet and then had something to eat and drink.

22While the Levite and those who were with him were enjoying themselves, some very bad men from the city surrounded the house. They began beating on the door. They shouted at the old man who owned the house. They said, "Bring out the man who came to your house. We want to have sex with him."

23The old man went outside and said to them, "My friends, don't do such an evil thing! This man is a guest in my house.*a* Don't commit this terrible sin. 24Look, here is my daughter. She has never had sex before. I will bring her out to you now. This man also has a slave woman. You can use them any way you want, but don't do such a terrible sin against this man."

25But those evil men would not listen to the old man. So the Levite took his slave woman and put her outside with them. They hurt her and raped her all night long. Then, at dawn, they let her go. 26At dawn, the woman came back to the house where her master was staying. She fell down at the front door and lay there until it was daylight.

27The Levite got up early the next morning. He wanted to go home. He opened the door to go outside, and a hand fell across the threshold of the door. There was his slave woman. She had fallen down against the door. 28The Levite said to her, "Get up, let's go." But there was no answer.

The Levite put her body on his donkey and went home. 29When he arrived at his house, he took a knife and cut her body into 12 parts. Then he sent the 12 parts of the woman to each of the areas where the Israelites lived. 30Everyone who saw this said, "Nothing like this has ever happened in Israel before. We haven't seen anything like this from the time we came out of Egypt. Discuss this and tell us what to do."

The War Between Israel and Benjamin

20¹So all the Israelites joined together. They all came together to stand before the LORD in the city of Mizpah. People came from everywhere in Israel.*b* Even the Israelites from Gilead*c* were there. 2The leaders of all the tribes of Israel were there. They took their places in the public meeting of God's people. There were 400,000 soldiers with swords in that place. 3The people from the tribe of Benjamin heard that the Israelites were meeting together in Mizpah. The Israelites said, "Tell us how this terrible thing happened."

4So the Levite, the husband of the woman

who had been murdered, told them the story. He said, "My slave woman* and I came to the city of Gibeah in the area of Benjamin. We spent the night there. 5But during the night the men of the city of Gibeah came to the house where I was staying. They surrounded the house, and they wanted to kill me. They raped my slave woman, and she died. 6So I took her and cut her into pieces. Then I sent one piece to each of the tribes of Israel. I sent the 12 pieces to the lands we have received. I did that because the people of Benjamin have done this terrible thing in Israel. 7Now, all you men of Israel, speak up. Give your decision about what we should do."

8Then all the people stood up at the same time. They said together, "None of us will go home. No, not one of us will go back to his house. 9Now this is what we will do to the city of Gibeah. We will throw lots* to let God show us who will lead the attack. 10We will choose ten men from every 100 from all the tribes of Israel. And we will choose 100 men from every 1000. We will choose 1000 men from every 10,000. These men we have chosen will get supplies for the army. Then the army will go to the city of Gibeah in the area of Benjamin. The army will punish those people for the terrible thing they did among the Israelites."

11So all the men of Israel gathered together at the city of Gibeah, united together and in agreement as to what they were doing. 12The tribes of Israel sent men to the tribe of Benjamin with this message: "What about this terrible thing that some of your men have done? 13Send the bad men from the city of Gibeah to us so that we can put them to death. We must remove the evil from among the Israelites."

But the people from the tribe of Benjamin would not listen to the messengers from their relatives, the other Israelites. 14The people from the tribe of Benjamin left their cities and went to the city of Gibeah. They went to Gibeah to fight against the other tribes of Israel. 15The people from the tribe of Benjamin got 26,000 soldiers together who were trained for war. They also had 700 trained soldiers from the city of Gibeah. 16There were also 700 trained soldiers who were trained to fight with their left hand.*d* Each one of them could use a sling* with great skill. They all could use a sling to throw a stone at a hair and not miss!

17All the tribes of Israel, except Benjamin, gathered together 400,000 fighting men with swords. Each one was a trained soldier. 18The Israelites went up to the city of Bethel. At Bethel they asked God, "Which tribe will be first to attack the tribe of Benjamin?"

The LORD answered, "The tribe of Judah will go first."

---

a **19:23** *This man ... my house* At this time, it was a custom that if you invited people to be your guests, you had to protect and care for those people.
b **20:1** *from everywhere in Israel* Literally, "from Dan to Beersheba."
c **20:1** *Gilead* This area was east of the Jordan River.

d **20:16** *trained ... left hand* Literally, "restrained in their right hand."

19The next morning the Israelites got up. They made a camp near the city of Gibeah. 20Then the army of Israel took their positions for battle against the army of Benjamin at the city of Gibeah. 21Then the army of Benjamin came out of the city of Gibeah. The army of Benjamin killed 22,000 men in the army of Israel during the battle that day.

22-23The Israelites went to the LORD and cried until evening. They asked the LORD, "Should we go to fight the people of Benjamin again? They are our relatives."

The LORD answered, "Go fight against them." The men of Israel encouraged each other. So they again went out to fight, as they had done the first day.

24Then the army of Israel came near the army of Benjamin. This was the second day of the war. 25The army of Benjamin came out of the city of Gibeah to attack the army of Israel on the second day. This time, the army of Benjamin killed another 18,000 men from the army of Israel. All the men in the army of Israel were trained soldiers.

26Then all the Israelites went up to the city of Bethel. There they sat down and cried to the LORD. They did not eat anything all day, until evening. They also offered burnt offerings* and fellowship offerings* to the LORD. 27The men of Israel asked the LORD a question. (In those days God's Box of the Agreement* was there at Bethel. 28Phinehas was the priest who served God there. Phinehas was the son of Eleazar. Eleazar was the son of Aaron.) The Israelites asked, "The people of Benjamin are our relatives. Should we again go to fight against them? Or should we stop fighting?"

The LORD answered, "Go. Tomorrow I will help you defeat them."

29Then the army of Israel hid some men all around the city of Gibeah. 30The army of Israel went to fight against the city of Gibeah on the third day. They got ready for battle as they had done before. 31The army of Benjamin came out of the city of Gibeah to fight the army of Israel. The army of Israel backed up and let the army of Benjamin chase them. In this way the army of Benjamin was tricked into leaving the city far behind them.

The army of Benjamin began to kill some of the men in the army of Israel, as they had done before. They killed about 30 men from Israel. They killed some of them in the fields, and they killed some of them on the roads. One road led to the city of Bethel. The other road led to the city of Gibeah. 32The men of Benjamin said, "We are winning as before!"

The men of Israel were running away, but it was a trick. They wanted to lead the men of Benjamin away from their city and onto the roads. 33So all the men ran away. They stopped at a place named Baal Tamar. Some of the men of Israel were hiding west of Gibeah. They ran from their hiding places. 3410,000

of Israel's best-trained soldiers attacked the city of Gibeah. The fighting was very heavy. But the army of Benjamin did not know that a terrible thing was about to happen to them.

35The LORD used the army of Israel and defeated the army of Benjamin. On that day, the army of Israel killed 25,100 soldiers from Benjamin. All of them had been trained for war. 36So the people of Benjamin saw that they were defeated.

The army of Israel had moved back because they were depending on the surprise attack. They had men hiding near Gibeah. 37The men who were hiding rushed into the city of Gibeah. They spread out and killed everyone in the city with their swords. 38Now the men of Israel had made a plan with the men who were hiding. The men who were hiding were supposed to send a special signal. They were supposed to make a big cloud of smoke.

39-41The army of Benjamin had killed about 30 Israelite soldiers. So the men of Benjamin were saying, "We are winning, as before." But then a big cloud of smoke began to rise from the city. The men of Benjamin turned around and saw the smoke. The whole city was on fire. Then the army of Israel stopped running away. They turned around and began to fight. The men of Benjamin were afraid because they knew that a terrible thing had happened to them.

42So the army of Benjamin ran away from the army of Israel. They ran toward the desert. But they could not escape the fighting. And the men of Israel came out of the cities and killed them. 43The men of Israel surrounded the men of Benjamin and began chasing them. They did not let them rest. They defeated them in the area east of Gibeah. 44So 18,000 brave and strong fighters from the army of Benjamin were killed.

45The army of Benjamin turned around and ran toward the desert. They ran to a place called the Rock of Rimmon, but the army of Israel killed 5000 soldiers from Benjamin along the roads. They kept chasing the men of Benjamin. They chased them as far as a place named Gidom. The army of Israel killed 2000 more men from Benjamin in that place.

46On that day, 25,000 men of the army of Benjamin were killed. All of them fought bravely with their swords. 47But 600 men from Benjamin ran into the desert to the place called the Rock of Rimmon and stayed there for four months. 48The men of Israel went back to the land of Benjamin. They killed the people and all the animals in every city. They destroyed everything they could find and burned every city they came to.

Getting Wives for the Men of Benjamin

21 1At Mizpah, the men of Israel made a promise. This was their promise: "Not one of us will let his daughter marry a man from the tribe of Benjamin."

²The Israelites went to the city of Bethel. There they sat before God until evening. They cried loudly as they sat there. ³They said to God, "LORD, you are the God of the Israelites. Why has this terrible thing happened to us? Why has one tribe of the Israelites been taken away?"

⁴Early the next day, the Israelites built an altar.* They put burnt offerings* and fellowship offerings* to God on that altar. ⁵Then the Israelites said, "Are there any tribes of Israel who did not come here to meet with us before the LORD?" They asked this question because they had made a serious promise. They had promised that anyone who did not come together with the other tribes at the city of Mizpah would be killed.

⁶Then the Israelites felt sorry for their relatives, the people of Benjamin. They said, "Today, one tribe has been separated from Israel. ⁷We made a promise before the LORD. We promised not to allow our daughters to marry a man from Benjamin. How can we make sure that the men of Benjamin will have wives?"

⁸Then the Israelites asked, "Which one of the tribes of Israel did not come here to Mizpah? We have come together before the LORD. Surely one family was not here!" Then they found that no one from the city of Jabesh Gilead had met together with the other Israelites. ⁹The Israelites counted everyone to see who was there and who was not. They found that no one from Jabesh Gilead was there. ¹⁰So the Israelites sent 12,000 soldiers to the city of Jabesh Gilead. They told the soldiers, "Go to Jabesh Gilead, and use your swords to kill everyone who lives there, even the women and children. ¹¹You must do this! You must kill every man in Jabesh Gilead and every woman who has had sexual relations with a man. But do not kill any woman who has never had sex with a man." So the soldiers did these things.ᵃ ¹²The 12,000 soldiers found 400 young women in the city of Jabesh Gilead who had never had sex with a man. They brought these women to the camp at Shiloh in the land of Canaan.*

¹³Then the Israelites sent a message to the men of Benjamin. They offered to make peace with the men of Benjamin. The men of Benjamin were at the place named the Rock of Rimmon. ¹⁴So the men of Benjamin came back to Israel. The Israelites gave them the women from Jabesh Gilead who they had not killed. But there were not enough women for all the men of Benjamin.

¹⁵The Israelites felt sorry for the men of Benjamin. They felt sorry for them because the LORD had separated them from the other tribes of Israel. ¹⁶The elders of the Israelites said, "The women of the tribe of Benjamin have been killed. Where can we get wives for the men of Benjamin who are still alive? ¹⁷The men of Benjamin who are still alive must have children to continue their families. This must be done so that a tribe in Israel will not die out! ¹⁸But we cannot allow our daughters to marry the men of Benjamin. We have made this promise: 'Bad things will happen to anyone who gives a wife to a man of Benjamin.' ¹⁹We have an idea! This is the time for the festival of the LORD at the city of Shiloh. This festival is celebrated every year there." (The city of Shiloh is north of the city of Bethel and east of the road that goes from Bethel to Shechem. And it is also to the south of the city of Lebonah.)

²⁰So the elders* told the men of Benjamin about their idea. They said, "Go and hide in the vineyards.* ²¹Watch for the time during the festival when the young women from Shiloh come out to join the dancing. Then run out from where you are hiding in the vineyards. Each of you should take one of the young women from the city of Shiloh. Take them to the land of Benjamin and marry them. ²²The fathers or brothers of the young women will come and complain to us. But we will say, 'Be kind to the men of Benjamin. Let them marry the women. We could not get wives for each of them during the war. And you did not willingly give the women to the men of Benjamin, so you did not break your promise.'"

²³So that is what the men of the tribe of Benjamin did. While the young women were dancing, each man caught one of them. They took them away and married them. Then they went back to their land. The men of Benjamin built cities again in that land, and they lived in them. ²⁴Then the Israelites went home. They went to their own land and tribe.

²⁵In those days the Israelites did not have a king, so everyone did whatever they thought was right.

ᵃ21:11 *But do not kill … these things* This is from the ancient Greek version.

Ruth

Famine in Judah

1 ¹Long ago, during the time the judges* ruled, there was a famine* in the land, and a man named Elimelech left the town of Bethlehem in Judah. He, his wife, and his two sons moved to the country of Moab.* ²The man's wife was named Naomi, and his two sons were named Mahlon and Kilion. They were from the Ephrathah family of Bethlehem in Judah. The family traveled to the hill country of Moab and stayed there.

³Later, Naomi's husband, Elimelech, died, so only Naomi and her two sons were left. ⁴Her sons married women from the country of Moab. One wife's name was Orpah, and the other wife's name was Ruth. They lived in Moab about ten years; ⁵then Mahlon and Kilion also died. So Naomi was left alone without her husband or her two sons.

Naomi Goes Home

⁶While Naomi was in the country of Moab, she heard that the LORD had helped his people. He had given food to his people in Judah. So Naomi decided to leave the hill country of Moab and go back home. Her daughters-in-law also decided to go with her. ⁷They left the place where they had been living and started walking back to the land of Judah.

⁸Then Naomi told her daughters-in-law, "Each of you should go back home to your mother. You have been very kind to me and my sons who are now dead. So I pray the LORD will be just as kind to you. ⁹I pray that he helps each of you find a husband and a good home." Naomi kissed her daughters-in-law, and they all started crying.

¹⁰Then the daughters said, "But we want to come with you and go to your family."

¹¹But Naomi said, "No, daughters, go back to your own homes. Why should you go with me? I can't have any more sons to be your husbands. ¹²Go back home. I am too old to have a new husband. Even if I thought I could be married again, I could not help you. If I became pregnant tonight and had two sons, ¹³you would have to wait until they grew to become men before you could marry them. I cannot make you wait that long for husbands. That would make me very sad. And I am already sad enough—the LORD has done many things to me!"

¹⁴So again they cried very much. Then Orpah kissed Naomi goodbye, but Ruth hugged her and stayed.

¹⁵Naomi said, "Look, your sister-in-law has gone back to her own people and her own gods. You should do the same."

¹⁶But Ruth said, "Don't force me to leave you! Don't force me to go back to my own people. Let me go with you. Wherever you go, I will go. Wherever you sleep, I will sleep. Your people will be my people. Your God will be my God. ¹⁷Where you die, I will die, and that is where I will be buried. I ask the LORD to punish me if I don't keep this promise: Only death will separate us."*a*

The Homecoming

¹⁸Naomi saw that Ruth wanted very much to go with her. So Naomi stopped arguing with her. ¹⁹Naomi and Ruth traveled until they came to the town of Bethlehem. When the two women entered Bethlehem, all the people were very excited. They said, "Is this Naomi?"

²⁰But Naomi told the people, "Don't call me Naomi*b*; call me Marah.*c* Use this name because God All-Powerful has made my life very sad. ²¹I had everything I wanted when I left, but now, the LORD brings me home with nothing. The LORD has made me sad, so why should you call me 'Happy'*d*? God All-Powerful has given much trouble to me."

²²So Naomi and her daughter-in-law Ruth, the Moabite, came back from the hill country of Moab. These two women came to Bethlehem at the beginning of the barley harvest.

Ruth Meets Boaz

2 ¹There was a rich man named Boaz living in Bethlehem. Boaz was one of Naomi's close relatives*e* from Elimelech's family.

²One day Ruth, the Moabite, said to Naomi, "I think I will go to the fields. Maybe I can find someone who will be kind to me and let me

a 1:17 I ask ... separate us Literally, "May the LORD do this to me, and even more, unless death separates us!"

b 1:20 Naomi This name means "Happy" or "Pleasant."

c 1:20 Marah This name means "Bitter" or "Sad."

d 1:21 Happy This is the name Naomi.

e 2:1 close relatives If a man died without children, one of his close relatives would take the dead man's wife so that she could have children. He would care for this family, but this family and their property would not belong to him. They would all be in the dead man's name.

gather the grain they leave in their field."

Naomi said, "Fine, daughter, go ahead."

³So Ruth went to the fields. She followed the workers who were cutting the grain and gathered the grain that was left.ᵃ It happened that part of the field belonged to Boaz, the man from Elimelech's family.

⁴Later, Boaz came to the field from Bethlehem and greeted his workers. He said, "The LORD be with you!"

And the workers answered, "And may the LORD bless you!"

⁵Then Boaz spoke to his servant who was in charge of the workers. He asked, "Whose girl is that?"

⁶The servant answered, "She is the Moabite woman who came with Naomi from the country of Moab. ⁷She came early this morning and asked me if she could follow the workers and gather the grain that was left on the ground. She rested only a short time in that shelter."ᵇ

⁸Then Boaz said to Ruth, "Listen, child. Stay here in my field to gather grain for yourself. There is no need for you to go to any other field. Continue following behind my women workers. ⁹Watch to see which fields they go into to cut the grain and follow them. I have warned the young men not to bother you. When you are thirsty, go and drink from the same water jug my men drink from."

¹⁰Then Ruth bowed very low to the ground. She said to Boaz, "I am a foreigner, so I am surprised you even noticed me."

¹¹Boaz answered her, "I know about all the help you have given to your mother-in-law Naomi. I know you helped her even after your husband died. And I know that you left your father and mother and your own country and came here to this country. You did not know anyone from this country, but you came here with Naomi. ¹²The LORD will reward you for all the good things you have done. The LORD, the God of Israel, will pay you in full. You have come to him for safety,ᶜ and he will protect you."

¹³Then Ruth said, "I hope I can continue to please you, sir. You are very kind. I am only a servant and not even one of your own servants. But you have said kind words to me and comforted me."

¹⁴At mealtime, Boaz told Ruth, "Come and eat some of our bread. Here, dip your bread in our vinegar."

So Ruth sat down with the workers. Boaz gave her some roasted grain. Ruth ate until she was full, and there was some food left. ¹⁵Then Ruth got up and went back to work.

Then Boaz told his servants, "Let Ruth gather even around the piles of grain. Don't stop her. ¹⁶And make her work easier by dropping some full heads of grain for her. Let her gather that grain. Don't tell her to stop."

Naomi Hears About Boaz

¹⁷Ruth worked in the fields until evening. Then she separated the grain from the chaff.* There was about one-half bushelᵈ of barley. ¹⁸Ruth carried the grain into town to show her mother-in-law what she had gathered. She also gave her the food that was left from lunch.

¹⁹Her mother-in-law asked her, "Where did you gather all this grain? Where did you work? Bless the man who noticed you."

Then Ruth told her who she had worked with. She said, "The man I worked with today is a man named Boaz."

²⁰Naomi told her daughter-in-law, "LORD bless him! He has continued showing his kindness to the living as well as the dead." Then Naomi told her daughter-in-law, "Boaz is one of our relatives. He is one of our protectors.ᵉ"

²¹Then Ruth said, "Boaz also told me to come back and continue working. He said that I should work closely with his servants until the harvest is finished."

²²Then Naomi said to her daughter-in-law Ruth, "It is good for you to continue working with his women servants. If you work in another field, some man might hurt you." ²³So Ruth continued working closely with the women servants of Boaz. She gathered grain until the barley harvest was finished. She also worked there through the end of the wheat harvest. Ruth continued living with her mother-in-law Naomi.

The Threshing Floor

3 ¹Then Naomi, Ruth's mother-in-law, said to her, "My daughter, maybe I should find a husband and a good home for you. That would be good for you. ²Boaz is our close relative.ᶠ You worked with his women servants. Tonight he will be working at the threshing* floor. ³Go wash yourself and get dressed. Put on a nice dress, and go down to the threshing floor. But don't let Boaz see you until he has finished eating his dinner. ⁴After he eats, he will lie down to rest. Watch him so that you will know where he lies down. Go

ᵃ2:3 There was a law that a farmer must leave some grain in his field during harvest, so poor people and travelers could find something to eat. See Lev. 19:9; 23:22.
ᵇ2:7 She ... shelter Or "That is her house over there."
ᶜ2:12 You have ... for safety Literally, "You have come under his wings for safety."

ᵈ2:17 one-half bushel Literally, "one ephah" (22 l).
ᵉ2:20 protectors Or "redeemers," those who cared for and protected the family of a dead relative. Often they bought back (redeemed) the poor relatives from slavery, making them free again.
ᶠ3:2 close relative, protector A close relative who could marry Ruth so that she could have children. This man would care for this family, but this family and their property would not belong to him. They would belong to Ruth's dead husband. Also in 3:9, 12; 4:1, 3, 6.

there and lift the cover off his feet.[a] Then lie down there with Boaz. He will tell you what you should do about marriage."

[5]Then Ruth answered, "I will do what you say."

[6]So Ruth went down to the threshing floor and did everything that her mother-in-law told her to do. [7]After eating and drinking, Boaz was very satisfied. He went to lie down near the pile of grain. Then Ruth went to him very quietly and lifted the cover from his feet and lay down by his feet.

[8]About midnight, Boaz rolled over in his sleep and woke up. He was very surprised. There was a woman lying near his feet. [9]Boaz said, "Who are you?"

She said, "I am Ruth, your servant girl. Spread your cover over me.[b] You are my protector."

[10]Then Boaz said, "May the Lord bless you, young woman. You have been very kind to me. Your kindness to me is greater than the kindness you showed to Naomi in the beginning. You could have looked for a young man to marry, rich or poor. But you did not. [11]Now, young woman, don't be afraid. I will do what you ask. All the people in our town know that you are a very good woman. [12]And it is true, I am a close relative. But there is a man who is a closer relative to you than I am. [13]Stay here tonight. In the morning we will see if he will help[c] you. If he decides to help you, that is fine. If he refuses to help, I promise, as the Lord lives, I will marry you and buy back Elimelech's land for you.[d] So lie here until morning."

[14]So Ruth lay near Boaz's feet until morning. She got up while it was still dark, before it was light enough for people to recognize each other.

Boaz said to her, "We will keep it a secret that you came here to me last night." [15]Then he said, "Bring me your coat. Now, hold it open."

So Ruth held her coat open, and Boaz measured out about a bushel of barley[e] as a gift to Naomi, her mother-in-law. Boaz then wrapped it in Ruth's coat, and put it on her back. Then he went to the city.

[16]Ruth went to the home of her mother-in-law, Naomi. Naomi went to the door and asked, "Who's there?"

Ruth went in telling Naomi everything that Boaz did for her. [17]She said, "Boaz gave me this barley as a gift for you. He said that I must not go home without bringing a gift for you."

[18]Naomi said, "Daughter, be patient until we hear what happens. Boaz will not rest until he has finished doing what he should do. We will know what will happen before the day is ended."

Boaz and the Other Relative

4 [1]Boaz went to the place where people gather near the city gates. He sat there until the close relative Boaz had mentioned passed by. Boaz called to him, "Come here, friend. Sit here."

[2]Boaz gathered ten of the elders* of the city. He told them, "Sit here!" So they sat down.

[3]Then Boaz spoke to the close relative. He said, "Naomi came back from the hill country of Moab. She is selling the land[f] that belonged to our relative Elimelech. [4]I decided to tell you about this in front of the people living here and in front of the elders of my people. If you want to buy back the land, buy it. If you don't want to redeem the land, tell me. I know that I am the next one after you who can redeem the land. If you don't buy the land back, I will."

[5]Then Boaz said, "If you buy the land from Naomi, you also get the dead man's wife, Ruth, the Moabite woman, and the first child will get the land. That way, the land will stay in the dead man's family."

[6]The close relative answered, "I cannot buy back the land. That land should belong to me, but I cannot buy it. If I do, I might lose my own land. So you can buy the land." [7](Long ago in Israel, when people bought or redeemed property, one person took off a sandal and gave it to the other person. This was their proof of purchase.) [8]So the close relative said to Boaz, "Buy the land." And then the close relative took off his sandal and gave it to Boaz.[g]

[9]Then Boaz said to the elders and all the people, "You are witnesses today that I am buying from Naomi everything that belonged to Elimelech, Kilion, and Mahlon. [10]I am also taking Ruth to be my wife. I am doing this so that the dead man's property will stay with his family. This way, the dead man's name will not be separated from his family and his land. You are witnesses this day."

[11]So all the people and elders that were near the city gates were witnesses. They said,

> "May the Lord make this woman
>   who is coming into your home
>   like Rachel and Leah
>   who built the house of Israel.[h]

---

[a]**3:4** *lift the cover off his feet* Literally, "uncover his legs." This showed that Ruth was asking Boaz to be her protector.

[b]**3:9** *Spread your cover over me* Or "Spread your wing over me." This showed that Ruth was asking for help and protection. See Ruth 2:12.

[c]**3:13** *help* Or "redeem." This meant the close relative would care for and protect the dead man's family and property, but that property would not be his.

[d]**3:13** *I will marry … you* Literally, "I will redeem you."

[e]**3:15** *bushel of barley* Literally, "six ⌊measures⌋ of barley."

[f]**4:3** *She is selling the land* Or "She has sold the land."

[g]**4:8** *and gave it to Boaz* This is from the ancient Greek version.

[h]**4:11** *built the house of Israel* The Hebrew word "built" is like the word meaning "gave birth to sons."

Become powerful in Ephrathah*a*!
Be famous in Bethlehem!
12 Tamar gave birth to Judah's son Perez.*b*
And his family became great.
In the same way may the LORD give you
many children through Ruth,
and may your family be great like his."

13So Boaz married Ruth. The LORD allowed Ruth to become pregnant, and she had a son. 14The women told Naomi,

"Praise the LORD who gave you this child.*c*
He will become famous in Israel.
15 He will make you alive again
and care for you in your old age.
Your daughter-in-law made it happen.
She bore this child for you.

*a***4:11** *Ephrathah* Another name for Bethlehem.
*b***4:12** *Perez* One of Boaz's ancestors.
*c***4:14** *child* Literally, "protector" or "redeemer." This might refer to Boaz, or the women might have used this name for the baby because he would be the one to care for Naomi and her family and to carry on the name of Elimelech.

She loves you,
and she is better for you than seven
sons."

16Naomi took the boy, held him in her arms, and cared for him. 17The neighbors gave the boy his name. These women said, "Naomi has a son now!"*d* They named him Obed. Obed was the father of Jesse, and Jesse was the father of David.*

Ruth and Boaz's Family

18This is the family history of Perez:

Perez was the father of Hezron.
19 Hezron was the father of Ram.
Ram was the father of Amminadab.
20 Amminadab was the father of Nahshon.
Nahshon was the father of Salmon.
21 Salmon was the father of Boaz.
Boaz was the father of Obed.
22 Obed was the father of Jesse.
Jesse was the father of David.

*d***4:17** *Naomi … now* Literally, "A son was born for Naomi."

1 Samuel

Elkanah's Family Worships at Shiloh

1 1There was a man named Elkanah from the Zuph family who lived in Ramah in the hill country of Ephraim. Elkanah was the son of Jeroham, the son of Elihu, the son of Tohu, the son of Zuph from the tribe of Ephraim. 2Elkanah had two wives. One wife was named Hannah and the other wife was named Peninnah. Peninnah had children, but Hannah did not.

3Every year Elkanah left his town of Ramah and went up to Shiloh. He worshiped the LORD All-Powerful at Shiloh and offered sacrifices* to the Lord there. Shiloh was where Eli's sons, Hophni and Phinehas, served as priests of the LORD. 4Whenever Elkanah offered his sacrifices, he always gave one share of the food to his wife Peninnah and a share of the food to each of Peninnah's children. 5Elkanah always gave an equal share*e* of the food to Hannah. He did this because he loved her very much, even though the LORD had not let Hannah have any children.

Peninnah Upsets Hannah

6Peninnah always upset Hannah and made her feel bad because the LORD had not made her able to have children. 7This happened every year when their family went to the LORD's house at Shiloh. Peninnah would upset Hannah so much that she would begin to cry and would not eat anything. One year when this happened, 8her husband Elkanah said to her, "Hannah, why are you crying? Why won't you eat? Why are you so sad? You have me. Isn't that better than having even ten sons?"

Hannah's Prayer

9After eating and drinking, Hannah quietly got up and went to pray to the Lord.*f* Eli the priest was sitting on a chair near the door of the LORD's Holy Building.*g* 10Hannah was so sad that she cried the whole time she was praying to the LORD. 11She made a special promise to God and said, "LORD All-Powerful, you can see how sad I am. Remember me.

*f***1:9** *went to pray to the Lord* This is from the ancient Greek version.
*g***1:9** *Holy Building* This could mean the Holy Tent at Shiloh where people went to worship the Lord or a larger area where they put the Holy Tent.

*e***1:5** *equal share* Or "double share."

Don't forget me. If you will give me a son, I will give him to you. He will be yours his whole life, and as a Nazirite,* he will not drink wine or strong drink,[a] and no one will ever cut his hair."

[12]Hannah prayed to the LORD a long time. Eli was watching her mouth while she was praying. [13]Hannah was praying in her heart. Her lips were moving, but since she did not say the words out loud, Eli thought she was drunk. [14]He said to her, "You have had too much to drink. It is time to put away the wine."

[15]Hannah answered, "Sir, I have not drunk any wine or beer. I am deeply troubled, and I was telling the LORD about all my problems. [16]Don't think I am a bad woman. I have been praying so long because I have so many troubles and am very sad."

[17]Eli answered, "Go in peace. May the God of Israel give you what you asked for."

[18]Hannah said, "May you be happy with me." Then she left and ate something. She was not sad anymore.

[19]Early the next morning Elkanah's family got up. They worshiped the LORD and then went back home to Ramah.

Samuel's Birth

Elkanah had sexual relations with his wife Hannah, and the LORD remembered Hannah. [20]By that time the following year, Hannah had become pregnant and had a son. She named him Samuel.[b] She said, "His name is Samuel because I asked the LORD for him."

[21]That year Elkanah went to Shiloh to offer sacrifices and to keep the promises he made to God. He took his family with him. [22]But Hannah did not go. She told Elkanah, "When the boy is old enough to eat solid food, I will take him to Shiloh. Then I will give him to the LORD. He will become a Nazirite.[c] He will stay there at Shiloh."

[23]Hannah's husband Elkanah said to her, "Do what you think is best. You may stay home until the boy is old enough to eat solid food. May the LORD do what you have said." So Hannah stayed at home to nurse her son until he was old enough to eat solid food.

Hannah Takes Samuel to Eli at Shiloh

[24]When the boy was old enough to eat solid food, Hannah took him to the LORD's house at Shiloh. She also took a bull that was three years old, 20 pounds[d] of flour, and a bottle of wine.

[25]They went before the Lord. Elkanah killed the bull as a sacrifice to the Lord as he usually did.[e] Then Hannah gave the boy to Eli. [26]She said to him, "Pardon me, sir. I am the same woman who stood near you praying to the LORD. I promise that I am telling the truth. [27]I prayed for this child, and the LORD answered my prayer. He gave me this child. [28]And now I give this child to the LORD. He will serve[f] the LORD all his life."

Then Hannah left the boy there[g] and worshiped the LORD.

Hannah Gives Thanks

2 [1]Hannah said,

"My heart is happy in the LORD.
    I feel very strong[h] in my God.
I laugh at my enemies.[i]
    I am very happy in my victory.
[2] There is no holy God like the LORD.
    There is no God but you.
    There is no Rock* like our God.
[3] Don't continue bragging.
Don't speak proud words,
    because the LORD God knows
        everything.
He leads and judges people.
[4] The bows of strong soldiers break,
    and weak people become strong.
[5] People who had plenty of food in the past
    must now work to get food.
But those who were hungry in the past
    now grow fat on food.
The woman who was not able to have
        children
    now has seven children.
But the woman who had many children
    is sad because her children are gone.
[6] The LORD causes people to die,
    and he causes them to live.
He sends people down to the grave,*
    and he can raise them up to live again.
[7] The LORD makes some poor,
    and he makes others rich.
He humbles some people,
    and he honors others.
[8] He raises the poor from the dust,
    and he takes away their sadness.[j]
He makes them important
    and seats them with princes and at the
        places for honored guests.

[e]**1:25 They went … he usually did** This is found in the ancient Greek version and a Hebrew scroll from Qumran but not in the standard Hebrew text.
[f]**1:28 serve** Or "belong to."
[g]**1:28 left the boy there** This is found in a Hebrew scroll from Qumran but not in the standard Hebrew text.
[h]**2:1 I feel very strong** Literally, "In the LORD my horn is lifted high." The horn is a symbol of strength.
[i]**2:1 I laugh at my enemies** Literally, "My mouth is wide open over my enemies."
[j]**2:8 he … sadness** Literally, "he picks up the poor from the ashes."

[a]**1:11 he … strong drink** This is found in the ancient Greek version and a Hebrew scroll from Qumran but not in the standard Hebrew text.
[b]**1:20 Samuel** This name means "His name is El (God)." But in Hebrew it is like "heard by God."
[c]**1:22 He will become a Nazirite** This is found in the ancient Greek version and a Hebrew scroll from Qumran but not in the standard Hebrew text.
[d]**1:24 20 pounds** Literally, "an ephah" (22 l).

The Lord made the whole world,
and the whole world belongs to him.*a*
9 The Lord protects his holy people.
He keeps them from stumbling.
But evil people will be destroyed.
They will fall in the darkness.
Their power won't help them win.
10 The Lord destroys his enemies.
God Most High will thunder in heaven
against people.
The Lord will judge even the lands that
are far away.
He will give power to his king.
He will make his chosen king*b* strong."

11Elkanah and his family went home to
Ramah, but the boy stayed in Shiloh and
served the Lord under Eli the priest.

Eli's Evil Sons

12Eli's sons were evil men who did not care
about the Lord. 13They did not care about
how priests were supposed to treat people.
Whenever someone brings a sacrifice, priests
are supposed to put the meat in a pot of boiling water. Then their servant is supposed
get the three-pronged fork 14and use it to
get some meat out of the pot or kettle. The
priest is supposed to take whatever his helper
removes from the pot with the special fork.
This is what the priests should have done for
the Israelites who came to offer sacrifices at
Shiloh. 15But that is not what the sons of Eli
did. Even before the fat was burned on the
altar, their servant would go to the people
offering sacrifices and say, "Give the priest
some meat to roast. The priest won't accept
boiled meat from you."

16Maybe the man offering the sacrifice
would say, "Burn the fat*c* first, and then you
can take whatever you want." But the servant
would answer: "No, give me the meat now. If
you don't give it to me, I'll take it from you!"

17In this way Hophni and Phinehas showed
that they did not respect the offerings made
to the Lord. This was a terrible sin against
the Lord.

18But Samuel served the Lord. He was a
helper who wore the linen ephod.* 19Every
year Samuel's mother made a robe for Samuel. She took the little robe to Samuel when
she went up to Shiloh with her husband for
the sacrifice every year.

20Eli would bless Elkanah and his wife.
He would say, "May the Lord give you more
children through Hannah who will take the
place of the boy she prayed for and gave to
the Lord."

Elkanah and Hannah went home. 21The
Lord was kind to Hannah, and she had three
sons and two daughters. The boy Samuel grew
up at the holy place near the Lord.

Eli Fails to Control His Evil Sons

22Eli was very old. He heard about the bad
things his sons were doing to the Israelites at
Shiloh and how his sons were having sexual
relations with the women who served at the
door of the Meeting Tent.*

23Eli said to his sons, "The people here
told me about the evil things you have done.
Why are you doing such things? 24Sons, stop
that! The Lord's people are saying bad things
about you. 25If you sin against other people,
God might protect you. But who can help you
if you sin against the Lord?"

Eli's sons refused to listen to him, so the
Lord decided to kill them.

26The boy Samuel kept growing. He was
pleasing to God and to the people.

The Terrible Prophecy About Eli's Family

27A man of God* came to Eli and said, "The
Lord says, 'I appeared to your ancestors*d*
when they were slaves of Pharaoh. 28From all
the tribes of Israel, I chose your tribe to be my
priests. I chose them to offer sacrifices on my
altar, to burn incense,* and wear the ephod.*
I also let your tribe have the meat from the
sacrifices that the Israelites give to me. 29So
why don't you respect these gifts and sacrifices? You honor your sons more than me. You
become fat eating the best parts of the meat
that the Israelites bring to me.'

30"The Lord, the God of Israel, promised
that your father's family would serve him forever. But now the Lord says, 'That will never
be! I will honor people who honor me, but
bad things will happen to those who refuse
to respect me. 31The time is coming when I
will destroy all your descendants. No one in
your family will live to be an old man. 32Good
things will happen to Israel, but you will see
bad things happening at home.*e* No one in
your family will live to be an old man. 33There
is only one man I will save to serve as priest
at my altar. He will live until his eyes wear
out and his strength is gone. But all of your
descendants will die by the sword. 34I will
give you a sign to show that these things will
come true. Your two sons, Hophni and Phinehas, will die on the same day. 35I will choose
a priest I can trust. This priest will listen to
me and do what I want. I will make his family
strong, and he will always serve before my
chosen king.*f* 36Then whoever is left in your
family will come and bow down before this

---

a2:8 The Lord made ... to him Literally, "The whole
world, even to its foundations, belongs to the Lord.
He set the world on those pillars."

b2:10 chosen king Literally, "anointed one."

c2:16 Burn the fat The fat was the part of the animal
that belonged only to God. It was supposed to be
burned first as an offering to him.

d2:27 ancestors Literally, "father's house." See
"ancestor" in the Word List.

e2:32 but you ... at home These words are not in
the ancient Greek version or the Hebrew scrolls
from Qumran.

f2:35 chosen king Literally, "anointed one."

priest and beg for a little money or a piece of bread. They will say, "Please give me a job as priest so that I can have some food to eat."'"

God Calls Samuel

3 [1]The boy Samuel was Eli's helper and served the LORD with him. At that time the LORD did not speak directly to people very often. There were very few visions.*

[2]Eli's eyes were getting so weak that he was almost blind. One night he went to his room to go to bed. [3]The special lamp in the temple[a] was still burning, so Samuel lay down in the temple near where the Holy Box* was. [4]The LORD called Samuel, and Samuel answered, "Here I am." [5]Samuel thought Eli was calling him, so he ran to Eli and said, "Here I am. You called me."

But Eli said, "I didn't call you. Go back to bed."

So Samuel went back to bed. [6]Again the LORD called, "Samuel!" Again Samuel ran to Eli and said, "Here I am. You called me."

Eli said, "I didn't call you. Go back to bed."

[7]Samuel did not yet know the LORD because the LORD had not spoken directly to him before.[b]

[8]The LORD called Samuel the third time. Again Samuel got up and went to Eli and said, "Here I am. You called me."

Finally, Eli understood that the LORD was calling the boy. [9]Eli told Samuel, "Go to bed. If he calls you again, say, 'Speak, LORD. I am your servant, and I am listening.'"

So Samuel went back to bed. [10]The LORD came and stood there. He called as he did before, saying, "Samuel, Samuel!"

Samuel said, "Speak. I am your servant, and I am listening."

[11]The LORD said to Samuel, "I will soon do things in Israel that will shock anyone who hears about them. [12]I will do everything I said I would do against Eli and his family, everything from the beginning to the end. [13]I told Eli I would punish his family forever. I will do this because Eli knew his sons were saying and doing bad things against God. But he failed to control them. [14]That is why I swore an oath* that sacrifices and offerings will never take away the sins of the people in Eli's family.[c]"

[15]Samuel lay down in bed until the morning came. He got up early and opened the doors of the LORD's house. Samuel was afraid to tell Eli about the vision.

[16]But Eli said to Samuel, "Samuel, my son."

Samuel answered, "Yes, sir."

[17]Eli asked, "What did the LORD say to you? Don't hide it from me. God will punish you if you hide anything from the message he spoke to you."

[18]So Samuel told Eli everything. He did not hide anything from Eli.

Eli said, "He is the LORD. Let him do whatever he thinks is right."

[19]The LORD was with Samuel while he grew up. He did not let any of Samuel's messages prove false. [20]Then all Israel, from Dan to Beersheba, knew that Samuel was a true prophet of the LORD. [21]And the LORD continued to appear to Samuel at Shiloh. He revealed himself to Samuel as the word of the LORD.[d]

4 [1]News about Samuel spread throughout Israel. Eli was very old. His sons kept doing bad things before the LORD.[e]

The Philistines Defeat the Israelites

At that time the Israelites went out to fight against the Philistines. The Israelites made their camp at Ebenezer. The Philistines made their camp at Aphek. [2]The Philistines lined up their soldiers in front of the Israelites and began the attack.

The Philistines defeated the Israelites. They killed about 4000 soldiers from Israel's army. [3]The rest of the Israelite soldiers went back to their camp. The elders* of Israel asked, "Why did the LORD let the Philistines defeat us? Let's bring the LORD's Box of the Agreement* from Shiloh. God will go with us into battle and save us from our enemies."

[4]So the people sent men to Shiloh. The men brought back the LORD All-Powerful's Box of the Agreement. On top of the Box are the Cherub angels. They are like the throne that the LORD sits on. Eli's two sons, Hophni and Phinehas, came with the Box.

[5]When the LORD's Box of the Agreement came into the camp, all the Israelites gave a great shout loud enough to make the ground shake. [6]The Philistines heard Israel's shout and asked, "Why are the people so excited in the Hebrew[f] camp?"

Then the Philistines learned that the LORD's Holy Box* had been brought into Israel's camp. [7]They became afraid and said, "Gods have come to their camp! We're in trouble. This has never happened before. [8]We are worried. Who can save us from these powerful gods? These gods are the same ones that gave the Egyptians those diseases and terrible sicknesses. [9]Be brave, Philistines. Fight like men. In the past they were our slaves, so fight like men or you will become their slaves."

[10]So the Philistines fought very hard and

---

[a]3:3 **temple** This could mean the Holy Tent at Shiloh where people went to worship the Lord or a larger area where they put the Holy Tent.

[b]3:7 **the LORD ... him before** Literally, "the word of the LORD had not yet been revealed to him."

[c]3:14 Or "That is why I swore an oath that Eli's family would not be forgiven for their sins against the offerings and sacrifices."

[d]3:21 **word of the LORD** This often means simply "a message from God." But sometimes it may mean a special way God spoke to his prophets.

[e]4:1 **Eli ... the LORD** This is from the ancient Greek version.

[f]4:6 **Hebrew** Or "Israelite."

defeated the Israelites. The Israelite soldiers ran away and went home. It was a terrible defeat for Israel. 30,000 Israelite soldiers were killed. [11]The Philistines took God's Holy Box and killed Eli's two sons, Hophni and Phinehas.

[12]One of the men who ran from the battle was a man from the tribe of Benjamin. He tore his clothes and put dust on his head to show his great sadness. [13]Eli was worried about the Holy Box, so he was sitting there by the city gate waiting and watching when the Benjamite man came into Shiloh and told the bad news. All the people in town began to cry loudly. [14-15]Eli was 98 years old. He was blind, so he could not see what was happening, but he could hear the loud noise of the people crying. Eli asked, "Why are the people making this loud noise?"

The Benjamite man ran to Eli and told him what happened. [16]He said, "I am the man who just came from the battle. I ran away from the battle today."

Eli asked, "What happened, son?"

[17]The Benjamite man answered, "Israel ran away from the Philistines. The Israelite army has lost many soldiers. Your two sons are both dead, and the Philistines took God's Holy Box."

[18]When the Benjamite man mentioned God's Holy Box, Eli fell backward off his chair near the gate and broke his neck. Eli was old and fat, so he died. He had led Israel for 20 years.[a]

The Glory Is Gone

[19]Eli's daughter-in-law, the wife of Phinehas, was pregnant. It was nearly time for her baby to be born. She heard the news that God's Holy Box* was taken. She also heard that her father-in-law Eli and her husband Phinehas were both dead. As soon as she heard the news, her pain started and she began giving birth to her baby. [20]She was about to die when the women who were helping her said, "Don't worry, you have given birth to a son."

But she did not answer or pay attention. [21]She named the baby Ichabod,[b] that is to say, "Israel's glory has been taken away."[c] She did this because God's Holy Box was taken away and because both her father-in-law and her husband were dead. [22]She said, "Israel's glory has been taken away" because the Philistines had taken God's Holy Box.

The Holy Box Troubles the Philistines

5 [1]The Philistines carried God's Holy Box,* from Ebenezer to Ashdod. [2]They carried God's Holy Box into the temple of Dagon* and put it next to the statue of Dagon. [3]The next morning, the people of Ashdod got up and found Dagon lying face down on the ground before the LORD's Box.

The people of Ashdod put the statue of Dagon back in its place. [4]But the next morning when the people of Ashdod got up, they found Dagon on the ground again. Dagon had fallen down before the LORD's Holy Box. This time, Dagon's head and hands were broken off and were lying in the doorway. Only his body was still in one piece. [5]That is why, even today, the priests or other people refuse to step on the threshold when they enter Dagon's temple at Ashdod.

[6]The LORD made life hard for the people of Ashdod and their neighbors. He gave them many troubles and caused them to get tumors. He also sent mice to them. The mice ran all over their ships and then onto their land. The people in the city were very afraid.[d] [7]They saw what was happening and said, "The Holy Box of the God of Israel can't stay here. God is punishing us and Dagon our god."

[8]The people of Ashdod called the five Philistine rulers together and asked them, "What must we do with the Holy Box of the God of Israel?"

The rulers answered, "Move the Holy Box of the God of Israel to Gath." So the Philistines moved God's Holy Box.

[9]But after the Philistines had moved God's Holy Box to Gath, the LORD punished that city. The people became very frightened. God caused many troubles for all the people—young and old. He caused the people in Gath to have tumors. [10]So the Philistines sent God's Holy Box to Ekron.

But when God's Holy Box came into Ekron, the people of Ekron complained. They said, "Why are you bringing the Box of the God of Israel to our city Ekron? Do you want to kill us and our people?" [11]The people of Ekron called all the Philistine rulers together and said to the rulers, "Send the Box of the God of Israel back home before it kills us and our people!"

The people of Ekron were deathly afraid because God severely punished them there. [12]Many people died, and those who did not, had tumors. The people of Ekron cried loudly to heaven.

God's Holy Box Is Sent Back Home

6 [1]The Philistines kept the Holy Box* in their land for seven months. [2]The Philistines called their priests and magicians and said, "What must we do with the LORD's Box? Tell us how to send the Box back home."

[3]The priests and magicians answered, "If you send back the Holy Box of the God of

---

[a]**4:18** *20 years* This is found in the ancient Greek version and Josephus. The standard Hebrew text has "40 years."

[b]**4:21** *Ichabod* This name means "No glory." The Greek has "Ouai Barchaboth."

[c]**4:21** *that is ... taken away* This is not in the ancient Greek version.

[d]**5:6** *He also sent ... afraid* This is from the ancient Greek version.

Israel, don't send it away empty. You must offer gifts to the God of Israel. Then you will be healed. You must do this so that God will stop punishing you."[a]

4The Philistines asked, "What kind of gifts should we send for Israel's God to forgive us?"

The priests and magicians answered, "There are five Philistine leaders, one leader for each city. All of you and your leaders had the same problems. So you must make five gold models to look like five tumors. And you must make five gold models to look like five mice. 5So make models of the tumors and models of the mice that are ruining the country. Give these gold models to the God of Israel as payment. Then maybe the God of Israel will stop punishing you, your gods, and your land. 6Don't be stubborn like Pharaoh and the Egyptians. God punished the Egyptians. That is why the Egyptians let the Israelites leave Egypt.

7"You must build a new wagon and get two cows that just had calves. These must be cows that have never worked in the fields. Tie the cows to the wagon so that they can pull it. Then take the calves back home and put them in their pen. Don't let them follow their mothers.[b] 8Put the Lord's Holy Box on the wagon. You must put the golden models in the bag beside the Box. They are your gifts for God to forgive your sins. Send the wagon straight on its way. 9Watch the wagon. If the wagon goes toward Beth Shemesh in Israel's own land, the Lord has given us this great sickness. But if the cows don't go straight to Beth Shemesh, we will know it was not their God who brought this sickness to us. It was just one of those things that sometimes happen."

10The Philistines did what the priests and magicians said. They found two cows that had just had calves and tied the cows to the wagon and put the calves in their pens at home. 11Then the Philistines put the Lord's Holy Box on the wagon along with the bag with the golden models of the tumors and mice. 12The cows went straight to Beth Shemesh. The cows stayed on the road, mooing all the way. They did not turn right or left. The Philistine rulers followed the cows as far as the city limits of Beth Shemesh.

13The people of Beth Shemesh were harvesting their wheat in the valley. They looked up and saw the Holy Box. They were very happy to see it again. They ran to get it. 14-15The wagon came to the field that belonged to Joshua of Beth Shemesh and stopped there near a large rock.

Some Levites* took down the Lord's Holy Box and the bag that had the golden models. The Levites put the Lord's Box and the bag that was with it on the large rock.

The people of Beth Shemesh cut up the wagon and killed the cows. That day, they sacrificed the cows as burnt offerings to the Lord.

16The five Philistine rulers watched the people of Beth Shemesh do this and then went back to Ekron that same day.

17In this way the Philistines sent golden models of tumors as gifts for their sins to the Lord. They sent one golden model of a tumor for each of the Philistine towns of Ashdod, Gaza, Ashkelon, Gath, and Ekron. 18The Philistines also sent golden models of mice. The number of these golden mice was the same number as the towns that belonged to the five Philistine rulers. These towns had walls around them, and each town had villages around it.

The people of Beth Shemesh put the Lord's Holy Box on a rock. That rock is still in the field of Joshua from Beth Shemesh. 19But there were no priests[c] there, and the men of Beth Shemesh looked at the Lord's Holy Box. So the Lord killed 70 men from Beth Shemesh. The people of Beth Shemesh cried because the Lord punished them so severely. 20They said, "Where is a priest who can care for the Holy Box? Where should the Box go from here?"

21There was a priest at Kiriath Jearim. The people of Beth Shemesh sent messengers to the people of Kiriath Jearim. The messengers said, "The Philistines have brought back the Lord's Holy Box. Come down and take it to your city."

7 1The men of Kiriath Jearim came and took the Lord's Holy Box up the hill to the house of Abinadab the priest. They performed a special ceremony to prepare Abinadab's son, Eleazar, to guard the Lord's Holy Box. 2The Box stayed there at Kiriath Jearim for a long time.

The Lord Saves the Israelites

Twenty years passed while the Holy Box was in Kiriath Jearim, and the Israelites began to follow the Lord again. 3Samuel told the Israelites, "If you are really coming back to the Lord with all your heart, you must throw away your foreign gods and your idols* of Ashtoreth.* You must give yourselves fully to the Lord and serve only him. Then he will save you from the Philistines."

4So the Israelites threw away their statues of Baal* and Ashtoreth. The Israelites served only the Lord.

5Samuel said, "All Israel must meet at Mizpah. I will pray to the Lord for you."

[a]6:3 You must do … punishing you This is found in the ancient Greek version and a Hebrew scroll from Qumran. The standard Hebrew text has "Then you will know why God did not stop punishing you."
[b]6:7 Don't let … mothers The Philistines thought if the cows did not try to find their calves it would prove that God was leading them and that he had accepted their gifts.

[c]6:19 no priests Only priests were allowed to carry the Box of the Agreement.

⁶The Israelites met together at Mizpah. They got water and poured it out before the LORD. In this way they began a time of fasting. They did not eat any food that day, and they confessed their sins. They said, "We have sinned against the LORD." So Samuel served as a judge* of Israel at Mizpah.

⁷When the Philistines heard that the Israelites were meeting at Mizpah, they went to fight them. The Israelites were frightened when they heard the Philistines were coming ⁸and said to Samuel, "Don't stop praying to the LORD our God for us. Ask the LORD to save us from the Philistines."

⁹Samuel took a baby lamb and offered it as a whole burnt offering to the LORD. He prayed to the LORD for Israel, and the LORD answered his prayer. ¹⁰The Philistines came closer and closer to fight the Israelites while Samuel offered the sacrifice. But then, the LORD caused a loud clap of thunder to hit near the Philistines. The thunder scared the Philistines, and they became confused, so the Israelites defeated them in battle. ¹¹The men of Israel ran out of Mizpah and chased the Philistines all the way to Beth Car. They killed Philistine soldiers all along the way.

Peace Comes to Israel

¹²After this Samuel set up a special stone to help people remember what God did. Samuel put the stone between Mizpah and Shen*ᵃ* and named the stone "Stone of Help."*ᵇ* Samuel said, "The LORD helped us all the way to this place."

¹³The Philistines were defeated and did not enter the land of Israel again. The LORD was against the Philistines during the rest of Samuel's life. ¹⁴The Philistines had taken some cities from Israel, but the Israelites won them back. They recovered those cities throughout the Philistine area, from Ekron to Gath.

There was also peace between Israel and the Amorites.

¹⁵Samuel led Israel all his life. ¹⁶He went from place to place judging the Israelites. Every year he traveled around the country. He went to Bethel, Gilgal, and Mizpah and he judged the Israelites in all these places. ¹⁷But Samuel always went back to his home in Ramah. There he built an altar to the LORD and judged Israel.

Israel Asks for a King

8 ¹When Samuel was old, he appointed his sons to be judges* for Israel. ²Samuel's first son was named Joel. His second son was named Abijah. Joel and Abijah were judges in Beersheba. ³But Samuel's sons did not live the same way he did. Joel and Abijah accepted bribes. They took money secretly and changed their decisions in court. They cheated people in court. ⁴So all the elders* of Israel met together and went to Ramah to meet with Samuel. ⁵The elders said to Samuel, "You're old, and your sons don't live right. They are not like you. Now, give us a king to rule us like all the other nations."

⁶So the elders asked for a king to lead them. Samuel thought this was a bad idea, so he prayed to the LORD. ⁷The LORD told Samuel, "Do what the people tell you. They have not rejected you. They have rejected me. They don't want me to be their king. ⁸They are doing the same thing they have always done. I took them out of Egypt, but they left me and served other gods. They are doing the same to you. ⁹So listen to the people and do what they say. But give them a warning. Tell the people what a king will do to them. Tell them how a king rules people."

¹⁰Those people asked for a king. So Samuel told them everything the LORD said. ¹¹Samuel said, "If you have a king ruling over you, this is what he will do: He will take away your sons and force them to serve him. He will force them to be soldiers—they must fight from his chariots* and become horse soldiers in his army. Your sons will become guards running in front of the king's chariot.

¹²"A king will force your sons to become soldiers. He will choose which of your sons will be officers over 1000 men and which will be officers over 50 men.

"A king will force some of your sons to plow his fields and gather his harvest. He will force some of your sons to make weapons for war and to make things for his chariots.

¹³"A king will take your daughters and force some of them to make perfume for him and some to cook and bake for him.

¹⁴"A king will take your best fields, vineyards,* and olive groves. He will take them from you and give them to his officers. ¹⁵He will take one-tenth of your grain and grapes, and he will give them to his officers and servants.

¹⁶"A king will take your men and women servants. He will take your best cattleᶜ and your donkeys. He will use them all for his own work. ¹⁷He will take one-tenth of your flocks.

"And you yourselves will become slaves of this king. ¹⁸When that time comes, you will cry because of the king you chose. But the LORD won't answer you at that time."

¹⁹But the people would not listen to Samuel. They said, "No, we want a king to rule over us. ²⁰Then we will be the same as all the other nations. Our king will lead us. He will go before us and fight our battles."

²¹Samuel listened to the people and then repeated their words to the LORD. ²²The LORD

---

*ᵃ*7:12 *Shen* Or "Jeshanah," a town about 17 miles north of Jerusalem.
*ᵇ*7:12 *Stone of Help* Or "Ebenezer."

*ᶜ*8:16 *cattle* This is from the ancient Greek version. The standard Hebrew text has "young men."

answered, "Listen to them and give them a king."

Then Samuel told the Israelites, "You will have a king. Now go home."

Saul Looks for His Father's Donkeys

9 ¹Kish was an important man from the tribe of Benjamin. He was the son of Abiel. Abiel was the son of Zeror. Zeror was the son of Becorath. Becorath was the son of Aphiah, a man from Benjamin. ²Kish had a son named Saul, who was a handsome young man. There was no one more handsome than Saul. He stood a head taller than any other man in Israel.

³One day, Kish's donkeys got lost. So he said to his son Saul, "Take one of the servants and go look for the donkeys." ⁴Saul went to look for the donkeys. He walked through the hills of Ephraim and through the area around Shalisha. But Saul and the servant could not find Kish's donkeys. So they went to the area around Shaalim, but the donkeys were not there either. Then Saul traveled through the land of Benjamin, but he and the servant still could not find the donkeys.

⁵Finally, Saul and the servant came to the town named Zuph. Saul said to his servant, "Let's go back. My father will stop worrying about the donkeys and start worrying about us."

⁶But the servant answered, "A man of God* is in this town. People respect him. Everything he says comes true, so let's go into town. Maybe the man of God will tell us where we should go next."

⁷Saul said to his servant, "Sure, we can go into town, but what can we give to him? We have no gift to give the man of God. Even the food in our bags is gone. What can we give him?"

⁸Again the servant answered Saul. "Look, I have a little bit of money.ᵃ Let's give it to the man of God. Then he will tell us where we should go."

⁹⁻¹¹Saul said to his servant, "That is a good idea. Let's go." So they went to the town where the man of God was.

Saul and the servant were walking up the hill toward town when they met some young women on the road. The young women were coming out to get water. Saul and the servant asked the young women, "Is the seer* here?" (In the past, people in Israel called a prophet a "seer." So if they wanted to ask something from God, they would say, "Let's go to the seer.")

¹²The young women answered, "Yes, the seer is here. He is just up the road. He came to town today. Some people are meeting together today to share in a fellowship offering at the place for worship.ᵇ ¹³So go into town and you will find him. If you hurry, you can catch him before he goes up to eat at the place for worship. The seer blesses the sacrifice, so the people won't begin eating until he gets there. If you hurry, you can find him."

¹⁴Saul and the servant started walking up the hill to town. Just as they came into town, they saw Samuel coming out of town, walking toward them. He was on his way to the place for worship.

¹⁵The day before, the LORD had told Samuel, ¹⁶"At this time tomorrow I will send a man to you. He will be from the tribe of Benjamin. You must anoint* him and make him the new leader over my people Israel. This man will save my people from the Philistines. I have seen my people suffering,ᶜ and I have heard their cries for help."

¹⁷When Samuel saw Saul, the LORD said to Samuel, "This is the man I told you about. He will rule my people."

¹⁸Saul went up to a man near the gate to ask directions. This man just happened to be Samuel. Saul said, "Excuse me. Could you tell me where the seer's house is?"

¹⁹Samuel answered, "I am the seer. Go on up ahead of me to the place for worship. You and your servant will eat with me today. I will let you go home tomorrow morning. I will answer all your questions. ²⁰And don't worry about the donkeys that you lost three days ago. They have been found. Now, there is something that everyone in Israel is looking for and that something is you and your family."

²¹Saul answered, "But I am a member of the tribe of Benjamin. It is the smallest tribe in Israel. And my family is the smallest in the tribe of Benjamin. Why do you say Israel wants me?"

²²Then Samuel took Saul and his servant to the eating area. About 30 people had been invited to eat together and share the sacrifice. Samuel gave Saul and his servant the most important place at the table. ²³Samuel said to the cook, "Bring the meat I gave you. It is the share I told you to save."

²⁴The cook brought out the thighᵈ and put it on the table in front of Saul. Samuel said, "Eat the meat that was put in front of you. It was saved for you for this special time when I called the people together." So Saul ate with Samuel that day.

²⁵After they finished eating, they came down from the place for worship and went

---

ᵇ**9:12** *place for worship* Or "high place." See "high place" in the Word List. Also in verses 14, 19, 25.
ᶜ**9:16** *suffering* This is from the ancient Greek version.
ᵈ**9:24** *thigh* This was probably the left thigh that was reserved for important guests. The right thigh was reserved for the priest who sacrificed the animal. This priest helped kill the animal and put the fat from the animal on the altar as a gift to God.

ᵃ**9:8** *a little bit of money* Literally, "1/4 shekel of silver" (about 1/10 of an ounce).

back to town. Samuel made a bed for Saul on the roof, [26]and Saul went to sleep.[a]

Early the next morning, Samuel shouted to Saul on the roof and said, "Get up. I will send you on your way." Saul got up and went out of the house with Samuel.

[27]Saul, his servant, and Samuel were walking together near the edge of town. Samuel said to Saul, "Tell your servant to go on ahead of us. I have a message for you from God." So the servant walked ahead of them.

Samuel Anoints Saul

10 [1]Samuel took a jar of the special oil and poured the oil on Saul's head. Samuel kissed Saul and said, "The Lord has anointed* you to be the leader over the people who belong to him. You will control the people. You will save them from the enemies that are all around them. He has anointed you to be ruler over his people. Here is a sign that will prove this is true:[b] [2]After you leave me today, you will meet two men near Rachel's tomb on the border of Benjamin at Zelzah. The two men will say to you, 'Someone found the donkeys you were looking for. Your father stopped worrying about his donkeys. Now he is worrying about you. He is saying: What will I do about my son?'"

[3]Samuel said, "Then you will go until you come to the large oak tree at Tabor. Three men will meet you there. They will be on their way to worship God at Bethel. One man will be carrying three young goats. The second man will be carrying three loaves of bread. And the third man will have a leather bag full of wine. [4]These three men will say hello to you. They will offer you two loaves of bread, and you will accept the two loaves. [5]Then you will go to Gibeath Elohim. There is a Philistine fort in that place. When you come to this town, a group of prophets will come out. These prophets will come down from the place for worship.[c] They will be prophesying.[d] They will be playing harps, tambourines, flutes, and lyres. [6]Then the Lord's Spirit will come on you with great power. You will be changed. You will be like a different man. You will begin to prophesy with these prophets. [7]After that happens, you can do whatever you choose to do, because God will be with you.

[8]"Go to Gilgal before me. Then I will come

there to you. And I will offer burnt offerings and fellowship offerings. But you must wait seven days. Then I will come and tell you what to do."

Saul Becomes Like the Prophets

[9]Just as Saul turned to leave Samuel, God turned Saul's life around. All these things happened that day. [10]When Saul and his servant came to Gibeath Elohim, Saul met a group of prophets. God's Spirit came on Saul with great power, and Saul prophesied with the prophets. [11]Some of the people who had known Saul before saw him prophesying with the prophets. So they asked each other, "What has happened to Kish's son? Is Saul also one of the prophets?"

[12]A man living in Gibeath Elohim said, "Yes, and it seems that he is their leader."[e] That is why this became a famous saying: "Is Saul also one of the prophets?"

Saul Arrives Home

[13]After Saul finished prophesying, he went to the place of worship.

[14]Saul's uncle asked Saul and his servant, "Where have you been?"

Saul said, "We were looking for the donkeys. When we couldn't find them, we went to see Samuel."

[15]Saul's uncle said, "Please tell me, what did Samuel say to you?"

[16]Saul answered, "Samuel told us the donkeys were already found." He did not tell his uncle everything. Saul did not tell him what Samuel said about the kingdom.

Samuel Announces Saul as King

[17]Samuel told all the Israelites to meet together with the Lord at Mizpah. [18]Samuel told the Israelites, "The Lord, the God of Israel says, 'I led Israel out of Egypt. I saved you from Egypt's control and from the other kingdoms that tried to hurt you.' [19]But today you have rejected your God. Your God saves you from all your troubles and problems. But you said, 'No, we want a king to rule us.' Now come, stand before the Lord in your family groups and tribes."

[20]Samuel brought all the tribes of Israel near. Then Samuel began to choose the new king. First, the tribe of Benjamin was chosen. [21]Samuel told each family in the tribe of Benjamin to pass by. Matri's family was chosen. Then Samuel told each man in Matri's family to walk by. Saul son of Kish was chosen.

But when the people looked for Saul, they could not find him. [22]Then they asked the Lord, "Has Saul come here yet?"

The Lord said, "Saul is hiding behind the supplies."

---

[a]**9:25–26 made ... to sleep** This is from the ancient Greek version. The standard Hebrew text has "Samuel spoke with Saul on the roof." In ancient Israel, houses had flat roofs that were used as an extra room.

[b]**10:1 You will control ... true** This is from the ancient Greek version.

[c]**10:5 place for worship** Or "high places," places for worshiping God or false gods. These places were often on the hills and mountains.

[d]**10:5 prophesying** This usually means "speaking for God." But here, this also means that the Spirit of God took control of people, causing them to sing and dance. Also in verses 11, 13.

[e]**10:12 Yes ... leader** Literally, "And who is their father?" Often the man who taught and led other prophets was called "father."

23The people ran and took Saul out from behind the supplies. Saul stood up among the people. He was a head taller than anyone else.

24Samuel said to all the people, "See the man the LORD has chosen. There is no one like Saul among the people."

Then the people shouted, "Long live the king!"

25Samuel explained the rules of the kingdom to the people. He wrote the rules in a book and put the book before the LORD. Then Samuel told the people to go home.

26Saul also went to his home in Gibeah. God touched the hearts of brave men who then began to follow Saul. 27But some troublemakers said, "How can this man save us?" They said bad things about Saul and refused to bring gifts to him. But Saul said nothing.

Nahash, King of the Ammonites

King Nahash of the Ammonites had been hurting the tribes of Gad and Reuben. Nahash poked out the right eye of each of the men and did not allow anyone to help them. He poked out the right eye of every Israelite man living in the area east of the Jordan River. But 7000 Israelite men ran away from the Ammonites and came to Jabesh Gilead.a

11 1About a month later, Nahash the Ammonite and his army surrounded Jabesh Gilead. All the people of Jabesh said to Nahash, "If you will make a treaty with us, we will serve you."

2But he answered, "I will make a treaty with you people only if I can poke out the right eye of each person. Then all Israel will be ashamed."

3The leaders of Jabesh said to Nahash, "Let us have seven days. We will send messengers through all Israel. If no one comes to help us, we will come up to you and surrender to you."

Saul Saves Jabesh Gilead

4The messengers came to Gibeah where Saul lived. They told the news to the people. The people cried loudly. 5Saul had been out in the field with his oxen. When he came in from the field he heard the people crying and asked, "What's wrong with the people? Why are they crying?"

Then the people told Saul what the messengers from Jabesh said. 6Saul listened to their story. Then God's Spirit came on him with great power. Saul became very angry. 7He took a pair of oxen and cut them in pieces. Then he gave the pieces of the oxen to messengers. He ordered the messengers to carry the pieces throughout the land of Israel. He

told them to give this message to the Israelites: "Come follow Saul and Samuel. If anyone doesn't come and help them, this same thing will happen to his oxen."

A great fear from the LORD came on the people. They all came together like one person. 8Saul gathered the men together at Bezek. There were 300,000 men from Israel and 30,000 men from Judah.

9Saul and his army told the messengers from Jabesh, "Tell the people at Jabesh in Gilead that by noon tomorrow, you will be saved."

The messengers told Saul's message to the people at Jabesh, and they were very happy. 10Then the people of Jabesh said to Nahash the Ammonite, "Tomorrow we will come to you, and you can do whatever you want to us."

11The next morning Saul separated his soldiers into three groups. At sunrise, Saul and his soldiers entered the Ammonite camp. Saul attacked while they were changing guards that morning. He and his soldiers defeated the Ammonites before noon. The Ammonite soldiers all ran away in different directions—no two soldiers stayed together.

12Then the people said to Samuel, "Where are the people who said they didn't want Saul to rule as king? Bring them here, and we will kill them."

13But Saul said, "No, don't kill anyone today! The LORD saved Israel today."

14Then Samuel said to the people, "Come, let's go to Gilgal. At Gilgal we will again make Saul the king."

15All the people went to Gilgal. There, in front of the LORD, the people made Saul king. They offered fellowship offerings to the LORD. Saul and all the Israelites had a great celebration.

Samuel Speaks About the King

12 1Samuel said to all Israel: "I have done everything you wanted me to do. I have put a king over you. 2Now you have a king to lead you. I am old and gray, but my sons are here with you. I have been your leader since I was young. 3Here I am. If I have done anything wrong, you must tell these things to the LORD and his chosen king.b Did I steal anyone's ox or donkey? Did I hurt or cheat anyone? Did I ever take money, or even a pair of sandals, to do something wrong? If I did any of these things, I will make it right."

4The Israelites answered, "No, you never did anything bad to us. You never cheated us or took things from us."

5Samuel said to the Israelites, "The LORD and his chosen king are witnesses today. They heard what you said. They know that you could find nothing wrong with me."

---

a10:27 Nahash ... came to Jabesh Gilead This is found in some ancient versions and in a Hebrew scroll from Qumran but not in the standard Hebrew text.

b12:3 chosen king Literally, "anointed one." Also in verse 5.

The people answered, "Yes, the LORD is our witness!"

[6]Then Samuel said to the people, "The LORD has seen what happened. The LORD is the one who chose Moses and Aaron and brought your ancestors* out of Egypt. [7]Now, stand there, and I will tell you about the good things the LORD did for you and your ancestors.

[8]"Jacob went to Egypt. Later, the Egyptians made life hard for his descendants. So they cried to the LORD for help. The LORD sent Moses and Aaron, and they took your ancestors out of Egypt and led them to live in this place.

[9]"But your ancestors forgot the LORD their God. So he let them become the slaves of Sisera, the commander of the army at Hazor. Then the Lord let them become the slaves of the Philistines and the king of Moab. They all fought against your ancestors. [10]But your ancestors cried to the LORD for help. They said, 'We have sinned. We left the LORD, and we served the false gods Baal* and Ashtoreth.* But now save us from our enemies, and we will serve you.'

[11]"So the LORD sent Jerub Baal *(Gideon)*, Barak, Jephthah, and Samuel. He saved you from your enemies around you, and you lived in safety. [12]But then you saw King Nahash of the Ammonites coming to fight against you. You said, 'No, we want a king to rule over us!' You said that, even though the LORD your God was already your king. [13]Now, here is the king you chose. The LORD put this king over you. [14]You must fear and respect the LORD. You must serve him and obey his commands. You must not turn against him. You and the king ruling over you must follow the LORD your God. If you do, God will save you.*a* [15]But if you don't obey the LORD, and if you turn against him, he will be against you. The LORD will destroy you and your king.

[16]"Now stand still and see the great thing the LORD will do before your eyes. [17]Now is the time of the wheat harvest.*b* I will pray to the LORD and ask him to send thunder and rain. Then you will know you did a very bad thing against the LORD when you asked for a king."

[18]So Samuel prayed to the LORD. That same day the LORD sent thunder and rain. And the people became very afraid of the LORD and Samuel. [19]All the people said to Samuel, "Pray to the LORD your God for us, your servants. Don't let us die! We have sinned many times. And now we have added to these sins—we have asked for a king."

[20]Samuel answered, "Don't be afraid. It is true that you did all these bad things, but don't stop following the LORD. Serve the LORD with

all your heart. [21]Idols* are only statues—they can't help you. So don't worship them. Idols can't help you or save you. They are nothing! [22]"But the LORD won't leave his people. No, the LORD was pleased to make you his own people. So for his own good name, he won't leave you. [23]And as for me, I would never stop praying for you. If I stopped praying for you, I would be sinning against the LORD. I will continue to teach you the right way to live a good life. [24]But you must honor the LORD. You must sincerely serve the LORD with all your heart. Remember the wonderful things he did for you. [25]But if you are stubborn and do evil, God will throw you and your king away—like sweeping dirt out with a broom."

Saul Makes His First Mistake

13 [1]Saul was 30*c* years old when he became king. He ruled over Israel 42 years.*d* [2]Saul chose 3000 men from Israel. There were 2000 men who stayed with him at Micmash in the hill country of Bethel. There were 1000 men who stayed with Jonathan at Gibeah in Benjamin. Saul sent the other men in the army back home.

[3]Jonathan defeated the Philistines at their camp in Geba. The Philistines heard about this. They said, "The Hebrews have rebelled."*e*

Saul said, "Let the Hebrew people hear what happened." So Saul told the men to blow trumpets through all the land of Israel. [4]All the Israelites heard this news: "Saul has killed the Philistine leader. Now the Philistines will really hate the Israelites!"

The Israelites were called to join Saul at Gilgal. [5]The Philistines gathered to fight Israel. The Philistines camped at Micmash, east of Beth Aven. They had 3000*f* chariots* and 6000 horse soldiers. There were so many Philistines that they were like sand on the seashore.

[6]The Israelites saw that they were in trouble. They felt trapped. They ran away to hide in caves and cracks in the rock. They hid among the rocks, in wells, and in other holes in the ground. [7]Some Hebrews even went across the Jordan River to the land of Gad and Gilead. Saul was still at Gilgal. All the men in his army were shaking with fear.

[8]Samuel said he would meet Saul at Gilgal. Saul waited there seven days. But Samuel had not yet come to Gilgal, and the soldiers began

---

*a***12:14** *If you do, God will save you* This is from the ancient Greek version.

*b***12:17** *time of … harvest* This was the dry time of year when no rains fell.

*c***13:1** *30* This first number and part of the second number in this verse are missing in the Hebrew text. The whole verse is missing from most copies of the ancient Greek version, but a few late Greek copies have the numbers 30 and 42. Acts 13:21 says that Saul was king for forty years.

*d***13:1** *He ruled … 42 years* Or "After he had ruled over Israel for 2 years, …."

*e***13:3** *They said … rebelled* This is from the ancient Greek version.

*f***13:5** *3000* This is found in some copies of the ancient Greek version and the Syriac version. The standard Hebrew text has "30,000."

to leave Saul. ⁹So Saul said, "Bring me the burnt offerings and the fellowship offerings." Then Saul offered the burnt offering. ¹⁰As soon as Saul finished offering that sacrifice, Samuel arrived. Saul went out to meet him.

¹¹Samuel asked, "What have you done?"

Saul answered, "I saw the soldiers leaving me. You were not here on time, and the Philistines were gathering at Micmash. ¹²I thought to myself, 'The Philistines will come here and attack me at Gilgal, and I haven't asked the Lord to help us yet. So I forced myself to offer the burnt offering.'"

¹³Samuel said, "You did a foolish thing. You did not obey the Lord your God. If you had obeyed God's command, he would have let your family rule Israel forever. ¹⁴But now your kingdom won't continue. The Lord was looking for a man who wants to obey him. He has found that man—and the Lord has chosen him to be the new leader of his people, because you didn't obey his command." ¹⁵Then Samuel got up and left Gilgal.

The Battle at Micmash

Saul and the rest of his army left Gilgal and went to Gibeah in Benjamin. Saul counted the men who were still with him. There were about 600. ¹⁶Saul, his son Jonathan, and the soldiers went to Geba in Benjamin.

The Philistines were camped at Micmash. ¹⁷So their best soldiers began the attack. The Philistine army split into three groups. One group went north on the road to Ophrah, near Shual. ¹⁸The second group went southeast on the road to Beth Horon, and the third group went east on the road to the border. That road looks over the Valley of Zeboim toward the desert.

¹⁹There were no blacksmiths* in Israel. The Philistines would not allow them because they were afraid the Israelites would make iron swords and spears. ²⁰Only the Philistines could sharpen iron tools. So if the Israelites needed to sharpen their plows, hoes, axes, or sickles,* they had to go to the Philistines. ²¹The Philistine blacksmiths charged ⅓ ounce*ᵃ of silver for sharpening plows and hoes and ⅙ ounceᵇ of silver for sharpening picks, axes, and the iron tip on ox goads.* ²²So on the day of battle, none of the Israelite soldiers with Saul had iron swords or spears. Only Saul and his son Jonathan had such weapons.

²³A group of Philistine soldiers guarded the mountain pass at Micmash.

Jonathan Attacks the Philistines

14¹That day, Saul's son Jonathan was talking with the young man who carried his weapons. Jonathan said, "Let's go to the Philistine camp on the other side of the

valley." But Jonathan did not tell his father.

²Saul was sitting under a pomegranate* tree at the threshing* floorᶜ at the edge of the hill.ᵈ Saul had about 600 men with him. ³One of the men was named Ahijah. Ahijah was a son of Ichabod's brother Ahitub. Ahitub was the son of Phinehas. Phinehas was the son of Eli. Eli had been the Lord's priest at Shiloh. Now Ahijah was the priest who wore the ephod.*

These men did not know that Jonathan had left. ⁴Jonathan was planning to go through a pass to get to the Philistine camp. There was a large rock on each side of the pass. The large rock on one side was named Bozez. The large rock on the other side was named Seneh. ⁵One of the rocks faced north toward Micmash, and the other faced south toward Geba.

⁶Jonathan said to his young helper who carried his weapons, "Come on, let's go to the camp of those foreigners.ᵉ Maybe the Lord will use us to defeat them. Nothing can stop the Lord—it doesn't matter if we have many soldiers or just a few soldiers."

⁷The young man who carried Jonathan's weapons said to him, "Do what you think is best. Whatever you decide, I am with you all the way."

⁸Jonathan said, "Let's go! We'll cross the valley and go to the Philistine guards. We'll let them see us. ⁹If they say to us, 'Stay there until we come to you,' we will stay where we are. We won't go up to them. ¹⁰But if the Philistine men say, 'Come up here,' then we will climb up to them. That will be a sign from God. That will mean that the Lord will allow us to defeat them."

¹¹So Jonathan and his helper let the Philistines see them. The Philistine guards said, "Look! The Hebrews are coming out of the holes they were hiding in." ¹²The Philistines in the fort shouted to Jonathan and his helper, "Come up here. We'll teach you a lesson."

Jonathan said to his helper, "Follow me up the hill. The Lord is letting Israel defeat the Philistines."

¹³⁻¹⁴So Jonathan climbed up the hill with his hands and feet, and his helper was right behind him. Jonathan and his helper attacked them. In the first attack, they killed 20 Philistines in an area about one-half acre in size. Jonathan fought the men who attacked from the front. His helper came behind him and killed the men who were only wounded.

¹⁵Great fear spread among the Philistine soldiers—those in the field, in the camp, and at the fort. Even the bravest soldiers were afraid. The ground began to shake, and they were completely overcome with fear.

ᶜ**14:2** *at the threshing floor* Or "in Migron."
ᵈ**14:2** *edge of the hill* Or "the edge of Gibeah."
ᵉ**14:6** *foreigners* Literally, "uncircumcised." This means people who did not share in the agreement God made with Israel. See "circumcise, circumcision" in the Word List.

ᵃ**13:21** *1/3 ounce* Literally, "1 *pim*" (7.8 g).
ᵇ**13:21** *1/6 ounce* Literally, "1/3 shekel" (3.8 g).

16Saul's guards at Gibeah in the land of Benjamin saw the Philistine soldiers running away in different ways. 17Saul said to the army with him, "Count the men. I want to know who left camp."

They counted the men. Jonathan and his helper were gone.

18Saul said to Ahijah, "Bring God's Holy Box*!" (At that time God's Holy Box was there with the Israelites.)a 19Saul was talking to Ahijah the priest ⌊waiting for advice from God⌋. But the noise and confusion in the Philistine camp was growing and growing. Saul was becoming impatient. Finally, he said to Ahijah the priest, "That's enough. Put your hand down ⌊and stop praying⌋."

20Saul gathered his army together and went to the battle. The Philistine soldiers were very confused. They were even fighting each other with their swords. 21There were Hebrews who served the Philistines in the past and who stayed in the Philistine camp. But now these Hebrews joined the Israelites with Saul and Jonathan. 22All the Israelites who had hidden in the hill country of Ephraim heard the Philistine soldiers were running away. So these Israelites also joined in the battle and began chasing the Philistines.

23So the LORD saved the Israelites that day. The battle moved on past Beth Aven. The whole army was with Saul—he now had about 10,000 men. The battle spread to every city in the hill country of Ephraim.b

Saul Makes Another Mistake

24But Saul made a big mistake that day.c He made this oath*: "If any man eats food before evening comes, before I finish defeating my enemies, he will be under a curse." He made the soldiers promise not to eat. So none of them ate anything.

25-26Because of the fighting, the people went into some woods. Then they saw a honeycomb on the ground. The Israelites went up to the honeycomb, but they didn't eat any of it. They were afraid to break the promise. 27But Jonathan didn't know about the oath. He didn't hear his father make the soldiers promise not to eat. Jonathan had a stick in his hand, so he dipped the end of the stick into the honeycomb and pulled out some honey. He ate the honey and began to feel much better.

28One of the soldiers told Jonathan, "Your father forced the soldiers to make a special promise. He said that any man who eats today will be under a curse. So the men have not eaten anything. That's why they are weak."

29Jonathan said, "My father has brought a lot of trouble to the land. See how much better I feel after tasting just a little of this honey. 30It would have been much better for the men to eat the food that they took from their enemies today. We could have killed more Philistines."

31That day the Israelites defeated the Philistines. They fought them all the way from Micmash to Aijalon. So the people were very tired and hungry. 32They had taken sheep, cattle, and calves from the Philistines. Now they were so hungry that they killed the animals on the ground and ate them. And the blood was still in the animals.

33Someone said to Saul, "Look, the men are sinning against the LORD. They're eating meat that still has blood in it!"

Saul said, "You have sinned. Roll a large stone over here now!" 34Then Saul said, "Go to the men and tell them that each one must bring his bull and sheep to me. Then the men must kill their bulls and sheep here. Don't sin against the LORD! Don't eat meat that still has blood in it."

That night everyone brought their animals and killed them there. 35Then Saul built an altar for the LORD. Saul himself began building that altar for the LORD.

36Saul said, "Let's go after the Philistines tonight. We will take everything from them. We will kill them all!"

The army answered, "Do whatever you think is best."

But the priest said, "Let's ask God."

37So Saul asked God, "Should I go chase the Philistines? Will you let us defeat the Philistines?" But God did not answer Saul that day.

38So Saul said, "Bring all the leaders to me! Let's find who committed the sin today. 39I swear by the LORD who saves Israel, that even if my own son Jonathan sinned, he must die." None of the people said a word.

40Then Saul said to all the Israelites, "You stand on this side. I and my son Jonathan will stand on the other side."

The soldiers answered, "As you wish, sir."

41Then Saul prayed, "LORD, God of Israel, why haven't you answered your servant today? If I or my son Jonathan have sinned, LORD, God of Israel, give Urim.* If your people Israel have sinned, give Thummim.*"d

Saul and Jonathan were chosen, and the people went free. 42Saul said, "Throw them again to show who is guilty—me or my son Jonathan." Jonathan was chosen.

43Saul said to Jonathan, "Tell me what you have done."

Jonathan told Saul, "I only tasted a little honey from the end of my stick. Should I die for doing that?"

---

a14:18 The ancient Greek and Latin versions have "Saul said to Ahijah, 'Bring the ephod!' (At that time Ahijah was wearing the ephod.)"

b14:23 The whole army … Ephraim This is from the ancient Greek version.

c14:24 But Saul … that day This is from the ancient Greek version. The standard Hebrew text has "The Israelites were very tired and hungry that day."

d14:41 Then Samuel prayed … give Thummim This is found in the ancient Greek version. The standard Hebrew text has "Then Samuel prayed to the Lord, God of Israel, 'Give the right answer.'"

44Saul said, "I made an oath and asked God to punish me if I didn't keep it. Jonathan, you must die."

45But the soldiers said to Saul, "Jonathan led Israel to a great victory today. Must Jonathan die? Never! We swear by the living God that not one hair of Jonathan's head will fall to the ground! God helped Jonathan fight against the Philistines today." So the people saved Jonathan. He was not put to death.

46Saul did not chase the Philistines. The Philistines went back to their place.

Saul Fights Israel's Enemies

47Saul took full control of Israel and fought all the enemies who lived around Israel. Saul fought Moab, the Ammonites, Edom, the king of Zobah, and the Philistines. He defeated Israel's enemies wherever he went. 48Saul was very brave. He saved Israel from all the enemies who tried to take things from the Israelites. He even defeated the Amalekites.

49Saul's sons were Jonathan, Ishvi, and Malki Shua. Saul's older daughter was named Merab. Saul's younger daughter was named Michal. 50Saul's wife was named Ahinoam. Ahinoam was the daughter of Ahimaaz.

The commander of Saul's army was named Abner son of Ner. Ner was Saul's uncle. 51Saul's father Kish and Abner's father Ner were sons of Abiel.

52Saul was brave all his life. He fought hard against the Philistines. Any time Saul saw a man who was strong or brave, he took that man and put him into the group of soldiers who stayed near the king and protected him.

Saul Destroys the Amalekites

15 1One day Samuel said to Saul, "The Lord sent me to anoint* you king over his people Israel. Now listen to his message. 2The Lord All-Powerful says: 'When the Israelites came out of Egypt, the Amalekites tried to stop them from going to Canaan.* I saw what the Amalekites did. 3Now go fight against the Amalekites. You must completely destroy the Amalekites and everything that belongs to them. Don't let anything live; you must kill all the men and women and all of their children and little babies. You must kill all of their cattle and sheep and all of their camels and donkeys.'"

4Saul gathered the army together at Telaim. There were 200,000 foot soldiers and 10,000 other men, including the men from Judah. 5Then Saul went to the city of Amalek and waited in the valley. 6He said to the Kenites, "Go away, leave the Amalekites. Then I won't destroy you with the Amalekites. You showed kindness to the Israelites when they came out of Egypt." So the Kenites left the Amalekites.

7Saul defeated the Amalekites. He fought them and chased them all the way from Havilah to Shur, at the border of Egypt. 8Agag was the king of the Amalekites. Saul captured Agag alive. Saul let Agag live, but he killed all the men in Agag's army. 9Saul and the Israelite soldiers felt bad about destroying everything. So they let Agag live. They also kept the fat cattle, the best sheep, and the lambs. They kept everything that was worth keeping. They didn't want to destroy those things. They destroyed only what was not worth keeping.

Samuel Tells Saul About His Sin

10Then Samuel received a message from the Lord. 11The Lord said, "Saul has stopped following me, so I am sorry that I made him king. He is not doing what I tell him." Samuel became angry and cried to the Lord all night.

12Samuel got up early the next morning and went to meet Saul. But the people told Samuel, "Saul went to Carmel. He went there to set up a stone monument to honor himself. Then he left there and went down to Gilgal."

So Samuel went to Saul. Saul had just offered the first part of the things he took from the Amalekites as a burnt offering to the Lord.a 13When Samual came near to Saul, Saul greeted him and said, "The Lord bless you! I have obeyed the Lord's commands."

14But Samuel said, "Then what is that sound I hear? Why do I hear sheep and cattle?"

15Saul said, "The soldiers took them from the Amalekites. They saved the best sheep and cattle to burn as sacrifices* to the Lord your God. But we destroyed everything else."

16Samuel said to Saul, "Stop! Let me tell you what the Lord told me last night."

Saul answered, "Tell me what he said."

17Samuel said, "In the past you didn't think that you were important, but the Lord chose you to be the king. So you became the leader of the tribes of Israel. 18The Lord sent you on a special mission. He said, 'Go and destroy all the Amalekites. They are evil people. Destroy them all! Fight them until they are completely finished' 19So why didn't you listen to the Lord? You did what the Lord said is wrong because you wanted to keep what you took in battle."

20Saul said, "But I did obey the Lord! I went where the Lord sent me. I destroyed all the Amalekites. I brought back only one—their king Agag. 21And the soldiers took the best sheep and cattle to sacrifice to the Lord your God at Gilgal."

22But Samuel answered, "Which pleases the Lord more: burnt offerings and sacrifices or obeying his commands? It is better to obey God than to offer sacrifices to him. It is better to listen to him than to offer the fat from rams. 23Refusing to obey is as bad as the sin of sorcery.* Being stubborn and doing what you want is like the sin of worshiping idols.* You

a15:12 *Saul had just offered ... Lord* This is from the ancient Greek version.

refused to obey the LORD's command, so he now refuses to accept you as king."

24Then Saul said to Samuel, "I have sinned. I did not obey the LORD's commands, and I did not do what you told me. I was afraid of the people, and I did what they said. 25Now I beg you, forgive me for doing this sin. Come back with me, so I may worship the LORD."

26But Samuel said to Saul, "I won't go back with you. You rejected the LORD's command, and now he rejects you as king of Israel."

27When Samuel turned to leave, Saul caught Samuel's robe. The robe tore. 28Samuel said to Saul, "Just as you tore my robe, the LORD has torn the kingdom of Israel from you today. The LORD has given the kingdom to one of your friends. This man is a better person than you are. 29The LORD is the God of Israel. He lives forever. He does not lie or change his mind. He is not like a man who changes his mind."

30Saul answered, "All right, I sinned! But please come back with me. Show me some respect in front of the leaders and the Israelites. Come back with me so that I may worship the LORD your God." 31Samuel went back with Saul, and Saul worshiped the LORD.

32Samuel said, "Bring King Agag of the Amalekites to me."

Agag came to Samuel. Agag was tied with chains and thought, "Surely he won't kill me."a

33But Samuel said to Agag, "Your sword took babies from their mothers. So now, your mother will have no children." And Samuel cut Agag to pieces before the LORD at Gilgal.

34Then Samuel left and went to Ramah. And Saul went up to his home in Gibeah. 35After that, Samuel never saw Saul again. Samuel was very sad for Saul. And the LORD was very sorry that he had made Saul king of Israel.

Samuel Goes to Bethlehem

16 1The LORD said to Samuel, "How long will you feel sorry for Saul? I have rejected him as king of Israel. Fill your hornb with oil and go to Bethlehem. I am sending you to Jesse who lives in Bethlehem, because I have chosen one of his sons to be the new king."

2But Samuel said, "If I go, Saul will hear the news and try to kill me."

The LORD said, "Go to Bethlehem. Take a young calf with you and tell them, 'I have come to make a sacrifice* to the LORD.' 3Invite Jesse to the sacrifice. Then I will show you what to do. You must anoint* the person I show you."

4Samuel did what the LORD told him to do and went to Bethlehem. The elders* of

Bethlehem shook with fear. They met Samuel and asked, "Do you come in peace?"

5Samuel answered, "Yes, I come in peace. I come to make a sacrifice to the LORD. Prepare yourselves and come to the sacrifice with me." Samuel prepared Jesse and his sons. Then he invited them to come and share the sacrifice.

6When Jesse and his sons arrived, Samuel saw Eliab and thought, "Surely this is the man who the LORD has chosen."

7But the LORD said to Samuel, "Eliab is tall and handsome, but don't judge by things like that. God doesn't look at what people see. People judge by what is on the outside, but the LORD looks at the heart. Eliab is not the right man."

8Then Jesse called his second son, Abinadab. Abinadab walked by Samuel. But Samuel said, "No, this is not the man who the LORD chose."

9Then Jesse told Shammah to walk by Samuel. But Samuel said, "No, the LORD did not choose this man, either."

10Jesse showed seven of his sons to Samuel. But Samuel said to Jesse, "The LORD has not chosen any of these men."

11Then he asked Jesse, "Are these all the sons you have?"

Jesse answered, "No, I have another son—my youngest, but he is out taking care of the sheep."

Samuel said, "Send for him. Bring him here. We won't sit down to eat until he arrives."

12Jesse sent someone to get his youngest son. This son was a good-looking, healthyc young man. He was very handsome.

The LORD said to Samuel, "Get up and anoint him. He is the one."

13Samuel took the horn with the oil in it, and poured the special oil on Jesse's youngest son in front of his brothers. The Spirit of the LORD came on David with great power from that day on. Then Samuel went back home to Ramah.

An Evil Spirit Bothers Saul

14The LORD's Spirit left Saul. Then the LORD sent an evil spirit to Saul that caused him much trouble. 15Saul's servants said to him, "An evil spirit from God is bothering you. 16Give us the command and we will look for someone who can play the harp. If the evil spirit from God comes on you, this person will play music for you. Then you will feel better."

17So Saul said to his servants, "Find someone who plays music well and bring him to me."

18One of the servants said, "There is a man named Jesse living in Bethlehem. I saw Jesse's son. He knows how to play the harp. He is

---

a15:32 *Surely ... kill me* The ancient Greek version has "This treatment is worse than death."

b16:1 *horn* An animal's horn is hollow and often used like a bottle.

c16:12 *healthy* The Hebrew word means "red," "ruddy," or "red-haired."

also a brave man and fights well. He is smart and handsome, and the LORD is with him."

¹⁹So Saul sent messengers to Jesse. They told Jesse, "You have a son named David. He takes care of your sheep. Send him to me."

²⁰So Jesse got some things as a gift for Saul. Jesse got a donkey, some bread and a leather bag full of wine, and a young goat. He gave them to David and sent him to Saul. ²¹So David went to Saul and stood in front of him. Saul loved David very much. David became the helper who carried Saul's weapons. ²²Saul sent a message to Jesse. "Let David stay and serve me. I like him very much."

²³Any time the evil spirit from God came on Saul, David would take his harp and play it. The evil spirit would leave Saul and he would begin to feel better.

Goliath Challenges Israel

17 ¹The Philistines gathered their armies together for war. They met at Socoh in Judah. Their camp was between Socoh and Azekah, at a town called Ephes Dammim.

²Saul and the Israelite soldiers also gathered together. Their camp was in the Valley of Elah. Saul's soldiers were lined up and ready to fight the Philistines. ³The Philistines were on one hill. The Israelites were on the other hill. The valley was between them.

⁴The Philistines had a champion fighter named Goliath, who was from Gath. He was over 9 feet* tall. Goliath came out of the Philistine camp. ⁵He had a bronze helmet on his head. He wore a coat of armor* that was made like the scales on a fish. This armor was made of bronze and weighed about 125 pounds.* ⁶Goliath wore bronze protectors on his legs. He had a bronze javelin tied on his back. ⁷The wooden part of his spear was as big as a weaver's rod. The spear's blade weighed 15 pounds.* Goliath's helper walked in front of him, carrying Goliath's shield.

⁸Each day Goliath would come out and shout a challenge to the Israelite soldiers. He would say, "Why are all of your soldiers lined up ready for battle? You are Saul's servants. I am a Philistine. So choose one man and send him to fight me. ⁹If that man kills me, he wins and we Philistines will become your slaves. But if I kill your man, then I win, and you will become our slaves. You will have to serve us."

¹⁰The Philistine also said, "Today I stand and make fun of the army of Israel. I dare you to send me one of your men and let us fight."

¹¹Saul and the Israelite soldiers heard what Goliath said, and they were very afraid.

David Goes to the Battle Front

¹²David was the son of Jesse. Jesse was from the Ephrathah family in Bethlehem, Judah. Jesse had eight sons. In Saul's time Jesse was an old man. ¹³Jesse's three oldest sons went with Saul to the war. The first son was Eliab, the second was Abinadab, and the third was Shammah. ¹⁴David was the youngest son. The three oldest sons were in Saul's army, ¹⁵but David left Saul from time to time to take care of his father's sheep at Bethlehem.

¹⁶The Philistine came out every morning and evening and stood before the Israelite army. Goliath insulted Israel like this for 40 days.

¹⁷One day Jesse said to his son David, "Take this basket* of cooked grain and these ten loaves of bread to your brothers in the camp. ¹⁸Also take these ten pieces of cheese for the officer who commands your brothers' group of 1000 soldiers. See how your brothers are doing. Bring back something to show me your brothers are all right. ¹⁹Your brothers are with Saul and all the Israelite soldiers in the Valley of Elah. They are there to fight against the Philistines."

²⁰Early in the morning, David had another shepherd take care of the sheep while he took the food and left as Jesse had told him to. David drove their wagon to the camp. The soldiers were going out to their battle positions just as David arrived. The soldiers began shouting their war cry. ²¹The Israelites and Philistines were lined up and ready for battle.

²²David left the food with the man who kept supplies. Then he ran to the place where the Israelite soldiers were and asked about his brothers. ²³While David was talking with his brothers, the Philistine champion fighter came out from the Philistine army. This was Goliath, the Philistine from Gath. Goliath shouted things against Israel as usual. David heard what he said.

²⁴The Israelite soldiers saw Goliath and ran away. They were all afraid of him. ²⁵One of the Israelite men said, "Did you see that man? Look at him! He comes out each day and makes fun of Israel. Whoever kills him will get rich. King Saul will give him a lot of money. Saul will also let his daughter marry the man who kills Goliath. He will also make that man's family free from taxes in Israel."

²⁶David asked the men standing near him, "What did he say? What is the reward for killing this Philistine and taking away this shame from Israel? Who is this Goliath anyway? He is only some foreigner,* nothing but a Philistine.

---

*a*17:4 *over 9 feet* Literally, "6 cubits and 1 span" (2.9 m). Josephus, most copies of the ancient Greek version, and a Hebrew scroll from Qumran all have "4 cubits and 1 span." This is 6' 6" (2 m) for the short cubit or 7' 7" (2.33 m) for the long cubit.

*b*17:5 *125 pounds* Literally, "5000 shekels" (57.5 kg).

*c*17:7 *15 pounds* Literally, "600 shekels" (6.9 kg).

*d*17:17 *basket* Literally, "ephah."

*e*17:26 *foreigner* Literally, "uncircumcised." This means a person who did not share in the agreement God made with Israel. See "circumcise, circumcision" in the Word List. Also in verse 36.

Why does he think he can speak against the army of the living God?"

27So the Israelite told David about the reward for killing Goliath. 28David's oldest brother Eliab heard David talking with the soldiers and became angry. Eliab asked David, "Why did you come here? Who did you leave those few sheep with in the desert? I know why you came down here. You didn't want to do what you were told to do. You just wanted to come down here to watch the battle."

29David said, "What did I do now? I didn't do anything wrong! I was only talking." 30He turned to some other people and asked them the same questions. They gave him the same answers as before.

31Some men heard David talking. They took David to Saul and told him what David had said. 32David said to Saul, "People shouldn't let Goliath discourage them. I am your servant. I will go fight this Philistine."

33Saul answered, "You can't go out and fight against this Philistine. You're not even a soldier!a Goliath has been fighting in wars since he was a boy."

34But David said to Saul, "There were times when I was taking care of my father's sheep that wild animals came to take some sheep from the flock. Once there was a lion and another time, a bear. 35I chased that wild animal, attacked it, and took the sheep from its mouth. The wild animal jumped on me, but I caught it by the fur under its mouth. And I hit it and killed it. 36I killed both a lion and a bear like that! And I will kill that foreigner, Goliath, just like them. Goliath will die because he made fun of the army of the living God. 37The LORD saved me from the lion and the bear. He will also save me from this Philistine."

Saul said to David, "Go and may the LORD be with you." 38Saul put his own clothes on David. He put a bronze helmet on David's head and armor* on his body. 39David put on the sword and tried to walk around. He tried to wear Saul's uniform, but David was not used to all those heavy things.

David said to Saul, "I can't fight in these things. I'm not used to them." So David took them all off. 40He took his walking stick in his hand and went to find five smooth stones from the stream. He put the five stones in his shepherd's bag and held his sling* in his hand. Then he went out to meet the Philistine.

David Kills Goliath

41The Philistine slowly walked closer and closer to David. Goliath's helper walked in front of him, carrying a large shield. 42Goliath looked at David with disgust. He saw that David was only a handsome, healthyb boy.c 43Goliath said to David, "What is that stick for? Did you come to chase me away like a dog?" Then Goliath used the names of his gods to say curses against David. 44He said to David, "Come here, and I'll feed your body to the birds and wild animals."

45David said to the Philistine, "You come to me using sword, spear, and javelin. But I come to you in the name of the LORD All-Powerful, the God of the armies of Israel. You have said bad things about him. 46Today the LORD will let me defeat you. I will kill you. I will cut off your head and feed your body to the birds and wild animals. And we will do the same thing to all the other Philistines too. Then all the world will know there is a God in Israel. 47All the people gathered here will know that the LORD doesn't need swords or spears to save people. The battle belongs to the LORD, and he will help us defeat all of you."

48Goliath the Philistine started to attack David. He slowly walked closer and closer toward David, but David ran out to meet Goliath.

49David took out a stone from his bag. He put it in his sling* and swung the sling. The stone flew from the sling and hit Goliath right between the eyes. The stone sank deep into his head, and Goliath fell to the ground—face down.

50So David defeated the Philistine with only a sling and one stone! He hit the Philistine and killed him. David didn't have a sword, 51so he ran and stood beside the Philistine. Then David took Goliath's own sword out of its sheath* and used it to cut off his head. That is how David killed the Philistine.

When the other Philistines saw their hero was dead, they turned and ran. 52The soldiers of Israel and Judah shouted and started chasing the Philistines. The Israelites chased them all the way to the city limits of Gath and to the gates of Ekron. They killed many of the Philistines. Their bodies were scattered along the Shaaraim road all the way to Gath and Ekron. 53After chasing the Philistines, the Israelites came back to the Philistine camp and took many things from that camp.

54David took the Philistine's head to Jerusalem, but he kept the Philistine's weapons at home.

Saul Begins to Fear David

55Saul watched David go out to fight Goliath. Saul spoke to Abner, the commander of the army. "Abner, who is that young man's father?"

Abner answered, "I swear I don't know, sir."

---

a17:33 You're not even a soldier Or "You are only a boy!" The Hebrew word for "boy" often means "servant" or "the helper who carries a soldier's weapons."

b17:42 healthy The Hebrew word means "red," "ruddy," or "red-haired."

c17:42 boy Or "teenager" or "soldier's helper."

⁵⁶King Saul said, "Find out who his father is."

⁵⁷When David came back after killing Goliath, Abner brought him to Saul. David was still holding the Philistine's head.

⁵⁸Saul asked him, "Young man, who is your father?"

David answered, "I am the son of your servant Jesse, from Bethlehem."

David and Jonathan Become Friends

18 ¹⁻²Saul decided to take David with him. He would not let David go back home to his father. After David finished talking with Saul, Jonathan developed a strong friendship with David.ᵃ ³Jonathan loved David as much as himself, so they made a special agreement. ⁴Jonathan took off the coat he was wearing and gave it to David. In fact, Jonathan gave David his whole uniform—including his sword, his bow, and even his belt.

Saul Notices David's Success

⁵David went to fight wherever Saul sent him. He was very successful, so Saul put him in charge of the soldiers. This pleased everyone, even Saul's officers. ⁶David would go out to fight against the Philistines. On the way home after the battles, women in every town in Israel would come out to meet him. They sang and danced for joy as they played their tambourines and lyres.* They did this right in front of Saul! ⁷The women sang,

"Saul has killed his thousands,
    but David has killed tens of thousands."

⁸This song upset Saul and he became very angry. Saul thought, "The women give David credit for killing tens of thousands of the enemy, and they give me credit for only thousands. A little more of this and they will give him the kingdom itself!ᵇ" ⁹So from that time on, Saul watched David very closely.

Saul Is Afraid of David

¹⁰The next day, an evil spirit from God took control of Saul and he went wildᶜ in his house. David played the harp to calm him as he usually did, ¹¹but Saul had a spear in his hand. He thought, "I'll pin David to the wall." Saul threw the spear twice, but David jumped out of the way both times.

¹²The Lord had left Saul and was now with David, so Saul was afraid of David. ¹³Saul sent David away and made him a commander over 1000 soldiers. This put David out among the men even more as they went into battle and returned. ¹⁴The Lord was with David, so he was successful in everything. ¹⁵Saul saw how successful David was and became even more afraid of him. ¹⁶But all the people in Israel and Judah loved David because he was out among them and led them into battle.

Saul Wants His Daughter to Marry David

¹⁷One day, Saul said to David, "Here is my oldest daughter, Merab. I will let you marry her. Then you will be like a son to me and you will be a real soldier.ᵈ Then you will go and fight the Lord's battles." Saul was really thinking, "Now I won't have to kill David. I will let the Philistines kill him for me."

¹⁸But David said, "I am not an important man from an important family. I can't marry the king's daughter."

¹⁹So when the time came for David to marry Saul's daughter, Saul let her marry Adriel from Meholah.

²⁰People told Saul that his daughter Michal loved David. This made Saul happy. ²¹He thought, "I will use Michal to trap David. I will let Michal marry David, and then I will let the Philistines kill him." So Saul said to David a second time, "You can marry my daughter today."

²²Saul commanded his officers to speak to David in private. He told them to say, "Look, the king likes you. His officers like you. You should marry his daughter."

²³Saul's officers said these things to David, but David answered, "Do you think it is easy to become the king's son-in-law? I am just a poor, ordinary man."

²⁴Saul's officers told Saul what David said. ²⁵Saul told them, "Say this to David, 'David, the king doesn't want you to pay money for his daughter.ᵉ He wants to get even with his enemy, so the price for marrying his daughter is 100 Philistine foreskins.'" That was Saul's secret plan. He thought the Philistines would kill David.

²⁶Saul's officers told this to David. David was happy that he had a chance to become the king's son-in-law, so immediately ²⁷he and his men went out to fight the Philistines. They killed 200ᶠ Philistines. David took these Philistine foreskins and gave them to Saul. He did this because he wanted to become the king's son-in-law.

Saul let David marry his daughter Michal. ²⁸He saw that the Lord was with David and he also saw that his daughter, Michal, loved

---

ᵃ**18:1-2** *Jonathan ... with David* Literally, "Jonathan's soul was tied to David's soul."
ᵇ**18:8** *A little more ... itself* This is not in one of the oldest and best copies of the ancient Greek version.
ᶜ**18:10** *Saul ... wild* Or "Saul prophesied." The Hebrew word means that the person lost control of what they said and did. Usually this meant God was using them to give a special message to other people.

ᵈ**18:17** *real soldier* That is, a member of the warrior class. They were free from certain duties of ordinary citizens.
ᵉ**18:25** *money for his daughter* In Bible times a man usually had to give money to a woman's father before he could marry her.
ᶠ**18:27** *200* The ancient Greek version has "100."

David. ²⁹So Saul became even more afraid of David and was against him all that time.

³⁰The Philistine commanders continued to go out to fight the Israelites, but David defeated them every time. He became famous as Saul's best officer.

Jonathan Helps David

19 ¹Saul told his son Jonathan and his officers to kill David. But Jonathan liked David very much, ^{2–3}so he warned him. "Be careful! Saul is looking for a chance to kill you. In the morning go into the field and hide. I will go out into the field with my father. We will stand in the field where you are hiding. I will talk to my father about you, and I will tell you what I learn."

⁴Jonathan talked to his father Saul. Jonathan said good things about David. He said, "You are the king. David is your servant. David hasn't done anything wrong to you, so don't do anything wrong to him. He has always been good to you. ⁵He risked his life when he killed the Philistine. The LORD won a great victory for all Israel. You saw it, and you were happy. Why do you want to hurt David? He's innocent. There is no reason to kill him."

⁶Saul listened to Jonathan and made a promise. He said, "As surely as the LORD lives, David won't be put to death."

⁷So Jonathan called David and told him everything that was said. Then Jonathan brought David to Saul, and David was with Saul as before.

Saul Tries Again to Kill David

⁸Once again there was war with the Philistines, and David went out to fight. He defeated them badly, and they ran away. ⁹Later, in Saul's house, David was playing the harp. Saul was there with his spear in his hand. Then an evil spirit from the LORD came on Saul. ¹⁰Saul threw his spear at David and tried to pin him to the wall. David jumped out of the way, so the spear missed him and stuck in the wall. That night, David ran away.

¹¹Saul sent men to watch David's house. They stayed there all night. They were waiting to kill David in the morning, but David's wife Michal warned him. She said, "You must run away tonight and save your life. If you don't, you will be killed tomorrow." ¹²Then Michal let David down out of a window, and he escaped and ran away. ¹³Michal took the household god, put clothes on it, and put goats' hair on its head. Then she put the statue in the bed.

¹⁴Saul sent messengers to take David prisoner. But Michal said, "David is sick."

¹⁵The men went and told Saul, but he sent the messengers back to see David. Saul told these men, "Bring David to me. Bring him lying on his bed if you must, even if it kills him."

¹⁶The messengers went to David's house. They went inside to get him, but they saw it was only a statue and that its hair was only goat's hair.

¹⁷Saul said to Michal, "Why did you trick me like this? You let my enemy escape, and now he is gone."

Michal answered Saul, "David told me he would kill me if I didn't help him escape."

David Goes to the Camps at Ramah

¹⁸David escaped and ran away to Samuel at Ramah. He told Samuel everything that Saul had done to him. Then David and Samuel went to the camps where the prophets stayed. David stayed there.

¹⁹Saul heard that David was there in the camps near Ramah. ²⁰So he sent some men to arrest David. But when they came to the camps, there was a group of prophets prophesying.^a Samuel was standing there leading the group. The Spirit of God came on Saul's messengers and they began prophesying. ²¹Saul heard about this, so he sent other messengers, but they also began prophesying. So Saul sent messengers a third time, and they also began prophesying. ²²Finally, Saul himself went to Ramah. Saul came to the big well by the threshing* floor at Secu. He asked, "Where are Samuel and David?"

The people answered, "In the camps near Ramah."

²³So Saul went out to the camps near Ramah. The Spirit of God came on Saul, and he also began prophesying. He prophesied all the way to the camps at Ramah. ²⁴Saul even took off his clothes. He lay there naked all day and through the night. So even Saul prophesied there in front of Samuel.

That is why people say, "Is Saul also one of the prophets?"

David and Jonathan Make an Agreement

20 ¹David ran away from the camps at Ramah and went to Jonathan and asked him, "What have I done wrong? What is my crime? Why is your father trying to kill me?"

²Jonathan answered, "That can't be true! My father isn't trying to kill you. My father doesn't do anything without first telling me. It doesn't matter how important it is, my father always tells me. Why would my father refuse to tell me that he wants to kill you? No, it is not true!"

³But David answered, "Your father knows very well that I am your friend. Your father said to himself, 'Jonathan must not know about it. If he knows, he will tell David.'^b But

^a**19:20 prophesying** This usually means "speaking for God." But here, this also means that the Spirit of God took control of the people, causing them to sing and dance. Also in verse 23.
^b**20:3 he will tell David** This is from the ancient Greek version. The standard Hebrew text here has "he will be upset."

as surely as you and the LORD are alive, I am very close to death."

⁴Jonathan said to David, "I will do anything you want me to do."

⁵Then David said, "Look, tomorrow is the New Moon* celebration. I am supposed to eat with the king, but let me hide in the field until the evening. ⁶If your father notices I am gone, tell him, 'David wanted to go home to Bethlehem. His family is having its own feast for this monthly sacrifice. David asked me to let him run down to Bethlehem and join his family.' ⁷If your father says, 'Fine,' then I am safe. But if your father becomes angry, you will know that he wants to hurt me. ⁸Jonathan, be kind to me. I am your servant. You have made an agreement with me before the LORD. If I am guilty, you may kill me yourself, but don't take me to your father."

⁹Jonathan answered, "No, never! If I learn that my father plans to hurt you, I will warn you."

¹⁰David said, "Who will warn me if your father says bad things to you?"

¹¹Then Jonathan said, "Come, let's go out into the field." So Jonathan and David went together into the field.

¹²Jonathan said to David, "I make this promise before the LORD, the God of Israel. I promise that I will learn how my father feels about you. I will learn if he feels good about you or not. Then, in three days, I will send a message to you in the field. ¹³If my father wants to hurt you, I will let you know. I will let you leave in safety. May the LORD punish me if I don't do this. May the LORD be with you as he has been with my father. ¹⁴⁻¹⁵As long as I live, show me the same kindness the LORD does. And if I die, never stop showing this kindness to my family. Be faithful to us, even when the LORD destroys all your enemiesᵃ from the earth." ¹⁶So Jonathan made this agreement with David and his family, and he asked the LORD to hold them responsible for keeping it.ᵇ

¹⁷Jonathan loved David as himself, and because of this love, he asked David to repeat this agreement for himself.

¹⁸Jonathan said to David, "Tomorrow is the New Moon celebration. Your seat will be empty, so my father will see that you are gone. ¹⁹On the third day go to the same place you hid when this trouble began. Wait by that hill. ²⁰On the third day I will go to that hill and shoot three arrows as if I am shooting at a target. ²¹Then I will tell the boy to go find the arrows. If everything is fine, I will tell the boy, 'You went too far! The arrows are closer to me. Come back and get them.' If I say that, you can come out of hiding. I promise, as surely as the LORD lives, you are safe. There is

no danger. ²²But if there is trouble, I will say to the boy, 'The arrows are farther away. Go get them.' If I say that, you must leave. The LORD is sending you away. ²³Remember this agreement between you and me. The LORD is our witness forever."

²⁴Then David hid in the field.

Saul's Attitude at the Celebration

The time for the New Moon* celebration came, and the king sat down to eat. ²⁵He sat next to the wall where he usually sat, and Jonathan sat across from him. Abner sat next to Saul, but David's place was empty. ²⁶That day Saul said nothing. He thought, "Maybe something happened to David so that he is not clean.*"

²⁷On the next day, the second day of the month, David's place was empty again. Then Saul said to his son Jonathan, "Why didn't Jesse's son come to the New Moon celebration yesterday or today?"

²⁸Jonathan answered, "David asked me to let him go to Bethlehem. ²⁹He said, 'Let me go. Our family is having a sacrifice* in Bethlehem. My brother ordered me to be there. Now if I am your friend, please let me go and see my brothers.' That is why David has not come to the king's table."

³⁰Saul was very angry with Jonathan and said to him, "You son of a twisted, rebellious woman! I know that you have chosen to support that son of Jesse—it will bring shame to you and to your mother. ³¹As long as Jesse's son lives, you will never be king and have a kingdom. Now, bring David to me! He is a dead man."

³²Jonathan asked his father, "Why should David be killed? What did he do wrong?"

³³But Saul threw his spear at Jonathan and tried to kill him. So Jonathan knew that his father wanted very much to kill David. ³⁴Jonathan became angry and left the table. He was so upset and angry with his father that he refused to eat any food on the second day of the festival. He was angry because Saul humiliated him and because Saul wanted to kill David.

David and Jonathan Say Goodbye

³⁵The next morning Jonathan went out to the field to meet David as they had agreed. Jonathan brought a little boy with him. ³⁶He said to the boy, "Run. Go find the arrows I shoot." The boy began to run, and Jonathan shot the arrows over his head. ³⁷The boy ran to the place where the arrows fell, but Jonathan called, "The arrows are farther away." ³⁸Then he shouted, "Hurry! Go get them. Don't just stand there." The boy picked up the arrows and brought them back to his master. ³⁹The boy knew nothing about what went on. Only Jonathan and David knew. ⁴⁰Jonathan gave his bow and arrows to the boy and told him to go back to town.

ᵃ20:14–15 *enemies* Or "descendants."
ᵇ20:14–16 The Hebrew text here is unclear, and several different translations are possible.

⁴¹When the boy left, David came out from his hiding place on the other side of the hill. David gave a formal greeting by bowing to the ground three times to show his respect for Jonathan. But then David and Jonathan kissed each other and cried together. It was a very sad goodbye, especially for David.

⁴²Then Jonathan said to David, "Go in peace. We have taken an oath* in the LORD's name to be friends forever. We have asked the LORD to be a witness between us and our descendants forever."

David Goes to See Ahimelech the Priest

21 ¹Then David left and Jonathan went back to the town. David went to the town named Nob*ᵃ* to see Ahimelech the priest.

Ahimelech went out to meet David. He was afraid of David and asked, "Why are you alone? Why isn't anyone with you?"

²David answered him, "The king gave me a special order. He told me, 'Don't let anyone know about this mission. No one must know what I told you to do.' I told my men where to meet me. ³Now, what food do you have with you? Give me five loaves of bread or whatever you have to eat."

⁴The priest said to David, "I don't have any ordinary bread here, but I do have some of the holy bread.* Your officers can eat it if they have not had sexual relations with any women."*ᵇ*

⁵David answered the priest, "We have not been with any women. My men keep their bodies*ᶜ* holy every time we go out to fight, even on ordinary missions.*ᵈ* And this is especially true today."

⁶There was no bread except the holy bread, so the priest gave David this bread. This was the bread that the priests put on the holy table before the LORD. Each day they took this bread away and put fresh bread in its place.

⁷One of Saul's officers was there that day. He was Doeg the Edomite, the leader of Saul's shepherds.*ᵉ* He had been kept there before the LORD.*ᶠ*

⁸David asked Ahimelech, "Do you have a spear or sword here? The king's business is very important. I had to leave quickly, and I didn't bring my sword or any other weapon."

⁹The priest answered, "The only sword here is the sword of Goliath the Philistine. It is the sword you took from him when you killed him in the Valley of Elah. That sword is behind the ephod,* wrapped in a cloth. You may take it if you want to."

David said, "Goliath's sword—there's not another one like it. Give it to me."

David Runs Away to the Enemy at Gath

¹⁰That day David ran away from Saul and went to King Achish of Gath. ¹¹Achish's officers said, "Isn't this David, the king of the land of Israel? He is the one the Israelites sing about. They dance and sing this song about him:

> "Saul has killed thousands of enemies,
>   but David has killed tens of thousands."

¹²David paid close attention to what they said. He was afraid of King Achish of Gath, ¹³so he pretended to be crazy in front of Achish and his officers. While David was with them, he acted like a crazy man. He spat on the doors of the gate. He let spit fall down his beard.

¹⁴Achish said to his officers, "Look at the man! He is crazy. Why did you bring him to me? ¹⁵I have enough crazy men. I don't need you to bring this man to my house to act crazy in front of me. Don't let this man come into my house again."

David Goes to Different Places

22 ¹David left Gath and ran away to the cave*ᵍ* of Adullam. David's brothers and relatives heard that David was at Adullam and went to see him there. ²Many people joined David. There were men who were in some kind of trouble, men who owed a lot of money, and men who were just not satisfied with life. All kinds of people joined David, and he became their leader. He had about 400 men with him.

³David left Adullam and went to Mizpah in Moab. David said to the king of Moab, "Please let my father and mother come and stay with you until I learn what God is going to do to me." ⁴So David left his parents with the king of Moab. They stayed with the king of Moab as long as David was at the fort.

⁵But the prophet Gad said to David, "Don't stay in the fort. Go to the land of Judah." So David left and went to Hereth Forest.

Saul Destroys Ahimelech's Family

⁶Saul heard the report about David and his men while sitting under the tree on the hill at Gibeah. Saul had his spear in his hand. All of his officers were standing around him. ⁷Saul said to his officers who were standing around him, "Listen, men of Benjamin. Do you think

---

*ᵃ***21:1 Nob** A city near Ranah where many priests lived. See 1 Sam. 22:19.

*ᵇ***21:4 Your officers ... women** This would make the men unclean and not able to eat any food that had been made holy by offering it to God. See Lev. 7:21; 15:1–33.

*ᶜ***21:5 bodies** Literally, "vessels" or "weapons."

*ᵈ***21:5 My men ... missions** See 2 Sam. 11:11 and the rules in Deut. 23:9–14.

*ᵉ***21:7 shepherds** Or "messengers."

*ᶠ***21:7 kept there before the LORD** This might mean that Doeg was there as part of a special promise to God or some other religious reason. Or it might mean he was being held there because of some crime, such as accidentally killing a man.

*ᵍ***22:1 cave** Or possibly, "fortress."

the son of Jesse *(David)* will give you fields and vineyards*? Do you think he will promote you and make you officers over 1000 men and officers over 100 men? [8]No, but all of you are plotting against me. None of you told me about my son Jonathan and the agreement he made with the son of Jesse. None of you cares enough about me to tell me that my own son Jonathan encouraged David to turn against me and attack me. And that is what David is doing now."

[9]Doeg the Edomite was standing there with Saul's officers. Doeg said, "I saw Jesse's son at Nob. David came to see Ahimelech son of Ahitub. [10]Ahimelech prayed to the LORD for David and gave him some food. He even gave David the sword of Goliath the Philistine."

[11]Then King Saul ordered some men to bring the priest to him. Saul told them to bring Ahimelech son of Ahitub and all his relatives who were priests at Nob. So all of them came to the king. [12]Saul said to Ahimelech, "Listen now, son of Ahitub."

Ahimelech answered, "Yes, sir."

[13]Saul said to him, "Why did you and Jesse's son make secret plans against me? You gave David bread and a sword. You prayed to God for him. And right now, David is waiting to attack me."

[14]Ahimelech answered, "David is very faithful to you. Not one of your other officers is as faithful as David. He is your own son-in-law and the captain of your bodyguards. Your own family respects David. [15]That was not the first time I prayed to God for David. Not at all! Don't blame me or any of my relatives. We are your servants. I know nothing about what is happening."

[16]But the king said, "Ahimelech, you and all your relatives must die." [17]Then the king told the guards at his side, "Go and kill the priests of the LORD because they are on David's side too. They knew he was running away, but they didn't tell me."

The king's officers refused to hurt the priests of the LORD. [18]So the king gave the order to Doeg. Saul said, "Doeg, you go kill the priests." So Doeg the Edomite went and killed the priests. That day he killed 85 men who were priests.[a] [19]Nob was the city of the priests. Doeg killed all the people of Nob. He used his sword and killed men, women, children and small babies. He even killed their cattle, donkeys, and sheep.

[20]But Abiathar son of Ahimelech escaped. He ran away and joined David. [21]Abiathar told David that Saul had killed the LORD's priests. [22]Then David told Abiathar, "I saw Doeg the Edomite at Nob that day. I knew he would tell Saul! I am responsible for the death of your father's family. [23]Stay with me. Don't be afraid, because the man *(Saul)* who tried

to kill you is the same man who wants to kill me. I will protect you if you stay with me."

David at Keilah

23 [1]People told David, "Look, the Philistines are fighting against the city of Keilah. They are robbing grain from the threshing* floors."

[2]David asked the LORD, "Should I go and fight these Philistines?"

The LORD answered David, "Yes, go attack the Philistines. Save Keilah."

[3]But David's men said to him, "Look, our men are afraid here in Judah. Just think how afraid we will be if we go to Keilah, where the Philistine army is lined up and ready for battle."

[4]David again asked the LORD. And the LORD answered David, "Go down to Keilah. I will help you defeat the Philistines." [5]So David and his men went to Keilah. David's men fought the Philistines. They defeated them and took their cattle. In this way David saved the people of Keilah. [6](When Abiathar ran away to David, Abiathar took an ephod* with him.[b])

[7]People told Saul that David was now at Keilah. Saul said, "God has given David to me. David trapped himself when he went into a city surrounded by a wall with gates and bars to lock them." [8]Saul called all his army together for battle. They prepared to go down to Keilah to attack David and his men.

[9]David learned that Saul was making plans against him. David then said to Abiathar the priest, "Bring the ephod."

[10]David prayed, "LORD, God of Israel, I have heard that Saul plans to come to Keilah and destroy the town because of me. [11]Will Saul come to Keilah? Will the people of Keilah give me to Saul? LORD, God of Israel, I am your servant. Please tell me!"

The LORD answered, "Saul will come."

[12]Again David asked, "Will the people of Keilah give me and my men to Saul?"

The LORD answered, "They will."

[13]So David and his men left Keilah. There were about 600 men who went with David. They kept moving from place to place. Saul learned that David had escaped from Keilah, so he did not go to that city.

Saul Chases David

[14]David went into the Desert of Ziph and stayed in the mountains and fortresses* there. Saul looked for David the whole time, but the LORD didn't let Saul catch him.

[15]David was at Horesh in the Desert of Ziph. He was afraid because Saul was coming to kill him. [16]But Saul's son Jonathan went to see David at Horesh and encouraged him to

---

[a]22:18 **priests** Literally, "men who wore the linen ephod."

[b]23:6 **When Abiathar ... him** This means that Abiathar could go before God for David and ask for advice.

have a stronger faith in God. [17]Jonathan told David, "Don't be afraid. My father Saul won't hurt you. You will become the king of Israel, and I will be second to you. Even my father knows this."

[18]Jonathan and David both made an agreement before the LORD. Then Jonathan went home, and David stayed at Horesh.

The People of Ziph Tell Saul About David

[19]Some people from Ziph went to Saul at Gibeah and told him, "David is hiding in our area. He is at the fortresses* of Horesh on Hakilah Hill, south of Jeshimon. [20]Now, King, come down any time you want. It is our duty to give David to you."

[21]Saul answered, "May the LORD bless you for helping me. [22]Go and learn more about David. Keep track of where he goes and who goes to see him. I am told that David is smart and that he is trying to trick me. [23]Find all the hiding places that David uses. Then come back to me and tell me everything. Then I'll go with you. If David is in the area, I will find him, even if I must go to every family group in Judah."

[24]So those people went back to Ziph before Saul.

David and his men were in the Desert of Maon, south of Jeshimon. [25]Saul and his men went to look for David, but the people warned him. They told David that Saul was looking for him. So David then went down to "The Rock" in the Desert of Maon. Saul heard that David had gone to the Desert of Maon, so Saul went to that place to find him.

[26]Saul was on one side of the mountain. David and his men were on the other side of the same mountain. David was moving as quickly as possible to get away from Saul. But Saul and his soldiers were going around the mountain to cut them off and trap David and his men.

[27]Then a messenger arrived and told Saul, "Come quickly! The Philistines are attacking."

[28]So Saul stopped chasing David and went to fight the Philistines. That is why people call this place "Slippery Rock."[a] [29]David left the Desert of Maon and went to the fortresses near En Gedi.

David Shames Saul

24 [1]After Saul had chased the Philistines away, people told him, "David is in the desert area near En Gedi."

[2]So Saul chose 3000 men from all over Israel and began searching for David and his men. They looked near Wild Goat Rocks. [3]Saul came to some sheep pens beside the road. There was a cave near there, so Saul went in to relieve himself. David and his men were deep inside that same cave. [4]David's

men told him, "This is day the LORD told you about when he said, 'I will give your enemy to you, and you can do whatever you want to him.'"

So David crawled closer and closer to Saul and cut off a corner of Saul's robe. Saul didn't notice what happened. [5]Later, David felt bad about what he did. [6]He said to his men, "I pray the LORD never lets me do anything like that to my master again. I must not do anything against Saul, because he is the LORD's chosen king.[b]" [7]David said these things to stop his men. He would not let his men hurt Saul.

Saul left the cave and went on his way. [8]Later, David came out of the cave and called out to Saul, "My lord the king!"

Saul looked back. David bowed with his face to the ground to show his respect. [9]David said to Saul, "Why do you listen when people say, 'David plans to hurt you'? [10]You can see that with your own eyes that is not true. The LORD put you within my grasp today in the cave, but I refused to kill you. I was merciful to you. I said, 'I won't hurt my master. Saul is the LORD's chosen king.' [11]Look at this piece of cloth in my hand. I cut off the corner of your robe. I could have killed you, but I didn't. Now, I want you to understand this. I want you to know that I am not planning anything against you. I did nothing wrong to you, but you are hunting me and trying to kill me. [12]Let the LORD be the judge. He might punish you for the wrong you did to me, but I won't fight you myself. [13]There is an old saying:

'Bad things come from bad people.'

"I haven't done anything bad, and I won't hurt you. [14]Who are you chasing? Did the king of Israel bring an army to chase a single flea or a dying dog? [15]Let the LORD be the judge. Let him decide between you and me. He will support me and show that I am right. He will save me from you."

[16]When David finished speaking, Saul asked, "Is that your voice, David my son?" Then Saul lifted his voice and began to cry. [17]He said, "You are right, and I am wrong. You were good to me, even though I have been bad to you. [18]You yourself said it when you told me about the good things you did. The LORD put my life in your hands, but you did not kill me. [19]This shows that you are not my enemy. A man doesn't catch his enemy and then just let him go. He doesn't do good things for his enemy. May the LORD reward you for being good to me today. [20]Now, I know that you will become the new king. You will rule the kingdom of Israel. [21]Now make a promise to me. Use the LORD's name and promise that you will not kill my descendants,

---

[a]**23:28 Slippery Rock** Or "Sela Hammahlekoth."

[b]**24:6 chosen king** Literally, "anointed one." Also in verse 10.

even after I die. Promise me that you will not erase my name from my father's family."

²²So David made a promise to Saul. He promised that he would not kill Saul's family. Then Saul went back home. David and his men went back up to the fort.

David and Nabal the Fool

25 ¹Samuel died. All the Israelites met together and mourned* his death. They buried him at his home in Ramah.

Then David moved to the Desert of Maon.ᵃ ²There was a very rich man living in Maon. He had 3000 sheep and 1000 goats. That man was in Carmel taking care of some business. He went there to cut the wool from his sheep. ³This man's name was Nabal.ᵇ He was from Caleb's family. Nabal's wife was named Abigail. She was a wise and beautiful woman, but Nabal was a mean and cruel man.

⁴David was in the desert when he heard that Nabal was cutting the wool from his sheep. ⁵David sent ten young men to talk to Nabal. He told them, "Go to Carmel. Find Nabal and tell him 'Hello' for me." ⁶David gave them this message for Nabal: "May you and your family be well and all that you own be well. ⁷I heard that you are cutting wool from your sheep. Your shepherds were with us for a while, and we did nothing wrong to them. We never took anything from your shepherds while they were at Carmel. ⁸Ask your servants and they will tell you this is true. Please be kind to my young men. We come to you now, at this happy time. Please give these young men anything you can. Please do this for me, your friendᶜ David."

⁹David's men went to Nabal. They gave his message to Nabal, ¹⁰but Nabal said, "Who is David? Who is this son of Jesse? There are many slaves who have run away from their masters these days. ¹¹I have bread and water, and I have the meat I killed for my servants who cut the wool from my sheep. But I won't give them to men I don't even know."

¹²David's men went back and told him everything that Nabal had said. ¹³David's response was, "Put on your swords." So David and his men put on their swords. About 400 men went with David while 200 of them stayed with the supplies.

Abigail Prevents Trouble

¹⁴One of Nabal's servants spoke to Nabal's wife Abigail. The servant said, "David sent messengers from the desert to meet our master, but Nabal was rude to them. ¹⁵These men were very good to us while we were out in the fields with the sheep. David's men were with us the whole time, and they never did anything wrong to us. They did not take anything

from us. ¹⁶His men protected us night and day. They were like a wall around us—they protected us while we were with them caring for the sheep. ¹⁷Nabal was foolish to say what he did. Terrible trouble is coming to our master and all his family. You need to think of something to do."

¹⁸Abigail quickly gathered up 200 loaves of bread, two full wine bags, five cooked sheep, about a bushelᵈ of cooked grain, about 2 quartsᵉ of raisins, and 200 cakes of pressed figs. She put them on donkeys. ¹⁹Then Abigail told her servants, "Go on. I'll follow you." But she did not tell her husband.

²⁰Abigail rode her donkey down to the other side of the mountain. She met David and his men coming from the other direction.

²¹David was saying, "I protected Nabal's property in the desert. I made sure not one of his sheep was missing. I did all that for nothing. I was good to him, but he was rude to me. ²²I swear,ᶠ I won't let even one man in Nabal's family live until tomorrow morning."

²³Just then Abigail arrived. When she saw David, she quickly got off her donkey and bowed down with her face to the ground in front of him. ²⁴Abigail fell at his feet and said, "Sir, please let me talk to you. Listen to what I say. Blame me for what happened. ²⁵I didn't see the men you sent. Sir, don't pay any attention to that worthless man, Nabal. His name means 'Foolish,' and that is what he is. ²⁶The LORD has kept you from killing innocent people. As surely as the LORD lives and you as well, may your enemies and anyone else who wants to harm you be as cursed as Nabal is. ²⁷Now, I am bringing this gift to you. Please give these things to your men. ²⁸Please forgive me for doing wrong. I know the LORD will make your family strong because you fight his battles. People will never find anything bad about you as long as you live. ²⁹If someone chases you to kill you, the LORD your God will save your life. But he will throw away your enemies like a stone from a sling.* ³⁰The LORD promised to do many good things for you, and he will keep his promises. He will make you leader over Israel. ³¹So don't do anything that would make you guilty of killing innocent people. Please don't fall into that trap. Please remember me when the LORD blesses you."

³²David answered Abigail, "Praise the LORD, the God of Israel. Praise God for sending you to meet me. ³³God bless you for your good judgment. You kept me from killing innocent people today. ³⁴As surely as the LORD, the God of Israel, lives, if you hadn't come quickly to meet me, not one man in Nabal's family would have lived until tomorrow morning. But the Lord prevented me from hurting you."

ᵃ**25:1** *Maon* This is from the ancient Greek version. The standard Hebrew text has "Paran."
ᵇ**25:3** *Nabal* This name means "foolish."
ᶜ**25:8** *friend* Literally, "son."

ᵈ**25:18** *about a bushel* Literally, "5 seahs" (36.5 l).
ᵉ**25:18** *2 quarts* Literally, "1 omer" (2.2 l).
ᶠ**25:22** *I swear* Literally, "May God do so and so for David's enemies if …."

35Then David accepted Abigail's gifts. He told her, "Go home in peace. I have listened to your request, and I will do what you asked."

Nabal's Death

36Abigail went back to Nabal, who was in the house. He had been eating like a king, and he was drunk and feeling good. So Abigail told Nabal nothing until the next morning. 37The next morning, Nabal was sober, so his wife told him everything. He had a heart attack and became as stiff as a rock. 38About ten days later, the LORD gave him a stroke and Nabal died.

39When David heard that Nabal was dead, he said, "Praise the LORD! Nabal insulted me, but the LORD defended my honor. The LORD kept me from doing wrong and made Nabal pay for what he did."

Then David sent a message to Abigail and asked her to be his wife. 40His servants went to Carmel with this message, "David sent us to get you. He wants you to be his wife."

41Abigail bowed her face to the ground. She said, "I am willing to be your slave woman,* even if it is only to wash the feet of my master's servants."

42Abigail quickly got on a donkey and brought five of her maids with her. They followed David's messengers. So Abigail became David's wife. 43David had also married Ahinoam of Jezreel. Both Ahinoam and Abigail were David's wives. 44David was also married to Saul's daughter Michal, but Saul had taken her away from him and had given her to a man named Palti, son of Laish. Palti was from the town named Gallim.

David and Abishai Enter Saul's Camp

26 1The people of Ziph went to see Saul at Gibeah and said to him, "David is hiding on Hakilah Hill, across from Jeshimon."

2Saul gathered 3000 of the best soldiers in Israel and went down to the desert of Ziph to search for David in the desert of Ziph. 3Saul set up his camp by the road at Hakilah Hill, across from Jeshimon.

David was out in the desert and saw that Saul had come out into the desert after him. 4So David sent out spies to know for certain that Saul had come after him again. 5Then David went to where Saul had set up his camp. David saw where Saul and Abner were sleeping. (Abner son of Ner was the commander of Saul's army.) Saul was sleeping in the center of a circle of men that surrounded him.

6David talked to Ahimelech the Hittite and Abishai son of Zeruiah. (Abishai was Joab's brother.) He asked them, "Who would like to go down into the camp with me after Saul?"

Abishai answered, "I'll go with you."

7When night came, David and Abishai went into Saul's camp. Saul was asleep in the middle of the circle of men. His spear was stuck in the ground near his head. Abner and the other soldiers were asleep around Saul. 8Abishai said to David, "Today God has given your enemy to you. Let me pin Saul to the ground with his spear. I'll only do it once!"

9But David said to Abishai, "Don't kill Saul! Anyone who hurts the LORD's chosen king*a* must be punished. 10As surely as the LORD lives, the LORD himself will punish Saul. Maybe Saul will die naturally or maybe he will be killed in battle. 11But I pray that the LORD never lets me hurt the LORD's chosen king. Now pick up the spear and water jug by Saul's head and then let's go."

12So David took the spear and water jug that were near Saul's head, and then David and Abishai left Saul's camp. No one knew what had happened. No one saw it. No one even woke up. Saul and all of his soldiers slept because the LORD had put them into a deep sleep.

David Shames Saul Again

13David crossed over to the other side of the valley. He stood on top of the mountain across the valley from Saul's camp. David and Saul's camp were far apart. 14David shouted to the army and to Abner son of Ner, "Answer me, Abner!"

Abner answered, "Who are you? Why are you calling the king?"

15David said, "You are an important man, aren't you? You are better than any other man in Israel. Is that right? So why didn't you guard your master, the king? An ordinary man came into your camp to kill your master, the king. 16You made a big mistake. As surely as the LORD is alive, you and your men should die, because you didn't protect your master, the LORD's chosen king. Look for the king's spear and the water jug that was near Saul's head. Where are they?"

17Saul knew David's voice and said, "Is that your voice, David my son?"

David answered, "Yes, it is my voice, my lord the king. 18Sir, why are you chasing me? What wrong have I done? What am I guilty of? 19My lord the king, listen to me. If the LORD caused you to be angry with me, let him accept an offering. But if men caused you to be angry with me, I ask the LORD to curse them because they forced me to leave the land that the LORD gave me and told me to go serve other gods. 20Now don't make me die far away from the LORD's presence. The king of Israel has come out looking for a flea. You are like a man hunting partridges in the mountains."*b*

---

*a***26:9 chosen king** Literally, "anointed one." Also in verses 16, 23.

*b***26:20 hunting partridges in the mountains** People hunted these birds until the birds became too tired to go on. Then they killed the birds. Saul was chasing David the same way. This is also a wordplay. The Hebrew word for "partridge" is like the word for "calling" in verse 14.

21Then Saul said, "David, my son! I have sinned. Come back. Today you showed me that my life is important to you, so I won't try to hurt you. I have acted foolishly. I have made a big mistake."

22David answered, "Here is the king's spear. Let one of your young men come here and get it. 23The LORD pays every man for what he does—he rewards him if he does right, and he punishes him if he does wrong. The LORD gave you to me today, but I wouldn't hurt his chosen king. 24Today I showed you that your life is important to me. In the same way the LORD will show that my life is important to him. He will save me from every trouble."

25Then Saul said to David, "God bless you, David my son. You will do great things and you will win."

David went on his way, and Saul went back home.

David Lives With the Philistines

27 1But David thought to himself, "Saul will catch me some day. The best thing I can do is to escape to the land of the Philistines. Then Saul will give up looking for me in Israel. That way I will escape from Saul."

2So David and his 600 men left Israel and went to Achish son of Maoch. Achish was king of Gath. 3David, his men, and their families lived in Gath with Achish. David had his two wives with him—Ahinoam of Jezreel and Abigail of Carmel. Abigail was the widow of Nabal. 4People told Saul that David had run away to Gath, so Saul stopped looking for him.

5David said to Achish, "If you are pleased with me, give me a place in one of the country towns. I am only your servant. I should live there, not here with you in this royal city."

6That day Achish gave David the town of Ziklag. And Ziklag has belonged to the kings of Judah ever since. 7David lived with the Philistines one year and four months.

David Fools King Achish

8David and his men went to fight the Amalekites and Geshurites who lived in the area from Telem near Shur all the way to Egypt. David's men defeated them and took their wealth. 9David defeated the people in that area. He took all their sheep, cattle, donkeys, camels, and clothes and brought them back to Achish. But David didn't let any of those people live.

10David did this many times. Each time Achish asked David where he fought and took those things. David said, "I fought against the southern part of Judah," or "I fought against the southern part of Jerahmeel," or "I fought against the southern part of the Kenizzites."a 11David never brought a man or woman alive

to Gath. He thought, "If we let anyone live, they might tell Achish what I really did."

David did this all the time he lived in the Philistine land. 12Achish began to trust David and said to himself, "Now David's own people hate him. The Israelites hate him very much. Now he will serve me forever."

The Philistines Prepare for War

28 1Later, the Philistines gathered their armies to fight against Israel. Achish said to David, "Do you understand that you and your men must go with me to fight against Israel?"

2David answered, "Certainly, then you can see for yourself what I can do."

Achish said, "Fine, I will make you my permanent bodyguard."

Saul and the Woman at Endor

3After Samuel died, all the Israelites mourned* for him and buried him in Ramah, his hometown.

Saul had removed the mediums* and fortunetellers* from Israel.

4The Philistines prepared for war. They came to Shunem and made their camp at that place. Saul gathered all the Israelites together and made his camp at Gilboa. 5Saul saw the Philistine army, and he was afraid. His heart pounded with fear. 6He prayed to the LORD, but the LORD did not answer him. God did not talk to Saul in dreams. God did not use the Urim* to give him an answer, and God did not use prophets to speak to Saul. 7Finally, Saul said to his officers, "Find me a woman who is a medium. Then I can go ask her what will happen."

His officers answered, "There is a medium at Endor.b"

8That night, Saul put on different clothes so that no one would know who he was. Then Saul and two of his men went to see the woman. Saul said to her, "I want you to bring up a ghost who can tell me what will happen in the future. You must call for the ghost of the person I name."

9But the woman said to him, "You know that Saul forced all the mediums and fortunetellers to leave the land of Israel. You are trying to trap me and kill me."

10Saul used the LORD's name to make a promise to the woman. He said, "As surely as the LORD lives, you won't be punished for doing this."

11The woman asked, "Who do you want me to bring up for you?"

Saul answered, "Bring up Samuel."

12And it happened—the woman saw Samuel and screamed. She said to Saul, "You tricked me! You are Saul."

a27:10 *Judah, Jerahmeel, Kenizzites* All these places belonged to Israel. David made Achish think he had fought against his own people, the Israelites.

b28:7 *Endor* A town around the mountain from Shunem, where the Philistines were camped. Saul had to go around them to get to Endor.

13The king said to the woman, "Don't be afraid! What do you see?"

The woman said, "I see a spirit coming up out of the ground.*a*"

14Saul asked, "What does he look like?"

The woman answered, "He looks like an old man wearing a special robe."

Then Saul knew it was Samuel, and he bowed down. His face touched the ground. 15Samuel said to Saul, "Why did you bother me? Why did you bring me up?"

Saul answered, "I am in trouble! The Philistines have come to fight me, and God has left me. God won't answer me anymore. He won't use prophets or dreams to answer me, so I called you. I want you to tell me what to do."

16Samuel said, "The LORD left you and is now your enemy, so why are you asking me for advice? 17The LORD used me to tell you what he would do, and now he is doing what he said he would do. He is tearing the kingdom out of your hands and giving it to your neighbor, David. 18The reason this is happening is because you did not obey the LORD and destroy the Amalekites. 19The LORD will let the Philistines defeat you and the army of Israel today. Tomorrow, you and your sons will be here with me."

20Saul quickly fell to the ground and lay stretched out there. Saul was afraid because of what Samuel said. Saul was also very weak because he had not eaten any food all that day and night.

21The woman came over to Saul and saw how afraid he was. She said, "Look, I am your servant. I have obeyed you. I risked my life and did what you told me to do. 22Please, listen to me. You need to eat. Let me get you some food. Then you will have enough strength to go on your way."

23But Saul refused. He said, "I won't eat."

Saul's officers joined the woman and begged him to eat. Finally, Saul listened to them. He got up from the ground and sat on the bed. 24The woman had a calf that she had been fattening. She quickly killed the calf. She took some flour and pressed it with her hands. Then she baked some bread without yeast. 25The woman put the food before Saul and his officers and they ate. Then they got up and left during the night.

David Can't Come With Us

29 1Meanwhile, the Philistines had gathered all of their army camps at Aphek. The Israelites were camped by the spring near Jezreel. 2The Philistine rulers were marching in divisions of 100 and 1000 men. David and his men were at the back with Achish.

3The Philistine captains asked, "What are these Hebrews doing here?"

Achish told the Philistine captains, "This is David. He was one of Saul's officers, but he has been with me for a long time. I found nothing wrong in David since the time he left Saul and came to me."

4But the Philistine captains were angry with Achish. They said, "Send him back. Let him go back to the city you gave him, but he can't go into battle with us. As long as he is here, we have an enemy in our own camp. He would make his king happy by killing our men. 5Isn't David the one the Israelites sing about? They dance and sing this song:

'Saul has killed thousands of enemies,
     but David has killed tens of thousands.'"

6So Achish called David and said, "As surely as the LORD lives, you are loyal to me. I would be pleased to have you serve in my army. I haven't found anything wrong with you since the day you came to me. The Philistine rulers also think you are a good man.*b* 7Go back in peace. Don't do anything against the Philistine rulers."

8David asked, "What have I done wrong? Have you found anything wrong with me since the day I came to you? So why won't you let me go to fight the enemies of my lord the king?"

9Achish answered, "I believe that you are a good man. You are like an angel from God. But the Philistine captains still say, 'David can't go with us into battle.' 10Early in the morning, you and your men should go back to the city I gave you. Don't pay attention to the bad things the captains say about you. You are a good man, but you must leave as soon as there is enough light in the morning."

11So David and his men got up early in the morning and went back to the country of the Philistines, and the Philistines went up to Jezreel.

The Amalekites Attack Ziklag

30 1As soon as David and his men arrived at Ziklag on the third day, they saw that the Amalekites had attacked Ziklag. The Amalekites invaded the Negev area, attacked Ziklag, and burned the city. 2They took all the women in Ziklag, both young and old, as prisoners. They didn't kill anyone; they only took them as prisoners.

3When David and his men came to Ziklag, they found the city burning. Their wives, sons, and daughters were all gone. The Amalekites had taken them. 4David and the other men in his army cried loudly until they were too weak to cry anymore. 5The Amalekites had taken David's two wives, Ahinoam of Jezreel and Abigail, who had been the wife of Nabal from Carmel.

*b*29:6 *The Philistine ... man* This is from the ancient Greek version. The Philistine rulers were pleased with David. It was the Philistine army commanders who were against him. The standard Hebrew text has "The Philistine rulers do not think you are a good man."

*a*28:13 *ground* Or "Sheol, the place of death."

[6]All the men in the army were sad and angry because their sons and daughters were taken as prisoners. The men were talking about killing David with stones. This upset David very much, but he found strength in the LORD his God. [7]David said to Abiathar the priest, "Bring the ephod.*"

[8]Then David prayed to the LORD. "Should I chase the people who took our families? Will I catch them?"

The LORD answered, "Chase them. You will catch them, and you will save your families."

David Finds an Egyptian Slave

[9-10]David took the 600 men with him and went to Besor Ravine. About 200 of his men stayed there because they were too weak and tired to continue. But David and the other 400 men continued to chase the Amalekites. [11]David's men found an Egyptian in a field and took him to David. They gave the Egyptian some water to drink and some food to eat. [12]The Egyptian had not had any food or water for three days and nights, so they gave him a piece of fig cake and two clusters of raisins. He felt better after eating.

[13]David asked the Egyptian, "Who is your master? Where do you come from?"

The Egyptian answered, "I am an Egyptian, the slave of an Amalekite. Three days ago I got sick, and my master left me behind. [14]We had attacked the Negev area where the Kerethites[a] live. We also attacked Judah and the Negev area where Caleb's people live. We burned Ziklag."

[15]David asked the Egyptian, "Will you lead me to the people who took our families?"

The Egyptian answered, "If you make a special promise before God, I will help you find them. But you must promise that you will not kill me or give me back to my master."

David Defeats the Amalekites

[16]The Egyptian led David to the Amalekites. They were lying around on the ground, eating and drinking. They were celebrating with the many things they had taken from the Philistines and from Judah. [17]David attacked them and killed them. They fought from sunrise until the evening of the next day. None of the Amalekites escaped, except for 400 young men who jumped onto their camels and rode away.

[18]David got back everything the Amalekites had taken, including his two wives. [19]Nothing was missing. They found all the children and old people, all their sons and daughters, and all their valuables. They got back everything the Amalekites had taken. David brought everything back. [20]He took all the sheep and cattle. His men led these animals

to the front of the group and said, "This is David's prize."

All Men Will Share Equally

[21]David came to the 200 men who had stayed at Besor Ravine. These were the men who were too weak and tired to follow David. They came out to meet him and the soldiers who went with him. They greeted David and his army as they approached. [22]There were some troublemakers in the group who went with David who started complaining, "These 200 men didn't go with us, so why should we give them any of the things we took. These men get nothing but their own wives and children."

[23]David answered, "No, my brothers. Don't do that! Think about what the LORD gave us. He let us defeat the enemy that attacked us. [24]No one will listen to what you say. The share will be the same for the man who stayed with the supplies and for the man who went into battle. Everyone will share alike." [25]David made this an order and rule for Israel. This rule continues even today.

[26]When David got to Ziklag, he sent some of the things he took from the Amalekites to his friends, the leaders of Judah. David said, "Here is a present for you that we took from the LORD's enemies."

[27]David sent some of the gifts to the leaders in Bethel, Ramoth in the Negev, Jattir, [28]Aroer, Siphmoth, Eshtemoa, [29]Racal, the cities of the Jerahmeelites and the cities of the Kenites, [30]Hormah, Bor Ashan, Athach, [31]and Hebron, and to all the other places where David and his men had stayed.

The Death of Saul

31 [1]Meanwhile, the Philistines fought against the Israelites, and the Israelites ran from them. There were many dead bodies that fell at Mount Gilboa. [2]The Philistines fought hard against Saul and his sons. They killed Jonathan, Abinadab, and Malki Shua.

[3]The battle grew even more intense around Saul. The archers* closed in on Saul and wounded him with many arrows. [4]Saul told the boy who carried his armor,* "Take your sword and kill me or else these foreigners will do it and torment me as well!" But Saul's helper was afraid and refused to kill him. So Saul took out his own sword and fell on it. [5]When the helper saw that Saul was dead, he took out his own sword, fell on it, and died there with Saul. [6]So Saul, his three sons, and the boy who carried his armor all died together that day.

The Philistines Rejoice at Saul's Death

[7]The Israelites who lived on the other side of the valley saw the Israelite army running away. They saw that Saul and his sons were dead, so they left their cities and ran away. Then the Philistines came and lived in their cities.

---

[a]**30:14** Kerethites Or "people from Crete." These were one of the groups of Philistines. Some of David's best soldiers were Kerethites.

⁸The next day, the Philistines went back to take things from the dead bodies. They found Saul and his three sons dead on Mount Gilboa. ⁹The Philistines cut off Saul's head and took all his armor.* They carried the news to the Philistines and to all the temples of their idols.* ¹⁰They put Saul's armor in the temple of Ashtoreth.* The Philistines also hung Saul's body on the wall of Beth Shan.ᵃ

ᵃ**31:10 Beth Shan** Or possibly, "Beth Shean." Also in verse 12.

¹¹The people living in Jabesh Gilead heard what the Philistines did to Saul. ¹²So all the soldiers of Jabesh went to Beth Shan. They marched all night, went to the wall of Beth Shan, and took down the bodies of Saul and his sons. Then they carried them to Jabesh. There the people of Jabesh burned the bodies of Saul and his three sons. ¹³Later, they buried the bones of Saul and his three sons under the big tree in Jabesh. Then the people of Jabesh showed their sadness—they did not eat for seven days.

2 Samuel

David Learns About Saul's Death

1 ¹After David defeated the Amalekites, he went back to Ziklag. This was just after Saul had been killed. David had been there two days. ²Then, on the third day, a young soldier from Saul's camp came to Ziklag. His clothes were torn, and he had dirt on his head.ᵇ He came to David and bowed with his face to the ground.

³David asked him, "Where have you come from?"

The man answered, "I just came from the Israelite camp."

⁴David asked him, "Please tell me, who won the battle?"

The man answered, "Our people ran away from the battle. Many of them were killed in the battle. Even Saul and his son Jonathan are dead."

⁵David said to the young soldier, "How do you know Saul and his son Jonathan are dead?"

⁶The young soldier said, "I happened to be on Mount Gilboa. I saw Saul leaning on his spear. The Philistine chariots* and horse soldiers were coming closer and closer to Saul. ⁷Saul looked back and saw me. He called to me and I answered him. ⁸Then Saul asked me who I was. I told him that I was an Amalekite. ⁹Then Saul said, 'Please kill me. I am hurt badly. And I am about to die anyway.' ¹⁰He was hurt so badly that I knew he wouldn't live. So I stopped and killed him. Then I took the crown from his head and the bracelet from his arm and brought them here to you, my lord."

¹¹Then David tore his clothes to show he was very sad. All the men with him did the same thing. ¹²They were very sad and cried. They did not eat until evening. They

cried because Saul and his son Jonathan were dead. David and his men cried for the LORD's people, and they cried for Israel. They cried because Saul, his son Jonathan, and many Israelites had been killed in battle.

David Orders the Amalekite Killed

¹³Then David talked with the young soldier who had told him about Saul's death. David asked, "Where are you from?"

The young soldier answered, "I am the son of a foreigner. I am an Amalekite."

¹⁴David said to the young soldier, "Why were you not afraid to kill the LORD's chosen king?"

¹⁵⁻¹⁶Then David told the Amalekite, "You are responsible for your own death. You said you killed the LORD's chosen king, so your own words prove you are guilty." Then David called one of his young servants and told him to kill the Amalekite. So the young Israelite killed him.

David's Song About Saul and Jonathan

¹⁷David sang a sad song about Saul and his son Jonathan. ¹⁸David told his men to teach the song to the people of Judah. This song is called *The Bow*, and it is written in the *Book of Jashar*.ᵈ

¹⁹"Israel, your beauty was ruined on your
    hills.
    Oh, how those heroes fell!

²⁰ Don't tell the news in Gath.ᵉ
    Don't announce it in the streets of
    Ashkelon.ᶠ

ᵇ**1:2 clothes … head** This showed that the man was very sad.

ᶜ**1:14 chosen king** Literally, "anointed one."
ᵈ**1:18 Book of Jashar** An ancient book about the wars of Israel.
ᵉ**1:20 Gath** The Philistine capital city.
ᶠ**1:20 Ashkelon** One of the five major Philistine cities.

Those Philistine cities would be happy!
Those foreigners[a] would be glad.

21"May no rain or dew fall
    on you, mountains of Gilboa.
May there be no offerings
    coming from your fields.
The shields of the heroes rusted there.
    Saul's shield was not rubbed with oil.
22 Jonathan's bow killed its share of enemies,
    and Saul's sword killed its share!
They have spilled the blood of men now
        dead.
They cut into the fat of strong men.

23"Saul and Jonathan—how dear they were
        to us!
    In life they loved being together,
    and even death did not separate them!
They were faster than eagles
    and stronger than lions.
24 Daughters of Israel, cry for Saul!
    Saul gave you beautiful red dresses
    and covered them with gold jewelry!

25"Strong men have fallen in the battle.
    Jonathan is dead on Gilboa's hills.
26 Jonathan, my brother, I miss you!
    I enjoyed your friendship so much.
Your love for me was wonderful,
    stronger than the love of women.
27 Heroes have fallen in battle.
    Their weapons of war are lost."

David Is Anointed King of Judah

2 ¹Later David asked the LORD for advice. David said, "Should I take control[b] of any of the cities of Judah?"

The LORD said to David, "Yes."

David asked, "Where should I go?"

The LORD answered, "To Hebron."

²So David and his two wives moved to Hebron. (His wives were Ahinoam from Jezreel and Abigail, who had been the wife of Nabal from Carmel.) ³David also brought his men and their families. All of them made their homes in Hebron and the towns nearby.

⁴The men of Judah came to Hebron and anointed* David to be the king of Judah. Then they told David, "The men of Jabesh Gilead buried Saul."

⁵David sent messengers to the men of Jabesh Gilead. These messengers told the men in Jabesh: "The LORD bless you, because you have shown kindness to your lord Saul by burying him.[c] ⁶The LORD will be kind and true to you, and so will I. ⁷Now be strong and

brave. Your lord, Saul, is dead, but the tribe of Judah has anointed me to be their king."

Ish Bosheth Becomes King

⁸Abner son of Ner was the captain of Saul's army. Abner took Ish Bosheth son of Saul to Mahanaim ⁹and made him king of Gilead, Asher, Jezreel, Ephraim, Benjamin, and all Israel.[d]

¹⁰Ish Bosheth son of Saul was 40 years old when he began to rule over Israel. He ruled Israel two years, but the tribe of Judah followed David. ¹¹David ruled over the tribe of Judah from Hebron for seven years and six months.

The Deadly Contest

¹²Abner son of Ner and the officers of Ish Bosheth son of Saul left Mahanaim and went to Gibeon. ¹³Joab, Zeruiah's son, and the officers of David also went to Gibeon. They met Abner and Ish Bosheth's officers at the pool of Gibeon. Abner's group sat on one side of the pool. Joab's group sat on the other side.

¹⁴Abner said to Joab, "Let's have the young soldiers get up and have a contest here."

Joab said, "Yes, let's have a contest."

¹⁵So the young soldiers got up. The two groups counted their men for the contest. They chose twelve men from the tribe of Benjamin to fight for Ish Bosheth son of Saul, and they chose twelve men from David's officers. ¹⁶Each of the men grabbed his opponent's head and stabbed him in the side with his sword, and then they fell down together. That is why this place in Gibeon is called "The Field of the Sharp Knives."[e]

Abner Kills Asahel

¹⁷That contest turned into a terrible battle and David's officers defeated Abner and the Israelites that day. ¹⁸Zeruiah had three sons, Joab, Abishai, and Asahel. Asahel was a fast runner, as fast as a wild deer. ¹⁹Asahel ran straight toward Abner and began chasing him. ²⁰Abner looked back and asked, "Is that you, Asahel?"

Asahel said, "Yes, it's me."

²¹Abner didn't want to hurt Asahel, so he said to Asahel, "Stop chasing me—go after one of the young soldiers. You could easily take his armor* for yourself." But Asahel refused to stop chasing Abner.

²²Abner again said to Asahel, "Stop chasing me, or I will have to kill you. Then I will not be able to look your brother Joab in the face again."

²³But Asahel refused to stop chasing Abner. So Abner used the back end of his spear and

---

*a*1:20 *foreigners* Literally, "uncircumcised." This shows that the Philistines had not shared in Israel's agreement with God.
*b*2:1 *take control* Literally, "go up against."
*c*2:5 *burying him* The bodies of both Saul and Jonathan were burned and their bones were buried. See 1 Sam. 31:12.

*d*2:9 *Israel* Sometimes this means the whole country, Judah and Israel. Here, it means only the tribes that were not united with Judah.
*e*2:16 *The Field of the Sharp Knives* Or "Helkath Hazzurim."

pushed it into Asahel's stomach. The spear went deep into Asahel's stomach and came out of his back. Asahel died right there.

Joab and Abishai Chase Abner

Asahel's body lay on the ground. Everyone who came that way stopped to look at Asahel, 24but Joab and Abishai*a* continued chasing Abner. The sun was just going down when they came to Ammah Hill. (Ammah Hill is in front of Giah on the way to the Gibeon Desert.) 25The men from the tribe of Benjamin gathered around Abner at the top of the hill.

26Abner shouted to Joab and said, "Must we fight and kill each other forever? Surely you know that this will only end in sadness. Tell the people to stop chasing their own brothers."

27Then Joab said, "As surely as God is alive, if you had not said something, people would still be chasing their brothers in the morning." 28So Joab blew a trumpet, and his people stopped chasing the Israelites. They did not try to fight the Israelites anymore.

29Abner and his men marched all night through the Jordan Valley. They crossed the Jordan River and then marched all day until they came to Mahanaim.

30Joab stopped chasing Abner and turned back. Joab had gathered his men and learned that 19 of David's officers were missing, including Asahel. 31But David's officers had killed 360 of Abner's men from the tribe of Benjamin. 32David's officers took Asahel and buried him in the tomb of his father at Bethlehem.

Joab and his men marched all night. The sun came up just as they reached Hebron.

War Between Israel and Judah

3 1There was war for a long time between Saul's family and David's family. David became stronger and stronger, but Saul's family became weaker and weaker.

David's Six Sons Born at Hebron

2Several of David's sons were born at Hebron. The first son was Amnon. Amnon's mother was Ahinoam from Jezreel. 3The second son was Kileab. Kileab's mother was Abigail, who had been the wife of Nabal from Carmel. The third son was Absalom. His mother was Maacah daughter of King Talmai of Geshur. 4The fourth son was Adonijah. Adonijah's mother was Haggith. The fifth son was Shephatiah. Shephatiah's mother was Abital. 5The sixth son was Ithream. Ithream's mother was David's wife Eglah. These sons were all born at Hebron.

Abner Decides to Join David

6As the families of Saul and David fought each other, Abner became more and more powerful in Saul's army. 7Saul had a slave woman* named Rizpah daughter of Aiah. Ish Bosheth said to Abner, "Why did you have sexual relations with my father's servant woman?"

8This made Abner very angry. He said, "I have been loyal to Saul and his family. I did not give you to David. I am not a traitor working for Judah.*b* But now you are saying that I did this bad thing. 9-10The LORD said he would take the kingdom away from Saul's family and give it to David. I swear, I will make sure that happens. The LORD will make David king of Judah and Israel. He will rule from Dan to Beersheba.*c*" 11Ish Bosheth was too afraid of Abner to say anything in response.

12Abner sent messengers to David and said, "Who do you think should rule this country? Make an agreement with me, and I will help you become the ruler of all the people of Israel."

13David answered, "Good! I will make an agreement with you. But I ask you only one thing: I will not meet with you until you bring Saul's daughter Michal to me."

14David sent messengers to Saul's son Ish Bosheth. David said, "Give me my wife Michal. She was promised to me. I killed 100 Philistines to get her."*d*

15Then Ish Bosheth told the men to go and take Michal from a man named Paltiel son of Laish. 16Michal's husband, Paltiel, followed them, crying all the way to Bahurim. Finally Abner said to him, "Go back home." So Paltiel went back home.

17Abner sent this message to the leaders of Israel. He said, "You have been wanting to make David your king. 18Now do it! The LORD was talking about David when he said, 'I will save my people the Israelites from the Philistines and all their other enemies. I will do this through my servant David.'"

19Abner said these things to David in Hebron, and he said these things to the people of the tribe of Benjamin. The things Abner said sounded good to the tribe of Benjamin and to all the people of Israel.

20Then Abner came up to David at Hebron. Abner brought 20 men with him. David gave a party for Abner and for all the men who came with him.

21Abner said to David, "My lord and king, let me go bring all the Israelites to you. Then they will make an agreement with you, and you will rule over all Israel, as you wanted."

So David let Abner leave in peace.

*b*3:8 *I am not ... Judah* Literally, "Am I a dog's head of Judah?"
*c*3:9–10 *Dan to Beersheba* This means the whole nation of Israel, north and south. Dan was a town in the northern part of Israel and Beersheba was in the southern part of Judah.
*d*3:14 *I killed ... to get her* Literally, "I paid for her with 100 Philistine foreskins." See 1 Sam. 18:20–30; 25:44.

*a*2:24 *Joab and Abishai* Brothers of Asahel, the man who Abner killed. See verse 18.

Abner's Death

22Joab and David's officers came back from battle. They had many valuable things that they had taken from the enemy. David had just let Abner leave in peace. So Abner was not there in Hebron with David. 23Joab and all his army arrived at Hebron. The army said to Joab, "Abner son of Ner came to King David, and David let Abner leave in peace."

24Joab came to the king and said, "What have you done? Abner came to you, but you sent him away without hurting him! Why? 25You know Abner son of Ner. He came to trick you. He came to learn all about what you are doing."

26Joab left David and sent messengers to Abner at the well of Sirah. The messengers brought Abner back, but David did not know this. 27When Abner arrived at Hebron, Joab met him in the gateway, pulled him aside to talk in private, and then stabbed him in the stomach. So he got his revenge against Abner. Joab killed Abner because Abner had killed Joab's brother Asahel.

David Cries for Abner

28Later David heard the news and said, "My kingdom and I are innocent of the death of Abner son of Ner. The LORD knows this. 29Joab and his family are responsible for this, and they will be cursed. Many troubles will come to his family. His people will be sick with leprosy,* crippled, killed in war, and not have enough food to eat!"

30Joab and his brother Abishai killed Abner because Abner had killed their brother Asahel in the battle at Gibeon.

31-32David said to Joab and to all the people with Joab, "Tear your clothes and put on sackcloth.* Cry for Abner." They buried Abner in Hebron. David went to the funeral. King David and all the people cried at Abner's grave.

33King David sang this sad song at Abner's funeral:

"Did Abner die like some foolish criminal?
34   Abner, your hands were not tied.
      Your feet were not put in chains.
   No, Abner, evil men killed you!"

Then all the people cried again for Abner. 35All day long people came to encourage David to eat food. But David had made a special promise. He said, "May God punish me and give me many troubles if I eat bread or any other food before the sun goes down." 36All the people saw what happened, and they were pleased with what King David had done. 37All the people of Judah and Israel understood that King David had not killed Abner son of Ner.

38King David said to his officers, "You know that a very important leader died today in Israel. 39And it was on the very same day that I was anointed* to be the king. These sons of Zeruiah have caused me a lot of trouble. May the LORD give them the punishment they deserve."

Troubles Come to Saul's Family

4 1Saul's son Ish Bosheth heard that Abner had died at Hebron. Ish Bosheth and all his people became very afraid. 2Two men went to see to Saul's son. These two men were captains in the army. They were Recab and Baanah, the sons of Rimmon from Beeroth. (They were Benjamites because the town Beeroth belonged to the tribe of Benjamin. 3But all the people in Beeroth ran away to Gittaim, and they are still living there today.)

4Saul's son Jonathan had a son named Mephibosheth. He was five years old when the news came from Jezreel that Saul and Jonathan had been killed. The woman who cared for Mephibosheth picked him up and ran away. But while running away, she dropped the boy, and he became crippled in both feet.

5Recab and Baanah, sons of Rimmon from Beeroth, went to Ish Bosheth's house at noon. Ish Bosheth was resting because it was hot. 6-7Recab and Baanah came into the house as if they were going to get some wheat. Ish Bosheth was lying on his bed in his bedroom, and they stabbed and killed him. Then they cut off his head and took it with them. They traveled all night on the road through the Jordan Valley. 8When they arrived at Hebron, they gave Ish Bosheth's head to David.

Recab and Baanah said to King David, "Here is the head of your enemy, Ish Bosheth son of Saul. He tried to kill you, but the LORD has punished Saul and his family for you today."

9But David told Recab and his brother Baanah, "As surely as the LORD lives, it is the LORD who has rescued me from all my troubles! 10Once before a man thought he would bring me good news. He told me, 'Look! Saul is dead.' He thought I would reward him for bringing me the news. But I grabbed this man and killed him at Ziklag. 11I will kill you too and remove this evil from our land because you evil men killed a good man sleeping on his own bed, in his own house."

12So David commanded his young helpers[a] to kill Recab and Baanah. The young men cut off the hands and feet of Recab and Baanah and hanged them by the pool of Hebron. Then they took the head of Ish Bosheth and buried it where Abner was buried at Hebron.

The Israelites Make David King

5 1All the tribes of Israel came to David at Hebron. They said to David, "Look, we are one family[b]! 2Even when Saul was

---

a4:12 young helpers Young men who carried a soldier's weapons into battle but were not yet soldiers themselves.
b5:1 one family Literally, "your flesh and blood."

our king, you were the one who led us into battle. And you were the one who brought Israel back home from war. The Lᴏʀᴅ himself said to you, 'You will be the shepherd of my people, the Israelites. You will be the ruler over Israel.'"

³So all the leaders of Israel came to meet with King David at Hebron. He made an agreement with them in Hebron in front of the Lᴏʀᴅ, and they anointed* David to be the king of Israel.

⁴David was 30 years old when he began to rule. He was king for 40 years. ⁵In Hebron he ruled over Judah for 7 years and 6 months, and in Jerusalem he ruled over all Israel and Judah for 33 years.

David Captures Jerusalem

⁶The king and his men went to fight against the Jebusites living in Jerusalem. The Jebusites said to David, "You cannot come into our city.ᵃ Even our blind and crippled people can stop you." (They said this because they thought that David would not be able to enter into their city. ⁷But David did take the fort of Zion. This fort became the City of David.*)

⁸That day David said to his men, "Whenever you strike at the Jebusites, aim for the throat and kill them."ᵇ David said this because he hates to have people left who are crippled and blind. That is why people now say, "The lame and blind are not allowed in the temple.ᶜ"

⁹David lived in the fort and called it "The City of David." David built up the city from the Milloᵈ inward.ᵉ ¹⁰He became stronger and stronger because the Lᴏʀᴅ All-Powerful was with him.

¹¹King Hiram of Tyre sent messengers to David. He also sent cedar trees, carpenters, and stonemasons. They built a house for David. ¹²Then David knew that the Lᴏʀᴅ had really made him king of Israel and had made him ruler over his kingdom for the good of his people, Israel.

¹³David moved from Hebron to Jerusalem. In Jerusalem, he got more slave women* and wives. So David had more children who were born in Jerusalem. ¹⁴David's sons who were born in Jerusalem are Shammua, Shobab, Nathan, Solomon, ¹⁵Ibhar, Elishua, Nepheg, Japhia, ¹⁶Elishama, Eliada, and Eliphelet.

David Fights Against the Philistines

¹⁷When the Philistines heard that the Israelites had anointed* David to be the king of Israel, all the Philistines went up to kill him. David heard about this and went down into the fort at Jerusalem. ¹⁸The Philistines came and camped in Rephaim Valley.

¹⁹David asked the Lᴏʀᴅ, saying, "Should I go up to fight against the Philistines? Will you help me defeat them?"

The Lᴏʀᴅ answered, "Yes, I certainly will help you defeat the Philistines."

²⁰Then David went to Baal Perazim and defeated the Philistines in that place. He said, "The Lᴏʀᴅ broke through my enemies like water breaking through a dam." That is why David named that place "Baal Perazim."ᶠ ²¹The Philistines left the statues of their gods behind at Baal Perazim. David and his men took them away.

²²Again the Philistines came up and camped in Rephaim Valley.

²³David prayed to the Lᴏʀᴅ. This time the Lᴏʀᴅ told him, "Don't go up the valley. Go around them to the other side of their army. Attack them from the other side of the balsam trees. ²⁴When you hear the sound of marching in the tops of the balsam trees, you must act quickly because that is the sign that the Lᴏʀᴅ has gone out in front of you to defeat the Philistines.ᵍ"

²⁵David did what the Lᴏʀᴅ commanded him to do, and he defeated the Philistines. He chased them from Geba to Gezer, killing them all along the way.

God's Holy Box Is Moved to Jerusalem

6 ¹David again gathered all the best soldiers in Israel. There were 30,000 men. ²Then David and all his men went to Baalah in Judahʰ to take God's Holy Box* there. ⌊The Holy Box is like God's throne⌋—people go there to call on the name of the Lᴏʀᴅ who sits as king above the Cherub angels* that are on that Box. ³David's men brought the Holy Box out of Abinadab's house on the hill. Then they put God's Holy Box on a new wagon. Uzzah and Ahio, sons of Abinadab, were driving the new wagon.

⁴So they carried the Holy Box out of Abinadab's house on the hill. The sons of Abinadab, Uzzah and Ahio, drove the new wagon. Ahio was walking in front of the Holy Box. ⁵David and all the Israelites were dancing in front of the Lᴏʀᴅ and playing all kinds of musical instruments. There were lyres,*

ᵃ**5:6** *You cannot come … city* The city of Jerusalem was built on a hill. It had high walls around it, making it hard to capture.

ᵇ**5:8** *Whenever … throat* Or "Whoever wants to attack the Jebusites must go through the shaft." This might refer to a tunnel or shaft leading up into the city through Gihon Spring, which was outside the city walls.

ᶜ**5:8** *temple* Or "the king's palace."

ᵈ**5:9** *Millo* This is probably the stone foundation walls that were built on the steep slopes on the east side of the City of David.

ᵉ**5:9** *inward* Or "toward the Temple."

ᶠ**5:20** *Baal Perazim* This name means "the Lord breaks through."

ᵍ**5:24** Or "From the top of the balsam trees you will be able to hear them marching into battle. Then you must act quickly, because at that time the Lᴏʀᴅ will go ahead of you and defeat the Philistines for you."

ʰ**6:2** *Baalah in Judah* Another name for Kiriath Jearim. See 1 Chron. 13:6.

harps, drums, rattles, instruments made from cypress wood, and cymbals.* 6When David's men came to the threshing* floor of Nacon, the oxen stumbled, and God's Holy Box began to fall off the wagon. Uzzah caught the Holy Box. 7But the Lord was angry with Uzzah and killed him for that mistake. Uzzah showed he did not honor God when he touched the Holy Box, so he died there by God's Holy Box. 8David was upset because the Lord had killed Uzzah. David called that place "Perez Uzzah."a It is still called Perez Uzzah today.

9David became afraid of the Lord that day, and he said, "How can I bring God's Holy Box here now?" 10So David would not move the Lord's Holy Box into the City of David.* He put the Holy Box at the house of Obed Edom from Gath.b 11The Lord's Holy Box stayed in Obed Edom's house for three months. The Lord blessed Obed Edom and all his family.

12Later people told David, "The Lord has blessed the family of Obed Edom and everything he owns, because God's Holy Box is there." So David went and brought God's Holy Box from Obed Edom's house. David was very happy and excited. 13When the men who carried the Lord's Holy Box had walked six steps, they stopped and David sacrificed a bull and a fat calf. 14David was dancing in front of the Lord. He was wearing a linen ephod.*

15David and all the Israelites were excited—they shouted and blew the trumpet as they brought the Lord's Holy Box into the city. 16Saul's daughter Michal was looking out the window. While the Lord's Holy Box was being carried into the city, David was jumping and dancing before the Lord. Michal saw this, and she was upset at David.

17David put up a tent for the Holy Box. The Israelites put the Lord's Holy Box in its place under the tent. Then David offered burnt offerings* and fellowship offerings* before the Lord. 18After David had finished offering the burnt offerings and the fellowship offerings, he blessed the people in the name of the Lord All-Powerful. 19He also gave a share of bread, a raisin cake, and some date bread to every man and woman of Israel. Then all the people went home.

Michal Scolds David

20David went back to bless his house, but Saul's daughter Michal came out to meet him. She said, "The king of Israel did not honor himself today! You took off your clothes in front of your servants' girls. You were like a fool who takes off his clothes without shame!"

21Then David said to Michal, "The Lord chose me, not your father or anyone from his family. The Lord chose me to be leader of his people, the Israelites. So I will continue dancing and celebrating in front of the Lord. 22I might do things that are even more embarrassing! Maybe you will not respect me, but the girls you are talking about are proud of me!"

23Saul's daughter Michal never had a child. She died without having any children.

David Wants to Build a Temple

7 1After King David moved into his new house the Lord gave him some relief from all of his enemies around him. 2King David said to Nathan the prophet, "Look, I am living in a fancy house made of cedar wood, but God's Holy Box* is still kept in a tent!"

3Nathan said to King David, "Do whatever you want to do. The Lord will be with you."

4But that night, the Lord's word came to Nathan: 5"Go and tell my servant David, 'This is what the Lord says: You are not the one to build a house for me to live in. 6I did not live in a house at the time I took the Israelites out of Egypt. No, I traveled around in a tent. I used the tent for my home. 7I never told any of the tribes of Israel to build me a fancy house made from cedar wood.'

8"You must say this to my servant David: 'This is what the Lord All-Powerful says: I chose you while you were out in the pasture following the sheep. I took you from that job and made you the leader of my people, the Israelites. 9I have been with you every place you went. I have defeated your enemies for you. I will make you one of the most famous people on earth. 10-11And I chose a place for my people, the Israelites. I planted the Israelites. I gave them their own place to live so that they will not have to move from place to place anymore. In the past, I sent judges to lead my people, but evil people gave them many troubles. That will not happen now. I am giving you peace from all of your enemies. I promise that I will make your family a family of kings.c

12"'When your life is finished, you will die and be buried with your ancestors. But then I will make one of your own children become the king. 13He will build a house for my name, and I will make his kingdom strong forever. 14I will be his father, and he will be my son.d When he sins, I will use other people to punish him. They will be my whips. 15But I will never stop loving him. I will continue to be loyal to him. I took away my love and kindness from Saul. I pushed Saul away when I turned to you. 16Your family of kings will continue—you can depend on that! For you, your

---

a6:8 Perez Uzzah This name means "The Punishment of Uzzah."

b6:10 Obed Edom from Gath A person from the tribe of Levi who lived near Jerusalem.

c7:10-11 make … family of kings Literally, "make a house for you."

d7:14 father … son God "adopted" the kings from David's family, and they became his "sons." See Ps. 2:7.

kingdom will continue forever! Your throne will stand forever!'"

¹⁷Nathan told David about that vision.* He told David everything God had said.

David Prays to God

¹⁸Then King David went in and sat in front of the Lord. David said, "Lord God, why am I so important to you? Why is my family important? Why have you made me so important? ¹⁹I am nothing but a servant, but Lord God, you have also said these kind things about my future family. Lord God, you don't always talk like this to people, do you? ²⁰How can I continue talking to you? Lord God, you know that I am only a servant. ²¹You will do all these wonderful things because you said you would do them and because you want to do them. And you decided to let me know about all these things. ²²Lord God, this is why you are so great! There is no one like you. There is no god except you! We know that because of what we ourselves have heard about what you did.

²³"And there is no nation on earth like your people, Israel. They are a special people. They were slaves, but you took them out of Egypt and made them free. You made them your people. You did great and wonderful things for the Israelites and for your land. ²⁴You made the people of Israel your very own people forever, and Lord, you became their God.

²⁵"Now, Lord God, you promised to do something for me, your servant, and for my family. Now please do what you promised—make my family a family of kings forever! ²⁶Then your name will be honored forever. People will say, 'The Lord God All-Powerful rules Israel! And may the family of your servant David continue to be strong in serving you.'

²⁷"You, Lord All-Powerful, the God of Israel, have shown things to me. You said, 'I will make your family great.' That is why I, your servant, decided to pray this prayer to you. ²⁸Lord God, you are God, and I can trust what you say. And you said that these good things will happen to me, your servant. ²⁹Now, please, bless my family. Let them stand before you and serve you forever. Lord God, you yourself said these things. You yourself blessed my family with a blessing that will continue forever."

David Wins Many Wars

8 ¹Later David defeated the Philistines and took control of a large area of land around Gath.ᵃ ²He also defeated the Moabites. He forced them to lie on the ground in a long row. Using a rope to measure, those within two lengths of the rope were killed and those within every third length were allowed to live. So the Moabites became servants of David and paid tribute* to him.

³David went to an area near the Euphrates to set up a monument for himself.ᵇ At that time he defeated the king of Zobah, Hadadezer son of Rehob. ⁴David took 1000 chariots, 7000 horse soldiers,ᶜ and 20,000 foot soldiers from Hadadezer. He crippled all but 100 of the chariot horses.ᵈ

⁵Arameans from Damascus came to help King Hadadezer of Zobah, but David defeated those 22,000 Arameans. ⁶Then David put his soldiers in Damascus, Aram. The Arameans became David's servants and brought tribute. The Lord gave victory to David wherever he went.

⁷David took the gold shieldsᵉ that had belonged to Hadadezer's servants and brought them to Jerusalem. ⁸David also took many things made of bronze from Tebahᶠ and Berothai. (Tebah and Berothai were cities that had belonged to Hadadezer.)

⁹King Toi of Hamath heard that David had defeated Hadadezer's whole army. ¹⁰Hadadezer had fought against Toi in the past, so Toi sent his son Joram to King David. Joram greeted him and blessed him because David had fought against Hadadezer and defeated him. Joram brought gifts of silver, gold, and bronze. ¹¹David took these things and dedicated* them to the Lord. He put them with the other things he had taken and dedicated to the Lord. ¹²David defeated Aram, Moab, Ammon, Philistia, and Amalek. He also defeated Hadadezer son of Rehob, king of Zobah. ¹³David defeated 18,000 Edomitesᵍ in Salt Valley. He was famous when he came home. ¹⁴David put groups of soldiers throughout Edom and the whole nation became his servants. The Lord gave victory to him wherever he went.

David's Rule

¹⁵David ruled over all Israel, and he made good and fair decisions for all of his people. ¹⁶Joab son of Zeruiah was the captain over the army. Jehoshaphat son of Ahilud was the historian. ¹⁷Zadok son of Ahitub and Ahimelech son of Abiathar were priests. Seraiah was secretary. ¹⁸Benaiah son of Jehoiada was

---

ᵇ**8:3 David went … for himself** Or "David went to take control of the area near the Euphrates River."
ᶜ**8:4 David … soldiers** This is found in the ancient Greek version and a Hebrew scroll from Qumran. The standard Hebrew text has "1700 horse soldiers."
ᵈ**8:4 He cripples … horses** Or "He destroyed all but 100 chariots."
ᵉ**8:7 shields** Or "bow cases."
ᶠ**8:8 Tebah** This is found in some ancient Greek copies. The standard Hebrew text has "Betah." See 1 Chron. 18:8.
ᵍ**8:13 Edomites** This is found in the ancient Greek and Syriac versions and a few Hebrew copies. The standard Hebrew text has "Arameans."

ᵃ**8:1 area of land around Gath** Or "villages controlled by the mother city" or "Metheg-Ammah." See 1 Chron. 18:1.

in charge of the Kerethites and Pelethites,[a] and David's sons were priests.[b]

David Is Kind to Saul's Family

9 ¹David asked, "Is there anyone still left in Saul's family? I want to show kindness to this person. I want to do it for Jonathan."

²There was a servant named Ziba from Saul's family. David's servants called Ziba to David. King David said to Ziba, "Are you Ziba?"

Ziba said, "Yes, I am your servant Ziba."

³The king said, "Is there anyone left in Saul's family? I want to show God's kindness to this person."

Ziba said to King David, "Jonathan has a son still living. He is crippled in both feet."

⁴The king said to Ziba, "Where is this son?"

Ziba said to the king, "He is at the house of Makir son of Ammiel in Lo Debar."

⁵Then King David sent some of his officers to Lo Debar to bring Jonathan's son from the house of Makir son of Ammiel. ⁶Jonathan's son Mephibosheth came to David and bowed with his face low to the floor.

David said, "Mephibosheth?"

Mephibosheth said, "Yes sir, it is I, your servant Mephibosheth."

⁷David said to Mephibosheth, "Don't be afraid. I will be kind to you because of your father Jonathan. I will give back to you all the land of your grandfather Saul. And you will always be able to eat at my table."

⁸Mephibosheth bowed to David again and he said, "I am no better than a dead dog, but you are being very kind to me."

⁹Then King David called Saul's servant Ziba and said, "I have given Saul's family and everything he owns to your master's grandson, Mephibosheth. ¹⁰You will farm the land for Mephibosheth. Your sons and servants will do this for him. You will harvest the crops. Then your master's grandson will have plenty of food to eat, but Mephibosheth will always be allowed to eat at my table."

Ziba had 15 sons and 20 servants. ¹¹He said to King David, "I am your servant. I will do everything that my lord the king commands."

So Mephibosheth ate at David's table like one of the king's sons. ¹²Mephibosheth had a young son named Mica. All the people in Ziba's family became Mephibosheth's servants. ¹³Mephibosheth lived in Jerusalem. He was crippled in both feet, and every day he ate at the king's table.

Hanun Shames David's Men

10 ¹Later King Nahash of the Ammonites died. His son Hanun became the new king after him. ²David said, "Nahash was kind to me, so I will be kind to his son Hanun." So David sent his officers to comfort Hanun about his father's death.

David's officers went to the land of the Ammonites. ³But the Ammonite leaders said to Hanun, their lord, "Do you think that David is trying to honor your father by sending some men to comfort you? No, David sent these men to spy on your city. They plan to make war against you."

⁴So Hanun took David's officers and shaved off one half of their beards. He cut off their clothes at the hips. Then he sent them away.

⁵When the people told David, he sent messengers to meet his officers. He did this because these men were very ashamed. King David said, "Wait at Jericho until your beards grow again. Then come back home."

War Against the Ammonites

⁶The Ammonites saw that they had become David's enemies, so they hired Arameans from Beth Rehob and Zobah. There were 20,000 Aramean foot soldiers. The Ammonites also hired the king of Maacah with 1000 men and 12,000 men from Tob.

⁷David heard about this, so he sent Joab and the whole army of powerful men. ⁸The Ammonites came out and got ready for the battle. They stood at the city gate. The Arameans from Zobah and Rehob and the men from Tob and Maacah did not stand together with the Ammonites in the field.

⁹Joab saw that there were enemies in front of him and behind him. So he chose some of the best Israelite soldiers and lined them up for battle against the Arameans. ¹⁰Then Joab gave the other men to his brother Abishai to lead against the Ammonites. ¹¹Joab said to Abishai, "If the Arameans are too strong for me, you will help me. If the Ammonites are too strong for you, I will come and help you. ¹²Be strong, and let us fight bravely for our people and for the cities of our God. The LORD will do what he decides is right."

¹³Then Joab and his men attacked the Arameans. The Arameans ran away from Joab and his men. ¹⁴The Ammonites saw that the Arameans were running away, so they ran away from Abishai and went back to their city.

So Joab came back from the battle with the Ammonites and went back to Jerusalem.

The Arameans Decide to Fight Again

¹⁵When the Arameans saw that the Israelites had defeated them, they came together into one big army. ¹⁶Hadadezer[c] sent messengers

---

[a]**8:18** *Kerethites and Pelethites* These were David's special bodyguards. An ancient Aramaic version has "the archers and stone throwers." This would mean these men were specially trained in using bows and arrows and slings.

[b]**8:18** *priests* Or "important leaders."

[c]**10:16** *Hadadezer* The ancient Greek version has "Hadarezer." Also in verse 19.

to bring the Arameans who lived on the other side of the Euphrates River. These Arameans came to Helam. Their leader was Shobach, the captain of Hadadezer's army.

[17]When David heard about this, he gathered all the Israelites together. They crossed over the Jordan River and went to Helam.

There the Arameans prepared for battle and attacked, [18]but David defeated them, and they ran from the Israelites. David killed 700 chariot drivers and 40,000 horse soldiers as well as Shobach, the captain of the Aramean army.

[19]The kings who served Hadadezer saw that the Israelites had defeated them, so they made peace with the Israelites and became their servants. The Arameans were afraid to help the Ammonites again.

David Meets Bathsheba

11 [1]In the spring, when kings go out to war, David sent Joab, his officers, and all the Israelites out to destroy the Ammonites. Joab's army surrounded their capital city, Rabbah.

David stayed in Jerusalem. [2]One evening he got up from his bed and walked around on the roof of his house. From there, he saw a woman bathing. She was very beautiful, [3]so David sent for his officers and asked them who she was. An officer answered, "That is Bathsheba, daughter of Eliam. She is the wife of Uriah the Hittite."

[4]David sent messengers to go and bring Bathsheba to him. She had just purified herself after her monthly time of bleeding. She went to David, he had sexual relations with her, and then she went back to her house. [5]Later, Bathsheba became pregnant. She sent word to him saying, "I am pregnant."

David Tries to Hide His Sin

[6]David sent a message to Joab. "Send Uriah the Hittite to me."

So Joab sent Uriah to David. [7]When Uriah came, David asked him how Joab was, how the soldiers were, and how the war was going. [8]Then David said to Uriah, "Go home and relax.[a]"

So Uriah left the king's palace. The king also sent a gift to Uriah. [9]But Uriah did not go home. He slept outside the door of the king's palace, as the rest of the king's servants did. [10]The servants told David, "Uriah did not go home."

Then David said to Uriah, "You came from a long trip. Why did you not go home?"

[11]Uriah said to David, "The Holy Box* and the soldiers of Israel and Judah are staying in tents. My lord Joab and my lord's officers are camping out in the field. So it is not right for me to go home to eat and drink and sleep with my wife. As surely as you live, I will not do this."

[12]David said to Uriah, "Stay here today. Tomorrow I will send you back to the battle."

Uriah stayed in Jerusalem until the next morning. [13]Then David called Uriah to come and see him. Uriah ate and drank with David. David got him drunk, but Uriah still did not go home. That evening, Uriah again slept at the palace with the rest of the king's servants.

David Plans Uriah's Death

[14]The next morning David wrote a letter to Joab and made Uriah carry the letter. [15]In the letter David wrote: "Put Uriah on the front lines where the fighting is the hardest. Then leave him there alone, and let him be killed in battle."

[16]Joab watched the city and saw where the bravest Ammonites were. He chose Uriah to go to that place. [17]The men of the city came out to fight against Joab. Some of David's men were killed. Uriah the Hittite was one of them.

[18]Then Joab sent a report to David about what happened in the battle. [19]Joab told the messenger to tell King David what had happened in the battle. [20]"The king might get upset and ask, 'Why did Joab's army go that close to the city to fight? Surely he knows that there are men on the city walls who can shoot arrows down at his men? [21]Surely he remembers that at Thebez a woman killed Abimelech son of Jerub Besheth when she threw the top part of a grinding stone down from the wall. So why did he go that close to the wall?' If King David says something like that, tell him, 'Your officer, Uriah the Hittite, also died.'"

[22]The messenger went in and told David everything Joab told him to say. [23]The messenger told David, "The men of Ammon attacked us in the field. We fought them and chased them all the way to the city gate. [24]Then the men on the city wall shot arrows at your officers. Some of your officers were killed, including Uriah the Hittite."

[25]David said to the messenger, "Give this message to Joab: 'Don't be too upset about this. A sword can kill one person as well as the next. Make a stronger attack against Rabbah and you will win.' Encourage Joab with these words."

David Marries Bathsheba

[26]Bathsheba heard that her husband Uriah had died, so she mourned* for him. [27]After her time of sadness, David sent servants to bring her to his house. She became David's wife and gave birth to a son for David. But the LORD did not like what David had done.

Nathan Speaks to David

12 [1]The LORD sent Nathan to David. Nathan went to him and said, "There were two men in a city. One man was rich,

[a]11:8 *relax* Literally, "wash your feet."

but the other man was poor. ²The rich man had lots of sheep and cattle. ³But the poor man had nothing except one little female lamb that he bought. The poor man fed the lamb, and the lamb grew up with this poor man and his children. She ate from the poor man's food and drank from his cup. The lamb slept on the poor man's chest. The lamb was like a daughter to the poor man.

⁴"Then a traveler stopped to visit the rich man. The rich man wanted to give food to the traveler, but he did not want to take any of his own sheep or cattle to feed the traveler. No, the rich man took the lamb from the poor man and cooked it for his visitor."

⁵David became very angry with the rich man. He said to Nathan, "As the LORD lives, the man who did this should die! ⁶He must pay four times the price of the lamb because he did this terrible thing and because he had no mercy."

Nathan Tells David About His Sin

⁷Then Nathan said to David, "You are that rich man! This is what the LORD, the God of Israel, says: 'I choseᵃ you to be the king of Israel. I saved you from Saul. ⁸I let you take his family and his wives, and I made you king of Israel and Judah. As if that had not been enough, I would have given you more and more. ⁹So why did you ignore my command? Why did you do what I say is wrong? You let the Ammonites kill Uriah the Hittite, and you took his wife. It is as if you yourself killed Uriah in war. ¹⁰So your family will never have peace! When you took Uriah's wife, you showed that you did not respect me.'

¹¹"This is what the LORD says: 'I am bringing trouble against you. This trouble will come from your own family. I will take your wives from you and give them to someone who is very close to you. He will have sexual relations with your wives, and everyone will know it!ᵇ ¹²You had sexual relations with Bathsheba in secret, but I will punish you so that all the people of Israel can see it.'"ᶜ

¹³Then David said to Nathan, "I have sinned against the LORD."

Nathan said to David, "The LORD will forgive you, even for this sin. You will not die. ¹⁴But you did things that made the LORD's enemies lose their respect for him, so your new baby son will die."

David and Bathsheba's Baby Dies

¹⁵Then Nathan went home. And the LORD caused the baby boy who was born to David and Uriah's wife to become very sick. ¹⁶David prayed to God for the baby. David refused

to eat or drink. He went into his house and stayed there and lay on the ground all night.

¹⁷The leaders of David's family came and tried to pull David up from the ground, but he refused to get up. He refused to eat with these leaders. ¹⁸On the seventh day the baby died. David's servants were afraid to tell him that the baby was dead. They said, "Look, we tried to talk to David while the baby was alive, but he refused to listen to us. If we tell David that the baby is dead, he might do something bad to himself."

¹⁹David saw his servants whispering and understood that the baby was dead. So David asked his servants, "Is the baby dead?"

The servants answered, "Yes, he is dead."

²⁰Then David got up from the floor. He washed himself. He changed his clothes and got dressed. Then he went into the LORD's house to worship. After that he went home and asked for something to eat. His servants gave him some food, and he ate.

²¹David's servants asked him, "Why are you doing this? When the baby was alive, you cried and refused to eat. But when the baby died you got up and ate food."

²²David said, "While the baby was still living, I cried and refused to eat because I thought, 'Who knows? Maybe the LORD will feel sorry for me and let the baby live.' ²³But now the baby is dead, so why should I refuse to eat? Can I bring the baby back to life? No. Some day I will go to him, but he cannot come back to me."

Solomon Is Born

²⁴Then David comforted Bathsheba his wife. He slept with her and had sexual relations with her. Bathsheba became pregnant again and had another son. David named the boy Solomon. The LORD loved Solomon. ²⁵The LORD sent word through Nathan the prophet. Nathan gave Solomon the name, Jedidiah.ᵈ Nathan did this for the LORD.

David Captures Rabbah

²⁶Rabbah was the capital city of the Ammonites. Joab fought against Rabbah and captured it. ²⁷Joab sent messengers to David and said, "I have fought against Rabbah and have captured its water supply. ²⁸Now bring the rest of the army together and attack Rabbah. Capture this city before I do, or else it will be called by my name."

²⁹So David gathered all the soldiers together and went to Rabbah. He fought against Rabbah and captured the city. ³⁰David took the crown off their king's head.ᵉ The crown was gold and weighed about 75 pounds.ᶠ This crown had precious stones in it. They put

---

ᵃ**12:7 chose** Literally, "anointed." See the Word List.
ᵇ**12:11 and everyone will know it** Literally, "in the sight of the sun."
ᶜ**12:12 so that all … can see it** Literally, "before all Israel and before the sun."

ᵈ**12:25 Jedidiah** This name means "loved by the LORD."
ᵉ**12:30 their king's head** Or "Milcom's head." Milcom was a false god that the Ammonites worshiped.
ᶠ**12:30 75 pounds** Literally, "1 talent" (34.5 kg).

the crown on David's head. David took many valuable things out of the city.

³¹David also brought out the people of the city of Rabbah and made them work with saws, iron picks, and axes. He also forced them to build things with bricks. He did the same thing to all the Ammonite cities. Then David and the army went back to Jerusalem.

Amnon and Tamar

13 ¹David had a son named Absalom. Absalom had a very beautiful sister named Tamar. Another one of David's sons, Amnon,ᵃ was in love with Tamar. ²She was a virgin.* Amnon wanted her very much, but he did not think it was possible for him to have her. He thought about her so much that he made himself sick.ᵇ

³Amnon had a friend named Jonadab son of Shimeah. (Shimeah was David's brother.) Jonadab was a very clever man. ⁴He said to Amnon, "Every day you look thinner and thinner. You are the king's son. ⌊You have plenty to eat, so why are you losing weight?⌋ Tell me!"

Amnon told Jonadab, "I love Tamar. But she is the sister of my half-brother Absalom."

⁵Jonadab said to Amnon, "Go to bed. Act like you are sick. Then your father will come to see you. Tell him, 'Please let my sister Tamar come in and give me food to eat. Let her make the food in front of me. Then I will see it, and eat it from her hand.'"

⁶So Amnon lay down in bed and acted like he was sick. King David came in to see Amnon. He said to King David, "Please let my sister Tamar come in. Let her make two cakes for me while I watch. Then I can eat from her hands."

⁷David sent messengers to Tamar's house. They told her, "Go to your brother Amnon's house and make some food for him."

⁸So Tamar went to the house of her brother Amnon. He was in bed. Tamar took some dough, pressed it together with her hands, and cooked the cakes. She did this while he watched. ⁹Then Tamar took the cakes out of the pan and set them out for him. But he refused to eat. He said to his servants, "Get out of here. Leave me alone!" So all of his servants left the room.

Amnon Rapes Tamar

¹⁰Then Amnon said to Tamar, "Bring the food into the bedroom and feed me by hand."

So Tamar took the cakes she had made and went into her brother's bedroom. ¹¹She started to feed Amnon, but he grabbed her hand. He said to her, "Sister, come and sleep with me."

¹²Tamar said to Amnon, "No, brother! Don't force me to do this. Don't do this shameful thing! Terrible things like this should never be done in Israel! ¹³I would never get rid of my shame, and people would think that you are just a common criminal. Please, talk with the king. He will let you marry me."

¹⁴But Amnon refused to listen to Tamar. He was stronger than she was, so he forced her to have sexual relations with him. ¹⁵Then Amnon began to hate Tamar. He hated her much more than he had loved her before. Amnon said to her, "Get up and get out of here!"

¹⁶Tamar said to Amnon, "No! Don't send me away like this. That would be even worse than what you did before!"

But Amnon refused to listen to Tamar. ¹⁷He called his servant and said, "Get this girl out of this room, now! And lock the door after her."

¹⁸So Amnon's servant led Tamar out of the room and locked the door.

Tamar was wearing a long robe with many colors.ᶜ The king's virgin daughters wore robes like this. ¹⁹Tamar tore her robe of many colors and put ashes on her head. Then she put her hand on her head and began crying.ᵈ

²⁰Then Tamar's brother Absalom said to her, "Have you been with your brother Amnon? Did he hurt you? Now, calm down, sister. Amnon is your brother, ⌊so we will take care of this⌋. Don't let it upset you too much." So Tamar did not say anything. She quietly went to live at Absalom's house.ᵉ

²¹King David heard the news and became very angry, but he did not want to say anything to upset Amnon, because he loved him since he was his firstborn son.ᶠ ²²Absalom began to hate Amnon. Absalom did not say one word, good or bad, to Amnon, but he hated him because Amnon had raped his sister Tamar.

Absalom's Revenge

²³Two years later, Absalom had some men come to Baal Hazor to cut the wool from his sheep. He invited all the king's sons to come and watch. ²⁴Absalom went to the king and said, "I have some men coming to cut the wool from my sheep. Please come with your servants and watch."

²⁵King David said to Absalom, "No, son. We will not all go. It will be too much trouble for you."

Absalom begged David to go. David did not go, but he did give his blessing.

ᵃ**13:1** *Amnon* Amnon was half-brother to Absalom and Tamar. They all had David as their father, but Amnon had a different mother. See 2 Sam. 3:2, 3.
ᵇ**13:2** *He thought ... sick* Or "Amnon thought of a plan to pretend he was sick."
ᶜ**13:18** *many colors* Or "stripes."
ᵈ**13:19** *Tamar tore ... crying* This was the way people showed how very sad and upset they were.
ᵉ**13:20** *She ... Absalom's house* Or "She lived in her brother Absalom's house, a ruined woman."
ᶠ**13:21** *but he did not ... son* This is found in the ancient Greek version and a Hebrew scroll from Qumran but not in the standard Hebrew text.

26Absalom said, "If you don't want to go, please let my brother Amnon go with me."

King David asked Absalom, "Why should he go with you?"

27Absalom kept begging David. Finally, David let Amnon and all the king's other sons go with Absalom.

Amnon Is Murdered

28Then Absalom gave this command to his servants, "Watch Amnon. When he is drunk and feeling good from the wine, I will give you the command. You must attack Amnon and kill him. Don't be afraid of being punished. After all, you will only be obeying my command. Now, be strong and brave."

29So Absalom's young soldiers did what he said. They killed Amnon. But all of David's other sons escaped. Each son got on his mule and escaped.

David Hears About Amnon's Death

30The king's sons were still on their way into town. But King David got a message about what happened. But the message was, "Absalom has killed all the king's sons! Not one of the sons was left alive."

31King David tore his clothes and lay on the ground.a All of David's officers standing near him also tore their clothes.

32But then Jonadab, the son of David's brother Shimeah, said, "Don't think that all the king's sons were killed! Only Amnon is dead. Absalom has been planning this from the day that Amnon raped his sister Tamar. 33My lord and king, don't think that all of your sons are dead. Only Amnon is dead."

34Absalom ran away.

There was a guard standing on the city wall. He saw many people coming from the other side of the hill, and went to tell the king. 35So Jonadab said to King David, "Look, I was right! The king's sons are coming."

36The king's sons came in just after Jonadab said that. They were crying loudly. David and all of his officers began crying. They all cried very hard. 37David cried for his son every day.

Absalom Escapes to Geshur

Absalom ran away to Talmai son of Ammihud, the king of Geshur.b 38After Absalom had run away to Geshur, he stayed there for three years. 39King David was comforted after Amnon died, but he missed Absalom very much.

Joab Sends a Wise Woman to David

14 1Joab son of Zeruiah knew that King David missed Absalom very much. 2So Joab sent messengers to Tekoa to bring

a wise woman from there. Joab said to this wise woman, "Please pretend to be very sad. Put on sackcloth.* Don't dress up. Act like a woman who has been crying many days for someone who died. 3Go to the king and talk to him using these words that I tell you." Then Joab told the wise woman what to say.

4Then the woman from Tekoa talked to the king. She bowed with her face to the ground. Then she said, "King, please help me!"

5King David said to her, "What's your problem?"

The woman said, "I am a widow. My husband is dead. 6I had two sons. They were out in the field fighting. There was no one to stop them. One son killed the other son. 7Now the whole family is against me. They said to me, 'Bring us the son who killed his brother and we will kill him, because he killed his brother.' My son is like the last spark of a fire. If they kill my son, that fire will burn out and be finished. He is the only son left alive to get his father's property. So my dead husband's property will go to someone else and his name will be removed from the land."

8Then the king said to the woman, "Go home. I will take care of things for you."

9The woman of Tekoa said to the king, "Let the blame be on me, my lord and king. You and your kingdom are innocent."

10King David said, "If anyone is saying bad things to you, bring them to me. They will not bother you again."

11The woman said, "Please, use the name of the LORD your God and swear that you will stop these people. They want to punish my son for murdering his brother. Swear that you will not let them destroy my son."

David said, "As the LORD lives, no one will hurt your son. Not even one hair from your son's head will fall to the ground."

12The woman said, "My lord and king, please let me say something else to you."

The king said, "Speak."

13Then the woman said, "Why have you planned these things against the people of God? When you say these things, you show you are guilty because you have not brought back the son who you forced to leave home. 14We will all die some day. We will be like water that is spilled on the ground. No one can gather this water back from the ground. You know God forgives people. God made plans for people who are forced to run away for safety—God does not force them to run away from him! 15My lord and king, I came to say these words to you, because the people made me afraid. I said to myself, 'I will talk to the king. Maybe the king will help me. 16The king will listen to me and save me from the man who wants to kill me and my son. That man just wants to keep us from getting what God gave us.' 17I know that the words of my lord the king will give me rest, because you are like an angel from God. You know what is

---

a13:31 tore his clothes ... ground This showed that he was very sad and upset.

b13:37 Talmai ... king of Geshur Talmai was Absalom's grandfather. See 2 Sam. 3:3.

good and what is bad. And the LORD your God is with you."

18King David answered the woman, "You must answer the question I will ask you."

The woman said, "My lord and king, please ask your question."

19The king said, "Did Joab tell you to say all these things?"

The woman answered, "As you live, my lord and king, you are right. Your officer Joab did tell me to say these things. 20Joab did this so that you would see things differently. My lord, you are as wise as God's angel. You know everything that happens on earth."

Absalom Returns to Jerusalem

21The king said to Joab, "Look, I will do what I promised. Now please bring back the young man Absalom."

22Joab bowed with his face on the ground. He blessed King David, and said, "Today I know that you are pleased with me. I know because you have done what I asked."

23Then Joab got up and went to Geshur and brought Absalom to Jerusalem. 24But King David said, "Absalom must go back to his own house. He cannot come to see me." So Absalom went back to his own house, but he could not go to see the king.

25People really bragged about how good-looking Absalom was. No man in Israel was as handsome as Absalom. Every part of his body was perfect—from his head to his feet. 26At the end of every year, Absalom cut the hair from his head and weighed it. The hair weighed about five pounds.a 27Absalom had three sons and one daughter. Her name was Tamar, and she was a beautiful woman.

Absalom Forces Joab to Come See Him

28Absalom lived in Jerusalem for two full years without being allowed to visit King David. 29Absalom sent a message to Joab, asking for permission to see the king, but Joab refused to come see him. So Absalom sent a second message to Joab. Again, Joab refused to come see him.

30Then Absalom said to his servants, "Look, Joab's field is next to my field. He has barley growing in that field. Go burn the barley."

So Absalom's servants went and started a fire in Joab's field. 31Joab got up and came to Absalom's house and said to Absalom, "Why did your servants burn my field?"

32Absalom said to Joab, "I sent a message to you. I asked you to come here. I wanted to send you to the king to ask him why he asked me to come home from Geshur. I cannot see him, so it would have been better for me to stay in Geshur. Now let me see the king. If I have sinned, he can kill me!"

Absalom Visits King David

33Then Joab came to the king and told him what Absalom said. The king called for Absalom. Absalom came to the king and bowed low on the ground before the king. The king kissed him.

Absalom Makes Many Friends

15 1After this, Absalom got a chariot* and horses for himself. He had 50 men run in front of him while he drove the chariot. 2Absalom would get up early and stand near the gate.b He would watch for anyone with problems who was going to King David for judgment. Then Absalom would talk to them and say, "What city are you from?" They would say they were from such and such tribe in Israel. 3Then Absalom would say, "Look, you are right, but King David will not listen to you."

4Absalom would also say, "Oh, I wish someone would make me a judge in this country! Then I could help everyone who comes to me with a problem. I would help them get a fair solution to their problem."

5And if anyone came to Absalom and started to bow down to him, Absalom would treat him like a close friend—he would reach out and touch him and kiss him. 6Absalom did that to all the Israelites who came to King David for judgment. In this way Absalom won the hearts of all the people of Israel.

Absalom Plans to Take David's Kingdom

7After four years,c Absalom said to King David, "Please let me go to Hebron to complete a special promise that I made to the LORD. 8I made that promise while I was still living in Geshur in Aram. I said, 'If the LORD brings me back to Jerusalem, I will serve the LORD in a special way.'"

9King David said, "Go in peace."

Absalom went to Hebron. 10But he also sent spies to all the tribes of Israel. They told the people, "When you hear the trumpet, say, 'Absalom is king in Hebron!'"

11Absalom invited 200 men to go with him. They left Jerusalem with him, but they did not know what he was planning. 12Ahithophel was one of David's advisors. He was from the town of Giloh. While Absalom was offering sacrifices,* he invited Ahithophel to join. Absalom's plans were working very well and more and more people began to support him.

David Learns About Absalom's Plans

13A man came in to tell the news to David. The man said, "The people of Israel are beginning to follow Absalom."

b15:2 gate This was where people came to do all of their business. This was also where many court cases were held.
c15:7 four years This is found in several ancient versions. The standard Hebrew text has "40 years."

a14:26 five pounds Literally, "200 shekels by the king's weight."

¹⁴Then David said to all of his officers who were still in Jerusalem with him, "Come on, we cannot let him trap us here in Jerusalem. Hurry up, before he catches us. He will destroy us all, and Jerusalem will be destroyed in the battle."

¹⁵The king's officers told him, "We will do whatever you tell us."

David and His People Escape

¹⁶King David left with everyone in his family, except ten of his slave women.* He left them to take care of the house. ¹⁷The king left with everyone in his house following him on foot. They stopped at the last house. ¹⁸All the king's officers passed by him. And all the Kerethites, all the Pelethites, and the Gittites (600 men from Gath) passed by the king.

¹⁹The king said to Ittai from Gath, "Why are you also going with us? You are a foreigner; this is not your homeland. Go back and stay with the new king. ²⁰You came to join me only yesterday. You don't need to wander from place to place with me. Take your brothers and go back. Go with my faithful, loving kindness."

²¹But Ittai answered the king, "As the LORD lives, and as long as you live, I will stay with you, in life or death!"

²²David said to Ittai, "Then come, let's go cross Kidron Brook."

So Ittai from Gath and all of his people and their children crossed over Kidron Brook. ²³All the people*a* were crying loudly. Then King David crossed over Kidron Brook, and all the people went out to the desert. ²⁴Zadok and all the Levites with him were carrying the Box of God's Agreement.* They set down God's Holy Box, and Abiathar said prayers*b* until all the people had left Jerusalem.

²⁵King David said to Zadok, "Take God's Holy Box back to Jerusalem. If the LORD is pleased with me, he will bring me back and let me see Jerusalem and his Temple. ²⁶But if the LORD says that he is not pleased with me, let him do whatever he wants to me."

²⁷The king said to Zadok the priest, "You are a seer.* Go back to the city in peace.*c* Take your son Ahimaaz and Jonathan the son of Abiathar. ²⁸I will be waiting near the places where people cross the river into the desert. I will wait there until I hear from you."

²⁹So Zadok and Abiathar took God's Holy Box back to Jerusalem and stayed there.

David's Prayer Against Ahithophel

³⁰David walked up the path to the Mount of Olives. He was crying, his head was covered, and he went without sandals on his feet. All the people with David also covered their heads and were crying as they walked with him.

³¹Someone told David, "Ahithophel is one who joined in Absalom's plot against you." Then David prayed, "LORD, I ask you to make Ahithophel give only foolish advice." ³²When David got to the top of the mountain, he bowed down to worship God. Then David noticed Hushai the Arkite. Hushai's coat was torn, and there was dust on his head.*d*

³³David said to Hushai, "If you go with me, you will be just one more person to care for. ³⁴But if you go back to Jerusalem, you can disagree with Ahithophel and make his advice useless. Tell Absalom, 'King, I am your servant. I served your father, but now I will serve you.' ³⁵The priests Zadok and Abiathar will be with you. You must tell them everything you hear in the king's palace. ³⁶Zadok's son Ahimaaz and Abiathar's son Jonathan will be with them. You can send them to tell me everything you hear."

³⁷So David's friend Hushai went back to the city, just as Absalom arrived in Jerusalem.

Ziba Meets David

16 ¹David went a short way over the top of the Mount of Olives and met Ziba, the servant of Mephibosheth. Ziba had two donkeys with saddles on them. The donkeys also carried 200 loaves of bread, 100 bunches of raisins, 100 summer fruits, and a wineskin full of wine. ²King David said to Ziba, "What are these things for?"

Ziba answered, "The donkeys are for the king's family to ride on. The bread and the summer fruit are for the servants to eat. And the wine is refreshment for whoever begins to feel weak in the desert."

³Then the king asked, "And where is Mephibosheth*e*?"

Ziba answered the king, "Mephibosheth is staying in Jerusalem. He said, 'Today the Israelites will give my father's kingdom back to me.'"

⁴Then the king said to Ziba, "All right, I now give you everything that belonged to Mephibosheth."

Ziba said, "I bow to you. I pray I will always be able to please you."

Shimei Curses David

⁵As David came to Bahurim, a man from Saul's family, Shimei son of Gera, came out cursing David again and again.

---

*a***15:23** *people* Literally, "country."

*b***15:24** *said prayers* Literally, "went up." This could mean "burn incense," "offer sacrifices," or it might mean simply that Abiathar stood to one side, by the Holy Box, until all the people passed by.

*c***15:27** *You are a seer ... peace* Or "You do see, don't you, that you should go back to the city in peace."

*d***15:32** *coat was torn ... head* This showed that he was very sad.

*e***16:3** *Mephibosheth* Literally, "your master's grandson."

⁶Shimei began throwing stones at David and his officers. Both the people and the soldiers gathered around David to protect him—they were all around him. ⁷Shimei cursed David. He said, "Get out, get out, you no-good murderer*ᵃ*! ⁸The Lᴏʀᴅ is punishing you because you killed people in Saul's family. You stole Saul's place as king. But now the same bad things are happening to you. The Lᴏʀᴅ has given the kingdom to your son Absalom, because you are a murderer."

⁹Abishai son of Zeruiah said to the king, "Why should this dying dog curse you, my lord the king? Let me go over and cut off Shimei's head."

¹⁰But the king answered, "What can I do, sons of Zeruiah? Yes, Shimei is cursing me, but the Lᴏʀᴅ told him to curse me. And who can ask him why he did that?" ¹¹David also said to Abishai and all his servants, "Look, my very own son is trying to kill me, so why shouldn't this man from the tribe of Benjamin want to do the same? Leave him alone. Let him continue to curse me. The Lᴏʀᴅ told him to do this. ¹²Maybe the Lᴏʀᴅ will see the wrong things that are happening to me and give me something good for every bad thing that Shimei says today."

¹³So David and his men went on their way down the road. Shimei kept following David. He walked on the other side of the road by the side of the hill. He kept cursing David on his way. Shimei also threw stones and dirt at David.

¹⁴King David and all his people came to the Jordan River. They were tired, so they rested and refreshed themselves there.

¹⁵Meanwhile, Absalom, Ahithophel, and all the Israelites came to Jerusalem. ¹⁶David's friend, Hushai the Arkite, came to Absalom and told him, "Long live the king! Long live the king!"

¹⁷Absalom answered, "Why are you not loyal to your friend David? Why did you not leave Jerusalem with your friend?"

¹⁸Hushai said, "I belong to the one that the Lᴏʀᴅ chooses. These people and the people of Israel chose you. I will stay with you. ¹⁹In the past, I served your father. So now I will serve you, David's son."

Absalom Asks Ahithophel for Advice

²⁰Absalom said to Ahithophel, "Please tell us what we should do."

²¹Ahithophel said to Absalom, "Your father left some of his slave women* here to take care of the house. Go and have sexual relations with them. Then all the Israelites will hear how you humiliated your father, and they will be encouraged to give you more support."

²²Then they put up a tent for Absalom up on the roof of the house. Absalom had sexual relations with his father's wivesᵇ so that all the Israelites could see what happened. ²³So in those days, Ahithophel's advice was very important. Both David and Absalom accepted his advice as though it were the word of God.

Ahithophel's Advice About David

17 ¹Ahithophel also said to Absalom, "Now, let me choose 12,000 men to chase David tonight. ²I will catch him while he is tired and weak. I will frighten him, and all his people will run away. But I will kill only King David. ³Then I will bring all the people back to you. If David is dead, all the people will come back in peace."

⁴This plan seemed good to Absalom and all the leaders of Israel. ⁵But Absalom said, "Now call Hushai the Arkite. I also want to hear what he says."

Hushai Ruins Ahithophel's Advice

⁶Hushai came to Absalom. Absalom said to Hushai, "This is the plan Ahithophel gave. Should we follow it? If not, tell us."

⁷Hushai said to Absalom, "Ahithophel's advice is not good this time." ⁸Hushai added, "You know that your father and his men are strong men. They are as dangerous as a wild bear when something has taken its cubs. Your father is a skilled fighter. He will not stay all night with the people. ⁹He is probably already hiding in a cave or some other place. If your father attacks your men first, people will hear the news and think, 'Absalom's followers are losing!' ¹⁰Then even your bravest men will be frightened, because all the Israelites know that your father is a powerful soldier and that his men are very brave.

¹¹"This is what I suggest: You must gather all the Israelites together from Dan to Beersheba.ᶜ Then there will be many people, like the sand by the sea. Then you yourself must go into the battle. ¹²We will catch David wherever he is hiding and attack him with so many soldiers that they will be like the dew that covers the ground. We will kill David and all of his men—no one will be left alive. ¹³But if David escapes into a city, all the Israelites can bring ropes to that city and pull its walls down into the valley. Not even a small stone will be left in that city."

¹⁴Absalom and all the Israelites said, "Hushai's advice is better than Ahithophel's." Actually, Ahithophel's advice was good, but they said this because the Lᴏʀᴅ had decided to make Ahithophel's advice useless. He did this to punish Absalom.

ᵃ**16:7** *murderer* Literally, "man of blood."

ᵇ**16:22** *wives* Or "concubines." See "slave woman" in the Word List.

ᶜ**17:11** *Dan to Beersheba* This means the whole nation of Israel, north and south. Dan was a town in the northern part of Israel, and Beersheba was in the southern part of Judah.

Hushai Sends a Warning to David

¹⁵Hushai told the priests, Zadok and Abiathar, what was said. He told them what Ahithophel suggested to Absalom and the leaders of Israel. Hushai also told them what he himself had suggested. He said, ¹⁶"Send a message to David now! Tell him not to spend the night at the places where people cross into the desert. Tell him to go across the Jordan River at once. If he crosses the river, the king and all his people will not be caught."

¹⁷The priests' sons, Jonathan and Ahimaaz, did not want to be seen going into the town, so they waited at En Rogel. A servant girl went out to them and gave them the message. Then Jonathan and Ahimaaz carried the message to King David.

¹⁸But a boy saw Jonathan and Ahimaaz and ran to tell Absalom. Jonathan and Ahimaaz ran away quickly. They arrived at a man's house in Bahurim. The man had a well in his courtyard.ᵃ Jonathan and Ahimaaz went down into this well. ¹⁹The man's wife spread a sheet over the mouth of the well and covered it with grain. The well looked like a pile of grain, so no one would know to look there. ²⁰Absalom's servants came to the woman at the house. They asked, "Where are Ahimaaz and Jonathan?"

The woman said to Absalom's servants, "They have already crossed over the brook."

Absalom's servants then went to look for Jonathan and Ahimaaz, but they could not find them. So Absalom's servants went back to Jerusalem.

²¹After Absalom's servants left, Jonathan and Ahimaaz climbed out of the well and went to King David. They said to David, "Hurry, go across the river. Ahithophel is planning to do something to you."

²²So David and his people crossed over the Jordan River. By sunrise, all of David's people had crossed the Jordan River. No one was left behind.

Ahithophel Kills Himself

²³When Ahithophel saw that the Israelites did not do what he suggested, he saddled his donkey and went back to his hometown. He made plans for his family and then hanged himself. They buried him in his father's tomb.*

Absalom Crosses the Jordan River

²⁴David arrived at Mahanaim just as Absalom and the Israelites who were with him crossed over the Jordan River. ²⁵⁻²⁶Absalom and the Israelites made their camp in the land of Gilead. Absalom had made Amasa the new captain of the army. He took Joab's place.ᵇ

Amasa was the son of Ithra the Ishmaelite.ᶜ His mother was Abigail, the daughter of Nahash, the sister of Joab's mother, Zeruiah.ᵈ

Shobi, Makir, and Barzillai

²⁷When David arrived at Mahanaim, Shobi, Makir, and Barzillai were there. Shobi son of Nahash was from the Ammonite town of Rabbah. Makir son of Ammiel was from Lo Debar. Barzillai was from Rogelim in Gilead. ²⁸⁻²⁹These three men said, "The people are tired, hungry, and thirsty from the desert." So they brought many things to David and those with him. They brought beds, bowls, and other kinds of dishes. They also brought wheat, barley, flour, roasted grain, beans, lentils, dried seeds, honey, butter, sheep, and cheese made from cow's milk.

David Gets Ready for Battle

18 ¹David counted his men and chose captains over 1000 and captains over 100 to lead them. ²He separated the people into three groups and sent them out. Joab led a third of the men. Joab's brother, Abishai son of Zeruiah, led another third. And Ittai from Gath led the last third.

King David said to the people, "I will also go with you."

³But they said, "No! You must not go with us. If we run away in the battle, Absalom's men will not care. No, even if only half of us are killed, Absalom's men will not care. But you are worth 10,000 of us! It is better for you to stay in the city. Then, if we need help, you can come to help us."

⁴The king said to them, "I will do what you think is best."

Then the king stood by the gate as the army went out in groups of 100 and 1000.

⁵The king gave a command to Joab, Abishai, and Ittai. He said, "Do this for me: Be gentle with young Absalom!" Everyone heard the king's orders about Absalom to the captains.

David's Army Defeats Absalom's Army

⁶David's army went out into the field against Absalom's Israelites. They fought in the forest of Ephraim. ⁷David's army defeated the Israelites. It was a great defeat because 20,000 men were killed that day. ⁸The battle spread throughout the country, but more men died in the forest than by the sword.

⁹It so happened that David's officers found Absalom. Absalom jumped on his mule and tried to escape, but the mule went under the branches of a large oak tree. The branches were thick, and Absalom's head got caught in

ᵃ**17:18 courtyard** An open area outside the house. Many houses were built around courtyards so that people could work, cook, or eat outside.
ᵇ**17:25–26 He took Joab's place** Joab still supported David. Joab was one of the three captains in David's army when David was running away from Absalom. See 2 Sam. 18:2.

ᶜ**17:25–26 Ishmaelite** This is from the ancient Greek version. The standard Hebrew text has "Israelite," but see 1 Chron 2:17.
ᵈ**17:25–26 His mother … Zeruiah** Literally, "Ithra had sexual relations with Abigail, the daughter of Nahash sister of Zeruiah."

the tree. His mule ran out from under him, so Absalom was left hanging above the ground.*

[10]Someone saw this happen and told Joab, "I saw Absalom hanging in an oak tree."

[11]Joab said to the man, "Why didn't you kill him and let him fall to the ground? I would have given you a belt and ten pieces of silver!"

[12]The man said to Joab, "I would not try to hurt the king's son even if you gave me 1000 pieces of silver. We heard the king's command to you, Abishai, and Ittai. The king said, 'Be careful not to hurt young Absalom.' [13]If I had killed Absalom, the king himself would find out, and you would punish me.*"

[14]Joab said, "I will not waste my time here with you!"

Absalom was still alive and hanging in the oak tree. Joab took three sticks in his hand and hit him in the heart. [15]Ten of Joab's young helpers gathered around Absalom and killed him.

[16]Joab blew the trumpet and called the people to stop chasing Israelites. [17]Then Joab's men took Absalom's body and threw it into a large hole in the forest and covered it with stones.

All the Israelites ran away and went home. [18]While Absalom was alive he put up a memorial stone in King's Valley. He said, "I have no son to keep my name alive." So he named that monument after himself. It is called "Absalom's Monument" even today.

Joab Sends the News to David

[19]Ahimaaz the son of Zadok said to Joab, "May I run and take the news to King David? I'll tell him the LORD has destroyed the enemy for him."

[20]Joab answered Ahimaaz, "No, you will not carry the message today. You can do it some other time, but not today because it is the king's son who is dead."

[21]Then Joab said to a man from Ethiopia, "Go, tell the king what you have seen."

So the Ethiopian bowed to Joab and ran to tell David.

[22]But Ahimaaz son of Zadok begged Joab again, "No matter what happens, please let me also run after the Ethiopian!"

Joab said, "Son, why do you want to carry the news? You will not get any reward for the news you bring."

[23]Ahimaaz answered, "No matter what happens, I will run to David."

Joab said to Ahimaaz, "All right, run to David!"

Then Ahimaaz ran through Jordan Valley and passed the Ethiopian.

David Hears the News

[24]David was sitting between the two gates of the city. The watchman went up to the roof over the gate walls and saw a man running alone. [25]The watchman shouted to tell King David.

King David said, "If the man is alone, he is bringing news."

The man came closer and closer to the city. [26]But then the watchman saw another man running. He called to the gatekeeper, "Look! Another man is running alone."

The king said, "He is also bringing news."

[27]The watchman said, "I think the first man runs like Ahimaaz son of Zadok."

The king said, "Ahimaaz is a good man, he must be bringing good news."

[28]Ahimaaz called to the king, "All is well!" Ahimaaz bowed with his face to the ground in front of the king and said, "Praise the LORD your God! The LORD has defeated the men who were against you, my lord and king."

[29]The king asked, "Is young Absalom all right?"

Ahimaaz answered, "When Joab sent me, I saw some great excitement, but I don't know what it was."

[30]Then the king said, "Step over here and wait." Ahimaaz went there and stood waiting.

[31]The Ethiopian arrived and said, "News for my lord and king. Today the LORD has punished all those who were against you!"

[32]The king asked the Ethiopian, "Is young Absalom all right?"

The Ethiopian answered, "May your enemies, or whoever tries to hurt you, suffer the same as this young man did."

[33]So the king knew Absalom was dead and he became very upset. He went upstairs to the room over the gate, crying, "O my son Absalom! My son Absalom, I wish I had died instead of you! O Absalom, my son, my son!"

Joab Scolds David

19 ^[1]People told Joab what had happened, "Look, the king is crying and mourning* for Absalom." [2]So the joy of victory turned to sadness for everyone. It was a very sad day because the people heard, "The king is mourning for his son."

[3]The people came into the city quietly as if they were the ones who had been defeated in battle. [4]The king had covered his face and was crying loudly, "O my son Absalom, O Absalom, my son, my son!"

[5]Joab came into the king's palace and said to the king, "You are humiliating every one of your officers! Look, they saved your life today and the lives of your sons and daughters and your wives and slave women.* [6]It seems that you love those who hate you, and you hate those who love you! Today you have made it clear to your officers and men that they mean nothing to you. It appears as if you would

---

a18:9 above the ground Literally, "between heaven and earth."

b18:13 you would punish me Or "you would have opposed me."

have been perfectly happy if Absalom had lived and the rest of us had been killed today! 7Now get up and go encourage your officers. I swear by the LORD, if you don't go out and do that right now, not one man will be with you tonight. And that will be worse for you than all the trouble you have had since you were a child."

8So the king went to the city gate.a The news spread that the king was at the gate, so all the people came to see him, except for the Israelites who had run away to their homes.

David Is King Again

9The tribes of Israel began discussing what to do next. They said, "King David saved us from the Philistines and our other enemies. David left the country because he was running away from Absalom. 10We anointed* Absalom to be the king, but he was killed in battle. So we should bring David back to be the king again."

11King David sent a message to Zadok and Abiathar the priests. David said, "Speak to the leaders of Judah and tell them, 'Why are you the last tribe to bring King David back home? See, all the Israelites are talking about bringing the king back home. 12You are my brothers, my family, so why are you the last tribe to bring the king back?' 13Also tell Amasa, 'You are part of my family. I swear that I will make you captain of the army in Joab's place.'"

14David touched the hearts of the people of Judah, and they all agreed as one. The people of Judah sent a message to the king, saying, "You and all your officers come back!"

15King David came to the Jordan River. The people of Judah came to Gilgal to meet the king and take him across the Jordan River.

Shimei Asks David to Forgive Him

16Shimei son of Gera, from the tribe of Benjamin, lived in Bahurim. Shimei rushed down to meet King David, with the rest of the people of Judah. 17About 1000 people from the tribe of Benjamin came with Shimei. Ziba the servant from Saul's family also came. Ziba brought his 15 sons and 20 servants with him. All these people hurried to the Jordan River to meet King David.

18The people went across the Jordan River to help bring the king's family back to Judah. They did whatever the king wanted. While the king was crossing the river, Shimei son of Gera came to meet him. He bowed down to the ground in front of the king. 19Shimei said to the king, "My lord, don't think about the wrong things I did. My lord and king, don't remember the bad things I did when you left Jerusalem. 20I know that I sinned. That is why today I am the first person from Joseph's

family b to come down and meet you, my lord and king."

21Abishai son of Zeruiah said, "Let's kill him for all the bad things he said about the LORD's chosen king.c"

22David said, "What should I do with you, sons of Zeruiah? Are you trying to cause me trouble? No one will be put to death in Israel today! Today I know that I am king over Israel."

23Then the king said to Shimei, "You will not die." The king made a promise to Shimei that he himself would not kill Shimei.d

Mephibosheth Goes to See David

24Saul's grandson,e Mephibosheth, came down to meet King David. Mephibosheth had not cared for his feet, trimmed his mustache, or washed his clothes since the day the king left Jerusalem. 25When he met the king at Jerusalem, the king said, "Mephibosheth, why didn't you go with me when I ran away from Jerusalem?"

26Mephibosheth answered, "My lord and king, my servant tricked me. I am crippled so I said to my servant, Ziba, 'Go saddle a donkey for me so that I can go with the king.' 27But my servant tricked me and said bad things about me. My lord and king, you are like an angel from God. Do whatever you think is right. 28You could have killed all my grandfather'sf family, but you did not do that. Instead, you included me among the people who eat at your own table. So I don't have a right to complain to the king about anything."

29The king said to Mephibosheth, "Don't say anything more about your problems. This is what I have decided: You and Ziba will divide the land."

30Mephibosheth said to the king, "My lord and king, it is enough that you have come home in peace. Let Ziba have the land."

David Asks Barzillai to Come With Him

31Barzillai of Gilead came down from Rogelim to cross the Jordan River with King David and send him on his way home. 32Barzillai was a very old man, 80 years old. He had given the king food and other things when David was staying at Mahanaim. Barzillai could do this because he was a very rich man. 33David said to Barzillai, "Come across the river with me. I will take care of you if you will live in Jerusalem with me."

---

a19:8 city gate This was where the public meetings were held.

b19:20 Joseph's family This probably means the Israelites who followed Absalom. Many times the name Ephraim (a son of Joseph) is used for all the tribes in northern Israel.

c19:21 chosen king Literally, "anointed one."

d19:23 David did not kill Shimei. But a few years later, David's son Solomon ordered Shimei to be put to death. See 1 Kings 2:44–46.

e19:24 grandson Literally, "son."

f19:28 grandfather's Literally, "father's."

34But Barzillai said to the king, "Do you know how old I am? Do you think I can go with you to Jerusalem? 35I am 80 years old! I am too old to tell what is bad or good. I cannot taste what I eat or drink or hear the voices of men and women singers. Why should you want to be bothered with me? 36I don't need any of the things that you want to give me. I will cross the Jordan River with you. 37Then please let me go back so that I can die in my own town and be buried in the grave of my father and mother. But here is Kimham; take him back with you as a servant, my lord and king. Do whatever you want with him."

38The king answered, "Kimham will go back with me. I will be kind to him for you. I will do anything for you."

David Goes Back Home

39The king kissed Barzillai and blessed him. Barzillai went back home, and the king and all the people went across the river.

40The king crossed the Jordan River to Gilgal. Kimham went with him. All the people of Judah and half the people of Israel led David across the river.

Israelites Argue With the People of Judah

41All the Israelites came to the king and said to him, "Why did our brothers, the people of Judah, steal you away? Why did they bring you and your family back across the Jordan River with your men?"

42All the people of Judah answered the Israelites, "We did it because the king is our close relative. Why are you angry with us about this? We have not eaten food at the king's expense. The king did not give us any gifts."

43The Israelites answered, "We have ten shares in David,a so we have more right to David than you do. Why did you ignore us? We were the first ones to talk about bringing our king back."

But the people of Judah replied with words that were even louder and angrier than those of the Israelites.

Sheba Leads Israel Away From David

20 1At that place there was a man named Sheba son of Bicri. Sheba was a worthless troublemaker from the tribe of Benjamin. He blew a trumpet to gather the people together and said,

"We have no share in David.
    We have no part in the son of Jesse.
Israel, let's all go home."

2So all the Israelitesb left David and followed Sheba son of Bicri. But the people from Judah stayed with their king all the way from the Jordan River to Jerusalem.

3David went back to his house in Jerusalem. He had left ten of his slave women* to take care of the house. He put these women in a special house.c Then he put guards around the house. They stayed in this house until they died. David took care of the women and gave them food, but he did not have sexual relations with them. They lived like widows until they died.

4The king told Amasa, "Tell the people of Judah to meet with me in three days. You must be here, too."

5So Amasa called the people of Judah together, but he took longer than the king had told him.

David Tells Abishai to Kill Sheba

6David said to Abishai, "Sheba son of Bicri is more dangerous to us than Absalom was. So take my officers and chase Sheba. Hurry before he gets into cities with walls. If he gets into the well-protected cities, we will not be able to get him."

7So Joab took the Kerethites and Pelethitesd and the other soldiers with him and left Jerusalem to chase after Sheba son of Bicri.

Joab Kills Amasa

8When Joab and the army came to Big Rock at Gibeon, Amasa came out to meet them. Joab was wearing his uniform. He had on a belt, and his sword was in its sheath.* As he was walking toward Amasa, Joab's sword fell out of its sheath. He picked up the sword and was holding it in his hand. 9Joab asked Amasa, "How are you doing, brother?"

Then Joab reached out with his right hand and grabbed Amasa by the beard to kiss him hello. 10Amasa didn't pay any attention to the sword that was in Joab's hand. Joab stabbed Amasa in the belly with his sword. Amasa's intestines spilled out on the ground. Joab didn't have to stab him again—he was already dead.

David's Men Continue to Look for Sheba

Then Joab and his brother Abishai resumed the chase after Sheba son of Bicri. 11One of Joab's young soldiers stood by Amasa's body and said, "All of you who support Joab and David, let's follow Joab."

12Amasa was there in the middle of road, lying in his own blood. The young soldier noticed that all the people kept stopping to look at the body, so he rolled the body off the road and into the field and covered it with a cloth. 13Once the body was out of the way,

a19:43 ten shares in David Judah and Benjamin were two of the tribes that later became the kingdom of Judah after the kingdom split. The other ten tribes were in the kingdom of Israel.
b20:2 Israelites Here, this means the tribes not united with Judah.

c20:3 David ... special house David's son Absalom had ruined David's concubines by having sexual relations with them. See 2 Sam. 16:21-22.
d20:7 Kerethites and Pelethites David's special group of fighting men. Also in verse 23.

the people simply passed it by and joined up with Joab to go after Sheba son of Bicri.

Sheba Escapes to Abel Beth Maacah

[14]Sheba son of Bicri passed through all the tribes of Israel on his way to Abel Beth Maacah. All the Berites[a] joined together and followed Sheba.

[15]When Joab and his men came to Abel Beth Maacah, they surrounded the town. They piled dirt up against the city wall and began breaking stones out of the wall to make it fall down.

[16]But there was a very wise woman in that city who shouted out to them and said, "Listen to me! Tell Joab to come here. I want to talk with him."

[17]Joab went to talk with the woman. She asked him, "Are you Joab?"

Joab answered, "Yes, I am."

Then the woman said, "Listen to me."

Joab said, "I am listening."

[18]Then the woman said, "In the past people would say, 'Ask for help in Abel and you will get what you need.' [19]I am one of many peaceful, loyal people in this town. You are trying to destroy an important city of Israel. Why do you want to destroy something that belongs to the Lord?"

[20]Joab answered, "I don't want to destroy anything. I don't want to ruin your city. [21]But there is a man in your city from the hill country of Ephraim. He is named Sheba son of Bicri. He rebelled against King David. Bring him to me, and I will leave the city alone."

The woman said to Joab, "All right. His head will be thrown over the wall to you."

[22]Then the woman spoke very wisely to all the people of the city. They cut off the head of Sheba son of Bicri and threw it over the city wall to Joab.

So Joab blew the trumpet and the army left the city. The soldiers went home, and Joab went back to the king in Jerusalem.

The People on David's Staff

[23]Joab was captain of the whole army of Israel. Benaiah son of Jehoiada led the Kerethites and Pelethites. [24]Adoniram led the men who were forced to do hard work. Jehoshaphat son of Ahilud was the historian. [25]Sheva was the secretary. Zadok and Abiathar were the priests. [26]And Ira from Jair was David's personal priest.[b]

Saul's Family Punished

21 [1]While David was king, there was a famine* that continued for three years. So David prayed to the Lord. And the Lord answered, "Saul and his family of murderers[c] are the reason for the famine, because he killed

the Gibeonites." [2](The Gibeonites were not Israelites. They were a group of Amorites. The Israelites had promised not to hurt them,[d] but Saul tried to kill the Gibeonites. He did this because of his strong feelings for the people of Israel and Judah.)

King David called the Gibeonites together and talked to them. [3]David said to the Gibeonites, "What can I do for you? What can I do to take away Israel's sin, so that you can bless the Lord's people?"

[4]The Gibeonites said to David, "There isn't enough gold and silver for Saul's family to pay for what they did. But we don't have the right to kill anyone else in Israel."

David said, "Well, what can I do for you?"

[5]The Gibeonites said to King David, "The person who plotted against us was Saul. He is the one who tried to destroy all our people living in the land of Israel. [6]Give us seven of Saul's sons. Saul was the Lord's chosen king,[e] so we will hang his sons in front of the Lord on Mount Gibeah of Saul."

King David said, "All right, I will give them to you." [7]But the king protected Jonathan's son, Mephibosheth. Jonathan was Saul's son, and David had made a promise in the Lord's name to Jonathan.[f] So the king did not let them hurt Mephibosheth. [8]David gave them Armoni and Mephibosheth.[g] These were the sons of Saul and Rizpah. Saul also had a daughter named Merab who was married to Adriel son of Barzillai, from Meholah. David took the five sons of Merab and Adriel. [9]David gave these seven men to the Gibeonites who then brought them to Mount Gibeah and hanged them in front of the Lord. Those seven men died together in the spring, during the first days of the barley harvest.

David and Rizpah

[10]Rizpah the daughter of Aiah took a mourning* cloth and put it on the rock.[h] That cloth stayed on the rock from the time the harvest began until the rains came. Rizpah watched the bodies day and night. She protected them from the wild birds during the day and the wild animals at night.

[11]People told David what Saul's slave woman* Rizpah was doing. [12]Then David took the bones of Saul and Jonathan from the men of Jabesh Gilead. (The men of Jabesh Gilead got these bones after Saul and Jonathan were

---

[a]20:14 *Berites* The Greek and Latin versions have "Bicrites."

[b]20:26 *personal priest* Or "chief servant" or "advisor."

[c]21:1 *family of murderers* Literally, "house of blood."

[d]21:2 *The Israelites ... them* This happened in Joshua's time when the Gibeonites tricked the Israelites. Read Josh. 9:3–15.

[e]21:6 *chosen king* Literally, "anointed one."

[f]21:7 *David had made ... to Jonathan* David and Jonathan promised each other they would not harm each other's families. Read 1 Sam. 20:12–23, 42.

[g]21:8 *Mephibosheth* This is another man named Mephibosheth, not Jonathan's son.

[h]21:10 *rock* This might be the Big Rock at Gibeon (read 2 Sam. 20:8), the rock that the bodies were lying on, or a rock that marked the place where her sons were buried.

killed at Gilboa. The Philistines had hanged the bodies of Saul and Jonathan on a wall in Beth Shan.[a] But the men of Beth Shan went there and stole the bodies from that public area.) [13]David brought the bones of Saul and his son Jonathan from Jabesh Gilead and buried them with the bodies of the seven men who were hanged. [14]They buried the bones of Saul and his son Jonathan in the area of Benjamin, in one of the tunnels in the grave of Saul's father Kish, as the king commanded. After that God again listened to the prayers of the people in that land.

War With the Philistines

[15]The Philistines started another war with Israel. David and his men went out to fight the Philistines, but David became very tired and weak. [16]Ishbi Benob was one of the giants.[b] His spear weighed about 7½ pounds.[c] Ishbi Benob was wearing his new weapons and tried to kill David, [17]but Abishai son of Zeruiah killed the Philistine and saved David's life.

Then David's men made a special promise to him. They said, "You cannot go out with us to battle anymore. If you do, Israel might lose its greatest leader."

[18]Later, there was another battle with the Philistines at Gob. Sibbecai the Hushathite killed Saph, another one of the giants.

[19]Later, there was another battle at Gob against the Philistines. Elhanan the son of Jaare Oregim from Bethlehem killed ⌊Lahmi, the brother of⌋ Goliath from Gath.[d] His spear was as big as a post.[e]

[20]There was another battle at Gath. There was a very large man who had six fingers on each hand and six toes on each foot. He had 24 fingers and toes in all. This man was also one of the giants. [21]This man challenged Israel and made fun of them, but Jonathan killed this man. (This was Jonathan, the son of David's brother Shimei.)

[22]All four of these men were giants from Gath. They were killed by David and his men.

David's Song of Praise to the Lord

22

[1][f] David sang this song to the LORD when the LORD saved him from Saul and all his other enemies.

2 The LORD is my Rock,* my fortress,* my place of safety.
3 He is my God, the Rock I run to for protection.

He is my shield; by his power I am saved.[g]
   He is my hiding place, my place of safety, high in the hills.
He is my savior, the one who rescues me from the cruel enemy.
4 I called to the LORD for help, and he saved me from my enemies.
   He is worthy of my praise!

5 Waves of death were crashing around me.
   A deadly flood was carrying me away.
6 The ropes of the grave wrapped around me.
   Death set its trap right there in front of me.
7 In my trouble I called to the LORD.
   Yes, I cried out to my God for help.
   There in his temple he heard my voice.
   He heard my cry for help.
8 The earth shook and shivered.
   The foundations of heaven trembled.
   They shook because he was angry!
9 Smoke came from his nose.
   Burning flames came from his mouth.
   Red-hot coals fell from him.
10 He tore open the sky and came down.
   He stood on a thick, dark cloud.
11 He flew across the sky, riding on a Cherub angel,*
   gliding on the wings of the wind.
12 He wrapped himself in darkness that covered him like a tent.
   He was hidden by dark clouds filled with water.
13 Out of the brightness before him, flashes of lightning came down.
14 The LORD thundered from the sky.
   God Most High let his voice be heard.
15 He scattered the enemy with his arrows—
   the lightning bolts that threw them into confusion.

16 The LORD shouted his command, and a powerful wind began to blow.[h]
   Then the bottom of the sea could be seen, and the earth's foundations were uncovered.

17 The Lord reached down from above and grabbed me.
   He pulled me from the deep water.
18 He saved me from my powerful enemies, who hated me.
   They were too strong for me, so he saved me.
19 They attacked me in my time of trouble, but the LORD was there to support me.
20 He was pleased with me, so he rescued me.
   He took me to a safe place.

---

[a]**21:12 Beth Shan** Or possibly, "Beth Shean."
[b]**21:16 one of the giants** Or "a son of Rapha (Rephaim)." Also in verses 18, 20, 22.
[c]**21:16 7 1/2 pounds** Literally, "300 shekels of bronze" (3.45 kg).
[d]**21:19 Lahmi ... Gath** See 1 Chron. 20:5.
[e]**21:19 post** Literally, "a weaver's rod," the large beam across a loom.
[f]**22:1 Chapter 22** This song is also found in Ps. 18.

[g]**22:3 by his power I am saved** Literally, "He is the horn of my salvation."
[h]**22:16 and ... blow** Or "and a blast of breath came from his nose."

²¹ The Lᴏʀᴅ rewarded me for doing what is
    right.
    He was good to me because I am
        innocent.
²² The Lᴏʀᴅ did this because I have obeyed
    him.
    I have not turned against my God.
²³ I always remembered his laws.
    I never stopped following his rules.
²⁴ He knows I did nothing that was wrong.
    I have kept myself from sinning.
²⁵ So the Lord rewarded me for doing what
    is right.
    He could see that I am innocent.

²⁶ Lord, you are faithful to those who are
    faithful.
    You are good to those who are good.
²⁷ You never do wrong to those who have
    done no wrong.
    But you outsmart the wicked, no matter
        how clever they are.
²⁸ You help those who are humble,
    but as soon as you see the proud, you
        humiliate them.
²⁹ Lᴏʀᴅ, you are my lamp.
    You, Lᴏʀᴅ, turn the darkness around me
        into light.
³⁰ With your help I can defeat an army.
    If my God is with me, I can climb over
        enemy walls.

³¹ God's way is perfect.
    The Lᴏʀᴅ's promise always proves to be
        true.
    He protects those who trust in him.
³² There is no God except the Lᴏʀᴅ.
    There is no Rock except our God.
³³ God is my strong fortress.*
    He clears the path I need to take.
³⁴ He makes my feet as steady as those of a
    deer.
    Even on steep mountains he keeps me
        from falling.
³⁵ He trains me for war
    so that my arms can bend the most
        powerful bow.

³⁶ Lord, you have given me your shield to
    protect me.
    It is your help that has made me great.
³⁷ You cleared a path for my feet
    so that I could walk without stumbling.
³⁸ I chased my enemies and defeated them.
    I did not stop until they were destroyed.
³⁹ I destroyed my enemies.
    I struck them down.
    They did not get up again.
    They fell under my feet.

⁴⁰ Lord, you made me strong in battle.
    You made my enemies fall before me.
⁴¹ You made my enemies turn and run
    away.
    I destroyed those who hated me.

⁴² They looked for help,
    but there was no one to save them.
    They cried out to the Lᴏʀᴅ,
    but he did not answer them.
⁴³ I beat my enemies to pieces
    like dust on the ground.
    I smashed them and walked on them
    like mud in the streets.

⁴⁴ You saved me from those who fought
    against me.
    You made me the ruler over nations.
    People I never knew now serve me.
⁴⁵ Foreigners fall helpless before me!
    As soon as they heard about me, they
        were ready to obey.
⁴⁶ They lose all their courage
    and come out of their hiding places
        shaking with fear.

⁴⁷ The Lᴏʀᴅ lives!
    I praise my Rock!
    How great is my God, the Rock who
        saves me!
⁴⁸ He is the God who punishes my enemies
    for me,
    the one who puts people under my rule.
⁴⁹ He saves me from my enemies!

    You help me defeat those who attack me.
    You save me from cruel people.
⁵⁰ Lᴏʀᴅ, that is why I praise you among the
    nations.
    That is why I sing songs of praise to
        your name.

⁵¹ The Lᴏʀᴅ helps his king win battle after
    battle.
    He shows his faithful love to the one he
        has chosen,ᵃ
    to David and his descendants forever!

David's Last Words

23 ¹These are the last words of David:

"This message is from David son of Jesse.
    This message is from the man God
        made great.
    He is the king chosen by the God of
        Jacob,*
    the sweet singer of Israel.ᵇ
² The Lᴏʀᴅ's Spirit spoke through me.
    His word was on my tongue.
³ The God of Israel spoke.
    The Rock of Israel said to me,
'Whoever rules people fairly,
    who rules with respect for God,
⁴ is like the morning light at dawn,
    like a morning without clouds.

ᵃ**22:51** *to the one he has chosen* Literally, "his
anointed one."
ᵇ**23:1** *the sweet singer of Israel* Or "The most pleasant of the songs of Israel."

He is like sunshine after a rain
    that makes tender grass grow from the
        ground.'

5 "God made my family strong and secure.[a]
    He made an agreement with me forever.
    God made sure this agreement was
        good and secure in every way.
    So surely he will give me every victory.
    He will give me everything I want!

6 "But evil people are like thorns.
    People don't hold thorns.
    They throw them away.
7 If someone touches them,
    it hurts like a spear made of wood and
        iron.
Yes, evil people are like thorns.
    They will be thrown into the fire,
    and they will be completely burned."

The Three Heroes

8 These are the names of David's special soldiers:

Josheb Basshebeth the Tahkemonite[b] was captain of the king's special forces.[c] He used his spear to kill 800 men at one time.[d]

9 Next, there was Eleazar son of Dodai[e] who was there with David when he challenged the Philistines who had gathered for battle. The Israelites ran away, 10 but Eleazar stood and fought the Philistines until his hand became so tired that it cramped around his sword handle. The LORD won a great victory that day. The people of Israel came back, but only to take things from the dead.

11 Next there was Shammah son of Agee from Harar. The Philistines came together to fight. They fought in a field of lentils.[f] The people ran away from the Philistines. 12 But Shammah stood in the middle of the field and defended it. He defeated the Philistines. The LORD gave Israel a great victory that day.

13 Once during harvest time David was at the cave of Adullam, and three of the Thirty Heroes[g] went down to meet him there. At the same time the Philistine army was camped in the Valley of Rephaim.[h]

14 Another time David was in the fortress,* and a group of Philistines soldiers was stationed in Bethlehem. 15 David was thirsty for some water from his hometown, so he said, "Oh, if only I could have some water from that well by the gate in Bethlehem." 16 So the Three Heroes[i] fought their way through the Philistine army and got some water from the well near the city gate in Bethlehem. They took it to David, but he refused to drink it. He poured it on the ground as an offering to the LORD. 17 David said, "LORD, I cannot drink this water. It would be like drinking the blood of the men who risked their lives for me." This is why David refused to drink the water. The Three Heroes did many brave things like that.

Other Brave Soldiers

18 Abishai was the brother of Joab son of Zeruiah. Abishai was the leader of the Three Heroes. He used his spear against 300 enemies and killed them. He became as famous as the Three. 19 Abishai was as famous as the Three Heroes. He became their leader, even though he was not one of them.

20 Then there was Benaiah son of Jehoiada, from Kabzeel. He was the son of a powerful man.[j] Benaiah did many brave things. He killed two of the best soldiers in Moab. One day when it was snowing, Benaiah went down into a hole in the ground and killed a lion. 21 Benaiah also killed a big Egyptian soldier. The Egyptian had a spear in his hand, and Benaiah only had a club. He grabbed the spear in the Egyptian's hands and took it away from him. Then Benaiah killed the Egyptian with his own spear. 22 Benaiah son of Jehoiada did many more brave things like that. He was as famous as the Three Heroes. 23 Benaiah was even more famous than the Thirty Heroes, but he did not become a member of the Three Heroes. David made Benaiah the leader of his bodyguards.

The Thirty Heroes

24 The following men were among the Thirty Heroes: Asahel, the brother of Joab; Elhanan son of Dodo from Bethlehem; 25 Shammah the Harodite; Elika the Harodite; 26 Helez the Paltite; Ira son of Ikkesh from Tekoa; 27 Abiezer from Anathoth; Mebunnai the Hushathite; 28 Zalmon the Ahohite; Maharai from Netophah; 29 Heled son of Baanah from Netophah; Ithai son of Ribai from Gibeah of Benjamin; 30 Benaiah the Pirathonite; Hiddai from the Brooks of Gaash; 31 Abi Albon the Arbathite; Azmaveth the Barhumite; 32 Eliahba the Shaalbonite; the sons of Jashen; Jonathan 33 the son of Shammah from Harar; Ahiam son of Sharar from Harar; 34 Eliphelet son of Ahasbai the Maacathite; Eliam son of

---

[a] 23:5 God ... secure Or "Hasn't God made my family strong?"

[b] 23:8 Josheb Basshebeth the Tahkemonite Or "Jashobeam the Hacmonite." See 1 Chron. 11:11.

[c] 23:8 king's special forces A special group of soldiers who formed three-man squads and went on special missions for the king.

[d] 23:8 Josheb Basshebeth ... time The Hebrew text here is unclear. The translation follows 1 Chron. 11:11 and the ancient Greek version.

[e] 23:9 Eleazar son of Dodai Or "Eleazar his cousin."

[f] 23:11 lentils Small round beans.

[g] 23:13 Thirty Heroes Or "the king's special forces." These men were David's famous group of very brave soldiers. Also in verses 23, 24.

[h] 23:13 three ... Rephaim The Hebrew text here is hard to understand, but compare 1 Chron. 11:15.

[i] 23:16 Three Heroes These were David's three bravest soldiers. Also in verses 18, 22.

[j] 23:20 powerful man That is, a man from the warrior class. He is ready to protect his people in war.

Ahithophel the Gilonite; [35]Hezro the Carmelite; Paarai the Arbite; [36]Igal son of Nathan of Zobah; Bani the Gadite; [37]Zelek the Ammonite; Naharai from Beeroth (Naharai carried the armor* for Joab son of Zeruiah); [38]Ira the Ithrite; Gareb the Ithrite; [39]and Uriah the Hittite. There were 37 in all.

David Decides to Count His Army

24 [1]The LORD was angry with Israel again. He caused David to turn against the Israelites. He told David, "Go count the people of Israel and Judah."

[2]King David said to Joab, the captain of the army, "Go through all the tribes of Israel from Dan to Beersheba,[a] and count the people. Then I will know how many people there are."

[3]But Joab said to the king, "May the LORD your God give you 100 times as many people, no matter how many there are! And may your eyes see this thing happen. But why do you want to do this?"

[4]King David strongly commanded Joab and the other captains of the army to count the people. So they went out from the king to count the people of Israel. [5]After they crossed over the Jordan River, they made their camp in Aroer on the right side of the city. (The city is in the middle of the valley of Gad, on the way to Jazer.)

[6]Then they went east to Gilead, all the way to Tahtim Hodshi. Then they went north to Dan Jaan and around to Sidon. [7]They went to the fort of Tyre. They went to all the cities of the Hivites and of the Canaanites. Then they went south to Beersheba in the southern part of Judah. [8]It took them nine months and 20 days for them to go through the country. After nine months and 20 days they came back to Jerusalem.

[9]Joab gave the list of the people to the king. There were 800,000 men in Israel who could use the sword. And there were 500,000 men in Judah.

The Lord Punishes David

[10]David felt ashamed after he had counted the people and said to the LORD, "I have sinned greatly in what I did! LORD, I beg you, forgive me for my sin. I have been very foolish."

[11]When David got up in the morning, the LORD's word came to Gad, David's seer.* [12]The LORD told Gad, "Go and tell David, 'This is what the LORD says: I offer you three things. Choose the one that I will do to you.'"

[13]So Gad went to David and said to him, "Choose one of these three things: seven years of famine for you and your country, or your enemies will chase you for three months, or three days of disease in your country. Think about it, and choose one of these things. Then I will tell the LORD who sent me about your choice."

[14]David said to Gad, "I am really in trouble, but the LORD is very merciful. So I choose to let the LORD punish us. Don't let my punishment come from people."

[15]So the LORD sent a disease against Israel. It began in the morning and continued until the chosen time to stop. From Dan to Beersheba 70,000 people died. [16]The angel raised his arm over Jerusalem and was ready to destroy it, but the LORD felt very sorry about the bad things that had happened. He said to the angel who destroyed the people, "That's enough! Put down your arm." The LORD's angel was by the threshing* floor of Araunah[b] the Jebusite.[c]

David Buys Araunah's Threshing Floor

[17]When he saw the angel who killed the people, David spoke to the LORD. David said, "I sinned! I did wrong! And these people only did what I told them—they only followed me like sheep. They did nothing wrong. Please let your punishment be against me and my father's family."

[18]That day Gad came to David and said, "Go and build an altar* to the LORD on the threshing* floor of Araunah the Jebusite." [19]So David did what Gad told him to. David did what the LORD wanted and went to see Araunah. [20]Araunah looked and saw King David and his officers coming to him. Araunah went out and bowed his face to the ground. [21]He said, "Why has my lord and king come to me?"

David answered, "I came to buy the threshing floor from you. Then I can build an altar to the LORD. Then the disease will stop."

[22]Araunah said to David, "My lord and king, you can take anything you want for a sacrifice.* Here are some oxen for the burnt offering, and the threshing boards and the yokes* for the wood. [23]O King, I give everything to you!" Araunah also said to the king, "May the LORD your God be pleased with you."

[24]But the king said to Araunah, "No! I tell you the truth, I will pay you for these things. I will not offer burnt offerings to the LORD my God that cost me nothing."

So David bought the threshing floor and the oxen for 50 shekels of silver. [25]Then David built an altar to the LORD there and offered burnt offerings and peace offerings.

The LORD answered his prayer for the country. He stopped the disease in Israel.

[a]24:2 *Dan to Beersheba* This means the whole nation of Israel, north and south. Dan was a town in the northern part of Israel, and Beersheba was in the southern part of Judah. Also in verse 15.

[b]24:16 *Araunah* Also spelled "Ornan." Also in verses 18, 22, 24.
[c]24:16 *Jebusite* A person who lived in Jerusalem before the Israelites took the city. "Jebus" was the old name for Jerusalem.

1 Kings

Adonijah Wants to Be King

1 ¹King David was very old and could not keep warm. His servants covered him with blankets, but he was still cold. ²So they said to him, "We will find a young woman to care for you. She will lie next to you and keep you warm." ³So the king's servants began looking everywhere in the country of Israel for a beautiful young woman to keep the king warm. They found a young woman named Abishag, from the town of Shunem, and brought her to the king. ⁴She was very beautiful. She cared for the king and served him, but King David did not have sexual relations with her.

⁵⁻⁶Adonijah was the son of King David and his wife Haggith. He was born after Absalom. Adonijah was a very handsome man. King David never corrected his son Adonijah, and he never made him explain his actions. Adonijah became very proud and decided that he would be the next king. He wanted very much to be the king, so he got himself a chariot,* horses, and 50 men to run ahead of him.

⁷Adonijah talked with Joab son of Zeruiah and Abiathar the priest. They decided to help make him the new king, ⁸but several important men did not join Adonijah. They were Zadok the priest, Benaiah son of Jehoiada, Nathan the prophet, Shimei, Rei, and King David's special guard.ᵃ

⁹One day, at Zoheleth Rock near En Rogel,ᵇ Adonijah sacrificed some sheep, cattle, and fat calves as a fellowship offering.* He invited his brothers (the other sons of King David) and all the officers from Judah. ¹⁰But he did not invite his brother Solomon, Nathan the prophet, Benaiah, or the men in the king's special guard.

Nathan Advises Bathsheba

¹¹When Nathan heard about this, he went to Solomon's mother Bathsheba and asked her, "Have you heard what Haggith's son, Adonijah, is doing? He is making himself king. And our master, King David, knows nothing about it. ¹²You and your son Solomon are in danger, but I will tell you what to do to save yourself. ¹³Go to King David and tell

him, 'My lord and king, you promised me that my son Solomon would be the next king after you. So why is Adonijah becoming the new king?' ¹⁴Then while you are still talking with him, I will come in. After you leave I will tell the king what has happened. This will show that what you said is true."

¹⁵So Bathsheba went in to see the king in his bedroom. The king was very old. Abishag, the girl from Shunem, was caring for him there. ¹⁶Bathsheba bowed down before the king. The king asked, "What can I do for you?"

¹⁷Bathsheba answered, "Sir, you used the name of the LORD your God and made a promise to me. You said, 'Your son Solomon will be the next king after me. He will sit on my throne.' ¹⁸Now, you don't know this, but Adonijah is making himself king. ¹⁹He is giving a big fellowship meal. He has killed many cattle and the best sheep, and he has invited all of your sons to the meal. He also invited Abiathar the priest and Joab, the commander of your army, but he did not invite your faithful son Solomon. ²⁰Now, my lord and king, all the Israelites are watching you. They are waiting for you to decide who will be the next king after you. ²¹If you don't decide, then after you are buried, these men will say that Solomon and I are criminals."

²²While Bathsheba was still talking with the king, Nathan the prophet came to see him. ²³The servants told the king, "Nathan the prophet is here." Nathan went in to speak to the king. He bowed down before the king ²⁴and said, "My lord and king, did you announce that Adonijah will be the new king after you? Have you decided that he will rule the people now? ²⁵Today he went down into the valley to offer many cattle and the best sheep as fellowship offerings. He invited all your other sons, the commanders of the army, and Abiathar the priest. They are now eating and drinking with him. And they are saying, 'Long live King Adonijah!' ²⁶But he did not invite me, or Zadok the priest, or Benaiah son of Jehoiada, or your son Solomon. ²⁷My lord and king, did you do this without telling us? Please tell us, who will be the next king after you?"

²⁸Then King David said, "Tell Bathsheba to come in!" So she came in and stood before the king.

²⁹Then the king made a promise: "The LORD God has saved me from every danger. As

ᵃ1:8 Shimei, Rei ... guard Or "Shimei and his friends, the Heroes."
ᵇ1:9 En Rogel A spring of water in the valley south of Jerusalem, about 1/4 mile from Gihon Spring.

surely as he lives, I make this promise to you. ³⁰Today I will do what I promised you in the past. I made that promise by the power of the Lord, the God of Israel. I promised that your son Solomon would be the next king after me. I promised that he would take my place on my throne, and I will keep my promise!"

³¹Then Bathsheba bowed down before the king and said, "Long live King David!"

Solomon Is Anointed King

³²Then King David said, "Tell Zadok the priest, Nathan the prophet, and Benaiah son of Jehoiada to come in here." So the three men came in to meet with the king. ³³Then the king said to them, "Take my officers with you. Put my son Solomon on my mule and take him to Gihon Spring.ᵃ ³⁴There Zadok the priest and Nathan the prophet will anoint* him to be the new king of Israel. Blow the trumpet and announce, 'This is the new king, Solomon!' ³⁵Then come back here with him. Solomon will sit on my throne and be the new king in my place. I have chosen him to be the ruler of Israel and Judah."

³⁶Benaiah son of Jehoiada answered the king, "Amen! It is as true as if the Lord God himself had said it, my lord and king. ³⁷My lord and king, the Lord has been with you, and now I pray the Lord will be with Solomon! And I pray King Solomon's kingdom will grow and be even more powerful than yours, my lord and king."

³⁸So Zadok, Nathan, Benaiah, and the king's officers obeyed King David. They put Solomon on David's mule and went with him down to Gihon Spring. ³⁹Zadok the priest carried the oil from the Holy Tent* and poured it on Solomon's head to show that he was the new king. They blew the trumpet and all the people shouted, "Long live King Solomon!" ⁴⁰Then all the people followed Solomon back into the city. They were very happy and excited. They were playing flutes and making so much noise that the ground shook.

⁴¹Meanwhile, Adonijah and his guests were just finishing their meal. They heard the sound of the trumpet, and Joab asked, "What is that noise? What is happening in the city?"

⁴²While Joab was still speaking, Jonathan, son of Abiathar the priest, arrived. Adonijah said, "Come here! You are a good man,ᵇ so you must be bringing good news."

⁴³But Jonathan answered, "No, it is not good news for you! King David has made Solomon the new king. ⁴⁴King David sent Zadok the priest, Nathan the prophet, Benaiah son of Jehoiada, and all the king's officers with Solomon out to Gihon Spring. They put Solomon on the king's mule. ⁴⁵Zadok the

priest and Nathan the prophet anointed Solomon at Gihon Spring and then went back into the city. The people followed them, and now everyone in the city is celebrating. That is the noise you hear. ⁴⁶⁻⁴⁷Solomon is sitting on the king's throne and the king's officers are congratulating King David, saying, 'King David, you are a great king!' And now we pray that your God will make Solomon a great king too. We pray your God will make him even more famous than you. And we pray that his kingdom will be even greater than yours is! Even King David was there. From his bed, the king bowed before Solomon ⁴⁸and said, 'Praise the Lord, the God of Israel. The Lord put one of my own sons on my throne, and he let me live to see it.'"

⁴⁹All of Adonijah's guests were afraid and left very quickly. ⁵⁰Adonijah was also afraid of Solomon, so he went to the altar and held onto the horns of the altar.* ⁵¹Then someone told Solomon, "Adonijah is afraid of you, King Solomon. He is at the Holy Tent holding onto the horns of the altar, and he refuses to leave. Adonijah says, 'Tell King Solomon to promise that he will not kill me.'"

⁵²So Solomon answered, "If Adonijah shows that he is a good man, I promise that not a hair on his head will be hurt. But if he does anything wrong, he will die." ⁵³Then King Solomon sent some men to get Adonijah and brought him in. He approached the king and bowed before him. Then Solomon said, "Go home."

King David Dies

2 ¹The time came for David to die, so he gave these commands to Solomon, ²"I am about to die, like all men must. But you are growing stronger and becoming a man. ³Now, carefully obey all the commands of the Lord your God. Carefully obey all his laws, commands, decisions, and agreements. Obey everything that is written in the Law of Moses. If you do this, you will be successful at whatever you do and wherever you go. ⁴And if you obey the Lord, he will keep his promise about me. He said, 'If your sons carefully live the way I tell them, sincerely, with all their heart, the king of Israel will always be a man from your family.'"

⁵David also said, "You remember what Joab son of Zeruiah did to me. He killed two of the commanders of Israel's army, Abner son of Ner and Amasa son of Jether. Remember, it was during a time of peace when he spilled the blood that splattered onto his sword belt and army boots. I should have punished him then. ⁶Use your wisdom, but don't let him die peacefully of old age.

⁷"Also, be kind to the children of Barzillai from Gilead. Be friends with them, and let them eat at your table, because they helped me when I ran away from your brother Absalom.

8"And remember, Shimei son of Gera is still around. He is the Benjamite from Bahurim who cursed me when I ran away to Mahanaim. But when he came down to meet me at the Jordan River, I made a promise to him before the Lord that I would not kill him. 9Now, don't leave him unpunished. You are a wise man. You will know what you must do, but don't let him die peacefully of old age."

10Then David died and was buried in the City of David.* 11David ruled Israel 40 years. He ruled seven years in Hebron and 33 years in Jerusalem.

Solomon and Adonijah

12Now Solomon was king. He sat on the throne of his father David and was in complete control of his kingdom.

13One day Adonijah, the son of Haggith, went to Solomon's mother, Bathsheba. She asked him, "Do you come in peace?"

Adonijah answered, "Yes, this is a peaceful visit. 14I have something to ask you."

Bathsheba said, "Then speak."

15Adonijah said, "You know that at one time the kingdom was mine. All the people of Israel wanted me to be their king. But things have changed, and now my brother is the king. The Lord chose him to be king. 16But now I have one thing to ask you. Please don't refuse me."

Bathsheba answered, "What do you want?"

17Adonijah said, "I know that King Solomon will do whatever you ask. So please ask him to let me marry Abishag, the woman from Shunem."

18Then Bathsheba said, "Very well, I will speak to the king for you."

19So Bathsheba went to King Solomon to talk with him. When the king saw her, he stood up, bowed before her, and then sat back down. He told some servants to bring another throne for his mother, and she sat down at his right side.

20Bathsheba said to him, "I have one small thing to ask you. Please don't refuse me."

The king answered, "Ask whatever you want, mother. I will not refuse you."

21So Bathsheba said, "Let your brother Adonijah marry Abishag, the woman from Shunem."

22King Solomon answered his mother, "Why are you asking me to give Abishag to Adonijah? Why don't you just ask me to give him the whole kingdom! After all, he is my older brother, and both Abiathar the priest and Joab support him!"

23Then Solomon said, "By the Lord, I swear I'll make Adonijah pay for this with his life! 24The Lord made me the king of Israel. He gave me the throne of my father David. The Lord kept his promise and gave the kingdom to me and my family. Now, as surely as the Lord lives, I swear Adonijah will die today!"

25King Solomon gave the command to Benaiah, and Benaiah went out and killed Adonijah.

26Then King Solomon said to Abiathar the priest, "I should kill you, but I will let you go back to your home in Anathoth. I will not kill you now because you helped carry the Holy Box* of the Lord while marching with my father David. And I know that you shared in the hard times with my father." 27So Solomon told Abiathar that he could not continue to serve as a priest of the Lord. This happened as the Lord said it would when he told Eli the priest what would happen to him and his family.ᵃ

28Joab had supported Adonijah, but not Absalom. But when Joab heard what happened to Abiathar, he was frightened and ran to the tent of the Lord to hold onto the horns of the altar.* 29Someone told King Solomon that Joab was at the altar in the Lord's Tent. So Solomon ordered Benaiah to go and kill him.

30Benaiah went into the Lord's Tent and said to Joab, "The king says, 'Come out!'"

But Joab answered, "No, I will die here."

Benaiah went back to the king and told him what Joab had said. 31The king commanded Benaiah, "Do as he says! Kill him there and take him out to bury him. Then my family and I will be free of Joab's guilt from killing innocent people. 32Joab killed two men who were much better than he was. He killed Abner son of Ner, the commander of the army of Israel, and Amasa son of Jether, the commander of the army of Judah. He did this without my father's knowledge. But now the Lord will punish Joab for the men he killed. 33He and his family will always be guilty for their deaths. But the Lord will bring peace to David, his descendants, his family of kings, and his kingdom forever."

34So Benaiah son of Jehoiada killed Joab, and he was buried near his home in the desert. 35Solomon then made Benaiah son of Jehoiada the commander of the army in Joab's place. Solomon also made Zadok the new high priest in Abiathar's place. 36Next, the king sent for Shimei and said to him, "Build yourself a house here in Jerusalem to live in and don't leave the city. 37If you leave the city and go any further than Kidron Brook, you will be killed, and it will be your own fault."

38Shimei answered, "Yes, my king. I will obey you." So Shimei lived in Jerusalem for a long time. 39But three years later, two of Shimei's slaves ran away. They went to King Achish of Gath, who was the son of Maacah. Shimei heard that his slaves were in Gath, 40so he saddled his donkey and went to King Achish at Gath to find them. He found them there and brought them back home.

41But someone told Solomon that Shimei had left Jerusalem and gone to Gath and back.

ᵃ2:27 This … family See 1 Samuel 2:27-36.

⁴²So Solomon sent for him and said, "I made you promise in the LORD's name not to leave Jerusalem. And I warned you that if you went anywhere, you would die. And you agreed to what I said. You said that you would obey me. ⁴³So why didn't you obey me? Why did you break your promise? ⁴⁴You know all the bad things you did to my father David. Now the LORD will punish you for it. ⁴⁵But the LORD will bless me and keep David's throne before him forever."

⁴⁶Then the king ordered Benaiah to kill Shimei, and he did. So Solomon had full control of his kingdom.

Solomon Asks for Wisdom

3 ¹Solomon made a peace treaty with Pharaoh, the king of Egypt, by marrying his daughter. Solomon brought her to the City of David.* This was when Solomon was still building his palace, the Temple of the LORD, and the wall around Jerusalem. ²The Temple had not yet been finished, so people were still making animal sacrifices* on altars at the high places.* ³Solomon showed that he loved the LORD by obeying everything his father David told him to do, except that Solomon continued to go to the high places to offer sacrifices and to burn incense.*

⁴King Solomon went to Gibeon to offer a sacrifice because that was the most important high place. He offered a thousand burnt offerings* on that altar. ⁵While Solomon was at Gibeon, the LORD came to him at night in a dream. God said, "Solomon, ask me what you want me to give you."

⁶Solomon answered, "You were very kind and loyal to your servant, my father David. He was faithful to you and lived a good, honest life. And you showed him the greatest kindness when you let his son take his place as king. ⁷LORD my God, you have made me the king in my father's place, but I am like a small child. I don't have the wisdom I need to do what I must do. ⁸I am your servant here among your chosen people. There are so many that they cannot be counted. ⁹So I ask you to give me the wisdom to rule and judge them well and to help me know the difference between right and wrong. Without such great wisdom, it would be impossible to rule this great nation."

¹⁰The Lord was happy that Solomon asked for wisdom. ¹¹So God said to him, "You did not ask for long life and riches for yourself. You did not ask for the death of your enemies. You asked for the wisdom to listen and make the right decisions. ¹²So I will give you what you asked for. I will make you wise and intelligent. I will make you wiser than anyone who ever lived or ever will live. ¹³And I will also give you what you did not ask for. You will have riches and honor all your life. There will be no other king in the world as great as you. ¹⁴And I will give you a long life if you follow me and obey my laws and commands as your father David did."

¹⁵Solomon woke up and knew that God had spoken to him in the dream. Then Solomon went to Jerusalem and stood before the Box of the LORD's Agreement.* He offered a burnt offering and fellowship offerings* to the LORD and then gave a party for all of his officials.

Proof of Solomon's Wisdom

¹⁶One day two prostitutes came to Solomon and stood before the king. ¹⁷One of the women said, "Sir, this woman and I live in the same house. We were both pregnant and ready to give birth to our babies. I had my baby while she was there with me. ¹⁸Three days later she also gave birth to her baby. There was no one else in the house with us, just the two of us. ¹⁹One night while this woman was asleep with her baby, the baby died. ²⁰That night while I was asleep, she took my son from my bed and carried him to her bed. Then she put the dead baby in my bed. ²¹In the morning I woke up and was about to feed the baby when I saw he was dead. When I looked at him more closely, I saw that he was not my baby."

²²But the other woman said, "No! The dead baby is yours, and the one still alive is mine!"

But the first woman said, "No, you are wrong! The dead baby is yours! The one that is still alive is mine." So the two women argued in front of the king.

²³Then King Solomon said, "Each of you says that the living baby is your own and that the dead baby belongs to the other woman." ²⁴Then King Solomon sent his servant to get a sword. ²⁵He told the servant, "Cut the living baby in two and give one half of the baby to each woman."

²⁶The second woman said, "Yes, cut him in two. Then neither of us will have him." But the first woman, the real mother, loved her son and said to the king, "Please, sir, don't kill the baby! Give him to her."

²⁷Then King Solomon said, "Stop, don't kill the baby. Give him to this woman. She is the real mother."

²⁸The people of Israel respected the king when they heard about this decision. They saw he had the wisdom of God*ᵃ* to make the right decisions.

Solomon's Kingdom

4 ¹King Solomon ruled over all Israel. ²These are the names of his leading officials:

Azariah son of Zadok was the priest;
³ Elihoreph and Ahijah, sons of Shisha, had the job of writing notes about what happened in the courts;
Jehoshaphat son of Ahilud wrote notes about the history of the people;

ᵃ**3:28** *the wisdom of God* Or "very great wisdom."

4 Benaiah son of Jehoiada was the
   commander of the army;
   Zadok and Abiathar were priests;
5 Azariah son of Nathan was in charge of
   the district governors;
   Zabud son of Nathan was a priest and an
   advisor to King Solomon;
6 Ahishar was responsible for everything in
   the king's palace;
   Adoniram son of Abda was in charge of
   the slaves.

7Israel was divided into twelve districts.
Solomon chose governors to rule over each
district. These governors were ordered to
gather food from their districts and give it to
the king and his family. Each of the twelve
governors was responsible for giving food to
the king one month each year. 8These are the
names of the twelve governors:

Ben Hur was governor of the hill country
   of Ephraim.
9 Ben Deker was governor of Makaz,
   Shaalbim, Beth Shemesh, and Elon
   Bethhanan.
10 Ben Hesed was governor of Arubboth,
   Socoh, and Hepher.
11 Ben Abinadab was governor of Naphoth
   Dor. He was married to Taphath,
   daughter of Solomon.
12 Baana son of Ahilud was governor of
   Taanach and Megiddo and all of Beth
   Shean next to Zarethan. This was
   below Jezreel, from Beth Shean to Abel
   Meholah across from Jokmeam.
13 Ben Geber was governor of Ramoth
   Gilead. He was governor of all the
   towns and villages of Jair son of
   Manasseh in Gilead. He was also
   governor of the district of Argob in
   Bashan. In this area there were 60
   cities with big walls around them.
   These cities also had bronze bars on the
   gates.
14 Ahinadab son of Iddo was governor of
   Mahanaim.
15 Ahimaaz was governor of Naphtali. He
   was married to Basemath the daughter
   of Solomon.
16 Baana son of Hushai was governor of
   Asher and Aloth.
17 Jehoshaphat son of Paruah was governor
   of Issachar.
18 Shimei son of Ela was governor of
   Benjamin.
19 Geber son of Uri was governor of Gilead.
   There had been two kings in this area,
   King Sihon of the Amorites and King Og
   of Bashan, but Solomon appointed only
   one governor for that district.

20In Judah and Israel there were as many
people as sand on the seashore. The people
were happy and had plenty to eat and drink.

21Solomon ruled over all the kingdoms from
the Euphrates River to the land of the Philistines. His kingdom went as far as the border
of Egypt. These countries sent gifts to Solomon, and they obeyed him all of his life.ᵃ

22-23This is the amount of food that Solomon needed each day for himself and for
everyone who ate at his table: 150 bushelsᵇ
of fine flour, 300 bushelsᶜ of flour, 10 cattle
that were fed grain, 20 cattle that were raised
in the fields, 100 sheep, wild animals such as
deer, gazelles, roebucks,ᵈ and game birds.

24Solomon ruled over all the countries west
of the Euphrates River, from Tiphsah to Gaza.
And Solomon had peace along all the borders of his kingdom. 25During Solomon's life
everyone in Judah and Israel, all the way from
Dan to Beersheba, lived in peace and security.
The people were at peace sitting under their
own fig trees and grapevines.

26Solomon had places to keep 4000ᵉ
horses for his chariots* and he had 12,000
horse soldiers. 27And each month one of the
twelve district governors gave King Solomon
everything he needed for all the people who
ate at the king's table. 28The district governors also gave the king enough straw and
barley for the chariot horses and the riding
horses. Everyone brought this grain to the
necessary places.

Solomon's Wisdom

29God made Solomon very wise. Solomon
could understand more than you can imagine. 30He was wiser than anyone in the Eastᶠ
or in Egypt. 31He was wiser than anyone on
earth, even Ethan the Ezrahite and the sons
of Mahol—Heman, Calcol, and Darda. King
Solomon became famous in all the surrounding countries. 32By the end of his life, he had
writtenᵍ 3000 proverbs* and 1005 songs.

33Solomon also knew very much about
nature. He taught about many different kinds
of plants—everything from the great cedar
trees of Lebanon to the little vines that grow
out of the walls. He also taught about animals, birds, and snakes.ʰ 34People from every
nation came to listen to Solomon's wisdom.
Kings all over the world sent their people to
listen to him.

ᵃ4:21 sent gifts ... life This showed that these countries had made peace agreements with Solomon
because of his great power.
ᵇ4:22-23 150 bushels Literally, "30 cors" (6600 l).
ᶜ4:22-23 300 bushels Literally, "60 cors" (13,200 l).
ᵈ4:22-23 deer, gazelles, roebucks Different kinds
of wild deer.
ᵉ4:26 4000 This is found in some copies of the
ancient Greek version. The standard Hebrew text
has 40,000, but see 2 Chron. 9:25.
ᶠ4:30 East The area between the Tigris and Euphrates rivers as far east as the Persian Gulf.
ᵍ4:32 written Literally, "spoken."
ʰ4:33 snakes Literally, "creeping things." These can
be anything: insects, lizards, snakes, or fish.

Solomon and Hiram

5 [1]Hiram was the king of Tyre. He had always been David's friend. So when Hiram heard that Solomon had become the new king after David, he sent his servants to Solomon. [2]This is what Solomon said to King Hiram: [3]"You remember that my father, King David, had to fight many wars all around him. So he was never able to build a temple to honor the LORD his God. King David was waiting until the LORD allowed him to defeat all his enemies. [4]But now the LORD my God has given me peace along all the borders of my country. I have no enemies, and my people are in no danger.

[5]"The LORD made a promise to my father David. He said, 'I will make your son king after you, and he will build a temple to honor me.' Now, I plan to build that temple to honor the LORD my God. [6]And so I ask you to help me. Send your men to Lebanon to cut down cedar trees for me. My servants will work with yours. I will pay you any price that you decide as your servants' wages, but I need your help. Our carpenters[a] are not as good as the carpenters of Sidon."

[7]Hiram was very happy when he heard what Solomon asked. He said, "I praise the LORD today for giving David a wise son to rule this great nation!" [8]Then Hiram sent this message to Solomon, "I heard what you asked for. I will give you all the cedar trees and the fir trees you want. [9]My servants will bring them down from Lebanon to the sea. Then I will tie them together and float them down the shore to the place you choose. There I will separate the logs, and you can take them from there. As payment for this, you will give food to all those who live in my palace." [10]So Hiram gave Solomon all the cedar and fir logs that he wanted.

[11]Solomon gave Hiram about 120,000 bushels[b] of wheat and about 120,000 gallons[c] of pure olive oil every year for his family. [12]The LORD made Solomon wise as he had promised. Hiram and Solomon made a treaty between themselves and were at peace with one another.

[13]King Solomon forced 30,000 men of Israel to help in this work. [14]He chose a man named Adoniram to be in charge of them. Solomon divided the men into three groups with 10,000 men in each group. Each group worked one month in Lebanon and then went home for two months. [15]Solomon also forced 80,000 men to work in the hill country cutting stone. There were also 70,000 men to carry the stones. [16]There were 3300 men to supervise the workers. [17]King Solomon commanded them to cut large, expensive stones for the foundation of the Temple. [18]Then Solomon and Hiram's builders and the men from Byblos[d] carved the stones and prepared them and the logs for use in building the Temple.

Solomon Builds the Temple

6 [1]So in the month of Ziv, the second month of the year, during Solomon's fourth year as king, he began work on the Temple. This was 480 years after the Israelites left Egypt.[e] [2]The Temple was 60 cubits[f] long, 20 cubits[g] wide, and 30 cubits[h] high. [3]The porch of the Temple was 20 cubits long and 10 cubits[i] wide. The porch ran along the front of the main part of the Temple itself. Its length was equal to the width of the Temple. [4]There were narrow windows in the Temple. These windows were smaller on the inside of the wall than on the outside.[j] [5]Then Solomon built a row of rooms around the main part of the Temple. This row of rooms was three stories tall with the rooms built one above the other. [6]The rooms touched the Temple wall, but their beams were not built into that wall. The Temple wall became thinner at the top, so the rooms on the upper floors were larger than the ones below them. The rooms on the bottom floor were 5 cubits[k] wide. The rooms on the middle floor were 6 cubits[l] wide. The rooms above that were 7 cubits[m] wide. [7]The stones were completely finished before they were brought into the Temple area, so there was no noise of hammers, axes, or any other iron tools in the Temple.

[8]The entrance to these rooms was on bottom floor at the south side of the Temple. Inside there were stairs that went up to the second floor and from there to the third floor.

[9]Solomon finished building the main part of the Temple and then covered it inside with cedar boards. [10]Then he finished building the rooms around the Temple. Each story was 5 cubits tall. The cedar beams in these rooms rested on a ledge of the Temple wall.

[11]The LORD said to Solomon, [12]"If you obey all my laws and commands, I will do for you what I promised your father David. [13]I will live among the children of Israel in this Temple that you are building, and I will never leave the people of Israel."

---

[d]**5:18** *Byblos* Literally, "Gebal."

[e]**6:1** *480 years ... Egypt* This was about 960 B.C.

[f]**6:2** *60 cubits* 102' 3/8" (31.1 m).

[g]**6:2** *20 cubits* 34' 1/8" (10.37 m). Also in verses 16, 20.

[h]**6:2** *30 cubits* 51' 3/16" (15.55 m). The ancient Greek version has "25 cubits."

[i]**6:3** *10 cubits* 17' 1/16" (5.18 m). Also in verses 23, 24–26.

[j]**6:4** *These windows ... outside* Or "These windows had lattice work over them."

[k]**6:6** *5 cubits* 8' 6" (2.6 m). Also in verses 10, 24–26.

[l]**6:6** *6 cubits* 10' 2 7/16" (3.11 m).

[m]**6:6** *7 cubits* 11' 10 13/16" (3.63 m).

---

[a]**5:6** *carpenters* People who work with wood. In ancient times, this also meant that they cut the trees.

[b]**5:11** *120,000 bushels* Literally, "20,000 *cors*" (4,400,000 l).

[c]**5:11** *120,000 gallons* Literally, "20,000 *baths*" (440,000 l).

¹⁴When Solomon finished the stonework on the Temple, ¹⁵the stone walls inside the Temple were covered with cedar boards from floor to ceiling. Then the stone floor was covered with pine boards. ¹⁶They built an inner room 20 cubits long in the back part of the Temple. This room was called the Most Holy Place. They covered the walls in this room with cedar boards, from floor to ceiling. ¹⁷In front of the Most Holy Place was the main part of the Temple. This room was 40 cubits*a* long. ¹⁸They covered the walls in this room with cedar boards—none of the stones in the walls could be seen. They carved pictures of flowers and gourds into the cedar.

¹⁹Solomon finished the inner room in the back part of the Temple. This room was for the LORD's Box of the Agreement.* ²⁰This room was 20 cubits long, 20 cubits wide, and 20 cubits high. Solomon covered this room with pure gold. He also covered the cedar altar with gold. ²¹He covered the inside of the Temple with pure gold and wrapped gold chains around it. ²²The inside of the Temple was covered with gold, and the altar in front of the Most Holy Place was covered with gold.

²³The workers made two statues of Cherub angels* with wings. They made the statues from olive wood and put them in the Most Holy Place. Each angel was 10 cubits tall. ²⁴⁻²⁶Both Cherub angels were the same size and built the same way. Each one had two wings. Each wing was 5 cubits long. From the end of one wing to the end of the other wing was 10 cubits. And each Cherub angel was 10 cubits tall. ²⁷They put the Cherub angels beside one another in the Most Holy Place. Their wings touched each other in the middle of the room. The other two wings touched each side wall. ²⁸The two Cherub angels were covered with gold.

²⁹The walls around the main room and the inner room were carved with pictures of Cherub angels, palm trees, and flowers. ³⁰The floor of both rooms was covered with gold.

³¹The workers made two doors from olive wood. They put these doors at the entrance of the Most Holy Place. The frame around the doors was made with five sides.*b* ³²They made the two doors from olive wood. The workers carved pictures of Cherub angels, palm trees, and flowers on the doors. Then they covered the doors with gold.

³³They also made doors for the entrance to the main room. They used olive wood to make a square doorframe. ³⁴There were two doors made from pine. Each door had two parts that folded together. ³⁵They carved pictures of Cherub angels, palm trees, and flowers on the doors. Then they covered them with gold.

³⁶Then they built a wall around the inner yard. Each wall was made from three rows of cut stones and one row of cedar timbers.

³⁷They started working on the Temple in the month of Ziv, the second month of the year. This was during Solomon's fourth year as king of Israel. ³⁸The Temple was finished in the month of Bul, the eighth month of the year, in Solomon's eleventh year as king. It took seven years to build the Temple. It was built exactly as planned.

Solomon's Palace

7 ¹King Solomon also built a palace for himself. It took 13 years to build Solomon's palace. ²He also built the building called the "Forest of Lebanon." It was 100 cubits*c* long, 50 cubits*d* wide, and 30 cubits*e* high. It had four rows of cedar columns. On top of each column was a cedar capital.* ³There were cedar beams going across the rows of columns. There were 15 beams for each section of columns. There was a total of 45 beams. On top of these beams there were cedar boards for the ceiling. ⁴There were three rows of windows across from each other on the side walls. ⁵There were three doors at each end. All the door openings and frames were square.

⁶Solomon also built the Porch of Columns. It was 50 cubits long and 30 cubits wide. Along the front of the porch, there was a covering supported by columns.

⁷He also built a throne room where he judged people. He called this the Judgment Hall. The room was covered with cedar from floor to ceiling.

⁸Behind the Judgment Hall was a courtyard. The palace where Solomon lived was built around that courtyard and looked like the Judgment Hall. He also built the same kind of palace for his wife, the daughter of the king of Egypt.

⁹All these buildings were made with expensive blocks of stone. The stones were cut to the right size with a saw and then smoothed on front and back. These expensive stones went from the foundation all the way up to the top layer of the wall. Even the wall around the yard was made with expensive blocks of stone. ¹⁰The foundations were made with large, expensive stones. Some of the stones were 10 cubits*f* long and the others were 8 cubits*g* long. ¹¹On top of these stones there were other expensive stones and cedar beams. ¹²There were walls around the palace yard, the Temple yard, and the porch of the Temple. The walls were built with three rows of stone and one row of cedar timbers.

¹³King Solomon sent for a man named

---

*a*6:17 40 cubits 68' 1/4" (20.73 m).
*b*6:31 The frame ... sides This probably means there were three sections that formed an arch at the top of the door.

*c*7:2 100 cubits 170' 5/8" (51.83 m).
*d*7:2 50 cubits 85' 5/16" (25.92 m). Also in verse 6.
*e*7:2 30 cubits 51' 3/16" (15.55 m). Also in verses 6, 23.
*f*7:10 10 cubits 17' 1/16" (5.18 m). Also in verse 23.
*g*7:10 8 cubits 13' 7 1/4" (4.2 m).

Huram[a] who lived in Tyre and brought him to Jerusalem. [14]Huram's mother was an Israelite from the tribe of Naphtali. His dead father was from Tyre. Huram made things from bronze.* He was a very skilled and experienced builder. So King Solomon asked him to come, and Huram accepted. King Solomon put him in charge of all the bronze work, and Huram did all the work he was given to do.

[15]Huram made two bronze columns for the porch. Each column was 18 cubits[b] tall and 12 cubits[c] around. The columns were hollow and their metal walls were 3 inches[d] thick.[e] [16]He also made two bronze capitals that were 5 cubits[f] tall. He put these capitals on top of the columns. [17]He made two nets of chain to cover the capitals on top of the two columns. [18]Then he made two rows of bronze pomegranates.* He put the bronze pomegranates on the nets of each column to cover the capitals at the top of the columns. [19]The capitals on top of the columns were shaped like flowers. [20]The capitals were on top of the columns, above the bowl-shaped net. There were 200 pomegranates in rows all around the capitals. [21]Huram put these two bronze columns at the porch of the Temple. One column was put on the south side of the entrance and one was put on the north side of it. The column on the south was named Jakin. The column on the north was named Boaz. [22]They put the flower-shaped capitals on top of the columns, and the work on the two columns was finished.

[23]Then Huram melted bronze and poured it into a huge mold to make a tank,[g] which was called "The Sea." The tank was about 30 cubits around. It was 10 cubits across and 5 cubits deep. [24]There was a rim around the outer edge of the tank. Under this rim there were two rows of bronze gourds all around the tank. The bronze gourds were made in one piece as part of the tank. [25]The tank rested on the backs of 12 bronze bulls. All 12 of the bulls were looking out, away from the tank. Three were looking north, three east, three south, and three west. [26]The sides of the tank were 3 inches thick. The rim around the tank was like the rim of a cup or like the petals on a flower. The tank held about 11,000 gallons[h] of water

[27]Then Huram made ten bronze carts. Each cart was 4 cubits[i] long, 4 cubits wide,

and 3 cubits[j] high. [28]The carts were made with square panels set in frames. [29]On the panels and frames were bronze bulls, lions, and Cherub angels.* There were designs of flowers hammered into the bronze above and below the bulls and lions. [30]Each cart had four bronze wheels with bronze axles. At the corners there were bronze supports for a large bowl. The supports had designs of flowers hammered into the bronze. [31]There was a frame around the top with an opening for the bowl. The frame was 1 cubit[k] tall, and the opening was 1½ cubits[l] in diameter. There were designs carved into the bronze on the frame. The frame was square, not round. [32]There were four wheels under the frame. The wheels were 1½ cubits in diameter. The axles between the wheels were made as one piece with the cart. [33]The wheels were like the wheels on a chariot.* Everything on the wheels—the axles, the rims, the spokes, and the hubs were made from bronze.

[34]There were supports at each of the four corners of the carts. They were made as one piece with the cart. [35]There was a strip of bronze around the top of each cart. It was made as one piece with the cart. [36]The sides of the cart and the frames had pictures of Cherub angels, lions, and palm trees carved into the bronze. These pictures were carved all over the carts—wherever there was room. And there were flowers carved on the frame around the cart. [37]Huram made ten carts, and they were all the same. Each cart was made from bronze. The bronze was melted and poured into a mold. So all the carts were the same size and shape.

[38]Huram also made ten bowls. There was one bowl for each of the ten carts. Each bowl was 4 cubits across and could hold about 230 gallons.[m] [39]He put five carts on the south side of the Temple and five carts on the north side. He put the large tank in the southeast corner of the Temple. [40-45]Huram also made pots, small shovels, and small bowls. He finished making all the things King Solomon wanted him to make. This is a list of the things that Huram made for the Temple of the LORD:

2 columns;

2 capitals shaped like bowls for the top of the columns;

2 nets to go around the capitals;

400 pomegranates for the two nets (two rows of pomegranates for each net to cover the two bowls for the capitals on top of the columns);

10 carts with a bowl on each cart;

the large tank with 12 bulls under it;

the pots, small shovels, small bowls, and all the dishes for the LORD's Temple.

---

[a]7:13 *Huram* Or "Hiram." Also in verses 15, 23, 27, 37, 38, 40–45.

[b]7:15 *18 cubits* 30' 7 5/16" (9.33 m).

[c]7:15 *12 cubits* 20' 4 7/8" (6.22 m).

[d]7:15 *3 inches* Literally, "1 handbreadth" (7.4 cm).
Also in verse 26.

[e]7:15 *The columns ... 3 inches thick* This is from the ancient Greek version.

[f]7:16 *5 cubits* 8' 6" (2.6 m). Also in verses 19, 23.

[g]7:23 *tank* A very large container for water.

[h]7:26 *11,000 gallons* Literally, "2000 baths" (44,000 l).

[i]7:27 *4 cubits* 6' 9 5/8" (2.1 m). Also in verse 38.

[j]7:27 *3 cubits* 5' 1 3/16" (1.55 m).

[k]7:31 *1 cubit* 20 3/8" (51.83 cm).

[l]7:31 *1 1/2 cubits* 30 5/8" (77.75 cm).

[m]7:38 *230 gallons* Literally, "40 baths" (880 l).

Huram made everything King Solomon wanted. They were all made from polished bronze. [46-47]Solomon never weighed the bronze that was used to make these things. There was too much to weigh. So the total weight of all the bronze was never known. The king ordered these things to be made near the Jordan River between Succoth and Zarethan. They made them by melting the bronze and pouring it into molds in the ground.

[48-50]Solomon also commanded that all these things be made from gold for the Temple:

the golden altar;
the golden table which held the special bread that was offered to God;
the lampstands of pure gold (five on the south side and five on the north side in front of the Most Holy Place);
the gold flowers, lamps, and tongs;
the pure gold bowls, lamp snuffers,* small bowls, pans, and dishes for carrying coals;
the gold hinges for the doors to the inner room (the Most Holy Place) and for the doors to the main room of the Temple.

[51]So King Solomon finished all the work he wanted to do for the Lord's Temple. Then he took everything his father David had saved for this special purpose and put them in the Temple. He put the silver and gold in the special storage rooms in the Lord's Temple.

The Box of the Agreement in the Temple

8 [1]Then King Solomon told all the elders of Israel, the heads of the tribes, and the leaders of the families of Israel to come together in Jerusalem. Solomon wanted them to join in moving the Box of the Agreement* from the City of David* up to the Temple. [2]So during the special festival[a] in the month of Ethanim, the seventh month of the year, all the men of Israel came to the meeting with King Solomon.

[3-4]When all the elders of Israel arrived, the priests and Levites* carried the Holy Box* of the Lord up to the Temple. They also carried the Meeting Tent* and all the holy things that were in it up to the Temple. [5]King Solomon and all Israel met together before the Box of the Agreement and sacrificed so many sheep and cattle that no one was able to count them all. [6]The priests carried the Box of the Agreement of the Lord to its proper place inside the Most Holy Place in the Temple, under the wings of the Cherub angels.* [7]The wings of the Cherub angels spread out over the Holy Box, and they covered the Holy Box and its carrying poles. [8]The poles are still there today. They are too long for the Most Holy Place, so anyone standing in the Holy Place

can see the ends of the poles, although no one outside can see them. [9]The only things inside the Holy Box are the two tablets that Moses put there at Mt. Horeb. This is where the Lord made his agreement* with the Israelites after they came out of Egypt.

[10]When the priests came out of the Holy Place, the cloud[b] filled the Lord's Temple. [11]The priests could not continue their work because the Temple was filled with the Glory of the Lord.* [12]Then Solomon said,

"The Lord caused the sun to shine in the sky,
    but he chose to live in a dark cloud.[c]
[13] Now, Lord, I have built a beautiful Temple for you,
    where you may live forever."

[14]Then King Solomon turned toward all the Israelites who were standing there and asked God to bless them. [15]He prayed this long prayer to the Lord:

"The Lord, the God of Israel, is great.
He has done what he promised my father David.
He told my father,
[16] 'I brought my people, Israel, out of Egypt,
    but I had not yet chosen a city from among the tribes of Israel for a temple to honor me.
And I had not chosen a man
    to be leader over my people, Israel.
But now I have chosen Jerusalem
    to be the city where I will be honored.[d]
And I have chosen David
    to rule over my people, Israel.'

[17]"My father David wanted very much to build a temple to honor the Lord, the God of Israel. [18]But the Lord said to my father, 'I know that you want very much to build a temple to honor me, and it is good that you want to build it. [19]But you are not the one to build my temple. Your son will build my temple.'

[20]"So the Lord has kept his promises. I am the king now in place of my father David. I rule the people of Israel as the Lord promised. And I have built the Temple for the Lord, the God of Israel. [21]I have made a place in the Temple for the Holy Box. Inside that Holy Box is the agreement that the Lord made with our ancestors when he brought them out of Egypt."

---

[b]8:10 cloud The special sign that showed God was with his people.
[c]8:12 The Lord ... dark cloud This is from the ancient Greek version, which places verses 12–13 after verse 53. In verse 12 the standard Hebrew text has only "The Lord said he would live in darkness."
[d]8:16 And I ... honored This is from the ancient Greek version. It is found in the standard Hebrew text of 2 Chron. 6:5–6, but not here.

[a]8:2 the special festival That is, the Festival of Shelters. See "Festival of Shelters" in the Word List.

22Then Solomon stood in front of whole assembly of Israel and faced the LORD's altar.* Solomon spread his hands and looked toward heaven 23and said,

"LORD, God of Israel, there is no other god like you in heaven or on the earth. You keep the agreement that you made with your people. You are kind and loyal to those who follow you with all their heart. 24You made a promise to your servant, my father David, and you kept that promise. You made that promise with your own mouth, and with your own hands you made it come true today. 25Now, LORD, God of Israel, keep the other promises you made to your servant David, my father. You said, 'David, if your sons carefully obey me as you did, you will always have someone from your family ruling the people of Israel.' 26Again, LORD, God of Israel, I ask you to keep the promise you made to your servant, my father David.

27"But, God, will you really live here with us on the earth? The whole sky and the highest heaven cannot contain you. Certainly this Temple that I built cannot contain you either. 28But please listen to my prayer and my request. I am your servant, and you are the LORD my God. Hear this prayer that I am praying to you today. 29In the past you said, 'I will be honored there.' So please watch over this Temple, night and day. And please listen to my prayer as I turn toward this Temple and pray to you. 30And LORD, please listen to our prayers in the future when I and your people Israel turn to this place and pray to you. We know that you live in heaven. We ask you to hear our prayer there and forgive us.

31"Those who wrong others will be brought to this altar. If they are not guilty, they will make an oath* and promise that they are innocent. 32Please listen from heaven and judge them. If they are guilty, please show us that they are guilty. And if they are innocent, please show us that they are not guilty.

33"Sometimes your people Israel will sin against you, and their enemies will defeat them. Then the people will come back to you and praise you. They will pray to you in this Temple. 34Please listen in heaven, please listen to the prayers of your people Israel. Forgive them for their sins and let them have their land again. You gave this land to their ancestors.

35"Sometimes they will sin against you, and you will stop the rain from falling on their land. Then they will pray toward this place and praise your name. You make them suffer, and they will be sorry for their sins. 36So please listen in heaven to their prayer. Then forgive us for our sins. Teach the people to live right. Then, LORD, please send rain to the land you gave them.

37"The land might become very dry and no food will grow on it. Or maybe a great sickness will spread among the people. Maybe all the food that is growing will be destroyed by insects. Or your people might be attacked in some of their cities by their enemies. Or many of your people might get sick. 38When any of these things happen, and people feel compelled in their hearts to spread their hands in prayer toward this Temple, 39please listen to their prayer. Listen while you are in your home in heaven and forgive them and help them. Only you know what people are really thinking, so only you can judge then fairly. 40Do this so that your people will fear and respect you all the time that they live in this land that you gave to our ancestors.

41-42"People from other places will hear about your greatness and your power. They will come from far away to pray at this Temple. 43From your home in heaven please listen to their prayers. Please do everything the people from other places ask you. Then they will fear and respect you the same as your people in Israel. Then all people everywhere will know that I built this Temple to honor you.

44"Sometimes you will command your people to go and fight against their enemies. Then your people will turn toward the city that you have chosen and the Temple that I built in your honor, and they will pray to you. 45Listen to their prayers from your home in heaven, and help them.

46"Your people will sin against you. I know this because everyone sins. And you will be angry with your people. You will let their enemies defeat them. Their enemies will make them prisoners and carry them to some faraway land. 47In that faraway land, your people will think about what happened. They will be sorry for their sins, and they will pray to you. They will say, 'We have sinned and done wrong.' 48They will be in that faraway land of their enemies, but they will turn back to you. They will feel sorry for their sins with their whole heart and soul. They will turn toward the land you gave their ancestors.* They will look toward the city you chose and toward the Temple I built, and they will pray to you. 49Please listen to their prayers from your home in heaven, and do what is right. 50Forgive your sinful people for all the things they have done against you. Make their enemies be kind to them. 51Remember that they are your people and that you brought them out of Egypt. It was as if you saved them by pulling them out of a hot oven!

52"LORD God, please listen to my prayers and to the prayers of your people Israel. Listen to their prayers any time that they ask you for help. 53You have chosen them from all the peoples of the earth to be your own special people. LORD, you promised to do that for us. You used your servant Moses to make that promise when you brought our ancestors out of Egypt."

54Solomon prayed that prayer to God. He was on his knees in front of the altar. He prayed with his arms raised toward heaven. When he finished praying, he stood up. [55]Then, in a loud voice, he asked God to bless all the people of Israel. Solomon said,

[56]"Praise the LORD! He promised to give rest to his people, Israel. And he has given us rest! He used his servant Moses and made many good promises to the people of Israel. And he has kept every one of them! [57]I pray that the LORD our God will be with us, as he was with our ancestors. I pray that he will never leave us. [58]I pray that we will turn to him and follow him. Then we will obey all the laws, decisions, and commands that he gave our ancestors. [59]I pray that the LORD our God will always remember this prayer and what I have asked. I pray that he will do these things for his servant, the king, and for his people, Israel. I pray that he will do this every day. [60]If he will do these things, all the people of the world will know that the LORD is the only true God. [61]You people must be loyal and true to the LORD our God. You must always follow and obey all of his laws and commands. You must continue to obey in the future as you do now."

[62]Then King Solomon and all the Israelites with him offered sacrifices to the LORD. [63]Solomon killed 22,000 cattle and 120,000 sheep for fellowship offerings.* In this way the king and the people showed that they had dedicated* the Temple to the LORD.

[64]King Solomon also dedicated the yard in front of the Temple. He offered burnt offerings,* grain offerings, and the fat from the animals that were used as fellowship offerings. King Solomon made these offerings there in the yard. He did this because the bronze altar in front of the LORD was too small to hold them all.

[65]So there at the Temple, King Solomon and all the people of Israel celebrated the festival.[a] People came from as far away as Hamath Pass in the north and the border of Egypt in the south. This huge crowd of people ate, drank, and enjoyed themselves together with the LORD for seven days. Then they stayed for another seven days. They celebrated for a total of 14 days.[b] [66]The next day Solomon told the people to go home. All the people thanked the king, said goodbye, and went home. They were happy because of all the good things that the LORD had done for David his servant and for his people Israel.

God Comes to Solomon Again

9 [1]So Solomon finished building the LORD's Temple and his own palace. Solomon built everything that he wanted to build. [2]Then the LORD appeared to Solomon again, just as he did at Gibeon. [3]The LORD said to him, "I heard your prayer and what you asked me to do. You built this Temple, and I have made it a holy place. So I will be honored there forever. I will watch over it and think of it always. [4]You must serve me with a pure and honest heart, just as your father David did. You must obey my laws and do everything that I commanded you. [5]If you do, I will make sure that your family will always rule Israel, just as I promised your father David when I told him that Israel would always be ruled by one of his descendants.

[6-7]"But if you or your children stop following me, and don't obey the laws and commands that I have given you, and if you serve and worship other gods, I will force Israel to leave the land that I have given to them. Israel will be an example to other people. Other people will make jokes about Israel. I made the Temple holy. It is the place where people honor me. But I will tear it down. [8]This Temple will be destroyed. Everyone who sees it will be amazed. They will ask, 'Why did the LORD do this terrible thing to this land and to this temple?' [9]People will say, 'This happened because they left the LORD their God. He brought their ancestors out of Egypt, but they decided to follow other gods. They began to worship and serve those gods. That is why the LORD caused all these bad things to happen to them.'"

[10]It took 20 years for King Solomon to build the LORD's Temple and the king's palace. [11]Hiram supplied Solomon with all the cedar, pine and gold that he wanted, so Solomon gave him 20 cities in Galilee. [12]So Hiram traveled from Tyre to see the cities that Solomon had given him. But Hiram was not pleased when he saw them. [13]King Hiram said, "What are these towns that you have given me, my brother?" King Hiram named that land the Land of Cabul.[c] And that area is still called Cabul today. [14]Hiram had sent King Solomon about 9000 pounds[d] of gold to use in building the Temple.

[15]King Solomon forced slaves to work for him to build the Temple and his palace. Then he used these slaves to build many other things. He built the Millo* and the city wall around Jerusalem. Then he rebuilt the cities of Hazor, Megiddo, and Gezer.

[16]In the past the king of Egypt had fought against the city of Gezer and burned it. He killed the Canaanites who lived there. When Solomon married Pharaoh's daughter, Pharaoh gave him that city as a wedding present. [17]Solomon rebuilt Gezer and the city of Lower Beth Horon. [18]He also built the cities of Baalath and Tamar in the Judean desert. [19]He also built cities where he could store grain, and he built places for his chariots* and his horses.

---

[a]8:65 *festival* The Festival of Shelters. See verse 2.
[b]8:65 *Then … 14 days* This is not in the ancient Greek version.

[c]9:13 *Cabul* This name is like the Hebrew word meaning "worthless."
[d]9:14 *9000 pounds* Literally, "120 talents" (4140 kg).

King Solomon also built whatever he wanted in Jerusalem, Lebanon, and all the places he ruled.

²⁰There were people left in the land who were not Israelites. There were Amorites, Hittites, Perizzites, Hivites, and Jebusites. ²¹The Israelites had not been able to destroy them, but Solomon forced them to work for him as slaves. They are still slaves today. ²²Solomon did not force any Israelites to be his slaves. The Israelites were soldiers, government officials, officers, captains, and chariot commanders and drivers. ²³There were 550 supervisors over Solomon's projects. They supervised the men who did the work.

²⁴Pharaoh's daughter moved from the City of David* to the palace that Solomon had built for her. Then he built the Millo.

²⁵Three times each year Solomon offered burned sacrifices and fellowship offerings* on the altar* that he built for the LORD. King Solomon also burned incense before the LORD and supplied what was needed for the Temple.

²⁶King Solomon also built ships at Ezion Geber. This town is near Elath on the shore of the Red Sea, in the land of Edom. ²⁷King Hiram had some skilled sailors who knew the sea well. He sent them to serve in Solomon's navy and work with Solomon's men. ²⁸Solomon's ships went to Ophir and brought back about 16 tons*ᵃ* of gold for him.

The Queen of Sheba Visits Solomon

10 ¹The queen of Sheba heard about Solomon, so she came to test him with hard questions. ²She traveled to Jerusalem with a very large group of servants. There were many camels carrying spices, jewels, and a lot of gold. She met Solomon and asked him all the questions that she could think of. ³Solomon answered all the questions. None of her questions was too hard for him to explain. ⁴The queen of Sheba saw that Solomon was very wise. She also saw the beautiful palace he had built. ⁵She saw the food at the king's table. She saw his officials meeting together. She saw the servants in the palace and the good clothes they wore. She saw his parties and the sacrifices that he offered in the Temple. She was so amazed that it took her breath away.

⁶Then she said to King Solomon, "The stories I heard in my country about your great works and your wisdom are true. ⁷I did not believe it until I came and saw it with my own eyes. Now I see that it is even greater than what I heard. Your wealth and wisdom are much greater than people told me. ⁸Your wives*ᵇ* and officers are very fortunate, because they serve you and hear your wisdom every day. ⁹Praise the LORD your God! He was

pleased to make you king of Israel. Because of the LORD's unending love for Israel, he has made you king to rule with justice and fairness."

¹⁰Then the Queen of Sheba gave King Solomon 4½ tons*ᶜ* of gold, a great many spices, and valuable stones. She gave him more spices than anyone has ever brought into Israel.

¹¹Hiram's ships brought gold from Ophir. They also brought jewels and a special kind of wood.*ᵈ* ¹²Solomon used this special wood to build supports in the Temple and the palace as well as harps and lyres* for the singers. That was the last time such a large shipment of that kind of wood was brought to Israel. There hasn't been any seen around here since then.*ᵉ*

¹³King Solomon gave the Queen of Sheba everything she asked for. He gave her more than she brought to give him. Then the Queen of Sheba and her servants left and went back to their own country.

Solomon's Great Wealth

¹⁴Every year King Solomon received almost 25 tons*ᶠ* of gold. ¹⁵In addition to the gold brought in by the traveling merchants* and traders, all the kings of Arabia and the governors of the land also brought gold and silver to Solomon.

¹⁶King Solomon made 200 large shields of hammered gold. Each shield contained about 15 pounds*ᵍ* of gold. ¹⁷He also made 300 smaller shields of hammered gold. Each shield contained about 4 pounds*ʰ* of gold. The king put them in the building called the "Forest of Lebanon."

¹⁸King Solomon also built a large throne with ivory decorations. It was covered with pure gold. ¹⁹There were six steps leading up to the throne. The back of the throne was round at the top. There were armrests on both sides of the throne, and there were lions in the sides of the throne under the armrests. ²⁰There were also two lions on each of the six steps, one at each end. There was nothing like it in any other kingdom.

²¹All of Solomon's cups and glasses were made of gold, and all the dishes*ⁱ* in the building called the Forest of Lebanon were made from pure gold. Nothing in the palace was made from silver. There was so much gold

---

*ᶜ***10:10** *4 1/2 tons* Literally, "120 talents" (4140 kg).
*ᵈ***10:11** *special ... wood* Literally, "almug." No one knows exactly what kind of wood this was, but it might have been sandalwood.
*ᵉ***10:12** *since then* Literally, "to this day," that is, when the book of Kings was written.
*ᶠ***10:14** *almost 25 tons* Literally, "666 talents" (22,977 kg).
*ᵍ***10:16** *15 pounds* Hebrew, "600 ₗshekelsⱼ" (6.9 kg). Also in verse 29.
*ʰ***10:17** *4 pounds* Literally, "3 minas" (1.7 kg).
*ⁱ***10:21** *dishes* The Hebrew word can mean "dishes," "tools," or "weapons."

---

*ᵃ***9:28** *16 tons* Literally, "420 talents" (14,490 kg).
*ᵇ***10:8** *wives* This is from the ancient Greek version. The Hebrew text has "men."

that in Solomon's time people did not think silver was important.

22The king also had many cargo ships*a* that he sent out to trade things with other countries. These were Hiram's ships. Every three years the ships would come back with a new load of gold, silver, ivory, and apes and baboons.

23King Solomon became greater in riches and wisdom than any other king on earth. 24People everywhere wanted to see King Solomon and listen to the great wisdom that God had given him. 25Every year people came to see the king and brought gifts made from gold and silver, clothes, weapons, spices, horses, and mules.

26Solomon had a great number of chariots* and horses. He had 1400 chariots and 12,000 horse soldiers. He built special cities for these chariots. So the chariots were kept in these cities. King Solomon also kept some of the chariots with him in Jerusalem. 27The king made Israel very rich. In the city of Jerusalem, silver was as common as rocks and cedar wood was as common as the many fig trees growing on the hills. 28Solomon brought horses from Egypt and Kue. His traders bought them in Kue and brought them to Israel. 29A chariot from Egypt cost about 15 pounds of silver, and a horse cost almost 4 pounds*b* of silver. Solomon sold horses and chariots to the kings of the Hittites and the Arameans.

Solomon and His Many Wives

11 1King Solomon loved many foreign women, including the daughter of Pharaoh and women from Moab, Ammon, Edom, Sidon, and the Hittites. 2In the past the LORD had said to the Israelites, "You must not marry people from other nations. If you do, they will cause you to follow their gods." But Solomon fell in love with these women. 3He had 700 wives who were the daughters of leaders from other nations. He also had 300 slave women who were like wives to him. His wives caused him to turn away from God. 4When Solomon was old, his wives caused him to follow other gods, so he did not follow the LORD completely as his father David did. 5Solomon worshiped Ashtoreth,* the goddess of Sidon, and Milcom,* the horrible god of the Ammonites. 6So Solomon did what the LORD said was wrong. He did not follow the LORD completely as his father David did.

7On the mountain next to Jerusalem, Solomon built a place for worshiping Chemosh, that horrible idol* of the Moabites. On the same mountain, Solomon built a place for worshiping Molech, that horrible idol of the Ammonites. 8Solomon did the same thing for all of his other foreign wives who burned incense* and gave sacrifices to their gods.

9So Solomon did not remain faithful to the LORD, the God of Israel, even though God had appeared to him twice. The LORD became angry with him. 10He had told Solomon that he must not follow other gods, but Solomon did not obey the LORD's command. 11So the LORD said to Solomon, "You have chosen to break your agreement with me. You have not obeyed my commands. So I promise that I will tear your kingdom away from you and give it to one of your servants. 12But I loved your father David, so I will not take your kingdom away from you while you are alive. I will wait until your son becomes king. Then I will take it from him. 13Still, I will not tear away all the kingdom from your son. I will leave him one tribe to rule. I will do this for my servant David and for Jerusalem, the city I chose."

Solomon's Enemies

14Then the LORD raised up Hadad the Edomite to become Solomon's enemy. Hadad was from the royal family of Edom. 15This is how it happened. In the past David fought against Edom. Joab was the commander of David's army. Joab went to Edom to bury his dead soldiers. While there Joab killed all the Edomite men who were still alive. 16Joab and the men of Israel stayed in Edom for six months until they killed all the men of Edom. 17At the time Hadad was only a young boy. He and some of his father's servants ran away to Egypt. 18They left Midian and went to Paran. In Paran some other people joined them and the whole group went to Egypt. They went to Pharaoh, the king of Egypt, and asked for help. Pharaoh gave Hadad a house, some land, and food to eat.

19Pharaoh liked Hadad so much that he gave Hadad a wife. She was Pharaoh's sister-in-law. (Pharaoh's wife was Queen Tahpenes.) 20Hadad and the sister of Tahpenes had a son named Genubath. Queen Tahpenes let Genubath grow up in Pharaoh's house with his children.

21In Egypt Hadad heard that David had died and that Joab, the commander of the army, was dead. So Hadad said to Pharaoh, "Let me go home to my own country."

22But Pharaoh answered, "I have given you everything you need here. Why do you want to go back to your own country?"

Hadad answered, "Please, just let me go home."

23God also raised up another man to become one of Solomon's enemies. This man was Rezon, son of Eliada. Rezon ran away from his master, King Hadadezer of Zobah. 24After David defeated the army of Zobah, Rezon gathered some men and became the leader of a small army. He went to Damascus and stayed there to rule from Damascus. 25Rezon became the king of Aram. He was an enemy of Israel throughout Solomon's life and

---

*a***10:22** *cargo ships* Literally, "ships of Tarshish."
*b***10:29** *almost 4 pounds* Literally, "150 shekels" (1.725 kg).

added to the trouble that Hadad created for Israel.

²⁶There was also another person who became an enemy of Solomon. He was Jeroboam son of Nebat. He was an Ephraimite from the town of Zeredah. His mother was a widow named Zeruah. He was one of Solomon's servants, but he rebelled against the king.

²⁷This is the story about how Jeroboam turned against the king. Solomon was building the Millo* and repairing the wall around the city of David, his father. ²⁸Jeroboam was a free man.ᵃ Solomon saw that this young man was a skilled worker, so he made him the supervisor over all the workers from the tribes that descended from Joseph. ²⁹One day as Jeroboam was leaving Jerusalem, the prophet Ahijah from Shiloh met him on the road. They were alone out in the country, and Ahijah was wearing a new coat.

³⁰Ahijah took his new coat and tore it into twelve pieces. ³¹Then he said to Jeroboam, "Take ten pieces of this coat for yourself because the Lord, the God of Israel, says: 'I will tear the kingdom away from Solomon, and I will give you ten of the tribes. ³²I will let David's family keep only one tribe. I will do this because of my servant David and because of Jerusalem, the city that I chose from among all the tribes of Israel. ³³I will take the kingdom from Solomon because he stopped following me and began worshiping Ashtoreth, the goddess of Sidon; Chemosh, the god of Moab; and Milcom, the god of the Ammonites. Solomon stopped following my ways and doing what I say is right. He does not obey my laws and commands as his father David did. ³⁴So I will take the kingdom away from Solomon's family. I chose David because he obeyed all my laws and commands. So for my servant David, I will let Solomon be the king for the rest of his life. ³⁵But Jeroboam, I will take the ten tribes away from his son and give them to you. ³⁶I will let Solomon's son keep one tribe to rule over. I will do this for my servant David, so he will always have someone to rule near me in Jerusalem, the city that I chose to be my own. ³⁷But I will make you king of Israel.ᵇ You will rule over everything you want. ³⁸If you live right and obey all my commands as David did, I will be with you and make your family a family of kings, just as I did for David. And you will have Israel as your kingdom. ³⁹I will punish David's descendants because of what Solomon did, but not forever.'"

Solomon's Death

⁴⁰Solomon tried to kill Jeroboam, but Jeroboam ran away to Egypt. He went to King Shishak of Egypt and stayed there until Solomon died.

⁴¹Everything else Solomon did, from the beginning to the end, is written in the book, *The History of Solomon*. ⁴²Solomon ruled in Jerusalem over all Israel for 40 years. ⁴³Then he diedᶜ and was buried in the city of David, his father. Then Solomon's son, Rehoboam, became the next king after him.

Civil War

12 ¹⁻³Jeroboam son of Nebat was still in Egypt where he had run away from Solomon. When he heard about Solomon's death, he returned to his city, Zeredah, in the hills of Ephraim.ᵈ

Rehoboam and all the Israelites went to Shechem to make him the king. The people said to Rehoboam, ⁴"Your father forced us to work very hard. Now, make it easier for us. Stop the heavy work that your father forced us to do and we will serve you."

⁵Rehoboam answered, "Come back to me in three days, and I will answer you." So the people left.

⁶There were some older men who had helped Solomon make decisions when he was alive. So King Rehoboam asked these men what he should do. He said, "How do you think I should answer the people?"

⁷They answered, "If you are like a servant to them today, they will sincerely serve you. If you speak kindly to them, they will always work for you."

⁸But Rehoboam did not listen to the advice from the older men. He asked the young men who were his friends. ⁹Rehoboam asked them, "The people said, 'Give us easier work than your father gave us.' How do you think I should answer them? What should I tell them?"

¹⁰Then the young men who grew up with him answered, "Those people came to you and said, 'Your father forced us to work very hard. Now make our work easier.' So you should tell them, 'My little finger is stronger than my father's whole body. ¹¹My father forced you to work hard, but I will make you work much harder! My father punished you with whips, but I will punish you with whips that have sharp metal tips.'"

¹²Three days later, Jeroboam and all the people came back as Rehoboam had said. ¹³King Rehoboam did not listen to the advice from the older men, and he was rude to the people. ¹⁴He did what his friends told him to do and said, "My father forced you to work hard, but I will make you work much harder! My father punished you with whips, but I will punish you with whips that have sharp metal tips." ¹⁵So the king did not do what the

---

ᵃ**11:28** *free man* Or "a nobleman," someone who could be called to war to protect his people.
ᵇ**11:37** *Israel* That is, the northern ten tribes.
ᶜ**11:43** *died* Literally, "slept with his ancestors."
ᵈ**12:1–3** *to his city ... Ephraim* This is from the ancient Greek version.

people wanted. The LORD caused this to happen. He did this in order to keep the promise he made to Jeroboam son of Nebat when he sent the prophet Ahijah from Shiloh to speak to him.

16The Israelites saw that the new king refused to listen to them, so they said to him, "We are not part of David's family are we? We don't get any of Jesse's land, do we? So, people of Israel, let's go home and let David's son rule his own people!" So the Israelites went home. 17But Rehoboam still ruled over the Israelites who lived in the cities of Judah.

18A man named Adoniram was one of the men who directed the workers. King Rehoboam sent Adoniram to talk to the people, but the Israelites threw stones at him until he died. King Rehoboam ran to his chariot* and escaped to Jerusalem. 19So Israel rebelled against the family of David, and this is how things are even today.

20When all the Israelites heard that Jeroboam had come back, they called him to a meeting and made him king over all Israel. The tribe of Judah was the only tribe that continued to follow the family of David.

21Rehoboam went back to Jerusalem and gathered together an army of 180,000 men from the families of Judah and the tribe of Benjamin. Rehoboam wanted to go fight against the Israelites and take back his kingdom. 22But the LORD spoke to a man of God* named Shemaiah. He said, 23"Talk to Rehoboam, the son of Solomon, king of Judah, and to men of Judah and Benjamin. 24Say to them, 'The LORD says that you must not go to war against your brothers. Everyone, go home! I made all this happen.'" So all the men in Rehoboam's army obeyed the LORD and went home.

25Jeroboam rebuilt the city of Shechem, in the hill country of Ephraim, and lived there. Later he went to the city of Penuel*a* and rebuilt it.

26-27Jeroboam said to himself, "If the people keep going to Jerusalem to offer sacrifices at the LORD's Temple, someday they will want to be ruled by their old masters. They will want to be ruled by King Rehoboam of Judah. And then they will kill me." 28So the king asked his advisors what to do. They gave him their advice, and King Jeroboam made two golden calves. He said to the people, "You don't have to go to Jerusalem to worship anymore. Israel, these are the gods that brought you out of Egypt."*b* 29King Jeroboam put one golden calf in Bethel and the other one in the city of Dan.*c* 30What a terrible sin this was, because

the Israelites started going to the cities of Dan and Bethel*d* to worship the calves.

31Jeroboam also built temples at the high places* and chose priests from among the different tribes of Israel. (He did not choose priests only from the tribe of Levi.) 32Then King Jeroboam started a new festival that was like the festival*e* in Judah, but it was on the 15th day of the eighth month. At this time the king offered sacrifices on the altar at Bethel. He and the priests he chose offered the sacrifices to the calves that he had set up at the high places he had made. 33So King Jeroboam chose his own time for a festival for the Israelites, the 15th day of the eighth month. And during that time he offered sacrifices and burned incense* on the altar he had built at Bethel.

God Speaks Against Bethel

13 1The LORD commanded a man of God* from Judah to go to the city of Bethel. King Jeroboam was standing at the altar offering incense when the man of God arrived. 2The LORD had commanded the man of God to speak against the altar. He said,

"Altar, the LORD says to you: 'David's family will have a son. His name will be Josiah. The priests of the high places are now burning incense on you, but Josiah will offer the priests on you and burn human bones on you, so you can never be used again!'"

3The man of God gave proof to the people that this would happen. He said, "This is the proof that the LORD told me about. He said, 'This altar will break apart, and the ashes on it will fall onto the ground.'"

4When King Jeroboam heard the message from the man of God about the altar in Bethel, he took his hand off the altar and pointed at the man. He said, "Arrest that man!" But when the king said this, his arm became paralyzed. He could not move it. 5Then the altar broke into pieces, and all its ashes fell onto the ground. This proved that what the man of God had said came from God. 6Then King Jeroboam said to the man of God, "Please pray to the LORD your God for me. Ask him to heal my arm."

So the man of God prayed to the LORD, and the king's arm was healed, as it was before. 7Then the king said to the man of God, "Please come home with me. Come and eat with me. I will give you a gift."

8But the man of God said to the king, "I will not go home with you, even if you give me half of your kingdom! I will not eat or drink anything in this place. 9The LORD commanded me not to eat or drink anything here. He also commanded me not to go back the same way I came." 10So he took a different

---

*a*12:25 *Penuel* Or "Peniel."

*b*12:28 *Israel … out of Egypt* This is exactly the same thing that Aaron said at the time he made the golden calf in the desert. See Ex. 32:4.

*c*12:29 *Bethel, Dan* Bethel was a city in the southern part of Israel, near Judah. Dan was in the northern part of Israel.

*d*12:30 *and Bethel* This is from the ancient Greek version.

*e*12:32 *the festival* Probably the Festival of Shelters. See "Festival of Shelters" in the Word List.

road home. He did not go back the same way he came to Bethel.

¹¹There was an old prophet* living in Bethel. His sons came and told him what the man of God did in Bethel and what he said to King Jeroboam. ¹²The old prophet said, "Which way did he go when he left?" So the sons showed their father which road the man of God from Judah had taken. ¹³The old prophet told his sons to saddle his donkey. They put the saddle on the donkey, and the prophet left.

¹⁴The old prophet went after the man of God. He found him sitting under an oak tree and asked him, "Are you the man of God who just came from Judah?"

The man of God answered, "Yes, I am."

¹⁵So the old prophet said, "Please come home and eat with me."

¹⁶But the man of God said, "I cannot go home with you. I cannot eat or drink anything in this place. ¹⁷The LORD said to me, 'You must not eat or drink anything in that place, and you must go back on a different road.'"

¹⁸The old prophet lied to him and said, "But I am a prophet like you. And an angel from the LORD came to me and told me to bring you home and give you something to eat and drink."

¹⁹So the man of God went to the old prophet's house and ate and drank with him. ²⁰While they were sitting at the table, the LORD spoke to the old prophet, ²¹and the old prophet spoke to the man of God from Judah. He said, "The LORD said that you did not obey him! You did not do what he commanded. ²²The LORD commanded you not to eat or drink anything in this place, but you came back here and ate and drank. So your body will not be buried in your family grave."

²³The man of God finished eating and drinking. Then the old prophet saddled the man's donkey for him and the man left. ²⁴On the way home, a lion attacked and killed the man of God. His body was lying on the road while the lion stood next to it. The donkey stood nearby. ²⁵Some people came walking by and saw the body and the lion standing by it. They went into the city where the old prophet lived and told people what they had seen on the road.

²⁶The old prophet heard the story and said, "This is the man of God who did not obey the LORD's command, so the LORD sent a lion to kill him, just as he said he would." ²⁷Then the prophet told his sons to saddle his donkey, and they did so. ²⁸The old prophet went to find the body lying on the road. The donkey and the lion were still standing near it. The lion had not eaten the body or hurt the donkey.

²⁹The old prophet put the body on his donkey and carried it back to the city to cry for him and bury him. ³⁰The old prophet buried the man in his own family grave. The old prophet cried for him and said, "Oh, my brother, I am

sorry for you." ³¹So the old prophet buried the body. Then he said to his sons, "When I die, bury me in this same grave. Put my bones next to his. ³²What the LORD spoke through him will certainly come true. The LORD used him to speak against the altar at Bethel and against the high places* in the other towns in Samaria."

³³King Jeroboam did not change. He continued doing evil. He continued to choose people from different tribes to serve as priestsᵃ at the high places. Whoever wanted to be a priest was allowed to be one. ³⁴This is the sin that caused the ruin and destruction of his kingdom.

Jeroboam's Son Dies

14 ¹At that time Jeroboam's son Abijah became very sick. ²Jeroboam said to his wife, "Go to Shiloh and see the prophet Ahijah. He is the one who said that I would become king of Israel. Dress yourself so that people will not know that you are my wife. ³Give the prophet ten loaves of bread, some cakes, and a jar of honey. Then ask him what will happen to our son, and he will tell you."

⁴So the king's wife did what he said. She went to the home of Ahijah the prophet in Shiloh. Ahijah was very old and had become blind. ⁵But the LORD said to him, "Jeroboam's wife is coming to ask you about her son. He is sick." Then the LORD told Ahijah what he should say.

Jeroboam's wife came to Ahijah's house. She was trying not to let people know who she was. ⁶Ahijah heard her coming to the door. So he said, "Come in, Jeroboam's wife. Why are you trying to make people think you are someone else? I have some bad news for you. ⁷Go back and tell Jeroboam that this is what the LORD, the God of Israel, says: 'Jeroboam, I chose you from among all the Israelites. I made you the ruler of my people. ⁸David's family was ruling the kingdom of Israel, but I took the kingdom away from them and gave it to you. But you are not like my servant David. He always obeyed my commands and followed me with his whole heart. He did only what I accepted. ⁹But you have sinned worse than anyone who ruled before you. You stopped following me and made other gods for yourself. You made those statues to make me angry. ¹⁰So Jeroboam, I will bring troubles to your family. I will kill all the men in your family. I will destroy your family completely, like fire burning up dung. ¹¹Anyone from your family who dies in the city will be eaten by dogs. And anyone from your family who dies in the fields will be eaten by birds. The LORD has spoken.'"

¹²Then Ahijah said, "Now, go home. Your son will die as soon as your enter the city.

ᵃ**13:33** *people … priests* The Law taught that only people from the tribe of Levi could become priests.

¹³All Israel will cry for him. They will bury him, but he is the only one from Jeroboam's family who will be buried. This is because he is the only one in Jeroboam's family who pleased the Lord, the God of Israel. ¹⁴Soon, the Lord will put a new king over Israel who will destroy Jeroboam's family. ¹⁵Then the Lord will punish Israel. The Israelites will be so full of fear that they will shake like tall grass in the water. He will pull Israel up from this good land that he gave their ancestors. He will scatter them to the other side of the Euphrates River. The Lord will do this because the people made him angry when they built sacred poles.ᵃ ¹⁶Jeroboam sinned, and then he made the Israelites sin. So the Lord will let the Israelites be defeated."

¹⁷Jeroboam's wife went back to Tirzah. As soon as she stepped into the house, the boy died. ¹⁸All the people of Israel buried him and cried for him. This happened just as the Lord said it would through his servant, the prophet Ahijah.

¹⁹The rest of what King Jeroboam did is written in the book, *The History of the Kings of Israel*. It includes the wars he fought and the way he ruled. ²⁰Jeroboam ruled as king for 22 years. Then he died and was buried with his ancestors.ᵇ His son Nadab became the new king after him.

Rehoboam, King of Judah

²¹Solomon's son, Rehoboam, was 41 years old when he became king of Judah. Rehoboam ruled 17 years in Jerusalem, the city the Lord chose for his own. He chose this city from all the other tribes of Israel. Rehoboam's mother was Naamah. She was an Ammonite.

²²The people of Judah also sinned and did what that the Lord said was wrong. They made the Lord angry. They were worse than their fathers who lived before them. ²³They built high places, memorial stones, and sacred poles.ᶜ They built them on every high hill and under every green tree. ²⁴There were also men who served other gods by selling their bodies for sex.ᵈ So the people of Judah were worse than the people who had lived in the land before them. And the Lord took the land away from those people to give it to the Israelites.

²⁵In the fifth year that Rehoboam was king, King Shishak of Egypt came to attack Jerusalem. ²⁶He took the treasures from the Lord's Temple and from the king's palace. He even

took the gold shields that David had taken from the officers of King Hadadezer of Aram and put on the walls of Jerusalem.ᵉ ²⁷King Rehoboam made more shields to put in their places, but they were made from bronze. He gave them to the guards on duty at the palace gates. ²⁸Every time the king went to the Lord's Temple, the guards took out the shields and went with him. After they were finished, they put the shields back on the wall in the guardroom.

²⁹The rest of what King Rehoboam did is written in the book, *The History of the Kings of Judah*. ³⁰Rehoboam and Jeroboam were always fighting against each other.

³¹Rehoboam diedᶠ and was buried with his ancestors in the City of David.* (His mother was Naamah. She was an Ammonite.) Rehoboam's son Abijah became the next king after him.

Abijah, King of Judah

15 ¹Abijah became the new king of Judah during the 18th year that Jeroboam son of Nebat ruled Israel. ²Abijah ruled in Jerusalem for three years. His mother's name was Maacah. She was Absalom's daughter.

³He did all the same sins that his father before him had done. Abijah was not faithful to the Lord his God. In this way he was not like his grandfather, David. ⁴But for David's sake, the Lord gave Abijah a kingdom in Jerusalem and allowed him to have a son. He also kept Jerusalem safe. ⁵David had always done what the Lord said was right. He had always obeyed his commands. The only time David did not obey him was when he sinned against Uriah the Hittite.

⁶Rehoboam and Jeroboam were always fighting against each other.ᵍ ⁷The rest of what Abijah did is written in the book, *The History of the Kings of Judah*.

There was war between Abijah and Jeroboam during the whole time that Abijah was king. ⁸When Abijah died, he was buried in the City of David.* Abijah's son Asa became the new king after him.

Asa, King of Judah

⁹During Jeroboam's 20th year as king over Israel, Asa became king of Judah. ¹⁰He ruled in Jerusalem for 41 years. His grandmother's name was Maacah, and she was the daughter of Absalom.

¹¹Asa did what the Lord said is right, as his ancestor* David did. ¹²During Asa's time there were men who served other gods by selling their bodies for sex. Asa forced them to leave the country. He took away the idols* that his ancestors had made. ¹³King Asa also

---

ᵃ**14:15 sacred poles** People used these things to worship false gods.

ᵇ**14:20 died … ancestors** Literally, "slept with his ancestors."

ᶜ**14:23 high places, memorial stones, and sacred poles** People used these things to worship false gods.

ᵈ**14:24 men … for sex** Sexual sins like this were a part of the way people worshiped the Canaanite gods.

ᵉ**14:26 He even took … Jerusalem** This is from the ancient Greek version. The standard Hebrew text has "He even took the gold shields that Solomon had made."

ᶠ**14:31 died** Literally, "slept with his ancestors."

ᵍ**15:6** This is not in the ancient Greek version.

took away the right of his mother Maacah to be queen mother. He did this because she had set up one of those awful poles to honor the goddess Asherah. Asa cut down that Asherah pole* and smashed it into small pieces and burned the pieces in the Kidron Valley. ¹⁴Asa did not destroy the high places,* even though he was faithful to the Lord all his life. ¹⁵Asa and his father had given some special gifts to God. Asa put these gifts of gold, silver, and other things into the Temple.

¹⁶The whole time that King Asa was king of Judah, he fought a war against King Baasha of Israel. ¹⁷Once Baasha attacked Judah and then built up the city of Ramah to keep Asa from leaving Judah on any kind of military campaign. ¹⁸So Asa took gold and silver from the treasuries of the Lord's Temple and the king's palace. He gave it to his officials and sent them to King Ben-Hadad of Aram. Ben-Hadad was the son of Tabrimmon. Tabrimmon was the son of Hezion. Damascus was Ben-Hadad's capital city. ¹⁹Asa sent this message: "My father and your father had a peace agreement. Now I want to make a peace agreement with you. I am sending you this gift of gold and silver. Please break your treaty with King Baasha of Israel and make him leave us alone."

²⁰King Ben-Hadad made the agreement with King Asa and sent his army to fight against the Israelite towns of Ijon, Dan, Abel Beth Maacah, the towns near Lake Galilee, and the area of Naphtali. ²¹When Baasha heard about these attacks, he stopped building up Ramah and went back to Tirzah. ²²Then King Asa gave an order to all the men in Judah. Everyone had to help. They had to go to Ramah and carry out all the stone and wood that Baasha was using to build up the city. They carried the material to Geba in Benjamin and to Mizpah and used it to strengthen those two cities.

²³All the other things about Asa—the great things he did and the cities he built—are written in the book, *The History of the Kings of Judah*. When Asa became old, his feet became infected. ²⁴He died and was buried in the City of David,* his ancestor. Then Asa's son Jehoshaphat became the new king after him.

Nadab, King of Israel

²⁵During Asa's second year as king of Judah, Jeroboam's son Nadab became king of Israel. Nadab ruled over Israel for two years. ²⁶He did what the Lord said was wrong. He sinned just as his father Jeroboam did when he caused the Israelites to sin.

²⁷Baasha was the son of Ahijah. They were from the tribe of Issachar. Baasha made a plan to kill King Nadab. Nadab and all Israel were fighting against the Philistine town of Gibbethon. And that is where Baasha killed Nadab. ²⁸This happened during Asa's third year as king of Judah. So Baasha became the next king of Israel.

Baasha, King of Israel

²⁹When Baasha became the new king, he killed everyone in Jeroboam's family. He left no one in Jeroboam's family alive. This happened just as the Lord said it would when he spoke through his servant Ahijah at Shiloh. ³⁰This happened because King Jeroboam had committed many sins and had caused the Israelites to sin. This made the Lord, the God of Israel, very angry.

³¹The other things that Nadab did are written in the book, *The History of the Kings of Israel*. ³²All during the time that Baasha ruled over Israel, he was fighting wars against King Asa of Judah.

³³Ahijah's son Baasha became king of Israel during the third year that Asa ruled over Judah. Baasha ruled in Tirzah for 24 years, ³⁴but he did what the Lord said was wrong. He did the same sins that Jeroboam had done that caused the Israelites to sin.

16 ¹Then the Lord spoke against King Baasha through the prophet, Jehu son of Hanani. He said, ²"I made you an important prince over my people Israel. But you have done the same things Jeroboam did. You have caused my people Israel to sin. Their sins have made me angry. ³So Baasha, I will destroy you and your family, just as I did Jeroboam son of Nebat and his family. ⁴Dogs will eat the bodies of those in your family who die in the city. And wild birds will eat the bodies of those who die out in the fields."

⁵The rest of the story about Baasha and the great things he did are written in the book, *The History of the Kings of Israel*. ⁶Baasha died and was buried in Tirzah. His son Elah became the new king after him.

⁷That book also has the story of the time the Lord gave the message to Jehu the prophet about Baasha and his family. Baasha did many things the Lord said were wrong, just as Jeroboam and his family had done. This and the fact that Baasha had killed everyone in Jeroboam's family made the Lord very angry.

Elah, King of Israel

⁸Elah son of Baasha became king during the 26th year that Asa was the king of Judah. He ruled in Tirzah for two years.

⁹Zimri was one of King Elah's officers. Zimri commanded half of Elah's chariots,* but Zimri plotted against Elah. King Elah was in Tirzah, drinking and getting drunk at Arza's home. Arza was the man in charge of the palace at Tirzah. ¹⁰Zimri went into the house and killed King Elah. Then Zimri became the new king of Israel after Elah. This was during the 27th year that Asa was king in Judah.

Zimri, King of Israel

¹¹After Zimri became the new king, he killed all of Baasha's family and friends. He did not let any male in Baasha's family live. ¹²So Zimri destroyed Baasha's family just as the

LORD said he would when he spoke against Baasha through the prophet Jehu. ¹³This happened because of all the sins of Baasha and his son, Elah. They sinned and they caused the Israelites to sin. They worshiped worthless idols,* and this made the LORD angry.

¹⁴The rest of what that Elah did is written in the book, *The History of the Kings of Israel*.

¹⁵Zimri became king of Israel during the 27th year that Asa was king of Judah. Zimri ruled in Tirzah only seven days. This is what happened: The army of Israel was at Gibbethon, which was under Philistine control. ¹⁶Omri was the commander of the army of Israel. The men in the camp heard that Zimri had made secret plans against the king and killed him. So in the camp all the soldiers made Omri the new king. ¹⁷Then Omri and all the soldiers of Israel left Gibbethon and went to Tirzah. They surrounded the city and attacked it. ¹⁸When Zimri saw the city had been captured, he ran to the palace fortress, but the soldiers burned it down with him still in it. ¹⁹So Zimri died because he sinned and did what the LORD said was wrong, just as Jeroboam did when he caused the Israelites to sin.

²⁰The story about Zimri's secret plans and the other things that he did are written in the book, *The History of the Kings of Israel*.

Omri, King of Israel

²¹Then the Israelites were divided. Half of the people followed Tibni the son of Ginath and wanted to make him king. The other half of the people followed Omri. ²²But Omri's followers were stronger than the followers of Tibni son of Ginath. Tibni died, and Omri became king.

²³Omri became king of Israel during Asa's 31st year as the king of Judah. Omri ruled over Israel for 12 years. Six of those years he ruled from Tirzah. ²⁴Then Omri bought the hill of Samaria from Shemer for about 150 pounds*ᵃ* of silver. Omri built a city on that hill. He named the city Samaria after the name of its owner, Shemer.

²⁵Omri did what the LORD said was wrong. He was worse than all the kings who were before him. ²⁶He committed all the sins that Jeroboam son of Nebat had committed when he caused the Israelites to sin. They worshiped worthless idols, and this made the LORD, the God of Israel, very angry.

²⁷The rest of the story about Omri and the great things he did are written in the book, *The History of the Kings of Israel*. ²⁸Omri died and was buried in Samaria. His son Ahab became the new king after him.

Ahab, King of Israel

²⁹Ahab son of Omri became king of Israel during the 38th year that Asa was king of Judah. Ahab ruled Israel from the town of Samaria for 22 years. ³⁰He did what the LORD said was wrong. Ahab was worse than all the kings who were before him. ³¹It was not enough for Ahab to commit the same sins that Jeroboam, son of Nebat, had done. Ahab also married Jezebel, daughter of King Ethbaal of Sidon. Then Ahab began to serve and worship Baal.* ³²He built a temple and an altar in Samaria for worshiping Baal. ³³He also set up a sacred pole.*ᵇ* Ahab did more to make the LORD, the God of Israel, angry than all the other kings who were before him.

³⁴During Ahab's time, Hiel from Bethel rebuilt the town of Jericho. When Hiel started work on the city, his oldest son Abiram died. And when Hiel built the gates of the city, his youngest son Segub died. This happened just as the LORD said it would happen when he spoke through Joshua son of Nun.*ᶜ*

Elijah and the Time Without Rain

17 ¹Elijah was a prophet from the town of Tishbe in Gilead. He said to King Ahab, "I serve the LORD, the God of Israel. By his power, I promise that no dew or rain will fall for the next few years. The rain will fall only when I command it to fall."

²Then the LORD said to Elijah, ³"Leave this place and go east. Hide near Kerith Ravine, east of the Jordan River. ⁴You can get your water from that stream, and I have commanded ravens to bring food to you there." ⁵So Elijah did what the LORD told him to do. He went to live near Kerith Ravine, east of the Jordan River. ⁶Ravens brought Elijah food every morning and every evening, and he drank water from the stream.

⁷There was no rain, so after a while the stream became dry. ⁸Then the LORD said to Elijah, ⁹"Go to Zarephath in Sidon and stay there. There is a widow there that I commanded to take care of you."

¹⁰So Elijah went to Zarephath. He went to the town gate and saw a woman there gathering wood for a fire. She was a widow. Elijah said to her, "Would you bring me a small cup of water to drink?" ¹¹As she was going to get the water, Elijah said, "Bring me a piece of bread too, please."

¹²The woman answered, "I promise you, before the LORD your God, that I have nothing but a handful of flour in a jar and a little bit of olive oil in a jug. I came here to gather a few pieces of wood for a fire to cook our last meal. My son and I will eat it and then die from hunger."

¹³Elijah said to the woman, "Don't worry. Go home and cook your food as you said. But first make a small piece of bread from the flour that you have and bring it to me. Then

ᵃ**16:24** *150 pounds* Literally, "2 talents" (69 kg).

ᵇ**16:33** *sacred pole* People used these to worship false gods.

ᶜ**16:34** *This happened ... Joshua son of Nun* See Josh. 6:26.

cook some for yourself and your son. ¹⁴The Lord, the God of Israel, says, 'That jar of flour will never be empty and the jug will always have oil in it. This will continue until the day the Lord sends rain to the land.'"

¹⁵So the woman went home and did what Elijah told her to do. And Elijah, the woman, and her son had enough food for a long time. ¹⁶The jar of flour and the jug of oil were never empty. This happened just as the Lord said through Elijah.

¹⁷Some time later the woman's son became sick. He became worse and worse until he stopped breathing. ¹⁸Then the woman said to Elijah, "You are a man of God.* Can you help me? Or did you come here only to remind me of my sins and to make my son die?"

¹⁹Elijah said to her, "Give me your son." He took the boy from her and carried him upstairs. He laid him on the bed in the room where he was staying. ²⁰Then Elijah prayed, "Lord my God, this widow is letting me stay in her house. Will you do this bad thing to her? Will you cause her son to die?" ²¹Then Elijah lay on top of the boy three times. He prayed, "Lord my God, let this boy live again!"

²²The Lord answered Elijah's prayer. The boy began breathing again and was alive. ²³Elijah carried the boy downstairs, gave him to his mother, and said, "Look, your son is alive!"

²⁴The woman answered, "Now I know that you really are a man from God. I know that the Lord really speaks through you!"

Elijah and the Prophets of Baal

18 ¹During the third year that no rain fell, the Lord said to Elijah, "Go meet with King Ahab, and I will make it rain." ²So Elijah went to meet with Ahab.

The famine was very bad in Samaria. ³So King Ahab told Obadiah to come to him. Obadiah was the man in charge of the king's palace. (Obadiah was a true follower of the Lord. ⁴One time when Jezebel was killing all the Lord's prophets, Obadiah hid 100 prophets in two caves. He put 50 prophets in one cave and 50 prophets in another cave. Then he brought them food and water.) ⁵King Ahab said to Obadiah, "Come with me. We will look at every spring and every stream in the land. We will see if we can find enough grass to keep our horses and mules alive. Then we will not have to kill our animals." ⁶They decided where each of them would go to look for water. Ahab went in one direction by himself, and Obadiah went in another direction by himself. ⁷As Obadiah was walking along the road by himself, he looked up, and there was Elijah. Obadiah recognized him and bowed down to show his respect. He said, "Elijah? Is it really you, master?"

⁸Elijah answered, "Yes, it is me. Now, go and tell your master, the king, that I am here."

⁹Obadiah said, "If I tell Ahab that I know where you are, he will kill me! I have done nothing wrong to you. Why do you want me to die? ¹⁰As surely as the Lord your God lives, the king has been looking for you everywhere. He has sent people to every country to find you. He even made the rulers of those countries swear that you were not there. ¹¹Now you want me to go and tell him that you are here! ¹²If I go tell King Ahab that you are here, the Lord might carry you away. Then when King Ahab comes here and cannot find you, he will kill me! I have followed the Lord since I was a boy. ¹³You heard what I did. When Jezebel was killing the Lord's prophets, I hid 100 of them in caves. I put 50 prophets in one cave and 50 prophets in another cave. I brought them food and water. ¹⁴Now you want me to go and tell the king that you are here. The king will kill me!"

¹⁵Elijah answered, "I serve the Lord All-Powerful. As surely as he lives, I promise that I will stand before the king today."

¹⁶So Obadiah went to King Ahab and told him where Elijah was. King Ahab went to meet Elijah.

¹⁷When Ahab saw Elijah he said, "Is that really you, the troublemaker of Israel?"

¹⁸Elijah answered, "I have not made trouble for Israel. You and your father's family caused all the problems when you stopped obeying the Lord's commands and began following the false gods. ¹⁹Now tell all the people of Israel to meet me at Mount Carmel. Also bring the 450 prophets of Baal* and the 400 prophets of the goddess Asherah* that Queen Jezebel supports."ᵃ

²⁰So Ahab called all the Israelites and those prophets to Mount Carmel. ²¹Elijah came to all the people and said, "You must decide what you are going to do. How long will you keep jumping from one side to the other? If the Lord is the true God, follow him. But if Baal is the true God, then follow him!"

The people said nothing. ²²So Elijah said, "I am the only prophet of the Lord here, but there are 450 prophets of Baal. ²³So bring us two bulls. Let the prophets of Baal have one bull. Let them kill it and cut it into pieces and then put the meat on the wood. But don't start the fire. I will do the same with the other bull, and I will not start the fire either. ²⁴Prophets of Baal, pray to your god, and I will pray to the Lord. Whichever god answers the prayer and starts the fire is the true God."

All the people agreed that this was a good idea.

²⁵Then Elijah said to the prophets of Baal, "There are many of you, so you go first. Choose a bull and prepare it, but don't start your fire."

ᵃ**18:19 Queen Jezebel ... supports** Literally, "Those prophets eat at Jezebel's table."

²⁶So the prophets took the bull that was given to them and prepared it. They started praying to Baal and prayed until noon. They said, "Baal, please answer us!" But there was no sound. No one answered. Then they began jumping around on the altar they had built.

²⁷At noon Elijah began to make fun of them. He said, "If Baal really is a god, maybe you should pray louder! Maybe he is busy. Maybe he is thinking about something, or maybe he stepped out for a moment! He could be sleeping! Maybe you should pray louder and wake him up!" ²⁸So the prophets prayed louder. They cut themselves with swords and spears. (This was the way they worshiped.) They cut themselves until they were bleeding all over. ²⁹The afternoon passed but the fire still had not started. The prophets were out of control and continued to act this way until the time came for the evening sacrifice. But nothing happened—there was no answer from Baal. There was no sound. There was no one listening.

³⁰Then Elijah said to all the people, "Now come here." So they gathered around Elijah. The LORD's altar* had been torn down, so Elijah repaired it. ³¹Elijah found twelve stones. There was one stone for each of the twelve tribes. These twelve tribes were named for the twelve sons of Jacob, the man who the LORD had named Israel. ³²Elijah used these stones to repair the altar to honor the LORD. He dug a small ditch around the altar. It was wide enough and deep enough to hold about 4 gallons*a* of water. ³³Then Elijah put the wood on the altar. He cut the bull into pieces and laid the pieces on the wood. ³⁴Then he said, "Fill four jars with water. Pour the water on the pieces of meat and on the wood." Then Elijah said, "Do it again." Then he said, "Do it a third time." ³⁵The water ran down off the altar and filled the ditch.

³⁶At about the time for the afternoon sacrifice, the prophet Elijah approached the altar and prayed, "LORD, the God of Abraham, Isaac, and Jacob, I ask you now to prove that you are the God of Israel and that I am your servant. Show these people that it was you who commanded me to do all these things. ³⁷LORD, answer my prayer. Show these people that you, LORD, are God and that you are the one who is bringing them back to you."

³⁸Then fire came down from the LORD and burned the sacrifice, the wood, the stones, and the ground around the altar. Then it dried up all the water in the ditch. ³⁹All the people saw this happen and bowed down to the ground and began saying, "The LORD is God! The LORD is God!"

⁴⁰Then Elijah said, "Get the prophets of Baal! Don't let any of them escape!" So the people captured all the prophets. Then Elijah led them down to Kishon Creek and killed them all.

The Rain Comes Again

⁴¹Then Elijah said to King Ahab, "Now go eat and drink. A heavy rain is coming." ⁴²So King Ahab went to eat. At the same time Elijah climbed to the top of Mount Carmel. At the top of the mountain Elijah bent down. He put his head between his knees. ⁴³Then Elijah said to his servant, "Go up higher and look toward the sea."

The servant went and looked. He came back and said, "I saw nothing." Elijah told him to go look again. This happened seven times. ⁴⁴The seventh time, the servant came back and said, "I saw a small cloud the size of a man's fist that was coming in from the sea."

Elijah told the servant, "Go tell King Ahab to get his chariot* ready and go home now. If he does not leave now, the rain will stop him."

⁴⁵After a short time the sky was covered with dark clouds. The wind began to blow, and a heavy rain began to fall. Ahab got in his chariot and started back to Jezreel. ⁴⁶The power of the LORD came to Elijah. He used his belt to hold up the bottom of his robe away from his feet. Then he ran ahead of King Ahab all the way to Jezreel.

Elijah at Mount Horeb (Sinai)

19 ¹King Ahab told Jezebel everything that Elijah did and how Elijah had killed all the prophets of Baal* with a sword. ²So Jezebel sent a messenger to Elijah and said, "I swear that by this time tomorrow, you will be just as dead as those prophets. If I don't succeed, may the gods do the same or worse to me."

³When Elijah heard this, he was afraid. So he ran away to save his life. He took his servant with him, and they went to Beersheba in Judah. Then Elijah left his servant in Beersheba ⁴and walked for a whole day into the desert. Then he sat down under a bush and asked to die. He said, "I have had enough, LORD! Take my life. I am no better than my ancestors.*"

⁵Then Elijah lay down under the bush and went to sleep. An angel came to him and touched him. The angel said, "Get up and eat!" ⁶Elijah looked around, and by his head there was a cake that had been baked over coals and a jar of water. He ate and drank and then went back to sleep.

⁷Later the LORD's angel came to him again, touched him, and said, "Get up and eat! If you don't, you will not be strong enough to make the long trip." ⁸So Elijah got up. He ate and drank and felt strong. Then Elijah walked for 40 days and nights to Mount Horeb, the mountain of God. ⁹There Elijah went into a cave and spent the night.

---

*a***18:32** *about 4 gallons* Literally, "2 *seahs* of seed" (14.6 l).

Then the LORD said to him, "Elijah, why are you here?"

¹⁰Elijah answered, "LORD God All-Powerful, I have always served you the best I can, but the Israelites have broken their agreement with you. They destroyed your altars* and killed your prophets. I am the only prophet left alive, and now they are trying to kill me!"

¹¹Then the LORD said to Elijah, "Go, stand in front of me on the mountain. I will pass by you."ᵃ Then a very strong wind blew. The wind caused the mountains to break apart. It broke large rocks in front of the LORD. But that wind was not the LORD. After that wind, there was an earthquake. But that earthquake was not the LORD. ¹²After the earthquake, there was a fire. But that fire was not the LORD. After the fire, there was a quiet, gentle voice.ᵇ

¹³When Elijah heard the voice, he used his coat to cover his face and went to the entrance to the cave and stood there. Then a voice said to him, "Elijah, why are you here?"

¹⁴Elijah said, "LORD God All-Powerful, I have always served you the best that I can, but the Israelites broke their agreement with you. They destroyed your altars and killed your prophets. I am the only prophet left alive, and now they are trying to kill me."

¹⁵The LORD said, "Go back. Take the road that leads to the desert around Damascus. Go into Damascus and anoint* Hazael as king over Aram. ¹⁶Then anoint Jehu son of Nimshi as king over Israel. Next, anoint Elisha son of Shaphat from Abel Meholah. He will be the prophet who takes your place. ¹⁷Jehu will kill anyone who escapes Hazael's sword, and Elisha will kill anyone who escapes from Jehu's sword. ¹⁸I still have 7000 people in Israel who have never bowed down to Baal or kissed that idol.*"

Elisha Becomes a Prophet

¹⁹So Elijah left that place and went to find Elisha son of Shaphat. Elisha was plowing 12 acres of land and was working on the last acre when Elijah came.ᶜ Elijah went to Elisha and put his coatᵈ on Elisha. ²⁰Elisha immediately left his oxen and ran after Elijah. Elisha said, "Let me kiss my mother and father goodbye. Then I will follow you."

Elijah answered, "You can do that. I will not stop you.ᵉ"

²¹Elisha turned away from him and went back. He killed the oxen and used the yoke* for firewood. He boiled the meat, gave it to the people, and they all ate together. Then Elisha went to follow Elijah and became his helper.

Ben-Hadad and Ahab Go to War

20 ¹King Ben-Hadad of Aram gathered his army together. There were 32 kings with him and many horses and chariots.* They surrounded Samaria and attacked it. ²The king sent messengers to King Ahab of Israel who was inside the city. ³The message was, "Ben-Hadad says, 'Your silver and your gold are mine, and so are the best of your wives and children.'"

⁴The king of Israel answered, "Yes, my lord and king, I am yours now, and everything I have belongs to you."

⁵Then the messengers came back to Ahab. They said, "Ben-Hadad says, 'I told you before that all of your silver and gold and your wives and children belong to me. So give them to me! ⁶Tomorrow I will send my men to search through your house and through the houses of your officials. Give my men all of your valuables, and they will bring them back to me.'"

⁷So King Ahab called a meeting of all the elders* of his country and said, "Look, Ben-Hadad is looking for trouble. First he told me that I must give him my wives and children and my silver and gold. I agreed to give them to him."

⁸But the elders and all the people said, "Don't obey him or do what he says."

⁹So Ahab sent a message to Ben-Hadad that said, "I will do what you said at first, but I cannot obey your second command."

King Ben-Hadad's men carried the message to the king. ¹⁰Then they came back with another message from Ben-Hadad that said, "I will completely destroy Samaria. I promise that there will be nothing left of that city! There will not be enough of that city left for my men to find any souvenirsᶠ to take home. May the gods destroy me if I don't do this!"

¹¹King Ahab answered, "Tell Ben-Hadad that the man who puts on his armor* should not boast as much as the man who lives long enough to take it off."

¹²King Ben-Hadad was drinking in his tent with the other rulers when the messengers came back and gave him the message from King Ahab. King Ben-Hadad commanded his men to prepare to attack the city, so the men moved into their places for the battle.

¹³Then a prophet went to King Ahab and said, "King Ahab, the LORD says to you, 'Do you see that great army? I, the LORD, will defeat that army for you today. Then you will know that I am the LORD.'"

ᵃ**19:11 Go, stand ... you** This is like the time God appeared to Moses. See Ex. 33:12–23.

ᵇ**19:12 voice** Or "sound."

ᶜ**19:19 Elisha was plowing ... came** Or "Elijah was plowing. There were 11 pair of oxen before him, and he was on the twelfth."

ᵈ**19:19 coat** A special robe that prophets wore. Elijah put his coat on Elisha to show that Elisha would take his place as a prophet.

ᵉ**19:20 I will not stop you** Literally, "What have I done to you?" or "What will I do to you?"

ᶠ**20:10 souvenirs** Things that help people remember places they have been. Literally, the Hebrew text has "handfuls of dust."

¹⁴Ahab said, "Who will you use to defeat them?"

The prophet answered, "The LORD says, 'The young men who carry the weapons for the government officials.'"

Then the king asked, "Who should command the main army?"

The prophet answered, "You will."

¹⁵So Ahab gathered the young helpers of the government officials. There were 232 of these young men. Then the king called together the army of Israel. The total number was 7000.

¹⁶King Ahab began his attack at noon, while King Ben-Hadad and the 32 kings were drinking and getting drunk in their tents. ¹⁷The young helpers went out first. King Ben-Hadad's men told him that some soldiers had come out of Samaria. ¹⁸So Ben-Hadad said, "They might be coming to fight or they might be coming to ask for peace. Capture them alive."

¹⁹The young men of King Ahab were the first to come out, but the rest of the army of Israel was following them. ²⁰Each of the men of Israel killed the man who had come against him. So the men from Aram began to run away and the army of Israel chased them. King Ben-Hadad escaped on a horse with the chariots. ²¹King Ahab led the army and attacked all the horses and chariots. So King Ahab made the Arameans suffer a great defeat.

²²Then the prophet went to King Ahab and said, "The king of Aram will come back to fight again next spring. So go back and strengthen your army and make careful plans to defend yourself against him."

Ben-Hadad Attacks Again

²³King Ben-Hadad's officers said to him, "The gods of Israel are mountain gods. We fought in a mountain area, so the Israelites won. If we fight them on level ground, we will win. ²⁴Also, don't let the 32 kings command the armies. Put your commanders in charge of the armies. ²⁵Let's gather an army like the one that was destroyed. Gather as many men, horses, and chariots* as before, and fight the Israelites on level ground. Then we will win." Ben-Hadad followed their advice and did what they said.

²⁶So in the spring, Ben-Hadad gathered the men of Aram and went to Aphek to fight against Israel.

²⁷The Israelites also prepared for war and went to fight the army of Aram. They made their camp opposite the camp of Aram. The Aramean soldiers filled the land, but Israel's army looked like two small flocks of goats.

²⁸A man of God* came to the king of Israel with this message: "The LORD said, 'The people of Aram said that I, the LORD, am a god of the mountains and not a god of the valleys. So I will let you defeat this great army. Then all of you will know that I am the LORD, wherever you are!'"

²⁹The armies were camped across from each other for seven days. On the seventh day the battle began. The Israelites killed 100,000 Aramean soldiers in one day. ³⁰The survivors ran away to the city of Aphek. The wall of the city fell on 27,000 of those soldiers. Ben-Hadad also ran away to the city and hid in a room. ³¹His servants said to him, "We heard that the kings of Israel are merciful. Let's dress in rough cloth with ropes on our heads.ᵃ Then let's go to the king of Israel. Maybe he will let us live."

³²They dressed in rough cloth with ropes on their heads. They came to the king of Israel. They said, "Your servant, Ben-Hadad, says, 'Please let me live.'"

Ahab said, "Is he still alive? He is my brother.ᵇ"

³³Ben-Hadad's men wanted King Ahab to say something to show that he would not kill King Ben-Hadad. When Ahab called Ben-Hadad his brother, the advisors quickly said, "Yes! Ben-Hadad is your brother."

Ahab said, "Bring him to me." So Ben-Hadad came to King Ahab. King Ahab asked him to get in the chariot with him.

³⁴Ben-Hadad said to him, "Ahab, I will give you the towns that my father took from your father. And you can put shops in Damascus, as my father did in Samaria."

Ahab answered, "If you agree to this, I will let you go free." So the two kings made a peace agreement. Then King Ahab let King Ben-Hadad go free.

A Prophet Speaks Against Ahab

³⁵One of the prophets told another prophet, "Hit me!" He said that because the LORD had commanded it. But the other prophet refused to hit him. ³⁶So the first prophet said, "You did not obey the LORD's command. So a lion will kill you when you leave this place." When the second prophet left, a lion killed him.

³⁷The first prophet went to another man and said, "Hit me!"

This man hit him and hurt the prophet. ³⁸So the prophet wrapped his face with a cloth. This way no one could see who he was. The prophet went and waited for the king by the road. ³⁹The king came by and the prophet said to him, "I went to fight in the battle. One of our men brought an enemy soldier to me. The man said, 'Guard this man. If he runs away, you will have to give your life in his place or you will have to pay a fine of 75 poundsᶜ of silver.' ⁴⁰While I was busy doing other things, the man ran away."

The king of Israel answered, "You admitted

ᵃ**20:31** *rough cloth ... heads* This showed that they were being humble and that they wanted to surrender.
ᵇ**20:32** *brother* People who signed peace agreements often called each other "brother." It was as if they were one family.
ᶜ**20:39** *75 pounds* Literally, "1 talent" (34.5 kg).

that you are guilty, so you know the answer. You must do what the man said."

⁴¹Then the prophet quickly took the cloth from his face, and the king of Israel saw that he was one of the prophets. ⁴²Then the prophet said to the king, "The LORD says to you, 'You set free the man I said should die. So you will take his place—you and your people will die!'"

⁴³Then the king went back home to Samaria. He was worried and upset.

Naboth's Vineyard

21 ¹There was a vineyard* near King Ahab's palace in Samaria. A man from Jezreel named Naboth owned it. ²One day Ahab said to Naboth, "Give me your vineyard that is near my palace. I want to make it a vegetable garden. I will give you a better vineyard in its place. Or, if you prefer, I will pay you for it."

³Naboth answered, "By the LORD, I will never give my land to you. This land belongs to my family."

⁴So Ahab went home angry and upset because Naboth told him, "I will not give you my family's land." Ahab went to bed, turned away from everyone, and refused to eat.

⁵His wife Jezebel went to him and asked him, "Why are you upset? Why do you refuse to eat?"

⁶Ahab answered, "I asked Naboth from Jezreel to give me his vineyard. I told him that I would pay him the full price. Or, if he preferred, I would give him another vineyard. But he refused to give it to me."

⁷Jezebel answered, "But you are the king over Israel! Get out of bed and eat something, and you will feel better. I will get Naboth's vineyard for you."

⁸Then Jezebel wrote some letters. She signed Ahab's name to them and used his seal to seal the letters. Then she sent them to the elders* and important men who lived in the same town as Naboth. ⁹This is what the letter said:

"Announce that there will be a day of fasting when the people will eat nothing. Then call all the people of the town together for a meeting. At the meeting we will talk about Naboth. ¹⁰Find some men who will tell lies about Naboth. They should say that they heard Naboth speak against the king and against God. Then take Naboth out of the city and kill him with stones."

¹¹So the elders and important men of Jezreel obeyed the command. ¹²The leaders announced that there would be a day when all the people would eat nothing. On that day they called all the people together for a meeting. They put Naboth in a special place before the people. ¹³Then two men told the people that they heard Naboth speak against God and the king. So the people carried Naboth out of the city and killed him with stones. ¹⁴Then the leaders sent a message to Jezebel that said: "Naboth has been killed."

¹⁵When Jezebel heard this, she said to Ahab, "Naboth is dead. Now you can go and take the vineyard that you wanted." ¹⁶So Ahab went to the vineyard and took it for his own.

¹⁷Then the LORD spoke to Elijah, the prophet from Tishbe. The LORD said, ¹⁸"Go to King Ahab in Samaria. He will be at Naboth's vineyard. He is there to take the vineyard as his own. ¹⁹Tell Ahab that I, the LORD, say to him, 'Ahab! You killed the man Naboth and now you are taking his land. I tell you this: Where the dogs licked up the blood of Naboth, they will lick up your blood as well.'"

²⁰So Elijah went to Ahab. When Ahab saw him, he said, "Well, my enemy has found me again!"

Elijah answered, "Yes, I found you, because you have again sold yourself out to do what the LORD says is evil. ²¹So the LORD says to you, 'I will make something bad happen to you. I will kill you and every male in your family. ²²I will destroy your family just as I destroyed the families of King Jeroboam son of Nebat and King Baasha. I will do this to you because you have made me angry and you have caused the Israelites to sin.' ²³The LORD also says this about your wife Jezebel: 'Dogs will eat the body of Jezebel by the wall of the city of Jezreel. ²⁴As for the family of Ahab, whoever dies in the city will be eaten by dogs, and whoever dies in the fields will be eaten by birds.'"

²⁵So Ahab sold himself out to do what the LORD says is evil. There is no one who did as much evil as Ahab and his wife Jezebel, who caused him to do these things. ²⁶Ahab committed the terrible sin of worshiping those filthy idols,* just as the Amorites did. And that is why the LORD took the land from them and gave it to the Israelites.

²⁷When Ahab heard what Elijah said, he tore his clothes to show how sad he was. Then he put on sackcloth* and refused to eat. He even slept in these clothes. He was very sad and upset.

²⁸The LORD said to the prophet Elijah from Tishbe, ²⁹"Look, Ahab has humbled himself before me. So I will not make that disaster happen during his lifetime. I will wait until his son is king. Then I will destroy his family."

Micaiah Warns King Ahab

22 ¹For the next two years there was peace between Israel and Aram. ²Then during the third year, King Jehoshaphat of Judah went to visit King Ahab of Israel.

³Ahab asked his officials, "Remember when the king of Aram took Ramoth Gilead from us? That city is ours, so why have we

done nothing to get it back?" ⁴So Ahab asked King Jehoshaphat, "Will you join with us to go fight the Arameans at Ramoth Gilead?"

Jehoshaphat answered, "Yes, you and I will be as one—my men and my horses will be as yours. ⁵But first let's ask the LORD for advice."

⁶So Ahab called a meeting of the prophets. There were about 400 prophets at that time. Ahab asked the prophets, "Should I go and attack the Arameans at Ramoth Gilead or not?"

The prophets answered Ahab, "Yes, because the LORD will let you defeat Ramoth Gilead."

⁷But Jehoshaphat said, "Doesn't the LORD have another prophet here? Let's ask him what God says."

⁸King Ahab answered, "Yes, there is another prophet. His name is Micaiah son of Imlah. But I hate him because he will not say anything good about me when he speaks for the LORD. He always says things that I don't like."

Jehoshaphat said, "The king should not say that!"

⁹So King Ahab told one of his officers to go and find Micaiah.

¹⁰At that time the two kings were sitting on their thrones, with their royal robes on, at the judgment place near the gates of Samaria. All the prophets were standing before them, prophesying.* ¹¹One of the prophets was named Zedekiah son of Kenaanah. Zedekiah made some iron horns*ᵃ* and said to Ahab, "The LORD says, 'You will use these iron horns to fight against the army of Aram. You will defeat them and destroy them.'" ¹²All the other prophets agreed with Zedekiah and said, "Your army should march now to go fight against the Arameans at Ramoth Gilead. You will win the battle. The LORD will let you defeat them."

¹³While this was happening, the officer went to find Micaiah. When he found him, the officer told him, "All the other prophets have said that the king will succeed, so you should say the same thing."

¹⁴But Micaiah answered, "As surely as the LORD lives, I can say only what the LORD says."

¹⁵Micaiah went and stood before King Ahab. The king asked him, "Micaiah, should we go and attack the Arameans at Ramoth Gilead or not?"

Micaiah answered, "Yes, go and be successful! The LORD will let you take the city."

¹⁶But Ahab answered, "How many times do I have to tell you? Tell me the truth. What does the LORD say?"

¹⁷So Micaiah answered, "I can see the army of Israel scattered all over the hills, like sheep with no one to lead them. This is what the LORD says, 'These men have no leaders. Let them go home in peace.'"

¹⁸Then Ahab said to Jehoshaphat, "See, I told you! This prophet never says anything good about me. He always says something bad."

¹⁹But Micaiah said, "Listen to this message from the LORD: I saw the LORD sitting on his throne. All of heaven's army was standing around him, some on his left side and some on his right side. ²⁰The LORD said, 'Which of you will go fool Ahab into attacking the Arameans at Ramoth Gilead so that he will be killed?' The angels discussed many different plans. ²¹Then a spiritᵇ went and stood before the LORD and said, 'I will fool him!' The LORD asked, 'How will you do it?' ²²The angel answered, 'I will go out and become a spirit of lies in the mouths of Ahab's prophets—they will all speak lies.' So the LORD said, 'Yes, that will fool Ahab. Go out and do that.'

²³"So that is what has happened here. The LORD made your prophets lie to you. The LORD himself decided to bring this disaster to you."

²⁴Then the prophet Zedekiah went to Micaiah and hit him on the face. Zedekiah said, "How is it that the Spirit of the LORD left me to speak through you?"

²⁵Micaiah answered, "Look, what I said will happen! And you will see it one day when you are in a secret room somewhere hiding."

²⁶Then King Ahab ordered one of his officers to arrest Micaiah. Ahab said, "Arrest him and take him to Amon the governor of the city and prince Joash. ²⁷Tell them to put Micaiah in prison. Give him nothing but bread and water to eat. Keep him there until I come home from the battle."

²⁸Micaiah said, "Listen to me, everyone! Ahab, if you come back alive from the battle, the LORD has not spoken through me."

The Battle at Ramoth Gilead

²⁹King Ahab of Israel and King Jehoshaphat of Judah went to fight the Arameans at Ramoth Gilead. ³⁰Ahab said to Jehoshaphat, "Disguise yourself when you go into battle, but wear your own clothes. And I will disguise myself." The king of Israel went into battle dressed like an ordinary soldier.

³¹The king of Aram had 32 chariot commanders. He gave them this command, "Don't go after anyone except the king of Israel, no matter how important they are." ³²When the commanders saw King Jehoshaphat, they thought he was the king of Israel, and so they went to kill him. Jehoshaphat started shouting. ³³When the commanders saw that he was not King Ahab, they stopped chasing him.

³⁴Then a soldier in the distance pulled back as far as he could on his bow and shot

---

ᵃ**22:11** *iron horns* These were a symbol of great strength.

ᵇ**22:21** *a spirit* Or "the Spirit."

an arrow into the air. The arrow happened to hit the king of Israel in a small hole where his armor was fastened together. King Ahab said to his chariot driver, "I've been hit! Turn the chariot* around and take me off the battlefield!"

35The armies continued to fight while King Ahab was propped up in his chariot. He was leaning against the sides of the chariot, looking out toward the Arameans. His blood ran down onto the floor of the chariot. Later in the evening, he died. 36At sunset all the Israelites cheered when they were told to go home. So they all went back to their hometowns.

37And that is how King Ahab died. Some men carried his body to Samaria and buried him there. 38They took his chariot to the large pool in Samaria to clean it. The dogs licked up Ahab's blood while the prostitutes washed the chariot. This happened just as the Lord said it would.

39The rest of what King Ahab did during the time he ruled is written in the book, *The History of the Kings of Israel*. That book tells about all the cities he built and about all the ivory that he used to decorate his palace. 40Ahab died and was buried with his ancestors. His son Ahaziah became the next king after him.

Summary of Jehoshaphat's Rule

41Jehoshaphat son of Asa became the king of Judah in Ahab's fourth year as king of Israel. 42Jehoshaphat was 35 years old when he became king, and he ruled in Jerusalem for 25 years. His mother was Azubah, the daughter of Shilhi. 43Like his father Asa, Jehoshaphat was good and did everything that the Lord wanted, but he did not destroy the high places.* The people continued offering sacrifices* and burning incense* there.

44Jehoshaphat made a peace agreement with the king of Israel. 45Jehoshaphat was very brave and fought many wars. The rest of what he did is written in the book, *The History of the Kings of Judah*.

46Jehoshaphat forced all the men and women who sold their bodies for sex to leave the places of worship. They had served in these places of worship while his father Asa was king.

47In those days Edom did not have a king; it was ruled by a governor who was chosen by the king of Judah.

48King Jehoshaphat built some cargo ships. He wanted the ships to sail to Ophir for gold, but they never went there—they were destroyed in their home port at Ezion Geber. 49Then King Ahaziah of Israel offered to put some of his own sailors with Jehoshaphat's men on the ships,*a* but Jehoshaphat refused to accept his help.

50Jehoshaphat died and was buried with his ancestors in the City of David.* Then his son Jehoram became the next king.

Ahaziah, King of Israel

51Ahaziah was the son of Ahab. He became king of Israel during the 17th year that King Jehoshaphat ruled Judah. Ahaziah ruled in Samaria for two years. 52He sinned against the Lord just as his parents, Ahab and Jezebel, did. He caused Israel to sin just as Jeroboam son of Nabat did. 53Ahaziah served the false god Baal* and worshiped him, just as his father did before him. He did all the things that his father did to make the Lord, the God of Israel, angry.

*a*22:49 *King Ahaziah … ships* Jehoshaphat controlled the port of Ezion Geber which was Israel's only way to the Red Sea and the coasts of Africa, the Arabian Peninsula, and the coasts leading to the Persian Gulf and India. Ahaziah thought he could get control of that area by "helping" Jehoshaphat.

2 Kings

A Message for Ahaziah

1 1After King Ahab died, Moab broke away from Israel's rule.

2One day Ahaziah was on the roof of his house in Samaria. He fell down through the wooden bars on top of his house and was badly hurt. He called messengers and told them, "Go to ₁the priests of₁ Baal Zebub, the god of Ekron, and ask them if I will get well from my injuries."

3But the Lord's angel said to Elijah the Tishbite, "King Ahaziah has sent some messengers from Samaria. Go meet those men and ask them, 'There is a God in Israel, so why are you men going to ask questions of Baal Zebub, the god of Ekron? 4Since you did this, the Lord says, You will not get up from your bed. You will die!'" Then Elijah left.

5When messengers came back to Ahaziah, he asked them, "Why did you come back so soon?"

6The messengers said to Ahaziah, "A man came up to meet us and told us to go back to the king who sent us and tell him what the

LORD says: 'There is a God in Israel, so why did you send messengers to ask questions of Baal Zebub, the god of Ekron? Since you did this, you will not get up from your bed. You will die!'"

[7]Ahaziah said to the messengers, "What did the man look like who met you and told you this?"

[8]They answered Ahaziah, "This man was wearing a hairy coat[a] with a leather belt around his waist."

Then Ahaziah said, "That was Elijah the Tishbite."

Ahaziah Calls for Elijah

[9]Ahaziah sent a captain and 50 men to Elijah. The captain went to Elijah, who was sitting on top of a hill. The captain said to Elijah, "Man of God,* the king says, 'Come down!'"

[10]Elijah answered the captain of 50, "If I am a man of God, let fire come down from heaven and destroy you and your 50 men!"

So fire came down from heaven and destroyed the captain and his 50 men.

[11]Ahaziah sent another captain with 50 men to Elijah. He said to Elijah, "Man of God, the king says, 'Come down quickly!'"

[12]Elijah told the captain and his 50 men, "If I am a man of God, let fire come down from heaven and destroy you and your 50 men!"

Then God's fire came down from heaven and destroyed the captain and his 50 men.

[13]Ahaziah sent a third captain with 50 men. The third captain came to Elijah. He fell down on his knees and begged Elijah, saying to him, "Man of God, I ask you, please let my life and the lives of your 50 servants be valuable to you. [14]Fire came down from heaven and destroyed the first two captains and their 50 men. But now, have mercy and let us live!"

[15]The LORD's angel said to Elijah, "Go with the captain. Don't be afraid of him."

So Elijah went with the captain to see King Ahaziah.

[16]Elijah told Ahaziah, "This is what the LORD says: 'There is a God in Israel, so why did you send messengers to ask questions of Baal Zebub, the god of Ekron? Since you did this, you will not get up from your bed. You will die!'"

Joram Takes Ahaziah's Place

[17]Ahaziah died, just as the LORD said through Elijah. Ahaziah did not have a son, so Joram became the new king after Ahaziah. He began to rule during the second year that Jehoram son of Jehoshaphat was the king of Judah.

[18]The other things that Ahaziah did are written in the book, *The History of the Kings of Israel*.

The Lord Makes Plans to Take Elijah

2 [1]It was near the time for the LORD to take Elijah by a whirlwind up into heaven. Elijah and Elisha started to leave Gilgal.

[2]Elijah said to Elisha, "Please stay here, because the LORD told me to go to Bethel."

But Elisha said, "I promise, as the LORD lives and as you live, I will not leave you." So the two men went down to Bethel.

[3]The group of prophets[b] at Bethel came to Elisha and said to him, "Do you know that the LORD will take your master away from you today?"

Elisha said, "Yes, I know. Don't talk about it."

[4]Elijah said to Elisha, "Please stay here, because the LORD told me to go to Jericho."

But Elisha said, "I promise, as the LORD lives and as you live, I will not leave you!" So the two men went to Jericho.

[5]The group of prophets at Jericho came to Elisha and said to him, "Do you know that the LORD will take your master away from you today?"

Elisha answered, "Yes, I know. Don't talk about it."

[6]Elijah said to Elisha, "Please stay here, because the LORD told me to go to the Jordan River."

Elisha answered, "I promise, as the LORD lives and as you live, I will not leave you!" So the two men went on.

[7]There were 50 men from the group of prophets who followed them. Elijah and Elisha stopped at the Jordan River. The 50 men stood far away from Elijah and Elisha. [8]Elijah took off his coat, folded it, and hit the water with it. The water separated to the right and to the left. Then Elijah and Elisha crossed the river on dry ground.

[9]After they crossed the river, Elijah said to Elisha, "What do you want me to do for you before God takes me away from you?"

Elisha said, "I ask you for a double share of your spirit on me."

[10]Elijah said, "You have asked a hard thing. If you see me when I am taken from you, it will happen. But if you don't see me when I am taken from you, it will not happen."

The Lord Takes Elijah Into Heaven

[11]Elijah and Elisha were walking and talking together. Suddenly, some horses and a chariot* came and separated Elijah from Elisha. The horses and the chariot were like fire. Then Elijah was carried up into heaven in a whirlwind.

[12]Elisha saw it, and shouted, "My father! My father! The chariot of Israel and his horses!c"

---

[b]**2:3 group of prophets** Literally, "sons of the prophets." These were prophets and people studying to become prophets. Also in verses 5, 7, 15, 17.

[c]**2:12 chariot ... horses** Or "the Chariot of Israel and his horse soldiers." This may mean "God and his heavenly army *(angels)*."

[a]**1:8 This man ... coat** Or "This man was a hairy man."

Elisha never saw Elijah again. Elisha grabbed his own clothes and tore them in two to show his sadness. [13]Elijah's coat had fallen to the ground, so Elisha picked it up. He went back and stood at the edge of the Jordan River. [14]He hit the water and said, "Where is the LORD, the God of Elijah?" Just as Elisha hit the water, the water separated to the right and to the left! Then Elisha crossed the river.

The Prophets Ask for Elijah

[15]When the group of prophets at Jericho saw Elisha, they said, "Elijah's spirit is now on Elisha!" They came to meet Elisha. They bowed very low to the ground before him. [16]They said, "Look, we have 50 good men. Please let them go and look for your master. Maybe the LORD's Spirit has taken Elijah up and dropped him on some mountain or in some valley."

But Elisha answered, "No, don't send men to look for Elijah!"

[17]The group of prophets begged Elisha until he was embarrassed. Then Elisha said, "Send the men to look for Elijah."

The group of prophets sent the 50 men to look for Elijah. They looked three days, but they could not find him. [18]So the men went to Jericho where Elisha was staying and told him. Elisha said to them, "I told you not to go."

Elisha Makes the Water Good

[19]The men of the city said to Elisha, "Sir, you can see this city is in a nice place, but the water is bad. That is why the land cannot grow crops."

[20]Elisha said, "Bring me a new bowl and put salt in it."

They brought the bowl to Elisha. [21]Then he went out to the place where the water began flowing from the ground. Elisha threw the salt into the water and said, "The LORD said, 'I am making this water pure! From now on this water will not cause any more death or keep the land from growing crops.'"

[22]The water became pure and is still good today. It happened just as Elisha had said.

Some Boys Make Fun of Elisha

[23]Elisha went from that city to Bethel. He was walking up the hill to the city, and some boys were coming down out of the city. They began making fun of him. They said, "Go away, you bald-headed man! Go away, you bald-headed man!"

[24]Elisha looked back and saw them. He asked the LORD to cause bad things to happen to them. Then two bears came out of the forest and attacked the boys. There were 42 boys ripped apart by the bears.

[25]Elisha left Bethel and went to Mount Carmel and from there he went back to Samaria.

Joram Becomes King of Israel

3 [1]Joram son of Ahab became king over Israel at Samaria. He began to rule during Jehoshaphat's 18th year as king of Judah. Joram ruled 12 years. [2]He did what the LORD said was wrong. But he was not like his father and mother, because he removed the pillar that his father had made for worshiping Baal.* [3]But he continued to do the sins of Jeroboam son of Nebat who had caused the Israelites to sin. Joram did not stop committing the sins of Jeroboam.

Moab Breaks Away From Israel

[4]Mesha was the king of Moab. He owned many sheep. He gave the wool of 100,000 lambs and 100,000 rams to the king of Israel. [5]But when Ahab died, the king of Moab broke away from the rule of the king of Israel.

[6]Then King Joram went out of Samaria and gathered together all the men of Israel. [7]Joram sent messengers to Jehoshaphat, the king of Judah. Joram said, "The king of Moab has broken away from my rule. Will you go with me to fight against Moab?"

Jehoshaphat said, "Yes, I will go with you. We will join together as one army. My people will be like your people, and my horses will be like your horses."

The Three Kings Ask Elisha for Advice

[8]Jehoshaphat asked Joram, "Which way should we go?"

Joram answered, "We should go through the Desert of Edom."

[9]So the king of Israel went with the king of Judah and the king of Edom. They traveled around for seven days. There was not enough water for the army or for their animals. [10]Finally the king of Israel said, "Oh, I think the LORD really brought us three kings together only to let the Moabites defeat us!"

[11]But Jehoshaphat said, "Surely one of the LORD's prophets is here. Let's ask the prophet what the LORD says we should do."

One of the servants of the king of Israel said, "Elisha son of Shaphat is here. Elisha was Elijah's servant.*"

[12]Jehoshaphat said, "The LORD's word is with Elisha."

So the king of Israel, Jehoshaphat, and the king of Edom went down to see Elisha.

[13]Elisha said to the king of Israel, "What do you want from me? Go to the prophets of your father and mother."

The king of Israel said to Elisha, "No, we have come to see you because the LORD called us three kings together to let the Moabites defeat us."

[14]Elisha said, "I respect King Jehoshaphat of Judah, and I serve the LORD All-Powerful. As surely as he lives, I came here only because of Jehoshaphat. I tell you the truth, if he were not here, I would not pay any attention to you. I would ignore you completely.

3:11 Elisha was Elijah's servant Literally, "Elisha poured water over Elijah's hands."

[15]But now bring me someone who plays the harp."

When the person played the harp, the LORD's power[a] came on Elisha. [16]Then Elisha said, "This is what the LORD says: 'Dig holes in the valley.' [17]Yes, this is what the LORD says: 'You will not see wind or rain, but that valley will be filled with water. Then you and your cattle and other animals will have water to drink.' [18]This is an easy thing for the LORD to do. He will also help you defeat the Moabites. [19]You will attack every strong city and every good city. You will cut down every good tree. You will stop up all the springs of water. You will ruin every good field with stones."

[20]In the morning, at the time for the morning sacrifice, water began flowing from the direction of Edom and filled the valley.

[21]The Moabites heard that the kings had come up to fight against them. So they gathered together all the men old enough to wear armor* and waited at the border. [22]The Moabites got up early that morning. The rising sun was shining on the water in the valley, and it looked like blood to the Moabites. [23]They said, "Look at the blood! The kings must have fought against each other. They must have destroyed each other. Let's go take the valuable things from the dead bodies!"

[24]The Moabites came to the Israelite camp, but the Israelites came out and attacked the Moabite army. The Moabites ran away from the Israelites. The Israelites followed them into Moab to fight them. [25]The Israelites destroyed the cities. They threw their stones[b] at every good field in Moab. They stopped up all the springs of water and cut down all the good trees. The Israelites fought all the way to Kir Hareseth. The soldiers surrounded Kir Hareseth and attacked it too.

[26]The king of Moab saw that the battle was too strong for him, so he took 700 men with swords to break through to the king of Edom. But they were not able to do it. [27]Then the king of Moab took his oldest son, who would become the next king after him. On the wall around the city, the king of Moab offered his son as a burnt offering. This upset the Israelites very much. So the Israelites left the king of Moab and went back to their own land.

A Prophet's Widow Asks Elisha for Help

4 [1]A man from the group of prophets[c] had a wife. This man died, and his wife cried out to Elisha, "My husband was like a servant to you. Now he is dead! You know he honored the LORD. But he owed money to a man. Now that man is coming to take my two boys and make them his slaves!"

[2]Elisha answered, "How can I help you? Tell me, what do you have in your house?"

The woman said, "I don't have anything in the house except a jar of olive oil."

[3]Then Elisha said, "Go and borrow bowls from all your neighbors. They must be empty. Borrow plenty of bowls. [4]Then go to your house and close the doors. Only you and your sons will be in the house. Then pour the oil into all the bowls. Fill them, and put them in a separate place."

[5]So the woman left Elisha, went into her house, and shut the door. Only she and her sons were in the house. Her sons brought the bowls to her and she poured oil. [6]She filled many bowls. Finally, she said to her son, "Bring me another bowl."

But all the bowls were full. One of the sons said to her, "There aren't any more bowls." Then the oil in the jar was finished!

[7]When she told the man of God* what had happened, Elisha said to her, "Go, sell the oil and pay your debt. You and your sons can live on the money that is left."

A Woman in Shunem Gives Elisha a Room

[8]One day Elisha went to Shunem, where an important woman lived. She asked Elisha to stop and eat at her house. So every time Elisha went through that place, he stopped there to eat.

[9]The woman said to her husband, "Look, I can see that Elisha is a holy man of God. He passes by our house all the time. [10]Please, let's make a little room on the roof[d] for him. Let's put a bed in this room and a table, a chair, and a lampstand. Then when he comes to our house, he can have this room for himself."

[11]One day Elisha came to the woman's house. He went to this room and rested there. [12]Elisha said to his servant Gehazi, "Call this Shunammite woman."

The servant called the Shunammite woman, and she stood in front of Elisha. [13]Elisha told his servant, "Now say to her, 'Look, you have done your best to take care of us. What can we do for you? Do you want us to speak to the king for you, or to the captain of the army?'"

She answered, "I am fine living here among my own people."

[14]Elisha said to Gehazi, "What can we do for her?"

He answered, "I know! She does not have a son, and her husband is old."

[15]Then Elisha said, "Call her."

So Gehazi called the woman. She came and stood at his door. [16]Elisha said, "About this time next spring, you will be holding your own baby boy in your arms."

The woman said, "No, sir! Man of God,* don't lie to me!"

---

[a]3:15 *power* Literally, "hand."

[b]3:25 *threw their stones* These were probably the stones soldiers threw with slings in war.

[c]4:1 *group of prophets* Literally, "sons of the prophets." These were prophets and those studying to become prophets. Also in verses 38, 39, 44.

[d]4:10 *room on the roof* In ancient Israel, houses had flat roofs that were used as an extra room.

The Woman in Shunem Has a Son

17But the woman did become pregnant and gave birth to a son that next spring, just as Elisha had said.

18The boy grew. One day the boy went out into the fields to see his father and the men cutting the grain. 19The boy said to his father, "Oh, my head! My head hurts!"

The father said to his servant, "Carry him to his mother!"

20The servant took the boy to his mother. The boy sat on his mother's lap until noon. Then he died.

The Woman Goes to See Elisha

21The woman laid the boy on the bed of Elisha, the man of God.* Then she shut the door to that room and went outside. 22She called to her husband and said, "Please send me one of the servants and a donkey. Then I will go quickly to get the man of God and come back."

23The woman's husband said, "Why would you want to go to the man of God today? It isn't the New Moon* or Sabbath* day."

She said, "Goodbye!"*a*

24Then she put a saddle on a donkey and said to her servant, "Let's go, and hurry! Go slow only when I tell you."

25The woman went to Mount Carmel to get the man of God.

The man of God saw the Shunammite woman coming from far away and said to his servant Gehazi, "Look, there's the Shunammite woman! 26Please run now to meet her! Say to her, 'Are you all right? Is your husband all right? Is the child all right?'"

She answered, "Everything is all right."*b*

27But the Shunammite woman went up the hill to the man of God. She bowed down and touched Elisha's feet. Gehazi came near to pull her away. But the man of God said to Gehazi, "Leave her alone! She's very upset, and the LORD didn't tell me about it. The LORD hid this news from me."

28Then she said, "Sir, I never asked for a son. I told you, 'Don't trick me!'"

29Then Elisha said to Gehazi, "Get ready to go. Take my walking stick and go! If you meet anyone along the way, don't even stop to say hello to him. If anyone says hello to you, don't answer. Put my walking stick on the child's face."

30But the child's mother said, "I promise, as the LORD lives and as you live, I will not leave without you!"

So Elisha got up and followed her.

31Gehazi arrived at the house before Elisha and the Shunammite woman. Gehazi laid the walking stick on the child's face, but the child did not talk or show any sign that he heard

a4:23 Goodbye Or "Everything is all right." Literally, "Peace."

b4:26 Everything is all right Or "Hello." Literally, "Peace."

anything. Then Gehazi came back to meet Elisha and said, "The child will not wake up!"

The Woman's Son Comes Back to Life

32Elisha went into the house, and there was the child, lying dead on his bed. 33Elisha went into the room and shut the door. He and the child were alone in the room now. Then he prayed to the LORD. 34Elisha went to the bed and lay on the child. He put his eyes on the child's eyes, his mouth on the child's mouth, and his hands on the child's hands. He lay there on top of the child until the child's body became warm.

35Then Elisha turned away and walked around the room. He went back and lay on the child until the child sneezed seven times and opened his eyes.

36Elisha called Gehazi and said, "Call the Shunammite woman!"

Gehazi called her, and she came to Elisha. Elisha said, "Pick up your son."

37Then the Shunammite woman went into the room and bowed down at Elisha's feet. Then she picked up her son and went out.

Elisha and the Poisoned Soup

38Elisha went to Gilgal again. There was a famine* in the land. The group of prophets was sitting in front of Elisha. Elisha said to his servant, "Put the large pot on the fire, and make some soup for the group of prophets."

39One man went out into the field to gather herbs. He found a wild vine and picked the fruit from it. He put that fruit in his robe and brought it back. He cut up the wild fruit and put it into the pot. But the group of prophets did not know what kind of fruit it was.

40Then they poured some of the soup for the men to eat. But when they began to eat the soup, they shouted out, "Man of God*! There's poison in the pot!" The food tasted like poison, so they could not eat that food.

41But Elisha said, "Bring some flour." He threw the flour into the pot. Then he said, "Pour the soup for the people so that they can eat."

And there was nothing wrong with the soup.

Elisha Feeds the Group of Prophets

42A man from Baal Shalishah came and brought bread from the first harvest to the man of God.* This man brought 20 loaves of barley bread and fresh grain in his sack. Then Elisha said, "Give this food to the people, so that they can eat."

43Elisha's servant said, "What? There are 100 men here. How can I give this food to all those men?"

But Elisha said, "Give the food to the people to eat. The LORD says, 'They will eat and there will still be food left over.'"

44Then Elisha's servant put the food in front of the group of prophets. The group of prophets had enough to eat, and they even had food left over. This happened just as the LORD had said.

Naaman's Problem

5 ¹Naaman was the captain of the army of the king of Aram. He was very important to his king*ᵃ* because the LORD used him to lead Aram to victory. Naaman was a great and powerful man, but he was also sick with leprosy.*

²The Aramean army sent many groups of soldiers to fight in Israel. One time they took a little girl from the land of Israel. This girl became a servant of Naaman's wife. ³She said to his wife, "I wish that my master· would meet the prophet who lives in Samaria. He could heal Naaman of his leprosy."

⁴Naaman went to the king and told him what the Israelite girl said.

⁵Then the king of Aram said, "Go now, and I will send a letter to the king of Israel."

So Naaman went to Israel. He took 750 pounds*ᵇ* of silver, 6000 pieces of gold and ten changes of clothes as gifts. ⁶Naaman took the letter from the king of Aram to the king of Israel. The letter said: "Now this letter is to show that I am sending my servant Naaman to you. Cure his leprosy."

⁷When the king of Israel had read the letter, he tore his clothes to show he was sad and upset. He said, "Am I God? I don't have the power over life and death. So why did the king of Aram send a man sick with leprosy for me to heal? Think about it, and you will see that it is a trick. The king of Aram is trying to start a fight."

⁸Elisha, the man of God,* heard that the king of Israel had torn his clothes. So Elisha sent this message to the king: "Why did you tear your clothes? Let Naaman come to me. Then he will know there is a prophet in Israel."

⁹So Naaman came with his horses and chariots* to Elisha's house and stood outside the door. ¹⁰Elisha sent a messenger to Naaman who said, "Go and wash in the Jordan River seven times. Then your skin will be healed, and you will be pure and clean."

¹¹Naaman became angry and left. He said, "I thought Elisha would at least come out and stand in front of me and call on the name of the LORD his God. I thought he would wave his hand over my body and heal the leprosy. ¹²Abana and Pharpar, the rivers of Damascus, are better than all the water in Israel. Why can't I wash in those rivers in Damascus and become clean?" He was very angry and turned to leave.

¹³But Naaman's servants went to him and talked to him. They said, "Father,*ᶜ* if the prophet told you to do some great thing, you would do it, isn't that right? But he said, 'Wash, and you will be pure and clean.'"

¹⁴So Naaman did what the man of God said. He went down and dipped himself in the Jordan River seven times, and he became pure and clean. His skin became soft like the skin of a baby.

¹⁵Naaman and his whole group came back to the man of God. He stood before Elisha and said, "Look, I now know there is no God in all the earth except in Israel. Now please accept a gift from me."

¹⁶But Elisha said, "I serve the LORD. And I promise, as the LORD lives, I will not accept any gift."

Naaman tried hard to make Elisha take the gift, but he refused. ¹⁷Then Naaman said, "If you will not accept this gift, at least do this for me. Let me have enough dirt from Israel to fill the baskets on two of my mules.*ᵈ* I ask this because I will never again offer any burnt offering* or sacrifice to any other gods. I will offer sacrifices only to the LORD! ¹⁸And I pray that the LORD will forgive me for this: When my master goes to the temple of Rimmon to worship that false god, he will want to lean on me for support. So I must bow down in the temple of Rimmon. I ask the LORD now to forgive me when that happens."

¹⁹Then Elisha said to Naaman, "Go in peace."

So Naaman left Elisha and went a short way. ²⁰But Gehazi, the servant of Elisha the man of God, said, "Look, my master has let Naaman the Aramean go without accepting the gift that he brought. As the LORD lives, I will run after Naaman and get something from him." ²¹So Gehazi ran to Naaman.

Naaman saw someone running after him. He stepped down from the chariot to meet Gehazi. Naaman said, "Is everything all right?"

²²Gehazi said, "Yes, everything is all right. My master has sent me. He said, 'Look, two young men came to me from the group of prophets*ᵉ* in the hill country of Ephraim. Please give them 75 pounds*ᶠ* of silver and two changes of clothes.'"

²³Naaman said, "Please, take 150 pounds.*ᵍ*" He persuaded Gehazi to take the silver. Naaman put 150 pounds of silver in two bags and took two changes of clothes. Then he gave these things to two of his servants. The servants carried these things for Gehazi. ²⁴When Gehazi came to the hill, he took these things

---

*ᵈ***5:17** *Let me have … my mules* Naaman probably thought the ground in Israel was holy, so he wanted to take some with him to help him worship the Lord in his own country.

*ᵉ***5:22** *group of prophets* Literally, "sons of the prophets." These were prophets and people studying to become prophets. Also in 6:1, 4.

*ᶠ***5:22** *75 pounds* Literally, "1 talent" (34.5 kg).

*ᵍ***5:23** *150 pounds* Literally, "2 talents" (69 kg).

*ᵃ***5:1** *king* Literally, "master."

*ᵇ***5:5** *750 pounds* Literally, "10 talents" (345 kg).

*ᶜ***5:13** *Father* Slaves often called their masters "father," and the masters often called their slaves "children."

from the servants. He sent the servants away, and they left. Then he hid those things in the house.

25Gehazi came in and stood before his master. Elisha said to Gehazi, "Where have you been Gehazi?"

Gehazi answered, "I didn't go anywhere."

26Elisha said to him, "That is not true! My heart was with you when the man turned from his chariot to meet you. This is not the time to take money, clothes, olives, grapes, sheep, cattle, or men and women servants. 27Now you and your children will catch Naaman's disease. You will have leprosy forever!"

When Gehazi left Elisha, his skin was as white as snow! He was sick with leprosy.

Elisha and the Ax Head

6 1The group of prophets said to Elisha, "We are staying in that place over there, but it is too small for us. 2Let's go to the Jordan River and cut some wood. Each of us will get a log and we will build us a place to live there."

Elisha answered, "Go and do it."

3One of them said, "Please go with us."

Elisha said, "Yes, I will go with you."

4So Elisha went with the group of prophets. When they arrived at the Jordan River, they began to cut down some trees. 5But when one man was cutting down a tree, the iron ax head slipped from the handle and fell into the water. He shouted, "Oh, master! I borrowed that ax!"

6The man of God* said, "Where did it fall?"

The man showed Elisha the place where the ax head fell. Then Elisha cut a stick and threw the stick into the water. The stick made the iron ax head float. 7Elisha said, "So pick up the ax head." Then the man reached out and took the ax head.

Aram Tries to Trap Israel

8The king of Aram was making war against Israel. He had a council meeting with his army officers. He said, "Go to such and such a place and prepare to attack the Israelites when they come by."

9But the man of God* sent a message to the king of Israel. Elisha said, "Be careful! Don't go by that place, because the Aramean soldiers are hiding there!"

10The king of Israel sent a message to his men at the place that the man of God warned him about. And the king of Israel saved quite a few men.*a*

11The king of Aram was very upset about this. He called his army officers and said to them, "Tell me who is spying for the king of Israel!"

12One of the officers of the king of Aram said, "My lord and king, not one of us is a spy. Elisha, the prophet from Israel, can tell the

king of Israel many secret things—even the words that you speak in your bedroom!"

13The king of Aram said, "Find Elisha, and I will send men to catch him."

The servants told the king of Aram, "Elisha is in Dothan."

14Then the king of Aram sent horses, chariots,* and a large army to Dothan. They arrived at night and surrounded the city. 15Elisha's servant got up early that morning. When he went outside, he saw an army with horses and chariots all around the city.

The servant said to Elisha, "Oh, my master, what can we do?"

16Elisha said, "Don't be afraid. The army that fights for us is larger than the army that fights for Aram."

17Then Elisha prayed and said, "LORD, I ask you, open my servant's eyes so that he can see."

The LORD opened the eyes of the young man, and the servant saw the mountain was full of horses and chariots of fire. They were all around Elisha.

18These horses and chariots of fire came down to Elisha. He prayed to the LORD and said, "I pray that you will cause these people to become blind."

Then the LORD did what Elisha asked. He caused the Aramean army to become blind. 19Elisha said to the Aramean army, "This is not the right way. This is not the right city. Follow me. I will lead you to the man you are looking for." Then Elisha led them to Samaria.*b*

20When they arrived at Samaria, Elisha said, "LORD, open the eyes of these men so that they can see."

Then the LORD opened their eyes, and the Aramean army saw they were in the city of Samaria! 21The king of Israel saw the Aramean army and said to Elisha, "My father, should I kill them? Should I kill them?"

22Elisha answered, "No, don't kill them. You would not kill people who you captured in war with your sword and with your bow. Give the Aramean army some bread and water. Let them eat and drink. Then let them go home to their master."

23The king of Israel prepared much food for the Aramean army. After they ate and drank, he sent them back home to their master. The Arameans did not send any more soldiers into the land of Israel to make raids.

A Time of Terrible Hunger Hits Samaria

24After this happened, King Ben-Hadad of Aram gathered all his army and went to surround and attack the city of Samaria. 25The soldiers would not let people bring food into the city, so there was a time of terrible hunger in Samaria. It was so bad in Samaria that a

*a***6:10** *quite a few men* Literally, "not one or two."

*b***6:19** *Samaria* This was the capital city of Israel—the enemy of Aram.

donkey's head was sold for 80 pieces of silver and one pint[a] of dove's dung sold for five pieces of silver.

26The king of Israel was walking on the wall around the city. A woman shouted out to him. She said, "My lord and king, please help me!"

27The king of Israel said, "If the LORD does not help you, how can I help you? I cannot give you grain from the threshing* floor or wine from the winepress.*" 28Then he said to her, "What is your trouble?"

She answered, "This woman said to me, 'Give me your son so that we can eat him today. Then we will eat my son tomorrow.' 29So we boiled my son and ate him. Then the next day, I said to this woman, 'Give me your son so that we can eat him.' But she has hidden her son!"

30When the king heard the woman's words, he tore his clothes to show he was upset. As he passed by on the wall, the people saw the king was wearing the rough cloth under his clothes to show he was sad and upset.

31The king said, "May God punish me if the head of Elisha son of Shaphat is still on his body at the end of this day!"

32The king sent a messenger to Elisha. Elisha was sitting in his house, and the elders* were sitting with him. Before the messenger arrived, Elisha said to the elders, "Look, that son of a murderer is sending men to cut off my head. When the messenger arrives, shut the door. Hold the door and don't let him in. I hear the sound of his master's feet coming behind him."

33While Elisha was still talking with the elders, the messenger[b] came to him. This was the message: "This trouble has come from the LORD. Why should I wait for the LORD any longer?"

7 1Elisha said, "Listen to the message from the LORD! The LORD says, 'About this time tomorrow, there will be plenty of food, and it will be cheap again. A person will be able to buy a basket[c] of fine flour or two baskets of barley for only one shekel[d] in the marketplace by the city gates of Samaria.'"

2Then the officer who was close to the king[e] answered the man of God.* The officer said, "Even if the LORD made windows in heaven, this could not happen."

Elisha said, "You will see it with your own eyes, but you will not eat any of that food."

Lepers Find the Aramean Camp Empty

3There were four men sick with leprosy* near the city gate. They said to each other,

"Why are we sitting here waiting to die? 4There is no food in Samaria. If we go into the city, we will die there. If we stay here, we will also die. So let's go to the Aramean camp. If they let us live, we will live. If they kill us, we will just die."

5So that evening the four lepers* went to the Aramean camp. When they came to the edge of the camp, no one was there! 6The LORD had caused the Aramean army to hear the sound of chariots,* horses, and a large army. So the Aramean soldiers said to each other, "The king of Israel has hired the kings of the Hittites and Egyptians to come against us."

7The Arameans ran away early that evening. They left everything behind. They left their tents, horses, and donkeys and ran for their lives.

The Lepers in the Enemy Camp

8When these lepers* came to where the camp began, they went into one tent. They ate and drank. Then they carried silver, gold, and clothes out of the camp and hid them. Then they came back and entered another tent. They carried things out from this tent and went out and hid them. 9Then they said to each other, "We are doing wrong! Today we have good news, but we are silent. If we wait until the sun comes up, we will be punished. Now let's go and tell the people who live in the king's palace."

The Lepers Tell the Good News

10So the lepers* came and called to the gatekeepers of the city. They told the gatekeepers, "We went to the Aramean camp, but we did not hear anyone. No one was there, but the horses and donkeys were still tied up, and the tents were still standing."

11Then the gatekeepers of the city shouted out and told the people in the king's palace. 12It was night, but the king got up from bed and said to his officers, "I will tell you what the Aramean soldiers are doing to us. They know we are hungry. They left the camp to hide in the field. They are thinking, 'When the Israelites come out of the city, we will capture them alive. And then we will enter the city.'"

13One of the king's officers said, "Let some men take five of the horses that are still left in the city. The horses will soon die anyway, just as all the Israelites who are still left in the city.[f] Let's send these men to see what happened."

14So the men took two chariots* with horses. The king sent these men after the Aramean army. He told them, "Go and see what happened."

15The men went after the Aramean army as far as the Jordan River. All along the road

---

[a]6:25 one pint Literally, "1/4 cab" (about .3 l).

[b]6:33 messenger Or possibly, "king."

[c]7:1 basket Literally, "seah." Also in verses 16, 18.

[d]7:1 shekel 2/5 of an ounce (11.5 g). Also in verses 16, 18.

[e]7:2 that was close to the king Literally, "on whose arm the king leaned."

[f]7:13 The horses ... city The Hebrew text here is hard to understand.

there were clothes and weapons. The Arameans had thrown these things down when they hurried away. The messengers went back to Samaria and told the king.

16Then the people ran out to the Aramean camp and took valuable things from there. So it happened just as the LORD had said. A person could buy a basket of fine flour or two baskets of barley for only one shekel.

17There was one officer who always stayed close by the king to help him. The king sent this officer to guard the gate, but the people knocked him down and trampled him, and he died. So everything happened just as the man of God* had said when the king came to Elisha's house. 18Elisha had said, "A person will be able to buy a basket of fine flour or two baskets of barley for only one shekel in the marketplace by the city gates of Samaria." 19But that officer had answered the man of God, "Even if the LORD made windows in heaven, this could not happen!" And Elisha had told the officer, "You will see it with your own eyes, but you will not eat any of that food." 20It happened to the officer just that way. The people knocked him down at the gate and trampled him, and he died.

The King and the Shunammite Woman

8 1Elisha talked to the woman whose son he had brought back to life. He said, "You and your family should move to another country, because the LORD has decided that there will be a famine* here. It will last for seven years."

2So the woman did what the man of God* said. She went with her family to stay in the land of the Philistines for seven years. 3After seven years she returned from the land of the Philistines.

She went to speak with the king to ask him to help her get back her house and land.

4The king was talking with Gehazi, the servant of the man of God. The king said to Gehazi, "Please tell me all the great things Elisha has done."

5Gehazi was telling the king about Elisha bringing a dead person back to life. At that same time the woman whose son Elisha brought back to life went to the king. She wanted to ask him to help her get back her house and land. Gehazi said, "My lord and king, this is the woman, and this is the son who Elisha brought back to life."

6The king asked the woman what she wanted, and she told him.

Then the king chose an officer to help her. The king said, "Give to the woman all that belongs to her. And give her all the harvest of her land from the day she left the country until now."

Ben-Hadad Sends Hazael to Elisha

7Elisha went to Damascus. King Ben-Hadad of Aram was sick. Someone told Ben-Hadad, "The man of God* has come here."

8Then the King Ben-Hadad said to Hazael, "Take a gift and go meet the man of God. Ask him to ask the LORD if I will get well from my sickness."

9So Hazael went to meet Elisha. Hazael brought a gift with him. He brought all kinds of good things from Damascus. It took 40 camels to carry everything. Hazael came to Elisha and said, "Your follower,a King Ben-Hadad of Aram, sent me to you. He asks if he will get well from his sickness."

10Then Elisha said to Hazael, "Go and tell Ben-Hadad, 'You will live.' But really the LORD told me, 'He will die.'"

Elisha Makes a Prophecy About Hazael

11Elisha began to stare. He stared for an embarrassingly long time. Then the man of God* began to cry. 12Hazael said, "Sir, why are you crying?"

Elisha answered, "I am crying because I know the bad things you will do to the Israelites. You will burn their strong cities and kill their young men with swords. You will kill their babies and split open their pregnant women."

13Hazael said, "I am not a powerful man!b How can I do these great things?"

Elisha answered, "The LORD showed me that you will be king over Aram." 14Then Hazael left Elisha and went to his king.c Ben-Hadad said to Hazael, "What did Elisha say to you?"

He answered, "Elisha told me that you will live."

Hazael Murders Ben-Hadad

15But the next day Hazael took a thick cloth and dipped it in water. Then he held it on Ben-Hadad's face until he died. Then Hazael became the new king.

Jehoram Begins His Rule

16Jehoram son of Jehoshaphat was the king of Judah. He began to rule in the fifth year that Joram son of Ahab was king of Israel.d 17Jehoram was 32 years old when he began to rule. He ruled eight years in Jerusalem. 18But Jehoram lived like the kings of Israel and did what the LORD saw as evil. He lived like the people from Ahab's family, because his wife was Ahab's daughter. 19But the LORD would not destroy Judah because of the promise to his servant David. The LORD had promised

---

a8:9 follower Literally, "son."
b8:13 I ... powerful man Literally, "Your servant is only a dog!"
c8:14 king Literally, "master."
d8:16 This is found in the ancient Greek and Syriac versions. The standard Hebrew text also adds "while Jehoshaphat was still king of Judah." That is, according to the Hebrew, father and son ruled Judah together for a time.

David that someone from his family would always be king.

20In Jehoram's time Edom broke away from Judah's rule. The people of Edom chose a king for themselves.

21Then Jehoram and all his chariots* went to Zair. The Edomite army surrounded them, but Jehoram and his officers attacked them and escaped. Jehoram's soldiers all ran away and went home. 22So the Edomites broke away from the rule of Judah. And they have been free from the rule of Judah until today.

At the same time Libnah also broke away from Judah's rule.

23All the things Jehoram did are written in the book, *The History of the Kings of Judah*.

24Jehoram died and was buried with his ancestors* in the City of David.* Jehoram's son Ahaziah became the new king.

Ahaziah Begins His Rule

25Ahaziah son of Jehoram became the king of Judah in the 12th year that Joram son of Ahab was king of Israel. 26Ahaziah was 22 years old when he began to rule. He ruled one year in Jerusalem. His mother's name was Athaliah. She was the daughter of King Omri of Israel. 27Ahaziah did what the LORD said was wrong. He did many bad things, just as the people from Ahab's family had done. He lived like this because his wife was from Ahab's family.

Joram Is Hurt in the War Against Hazael

28Joram was from Ahab's family. Ahaziah went with Joram to fight against King Hazael of Aram at Ramoth Gilead. The Arameans wounded Joram. 29King Joram went back to Israel so that he could get well from those wounds. He went to the area of Jezreel. Ahaziah son of Jehoram was the king of Judah. Ahaziah went to Jezreel to see Joram.

Elisha Tells a Prophet to Anoint Jehu

9　1Elisha the prophet called one of the men from the group of prophets*a* and said to him, "Get ready and take this small bottle of oil in your hand. Go to Ramoth Gilead. 2When you arrive, find Jehu son of Jehoshaphat, the son of Nimshi. Then go in and make him get up from among his brothers. Take him to an inner room. 3Take the small bottle of oil and pour the oil on Jehu's head. Say, 'This is what the LORD says: I have anointed* you to be the new king over Israel.' Then open the door and run away. Don't wait!"

4So this young man, the prophet, went to Ramoth Gilead. 5When the young man arrived, he saw the captains of the army sitting. He said, "Captain, I have a message for you."

Jehu asked, "Which one of us is the message for?"

The young man said, "For you, sir."

6Jehu got up and went into the house. Then the young prophet poured the oil on Jehu's head and said to him, "The LORD, the God of Israel, says, 'I am anointing you to be the new king over the LORD's people, Israel. 7You must destroy the family of Ahab your king. In this way I will punish Jezebel for the deaths of my servants, the prophets, and the deaths of all the LORD's servants who were murdered. 8So all Ahab's family will die. I will not let any male child in Ahab's family live. It doesn't matter if that male child is a slave or a free person in Israel. 9I will make Ahab's family like the family of Jeroboam son of Nebat and like the family of Baasha son of Ahijah. 10The dogs will eat Jezebel in the area of Jezreel, and she will not be buried.'"

Then the young prophet opened the door and ran away.

The Servants Announce Jehu as King

11Jehu went back to his king's officers. One of the officers said to Jehu, "Is everything all right? Why did this crazy man come to you?"

Jehu answered the servants, "You know the man and the crazy things he says."

12The officers said, "No, tell us the truth. What did he say?" Jehu told the officers what the young prophet said. Jehu said, "He said a few things and then he said, 'This is what the LORD says: I have anointed you to be the new king over Israel.'"

13Then each officer quickly took his robe off and put it on the steps in front of Jehu. Then they blew the trumpet and made the announcement, "Jehu is king!"

Jehu Goes to Jezreel

14So Jehu son of Jehoshaphat, son of Nimshi, made plans against Joram.

At that time Joram and the Israelites had been trying to defend Ramoth Gilead from King Hazael of Aram. 15King Joram had fought against King Hazael of Aram. But the Arameans wounded King Joram, and he went to Jezreel to get well from those injuries.

So Jehu told the officers, "If you agree that I am the new king, don't let anyone escape from the city to tell the news in Jezreel."

16Joram was resting in Jezreel, so Jehu got in his chariot* and drove to Jezreel. King Ahaziah of Judah had also come to Jezreel to see Joram.

17A guard was standing on the tower in Jezreel. He saw Jehu's large group coming. He said, "I see a large group of people!"

Joram said, "Send someone on a horse to meet them. Tell this messenger to ask if they come in peace."

18So the messenger rode on a horse to meet Jehu. The messenger said, "King Joram says, 'Do you come in peace?'"

---

*a***9:1** *group of prophets* Literally, "sons of the prophets." These were prophets and people studying to become prophets.

Jehu said, "You have nothing to do with peace. Come and follow me."

The guard told Joram, "The messenger went to the group, but he has not come back yet."

¹⁹Then Joram sent out a second messenger on a horse. This man came to Jehu's group and said, "King Joram says, 'Peace.'ᵃ"

Jehu answered, "You have nothing to do with peace. Come and follow me."

²⁰The guard told Joram, "The second messenger went to the group, but he has not come back yet. There is a man driving his chariot like a mad man. He is driving like Jehu son of Nimshi."

²¹Joram said, "Get me my chariot!"

So the servant got Joram's chariot. Both King Joram of Israel and King Ahaziah of Judah got their chariots and drove out to meet Jehu. They met him at the property of Naboth from Jezreel.

²²Joram saw Jehu and asked, "Do you come in peace, Jehu?"

Jehu answered, "There is no peace as long as your mother Jezebel does many acts of prostitution and witchcraft.*"

²³Joram turned the horses to run away. He said to Ahaziah, "It is a trick, Ahaziah!"

²⁴But Jehu grabbed his bow and shot Joram in the middle of his back, through the heart. Joram fell dead in his chariot.

²⁵Jehu said to his chariot driver Bidkar, "Take Joram's body up and throw it into the field of Naboth from Jezreel. Remember when you and I rode together with Joram's father Ahab, the LORD said this would happen to him. ²⁶The LORD said, 'Yesterday I saw the blood of Naboth and his sons. So I will punish Ahab in this field.' The LORD said that. So take Joram's body and throw it into the field, just as he said."

²⁷King Ahaziah of Judah saw this and ran away. He tried to escape through the garden house, but Jehu followed him. Jehu had said, "Shoot Ahaziah too!"

Ahaziah was wounded when he was in his chariot on the road to Gur near Ibleam. He got as far as Megiddo, but he died there. ²⁸Ahaziah's servants carried his body in the chariot to Jerusalem. They buried him in his tomb with his ancestors* in the City of David.*

²⁹Ahaziah had become king over Judah during Joram'sᵇ eleventh year as king of Israel.

The Terrible Death of Jezebel

³⁰When Jehu came to Jezreel, Jezebel heard the news. She put her makeup on and fixed her hair. Then she stood by the window and looked out. ³¹Jehu entered the city. Jezebel said, "Hello, you Zimri.ᶜ You killed your master just as he did."

³²Jehu looked up at the window and said, "Who is on my side? Who?"

Two or three eunuchs* looked out at Jehu. ³³Jehu said, "Throw Jezebel down!"

Then the eunuchs threw her down. Some of her blood splashed on the wall and on the horses that trampled her body. ³⁴Jehu went into the house and ate and drank. Then he said, "Now see about this cursed woman. Bury her, because she is a king's daughter."

³⁵The men went to bury Jezebel, but they could not find her body. They could only find her skull, her feet, and the palms of her hands. ³⁶When the men came back and told Jehu, he said, "The LORD told his servant Elijah the Tishbite to give this message: 'Dogs will eat the body of Jezebel in the area of Jezreel. ³⁷Her body will be like dung on the field in the area of Jezreel. No one will be able to recognize her body!'"

Jehu Writes the Leaders of Samaria

10 ¹Ahab had 70 sons in Samaria. Jehu wrote letters and sent them to Samaria to the rulers and leaders of Jezreel.ᵈ He also sent the letters to the people who raised Ahab's sons saying, ²⁻³"As soon as you get this letter, choose the one who is the best and most worthy among your master's sons. You have chariots* and horses. And you are living in a strong city. You also have weapons. Put the son you choose on his father's throne. Then fight for your master's family."

⁴But the rulers and leaders of Jezreel were very afraid. They said, "The two kings could not stop Jehu. So we cannot stop him either!"

⁵The palace manager, the official in charge of the city, the elders, and the people who raised the king's children sent a message to Jehu. "We are your servants and we will do whatever you tell us. We will not make anyone king; you may do whatever you think is best."

Leaders of Samaria Kill Ahab's Children

⁶Then Jehu wrote a second letter to these leaders. He said, "If you support me and obey me, cut off the heads of Ahab's sons. Bring them to me at Jezreel about this time tomorrow."

Ahab had 70 sons. They were with the leaders of the city who raised them. ⁷When the leaders of the city received the letter, they took the king's sons and killed all 70 of them. Then the leaders put the heads of the king's sons in baskets and sent the baskets to Jehu at Jezreel. ⁸The messenger came to Jehu and told him, "They have brought the heads of the king's sons."

Then Jehu said, "Lay the heads in two piles at the city gate until morning."

ᵃ**9:19** *Peace* A way of saying "hello."
ᵇ**9:29** *Joram's* Literally, "Joram son of Ahab."
ᶜ**9:31** *Zimri* Zimri killed Elah and the family of Baasha in Israel many years before. Read 1 Kings 16:8–12.

ᵈ**10:1** *leaders of Jezreel* The ancient Greek and Latin versions have "leaders of the city (Samaria)."

9In the morning Jehu went out and stood before the people. He said to them, "You are innocent. Look, I made plans against my master. I killed him. But who killed all these sons of Ahab? You killed them. 10You should know that everything the LORD says will happen. The LORD used Elijah to say these things about Ahab's family. Now the LORD has done what he said he would do."

11So Jehu killed all the people in Ahab's family living in Jezreel. He killed all the important men, close friends, and priests. None of Ahab's people were left alive.

Jehu Kills Ahaziah's Relatives

12Jehu left Jezreel and went to Samaria. On the way he stopped at a place called Shepherd's Camp. 13There he met with the relatives of King Ahaziah of Judah. Jehu asked, "Who are you?"

They answered, "We are the relatives of King Ahaziah of Judah. We have come down to visit the king's children and the queen mother's*a* children."

14Then Jehu said, "Take them alive!"

Jehu's men captured Ahaziah's relatives alive. There were 42 of them. Jehu killed them at the well near Beth Eked. He did not leave anyone alive.

Jehu Meets Jehonadab

15After Jehu left there, he met Jehonadab son of Recab. Jehonadab was on his way to meet Jehu. Jehu greeted Jehonadab and said to him, "Are you a faithful friend to me, as I am to you?"*b*

Jehonadab answered, "Yes, I am a faithful friend to you."

Jehu said, "If you are, give me your hand." Then Jehu reached out and pulled Jehonadab up into the chariot.*

16Jehu said, "Come with me. You can see how strong my feelings are for the LORD."

So Jehonadab rode in Jehu's chariot. 17Jehu came to Samaria and killed all Ahab's family who were still alive in Samaria. He killed them all. He did what the LORD had told Elijah.

Jehu Calls the Worshipers of Baal

18Then Jehu gathered all the people together and said to them, "Ahab served Baal* a little, but Jehu will serve Baal much. 19Now call together all the priests and prophets of Baal. And call together everyone who worships Baal. Don't let anyone miss this meeting. I have a great sacrifice to give to Baal. I will kill anyone who does not come to this meeting."

But Jehu was tricking them. He wanted to destroy the worshipers of Baal. 20Jehu said, "Prepare a holy meeting for Baal." So the priests announced the meeting. 21Then Jehu sent a message through all the land of Israel. All the worshipers of Baal came. Not one stayed home. The Baal worshipers came into the temple of Baal. The temple was filled with people.

22Jehu said to the man who kept the robes, "Bring out the robes for all the worshipers of Baal." So that man brought out the robes for the Baal worshipers.

23Then Jehu and Jehonadab son of Recab went into the temple of Baal. Jehu said to the worshipers of Baal, "Look around and be sure that there are no servants of the LORD with you. Be sure there are only people who worship Baal." 24The worshipers of Baal went into the temple of Baal to offer sacrifices and burnt offerings.

But outside, Jehu had 80 men waiting. He told them, "Don't let anyone escape. If any man lets one person escape, that man must pay with his own life."

25Quickly after Jehu had finished offering the burnt offering,* he said to the guards and to the captains, "Go in and kill the worshipers of Baal! Don't let anyone come out of the temple alive!"

So the captains used thin swords and killed the worshipers of Baal. They threw the bodies of the worshipers of Baal out. Then the guards and the captains went to the inner room*c* of the temple of Baal. 26They brought out the memorial stones* that were in the temple of Baal and burned that temple. 27Then they smashed the memorial stones of Baal. They also smashed the temple of Baal. They made the temple of Baal into a public toilet, which is still used today.

28So Jehu destroyed Baal worship in Israel, 29but he did not completely turn away from the sins of Jeroboam son of Nebat that caused Israel to sin. Jehu did not destroy the golden calves in Bethel and in Dan.

Jehu's Rule Over Israel

30The LORD said to Jehu, "You have done well. You have done what I say is good. You destroyed Ahab's family the way I wanted you to, so your descendants will rule Israel for four generations."

31But Jehu was not careful to follow the law of the LORD with all his heart. Jehu did not stop committing the sins of Jeroboam that caused Israel to sin.

Hazael Defeats Israel

32At that time the LORD began to cut away sections of Israel and give them to other nations. King Hazael of Aram defeated the Israelites on every border of Israel. 33He won the land east of the Jordan River—all the land

---

*a*10:13 *queen mother* The mother of the king.

*b*10:15 *Are you a faithful friend ... you* Literally, "Is your heart true to me? My heart is true to your heart."

*c*10:25 *inner room* Literally, "the city of the temple of Baal."

of Gilead, including the land that belonged to the tribes of Gad, Reuben, and Manasseh. He won all the land from Aroer by the Arnon Valley to Gilead and Bashan.

The Death of Jehu

³⁴All the other great things that Jehu did are written in the book, *The History of the Kings of Israel*. ³⁵Jehu died and was buried with his ancestors.* The people buried him in Samaria. His son Jehoahaz became the new king of Israel after him. ³⁶Jehu ruled over Israel in Samaria for 28 years.

Athaliah Kills the King's Sons in Judah

11 ¹Athaliah was Ahaziah's mother. She saw that her son was dead, so she got up and killed all the king's family.

²Jehosheba was King Joram's daughter and Ahaziah's sister. Joash was one of the king's sons. While the other children were being killed, Jehosheba took Joash and hid him. She put him and his nurse in her bedroom, so Jehosheba and the nurse hid Joash from Athaliah. That way Joash was not killed.

³Then Joash and Jehosheba hid in the LORD's Temple.* Joash hid there for six years. During that time Athaliah ruled over the land of Judah.

⁴In the seventh year Jehoiada the high priest sent for the captains of the Carites*a* and guards.*b* He brought them together in the LORD's Temple and made an agreement with them. In the Temple he forced them to make a promise. Then he showed the king's son to them.

⁵Then Jehoiada gave them a command. He said, "This is what you must do. One-third of you, from those who go on duty on the Sabbath* day, must stand guard at the royal palace. ⁶Another third will be at the Sur Gate, and the other third will be at the gate behind the guard. This way you will stand guard over the palace on all sides. ⁷Your two divisions who go off duty on the Sabbath day will stand guard at the LORD's Temple and protect King Joash. ⁸You must stay with him wherever he goes. The whole group must surround the king. Each guard must have his weapon in his hand, and you must kill anyone who comes too close to you."

⁹The captains obeyed everything that Jehoiada the priest commanded. Each captain took his men, both those who were going on duty on the Sabbath day and those who were going off duty. All these men went to Jehoiada the priest, ¹⁰and he gave spears and shields to the captains. These were the spears and shields David put in the LORD's Temple. ¹¹These guards stood with their weapons in their hands from the right corner of the Temple to the left corner. They stood around the altar* and the Temple and around the king when he went to the Temple. ¹²These men brought out Joash. They put the crown on him and gave him a copy of the agreement.*c* Then they anointed* him and made him the new king. They clapped their hands and shouted, "Long live the king!"

¹³Queen Athaliah heard the noise from the guards and the people, so she went to them at the LORD's Temple. ¹⁴Athaliah saw the king by the column where new kings usually stood. She also saw the leaders and men playing the trumpets for him. She saw that all the people were very happy. She heard the trumpets, and she tore her clothes to show she was upset. Then Athaliah shouted, "Treason! Treason!"

¹⁵Jehoiada the priest gave a command to the captains who were in charge of the soldiers. Jehoiada told them, "Take Athaliah outside of the Temple area. Kill any of her followers, but don't kill them in the LORD's Temple."

¹⁶So the soldiers grabbed Athaliah and killed her as soon as she went through the horse's entrance to the palace.

¹⁷Then Jehoiada made the agreement between the LORD and the king and the people. This agreement showed that the king and the people belonged to the LORD. Jehoiada also made the agreement between the king and the people.

¹⁸Then all the people went to the temple of Baal.* They destroyed the statue of Baal and his altars. They broke them into many pieces. They also killed Baal's priest, Mattan, in front of the altars.

So Jehoiada the priest put men in charge of maintaining the LORD's Temple. ¹⁹The priest led all the people. They went from the LORD's Temple to the king's palace. The king's special guards and the captains went with the king, and all the other people followed them. They went to the entrance to the king's palace. Then King Joash sat on the throne. ²⁰All the people were happy, and the city was peaceful. And Queen Athaliah was killed with a sword near the king's palace.

²¹Joash was seven years old when he became king.

Joash Begins His Rule

12 ¹Joash began to rule during Jehu's seventh year as king of Israel. Joash ruled 40 years in Jerusalem. His mother was named Zibiah of Beersheba. ²Joash did what the LORD said was right. He obeyed the LORD all his life. He did what Jehoiada the priest taught him, ³but he did not destroy the high places.* The people still made sacrifices and burned incense at those places of worship.

---

*a***11:4** *Carites* Or "Kerethites," special soldiers hired to serve the king.

*b***11:4** *guards* Literally, "runners" or "messengers."

*c***11:12** *a copy of the agreement* Literally, "testimony." This could be a copy of the Law of Moses (see Deut. 17:18) or a special agreement between God and the king (see verse 17 and 1 Sam. 10:25).

Joash Orders the Temple Repaired

⁴⁻⁵Joash said to the priests, "There is much money in the LORD's Temple.* People have given things to the Temple and have paid the Temple tax when they were counted. And they have given money simply because they wanted to. You priests should take that money and repair the LORD's Temple. Each priest should use the money he gets from the people he serves. He should use that money to repair the damage to the Temple."

⁶In the 23rd year that Joash was king, the priests still had not repaired the Temple, ⁷so King Joash called for Jehoiada the priest and the other priests. Joash said to them, "Why haven't you repaired the Temple? Stop taking money from the people you serve. That money must be used to repair the Temple."

⁸The priests agreed to stop taking money from the people, but they also decided not to repair the Temple. ⁹So Jehoiada the priest took a box and made a hole in the top of it. Then Jehoiada put the box on the south side of the altar.* This box was by the door where people came into the LORD's Temple. Some of the priests guarded the doorway*ᵃ of the Temple. They took the money people had given to the LORD, and they put that money into that box.

¹⁰Whenever the king's secretary and the high priest saw there was a lot of money in the box, they came and took the money from the box. They put the money in bags and counted it. ¹¹Then they paid the workers who worked on the LORD's Temple. They paid the carpenters and other builders who worked on the Temple. ¹²They used that money to pay the stoneworkers and stonecutters, and they used it to buy timber, cut stone, and everything else to repair the LORD's Temple.

¹³⁻¹⁴People gave money for the LORD's Temple, but the priests could not use that money to make silver cups, snuffers,* basins, trumpets, or any gold and silver dishes. That money was used to pay the workers who repaired the LORD's Temple. ¹⁵No one counted all the money or forced the workers to tell what happened to the money, because those workers could be trusted.

¹⁶People gave money when they offered guilt offerings and sin offerings,* but that money was not used to pay the workers. It belonged to the priests.

Joash Saves Jerusalem From Hazael

¹⁷Hazael was the king of Aram. He went to fight against the city of Gath and defeated it. Then he made plans to go fight against Jerusalem.

¹⁸Jehoshaphat, Jehoram, and Ahaziah had been kings of Judah. They were Joash'sᵇ ancestors.* They had given many things to the LORD that were kept in the Temple.* Joash also had given many things to the LORD. He took all these things and all the gold that was in the Temple and in his palace. Joash sent all these expensive things to King Hazael of Aram, so the king and his army left Jerusalem.

The Death of Joash

¹⁹All the great things that Joash did are written in the book, *The History of the Kings of Judah.*

²⁰Joash's officers made plans against him. They killed Joash at the house of Millo* on the road that goes down to Silla. ²¹Jozabad son of Shimeath and Jehozabad son of Shomer were Joash's officers. These men killed Joash.

The people buried Joash with his ancestors* in the City of David.* His son Amaziah became the new king after him.

Jehoahaz Begins His Rule

13 ¹Jehoahaz son of Jehu became king over Israel in Samaria. This was during the 23rd year that Joash son of Ahaziah was king in Judah. Jehoahaz ruled 17 years.

²Jehoahaz did what the LORD said was wrong. He followed the sins of Jeroboam son of Nebat who caused Israel to sin. Jehoahaz did not stop doing those things. ³Then the LORD was angry with Israel. He let King Hazael of Aram and Hazael's son Ben-Hadad gain control of Israel.

The Lord Has Mercy on Israel

⁴Then Jehoahaz begged the LORD to help them, and the LORD listened to him. The LORD had seen the troubles of Israel and how the king of Aram troubled the Israelites.

⁵So the LORD sent a man to save Israel. The Israelites were free from the Arameans. So the Israelites went to their own homes, as they did before.

⁶But the Israelites still did not stop committing the sins of the family of Jeroboam that caused Israel to sin. The Israelites continued committing the sins of Jeroboam. They also kept the Asherah poles* in Samaria.

⁷The king of Aram defeated Jehoahaz's army and destroyed most of the men in the army. He left only 50 horse soldiers, 10 chariots,* and 10,000 foot soldiers. Jehoahaz's soldiers were like chaff* blown away by the wind at the time of threshing.*

⁸All the great things that Jehoahaz did are written in the book, *The History of the Kings of Israel.* ⁹Jehoahaz died and was buried with his ancestors.* The people buried Jehoahaz in Samaria. His son Jehoash became the new king after him.

Jehoash's Rule Over Israel

¹⁰Jehoash son of Jehoahaz became king over Israel in Samaria. This was during the 37th year that Joash was king of Judah. Jehoash

---

ᵃ**12:9 doorway** Literally, "threshold."
ᵇ**12:18 Joash** Or "Jehoash," the long form of the name "Joash."

ruled Israel for 16 years. [11]He did what the LORD said was wrong. He did not stop committing the sins of Jeroboam son of Nebat who caused Israel to sin. Jehoash continued to commit those sins. [12]All the great things that Jehoash did and his wars against King Amaziah of Judah are written in the book, *The History of the Kings of Israel.* [13]Jehoash died and was buried with his ancestors.* Jeroboam became the new king and sat on Jehoash's throne. Jehoash was buried at Samaria with the kings of Israel.

Jehoash Visits Elisha

[14]Elisha became sick, and later he died from this sickness. King Jehoash of Israel went to visit Elisha. Jehoash cried for him and said, "My father, my father! Is it time for the chariot of Israel and its horses?[a]"

[15]Elisha said to Jehoash, "Take a bow and some arrows."

Jehoash took a bow and some arrows. [16]Then Elisha said to the king of Israel, "Put your hand on the bow." Jehoash put his hand on the bow. Then Elisha put his hands on the king's hands. [17]Elisha said, "Open the east window." Jehoash opened the window. Then Elisha said, "Shoot."

Jehoash shot. Then Elisha said, "This is the LORD's arrow of victory over Aram! You will defeat the Arameans at Aphek until you destroy them."

[18]Elisha said, "Take the arrows." Jehoash took the arrows. Then Elisha said to him, "Hit on the ground."

Jehoash hit the ground three times. Then he stopped. [19]The man of God* was angry with Jehoash. Elisha said, "You should have hit five or six times! Then you would have defeated Aram until you destroyed it! But now, you will defeat Aram only three times."

An Amazing Thing at Elisha's Grave

[20]Elisha died, and the people buried him.

One time in the spring a group of Moabite soldiers came to fight against Israel. [21]Some Israelites were burying a dead man when they saw that group of soldiers. The Israelites quickly threw the dead man into Elisha's grave. As soon as the dead man touched the bones of Elisha, he came back to life and stood up on his feet.

Jehoash Wins Back Cities of Israel

[22]During all the days that Jehoahaz ruled, King Hazael of Aram caused trouble to Israel. [23]But the LORD was kind to the Israelites. The LORD had mercy and turned to the Israelites, because of his agreement* with Abraham, Isaac, and Jacob. The LORD would not destroy the Israelites or throw them away yet.

[24]King Hazael of Aram died, and Ben-Hadad

became the new king after him. [25]Before he died, Hazael had taken some cities in war from Jehoahaz, Jehoash's father. But now Jehoash took back these cities from Hazael's son Ben-Hadad. Jehoash defeated Ben-Hadad three times and took back the cities of Israel.

Amaziah Begins His Rule in Judah

14 [1]Amaziah son of King Joash of Judah became king in the second year that Jehoash son of Jehoahaz was king of Israel. [2]Amaziah was 25 years old when he began to rule. He ruled 29 years in Jerusalem. His mother was Jehoaddin from Jerusalem. [3]Amaziah did what the LORD said was right, but he did not follow God completely like David his ancestor.* Amaziah did everything that Joash his father had done. [4]He did not destroy the high places.* The people still sacrificed and burned incense* at those places of worship.

[5]At the time that Amaziah had strong control of the kingdom, he killed the officers who had killed his father. [6]But he did not kill the children of the murderers because of the rules written in the book, *The Law of Moses.* The LORD gave this command in there: "Parents must not be put to death for something their children did. And children must not be put to death for something their parents did. People should be put to death only for what that they themselves did."[b]

[7]Amaziah killed 10,000 Edomites in the Valley of Salt. In war Amaziah took Sela and called it "Joktheel." It is still called "Joktheel" today.

Amaziah Wants War Against Jehoash

[8]Amaziah sent messengers to Jehoash son of Jehoahaz, son of King Jehu of Israel. Amaziah's message said, "Come on, let's meet together face to face and fight."

[9]King Jehoash of Israel sent an answer to King Amaziah of Judah. Jehoash said, "The thornbush in Lebanon sent a message to the cedar tree in Lebanon. It said, 'Give your daughter for my son to marry.' But a wild animal from Lebanon passed by and trampled down the thornbush. [10]True, you have defeated Edom. But you have become proud because of your victory over Edom. But stay at home and brag! Don't make trouble for yourself. If you do this, you will fall, and Judah will fall with you!"

[11]But Amaziah would not listen to Jehoash's warning. So King Jehoash of Israel went to fight against King Amaziah of Judah at Beth Shemesh in Judah.[c] [12]Israel defeated Judah. Every man of Judah ran home. [13]At Beth Shemesh, King Jehoash of Israel captured King Amaziah of Judah, the son of Joash, the son of Ahaziah. Jehoash took Amaziah to Jerusalem.

---

[b]**14:6** *Parents must ... did* See Deut. 24:16.
[c]**14:11** *Jehoash ... Judah* Literally, "He and King Amaziah of Judah looked at each other in the face at Beth Shemesh in Judah."

[a]**13:14** *Is it time ... horses* This means "Is it time for God to come and take you?" See 2 Kings 2:12.

Jehoash broke down the wall of Jerusalem from the Gate of Ephraim to the corner gate, about 600 feet.*a* ¹⁴Then Jehoash took all the gold and silver and all the dishes in the LORD's Temple and in the treasures of the king's palace. Jehoash also took people to be his prisoners. Then he went back to Samaria.

¹⁵All the great things that Jehoash did, including how he fought against King Amaziah of Judah, are written in the book, *The History of the Kings of Israel.* ¹⁶Jehoash died and was buried with his ancestors.* He was buried in Samaria with the kings of Israel. Jehoash's son Jeroboam became the new king after him.

The Death of Amaziah

¹⁷King Amaziah son of Joash of Judah lived 15 years after the death of King Jehoash son of Jehoahaz of Israel. ¹⁸All the great things that Amaziah did are written in the book, *The History of the Kings of Judah.* ¹⁹The people made a plan against Amaziah in Jerusalem, so he ran away to Lachish. But the people sent men after Amaziah to Lachish, and they killed him there. ²⁰The people brought Amaziah's body back on horses. He was buried at Jerusalem with his ancestors* in the City of David.*

Azariah Begins His Rule Over Judah

²¹Then all the people of Judah made Azariah the new king. Azariah was 16 years old. ²²So King Amaziah died and was buried with his ancestors.* Then Azariah rebuilt Elath and got it back for Judah.

Jeroboam II Begins His Rule Over Israel

²³King Jeroboam son of Jehoash of Israel began to rule in Samaria during the 15th year that Amaziah son of Joash was king of Judah. Jeroboam ruled 41 years. ²⁴Jeroboam did what the LORD said was wrong. He did not stop committing the sins of Jeroboam son of Nebat who caused Israel to sin. ²⁵Jeroboam took back Israel's land, which ran from the Lebo Hamath to the Arabah Sea.*b* This happened as the LORD of Israel had told his servant Jonah son of Amittai, the prophet from Gath Hepher. ²⁶The LORD saw that all the Israelites, both slaves and free men, had many troubles. No one was left who could help Israel. ²⁷The LORD did not say that he would take away the name of Israel from the world. So he used Jeroboam son of Jehoash to save the Israelites.

²⁸All the great things that Jeroboam did are written in the book, *The History of the Kings of Israel.* This includes the story about Jeroboam winning back Damascus and Hamath for Israel. (These cities had belonged to Judah.) ²⁹Jeroboam died and was buried with his ancestors,* the kings of Israel. Jeroboam's son Zechariah became the new king after him.

Azariah's Rule Over Judah

15 ¹King Azariah son of Amaziah of Judah became king in the 27th year that Jeroboam was king of Israel. ²Azariah was 16 years old when he began to rule. He ruled 52 years in Jerusalem. His mother was named Jecoliah of Jerusalem. ³Azariah did what the LORD said was right, just as his father Amaziah had done. ⁴But he did not destroy the high places.* People still made sacrifices and burned incense* in these places of worship.

⁵The LORD caused King Azariah to become sick with leprosy.* He was a leper until the day he died. Azariah lived in a separate house. His son Jotham was in charge of the king's palace, and he ruled the people.

⁶All the great things that Azariah did are written in the book, *The History of the Kings of Judah.* ⁷Azariah died and was buried with his ancestors* in the City of David.* Azariah's son Jotham became the new king after him.

Zechariah's Short Rule Over Israel

⁸Zechariah son of Jeroboam ruled over Samaria in Israel for six months. This was during the 38th year that Azariah was king of Judah. ⁹Zechariah did what the LORD said was wrong. He did the same things his ancestors* did. He did not stop committing the sins of Jeroboam son of Nebat who caused Israel to sin.

¹⁰Shallum son of Jabesh made plans against Zechariah. Shallum killed Zechariah in Ibleam.*c* Shallum became the new king. ¹¹All the other things that Zechariah did are written in the book, *The History of the Kings of Israel.* ¹²In this way the LORD's word came true. He had told Jehu that four generations of his descendants would be kings of Israel.

Shallum's Short Rule Over Israel

¹³Shallum son of Jabesh became king of Israel during the 39th year that Uzziah was king of Judah. Shallum ruled for one month in Samaria. ¹⁴Menahem son of Gadi came up from Tirzah to Samaria and killed Shallum son of Jabesh. Then Menahem became the new king after him.

¹⁵All the things Shallum did, including his plans against Zechariah, are written in the book, *The History of the Kings of Israel.*

Menahem's Rule Over Israel

¹⁶Menahem defeated Tiphsah and the area around it. The people refused to open the city gate for him. So Menahem defeated them and ripped open all the pregnant women in that city.

¹⁷Menahem son of Gadi became king over Israel during the 39th year that Azariah was

---

*a***14:13** *about 600 feet* Literally, "400 cubits" (177.6 m).
*b***14:25** *Arabah Sea* The Dead Sea.

*c***15:10** *in Ibleam* This is found in some copies of the ancient Greek version. The standard Hebrew text has "in public."

king of Judah. Menahem ruled ten years in Samaria. ¹⁸Menahem did what the LORD said was wrong. He did not stop committing the sins of Jeroboam son of Nebat who caused Israel to sin.

¹⁹King Pul of Assyria came to fight against Israel. Menahem gave Pul 75,000 pounds[a] of silver so that Pul would support him and help him gain complete control of the kingdom. ²⁰Menahem raised the money by making all the rich and powerful men pay taxes. He taxed each man 20 ounces[b] of silver and gave the money to the king of Assyria. So the king of Assyria left and did not stay there in Israel.

²¹All the great things that Menahem did are written in the book, *The History of the Kings of Israel.* ²²Menahem died and was buried with his ancestors.* His son Pekahiah became the new king after him.

Pekahiah's Rule Over Israel

²³Pekahiah son of Menahem became king over Israel in Samaria during the 50th year that Azariah was king of Judah. Pekahiah ruled two years. ²⁴He did what the LORD said was wrong. He did not stop committing the sins of Jeroboam son of Nebat that caused Israel to sin.

²⁵The commander of Pekahiah's army was Pekah son of Remaliah. Pekah killed Pekahiah in Samaria at the king's palace. Pekah had 50 men from Gilead with him when he killed Pekahiah. Then Pekah became the new king after him.

²⁶All the great things Pekahiah did are written in the book, *The History of the Kings of Israel.*

Pekah's Rule Over Israel

²⁷Pekah son of Remaliah began to rule over Israel in Samaria during the 52nd year that Azariah was king of Judah. Pekah ruled 20 years. ²⁸Pekah did what the LORD said was wrong. He did not stop committing the sins of Jeroboam son of Nebat who caused Israel to sin.

²⁹King Tiglath Pileser of Assyria came to fight against Israel while Pekah was king of Israel. Tiglath Pileser captured Ijon, Abel Bethmaacah, Janoah, Kedesh, Hazor, Gilead, Galilee, and all the area of Naphtali. He took the people from these places as prisoners to Assyria.

³⁰Hoshea son of Elah made plans against Pekah son of Remaliah and killed him. Then Hoshea became the new king. This was during the 20th year that Jotham son of Uzziah was king of Judah.

³¹All the great things that Pekah did are written in the book, *The History of the Kings of Israel.*

Jotham's Rule Over Judah

³²Jotham son of Uzziah became king of Judah. This was during the second year that Pekah son of Remaliah was king of Israel. ³³Jotham was 25 years old when he became king. He ruled 16 years in Jerusalem. His mother was named Jerusha, the daughter of Zadok. ³⁴Jotham did what the LORD said was right, just as his father Uzziah had done. ³⁵But he did not destroy the high places.* The people still made sacrifices and burned incense* at those places of worship. Jotham built the upper gate of the LORD's Temple.* ³⁶All the great things that Jotham did are written in the book, *The History of the Kings of Judah.*

³⁷At that time the LORD sent King Rezin of Aram and Pekah son of Remaliah to fight against Judah.

³⁸Jotham died and was buried with his ancestors* in the City of David,* his ancestor. Jotham's son Ahaz became the new king after him.

Ahaz Becomes King Over Judah

16 ¹Ahaz son of Jotham became king of Judah during the 17th year that Pekah son of Remaliah was king of Israel. ²Ahaz was 20 years old when he became king. He ruled 16 years in Jerusalem. Unlike his ancestor* David, Ahaz did not do what the LORD said was right. ³He did the same bad things the kings of Israel had done. He even burned his son as a sacrifice.[c] He copied the terrible sins of the nations that the LORD had forced to leave the country when the Israelites came. ⁴Ahaz made sacrifices and burned incense* at the high places* and on the hills and under every green tree.

⁵King Rezin of Aram and King Pekah son of Remaliah of Israel came to fight against Jerusalem. Rezin and Pekah surrounded Ahaz, but could not defeat him. ⁶At that time King Rezin of Aram took back Elath for Aram. Rezin took all the people of Judah who were living in Elath. The Arameans settled in Elath, and they still live there today.

⁷Ahaz sent messengers to King Tiglath Pileser of Assyria with this message: "I am your servant. I am like a son to you. Come and save me from the king of Aram and the king of Israel. They have come to fight me." ⁸Ahaz also took the silver and gold that was in the Temple* of the LORD and in the treasuries of the king's palace. Then Ahaz sent a gift to the king of Assyria. ⁹The king of Assyria listened to Ahaz and went to fight against Damascus. The king captured that city and took the people from Damascus as prisoners to Kir. He also killed Rezin.

---

[a]**15:19** *75,000 pounds* Literally, "1000 talents" (34,500 kg).
[b]**15:20** *20 ounces* Literally, "50 shekels" (575 g).

[c]**16:3** *burned his son as a sacrifice* Literally, "made his son pass through the fire."

¹⁰King Ahaz went to Damascus to meet King Tiglath Pileser of Assyria. Ahaz saw the altar* at Damascus. He sent a model and pattern of this altar to Uriah the priest. ¹¹Then Uriah the priest built an altar just like the model King Ahaz had sent him from Damascus. Uriah the priest built the altar this way before King Ahaz came back from Damascus.

¹²When the king arrived from Damascus, he saw the altar. He offered sacrifices on the altar. ¹³Ahaz burned his burnt offerings* and grain offerings on it. He poured his drink offering and sprinkled the blood of his fellowship offerings* on this altar.

¹⁴Ahaz took the bronze altar that was before the LORD from the front of the Temple. This bronze altar was between Ahaz's altar and the Temple of the LORD. Ahaz put the bronze altar on the north side of his own altar. ¹⁵He commanded Uriah the priest, "Use the large altar to burn the morning burnt offerings, the evening grain offerings, and the drink offerings from all the people of this country. Sprinkle all the blood from the burnt offering and other sacrifices on the large altar. But I will use the bronze altar to get answers from God." ¹⁶Uriah the priest did everything that King Ahaz commanded him to do.

¹⁷There were carts with bronze panels and basins for the priests to wash their hands. King Ahaz removed the panels and basins and cut up the carts. He also took the large tankᵃ off the bronze bulls that stood under it. He put the large tank on a stone pavement. ¹⁸Workers had built a covered place inside the Temple area for the Sabbath* meetings. But Ahaz removed the covered place and the outside entrance for the king. He removed all these from the LORD's Temple. Ahaz did this because of the king of Assyria.

¹⁹All the great things that Ahaz did are written in the book, *The History of the Kings of Judah*. ²⁰Ahaz died and was buried with his ancestors in the City of David.* Ahaz's son Hezekiah became the new king after him.

Hoshea Begins His Rule Over Israel

17 ¹Hoshea son of Elah began to rule in Samaria over Israel. This was during the 12th year that Ahaz was king of Judah. Hoshea ruled nine years. ²He did what the LORD said was wrong, but he was not as bad as the kings of Israel who had ruled before him.

³King Shalmaneser of Assyria came to fight against Hoshea and defeated him. So Hoshea paid tribute* to Shalmaneser.

⁴Later, Hoshea sent messengers to the king of Egypt to ask for help. That king's name was So. That year Hoshea did not pay tribute to the king of Assyria as he did every other year. The king of Assyria learned that Hoshea had made plans against him. So he arrested Hoshea and put him in jail.

⁵The king of Assyria attacked many places in Israel. Then he came to Samaria and fought against it for three years. ⁶The king of Assyria took Samaria during the ninth year that Hoshea was king of Israel. He captured many Israelites and took them as prisoners to Assyria. He made them live in Halah by the Habor River at Gozan and in other cities of the Medes.*

⁷These things happened because the Israelites had sinned against the LORD their God. And it was the Lord who brought the Israelites out of the land of Egypt! He saved them from the power of Pharaoh, the king of Egypt. But the Israelites began worshiping other gods. ⁸They began doing the same things that other people did. And the LORD had forced those people to leave their land when the Israelites came. The Israelites also chose to be ruled by kings. ⁹The Israelites secretly did things against the LORD their God, and those things were wrong!

The Israelites built high places* in all their cities—from the smallest town to the largest city. ¹⁰They put up memorial stones* and Asherah poles* on every high hill and under every green tree. ¹¹They burned incense* there in all those places for worship.ᵇ They did these things like the nations that the LORD forced out of the land before them. The Israelites did evil things that made the LORD angry. ¹²They served idols,* and the LORD had said to them, "You must not do this."

¹³The LORD used every prophet and every seer* to warn Israel and Judah. He said, "Turn away from the evil things you do. Obey my commands and laws. Follow all the law that I gave to your ancestors.* I used my servants the prophets to give this law to you."

¹⁴But the people would not listen. They were very stubborn like their ancestors. Their ancestors did not believe the LORD their God. ¹⁵They refused the LORD's laws and the agreement* that he made with their ancestors. They refused to listen to the Lord's warnings. They worshiped idols that were worth nothing and they themselves became worth nothing. They lived like the people in the nations around them. They did those bad things. And the Lord had warned the Israelites. The LORD told them not to do those bad things.

¹⁶The people stopped following the commands of the LORD their God. They made two gold statues of calves. They made Asherah poles. They worshiped all the stars of heaven and served Baal.* ¹⁷They sacrificed their sons and daughters in the fire. They used magic and witchcraft* to try to learn the future. They sold themselves to do what the LORD said was evil. They did this to make the LORD angry. ¹⁸So the LORD became very angry with Israel

---

ᵃ16:17 *tank* A very large container for water.

ᵇ17:11 *places for worship* Or "high places," places for worshiping God or false gods. These places were often on the hills and mountains.

and removed them from his sight. There were no Israelites left, except the tribe of Judah.

The People of Judah Are Also Guilty

¹⁹But even the people of Judah did not obey the commands of the LORD their God. They lived just as the Israelites had.

²⁰The LORD rejected all the Israelites. He brought them many troubles. He let people destroy them. Finally he threw them away and removed them from his sight. ²¹The LORD tore them from the family of David, and they made Jeroboam son of Nebat their king. Jeroboam pulled the Israelites away from following the LORD. He caused them to commit a great sin. ²²So the Israelites sinned in all the ways Jeroboam did. And they did not stop committing these sins ²³until the LORD took Israel away from his sight. And he said this would happen. He sent his prophets to tell the people this would happen. So the Israelites were taken out of their country into Assyria. And they have been there to this day.

Foreigners Settle in Israel

²⁴The king of Assyria took the Israelites out of Samaria and brought in other people from Babylon, Cuthah, Avva, Hamath, and Sepharvaim. They took over Samaria and lived in the cities around it. ²⁵When these people began to live in Samaria, they did not honor the LORD, so the LORD sent lions to attack them. The lions killed some of them. ²⁶Some people said to the king of Assyria, "The people who you took away and put in the cities of Samaria don't know the law of the god of that country. So that god sent lions to attack them. The lions killed them because they don't know the law of the god of that country."

²⁷So the king of Assyria gave this command: "You took some priests from Samaria. Send one of them who I captured back to Samaria. Let that priest go and live there. Then he can teach the people the law of the god of that country."

²⁸So one of the priests who the Assyrians had carried away from Samaria came to live in Bethel. He taught the people how they should honor the LORD.

²⁹But all those people made gods of their own. They put them in the temples at the high places* that the people of Samaria had made. They did this wherever they lived. ³⁰The people of Babylon made the false god Succoth Benoth. The people of Cuthah made the false god Nergal. The people of Hamath made the false god Ashima. ³¹The people of Avva made the false gods Nibhaz and Tartak. The people from Sepharvaim also burned their children in the fire to honor their false gods, Adrammelech and Anammelech.

³²But they also worshiped the LORD. They chose priests for the high places from among the people. These priests made sacrifices for the people in the temples at those places of worship. ³³They respected the LORD but also served their own gods, just as they did in their own countries.

³⁴Even today they live like they did in the past. They don't honor the LORD. They don't obey the rules and commands of the Israelites. They don't obey the law or the commands that the LORD gave to the children of Jacob. ³⁵The LORD made an agreement* with the Israelites. The LORD commanded them, "You must not honor other gods. You must not worship them or serve them or offer sacrifices to them. ³⁶But you must follow the LORD, who brought you out of Egypt. He used his great power to save you. You must worship him and make sacrifices to him. ³⁷You must obey the rules, laws, teachings, and commands that he wrote for you. You must obey these things all the time. You must not respect other gods. ³⁸You must not forget the agreement that I made with you. You must not respect other gods. ³⁹No, you must respect only the LORD your God. Then he will save you from all your enemies."

⁴⁰But the Israelites did not listen. They kept on doing the same things they did before. ⁴¹So now those other nations respected the LORD, but they also served their own idols.* Their children and grandchildren did the same thing their ancestors* did. They still do these things to this day.

Hezekiah Begins His Rule Over Judah

18 ¹Hezekiah son of Ahaz was king of Judah. Hezekiah began to rule during the third year that Hoshea son of Elah was king of Israel. ²Hezekiah was 25 years old when he began to rule. He ruled 29 years in Jerusalem. His mother's name was Abi,ᵃ the daughter of Zechariah.

³Hezekiah did what the LORD said was right, just as David his ancestor* had done.

⁴Hezekiah destroyed the high places.* He broke the memorial stones* and cut down the Asherah poles.* At that time the Israelites burned incense* to the bronze snake made by Moses. This bronze snake was called "Nehushtan."ᵇ Hezekiah broke this bronze snake into pieces.

⁵Hezekiah trusted in the LORD, the God of Israel. There was no one like Hezekiah among all the kings of Judah before him or after him. ⁶He was very faithful to the LORD and did not stop following him. He obeyed the commands that the LORD had given to Moses. ⁷The LORD was with Hezekiah, so he was successful in everything he did.

Hezekiah broke away from the king of Assyria and stopped serving him. ⁸Hezekiah defeated the Philistines all the way to Gaza and the area around it. He defeated all the

---

ᵃ**18:2 Abi** Or "Abijah."
ᵇ**18:4 Nehushtan** This Hebrew name is like the words meaning "bronze" and "snake."

Philistine cities—from the smallest town to the largest city.

The Assyrians Capture Samaria

9King Shalmaneser of Assyria went to fight against Samaria. His army surrounded the city. This happened during the fourth year that Hezekiah was king of Judah. (This was also the seventh year that Hoshea son of Elah was king of Israel.) 10At the end of the third year Shalmaneser captured Samaria. He took Samaria during the sixth year that Hezekiah was king of Judah. (This was also the ninth year that Hoshea was king of Israel.) 11The king of Assyria took the Israelites as prisoners to Assyria. He made them live in Halah, on the Habor (the river of Gozan), and in the cities of the Medes.* 12This happened because the Israelites did not obey the LORD their God. They broke his agreement* and did not obey everything that Moses, the LORD's servant, had commanded. The Israelites would not listen to the Lord's agreement, or do what it taught them to do.

Assyria Gets Ready to Take Judah

13During Hezekiah's 14th year as king, King Sennacherib of Assyria went to fight against all the strong cities of Judah. Sennacherib defeated them all. 14Then King Hezekiah of Judah sent a message to the king of Assyria at Lachish. Hezekiah said, "I have done wrong. Leave me alone, and I will pay whatever you want."

Then the king of Assyria told King Hezekiah of Judah to pay over 11 tons*a* of silver and over 1 ton*b* of gold. 15Hezekiah gave all the silver that was in the LORD's Temple* and in the king's treasuries. 16That is when Hezekiah cut off the gold that he had put on the doors and doorposts of the LORD's Temple and gave it to the king of Assyria.

King of Assyria Sends Men to Jerusalem

17The king of Assyria sent his three most important officers with a large army to King Hezekiah in Jerusalem. They left Lachish and went to Jerusalem. They stood near the aqueduct* by the Upper Pool,*c* on the street that leads up to Laundryman's Field. 18These men called for the king, but Eliakim son of Hilkiah, Shebna, and Joah son of Asaph went out to meet them. Eliakim was the palace manager, Joah was the record keeper, and Shebna was the royal secretary.

19The commander said to them, "Tell Hezekiah this is what the great king, the king of Assyria says:

'What are you trusting in to help you? 20If you say, "I trust in power and great battle plans," then that is useless. Now I ask you, who do you trust so much that you are willing to rebel against me? 21Are you depending on Egypt to help you? Egypt is like a broken walking stick. If you lean on it for support, it will only hurt you and make a hole in your hand. Pharaoh, the king of Egypt, cannot be trusted by anyone who depends on him for help. 22Maybe you will say, "We trust the LORD our God to help us." But I know that Hezekiah destroyed the altars* and high places* where people worshiped the Lord. Hezekiah told the people of Judah and Jerusalem, "You must worship only at this one altar here in Jerusalem."

23'If you still want to fight my master, the king of Assyria, I will make this agreement with you. I promise that I will give you 2000 horses if you can find enough men to ride them into battle. 24But even then you couldn't beat one of my master's lowest ranking officers. So why do you still depend on Egypt's chariots* and horse soldiers?

25'Now, do you think I came to this country to destroy it without the LORD's help? No, the LORD said to me, "Go up against this country and destroy it!"'"

26Then Eliakim son of Hilkiah, Shebna, and Joah said to the commander, "Please speak to us in Aramaic.* We understand that language. Don't speak to us in the language of Judah because the people on the wall will understand you."

27But the commander said to them, "My master did not send me to speak only to you and your master. I was also sent to speak to those people sitting on the wall. They, too, will not have enough food or water; they, too, will eat their own waste and drink their own urine like you!*d*"

28Then the commander shouted loudly in Hebrew,*e* "Hear this message from the great king, the king of Assyria! 29The king says, 'Don't let Hezekiah fool you, because he cannot save you from my power.' 30Don't let Hezekiah make you trust in the LORD.' Hezekiah says, 'The LORD will save us. The king of Assyria will not defeat this city.' 31But don't listen to Hezekiah. The king of Assyria says this:

---

*a*18:14 *11 tons* Literally, "300 talents" (10,350 kg).
*b*18:14 *1 ton* Literally, "30 talents" (1035 kg).
*c*18:17 *Upper Pool* The Pool of Siloam at the southern tip of the City of David (Jerusalem), just above the older pool now called Birket al Hamrah.

*d*18:27 *eat … like you* The Assyrian army planned to surround Jerusalem and not let people bring any food or water into the city. They thought the people would become hungry enough to eat their own waste.
*e*18:28 *Hebrew* Literally, "Judean," the language of Judah and Israel.

'Do this favor for me; come out to me and then everyone will be free to have grapes from their own vines, figs from their own trees, and water from their own well. 32You can do this until I come and take you away to a land like your own. In that new land, you will have good grain and new wine, bread, vineyards,* olive oil, and honey. Then you can live and not die. But don't listen to Hezekiah. He is trying to change your mind. He is saying, "The LORD will save us." 33Did any of the gods of the other nations save their land from the king of Assyria? 34Where are the gods of Hamath and Arpad? Where are the gods of Sepharvaim, Hena, and Ivvah? Did they save Samaria from me? 35Did any of the gods in the other countries save their land from me? No! So do you think the LORD will save Jerusalem from me?'"

36But the people were silent. They did not say a word to the commander because King Hezekiah had commanded them, "Don't say anything to him."

37Then the palace manager (Eliakim son of Hilkiah), the royal secretary (Shebna), and the record keeper (Joah son of Asaph) went to Hezekiah. Their clothes were torn to show they were upset. They told Hezekiah everything the Assyrian commander had said.

Hezekiah Talks With Isaiah the Prophet

19 1When King Hezekiah heard this, he tore his clothes to show he was upset. Then he put on sackcloth* and went to the LORD's Temple.*

2Hezekiah sent Eliakim the palace manager, Shebna the royal secretary, and the elders of the priests to the prophet Isaiah son of Amoz. They wore the special clothes that showed they were sad and upset. 3They said to Isaiah, "King Hezekiah has commanded that today will be a special day for sorrow and sadness. It will be a very sad day, like the time a child should be born, but is not strong enough to come from its mother's womb. 4The commander's master, the king of Assyria, has sent him to say bad things about the living God. Maybe the LORD your God will hear all those things. Maybe he will prove the enemy is wrong! So pray for the people who are still left alive."

5King Hezekiah's officers went to Isaiah. 6Isaiah said to them, "Give this message to your master, Hezekiah: The LORD says, 'Don't be afraid of what you heard from the commanders. Don't believe what those "boys" from the king of Assyria said to make fun of me. 7Look, I will send a spirit against the king of Assyria. He will get a report warning him about a danger, so he will return to his own country. And I will cut him down with a sword in his own country.'"

The Assyrian Army Leaves Jerusalem

8The commander heard that the king of Assyria had left Lachish. He found him at Libnah, fighting against that city. 9Then the king of Assyria heard a report that said, "Tirhakah,a the king of Ethiopia,* has come to fight against you."

So the king of Assyria sent messengers to Hezekiah again. 10He told them, "Tell King Hezekiah of Judah these things:

'Don't be fooled by the god you trust when he says Jerusalem will not be defeated by the king of Assyria. 11You have heard what the kings of Assyria did to all the other countries. We completely destroyed them! Will you be saved? No! 12Did the gods of those nations save their people? No, my ancestors* destroyed them all. They destroyed Gozan, Haran, Rezeph, and the people of Eden living in Tel Assar. 13Where is the king of Hamath? The king of Arpad? The king of the city of Sepharvaim? The kings of Hena and Ivvah?'"

Hezekiah Prays to the Lord

14Hezekiah received the letters from the messengers and read them. Then he went up to the LORD's Temple* and laid the letters out in front of the LORD. 15Hezekiah prayed before the LORD and said, "LORD, God of Israel, you sit as King above the Cherub angels.* You alone are the God who rules all the kingdoms on earth. You made heaven and earth. 16LORD, please listen to me. LORD, open your eyes and look at this message. Hear the words that Sennacherib sent to insult the living God. 17It is true, LORD. The kings of Assyria did destroy all those nations. 18They did throw the gods of those nations into the fire. But they were not real gods. They were only wood and stone—statues that people made. That is why the kings of Assyria could destroy them. 19But you are the LORD our God, so please save us from the king of Assyria. Then all the other nations will know that you, LORD, are the only God."

God Answers Hezekiah

20Then Isaiah son of Amoz sent this message to Hezekiah. Isaiah said, "The LORD, the God of Israel, says this: You prayed to me about the message that came from King Sennacherib of Assyria. I have heard you. 21"This is the LORD's message against Sennacherib:

'The virgin daughter Zionb does not think you are important.

---

a**19:9** *Tirhakah* This is probably Taharqa, the Pharaoh of Egypt about 690–664 B.C.
b**19:21** *The virgin daughter Zion* The city of Jerusalem. See "Zion" in the Word List.

She makes fun of you.
Daughter Jerusalem shakes her head at
  you
and laughs behind your back.
22 But who did you insult and make fun of?
  Who did you speak against?
You were against the Holy One of Israel.
  You acted like you were better than he
    was!
23 You sent your messengers to insult the
    Lord.
You said, "I came with my many
    chariots* to the high mountains deep
    inside Lebanon.
I cut down the tallest cedar trees and
    the best fir trees of Lebanon.
I went to its highest mountains, its
    thickest forests.
24 I dug wells, and drank water from new
    places.
I dried up the rivers of Egypt
and walked on the land there."
25 That is what you said, but haven't you
    heard what I said?
I planned it long ago;
  from ancient times I planned it.
And now I have made it happen.
I let you tear down the strong cities
  and change them into piles of rocks.
26 The people in the cities had no power.
  They were afraid and confused.
They were about to be cut down
  like grass and plants in the field.
They were like grass growing on the
    housetops,
  dying before it grows tall.
27 I know all about your battles;
I know when you rested,
  when you went out to war,
  and when you came home.
I also know when you got upset at me.
28 Yes, you were upset at me.
I heard your proud insults.
So I will put my hook in your nose
  and my bit in your mouth.
Then I will turn you around
  and lead you back the way you came.'"

The Lord's Message for Hezekiah
29Then the Lord said, "I will give you a sign
to show that these words are true. You were
not able to plant seeds this year, so next year
you will eat grain that grows wild from the
previous year's crop. But in the third year, you
will eat grain from seeds that you planted. You
will harvest your crops and have plenty to eat.
You will plant grapevines and eat their fruit.
You will plant vineyards* and eat the grapes
from them. 30The people from the family of
Judah who have escaped and are left alive
will be like plants that send their roots deep
into the ground and produce fruit above
the ground. 31That is because a few people
will come out of Jerusalem alive. There will
be survivors coming from Mount Zion. The

strong love^a of the LORD God will do this.
32"So the LORD says this about the king of
Assyria:

'He will not come into this city
  or shoot an arrow at this city.
He will not bring his shields up against
    this city
  or build up a hill of dirt to attack its
    walls.
33 He will go back the way he came,
  and he will not come into this city.
The LORD says this.
34 I will protect this city and save it.
I will do this for myself and for my
    servant David.'"

The Assyrian Army Is Destroyed
35That night the angel of the LORD went
out and killed 185,000 people in the Assyrian
camp. When the others got up in the morning, they saw all the dead bodies.
36So King Sennacherib of Assyria left and
went back to Nineveh where he stayed.
37One day Sennacherib was in the temple of
his god Nisroch, worshiping him. His sons
Adrammelech and Sharezer killed him with
a sword and ran away to Ararat.* So his son
Esarhaddon became the new king of Assyria.

Hezekiah's Illness
20 1At that time Hezekiah became sick
and almost died. The prophet Isaiah
son of Amoz went to see him and told him,
"The LORD says, 'You will die soon, so you
should tell your family what they should do
when you die. You will not get well.'"
2Hezekiah turned his face to the wall ₍that
faced the Temple₎ and began praying to the
LORD. 3"LORD, remember that I have sincerely
served you with all my heart. I have done
what you say is good." Then Hezekiah cried
very hard.
4Before Isaiah had left the middle courtyard, he received this message from the LORD,
5"Go back and speak to Hezekiah, the leader
of my people. Tell him, 'The LORD, the God
of your ancestor* David, says: I heard your
prayer and I saw your tears, so I will heal
you. On the third day you will go up to the
Temple* of the LORD. 6I will add 15 years to
your life. I will save you and this city from the
king of Assyria. I will protect this city. I will
do this for myself and because of the promise
I made to my servant David.'"
7Then Isaiah said, "Crush figs together and
put them on your sore; you will get well."
So they took the mixture of figs and put it
on Hezekiah's sore, and he got well.
8Hezekiah asked Isaiah, "What will be the
sign that the LORD will heal me, and that I

---

^{a}**19:31 strong love** The Hebrew word can mean
strong feelings such as zeal, jealousy, or love.

will go up to the Temple of the LORD on the third day?"

⁹Isaiah said, "Which do you want? Should the shadow go forward ten steps or go back ten steps?ᵃ This is the sign for you from the LORD to show that the LORD will do what he said he would do."

¹⁰Hezekiah answered, "It is an easy thing for the shadow to go down ten steps. No, make the shadow go back ten steps."

¹¹Then Isaiah prayed, and the LORD made the shadow move back ten steps. It went back up the steps that it had already been on.

Messengers From Babylon

¹²At that time Merodach Baladan son of Baladan was king of Babylon. He sent letters and a gift to Hezekiah when he heard that Hezekiah had been sick. ¹³Hezekiah listened to the messengers and then showed them all the valuable things he owned. He showed them the silver, the gold, the spices, the expensive perfume, and the building where he stored the weapons. He showed them everything in his treasuries, in his palace, and in his kingdom.

¹⁴Then Isaiah the prophet came to King Hezekiah and asked him, "What did these men say? Where did they come from?"

Hezekiah said, "These men came from a faraway country, from Babylon."

¹⁵Isaiah said, "What did they see in your palace?"

Hezekiah answered, "They saw everything I own. I showed them all my wealth."

¹⁶Then Isaiah said to Hezekiah, "Listen to this message from the LORD. ¹⁷The time is coming when everything in your palace and everything your ancestors* have saved until today will be carried away to Babylon. Nothing will be left! The LORD said this. ¹⁸The Babylonians will take your sons, and your sons will become officersᵇ in the palace of the king of Babylon."

¹⁹Then Hezekiah told Isaiah, "This message from the LORD is good." (Hezekiah said this because he thought, "There will be real peace and security during my lifetime.")

²⁰All the great things that Hezekiah did, including his work on the pool and the aqueduct* to bring water into the city, are written in the book, *The History of the Kings of Judah.* ²¹Hezekiah died and was buried with his ancestors. And his son Manasseh became the new king after him.

Manasseh Begins His Evil Rule Over Judah

21 ¹Manasseh was twelve years old when he began to rule. He ruled 55 years in Jerusalem. His mother's name was Hephzibah.

²Manasseh did what the LORD said was wrong. He did the terrible things the other nations did. (And the LORD forced those nations to leave their country when the Israelites came.) ³Manasseh rebuilt the high places* that his father Hezekiah had destroyed. He also built altars* for Baal* and made an Asherah pole,* just as King Ahab of Israel had done. Manasseh worshiped and served the stars of heaven. ⁴He built altars ₍to honor false gods₎ in the LORD's Temple. (This is the place the LORD was talking about when he said, "I will put my name in Jerusalem.") ⁵Manasseh built altars for the stars of heaven in the two courtyards of the LORD's Temple. ⁶He sacrificed his own son and burned him on the altar.ᶜ He used different ways of trying to know the future. He visited mediums* and wizards.*

Manasseh did more and more things that the LORD saw as evil, which made the Lord angry. ⁷Manasseh made a carved statue of Asherah.* He put this statue in the Temple.* The LORD had said to David and to David's son Solomon about this Temple: "I have chosen Jerusalem from all the cities in Israel. I will put my name in the Temple in Jerusalem forever. ⁸I will not cause the Israelites to leave the land that I gave to their ancestors.* I will let the people stay in their land if they obey everything I commanded them and all the teachings that my servant Moses gave them." ⁹But the people did not listen to God. Manasseh did more evil things than all the nations that lived in Canaan* before Israel came. And the LORD destroyed those nations when the Israelites came to take their land.

¹⁰The LORD used his servants the prophets to say this: ¹¹"King Manasseh of Judah has done these hated things and has done more evil than the Amorites before him. He also has caused Judah to sin because of his idols.* ¹²So the LORD, the God of Israel, says, 'Look! I will bring so much trouble against Jerusalem and Judah that anyone who hears about it will be shocked.ᵈ ¹³I will stretch the measuring line of Samariaᵉ and the plumb lineᶠ of Ahab's family over Jerusalem. A man wipes a dish, and then he turns it upside down. I will do that to Jerusalem. ¹⁴There will still be a few of my people left, but I will leave

---

ᶜ**21:6 sacrificed ... on the altar** Literally, "made his son pass through the fire."

ᵈ**21:12 will be shocked** Literally, "both his ears will tingle."

ᵉ**21:13 measuring line of Samaria** Workers used a string with a weight to mark a straight line at the end of a stone wall. The pieces of stone that were outside the line were chipped off and thrown away. This shows that God was "throwing away" Samaria and Ahab's family of kings.

ᶠ**21:13 plumb line** A string with a weight on one end used to show that a wall or building was not straight.

ᵃ**20:9 the shadow ... steps** This may mean the steps of a special building that Hezekiah used like a clock. When the sun shone on the steps, the shadows showed what time of the day it was.

ᵇ**20:18 officers** Or "eunuchs." See "eunuch" in the Word List.

them. I will give them to their enemies. Their enemies will take them as prisoners—they will be like the valuable things soldiers take in war. ¹⁵This is because my people did what I said was wrong. They have made me angry with them since the day their ancestors came up out of Egypt. ¹⁶And Manasseh killed many innocent people. He filled Jerusalem from one end to another with blood. And all these sins are in addition to the sins that caused Judah to sin. Manasseh caused Judah to do what the LORD said was wrong.'"

¹⁷All the things that Manasseh did, including the sins that he committed, are written in the book, *The History of the Kings of Judah*. ¹⁸Manasseh died and was buried with his ancestors. He was buried in the garden at his house. It was called the "Garden of Uzza." His son Amon became the new king after him.

Amon's Short Rule

¹⁹Amon was 22 years old when he began to rule. He ruled two years in Jerusalem. His mother's name was Meshullemeth daughter of Haruz from Jotbah.

²⁰Amon did what the LORD said was wrong, just as his father Manasseh had done. ²¹Amon lived just as his father had lived. He worshiped and served the same idols* his father had worshiped. ²²Amon left the LORD, the God of his ancestors,* and did not live the way the LORD wanted.

²³Amon's servants made plans against him and killed him in his palace. ²⁴The common people killed all the officers who made plans against King Amon. Then the people made Amon's son Josiah the new king after him.

²⁵The other things that Amon did are written in the book, *The History of the Kings of Judah*. ²⁶Amon was buried in his grave at the Garden of Uzza. His son Josiah became the new king.

Josiah Begins His Rule Over Judah

22 ¹Josiah was eight years old when he began to rule. He ruled 31 years in Jerusalem. His mother's name was Jedidah the daughter of Adaiah of Bozkath. ²Josiah did what the LORD said was right. He followed God like his ancestor* David. Josiah obeyed God's teachings—he did exactly what God wanted.

Josiah Orders the Temple Repaired

³During the 18th year that Josiah was king, he sent Shaphan son of Azaliah son of Meshullam, the secretary, to the LORD's Temple.* Josiah said, ⁴"Go up to Hilkiah the high priest. Tell him that he must get the money that people brought to the LORD's Temple. The gatekeepers collected that money from the people. ⁵The priests must use that money to pay the workers to repair the LORD's Temple. They must give that money to the men who supervise the work on the LORD's Temple. ⁶Use that money for the carpenters, stonemasons, and stonecutters. Also use that money to buy the timber and cut stones that are needed to repair the Temple. ⁷Don't count the money that you give to the workers. They can be trusted."

Book of the Law Found in the Temple

⁸Hilkiah the high priest said to Shaphan the secretary, "Look, I found the *Book of the Law*ᵃ in the LORD's Temple*!" Hilkiah gave the book to Shaphan, and Shaphan read it.

⁹He went to King Josiah and told him what happened. Shaphan said, "Your servants have gathered all the money that was in the Temple. They gave it to the men who supervise the work on the LORD's Temple." ¹⁰Then he told the king, "And Hilkiah the priest also gave this book to me." Then Shaphan read the book to the king.

¹¹When the king heard the words of the *Book of the Law*, he tore his clothes to show he was sad and upset. ¹²Then he gave a command to Hilkiah the priest, Ahikam son of Shaphan, Acbor son of Micaiah, Shaphan the secretary, and Asaiah the king's servant. ¹³King Josiah said, "Go and ask the LORD what we should do. Ask for me, for the people, and for all Judah.* Ask about the words of this book that was found. The LORD is angry with us, because our ancestors* did not listen to the words of this book. They did not obey all the commands that were written for us."

Josiah and Huldah the Prophetess

¹⁴So Hilkiah the priest, Ahikam, Acbor, Shaphan, and Asaiah went to Huldah the woman prophet.* Huldah was the wife of Shallum son of Tikvah, son of Harhas. He took care of the priests' clothes. Huldah was living in the second quarter in Jerusalem. They went and talked with Huldah.

¹⁵Then Huldah said to them, "The LORD, the God of Israel, says: Tell the man who sent you to me: ¹⁶'The LORD says this: I am bringing trouble on this place and on the people who live here. These are the troubles that are mentioned in the book that the king of Judah read. ¹⁷The people of Judah have left me and have burned incense* to other gods. They made me very angry. They made many idols.* That is why I will show my anger against this place. My anger will be like a fire that cannot be stopped!'

¹⁸⁻¹⁹"King Josiah of Judah sent you to ask advice from the LORD. Tell Josiah this: 'The LORD, the God of Israel, said the words that you heard. You heard what I said about this place and those who live here. Your heart was soft, and you felt sorry when you heard those things. I said that terrible things would happen to this place. You tore your clothes

---

ᵃ**22:8** *Book of the Law* This is probably the book of Deuteronomy. Also in 23:2.

to show your sadness and you began to cry. That is why I heard you.' The LORD says this. [20]'I will bring you to be with your ancestors.* You will die and go to your grave in peace. So your eyes will not see all the trouble that I am bringing on this place.'"

Then Hilkiah the priest, Ahikam, Acbor, Shaphan, and Asaiah gave that message to the king.

The People Hear the Law

23 [1]King Josiah told all the leaders of Judah and Jerusalem to come and meet with him. [2]Then the king went up to the LORD's Temple.* All the people of Judah and the people who lived in Jerusalem went with him. The priests, the prophets, and all the people—from the least important to the most important—went with him. Then he read the *Book of the Agreement*. This was the *Book of the Law* that was found in the Lord's Temple. Josiah read the book so that all the people could hear it.

[3]The king stood by the column and made an agreement with the LORD. He promised to follow the LORD and to obey his commands, the laws, and his rules. He promised to do this with all his heart and soul. He promised to obey the agreement written in this book. All the people stood to show that they promised to follow the agreement.

[4]Then the king commanded Hilkiah the high priest, the other priests, and the gate-keepers to bring out of the LORD's Temple all the dishes and things that were made to honor Baal,* Asherah,* and the stars of heaven. Then Josiah burned those things outside Jerusalem in the fields in Kidron Valley. Then they carried the ashes to Bethel.

[5]The kings of Judah had chosen some ordinary men to serve as priests. These false priests were burning incense* at the high places* in every city of Judah and all the towns around Jerusalem. They burned incense to honor Baal, the sun, the moon, the constellations, and all the stars in the sky. But Josiah stopped those false priests.

[6]Josiah removed the Asherah pole* from the LORD's Temple. He took the Asherah pole outside the city to the Kidron Valley and burned it there. Then he beat the burned pieces into dust and scattered the dust over the graves of the common people.[a]

[7]Then King Josiah broke down the houses of the male prostitutes who were in the LORD's Temple. Women also used these houses and made little tent covers to honor the false goddess Asherah.

[8-9]At that time the priests did not bring the sacrifices to Jerusalem and offer them on the altar* in the Temple. The priests lived in cities all over Judah. They burned incense and offered sacrifices at the high places in those cities. The high places were everywhere, from Geba to Beersheba. And the priests ate their unleavened* bread in those towns with the ordinary people—⸢not at the special place for priests in the Temple in Jerusalem⸣. But King Josiah ruined the high places and brought the priests to Jerusalem. Josiah also destroyed the high places that were on the left side of the city gate, by the Gate of Joshua. (Joshua was the ruler of the city.)

[10]Topheth was a place in the Valley of Hinnom's Son where people killed their children and burned them on an altar to honor the false god Molech.[b] Josiah ruined that place so that no one could use it again. [11]In the past the kings of Judah had put some horses and a chariot* near the entrance to the LORD's Temple. This was near the room of an important official named Nathan Melech. The horses and chariot were to honor the sun god.[c] Josiah removed the horses and burned the chariot.

[12]In the past the kings of Judah had built altars on the roof of Ahab's building. King Manasseh had also built altars in the two courtyards of the LORD's Temple. Josiah destroyed all the altars and threw the broken pieces into the Kidron Valley.

[13]In the past King Solomon built some high places on Destroyer Hill near Jerusalem. The high places were on the south side of that hill. King Solomon built one of these places of worship to honor Ashtoreth, that horrible thing the people of Sidon worship. He also built one to honor Chemosh, that horrible thing the Moabites worship. And King Solomon built one high place to honor Milcom, that horrible thing the Ammonites worship. But King Josiah ruined all these places of worship. [14]He broke all the memorial stones* and Asherah poles. Then he scattered dead men's bones over that place.[d]

[15]Josiah also broke down the altar and high place at Bethel. Jeroboam son of Nebat had made this altar. Jeroboam caused Israel to sin.[e] Josiah broke down both that altar and the high place. He broke the stones of the altar to pieces. Then he beat it into dust and he burned the Asherah pole. [16]Josiah looked around and saw graves on the mountain. He sent men, and they took the bones from the graves. Then he burned the bones on the altar. In this way Josiah ruined the altar. This happened according to the message from the

---

[a]**23:6** *scattered ... common people* This was a strong way of showing that the Asherah pole could never be used again.

[b]**23:10** *people ... Molech* Literally, "people made their son or daughter pass through fire to Molech."
[c]**23:11** *horses ... sun god* The people thought the sun was a god who drove his chariot (the sun) across the sky each day.
[d]**23:14** *scattered ... place* This was the way he defiled (ruined) those places so that they could not be used for places of worship.
[e]**23:15** *Jeroboam ... sin* See 1 Kings 12:26–30.

Lord that the man of God* announced.ᵃ The man of God announced these things when Jeroboam stood beside the altar at the feast.

Then Josiah looked around and saw the grave of the man of God.ᵇ

17Josiah said, "What is that monument I see?"

The people of the city told him, "It is the grave of the man of God who came from Judah. This man of God told about the things you have done to the altar at Bethel. He said them a long time ago."

18Josiah said, "Leave the man of God alone. Don't move his bones." So they left his bones and the bones of the man of God from Samaria.

19Josiah also destroyed all the temples at the high places in the cities of Samaria. The kings of Israel had built those temples, which had made the Lord very angry. Josiah destroyed them, just as he had destroyed the place of worship at Bethel.

20Josiah killed all the priests of the high places that were in Samaria. He killed the priests on those altars and burned men's bones on the altars so that they could never be used again. Then he went back to Jerusalem.

The People of Judah Celebrate Passover

21Then King Josiah gave a command to all the people. He said, "Celebrate Passover* for the Lord your God. Do this just as it is written in the Book of the Agreement."

22The people had not celebrated a Passover like this since the days when the judges ruled Israel. None of the kings of Israel or the kings of Judah ever had such a big celebration for Passover. 23They celebrated this Passover for the Lord in Jerusalem during Josiah's 18th year as king.

24Josiah destroyed the mediums,* wizards,* the house gods, the idols,* and all the horrible things people worshiped in Judah and Jerusalem. He did this to obey the law written in the book that Hilkiah the priest found in the Lord's Temple.*

25There had never been a king like Josiah before. Josiah turned to the Lord with all his heart, with all his soul, and with all his strength.ᶜ No king had followed all the Law of Moses like Josiah. And there has never been another king like Josiah since that time.

26But the Lord did not stop being angry with the people of Judah. He was still angry with them for everything that Manasseh had done. 27The Lord said, "I forced the Israelites to leave their land. I will do the same to Judah. I will take Judah out of my sight. I will not accept Jerusalem. Yes, I chose that city. I was talking about Jerusalem when I said, 'My name will be there.' But I will destroy the Temple that is in that place."

28All the other things that Josiah did are written in the book, The History of the Kings of Judah.

The Death of Josiah

29While Josiah was king, Pharaoh Neco, the king of Egypt, went to fight against the king of Assyria at the Euphrates River. Josiah went out to meet Neco at Megiddo. Pharaoh saw Josiah and killed him. 30Josiah's officers put his body in a chariot* and carried him from Megiddo to Jerusalem. They buried Josiah in his own grave.

Then the common people took Josiah's son Jehoahaz and anointed* him. They made Jehoahaz the new king.

Jehoahaz Becomes King of Judah

31Jehoahaz was 23 years old when he became king. He ruled three months in Jerusalem. His mother's name was Hamutal, daughter of Jeremiah from Libnah. 32Jehoahaz did what the Lord said was wrong. He did all the same things that his ancestors* had done.

33Pharaoh Neco put Jehoahaz in prison at Riblah in the land of Hamath. So Jehoahaz could not rule in Jerusalem. Pharaoh Neco forced Judah to pay 7500 poundsᵈ of silver and 75 poundsᵉ of gold. 34Pharaoh Neco made Josiah's son Eliakim the new king. Eliakim took the place of Josiah his father. Pharaoh Neco changed Eliakim's name to Jehoiakim. And Pharaoh Neco took Jehoahaz away to Egypt where he died. 35Jehoiakim gave the silver and the gold to Pharaoh. But Jehoiakim made the common people pay taxes and used that money to give to Pharaoh Neco. So everyone paid their share of silver and gold, and King Jehoiakim gave the money to Pharaoh Neco.

36Jehoiakim was 25 years old when he became king. He ruled eleven years in Jerusalem. His mother's name was Zebidah daughter of Pedaiah from Rumah. 37Jehoiakim did what the Lord said was wrong. He did all the same things his ancestors had done.

King Nebuchadnezzar Comes to Judah

24 1In the time of Jehoiakim, King Nebuchadnezzar of Babylon came to the country of Judah. Jehoiakim served Nebuchadnezzar for three years. Then Jehoiakim turned against Nebuchadnezzar and broke away from his rule. 2The Lord sent groups of Babylonians, Arameans, Moabites, and Ammonites to fight against Jehoiakim. He sent them to destroy Judah. This happened just as the Lord had said. He used his servants the prophets to say those things.

ᵃ23:16 announced See 1 Kings 13:1–3.
ᵇ23:16 The man of God ... the grave of the man of God This is from the ancient Greek version.
ᶜ23:25 with all his heart ... strength See Deut. 6:4, 5.

ᵈ23:33 7500 pounds Literally, "100 talents" (3450 kg).
ᵉ23:33 75 pounds Literally, "1 talent" (34.5 kg).

[3]The LORD commanded this to happen to Judah. In this way he would remove them from his sight. He did this because of all the sins that Manasseh committed. [4]He did this because Manasseh killed many innocent people and filled Jerusalem with their blood. The LORD would not forgive these sins.

[5]The other things that Jehoiakim did are written in the book, *The History of the Kings of Judah*. [6]Jehoiakim died and was buried with his ancestors.* His son Jehoiachin became the new king after him.

[7]The king of Babylon captured all the land between the Brook of Egypt and the Euphrates River. This land was previously controlled by Egypt. So the king of Egypt did not leave Egypt anymore.

Nebuchadnezzar Captures Jerusalem

[8]Jehoiachin was 18 years old when he began to rule. He ruled three months in Jerusalem. His mother's name was Nehushta daughter of Elnathan from Jerusalem. [9]Jehoiachin did what the LORD said was wrong. He did all the same things that his father had done.

[10]At that time the officers of King Nebuchadnezzar of Babylon came to Jerusalem and surrounded it. [11]Then King Nebuchadnezzar of Babylon came to the city. [12]King Jehoiachin of Judah went out to meet the king of Babylon. His mother, his officers, leaders, and officials also went with him. Then the king of Babylon captured Jehoiachin. This was during the eighth year of Nebuchadnezzar's rule.

[13]Nebuchadnezzar took from Jerusalem all the treasures in the LORD's Temple* and all the treasures in the king's palace. He cut up all the golden dishes that King Solomon of Israel had put in the LORD's Temple. This happened just as the LORD had said.

[14]Nebuchadnezzar captured all the people of Jerusalem, including the leaders and other wealthy people. He took 10,000 people and made them prisoners. He took all the skilled workers and craftsmen. No one was left, except the poorest of the common people. [15]Nebuchadnezzar took Jehoiachin to Babylon as a prisoner. He also took the king's mother, his wives, officers, and the leading men of the land. He took them from Jerusalem to Babylon as prisoners. [16]There were 7000 soldiers. Nebuchadnezzar took all the soldiers and 1000 of the skilled workers and craftsmen. All these men were trained soldiers, ready for war. The king of Babylon took them to Babylon as prisoners.

King Zedekiah

[17]The king of Babylon made Mattaniah the new king. Mattaniah was Jehoiachin's uncle. He changed his name to Zedekiah. [18]Zedekiah was 21 years old when he began to rule. He ruled 11 years in Jerusalem. His mother's name was Hamutal daughter of Jeremiah from Libnah. [19]Zedekiah did what the LORD said

was wrong. He did all the same things that Jehoiakim did. [20]The LORD became so angry with Jerusalem and Judah that he threw them away.

Nebuchadnezzar Ends Zedekiah's Rule

Zedekiah rebelled and refused to obey the king of Babylon.

25 [1]So King Nebuchadnezzar of Babylon and all his army came to fight against Jerusalem. This happened on the 10th day of the tenth month of Zedekiah's ninth year as king. Nebuchadnezzar put his army around Jerusalem to stop people from going in and out of the city. Then he built a wall of dirt around the city. [2]His army stayed around Jerusalem until Zedekiah's eleventh year as king of Judah. [3]The famine was getting worse and worse in the city. By the 9th day of the fourth month there was no more food for the common people in the city.

[4]Nebuchadnezzar's army finally broke through the city wall. That night King Zedekiah and all his soldiers ran away. They used the secret gate that went through the double walls. It was by the king's garden. The enemy soldiers were all around the city, but Zedekiah and his men escaped on the road to the desert. [5]The Babylonian army chased King Zedekiah and caught him near Jericho. All of Zedekiah's soldiers left him and ran away.

[6]The Babylonians took King Zedekiah to the king of Babylon at Riblah. The Babylonians decided to punish Zedekiah. [7]They killed Zedekiah's sons in front of him. Then they put out Zedekiah's eyes. They put chains on him and took him to Babylon.

Jerusalem Is Destroyed

[8]Nebuchadnezzar came to Jerusalem on the 7th day of the fifth month of his nineteenth year as king of Babylon. The captain of Nebuchadnezzar's best soldiers was Nebuzaradan. [9]Nebuzaradan burned the LORD's Temple,* the king's palace, and all the houses in Jerusalem. He destroyed even the largest houses.

[10]Then the Babylonian army that was with Nebuzaradan pulled down the walls around Jerusalem. [11]Nebuzaradan captured all the people who were still left in the city. He took all the people as prisoners, even those who had tried to surrender. [12]He let only the poorest of the common people stay there. He let them stay so that they could take care of the grapes and other crops.

[13]The Babylonian soldiers broke into pieces all the bronze things in the LORD's Temple. They broke the bronze columns, the bronze carts, and the large bronze tank.[a] Then they took all of that bronze to Babylon. [14]The Babylonians also took the pots, the shovels, the tools for trimming the lamps, the spoons, and all the bronze dishes that were used in the LORD's

a25:13 tank A very large container for water.

Temple. ¹⁵Nebuzaradan took all the firepans* and bowls. He took all the things made of gold for the gold. And he took everything made of silver for the silver. ¹⁶⁻¹⁷So Nebuzaradan took the large bronze tank and the 2 bronze columns. (Each column was about 31 feet*ᵃ tall. The capitals* on the columns were over 5 feetᵇ tall. They were made from bronze and had a design like a net and pomegranates. Both columns had the same kind of design.) He also took the carts that Solomon made for the LORD's Temple. The bronze from these things was too heavy to be weighed.

The People of Judah Taken as Prisoners

¹⁸⌊From the Temple⌋ Nebuzaradan took Seraiah the high priest, Zephaniah the second priest, and the three men who guarded the entrance. ¹⁹From the city Nebuzaradan took one official who was in charge of the army and five of the king's advisorsᶜ who were still in the city. He took one secretary of the commander of the army who was in charge of counting the common people and choosing some of them to be soldiers and 60 people who just happened to be in the city. ²⁰⁻²¹Then Nebuzaradan took all these people to the king of Babylon at Riblah in the area of Hamath. The king of Babylon killed them there at Riblah. And the people of Judah were led away as prisoners from their land.

Gedaliah, Governor of Judah

²²King Nebuchadnezzar of Babylon left some people in the land of Judah. There was

a man named Gedaliah son of Ahikam son of Shaphan. Nebuchadnezzar made Gedaliah governor over the people in Judah.

²³The army captains were Ishmael son of Nethaniah, Johanan son of Kareah, Seraiah son of Tanhumeth from Netophah, and Jaazaniah son of the Maachathite. These army captains and their men heard that the king of Babylon had made Gedaliah governor, so they went to Mizpah to meet with him. ²⁴Gedaliah made promises to these officers and their men. He said to them, "Don't be afraid of the Babylonian officers. Stay here and serve the king of Babylon. Then everything will be all right with you."

²⁵Ishmael son of Nethaniah son of Elishama was from the king's family. In the seventh month Ishmael and ten of his men attacked Gedaliah and killed all the men of Judah and Babylonians who were with Gedaliah at Mizpah. ²⁶Then the army officers and all the people ran away to Egypt. Everyone, from the least important to the most important, ran away because they were afraid of the Babylonians.

²⁷Later, Evil Merodach became the king of Babylon. He let King Jehoiachin of Judah out of prison. This happened in the 37th year after Jehoiachin was captured. This was on the 27th day of the twelfth month from the time that Evil Merodach began to rule. ²⁸Evil Merodach was kind to Jehoiachin. He gave him a more important place to sit than the other kings who were with him in Babylon. ²⁹Evil Merodach let Jehoiachin stop wearing prison clothes. And every day for the rest of his life he ate at the same table with the king. ³⁰And each day, for as long as Jehoiachin lived, the king gave him enough money to pay for whatever he needed.

ᵃ**25:16–17** *31 feet* Literally, "18 cubits" (9.33 m).
ᵇ**25:16–17** *5 feet* Literally, "3 cubits" (1.55 m).
ᶜ**25:19** *king's advisors* Literally, "men who saw the king's face."

1 Chronicles

Family History From Adam to Noah

1 ¹⁻³The first generations of people were Adam, Seth, Enosh, Kenan, Mahalalel, Jared, Enoch, Methuselah, Lamech, and Noah.ᵈ

⁴The sons of Noah were Shem, Ham, and Japheth.

Japheth's Descendants

⁵The sons of Japheth were Gomer, Magog, Madai, Javan, Tubal, Meshech, and Tiras.

⁶The sons of Gomer were Ashkenaz, Riphath,ᵉ and Togarmah.

⁷The sons of Javan were Elishah, Tarshish, Kittim, and Rodanim.

Ham's Descendants

⁸The sons of Ham were Cush,ᶠ Mizraim,ᵍ Put, and Canaan.

⁹The sons of Cush were Seba, Havilah, Sabtah, Raamah, and Sabtecah.

ᵈ**1:1–3** This list of names gives the name of a man, followed by his descendants.

ᵉ**1:6** *Riphath* Or "Diphath."
ᶠ**1:8** *Cush* That is, Ethiopia.
ᵍ**1:8** *Mizraim* That is, Egypt.

The sons of Raamah were Sheba and Dedan.

¹⁰Nimrod, a descendant of Cush, grew up to become the strongest and bravest soldier in the world.

¹¹Mizraim was the father of the people of Lud, Anam, Lehab, Naphtuh, ¹²Pathrus, Casluh, and Caphtor. (The Philistines came from Casluh.)

¹³Canaan was the father of Sidon. Sidon was his first child. Canaan was also the father of the Hittites, ¹⁴Jebusites, Amorites, Girgashites, ¹⁵Hivites, Arkites, Sinites, ¹⁶Arvadites, Zemarites, and the people from Hamath.

Shem's Descendants

¹⁷Shem's sons were Elam, Asshur, Arphaxad, Lud, and Aram. Aram's sons were[a] Uz, Hul, Gether, and Meshech.[b]

¹⁸Arphaxad was the father of Shelah. Shelah was the father of Eber.

¹⁹Eber had two sons. One son was named Peleg,[c] because the people on the earth were divided into different languages during his lifetime. Peleg's brother was named Joktan. ²⁰(Joktan was the father of Almodad, Sheleph, Hazarmaveth, Jerah, ²¹Hadoram, Uzal, Diklah, ²²Ebal,[d] Abimael, Sheba, ²³Ophir, Havilah, and Jobab. All these men were Joktan's sons.)

²⁴Shem's descendants were Arphaxad, Shelah, ²⁵Eber, Peleg, Reu, ²⁶Serug, Nahor, Terah, ²⁷and Abram. (Abram is also called Abraham.)

Abraham's Family

²⁸Abraham's sons were Isaac and Ishmael. ²⁹These are their descendants:

Ishmael's first son was Nebaioth. His other sons were Kedar, Adbeel, Mibsam, ³⁰Mishma, Dumah, Massa, Hadad, Tema, ³¹Jetur, Naphish, and Kedemah. These were Ishmael's sons.

³²Abraham also had sons by Keturah, his slave woman.* They were Zimran, Jokshan, Medan, Midian, Ishbak, and Shuah.

Jokshan's sons were Sheba and Dedan.

³³Midian's sons were Ephah, Epher, Hanoch, Abida, and Eldaah.

These men were the descendants of Keturah.

Isaac's Descendants

³⁴Abraham was the father of Isaac. Isaac's sons were Esau and Israel.*

³⁵Esau's sons were Eliphaz, Reuel, Jeush, Jalam, and Korah.

³⁶Eliphaz's sons were Teman, Omar, Zepho,[e] Gatam, and Kenaz. Also Eliphaz and Timna had a son named Amalek.

³⁷Reuel's sons were Nahath, Zerah, Shammah, and Mizzah.

The Edomites From Seir

³⁸Seir's sons were Lotan, Shobal, Zibeon, Anah, Dishon, Ezer, and Dishan.

³⁹Lotan's sons were Hori and Homam.[f] Lotan had a sister named Timna.

⁴⁰Shobal's sons were Alvan, Manahath, Ebal, Shepho, and Onam.

Zibeon's sons were Aiah and Anah.

⁴¹Anah's son was Dishon.

Dishon's sons were Hemdan, Eshban, Ithran, and Keran.

⁴²Ezer's sons were Bilhan, Zaavan, and Akan.

Dishan's sons were Uz and Aran.

The Kings of Edom

⁴³There were kings in Edom long before there were kings in Israel. These are the names of the kings of Edom:

Bela was the son of Beor. The name of Bela's city was Dinhabah.

⁴⁴When Bela died, Jobab son of Zerah became the new king. Jobab came from Bozrah.

⁴⁵When Jobab died, Husham became the new king. Husham was from the country of the Temanites.

⁴⁶When Husham died, Hadad son of Bedad became the new king. Hadad defeated Midian in the country of Moab. Hadad's city was named Avith.

⁴⁷When Hadad died, Samlah became the new king. Samlah was from Masrekah.

⁴⁸When Samlah died, Shaul became the new king. Shaul was from Rehoboth by the Euphrates River.

⁴⁹When Shaul died, Baal Hanan son of Acbor became the new king.

⁵⁰When Baal Hanan died, Hadad became the new king. Hadad's city was named Pau.[g] Hadad's wife was named Mehetabel. Mehetabel was Matred's daughter. Matred was Mezahab's daughter. ⁵¹Then Hadad died.

The leaders of Edom were Timna, Alvah, Jetheth, ⁵²Oholibamah, Elah, Pinon, ⁵³Kenaz, Teman, Mibzar, ⁵⁴Magdiel, and Iram. This is a list of the leaders of Edom.

Israel's Sons

2 ¹Israel's* sons were Reuben, Simeon, Levi, Judah, Issachar, Zebulun, ²Dan, Joseph, Benjamin, Naphtali, Gad, and Asher.

---

[a]1:17 Aram's sons were This is found in one Hebrew copy and some copies of the ancient Greek version. It is also found in the standard Hebrew text of Gen. 10:23, but not here.

[b]1:17 Meshech Or "Mash." See Gen. 10:23.

[c]1:19 Peleg This name means "division."

[d]1:22 Ebal Or "Obal." See Gen. 10:28.

[e]1:36 Zepho Or "Zephi."

[f]1:39 Homam Or "Heman." See Gen. 36:22.

[g]1:50 Pau Or "Pai."

Judah's Sons

³Judah's sons were Er, Onan, and Shelah. Bathshua*ᵃ* was their mother. She was a woman from Canaan.* The Lᴏʀᴅ saw that Judah's first son, Er, was evil. That is why the Lᴏʀᴅ killed Er. ⁴Judah's daughter-in-law Tamar gave birth to Perez and Zerah.*ᵇ* So Judah had five sons.

⁵Perez's sons were Hezron and Hamul.

⁶Zerah had five sons. They were Zimri, Ethan, Heman, Calcol, and Darda.

⁷Zimri's son was Carmi. Carmi's son was Achar.*ᶜ* Achar was the man who brought many troubles to Israel. Achar kept the things he took in battle, but he was supposed to give them all to God.

⁸Ethan's son was Azariah.

⁹Hezron's sons were Jerahmeel, Ram, and Caleb.*ᵈ*

Ram's Descendants

¹⁰Ram was Amminadab's father, and Amminadab was Nahshon's father. Nahshon was the leader of the people of Judah.*ᵉ* ¹¹Nahshon was Salmon's father. Salmon was Boaz's father. ¹²Boaz was Obed's father. Obed was Jesse's father. ¹³Jesse was Eliab's father. Eliab was Jesse's first son. Jesse's second son was Abinadab. His third son was Shimea. ¹⁴Nethanel was Jesse's fourth son. Jesse's fifth son was Raddai. ¹⁵Ozem was Jesse's sixth son, and David was his seventh son. ¹⁶Their sisters were Zeruiah and Abigail. Zeruiah's three sons were Abishai, Joab, and Asahel. ¹⁷Abigail was Amasa's mother. Amasa's father was Jether. Jether was from the Ishmaelites.

Caleb's Descendants

¹⁸Caleb was Hezron's son. Caleb had children with his wife Azubah. Azubah was the daughter of Jerioth.*ᶠ* Azubah's sons were Jesher, Shobab, and Ardon. ¹⁹When Azubah died, Caleb married Ephrath. Caleb and Ephrath had a son. They named him Hur. ²⁰Hur was Uri's father. Uri was Bezalel's father.

²¹Later when Hezron was 60 years old, he married Makir's daughter. Makir was the father of Gilead. Hezron had sexual relations with Makir's daughter, and she gave birth to Segub. ²²Segub was Jair's father. Jair had 23 cities in the country of Gilead. ²³But Geshur and Aram took Jair's villages. Among them were Kenath and the small towns around it. There were 60 small towns in all. All these towns belonged to the sons of Makir, the father of Gilead.

²⁴After Hezron died in the town of Caleb Ephrathah, his wife Abijah had his son, who was named Ashhur. Ashhur was the father of Tekoa.

Jerahmeel's Descendants

²⁵Jerahmeel was Hezron's first son. Jerahmeel's sons were Ram, Bunah, Oren, Ozem, and Ahijah. Ram was Jerahmeel's first son. ²⁶Jerahmeel had another wife named Atarah. Onam's mother was Atarah.

²⁷Jerahmeel's first son, Ram, had sons. They were Maaz, Jamin, and Eker.

²⁸Onam's sons were Shammai and Jada. Shammai's sons were Nadab and Abishur. ²⁹Abishur's wife was named Abihail. They had two sons. Their names were Ahban and Molid.

³⁰Nadab's sons were Seled and Appaim. Seled died without having children.

³¹Appaim's son was Ishi. Ishi's son was Sheshan. Sheshan's son was Ahlai.

³²Jada was Shammai's brother. Jada's sons were Jether and Jonathan. Jether died without having children.

³³Jonathan's sons were Peleth and Zaza. This was the list of Jerahmeel's children.

³⁴Sheshan did not have sons. He only had daughters. Sheshan had a servant from Egypt named Jarha. ³⁵Sheshan let his daughter marry Jarha. They had a son. His name was Attai.

³⁶Attai was Nathan's father. Nathan was Zabad's father. ³⁷Zabad was Ephlal's father. Ephlal was Obed's father. ³⁸Obed was Jehu's father. Jehu was Azariah's father. ³⁹Azariah was Helez's father. Helez was Eleasah's father. ⁴⁰Eleasah was Sismai's father. Sismai was Shallum's father. ⁴¹Shallum was Jekamiah's father, and Jekamiah was Elishama's father.

Caleb's Family

⁴²Caleb was Jerahmeel's brother. Caleb had some sons. His first son was Mesha. Mesha was Ziph's father. There was also Caleb's son Mareshah. Mareshah was the father of Hebron.

⁴³Hebron's sons were Korah, Tappuah, Rekem, and Shema. ⁴⁴Shema was Raham's father. Raham was Jorkeam's father. Rekem was Shammai's father. ⁴⁵Shammai's son was Maon. Maon was Beth Zur's father.

⁴⁶Caleb's slave woman* was named Ephah. Ephah was the mother of Haran, Moza, and Gazez. Haran was Gazez's father.

⁴⁷Jahdai's sons were Regem, Jotham, Geshan, Pelet, Ephah, and Shaaph.

⁴⁸Maacah was another slave woman of Caleb. Maacah was the mother of Sheber and Tirhana. ⁴⁹Maacah was also the mother of Shaaph and Sheva. Shaaph was Madmannah's father. Sheva was the father of Macbenah and Gibea. Caleb's daughter was Acsah.

---

*ᵃ***2:3** *Bathshua* This name means "the daughter of Shua." See Gen. 38:2.

*ᵇ***2:4** Judah had sexual relations with his own daughter-in-law, Tamar, and caused her to be pregnant. See Gen. 38:12–30.

*ᶜ***2:7** *Achar* Or "Achan." See Josh. 7:11.

*ᵈ***2:9** *Caleb* Literally, "Kelubai."

*ᵉ***2:10** *Nahshon … Judah* Nahshon was leader of the tribe of Judah at the time the Israelites came out of Egypt. See Num. 1:7; 2:3; 7:12.

*ᶠ***2:18** Or "Caleb had children with Azubah his wife and with Jerioth."

⁵⁰This is a list of Caleb's descendants: Hur was Caleb's first son. He was born to Ephrathah. Hur's sons were Shobal, the founder*ᵃ* of Kiriath Jearim, ⁵¹Salma, the founder of Bethlehem, and Hareph, the founder of Beth Gader.

⁵²Shobal was the founder of Kiriath Jearim. This is a list of Shobal's descendants: Haroeh, half the people in Manahti, ⁵³and the tribes from Kiriath Jearim. These are the Ithrites, Puthites, Shumathites, and Mishraites. The Zorathites and the Eshtaolites came from the Mishraites.

⁵⁴This is a list of Salma's descendants: the people from Bethlehem, Netophah, Atroth Beth Joab, half the people from Manahti, the Zorites, ⁵⁵and the families of scribes* who lived at Jabez, Tirath, Shimeath, and Sucah. These scribes are the Kenites who came from Hammath. Hammath was the founder of Beth Recab.

David's Sons

3 ¹Some of David's sons were born in the town of Hebron. This is a list of David's sons:

David's first son was Amnon. Amnon's mother was Ahinoam. She was from the town of Jezreel.

The second son was Daniel. His mother was Abigail from Carmel in Judah.

²The third son was Absalom. His mother was Maacah, daughter of Talmai. Talmai was the king of Geshur.

The fourth son was Adonijah. His mother was Haggith.

³The fifth son was Shephatiah. His mother was Abital.

The sixth son was Ithream. His mother was Eglah, David's wife. ⁴These six sons were born to David in Hebron.

David ruled as king in Hebron for seven years and six months. He ruled as king in Jerusalem 33 years.

⁵These are the children born to David in Jerusalem:

There were four sons from Bathsheba,*ᵇ* the daughter of Ammiel. They were Shimea, Shobab, Nathan, and Solomon. ⁶⁻⁸There were nine other sons. They were Ibhar, Elishua, Eliphelet, Nogah, Nepheg, Japhia, Elishama, Eliada, and Eliphelet. ⁹They were all David's sons. Their sister was named Tamar. David also had other sons by his slave women.*

Kings of Judah After David's Time

¹⁰Solomon's son was Rehoboam. Rehoboam's son was Abijah. Abijah's son was Asa. Asa's son was Jehoshaphat. ¹¹Jehoshaphat's son was Jehoram. Jehoram's son was Ahaziah. Ahaziah's son was Joash. ¹²Joash's son was Amaziah. Amaziah's son was Azariah. Azariah's

son was Jotham. ¹³Jotham's son was Ahaz. Ahaz's son was Hezekiah. Hezekiah's son was Manasseh. ¹⁴Manasseh's son was Amon. Amon's son was Josiah.

¹⁵This is a list of Josiah's sons: The first son was Johanan. The second son was Jehoiakim. The third son was Zedekiah. The fourth son was Shallum.

¹⁶Jehoiakim's sons were Jehoiachin, his son, and Zedekiah, his son.*ᶜ*

David's Family After Babylonian Captivity

¹⁷This is a list of Jehoiachin's children after Jehoiachin became a prisoner in Babylon: His children were Shealtiel, ¹⁸Malkiram, Pedaiah, Shenazzar, Jekamiah, Hoshama, and Nedabiah.

¹⁹Pedaiah's sons were Zerubbabel and Shimei. Zerubbabel's sons were Meshullam and Hananiah. Shelomith was their sister. ²⁰Zerubbabel had five other sons also. Their names were Hashubah, Ohel, Berekiah, Hasadiah, and Jushab Hesed.

²¹Hananiah's son was Pelatiah. His son was Jeshaiah.*ᵈ* His son was Rephaiah. His son was Arnan. His son was Obadiah. His son was Shecaniah.*ᵉ*

²²This is a list of Shecaniah's descendants: Shemaiah. Shemaiah had six sons: Shemaiah, Hattush, Igal, Bariah, Neariah, and Shaphat.

²³Neariah had three sons. They were Elioenai, Hizkiah, and Azrikam.

²⁴Elioenai had seven sons. They were Hodaviah, Eliashib, Pelaiah, Akkub, Johanan, Delaiah, and Anani.

Other Family Groups of Judah

4 ¹This is a list of Judah's sons: They were Perez, Hezron, Carmi, Hur, and Shobal.

²Shobal's son was Reaiah. Reaiah was Jahath's father. Jahath was the father of Ahumai and Lahad. The Zorathites are descendants of Ahumai and Lahad.

³Etam's sons were Jezreel, Ishma, and Idbash. And they had a sister named Hazzelelponi.

⁴Penuel was Gedor's father, and Ezer was Hushah's father.

These were Hur's sons. Hur was Ephrathah's first son, and Ephrathah was the founder*ᶠ* of Bethlehem.

⁵Tekoa's father was Ashhur. Ashhur had two wives. Their names were Helah and Naarah. ⁶Naarah had Ahuzzam, Hepher, Temeni, and Haahashtari. These were the sons Naarah had with Ashhur. ⁷The sons of Helah were Zereth, Zohar, Ethnan, and Koz. ⁸Koz was the father

---

*ᶜ*3:16 This can be interpreted in two ways: "This Zedekiah was the son of Jehoiakim and the brother of Jehoiachin" or "This Zedekiah is the son of Jehoiachin and the grandson of Jehoiakim."

*ᵈ*3:21 *Jeshaiah* Or "Isaiah."

*ᵉ*3:21 The Hebrew text here is hard to understand.

*ᶠ*4:4 *founder* Literally, "father." The person who started the city. Also in verse 14.

*ᵃ*2:50 *founder* Literally, "father." The person who started the city.

*ᵇ*3:5 *Bathsheba* The standard Hebrew text has "Bathshua."

of Anub and Hazzobebah. Koz also was the father of the tribes of Aharhel. Aharhel was Harum's son.

⁹Jabez was a very good man, who was better than his brothers. His mother said, "I have named him Jabez*ᵃ* because I was in much pain when I had him." ¹⁰Jabez prayed to the God of Israel and said, "I pray that you would bless me and give me more land! Be near me and don't let anyone hurt me! Then I will not have any pain." God gave Jabez what he asked for.

¹¹Kelub was Shuhah's brother. Kelub was Mehir's father. Mehir was Eshton's father. ¹²Eshton was the father of Beth Rapha, Paseah, and Tehinnah. Tehinnah was the father of Ir Nahash.*ᵇ* These men were from Recah.

¹³The sons of Kenaz were Othniel and Seraiah. Othniel's sons were Hathath and Meonothai. ¹⁴Meonothai was Ophrah's father.

And Seraiah was Joab's father. Joab was the founder of the Ge Harashim.*ᶜ* The people used that name because they were skilled workers.

¹⁵Caleb was Jephunneh's son. Caleb's sons were Iru, Elah, and Naam. Elah's son was Kenaz.

¹⁶Jehallelel's sons were Ziph, Ziphah, Tiria, and Asarel.

¹⁷⁻¹⁸Ezrah's sons were Jether, Mered, Epher, and Jalon. Mered was the father of Miriam, Shammai, and Ishbah. Ishbah was the father of Eshtemoa. Mered had a wife from Egypt. She had Jered, Heber, and Jekuthiel. Jered was Gedor's father. Heber was Soco's father. And Jekuthiel was Zanoah's father. These were the sons of Bithiah. Bithiah was Pharaoh's daughter. She was Mered's wife from Egypt.

¹⁹Mered's wife was Naham's sister. Mered's wife was from Judah.*ᵈ* The sons of Mered's wife were the father of Keilah and Eshtemoa. Keilah was from the Garmites. And Eshtemoa was from the Maacathites. ²⁰Shimon's sons were Amnon, Rinnah, Ben Hanan, and Tilon.

Ishi's sons were Zoheth and Ben Zoheth.

²¹⁻²²Shelah was Judah's son. Shelah's sons were Er, Laadah, Jokim, the men from Cozeba, Joash, and Saraph. Er was the father of Lecah. Laadah was the father of Mareshah and the tribes of linen* workers at Beth Ashbea. Joash and Saraph married Moabite women. Then they went back to Bethlehem.*ᵉ* The writings about this family are very old. ²³These sons of Shelah were workers who made things from clay. They lived in Netaim and Gederah and worked for the king.

Simeon's Children

²⁴Simeon's sons were Nemuel, Jamin, Jarib, Zerah, and Shaul. ²⁵Shaul's son was Shallum. Shallum's son was Mibsam. Mibsam's son was Mishma.

²⁶Mishma's son was Hammuel. Hammuel's son was Zaccur. Zaccur's son was Shimei. ²⁷Shimei had sixteen sons and six daughters, but Shimei's brothers did not have many children. Shimei's brothers did not have large families. Their families were not as large as the other tribes in Judah.

²⁸Shimei's descendants lived in Beersheba, Moladah, Hazar Shual, ²⁹Bilhah, Ezem, Tolad, ³⁰Bethuel, Hormah, Ziklag, ³¹Beth Marcaboth, Hazar Susim, Beth Biri, and Shaaraim. They lived in these towns until David became king. ³²The five villages near these towns were Etam, Ain, Rimmon, Token, and Ashan. ³³There were also other villages as far away as Baalath. This is where they lived. And they also wrote the history about their family.

³⁴⁻³⁸This is the list of men who were leaders of their tribes: They were Meshobab, Jamlech, Joshah (Amaziah's son), Joel, Jehu son of Joshibiah, Joshibiah son of Seraiah, Seraiah son of Asiel, Elioenai, Jaakobah, Jeshohaiah, Asaiah, Adiel, Jesimiel, Benaiah, and Ziza (Shiphi's son). Shiphi was Allon's son, and Allon was Jedaiah's son. Jedaiah was Shimri's son, and Shimri was Shemaiah's son.

These men's families grew to be very large. ³⁹They went to the area outside the town of Gedor to the east side of the valley. They went to that place to look for fields for their sheep and cattle. ⁴⁰They found good fields with plenty of grass. They found plenty of good land there. The land was peaceful and quiet. Ham's descendants lived there in the past. ⁴¹This happened during the time that Hezekiah was king of Judah. These men came to Gedor and fought against the Hamites. They destroyed the tents of the Hamites. They also fought against the Meunites who lived there. These men destroyed all the Meunites. There are no Meunites in this place even today. So these men began to live there. They lived there because the land had grass for their sheep.

⁴²Five hundred people from the tribe of Simeon went to the hill country of Seir. Ishi's sons led these men. The sons were Pelatiah, Neariah, Rephaiah, and Uzziel. The Simeonite men fought against the people living in that place. ⁴³There were only a few Amalekites still living, and these Simeonites killed them. Since that time until now, the Simeonites have lived in Seir.

Reuben's Descendants

5 ¹⁻³Reuben was Israel's first son. Reuben should have received the special privileges of the oldest son. But he had sexual relations with his father's wife. So those privileges were given to Joseph's sons. In the family history, Reuben's name is not listed as the first son. Judah became stronger than his brothers, so the leaders came from his family. But Joseph's family got the other privileges that belong to the oldest son. Reuben's sons were Hanoch, Pallu, Hezron, and Carmi.

4These are the names of Joel's descendants: Shemaiah was Joel's son. Gog was Shemaiah's son. Shimei was Gog's son. 5Micah was Shimei's son. Reaiah was Micah's son. Baal was Reaiah's son. 6Beerah was Baal's son. King Tiglath Pileser of Assyria forced Beerah to leave his home. So Beerah became the king's prisoner. Beerah was a leader of the tribe of Reuben.

7Joel's brothers and all his tribes are listed just as they are written in the family histories: Jeiel was the first son, then Zechariah, 8and Bela. Bela was Azaz's son. Azaz was Shema's son. Shema was Joel's son. They lived in the area of Aroer all the way to Nebo and Baal Meon. 9Bela's people lived to the east as far as the edge of the desert, near the Euphrates River. They lived there because they had many cattle in the land of Gilead. 10When Saul was king, Bela's people fought a war against the Hagrites. They defeated the Hagrites. Bela's people lived in the tents that had belonged to the Hagrites. They lived in those tents and traveled throughout the area east of Gilead.

Gad's Descendants

11The people of Gad lived across the river from Reuben, in the area of Bashan. They spread all the way to the town of Salecah. 12Joel was the first leader in Bashan. Shapham was the second leader. Then Janai became the leader.a 13The seven brothers in their families were Michael, Meshullam, Sheba, Jorai, Jacan, Zia, and Eber. 14They were the descendants of Abihail. Abihail was Huri's son. Huri was Jaroah's son. Jaroah was Gilead's son. Gilead was Michael's son. Michael was Jeshishai's son. Jeshishai was Jahdo's son. Jahdo was Buz's son. 15Ahi was Abdiel's son. Abdiel was Guni's son. Ahi was the leader of their family.

16The people in the tribe of Gad lived in the area of Gilead. They lived in the area of Bashan, in the small towns around Bashan, and in all the pastures in the area of Sharon all the way to the borders.

17During the time of Jotham and Jeroboam, all these people's names were written in the family history of Gad. Jotham was the king of Judah and Jeroboam was the king of Israel.

Some Soldiers Skilled in War

18From half the tribe of Manasseh and from the tribes of Reuben and Gad there were 44,760 brave men ready for war. They were skilled in war. They carried shields and swords. And they were also good with bows

and arrows. 19They started a war against the Hagrites and the people of Jetur, Naphish, and Nodab. 20The men from the tribes of Manasseh, Reuben, and Gad prayed to God during the war. They asked God to help them because they trusted him, so God helped them. He allowed them to defeat the Hagrites and those who were with the Hagrites. 21They took the animals that belonged to the Hagrites. They took 50,000 camels, 250,000 sheep, 2000 donkeys, and 100,000 people. 22Many Hagrites were killed because God helped the people of Reuben win the war. Then the tribes of Manasseh, Reuben, and Gad settled in the land of the Hagrites. They lived there until the time when the Israelites were taken into captivity.

23Half the tribe of Manasseh lived in the area of Bashan all the way to Baal Hermon, Senir, and Mount Hermon. They became a very large group of people.

24These were the family leaders from half the tribe of Manasseh: Epher, Ishi, Eliel, Azriel, Jeremiah, Hodaviah, and Jahdiel. They were all strong, brave, and famous men, and they were leaders in their families. 25But they sinned against the God who their ancestors* worshiped. They began worshiping the false gods of the people living there—and those were the people God destroyed.

26The God of Israel made King Pul of Assyria want to go to war. He was also called Tiglath Pileser. He fought against the tribes of Manasseh, Reuben, and Gad. He forced them to leave their homes and made them prisoners. Pul took them to Halah, Habor, Hara, and near the Gozan River. Those tribes from Israel have lived in those places since that time until today.

Levi's Descendants

6 1Levi's sons were Gershon, Kohath, and Merari.

2Kohath's sons were Amram, Izhar, Hebron, and Uzziel.

3Amram's children were Aaron, Moses, and Miriam.

Aaron's sons were Nadab, Abihu, Eleazar, and Ithamar. 4Eleazar was Phinehas' father. Phinehas was Abishua's father. 5Abishua was Bukki's father. Bukki was Uzzi's father. 6Uzzi was Zerahiah's father. Zerahiah was Meraioth's father. 7Meraioth was Amariah's father. Amariah was Ahitub's father. 8Ahitub was Zadok's father. Zadok was Ahimaaz's father. 9Ahimaaz was Azariah's father. Azariah was Johanan's father. 10Johanan was Azariah's father. (Azariah is the one who served as priest in the Temple that Solomon built in Jerusalem.) 11Azariah was Amariah's father. Amariah was Ahitub's father. 12Ahitub was Zadok's father. Zadok was Shallum's father. 13Shallum was Hilkiah's father. Hilkiah was Azariah's father. 14Azariah was Seraiah's father. Seraiah was Jehozadak's father.

---

a5:12 Then Janai became the leader Or "Then there was Janai, and then Shaphat was in Bashan."

[15]Jehozadak was forced to leave his home when the LORD sent the people of Judah and Jerusalem away. Through Nebuchadnezzar the Lord caused them all to be made prisoners in another country.

Other Descendants of Levi

[16]Levi's sons were Gershon, Kohath, and Merari.

[17]The names of Gershon's sons were Libni and Shimei.

[18]Kohath's sons were Amram, Izhar, Hebron, and Uzziel.

[19]Merari's sons were Mahli and Mushi.

This is a list of the families in the tribe of Levi. They are listed with their fathers' names first:

[20]These were Gershon's descendants: Libni was Gershon's son. Jahath was Libni's son. Zimmah was Jahath's son. [21]Joah was Zimmah's son. Iddo was Joah's son. Zerah was Iddo's son. Jeatherai was Zerah's son.

[22]These were Kohath's descendants: Amminadab was Kohath's son. Korah was Amminadab's son. Assir was Korah's son. [23]Elkanah was Assir's son. Ebiasaph was Elkanah's son. Assir was Ebiasaph's son. [24]Tahath was Assir's son. Uriel was Tahath's son. Uzziah was Uriel's son. Shaul was Uzziah's son.

[25]Elkanah's sons were Amasai and Ahimoth. [26]Zophai was Elkanah's son. Nahath was Zophai's son. [27]Eliab was Nahath's son. Jeroham was Eliab's son. Elkanah was Jeroham's son. Samuel was Elkanah's son. [28]Samuel's sons were his oldest son Joel, and Abijah.

[29]These are Merari's sons: Mahli was Merari's son, Libni was Mahli's son, Shimei was Libni's son, and Uzzah was Shimei's son. [30]Shimea was Uzzah's son. Haggiah was Shimea's son. Asaiah was Haggiah's son.

The Temple Musicians

[31]These are the men David chose to take care of the music at the tent of the LORD's house after the Box of the Agreement* was put there. [32]These men served by singing at the Holy Tent.* The Holy Tent is also called the Meeting Tent. These men served until Solomon built the LORD's Temple* in Jerusalem. They served by following the rules given to them for their work.

[33]These are the names of the men and their sons who served with music:

The descendants from the Kohath family were Heman the singer who was Joel's son; Joel was Samuel's son; [34]Samuel was Elkanah's son; Elkanah was Jeroham's son; Jeroham was Eliel's son; Eliel was Toah's son; [35]Toah was Zuph's son; Zuph was Elkanah's son; Elkanah was Mahath's son; Mahath was Amasai's son; [36]Amasai was Elkanah's son; Elkanah was Joel's son; Joel was Azariah's son; Azariah was Zephaniah's son; [37]Zephaniah was Tahath's son; Tahath was Assir's son; Assir was Ebiasaph's son; Ebiasaph was

Korah's son; [38]Korah was Izhar's son; Izhar was Kohath's son; Kohath was Levi's son; Levi was Israel's* son.

[39]Heman's relative was Asaph. Asaph served by Heman's right side. Asaph was Berekiah's son. Berekiah's was Shimea's son. [40]Shimea was Michael's son. Michael was Baaseiah's son. Baaseiah was Malkijah's son. [41]Malkijah was Ethni's son. Ethni was Zerah's son. Zerah was Adaiah's son. [42]Adaiah was Ethan's son. Ethan was Zimmah's son. Zimmah was Shimei's son. [43]Shimei was Jahath's son. Jahath was Gershon's son. Gershon was Levi's son.

[44]Merari's descendants were the relatives of Heman and Asaph. They were the singing group on Heman's left side. Ethan was Kishi's son. Kishi was Abdi's son. Abdi was Malluch's son. [45]Malluch was Hashabiah's son. Hashabiah was Amaziah's son. Amaziah was Hilkiah's son. [46]Hilkiah was Amzi's son. Amzi was Bani's son. Bani was Shemer's son. [47]Shemer was Mahli's son. Mahli was Mushi's son. Mushi was Merari's son. Merari was Levi's son.

[48]Heman and Asaph's brothers were from the tribe of Levi. The tribe of Levi was also called Levites.* The Levites were chosen to do the work in the Holy Tent. The Holy Tent was God's house. [49]But only Aaron's descendants were permitted to burn incense* on the altar* of burnt offering* and on the altar of incense. Aaron's descendants did all the work in the Most Holy Place* in God's house. They also did the ceremonies to make the Israelites pure.* They followed all the rules and laws that Moses, God's servant, commanded.

Aaron's Descendants

[50]These were Aaron's sons: Eleazar was Aaron's son. Phinehas was Eleazar's son. Abishua was Phinehas' son. [51]Bukki was Abishua's son. Uzzi was Bukki's son. Zerahiah was Uzzi's son. [52]Meraioth was Zerahiah's son. Amaraiah was Meraioth's son. Ahitub was Amariah's son. [53]Zadok was Ahitub's son. Ahimaaz was Zadok's son.

Homes for the Levite Families

[54]These are the places where Aaron's descendants lived. They lived in their camps in the land that was given to them. The Kohath families got the first share of the land that was given to the Levites.* [55]They were given the town of Hebron and the fields around it. This was in the area of Judah. [56]But the fields farther from town and the villages near the town of Hebron were given to Caleb son of Jephunneh. [57]The descendants of Aaron were given the city of Hebron. Hebron was a city of safety.[a] They were also given the cities

---

[a]6:57 *city of safety* A special city where an Israelite could run to in order to escape the angry relatives of a person who was accidentally killed by that Israelite. See Num. 35:6–34 and Josh. 20:1–9. Also in verse 67.

of Libnah, Jattir, Eshtemoa, ⁵⁸Hilen, Debir, ⁵⁹Ashan, Juttah, and Beth Shemesh. They got all the cities and the fields around them. ⁶⁰From the tribe of Benjamin they got the cities of Gibeon, Geba, Alemeth, and Anathoth. They got all the cities and the fields around them.

Thirteen cities were given to the Kohath families.

⁶¹The rest of Kohath's descendants got ten towns from half the tribe of Manasseh.

⁶²The tribes that were the descendants of Gershon got 13 cities. They got the cities from the tribes of Issachar, Asher, Naphtali, and the part of Manasseh living in the area of Bashan.

⁶³The tribes that were the descendants of Merari got 12 cities. They got the cities from the tribes of Reuben, Gad, and Zebulun. They got them by throwing lots.*

⁶⁴So the Israelites gave those towns and fields to the Levites. ⁶⁵All those cities came from the tribes of Judah, Simeon, and Benjamin. They decided which Levite family got which city by throwing lots.

⁶⁶The tribe of Ephraim gave some of the Kohath families some towns. Those towns were chosen by throwing lots. ⁶⁷They were given the city of Shechem. Shechem is a city of safety. They were also given the towns of Gezer, ⁶⁸Jokmeam, Beth Horon, ⁶⁹Aijalon, and Gath Rimmon. They also got fields with those towns. Those towns were in the hill country of Ephraim. ⁷⁰And from half the tribe of Manasseh, the Israelites gave the towns of Aner and Bileam to the Kohath families. The Kohath families also got fields with those towns.

Other Levite Families Get Homes

⁷¹The Gershon families got the towns of Golan in the area of Bashan and Ashtaroth from half the tribe of Manasseh. They also got the fields near those towns.

⁷²⁻⁷³The Gershon families also got the towns of Kedesh, Daberath, Ramoth, and Gannim from the tribe of Issachar. They also got the fields near those towns.

⁷⁴⁻⁷⁵The Gershon families also got the towns of Mashal, Abdon, Hukok, and Rehob from the tribe of Asher. They also got the fields near those towns.

⁷⁶The Gershon families also got the towns of Kedesh in Galilee, Hammon, and Kiriathaim from the tribe of Naphtali. They also got the fields near those towns.

⁷⁷The rest of the Levites,* from the Merari families, got the towns of Jokneam, Kartah, Rimmono, and Tabor from the tribe of Zebulun. They also got the fields near those towns.

⁷⁸⁻⁷⁹The Merari families also got the towns of Bezer in the desert, Jahzah, Kedemoth, and Mephaath from the tribe of Reuben. The tribe of Reuben lived on the east side of the Jordan

River, east of the city of Jericho. These Merari families also got the fields near those towns.

⁸⁰⁻⁸¹And the Merari families got the towns of Ramoth in Gilead, Mahanaim, Heshbon, and Jazer from the tribe of Gad. They also got the fields near those towns.

Issachar's Descendants

7 ¹Issachar had four sons. Their names were Tola, Puah, Jashub, and Shimron.

²Tola's sons were Uzzi, Rephaiah, Jeriel, Jahmai, Ibsam, and Samuel. They were all leaders of their families. Those men and their descendants were strong soldiers. Their families grew. By the time David was king, there were 22,600 men ready for war.

³Uzzi's son was Izrahiah. Izrahiah's sons were Michael, Obadiah, Joel, and Isshiah. All five of them were leaders of their families. ⁴Their family history shows they had 36,000 soldiers ready for war. They had a large family because they had many wives and children.

⁵The family history shows there were 87,000 strong soldiers in all the tribes of Issachar.

Benjamin's Descendants

⁶Benjamin had three sons. Their names were Bela, Beker, and Jediael.

⁷Bela had five sons. Their names were Ezbon, Uzzi, Uzziel, Jerimoth, and Iri. They were leaders of their families. Their family history shows they had 22,034 soldiers.

⁸Beker's sons were Zemirah, Joash, Eliezer, Elioenai, Omri, Jeremoth, Abijah, Anathoth, and Alemeth. They all were Beker's children. ⁹Their family history shows who the family leaders were. And it also shows they had 20,200 soldiers.

¹⁰Jediael's son was Bilhan. Bilhan's sons were Jeush, Benjamin, Ehud, Kenaanah, Zethan, Tarshish, and Ahishahar. ¹¹All of Jediael's sons were leaders of their families. They had 17,200 soldiers ready for war.

¹²The Shuppites and Huppites were the descendants of Ir. Hushim was the son of Aher.

Naphtali's Descendants

¹³Naphtali's sons were Jahziel, Guni, Jezer, and Shallum.

And these are the descendants of Bilhah.ᵃ

Manasseh's Descendants

¹⁴These are Manasseh's descendants:

Manasseh's Aramean slave woman* had a son named Asriel. She also bore Makir, the father of Gilead. ¹⁵Makir married a woman from the Huppites and Shuppites. Makir's sister was named Maacah. The name of the second was Zelophehad, who had only daughters. ¹⁶Makir's wife Maacah had a son.

ᵃ**7:13** *Bilhah* Jacob's slave woman and the mother of Dan and Naphtali. See Gen. 30:4–8.

She named this son Peresh. His brother was named Sheresh. The sons of Sheresh were Ulam and Rakem.

[17]Ulam's son was Bedan.

These were the descendants of Gilead. Gilead was Makir's son. Makir was Manasseh's son. [18]Makir's sister Hammoleketh[a] had Ishhod, Abiezer, and Mahlah.

[19]Shemida's sons were Ahian, Shechem, Likhi, and Aniam.

Ephraim's Descendants

[20]These were the names of Ephraim's descendants. Ephraim's son was Shuthelah. Shuthelah's son was Bered. Bered's son was Tahath. [21]Tahath's son was Eleadah. Eleadah's son was Tahath. Tahath's son was Zabad. Zabad's son was Shuthelah.

Some men who grew up in the city of Gath killed Ezer and Elead. This happened because Ezer and Elead went there to steal cattle and sheep from those men in Gath. [22]Ephraim was the father of Ezer and Elead. He cried for many days because Ezer and Elead were dead. Ephraim's family came to comfort him. [23]Then Ephraim had sexual relations with his wife. She became pregnant and had a son. Ephraim named this new son Beriah[b] because something bad had happened to his family. [24]Ephraim's daughter was Sheerah. Sheerah built Lower Beth Horon and Upper Beth Horon and Lower Uzzen Sheerah and Upper Uzzen Sheerah.

[25]Rephah was Ephraim's son. Resheph was Rephah's son. Telah was Resheph's son. Tahan was Telah's son. [26]Ladan was Tahan's son. Ammihud was Ladan's son. Elishama was Ammihud's son. [27]Nun was Elishama's son. Joshua was Nun's son.

[28]These are the cities and lands where Ephraim's descendants lived: Bethel and the villages near it, Naaran to the east, Gezer and the villages near it on the west, and Shechem and the villages near it all the way to Ayyah and the villages near it. [29]Along the borders of Manasseh's land were the towns of Beth Shan, Taanach, Megiddo, and Dor, and the small towns near them. The descendants of Joseph lived in these towns. Joseph was the son of Israel.*

Asher's Descendants

[30]Asher's sons were Imnah, Ishvah, Ishvi, and Beriah. Their sister was named Serah.

[31]Beriah's sons were Heber and Malkiel. Malkiel was Birzaith's father.

[32]Heber was the father of Japhlet, Shomer, Hotham, and of their sister Shua.

[33]Japhlet's sons were Pasach, Bimhal, and Ashvath. These were Japhlet's children.

[34]Shomer's sons were Ahi, Rohgah, Jehubbah,[c] and Aram.

[35]Shomer's brother was Helem. Helem's sons were Zophah, Imna, Shelesh, and Amal.

[36]Zophah's sons were Suah, Harnepher, Shual, Beri, Imrah, [37]Bezer, Hod, Shamma, Shilshah, Ithran, and Beera.

[38]Jether's sons were Jephunneh, Pispah, and Ara.

[39]Ulla's sons were Arah, Hanniel, and Rizia.

[40]All these men were descendants of Asher. They were leaders of their families. They were the best men. They were soldiers and great leaders. Their family history shows 26,000 soldiers ready for war.

The Family History of King Saul

8 [1]Benjamin was Bela's father. Bela was Benjamin's first son. Ashbel was Benjamin's second son. Aharah was Benjamin's third son. [2]Nohah was Benjamin's fourth son. And Rapha was Benjamin's fifth son.

[3-5]Bela's sons were Addar, Gera, Abihud, Abishua, Naaman, Ahoah, Gera, Shephuphan, and Huram.

[6-7]These were the descendants of Ehud. They were leaders of their families in Geba. They were forced to leave their homes and move to Manahath. Ehud's descendants were Naaman, Ahijah, and Gera. Gera forced them to leave their homes. He was the father of Uzza and Ahihud.

[8]Shaharaim divorced his wives Hushim and Baara in Moab. After he did this he had some children with another wife. [9-10]Shaharaim had Jobab, Zibia, Mesha, Malcam, Jeuz, Sakia, and Mirmah with his wife Hodesh. They were leaders of their families. [11]Shaharaim and Hushim had two sons named Abitub and Elpaal.

[12-13]Elpaal's sons were Eber, Misham, Shemed, Beriah, and Shema. Shemed built the towns of Ono and Lod and the small towns around Lod. Beriah and Shema were the leaders of the families living in Aijalon. They forced the people who lived in Gath to leave.

[14]Beriah's sons were Shashak and Jeremoth, [15]Zebadiah, Arad, Eder, [16]Michael, Ishpah, and Joha. [17]Elpaal's sons were Zebadiah, Meshullam, Hizki, Heber, [18]Ishmerai, Izliah, and Jobab.

[19]Shimei's sons were Jakim, Zicri, Zabdi, [20]Elienai, Zillethai, Eliel, [21]Adaiah, Beraiah, and Shimrath.

[22]Shashak's sons were Ishpan, Eber, Eliel, [23]Abdon, Zicri, Hanan, [24]Hananiah, Elam, Anthothijah, [25]Iphdeiah, and Penuel.

[26]Jeroham's sons were Shamsherai, Shehariah, Athaliah, [27]Jaareshiah, Elijah, and Zicri.

[28]All these men were leaders of their families. They were listed in their family histories

*a***7:18** *Hammoleketh* Or "the woman who ruled" or "queen."

*b***7:23** *Beriah* This is like the Hebrew word meaning "bad" or "trouble."

*c***7:34** *Jehubbah* Or "Hubbah."

as leaders. They lived in Jerusalem.

²⁹Jeiel was Gibeon's father. He and his wife, Maacah, lived in the town of Gibeon. ³⁰His oldest son was Abdon. Other sons were Zur, Kish, Baal, Ner, Nadab, ³¹Gedor, Ahio, Zeker, ⌊and Mikloth⌋. ³²Mikloth was the father of Shimeah. These sons also lived near their relatives in Jerusalem.

³³Ner was Kish's father. Kish was Saul's father, and Saul was the father of Jonathan, Malki Shua, Abinadab, and Esh Baal.

³⁴Jonathan's son was Merib Baal. Merib Baal was Micah's father.

³⁵Micah's sons were Pithon, Melech, Tarea, and Ahaz.

³⁶Ahaz was Jehoaddah's father. Jehoaddah was the father of Alemeth, Azmaveth, and Zimri. Zimri was Moza's father. ³⁷Moza was Binea's father. Raphah was Binea's son. Eleasah was Raphah's son. And Azel was Eleasah's son.

³⁸Azel had six sons. Their names were Azrikam, Bokeru, Ishmael, Sheariah, Obadiah, and Hanan. All these sons were Azel's children.

³⁹Azel's brother was Eshek. Eshek had some sons. These were Eshek's sons: Ulam was Azel's oldest son. Jeush was Eshek's second son. Eliphelet was Eshek's third son. ⁴⁰Ulam's sons were strong soldiers who were very good with bows and arrows. They had many sons and grandsons. In all, there were 150 sons and grandsons.

All these men were descendants of Benjamin.

9 ¹The names of all the Israelites were listed in their family histories. Those family histories were put in the book, *The History of the Kings of Israel.*

The People in Jerusalem

The people of Judah were made prisoners and forced to go to Babylon. They were taken there because they were not faithful to God. ²The first people to come back and live in their own lands and towns were some Israelites, priests, Levites,* and servants who work in the Temple.*

³These are the people from the tribes of Judah, Benjamin, Ephraim, and Manasseh who lived in Jerusalem:

⁴Uthai was Ammihud's son. Ammihud was Omri's son. Omri was Imri's son. Imri was Bani's son. Bani was a descendant of Perez. Perez was Judah's son.

⁵The Shilonites who lived in Jerusalem were Asaiah the oldest son and his sons.

⁶The Zerahites who lived in Jerusalem were Jeuel and their relatives. There were 690 of them in all.

⁷These are the people from the tribe of Benjamin who lived in Jerusalem: Sallu was Meshullam's son. Meshullam was Hodaviah's son. Hodaviah was Hassenuah's son. ⁸Ibneiah was Jeroham's son. Elah was Uzzi's son. Uzzi

was Micri's son. And Meshullam was Shephatiah's son. Shephatiah was Reuel's son. Reuel was Ibnijah's son. ⁹The family history of Benjamin shows there were 956 of them living in Jerusalem. All these men were leaders in their families.

¹⁰These are the priests who lived in Jerusalem: Jedaiah, Jehoiarib, Jakin, and ¹¹Azariah. Azariah was Hilkiah's son. Hilkiah was Meshullam's son. Meshullam was Zadok's son. Zadok was Meraioth's son. Meraioth was Ahitub's son. Ahitub was the important official responsible for God's Temple. ¹²Also there was Jeroham's son, Adaiah. Jeroham was Pashhur's son. Pashhur was Malkijah's son. And there was Adiel's son, Maasai. Adiel was Jahzerah's son. Jahzerah was Meshullam's son. Meshullam was Meshillemith's son. Meshillemith was Immer's son.

¹³There were 1760 priests. They were leaders of their families. They were responsible for the work of serving in God's Temple.

¹⁴These are the people from the tribe of Levi who lived in Jerusalem: Hasshub's son, Shemaiah. Hasshub was Azrikam's son. Azrikam was Hashabiah's son. Hashabiah was a descendant of Merari. ¹⁵Also living in Jerusalem were Bakbakkar, Heresh, Galal, and Mattaniah. Mattaniah was Mica's son. Mica was Zicri's son. Zicri was Asaph's son. ¹⁶Obadiah was Shemaiah's son. Shemaiah was Galal's son. Galal was Jeduthun's son. Berekiah was Asa's son. Asa was Elkanah's son. Berekiah lived in the small towns near the people of Netophah.

¹⁷These are the gatekeepers who lived in Jerusalem: Shallum, Akkub, Talmon, Ahiman, and their relatives. Shallum was their leader. ¹⁸Now these men stand next to the King's Gate on the east side. They were the gatekeepers from the tribe of Levi. ¹⁹Shallum was Kore's son. Kore was Ebiasaph's son. Ebiasaph was Korah's son. Shallum and his brothers were gatekeepers. They were from the family of Korah. They had the job of guarding the gates to the Holy Tent.* They did this just as their ancestors* had done before them. Their ancestors had the job of guarding the entrance to the Holy Tent. ²⁰In the past, Phinehas was in charge of the gatekeepers. Phinehas was Eleazar's son. The Lᴏʀᴅ was with Phinehas. ²¹Zechariah son of Meshelemiah was the gatekeeper at the entrance to the Holy Tent.

²²In all there were 212 men who were chosen to guard the gates of the Holy Tent. Their names were written in their family histories in their small towns. David and Samuel the seer* chose these men because they could be trusted. ²³The gatekeepers and their descendants had the responsibility of guarding the gates of the Lᴏʀᴅ's house, the Holy Tent. ²⁴There were gates on the four sides: east, west, north, and south. ²⁵The gatekeepers' relatives who lived in the small towns had to come and help them at certain times. They

came and helped the gatekeepers for seven days each time.

²⁶There were four gatekeepers who were the leaders of all the gatekeepers. They were Levites. They had the job of caring for the rooms and treasures in God's Temple. ²⁷They stayed up all night guarding God's Temple, and they had the job of opening God's Temple every morning.

²⁸Some of the gatekeepers had the job of caring for the dishes used in the Temple services. They counted them when they were brought in. They also counted these dishes when they were taken out. ²⁹Other gatekeepers were chosen to care for the furniture and the special dishes. They also took care of the flour, wine, oil, incense,* and special oil.^a ³⁰But it was the priests who had the job of mixing the special oil.

³¹There was a Levite named Mattithiah who had the job of baking the bread used for the offerings. Mattithiah was Shallum's oldest son. Shallum was from the Korah family. ³²Some of the gatekeepers who were in the Korah family had the job of preparing the bread put on the table every Sabbath.*

³³The Levites who were singers and leaders of their families stayed in the rooms at the Temple. They did not have to do other work because they were responsible for the work in the Temple day and night. ³⁴All these Levites were leaders of their families. They were listed as leaders in their family histories. They lived in Jerusalem.

The Family History of King Saul

³⁵Jeiel was Gibeon's father. Jeiel lived in the town of Gibeon. His wife was named Maacah. ³⁶Jeiel's oldest son was Abdon. Other sons were Zur, Kish, Baal, Ner, Nadab, ³⁷Gedor, Ahio, Zechariah, and Mikloth. ³⁸Mikloth was Shimeam's father. Jeiel's family lived near their relatives in Jerusalem.

³⁹Ner was Kish's father. Kish was Saul's father. And Saul was the father of Jonathan, Malki Shua, Abinadab, and Esh Baal.

⁴⁰Jonathan's son was Merib Baal. Merib Baal was Micah's father.

⁴¹Micah's sons were Pithon, Melech, Tahrea, and Ahaz. ⁴²Ahaz was the father of Jadah.^b Jadah was the father of Alemeth, Azmaveth, and Zimri. Zimri was Moza's father. ⁴³Moza was the father of Binea. Rephaiah was Binea's son. Eleasah was Rephaiah's son. And Azel was Eleasah's son.

⁴⁴Azel had six sons. Their names were Azrikam, Bokeru, Ishmael, Sheariah, Obadiah, and Hanan. They were Azel's children.

The Death of King Saul

10 ¹The Philistines fought against the Israelites. The Israelites ran away from the Philistines. Many Israelites were killed on Mount Gilboa. ²The Philistines continued chasing Saul and his sons. They caught them and killed them. The Philistines killed Saul's sons Jonathan, Abinadab, and Malki Shua. ³The fighting was heavy around Saul. The archers* shot Saul with their arrows and wounded him.

⁴Then Saul said to his armor bearer,* "Pull out your sword and use it to kill me. Then these foreigners^c will not hurt me and make fun of me when they come."

But Saul's armor bearer was afraid. He refused to kill Saul. Then Saul used his own sword to kill himself—he fell on his sword. ⁵When the armor bearer saw that Saul was dead, he killed himself—he fell on his own sword and died. ⁶So Saul and three of his sons died. All of Saul's family died together.

⁷When all the Israelites living in the valley saw that their own army had run away and that Saul and his sons were dead, they left their towns and ran away. Then the Philistines came into the towns and lived in them.

⁸The next day, the Philistines came to take valuable things from the dead bodies. They found Saul's body and the bodies of his sons on Mount Gilboa. ⁹The Philistines took things from Saul's body. They took Saul's head and armor.* They sent messengers through all their country to tell the news to their false gods and to their people. ¹⁰The Philistines put Saul's armor in the temple of their false gods. They hung Saul's head in the temple of Dagon.*

¹¹All the people living in the town of Jabesh Gilead heard everything that the Philistines had done to Saul. ¹²All the brave men from Jabesh Gilead went to get the bodies of Saul and his sons. They brought them back to Jabesh Gilead. They buried the bones of Saul and his sons under the large tree in Jabesh. Then they showed their sadness and fasted for seven days.

¹³Saul died because he was not faithful to the LORD. He did not obey the LORD's word. Saul also went to a medium* and asked her for advice ¹⁴instead of asking the LORD. That is why the LORD killed Saul and gave the kingdom to Jesse's son David.

David Becomes King Over Israel

11 ¹All the Israelites came to David at the town of Hebron. They said to David, "We are your own flesh and blood.^d ²In the past you led us in war. You led us even

---

^a**9:29** *special oil* Or "perfume." This might be the oil used to anoint priests, prophets, and kings. See Ex. 30:22-38.

^b**9:42** *Jadah* This is from the ancient Greek translation and some Hebrew copies. Most Hebrew copies have "Jarah" for "Jadah" in this verse.

^c**10:4** *foreigners* Literally, "uncircumcised." This means people who did not share in the agreement God made with Israel. See "circumcise, circumcision" in the Word List.

^d**11:1** *We are … blood* A way of saying they were David's relatives.

though Saul was the king. The LORD said to you 'David, you will be the shepherd of my people, the Israelites. You will become the leader over my people.'"

[3] All the leaders of Israel came to King David at the town of Hebron. David made an agreement with them in Hebron before the LORD. The leaders anointed* David. That made him king over Israel. The LORD promised this would happen. The LORD had used Samuel to make that promise.

David Captures Jerusalem

[4] David and all the Israelites went to the city of Jerusalem. Jerusalem was called Jebus at that time. The people living in that city were named Jebusites. They [5] said to David, "You cannot get inside our city." But David did defeat them. He took over the fortress* of Zion,* and it became the City of David.*

[6] David said, "The one who leads the attack on the Jebusites will become the commander over all my army." So Joab led the attack. He was Zeruiah's son. Joab became the commander of the army.

[7] Then David made his home in the fortress. That is why it is named the City of David. [8] David built the city around the fort. He built it from the Millo* to the wall around the city. Joab repaired the other parts of the city. [9] David continued to grow greater, and the LORD All-Powerful was with him.

The Three Heroes

[10] This is a list of the leaders over David's special soldiers. These heroes became very powerful with David in his kingdom. They and all the Israelites supported David and made him king, just as God had promised.

[11] This is a list of David's special soldiers:
Jashobeam the Hacmonite[a] was the leader of the king's special forces.[b] Jashobeam used his spear to kill 300 men at one time.

[12] Next there was Eleazar son of Dodai[c] from Ahoah. Eleazar was one of the Three Heroes.[d] [13] Eleazar was with David at Pasdammim. The Philistines had come to that place to fight a war. There was a field full of barley there. The Israelites ran away from the Philistines. [14] But the Three Heroes stood there in that field and defended it. They defeated the Philistines. The LORD gave the Israelites a great victory.

[15] Once David was at the cave of Adullam, and three of the Thirty Heroes[e] went down

to meet him by a rock near the cave. At the same time the Philistine army was camped in the Valley of Rephaim.

[16] Another time David was in the fortress,* and a group of Philistine soldiers was stationed in Bethlehem. [17] David was thirsty for some water from his hometown, so he said, "Oh, if only I could have some water from that well by the gate in Bethlehem." [18] So the Three Heroes[f] fought their way through the Philistine army and got some water from the well near the city gate in Bethlehem. They took it to David, but he refused to drink it. He poured it on the ground as an offering to the LORD. [19] David said, "God, I cannot drink this water. It would be like drinking the blood of the men who risked their lives to get this water for me." That is why David refused to drink the water. The Three Heroes did many brave things like that.

Other Brave Soldiers

[20] Joab's brother, Abishai, was the leader of the Three Heroes. Abishai used his spear against 300 enemies and killed them. He was as famous as the Three Heroes. [21] Abishai was even more famous than the Three Heroes.[g] He became their leader, even though he was not one of the Three Heroes.

[22] Then there was Benaiah son of Jehoiada, from Kabzeel. He was the son of a powerful man.[h] Benaiah did many brave things. He killed two of the best soldiers in Moab. One day when it was snowing, Benaiah went down into a hole in the ground and killed a lion. [23] And Benaiah killed a big Egyptian soldier. That man was about 7½ feet[i] tall. The Egyptian had a spear that was very large and heavy. It was as big as the pole on a weaver's loom.* Benaiah had only a club. He grabbed the spear in the Egyptian's hands and took it away from him. Then Benaiah killed the Egyptian with his own spear. [24] Benaiah son of Jehoiada did many brave things like that. He was as famous as the Three Heroes. [25] Benaiah was even more famous than the Thirty Heroes, but he was not one of the Three Heroes. David made Benaiah the leader of his bodyguards.

The Thirty Heroes

[26] The following men were among the king's special forces: Asahel, Joab's brother; Elhanan son of Dodai from Bethlehem; [27] Shammoth the Harodite; Helez the Pelonite; [28] Ira son of Ikkesh from Tekoa; Abiezer from Anathoth; [29] Sibbecai the Hushathite; Ilai from Ahoah; [30] Maharai from Netophah; Heled son of

---

[a] 11:11 Jashobeam the Hacmonite This is "Josheb Basshebeth the Tahkemonite" in 2 Sam. 23:8.
[b] 11:11 king's special forces A special group of soldiers who formed three-man squads and went on special missions for the king.
[c] 11:12 Eleazar son of Dodai Or "Eleazar his cousin."
[d] 11:12 Three Heroes These were David's three bravest soldiers. Also in verses 18, 20, 24.
[e] 11:15 Thirty Heroes Or "the king's special forces." These men were David's famous group of very brave soldiers. Also in verses 25, 42.

[f] 11:18 Three Heroes These were David's three bravest soldiers. Also in verses 19–21.
[g] 11:21 Three Heroes Or possibly, "The Thirty Heroes."
[h] 11:22 powerful man That is, a man from the warrior class ready to protect his people in war.
[i] 11:23 7 1/2 feet Literally, "5 [short] cubits" (2.22 m).

Baanah from Netophah; ³¹Ithai son of Ribai from Gibeah in Benjamin; Benaiah the Pirathonite; ³²Hurai from the Brooks of Gaash; Abiel the Arbathite; ³³Azmaveth the Baharumite; Eliahba the Shaalbonite; ³⁴the sons of Hashem the Gizonite; Jonathan son of Shagee the Hararite; ³⁵Ahiam son of Sacar the Hararite; Eliphal son of Ur; ³⁶Hepher the Mekerathite; Ahijah the Pelonite; ³⁷Hezro the Carmelite; Naarai son of Ezbai; ³⁸Joel, Nathan's brother; Mibhar son of Hagri; ³⁹Zelek the Ammonite; Naharai, the officer from Beeroth, who carried the armor* for Joab son of Zeruiah; ⁴⁰Ira the Ithrite; Gareb the Ithrite; ⁴¹Uriah the Hittite; Zabad son of Ahlai; ⁴²Adina who was the son of Shiza from the tribe of Reuben and was the leader of the tribe and one of the Thirty Heroes; ⁴³Hanan son of Maacah; Joshaphat the Mithnite; ⁴⁴Uzzia the Ashterathite; Shama and Jeiel sons of Hotham from Aroer; ⁴⁵Jediael son of Shimri and his brother Joha the Tizite; ⁴⁶Eliel the Mahavite; Jeribai and Joshaviah the sons of Elnaam; Ithmah the Moabite; ⁴⁷Eliel; Obed; and Jaasiel the Mezobaite.

The Brave Men Who Joined David

12 ¹This is a list of the men who came to David while he was at Ziklag. This was when David was hiding from Saul son of Kish. These men helped David in battle. ²They could shoot arrows from their bows with either their right or left hand. They could also throw stones from their slings* with either their right or left hand. They were Saul's relatives from the tribe of Benjamin. They were ³Ahiezer, their leader, and Joash (sons of Shemaah the Gibeathite); Jeziel and Pelet (sons of Azmaveth); Beracah and Jehu from the town of Anathoth; ⁴Ishmaiah the Gibeonite (a hero and leader of the Thirty Heroes); Jeremiah, Jahaziel, Johanan, and Jozabad from the Gederathites; ⁵Eluzai, Jerimoth, Bealiah, and Shemariah; Shephatiah from Haripha; ⁶Elkanah, Isshiah, Azarel, Joezer, and Jashobeam, all from the tribe of Korah; ⁷and Joelah and Zebadiah, the sons of Jeroham from the town of Gedor.

The Gadites

⁸Part of the tribe of Gad joined David at his fortress* in the desert. They were brave soldiers trained for war and skilled with the shield and spear. They looked as fierce as lions, and they could run as fast as gazelles* through the mountains.

⁹Ezer was the leader of the army from the tribe of Gad. Obadiah was the second in command. Eliab was the third in command. ¹⁰Mishmannah was the fourth in command. Jeremiah was the fifth in command. ¹¹Attai was the sixth in command. Eliel was the seventh in command. ¹²Johanan was the eighth in command. Elzabad was the ninth in command. ¹³Jeremiah was the tenth in command. Macbannai was the eleventh in command.

¹⁴These men were leaders of the Gadite army. The weakest from that group was worth 100 men, and the strongest was worth 1000 men.ᵃ ¹⁵They were the soldiers who crossed the Jordan River in the first month of the year, when it was flooded over its banks. They chased away the people in the valley who were on both sides of the river.

Other Soldiers Join David

¹⁶Other men from the tribes of Benjamin and Judah also came to David at the fortress.* ¹⁷David went out to meet them and said, "If you have come in peace to help me, I welcome you. Join me. But if you have come to spy on me when I have done nothing wrong, may the God of our ancestors* see what you did and punish you."

¹⁸Amasai was the leader of the Thirty Heroes.ᵇ Then the Spirit came on Amasai, and he said,

"We are yours, David!
　We are with you, son of Jesse.
　Peace, peace to you.
　Peace to those who help you, because
　　your God helps you."

So David welcomed these men into his group and put them in charge of the troops.

¹⁹Some of the men from the tribe of Manasseh also joined David. They joined him when he went with the Philistines to fight Saul. But David and his men did not really help the Philistines. The Philistine leaders talked about David helping them, but then they decided to send him away. They said, "If David goes back to his master Saul, our heads will be cut off!" ²⁰These were the men from Manasseh who joined David when he went to the town of Ziklag: Adnah, Jozabad, Jediael, Michael, Jozabad, Elihu, and Zillethai. All of them were generalsᶜ from the tribe of Manasseh. ²¹They helped David fight against bad men who were going around the country and stealing things from people. All these men of Manasseh were brave soldiers. They became leaders in David's army.

²²More and more men came every day to help David. So he had a large and powerful army.

Other Men Join David at Hebron

²³These are the numbers of the men who came to David at the town of Hebron. These men were ready for war. They came to give Saul's kingdom to David. That is what the LORD said would happen. This is their number:

ᵃ**12:14** *The weakest ... 1000 men* Or "The smallest was commander over 100 men, the greatest over 1000 men."

ᵇ**12:18** *Thirty Heroes* Or "The Three" or "the chariot officers."

ᶜ**12:20** *generals* Literally, "leaders over 1000 men."

²⁴From the tribe of Judah there were 6800 men ready for war. They carried shields and spears.

²⁵From the tribe of Simeon there were 7100 men. They were brave soldiers ready for war.

²⁶From the tribe of Levi there were 4600 men. ²⁷Jehoiada was in that group. He was a leader from Aaron's family. There were 3700 men with Jehoiada. ²⁸Zadok was also in that group. He was a brave young soldier. He came with 22 officers from his family.

²⁹From the tribe of Benjamin there were 3000 men. They were Saul's relatives. Most of them stayed faithful to Saul's family until that time.

³⁰From the tribe of Ephraim there were 20,800 men. They were brave soldiers. They were famous men in their own families.

³¹From half the tribe of Manasseh there were 18,000 men. They were called by name to come and make David king.

³²From the family of Issachar there were 200 wise leaders. These men understood the right thing for Israel to do at the right time. Their relatives were with them and under their command.

³³From the tribe of Zebulun there were 50,000 trained soldiers. They were trained to use all kinds of weapons and were very loyal to David.

³⁴From the tribe of Naphtali there were 1000 officers. They had 37,000 men with them. These men carried shields and spears.

³⁵From the tribe of Dan there were 28,600 men ready for war.

³⁶From the tribe of Asher there were 40,000 trained soldiers ready for war.

³⁷From the east side of the Jordan River, there were 120,000 men from the tribes of Reuben, Gad, and half of Manasseh. They had all kinds of weapons.

³⁸All these men were brave fighters. They came to the town of Hebron for one reason—to make David king of all Israel. All the other Israelites also agreed that David should be king. ³⁹The men spent three days at Hebron with David. They ate and drank, because their relatives had prepared food for them. ⁴⁰Also, their neighbors from the areas where the tribes of Issachar, Zebulun, and Naphtali live brought food on donkeys, camels, mules, and cattle. They brought much flour, fig cakes, raisins, wine, oil, cattle, and sheep. The people in Israel were very happy.

Bringing Back the Box of the Agreement

13 ¹David talked with all the officers of his army. ²Then he called the Israelites together and said, "If you think it is a good idea, and if it is what the LORD wants, let us send a message to our brothers in all the areas of Israel. Let's also send the message to the priests and Levites* who live with our brothers in their towns and the fields near those towns. Let the message tell them to come and join us. ³Let's bring the Box of the Agreement* back to us in Jerusalem. We did not take care of the Box of the Agreement while Saul was king." ⁴So all the Israelites agreed with David. They all thought it was the right thing to do.

⁵So David gathered all the Israelites from the Shihor River in Egypt to the town of Lebo Hamath. They came together to bring the Box of the Agreement back from the town of Kiriath Jearim. ⁶David and all the Israelites with him went to Baalah of Judah. (Baalah is another name for Kiriath Jearim.) They went there to bring out the Box of the Agreement, that is, the Box of God the LORD who sits above the Cherub angels.* It is the Box that is called by his name.

⁷The people moved the Box of the Agreement from Abinadab's house and put it on a new wagon. Uzzah and Ahio were driving the wagon.

⁸David and all the Israelites were celebrating before God. They were praising God and singing songs. They were playing harps, lyres,* drums, cymbals,* and trumpets.

⁹They came to Kidon's threshing* floor. The oxen pulling the wagon stumbled, and the Box of the Agreement almost fell. Uzzah reached out with his hand to catch the Box. ¹⁰The LORD became very angry with Uzzah and killed him because he touched the Box. So Uzzah died there in front of God. ¹¹God showed his anger at Uzzah, and this made David angry. Since that time until now that place has been called "Perez Uzzah."ᵃ

¹²David was afraid of God that day. David said, "I cannot bring the Box of the Agreement here to me!" ¹³So he did not take the Box of the Agreement with him to the City of David.* He left the Box of the Agreement at Obed Edom's house. Obed Edom was from the city of Gath. ¹⁴The Box of the Agreement stayed with Obed Edom's family in his house for three months. The LORD blessed Obed Edom's family and everything Obed Edom owned.

David's Kingdom Grows

14 ¹Hiram was king of the city of Tyre. He sent messengers to David. He also sent logs from cedar trees, stonecutters, and carpenters to David. Hiram sent them to build a house for David. ²Then David could see that the LORD had really made him king of Israel. The LORD made David's kingdom very large and powerful. God did this because he loved David and the Israelites.

³David married more women in the city of Jerusalem and had more sons and daughters. ⁴These are the names of David's children born in Jerusalem: Shammua, Shobab,

ᵃ**13:11 Perez Uzzah** This name means "the outburst at Uzzah."

Nathan, Solomon, [5]Ibhar, Elishua, Elpelet, [6]Nogah, Nepheg, Japhia, [7]Elishama, Beeliada, and Eliphelet.

David Defeats the Philistines

[8]The Philistines heard that David had been chosen to be the king of Israel, so all the Philistines went to look for him. When David heard about it, he went out to fight them. [9]The Philistines attacked the people living in the Valley of Rephaim and stole their things. [10]David asked God, "Should I go and fight the Philistines? Will you let me defeat them?"

The LORD answered David, "Go. I will let you defeat the Philistines."

[11]Then David and his men went up to the town of Baal Perazim. There David and his men defeated the Philistines. David said, "Waters break out from a broken dam. In the same way God has broken through my enemies! God has done this through me." That is why that place is named Baal Perazim.[a] [12]The Philistines had left their idols* at Baal Perazim. David ordered his men to burn the idols.

Another Victory Over the Philistines

[13]The Philistines attacked the people living in the Valley of Rephaim again. [14]David prayed to God again, and God answered his prayer. God said, "David, don't follow the Philistines up the hill when you attack. Instead, go around them and hide on the other side of the balsam trees. [15]When you hear the sound of marching in the tops of the balsam trees, go out to battle because that is the sign that God has gone out in front of you to defeat the Philistines." [16]David did what God told him to do. So David and his men defeated the Philistine army. They killed Philistine soldiers all the way from the town of Gibeon to the town of Gezer. [17]So David became famous in all the countries. The LORD made all nations afraid of him.

The Box of the Agreement in Jerusalem

15 [1]David built houses for himself in the City of David.* Then he built a place to put the Box of the Agreement.* He set up a tent for it. [2]Then he said, "Only the Levites* are permitted to carry the Box of the Agreement. The LORD chose them to carry it and to serve him forever."

[3]David told all the Israelites to meet together at Jerusalem ⌊while the Levites carried⌋ the Box of the Agreement to the place he had made for it. [4]He called together the descendants of Aaron and the Levites. [5]There were 120 people from the tribe of Kohath. Uriel was their leader. [6]There were 220 people from the tribe of Merari. Asaiah was their leader. [7]There were 130 people from the tribe of Gershon. Joel was their leader. [8]There were 200 people from the tribe of Elizaphan. Shemaiah was their leader. [9]There were 80 people from the tribe of Hebron. Eliel was their leader. [10]There were 112 people from the tribe of Uzziel. Amminadab was their leader.

David Talks to the Priests and Levites

[11]Then David asked the priests, Zadok and Abiathar, to come to him. David also asked these Levites* to come to him: Uriel, Asaiah, Joel, Shemaiah, Eliel, and Amminadab. [12]David said to them, "You are the leaders from the tribe of Levi. You and the other Levites must make yourselves holy.[b] Then bring the Box of the Agreement* to the place I have made for it. [13]The last time we did not ask the LORD how to carry the Box of the Agreement. You Levites did not carry it, and that is why the LORD punished us."

[14]Then the priests and Levites made themselves holy so that they could carry the Box of the Agreement of the LORD, the God of Israel. [15]The Levites used the special poles to carry the Box of the Agreement on their shoulders, the way Moses commanded. They carried the Box just as the LORD had said.

The Singers

[16]David told the Levite* leaders to get their brothers, the singers. The singers were to take their lyres,* harps, and cymbals* and sing happy songs.

[17]Then the Levites got Heman and his brothers, Asaph and Ethan. Heman was Joel's son. Asaph was Berekiah's son. Ethan was Kushaiah's son. These men were from the Merari tribe. [18]There was also a second group of Levites. They were Zechariah, Jaaziel, Shemiramoth, Jehiel, Unni, Eliab, Benaiah, Maaseiah, Mattithiah, Eliphelehu, Mikneiah, Obed Edom, and Jeiel. These men were the Levite guards.

[19]The singers Heman, Asaph, and Ethan played bronze cymbals. [20]Zechariah, Jaaziel, Shemiramoth, Jehiel, Unni, Eliab, Maaseiah, and Benaiah played the alamoth[c] harps. [21]Mattithiah, Eliphelehu, Mikneiah, Obed Edom, Jeiel, and Azaziah played the sheminith harps. This was their job forever. [22]The Levite leader Kenaniah was in charge of the singing. Kenaniah had this job because he was very skilled at singing.

[23]Berekiah and Elkanah were two of the guards for the Box of the Agreement.* [24]The priests Shebaniah, Joshaphat, Nethanel, Amasai, Zechariah, Benaiah, and Eliezer had the job of blowing trumpets as they walked in front of the Box of the Agreement. Obed

---

[a]**14:11** *Baal Perazim* This name means "the Lord breaks through."

[b]**15:12** *holy* Here, this means "prepared to serve the LORD." Also in verse 14.

[c]**15:20, 21** *alamoth, sheminith* The meaning of these words is uncertain, but they may refer to types of instruments, special ways of tuning an instrument, or two different groups that played harps in the Temple orchestra.

Edom and Jehiah were the other guards for the Box of the Agreement.

25David, the elders* of Israel, and the generals*a went to get the Box of the Agreement. They brought it out from Obed Edom's house. Everyone was very happy! 26God helped the Levites who carried the Box of the Agreement. They sacrificed* seven bulls and seven rams. 27All the Levites who carried the Box wore robes made from fine linen.* Kenaniah, the man in charge of the singing, and all the singers had robes made from fine linen. David also wore a robe made from fine linen and an ephod* made of fine linen.

28So all the Israelites brought up the Box of the Agreement. They shouted, they blew rams' horns and trumpets, and they played cymbals, lyres, and harps.

29When the Box of the Agreement arrived at the City of David,* Saul's daughter Michal looked through a window. When she saw King David dancing and playing, she lost her respect for him.

16 1The Levites brought the Box of the Agreement and put it inside the tent David had set up for it. Then they offered burnt offerings* and fellowship offerings* to God. 2After David had finished giving the burnt offerings and fellowship offerings, he used the LORD's name to bless the people. 3Then he gave a loaf of bread, some dates, and raisins to every Israelite man and woman.

4Then David chose some of the Levites to serve before the Box of the Agreement. They had the job of celebrating and giving thanks and praise to the LORD, the God of Israel. 5Asaph was the leader of the first group. His group played the cymbals. Zechariah was the leader of the second group. The other Levites were Uzziel, Shemiramoth, Jehiel, Mattithiah, Eliab, Benaiah, Obed Edom, and Jeiel. These men played the lyres and harps. 6Benaiah and Jahaziel were the priests who always blew the trumpets before the Box of the Agreement. 7This was when David first gave Asaph and his brothers the job of singing praises to the LORD.

David's Song of Thanks

8 Give thanks to the LORD and call out to him!
  Tell the nations what he has done!
9 Sing to him; sing praises to him.
  Tell about the amazing things he has done.
10 Be proud of his holy name.
  You followers of the LORD, be happy!
11 Depend on the LORD for strength.
  Always go to him for help.
12 Remember the amazing things he has done.
  Remember his miracles* and his fair decisions.

13 The people of Israel* are his servants.
  The descendants of Jacob* are his chosen people.
14 The LORD is our God.
  He rules the whole world.
15 Remember his agreement* forever,
  the promise he gave that will never end.
16 Remember the agreement he made with Abraham*
  Remember his promise to Isaac.*
17 He gave it as a law for Jacob,
  as an agreement with Israel that will last forever.
18 He said, "I will give you the land of Canaan.*
  It will be your very own."

19 At the time God said this, there were only a few of his people,
  and they were strangers there.
20 They traveled around from nation to nation,
  from one kingdom to another.
21 But the Lord did not let anyone mistreat them.
  He warned kings not to harm them.
22 He said, "Don't hurt my chosen people.
  Don't hurt my prophets.*"
23 Let the whole world sing to the LORD!
  Tell the good news every day about how he saves us.
24 Tell all the nations how wonderful he is!
  Tell people everywhere about the amazing things he does.
25 The LORD is great and worthy of praise.
  He is more awesome than any of the "gods."
26 All the "gods" in other nations are nothing but statues,
  but the LORD made the heavens!
27 He lives in the presence of glory* and honor.
  His Temple* is a place of power and joy.
28 Praise the LORD, all people of every nation;
  praise the LORD's glory and power!
29 Give the LORD praise worthy of his glory.
  Come into his presence with your offerings.
  Worship the LORD in all his holy beauty.
30 Everyone on earth should tremble before him!
  But the world stands firm and cannot be moved.
31 Let the heavens rejoice and the earth be happy!
  Let people everywhere say, "The LORD rules!"
32 Let the sea and everything in it shout for joy!
  Let the fields and everything in them be happy!
33 The trees of the forest will sing for joy when they see the LORD,
  because he is coming to rule the world.

---

a15:25 generals Literally, "leaders over 1000 men."

34 Give thanks to the LORD because he is
　　　good.
　　His faithful love will last forever.
35 Say to him,
　　"Save us, God our Savior.
　　Bring us back together,
　　　and save us from the other nations.
　　Then we will give thanks to your holy
　　　name
　　　and joyfully praise you."
36 Praise the LORD, the God of Israel!
　　He always was and will always be
　　　worthy of praise!

All the people praised the LORD and said
"Amen!"

37Then David left Asaph and his brothers
there in front of the Box of the Agreement.*
David left them there to serve in front of it
every day. 38He also left Obed Edom and 68
other Levites* to serve with Asaph and his
brothers. Obed Edom and Hosah were guards.
Obed Edom was Jeduthun's son.

39David left Zadok the priest and the other
priests who served with him in front of the
LORD's Tent*a at the high place* in Gibeon.
40Every morning and evening Zadok and the
other priests offered burnt offerings on the
altar* of burnt offerings. They did this to follow the rules written in the law of the LORD,
which the LORD had given Israel. 41Heman,
Jeduthun, and all the other Levites were chosen by name to sing the songs of praise such
as, *Praise the LORD Because His Faithful Love
Will Last Forever.b* 42Heman and Jeduthun
were with them. They had the job of blowing
the trumpets and playing cymbals.* They also
had the job of playing other musical instruments when songs were sung to God. Jeduthun's sons guarded the gates.

43After the celebration, all the people left
and went home. David also went home to
bless his family.

God's Promise to David

17 1After David had moved into his palace, he said to Nathan the prophet,
"Look, I am living in this nice palace made
of cedar, but the Box of the Agreement* sits
in a tent."

2Nathan answered David, "You may do
what you want to do. God is with you."

3But that night the word of God came to
Nathan. 4God said, "Go and tell this to my
servant David: The LORD says, 'David, you are
not the one to build a house for me to live
in. 5-6Since the time I brought Israel out of
Egypt until now, I have not lived in a house. I
have moved around in a tent. I chose people

to be special leaders for the Israelites. They
were like shepherds for my people. While I
was going around in Israel to different places,
I never said to any of them: Why haven't you
built a house of cedar wood for me?'

7"Now, tell this to my servant David: The
LORD All-Powerful says, 'I took you from the
fields and from taking care of the sheep. I
made you king of my people Israel. 8I have
been with you everywhere you went. I went
ahead of you and I killed your enemies. Now
I will make you one of the most famous men
on earth. 9I am giving this place to my people
Israel. They will plant their trees, and they
will sit in peace under those trees. They will
not be bothered anymore. Evil people will not
hurt them as they did at first. 10Those bad
things happened, but I chose leaders to care
for my people Israel. And I will also defeat all
your enemies.

"'I tell you that the LORD will build a house
for you.c 11When you die, and you join your
ancestors,* then I will let your own son be the
new king. The new king will be one of your
sons, and I will make his kingdom strong.
12Your son will build a house for me. I will
make your son's family rule forever. 13I will be
his father, and he will be my son. Saul was the
king before you, and I took away my support
from Saul. But I will never stop loving your
son. 14I will put him in charge of my house
and kingdom forever. His rule will continue
forever!'"

15Nathan told David about the vision* and
everything God had said.

David's Prayer

16Then King David went to the Holy Tent
and sat before the LORD. David said, "LORD
God, you have done so much for me and my
family. And I don't understand why. 17Besides
all these things, you let me know what will
happen to my family in the future. You have
treated me like a very important man. 18What
more can I say? You have done so much for
me. And I am only your servant. You know
that. 19LORD, you have done this wonderful
thing for me and because you wanted to.
20There is no one like you, LORD. There is no
God except you. We have never heard of any
god doing wonderful things like those! 21Is
there any other nation like Israel? No, Israel
is the only nation on earth that you have done
these wonderful things for. You took us out of
Egypt and you made us free. You made yourself famous. You went in front of your people,
and forced other people to leave their land for
us. 22You took Israel to be your people forever, and LORD, you became their God!

23"LORD, you made this promise to me and
my family. Now, keep your promise forever.

---

a16:39 *LORD's Tent* Or "Tabernacle." Also called the
"Meeting Tent." The people would go to this tent to
meet with God. They used this tent until Solomon
built the Temple in Jerusalem.

b16:41 *Praise ... Forever* See 2 Chron. 7:6, Ps. 118
and 136.

c17:10 *build a house for you* This does not mean a
real house. It means the Lord would make men from
David's family kings for many years.

Do what you said you would. ²⁴Keep your promise so that people will honor your name forever. Then people will say, 'The LORD All-Powerful is Israel's God!' I am your servant. Please let my family be strong and continue to serve you.

²⁵"My God, you spoke to me, your servant. You made it clear that you would make my family a family of kings. That is why I am being so bold—that is why I am asking you to do these things. ²⁶LORD, you are God, and you yourself promised to do these good things for me. ²⁷LORD, you have been kind enough to bless my family. You were kind enough to promise that my family will serve you forever. LORD, you yourself blessed my family, so my family really will be blessed forever."

David Wins Over Different Nations

18 ¹Later, David attacked the Philistines and defeated them. He took the town of Gath and the other small towns around it from the Philistines.

²Then David defeated the country of Moab. The Moabites became David's servants and brought tribute* to him.

³David also fought against Hadadezer's army. Hadadezer was the king of Zobah. David fought against that army all the way to the town of Hamath. David did this when he went to set up a monument for himself at the Euphrates River.ᵃ ⁴David took 1000 chariots,* 7000 chariot drivers, and 20,000 soldiers from Hadadezer. David also crippled most of Hadadezer's horses that were used for pulling chariots. But David saved enough horses to pull 100 chariots.

⁵The Arameans from the city of Damascus came to help King Hadadezer of Zobah. But David defeated and killed 22,000 Aramean soldiers. ⁶Then David put fortresses* in the city of Damascus in Aram. The Arameans became David's servants and brought tribute to him. So the LORD gave victory to David everywhere he went.

⁷David took the gold shields from Hadadezer's army leaders and brought them to Jerusalem. ⁸David also took much bronze from the towns of Tebah and Cun. These towns belonged to Hadadezer. Later, Solomon used this bronze to make the bronze tank,ᵇ the bronze columns, and other things made from bronze for the Temple.*

⁹Tou was king of the city of Hamath. Hadadezer was the king of Zobah. Tou heard that David had defeated all of Hadadezer's army. ¹⁰So Tou sent his son Hadoram to King David to ask for peace and to bless him. He did this because David had fought against Hadadezer and defeated him. Hadadezer had been at war with Tou before. Hadoram gave David

all kinds of things made of gold, silver, and bronze. ¹¹King David made these things holy* and gave them to the LORD. David did the same thing with all the silver and gold he had gotten from Edom, Moab, the Ammonites, the Philistines, and Amalekites.

¹²Abishai son of Zeruiah killed 18,000 Edomites in the Valley of Salt. ¹³Abishai also put fortresses in Edom and all the Edomites became David's servants. The LORD gave David victory everywhere he went.

David's Important Officials

¹⁴David was king over all Israel. He did what was right and fair for everyone. ¹⁵Joab son of Zeruiah was the commander of David's army. Jehoshaphat son of Ahilud wrote about the things David did. ¹⁶Zadok and Abimelech were the priests. Zadok was Ahitub's son, and Abimelech was Abiathar's son. Shavsha was the scribe.* ¹⁷Benaiah was responsible for leading the Kerethite and Pelethites.ᶜ Benaiah was Jehoiada's son. And David's sons were important officials. They served at King David's side.

The Ammonites Shame David's Men

19 ¹Nahash was king of the Ammonites. When Nahash died, his son became the new king. ²Then David said, "Nahash was kind to me, so I will be kind to Hanun, Nahash's son." So David sent messengers to comfort Hanun about the death of his father. David's messengers went to the country of Ammon to comfort Hanun.

³But the Ammonite leaders said to Hanun, "Don't be fooled. David didn't really send these men to comfort you or to honor your dead father! No, David sent his servants to spy on you and your land. He really wants to destroy your country!" ⁴So Hanun arrested David's servants and cut off their beards.ᵈ Hanun also cut their clothes off at the hip and sent them away.

⁵David's men were too embarrassed to go home. Some people went to David and told him what happened to his men. So King David sent this message to his men: "Stay in the town of Jericho until your beards grow again. Then you can come back home."

⁶The Ammonites saw they had caused themselves to become hated enemies of David. Then Hanun and the Ammonites used 75,000 poundsᵉ of silver to buy chariots* and chariot drivers from Mesopotamia.ᶠ They also got chariots and chariot drivers from the towns of Maacah and Zobah in Aram. ⁷The

---

ᵃ**18:3** *David did this ... the Euphrates River* Or "David did this because Hadadezer tried to spread his kingdom all the way to the Euphrates River."

ᵇ**18:8** *tank* A very large container for water.

ᶜ**18:17** *Kerethites and Pelethites* These were the king's bodyguards.

ᵈ**19:4** *cut off their beards* This was an insult to an Israelite man, who was forbidden to cut the corners of his beard. See Lev. 19:27.

ᵉ**19:6** *75,000 pounds* Literally, "1000 talents" (34,500 kg).

ᶠ**19:6** *Mesopotamia* Literally, "Aram Naharaim."

Ammonites bought 32,000 chariots. They also paid the king of Maacah and his army to come and help them. The king of Maacah and his people came and set up a camp near the town of Medeba. The Ammonites themselves came out of their towns and got ready for battle.

8David heard that the Ammonites were getting ready for war. So he sent Joab and the whole army of Israel to fight the Ammonites. 9The Ammonites came out and got ready for battle. They were near the city gate. The kings who had come to help stayed out in the fields by themselves.

10Joab saw that there were two army groups ready to fight against him. One group was in front of him and the other group was behind him. So Joab chose some of the best soldiers of Israel and sent them out to fight against the Aramean army. 11He put the rest of the Israelite army under his brother Abishai's command. These soldiers went out to fight against the Ammonite army. 12Joab said to Abishai, "If the Arameans are too strong for me, you must help me. But if the Ammonites are too strong for you, I will help you. 13Let's be brave and strong while we fight for our people and for the cities of our God! May the LORD do what he thinks is right."

14Joab and the army with him attacked the Aramean army. The Arameans ran away from Joab and his army. 15When the Ammonite army saw that the Aramean army was running away, they also ran away. They ran away from Abishai and his army. The Ammonites went back to their city, and Joab went back to Jerusalem.

16The Aramean leaders saw that Israel had defeated them. So they sent messengers to get help from the Arameans living east of the Euphrates River. Shophach was the commander of Hadadezer's army from Aram. Shophach also led the other Aramean soldiers.

17David heard the news that the Arameans were gathering for battle, so he gathered all the Israelites. David led them across the Jordan River, and they came face to face with the Arameans. David got his army ready for battle and they attacked the Arameans. 18The Arameans ran away from the Israelites. David and his army killed 7000 Aramean chariot drivers and 40,000 Aramean soldiers. David and his army also killed Shophach, the commander of the Aramean army.

19When Hadadezer's officers saw that Israel had defeated them, they made peace with David. They became his servants. So the Arameans refused to help the Ammonites again.

Joab Destroys the Ammonites

20 1In the spring,a Joab led the army of Israel out to battle. That was the time of year when kings went out to battle, but David stayed in Jerusalem. The army of Israel went to the country of Ammon and destroyed it. Then they went to the city of Rabbah. The army camped around the city—they stayed there to keep people from going in or out of the city. Joab and the army of Israel fought against the city of Rabbah until they destroyed it.

2David took the crown from their king'sb head. That gold crown weighed about 75 poundsc and there were valuable stones in it. The crown was put on David's head. Then David had a great many valuable things brought out of the city of Rabbah. 3He brought out the people in Rabbah and forced them to work with saws, iron picks, and axes. He did the same thing to all the cities of the Ammonites. Then David and all the army went back to Jerusalem.

Philistine Giants Are Killed

4Later, the Israelites went to war with the Philistines at the town of Gezer. At that time Sibbecai from Hushah killed Sippai, who was one of the sons of the giants. So those Philistines became like slaves to the Israelites.

5Another time when the Israelites fought against the Philistines, Elhanan son of Jair killed Lahmi. Lahmi was Goliath's brother. Goliath was from the town of Gath. Lahmi's spear was very big and heavy. It was like the large pole on a loom.*

6Later, the Israelites fought another war with the Philistines at the town of Gath. In this town there was a very large man. He had 24 fingers and toes. He had six fingers on each hand and six toes on each foot. He also was a son of the giants. 7So when that man made fun of Israel, Jonathan killed him. Jonathan was Shimea's son. Shimea was David's brother.

8These Philistine men were sons of the giants from the town of Gath. David and his servants killed those giants.

David Sins by Counting Israel

21 1Satand was against the Israelites. He encouraged David to count the Israelites. 2So David said to Joab and the leaders of the people, "Go and count all the Israelites. Count everyone in the country—from the town of Beersheba all the way to the town of Dan. Then tell me, so I will know how many people there are."

3But Joab answered, "May the LORD make his nation 100 times as large! Sir, all the Israelites are your servants. Why do you want to do this thing, my lord and king? You will make all the Israelites guilty of sin!"

---

a20:1 In the spring Literally, "At the return of the year."

b20:2 their king's Or "Milcom," the god of the Ammonite people.

c20:2 75 pounds Literally, "1 talent" (34.5 kg).

d21:1 Satan Or "An adversary," someone who was against the king.

⁴But King David was stubborn. Joab had to do what the king said. So Joab left and went through all the country of Israel counting the people. Then he came back to Jerusalem ⁵and told David how many people there were. In Israel there were 1,100,000 men who could use a sword. And there were 470,000 men in Judah who could use a sword. ⁶Joab did not count the tribes of Levi and Benjamin because he did not like King David's order. ⁷David had done a bad thing in God's sight, so God punished Israel.

God Punishes Israel

⁸Then David said to God, "I have done something very foolish. I have committed a terrible sin by counting the Israelites. Now, I beg you to take the sin away from me, your servant."

⁹⁻¹⁰Gad was David's seer.* The LORD said to Gad, "Go and tell David: 'This is what the LORD says: I am going to give you three choices. You must choose one of them. Then I will punish you the way you choose.'"

¹¹⁻¹²Then Gad went to David. He said to David, "The LORD says, 'David, choose which punishment you want: three years without enough food, or three months of running away from your enemies while they use their swords to chase you, or three days of punishment from the LORD. Terrible sicknesses will spread through the country, and the LORD's angel will go through Israel destroying the people.' David, God sent me. Now, you must decide which answer I will give to him."

¹³David said to Gad, "I am in trouble! I don't want some man to decide my punishment. The LORD is very merciful, so let the LORD decide how to punish me."

¹⁴So the LORD sent terrible sicknesses to Israel, and 70,000 people died. ¹⁵God sent an angel to destroy Jerusalem. But when the angel started to destroy Jerusalem, the LORD saw it and felt sorry. So the LORD decided not to destroy Jerusalem. The LORD said to the angel who was destroying, "Stop! That is enough!" The angel of the LORD was standing at the threshing* floor of Araunahᵃ the Jebusite.ᵇ

¹⁶David looked up and saw the LORD's angel in the sky. The angel was holding his sword over the city of Jerusalem. Then David and the elders* bowed with their faces touching the ground. They were wearing the special clothes to show their sadness. ¹⁷David said to God, "I am the one who sinned. I gave the order for the people to be counted! I was wrong. The Israelites did not do anything wrong. LORD my God, punish me and my family, but stop the terrible sicknesses that are killing your people."

¹⁸Then the angel of the LORD spoke to Gad. He said, "Tell David to build an altar* to worship the LORD. David must build that altar near the threshing floor of Araunah the Jebusite." ¹⁹Gad told David this, and David went to Araunah's threshing floor.

²⁰Araunah was threshing the wheat. He turned around and saw the angel. His four sons ran away to hide. ²¹David walked up the hill to Araunah. Araunah saw him and left the threshing floor. He walked to David and bowed with his face to the ground in front of him.

²²David said to Araunah, "Sell me your threshing floor. I will pay you the full price. Then I can use the area to build an altar to worship the LORD. Then the terrible sicknesses will be stopped."

²³Araunah said to David, "Take this threshing floor. You are my LORD and king. Do anything you want. Look, I will also give you cattle for the burnt offering.* You can have the wooden threshing tools to burn for the fire on the altar. And I will give the wheat for the grain offering. I will give all this to you."

²⁴But King David answered Araunah, "No, I will pay you the full price. I will not take anything that is yours and give it to the LORD. I will not give offerings that cost me nothing."

²⁵So David gave Araunah about 15 poundsᶜ of gold for the place. ²⁶David built an altar for worshiping the LORD there. David offered burnt offerings and fellowship offerings.* He prayed to the LORD. The LORD answered David by sending fire down from heaven. The fire came down on the altar of burnt offering. ²⁷Then the LORD commanded the angel to put his sword back into its sheath.*

²⁸David saw that the LORD had answered him on the threshing floor of Araunah, so David offered sacrifices to the LORD. ²⁹(The Holy Tent* and the altar of burnt offering were at the high place* in the town of Gibeon. Moses had made the Holy Tent while the Israelites were in the desert. ³⁰David could not go to the Holy Tent to speak with God because he was afraid. He was afraid of the angel of the LORD and his sword.)

22 ¹David said, "The Temple* of the LORD God and the altar for burning offerings for the Israelites will be built here."

David Makes Plans for the Temple

²David gave an order for all foreigners living in Israel to be gathered together. He chose stonecutters from that group of foreigners. Their job was to cut stones ready to be used for building God's Temple.* ³David got iron for making nails and hinges for the gate doors. He also got more bronze than could be weighed ⁴and more cedar logs than could be counted. The people from the cities of Sidon and Tyre brought many cedar logs to David.

ᵃ21:15 Araunah In Hebrew, "Ornan." Also in verses 18-25, 28.
ᵇ21:15 Jebusite A person who lived in Jerusalem before the Israelites took the city. "Jebus" was the old name for Jerusalem.
ᶜ21:25 15 pounds Literally, "600 shekels" (6.9 kg).

⁵David said, "We should build a very great Temple for the LORD, but my son Solomon is young and he hasn't learned what he needs to know. The LORD's Temple should be very great. It should be famous in all the nations because of its greatness and beauty. That is why I will make plans for building the LORD's Temple." So David made many plans for building the Temple before he died.

⁶Then David called for his son Solomon and told him to build the Temple for the LORD, the God of Israel. ⁷David said to Solomon, "My son, I wanted to build a temple for the name of the LORD my God. ⁸But the LORD said to me, 'David, you have fought many wars and you have killed many people. So you cannot build a temple for my name. ⁹But you have a son who is a man of peace. I will give your son a time of peace. His enemies around him will not bother him. His name is Solomon.ᵃ And I will give Israel peace and quiet during the time that he is king. ¹⁰Solomon will build a temple for my name. He will be my son, and I will be his Father. I will make his kingdom strong, and someone from his family will rule Israel forever!'"

¹¹David also said, "Now, son, may the LORD be with you. May you be successful and build the Temple for the LORD your God, as he said you would. ¹²He will make you the king of Israel. May the LORD give you wisdom and understanding so that you can lead the people and obey the law of the LORD your God. ¹³And you will have success, if you are careful to obey the rules and laws that the LORD gave Moses for Israel. Be strong and brave. Don't be afraid.

¹⁴"Solomon, I have worked hard making plans for building the LORD's Temple. I have given 3750 tonsᵇ of gold and about 37,500 tonsᶜ of silver. I have given so much bronze and iron that it cannot be weighed. And I have given wood and stone. Solomon, you can add to them. ¹⁵You have many stonecutters and carpenters. You have men skilled in every kind of work. ¹⁶They are skilled in working with gold, silver, bronze, and iron. You have more skilled workers than can be counted. Now begin the work. And may the LORD be with you."

¹⁷Then David ordered all the leaders of Israel to help his son Solomon. ¹⁸David said to these leaders, "The LORD your God is with you. He has given you a time of peace. He helped me defeat the people living around us. The LORD and his people are now in control of this land. ¹⁹Now give your heart and soul to the LORD your God, and do what he says. Build the holy* place of the LORD God. Build the Temple for the LORD's name. Then bring the Box of the Agreement* and all the other holy things into the Temple."

The Levites Work in the Temple

23 ¹David became an old man, so he made his son Solomon the new king of Israel. ²David gathered all the leaders of Israel and also the priests and Levites.* ³David counted the Levites who were 30 years old and older. All together there were 38,000 Levites. ⁴David said, "24,000 will supervise the work of building the LORD's Temple.* 6000 will be court officers and judges. ⁵4000 will be gatekeepers, and 4000 will be musicians. I made special musical instruments for them. They will use them to praise the LORD."

⁶David separated the Levites into three groups. They were the tribes of Levi's three sons, Gershon, Kohath, and Merari.

The Gershon Family Group

⁷From the tribe of Gershon there were Ladan and Shimei. ⁸Ladan had three sons. His oldest son was Jehiel. His other sons were Zethan and Joel. ⁹Shimei's sons were Shelomoth, Haziel, and Haran. These three sons were leaders in Ladan's families.

¹⁰Shimei had four sons. They were Jahath, Ziza, Jeush, and Beriah. ¹¹Jahath was the oldest son and Ziza was the second son. But Jeush and Beriah did not have many children. So Jeush and Beriah were counted like one family.

The Kohath Family Group

¹²Kohath had four sons. They were Amram, Izhar, Hebron, and Uzziel. ¹³Amram's sons were Aaron and Moses. Aaron was chosen to be very special. Aaron and his descendants were chosen to be special forever. They were chosen to prepare the holy* things for the LORD's service. Aaron and his descendants were chosen to burn the incense* before the LORD. They were chosen to serve the LORD as priests. They were chosen to use the LORD's name and give blessings to the people forever.

¹⁴Moses was the man of God,* and his sons were part of the tribe of Levi. ¹⁵Moses' sons were Gershom and Eliezer. ¹⁶Gershom's oldest son was Shubael. ¹⁷Eliezer's oldest son was Rehabiah. Eliezer had no other sons. But Rehabiah had very many sons.

¹⁸Izhar's oldest son was Shelomith.

¹⁹Hebron's oldest son was Jeriah. Hebron's second son was Amariah. Jahaziel was the third son, and Jekameam was the fourth son.

²⁰Uzziel's oldest son was Micah, and Isshiah was his second son.

The Merari Family Group

²¹Merari's sons were Mahli and Mushi. Mahli's sons were Eleazar and Kish. ²²Eleazar died without having sons. He only had

---

ᵃ**22:9 Solomon** This name is like the Hebrew word meaning "peace."
ᵇ**22:14 3750 tons** Literally, "100,000 talents" (3450 metric tons).
ᶜ**22:14 37,500 tons** Literally, "1,000,000 talents" (34,500 metric tons).

daughters. Eleazar's daughters married their own relatives. Their relatives were Kish's sons. ²³Mushi's sons were Mahli, Eder, and Jeremoth. There were three sons in all.

The Levites' Work

²⁴These were Levi's descendants. They were listed by their families. They were the leaders of families. Each person's name was listed. The people who were listed were 20 years old or older. They served in the LORD's Temple.*

²⁵David had said, "The LORD, the God of Israel, has given peace to his people. The LORD has come to Jerusalem to live there forever. ²⁶So the Levites* don't need to carry the Holy Tent* or any of the things used in its services anymore."

²⁷David's last instructions for the Israelites were to count the descendants from the tribe of Levi. They counted the Levite men who were 20 years old and older.

²⁸The Levites had the job of helping Aaron's descendants in the service of the LORD's Temple. They also cared for the Temple courtyard and the side rooms in the Temple. And they made sure all the holy* things were kept pure. It was their job to serve in God's Temple. ²⁹They were responsible for putting the special bread on the table in the Temple and for the flour, the grain offerings, and the bread made without yeast. They were also responsible for the baking pans and the mixed offerings. They did all the measuring. ³⁰The Levites stood every morning and gave thanks and praise to the LORD. They also did this every evening. ³¹The Levites prepared all the burnt offerings* to the LORD on the Sabbath days, during New Moon* celebrations, and on the other special meeting days. They served before the LORD every day. There were special rules for how many Levites should serve each time. ³²So the Levites did everything that they were supposed to do. They took care of the Holy Tent and the Holy Place.* And they helped their relatives, the priests, Aaron's descendants, with the services at the LORD's Temple.

The Groups of the Priests

24 ¹These were the groups of Aaron's sons: Aaron's sons were Nadab, Abihu, Eleazar, and Ithamar. ²But Nadab and Abihu died before their father did. Nadab and Abihu had no sons, so Eleazar and Ithamar served as the priests. ³David separated the tribes of Eleazar and Ithamar into two different groups. He did this so that these groups could do the duties of work they were given to do. David did this with the help of Zadok and Ahimelech. Zadok was a descendant of Eleazar, and Ahimelech was a descendant of Ithamar. ⁴There were more leaders from Eleazar's family than from Ithamar's. There were 16 leaders from Eleazar's family and

there were eight leaders from Ithamar's family. ⁵Men were chosen from each family. They were chosen by throwing lots.* Some of the men were chosen to be in charge of the Holy Place.* And other men were chosen to serve as priests. All these men were from the families of Eleazar and Ithamar.

⁶Shemaiah was the secretary.ᵃ He was Nethanel's son. Shemaiah was from the tribe of Levi. Shemaiah wrote the names of those descendants. He wrote their names in front of King David and these leaders: Zadok the priest, Ahimelech, and the leaders from the families of the priests and of the Levites.* Ahimelech was Abiathar's son. Each time they threw the lots a man was chosen, and Shemaiah wrote down that man's name. So they divided the work among groups of men from the families of Eleazar and Ithamar.

⁷ The first was Jehoiarib's group.
   The second was Jedaiah's group.
⁸ The third was Harim's group.
   The fourth was Seorim's group.
⁹ The fifth was Malkijah's group.
   The sixth was Mijamin's group.
¹⁰ The seventh was Hakkoz's group.
    The eighth was Abijah's group.
¹¹ The ninth was Jeshua's group.
    The tenth was Shecaniah's group.
¹² The eleventh was Eliashib's group.
    The twelfth was Jakim's group.
¹³ The thirteenth was Huppah's group.
    The fourteenth was Jeshebeab's group.
¹⁴ The fifteenth was Bilgah's group.
    The sixteenth was Immer's group.
¹⁵ The seventeenth was Hezir's group.
    The eighteenth was Happizzez's group.
¹⁶ The nineteenth was Pethahiah's group.
    The twentieth was Jehezkel's group.
¹⁷ The twenty-first was Jakin's group.
    The twenty-second was Gamul's group.
¹⁸ The twenty-third was Delaiah's group.
    The twenty-fourth was Maaziah's group.

¹⁹These were the groups chosen to serve in the LORD's Temple.* They obeyed Aaron's rules for serving in the Temple. The LORD, the God of Israel, had given them to Aaron.

The Other Levites

²⁰These are the names of the rest of Levi's descendants:

Shubael was a descendant of Amram.
Jehdeiah was a descendant of Shubael.
²¹ Isshiah was the oldest son of Rehabiah.
²² From the Izhar family group there was Shelomoth.
Jahath was a descendant of Shelomoth.
²³ Jeriah was the oldest son of Hebron.
Amariah was Hebron's second son.

ᵃ**24:6 secretary** A man who wrote down and copied books and letters.

Jahaziel was his third son,
and Jekameam was his fourth son.
24 Uzziel's son was Micah.
Micah's son was Shamir.
25 Isshiah was Micah's brother.
Isshiah's son was Zechariah.
26 *a* Merari's descendants were Mahli, Mushi,
and Jaaziah his son.
27 Jaaziah son of Merari had sons named
Shoham, Zaccur, and Ibri.
28 Mahli's son was Eleazar, but Eleazar did
not have sons.
29 Kish's son was Jerahmeel.
30 Mushi's sons were Mahli, Eder, and
Jerimoth.

These are the leaders of the Levite* families. They are listed by their families. 31They were chosen for special jobs by throwing lots,* like their relatives, the priests. The priests were Aaron's descendants. They threw lots in front of King David, Zadok, Ahimelech, and the leaders of the priests' and Levite families. The older families and the younger families were treated the same when their jobs were chosen.

The Music Groups

25 ¹David and the leaders of the army separated the sons of Asaph, Heman, and Jeduthun for special service. Their special service was to prophesy* God's message with harps, lyres,* and cymbals.* Here is a list of the men who served this way:

²From Asaph's family: Zaccur, Joseph, Nethaniah, and Asarelah. King David chose Asaph to prophesy. And Asaph led his sons.

³From Jeduthun's family: Gedaliah, Zeri, Jeshaiah, Shimei, Hashabiah, and Mattithiah. There were six of them. Jeduthun led his sons. Jeduthun used harps to prophesy and give thanks and praise to the LORD.

⁴Heman's sons who served were Bukkiah, Mattaniah, Uzziel, Shubael, and Jerimoth; Hananiah, Hanani, Eliathah, Giddalti, and Romamti Ezer; Joshbekashah, Mallothi, Hothir, and Mahazioth. ⁵All these men were Heman's sons. Heman was David's seer.* God promised to make Heman strong. So Heman had many sons. God gave Heman fourteen sons and three daughters. ⁶Heman led all his sons in singing in the LORD's temple.*ᵇ His sons used cymbals, lyres, and harps. That was their way of serving in God's temple. King David chose these men. ⁷These men and their relatives from the tribe of Levi were trained to sing. There were 288 men who learned to sing praises to the LORD. ⁸They threw lots* to choose the different kinds of work each person was to do. Everyone was treated the same. Young and old were treated the same. And the teacher was treated the same as the student.

⁹The first one chosen was Asaph (Joseph). Second, there were 12 men chosen from Gedaliah's sons and relatives.

¹⁰Third, there were 12 men chosen from Zaccur's sons and relatives.

¹¹Fourth, there were 12 men chosen from Izri's sons and relatives.

¹²Fifth, there were 12 men chosen from Nethaniah's sons and relatives.

¹³Sixth, there were 12 men chosen from Bukkiah's sons and relatives.

¹⁴Seventh, there were 12 men chosen from Asarelah's sons and relatives.

¹⁵Eighth, there were 12 men chosen from Jeshaiah's sons and relatives.

¹⁶Ninth, there were 12 men chosen from Mattaniah's sons and relatives.

¹⁷Tenth, there were 12 men chosen from Shimei's sons and relatives.

¹⁸Eleventh, there were 12 men chosen from Azarel's sons and relatives.

¹⁹Twelfth, there were 12 men chosen from Hashabiah's sons and relatives.

²⁰Thirteenth, there were 12 men chosen from Shubael's sons and relatives.

²¹Fourteenth, there were 12 men chosen from Mattithiah's sons and relatives.

²²Fifteenth, there were 12 men chosen from Jeremoth's sons and relatives.

²³Sixteenth, there were 12 men chosen from Hananiah's sons and relatives.

²⁴Seventeenth, there were 12 men chosen from Joshbekashah's sons and relatives.

²⁵Eighteenth, there were 12 men chosen from Hanani's sons and relatives.

²⁶Nineteenth, there were 12 men chosen from Mallothi's sons and relatives.

²⁷Twentieth, there were 12 men chosen from Eliathah's sons and relatives.

²⁸Twenty-first, there were 12 men chosen from Hothir's sons and relatives.

²⁹Twenty-second, there were 12 men chosen from Giddalti's sons and relatives.

³⁰Twenty-third, there were 12 men chosen from Mahazioth's sons and relatives.

³¹Twenty-fourth, there were 12 men chosen from Romamti Ezer's sons and relatives.

The Gatekeepers

26 ¹These are the groups of the gatekeepers from the Korah family: There was Meshelemiah, son of Kore. Kore was from the family of Asaph. ²Meshelemiah had sons. Zechariah was the oldest son. Jediael was the second son. Zebadiah was the third son. Jathniel was the fourth son. ³Elam was the fifth son. Jehohanan was the sixth son. And Eliehoenai was the seventh son.

⁴Obed Edom had sons. Obed Edom's oldest son was Shemaiah. Jehozabad was his second son. Joah was his third son. Sacar was his fourth son. Nethanel was his fifth son. ⁵Ammiel was his sixth son, Issachar his seventh son, and Peullethai his eighth son. God

*a*24:26, 27 The Hebrew text here is hard to understand.
*b*25:6 *temple* Here, this means the Holy Tent where people went to worship the Lord.

really blessed Obed Edom.*a* 6Obed Edom's son was Shemaiah. Shemaiah also had sons. His sons were leaders in their father's family because they were brave soldiers. 7Shemaiah's sons were Othni, Rephael, Obed, Elzabad, Elihu, and Semakiah. Elzabad's relatives were skilled workers. 8All these men were Obed Edom's descendants. These men and their sons and relatives were powerful men. They were good guards. Obed Edom had 62 descendants.

9Meshelemiah had sons and relatives who were powerful men. In all there were 18 sons and relatives.

10These are the gatekeepers from the Merari family. There was Hosah. Shimri was chosen to be the first son. He was not really the oldest, but his father chose him to be the firstborn* son. 11Hilkiah was his second son, Tebaliah his third, and Zechariah his fourth. In all Hosah had 13 sons and relatives.

12These were the leaders of the groups of the gatekeepers. The gatekeepers had a special way to serve in the LORD's Temple,* just as their relatives did. 13Each family was given a gate to guard. Lots* were thrown to choose a gate for a family. Young and old were treated the same.

14Meshelemiah was chosen to guard the East Gate. Then lots were thrown for Meshelemiah's son Zechariah. Zechariah was a wise counselor. Zechariah was chosen for the North Gate. 15Obed Edom was chosen for the South Gate. And Obed Edom's sons were chosen to guard the house where the valuable things were kept. 16Shuppim and Hosah were chosen for the West Gate and the Shalleketh Gate on the upper road.

Guards stood side by side. 17Six Levites* stood guard every day at the East Gate. Four Levites stood guard every day at the North Gate. Four Levites stood guard at the South Gate. And two Levites guarded the house where the valuable things were kept. 18There were four guards at the western court*b* and two guards on the road to the court.

19These were the groups of the gatekeepers from the families of Korah and Merari.

The Treasurers and Other Officials

20Ahijah was from the tribe of Levi. Ahijah was responsible for taking care of the valuable things in God's Temple.* Ahijah also was responsible for the places where the holy* things were kept.

21Ladan was from Gershon's family. Jehieli was one of the leaders of the tribe of Ladan. 22Jehieli's sons were Zetham and Zetham's brother Joel. They were responsible for the valuable things in the LORD's Temple.

23Other leaders were chosen from the tribes of Amram, Izhar, Hebron, and Uzziel. 24Shubael was the leader responsible for the valuable things in the LORD's Temple. Shubael was Gershom's son. Gershom was Moses' son. 25These were Shubael's relatives: His relatives from Eliezer were Rehabiah, Eliezer's son; Jeshaiah, Rehabiah's son; Joram, Jeshaiah's son; Zicri, Joram's son; and Shelomith, Zicri's son. 26Shelomith and his relatives were responsible for everything that David had collected for the Temple.

The officers of the army also gave things for the Temple. 27They gave some of the things taken in wars. They gave these things to be used in building the LORD's Temple. 28Shelomith and his relatives also took care of all the holy things given by Samuel the seer,* Saul son of Kish, Abner son of Ner, and Joab son of Zeruiah. Shelomith and his relatives took care of all the holy things that people gave to the LORD.

29Kenaniah was from the Izhar family. Kenaniah and his sons had work outside the Temple. They worked as court officers and judges in different places in Israel. 30Hashabiah was from the Hebron family. Hashabiah and his relatives were responsible for all the LORD's work and for the king's business in Israel west of the Jordan River. There were 1700 powerful men in Hashabiah's group. 31The family history of the Hebron family shows that Jeriah was their leader. When David had been king for 40 years, he ordered his people to search through the family histories for strong and skilled men. Some of them were found among the Hebron family living in the town of Jazer in Gilead. 32Jeriah had 2700 relatives who were powerful men and leaders of families. King David gave these 2700 relatives the responsibility of leading the tribes of Reuben, Gad, and half of Manasseh in taking care of God's work and the king's business.

Army Groups

27 1This is the list of the Israelites who served the king in the army. Each group was on duty one month each year. There were rulers of families, captains, generals, and the court officers who served the king. Each army group had 24,000 men.

2Jashobeam son of Zabdiel was in charge of the first group for the first month. There were 24,000 men in Jashobeam's group. 3Jashobeam, one of Perez's descendants, was leader of all the army officers for the first month.

4Dodai, from the Ahoahites, was in charge of the army group for the second month. Mikloth was a leader in that group. There were 24,000 men in Dodai's group.

5The third commander, for the third month, was Benaiah son of Jehoiada the leading priest. There were 24,000 men in Benaiah's group. 6He was the same Benaiah who was a brave soldier from the Thirty Heroes. He led

---

*a*26:5 *Obed Edom* God blessed Obed Edom when the Box of the Agreement stayed at his house. See 1 Chron. 21.
*b*26:18 *court* The meaning of this word is uncertain.

these men. His son Ammizabad was in charge of Banaiah's group.

7The fourth commander, for the fourth month, was Asahel the brother of Joab. Later, Asahel's son Zebadiah took his place as commander. There were 24,000 men in Asahel's group.

8The fifth commander, for the fifth month, was Shamhuth from Zerah's family. There were 24,000 men in Shamhuth's group.

9The sixth commander, for the sixth month, was Ira son of Ikkesh from the town of Tekoa. There were 24,000 men in Ira's group.

10The seventh commander, for the seventh month, was Helez from the Pelonites and a descendant of Ephraim. There were 24,000 men in Helez' group.

11The eighth commander, for the eighth month, was Sibbecai from Hushah and from Zerah's family. There were 24,000 men in Sibbecai's group.

12The ninth commander, for the ninth month, was Abiezer from the town of Anathoth and the tribe of Benjamin. There were 24,000 men in Abiezer's group.

13The tenth commander, for the tenth month, was Maharai from Netophah and from Zerah's family. There were 24,000 men in Maharai's group.

14The eleventh commander, for the eleventh month, was Benaiah from Pirathon and the tribe of Ephraim. There were 24,000 men in Benaiah's group.

15The twelfth commander, for the twelfth month, was Heldai from Netophah and from Othniel's family. There were 24,000 men in Heldai's group.

Leaders of the Tribes of Israel

16These were the leaders of the tribes of Israel:

Eliezer son of Zicri, leader of the tribe of Reuben;

Shephatiah son of Maacah, leader of the tribe of Simeon;

17 Hashabiah son of Kemuel, leader of the tribe of Levi;

Zadok, leader of the people of Aaron;

18 Elihu, one of David's brothers, leader of the tribe of Judah;

Omri son of Michael, leader of the tribe of Issachar;

19 Ishmaiah son of Obadiah, leader of the tribe of Zebulun;

Jeremoth son of Azriel, leader of the tribe of Naphtali;

20 Hoshea son of Azaziah, leader of the tribe of Ephraim;

Joel son of Pedaiah, leader of West Manasseh;

21 Iddo son of Zechariah, leader of East Manasseh;

Jaasiel son of Abner, leader of the tribe of Benjamin;

22 Azarel son of Jeroham, leader of the tribe of Dan.

David Counts the Israelites

23David decided to count the men in Israel. There were very many people because God promised to make the Israelites as many as the stars in the sky. So David only counted the men who were 20 years old and older. 24Joab son of Zeruiah began to count the people, but he did not finish.*a* God became angry with the Israelites. That is why the number of the people was not put in the book, *The History of King David*.

The King's Administrators

25This is the list of men who were responsible for the king's property:

Azmaveth son of Adiel was in charge of the king's storerooms.

Jonathan son of Uzziah was in charge of the storerooms in the small towns, villages, fields, and towers.

26 Ezri son of Kelub was in charge of the field workers.

27 Shimei from Ramah was in charge of the vineyards.*

Zabdi from Shepham was in charge of the storage and care of the wine that came from the vineyards.

28 Baal Hanan from Geder was in charge of the olive trees and sycamore trees in the western hill country.

Joash was in charge of storing the olive oil.

29 Shitrai from Sharon was in charge of the cattle around Sharon.

Shaphat son of Adlai was in charge of the cattle in the valleys.

30 Obil the Ishmaelite was in charge of the camels.

Jehdeiah the Meronothite was in charge of the donkeys.

31 Jaziz the Hagrite was in charge of the sheep.

All these men were the leaders who took care of King David's property.

32Jonathan was a wise counselor and a scribe.* He was David's uncle. Jehiel son of Hacmoni took care of the king's sons. 33Ahithophel was the king's counselor. Hushai was the king's friend. Hushai was from the Arkites. 34Jehoiada and Abiathar later took Ahithophel's place as the king's counselor. Jehoiada was Benaiah's son. Joab was the commander of the king's army.

David's Plans for the Temple

28 1David gathered all the leaders of the Israelites and commanded them to

---

*a*27:24 *Joab ... did not finish* God stopped him. See 1 Chron. 21:1–30.

come to Jerusalem. David called all the leaders of the tribes, the commanders of the army groups serving the king, the captains, the generals, the officials taking care of the property and animals that belonged to the king and his sons, the king's important officials, the powerful heroes, and all the brave soldiers.

²King David stood up and said, "Listen to me, my brothers and my people. In my heart I wanted to build a place to keep the Box of the LORD's Agreement.* I wanted to build a place that would be God's footstool.ᵃ And I made the plans for building that house for God. ³But God said to me, 'No David, you must not build a house for my name. You must not do that because you are a soldier, and you have killed many men.'

⁴"The LORD, the God of Israel, chose the tribe of Judah to lead the twelve tribes of Israel. Then from that tribe, the LORD chose my father's family. And from that family, God chose me to be the king of Israel forever. God wanted to make me king of Israel. ⁵The LORD has given me many sons. And from all those sons, he chose Solomon to be the new king of Israel. But really, Israel is the LORD's kingdom. ⁶The LORD said to me, 'David, your son Solomon will build my Temple* and the area around it, because I have chosen Solomon to be my son, and I will be his father.ᵇ ⁷Solomon is obeying my laws and commands now. If he continues to obey my laws, I will make Solomon's kingdom strong forever.'"

⁸David said, "Now, in front of all Israel and God, I tell you these things: Be careful to obey all the commands of the LORD your God. Then you can keep this good land and pass it on to your descendants forever.

⁹"And you, my son Solomon, know the God of your father. Serve God with a pure heart. Be happy to serve him, because the LORD knows what is in everyone's heart. He knows what you are thinking. If you go to him for help, you will get an answer. But if you turn away from him, he will leave you forever. ¹⁰Solomon, you must understand that the LORD has chosen you to build his holy* place—the Temple. Be strong and finish the job."

¹¹Then David gave his son Solomon the plans for building the Temple. They included plans for the porch around the Temple, its buildings, its storerooms, its upper rooms, its inside rooms, and the room for the mercy-cover.* ¹²David had made plans for all parts of the Temple. He gave them to Solomon. David gave him all the plans for the courtyard around the LORD's Temple and for all the rooms around it. He gave him the plans for the Temple storerooms and for the storerooms where they kept the holy things used in the Temple. ¹³David told Solomon about the groups of the priests and Levites.* He told Solomon about all the work of serving in the LORD's Temple and about all the things to be used in the Temple service. ¹⁴David told Solomon how much gold and silver should be used to make all the things to be used in the Temple. ¹⁵There were plans for gold lamps and lampstands, and there were plans for silver lamps and lampstands. David told Solomon how much gold or silver to use for each lampstand and its lamps. The different lampstands were to be used where needed. ¹⁶David told him how much gold should be used for each table for the holy bread.* He told how much silver should be used for the silver tables. ¹⁷He told how much pure gold should be used to make the forks, sprinkling bowls, and pitchers. He told him how much gold should be used to make each gold dish and how much silver should be used to make each silver dish. ¹⁸He told him how much pure gold should be used for the altar of incense.* David also gave Solomon the plans for ₍God's₎ chariot—the mercy-cover with the Cherub angels* spreading their wings over the Box of the LORD's Agreement. The Cherub angels were made of gold.

¹⁹David said, "All these plans were written with the LORD guiding me. He helped me understand everything in the plans."

²⁰David also said to his son Solomon, "Be strong and brave and finish this work. Don't be afraid, because the LORD God, my God, is with you. He will help you until all the work is finished. He will not leave you. You will build the LORD's Temple. ²¹The groups of the priests and Levites are ready for all the work on God's Temple. Every skilled worker is ready to help you with all the work. The officials and all the people will obey every command you give."

Gifts for Building the Temple

29 ¹King David said to all the Israelites who were gathered together, "God chose my son Solomon. Solomon is young and does not know all that he needs to do this work. But the work is very important. This house isn't for people; this house is for the LORD God. ²I have done my best to make plans to build my God's Temple.* I have given gold for the things made of gold. I have given silver for the things made of silver. I have given bronze for the things made of bronze. I have given iron for the things made of iron. I have given wood for the things made of wood. I have also given onyx* stones for the settings,ᶜ mosaic tiles,ᵈ all kinds of valuable stones in many different colors, and white marble stones. I have given many of these

---

ᵃ**28:2** *footstool* Usually this was a small stool in front of a chair, but here, it means the Temple. It is as if God were the king sitting in his chair and resting his feet on the building David wanted to build.
ᵇ**28:6** *I will be his father* This showed that God was making Solomon the king. See Ps. 2:7.

ᶜ**29:2** *settings* The frames in which stones are mounted.
ᵈ**29:2** *mosaic tiles* Literally, "stones set in mortar."

things for the building of the LORD's Temple. ³I am making a special gift of gold and silver things for my God's Temple. I am doing this because I really want the Temple of my God to be built. I am giving all these things to build this holy* Temple. ⁴I have given 110 tons*a* of pure gold from Ophir. I have given 263 tons*b* of pure silver. The silver is for covering the walls of the buildings in the Temple. ⁵I have given gold and silver for all the things made of gold and silver. I have given gold and silver so that skilled men can make all different kinds of things for the Temple. Now, how many of you Israelites are ready to give yourselves to the LORD today?"

⁶The family leaders, the leaders of the tribes of Israel, the generals, the captains, and the officials responsible for the king's work, were all ready and gave their valuable things. ⁷These are the things they gave for God's house: 190 tons*c* of gold; 375 tons*d* of silver; 675 tons*e* of bronze; and 3750 tons*f* of iron. ⁸People who had valuable stones gave them to the LORD's Temple. Jehiel took care of the valuable stones. He was from the Gershon family. ⁹The people were very happy because their leaders were happy to give so much. The leaders were happy to give freely from good hearts. King David was also very happy.

David's Beautiful Prayer

¹⁰Then David praised the LORD in front of all the people who were gathered together. David said,

"LORD, the God of Israel, our Father,
may you be praised forever and ever!
¹¹ Greatness, power, glory, victory, and
honor belong to you,
because everything in heaven and on
earth belongs to you!
The kingdom belongs to you, LORD!
You are the head, the Ruler over
everything.
¹² Riches and honor come from you.
You rule everything.
You have the power and strength in your
hand!
And in your hand is the power to make
anyone great and powerful!
¹³ Now, our God, we thank you,
and we praise your glorious name!
¹⁴ All these things didn't come from me and
my people.
All these things come from you.

We are only giving back to you things
that came from you.
¹⁵ We are only strangers traveling through
this world like our ancestors.*
Our time on earth is like a passing
shadow,
and we cannot stop it.
¹⁶ LORD our God, we gathered all these
things to build your Temple.*
We build it to honor your name.
But all these things have come from you.
Everything belongs to you.
¹⁷ My God, I know that you test people,
and that you are happy when people do
what is right.
I gladly give you all these things
with a pure, honest heart.
I see your people gathered here,
and I see that they are happy about
giving these things to you.
¹⁸ LORD, you are the God of our ancestors,
Abraham, Isaac, and Jacob.*
Please help your people plan the right
things.
Help them be loyal and true to you.
¹⁹ And help my son Solomon be true to you.
Help him always obey your commands,
laws, and rules.
Help Solomon do these things.
And help him build this Temple that I
have planned."

²⁰Then David said to all the group of people gathered together, "Now give praise to the LORD your God." So all the people gave praise to the LORD God, the God their ancestors worshiped. They bowed to the ground to give honor to the LORD and to the king.

Solomon Becomes King

²¹The next day the people made sacrifices* to the LORD. They offered burnt offerings* to him. They offered 1000 bulls, 1000 rams, 1000 lambs, and the drink offerings that go with them. They offered many sacrifices for all the Israelites. ²²That day the people were very happy as they ate and drank there together with the LORD.

And they made David's son Solomon king the second time.*g* They anointed* Solomon to be king, and they anointed Zadok to be priest. They did this in the place where the LORD was.

²³Then Solomon sat on the LORD's throne as king. Solomon took his father's place. He was very successful. All the Israelites obeyed him. ²⁴All the leaders, soldiers, and all of King David's sons accepted Solomon as king and obeyed him. ²⁵The LORD made Solomon very great. All the Israelites knew that the

---

*a*29:4 *110 tons* Literally, "3000 talents" (103,500 kg).
*b*29:4 *263 tons* Literally, "7000 talents" (241,500 kg).
*c*29:7 *190 tons* Literally, "5000 talents and 10,000 darics" (172.59 metric tons).
*d*29:7 *375 tons* Literally, "10,000 talents" (345 metric tons).
*e*29:7 *675 tons* Literally, "18,000 talents" (621 metric tons).
*f*29:7 *3750 tons* Literally, "100,000 talents" (3450 metric tons).

*g*29:22 *And they made ... time* Solomon was chosen to be king the first time when his half-brother Adonijah tried to make himself king. See 1 Kings 1:5-39.

Lord was making him great. He gave Solomon the honor that a king should have. No king in Israel before Solomon had such honor.

David's Death

²⁶⁻²⁷David son of Jesse was king over all Israel for 40 years. He was king in the city of Hebron for seven years. Then he was king in the city of Jerusalem for 33 years. ²⁸David died when he was old. He had lived a good, long life and had many riches and honors. His son Solomon became the new king after him. ²⁹The things that King David did, from beginning to end, are in the books written by Samuel the seer,* Nathan the prophet,* and Gad the seer. ³⁰Those writings tell all about what David did as king of Israel. They tell about David's power and what happened to him and to Israel and to all the kingdoms around them.

2 Chronicles

Solomon Asks for Wisdom

1 ¹Solomon, the son of David, became a very strong king, because the Lord his God was with him and made him very great.

²⁻³The people of Israel and the captains, generals, judges, leaders, and heads of the families were all gathered together. Solomon spoke to them, and then they all went to the high place* at Gibeon. They went there because God's Meeting Tent* was there. The Lord's servant Moses made this tent when he and the Israelites were in the desert. ⁴David had carried God's Box of the Agreement* from Kiriath Jearim to Jerusalem where he had set up another tent for it. ⁵But the bronze altar* that Bezalel son of Uri, who was the son of Hur, had made was in front of the Holy Tent* at Gibeon. So Solomon and the people went there to ask the Lord for advice. ⁶Solomon went up to the bronze altar and offered a thousand burnt offerings* on it.

⁷That night God came to Solomon and said, "Ask me for whatever you want me to give you."

⁸Solomon said to God, "You were very kind to my father David when you allowed me to rule on his throne after him. ⁹Now, Lord God, continue to keep your promise to my father David. You made me king over so many people that they are like the dust of the earth. ¹⁰Now give me wisdom and knowledge so that I can lead these people in the right way. No one could rule this great nation without your help."

¹¹God said to Solomon, "You have the right attitude. You did not ask for long life and riches for yourself. You did not ask for the death of your enemies. You asked for the wisdom and knowledge so that you can make the right decisions. ¹²So I will give you wisdom and knowledge, but I will also give you wealth, riches, and honor. No king who lived before you has ever had so much wealth and honor, and no king in the future will have as much wealth and honor."

¹³Solomon left the Meeting Tent that was at the high place in Gibeon and went back to Jerusalem to rule as the king of Israel.

Solomon Strengthens His Army

¹⁴Solomon started gathering horses and chariots* for his army. He had 1400 chariots and 12,000 horse soldiers. He kept them in the chariot cities*ᵃ* and in Jerusalem where he lived. ¹⁵In Jerusalem Solomon gathered so much gold and silver that it was as common as rocks. He gathered so much cedar wood that it was as common as sycamore trees in the western hill country. ¹⁶Solomon imported horses from Egypt and Kue.ᵇ His merchants* bought the horses in Kue for a set price. ¹⁷They also bought chariots from Egypt for 600 shekelsᶜ of silver each and horses for 150 shekelsᵈ of silver each. They then sold the horses and chariots to the kings of the Hittites and Arameans.

Plans for the Temple and Palace

2 ¹Solomon planned to build a Temple* to give honor to the Lord's name. He also planned to build a palace for himself. ²He got 70,000 laborers and 80,000 stonemasons to cut stones in the mountains. He chose 3600 foremen to supervise the workers.

³Then Solomon sent this message to King Hiram of Tyre: "Help me as you helped my father David. You sent him cedar logs so that he could build a palace for himself to live in. ⁴I will build a Temple to honor the name of the Lord my God. At the Temple we will burn incense* in front of him, and we will always put the holy bread* on the special table. We

---

ᵃ1:14 *chariot cities* Cities with special places to keep the horses and chariots.
ᵇ1:16 *Kue* Or "Cilicia," a country in what is now southern Turkey.
ᶜ1:17 *600 shekels* 15 pounds (6.9 kg).
ᵈ1:17 *150 shekels* 3 3/4 pounds (1.725 kg).

will offer burnt offerings every morning and evening, on the Sabbath* days, during New Moon* celebrations, and on the other special meeting days that the Lord our God has commanded us to celebrate. This is a rule for the people of Israel to obey forever.

5"I will build a great temple because our God is greater than all the other gods. 6No one can really build a house to put our God in. The whole sky and the highest heaven cannot contain our God, so I cannot build a temple to put him in. I can only build a place to burn incense to honor him.

7"Now I would like you to send me a man who is skilled in working with gold, silver, bronze, and iron. He must know how to work with purple, red, and blue cloth. He will work here in Judah and Jerusalem with the craftsmen my father chose. 8Also send me wood from cedar trees, pine trees, and algum trees[a] from the country of Lebanon. I know your servants are experienced at cutting down trees from Lebanon. My servants will help your servants. 9I will need lots of wood because the Temple I am building will be very large and beautiful. 10This is what I will pay for your servants to cut down the trees for wood. I will give them 125,000 bushels[b] of wheat for food, 125,000 bushels of barley, 115,000 gallons[c] of wine, and 115,000 gallons of oil."

11Then Hiram answered Solomon and sent this message to him: "Solomon, the Lord loves his people. That is why he chose you to be their king." 12Hiram also said, "Praise the Lord, the God of Israel! He made heaven and earth. He gave a wise son to King David. Solomon, you have wisdom and understanding. You are building a Temple for the Lord. You are also building a palace for yourself. 13I will send you a skilled craftsman named Huram Abi.[d] 14His mother was from the tribe of Dan, and his father was from the city of Tyre. Huram Abi has skill in working with gold, silver, bronze, iron, stone, and wood. He also has skill in working with purple, blue, and red cloth and expensive linen.* Huram Abi can design and build anything you tell him. He will work with your craftsmen and with the craftsmen of your father King David.

15"Now, sir, you offered to give us wheat, barley, oil, and wine. Give them to my servants, 16and we will cut as much wood as you need from Lebanon. We will tie the logs together and float them by sea to the town of Joppa. Then you can carry the wood to Jerusalem."

17So Solomon counted all the foreigners living in Israel. (This was after the time when his father David counted the people.) They found 153,600 strangers in the country. 18Solomon chose 70,000 men to carry the stones, 80,000 men to cut the stone in the mountains, and 3600 men to supervise the workers.

Solomon Builds the Temple

3 1Solomon began building the Lord's Temple* at Jerusalem on Mount Moriah, where the Lord appeared to David, Solomon's father. This was the place David had prepared for the Temple. It had been the threshing* floor of Araunah[e] the Jebusite. 2Solomon started to build on the second day of the second month of his fourth year as king of Israel.

3These are the measurements he used for building the foundation of God's Temple, using the old cubit.[f] The foundation was 60 cubits[g] long and 20 cubits[h] wide. 4The porch in front of the Temple was 20 cubits long and 20 cubits high.[i] He covered the inside of the porch with pure gold. 5He put panels made of cypress wood on the walls of the larger room. Then he put pure gold over the cypress panels and then put pictures of palm trees and chains on the gold. 6He put valuable stones in the Temple for beauty. The gold he used was gold from Parvaim.[j] 7He covered the inside of the Temple with the gold. He put the gold on the ceiling beams, doorposts, walls, and doors. He carved Cherub angels* on the walls.

8Then he made the Most Holy Place.* This room was 20 cubits long and 20 cubits wide. It was as wide as the Temple was. He put pure gold on the walls of the Most Holy Place. The gold weighed about 22½ tons.[k] 9The gold nails weighed 1¼ pounds.[l] He covered the upper rooms with gold. 10He made two Cherub angels to put in the Most Holy Place. The workers covered the Cherub angels with gold. 11Each wing of the Cherub angels was 5 cubits[m] long. The total length of the wings was 20 cubits. One wing of the first Cherub angel touched the wall on one side of the room. The other wing touched one wing of the second Cherub angel. 12And the other wing of the second Cherub angel touched the other wall on the other side of the room. 13The wings of the Cherub angels covered a

---

[e]3:1 *Araunah* In Hebrew, "Ornan."

[f]3:3 *the old cubit* This was the Egyptian cubit, measuring about 20 3/8" (51.83 cm).

[g]3:3 *60 cubits* 102' 3/8" (31.1 m).

[h]3:3 *20 cubits* 34' 1/8" (10.37 m). Also in verses 4, 8, 11, 13.

[i]3:4 *20 cubits high* 34' 1/8" (10.37 m). Some of the Hebrew texts have "120 cubits high."

[j]3:6 *Parvaim* This was a place where there was much gold. It was probably in the country of Ophir.

[k]3:8 *22 1/2 tons* Literally, "600 talents" (20,700 kg).

[l]3:9 *1 1/4 pounds* Literally, "50 shekels" (575 g).

[m]3:11 *5 cubits* 8' 6" (2.6 m). Also in verse 15.

[a]2:8 *algum trees* Or "Almug," as in 1 Kings. No one knows exactly what type of wood this was, but it might have been sandalwood.

[b]2:10 *125,000 bushels* Literally, "20,000 *cors*" (4,400,000 l).

[c]2:10 *115,000 gallons* Literally, "20,000 *baths*" (440,000 l).

[d]2:13 Or "I will send one of the craftsmen of my father Hiram."

total of 20 cubits. The Cherub angels stood facing the Holy Place.[a]

[14]He made the curtain[b] from blue, purple, and red materials and expensive linen.* There were Cherub angels on the curtain.

[15]He put two columns in front of the Temple. The columns were 35 cubits[c] tall. The top part of the two columns was 5 cubits long. [16]He made chains in a necklace and put them on the tops of the columns. He made 100 pomegranates[d] and put them on the chains. [17]Then he put the columns up in front of the Temple. One column stood on the right side. The other column stood on the left side. He named the column on the right side "Jakin."[e] And he named the column on the left side "Boaz."[f]

Furniture for the Temple

4 [1]He made a bronze altar* that was 20 cubits[g] long, 20 cubits wide, and 10 cubits[h] tall. [2]Then he made a large tank[i] from melted bronze. It was round and it measured 10 cubits across from edge to edge. It was 5 cubits[j] tall and about 30 cubits[k] around. [3]There were images of bulls under the lip of the large bronze tank.[l] They were in two rows that went 10 cubits around the tank. The bulls were molded in place when the tank was shaped. [4]The large bronze tank was on top of twelve large statues of bulls. Three bulls looked toward the north. Three bulls looked toward the west. Three bulls looked toward the south. Three bulls looked toward the east. The large bronze tank was on top of these bulls. All the bulls stood with their rear ends to each other and to the center. [5]The large bronze tank was 3 inches[m] thick. The edge of the large tank was like the edge of a cup. The edge looked like a lily blossom. The tank could hold about 17,400 gallons.[n]

[6]He made ten basins. He put five basins on the right side of the large bronze tank and five basins on the left side. These ten basins were to be used to wash the things offered for the burnt offerings.* But the large bronze tank was to be used by the priests for washing before they offered sacrifices.*

[7]He made ten lampstands of gold. He followed the plans made for these lampstands. He put the lampstands in the Temple.* There were five lampstands on the right side and five lampstands on the left side. [8]He made ten tables and put them in the Temple. Five tables were on the right side and five tables on the left side in the Temple. And he used gold to make 100 basins. [9]He also made the priests' courtyard, the large courtyard, and the doors that open to them. He used bronze to cover these doors. [10]Then he put the large bronze tank on the right side of the Temple on the southeast side.

[11]Huram made the pots, shovels, and basins. Then he finished his work for King Solomon on God's Temple. [12]Huram had made the two columns and the large bowls on the top parts of the two columns. He also made the two net decorations to cover the two large bowls on the top parts of the two columns. [13]Huram made 400 pomegranates for the two net decorations. There were two rows of pomegranates for each net. The nets covered the large bowls on the top parts on the two columns. [14]He also made the stands and the bowls on the stands. [15]He made the one large bronze tank and twelve bulls under the tank. [16]Huram made the pots, shovels, forks, and all the things for King Solomon for the LORD's Temple. These things were made of polished bronze. [17]King Solomon first poured these things in clay molds. The molds were made in the Jordan Valley between the towns of Succoth and Zeredah. [18]Solomon made so many of them that no one tried to weigh the bronze used.

[19]Solomon also made the dishes and things for God's Temple. He made the golden altar and the tables where they put the bread of the Presence. [20]He made the lamps and lampstands of pure gold. These were put inside the Holy Place in front of the Most Holy Place. [21]He used pure gold to make the flowers, lamps, and tongs.[o] [22]He used pure gold to make the lamp snuffers,* bowls, pans, and the censers.[p] He used pure gold to make the doors for the Temple, the inside doors for the Most Holy Place* and the doors for the main hall.

5 [1]When all the work was completed on the LORD's Temple, Solomon brought in everything his father David had set aside for the Temple. Solomon put all the furniture and all the things made of silver and gold into the storage rooms in God's Temple.

---

[a]**3:13** *facing the Holy Place* Or "facing one another." The Holy Place is the room in the Temple that was used by the priests to do their daily service to God.
[b]**3:14** *curtain* This curtain was a large piece of cloth that hung between the Holy Place and the Most Holy Place so that no one could see the LORD's Box of the Agreement and Cherub angels that were in there.
[c]**3:15** *35 cubits* 59' 6 3/16" (18.14 m).
[d]**3:16** *pomegranates* Small bells shaped like pomegranates, a red fruit with many tiny seeds covered with a soft, juicy part of the fruit. Also in 4:13.
[e]**3:17** *Jakin* In Hebrew, Jakin seems to mean "he establishes."
[f]**3:17** *Boaz* In Hebrew, Boaz seems to mean "in him is strength."
[g]**4:1** *20 cubits* 34' 1/8" (10.37 m).
[h]**4:1** *10 cubits* 17' 1/16" (5.18 m).
[i]**4:2** *large tank* Literally, "sea."
[j]**4:2** *5 cubits* 8' 6" (2.6 m).
[k]**4:2** *30 cubits* 51' 3/16" (15.55 m).
[l]**4:3** *large bronze tank* Literally, "sea." Also in verses 10, 14.
[m]**4:5** *3 inches* Literally, "1 handbreadth" (7.4 cm).
[n]**4:5** *17,400 gallons* Literally, "3000 baths" (66,000 l).

[o]**4:21** *tongs* A tool used to hold hot coals.
[p]**4:22** *censers* Bowls used to carry fire.

The Holy Box Carried Into the Temple

²Solomon commanded the elders of Israel, the leaders of the tribes, and the heads of families to meet together in Jerusalem. He did this so that they could bring the Box of the Lord's Agreement* up to the Temple from the City of David,* that is, Zion. ³All the men of Israel met together before King Solomon during the special festival*ᵃ* in the seventh month of the year.

⁴When all the elders of Israel arrived, the Levites*ᵇ* lifted the Box of the Agreement* ⁵and carried it up to the Temple. The priests and the Levites*ᶜ* also brought the Meeting Tent* and all the holy things that were in it to the Temple in Jerusalem. ⁶Then King Solomon and all the Israelites met in front of the Box of the Agreement to offer sheep and bulls as sacrifices.* There were so many offerings that no one could count them. ⁷Then the priests carried the Box of the Lord's Agreement to the place that was prepared for it in the Most Holy Place* inside the Temple.* They put the Box of the Agreement under the wings of the Cherub angels.* ⁸The Cherub angels stood with their wings spread over the Box of the Agreement and the poles that were used to carry it. ⁹The poles are still there today. They were too long for the Most Holy Place, so their ends could be seen by anyone standing in the Holy Place, although no one outside could see them. ¹⁰The only things inside the Holy Box are the two tablets that Moses put there at Mt. Horeb. This is where the Lord made his agreement* with the Israelites after they came out of Egypt.

¹¹All the priests who were there did the ceremony to make themselves holy. Then, as they came out of the Holy Place,* they stood together, but not in their special groups. ¹²The Levite singers stood at the east side of the altar.* All the singing groups of Asaph, Heman, and Jeduthun were there. And their sons and relatives were there. The Levite singers were dressed in white linen.* They had cymbals,* lyres,* and harps. There were 120 priests there with the Levite singers. The 120 priests blew trumpets. ¹³Those who blew the trumpets and those who sang were like one person. They made one sound when they praised and thanked the Lord. They made a loud noise with the trumpets, cymbals, and instruments of music. They sang the song,*ᵈ* *Praise the Lord Because He Is Good. His Faithful Love Will Last Forever.*

Then the Lord's Temple was filled with a cloud. ¹⁴The priests could not continue to serve because of the cloud, because the Glory of the Lord* filled the Temple.

6 ¹Then Solomon said, "The Lord chose to live in a dark cloud. ²But, Lord, I have built a beautiful house for you to live in forever."

Solomon's Speech

³King Solomon turned around and blessed all the Israelites gathered in front of him. ⁴He said, "Praise the Lord, the God of Israel, who has done what he promised my father David. The Lord said, ⁵'I led Israel out of Egypt long ago. And in all that time, I have not chosen a city from any tribe of Israel for a place to build a house for my name. I have not chosen a man to lead my people, the people of Israel. ⁶But now I have chosen Jerusalem as a place for my name, and I have chosen David to lead my people Israel.'

⁷"My father David wanted to build a temple for the name of the Lord, the God of Israel. ⁸But the Lord said to my father, 'David, it is good that you want to build a temple for my name, ⁹but you cannot build the Temple.* Your son will build the Temple for my name.' ¹⁰Now, the Lord has done what he said he would do. I am the new king in my father's place. David was my father. Now I am Israel's king. That is what the Lord promised, and I have built the Temple for the name of the Lord, the God of Israel. ¹¹I put the Holy Box* in the Temple. The Lord's Agreement with Israel is in that box."

Solomon's Prayer

¹²⁻¹³Solomon had made a bronze platform and placed it in the middle of the outer courtyard.* The platform was 5 cubits*ᵉ* long, 5 cubits wide, and 3 cubits*ᶠ* tall. Solomon stood on the platform and faced the Lord's altar.* In front of all the Israelites who were gathered together, Solomon kneeled, spread his hands out toward heaven, ¹⁴and said,

"Lord, God of Israel, there is no god like you in heaven or on earth. You keep the agreement* that you made with your people. You are kind and loyal to those who follow you with all their heart. ¹⁵You made a promise to your servant, my father David, and you kept that promise. You made that promise with your own mouth, and with your own hands you made it come true today. ¹⁶Now, Lord, God of Israel, keep the other promises you made to your servant David, my father. You said, 'David, if your sons carefully obey me as you did, you will always have someone from your family ruling the people of Israel.' ¹⁷Again, Lord, God of Israel, I ask you to keep the promise you made to your servant, my father David.

---

*ᵃ***5:3** *the special festival* That is, the Festival of Shelters. See "Festival of Shelters" in the Word List.
*ᵇ***5:4** *Levites* Or "priests from the tribe of Levi."
*ᶜ***5:5** *the priests and the Levites* Or "The priests from the tribe of Levi."
*ᵈ***5:13** *They sang the song* Or "They sang the Hallel and ...." See Ps. 111–118 and 136.

*ᵉ***6:12–13** *5 cubits* 8' 6" (2.6 m).
*ᶠ***6:12–13** *3 cubits* 5' 1 3/16" (1.55 m).

[18]"But, God, will you really live here with us on the earth? The whole sky and the highest heaven cannot contain you. Certainly this house that I built cannot contain you either. [19]But please listen to my prayer and my request. I am your servant, and you are the Lord my God. Hear this prayer that I am praying to you today. [20]In the past you said, 'I will be honored there.' So please watch over this Temple, night and day. And please listen to my prayer as I turn toward this Temple and pray to you. [21]And Lord, please listen to our prayers in the future when I and your people Israel turn to this place and pray to you. We know that you live in heaven. We ask you to hear our prayer there and forgive us.

[22]"Whoever does wrong to someone will be brought to this altar. If they are not guilty, they will make an oath* and promise that they are innocent. [23]Please listen from heaven and judge them. If they are guilty, please show us that they are guilty. And if they are innocent, please show us that they are not guilty.

[24]"Sometimes your people Israel will sin against you, and their enemies will defeat them. Then the people will come back to you and praise you. They will pray to you in this Temple. [25]In heaven, please listen to the prayers of your people Israel. Forgive them for their sins and let them have their land again. You gave this land to their ancestors.

[26]"Sometimes they will sin against you, and you will stop the rain from falling on their land. Then they will pray toward this place and praise your name. You will make them suffer, and they will be sorry for their sins. [27]So please listen in heaven to their prayer. Then forgive us for our sins. Teach the people to live right. Then, Lord, please send rain to the land you gave them.

[28]"The land might become very dry so that no food will grow on it. Or maybe a great sickness will spread among the people. Maybe all the food that is growing will be destroyed by insects. Or your people might be attacked in some of their cities by their enemies. Or many of your people might get sick. [29]When any of these things happen, people feel the need to spread their hands in prayer toward this Temple. [30]Please listen to their prayer while you are in your home in heaven and forgive them and help them. Only you know what people are really thinking, so only you can judge them fairly. [31]Do this so that your people will fear and respect you all the time that they live in this land you gave to our ancestors.

[32]"People from other places will hear about your greatness and your power. They will come from far away to pray at this Temple. [33]From your home in heaven please listen to their prayers. Please do everything those from other places ask you. Then they will fear and respect you the same as your people in Israel. Then all people everywhere will know that I built this Temple to honor you.

[34]"Sometimes you will command your people to go and fight against their enemies. Then your people will turn toward this city that you have chosen and the Temple that I built in your honor, and they will pray to you. [35]Listen to their prayers from your home in heaven, and help them.

[36]"Your people will sin against you. I know this because everyone sins. And you will be angry with your people. You will let their enemies defeat them. Their enemies will make them prisoners and carry them to some faraway land. [37]In that faraway land, your people will think about what happened. They will be sorry for their sins, and they will pray to you. They will say, 'We have sinned and done wrong.' [38]They will be in that faraway land of their enemies, but they will turn back to you. They will feel sorry for their sins with their whole heart and soul. They will turn toward the land you gave their ancestors.* They will look toward the city you chose and toward the Temple I built, and they will pray to you. [39]Please listen from your home in heaven. Accept their prayers when they beg for help, and help them. Forgive your people who have sinned against you. [40]Now, my God, I ask you, open your eyes and your ears. Listen and pay attention to the prayers we are praying in this place.

[41]"Now, Lord God, get up and come to your
    special place,
   the Box of the Agreement* that shows
    your strength.
May your priests be dressed with
    salvation,
   and may your true followers be happy
    about these good things.
[42] Lord God, accept your anointed* king.
   Remember your loyal servant David."

The Temple Dedicated to the Lord

7 [1]When Solomon finished praying, fire came down from the sky and burned up the burnt offering* and the sacrifices.* The Glory of the Lord* filled the Temple.* [2]The priests could not enter the Lord's Temple because the Glory of the Lord filled it. [3]When all the Israelites saw the fire come down from heaven and the Glory of the Lord on the Temple, they bowed their faces down low to the ground on the pavement. They worshiped and thanked the Lord. They sang the song, *He Is Good. His Faithful Love Will Last Forever.*[a]

[4]Then King Solomon and all the Israelites offered sacrifices to the Lord. [5]King Solomon offered 22,000 bulls and 120,000 sheep. So the king and the people showed that they had dedicated* the Temple to the Lord. [6]The priests stood ready to do their work. The Levites stood with the instruments they would use

[a]**7:3 The Lord ... Forever** See Ps. 118 and 136.

to play music to the LORD. King David made these instruments to use in giving thanks to the LORD. The priests and Levites sang the song, *Praise the Lord Because His Faithful Love Will Last Forever.*[a] The priests blew their trumpets as they stood across from the Levites. And all the Israelites were standing.

[7]King Solomon also dedicated the middle of the courtyard, the part that is in front of the Temple of the LORD. There he offered burnt offerings, grain offerings, and the fat from the animals that were used as fellowship offerings.* He did this because the bronze altar* he had built was too small to hold all these offerings.

[8]So there at the Temple, King Solomon and all the people of Israel celebrated the festival.[b] People came from as far away as Hamath Pass in the north and the border of Egypt in the south. This huge crowd of people ate, drank, and enjoyed themselves together with the LORD for seven days. [9]On the eighth day they had a holy meeting because they had celebrated for seven days. They made the altar holy and it was to be used only for worshiping the Lord. And they celebrated the festival for seven days. [10]On the 23rd day of the seventh month Solomon told the people to go home. All the people thanked the king, said goodbye, and went home. They were happy because of all the good things that the LORD had done for David his servant and for his people Israel.

The Lord Comes to Solomon

[11]So Solomon finished building the LORD's Temple and his own palace. Solomon built everything that he wanted to build. [12]Then the LORD appeared to Solomon at night and said to him, "Solomon, I have heard your prayer, and I have chosen this place for myself to be a house for sacrifices.* [13]When I close the sky so that there is no rain, or command the locusts to destroy the land, or send sicknesses to my people [14]and if my people who are called by my name become humble and pray, and look for me, and turn away from their evil ways, then I will hear them from heaven. I will forgive their sin and heal their land. [15]Now, my eyes are open, and my ears will pay attention to the prayers prayed in this place. [16]I have chosen this Temple, and I have made it a holy place. So I will be honored there forever. I will watch over it and think of it always. [17]You must serve me with a pure and honest heart, just as your father David did. You must obey my laws and do everything that I commanded you. If you obey all I have commanded, and if you obey my laws and rules, [18]then I will make you a strong king and your kingdom will be great. That is the agreement I made with David your father

when I told him that Israel would always be ruled by one of his descendants.

[19]"But if you don't obey my laws and commands that I gave you, and if you worship other gods and serve them, [20]then I will take the Israelites out from my land that I gave them. And I will leave this Temple* that I have made holy for my name. I will make this Temple something that all the nations will speak evil about. [21]Everyone who sees it will be amazed. They will ask, 'Why did the LORD do this terrible thing to this land and to this temple?' [22]People will say, 'This happened because they left the LORD their God. He brought their ancestors out of Egypt, but they decided to follow other gods. They began to worship and to serve those gods. That is why the LORD caused all these bad things to happen to them.'"

The Cities Solomon Built

8 [1]It took 20 years for King Solomon to build the LORD's Temple and the king's palace. [2]Then Solomon rebuilt the towns that Hiram gave him and then moved Israelites into those towns to live there. [3]After this Solomon went to Hamath of Zobah and captured it. [4]He also built the town of Tadmor in the desert. He built all the towns in Hamath to store things in. [5]He rebuilt the towns of Upper Beth Horon and Lower Beth Horon. He made them into strong forts with strong walls, gates, and bars in the gates. [6]He also rebuilt the town of Baalath and all the other towns where he stored things. He built all the cities where the chariots* were kept and where the horse riders lived. Solomon built all he wanted in Jerusalem, Lebanon, and in all the country where he was king.

[7-8]There were many people left in the land who were not Israelites. There were Hittites, Amorites, Perizzites, Hivites, and Jebusites. The Israelites had not been able to destroy them, but Solomon forced them to work for him as slaves. They are still slaves today. [9]Solomon did not force any of the Israelites to be his slaves. They were soldiers, government officials, officers, captains, and chariot commanders and drivers. [10]There were 250 supervisors over Solomon's projects. They supervised the men.

[11]Solomon brought Pharaoh's daughter up from the City of David* to the house he built for her. He said, "My wife must not live in King David's palace because the places where the Box of the Agreement* has been are holy places."

[12]Then Solomon offered burnt offerings* to the LORD on the LORD's altar.* He built that altar in front of the Temple* porch. [13]Solomon offered sacrifices* every day the way Moses commanded. Sacrifices were to be offered on Sabbath* days, during New Moon* celebrations, and at the three yearly festivals. The three yearly festivals were the Festival of

---

[a]**7:6** *Praise ... Forever* See 1 Chron. 16:41, Ps. 118 and 136.

[b]**7:8** *festival* This was probably Passover.

Unleavened Bread,* the Festival of Harvest,* and the Festival of Shelters.* [14]Solomon followed his father David's instructions. He chose the groups of priests for their service and the Levites for their duties. The Levites were to lead the praise and help the priests from day to day to do what needed to be done in the Temple service. And he chose the gatekeepers by their groups to serve at each gate. This is the way David, the man of God, instructed. [15]The Israelites did not change or disobey any of Solomon's instructions to the priests and Levites. They did not change any of the instructions, even in the way they should keep the valuable things.

[16]So Solomon completed his work on the Lord's Temple. Work began the day they laid the foundation and continued without stopping until the day the Temple was finished.

[17]King Solomon also built ships at Ezion Geber. This town is near Elath on the shore of the Red Sea, in the land of Edom. [18]Hiram sent ships to Solomon. Hiram's own men sailed the ships. They were skilled at sailing on the sea. His men went with Solomon's servants to Ophir[a] and brought back 17 tons[b] of gold to King Solomon.

The Queen of Sheba Visits Solomon

9 [1]The queen of Sheba heard about Solomon, so she came to test him with hard questions. She had a very large group with her. She had camels that carried spices, much gold, and valuable stones. She traveled to Jerusalem with a very large group of servants. There were many camels carrying spices, jewels, and a lot of gold. She met Solomon and asked him all the questions that she could think of. [2]Solomon answered all the questions. None of her questions was too hard for him to explain. [3]The queen of Sheba saw that Solomon was very wise. She also saw the beautiful palace he had built. [4]She saw the food at the king's table. She saw his officials meeting together. She saw the servants in the palace and the good clothes they wore. She saw his parties and the sacrifices that he offered in the Temple. She was so amazed that it took her breath away!

[5]Then she said to King Solomon, "The stories I heard in my country about your great works and your wisdom are true. [6]I did not believe it until I came and saw it with my own eyes. Now I see that it is even greater than what I heard. Your wealth and wisdom is much greater than people told me. [7]Your wives[c] and officers are very fortunate! They can serve you and hear your wisdom every day. [8]Praise the Lord your God! He was pleased to make you king of Israel. The Lord God loves Israel, so he made you the king. You follow the law and treat people fairly."

[9]Then the Queen of Sheba gave King Solomon 4½ tons[d] of gold, a great many spices, and valuable stones. She gave Solomon more spices than anyone has ever brought into Israel.

[10]Hiram's servants brought gold from Ophir. They also brought in jewels and a special kind of wood.[e] [11]King Solomon used this special wood to make steps for the Lord's Temple* and the king's palace. Solomon also used the algum wood to make lyres* and harps for the singers. No one ever saw such beautiful things like those made from the algum wood in the country of Judah.

[12]King Solomon gave the Queen of Sheba everything she asked for. He gave her more than she brought to give him. Then the Queen of Sheba and her servants left and went back to their own country.

Solomon's Great Wealth

[13]Every year Solomon got almost 25 tons[f] of gold. [14]In addition to the gold brought in by the traveling merchants* and traders, all the kings of Arabia and the governors of the land also brought gold and silver to Solomon.

[15]King Solomon made 200 large shields from hammered gold. He used about 15 pounds[g] of gold for each shield. [16]He also made 300 small shields of hammered gold. He used about 7½ pounds[h] of gold for each shield. The king put them in his palace called the "Forest of Lebanon."

[17]King Solomon also built a large throne with ivory decorations. It was covered with pure gold. [18]There were six steps leading up to the throne. The back of the throne was round at the top. There were armrests on both sides of the throne, and there were lions in the sides of the throne under the armrests. [19]There were also two lions on each of the six steps, one at each end. There was nothing like it in any other kingdom.

[20]All of Solomon's cups and glasses were made of gold. And all the dishes[i] in the building called the "Forest of Lebanon" were made from pure gold. Nothing in the palace was made from silver. There was so much gold that in Solomon's time people did not think silver was important!

---

[a]**8:18** *Ophir* A place where there was much gold. Today no one knows where Ophir really was. Also in 9:10.

[b]**8:18** *17 tons* Literally, "450 talents" (15,525 kg).

[c]**9:7** *wives* This is from the ancient Greek version. The standard Hebrew text has "men."

[d]**9:9** *4 1/2 tons* Literally, "120 talents" (4140 kg).

[e]**9:10** *special ... wood* Literally, "algum" or "Almug," as in 1 Kings. No one knows exactly what type of wood this was, but it might have been sandalwood.

[f]**9:13** *25 tons* Literally, "666 talents" (22,977 kg).

[g]**9:15** *About 15 pounds* Hebrew, "600 ͺshekels,ͺ" (6.9 kg).

[h]**9:16** *About 7 1/2 pounds* Hebrew, "300 ͺshekels,ͺ" (3.45 kg).

[i]**9:20** *dishes* The Hebrew word can mean "dishes," "tools," or "weapons."

²¹The king also had cargo ships that went to Tarshish to trade things with other countries. Hiram's men were on these ships. Every three years the ships would come back with a new load of gold, silver, ivory, and apes and baboons.

²²King Solomon became greater in riches and wisdom than any other king on earth. ²³People everywhere wanted to see King Solomon. They wanted to hear the great wisdom that God had given him. ²⁴Every year people came to see the king, and everyone brought a gift. They brought things made from gold and silver, clothes, weapons, spices, horses, and mules.

²⁵Solomon had 4000 stalls to keep horses and chariots.* He had 12,000 horse soldiers. Solomon built special cities for these chariots. So the chariots were kept in these cities. King Solomon also kept some of the chariots with him in Jerusalem. ²⁶Solomon was the king over all the kings from the Euphrates River all the way to the land of the Philistines, and to the border of Egypt. ²⁷King Solomon had so much silver that it was as common as rocks in Jerusalem. And he had so much cedar wood that it was as common as sycamore trees in the hill country. ²⁸The people brought horses to Solomon from Egypt and from all the other countries.

Solomon's Death

²⁹Everything else Solomon did, from the beginning to the end, is written in the writings of Nathan the Prophet, in *The Prophecy of Ahijah* from Shiloh, and in *The Visions of Iddo the Seer*. Iddo was a seer* who wrote about Jeroboam son of Nebat. ³⁰Solomon ruled in Jerusalem over all Israel for 40 years. ³¹Then he died*a* and was buried in the city of David, his father. Then Solomon's son Rehoboam became the next king.

Rehoboam Acts Foolishly

10 ¹⁻³Jeroboam son of Nebat was still in Egypt where he had run away from Solomon. When he heard about Solomon's death, he returned to his city, Zeredah, in the hills of Ephraim.

Rehoboam and all the Israelites went to Shechem to make Rehoboam the king. The people said to Rehoboam, ⁴"Your father forced us to work very hard. Now, make it easier for us. Stop the heavy work that your father forced us to do and we will serve you."

⁵Rehoboam answered, "Come back to me in three days, and I will answer you." So the people left.

⁶There were some older men who had helped Solomon make decisions when he was alive. So King Rehoboam asked these men what he should do. He said, "How do you think I should answer the people?"

⁷They answered, "If you do what is good for the people, you will please them. If you speak kindly to them, they will always work for you."

⁸But Rehoboam did not listen to the advice from the older men. He asked the young men who were his friends. ⁹Rehoboam said, "The people said, 'Give us easier work than your father gave us.' How do you think I should answer them? What should I tell them?"

¹⁰Then the young men who grew up with him answered, "Those people came to you and said, 'Your father forced us to work very hard. Now make our work easier.' So you should tell them, 'My little finger is stronger than my father's whole body. ¹¹My father forced you to work hard, but I will make you work much harder! My father punished you with whips, but I will punish you with whips that have sharp metal tips.'"

¹²Three days later, Jeroboam and all the people came back like Rehoboam had said. ¹³King Rehoboam did not listen to the advice from the older men, and he was rude to the people. ¹⁴He did what his friends told him to do and said, "My father forced you to work hard, but I will make you work much harder! My father punished you with whips, but I will punish you with whips that have sharp metal tips." ¹⁵So the king did not do what the people wanted. The LORD caused this to happen. He did this in order to keep the promise he made to Jeroboam son of Nebat when he sent Ahijah, the prophet from Shiloh, to speak to him.

¹⁶The Israelites saw that the new king refused to listen to them, so they said to the king, "Are we part of David's family? No. Do we get any of Jesse's land? No. So Israel, let's go home and let David's son rule his own people!" So the Israelites went home. ¹⁷But Rehoboam still ruled over the Israelites who lived in the cities of Judah.

¹⁸A man named Adoniram was one of the men who directed the workers. King Rehoboam sent Adoniram to talk to the people, but the Israelites threw stones at him until he died. King Rehoboam ran to his chariot* and escaped to Jerusalem. ¹⁹So Israel rebelled against the family of David, and that is how things are even today.

11 ¹Rehoboam went back to Jerusalem and gathered together an army of 180,000 men from the families of Judah and the tribe of Benjamin. Rehoboam wanted to go fight against the Israelites and take back his kingdom. ²But the LORD spoke to a man of God* named Shemaiah. He said, ³"Talk to Rehoboam, the son of Solomon, king of Judah, and to men of Judah and Benjamin. ⁴Say to them, 'The LORD says that you must not go to war against your brothers. Everyone, go home! I made all this happen.'" So all the men in Rehoboam's army obeyed the LORD and went home. They did not attack Jeroboam.

Rehoboam Strengthens Judah

[5]Rehoboam lived in Jerusalem and built strong cities in Judah to defend against attacks. [6]He repaired the cities of Bethlehem, Etam, Tekoa, [7]Beth Zur, Soco, Adullam, [8]Gath, Mareshah, Ziph, [9]Adoraim, Lachish, Azekah, [10]Zorah, Aijalon, and Hebron. These cities in Judah and Benjamin were made strong. [11]When Rehoboam made these cities strong, he put commanders in them. He also put supplies of food, oil, and wine in them. [12]Also, he put shields and spears in every city and made the cities very strong. He kept the peoples and cities of Judah and Benjamin under his control.

[13]The priests and the Levites from all over Israel agreed with Rehoboam and joined him. [14]The Levites left their grasslands and their own fields and came to Judah and Jerusalem. The Levites did this because Jeroboam and his sons refused to let them serve as priests to the Lord. [15]Jeroboam chose his own priests to serve in the high places,* where he set up the goat and calf idols* he had made. [16]When the Levites left Israel, the people in all the tribes of Israel who were faithful to the Lord, the God of Israel, came to Jerusalem to sacrifice* to the Lord, the God of their fathers. [17]These people made the kingdom of Judah strong, and they supported Solomon's son Rehoboam for three years. They did this because during that time they lived the way David and Solomon had lived.

Rehoboam's Family

[18]Rehoboam married Mahalath. Her father was Jerimoth. Her mother was Abihail. Jerimoth was David's son. Abihail was Eliab's daughter, and Eliab was Jesse's son. [19]Mahalath gave Rehoboam these sons: Jeush, Shemariah, and Zaham. [20]Then Rehoboam married Maacah. Maacah was Absalom's granddaughter.[a] And Maacah gave Rehoboam these children: Abijah, Attai, Ziza, and Shelomith. [21]Rehoboam loved Maacah more that he loved all his other wives and slave women.* Rehoboam had 18 wives and 60 slave women. He was the father of 28 sons and 60 daughters.

[22]Rehoboam chose Abijah to be the leader among his own brothers. He did this because he planned to make Abijah king. [23]Rehoboam acted wisely and spread all his sons through all the areas of Judah and Benjamin to every strong city. And Rehoboam gave plenty of supplies to his sons. He also looked for wives for them.

Shishak, King of Egypt Attacks Jerusalem

12 [1]Rehoboam became a strong king and made his kingdom strong. Then Rehoboam and the whole tribe of Judah[b] refused to obey the law of the Lord.

[2]During the fifth year that Rehoboam was king, Shishak king of Egypt came to attack Jerusalem. This happened because Rehoboam and the people of Judah rebelled against the Lord. [3]Shishak had 12,000 chariots,* 60,000 horse riders, and an army that no one could count. In Shishak's large army there were Libyan soldiers, Sukkite soldiers, and Ethiopian soldiers. [4]Shishak defeated the strong cities of Judah. Then Shishak brought his army to Jerusalem.

[5]Then Shemaiah the prophet came to Rehoboam and the leaders of Judah. The leaders of Judah had gathered together in Jerusalem because they all were afraid of Shishak. Shemaiah said to Rehoboam and the leaders of Judah, "This is what the Lord says: 'Rehoboam, you and the people of Judah have left me and refused to obey my law. So now I will leave you to face Shishak without my help.'"

[6]Then the leaders of Judah and King Rehoboam were sorry and humbled themselves. They said, "The Lord is right."

[7]The Lord saw that the king and the leaders of Judah had humbled themselves. Then the message from the Lord came to Shemaiah. The Lord said, "The king and the leaders humbled themselves. So I will not destroy them, but I will save them soon. I will not use Shishak to pour out my anger on Jerusalem. [8]But the people of Jerusalem will become Shishak's servants. This will happen so that they may learn that serving me is different from serving the kings of other nations."

[9]Shishak took the treasures from the Lord's Temple and from the king's palace. He also took the gold shields that Solomon had made. [10]King Rehoboam made more shields to put in their places, but they were made from bronze. He gave them to the guards on duty at the palace gates. [11]Every time the king went to the Lord's Temple, the guards took out the shields and went with him. After they were finished, they put the shields back on the wall in the guardroom.

[12]Rehoboam humbled himself, and the Lord stopped being angry with him. So he did not completely destroy Rehoboam. There was some good in Judah.

[13]King Rehoboam made himself a strong king in Jerusalem. He was 41 years old when he became king of Judah. Rehoboam ruled 17 years in Jerusalem, the city the Lord chose for his own. He chose this city from all the other cities of Israel. Rehoboam's mother was Naamah. She was an Ammonite. [14]Rehoboam did evil because he didn't decide in his heart to obey the Lord.

[15]All the things Rehoboam did when he was king, from the beginning to the end of his rule, are written in the writings of Shemaiah the prophet and in the writings of Iddo the seer.* Those men wrote family histories.

---

[a]**11:20 granddaughter** Literally, "daughter."
[b]**12:1 Judah** Literally, "Israel."

And there were wars between Rehoboam and Jeroboam all the time both kings ruled. [16]Rehoboam rested with his ancestors* and was buried in the City of David.* Then Rehoboam's son Abijah became the next king after him.

Abijah, King of Judah

13 [1]Abijah became the new king of Judah. This was during the 18th year that Jeroboam son of Nebat ruled Israel. [2]Abijah ruled in Jerusalem for three years. His mother's name was Maacah. She was the daughter of Uriel, from the town of Gibeah. And there was war between Abijah and Jeroboam. [3]Abijah's army had 400,000 brave soldiers. Abijah led that army into battle. Jeroboam's army had 800,000 brave soldiers. Jeroboam got ready to have a war with Abijah.

[4]Then Abijah stood on Mount Zemaraim in the hill country of Ephraim and said, "Jeroboam and all Israel, listen to me! [5]You should know that the Lord, the God of Israel, gave David and his sons the right to be king over Israel forever. God gave this right to David with an agreement of salt.[a] [6]But Jeroboam turned against his master. Jeroboam son of Nebat was one of the servants of David's son Solomon. [7]Then worthless, evil men became friends with Jeroboam. Then Jeroboam and the bad men turned against Rehoboam, Solomon's son. Rehoboam was young and did not have experience. So he could not stop Jeroboam and his bad friends.

[8]"Now, you people have decided to defeat the Lord's kingdom—the kingdom that is ruled by David's sons. You have so many people with you and you have the golden calves—the 'gods' that Jeroboam made for you. [9]You threw out the Lord's priests, the descendants of Aaron. And you threw out the Levites. Then you chose your own priests, as every other nation on earth does. And now, anyone who will bring a young bull and seven rams can become a priest to serve these 'no-gods.'

[10]"But as for us, the Lord is our God. We people of Judah have not refused to obey God. We have not left him. The priests who serve the Lord are Aaron's sons, and the Levites help the priests in their work. [11]They offer burnt offerings* and burn incense* of spices to the Lord every morning and every evening. They put the bread in rows on the special table in the Temple.* And they take care of the lamps on the golden lampstand so that it shines bright each and every evening. We very carefully serve the Lord our God, but you people have abandoned him. [12]God himself is with us. He is our ruler, and his priests

are with us. God's priests blow his trumpets to wake you up and make you excited about coming to him. Men of Israel, don't fight against the Lord, God of your ancestors,* because you will not succeed!"

[13]But Jeroboam sent a group of soldiers to sneak behind Abijah's army. Jeroboam's army was in front of Abijah's army. The hidden soldiers from Jeroboam's army were behind Abijah's army. [14]When the soldiers in Abijah's army from Judah looked around, they saw Jeroboam's army attacking both in front and in back.[b] The men of Judah shouted out to the Lord and the priests blew the trumpets. [15]Then the men in Abijah's army shouted. When the men of Judah shouted, God defeated Jeroboam's army. Jeroboam's whole army from Israel was defeated by Abijah's army from Judah. [16]The men of Israel ran away from the men of Judah. God let the army from Judah defeat the army from Israel. [17]Abijah's army greatly defeated the army of Israel, and 500,000 of the best men of Israel were killed. [18]So at that time the Israelites were defeated, and the people of Judah won. The army from Judah won because they depended on the Lord, the God of their ancestors.

[19]Abijah's army chased Jeroboam's army, and they captured the towns of Bethel, Jeshanah, and Ephron from Jeroboam. They captured the towns and the small villages near them.

[20]Jeroboam never became strong again while Abijah lived. The Lord killed Jeroboam, [21]but Abijah became strong. He married 14 women and was the father of 22 sons and 16 daughters. [22]Everything else Abijah did is written in the books of the prophet Iddo.

14 [1]When Abijah died, they buried him in the City of David.* Abijah's son Asa became the new king after him. There was peace in the country for ten years in Asa's time.

Asa, King of Judah

[2]Asa did what the Lord his God said was good and right. [3]He took away the altars of the foreigners and the high places.* He also smashed the memorial stones* and cut down the Asherah poles.* [4]He commanded the people of Judah to follow the Lord, the God their ancestors* followed. And he commanded them to obey the Lord's laws and commandments. [5]He also removed all the high places and incense* altars from all the towns in Judah. So the kingdom had peace when Asa was king. [6]Asa built strong cities in Judah while there was peace in Judah. He had no war in these years because the Lord gave him peace.

---

*a***13:5** *agreement of salt* When people ate salt together, it meant their agreement of friendship would never be broken. Abijah was saying here that God had made an agreement with David that would never be broken.

*b***13:14** *When the soldiers ... in back* The standard Hebrew text has "The battle was in front and in the back."

7Asa said to the people of Judah, "Let's build these towns and make walls around them. Let's make towers, gates, and bars in the gates. Let's do this while we still live in this country. This country is ours because we have followed the LORD our God. He has given us peace all around us." So they built and had success.

8Asa had an army of 300,000 men from the tribe of Judah and 280,000 men from the tribe of Benjamin. The men from Judah carried large shields and spears. The men from Benjamin carried small shields and shot arrows from bows. All of them were strong and brave soldiers.

9Then Zerah from Ethiopia*a* came out against Asa's army. He had 1,000,000 men and 300 chariots* in his army. His army went as far as the town of Mareshah. 10Asa went out to fight against Zerah. Asa's army got ready for battle in the Valley of Zephathah at Mareshah.

11Asa called out to the LORD his God and said, "LORD, only you can help weak people against strong people! Help us, LORD our God! We depend on you. We fight against this large army in your name. LORD, you are our God! Don't let anyone win against you!"

12Then the LORD used Asa's army from Judah to defeat the Ethiopian army. And the army ran away. 13Asa's army chased the Ethiopian army all the way to the town of Gerar. So many Ethiopians were killed that they could not get together as an army to fight again. They were crushed by the LORD and his army. Asa and his army carried many valuable things away from the enemy. 14Asa and his army defeated all the towns near Gerar. The people living in those towns were afraid of the LORD. Those towns had very many valuable things. Asa's army took those valuable things away from those towns. 15His army also attacked the camps where the shepherds lived and took many sheep and camels. Then they went back to Jerusalem.

Asa's Changes

15 1The Spirit of God came on Azariah, who was Obed's son. 2Azariah went to meet Asa and said, "Listen to me, Asa, and all you people of Judah and Benjamin. The LORD is with you when you are with him. If you look for the LORD, you will find him. But if you leave him, he will leave you. 3For a long time Israel was without the true God. And they were without a teaching priest, and without the law. 4But when the Israelites had trouble, they turned to the LORD God again. He is the God of Israel. They looked for the LORD and they found him. 5In those times of trouble, no one could travel safely. There was much trouble in all the nations. 6One nation

would destroy another nation and one city would destroy another city. This was happening because God gave them all kinds of trouble. 7But Asa, you and the people of Judah and Benjamin, be strong. Don't be weak and don't give up, because you will get a reward for your good work!"

8Asa felt encouraged when he heard these words and the message from Obed the prophet. Then he removed the hated idols from the whole area of Judah and Benjamin. He also removed the hated idols* from the towns he had captured in the hill country of Ephraim. And he repaired the LORD's altar* that was in front of the porch of the LORD's Temple.*

9Then Asa gathered all the people from Judah and Benjamin and the people from the tribes of Ephraim, Manasseh, and Simeon who had moved from the country of Israel to live in the country of Judah. A great many of these people came to Judah because they saw that the LORD, Asa's God, was with him.

10Asa and these people gathered together in Jerusalem on the third month in the 15th year of Asa's rule. 11At that time they sacrificed* 700 bulls and 7000 sheep and goats to the LORD. Asa's army had taken the animals and other valuable things from their enemies. 12Then they made an agreement to serve the LORD God with all their heart and with all their soul. He is the God their ancestors* served. 13Anyone who refused to serve the LORD God was to be killed. It did not matter if that person was important or not or if that person was a man or woman. 14Then Asa and the people made an oath* to the LORD. They shouted it out loudly and blew their trumpets and rams' horns. 15All the people of Judah were happy about the oath, because they had promised with all their heart. They followed God with all their heart. They looked for God and found him, so the LORD gave them peace in all the country.

16King Asa also removed Maacah, his mother, from being queen mother. He did this because she had set up one of those awful poles to honor the goddess Asherah. Asa cut down that Asherah pole,* smashed it into small pieces, and burned the pieces in the Kidron Valley. 17Asa did not destroy the high places,* even though he was faithful to the LORD all his life.

18Asa and his father had given some special gifts to God. Asa put these gifts of gold, silver, and other things into the Temple. 19There was no more war until the 35th year of Asa's rule.*b*

Asa's Last Years

16 1In Asa's 36th year as king,*c* Baasha attacked Judah and then built up the city of Ramah to keep Asa from leaving Judah on any kind of military campaign. 2So

---

*a***14:9** *Ethiopia* Or "Cush."

*b***15:19** *35th year of Asa's rule* About the year 880 B.C.
*c***16:1** *36th year as king* About the year 879 B.C.

Asa took gold and silver from the treasuries of the LORD's Temple and the king's palace. He gave it to his officials and sent them to King Ben-Hadad of Aram. Ben-Hadad was the son of Tabrimmon. Tabrimmon was the son of Hezion. Damascus was Ben-Hadad's capital city. [3]Asa sent this message, "My father and your father had a peace agreement. Now I want to make a peace agreement with you. I am sending you this gift of gold and silver. Please break your treaty with King Baasha of Israel and make him leave us alone."

[4]King Ben-Hadad made that agreement with King Asa and sent his army to fight against the Israelite towns of Ijon, Dan, Abel Maim, and the storage cities in the area of Naphtali. [5]When Baasha heard about these attacks, he stopped building up Ramah and went back to Tirzah. He stopped all the work he was doing. [6]Then King Asa gave an order for all the men in Judah, with no exceptions. They had to go to Ramah and carry out all the stone and wood that Baasha was using to build up the city. They carried the material to Geba in Benjamin and to Mizpah and used it to strengthen those two cities.

[7]At that time Hanani the seer* came to King Asa of Judah and said to him, "Asa, you depended on the king of Aram to help you and not the LORD your God. You should have depended on the LORD. But, because you did not depend on the LORD for help, the king of Aram's army escaped from you. [8]The Ethiopians and the Libyans had a very large and powerful army. They had many chariots* and chariot drivers. But Asa, you depended on the LORD to help you defeat that large powerful army, and the LORD let you defeat them. [9]The eyes of the LORD go around looking in all the earth for people who are faithful to him so that he can make them strong. Asa, you did a foolish thing. So from now on you will have wars."

[10]Asa was angry with Hanani because of what he said. He was so mad that he put Hanani in prison. He was also very rough and cruel to some of the people then.

[11]Everything Asa did, from the beginning to the end, is written in the book, *The History of the Kings of Judah and Israel.* [12]Asa's feet became infected in his 39th year as king.*a* Even though the infection was very serious, Asa did not go to the LORD for help. He went to the doctors instead. [13]Asa died in the 41st year as king*b* and rested with his ancestors.* [14]The people buried Asa in his own tomb that he made for himself in the City of David.* They laid him in a bed that was filled with spices and different kinds of mixed perfumes, and they burned a large fire for him.*c*

*a***16:12** *39th year as king* About the year 875 B.C.
*b***16:13** *41st year as king* About the year 873 B.C.
*c***16:14** This probably means the people burned spices in honor of Asa, but it could also mean they burned his body.

Jehoshaphat, King of Judah

17 [1]Asa's son Jehoshaphat became the new king after him. Jehoshaphat made Judah strong so that they could fight against Israel. [2]He put groups of soldiers in all the towns of Judah that were made into fortresses.* He built fortresses in Judah and in the towns of Ephraim that his father Asa had captured.

[3]The LORD was with Jehoshaphat because in his young life he did the good things his ancestor* David did. Jehoshaphat did not follow the Baal* idols.* [4]He looked for the God his ancestors followed. He followed God's commands and did not live the same way the Israelites lived. [5]The LORD made Jehoshaphat a strong king over Judah. All the people of Judah brought gifts to Jehoshaphat. So he had much wealth and honor. [6]His heart found pleasure in the ways of the LORD. He removed the high places* and the Asherah poles* from the country of Judah.

[7]During the third year of Jehoshaphat's rule,*d* he sent his leaders to teach in the towns of Judah. These leaders were Ben Hail, Obadiah, Zechariah, Nethanel, and Micaiah. [8]Jehoshaphat also sent Levites with these leaders. These Levites were Shemaiah, Nethaniah, Zebadiah, Asahel, Shemiramoth, Jehonathan, Adonijah, and Tobijah. He also sent the priests Elishama and Jehoram. [9]These leaders, Levites, and priests taught the people in Judah. They had the *Book of the Law of the LORD* with them. They went through all the towns of Judah and taught the people.

[10]The nations near Judah were afraid of the LORD, so they did not start a war against Jehoshaphat. [11]Some of the Philistines brought gifts to Jehoshaphat. They also brought silver to him because they knew he was a very powerful king. Some Arabian people brought flocks to Jehoshaphat. They brought 7700 rams and 7700 goats to him.

[12]Jehoshaphat became more and more powerful. He built fortresses and storage towns in the country of Judah. [13]He kept many supplies in the storage towns. And Jehoshaphat kept trained soldiers in Jerusalem. [14]These soldiers were listed in their tribes. This is the list of these soldiers in Jerusalem:

From the tribe of Judah, these were the generals: Adnah was the general of 300,000 soldiers. [15]Jehohanan was the general of 280,000 soldiers. [16]Amasiah was the general of 200,000 soldiers. Amasiah was Zicri's son. Amasiah was happy to give himself to serve the LORD.

[17]From the tribe of Benjamin these were the generals: Eliada had 200,000 soldiers who used bows, arrows, and shields. Eliada was a very brave soldier. [18]Jehozabad had

*d***17:7** *third year of Jehoshaphat's rule* About the year 871 B.C.

180,000 men ready for war. ¹⁹All these soldiers served King Jehoshaphat. The king also had other men in the fortresses in all the country of Judah.

Micaiah Warns King Ahab

18 ¹Jehoshaphat became very rich and famous. He made an agreement with King Ahab through marriage.ᵃ ²A few years later, Jehoshaphat visited Ahab in the town of Samaria. Ahab sacrificed* many sheep and cattle for Jehoshaphat and the people with him. Ahab encouraged Jehoshaphat to join in an attack on the city of Ramoth Gilead. ³Ahab said to Jehoshaphat, "Will you go with me to attack Ramoth Gilead?" Ahab was the king of Israel and Jehoshaphat was the king of Judah. Jehoshaphat answered, "Yes, you and I will be as one—my men will be as yours in battle. ⁴But first let's ask the Lord for advice."

⁵So Ahab called a meeting of the prophets. There were about 400 prophets at that time. Ahab asked the prophets, "Should we go and attack Ramoth Gilead or not?"

The prophets answered Ahab, "Yes, because God will let you defeat Ramoth Gilead."

⁶But Jehoshaphat said, "Doesn't the Lord have another prophet here? Let's ask him what God says."

⁷King Ahab answered, "Yes, there is another prophet. His name is Micaiah son of Imlah. But I hate him. He never says anything good about me when he speaks for the Lord. He always says things that I don't like."

Jehoshaphat said, "The king shouldn't say things like that!"

⁸So King Ahab told one of his officers to go and find Micaiah.

⁹At that time the two kings were sitting on their thrones, with their royal robes on, at the judgment place near the gates of Samaria. All the prophets were standing before them, prophesying.* ¹⁰One of the prophets was named Zedekiah son of Kenaanah. Zedekiah made some iron hornsᵇ and said to Ahab, "The Lord says, 'You will use these iron horns to fight against the army of Aram. You will defeat them and destroy them.'" ¹¹All the other prophets agreed with Zedekiah and said, "Your army should march now to go fight the Arameans at Ramoth Gilead. You will win the battle. The Lord will let you defeat them."

¹²While this was happening, the officer went to find Micaiah. When he found him, the officer told him, "All the other prophets have said that the king will succeed, so you should say the same thing."

¹³But Micaiah answered, "As surely as the Lord lives, I can say only what my God says."

¹⁴Micaiah went and stood before King Ahab. The king asked him, "Micaiah, should we go and attack the Arameans at Ramoth Gilead or not?"

Micaiah answered, "Yes, go and be successful! You will take the city."

¹⁵But Ahab answered, "How many times do I have to tell you? Tell me the truth. What does the Lord say?"

¹⁶So Micaiah answered, "I can see the army of Israel scattered all over the hills, like sheep with no one to lead them. This is what the Lord says, 'These men have no leaders. Let them go home in peace.'"

¹⁷Then Ahab said to Jehoshaphat, "See, I told you! This prophet never says anything good about me. He always says something bad."

¹⁸Micaiah said, "Hear the message from the Lord: I saw the Lord sitting on his throne. All of heaven's army was standing around him, some on his left side and some on his right side. ¹⁹The Lord said, 'Which of you will go fool Ahab into attacking the Arameans at Ramoth Gilead so that he will be killed?' The angels discussed many different plans. ²⁰Then a spiritᶜ went and stood before the Lord. He said, 'I will fool him!' The Lord asked, 'How will you do it?' ²¹He answered, 'I will go out and become a spirit of lies in the mouths of Ahab's prophets—they will all speak lies.' So the Lord said, 'Yes, that will fool Ahab. Go out and do that!'

²²"So that is what has happened here. The Lord made your prophets lie to you. The Lord himself decided to bring this disaster to you."

²³Then the prophet Zedekiah went to Micaiah and hit him on the face. Zedekiah said, "How is it that the Spirit of the Lord left me to speak through you?"

²⁴Micaiah answered, "Look, what I said will happen! And when you see it, you will go into the deepest part of your house to hide!"

²⁵Then King Ahab ordered one of his officers to arrest Micaiah. Ahab said, "Arrest him and take him to Amon the governor of the city and prince Joash. ²⁶Tell them to put Micaiah in prison. Give him nothing but bread and water to eat. Keep him there until I come home from the battle."

²⁷Micaiah said, "Listen to me, everyone! Ahab, if you come back alive from the battle, the Lord has not spoken through me."

The Battle at Ramoth Gilead

²⁸King Ahab of Israel and King Jehoshaphat of Judah went to fight the Arameans at Ramoth Gilead. ²⁹Ahab said to Jehoshaphat, "Disguise yourself when you go into battle, but wear your own clothes. And I will disguise myself." The king of Israel went into battle dressed like an ordinary soldier.

ᵃ**18:1** Jehoshaphat's son, Jehoram, married Athaliah, Ahab's daughter. See 2 Chron. 21:6.
ᵇ**18:10** *iron horns* These were a symbol of great strength.
ᶜ**18:20** *a spirit* Or "The Spirit."

³⁰The king of Aram had 32 chariot commanders. He gave them this command, "Don't go after anyone except the king of Israel, no matter how important they are!" ³¹During the battle, the commanders saw King Jehoshaphat and thought he was the king of Israel. So they went to kill him. Jehoshaphat started shouting, and the LORD helped him. God made the chariot commanders turn away from Jehoshaphat. ³²When the commanders saw that he was not King Ahab, they stopped chasing him.

³³Then a soldier pulled back on his bow and shot an arrow into the air. By chance it hit the king of Israel between two pieces of his armor. King Ahab said to his chariot driver, "I've been hit! Turn the chariot* around and take me off the battlefield!"

³⁴The armies continued fighting all that day. King Ahab leaned against the side of his chariot to hold himself up, facing the Arameans. He watched until evening. Then, just as the sun was setting, he died.

19 ¹King Jehoshaphat of Judah came back safely to his house in Jerusalem. ²Jehu the seer* went out to meet him. Jehu's father's name was Hanani. Jehu said to King Jehoshaphat, "Did you just help wicked people? Do you love those who hate the LORD? The LORD is angry with you now. ³Fortunately, you did some good things in your life. You did remove the Asherah poles* from this country, and you did decide to ask God for his advice."

Jehoshaphat Chooses Judges

⁴Jehoshaphat lived in Jerusalem, but he would go out among the people throughout Judah, from Beersheba to the hill country of Ephraim. He helped the people turn back to the LORD, the God their ancestors* worshiped. ⁵Jehoshaphat went from town to town and appointed judges in each of the fortresses* of Judah. ⁶He told the judges, "Be careful in what you are doing, because you are not judging for people, but for the LORD. The LORD will be with you when you make decisions. ⁷You must fear the LORD. Protect justice and do what is right because the LORD our God is fair. He does not treat some people as if they are more important than others, and he does not accept bribes to change his judgments."

⁸In Jerusalem, Jehoshaphat chose some of the Levites, priests, and heads of the families of Israel to be judges. These men lived in Jerusalem and used the law of the LORD to settle problems among the people. ⁹Jehoshaphat commanded them, "You must serve faithfully with all your heart. You must fear the LORD. ¹⁰People from cities around the country will bring their problems to you. You will listen to cases where people have broken a law or a command or maybe killed someone. In all these cases you must warn the people not to sin against the LORD. You must do this so that

the LORD will not become angry and punish you and the people.

¹¹"Amariah is the high priest, so he will make the final decision about the people's responsibilities to the LORD. Zebadiah son of Ishmael is the leader of the tribe of Judah, so he will make the final decision about the people's responsibilities to the king. The Levites will serve as scribes* for you. Be brave and do what is right! May the LORD be with those of you who are good judges."

Jehoshaphat Faces War

20 ¹Later, the Moabites, the Ammonites, and some Meunites*ᵃ* came to start a war with Jehoshaphat. ²Some men came and told Jehoshaphat, "There is a large army coming against you from Edom. They are coming from the other side of the Dead Sea. They are already in Hazazon Tamar!" (Hazazon Tamar is also called En Gedi.) ³Jehoshaphat became afraid, and he decided to ask the LORD what to do. He announced a time of fasting* for everyone in Judah. ⁴The people of Judah came together to ask the LORD for help. They came from out of all the towns of Judah to ask for the LORD's help. ⁵Jehoshaphat was in the new courtyard of the LORD's Temple.* He stood up in the meeting of the people from Judah and Jerusalem ⁶and said, "LORD God of our ancestors,* you are the God in heaven. You rule over all the kingdoms in all the nations. You have power and strength. No one can stand against you. ⁷You are our God! You forced the people living in this land to leave. You did this in front of your people Israel. You gave this land to the descendants of Abraham forever. Abraham was your friend. ⁸His descendants lived in this land, and built a Temple for your name. ⁹They said, 'If trouble comes to us— the sword, punishment, sicknesses, or famine—we will stand in front of this Temple and in front of you. Your name is on this Temple. We will shout to you when we are in trouble. Then you will hear and save us.'

¹⁰"But now, here are men from Ammon, Moab, and Mount Seir. You would not let the Israelites enter their lands when they came out of Egypt.ᵇ So the Israelites turned away and didn't destroy them. ¹¹But see the kind of reward those people give us for not destroying them. They have come to force us out of your land that you gave to us. ¹²Our God, punish those people. We don't have the strength to stop this large army that is coming against us. We don't know what to do! We are looking to you for help."ᶜ

ᵃ**20:1** *Meunites* In some copies of the ancient Greek version. The standard Hebrew text has "Ammonites."
ᵇ**20:10** *You would not let … Egypt* See Deut. 2:4–9, 19.
ᶜ**20:12** *We are … help* Literally, "But our eyes are on you!"

¹³All the men of Judah stood before the LORD with their wives, babies, and children. ¹⁴Then the Spirit of the LORD came on Jahaziel son of Zechariah. (Zechariah was the son of Benaiah, the son of Jeiel, the son of Mattaniah.) Jahaziel was a Levite from the family of Asaph. In the middle of the meeting, ¹⁵Jahaziel said, "Listen to me King Jehoshaphat and everyone living in Judah and Jerusalem! The LORD says this to you: 'Don't be afraid or worry about this large army, because the battle is not your battle. It is God's battle! ¹⁶Tomorrow, they will come up through the Ziz Pass. You must go down to them. You will find them at the end of the valley on the other side of Jeruel Desert. ¹⁷You will not have to fight this battle. Just stand there and watch the LORD save you. Judah and Jerusalem, don't be afraid. Don't worry, the LORD is with you. So go out to stand against those people tomorrow.'"

¹⁸Jehoshaphat bowed with his face to the ground. And all the people of Judah and Jerusalem bowed down before the LORD and worshiped him. ¹⁹The Levites from the Kohath family groups and the Korah family stood up to praise the LORD, the God of Israel. They sang very loudly.

²⁰Early the next morning, Jehoshaphat's army went out into Tekoa Desert. As they marched out, Jehoshaphat stood there saying, "Listen to me, men of Judah and Jerusalem. Have faith in the LORD your God, and you will stand strong! Have faith in the LORD's prophets, and you will succeed!"

²¹Jehoshaphat encouraged the men and gave them instructions. Then he had the temple singers stand up in their special clothes to praise the LORD. They marched in front of the army and sang praises. They sang the song, *Praise the LORD Because His Faithful Love Will Last Forever!*^a ²²As they began to sing and to praise God, the LORD set an ambush for the army from Ammon, Moab, and Mount Seir who had come to attack Judah. The enemy was defeated! ²³The Ammonites and the Moabites started to fight the men from Mount Seir. After they killed them, the Ammonites and Moabites turned on themselves and killed each other.

²⁴The men from Judah arrived at the lookout point in the desert. They looked for the enemy's large army, but all they saw were dead bodies lying on the ground. There were no survivors. ²⁵Jehoshaphat and his army came to take things from the bodies. They found many animals, riches, clothes, and other valuable things. It was more than Jehoshaphat and his men could carry away. There was so much that they spent three days taking everything from the dead bodies. ²⁶On the fourth day Jehoshaphat and his army met in the Valley of Beracah.^b They praised the

LORD. That is why people still call that place, "The Valley of Beracah."

²⁷All the men from Judah and Jerusalem were very happy as they marched back to Jerusalem with Jehoshaphat in the front. The LORD made them very happy when he defeated their enemy. ²⁸They entered Jerusalem with lyres,* harps, and trumpets and went to the Temple of the LORD.

²⁹People in all the surrounding kingdoms became afraid of God when they heard that the LORD fought against the enemies of Israel. ³⁰That is why there was peace for Jehoshaphat's kingdom—his God brought him rest from the enemies that were all around him.

Summary of Jehoshaphat's Rule

³¹Jehoshaphat ruled over the country of Judah. He was 35 years old when he became king, and he ruled 25 years in Jerusalem. His mother's name was Azubah, the daughter of Shilhi. ³²⁻³³Like his father Asa, Jehoshaphat was good and did everything that the LORD wanted, except he did not destroy the high places.* Also, the people did not turn back to the God that their ancestors* worshiped.

³⁴Everything else Jehoshaphat did, from beginning to end, is written in *The Official Records of Jehu Son of Hanoni.* It was copied and included in the book, *The History of the Kings of Israel.*

³⁵Later on, King Jehoshaphat of Judah made an agreement with King Ahaziah of Israel. Ahaziah was very evil. ³⁶Jehoshaphat joined with Ahaziah to make ships to go to the town of Tarshish.* They built some ships at Ezion Geber. ³⁷There was a man from the town of Mareshah named Eliezer son of Dodavahu. He spoke against Jehoshaphat and said, "Jehoshaphat, since you have joined with Ahaziah, the LORD will destroy what you have built." The ships were wrecked, so Jehoshaphat and Ahaziah were not able to send them to Tarshish.

21 ¹Then Jehoshaphat died and was buried with his ancestors in the City of David.* Then his son, Jehoram became the next king. ²Jehoram's brothers were Azariah, Jehiel, Zechariah, Azariah, Michael, and Shephatiah. They were the sons of King Jehoshaphat of Judah.^c ³Jehoshaphat gave his sons many gifts of silver, gold, and precious things. He also gave them strong fortresses* in Judah. But Jehoshaphat gave the kingdom to Jehoram because he was his oldest son.

Jehoram, King of Judah

⁴Jehoram took over his father's kingdom and made himself strong. Then he used a sword to kill all his brothers. He also killed some of the leaders of Israel. ⁵Jehoram was 32 years old when he began to rule. He

^a**20:21** *Praise ... Forever* See Ps. 118 and 136.
^b**20:26** *Beracah* This word means "blessing" or "praise."
^c**21:2** *Judah* Literally, "Israel."

ruled eight years in Jerusalem. ⁶He lived the same way the kings of Israel lived. He lived the same way Ahab's family lived. This was because Jehoram married Ahab's daughter. And Jehoram did evil in the LORD's sight. ⁷But the LORD would not destroy David's family because of the agreement he made with David. He had promised to keep a lamp burning for David and his children forever.ᵃ

⁸In Jehoram's time, Edom broke away from under Judah's authority. The people of Edom chose their own king. ⁹So Jehoram went to Edom with all his commanders and chariots.* The Edomite army surrounded Jehoram and his chariot commanders. But Jehoram fought his way out at night. ¹⁰Since that time and until now the country of Edom has been rebellious against Judah. The people from the town of Libnah also turned against Jehoram. This happened because Jehoram left the LORD God. He is the God Jehoram's ancestors* followed. ¹¹Jehoram also built high places* on the hills in Judah. He caused the people of Jerusalem to stop doing what God wanted. He led the people of Judah away from the LORD.

¹²Jehoram received this message from Elijah the prophet: "This is what the LORD, the God your father David followed, says, 'Jehoram, you have not lived the way your father Jehoshaphat lived. You have not lived the way King Asa of Judah lived. ¹³But you have lived the way the kings of Israel lived. You have caused the people of Judah and Jerusalem to stop doing what God wants. That is what Ahab and his family did. They were unfaithful to God. You have killed your brothers, and they were better than you. ¹⁴So now, the LORD will soon punish your people with much punishment. The LORD will punish your children, wives, and all your property. ¹⁵You will have a terrible sickness that will get worse and worse. The sickness will be in your intestines and eventually they will fall out.'"

¹⁶The LORD caused the Philistines and the Arabs living near the Ethiopians to be angry with Jehoram. ¹⁷They attacked Judah and carried away all the riches in the king's palace. They also took Jehoram's sons and wives. Only Jehoram's youngest son, Ahaziah,ᵇ was left.

¹⁸After this happened, the LORD made Jehoram sick with a disease in his intestines that could not be cured. ¹⁹His intestines fell out two years later because of his sickness. He died in very bad pain. The people did not make a large fire to honor Jehoram as they did for his father. ²⁰Jehoram was 32 years old when he became king. He ruled eight years in Jerusalem. No one was sad when he died. The people buried Jehoram in the City of David,* but not in the graves where the kings are buried.

Ahaziah, King of Judah

22 ¹The people of Jerusalem chose Ahaziah to be the new king in Jehoram's place. Ahaziah was Jehoram's youngest son. The people who came with the Arabs to attack Jehoram's camp killed all of Jehoram's older sons. So Ahaziah began to rule in Judah. ²Ahaziah was 22 years old when he began to rule.ᶜ He ruled one year in Jerusalem. His mother's name was Athaliah. Her father's name was Omri. ³Ahaziah also lived the way Ahab's family lived because his mother encouraged him to do wrong things. ⁴Ahaziah did evil in the LORD's sight. That is what Ahab's family did. Ahab's family gave advice to Ahaziah after Ahaziah's father died. They gave Ahaziah bad advice that led to his death. ⁵Ahaziah followed the advice Ahab's family gave him and went with King Joram to fight against King Hazael from Aram at the town of Ramoth Gilead. Joram's father's name was King Ahab of Israel. But the Arameans wounded Joram in the battle. ⁶He went back to the town of Jezreel to get well. He was wounded at Ramoth when he fought against King Hazael of Aram.

Then Ahaziahᵈ went to the town of Jezreel to visit Joram. Ahaziah's father's name was Jehoram, the king of Judah. Joram's father's name was Ahab. Joram was in the town of Jezreel because he was wounded.

⁷God caused Ahaziah's death when he went to visit Joram. Ahaziah arrived and went out with Joram to meet Jehu. Jehu's father's name was Nimshi. The LORD chose Jehu to destroy Ahab's family. ⁸Jehu was punishing Ahab's family. He found the leaders of Judah and Ahaziah's relatives who served Ahaziah. He killed the leaders of Judah and Ahaziah's relatives. ⁹Then Jehu looked for Ahaziah. Jehu's men caught him when he tried to hide in the town of Samaria. They brought him to Jehu. They killed Ahaziah and buried him. They said, "Ahaziah is the descendant of Jehoshaphat. Jehoshaphat followed the LORD with all his heart." Ahaziah's family had no power to hold the kingdom of Judah together.

Queen Athaliah

¹⁰Athaliah was Ahaziah's mother. When she saw that her son was dead, she killed all the king's children in Judah. ¹¹But Jehosheba took Ahaziah's son Joash and hid him. Jehosheba put Joash and his nurse in the inside bedroom. Jehosheba was King Jehoram's daughter. She was also Jehoiada's wife. Jehoiada was a priest, and Jehosheba was Ahaziah's sister.

ᵃ**21:7 He ... forever** Here, the writer means that one of David's descendants would always rule.
ᵇ**21:17 Ahaziah** Literally, "Jehoahaz."
ᶜ**22:2 He was ... rule** The standard Hebrew text has "42 years old." 2 Kings 8:26 says Ahaziah was 22 years old when he began to rule.
ᵈ**22:6 Ahaziah** Literally, "Azariah."

Athaliah did not kill Joash, because Jehosheba hid him. [12]Joash was hidden with the priests in God's Temple* for six years. During that time, Athaliah ruled over the land as queen.

Priest Jehoiada and King Joash

23 [1]After six years, Jehoiada showed his strength and made an agreement with the captains. These captains were Azariah son of Jeroham, Ishmael son of Jehohanan, Azariah son of Obed, Maaseiah son of Adaiah, and Elishaphat son of Zicri. [2]They went around in Judah and gathered the Levites from all the towns of Judah. They also gathered the leaders of the families of Israel. Then they went to Jerusalem. [3]All the people meeting together made an agreement with the king in God's Temple.*

Jehoiada said to the people, "The king's son will rule. That is what the LORD promised about David's descendants. [4]Now, this is what you must do: One-third of you priests and Levites who go on duty on the Sabbath* will guard the doors. [5]And one-third of you will be at the king's palace, and one-third of you will be at the Foundation Gate. But all the other people will stay in the yards of the LORD's Temple. [6]Don't let anyone come into the LORD's Temple. Only the priest and Levites who serve are permitted to come into the LORD's Temple because they are holy. But all the other men must do the job the LORD has given them. [7]The Levites must stay near the king. Every man must have his sword with him. If anyone tries to enter the Temple, kill that person. You must stay with the king everywhere he goes."

[8]The Levites and all the people of Judah obeyed all that Jehoiada the priest commanded. Jehoiada the priest did not excuse anyone from the groups of the priests. So each captain and all his men came in on the Sabbath with those who went out on the Sabbath. [9]Jehoiada the priest gave the spears and the large and small shields that belonged to King David to the officers. The weapons were kept in God's Temple. [10]Then Jehoiada told the men where to stand. Every man had his weapon in his hand. The men stood all the way from the right side of the Temple to the left side of the Temple. They stood near the altar* and the Temple, and near the king. [11]They brought out the king's son and put the crown on him. They gave him a copy of the agreement.[a] Then they made Joash king. Jehoiada and his sons anointed* Joash and said, "Long live the king!"

[12]Athaliah heard the noise of the people running to the Temple and praising the king. She came into the LORD's Temple to the people. [13]She looked and saw the king standing by his column at the front entrance. The officers and the men who blew trumpets were near the king. The people of the land were happy and blowing trumpets. The singers were playing on instruments of music. They led the people in singing praises. Then Athaliah tore her clothes[b] and said, "Treason! Treason!"[c]

[14]Jehoiada the priest brought out the army captains. He said to them, "Take Athaliah outside among the army. Use your swords to kill anyone who follows her." Then the priest warned the soldiers, "Don't kill Athaliah in the LORD's Temple." [15]Then those men grabbed Athaliah when she came to the entrance of the Horse Gate at the king's palace. Then they killed her there.

[16]Then Jehoiada made an agreement with all the people and the king. They all agreed that they all would be the LORD's people. [17]All the people went into the temple of the idol* Baal* and tore it down. They also broke the altars and idols that were in Baal's temple. They killed Mattan the priest of Baal in front of the altars of Baal. [18]Then Jehoiada chose the priests to be responsible for the LORD's Temple. The priests were Levites, and David had given them the job of being responsible for the LORD's Temple. They were to offer the burnt offerings* to the LORD the way the Law of Moses commanded. They offered the sacrifices* with much joy and singing the way David commanded. [19]Jehoiada put guards at the gates of the LORD's Temple to prevent any unclean person from entering the Temple.

[20]Jehoiada took the army captains, the leaders, the rulers of the people, and all the people of the land with him. Then Jehoiada took the king out of the LORD's Temple. They went through the Upper Gate to the king's palace and put the king on the throne. [21]All the people of Judah were very happy, and the city of Jerusalem had peace because Athaliah was killed with a sword.

Joash Rebuilds the Temple

24 [1]Joash was seven years old when he became king. He ruled 40 years in Jerusalem. His mother's name was Zibiah. Zibiah was from the town of Beersheba. [2]Joash did right in front of the LORD as long as Jehoiada the priest was living. [3]Jehoiada chose two wives for Joash. Joash had sons and daughters.

[4]Then later on, Joash decided to rebuild the LORD's Temple.* [5]Joash called the priests and the Levites together. He said to them, "Go out

---

[a]**23:11** *a copy of the agreement* Literally, "testimony." This could be a copy of the Law of Moses (see Deut. 17:18) or a special agreement between God and the king (see 1 Sam. 10:25; 2 Kings 11:17).

[b]**23:13** *tore her clothes* A way to show that she was very upset.

[c]**23:13** *Treason* Turning against the government. Here, Athaliah was blaming the people for turning against her government.

to the towns of Judah and gather the money all the Israelites pay every year. Use that money to rebuild your God's Temple. Hurry and do this." But the Levites didn't hurry.

⁶So King Joash called Jehoiada the leading priest. The king said, "Jehoiada, why haven't you made the Levites bring in the tax money from Judah and Jerusalem? Moses the LORD's servant and the Israelites used that tax money for the Tent of the Agreement.*"

⁷In the past, Athaliah's sons broke into God's Temple and used the holy things in the LORD's Temple for their worship of the Baal* gods. Athaliah was a very wicked woman.

⁸King Joash gave a command for a box to be made and put outside the gate at the LORD's Temple. ⁹Then the Levites made an announcement in Judah and Jerusalem. They told the people to bring in the tax money for the LORD. That tax money is what Moses the servant of God had required the Israelites to give while they were in the desert. ¹⁰All the leaders and the people were happy. They brought their money and put it in the box. They continued giving until the box was full. ¹¹Then the Levites would take the box to the king's officials. They saw that the box was full of money. The king's secretary and the leading priest's officer came and took the money out of the box. Then they took the box back to its place again. They did this often and gathered much money. ¹²Then King Joash and Jehoiada gave the money to the people who worked on the LORD's Temple. And the people who worked on the LORD's Temple hired skilled woodcarvers and carpenters to rebuild the LORD's Temple. They also hired workers who knew how to work with iron and bronze to rebuild the LORD's Temple.

¹³The men who supervised the work were very faithful. The work to rebuild the LORD's Temple was successful. They built God's Temple the way it was before and they made it stronger. ¹⁴When the workers finished, they brought the money that was left to King Joash and Jehoiada. They used that money to make things for the LORD's Temple. These things were used for the service in the Temple and for offering burnt offerings.* They also made bowls and other things from gold and silver. The priests offered burnt offerings in the LORD's Temple every day while Jehoiada was alive.

¹⁵Jehoiada became old. He had a very long life, and he died when he was 130 years old. ¹⁶The people buried Jehoiada in the City of David* where the kings are buried. The people buried Jehoiada there because in his life he did much good in Israel for God and for God's Temple.

¹⁷After Jehoiada died, the leaders of Judah came and bowed to King Joash. The king listened to the leaders. ¹⁸The king and these leaders rejected the Temple of the LORD God. Their ancestors* followed the LORD God.

They worshiped the Asherah poles* and other idols.* God was angry with the people of Judah and Jerusalem because the king and those leaders were guilty. ¹⁹God sent prophets to the people to bring them back to the LORD. The prophets warned them, but they refused to listen.

²⁰The Spirit of God filled Zechariah the son of Jehoiada the priest, and he stood in front of the people and said, "This is what God says: 'Why do you people refuse to obey the LORD's commands? You will not be successful. You have left the LORD. So he has also left you!'"

²¹But the people made plans against Zechariah. The king commanded the people to kill Zechariah, so they threw rocks at him until he was dead. They did this in the Temple courtyard. ²²Joash the king didn't remember Jehoiada's kindness to him. Jehoiada was Zechariah's father. But Joash killed Zechariah, Jehoiada's son. Before Zechariah died, he said, "May the LORD see what you are doing and punish you!"

²³At the end of the year, the Aramean army came against Joash. They attacked Judah and Jerusalem and killed all the leaders of people. They sent all the valuable things to the king of Damascus. ²⁴The Aramean army came with a small group of men, but the LORD let them defeat a very large army from Judah. The LORD did this because the people of Judah left the LORD God their ancestors followed. So Joash was punished. ²⁵When the Arameans left Joash, he was badly wounded. His own servants made plans against him. They did this because Joash killed Zechariah the son of Jehoiada the priest. The servants killed Joash on his own bed. After he died, the people buried him in the City of David, but not in the place where the kings are buried.

²⁶These are the servants who made plans against Joash: Zabad and Jehozabad. Zabad's mother's name was Shimeath. Shimeath was from Ammon. And Jehozabad's mother's name was Shimrith. Shimrith was from Moab. ²⁷The story about Joash's sons, the great prophecies against him, and how he rebuilt God's Temple are written in the book, *Commentary on the Kings*. Joash's son Amaziah became the new king after him.

Amaziah, King of Judah

25 ¹Amaziah was 25 years old when he became king. He ruled for 29 years in Jerusalem. His mother's name was Jehoaddin. Jehoaddin was from Jerusalem. ²Amaziah did what the LORD wanted him to do, but not with all his heart. ³He became a strong king and killed the officials who had killed his father the king. ⁴But Amaziah obeyed the law written in the *Book of Moses* and did not kill the official's children. The LORD commanded, "Parents must not be put to death for something their children did, and children must not be put to death for something their parents did. People should be put to death only for what they themselves did."[a]

5Amaziah gathered the people of Judah together. He grouped them by families and he put generals and captains in charge of these groups. The leaders were in charge of all the soldiers from Judah and Benjamin. All the men who were chosen to be soldiers were 20 years old and older. In all there were 300,000 skilled soldiers ready to fight with spears and shields. 6Amaziah also hired 100,000 soldiers from Israel. He paid 3¾ tons[b] of silver to hire these soldiers. 7But a man of God* came to Amaziah and said, "King, don't let the army of Israel go with you. The LORD is not with Israel or the people of Ephraim.* 8Maybe you will make yourself strong and ready for war, but God can help you win or help you lose." 9Amaziah said to the man of God, "But what about the money I already paid to the Israelite army?" The man of God answered, "The LORD has plenty. He can give you much more than that."

10So Amaziah sent the Israelite army back home to Ephraim. These men were very angry with the king and the people of Judah. They went back home very angry.

11Then Amaziah became very brave and led his army to the Salt Valley in the country of Edom. There his army killed 10,000 men from Seir.[c] 12They also captured 10,000 men from Seir and took them to the top of a cliff. Then the army of Judah threw them from the top of the cliff while they were still alive and their bodies were broken on the rocks below.

13Meanwhile, the Israelite army was attacking towns in Judah. They attacked the towns from Beth Horon all the way to Samaria. They killed 3000 people and took many valuable things. They were angry because Amaziah didn't let them join him in the war.

14Amaziah came home after he defeated the Edomites. He brought the idols* that the people of Seir worshiped. He started to worship those idols. He bowed down in front of them and burned incense* to them. 15The LORD was very angry with Amaziah, so he sent a prophet to him. The prophet said, "Amaziah, why have you worshiped the gods those people worship? Those gods could not even save their own people from you!"

16When the prophet spoke, Amaziah said to the prophet, "We never made you an advisor to the king. Be quiet! If you don't be quiet, you will be killed." The prophet became quiet, but then said, "God has decided to destroy you because you did this and didn't listen to my advice."

17King Amaziah of Judah talked with his advisors. Then he sent a message tò King Jehoash of Israel. Amaziah said to Jehoash,

"Let's meet face to face." Jehoash was Jehoahaz's son. Jehoahaz was Jehu's son.

18Then Jehoash sent his answer to Amaziah. Jehoash was the king of Israel and Amaziah was the king of Judah. Jehoash told this story: "A little thornbush of Lebanon sent a message to a big cedar tree of Lebanon. The little thornbush said, 'Let your daughter marry my son.' But a wild animal came and walked over the thornbush and destroyed it. 19You say to yourself, 'I have defeated Edom!' You are proud and you brag. But you should stay at home. There is no need for you to get into trouble. If you fight me, you and Judah will be destroyed."

20But Amaziah refused to listen. God made this happen. God planned to let Israel defeat Judah, because the people of Judah followed the gods the people of Edom followed. 21So King Jehoash of Israel met King Amaziah of Judah face to face at the town of Beth Shemesh in Judah. 22Israel defeated Judah. Every man of Judah ran away to his home. 23Jehoash captured Amaziah at Beth Shemesh and took him to Jerusalem. Amaziah's father's name was Joash. Joash's father's name was Jehoahaz. Jehoash tore down the wall of Jerusalem from the Ephraim Gate to the Corner Gate, a section about 600 feet[d] long. 24He took the gold and silver and all the other things in God's Temple* that Obed Edom was responsible for. Jehoash also took the treasures from the king's palace and some people as hostages. Then he went back to Samaria.

25Amaziah lived 15 years after Jehoash died. Amaziah's father was King Joash of Judah. 26Everything else Amaziah did, from beginning to end, is written in the book, *The History of the Kings of Judah and Israel.* 27When Amaziah stopped obeying the LORD, the people in Jerusalem made plans against Amaziah. He ran away to the town of Lachish. But the people sent men to Lachish and they killed Amaziah there. 28Then they carried his body on horses and buried him with his ancestors* in the City of Judah.

Uzziah, King of Judah

26 1Then the people of Judah chose Uzziah to be the new king in place of Amaziah. Amaziah was Uzziah's father. Uzziah was 16 years old when he became king. 2Uzziah rebuilt the town of Elath and gave it back to Judah. He did this after Amaziah died and was buried with his ancestors.*

3Uzziah was 16 years old when he became king. He ruled 52 years in Jerusalem. His mother's name was Jecoliah. Jecoliah was from Jerusalem. 4Uzziah did what the LORD wanted him to do. He obeyed God the same as his father Amaziah had done. 5Uzziah followed God in the time of Zechariah's life. Zechariah taught Uzziah how to respect and

---

[a]25:4 *Parents … did* See Deut. 24:16.
[b]25:6 *3 3/4 tons* Literally, "100 talents" (3450 kg).
[c]25:11 *Seir* Or "Edom," a country east of Judah.

[d]25:23 *600 feet* Literally, "400 cubits" (207.33 m).

obey God. When Uzziah was obeying the LORD, God gave him success.

6Uzziah fought a war against the Philistines. He tore down the walls around the towns of Gath, Jabneh, and Ashdod. Uzziah built towns near the town of Ashdod and in other places among the Philistines. 7God helped Uzziah fight the Philistines, the Arabs living in the town of Gur Baal, and the Meunites. 8The Ammonites paid tribute* to Uzziah. His name became famous all the way to the border of Egypt. He was famous because he was very powerful.

9Uzziah built towers in Jerusalem at the Corner Gate, at the Valley Gate, and at the place where the wall turned. He made them strong. 10He built towers in the desert. He also dug many wells. He had many cattle in the hill country and in the flat lands. He had farmers in the mountains and in the lands where growth was good. He also had men who took care of vineyards.* He loved farming.

11Uzziah had an army of trained soldiers. They were put in groups by Jeiel the secretary and Maaseiah the officer. Hananiah was their leader. Jeiel and Maaseiah counted the soldiers and put them into groups. Hananiah was one of the king's officers. 12There were 2600 leaders over the soldiers. 13These family leaders were in charge of an army of 307,500 men who fought with great power. These soldiers helped the king against the enemy. 14Uzziah gave the army shields, spears, helmets, armor,* bows, and stones for the slings.* 15In Jerusalem, Uzziah made machines that were invented by clever men. These machines were put on the towers and corner walls. They shot arrows and large rocks. Uzziah became famous. People knew his name in far away places. He had much help and became a powerful king.

16But when Uzziah became strong, his pride caused him to be destroyed. He was not faithful to the LORD his God. He went into the LORD's Temple* to burn incense* on the altar* for burning incense. 17Azariah the priest and 80 brave priests who served the LORD followed Uzziah into the Temple. 18They told Uzziah he was wrong and said to him, "Uzziah, it is not your job to burn incense to the LORD. It is not good for you to do this. The priests and Aaron's descendants are the ones who burn incense to the LORD. These priests were trained for holy service to burn incense. Go out of the Most Holy Place.* You have not been faithful. The LORD God will not honor you for this."

19But Uzziah was angry. He had a bowl in his hand for burning incense. While Uzziah was very angry with the priests, leprosy* broke out on his forehead. This happened in front of the priests in the LORD's Temple by the altar for burning incense. 20Azariah the leading priest and all the priests looked at Uzziah. They could see the leprosy on his forehead. The priests quickly forced him out from the Temple. Uzziah himself hurried out because the LORD had punished him. 21So Uzziah the king was a leper.* He could not enter the LORD's Temple. His son Jotham controlled the king's palace and became governor for the people.

22Everything else Uzziah did, from beginning to end, is written by the prophet Isaiah son of Amoz. 23Uzziah died and was buried near his ancestors in the field near the king's burial places. This was because the people said, "Uzziah has leprosy." And Uzziah's son Jotham became the new king in his place.

Jotham, King of Judah

27 1Jotham was 25 years old when he became king. He ruled 16 years in Jerusalem. His mother's name was Jerusha. Jerusha was Zadok's daughter. 2Jotham did what the LORD wanted him to do. He obeyed God just as his father Uzziah had done. But Jotham did not enter the LORD's Temple* to burn incense* as his father had. But the people continued doing wrong. 3Jotham rebuilt the Upper Gate of the LORD's Temple. He did much building on the wall at the place named Ophel. 4He also built towns in the hill country of Judah. He built fortresses* and towers in the forests. 5Jotham also fought against the king of the Ammonites and his army and defeated them. So each year for three years the Ammonites gave Jotham 3¾ tons*a* of silver, 62,000 bushels*b* of wheat, and 62,000 bushels of barley.

6Jotham became powerful because he faithfully obeyed the LORD his God. 7Everything else Jotham did and all his wars are written in the book, *The History of the Kings of Israel and Judah*. 8Jotham was 25 years old when he became king. He ruled 16 years in Jerusalem. 9Then Jotham died and was buried with his ancestors.* The people buried him in the City of David.* Jotham's son Ahaz became king in his place.

Ahaz, King of Judah

28 1Ahaz was 20 years old when he became king. He ruled 16 years in Jerusalem. He did not live right, as David his ancestor* had done. Ahaz did not do what the LORD wanted him to do. 2He followed the bad example of the kings of Israel. He used molds to make idols* to worship the Baal* gods. 3He burned incense* in the Valley of Ben Hinnom*c* and sacrificed* his own sons by burning them in the fire. He did the same terrible sins that

---

a27:5 3 3/4 tons Literally, "100 talents" (3450 kg).
b27:5 62,000 bushels Literally, "10,000 cors" (2,200,000 l).
c28:3 Valley of Ben Hinnom Later, called "Gehenna." This valley was west and south of Jerusalem. Many babies and young children were sacrificed to false gods in this valley.

the peoples living in that land did. The Lord had forced them out when the Israelites entered that land. ⁴Ahaz offered sacrifices and burned incense in the high places,* on the hills, and under every green tree.

⁵⁻⁶Ahaz sinned, so the Lord his God let the king of Aram defeat him. The king of Aram and his army defeated Ahaz and made many people of Judah prisoners. The king of Aram took the prisoners to the city of Damascus. The Lord also let King Pekah of Israel defeat Ahaz. Pekah's father's name was Remaliah. Pekah and his army killed 120,000 brave soldiers from Judah in one day. He defeated the men from Judah because they stopped obeying the Lord, the God their ancestors obeyed. ⁷Zicri was a brave soldier from Ephraim.* He killed the king's son Maaseiah. He also killed Azrikam, the officer in charge of the king's palace, and Elkanah, who was second in command to the king.

⁸The Israelite army captured 200,000 of their own relatives living in Judah. They took women, children, and many valuable things from Judah and carried them back to Samaria. ⁹But one of the Lord's prophets named Oded was there. Oded met the Israelite army that came back to Samaria. He said to the Israelite army, "The Lord, the God your ancestors worshiped, let you defeat the people of Judah because he was angry with them. But now he is angry with you, because he has seen how cruel you were in killing them. ¹⁰And now you plan to keep the people of Judah and Jerusalem as slaves. But you are as guilty as they are for sinning against the Lord your God. ¹¹Now listen to me. Send back all those you captured, your own brothers and sisters, because the Lord's terrible anger is against you."

¹²Then some of the leaders in Ephraim saw the Israelite soldiers coming home from war. They met the Israelite soldiers and warned them. The leaders were Azariah son of Jehohanan, Berekiah son of Meshillemoth, Jehizkiah son of Shallum, and Amasa son of Hadlai. ¹³They said to the Israelite soldiers, "Don't bring the prisoners from Judah here. If you do that, it will make us sin worse against the Lord. That will make our sin and guilt worse and the Lord will be very angry with Israel!"

¹⁴So the soldiers gave the prisoners and valuable things to the leaders and to the people. ¹⁵The leaders (Azariah, Berekiah, Jehizkiah, and Amasa) stood up and helped the prisoners. These four men got the clothes that the Israelite army took and gave them to the people who were naked. The leaders also gave them sandals. They gave the prisoners from Judah something to eat and drink. They rubbed oil on them to soften and heal their wounds. Then the leaders from Ephraim put the weak prisoners on donkeys and took them back home to their families in Jericho, the city of palm trees. Then the four leaders went back home to Samaria.

¹⁶⁻¹⁷At that same time, the people from Edom came again and defeated the people of Judah. The Edomites captured people and took them away as prisoners. So King Ahaz asked the king of Assyria to help him. ¹⁸The Philistines also attacked the towns in the hills and in south Judah. The Philistines captured the towns of Beth Shemesh, Aijalon, Gederoth, Soco, Timnah, and Gimzo. They also captured the villages near these towns. Then the Philistines lived in them. ¹⁹The Lord gave troubles to Judah because King Ahaz of Judah encouraged the people of Judah to sin. He was very unfaithful to the Lord. ²⁰King Tiglath Pileser of Assyria came and gave Ahaz trouble instead of helping him. ²¹Ahaz took some valuable things from the Lord's Temple* and from the king's palace and from the prince's house. Ahaz gave them to the king of Assyria, but that didn't help him.

²²In Ahaz's troubles, he sinned worse and became more unfaithful to the Lord. ²³He offered sacrifices to the gods the people of Damascus worshiped. The people of Damascus had defeated Ahaz. So he thought to himself, "The gods the people of Aram worship helped them. So if I offer sacrifices to them, maybe they will help me also." Ahaz worshiped these gods. In this way he sinned, and he made the people of Israel sin.

²⁴Ahaz gathered the things from God's Temple and broke them to pieces. Then he closed the doors of the Lord's Temple. He made altars* and put them on every street corner in Jerusalem. ²⁵In every town in Judah Ahaz made high places for burning incense to worship other gods. Ahaz made the Lord, the God his ancestors obeyed, very angry.

²⁶Everything else Ahaz did, from the beginning to the end, is written in the book, *The History of the Kings of Judah and Israel.* ²⁷Ahaz died and was buried with his ancestors. The people buried him in the city of Jerusalem. But they didn't bury him in the same burial place where the kings of Israel were buried. Ahaz's son Hezekiah became the new king in his place.

Hezekiah, King of Judah

29 ¹Hezekiah became king when he was 25 years old. He ruled 29 years in Jerusalem. His mother's name was Abijah. Abijah was Zechariah's daughter. ²Hezekiah did what the Lord wanted him to do. He did what was right just as David his ancestor* had done.

³Hezekiah repaired the doors of the Lord's Temple* and made them strong. He opened the Temple again. He did this in the first month of the first year after he became king. ⁴⁻⁵Hezekiah called the priests and Levites together in one assembly. He had a meeting with them in the courtyard on the east side of the Temple. Hezekiah said to them, "Listen to me, Levites! Make yourselves ready for

holy service. Make the Temple of the LORD God ready for holy service. He is the God your ancestors obeyed. Take away the things from the Temple that don't belong in there. These things make the Temple unclean.* ⁶Our ancestors left the LORD and turned their faces away from the LORD's house.ᵃ ⁷They shut the doors of the porch of the Temple and let the fire go out in the lamps. They stopped burning incense* and offering burnt offerings* in the Holy Place* to the God of Israel. ⁸So the LORD became very angry with the people of Judah and Jerusalem. The LORD punished them. Other peoples became afraid and were shocked when they saw what the LORD did to the people of Judah and Jerusalem. They shook their heads with hate and shame for the people of Judah. You know this is true. You can see with your own eyes. ⁹That is why our ancestors were killed in battle. Our sons, daughters, and wives were made prisoners. ¹⁰So now I, Hezekiah, have decided to make an agreement with the LORD, the God of Israel. Then he will not be angry with us anymore. ¹¹So my sons,ᵇ don't be lazy or waste any more time. The LORD chose you to serve him ₍in the Temple₎ and to burn incense."

¹²⁻¹⁴This is a list of the Levites who started to work: From the Kohath family there were Mahath son of Amasai and Joel son of Azariah. From the Merari family there were Kish son of Abdi and Azariah son of Jehallelel. From the Gershon family there were Joah son of Zimmah and Eden son of Joab. From Elizaphan's descendants there were Shimri and Jeiel. From Asaph's descendants there were Zechariah and Mattaniah. From Heman's descendants there were Jehiel and Shimei. From Jeduthun's descendants there were Shemaiah and Uzziel. ¹⁵Then these Levites gathered their brothers together and made themselves ready for holy service in the Temple. They obeyed the king's command that came from the LORD. They went into the LORD's Temple to clean it. ¹⁶The priests went into the inside part of the LORD's Temple to clean it. They took out all the unclean things they found there. They brought the unclean things out to the courtyard of the LORD's Temple. Then the Levites took these things out to the Kidron Valley. ¹⁷On the first day of the first month, the Levites began to make themselves ready for holy service. On the eighth day of the month, the Levites came to the porch of the LORD's Temple. For eight more days they cleaned the LORD's Temple to make it ready for holy use. They finished on the 16th day of the first month.

¹⁸Then they went to King Hezekiah and said to him, "King Hezekiah, we cleaned all the LORD's Temple and the altar* for burning offerings and all the things in the Temple. We cleaned the table for the rows of bread with all the things used for that table. ¹⁹During the time that Ahaz was king, he rebelled against God. He threw away many of the things that were in the Temple. But we repaired all those things and made them ready for their special use. They are now in front of the LORD's altar."

²⁰King Hezekiah gathered the city officials and went up to the Temple of the LORD early the next morning. ²¹They brought seven bulls, seven rams, seven lambs, and seven young male goats. These animals were for a sin offering* for the kingdom of Judah, for the Holy Place to make it clean, and for the people of Judah. King Hezekiah commanded the priests who were descendants of Aaron to offer these animals on the LORD's altar. ²²So the priests killed the bulls and kept the blood. Then they sprinkled the bulls' blood on the altar. Then they killed the rams and sprinkled the rams' blood on the altar. Then they killed the lambs and sprinkled the lambs' blood on the altar. ²³⁻²⁴Then the priests brought the male goats in front of the king, and the people gathered together. The goats were the sin offering. The priests put their hands on the goats and killed the goats. They made a sin offering with the goats' blood on the altar. They did this so that God would forgive the sins of the Israelites. The king said that the burnt offering and the sin offering should be made for all the Israelites.

²⁵King Hezekiah put the Levites in the LORD's Temple with cymbals,* harps, and lyres* as David, Gad, the king's seer,* and the prophet Nathan had commanded. This command came from the LORD through his prophets. ²⁶So the Levites stood ready with David's instruments of music, and the priests stood ready with their trumpets. ²⁷Then Hezekiah gave the order to sacrifice* the burnt offering on the altar. When the burnt offering began, singing to the LORD also began. The trumpets were blown, and the instruments of David king of Israel were played. ²⁸All the assembly bowed down, the musicians sang, and the trumpet players blew their trumpets until the burnt offering was finished.

²⁹After the sacrifices were finished, King Hezekiah and all the people with him bowed down and worshiped. ³⁰King Hezekiah and his officials ordered the Levites to give praise to the LORD. They sang songs that David and Asaph the seer had written. They praised God and became happy. They all bowed and worshiped God. ³¹Hezekiah said, "Now you people of Judah have given yourselves to the LORD. Come near and bring sacrifices and thank offerings to the LORD's Temple." Then the people brought sacrifices and thank offerings. Anyone who wanted to, also brought burnt offerings. ³²This is how many

ᵃ29:6 LORD's house Another name for the Temple in Jerusalem.

ᵇ29:11 my sons Here, Hezekiah is speaking to the priests like a father to his sons. They are not really his children.

burnt offerings the assembly brought to the Temple: 70 bulls, 100 rams, and 200 lambs. All these animals were sacrificed. 33The holy offerings for the LORD were 600 bulls and 3000 sheep and goats. 34But there were not enough priests to skin and cut up all the animals for the burnt offerings. So their relatives, the Levites, helped them until the work was finished and until other priests could make themselves ready for holy service. The Levites were more serious about making themselves ready to serve the LORD. They were more serious than the priests. 35There were many burnt offerings, and the fat of fellowship offerings,* and drink offerings. So the service in the LORD's Temple began again. 36Hezekiah and the people were very happy about the things God prepared for his people. And they were happy he did it so quickly!

Hezekiah Celebrates the Passover

30 1King Hezekiah sent messages to all the people of Israel and Judah. He wrote letters to the people of Ephraim and Manasseh*a* also. He invited all these people to come to the LORD's Temple* in Jerusalem so that they all could celebrate the Passover* for the LORD, the God of Israel. 2King Hezekiah agreed with all his officials and all the assembly in Jerusalem to have the Passover in the second month. 3They could not celebrate the Passover Festival at the regular time, because not enough priests had made themselves ready for holy service and the people had not gathered in Jerusalem. 4The agreement satisfied King Hezekiah and all the assembly. 5So they sent the announcement throughout Israel, from the town of Beersheba all the way to the town of Dan. They told the people to come to Jerusalem to celebrate the Passover for the LORD, the God of Israel. Not many people had been celebrating it as it was described in the law. 6So the messengers took the king's letters all through Israel and Judah. This is what the letters said:

"Children of Israel, turn back to the LORD, the God who Abraham, Isaac, and Israel* obeyed. Then God will come back to you who are still alive and have escaped from the kings of Assyria. 7Don't be like your fathers or your brothers. The LORD was their God, but they turned against him. So the LORD made people hate them and speak evil about them. You can see with your own eyes that this is true. 8Don't be stubborn as your ancestors* were. But obey the LORD with a willing heart. Come to the Temple. The LORD has made the Temple to be

holy forever. Serve the LORD your God. Then the LORD's fearful anger will turn away from you. 9If you come back and obey the LORD, your relatives and your children will find mercy from the people who captured them. And your relatives and your children will come back to this land. The LORD your God is kind and merciful. He will not turn away from you if you come back to him."

10The messengers went to every town in the area of Ephraim and Manasseh. They went all the way to the area of Zebulun, but the people laughed at the messengers and made fun of them. 11But, some men from the areas of Asher, Manasseh, and Zebulun humbled themselves and went to Jerusalem. 12Also, in Judah God's power united the people so that they would obey the king and his officials concerning the word of the LORD.

13Many people came together in Jerusalem to celebrate the Festival of Unleavened Bread* in the second month. It was a very large crowd. 14The people took away the altars in Jerusalem that were for false gods and all the incense altars that were for false gods. They threw them into the Kidron Valley. 15Then they killed the Passover lamb on the 14th day of the second month. The priests and the Levites felt ashamed. They made themselves ready for holy service. The priests and the Levites brought burnt offerings* into the LORD's Temple. 16They took their regular places in the Temple as described in the Law of Moses, the man of God.* The Levites gave the blood to the priests. Then the priests sprinkled the blood on the altar.* 17There were many people in the group who had not made themselves ready for holy service, so they were not permitted to kill the Passover lambs. That is why the Levites were responsible for killing the Passover lambs for everyone who was not clean. The Levites made each lamb holy for the LORD.

18-19Many people from Ephraim, Manasseh, Issachar, and Zebulun had not prepared themselves in the right way for the Passover Festival. They did not celebrate the Passover the right way, as the Law of Moses says. But Hezekiah prayed for the people. So he said this prayer, "LORD God, you are good. These people sincerely wanted to worship you in the right way, but they did not make themselves clean as the law says. Please forgive these people. You are the God who our ancestors obeyed. Forgive, even if someone did not make himself clean as the rules of the Most Holy Place say." 20The LORD listened to King Hezekiah's prayer and forgave the people. 21The children of Israel at Jerusalem celebrated the Festival of Unleavened Bread for seven days. They were very happy. The Levites and the priests gave praise to the LORD every day with all their strength. 22King Hezekiah encouraged all the Levites who understood very well how to do the service of the Lord. The people celebrated the festival for seven days and offered fellowship offerings.* They gave thanks and praise to the Lord, the God of their ancestors.

23All the people agreed to stay seven more days. They were joyful as they celebrated the Passover for seven more days. 24King Hezekiah of Judah gave 1000 bulls and 7000 sheep to the assembly to kill and eat. The leaders gave 1000 bulls and 10,000 sheep to the assembly. Many priests prepared themselves for holy service. 25All the assembly of Judah, the priests, the Levites, all the assembly who came from Israel, and the travelers who came from Israel and moved to Judah—all these people were very happy. 26So there was much joy in Jerusalem. There had not been a celebration like this since the time of Solomon son of King David of Israel. 27The priests and the Levites stood up and asked the Lord to bless the people. God heard them. Their prayer came up to the Lord's holy home in heaven.

King Hezekiah Makes Improvements

31 1When the Passover* celebration was finished, the Israelites who were in Jerusalem for Passover went out to the towns of Judah. Then they smashed the stone idols* that were in the towns. These stone idols were used to worship false gods. They also cut down the Asherah poles.* And they destroyed the high places* and the altars all through the areas of Judah and Benjamin. They did the same things in the area of Ephraim and Manasseh. They did these things until they destroyed all the things used for worshiping the false gods. Then all the Israelites went back home to their own towns.

2The priests and Levites had been divided into groups, and each group had its own special job to do. So King Hezekiah told these groups to begin doing their jobs again. So the priests and Levites again had the job of offering the burnt offerings* and the fellowship offerings.* And they had the job of serving in the Temple* and singing and praising God by the doors to the Lord's house.ᵃ 3Hezekiah gave some of his own animals to be offered as the burnt offerings. These animals were used for the daily burnt offerings that were given each morning and each evening. They were offered on the Sabbath* days, during New Moon* celebrations, and on the other special meeting days, as law of the Lord commands.

4The people were supposed to give a part of their crops and things to the priests and Levites. So Hezekiah commanded the people living in Jerusalem to give them their share. In that way the priests and Levites could spend all of their time doing what the law told

them to do. 5People all around the country heard about this command. So the Israelites gave the first part of their harvest of grain, grapes, oil, honey, and all the things they grew in their fields. They brought one-tenth of all these many things. 6The men of Israel and Judah living in the towns of Judah also brought one-tenth of their cattle and sheep. They also brought one-tenth of the things that were put in a special place that was only for the Lord. They brought all these things to the Lord their God, and they put them in piles.

7The people began to bring these things in the third month and they finished bringing the collection in the seventh month. 8When Hezekiah and the leaders came, they saw the piles of things that were collected. They praised the Lord and his people, the Israelites.

9Then Hezekiah asked the priests and the Levites about the piles of things. 10Azariah the high priest from Zadok's family said to Hezekiah, "From the time that the people started bringing the offerings into the Lord's house, we have had plenty to eat. We have eaten until we are full and there is still plenty left over! The Lord has really blessed his people. That is why we have so much left over."

11Then Hezekiah commanded the priests to make storerooms ready in the Lord's Temple. So this was done. 12Then the priests brought the offerings, tithes,ᵇ and other things that were to be given only to the Lord. All these things collected were put in the storerooms in the Temple. Conaniah the Levite was in charge of everything that was collected. Shimei was second in charge of these things. Shimei was Conaniah's brother. 13Conaniah and his brother Shimei were supervisors of these men: Jehiel, Azaziah, Nahath, Asahel, Jerimoth, Jozabad, Eliel, Ismakiah, Mahath, and Benaiah. King Hezekiah and Azariah the official in charge of God's Temple chose these men.

14Kore was in charge of the offerings that the people freely gave to God. He was responsible for giving out the collections that were given to the Lord. And he was responsible for giving out the gifts that were made holy for the Lord. Kore was the gatekeeper at the East Gate. His father's name was Imnah the Levite. 15Eden, Miniamin, Jeshua, Shemaiah, Amariah, and Shecaniah helped Kore. These men served faithfully in the towns where the priests were living. They gave the collection of things to their relatives in each group of priests. They gave the same things to the more important people and to the less important.

16These men also gave the collection of things to the males three years old and older who had their names in the Levite family histories. All these males were to enter the

---

ᵃ31:2 Lord's house Or "Lord's Camp," that is, the courtyard of the Temple in Jerusalem.

ᵇ31:12 tithes One-tenth of a person's crops or animals.

LORD's Temple for daily service to do the things they were responsible to do. Each group of Levites had their own responsibility. [17]The priests were given their part of the collection. This was done by families, in the way they were listed in the family histories. The Levites who were 20 years old and older were given their part of the collection, according to their groups and responsibilities. [18]The Levites' babies, wives, sons, and daughters also got part of the collection. This was done for all the Levites who were listed in the family histories. This was because the Levites were faithful to always keep themselves holy and ready for service.

[19]Some of Aaron's descendants, the priests, lived in the towns or on farms near the towns where the Levites were living. Men were chosen by name in each of these towns to give part of the collection to these descendants of Aaron. All the males and those named in the family histories of the Levites got part of the collection.

[20]So King Hezekiah did those good things in all Judah. He did what was good and right and faithful before the LORD his God. [21]He had success in every work he began—the service of God's Temple and in obeying the law and commands, and in following his God. Hezekiah did all these things with all his heart.

The King of Assyria Troubles Hezekiah

32 [1]After all these things that Hezekiah had faithfully done happened, King Sennacherib of Assyria came to attack the country of Judah. Sennacherib and his army camped outside the fortresses.* He did this so that he could make plans to defeat these towns. Sennacherib wanted to win them for himself. [2]Hezekiah knew that Sennacherib came to Jerusalem to attack it. [3]Then Hezekiah talked to his officials and army officers. They all agreed to stop the waters of the water springs outside the city. The officials and army officers helped Hezekiah. [4]Many people came together and stopped all the springs and the stream that flowed through the middle of the country. They said, "The king of Assyria will not find much water when he comes here!" [5]Hezekiah made Jerusalem stronger. This is how he did it: He rebuilt all the parts of the wall that were broken down. He also built towers on the wall. He also built another wall outside the first wall. He rebuilt the strong places on the east side of the old part of Jerusalem. He made many weapons and shields. [6-7]Hezekiah chose officers of war to be in charge of the people. He met with these officers at the open place near the city gate. He talked to the officers and encouraged them. He said, "Be strong and brave. Don't be afraid or worry about the king of Assyria or the large army with him. There is a greater power with us than the king of Assyria has with him! [8]The king of Assyria only has men. But we have the

LORD our God with us! Our God will help us. He will fight our battles!" So King Hezekiah of Judah encouraged the people and made them feel stronger.

[9]King Sennacherib of Assyria and all his army were camped near the town of Lachish so that they could defeat it. Then Sennacherib sent his officers to King Hezekiah of Judah and to all the people of Judah in Jerusalem. His officers had a message for Hezekiah and all the people in Jerusalem. [10]They said, "King Sennacherib of Assyria says this: 'What do you trust in that makes you stay under attack in Jerusalem? [11]Hezekiah is fooling you. You are being tricked into staying in Jerusalem so that you will die from hunger and thirst. Hezekiah says to you, "The LORD our God will save us from the king of Assyria." [12]Hezekiah himself took away the LORD's high places* and altars.* He told you people of Judah and Jerusalem that you must worship and burn incense* on only one altar. [13]Of course, you know what my ancestors* and I have done to all the peoples in other countries. The gods of the other countries could not save their people. Those gods could not stop me from destroying their people. [14]My ancestors destroyed those countries. There is no god that can stop me from destroying his people. So you think your god can save you from me? [15]Don't let Hezekiah fool you or trick you. Don't believe him because no god of any nation or kingdom has ever been able to keep his people safe from me or my ancestors. Don't think your god can stop me from destroying you.'"

[16]The officers of the king of Assyria said worse things against the LORD God and against Hezekiah, God's servant. [17]The king of Assyria also wrote letters that insulted the LORD, the God of Israel. This is what the king of Assyria said in those letters: "The gods of the other nations could not stop me from destroying their people. In the same way Hezekiah's god will not be able to stop me from destroying his people." [18]Then the Assyrian officers shouted loudly to the people of Jerusalem who were on the city wall. They spoke in the language of Judah so that the people on the wall could understand and be frightened enough that the Assyrians could capture the city of Jerusalem. [19]Then they insulted the God of Jerusalem just as they had insulted all the gods of the people from other nations—even though those gods are only things people made with their hands.

[20]Hezekiah the king and the prophet Isaiah son of Amoz prayed about this problem. They prayed very loudly to heaven. [21]Then the LORD sent an angel to the king of Assyria's camp. That angel killed all the soldiers, leaders, and officers in the Assyrian army. So the king of Assyria went back home to his own country, and his people were ashamed of him. He went into the temple of his god and some of his own sons killed him there with a

sword. ²²So the LORD saved Hezekiah and the people in Jerusalem from King Sennacherib of Assyria and from all other people. The LORD cared for Hezekiah and the people of Jerusalem. ²³Many people brought gifts for the LORD to Jerusalem. They brought valuable things to King Hezekiah of Judah. From that time on, all the nations respected Hezekiah.

²⁴It was in those days that Hezekiah became very sick and near death. He prayed to the LORD, and he spoke to Hezekiah and gave him a sign.ª ²⁵But Hezekiah's heart was proud, so he did not give God thanks for his kindness. This is why God was angry with Hezekiah and with the people of Judah and Jerusalem. ²⁶But Hezekiah and the people living in Jerusalem changed their hearts and lives. They became humble and stopped being proud. So the LORD's anger didn't come on them while Hezekiah was alive.

²⁷Hezekiah had many riches and much honor. He made places to keep silver, gold, valuable jewels, spices, shields, and all kinds of things. ²⁸Hezekiah had storage buildings for the grain, new wine, and oil that people sent to him. He had stalls for all the cattle and stalls for the sheep. ²⁹Hezekiah also built many towns, and he got many flocks of sheep and cattle. God gave him much wealth. ³⁰It was Hezekiah who stopped up the upper source of the waters of the Gihon Spring in Jerusalem and made the waters flow straight down on the west side of the City of David.* And he was successful in everything he did.

³¹One time the leaders of Babylon sent messengers to Hezekiah. The messengers asked about a strange sign that had happened in the nations.ᵇ When they came, God left Hezekiah alone to test him and to know everything that was in Hezekiah's heart.ᶜ

³²Everything else Hezekiah did and how he loved the LORD are written in the book, *The Vision of the Prophet Isaiah Son of Amoz* and in the book, *The History of the Kings of Judah and Israel*. ³³Hezekiah died and was buried with his ancestors. The people buried him on the hill where the graves of David's ancestors are. All the people of Judah and those living in Jerusalem gave honor to Hezekiah when he died. Hezekiah's son Manasseh became the new king in his place.

Manasseh, King of Judah

33 ¹Manasseh was twelve years old when he became king of Judah. He was king for 55 years in Jerusalem. ²Manasseh did what the LORD said was wrong. He followed the terrible and sinful ways of the nations that the LORD had forced out of the land before the Israelites. ³Manasseh rebuilt the high places* that his father Hezekiah had broken down. Manasseh built altars for the Baal* gods and made Asherah poles.* He bowed down to the constellationsᵈ and worshiped those groups of stars. ⁴Manasseh built altars for false gods in the LORD's Temple.* The LORD said about the Temple, "My name will be in Jerusalem forever." ⁵He built altars for all the groups of stars in the two yards of the LORD's Temple. ⁶He also burned his own children for a sacrifice* in the Valley of Ben Hinnom.ᵉ He also used magic by doing soothsaying, divination, and sorcery.ᶠ He talked with mediums* and wizards.* He did many things that the LORD said were wrong, and this made the LORD angry. ⁷Manasseh also made a statue of an idol* and put it in God's Temple—the very same Temple that God had talked about to David and his son Solomon. God had said, "I will put my name in this house and in Jerusalem—the city that I chose from all the cities in all the tribes—and my name will be there forever! ⁸I will not continue to keep the Israelites off the land that I chose to give to their ancestors.* But they must obey everything I commanded them. The Israelites must obey all the laws, rules, and commands that I gave Moses to give to them."

⁹Manasseh encouraged the people of Judah and the people living in Jerusalem to do wrong. They were worse than the nations that were in the land before the Israelites—and the LORD destroyed those people.

¹⁰The LORD spoke to Manasseh and to his people, but they refused to listen. ¹¹So the LORD brought commanders from the king of Assyria's army to attack Judah. These commanders captured Manasseh and made him their prisoner. They put hooks in him and brass chains on his hands and took him to the country of Babylon.

¹²When these troubles came to him, Manasseh begged for help from the LORD his God. He humbled himself before the God of his ancestors. ¹³Manasseh prayed to God and begged him for help. God heard his begging and felt sorry for him, so he let Manasseh return to Jerusalem and to his throne. Then Manasseh knew that the LORD was the true God.

¹⁴After that happened, Manasseh built an outer wall for the City of David.* This wall went to the west of Gihon Spring in Kidron

---

ª**32:24** *The LORD spoke … sign* See Isa. 38:1–8 for the story about Hezekiah and how the LORD gave him 15 more years to live.

ᵇ**32:31** *a strange sign … nations* See Isa. 38:1–8.

ᶜ**32:31** *in Hezekiah's heart* See 2 Kings 20:12–19.

ᵈ**33:3** *constellations* Groups of stars. These are probably the twelve "signs of the Zodiac." Some people thought the stars, not God, controlled their life.

ᵉ**33:6** *Valley of Ben Hinnom* Later, called "Gehenna." This valley was west and south of Jerusalem. Many babies and young children were sacrificed to false gods in this valley.

ᶠ**33:6** *soothsaying, divination, and sorcery* Different ways people try to do magic or tell what will happen in the future.

Valley, to the entrance of the Fish Gate, and around the hill of Ophel.ᵃ He made the wall very tall. Then he put officers in all the fortresses* in Judah. ¹⁵Manasseh took away the strange idol gods, and he took the idol out of the Lord's Temple. He took away all the altars he had built on the Temple hill, and in Jerusalem. Manasseh threw all the altars out of the city of Jerusalem. ¹⁶Then he set up the Lord's altar* and offered fellowship offerings* and thank offerings on it. He gave a command for all the people of Judah to serve the Lord, the God of Israel. ¹⁷The people continued to offer sacrifices at the high places, but their sacrifices were only to the Lord their God.

¹⁸Everything else Manasseh did, his prayer to his God and the words of the seers* who spoke to him in the name of the Lord, the God of Israel, are all written in the book, *The Official Records of the Kings of Israel*. ¹⁹Manasseh's prayer and how God listened and felt sorry for him are written in *The Book of the Seers*. Also all his sins, the wrongs he did before he humbled himself, and the places where he built high places and set up the Asherah poles are written in *The Book of the Seers*. ²⁰So Manasseh died and was buried with his ancestors. The people buried Manasseh in his own palace. Manasseh's son Amon became the new king in his place.

Amon, King of Judah

²¹Amon was 22 years old when he became king of Judah. He was king for two years in Jerusalem. ²²Amon did evil before the Lord, just as his father Manasseh had done. Amon offered sacrifices* for all the carved idols* and statues that Manasseh his father made. Amon worshiped those idols. ²³Amon did not humble himself in front of the Lord like Manasseh his father humbled himself. But Amon sinned more and more. ²⁴His servants made plans against him. They killed Amon in his own house. ²⁵But the people of Judah killed all the servants who planned against King Amon. Then the people chose Amon's son Josiah to be the new king.

Josiah, King of Judah

34 ¹Josiah was eight years old when he became king. He was king for 31 years in Jerusalem. ²He lived in a way that pleased the Lord, always doing what was right, as his ancestor* David had done. Josiah never changed this way of life. ³When Josiah was in his eighth year as king, he began to follow the God that David his ancestor followed. He was still young when he began to obey God. When he was in his twelfth year as king he began to destroy the high places,* the Asherah poles,* and idols* that were carved and idols that were made from molds from Judah

and Jerusalem. ⁴As Josiah watched, the people broke down the altars for the Baal gods. Then he cut down the incense* altars that stood high above the people. He broke the idols that were carved and the idols that were made from molds. He beat the idols into powder and sprinkled the powder on the graves of the people who had offered sacrifices* to the Baal gods. ⁵Josiah even burned the bones of the priests who had served the Baal gods on their own altars. This is how he destroyed idols and idol worship from Judah and Jerusalem. ⁶Josiah did the same for the towns in the areas of Manasseh, Ephraim, Simeon, and all the way to Naphtali. He did the same for the ruins near all these towns.ᵇ ⁷Josiah broke down the altars and the Asherah poles. He beat the idols into powder. He cut down all the incense altars used for Baal worship in all the country of Israel. Then he went back to Jerusalem.

⁸When Josiah was in his 18th year as king of Judah, he sent Shaphan, Maaseiah, and Joah to rebuild and repair the Temple* of the Lord his God. Shaphan's father's name was Azaliah. Maaseiah was the city leader, and Joah's father's name was Joahaz. Joah was the man who wrote about what happened.

So Josiah commanded the Temple to be repaired so that he could make Judah and the Temple clean. ⁹These men came to Hilkiah the high priest. They gave him the money that people gave for God's Temple. The Levite doorkeepers had collected this money from the people of Manasseh, Ephraim, and from all the Israelites who were left. They also collected this money from all Judah, Benjamin, and all the people living in Jerusalem. ¹⁰Then the Levites paid the men who supervised the work on the Lord's Temple. And the supervisors paid the workers who repaired the Lord's Temple. ¹¹They gave the money to carpenters and builders to buy large rocks that were already cut, and to buy wood. The wood was used to rebuild the buildings and to make beams for the buildings. In the past, the kings of Judah did not take care of the Temple buildings. The buildings had become old and ruined. ¹²⁻¹³The men worked faithfully. Their supervisors were Jahath and Obadiah. Jahath and Obadiah were Levites, and they were descendants of Merari. Other supervisors were Zechariah and Meshullam. They were descendants of Kohath. The Levites who were skilled in playing instruments of music also supervised the laborers and all the other workers. Some Levites worked as secretaries, officials, and doorkeepers.

The Book of the Law Found

¹⁴The Levites brought out the money that was in the Lord's Temple.* At that time

---

ᵃ33:14 *Ophel* The upper part of the City of David, just south of the Temple area.

ᵇ34:6 *ruins near all these towns* The Hebrew text here is hard to understand.

Hilkiah the priest found the *Book of the Law of the* Lord that was given through Moses. ¹⁵Hilkiah said to Shaphan the secretary, "I found the *Book of the Law* in the Lord's house.ª" Hilkiah gave the book to Shaphan. ¹⁶Shaphan brought the book to King Josiah. Shaphan reported to the king, "Your servants are doing everything you told them to do. ¹⁷They got the money that was in the Lord's Temple and are paying the supervisors and the workers." ¹⁸Then Shaphan said to King Josiah, "Hilkiah the priest gave a book to me." Then Shaphan read from the book in front of the king. ¹⁹When King Josiah heard the words of the law being read, he tore his clothes.ᵇ ²⁰Then the king gave a command to Hilkiah, Ahikam son of Shaphan, Abdon son of Micah, Shaphan the secretary, and Asaiah the servant. ²¹The king said, "Go, ask the Lord for me, and for the people who are left in Israel and in Judah. Ask about the words in the book that was found. The Lord is very angry with us because our ancestors* did not obey the Lord's word. They did not do everything this book says to do."

²²Hilkiah and the king's servantsᶜ went to Huldah the prophetess.* Huldah was Shallum's wife. Shallum was Tokhath's son. Tokhath was Hasrah's son. Shallum took care of the king's clothes. Huldah lived in the newer part of Jerusalem. Hilkiah and the king's servants told Huldah what had happened. ²³Huldah said to them, "This is what the Lord, the God of Israel, says: Tell King Josiah: ²⁴This is what the Lord says, 'I will bring trouble to this place and to the people living here. I will bring all the terrible things that are written in the book that was read in front of the king of Judah. ²⁵I will do this because the people left me and burned incense* to other gods. They made me angry because of all the bad things they have done. So I will pour out my anger on this place. Like a hot burning fire, my anger will not be put out!'

²⁶"But tell this to King Josiah of Judah. He sent you to ask the Lord: This is what the Lord, the God of Israel, says about the words you heard a little while ago: ²⁷'Josiah, you repented and you humbled yourself. You tore your clothes, and you cried before me. So because your heart was tender, ²⁸I will take you to be with your ancestors.ᵈ You will go to your grave in peace. You will not have to see any of the trouble that I will bring on this place and on the people living here.'" Hilkiah and the king's servants brought back this message to King Josiah.

²⁹Then King Josiah called for all the elders of Judah and Jerusalem to come and meet with him. ³⁰The king went up to the Lord's Temple. All the people from Judah, the people living in Jerusalem, the priests, the Levites, and all the people, both important and not important, were with Josiah. He read to them all the words in the *Book of the Agreement*. That book was found in the Lord's Temple. ³¹Then the king stood up in his place. He made an agreement with the Lord. He agreed to follow the Lord and to obey the Lord's commands, laws, and rules. He agreed to obey with all his heart and soul the words of the agreement* written in this book. ³²Then Josiah made all the people in Jerusalem and Benjamin promise to accept the agreement. The people of Jerusalem obeyed the agreement of God, the God their ancestors obeyed. ³³The Israelites had idols from many different countries, but Josiah destroyed all the terrible idols.* He made all the people in Israel serve the Lord their God. And as long as Josiah was alive, the people continued to serve the Lord, the God of their ancestors.

Josiah Celebrates Passover

35 ¹King Josiah celebrated the Passover* to the Lord in Jerusalem. The Passover lamb was killed on the 14th day of the first month. ²Josiah chose the priests to do their duties. He encouraged the priests while they were serving in the Lord's Temple.* ³He spoke to the Levites who taught the Israelites and who were made holy* for service to the Lord. He said to the Levites, "Put the Holy Box* in the Temple that Solomon built. Solomon was David's son. David was king of Israel. Don't carry the Holy Box from place to place on your shoulders again. Now serve the Lord your God and his people, the Israelites. ⁴Make yourselves ready for service in the Temple by your tribes. Do the jobs that King David and his son King Solomon gave you to do. ⁵Stand in the Holy Place* with a group of Levites. Do this for each different tribe of the people so that you can help them. ⁶Kill the Passover lambs and make yourselves holy to the Lord. Get ready to help your fellow Israelites. Do everything the Lord commanded us in the laws he gave to Moses."

⁷Josiah gave the Israelites 30,000 sheep and goats to kill for the Passover sacrifices.* He also gave 3000 cattle to the people. All these animals were from King Josiah's own animals. ⁸Josiah's officials also freely gave animals and things to the people, to the priests, and Levites to use for the Passover. Hilkiah the high priest, Zechariah, and Jehiel were the officials in charge of the Temple. They gave the priests 2600 lambs and goats and 300 bulls for Passover sacrifices. ⁹Also Conaniah with Shemaiah and Nethanel, his brothers, and Hashabiah, Jeiel and Jozabad

---

ª**34:15** Lord's *house* Another name for the Temple in Jerusalem.

ᵇ**34:19** *tore his clothes* A way of showing that a person was upset. Josiah was upset because his people had not obeyed the Lord's laws. Also in verse 27.

ᶜ**34:22** *the king's servants* Literally, "those ... of the king."

ᵈ**34:28** *take you to be with your ancestors* This means that Josiah would die.

gave 500 sheep and goats and 500 bulls for Passover sacrifices to the Levites. These men were leaders of the Levites.

¹⁰When everything was ready for the Passover service to begin, the priests and Levites went to their places. This is what the king commanded. ¹¹The Passover lambs were killed. Then the Levites skinned the animals and gave the blood to the priests. The priests sprinkled the blood on the altar.* ¹²Then they gave the animals to be used for burnt offerings to the different tribes. This was done so that the burnt offerings could be offered the way the Law of Moses taught. ¹³The Levites roasted the Passover sacrifices over the fire in the way they were commanded. And they boiled the holy offerings in pots, kettles, and pans. Then they quickly gave the meat to the people. ¹⁴After this was finished, the Levites got meat for themselves and for the priests who were descendants of Aaron. These priests were kept very busy, working until it got dark. They worked hard burning the burnt offerings and the fat of the sacrifices. ¹⁵The Levite singers from Asaph's family got in the places that King David had chosen for them to stand. They were Asaph, Heman, and Jeduthun the king's prophet. The gatekeepers at each gate did not have to leave their places because their brother Levites made everything ready for them for the Passover.

¹⁶So everything was done that day for the worship of the LORD as King Josiah commanded. The Passover was celebrated and the burnt offerings* were offered on the LORD's altar. ¹⁷The Israelites who were there celebrated Passover and the Festival of Unleavened Bread* for seven days. ¹⁸Passover hadn't been celebrated like this since the time of Samuel the prophet! None of the kings of Israel had ever celebrated a Passover like this. King Josiah, the priests, the Levites, and the people of Judah and Israel who were there with all the people in Jerusalem celebrated the Passover in a very special way. ¹⁹They celebrated this Passover in Josiah's 18th year as king.

The Death of Josiah

²⁰Josiah did all these good things for the Temple.* Later, King Neco of Egypt led an army to fight against the town of Carchemish on the Euphrates River. King Josiah went out to fight against Neco. ²¹But Neco sent messengers to Josiah. They said, "King Josiah, this war is not your problem. I didn't come to fight against you. I came to fight my enemies. God told me to hurry. He is on my side, so don't bother me. If you fight against me, God will destroy you!" ²²But Josiah did not go away. He put on different clothes to hide who he was and went to fight the battle. Josiah refused to listen to the warning Neco had received from God and went to fight on the plain of Megiddo. ²³Then King Josiah was shot by arrows while he was in the battle. He told his servants, "Take me

away, I am wounded badly!"

²⁴So the servants took Josiah out of his chariot* and put him in another chariot he had brought with him to the battle. Then they took Josiah to Jerusalem. He died there and was buried in the tombs where his ancestors* were buried. All the people of Judah and Jerusalem were very sad because Josiah was dead. ²⁵Jeremiah wrote and sang some funeral songs for Josiah. And the men and women singers still sing these sad songs today. It became something the people of Israel always do—they sing a sad song for Josiah. These songs are written in the book, *Funeral Songs*.

²⁶⁻²⁷Everything else Josiah did while he was king, from beginning to the end of his rule, is written in the book, *The History of the Kings of Israel and Judah*. The book tells about his loyalty to the LORD and how he obeyed the LORD's law.

Jehoahaz, King of Judah

36 ¹The people of Judah chose Jehoahaz to be the new king in Jerusalem. Jehoahaz was Josiah's son. ²He was 23 years old when he became king of Judah. He was king in Jerusalem for three months. ³Then King Neco from Egypt made Jehoahaz a prisoner. Neco made the people of Judah pay 3¾ tons*a* of silver and 75 pounds*b* of gold for a fine. ⁴Neco chose Jehoahaz's brother to be the new king of Judah and Jerusalem. Jehoahaz's brother's name was Eliakim. Then Neco gave Eliakim a new name. He named him Jehoiakim. But Neco took Jehoahaz to Egypt.

Jehoiakim, King of Judah

⁵Jehoiakim was 25 years old when he became the new king of Judah. He was king in Jerusalem for eleven years. Jehoiakim didn't do what the LORD wanted him to do. He sinned against the LORD his God.

⁶King Nebuchadnezzar from Babylon attacked Judah. He made Jehoiakim a prisoner and put bronze chains on him. Then Nebuchadnezzar took King Jehoiakim to Babylon. ⁷Nebuchadnezzar took some of the things from the LORD's Temple.* He carried them to Babylon and put them in his own house. ⁸Everything else Jehoiakim did, the terrible sins he did, and everything he was guilty of doing, are written in the book, *The History of the Kings of Israel and Judah*. Jehoiakim's son Jehoiachin became the new king in his place.

Jehoiachin, King of Judah

⁹Jehoiachin was 18 years old when he became king of Judah. He was king in Jerusalem for three months and ten days. He didn't do what the LORD wanted him to do. He sinned against the LORD. ¹⁰In the spring, King Nebuchadnezzar sent some servants

---

*a***36:3** *3 3/4 tons* Literally, "100 talents" (3450 kg).
*b***36:3** *75 pounds* Literally, "1 talent" (34.5 kg).

to get Jehoiachin. They brought Jehoiachin and some valuable treasures from the LORD's Temple* to Babylon. Nebuchadnezzar chose Zedekiah to be the new king of Judah and Jerusalem. Zedekiah was one of Jehoiachin's relatives.

Zedekiah, King of Judah

¹¹Zedekiah was 21 years old when he became king of Judah. He was king in Jerusalem for eleven years. ¹²Zedekiah didn't do what the LORD wanted him to do. He sinned against the LORD. Jeremiah the prophet spoke messages from the LORD. But Zedekiah didn't humble himself and obey what Jeremiah said.

Jerusalem Is Destroyed

¹³Zedekiah turned against King Nebuchadnezzar. In the past Nebuchadnezzar forced Zedekiah to make a promise to be faithful to him. Zedekiah used God's name and promised to be faithful to Nebuchadnezzar. But Zedekiah was stubborn and would not change his life. He refused to obey the LORD, the God of Israel. ¹⁴Also, all the leaders of the priests and the leaders of the people of Judah sinned worse and became more unfaithful to the Lord. They followed the evil example of the other nations. They ruined the Temple* that the LORD had made holy in Jerusalem. ¹⁵The LORD, the God of their ancestors,* sent prophets again and again to warn his people. He did this because he felt sorry for them and for his Temple. He didn't want to destroy them or his Temple. ¹⁶But they made fun of God's prophets and refused to listen to them. They hated God's messages. Finally, God could not hold his anger any longer. He became angry with his people and there was nothing that could be done to stop it. ¹⁷So God brought the king of Babylon to attack the people of Judah and Jerusalem.ᵃ The king of Babylon killed the young men even when they were in the Temple. He didn't have mercy on the people of Judah and Jerusalem. The king of Babylon killed young and old people. He killed men and women. He killed sick and healthy people. God permitted Nebuchadnezzar to punish the people of Judah and Jerusalem. ¹⁸Nebuchadnezzar carried all the things in God's Temple away to Babylon. He took all the valuable things from the Temple, from the king, and from the king's officials. ¹⁹Nebuchadnezzar and his army burned the Temple. They broke down Jerusalem's wall and burned all the houses that belonged to the king and his officials. They took or destroyed every valuable thing in Jerusalem. ²⁰Nebuchadnezzar took the people who were still alive back to Babylon and forced them to be slaves. They stayed in Babylon as slaves until the Persian kingdom defeated the kingdom of Babylon. ²¹And so what the LORD told the people of Israel through the prophet Jeremiah really happened. He had said through Jeremiah: "This place will be an empty wasteland for 70 years.ᵇ This will happen to make up for the Sabbath restsᶜ that the people had not kept."

²²During the first year that Cyrusᵈ was king of Persia, the LORD caused Cyrus to make a special announcement. He did this so that what the LORD promised through Jeremiah the prophet would really happen. Cyrus sent messengers to every place in his kingdom. They carried this message:

²³"This is what King Cyrus of Persia says: The LORD, the God of heaven, made me king over the whole earth. He gave me the responsibility of building a Temple for him in Jerusalem. Now, all of you who are his people are free to go to Jerusalem. And may the LORD your God be with you."

ᵇ**36:21** *This place ... for 70 years* See Jer. 25:11; 29:10.
ᶜ**36:21** *Sabbath rests* The Law said that every seventh year the land was not to be farmed. See Lev. 25:1–7.
ᵈ**36:22** *the first year ... Cyrus* This was about 539–538 B.C.

ᵃ**36:17** This happened in the year 586 B.C., when Jerusalem was finally destroyed by King Nebuchadnezzar from Babylon.

Ezra

Cyrus Helps the Prisoners Return

1 [1]During the first year[a] that Cyrus was king of Persia, the LORD caused him to make an announcement. It was written down, and Cyrus ordered that it be read throughout his kingdom. This was done so that what the LORD had told Jeremiah[b] years before would now happen. This was the announcement:

[2]"From King Cyrus of Persia:

The LORD, the God of heaven, gave all the kingdoms on earth to me. And he chose me to build a temple for him at Jerusalem in the country of Judah. [3]The LORD is the God of Israel, the God who is in Jerusalem. If any of God's people are living among you, I pray God will bless them. You must let them go to Jerusalem in the country of Judah. You must let them go build the LORD's Temple.* [4]And so in any place where there might be survivors* of Israel, the men in that place must support these survivors. Give them silver, gold, animals, and other things. Give them gifts for God's Temple in Jerusalem."

[5]So the family leaders from the tribes of Judah and Benjamin prepared to go up to Jerusalem. They were going to Jerusalem to build the LORD's Temple. Also everyone who God had encouraged prepared to go to Jerusalem. [6]All their neighbors gave them many gifts. They gave them silver, gold, animals, and other expensive things. Their neighbors freely gave them all those things. [7]Also, King Cyrus brought out the things that belonged in the LORD's Temple that Nebuchadnezzar had taken away from Jerusalem. He had put them in his temple where he kept his false gods. [8]King Cyrus of Persia told Mithredath, the man who keeps his money, to bring those things out. So Mithredath brought them out to Sheshbazzar,* the leader of Judah.

[9]This is what Mithredath brought out of the Lord's Temple: 30 gold dishes, 1000 silver dishes, 29 knives and pans, [10]30 gold bowls, 410 silver bowls similar to the gold bowls, and 1000 other dishes. [11]All together, there were 5400 things

made from gold and silver. Sheshbazzar brought them all with him when the prisoners left Babylon and went back to Jerusalem.

The List of the Prisoners Who Returned

2 [1]These are the people of the province who returned from captivity. King Nebuchadnezzar of Babylon had taken these people as prisoners to Babylon. They now returned to Jerusalem and Judah, everyone to their own town. [2]These are the people who returned with Zerubbabel[c]: Jeshua, Nehemiah, Seraiah, Reelaiah, Mordecai, Bilshan, Mispar, Bigvai, Rehum, and Baanah. This is the list of names and numbers of men from Israel who returned:

[3]	the descendants of Parosh	2172
[4]	the descendants of Shephatiah	372
[5]	the descendants of Arah	775
[6]	the descendants of Pahath Moab of the family of Jeshua and Joab	2812
[7]	the descendants of Elam	1254
[8]	the descendants of Zattu	945
[9]	the descendants of Zaccai	760
[10]	the descendants of Bani	642
[11]	the descendants of Bebai	623
[12]	the descendants of Azgad	1222
[13]	the descendants of Adonikam	666
[14]	the descendants of Bigvai	2056
[15]	the descendants of Adin	454
[16]	the descendants of Ater through the family of Hezekiah	98
[17]	the descendants of Bezai	323
[18]	the descendants of Jorah	112
[19]	the descendants of Hashum	223
[20]	the descendants of Gibbar	95
[21]	from the town of Bethlehem	123
[22]	from the town of Netophah	56
[23]	from the town of Anathoth	128
[24]	from the town of Azmaveth	42
[25]	from the towns of Kiriath Jearim, Kephirah, and Beeroth	743
[26]	from the towns of Ramah and Geba	621
[27]	from the town of Micmash	122
[28]	from the towns of Bethel and Ai	223
[29]	from the town of Nebo	52
[30]	from the town of Magbish	156
[31]	from the other town named Elam	1254
[32]	from the town of Harim	320

[a]1:1 *first year* That is, 538 B.C.
[b]1:1 *what the LORD had told Jeremiah* See Jer. 25:12–14.

[c]2:2 *Zerubbabel* Possibly Sheshbazzar, the leader mentioned in 1:8, 11. See "Sheshbazzar" in the Word List.

33 from the towns of Lod, Hadid, and
Ono   725
34 from the town of Jericho   345
35 from the town of Senaah   3630

36These are the priests:

the descendants of Jedaiah through
the family of Jeshua   973
37 the descendants of Immer   1052
38 the descendants of Pashhur   1247
39 the descendants of Harim   1017

40These are the people from the tribe of Levi:

the descendants of Jeshua and Kadmiel
through the family of Hodaviah   74

41These are the singers:

the descendants of Asaph   128

42These are the descendants of the Temple*
gatekeepers:

the descendants of Shallum, Ater,
Talmon, Akkub, Hatita, and Shobai 139

43These are the descendants of the special
Temple servants:

Ziha, Hasupha, Tabbaoth,
44 Keros, Siaha, Padon,
45 Lebanah, Hagabah, Akkub,
46 Hagab, Shalmai, Hanan,
47 Giddel, Gahar, Reaiah,
48 Rezin, Nekoda, Gazzam,
49 Uzza, Paseah, Besai,
50 Asnah, Meunim, Nephussim,
51 Bakbuk, Hakupha, Harhur,
52 Bazluth, Mehida, Harsha,
53 Barkos, Sisera, Temah,
54 Neziah, and Hatipha.

55These are the descendants of Solomon's
servants:

Sotai, Hassophereth, Peruda,
56 Jaala, Darkon, Giddel,
57 Shephatiah, Hattil, Pokereth Hazzebaim,
and Ami,
58 the Temple servants and descendants
of Solomon's servants   392

59Some people came to Jerusalem from the
towns of Tel Melah, Tel Harsha, Kerub,
Addon, and Immer. But these people could
not prove that their families were from the
family of Israel:

60 the descendants of Delaiah, Tobiah,
and Nekoda   652

61From the family of priests there were
descendants of

Hobaiah, Hakkoz, and Barzillai (If a man
married a daughter of Barzillai from
Gilead, he was counted as a descendant
of Barzillai.)

62These people searched for their family histories, but they could not find them.
Their names were not included in the list of
priests. They could not prove that their ancestors* were priests, so they could not serve as
priests. 63The governor ordered them not
to eat any of the holy food until there was a
priest who could use the Urim* and Thummim* to ask God what to do.

64-65All together, there were 42,360 people in the group who came back. This is not
counting their 7337 men and women slaves.
They also had 200 men and women singers
with them. 66-67They had 736 horses, 245
mules, 435 camels, and 6720 donkeys.
68When the group arrived at the place in
Jerusalem where the LORD's Temple had been,
the family leaders gave their gifts for building
this house of God again. They wanted to build
it in this same place. 69They gave as much
as they were able. These are the things they
gave for building the Temple: 1100 pounds*a*
of gold, about 4 tons*b* of silver, and 100 coats
that priests wear.
70So the priests, Levites, and some of the
other people moved to Jerusalem and the area
around it. This group included the Temple
singers, gatekeepers, and the Temple servants. The other Israelites settled in their
own hometowns.

Rebuilding the Altar

3 1So by the seventh month,*c* the Israelites
had moved back to their own hometowns.
At that time all the people met together in
Jerusalem. They were all united as one people. 2Then Jeshua son of Jozadak and the
priests with him, along with Zerubbabel son
of Shealtiel, and the people with him, built
the altar of the God of Israel. They built the
altar of the God of Israel so that they could
offer sacrifices on it. They built it just as it
says in the Law of Moses. Moses was God's
special servant.
3They were afraid of the other people living near them, but that didn't stop them.
They built the altar on its old foundation and
offered burnt offerings* on it to the LORD. They
offered sacrifices in the morning and in the
evening. 4Then they celebrated the Festival of
Shelters* just as the Law of Moses said. They
offered the right number of burnt offerings
for each day of the festival. 5After that, they
began offering the continual burnt offerings
each day and the offerings for the New Moon*

*a*2:69 *1100 pounds* Literally, "61,000 drachmas"
(about 526 kg).
*b*2:69 *4 tons* Literally, "5000 minas" (3450 kg).
*c*3:1 *seventh month* That is, September–October,
538 B.C.

and all the other festivals that were commanded by the LORD. The people also began giving any other gifts they wanted to give to the LORD. [6]So on the first day of the seventh month, these Israelites again began offering sacrifices to the LORD. This was done, even though the Temple* had not been rebuilt.

Rebuilding the Temple

[7]Then those who had come back from captivity gave money to the stonecutters and carpenters. They also gave food, wine, and olive oil. They used these things to pay the people of Tyre and Sidon to bring cedar logs from Lebanon. They wanted to bring the logs in ships to the seacoast town of Joppa as they did for the first Temple.* King Cyrus of Persia gave permission for them to do this.

[8]So in the second month[a] of the second year after they came to the Temple in Jerusalem, Zerubbabel son of Shealtiel and Jeshua son of Jozadak began the work. Their brothers, the priests, Levites, and everyone who came back to Jerusalem from captivity began working with them. They chose Levites who were 20 years old and older to be the leaders in the building of the LORD's Temple. [9]These were the men who supervised the work of building the LORD's Temple: Jeshua and his sons, Kadmiel and his sons (the descendants of Judah), the sons of Henadad and their brothers, the Levites. [10]The builders finished laying the foundation for the LORD's Temple. When the foundation was finished, the priests put on their special clothing. Then they got their trumpets, and the sons of Asaph got their cymbals. They all took their places to praise the LORD. This was done the way King David of Israel had ordered in the past. [11]They sang the response songs,[b] *Songs of Praise* and *Praise the LORD Because He is Good. His Faithful Love Will Last Forever.* Then all the people cheered—they gave a loud shout and praised the LORD because the foundation of the LORD's Temple had been laid.

[12]But many of the older priests, Levites, and family leaders, who could remember seeing the first Temple, began to cry aloud. They cried while the others there shouted for joy. [13]The sound could be heard far away. All of them made so much noise that no one could tell the difference between the shouts of joy and the crying.

Enemies Against Rebuilding the Temple

4 [1-2]Many people living in the area were against the people of Judah and Benjamin. These enemies heard that the people who had come from captivity were building a temple for the LORD, the God of Israel. So they came to Zerubbabel and to the family leaders and said, "Let us help you build. We are the same as you, we ask your God for help. We have offered sacrifices to your God since the time King Esarhaddon of Assyria brought us here."

[3]But Zerubbabel, Jeshua, and the other family leaders of Israel answered, "No, you people cannot help us build a temple for our God. Only we can build the Temple* for the LORD. He is the God of Israel. This is what King Cyrus of Persia commanded us to do."

[4]So the enemies began to discourage them and tried to frighten them in order to stop them from building the Temple. [5]These enemies hired government officials to work against the people of Judah. The officials constantly did things to stop the Jews' plans to build the Temple. This continued the whole time that Cyrus was the king until Darius became the king of Persia.

[6]These enemies even wrote letters to the king of Persia trying to stop the Jews. They wrote a letter the year that Xerxes[c] became the king of Persia.

Enemies Against Rebuilding Jerusalem

[7]Later, when Artaxerxes* became the new king of Persia, some of these men wrote another letter complaining about the Jews. The men who wrote the letter were Bishlam, Mithredath, Tabeel, and the other people in their group. The letter was written in Aramaic* and translated.[d]

[8][e] Then Rehum the commanding officer and Shimshai the secretary wrote a letter against the people of Jerusalem. They wrote the letter to Artaxerxes the king. This is what they wrote:

[9]From Rehum the commanding officer and Shimshai the secretary, and from the judges and important officials over the men from Tripolis, Persia, Erech, and Babylon, and from the Elamites from Susa, [10]and from the other people who the great and powerful Ashurbanipal moved to the city of Samaria and other places in the country west of the Euphrates River.

[11]This is the copy of the letter sent to King Artaxerxes:

From your servants living in the area west of the Euphrates River.

---

[a]**3:8** *second month* That is, April–May, 536 B.C.

[b]**3:11** *response songs* Songs sung in two parts. One group (the Levites) sang the first part and the other group (the people) responded with the second part. Here, these are probably Ps. 111–118 and Ps. 136.

[c]**4:6** *Xerxes* King of Persia about 485–465 B.C.

[d]**4:7** *The letter … translated* Or "The letter was written in the local language, but with Aramaic characters, and then translated into Aramaic." This would mean the scribe used the "modern" Aramaic alphabet rather than the older alphabet that was still being used in Judah.

[e]**4:8** Here, the original language changes from Hebrew to Aramaic.

¹²King Artaxerxes, we wish to inform you that the Jews you sent from there are now in Jerusalem. They are trying to rebuild that terrible city. The people there have always rebelled against other kings. Now they have almost finished repairing the foundations and building the walls.ᵃ

¹³Also, King Artaxerxes, you should know that if Jerusalem and its walls are rebuilt, the people of Jerusalem will stop paying their taxes. They will stop sending money to honor you. They also will stop paying customs fees, and the king will lose all that money.

¹⁴We have a responsibility to the king. We don't want to see this happen, so we are sending this letter to inform the king.

¹⁵King Artaxerxes, we suggest that you search the writings of the kings who ruled before you. You will see in the writings that Jerusalem always rebelled against other kings. It has caused much trouble for other kings and nations. Many rebellions have started in this city since ancient times. That is why Jerusalem was destroyed.

¹⁶King Artaxerxes, we wish to inform you that if this city and its walls are rebuilt, you will lose control of the area west of the Euphrates River.

¹⁷Then King Artaxerxes sent this answer:

To Rehum the commanding officer, Shimshai the secretary, and all the people with them living in Samaria and other places west of the Euphrates River.

Greetings:
¹⁸The letter you sent us has been translated and read to me. ¹⁹I gave an order for the writings of the kings before me to be searched. The writings were read, and we found out that Jerusalem has a long history of rebellion against kings. Jerusalem has been a place where rebellion and revolt has happened often. ²⁰Jerusalem has had powerful kings ruling over it and over the whole area west of the Euphrates River. Their kings received taxes, customs, fees, and tribute.*

²¹Now, you must give an order for these men to stop work. That order must be given to keep Jerusalem from being rebuilt until I say so. ²²Be careful not to overlook this matter. We should not let the building of Jerusalem continue. If that work continues, I will not get any more money from Jerusalem.

²³So a copy of the letter that King Artaxerxes sent was read to Rehum, Shimshai the secretary, and the people with them. They went very quickly to the Jews in Jerusalem and forced them to stop building.

The Work on the Temple Stopped

²⁴So the work stoppedᵇ on God's Temple* in Jerusalem. The work did not continue until the second yearᶜ that Darius was king of Persia.

5 ¹At that time the prophets Haggaiᵈ and Zechariah son of Iddoᵉ began to prophesy* in the name of God. They encouraged the Jews in Judah and Jerusalem. ²So Zerubbabel son of Shealtiel and Jeshua son of Jozadak again started working on the Temple in Jerusalem. All of God's prophets were with them and were supporting the work. ³At that time Tattenai was the governor of the area west of the Euphrates River. Tattenai, Shethar Bozenai, and the men with them went to Zerubbabel, Jeshua, and the others who were building. Tattenai and the people with him asked Zerubbabel and the people with him, "Who gave you permission to rebuild this Temple and repair it like new?" ⁴They also asked Zerubbabel, "What are the names of the men who are working on this building?"

⁵But God was watching over the Jewish leaders. The builders didn't have to stop working until a report could be sent to King Darius. They continued working until the king sent his answer back.

⁶Tattenai the governor of the area west of the Euphrates River, Shethar Bozenai, and important people with them sent a letter to King Darius. ⁷This is a copy of that letter:

To King Darius.

Greetings:
⁸King Darius, you should know that we went to the province of Judah. We went to the Temple of the great God. The people in Judah are building that Temple with large stones. They are putting big wooden timbers in the walls. The work is being done with much care and the people of Judah are working very hard. They are building very fast; it will soon be done.

⁹We asked their leaders some questions about the work they are doing. We asked them, "Who gave you permission to rebuild this temple and repair it like new?" ¹⁰We also asked for their names. We wanted to write down the names of

ᵇ4:24 the work stopped Here, this refers to the time of Xerxes, when work on the Temple was stopped, not to the time of Artaxerxes, when work on the walls around Jerusalem was stopped.
ᶜ4:24 second year That is, 520 B.C.
ᵈ5:1 Haggai See Hag. 1:1.
ᵉ5:1 Zechariah son of Iddo See Zech. 1:1.

their leaders so that you would know who they are.

¹¹This is the answer they gave us:

"We are the servants of the God of heaven and earth. We are rebuilding the Temple that a great king of Israel built and finished many years ago. ¹²But our ancestors* made the God of heaven angry, so God gave our ancestors to King Nebuchadnezzar of Babylon. Nebuchadnezzar destroyed this Temple, and he forced the people to go to Babylon as prisoners. ¹³But, in the first year that Cyrus was king of Babylon, King Cyrus gave a special order for God's Temple to be rebuilt. ¹⁴And Cyrus brought out from his false god's temple in Babylon the gold and silver things that were taken from God's Temple in the past. Nebuchadnezzar took them from the Temple in Jerusalem and brought them to his false god's temple in Babylon. Then King Cyrus gave those gold and silver things to Sheshbazzar.*" Cyrus chose Sheshbazzar to be governor.

¹⁵Then Cyrus said to Sheshbazzar, "Take these gold and silver things and put them back in the Temple in Jerusalem. Rebuild God's Temple in the same place it was in the past."

¹⁶So Sheshbazzar came and built the foundations of God's Temple in Jerusalem. From that day until now, the work has continued, but it is not yet finished.

¹⁷Now, if it pleases the king, please search the official records of the king. See if it is true that King Cyrus gave an order to rebuild God's Temple in Jerusalem. And then, sir, please send us a letter to let us know what you have decided to do about this.

The Order of Darius

6 ¹So King Darius gave an order to search the writings of the kings before him. The writings were kept in Babylon in the same place the money was kept. ²A scroll* was found in the fortress* of Ecbatana. (Ecbatana is in the province of Media.) This is what was written on that scroll:

Official Note: ³During the first year that Cyrus was king, he gave an order about the Temple* of God in Jerusalem. The order said:

Let the Temple of God be rebuilt. It will be a place to offer sacrifices. Let its foundations be built. The Temple must be 60 cubits*ᵃ high and 60 cubits wide. ⁴Its wall will be in layers that have three

rows of large stones*ᵇ and one row of wooden timbers. The cost of building the Temple must be paid for from the king's treasury. ⁵Also, the gold and silver things from God's Temple must be put back in their places. Nebuchadnezzar took them from the Temple in Jerusalem and brought them to Babylon. They must be put back in God's Temple.

⁶Now then, I, Darius, order you Tattenai, governor of the area west of the Euphrates River, and Shethar Bozenai,. and all the officials living in that province, to stay away from Jerusalem. ⁷Don't bother the workers. Don't try to stop the work on this Temple of God. Let the Jewish governor and the Jewish leaders rebuild it. Let them rebuild God's Temple in the same place it was in the past.

⁸Now I give this order. You must do this for the Jewish leaders building God's Temple: The cost of the building must be fully paid from the king's treasury. The money will come from the taxes collected from the provinces in the area west of the Euphrates River. Do these things quickly, so the work will not stop. ⁹Give them anything they need. If they need young bulls, rams, or male lambs for sacrifices to the God of Heaven, give these things to them. If the priests of Jerusalem ask for wheat, salt, wine, and oil, give these things to them every day without fail. ¹⁰Give them to the Jewish priests so that they may offer sacrifices that please the God of Heaven. Give these things so that the priests may pray for me and my sons.

¹¹Also, I give this order: If anyone changes this order, a wooden beam must be pulled from their house and pushed through their body. Then their house must be destroyed until it is only a pile of rocks.

¹²God put his name there in Jerusalem. May God defeat any king or other person who tries to change this order. If anyone tries to destroy this Temple in Jerusalem, may God destroy that person.

I, Darius, have ordered it. This order must be obeyed quickly and completely.

The Temple Completed and Dedicated

¹³So Tattenai the governor of the area west of the Euphrates River, Shethar Bozenai, and the men with them obeyed King Darius' order. They obeyed the order quickly and completely. ¹⁴So the Jewish leaders continued to build. Encouraged by the preaching of Haggai the prophet and Zechariah son of Iddo, they had great success. They finished

---

ᵃ**6:3** *60 cubits* 102' 3/8" (31.1 m).   ᵇ**6:4** *large stones* Or "marble stones."

building the Temple* as the God of Israel had commanded and as Cyrus, Darius, and Artaxerxes, the kings of Persia, had ordered. ¹⁵The Temple was finished on the third day of the month of Adar.ᵃ That was in the sixth year of the rule of King Darius.ᵇ

¹⁶Then the Israelites celebrated the dedication* of God's Temple with much happiness. The priests, the Levites, and all the other people who came back from captivity joined in the celebration.

¹⁷This is the way they dedicated God's Temple: They offered 100 bulls, 200 rams, and 400 male lambs. And they offered twelve male goats for all Israel for a sin offering.* That is one goat for each of the twelve tribes of Israel. ¹⁸Then they chose the priests in their groups and the Levites in their groups to serve in God's Temple in Jerusalem. They did these things as it is written in the *Book of Moses*.

The Passover

¹⁹ᶜ On the fourteenth day of the first month,ᵈ the Jews who came back from captivity celebrated the Passover.* ²⁰The priests and Levites made themselves pure. They all made themselves clean and ready to celebrate the Passover. The Levites killed the Passover lamb for all the Jews who came back from captivity. They did that for their brothers the priests, and for themselves. ²¹So all the Israelites who came back from captivity ate the Passover meal. Other people washed themselves and made themselves pure from the unclean* things of the people living in that country. These pure people also shared in the Passover meal. They did this so that they could go to the LORD, the God of Israel, for help. ²²They celebrated the Festival of Unleavened Bread* with much joy for seven days. The LORD made them very happy because he had changed the attitude of the king of Assyria.ᵉ So the king of Assyria had helped them do the work on God's Temple.*

Ezra Comes to Jerusalem

7 ¹After these things,ᶠ during the rule of King Artaxerxes* of Persia, Ezra came to Jerusalem from Babylon. Ezra was the son of Seraiah. Seraiah was the son of Azariah. Azariah was the son of Hilkiah. ²Hilkiah was the son of Shallum. Shallum was the son of Zadok. Zadok was the son of Ahitub. ³Ahitub

was the son of Amariah. Amariah was the son of Azariah. Azariah was the son of Meraioth. ⁴Meraioth was the son of Zerahiah. Zerahiah was the son of Uzzi. Uzzi was the son of Bukki. ⁵Bukki was the son of Abishua. Abishua was the son of Phinehas. Phinehas was the son of Eleazar. Eleazar was the son of Aaron the high priest.

⁶Ezra came to Jerusalem from Babylon. He was a teacherᵍ and knew the Law of Moses very well. The Law of Moses was given by the LORD, the God of Israel. King Artaxerxes gave Ezra everything he asked for because the LORD was with Ezra. ⁷Among the people who came with Ezra were Israelites, priests, Levites, singers, gatekeepers, and Temple* servants. They arrived in Jerusalem during the seventh year of King Artaxerxes. ⁸Ezra arrived in Jerusalem in the fifth monthʰ of the seventh year that Artaxerxes was king. ⁹Ezra left Babylon on the first day of the first month and arrived in Jerusalem on the first day of the fifth month. The LORD God was with Ezra. ¹⁰Ezra gave all his time and attention to studying and obeying the law of the LORD. He wanted to teach the rules and commandments of the LORD to the Israelites. And he also wanted to help the people follow these laws in Israel.

King Artaxerxes' Letter to Ezra

¹¹Ezra was a priest and teacher. He knew much about the commands and laws the LORD gave Israel. This is a copy of the letter King Artaxerxes* gave to Ezra the teacher:

¹²ⁱ From King Artaxerxes.
To Ezra the priest, a teacher of the law of the God of Heaven.

Greetings!

¹³I give this order: Any of the Israelites living in my kingdom, including priests and Levites, who want to go with you to Jerusalem, may go.

¹⁴I and my seven advisors send you to Judah and Jerusalem. Go and see how your people are doing in obeying the law of your God. You have that law with you.

¹⁵I and my advisors are giving gold and silver to the God of Israel, who lives in Jerusalem. You must take this gold and silver with you. ¹⁶You must also go through all the provinces of Babylonia. Collect the gifts from your people, from the priests, and from the Levites. The gifts are for the Temple* of their God in Jerusalem.

¹⁷Use this money to buy bulls, rams,

ᵃ**6:15** *third ... Adar* That is, February–March. Some ancient writers have "23rd of Adar."
ᵇ**6:15** *the sixth year ... Darius* That is, 515 B.C.
ᶜ**6:19** Here, the original language changes from Aramaic back to Hebrew.
ᵈ**6:19** *first month* That is, March–April, 515 B.C.
ᵉ**6:22** *king of Assyria* This probably means King Darius of Persia.
ᶠ**7:1** *After these things* There is a time period of 58 years between Ezra 6 and Ezra 7. The story of Esther takes place at this time.

ᵍ**7:6** *teacher* Literally, "scribe." This was a person who made copies of books. These men studied those books and became teachers.
ʰ**7:8** *fifth month* That is, July–August, 458 B.C.
ⁱ**7:12** Here, the text changes from Hebrew to Aramaic.

and male lambs. Buy the grain offerings and drink offerings that go with these sacrifices. Then sacrifice them on the altar in the Temple of your God in Jerusalem. ¹⁸Then you and the other Jews may spend the silver and gold left over any way you want to. Use it in a way that is pleasing to your God. ¹⁹Take all these things to the God of Jerusalem. They are for the worship in the Temple of your God. ²⁰And you may get any other things that you need for the Temple of your God. Use the money in the king's treasury to buy anything you need.

²¹Now I, King Artaxerxes, give this order: I order all the men who keep the king's money in the area west of the Euphrates River to give Ezra anything he wants. Ezra is a priest and a teacher of the Law of the God of Heaven. Do this quickly and completely. ²²Give this much to Ezra: 3¾ tons[a] of silver, 600 bushels[b] of wheat, 600 gallons[c] of wine, 600 gallons of olive oil, and as much salt as Ezra wants. ²³Anything that the God of Heaven has ordered for Ezra to get, you must give to Ezra quickly and completely. Do this for the Temple of the God of Heaven. We don't want God to be angry with my kingdom or my sons.

²⁴I want you men to know that it is against the law to make the priests, Levites, singers, gatekeepers, Temple servants, and other workers in God's Temple pay taxes. They don't have to pay taxes, money to honor the king, or any customs fees. ²⁵Ezra, I give you the authority to use the wisdom you have from your God and choose civil and religious judges. These men will be judges for all the people living in the area west of the Euphrates River. They will judge all the people who know the laws of your God and they will teach those who don't know those laws. ²⁶Anyone who does not obey the law of your God, or the law of the king, must be punished. Depending on the crime, they must be punished with death, or sent away to another country, or their property taken away, or put into prison.

Ezra Praises God

²⁷ᵈ Blessed is the LORD, the God of our
    ancestors.*
  He put the idea into the king's heart
    to honor the LORD's Temple* in
    Jerusalem.

²⁸ The LORD showed his faithful love to me
    in front of the king, his advisors, and
    the king's important officials.
  The LORD God was with me, so I was
    brave.
  I gathered together the leaders of Israel
    to go with me to Jerusalem.

List of Leaders Returning With Ezra

8 ¹These are the names of the family leaders and the other people who came with me to Jerusalem from Babylon. We came to Jerusalem during the rule of King Artaxerxes. Here is the list of names: ²from the descendants of Phinehas: Gershom; from the descendants of Ithamar: Daniel; from the descendants of David: Hattush; ³from the descendants of Shecaniah: the descendants of Parosh, Zechariah, and 150 other men; ⁴from the descendants of Pahath Moab: Eliehoenai son of Zerahiah, and 200 other men; ⁵from the descendants of Zattu: Shecaniah son of Jahaziel, and 300 other men; ⁶from the descendants of Adin: Ebed son of Jonathan, and 50 other men; ⁷from the descendants of Elam: Jeshaiah son of Athaliah, and 70 other men; ⁸from the descendants of Shephatiah: Zebadiah son of Michael, and 80 other men; ⁹from the descendants of Joab: Obadiah son of Jehiel, and 218 other men; ¹⁰from the descendants of Bani: Shelomith son of Josiphiah, and 160 other men; ¹¹from the descendants of Bebai: Zechariah son of Bebai, and 28 other men; ¹²from the descendants of Azgad: Johanan son of Hakkatan, and 110 other men; ¹³from the last of the descendants of Adonikam: Eliphelet, Jeuel, Shemaiah, and 60 other men; ¹⁴from the descendants of Bigvai: Uthai, Zaccur, and 70 other men.

The Return to Jerusalem

¹⁵I called all these people to meet together at the river that flows toward Ahava. We camped at that place for three days. I learned there were priests in the group, but there were no Levites. ¹⁶So I called these leaders: Eliezer, Ariel, Shemaiah, Elnathan, Jarib, Elnathan, Nathan, Zechariah, and Meshullam, and I called Joiarib and Elnathan. (These men were teachers.) ¹⁷I sent the men to Iddo, leader in the town of Casiphia. I told them what to say to Iddo and his relatives, who are the Temple* workers in Casiphia. I told the men to ask Iddo and his relatives to send us workers to serve in God's Temple. ¹⁸Because God was with us, they sent Sherebiah, a skilled man from the descendants of Mahli (Mahli was a son of Levi, one of Israel's sons.) They also sent his sons and brothers, 18 men in all. ¹⁹They also sent Hashabiah and Jeshaiah from the descendants of Merari, along with their brothers and nephews. In all there were 20 men. ²⁰Besides these, there were 220 Temple workers whose ancestors* had been chosen by David and his officials to help

---

ᵃ7:22 *3 3/4 tons* Literally, "100 talents" (3450 kg).
ᵇ7:22 *600 bushels* Literally, "100 cors" (22,000 l).
ᶜ7:22 *600 gallons* Literally, "100 baths" (2200 l).
ᵈ7:27 Here, the text changes from Aramaic back to Hebrew.

the Levites. The names of all these men were written on the list.

21There near the Ahava River, I announced that we all should fast.* We should fast to make ourselves humble before our God. We wanted to ask God for a safe trip for ourselves, our children, and for everything we owned. 22I was embarrassed to ask King Artaxerxes for soldiers and horsemen to protect us as we traveled. There were enemies on the road. The reason I was embarrassed to ask for protection was because of what we had told the king. We had said to King Artaxerxes, "Our God is with everyone who trusts him, but he is very angry with everyone who turns away from him." 23So we fasted and prayed to our God about our trip. He answered our prayers.

24Then I chose twelve of the priests who were leaders. I chose Sherebiah, Hashabiah, and ten of their brothers. 25I weighed the silver, gold, and the other things that were given for God's Temple. I gave them to the twelve priests I had chosen. King Artaxerxes, his advisors, his important officials, and all the Israelites in Babylon gave those things for God's Temple. 26I weighed all these things. There were 25 tonsᵃ of silver. There were also 7500 poundsᵇ of silver dishes and things. There were 3¾ tons of gold. 27And I gave them 20 gold bowls. The bowls weighed about 19 pounds.ᶜ And I gave them two beautiful dishes made from polished bronze that were as valuable as gold. 28Then I said to the twelve priests: "You and these things are holy to the LORD. People gave this silver and gold to the LORD, the God of your ancestors. 29So guard these things carefully. You are responsible for them until you give them to the Temple leaders in Jerusalem. You will give them to the leading Levites and the family leaders of Israel. They will weigh them and put them in the rooms of the LORD's Temple in Jerusalem."

30So the priests and Levites accepted the silver, gold, and special things that Ezra had weighed and given to them. They were told to take them to God's Temple in Jerusalem.

31On the twelfth day of the first monthᵈ we left the Ahava River and started toward Jerusalem. God was with us, and he protected us from enemies and robbers along the way. 32Then we arrived in Jerusalem. We rested there for three days. 33On the fourth day, we went to the Temple and weighed the silver, gold, and special things. We gave them to Meremoth son of Uriah the priest. Eleazar son of Phinehas was with Meremoth. The Levites, Jozabad son of Jeshua, and Noadiah son of Binnui were with them also. 34We counted and weighed everything and we wrote down the total weight.

35Then the Jewish people who came back from captivity offered burnt offerings to the God of Israel. They offered twelve bulls for all Israel, 96 rams, 77 male lambs, and twelve male goats for a sin offering.* All this was a burnt offering to the LORD.

36Then the people gave the letter from King Artaxerxes to the royal satraps* and to the governors of the area west of the Euphrates River. Then the leaders gave their support to the Israelites and to the Temple.

Marriages to Non-Jewish People

9 1After we finished all these things, the leaders of the Israelites came to me and said, "Ezra, the Israelites have not kept themselves separate from the other people living around us. And the priests and the Levites have not kept themselves separate. The Israelites are being influenced by evil things done by the Canaanites, Hittites, Perizzites, Jebusites, Ammonites, Moabites, Egyptians, and Amorites. 2The Israelites have married the people living around us. The Israelites are supposed to be special, but now they are mixed with the other people living around them. The leaders and important officials of the Israelites have set a bad example in this thing." 3When I heard about this, I tore my robe and my coat to show I was upset. I pulled hair from my head and beard. I sat down, shocked and upset. 4Then everyone who respected God's Law shook with fear. They were afraid because the Israelites who came back from captivity were not faithful to God. I was shocked and upset. I sat there until the evening sacrifice, and the people gathered around me.

5Then, when it was time for the evening sacrifice, I got up. I had made myself look shameful while I was sitting there. My robe and coat were torn, and I fell on my knees with my hands spread out to the LORD my God. 6Then I prayed this prayer:

"My God, I am too ashamed and embarrassed to look at you. I am ashamed because our sins are higher than our heads. Our guilt has reached all the way up to the heavens. 7We have been guilty of many sins from the days of our ancestors* until now. We sinned so our kings and priests were punished. Foreign kings attacked us and took our people away. They took away our wealth and made us ashamed. It is the same even today.

8"But now, finally, you have been kind to us. You have let a few of us escape captivity and come to live in this holy place. LORD, you gave us new life and relief from our slavery. 9Yes, we were slaves, but you would not let us be slaves forever. You were kind to us. You made the kings of Persia be kind to us. Your Temple* was ruined, but you gave us new life so that we can rebuild your Temple and repair it like new. God, you helped us build a wall to protect Judah and Jerusalem.

ᵃ8:26 25 tons Literally, "650 talents" (22,425 kg).
ᵇ8:26 7500 pounds Literally, "100 talents" (3450 kg).
ᶜ8:27 19 pounds Literally, "1000 darics" (about 8.63 kg).
ᵈ8:31 first month That is, March–April, 458 B.C.

10"Now, God, what can we say to you? We have stopped obeying you again. 11You used your servants the prophets to give these commands to us. You said, "The land you are going to live in and own is a ruined land. It has been ruined by evil things the people living there have done. They have done very bad things in every place in this land. They have made this land dirty with their sins. 12So Israelites, don't let your children marry their children. Don't join them. Don't want the things they have. Obey my commands so that you will be strong and enjoy the good things of the land. And then you can keep this land and give it to your children."

13"What has happened to us is our own fault. We have done evil things, and we have much guilt. But you, our God, have punished us much less than we should have been. We have done many terrible sins, and we should have been punished worse. And you have even let some of our people escape captivity. 14So we know that we must not break your commands. We must not marry those people. They do very bad things. God, if we continue to marry these bad people, we know you will destroy us. Then there would be no one from the Israelites left alive.

15"LORD, God of Israel, you are good, and you still have let some of us live. Yes, we are guilty, and because of our guilt, not one of us should be allowed to stand in front of you."

The People Confess Their Sin

10 1Ezra was praying and confessing. He was crying and bowing down in front of God's Temple. While Ezra was doing that, a large group of the Israelites—men, women, and children—gathered around him. They were crying. 2Then Shecaniah son of Jehiel, one of the descendants of Elam, spoke to Ezra and said, "We have not been faithful to our God. We have married the people living around us. But, even though we have done this, there is still hope for Israel. 3Now let us make an agreement before our God to send away all these women and their children. We will do that to follow the advice of Ezra and the people who respect the laws of our God. We will obey God's law. 4Get up, Ezra. This is your responsibility, but we will support you. So be brave and do it."

5So Ezra got up. He made the leading priests, the Levites, and all the Israelites promise to do what he said. 6Then Ezra went away from the front of God's house. He went to the room of Jehohanan son of Eliashib. While Ezra was there, he didn't eat food or drink water. He did that because he was still very sad. He was very sad about the Israelites who came back to Jerusalem. 7Then he sent a message to every place in Judah and Jerusalem. The message told all the Jewish people who had come back from captivity to meet together in Jerusalem. 8Those who did not

come to Jerusalem in three days like the officials and elders said would lose their property and be removed from the group.

9So in three days all the men from the families of Judah and Benjamin gathered in Jerusalem. And on the twentieth day of the ninth month,a all the people met together in the Temple yard. They were very upset because of the reason for the meeting and because of the heavy rain. 10Then Ezra the priest stood and said to them, "You people have not been faithful to God. You have married foreign women. You have made Israel more guilty by doing that. 11Now you must confess your sins to the LORD, the God of your ancestors.* You must obey his command. Separate yourselves from the people living around you and from your foreign wives."

12Then the whole group who met together answered Ezra. They shouted, "Ezra, you are right! We must do what you say. 13But there are many people here. And it is the rainy time of year, so we cannot stay outside. This problem cannot be solved in a day or two because we have sinned in a very bad way. 14Let our leaders decide for the whole group meeting here. Then let every man in our towns who married a foreign woman come here to Jerusalem at a planned time. Let them come here with the elders* and judges of their towns. Then God will stop being angry with us."

15Only a few men were against this plan. They were Jonathan son of Asahel and Jahzeiah son of Tikvah. Meshullam and Shabbethai the Levite also were against the plan.

16So the Israelites who came back to Jerusalem accepted the plan. Ezra the priest chose men who were family leaders. He chose one man from each tribe. Each man was chosen by name. On the first day of the tenth month,b the men who were chosen sat down to study each of the cases. 17And by the first day of the first month,c they finished discussing all the men who had married foreign women.

List of Men Who Married Foreign Women

18These are the names of the descendants of the priests who married foreign women:

From the descendants of Jeshua son of Jozadak and Jeshua's brothers, these men: Maaseiah, Eliezer, Jarib, and Gedaliah. 19All of them promised to divorce their wives. And then each one of them offered a ram from the flock for a guilt offering. They did that because of their guilt.

20From the descendants of Immer, these men: Hanani and Zebadiah.

21From the descendants of Harim, these men: Maaseiah, Elijah, Shemaiah, Jehiel, and Uzziah.

---

a 10:9 ninth month That is, November–December.
b 10:16 tenth month That is, December–January.
c 10:17 first month That is, March–April.

²²From the descendants of Pashhur, these men: Elioenai, Maaseiah, Ishmael, Nethanel, Jozabad, and Elasah.

²³Among the Levites, these are the men who married foreign women: Jozabad, Shimei, Kelaiah (also called Kelita), Pethahiah, Judah, and Eliezer.

²⁴Among the singers, this is the man who had married a foreign woman: Eliashib.

Among the gatekeepers, these are the men who had married foreign women: Shallum, Telem, and Uri.

²⁵Among the Israelites, these men married foreign women:

From the descendants of Parosh, these men: Ramiah, Izziah, Malkijah, Mijamin, Eleazar, Malkijah, and Benaiah.

²⁶From the descendants of Elam, these men: Mattaniah, Zechariah, Jehiel, Abdi, Jeremoth, and Elijah.

²⁷From the descendants of Zattu, these men: Elioenai, Eliashib, Mattaniah, Jeremoth, Zabad, and Aziza.

²⁸From the descendants of Bebai, these men: Jehohanan, Hananiah, Zabbai, and Athlai.

²⁹From the descendants of Bani, these men: Meshullam, Malluch, Adaiah, Jashub, Sheal, and Jeremoth.

³⁰From the descendants of Pahath Moab, these men: Adna, Kelal, Benaiah, Maaseiah, Mattaniah, Bezalel, Binnui, and Manasseh.

³¹From the descendants of Harim, these men: Eliezer, Ishijah, Malkijah, Shemaiah, Shimeon, ³²Benjamin, Malluch, and Shemariah.

³³From the descendants of Hashum, these men: Mattenai, Mattattah, Zabad, Eliphelet, Jeremai, Manasseh, and Shimei.

³⁴From the descendants of Bani, these men: Maadai, Amram, Uel, ³⁵Benaiah, Bedeiah, Keluhi, ³⁶Vaniah, Meremoth, Eliashib, ³⁷Mattaniah, Mattenai, and Jaasu.

³⁸From the descendants of Binnui, these men: Shimei, ³⁹Shelemiah, Nathan, Adaiah, ⁴⁰Macnadebai, Shashai, Sharai, ⁴¹Azarel, Shelemiah, Shemariah, ⁴²Shallum, Amariah, and Joseph.

⁴³From the descendants of Nebo, these men: Jeiel, Mattithiah, Zabad, Zebina, Jaddai, Joel, and Benaiah.

⁴⁴All these men had married foreign women, and some of them had children with these wives.

Nehemiah

Nehemiah's Prayer

1 ¹These are the words of Nehemiah son of Hacaliah: I, Nehemiah, was in the capital city of Susa in the month of Kislev. This was in the 20th year[a] that Artaxerxes was king. ²While I was in Susa, one of my brothers named Hanani and some other men came from Judah. I asked them about the Jews who had escaped captivity and still lived in Judah. I also asked them about the city of Jerusalem.

³They answered, "Nehemiah, the Jews who escaped captivity and are in the land of Judah are in much trouble. They are having many problems and are full of shame because the wall of Jerusalem is broken down, and its gates have been burned with fire."

⁴When I heard this about the people of Jerusalem and about the wall, I sat down and cried. I was very sad. I fasted* and prayed to the God of Heaven for several days. ⁵Then I prayed this prayer:

"Lord, God of Heaven, you are the great and powerful God. You are the God who keeps his agreement of love with people who love you and obey your commands.

⁶"Please open your eyes and ears and listen to the prayer your servant is praying before you day and night. I am praying for your servants, the Israelites. I confess the sins we Israelites have done against you. I am confessing that I have sinned against you and that the other people in my father's family have sinned against you. ⁷We Israelites have been very bad to you. We have not obeyed the commands, rules, and laws you gave your servant Moses.

⁸"Please remember the teaching you gave your servant Moses. You said to him, 'If you Israelites are not faithful, I will force you to be scattered among the other nations. ⁹But if you Israelites come back to me and obey my commands, this is what I will do: Even if your people have been forced to leave their homes and go to the ends of the earth, I will gather them from there. And I will bring them back to the place I have chosen to put my name.'

*a*1:1 *Kislev ... 20th year* This was about December, 444 B.C.

[10]"The Israelites are your servants and your people. You used your great power and rescued them. [11]So, Lord, please listen to my prayer. I am your servant. Please listen to the prayers of your servants who want to show respect for your name. You know I am the king's wine servant,[a] so please help me today. Help me as I ask the king for help. Give me success and help me to be pleasing to the king."

The King Sends Nehemiah to Jerusalem

2 [1]In the month of Nisan* in the 20th year[b] of King Artaxerxes, some wine was brought to the king. I took the wine and gave it to the king. I had never before been sad when I was with him, but now I was sad. [2]So the king asked me, "Are you sick? Why do you look sad? I think your heart is full of sadness."

Then I was very afraid. [3]But even though I was afraid, I said to the king, "May the king live forever! I am sad because the city where my ancestors* are buried lies in ruins, and the gates of that city have been destroyed by fire."

[4]Then the king said to me, "What do you want me to do?"

Before I answered, I prayed to the God of Heaven. [5]Then I answered the king, "If it would please the king, and if I have been good to you, please send me to Jerusalem, the city in Judah where my ancestors are buried. I want to go there and rebuild that city."

[6]The king and the queen who was sitting next to him asked me, "How long will your trip take? When will you get back here?"

The king was happy to send me, so I gave him a certain time. [7]I also said to the king, "If it would please the king to do something else for me, let me ask. Please give me some letters to show the governors of the area west of the Euphrates River. I need these letters so that the governors will give me permission to pass safely through their lands on my way to Judah. [8]I also need lumber for the heavy wooden beams for the gates, the walls, the walls around the Temple,* and my house. So I need a letter from you to Asaph, who is in charge of your forests."

The king gave me the letters and everything I asked for. The king did that because God was kind to me.

[9]So I went to the governors of the area west of the Euphrates River and gave them the letters from the king. The king had also sent army officers and soldiers on horses with me. [10]Sanballat from Horon and Tobiah the Ammonite official heard about what I was doing. They were very upset and angry that someone had come to help the Israelites.

Nehemiah Inspects the Walls of Jerusalem

[11-12]I went to Jerusalem and stayed there three days. Then at night I started out with a few men. I had not said anything to anyone about what God had put on my heart to do for Jerusalem. There were no horses with me except the horse I was riding. [13]While it was dark I went out through the Valley Gate. I rode toward the Dragon Well and the Gate of the Ash Piles. I was inspecting the walls of Jerusalem that had been broken down and the gates in the wall that had been burned with fire. [14]Then I rode on toward the Fountain Gate and the King's Pool. As I got close, I could see there was not enough room for my horse to get through. [15]So I went up the valley in the dark, inspecting the wall. Finally, I turned back and went back in through the Valley Gate. [16]The officials and important Israelites didn't know where I had gone. They didn't know what I was doing. I had not yet said anything to the Jews, the priests, the king's family, the officials, or any of the other people who would be doing the work.

[17]Then I said to them, "You can see the trouble we have here: Jerusalem is a pile of ruins, and its gates have been burned with fire. Come, let's rebuild the wall of Jerusalem. Then we will not be ashamed anymore."

[18]I also told them that God had been kind to me. I told them what the king had said to me. Then they answered, "Let's start to work, now!" So we began this good work. [19]But Sanballat from Horon, Tobiah the Ammonite official, and Geshem the Arab heard that we were building again. They made fun of us in a very ugly way. They said, "What are you doing? Are you turning against the king?"

[20]But this is what I said to them: "The God of Heaven will help us succeed. We are God's servants and we will rebuild this city. You cannot help us in this work because none of your family lived here in Jerusalem. You don't own any of this land, and you have no right to be in this place."

Builders of the Wall

3 [1]The name of the high priest was Eliashib. He and his brothers the priests went to work and built the Sheep Gate. They prayed and made that gate holy to the Lord. They set its doors in place in the wall. The priests worked on the wall of Jerusalem as far as the Tower of the Hundred and the Tower of Hananel. They prayed and made their work holy to the Lord.

[2]The men from Jericho built the wall next to the priests. And Zaccur son of a man named Imri built the wall next to the men of Jericho.

[3]The sons of a man named Hassenaah built the Fish Gate. They set the beams in place.

---

[a]*1:11 wine servant* A very important job. This official was always close to the king and tasted the king's wine to make sure no one was trying to poison the king.
[b]*2:1 20th year* That is, 443 B.C.

They put doors on the building. Then they put the locks and bolts on the doors.

[4]Meremoth son of Uriah repaired the next section of the wall. (Uriah was the son of Hakkoz.)

Meshullam son of Berekiah repaired the next section of the wall. (Berekiah was the son of Meshezabel.)

Zadok son of Baana repaired the next section of the wall.

[5]The men from Tekoa repaired the next section of the wall, but the leaders from Tekoa refused to work for Nehemiah their governor.

[6]Joiada and Meshullam fixed the Old Gate. Joiada is the son of Paseah and Meshullam is the son of Besodeiah. They set the beams in place. They put the doors on the hinges. Then they put the locks and bolts on the doors.

[7]The men from Gibeon and Mizpah fixed the next section of the wall. Melatiah from Gibeon and Jadon from Meronoth did the work. Gibeon and Meronoth are places that are controlled by the governors of the area west of the Euphrates River.

[8]Uzziel son of Harhaiah repaired the next section of the wall. Uzziel was a goldsmith.* Hananiah was one of the perfume makers. These men built and repaired Jerusalem as far as the Broad Wall.

[9]Rephaiah son of Hur repaired the next section of the wall. Rephaiah was the governor of half of Jerusalem.

[10]Jedaiah son of Harumaph repaired the next section of the wall. Jedaiah repaired the wall next to his own house. Hattush son of Hashabneiah repaired the next section.

[11]Malkijah son of Harim and Hasshub son of Pahath-Moab repaired the next section. They also repaired Oven Tower.

[12]Shallum son of Hallohesh repaired the next section of the wall. His daughters helped him. Shallum was the governor of the other half of Jerusalem.

[13]The Valley Gate was repaired by Hanun and the people who live in the town of Zanoah. They built the Valley Gate. They put the doors on their hinges. Then they put the locks and bolts on the doors. They also repaired 500 yards[a] of the wall. They worked on the wall all the way to the Gate of Ash Piles.

[14]Malkijah son of Recab repaired the Gate of Ash Piles. Malkijah was the governor of the district of Beth Hakkerem. He repaired the gate. He put the doors on the hinges. Then he put the locks and bolts on the doors.

[15]Shallun son of Col-Hozeh repaired the Fountain Gate. Shallun was the governor of the district of Mizpah. He repaired the gate and put a roof over it. He put the doors on the hinges. Then he put the locks and bolts on the doors. He also repaired the wall of the Pool of Siloam that is next to the King's Garden. He

repaired the wall all the way to the steps that go down from the City of David.*

[16]Nehemiah son of Azbuk repaired the next section. This Nehemiah was the governor of half the district of Beth Zur. He made repairs up to a place that is across from the tombs of David. And he worked as far as the man-made pool and the House of Heroes.

[17]The men from the tribe of Levi repaired the next section. They worked under Rehum son of Bani. Hashabiah repaired the next section. Hashabiah was governor of half the district of Keilah. He made repairs for his own district.

[18]Their brothers repaired the next section. They worked under Binnui son of Henadad. Binnui was the governor of the other half of the district of Keilah.

[19]Ezer son of Jeshua repaired the next section. Ezer was governor of Mizpah. He repaired the section of wall from the room for weapons to the corner of the wall. [20]Baruch son of Zabbai repaired the next section. Baruch worked very hard and repaired the section of wall from the corner to the entrance to the house of Eliashib the high priest. [21]Meremoth son of Uriah, the son of Hakkoz, repaired the next section of wall from the entrance to Eliashib's house to the end of that house. [22]The next section of walls was repaired by the priests who lived in that area.[b]

[23]Benjamin and Hasshub repaired the wall in front of their own house. And Azariah son of Maaseiah, the son of Ananiah, repaired the wall next to his house.

[24]Binnui son of Henadad repaired the section of wall from Azariah's house to the bend in the wall and then to the corner.

[25]Palal son of Uzai worked across from the bend in the wall near the tower. This is the tower at the king's upper house. That is near the courtyard of the king's guard. Pedaiah son of Parosh worked next to Palal.

[26]The Temple* servants lived on Ophel Hill. They repaired the next section all the way to the east side of the Water Gate and the tower near it.

[27]The men from Tekoa repaired the rest of that section from the big tower all the way to the Ophel wall.

[28]The priests repaired the section over the Horse Gate. Each priest repaired the wall in front of his own house. [29]Zadok son of Immer repaired the section in front of his house. Shemaiah son of Shecaniah repaired the next section. Shemaiah was the guard of the East Gate.

[30]Hananiah son of Shelemiah and Hanun son of Zalaph repaired the rest of that section of wall. (Hanun was Zalaph's sixth son.)

Meshullam son of Berekiah repaired the section in front of his house. [31]Malkijah repaired the next section of wall all the way

---

[a]**3:13** *500 yards* Literally, "1000 cubits" (444 m).   [b]**3:22** *that area* Or possibly, "the Jordan Valley."

to the houses of the Temple servants and the merchants.* That is across from the Inspection Gate. Malkijah repaired the section all the way to the room over the corner of the wall. Malkijah was a goldsmith. ³²The goldsmiths and the merchants repaired the section of wall between the room over the corner to the Sheep Gate.

Sanballat and Tobiah

4 ¹When Sanballat heard that we were building the wall of Jerusalem, he was very angry and upset. He started making fun of the Jews. ²Sanballat talked with his friends and the army at Samaria and said, "What are these weak Jews doing? Do they think we will leave them alone? Do they think they will offer sacrifices*? Maybe they think they can finish building in only one day. They cannot bring stones back to life from these piles of trash and dirt. These are just piles of ashes and dirt!"

³Tobiah the Ammonite was with Sanballat. Tobiah said, "What do these Jews think they are building? If even a small fox climbed up on it, he would break down their wall of stones!"

⁴Nehemiah prayed and said, "Our God, listen to our prayer. These men hate us. Sanballat and Tobiah are insulting us. Make bad things happen to them. Make them ashamed, like people taken away as prisoners. ⁵Don't take away their guilt or forgive the sins they have done in your sight. They have insulted and discouraged the builders."

⁶We built the wall of Jerusalem all the way around the city. But it was only half as tall as it should be. We did this much because the people worked with all their heart.

⁷But Sanballat, Tobiah, the Arabs, the Ammonites, and the men from Ashdod were very angry. They heard that the people continued working on the walls of Jerusalem. They heard the people were repairing the holes in the wall. ⁸So all these men got together and made plans against Jerusalem. They planned to stir up trouble against Jerusalem. They planned to come and fight against the city. ⁹But we prayed to our God. And we put guards on the walls to watch day and night so that we could be ready to meet them.

¹⁰And so at that time the people of Judah said, "The workers are becoming tired. There is too much dirt and trash in the way. We cannot continue to build the wall. ¹¹And our enemies are saying, 'Before the Jews know it or see us, we will be right there among them. We will kill them and that will stop the work.'"

¹²Then the Jews living among our enemies came and said this to us ten times, "Our enemies are all around us. They are everywhere we turn."

¹³So I put some of the people behind the lowest places along the wall, and I put them by the holes in the wall. I put families together, with their swords, spears, and bows. ¹⁴After looking over everything, I stood up and spoke to the important families, the officials, and the rest of the people. I said, "Don't be afraid of our enemies. Remember the Lord, who is great and powerful! You must fight for your brothers, your sons, and your daughters! You must fight for your wives and your homes!"

¹⁵Then our enemies heard that we knew about their plans. They knew that God ruined their plans. So we all went back to work on the wall. Everyone went back to their own place and did their part. ¹⁶From that day on, half of my men worked on the wall. The other half of my men were on guard, ready with spears, shields, bows, and armor.* The army officers stood behind all the people of Judah who were building the wall. ¹⁷The builders and their helpers had their tools in one hand and a weapon in the other hand. ¹⁸Each of the builders wore his sword at his side as he worked. The man who blew the trumpet to warn the people stayed next to me. ¹⁹Then I spoke to the leading families, the officials, and the rest of the people. I said, "This is a very big job and we are spread out along the wall. We are far from one another. ²⁰So if you hear the trumpet, run to that place. We will all meet together there, and God will fight for us!"

²¹So we continued to work on the wall of Jerusalem, and half the men held spears. We worked from the first light of the morning until the stars came out at night.

²²At that time I also said this to the people, "Every builder and his helper must stay inside Jerusalem at night. Then they can be guards at night and workers during the day." ²³So none of us took off our clothes—not me, not my brothers, not my men, and not the guards. Each of us had our weapon ready at all times, even when we went to get water.

Nehemiah Helps the Poor

5 ¹Many of the poor people began to complain against their fellow Jews. ²Some of them were saying, "We have many children. We must get some grain if we are going to eat and stay alive."

³Other people were saying, "This is a time of famine.* We have to use our fields, vineyards,* and homes to pay for grain."

⁴And still other people were saying, "We have to pay the king's tax on our fields and vineyards. But we cannot afford to pay, so we are borrowing money to pay the tax. ⁵We are as good as the others. Our sons are as good as their sons. But we will have to sell our sons and daughters as slaves. Some of us have already had to sell our daughters as slaves. There is nothing we can do. We have already lost our fields and vineyards. Other people own them now."

⁶When I heard their complaints, I was very

angry. ⁷I calmed myself down, and then I went to the rich families and the officials. I told them, "You are forcing your own people to pay interest on the money you loan them. You must stop doing that!" Then I called for all the people to meet together ⁸and said to them, "Our fellow Jews were sold as slaves to people in other countries. We did our best to buy them back and make them free. And now, you are selling them like slaves again!"

The rich people and officials kept quiet. They could not find anything to say. ⁹So I continued speaking. I said, "What you people are doing is not right! You know that you should fear and respect God. You should not do the shameful things other people do! ¹⁰My men, my brothers, and I are also lending money and grain to the people. But let's stop forcing them to pay interest on these loans. ¹¹You must give their fields, vineyards, olive fields, and houses back to them, right now! And you must give back the interest you charged them. You charged them one percent for the money, grain, new wine, and oil that you loaned them."

¹²Then the rich people and the officials said, "We will give it back and not demand anything more from them. Nehemiah, we will do as you say."

Then I called the priests. I made the rich people and the officials promise to God that they would do what they said. ¹³Then I shook out the folds of my clothes. I said, "God will do the same thing to everyone who does not keep their promise. God will shake them out of their houses and they will lose everything they worked for. They will lose everything!"

I finished saying these things and all the people agreed. They all said, "Amen" and praised the LORD. So the people did as they had promised.

¹⁴And also, during the whole time that I was appointed to be governor in the land of Judah, neither my brothers nor I ate the food that was allowed for the governor. I never forced the people to pay taxes to buy my food. I was governor from the 20th year until the 32nd year that Artaxerxes was king.ᵃ I was governor of Judah for twelve years. ¹⁵But the governors who ruled before me made life hard for the people. The governors forced everyone to pay 1 poundᵇ of silver. They also made the people give them food and wine. The leaders under these governors also ruled over the people and made life even harder. But I respected and feared God, so I didn't do things like that. ¹⁶I worked hard at building the wall of Jerusalem. All my men gathered there to work on the wall. We didn't take any land from anyone.

¹⁷Also, I regularly fed 150 Jews who were always welcome at my table, and I fed those who came to us from the nations around us. ¹⁸Every day I prepared this much food for the people who ate at my table: one ox, six good sheep, and different kinds of birds. Every ten days all kinds of wine were brought to my table. But I never demanded that they give me the food that was allowed for the governor. I knew that the work the people were doing was very hard. ¹⁹God, remember all the good I have done for these people.

More Problems

6 ¹Then Sanballat, Tobiah, Geshem the Arab, and our other enemies heard that I had built the wall. We repaired all the holes in the wall, but we had not yet put the doors in the gates. ²So Sanballat and Geshem sent me this message: "Come Nehemiah, let's meet together. We can meet in the town of Kephirim on the plain of Ono." But they were planning to hurt me.

³So I sent messengers to them with this answer: "I am doing important work, so I cannot come down. I don't want the work to stop just so I can come down and meet with you."

⁴Sanballat and Geshem sent the same message to me four times, and I sent the same answer back to them each time. ⁵Then, the fifth time, Sanballat sent his helper to me with the same message. And he had a letter in his hand that was not sealed. ⁶This is what the letter said: "There is a rumor going around. People are talking about it everywhere. And, by the way, Geshem says it is true. People are saying that you and the Jews are planning to turn against the king. This is why you are building the wall of Jerusalem. People are also saying that you will be the new king of the Jews. ⁷And the rumor is that you have chosen prophets to announce this about you in Jerusalem: 'There is a king in Judah!'

"Now I warn you, Nehemiah, King Artaxerxes will hear about this. So come, let's meet and talk about this together."

⁸So I sent this answer back to Sanballat: "Nothing you are saying is happening. You are just making all that up in your own head."

⁹Our enemies were only trying to make us afraid. They are thinking to themselves, "The Jews will be afraid and too weak to keep on working. Then the wall will not be finished."

But I prayed, "God, make me strong."

¹⁰One day I went to the house of a man named Shemaiah son of Delaiah. Delaiah was the son of Mehetabel. Shemaiah had to stay in his house. He said,

"Nehemiah, let's meet in God's Temple.*
    Let's go inside the Holy Placeᶜ and lock
    the doors.

ᵃ5:14 *the 20th year ... king* This was from 444–432 B.C.

ᵇ5:15 *1 pound* Literally, "40 shekels" (460 g).

ᶜ6:10 *Holy Place* Literally, "palace." Only priests were allowed to go into this part of the Temple.

Men are coming to kill you.
Tonight they are coming to kill you."

[11]But I said to Shemaiah, "Should a man like me run away? You know that an ordinary man like me cannot go into the Holy Place without being put to death. I will not go!"

[12]I knew that God had not sent Shemaiah. I knew that he had prophesied against me because Tobiah and Sanballat had paid him to do that. [13]They hired Shemaiah to scare me and make me sin ⌊by going into that part of the Temple⌋. They were planning those bad things against me so that they could shame me.

[14]God, please remember Tobiah and Sanballat and the bad things they have done. Also remember the woman prophet Noadiah and the other prophets who have been trying to scare me.

The Wall Is Finished

[15]So the wall of Jerusalem was completed on the 25th day of the month of Elul.[a] It had taken 52 days to finish building the wall. [16]Then all our enemies heard that we had completed the wall, and all the nations around us saw that it was finished. So they lost their courage, because they understood that this work had been done with the help of our God.

[17]Also in those days after the wall had been completed, the rich people of Judah were sending many letters to Tobiah, and he was answering their letters. [18]They sent those letters because many people in Judah had promised to be loyal to him. The reason for this is because Tobiah was son-in-law to Shecaniah son of Arah. And Tobiah's son Jehohanan had married the daughter of Meshullam. Meshullam is the son of Berekiah. [19]And in the past, those people had made a special promise to Tobiah. So they kept telling me how good Tobiah was. And they kept telling Tobiah what I was doing. Tobiah kept sending me letters to make me afraid.

7 [1]After we finished building the wall and put the doors in the gates, we chose the men who would guard the gates and the men to sing in the Temple* and help the priests. [2]Next, I put my brother Hanani in charge of Jerusalem. I chose another man named Hananiah to be the commander of the fort. I picked Hanani because he was a very honest man and he feared God more than most people do. [3]Then I said to Hanani and Hananiah, "Each day you must wait until the sun has been up for several hours before you open the gates of Jerusalem. You must shut and lock the gates before the sun goes down. Also choose people who live in Jerusalem as guards. Put some of them at special places to guard the city, and put the other people near their own houses."

The List of Captives Who Returned

[4]Now the city was large and there was plenty of room. But there were few people in it, and the houses had not yet been rebuilt. [5]So my God put it in my heart to have all the people meet together. I called together all the important people, the officials, and the common people. I did this so that I could make a list of all the families. I found the family lists[b] of the people who had been the first to return from captivity. This is what I found written there:

[6]These are the people of the province who came back from captivity. In the past, King Nebuchadnezzar of Babylon took them as prisoners to Babylon. These people came back to Jerusalem and Judah. They all went to their own towns. [7]They returned with Zerubbabel, Jeshua, Nehemiah, Azariah, Raamiah, Nahamani, Mordecai, Bilshan, Mispereth, Bigvai, Nehum, and Baanah. This is the list of names and numbers of men from Israel who came back:

8	the descendants of Parosh	2172
9	the descendants of Shephatiah	372
10	the descendants of Arah	652
11	the descendants of Pahath Moab of the family line of Jeshua and Joab	2818
12	the descendants of Elam	1254
13	the descendants of Zattu	845
14	the descendants of Zaccai	760
15	the descendants of Binnui	648
16	the descendants of Bebai	628
17	the descendants of Azgad	2322
18	the descendants of Adonikam	667
19	the descendants of Bigvai	2067
20	the descendants of Adin	655
21	the descendants of Ater through the family of Hezekiah	98
22	the descendants of Hashum	328
23	the descendants of Bezai	324
24	the descendants of Hariph	112
25	the descendants of Gibeon	95
26	from the towns of Bethlehem and Netophah	188
27	from the town of Anathoth	128
28	from the town of Beth Azmaveth	42
29	from the towns of Kiriath Jearim, Kephirah, and Beeroth	743
30	from the towns of Ramah and Geba	621
31	from the town of Micmash	122
32	from the towns of Bethel and Ai	123
33	from the other town of Nebo	52
34	from the other town of Elam	1254
35	from the town of Harim	320
36	from the town of Jericho	345
37	from the towns of Lod, Hadid, and Ono	721
38	from the town of Senaah	3930

[a]6:15 Elul That is, August–September, 443 B.C.   [b]7:5 family lists See Ezra 2.

39These are the priests:

the descendants of Jedaiah through
the family of Jeshua   973
40 the descendants of Immer   1052
41 the descendants of Pashhur   1247
42 the descendants of Harim   1017

43These are the people from the tribe of Levi:

the descendants of Jeshua through
Kadmiel through the family of
Hodeiah[a]   74

44These are the singers:

the descendants of Asaph   148

45These are the gatekeepers:

the descendants of Shallum, Ater, Talmon,
Akkub, Hatita, and Shobai   138

46These are the special Temple* servants:

the descendants of Ziha, Hasupha,
Tabbaoth,
47 Keros, Sia, Padon,
48 Lebana, Hagaba, Shalmai,
49 Hanan, Giddel, Gaher,
50 Reaiah, Rezin, Nekoda,
51 Gazzam, Uzza, Paseah,
52 Besai, Meunim, Nephussim,
53 Bakbuk, Hakupha, Harhur,
54 Bazluth, Mehida, Harsha,
55 Barkos, Sisera, Temah,
56 Neziah, and Hatipha.

57These are the descendants of the servants
of Solomon:

Sotai, Sophereth, Perida,
58 Jaala, Darkon, Giddel,
59 Shephatiah, Hattil, Pokereth Hazzebaim,
and Amon,
60 the Temple servants and the
descendants of Solomon's servants 392

61Some people came to Jerusalem from
these towns of Tel Melah, Tel Harsha, Kerub,
Addon, and Immer. But these people could
not prove that their families really came from
the Israelites:

62 the descendants of Delaiah, Tobiah,
and Nekoda   642

63From the family of priests there were the
descendants of

Hobaiah, Hakkoz, and Barzillai (If a man
married a daughter of Barzillai from
Gilead, he was counted as a descendant
of Barzillai.)
[a]7:43 Hodeiah Or "Hodaviah."

64These people searched for their family
histories, but they could not find them. They
could not prove that their ancestors* were
priests, so they could not serve as priests.
Their names were not included in the list of
priests. 65The governor ordered them not to
eat any of the most holy food until a priest
could use the Urim* and Thummim* to ask
God what to do.

66-67All together, there were 42,360 people in the group who came back. This is not
counting their 7337 men and women slaves.
They also had 245 men and women singers
with them. 68-69They had 736 horses, 245
mules, 435 camels, and 6720 donkeys.

70Some of the family leaders gave money
to support the work. The governor gave 19
pounds[b] of gold to the treasury. He also gave
50 bowls and 530 pieces of clothing for the
priests. 71The family leaders gave 375 pounds[c]
of gold to the treasury to support the work.
They also gave 2750 pounds[d] of silver. 72All
together the other people gave 375 pounds of
gold, 2500 pounds[e] of silver, and 67 pieces of
clothing for the priests.

73So the priests, the people from the tribe
of Levi, the gatekeepers, the singers, and the
Temple servants settled down in their own
towns. And all the other Israelites settled
down in their own towns. By the seventh
month[f] of the year, all the Israelites had settled down in their own towns.

Ezra Reads the Law

8 ¹So all the Israelites met together in the
seventh month of the year. They were
united and in complete agreement. They all
met together in the open place in front of
the Water Gate. All the people asked Ezra
the teacher to bring out the *Book of the Law
of Moses*, which the LORD had given to the
Israelites. ²So Ezra the priest brought the law
before those who had met together. This was
on the first day of the month.[g] It was the seventh month of the year. Men, women, and
anyone old enough to listen and understand
were at the meeting. ³Ezra read in a loud
voice from the *Book of the Law* from early
morning until noon. He was facing the open
place that was in front of the Water Gate. He
read to all the men and women, and to everyone old enough to listen and understand. All
the people listened carefully and paid attention to the *Book of the Law*.

⁴Ezra stood on a high wooden stage. It had

[b]7:70 19 pounds Literally, "1000 drachmas" (8.63 kg).
[c]7:71 375 pounds Literally, "20,000 drachmas"
(172.5 kg).
[d]7:71 2750 pounds Literally, "2200 minas" (1265 kg).
[e]7:72 2500 pounds Literally, "2000 minas" (1150 kg).
[f]7:73 seventh month That is, September–October.
Also in 8:1, 14–15.
[g]8:2 first day of the month This was a special day
of worship. The people met together and shared a
fellowship meal.

been built just for this special time. On his right side stood Mattithiah, Shema, Anaiah, Uriah, Hilkiah, and Maaseiah. And on his left side stood Pedaiah, Mishael, Malkijah, Hashum, Hashbaddanah, Zechariah, and Meshullam.

⁵So Ezra opened the book. All the people could see him because he was standing above them on the high stage. As he opened the *Book of the Law*, all the people stood up. ⁶Ezra praised the LORD, the great God, and all the people held up their hands and said, "Amen! Amen!" Then all the people bowed down and put their faces low to the ground and they worshiped the LORD.

⁷These men from the tribe of Levi taught the people about the law as they were all standing there. The Levites were Jeshua, Bani, Sherebiah, Jamin, Akkub, Shabbethai, Hodiah, Maaseiah, Kelita, Azariah, Jozabad, Hanan, and Pelaiah. ⁸They read the *Book of the Law of God*. They made it easy to understand, and explained what it meant. They did this so that the people could understand what was being read.

⁹Then Nehemiah the governor, Ezra the priest and teacher, and the Levites who were teaching the people spoke. They said, "Today is a special day*ᵃ* to the LORD your God. Don't be sad and cry." They said that because all the people had begun to cry as they were listening to the messages of God in the law.

¹⁰Nehemiah said, "Go and enjoy the good food and sweet drinks. Give some food and drinks to those who didn't prepare any food. Today is a special day to the LORD. Don't be sad, because the joy of the LORD will make you strong."

¹¹The Levites helped the people to calm down. They said, "Be quiet, calm down, this is a special day. Don't be sad."

¹²Then all the people went to eat the special meal. They shared their food and drinks. They were very happy and celebrated that special day. They finally understood the lessons from the LORD that the teachers had been trying to teach them.

¹³Then on the second day of the month,*ᵇ* the leaders of all the families went to meet with Ezra, the priests, and the Levites. They all gathered around Ezra the teacher to study the words of the law.

¹⁴⁻¹⁵They studied and found these commands in the law. The LORD gave this command to the people through Moses: In the seventh month of the year, the Israelites must go to Jerusalem to celebrate a special festival. They must live in temporary shelters. And the people are supposed to go through all of their towns and Jerusalem and say this: "Go out

into the hill country and get branches from different kinds of olive trees. Get branches from myrtle trees, palm trees, and shade trees. Use the branches to make temporary shelters. Do what the law says."

¹⁶So the people went out and got tree branches. Then they built temporary shelters for themselves. They built shelters on their own roofs and in their own yards. And they built shelters in the Temple* yard, in the open place near the Water Gate, and near Ephraim Gate. ¹⁷The whole group that had come back from captivity built shelters. They lived in the shelters they had built. Since the days of Joshua son of Nun up until that day, the Israelites had not celebrated the Festival of Shelters* like this. Everyone was very happy!

¹⁸Ezra read to them from the *Book of the Law* every day of the festival from the first day of the festival to the last day. The Israelites celebrated the festival for seven days. Then on the eighth day the people met together for a special meeting, as the law says.

The People of Israel Confess Their Sins

9 ¹Then on the 24th day of that same month, the Israelites gathered together for a day of fasting.* They wore sackcloth* and put ashes on their heads to show they were sad and upset. ²Those people who were true Israelites separated themselves from foreigners. The Israelites stood and confessed their sins and the sins of their ancestors.* ³They stood there for about three hours, and the people read the *Book of the Law* of the LORD their God. Then for three more hours they confessed their sins and bowed down to worship the LORD their God.

⁴Then these Levites stood on the stairs: Jeshua, Bani, Kadmiel, Shebaniah, Bunni, Sherebiah, Bani, and Kenani. They called out to the LORD their God with loud voices. ⁵Then these Levites spoke again: Jeshua, Bani, Kadmiel, Bani, Hashabneiah, Sherebiah, Hodiah, Shebaniah, and Pethahiah. They said, "Stand up and praise the LORD your God!

"God has always lived and will live forever.
  People should praise your glorious name.
    May your name be lifted above all
      blessing and praise.
6 You are God.
    LORD, only you are God.
  You made the sky and the highest heavens
    and everything in them.
  You made the earth
    and everything on it.
  You made the seas
    and everything in them.
  You give life to everything.
    All the heavenly angels bow down and
      worship you.
7 You are the LORD God.
  You chose Abram.

---

*ᵃ***8:9** *special day* The first and second days of each month were special days of worship. The people met together and shared a fellowship meal.

*ᵇ***8:13** *second day of the month* The first and second days of each month were special days of worship. The people met together and shared a fellowship meal.

You led him from Ur in Babylonia.
You changed his name to Abraham.
8 You saw he was true and loyal to you,
and you made an agreement with him.
You promised to give him the land
of the Canaanites, Hittites, Amorites,
Perizzites, Jebusites, and the
Girgashites.
But you promised to give that land to
Abraham's descendants.
And you kept your promise because you
are good.

9 You saw our ancestors suffering in Egypt
and heard them call for help by the Red
Sea.
10 You showed the miracles to Pharaoh.
You did amazing things to his officials
and his people.
You knew that the Egyptians thought
they were better than our ancestors.
But you proved how great you are,
and they remember that even today.
11 You split the Red Sea in front of them,
and they walked through on dry land.
The Egyptian soldiers were chasing them,
but you threw that enemy into the
sea.
And they sank like a rock into the sea.
12 With the tall cloud, you led them by day,
and at night you used the column of
fire.
That is the way you lit their path
and showed them where to go.
13 Then you came down to Mount Sinai.
You spoke to them from heaven.
You gave them good laws.
You gave them true teachings.
You gave them laws and commands that
were very good.
14 You told them about your special day of
rest—the Sabbath.
Through your servant Moses, you gave
them commands, laws, and teachings.
15 They were hungry,
so you gave them food from heaven.
They were thirsty,
so you gave them water from a rock.
You told them,
'Come, take this land.'
You used your power,
and took the land for them.
16 But our ancestors became proud and
stubborn.
They refused to obey your commands.
17 They refused to listen.
They forgot the amazing things you did
with them.
They became stubborn.
They decided to return to Egypt and
become slaves again.

"But you are a forgiving God!
You are kind and full of mercy.
You are patient and full of love.
So you didn't leave them!

18 You didn't leave them even when they
made golden calves and said,
'These are the gods that led us out of
Egypt.'
19 You are very kind,
so you didn't leave them in the desert.
You didn't take the tall cloud
away from them by day.
You continued to lead them.
You didn't take the column of fire
away from them at night.
You continued to light their path
and show them which way to go.
20 You gave them your good Spirit to make
them wise.
You gave them manna* for food.
You gave them water for their thirst.
21 You took care of them for 40 years.
They had all they needed in the desert.
Their clothes didn't wear out,
and their feet didn't swell and hurt.
22 You gave them kingdoms and nations,
and you gave them faraway places
where few people live.
They got the land of King Sihon of
Heshbon.
They got the land of King Og of Bashan.
23 You made their descendants
as many as the stars in the sky.
You brought them to the land
you promised to give their ancestors.
They went in and took that land.
24 Their children took the land.
They defeated the Canaanites living there.
You let them defeat those people.
You let them do whatever they wanted
to those nations, people, and kings.
25 They defeated powerful cities.
They took the fertile land.
They got houses filled with good things.
They got wells that were already dug.
They got vineyards,* olive trees, and
plenty of fruit trees.
They ate until they were full and fat.
They enjoyed all the wonderful things you
gave them.
26 And then they turned against you.
They threw away your teachings.
They killed your prophets.
Those prophets warned the people.
They tried to bring them back to you.
But our ancestors said terrible things
against you.
27 So you let their enemies have them.
The enemy caused them much trouble.
When trouble came, our ancestors called
to you for help.
And in heaven, you heard them.
You are very kind,
so you sent people to save them.
And they rescued them from their
enemies.
28 Then as soon as our ancestors were
rested,
they started doing terrible things again!

So you let the enemy defeat them and
    punish them.
They called to you for help,
    and in heaven you heard them and
    helped them.
You are so kind.
    That happened so many times.
29 You warned them.
You told them to come back,
    but they were too proud.
They refused to listen to your
    commands.
If people obey your laws,
    they will live.
But our ancestors broke your laws.
They were stubborn.
    They turned their backs on you.
    They refused to listen.

30"You were very patient with our ancestors.
You let them mistreat you for many
    years.
You warned them with your Spirit.
    You sent the prophets to warn them.
But our ancestors didn't listen.
    So you gave them to people in other
    countries.

31"But you are so kind!
You didn't completely destroy them.
You didn't leave them.
    You are such a kind and merciful God!
32 Our God, you are the great God,
    the awesome, powerful soldier!
You are kind and loyal.
    You keep your agreement.
We have had many troubles,
    and our troubles are important to you.
Bad things happened to all our people,
    and to our kings and leaders,
    and to our priests and prophets.
Those terrible things have happened
    from the days of the king of Assyria
    until today!
33 But God, you were right
    about everything that happened to us.
You were right,
    and we were wrong.
34 Our kings, leaders, priests, and fathers did
    not obey your law.
They didn't listen to your commands.
    They ignored your warnings.
35 Our ancestors didn't serve you even
    when they were living in their own
    kingdom.
They didn't stop doing evil.
They enjoyed all the wonderful things
    you gave them.
They enjoyed the rich land and had plenty
    of room,
    but they didn't stop their evil ways.
36 And now, we are slaves.
We are slaves in this land,
    the land you gave our ancestors
    so they could enjoy its fruit

and all the good things that grow here.
37 The harvest is big in this land.
    But we sinned, so that harvest goes to
    the kings you put over us.
They control us and our cattle.
    They do anything they want.
    We are in a lot of trouble.
38 Because of all these things,
    we are making an agreement that
    cannot be changed.
We are putting this agreement in
    writing.
Our leaders, Levites, and priests are
    signing their names to this agreement
    and sealing it with a seal.*"

10

1These are the names on the sealed
agreement: Nehemiah the governor,
son of Hacaliah. Zedekiah, 2Seraiah, Azariah, Jeremiah, 3Pashhur, Amariah, Malkijah, 4Hattush, Shebaniah, Malluch, 5Harim,
Meremoth, Obadiah, 6Daniel, Ginnethon,
Baruch, 7Meshullam, Abijah, Mijamin, 8Maa-
ziah, Bilgai, and Shemaiah. These were the
priests who put their names on the sealed
agreement.

9And these are the Levites who put their
names on the sealed agreement: Jeshua son
of Azaniah, Binnui from the family of Henadad, Kadmiel, 10and their brothers: Shebaniah, Hodiah, Kelita, Pelaiah, Hanan, 11Mica,
Rehob, Hashabiah, 12Zaccur, Sherebiah, Shebaniah, 13Hodiah, Bani, and Beninu.

14And these are the names of the leaders
who put their names on the sealed agreement: Parosh, Pahath-Moab, Elam, Zattu,
Bani, 15Bunni, Azgad, Bebai, 16Adonijah, Bigvai, Adin, 17Ater, Hezekiah, Azzur, 18Hodiah,
Hashum, Bezai, 19Hariph, Anathoth, Nebai,
20Magpiash, Meshullam, Hezir, 21Meshe-
zabel, Zadok, Jaddua, 22Pelatiah, Hanan,
Anaiah, 23Hoshea, Hananiah, Hasshub, 24Hal-
lohesh, Pilha, Shobek, 25Rehum, Hashabnah,
Maaseiah, 26Ahiah, Hanan, Anan, 27Malluch,
Harim, and Baanah.

28-29So all these people now make this
special promise to God. And they all ask for
bad things to happen if they don't keep their
promise. All these people promise to follow
the law of God. That law of God was given to
us through Moses his servant. These people
promise to carefully obey all the commands,
rules, and teachings of the LORD our God.
Now, these are the people who are making
this promise: The rest of the people—the
priests, Levites, gatekeepers, singers, Temple*
servants, and all the Israelites who separated
themselves from the people living around
them. They have separated themselves to
obey God's law. Their wives, sons, and daughters who are able to listen and understand
also did this. All these people joined their
brothers and the important people to accept
for themselves the promise to obey God's law.
And they accepted the curse that asks for bad

things to happen to them if they don't obey God's law.

30"We promise not to let our daughters marry the people living around us. And we promise not to let our sons marry their daughters.

31"We promise not to work on the Sabbath* day. If the people living around us bring grain or other things to sell on the Sabbath, we will not buy them on that special day or on any other festival. Every seventh year,*a* we will not plant or work the land. And every seventh year, we will cancel every debt that other people owe to us.

32"We will accept the responsibility for obeying the commands to take care of God's Temple. We will give ⅓ shekel*b* of silver each year to support the Temple service to honor our God. 33This money will pay for the special bread that the priests put on the table in the Temple. It will pay for the daily grain offerings and burnt offerings.* It will pay for the offerings on the Sabbaths, New Moon* celebrations, and other special meeting days. It will pay for the holy offerings and for the sin offerings* that make the Israelites pure.* It will pay for any work needed on the Temple of our God.

34"We, the priests, the Levites, and the people have thrown lots* to decide when each of our families is to bring a gift of wood to the Temple of our God at certain times each year. The wood is to burn on the altar of the LORD our God. We must do that just as it is written in the law.

35"We also accept the responsibility of bringing the first part of our harvest, whether from the grain in our fields or the fruit from our trees. We will bring them to the LORD's Temple each year.

36"Just as it is also written in the law, this is what we will do: We will bring our firstborn* sons and our firstborn cattle, sheep, and goats. We will bring these to the Temple of our God, to the priests who are serving there.

37"And we will also bring the first part of our harvest to priests to put in the storage rooms of the LORD's Temple. We will bring the first of our ground meal, the first of our grain offerings, the first fruit from our trees, and the first of our new wine and oil. And we will bring a tenth of our crops to the Levites, because they are the ones who collect these things in all the towns where we work. 38A priest from the family of Aaron must be with the Levites when they receive the crops. Then the Levites must bring the crops to the Temple of our God and put them in the storerooms of the Temple treasury. 39The Israelites and the Levites must bring their gifts to the storerooms. They are to bring their gifts of grain, new wine, and oil. All the things for the Temple are kept in the storerooms, and that is where the priests who are on duty stay. The singers and gatekeepers also stay there.

"We all promise that we will take care of the Temple of our God."

New People Move Into Jerusalem

11 1Now the leaders of the Israelites moved into the city of Jerusalem. The other Israelites had to decide who would move into the city. So they threw lots,* and one out of every ten people had to live in Jerusalem, the holy city. The other nine people could live in their own hometowns. 2Some people volunteered to live in Jerusalem. The other people thanked and blessed them for volunteering.

3Here are the leaders of the provinces who lived in Jerusalem. (Some of the Israelites, priests, Levites, Temple* servants, and descendants of Solomon's servants lived in the towns of Judah. Everyone lived on their own land in the different towns. 4And other people from the families of Judah and Benjamin lived in the city of Jerusalem.)

These are the descendants of Judah who moved into Jerusalem: Athaiah son of Uzziah (the son of Zechariah, who was the son of Amariah, who was the son of Shephatiah, who was the son of Mahalalel, who was a descendant of Perez) 5and Maaseiah son of Baruch (the son of Col-Hozeh, who was the son of Hazaiah, who was the son of Adaiah, who was the son of Joiarib, who was the son of Zechariah, who was a descendant of Shelah). 6The number of Perez's descendants living in Jerusalem was 468. All of them were brave men.

7These are the descendants of Benjamin who moved into Jerusalem: Sallu son of Meshullam (the son of Joed, who was the son of Pedaiah, who was the son of Kolaiah, who was the son of Maaseiah, who was the son of Ithiel, who was the son of Jeshaiah), 8and those who followed Jeshaiah were Gabbai and Sallai. All together there were 928 men. 9Joel son of Zicri was in charge of them. And Judah son of Hassenuah was in charge of the Second District of the city of Jerusalem.

10These are the priests who moved into Jerusalem: Jedaiah son of Joiarib, Jakin, 11and Seraiah son of Hilkiah (the son of Meshullam, who was the son of Zadok, who was the son of Meraioth, who was the son of Ahitub), who was the supervisor in the Temple of God, 12and 822 men of their brothers that did the work for the Temple, and Adaiah son of Jeroham (the son of Pelaliah, who was the son of Amzi, who was the son of Zechariah, who was the son of Pashhur, who was the son of Malkijah), 13and 242 men who were Adaiah's brothers (leaders of their families), Amashsai son of Azarel (the son of Ahzai, who was the son of Meshillemoth, who was the son of Immer), 14and 128 of Amashsai's brothers.

---

*a*10:31 *seventh year* See Ex. 23:10, 11.

*b*10:32 *1/3 shekel* This was probably a coin at this time, but 1 shekel is 2/5 of an ounce (11.5 g).

(These men were brave soldiers. The officer over them was Zabdiel son of Haggedolim.)

15These are the Levites who moved into Jerusalem: Shemaiah son of Hasshub (the son of Azrikam, who was the son of Hashabiah, who was the son of Bunni), 16Shabbethai and Jozabad (two of the leaders of the Levites in charge of the outside work of God's Temple), 17Mattaniah (the son of Mica, who was the son of Zabdi, who was the son of Asaph), the director who led the people in singing songs of praise and prayer, Bakbukiah (the second in charge over his brothers), and Abda son of Shammua (the son of Galal, who was the son of Jeduthun). 18So there were 284 Levites who moved into Jerusalem, the holy city.

19These are the gatekeepers who moved into Jerusalem: Akkub, Talmon, and 172 of their brothers. They watched and guarded the gates of the city.

20The other Israelites, and the other priests and Levites, lived in all the towns of Judah. Everyone lived on the land that their ancestors* had owned. 21The Temple servants lived on the hill of Ophel. Ziha and Gishpa were in charge of the Temple servants.

22The officer over the Levites in Jerusalem was Uzzi. Uzzi was the son of Bani (the son of Hashabiah, who was the son of Mattaniah, who was the son of Mica). Uzzi was a descendant of Asaph. Asaph's descendants were the singers who were responsible for the service in God's Temple. 23The singers obeyed orders from the king, which told them what to do from day to day. 24Pethahiah son of Meshezabel told the people what the king wanted done. (Meshezabel was one of the descendants of Zerah. Zerah was Judah's son.)

25The people of Judah lived in these towns: In Kiriath Arba and the small towns around it, in Dibon and the small towns around it, in Jekabzeel and the small towns around it, 26and in Jeshua, in Moladah, in Beth Pelet, 27in Hazar Shual, in Beersheba and the small towns around it, 28and in Ziklag, in Meconah and the small towns around it, 29and in En Rimmon, in Zorah, in Jarmuth, 30and in Zanoah and Adullam and the small towns around them, in Lachish and the fields around it, and in Azekah and the small towns around it. So the people of Judah were living all the way from Beersheba to the Valley of Hinnom.

31The descendants of the family of Benjamin from Geba lived in Micmash, Aija, Bethel, and the small towns around it, 32in Anathoth, Nob, and Ananiah, 33in Hazor, Ramah, and Gittaim, 34in Hadid, Zeboim, and Neballat, 35in Lod and Ono, and in the Valley of the Craftsmen. 36Some of the groups from the family of Levi moved to the land of Benjamin.

Priests and Levites

12 1These are the priests and Levites who came back to the land of Judah. They came back with Zerubbabel son of Shealtiel and Jeshua. This is a list of their names: Seraiah, Jeremiah, Ezra, 2Amariah, Malluch, Hattush, 3Shecaniah, Rehum, Meremoth, 4Iddo, Ginnethon, Abijah, 5Mijamin, Maadiah, Bilgah, 6Shemaiah, Joiarib, Jedaiah, 7Sallu, Amok, Hilkiah, and Jedaiah. These men were the leaders of the priests and their relatives in the days of Jeshua.

8The Levites were Jeshua, Binnui, Kadmiel, Sherebiah, Judah, and also Mattaniah. These men, with Mattaniah's relatives, were in charge of the songs of praise to God. 9Bakbukiah and Unni were the relatives of those Levites. These two men stood across from them in the services. 10Jeshua was the father of Joiakim. Joiakim was the father of Eliashib. Eliashib was the father of Joiada. 11Joiada was the father of Jonathan, and Jonathan was the father of Jaddua.

12In the days of Joiakim, these men were the leaders of the families of priests:

The leader of Seraiah's family was Meraiah.
The leader of Jeremiah's family was Hananiah.
13 The leader of Ezra's family was Meshullam.
The leader of Amariah's family was Jehohanan.
14 The leader of Malluch's family was Jonathan.
The leader of Shecaniah's family was Joseph.
15 The leader of Harim's family was Adna.
The leader of Meremoth's family was Helkai.
16 The leader of Iddo's family was Zechariah.
The leader of Ginnethon's family was Meshullam.
17 The leader of Abijah's family was Zicri.
The leader of Miniamin and Maadiah's families was Piltai.
18 The leader of Bilgah's family was Shammua.
The leader of Shemaiah's family was Jehonathan.
19 The leader of Joiarib's family was Mattenai.
The leader of Jedaiah's family was Uzzi.
20 The leader of Sallu's family was Kallai.
The leader of Amok's family was Eber.
21 The leader of Hilkiah's family was Hashabiah.
The leader of Jedaiah's family was Nethanel.

22The names of the leaders of the families of the Levites and the priests in the days of Eliashib, Joiada, Johanan, and Jaddua were written down during the rule of Darius the Persian king. 23The family leaders among the descendants of the Levites and up to the time of Johanan son of Eliashib were written in the history book. 24And these were the leaders of the Levites: Hashabiah, Sherebiah, Jeshua the son of Kadmiel, and their brothers. Their brothers stood across from them to sing praise and honor to God. One group answered the other group. That is what was commanded by David the man of God.

25The gatekeepers who guarded the storerooms next to the gates were Mattaniah, Bakbukiah, Obadiah, Meshullam, Talmon, and Akkub. 26They served in the days of Joiakim. Joiakim was the son of Jeshua, who was the son of Jozadak. And the gatekeepers also served in the days of Nehemiah the governor and in the days of Ezra the priest and teacher.

Dedication of the Wall of Jerusalem

27The people dedicated* the wall of Jerusalem. They brought all the Levites to Jerusalem. The Levites came from the towns they lived in. They came to Jerusalem to celebrate the dedication of the wall of Jerusalem. They came to sing songs of praise and thanks to God. They played their cymbals,* harps, and lyres.* 28-29And all the singers also came to Jerusalem. They came from the towns all around Jerusalem. They came from the town of Netophah, from Beth Gilgal, Geba, and Azmaveth. The singers had built small towns for themselves in the area around Jerusalem. 30So the priests and Levites made themselves pure in a ceremony. Then they also made the people, the gates, and the wall of Jerusalem pure in a ceremony.

31I told the leaders of Judah to go up and stand on top of the wall. I also chose two large singing groups to give thanks to God. One group was to start going up on top of the wall on the right side, toward the Ash Pile Gate. 32Hoshaiah and half of the leaders of Judah followed the singers. 33Also following them were Azariah, Ezra, Meshullam, 34Judah, Benjamin, Shemaiah, and Jeremiah. 35And some of the priests with trumpets also followed them up to the wall. Zechariah also followed them. (Zechariah was the son of Jonathan, who was the son of Shemaiah, who was the son of Mattaniah, who was the son of Micaiah, who was the son of Zaccur, who was the son of Asaph.) 36There were also Asaph's brothers, who were Shemaiah, Azarel, Milalai, Gilalai, Maai, Nethanel, Judah, and Hanani. They had the musical instruments that David, the man of God, had made. Ezra the teacher led the group of people who were there to dedicate the wall. 37They went to the Fountain Gate and walked up the stairs all the way to the City of David.* They were on top of the city wall. They walked over the house of David and went toward the Water Gate.

38The second group of singers started out in the other direction, to the left. I followed them as they went up to the top of the wall. Half of the people also followed them. They went past the Tower of Ovens to the Broad Wall. 39Then they went over these gates: the Gate of Ephraim, the Old Gate, and the Fish Gate. And they went over the Tower of Hananel and the Tower of the Hundred. They went as far as the Sheep Gate and stopped at the Guard Gate. 40Then the two singing groups went to their places in God's Temple.* And I stood in my place. And half the officials stood in their places in the Temple. 41Then these priests stood in their places: Eliakim, Maaseiah, Mijamin, Micaiah, Elioenai, Zechariah, and Hananiah. These priests had their trumpets with them. 42Then these priests stood in their places in the Temple: Maaseiah, Shemaiah, Eleazar, Uzzi, Jehohanan, Malkijah, Elam, and Ezer.

Then two singing groups began singing with Jezrahiah leading them. 43So on that special day, the priests offered many sacrifices.* Everyone was very happy because God had made them happy. Even the women and children were excited and happy. People far away could hear the happy sounds coming from Jerusalem.

44Men were chosen to be in charge of the storerooms on that day. People brought the first part of the harvest and a tenth of their crops. So the men in charge put these things in the storerooms. The Jewish people were very happy about the priests and Levites on duty. So they brought many things to be put in the storerooms. 45The priests and Levites did their work for their God. They did the ceremonies that made people pure, and the singers and gatekeepers did their part. They did everything that David and Solomon had commanded. 46(Long ago, in the days of David, Asaph had been the director. And he had many songs of praise and thanks to God.)

47So in the days of Zerubbabel and of Nehemiah, all the Israelites gave every day to support the singers and gatekeepers. The people also set aside the money for the other Levites. And the Levites set aside the money for the descendants of Aaron.

Nehemiah's Last Commands

13 1On that day the *Book of Moses* was read out loud, so that all the people could hear. They found this law written there: No Ammonite and no Moabite would be permitted to join in the meetings with God. 2That law was written because those people didn't give the Israelites food and water. And they had paid Balaam to say a curse* against the Israelites. But our God changed that curse and made it a blessing for us. 3So when the Israelites heard that law, they obeyed it. They separated themselves from the people who were descendants of foreigners.

4-5But, before that happened, Eliashib had given a room in the Temple* to Tobiah. Eliashib was the priest in charge of the storerooms in God's Temple. And he was a close friend of Tobiah. That room had been used for storing the grain offerings, incense, and the Temple dishes and things. They also kept the tenth of grain, new wine, and oil for the Levites, singers, and gatekeepers in that room. And they also kept the gifts for the priests in that room. But Eliashib gave that room to Tobiah.

⁶I was not in Jerusalem while all of this was happening. I had gone back to the king of Babylon. I went back to Babylon in the 32nd year that Artaxerxes was king of Babylon.ᵃ Later, I asked the king for permission to go back to Jerusalem. ⁷So I came back to Jerusalem. There I heard about the sad thing that Eliashib had done. He had given Tobiah a room in the Temple of our God! ⁸I was very angry about what Eliashib had done, so I threw all of Tobiah's things out of the room. ⁹I gave commands for the rooms to be made pure and clean. Then I put the Temple dishes and things, the grain offerings, and the incense back into the rooms.

¹⁰I also heard that the people had not given the Levites their share. So the Levites and singers had gone back to work in their own fields. ¹¹So I told the officials that they were wrong. I asked them, "Why didn't you take care of God's Temple?" Then I called all Levites together and told them to go back to their places and duties in the Temple. ¹²Then everyone in Judah brought their tenth of grain, new wine, and oil to the Temple. These things were put into the storerooms.

¹³I put these men in charge of the storerooms: Shelemiah the priest, Zadok the teacher, and a Levite named Pedaiah. And I made Hanan son of Zaccur, son of Mattaniah, their helper. I knew I could trust these men. They were responsible for giving the supplies to their relatives.

¹⁴God, please remember me for these things I have done. Don't forget all I have faithfully done for the Temple of my God and for its services.

¹⁵In those days in Judah, I saw people working on the Sabbath* day. I saw people pressing grapes to make wine. I saw people bringing in grain and loading it on donkeys. I saw people carrying grapes, figs, and all kinds of things in the city. They were bringing all these things into Jerusalem on the Sabbath day, so I warned them about this. I told them they must not sell food on the Sabbath day.

¹⁶There were some men from the city of Tyre living in Jerusalem. They were bringing fish and all kinds of things into Jerusalem and selling them on the Sabbath day. And the Jews were buying them. ¹⁷I told the important people of Judah that they were wrong. I said, "You are doing a very bad thing. You are ruining the Sabbath day. ¹⁸You know that your ancestors* did the same thing. That is why our God brought all the troubles and disaster to us and to this city. Now you people are

making it so that more of these bad things will happen to Israel. They are doing this because you are breaking the Sabbath by treating it just as if it were any other day."

¹⁹So this is what I did: Every Friday evening, just before dark, I commanded the gatekeepers to shut and lock the gates to Jerusalem. They were not to be opened until the Sabbath day was over. I put some of my own men at the gates. They were commanded to make sure that no load was brought into Jerusalem on the Sabbath day.

²⁰One or two times, traders and merchants* had to stay the night outside Jerusalem. ²¹But I warned them, "Don't stay the night in front of the wall. If you do that again, I will arrest you." So from that time on they didn't come on the Sabbath day to sell their things.

²²Then I commanded the Levites to make themselves pure. After they did that, they were to go and guard the gates. This was done to make sure the Sabbath day was kept a holy day.

God, please remember me for doing this. Be kind to me and show me your great love!

²³In those days I also noticed that some Jewish men had married women from the countries of Ashdod, Ammon, and Moab. ²⁴And half of the children from those marriages didn't know how to speak the Jewish language. They spoke the language of Ashdod, Ammon, or Moab. ²⁵So I told the men that they were wrong. I said bad things to them. I hit some of them, and I pulled out their hair. I forced them to make a promise in God's name. I said to them, "You must not marry the daughters of these foreigners. Don't let their daughters marry your sons, and don't let your daughters marry the sons of these foreigners. ²⁶You know that marriages like this caused Solomon to sin. In all the many nations, there was not a king as great as Solomon. God loved him and made him king over the whole nation of Israel. But even Solomon was made to sin because of foreign women. ²⁷And now, we hear that you also are doing this terrible sin. You are not being true to God. You are marrying foreign women."

²⁸Joiada was the son of Eliashib the high priest. One of Joiada's sons was a son-in-law of Sanballat from Horon. I forced him to leave this place. I forced him to run away.

²⁹My God, punish these people. They made the priesthood unclean. They treated it as if it was not important. They did not obey the agreement that you made with the priests and Levites. ³⁰So I made the priests and Levites clean and pure. I took away all the foreigners and the strange things they taught. And I gave the Levites and priests their own duties and responsibilities. ³¹And I made sure that people will bring gifts of wood and the first part of their harvest at the right times.

My God, remember me for doing these good things.

ᵃ13:6 *the 32nd year … Babylon* That is, 432 B.C.

Esther

Queen Vashti Disobeys the King

1 ¹This is what happened during the time when Xerxes was king. Xerxes ruled over the 127 provinces from India to Ethiopia. ²King Xerxes ruled from his throne in the capital city of Susa.

³In the third year of Xerxes' rule, he gave a party for his officers and leaders. The army leaders and important leaders from all of Persia and Media were there. ⁴The party continued for 180 days. All during this time, King Xerxes was showing the great wealth of his kingdom and the majestic beauty and wealth of his palace. ⁵And when the 180 days were over, King Xerxes gave another party that continued for seven days. It was held in the inside garden of the palace. All the people who were in the capital city of Susa were invited, from the most important to the least important. ⁶The inside garden had white and blue linen* hangings around the room. They were held in place with cords of white linen and purple material on silver rings and marble pillars. There were couches made of gold and silver. They were sitting on mosaic pavement made of porphyry,ᵃ marble, mother-of-pearl, and other expensive stones. ⁷Wine was served in golden cups, and every cup was different. There was plenty of the king's wine, because the king was very generous. ⁸The king had given a command to his servants. He told them that each guest must be given as much wine as he wanted, and the wine server obeyed the king.

⁹Queen Vashti also gave a party for the women in the king's palace.

¹⁰⁻¹¹On the seventh day of the party, King Xerxes was in high spirits from drinking wine. He gave a command to the seven eunuchs* who served him. The eunuchs were Mehuman, Biztha, Harbona, Bigtha, Abagtha, Zethar, and Carcas. He commanded them to bring Queen Vashti to him wearing her royal crown. She was to come so that she could show her beauty to the leaders and important people. She was very beautiful.

¹²But when the eunuchs told Queen Vashti about the king's command, she refused to come. Then the king was very angry. ¹³⁻¹⁴It was the custom for the king to ask the advice of the experts about the law and punishments. So King Xerxes spoke with the wise men who

understood the laws. They were very close to the king. Their names were Carshena, Shethar, Admatha, Tarshish, Meres, Marsena, and Memucan. They were the seven most important officials of Persia and Media. They had special privileges to see the king. They were the highest officials in the kingdom. ¹⁵The king asked them, "What does the law say must be done to Queen Vashti? She has not obeyed the command of King Xerxes that the eunuchs had taken to her."

¹⁶Then Memucan answered the king with the other officials listening, "Queen Vashti has done wrong. She has done wrong against the king and also against all the leaders and people of all the provinces of King Xerxes. ¹⁷I say this, because all the other women will hear about what Queen Vashti did. Then they will stop obeying their husbands. They will say to their husbands, 'King Xerxes commanded Queen Vashti to be brought to him, but she refused to come.'

¹⁸"Today the wives of the Persian and Median leaders have heard what the queen did, and these women will be influenced by what she did. They will do the same thing to the king's important leaders. And there will be plenty of disrespect and anger.

¹⁹"So if it pleases the king, here is a suggestion: Let the king give a royal command and let it be written in the laws of Persia and Media. The laws of Persia and Media cannot be changed. The royal command should be that Vashti is never again to enter the presence of King Xerxes. Let the king also give her royal position to someone else who is better than she is. ²⁰Then when the king's command is announced in all parts of his large kingdom, all the women will respect their husbands. From the most important to the least important, all the women will respect their husbands."

²¹The king and his important officials were happy with this advice, so King Xerxes did as Memucan suggested. ²²King Xerxes sent letters to all parts of the kingdom. He sent them to each province, written in its own language. He sent them to each nation in its own language. These letters announced in each person's language that every man was to be the ruler over his own family.

Esther Made Queen

2 ¹Later, King Xerxes stopped being angry. Then he remembered Vashti and what

---

ᵃ**1:6** *porphyry* A dark red or purple stone.

she had done. He remembered his commands about her. ²Then the king's personal servants had a suggestion. They said, "Search for beautiful young virgins* for the king. ³Let the king choose leaders in every province of his kingdom. Then let the leaders bring every beautiful young virgin to the capital city of Susa. These young women will be put with the group of the king's women. They will be under the care of Hegai, the king's eunuch,* who is in charge of the women. Then give beauty treatments to all of them. ⁴Then let the one who is pleasing to the king become the new queen in Vashti's place." The king liked this suggestion, so he accepted it.

⁵Now there was a Jew from the tribe of Benjamin named Mordecai. Mordecai was the son of Jair, and Jair was the son of Shimei, and Shimei was the son of Kish. Mordecai was in the capital city, Susa. ⁶Mordecai had been carried into captivity from Jerusalem by King Nebuchadnezzar of Babylon. He was with the group that was taken into captivity with King Jehoiachin of Judah. ⁷Mordecai had a cousin named Hadassah. She didn't have a father or a mother, so Mordecai took care of her. Mordecai had adopted her as his own daughter when her father and mother died. Hadassah was also called Esther. She had a very pretty face and a good figure.

⁸When the king's command had been heard, many young women were brought to the capital city of Susa. They were put under the care of Hegai. Esther was one of these women. She was taken to the king's palace and put into Hegai's care. Hegai was in charge of the king's women. ⁹He liked Esther. She became his favorite, so he quickly gave Esther beauty treatments and special food. He chose seven slave women from the king's palace and gave them to Esther. Then he moved Esther and her seven women servants into the best place where the king's women lived. ¹⁰Esther didn't tell anyone she was a Jew. She didn't tell anyone about her family background, because Mordecai had told her not to. ¹¹Every day Mordecai walked back and forth near the area where the king's women lived. He did this because he wanted to find out how Esther was, and what was happening to her.

¹²Before a young woman could take her turn to go in before King Xerxes, she had to complete twelve months of beauty treatments—six months with oil of myrrh* and six months with perfumes and cosmetics. ¹³When her time came to go in to the king, she could choose to wear or take whatever she wanted from the women's living area. ¹⁴In the evening the young woman would go to the king's palace. And in the morning she would return to another area where the king's women lived. Then she would be placed under the care of a man named Shaashgaz. He was the king's eunuch in charge of the slave women.* She would not go back to the king again unless he

was pleased with her. Then he would call her by name to come back to him.

¹⁵The time came for Esther to go to the king. She was the one Mordecai had adopted, the daughter of his uncle Abihail. All she wanted to take with her was what Hegai, the king's officer in charge of the women, suggested. Everyone who saw Esther liked her. ¹⁶So Esther was taken to King Xerxes in the palace. This happened in the tenth month, the month of Tebeth, in the seventh year of his rule.

¹⁷The king loved Esther more than any of the other young women, and she became his favorite. He approved of her more than any of the others. So King Xerxes put a crown on Esther's head and made her the new queen in place of Vashti. ¹⁸And the king gave a big party for Esther. It was for all his important people and leaders. He announced a festival in all the provinces and sent out gifts to people, because he was a generous king.

Mordecai Learns About an Evil Plan

¹⁹Mordecai was sitting next to the king's gate at the time the young women were gathered together the second time. ²⁰Esther had still kept it a secret that she was a Jew. She had not told anyone about her family background. This is what Mordecai had told her to do. She still obeyed Mordecai just as she had done when he was taking care of her.

²¹During the time Mordecai was sitting next to the king's gate, this happened: Bigthana and Teresh, two of the king's officers who guarded the doorway, became angry with the king. They began to make plans to kill King Xerxes. ²²But Mordecai learned about these plans and told Queen Esther. Then she told the king. She also told him that Mordecai was the one who had learned about the evil plan. ²³Then the report was checked out. It was learned that Mordecai's report was true. The two guards who had planned to kill the king were hanged on a post. All these things were written down in a book of the king's histories in front of the king.

Haman's Plan to Destroy the Jews

3 ¹After these things happened, King Xerxes honored Haman son of Hammedatha the Agagite. The king promoted Haman and gave him a place of honor more important than any of the other leaders. ²All the king's leaders at the king's gate would bow down and give honor to Haman. This is what the king commanded them to do. But Mordecai refused to bow down or give honor to Haman. ³Then the king's leaders at the gate asked Mordecai, "Why don't you obey the king's command to bow down to Haman?"

⁴Day after day, the king's leaders spoke to Mordecai, but he refused to obey the command to bow down to Haman. So they told Haman about it. They wanted to see what

Haman would do about Mordecai. Mordecai had told them that he was a Jew. ⁵When Haman saw that Mordecai refused to bow down to him or give him honor, he was very angry. ⁶Haman had learned that Mordecai was a Jew. But he was not satisfied to only kill Mordecai. He also wanted to find a way to destroy all of Mordecai's people, the Jews, in all of Xerxes' kingdom.

⁷In the twelfth year of King Xerxes' rule, in the first month, the month of Nisan,* Haman threw lots* to choose a special day and month. And the twelfth month, the month of Adar was chosen. (At that time the lot was called "pur.") ⁸Then Haman came to King Xerxes and said, "King Xerxes, there is a certain group of people scattered among the people in all the provinces of your kingdom. They keep themselves separate from other people. Their customs are different from those of all other people. And they don't obey the king's laws. It is not right for the king to allow them to continue to live in your kingdom.

⁹"If it pleases the king, I have a suggestion: Give a command to destroy these people. And I will put 750,000 pounds*ᵃ* of silver into the king's treasury. This money could be used to pay the men who do these things."

¹⁰So the king took the official ring off his finger and gave it to Haman son of Hammedatha the Agagite. Haman was the enemy of the Jews. ¹¹Then the king said to Haman, "Keep the money. Do what you want with them."

¹²Then on the 13th day of the first month the king's secretaries were called. They wrote out all of Haman's commands in the language of each province. And they wrote them in the language of each group of people. They wrote to the king's satraps,* the governors of the different provinces, and the leaders of the different groups of people. They wrote with the authority of King Xerxes himself, and sealed the commands with the king's own ring.

¹³Messengers carried the letters to all the king's provinces. The letters were the king's command to ruin, kill, and completely destroy all the Jews. This meant young people and old people, women, and little children too. The command was to kill all the Jews on a single day. The day was to be the 13th day of the twelfth month, the month of Adar. And the command was to take everything that belonged to the Jews.

¹⁴A copy of the letters with the command was to be given as a law. It was to be a law in every province and announced to the people of every nation living in the kingdom. Then everyone would be ready for that day. ¹⁵At the king's command the messengers hurried off. The command was given in the capital city of Susa. The king and Haman sat down to drink, but the city of Susa was in confusion.

ᵃ3:9 750,000 pounds Literally, "10,000 talents" (340,000 kg).

Mordecai Persuades Esther to Help

4 ¹When Mordecai heard about all that had been done, he tore his clothes. Then he put on sackcloth,* put ashes on his head, and went out into the city crying loudly. ²But Mordecai went only as far as the king's gate. No one was allowed to enter the gate dressed in sackcloth. ³In every province where the king's command had come, there was much crying and sadness among the Jews. They were fasting* and crying loudly. Many Jews were lying on the ground dressed in sackcloth with ashes on their heads.

⁴Esther's slave women and eunuchs* came to her and told her about Mordecai. This made Queen Esther very sad and upset. She sent clothes for Mordecai to put on instead of the sackcloth, but he would not accept them. ⁵Then Esther called Hathach, one of the king's eunuchs who had been chosen to serve her. She commanded him to find out what was bothering Mordecai, and why. ⁶So Hathach went out to where Mordecai was in the open place of the city in front of the king's gate. ⁷Then Mordecai told Hathach everything that had happened to him. Mordecai told him about the exact amount of money Haman had promised to put into the king's treasury for killing Jews. ⁸Mordecai also gave Hathach a copy of the king's command to kill the Jews. The command had been sent out all over the city of Susa. He wanted Hathach to show it to Esther and tell her everything. And he told him to encourage Esther to go to the king and beg him for mercy for Mordecai and her people.

⁹Hathach went back and told Esther everything Mordecai had said.

¹⁰Then Esther told Hathach to say this to Mordecai: ¹¹"Mordecai, all the king's leaders and all the people of the king's provinces know this: The king has one law for any man or woman who goes to the king without being called. That person must be put to death unless the king holds out his gold scepter* to them. If the king does this, that person's life will be saved. And I have not been called to go see the king for 30 days."

¹²⁻¹³Then Esther's message was given to Mordecai. When he got her message, Mordecai sent his answer back: "Esther, don't think that just because you live in the king's palace you will be the only Jew to escape. ¹⁴If you keep quiet now, help and freedom for the Jews will come from another place. But you and your father's family will all die. And who knows, maybe you have been chosen to be the queen for such a time as this."

¹⁵⁻¹⁶Then Esther sent this answer to Mordecai: "Mordecai, go and get all the Jews in Susa together, and fast for me. Don't eat or drink for three days and nights. I and my women servants will fast too. After we fast, I will go to the king. I know it is against the law to go to the king if he didn't call me, but I will

do it anyway. If I die, I die."

¹⁷So Mordecai went away and did everything Esther told him to do.

Esther Speaks to the King

5 ¹On the third day, Esther put on her special robes. Then she stood in the inside area of the king's palace, in front of the king's hall. The king was sitting on his throne in the hall, facing the place where people enter the throne room. ²When the king saw Queen Esther standing in the court, he was very pleased. He held out to her the gold scepter* that was in his hand. So Esther went in to the room and went near the king. Then she touched the end of the king's gold scepter.

³Then the king asked, "What is bothering you Queen Esther? What do you want to ask me? I will give you anything you ask for, even half my kingdom."

⁴Esther said, "I have prepared a party for you and Haman. Will you and Haman please come to the party today?"

⁵Then the king said, "Bring Haman quickly so that we may do what Esther asks."

So the king and Haman went to the party Esther had prepared for them. ⁶While they were drinking wine, the king asked her again, "Now Esther, what do you want to ask for? Ask for anything, I will give it to you. So what is it you want? I will give you anything you want, up to half my kingdom."

⁷Esther answered, "This is what I want to ask for: ⁸If the king is pleased with me and thinks it good to give me what I ask for, let the king and Haman come tomorrow. I will prepare another party for them. Then I will tell what I really want."

Haman's Anger at Mordecai

⁹Haman left the king's palace that day very happy and in a good mood. But when he saw Mordecai at the king's gate, he became very angry. Haman was very mad at him because Mordecai didn't show any respect when Haman walked by. Mordecai was not afraid of Haman, and this made Haman mad. ¹⁰But Haman controlled his anger and went home. Then Haman called together his friends and his wife, Zeresh. ¹¹Haman started bragging about how rich he was. He was bragging to his friends about his many sons, and about all the ways the king had honored him. And he was bragging about how the king had promoted him higher than all the other leaders. ¹²"And that's not all," Haman added. "I'm the only one Queen Esther invited to be with the king at the party she gave. And the Queen also has invited me to be with the king again tomorrow. ¹³But all these things don't really make me happy. I'm not really happy as long as I see that Jew Mordecai sitting at the king's gate."

¹⁴Then Haman's wife Zeresh and all his friends had a suggestion. They said, "Tell someone to build a post to hang him on. Make it 75 feet*ᵃ* tall. In the morning, ask the king to hang Mordecai on it. Then go to the party with the king and you can be happy."

Haman liked this suggestion, so he ordered someone to build the hanging post.

Mordecai Is Honored

6 ¹That same night, the king could not sleep. So he told a servant to bring the history book and read it to him. (*The Book of History of the Kings* lists everything that happens during a king's rule.) ²The servant read the book to the king. He read about the evil plan to kill King Xerxes. That was when Mordecai had learned about Bigthana and Teresh. These two men were the king's officers who guarded the doorway. They had planned to kill the king, but Mordecai learned about the plan and told someone about it.

³Then the king asked, "What honor and good things have been given to Mordecai for this?"

The servants answered the king, "Nothing has been done for Mordecai."

⁴Haman had just entered the outer area of the king's palace. He had come to ask the king to hang Mordecai on the hanging post Haman had commanded to be built. The king said, "Who just came into the courtyard?" ⁵The king's servants said, "Haman is standing in the courtyard."

So the king said, "Bring him in."

⁶When Haman came in, the king asked him a question. He said, "Haman, what should be done for a man the king wants to honor?"

Haman thought to himself, "Who is there that the king would want to honor more than me? I'm sure that the king is talking about honoring me."

⁷So Haman answered the king, "Do this for the man the king loves to honor: ⁸Have the servants bring a special robe the king himself has worn and a horse the king himself has ridden. Have the servants put the king's special mark on the horse's head. ⁹Then put one of the king's most important leaders in charge of the robe and the horse, and let the leader put the robe on the man the king wants to honor. Then let him lead him on the horse through the city streets. As he leads him, let him announce, 'This is done for the man the king wants to honor!'"

¹⁰"Go quickly," the king commanded Haman. "Get the robe and the horse and do just as you have suggested for Mordecai the Jew. He is sitting near the king's gate. Do everything that you suggested."

¹¹So Haman got the robe and the horse. Then he put the robe on Mordecai and led him on horseback through the city streets. Haman announced ahead of Mordecai, "This is done for the man the king wants to honor!"

ᵃ**5:14 75 feet** Literally, "50 cubits" (22 m).

¹²After that Mordecai went back to the king's gate, but Haman hurried home with his head covered because he was embarrassed and ashamed. ¹³Then Haman told his wife Zeresh and all his friends everything that had happened to him. His wife and the men who gave him advice said, "If Mordecai is a Jew, you cannot win. You have already started to fall. Surely you will be ruined!"

¹⁴While they were still talking to Haman, the king's eunuchs* came to Haman's house. They made Haman hurry to the party that Esther had prepared.

Haman Is Hanged

7 ¹So the king and Haman went to eat with Queen Esther. ²Then as they were drinking wine on the second day of the party, the king again asked Esther a question, "Queen Esther, what is it you want to ask for? Ask anything and it will be given to you. What do you want? I will give you anything, even half my kingdom."

³Then Queen Esther answered, "King, if you like me and it pleases you, please let me live. And I ask you to let my people live too. This is what I ask for. ⁴I ask this because my people and I have been sold to be destroyed— to be killed and wiped out completely. If we had just been sold as slaves, I would have kept quiet, because that would not be enough of a problem to bother the king."

⁵Then King Xerxes asked Queen Esther, "Who did this to you? Where is the man who dared to do such a thing to your people?"

⁶Esther said, "The man against us, our enemy, is this wicked Haman."

Then Haman was filled with terror before the king and queen. ⁷The king was very angry. He got up, left his wine, and went out into the garden. But Haman stayed inside to beg Queen Esther to save his life. He begged for his life because he knew that the king had already decided to kill him. ⁸Just as the king was coming back in from the garden to the party room, he saw Haman falling on the couch where Esther was lying. The king said with anger in his voice, "Will you attack the queen even while I am in the house?"

As soon as the king had said this, servants came in and killed Haman.ᵃ ⁹One of the eunuchs* who served the king was named Harbona. He said, "A hanging post 75 feetᵇ tall has been built near Haman's house. Haman had it made so that he could hang Mordecai on it. Mordecai is the man who helped you when he told about the evil plans to kill you."

The king said, "Hang Haman on that post!"

¹⁰So they hanged Haman on the hanging post he had built for Mordecai. Then the king stopped being angry.

The King's Order to Help the Jews

8 ¹That same day King Xerxes gave Queen Esther everything that belonged to Haman, the enemy of the Jews. Esther told the king that Mordecai was her cousin. Then Mordecai came to see the king. ²The king had gotten his ring back from Haman. The king took the ring off his finger and gave it to Mordecai. Then Esther put Mordecai in charge of everything that belonged to Haman.

³Then Esther spoke to the king again. She fell at the king's feet and began crying. She begged the king to cancel the evil plan of Haman the Agagite. Haman had thought up the plan to hurt the Jews.

⁴Then the king held out the gold scepter* to Esther. Esther got up and stood in front of the king. ⁵Then she said, "King, if you like me and if it pleases you, please do this for me. Please do this if you think it is a good idea. If the king is happy with me, please write a command that would stop the command Haman sent out. Haman the Agagite thought of a plan to destroy the Jews in all the king's provinces, and he sent out commands for this to happen. ⁶I am begging the king because I could not bear to see these terrible things happen to my people. I could not bear to see my family killed."

⁷King Xerxes answered Queen Esther and Mordecai the Jew, "Because Haman was against the Jews, I have given his property to Esther. And my soldiers have hanged him on the hanging post. ⁸Now write another command by the authority of the king. Write it to help the Jews in a way that seems best to you. Then seal the order with the king's special ring. No official letter written by the authority of the king and sealed with the king's ring can be canceled."

⁹Very quickly the king's secretaries were called. This was done on the 23rd day of the third month, the month of Sivan. They wrote out all of Mordecai's commands to the Jews, and to the satraps,* the governors, and officials of the 127 provinces. These provinces reached from India to Ethiopia. The commands were written in the language of each province and translated into the language of each group of people. The commands were written to the Jews in their own language and alphabet. ¹⁰Mordecai wrote commands by the authority of King Xerxes. Then he sealed the letters with the king's ring and sent them by messengers on horses. The messengers rode fast horses, which were raised especially for the king.

¹¹The king's commands in the letters said this:

The Jews in every city have the right to gather together to protect themselves.

ᵃ**7:8 killed Haman** Literally, "covered Haman's face."
ᵇ**7:9 75 feet** Literally, "50 cubits" (22 m).

They have the right to ruin, kill, and completely destroy any army from any group who might attack them and their women and children. And the Jews have the right to take and destroy the property of their enemies.

12The day set for the Jews to do this was the 13th day of the twelfth month, the month of Adar. They were permitted to do this in all King Xerxes' provinces. 13A copy of the letter with the king's command was to be sent out. It became a law in every province. They announced it to all the people of every nation living in the kingdom. They did this so that the Jews would be ready for that special day. They would be allowed to pay their enemies back. 14The messengers hurried out, riding on the king's horses. The king commanded them to hurry. And the command was also put in the capital city of Susa.

15Mordecai left the king. He was wearing special clothes from the king. His clothes were blue and white, and he had on a large gold crown. He also had a purple robe made of the best linen.* There was a special celebration in Susa. The people were very happy. 16It was an especially happy day for the Jews, a day of great joy and happiness.

17Wherever the king's command went in every province and every city, there was joy and gladness among the Jews. They were having parties and celebrating. Many of the common people from other groups became Jews. They did this because they were very afraid of the Jews.

Victory for the Jews

9 1On the 13th day of the twelfth month (Adar), the people were supposed to obey the king's command. This was the day the enemies of the Jews hoped to defeat them, but now things had changed. The Jews were stronger than their enemies who hated them. 2The Jews met together in their cities in all the provinces of King Xerxes so that they would be strong enough to attack the people who wanted to destroy them. No one was strong enough to stand against them. They were afraid of the Jews. 3And all the officials of the provinces, the satraps,* the governors, and the king's administrators helped the Jews. All the leaders helped them because they were afraid of Mordecai. 4Mordecai had become a very important man in the king's palace. Everyone in the provinces knew his name and knew how important he was. And Mordecai became more and more powerful.

5The Jews defeated all their enemies. They used swords to kill and destroy them. They did what they wanted to the people who hated them. 6They killed and destroyed 500 men in the capital city of Susa. 7They also killed these men: Parshandatha, Dalphon, Aspatha, 8Poratha, Adalia, Aridatha, 9Parmashta, Arisai,

Aridai, and Vaizatha. 10These men were the ten sons of Haman. Haman son of Hammedatha was the enemy of the Jews. The Jews killed all the men, but they didn't take anything that belonged to them.

11That day the king heard how many men had been killed in the capital city of Susa. 12So the king said to Queen Esther, "The Jews have killed 500 men in Susa, including Haman's ten sons. Now, what do you want done in the other provinces of the king? Tell me, and I will have it done. Ask, and I will do it."

13Esther said, "If it pleases the king, please let the Jews in Susa do the same thing again tomorrow. Also, hang the bodies of Haman's ten sons on posts."

14So the king gave the command that it should be done. So the law was given in Susa, and they hanged Haman's ten sons. 15The Jews in Susa met together on the 14th day of the month of Adar. They killed 300 men in Susa, but they didn't take the things that belonged to them.

16At the same time, the Jews living in the other provinces also met together. They met together so that they would be strong enough to protect themselves. And so they got rid of their enemies. They killed 75,000 of their enemies. But the Jews didn't take anything that belonged to them. 17This happened on the 13th day of the month Adar. On the 14th day the Jews rested and made that day a happy day of feasting.

The Festival of Purim

18The Jews in Susa had met together on the 13th and 14th days of the month of Adar. And then on the 15th day they rested. So they made the 15th day a happy day of feasting. 19So those who live in the country and small villages celebrate Purim on the 14th day of Adar. They keep the 14th day as a happy day of feasting. On this day they have parties and give presents to each other.

20Mordecai wrote everything down that had happened, and then he sent letters to all the Jews in all of King Xerxes' provinces. He sent letters far and near. 21He did this to tell the Jews to celebrate Purim every year on the 14th and 15th days of the month of Adar. 22They were to celebrate those days because on those days the Jews got rid of their enemies. And they were also to celebrate that month as the month when their sadness was turned into joy. It was a month when their crying was changed into a day of celebration. Mordecai wrote letters to all the Jews and told them to celebrate those days as a happy day of feasting. They should have parties, give gifts to each other, and give presents to the poor.

23So the Jews agreed to do what Mordecai had written to them. And they agreed to continue the celebration they had begun.

24Haman son of Hammedatha the Agagite was the enemy of all the Jews. He had made an evil plan against the Jews to destroy them. And Haman had thrown the lot* to choose a day to ruin and to destroy the Jews. At that time the lot was called a "pur." ²⁵Haman did this, but Esther went to talk to the king. So he sent out new commands. These commands not only ruined Haman's plans, but these commands caused those bad things to happen to Haman and his family! So Haman and his sons were hanged on the posts.

²⁶⁻²⁷At this time, lots were called "purim." So this festival is called "Purim." Mordecai wrote a letter and told the Jews to celebrate this festival. And so the Jews started the custom of celebrating these two days every year. ²⁸They do this to help them remember what they had seen happen to them. The Jews and all the people who join them celebrate these two days every year at the right time in just the right way. Every generation and every family remembers these two days. They celebrate this festival in each and every province and in each and every town. And the Jews will never stop celebrating the days of Purim. Their descendants will always remember this festival.

²⁹So Queen Esther daughter of Abihail, along with Mordecai the Jew, wrote an official letter about Purim. They wrote with full authority of the king to prove that the second letter was true. ³⁰So Mordecai sent letters to all the Jews in the 127 provinces of King Xerxes' kingdom. He told the people that the festival should bring peace and make people trust*ᵃ* each other. ³¹He wrote these letters to tell the people to start celebrating Purim. And he told them when to celebrate this new festival. Mordecai the Jew and Queen Esther had sent out the command for the Jews to establish this two-day festival for themselves and their descendants. They will remember this festival just as they remember the other festivals when they fast* and cry about the bad things that had happened. ³²Esther's letter made the rules for Purim official, and these things were written down in a book.

Mordecai Honored

10 ¹King Xerxes made people pay taxes. All the people in the kingdom, even the faraway cities on the seacoast, had to pay taxes. ²And all the great things Xerxes did are written in the *Book of History of the Kings of Media and Persia.* Also written in those history books are all the things Mordecai did. The king made Mordecai a great man. ³Mordecai the Jew was second in importance to King Xerxes. He was the most important man among the Jews. His fellow Jews respected him very much, because he worked hard for the good of his people and brought peace to all the Jews.

*ᵃ***9:30** *peace … trust* Or "fellowship and truth." Zech. 8:19 teaches that this is how people should celebrate the festivals and why God gave them.

Job

Job, the Good Man

1 ¹There was a man named Job who lived in the country of Uz. He was a good, honest man. He respected God and refused to do evil. ²Job had seven sons and three daughters. ³He owned 7000 sheep, 3000 camels, 1000 oxen, and 500 female donkeys. He had many servants. He was the richest man in the east.

⁴Job's sons took turns having dinner parties in their homes, and they invited their sisters. ⁵The day after each of these parties, Job got up early in the morning, sent for his children, and offered a burnt offering* for each of them. He thought, "Maybe my children were careless and sinned against God at their party." Job always did this so that his children would be forgiven of their sins.

⁶Then the day came for the angels*ᵇ* to meet with the Lord. Even Satan* was there with them. ⁷The Lord said to Satan, "Where have you been?"

Satan answered the Lord, "I have been roaming around the earth, going from place to place."

⁸Then the Lord said to Satan, "Have you noticed my servant Job? There is no one on earth like him. He is a good, faithful man. He respects God and refuses to do evil."

⁹Satan answered, "But Job has a good reason to respect you. ¹⁰You always protect him, his family, and everything he has. You have blessed him and made him successful in everything he does. He is so wealthy that his herds and flocks are all over the country. ¹¹But if you were to destroy everything he has, I promise you that he would curse* you to your face."

¹²The Lord said to Satan, "All right, do whatever you want with anything that he has, but don't hurt Job himself."

Then Satan left the meeting.

*ᵇ***1:6** *angels* Literally, "sons of God."

Job Loses Everything

¹³One day Job's sons and daughters were eating and drinking wine at the oldest brother's house. ¹⁴A messenger came to Job and said, "We were plowing the fields with the oxen and the donkeys were eating grass nearby, ¹⁵when some Sabeans*ᵃ* attacked us and took your animals! They killed the other servants. I am the only one who escaped to come and tell you the news!"

¹⁶That messenger was still speaking when another one came in and said, "A bolt of lightning*ᵇ* struck your sheep and servants and burned them up. I am the only one who escaped to come and tell you the news!"

¹⁷That messenger was still speaking when another one came in and said, "The Chaldeans*ᶜ* sent out three raiding parties that attacked us and took the camels! They killed the other servants. I am the only one who escaped to come and tell you the news!"

¹⁸That messenger was still speaking when another one came in and said, "Your sons and daughters were eating and drinking wine at the oldest brother's house. ¹⁹A strong wind suddenly came in from across the desert and blew the house down. It fell on your sons and daughters, and they are all dead. I am the only one who escaped to come and tell you the news!"

²⁰When Job heard this, he got up, tore his clothes, and shaved his head to show his sadness. Then he fell to the ground to bow down before God ²¹and said,

"When I was born into this world,
  I was naked and had nothing.
When I die and leave this world,
  I will be naked and have nothing.
The LORD gives,
  and the LORD takes away.
Praise the name of the LORD!"

²²Even after all this, Job did not sin. He did not accuse God of doing anything wrong.

Satan Bothers Job Again

2 ¹Then another day came for the angels*ᵈ* to meet with the LORD. Satan* was also there with them. ²The LORD said to Satan, "Where have you been?"

Satan answered the LORD, "I have been roaming around the earth, going from place to place."

³Then the LORD said to Satan, "Have you noticed my servant Job? There is no one on earth like him. He is a good, faithful man. He respects God and refuses to do evil. He is still faithful, even though you asked me to let you destroy, without reason, everything he has."

⁴Satan answered, "Skin for skin!*ᵉ* A man will give everything he has to protect himself. ⁵I swear, if you attack his flesh and bones, he will curse* you to your face!"

⁶So the LORD said to Satan, "All right, Job is in your hands, but you are not allowed to kill him."

⁷So Satan left the meeting with the LORD and gave Job painful sores all over his body, from the bottom of his feet to the top of his head. ⁸Job sat on the pile of ashes where he was mourning* and used a piece of broken pottery to scrape his sores. ⁹His wife said to him, "Are you still holding on to your faith? Why don't you just curse God and die!"

¹⁰Job answered, "You sound like one of those fools on the street corner! How can we accept all the good things that God gives us and not accept the problems?" So even after all that happened to Job, he did not sin. He did not accuse God of doing anything wrong.

Job's Three Friends Come to See Him

¹¹Job's three friends heard about all the bad things that happened to him, so Eliphaz came from Teman, Bildad from Shuah, and Zophar from Naamah. They met together and went to comfort Job and show him their sympathy. ¹²But his friends didn't even recognize him when they first saw him in the distance! They began to cry loudly. They tore their clothes and threw dirt in the air over their heads to show how sad they were. ¹³Then they sat on the ground with Job for seven days and seven nights. They didn't say a word, because they saw he was in so much pain.

Job Curses the Day He Was Born

3 ¹Then Job opened his mouth and cursed* the day he was born. ²He said,

³"I wish the day I was born would be lost forever.
  I wish the night they said, 'It's a boy!'
    had never happened.
⁴ I wish that day had remained dark.
  I wish God above had forgotten that day
    and not let any light shine on it.
⁵ I wish that bitter day had remained as dark as death,
    covered with the darkest clouds.
⁶ I wish the darkness had carried away that night,
    that it was left off the calendar
    and not included in any of the months.
⁷ I wish that night had produced nothing
    and no happy shouts had been heard.

---

*ᵃ*1:15 *Sabeans* A group of people from the Arabian Desert, probably south of Uz.

*ᵇ*1:16 *A bolt of lightning* Or "God's fire fell from the sky."

*ᶜ*1:17 *Chaldeans* Tribes of people who moved from place to place in the area between the Euphrates and Jordan rivers.

*ᵈ*2:1 *angels* Literally, "sons of God."

*ᵉ*2:4 *Skin for skin* This means a person will do anything to avoid pain.

8 Some magicians think they can wake
   Leviathan.[a]
   So let them say their curses and curse
   the day I was born.
9 Let that day's morning star be dark.
   Let that night wait for a morning that
   never comes.
   I wish it had never seen the first rays of
   sunlight.
10 I wish it had stopped me from being born
   and kept me from seeing all these
   troubles.
11 Why didn't I die when I was born?
   Why didn't I die as I came from my
   mother's womb?
12 Why did my mother hold me on her
   knees?
   Why did her breasts feed me?
13 If I had died when I was born,
   I would be at peace now.
   I wish I were asleep and at rest
14 with the kings and their advisors
   who built palaces that are now in ruins.
15 I wish I were buried with rulers
   who filled their graves with gold and
   silver.
16 Why wasn't I a child who died at birth
   and was put in the ground?
   I wish I had been buried like a baby
   who never saw the light of day.
17 There the wicked stop causing trouble,
   and the weary find rest.
18 Even prisoners find relief there;
   they no longer hear their guards
   shouting at them.
19 Everyone—from the greatest to the least
   important—will be there,
   and even the slave is free from his
   master.

20 "Why must a suffering person continue to
   live?
   Why let anyone live such a bitter life?
21 Such people want to die, but death does
   not come.
   They search for death more than for
   hidden treasure.
22 They would be happy to find their grave.
   They would rejoice to find their tomb.
23 But God keeps their future a secret
   and builds a wall around them to
   protect them.
24 When it is time to eat, all I can do is sigh
   with sadness, not joy.
   My groans pour out like water.
25 I was afraid something terrible would
   happen,
   and what I feared most has happened.
26 I cannot calm down or relax.
   I am too upset to rest!"

Eliphaz Speaks

4 [1]Eliphaz from Teman answered:

2 "I must say something.
   Would it upset you if I speak?
3 Job, you have taught many people.
   You encouraged those who were ready
   to quit.
4 Your words helped those who were ready
   to fall.
   You gave strength to those who could
   not stand by themselves.
5 But now trouble comes to you,
   and you are discouraged.
   Trouble hits you,
   and you are upset.
6 You worship God.
   You trust him.
   You are a good man,
   so let that be your hope.
7 Can you think of any innocent person
   who was ever destroyed?
   Do you know of any place where good
   people are punished?
8 Yes, I have seen people whose lives were
   cut short,
   but they were evil troublemakers.
9 They lost the breath God gave them.
   They were cut off from his breath of
   life.
10 They were like roaring lions,
   like growling lions with broken teeth—
11 like a lioness that cannot find prey.
   They died, and their cubs starved to
   death.

12 "I happened to hear a message.
   My ears caught a whisper of it.
13 Like a bad dream[b] in the night,
   it ruined my sleep.
14 It frightened me,
   and I trembled down to my bones.
15 A spirit passed by my face.
   The hair on my body stood up!
16 The spirit stood still,
   but I could not see what it was.
   A shape stood before my eyes,
   and there was silence.
   Then I heard a quiet voice:
17 'A person cannot be more right than God.
   People cannot be more pure than their
   Maker.
18 Look, God cannot even trust his heavenly
   servants.
   He sees faults even in his angels.
19 So surely people are worse!
   They live in houses of clay[c] built on
   dust.
   They can be crushed as easily as a moth!
20 From dawn to sunset people are
   destroyed.

---

[a]3:8 *Leviathan* Here, this is probably a giant sea
monster. Some people thought magicians were
able to make it "swallow the sun," that is, cause an
eclipse.

[b]4:13 *bad dream* Or "vision of the night."
[c]4:19 *houses of clay* This means the human body.

They die—gone forever—and no one
even notices.

²¹ The ropes of their tent are pulled up,
and they die before gaining wisdom.'

5 ¹"Job, call out if you want, and see if
anyone answers!
But to which of the angels will you
turn?

² A fool's anger will kill him.
His jealousy will destroy him.

³ I saw a fool who thought he was safe,
but suddenly he died.ᵃ

⁴ There was no one to help his children.
No one defended them in court.

⁵ Hungry people ate all his crops, even the
grain growing among the thorns,
and greedy people took all he had.

⁶ Bad times don't come up from the dirt.
Trouble does not grow from the ground.

⁷ But people are born to have trouble,
as surely as sparks rise from a fire.

⁸ If I were you, I would turn to God
and tell him about my problems.

⁹ People cannot understand the wonderful
things God does.
His miracles are too many to count.

¹⁰ He sends rain all over the earth
and waters the fields.

¹¹ He raises up the humble
and makes sad people happy.

¹² He spoils the plans of even the smartest
people
so that they will not succeed.

¹³ He catches those who think they are wise
in their own clever traps
and brings to an end their evil plans.

¹⁴ Daylight will be like darkness for them.
Even at noon they will have to feel their
way as in the dark.

¹⁵ God saves the poor from the hurtful
words of the wicked.
He saves them from those who are
powerful.

¹⁶ So the poor have hope;
God shuts the mouths of those who
would cause them harm.

¹⁷"You are fortunate when God corrects you.
So don't complain when God All-
Powerful punishes you.

¹⁸ God might injure you,
but he will bandage those wounds.
He might hurt you,
but his hands also heal.

¹⁹ He will save you again and again.
No evil will harm you.ᵇ

²⁰ God will save you from death
when there is famine.*

He will protect you from the sword
when there is war.

²¹ People might say bad things about you
with their sharp tongues.
But God will protect you.
You will not be afraid
when bad things happen!

²² You will laugh at destruction and famine.
You will not be afraid of wild animals!

²³ It is as if you have a peace treaty
with the wild animals and the rocks in
the field.

²⁴ You will live in peace
because your tent is safe.
You will count your property
and find nothing missing.

²⁵ You will have many children.
They will be as many as the blades of
grass on the earth.

²⁶ You will be like the wheat that grows
until harvest time.
Yes, you will live to a ripe old age.

²⁷"We have studied this and know it is true.
So listen to us, and learn for yourself."

Job Answers Eliphaz

6 ¹Then Job answered:

²"I wish my suffering could be weighed
and all my trouble be put on the scales.

³ They would be heavier than all the sand
of the sea!
That is why my words are so crazy.

⁴ God All-Powerful has shot me with his
arrows.
My spirit feels their poison!
God's terrible weapons are lined up
against me.

⁵ Even a wild donkey does not complain
when it has grass to eat.
And a cow is quiet when it has food.

⁶ Food without salt does not taste good,
and the white of an egg has no taste.

⁷ I refuse to touch that kind of food;
it makes me sick!

⁸"I wish I could have what I ask for.
I wish God would give me what I want.

⁹ I wish he would crush me—
just go ahead and kill me!

¹⁰ Then I would be comforted by this one
thing:
Even through all this pain I never refused
to obey the commands of the Holy One.

¹¹"With my strength gone, I have no hope to
go on living.
With nothing to look forward to, why
should I be patient?

¹² I am not strong like a rock.
My body is not made from bronze.

¹³ I don't have the power to help myself,
because all hope of success has been
taken away from me.

ᵃ5:3 *suddenly he died* Or "suddenly his home was
cursed."
ᵇ5:19 Literally, "In six troubles, he will rescue you,
and in seven, evil will not touch you."

14"Friends should be loyal to you in times of
    trouble,
        even if you turn away from God
        All-Powerful.ᵃ
15 But I cannot depend on you, my brothers.
    You are like a stream that has no water
        when the weather is dry but is
        flooded when the rains come.
16 In the winter, it is choked with ice and
    melting snow.
17 But when the weather is hot and dry,
    the water stops flowing,
        and the stream disappears.
18 It twists and turns along the way
    and then disappears into the desert.
19 Traders from Tema search for it.
    Travelers from Sheba hope to find it.
20 They are sure they can find water,
    but they will be disappointed.
21 Now, you are like those streams.
    You see my troubles and are afraid.
22 But have I ever asked you to help me?
    Did I ask you to offer a bribe for me
        from your wealth?
23 No, and I never said, 'Save me from my
    enemies!'
        or 'Save me from those who are cruel!'

24"So now, teach me, and I will be quiet.
    Show me what I have done wrong.
25 Honest words are powerful,
    but your arguments prove nothing.
26 Do you plan to criticize me?
    Will you speak more tiring words?
27 Are you the kind of people
    who would gamble for orphans
        and sell out your own friends?
28 Now, look me in the face,
    and see that I am telling the truth!
29 You need to start over and stop being so
    unfair!
        Think again, because I am innocent.
30 I am not lying.
    I know right from wrong.

7 ¹"People have a hard struggle on earth.
    Their life is like that of a hired
    worker.
2 They are like a slave looking for cool
    shade
        or a hired worker waiting for payday.
3 Month after frustrating month has gone
    by.
        I have suffered night after night.
4 When I lie down, I think,
    'How long before it's time to get up?'
        The night drags on.
        I toss and turn until the sun comes up.
5 My skin is covered with worms and scabs.
    It is cracked and covered with sores.

6"My days pass by faster than a weaver's
    shuttle,ᵇ
        and my life will end without hope.
7 God, remember, my life is like a breath.
    I will not get a second chance to enjoy
        it.
8 Those who see me now will never see me
    again.
        You watch me for a while, but then I am
        gone.
9 Just as clouds that come and go,
    people are put in the grave, never to
        rise again.
10 They don't come back to their old homes.
    The people there would not know them.

11"So I will not be quiet!
    I will let my suffering spirit speak!
    I will let my bitter soul complain!
12 Am I one of your enemies?
    Is that why you put a guard over me?ᶜ
13 My bed should bring me comfort.
    My couch should give me rest and
        relief.
14 But when I lie down, you scare me with
    dreams;
        you frighten me with visions.*
15 So I would rather be choked to death
    than to live like this.
16 I hate my life—I give up.
    I don't want to live forever.
    Leave me alone!
        My life means nothing.
17 God, why are people so important to you?
    Why do you even notice them?
18 Why do you visit them every morning
    and test them at every moment?
19 You never look away from me
    or leave me alone for a second.
20 You are always watching us!
    If I sinned, would that hurt you?
    Why have you made me your target?
    Have I become a problem for you?
21 Why don't you just pardon me for doing
    wrong?
        Why don't you just forgive me for my
        sins?
    Soon I will die and be in my grave.
        You will search for me, but I will be
        gone."

Bildad Speaks to Job

8 ¹Then Bildad from Shuah answered:

2"How long will you talk like that?
    Your words are nothing but hot air!
3 God is always fair.
    God All-Powerful does what is right.

ᵇ**7:6** *weaver's shuttle* The tool a person who makes
cloth uses to pass the thread between the other
threads.
ᶜ**7:12** Literally, "Am I Yam or Tannin that you should
appoint a guard to watch me?" In ancient Canaanite
stories, Yam was the god of the sea, and Tannin was
a sea monster.

ᵃ**6:14** Or "People who fail to be loyal to their friends
have also failed to respect God All-Powerful."

4 If your children sinned against God, he
   punished them.
   They paid for their sins.
5 But now, look to God
   and pray to the All-Powerful.
6 If you are pure and good, he will quickly
   come to help you.
   He will give your family back to you.
7 Then you will have a lot more
   than you had in the beginning!

8 "Ask those who are now old.
   Find out what their ancestors* learned.
9 It seems as though we were born
   yesterday.
   We are too young to know anything.
   Our days on earth are very short, like a
   shadow.
10 Maybe the old people can tell you
   something.
   Maybe they will teach you what they
   learned.

11 "Can papyrus* grow tall on a dry land?
   Can reeds grow without water?
12 No, they will dry up before harvest.
   They will be too small to cut and use.
13 People who forget God are like that.
   Those who oppose him have no hope.
14 They have put their trust in something
   weak.
   It is like a spider's web.
15 When they lean against it,
   it will break.
   When they reach out for it,
   it will not hold them up.
16 Such people are like a vine that gets
   plenty of water and sunshine,
   and its branches spread throughout the
   garden.
17 Its roots spread among the rocks,
   searching for good soil.
18 But if you move it, it will die,
   and no one can tell it was ever there.
19 Everything might have been going well,
   but another vine will take its place.
20 God does not support evil people,
   and he does not abandon the innocent.
21 So perhaps you might laugh again.
   Maybe shouts of joy will come from
   your lips.
22 Maybe your enemies will be humiliated
   and the homes of the wicked
   destroyed."

Job Answers Bildad

9 ¹Then Job answered:

2 "Of course, I know that this is true.
   But how can a human being win an
   argument with God?
3 Anyone who chose to argue with him
   could not answer one question in a
   thousand!
4 God is so wise and powerful that

no one could oppose him and survive.
5 When God is angry, he moves mountains
   before they know what happened.
6 He can shake the earth,
   and it will tremble down to its
   foundations.
7 With one command he can stop the sun
   from rising.
   He can lock up the stars and keep them
   from shining.
8 He alone made the skies,
   and he walks on the ocean waves.

9 "God made the Bear, Orion, and the
   Pleiades.ᵃ
   He made the planets that cross the
   southern sky.ᵇ
10 He does things too marvelous for people
   to understand.
   He does too many miracles to count!
11 When he passes by, I cannot see him.
   He goes right past me, and I don't
   notice.
12 If he takes something away,
   no one can stop him.
   No one can say to him,
   'What are you doing?'
13 God will not hold back his anger.
   Even Rahab's* helpers are afraid of him.
14 So I cannot argue with God.
   I would not know what to say to him.
15 I am innocent, but I cannot give him an
   answer.
   All I can do is beg my Judge for mercy.
16 Even if I called and he answered,
   I cannot believe he would listen to me.
17 He would just send storms to crush me.
   He would give me more wounds for no
   reason.
18 He would not let me catch my breath
   again.
   He would just give me more trouble.
19 I cannot defeat God.
   He is too powerful!
   I cannot take him to court for justice.
   Who could force him to come?
20 I am innocent, but anything I say makes
   me seem guilty.
   I am innocent, but if I speak, my mouth
   proves me wrong.
21 I am innocent, but I don't know what to
   think.
   I hate my own life.
22 So I say, 'Does it make any difference?
   God destroys the innocent as well as the
   guilty.'

ᵃ9:9 Bear, Orion, and the Pleiades Names of well-
known constellations (groups of stars) in the night
sky.
ᵇ9:9 planets ... sky Literally, "Rooms of the South"
or "Rooms of Teman." This might be the planets or
the twelve constellations of the Zodiac. North of the
equator, these seem to move across the southern
sky.

23 Is it God who laughs when a disaster kills
    innocent people?
24 Is it God who keeps the leaders from
    seeing when an evil person takes
    control?
    If it is not God, then who is it?

25 "My days are passing faster than a runner.
    They are flying by without any joy.
26 They go by as quickly as papyrus* boats,
    as fast as an eagle swooping down on its
    prey.

27 "I could say, 'I will not complain.
    I will forget my pain and put a smile on
    my face.'
28 But the suffering still frightens me.
    I know that God will not see me as
    innocent.
29 I will be found guilty,
    so why should I even think about it?
30 Even if I scrubbed my hands with soap
    and washed myself whiter than snow,
31 God would still push me into the slime
    pit,*a*
    and even my clothes would hate to
    touch me.
32 God is not a human like me, so I cannot
    argue with him.
    I cannot take him to court.
33 I wish there were someone who could
    listen to both sides,*b*
    someone to judge both of us in a fair
    way.
34 I wish someone could take away the
    threat of God's punishment.
    Then he would not frighten me
    anymore.
35 Then I could say what I want without
    being afraid of him.
    But I cannot do that now.

10 ¹"I hate my own life, so I will
    complain freely.
    I am very bitter, so now I will speak.
2 I will say to God: 'Don't just say I am
    guilty!
    Tell me what you have against me.
3 Do you enjoy hurting me?
    Do you enjoy ignoring me while smiling
    at what evil people say?
4 Do you have human eyes?
    Do you see things the way people do?
5 Is your life as short as ours?
    Is your life as short as a man's life?
6 You look for my wrong
    and search for my sin.
7 You know I am innocent,
    but no one can save me from your
    power!

8 Your hands made me
    and shaped my body.
    But now they are closing around me
    and squeezing me to death!
9 Remember, you molded me like clay.
    Will you turn me into clay again?
10 You poured me out like milk.
    You spun me around and squeezed me
    like someone making cheese.
11 You put me together with bones and
    muscles,
    and then you clothed me with skin and
    flesh.
12 You gave me life and were very kind to
    me.
    You cared for me and watched over my
    spirit.
13 But this is what you hid in your heart.
    Now I know what you were planning
    for me.
14 If I sinned, you would be watching me
    so that you could punish me for doing
    wrong.
15 If I sin, I am guilty
    and should be cursed.
    But even when I am innocent,
    I cannot lift up my head.
    I am so ashamed
    because of all the troubles I have.
16 If I have any success and feel proud,
    you hunt me down like a lion
    and show your power over me.
17 You bring witness after witness
    to prove that I am wrong.
    Again and again you show your anger
    as you send army after army against me.
18 So why did you let me be born?
    I wish I had died before anyone saw me.
19 I wish I had never lived.
    I wish they had carried me from my
    mother's womb straight to the grave.
20 My life is almost finished.
    So leave me alone!
    Let me enjoy the little time I have left.
21 I am going soon to the land of no return,
    the place of death and darkness—
22 that land of darkest night, of shadows and
    confusion,
    where even the light is darkness.'"

Zophar Speaks to Job

11 ¹Then Zophar from Naamah answered
    Job and said,

2 "This flood of words should be answered!
    Does all this talking make Job right?
3 Do you think we don't have
    an answer for you?
    Do you think no one will warn you
    when you laugh at God?
4 You say to God,
    'My arguments are right,
    and you can see I am pure.'
5 I wish God would answer you
    and tell you that you are wrong.

---

a 9:31 *slime pit* The grave, a place where bodies rot.
b 9:33 *someone … sides* Literally, "a mediator" or "an
umpire."

6 He could tell you the secret of wisdom.
   He would tell you that every story has
      two sides.
   You can be sure of this:
      God is not punishing you as much as he
         should.

7 "Do you think you really understand God?
   Do you completely understand God
      All-Powerful?
8 That knowledge is higher than the
      heavens
   and deeper than the place of death.
   So what can you do?
   How can you learn it all?
9 It is greater than the earth
   and bigger than the seas.

10 "If God decides to arrest you and take you
      to court,
   no one could stop him.
11 God knows who is worthless.
   When he sees evil, he remembers it.
12 A wild donkey cannot give birth to a man,
   and a stupid person will never become
      wise.
13 Prepare your heart to serve only God.
   Lift your arms and pray to him.
14 Put away the sin that you still hold on to.
   Don't keep evil in your tent.
15 If you will do that, you could look to God
      without shame.
   You can stand strong and not be afraid.
16 Then you can forget your troubles,
   like water that has already passed by.
17 Your life will be brighter than the
      sunshine at noon.
   Life's darkest hours will shine like the
      morning sun.
18 You will feel safe because there is hope.
   God will protect you and give you rest.
19 You will lie down without fear of anyone.
   Many people will come to you for help.
20 Evil people might look for help,
   but they will not escape their troubles.
   Their hope leads only to death."

Job Answers His Friends

12 1 Then Job answered them:

2 "I'm sure you think you are
   the only wise people left.
   You think that when you die,
      wisdom will be gone with you.
3 But my mind is as good as yours.
   You aren't any smarter than I am.
   You haven't said anything
      that people don't already know.

4 "My friends laugh at me now.
   They say, 'He prayed to God and got his
      answer.'
   I am a good, innocent man, but still
      they laugh at me.
5 Those who have no troubles make fun of

those who do.
   They hit a man when he is down.
6 But robbers' tents are not bothered.
   Those who make God angry live in
      peace,
   even though God has them in his
      power.

7 "But ask the animals,
   and they will teach you.
   Or ask the birds of the air,
      and they will tell you.
8 Or speak to the earth,
   and it will teach you.
   Or let the fish in the sea
      tell you their wisdom.
9 Everyone knows the LORD made these
      things.
10 Every animal that lives and everyone who
      breathes—
   they are all under God's power.
11 But just as the tongue tastes food,
   the ears test the words they hear.
12 People say, 'Wisdom is to be found in
      those who are old.
   Long life brings understanding.'
13 But wisdom and power belong to God.
   Good advice and understanding are his.
14 Anything God tears down cannot be
      rebuilt.
   Anyone he puts in prison cannot be set
      free.
15 If he holds back the rain, the earth will
      dry up.
   If he lets the rain loose, it will flood the
      land.
16 God is strong and always wins.
   He controls those who fool others and
      those who are fooled.
17 He strips advisors of their wisdom
   and makes leaders act like fools.
18 He strips kings of their authority
   and makes them slaves.
19 He strips priests of their power
   and removes those who feel so secure
      in their position.
20 He makes trusted advisors be silent.
   He takes away the wisdom of the older
      leaders.
21 He brings disgrace to important people.
   He takes power away from rulers.
22 He exposes even the darkest secrets.
   He sends light into places that are as
      dark as death.
23 God makes nations great,
   and then he destroys them.
   He makes nations grow large,
      and then he scatters their people.
24 He makes their leaders foolish.
   He makes them wander around in the
      desert.
25 They are like someone feeling their way
      in the dark.
   They are like drunks who don't know
      where they are going.

13

1 "I have seen all this before.
I have already heard everything you
say.
I understand all these things.

2 I know as much as you do.
I am as smart as you are.

3 But I don't want to argue with you.
I want to speak to God All-Powerful.
I want to argue with God about my
troubles.

4 But you men try to cover up your
ignorance with lies.
You are like worthless doctors who
cannot heal anyone.

5 I wish you would just be quiet.
That would be the wisest thing you
could do.

6 "Now, listen to my argument.
Listen to what I have to say.

7 Will you speak lies for God?
Do you really believe your lies are what
God wants you to say?

8 Are you trying to defend God against me?
You are not being fair.
You are choosing God's side simply
because he is God.

9 If God checked you very closely,
would he see that you are right?
Do you really think you can fool God
the same as you fool people?

10 You know that God would criticize you
if you chose someone's side simply
because they were important.

11 God's majesty frightens you.
You are afraid of him.

12 The wise sayings you quote are worthless.
Your arguments are as weak as clay.

13 "Be quiet and let me talk!
I accept whatever happens to me.

14 I will put myself in danger
and take my life in my own hands.

15 I will continue to trust God even if he
kills me.[a]
But I will defend myself to his face.

16 And if he lets me live, it will be because I
had the confidence to speak.
No guilty person would dare meet God
face to face.

17 Listen carefully to what I say.
Let me explain.

18 I am ready now to defend myself.
I will carefully present my arguments.
I know I will be shown to be right.

19 If anyone can prove I am wrong,
I will shut up and wait to die.

20 "God, just give me two things,
and then I will not hide from you:

21 Stop punishing me,
and don't frighten me with your terrors.

22 Then call to me, and I will answer you.
Or let me speak, and you answer me.

23 How many sins have I committed?
What wrongs have I done?
Show me where I went wrong or how I
sinned.

24 God, why do you avoid me
and treat me like your enemy?

25 Are you trying to scare me?
I am only a leaf blowing in the wind.
You are attacking a piece of straw!

26 You have a list of terrible charges against
me.
Are you making me suffer for the sins I
did when I was young?

27 You have put chains on my feet.
You watch every step I take.
You see every move I make.

28 So I am becoming weaker and weaker,
like a piece of wood rotting away,
like a piece of cloth eaten by moths.

14

1 "We are all human beings.[b]
Our life is short and full of trouble.

2 Our life is like a flower.
It grows quickly and then dies away.
Our life is like a shadow that is here for a
short time and then is gone.

3 God, do you need to keep an eye on
something so small?
Why bother to bring charges against
me?

4 "No one can make something clean from
something so dirty.

5 The length of our life has been decided.
You alone know how long that is.
You have set the limits for us and
nothing can change them.

6 So stop watching us; leave us alone,
and let us enjoy this hard life until we
have put in our time.

7 "There is always hope for a tree.
If it is cut down, it can grow again.
It will keep sending out new branches.

8 Its roots might grow old in the ground
and its stump die in the dirt,

9 but with water, it will grow again.
It will grow branches like a new plant.

10 But when a man dies,
he becomes weak and sick, and then he
is gone!

11 Like a lake that goes dry
or a river that loses its source,

12 so people lose their lives,
never to live again.
The skies will all pass away
before they rise from death.
The skies will all disappear before
anyone wakes up from that sleep!

---

[a] 13:15 I will … kills me Or "If he decides to kill me, I
have no hope."

[b] 14:1 human beings Literally, "born of woman."

13"I wish you would hide me in my grave.
 I wish you would hide me there, until
     your anger is gone.
 Then you could pick a time to remember
     me.
14 If a man dies, will he live again?
 If so, I would gladly suffer through this
     time waiting for my release.*a*
15 God, you would call me,
 and I would answer you.
 Then I, the one you made,
     would be important to you.
16 You would still watch every step I take,
 but you would not remember my sins.
17 It would be as if you had sealed my sins in
     a bag.
 It would be as if you had covered my
     guilt with plaster.

18"Mountains fall and crumble away.
 Large rocks break loose and fall.
19 Water flowing over stones wears them
     down.
 Floods wash away the soil on the
     ground.
 In the same way, God, you destroy the
     hope people have.
20 You defeat them completely
 and then they are gone.
 You change the way they look
 and send them away forever to the
     place of death.
21 If their sons are honored, they will never
     know it.
 If their sons do wrong, they will never
     see it.
22 They only feel the pain in their bodies,
 and they alone cry for themselves."

Eliphaz Answers Job

15 ¹Then Eliphaz from Teman answered
Job:

2"If you were really wise,
 you would not answer with your
     worthless personal opinions!
 A wise man would not be so full of hot
     air.
3 Do you think a wise man would use
     empty words
 and meaningless speeches to win his
     arguments?
4 If you had your way,
 no one would respect God and pray to
     him.
5 What you say clearly shows your sin.
 Job, you are trying to hide your sin by
     using clever words.
6 I don't need to prove to you that you are
     wrong.

The words from your own mouth show
     that you are wrong.
 Your own lips speak against you.

7"Do you think you were the first person
     ever to be born?
 Were you born before the hills?
8 Did you listen to God's secret plans?
 Do you think you are the only wise
     person?
9 We know as much as you do!
 We understand as well as you.
10 The old, gray-haired men agree with us.
 People older than your father are on our
     side.
11 God tries to comfort you,
 but that is not enough for you.
 We have spoken his message to you in a
     gentle way.
12 Why will you not understand?
 Why can you not see the truth?
13 You are expressing your anger against God
 when you say these things.

14"People cannot really be pure.
 They*b* cannot be more right than God!
15 God does not even trust his angels.*c*
 He does not even think the sky is pure.
16 People are even worse.
 They are disgusting and dirty.
 They drink up evil like water.

17"Listen to me, and I will explain it to you.
 Let me tell you what I have seen.
18 I will tell you what wise men would say,
 things they heard from their fathers
 and then freely passed on.
 They didn't hide any secrets from me.
19 These are important people in our
     country!
 Everyone knows who they are.
20 And they said that an evil man suffers all
     his life.
 A cruel man suffers all his numbered
     years.
21 Every noise scares him.
 His enemy will attack him when he
     thinks he is safe.
22 An evil man has no hope of escaping the
     darkness.
 There is a sword somewhere waiting to
     kill him.
23 He wanders from place to place, looking
     for food.
 But he knows a dark day is coming,
 which he brought on himself.
24 He lives in fear, with worry and suffering
     threatening him
 like a king ready to attack.
25 That is because that evil man shook his
     fist at God, refusing to obey.
 He dared to attack God All-Powerful,

---

*a*14:14 *I would … release* Or "I would wait my whole
tour of duty for my replacement to come."

*b*15:14 *They* Literally, "a man born of woman."
*c*15:15 *angels* Literally, "holy ones."

26 like a soldier with a thick, strong shield
    who runs at his enemy to strike him in
        the neck.
27 He might be rich and fat,
28 but his town will be ruined;
    his home will be destroyed;
    his house will be empty.
29 He will not be rich for long.
    His wealth will not last.
    His crops will not grow large.
30 He will not escape the darkness.
    He will be like a tree whose leaves die
        from disease
    and are blown away by the wind.
31 That evil man should not fool himself by
        trusting in worthless things,
    because he will keep nothing.
32 He will die before his time,
    like a tree whose top branches have
        already begun to die.
33 He will be like a vine that loses its grapes
        before they ripen.
    He will be like an olive tree that loses
        its buds.
34 That is because people without God have
        nothing.
    Those who take bribes will have their
        homes destroyed by fire.
35 They are always thinking of ways to do
        evil and cause trouble.
    They are always planning how they
        might cheat others."

Job Answers Eliphaz

16 ¹Then Job answered:

²"I have heard all these things before.
    You men give me trouble, not comfort.
3 Your long speeches never end!
    Why do you continue arguing?
4 I also could say the same things you say,
        if you had my troubles.
    I could say wise things against you
    and shake my head at you.
5 But I would say things to encourage you
        and give you hope.

6"Nothing I say makes my pain go away.
    But keeping quiet does not help either.
7 God, you surely took away my strength.
    You destroyed my whole family.
8 You have made me thin and weak,
    and people think that means I am guilty.

9"God attacks me;
    he is angry with me and tears my body
        apart.
    He grinds his teeth against me.
    My enemy looks at me with hate.
10 People have crowded around me.
    They make fun of me and slap my face.
11 God has given me to evil people.
    He let the wicked hurt me.
12 I was enjoying a quiet, peaceful life,
    but then God crushed me.

Yes, he took me by the neck
    and broke me into pieces.
He has made me his target.
13 With his archers* all around me,
    he shoots arrows into my kidneys.
He shows no mercy
    and spills my gallᵃ on the ground.
14 Again and again he attacks me.
    He runs at me like a soldier in battle.

15"I am very sad,
    so I wear this sackcloth.*
I sit here in dust and ashes,
    feeling defeated.
16 My face is red from crying.
    There are dark rings around my eyes.
17 I was never cruel to anyone,
    and my prayers are pure.

18"Earth, don't hide the wrong things that
        were done to me.ᵇ
    Don't let my begging for fairness be
        stopped.
19 Even now there is someone in heaven
    who will speak for me.
    There is someone above who will testify
        for me.
20 My friend speaks for me,
    while my eyes pour out tears to God.
21 He speaks to God for me,
    like someoneᶜ presenting an argument
        for a friend.

22"In only a few years I will go to that place
        of no return.

17 ¹My spirit is broken;
    I am ready to give up.
My life is almost gone;
    the grave is waiting for me.
2 People stand around me and laugh at me.
    I watch them as they tease and insult
        me.

3"God, give me some support.
    No one else will!
4 You have closed my friends' minds,
    and they don't understand.
    Please don't let them win.
5 You know what people say:
    'A man neglects his own children to help
        his friends.'ᵈ
    But my friends have turned against me.
6 God has made my name a bad word to
        everyone.
    People spit in my face.
7 My eyes are almost blind from my grief.
    My whole body is as thin as a shadow.

ᵃ**16:13** *gall* The bitter contents of the gall bladder,
which is near the liver. Here, it means something
bitter and painful.
ᵇ**16:18** *Earth ... done to me* Literally, "Earth, don't
cover my blood." See Gen. 4:10–11.
ᶜ**16:21** *someone* Literally, "son of man."
ᵈ**17:5** *You know ... friends* Literally, "He promises a
share to his friends and his children's eyes go blind."

8 Good people wonder how this could
   happen.
   The innocent are upset with anyone
   who is against God.
9 But those who do right will continue to
   do what is right.
   Those who are not guilty grow stronger
   and stronger.

10"But come on, all of you, and try to prove
   me wrong.
   I don't find any of you to be wise.
11 My life is passing away, and my plans are
   destroyed.
   My hope is gone.
12 Everything is confused—
   night is day, and evening comes when it
   should be dawn.

13"I might hope for the grave to be my new
   home.
   I might hope to make my bed in the
   dark grave.
14 I might say to the grave, 'You are my
   father,'
   and to the worms, 'my mother' or 'my
   sister.'
15 But you can't really call that hope, can
   you?
   Does anyone see any hope for me?
16 Will hope go down with me to the place
   of death?
   Will we go down into the dirt
   together?"

Bildad Answers Job

18 ¹Then Bildad from Shuah answered:

2"When will you stop talking?
   Be sensible; let us say something.
3 Why do you think we are stupid, like
   dumb cows?
4 Your anger is hurting no one but you.
   Do you think this world was made for
   you alone?
   Do you think God should move
   mountains just to satisfy you?

5"Yes, the light of those who are evil will go
   out.
   Their fire will stop burning.
6 The light in their houses will become
   dark.
   The lamps next to them will go out.
7 Their steps, once strong and fast, become
   weak.
   Their own evil plans make them fall.
8 Their own feet lead them into a net.
   They fall into its hidden pit and are
   caught.
9 A trap catches them by the heel,
   and it holds them tight.
10 A rope is hidden on the ground to trip
   them.
   A trap is waiting in their path.

11 On every side terrors frighten them.
   Fears follow every step they take.
12 Disaster is hungry for them.
   Ruin stands close by, waiting for them
   to fall.
13 Diseases will eat away their skin.
   Death itself[a] will eat their arms and
   legs.
14 They will be taken away from the safety
   of their tents
   and be led away to meet death, the king
   of terrors.
15 Nothing will be left in their tents,
   which will be sprinkled with burning
   sulfur.
16 Their roots below will dry up,
   and their branches above will die.
17 People on earth will not remember them.
   Their names will be forgotten.
18 They will be forced from light into
   darkness.
   They will be chased out of this world.
19 They will leave behind no children, no
   descendants.
   None of their people will be left alive.
20 People in the west will be shocked at
   what happened to them.
   People in the east will be numb with
   fear.
21 This is what will happen to the homes of
   those who are evil.
   This is the place of those who don't
   know God!"

Job Answers

19 ¹Then Job answered:

2"How long will you hurt me
   and crush me with your words?
3 You have insulted me ten times now.
   You have attacked me without shame!
4 Even if I have sinned,
   it is my problem, not yours!
5 You want me to look bad to make
   yourselves look good.
   You say my troubles are proof that I did
   wrong.
6 I want you to know it was God who did
   this.
   He set this trap for me.
7 I shout, 'He hurt me!' but get no answer.
   No one hears my cry for fairness.
8 God has blocked my way to keep me from
   getting through.
   He has hidden my path in darkness.
9 He took away my honor.
   He took the crown from my head.
10 He hits me on every side until I am worn
   out.
   He takes away my hope.
   It is like a tree pulled up by the roots.

---

a **18:13** *Death itself* Literally, "Death's firstborn," a
name for a deadly disease, or the worms that eat a
dead body.

11 His anger burns against me.
His treats me like an enemy.
12 He sends his army to attack me.
They build attack towers around me.
They camp around my tent.

13 "God has made my brothers hate me.
Those who knew me have become
strangers.
14 My relatives have left me.
My friends have forgotten me.
15 My servant girls and visitors in my home
look at me as if I am a stranger and a
foreigner.
16 I call for my servant, but he does not
answer.
Even if I beg for help, he will not
answer.
17 My wife hates the smell of my breath.
My own brothers hate me.
18 Even little children make fun of me.
When I get up, they say bad things
about me.
19 All my close friends hate me.
Even my loved ones have turned against
me.

20 "I am so thin, my skin hangs loose on my
bones.
I have little life left in me.

21 "Pity me, my friends, pity me,
because God is against me.
22 Why do you persecute me like God does?
Don't you get tired of hurting me?

23 "I wish someone would write down
everything I say.
I wish my words were written on a
scroll.
24 I wish they were carved with an iron tool
into lead
or scratched on a rock so that they
would last forever.
25 I know that there is someone to defend
me and that he lives!
And in the end, he will stand here on
earth and defend me.
26 After I leave my body and my skin has
been destroyed,
I know I will still see God.
27 I will see him with my own eyes.
I myself, not someone else, will see God.
And I cannot tell you how excited that
makes me feel!^{a}

28 "Maybe you will say, 'How can we push
Job a little harder

and make him realize that he is the
source of his problems?'
29 But you need to worry about your own
punishment.
God might use the sword against you!
Then you will know there is a time for
judgment."

Zophar Answers Job

20 ^{1}Then Zophar from Naamah answered:

2 "You upset me, so I must answer you.
I must tell you what I am thinking.
3 You insulted me with your answers!
But I am wise and know how to answer
you.

4-5 "You know that the joy of the wicked does
not last long.
That has been true a long time, ever
since Adam was^b put on earth.
Those who don't know God are happy
for only a short time.
6 Maybe an evil man's pride will reach up
to the sky,
and his head will touch the clouds.
7 But he will be gone forever like his own
body waste.
People who knew him will say, 'Where
is he?'
8 Like a dream, he will fly away, never to
be found.
He will be chased away like a bad
dream.^{c}
9 Those who knew him before will not see
him again.
His family will never again get to see
him.
10 His children will have to give back what
he took from the poor.
His own hands will give up his wealth.
11 When he was young, his bones were
strong,
but, like the rest of his body, they will
soon lie in the dirt.

12 "Evil tastes sweet in his mouth.
He keeps it under his tongue to enjoy it
fully.
13 He hates to let it go
and holds it in his mouth.
14 But that evil will turn sour in his stomach.
It will be like a snake's bitter poison
inside him.
15 The evil man will spit out the riches he
has swallowed.
God will make him vomit them up.
16 What he drank will be like a snake's
poison;
it will kill him like the bite of a deadly
snake.

^{a}**19:25–27** Or "And in the end, he will stand here on
earth and defend me, ^{26}even after my skin has been
destroyed. But I want to see God while I am still in
my body. ^{27}I want to see him with my own eyes, not
through someone else's eyes. And I cannot tell you
how much I want this to happen!"

^{b}**20:4–5** *Adam was* Or "people were."
^{c}**20:8** *bad dream* Or "vision of the night."

17 He will never again enjoy so much
       wealth—
    rivers flowing with honey and cream.*a*

18 He will be forced to give back his profits.
    He will not be allowed to enjoy what he
       worked for,
19 because he hurt the poor and left them
       with nothing.
    He took houses he did not build.

20 "The evil man is never satisfied.
    But the things he wants cannot save him.
21 After filling himself, there is nothing left.
    His success will not continue.
22 Even while he has plenty, he will be
       pressed down with trouble.
    His problems will come down on him!
23 If he does get all he wants,
    God will throw his burning anger
       against him.
    God will attack him and rain down
       punishment on him.
24 Maybe he will run away from an iron
       sword,
    but then a bronze arrow*b* will strike him
       down.
25 It will go through his body and stick out
       of his back.
    Its shining point will pierce his liver,
    and he will be shocked with terror.
26 All his treasures will be lost in darkness.
    He will be destroyed by a fire, a fire that
       no human started.
    It will destroy everything left in his
       house.
27 Heaven will prove that he is guilty.
    The earth will be a witness against him.
28 His house and everything in it will be
       carried away
    in the flood of God's anger.
29 That is what God will do to those who are
       evil.
    That is what he plans to give them."

Job Answers

21 ¹Then Job answered:

2 "Listen to what I say.
    Let this be your way of comforting me.
3 Be patient while I speak.
    Then after I have finished speaking, you
       may make fun of me.

4 "My complaint is not against people.
    There is a good reason why I am not
       patient.
5 Look at me and be shocked.
    Put your hand over your mouth, and
       stare at me in shock!

6 When I think about what happened to
       me,
    I feel afraid and my body shakes!
7 Why do evil people live long lives?
    Why do they grow old and successful?
8 They watch their children grow up
    and live to see their grandchildren.
9 Their homes are safe and free from fear.
    God does not punish them.
10 Their bulls never fail to mate.
    Their cows have healthy calves.
11 They send their children out to play like
       lambs.
    Their children dance around.
12 They sing and dance to the sound of harps
       and flutes.
13 Evil people enjoy success during their
       lives
    and then go to the grave without
       suffering.
14 They say to God, 'Leave us alone!
    We don't care what you want us to do!'
15 And they say, 'Who is God All-Powerful?
    We don't need to serve him!
    It will not help to pray to him!'

16 "Of course, evil people don't make their
       own success.
    I would never follow their advice.
17 But how often does God blow out their
       light?
    How often does trouble come to them?
    How often does God get angry with
       them and punish them?
18 Does God blow them away, like the wind
       blows straw
    or like strong winds blow the grain
       husks?
19 But you say, 'God is saving their
       punishment for their children.'
    No! Let God punish the evil people
       themselves so that they will know
       what they have done!
20 Let them see their own punishment.
    Let them feel the anger of God
       All-Powerful.
21 When their life is finished and they are
       dead,
    they will not care about the family they
       leave behind.

22 "No one can teach God anything he
       doesn't already know.
    God judges even those in high places.
23 One person dies after living a full and
       successful life,
    a life completely safe and comfortable,
24 with a body that was well fed
    and bones that were still strong.
25 But another person dies after a hard life
       that has made them bitter,
    never having enjoyed anything good.
26 In the end, both of these people will lie
       together in the dirt.
    The worms will cover them both.

a20:17 rivers ... cream A figure meaning a plentiful
supply of rich food. The word translated "cream"
could mean butter, curds, or yogurt.
b20:24 bronze arrow Literally, "bronze bow." Or
"powerful bow," possibly a bow made of sinew,
wood and horn.

27 "But I know what you are thinking,
and I know you want to hurt me.
28 You might say: 'Show me a good man's
house.
Now, show me where evil people live.'[a]

29 "Surely you have talked with travelers.
Surely you will accept their stories.
30 Evil people are spared when disaster
comes.
They survive when God shows his
anger.
31 No one criticizes them to their faces for
how they lived.
No one punishes them for the evil they
have done.
32 When they are carried to the grave,
they will have someone to watch over
the place they are buried.
33 So even the soil in the valley will be
pleasant for them,
and thousands of people will join their
funeral procession.

34 "So your empty words are no comfort to
me.
There is no truth at all in your
answers!"

Eliphaz Answers Job

22 ¹Then Eliphaz from Teman answered:

2 "Does God need our help?
Even the wisest of us is not really useful
to him.
3 Does your living right benefit him?
Does God All-Powerful gain anything if
you follow him?
4 Why does God blame and punish you?
Is it because you worship him?
5 No, it is because you sin so much.
You never stop sinning.
6 Maybe to guarantee loans you took things
from people for no reason.
Maybe you took a poor man's clothes to
make sure he paid you back.[b]
7 Maybe you failed to give water or food
to people who were tired or hungry.
8 You have a lot of farmland,
and people respect you.
9 But maybe you sent widows away without
giving them anything.
And maybe you took advantage of
orphans.
10 That is why traps are all around you,
and sudden trouble makes you afraid.
11 That is why it is so dark you cannot see,
and why a flood of water covers you.

12 "God lives in the highest part of heaven
and looks down on the highest stars.

13 But you might say, 'What does God know?
Can he see through the dark clouds to
judge us?
14 Thick clouds hide us from his eyes,
so he cannot see us as he walks around
the edge of the sky.'

15 "Job, you are walking on the old path
that evil people walked on long ago.
16 They were destroyed before it was their
time to die.
They were washed away by the flood.
17 They told God, 'Leave us alone!'
and said, 'God All-Powerful cannot do
anything to us!'
18 And it was God who filled their houses
with good things.
No, I would never follow the advice of
evil people.
19 Those who do what is right are happy to
see them destroyed.
The innocent laugh at them and say,
20 'Surely our enemies are destroyed!
Their wealth burned up in the fire!'

21 "Now, Job, give yourself to God and make
peace with him.
Do this, and you will get many good
things.
22 Accept his teaching.
Pay attention to what he says.
23 If you return to God All-Powerful, you
will be restored.
But remove the evil from your house.
24 Think of your gold as nothing but dirt.
Think of your finest gold as rocks from a
stream.
25 And let God All-Powerful be your gold.
Let him be your pile of silver.
26 Then you will enjoy God All-Powerful,
and you will look up to him.
27 When you pray, he will hear you.
And you will be able to do all that you
promised him.
28 If you decide to do something, it will be
successful.
And your future will be very bright!
29 When people are brought down and you
ask God to help them,
he will rescue those who have been
humbled.
30 Even those who are guilty will be
forgiven.
They will be saved because you did
what was right."

Job Answers

23 ¹Then Job answered:

2 "I am still complaining today.
I groan because God is still making me
suffer.
3 I wish I knew where to find him.
I wish I knew how to go to where he
lives.

---

[a]21:28 Show me … live Or "Show me a wicked
ruler's house. Show me where evil people live."
[b]22:6 paid you back See Deut. 24:12-13 for rules
about making loans to the poor.

4 I would present my case to him.
  I would make my arguments to show
    that I am innocent.
5 He could give his response, and I would
    understand.
  I would listen closely to what he says.
6 Would God use his power against me?
  No, he would listen to me!
7 Since I am an honest man, he would let
    me tell my story.
  Then my Judge would set me free!

8 "If I go to the east, God is not there.
  If I go to the west, I still don't see him.
9 When he is working in the north, I don't
    see him.
  When he turns to the south, I still don't
    see him.
10 But God knows me.
  He is testing me and will see that I am
    as pure as gold.
11 I have always lived the way God wants.
  I have never stopped following him.
12 I always obey his commands.
  I love the words from his mouth more
    than I love my food.

13 "But God never changes,
  and who can stand against him?
  He does anything he wants.
14 He will do to me what he planned,
  and he has many other plans for me.
15 That is why I am terrified to stand before
    him.
  Just thinking about it makes me afraid.
16 The fear of God has made me lose my
    courage.
  God All-Powerful makes me afraid.
17 What has happened to me is like a dark
    cloud over my face.
  But the darkness will not keep me
    quiet.

24

1 "Why doesn't God All-Powerful set
    times for judgment?
  And why can't his followers know when
    those times will be?

2 "People move property markers to get
    more of their neighbor's land.
  People steal flocks and lead them to
    other grasslands.
3 They steal a donkey that belongs to an
    orphan.
  They take a widow's cow until she pays
    what she owes them.
9a They take a nursing baby from its mother.
  They take a poor person's child to
    guarantee a loan.
4 They force the poor to move out of their
    way
  and get off the road.

5 "The poor are like wild donkeys that go
    out to the desert to find food.
  From morning to night they work to
    gather food for their children.
6 They have to work in the fields,
    harvesting grain.
  They work for the rich,b gathering
    grapes in their vineyards.*
7 They must sleep all night without clothes.
  They have no covers to protect them
    from the cold.
8 They are soaked with rain in the
    mountains.
  They stay close to the large rocks for
    shelter.
10 They have no clothes, so they work
    naked.
  They carry piles of grain for others, but
    they go hungry.
11 They press out olive oil
  and walk on grapes in the winepress,*
  but they have nothing to drink.
12 In the city you can hear the sad sounds of
    dying people.
  Those who are hurt cry out for help, but
    God does not listen.

13 "Some people rebel against the light.
  They don't know what God wants.
  They don't live the way he wants.
14 A murderer gets up at dawn and kills
    poor, helpless people.
  And at night he becomes a thief.
15 A man who commits adultery* waits for
    the night to come.
  He thinks, 'No one will see me,' but
    still, he covers his face.
16 When it is dark, evil people go out and
    break into houses.
  But during the day they lock themselves
    in their homes to avoid the light.
17 The darkest night is their morning.
  They are friends with the terrors of
    darkness.

18 "You say, 'Evil people are taken away like
    things carried away in a flood.
  The land they own is cursed,* so no one
    goes to work in their vineyards.
19 As hot, dry weather melts away the
    winter snows,
  so the grave takes away those who have
    sinned.
20 Their own mothers will forget them.
  Only the worms will want them.
  No one will remember them.
  They will be broken like a rotten stick!
21 These evil people hurt women who have
    no children to protect them,
  and they refuse to help widows.
22 By his power God removes the powerful.
  Even if they have a high position, they
    cannot be sure of their lives.

---

a24:9 In the Hebrew text this verse follows verse 8.   b24:6 the rich Or "the wicked."

23 They might feel safe and secure,
   but God is watching how they live.
24 They might be successful for a while, but
   then they will be gone.
   Like everyone else, they will be cut
   down like grain.'

25"I swear these things are true!
   Who can prove that I lied?
   Who can show that I am wrong?"

Bildad Answers Job

25 ¹Then Bildad from Shuah answered:

2"God is the ruler.
   He makes people fear and respect him.
   He keeps peace in his kingdom above.
3 No one can count his stars.ᵃ
   His sun rises on all people.
4 How can anyone claim to be right before
   God?
   No human beingᵇ can really be pure.
5 In God's eyes even the moon is not pure
   and bright;
   even the stars are not pure.
6 People are much less pure.
   They are like maggots, as worthless as
   worms!"

Job Answers Bildad

26 ¹Then Job answered:

2"Bildad, what a great help you are to this
   tired, weary man!
   You have really supported me!
3 You have given such wonderful advice to
   this foolish man!
   You have provided so much useful
   information!ᶜ
4 Who helped you say these things?
   Whose spirit inspired you to speak?

5"The ghosts and their neighbors
   in the underworldᵈ shake with fear.
6 But God can see clearly into that place of
   death.
   Deathᵉ is not hidden from God.
7 God stretched the northern sky over
   empty space.
   He hung the earth on nothing.
8 He fills the thick clouds with water.

But he does not let its heavy weight
   break the clouds open.
9 He covers the face of the full moon.
   He spreads his clouds over it and hides
   it.
10 He drew the horizon on the ocean,
   like a circle where light and darkness
   meet.
11 The foundations that hold up the sky
   shake with fear when God threatens
   them.
12 With his own power God calmed the sea.
   With his wisdom he destroyed Rahab.*
13 His breath made the skies clear.
   His hand destroyed the snake that tried
   to get away.ᶠ
14 These are only a few of the amazing
   things God has done.
   We hear only a small whisper of God's
   thundering power."

27 ¹Job continued his answer:

2"God All-Powerful has been unfair to me;
   he has made my life bitter.
   But I swear by his life,
3   as long as I have life in me,
   as long as breath from God is in my
   nostrils,
4 I will not be a hypocrite.*
   I will not lie.
5 You will never hear me say you men are
   right!
   Until the day I die I will not be untrue
   to myself.
6 I will hold on to my innocence and never
   let go!
   My conscience will always be clear!
7 May my enemies be punished like those
   who are evil.
   May those who stood against me end up
   like all who have done wrong.
8 What hope do people without God have
   when it is time to die,
   when God takes their life away?
9 When they have troubles and cry out for
   help,
   God will not listen to them!
10 It will be too late for them to enjoy talking
   with God All-Powerful.
   They should have prayed to God all the
   time.

11"I will teach you about God's power.
   I will not hide anything about God
   All-Powerful.
12 But you have seen it all with your own
   eyes.
   So why do you say such useless things?

ᵃ**25:3 his stars** Or "his troops." This means God's
heavenly army. It could be all the angels or all the
stars in the sky.
ᵇ**25:4 No human being** Literally, "No one born from
woman."
ᶜ**26:2-3** Job is being sarcastic here—showing by
the way he speaks that he does not really mean it.
ᵈ**26:5 The ghosts ... underworld** Literally, "The
ghosts under the water." This refers to Sheol, the
place of death.
ᵉ**26:6 Death** Or "Abaddon," a Hebrew name meaning "death" or "destruction." See Rev. 9:11.

ᶠ**26:13 snake ... get away** Or "the escaping monster." This might be another name for Rahab. See
Isa. 27:1.

13[a] "Here is what God has planned for those
        who are evil.
    This is what cruel people will get from
        God All-Powerful.
14 They may have many children, but all of
        them will be killed in war.
    Or their children will not have enough
        to eat.
15 All those who are left will die,
    and the widows will not even cry for
        them.
16 Evil people collect silver as easily as dirt.
    They may have so many clothes that
        they are piled up like clay.
17 But their piles of clothes will be worn by
        those who have lived right.
    All that silver will be given to those
        who have done no wrong.
18 Evil people might build houses, but they
        will not last long.
    They will be like a spider's web or a
        guard's tent.
19 They might be rich when they go to bed,
    but when they open their eyes, all their
        riches will be gone.
20 Terrible fears will come over them like a
        flood,
    like a storm in the night that blows
        everything away.
21 The east wind will carry them away, and
        they will be gone.
    The storm will sweep them out of their
        homes.
22 They may try to run away from the power
        of the storm,
    but it will come down on them without
        mercy.
23 It will make a sound like clapping hands
        as they run away.
    It will whistle at them as they run from
        their homes."

The Value of Wisdom

28 1 "There are mines where people get
            silver
    and places where people melt gold to
        make it pure.
2 Iron is dug out of the ground,
    and copper is melted out of the rocks.
3 Miners carry lights deep into caves
    to search for these rocks in the deepest
        darkness.
4 Far from where people live, they dig deep
        into the ground,
    down where no one else has been
        before.
    There they work all alone, hanging from
        ropes.
5 Food grows on the ground above.
    But underground it is different,
        as if everything were melted by fire.

6 In the rocks there are sapphires*
    and grains of pure gold.
7 Wild birds know nothing about the way to
        these places.
    No falcon[b] has ever seen it.
8 Wild animals have never been there.
    Lions have not traveled that way.
9 Miners dig the hardest rocks.
    They dig away at the mountains and
        make them bare.
10 They cut tunnels through the rocks
    and see all the treasures they hold.
11 They even find places where rivers begin.
    They bring to light what once was
        hidden.

12 "But where can anyone find wisdom?
    Where can we get understanding?
13 People don't know where wisdom is.
    It cannot be found by anyone on earth.
14 The deep ocean says, 'It's not here with
        me.'
    The sea says, 'It's not here with me.'
15 You cannot buy wisdom with even the
        purest gold.
    There's not enough silver in the world
        to pay for it.
16 You cannot buy it with gold from Ophir
    or with precious onyx* or sapphires.
17 Wisdom is worth more than gold or
        crystal.
    It cannot be bought with expensive
        jewels set in gold.
18 It is far more valuable than coral* and
        jasper,
    more precious than rubies.
19 The topaz from Ethiopia cannot match its
        value,
    which is greater than the purest gold.

20 "So where does wisdom come from?
    Where can we find understanding?
21 Wisdom is hidden from every living thing
        on earth.
    Even birds in the sky cannot see it.
22 Death and destruction[c] say,
    'We have never seen wisdom;
        we have only heard rumors about it.'

23 "Only God knows the way to wisdom.
    Only he knows where wisdom is.
24 He can see to the very ends of the earth.
    He sees everything under the sky.
25 God gave the wind its power.
    He decided how big to make the oceans.
26 He decided where to send the rain
    and where the thunderstorms should
        go.
27 He looked at wisdom and discussed it.
    He examined it and saw how much it is
        worth.

[b]**28:7 falcon** A kind of bird, like a hawk.
[c]**28:22 Death and destruction** Or "Abaddon," a
Hebrew name meaning "death" or "destruction." See
Rev. 9:11.

[a]**27:13** Though Zophar is not mentioned in the text,
many scholars think he answers Job in verses 13–23.

28 Then he said to humans, 'To fear and
respect the LORD is wisdom.
To turn away from evil is
understanding.'"

Job Continues His Speech

29

¹Job continued to speak:

²"I wish my life could be the same as it was
a few months ago,
when God watched over me and cared
for me.
³ God's light shined above me,
so I could walk through the darkness.
⁴ I wish for the days when I was successful,
when I enjoyed God's friendship and
blessing in my home.
⁵ God All-Powerful was still with me then,
and my children were all around me.
⁶ Life was so good that I washed my feet in
cream
and had plenty of the finest oils.ᵃ

⁷"Those were the days when I went to the
city gate
and sat in the public meeting of the
elders.
⁸ When the young men saw me coming,
they stepped out of my way.
And the old men stood up to show they
respected me.
⁹ The leaders of the people stopped talking
and put their hands over their mouths.
¹⁰ Even the most important leaders were
quiet,
as if their tongues were stuck to the roof
of their mouths.
¹¹ All who heard me said good things about
me.
Those who saw what I did praised me,
¹² because I helped the poor when they
cried out.
I helped the orphans who had no one to
care for them.
¹³ People who were dying asked God to
bless me.
My help brought joy to widows in need.
¹⁴ Right living was my clothing.
Fairness was my robe and turban.*
¹⁵ I was like eyes for the blind,
like feet for the crippled.
¹⁶ I was like a father to the poor.
I helped people I didn't even know win
their case in court.
¹⁷ I stopped evil people from abusing their
power
and saved innocent people from them.ᵇ

¹⁸"I always thought I would live a long life,
growing old with my family around me.
¹⁹ I was like a healthy plant with roots that
have plenty of water
and branches that are wet with dew.
²⁰ I thought each new day would bring more
honor
and be full of new possibilities.ᶜ

²¹"In the past people listened to me.
They waited quietly for my advice.
²² When I finished speaking, they had
nothing more to say.
My words fell gently on their ears.
²³ They waited for my words as they would
for rain.
They drank them in like rain in the
springtime.
²⁴ I smiled at them, and they could hardly
believe it.
My smile made them feel better.
²⁵ I was their leader and made decisions
about their future.
I was like a king among his troops,
comforting those who were sad.

30

¹But now men younger than I make
fun of me—
men whose fathers were too worthless
to put with my sheep dogs.
² Their fathers are still too weak to be of
any use to me.
All their strength is gone.
³ They are starving with nothing to eat,
so they chew on the dry, ruined land.
⁴ They pull up salt plants in the desert
and eat the roots from the broom tree.
⁵ They are forced away from other people,
who shout at them as if they were
thieves.
⁶ They must live in the dry riverbeds,
hillside caves, and holes in the ground.
⁷ They howl in the bushes
and huddle together under thornbushes.
⁸ They are a bunch of worthless people
without names,
who were forced to leave their country.

⁹"Now their sons sing songs to make fun of
me.
My name has become a bad word to
them.
¹⁰ They hate me and stay far away from me,
except when they come to spit in my
face!
¹¹ God has taken the string from my bow
and made me weak,
so they feel free to do whatever they
want to me.

ᵃ**29:6 I had plenty of the finest oils** Literally, "Around
the anointed rock near me were streams of oil." This
probably means Job had so much olive oil that
there were streams of oil running down the altar
from the part Job gave as a gift to God.
ᵇ**29:17** Literally, "I shattered the teeth of the
crooked and snatched the victims from their teeth."

ᶜ**29:20** Literally, "My glory is new with me and my
bow in my hand renewed." The words "glory" and
"bow" might both refer to a rainbow—the promise
of good weather after a storm. Or this might be
understood as, "My soul feels new every day, my
hand always strong enough to shoot a new bow."

12 They attack me on my right side.
   They knock my feet out from under me.
   They build ramps to attack and destroy
     me like a city.
13 They guard the road so that I cannot
     escape.
   They succeed in destroying me, without
     help from anyone.
14 They break a hole in the wall and come
     rushing through it,
   and the crashing rocks fall on me.
15 I am shaking with fear.
   They chased my honor away like dust in
     the wind.
   My safety disappears like a cloud.

16"Now my life is almost gone, and soon I
     will die.
   Days of suffering have grabbed me.
17 All my bones ache at night.
   Pain never stops chewing on me.
18 God grabbed the collar of my coat
   and twisted my clothes out of shape.
19 He threw me into the mud,
   and I became like dust and ashes.

20"God, I cry out to you for help,
     but you don't answer.
   I stand up and pray,
     but you don't pay attention to me.
21 You have become cruel to me;
   you use your power to hurt me.
22 You let the strong wind blow me away.
   You throw me around in the storm.
23 I know you will lead me to my death,
   to that place where all the living must
     go.

24"Surely no one would attack a man who is
     already ruined,
   when he is hurt and crying for help.
25 God, you know that I cried for those who
     were in trouble.
   You know that I mourned* for the poor.
26 But when I hoped for good, trouble came
     instead.
   When I looked for light, darkness came.
27 I constantly feel upset.
   And my suffering has only just begun.
28 I am always sad and depressed, without
     any relief.
   I stand up in the public meeting and cry
     for help,
29 making sad sounds like the wild dogs,
   like the ostriches* in the desert.
30 My skin is burned and peeling away.
   My body is hot with fever.
31 My harp is tuned to play songs of sorrow.
   My flute makes sad sounds like
     someone crying.

31 1"I made an agreement with my eyes
         not to look at a young woman in a
   way that would make me want her.
2 What does God above have for us?

How does God All-Powerful repay
   people from his home high in
   heaven?ᵃ
3 He sends trouble to the wicked
   and disaster to those who do wrong.
4 God is the one who knows what I do
   and sees every step I take.

5"I have not lied to anyone.
   I never tried to cheat people.
6 If God would use accurate scales,ᵇ
   he would know that I am innocent.
7 If I ever stepped off the right path,
   if my eyes led my heart to do evil,
   or if my hands are dirty with sin,
8 then let others eat what I planted.
   Let my crops be pulled up by the roots.

9"If I have desired another woman
   or waited at my neighbor's door to sin
     with his wife,
10 then let my wife serve someone else,
   and let other men sleep with her.
11 To do such a thing would be shameful,
   a sin that must be punished.
12 Such sin is like a fire that burns until it
     destroys everything.
   It would completely ruin my life's work.

13"If I refused to be fair to my slaves
   when they had a complaint against me,
14 then what will I do when I must face
     God?
   What will I say when he asks me to
     explain what I did?
15 The one who made me in my mother's
     womb also made them.
   God shaped us all inside our mothers.

16"I have never refused to help the poor.
   I always gave widows what they
     needed.
17 I have never been selfish with my food.
   I shared what I had with orphans.
18 All my life I have been like a father to
     orphans
   and have taken care of widows.
19 Whenever I found people suffering
     because they didn't have clothes
   or saw a poor man with no coat,
20 I always gave them something to wear.
   I used the wool from my own sheep to
     make them warm.
   And they thanked me with all their
     heart.
21 I never threatened an orphan,

ᵃ31:1-2 Or possibly, "I made an agreement with
my eyes not to look with desire at the Virgin or the
sacred things that belong to God All-Powerful."
Here, "the Virgin" refers to a goddess worshiped by
the Canaanites.
ᵇ31:6 *accurate scales* Literally, "scales of righteousness." As a wordplay, this could mean either "accurate scales" or "scales that show a person is good."

even when I knew I had support in
court.[a]

²² If I ever did that, may my arm be pulled
from its socket
and fall from my shoulder!

²³ But I didn't do any of these bad things.
I fear God's punishment too much.
His majesty scares me.[b]

²⁴"I have never trusted in riches.
I never said even to pure gold, 'You are
my hope.'

²⁵ I have been wealthy,
but that didn't make me proud.
I earned a lot of money,
but that is not what made me happy.

²⁶ I have never worshiped the bright sun
or the beautiful moon.

²⁷ I was never foolish enough
to worship the sun and the moon.

²⁸ This is also a sin that must be punished.
If I had worshiped them, I would have
been unfaithful to God All-Powerful.

²⁹"I have never been happy
when my enemies were destroyed.
I have never laughed at my enemies
when bad things happened to them.

³⁰ I have never let my mouth sin by cursing*
my enemies
and wishing for them to die.

³¹ The people in my house know that
I have never let anyone go hungry.

³² I always invited strangers into my home
so that they would not have to sleep in
the streets.

³³ I have not tried to hide my sins as some
people do.
I have never hidden my guilt.

³⁴ I was never so afraid of what people
might say or of making enemies
that I kept my sins secret and avoided
going out.

³⁵"How I wish someone would listen to me!
I will sign my name to all I have said.
Now let God All-Powerful answer me.
Let him make a list of what he thinks I
did wrong.

³⁶ I would wear it around my neck.
I would put it on my head like a crown.

³⁷ Then I could explain everything I have
done.
I could come to God with my head held
high like a prince.

³⁸"I did not use my land in a wrong way.
I never caused it to suffer.

³⁹ I always paid the workers for the food I
got from the land.
I never let any of them starve.

[a]31:21 Or "I never shook my fist at an orphan who
was at the gate asking for help."
[b]31:23 *His majesty ... me* Or "I could not stand
before his majesty."

⁴⁰ If I ever did any of these bad things,
let thorns and weeds grow in my fields
instead of wheat and barley!"

Job's words are finished.

Elihu Adds to the Argument

32 ¹Then Job's three friends gave up trying to answer him, because he was so
sure that he was innocent. ²But there was a
young man there named Elihu son of Barakel. He was a descendant of a man named
Buz. Elihu was from the family of Ram. He
became very angry because Job kept saying
he was innocent—that he was right and God
was wrong. ³Elihu was also angry with Job's
three friends because they could not answer
him, and yet they still considered him guilty
of doing wrong. ⁴Elihu was the youngest one
there, so he had waited until everyone finished talking. ⁵But when he saw that Job's
three friends had nothing more to say, his
anger forced him to speak. ⁶So here's what
Elihu son of Barakel the Buzite said:

"I am only a young man, and you are all
older.
That is why I was afraid to tell you what
I think.

⁷ I thought to myself, 'Older people should
speak first.
They have lived many years, so they
have learned many things.'

⁸ But it is the spirit in people, the breath
from God All-Powerful,
that makes them understand.

⁹ Old men are not the only wise people.
They are not the only ones who
understand what is right.

¹⁰"So please listen to me,
and I will tell you what I think.

¹¹ I waited patiently while you men talked.
I listened to the answers you gave as
you searched for the right words.

¹² I listened carefully to what you said.
Not one of you proved Job wrong.
Not one of you answered his arguments.

¹³ You men cannot say that you have found
wisdom.
The answer to Job's arguments must
come from God, not people.

¹⁴ Job was arguing with you, not me,
so I will not use your arguments to
answer him.

¹⁵"Job, these men lost the argument.
They don't have anything more to say.
They don't have any more answers.

¹⁶ I waited for them to answer you.
But now they are quiet.
They stand there with nothing more to
say.

¹⁷ So now I will give you my answer.
Yes, I will tell you what I think.

18 I have so much to say
    that I cannot hold it in.
19 I feel like a jar of wine that has never
    been opened.
  I am like a new wineskin ready to burst.
20 I must speak so that I will feel better.
  I must answer your arguments.
21 I will treat you the same as I would treat
    anyone else.
  I will not praise you to win your favor.
22 I cannot treat one person better than
    another.
  If I did, God my Maker would punish
    me!

33

1 "Now, Job, listen to me.
  Listen carefully to what I say.
2 I am ready to speak.
3 My heart is honest, so my words are
    sincere.
  I will speak the truth about what I
    know.
4 God's Spirit made me.
  My life comes from God All-Powerful.
5 Listen to me and answer if you can.
  Get your arguments ready to face me.
6 You and I are the same before God.
  He used clay to make us both.
7 Don't be afraid of me.
  I will not be hard on you.

8 "But, Job, I heard what you said.
  These were your very words:
9 'I am pure and innocent;
  I did nothing wrong; I am not guilty!
10 But God found an excuse to attack me.
  He treats me like an enemy.
11 He put chains on my feet
  and watches everything I do.'

12 "But you are wrong about this, and I will
    prove it to you.
  God knows more than any of us.*a*
13 You are arguing with God!
  Why do you think he should explain
    everything to you?
14 But maybe God does explain what he
    does
  but speaks in ways that people don't
    understand.
15 He may speak in a dream, or in a vision*
    at night,
  when people are in a deep sleep lying in
    their beds.
16 He may whisper something in their ear,
  and they are frightened when they hear
    his warnings.
17 God warns people to stop them from
    doing wrong
  and to keep them from becoming proud.
18 He does this to save them from death.*b*

a 33:12 God … any of us Or "God is much greater
than anyone."
b 33:18 death Literally, "the Pit," the place where
people go when they die. Also in verse 22.

  He wants to keep them from being
    destroyed.

19 "Or those who are sick in bed might be
    suffering punishment from God.
  The pain that makes their bones ache
    might be a warning from him.
20 They feel so bad they cannot eat.
  Even the best food makes them sick.
21 Their bodies might waste away until they
    become thin
  and all their bones stick out.
22 They might be close to death,
  their lives about to end.
23 But maybe one of God's thousands of
    angels is watching over them,
  to speak for them and tell about the
    good things they have done.
24 Maybe the angel will be kind and say to
    God,
  'Save this one from the place of death!
  I have found a way to pay for his life.'
25 Then that person's body will become
    young and strong again.
  He will be as he was when he was
    young.
26 He will pray and God will answer.
  He will worship God and shout with joy.
  He will again stand as right before God.
27 He will tell everyone, 'I sinned.
  I changed good into bad,
  but God didn't give me the punishment
    I deserved!
28 God saved me from going down to the
    place of death.
  Now I can enjoy life again.'

29 "God does all these things for people again
    and again.
30 He wants them to be saved from death
  so that they can enjoy life.

31 "Job, pay attention and listen to me.
  Be quiet and let me talk.
32 But if you have an answer, go ahead and
    speak.
  Tell me your argument.
  I would be happy to know that you are
    innocent!
33 But if you have nothing to say, then listen
    to me.
  Be quiet, and I will teach you wisdom."

34

1 Then Elihu continued his speech:

2 "Listen to what I say, you wise men.
  Pay attention, you who know so much.
3 Your tongue tastes the food it touches,
  and your ear tests the words it hears.
4 So let us test these arguments and decide
    for ourselves what is right.
  Together we will learn what is good.
5 Job says, 'I am innocent,
  and God is not being fair to me.
6 I am right, but I am judged to be a liar.

I have done no wrong, but I am badly
hurt.'

7 "Would anyone but Job say such things?
He has more thirst for insulting God
than for water.
8 He is a friend of evil people.
He likes to spend time with the wicked.
9 I know this because he says,
'You will gain nothing if you try to please
God.'

10 "You men can understand, so listen to me.
God would never do what is evil!
God All-Powerful would never do
wrong.
11 He pays us back for what we have done.
He gives us what we deserve.
12 The truth is that God does no wrong.
God All-Powerful is always fair.
13 No one chose God to be in charge of the
earth.
No one gave him responsibility for the
whole world.
14 If God decided to take away his spirit
and the breath of life he gave us,
15 then everything on earth would die.
We would all become dust again.

16 "If you men are wise,
you will listen to what I say.
17 Can someone be a ruler if he hates
justice?
Job, God is not only powerful, but he is
fair.
Do you think you can judge him guilty?
18 God is the one who says to kings, 'You are
worthless!'
He says to leaders, 'You are evil!'
19 He does not respect leaders more than
other people.
And he does not respect the rich more
than the poor.
God made everyone.
20 Any of us can die suddenly, in the middle
of the night.
Anyone can get sick and pass away.
Even powerful people die for no reason
we can see.

21 "God watches what people do.
He sees every step they take.
22 There is no place dark enough
for evil people to hide from God.
23 God does not need to set a time
for people to come before him and be
judged.
24 He does not have to ask questions when
people do wrong,
even if they are powerful leaders.
He simply destroys them
and chooses others to take their place.
25 When he learns what people have done,
he defeats them, and overnight they are
gone.

26 He will punish them for the evil they
have done,
and he will do it where everyone can
see.
27 He will do this because they rebelled
against him
and ignored what he wanted.
28 They hurt the poor and made them cry to
God for help.
And he hears their cry!
29 But if God decides not to help them,
no one can judge him guilty.
If he hides himself, no one can find him.
He is the ruler over every person and
nation.
30 And if a ruler causes people to sin,
God will remove him from power.

31 "But what if someone says to God,
'I am guilty; I will not sin anymore'?
32 What if that person says, 'Show me the
sins I am not able to see.
If I have done wrong, I will not do it
again'?
33 Job, you want God to reward you,
but you refuse to change.
It is your decision, not mine.
Tell me what you think.
34 A wise person would listen to me.
A wise person would say,
35 'Job talks like an ignorant person.
What he says doesn't make sense!'
36 I think Job should be punished even
more,
because he answers us like someone
who is evil!
37 He adds rebellion to his other sins.
He sits there insulting us and arguing
with God!"

35

1 Elihu continued talking and said,

2 "Job, it is not fair for you to say,
'I am more right than God,'
3 because you also ask him,
'What's the use of trying to please you?
What good will it do me if I don't sin?'

4 "Job, I want to answer you and your
friends here with you.
5 Look up at the sky.
Look at the clouds, which are so much
higher than you.
6 If you sin, it does not hurt God.
Even if your sins are too many to count,
that does nothing to God.
7 And if you are good, that does not help
God.
He gets nothing from you.
8 Job, the good and bad things you do
affect only other people like yourself.

9 "If people are being hurt, they cry out
and beg for protection from those who
hurt them.

10 But they forget to say, 'Where is God, the
   one who made me?
   He is the one who gives us songs to sing
   in the night.
11 He is the one who makes us smarter than
   any animal on earth
   and wiser than any bird.'

12 "Or if evil people ask God for help, he will
   not answer them,
   because they are too proud.
13 God will not listen to their worthless
   begging.
   God All-Powerful will not pay attention
   to them.
14 So, Job, God will not listen to you
   when you say that you don't see him.
   You say you are waiting for your chance to
   meet with him
   and prove that you are innocent.

15 "Job thinks that God does not punish evil
   and that he pays no attention to sin.
16 So he continues his worthless talking.
   Everything he has said shows he does
   not know what he is talking about."

36

¹Elihu continued talking and said,

2 "Be patient with me a little longer.
   God has a few more words that he
   wants me to say.
3 I will share my knowledge with everyone.
   I will prove that my Maker is right.
4 Job, I am telling the truth.
   I know what I am talking about.

5 "God is very powerful,
   but he does not hate people.
   He is very powerful,
   but he is also very wise.
6 He will not let evil people live.
   He brings justice to the poor.
7 He watches over those who live right.
   He lets them rule in high places.
8 So if people are punished,
   if they are tied with chains and ropes,
   they did something wrong.
9 And God will tell them what they did,
   that they sinned and were proud.
10 He will force them to listen to his warning.
   He will command them to stop sinning.
11 If they serve and obey him, he will make
   them successful
   and they will live a happy life.
12 But if they refuse to obey him, they will
   be destroyed.
   They will die like fools.

13 "People who don't care about God are
   always bitter.
   Even when he punishes them, they
   refuse to pray to him for help.
14 They will die while they are still young,
   like the male prostitutes.

15 God saves those who suffer by using their
   suffering.
   He uses their troubles to speak in a way
   that makes them listen.

16 "In fact, God wants to help you out of your
   troubles.
   He wants to take away your burdens
   that are crushing you.
   He wants to load your table with plenty
   of food.
17 But you are full of this talk about guilt,
   judgment, and justice!
18 Job, don't let your anger fill you with
   doubt about God.
   And don't let the price of forgiveness
   turn you away.
19 Do you think your wealth will keep you
   out of trouble?
   Will your great strength be of any help
   to you now?
20 Don't be like those who wish darkness
   would come and hide them.
   They try to disappear into the night.ᵃ
21 Job, don't let your suffering cause you to
   choose evil.
   Be careful not to do wrong.

22 "Look, God's power makes him great!
   He is the greatest teacher of all.
23 No one can tell him what to do.
   No one can say, 'God, you have done
   wrong.'
24 Remember to praise him for what he has
   done,
   as many others have done in song.
25 Everyone can see what he has done,
   even people in faraway countries.
26 Yes, God is great, but we cannot
   understand his greatness.
   We don't know how long he has lived.

27 "God takes up water from the earth
   and changes it into mist and rain.
28 So the clouds pour out the water,
   and the rain falls on many people.
29 No one can understand how he spreads
   the clouds out
   or how the thunder rumbles from his
   home in the sky.
30 Look, he spreads lightning all over the sky
   and covers the deepest part of the
   ocean.
31 He uses them to control the nations
   and to give them plenty of food.
32 He grabs the lightning with his hands,
   and commands it to strike where he
   wants.
33 The thunder warns that a storm is
   coming.
   So even the cattle know it is near.

ᵃ36:19–20 The Hebrew text here is hard to
understand.

37

¹"The thunder and lightning frighten me;
my heart pounds in my chest.
² Listen to God's thundering voice!
Listen to the sound coming from his mouth.
³ He sends his lightning to flash across the whole sky.
It lights up the earth from one end to the other.
⁴ After the flashes of lightning you can hear his roaring voice.
He thunders with his wonderful voice!
And while his voice thunders, the lightning flashes continue.
⁵ God's thundering voice is amazing!
He does great things that we cannot understand.
⁶ He says to the snow,
'Fall on the earth.'
And he says to the rain,
'Pour down on the earth.'
⁷ God does this to stop everyone's work
and to show the people he made what he can do.
⁸ The animals run into their dens and stay there.
⁹ Whirlwinds come from the south.
The cold winds come from the north.
¹⁰ God's breath makes ice
and freezes even large bodies of water.
¹¹ He fills the clouds with water
and scatters his lightning through them.
¹² He orders the clouds to be blown all around the earth.
The clouds do whatever he commands.
¹³ He causes the clouds to punish people with floods
or to water his earth and show his love.

¹⁴"Job, stop for a minute and listen.
Think about the wonderful things God does.
¹⁵ Do you know how God controls the clouds?
Do you know how he makes his lightning flash?
¹⁶ Do you know how the clouds hang in the sky?
This is just one of the amazing works of the one who knows everything.
¹⁷ All you know is that you sweat, your clothes stick to you,
and all is still and quiet when the heat wave comes from the south.
¹⁸ Can you help God spread out the sky
and make it shine like polished brass?

¹⁹"Job, tell us what we should say to God!
We cannot think of what to say because of our ignorance.*ᵃ*

²⁰ I would not tell God that I wanted to talk to him.
That would be like asking to be destroyed.
²¹ A person cannot look at the sun.
It is too bright as it shines in the sky
after the wind blows the clouds away.
²² In the same way God's golden glory
shines from the Holy Mountain.*ᵇ*
He is surrounded by the brightest light.
²³ We have seen that God All-Powerful really is all powerful!
But he is just and never treats anyone unfairly.*ᶜ*
²⁴ That is why people fear and respect him.
He shows no respect for those who think they are wise."

God Speaks to Job

38

¹Then the LORD spoke to Job from a whirlwind and said,

²"Who is this ignorant person
saying these foolish things?"*ᵈ*
³ Brace yourself*ᵉ* and get ready to answer the questions I will ask you.

⁴"Where were you when I made the earth?
If you are so smart, answer me.
⁵ And who decided how big the earth should be?
Who measured it with a measuring line?
⁶ What is the earth resting on?
Who put the first stone in its place
⁷ when the morning stars sang together
and the angels*ᶠ* shouted with joy?

⁸"Who closed the flood gates
as the sea gushed from the womb?
⁹ Who covered it with clouds
and wrapped it in darkness?
¹⁰ I set the limits for the sea
and put it behind locked gates.
¹¹ I said to the sea, 'You can come this far, but no farther.
This is where your proud waves will stop.'

¹²"Did you ever in your life command the morning to begin
or the day to dawn?
¹³ Did you ever tell the morning light to grab the earth
and shake those who are evil out of their hiding places?
¹⁴ The morning light makes the hills
and valleys easy to see.

---

*ᵇ*37:22 *Holy Mountain* Or "the north" or "Zaphon."
*ᶜ*37:23 *But he ... unfairly* Or "He does not answer us when we try to sue him for justice."
*ᵈ*38:2 Or "Who is this person darkening advice with ignorant words."
*ᵉ*38:3 *brace yourself* Literally, "gird yourself like a man." This means "get ready for battle."
*ᶠ*38:7 *angels* Literally, "sons of God."

*ᵃ*37:19 *We cannot ... ignorance* Literally, "We cannot arrange ₍our thoughts₎ because of the darkness."

When the daylight comes to the earth,
  the shapes of these places stand out like
    the folds of a coat.
They take shape like soft clay
  that is pressed with a stamp.
15 Evil people don't like the daylight.
  When it shines bright, it keeps them
    from doing the bad things they do.

16 "Have you ever gone to the deepest parts
    of the sea?
  Have you ever walked on the ocean
    bottom?
17 Has anyone shown you the gates to the
    world of the dead?
  Have you ever seen those gates that lead
    to the dark place of death?
18 Do you really understand how big the
    earth is?
  Tell me, if you know all this.

19 "Where does light come from?
  Where does darkness come from?
20 Can you take them back to where they
    belong?
  Do you know how to get there?
21 Surely you know these things, since you
    are so old and wise.
  You were alive when I made them,
    weren't you?^{a}

22 "Have you ever gone into the storerooms
    where I keep the snow and the hail?
23 I save them there for times of trouble,
  for the times of war and battle.
24 Have you ever gone to the place where
    the sun comes up,
  where it makes the east wind blow all
    over the earth?^{b}
25 Who dug ditches in the sky for the heavy
    rain?
  Who made a path for the thunderstorm?
26 Who makes it rain even in desert places
    where no one lives?
27 The rain gives that dry empty land all the
    water it needs,
  and grass begins to grow.
28 Does the rain have a father?
  Who produces the drops of dew?
29 Does ice have a mother?
  Who gives birth to the frost?
30 That's when the water freezes as hard as
    a rock.
  Even the deep sea freezes over!

31 "Can you tie up the Pleiades^c?
  Can you unfasten the belt of Orion^d?

32 Can you bring out the other
    constellations^e at the right times?
  Can you lead out the Bear^f with its
    cubs?
33 Do you know the laws that control the
    sky?
  Can you put each star in its place above
    the earth?^{g}

34 "Can you shout at the clouds
  and command them to cover you with
    rain?
35 Can you give a command to the lightning?
  Will it come to you and say, 'Here we
    are; what do you want, sir?'
  Will it go wherever you want it to go?

36 "Who makes people wise?
  Who puts wisdom deep inside them?
37 Who is wise enough to count the clouds
  and tip them over to pour out their
    rain?
38 The rain makes the dust become mud,
  and the clumps of dirt stick together.

39 "Do you find food for the lions?
  Do you feed their hungry babies?
40 No, they hide in their caves
  or wait in the grass, ready to attack
    their prey.
41 Who feeds the ravens when their babies
    cry out to God
  and wander around without food?

39

1 "Do you know when the mountain
    goats are born?
  Do you watch when the mother deer
    gives birth?
2 Do you know how many months they
    must carry their babies?
  Do you know when it is the right time
    for them to be born?
3 These animals lie down, they feel their
    birth pains,
  and their babies are born.
4 Their babies grow strong out in the wild.
  Then they leave their mothers and
    never come back.

5 "Who let the wild donkeys go free?
  Who untied their ropes and let them
    loose?

---

^{a}38:19–21 This is sarcasm—saying something in
a way that everyone understands it is not really true.
^{b}38:24 Or "Where is the place that the fog disperses
and the place where the east wind scatters it all
over the earth?"
^{c}38:31 *Pleiades* A famous group of stars. It is often
called, "The Seven Sisters."
^{d}38:31 *Orion* A famous group of stars. It looks like a

hunter or powerful soldier.
^{e}38:32 *constellations* Groups of stars in the night
sky. Here, this probably means the twelve constellations of the Zodiac. They seem to pass through the
sky so that a new constellation is in a certain part of
the sky each month.
^{f}38:32 *Bear* A famous group of stars. It looks like a
bear. It is often called, "the Big Dipper." Near it is a
smaller constellation that looks like a small bear. It is
often called, "the Little Dipper."
^{g}38:33 *Can you ... earth* Or "Can you put it in
charge over the earth?"

6 I let the wild donkey have the desert for a
home.
I gave the salt lands to them for a place
to live.
7 They are happy to be away from the noise
of the city.
They never have to listen to their
drivers shouting at them.
8 They live in the mountains.
That is their pasture.
That is where they look for food to eat.

9 "Will a wild bull agree to serve you?
Will he stay in your barn at night?
10 Will he let you put ropes on him
to plow your fields?
11 A wild bull is very strong,
but can you trust him to do your work?
12 Can you trust him to gather your grain
and bring it to your threshing* place?

13 "An ostrich* gets excited and flaps its
wings, but it cannot fly.
Its wings and feathers are not like the
wings of a stork.
14 An ostrich lays her eggs on the ground
and lets the sand keep them warm.
15 The ostrich forgets that someone might
step on her eggs
or that a wild animal might break them.
16 An ostrich leaves her little babies.
She treats them as if they were not her
own.
If her babies die, she does not care that
all her work was for nothing.
17 That's because I did not give wisdom to
the ostrich.
She is foolish, and I made her that way.
18 But when the ostrich gets up to run, she
laughs at the horse and its rider,
because she can run faster than any
horse.

19 "Did you give the horse its strength?
Did you put the mane[a] on its neck?
20 Did you make it able to jump like a locust
or snort[b] so loudly that it scares people?
21 A horse is happy to be so strong.
It scratches the ground with its foot and
runs into battle.
22 It laughs at fear; nothing makes it afraid!
It does not run away from battle.
23 The soldier's quiver* shakes on the
horse's side.
The spear and weapons its rider carries
shine in the sun.
24 The horse gets very excited and races
over the ground.[c]
When it hears the trumpet blow, it
cannot stand still.

25 When the trumpet sounds, it snorts,
'Hurray!'
It can smell the battle from far away
and hear the shouts of commanders
with all the other sounds of battle.

26 "Did you teach the hawk how to spread its
wings and fly south[d]?
27 Are you the one who told the eagle[e] to fly
high into the sky?
Did you tell it to build its nest high in
the mountains?
28 It lives high on a peak at the top of a cliff.
That is its fortress.*
29 From there it looks far into the distance,
searching for its food.
30 The eagles gather around dead bodies,
and their young eat the blood."

40 ¹Then the LORD said to Job,

2 "You wanted to argue with God
All-Powerful.
You wanted to correct me and prove
that I was wrong.
So give me your answer!"

3 Then Job answered the LORD:

4 "I am not worthy to speak!
What can I say to you?
I cannot answer you!
I will put my hand over my mouth.
5 I spoke once, but I will not speak again.
I spoke twice, but I will not say
anything more."

6 Then the LORD spoke to Job again from the
storm:

7 "Brace yourself[f] and get ready to answer
the questions I will ask you.
8 "Are you trying to show that I am unfair?
Are you trying to look innocent by
saying that I am guilty?
9 Are your arms as strong as mine?
Do you have a voice like mine that is as
loud as thunder?
10 If so, you can be proud and wear glory
and honor like clothes.
11 If you are as powerful as God, then show
your anger!
Punish those who are proud and
humble them.
12 Yes, just look at the proud and make them
humble.
Crush those evil people where they
stand.
13 Bury them all in the dirt.
Wrap their bodies up and put them in
their graves.

---

[a]39:19 mane The hair on a horse's neck.
[b]39:20 snort The sound a horse makes by blowing
air very hard through the nose.
[c]39:24 races over the ground Literally, "swallows up
the ground."

[d]39:26 south Or "to Teman."
[e]39:27 eagle Or "vulture."
[f]40:7 Brace yourself Literally, "Gird yourself like a
man." This means "get ready for battle."

14 If you can do any of these things, then
    even I will praise you.
    And I will admit that you can save
      yourself by your own power.

15 "Look at the behemoth.ᵃ
    I made the behemoth, and I made you.
    He eats grass like a cow.
16 But he has great strength in his body.
    The muscles in his stomach are
      powerful.
17 His tail stands strong like a cedar tree.
    His leg muscles are very strong.
18 His bones are as strong as bronze.
    His legs are like iron bars.
19 The behemoth is the most amazing
      animal I made,
    but I can defeat him.
20 He eats the grass that grows on the hills
    where the wild animals play.
21 He lies under the lotus plants.
    He hides among the reeds of the swamp.
22 The lotus plants hide him in their shade.
    He lives under the willow trees that
      grow near the river.
23 If the river floods, the behemoth will not
      run away.
    He is not afraid if the Jordan River
      splashes on his face.
24 No one can blind his eyes and capture
      him.
    No one can catch him in a trap.

41

1 "Can you catch Leviathanᵇ with a
      fishhook?
    Can you tie his tongue with a rope?
2 Can you put a rope through his nose
    or a hook through his jaw?
3 Will he beg you to let him go free?
    Will he speak to you with gentle words?
4 Will he make an agreement with you
    and promise to serve you forever?
5 Will you play with Leviathan as you
      would play with a bird?
    Will you put a rope on him so that your
      girls can play with him?
6 Will fishermen try to buy him from you?
    Will they cut him into pieces and sell
      him to the merchants*?
7 Can you throw spears into his skin or
      head?

8 "If you ever lay a hand on Leviathan, you
      will never do it again!
    Just think about the battle that would
      be!
9 Do you think you can defeat him?
    Well, forget it! There is no hope.
    Just looking at him will scare you!
10 No one is brave enough to wake him up
    and make him angry.

"Well, no one can challenge me either!ᶜ
11 I owe nothing to anyone.
    Everything under heaven belongs to
      me.ᵈ

12 "I will tell you about Leviathan's legs,
    his strength, and his graceful shape.
13 No one can pierce his skin.
    It is like armor!ᵉ
14 No one can force him to open his jaws.
    The teeth in his mouth scare people.
15 His back has rows of shields
    tightly sealed together.
16 They are so close to each other
    that no air can pass between them.
17 The shields are joined to each other.
    They hold together so tightly that they
      cannot be pulled apart.
18 When Leviathan sneezes, it is like
      lightning flashing out.
    His eyes shine like the light of dawn.
19 Burning torches come from his mouth.
    Sparks of fire shoot out.
20 Smoke pours from his nose
    like burning weeds under a boiling pot.
21 His breath sets coals on fire,
    and flames shoot from his mouth.
22 His neck is very powerful.
    People are afraid and run away from
      him.
23 There is no soft spot in his skin.
    It is as hard as iron.
24 His heart is like a rock; he has no fear.
    It is as hard as a millstone.*
25 When he gets up, even the strongest
      peopleᶠ are afraid.
    They run away when he swings his tail.
26 Swords, spears, and darts only bounce off
      when they hit him.
    These weapons don't hurt him at all!
27 He breaks iron as easily as straw.
    He breaks bronze like rotten wood.
28 Arrows don't make him run away.
    Rocks thrown at him seem as light as
      chaff.*
29 When a wood club hits him, it feels to
      him like a piece of straw.
    He laughs when anyone throws a spear
      at him.
30 The skin on his belly is like sharp pieces
      of broken pottery.
    He leaves tracks in the mud like a
      threshing* board.
31 He stirs up the water like a boiling pot.
    He makes it bubble like a pot of boiling
      oil.
32 When he swims, he leaves a sparkling
      path behind him.

ᶜ**41:10** *Well, no one ... either* Or "No one can stand
and fight him."
ᵈ**41:11** Or "No one has come near to Leviathan and
survived—no one under heaven!"
ᵉ**41:13** *It is like armor* Or "No one can approach him
with a bridle."
ᶠ**41:25** *strongest people* Or "gods."

ᵃ**40:15** *behemoth* This might be a hippopotamus, a
rhinoceros, or possibly an elephant.
ᵇ**41:1** *Leviathan* This animal might be a crocodile or
a giant sea monster.

He stirs up the water and makes it
white with foam.

33 No animal on earth is like him.
He is an animal made without fear.

34 He looks down on the proudest of
creatures.
He is king over all the wild animals."

Job Answers the Lord

42 ¹Then Job answered the LORD:

2 "I know you can do everything.
You make plans, and nothing can
change or stop them.

3 You asked, 'Who is this ignorant person
saying these foolish things?'ᵃ
I talked about things I did not
understand.
I talked about things too amazing for me
to know.

4 "You said to me, 'Listen, and I will speak.
I will ask you questions, and you will
answer me.'

5 In the past I heard about you,
but now I have seen you with my own
eyes.

6 And I am ashamed of myself.ᵇ
I am so sorry.
As I sit in the dust and ashes,ᶜ
I promise to change my heart and my
life."

The Lord Gives Job's Wealth Back

7 After the LORD finished talking to Job, he
spoke to Eliphaz from Teman. He said, "I am
angry with you and your two friends, because

ᵃ**42:3 Who … things** Or "Who is this person darkening advice with ignorant words."
ᵇ**42:6 I am ashamed of myself** Or "I take back what
I said."
ᶜ**42:6 dust and ashes** People sat in dust and ashes
to show that they were very sad about something.

---

you did not tell the truth about me, as my servant Job did. ⁸So now, Eliphaz, get seven bulls
and seven rams. Take them to my servant Job.
Kill them and offer them as a burnt offering*
for yourselves. My servant Job will pray for
you, and I will answer his prayer. Then I will
not give you the punishment you deserve.
You should be punished, because you were
very foolish. You did not say what is right
about me, as my servant Job did."

9 So Eliphaz from Teman, Bildad from
Shuah, and Zophar from Naamah obeyed the
LORD. Then the LORD answered Job's prayer.

10 Job prayed for his friends, and the LORD
made Job successful again. God gave him
twice as much as he had before. ¹¹Then all his
brothers and sisters and all the people who
knew him before came to his house. They all
ate a big meal with him. They comforted him
and were sorry that the LORD had brought
him so much trouble. Each person gave Job a
piece of silver and a gold ring.

12 The LORD blessed Job with even more
than he had in the beginning. Job got 14,000
sheep, 6000 camels, 2000 oxen, and 1000
female donkeys. ¹³He also got seven sons and
three daughters. ¹⁴He named the first daughter Jemimah and the second daughter Keziah.
He named the third daughter Keren Hap-
puch. ¹⁵Job's daughters were among the most
beautiful women in all the country. And, like
their brothers, they each got a share of their
father's property.ᵈ

16 So Job lived for 140 years more. He
lived to see his children, his grandchildren,
his great-grandchildren, and his great-great-
grandchildren. ¹⁷Job lived to be a very old
man who had lived a good, long life.

ᵈ**42:15 And … property** Usually a person's property
was divided only among the sons, but here, even
Job's daughters got part of his property.

Psalms

BOOK 1 *(Psalms 1-41)*

1 ¹Great blessings belong to those who
don't listen to evil advice,
who don't live like sinners,
and who don't join those who make fun
of God.ᵉ

2 Instead, they love the LORD's teachings
and think about them day and night.

3 So they grow strong, like a tree planted by
a stream—
a tree that produces fruit when it should
and has leaves that never fall.
Everything they do is successful.

4 But the wicked are not like that.
They are like chaff* that the wind blows
away.

ᵉ**1:1** Or "The one who does not follow the advice
of the wicked or turn onto Sinners Road or stay at
Scoffers' House is blessed."

5 When the time for judgment comes, the
    wicked will be found guilty.
    Sinners have no place among those who
    do what is right.[a]
6 The LORD shows his people how to live,
    but the wicked have lost their way.

2 ¹Why are the nations so angry?
    Why are the people making such
    foolish plans?
2 Their kings and leaders join together
    to fight against the LORD and his chosen
    king.[b]
3 They say, "Let's rebel against them.
    Let's break free from them!"

4 But the one who rules in heaven laughs at
    them.
    The LORD makes fun of them.
5 He speaks to them in anger,
    and it fills them with fear.
6 He says, "I have chosen this man to be
    king,
    and he will rule on Zion,* my holy
    mountain."

7 Let me tell you about the LORD's
    agreement*:
    He said to me, "Today I have become
    your father,[c]
    and you are my son.
8 If you ask, I will give you the nations.
    Everyone on earth will be yours.
9 You will rule over them with great power.
    You will scatter your enemies like
    broken pieces of pottery!"

10 So, kings and rulers, be smart
    and learn this lesson.
11 Serve the LORD with fear and trembling.
12 Show that you are loyal to his son,[d]
    or the Lord will be angry and destroy
    you.
    He is almost angry enough to do that now,
    but those who go to him for protection
    will be blessed.

3 A song of David* written during the time he
    was running from his son Absalom.
1 LORD, I have so many enemies.
    So many people have turned against me.
2 They say to themselves, "God will not
    rescue him!"   Selah*

3 But you, LORD, protect me.
    You bring me honor;
    you give me hope.

4 I will pray to the LORD,
    and he will answer me from his holy
    mountain.   Selah
5 I can lie down to rest and know that I will
    wake up,
    because the LORD covers and protects
    me.
6 So I will not be afraid of my enemies,
    even if thousands of them surround me.

7 LORD, get up![e]
    My God, come rescue me!
    If you hit my enemies on the cheek,
    you will break all their teeth.

8 LORD, the victory[f] is yours!
    You are so good to your people.   Selah

4 To the director*: With stringed instruments.
    A song of David.*
1 God, you showed that I was innocent.
    You gave me relief from all my troubles.
    So listen to me now when I call to you for
    help.
    Be kind to me and hear my prayer.

2 Men,[g] how long will you try to dishonor
    me?
    Do you enjoy wasting your time
    searching for new lies against me?
                                    Selah*

3 You can be sure that anyone who serves
    the LORD faithfully is special to him.
    The LORD listens when I pray to him.

4 Tremble with fear, and stop sinning.[h]
    Think about this when you go to bed,
    and calm down.   Selah
5 Give the right sacrifices* to the LORD,
    and put your trust in him!

6 Many people say, "I wish I could enjoy
    the good life.
    LORD, give us some of those blessings."[i]
7 But you have made me happier than they
    will ever be with all their wine and
    grain.
8 When I go to bed, I sleep in peace,
    because, LORD, you keep me safe.

[e]3:7 *LORD, get up* The people said this when they
lifted the Box of the Agreement and took it into
battle, showing that God was with them. See Num.
10:35–36.
[f]3:8 *victory* Or "salvation."
[g]4:2 *Men* Literally, "Sons of man." This may be a term
of respect spoken to the leaders who were judging
the writer of this psalm.
[h]4:4 Or "Be angry, but don't sin." See Eph. 4:26,
which is based on the ancient Greek version.
[i]4:6 *I wish … blessings* Or "Who will show us good.
Lift up on us the light of your face, LORD."

[a]1:5 Or "The wicked will not be allowed to sit as
judges nor sinners in the meeting of good people."
[b]2:2 *his chosen king* Or "his anointed one."
[c]2:7 *I have become your father* Literally, "I fathered
you." Originally, this probably meant God was
"adopting" the king as his son.
[d]2:12 *Show … his son* Literally, "Kiss the son."

5 *To the director*: With flutes.*[a]
A song of David.*

1 LORD, listen to me
    and understand what I am trying to say.
2 My God and King,
    listen to my prayer.
3 Every morning, LORD, I lay my gifts before
    you
    and look to you for help.
    And every morning you hear my prayers.

4 God, you don't want evil people near you.
    They cannot stay in your presence.[b]
5 Fools[c] cannot come near you.
    You hate those who do evil.
6 You destroy those who tell lies.
    LORD, you hate those who make secret
    plans to hurt others.

7 But by your great mercy, I can enter your
    house.
    I can worship in your holy Temple* with
    fear and respect for you.
8 LORD, show me your right way of living,
    and make it easy for me to follow.
    People are looking for my weaknesses,
    so show me how you want me to live.
9 My enemies never tell the truth.
    They only want to destroy people.
    Their words come from mouths that are
    like open graves.
    They use their lying tongues to deceive
    others.[d]
10 Punish them, God!
    Let them be caught in their own traps.
    They have turned against you,
    so punish them for their many crimes.
11 But let those who trust in you be happy
    forever.
    Protect and strengthen those who love
    your name.
12 LORD, when you bless good people,
    you surround them with your love, like
    a large shield that protects them.

6 *To the director*: With stringed instruments,
on the sheminith.* A song of David.**

1 LORD, don't punish me.
    Don't correct me when you are so
    angry.
2 LORD, be kind to me.
    I am sick and weak.
    Heal me, LORD!
    My bones are shaking.
3 I am trembling all over.

LORD, how long until you heal me?[e]
4 LORD, come back and make me strong
    again.
    Save me because you are so loyal and
    kind.
5 If I am dead, I cannot sing about you.
    Those in the grave don't praise you.

6 LORD, I am so weak.
    I cried to you all night.
    My pillow is soaked;
    my bed is dripping wet from my tears.
7 My enemies have caused me such sorrow
    that my eyes are worn out from crying.

8 Go away, you wicked people,
    because the LORD has heard my cries.
9 The LORD has heard my request for mercy.
    The LORD has accepted my prayer.

10 All my enemies will be filled with fear
    and shame.
    They will be sorry when disgrace
    suddenly comes upon them.

7 *A song[f] of David* that he sang to the LORD
about Cush from the tribe of Benjamin.*

1 LORD my God, I come to you for
    protection.
    Save me from those who are chasing
    me.
2 If you don't help me, I will be torn apart
    like an animal caught by a lion.
    I will be carried away with no one to
    save me.

3 LORD my God, I have done nothing wrong.
4 I have done nothing to hurt a friend[g]
    or to help his enemies.
5 If that is not the truth, then punish me.
    Let an enemy chase me, catch me, and
    kill me.
    Let him grind me into the dirt and put
    me in my grave.   *Selah**

6 LORD, get up[h] and show your anger!
    My enemy is angry, so stand and fight
    against him.
    Get me the justice that you demand.
7 Gather the nations around you,
    and take your place as judge.
8 LORD, judge the people.
    LORD, judge me.
    Prove that I am right and that I am
    innocent.

---

[a]**Psalm 5** *For the flutes* This might be the name of a
tune instead of a type of instrument.
[b]**5:4** Or "You are not a God who likes evil people,
and they don't respect you."
[c]**5:5** *Fools* Here, this means people who do not
follow God and his wise teachings.
[d]**5:9** *They use ... others* Or "They say nice things to
others, but only to trap them."

[e]**6:3** *LORD ... heal me* Literally, "As for you, LORD, how
long?"
[f]**Psalm 7** *song* Literally, "shiggayon," which may
mean a special kind of song, perhaps one that is sad
or full of emotion.
[g]**7:4** *friend* Or "ally."
[h]**7:6** *LORD, get up* The people said this when they
lifted the Box of the Agreement and took it into
battle, showing that God was with them. See Num.
10:35–36.

9 Stop those who do evil.
  Support those who do good.
  God, you are fair.
  You know what people are thinking.

10 God helps people who want to do right,
   so he will protect me.
11 God is a good judge.
   He always condemns evil.
12-13If the wicked will not change,
   then God is ready to punish them.
   He has prepared his deadly weapons.
   His sword is sharp.
   His bow is strung, drawn back, and
     ready to shoot its flaming arrow.

14 The minds of the wicked are full of evil;
   they are pregnant with wicked plans,
   which give birth to lies.
15 They dig a pit to trap others,
   but they are the ones who will fall into
     it.
16 The trouble they cause will come back on
     them.
   They plan harm for others,
   but they are the ones who will be hurt.

17 I praise the LORD because he is good.
   I praise the name of the LORD Most High.

8 *To the director*: With the gittith.**
  A song of David.*
1 LORD our Lord, your name is the most
     wonderful in all the earth!
   It brings you praise everywhere in
     heaven.

2 From the mouths of children and babies
     come songs of praise to you.
   They sing of your power to silence your
     enemies who were seeking revenge.

3 I look at the heavens you made with your
     hands.
   I see the moon and the stars you
     created.
4 And I wonder, "Why are people so
     important to you?
   Why do you even think about them?
   Why do you care so much about
     humans*a*?
   Why do you even notice them?"

5 But you made people*b* almost like gods
     and crowned them with glory and honor.
6 You put them in charge of everything you
     made.

You put everything under their control.
7 People rule over the sheep and cattle and
     all the wild animals.
8 They rule over the birds in the sky
     and the fish that swim in the sea.
9 LORD our Lord, your name is the most
     wonderful name in all the earth!

9 *c To the director*: Use the Alamoth of Ben.d*
  A song of David.*
1 I will praise you, LORD, with all my heart.
   I will tell about the wonderful things
     you have done.
2 You make me happy, so I will rejoice in
     you.
   God Most High, I praise your name.
3 My enemies turned to run from you,
   but they fell and were destroyed.

4 You listened to me from your throne like
     a good judge,
   and you decided that I was right.
5 You told the nations how wrong they
     were.
   You destroyed those evil people.
   You erased their names from our
     memory forever and ever.
6 The enemy is finished!
   You destroyed their cities.
   There is nothing left to remind us of
     them.

7 The LORD set up his throne to bring
     justice,
   and he will rule forever.
8 He judges everyone on earth fairly.
   He judges all nations honestly.
9 Many people are suffering—
   crushed by the weight of their troubles.
   But the LORD is a refuge for them,
   a safe place they can run to.

10 LORD, those who know your name
   come to you for protection.
   And when they come,
     you do not leave them without help.

11 Sing praises to the LORD, who sits as King
     in Zion.e
   Tell the nations about the great things
     he has done.
12 He punishes murderers
   and remembers those who are in need.
   When suffering people cry for help,
   he does not ignore them.

---

*a*8:4 *people ... humans* Literally, "man ... son of
man" or "Enosh ... son of Adam." These are Hebrew
ways of saying humans—descendants of Adam
and Enosh.
*b*8:5, 6 *people, them, their* Literally, "him, him, his."
The writer is still talking about "man" and "son of
man," which can be understood as one person or as
all people.

*c*Psalm 9 In many Hebrew copies and in the ancient
Greek version, Psalms 9 and 10 are combined as
one psalm.
*d*Psalm 9 *Alamoth of Ben* This might be the name
of a tune, "On the Death of the Son," a music style,
or one of the orchestral groups in the Temple. See 1
Chron. 15:20.
*e*9:11 *Sing ... Zion* Or "Inhabitants of Zion, sing
praises to the LORD." See "Zion" in the Word List.

13 I said this prayer: "LORD, be kind to me.
   See how my enemies are hurting me.
   Save me from the 'gates of death.'
14 Then, at the gates of Jerusalem,[a] I can
      sing praises to you.
   I will be so happy because you saved
      me."

15 Those other nations have fallen into the
      pit they dug to catch others.
   They have been caught in their own
      trap.
16 The LORD showed that he judges fairly.
   The wicked were caught by what they
      did to hurt others.   *Higgayon[b] Selah**

17 The wicked will go to the place of death,
   as will all the nations that forget God.
18 It may seem that those who are poor and
      needy have been forgotten,
   but God will not forget them.
   He will not leave them without hope.

19 LORD, get up[c] and judge the nations.
   Don't let anyone think they can win
      against you.
20 Teach them a lesson.
   Let them know they are only human.
                                      Selah

10

1 LORD, why do you stay so far away?
   Why do you hide from people in
      times of trouble?
2 The wicked are proud and make evil plans
      to hurt the poor,
   who are caught in their traps and made
      to suffer.
3 Those greedy people brag about the
      things they want to get.
   They curse* the LORD and show that
      they hate him.
4 The wicked are too proud to ask God for
      help.
   He does not fit into their plans.
5 They succeed in everything they do.
   They don't understand how you can
      judge them.
   They make fun of all their enemies.
6 They say to themselves, "Nothing bad will
      ever happen to us.
   We will have our fun and never be
      punished."
7 They are always cursing, lying,
   and planning evil things to do.
8 They hide just outside the villages,
   waiting to kill innocent people,

always looking for any helpless person
   they can hurt.
9 They are like lions hiding in the bushes
   to catch weak and helpless animals.
   They lay their traps for the poor,
   who are caught in their nets.
10 Again and again they hurt people
   who are already weak and suffering.
11 They say to themselves, "God has
      forgotten about us.
   He is not watching.
   He will never see what we are doing."

12 LORD, get up and do something.
   Punish those who are wicked, God.
   Don't forget those who are poor and
      helpless.

13 The wicked turn against God
   because they think he will not punish
      them.
14 But, Lord, you do see the pain and
      suffering they cause.
   You see it, so punish them.
   Those who were left helpless put their
      trust in you.
   After all, you are the one who cares for
      orphans.

15 Break the arms of those who are wicked
      and evil.
   Punish them for the evil they have
      done,
   and stop them from doing any more.
16 LORD, you are King forever and ever,
   so I know you will remove the wicked
      nations from your land.
17 LORD, you have heard what the poor want.
   Listen to their prayers, and do what
      they ask.
18 Protect the orphans and those who have
      been hurt.
   Don't let powerful people drive us from
      our land!

11

To the director:
*A song of David.**
1 I trust in the LORD, so why did you tell me
      to run and hide?
   Why did you say, "Fly like a bird to your
      mountain?"

2 Like hunters, the wicked hide in the dark.
   They get their bows ready and aim their
      arrows.
   They shoot at good, honest people.
3 What would good people do
   if the wicked destroyed all that is good?[d]

4 The LORD is in his holy temple.
   The LORD sits on his throne in heaven.
   He sees everything that happens.

---

[a]9:14 *Jerusalem* Literally, "daughter Zion." See "Zion"
in the Word List.
[b]9:16 *Higgayon* Or "Meditation." Together with
Selah this may mean a time to pause and think
quietly.
[c]9:19 *LORD, get up* The people said this when they
lifted the Box of the Agreement and took it into
battle, showing that God was with them. See Num.
10:35–36. Also in Ps. 10:12.
[d]11:3 Or "What if the foundations of society were
really destroyed?

He watches people closely.
5 The LORD examines those who are good
    and those who are wicked;
  he hates those who enjoy hurting others.
6 He will make hot coals and burning sulfur
    fall like rain on the wicked.
  They will get nothing but a hot, burning
    wind.
7 The LORD always does what is right, and
    he loves seeing people do right.
  Those who live good lives will be with
    him.*a*

12 *To the director*: With the sheminith.*
*A song of David.**
1 Save me, LORD!
  We can no longer trust anyone!
  All the good, loyal people are gone.
2 People lie to their neighbors.
  They say whatever they think people
    want to hear.
3 The LORD should cut off their lying lips
    and cut out their bragging tongues.
4 Those people think they can win any
    argument.
  They say, "We are so good with words,
    no one will be our master."

5 They took advantage of the poor
    and stole what little they had.
  But the LORD knows what they did, and
    he says,
  "I will rescue those who are poor and
    helpless,
    and I will punish those who hurt
      them."*b*

6 The LORD's words are true and pure,
    like silver purified by fire,
  like silver melted seven times to make it
    perfectly pure.

7 LORD, take care of the helpless.
  Protect them forever from the wicked
    people in this world.
8 The wicked are all around us,
    and everyone thinks evil is something to
      be praised!

13 *To the director*:
*A song of David.**
1 How long will you forget me, LORD?
  Will you forget me forever?
  How long will you refuse to accept me?*c*
2 How long must I wonder if you have
    forgotten me?
  How long must I feel this sadness in my
    heart?
  How long will my enemy win against me?

3 LORD my God, look at me and give me an
    answer.
  Make me feel strong again, or I will die.
4 If that happens, my enemy will say, "I
    beat him!"
  He will be so happy that he won.

5 But, LORD, I trust in your faithful love,
    so let me rejoice because you saved me.
6 Then I will sing to the LORD
    because he was so good to me.

14 *To the director*:
*A song of David.**
1 Only fools think there is no God.
  People like that are evil and do terrible
    things.
  They never do what is right.

2 The LORD looks down from heaven
    to see if there is anyone who is wise,
    anyone who looks to him for help.
3 But everyone has gone the wrong way.
  Everyone has turned bad.
  No one does anything good.
    No, not one person!

4 Those who are evil treat my people like
    bread to be eaten.
  And they never ask for the Lord's help.
  Don't they know what they are doing?
5 They will have plenty to fear,
    because God is with those who do what
      is right.
6 You wicked people want to spoil the
    hopes of the poor,
    but the LORD will protect them.

7 I wish the one who lives on Mount Zion*
    would bring victory to Israel*!
  When the LORD makes his people
    successful again,
    the people of Jacob* will be happy;
    the people of Israel will be glad.

15 *A song of David.**
1 LORD, who can live in your Holy Tent*d*?
  Who can live on your holy mountain?
2 Only those who live pure lives, do what is
    right,
    and speak the truth from their hearts.
3 Such people don't say bad things about
    others.
  They don't do things to hurt their
    neighbors.
  They don't tell shameful things about
    those close to them.
4 They hate those who fail to please God
    and honor those who respect the LORD.

---

*a*11:7 *Those ... him* Literally, "They will see his face."
*b*12:5 *I will rescue ... hurt them* Or "I will rescue
poor, helpless people who were hurt and asked me
for help."
*c*13:1 *refuse to accept me* Literally, "hide your face
from me."

*d*15:1 *Holy Tent* The special tent where the people
of Israel worshiped God. Here, it is probably the
Temple on the "holy mountain" (see "Zion" in the
Word List) in Jerusalem.

If they make a promise to their neighbor,
    they do what they promised.[a]
5 If they loan money to someone,
    they do not charge them interest.
And they refuse to testify against an
      innocent person,
    even if someone offers them money to
      do it.

Whoever lives like this will always stand
    strong.

16   *A miktam* of David.*

1 Protect me, God, because I depend on you.
2 Some of you[b] have said to the LORD,
    "You are my Lord.
    Every good thing I have comes from you."
3 But you have also said about the gods[c] of
      this land,
    "They are my powerful gods.
    They are the ones who make me happy."

4 But those who worship other gods will
      have many troubles.
    I will not share in the gifts of blood they
      offer to their idols.
    I will not even say their names.
5 LORD, you give me all that I need.
    You support me.
    You give me my share.
6 My share[d] is wonderful.
    My inheritance[e] is very beautiful.
7 I praise the LORD because he taught me
      well.
    Even at night he put his instructions
      deep inside my mind.[f]

8 I always remember that the LORD is with
      me.[g]
    He is here, close by my side,
    so nothing can defeat me.
9 So my heart and soul will be very happy.
    Even my body will live in safety,
10 because you will not leave me in the
      place of death.
    You will not let your faithful one rot in
      the grave.
11 You will teach me the right way to live.
    Just being with you will bring complete
      happiness.
    Being at your right side will make me
      happy forever.

17   *A prayer of David.[h]*

1 LORD, hear my prayer for justice.
    I am calling loudly to you.
I am being honest in what I say,
    so please listen to my prayer.
2 You will make the right decision,
    because you can see the truth.
3 You were with me all night
    and looked deep into my heart.
You questioned me and found that
    I did not say or do anything wrong.
4 Unlike most people, I have obeyed your
      commands,
    so I have never been like those who are
      cruel and evil.
5 I have followed your way.
    My feet never left your path.
6 Every time I call to you, God, you answer
      me.
    So listen to me now, and hear what I
      say.
7 Show your amazing kindness
    and rescue those who depend on you.
Use your great power
    and protect them from their enemies.
8 Protect me like the pupil[i] of your eye.
    Hide me in the shadow of your wings.
9 Save me from the wicked people who are
      trying to destroy me.
    Protect me from those who come to hurt
      me.
10 They think only of themselves
    and brag about what they will do.
11 They have been following me,
    and now they are all around me.
They watch me, waiting to throw me to
      the ground.
12 Like hungry lions, they want to kill and
      eat.
    Like young lions, they hide, ready to
      attack.

13 LORD, get up[j] and face the enemy.
    Make them surrender.
    Use your sword and save me from these
      wicked people.
14 Use your power, LORD, and remove
      them from this life.
But as for the people you treasure, fill
      them with food.
    Give them plenty for their children and
      their grandchildren.

---

[a] **15:4** *If they ... promised* Or "They promised not to
do bad things, and they do not do bad things."
[b] **16:2** *Some of you* Literally, "you" (singular). Most
translations assume it should be "I," giving a different meaning to verses 2 and 3, which are very
difficult in the Hebrew text.
[c] **16:3** *gods* Literally, "holy ones."
[d] **16:6** *share* Or "section of land."
[e] **16:6** *inheritance* Here, this probably means the
land each Israelite received.
[f] **16:7** *mind* Literally, "my kidneys."
[g] **16:8** Literally, "I set the LORD before me always."

[h] **Psalm 17** *A prayer of David* Or "A prayer dedicated
to David."
[i] **17:8** *pupil* The center of the eye, which everyone
wants to protect.
[j] **17:13** *LORD, get up* The people said this when they
lifted the Box of the Agreement and took it into
battle, showing that God was with them. See Num.
10:35–36.

15 I have done only what is right, so I will
see your face.
And seeing you,[a] I will be fully satisfied.

18 [b] *To the director*: A song of David,* the*
Lord's *servant. He sang this song to the*
Lord *when the* Lord *saved him from Saul and all
his other enemies.*

1 I love you, Lord!
You are my strength.

2 The Lord is my Rock,* my fortress,* my
place of safety.
He is my God, the Rock I run to for
protection.
He is my shield; by his power I am
saved.[c]
He is my hiding place high in the hills.

3 I called to the Lord for help,
and he saved me from my enemies!
He is worthy of my praise!

4 Death had its ropes wrapped around me.
A deadly flood was carrying me away.

5 The ropes of the grave wrapped around
me.
Death set its trap right there in front of
me.

6 In my trouble I called to the Lord.
Yes, I cried out to my God for help.
There in his temple he heard my voice.
He heard my cry for help.

7 The earth shook and shivered.
The foundations of the mountains
trembled.
They shook because he was angry.

8 Smoke came from his nose.
Burning flames came from his mouth.
Red-hot coals fell from him.

9 He tore open the sky and came down!
He stood on a thick, dark cloud.

10 He flew across the sky, riding on a Cherub
angel*
racing on the wings of the wind.

11 He wrapped himself in darkness that
covered him like a tent.
He was hidden by dark clouds heavy
with water.

12 Out of the brightness before him,
hail broke through the clouds with
flashes of lightning.

13 The Lord thundered from the sky;
God Most High let his voice be heard.[d]

14 He scattered his enemies with his
arrows—
the lightning bolts that threw them into
confusion.

15 Lord, you shouted your command,
and a powerful wind began to blow.[e]
Then the bottom of the sea could be seen,
and the earth's foundations were
uncovered.

16 He reached down from above and grabbed
me.
He pulled me from the deep water.

17 He saved me from my powerful enemies,
who hated me.
They were too strong for me, so he
saved me.

18 They attacked me in my time of trouble,
but the Lord was there to support me.

19 He was pleased with me, so he rescued
me.
He took me to a safe place.

20 The Lord rewarded me for doing what is
right.
He was good to me because I am
innocent.

21 The Lord did this because I have obeyed
him.
I have not turned against my God.

22 I always remembered his laws.
I never rejected his rules.

23 He knows I did nothing that was wrong.
I have kept myself from sinning.

24 So the Lord rewarded me for doing what
is right.
He could see that I am innocent.

25 Lord, you are faithful to those who are
faithful.
You are good to those who are good.

26 You never do wrong to those who have
done no wrong.
But you outsmart the wicked, no matter
how clever they are.

27 You help those who are humble,
but you humiliate the proud.

28 Lord, you provide the flame for my lamp.
You, God, turn the darkness around me
into light.

29 With your help I can defeat an army.
If my God is with me, I can climb over
enemy walls.

30 God's way is perfect.
The Lord's promise always proves to be
true.
He protects those who trust in him.

31 There is no God except the Lord.
There is no Rock except our God.

32 God is the one who gives me strength.
He clears the path I need to take.

33 He makes my feet as steady as those of a
deer.
Even on steep mountains he keeps me
from falling.

---

[a]**17:15** *you* Literally, "your likeness."
[b]**Psalm 18** This song is also found in 2 Sam. 22.
[c]**18:2** *by his power I am saved* Literally, "He is the
horn of my salvation."
[d]**18:13** The ancient Greek version and some Hebrew
copies add "with hailstones and bolts of lightning."

[e]**18:15** *and ... blow* Or "and a blast of breath came
from your nose."

34 He trains me for war
    so that my arms can bend the most
        powerful bow.

35 Lord, you have given me your shield to
        protect me.
    You support me with your right hand.
    It is your help that has made me great.
36 You cleared a path for my feet
    so that I could walk without stumbling.

37 I chased my enemies and caught them.
    I did not stop until they were destroyed.
38 I struck them down, and they could not
        get up again.
    They fell under my feet.
39 God, you made me strong in battle.
    You made my enemies fall before me.
40 You made my enemies turn and run away.
    I destroyed those who hated me.
41 They cried out for help,
        but there was no one to save them.
    They cried out to the LORD,
        but he did not answer them.
42 I beat them to pieces like dust blown by
        the wind.
    I smashed them like mud in the streets.

43 You saved me from those who fought
        against me.
    You made me the ruler over nations.
    People I never knew now serve me.
44 As soon as they heard about me, they
        were ready to obey.
    Those foreigners fall helpless before me!
45 They lose all their courage
    and come out of their hiding places
    .shaking with fear.

46 The LORD lives!
    I praise my Rock, the God who saves
        me.
    How great he is!
47 He is the God who punishes my enemies
        for me,
    the one who puts people under my
        control.
48 He saves me from my enemies!

    You, Lord, help me defeat those who
        attack me.
    You save me from cruel people.
49 LORD, that is why I praise you among the
        nations.
    That is why I sing songs of praise to
        your name.

50 The Lord helps his king win battle after
        battle.
    He shows his faithful love to his chosen
        one,[a]
    to David* and his descendants forever.

19

To the director*:
A song of David.*

1 The heavens tell about the glory* of God.
    The skies announce what his hands
        have made.
2 Each new day tells more of the story,
    and each night reveals more and more
        about God's power.[b]
3 You cannot hear them say anything.
    They don't make any sound we can
        hear.
4 But their message goes throughout the
        world.
    Their teaching reaches the ends of the
        earth.

    The sun's tent is set up in the heavens.
5   It comes out like a happy bridegroom
        from his bedroom.
    It begins its path across the sky
        like an athlete eager to run a race.
6   It starts at one end of the sky
    and runs all the way to the other end.
    Nothing can hide from its heat.

7 The LORD's teachings are perfect.
    They give strength to his people.
    The LORD's rules can be trusted.
    They help even the foolish become
        wise.
8 The LORD's laws are right.
    They make people happy.
    The LORD's commands are good.
    They show people the right way to live.

9 Learning respect for the LORD is good.
    It will last forever.
    The LORD's judgments are right.
    They are completely fair.
10 His teachings are worth more than pure
        gold.
    They are sweeter than the best honey
        dripping from the honeycomb.
11 His teachings warn his servants,
    and good things come to those who
        obey them.

12 People cannot see their own mistakes,
    so don't let me commit secret sins.
13 Don't let me do what I know is wrong.
    Don't let sin control me.
    If you help me, I can be pure and free
        from sin.
14 May my words and thoughts please you.
    LORD, you are my Rock*—the one who
        rescues me.

20

To the director*:
A song of David.*

1 May the LORD answer you in times of
    trouble.

---

[a]18:50 his chosen one Literally, "his anointed one."

[b]19:2 Or "Like the changing of the guards, each
day passes the news to the next day and each night
passes information to the next night."

May the God of Jacob* protect you.

2 May he send you help from his Holy
Place.*
May he support you from Zion.*

3 May he remember all the gifts you have
offered.
May he accept all your sacrifices.* *Selah**

4 May he give you what you really want.
May he make all your plans successful.

5 We will celebrate when he helps you.
We will praise the name of God.
May the LORD give you everything you ask
for.

6 Now I know the LORD helps his chosen
king.
From his holy heaven he answered.
With his great power he saved him.

7 Some give the credit for victory to their
chariots* and soldiers,
but we honor the LORD our God.

8 They fall in battle, totally defeated,
but we survive and stand strong!

9 LORD, save the king!
Answer us when we call to you for help.

21 *To the director*:*
*A song of David.**

1 LORD, your strength makes the king happy.
He is so happy when you give him
victory.

2 And you gave him what he wanted.
You gave him what he asked for.   *Selah**

3 You gave the king such wonderful
blessings.
You put a golden crown on his head.

4 He asked for life, and you gave it.
You gave him life that goes on forever.

5 You led him to victory that brought him
great glory.
You gave him honor and fame.

6 You have given him blessings that will last
forever.
You have given him the joy of being
near you.

7 The king trusts in the LORD,
and the faithful love of God Most High
will keep him from falling.

8 Lord, you will show all your enemies that
you are strong.
Your power will defeat those who hate
you.

9 When you appear,
you will burn them up like a blazing
furnace.
In your anger, LORD, you will completely
destroy them;
they will be swallowed by flames of
fire.*

10 Their families will be destroyed.
They will be removed from the earth.

11 That is because they made evil plans
against you.
They wanted to do things they could not
do.

12 You will make them turn and run away
when you aim your arrows at their faces.

13 LORD, we lift you up with our songs of
praise.
We sing and play songs about your
power!

22 *To the director*: To the tune "The Deer of
Dawn."* A song of David.**

1 My God, my God, why have you left me?
You seem too far away to save me,
too far to hear my cries for help!

2 My God, I kept calling by day,
and I was not silent at night.
But you did not answer me.

3 God, you are the Holy One.
You sit as King upon the praises of
Israel.*

4 Our ancestors* trusted you.
Yes, they trusted you, and you saved
them.

5 They called to you for help and escaped
their enemies.
They trusted you and were not
disappointed!

6 But I feel like a worm, less than human!
People insult me and look down on me.

7 Everyone who sees me makes fun of me.
They shake their heads and stick out
their tongues at me.

8 They say, "Call to the LORD for help.
Maybe he will save you.
If he likes you so much, surely he will
rescue you!"

9 God, the truth is, you are the one who
brought me into this world.
You made me feel safe while I was still
at my mother's breasts.

10 You have been my God since the day I
was born.
I was thrown into your arms as I came
from my mother's womb.

11 So don't leave me!
Trouble is near, and there is no one to
help me.

12 My enemies have surrounded me like
angry bulls.
They are like the powerful bulls of
Bashan, and they are all around me.

13 Their mouths are opened wide,
like a lion roaring and tearing at its prey.

---

a **21:9** Or "You will make your king like a burning
oven when you come to help him, LORD. And in his
anger, he will completely destroy them."

b **Psalm 22** *The Deer of Dawn* This is probably the
name of the tune for this song, but it might refer to
a music style or type of instrument.

14 My strength is gone,
    like water poured out on the ground.
  My bones have separated.
    My courage is gone.*ᵃ*

15 My mouth*ᵇ* is as dry as a piece of baked
      pottery.
  My tongue is sticking to the roof of my
      mouth.
  You have left me dying in the dust.

16 The "dogs" are all around me—
    a pack*ᶜ* of evil people has trapped me.
  They have pierced my hands and feet.*ᵈ*

17 I can see each one of my bones.
  My enemies are looking at me;
    they just keep staring.

18 They divide my clothes among
      themselves,
  and they throw lots* for what I am
      wearing.

19 Lᴏʀᴅ, don't leave me!
  You are my strength—hurry and help
      me!

20 Save me from the sword.
  Save my precious life from these dogs.

21 Rescue me from the lion's mouth.
  Protect me from the horns of the bulls.*ᵉ*

22 I will tell my people about you.
  I will praise you in the great assembly.

23 Praise the Lᴏʀᴅ, all you who worship him!
  Honor him, you descendants of Jacob*!
  Fear and respect him, all you people of
      Israel*!

24 He does not ignore those who need help.
  He does not hate them.
  He does not turn away from them.
  He listens when they cry for help.

25 Lord, because of you I offer praise in the
      great assembly.
  In front of all these worshipers I will do
      all that I promised.

26 Poor people, come eat and be satisfied.*ᶠ*
  You who have come looking for the
      Lᴏʀᴅ, praise him!
  May your hearts be happy*ᵍ* forever.

27 May those in faraway countries remember
      the Lᴏʀᴅ
  and come back to him.
  May those in distant lands worship him,

28 because the Lᴏʀᴅ is the King.
  He rules all nations.

29 The people have eaten all they wanted
  and bowed down to worship him.
  Yes, everyone will bow down to him—
  all who are on the way to the grave,
      unable to hold on to life.

30 Our descendants will serve him.
  Those who are not yet born will be told
      about him.

31 Each generation will tell their children
  about the good things the Lord has
      done.

23 *A song of David.**

1 The Lᴏʀᴅ is my shepherd.
  I will always have everything I need.*ʰ*

2 He gives me green pastures to lie in.
  He leads me by calm pools of water.

3 He restores my strength.
  He leads me on right paths*ⁱ* to show
      that he is good.

4 Even if I walk through a valley as dark as
      the grave,*ʲ*
  I will not be afraid of any danger,
      because you are with me.
  Your rod and staff*ᵏ* comfort me.

5 You prepared a meal for me in front of my
      enemies.
  You welcomed me as an honored guest.*ˡ*
  My cup is full and spilling over.

6 Your goodness and mercy will be with me
      all my life,
  and I will live in the Lᴏʀᴅ's house*ᵐ* a
      long, long time.*ⁿ*

24 *A song of David.**

1 The earth and everything on it belong to
      the Lᴏʀᴅ.
  The world and all its people belong to
      him.

2 He built the earth on the water.
  He built it over the rivers.

3 Who can go up on the Lᴏʀᴅ's mountain*ᵒ*?
  Who can stand in his holy Temple*?

---

*ᵃ*22:14 *My courage is gone* Literally, "My heart is
melted in me like wax."
*ᵇ*22:15 *mouth* Or "strength."
*ᶜ*22:16 *pack* A group of dogs. Dogs travel together
in packs to hunt and kill other animals for food.
*ᵈ*22:16 *They … feet* Literally, "Like a lion, my hands
and feet."
*ᵉ*22:21 *Protect me … bulls* Or "You have answered
me and protected me from the horns of the bulls."
This could be both a prayer for help (like the first
half of the psalm) and also a statement that God
had answered this prayer (like the second half of
the psalm).
*ᶠ*22:26 *come eat … satisfied* This person was giving
a thank offering that would be shared with other
people at the Temple. This was how someone
shared their happiness when God blessed them.
See Lev. 3:1–5 and Deut. 14:22–29.
*ᵍ*22:26 *be happy* Literally, "live."
*ʰ*23:1 *I will … need* Literally, "I will lack nothing."
*ⁱ*23:3 *right paths* Or "paths of goodness."
*ʲ*23:4 *valley … grave* Or "death's dark valley" or "a
very dark valley."
*ᵏ*23:4 *rod and staff* The club and walking stick a
shepherd uses to protect and guide his sheep.
*ˡ*23:5 *You welcomed … guest* Literally, "You
anointed my head with oil."
*ᵐ*23:6 *house* Or "Temple." See "Temple" in the Word
List.
*ⁿ*23:6 *I … long time* Or "I will return again and again
to the Lᴏʀᴅ's Temple for as long as I live."
*ᵒ*24:3 *Lᴏʀᴅ's mountain* Mount Zion, the hill in
Jerusalem where the Temple was built.

4 Only those who have not done evil,
  who have pure hearts,
  who have not used my name*a* to hide
    their lies,
  and who have not made false promises.

5 Good people ask the Lord to bless others.
  They ask God, their Savior, to do good
    things.
6 They try to follow God.
  They go to the God of Jacob* for help.
                                      *Selah**

7 Gates, proudly lift your heads!
  Open, ancient doors,
  and the glorious King will come in.
8 Who is the glorious King?
  He is the Lord, the powerful soldier.
  He is the Lord, the war hero.

9 Gates, proudly lift your heads!
  Open, ancient doors,
  and the glorious King will come in.
10 Who is the glorious King?
  The Lord All-Powerful is the glorious
    King.

25 *b A song of David.**

1 Lord, I put my life in your hands.*c*
2 I trust in you, my God,
  and I will not be disappointed.
  My enemies will not laugh at me.
3 No one who trusts in you will be
    disappointed.
  But disappointment will come to those
    who try to deceive others.
  They will get nothing.

4 Lord, help me learn your ways.
  Show me how you want me to live.
5 Guide me and teach me your truths.
  You are my God, my Savior.
  You are the one I have been waiting for.
6 Remember to be kind to me, Lord.
  Show me the tender love that you have
    always had.
7 Don't remember the sinful things I did
    when I was young.
  Because you are good, Lord, remember
    me with your faithful love.

8 The Lord is good and does what is right.
  He shows sinners the right way to live.
9 He teaches his ways to humble people.
  He leads them with fairness.
10 The Lord is kind and true to those
    who obey what he said in his
    agreement.*

11 Lord, I have done many wrong things.
  But I ask you to forgive them all to show
    your goodness.

12 When people choose to follow the Lord,
  he shows them the best way to live.
13 They will enjoy good things,
  and their children will get the land God
    promised.
14 The Lord tells his secrets to his followers.
  He teaches them about his agreement.
15 I always look to the Lord for help.
  Only he can free me from my troubles.*d*

16 I am hurt and lonely.
  Turn to me, and show me mercy.
17 Free me from my troubles.
  Help me solve my problems.
18 Look at my trials and troubles.
  Forgive me for all the sins I have done.
19 Look at all the enemies I have.
  They hate me and want to hurt me.
20 Protect me! Save me from them!
  I come to you for protection, so don't let
    me be disappointed.
21 You are good and do what is right.
  I trust you to protect me.
22 God, save the people of Israel* from all
    their enemies.

26 *A song of David.**

1 Lord, judge me and prove that I have
    lived a pure life
  and have depended on you to keep me
    from falling.
2 Look closely at me, Lord, and test me.
  Judge my deepest thoughts and
    emotions.
3 I always remember your faithful love.
  I depend on your faithfulness.
4 I don't run around with troublemakers.
  I have nothing to do with hypocrites.*
5 I hate being around evil people.
  I refuse to join those gangs of crooks.

6 Lord, I wash my hands to make myself
    pure,
  so that I can come to your altar.
7 I sing a song to give you thanks,
  and I tell about all the wonderful things
    you have done.
8 Lord, I love the house*e* where you live,
  the place where your glory* is.

9 Lord, don't treat me like one of those
    sinners.
  Don't kill me with those murderers.
10 They are guilty of cheating people.
  They take bribes to do wrong.

---

*a***24:4 *my name** Literally, "my soul."
*b***Psalm 25** In Hebrew, each verse in this psalm
begins with the next letter of the alphabet.
*c***25:1 *I put … hands** Literally, "I lift my soul to you."

*d***25:15 *Only … troubles** Literally, "For he will
remove my feet from the net."
*e***26:8 *house** Or "Temple." See "Temple" in the Word
List.

11 But I am innocent,
    so be kind to me and save me.
12 I am safe from all danger
    as I stand here praising you, Lord, in
      the assembly of your people.

27 A song of David.*

1 Lord, you are my Light and my Savior,
    so why should I be afraid of anyone?
  The Lord is where my life is safe,
    so I will be afraid of no one!
2 Evil people might attack me.
    They might try to destroy my body.
  Yes, my enemies might attack me and try
      to destroy me,
    but they will stumble and fall.
3 Even if an army surrounds me, I will not
      be afraid.
    Even if people attack me in war, I will
      trust in the Lord.

4 I ask only one thing from the Lord.
    This is what I want most:
  Let me live in the Lord's house all my life,
    enjoying the Lord's beauty
    and spending time in his palace.a

5 He will protect me when I am in danger.
    He will hide me in his tent.b
  He will take me up to his place of safety.
6 If he will help me defeat the enemies
      around me,
    I will offer sacrifices* in his tent with
      shouts of joy.
    I will sing and play songs to honor the
      Lord.

7 Lord, hear my voice.
    Be kind and answer me.
8 My heart told me to come to you, Lord,
    so I am coming to ask for your help.
9 Don't turn away from me.
    Don't be angry with your servant.
    You are the only one who can help me.
  My God, don't leave me all alone.
    You are my Savior.
10 Even if my mother and father leave me,
    the Lord will take me in.
11 I have enemies, Lord, so teach me your
      ways.
    Show me the right way to live.
12 My enemies have attacked me.
    They have told lies about me and have
      tried to hurt me.
13 But I really believe that I will see the
    Lord's goodness before I die.c

14 Wait for the Lord's help.
    Be strong and brave,
    and wait for the Lord's help.

28 A song of David.*

1 Lord, you are my Rock.*
    I am calling to you for help.
    Don't close your ears to my prayers.
  If you don't answer me,
    I will be counted among the dead.
2 I lift my hands and pray toward your Most
      Holy Place.*
    Hear me when I call to you.
    Show mercy to me.
3 Don't treat me like the evil people who
      do wicked things.
    They greet their neighbors like friends,
    but secretly plan to hurt them.
4 They do bad things to others,
    so make bad things happen to them.
    Give them the punishment they
      deserve.
5 They don't notice what the Lord does.
    They ignore all the good things he has
      made.
    So instead of building them up, he will
      destroy them.

6 Praise the Lord!
    He has heard my prayer for mercy.
7 The Lord is my strength and shield.
    I trusted him with all my heart.
  He helped me, so I am happy.
    I sing songs of praise to him.
8 The Lord protects his chosen one.d
    He saves him and gives him strength.

9 Save your people.
    Bless those who belong to you.
    Lead them and honor theme forever.

29 A song of David.*

1 Praise the Lord, you heavenly angelsf!
    Praise the Lord's glory* and power.
2 Praise the Lord and honor his name!
    Worship the Lord in all his holy beauty.
3 The Lord's voice can be heard over the
      sea.
    The voice of our glorious Lord God is
      like thunder over the great ocean.
4 The Lord's voice is powerful.
    It shows the Lord's glory.
5 The Lord's voice shatters great cedar
      trees.
    He breaks the great cedars of Lebanon.

a27:4 palace A large house built for a king. Here, it
is the Temple. See "Temple" in the Word List.
b27:5 tent The place where God lives among his
people. Here, it is the Temple in Jerusalem. See
"Holy Tent" and "Temple" in the Word List.
c27:13 before I die Literally, "in the land of the
living."

d28:8 his chosen one Or "his anointed one." This
might be anyone God chose to serve in a special
way, but it is usually the king he has chosen.
e28:9 honor them Or "forgive them." Literally, "lift
them up."
f29:1 heavenly angels Literally, "sons of gods." This
probably means God's angels who are pictured here
as priests worshiping him in heaven.

6 He makes Lebanon shake like a young calf
    dancing.
  Sirion*a* trembles like a young bull
    jumping up and down.
7 The LORD's voice cuts the air with flashes
    of lightning.
8 The LORD's voice shakes the desert.
  Kadesh Desert*b* trembles at the LORD's
    voice.
9 The LORD's voice frightens the deer.*c*
  He destroys the forests.
  In his temple everyone shouts, "Glory to
    God!"

10 The LORD ruled as king at the time of the
     flood,
   and he will rule as king forever.
11 May the LORD make his people strong.
   May the LORD bless his people with
     peace.

30 *A song of David for the dedication* of the
       Temple.*d*
1 LORD, you lifted me out of my troubles.
    You did not give my enemies a reason to
      laugh,
    so I will praise you.
2 LORD my God, I prayed to you,
    and you healed me.
3 LORD, you lifted me out of the grave.
    I was falling into the place of death, but
      you saved my life.

4 Praise the LORD, you who are loyal to him!
    Praise his holy name*e*!
5 His anger lasts for a little while,
    but then his kindness brings life.
  The night may be filled with tears,
    but in the morning we can sing for joy!

6 When I was safe and secure,
    I thought nothing could hurt me.
7 Yes, LORD, while you were kind to me,
    I felt that nothing could defeat me.*f*
  But when you turned away from me,
    I was filled with fear.
8 So, LORD, I turned and prayed to you.
    I asked you to show me mercy.
9 I said, "What good is it if I die
    and go down to the grave?
  The dead just lie in the dirt.
    They cannot praise you.
    They cannot tell anyone how faithful
      you are.
10 LORD, hear my prayer, and be kind to me.
   LORD, help me!"

11 You have changed my sorrow into dancing.
   You have taken away my sackcloth*
     and clothed me with joy.
12 You wanted me to praise you and not be
     silent.
   LORD my God, I will praise you forever!

31 *To the director*:
       A song of David.*
1 LORD, I come to you for protection.
    Don't let me be disappointed.
  You always do what is right, so save me.
2 Listen to me.
   Come quickly and save me.
  Be my Rock,* my place of safety.
  Be my fortress* and protect me!
3 Yes, you are my Rock and my protection.
    For the good of your name, lead me and
      guide me.
4 Save me from the traps my enemy has set.
    You are my place of safety.
5 LORD, you are the God we can trust.
    I put my life*g* in your hands.
    Save me!
6 I hate those who worship false gods.
    I trust only in the LORD.
7 Your kindness makes me so happy.
    You have seen my suffering.
    You know about the troubles I have.
8 You will not let my enemies take me.
    You will free me from their traps.
9 LORD, I have many troubles, so be kind to
     me.
   I have cried until my eyes hurt.
   My throat and stomach are aching.
10 Because of my sin, my life is ending in
     grief;
   my years are passing away in sighs of
     pain.
   My life is ending in weakness.
   My strength is draining away.
11 My enemies despise me,
     and even my neighbors have turned
       away.
   When my friends see me in the street,
     they turn the other way.
   They are afraid to be around me.
12 People want to forget me like someone
     already dead,
     thrown away like a broken dish.
13 I hear them whispering about me.
   They have turned against me and plan
     to kill me.

14 LORD, I trust in you.
   You are my God.
15 My life is in your hands.
   Save me from those who are
     persecuting me.
16 Please welcome and accept your servant.*h*
   Be kind to me and save me.

*a***29:6** *Sirion* Or "Mount Hermon."
*b***29:8** *Kadesh Desert* A desert in Syria. This might
also mean "the holy desert."
*c***29:9** *deer* Or "oak trees."
*d***Psalm 30** *A song … Temple* Or "A psalm. The song
for the dedication of the house. Dedicated to David."
*e***30:4** *name* Literally, "memory" or "memorial."
*f***30:7** *I felt … defeat me* Literally, "You placed me on
the strong mountains."

*g***31:5** *life* Literally, "spirit."
*h***31:16** *Please … servant* Literally, "Let your face
shine on your servant."

17 LORD, I am praying to you.
  Don't let me be disappointed.
The wicked are the ones who should be
    disappointed.
  Let them go to the grave in silence.
18 Those evil people brag
    and tell lies about those who do right.
  They are so proud now,
    but their lying lips will be silent.

19 Lord, you have hidden away many
      wonderful things for your followers.
  You have done so many good things for
    those who trust in you.
  You have blessed them so that all the
    world can see.
20 Others make plans to hurt them.
  They say such bad things about them.
  But you hide your people in your shelter
    and protect them.
21 Praise the LORD, because he showed me
      how wonderful his faithful love is
  when the city was surrounded by
    enemies.
22 I was afraid and said, "I am in a place
    where he cannot see me."
  But I prayed to you, and you heard my
    loud cries for help.

23 Love the LORD, all of you who are his
    loyal followers.
  The LORD protects those who are loyal
    to him.
  But he punishes those who brag about
    their own power.
  He gives them all the punishment they
    deserve.
24 Be strong and brave, all of you who are
    waiting for the LORD's help.

32 A maskil* of David.

1 It is a great blessing
    when people are forgiven for the
      wrongs they have done,
    when their sins are erased.ᵃ
2 It is a great blessing
    when the LORD says they are not guilty,
    when they don't try to hide their sins.

3 Lord, I prayed to you again and again,
    but I did not talk about my sins.
  So I only became weaker and more
    miserable.
4 Every day you made life harder for me.
  I became like a dry land in the hot
    summertime.   Selah*

5 But then I decided to confess my sins to
    the LORD.
  I stopped hiding my guilt and told you
    about my sins.
  And you forgave them all!   Selah

ᵃ32:1 erased Or "covered over" or "atoned."

6 That is why your loyal followers pray to
    you while there is still time.
  Then when trouble rises like a flood, it
    will not reach them.
7 You are a hiding place for me.
  You protect me from my troubles.
  You surround me and protect me,
    so I sing about the way you saved me.
                                 Selah
8 The Lord says, "I will teach you
    and guide you in the way you should
      live.
  I will watch over you and be your guide.
9 Don't be like a stupid horse or mule that
    will not come to you
  unless you put a bit in its mouth and
    pull it with reins."

10 Many pains will come to the wicked,
    but the LORD's faithful love will
  surround those who trust in him.
11 Good people, rejoice and be very happy in
    the LORD.
  All you who want to do right, rejoice!

33 1 Rejoice in the LORD, good people!
  It is only right for good people to
    praise him.
2 Play the lyre* and praise the LORD.
  Play the ten-stringed harp for him.
3 Sing a new songᵇ to him.
  Play it well and sing it loud!
4 The LORD's word is true,
    and he is faithful in everything he does.
5 He loves goodness and justice.
  The LORD's faithful love fills the earth.
6 The LORD spoke the command, and the
    world was made.
  The breath from his mouth created
    everything in the heavens.
7 He gathered together the water of the sea.
  He put the ocean in its place.
8 Everyone on earth should fear and respect
    the LORD.
  All the people in the world should fear
    him,
9 because when he speaks, things happen.
  And if he says, "Stop!"—then it stops.ᶜ
10 The LORD can ruin every decision the
    nations make.
  He can spoil all their plans.
11 But the LORD's decisions are good forever.
  His plans are good for generation after
    generation.
12 Great blessings belong to those who have
    the LORD as their God!
  He chose them to be his own special
    people.

ᵇ33:3 new song Whenever God did a new and
wonderful thing for his people, they would write a
new song about it.
ᶜ33:9 And if … stops Or "He gives the command,
and it stands!" The word "stand" can mean "stand
forever" or "stop."

13 The LORD looked down from heaven
　　and saw all the people.
14 From his high throne he looked down
　　at all the people living on earth.
15 He created every person's mind,
　　and he knows what each one is doing.
16 A king is not saved by the power of his
　　army.
　　A soldier does not survive by his own
　　great strength.
17 Horses don't really bring victory in war.
　　Their strength cannot help you escape.
18 The LORD watches over his followers,
　　those who wait for him to show his
　　faithful love.
19 He saves them from death.
　　He gives them strength when they are
　　hungry.
20 So we will wait for the LORD.
　　He helps us and protects us.
21 He makes us happy.
　　We trust his holy name.
22 LORD, we worship you,
　　so show your great love for us.

34 *a A song of David* when he pretended to be crazy so that Abimelech would send him away, which he did.*

1 I will praise the LORD at all times.
　　I will never stop singing his praises.
2 Humble people, listen and be happy,
　　while I brag about the LORD.
3 Praise the LORD with me.
　　Let us honor his name.
4 I went to the LORD for help, and he
　　listened.
　　He saved me from all that I fear.
5 Look to the LORD for help.
　　You will be accepted.
　　You have no need to be ashamed.*b*
6 This poor man called to the LORD for help,
　　and he heard me.
　　He saved me from all my troubles.
7 The LORD's angel builds a camp around
　　his followers,
　　and he protects them.
8 Give the LORD a chance to show you*c*
　　how good he is.
　　Great blessings belong to those who
　　depend on him!
9 The LORD's holy people should fear and
　　respect him.
　　Those who respect him will always have
　　what they need.
10 Even strong lions get weak and hungry,
　　but those who go to the LORD for help
　　will have every good thing.
11 Children, come and listen to me;
　　I will teach you to respect the LORD.

12 Do you want to enjoy life?
　　Do you want to have many happy days?
13 Then avoid saying anything hurtful,
　　and never let a lie come out of your
　　mouth.
14 Stop doing anything evil, and do good.
　　Look for peace, and do all you can to
　　help people live peacefully.
15 The LORD watches over those who do
　　what is right,
　　and he hears their prayers.
16 But the LORD is against those who do evil,
　　so they are forgotten soon after they die.

17 Pray to the LORD, and he will hear you.
　　He will save you from all your troubles.
18 The LORD is close to those who have
　　suffered disappointment.
　　He saves those who are discouraged.
19 Good people might have many problems,
　　but the LORD will take them all away.
20 He will protect them completely.
　　Not one of their bones will be broken.
21 But troubles will kill the wicked.
　　The enemies of those who live right will
　　all be punished.
22 The LORD saves his servants.
　　All who go to him for protection will
　　escape punishment.

35 *A song of David.**

1 LORD, oppose those who oppose me.
　　Fight those who fight me.
2 Pick up your shields, large and small.
　　Get up and help me!
3 Take a spear and javelin
　　and fight those who are chasing me.
　　Tell me, "I will rescue you."

4 Some people are trying to kill me.
　　Disappoint them and make them
　　ashamed.
　　Make them turn and run away.
　　They are planning to hurt me.
　　Defeat and embarrass them.
5 Make them like chaff* blown by the
　　wind.*d*
　　Let them be chased by the LORD's angel.
6 Make their road dark and slippery.
　　Let the LORD's angel chase them.
7 I did nothing wrong, but they tried to trap
　　me.
　　For no reason at all, they dug a pit to
　　catch me.
8 So let them fall into their own traps.
　　Let them stumble into their own nets.
　　Let some unknown danger catch them.
9 Then I will rejoice in the LORD.
　　I will be happy when he saves me.
10 With my whole self I will say,
　　"LORD, there is no one like you."

*a*Psalm 34 In Hebrew, each verse in this psalm
begins with the next letter of the alphabet.
*b*34:5 *You will be accepted … be ashamed* Literally,
"Look at him and shine. Don't let your face be pale."
*c*34:8 *Give … show you* Literally, "Taste and see."

*d*35:5 *wind* This may be a wordplay, because the
Hebrew word also means "spirit."

You protect the poor from those who are
stronger.
You save the poor and helpless from
those who try to rob them."

11 There are witnesses[a] trying to harm me.
They ask me questions that I know
nothing about.

12 They pay me back evil for the good I have
done.
They make me so very sad.

13 When they were sick, I was sad and wore
sackcloth.*
I went without eating to show my
sorrow.
(May my prayers for them not be
answered!)

14 I mourned* for them as I would for a
friend or a brother.
I bowed low with sadness, crying as I
would for my own mother.

15 But when I had troubles, they laughed at
me.
They were not really friends.
I was surrounded and attacked by people I
didn't even know.

16 They made fun of me, using the worst
language.
They ground their teeth to show their
anger.

17 My Lord, how long will you watch this
happen?
Save my life from these people who are
attacking me like lions and trying to
destroy me.

18 I will praise you in the great assembly.
I will praise you there among the
crowds.

19 Don't let my lying enemies keep on
laughing at me.
They have no reason to hate me.
Surely they will be punished for their
secret plans.[b]

20 They have no friendly words for others,
but plan ways to hurt those who want
to live in peace.

21 They are telling lies about me.
They say, "Aha! We know what you
did!"

22 Lord, surely you can see what is
happening.
So don't keep quiet.
Lord, don't leave me.

23 Wake up! Get up!
My God and my Lord, fight for me, and
bring me justice.

24 Lord my God, judge me with your
fairness.
Don't let those people laugh at me.

25 Don't let them think, "Aha! We got what
we wanted!"
Don't let them say, "We destroyed
him!"

26 Let my enemies be ashamed and
embarrassed—
all those who were happy about my
troubles.
Proud of themselves, they treated me as
worthless.
So let them be covered with shame and
disgrace.

27 To those who want the best for me,
I wish them joy and happiness.
May they always say, "Praise the Lord,
who wants what is best for his
servant."

28 So, Lord, I will tell people how good you
are.
I will praise you all day long.

36 To the director*:
A song of David,* the Lord's servant.

1 Deep in the hearts of the wicked a voice
tells them to do wrong.
They have no respect for God.

2 They lie to themselves.
They don't see their own faults,
so they are not sorry for what they do.

3 Their words are wicked lies.
They have stopped doing anything wise
or good.

4 They make wicked plans in bed at night.
They choose a way of life that does no
good.
And they never say no to anything evil.

5 Lord, your faithful love reaches to the sky.
Your faithfulness is as high as the
clouds.

6 Your goodness is higher than the highest
mountains.
Your fairness is deeper than the deepest
ocean.
Lord, you protect people and animals.

7 Nothing is more precious than your loving
kindness.
All people can find protection close to
you.

8 They get strength from all the good things
in your house.
You let them drink from your wonderful
river.

9 The fountain of life flows from you.
Your light lets us see light.

10 Continue to love those who really know
you,
and do good to those who are true to
you.[c]

11 Don't let proud people trap me.
Don't let the wicked force me to run
away.

[a]**35:11** *witnesses* People who tell what they have
seen or heard. Here, these people were probably
telling lies.

[b]**35:19** *Surely … plans* Literally, "Will the people
who hate me freely wink their eyes?"

[c]**36:10** *true to you* Or "honest hearted."

12 Put this on their grave markers:
   "Here fell the wicked.
   They were crushed.
   They will never stand up again."

37 [a] A song of David.*

1 Don't get upset about evil people.
   Don't be jealous of those who do wrong.
2 They are like grass and other green plants
   that dry up quickly and then die.
3 So trust in the Lord and do good.
   Live on your land and be dependable.[b]
4 Enjoy serving the Lord,
   and he will give you whatever you ask
   for.
5 Depend on the Lord.
   Trust in him, and he will help you.
6 He will make it as clear as day that you
   are right.
   Everyone will see that you are being
   fair.
7 Trust in the Lord and wait quietly for his
   help.
   Don't be angry when people make evil
   plans and succeed.
8 Don't become so angry and upset that
   you, too, want to do evil.
9 The wicked will be destroyed,
   but those who call to the Lord for help
   will get the land he promised.
10 In a short time there will be no more evil
   people.
   You can look for them all you want, but
   they will be gone.
11 Humble people will get the land God
   promised,
   and they will enjoy peace.

12 The wicked plan bad things for those who
   are good.
   They show their teeth in anger at them.
13 But our Lord will laugh at them.
   He will make sure they get what they
   deserve.
14 The wicked draw their swords to kill the
   poor and the helpless.
   They aim their arrows to murder all
   who live right.
15 But their bows will break,
   and their swords will pierce their own
   hearts.
16 A few good people are better
   than a large crowd of those who are
   evil.
17 The wicked will be destroyed,
   but the Lord cares for those who are
   good.

18 The Lord protects pure people all their
   life.
   Their reward will continue forever.
19 When trouble comes,
   good people will not be destroyed.
   When times of hunger come,
   good people will have plenty to eat.
20 But evil people are the Lord's enemies,
   and they will be destroyed.
   Their valleys will dry up and burn.
   They will be destroyed completely.
21 The wicked borrow money and never pay
   it back.
   But good people are kind and generous.
22 Everyone the Lord blesses will get the
   land he promised.
   Everyone he curses* will be destroyed.
23 The Lord shows us how we should live,
   and he is pleased when he sees people
   living that way.
24 If they stumble, they will not fall,
   because the Lord reaches out to steady
   them.
25 I was young, and now I am old,
   but I have never seen good people left
   with no one to help them;
   I have never seen their children begging
   for food.
26 They are kind and generous,
   and their children are a blessing.
27 Stop doing anything evil and do good,
   and you will always have a place to live.
28 The Lord loves what is right,
   and he will never leave his followers
   without help.
   He will always protect them,
   but he will destroy the families of the
   wicked.
29 Good people will get the land God
   promised
   and will live on it forever.
30 Those who do what is right give good
   advice.
   Their decisions are always fair.
31 They have learned God's teachings,
   and they will never stop living right.[c]

32 The wicked are always looking for ways to
   kill good people.
33 But the Lord will not let the wicked
   defeat them.
   He will not let good people be judged
   guilty.
34 Do what the Lord says, and wait for his
   help.
   He will reward you and give you the
   land he promised.
   You will see the wicked being forced to
   leave.

35 I once saw a wicked man who was
   powerful.
   He was like a strong, healthy tree.

---

[a]**Psalm 37** In Hebrew, about every other verse
in this psalm begins with the next letter of the
alphabet.
[b]**37:3 be dependable** Literally, "shepherd
faithfulness."
[c]**37:31 they ... right** Literally, "his steps will not slip."

36 But then he was gone.
   I looked for him, but I could not find
      him.
37 Be pure and honest.
   Peace loving people will have many
      descendants.
38 But those who break the law will be
      destroyed completely.
   And their descendants will be forced to
      leave the land.[a]
39 The LORD saves those who are good.
   When they have troubles, he is their
      strength.
40 The LORD helps good people and rescues
      them.
   They depend on him, so he rescues
      them from the wicked.

38

*A song of David[*] for the day of
remembrance.[b]*

1 LORD, don't criticize me when you are
      angry.
   Don't discipline me in anger.
2 You have hurt me.
   You punished me and hurt me deeply.
3 You punished me severely, so my whole
      body is sore.
   I sinned, and now all my bones hurt.
4 My guilt is like a heavy burden.
   I am sinking beneath its weight.
5 I did a foolish thing,
   and now I have infected sores that stink.
6 I am bent and bowed down.
   I am depressed all day long.
7 I am burning with fever,
   and my whole body hurts.
8 I hurt so much I cannot feel anything.
   My pounding heart makes me scream!
9 My Lord, you heard my groaning.
   You can hear my sighs.
10 My heart is pounding.
   My strength is gone, and I am going
      blind.[c]
11 Because of my sickness,
   my friends and neighbors will not visit
      me;
   my family will not come near me.
12 My enemies say bad things about me.
   They are spreading lies and rumors.
   They talk about me all the time.
13 But I am like a deaf man and cannot hear.
   I am like someone who cannot speak.
14 I am like those who cannot hear what
      people are saying about them.
   I cannot answer to prove my enemies
      wrong.
15 LORD, you must defend me.
   Lord my God, you must speak for me.

16 That's why I prayed, "Don't let my
      enemies smile at my pain.
   Full of pride, they will laugh if I stumble
      and fall."
17 I know I am guilty of doing wrong.
   I cannot forget my pain.
18 LORD, I told you about the bad things I
      did.
   I am worried about my sins.
19 But my enemies are alive and healthy,
   and they have told many lies.
20 I did nothing but good,
   and they paid me back with evil.
   I try to do what is right,
   but that only makes them turn against
      me.
21 LORD, don't leave me.
   My God, stay close to me.
22 Come quickly and help me.
   My Lord, you are the one who saves
      me.

39

*To the director,[*] Jeduthun.[d]
A song of David.[*]*

1 I said, "I will be careful about what I say.
   I will not let my tongue cause me to sin.
   I will keep my mouth closed[e] when I
      am around wicked people."

2 So I didn't say anything.
   I didn't even say anything good,
   but I became even more upset.
3 I was very angry,
   and the more I thought about it, the
      angrier I became.
   So I said something.

4 LORD, tell me, what will happen to me
      now?
   Tell me, how long will I live?
   Let me know how short my life really is.
5 You gave me only a short life.
   Compared to you, my whole life is
      nothing.
   The life of every human is like a cloud
      that quickly disappears.   *Selah[*]*

6 Our life is like an image in a mirror.[f]
   We rush through life collecting things,
   but we don't know who will get them
      after we die.

7 So, Lord, what hope do I have?
   You are my hope!
8 Save me from the bad things I did.
   Don't let me be treated like a fool.
9 I will not open my mouth.

---

[a]**37:38 forced to leave the land** Or "destroyed." Literally, "cut off."
[b]**Psalm 38 for ... remembrance** The ancient Greek version has "for the Sabbath."
[c]**38:10 I am going blind** Or "My eyes have lost their sparkle." Literally, "Even the light of my eyes is no longer with me."

[d]**Psalm 39 Jeduthun** Or "and to Jeduthun," one of the three main temple musicians. See 1 Chron. 9:16; 16:38–42.
[e]**39:1 will keep ... closed** Literally, "guard my mouth with a muzzle."
[f]**39:6 Our life ... mirror** Or "This life is not real—it is only a shadow" or "People wander around in the dark—not knowing what will happen."

I will not say anything.
You did what should have been done.
10 But please stop punishing me.
You will destroy me if you do not stop.
11 You punish people for doing wrong to
teach them the right way to live.
As a moth destroys cloth, you destroy
what people love.
Yes, our lives are like a small cloud that
quickly disappears.   *Selah*

12 LORD, hear my prayer!
Listen to the words I cry to you.
Look at my tears.
I am only a traveler passing through this
life with you.
Like all my ancestors, I will live here
only a short time.*a*
13 Leave me alone*b* and let me be happy
before I am dead and gone.

40

To the director:*
*A song of David.**

1 I called*c* to the LORD, and he heard me.
He heard my cries.
2 He lifted me out of the grave.*d*
He lifted me from that muddy place.*e*
He picked me up, put me on solid ground,
and kept my feet from slipping.
3 He put a new song*f* in my mouth,
a song of praise to our God.
Many will see what he did and worship
him.
They will put their trust in the LORD.
4 Great blessings belong to those who trust
in the LORD,
for those who do not turn to demons
and false gods*g* for help.
5 LORD my God, you have done many
amazing things!
You have made great plans for us—too
many to list.
I could talk on and on about them,
because there are too many to count.

6 Lord, you made me understand this:*h*
You don't really want sacrifices* and
grain offerings.
You don't want burnt offerings* and sin
offerings.*

7 So I said, "Here I am,
ready to do what was written about me
in the book.
8 My God, I am happy to do whatever you
want.
I never stop thinking about your
teachings."
9 I told the good news of victory*i* to the
people in the great assembly.
And, LORD, you know that I will never
stop telling that good news.
10 I told about the good things you did.
I did not hide these things in my heart.
I spoke of how you can be trusted to save
us.
I did not hide your love and loyalty from
those in the great assembly.
11 LORD, do not hide your mercy from me.
Let your love and loyalty always protect
me.

12 Troubles have surrounded me.
They are too many to count!
My sins have caught me,
and I cannot escape them.
They are more than the hairs on my head.
I have lost my courage.
13 Please, LORD, rescue me!
LORD, hurry and help me!
14 People are trying to kill me.
Please disappoint them.
Humiliate them completely!
They wanted to hurt me.
Make them run away in shame!
15 May those who make fun of me
be too embarrassed to speak!
16 But may those who come to you be happy
and rejoice.
May those who love being saved by
you always be able to say, "Praise the
LORD!"*j*

17 My Lord, I am only a poor, helpless man,
but please pay attention to me.
You are my helper, the one who can save
me.
My God, don't be too late.

41

To the director:*
*A song of David.**

1 Those who help the poor succeed will get
many blessings.*k*
When trouble comes, the LORD will save
them.
2 The LORD will protect them and save their
lives.
He will bless them in this land.
He will not let their enemies harm
them.

---

a **39:12** *I live … time* Literally, "I am a settler."
b **39:13** *Leave me alone* Or "Stop looking at me."
c **40:1** *called* Or "waited patiently."
d **40:2** *grave* Literally, "pit of destruction." That is,
"Sheol," the place of death.
e **40:2** *muddy place* In many ancient stories, Sheol,
the place of death, is a dark place with mud all
around, like a grave.
f **40:3** *new song* Whenever God did a new and
wonderful thing for his people, they would write a
new song about it.
g **40:4** *demons and false gods* Or "proud and decep-
tive people."
h **40:6** *you made … this* Literally, "you have dug my
ears." The ancient Greek version has "you prepared
a body for me."

i **40:9** *victory* Or "goodness" or "righteousness."
j **40:16** *Praise the LORD* Literally, "The LORD is great"
or "May the LORD be magnified."
k **41:1** Or "Those who teach the poor will be very
fortunate."

3 When they are sick in bed,
    the Lord will give them strength and
        make them well!

4 I say, "Lord, be kind to me.
    I sinned against you, but forgive me and
        make me well."

5 My enemies say bad things about me.
    They ask, "When will he die and be
        forgotten?"

6 If they come to see me,
    they don't say what they are really
        thinking.
    They come to gather a little gossip
        and then go to spread their rumors.

7 Those who hate me whisper about me.
    They think the worst about me.

8 They say, "He did something wrong.
    That is why he is sick.
    He will never get well."

9 My best friend, the one I trusted,
    the one who ate with me—even he has
        turned against me.

10 Lord, please be kind to me.
    Let me get up, and I will pay them back.

11 Don't let my enemy defeat me.
    Then I will know that you care for me.

12 I was innocent and you supported me.
    You let me stand and serve you forever.

13 Praise the Lord, the God of Israel.*
    He always was, and he always will be.

    Amen* and Amen!

BOOK 2 (Psalms 42-72)

42 *To the director*:
A maskil from the Korah family.

1 Like a deer drinking from a stream,
    I reach out to you, my God.*

2 My soul thirsts for the living God.
    When can I go to meet with him?

3 Instead of food, I have only tears day and
        night,
    as my enemies laugh at me and say,
    "Where is your God?"

4 My heart breaks as I remember the
        pleasant times in the past,
    when I walked with the crowds as I led
        them up to God's Temple.*
    I remember the happy songs of praise
        as they celebrated the festival.

5-6 Why am I so sad?
    Why am I so upset?
    I tell myself, "Wait for God's help!
    You will again be able to praise him,
        your God, the one who will save you."

In my sadness I say, "I will remember you
    from here on this small hill,*
    where Mount Hermon and the Jordan
        River meet."

7 I hear the roar of the water coming from
        deep within the earth.
    It shouts to the water below as it
        tumbles down the waterfall.
    God, your waves come one after another,
        crashing all around and over me.*

8 By day the Lord shows his faithful love,
    and at night I have a song for him—a
        prayer for the God of my life.*

9 I say to God, my Rock,*
    "Why have you forgotten me?
    Why must I suffer this sadness that my
        enemies have brought me?"

10 Their constant insults are killing me.
    They never stop asking, "Where is your
        God?"

11 Why am I so sad?
    Why am I so upset?
    I tell myself, "Wait for God's help!
    You will again be able to praise him,
        your God, the one who will save you."

43 1 Defend me, God.
    Argue my case against those people
        who don't know you.
    Protect me from those evil liars.

2 God, you are my place of safety.
    Why have you turned me away?
    Why must I suffer this sadness
        that my enemies have brought me?

3 Send your light and your truth to guide me,
    to lead me to your holy mountain, to
        your home.

4 I want to go to God's altar,
    to the God who makes me so very happy.
    God, my God, I want to play my harp
        and sing praises to you!

5 Why am I so sad?
    Why am I so upset?
    I tell myself, "Wait for God's help!
    You will again have a chance to praise
        him,
    your God, the one who will save you."

44 *To the director*:
A maskil from the Korah family.

1 God, we have heard about you.
    Our fathers* told us what you did in
        their lifetime.
    They told us what you did long ago.

2 With your great power you took this land
        from other people,
    and you gave it to us.

---

*b*42:5-6 *small hill* Or "Mount Mizar."
*c*42:7 *God, your waves ... over me* These word pictures describe the psalmist's feelings about the many troubles the Lord has allowed him to experience."
*d*42:8 *the God of my life* Or "my living God."

*a*42:1 Or "As a deer stretches out to drink water from a stream, so my soul thirsts for you, God."

You crushed those foreigners
and forced them to leave this land.
3 It was not our fathers' swords that took
the land.
It was not their strong arms that
brought them victory.
It was your power.
It was because you accepted them and
smiled down on them.
4 God, you are my king.
Give the command and lead Jacob's*
people to victory.
5 We need your help to push our enemies
back.
Only in your name can we trample
those who attacked us.
6 I don't put my trust in my bow.
My sword cannot save me.
7 You are the one who saved us from our
enemies.
You are the one who put our enemies to
shame.
8 We have praised you all day long,
and we will praise your name forever.
Selah*

9 But you left us and put us to shame.
You did not go with us into battle.
10 You let our enemies push us back.
You let them take our wealth.
11 You gave us away like sheep to be killed
and eaten.
You scattered us among the nations.
12 You sold your people for nothing.
You did not even argue over the price.
13 You made us a joke to our neighbors.
They laugh and make fun of us.
14 You made us one of the stories that people
love to tell.
People all over the world laugh at us
and shake their heads.
15 All I can think about is my shame.
Just look at my face, and you will see it.
16 All I can hear are the jokes and insults of
my enemies,
as I watch them take their revenge.
17 We have not forgotten you.
But you do all those things to us.
We did not break the agreement* you
gave us.
18 We did not turn away from you.
We did not stop following you.
19 But you crushed us in this home of
jackals.*
You left us in this place as dark as death.
20 Did we forget the name of our God?
Did we pray to foreign gods?
21 If we did, then God knows it,
because he knows our deepest secrets.
22 All day long we died for you.
We are like sheep being led away to be
killed.
23 Lord, wake up!
Why are you sleeping?
Get up! Don't ignore us forever!

24 Why are you hiding from us?
Have you forgotten our pain and
troubles?
25 We have been pushed down into the dirt.
We are lying face down in the dust.*a*
26 Get up and help us!
Rescue us because of your faithful love.

45 *To the director*: To the tune
"Shoshanim."b A maskil* from the Korah
family. A love song.*
1 Beautiful thoughts fill my mind
as I speak these lines for the king.
These words come from my tongue
as from the pen of a skilled writer.

2 You are more handsome than anyone,
and you say such pleasant things.
So God will always bless you.
3 Put on your sword, mighty warrior,
so impressive in your splendid uniform.
4 Go out in your greatness to win the
victory for what is true and right.
Let us see the amazing things you can
do with your powerful right arm.*c*
5 Your sharp arrows will go deep into the
hearts of your enemies,
who will fall to the ground in front of
you.
6 God,*d* your throne will last forever.
Your justice is a sign of your power to
rule.
7 You love what is right and hate what is
evil.
So God, your God, chose you to be king
and made you happier than any of your
friends.*e*
8 From your clothes comes the wonderful
smell of myrrh,* aloes,* and cassia.*
In palaces decorated with ivory,
you enjoy the music of stringed
instruments.
9 Here are ladies of honor, daughters of
kings.
Your bride*f* stands at your right side,
wearing a gown decorated with the
finest gold.

---

*a*44:25 This shows that the people were being
treated like slaves who must bow down to their
masters.
*b*Psalm 45 *To the tune Shoshanim* Or "On the
Shoshanim."
*c*45:4 *right arm* This pictures God as a warrior-
king. The right arm is a symbol of his power and
authority.
*d*45:6 *God* This might be a song to God as king. Or
here, the writer might be using the word "God" as a
title for the king.
*e*45:7 *chose ... friends* Literally, "poured the oil
of rejoicing on you over your friends." This refers
to the special oil kept in the Temple and used in
dedications.
*f*45:9 *bride* Or "queen."

10 My lady,[a] listen to me.
    Listen carefully and understand me.
    Forget your people and your father's
        family,
11 so that the king will be pleased with
        your beauty.
    He will be your new husband,[b]
        so you must honor him.
12 People from Tyre will bring you gifts.
    Their richest people will try to win your
        friendship.

13 The princess is so beautiful in her gown,
    like a pearl set in gold.
14 Clothed in beauty, she is led to the king,
    followed by her bridesmaids.
15 Filled with joy and excitement,
    they enter into the king's palace.

16 Your sons will be kings like their
        ancestors.*
    You will make them rulers throughout
        the land.
17 You will be famous for generations.
    People will praise you forever and ever.

46 To the director*: A song from the Korah
family. Use the alamoth.[c] A song.
1 God is our protection and source of
        strength.
    He is always ready to help us in times of
        trouble.
2 So we are not afraid when the earth
        quakes
    and the mountains fall into the sea.
3 We are not afraid when the seas become
        rough and dark
    and the mountains tremble.   Selah*

4 There is a river whose streams bring
        happiness to God's city,
    to the holy city of God Most High.
5 God is in that city, so it will never be
        destroyed.
    He is there to help even before sunrise.
6 Nations will shake with fear and
        kingdoms will fall
    when God shouts and makes the earth
        move.
7 The LORD All-Powerful is with us.
    The God of Jacob* is our place of safety.
                                    Selah

8 Look at the powerful things the LORD has
        done.
    See the awesome things he has done on
        earth.
9 He stops wars all over the world.

He breaks the soldiers' bows, shatters
    their spears, and burns their shields.[d]
10 God says, "Stop fighting and know that I
        am God!
    I am the one who defeats the nations;
    I am the one who controls the world."
11 The LORD All-Powerful is with us.
    The God of Jacob is our place of safety.
                                    Selah

47 To the director*:
A song from the Korah family.
1 Everyone, clap your hands.
    Shout with joy to God!
2 The LORD Most High is awesome.
    He is the great King over all the earth.
3 He helped us defeat other nations.
    He put those people under our control.
4 He chose our land for us.
    He chose that wonderful land for Jacob,*
        the one he loved.   Selah*

5 The LORD God goes up to his throne
    at the sound of the trumpet and horn.
6 Sing praises to God, sing praises!
    Sing praises to our King, sing praises!
7 God is the King of the whole world.
    Sing songs of praise![e]
8 God sits on his holy throne;
    he rules all the nations.
9 The leaders of the nations have come
        together
    with the people of the God of
        Abraham.*
All the rulers of the world belong to God.
    He is over them all!

48 A song of praise from the Korah family.
1 The LORD is great!
    He is praised throughout the city of our
        God, his holy mountain.
2 His city is such a pleasant place.
    It brings joy to people from around the
        world.
Mount Zion* is the true mountain of
        God.[f]
    It is the city of the great King.
3 In the palaces of that city,
    God is known as the fortress.*
4 Once some kings met together
    and planned an attack against this city.
They marched toward the city,
5 but when they saw it, they were
        amazed.
    They all panicked and ran away.

a45:10 My lady Literally, "Daughter."
b45:11 husband Or "master."
cPsalm 46 alamoth This might be a musical instrument, a special way of tuning an instrument, a
music style, or one of the groups that played harps
in the Temple orchestra. See 1 Chron. 15:21.

d46:9 shields Or "chariots."
e47:7 songs of praise Literally, "maskil." See "maskil"
in the Word List.
f48:2 true mountain of God Literally, "the summit
of Zaphon." In Canaanite stories, Mt. Zaphon was
where the gods lived.

6 Fear grabbed them;
  they trembled like a woman giving
    birth.
7 God, with a strong east wind,
  you wrecked their big ships.
8 Yes, we heard the stories about your
    power.
  But we also saw it in the city of our God,
    the city of the LORD All-Powerful.
  God makes that city strong forever. *Selah**

9 God, in your Temple* we remember your
    loving kindness.
10 Your name is known everywhere, God,
  and people throughout the earth praise
    you.
  You have shown that you do what is
    right.
11 Mount Zion is happy,
  and the towns of Judah rejoice, because
    your decisions are fair.
12 Walk around Jerusalem,
  and count its towers.
13 Look at the tall walls,
  and see the palaces.
  Then you can tell the next generation
    about them.
14 This God is our God forever and ever.
  He will lead us from now to the end of
    time!

49 *To the director*:*
       A song from the Korah family.
1 Listen to this, all you nations.
  Pay attention, all you people on earth.
2 Everyone, rich and poor, listen to me.
3 I have some very wise words for you.
  My thoughts will give you
    understanding.
4 I listened to these sayings.
  And now, with my harp, I will sing and
    make the hidden meaning clear.

5 Why should I be afraid when trouble
    comes?
  There is no need to fear when evil
    enemies surround me.
6 They think their wealth will protect them.
  They brag about how rich they are.
7 But no one has enough to buy back a life,
  and you cannot bribe*a* God.
8 You will never get enough money
  to pay for your own life.
9 You will never have enough
  to buy the right to live forever
  and keep your body out of the grave.
10 Look, the wise die the same as fools and
    stupid people.*b*
  They die and leave their wealth to
    others.

11 The grave will be their new home forever.
  And how much land they owned will
    not make any difference.
12 People might be wealthy, but they cannot
    stay here forever.
  They will die like the animals.
13 That is what happens to all who trust in
    themselves
  and to anyone who accepts their way of
    life.   *Selah**
14 They are just like sheep, but the grave
    will be their pen.
  Death will be their shepherd.
  When morning comes, the good people
    will enjoy victory,
    as the bodies of the proud slowly rot in
    the grave, far away from their fancy
    houses.

15 But God will pay the price to save me
    from the grave.
  He will take me to be with him.   *Selah*

16 Don't be afraid of people just because
    they are rich.
  Don't be afraid of people just because
    they have big, fancy houses.
17 They will not take anything with them
    when they die.
  They will not take their wealth with
    them.
18 A wealthy man might tell himself how
    well he has done in life.
  And other people might praise him.
19 But the time will come for him to die
    and go to his ancestors.
  And he will never again see the light of
    day.
20 Wealthy people don't seem to understand
    that they will die like the animals.

50 *One of Asaph's songs.*
1 The LORD God Most Powerful has spoken.
  He calls to everyone on earth, from
    where the sun rises to where it sets.
2 God appeared from Zion,* the city of
    perfect beauty.*c*
3 Our God is coming and will not keep
    quiet.
  Fire burns in front of him.
  There is a great storm around him.
4 He tells the sky and the earth to be
    witnesses
  as he judges his people.
5 He says, "My followers, gather around
    me.
  Come, my worshipers, who made an
    agreement with me."

6 God is the judge,
  and the skies tell how fair he is.   *Selah**

---

*a***49:7** *bribe* Here, this means offering a gift or sacrifice so that God will not punish a guilty person.
*b***49:10** *stupid people* Or "animals."

*c***50:2** *God … beauty* Or "God shining from Zion is
absolutely beautiful."

7 God says, "My people, listen to me!
  People of Israel,* I will show my
    evidence against you.
  I am God, your God.
8 The problem I have with you is not your
    sacrifices*
  or the burnt offerings* you bring to me
    everyday.
9 Why would I want more bulls from your
    barns
  or goats from your pens?
10 I already own all the animals in the forest.
  I own all the animals on a thousand
    hills.
11 I know every bird in the mountains.
  Everything that moves in the fields is
    mine.
12 If I were hungry, I would not ask you for
    food.
  I already own the world and everything
    in it.
13 I don't eat the meat of bulls or drink the
    blood of goats."

14 You made promises to God Most High, so
    give him what you promised.
  Bring your sacrifices and thank
    offerings.*
15 God says, "Call me when trouble comes.
  I will help you, and you will honor me."

16 But God says to the wicked,
  "Stop quoting my laws!
  Stop talking about my agreement*!
17 You hate for me to tell you what to do.
  You ignore what I say.
18 You see a thief and run to join him.
  You jump into bed with those who
    commit adultery.*
19 You say evil things and tell lies.
20 You sit around talking about people,
  finding fault with your own brothers.
21 When you did these things, I said
    nothing.
  So you thought that I* was just like you.
  But I will not be quiet any longer.
  I will correct you and make clear what I
    have against you.
22 You people who have forgotten God,
  understand what I am telling you,
  or I will tear you apart,
  and no one will be able to save you!
23 Whoever gives a thank offering shows me
    honor.
  And whoever decides to live right will
    see my power to save."

51 *To the director*: A song of David* written
    when Nathan the prophet came to him
after David's sin with Bathsheba.*
1 God, be merciful to me
  because of your faithful love.

Because of your great compassion,
  erase all the wrongs I have done.
2 Scrub away my guilt.
  Wash me clean from my sin.
3 I know I have done wrong.
  I remember that sin all the time.
4 I did what you said is wrong.
  You are the one I have sinned against.
  I say this so that people will know
    that I am wrong and you are right.
  What you decided is fair.
5 I was born to do wrong,
  a sinner before I left my mother's
    womb.
6 You want me to be completely loyal,
  so put true wisdom deep inside of me.
7 Remove my sin and make me pure.*b*
  Wash me until I am whiter than snow!
8 Let me hear sounds of joy and happiness
    again.
  Let the bones you crushed be happy
    again.
9 Don't look at my sins.
  Erase them all.
10 God, create a pure heart in me,
  and make my spirit strong again.
11 Don't push me away
  or take your Holy Spirit* from me.
12 Your help made me so happy.
  Give me that joy again.
  Make my spirit strong and ready to obey
    you.
13 I will teach the guilty how you want them
    to live,
  and the sinners will come back to you.
14 God, spare me from the punishment of
    death.*c*
  My God, you are the one who saves me!
  Let me sing about all the good things you
    do for me!
15 My Lord, I will open my mouth and sing
    your praises!
16 You don't really want sacrifices,*
  or I would give them to you.
17 The sacrifice that God wants is a humble
    spirit.
  God, you will not turn away someone
    who comes with a humble heart and
    is willing to obey you.*d*

18 God, please be good to Zion.*
  Rebuild the walls of Jerusalem.
19 Then you can enjoy the kind of sacrifices
    you want.*e*
  You will receive whole burnt offerings,*
    and people will again offer bulls on your
    altar.

---

*b***51:7 Remove ... pure** Literally, "Cleanse me with
hyssop." See "hyssop" in the Word List.
*c***51:14 spare ... death** Or "don't consider me guilty
of murder."
*d***51:17 someone ... obey you** Literally, "a broken
and crushed heart."
*e***51:19 the kind ... you want** Or "the offering of
righteousness."

*a***50:21 that I** Or "that the 'I AM.'"

52 To the director*: A maskil* of David written when Doeg the Edomite went to Saul and told him, "David is in Ahimelech's house."

1 Great warrior, why are you bragging about
    the evil you did?
    You are a disgrace to God.
2 You are nothing but a hired killer,a
    making plans to hurt people and making
    up lies!
3 You love evil more than goodness.
    You love lies more than truth.   Selah*

4 You and your lying tongue love to hurt
    people.
5 So God will ruin you forever!
    He will grab you and pull you from your
    home,b like someone pulling up a
    plant by the roots!c
6 Good people will see this
    and learn to fear and respect God.
    They will laugh at you and say,
7 "Look what happened to the warrior who
    did not depend on God.
    That fool thought his wealth and lies
    would protect him."

8 But I am like a green olive tree growing in
    God's Temple.*
    I will trust God's faithful love forever
    and ever.
9 God, I praise you forever for what you
    have done.
    I will speak your named before your
    followers because it is so good!

53 To the director*: Use the mahalath.e
A maskil* of David.

1 Only fools think there is no God.
    People like that are evil and do terrible
    things.
    They never do what is right.
2 God looks down from heaven to see
    if there is anyone who is wise,
    anyone who looks to him for help.
3 But everyone has turned away from him.
    Everyone has become evil.
    No one does anything good.
    No, not one person!

4 Those who are evil treat my people like
    bread to be eaten.
    And they never ask for God's help.
    Don't they understand what they are
    doing?

5 They will be filled with fear—
    a fear like they have never felt before!
    People of Israel,* you will defeat those
    who attacked you,
    because God has rejected them.
    And he will scatter their bones.

6 I wish the one who lives on Mount Zion*
    would bring victory to Israel!
    When God makes Israel successful again,
    the people of Jacob* will be very happy;
    the people of Israel will be glad.

54 To the director*: With instruments. A
maskil* of David written when the Ziphites
went to Saul and told him, "We think David is
hiding among our people."

1 God, use your power and save me.
    Use your great power to set me free.f
2 God, listen to my prayer.
    Listen to what I say.
3 Strangers who don't even think about
    God have turned against me.
    Those powerful men are trying to kill
    me.   Selah*

4 Look, my God will help me.
    My Lord will support me.
5 He will punish the people who turned
    against me.
    God, be faithful to me and destroy
    them.

6 Lord, I will give freewill offerings to you.
    I will praise your good name.
7 You saved me from all my troubles.
    I saw my enemies defeated.

55 To the director*: With instruments.
A maskil* of David.

1 God, hear my prayer.
    Don't ignore my cry for help.
2 Please listen and answer me.
    Let me speak to you and tell you what
    upsets me.
3 My enemies shout at me and threaten
    me.
    In their anger they attack me.
    They bring troubles crashing down on
    me.
4 My heart is pounding inside me.
    I am afraid to die.
5 I am trembling with fear.
    I am terrified!
6 Oh, I wish I had wings like a dove.
    I would fly away and find a place to rest.
7 I would go far into the desert and stay
    there.   Selah*

8 I would run away.
    I would escape from this storm of
    trouble.

a**52:2 hired killer** Literally, "sharpened razor."
b**52:5 home** This means the body. This is a poetic
way of saying, "God will end your life here on earth."
c**52:5 like someone … roots** Literally, "He will root
you up from the land of the living." This also means
"He will kill you and your descendants."
d**52:9 speak your name** Or "I will trust your name."
e**Psalm 53 mahalath** Probably a musical term. It
might be the name of an instrument or a tune, or it
might mean a certain musical style.

f**54:1** Literally, "God, save me with your name, judge
me with your might."

9 My Lord, confuse their words and stop
        their plans.
    I see so much cruelty and fighting in
        this city.
10 Day and night, in every neighborhood,
        the city is filled with evil and trouble.
11 There is so much crime in the streets.
    People who hurt and cheat others are
        everywhere.

12 If it were an enemy insulting me,
        I could bear it.
    If it were my enemies attacking me,
        I could hide.
13 But it is you, the one so close to me,
        my companion, my good friend, who
            does this.
14 We used to share our secrets with one
            another,
        as we walked through the crowds
            together in God's Temple.*

15 I wish death would take my enemies by
            surprise!
    I wish the earth would open up and
        swallow them alive,*
    because they plan such terrible things
        together.

16 I will call to God for help,
        and the LORD will save me.
17 I speak to God morning, noon, and night.
    I tell him what upsets me, and he
        listens to me!
18 I have fought in many battles,
        but he has always rescued me and
            brought me back safely.
19 God, who has always ruled as king,
        will hear me and punish my enemies.
                                            Selah

    But they will never change.
    They don't fear and respect God.
20 This one who was once my friend now
            attacks his friends.
    He is breaking every promise he made.
21 His words about peace are as smooth as
            butter,
    but he has only war on his mind.
    His words are as slick as oil,
        but they cut like a knife.

22 Give your worries to the LORD,
        and he will care for you.
    He will never let those who are good be
        defeated.

23 But, God, you will send those liars and
            murderers to the grave.
    They will die before their life is half
        finished!
    As for me, I will put my trust in you.

56 *To the director*: To the tune "The Dove
        in the Distant Oak." A miktam* of David
written when the Philistines* captured him in
Gath.*
1 God, people have attacked me, so be
        merciful to me.
    They have been chasing me all day,
        closing in to attack me.
2 My enemies come at me constantly.
    There are too many fighters to count.*
3 When I am afraid, I put my trust in you.
4 I trust God, so I am not afraid of what
        people can do to me!
    I praise God for his promise to me.
5 My enemies are always twisting my
        words.
    They are always making plans against
        me.
6 They hide together and watch every move
        I make,
    hoping for some way to kill me.
7 God, send them away because of the bad
        things they did.
    Show your anger and defeat those
        people.
8 You know I am very upset.
    You know how much I have cried.
    Surely you have kept an account of all my
        tears.

9 I know that when I call for help, my
        enemies will turn and run.
    I know that because God is with me!

10 I praise God for his promise.
    I praise the LORD for his promise to me.
11 I trust God, so I am not afraid
        of what people can do to me!
12 God, I will keep the special promises I
        made to you.
    I will give you my thank offering.
13 You saved me from death.
    You kept me from being defeated.
    So I will serve you in the light
        that only the living can see.

57 *To the director*: To the tune "Don't
        Destroy." A miktam* of David written
when he escaped from Saul and went into the cave.
1 God, be merciful to me.
    Be kind because my soul trusts in you.
    I have come to you for protection,
        while the trouble passes.
2 I pray to God Most High for help,
    and he takes care of me completely!
3 From heaven he helps me and saves me.
    He will punish the one who attacks me.
                                            Selah*
    God will remain loyal to me
        and send his love to protect me.

55:15 I wish ... alive Literally, "I wish they would go
down into Sheol alive." See Num. 16:31–33.

56:2 There are ... count Or "There are many attacking me from above."

4 My life is in danger.
  My enemies are all around me.
  They are like man-eating lions,
  with teeth like spears or arrows
  and tongues like sharp swords.

5 God, rise above the heavens!
  Let all the world see your glory.*
6 My enemies set a trap for my feet
  to bring me down.
  They dug a deep pit to catch me,
  but they fell into it.   Selah

7 God, I am ready, heart and soul,
  to sing songs of praise.
8 Wake up, my soul!
  Harps and lyres,* wake up, and let's
  wake the dawn!
9 My Lord, I will praise you before all
  people.
  I will sing praises about you to every
  nation.
10 Your faithful love is higher than the
   highest clouds in the sky!
11 Rise above the heavens, God.
   Let all the world see your glory.*

58 To the director*: To the tune "Don't
Destroy." A miktam* of David.
1 You judges are not being fair in your
  decisions.
  You are not judging people fairly.
2 No, you only think of evil things to do.
  You do violent crimes in this country.
3 Those wicked people started doing wrong
  as soon as they were born.
  They have been liars from birth.
4 Their anger is as deadly as the poison of a
  snake.a
  They shut their ears like a deaf cobra
5 that does not listen to the music of the
  snake charmers,
  no matter how well they play.

6 God, they are like lions.
  So Lord, break their teeth.
7 May they disappear like water down a
  drain.
  May they be crushed like weeds on a
  path.b
8 May they be like snails melting away as
  they move.
  May they be like a baby born dead, who
  never saw the light of day.
9 May they be destroyed suddenly,
  like the thorns that are burned to
  quickly heat a pot.

10 Good people will be happy
   when they see the wicked getting the

punishment they deserve.
They will feel like soldiers walking
  through the blood of their enemies!c
11 Then people will say, "Good people really
   are rewarded.
   Yes, there is a God judging the world!"d

59 To the director*: To the tune "Don't
Destroy." A miktam* of David written
when Saul sent people to watch David's house to
try to kill him.
1 God, save me from my enemies.
  Protect me from those who stand
  against me.
2 Save me from those who do wrong.
  Save me from those murderers.
3 Look, powerful men are waiting for me.
  Lord, they are waiting to kill me,
  even though I did not sin or commit
  a crime.
4 I have done nothing wrong, but they are
  rushing to attack me.
  Come and see for yourself!
5 You are the Lord God All-Powerful, the
  God of Israel*!
  Get up and punish them.
  Don't show any mercy to those traitors.
                                    Selah*

6 Those evil men are like dogs
  that come into town in the evening,
  growling and roaming the streets.
7 Listen to their threats and insults.
  They say such cruel things,
  and they don't care who hears them.

8 Lord, laugh at them.
  Make fun of them all.
9 I will sing my songs of praise to you.e
  God, you are my place of safety, high in
  the mountains.
10 God loves me, and he will help me win.
   He will help me defeat my enemies.
11 Don't just kill them, or my people might
   forget.
   My Lord and Protector, scatter and
   defeat them with your strength.
12 Those evil people curse* and tell lies.
   Punish them for what they said.
   Let their pride trap them.
13 Destroy them in your anger.
   Destroy them completely!
   Then people all over the world will know
   that God rules over the people of
   Jacob.*   Selah

14 Those evil men are like dogs
   that come into town in the evening,
   growling and roaming the streets.

a58:4 anger ... snake A wordplay in Hebrew. The
word meaning "anger" can also mean "venom"
(poison).
b58:7 Or "May he shoot his arrows, ⌊cutting them
down⌋ as if they were withering ⌊grass⌋."
c58:10 They ... enemies Literally, "They will wash
their feet in the blood of the wicked."
d58:11 Yes ... world Or "There really are judges in
this land doing their job."
e59:9 I will sing ... to you Or "My Strength, I am
waiting for you." See Ps. 59:17.

15 They roam around looking for food,
     but even if they eat their fill, they still
        growl and complain.
16 But I will sing about your strength.
     I will rejoice in your love every
        morning.
   You have been my place of safety,
     the place I can run to when troubles
        come.
17 I will sing praises to you, my source of
        strength.
   You, God, are my place of safety.
   You are the God who loves me!

60

To the director*: To the tune "Lily of the Agreement." A miktam* of David for teaching. Written when David fought Aram Naharaim and Aram Zobah, and Joab came back and defeated 12,000 Edomite soldiers at Salt Valley.

1 God, you were angry with us.
     You rejected us and destroyed our
        defenses.
     Please make us strong again.
2 You shook the earth and split it open.
     It is falling apart like a broken wall.
     Please put it back together.
3 You have given your people many
        troubles.
     We are dizzy and fall down like drunks.
4 But you have provided a flag to show your
        faithful followers
     where to gather to escape the enemy's
        attack.   *Selah**

5 Use your great power and give us victory!
     Answer our prayer and save the people
        you love.

6 God has spoken in his Temple*a*:
     "I will win the war and rejoice in victory!
     I will divide this land among my people.
     I will give them Shechem.
     I will give them Succoth Valley.
7 Gilead and Manasseh will be mine.
     Ephraim* will be my helmet.
     Judah* will be my royal scepter.*
8 Moab will be the bowl for washing my
        feet.
     Edom will be the slave who carries my
        sandals.
     I will defeat the Philistines* and shout
        in victory!"

9-10 But, God, it seems that you have left us!
     You do not go out with our army.
   So who will lead me into the strong,
        protected city?
   Who will lead me into battle against
        Edom?
11 Help us defeat the enemy!
     No one on earth can rescue us.
12 Only God can make us strong.
     Only God can defeat our enemies!

a60:6 in his Temple Or "in his holiness."

61

To the director*: With stringed instruments. A song of David.*

1 God, hear my cry for help.
     Listen to my prayer.
2 From a faraway land I call to you for help.
     I feel so weak and helpless!
   Carry me to a high rock
     where no one can reach me.
3 You are my place of safety,
     a strong tower that protects me from my
        enemies.
4 I want to live in your tent*b* forever.
     I want to hide where you can protect
        me.   *Selah**

5 God, you heard what I promised to give
        you,
     but everything your worshipers have
        comes from you.
6 Give the king a long life.
     Let him live forever!
7 Let him rule in your presence forever.
     Protect him with your faithful love.
8 Then I will praise your name forever.
     Every day I will do what I promised.

62

To the director,* Jeduthun.c A song of David.*

1 I must calm down and turn to God;
     only he can rescue me.
2 He is my Rock,* the only one who can
        save me.
   He is my high place of safety, where no
        army can defeat me.

3 How long will you people attack me?
     Do you all want to kill me?
   I am like a leaning wall,
     like a fence ready to fall.
4 You want only to destroy me,
     to bring me down from my important
        position.
   It makes you happy to tell lies about me.
     In public, you say nice things,
     but in private, you curse* me.   *Selah**

5 I must calm down and turn to God;
     he is my only hope.
6 He is my Rock, the only one who can save
        me.
   He is my high place of safety, where no
        army can defeat me.
7 My victory and honor come from God.
     He is the mighty Rock, where I am safe.
8 People, always put your trust in God!
     Tell him all your problems.
     God is our place of safety.   *Selah*

---

b61:4 tent The place where God lives among his people. Here, it is the Temple in Jerusalem. See "Holy Tent" and "Temple" in the Word List.
cPsalm 62 Jeduthun Or "and to Jeduthun," one of the three main temple musicians. See 1 Chron. 9:16; 16:38–42.

9 People cannot really help.
   You cannot depend on them.
   Compared to God, they are nothing—
   no more than a gentle puff of air!
10 Don't trust in your power to take things
   by force.
   Don't think you will gain anything by
   stealing.
   And if you become wealthy,
   don't put your trust in riches.
11 God says there is one thing you can really
   depend on, and I believe it:
   "Strength comes from God!"

12 My Lord, your love is real.
   You reward all people for what they do.

63
A song of David* written when he was in the desert of Judah.
1 God, you are my God.
   I am searching so hard to find you.
   Body and soul, I thirst for you
   in this dry and weary land without
   water.
2 Yes, I have seen you in your Temple.*a*
   I have seen your strength and glory.*
3 Your faithful love is better than life,
   so my lips praise you.
4 By my life, I will praise you.
   In your name, I lift my hands in prayer.
5 When I sit down to satisfy my hunger,
   my joyful lips hunger to praise you!
6 I remember you while lying on my bed.
   I think about you in the middle of the
   night.
7 That is because you are the one who
   helps me.
   It makes me happy to be under your
   protection!
8 I stay close to you,
   and you hold me with your powerful
   arm.

9 Those who are trying to kill me will be
   destroyed.
   They will go down to their graves.
10 They will be killed with swords.
   Wild dogs will eat their dead bodies.
11 But the king will be happy with his God,
   and those who promised to obey him
   will praise him when he defeats those
   liars.

64
To the director:
A song of David.**
1 God, listen to my complaint.
   Save me from the terrible threats of my
   enemies!
2 Protect me from the secret plans of the
   wicked.
   Hide me from that gang of evil people.
3 They sharpen their tongues to use like
   swords.

They aim their poisonous words like
   arrows.
4 Suddenly, from their hiding places, they
   let their arrows fly.
   They shoot to kill innocent people.
5 They encourage each other to do wrong.
   They talk about setting traps and say,
   "No one will see them here!
6 No one will discover our crime.
   We have the perfect plan!"
   Yes, people can be very tricky and hard to
   understand.
7 But suddenly, God will shoot his arrows,
   and those wicked people will be hit.
8 He will use their own words against
   them,
   and they will be destroyed.
   Then everyone who sees them
   will shake their heads in amazement.
9 People will see what God has done.
   They will tell other people about him.
   Then everyone will learn more about God.
   They will learn to fear and respect him.
10 Good people are happy to serve the Lord.
   They depend on him to protect them.
   All those who want to do right will praise
   him!

65
To the director:
A praise song of David.**
1 God in Zion,* we praise you
   and give you what we promised.
2 Anyone can come to you,
   and you will listen to their prayers.
3 When our sins become too heavy for us,
   you wipe them away.
4 Oh, how wonderful it is to be the people
   you chose
   to come and stay in your Temple.*
   And we are so happy to have the
   wonderful things
   that are in your Temple, your holy
   palace.
5 God, you answer our prayers and do what
   is right.
   You do amazing things to save us.
   People all over the world know they can
   trust in you,
   even those who live across the sea.
6 You made the mountains.
   We see your power all around us.
7 You can calm the roughest seas
   or the nations raging around us.
8 People all around the world are amazed at
   the wonderful things you do.
   You make all people, east and west, sing
   with joy.
9 You take care of the land.
   You water it and make it fertile.
   Your streams are always filled with water.
   That's how you make the crops grow.
10 You pour rain on the plowed fields;
   you soak the fields with water.
   You make the ground soft with rain,
   and you make the young plants grow.

a63:2 your Temple Or "your holiness."

11 You start the new year with a good
  harvest.
  You end the year with many crops.[a]
12 The desert and hills are covered with
  grass.
13 The pastures are covered with sheep.
  The valleys are filled with grain.
  Everything is singing and shouting for joy.

66 *To the director**:
A song of praise.
1 Everything on earth, shout with joy to
  God!
2 Praise his glorious name!
  Honor him with songs of praise!
3 Tell God, "Your works are wonderful!
  Your great power makes your enemies
  bow down in fear before you.
4 Let the whole world worship you.
  Let everyone sing praises to your
  name."   *Selah**

5 Look at what God has done!
  These things amaze us.
6 He changed the sea to dry land,[b]
  and his people went across the water[c]
  on foot.
  So let's celebrate because of what he has
  done!
7 He rules the world with his great power.
  He watches people everywhere.
  No one can rebel against him. *Selah*

8 People, praise our God.
  Sing loud songs of praise to him.
9 He continues to give us life,
  and he keeps us from falling.
10 God, you have tested us, as people test
  silver with fire.
11 You let us be trapped.
  You put heavy burdens on us.
12 You let our enemies run over us.
  We went through fire and water,
  but you brought us to a safe place.
13-14 So I bring sacrifices* to your Temple.*
  When I was in trouble, I asked for help
  and made promises to you.
  Now I am giving you what I promised.
15 I bring my best sheep as burnt
  offerings.*
  I offer the smoke from them up to you.
  I give you sacrifices of bulls and goats.
         Selah

16 All you people who worship God,
  come and I will tell you what he has
  done for me.
17-18 I cried out to him for help,
  and I praised him.
  If I had been hiding sin in my heart,
  the Lord would not have listened to me.
19 But God did listen to me;
  he heard my prayer.
20 Praise God!
  He did not turn away from me—he
  listened to my prayer.
  He continues to show his love to me!

67 *To the director**: *With instruments.*
A song of praise.
1 God, show mercy to us and bless us.
  Please accept us!   *Selah**

2 Let everyone on earth learn about you.
  Let every nation see how you save
  people.
3 May people praise you, God!
  May all people praise you.
4 May all nations rejoice and be happy
  because you judge people fairly.
  You rule over every nation.
5 May the people praise you, God!
  May all people praise you.
6 God, our God, bless us.
  Let our land give us a great harvest.
7 May God bless us,
  and may all people on earth fear and
  respect him.

68 *To the director**:
A praise song of David.*
1 God, get up and scatter your enemies!
  May all your enemies run from you.
2 May your enemies be scattered
  like smoke blown away by the wind.
  May your enemies be destroyed
  like wax melting in a fire.
3 But let good people be happy.
  Let them gather before God and enjoy
  themselves together.
4 Sing to God! Sing praises to his name!
  Prepare the way for the one who rides
  on the clouds.
  His name is YAH.[d]
  Worship before him with joy.
5 God, who lives in his holy palace, is a
  father to orphans,
  and he takes care of widows.
6 God provides homes for those who are
  lonely.
  He frees people from prison and makes
  them happy.
  But those who turn against him will live
  in the desert.

---

[a]**65:11** In ancient Israel there were two calendars.
The calendar for religious festivals began in the
spring, at the barley harvest. The other calendar
started in the fall, when they gathered other crops.
[b]**66:6** *changed the sea to dry land* This was with
Moses at the Red Sea. See Ex. 14.
[c]**66:6** *water* Literally, "river." Although this word is
not used for the Jordan River elsewhere, some think
this line may refer to the later crossing there. See
Josh. 3:14–17.

[d]**68:4** *YAH* This is a Hebrew name for God. It is like
the Hebrew name usually translated "LORD." Also in
verse 18.

7 God, you led your people out of Egypt.
   You marched across the desert.   *Selah**

8 The ground shook and rain poured from
      the sky
   when God, the God of Israel,* came to
      Sinai.

9 God, you sent the rain
   to make a tired, old land strong again.

10 Your people*a* came back to live there,
   and you provided good things for the
      poor.

11 My Lord gave the command,
   and many people went to tell the good
      news:

12 "The armies of powerful kings ran away!
   At home, the women divide the things
      brought from the battle.

13 Those who stayed home will share in the
      wealth—
   metal doves with wings covered in
      silver and feathers sparkling with
      gold."

14 God All-Powerful scattered the kings
   like snow falling on Mount Zalmon.

15 Mount Bashan is a great mountain with
      many high peaks.

16 But, Bashan, why are you jealous of
      Mount Zion*?
   That is where God has chosen to live.
   The LORD will live there forever.

17 With his millions of chariots*
   the Lord came from Sinai into the holy
      place.

18 You went up to your high place,
      leading a parade of captives.
   You received gifts from people,*b*
   even those who turned against you.
   The LORD God went up there to live.

19 Praise the Lord!
   Every day he helps us with the loads we
      must carry.
   He is the God who saves us.   *Selah*

20 He is our God, the God who saves us.
   My Lord GOD saves us from death.

21 God will smash the heads of his enemies.
   He will punish those who fight against
      him.*c*

22 My Lord said, "If they run up to Bashan
      or down to the depths of the sea,
   I will bring them back.

23 So you will march through pools of their
      blood,
   and there will be plenty left for your
      dogs."

24 God, everyone can see your victory
      parade—
   the victory march of my God and King
      into his holy place!*d*

25 Singers come marching in front, followed
      by the musicians;
   they are surrounded by young girls
      playing tambourines.

26 Praise God in the meeting place.*e*
   Praise the LORD, people of Israel*!

27 There is the smallest tribe, Benjamin,
      leading them.
   And there comes a large group of
      leaders from Judah.
   Following them are the leaders of
      Zebulun and Naphtali.

28 God, show us your power!
   Show us the power you used for us in
      the past.

29 Kings will bring their wealth to you,
   to your Temple* in Jerusalem.

30 Punish the people in Egypt.
   They are like cattle in the marshes, like
      bulls among the calves.
   You humiliated them.
   You scattered them in war.
   Now let them come crawling to you,
      bringing their pieces of silver.

31 Messengers from Egypt will come bearing
      gifts.
   Ethiopia will offer God their tribute.*

32 Kings on earth, sing to God!
   Sing songs of praise to our Lord!   *Selah*

33 Sing to him who rides his chariot through
      the ancient skies.
   Listen to his powerful voice!

34 Tell everyone how powerful he is!
   He rules over Israel.
   His power fills the skies.

35 God, you are awesome in your Temple!
   The God of Israel is the one who gives
      strength and power to his people.
   Praise God!

69 *To the director*: To the tune "The Lilies." A song of David.**

1 God, save me from all my troubles!
   The rising water has reached my neck.

2 I have nothing to stand on.
   I am sinking down, down into the mud.
   I am in deep water,
   and the waves are about to cover me.

3 I am getting weak from calling for help.
   My throat is sore.
   I have waited and looked for your help
      until my eyes are hurting.

4 I have more enemies than the hairs on
      my head.
   They hate me for no reason.

---

*a*68:10 *people* Or "animals" or "living things."
*b*68:18 *received gifts from people* Or "took people
as gifts." Or "gave gifts to people," as in the ancient
Syriac and Aramaic versions and in Eph. 4:8.
*c*68:21 Literally, "God will smash the heads of his
enemies. He will smash the hairy skull walking in
guilt."

*d*68:24 *of my God ... holy place* Or "led by my holy
God and King!"
*e*68:26 *in the meeting place* Or "with the trumpets
that announce the assembly!"

They try hard to destroy me.
My enemies tell lies about me.
    They say I stole from them
    and they demand that I pay for things I
        did not steal.

5 God, you know my faults.
    I cannot hide my sins from you.

6 My Lord GOD All-Powerful, don't let me
        embarrass your followers.
    God of Israel,* don't let me bring
        disgrace to those who worship you.

7 My face is covered with shame.
    I carry this shame for you.

8 My own brothers treat me like a stranger.
    They act as if I came from a foreign
        land.

9 My strong devotion to your Temple* is
        destroying me.
    Those who insult you are also insulting
        me.

10 When I spend time crying and fasting,*
    they make fun of me.

11 When I wear sackcloth* to show my
        sorrow,
    they tell jokes about me.

12 They talk about me in public places.
    The beer drinkers make up songs about
        me.

13 As for me, LORD, this is my prayer to you:
    Please accept me!
    God, I want you to answer me with love.
    I know I can trust you to save me.

14 Pull me from the mud,
    and don't let me sink down deeper.
    Save me from those who hate me.
    Save me from this deep water.

15 Don't let the waves drown me.
    Don't let the deep sea swallow me
    or the grave close its mouth on me.

16 Answer me, LORD, from the goodness of
        your faithful love.
    Out of your great kindness turn to me
        and help me!

17 Don't turn away from your servant.
    I am in trouble, so hurry and help me!

18 Come save my soul.
    Rescue me from my enemies.

19 You know the shame I have suffered.
    You know all my enemies.
    You saw how they humiliated me.

20 I feel the pain of their insults.
    The shame makes me feel like dying!
    I wanted some sympathy,
        but there was none.
    I waited for someone to comfort me,
        but no one came.

21 They gave me poison, not food.
    They gave me vinegar, not wine.

22 Their tables are covered with food.
    Let their fellowship meals destroy them.

23 Let them go blind and their backs become
        weak.

24 Show them how angry you are.
    Let them feel what your anger can do.

25 Make their homes empty.

Don't let anyone live there.

26 They try to hurt people you have already
        punished.
    They tell everyone about the suffering
        you gave them.

27 Punish them for the bad things they have
        done.
    Don't show them how good you can be.

28 Erase their names from the book of life.
    Don't let their names appear on the list
        of those who do what is right.

29 I am sad and hurting.
    God, lift me up and save me!

30 I will praise God's name in song.
    I will honor him by giving him thanks.

31 The LORD will be happier with this
    than with the offering of an ox or a full-
        grown bull as a sacrifice.*

32 Poor people, you came to worship God.
    You will be happy to know these things.

33 The LORD listens to poor, helpless people.
    He does not turn away from those who
        are in prison.

34 Praise him, heaven and earth!
    Sea and everything in it, praise him!

35 God will save Zion.*
    He will rebuild the cities of Judah.
    The people will settle there again and
        own the land.

36   The descendants of his servants will get
        that land.
    Those who love his name will live
        there.

70
To the director:*
A song of David to help people remember.*

1 Please, God, rescue me!
    LORD, hurry and help me!

2 People are trying to kill me.
    Please disappoint them.
    Humiliate them!
    They want to hurt me.
    Make them run away in shame.

3 May those who make fun of me
    be too embarrassed to speak.

4 But may those who come to you be happy
        and rejoice.
    May those who love being saved by you
        always be able to say, "Praise God!"*a*

5 I am only a poor, helpless man.
    God, please hurry to me.
    You are my helper, the one who can save
        me.
    LORD, don't be too late!

71
1LORD, I depend on you for
        protection.
    Don't let me be disappointed.

2 You always do what is right, so come and
        save me.
    Listen to me and save me.

a70:4 Praise God Literally, "God is great" or "May
God be magnified."

3 Be my Rock,* my place of safety.
  Be my fortress,* and protect me!
  You are my Rock and my protection.
4 My God, save me from wicked people.
  Save me from cruel, evil people.
5 Lord GOD, you are my hope.
  I have trusted you since I was a young
    boy.
6 I depended on you even before I was
    born.
  I relied on you even in my mother's
    womb.
  I have always prayed to you.*a*
7 You are my source of strength,
  so I have been an example to others.
8 I am always singing about the wonderful
    things you do.
9 Don't throw me away just because I am
    old.
  Don't leave me as I lose my strength.
10 My enemies make plans against me.
  They have met together and are making
    plans to kill me.
11 They say, "Go get him!
  God has left him, so there is no one to
    help him."
12 God, don't leave me!
  My God, hurry and help me!
13 Defeat my enemies.
  Destroy them completely!
  They are trying to hurt me.
  Let them suffer shame and disgrace.
14 Then I will always trust in you
  and praise you more and more.
15 I will tell people how good you are.
  I will tell about all the times you saved
    me—
  too many times to count.
16 I will tell about your greatness, my Lord
    GOD.
  I will talk only about you and your
    goodness.
17 God, you have taught me since I was a
    young boy.
  And to this day I have told people about
    the wonderful things you do.
18 Now that I am old and my hair is gray,
    don't leave me, God.
  I must tell the next generation about
    your power and greatness.
19 God, your goodness reaches far above the
    skies.
  You have done wonderful things.
  God, there is no one like you.
20 You have let me see troubles and hard
    times,
  but you will give me new life;
  you will lift me up from this pit of death!
21 You will help me do even greater things.
  You will comfort me again!
22 I will play the harp and praise you.
  My God, I will sing about your
    faithfulness.

I will play songs on my lyre* for the
  Holy One of Israel.*
23 I will shout for joy,
  singing songs of praise to you for saving
    me.
24 My tongue will sing about your goodness
    all the time,
  because those who wanted to kill me
  have been defeated and disgraced.

72 To Solomon.*b*

1 God, help the king be like you and make
    fair decisions.
  Help the king's son know what justice
    is.
2 Help the king judge your people fairly.
  Help him make wise decisions for your
    poor people.
3 Let there be peace and justice throughout
    the land,
  known on every mountain and hill.
4 May the king be fair to the poor.
  May he help the helpless and punish
    those who hurt them.
5 May people always fear and respect you,
    God,
  as long as the sun shines and the moon
    is in the sky.
6 Help the king be like rain falling on the
    fields,
  like showers falling on the land.
7 Let goodness grow everywhere while he
    is king.
  Let peace continue as long as there is a
    moon.
8 Let his kingdom grow from sea to sea,
  from the Euphrates River to the faraway
    places on earth.*c*
9 May all the people living in the desert
    bow down to him.
  May all his enemies bow before him
    with their faces in the dirt.
10 May the kings of Tarshish* and all the
    faraway lands by the sea bring gifts to
    him.
  May the kings of Sheba and Seba bring
    their tribute* to him.
11 May all kings bow down to our king.
  May all nations serve him.
12 Our king helps the poor who cry out to
    him—
  those in need who have no one to help
    them.
13 He feels sorry for all who are weak and
    poor.
  He protects their lives.
14 He saves them from the cruel people who
    try to hurt them.
  Their lives are important to him.

---

*b***Psalm 72** *To Solomon* This might mean that this
song was written by Solomon or dedicated to him,
or that it is from some special collection of songs.
*c***72:8** *faraway places on earth* This usually means
the countries around the Mediterranean Sea.

15 Long live the king!
   Let him receive gold from Sheba.
   Always pray for the king.
   Ask God to bless him every day.
16 May the fields grow plenty of grain
   and the hills be covered with crops.
   May the fields be as fertile as Lebanon,
   and may people fill the cities as grass
   covers a field.
17 May the king be famous forever.
   May people remember his name as long
   as the sun shines.
   May all nations be blessed through him,
   and may they all bless him.

18 Praise the Lord God, the God of Israel*!
   Only he can do such amazing things.
19 Praise his glorious name forever!
   Let his glory* fill the whole world.
   Amen* and Amen!

20(This ends the prayers of David* son of
Jesse.)

BOOK 3 *(Psalms 73–89)*

73 *Asaph's song of praise.*

1 God is so good to Israel,*
   to those whose hearts are pure.
2 But I almost slipped and lost my balance.
   I almost fell into sin.
3 I saw that wicked people were successful,
   and I became jealous of those proud
   people.
4 They are healthy.
   They don't have to struggle to survive.*a*
5 They don't suffer like the rest of us.
   They don't have troubles like other
   people.
6 So they are proud and hateful.
   This is as easy to see as the jewels and
   fancy clothes they wear.
7 If they see something they like, they go
   and take it.
   They do whatever they want.
8 They make fun of others and say cruel
   things about them.
   In their pride they make plans to hurt
   people.
9 They think they are gods!
   They think they are the rulers of the
   earth.
10*b* Even God's people turn to them
   and do what they say.
11 Those evil people say, "God does not
   know what we are doing!
   God Most High does not know!"

12 Those proud people are wicked,
   but they are rich and getting richer.
13 Clearly, then, I gain nothing by keeping

   my thoughts pure!
   What good is it to keep myself from sin?
14 God, I suffer all day long,
   and you punish me every morning.

15 I wanted to tell others these things,
   but that would have made me a traitor*
   to your people.
16 I tried hard to understand all this,
   but it was too hard for me.
17 But then, God, I went to your Temple,*
   and I understood what will happen to
   the wicked.
18 Clearly, you have put them in danger.
   You make it easy for them to fall and be
   destroyed.
19 Trouble can come suddenly,
   and they will be ruined.
   Terrible things can happen to them,
   and they will be finished.
20 Then they will be like a dream
   that we forget when we wake up.
   You will make them disappear
   like the monsters in our dreams.

21-22I was so stupid.
   I thought about such people and became
   upset.
   God, I was upset and angry with you!
   I acted like a senseless animal.
23 But I am always with you.
   You hold my hand.
24 You lead me and give me good advice,
   and later you will lead me to glory.*c*
25 In heaven, God, I have only you.
   And if I am with you, what on earth
   could I want?
26 Maybe my mind*d* and body will become
   weak,
   but God is my source of strength.*e*
   He is mine forever!
27 God, people who leave you will be lost.
   You will destroy all who are not faithful
   to you.
28 As for me, all I need is to be close to God.
   I have made the Lord God my place of
   safety.
   And, God, I will tell about all that you
   have done.

74 *A maskil* of Asaph.*

1 God, why have you turned away from us
   for so long?
   Why are you still angry with us, your
   own flock?
2 Remember the people you bought so long
   ago.
   You saved us, and we belong to you.
   And remember Mount Zion,* the place
   where you lived.

---

*c*73:24 *lead me to glory* Or "receive me in honor."
*d*73:26 *mind* Literally, "heart."
*e*73:26 *my ... strength* Literally, "the Rock of my
heart."

---

*a*73:4 Literally, "They have no bonds to their death."
*b*73:10 The Hebrew text here is hard to understand.

3 God, come walk through these ancient
ruins.
Come back to the Holy Place* that the
enemy destroyed.

4 The enemy shouted their war cries in the
Temple.*
They put up their flags there to show
they had won the war.

5 Their soldiers attacked the doors,
like workmen chopping down trees.

6 Using axes and hatchets,
they smashed the carved panels inside.

7 They burned down your Holy Place.
It was built to honor your name,
but they pulled it down to the ground.

8 The enemy decided to crush us
completely.
They burned every holy place*a* in the
country.

9 We do not see any of our signs.*b*
There are no more prophets.
And no one knows how long this will
last.

10 God, how much longer will the enemy
make fun of us?
Will you let them insult your name
forever?

11 Why won't you help us?
Use your power to defeat our enemies!

12 God, you have been our King for a long
time.
You have saved us many times on this
earth.

13 With your great power you split open the
sea
and broke the heads of the sea monster.

14 Yes, you smashed the heads of Leviathan*c*
and left his body for animals to eat.

15 You make the springs and rivers flow,
and you make the rivers dry up.

16 You control the day and the night.
You made the sun and the moon.

17 You set the limits for everything on earth.
And you created summer and winter.

18 LORD, remember, the enemy insulted you!
Those foolish people hate your name!

19 Don't give us like a helpless dove to those
wild animals.
Never forget your poor, suffering people.

20 Remember the agreement you gave us,
because violence fills every dark place
in this land.

21 Your people were treated badly.
Don't let them be hurt anymore.
Let your poor, helpless people praise
you.

22 God, get up and defend yourself!
Remember, those fools challenged you.

23 Don't forget the shouts of your enemies.
They insulted you again and again.

75 To the director*: To the tune "Don't
Destroy." One of Asaph's songs of praise.

1 We praise you, God!
We praise you because you*d* are near to
us.
We tell about the amazing things you
have done.

2 God says, "I have chosen a time for
judgment,
and I will judge fairly.

3 The earth and all its people may shake,
but I am the one who keeps it steady.
*Selah**

4 "To those who are proud I say, 'Stop your
boasting.'
I warn the wicked, 'Don't brag about
how strong you are.

5 Don't be so sure that you will win.
Don't boast that victory is yours!'"

6 There is no power on earth
that can make a person important.*e*

7 God is the judge.
He decides who will be important.
He lifts one person up and brings
another down.

8 The LORD has a cup in his hand.
It is filled with the poisoned wine of his
anger.
He will pour out this wine,
and the wicked will drink it to the last
drop.

9 I will always tell people how great God is.
I will sing praise to the God of Jacob.*

10 He*f* will take away any power the wicked
have
and give it to those who are good.

76 To the director*: With instruments.
One of Asaph's songs of praise.

1 People in Judah* know God.
People in Israel* respect his name.

2 His Temple* is in Salem.*g*
His house is on Mount Zion.*

3 There he shattered the arrows,
shields, swords, and other weapons of
war.
*Selah**

*a*74:8 *holy place* Or "El meeting place." This means
every place where people went to meet with God.
*b*74:9 *signs* These were probably signal fires that
people burned as a way of passing messages from
one town to the next. In war, this was a way people
showed other towns that the enemy had not yet
destroyed their own town.
*c*74:13–14 *sea monster ... Leviathan* These were
creatures from ancient stories. People believed that
they kept the world from being a safe, orderly place.
So this verse means that God controls every part of
the world and everything in it.

*d*75:1 *you* Literally, "your name."
*e*75:6 Literally, "Not from the east or the west and
not from the desert mountains."
*f*75:10 *He* Or "I."
*g*76:2 *Salem* Another name for Jerusalem. This
name means "Peace."

4 God, you are glorious coming back
   from the hills where you defeated your
      enemies.
5 They thought they were strong, but now
      they lie dead in the fields.
   Their bodies are stripped of all they
      owned.
   They could not defend themselves.[a]
6 The God of Jacob* shouted at them,
   and their army of chariots* and horses
      fell dead.
7 God, you are awesome!
   No one can stand against you when you
      are angry.
8-9 You stood as judge and announced your
      decision.
   You saved the humble people of the land.
   From heaven you gave the decision,
   and the whole earth was silent and
      afraid.
10 Even human anger can bring you honor
   when you use it to punish your
      enemies.[b]

11 People, you made promises to the LORD
      your God.
   Now give him what you promised.
   People everywhere fear and respect God,
   and they will bring gifts to him.
12 God defeats great leaders;
   all the kings on earth fear him.

77 To the director,* Jeduthun.[c]
One of Asaph's songs.

1 I cry out to God for help.
   I cry out to you, God; listen to me!
2 My Lord, in my time of trouble I came to
      you.
   I reached out for you all night long.
   My soul refused to be comforted.
3 I thought about you, God,
   and tried to tell you how I felt, but I
      could not.
4 You would not let me sleep.
   I tried to say something, but I was too
      upset.
5 I kept thinking about the past,
   about things that happened long ago.
6 During the night, I thought about my
      songs.
   I talked to myself, trying to understand
      what is happening.
7 I wondered, "Has our Lord rejected us
      forever?
   Will he ever accept us again?
8 Is his love gone forever?
   Will he never again speak to us?

9 Has God forgotten what mercy is?
   Has his compassion changed to anger?"
                                    Selah*

10 Then I said to myself, "What bothers me
      most is the thought
   that God Most High has lost his power."
11 LORD, I remember what you have done.
   I remember the amazing things you did
      long ago.
12 I think about those things.
   I think about them all the time.
13 God, all that you do is holy.*
   No god is as great as you are.
14 You are the God who does amazing
      things.
   You showed the nations your great
      power.
15 By your power you saved your people,
   the descendants of Jacob* and Joseph.
                                    Selah

16 God, the water saw you and became
      afraid.
   The deep water shook with fear.
17 The thick clouds dropped their water.
   Thunder roared in the sky above.
   Your arrows of lightning flashed through
      the clouds.
18 There were loud claps of thunder.
   Lightning lit up the world.
   The earth shook and trembled.
19 You walked through the water and
      crossed the deep sea,
   but you left no footprints.
20 You led your people like sheep,
   using Moses* and Aaron* to guide them.

78 One of Asaph's maskils.*

1 My people, listen to my teachings.
   Listen to what I say.
2 I will tell you a story.
   I will tell you about things from the past
      that are hard to understand.
3 We have heard the story, and we know it
      well.
   Our fathers told it to us.
4 And we will not forget it.
   Our people will be telling this story to
      the last generation.
   We will all praise the LORD
   and tell about the amazing things he did.
5 He made an agreement* with Jacob.*
   He gave the law to Israel.*
   He gave the commands to our
      ancestors.*
   He told them to teach the law to their
      children.
6 Then the next generation, even the
      children not yet born, would learn the
      law.
   And they would be able to teach it to
      their own children.

[a]76:5 They ... themselves Literally, "The warriors
could not find their hands."
[b]76:7–10 The Hebrew text here is hard to
understand.
[c]Psalm 77 Jeduthun Or "and to Jeduthun," one of
the three main temple musicians. See 1 Chron. 9:16;
16:38–42.

7 So they would all trust in God,
    never forgetting what he had done
    and always obeying his commands.
8 They would not be like their ancestors,
    who were stubborn and refused to obey.
  Their hearts were not devoted to God,
    and they were not faithful to him.

9 The men from Ephraim* had their
    weapons,
    but they ran from the battle.
10 They did not keep their agreement with
    God.
    They refused to obey his teachings.
11 They forgot the great things he had done
    and the amazing things he had shown
    them.
12 While their ancestors watched,
    he showed his great power at Zoan in
    Egypt.
13 He split the Red Sea and led the people
    across.
    The water stood like a solid wall on
    both sides of them.
14 Each day God led them with the tall
    cloud,
    and each night he led them with the
    light from the column of fire.
15 He split the rocks in the desert
    and gave them an ocean of fresh water.
16 He brought a stream of water out of the
    rock
    and made it flow like a river!
17 But they continued sinning against him.
    They rebelled against God Most High in
    the desert.
18 Then they decided to test God
    by telling him to give them the food
    they wanted.
19 They complained about him and said,
    "Can God give us food in the desert?
20 Yes, he struck the rock and a flood of
    water came out.
    But can he give us bread and meat?"
21 The LORD heard what they said
    and became angry with Jacob's people.
  He was angry with Israel,
22   because they did not trust in him.
    They did not believe that God could save
    them.
23-24 But then God opened the clouds above,
    and manna* rained down on them for
    food.
  It was as if doors in the sky opened,
    and grain poured down from a
    storehouse in the sky.
25 These people ate the food of angels.
    God sent plenty of food to satisfy them.
26 He sent a strong wind from the east,
    and by his power he made the south
    wind blow.
27 He made quail fall like rain until they
    covered the ground.
    There were so many birds that they
    were like sand on the seashore.

28 The birds fell in the middle of the camp,
    all around their tents.
29 The people ate until they were full.
    God had given them what they wanted.
30 But before they were fully satisfied,
    while the food was still in their mouths,
31 God became angry and killed even the
    strongest of them.
    He brought down Israel's best young
    men.
32 But the people continued to sin!
    They did not trust in the amazing things
    God could do.
33 So he ended their worthless lives;
    he brought their years to a close with
    disaster.
34 When he killed some of them, the others
    would turn back to him.
    They would come running back to God.
35 They would remember that God was their
    Rock.*
    They would remember that God Most
    High had saved them.
36 But they tried to fool him with their
    words;
    they told him lies.
37 Their hearts were not really with him.
    They were not faithful to the agreement
    he gave them.
38 But God was merciful.
    He forgave their sins and did not
    destroy them.
  Many times he held back his anger.
    He never let it get out of control.
39 He remembered that they were only
    people,
    like a wind that blows and then is gone.
40 Oh, they caused him so much trouble in
    the desert!
    They made him so sad.
41 Again and again they tested his patience.
    They really hurt the Holy One of Israel.
42 They forgot about his power.
    They forgot the many times he saved
    them from the enemy.
43 They forgot the miracles in Egypt,
    the miracles in the fields of Zoan.
44 God turned the rivers into blood,
    and the Egyptians could not drink the
    water.
45 He sent swarms of flies that bit them.
    He sent the frogs that ruined their
    lives.
46 He gave their crops to grasshoppers
    and their other plants to locusts.
47 He destroyed their vines with hail
    and their trees with sleet.
48 He killed their animals with hail
    and their cattle with lightning.
49 He showed the Egyptians his anger.
    He sent his destroying angels against
    them.
50 He found a way to show his anger.
    He did not spare their lives.
    He let them die with a deadly disease.

51 He killed all the firstborn* sons in Egypt.
   He killed every firstborn in Ham's[a]
   family.
52 Then he led Israel like a shepherd.
   He led his people like sheep into the
   desert.
53 He guided them safely.
   They had nothing to fear.
   He drowned their enemies in the sea.
54 He led his people to his holy land,
   to the mountain he took with his own
   power.
55 He forced the other nations out before
   them
   and gave each family its share of the
   land.
   He gave each tribe of Israel a place to
   live.
56 But they tested God Most High and made
   him very sad.
   They didn't obey his commands.
57 They turned against him and were
   unfaithful just like their ancestors.
   They changed directions like a
   boomerang.*
58 They built high places* and made God
   angry.
   They built statues of false gods and
   made him jealous.
59 God heard what they were doing and
   became very angry.
   So he rejected Israel completely!
60 He abandoned his place at Shiloh,[b]
   the Holy Tent* where he lived among
   the people.
61 He let foreigners capture the Box of the
   Agreement,*
   the symbol of his power and glory.*
62 He showed his anger against his people
   and let them be killed in war.
63 Their young men were burned to death,
   and there were no wedding songs for
   their young women.
64 Their priests were killed,
   but the widows had no time to mourn*
   for them.
65 Finally, our Lord got up
   like a man waking from his sleep,
   like a soldier after drinking too much
   wine.
66 He forced his enemies to turn back
   defeated.
   He brought them shame that will last
   forever.
67 Then he rejected Joseph's family.
   He did not accept Ephraim's family.
68 No, he chose the tribe of Judah,*
   and he chose Mount Zion,* the place he
   loves.
69 He built his holy Temple* high on that
   mountain.

Like the earth, God built his Temple to
   last forever.
70 He chose David* to be his special servant.
   He took him from the sheep pens.
71 He took him away from the job of caring
   for sheep
   and gave him the job of caring for the
   descendants of Jacob—Israel, his
   chosen people.
72 And David led them with a pure heart
   and guided them very wisely.

79 One of Asaph's songs of praise.

1 God, some people from other nations
   came to fight your people.
   They ruined your holy Temple.*
   They left Jerusalem in ruins.
2 They left the bodies of your servants for
   the wild birds to eat.
   They let wild animals eat the bodies of
   your followers.
3 Blood flowed like water all over
   Jerusalem.
   No one is left to bury the bodies.
4 The countries around us insult us.
   The people around us laugh at us and
   make fun of us.
5 LORD, will you be angry with us forever?
   Will your strong feelings[c] continue to
   burn like a fire?
6 Turn your anger against the nations that
   do not know you,
   against the people who do not honor
   you as God.
7 Those nations killed Jacob's* family
   and destroyed their land.
8 Please don't punish us for the sins of our
   ancestors.*
   Hurry, show us your mercy!
   We need you so much!
9 Our God and Savior, help us!
   That will bring glory to your name.
   Save us and forgive our sins
   for the good of your name.
10 Don't give the other nations a reason to
   say,
   "Where is their God? Can't he help
   them?"
   Let us see you punish those people.
   Punish them for killing your servants.
11 Listen to the sad cries of the prisoners!
   Use your great power to free those who
   are sentenced to die.
12 Punish the nations around us!
   Pay them back seven times for what
   they did to us.
   Punish them for insulting you.
13 We are your people, the sheep of your
   flock.
   We will praise you forever.
   We will praise you forever and ever!

[a]78:51 Ham The Egyptians were Ham's descendants. See Gen. 10:6–10.
[b]78:60 Holy Tent at Shiloh See 1 Sam. 4:4–11; Jer. 7:17.

[c]79:5 strong feelings The Hebrew word can mean any strong feelings such as zeal, jealousy, or love.

80

To the director*: To the tune "Lilies of the Agreement." One of Asaph's songs of praise.

1 Shepherd of Israel,* listen to us.
  You lead your people*a* like sheep.
  You sit on your throne above the Cherub angels.*
  Let us see you.
2 Shepherd of Israel, show your greatness to the tribes of Ephraim, Benjamin, and Manasseh.
  Come and save your people.
3 God, accept us again.
  Smile down on us and save us!
4 Lord God All-Powerful, when will you listen to our prayers?
  How long will you be angry with us?
5 Instead of bread and water,
  you gave your people tears.
6 You made us the target of everyone's hatred.
  Our enemies make fun of us.
7 God All-Powerful, accept us again.
  Smile down on us and save us!

8 When you brought us out of Egypt,
  we were like your special vine.
  You forced other nations to leave this land,
  and you planted that vine here.
9 You prepared the ground for it,
  and it sent its roots down deep and spread throughout the land.
10 It covered the mountains,
  and its leaves shaded even the giant cedar trees.
11 Its branches spread to the Mediterranean Sea,
  its shoots to the Euphrates River.
12 God, why did you pull down the walls that protect your vine?
  Now everyone who passes by picks its grapes.
13 Wild pigs come and ruin it.
  Wild animals eat the leaves.
14 God All-Powerful, come back.
  Look down from heaven at your vine and protect it.
15 Look at the vine you planted with your own hands.
  Look at the young plant*b* you raised.
16 Our enemies have cut it down and burned it up.
  Show them how angry you are and destroy them.

17 Reach out and help your chosen one.*c*
  Reach out to the people*d* you raised up.

18 Then we will never leave you.
  Let us live, and we will worship you.
19 Lord God All-Powerful, accept us again.
  Smile down on us and save us!

81

To the director*: On the gittith.* One of Asaph's songs.

1 Be happy and sing to God, our strength.
  Shout with joy to the God of Jacob.*
2 Begin the music.
  Play the tambourines.
  Play the pleasant harps and lyres.*
3 Blow the ram's horn at the time of the new moon*e*
  and at the time of the full moon,*f* when our festival begins.
4 This is the law for the people of Israel.*
  The God of Jacob gave the command.
5 God made this agreement with Joseph's people,
  when he led them out of Egypt.
  In a language we didn't understand, God said,
6 "I took the load from your shoulder.
  I let you drop the worker's basket.
7 When you were in trouble, you called for help, and I set you free.
  I was hidden in the storm clouds, and I answered you.
  I tested you by the water at Meribah.*g*"
  Selah*

8 "My people, I am warning you.
  Israel, listen to me!
9 Don't worship any of the false gods that the foreigners worship.
10 I, the Lord, am your God.
  I brought you out of Egypt.
  Israel, open your mouth,
  and I will feed you.

11 "But my people did not listen to me.
  Israel did not obey me.
12 So I let them go their own stubborn way and do whatever they wanted.
13 If my people would listen to me and would live the way I want,
14 then I would defeat their enemies.
  I would punish those who cause them trouble.
15 Those who hate the Lord would shake with fear.
  They would be punished forever.

16 I would give the best wheat to my people.
  I would give them the purest honey,
  until they were satisfied."

---

*a*80:1 *your people* Literally, "Joseph," the father of Ephraim and Manasseh, whose names are often used to mean all the tribes in northern Israel.
*b*80:15 *young plant* Literally, "son."
*c*80:17 *chosen one* Literally, "the man of your right hand."
*d*80:17 *people* Literally, "son of man."

*e*81:3 *new moon* The first day of the Hebrew month. There were special meetings on these days when the people shared fellowship offerings as part of their worship to God.
*f*81:3 *full moon* The middle of the Hebrew month. Many of the special meetings and festivals started at the time of a full moon.
*g*81:7 *Meribah* See Ex. 17:1–7.

82
One of Asaph's songs of praise.

1 God stands in the assembly of the gods.[a]
  He stands as judge among the judges.
2 He says, "How long will you judge unfairly
  and show special favors to the wicked?"
                                        *Selah**

3 "Defend the poor and orphans.
  Protect the rights of the poor.
4 Help those who are poor and helpless.
  Save them from those who are evil.

5 "They[b] don't know what is happening.
  They don't understand!
  They don't know what they are doing.
  Their world is falling down around
  them!"
6 I, God Most High, say,
  "You are gods,[c] my own sons.
7 But you will die as all people must die.
  Your life will end like that of any ruler."

8 Get up, God! You be the judge!
  You be the leader over all the nations!

83
One of Asaph's songs of praise.

1 God, don't keep quiet!
  Don't close your ears!
  Please say something, God.
2 Your enemies are getting ready to do
  something.
  Those who hate you will soon attack.
3 They are making secret plans against your
  people.
  Your enemies are discussing plans
  against the people you love.
4 They say, "Come, let us destroy them
  completely.
  Then no one will ever again remember
  the name Israel.*"
5 God, they have all joined together.
  They have united against you.
6-7 Their army includes the Edomites,
  Ishmaelites, Moabites, and Hagar's
  descendants,
  the people of Byblos, Ammon, and
  Amalek,
  the Philistines,* and the people of Tyre.
8 Even the Assyrians have joined them.
  They have made Lot's descendants very
  powerful.   *Selah**

9 God, defeat them just as you defeated
  Midian.
  Do what you did to Sisera and Jabin at
  the Kishon River.
10 You destroyed the enemy at Endor,
  and their bodies rotted on the ground.
11 Punish their leaders as you did Oreb and
  Zeeb.
  Do what you did to Zebah and
  Zalmunna.
12 They said, "Let's make this land our
  own—
  these fields of grass that belong to God!"
13 Make them like weeds blown by the
  wind.
  Scatter them, like the wind scatters
  straw.
14 Be like a fire that destroys a forest
  or like a flame that sets the hills on fire.
15 Chase them away with your blasts of
  wind;
  frighten them with your storms.
16 Lord, cover them with shame
  until they come to you for help.
17 May they be forever ashamed and afraid.
  Disgrace and defeat them.
18 Then they will know that your name is
  Yahweh*—
  that you alone are the Lord.
  They will know that you are God Most
  High,
  ruler over all the earth!

84
To the director: On the gittith.*
A song of praise from the Korah family.*

1 Lord All-Powerful, the place where you
  live is so beautiful!
2 Lord, I cannot wait to enter your Temple.*
  I am so excited!
  Every part of me cries out to be with the
  Living God.
3 Lord All-Powerful, my King, my God,
  even the birds have found a home in
  your Temple.
  They make their nests near your altar,
  and there they have their babies.
4 Great blessings belong to those who live
  at your Temple!
  They continue to praise you.   *Selah**

5 Great blessings belong to those who
  depend on you for strength!
  Their heart's desire is to make the trip
  to your Temple.
6 They travel through Baca Valley,
  which God has made into a place of
  springs.
  Autumn rains form pools of water there.
7 The people travel from town to town[d]
  on their way to Zion,* where they will
  meet with God.

---

[a] 82:1 *assembly of the gods* Other nations taught
that El (God) and the other gods met together to
decide what to do with the people on earth. But
many times kings and leaders were also called
"gods." So this psalm may be God's warning to the
leaders of Israel.
[b] 82:5 *They* This might mean that the poor don't
understand what is happening. Or it might mean
that the "gods" or leaders don't understand that
they are ruining the world by not being fair and by
not doing what is right.
[c] 82:6 *gods* Or "judges."

[d] 84:7 *town to town* Or "wall to wall."

8 Lᴏʀᴅ God All-Powerful, listen to my
prayer.
God of Jacob,* listen to me.   *Selah*

9 God, watch over the king, our protector.ᵃ
Be kind to him, the one you have
chosen.

10 One day in your Temple is better
than a thousand days anywhere else.
Serving as a guard at the gate of my God's
house is better
than living in the homes of the wicked.

11 The Lᴏʀᴅ God is our protector and
glorious king.ᵇ
He blesses us with kindness and honor.
The Lᴏʀᴅ freely gives every good thing
to those who do what is right.

12 Lᴏʀᴅ All-Powerful, great blessings belong
to those who trust in you!

85 *To the director*:*
A song of praise from the Korah family.

1 Lᴏʀᴅ, you have been so kind to your land.
You have brought success again to the
people of Jacob.*

2 You have forgiven the bad things your
people did.
You have taken away the guilt of their
sins!   *Selah**

3 You stopped being angry with them.
Your terrible anger has gone away.

4 Our God and Savior, accept us again.
Don't be angry with us anymore.

5 Will you be angry with us forever?
Will your anger reach to our children
and to their children?

6 Please, give us new life!
Make your people happy to be yours.

7 Lᴏʀᴅ, save us
and show us your love.

8 I heard what the Lᴏʀᴅ God said.
He said there would be peace for his
people and his loyal followers.
So they must not go back to their foolish
way of living.

9 He will soon save his faithful followers.
His glory will again live in our land.ᶜ

10 God's love will come together with his
faithful people.
Goodness and peace will greet them
with a kiss.

11 People on earth will be loyal to God,
and God in heaven will be good to
them.ᵈ

12 The Lᴏʀᴅ will give us many good things.
The ground will grow many good
crops.

13 Goodness will go before the Lord
and prepare the way for him.

86 *A prayer of David.*

1 I am a poor, helpless man.
Lᴏʀᴅ, please listen to me and answer
my prayer!

2 I am your follower, so please protect me.
I am your servant, and you are my God.
I trust in you, so save me.

3 My Lord, be kind to me.
I have been praying to you all day.

4 My Lord, I put my life in your hands.
I am your servant, so make me happy.

5 My Lord, you are good and merciful.
You love all those who call to you for
help.

6 Lᴏʀᴅ, hear my prayer.
Listen to my cry for mercy.

7 I am praying to you in my time of trouble.
I know you will answer me.

8 My Lord, there is no God like you.
No one can do what you have done.

9 My Lord, you made everyone.
I wish they all would come worship you
and honor your name.

10 You are great and do amazing things.
You and you alone are God.

11 Lᴏʀᴅ, teach me your ways,
and I will live and obey your truths.
Help me make worshiping your name
the most important thing in my life.

12 My Lord God, I praise you with all my
heart.
I will honor your name forever!

13 You have such great love for me.
You save me from the place of death.

14 Proud people are attacking me, God.
A gang of cruel men is trying to kill me.
They don't respect you.

15 My Lord, you are a kind and merciful
God.
You are patient, loyal, and full of love.

16 Show that you hear me and be kind to
me.
I am your servant, so give me strength.
I am your slave, as my mother was, so
save me!

17 Lᴏʀᴅ, show me a sign that you care for
me.
My enemies will see it and be
disappointed,
because you helped and comforted me.

87 *A song of praise from the Korah family.*

1 The Lᴏʀᴅ built his city on the holy hills.

2 He loves the gates of Zion* more than
any other place in Israel.*

3 Wonderful things are said about you, City
of God.   *Selah**

ᵃ**84:9 the king, our protector** Literally, "our shield."
This line could also mean "God, our Shield, look!"
ᵇ**84:11 protector and glorious king** Literally, "sun
and shield."
ᶜ**85:9 We … land** Or "We will soon live with honor
in our land."
ᵈ**85:11** Literally, "Loyalty will sprout from the
ground, and goodness will look down from the sky."

⁴ God says, "Some of my people live in
    Egypt* and Babylon.
  Some of them were born in Philistia,
    Tyre, and even Ethiopia."
⁵ But about Zion he says,
  "I know each and every person born
    there."
  It is the city built by God Most High.
⁶ The LORD keeps a list of all his people,
  and he knows where each of them was
    born.   *Selah*

⁷ At the festivals, people will dance and
    sing,
  "All good things come from Zion."

88

*A song from the Korah family. To the
director*: About a painful sickness. A
maskil* of Heman the Ezrahite.*

¹ LORD God, you are my Savior.
  I have been praying to you day and
    night.
² Please pay attention to my prayers.
  Listen to my prayers for mercy.
³ My soul has had enough of this pain!
  I am ready to die.
⁴ People already treat me like a dead man,
  like someone too weak to live.
⁵ Look for me among the dead,
    like a body in the grave.
  I am one of those you have forgotten,
    cut off from you and your care.
⁶ You put me in that hole in the ground.
  Yes, you put me in that dark place.
⁷ Your anger presses down on me like a
    heavy weight.
  It's like one wave after another
    pounding against me.   *Selah*

⁸ You made my friends leave me.
  They all avoid me like someone no one
    wants to touch.
  Like a prisoner in my house, I cannot go
    out.
⁹ My eyes hurt from crying.
  LORD, I pray to you constantly!
  I lift my arms in prayer to you.
¹⁰ Do you do miracles for the dead?
  Do ghosts rise up and praise you? No!
                                    Selah

¹¹ The dead in their graves cannot talk about
    your faithful love.
  People in the world of the dead* cannot
    talk about your faithfulness.
¹² The dead who lie in darkness cannot see
    the amazing things you do.
  Those in the world of the forgotten
    cannot talk about your goodness.
¹³ LORD, I am asking you to help me!

87:4 Egypt Literally, "Rahab." This name means the
"Dragon." It became a popular name for Egypt.
88:11 the world of the dead Or "Abaddon," a
Hebrew name meaning "death" or "destruction." See
Rev. 9:11.

  Early each morning I pray to you.
¹⁴ LORD, why have you abandoned me?
  Why do you refuse to listen to me?
¹⁵ I have been sick and weak since I was
    young.
  I have suffered your anger, and I am
    helpless.
¹⁶ Your anger covers me like a flood.
  Your attacks are killing me.
¹⁷ They surround me on every side.
  I feel like a drowning man.
¹⁸ You caused my friends and loved ones to
    leave me.
  Now darkness is my closest friend.

89

A maskil from Ethan the Ezrahite.*

¹ I will sing forever about the LORD's love.
  I will sing about his faithfulness forever
    and ever!
² I will say, "Your faithful love will last
    forever.
  Your loyalty is like the sky—there is no
    end to it!"

³ You said, "I made an agreement with my
    chosen king.
  I made this promise to my servant
    David*:
⁴ 'There will always be someone from your
    family to rule.
  I will make your kingdom continue
    forever and ever.'"   *Selah**

⁵ LORD, the heavens praise you for the
    amazing things you do.
  The assembly of holy ones sings about
    your loyalty.
⁶ No one in heaven is equal to the LORD.
  None of the "gods" can compare to the
    LORD.
⁷ When God's holy ones—the angels
    around his throne—meet together,
    they fear and respect him;
  he is more awesome than all those
    around him.
⁸ LORD God All-Powerful, there is no one
    like you.
  You are strong, LORD, and always
    faithful.
⁹ You rule the stormy sea.
  You can calm its angry waves.
¹⁰ You defeated Rahab.*
  You scattered your enemies with your
    own powerful arm.
¹¹ Everything in heaven and earth belongs
    to you.
  You made the world and everything in
    it.
¹² You created everything north and south.
  Mount Tabor and Mount Hermon sing
    praises to your name.
¹³ You have the power!
  Your power is great!
  Victory is yours!

14 Your kingdom is built on truth and justice.
   Love and faithfulness are servants
      before your throne.
15 LORD, your loyal followers are happy.
   They live in the light of your kindness.
16 Your name always makes them happy.
   They praise your goodness.
17 You are their amazing strength.
   Their power comes from you.
18 The king, our protector, belongs to the
      LORD,
   who is the Holy One of Israel.*
19 Lord, you once spoke in a vision to your
      followers:
   "I have made a young soldier strong.
      From among my people I chose him for
      an important position.
20 I have found my servant David
   and anointed* him as king with my
      special oil.
21 I will support him with my right hand,
   and my arm will make him strong.
22 So no enemy will ever control him.
   The wicked will never defeat him.
23 I will destroy his enemies before his eyes.
   I will defeat those who hate him.
24 I will always love and support him.
   I will always make him strong.
25 I will put him in charge of the sea.
   He will control the rivers.
26 He will say to me, 'You are my father.
   You are my God, my Rock,* my Savior.'
27 And I will make him my firstborn* son.
   He will be the great king on earth.
28 My love will protect him forever.
   My agreement with him will never end.
29 I will make his family continue forever.
   His kingdom will last as long as the
      skies.
30 If his descendants stop following my law
   and stop obeying my commands,
31 if they break my laws
   and ignore my commands,
32 I will punish them severely for their sins
      and wrongs.
33 But I will never take my love from him.
   I will never stop being loyal to him.
34 I will not break my agreement with
      David.
   I will never change what I said.
35 By my holiness, I made a promise to him,
   and I would not lie to David.
36 His family will continue forever.
   His kingdom will last as long as the sun.
37 Like the moon, it will continue forever.
   The sky is a witness to the agreement that
      can be trusted."   Selah

38 But now, Lord, you have become angry
      with your chosen king,*a*
   and you have left him all alone.
39 You ended the agreement you made with
      your servant.

*a*89:38 *chosen king* Literally, "anointed one."

You threw the king's crown into the dirt.
40 You pulled down the walls of his city.
   You destroyed all his fortresses.*
41 Everyone passing by steals from him.
   His neighbors laugh at him.
42 You made all the king's enemies happy
   and let his enemies win the war.
43 You helped them defend themselves.
   You did not help your king win the
      battle.
44 You did not let him win.
   You threw his throne to the ground.
45 You cut his life short.
   You shamed him.   Selah

46 LORD, how long will this continue?
   Will you ignore us forever?
   Will your anger burn like a fire forever?
47 Remember how short my life is.
   You created us to live a short life and
      then die.
48 Is there anyone alive who will never die?
   Will anyone escape the grave?   Selah

49 Lord, where is the love you showed in the
      past?
   You promised David that you would be
      loyal to his family.
50-51 My Lord, please remember how people
      insulted your servant.
   LORD, I had to listen to all the insults from
      your enemies.
   They insulted your chosen king
      wherever he went.

52 Praise the LORD forever!
   Amen* and Amen!

BOOK 4 *(Psalms 90–106)*

90 *The prayer of Moses,* the man of God.*

1 My Lord, you have been our home forever
      and ever.
2 You were God before the mountains were
      born,
   before the earth and the world were
      made.
   You have always been and will always
      be God!

3 You bring people into this world,
   and you change them into dust again.
4 To you, a thousand years is like yesterday,
   like a few hours in the night.
5 Our life is like a dream that ends when
      morning comes.
   We are like grass
6   that grows and looks so fresh in the
      morning,
   but in the evening it is dry and dying.
7 Your anger could destroy us.
   Your anger frightens us!
8 You know about all our sins.
   You see every one of our secret sins.

9 Your anger can end our life.
  Our lives fade away like a whisper.
10 We live about 70 years
   or, if we are strong, 80 years.
   But most of them are filled with hard
     work and pain.
   Then, suddenly, the years are gone, and
     we fly away.
11 No one really knows the full power of
     your anger,
   but our fear and respect for you is as
     great as your anger.
12 Teach us how short our lives are
   so that we can become wise.
13 LORD, come back to us.
   Be kind to your servants.
14 Fill us with your love every morning.
   Let us be happy and enjoy our lives.
15 For years you have made life hard for us
   and have given us many troubles.
   Now make us happy for just as long.
16 Let your servants see the wonderful
     things you can do for them.
   And let their children see your glory.*
17 Lord, our God, be kind to us.
   Make everything we do successful.
   Yes, make it all successful.

91 ¹You can go to God Most High to
  hide.
   You can go to God All-Powerful for
     protection.
2 I say to the LORD, "You are my place of
     safety, my fortress.*
   My God, I trust in you."
3 God will save you from hidden dangers
   and from deadly diseases.
4 You can go to him for protection.
   He will cover you like a bird spreading
     its wings over its babies.
   You can trust him to surround and
     protect you like a shield.
5 You will have nothing to fear at night
   and no need to be afraid of enemy
     arrows during the day.
6 You will have no fear of diseases that
     come in the dark
   or terrible suffering that comes at noon.
7 A thousand people may fall dead at your
     side
   or ten thousand right beside you,
   but nothing bad will happen to you!
8 All you will have to do is watch,
   and you will see that the wicked are
     punished.
9 You trust in the LORD for protection.
   You have made God Most High your
     place of safety.
10 So nothing bad will happen to you.
   No diseases will come near your home.
11 He will command his angels to protect
     you wherever you go.
12 Their hands will catch you
   so that you will not hit your foot on a
     rock.

13 You will have power to trample on lions
   and poisonous snakes.
14 The LORD says, "If someone trusts me, I
     will save them.
   I will protect my followers who call to
     me for help.
15 When my followers call to me, I will
     answer them.
   I will be with them when they are in
     trouble.
   I will rescue them and honor them.
16 I will give my followers a long life
   and show them my power to save."

92 A song of praise for the Sabbath.*

1 It is good to praise the LORD.
   God Most High, it is good to praise your
     name.
2 It is good to sing about your love in the
     morning
   and about your faithfulness at night.
3 It is good to play for you on the ten-
     stringed instrument and lyre*
   and to add the soft sounds of the harp to
     my praise.
4 LORD, you make us very happy because of
     what you did.
   I gladly sing about it.
5 LORD, you did such great things.
   Your thoughts are too hard for us to
     understand.
6 Stupid people don't know this.
   Fools don't understand.
7 The wicked may sprout like grass,
   and those who do evil may blossom like
     flowers,
   but they will be destroyed, never to be
     seen again.
8 But, LORD, you will be honored forever.
9 LORD, all your enemies will be destroyed,
   and all who do evil will be scattered.
10 But you have made me as strong as a wild
     ox.
   You have given me your blessing.*a*
11 My eyes will see the defeat of those
     waiting to attack me.
   My ears will hear the cries of my evil
     enemies.

12 Good people are like budding palm trees.
   They grow strong like the cedar trees of
     Lebanon.
13 They are planted in the LORD's house.*b*
   They grow strong there in the
     courtyards of our God.
14 Even when they are old,
   they will continue producing fruit like
     young, healthy trees.

---

*a*92:10 You ... blessing Or "You poured your refreshing oil over me."
*b*92:13 house Or "Temple." See "Temple" in the Word List.

¹⁵ They are there to show everyone
that the Lᴏʀᴅ is good.^a
He is my Rock,*
and he does nothing wrong.^b

93 ¹The Lᴏʀᴅ is King.
The Lᴏʀᴅ wears majesty and strength
like clothes.
He is ready, so the whole world is safe.
It will not be shaken.
² Your kingdom has continued forever.
You have lived forever!
³ Lᴏʀᴅ, the ocean roars.
The mighty ocean sounds like thunder
as the waves crash on the shore.
⁴ The crashing waves of the sea are loud
and powerful,
but the Lᴏʀᴅ above is even more
powerful.
⁵ Lᴏʀᴅ, your laws will continue forever.^c
Your holy Temple* will stand for a long
time.

94 ¹The Lᴏʀᴅ is a God who punishes
people.
God, come punish them.
² You are the judge of the whole earth.
Give proud people the punishment they
deserve.
³ Lᴏʀᴅ, how long will the wicked have
their fun?
How much longer?
⁴ How much longer will those criminals
brag about the evil they did?
⁵ Lᴏʀᴅ, they hurt your people
and make them suffer.
⁶ They kill widows and foreigners living in
our country.
They murder orphans.
⁷ And they say the Lᴏʀᴅ does not see them
doing these evil things!
They say the God of Jacob* does not
know what is happening.

⁸ You evil people are foolish.
When will you learn your lesson?
You are so stupid!
You must try to understand.
⁹ God made our ears,
so surely he can hear what is
happening!
He made our eyes,
so surely he can see you!
¹⁰ The one who disciplines nations will
surely correct you.
He is the one who teaches us
everything.

¹¹ He knows what people are thinking.
He knows that their thoughts are like a
puff of wind.

¹² Lᴏʀᴅ, great blessings belong to those you
discipline,
to those you teach from your law.
¹³ You help them stay calm when trouble
comes.
You will help them until the wicked are
put in their graves.
¹⁴ The Lᴏʀᴅ will not leave his people.
He will not leave them without help.
¹⁵ Justice will return and bring fairness.
And those who want to do right will be
there to see it.

¹⁶ No one helped me fight against the
wicked.
No one stood with me against those
who do evil.
¹⁷ And if the Lᴏʀᴅ had not helped me,
I would have been silenced by death.
¹⁸ I know I was ready to fall,
but, Lᴏʀᴅ, your faithful love supported
me.
¹⁹ I was very worried and upset,
but you comforted me and made me
happy!

²⁰ You don't help crooked judges.
They use the law to make life hard for
the people.
²¹ They attack those who do right.
They say innocent people are guilty and
put them to death.
²² But the Lᴏʀᴅ is my place of safety, high
on the mountain.
God, my Rock,* is my safe place!
²³ He will punish those evil judges for the
bad things they did.
He will destroy them because they
sinned.
The Lᴏʀᴅ our God will destroy them.

95 ¹Come, let us praise the Lᴏʀᴅ!
Let us shout praises to the Rock* who
saves us.
² Let us go to worship the Lᴏʀᴅ.
Let us approach him with songs of
thanks.^d
Let us sing happy songs of praise to him.
³ For the Lᴏʀᴅ is a great God,
the great King ruling over all the other
"gods."
⁴ The deepest caves and the highest
mountains belong to him.
⁵ The ocean is his—he created it.
He made the dry land with his own
hands.
⁶ Come, let us bow down and worship him!
Let us kneel before the Lᴏʀᴅ who made
us.

^a**92:15 good** This is a wordplay. The Hebrew word means "straight" (like the trees) and "good" or "honest."
^b**92:15 he ... wrong** Or "there is no crookedness in him."
^c**93:5 your laws ... forever** Or "your agreement can really be trusted."

^d**95:2 songs of thanks** Or "thank offerings."

7 He is our God,
    and we are the people he cares for,
    his sheep that walk by his side.

Listen to his voice today:
8 "Don't be stubborn, as you were at
    Meribah,
    as you were at Massah*a* in the desert.
9 Your ancestors* doubted and tested me,
    even after they saw what I could do!
10 I was angry with them for 40 years.
    I said, 'They are not faithful to me.
    They refuse to do what I say.'
11 So in my anger I made this vow*:
    'They will never enter my land of rest.'"

96

1 Sing a new song*b* to the LORD!
    Let the whole world sing to the LORD!
2 Sing to the LORD and praise his name!
    Tell the good news every day about how
    he saves us!
3 Tell all the nations how wonderful he is!
    Tell people everywhere about the
    amazing things he does.
4 The LORD is great and worthy of praise.
    He is more awesome than any of the
    "gods."
5 All the "gods" in other nations are
    nothing but statues,
    but the LORD made the heavens.
6 He lives in the presence of glory* and
    honor.
    His Temple* is a place of power and
    beauty.
7 Praise the LORD, all people of every
    nation;
    praise the LORD's glory and power.
8 Give the LORD praise worthy of his glory!
    Come, bring your offerings into his
    courtyard.
9 Worship the LORD in all his holy beauty.
    Everyone on earth should tremble before
    him.
10 Tell the nations that the LORD is King!
    The world stands firm and cannot be
    moved.
    He will judge all people fairly.
11 Let the heavens rejoice and the earth be
    happy!
    Let the sea and everything in it shout
    for joy!
12 Let the fields and everything in them be
    happy!
    Let the trees in the forest sing for joy
13 when they see the LORD coming!
    He is coming to rule*c* the world.
    He will rule all the nations of the world
    with justice and fairness.

97

1 The LORD rules, and the earth is
    happy.
    All the faraway lands are happy.
2 Thick, dark clouds surround the LORD.
    Goodness and justice make his kingdom
    strong.
3 A fire goes in front of the LORD
    and destroys his enemies.
4 His lightning flashes in the sky.
    The people see it and are afraid.
5 The mountains melt like wax before the
    LORD,
    before the Lord of all the earth.
6 The skies tell about his goodness,
    and the nations see his glory.*
7 People worship their idols.
    They brag about their "gods."
    But they will be embarrassed.
    And all their "gods" will bow down
    before the LORD.
8 Zion,* listen and be happy!
    Cities of Judah,* be glad!
    Rejoice because the LORD's decisions are
    fair.
9 LORD Most High, you really are the ruler
    of the earth.
    You are much better than the "gods."
10 Hate evil, you who love the LORD.
    He protects his followers and saves
    them from evil people.
11 Light and happiness shine on those who
    want to do right.
12 Good people, be happy in the LORD!
    Praise his holy name!

98

A song of praise.

1 Sing a new song*d* to the LORD,
    because he has done amazing things!
    His powerful and holy right arm*e*
    has brought him another victory.
2 The LORD showed the nations his power
    to save.
    He showed them his goodness.
3 He has kept his promise of love and
    loyalty to the people of Israel.*
    People everywhere have seen our God's
    power to save.
4 Everyone on earth, shout with joy to the
    LORD.
    Start singing happy songs of praise!
5 Praise the LORD with harps.
    Yes, praise him with music from the
    harps.
6 Blow the pipes and horns,
    and shout for joy to the LORD our King!

---

*a***95:8 *Meribah ... Massah*** See Ex. 17:1–7.
*b***96:1 *new song*** Whenever God did a new and
wonderful thing for his people, they would write a
new song about it.
*c***96:13 *rule*** Or "judge." Also in 98:9.

*d***98:1 *new song*** Whenever God did a new and
wonderful thing for his people, they would write a
new song about it.
*e***98:1 *holy right arm*** This pictures God as a war-
rior-king. The right arm symbolizes his power and
authority. "Holy" may refer to the special cleansing
and dedication that Israelites performed before
going into battle.

7 Let the sea and everything in it,
  the earth and all who live in it shout his
    praise!
8 Rivers, clap your hands!
  All together now, mountains sing out!
9 Sing before the LORD
  because he is coming to judge the
    world.
  He will rule the world fairly.
  He will rule the people with goodness.

99

1 The LORD is King,
  so let the nations shake with fear.
  He sits as King above the Cherub angels,*
  so let the whole earth shake.
2 The LORD in Zion* is great!
  He is the great leader over all people.
3 Let all the nations praise your name.
  Your name is great and awesome.
  Your name is holy.
4 You are the powerful King who loves
    justice.
  You have made things right.
  You have brought goodness and fairness
    to Jacob.*
5 Praise the LORD our God,
  and bow down before his footstool,a for
    he is holy.
6 Moses* and Aaron* were some of his
    priests,
  and Samuel was one of the men who
    called on his name.
  They prayed to the LORD,
  and he answered them.
7 God spoke from the tall cloud,
  and they obeyed his commands
  and the law he gave them.
8 LORD our God, you answered their
    prayers.
  You showed them that you are a
    forgiving God
  and that you punish people for the evil
    they do.
9 Praise the LORD our God.
  Bow down toward his holy mountain
  and worship him.
  The LORD our God is holy!

100
A song of thanks.

1 Earth, sing to the LORD!
2 Be happy as you serve the LORD!
  Come before him with happy songs!
3 Know that the LORD is God.
  He made us, and we belong to him.
  We are his people, the sheep he takes
    care of.
4 Come through the gates to his Temple*
    giving thanks to him.
  Enter his courtyards with songs of
    praise.
  Honor him and bless his name.

5 The LORD is good!
  There is no end to his faithful love.
  We can trust him forever and ever!

101
*A song of David.**

1 I will sing about love and justice.
  LORD, I will sing to you.
2 I will be careful to live a pure life.
  I will live in my house with complete
    honesty.
  When will you come to me?
3 I will not even look at anything
    shameful.b
  I hate all wrongdoing.
  I want no part of it!
4 I will not be involved in anything
    dishonest.
  I will have nothing to do with evil.
5 I will stop anyone who secretly
  says bad things about a neighbor.
  I will not allow people to be proud
  and think they are better than others.

6 I will look throughout the land for those
    who can be trusted.
  Only such people can live with me.
  Only those who live pure lives can be
    my servants.
7 I will never let a dishonest person live in
    my house.
  I will not let liars stay near me.
8 My goal each day will be to destroy the
    wicked living in our land.
  I will force all who do evil to leave the
    city of the LORD.

102
*A prayer for a time of suffering, when
anyone feels weak and wants to tell
their complaints to the LORD.*

1 LORD, hear my prayer.
  Listen to my cry for help.
2 Don't turn away from me when I have
    troubles.
  Listen to me, and answer me quickly
    when I cry for help.
3 My life is passing away like smoke.
  My life is like a fire slowly burning out.
4 My strength is gone—
  I am like dry, dying grass.
  I even forget to eat.
5 Because of my sadness, I am losing so
    much weight
  that my skin hangs from my bones.
6 I am lonely, like an owl living in the
    desert,
  like an owl living among old ruined
    buildings.
7 I cannot sleep.
  I am like a lonely bird on the roof.
8 My enemies insult me all the time.
  They make fun of me and use me as an
    example in their curses.*

---

a99:5 *footstool* This probably means the Temple.
See "Temple" in the Word List.

b101:3 *anything shameful* Or "an idol."

9 My great sadness is my only food.
   My tears fall into my drink.
10 You were angry with me,
   so you picked me up and threw me
   away.

11 My life is almost finished, like the long
   shadows at the end of the day.
   I am like dry and dying grass.
12 But you, Lord, will rule as king forever!
   Your name will continue forever and
   ever!
13 You will rise up and comfort Zion.*
   The time has come for you to be kind to
   Zion.
14 Your servants love her stones.
   They love even the dust of that city!
15 The nations will worship the Lord's name.
   All the kings on earth will honor you.
16 The Lord will rebuild Zion,
   and people will again see her glory.*
17 He will listen to the prayers of those in
   poverty.
   He will not ignore them.
18 Write these things for future generations,
   so that they will praise the Lord.
19 The Lord will look down from his Holy
   Place* above.
   He will look down at the earth from
   heaven.
20 And he will hear the prisoner's prayers.
   He will free those who were
   condemned to die.
21 Then people in Zion will tell about the
   Lord.
   They will praise his name in Jerusalem
22 when nations gather together
   and kingdoms come to serve the Lord.

23 My strength failed me.
   My life is cut short.
24 So I said, "Don't let me die while I am
   still young.
   God, you will live forever and ever!
25 Long ago, you made the world.
   You made the sky with your own hands!
26 The earth and sky will end,
   but you will live forever!
   They will wear out like clothes,
   and like clothes, you will change them.
27 But you never change.
   You will live forever!
28 We are your servants today.
   Our children will live here,
   and their descendants will come here to
   worship you."

103 *A song of David.**

1 My soul, praise the Lord!
   Every part of me, praise his holy* name!
2 My soul, praise the Lord
   and never forget how kind he is!
3 He forgives all our sins
   and heals all our sicknesses.

4 He saves us from the grave,
   and he gives us love and compassion.
5 He gives us plenty of good things.
   He makes us young again,
   like an eagle that grows new feathers.
6 The Lord does what is fair.
   He brings justice to all who have been
   hurt by others.
7 He taught his laws to Moses.*
   He let Israel* see the powerful things he
   can do.
8 The Lord is kind and merciful.
   He is patient and full of love.
9 He does not always criticize.
   He does not stay angry with us forever.
10 We sinned against him,
   but he didn't give us the punishment
   we deserved.
11 His love for his followers is
   as high above us as heaven is above the
   earth.
12 And he has taken our sins
   as far away from us as the east is from
   the west.
13 The Lord is as kind to his followers
   as a father is to his children.
14 He knows all about us.
   He knows we are made from dust.
15 He knows our lives are short,
   that they are like grass.
   He knows we are like a little wildflower
   that grows so quickly,
16 but when the hot wind blows, it dies.
   Soon, you cannot even see where the
   flower was.
17 But the Lord has always loved his
   followers,
   and he will continue to love them
   forever and ever!
   He will be good to all their descendants,
18 to those who are faithful to his
   agreement*
   and who remember to obey his
   commands.
19 The Lord set his throne up in heaven,
   and he rules over everything.
20 Angels, praise the Lord!
   You angels are the powerful soldiers
   who obey his commands.
   You listen to him and obey his
   commands.
21 Praise the Lord, all his armies.*a*
   You are his servants,
   and you do what he wants.
22 Everything the Lord has made should
   praise him
   throughout the world that he rules!
   My soul, praise the Lord!

---

*a*103:21 *armies* This word can mean "armies,"
"angels," or the "stars and planets." This word is
part of the name translated "Lord All-Powerful." It
shows that God is in control of all the powers in the
universe.

104

¹My soul, praise the LORD!
LORD my God, you are very great!
You are clothed with glory* and honor.
² You wear light like a robe.
You spread out the skies like a curtain.
³ You built your home above them.ᵃ
You use the thick clouds like a chariot*
and ride across the sky on the wings of
the wind.
⁴ You make the winds your messengers
and flames of fire your servants.ᵇ
⁵ You built the earth on its foundations,
so it can never be moved.
⁶ You covered it with water like a blanket.
The water covered even the mountains.
⁷ But you gave the command, and the water
turned back.
You shouted at the water, and it rushed
away.
⁸ The water flowed down from the
mountains into the valleys,
to the places you made for it.
⁹ You set the limits for the seas,
and the water will never again rise to
cover the earth.

¹⁰ Lord, you cause water to flow from
springs into the streams
that flow down between the mountains.
¹¹ The streams provide water for all the wild
animals.
Even the wild donkeys come there to
drink.
¹² Wild birds come to live by the pools;
they sing in the branches of nearby
trees.
¹³ You send rain down on the mountains.
The earth gets everything it needs from
what you have made.
¹⁴ You make the grass grow to feed the
animals.
You provide plants for the crops we
grow—the plants that give us food
from the earth.
¹⁵ You give us the wine that makes us happy,
the oil that makes our skin soft,ᶜ
and the food that makes us strong.

¹⁶ The great cedar trees of Lebanon belong
to the LORD.
He planted them and gives them the
water they need.
¹⁷ That's where the birds make their nests,
and the storks live in the fir trees.

¹⁸ The high mountains are a home for wild
goats.
The large rocks are hiding places for
rock badgers.

¹⁹ Lord, you made the moon to show us
when the festivals begin.
And the sun always knows when to set.
²⁰ You made darkness to be the night—
the time when wild animals come out
and roam around.
²¹ Lions roar as they attack,
as if they are asking God for the food he
gives them.
²² When the sun rises, they leave
and go back to their dens to rest.
²³ Then people go out to do their work,
and they work until evening.

²⁴ LORD, you created so many things!
With your wisdom you made them all.
The earth is full of the living things you
made.
²⁵ Look at the ocean, so big and wide!
It is filled with all kinds of sea life.
There are creatures large and small—
too many to count!
²⁶ Ships sail over the ocean,
and playing there is Leviathan,ᵈ
the great sea creature you made.

²⁷ Lord, all living things depend on you.
You give them food at the right time.
²⁸ You give it, and they eat it.
They are filled with good food from your
open hands.
²⁹ When you turn away from them,
they become frightened.
When you take away their breath,ᵉ
they die, and their bodies return to the
dust.
³⁰ But when you send out your life-giving
breath,ᶠ
things come alive, and the world is like
new again!

³¹ May the LORD's glory continue forever!
May the LORD enjoy what he made.
³² He just looks at the earth,
and it trembles.
He just touches the mountains,
and smoke rises from them.

³³ I will sing to the LORD for the rest of my
life.
I will sing praises to my God as long as I
live.
³⁴ May my words be pleasing to him.

ᵃ**104:3 above them** Literally, "on the water above."
This is like the picture of the world in Gen. 1. There
the sky was like a bowl turned upside down on the
earth. There was water below the bowl and water
above it.
ᵇ**104:4** Or "You make your angels spirits and your
servants flames of fire." This may be a wordplay
referring to the Cherub and Seraph angels.
ᶜ**104:15 makes our skin soft** Literally, "makes our
face shine." This can also mean "makes us happy."

ᵈ**104:26 Leviathan** This might mean any large sea
animal, like a whale. But it probably means "the
sea monster," the "Dragon," or "Rahab." This creature
represents the great power of the ocean, the power
that God controls.
ᵉ**104:29 breath** Or "spirit."
ᶠ**104:30 life-giving breath** Or "Spirit."

The LORD is the one who makes me happy.

35 I wish sinners would disappear from the earth.
I wish the wicked would be gone forever.
My soul, praise the LORD!

Praise the LORD!

105

¹Give thanks to the LORD and call out to him!
Tell the nations what he has done!
2 Sing to him; sing praises to him.
Tell about the amazing things he has done.
3 Be proud of his holy name.
You followers of the LORD, be happy!
4 Depend on the LORD for strength.
Always go to him for help.
5 Remember the amazing things he has done.
Remember his miracles* and his fair decisions.
6 You belong to the family of his servant Abraham.*
You are descendants of Jacob,* the people God chose.
7 The LORD is our God.
He rules the whole world.
8 He will remember his agreement* forever.
He will always keep the promises he made to his people.
9 He will keep the agreement he made with Abraham
and the promise he made to Isaac.*
10 He gave it as a law to Jacob.
He gave it to Israel* as an agreement that will last forever!
11 He said, "I will give you the land of Canaan.*
It will be your very own."
12 At the time God said this, there were only a few of his people,
and they were strangers there.
13 They traveled around from nation to nation,
from one kingdom to another.
14 But the Lord did not let anyone mistreat them.
He warned kings not to harm them.
15 He said, "Don't hurt my chosen people.
Don't harm my prophets.*"
16 He caused a famine* in that country,
and people did not have enough food.
17 But he sent a man named Joseph to go ahead of them.
Joseph was sold like a slave.
18 They tied a rope around his feet
and put an iron ring around his neck.
19 Joseph was a slave until what he said had really happened.
The LORD's message proved that Joseph was right.
20 So the king of Egypt set him free.

That nation's leader let him out of jail.
21 He put Joseph in charge of his house.
Joseph took care of everything the king owned.
22 Joseph gave instructions to the other leaders.
He taught the older men.
23 Then Israel came to Egypt.
Jacob lived there in Ham's country.ᵃ
24 Jacob's family became very large
and more powerful than their enemies.
25 So the Egyptians began to hate his people.
They made plans against his servants.
26 So the Lord sent Moses,* his servant,
and Aaron,* his chosen priest.
27 He used Moses and Aaron
to do many miracles in Ham's country.
28 He sent darkness to cover their land,
but the Egyptians did not listen to him.
29 So he changed the water into blood,
and all their fish died.
30 Their country was filled with frogs,
even in the king's bedroom.
31 The Lord gave the command,
and the flies and gnats came.
They were everywhere!
32 He made the rain become hail.
Lightning struck throughout their land.
33 He destroyed their vines and fig trees.
He destroyed every tree in their country.
34 He gave the command, and the locusts and grasshoppers came.
There were too many to count!
35 They ate all the plants in the country,
including all the crops in their fields.
36 Then the Lord killed every firstborn* in their country.
He killed their oldest sons.
37 He led his people out of Egypt.
They were carrying gold and silver,
and none of them stumbled or fell behind.
38 Egypt was happy to see his people go,
because they were afraid of them.
39 The Lord spread out his cloud like a blanket.
He used his column of fire to give his people light at night.
40 They asked for food, and he sent them quail.
He also gave them plenty of bread from heaven.
41 He split the rock, and water came bubbling out.
A river began flowing in the desert!

42 The Lord remembered his holy promise
that he had made to his servant Abraham.
43 He brought his people out of Egypt.
They came out rejoicing and singing their happy songs!

ᵃ105:23 Ham's country Or "Egypt." The Egyptians were Ham's descendants. See Gen. 10:6–20.

44 Then he gave his people the lands of
    other nations.
    His people got what others had worked
    for.
45 He did this so that his people would obey
    his laws
    and follow his teachings.

Praise the Lord!

106
1Praise the Lord!
Give thanks to the Lord because
he is good!
His faithful love will last forever!
2 No one can describe how great the Lord
    really is.
    No one can praise him enough.
3 Those who obey his commands are happy.
    They do good things all the time.

4 Lord, remember me when you show
    kindness to your people.
    Remember to save me too!
5 Let me share in the good things
    that you do for your chosen people.
    Let me rejoice with your nation.
    Let me join with your people in praise.

6 We sinned just as our ancestors* did.
    We were wrong; we did bad things!
7 Lord, our ancestors learned nothing
    from the miracles* you did in Egypt.
    They forgot your kindness at the Red Sea
    and rebelled against you.

8 But the Lord saved our ancestors for the
    honor of his name.
    He saved them to show his great power.
9 He gave the command, and the Red Sea
    became dry.
    He led them through the deep sea on
    land as dry as the desert.
10 He saved our ancestors
    and rescued them from their enemies.
11 He covered their enemies with the sea.
    Not one of them escaped!

12 Then our ancestors believed what he said.
    They sang praises to him.
13 But they quickly forgot about what he did.
    They did not listen to his advice.
14 They became hungry in the desert,
    and they tested him in the wilderness.
15 He gave them what they asked for,
    but he also gave them a terrible
    disease.
16 The people became jealous of Moses.*
    They became jealous of Aaron,* the
    Lord's holy priest.
17 The ground opened up and swallowed
    Dathan.
    Then the ground closed up and covered
    Abiram's group.
18 Then a fire burned that mob of people.
    It burned those wicked people.

19 The people made a golden calf at Mount
    Horeb.*
    They worshiped a statue!
20 They traded their glorious God
    for a statue of a grass-eating bull!
21 They forgot all about God, the one who
    saved them,
    the one who did the miracles in Egypt.
22 He did amazing things there in Ham's
    country*a!
    He did awesome things at the Red Sea!

23 God wanted to destroy those people,
    but Moses, the leader he chose, stood in
    the way.
    God was very angry, but Moses begged
    him to stop,
    so God did not destroy the people.*b

24 But then they refused to go into the
    wonderful land of Canaan.*
    They did not believe that God would
    help them defeat the people there.
25 Our ancestors complained in their tents
    and refused to obey the Lord.
26 So he swore that they would die in the
    desert.
27 He promised to scatter them among the
    nations
    and to let other people defeat their
    descendants.

28 At Baal Peor they joined in worshiping
    Baal*
    and ate sacrifices to honor the dead.*c
29 The Lord became angry with his people,
    so he made them sick.
30 But Phinehas prayed*d to God,
    and God stopped the sickness.
31 He considered what Phinehas did a good
    work,
    and it will be remembered forever and
    ever.

32 At Meribah the people made the Lord
    angry
    and created trouble for Moses.
33 They upset Moses,
    and he spoke without stopping to think.

34 The Lord told the people to destroy the
    other nations living in Canaan.

a106:22 Ham's country Or "Egypt." The Egyptians
were Ham's descendants. See Gen. 10:6–20.
*b106:23 Or "God said he would destroy them. But
Moses, his chosen one, stood in the breach and
repelled his anger from destroying." This compares
Moses to a soldier standing at a break in a wall
defending the city against enemy soldiers.
c106:28 the dead This might refer to "lifeless gods"
or to dead friends or relatives honored with meals
eaten at their graves.
d106:30 prayed Or "intervened," or "judged."
Phinehas not only prayed to God, but he also did
something to stop the people from doing these
sins. See Num. 25:1–16.

But the Israelites did not obey him.
35 They mixed with the other people
   and did what those people were doing.
36 They began worshiping the false gods
   those people worshiped.
   And their idols* became a trap.
37 They even offered their own children
   as sacrifices to demons.
38 They killed their innocent sons and
   daughters
   and offered them to the false gods of
   Canaan.
   So the land was polluted with the sin of
   murder.
39 They were unfaithful to him,
   and they became dirty with the sins of
   other nations.
40 So the LORD became angry with his
   people.
   He rejected those who belonged to him.
41 He gave his people to other nations
   and let their enemies rule over them.
42 Their enemies controlled them
   and made life hard for them.
43 He saved his people many times,
   but they turned against him and did
   what they wanted to do.
   His people did many bad things.
44 But whenever they were in trouble,
   he listened to their prayers.
45 He always remembered his agreement,*
   and because of his faithful love, he
   comforted them.
46 Other nations took them as prisoners,
   but he caused them to be kind to his
   people.
47 LORD our God, save us!
   Bring us back together from those
   nations.
   Then we will give thanks to your holy
   name
   and joyfully praise you.
48 Praise the LORD, the God of Israel!
   He always was and will always be
   worthy of praise.
   Let all the people say, "Amen*!"

   Praise the LORD!

BOOK 5 (Psalms 107–150)

107
¹Praise the LORD, because he is
good!
His faithful love will last forever!
2 Everyone the LORD has saved should
   repeat that word of thanks.
   Praise him, all who have been rescued
   from the enemy.
3 He gathered his people together from
   many different countries.
   He brought them from east and west,
   north and south.ᵃ

4 Some of them wandered in the dry desert.
   They were looking for a place to live,
   but they could not find a city.
5 They were hungry and thirsty
   and growing weak.
6 Then they called to the LORD for help,
   and he saved them from their troubles.
7 He led them straight to the city where
   they would live.
8 Thank the LORD for his faithful love
   and for the amazing things he does for
   people.
9 He satisfies those who are thirsty.
   He fills those who are hungry with good
   things.

10 Some of God's people were prisoners,
   locked behind bars in dark prisons.
11 That was because they had fought against
   what God said.
   They refused to listen to the advice of
   God Most High.
12 God made life hard for those people
   because of what they did.
   They stumbled and fell,
   and there was no one to help them.
13 They were in trouble, so they called to
   the LORD for help,
   and he saved them from their troubles.
14 He took them out of their dark prisons.
   He broke the ropes that held them.
15 Thank the LORD for his faithful love
   and for the amazing things he does for
   people.
16 He breaks down their bronze gates.
   He shatters their iron bars.

17 Some people became fools and turned
   against God,
   and they suffered for the evil they did.
18 They became so sick that they refused to
   eat,
   so they almost died.
19 They were in trouble, so they called to
   the LORD for help,
   and he saved them from their troubles.
20 He gave the command and healed them,
   so they were saved from the grave.
21 Thank the LORD for his faithful love
   and for the amazing things he does for
   people.
22 Offer sacrifices* of thanks to him.
   Sing with joy about all that he has done.

23 Some sailed the sea in ships.
   Their work carried them across the
   water.
24 They saw what the LORD can do.
   They saw the amazing things he did at
   sea.
25 He gave the command, and a strong wind
   began to blow.
   The waves became higher and higher.
26 The waves lifted them high into the sky
   and dropped them into the deep sea.

ᵃ107:3 south Or "the Sea." This might refer to all the
coastal areas around the Mediterranean Sea.

The storm was so dangerous that the men
  lost their courage.
27 They were stumbling and falling like
  someone who is drunk.
  Their skill as sailors was useless.
28 They were in trouble, so they called to
  the LORD for help,
  and he saved them from their troubles.
29 He stopped the storm
  and calmed the waves.
30 The sailors were happy that the sea was
  calm again,
  and the LORD led them safely to where
  they wanted to go.
31 Thank the LORD for his faithful love
  and for the amazing things he does for
  people.
32 Praise God in the great assembly.
  Praise him when the older leaders meet
  together.

33 He changed rivers into a desert.
  He stopped springs from flowing.
34 He made the fertile land become salty,
  because the people living there did such
  evil things.
35 He changed the desert into a land with
  pools of water.
  He caused springs to flow from dry
  ground.
36 He led the hungry to that good land,
  and they built a city to live in.
37 They planted seeds in their fields and
  grapes in their vineyards,*
  and they had a good harvest.
38 The LORD blessed them.
  Their families grew,
  and they had many animals.
39 But because of disaster and troubles,
  their families became small and weak.
40 The LORD shamed their leaders.
  He let them wander through the desert,
  where there are no roads.
41 But then he rescued the poor from their
  misery,
  and now their families are large like
  flocks of sheep.
42 Good people see this and are happy.
  But the wicked see it and don't know
  what to say.
43 Whoever is wise will remember these
  things
  and begin to understand the LORD's
  faithful love.

108 *A praise song of David.**

1 God, I am ready, heart and soul,
  to sing songs of praise.
  Wake up, my soul!
2 Harps and lyres,* wake up,
  and let's wake the dawn!
3 LORD, I will praise you before all people.
  I will sing praises about you to every
  nation.

4 Your faithful love is higher than the
  highest clouds in the sky!
5 Rise above the heavens, God.
  Let all the world see your glory.*
6 Use your great power and help us!
  Answer my prayer and save the people
  you love.

7 God has made this promise in his
  Temple*:
  "I will win the war and rejoice in victory!
  I will divide this land among my people.
  I will give them Shechem.
  I will give them Succoth Valley.
8 Gilead and Manasseh will be mine.
  Ephraim* will be my helmet.
  Judah* will be my royal scepter.*
9 Moab will be the bowl for washing my
  feet.
  Edom will be the slave who carries my
  sandals.
  I will defeat the Philistines* and shout
  in victory!"

10-11 But, God, it seems that you have left us!
  You do not go out with our army.
  So who will lead me into the strong,
  protected city?
  Who will lead me into battle against
  Edom?
12 Help us defeat the enemy!
  No one on earth can rescue us.
13 Only God can make us strong.
  Only God can defeat our enemies!

109 *To the director**:
*A praise song of David.**

1 God, I praise you!
  Hear my prayer and do something!
2 Wicked people are telling lies about me.
  They are saying things that are not true.
3 They are saying hateful things about me.
  They are attacking me for no reason.
4 I loved them, but they were against me.
  So I said a prayer.
5 I did good things to them,
  but they are doing bad things to me.
  I loved them,
  but they hated me.

6 They said, "Choose someone evil to
  represent him.
  Let the one at his side really be his
  accuser.
7 Let even his prayer be used as evidence
  against him,
  and let the court find him guilty.
8 Let his life be cut short,
  and let someone else take over his work.
9 Let his children become orphans and his
  wife a widow.
10 Make his children wander around as
  beggars,

*a***108:7** *in his Temple* Or "in his holiness."

forced from homes that lie in ruins.

11 Let the people he owes take everything
he owns.
Let strangers get everything he worked
for.
12 Let no one be kind to him.
Let no one show mercy to his children.
13 May his family come to an end.
May his name be unknown to future
generations.
14 May the LORD remember the sins of his
father,
and may his mother's sins never be
erased.
15 May the LORD remember their sins
forever,
and may he cause people to forget his
family completely.
16 He never did anything good.
He never loved anyone.
He made life hard for the poor and the
helpless.
17 He loved to curse* others,
so let those bad things happen to him.
He never blessed others,
so don't let good things happen to him.
18 Cursing was a daily part of his life,
like the clothes he wears.
Cursing others became a part of him,
like the water he drinks and the oil he
puts on his body.
19 So let curses cover him like the robe he
wears
and always surround him like a belt."

20 My enemies said these evil things against
me.
But may those curses be the way the
LORD punishes them.
21 My Lord GOD, treat me in a way that
brings honor to your name.
Save me because of your faithful love.
22 I am only a poor, helpless man.
I am so sad; my heart is broken.
23 I feel my life is over, fading like a shadow
at day's end.
I feel like a bug that someone brushed
away.
24 My knees are weak from fasting.*
I have lost weight and become thin.
25 My enemies insult me.
They look at me and shake their heads.
26 LORD my God, help me!
Show your faithful love and save me!
27 Then they will know that you did it.
They will know that it was your power,
LORD, that helped me.
28 They curse me, but you can bless me.
They attacked me, so defeat them.
Then I, your servant, will be happy.
29 Humiliate my enemies!
Let them wear their shame like a coat.
30 I give thanks to the LORD.
I praise him in front of everyone.
31 He stands by the helpless

and saves them from those who try to
put them to death.

110 *A praise song of David.**

1 The LORD said to my lord,*a*
"Sit at my right side, while I put your
enemies under your control."

2 The LORD will cause your kingdom to
grow, beginning at Zion,*
until you rule the lands of your
enemies!
3 Your people will gladly join you
when you gather your army together.
You will wear your special clothes
and meet together early in the morning.
Your young men will be all around you
like dew on the ground.*b*

4 The LORD has made a promise with an
oath*
and will not change his mind:
"You are a priest forever—
the kind of priest Melchizedek was."

5 My Lord is at your right side.
He will defeat the other kings when he
becomes angry.
6 He will judge the nations.
The ground will be covered with dead
bodies.
He will punish the leaders of powerful
nations all around the world.

7 The king will drink from a stream on the
way.
Then he will lift his head and become
strong!*c*

111 *d* 1Praise the LORD!
I thank the LORD with all my heart
in the assembly of his good people.
2 The LORD does wonderful things,
more than anyone could ask for.*e*
3 He does glorious and wonderful things!
There is no end to his goodness.
4 He does amazing things so that we will
remember
that the LORD is kind and merciful.
5 He gives food to his followers.
He remembers his agreement* forever.

---

*a*110:1 *my lord* That is, the king.
*b*110:3 The Hebrew text here is hard to understand.
Literally, "Your people will be freewill offerings on
your day of power. In holy splendor from the womb
of dawn your dew of youth will be yours."
*c*110:7 *lift his head and become strong* Literally,
"lift his head." Here, the poet probably means two
things: "he will raise his head after drinking the
water," and "he will become strong or important."
*d*Psalm 111 In Hebrew, each line of this psalm
begins with the next letter in the alphabet.
*e*111:2 *more ... for* Literally, "requested for all their
desires."

6 He has shown his people how powerful
    he is
    by giving them the land of other
    nations.
7 Everything he does is good and fair.
    All his commands can be trusted.
8 His commands will continue forever.
    They must be done with truth and
    honesty.
9 He rescued his people and made his
    agreement with them forever.
    His name is awesome and holy.
10 Wisdom begins with fear and respect for
    the LORD.
    Those who obey him are very wise.
    Praises will be sung to him forever.

112 *a* 1Praise the LORD!
    Great blessings belong to those
    who fear and respect the LORD,
    who are happy to do what he
    commands.
2 Their descendants will be given power on
    earth.
    Those who do right will be greatly
    blessed.
3 Their family will be very rich,
    and their goodness will continue
    forever.
4 A light shines in the dark for those who
    are good,
    for those who are merciful, kind, and
    fair.
5 It is good for people to be kind and
    generous
    and to be fair in business.
6 Such good people will never fall.
    They will always be remembered.
7 They will not be afraid of bad news.
    They are confident because they trust in
    the LORD.
8 They remain confident and without fear,
    so they defeat their enemies.
9 They freely give to the poor.
    Their goodness will continue forever.
    They will be honored with victory.
10 The wicked become angry when they see
    this.
    They grind their teeth in anger, but
    then they disappear.
    They will never get what they want
    most.

113 1Praise the LORD!
    Servants of the LORD, praise him!
    Praise the LORD's name.
2 May the LORD's name be praised now and
    forever.
3 May the LORD's name be praised
    from where the sun rises to where it
    goes down.

*a*Psalm 112 In Hebrew, each line of this psalm
begins with the next letter in the alphabet.

4 The LORD is higher than all nations.
    His glory* rises to the skies.
5 There is no one like the LORD our God.
    He sits on his throne high in heaven.
6 He is so high above us
    that he must look down to see the sky
    and the earth.
7 He lifts the poor out of the dirt
    and rescues beggars from the garbage
    dump.
8 He puts them in important positions,
    giving them a place among the leaders
    of his people.
9 He gives children to the woman whose
    home is empty.
    He makes her a happy mother.

Praise the LORD!

114 1The people of Israel* escaped
    from Egypt.
    Yes, Jacob's* descendants left that
    foreign country.
2 Then Judah* became God's special people,
    and Israel became his kingdom.
3 The Red Sea saw this and ran away.
    The Jordan River turned and ran.
4 The mountains danced like rams.
    The hills danced like lambs.

5 Red Sea, why did you run away?
    Jordan River, why did you turn and run
    away?
6 Mountains, why did you dance like rams?
    Hills, why did you dance like lambs?

7 The earth shook in front of the Lord, the
    God of Jacob.
8 He is the one who caused water to flow
    from a rock.
    He made a spring of water flow from
    that hard rock.

115 1Lord, you should receive the
    honor, not us.
    The honor belongs to you
    because of your faithful love and loyalty.
2 Why should the nations wonder where
    our God is?
3 Our God is in heaven, and he does
    whatever he wants.
4 The "gods" of those nations are only
    statues
    that some human made from gold and
    silver.
5 Those statues have mouths, but cannot
    talk.
    They have eyes, but cannot see.
6 They have ears, but cannot hear.
    They have noses, but cannot smell.
7 They have hands, but cannot feel.
    They have feet, but cannot walk.
    No sounds come from their throats.
8 The people who make and trust in those
    statues will become like them!

9 People of Israel,* trust in the LORD!
　　He is your strength and shield.
10 Aaron's* family, trust in the LORD!
　　He is your strength and shield.
11 Followers of the LORD, trust in the LORD!
　　He is your strength and shield.

12 The LORD remembers us.
　　He will bless us.
　　He will bless Israel.
　　He will bless Aaron's family.
13 The LORD will bless his followers, great
　　and small.

14 May the LORD give more and more to you
　　and to your children.
15 May you receive blessings from the
　　LORD,*a*
　　who made heaven and earth.
16 Heaven belongs to the LORD,
　　but he gave the earth to people.
17 The dead don't praise him.
　　Those in the grave don't praise the
　　LORD.
18 But we will praise the LORD now and
　　forever!

Praise the LORD!

116 1 I love the LORD for hearing me,
　　for listening to my prayers.
2 Yes, he paid attention to me,
　　so I will always call to him whenever I
　　need help.
3 Death's ropes were around me.
　　The grave was closing in on me.
　　I was worried and afraid.
4 Then I called on the LORD's name.
　　I said, "LORD, save me!"
5 The LORD is good and merciful;
　　our God is so kind.
6 The LORD takes care of helpless people.
　　I was without help, and he saved me.
7 My soul, relax!
　　The LORD is caring for you.
8 Lord, you saved my soul from death.
　　You stopped my tears.
　　You kept me from falling.
9 I will continue to serve the LORD in the
　　land of the living.

10 I continued believing even when I said,
　　"I am completely ruined!"
11 Yes, even when I was upset and said,
　　"There is no one I can trust!"

12 What can I give the LORD
　　for all that he has done for me?
13 He saved me,
　　so I will give him a drink offering,
　　and I will call on the LORD's name.

14 I will give the LORD what I promised.
　　I will go in front of all his people now.
15 Very dear to the LORD are the lives of his
　　followers.
　　He cares when they face death.
16 LORD, I am your servant!
　　Yes, I am your slave, as my mother was.
　　You set me free from the chains of
　　death.
17 I will give you a thank offering.
　　I will call on the LORD's name.
18 I will stand before the gathering of his
　　people
　　and give the LORD what I promised.
19 I will do this in Jerusalem,
　　in the courtyards of the LORD's Temple.*

Praise the LORD!

117 1 Praise the LORD, all you nations.
　　Praise him, all you people.
2 He loves us very much!
　　The LORD will be faithful to us forever!

Praise the LORD!

118 1 Praise the LORD because he is
　　good!
　　His faithful love will last forever!
2 Israel,* say it:
　　"His faithful love will last forever!"
3 Aaron's family,*b* say it:
　　"His faithful love will last forever!"
4 You people worshiping the LORD, say it:
　　"His faithful love will last forever!"

5 I was in trouble, so I called to the LORD
　　for help.
　　The LORD answered and made me free.
6 The LORD is with me, so I will not be
　　afraid.
　　No one on earth can do anything to
　　harm me.
7 The LORD is my helper.
　　I will see my enemies defeated.
8 It is better to trust in the LORD
　　than to trust in people.
9 It is better to trust in the LORD
　　than to trust in great leaders.

10 Many enemies surrounded me,
　　but with the LORD's power I defeated
　　them.
11 They surrounded me again and again,
　　but I defeated them with the LORD's
　　power.
12 They surrounded me like a swarm of
　　bees,
　　but they were quickly destroyed like a
　　fast-burning bush.
　　I defeated them with the LORD's power.

---

*a*115:15 *May ... the LORD* Or "The LORD welcomes
you with a blessing."

*b*118:3 *Aaron's family* That is, the priests.

13 My enemy attacked me and almost
      destroyed me,
      but the LORD helped me.
14 The LORD is my strength and my reason
      for singing.[a]
      He saved me!
15 You can hear the victory celebration in
      the homes of those who live right.
      The LORD has shown his great power
      again!
16 The LORD's arm is raised in victory.
      The LORD has shown his great power
      again.

17 I will live and not die,
      and I will tell what the LORD has done.
18 The LORD punished me,
      but he did not let me die.
19 Gates of goodness, open for me,
      and I will come in and worship the
      LORD.
20 Those are the LORD's gates,
      and only good people can go through
      them.
21 Lord, I thank you for answering my prayer.
      I thank you for saving me.

22 The stone that the builders rejected
      became the cornerstone.*
23 The LORD made this happen,
      and we think it is wonderful!
24 This is the day the LORD has made.
      Let us rejoice and be happy today!

25 ⌊The people say,⌋ "Praise the LORD!
      The LORD saved us!"[b]
26 Welcome to the one who comes in the
      name of the LORD."

⌊The priests answer,⌋ "We welcome you to
      the LORD's house!"
27 The LORD is God, and he accepts us.
      Tie up the lamb for the sacrifice* and
      carry it to the horns of the altar.*"

28 LORD, you are my God, and I thank you.
      My God, I praise you!
29 Praise the LORD because he is good.
      His faithful love will last forever.

Aleph[c]

119 ¹Great blessings belong to those
      who live pure lives!
      They follow the LORD's teachings.
2 Great blessings belong to those who
      follow his rules!

They seek him with all their heart.
3 They don't do wrong.
      They follow his ways.
4 Lord, you gave us your instructions
      and told us to always obey them.
5 How I wish I could be more faithful
      in obeying your laws!
6 Then I would never feel ashamed
      when I look closely at your commands.
7 The more I understand how fair your laws
      are,
      the more sincerely I will praise you.
8 I will obey your laws,
      so please don't leave me!

Beth

9 How can a young person live a pure life?
      By obeying your word.
10 I try with all my heart to serve you.
      Help me obey your commands.
11 I study your teachings very carefully
      so that I will not sin against you.
12 LORD, you are worthy of praise!
      Teach me your laws.
13 I will repeat the laws we have heard from
      you.
14 I enjoy following your rules
      as much as others enjoy great riches.
15 I will study your instructions.
      I will give thought to your way of life.
16 I enjoy your laws.
      I will not forget your word.

Gimel

17 Be good to me, your servant,
      so that I may live to obey your word.
18 Open my eyes so that I can see
      all the wonderful things in your
      teachings.
19 I feel like a stranger visiting here on earth.
      I need to know your commands.
      Don't keep them hidden from me.
20 I constantly feel a hunger
      to understand your laws.
21 You tell the proud how angry you are with
      them.
      All those who refuse to obey your word
      are cursed.*
22 Don't let me be ashamed and embarrassed.
      I have obeyed your rules.
23 Even if rulers say bad things about me,
      I am your servant,
      and I continue to study your laws.
24 Your rules make me happy.
      They give me good advice.

Daleth

25 I lie here like a dying man.
      Say the word, and I will live again.[d]
26 I told you about my life, and you
      answered me.
      Now, teach me your laws.

---

[a]**118:14** *my reason for singing* Or "my protection."
[b]**118:25** Literally, "LORD, please save us. LORD, please
make us successful." This was a shout of victory to
honor a king returning after winning a war.
[c]**Psalm 119** *Aleph* The first letter of the Hebrew
alphabet. This psalm has a section for each letter of
the Hebrew alphabet, and each of the eight verses
in each section begins with the Hebrew letter for
its section.

[d]**119:25** *Say ... again* Or "Give me life as you
promised."

27 Help me understand your instructions,
　　and I will think about your wonderful
　　　teachings.[a]
28 I am sad and tired.
　　Say the word, and make me strong
　　　again.
29 Don't let me live a lie.
　　Guide me with your teachings.
30 I have chosen to be loyal to you.
　　I respect your laws.
31 I follow your rules closely, Lord.
　　Don't let me be put to shame.
32 I do my best to follow your commands,
　　because you are the one who gives me
　　　the desire.

He

33 Lord, teach me your laws,
　　and I will always follow them.
34 Help me understand your teachings,
　　and I will follow them.
　　Obeying them will be my greatest
　　　desire.
35 Help me follow your commands,
　　because that makes me happy.
36 Give me the desire to follow your rules,
　　not the desire to get rich.
37 Don't let me look at worthless things.
　　Help me live your way.
38 Do what you promised me, your servant,
　　so that people will respect you.
39 Take away the shame I fear.
　　Your laws are good.
40 See how much I want to obey your
　　　instructions!
　　Be good to me, and let me live.

Waw

41 Lord, show me your faithful love.
　　Save me, as you promised.
42 Then I will have an answer for those who
　　　make fun of me
　　for trusting what you say.
43 Let me always say what is true.
　　I depend on your judgment to be fair.
44 I will follow your teachings forever and
　　　ever.
45 So I will live in freedom,
　　because I do my best to know your
　　　instructions.
46 I will discuss your rules with kings,
　　and no one will embarrass me.
47 What joy your commands give me!
　　How I love them!
48 Not only do I love your commands, but I
　　　also honor them.
　　I will study your laws.

Zain

49 Remember your promise to me, your
　　　servant.
　　It gives me hope.
50 You comfort me in my suffering,

because your promise gives me new life.
51 People full of pride are always making fun
　　　of me,
　　but I have not stopped following your
　　　teachings.
52 I remember the laws you gave us long
　　　ago, Lord,
　　and they bring me comfort.
53 I am overcome with anger when I see
　　　wicked people,
　　who have stopped following your
　　　teachings.
54 Your laws are the songs I sing
　　wherever I am living.
55 Lord, in the night I remembered your
　　　name,
　　and I obeyed your teachings.
56 This happened because I carefully obey
　　　your instructions.

Heth

57 Lord, I decided that my duty is to obey
　　　your commandments.
58 I beg you with all my heart,
　　be kind to me, as you promised.
59 I thought very carefully about my life,
　　and I decided to follow your rules.
60 Without wasting any time, I hurried back
　　　to obey your commands.
61 The wicked tried to trap me,
　　but I have not forgotten your teachings.
62 In the middle of the night, I get up to
　　　thank you
　　because your laws are so fair.
63 I am a friend to everyone who worships
　　　you.
　　I am a friend to everyone who obeys
　　　your instructions.
64 Lord, your faithful love fills the earth.
　　Teach me your laws.

Teth

65 Lord, you did good things for me, your
　　　servant.
　　You did what you promised to do.
66 Give me the knowledge to make wise
　　　decisions.
　　I trust your commands.
67 Before I suffered, I did many wrong
　　　things.
　　But now I carefully obey everything you
　　　say.
68 You are good, and you do good things.
　　Teach me your laws.
69 People full of pride made up lies about me.
　　But I keep obeying your instructions
　　　with all my heart.
70 Those people are so stupid that they care
　　　for nothing,
　　but I enjoy studying your teachings.
71 Suffering was good for me;
　　I learned your laws.
72 Your teachings are worth more to me
　　than a thousand pieces of silver and
　　　gold.

[a]**119:27** *teachings* Or "deeds."

Yod

73 With your hands you made me and
helped me become what I am.
Now help me learn and understand your
commands.
74 Your followers will see me and be happy,
because I trust in your word.
75 LORD, I know that your decisions are fair,
and you were right to punish me.
76 Now comfort me with your faithful love,
as you promised.
77 Comfort me and let me live.
I enjoy your teachings.
78 Bring shame on those proud people who
lied about me.
All I want to do is study your
instructions.
79 Let your followers come back to me
so that they may learn your rules.
80 Let me obey your laws perfectly
so that I will not be ashamed.

Kaph

81 I feel weaker and weaker as I wait for you
to save me.
But I put my trust in your word.
82 I keep looking for what you promised, but
my eyes are feeling tired.
When will you comfort me?
83 Even when I am like a dried wineskin on
the trash pile,
I will not forget your laws.
84 How long must I wait for you
to punish those who persecute me?
85 Proud people have tried to trap me
and make me disobey your teachings.
86 All your commands can be trusted.
Those people are wrong to persecute
me.
Help me!
87 They have almost destroyed me,
but I have not stopped obeying your
instructions.
88 Show me your faithful love and let me
live.
I will do whatever you say.

Lamedh

89 LORD, your word continues forever in
heaven.
90 You are loyal forever and ever.
You made the earth, and it still stands.
91 All things continue today because of your
laws.
Like slaves, they all obey you.
92 If I had not found joy in your teachings,
my suffering would have destroyed me.
93 I will never forget your commands,
because through them you gave me new
life.
94 I am yours, so save me!
I have done my best to know your
instructions.
95 The wicked tried to destroy me,
but your rules made me wise.

96 Everything has its limits,
except your commands.

Mem

97 Oh, how I love your teachings!
I talk about them all the time.
98 Your commands are always with me,
and they make me wiser than my
enemies.
99 I am wiser than all my teachers,
because I study your rules.
100 I understand more than those who are
older,
because I obey your instructions.
101 I have avoided every path that leads to
evil
so that I could obey your word.
102 You are my teacher,
so I will always do whatever you decide.
103 Your words are so sweet to me,
like the taste of honey!
104 I gain understanding from your
instructions,
so I hate anything that leads people the
wrong way.

Nun

105 Your word is like a lamp that guides my
steps,
a light that shows the path I should
take.
106 Your laws are good and fair.
I have promised to obey them, and I
will keep my promise.
107 LORD, I have suffered for a long time.
Say the word, and I will live again![a]
108 LORD, accept the praise I want to give you,
and teach me your laws.
109 My life is always in danger,
but I have not forgotten your teachings.
110 The wicked try to trap me,
but I have not disobeyed your
instructions.
111 The rules you have given me to follow
will be mine forever.
They give me great joy.
112 More than anything I want to obey your
laws always,
until the end of my life.

Samekh

113 Lord, I hate those who are not completely
loyal to you,
but I love your teachings.
114 Hide me and protect me.
I trust what you say.
115 You who are evil, don't come near me
so that I can obey my God's commands.
116 Support me, Lord, as you promised, and I
will live.
I trust in you, so don't disappoint me.
117 Help me and I will be saved.

---

[a] **119:107** *Say … again* Or "Give me life as you promised."

And I will always give attention to your
laws.
118You reject all who don't obey your laws,
because they are liars and did not do
what they said.
119You throw away the wicked of this world
like trash.
So I love your rules.
120I am shaking with fear before you.
I fear and respect your judgments.

Ain

121I have done what is right and good.
Don't let me fall into the hands of those
who want to hurt me.
122Promise to be good to me, your servant.
Don't let those proud people do harm to
me.
123I have worn out my eyes looking for your
help,
waiting for you to save me, as you
promised.
124Show your faithful love to me, your
servant.
Teach me your laws.
125I am your servant.
Give me wisdom to understand your
rules.
126Lord, it is time for you to do something.
The people do what is against your
teachings.
127I love your commands more than gold,
more than the purest gold.
128I carefully obey all your commands.
So I hate anything that leads people the
wrong way.

Pe

129Lord, your rules are wonderful.
That is why I follow them.
130As people understand your word, it brings
light to their lives.
Your word makes even simple people
wise.
131My desire to hear your commands is so
strong
that I wait with open mouth, gasping for
breath.
132Look at me, and be kind to me,
just as you always are to those who love
your name.
133Guide me, as you promised.
Don't let evil rule over me.
134Save me from those who want to hurt me,
and I will obey your instructions.
135Accept your servant,
and teach me your laws.
136I have cried a river of tears
because people don't obey your
teachings.

Tsadhe

137Lord, you do what is right,
and your decisions are fair.
138The rules you have given us are right.

We can trust them completely.
139Something that really upsets me is the
thought
that my enemies ignore your commands.
140I love your word.
Time and again it has been proven true.
141I am young, and people don't respect me.
But I have not forgotten your
instructions.
142Your goodness is forever,
and your teachings can be trusted.
143Even though I have troubles and hard
times,
your commands give me joy.
144Your rules are always right.
Help me understand them so that I can
live.

Qoph

145Lord, I call to you with all my heart.
Answer me, and I will obey your laws.
146I call to you.
Save me, and I will obey your rules.
147I get up early in the morning to pray to
you.
I trust what you say.
148Late into the night I stay awake
to think about your word.
149I know your love is true, so listen to me.
Lord, you always do what is right, so let
me live.
150Here come those who have evil plans to
hurt me.
They live far away from your teachings.
151But you are near me, Lord,
and all your commands can be trusted.
152Long ago, I learned from your rules
that you made them to last forever.

Resh

153Look at my suffering and rescue me.
I have not forgotten your teachings.
154Argue my case, and set me free.
Let me live, as you promised.
155The wicked have no hope of being saved,
because they don't follow your laws.
156Lord, you are very kind.
You always do what is right, so let me
live.
157I have many enemies trying to hurt me,
but I have not stopped following your
rules.
158I look at those traitors* and hate what I
see,
because they refuse to do what you say.
159See how much I love your instructions!
Lord, I know your love is true, so let
me live.
160Every word you say can be trusted.
Your laws are fair and will last forever.

Shin

161Powerful leaders attack me for no reason,
but the only thing I fear is your
command.

162Your word makes me happy,
    like someone who has found a great
      treasure.
163I hate lies; they make me sick!
    But I love your teachings.
164Seven times a day I praise you
    because your laws are fair.
165Those who love your teachings will find
      true peace.
    Nothing can make them fall.
166Lord, I am waiting for you to save me.
    I obey your commands.
167I follow your rules.
    I love them very much.
168I obey all your instructions and rules,
    because you know everything I do.

Taw

169Lord, listen to my cry for help.
    Make me wise, as you promised.
170Listen to my prayer.
    Save me, as you promised.
171I will burst into songs of praise,
    because you have taught me your laws.
172Let my voice sing about your word,
    because all your commands are good.
173I have chosen to follow your instructions,
    so reach out and help me!
174Lord, I want you to save me.
    Your teachings make me happy.
175Let me live to praise you.
    Let me find the help I need in your
      laws.
176I have wandered away like a lost sheep.
    Come and find me.
  I am your servant,
    and I have not forgotten your
      commands.

120 *A song for going up to the Temple.**

1 I was in trouble.
    I called to the Lord for help,
    and he answered me!
2 I said, "Lord, save me from liars,
    from those who say things that are not
      true."

3 Liars, do you know what the Lord has for
     you?
    Do you know what you will get?
4 You will get a soldier's sharp arrow and
    hot coals to punish you.

5 How I hate living here among these
     people!
    It's like living in Meshech or in the tents
     of Kedar.*a*
6 I have lived too long with those who hate
     peace.
7 I ask for peace, but they want war.

121 *A song for going up to the Temple.**

1 I look up to the hills,
    but where will my help really come from?
2 My help will come from the Lord,
    the Creator of heaven and earth.
3 He will not let you fall.
    Your Protector will not fall asleep.
4 Israel's* Protector does not get tired.
    He never sleeps.
5 The Lord is your Protector.
    The Lord stands by your side, shading
     and protecting you.
6 The sun cannot harm you during the day,
    and the moon cannot harm you at night.
7 The Lord will protect you from every
     danger.
    He will protect your soul.
8 The Lord will protect you as you come
     and go,*b*
  both now and forever!

122 *A song of David* for going up to the
Temple.**

1 I was happy when the people said,
    "Let us go to the Lord's Temple."
2 Here we are, standing at the gates of
     Jerusalem.
3 This is New Jerusalem!
    The city has been rebuilt as one united
     city.
4 This is where the tribes come, the tribes
     who belong to the Lord.
    The people of Israel* come here to
     praise the Lord's name.
5 The kings from David's* family put their
     thrones here.
    They set up their thrones to judge the
     people.

6 Pray for peace in Jerusalem:
    "May those who love you find peace.
7   May there be peace within your walls.
    May there be safety in your great
     buildings."

8 For the good of my family and neighbors,
    I pray that there will be peace here.
9 For the good of the Temple* of the Lord
     our God,
    I pray that good things will happen to
     this city.

123 *A song for going up to the Temple.**

1 Lord, I look up and pray to you.
    You sit as King in heaven.
2 A slave looks to his master to provide
     what he needs,
    and a servant girl depends on the
     woman she serves.
  So we depend on the Lord our God,
    waiting for him to have mercy on us.

---

*a*120:5 *Meshech ... Kedar* Places where the people
were known as wild and savage fighters.

*b*121:8 *come and go* This may refer to going to war.

³ Lᴏʀᴅ, be merciful to us,
      because we have been insulted much
            too long.
⁴ We have had enough of the hateful words
      of those proud people
      who make fun of us and show us no
            respect.

124 *A song of David* for going up to the Temple.**

¹ What would have happened to us if the
      Lᴏʀᴅ had not been on our side?
      Tell us about it, Israel.*

² What would have happened to us if the
      Lᴏʀᴅ had not been on our side
      when people attacked us?

³ They would have swallowed us alive
      when they became angry with us.

⁴ Their armies would have been
      like a flood washing over us,
      like a river drowning us.

⁵ Those proud people would have been
      like water rising up to our mouth and
            drowning us.

⁶ Praise the Lᴏʀᴅ!
      He did not let our enemies tear us apart.

⁷ We escaped like a bird from the net of a
      hunter.
      The net broke, and we escaped!

⁸ Our help came from the Lᴏʀᴅ,
      the one who made heaven and earth!

125 *A song for going up to the Temple.**

¹ Those who trust in the Lᴏʀᴅ are like
      Mount Zion.*
      They will never be shaken.
      They will continue forever.

² Like the mountains that surround
      Jerusalem,
      the Lᴏʀᴅ surrounds and protects his
            people now and forever.

³ The wicked will not always control the
      land of those who do right.
      If they did, even those who do right
            might start doing wrong.

⁴ Lᴏʀᴅ, be good to those who are good,
      to those who have pure hearts.

⁵ But, Lᴏʀᴅ, when you punish those who
      do evil,
      also punish those who have stopped
            following your way.

Let Israel* always enjoy peace!

126 *A song for going up to the Temple.**

¹ It will be like a dream
      when the Lᴏʀᴅ comes back with the
            captives of Zion.ᵃ

² We will laugh and sing happy songs!
      Then the other nations will say,
      "The Lᴏʀᴅ did a great thing for Zion!"

³ Yes, we will be happy because the Lᴏʀᴅ
      did a great thing for us.

⁴ So, Lᴏʀᴅ, bring back the good times,
      like a desert stream filled again with
            flowing water.

⁵ Then those who were sad when they
      planted
      will be happy when they gather the
            harvest!

⁶ Those who cried as they carried the
      seedsᵇ
      will be happy when they bring in the
            crops!

127 *A song from Solomon for going up to the Temple.**

¹ If it is not the Lᴏʀᴅ who builds a house,
      the builders are wasting their time.
      If it is not the Lᴏʀᴅ who watches over the
            city,
      the guards are wasting their time.

² It is a waste of time to get up early and
      stay up late,
      trying to make a living.
      The Lord provides for those he loves,
      even while they are sleeping.

³ Children are a giftᶜ from the Lᴏʀᴅ, a
      reward from a mother's womb.

⁴ A young man's sons are like the arrows in
      a soldier's hand.

⁵ The man who fills his quiver* with sons
      will be very blessed.
      He will never be defeated when he
            opposes his enemy at the city gates.ᵈ

128 *A song for going up to the Temple.**

¹ Great blessings belong to those who fear
      and respect the Lᴏʀᴅ
      and live the way he wants.

² You will get what you work for.
      You will enjoy the Lᴏʀᴅ's blessings, and
            all will go well for you.

³ At home, your wife will have many
      children, like a vine full of grapes.
      The children around your table will be
            like an orchard full of olive trees.

⁴ Yes, the Lᴏʀᴅ will really bless those who
      respect him.

Zion." See "Zion" in the Word List.
ᵇ**126:6** *carried the seeds* Or "carried all their
possessions."
ᶜ**127:3** *gift* Literally, "inheritance." This usually
means the land God gave to each family in Israel.
ᵈ**127:5** *city gates* This can refer to either a battle to
protect the city or to a court case held in this public
place.

ᵃ**126:1** *when ... Zion* Or "when the Lᴏʀᴅ restores

5 May the LORD bless you from Mount
   Zion.*
   May you enjoy the blessings of
   Jerusalem all your life.
6 And may you live to see your
   grandchildren.

   Let Israel* always enjoy peace!

129 *A song for going up to the Temple.**

1 All my life enemies have attacked me.
   Say it again, Israel.*
2 All my life enemies have attacked me,
   but they have never defeated me.
3 They beat me until I had deep cuts.
   My back looked like a freshly plowed
   field.
4 But the LORD does what is right;
   he cut the ropes and set me free from
   those wicked people.
5 May those who hate Zion* be put to
   shame.
   May they be stopped and chased away.
6 They will be like grass on a flat roof
   that dies before it has time to grow.
7 The one who goes to harvest it
   will not find enough to cut and stack.
8 May no one walking by those wicked
   people ever say,
   "May the LORD bless you! We bless you
   in the name of the LORD."

130 *A song for going up to the Temple.**

1 LORD, I am in deep trouble,
   so I am calling to you for help.
2 My Lord, listen to me.
   Listen to my cry for help.
3 LORD, if you punished people for all their
   sins,
   no one would be left alive.
4 But you forgive people,
   so they fear and respect you.

5 I am waiting for the LORD to help me.
   My soul waits for him.
   I trust what he says.
6 I am waiting for my Lord,
   like a guard waiting and waiting for the
   morning to come.
7 Israel,* trust in the LORD.
   The LORD is the one who is faithful and
   true.
   He saves us again and again,
8 and he is the one who will save the
   people of Israel from all their sins.

131 *A song of David* for going up to the Temple.**

1 LORD, I am not proud.
   I don't pretend to be more important
   than others.
   I am not interested in doing great things
   or trying to reach impossible goals.

2 But I am calm and quiet,
   like a child content in its mother's arms.

3 Israel,* trust in the LORD.
   Trust in him now and forever!

132 *A song for going up to the Temple.**

1 LORD, remember how David* suffered.
2 He made a promise to you, LORD,
   an oath to the Mighty God of Jacob.*
3 He said, "I will not go into my house
   or lie down on my bed.
4 I will not sleep
   or let my eyes rest,
5 until I find a home for the LORD,
   a tent for the Mighty God of Jacob!"

6 We heard about this in Ephrathah.*[a]
   We found the Box of the Agreement* at
   Kiriath Jearim.*[b]
7 Now, let's go to the Lord's house.
   Let's worship at his throne.*[c]
8 LORD, get up*[d] and go to your resting place;
   go with the Box that shows your power.
9 May your priests be clothed in victory
   and your loyal followers be filled with
   joy.
10 For the sake of your servant David,
   don't reject your chosen king.*[e]
11 The LORD made a promise to David, an
   oath* of loyalty to him:
   "I will always put one of your
   descendants on your throne.
12 If your descendants obey my agreement
   and the laws I teach them,
   then the king will always be someone
   from your family."

13 The LORD has chosen Zion* to be the
   place for his Temple,*
   the place he wanted for his home.
14 He said, "This will always be my place of
   rest.
   This is where I want to sit on my
   throne.
15 I will bless this city with plenty of food.
   Even the poor will have enough to eat.
16 I will clothe the priests with salvation,
   and my followers will be filled with joy.

[a] **132:6** *Ephrathah* Bethlehem, the town where
David was born.
[b] **132:6** *Kiriath Jearim* Literally, "fields of the forest."
The Hebrew word meaning "forest" is like the name
of this city.
[c] **132:7** *at his throne* Literally, "at his footstool."
This can mean the Box of the Agreement, the Holy
Tent, or the Temple. God is like a king sitting on
his throne and resting his feet on the place where
people worship him.
[d] **132:8** *LORD, get up* The people said this when they
lifted the Box of the Agreement and took it into
battle with them. This showed that God was with
them. See Num. 10:35-36.
[e] **132:10** *chosen king* Literally, "anointed one."

¹⁷ This is where I will make David's family
strong.
I will never let the lamp of my chosen
king stop burning.
¹⁸ I will cover his enemies with shame,
and on his head will be a shining
crown."

133

A song of David for going up to the
Temple.**

¹ Oh, how wonderful, how pleasing it is
when God's people all come together as
one*ᵃ*!
² It is like the sweet-smelling oil that is
poured over the high priest's*ᵇ* head,
that runs down his beard flowing over
his robes.
³ It is like a gentle rain*ᶜ* from Mount
Hermon falling on Mount Zion.*
It is there that the LORD has promised
his blessing of eternal life.

134

A song for going up to the Temple.*

¹ Praise the LORD, all his servants
who serve in the Temple* at night.
² Lift your hands toward the Temple,
and praise the LORD.
³ May the LORD, who made heaven and
earth,
bless you from Zion.*

135

¹Praise the LORD!
Praise the name of the LORD!
Praise him, you servants of the LORD,
² you who serve in the LORD's Temple,*
in the courtyard of the Temple of our
God.
³ Praise the LORD, because he is good.
Praise his name, because it brings such
joy!

⁴ The LORD chose Jacob* to be his own.
Yes, he chose Israel* to be his own
people.
⁵ I know the LORD is great!
Our Lord is greater than all the gods!
⁶ The LORD does whatever he wants,
in heaven and on earth, in the seas and
the deep oceans.
⁷ He brings the clouds from the other side
of the earth.
He sends the lightning and the rain,
and he opens the doors to release the
winds.
⁸ He destroyed the firstborn* males of the
people in Egypt and their animals.
⁹ He did great wonders and miracles* in
Egypt.

---

*ᵃ***133:1** *when ... as one* Or "when brothers live
together in peace."
*ᵇ***133:2** *high priest's* Literally, "Aaron's."
*ᶜ***133:3** *gentle rain* Or "mist" or "snow." The Hebrew
can mean either "the oil is like the mist ..." or
"Aaron's beard is like the snow ...."

He used them against Pharaoh* and his
officials.
¹⁰ He defeated many nations
and killed powerful kings.
¹¹ He defeated Sihon, king of the Amorites,
Og, king of Bashan,
and all the kingdoms in Canaan.*
¹² Then he gave their land to Israel, his
people.

¹³ LORD, your name will be famous forever!
LORD, people will remember you forever
and ever.
¹⁴ The LORD defends his people;
he is kind to his servants.
¹⁵ The gods of other nations are only gold
and silver idols
that people have made.
¹⁶ They have mouths, but cannot speak.
They have eyes, but cannot see.
¹⁷ They have ears, but cannot hear.
They have mouths, but no breath.
¹⁸ Those who make idols and trust in them
will become just like the idols they have
made.

¹⁹ Family of Israel, praise the LORD!
Aaron's* family, praise the LORD!
²⁰ Levi's family, praise the LORD!
All you who worship the LORD, praise
the LORD!
²¹ The LORD should be praised from Zion,*
from Jerusalem, his home.

Praise the LORD!

136

¹Praise the LORD because he is
good.
His faithful love will last forever.
² Praise the God of gods!
His faithful love will last forever.
³ Praise the Lord of lords!
His faithful love will last forever.
⁴ Praise him who alone does wonderful
miracles*!
His faithful love will last forever.
⁵ Praise the one who used wisdom to make
the skies!
His faithful love will last forever.
⁶ He spread the land over the sea.
His faithful love will last forever.
⁷ He made the great lights.
His faithful love will last forever.
⁸ He made the sun to rule the day.
His faithful love will last forever.
⁹ He made the moon and stars to rule the
night.
His faithful love will last forever.
¹⁰ He killed the firstborn* males in Egypt,
both men and animals.
His faithful love will last forever.
¹¹ He took Israel* out of Egypt.
His faithful love will last forever.
¹² He used his powerful arms and strong
hands.

His faithful love will last forever.
13 He split the Red Sea into two parts.
   His faithful love will last forever.
14 He led Israel through the sea.
   His faithful love will last forever.
15 He drowned Pharaoh* and his army in the
   Red Sea.
   His faithful love will last forever.
16 He led his people through the desert.
   His faithful love will last forever.
17 He defeated powerful kings.
   His faithful love will last forever.
18 He defeated strong kings.
   His faithful love will last forever.
19 He defeated Sihon king of the Amorites.
   His faithful love will last forever.
20 He defeated Og king of Bashan.
   His faithful love will last forever.
21 He gave their land to Israel.
   His faithful love will last forever.
22 He gave it as a gift to Israel, his servant.
   His faithful love will last forever.
23 He remembered us when we were
   defeated.
   His faithful love will last forever.
24 He saved us from our enemies.
   His faithful love will last forever.
25 He provides food for all living things.
   His faithful love will last forever.
26 Praise the God of heaven!
   His faithful love will last forever.

137

1 We sat by the rivers in Babylon
and cried as we remembered
Zion.*
2 We hung our harps nearby, there on the
   willow trees.[a]
3 There in Babylon, those who captured us
   told us to sing.
   Our enemies told us to entertain them.
   They said, "Sing us one of your songs
   about Zion."
4 But we cannot sing the LORD's songs
   in a foreign country!
5 Jerusalem, if I ever forget you,
   may I never play a song again.
6 If I fail to remember you,
   may I never sing again.
   I will always remember Jerusalem
   as my greatest joy!

7 LORD, be sure to punish the Edomites for
   what they did
   when Jerusalem was captured.
   They shouted, "Destroy its buildings!
   Pull them down to the ground!"
8 Babylon, you will be destroyed!
   Bless the one who pays you back for
   what you did to us.
9 Bless the one who grabs your babies
   and smashes them against a rock.

---

[a]137:2 These instruments were used to praise God
in the Temple in Jerusalem. Since it was destroyed,
the people had no reason to play the songs.

138

*A song of David.**
1 LORD, I praise you with all my heart.
   I sing songs of praise to you before the
   gods.
2 I bow down toward your holy Temple,*
   and I praise your name for your love
   and loyalty.
   You are famous, and doing what you
   promised will make you even more
   famous!
3 When I called to you for help,
   you answered me and gave me strength.

4 LORD, all the kings on earth will praise you
   when they hear what you say.
5 They will sing about what the LORD has
   done,
   because the glory* of the LORD is very
   great.
6 The LORD has the highest place above all
   others,
   but he still cares for the humble.
   Even from there, so high above,
   he knows what the proud do.
7 If I am in trouble, you keep me alive.
   If my enemies are angry, you save me
   from them.
8 LORD, I know you will do what you have
   promised.
   LORD, your faithful love will last forever.
   You are the one who made us, so don't
   leave us!

139

To the director:
A praise song of David.**
1 LORD, you have tested me,
   so you know all about me.
2 You know when I sit down and when I
   get up.
   You know my thoughts from far away.
3 You know where I go and where I lie
   down.
   You know everything I do.
4 LORD, you know what I want to say,
   even before the words leave my mouth.
5 You are all around me—in front of me and
   behind me.
   I feel your hand on my shoulder.
6 I am amazed at what you know;
   it is too much for me to understand.
7 Your Spirit is everywhere I go.
   I cannot escape your presence.
8 If I go up to heaven, you will be there.
   If I go down to the place of death, you
   will be there.
9 If I go east where the sun rises
   or go to live in the west beyond the sea,
10 even there you will take my hand and
   lead me.
   Your strong right hand will protect me.

11 Suppose I wanted to hide from you and
   said,
   "Surely the darkness will hide me.

The day will change to night and cover me."

12 Even the darkness is not dark to you.
   The night is as bright as the day.
   Darkness and light are the same.
13 You formed the way I think and feel.*a*
   You put me together in my mother's womb.
14 I praise you because you made me in such a wonderful way.
   I know how amazing that was!

15 You could see my bones grow as my body took shape,
   hidden in my mother's womb.*b*
16 You could see my body grow each passing day.*c*
   You listed all my parts, and not one of them was missing.
17 Your thoughts are beyond my understanding.*d*
   They cannot be measured!
18 If I could count them, they would be more than all the grains of sand.
   But when I finished, I would have just begun.*e*

19 You murderers, get away from me!
   God, kill those wicked people—
20   those who say bad things about you.
   Your enemies use your name falsely.*f*
21 Lord, I hate those who hate you.
   I hate those who are against you.
22 I hate them completely!
   Your enemies are also my enemies.
23 God, examine me and know my mind.
   Test me and know all my worries.
24 Make sure that I am not going the wrong way.*g*

   Lead me on the path that has always been right.*h*

140

To the director*:
A praise song of David.*

1 Lord, save me from people who are evil.
   Protect me from those who are cruel,
2   from those who plan to do evil and always cause trouble.
3 Their words are as harmful as the fangs of a snake,
   as deadly as its venom.   *Selah**

4 Lord, save me from the wicked!
   Protect me from these cruel people who plan to hurt me.
5 These proud people are trying to trap me.
   They spread nets to catch me;
   they set traps in my path.   *Selah*

6 Lord, you are my God.
   Lord, listen to my prayer.
7 My Lord God, you are the powerful one who saves me.
   You protect my head in battle.
8 Lord, don't let the wicked have what they want.
   Don't let their plans succeed.   *Selah*

9 My enemies are planning trouble for me.
   Lord, make that trouble fall on them.
10 Pour burning coals on their heads.
   Throw them into the fire.
   Throw them into pits they can never escape.
11 Don't let those cruel liars enjoy success here.
   Let disaster hunt them down.
12 I know the Lord will provide justice for the poor
   and will defend the helpless.
13 Those who do what is right will praise your name;
   those who are honest will live in your presence.

141

A praise song of David.*

1 Lord, I call to you for help.
   Listen to me as I pray.
   Please hurry and help me!
2 Accept my prayer like a gift of burning incense,
   the words I lift up like an evening sacrifice.*

3 Lord, help me control what I say.
   Don't let me say anything bad.
4 Take away any desire to do evil.
   Keep me from joining the wicked in doing wrong.
   Help me stay away from their feasts.
5 If good people correct me,
   I will consider it a good thing.
   If they criticize me,
   I will accept it like a warm welcome.*i*
   But my prayer will always be against the wicked and the evil they do.
6 Let their judges be put to death.*j*
   Then everyone will know that I told the truth.

---

a **139:13** *the way I think and feel* Literally, "my kidneys," which were thought to be the center of emotions.
b **139:15** *mother's womb* Literally, "deepest parts of the earth," meaning a place we know nothing about.
c **139:16** *You ... day* Or "You watched me every day."
d **139:17** *beyond my understanding* Or "precious to me."
e **139:18** *I ... begun* Or "I would still be with you."
f **139:20** *Your enemies ... falsely* The Hebrew text here is hard to understand.
g **139:24** *Make sure ... way* Or "See that I don't worship idols."
h **139:24** *Lead me ... right* Or "Guide me on the ancient path."

i **141:5** *a warm welcome* Or "like oil poured over my head."
j **141:6** *Let their judges ... to death* Or "Let their judges be thrown from the cliffs."

7 Like rocks in a field that a farmer has
      plowed,
   so our bones will be scattered in the
      grave.
8 My Lord GOD, I look to you for help.
   I look to you for protection; don't let me
      die.
9 Those evil people are trying to trap me.
   Don't let me fall into their traps.
10 Let the wicked fall into their own traps,
   while I walk away unharmed.

142 A maskil* of David written when he was in the cave. A prayer.

1 I cry out to the LORD.
   I beg the LORD to help me.
2 I tell him my problems;
   I tell him about my troubles.
3 I am ready to give up.
   But you, LORD, know the path I am on,
   and you know that my enemies have set
      a trap for me.

4 I look around,
   and I don't see anyone I know.
   I have no place to run.
   There is no one to save me.
5 LORD, I cry out to you for help:
   "You are my place of safety.
   You are all I need in life."
6 Listen to my prayer.
   I am so weak.
   Save me from those who are chasing me.
   They are stronger than I am.
7 Help me escape this trap,[a]
   so that I can praise your name.
   Then good people will celebrate with me,
   because you took care of me.

143 A praise song of David.*

1 LORD, hear my prayer.
   Listen to my call for help and answer
      my prayer.
   Show me how good and loyal you are.
2 Don't judge me, your servant.
   No one alive could be judged innocent
      by your standards.
3 My enemies are chasing me.
   They have crushed me into the dirt.
   They are pushing me into the dark grave,
   like people who died long ago.
4 I am ready to give up.
   I am losing my courage.
5 But I remember what happened long ago.
   I am thinking about all you have done.
   I am talking about what you made with
      your hands!
6 I lift my hands in prayer to you.
   I am waiting for your help, like a dry
      land waiting for rain.   Selah*

7 Hurry and answer me, LORD!
   I have lost my courage.
   Don't turn away from me.
   Don't let me die and become like the
      people lying in the grave.
8 Show me your faithful love this morning.
   I trust in you.
   Show me what I should do.
   I put my life in your hands!
9 LORD, I come to you for protection.
   Save me from my enemies.
10 Show me what you want me to do.
   You are my God.
   Let your good Spirit lead me over level
      ground.
11 LORD, let me live
   so that people will praise your name.
   Show me how good you are
   and save me from my trouble.
12 Show me your love
   and defeat my enemies.
   Destroy those who are trying to kill me
   because I am your servant.

144 A song of David.*

1 The LORD is my Rock.*
   Praise the LORD!
   He prepares me for war.
   He trains me for battle.
2 He loves me and protects me.
   He is my safe place high on the
      mountain.
   He rescues me.
   He is my shield.
   I trust in him.
   He helps me rule my people.

3 LORD, why are people important to you?
   Why do you even notice us?
4 Our life is like a puff of air.
   It is like a passing shadow.

5 LORD, tear open the skies and come down.
   Touch the mountains, and smoke will
      rise from them.
6 Send the lightning and make my enemies
      run away.
   Shoot your "arrows" and make them
      run away.
7 Reach down from heaven and save me!
   Don't let me drown in this sea of
      enemies.
   Save me from these foreigners.
8 They are all liars,
   even when they swear to tell the truth.

9 God, I will sing a new song[b] for you.
   I will play a ten-stringed harp and sing
      praise to you.

[a]142:7 trap Literally, "frame around my soul."

[b]144:9 new song Whenever God did a new and
wonderful thing for his people, they would write a
new song about it.

¹⁰ You are the one who gives victory to
   kings.
   You saved your servant David* from the
   sword of his enemy.

¹¹ Save me from these foreigners.
   They are all liars,
   even when they swear to tell the truth.

¹² Save us so that our sons will be as strong
   as trees,
   and our daughters as beautiful as the
   carved columns of a palace.

¹³ Save us so that our barns will be filled
   with crops,
   and there will be thousands of sheep in
   our fields.

¹⁴ Then our soldiers will be safe,
   and no enemy will try to break in.
   Then we will not go to war,
   and people will not be screaming in our
   streets.

¹⁵ How wonderful to have such blessings!
   Yes, great blessings belong to those who
   have the LORD as their God.

145 *A song of David.**

¹ I will tell of your greatness, my God and
   King.
   I will praise your name forever and ever.
² I will praise you every day.
   I will praise your name forever and
   ever.
³ The LORD is great and deserves all our
   praise!
   No one can fully understand his
   greatness!
⁴ Each generation will praise you
   and tell the next generation about the
   great things you do.
⁵ Your majesty and glory* are wonderful.
   I will tell about your miracles.*
⁶ People will tell about the amazing things
   you do.
   I will tell about the great things you do.
⁷ They will tell about the good things you
   do.
   They will sing about your goodness.
⁸ The LORD is kind and merciful,
   patient and full of love.
⁹ The LORD is good to everyone.
   He shows his mercy to everything he
   made.
¹⁰ LORD, all you have made will give thanks
   to you.
   Your loyal followers will praise you.
¹¹ They will tell how great your kingdom is.
   They will tell how great you are.
¹² So others will learn about the mighty
   things you do,
   about the glory of your kingdom—how
   marvelous it is!
¹³ Your kingdom will never end,
   and you will rule forever.

The LORD can be trusted in all that he
   says.
   He is loyal in all that he does.ᵃ
¹⁴ The LORD lifts up people who have fallen.
   He helps those who are in trouble.
¹⁵ All living things look to you for their food,
   and you give them their food at the
   right time.
¹⁶ You open your hands
   and give every living thing all that it
   needs.
¹⁷ Everything the LORD does is good.
   Everything he does shows how loyal he
   is.
¹⁸ The LORD is near to everyone
   who sincerely calls to him for help.
¹⁹ He listens to his followers and does what
   they want.
   He answers their prayers and saves
   them.
²⁰ The LORD protects everyone who loves
   him,
   but he destroys all who do evil.
²¹ I will praise the LORD!
   Let everyone praise his holy name
   forever and ever!

146 ¹Praise the LORD!
   My soul, praise the LORD!

² I will praise the LORD all my life.
   I will sing praises to him as long as I
   live.
³ Don't depend on your leaders for help.
   Don't depend on people, because they
   cannot save you.
⁴ People die and are buried.
   Then all their plans to help are gone.
⁵ It is a great blessing for people to have the
   God of Jacob* to help them.
   They depend on the LORD their God.
⁶ He made heaven and earth.
   He made the sea and everything in it.
   He can be trusted to do what he says.
⁷ He does what is right for those who have
   been hurt.
   He gives food to the hungry.
   The LORD frees people locked up in
   prison.
⁸ The LORD makes the blind see again.
   The LORD helps those who are in trouble.
   The LORD loves those who do right.
⁹ The LORD protects strangers in our
   country.
   He cares for widows and orphans,
   but he destroys the wicked.
¹⁰ The LORD will rule forever!
   Zion,* your God will rule forever and
   ever!

Praise the LORD!

ᵃ**145:13 The LORD ... he does** This is found in the
ancient Greek and Syriac versions and a Hebrew
scroll from Qumran, but not in the standard Hebrew
text.

147

¹Praise the Lord because he is good.
Sing praises to our God.
It is good and pleasant to praise him.

² The Lord rebuilds Jerusalem.
He brings back the Israelites who were taken as prisoners.

³ He heals their broken hearts
and bandages their wounds.

⁴ He counts the stars
and knows each of them by name.

⁵ Our Lord is great and powerful.
There is no limit to what he knows.

⁶ The Lord supports the humble,
but he shames the wicked.

⁷ Give thanks to the Lord.
Praise our God with harps.

⁸ He fills the sky with clouds.
He sends rain to the earth.
He makes the grass grow on the mountains.

⁹ He gives food to the animals.
He feeds the young birds.

¹⁰ War horses and powerful soldiers are not what he cares about.

¹¹ The Lord enjoys people who worship him
and trust in his faithful love.

¹² Jerusalem, praise the Lord!
Zion,* praise your God!

¹³ He makes your gates strong,
and he blesses the people in your city.

¹⁴ He brought peace to your country,
so you have plenty of grain for food.

¹⁵ He gives a command to the earth,
and it quickly obeys.

¹⁶ He makes the snow fall until the ground is as white as wool.
He makes sleet blow through the air like dust.

¹⁷ He makes hail fall like rocks from the sky.
No one can stand the cold he sends.

¹⁸ Then he gives another command, and warm air begins to blow.
The ice melts, and water begins to flow.

¹⁹ He gave his commands to Jacob.*
He gave his laws and rules to Israel.*

²⁰ He did not do this for any other nation.
He did not teach his laws to other people.

Praise the Lord!

148

¹Praise the Lord!
Angels above, praise the Lord from heaven!

² Praise him, all you angels!
Praise him, all his army*!

³ Sun and moon, praise him!
Stars and lights in the sky, praise him!

⁴ Praise the Lord, highest heaven!
Waters above the sky, praise him!

⁵ Let them praise the Lord's name,
because he gave the command and created them all!

⁶ He made all these continue forever.
He made the laws that will never end.

⁷ Everything on earth, praise him!
Great sea animals and all the oceans, praise the Lord!

⁸ Praise him, fire and hail, snow and clouds,
and the stormy winds that obey him.

⁹ Praise him, mountains and hills,
fruit trees and cedar trees.

¹⁰ Praise him, wild animals and cattle,
reptiles and birds.

¹¹ Praise him, kings of the earth and all nations,
princes and all rulers on earth.

¹² Praise him, young men and women,
old people and children.

¹³ Praise the Lord's name!
Honor his name forever!
His name is greater than any other.
He is more glorious than heaven and earth.

¹⁴ He made his people strong.
His loyal followers praise him.
Israel,* his precious people, praise the Lord!

149

¹Praise the Lord.
Sing a new song* to the Lord!
Sing his praise in the assembly of his followers.

² Let Israel* be happy with their Maker.
Let the people of Zion* rejoice with their King.

³ Let them praise him by dancing
and playing their tambourines and harps.

⁴ The Lord is happy with his people.
He did a wonderful thing for his humble people.
He saved them!

⁵ Let his followers rejoice in this victory!
Let them sing for joy, even in their beds!

⁶ Let the people shout praise to God.
And with a sharp sword in their hand,

⁷ let them take revenge on the other nations.
Let them go punish those people.

⁸ They will put their kings in chains
and their leaders in chains of iron.

⁹ They will punish those nations as God commanded.
This is an honor for all his followers.

Praise the Lord!

148:2 his army This can mean "angels," "stars and planets," or "soldiers in an army."

149:1 new song Whenever God did a new and wonderful thing for his people, they would write a new song about it.

150

¹Praise the LORD!
Praise God in his Temple*!
Praise him in heaven, his strong
  fortress*!
² Praise him for the great things he does!
  Praise him for all his greatness!
³ Praise him with trumpets and horns!
  Praise him with harps and lyres*!
⁴ Praise him with tambourines and dancing!

Praise him with stringed instruments
  and flutes!
⁵ Praise him with loud cymbals!
  Praise him with crashing cymbals!

⁶ Everything that breathes, praise the
  LORD!

Praise the LORD!

Proverbs

Introduction

1

¹These are the proverbs* of Solomon, the son of David* and king of Israel.* ²They will help you learn to be wise, to accept correction, and to understand wise sayings. ³They will teach you to develop your mind in the right way. You will learn to do what is right and to be honest and fair. ⁴These proverbs will make even those without education smart. They will teach young people what they need to know and how to use what they have learned. ⁵Even the wise could become wiser by listening to these proverbs. They will gain understanding and learn to solve difficult problems. ⁶These sayings will help you understand proverbs, stories with hidden meanings, words of the wise, and other difficult sayings.

⁷Knowledge begins with fear and respect for the LORD, but stubborn fools hate wisdom and refuse to learn.

Advice to a Son

⁸My son,ᵃ listen to your father when he corrects you, and don't ignore what your mother teaches you. ⁹What you learn from your parents will bring you honor and respect, like a crown or a gold medal.ᵇ

¹⁰My son, those who love to do wrong will try to trick you. Don't listen to them. ¹¹They will say, "Come with us. Let's hide and beat to death anyone who happens to walk by. ¹²We will swallow them whole, as the grave swallows the dying. ¹³We will take everything they have and fill our houses with stolen goods. ¹⁴So join us, and you can share everything we get."

¹⁵My son, don't follow them. Don't even take the first step along that path. ¹⁶They run to do something evil, and they cannot wait to kill someone.

¹⁷You cannot trap birds with a net if they see you spreading it out. ¹⁸But evil people cannot see the trap they set for themselves. ¹⁹This is what happens to those who are greedy. Whatever they get destroys them.

The Good Woman—Wisdom

²⁰Listen! Wisdomᶜ is shouting in the streets. She is crying out in the marketplace. ²¹She is calling out where the noisy crowd gathers:

²²"Fools, how long will you love being ignorant? How long will you make fun of wisdom? How long will you hate knowledge? ²³I wanted to tell you everything I knew and give you all my knowledge, but you didn't listen to my advice and teaching.

²⁴"I tried to help, but you refused to listen. I offered my hand, but you turned away from me. ²⁵You ignored my advice and refused to be corrected. ²⁶So I will laugh at your troubles and make fun of you when what you fear happens. ²⁷Disasters will strike you like a storm. Problems will pound you like a strong wind. Trouble and misery will weigh you down.

²⁸"Fools will call for me, but I will not answer. They will look for me, but they will not find me. ²⁹That is because they hated knowledge. They refused to fear and respect the LORD. ³⁰They ignored my advice and refused to be corrected. ³¹They filled their lives with what they wanted. They went their own way, so they will get what they deserve.

³²"Fools die because they refuse to follow wisdom. They are content to follow their foolish ways, and that will destroy them. ³³But those who listen to me will live in safety and comfort. They will have nothing to fear."

ᵃ**1:8 My son** The proverbs in this section may have been directed originally to a teenage boy, perhaps a prince, who was becoming a young man. They are intended to teach him how to be a responsible person and leader who loves and respects God.
ᵇ**1:9** Literally, "They are like a wreath of favor to your head and a necklace around your neck."

ᶜ**1:20 Wisdom** Wisdom is pictured here as a good woman trying to get the attention of this young man, calling him to be wise and obey God. In a later passage (9:13–18), Foolishness is represented as another woman who is urging him toward a life of sin.

Listen to Wisdom

2 ¹My son, pay attention to what I say. Remember my commands. ²Listen to wisdom, and do your best to understand. ³Ask for good judgment. Cry out for understanding. ⁴Look for wisdom like silver. Search for it like hidden treasure. ⁵If you do this, you will understand what it means to respect the LORD, and you will come to know God.

⁶The LORD is the source of wisdom; knowledge and understanding come from his mouth. ⁷He gives good advice to honest people and shields those who do what is right. ⁸He makes sure that people are treated fairly. He watches over his loyal followers.

⁹If you listen to him, you will understand what is just and fair and how to do what is right. ¹⁰You will gain wisdom, and knowledge will bring you joy.

¹¹Planning ahead will protect you, and understanding will guard you. ¹²These will keep you from following the wrong path and will protect you from those who have evil plans. ¹³Such people have left the straight path and now walk in darkness.* ¹⁴They enjoy doing evil and are happy with the confusion it brings. ¹⁵Their ways are crooked; they lie and cheat.

¹⁶Wisdom will save you from that other woman, another man's wife, who tempts you with sweet words. ¹⁷She married when she was young, but then she left her husband. She forgot the marriage vows she made before God. ¹⁸Going into her house leads to death. She will lead you to the grave. ¹⁹All who enter lose their life and never return.

²⁰Wisdom will help you follow the example of good people and stay on the right path. ²¹Honest people will live in the land, and those who do right will remain there. ²²But the wicked will be forced to leave. Those who lie and cheat will be thrown out of the land.

The Blessing of Wisdom

3 ¹My son, don't forget my teaching. Remember what I tell you to do. ²What I teach will give you a good, long life, and all will go well for you.

³Don't ever let love and loyalty leave you. Tie them around your neck, and write them on your heart. ⁴Then God will be pleased and think well of you and so will everyone else.

⁵Trust the LORD completely, and don't depend on your own knowledge. ⁶With every step you take, think about what he wants, and he will help you go the right way. ⁷Don't trust in your own wisdom, but fear and respect the LORD and stay away from evil. ⁸If you do this, it will be like a refreshing drink and medicine for your body.

⁹Honor the LORD with your wealth and the first part of your harvest. ¹⁰Then your barns will be full of grain, and your barrels will be overflowing with wine.

¹¹My son, don't reject the LORD's discipline, and don't be angry when he corrects you. ¹²The LORD corrects the one he loves, just as a father corrects a child he cares about.

¹³Those who find wisdom are fortunate; they will be blessed when they gain understanding. ¹⁴Profit that comes from wisdom is better than silver and even the finest gold. ¹⁵Wisdom is worth more than fine jewels. Nothing you desire has more value.

¹⁶With her right hand, Wisdom offers long life—with the other hand, riches and honor. ¹⁷Wisdom will lead you to a life of joy and peace. ¹⁸Wisdom is like a life-giving tree to those who hold on to her; she is a blessing to those who keep her close.

¹⁹With wisdom and understanding, the LORD created the earth and sky. ²⁰With his knowledge, he made the oceans and the clouds that produce rain.

²¹My son, don't ever let wisdom out of your sight. Hold on to wisdom and careful planning. ²²They will bring you a long life filled with honor. ²³As you go through life, you will always be safe and never fall. ²⁴When you lie down, you will not be afraid. When you rest, your sleep will be peaceful. ²⁵⁻²⁶You have no reason to fear some sudden disaster. The LORD will be your strength. Never fear the destruction that comes to the wicked. The LORD will protect you from that trap.

²⁷Do everything you possibly can for those who need help. ²⁸If your neighbor needs something you have, don't say, "Come back tomorrow." Give it to him immediately.

²⁹Don't make plans to harm your neighbor, who lives near you and trusts you.*a*

³⁰Don't take people to court without good reason, especially when they have done nothing to harm you.

³¹Don't envy those who are violent. Never choose to be like them. ³²Such crooked people are disgusting to the LORD. But he is a friend to those who are good and honest.

³³The LORD curses* a wicked family, but he blesses the homes of those who live right.

³⁴He will humiliate those who make fun of others, but he is kind to those who are humble.

³⁵The way the wise live will bring them honor, but the way fools live will bring them shame.

A Father's Advice About Wisdom

4 ¹Children, listen to your father's teaching. Pay attention and you will learn how to learn. ²The advice I give is good, so don't ever forget what I teach you.

³When I was my father's little boy and my mother's dear son,*b* ⁴my father taught me this: "Pay attention to what I say. Obey my commands and you will have a good life. ⁵Try

---

*a***3:29** *neighbor ... trusts you* Or "neighbor. After all, you live near one another for protection."
*b***4:3** *dear son* Or "only son."

to get wisdom and understanding. Don't forget my teaching or ignore what I say. 6Don't turn away from wisdom, and she will protect you. Love her, and she will keep you safe.

7"The first step to becoming wise is to look for wisdom, so use everything you have to get understanding. 8Love wisdom, and she will make you great. Hold on to wisdom, and she will bring you honor. 9Wisdom will reward you with a crown of honor and glory."

10Son, listen to me. Do what I say, and you will live a long time. 11I am teaching you about wisdom and guiding you on the right path. 12As you walk on it, you will not step into a trap. Even if you run, you will not trip and fall. 13Always remember this teaching. Don't forget it. It is the key to life, so guard it well.

14Don't take the path of the wicked; don't follow those who do evil. 15Stay away from that path; don't even go near it. Turn around and go another way. 16The wicked cannot sleep until they have done something evil. They will not rest until they bring someone down. 17Evil and violence are their food and drink.

18The path of those who live right is like the early morning light. It gets brighter and brighter until the full light of day. 19But the path of the wicked is like a dark night. They trip and fall over what they cannot see.

20My son, pay attention to what I say. Listen closely to my words. 21Don't let them out of your sight. Never stop thinking about them. 22These words are the secret of life and health to all who discover them. 23Above all, be careful what you think because your thoughts control your life.

24Don't bend the truth or say things that you know are not right. 25Keep your eyes on the path, and look straight ahead. 26Make sure you are going the right way, and nothing will make you fall. 27Don't go to the right or to the left, and you will stay away from evil.

The Wisdom of Avoiding Adultery

5 1Son, listen to this piece of wisdom from me. Pay attention to what I know to be true. 2Remember to live wisely, and what you learn will keep your lips from saying the wrong thing. 3Now, another man's wife might be very charming, and the words from her lips so sweet and inviting. 4But in the end, she will bring only bitterness and pain. It will be like bitter poison and a sharp sword. 5She is on a path leading to death, and she will lead you straight to the grave. 6Don't follow her. She has lost her way and does not even know it. Be careful. Stay on the road that leads to life.

7Now, my sons, listen to me. Don't forget the words I say. 8Stay away from the woman who commits adultery.* Don't even go near her house. 9If you do, others will get the honor you should have had. Some stranger will get

everything you worked years to get. 10People you don't know will take all your wealth. Others will get what you worked for. 11At the end of your life, you will be sad that you ruined your health and lost everything you had. 12-13Then you will say, "Why didn't I listen to my parents? Why didn't I pay attention to my teachers? I didn't want to be disciplined. I refused to be corrected. 14So now I have suffered through just about every kind of trouble anyone can have, and everyone knows it."

15Now, about sex and marriage: Drink only the water that comes from your own well, 16and don't let your water flow out into the streets. 17Keep it for yourself, and don't share it with strangers. 18Be happy with your own wife. Enjoy the woman you married while you were young. 19She is like a beautiful deer, a lovely fawn.* Let her love satisfy you completely. Stay drunk on her love, 20and don't go stumbling into the arms of another woman.

21The Lord clearly sees everything you do. He watches where you go. 22The sins of the wicked will trap them. Those sins will be like ropes holding them back. 23Evil people will die because they refuse to be disciplined. They will be trapped by their own desires.

Dangers of Debt

6 1My son, don't make yourself responsible for the debts of others. Don't make such deals with friends or strangers. 2If you do, your words will trap you. 3You will be under the power of other people, so you must go and free yourself. Beg them to free you from that debt. 4Don't wait to rest or sleep. 5Escape from that trap like a deer running from a hunter. Free yourself like a bird flying from a trap.

The Dangers of Being Lazy

6You lazy people, you should watch what the ants do and learn from them. 7Ants have no ruler, no boss, and no leader. 8But in the summer, ants gather all of their food and save it. So when winter comes, there is plenty to eat.

9You lazy people, how long are you going to lie there? When will you get up? 10You say, "I need a rest. I think I'll take a short nap." 11But then you sleep and sleep and become poorer and poorer. Soon you will have nothing. It will be as if a thief came and stole everything you owned.

Troublemakers

12Some people are just troublemakers. They are always thinking up some crooked plan and telling lies. 13They use secret signals to cheat people; they wink their eyes, shuffle their feet, and point a finger. 14They are always planning to do something bad. 15But they will be punished. Disaster will strike, and they will be destroyed. There will be no one to help them.

What the Lord Hates

16 The Lord hates these seven things:
17   eyes that show pride,
   tongues that tell lies,
   hands that kill innocent people,
18   hearts that plan evil things to do,
   feet that run to do evil,
19   witnesses in court who tell lies,
   and anyone who causes family members
     to fight.

Warning Against Adultery

20My son, remember your father's command, and don't forget your mother's teaching. 21Remember their words always. Tie them around your neck and keep them over your heart. 22Let this teaching lead you wherever you go. It will watch over you while you sleep. And when you wake up, it will give you good advice.

23Your parents give you commands and teachings that are like lights to show you the right way. This teaching corrects you and trains you to follow the path to life. 24It stops you from going to an evil woman, and it protects you from the smooth talk of another man's wife. 25Such a woman might be beautiful, but don't let that beauty tempt you. Don't let her eyes capture you. 26A prostitute might cost a loaf of bread, but the wife of another man could cost you your life. 27If you drop a hot coal in your lap, your clothes will be burned. 28If you step on one, your feet will be burned. 29If you sleep with another man's wife, you will be punished.

30-31A hungry man might steal to fill his stomach. If he is caught, he must pay seven times more than he stole. It might cost him everything he owns, but other people understand. They don't lose all their respect for him. 32But a man who commits adultery* is a fool. He brings about his own destruction. 33He will suffer disease and disgrace and never be free from the shame. 34The woman's husband will be jealous and angry and do everything he can to get revenge. 35No payment—no amount of money—will stop him.

Wisdom Will Keep You From Adultery

7 1My son, remember my words. Don't forget what I have told you. 2Consider my teaching as precious as your own eyes. Obey my commands, and you will have a good life. 3Tie them around your finger. Write them on your heart. 4Treat wisdom like the woman you love and knowledge like the one dearest to you. 5Wisdom will save you from that other woman, the other man's wife, who tempts you with such sweet words.

6One day I was looking out my window 7at some foolish teenagers and noticed one who had no sense at all. 8He was walking through the marketplace and came to the corner where a certain woman lived. He then turned up the road that goes by her house.

9The day was ending. The sun had set, and it was almost dark. 10Suddenly, there she was in front of him, dressed like a prostitute. She had plans for him. 11She was a wild and rebellious woman who would not stay at home. 12She walked the streets, always looking for someone to trap. 13She grabbed the young man and kissed him. Without shame, she looked him in the eye and said, 14"I offered a fellowship offering* today. I gave what I promised to give, 15and I still have plenty of food left. So I came out to find you, and here you are! 16I have clean sheets on my bed—special ones from Egypt. 17My bed smells wonderful with myrrh,* aloes,* and cinnamon. 18Come, let's enjoy ourselves all night. We can make love until dawn. 19My husband has gone on a business trip. 20He took enough money for a long trip and won't be home for two weeks.a"

21This is what the woman said to tempt the young man, and her smooth words tricked him. 22He followed her, like a bull being led to the slaughter. He was like a deer walking into a trap, 23where a hunter waits to shoot an arrow through its heart. The boy was like a bird flying into a net, never seeing the danger he was in.

24Now, sons, listen to me. Pay attention to what I say. 25Don't let your heart lead you to an evil woman like that. Don't go where she wants to lead you. 26She has brought down some of the most powerful men; she has left many dead bodies in her path. 27Her house is the place of death. The road to it leads straight to the grave.

Wisdom—the Good Woman

8 1Listen, Wisdom is calling.
   Yes, Understanding is shouting for us.
2 Wisdom stands at the top of the hill,
   by the road where the paths meet.
3 She is near the entrance to the city,
   calling from the open gates.

4"I am calling out to all of you.
   I am speaking to everyone.
5 You who are ignorant, learn to be wise.
   You who are foolish, get some common sense.
6 Listen, I have something important to say,
   and I am telling you what is right.
7 My words are true,
   and I will not say anything that is wrong.
8 Everything I say is right;
   there is nothing false or crooked about it.
9 These things are clear
   to any intelligent person.
   They are right
   to anyone with knowledge.
10 Choose discipline over silver
   and knowledge over the finest gold.

a7:20 won't be ... weeks Literally, "will not come home until the full moon." The fellowship meal shows that this happened at the time of the new moon, the first day of the Hebrew month.

11 Wisdom is better than pearls,
　　and nothing you desire compares with
　　her.

The Value of Wisdom

12 "I am Wisdom.
　　I live with Good Judgment.
　　I am at home with Knowledge and
　　　Planning.
13 To respect the LORD means to hate evil.
　　I hate pride and boasting,
　　evil lives and hurtful words.
14 I have good advice and common sense to
　　offer.
　　I have understanding and power.
15 With my help kings rule,
　　and governors make good laws.
16 With my help leaders govern,
　　and important officials make good
　　　decisions.*a*
17 I love those who love me,
　　and those who look for me will find me.
18 With me there are riches and honor.
　　I have lasting wealth to give to you.
19 What I give is better than fine gold.
　　What I produce is better than pure
　　　silver.
20 I lead people the right way—
　　along the paths of justice.
21 I give riches to those who love me,
　　and I fill their houses with treasures.

22 "The LORD made me in the beginning,
　　long before he did anything else.
23 I was formed a long time ago,
　　before the world was made.
24 I was born before there was an ocean,
　　before the springs began to flow.
25 I was born before the mountains and hills
　　were set into place,
26 before the earth and fields were made,
　　before the dust of this world was
　　　formed.
27 I was there
　　when he set up the skies,
　　when he drew a circle in the ocean to
　　　make a place for the land.
28 I was there
　　when he put the clouds in the sky and
　　　made the deep springs flow.
29 I was there
　　when he set the limits on the sea to
　　　make it stop where he said.
　　I was there
　　when he laid the foundations of the
　　　earth.
30 I grew up as a child by his side,*b*
　　laughing and playing all the time.
31 I played in the world he made
　　and enjoyed the people he put there.

32 "Now, children, listen to me.
　　If you follow my ways,
　　you will be happy too.
33 Listen to my teaching and be wise;
　　don't ignore what I say.
34 Whoever waits at my door
　　and listens for me will be blessed.
35 Those who find me find life,
　　and the LORD will reward them.
36 But those who do not find me
　　put their lives in danger.
　　Whoever hates me loves death."

Wisdom's Invitation

9 ¹Wisdom has built her house; she has made it strong with seven columns.*c* ²She has cooked meat, mixed wine, and put food on the table. ³She has sent her servant girls to announce from the highest hill in the city,*d* ⁴"Whoever needs instruction, come." She invites all the simple people and says, ⁵"Come, eat my food and drink the wine I have prepared. ⁶Leave your old, foolish ways and live! Advance along the path of understanding."

⁷Criticize a person who is rude and shows no respect, and you will only get insults. Correct the wicked, and you will only get hurt. ⁸Don't correct such people, or they will hate you. But correct those who are wise, and they will love you. ⁹Teach the wise, and they will become wiser. Instruct those who live right, and they will gain more knowledge.

¹⁰Wisdom begins with fear and respect for the LORD. Knowledge of the Holy One leads to understanding. ¹¹Wisdom will help you live longer; she will add years to your life. ¹²If you become wise, it will be for your own good. If you are rude and show no respect, you are the one who will suffer.

Foolishness—the Other Woman

¹³Foolishness is that other woman, who is loud, stupid, and knows nothing. ¹⁴She sits on her chair at the door of her house, up on the highest hill of the city. ¹⁵When people walk by, she calls out to them. They show no interest in her, but still she says, ¹⁶"Whoever needs instruction, come." She invites all the simple people and says, ¹⁷"Stolen water is sweet. Stolen bread tastes good." ¹⁸Those simple people don't realize that her house is full of ghosts and that her guests have entered the world of the dead.

Solomon's Proverbs

10 ¹These are the proverbs* of Solomon: A wise son makes his father happy; a foolish one makes his mother sad.

---

*c***9:1** *seven columns* In ancient Israel, a good house was one that had four main rooms with seven columns to support the roof.
*d***9:3** Or "She has sent out her servant girls and invited people to come to the highest hill in the city to eat with her."

*a***8:16** *and important … decisions* Or "as well as important officials, all the judges on earth."
*b***8:30** *I grew … his side* Or "I was beside him like a skilled worker."

²Wealth gained by doing wrong will not really help you, but doing right will save you from death.

³The LORD takes care of good people and gives them the food they need, but he keeps the wicked from getting what they want.

⁴Lazy hands will make you poor; hard-working hands will make you rich.

⁵A son who works hard while it is harvest time will be successful, but one who sleeps through the harvest is worthless.

⁶People say good things about those who live right, but the words of the wicked only hide their violent plans.

⁷Good people leave memories that bless us, but the wicked are soon forgotten.

⁸The wise accept instruction, but fools argue and bring trouble on themselves.

⁹Honest people can always feel secure, but lying cheaters will be caught.

¹⁰If you fail to speak the truth, trouble will follow. If you speak openly, peace will come.ᵃ

¹¹The words of good people are like a spring of fresh water,ᵇ but the words of the wicked only hide their violent plans.

¹²Hatred causes arguments, but love overlooks all wrongs.

¹³Intelligent people speak words of wisdom, but fools must be punished before they learn their lesson.ᶜ

¹⁴Wise people are quiet and learn new things, but fools talk and bring trouble on themselves.

¹⁵Wealth protects the rich, but poverty destroys the poor.

¹⁶What good people do brings life, but wicked people produce only sin.

¹⁷Those who accept correction show others how to live. Those who reject correction lead others the wrong way.

¹⁸You might have to lie to hide your hatred, but saying something hurtful could be even more foolish.ᵈ

¹⁹A person who talks too much gets into trouble. A wise person learns to be quiet.

²⁰Words from good people are like pure silver, but thoughts from the wicked are worthless.

²¹Good people say things that help others, but the wicked die from a lack of understanding.

²²It is the LORD's blessing that brings wealth, and no hard work can add to it.ᵉ

²³Fools enjoy doing wrong, but the wise enjoy wisdom.

²⁴The wicked will be defeated by what they fear, but good people will get what they want.

²⁵The wicked are destroyed when trouble comes, but good people stand strong forever.

²⁶Sending a lazy person to do anything is as irritating as vinegar on your teeth or smoke in your eyes.

²⁷Respect for the LORD will add years to your life, but the wicked will have their lives cut short.

²⁸What good people hope for brings happiness,ᶠ but what the wicked hope for brings destruction.

²⁹The LORD protects those who do right, but he destroys those who do wrong.

³⁰Good people will always be safe, but the wicked will be forced out of the land.

³¹Those who live right say wise things, but people stop listening to troublemakers.ᵍ

³²Good people know the right things to say, but the wicked say things to make trouble.

11 ¹The LORD hates false scales, but he loves accurate weights.

²Proud and boastful people will be shamed, but wisdom stays with those who are modest and humble.

³Good people are guided by their honesty, but crooks who lie and cheat will ruin themselves.

⁴Money is worthless when you face God's punishment, but living right will save you from death.

⁵Doing right makes life better for those who are good, but the wicked are destroyed by their own wicked ways.

⁶Doing right sets honest people free, but people who can't be trusted are trapped by their greed.

⁷When the wicked die, all their hopes are lost; everything they thought they could do comes to nothing.

⁸Good people escape from trouble, but the wicked come along and are trapped by it.

⁹With their words hypocrites* can destroy their neighbors. But with what they know, good people can escape.

¹⁰When good people are successful, the whole city is happy, and they all shout with joy when evil people are destroyed.

¹¹Blessings from the honest people living in a city will make it great, but the things evil people say can destroy it.

¹²Stupid people say bad things about their neighbors.ʰ Wise people know to be quiet.

ᵃ10:10 *If you ... come* This is from the ancient Greek version. The Hebrew text repeats the second half of verse 8.
ᵇ10:11 *spring of fresh water* Or "the source of life."
ᶜ10:13 Literally, "Wisdom can be found on the lips of the intelligent, but a rod on the back of fools." This is a wordplay. In Hebrew, "lip" sounds like "rod."
ᵈ10:18 Or "Sometimes it would be foolish to say something negative, but the only way to hide your opposition would be to lie."
ᵉ10:22 Or "A blessing from the LORD will bring you true wealth—wealth without troubles."

ᶠ10:28 *good people ... happiness* Or "Good people can look forward to happiness."
ᵍ10:31 Or "The mouth of a good man speaks wisdom, but the tongue of a troublemaker will be cut off."
ʰ11:12 *Stupid people ... neighbors* Or "The neighbors hate a stupid person."

¹³People who tell secrets about others cannot be trusted. Those who can be trusted keep quiet.

¹⁴A nation without wise leaders will fall. Many good advisors make a nation safe.

¹⁵You will be sorry if you promise to pay a stranger's debt. Refuse to make such promises and you will be safe.

¹⁶A kind and gentle woman gains respect, but violent men gain only wealth.

¹⁷People who are kind will be rewarded for their kindness, but cruel people will be rewarded with trouble.

¹⁸The work of evil people is all lies, but those who do right will receive a good reward.ᵃ

¹⁹People who do what is right are on their way to life, but those who always want to do wrong are on their way to death.

²⁰The LORD hates those who love to do evil, but he is pleased with those who try to do right.

²¹The truth is, evil people will be punished, and good people will be set free.

²²A beautiful woman without good sense is like a gold ring in a pig's nose.

²³What good people want brings more good. What evil people want brings more trouble.

²⁴Some people give freely and gain more; others refuse to give and end up with less.

²⁵Give freely, and you will profit. Help others, and you will gain more for yourself.

²⁶People curse* a greedy man who refuses to sell his grain, but they bless a man who sells his grain to feed others.

²⁷People are pleased with those who try to do good. Those who look for trouble will find it.

²⁸Those who trust in their riches will fall like dead leaves, but good people will blossom.

²⁹Those who cause trouble for their families will inherit nothing but the wind. A foolish person will end up as a servant to one who is wise.

³⁰What good people produce is like a life-giving tree. Those who are wise give new life to others.ᵇ

³¹If good people are rewarded here on earth, then surely those who do evil will also get what they deserve.

12 ¹Whoever loves discipline loves to learn; whoever hates to be corrected is stupid.

²It is good to learn what pleases the LORD, because he condemns those who plan to do wrong.

³Evil people are never safe, but good people remain safe and secure.

⁴A good wife is like a crown to her husband, but a shameful wife is like a cancer.

⁵Good people are honest and fair in all they do, but those who are evil lie and cannot be trusted.

⁶Evil people use their words to hurt others, but the words from good people can save others from danger.

⁷When evil people are destroyed, they are gone and forgotten, but good people are remembered long after they are gone.

⁸You praise people for their intelligence, but no one respects those who are stupid.

⁹It is better to appear unimportant and have a servant than to pretend to be important and have no food.

¹⁰Good people take good care of their animals, but the wicked know only how to be cruel.ᶜ

¹¹Farmers who work their land have plenty of food, but those who waste their time on worthless projects are foolish.

¹²The wicked want a share of what an evil man might catch. But like a plant with deep roots, a good man is the one who produces the most.ᵈ

¹³The wicked are trapped by their foolish words, but good people escape from such trouble.

¹⁴People get good things for the words they say, and they are rewarded for the work they do.

¹⁵Fools always think their own way is best, but wise people listen to what others tell them.

¹⁶Fools are easily upset, but wise people avoid insulting others.

¹⁷Good people speak the truth and can be trusted in court, but liars make bad witnesses.

¹⁸Speak without thinking, and your words can cut like a knife. Be wise, and your words can heal.

¹⁹Lies last only a moment, but the truth lasts forever.

²⁰People who work for evil make trouble, but those who plan for peace bring happiness.

²¹The Lord will keep good people safe, but evil people will have many troubles.

²²The LORD hates people who tell lies, but he is pleased with those who tell the truth.

²³Smart people don't tell everything they know, but fools tell everything and show they are fools.

²⁴Those who work hard will be put in charge of others, but lazy people will have to work like slaves.

²⁵Worry takes away your joy, but a kind word makes you happy.

ᵃ**11:18** This is a wordplay in Hebrew. The word "lies" sounds like the word "reward."

ᵇ**11:30** Or, according to one ancient version, "The fruit of a good man is a tree of life, but a violent man takes lives."

ᶜ**12:10** *but the wicked … cruel* Or "but even the 'kindness' of the wicked is still cruelty."

ᵈ**12:12** The Hebrew text here is hard to understand.

26Good people are careful about choosing their friends, but evil people always choose the wrong ones.

27Lazy people don't get what they want, but riches come to those who work hard.

28Along the path of goodness there is life; that is the way to live forever.*a*

13

1A wise son listens to his father's advice, but a proud son will not listen to correction.

2People get good things for the words they say, but those who cannot be trusted say only bad things.

3People who are careful about what they say will save their lives, but those who speak without thinking will be destroyed.

4Lazy people always want things but never get them. Those who work hard get plenty.

5Good people hate lies, but the wicked do evil, shameful things.

6Goodness protects honest people, but evil destroys those who love to sin.

7Some people pretend they are rich, but they have nothing. Others pretend they are poor, but they are really rich.

8The rich might have to pay a ransom to save their lives, but the poor never receive such threats.

9The light of those who do right shines brighter and brighter, but the lamp of the wicked becomes darker and darker.*b*

10Pride causes arguments, but those who listen to others are wise.

11Money gained by cheating others will soon be gone. Money earned through hard work will grow and grow.

12Hope that is delayed makes you sad, but a wish that comes true fills you with joy.

13Those who reject a command hurt themselves; those who respect a command will be rewarded.

14The teaching of the wise is a source of life; their words will save you from deadly traps.

15People like a person with good sense, but life is hard for someone who cannot be trusted.

16Wise people always think before they do anything, but fools show how stupid they are by what they do.

17Disaster will catch up to the wicked messenger, but a runner who can be trusted will bring peace.

18If you refuse to learn from your mistakes, you will be poor, and no one will respect you. If you listen when you are criticized, you will be honored.

19People are happy when they get what they want. But stupid people want nothing but evil, and they refuse to change.

20Be friends with those who are wise, and you will become wise. Choose fools to be your friends, and you will have trouble.

21Trouble chases sinners wherever they go, but good things happen to good people.

22It is good to have something to pass down to your grandchildren. But wealth hidden away by sinners will be given to those who live right.

23The poor might have good land that produces plenty of food, but bad decisions can take it away.*c*

24If you don't correct your children, you don't love them. If you love them, you will be quick to discipline them.

25Good people will have plenty to eat, but the wicked will go hungry.

14

1A wise woman makes her home what it should be, but the home of a foolish woman is destroyed by her own actions.*d*

2Those who live right respect the LORD, but dishonest people hate him.

3Foolish words cause you trouble; wise words protect you.

4A barn with no cattle might be clean, but strong bulls are needed for a good harvest.

5A good witness is one who does not lie. A bad witness is a liar who cannot be trusted.

6Anyone who makes fun of wisdom will never find it, but knowledge comes easily to those who understand its value.

7Stay away from fools, there is nothing they can teach you.

8Wisdom lets smart people know what they are doing, but stupid people only think they know.

9Fines are needed to make fools obey the law, but good people are happy to obey it.

10When you are sad, no one else feels the pain; and when you are happy, no one else can really feel the joy.

11An evil person's house will be destroyed, but a good person's family will do well.

12There is a way that people think is right, but it leads only to death.

13Laughter might hide your sadness. But when the laughter is gone, the sadness remains.

14Evil people will be paid back for the wrong they do, and good people will be rewarded for the good they do.

15Fools believe every word they hear, but wise people think carefully about everything.

16Wise people are careful and avoid trouble; fools are too confident and careless.

17A quick-tempered person does stupid things, but it is also true that people don't like anyone who quietly plans evil.

18Fools are rewarded with more foolishness. Smart people are rewarded with knowledge.

---

*a*12:28 *that is ... forever* Or "but there is a path that leads to death."

*b*13:9 Or "The light of those who do right is happy; the lamp of the wicked goes out."

*c*13:23 Or "The fields of the poor might produce plenty of food, but the unjust often take it away."

*d*14:1 Or "Wisdom builds her house, but Foolishness tears hers down with her own hands."

¹⁹Good people will defeat those who are evil, and the wicked will be forced to show respect to those who live right.

²⁰The poor have no friends, not even their neighbors, but the rich have many friends.

²¹It is wrong to say bad things about your neighbors. Be kind to the poor, and you will be blessed.

²²Whoever works to do good will find love and loyalty. It is a mistake to work at doing evil.

²³If you work hard, you will have plenty. If you do nothing but talk, you will not have enough.

²⁴A wise person's reward is wealth, but a fool's reward is foolishness.

²⁵A witness who tells the truth saves lives, but one who tells lies hurts others.

²⁶People who respect the LORD will be safe, and they will make their children feel secure.

²⁷Respect for the LORD gives true life and will save you from death's trap.

²⁸Kings of large nations have great honor. Rulers without a country have nothing.

²⁹A patient person is very smart. A quick-tempered person makes stupid mistakes.

³⁰Peace of mind makes the body healthy, but jealousy is like a cancer.

³¹Whoever takes advantage of the poor insults their Maker, but whoever is kind to them honors him.

³²The wicked will be defeated by their evil, but good people are protected by their honesty.ᵃ

³³A wise person is always thinking wise thoughts, but a fool knows nothing about wisdom.

³⁴Goodness makes a nation great, but sin is a shame to any people.

³⁵Kings are pleased with intelligent officials, but they will punish shameful ones.

15 ¹A gentle answer makes anger disappear, but a rough answer makes it grow.

²Listening to wise people increases your knowledge, but only nonsense comes from the mouths of fools.

³The LORD sees what happens everywhere. He watches everyone, good and evil.

⁴Kind words are like a life-giving tree, but lying words will crush your spirit.

⁵Fools refuse to listen to their father's advice, but those who accept discipline are smart.

⁶Good people are rich in many ways, but those who are evil get nothing but trouble.

⁷Wise people say things that give you new knowledge, but fools say nothing worth hearing.

⁸The LORD hates the offerings of the wicked, but he is happy to hear the prayers of those who live right.

⁹The LORD hates the way evil people live, but he loves those who try to do good.

¹⁰Whoever stops living right will be punished. Whoever hates to be corrected will be destroyed.

¹¹The LORD knows everything, even what happens in the place of death. So surely he knows what people are thinking.

¹²Fools hate to be told they are wrong, so they refuse to ask wise people for advice.

¹³If you are happy, your face shows it. If you are sad, your spirit feels defeated.

¹⁴Intelligent people want more knowledge, but fools only want more nonsense.

¹⁵Life is always hard for the poor, but the right attitude can turn it into a party.

¹⁶It is better to be poor and respect the LORD than to be rich and have many troubles.

¹⁷It is better to eat a little where there is love than to eat a lot where there is hate.

¹⁸A quick temper causes fights, but patience brings peace and calm.

¹⁹For lazy people, life is a path overgrown with thorns and thistles. For those who do what is right, it is a smooth highway.

²⁰Wise children make their parents happy. Foolish children bring them shame.

²¹Doing foolish things makes a fool happy, but a wise person is careful to do what is right.

²²If you don't ask for advice, your plans will fail. With many advisors, they will succeed.

²³People are happy when they give a good answer. And there is nothing better than the right word at the right time.

²⁴What wise people do leads to life here on earthᵇ and stops them from going down to the place of death.

²⁵The LORD destroys a proud man's house but protects a widow's property.

²⁶The LORD hates evil thoughts, but he is pleased with kind words.

²⁷Whoever takes money to do wrong invites disaster. Refuse such gifts, and you will live.

²⁸Good people think before they answer, but the wicked do not, and what they say causes trouble.

²⁹The LORD is far away from the wicked, but he always hears the prayers of those who do what is right.

³⁰A smileᶜ makes people happy. Good news makes them feel better.

³¹To be counted among the wise, you must learn to accept helpful criticism.

³²If you refuse to be corrected, you are only hurting yourself. Listen to criticism, and you will gain understanding.

ᵃ14:32 Or "The wicked will be crushed by their evil, and those who hope for their destruction are right to do so."

ᵇ15:24 *here on earth* Literally, "above," that is, "above the ground."

ᶜ15:30 *smile* Literally, "a sparkle in the eyes."

33Wisdom teaches you to respect the Lord. You must be humbled before you can be honored.

16 1People might plan what they want to say, but it is the Lord who gives them the right words.

2People think that whatever they do is right, but the Lord judges their reason for doing it.

3Turn to the Lord for help in everything you do, and you will be successful.

4The Lord has a plan for everything. In his plan, the wicked will be destroyed.

5The Lord hates those who are proud. You can be sure he will punish them all.

6Faithful love and loyalty will remove your guilt.*a* Respect the Lord, and you will stay far away from evil.

7When people live to please the Lord, even their enemies will be at peace with them.

8It is better to be poor and do right than to be rich and do wrong.

9People can plan what they want to do, but it is the Lord who guides their steps.

10When a king speaks, his words are law. So when he makes a decision, it is never a mistake.

11The Lord wants all scales and balances to be right; he wants all business agreements to be fair.

12Kings hate to see anyone doing wrong,*b* because kingdoms grow strong only when everyone is honest and fair.

13Kings want to hear the truth. They like those who are honest.

14When a king gets angry, he can put someone to death. So it is wise to keep the king happy.

15When the king is happy, life is better for everyone. When he is pleased, it is like a refreshing spring rain.

16Wisdom is worth much more than gold. Understanding is worth much more than silver.

17Good people try to avoid evil. They watch what they do and protect themselves.

18Pride is the first step toward destruction. Proud thoughts will lead you to defeat.

19It is better to be a humble person living among the poor than to share the wealth among the proud.

20Good things happen to those who learn from their experiences, and the Lord blesses those who trust him.

21People will know if someone is wise. Those who choose their words carefully can be very convincing.

22Good sense is a spring of fresh water to those who have it, but fools can offer only foolishness.

23Wise people always think before they speak, so what they say is worth listening to.

24Kind words are like honey; they are easy to accept and good for your health.

25There is a way that seems right to people, but that way leads only to death.

26The thought of hunger keeps the workers working so that they can eat.

27Troublemakers create disasters. Their advice destroys like a wildfire.

28Troublemakers are always causing problems. Their gossip breaks up the closest of friends.

29Cruel people trick their neighbors and make them do wrong. 30With a wink of the eye, they plan to trick someone. With a grin, they make plans to hurt their friends.

31Gray hair is a crown of glory on people who have lived good lives. It is earned by living right.

32It is better to be patient than to be a strong soldier. It is better to control your anger than to capture a city.

33People might throw lots* to make a decision, but the answer always comes from the Lord.

17 1It is better to have nothing but a dry piece of bread to eat in peace than a whole house full of food with everyone arguing.

2A smart servant will gain control over his master's foolish son. He will be treated like a son and get a share of the inheritance.

3Fire is used to make gold and silver pure, but a person's heart is made pure by the Lord.

4People who do evil listen to evil ideas. Liars listen to liars.

5Whoever makes fun of beggars insults their Maker. Whoever laughs at someone else's trouble will be punished.

6Grandchildren are the pride and joy of old age, and children take great pride in their parents.

7You wouldn't expect to hear a fine speech from a fool, and you shouldn't expect lies from a ruler.

8Some people think a bribe is like a lucky charm—it seems to work wherever they go.

9Forgive someone, and you will strengthen your friendship. Keep reminding them, and you will destroy it.

10Smart people learn more from a single correction than fools learn from a hundred beatings.

11Those who are evil only want to cause trouble. In the end, punishment without mercy will be sent to them.

12It is better to meet a bear robbed of her cubs than a fool who is busy doing foolish things.

13If you do wrong to those who were good to you, you will have trouble the rest of your life.

---

a **16:6** *remove your guilt* Or "make atonement." The Hebrew word means "to cover," or "to erase" a person's sins.

b **16:12** *Kings ... wrong* Or "It is disgusting when kings do wrong."

¹⁴The start of an argument is like a small leak in a dam. Stop it before a big fight breaks out.

¹⁵The Lord hates these two things: punishing the innocent and letting the guilty go free.

¹⁶Money is wasted on fools. They cannot buy wisdom when they have no sense.

¹⁷A friend loves you all the time, but a brother was born to help in times of trouble.

¹⁸Only a fool would promise to pay for someone else's debts.

¹⁹A troublemaker loves to start arguments. Anyone who likes to brag is asking for trouble.

²⁰Crooks will not profit from their crimes, and those who plan to cause trouble will be trapped when it comes.

²¹A man who has a fool for a son will be disappointed. A fool brings no joy to his father.

²²Happiness is good medicine, but sorrow is a disease.

²³A wicked judge will accept a bribe, and that keeps justice from being done.

²⁴Intelligent people think about what needs to be done here and now. Fools are always dreaming about faraway places.

²⁵Foolish children upset their parents and make them sad.

²⁶It is wrong to punish an innocent person or attack leaders for doing what is right.

²⁷Intelligent people choose their words carefully. Those who know what they are doing remain calm.ᵃ

²⁸Silent fools seem wise. They say nothing and appear to be smart.

18 ¹Some people like to do things their own way, and they get upset when people give them advice.

²Fools don't want to learn from others. They only want to tell their own ideas.

³Do something evil, and people will hate you. Do something shameful, and they will have no respect for you.

⁴Words from wise people are like water bubbling up from a deep well—the well of wisdom.

⁵You must be fair in judging others. It is wrong to favor the guilty and rob the innocent of justice.

⁶Fools say things to start arguments. They are just asking for a beating.

⁷Fools hurt themselves when they speak. Their own words trap them.

⁸People love to hear gossip. It is like tasty food on its way to the stomach.

⁹Someone who does careless work is as bad as someone who destroys things.

¹⁰The name of the Lord is like a strong tower. Those who do what is right can run to him for protection.

¹¹The rich think their wealth will protect them. They think it is a strong fortress.

¹²A proud person will soon be ruined, but a humble person will be honored.

¹³Let people finish speaking before you try to answer them. That way you will not embarrass yourself and look foolish.

¹⁴A good attitude will support you when you are sick, but if you give up, nothing can help.ᵇ

¹⁵Wise people want to learn more, so they listen closely to gain knowledge.

¹⁶Gifts can open many doors and help you meet important people.

¹⁷The first person to speak always seems right until someone comes and asks the right questions.

¹⁸The best way to settle an argument between two powerful people may be to use lots.*

¹⁹An insulted brother is harder to win back than a city with strong walls. Arguments separate people like the strong bars of a palace gate.

²⁰Your words can be as satisfying as fruit, as pleasing as the food that fills your stomach.

²¹The tongue can speak words that bring life or death. Those who love to talk must be ready to accept what it brings.

²²If you find a wife, you have found something good. She shows that the Lord is happy with you.

²³The poor are polite when they beg for help. The rich are rude with their answer.

²⁴Some friends are fun to be with,ᶜ but a true friend can be better than a brother.

19 ¹It is better to be poor and honest than to be a liar and a fool.

²Being excited about something is not enough. You must also know what you are doing. Don't rush into something, or you might do it wrong.

³People ruin their lives with the foolish things they do, and then they blame the Lord for it.

⁴Wealth will bring you many friends, but become poor and your friends will leave you.

⁵A witness who lies will be punished; that liar will not escape.

⁶Many people are nice to a generous person. Everyone wants to be friends with someone who gives gifts.

⁷If you are poor, your family will turn against you, and your friends will avoid you even more. You might beg them for help, but no one will come to help you.

⁸Be a friend to yourself; do all you can to be wise. Try hard to understand, and you will be rewarded.

⁹A witness who lies will be punished. That liar will be destroyed.

ᵇ**18:14** *help* Literally, "lift up" or "heal."
ᶜ**18:24** *Some friends ... with* Or "Some friends can bring disaster."

ᵃ**17:27** *remain calm* Literally, "have a cool spirit."

¹⁰A fool should not be rich, and a slave should not rule over princes.

¹¹Experience makes you more patient, and you are most patient when you ignore insults.

¹²The shouts of an angry king are like a roaring lion, but his kind words are like a gentle rain falling softly on the grass.

¹³A foolish son brings a flood of troubles to his father, and a complaining wife is like the constant dripping of water.

¹⁴People receive houses and money from their parents, but a good wife is a gift from the LORD.

¹⁵Laziness brings on sleep, and an appetite for rest brings on hunger.

¹⁶Obey the law and live; ignore it and die.

¹⁷Giving help to the poor is like loaning money to the LORD. He will pay you back for your kindness.

¹⁸Discipline your children while there is still hope. Avoiding it can be deadly.

¹⁹People who are quick to become angry must pay the price. Protect them from punishment, and they become worse.

²⁰Listen to advice and accept discipline; then you, too, will become wise.

²¹People might make many plans, but what the LORD says is what will happen.

²²People want a friend they can trust. It is better to be poor than to be a liar.

²³Respect the LORD and you will have a good life, one that is satisfying and free from trouble.

²⁴Some people are too lazy to take care of themselves. They will not even lift the food from their plate to their mouth.

²⁵Punish a rude, arrogant person, and even slow learners will become wiser. But just a little correction is enough to teach a person who has understanding.

²⁶Those who would steal from their father and chase away their mother are disgusting, shameful people.

²⁷My son, if you stop listening to instructions, you will keep making stupid mistakes.

²⁸Using a criminal as a witness makes a joke of justice. People like that only want to do wrong.

²⁹People who show no respect for anything must be brought to justice. You must punish such fools.

20 ¹Wine and beer make people lose control; they get loud and stumble around. And that is foolish.

²An angry king is like a roaring lion. If you make him angry, you could lose your life.

³People who refuse to argue deserve respect. Any fool can start an argument.

⁴Some people are too lazy to plant seeds. So at harvest time, they look for food and find nothing.

⁵Getting information from someone can be like getting water from a deep well. If you are smart, you will draw it out.

⁶You might call many people your "friends," but it is hard to find someone who can really be trusted.

⁷When people live good, honest lives, their children are blessed.

⁸When the king sits and judges people, he must look carefully to separate the evil from the good.

⁹Can anyone say their heart is pure? Who can say, "I am free from sin"?

¹⁰The LORD hates for people to use the wrong weights and measures to cheat others.

¹¹Even children show what they are like by the things they do. You can see if their actions are pure and right.

¹²It was the LORD who gave us eyes for seeing and ears for hearing.

¹³If you love to sleep, you will become poor. Use your time working and you will have plenty to eat.

¹⁴When buying something, people always say, "It's no good. It costs too much." Then they go away and tell others what a good deal they got.

¹⁵The right knowledge can bring you gold, pearls, and other expensive things.

¹⁶If someone promises to pay the debt of a stranger, get a coat or something from him to keep until the debt is paid.

¹⁷It may seem to be a good thing to get something by cheating, but in the end, it will be worth nothing.

¹⁸Get good advice when you make your plans. Before you start a war, find good advisors.

¹⁹You cannot trust someone who would talk about things told in private. So don't be friends with someone who talks too much.

²⁰Those who would curse their father or mother are like a lamp that goes out on the darkest night.

²¹If your wealth was easy to get, it will not be worth much to you.ᵃ

²²Don't ever say, "I'll pay them back for what they did to me!" Wait for the LORD. He will make things right.

²³The LORD hates for people to use the wrong weights to cheat others. It is wrong to use scales that are not accurate.

²⁴The LORD guides our steps, and we never know where he will lead us.ᵇ

²⁵Think carefully before you promise to give something to God. Later, you might wish you had not made that promise.

²⁶Like a farmer who separates wheat from the chaff,* a wise king will decide who is wrong and crush them.

²⁷Your spirit is like a lamp to the LORD. He is able to see into your deepest parts.ᶜ

ᵃ**20:21** Or "An inheritance greedily guarded in the beginning will not be blessed in the end."
ᵇ**20:24** Or "A man's steps are from the LORD, and people don't understand his way."
ᶜ**20:27** Or "The LORD examines your breath and searches your deepest thoughts."

²⁸A king who is loyal and true will keep his power. Loyalty will keep his kingdom strong.

²⁹We admire a young man for his strength, but we respect an old man for his gray hair.

³⁰A beating can remove evil and make you completely clean.*a*

21 ¹To the Lord, a king's mind is like a ditch used to water the fields. He can lead the king wherever he wants him to go.

²People think that whatever they do is right, but the Lord judges the reasons for everything they do.

³Do what is right and fair. The Lord loves that more than sacrifices.

⁴Proud looks and proud thoughts are sins. They show a person is evil.

⁵Careful planning leads to profit. Acting too quickly leads to poverty.

⁶Wealth that comes from telling lies disappears quickly and leads to death.

⁷The bad things that evil people do will destroy them, because they refuse to do what is right.

⁸Criminals cause trouble wherever they go, but good people are honest and fair.

⁹It is better to live in a small corner on the roof than to share the house with a woman who is always arguing.

¹⁰Evil people always want to do more evil, and they show no mercy to people around them.

¹¹When you punish a proud person who laughs at what is right, even fools will learn something.*b* But a little instruction is enough for the wise to learn what they should.

¹²God is good. He knows what the wicked are doing, and he will punish them.

¹³Those who refuse to help the poor will not receive help when they need it themselves.

¹⁴If anyone is angry with you, give them a gift in private. A gift given in secret will calm even the strongest anger.

¹⁵A decision that is fair makes good people happy, but it makes those who are evil very afraid.

¹⁶Whoever leaves the path of wisdom will be on their way to an early death.

¹⁷Loving pleasure leads to poverty. Wine and luxury will never make you wealthy.

¹⁸The wicked must pay for what happens to good people—the cheaters will be taken in exchange for the honest.

¹⁹It is better to live alone in the desert than with a quick-tempered wife who loves to argue.

²⁰Wise people save the nice things they have. Fools use up everything as soon as they get it.

²¹People who try hard to do good and be faithful will find life, goodness, and honor.

²²A wise person can defeat a city full of warriors and tear down the defenses they trust in.

²³People who are careful about what they say will save themselves from trouble.

²⁴Proud people think they are better than others. They show they are evil by what they do.

²⁵Lazy people will cause their own destruction because they refuse to work.

²⁶Some people are greedy and never have enough. Good people are generous and have plenty.

²⁷The Lord hates sacrifices from the wicked because they offer them for some evil purpose.

²⁸Witnesses who lie will be caught and punished. A careful listener will always be there to speak up.

²⁹Good people know they are right, but the wicked have to pretend.

³⁰There is no one wise enough to make a plan that can succeed if the Lord is against it.

³¹You can prepare your horses for battle, but only the Lord can give you the victory.

22 ¹It is better to be respected than to be rich. A good name is worth more than silver or gold.

²The rich and the poor are the same. The Lord made them all.

³Wise people see trouble coming and get out of its way, but fools go straight to it and suffer for it.

⁴Respect the Lord and be humble. Then you will have wealth, honor, and true life.

⁵Evil people are trapped by many troubles, but those who want to live avoid them.

⁶Teach children in a way that fits their needs, and even when they are old, they will not leave the right path.

⁷The rich rule over the poor. The one who borrows is a slave to the one who lends.

⁸Those who spread trouble will harvest trouble. In the end, they will be destroyed for the trouble they caused.

⁹Generous people will be blessed, because they share their food with the poor.

¹⁰Get rid of the proud who laugh at what is right, and trouble will leave with them. All arguments and insults will end.

¹¹Love a pure heart and kind words, and the king will be your friend.

¹²The Lord watches over true knowledge, and he opposes those who try to deceive others.

¹³A person who is lazy and wants to stay home says, "There is a lion outside, and I might be killed in the streets!"

¹⁴The sin of adultery* is a trap, and the Lord gets very angry with those who fall into it.

¹⁵Children do foolish things, but if you punish them, they will learn not to do them.

¹⁶These two things will make you poor: hurting the poor to make yourself rich and giving gifts to the rich.

---

*a***20:30** The Hebrew text here is hard to understand.
*b***21:11** Or "Punish a rude, arrogant person, and the others will become wise."

Thirty Wise Sayings

[17]Listen carefully to these words from the wise. Pay attention to what I have learned. [18]It will be good for you to remember these words and have them ready when they are needed. [19]I will teach you these things now. I want you to trust the LORD. [20]I have written 30 sayings for you.[a] These are words of advice and wisdom. [21]They will teach you things that you can know for sure to be true. Then you can give good answers to the one who sent you.

— 1 —

[22]It is easy to steal from the poor, but don't do it. And don't take advantage of them in court. [23]The LORD is on their side. He supports the poor, and he will take from those who take from them.

— 2 —

[24]Don't be friends with people who become angry easily. Don't stay around quick-tempered people. [25]If you do, you may learn to be like them. Then you will have the same problems they do.

— 3 —

[26]Don't promise to pay someone else's debt. [27]If you cannot pay, you will lose everything you have. So why should you lose the bed you sleep on?

— 4 —

[28]Never move an old property line that was marked long ago by your ancestors.*

— 5 —

[29]Skilled workers will always serve kings. They will never have to work for less important people.

— 6 —

23 [1]When you sit and eat with an important person, remember who you are with. [2]Never eat too much, even if you are very hungry. [3]Don't eat too much of his fine food. It might be a trick.

— 7 —

[4]Don't ruin your health trying to get rich. If you are smart, you will give it up. [5]In the blink of an eye, money can disappear, as if it grew wings and flew away like a bird.

— 8 —

[6]Don't eat with selfish people. Control any desire you have for their finest foods. [7]They might tell you to eat and drink all you want, but they don't really mean it. They are the kind of people who are only thinking about

the cost. [8]And if you eat their food, you will get sick and be embarrassed.

— 9 —

[9]Don't try to teach fools. They will make fun of your wise words.

— 10 —

[10]Never move an old property line, and don't take land that belongs to orphans. [11]The Lord will be against you. He is powerful and protects orphans.

— 11 —

[12]Listen to your teacher and learn all you can.

— 12 —

[13]Always correct children when they need it. If you spank them, it will not kill them. [14]In fact, you might save their lives.

— 13 —

[15]My son, it makes me happy when you make a wise decision. [16]It makes me feel good inside when you say the right things.

— 14 —

[17]Never envy evil people, but always respect the LORD. [18]This will give you something to hope for that will not disappoint you.

— 15 —

[19]So listen, my son, and be wise. Always be careful to follow the right path. [20]Don't make friends with people who drink too much wine and eat too much food. [21]Those who eat and drink too much become poor. They sleep too much and end up wearing rags.

— 16 —

[22]Listen to your father. Without him, you would never have been born. Respect your mother, even when she is old. [23]Truth, wisdom, learning, and understanding are worth paying money for. They are worth far too much to ever sell. [24]The father of a good person is very happy. A wise child brings him joy. [25]Make both of your parents happy. Give your mother that same joy.

— 17 —

[26]My son, listen closely to what I am saying. Let my life be your example. [27]Prostitutes and bad women are a trap. They are like a deep well that you cannot escape. [28]A bad woman waits for you like a thief, and she causes many men to be unfaithful to their wives.

— 18 —

[29-30]Who gets into fights and arguments? Who gets hurt for no reason and has red, bloodshot eyes? People who stay out too late drinking wine, staring into their strong drinks.

[a]22:20 *I have … for you* Or "I wrote this for you earlier."

³¹So be careful with wine. It is pretty and red as it sparkles in the cup. And it goes down so smoothly when you drink it. ³²But in the end, it will bite like a snake.

³³Wine will cause you to see strange things and to say things that make no sense. ³⁴When you lie down, you will think you are on a rough sea and feel like you are at the top of the mast.* ³⁵You will say, "They hit me, but I never felt it. They beat me, but I don't remember it. Now I can't wake up. I need another drink."

24

— 19 —

¹Don't be jealous of evil people. Have no desire to be around them. ²In their hearts they plan to do evil. All they talk about is making trouble.

— 20 —

³Good homes are built on wisdom and understanding. ⁴Knowledge fills the rooms with rare and beautiful treasures.

— 21 —

⁵Wisdom makes a man more powerful. Knowledge gives a man strength. ⁶Get good advice before you start a war. To win, you must have many good advisors.

— 22 —

⁷Fools cannot understand wisdom. They have nothing to say when people are discussing important things.

— 23 —

⁸If you start planning ways to do wrong, people will learn that you are a troublemaker. ⁹Such foolish plans are wrong, and people have no respect for someone who laughs at what is right.

— 24 —

¹⁰If you are weak in times of trouble, that is real weakness.

— 25 —

¹¹If you see someone on their way to death or in danger of being killed, you must do something to save them. ¹²You cannot say, "It's none of my business." The Lord knows everything, and he knows why you do things. He watches you, and he will pay you back for what you do.

— 26 —

¹³My son, eat honey; it is good. Honey straight from the honeycomb is the sweetest. ¹⁴In the same way, know that wisdom is good for you. Wisdom will give you something to hope for that will not disappoint you.

— 27 —

¹⁵Don't be like a criminal who makes plans to rob those who are good or take away their homes. ¹⁶Good people might fall again and again, but they always get up. It is the wicked who are defeated by their troubles.

— 28 —

¹⁷Don't be happy when your enemy has troubles. Don't be glad when they fall. ¹⁸The Lord will see this, and he might be upset with you and decide not to punish your enemy.

— 29 —

¹⁹Don't let those who are evil upset you, and don't be jealous of them. ²⁰They have no hope. Their light will burn out.

— 30 —

²¹Son, respect the Lord and the king, and don't join with those who are against them, ²²because people like that can quickly be destroyed. You have no idea how much trouble God and the king can make for their enemies.

More Wise Sayings

²³These are also words from the wise:

A judge must be fair. He must not support some people simply because he knows them. ²⁴The people will turn against a judge who lets the guilty go free. Even the people of other nations will curse* him. ²⁵But if a judge punishes the guilty, then people will be happy with him, and he will be a blessing to them.

²⁶An honest answer is as pleasing as a kiss on the lips.

²⁷First get your fields ready, next plant your crops, and then build your house.

²⁸Don't speak against someone without a good reason, or you will appear foolish.

²⁹Don't say, "You hurt me, so I will do the same to you. I will punish you for what you did to me."

³⁰I walked past a field that belonged to a lazy man. It was a vineyard that belonged to someone who understood nothing. ³¹Weeds were growing everywhere! Wild vines covered the ground, and the wall around the vineyard was broken and falling down. ³²I looked at this and thought about it. This is what I learned: ³³a little sleep, a little rest, folding your arms, and taking a nap— ³⁴these things will make you poor very quickly. Soon you will have nothing, as if a thief broke in and took everything away.

More Wise Sayings From Solomon

25

¹These are some more wise sayings from Solomon. These proverbs* were copied by servants of Hezekiah, the king of Judah.

²We honor God for the things he keeps secret. But we honor kings for the things they can discover.

³We cannot discover how high the sky is above us or how deep the earth is below. The

same is true with the minds of kings. We cannot understand them.

4Remove the worthless things from silver to make it pure, and a worker can make something beautiful. 5Take the evil advisors away from a king, and goodness will make his kingdom strong.

6Don't brag about yourself before the king and pretend you are someone important. 7It is much better for the king to invite you to take a more important position than to embarrass you in front of his officials.

8Don't be too quick to tell a judge about something you saw. You will be embarrassed if someone else proves you wrong.

9If you want to tell your friends about your own problems, tell them. But don't discuss what someone told you in private. 10Whoever hears it will lose their respect for you and will never trust you again.

11Saying the right thing at the right time is like a golden apple in a silver setting. 12Wise advice to a listening ear is like gold earrings or fine jewelry.

13To his master who sent him, a messenger who can be trusted is as refreshing as a drink of cold water on a hot summer day.a

14People who promise to give gifts but never give them are like clouds and wind that bring no rain.

15With patience, you can make anyone change their thinking, even a ruler. Gentle speech is very powerful.

16Honey is good, but don't eat too much of it, or you will be sick. 17And don't visit your neighbors' homes too often, or they will begin to hate you.

18A person who gives false testimony against a neighbor is as deadly as a club, a sword, or a very sharp arrow. 19Never depend on a liar in times of trouble. It's like chewing with a bad tooth or walking with a crippled foot.

20Singing happy songs to a sad person is as foolish as taking a coat off on a cold day or mixing soda and vinegar.

21If your enemies are hungry, give them something to eat. If they are thirsty, give them some water. 22This will make them feel the burning pain of shame,b and the LORD will reward you for being good to them.

23Just as wind blowing from the north brings rain, telling secrets brings anger.

24It is better to live in a small corner of the roof than to share the house with a woman who is always arguing.

25Good news from a faraway place is like a cool drink of water when you are hot and thirsty.

26Good people who don't stand strong against evil are like springs that have been polluted or pools that have turned dirty and muddy.

27Just as eating too much honey is not good, it is not good for people to always be looking for honor.

28People who cannot control themselves are like cities without walls to protect them.

Wise Sayings About Fools

26 1Just as snow should not fall in summer, nor rain at harvest time, so people should not honor a fool.

2Don't worry when someone curses* you for no reason. Nothing bad will happen. Such words are like birds that fly past and never stop.

3You have to whip a horse, you have to put a bridle on a mule, and you have to beat a fool.

4-5There is no good way to answer fools when they say something stupid. If you answer them, then you, too, will look like a fool. If you don't answer them, they will think they are smart.

6Never let a fool carry your message. If you do, it will be like cutting off your own feet. You are only asking for trouble.

7A fool trying to say something wise is like a crippled person trying to walk.

8Showing honor to a fool is as bad as tying a rock in a sling.*

9A fool trying to say something wise is like a drunk trying to pick a thorn out of his hand.

10Hiring a fool or a stranger who is just passing by is dangerous—you don't know who might get hurt.

11Like a dog that returns to its vomit, a fool does the same foolish things again and again.

12People who think they are wise when they are not are worse than fools.

13A person who is lazy and wants to stay home says, "What if there is a lion out there? Really, there might be a lion in the street!"

14Like a door on its hinges, a lazy man turns back and forth on his bed.

15Lazy people are too lazy to lift the food from their plate to their mouth.

16Lazy people think they are seven times smarter than the people who really have good sense.

17To step between two people arguing is as foolish as going out into the street and grabbing a stray dog by the ears.

18-19Anyone who would trick someone and then say, "I was only joking" is like a fool who shoots flaming arrows into the air and accidentally kills someone.

20Without wood, a fire goes out. Without gossip, arguments stop.

21Charcoal keeps the coals glowing, wood keeps the fire burning, and troublemakers keep arguments alive.

22People love to hear gossip. It is like tasty food on its way to the stomach.

---

a25:13 drink ... day Literally, "as the cold snow at harvest time." This probably refers to snow or ice brought down from Mt. Hermon in Lebanon.
b25:22 This ... shame Literally, "for you will heap coals of fire on his head."

²³Good words that hide an evil heart are like silver paint over a cheap, clay pot. ²⁴Evil people say things to make themselves look good, but they keep their evil plans a secret. ²⁵What they say sounds good, but don't trust them. They are full of evil ideas. ²⁶They hide their evil plans with nice words, but in the end, everyone will see the evil they do.

²⁷Whoever digs a pit can fall into it. Whoever rolls a large stone can be crushed by it.

²⁸Liars hate the people they hurt, and false praise can hurt people.

27 ¹Never brag about what you will do in the future; you have no idea what tomorrow will bring.

²Never praise yourself. Let others do it.

³A stone is heavy, and sand is hard to carry, but the irritation caused by a fool is much harder to bear.

⁴Anger is cruel and can destroy like a flood, but jealousy is much worse.

⁵Open criticism is better than hidden love.

⁶You can trust what your friend says, even when it hurts. But your enemies want to hurt you, even when they act nice.

⁷When you are full, you will not even eat honey. When you are hungry, even something bitter tastes sweet.

⁸A man away from home is like a bird away from its nest.

⁹Perfume and incense make you feel good, and so does good advice from a friend.

¹⁰Don't forget your own friends or your father's friends. If you have a problem, go to your neighbor for help. It is better to ask a neighbor who is near than a brother who is far away.

¹¹My son, be wise. This will make me happy. Then I will be able to answer those who criticize me.

¹²Wise people see trouble coming and get out of its way, but fools go straight to the trouble and suffer for it.

¹³When you make a deal with a stranger, get something from him and any other foreigners with him to make sure he will pay you.

¹⁴Don't wake up your neighbors early in the morning with a shout of "Good morning!" They will treat it like a curse,* not a blessing.

¹⁵A complaining wife is like water that never stops dripping on a rainy day. ¹⁶Stopping her is like trying to stop the wind or trying to hold oil in your hand.

¹⁷As one piece of iron sharpens another, so friends keep each other sharp.

¹⁸People who take care of fig trees are allowed to eat the fruit. In the same way, people who take care of their masters will be rewarded.

¹⁹Just as you can see your own face reflected in water, so your heart reflects the kind of person you are.

²⁰Just as the place of death and destruction is never full, people always want more and more.

²¹People use fire to purify gold and silver. In the same way, you are tested by the praise people give you.

²²Even if you pound fools to powder like grain in a bowl, you will never force the foolishness out of them.

²³Learn all you can about your sheep. Take care of your goats the best you can. ²⁴Neither wealth nor nations last forever. ²⁵Cut the hay, and new grass will grow. Then gather the new plants that grow on the hills. ²⁶Cut the wool from your lambs, and make your clothes. Sell some of your goats, and buy some land. ²⁷Then there will be plenty of goat's milk for you and your family, with enough to keep the servants healthy.

28 ¹The wicked are afraid of everything, but those who live right are as brave as lions.

²A lawless nation will have many bad leaders. But a smart leader will rule for a long time in a land where people obey the law.

³A leader who takes advantage of the poor is like a hard rain that destroys the crops.ᵃ

⁴Those who refuse to obey the law promote evil. Those who obey the law oppose evil.

⁵The wicked don't understand justice, but those who love the Lord understand it completely.

⁶It is better to be poor and honest than rich and evil.

⁷A smart son obeys the laws, but a son who spends time with worthless people brings shame to his father.

⁸If you get rich by charging high interest rates, your wealth will go to someone who is kind to the poor.

⁹When people do not listen to God's teachings, he does not listen to their prayers.

¹⁰Those who plan to hurt good people will fall into their own traps, but good things will happen to those who are good.

¹¹The rich always think they are wise, but a poor person who is wise can see the truth.

¹²When good people become leaders, everything is great, but when the wicked rise to power, everyone hides.

¹³Whoever hides their sins will not be successful, but whoever confesses their sins and stops doing wrong will receive mercy.

¹⁴People who respect others will be blessed, but stubborn people will have plenty of troubles.

¹⁵An evil ruler over those who are helpless is like an angry lion or a charging bear.

¹⁶A foolish ruler hurts the people under him, but a ruler who hates wrong will rule for a long time.

ᵃ**28:3** Or "A poor person who takes advantage of beggars is like a hard rain and no food."

¹⁷A murderer will never have peace. Don't support such a person.

¹⁸Honest people will be safe, but dishonest people will be ruined.

¹⁹Whoever works hard will have plenty to eat, but whoever wastes their time with dreams will always be poor.

²⁰People who can be trusted will have many blessings, but those who are just trying to get rich in a hurry will be punished.

²¹It is wrong for a judge to support someone simply because he knows them. But some judges will change their decisions for the price of a loaf of bread.

²²Selfish people only want to get rich. They do not realize that they are very close to being poor.

²³Correct someone, and later they will thank you. That is much better than just saying something to be nice.

²⁴Someone might steal from their parents and say, "I did nothing wrong." But that person is as bad as an enemy who smashes everything in the house.

²⁵Greedy people might sue you in court, but those who trust the Lord are rewarded.

²⁶It is foolish to be too confident. Those who ask for advice are wise and will escape disaster.

²⁷Whoever gives to the poor will have plenty. Whoever refuses to help them will get nothing but curses.*

²⁸When the wicked rise to power, everyone hides. When they are defeated, good people multiply.

29 ¹Some people refuse to bend when someone corrects them. Eventually they will break, and there will be no one to repair the damage.

²When the rulers are good, the people are happy. When the rulers are evil, the people complain.

³A son who loves wisdom makes his father happy. One who wastes his money on prostitutes will lose his wealth.

⁴A nation will be strong when it has a fair and just king. A nation will be weak when it has a king who is selfish and demands gifts.

⁵If you give false praise to others in order to get what you want, you are only setting a trap for yourself.

⁶Evil people are defeated by their sin, but good people will sing and be happy.

⁷Good people want to do what is right for the poor, but the wicked don't care.

⁸Proud people who laugh at what is right cause problems that divide whole cities, but people who are wise are able to calm those who are angry.

⁹If someone who is wise tries to settle a problem with a fool, the fool will argue and say stupid things, and they will never agree.

¹⁰If you always try to be honest, murderers will hate you, but those who do what is right will want you to be their friend.

¹¹Fools are quick to express their anger, but wise people are patient and control themselves.

¹²If a ruler listens to lies, all his officials will be evil.

¹³In one way the poor and those who steal from them are the same—the Lord made them both.

¹⁴If a king judges the poor fairly, he will rule for a long time.

¹⁵Punishment and discipline can make children wise, but children who are never corrected will bring shame to their mother.

¹⁶If the wicked are ruling the nation, sin will be everywhere, but those who live right will win in the end.

¹⁷Correct your children whenever they are wrong. Then you will always be proud of them. They will never make you ashamed.

¹⁸If a nation is not guided by God, the people will lose self-control, but the nation that obeys God's law will be happy.

¹⁹Servants will not learn a lesson if you only talk to them. They might understand you, but they will not obey.

²⁰There is more hope for a fool than for someone who speaks without thinking.

²¹Give your servants everything they want, and they will learn to be wasteful.

²²An angry person causes arguments, and someone who is quick-tempered is guilty of many sins.

²³Your pride can bring you down. Humility will bring you honor.

²⁴You are your own worst enemy if you take part in a crime. You will not be able to tell the truth even when people threaten you.

²⁵Fear can be a trap, but if you trust in the Lord, you will be safe.

²⁶Many people want the friendship of a ruler, but the Lord is the only one who judges people fairly.

²⁷Good people think the wicked are disgusting, and the wicked feel disgust for those who are honest.

Wise Sayings of Agur Son of Jakeh

30 ¹These are the wise sayings of Agur son of Jakeh from Massa. He says, "God, I am tired, so tired. How can I keep going?"*ᵃ*

²I am stupid. I am not as smart as other people are. ³I have not learned to be wise. I know nothing about the Holy One.*ᵇ* ⁴Who has ever gone up to heaven and come back down? Who gathered the winds in his hand? Who can gather up all the water in his lap? Who set the limits for the world? What is his name, and what is his son's name? Do you know?

⁵You can trust this: Every word that God speaks is true. God is a safe place for those

---

*ᵃ***30:1** *He says, "God, ... keep going?"* Or "This is his message to Ithiel and Ucal."
*ᵇ***30:3** *Holy One* Literally, "the holy ones."

who go to him. ⁶So don't try to change what God says. If you do, he will punish you and prove that you are a liar.

⁷LORD, I ask you to do two things for me before I die. ⁸Don't let me tell lies. And don't make me too rich or too poor—give me only enough food for each day. ⁹If I have too much, I might deny that I need you, LORD. But if I am too poor, I might steal and bring shame to the name of my God.

¹⁰Never say bad things about a slave to his master. If you do, he will curse* you, and you will suffer for it.

¹¹Some people curse their fathers and refuse to bless their mothers.

¹²Some people think they are pure, but they have done nothing to remove the filth of their sin.

¹³Some people are so proud of themselves, and they look down on everyone else.

¹⁴There are people whose teeth are like swords and their jaws like knives. They take everything they can from the poor.

¹⁵Greedy people know only two thingsᵃ: "Give me," and "Give me." There are three other things that are never satisfied—really, four things that have never enough: ¹⁶the place of death, a woman with no children, dry ground that needs rain, and a fire that will never stop by itself.

¹⁷People who make fun of their father or refuse to obey their mother should have their eyes plucked out by wild birds and be eaten by vultures.*

¹⁸There are three things that are hard for me to understand—really, four things that I don't understand: ¹⁹an eagle flying in the sky, a snake moving on a rock, a ship moving across the ocean, and a man in love with a woman.

²⁰A woman who is not faithful to her husband acts innocent. She eats, wipes her mouth, and says she has done nothing wrong.

²¹There are three things that make trouble on the earth—really, four that the earth cannot bear: ²²a slave who becomes a king, fools who have everything they need, ²³a woman whose husband hated her but still married her, and a servant girl who becomes ruler over the woman she serves.

²⁴There are four things on the earth that are small but very wise:

²⁵ Ants are small and weak, but they save their food all summer;

²⁶ badgers are small animals, but they make their homes in the rocks;

²⁷ locusts have no king, but they are able to work together;

²⁸ lizards are small enough to catch with your hands, but you can find them living in kings' palaces.

²⁹There are three things that act important when they walk—really, there are four:

³⁰ a lion—he is the warrior of the animals
      and runs from nothing,
³¹ a rooster walking proudly,ᵇ
      a goat,
      and a king among his people.

³²If you have been foolish enough to become proud and make plans against other people, stop and think about what you are doing.

³³Stirring milk causes butter to form. Hitting someone's nose causes blood to flow. And making people angry causes trouble.

Wise Words for a King

31 ¹These are the wise sayings that King Lemuel's mother taught him:

²I prayed for a son, and you are the son I gave birth to. ³Don't waste your strength on women. Women destroy kings, so don't waste yourself on them. ⁴Lemuel, it is not wise for kings to drink wine. It is not wise for rulers to want beer. ⁵They may drink too much and forget what the law says. Then they might take away the rights of the poor. ⁶Give beer to people without hope. Give wine to those who are in trouble. ⁷Let them drink to forget their troubles. Let them forget they are poor.

⁸Speak up for people who cannot speak for themselves. Help people who are in trouble. ⁹Stand up for what you know is right, and judge all people fairly. Protect the rights of the poor and those who need help.

The Perfect Wife

¹⁰ᶜ How hard it is to find the perfect wife.ᵈ
      She is worth far more than jewels.
¹¹ Her husband depends on her.
      He will never be poor.
¹² She does good for her husband all her life.
      She never causes him trouble.
¹³ She is always gathering wool and flaxᵉ
      and enjoys making things with her
      hands.
¹⁴ She is like a ship from a faraway place.
      She brings home food from everywhere.
¹⁵ She wakes up early in the morning,
      cooks food for her family, and gives the
      servants their share.
¹⁶ She looks at land and buys it.
      She uses the money she has earned and
      plants a vineyard.
¹⁷ She works very hard.

ᵃ**30:15** Literally, "A leech has two daughters."

ᵇ**30:31** *a rooster walking proudly* Or possibly, "a greyhound" or "a war horse."
ᶜ**31:10–31** In Hebrew, each verse of this poem starts with the next letter of the alphabet, so this poem shows all the good qualities of a woman "from A to Z."
ᵈ**31:10** *the perfect wife* Or "a noble woman."
ᵉ**31:13** *flax* A plant used to make linen cloth.

She is strong and able to do all her
work.
¹⁸ She works late into the night
　to make sure her business earns a profit.
¹⁹ She makes her own thread
　and weaves her own cloth.
²⁰ She always gives to the poor
　and helps those who need it.
²¹ She does not worry about her family
　when it snows.
　She has given them all good, warm
　clothes.
²² She makes sheets and spreads for the
　beds,
　and she wears clothes of fine linen.
²³ Her husband is a respected member of
　the city council,
　where he meets with the other leaders.
²⁴ She makes clothes and belts
　and sells them to the merchants.*

²⁵ She is a strong person,[a] and people
　respect her.
　She looks to the future with confidence.
²⁶ She speaks with wisdom
　and teaches others to be loving and
　kind.
²⁷ She oversees the care of her house.
　She is never lazy.
²⁸ Her children say good things about her.
　Her husband brags about her and says,
²⁹"There are many good women,
　but you are the best."
³⁰ Grace and beauty can fool you,
　but a woman who respects the LORD
　should be praised.
³¹ Give her the reward she deserves.
　Praise her in public for what she has
　done.

[a]**31:25** *She is a strong person* Or "She is praised."

Ecclesiastes

1 ¹These are the words from the Teacher, a
son of David and king of Jerusalem.

²Everything is so meaningless. The Teacher
says that it is all a waste of time![b] ³Do people
really gain anything from all the hard work
they do in this life[c]?

Things Never Change

⁴People live and people die, but the earth
continues forever. ⁵The sun rises and the sun
goes down, and then it hurries to rise again in
the same place.

⁶The wind blows to the south, and the
wind blows to the north. The wind blows
around and around. Then it turns and blows
back to the place it began.

⁷All rivers flow again and again to the same
place. They all flow to the sea, but the sea
never becomes full.

⁸Words cannot fully explain things,[d] but
people continue speaking.[e] Words come
again and again to our ears, but our ears don't
become full. And our eyes don't become full
of what we see.

Nothing Is New

⁹All things continue the way they have
been since the beginning. The same things
will be done that have always been done.
There is nothing new in this life.

¹⁰Someone might say, "Look, this is new,"
but that thing has always been here. It was
here before we were.

¹¹People don't remember what happened
long ago. In the future, they will not remember what is happening now. And later, other
people will not remember what the people
before them did.

Does Wisdom Bring Happiness?

¹²I, the Teacher, was king over Israel in
Jerusalem. ¹³I decided to study and to use
my wisdom to learn about everything that is
done in this life. I learned that it is a very
hard thing that God has given us to do. ¹⁴I
looked at everything done on earth, and I saw
that it is all a waste of time. It is like trying
to catch the wind.[f] ¹⁵If something is crooked,
you cannot say it is straight. And if something
is missing, you cannot say it is there.

¹⁶I said to myself, "I am very wise. I am
wiser than all the kings who ruled Jerusalem
before me. I know what wisdom and knowledge really are."

[b]**1:2** *meaningless … a waste of time* The Hebrew
word means "vapor or breath" or "something that
is useless, meaningless, empty, wrong, or a waste
of time."
[c]**1:3** *in this life* Literally, "under the sun." Also in
verses 9, 13.
[d]**1:8** *Words cannot fully explain things* Literally, "All
words are weak."
[e]**1:8** *but people continue speaking* The Hebrew
could also be translated, "People cannot speak."

[f]**1:14** *trying to catch the wind* Or "It is very troubling to the spirit." The word for "troubling" can also
mean "craving," and the word for "spirit" can also
mean "wind." Also in verse 17.

¹⁷I decided to learn how wisdom and knowledge are better than thinking foolish thoughts. But I learned that trying to become wise is like trying to catch the wind. ¹⁸With much wisdom comes frustration. The one who gains more wisdom also gains more sorrow.

Does "Having Fun" Bring Happiness?

2 ¹I said to myself, "I should have fun—I should enjoy everything as much as I can." But I learned that this is also useless. ²It is foolish to laugh all the time. Having fun does not do any good.

³So I decided to fill my body with wine while I filled my mind with wisdom. I tried this foolishness because I wanted to find a way to be happy. I wanted to see what was good for people to do during their few days of life.

Does Hard Work Bring Happiness?

⁴Then I began doing great things. I built houses, and I planted vineyards* for myself. ⁵I planted gardens, and I made parks. I planted all kinds of fruit trees. ⁶I made pools of water for myself, and I used them to water my growing trees. ⁷I bought men and women slaves, and there were slaves born in my house. I owned many great things. I had herds of cattle and flocks of sheep. I owned more things than any other person in Jerusalem did.

⁸I also gathered silver and gold for myself. I took treasures from kings and their nations. I had men and women singing for me. I had everything any man could want.

⁹I became very rich and famous. I was greater than anyone who lived in Jerusalem before me. My wisdom was always there to help me. ¹⁰Anything my eyes saw and wanted, I got for myself. My mind was pleased with everything I did. And this happiness was the reward for all my hard work.

¹¹But then I looked at everything I had done and the wealth I had gained. I decided it was all a waste of time! It was like trying to catch the wind.ᵃ There is nothing to gain from anything we do in this life.ᵇ

Maybe Wisdom Is the Answer

¹²Then I decided to think about what it means to be wise or to be foolish or to do crazy things. And I thought about the one who will be the next king. The new king will do the same as the kings before him.ᶜ ¹³I saw that wisdom is better than foolishness in the same way that light is better than darkness.

¹⁴Wise people use their minds like eyes to see where they are going. But for fools, it is as if they are walking in the dark.

I also saw that fools and wise people both end the same way. ¹⁵I thought to myself, "The same thing that happens to a fool will also happen to me. So why have I tried so hard to become wise?" I said to myself, "Being wise is also useless." ¹⁶Whether people are wise or foolish, they will still die, and no one will remember either one of them forever. In the future, people will forget everything both of them did. So the two are really the same.

Is There Real Happiness in Life?

¹⁷This made me hate life. It was depressing to think that everything in this life is useless, like trying to catch the wind.

¹⁸I began to hate all the hard work I had done, because I saw that the people who live after me will get the things that I worked for. I will not be able to take them with me. ¹⁹Some other person will control everything I worked and studied for. And I don't know if that person will be wise or foolish. This is also senseless.

²⁰So I became sad about all the work I had done. ²¹People can work hard using all their wisdom and knowledge and skill. But they will die and other people will get the things they worked for. They did not do the work, but they will get everything. That makes me very sad. It is also not fair and is senseless.

²²What do people really have after all their work and struggling in this life? ²³Throughout their life, they have pain, frustrations, and hard work. Even at night, a person's mind does not rest. This is also senseless.

²⁴⁻²⁵There is no one who has tried to enjoy life more than I have. And this is what I learned: The best thing people can do is eat, drink, and enjoy the work they must do. I also saw that this comes from God.ᵈ ²⁶If people do good and please God, he will give them wisdom, knowledge, and joy. But those who sin will get only the work of gathering and carrying things. God takes from the bad person and gives to the good person. But all this work is useless. It is like trying to catch the wind.

A Time for Everything

3 ¹There is a right time for everything, and everything on earth will happen at the right time.

² There is a time to be born
   and a time to die.
   There is a time to plant
   and a time to pull up plants.
³ There is a time to kill
   and a time to heal.

ᵃ2:11 *trying to catch the wind* Or "It is very troubling to the spirit." The word for "troubling" can also mean "craving," and the word for "spirit" can also mean "wind." Also in verses 17, 26.

ᵇ2:11 *in this life* Literally, "under the sun." Also in verses 17, 22.

ᶜ2:12 *And I thought … before him* The Hebrew text here is hard to understand.

ᵈ2:24–25 Or "²⁴The best people can do is eat, drink, and enjoy their work. I also saw that this comes from God. ²⁵No one can eat or enjoy life without God."

There is a time to destroy
and a time to build.
4 There is a time to cry
and a time to laugh.
There is a time to be sad
and a time to dance with joy.
5 There is a time to throw weapons down
and a time to pick them up.*a*
There is a time to hug someone
and a time to stop holding so tightly.
6 There is a time to look for something
and a time to consider it lost.
There is a time to keep things
and a time to throw things away.
7 There is a time to tear cloth
and a time to sew it.
There is a time to be silent
and a time to speak.
8 There is a time to love
and a time to hate.
There is a time for war
and a time for peace.

God Controls His World

9Do people really gain anything from their hard work? 10I saw all the hard work God gave us to do. 11God gave us the ability to think about his world,*b* but we can never completely understand everything he does. And yet, he does everything at just the right time.

12I learned that the best thing for people to do is to be happy and enjoy themselves as long as they live. 13God wants everyone to eat, drink, and enjoy their work. These are gifts from God.

14I learned that anything God does will continue forever. People cannot add anything to the work of God, and they cannot take anything away from it. God did this so that people would respect him. 15What happened in the past has happened, and what will happen in the future will happen. But God wants to help those who have been treated badly.*c*

16I also saw these things in this life*d*: I saw that the courts should be filled with goodness and fairness, but there is evil there now. 17So I said to myself, "God has planned a time for everything, and he has planned a time to judge everything people do. He will judge good people and bad people."

Are People Like Animals?

18I thought about what people do to each other. And I said to myself, "God wants people to see that they are like animals. 19The same thing happens to animals and to people—they die. People and animals have

the same 'breath.'*e* Is a dead animal different from a dead person? It is all so senseless! 20The bodies of people and animals end the same way. They came from the earth, and, in the end, they will go back to the earth. 21Who knows what happens to a person's spirit? Who knows if a human's spirit goes up to God while an animal's spirit goes down into the ground?"

22So I saw that the best thing people can do is to enjoy what they do, because that is all they have. Besides, no one can help another person see what will happen in the future.

Is It Better to Be Dead?

4 1Again I saw that many people are treated badly. I saw their tears, and I saw that there was no one to comfort them. I saw that cruel people had all the power, and I saw that there was no one to comfort the people they hurt. 2I decided that it is better for those who have died than for those who are still alive. 3And it is even better for those who die at birth, because they never saw the evil that is done in this world.*f*

Why Work So Hard?

4Then I thought, "Why do people work so hard?" I saw people try to succeed and be better than other people. They do this because they are jealous. They don't want other people to have more than they have. This is senseless. It is like trying to catch the wind.*g*

5Some people say, "It is foolish to fold your hands and do nothing. If you don't work, you will starve to death." 6Maybe that is true. But I say it is better to be satisfied with the few things you have than to always be struggling to get more.

7Again I saw something else that didn't make sense: 8I saw a man who has no family, not a son or even a brother. But he continues to work very hard. He is never satisfied with what he has. And he works so hard that he never stops and asks himself, "Why am I working so hard? Why don't I let myself enjoy my life?" This is also a very bad and senseless thing.

Friends and Family Give Strength

9Two people are better than one. When two people work together, they get more work done.

10If one person falls, the other person can reach out to help. But those who are alone when they fall have no one to help them.

11If two people sleep together, they will be warm. But a person sleeping alone will not be warm.

---

*a*3:5 Literally, "There is a time to throw stones away and a time to gather stones."
*b*3:11 *the ability ... world* Or "a desire to know the future."
*c*3:15 Or "What happens now also happened in the past. What happens in the future has also happened before. God makes things happen again and again."
*d*3:16 *in this life* Literally, "under the sun."

*e*3:19 *breath* Or "spirit."
*f*4:3 *in this world* Literally, "under the sun."
*g*4:4 *trying to catch the wind* Or "It is very troubling to the spirit." The word for "troubling" can also mean "craving," and the word for "spirit" can also mean "wind." Also in verse 16.

¹²An enemy might be able to defeat one person, but two people can stand back-to-back to defend each other. And three people are even stronger. They are like a rope that has three parts wrapped together—it is very hard to break.

People, Politics, and Popularity

¹³A young leader who is poor but wise is better than a king who is old but foolish. That old king does not listen to warnings. ¹⁴Maybe the young ruler was born a poor man in the kingdom. And maybe he came from prison to rule the country. ¹⁵But I have watched people in this life,ᵃ and I know this: People will follow that young man. He will become the new king. ¹⁶Many people will follow this young man. But later, those same people will not like him. This is also senseless. It is like trying to catch the wind.

Be Careful About Making Promises

5 ¹Be very careful when you go to worship God. It is better to listen to God than to give sacrifices* like fools. Fools often do bad things, and they don't even know it. ²Be careful when you make promises to God. Be careful about what you say to him. Don't let your feelings cause you to speak too soon. God is in heaven, and you are on the earth. So you need to say only a few things to him. This saying is true:

³ Bad dreams come from too many worries,
    and too many words come from the
      mouth of a fool.

⁴If you make a promise to God, keep your promise. Don't be slow to do what you promised. God is not happy with fools. Give God what you promised to give him. ⁵It is better to promise nothing than to promise something and not be able to do it. ⁶So don't let your words cause you to sin. Don't say to the priest,ᵇ "I didn't mean what I said." If you do this, God might become angry with your words and destroy everything you have worked for. ⁷You should not let your useless dreams and bragging bring you trouble. You should respect God.

For Every Ruler There Is a Ruler

⁸In some country you will see poor people who are forced to work very hard. You will see that this is not fair to them. It is against their rights. But don't be surprised! The ruler who forces them to work has another ruler who forces him. And there is still another ruler who forces both of these rulers. ⁹Even the king is a slave—his country owns him.ᶜ

Wealth Cannot Buy Happiness

¹⁰Those who love money will never be satisfied with the money they have. Those who love wealth will not be satisfied when they get more and more. This is also senseless.

¹¹The more wealth people have, the more "friends" they have to help spend it. So the rich really gain nothing. They can only look at their wealth.

¹²Those who work hard all day come home and sleep in peace. It is not important if they have little or much to eat. But the rich worry about their wealth and are not able to sleep.

¹³There is a very sad thing that I have seen happen in this life.ᵈ People save their money for the future.ᵉ ¹⁴Then something bad happens and they lose everything. So they have nothing to give to their children.

¹⁵People come into the world with nothing. And when they die, they leave with nothing. They might work hard to get things, but they cannot take anything with them when they die. ¹⁶It is very sad that people leave the world just as they came. So what does a person gain from "trying to catch the wind"? ¹⁷They only get days that are filled with sadness and sorrow. In the end, they are troubled, sick, and angry.

Enjoy Your Life's Work

¹⁸I have seen what is best for people to do on earth: They should eat, drink, and enjoy the work they have during their short time here. God has given them these few days, and that is all they have.

¹⁹If God gives some people wealth, property, and the power to enjoy those things, they should enjoy them. They should accept the things they have and enjoy their work—that is a gift from God. ²⁰People don't have many years to live, so they must remember these things all their life. God will keep them busy with the work they love to do.ᶠ

Wealth Does Not Bring Happiness

6 ¹I have seen another thing in this life that is not fair and is very hard to understand. ²God gives some people great wealth, riches, and honor. They have everything they need and everything they could ever want. But then God does not let them enjoy those things. Some stranger comes and takes everything. This is a very bad and senseless thing.

³A man might live a long time and have 100 children. But if he is not satisfied with those good things, and if no one remembers him after his death, I say that a baby who dies at birth is better off than that man. ⁴It is

---

ᵃ**4:15** *in this life* Literally, "under the sun."
ᵇ**5:6** *priest* Or "angel" or "messenger." This might be an angel, a priest, or a prophet.
ᶜ**5:8–9** *The ruler ... owns him* Or "One ruler is cheated by a higher ruler. And they are cheated by

an even higher ruler. ⁹Even the king gets his share of the profit. The wealth of the country is divided among them."
ᵈ**5:13** *in this life* Literally, "under the sun." Also in 6:1.
ᵉ**5:13** *for the future* Or "to their harm."
ᶠ**5:20** *God ... to do* Or "God will do whatever he wants to them."

senseless when a baby is born dead. The baby is quickly buried in a dark grave, without even a name. [5]The baby never saw the sun and never knew anything. But the baby finds more rest than the man who never enjoyed what God gave him. [6]He might live 2000 years. But if he does not enjoy life, then the baby who was born dead has found the easiest way to the same end.[a]

[7]People work and work to feed themselves, but they are never satisfied. [8]In the same way a wise person is no better than a fool. It is better to be a poor person who knows how to accept life as it is. [9]It is better to be happy with what you have than to always want more and more. Always wanting more and more is useless. It is like trying to catch the wind.[b]

[10-11]You are only what you were created to be—a human, and it is useless to argue about it. People cannot argue with God about this because he is more powerful than they are, and a long argument will not change that fact.

[12]Who knows what is best for people during their short life on earth? Their life passes like a shadow. No one can tell them what will happen later.

A Collection of Wise Teachings

7 [1]A good reputation is better than expensive pleasures.[c]

The day someone dies is better than the day they were born.

[2] It is better to go to a funeral than to a party,
because everyone must die,
and the living need to remember this.

[3] Sorrow is even better than laughter,
because when our face is sad, our heart becomes good.

[4] A wise person thinks about death,
but a fool thinks only about having a good time.

[5] It is better to be criticized by the wise than praised by the foolish.

[6] The laughter of fools is such a waste.
It is like thorns burning under a pot.
The thorns burn so quickly
that the pot does not get hot.[d]

[7] Even the wise will forget their wisdom,
if someone pays them enough.
That money destroys their understanding.

[8] It is better to finish something
than to start it.

It is better to be gentle and patient
than to be proud and impatient.

[9] Don't become angry quickly,
because anger is foolish.

[10] Don't say, "Life was better in the 'good old days.'
What happened?"
Wisdom does not lead us to ask that question.

[11]Wisdom is better if you also have property. Wise people[e] will get more than enough wealth. [12]Wisdom and money can protect you. But knowledge gained through wisdom is even better—it can save your life.

[13]Look at what God has made. You cannot change a thing, even if you think it is wrong. [14]When life is good, enjoy it. But when life is hard, remember that God gives us good times and hard times. And no one knows what will happen in the future.

People Cannot Really Be Good

[15]In my short life, I have seen everything. I have seen good people die young, and I have seen evil people live long lives. [16-17]So why ruin your life? Don't be too good or too bad, and don't be too wise or too foolish. Why should you die before your time?

[18]Try to be a little of this and a little of that.[f] Even God's followers will do some good things and some bad things. [19-20]Surely there is no one on earth who always does good and never sins. But wisdom can make one person stronger than ten leaders in a city.

[21]Don't listen to everything people say. You might hear your own servant saying bad things about you. [22]And you know that many times you too have said bad things about other people.

[23]I used my wisdom and thought about all these things. I wanted to be wise, but I couldn't do it. [24]I cannot understand why things are as they are. It is too hard for anyone to understand. [25]I studied and I tried very hard to find true wisdom. I tried to find a reason for everything.

I did learn that it is foolish to be evil, and it is crazy to act like a fool. [26]I also found that some women are dangerous like traps. Their hearts are like nets, and their arms are like chains. It is worse than death to be caught by these women. God's followers should run away from them. Let the sinners be caught by them.

[27-28]The Teacher says, "I added all this together to see what answer I could find. I am

---

[a]**6:6** *then the baby ... the same end* Or "Isn't it true that all go to the same place?"

[b]**6:9** Or "Having what you can see is better than chasing after the things you want. This is also like trying to catch the wind."

[c]**7:1** *A good reputation ... pleasures* Literally, "better a name than good perfume." This is a wordplay in Hebrew. The word for "name" and the word for "perfume" sound alike.

[d]**7:6** Or "The cackling of fools, like the crackling of thorns under a pot, is senseless."

[e]**7:11** *Wise people* Literally, "People who see the sun." This means wise people can see and plan what they should do.

[f]**7:18** *Try ... of that* Or "Hold onto this, but don't let go of that."

still looking for answers, but I did find this: I found one good man in a thousand. But I did not find even one good woman.

29"There is one other thing I have learned. God made people good, but they have found many ways to be bad."

Wisdom and Power

8 ¹No one can understand and explain things the way wise people can. Their wisdom makes them happy. It changes a sad face into a happy one.

²I say you should always obey the king's command. Do this because you made a promise to God. ³Don't be afraid to give suggestions to the king, and don't support something that is wrong. But remember, the king gives the commands that please him. ⁴He has the authority to give commands, and no one can tell him what to do. ⁵People will be safe if they obey his command. But wise people know the right time to do this, and they also know when to do the right thing.

⁶There is a right time and a right way to do everything. You must decide what you should do, even when it might cause problems ⁷and you are not sure what will happen. No one can tell you what will happen in the future.

⁸No one has the power to keep their spirit from leaving or to stop their death. During war, no soldier has the freedom to go wherever he wants. In the same way evil does not allow anyone who does wrong to go free.

⁹I saw all this. I thought very hard about the things that happen in this world. I saw that people always struggle for the power to rule others, and this is bad for them. ¹⁰I also saw great and beautiful funerals for evil people. While the people were going home after the funeral services, they said good things about the evil people who had died. This happened even in the same towns where the evil people had done many bad things. This is senseless.

Justice, Rewards, and Punishment

¹¹Sometimes people are not immediately punished for the bad things they do. Their punishment is slow to come, and that makes other people want to do bad things too.

¹²A sinner might do a hundred evil things and still live a long time. But I know that it is still better to obey and respect God. ¹³Evil people don't respect God, so they will not get good things or live long lives. Their lives will not be like the shadows that become longer and longer as the sun goes down.

¹⁴There is something else that happens on earth that does not seem fair. Bad things should happen to bad people, and good things should happen to good people. But sometimes bad things happen to good people, and good things happen to bad people. This is not fair. ¹⁵So I decided it was more important to enjoy life because the best thing people can do in this life*ᵃ* is to eat, drink, and enjoy life. At least that will help people enjoy the hard work God gave them to do during their life on earth.

We Cannot Understand All God Does

¹⁶I carefully studied the things people do in this life. I saw how busy people are. They work day and night, and they almost never sleep. ¹⁷I also saw the many things that God does, and I saw that people cannot understand all the work that God does on earth. You might try and try to understand, but you cannot. Even if some wise man says he understands what God does, it is not true. No one can understand all this.

Is Death Fair?

9 ¹I thought about all this very carefully. I saw that God controls what happens to the good and wise people and what they do. People don't know if they will be loved or hated, and they don't know what will happen in the future.

²But, there is one thing that happens to everyone—we all die! Death comes to good people and bad people. Death comes to those who are pure and to those who are not pure. Death comes to those who give sacrifices* and to those who don't give sacrifices. Good people will die just as sinners do. Those who make promises to God will die just as those who are afraid to make those promises.

³Of all the things that happen in this life, the worst thing is that all people end life the same way. But it is also very bad that people always think evil and foolish thoughts. And those thoughts lead to death. ⁴There is hope for those who are still alive—it does not matter who they are. But this saying is true:

A living dog is better than a dead lion.

⁵The living know that they will die, but the dead don't know anything. They have no more reward. People will soon forget them. ⁶After people are dead, their love, hate, and jealousy are all gone. And they will never again share in what happens on earth.

Enjoy Life While You Can

⁷So go and eat your food now and enjoy it. Drink your wine and be happy. It is all right with God if you do these things. ⁸Wear nice clothes and make yourself look good. ⁹Enjoy life with the wife you love. Enjoy every day of your short life. God has given you this short life on earth—and it is all you have. So enjoy the work you have to do in this life. ¹⁰Every time you find work to do, do it the best you can. In the grave there is no work. There is

ᵃ8:15 in this life Literally, "under the sun." Also in verse 16 and 9:3, 9, 11, 13.

no thinking, no knowledge, and there is no wisdom. And we are all going to the place of death.

Life Is Not Fair

[11] I also saw other things in this life that were not fair. The fastest runner does not always win the race; the strongest soldier does not always win the battle; wise people don't always get the food; smart people don't always get the wealth; educated people don't always get the praise they deserve. When the time comes, bad things can happen to anyone!

[12] You never know when hard times will come. Like fish in a net or birds in a snare, people are often trapped by some disaster that suddenly falls on them.

The Power of Wisdom

[13] I also saw a person doing a wise thing in this life, and it seemed very important to me. [14] There was a small town with a few people in it. A great king fought against that town and put his armies all around it. [15] But there was a wise man in that town. He was poor, but he used his wisdom to save his town. After everything was finished, the people forgot about the poor man. [16] But I still say that wisdom is better than strength. They forgot about the poor man's wisdom, and the people stopped listening to what he said. But I still believe that wisdom is better.

[17] Words spoken by the wise are heard more clearly
    than those shouted by a leader among fools.
[18] Wisdom is better than weapons of war,
    but one fool[a] can destroy much good.

10 [1] A few dead flies will make even the best perfume stink. In the same way, a little foolishness can ruin much wisdom and honor.

[2] The thoughts of the wise lead them the right way, but the thoughts of the foolish lead them the wrong way. [3] Fools show how foolish they are, just walking down the road. Their minds are empty, and everyone knows it.

[4] Don't quit your job simply because the boss is angry with you. If you remain calm and helpful, you can correct even great mistakes.[b]

[5] Here is something else that I have seen in this life[c] that isn't fair. It is the kind of mistake that rulers make. [6] Fools are given important positions, while the rich get jobs that are

not important. [7] I have seen servants riding on horses, while rulers were walking beside them like slaves.

Every Job Has Its Dangers

[8] If you dig a hole, you might fall into it. If you break down a wall, you might be bitten by a snake. [9] If you are moving large stones, you might be hurt by them. If you cut down a tree, you are in danger of it falling on you.

[10] But wisdom will make any job easier. It is very hard to cut with a dull knife. But if you sharpen the knife, the job is easier.

[11] Someone might know how to control snakes. But that skill is useless if a snake bites when that person is not around.

[12] Words from the wise bring praise,
    but words from a fool bring destruction.

[13] Fools begin by saying something foolish. But in the end, they speak nonsense. [14] Fools are always talking about what they will do, but you never know what will happen. People cannot tell what will happen in the future.

[15] Fools aren't smart enough to find their way home,
    so they must work hard all their lives.

The Value of Work

[16] It is very bad for a country if the king is like a child. And it is very bad for a country if its rulers use all their time eating. [17] But it is very good for a country if the king comes from a good family.[d] And it is very good for a country if the rulers control their eating and drinking. They eat and drink to become strong, not to become drunk.

[18] If someone is too lazy to work,
    their house will begin to leak, and the roof will fall in.

[19] People enjoy eating, and wine makes life happier. But money solves a lot of problems.

Gossip

[20] Don't say bad things about the king. Don't even think bad things about him. And don't say bad things about rich people, even if you are alone in your home. A little bird might fly and tell them everything you said.

Boldly Face the Future

11 [1] Do good wherever you go.[e] After a while, the good you do will come back to you.

---

[a] **9:18** *fool* Literally, "sinner."
[b] **10:4** *If you ... great mistakes* Literally, "A healer can put to rest great sins." The word "healer" means a person who is forgiving and tries to help other people.
[c] **10:5** *in this life* Literally, "under the sun."

[d] **10:17** *comes from a good family* Literally, "is a son of freedmen." This is a person who was never a slave and whose parents were not slaves.
[e] **11:1** *Do good ... go* Or "Throw your bread on the water."

[2]Invest what you have in several different things.[a] You don't know what bad things might happen on earth.

[3]There are some things you can be sure of. If clouds are full of rain, they will pour water on the earth. If a tree falls—to the south or to the north—then it will stay where it falls.

[4]But there are some things that you cannot be sure of. You must take a chance. If you wait for perfect weather, you will never plant your seeds. If you are afraid that every cloud will bring rain, you will never harvest your crops.

[5]You don't know where the wind blows. And you don't know how a baby grows in its mother's womb. In the same way, you don't know what God will do—and he makes everything happen.

[6]So begin planting early in the morning, and don't stop working until evening. You don't know what might make you rich. Maybe everything you do will be successful.

[7]It is good to be alive. It is nice to see the light from the sun. [8]You should enjoy every day of your life, no matter how long you live. But remember that you will die, and you will be dead much longer than you were alive. And after you are dead, you cannot do anything.

Serve God While You Are Young

[9]So young people, enjoy yourselves while you are young. Be happy. Do whatever your heart leads you to do. Do whatever you want, but remember that God will judge you for everything you do. [10]Don't let your anger control you, and don't let your body lead you to sin.[b] People do foolish things in the dawn of life while they are young.

The Problems of Old Age

12 [1]Remember your Creator while you are young, before the bad times come—before the years come when you say, "I have wasted my life."[c]

[2]Remember your Creator while you are young, before the time comes when the sun and the moon and the stars become dark to you—before problems come again and again like one storm after another.

[3]At that time your arms will lose their strength. Your legs will become weak and bent. Your teeth will fall out, and you will not be able to chew your food. Your eyes will not see clearly. [4]You will become hard of hearing. You will not hear the noise in the streets. Even the stone grinding your grain will seem quiet to you. You will not be able to hear the women singing. But even the sound of a bird singing will wake you early in the morning because you will not be able to sleep.

[5]You will be afraid of high places. You will be afraid of tripping over every small thing in your path. Your hair will become white like the flowers on an almond tree. You will drag yourself along like a grasshopper when you walk. You will lose your desire,[d] and then you will go to your eternal home. The mourners* will gather in the streets as they carry your body to the grave.

Death

[6] Remember your Creator
      while you are young,
      before the silver rope snaps
      and the golden bowl is crushed
      like a jar broken at the well,
      like a stone cover on a well that breaks
            and falls in.
[7] Your body came from the earth.
      And when you die, it will return to the
            earth.
      But your spirit came from God,
            and when you die, it will return to him.

[8]Everything is so meaningless. The Teacher says that it is all a waste of time![e]

Final Words of Advice

[9]The Teacher was very wise. He used his wisdom to teach the people. He very carefully studied and arranged[f] many wise teachings. [10]The Teacher tried very hard to find the right words, and he wrote the teachings that are true and dependable.

[11]Words from the wise are like sharp goads.* When these sayings are written down and saved, they can be used to guide people, just as a shepherd uses a sharp stick to make his sheep go the right way. [12]So, son, study these sayings, but be careful about other teachings. People are always writing books, and too much study will make you very tired.

[13-14]Now, what should we learn from everything that is written in this book?[g] The most important thing a person can do is to respect God and obey his commands, because he knows about everything people do—even the secret things. He knows about all the good and all the bad, and he will judge people for everything they do.

---

[a]**11:2 Invest ... different things** Or "Give a part to seven, or even eight."

[b]**11:10 Don't let ... sin** Or "Don't worry about things. Protect yourself from troubles."

[c]**12:1 I have wasted my life** Literally, "I take no pleasure in them." This might mean "I don't like the things I did when I was young" or "I don't enjoy life now that I am old."

[d]**12:5 desire** Or "appetite" or "sexual desire." The Hebrew text here is hard to understand.

[e]**12:8 meaningless ... a waste of time** The Hebrew word means "vapor," "breath," or "something that is useless, meaningless, empty, wrong, or a waste of time."

[f]**12:9 arranged** This Hebrew word means "to make straight," "arrange," "correct," or "edit."

[g]**12:13-14 Now ... book** Literally, "The sum of the matter, when all is heard, is ...."

Song of Songs

1

¹Solomon's Most Wonderful Song.

The Woman to the Man She Loves

² Cover me with kisses,
  for your love is better than wine.
³ Your perfume smells wonderful,
  but your name*a* is sweeter than the best
    perfume.
That is why the young women love you.
⁴ Take me with you.
  Let's run away.

The king took me into his room.

The Women of Jerusalem to the Man

We will rejoice and be happy for you.
Remember, your love is better than
  wine.
With good reason, the young women
  love you.

She Speaks to the Women

⁵ Daughters of Jerusalem,
  I am dark and beautiful,
  as black as the tents of Kedar and
    Salma.*b*

⁶ Don't look at how dark I am,
  at how dark the sun has made me.
My brothers were angry with me.
  They forced me to take care of their
    vineyards,*
  so I could not take care of myself.*c*

She Speaks to Him

⁷ I love you with all my soul!
Tell me, where do you feed your sheep?
  Where do you lay them down at noon?
₋I should come to be with you₋
  or I will be like a hired woman*d* caring
    for the sheep of your friends.

He Speaks to Her

⁸ You are such a beautiful woman.
  Surely you know what to do.
  Go, follow the sheep.

Feed your young goats near the
  shepherds' tents.

⁹ My darling, you are more exciting to me
  than any mare among the stallions*e*
    pulling Pharaoh's chariots.*f*
₋Those horses have beautiful decorations
  at the side of their faces and around
    their necks.₋
¹⁰⁻¹¹Here are the decorations made for you,
  a golden headband*g* and a silver
    necklace.
Your cheeks are so beautiful
  decorated with gold.
Your neck is so beautiful
  laced with silver.

She Speaks

¹² The smell of my perfume reaches out
  to the king lying on his couch.
¹³ My lover is like the small bag of myrrh*
  ₋around my neck₋,
  lying all night between my breasts.
¹⁴ My lover is like a bunch of henna flowers
  near the vineyards* of En Gedi.

He Speaks

¹⁵ My darling, you are so beautiful!
  Oh, you are beautiful!
Your eyes are like doves.

She Speaks

¹⁶ You are so handsome, my lover!
  Yes, and so charming!
Our bed is so fresh and pleasant.*h*
¹⁷ The beams of our house are cedar.
  The rafters are fir.

2

¹I am a rose on the plain of Sharon,*i* a
  lily*j* in the valleys.

---

*a*1:3 *name* In Hebrew this word sounds like the word "perfume."
*b*1:5 *Kedar and Salma* Arabian tribes. For "Salma" the standard Hebrew text has "Solomon," but compare "Salma, Salmon" in Ruth 4:20–21.
*c*1:6 *myself* Literally, "my own vineyard."
*d*1:7 *hired woman* Or "a woman wearing a veil." This might mean a prostitute.

*e*1:9 *mare ... stallions* Female and male horses. Only male horses were used to pull chariots.
*f*1:9 Literally, "To a mare among Pharaoh's chariots I compare you, my darling."
*g*1:10–11 *headband* The meaning of this Hebrew word here is uncertain. It might be a headband with decorations dangling at the cheeks.
*h*1:16 *fresh and pleasant* Or "lush and green" like a fresh field of grass.
*i*2:1 *rose ... Sharon* Or "a crocus on the plain."
*j*2:1 *lily* A kind of flower. Here, it is probably a red flower.

He Speaks

2 My darling, among other women,
   you are like a lily among thorns!

She Speaks

3 My lover, among other men,
   you are an apple tree among the wild
    trees in the forest!

She Speaks to the Women

I enjoy sitting in my lover's shadow;
   his fruit is so sweet to my taste.
4 My lover took me to the wine house;
   his intent toward me was love.
5 Strengthen me with raisins*a*;
   refresh me with apples, because I am
    weak with love.*b*
6 My lover's left arm is under my head,
   and his right arm holds me.

7 Women of Jerusalem, promise me by the
    gazelles* and wild deer,
   don't awaken love,
   don't arouse love, until I am ready.*c*

She Speaks Again

8 I hear my lover's voice.
   Here it comes,
    jumping over the mountains,
    skipping over the hills.
9 My lover is like a gazelle*
   or a young deer.
   Look at him standing behind our wall,
    staring out the window,
    looking through the lattice.*d*
10 My lover speaks to me,
 "Get up, my darling, my beautiful one.
   Let's go away!
11 Look, winter is past,
   the rains have come and gone.
12 The flowers are blooming in the fields.
   It's time to sing!*e*
   Listen, the doves have returned.
13 Young figs are growing on the fig trees.
   Smell the vines in bloom.
   Get up, my darling, my beautiful one.
   Let's go away!"

He Speaks

14 My dove,
   hiding in the caves high on the cliff,
   hidden here on the mountain,
   let me see you,
   let me hear your voice.
   Your voice is so pleasant,
   and you are so beautiful!

She Speaks to the Women

15 Catch the foxes for us—
   the little foxes that spoil the vineyard.*

Our vineyard is now in bloom.

16 My lover is mine,
   and I am his!
My lover feeds among the lilies,
17 while the day breathes its last breath
   and the shadows run away.
Turn, my lover,
   be like a gazelle* or a young deer on the
    cleft mountains!*f*

She Speaks

3 1At night on my bed,
   I look for the man I love.
I looked for him,
   but I could not find him.
2 I will get up now!
   I will go around the city.
In the streets and squares,
   I will look for the man I love.

I looked for him,
   but I could not find him.
3 The guards patrolling the city found me.
   I asked them, "Have you seen the man I
    love?"

4 I had just left the guards
   when I found the man I love!
I held him.
I would not let him go,
   while I took him to my mother's house,
   to the room of one who bore*g* me.

She Speaks to the Women

5 Women of Jerusalem, promise me by the
    gazelles* and wild deer,
   don't awaken love,
   don't arouse love, until I am ready.*h*

The Women of Jerusalem Speak

6 Who is this woman
   coming from the desert*i*
   ⌊with this large group of people⌋?
The dust rises behind them
   like clouds of smoke from burning
    myrrh* and frankincense* and other
    spices.*j*

7 Look, Solomon's traveling chair.*k*
   There are 60 soldiers guarding it,
   strong soldiers of Israel.
8 All of them are trained fighting men
   with their swords at their side,
   ready for any danger of the night.

---

f **2:17** *the cleft mountains* Or "the mountains of
Bether" or "the mountains of spice."
g **3:4** *bore* Or "taught." See 8:2.
h **3:5** *until I am ready* Literally, "until it desires."
i **3:6** *woman coming from the desert* See 8:5.
j **3:6** *spices* Literally, "powders of the trader." These
were imported spices and incense.
k **3:7** *traveling chair* A kind of chair that the rich
traveled in. These chairs were covered and had
poles that slaves used to carry them. Also in verse 9.

---

a **2:5** *raisins* Or "raisin cakes."
b **2:5** *I am weak with love* Or "I am lovesick."
c **2:7** *until I am ready* Literally, "until it desires."
d **2:9** *lattice* A wooden screen over a window.
e **2:12** *sing* Or "prune."

9 King Solomon made a traveling chair for
     himself.
     The wood came from Lebanon.
10 The poles were made from silver,
     and the supports were made from gold.
     The seat was covered with purple cloth.
     It was inlaid with love by the women of
     Jerusalem.

11 Women of Zion, come out
     and see King Solomon.
     See the crown*a* his mother put on him
     the day he was married,
     the day he was so happy!

He Speaks to Her

4 ¹My darling, you are so beautiful!
     Oh, you are beautiful!
Your eyes are like doves
     under your veil.
Your hair is long and flowing,
     like little goats dancing down the slopes
     of Mount Gilead.
2 Your teeth are white like ewes*b*
     just coming from their bath.
They all give birth to twins;
     not one of them has lost a baby.
3 Your lips are like a red silk thread.
     Your mouth is beautiful.
Your cheeks under your veil
     are like two slices of pomegranate.*
4 Your neck is long and thin
     like David's tower.
That tower was built to be decorated*c*
     with a thousand shields on its walls,
     with the shields of powerful soldiers.
5 Your breasts are
     like twin fawns,*
     like twins of a gazelle,* feeding among
     the lilies.
6 I will go to that mountain of myrrh*
     and to that hill of frankincense*
     while the day breathes its last breath,
     and the shadows run away.
7 My darling, you are beautiful all over.
     Every part of you is perfect.
8 Come with me, my bride, from Lebanon.
     Come with me from Lebanon.
Come from the peak of Amana,*d*
     from the top of Senir*e* and Hermon,
     from the lion's caves,
     from the mountain of the leopards.
9 My darling,*f* my bride,

you excite me!
You have stolen my heart
     with just one quick look from your eyes,
     with just one of the jewels from your
     necklace.
10 Your love is so beautiful, my darling, my
     bride!
     Your love is better than wine.
The smell of your perfume
     is better than any kind of spice!
11 My bride, your lips drip honey.
     Honey and milk are under your tongue.
     Your clothes smell as sweet as perfume.*g*
12 My darling, my bride, ⌊you are pure⌋
     like a locked garden.
You are like a locked pool,
     a closed fountain.
13 Your limbs are like a garden
     filled with pomegranates and other
     pleasant fruit,
     with all the best spices:
     henna,*h* ¹⁴nard,* saffron,*i* calamus,*j* and
     cinnamon.*k*
Your limbs are like a garden
     filled with trees of frankincense,*
     myrrh,* and aloe.*
15 You are like a garden fountain—
     a well of fresh water—
     flowing down from the mountains of
     Lebanon.

She Speaks

16 Wake up, north wind.
     Come, south wind.
Blow on my garden.
     Spread its sweet smell.
Let my lover enter his garden
     and eat its pleasant fruit.

He Speaks

5 ¹My darling my bride, I have entered my
     garden.
I have gathered my myrrh* and spice.
I have eaten my honey and honeycomb.
I have drunk my wine and milk.

The Women Speak to the Lovers

Dearest friends, eat, drink!
     Be drunk with love!

She Speaks

2 I am asleep,
     but my heart is awake.
I hear my lover knocking, saying,

---

*a***3:11** *crown* This might be a wreath of flowers he
wore on his head at his wedding.
*b***4:2** *ewes* Female goats.
*c***4:4** *Your neck ... decorated* Or "Your neck is like
David's tower, built with rows of stone." This would
mean she wore many necklaces, one above the
other, which looked like rows of stone in a tower.
*d***4:8** *Amana* The name of a mountain in Lebanon.
*e***4:8** *Senir* The Amorite word for "Snow Mountain."
This means Mount Hermon.
*f***4:9** *darling* Literally, "sister." Also in verses 10, 11;
5:1, 2.

*g***4:11** *perfume* Or "Lebanon."
*h***4:13–14** *henna* A plant with sweet-smelling,
blue-yellow flowers that grows in clusters (groups)
like grapes.
*i***4:13–14** *saffron* A kind of yellow flower used in
making perfume.
*j***4:13–14** *calamus* A kind of reed plant used in
making perfume.
*k***4:13–14** *cinnamon* A kind of plant used as a spice
and in making perfume.

"Open to me, my darling, my love, my
dove, my perfect one!
My head is soaked with dew.
My hair is wet with the mist of the
night."

3 "I have taken off my robe.*a*
I don't want to put it on again.
I have washed my feet.
I don't want to get them dirty again."

4 But my lover put his hand through the
opening,*b*
and I felt sorry for him.*c*

5 I got up to open for my lover,
myrrh* dripping from my hands,
myrrh scented lotion dripped from my
fingers onto the handles of the lock.

6 I opened for my lover,
but my lover had turned away and was
gone!
I nearly died
when he came and went.*d*
I looked for him,
but I couldn't find him.
I called for him,
but he didn't answer me.

7 The guards patrolling the city found me.
They hit me.
They hurt me.
The guards on the wall
took my robe from me.

8 I tell you, women of Jerusalem,
if you find my lover, tell him I am weak
with love.*e*

The Women of Jerusalem Answer Her

9 Beautiful woman, how is your lover
different from other lovers?
Is your lover better than other lovers?
Is that why you ask us to make this
promise?

She Answers the Women of Jerusalem

10 My lover is tanned and radiant.
He would stand out among 10,000
men.

11 His head is like the purest gold.
His hair is curly and as black as a raven.

12 His eyes are like doves by a stream,
like doves in a pool of milk,
like a jewel in its setting.

13 His cheeks are like a garden of spices,
like flowers used for perfume.
His lips are like lilies,*f*
dripping with liquid myrrh.*

14 His arms are like gold rods,
filled with jewels.
His body is like smooth ivory
with sapphires* set in it.

15 His legs are like marble pillars
on bases of fine gold.
He stands tall
like the finest cedar tree in Lebanon!

16 Yes, women of Jerusalem, my lover is
everything I desire.
His mouth is the sweetest of all.
This is my lover;
this is my darling.

The Women of Jerusalem Speak to Her

6 ¹Beautiful woman,
where has your lover gone?
Which way did your lover go?
Tell us so that we can help you look for
him.

She Answers the Women of Jerusalem

2 My lover has gone down to his garden,
to the flower beds of spices.
He went to feed in the gardens
and to gather the lilies.

3 I belong to my lover,
and my lover belongs to me.
He is the one feeding among the lilies.

He Speaks to Her

4 My darling, you are as beautiful as Tirzah,*g*
as pleasant as Jerusalem,
as awesome as the stars in the sky.*h*

5 Don't look at me!
Your eyes excite me too much!
And your hair ⌊is long and flowing⌋,
like little goats dancing down the slopes
of Mount Gilead.

6 Your teeth are white like ewes*i*
just coming from their bath.
They all give birth to twins.
Not one of them has lost a baby.

7 Your cheeks under your veil
are like slices of pomegranate.*

8 There might be 60 queens
and 80 slave women,*
and young women too many to count,

9 but there is only one ⌊woman for me⌋,
my dove, my perfect one.
She is the favorite of her mother,
her mother's favorite child.

---

*a*5:3 *robe* Or "veil," a piece of cloth used to cover a
person's face. Also in verse 7.
*b*5:4 *put ... opening* Or "pulled his hand from the
opening." In one sense, this might refer to a lock and
key. Some ancient keys were shaped like a hand.
The key was inserted through a hole in the door,
and the "fingers" fit into special holes that allowed
the bolt to slide, locking and unlocking the door.
*c*5:4 *I felt sorry for him* Literally, "My insides stirred
for him."
*d*5:6 *I nearly died ... went* Or "My soul left when he
spoke."
*e*5:8 *I am weak with love* Or "I am lovesick."

*f*5:13 *lily* A kind of flower. Here, it is probably a red
flower.
*g*6:4 *Tirzah* One of the capital cities of northern
Israel.
*h*6:4 *the stars in the sky* Or "an army ready for war."
The meaning of the Hebrew word here and in verse
10 is uncertain.
*i*6:6 *ewes* Female goats.

The young women see her and praise her.
  Even the queens and slave women
    praise her.

The Women Praise Her

10 Who is that young woman?
  She shines out like the dawn.
  She is as pretty as the moon.
  She is as bright as the sun.
  She is as awesome as the stars in the
    sky.

He Speaks to Her

11 I went down to the grove of walnut trees,
  to see the fruit of the valley,
  to see if the vines were in bloom,
  to see if the pomegranates* had budded.
12 I was so excited when she put me in the
  royal chariot.*a*

The Women of Jerusalem Call to Her

13 Come back, come back, Shulamith*b*!
  Come back, come back, so we may look
    at you.

Why are you staring at Shulamith,
  as she dances the Mahanaim dance*c*?

He Praises Her Beauty

7 ¹Princess,*d* your feet are beautiful in
    those sandals.
  The curves of your thighs are like jewelry
    made by an artist.
2 Your navel is like a round cup*e*;
  may it never be without wine.
  Your belly is like a pile of wheat
    surrounded by lilies.
3 Your breasts are like twin fawns*
  of a young gazelle.*
4 Your neck is like an ivory tower.
  Your eyes are like the pools in Heshbon
    near the gate of Bath Rabbim.
  Your nose is like the tower of Lebanon
    that looks toward Damascus.
5 Your head is like Carmel,
  and the hair on your head is like silk.
  Your long flowing hair
    captures even a king.
6 You are so beautiful and so pleasant,
  a lovely, delightful young woman!
7 You are tall—
  as tall as a palm tree.

And your breasts are like
  the clusters of fruit on that tree.
8 I would love to climb that tree
  and take hold of its branches.

May your breasts be like clusters of grapes
  and your fragrance*f* like apples.
9 May your mouth be like the best wine,
  flowing straight to my love,
  flowing gently to the sleeper's lips.

She Speaks to Him

10 I belong to my lover,
  and he wants me.
11 Come, my lover,
  let's go out into the field;
  let's spend the night in the villages.
12 Let's get up early and go to the vineyards.*
  Let's see if the vines are in bloom.
  Let's see if the blossoms have opened
    and if the pomegranates* are in bloom.
  There I will give you my love.

13 Smell the mandrakes*g*
  and all the pleasant flowers by our door.
  I have saved many pleasant things for you,
    my lover,
    pleasant things, new and old.

8 ¹If you were a baby, like my little brother
    nursing at his mother's breasts,
  and if I found you outside,
  I could kiss you,
  and no one would say it was wrong.
2 I would lead you into my mother's house,
  to the room of she who taught me.
  I would give you spiced wine
    squeezed from my pomegranate.*

She Speaks to the Women

3 His left arm is under my head,
  and his right hand holds me.

4 Women of Jerusalem, promise me,
  don't awaken love,
  don't arouse love, until I am ready.*h*

The Women of Jerusalem Speak

5 Who is this woman
  coming from the desert, leaning on her
    lover?

She Speaks to Him

I woke you under the apple tree,
  where your mother gave birth to you,
  where you were born.
6 Keep me near you like a seal* you wear
    over your heart,
  like a signet ring* you wear on your
    hand.

---

*a***6:12** *the royal chariot* Or "the chariots of my noble
people." See "chariot" in the Word List.
*b***6:13** *Shulamith* Or "Shulamite." The word might
be the feminine form of the name "Solomon." This
could mean she was or would become the bride of
Solomon. This name might also mean "perfect," "at
peace," or "woman from Shunem."
*c***6:13** *Mahanaim dance* Or "the victory dance" or
"the dance of the two camps."
*d***7:1** *Princess* Literally, "Daughter of a prince."
*e***7:2** *round cup* Or "turned bowl," a stone bowl
made on a lathe and used for mixing wine before
it is poured into cups. This might also mean a bowl
shaped like a crescent or half-moon.
*f***7:8** *fragrance* Literally, "breath of your nose."
*g***7:13** *mandrakes* Plants with roots that look like
people. People thought these plants had the power
to make people fall in love.
*h***8:4** *until I am ready* Literally, "until it desires."

Love is as strong as death.
    Passion is as strong as the grave.*a*
Its sparks become a flame,
    and it grows to become a great fire*b*!
7 A flood cannot put out love.
    Rivers cannot drown love.
Would people despise a man for giving
    everything he owns for love?

Her Brothers Speak

8 We have a little sister,
    and her breasts are not yet grown.
What should we do for our sister
    when a man comes asking to marry her?

9 If she were a wall,
    we would put silver trim*c* around her.
If she were a door,
    we would put a cedar board around her.

She Answers Her Brothers

10 I am a wall,
    and my breasts are my towers.

*a*8:6 *the grave* Or "Sheol," the place where dead people go.
*b*8:6 *great fire* Or "the flame of the LORD."
*c*8:9 *trim* Or "supports." Often horizontal beams and towers were built into walls to strengthen and support them. But here, this seems to be a decoration.

And he is satisfied with me!*d*

He Speaks

11 Solomon had a vineyard* at Baal Hamon.
    He put men in charge of the vineyard.
Each man brought in grapes worth 1000
    shekels*e* of silver.

12 Solomon, you can keep your 1000
    shekels.
Give 200 shekels to each man
    for the grapes he brought.
But I will keep my own vineyard.

He Speaks to Her

13 There you are, sitting in the garden.
    Friends are listening to your voice.
Let me hear it too!

She Speaks to Him

14 Hurry, my lover!
    Be like a gazelle* or a young deer on the
    mountains of spice.

*d*8:10 *he is satisfied with me* Literally, "in his eyes I find peace." In Hebrew this is also like the names "Solomon" and "Shulamith."
*e*8:11 *1000 shekels* About 25 pounds (11.5 kg). Also in verse 12.

Isaiah

1 ¹This is the vision* of Isaiah son of Amoz. God showed Isaiah what would happen to Judah and Jerusalem. Isaiah saw this during the time when Uzziah,* Jotham,* Ahaz,* and Hezekiah* were kings of Judah.

God's Case Against Israel

²Heaven and earth, listen! This is what the LORD says:

"I raised my children and helped them
    grow up,
    but they have turned against me.
3 A bull knows its master,
    and a donkey knows where its owner
        feeds it.
But Israel* does not know me.
    My people do not understand."

⁴Oh, what a sinful nation! Their guilt is like a heavy weight that they must carry. They are evil, destructive children.*f* They left the LORD

and insulted the Holy One of Israel. They turned away and treated him like a stranger.

⁵What good will it do to keep punishing you? You will continue to rebel. Your whole head and heart are already sick and aching.*g* ⁶From the bottom of your feet to the top of your head, every part of your body has wounds, cuts, and open sores. You have not taken care of them. Your wounds have not been cleaned and bandaged.

⁷Your land is in ruins, and your cities are in flames. Your enemies have taken your land, and foreigners are taking what it produces. It looks like some foreigners destroyed it.*h*

*f*1:4 *They ... children* Or "They are destructive children of evil parents."
*g*1:5 *Your whole ... aching* Or "Every head and heart is already sick and aching."
*h*1:7 *It looks ... destroyed it* Or "It looks like the land of the foreigners that was destroyed." This might refer to civil war in Israel or to some time when God destroyed foreign nations, such as Sodom and Gomorrah.

Warnings for Jerusalem

[8]The city of Jerusalem[a] is now like an empty shed left in a vineyard.* It is like an old straw hut abandoned in a field of cucumbers or like a city surrounded by enemies. [9]If the LORD All-Powerful had not allowed a few people to live, we would have been destroyed completely like the cities of Sodom* and Gomorrah.* And that almost happened!

[10]You officers of Sodom, listen to the LORD's message. You people of Gomorrah,[b] listen to God's teaching. [11]The LORD says, "Why do you continue giving me all these sacrifices*? I have had enough of your sacrifices of rams and the fat from well-fed animals. I don't want the blood of those bulls, sheep, and goats. [12]When you people come to meet with me, you trample everything in my yard. Who told you to do this?

[13]"Don't keep bringing me those worthless sacrifices. I hate the incense* you give me. I cannot stand your festivals for the New Moon,* the Sabbath,* and other special meeting days. I hate the evil you do during those holy* times together. [14]I hate your monthly meetings and councils. They have become like heavy weights to me, and I am tired of carrying them.

[15]"When you raise your arms to pray to me, I will refuse to look at you. You will say more and more prayers, but I will refuse to listen because your hands are covered with blood.

[16]"Wash yourselves and make yourselves clean. Stop doing the evil things I see you do. Stop doing wrong. [17]Learn to do good. Treat people fairly. Punish those who hurt others. Speak up for the widows and orphans. Argue their cases for them in court."

[18]"Come, let's discuss this. Even if your sins are as dark as red dye, that stain can be removed and you will be as pure as wool that is as white as snow.

[19]"If you listen to what I say, you will get the good things from this land. [20]But if you refuse to listen and rebel against me, your enemies will destroy you."

The LORD himself said this.

Unfaithful Jerusalem

[21]Look at Jerusalem. She was a faithful city. What made her become like a prostitute? In the past, Jerusalem was filled with justice, and goodness should live there now. Instead, there are murderers. [22]Once you were like pure silver, but now you are like the impurities that people throw away when the silver is purified. You are like good wine that has been weakened with water. [23]Your rulers are rebels and friends of thieves. They demand bribes and accept money for doing wrong. They take money to cheat people, and they don't speak up for widows and orphans. They will not even listen to their cries for help.

[24]Because of this, the Lord GOD All-Powerful, the Mighty One of Israel, says, "Look, I will get relief from my enemies. You will not cause me any more trouble. [25]People use lye to clean silver. In the same way, I will clean away all your wrongs. I will remove all the impurities from you. [26]I will bring back the kind of judges you had in the beginning. Your counselors will be like those you had long ago. Then you will be called 'The Good and Faithful City.'"

[27]God is good and does what is right, so he will rescue Zion* and the people who come back to him. [28]But all the criminals and sinners will be destroyed. Those who stopped following the LORD will be removed.

[29]In the future, you will be ashamed of the oak trees and special gardens[c] you chose to worship, [30]because you will be like an oak tree whose leaves are dying. You will be like a garden dying without water. [31]Powerful people will be like small, dry pieces of wood, and what they did will be like the sparks that start a fire. These people and their works will both burn up, and no one will be able to put out that fire.

God's Message to Judah and Jerusalem

2 [1]Isaiah son of Amoz saw this message about Judah and Jerusalem.

[2] In the last days the mountain of the
    LORD's Temple*
  will be the highest of all mountains.
It will be raised higher than the hills.
    There will be a steady stream of people
      from all nations going there.
[3] People from many places will go there
    and say,
  "Come, let's go up to the mountain of the
    LORD,
  to the Temple of the God of Jacob.*
Then God will teach us his way of living,
    and we will follow him."

His teaching, the LORD's message, will
    begin in Jerusalem on Mount Zion*
  and will go out to all the world.
[4] Then God will act as judge to end
    arguments between nations.
He will decide what is right for people
    from many lands.
They will stop using their weapons for
    war.
They will hammer their swords into
    plows
  and use their spears to make tools for
    harvesting.
All fighting between nations will end.
  They will never again train for war.

---

[a]**1:8** *city of Jerusalem* Literally, "daughter Zion." See "Zion" in the Word List.

[b]**1:10** *officers of Sodom … Gomorrah* Here, this refers to leaders and people from Judah.

[c]**1:29** *special gardens* Gardens where people worshiped false gods.

⁵Family of Jacob, let us follow the LORD.

⁶Family of Jacob, you have abandoned your people. This is clear because they have been filled with bad influences from the East,ᵃ and now your people try to tell the future like the Philistines.* They have completely accepted those strange ideas. ⁷Jacob's land has been filled with silver and gold from other places. There are many treasures there. His land has been filled with horses and many chariots.* ⁸His land is full of gods that the people bow down to worship. They made those idols* themselves. ⁹The people have become worse and worse. They have become very low, and you leaders did nothing to lift them up!ᵇ

¹⁰You should be afraid of the LORD! Go hide in the dirt and behind the rocks. Hide from his glorious power!

¹¹Proud people will stop being proud. They will bow down to the ground with shame, and only the LORD will still stand high.

¹²The LORD All-Powerful has a special day planned when he will punish the proud and boastful people. They will be brought down. ¹³They might be like the tall cedar trees from Lebanon* or the great oak trees from Bashan,* but they will be cut down. ¹⁴They might be like the tall mountains and high hills ¹⁵or like the tall towers and high walls, but they will be brought down. ¹⁶They might be like great ships from Tarshish,ᶜ filled with such wonderful cargo, but they will be brought down.

¹⁷At that time those proud people will fall. They will bow low to the ground, and only the LORD will stand high. ¹⁸All the idols will be gone. ¹⁹People will go into the holes in the ground and the cracks in the rocks because they fear the LORD and his great power as he stands to shake the earth.

²⁰At that time people will throw away their idols they made from gold and silver. They made these statues to worship, but they will throw them into holes in the ground where bats and moles live. ²¹They will go down into cracks in the rocks and boulders because they are afraid of the LORD and his glorious power as he stands to shake the earth.

²²Stop trusting other people to save you. Do not think too highly of them; they are only humans who have not stopped breathing yet.

3 ¹Understand what I am telling you: The Lord GOD All-Powerful will take away everything Judah and Jerusalem depend on. He will take away all the food and water. ²He will take away all the heroes and soldiers. He will take away all the judges,* the prophets,* the fortunetellers,* and the elders.* ³He will

take away the army officers and important officials. He will take away the skilled counselors, the magicians, and those who try to tell the future.

⁴The LORD says, "I will put young boys in charge of you. They will be your leaders. ⁵The people will turn against each other. Young people will not respect those who are older. The common people will not respect important leaders."

⁶At that time a man will grab one of his brothers from his own family and tell him, "You have a coat,ᵈ so you will be our leader. You will be the leader over all these ruins."

⁷But the brother will refuse and say, "I cannot help you. I don't have enough food or clothes for my own family. You will not make me your leader."

⁸This will happen because Jerusalem has stumbled, and Judah has fallen. They turned against the LORD. They said and did things against him, right in front of his glorious eyes.

⁹The look on their faces shows that they are guilty. They are like the people of Sodom; they don't care who sees their sin. But it will be very bad for them. They will get what they deserve.

¹⁰Tell the good people who do what is right that good things will happen to them. They will receive a reward for what they do. ¹¹But it will be very bad for wicked people, because they, too, will get what they deserve. They will get what they did to others. ¹²Even children will defeat my people, and women will rule over them.

My people, your guides lead you the wrong way, and they destroy the path you should follow.

God's Decision About His People

¹³Look, the LORD is standing to judge his people. ¹⁴The LORD is ready to present his case against the elders* and leaders of his people.

The LORD says, "You people have burned the vineyard,ᵉ and what you stole from the poor is still in your houses. ¹⁵What gives you the right to hurt my people? What gives you the right to push the faces of the poor into the dirt?" The Lord GOD All-Powerful said this.

¹⁶The LORD says, "The women in Zion* have become very proud. They walk around with their heads in the air, acting like they are better than other people. They flirt with their eyes and make tinkling sounds with their ankle bracelets as they take their quick little steps."

¹⁷The Lord will put sores on the heads of those women in Zion. The LORD will make their heads bald. ¹⁸Then the Lord will take

---

ᵃ2:6 *East* This usually refers to the area around Babylon.

ᵇ2:9 *They ... up* Or "The people have become very low. Surely you will not forgive them!"

ᶜ2:16 *ships from Tarshish* This is probably a special type of cargo ship.

ᵈ3:6 *coat* Or "robe." This showed that a person was a leader of the people.

ᵉ3:14 *vineyard* A garden for growing grapes. Here, this probably means Judah.

away everything they are proud of: the beautiful ankle bracelets, the necklaces that look like the sun and the moon, 19the earrings, bracelets, and veils, 20the scarves, the ankle chains, the cloth belts worn around their waists, the bottles of perfume, the charms,*a* 21the signet rings,* and the nose rings, 22the fine dresses, robes, veils, and purses, 23the mirrors, linen* dresses, turbans,* and long shawls.

24Those women now have sweet-smelling perfume, but it will get moldy and stink. Now they wear belts, but then they will have only ropes to wear. Now they have their hair fixed in fancy ways, but then their heads will be shaved—they will have no hair.*b* Now they have party dresses, but then they will have only mourning* clothes. They have beauty marks on their faces now, but then they will have another mark. It will be a mark burned into their skin to show that they are slaves.

25Your men will be killed with swords. Your heroes will die in war. 26There will be crying and sadness in the meeting places by the city gates. Jerusalem will sit there empty, like a woman who has lost everything to thieves and robbers and now just sits on the ground and cries.

4 1At that time seven women will grab one man and say, "Please marry us! We will supply our own food and make our own clothes. You won't have to do anything else if you let us wear your name and take away our shame."

2At that time the LORD's plant*c* will be very beautiful and glorious. The people in Israel who survived will be very proud of what the land grows. 3And all those who are left in Zion and Jerusalem will be called holy.* Their names were on the list of people in Jerusalem who were allowed to live.

4The LORD will wash away the filth*d* from the daughters of Zion.*e* He will wash away the blood from Jerusalem. With a spirit of judgment that burns like fire, he will make everything pure. 5Then the LORD will create a cloud of smoke in the day and a bright flame of fire*f* at night over every building and over every meeting of the people on the mountain of Zion. And there will be a covering over

everyone*g* for protection. 6It will be a shelter to protect the people from the heat of the sun and from all kinds of storms and rain.

Judah, God's Vineyard

5 1Now I will sing a song for my friend, my love song about his vineyard.*

My friend had a vineyard
  on a very fertile hill.
2 He dug and cleared the field
  and planted the best grapevines there.
He built a tower in the middle
  and cut a winepress into the stone.
He expected good grapes to grow there,
  but there were only rotten ones.

3 My friend said, "You people living in
    Jerusalem and you people of Judah,*h*
  think about me and my vineyard.
4 What more could I do for my vineyard?
  I did everything I could.
I hoped for good grapes to grow,
  but there were only rotten ones.
  Why did that happen?

5"Now I will tell you what I will do to my
    vineyard:
I will pull up the thornbushes that protect
    it,
  and I will burn them.
I will break down the stone wall
  and use the stones for a walkway.
6 I will turn my vineyard into useless land.
  No one will care for the plants or work
    in the field.
Weeds and thorns will grow there.
I will command the clouds not to rain on
    it."

7The vineyard that belongs to the LORD All-Powerful is the house of Israel. The grapevine, the plant he loves, is the man of Judah.*i*

The Lord hoped for justice,
  but there was only killing.
He hoped for fairness,
  but there were only cries from people
    being treated badly.

8Look at you people! You join houses to houses and fields to fields until there is no room for anyone else. But ⌞when the punishment comes,⌟ you will be forced to live alone. You will be the only people in the whole land. 9I heard the LORD All-Powerful make this oath*: "I swear, all these houses will be destroyed. These big, fancy houses will be empty. 10A ten-acre vineyard will make only a

---

*a*3:20 *charms* Things people wore on bracelets and necklaces. People thought these things would protect them from evil or danger.
*b*3:24 *they will have no hair* This means that they will become slaves.
*c*4:2 *the LORD's plant* This might refer to the country of Judah or to the future king or Messiah. See Isa. 5:7.
*d*4:4 *wash away the filth* This is like a special ceremony for washing away the blood after a menstrual period. After this a man and wife could have sexual relations.
*e*4:4 *daughters of Zion* This can refer either to the small towns around Jerusalem or to the women living there.
*f*4:5 *cloud of smoke ... fire* The signs God used to show that he was with his people.

*g*4:5 *everyone* Literally, "glory," but this can also mean "soul" or "person." See Ps. 16:9.
*h*5:3 *You people ... Judah* Or "Rulers of Jerusalem and leader of Judah ...."
*i*5:7 *man of Judah* This could mean either "the king of Judah" or simply, "people of Judah."

little wine,*a* and many sacks of seed will grow only a little grain.*b*"

¹¹How terrible it will be for you people who rise early in the morning and go looking for beer to drink. You stay awake late at night, getting drunk on wine. ¹²At your parties with your wine, harps, drums, flutes, and other musical instruments, you don't see what the Lord has done. You don't notice what his hands have made.

¹³My people don't really know God. So they will be captured and taken away. Everyone, the respected leaders and the common people as well, will be hungry and thirsty. ¹⁴They will die, and the place of death will open its mouth wide and swallow many of them. Then the noisy crowds and all the beautiful, happy people who are now so comfortable will go down into the grave.

¹⁵Everyone, common people and leaders alike, will be humbled. Those who are now so proud will bow their heads in shame. ¹⁶The Lord All-Powerful will judge fairly, and people will honor him. They will respect the Holy God when he brings justice. ¹⁷Then sheep will be able to go wherever they want and graze on the land that rich people once owned.

¹⁸Look at those people! They pull their guilt and sins behind them like people pull wagons with ropes.*c* ¹⁹They say, "We wish God would hurry and do what he plans to do, so we can know what is going to happen. We wish the Lord's plan would happen soon so that we can know what his plan is."

²⁰Look at those people! They say good is bad and bad is good. They think light is dark and dark is light. They think sour is sweet and sweet is sour. ²¹They think they are so smart. They think they are very intelligent. ²²They are famous for drinking wine and are heroes known for mixing drinks. ²³And if you pay them enough money, they will forgive a criminal. But they will not let good people be judged fairly. ²⁴So bad things will happen to them. Their descendants will be destroyed completely, just as fire burns straw and leaves. Their descendants will be like plants with rotten roots, whose flowers have all blown away like dust in the wind.

Those people refused to obey the teachings*d* of the Lord All-Powerful. They hated the message from the Holy One of Israel. ²⁵So

the Lord became angry with his people, and he raised his hand to punish them. Even the mountains shook with fear. Dead bodies were left in the streets like garbage. But even after all that, the Lord is still angry. His hand is still raised to punish the people.

God Will Bring Armies to Punish Israel

²⁶Look! God is giving a sign to the nations far away. He is raising a flag and whistling for them to come.

Now the enemy is coming from a faraway land and will soon enter the country. They are moving very quickly. ²⁷The enemy soldiers never get tired and stumble. They never get sleepy and fall asleep. Their weapon belts are always ready. Their sandal straps never break. ²⁸Their arrows are sharp. Their bows are strung and ready to shoot. The horses' hooves are as hard as flint. Clouds of dust rise from behind their chariots.*

²⁹The shouts of the enemy sound like the roar of lions. Like strong, young lions, they growl and grab their prey. The captives struggle and try to escape, but there is no one to save them. ³⁰Then there is a roar as loud as the ocean waves, and the captives turn their faces to the ground. And there is only darkness closing in as the light fades away in a black cloud.

God Calls Isaiah to Be a Prophet

6 ¹In the year that King Uzziah* died,*e* I saw the Lord sitting on a very high and wonderful throne. His long robe filled the Temple.* ²Seraph angels* stood around him. Each angel had six wings. They used two wings to cover their faces, two wings to cover their bodies, and two wings to fly. ³The angels were calling to each other, "Holy, holy, holy is the Lord All-Powerful. His Glory* fills the whole earth." ⁴The sound was so loud that it caused the frame around the door to shake, and the Temple was filled with smoke.*f*

⁵I was frightened and said, "Oh, no! I will be destroyed. I am not pure enough to speak to God, and I live among people who are not pure enough to speak to him.*g* But I have seen the King, the Lord All-Powerful."

⁶There was a fire on the altar.* One of the Seraph angels used a pair of tongs to take a hot coal from the fire. Then the angel flew to me with it in his hand. ⁷Then he touched my mouth with the hot coal and said, "When this hot coal touched your lips, your guilt was taken away, and your sins were erased.*h*"

⁸Then I heard the Lord's voice, saying, "Who can I send? Who will go for us?"

So I said, "Here I am. Send me!"

---

*a*5:10 *only a little wine* Literally, "one bath," a measure that equals about 6 gallons (22 l).
*b*5:10 *only a little grain* Literally, "A homer of seed will grow only an ephah of grain." A homer equals about 6 bushels (220 l). An ephah equals about 2/3 bushel (22 l).
*c*5:18 *ropes* Literally, "useless ropes." The Hebrew words here are like those meaning "useless things," that is, idols.
*d*5:24 *teachings* This can also mean "laws." Sometimes this means the laws God gave Moses to teach to the people of Israel.

*e*6:1 *year ... died* This was probably 740 b.c.
*f*6:4 *smoke* This showed that God was in the Temple. See Ex. 40:34–35.
*g*6:5 *I am not pure ... him* Literally, "I am a man of unclean lips and live among people of unclean lips."
*h*6:7 *erased* Or "atoned" or "covered over."

9Then the Lord said, "Go and tell the people, 'Listen closely, but don't understand. Look closely, but don't learn.' 10Confuse them. Make them unable to understand what they hear and see. If you don't do this, they might really look with their eyes, hear with their ears, and understand with their minds. Then they might come back to me and be healed!"

11Then I asked, "Lord, how long should I do this?"

He answered, "Do this until the cities are destroyed and all the people are gone. Do this until there is no one left living in the houses and the land is destroyed and empty."

12The Lord will make the people go far away, and there will be large areas of empty land in the country. 13A tenth of the people will be allowed to stay in the land, but it will be destroyed again. They will be like an oak tree. When the tree is chopped down, a stump is left. This stump will be a very special seed that will grow again.

Trouble With Aram

7 1Ahaz* was the son of Jotham,* who was the son of Uzziah.* Rezin* was the king of Aram,* Pekah son of Remaliah*a* was the king of Israel. When Ahaz was king of Judah, Rezin and Pekah went up to Jerusalem to attack it, but they were not able to defeat the city.*b*

2The family of David* received a message that said, "The armies of Aram and Ephraim* have joined together in one camp." When King Ahaz heard this message, he and the people became frightened. They shook with fear like trees of the forest blowing in the wind.

3Then the Lord told Isaiah, "You and your son Shear Jashub*c* should go out and talk to Ahaz. Go to the place where the water flows into the Upper Pool,*d* on the street that leads up to Laundryman's Field.

4"Tell Ahaz, 'Be careful, but be calm. Don't be afraid. Don't let those two men, Rezin and Remaliah's son,*e* frighten you! They are like two burning sticks. They might be hot now, but soon they will be nothing but smoke. Rezin, Aram, and Remaliah's son became angry 5and made plans against you. They said, 6"Let's go fight against Judah and divide it among ourselves. Then we will make Tabeel's son the new king of Judah."'"

7-9But the Lord God says, "Their plan will not succeed. Damascus is the capital of Aram, and Rezin is the ruler of Damascus for now. Samaria is the capital of Ephraim, and Remaliah's son is the ruler of Samaria for now. But their plan will not happen. If you don't believe this, you will not survive.*f*"

Immanuel—God Is With Us

10Then the Lord spoke to Ahaz* again 11and said, "Ask for a sign from the Lord your God to prove to yourself that this is true. You can ask for any sign you want. The sign can come from a place as deep as Sheol*g* or as high as the skies.*h*"

12But Ahaz said, "I will not ask for a sign as proof. I will not test the Lord."

13Then Isaiah said, "Family of David, listen very carefully! Is it not enough that you would test the patience of humans? Will you now test the patience of my God? 14But the Lord will still show you this sign:

The young woman is pregnant*i* and will
    give birth to a son.
She will name him Immanuel.*j*
15 He will eat milk curds and honey*k*
    as he learns to choose good and refuse
    evil.
16 But before he is old enough to make that
    choice,
    the land of the two kings you fear will
    be empty.

17"But the Lord will bring troubled times to you. These troubles will be worse than anything that has happened since the time Israel separated from Judah. This will happen to your people and to your father's family when God brings the king of Assyria* to fight against you.

18"At that time the Lord will call for the 'Fly' that is now near the streams of Egypt, and he will call for the 'Bee' that is now in the country of Assyria. Those enemies will come to your country. 19They will settle in the deep valleys and in the caves, by the thornbushes and watering holes. 20The Lord will use Assyria to punish Judah. Assyria will

---

*a***7:1** *Pekah son of Remaliah* A king of northern Israel. He ruled about 740–731 B.C.
*b***7:1** *Rezin and Pekah ... the city* Or "Rezin and Pekah went up to attack Jerusalem, but they were not able to fight."
*c***7:3** *Shear Jashub* This is a name that means "a few people will come back."
*d***7:3** *Upper Pool* Probably the Pool of Siloam at the southern tip of the City of David, just above the older pool now called the Red Pool.
*e***7:4** *Remaliah's son* Pekah, the king of northern Israel. He ruled about 740–731 B.C.

*f***7:7–9** *If you ... survive* This is a wordplay that can also mean "If you don't believe, you should not be trusted."
*g***7:11** *The sign ... Sheol* Or "Make your request deep." The Hebrew word for "request" is like the word for Sheol.
*h***7:11** *The sign ... skies* Literally, "make your request very high."
*i***7:14** *And here ... pregnant* Or "Look at this young woman. She is pregnant." The ancient Greek version (quoted in Mt. 1:23) translates "young woman" in this passage with a word meaning "virgin" and has "Look! The virgin will become pregnant."
*j***7:14** *Immanuel* This name means "God is with us."
*k***7:15** *milk curds and honey* This refers to some of the first solid foods, something like yogurt, that were fed to a baby. This is also the food that even the poor can find to eat. Also in verse 22.

be hired and used like a razor to shave off Judah's beard and to remove the hair from his head and body.[a]

21"At that time someone might keep only one young cow and two sheep alive. 22But there will be enough milk for them to eat milk curds. In fact, everyone left in the country will eat milk curds and honey. 23There are now fields that have 1000 grapevines, and each grapevine is worth 1000 pieces of silver. But those fields will be covered with weeds and thorns. 24That land will be wild and used only as a hunting ground where people go with bows and arrows. 25People once worked the soil and grew food on these hills, but at that time they will not go there, because the fields will be covered with weeds and thorns. It will be a place where cattle graze and sheep wander."

Assyria Is Coming Soon

8 ¹The LORD told me, "Get a large scroll,[b] and use an ordinary pen[c] to write these words: 'This is for Maher Shalal Hash Baz.'[d]"

²I found some men who could be trusted to serve as witnesses: Uriah the priest and Zechariah son of Jeberekiah. They watched me write those words. ³Then I went to my wife, the woman prophet. She became pregnant and had a son. The LORD told me, "Name the boy Maher Shalal Hash Baz." ⁴He said that because before the boy learns to say "Mama" and "Daddy," God will take all the wealth and riches from Damascus[e] and Samaria* and give them to the king of Assyria.*

⁵The LORD spoke to me again. ⁶He said, "These people[f] refuse to accept the slow-moving waters of Shiloah.[g] They prefer Rezin* and Remaliah's son." ⁷But the Lord will bring the king of Assyria and all his power against them. The Assyrians will come like their swift moving river, like water that rises and spills over its banks. ⁸This water will be like a flash flood as it passes through Judah. It will rise to Judah's throat and almost drown him.

But he will spread his wings over your whole country, Immanuel.[h]

9 All you nations, prepare for war.
    You will be defeated.
Listen, all you faraway countries!
    Prepare for battle.
    You will be defeated.
10 Make your plans for the fight.
    Your plans will be defeated.
Give orders to your armies,
    but your orders will be useless, because
    God is with us![i]

Warnings to Isaiah

¹¹The LORD spoke to me with his great power and warned[j] me not to be like these people.[k] He said, ¹²"Don't think there is a plan against you just because the people say there is. Don't be afraid of what they fear. Don't let them frighten you!"

¹³The LORD All-Powerful is the one you should fear. He is the one you should respect.[l] He is the one who should frighten you. ¹⁴If you people would respect the LORD, he would be a safe place[m] for you. But you don't respect him, so he is like a stone that you stumble over. He is a rock that makes the two families of Israel fall. The LORD has become a trap to all the people of Jerusalem. ¹⁵(Many people will trip over this rock. They will fall and be broken. They will be caught in the trap.)

¹⁶The Lord said, "Write this agreement.[n] Tie it up and seal it so that it cannot be changed. Give these teachings to my followers for safekeeping."

17 The LORD has turned away from the
        family of Jacob.*
    But I will wait for the LORD.
    I will wait for him to save us.

¹⁸My children and I are signs and proofs for the people of Israel. We have been sent by the LORD All-Powerful, who lives on Mount Zion.*

¹⁹The people will say, "Go to the fortune-tellers* and wizards* who mumble and chirp like birds. Ask them what to do." But I say, "Shouldn't people go to their God for help? Why go to the dead to get help for the living?" ²⁰You should follow the teachings and the agreement.[o] I swear, if you follow those other things, there is no future for you. ²¹When the enemy comes, there will be hard times

---

[a]7:20 *shave ... body* This means that the people of Judah would be humiliated and treated like slaves.
[b]8:1 *scroll* This Hebrew word might also mean a clay or stone tablet.
[c]8:1 *ordinary pen* Literally, "stylus of a man." This might be a pen for writing on clay.
[d]8:1 *Maher Shalal Hash Baz* This means "There will soon be looting and stealing."
[e]8:4 *Damascus* A city in the country of Aram (Syria).
[f]8:6 *These people* Probably Judeans who wanted to join Rezin and Pekah.
[g]8:6 *Shiloah* A channel that carried water from Gihon Spring to a pool at the south end of the City of David (Jerusalem). Men from David's family were anointed to be kings there.
[h]8:8 *But he ... Immanuel* Or "Immanuel, it will spread throughout your whole country." This might be a promise of God's protection, or it might be a warning about Assyria's power.

[i]8:10 *God is with us* In Hebrew this is like the name Immanuel.
[j]8:11 *warned* Or "prevented."
[k]8:11 *these people* Probably Judeans who wanted to join Rezin and Pekah.
[l]8:13 *respect* Literally, "consider holy."
[m]8:14 *safe place* Or "holy place."
[n]8:16 *Write this agreement* Or "Take a document." This could refer to the large scroll in verse 1 or to the promise that follows in verse 17.
[o]8:20 *agreement* This usually means the agreement God made with Israel through Moses. Here, it probably means the agreement in verse 17.

and hunger. And when he becomes hungry, he will become angry. He will say curses in the name of his king and his gods. Then he will lift his head upwards ₁like a roaring lion₁. ²²And when the captives turn their faces to the ground, there is only a depressing darkness closing in—the dark sadness of people forced to leave their country.

A New Day Is Coming

9 ¹But there will be an end to the gloom those people suffered. In the past, people thought the land of Zebulun and Naphtali was not important. But later, that land will be honored—the land along the sea, the land east of the Jordan River, and Galilee where people from other nations live. ²Those people lived in darkness, but they will see a great light. They lived in a place as dark as death, but a great light will shine on them.

³God, you will make the nation grow, and you will make the people happy. They will rejoice in your presence as they do at harvest time. It will be like the joy when people take their share of things they have won in war. ⁴That will happen because you will lift the heavy yoke* off their shoulders and take away their heavy burden. You will take away the rod that the enemy used to punish your people, as you did when you defeated Midian.ᵃ

⁵Every boot that marched in battle and every uniform stained with blood will be destroyed and thrown into the fire. ⁶This will happen when the special child is born. God will give us a son who will be responsible for leading the people. His name will be "Wonderful Counselor, Powerful God, Father Who Lives Forever, Prince of Peace." ⁷His power will continue to grow, and there will be peace without end. This will establish him as the king sitting on David's* throne and ruling his kingdom. He will rule with goodness and justice forever and ever. The strong loveᵇ that the LORD All-Powerful has for his people will make this happen!

God Will Punish Israel

⁸The Lord gave a command against Jacob* and someone in Israel fell.ᶜ ⁹So all the people in Ephraim, including the ruler in Samaria, learned their lesson.

Those people are very proud and boastful now. They say, ¹⁰"Yes, those bricks fell, but we will rebuild with strong stone. Yes, those little trees were chopped down, but we will plant new trees. And they will be large, strong trees."

¹¹The LORD found people to go up and fight against Rezin.* The Lord stirred up Rezin's

enemies. ¹²As for Israel, the Arameans are in front of him and the Philistines* are behind him. And they are both eating away at him. But even after all that, the LORD is still angry. His arm is still raised and ready to punish Israel.

¹³The LORD punished the people, but they did not stop sinning and come back to him. They did not come to the LORD All-Powerful for help. ¹⁴So the LORD cut off Israel's head and tail. He took away the branch and the stalk in one day. ¹⁵(The head means the elders* and important leaders. The tail means the prophets who told lies.)

¹⁶Their guides are leading them the wrong way, so those who follow them will be destroyed. ¹⁷All of them are evil. So the LORD is not happy with the young men, and he will not show mercy to their widows and orphans. That is because they are evil hypocrites.* They tell lies.

But even after all that, the LORD is still angry. His arm is still raised and ready to punish them.

¹⁸That evil was like a small fire that started among the weeds and thorns and then spread to the larger bushes in the forest. Finally, it became a giant fire, and everything went up in smoke.

¹⁹The LORD All-Powerful was angry, so the land was burned. The people were fuel for the fire. No one showed any compassion to anyone else. ²⁰People looked to the right and grabbed whatever they could, but they were still hungry. They grabbed whatever was on their left, but still they were not satisfied. So they turned on themselves and began to eat the bodies of their own children. ²¹Manasseh fought against Ephraim, and Ephraim fought against Manasseh. Then both of them turned on Judah.

But even after all that, the LORD is still angry. His arm is still raised and ready to punish them.

10 ¹Just look at those lawmakers who write evil laws and make life hard for the people. ²They are not fair to the poor. They take away the rights of the poor and allow people to steal from widows and orphans.

³Lawmakers, you will have to explain what you have done. What will you do then? Your destruction is coming from a faraway country. Where will you run for help? Your money and your riches will not help you. ⁴You will have to bow down like a prisoner. You will fall down like a dead man, but that will not help you. God will still be angry and ready to punish you.

God Will Punish Assyria's Pride

⁵The Lord says, "I will use Assyria* like a stick. In my anger I will use Assyria to punish Israel. ⁶I will send Assyria to fight against the people who do evil. I am angry with them,

---

ᵃ9:4 *as you ... Midian* See Judges 7:15–25.
ᵇ9:7 *strong love* The Hebrew word means strong feelings like love, hate, anger, zeal, or jealousy.
ᶜ9:8 Or "The Lord sent a command to Jacob and it happened to Israel."

and I will command Assyria to fight against them. Assyria will defeat them and take their wealth. Israel will be like dirt for Assyria to walk on in the streets.

⁷"But Assyria does not understand that I will use him. He does not think of himself as my tool. He only wants to destroy other people. He plans to destroy many nations. ⁸Assyria says to himself, 'All of my officers are like kings! ⁹The city of Calno is no better than the city of Carchemish. Arpad is like Hamath, and Samaria is like Damascus. ¹⁰I defeated those evil kingdoms and now I control them. The idols* those people worship are better than the idols of Jerusalem and Samaria. ¹¹I defeated Samaria and her gods. I will also defeat Jerusalem and the idols her people have made.'"

¹²When the Lord finishes doing what he planned to Jerusalem and Mount Zion,* he will punish Assyria. The king of Assyria is very proud. His pride made him do many bad things, so God will punish him.

¹³The king of Assyria said, "I am very wise. By my own wisdom and power I have done many great things. I have defeated many nations. I have taken their wealth and their people as slaves. I am a very powerful man. ¹⁴With my own hands I have taken the riches of all these people—like someone taking eggs from a bird's nest. A bird often leaves its nest and eggs, and there is nothing to protect the nest. There is no bird to chirp and fight with its wings and beak, so anyone can come take the eggs. And there is no one to stop me from taking all the people on earth."

¹⁵An ax is not better than the one who cuts with it. A saw is not better than the one who uses it. Is a stick stronger than the one who picks it up? It can't do anything to the person who is using it to punish someone! ¹⁶But Assyria doesn't understand this. So the Lord All-Powerful will send a terrible disease against him. He will lose his wealth and power like a sick man losing weight. Then Assyria's glory will be destroyed. It will be like a fire burning until everything is gone. ¹⁷The Light of Israel* will be like a fire. The Holy One will be like a flame. He will be like a fire that first begins to burn the weeds and thorns ¹⁸and then spreads to burn up the tall trees and vineyards.* Finally, everything will be destroyed—even the people. Assyria will be like a rotting log. ¹⁹There will be a few trees left standing in the forest—so few that even a child could count them.

²⁰Then the people from Jacob's* family who are left living in Israel will stop depending on the one who beat them. They will learn to depend on the Lord, the Holy One of Israel.

²¹Those who are left in Jacob's family will again follow the Powerful God.ᵇ

²²Your people are as many as the sands of the sea, but only a few of them will be left to come back to the Lord. They will return to God, but first, your country will be destroyed. God has announced that he will destroy the land, and then justice will come into the land; it will be like a river flowing full. ²³The Lord God All-Powerful really will destroy this land.

²⁴The Lord God All-Powerful says, "My people living in Zion,* don't be afraid of Assyria*! Yes, he will beat you, and it will be just as the time when Egypt beat you with a stick. ²⁵But after a short time my anger will stop. I will be satisfied that Assyria has punished you enough."

²⁶Then the Lord All-Powerful will beat Assyria with a whip, just as he defeated Midian at Raven Rock.ᶜ He will punish his enemies, as he did when he raised his stick over the seaᵈ and led his people from Egypt.

²⁷He will take away the troubles Assyria brought you—troubles that are like heavy weights carried with a yoke* on your neck. But that yoke will be taken off your neck. The burden will be lifted from your shoulders.

The Army of Assyria Invades Israel

²⁸ᵉ The army of Assyria will enter near the "Ruins" (Aiath). The army will walk on the "Threshing Floor" (Migron). It will keep its food in the "Storehouse" (Micmash). ²⁹The army will cross the river at the "Crossing" (Maabarah) and sleep at Geba. Ramah will be afraid. The people at Gibeah of Saulᶠ will run away.

³⁰Cry out, Bath Gallimᵍ! Laishah, listen! Anathoth, answer me! ³¹The people of Madmenah are running away. The people of Gebimʰ are hiding. ³²This day the army will stop at Nob and prepare to fight against Mount Zion,* the hill of Jerusalem.

³³Look, the Lord God All-Powerful will use his great power and chop down that great tree. Their highest officials will be brought down. Their most important leaders will be humbled. ³⁴The Lord will cut down his

---

ᵇ**10:21 Powerful God** See Isa. 9:6.

ᶜ**10:26 Midian at Raven Rock** Or "Midian at the Rock of Oreb." See Judges 7:25.

ᵈ**10:26 he raised … sea** See Ex. 14:1–15:21.

ᵉ**10:28–32** Isaiah uses names with double meanings to describe the different ways the Assyrian army would fight against Judah.

ᶠ**10:29 Geba, Ramah … Gibeah of Saul** Towns north of Jerusalem.

ᵍ**10:30 Bath Gallim** Gallim, a city south of Jerusalem. This name means "daughter of the waves," and might refer to birds that make loud noises by the shore.

ʰ**10:31 Gebim** An unknown city. This name is like the Hebrew word for "pit" or "cistern," a hole in the ground for storing water.

ᵃ**10:17 The Light of Israel** This is a name for God, like "The Holy One" in the next sentence. See "Israel" in the Word List.

enemies as an ax is used to cut down the tall trees in Lebanon.*

The King of Peace Is Coming

11 ¹A small tree*a* will begin to grow from the stump of Jesse.*b* That branch will grow from Jesse's roots. ²The Lord's Spirit* will always be with that new king to give him wisdom, understanding, guidance, and power. The Spirit will help him know and respect the Lord. ³He will find joy in obeying the Lord.

This king will not judge people by the way things look. He will not judge by listening to rumors. ⁴⁻⁵He will judge the poor fairly and honestly. He will be fair when he decides what to do for the poor of the land. If he decides people should be beaten, he will give the command, and they will be beaten. If he decides people must die, he will give the command, and those evil people will be killed. Goodness and fairness will be like a belt he wears around his waist.

⁶Then wolves will live at peace with lambs, and leopards will lie down in peace with young goats. Calves, lions, and bulls will all live together in peace. A little child will lead them. ⁷Bears and cattle will eat together in peace, and all their young will lie down together and will not hurt each other. Lions will eat hay like cattle. ⁸Even snakes will not hurt people. Babies will be able to play near a cobra's*c* hole and put their hands into the nest of a poisonous snake.

⁹People will stop hurting each other. People on my holy* mountain will not want to destroy things because they will know the Lord. The world will be full of knowledge about him, like the sea is full of water.

¹⁰At that time there will be someone special from Jesse's family. He will be like a flag that all the nations gather around. The nations will come to him and ask him what they should do. And the place where he is will be filled with glory.*

¹¹At that time the Lord will again reach out and take his people who are left in countries like Assyria, North Egypt, South Egypt, Ethiopia, Elam, Babylonia, Hamath, and other faraway countries around the world. ¹²The Lord will gather the people of Israel* and Judah who were forced to leave their country. They were scattered to all the faraway places on earth. But the Lord will raise the flag as a sign for the other nations, and he will gather his people together again.

¹³Then Ephraim* will not be jealous of Judah, and Judah will have no enemies left. And Judah will not cause trouble for Ephraim. ¹⁴But Ephraim and Judah will attack the Philistines.* These two nations will be like birds flying down to catch a small animal. Together, they will take the riches from the people in the East.*d* Ephraim and Judah will control Edom, Moab, and the people in Ammon.*e*

¹⁵Just as the Lord divided the Red Sea near Egypt,*f* he will raise his arm in anger over the Euphrates River and hit it. It will divide into seven small rivers. They will be so small that the people can walk across with their sandals on. ¹⁶Then God's people who are left in Assyria will have a way to leave. It will be just like the time God took the people out of Egypt.

A Song of Praise to God

12 ¹At that time you will say,
"I praise you, Lord!
You have been angry with me,
    but don't be angry with me now.
Show your love to me.
² God is the one who saves me.
    I trust him, and I am not afraid.
The Lord Yah is my strength.
    He saves me, and I sing songs of praise about him.*g*"

³ You people will get your water from the
        spring of salvation.
    Then you will be happy.
⁴ At that time you will say,
  "Praise the Lord and call out his name!
    Tell everyone what he has done
    and how wonderful he is."
⁵ Sing songs of praise about the Lord,
    because he has done great things.
  Spread this news about God throughout
        the whole world.
    Let all people know these things.
⁶ People of Zion,* shout about these things!
    The Holy One of Israel is with you in a
        powerful way.
    So sing and be happy!

God's Message to Babylon

13 ¹God showed Isaiah son of Amoz this message*h* about Babylon:

²"Raise a flag on that mountain*i* where
        nothing grows.
    Call out to the men.
  Wave your arms to let them know
    they should enter through the gates for
        important leaders.

---

*d*11:14 *East* This usually refers to the area around Babylon.

*e*11:14 *Edom, Moab, Ammon* Three countries east of Israel. They were Israel's enemies for many years.

*f*11:15 *the Lord … Egypt* Or "the Lord will dry up the tongue of the Sea of Egypt."

*g*12:2 *The Lord Yah … him* Literally, "Yah, Yahweh is my strength and praise. And he becomes my salvation." This comes from the victory song of Moses in Ex. 15:2.

*h*13:1 *message* Or "burden."

*i*13:2 *mountain* This probably means Babylon.

---

*a*11:1 *small tree* That is, a new king will come from the family of David.

*b*11:1 *Jesse* King David's father.

*c*11:8 *cobra* A very poisonous snake.

³"I have separated these men from the
　　people,
　and I myself will command them.
　I have gathered these proud, happy
　　soldiers of mine
　to show how angry I am.

⁴"Listen to that loud noise in the
　　mountains.
　It sounds like crowds of people.
　People from many kingdoms are gathering
　　together.
　The Lord All-Powerful is calling his
　　army together.
⁵　They are coming from a faraway land.
　They are coming from beyond the
　　horizon.
　The Lord will use this army as a weapon
　　to show his anger.
　They will destroy the whole country."

⁶The Lord's special day is near. So cry
and be sad for yourselves. A time is coming
when the enemy will steal your wealth. God
All-Powerful will make that happen.ᵃ ⁷People
will lose their courage. Fear will make them
weak. ⁸Everyone will be afraid. They will
stare at each other with shock on their faces.
Fear will grip them like the pains of a woman
in childbirth.

God's Judgment Against Babylon

⁹Look, the Lord's special day is coming! It
will be a terrible day. God will be very angry.
He will destroy the country and wipe out the
sinful people who live there. ¹⁰The skies will
be dark. The sun, the moon, and the stars will
not shine.
¹¹The Lord says, "I will cause bad things
to happen to the world. I will punish the evil
people for their sin. I will make proud people lose their pride. I will stop the bragging
of cruel people. ¹²There will be only a few
people left. They will be as rare as pure gold.
¹³In my anger I will shake the sky, and the
earth will be moved from its place."
That will happen on the day the Lord All-
Powerful shows his anger. ¹⁴Then the people
from Babylon will run away like wounded
deer or sheep that have no shepherd. Everyone will turn and run back to their own
country and people. ¹⁵Anyone caught by the
enemy will be killed with a sword. ¹⁶Every-
thing in their houses will be stolen. Their
wives will be raped, and their little children
will be beaten to death while they watch.
¹⁷The Lord says, "Look, I will cause the
armies of Media to attack Babylon. Nothing will stop them, even if someone offers
them gold and silver. ¹⁸They will walk on the
bows of the young soldiers of Babylon. The

enemy soldiers will not show any kindness or
mercy even to the babies and young children.
¹⁹Babylon will be destroyed like the time God
destroyed Sodom* and Gomorrah.*
　"Babylon is the most beautiful of all kingdoms. The Babyloniansᵇ are very proud of
their city. ²⁰But Babylon will not continue to
be beautiful. People will not continue to live
there in the future. Arabs will not put their
tents there. Shepherds will not bring their
sheep to let them eat there. ²¹The only animals living there will be wild animals from
the desert. People will not be living in their
houses in Babylon. The houses will be full of
owls and large birds. Wild goatsᶜ will play in
the houses. ²²Wild dogs and wolves will howl
in the great and beautiful buildings. Babylon
will be finished. The end is near, and it will
not be delayed."

Israel Will Return Home

14¹The Lord will again show his love to
Jacob.* He will again choose the people
of Israel.* He will give them their land. Then
the non-Israelitesᵈ will join the Israelites, and
both will become one family—Jacob's family.
²Those nations will bring the Israelites back
to their land. The men and women from the
other nations will become slaves to Israel. In
the past, those people forced the Israelites
to become their slaves. But in the future the
Israelites will defeat those nations, and Israel
will then rule over them. ³In the past, you
were slaves. People forced you to work hard.
But the Lord will take away the hard work
you were forced to do.

A Song About the King of Babylon

⁴At that time you will begin to sing this
song about the king of Babylon:

　The king was cruel when he ruled us,
　　but now his rule is finished.
⁵　The Lord breaks the scepter* of evil
　　rulers;
　he takes away their power.
⁶　In anger, the king of Babylon beat the
　　people.
　He never stopped beating them.
　He was an evil ruler who ruled in anger.
　He never stopped hurting people.
⁷　But now, the whole country rests and is
　　quiet.
　Now the people begin to celebrate.
⁸　You were an evil king,
　　and now you are finished.
　Even the pine trees are happy.
　The cedar trees of Lebanon rejoice.

ᵇ**13:19 Babylonians** Literally, "Chaldeans."
ᶜ**13:21 Wild goats** The Hebrew word means "hairy,"
"goat," or "goat-demon."
ᵈ**14:1 non-Israelites** This usually means those who
live in a country but are not yet citizens of that
country. Here, it is the non-Israelites who decided
to follow God.

ᵃ**13:6 A time ... happen** This is a wordplay in
Hebrew. The word meaning "stealing things in war"
sounds like the word meaning "God All-Powerful."

They say, "The king chopped us down,
    but now the king has fallen,
    and he will never stand again."
9 The place of death is excited that you are
        coming.
    Sheol* is waking the spirits of all the
        leaders of the earth for you.
    Sheol is making the kings stand up from
        their thrones to meet you.
10 They will make fun of you, saying,
    "Now you are as dead as we are.
    Now you are just like us."
11 Your pride has been sent down to Sheol.
    The music from your harps announces
        the coming of your proud spirit.
    Maggots will be the bed you lie on,
    and other worms will cover your body
        like a blanket.
12 You were like the morning star,
    but you have fallen from the sky.
    In the past, all the nations on earth
        bowed down before you,
    but now you have been cut down.
13 You always told yourself,
    "I will go to the skies above.
    I will put my throne above God's stars.
    I will sit on Zaphon,* the holy*
        mountain where the gods meet.
14 I will go up to the altar above the tops of
        the clouds.
    I will be like God Most High."

15 But that did not happen.
    You were brought down to the deep
        pit—Sheol, the place of death.
16 People will come to look at your dead
        body.
    They will think about you and say,
    "Is this the same man who caused great
        fear in all the kingdoms on earth,
17   who destroyed cities and turned the
        land into a desert,
    who captured people in war and would
        not let them go home?"
18 The kings of other nations lie buried with
        honor,
    each king with his own grave.
19 But you were thrown out of your grave
        like a branch cut from a tree and
        thrown away.
    You are like a dead man who fell in battle,
        trampled under the feet of other
        soldiers.
    Now you look like any other dead man
        wrapped in burial clothes.
20 Other kings have their own graves,
    but you will not join them,
    because you ruined your own country
        and killed your own people.
    So your wicked descendants will be
        stopped.

21 Prepare to kill his children,
    because their father is guilty.
    His children will never take control of the
        land.
    They will never fill the world with their
        cities.

22The Lord All-Powerful said, "I will stand
and fight against those people. I will destroy
the famous city, Babylon. I will destroy all
the people there. I will destroy their children, their grandchildren, and their great-
grandchildren." The Lord himself said this.
    23"I will change Babylon. It will be a place
for animals,b not people. It will be a swamp.
I will use the 'broom of destruction' to sweep
Babylon away." The Lord All-Powerful said
this.

God Will Also Punish Assyria

24The Lord All-Powerful made this promise: "This will happen exactly as I meant for
it to happen. It will happen just the way I
planned. 25I will destroy the king of Assyria in
my country. I will walk on him on my mountains. He forced my people to be his slaves;
he put a yoke* on their necks. But that pole
will be taken off Judah's neck, and that burden will be removed. 26This is what I plan to
do for this land. I will use my power to punish
all those nations."
    27When the Lord makes a plan, no one
can keep it from happening. When the Lord
raises his arm to punish people, no one can
stop him.

God's Message to Philistia

28This messagec was given the year King
Ahaz diedd:
    29Country of Philistia, don't be happy that
the king who beat you is now dead. It is true
that his rule has ended, but his son will come
and rule. It will be like one snake giving birth
to a more dangerous one. The new king will
be like a quick and dangerous snake to you.
30But even the poorest of my people will be
able to eat safely. And their children will be
able to lie down and feel safe. But I will make
your family die from hunger, and your enemy
will kill anyone who survives.

31 People near the city gates, cry!
    People in the city, cry out!
    Everyone in Philistia,
        your courage will melt like hot wax.

    Look to the north!
        There is a cloud of dust.
    An army is coming,
        and everyone in that army is strong.e

---

a14:13 *Zaphon* This Hebrew word literally means
"north" or "hidden."

b14:23 *animals* Literally, "porcupines."
c14:28 *message* Or "burden." Also in 15:1.
d14:28 *year King Ahaz died* About 727 B.C.
e14:31 *everyone ... strong* Or "there are no strag-
glers in that group."

32 But what will the messengers from that
　　nation report about us?
　　They will say, "The LORD made Zion*
　　　strong,
　　and his poor people went there for
　　　safety."

God's Message to Moab

15

¹This is a message about Moab*:

One night armies took the wealth from Ar
　　in Moab,
　　and the city was destroyed.
One night armies took the wealth from
　　Kir in Moab,
　　and the city was destroyed.
² The king's family and the people of Dibon[a]
　　go to the places of worship[b] to cry.
　　The people of Moab are crying for
　　　Nebo[c] and Medeba.[d]
　　They have shaved their heads and
　　　beards to show their sadness.
³ Everywhere in Moab, on the housetops
　　and in the streets,
　　people are wearing sackcloth.*
　　Everyone is crying.
⁴ In Heshbon and Elealeh they are crying
　　loudly.
　　You can hear their voices as far away as
　　　Jahaz.
　　Even the soldiers are frightened.
　　They are shaking with fear.

⁵ My heart cries, full of sorrow for Moab.
　　Its people run away to Zoar for safety.
　　They run to Eglath Shelishiyah.
　　The people are crying
　　as they go up the road to Luhith.
　　They are crying loudly
　　as they walk on the road to Horonaim.
⁶ But Nimrim Brook is as dry as a desert.
　　The grass has dried up,
　　and the plants are all dead.
　　Nothing is green.
⁷ So the people gather up everything they
　　　own
　　and cross the border at Arabah stream.

⁸ You can hear crying everywhere in
　　　Moab—
　　as far away as Eglaim and Beer Elim.
⁹ The water of Dimon[e] is full of blood,
　　and I will bring even more troubles to
　　　Dimon.

A few people living in Moab have escaped
　　the enemy,
　　but I will send lions to eat them.

16

¹You people should send a gift to the
king of the land. You should send a
lamb from Sela, through the desert, to the
mountain in the city of Jerusalem.[f]

² The women of Moab* try to cross the
　　river Arnon.
　　They run around looking for help,
　　like little birds that have fallen from
　　　their nest.
³ They say, "Help us!
　　Tell us what to do.
Protect us from our enemies
　　as shade protects us from the noon sun.
We are running from our enemies.
　　Hide us!
　　Don't give us to our enemies."
⁴ People from Moab were forced to leave
　　　their homes.
　　So let them live in your land.
　　Hide them from their enemies."

The robbing will stop.
　　The enemy will be defeated.
The men who hurt the people will be
　　gone from the land.
⁵ Then a new king will come.
　　He will be from David's family.[g]
　　He will be loyal, loving, and kind.
　　He will be a king who judges fairly.
　　He will do what is right and good.

⁶ We have heard that the people of Moab
　　are very proud and conceited.
　　They are hot-tempered braggers,
　　but their boasts are only empty words.
⁷ Because of their pride, everyone in Moab
　　will mourn.*
　　They will wish for the way things used to
　　　be.
　　They will wish for the raisin cakes from
　　　Kir Hareseth.[h]
⁸ The fields of Heshbon and the vines of
　　　Sibmah no longer grow grapes.
　　Foreign rulers have destroyed the vines.
　　The enemy has reached Jazer and has
　　　spread into the desert and down to
　　　the sea.[i]
⁹ I will cry with the people of Jazer and
　　　Sibmah,
　　because the grapes have been destroyed.

---

[a]15:2 *Dibon* A city in the country of Moab. This
name is like a Hebrew word meaning "to be very
sad."
[b]15:2 *places of worship* Or "high places." See "high
places" in the Word List.
[c]15:2 *Nebo* A city in the country of Moab and the
name of a false god.
[d]15:2 *Medeba* A city in the country of Moab. This
name is like a Hebrew word meaning "to be very sad."
[e]15:9 *Dimon* This is probably the city of Dibon.
Dimon is like the Hebrew word meaning "blood."

[f]16:1 *city of Jerusalem* Literally, "daughter Zion."
See "Zion" in the Word List.
[g]16:5 *David's family* The royal family of Judah. God
promised that men from David's family would be
kings in Judah.
[h]16:7 *Kir Hareseth* A city in the country of Moab.
[i]16:8 *Foreign rulers ... the sea* Or "These grapes
made many foreign rulers drunk. The vines spread
far to the city of Jazer, then into the desert and
down to the sea."

I will cry with the people of Heshbon and Elealeh
because there will be no harvest.
There will be no summer fruit,
and there will be no shouts of joy for
the harvest.
10 There will be no joy and happiness in the
orchard.
I will end the happy singing and
shouting in the vineyard.*
The grapes are ready to make wine,
but they will all be ruined.
11 So I will hum a sad song for Moab and Kir
Heres,*a*
like a harp playing a funeral song.
12 The people of Moab will go to their high
places* to worship.
They will go to their temple to pray,
but it will not help them.

13The LORD said these things about Moab
many times. 14And now the LORD says, "In
three years (counting as exactly as a hired
helper would) all those people and the things
they are proud of will be gone. Only a few of
their weakest people will be left."

God's Message to Aram

17 1This is a message*b* about Damascus*c*:

"Damascus is now a city, but it will be
destroyed.
Only ruined buildings will be left there.
2 People will leave the cities of Aroer.*d*
Flocks of sheep will wander freely in
those empty towns;
there will be no one to bother them.
3 The fort cities of Ephraim* will be
destroyed.
The government in Damascus will be
finished.
Those left in Aram* will lose everything,
just like the people of Israel," says the
LORD All-Powerful.

4"At that time Jacob's* wealth will all be
gone.
Yes, Israel* will be like a sick man who
has become weak and thin.

5"That time will be like the grain harvest
in Rephaim Valley.*e* The workers gather the
plants that grow in the field. Then they cut
the heads of grain from the plants and collect
the grain.

6"That time will also be like the olive harvest. People knock olives from the trees, but
a few olives are usually left at the top of each
tree. Four or five olives are left on some of
the top branches. It will be the same for those
cities," says the LORD All-Powerful.

7Then the people will look up to the one
who made them. Their eyes will see the
Holy One of Israel. 8They will not trust the
great things they have made. They will not
go to the special gardens*f* and altars*g* they
made for false gods. 9At that time all the
walled cities will be empty. They will be like
the mountains and the forests*h* in the land
before the Israelites came. In the past, all the
people ran away because the Israelites were
coming. In the future, the country will be
empty again. 10This will happen because you
have forgotten the God who saves you. You
have not remembered that God is your place
of safety.

You brought some very good grapevines
from faraway places. You might plant those
grapevines, but they will not grow. 11You will
plant your grapevines one day and try to make
them grow, and the next day they will blossom. But at harvest time, you will go to gather
the fruit from the plants, and you will see that
everything is dead. A sickness will kill all the
plants.

12 Listen to all these people!
Their loud crying sounds like the noise
from the sea.
Listen, it is like the crashing of waves in
the sea.
13 And like the waves,
they will rush away when God speaks
harshly to them.
They will be like chaff* blown away by
the wind.
They will be like weeds chased by a
storm.
14 That night, the people will be frightened.
By morning, nothing will be left.
So our enemies will get nothing.
They will come to our land, but nothing
will be there.

God's Message to Ethiopia

18 1Look at the land along the rivers of
Ethiopia* where you can hear the
buzzing of insect wings. 2That land sends
people down the Nile River in reed boats.*i*

*a*16:11 *Kir Heres* Kir Hareseth, a city in the country of Moab. Kir Heres means "a city chosen to be destroyed."
*b*17:1 *message* Or "burden."
*c*17:1 *Damascus* A city in the country of Aram (Syria).
*d*17:2 *Aroer* A place in the country of Aram (Syria).
*e*17:5 *Rephaim Valley* A valley southwest of Jerusalem.
*f*17:8 *special gardens* Gardens where people worshiped false gods.
*g*17:8 *altars* These might be altars for burning incense, or they might be altars for worshiping a special false god.
*h*17:9 *mountains and the forests* With a minor change in the Hebrew, this could be "the Horites and Amorites."
*i*18:2 *reed boats* These boats were made by tying many reeds (a type of water plant) together.

Fast messengers, go to the people
who are tall and smooth,
who are feared far and wide.
Go to that powerful nation
that defeats other countries
and whose land is divided by rivers.
Go warn them!
3 Like a flag on a hill,
everyone on earth will see what
happens.
Like a trumpet call,
everyone in the country will hear it.

4The Lord said, "I will be in the place prepared for me.ᵃ I will quietly watch these things happen: On a beautiful summer day, at noon, people will be resting. (It will be during the hot harvest time when there is no rain, but only early morning dew.) 5Then something terrible will happen. Earlier in the year, the flowers bloomed and the new grapes formed buds and began to grow. But before the crop is harvested, the enemy will come and cut the plants. They will break the vines and throw them away. 6The vines will be left for the birds from the mountains and the wild animals to eat. The birds will feed on them throughout the summer, and that winter the wild animals will eat the vines."

7At that time a special offering will be brought to the Lord All-Powerful from the people who are tall and smooth, from those who are feared far and wide, from that powerful nation that defeats other countries and whose land is divided by rivers.ᵇ This offering will be brought to the Lord's place on Mount Zion.*

God's Message to Egypt

19 1A messageᶜ about Egypt: Look, the Lord is coming on a fast cloud. He will enter Egypt, and all the false gods of Egypt will shake with fear. Egypt's courage will melt away like hot wax.

2The Lord says, "I will cause the Egyptians to fight against themselves. Men will fight their brothers. Neighbors will be against neighbors. Cities will be against cities. Kingdoms will be against kingdoms.ᵈ 3The Egyptians will be afraid and confused. They will ask their false gods and wise men what they should do. They will ask their wizards and magicians, but I will ruin their plans." 4The Lord God All-Powerful says, "I will give Egypt to a hard master. A powerful king will rule over the people."

5The water in the Nile River will dry up and disappear. 6All the rivers will smell very bad.ᵉ The canals in Egypt will be dry, and the water will be gone. All the water plants will rot. 7All the plants along the riverbanks will die and blow away. Even the plants at the widest part of the river will dry up, blow away, and disappear.

8The fishermen, all those who catch fish from the Nile River, will become sad and they will cry. They depend on the Nile River for their food, but it will be dry. 9Those who make cloth from flax, who weave it into linen, will all be sad. 10Those who weave cloth will be broken, and those who work for money will be depressed.

11The leaders of the city of Zoanᶠ are fools. Pharaoh's "wise advisors" give bad advice. They say they are wise. They say they are from the old family of the kings, but they are not as smart as they think. 12Egypt, where are your wise men? They should learn what the Lord All-Powerful has planned for Egypt. They should be the ones to tell you what will happen.

13The leaders of Zoan have been fooled. The leaders of Nophᵍ have believed lies, so they lead Egypt the wrong way. 14The Lord confused them, so they wander around and lead Egypt the wrong way. Everything they do is wrong. They are like drunks rolling in their vomit. 15There is nothing the leaders can do. (They are "the heads and the tails." They are "the tops and the stalks of plants."ʰ)

16At that time the Egyptians will be like frightened women. They will be afraid of the Lord All-Powerful, because he will raise his arm to punish the people. 17The land of Judah brings fear to everyone in Egypt. Anyone in Egypt who hears the name Judah will be afraid. This will happen because the Lord All-Powerful has planned terrible things to happen to Egypt. 18At that time there will be five cities in Egypt where people speak Hebrew.ⁱ One of these cities will be named "Destruction City."ʲ The people in these cities will promise to follow the Lord All-Powerful.

19At that time there will be an altar* for the Lord in the middle of Egypt. At the border of Egypt there will be a monument to show honor to the Lord. 20This will be a sign to show that the Lord All-Powerful does amazing things. Any time the people cry for help from the Lord, he will send help. He will send

---

ᵃ**18:4** *the place prepared for me* Probably the Temple in Jerusalem.
ᵇ**18:7** Or "At that time the people who are tall and smooth, who are feared far and wide, that powerful nation who defeats other countries and whose land is divided by rivers, those people will be brought to the Lord All-Powerful as a special gift."
ᶜ**19:1** *message* Or "burden."
ᵈ**19:2** *Kingdoms will be against kingdoms* Or "States will be against states." This means Egyptians will fight other Egyptians.

ᵉ**19:6** *smell very bad* In Hebrew this is like a name for the Nile River.
ᶠ**19:11** *Zoan* A city in Egypt. Also in verse 13.
ᵍ**19:13** *Noph* Or "Memphis," a city in Egypt.
ʰ**19:15** *the heads and … stalks of plants* See Isa. 9:14–15.
ⁱ**19:18** *Hebrew* Literally, "the language of Canaan."
ʲ**19:18** *Destruction City* This is a wordplay on the name meaning "Sun City," which is also called On or Heliopolis.

someone to save and defend the people—to rescue the people from those who hurt them.

²¹At that time the Lord will make himself known to the Egyptians, and they really will know the Lord. They will serve him and give him many sacrifices.* They will make promises*a* to the Lord, and they will do what they promise. ²²The Lord will punish the Egyptians, but then he will heal them, and they will come back to him. The Lord will listen to their prayers and heal them.

²³At that time there will be a highway from Egypt to Assyria.* Then the Assyrians will go to Egypt, and the Egyptians will go to Assyria. Egypt will work with Assyria.*b* ²⁴Then Israel, Assyria, and Egypt will join together and control the land. This will be a blessing for the land. ²⁵The Lord All-Powerful will bless these countries. He will say, "Egypt, you are my people. Assyria, I made you. Israel, I own you. You are all blessed!"

Assyria Will Defeat Egypt and Ethiopia

20 ¹Sargon*c* was the king of Assyria.* He sent his military commander to fight against Ashdod. The commander went there and captured the city. ²At that time the Lord spoke through Isaiah son of Amoz. He said, "Go, take the sackcloth* off your waist and the sandals off your feet." So Isaiah obeyed the Lord and went without clothes or sandals.

³Then the Lord said, "My servant Isaiah has gone without clothes or sandals for three years. This is a sign for Egypt and Ethiopia. ⁴The king of Assyria will defeat Egypt and Ethiopia. Assyria will take prisoners and lead them away from their countries. The people, young and old, will be led away without clothes or sandals. They will be completely naked. ⁵Those who looked to Ethiopia for help will be shattered. Those who were amazed by Egypt's glory will be ashamed."

⁶People living along the coast will say, "We trusted those countries to help us. We ran to them so that they would rescue us from the king of Assyria. But look at them. They have been captured, so how can we escape?"

God's Message About Babylon

21 ¹This is a message*d* about the Desert by the Sea*e*:

It is coming like a storm blowing through the Negev.*
It is coming in from the desert, from a frightening nation.

² I was given a vision of the hard times to come.
I see traitors turning against you.
I see people taking your wealth.

Elam, go against them!
Media, surround the city!
I will put an end to all their moaning.

³ I saw those terrible things, and now I am afraid.
My fear makes my stomach hurt like the pain of giving birth.
What I hear frightens me.
What I see makes me shake with fear.
⁴ I am worried and shaking with fear.
My pleasant evening has become a nightmare.

⁵ People are rushing around shouting their orders:
"Set the table!
Post the guard!
Get something to eat and drink!
Officers, get up!
Polish your shields!"

⁶The Lord said to me, "Go find someone to guard this city. He must report whatever he sees. ⁷Whether he sees a chariot and a team of horses or men riding donkeys or camels, he must listen carefully."*f*

⁸Then one day the watchman*g* called out,

"My master, every day I have been in the watchtower*h* watching.
Every night I have been standing on duty.
⁹ Look! I see a man in a chariot with a team of horses.*i*

The messenger said,
"Babylon has been defeated!
It has fallen to the ground!
All the statues of her false gods were thrown to the ground and broken to pieces."

¹⁰My people, you will be like the grain crushed on my threshing* floor. I have told you everything I heard from the Lord All-Powerful, the God of Israel.

*f*21:7 Or "Whether he sees a column of teams of horsemen, columns of donkeys, or columns of camels, he must listen carefully."
*g*21:8 *the watchman* Or "the seer," an ancient title for a prophet. The standard Hebrew text has "a lion."
*h*21:8 *watchtower* A tall building where guards stood and watched to see if anyone was coming near their city.
*i*21:9 *a man ... horses* Or "a column of teams of horsemen." This might be a team of horses pulling a war chariot or mounted archers in the Assyrian army who often worked in pairs.

*a*19:21 *promises* A special kind of promise to God. See Lev. 22:18–24.
*b*19:23 *Egypt will work with Assyria* Or "Egypt will serve Assyria."
*c*20:1 *Sargon* A king of Assyria. He was king about 721–705 B.C.
*d*21:1 *message* Or "burden." Also in verses 11, 13.
*e*21:1 *Desert by the Sea* Probably Babylon.

God's Message About Dumah

¹¹This is a message about Dumah*ᵃ*:

There is someone calling to me from
Seir,*ᵇ*
"Guard, how much of the night is left?
How much longer will it be night?"

¹² The guard answered,
"Morning is coming, but then night will
come again.
If you have something else to ask,
then come back*ᶜ* later and ask."

God's Message About Arabia

¹³This is a message about Arabia:

A caravan* from Dedan spent the night
near some trees in the Arabian Desert.
¹⁴ They gave water to some thirsty travelers.
The people of Tema gave them food.
¹⁵ They were running from swords
that were ready to kill.
They were running from bows
that were ready to shoot.
They were running from a hard battle.

¹⁶The Lord told me this would happen.
He said, "In one year, the way a hired helper
counts time, all Kedar's* glory will be gone.
¹⁷Only a few of the archers,* the great soldiers of Kedar, will be left alive." The LORD,
the God of Israel, told me this.

God's Message About Jerusalem

22 ¹This is a message*ᵈ* about the Valley
of Vision*ᵉ*:

Jerusalem, what is wrong?
Why has everyone gone up to hide in
their upper rooms?
² This city was so happy,
but now there is a terrible uproar.
There are bodies lying everywhere,
but they were not killed with swords.
The people died,
but not while fighting.
³ All your officers ran away together,
but they have all been captured without
bows.*ᶠ*
All the leaders ran away together,
but they were found and captured.

⁴ So I say, "Don't look at me!
Let me cry!

Don't rush to comfort me about the
destruction of Jerusalem."

⁵The LORD chose a special day for there to
be riots and confusion. People trampled on
each other in the Valley of Vision. The city
walls were pulled down. People in the valley
shouted up at those on the mountain. ⁶Horse
soldiers from Elam took their bags of arrows
and rode into battle. Soldiers from Kir rattled
their shields. ⁷Your favorite valley was filled
with chariots.* Horse soldiers were stationed
in front of the city gates. ⁸Then the cover protecting Judah*ᵍ* was removed, and the people
turned to the weapons they kept at the Forest
Palace.*ʰ*

⁹⁻¹¹Then you noticed how many cracks
there were in the walls around the City of
David,* so you began collecting water from
the Lower Pool.*ⁱ* You counted the houses and
used stones from them to repair the walls.
Then you built a pool between the double
walls*ʲ* for storing water from the Old Pool.*ᵏ*

You did all this to protect yourselves, but
you did not trust the God who made all these
things. You did not even notice the one who
made all these things so long ago. ¹²So the
Lord GOD All-Powerful told the people to cry
and mourn* for their dead friends. He told
them to shave their heads and wear mourning clothes. ¹³But look, everyone was happy.
The people rejoiced, saying,

"Kill the cattle and sheep, and let's
celebrate.
Let's eat meat and drink wine,
Eat and drink, for tomorrow we die."

¹⁴The LORD All-Powerful said this to me and
I heard it with my own ears: "You are guilty of
doing wrong, and I promise that you will die
before this guilt is forgiven." The Lord GOD
All-Powerful said these things.

God's Message to Shebna

¹⁵The Lord GOD All-Powerful told me this:
"Go to Shebna, the palace manager. ¹⁶Ask
him, 'What are you doing here? None of your
relatives are buried here, are they? Then
what right do you have to prepare a tomb*
for yourself in this high place? Why are you
cutting a tomb out of this rock?

¹⁷⁻¹⁸"What a big man you are! But the LORD
will crush you. He will roll you into a small ball

ᵍ **22:8 cover protecting Judah** This might be the wall
around Jerusalem, but see Isa. 4:4.
ʰ **22:8 Forest Palace** A part of Solomon's palace
where his weapons and wealth were stored.
ⁱ **22:9–11 Lower Pool** The pool at the southern tip
of the City of David, just below the Upper Pool (the
Pool of Siloam).
ʲ **22:9–11 pool between the double walls** This is
probably the Upper Pool (Pool of Siloam).
ᵏ **22:9–11 Old Pool** Probably the pool at Gihon
Spring on the eastern slopes of the city.

ᵃ **21:11 Dumah** This Hebrew word means "silence." It
may refer to Edom or to a city in Arabia.
ᵇ **21:11 Seir** A mountain in Edom or a city in Arabia.
ᶜ **21:12 come back** This can also mean "change your
heart" or "repent."
ᵈ **22:1 message** Or "burden."
ᵉ **22:1 Valley of Vision** This probably means one of
the valleys near Jerusalem. Also in verse 5.
ᶠ **22:3 but they have … bows** Or "but the archers
captured them."

and throw you far away into the open arms of another country, and there you will die.

"You are very proud of your chariots.* But in that faraway land, your new ruler will have better chariots. And your chariots will not look important in his palace." ¹⁹The Lord said, "I will force you out of your position here. Your new leader will take you away from your important job. ²⁰At that time I will call for my servant Eliakim son of Hilkiah. ²¹I will take your robe and put it on him. I will give him your scepter.* I will give him the important job you have, and he will be like a father to the people of Jerusalem and Judah's family.ᵃ

²²"I will put the key to David's* house around his neck. If he opens a door, no one will be able to close it. If he closes a door, no one will be able to open it. ²³He will be like a favorite chair in his father's house. I will make him like a strong peg in a solid board. ²⁴All the honored and important things of his father's house will hang on him. All the adults and little children will depend on him. They will be like little dishes and big water bottles hanging on him."

²⁵The Lord All-Powerful said, "At that time the peg that is now in the solid board will get weak and break. It will fall to the ground, and everything hanging on it will be destroyed. Then everything I said in this message will happen. It will happen because the Lord said it would."

God's Message About Tyre

23 ¹This is a messageᵇ about Tyre:

Ships traveling from Cyprus* heard this message:
"Cry, you ships from Tarshishᶜ!
Your harbor has been destroyed."

² You people living near the sea, mourn* in silence.
The merchants* of Sidon sent traders across the sea
and filled the city with riches.
³ They traveled the seas looking for grain.
The men from Tyre bought grain that
grows near the Nile River
and sold it to other nations.

⁴ Sidon, you should be very sad,
because now the Sea and the Fort of the Seaᵈ say,
"I have no children.
I have never felt the pain of birth;
I have never given birth to children.
I have never raised young men and women."

⁵ When Egypt hears the news about Tyre,
it will feel the pain of sorrow.
⁶ You ships, try to escape to Tarshish*!
Cry out, you people living near the sea!
⁷ Can this be that happy city that was
founded so long ago?
Is it that same city whose people
traveled so far to settle other lands?ᵉ
⁸ This city produced so many leaders.
Its merchants were like princes.
Its traders had the whole world's respect.
So who made these plans against Tyre?
⁹ It was the Lord All-Powerful.
He decided to destroy the great things
they were so proud of.
He wanted to disgrace those who were
so highly respected.
¹⁰ Ships from Tarshish, go back home.
Cross the sea as if it were a river.
No one will stop you now.
¹¹ The Lord raised his arm over the sea
to make the kingdoms angry enough to
fight against Tyre.
He commanded Canaan*
to destroy her place of safety.ᶠ
¹² He said, "Daughter Sidon,ᵍ you have been
hurt badly,
so you will no longer rejoice like a bride.
Go ahead, go to Cyprusʰ for help,
but you will not find a place to rest
there either."
¹³ As for Babylon, look at the land of the
Chaldeans*!
It is not even a country now.
Assyria* built war towers to attack it.
The soldiers took everything from the
beautiful houses.
Assyria destroyed Babylon.
They turned it into a pile of ruins
and made it a place for wild animals.
¹⁴ So be sad, you ships from Tarshish.
Your place of safety has been destroyed.

¹⁵People will forget about Tyre for 70 years—that is, about the length of a king's rule. After 70 years, Tyre will be like the prostitute in this song:

¹⁶"Oh, woman who men forgot,
take your harp and walk through the city.
Play your song well and sing it often.
Maybe someone will remember you."

ᵃ**22:21** *people of Jerusalem and Judah's family* Or "The king sitting on the throne in Jerusalem, the royal family of Judah."
ᵇ**23:1** *message* Or "burden."
ᶜ**23:1** *ships from Tarshish* This is probably a special type of cargo ship. Also in verse 14.
ᵈ**23:4** *Fort of the Sea* Another name for the city of Tyre.
ᵉ**23:7** *traveled … other lands?* Or "came from so far to live here?"
ᶠ**23:11** Or "He raised his arm over the sea and shook nations. He gave a command about Canaan to destroy its fortresses."
ᵍ**23:12** *Daughter Sidon* Another name for the city of Sidon.
ʰ**23:12** *Cyprus* Literally, "Kittim." This could also mean "Crete."

¹⁷After 70 years, the Lᴏʀᴅ will review Tyre's case, and he will give her a decision. Tyre will again have trade. She will be like a prostitute for all the nations on earth. ¹⁸But Tyre will not keep the money she earns. The profit from her trade will be saved for the Lᴏʀᴅ. Tyre will give that money to the people who serve the Lᴏʀᴅ to buy good food and nice clothes.

God Will Punish Israel

24 ¹Look, the Lᴏʀᴅ is destroying this land.^a He will clean out the land completely and force all the people to go far away. ²At that time whatever happens to the common people will also happen to the priests. Slaves and masters will be the same. Women slaves and their women masters will be the same. Buyers and sellers will be the same. Those who borrow and those who lend will be the same. Bankers and those who owe the bank will be the same. ³Everyone will be forced out of the land. All the wealth will be taken. This will happen because the Lᴏʀᴅ commanded it. ⁴The country will be empty and sad. The world will be empty and weak. The great leaders of the people in this land will become weak.

⁵The people have ruined the land. They did what God said was wrong. They did not obey God's laws. They made an agreement* with God a long time ago, but they broke their agreement with God. ⁶The people living in this land are guilty of doing wrong, so God promised to destroy the land. The people will be punished, and only a few of them will survive.

⁷The grapevines are dying. The new wine is bad. People who were happy are now sad. ⁸They have stopped showing their joy. The happy music from the drums and harps has ended. ⁹They no longer sing as they drink their wine. The beer now tastes bitter to those who drink it.

¹⁰"Total Confusion" is a good name for this city. The city has been destroyed. People cannot enter the houses. The doors are blocked. ¹¹People still ask for wine in the marketplaces, but all the joy is gone. It was carried off with everything else. ¹²All that is left is destruction. Even the gates are crushed.

¹³ At harvest time, people knock olives from the trees.
But a few olives are left in the trees.
It will be like that in this land and among the nations.

¹⁴ Those who are left will begin shouting louder than the ocean.
They will rejoice about the Lᴏʀᴅ's greatness.

¹⁵ They will say, "People in the east, praise the Lᴏʀᴅ!

People in faraway lands,
praise the name of the Lᴏʀᴅ, the God of Israel."

¹⁶ We hear songs of praise for God from every place on earth.
They praise the God who does what is right.
But I say, "Enough!
I have had enough.
What I see is terrible.
Traitors* are turning against people and hurting them."

¹⁷ I see troubles for you people living in this land.
I see fear, pits, and problems all around.

¹⁸ People will hear about the danger,
and they will be afraid.
Some of them will run away,
but they will fall into holes and be trapped.
Some of them will climb out of the holes,
but they will be caught in another trap.
The floodgates in the sky above will open,
and the floods will begin.
The foundations of the earth will shake.

¹⁹ There will be earthquakes,
and the earth will split open.

²⁰ The sins of the world are very heavy,
so the earth will fall under the weight.
It will shake like an old house.
It will fall like a drunk.
It will not be able to stand.

²¹ At that time the Lᴏʀᴅ will judge
the heavenly armies in heaven
and the earthly kings on earth.

²² Many people will be gathered together.
They have been locked in the Pit.
They have been in prison.^b
But finally, after a long time, they will be judged.

²³ The Lᴏʀᴅ will rule as king on Mount Zion* in Jerusalem.
His Glory* will be shown to the city leaders with such brightness that
the moon will be embarrassed
and the sun will be ashamed.

A Song of Praise to God

25 ¹Lᴏʀᴅ, you are my God.
I honor you and praise your name,
because you did amazing things.
The words you said long ago are completely true;
everything happened exactly as you said it would.

² And you destroyed the city that was protected by strong walls.
Now it is only a pile of rocks.
The foreign palace has been destroyed.
It will never be rebuilt.

---

^a**24:1** *land* Or "earth."

^b**24:22** *Pit ... prison* This is probably "Sheol," the grave.

³ That is why powerful nations will
    honor you.
  Powerful people from strong cities will
    fear you.
⁴ And, Lᴏʀᴅ, you are a safe place for poor
    people in trouble.
  You are like a shelter from floods and
    shade from the heat
    when powerful men attack.
  They are like rain streaming down the
    walls
    that protect us from the storm.
⁵ Like the heat of summer in a dry land,
    the angry shouts of those foreigners
    brought us to our knees.
  But like a thick cloud that blocks the
    summer heat,
    you answered their challenge.

God's Banquet for His Servants

⁶The Lᴏʀᴅ All-Powerful will give a feast for all the people on this mountain. At the feast, there will be the best foods and wines. The meat will be good and tender, the wine pure and clear.

⁷But now there is a veil covering all nations and people. This veil is called "death." ⁸But death will be destroyed forever.ᵃ And the Lord Gᴏᴅ will wipe away every tear from every face. In the past, all of his people were sad, but God will take away that sadness from the earth. All of this will happen because the Lᴏʀᴅ said it would.

⁹ At that time people will say,
  "Here is our God!
  He is the one we have been waiting for.
    He has come to save us.
  We have been waiting for our Lᴏʀᴅ.
    So we will rejoice and be happy when
    he saves us."
¹⁰ The Lᴏʀᴅ's power is on this mountain,
    and Moabᵇ will be defeated.
  The Lord will trample the enemy
    like someone walking on straw in a pile
    of waste.
¹¹ They will reach out their arms to escape
    like someone trying to swim.
  But their pride will sink
    with each stroke they take.
¹² He will destroy their high walls and safe
    places.
  He will throw them down into the dust
    on the ground.

A Song of Praise to God

26 ¹At that time people will sing this song in Judah:

  We have a strong city with strong walls
    and defenses.

  But the Lord gives us our salvation.ᶜ
² Open the gates for the good people to
    enter.
  They are the God's faithful followers.

³ Lᴏʀᴅ, you give true peace
  to people who depend on you,
  to those who trust in you.

⁴ So trust the Lᴏʀᴅ always,
    because in the Lᴏʀᴅ Yᴀʜᵈ you have a
    place of safety forever.
⁵ But he will destroy the proud city
    and punish those who live there.
  He will throw that high city down to the
    ground.
  It will fall into the dust.
⁶ Then poor and humble people will walk
    on those ruins.

⁷ Honesty is the path good people follow.
    They follow the path that is straight and
    true.
  And God, you make that way smooth
    and easy to follow.
⁸ But, Lᴏʀᴅ, we are waiting for your way of
    justice.
  We want to honor you and your name.
⁹ At night my soul longs to be with you,
    and the spirit in me wants to be with
    you at the dawn of every new day.
  When your way of justice comes to the
    world,
    people will learn the right way of living.
¹⁰ Evil people will not learn to do good,
    even if you show them only kindness.
  They will still do wrong, even if they live
    in a good world.
  They never see the Lᴏʀᴅ's greatness.
¹¹ Lᴏʀᴅ, your arm is raised to punish them,
    but they don't see it.
  Show them how strong your loveᵉ is for
    your people.
    Then those who are evil will be
    ashamed.
  Yes, your fire will destroy your enemies.
¹² Lᴏʀᴅ, you have succeeded in doing
    everything we tried to do,
    so give us peace.

God Will Give New Life to His People

¹³ Lᴏʀᴅ, you are our God, but in the past,
    we followed other lords.
  We belonged to other masters,ᶠ

ᵃ**25:8 But death ... forever** Some Greek versions have "But death will be swallowed in victory."
ᵇ**25:10 Moab** Or "the enemy." This name is like a Hebrew word meaning "enemy."
ᶜ**26:1** Or "We have a strong city that provides us with salvation. It has strong walls and defenses."
ᵈ**26:4 Lᴏʀᴅ Yᴀʜ** Or "Yᴀʜ Yᴀʜᴡᴇʜ," a Hebrew name for God.
ᵉ**26:11 strong ... love** The Hebrew word means strong feelings like love, hate, anger, zeal, or jealousy.
ᶠ**26:13 we followed ... masters** This is a wordplay. It could also be translated, "Husbands other than you married us." One word sounds like "Baal," the other like a title for God.

but now we want people to remember
only one name—yours.

14 Those dead lords will not come to life.
Those ghosts will not rise from death.
You decided to destroy them,
and you destroyed everything that
makes us think about them.

15 You helped the nation you love.
You made our nation bigger
and brought honor to yourself.*a*

16 LORD, people remember you
when they are in trouble.
So because of your punishment,
we called out to you.

17 LORD, because of you we were in pain,
like a woman giving birth,
who struggles and cries out when it is
time.

18 But we struggled in pain for nothing.
We gave birth only to wind.
We did nothing to save the land.
No one was born to live in the world.

19 ⌊But the Lord says,⌋
"Your people have died,
but they will live again.
The bodies of my people
will rise from death.
Dead people in the ground,
stand and be happy!
The dew covering you is like
the dew sparkling in the light of a new
day.
It shows that a new time is coming,
when the earth will give birth to the
dead who are in it."

Judgment: Reward or Punishment

20 My people, go into your rooms
and lock your doors.
Hide in there for a short time
until the LORD's anger is finished.

21 Look! The LORD is coming out from his
place*b*
to judge the people of the world for the
bad things they have done.
The earth will reveal the blood that has
been spilled on it.
It will no longer hide the proof of those
murders.

27 1 At that time the LORD will judge
Leviathan,*c* the crooked snake.
He will use his great sword, his hard and
powerful sword,
to punish Leviathan, that twisting,
turning snake.
He will kill the monster of the sea.*d*

2 At that time people will sing about the
pleasant vineyard.*

3 "I, the LORD, will care for the vineyard.
I will water it at the right time.
I will guard it day and night.
No one will hurt it.

4 I am not angry.
But if there is war and someone builds a
wall of thornbushes,*e*
then I will march to it and burn it.

5 But if anyone comes to me for safety and
wants to make peace with me,
then let them come and make peace.

6 In the future, Jacob* will take root firmly
on his soil.
Then Israel* will sprout and bloom,
and the world will be filled with his
fruit."

God Will Send Israel Away

7 Israel was not hurt as badly as the enemy
who tried to hurt it. Not as many of its people
were killed as those who tried to kill them.

8 The Lord will settle his argument with
Israel by sending the people far away. He will
speak harshly to Israel. His words will burn
like the hot desert wind.

9 How will Jacob's guilt be forgiven? What
will happen so his sins can be taken away?
The rocks of the altar* will be crushed to dust;
the statues*f* and altars for worshiping false
gods will all be destroyed.

10 The great city will be empty; it will be like
a desert. All the people will be gone—they
will run away. The city will be like an open
pasture. Young cattle will eat grass there. The
cattle will eat leaves from the branches of the
vines. 11 The vines will become dry, and the
branches will break off. Women will use them
for firewood.

The people refuse to understand. So God,
their Maker, will not comfort them or be kind
to them.

12 At that time the LORD will begin separating his people from others. He will begin at
the Euphrates River and will gather his people
from there*g* to the River of Egypt.*h*

You people of Israel will be gathered
together one by one. 13 Many of my people
are now lost in Assyria.* Some of my people
have run away to Egypt. But at that time a
great trumpet will be blown, and all those
people will come back to Jerusalem. They

---

*a*26:15 Or "You gathered together the nation you
love, the nation you drove into faraway lands."
*b*26:21 *his place* Probably the Temple in Jerusalem.
*c*27:1 *Leviathan* The Dragon or giant snake. Some
ancient stories say the Dragon was an enemy of God.
*d*27:1 *monster of the sea* This is probably Rahab.
Some ancient stories tell of Rahab fighting with
God.

*e*27:4 *a wall of thornbushes* Literally, "thorns and
thistles." Farmers planted walls of thornbushes
around vineyards to protect them from animals.
See Isa. 5:5.
*f*27:9 *statues* Or "idols." See "idol" in the Word List.
*g*27:12 *He will begin … from there* Literally, "He
will begin threshing at the stream of the river." This
Hebrew word for stream is like the word meaning
"head of grain."
*h*27:12 *Euphrates River … River of Egypt* These are
the borders of the land God promised to give Israel.

will bow down before the LORD on that holy* mountain.

Warnings to Northern Israel

28 ¹Look at Samaria!
The drunks of Ephraim* are proud of that city.
It sits on a hill with a rich valley around it.
The Samarians think their city is a beautiful crown of flowers.
But they are drunk with wine, and this "beautiful crown" is just a dying plant.

² Look, the Lord has someone who is strong and brave.
He will come into the country like a storm of hail and rain.
Like a powerful river of water flooding the country,
he will throw that crown*a* down to the ground.
³ The drunks of Ephraim are proud of their beautiful crown,
but that city will be trampled down.
⁴ That city sits on a hill with a rich valley around it.
But that beautiful crown of flowers is just a dying plant.
It will be like the first figs of summer.
As soon as someone sees a ripe one, they pick it and eat it.

⁵At that time the LORD All-Powerful will become the "Beautiful Crown." He will be the "Wonderful Crown of Flowers" for his people who are left. ⁶Then he will give wisdom to the judges who rule his people. He will give strength to the people who are in battles at the city gates. ⁷But now those leaders are drunk. The priests and prophets are all drunk with wine and beer. They stumble and fall down. The prophets are drunk when they see their dreams. The judges are drunk when they make their decisions. ⁸Every table is covered with vomit. There is not a clean place anywhere.

God Wants to Help His People

⁹ₗThe people say,ₗ "Who does he think he is trying to teach and explain his message to? Does he think we are babies who were at their mother's breast only a very short time ago? ¹⁰ₗHe speaks to us as though we were babies:ₗ

"Saw lasaw saw lasaw
Qaw laqaw qaw laqaw
Ze'er sham ze'er sham."*b*

---

a*28:2 that crown* That is, Samaria.
b*28:10 Saw lasaw ... ze'er sham* This is probably a Hebrew song to teach little children how to write. It sounds like baby talk or a foreign language, but it can also be translated, "A command here, a

¹¹So the LORD will use this strange way of talking, and he will use other languages to speak to these people.
¹²In the past, the Lord spoke to them and said, "Here is a resting place. This is the peaceful place. Let the tired people come and rest. This is the place of peace."
But the people did not want to listen to him. ¹³So the LORD's message will be as meaningless as a foreign language*c*:

"Saw lasaw saw lasaw.
Qaw laqaw qaw laqaw.
Ze'er sham ze'er sham."

When the people try to walk, they will fall backwards. They will be defeated, trapped, and captured.

No One Escapes God's Judgment

¹⁴You leaders in Jerusalem should listen to the LORD's message, but now you refuse to listen to him. ¹⁵You have said, "We have made an agreement with death. We have a contract with death. So we will not be punished. Punishment will pass us without hurting us. We will hide behind our tricks and lies."
¹⁶Because of these things, the Lord GOD says, "I will put a rock—a cornerstone—in the ground in Zion.* This will be a very precious stone.*d* Everything will be built on this very important rock. Anyone who trusts in that rock will not be disappointed.*e*
¹⁷"Workers use a string and weight to show their work is straight and true. I will use justice as the string and goodness as the weight when I lay that foundation. But your safe places were built on lies. So they will be destroyed and washed away when the troubles come against you like hail storms and floods. ¹⁸Your agreement with death will be erased. Your contract with Sheol* will not help you.
"Someone will come and punish you. He will make you like the dirt he walks on. ¹⁹He will come and take you away. Your punishment will be terrible. Your punishment will come early in the morning, and it will continue late into the night.
"Then you will understand this story: ²⁰A man tried to sleep on a bed that was too short for him. He had a blanket that was not wide enough to cover him. ₗThe bed and blanket were useless, and so were your agreements.ₗ"
²¹The LORD will fight as he did at Mount Perazim. He will be angry as he was in Gibeon

---

command there. A rule here, a rule there. A lesson here, a lesson there." Also in verse 13.
c*28:13 foreign language* Or "gibberish" or "baby talk."
d*28:16 very precious stone* This also means a stone has been tested and shown that it has no cracks.
e*28:16 Anyone ... disappointed* This is found in the ancient Greek version. The standard Hebrew text has "Whoever trusts will not panic."

Valley.*a* He will do what he must do. It will be what some stranger should do, but he will finish his work. Yes, this is a stranger's job. 22Now don't complain about these things. If you fight against them, you will only tighten the ropes around you.

The words I heard will not change. They came from the LORD All-Powerful, the ruler of all the earth, and these things will be done.

The Lord Punishes Fairly

23Listen closely to the message I am telling you. 24Does a farmer plow his field all the time? No, he doesn't work the soil all the time. 25A farmer prepares the ground, and then he plants the seed. He plants different kinds of seeds different ways. He scatters dill seeds, he throws cumin seeds on the ground, and he plants wheat in rows. A farmer plants barley in its special place, and he plants spelt* seeds at the edge of his field.

26Our God is using this to teach you a lesson. This example shows us that God is fair when he punishes his people. 27Does a farmer use large boards with sharp teeth to crush dill seeds? No, and he doesn't use a wagon to crush cumin seeds. A farmer uses a small stick to break the hulls from these seeds of grain. 28People grind grain to make flour, but they don't grind it forever. ⌐The Lord does the same thing when he punishes his people.⌐ He might frighten them with the wagon wheel, but he does not allow the horses*b* to walk on them. 29This lesson comes from the LORD All-Powerful, who gives wonderful advice. He is very wise.

God Punishes Jerusalem

29 1⌐God says,⌐ "Look at Ariel,*c* the city where David* camped. Keep on having your festivals, year after year. 2But I will punish Ariel. The city will be filled with sadness and crying, but it will always be my Ariel.

3"I will put armies all around you, Ariel. I will raise war towers against you. 4You will be pulled to the ground. Your voice will rise from the ground like the voice of a ghost. Your words come like a whisper from the dirt."

5There will be so many foreigners that they will be like dust. Cruel people will be like the chaff* blowing in the wind. Then suddenly, 6the LORD All-Powerful will punish you with earthquakes, thunder, and loud noises. There will be storms, strong winds, and a burning, destructive fire. 7Many nations will fight against Ariel. It will be a nightmare. Armies will surround Ariel and punish her. 8But it

will also be like a dream to those armies. They will not get what they want. It will be like a hungry man dreaming about food. When the man wakes up, he is still hungry. It will be like a thirsty man dreaming about water. When the man wakes up, he is still thirsty. The same thing is true about all the nations fighting against Zion.* Those nations will not get what they want.

9 Be surprised and amazed!
     You will become drunk, but not from
        wine.
   Look and be amazed!
     You will stumble and fall, but not from
        beer.
10 The LORD will make you sleepy.
     He will close your eyes. (The prophets
        are your eyes.)
     He will cover your heads. (The prophets
        are your heads.)

11To you my words are like the words in a book that is closed and sealed.*d* You can give the book to someone who can read and tell that person to read it. But that person will say, "I cannot read the book. It is closed and I cannot open it." 12Or you can give the book to someone who cannot read and tell that person to read it. That person will say, "I cannot read the book because I don't know how to read."

13The Lord says, "These people come to honor me with words, but I am not really important to them. The worship they give me is nothing but human rules they have memorized. 14So I will continue to amaze them by doing powerful and amazing things. Their wise men will lose their wisdom. Even the most intelligent among them will not be able to understand."

15Look at them! They try to hide things from the LORD. They think he will not understand. They do their evil things in darkness. They tell themselves: "No one can see us. No one will know who we are."

16You turn things upside down. You think the clay is equal to the potter.* You think that something that is made can tell the one who made it, "You did not make me!" This is like a pot telling its maker, "You know nothing."

A Better Time Is Coming

17This is the truth: After a very short time, Lebanon will become rich farmland, and the farmland will be like thick forests. 18The deaf will hear the words in the book. The blind will see through the darkness and fog. 19The LORD will make poor people happy. The poorest people will rejoice in the Holy One of Israel.*

---

*a*28:21 *Mount Perazim ... Gibeon Valley* See 1 Chron. 14:8–17.
*b*28:28 *horses* This word also means "horse soldiers."
*c*29:1 *Ariel* A name for the altar at the Temple in Jerusalem. This name means "hearth" or "fireplace" but sounds like the word meaning "Lion of God." Also in verse 7.

*d*29:11 *sealed* A piece of clay or wax was put on the closed book to show that the book should not be opened.

²⁰This will happen when the people who are mean and cruel have come to an end. It will happen when those who enjoy doing bad things are gone. ²¹(They lie about good people. They try to trap people in court. They try to destroy innocent people.)

²²So the Lord, who made Abraham free, speaks to Jacob's* family. He says, "Now the people of Jacob will not be embarrassed and ashamed. ²³They will look around at all the children they have I made with my hands, and they will say that my name is holy.* They will honor* the Holy One of Jacob. They will respect the God of Israel. ²⁴Many of these people did not understand, so they did what was wrong. They complained, but now they will learn their lesson."

Israel Should Trust in God, Not Egypt

30 ¹The Lord said, "Look at these children. They don't obey me. They make plans, but they don't ask me to help them. They make agreements with other nations, but my Spirit* does not want those agreements. These people are adding more and more sins to the ones they have already done. ²They are going down to Egypt for help, but they did not ask me if that was the right thing to do. They hope they will be saved by the Pharaoh.* They want Egypt to protect them.

³"But I tell you, hiding in Egypt will not help you. Pharaoh will not be able to protect you. ⁴Your leaders have gone to Zoan, and your representatives have gone to Hanes.ᵇ ⁵But they will be disappointed. They are depending on a nation that cannot help them. Egypt is useless—it will not help. Egypt will bring nothing but shame and embarrassment."

God's Message to Judah

⁶This is a messageᶜ about the Negev animalsᵈ:

There is a dangerous place full of lions, adders,ᵉ deadly snakes,ᶠ and useless people. And there are people who load their wealth onto donkeys and their treasures on the backs of camels. They carry them to a people who cannot help. ⁷That useless nation is Egypt. Egypt's help is worth nothing, so I call Egypt the "Do-Nothing Dragon."ᵍ

⁸Now write this on a sign so that all people can see it, and write this in a book. Write

these things for a future time. This will be far, far in the future:ʰ

⁹These people are like children who refuse to obey. They lie and refuse to listen to the Lord's teachings. ¹⁰They tell the prophets, "Don't see dreamsⁱ about things we should do. Don't tell us the truth. Say nice things to us and make us feel good. See only good things for us. ¹¹Stop seeing things that will really happen. Get out of our way. Stop telling us about the Holy One of Israel."

Judah's Help Comes Only From God

¹²The Holy One of Israel says, "You people have refused to accept this message from the Lord. You want to depend on fighting and lies to help you. ¹³You are guilty of these things. So you are like a tall wall with cracks in it. That wall will fall and break into small pieces. ¹⁴You will be like a large clay jar that breaks into many small, useless pieces. You cannot use them to get a hot coal from the fire or to get water from a pool in the ground."

¹⁵The Lord God, the Holy One of Israel, says, "If you come back to me you will be saved. Only by remaining calm and trusting in me can you be strong."

But you don't want to do that. ¹⁶You say, "No, we need fast horses for battle." That is true—you will need fast horses, but only to run away because your enemy will be faster than your horses. ¹⁷One enemy soldier will make threats, and a thousand of your men will run away. And when five of them make threats, all of you will run away. The only thing that will be left of your army will be a flagpole on a hill.

God Will Help His People

¹⁸So the Lord is waiting to show his mercy to you. He wants to rise and comfort you. The Lord is the God who does the right thing, so he will bless everyone who waits for his help.

¹⁹You people who live in Jerusalem on Mount Zion* will not continue crying. The Lord will hear your crying, and he will comfort you. When he hears you, he will help you.

²⁰The Lord might give you sorrow and pain like the bread and water you eat every day. But God is your teacher, and he will not continue to hide from you. You will see your teacher with your own eyes. ²¹If you wander from the right path, either to the right or to the left, you will hear a voice behind you saying, "You should go this way. Here is the right way."

ᵃ**29:23** *honor* Or "treat as holy."
ᵇ**30:4** *Zoan, Hanes* Cities in Egypt.
ᶜ**30:6** *message* Or "burden."
ᵈ**30:6** *Negev animals* Or "Creatures of the South," a phrase that can refer to Egypt.
ᵉ**30:6** *adders* Very poisonous snakes.
ᶠ**30:6** *deadly snakes* Literally, "flying snakes."
ᵍ**30:7** *Do-Nothing Dragon* Or "Resting Rahab," the great sea monster. Some ancient stories tell about Rahab fighting with God.

ʰ**30:8** *Write ... future* Or "Write this for the future as a witness forever."
ⁱ**30:10** *dreams* Or "visions." Special kinds of dreams God used to speak to his prophets.

²²Then you will take your idols* covered with gold and silver and make them unfit to be used again. You will throw them away like filthy rags*ª* and say, "Go away!"

²³At that time the LORD will send you rain. You will plant seeds, and the ground will grow food for you. You will have a very large harvest. You will have plenty of food in the fields for your animals. There will be large fields for your sheep. ²⁴Your cattle and donkeys will have all the food they need. There will be much food. You will have to use shovels and pitchforks to spread all the food*ᵇ* for your animals to eat. ²⁵Every mountain and hill will have streams filled with water. These things will happen after many people are killed and the enemy's towers are pulled down.

²⁶At that time the light from the moon will be as bright as the sun, and the light from the sun will be seven times brighter than it is now. One day of sunlight will be like a whole week's worth. This will happen when the LORD bandages his broken people and heals the hurts from their beatings.

²⁷Look! The LORD is coming from far away. His anger is like a fire with thick clouds of smoke. His mouth is filled with anger, and his tongue is like a burning fire. ²⁸His breath is like a great river that rises until it reaches the throat. He will judge the nations as if putting them through a strainer that separates the ones fit for destruction. He will put a bit in their mouths to lead them to the place they don't want to go.

²⁹You will sing happy songs, like the nights when you begin a festival. You will be very happy walking to the LORD's mountain and listening to the flute on the way to worship the Rock* of Israel.

³⁰The LORD will cause all people to hear his great voice and to see his powerful arm come down in anger. That arm will be like a great fire that burns everything. His power will be like a great storm with much rain and hail. ³¹Assyria* will be frightened by the LORD's voice and the stick that will beat him. ³²And as the LORD beats Assyria, his people will keep the rhythm with their drums and harps.

³³Topheth*ᶜ* has been made ready for a long time. It is ready for the king.*ᵈ* It was made very deep and wide. There is a very big pile of wood and fire there, and the LORD's breath will come like a stream of burning sulfur to start the fire.

Israel Should Depend on God's Power

31 ¹Look at the people going down to Egypt for help. They think the horses they get will save them. They hope the many chariots* and powerful soldiers will protect them. But the people don't trust the Holy One of Israel. They didn't ask the LORD for help. ²But he is the wise one who is bringing the disaster. And they will not be able to stop what he commanded. The Lord will attack those who are evil and all who try to help them.

³The Egyptians are only human, not God. The horses from Egypt are only animals, not spirit. The LORD will stretch out his arm, and the helper will be defeated. And those who wanted help will fall. They will all be destroyed together.

⁴The LORD told me: "When a lion or its cub catches an animal to eat, the lion stands over the dead animal and roars, and nothing can frighten it away. If men come and yell at the lion, the lion will not be afraid. They might make a lot of noise, but the lion will not run away."

In the same way, the LORD All-Powerful will come down to Mount Zion.* He will fight on that hill. ⁵Just as birds fly over their nest to protect it, so the LORD All-Powerful will defend*ᵉ* Jerusalem. He will save her. He will "pass over" and save Jerusalem.

⁶People of Israel, you should come back to the God you turned away from. ⁷That is because when those things happen, people will reject the gold and silver idols* you made when you sinned against me.

⁸It is true that Assyria* will be defeated with a sword, but it will not be a human sword that defeats him. Assyria will be destroyed, but that destruction will not come from a man's sword. Assyria will run away from God's sword, but the young men will be caught and made slaves. ⁹Their place of safety will be destroyed. Their leaders will be defeated, and they will abandon their flag.

The LORD, whose fireplace is on Zion and whose oven*ᶠ* is in Jerusalem, is the one who said this.

Leaders Should Be Good and Fair

32 ¹Listen to what I say! A king should rule in a way that brings justice. Leaders should make fair decisions when they lead the people. ²If this would happen, the king*ᵍ* would be like a shelter to hide from the wind and rain, like streams of water in a dry land, and like the cool shadow of a large rock in a hot land. ³Then people would actually see what they look at. They would actually listen to what they hear. ⁴People who are now confused would be able to understand. Those

---

*ª***30:22** *You ... rags* Or "You will throw those gods away like menstrual clothes."

*ᵇ***30:24** *food* This was special food that had been allowed to ferment. This made the meat of the animal tender and good.

*ᶜ***30:33** *Topheth* Gehenna, the Valley of Hinnom. In this valley people killed their children to honor the false god, "Molech."

*ᵈ***30:33** *king* This is like the name of the false god, "Molech."

*ᵉ***31:5** *defend* Literally, "fight on" or "fight against."

*ᶠ***31:9** *fireplace ... oven* That is, the altar in the Temple.

*ᵍ***32:2** *king* Literally, "man."

who cannot speak clearly now would be able to speak clearly and quickly. ⁵Fools would not be called great men. People would not respect men who make secret plans.

⁶Fools*ᵃ* say foolish things, and in their minds they plan evil things to do. They want to do what is wrong. They say bad things about the LORD. They don't let hungry people eat their food. They don't let thirsty people drink the water. ⁷They use evil like a tool and plan ways to steal from the poor. They tell lies about the poor and keep them from being judged fairly.

⁸But a good leader plans good things to do, and that will make him a leader over other leaders.

Hard Times Are Coming

⁹Some of you women are calm now; you feel safe. But you should stand and listen to the words I say. ¹⁰You feel safe now, but after one year you will be troubled. That is because you will not gather grapes next year—there will be no grapes to gather.

¹¹Women, you are calm now, but you should be afraid. You feel safe now, but you should be worried. Take off your nice clothes and put on sackcloth.* Wrap it around your waist. ¹²Beat your breasts in sorrow. Cry because your fields are empty. Your vineyards* once gave grapes, but now they are empty. ¹³Cry for the land of my people. Cry because only thorns and weeds will grow there. Cry for the city and for all the houses that were once filled with joy.

¹⁴People will leave the capital city. The palace and towers will be left empty. People will not live in houses—they will live in caves. Wild donkeys and sheep will live in the city—animals will go there to eat grass.

¹⁵This will continue until God gives us his Spirit* from above. Then the desert will become rich farmland and the farmland will be like thick forests. ¹⁶That is, what is now a desert will be filled with right decisions, and what is now a farmland will be filled with justice. ¹⁷That justice will bring peace and safety forever. ¹⁸My people will be safe in their homes and in their calm, peaceful fields.

¹⁹But before this happens, the forest must fall and the city must be torn down. ²⁰Some of you live away from the cities. You plant seeds by every stream and let your cattle and donkeys roam free. You will be very blessed.

The Lord Will Show His Power

33 ¹Look at you. You attack others when you have not been attacked. You turn against others when no one has turned against you. So when you stop your attacks, you will be attacked. When you stop turning against others, they will turn against you.

² LORD, be kind to us.
  We have waited for your help.
  Give us strength every morning.
  Save us when we are in trouble.
³ Your powerful voice makes people run
    away in fear.
  Your greatness causes the nations to run
    away.

⁴You people stole things in war. Those things will be taken from you. Many will come and take your wealth. It will be like the times when locusts* come and eat all your crops.

⁵The LORD is very great. He lives in a very high place. He fills Zion* with justice and goodness.

⁶Jerusalem, you are rich with wisdom and knowledge of God. You are rich with salvation. You respect the LORD, and that makes you rich.

⁷But listen! The messengers are crying outside. The messengers*ᵇ* who bring peace are crying very hard. ⁸The roads are empty. There is no one walking along the paths. People don't respect each other. They have broken the agreements they made, and they refuse to believe what witnesses*ᶜ* tell them. ⁹The land is sick and dying. Lebanon* is dying and Sharon Valley* is dry and empty. Bashan* and Carmel* once grew beautiful plants—but now those plants have stopped growing.

¹⁰The LORD says, "Now, I will stand and show people how great and powerful I am. ¹¹You people have done useless things. These things are like hay and straw. They are worth nothing! Your spirit*ᵈ* will be like a fire and burn you. ¹²People will be burned until their bones become lime.*ᵉ* They will burn quickly like thorns and dry bushes.

¹³"You people in faraway lands, listen to what I have done. You people who are near me, learn about my power."

¹⁴The sinners in Zion are afraid. Those who do wrong shake with fear. They say, "Can any of us live through this fire that destroys? Who can live near this fire that burns forever?"*ᶠ*

¹⁵Good, honest people who refuse to hurt others for money ₍will live through that fire₎. They refuse to take bribes or listen to plans to murder other people. They refuse to look at plans for doing bad things. ¹⁶They will live safely in high places. They will be protected in high rock fortresses. They will always have food and water.

---

*ᵇ***33:7 messengers … messengers** The Hebrew text has two different words that can also mean "angels."
*ᶜ***33:8 witnesses** Literally, "cities."
*ᵈ***33:11 spirit** Or "Spirit."
*ᵉ***33:12 lime** A white powder that is often used to make mortar or cement. It can be made by burning bones, shells, or limestone.
*ᶠ***33:14 fire that … burns forever** This might mean God, the Fire (Light) of Israel.

*ᵃ***32:6 Fools** Here, this means people who don't follow God and his wise teachings.

¹⁷Your eyes will see the King in his beauty. You will see the great land. ¹⁸⁻¹⁹When ,you think about the troubles you had in the past, you will wonder, "Where are those foreigners who spoke languages we could not understand. Where are the officials and tax collectors from other lands? Where are the spies who counted our defense towers?"

God Will Protect Jerusalem

²⁰Look at Zion,* the city of our religious festivals. Look at Jerusalem—that beautiful place of rest. Jerusalem is like a tent that will never be moved. The pegs that hold her in place will never be pulled up. Her ropes will never be broken, ²¹⁻²³because the LORD is our powerful leader there. That land is a place with streams and wide rivers, but there will be no enemy boats or powerful ships on those rivers. You men who work on such boats can stop your work with the ropes. You cannot make the mast* strong enough. You will not be able to open your sails, because the LORD is our judge.* He makes our laws. He is our king. He saves us. The LORD will give us our wealth. Even crippled people will get their share. ²⁴No one living there will say, "I am sick," because everyone living there has had their guilt removed.

God Will Punish His Enemies

34 ¹All you nations, come near and listen! Listen, all you people. The earth and everyone on it should listen to these things. Everything in this world should hear this. ²The LORD is angry with all the nations and their armies. He will destroy them all and put them to death. ³Their bodies will be thrown outside. The stink will rise from the bodies, and the blood will flow down the mountains. ⁴The skies will be rolled shut like a scroll,ᵃ and the stars will die and fall like leaves from a vine or a fig tree. All the starsᵇ in the sky will rot away. ⁵The LORD says, "This will happen when my sword in the sky is covered with blood."

Look, the LORD's sword will cut through Edom.* He judged them guilty, and they must die.ᶜ ⁶He decided there should be a time for killing in Bozrahᵈ and in Edom. So the LORD's sword is covered with blood and fat. The blood is from the "goats." The fat is from the kidneys of the "rams."ᵉ ⁷So the rams, the cattle, and the strong bulls will be killed. The land will be filled with their blood. The dirt will be covered with their fat.

⁸This will happen because the LORD has chosen a time for punishment. He has chosen a year when people must pay for the wrong they did to Zion.* ⁹Edom's rivers will be like hot tar.* Edom's ground will be like burning sulfur. ¹⁰The fires will burn day and night—no one will stop the fire. The smoke will rise from Edom forever. The land will be destroyed forever and ever. No one will ever travel through that land again. ¹¹Birds and small animals will own that land. Owls and ravens will live there. People will call it the "Empty Desert."ᶠ ¹²The freemenᵍ and leaders will all be gone, and there will be nothing left for them to rule.

¹³Thorns and wild bushes will grow in all the beautiful homes there. Wild dogs and owls will live in them. Wild animals will make their homes there. Big birds will live in the grasses that grow there. ¹⁴Wild cats will live there with hyenas.ʰ Wild goatsⁱ will call to their friends. Night animalsʲ will spend some time there and find a place to rest. ¹⁵Snakes will make their homes there and lay their eggs. The eggs will open, and small snakes will crawl from the dark places. Birds that eat dead things will gather there like women visiting their friends.

¹⁶Look at the LORD's scroll* and read what is written there. Nothing is missing. It is written in that scroll that these animals will be together. God said he will gather them together, so his Spirit* will gather them together. ¹⁷God decided what he should do with them, and then he chose a place for them. He drew a line and showed them their land. So the animals will own that land forever. They will live there year after year.

God Will Comfort His People

35 ¹The dry desert will rejoice. The desert will be glad and blossom. ²It will be covered with flowers and dance with joy. It will be as beautiful as the forest of Lebanon,* the hill of Carmel,* and the Sharon Valley.* This will happen because all people will see the Glory of the LORD.* They will see the beauty of our God.

³Make the weak arms strong again. Strengthen the weak knees. ⁴People are afraid and confused. Say to them, "Be strong! Don't be afraid!" Look, your God will come and punish your enemies. He will come and

---

ᶠ**34:11** *Empty Desert* Literally, "They will measure this city with the measuring string called 'emptiness' and stone weights called 'nothingness.'" These words described the empty earth in Gen. 1:2.

ᵍ**34:12** *freemen* Important citizens of a town or country. These people came from "good families" and had never been slaves.

ʰ**34:14** *hyenas* A kind of wild dog that often eats the meat of dead animals that other animals killed.

ⁱ**34:14** *Wild goats* The Hebrew word means "hairy," "goat," or "goat-demon."

ʲ**34:14** *Night animals* Or "Lilith, the night demon." This name is like the Hebrew word for night.

ᵃ**34:4** *rolled shut like a scroll* This is like someone closing a book when they have finished reading it.

ᵇ**34:4** *stars* Literally, "the armies of the skies."

ᶜ**34:5** *guilty, and they must die* The Hebrew means the people belonged completely to God, and if he does not get them, they must die.

ᵈ**34:6** *Bozrah* A city in the southern part of Edom.

ᵉ**34:6** *goats ... rams* This probably refers to the people and leaders of Edom.

give you your reward. The LORD will save you. ⁵Then the eyes of the blind will be opened so that they can see, and the ears of the deaf will be opened so that they can hear. ⁶Crippled people will dance like deer, and those who cannot speak now will use their voices to sing happy songs. This will happen when springs of water begin to flow in the dry desert. ⁷Now people see mirages*a* that look like water, but then there will be real pools of water. There will be wells in the dry land where water flows from the ground. Tall water plants will grow where wild animals once ruled.

⁸There will be a road there. This highway will be called "The Holy Road." Evil people will not be allowed to walk on that road. No fools*b* will walk on it. Only good people will walk there. ⁹There will be no dangers on that road. There will be no lions there to hurt people or any dangerous animals on it. That road will be for the people God saves.

¹⁰God will make his people free, and they will come back to him. They will come into Zion* rejoicing. They will be happy forever. Their happiness will be like a crown on their heads. Their gladness and joy will fill them completely. Sorrow and sadness will be gone far, far away.

The Assyrians Invade Judah

36 ¹During Hezekiah's* 14th year as king, Sennacherib* king of Assyria went to fight against all the strong cities of Judah. Sennacherib defeated those cities. ²He sent his commander with a large army to King Hezekiah in Jerusalem. The commander and his army left Lachish and went to Jerusalem. They stopped near the aqueduct*c* by the Upper Pool,*d* on the street that leads up to Laundryman's Field.

³Three men from Jerusalem went out to talk with the commander. These men were Eliakim son of Hilkiah, Joah son of Asaph, and Shebna. Eliakim was the palace manager, Joah was the record keeper, and Shebna was the royal secretary.

⁴The commander told them, "Tell Hezekiah this is what the great king, the king of Assyria says:

'What are you trusting in to help you? ⁵I tell you, if you are trusting in power and great battle plans, that is useless.

Those are nothing but empty words. Now I ask you, who do you trust so much that you are willing to rebel against me? ⁶Are you depending on Egypt to help you? Egypt is like a broken walking stick. If you lean on it for support, it will only stab you and hurt you. Pharaoh, the king of Egypt, cannot be trusted by anyone who depends on him for help.

⁷'But maybe you will say, "We trust the LORD our God to help us." But I know that Hezekiah destroyed the altars* and high places* where people worshiped the LORD. Hezekiah told the people of Judah and Jerusalem, "You must worship only at this one altar here in Jerusalem."

⁸'If you still want to fight, my master, the king of Assyria, will make this agreement with you. I promise that I will give you 2000 horses if you can find enough men to ride them into battle. ⁹But even then, you couldn't beat even one of my master's lowest ranking officers. So why do you still depend on Egypt's chariots* and horse soldiers?

¹⁰'Now, do you think I came to this country to destroy it without the LORD's help. No, the LORD said to me, "Go up against this country and destroy it!"'"

¹¹Then Eliakim, Shebna, and Joah said to the commander, "Please, speak to us in Aramaic.* We understand that language. Don't speak to us in Hebrew.*e* If you use our language, the people on the city walls will understand you."

¹²But the commander said, "My master did not send me to speak only to you and your master. I was also sent to speak to those people sitting there on the wall. They will not have enough food or water either; they, too, will eat their own waste and drink their own urine like you!*f*"

¹³Then the commander shouted loudly in Hebrew, ¹⁴"Hear this message from the great king, the king of Assyria:

'Don't let Hezekiah fool you. He cannot save you from my power. ¹⁵Don't believe Hezekiah when he says, "Trust in the LORD! The LORD will save us. He will not let the king of Assyria defeat the city."

¹⁶'Don't listen to Hezekiah. Listen to the king of Assyria. The king of Assyria says, "Do this favor for me; come out to me, and then everyone will be free to have grapes from their own vines, figs

---

*a***35:7** *mirages* In the desert, heat rising from the ground looks like water from far away. This is a mirage.

*b***35:8** *fools* Here, this means people who don't follow God and his wise teachings.

*c***36:2** *aqueduct* A ditch or pipe that carries water from one place to another. Here, this is the Shiloah, a channel that carried water from Gihon Spring to the Old Pool and the Pool of Siloam.

*d***36:2** *Upper Pool* The Pool of Siloam at the southern tip of the City of David (Jerusalem), just above the older pool now called Birket al Hamrah.

*e***36:11** *Hebrew* Literally, "Judean," the language of Judah and Israel.

*f***36:12** *They ... like you* The Assyrian army planned to surround Jerusalem and not let people bring any food or water into the city. They thought the people would become hungry enough to eat their own waste.

from their own trees, and water from their own well. [17]You can do this until I come and take you away to a land like your own. In that new land, you will have good grain, new wine, bread, and vineyards.*"

[18]'Don't let Hezekiah change your mind when he says, "The LORD will save us." Did any of the gods of other nations save their land from the king of Assyria? [19]Where are the gods of their cities, Hamath and Arpad? Where are the gods of Sepharvaim? Did they save Samaria* from my power? [20]Did any of the gods in the other countries save their land from me? So why do you think the LORD will save Jerusalem from me?'"

[21]But the people were silent. They did not say a word to the commander because King Hezekiah had given them a command. He said, "Don't say anything to him."

[22]Then the palace manager (Eliakim son of Hilkiah), the royal secretary (Shebna), and the record keeper (Joah son of Asaph) went to Hezekiah. Their clothes were torn to show they were upset. They told Hezekiah everything the Assyrian commander had said.

Hezekiah Asks God to Help

37 [1]When King Hezekiah listened to their message, he tore his clothes to show he was upset. Then he put on sackcloth* and went to the LORD's Temple.*

[2]Hezekiah sent Eliakim, the palace manager, Shebna, the royal secretary, and the elders of the priests to the prophet, Isaiah son of Amoz. They wore the special clothes that showed they were sad and upset. [3]They said to Isaiah, "King Hezekiah has commanded that today will be a special day for sorrow and sadness. It will be a very sad day—as sad as when a baby should be born, but there is not enough strength for the birth. [4]The commander's master, the king of Assyria, has sent him to say bad things about the living God. Maybe the LORD your God will hear it and prove the enemy is wrong. So pray for those who are still left alive."

[5]When King Hezekiah's officers came to Isaiah, [6]he said to them, "Give this message to your master, Hezekiah: The LORD says, 'Don't be afraid of what you heard from the commanders! Don't believe what those "boys" from the king of Assyria said to make fun of me. [7]Look, I will send a spirit against the king of Assyria. He will get a report that will make him return to his own country. And I will cut him down with a sword in his own country.'"

The Assyrian Army Leaves Jerusalem

[8]The commander heard that the king of Assyria had left Lachish. He found him at Libnah, fighting against that city. [9]Then the king of Assyria got a report that said, "King Tirhakah[a] of Ethiopia* is coming to fight you."

So the king of Assyria sent messengers to Hezekiah again. [10]He told them, "Tell King Hezekiah of Judah these things:

'Don't be fooled by the god you trust when he says, "Jerusalem will not be defeated by the king of Assyria." [11]You have heard what the kings of Assyria did to all the other countries. We destroyed them completely. Will you be saved? No! [12]Did the gods of those people save them? No, my ancestors* destroyed them all. They destroyed the cities of Gozan, Haran, Rezeph, and the people of Eden living in Tel Assar. [13]Where is the king of Hamath? The king of Arpad? The king of the city of Sepharvaim? The kings of Hena and Ivvah?'"

Hezekiah Prays to the Lord

[14]Hezekiah received the letters from the messengers and read them. Then he went up to the LORD's Temple* and laid the letters out in front of the LORD. [15]He prayed to the LORD: [16]"LORD All-Powerful, God of Israel, you sit as King above the Cherub angels.* You alone are the God who rules all the kingdoms on earth. You made heaven and earth. [17]LORD, please listen to me. LORD, open your eyes and look at this message. Hear the words that Sennacherib sent to insult the living God! [18]It is true, LORD. The kings of Assyria did destroy all those nations. [19]They did throw the gods of those nations into the fire, but they were not real gods. They were only wood and stone—statues that people made. That is why the kings of Assyria could destroy them. [20]But you are the LORD our God, so please save us from the king of Assyria. Then all the other nations will know that you are the LORD, the only God."

God's Answer to Hezekiah

[21]Then Isaiah son of Amoz sent this message to Hezekiah. Isaiah said, "The LORD, the God of Israel, says this, 'You prayed to me about the message that came from King Sennacherib of Assyria. I have heard you.[b]'

[22]"So this is the LORD's message against Sennacherib:

'The virgin daughter Zion[c] does not think
　　you are important.
She makes fun of you.

---

[a]**37:9 Tirhakah** This is probably Taharqa, the Pharaoh of Egypt about 690–664 B.C.
[b]**37:21 I have heard you** This is from the ancient Greek version and 2 Kings 19:20.
[c]**37:22 The virgin daughter Zion** The city of Jerusalem, which is in danger of attack by the Assyrians. See "Zion" in the Word List.

Daughter Jerusalem shakes her head at
   you
and laughs behind your back.
23 But who was it that you insulted and
   made fun of?
Who was it that you spoke against?
You were speaking against the Holy One
   of Israel.
You acted like you were great and he
   was nothing.
24 You sent your officers to insult the Lord.
   This is what you said:
"I took my many chariots* up the high
   mountains deep inside Lebanon.
I cut down its tallest cedars
   and its best fir trees.
I have been on its highest mountain
   and deep inside its forests.
25 I dug wells and drank water from new
   places.
I dried up the rivers of Egypt
   and walked where the water was."

26 'How could you say this, Sennacherib?
   Did no one ever tell you that I, the
   Lord, planned these things long ago?
From ancient times I decided what would
   happen.
And now I have made it happen.
I let you tear down strong cities
   and change them into piles of rocks.
27 The people living there had no power.
They were afraid and confused.
They were about to be cut down
   like grass and plants in the field.
They were like grass growing on the
   housetops,
   dying before it grows tall.
28 I know all about your battles;
I know when you rested,
   when you went out to war,
   and when you came home.
I also know when you got upset at me.
29 Yes, you were upset at me.
I heard your proud insults.
So I will put my hook in your nose
   and my bit in your mouth.
Then I will turn you around
   and lead you back the way you came.'"

The Lord's Message for Hezekiah

30Then the Lord said, "I will give you a sign
to show you that these words are true. You
will not be able to plant seeds this year, so
next year you will eat grain that grew wild
from the previous year's crop. But in the third
year, you will eat grain from seeds that you
planted. You will harvest your crops, and you
will have plenty to eat. You will plant vineyards* and eat grapes from them.
31"The people from the family of Judah
who have escaped and are left alive will be
like plants that send their roots deep into the
ground and produce fruit above the ground.
32That is because a few people will come out

of Jerusalem alive. There will be survivors
coming from Mount Zion.*" The strong love[a]
of the Lord All-Powerful will do this.
33So the Lord says this about the king of
Assyria:

"He will not come into this city
   or shoot an arrow here.
He will not bring his shields up against
   this city
   or build up a hill of dirt to attack its
   walls.
34 He will go back the way he came.
He will not come into this city.
The Lord says this!
35 I will protect this city and save it.
I will do this for myself and for my
   servant David.*"

The Assyrian Army Is Destroyed

36That night the angel of the Lord went
out and killed 185,000 men in the Assyrian
camp. When the people got up in the morning, they saw all the dead bodies. 37So King
Sennacherib of Assyria went back to Nineveh
and stayed there.
38One day Sennacherib was in the temple
of his god Nisroch, worshiping him. His sons
Adrammelech and Sharezer killed him with a
sword and ran away to Ararat.* So Sennacherib's son Esarhaddon became the new king
of Assyria.

Hezekiah's Illness

38 1At that time Hezekiah became sick
and almost died. The prophet Isaiah
son of Amoz went to see him and told him,
"The Lord told me to tell you this: 'You will
die soon. So you should tell your family what
they should do when you die. You will not
get well.'"
2Hezekiah turned toward the wall that
faced the Temple* and began praying to the
Lord. 3"Lord, remember that I have faithfully
served you with all my heart. I have done
what you say is good." Then Hezekiah cried
very hard.
4Then Isaiah received this message from the
Lord: 5"Go to Hezekiah and tell him that the
Lord, the God of your ancestor* David,* says,
'I heard your prayer, and I saw your tears. I
will add 15 years to your life. 6I will save you
and this city from the king of Assyria. I will
protect this city.'"
21 b Then Isaiah told Hezekiah, "Crush figs
together and put them on your sore. Then you
will get well."
22Hezekiah asked Isaiah, "What is the sign
that proves I will get well and go to the Lord's
Temple*?"

[a]37:32 *strong love* The Hebrew word can mean
strong feelings such as zeal, jealousy, or love.
[b]38:21, 22 These verses fit better here than at
the end of the chapter, where they appear in the
standard Hebrew text. See 2 Kings 20:6–9.

[7]This is the sign from the LORD to show you that he will do what he says: [8]"Look, I am causing the shadow that is on the steps of Ahaz[a] to move back ten steps. The sun's shadow will go back up the ten steps that it has already been on."

Hezekiah's Song

[9]This is the letter from Hezekiah when he became well:

[10] I thought I would live a full life.
   But now, in the middle of my life, the
      time has come for me to die.
[11] So I said, "I will not see the LORD YAH[b] in
      the land of the living again.
   I will not see the people living on earth.
[12] My home, my shepherd's tent, is being
      pulled down and taken from me.
   I am finished like the cloth someone
      rolls up and cuts from the loom.*
   You ended my life in such a short time.
[13] All night I cried as loud as a lion,
   but my hopes were crushed like a lion
      eating bones.
   You finished my life in such a short time.
[14] I cried like a bird
   and moaned like a dove.
   My eyes became tired,
      but I continued looking to the heavens.
   Lord, I am so depressed.
      Promise to help me."
[15] What can I say?
   He told me what would happen,
      and he will make it happen.
   I have had these troubles in my soul,
      so now I will be humble all my life.
[16] Lord, use this hard time to make my spirit
      live again.
   Help my spirit become strong and
      healthy.
   Help me become well!
   Help me live again!

[17] Look, my troubles are gone!
   I now have peace.
   You love me very much.
   You did not let me rot in the grave.
   You took my sins
      and threw them away.
[18] The dead cannot praise you.
   People in Sheol* cannot sing praises to
      you.
   Those who have died and gone below are
      not trusting in your faithfulness.
[19] People who are alive, people like me,
   are the ones who will praise you.
   Fathers should tell their children about
      how faithful you are.

[20] So I say, "The LORD saved me.
   So we will sing and play songs in the
      LORD's Temple* all our lives."

Messengers From Babylon

39 [1]At that time Merodach Baladan son of Baladan was king of Babylon. He sent some men with letters and a gift to Hezekiah when he heard that Hezekiah had been sick. [2]This made Hezekiah very happy, so he showed them all the valuable things in his storehouses. He showed them the silver, the gold, the spices, and the expensive perfumes. He showed them the building where he stored the weapons. He showed them everything in his treasuries and everything in his house and throughout his kingdom.

[3]Then Isaiah the prophet went to King Hezekiah and asked him, "What did these men say? Where did they come from?"

Hezekiah said, "These men came all the way from Babylon just to see me."

[4]So Isaiah asked him, "What did they see in your house?"

Hezekiah said, "They saw everything in my palace. I showed them all my wealth."

[5]Then Isaiah said this to Hezekiah, "Listen to this message from the LORD All-Powerful. [6]'The time is coming when everything in your house and everything your ancestors* have saved until today will be carried away to Babylon. Nothing will be left!' The LORD All-Powerful said this. [7]The Babylonians will take your own sons, and your sons will become officers[c] in the palace of the king of Babylon."

[8]Then Hezekiah told Isaiah, "This message from the LORD is good." (Hezekiah said this because he thought, "There will be real peace and security during my lifetime.")

Israel's Punishment Will End

40 [1]Your God says,
   "Comfort, comfort my people.
[2] Speak kindly to Jerusalem and tell her,
   'Your time of service is finished.
   You have paid the price for your sins.
   I, the LORD, have punished you twice for
      every sin you committed.'"

[3] Listen, there is someone shouting:
   "Prepare a way in the desert for the LORD.
   Make a straight road there for our God.
[4] Every valley must be filled.
   Every mountain and hill should be made
      flat.
   The crooked roads should be made
      straight,
   and the rough ground made smooth.
[5] Then the Glory of the LORD* will be
      shown to everyone.
   Together, all people will see it.
   Yes, this is what the LORD himself said!"

---

[a]**38:8 steps of Ahaz** The steps of a special building that Hezekiah used like a clock. When the sun shone on the steps, the shadows showed what time of the day it was.

[b]**38:11 LORD YAH** Or "YAHWEH," a Hebrew name for God. See "YAHWEH" in the Word List.

[c]**39:7 officers** Or "eunuchs." See "eunuch" in the Word List.

6 A voice said, "Speak!"
  So the man said, "What should I say?"
  The voice said, "People are like grass.
      Any glory they enjoy is like a
          wildflower.
7 When a wind from the LORD blows on
          them,
      the grass dies and the flower falls.
      Yes, all people are like grass.
8 Grass dies and flowers fall,
      but the word of our God lasts forever."

Salvation: God's Good News

9 Zion,* you have good news to tell.
      Go up on a high mountain and shout
          the good news.
  Jerusalem, you have good news to tell.
      Don't be afraid; speak loudly.
  Tell this news to all the cities of Judah:
      "Look, here is your God!"
10 The Lord GOD is coming with power.
      He will use his power to rule all the
          people.
  He will bring rewards for his people.
      He will have their payment with him.
11 Like a good shepherd, he takes care of his
          people.
  He gathers them like lambs in his arms.
      He holds them close, while their
          mothers walk beside him.

God Made the World; He Rules It

12 Who measured the oceans in the palm of
          his hand?
      Who used his hand to measure the sky?
  Who used a bowl to measure all the dust
          of the earth?
      Who used scales to measure the
          mountains and hills?
13 Who could know the LORD's mind?
      Who could be his teacher or give him
          advice?
14 Did the Lord ask for anyone's help?
      Did anyone teach him to be fair?
  Did anyone teach him knowledge?
      Did anyone teach him to be wise?
15 Look, all the nations in the world are like
          one small drop in the bucket.
  If the Lord took all the faraway nations
          and put them on his scales,
      they would be like small pieces of dust.
16 All the trees in Lebanon are not enough
          to burn on the altar* for the Lord.
  And all the animals in Lebanon
      are not enough to kill for a sacrifice.
17 Compared to God, all the nations of the
          world are nothing.
      Compared to him, they are worth
          nothing at all.

People Cannot Imagine What God Is Like

18 Can you compare God to anything?
      Can you make a picture of God?
19 No, but some people make statues from
          rock or wood,

and they call them gods.
  One worker makes a statue.
      Then another worker covers it with gold
          and makes silver chains for it.
20 For the base he chooses special wood,
      a kind of wood that will not rot.
  Then he finds a good wood worker,
      and the worker makes a "god" that will
          not fall over.
21 Surely you know the truth, don't you?
      Surely you have heard.
  Surely someone told you long ago.
      Surely you understand who made the
          earth.
22 It is the Lord who sits above the circle of
          the earth.
      And compared to him, people are like
          grasshoppers.
  He rolled open the skies like a piece of
          cloth.
      He stretched out the skies like a tent to
          sit under.
23 He takes away the power of rulers.
      He makes the world's leaders
          completely worthless.
24 They are like plants that are planted in
          the ground.
      But before they can send their roots into
          the ground,
  God blows on the "plants";
      they become dead and dry,
      and the wind blows them away like
          straw.
25 The Holy One says: "Can you compare
          me to anyone?
      No one is equal to me."

26 Look up to the skies.
      Who created all those stars?
  Who created all those "armies" in the
          sky?
      Who knows every star by name?
  He is very strong and powerful,
      so not one of these stars is lost.

27 People of Jacob,* this is true.
      Israel, you should believe it.
  So why do you say, "The LORD cannot see
          the way I live;
      he will not find me and punish me"*?

28 Surely you know the truth.
      Surely you have heard.
  The LORD is the God who lives forever!
      He created all the faraway places on
          earth.
  He does not get tired and weary.
      You cannot learn all he knows.
29 He helps tired people be strong.
      He gives power to those without it.
30 Young men get tired and need to rest.
      Even young boys stumble and fall.

---

*a***40:27 The LORD ... punish me** Or "My way is hidden
from the LORD; he ignores my case."

31 But those who trust in the LORD will
      become strong again—like eagles that
      grow new feathers.[a]
   They will run and not get weak.
   They will walk and not get tired.

The Lord Is the Eternal Creator

41 [1]The Lord says,
   "Faraway countries, be quiet and
      listen to me!
   Nations be brave.[b]
   Come to me and speak.
   We will meet together
      and decide who is right.

2 Who woke up the man who is coming
      from the east?
   He called Justice to march with him.
   He uses his sword to crush nations.
   He uses his bow and conquers kings—
      they run away like straw blown by the
      wind.

3 He chases armies and is never hurt.
   He goes places he has never been
      before.

4 Who was able to make all this happen?
   Who controlled the lives of everyone
      from the beginning?
   I, the LORD, am the one.
   I was here at the beginning,
      and I will be here when all things are
      finished.

5 People along the coast saw this,
      and they were frightened.
   Nations at the ends of the earth
      shook with fear.
   They have come near.
   They have arrived.

6"Workers help each other. They encourage each other to be strong. 7One worker cuts wood to make a statue. He encourages the man who works with gold. Another worker uses a hammer and makes the metal smooth. Then he encourages the man at the anvil.[c] This last worker says, 'This work is good; the metal will not come off.' Then he nails the statue to a base so that it will not fall over. And it never moves!"

Only the Lord Can Save Us

8 The Lord says, "You, Israel,* are my
      servant.
   Jacob,* I chose you.
   You are from the family of my friend,
      Abraham.
9 You were in a faraway country,

but I reached out to you.
   I called you from that faraway place.
   I said, 'You are my servant.'
   I chose you,
      and I have not rejected you.
10 Don't worry—I am with you.
   Don't be afraid—I am your God.
   I will make you strong.
   I will help you.
   I will support you with my right hand that
      brings victory.
11 Look, some people are angry with you,
      but they will be ashamed and disgraced.
   Your enemies will be lost and disappear.
12 You will look for the people who were
      against you,
      but you will not be able to find them.
   Those who fought against you
      will disappear completely.
13 I am the LORD your God,
      who holds your right hand.
   And I tell you, 'Don't be afraid!
   I will help you.'
14   People of Israel, descendants of Jacob,
      you may be weak and worthless,[d]
      but do not be afraid.
   I myself will help you."

   This is what the LORD himself says.

"I am the Holy One of Israel,
      the one who saves you.
15 Look, I have made you like a new
      threshing* board with many sharp
      teeth.
   You will trample mountains and crush
      them.
   You will make the hills[e] like chaff.*
16 You will throw them into the air,
      and the wind will blow them away and
      scatter them.
   Then you will be happy in the LORD.
   You will be proud of the Holy One of
      Israel.

17"The poor and needy look for water,
      but they cannot find any.
   Their tongues are dry with thirst.
   I, the LORD, will answer their prayers.
   I, the God of Israel, will not leave them
      to die.
18 I will make rivers flow on dry hills.
   I will make springs of water flow
      through the valleys.
   I will change the desert into a lake filled
      with water.
   There will be springs of water in that
      dry land.
19 I will make trees grow in the desert.
   There will be cedar, acacias, olive trees,
      cypress, fir trees, and pines.

[a]**40:31** *like ... feathers* This probably refers to the ancient belief that eagles regain their youth when they molt (lose and grow back their feathers). See Ps. 103:5. This line could also be translated, "They will rise up like eagles on their wings."
[b]**41:1** *be brave* Or "be strong again," as in Isa. 40:31.
[c]**41:7** *anvil* A heavy metal block. A worker puts hot metal on an anvil and beats the hot metal to change its shape.

[d]**41:14** *Jacob ... worthless* Literally, "Worm of Jacob, men of Israel."
[e]**41:15** *mountains ... hills* Symbols of the power of Israel's enemies.

20 I will do this so that people will see it and
    know who did it.
  They will notice what happened.
  Then they will understand
    that the LORD's hand made it happen,
    that the Holy One of Israel created it
    all."

The Lord Challenges the False Gods

21The LORD, the king of Jacob,* says, "Come,
present your arguments. Show me your proof.
22Let your idols* come in and tell us what will
happen. Idols, tell us what happened in the
beginning. We will listen closely so that we
can make a decision. Tell us what will happen in the future. 23What signs did you give in
the past to prove that you really are gods? Do
something! Do anything, good or bad, so that
we can see that you are alive. Then we might
fear and respect you.
24"Look, you false gods are worthless. You
cannot do anything. Only some horrible fool*
would want to worship you."

The Lord Proves He Is the Only God

25"I called someone in the north* to come.
  He is coming from the east where the
    sun rises,
  and he honors my name.
  He tramples kings the way a potter
    softens clay with his feet.

26"Who told us about this before it happened
    so that we could say he was right?
  None of your idols told us anything.
    They didn't say a word,
    and they cannot hear anything you say.
27 I, the LORD, was the first one to tell Zion*
    about these things.
  I sent a messenger to Jerusalem to say,
    'Look, your people are coming back!'"

28 I looked at those false gods.
  Not one of them said anything.
  They had no advice to offer.
  I asked them questions,
    but they didn't say a word.
29 Those gods are all less than nothing.
  They cannot do anything.
  They are worthless.

The Lord's Special Servant

42 1"Here is my servant,
  the one I support.
  He is the one I have chosen,
  and I am very pleased with him.
  I have filled him with my Spirit,*
  and he will bring justice to the nations.
2 He will not cry out or shout

or try to make himself heard in the
  streets.
3 He will not break even a crushed reed.*
  He will not put out even the weakest
    flame.
  He will bring true justice.
4 He will not grow weak or give up
  until he has brought justice to the
    world.
  And people in faraway places will hope to
    receive his teachings."

The Lord Is Ruler and Maker of the World

5The LORD, the true God, said these things.
(He created the sky and spread it out over the
earth. He formed the earth and everything it
produced. He breathes life into all the people
on earth. He gives a spirit to everyone who
walks on the earth.)

6"I, the LORD, was right to call you.
  I will hold your hand and protect you.
  You will be the sign of my agreement*
    with the people.
  You will be a light for the other nations.
7 You will make the blind able to see.
  You will free those who are held as
    captives.
  You will lead those who live in darkness
    out of their prison.

8"I am YAHWEH.*
  That is my name.
  I will not give my glory* to another.
  I will not let statues take the praise that
    should be mine.
9 In the past, I told you what would
    happen,
  and it happened!
  Now I am telling you something new,
  and I am telling you now, before it
    happens."

A Song of Praise to the Lord

10 Sing a new song* to the LORD;
  praise him everywhere on earth—
  all you who sail on the seas,
  everything in the sea,
  and all you people in faraway places!
11 Deserts and cities, villages of Kedar,*
  praise the Lord!
  People living in Sela, sing for joy!
  Sing from the top of your mountain.
12 Give glory to the LORD.
  Praise him, all you people in faraway
    lands!
13 The LORD will go out like a strong soldier.
  Like a man going into battle, he will be
    full of excitement.
  He will shout with a loud cry,
  and he will defeat his enemies.

---

a41:24 fool Literally, "horrible thing." The Hebrew
word usually describes idols and other wicked
things that God hates.
b41:25 someone in the north This probably means
Cyrus, a king of Persia. He ruled about 550–530 B.C.

c42:3 reed A plant that grows near water.
d42:10 new song Whenever God did a new and
wonderful thing for his people, they would write a
new song about it.

God Is Very Patient

14"For a long time I have said nothing.
   I have controlled myself and kept quiet.
   But now I will cry out like a woman
      giving birth.
   My breathing is getting faster and
      louder.
15 I will destroy the hills and mountains.
   I will dry up all the plants that grow
      there.
   I will change rivers to dry land
      and dry up pools of water.
16 Then I will lead the blind along a path
      they never knew
   to places where they have never been
      before.
   I will change darkness into light for them.
   I will make the rough ground smooth.
   I will do these things for them;
   I will not abandon my people.
17 But some of them have left me.
   They say to their gold statues, 'You are
      my gods.'
   They trust their false gods,
   but they will be disappointed and
      shamed.

Israel Refused to Listen to God

18"Deaf people, listen to me!
   Blind people, look and see!
19 In all the world, no one is more blind
      than my servant.*a*
   No one is more deaf than my
      messenger.
   No one is more blind than my chosen
      people, the servant of the LORD.
20 My people see what they should do,
   but they do not obey me.
   They can hear with their ears,
   but they refuse to listen to me."
21 The LORD wants them to do what is right.
   He wants them to honor his wonderful
      teachings.*b*
22 But look at his people.
   Others have defeated them and have
      stolen from them.
   The young men are afraid.
   They are locked in prisons.
   People have taken advantage of them,
   and there is no one to protect them.
   Others take their money,
   and there is no one to say, "Give it
      back!"

23If any of you listens to this message, you
should listen to what was said before. 24Who
let people defeat Jacob*? Who let them take
what belonged to Israel*? The LORD allowed
them to do this. We sinned against him, so
he let people take away our wealth. The people did not want to live the way he wanted.

They refused to listen to his teaching. 25So
he poured out his anger on them and brought
wars against them. It was as if there were
fires all around them, but they didn't know
what was happening. It was as if they were
burning, but they didn't try to understand.

God Is Always With His People

43 1Jacob,* the LORD created you. Israel,*
he made you, and now he says, "Don't
be afraid. I saved you. I named you. You are
mine. 2When you have troubles, I am with
you. When you cross rivers, you will not be
hurt. When you walk through fire, you will
not be burned; the flames will not hurt you.
3That's because I, the LORD, am your God. I,
the Holy One of Israel, am your Savior. I gave
Egypt to pay for you. I gave Ethiopia and Seba
to make you mine. 4You are precious to me,
and I have given you a special place of honor.
I love you. That's why I am willing to trade
others, to give up whole nations, to save your
life.

5"So don't be afraid, because I am with you.
I will gather your children and bring them to
you. I will gather them from the east and from
the west. 6I will tell the north: Give my people to me. I will tell the south: Don't keep my
people in prison. Bring my sons and daughters to me from the faraway places. 7Bring to
me all the people who are mine—the people
who have my name. I made them for myself.
I made them, and they are mine.

8"Bring out the people who have eyes but
are blind. Bring out the people who have
ears but are deaf.*c* 9All people and all nations
should also be gathered together. Which of
their gods said this would happen? Which
of their gods would tell what happened in
the beginning? They should bring their witnesses. The witnesses should speak the truth.
This will show they are right."

10The LORD says, "You people are my witnesses and the servant I chose. I chose you
so that you would help people believe me. I
chose you so that you would understand that
'I Am He'—⌐I am the true God⌐. There was
no God before me, and there will be no God
after me. 11I myself am the LORD, and there
is no other Savior. 12I am the one who spoke
to you, saved you, and told you those things.
It was not some stranger who was with you.
You are my witnesses, and I am God." (This is
what the LORD himself said.) 13"I have always
been God. When I do something, no one can
change what I have done. And no one can
save people from my power."

14The LORD, the Holy One of Israel, saves
you, and he says, "I will send armies to Babylon for you. Many people will be captured.
Those Chaldeans* will be taken away in
their own boats. (They are so proud of those

*a*42:19 *my servant* Here, this probably means the
people of Israel.
*b*42:21 Or "The LORD will make his teachings very
wonderful. He will do this because he is good."

*c*43:8 *blind ... deaf* This probably means the Israelites who would not believe God. See Isa. 6:9–10.

boats.)*ᵃ* ¹⁵I am the Lᴏʀᴅ your Holy One. I made Israel. I am your King."

God Will Save His People Again

¹⁶The Lord is making roads through the sea. He is making a path for his people, even through rough waters. The Lᴏʀᴅ says, ¹⁷"Those who fight against me with their chariots,* horses, and armies will be defeated. They will never rise again. They will be destroyed. They will be put out like the flame in a lamp. ¹⁸So don't remember what happened in earlier times. Don't think about what happened a long time ago, ¹⁹because I am doing something new! Now you will grow like a new plant. Surely you know this is true. I will even make a road in the desert, and rivers will flow through that dry land. ²⁰The wild animals will thank me. The large animals and birds will honor me when I put water in the desert and make rivers flow through that dry land. I will do this to give water to my chosen people. ²¹I made them, and they will sing songs of praise to me.

²²"Jacob,* you did not pray to me. Israel,* you became tired of me. ²³You have not brought your sheep as sacrifices* to me. You have not honored me with your sacrifices. I did not force you to give gifts to me like slaves. I did not force you to burn incense* until you became tired. ²⁴So you did not use your money to buy things to honor me. But you did force me to be like your slave. You sinned until the bad things you did made me very tired.

²⁵"I, I am the one who wipes away all your sins. I do this to please myself. I will not remember your sins. ²⁶But you should remember me. Let's meet together and decide what is right. Tell your story and prove that you are innocent. ²⁷Your first father sinned, and your lawyers*ᵇ* committed crimes against me. ²⁸I will make your Temple* leaders unfit to serve there. I will destroy Jacob.*ᶜ* Bad things will happen to Israel.

The Lord Is the Only God

44 ¹"Jacob,* you are my servant. Israel,* I chose you. Listen to me! ²I am the Lᴏʀᴅ, and I made you. I am the one who created you. I have helped you since you were in your mother's womb. Jacob, my servant, don't be afraid. Jeshurun,*ᵈ* I chose you.

³"I will pour water for thirsty people, and streams will flow through the desert. I will pour my Spirit* on your children, and I will bless*ᵉ* your family. ⁴They will sprout like grass in the spring and grow like trees by streams of water.

⁵"One man will call himself, 'I am the Lᴏʀᴅ's.' Another will use the name, 'Jacob.' Another man will sign his name as 'The Lᴏʀᴅ's Hand.' And another will use the name, 'Israel.'"

⁶The Lᴏʀᴅ is the king of Israel. The Lᴏʀᴅ All-Powerful is the one who will set Israel free. And he says, "I am the only God. There are no other gods. I am the Beginning and the End. ⁷There is no other God like me. If there is, that god should speak now. Let him lay out everything he has done since the time I made these ancient people. Let him show me the signs he gave long ago that prove he knew what would happen in the future.

⁸"Don't be afraid! Don't worry. I am the one who always told you what would happen. You are my proof.*ᶠ* There is no other God; I am the only one. There is no other 'Rock'*; I know I am the only one."

False Gods Are Useless

⁹Some people make idols,* but they are worthless. They love their statues, which are useless. Those who serve as witnesses for these statues cannot even see. They don't know enough to be ashamed.

¹⁰Who made these false gods? Who covered these useless statues? ¹¹Workers made them, and the workers are only human. If they all would come together before me, we could discuss this. Then they would all be ashamed and afraid.

¹²One worker uses his tools to heat iron over hot coals. Then he uses his hammer to beat the metal to shape it into a statue. He uses his own powerful arms, but when he gets hungry, he loses his strength. If he does not drink water, he becomes weak.

¹³Another worker uses his string line*ᵍ* and compass*ʰ* to draw lines on the wood to show where he should cut. Then he uses his chisels*ⁱ* and cuts a statue from the wood. He uses his calipers*ʲ* to measure the statue. In this way, the worker makes the wood look exactly like a man, and this statue of a man does nothing but sit in the house.

---

*ᵃ*43:14 *I will send ... boats* Or with minor changes to the Hebrew, "I will send someone against Babylon to break open the gates, and the shouts of victory from the Chaldeans will be changed to crying."

*ᵇ*43:27 *lawyers* Or "speakers," people who argue a person's case in court. This might refer to priests or prophets.

*ᶜ*43:28 *destroy Jacob* Or "I will make Jacob completely mine."

*ᵈ*44:2 *Jeshurun* Another name for Israel. It means "good" or "honest."

*ᵉ*44:3 *bless* This is a wordplay. This Hebrew word sounds like the word meaning "pool."

*ᶠ*44:8 *proof* Or "witnesses."

*ᵍ*44:13 *string line* In ancient times, this was a piece of string with wet paint on it. It was used to make straight lines on wood or stone.

*ʰ*44:13 *compass* A tool used to draw circles and copy measurements.

*ⁱ*44:13 *chisels* Sharp tools used to carve wood or stone.

*ʲ*44:13 *calipers* A special measuring tool, like a compass.

¹⁴To split the cedar tree, the worker took some oak or cypress ⌊wedges⌋. To make sure he had plenty of wood, he planted some pines. But it was the rain that made them grow.

¹⁵When the man wanted a fire, he took some of the wood to keep him warm. He also used some of it to bake his bread. But then he used that same wood to make a statue to worship as a god! That god is only a statue that he made, but he bows down to it! ¹⁶He burns half of the wood in the fire. He uses the fire to cook his meat, and he eats the meat until he is full. He burns the wood to keep himself warm. He says, "Good! Now I am warm, and I can see by the light of the fire." ¹⁷There is a little of the wood left, so he makes a statue and calls it his god. He bows down before it and worships it. He prays to it and says, "You are my god, save me!"

¹⁸People like that don't know what they are doing! They don't understand. It is as if they have mud in their eyes so they cannot see. Their minds cannot understand. ¹⁹They don't realize what they are doing. They aren't smart enough to think, "I burned half of the wood in the fire. I used the hot coals to bake my bread and cook the meat I ate. And I used the wood that was left to make this terrible thing. I am worshiping a block of wood!"

²⁰Someone like that is deceived. They don't know what they are doing.ᵃ They cannot save themselves, and they will not admit, "This statue I am holding is a lie!"

The Lord, the True God, Helps Israel

²¹"Jacob,* remember these things!
    Israel,* remember, you are my servant.
I made you, and you are my servant.
    So, Israel, don't forget me.
²² Your sins were like a big cloud,
    but I wiped them all away.
Your sins are gone,
    like a cloud that disappeared into thin
        air.
I rescued and protected you,
    so come back to me."

²³ The skies are happy because the LORD did
        great things.
    The earth is happy down to its deepest
        parts.
    The mountains sing with thanks to God.
    And all the trees in the forest are happy.
    They sing because the LORD has saved
        Jacob.
    He has done great things for Israel.
²⁴ The LORD made you what you are.
    He did this while you were still in your
        mother's womb.
    The LORD says, "I, the LORD, made
        everything.
    I put the skies there myself.
    I spread out the earth before me."

²⁵False prophets* tell lies, but the Lord shows that their lies are false. He makes fools of those who do magic. He confuses even the wise. They think they know a lot, but he makes them look foolish. ²⁶The Lord sends his servants to tell his messages to the people, and he makes those messages come true. He sends messengers to tell the people what they should do, and he proves that the advice is good.

God Chooses Cyrus to Rebuild Judah

The Lord says to Jerusalem, "People will
        live in you again."
    He says to the cities of Judah, "You will
        be rebuilt."
    He says to them, "I will repair your
        ruins."
²⁷ He tells the deep waters, "Become dry!
    I will make your streams dry too."
²⁸ He says to Cyrus,* "You are my shepherd.
    You will do what I want.
    You will say to Jerusalem, 'You will be
        rebuilt!'
    You will tell the Temple,* 'Your
        foundations will be put in place!'"

God Chooses Cyrus to Make Israel Free

45 ¹This is what the LORD said to Cyrus,*
        his chosen kingᵇ:

"I took you by your right hand
    to help you defeat nations,
    to strip other kings of their power,
    and to open city gates that will not be
        closed again.
² I will go in front of you
    and make the mountains flat.
    I will break the city gates of bronze
    and cut the iron bars on the gates.
³ I will give you the wealth that is stored in
        secret places.
    I will give you those hidden treasures.
    Then you will know that I am the LORD,
    the God of Israel,* who calls you by
        name.
⁴ I do this for my servant, Jacob.*
    I do it for my chosen people, Israel.
    Cyrus, I am calling you by name.
    You don't know me, but I know you.ᶜ
⁵ I am the LORD, the only God.
    There is no other God except me.
    I put your clothes on you,ᵈ
    but still you don't know me.
⁶ I am doing this so that everyone will
        know that I am the only God.
    From the east to the west people will
        know that I am the LORD
    and that there is no other God.
⁷ I made the light and the darkness.
    I bring peace, and I cause trouble.
    I, the LORD, do all these things.

ᵃ**44:20 They … doing** Literally, "They eat ashes."

ᵇ**45:1 chosen king** Literally, "the anointed one."
ᶜ**45:4 I know you** Or "I will give you a title."
ᵈ**45:5 I put … you** This also means "I made you strong."

⁸"May the clouds in the skies above
  drop goodness on the earth like rain.
May the earth open
  and let salvation grow.
And may victory*a* grow with it!
I, the Lord, created him.*b*

God Controls His Creation

⁹"Look at these people! They are arguing
with the one who made them. Look at them
argue with me. They are like pieces of clay
from a broken pot. Clay does not say to the
one molding it, 'Man, what are you doing?'
Things that are made don't have the power to
question the one who makes them. ¹⁰A father
gives life to his children, and they cannot ask,
'Why are you giving me life?' They cannot
question their mother and ask, 'Why are you
giving birth to me?'"

¹¹The Lord God is the Holy One of Israel.*
He created Israel, and he says,

"My children, you asked me to show you a
    sign.
  You told me to show you what I have
    done.*c*
¹² I made the earth,
    and I created the people on it.
  I used my own hands to make the skies.
  And I command all the armies in the
    sky.*d*
¹³ I was right to give power to Cyrus,*e*
    and I will make his work easy.
  He will rebuild my city,
    and he will set my people free without
      bribes or payment."
  The Lord All-Powerful said this.

¹⁴ The Lord says, "Egypt and Ethiopia are
    rich,
  but, Israel, you will get those riches.
  The tall people from Seba will be yours.
  They will walk behind you with chains
    around their necks.
  They will bow down before you
    and ask you to pray for them and say,
  'The true God really is with you,
    and there is no other God.'"

¹⁵ You are the God people cannot see.
  You are the God who saves Israel.
¹⁶ Many people make false gods,
    but they will be disappointed.
  All of them will go away ashamed.

¹⁷ But Israel will be saved by the Lord.
  That salvation will continue forever.
  Never again will Israel be shamed.
¹⁸ The Lord is God.
  He made the skies and the earth.
  He put the earth in its place.
  He did not want the earth to be empty
    when he made it.
  He created it to be lived on.
"I am the Lord.
  There is no other God.
¹⁹ I have spoken openly, not in secret.
  I did not hide my words in a dark and
    secret place.
  I did not tell the people of Jacob*
    to look for me in empty places.
  I am the Lord, and I speak the truth.
  I say only what is right.

The Lord Proves He Is the Only God

²⁰"You people who escaped from other
nations, gather together before me. (These
people carry statues of false gods. They pray
to useless gods, but they don't know what
they are doing. ²¹Tell them to come to me.
Let them present their case and discuss these
things.)

"Who told you about this before it happened? Who told you this so long ago? I, the
Lord, am the one who said these things. I
am the only God, the one who does what is
right. I am the one who saves, and there is no
other! ²²So all you people in faraway places,
turn to me and be saved, because I am God,
and there is no other.

²³"When I make a promise, that promise is
true. It will happen. And I swear by my own
power that everyone will bow before me and
will take an oath* to obey me. ²⁴They will say,
'Goodness and strength come only from the
Lord.'"

And all who show their anger against him
will be humiliated. ²⁵The Lord will help the
people of Israel live right*f* and praise their
God.

False Gods Are Useless

46 ¹The Lord says, "Bel* has fallen to the
ground. Nebo*g* is kneeling before me.
"Men put those idols* on the backs of animals. They are only heavy burdens that must
be carried. They do nothing but make people
tired. ²But they all bowed down and fell to the
ground. They couldn't escape; they were all
carried away like prisoners.

³"Family of Jacob,* listen to me! You who
are left from the family of Israel, listen! I have
carried you since you left your mother's womb.
I carried you when you were born, ⁴and I will
still be carrying you when you are old. Your
hair will turn gray, and I will still carry you. I
made you, and I will carry you to safety.

---

*a*45:8 *victory* Or "goodness."
*b*45:8 *I … created him* Or "I created it *(salvation or
victory)."*
*c*45:11 *My children … done* Or "Those who are coming asked for my children. They commanded me ⸢to
give them⸥ the people I made with my own hands."
*d*45:12 *armies in the sky* Sometimes this means the
angels, and sometimes it means the stars.
*e*45:13 *I was right … Cyrus* Or "I gave Cyrus power
to do something good."
*f*45:25 *live right* Or "find justice."
*g*46:1 *Nebo* A false god of Babylon.

⁵"Can you compare me to anyone? No one is equal to me. You cannot understand everything about me. There is nothing like me. ⁶Some people are rich with gold and silver. Gold falls from their purses, and they weigh their silver on scales. They pay an artist to make a false god from wood. Then they bow down and worship that false god. ⁷They put their false god on their shoulders and carry it. That false god is useless; people have to carry it! People set the statue on the ground, and it cannot move. That false god never walks away from its place. People can yell at it, but it will not answer. That false god is only a statue; it cannot save people from their troubles.

⁸"Sinners, change your heart and mind. Think about this again. Remember it and be strong. ⁹Remember what happened long ago. Remember, I am God and there is no other God. There is no other like me.

¹⁰"In the beginning, I told you what would happen in the end. A long time ago, I told you things that have not happened yet. When I plan something, it happens. I do whatever I want to do. ¹¹I am calling a man from the east to do what I want. He will come like an eagle from a faraway country. He will do all that I have planned. Everything I said will happen just as I said it would.

¹²"Listen to me, you stubborn*a* people! You are far from doing what is right. ¹³But I am close to making things right. Salvation will not be delayed much longer. I will bring salvation to Zion* and to my wonderful Israel."

God's Message to Babylon

47 ¹"Fall down and sit in the dirt,
  Virgin Daughter Babylon.
You have no throne, so sit on the ground,
  daughter of the Chaldeans.*b*
You are not the ruler now.
You are no longer the beautiful young
  princess that people said you were.
² Get the millstones ready
  and grind the grain into flour.
Take off your veil and fancy clothes.
  Lift your skirt and get ready to cross the
  rivers.*c*
³ Men will see your naked body
  and use you for sex.
I will make you pay for the bad things you
  did,
  and I will not let anyone help you.

⁴"My people say, 'God saves us.
  His name is the LORD All-Powerful, the
  Holy One of Israel.'"

⁵"So Babylon, sit down and shut up.

Daughter of the Chaldeans, go into the
  dark prison.
You will no longer be 'The Queen of the
  Kingdoms.'

⁶"I was angry with my people.
  They were mine, but I turned against
  them.
I let you punish them,
  but you showed them no mercy.
Even for those who were old
  you made the work hard.
⁷ You said, 'I will live forever.
  I will always be the queen.'
You didn't care what you did to my people.
  You didn't think about what might
  happen later.
⁸ So now listen, you who love only pleasure!
Feeling so safe, you tell yourself,
  'I alone am important, and no one else
  matters.
I will never be a widow or lose my
  children.'
⁹ These two things will happen to you:
  First, you will lose your children and
  then your husband.
  And none of your magic spells will help
  you.
¹⁰ You do bad things but still feel safe.*d*
  You say to yourself, 'No one sees the
  wrong I do.'
  You thought that your wisdom and
  knowledge would save you.
You tell yourself, 'I alone am important,
  and no one else matters.'

¹¹"But disaster is coming your way.
  You don't know when it will happen,
  but disaster is coming.
  And there is nothing you can do to stop
  it.
¹² You worked hard all your life
  learning magic and spells.
So start using that magic.
  Maybe those spells will help you.
  Maybe you will be able to frighten
  someone.
¹³ You have many advisors.
  Are you tired of the advice they give?
Then send out your men who read the
  stars.
  They can tell when the month starts,
  so maybe they can tell you when your
  troubles will come.
¹⁴ But they cannot even save themselves.
  They will burn like straw.
  They will burn so fast that there will be
  no coals left to cook bread.
  There will be no fire left to sit by.
¹⁵ That's what will happen to those you have
  worked with,
  the people you did business with all
  your life.

---

*a*46:12 **stubborn** Literally, "mighty of heart."
*b*47:1 **Virgin Daughter Babylon, daughter of the Chaldeans** Names for the city of Babylon.
*c*47:2 **rivers** The Tigris and Euphrates rivers. Babylon was between these two rivers.

*d*47:10 **You ... safe** Or "You put your trust in your evil."

They will all go their own way.
There will be no one left to save you."

God Rules His World

48 ¹The LORD says,
"Family of Jacob,* listen to me!
You people call yourself 'Israel,*'
  but you are from Judah's family.
You use the LORD's name to make promises.
You claim to worship the God of Israel,
  but you are not honest and sincere.

²"Yes, you call yourselves citizens of the
    holy city,ᵃ
  those who depend on the God of Israel.
The LORD All-Powerful is his name.

³"Long ago I told you what would happen.
  I told you about these things.
  And suddenly I made them happen.
⁴ I did that because I knew you were
    stubborn.
  You were like iron that will not bend,
  with heads as hard as bronze.
⁵ So long ago I told you what would happen.
  I told you about those things long before
    they happened.
I did this so that you could not say,
  'The gods we made did this.
  Our idols,* our statues, made this
    happen.'"

God Punishes Israel to Make Them Pure

⁶"You heard what I said would happen.
  And you can see it has all been done.
  Shouldn't you tell this to others?
Now I will tell you about new things,
  secrets you have not known before.
⁷ This is something that is happening now,
    not long ago.
  You have not heard about it before today.
So you cannot say, 'We already knew that.'
⁸ But even in the past you didn't listen.
  You didn't learn anything.
  You never listen to what I say.
I have always known that you would turn
    against me.
  You have rebelled against me from the
    time you were born.

⁹"But I will be patient.
  I will do this for myself.
People will praise me for not becoming
    angry and destroying you.
  You will praise me for waiting.

¹⁰"Look, I will make you pure,
  but not in the way you make silver pure.
  I will make you pure by giving you
    troubles.
¹¹ I will do this for myself—for me!
  I will not let you treat me as if I am not
    important.

I will not let some false god take my
    glory* and praise.

¹²"Jacob,* listen to me!
Israel,* I called you to be my people.
  So listen to me!
I am the Beginning,
  and I am the End.
¹³ I made the earth with my own hands.
  My right hand made the sky.
And if I call them,
  they will come to stand before me.

¹⁴"All of you, come here and listen to me.
  Did any of the false gods say these
    things would happen? No!
The LORD's friendᵇ will do what he wants
  to Babylon and the Chaldeans.*

¹⁵"I told you that I would call him.
  I will lead him,
  and I will make him succeed.
¹⁶ Come here and listen to me!
  I was there when Babylon began as a
    nation.
And from the beginning, I spoke clearly
  so that people could know what I said."

Now, the Lord GOD sends me and his
Spirit* to tell you these things. ¹⁷The LORD,
the Savior, the Holy One of Israel, says,

"I am the LORD your God.
  I teach you for your own good.
  I lead you in the way you should go.
¹⁸ If you had obeyed me,
  then peace would have come to you
    like a full flowing river.
Good things would have come to you
    again and again,
  like the waves of the sea.
¹⁹ If you had obeyed me,
  you would have had as many children as
    there are grains of sand.
And they would always have been mine
  and would never have been destroyed."

²⁰ My people, leave Babylon!
  My people, run from the Chaldeans!
Tell the news with joy.
  Spread the news around the world.
Tell them, "The LORD rescued his servant
  Jacob."
²¹ They never got thirsty as he led them
    through the desert,
  because he made water flow from a
    rock.
He split the rock,
  and water flowed out.

²² But the LORD also said,
  "There is no peace for evil people."

ᵃ**48:2** *holy city* That is, Jerusalem.

ᵇ**48:14** *friend* Or "partner." This probably means
Cyrus, king of Persia. He ruled about 550–530 B.C.

God Calls His Special Servant

49 [1]Hear me, people by the sea.
Listen to me, you faraway nations.
The LORD called me before I was born.
He called my name while I was still in
my mother's womb.
[2] He used me to speak for him.
He used me like a sharp sword,
but he also held me in his hand to
protect me.
He used me like a sharp arrow,
but he also kept me safe in his arrow
bag.

[3] He told me, "Israel,* you are my servant.
I will do wonderful things with you."

[4] I said, "I worked hard for nothing.
I wore myself out, but I did nothing
useful.
I used all my power, but I did not really
do anything.
So the LORD must decide what to do with
me.
He must decide my reward."

[5] The LORD is the one who made me in my
mother's womb,
so that I could be his servant.
He wanted me to lead Jacob* and Israel
back to him.
The LORD gives me honor.
I get my strength from my God.

[6] And now he says, "You are a very
important servant to me.
You must bring back to me the tribes of
Jacob.
You must bring back the people of Israel
who are still alive.
But I have something else for you to do
that is even more important:
I will make you a light for the other
nations.
You will show people all over the world
the way to be saved."

[7] The LORD, the Holy Protector of Israel,
speaks to his servant.
People hate that servant.
Nations despise him.
He is now a slave to rulers.
The Lord says to him,
"Kings will see you and stand to honor
you.
Great leaders will bow down to you."

This will happen for the LORD. The Holy
One of Israel is the one who chose you, and
he can be trusted.

The Day of Salvation

[8] This is what the LORD says,
"There will be a special time when I show
my kindness.
Then I will answer your prayers.

There will be a special day when I will
save you.
Then I will help you and protect you.
And you will be the proof of my
agreement* with the people.
The country is destroyed now,
but you will give the land back to the
people who own it.
[9] You will tell the prisoners,
'Come out of your prison!'
You will tell those who are in darkness,
'Come out of the dark!'
The people will eat along the road,
and they will have food even on empty
hills.
[10] They will not be hungry or thirsty.
The hot sun and wind will not hurt
them.
Their Comforter will lead them.
He will lead them by springs of water.
[11] I will make a road for my people.
The mountains will be made flat,
and the low roads will be raised.

[12]"Look! People are coming to me from
faraway places.
They are coming to me from the north
and from the west.
They are coming to me from Aswan in
Egypt."

[13] Heavens and earth, be happy!
Mountains, shout with joy!
The LORD comforts his people.
He is good to his poor people.

[14] But now Zion* says, "The LORD has left
me;
the Lord has forgotten me."

[15] But the Lord says,
"Can a woman forget her baby?
Can she forget the child who came from
her body?
Even if she can forget her children,
I cannot forget you.
[16] I drew a picture of you on my hand.
You are always before my eyes.*[a]*
[17] Your children will come back to you,
and those who destroyed you will
leave.
[18] Look up! Look all around you!
All of your children are gathering
together and coming to you."
The LORD says,
"On my life, I promise you this:
Your children will be like jewels that
you tie around your neck.
Your children will be like the necklace
that a bride wears.

*a**49:16 I . . . eyes** Or "I see your figure before me
always." This is a wordplay. The Hebrew word "figure"
also means "walls."*

19"You are destroyed and defeated now.
  Your land is useless.
But after a short time, you will have many
    people in your land.
  And those who destroyed you will be
    far, far away.
20 You were sad for the children you lost,
    but they will tell you,
  'This place is too small!
  Give us a bigger place to live!'
21 Then you will say to yourself,
  'Who gave me all these children?
I was sad and lonely.
  My children were taken away.
  They were gone.
  So who gave me these children?
Look, I was the only one left.
  Where did all these children come
    from?'"

22 This is what the Lord GOD says:
  "Look, I will wave my hand to the nations.
  I will raise my flag for everyone to see.
  Then they will bring your children to you.
  They will carry your children on their
    shoulders,
  and they will hold them in their arms.
23 Kings will be their teachers.
  The daughters of kings will care for
    them.
  The kings and their daughters will bow
    down to you.
  They will kiss the dirt at your feet.
  Then you will know that I am the LORD,
    and anyone who trusts in me will not be
    disappointed."

24 If a strong soldier takes a prisoner,
    can you set him free?
  If a powerful soldier guards someone,
    can the prisoner escape?
25 Here is the LORD's answer:
  "The prisoners will escape.
  Those captured by the strong soldier
    will be set free.
  That's because I will fight your battles,
    and I will save your children.
26 Those people hurt you,
    but I will force them to eat their own
    bodies.
  Their own blood will be the wine that
    makes them drunk.
  Then everyone will know that the LORD
    saved you.
  Everyone will know that the Powerful
    One of Jacob* saved you."

Israel Punished Because of Their Sin

50 ¹This is what the LORD says:
  "People of Israel, you say that I
    divorced your mother, Jerusalem.
  But where is the legal paper that proves
    I divorced her?
  My children, did I owe money to
    someone?

Did I sell you to pay a debt?
No, you were sold because of the bad
    things you did.
  Your mother was sent away because of
    the bad things you did.
2 I came home and found no one there.
  I called and called, but no one
    answered.
  Do you think I cannot get you back?
  Do you think I cannot save you?
  Look, if I gave the command, the ocean
    would dry up!
  I can turn rivers into a desert.
  The fish would die without water, and
    their bodies would rot.
3 I can make the skies dark.
  I can cover the skies in darkness as
    black as sackcloth.*"

God's Servant Depends on God

⁴The Lord GOD gave me the ability to teach, so now I teach these sad people. Every morning he wakes me and teaches me like a student. ⁵The Lord GOD helps me learn, and I have not turned against him. I will not stop following him. ⁶I will let those people beat me and pull the hair from my beard. I will not hide my face when they say bad things to me and spit at me. ⁷The Lord GOD will help me, so the bad things they say will not hurt me. I will be strong. I know I will not be disappointed.

⁸The LORD is with me. He shows that I am innocent, so no one will be able to show I am guilty. If someone wants to try to prove I am wrong, that person should come to me, and we will have a trial. ⁹But look, the Lord GOD helps me, so no one can prove me guilty. As for them, they will all be like worthless old clothes, eaten by moths.

¹⁰People who respect the LORD also listen to his servant. That servant lives completely trusting in God without knowing what will happen. He really trusts in the LORD's name and depends on his God.

¹¹The Lord says, "Look, you people want to do whatever you want. So light your own fires and torches, but you will be punished. You will fall into your fires and torches and be burned. I will make that happen."

Israel Should Be Like Abraham

51 ¹"Some of you people try hard to live good lives. You go to the LORD for help. Listen to me. You should look at Abraham your father. He is the rock you were cut from. ²Abraham is your father, so look at him. Look at Sarah, who gave birth to you. Abraham was alone when I called him. Then I blessed him, and he began a great family with many descendants."

³In the same way, the LORD will bless Zion.* He will feel sorry for her and her people, and he will do something great for her. He will turn the desert into a garden. It will be like

the Garden of Eden. The land was empty, but it will become like the LORD's garden. People there will be very happy. They will sing victory songs to thank God for what he did.

4 "My people, listen to me!
My decisions will be like lights showing
people how to live.
5 I will soon save you and show that I am
fair.
I will use my power and judge all
nations.
All the faraway places are waiting for
me.
They wait for my power to help them.
6 Look up to the heavens!
Look around you at the earth below!
The skies will disappear like clouds of
smoke.
The earth will become like worthless
old clothes.
The people on earth will die,
but my salvation will continue forever.
My goodness will never end.
7 You people who understand goodness
should listen to me.
You people who follow my teachings
should hear the things I say.
Don't be afraid of evil people.
Don't let their insults upset you.
8 They will be like old clothes eaten by
moths.
They will be like wool eaten by worms.
But my goodness will last forever.
My salvation will continue forever and
ever."

God's Own Power Will Save His People
9 Wake up! Wake up!
Arm of the LORD, clothe yourself with
strength.
Show your power the way you did long
ago,
as you have from ancient times.
You are the one who destroyed Rahab.*
You defeated the Dragon.*
10 You dried up the water that was in the
deep sea.
You made a road through the deepest
parts of the sea.
Your people crossed over and were
saved.
11 The LORD will save his people.
They will return to Zion* with joy.
They will be very happy.
Their happiness will be like a crown on
their heads forever.
They will be singing with joy.
All sadness will be gone far away.

12 The LORD says, "I am the one who
comforts you.
So why should you be afraid of people?
They are only humans who live and die
like the grass."

13 The LORD made you.
With his power he made the earth
and spread the sky over the earth.
But you forgot him,
so you are always afraid that angry men
will hurt you.
Those men planned to destroy you,
but where are they now?

14 People in prison will soon be made free.
They will not die and rot in prison.
They will have plenty of food.

15 "I am the LORD your God,
the one who stirs up the sea and makes
the waves roar."
(The LORD All-Powerful is his name.)

16 "My servant, I gave you the words I want you to say, and I covered you with my hands to protect you. I did this to make a new heaven and earth and so that you would say to Israel, 'You are my people.'"

God Punished Israel
17 Wake up! Wake up!
Jerusalem, get up!
The LORD was very angry with you.
So you were punished.
It was like a cup of poison you had to
drink,
and you drank it all.

18 Jerusalem had many people, but none of them became leaders for her. None of the children she raised became guides to lead her. 19 Troubles came to you, Jerusalem, in pairs: Your land was destroyed and lies in ruins, and your people suffered from famine and war. But no one felt sorry for you or showed you mercy. 20 Your people became weak. They fell on the ground and lay there. They were lying on every street corner, like animals caught in a net. They were punished by the LORD's anger until they could not accept any more punishment. When God said he would give them more punishment, they became very weak.

21 Listen to me, poor Jerusalem. You are weak like a drunk, but you are not drunk from wine. You are weak ₍from that "cup of poison"₎. 22 Your God will fight for his people. The LORD says to you, "Look, I am taking this 'cup of poison' away from you. I am taking my anger away from you. You will not be punished by my anger again. 23 I will now use my anger to punish the people who hurt you. They tried to kill you. They told you, 'Bow

---

a **51:9 Rahab ... Dragon** This is Rahab the great sea monster. Some ancient stories tell about Rahab fighting with God.

down before us, and we will walk on you.'
They forced you to bow down before them,
and then they walked on your back like dirt.
You were like a road for them to walk on."

Israel Will Be Saved

52 [1]Wake up! Wake up!
Zion,* clothe yourself with strength.
Holy city of Jerusalem, stand up
  and put on your beautiful clothes!
  Those filthy foreigners[a] will not enter
    you again.
[2] Jerusalem, get up and shake off the dust!
Daughter Zion,[b] you were a prisoner,
  but take the chains off your neck.
[3] The Lord says,
  "You were not sold for money.
  So I will not use money to set you free."

[4]The Lord God says, "First, my people
went down to Egypt and became slaves. Then
Assyria made them slaves. [5]Now look what
has happened. Another nation has taken my
people. That country did not pay to take my
people, but they rule over them and laugh at
them, and they say bad things about me all
the time."

[6]The Lord says, "This happened so that my
people will learn about me. My people will
know who I am. My people will know my
name, and they will know that I Am He[c] is
speaking to them."

[7]How wonderful it is to see someone coming over the hills to tell good news. How
wonderful to hear him announce, "There is
peace! We have been saved!" and to hear him
say to Zion, "Your God is the king!"

[8] The city guards[d] are shouting.
    They are all rejoicing together.
  They can all see the Lord returning to
    Zion.

[9] Ruins of Jerusalem, be happy again!
  Rejoice because the Lord
    comforted his people and set Jerusalem
      free.
[10] The Lord showed his holy strength to all
    the nations.
  All the faraway countries saw how God
    saved his people.

[11] So leave Babylon!
  Leave that place!
  Priests, you carry the things that are used
    in worship.

So make yourselves pure.
  Don't touch anything that is not pure.
[12] You will leave Babylon,
  but they will not force you to leave in a
    hurry.
  You will not be forced to run away.
  The Lord will be in front of you.
  The God of Israel will be behind you.[e]

God's Suffering Servant

[13]The Lord says, "Look, my servant will
succeed in what he has to do, and he will be
raised to a position of high honor. [14]It is true
that many were shocked when they saw him.
He was beaten so badly that he no longer
looked like a man. [15]But it is also true that
many nations will be amazed at him. Kings
will look at him and be unable to speak.
They will see what they had never been told.
They will understand what they had never
heard.[f]"

53 [1]Who really believed what we heard?
Who saw in it the Lord's great
power?[g]

[2]He was always close to the Lord. He grew
up like a young plant, like a root growing in
dry ground. There was nothing special or
impressive about the way he looked, nothing
we could see that would cause us to like him.
[3]People made fun of him, and even his friends
left him. He was a man who suffered a lot of
pain and sickness. We treated him like someone of no importance, like someone people
will not even look at but turn away from in
disgust.

[4]The fact is, it was our suffering he took
on himself; he bore our pain. But we thought
that God was punishing him, that God was
beating him for something he did. [5]But he
was being punished for what we did. He was
crushed because of our guilt. He took the
punishment we deserved; and this brought us
peace. We were healed because of his pain.
[6]We had all wandered away like sheep. We
had gone our own way. And yet the Lord put
all our guilt on him.

[7]He was treated badly, but he never protested. He said nothing, like a lamb being led
away to be killed. He was like a sheep that
makes no sound as its wool is being cut off.
He never opened his mouth to defend himself. [8]He was taken away by force and judged
unfairly. The people of his time did not even
notice that he was killed.[h] But he was put to

---

[a]**52:1** *filthy foreigners* Or "unclean men that have
not been circumcised."
[b]**52:2** *Daughter Zion* Another name for Jerusalem.
[c]**52:6** *I Am He* This is like YAHWEH, the Hebrew name
for God. It shows that God lives forever, and that he
is always with his people. See Ex. 3:13–17.
[d]**52:8** *guards* Men who stand on the city walls and
watch for messengers or trouble coming to the city.
Here, this probably means the prophets.

[e]**52:12** *The Lord ... behind you* This shows that God
will protect his people. Compare Ex. 14:19, 20.
[f]**52:15** *They will see ... heard* Or "Those who were
not told the message saw what happened. Those
who did not hear understood."
[g]**53:1** *Who ... power* Or "Upon whom was the arm
of the Lord revealed?"
[h]**53:8** *The people ... killed* Or "There is no story
about his descendants, because he was taken from
the land of the living."

death*a* for the sins of his*b* people. ⁹He had done no wrong to anyone. He had never even told a lie. But he was buried among the wicked. His tomb was with the rich.

¹⁰But the LORD was pleased with this humble servant who suffered such pain.*c* Even after giving himself as an offering for sin, he will see his descendants and enjoy a long life. He will succeed in doing what the LORD wanted. ¹¹After his suffering he will see the light,*d* and he will be satisfied with what he experienced.

The Lord says, "My servant, who always does what is right, will make his people right with me; he will take away their sins. ¹²For this reason I will treat him as one of my great people. I will give him the rewards of one who wins in battle, and he will share them with his powerful ones. I will do this because he gave his life for the people. He was considered a criminal, but the truth is, he carried away the sins of many. Now he will stand before me and speak for those who have sinned."

God Brings His People Home

54 ¹Woman, be happy!
You have not had any children,
but you should be very happy.

The LORD says,
"The woman who is alone*e*
will have more children than the
woman with a husband."

² Make your tent bigger.
Open your doors wide.
Don't think small!
Make your tent large and strong,
³ because you will grow in all directions.
Your children will take over many nations
and live in the cities that were
destroyed.
⁴ Don't be afraid!
You will not be disappointed.
People will not say bad things against you.
You will not be embarrassed.
When you were young, you felt shame.
But you will forget that shame now.
You will not remember the shame you felt
when you lost your husband.*f*

⁵ Your real husband is the one who made
you.
His name is the LORD All-Powerful.
The Holy One of Israel is your Protector,*g*
and he is the God of all the earth!

⁶ You were like a woman whose husband
had left her.
You were very sad in your spirit.
You were like a woman who married
young,
and then her husband left her.
But the Lord has called you back to him.

⁷ God says, "I left you,
but only for a short time.
But with all my love,
I will bring you back to me again.
⁸ I became angry
and turned away from you for a short
time.
But I will comfort you with kindness
forever."
The LORD your Savior said this.

⁹ God says, "Remember, in Noah's time I
punished the world with the flood.
But I made a promise to Noah that I
would never again destroy the world
with a flood.
In the same way, I promise that I will
never again be angry with you and say
bad things to you.

¹⁰"The mountains may disappear,
and the hills may become dust,
but my faithful love will never leave you.
I will make peace with you,
and it will never end."
The LORD who loves you said this.

¹¹"You poor city!
Enemies came against you like storms,
and no one comforted you.
But I will rebuild you.
I will use a beautiful mortar to lay the
stones of your walls.
I will use sapphire stones when I lay the
foundation.
¹² The stones on top of the wall will be
made from rubies.
I will use shiny jewels for the gates.
I will use precious stones to build the
walls around you.
¹³ Your children will all be followers of God.
And they will have real peace.
¹⁴ You will be built on goodness.
You will be safe from cruelty and fear.
So you will have nothing to fear.

*a*53:8 *put to death* Or "punished."
*b*53:8 *his* This is the reading in a Hebrew copy among the Dead Sea Scrolls. The standard Hebrew text has "my."
*c*53:10 *But the LORD … such pain* Or "The LORD decided to crush him. He decided that he must suffer."
*d*53:11 *the light* This is found in some Hebrew scrolls from Qumran and the ancient Greek version. Light is often used as a symbol for life.
*e*54:1 *The woman … alone* This Hebrew word is like the word "destroyed." This probably means "Jerusalem, the city that is destroyed."
*f*54:4 *husband* In Hebrew this word is like the name Baal. This means that the LORD is Jerusalem's true God, not the false god Baal.
*g*54:5 *Protector* Or "Redeemer," someone who cared for and protected the family of a dead relative. Often this person bought back (redeemed) the poor relatives from slavery, making them free again.

Nothing will come to hurt you.
15 I will never send anyone to attack you.
And if any army tries to attack you, you
will defeat them.

16"Look, I made the blacksmith.* He blows
on the fire to make it hotter. Then he takes
the hot iron and makes the kind of tool he
wants to make. In the same way, I made the
'Destroyer' to destroy things.
17"People will make weapons to fight
against you, but their weapons will not defeat
you. Some people will say things against you,
but anyone who speaks against you will be
proved wrong."
The Lord says, "That is what my servants
get! They get the good things*a* that come from
me.

God Gives "Food" That Really Satisfies

55 1"All you people who are thirsty,
come!
Here is water for you to drink.
Don't worry if you have no money.
Come, eat and drink until you are full!
You don't need money.
The milk and wine are free.
2 Why waste your money on something
that is not real food?
Why should you work for something
that does not really satisfy you?
Listen closely to me and you will eat what
is good.
You will enjoy the food that satisfies
your soul.
3 Listen closely to what I say.
Listen to me so that you will live.
I will make an agreement with you that
will last forever.
It will be an agreement you can trust,
like the one I made with David*—
a promise to love him and be loyal to
him forever.
4 I made David a witness of my power for
all nations.
I promised him that he would become
a ruler and commander of many
nations."

5 There are nations in places you don't
know,
but you will call for them to come.
They don't know you,
but they will run to you.
This will happen because the Lord, your
God, wants it.
It will happen because the Holy One of
Israel honors you.
6 So you should look for the Lord
before it is too late.
You should call to him now,
while he is near.

7 Evil people should stop living evil lives.
They should stop thinking bad thoughts.
They should come to the Lord again,
and he will comfort them.
They should come to our God
because he will freely forgive them.

People Cannot Understand God

8 The Lord says, "My thoughts are not like
yours.
Your ways are not like mine.
9 Just as the heavens are higher than the
earth,
so my ways are higher than your ways,
and my thoughts are higher than your
thoughts."
This is what the Lord himself said.

10"Rain and snow fall from the sky
and don't return until they have
watered the ground.
Then the ground causes the plants to
sprout and grow,
and they produce seeds for the farmer
and food for people to eat.
11 In the same way, my words leave my
mouth,
and they don't come back without
results.
My words make the things happen that I
want to happen.
They succeed in doing what I send
them to do.

12"So you will go out from there with joy.
You will be led out in peace.
When you come to the mountains and
hills, they will begin singing.
All the trees in the fields will clap their
hands.
13 Large cypress trees will grow where there
were thornbushes.
Myrtle trees will grow where there
were weeds.
All this will happen to make the Lord
known,
to be a permanent reminder of his
goodness and power."

All Nations Will Follow the Lord

56 1The Lord said these things, "Be
fair to all people. Do what is right,
because soon my salvation will come to you.
My goodness will soon be shown to the
whole world. 2I will bless those who refuse
to do wrong and who obey the law about the
Sabbath.*"
3Some foreigners will choose to follow the
Lord. They should not say, "The Lord will not
really accept me like the rest of his people." A
eunuch* should not say, "I am only a dry piece
of wood. ⌊I cannot have any children.⌋"
4They should not say that because the Lord
says, "Some eunuchs obey the laws about the
Sabbath. They choose to do what I want, and

*a*54:17 *good things* Or "victory."

they follow my agreement.[a] [5]So I will put a memorial stone in my Temple* for them. Their name will be remembered in my city! Yes, I will give those eunuchs something better than sons and daughters. I will give them a name that will last forever! They will not be cut off[b] from my people."

[6]"Some foreigners have chosen to follow the Lord. They do this so that they can serve him and love his name and be his servants. They keep the Sabbath as a special day of worship, and they will continue to follow closely my agreement.* [7]So I will bring them to my holy mountain and make them happy in my house of prayer. The offerings and sacrifices* they give me will please me, because my Temple will be called a house of prayer for all nations." [8]The Lord God said these things.

The Israelites were forced to leave their country, but the Lord will gather them together again. He says, "I will bring them back together again!"

[9] Wild animals in the forest, come and eat.
[10] The watchmen[c] are all blind.
　　They don't know what they are doing.
　　They are like dogs that will not bark.
　　　They lie on the ground and sleep.
　　　Oh, they love to sleep.
[11] They are like hungry dogs.
　　They are never satisfied.
　　The shepherds don't know what they are
　　　doing.
　　　Like their sheep, they have all
　　　　wandered away.
　　They are greedy.
　　All they want is to satisfy themselves.
[12] They come and say,
　　"I will drink some wine.
　　I will drink some beer.
　　I will do the same thing tomorrow,
　　but I will drink even more."

Israel Does Not Follow God

57 [1]All the good people are gone, and no one even noticed.
　The loyal followers were gathered up,
　　but no one knows why.

　The reason they were gathered up
　　is that trouble is coming.
[2] But peace will come too,
　　and those who trust him will get to rest
　　　in their own beds.

---

[3]"Come here, you children of witches.
　　Your father committed adultery,
　　and your mother was unfaithful.
[4] You are children out of control, full of lies.
　　You make fun of me.
　You make faces
　　and stick out your tongue at me.[d]
[5] All you want is to worship false gods
　　under every green tree.
　You kill children by every stream
　　and sacrifice them in the rocky places.
[6] You love to worship the smooth rocks in
　　the rivers.
　　You pour wine on them to worship
　　　them.
　You give sacrifices* to them, but those
　　rocks are all you get.
　Do you think this makes me happy?
　You make your bed on every hill
　　and high mountain.[e]
[7] You go up to those places
　　and offer sacrifices.
[8] You hide the things that help you
　　remember me
　　behind the doors and doorframes.[f]
　You were with me,
　　but you got up to go to them.
　You spread out your bed
　　and gave yourself to them.[g]
　You love their beds
　　and enjoy looking at their naked
　　　bodies.[h]
[9] You use your oils and perfumes
　　to look nice for Molech.*
　You sent your messengers to faraway
　　lands,
　　and this will bring you down to the
　　　place of death.[i]
[10] All of them made you tired,
　　but you never gave up.
　You found new strength,
　　because you enjoyed them.
[11] You did not remember me.
　　You did not even notice me!
　So who were you worrying about?
　　Who were you afraid of?
　　Why did you lie?
　Look, I have been quiet for a long time.
　　Is that why you didn't honor me?

---

[a]**56:4** *agreement* This usually means the agreement God made with Israel through Moses. (See "agreement" in the Word List.) Here, it might mean the agreement of Isaiah 55:3.

[b]**56:5** *cut off* To be removed from the list of the people of Israel. This included a person's being forced to leave family, land, and the people of Israel.

[c]**56:10** *The watchmen* Literally, "The seers," an ancient title for prophets.

[d]**57:4** *make faces … tongue* This probably refers to the god Bel, which is usually shown making a face and sticking out his tongue.

[e]**57:6** *every hill and high mountain* The people worshiped false gods in these places. The people thought these false gods would give them good crops and more children.

[f]**57:8** *doorframes* The Israelites were supposed to put special things on their doorframes to help them remember God. See Deut. 6:9.

[g]**57:8** *gave yourself to them* Or "And made agreements with them."

[h]**57:8** *naked bodies* This is a wordplay. The Hebrew word also means "memorial," as in Isaiah 56:5.

[i]**57:9** *this will … death* Or "You even send them down to Sheol."

12 I could tell about your 'good works' and
       all the 'religious' things you do,
   but that will not help you.
13 When you need help,
   you cry to those false gods that you have
       gathered around you.
   Let them help you!
   But I tell you, the wind will blow them all
       away.
   A puff of wind will blow them all away.
   But the one who depends on me
   will get the land I promised
   and enjoy my holy mountain.*"

The Lord Will Save His People

14 Clear the road! Clear the road!
   Make the way clear for my people!

15 God is high and lifted up.
   He lives forever.
   His name is holy.
   He says, "I live in a high and holy place,
   but I also live with people who are
       humble and sorry for their sins.
   I will give new life to those who are
       humble in spirit.
   I will give new life to those who are
       sorry for their sins.
16 I will not accuse my people forever.
   I will not always be angry.
   If I continued to show my anger,
       then the human spirit, the life I gave
       them, would die before me.
17 Israel's evil greed made me angry,
   so I punished them.
   I turned away from them
   because I was angry.
   But they continued to do wrong.
   They did whatever they wanted.
18 I have seen their way of life, but I will
       heal them.
   I will guide and comfort them and those
       who mourn* for them.
19 I will teach them a new word: peace.
   I will give peace to those who are near
   and to those who are far away.
   I will heal them."
   The LORD himself said this.

20 But evil people are like the angry ocean.
They cannot be quiet and peaceful. They are
angry, and like the ocean, they stir up mud.
My God says, 21 "There is no peace for evil
people."

People Must Be Told to Follow God

58 1 Shout as loud as you can and don't
       stop.
   Shout like a trumpet!
   Tell the people what they did wrong.
   Tell the family of Jacob* about their sins.
2 They still come every day to worship me.

They act just like they want to learn my
       ways.
They pretend to be a nation that lives right
   and obeys the commands of their God.
They ask me to judge them fairly.
They want their God to be near them.

3 They say, "We fast* to show honor to you.
Why don't you see us? We starve our bodies
to show honor to you. Why don't you notice
us?"
   But the LORD says, "You do things to please
yourselves on those special days of fasting.
And you punish your servants, not your own
bodies. 4 You are hungry, but not for food. You
are hungry for arguing and fighting, not for
bread. You are hungry to hit people with your
evil hands. This is not the way to fast if you
want your prayers to be heard in heaven! 5 Do
you think I want to see people punish their
bodies on those days of fasting? Do you think
I want people to look sad and bow their heads
like dead plants? Do you think I want people
to wear mourning* clothes and sit in ashes to
show their sadness? That is what you do on
your days of fasting. Do you think that is what
the LORD wants?
   6 "I will tell you the kind of day I want—a
day to set people free. I want a day that you
take the burdens off others. I want a day when
you set troubled people free and you take the
burdens from their shoulders. 7 I want you to
share your food with the hungry. I want you
to find the poor who don't have homes and
bring them into your own homes. When you
see people who have no clothes, give them
your clothes! Don't hide from your relatives
when they need help."
   8 If you do these things, your light will begin
to shine like the light of dawn. Then your
wounds will heal. Your "Goodness" will walk
in front of you, and the Glory of the LORD*
will come following behind you. 9 Then you
will call to the LORD, and he will answer you.
You will cry out to him, and he will say, "Here
I am."
   Stop causing trouble and putting burdens on
people. Stop accusing people of wrongdoing*b*
and saying hurtful things. 10 Feel sorry for
hungry people and give them food. Help those
who are troubled and satisfy their needs. Then
your light will shine in the darkness. You will
be like the bright sunshine at noon.
   11 The LORD will always lead you and satisfy
your needs in dry lands. He will give strength
to your bones. You will be like a garden that
has plenty of water, like a spring that never
goes dry.
   12 Your cities have been destroyed for many
years, but you will rebuild them and their
foundations will last for a long time. You will

---

*a*57:13 *holy mountain* Mount Zion, one of the
mountains Jerusalem was built on.

*b*58:9 *accusing people of wrongdoing* Literally,
"pointing of the finger." This might be a way of
cursing someone.

be called "Fence Fixer" and "Builder of Roads and Houses."

¹³That will happen when you stop sinning against God's law about the Sabbath* and when you stop doing things to please yourself on that special day. You should call the Sabbath a happy day. You should honor the Lord's special day by not saying and doing things that you do every other day of the week. ¹⁴Then you could enjoy the Lord. As the Lord himself says, "I could carry you up to the highest mountain and let you enjoy the land that I gave to your father Jacob."

Evil People Should Change Their Lives

59 ¹Look, the Lord's power is enough to save you. He can hear you when you ask him for help. ²It is your sins that separate you from your God. The Lord turns away from you when he sees them. ³That's because your hands are covered with blood from the people you murdered. You tell lies and say evil things. ⁴You can't be trusted, even in court. You lie about each other and depend on false arguments to win your cases. You create pain and produce wickedness. ⁵You hatch evil, like eggs from a poisonous snake. Anyone who eats the eggs will die. And if you break one of them open, a poisonous snake will come out.

Your lies are like spider webs. ⁶They cannot be used for clothes, and you cannot cover yourself with them.

Your hands are always busy sinning and hurting others. ⁷Your feet run toward evil. You are always ready to kill innocent people. You think of nothing but evil. Everywhere you go you cause trouble and ruin. ⁸You don't know how to live in peace. You don't do what is right and fair. You are crooked, and anyone who lives like that will never know true peace.

Israel's Sin Brings Trouble

⁹ All fairness and goodness is gone.
There is only darkness around us,
so we must wait for the light.
We hope for a bright light,
but all we have is darkness.
¹⁰ We are like people without eyes.
We walk into walls like blind people.
We stumble and fall as if it was night.
Even in the daylight, we cannot see.
At noontime, we fall like dead men.
¹¹ We are always complaining;
we growl like bears and moan like
doves.
We are waiting for justice,
but there is none.
We are waiting to be saved,
but salvation is still far away.
¹² That's because we committed crimes
against our God.
Our own sins speak out against us.
We know we are guilty.
We know we have sinned.

¹³ We rebelled against the Lord
and lied to him.
We turned away from our God
and left him.
We planned to hurt others
and to rebel against God.
From hearts filled with lies,
we talked about it and made our plans.
¹⁴ We pushed Justice away.
Fairness stands off in the distance.
Truth has fallen in the streets.
Goodness is not allowed in the city.
¹⁵ Loyalty is gone,
and people who try to do good are
robbed.

The Lord looked and saw there was no
justice.
He did not like what he saw.
¹⁶ He did not see anyone speak up for the
people.
He was shocked to see that no one
stood up for them.
So with his own power he saved them.
His desire to do what is right gave him
strength.
¹⁷ He put on
the armor of goodness,
the helmet of salvation,
the uniform of punishment, and
the coat of strong love.ᵃ
¹⁸ He will give his enemies the punishment
they deserve.
They will feel his anger.
He will punish all his enemies.
People along the coast will get the
punishment they deserve.
¹⁹ People from the west to the east will fear
the Lord and respect his Glory.*
He will come quickly, like a fast-flowing
river
driven by a windᵇ from the Lord.
²⁰ Then a redeemerᶜ will come to Zion*
to save the people of Jacob* who have
turned away from sin.

²¹The Lord says, "As for me, this is the agreement that I will make with these people. I promise my Spirit* that I put on you and my words that I put in your mouth will never leave you. They will be with you and your children and your children's children, for now and forever.

God Is Coming

60 ¹"Jerusalem, get up and shine!ᵈ
Your Light is coming!
The Glory of the Lord* will shine on you.

ᵃ**59:17 strong love** The Hebrew word means strong feelings like love, hate, anger, zeal, or jealousy.
ᵇ**59:19 wind** Or "spirit."
ᶜ**59:20 redeemer** Someone who sets a person free by paying their debt.
ᵈ**60:1 Jerusalem … shine** Or "Jerusalem, my light, get up!"

2 Darkness now covers the earth,
  and the people are in darkness.
But the Lord will shine on you,
  and his Glory will appear over you.
3 Then the nations will come to your light.
  Kings will come to your bright sunrise.
4 Look around you!
  See all the people gathering around.
  Those are your sons coming from far
    away,
  and your daughters are there beside
    them.

5 "At that time you will see your people,
  and your faces will shine with
    happiness.
First, you will be afraid,
  but then you will be excited.
All the riches from across the seas will be
  set before you.
  The riches of the nations will come to
    you.
6 Herds of camels from Midian and Ephah
  will cross your land.
Long lines of camels will come from
  Sheba.
  They will bring gold and incense.*
People will sing praises to the Lord.
7 People will collect all the sheep from
    Kedar and give them to you.
  They will bring you rams from
    Nebaioth.
You will offer those animals on my altar,*
  and I will accept them.
I will make my wonderful Temple*
  even more beautiful.
8 Look at the people.
  They are rushing toward you like clouds
    quickly crossing the sky.
  They are like doves flying to their nests.
9 The faraway lands are waiting for me.
  The great cargo ships are ready to sail.
They are ready to bring your children
  from faraway lands.
  They will bring silver and gold with
    them
  to honor the Lord your God, the Holy
    One of Israel.
The Lord does wonderful things for you.
10 Children from other lands will rebuild
  your walls.
  Their kings will serve you.

"When I was angry, I hurt you,
  but now I want to be kind to you.
  So I will comfort you.
11 Your gates will always be open.
  They will not be closed, day or night.
  Nations and kings will bring their wealth
    to you.
12 Any nation or kingdom that does not
    serve you will be destroyed.
13 All the great things of Lebanon* will be
  given to you.
  People will bring pine trees, fir trees,

and cypress trees to you.
These trees will be used for lumber
  to make my Holy Place* more beautiful.
This place is like a stool in front of my
    throne,
  and I will honor it.b
14 In the past, people hurt you,
  but they will bow down before you.
In the past, people hated you,
  but they will bow down at your feet.
They will call you 'The City of the Lord's,'
  'Zion* of the Holy One of Israel.'

15 "People hated you.
  You were left all alone with no one
    passing through.
But I will make you great from now on.
  You will be happy forever and ever.
16 Nations will give you what you need,
  like a child drinking milk from its
    mother.
But you will 'drink' riches from kings.
  Then you will know that it is I, the
    Lord, who saves you.
  You will know that I, the Great God of
    Jacob,* protect you.

17 "You now have copper,
  but I will bring you gold.
You now have iron,
  but I will bring you silver.
I will change your wood into copper
  and your rocks into iron.
I will change your punishment into peace.
And those who punished you
  will be replaced with those who are
    kind to you.
18 There will never again be news of
  violence in your country.
People will never again attack your
    country
  and steal from you.
You will name your walls, 'Salvation'
  and your gates, 'Praise.'

19 "The sun will no longer be your light
  during the day.
  The light from the moon will no longer
    be your light at night.
The Lord will be your light forever.
  Your God will be your glory.
20 Your sun will never go down again.
  Your moon will never again be dark.
That's because the Lord will be your light
    forever,
  and the dark days of mourning* will
    end.

21 "All your people will be good.
  They will get the land forever.
  They are the young plant in my gardenc

a 60:13 *my Holy Place* This probably means the
Temple in Jerusalem.
b 60:13 *I will honor it* Or "I will give it glory."
c 60:21 *young plant … garden* See Isa. 4:1 and 5:7.

that will grow to be a wonderful tree.
I made them with my own hands.ᵃ
22 The smallest family will become a large
    family group.
The smallest tribe will become a
    powerful nation.
When the time is right,
I, the Lᴏʀᴅ, will come quickly.
I will make these things happen."

The Lord's Message of Freedom

61 ¹The Spirit* of the Lord Gᴏᴅ is on me.
The Lᴏʀᴅ has chosen me to tell good
news to the poor and to comfort those who
are sad. He sent me to tell the captives and
prisoners that they have been set free. ²He
sent me to announce that the time has come
for the Lᴏʀᴅ to show his kindness, when our
God will also punish evil people. He has sent
me to comfort those who are sad, ³those in
Zion* who mourn.* I will take away the ashes
on their head, and I will give them a crown.
I will take away their sadness, and I will give
them the oil of happiness. I will take away
their sorrow, and I will give them celebration clothes. He sent me to name them 'Good
Trees' and 'The Lᴏʀᴅ's Wonderful Plant.'

⁴Then the old cities that were destroyed
will be rebuilt. Those ancient ruins will be
made new, as they were in the beginning.

⁵Then your enemies will come to care for
your sheep, and their children will work in
your fields and in your gardens. ⁶You will be
called, 'The Lᴏʀᴅ's Priests,' 'The Servants of
our God.' You will be proud of all the riches
that have come to you from all the nations
on earth.

⁷In the past, other people shamed you and
said bad things to you. You were shamed
much more than any other people. So in your
land you will get two times more than other
people. You will get the joy that continues
forever. ⁸That's because I am the Lᴏʀᴅ and
I love justice. I hate stealing and everything
that is wrong. So I will give the people what
they deserve. I will make an agreement with
my people forever. ⁹Their descendants will be
known throughout the earth, and everyone
will know their children. Whoever sees them
will know that the Lᴏʀᴅ has blessed them.

God's Servant Brings Salvation

10 The Lᴏʀᴅ makes me very happy.
I am completely happy with my God.
He dressed me in the clothes of salvation.
He put the victory coat on me.
I look like a man dressed for his wedding,
like a bride covered with jewels.
11 The earth causes plants to grow,
and a garden makes the seeds planted
    there rise up.

In the same way, the Lᴏʀᴅ will make
    goodness and praise
grow throughout the nations.

New Jerusalem: A City Full of Goodness

62 ¹I love Zion,*
so I will continue to speak for her.
I love Jerusalem,
so I will not stop speaking.
I will speak until goodnessᵇ shines like a
    bright light,
until salvation burns bright like a flame.
2 Then all nations will see your goodness.
All kings will see your honor.
Then you will have a new name
that the Lᴏʀᴅ himself will give you.
3 You will be like a beautiful crown that the
    Lᴏʀᴅ holds up,
like a king's crown in the hand of your
    God.
4 You will never again be called 'The People
    God Left.'
Your land will never again be called
    'The Land God Destroyed.'
You will be called 'The People God
    Loves.'
Your land will be called 'God's Bride,'
because the Lᴏʀᴅ loves you,
and your land will be his.ᶜ
5 As a young man takes a bride and she
    belongs to him,
so your land will belong to your
    children.ᵈ
As a man is happy with his new wife,
so your God will be happy with you.

6 Jerusalem, I put guards on your walls.
They will not be silent.
They will keep praying day and night.

Guards, keep praying to the Lᴏʀᴅ.
Remind him of his promise.
Don't ever stop praying.
7 Don't give him any rest until he rebuilds
    Jerusalem
and makes it a place that everyone on
    earth will praise.

8 The Lᴏʀᴅ made a promise and guaranteed
    it by his own power.
And he will use that power to keep his
    promise.
The Lord said, "I promise that I will never
    again give your food to your enemies.
I promise that they will never again take
    the wine you make.
9 Whoever gathers the food will eat it and
    praise the Lᴏʀᴅ.

ᵃ**60:21** *They ... hands* Or "They are the plant I
planted, which I made with my own hands, to show
how wonderful I am."

ᵇ**62:1** *goodness* Or "victory."

ᶜ**62:4** *your land ... his* Or "He will marry your land."
This is a wordplay. The Hebrew word also means "He
will be the lord of the land."

ᵈ**62:5** *your land ... children* Or "Your builders will
marry you."

Whoever gathers the grape will drink
the wine in the courtyards of my
Temple."

10 Come through the gates!
Clear the way for the people!
Prepare the road!
Move all the stones off the road!
Raise a flag as a sign for the nations!

11 Listen, the LORD is speaking to all the
faraway lands:
"Tell the people of Zion,
'Look, your Savior is coming.
He is bringing your reward to you.
He is bringing it with him.'"

12 His people will be called "The Holy
People,"
"The Saved People of the LORD."
And you, Jerusalem, will be called "The
City God Wants,"
"The City God Is With."

The Lord Punishes the Nations

63

1Who is this coming from Edom,*
from the city of Bozrah?
His clothes are stained bright red.
He is glorious in his clothes.
He is walking tall with his great power.
He says, "I have the power to save you,
and I speak the truth."

2"Why are your clothes bright red?
They are like the clothes of someone
who tramples grapes to make wine."

3 He answers, "I walked in the winepress*
by myself.
No one helped me.
I was angry, and I trampled the grapes.
The juice*a* splashed on my clothes, so
now they are stained.

4 I chose a time to punish people.
Now the time has come for me to save
and protect my people.

5 I looked around, but I saw no one to help
me.
I was surprised that no one supported
me.
So I used my own power to save my
people.
My own anger supported me.

6 In my anger I trampled down the nations.
I punished them in anger and spilled
their blood*b* on the ground."

The Lord Has Been Kind to His People

7 I will remember that the LORD is kind,
and I will remember to praise the LORD.
He gave many good things to the family of
Israel.*
He has been very kind to us.

He has shown us mercy.

8 He said, "These are my people.
These are my real children."
So he saved them.

9 The people had many troubles,
but he was not against them.
He loved them and felt sorry for them,
so he saved them.
He sent his special angel to save them.
He picked them up and carried them,
just as he did long ago.

10 But they turned against him
and made his Holy Spirit* very sad.
So the Lord became their enemy
and fought against them.

11 Then they remembered what happened
long ago.
They remembered Moses and those
with him.
So where is the one who brought them
through the sea
along with the shepherds who led his
flock?
Where is the one who sent his Holy Spirit
to live among them?

12 He was by Moses' side and led him with
his wonderful hand.
He divided the water,
so that the people could walk through
the sea.
He made his name famous
by doing those great things.

13 He led the people through the deep sea.
Like a horse running through the desert,
they walked without falling.

14 Like cattle going down to the valley,
The Spirit of the LORD led them.
This is how you led your people
and made your name wonderful.

A Prayer for God to Help His People

15 LORD, look down from the heavens.
See what is happening now.
Look down at us from your great and holy
home in heaven.
Where is your strong love*c* for us?
Where is your compassion?
Why are you hiding your kind love from
me?

16 Look, you are our father!
Abraham does not know us.
Israel* does not recognize us.
LORD, you are our father!
You are the one who has always saved
us!

17 LORD, why are you pushing us away from
you?
Why are you making it hard for us to
follow you?
Come back to us!
We are your servants.

---

*a***63:3** *juice* Or "strong drink" or "blood."
*b***63:6** *blood* Or "strong drink" or "strength."

*c***63:15** *strong love* The Hebrew word means strong
feelings like love, hate, anger, zeal, or jealousy.

Come to us and help us!
Our tribes belong to you.
18 Your holy people had their land only a
short time.
Then our enemies trampled down your
holy Temple.*
19 Some people don't follow you.
They don't wear your name.
And we have been like them
for a very long time.

64

1 If you would tear open the skies
and come down to earth, then
everything would change.
Mountains would melt before you.
2 The mountains would burst into flames
like burning bushes.
The mountains would boil like water on
the fire.
Then your enemies would learn about
you.
And all nations would shake with fear
when they see you.
3 But you have done awesome things that
we did not expect.
You came down, and mountains shook
in fear before you.
4 No one has ever heard of such a God.
No one has ever heard such a story.
No one has ever seen any God except
you,
who does such great things for those
who trust him.

5 You welcome people who enjoy doing
good and who remember you
by living the way you want them to.
But we sinned against you,
and you became angry with us.*a*
But you always saved us!
6 We are all dirty with sin.
Even our good works are not pure.
They are like bloodstained rags.
We are all like dead leaves.
Our sins have carried us away like
wind.
7 We don't call to you for help.
We aren't excited about following you,
so you have turned away from us.
We are helpless before you,
because we are full of sin.
8 But, LORD, you are our father.
We are like clay, and you are the potter.*
Your hands made us all.
9 LORD, don't continue to be angry with us!
Don't remember our sins forever!
Please, look at us!
We are all your people.
10 Your holy* cities are as empty as the
desert.
Zion* has become a desert.
Jerusalem is destroyed.

11 Our ancestors* worshiped you in our holy
Temple.*
That wonderful Temple has now been
burned.
All our precious possessions have been
destroyed.
12 Will these things always keep you from
helping?
Will you continue to say nothing?
Will you punish us forever?

All People Will Learn About God

65

1 The LORD says, "I helped people who
had not come to me for advice. Those
who found me were not looking for me.*b* I
spoke to a nation that does not use my name.
I said, 'Here I am! Here I am!'
2 "All day long I stood ready to accept those
who turned against me. But they kept doing
whatever they wanted to do, and all they did
was wrong. 3 They keep doing things, right in
front of me, that make me angry. They offer
sacrifices* and burn incense* in their special
gardens.*c* 4 They sit among the graves, waiting
to get messages from the dead. They eat the
meat of pigs, and their pots are full of soup
made from unclean meat. 5 But they tell others, 'Don't come near me! Don't touch me
because I am holy!' They are like smoke in
my eyes, and their fire burns all the time."

Israel Must Be Punished

6 "Look, here is a letter that lists all your
sins. It is a bill that must be paid. I will not
be quiet until I pay this bill, and I will pay it
by punishing you. 7 I am doing this because of
your sins and the sins of your ancestors.* They
did these sins when they burned incense* in
the mountains. They shamed me on those
hills, and I punished them first."

8 The LORD says, "When there is new wine
in the grapes, people squeeze out the wine.
But they don't completely destroy the grapes
because the grapes can still be used. I will
do the same thing to my servants. I will not
destroy them completely. 9 I will keep some
of the people of Jacob.* Some of the people
of Judah will get my mountains. I will choose
the people who will get the land. My servants
will live there. 10 Then Sharon Valley* will be
a field for sheep. The Valley of Achor*d* will
be a place for cattle to rest. All this will be
for my people—for the people who come to
me for help.

11 "But you people left the LORD, so you
will be punished. You forgot about my holy*

---

a 64:5 *we sinned ... us* Or "But you became angry
with us and we sinned."

b 65:1 *I helped ... me* Or "I was ready to answer
those who did not come to me for advice. I was
ready to be found by those who did not look for
me."
c 65:3 *special gardens* Gardens where people
worshiped false gods.
d 65:10 *Valley of Achor* A valley about ten miles
north of Jerusalem.

mountain.*a* You began to worship Luck. You held feasts for the false god, Fate.*b* 12But I decided what would happen to you: you will be killed with a sword. You will all be killed because I called to you, but you refused to answer me. I spoke to you, but you would not listen. You did what I said is evil and chose to do what I did not like."

13 So this is what the Lord GOD says:
"My servants will eat,
  but you evil people will be hungry.
My servants will drink,
  but you will be thirsty.
My servants will be happy,
  but you will suffer shame.
14 My servants will shout for joy,
  but you will cry out in pain.*c*
Your spirits will be broken,
  and you will be very sad.
15 Your names will be like curses to my
    chosen servants."
The Lord GOD will kill you,
  and then he will call his servants by a
    new name.
16 The Lord says, "People now ask blessings
    from the earth.
But in the future they will ask blessings
    from the faithful God.
People now trust in the power of the
    earth when they make a promise.
But in the future they will trust in the
    God who is faithful.
That's because the troubles in the past
    will all be forgotten.
They will be hidden from my sight."

A New Time Is Coming

17"I am creating a new heaven and a new
    earth.
The troubles of the past will be forgotten.
No one will remember them.
18 My people will be happy and rejoice
    forever and ever
  because of what I will make.
I will make a Jerusalem that is full of joy,
  and I will make her people happy.

19"Then I will rejoice with Jerusalem.
I will be happy with my people.
There will never again be crying
  and sadness in that city.
20 In that city there will never be a baby
    who lives only a few days,
  and every older person will live for a
    long, long time.
A person who lives 100 years will be
    called young.

And whoever doesn't live that long will
    be considered cursed.

21"In that city whoever builds a house will
    live there;
  whoever plants a vineyard* will eat the
    grapes from that garden.
22 Never again will one person build a house
    and another person live there.
Never again will one person plant a
    garden
  and another eat the fruit from it.
My people will live as long as the trees.
My chosen people will get full use of
    whatever they make.
23 Never again will a woman suffer
    childbirth and have her baby die.
Women will not fear childbirth.
I will bless all my people and their
    children.
24 I will answer them before they call for
    help.
I will help them before they finish
    asking.
25 Wolves and little lambs will eat together.
Lions will eat hay like cattle,
  and snakes will eat only dust.
They will not hurt or destroy each other
    on my holy mountain."
This is what the LORD said.

God Will Judge All Nations

66 1This is what the LORD says:
"Heaven is my throne,
  and the earth is where I rest my feet.
So do you think you can build a house for
    me?
Do I need a place to rest?
2 I am the one who made all things.
They are all here because I made them,"
  says the LORD.
"These are the people I care for:
  the poor, humble people who obey my
    commands.
3 Some people kill bulls as a sacrifice,
  but they also beat people.
They kill sheep as a sacrifice,*
  but they also break the necks of dogs.
They offer up grain offerings,
  but they also offer the blood of pigs.*d*
They burn incense,*
  but they also love their worthless idols.*
They choose their own ways,
  and they love their terrible idols.
4 So I decided to use their own tricks.
I will punish them using what they are
    most afraid of.
I will do this because I called to them,
  but they did not answer.
I spoke to them,
  but they did not listen.

---

*a*65:11 *my holy mountain* Mount Zion, the mountain Jerusalem is built on.
*b*65:11 *Luck … Fate* Two false gods. The people thought these gods controlled their futures.
*c*65:14 *My servants … pain* Literally, "My servants will rejoice with good hearts, and you will scream with painful hearts."

*d*66:3 *dogs … pigs* God did not want his people to offer dogs and pigs as sacrifices.

They did what I said is evil.
　　They chose to do what I did not like."

5 You who obey the LORD's commands,
　　listen to what he says:
"Your brothers hated you.
　　They turned against you because you
　　　followed me.
Your brothers said, 'When the LORD
　　shows his glory,*
then we will rejoice with you.'
　　But they will be punished."

Punishment and a New Nation

⁶Listen! There is a loud noise coming from the city and from the Temple.* It is the LORD punishing his enemies. He is giving them the punishment they deserve.

⁷⁻⁸"A woman does not give birth before she feels the pain. A woman must feel the pain of childbirth before she can see the boy she gives birth to. Who ever heard of such a thing? In the same way, no one ever saw a new world begin in one day. No one has ever heard of a new nation that began in one day. But when Zion feels the pain, she will give birth to her children. ⁹In the same way, I will not cause pain without allowing something new to be born."

The LORD says this: "I promise that if I cause you the pain of birth, I will not stop you from having your new nation." Your God said this.

10 Jerusalem and all her friends, be happy!
　　All of you who were sad for her, be
　　　happy and rejoice with her!
11 Be happy that you will receive mercy like
　　milk coming from her breast.
Jerusalem's "milk" will satisfy you!
　　You will drink it and enjoy her glory.*

12 This is what the LORD says:
"Look, I will give Jerusalem peace that will
　　flow in like a river.
Wealth from all the nations will come
　　flowing into her like a flood.
And like little babies, you will drink that
　　'milk.'
I will hold you in my arms,
　　and bounce you on my knees.
13 I will comfort you like a mother
　　comforting her child.
You will be comforted in Jerusalem."

14 When you see these things, you will be
　　happy.
You will be free and grow like grass.
The LORD's servants will see his power,
　　but his enemies will see his anger.
15 Look, the LORD is coming with fire.
　　His armies are coming with clouds of
　　　dust.
He is angry,
　　and he will punish his enemies with
　　　flames.

16 The LORD will judge the people.
　　Then he will destroy many people with
　　　his sword and with fire.

¹⁷These are the people who wash themselves and make themselves pure so that they can go into their special gardens*ᵃ* to worship their idols. They follow one another into the gardens to eat meat from pigs, rats, and other dirty things. But they will all be destroyed together.

¹⁸"They have evil thoughts and do evil things, so I am coming to punish them. I will gather all nations and all people. Everyone will be gathered together to see my Glory.*ᵇ* ¹⁹I will put a mark on some of these saved people. I will send some of these saved people to the nations of Tarshish,* Libya,*ᶜ* Lud*ᵈ* (the land of archers*), Tubal,*ᵉ* Greece, and all the faraway lands. Those people have never heard my teachings. They have never seen my Glory. So the saved people will tell the nations about my glory. ²⁰And they will bring all your brothers and sisters from those other nations to my holy mountain,*ᶠ* Jerusalem. Your brothers and sisters will ride on horses, mules, camels, and in chariots* and wagons. They will be like the gifts that the Israelites bring on clean plates to the Temple of the LORD. ²¹I will also choose some of these people to be priests and Levites.*" The LORD himself said this.

The New Heavens and the New Earth

²²"I will make a new world—new heavens and a new earth that will last forever. In the same way, your names and your children will always be with me. ²³Everyone will come to worship me on every worship day; they will come every Sabbath* and every first day of the month.*ᵍ*

²⁴"Whoever goes out of the city will see the dead bodies of those who sinned against me. The worms eating those bodies will never die, and the fires burning them will never go out. It will be horrible to anyone who sees it."

---

*ᵃ*66:17 *special gardens* Gardens where people worshiped false gods.
*ᵇ*66:18 *my Glory* See "Glory of the LORD" in the Word List.
*ᶜ*66:19 *Libya* A country in North Africa, west of Egypt.
*ᵈ*66:19 *Lud* This country was probably in the country that is now western Turkey.
*ᵉ*66:19 *Tubal* This country was probably in what is now eastern Turkey.
*ᶠ*66:20 *my holy mountain* This is probably Mount Zion, the mountain Jerusalem is built on.
*ᵍ*66:23 *first day of the month* Literally, "new moon." See "new moon" in the Word List.

Jeremiah

1 ¹These are the messages of Jeremiah, the son of Hilkiah. Jeremiah belonged to the family of priests who lived in the town of Anathoth.ᵃ That town is in the land that belongs to the tribe of Benjamin. ²The Lord began to speak to Jeremiah during the days when Josiah, son of Amon, was king of the nation of Judah.* The Lord began to speak to Jeremiah in the 13th year that Josiahᵇ was king. ³The Lord continued to speak to Jeremiah while Jehoiakim, son of Josiah, was king of Judah. He continued to speak to Jeremiah during the eleven years and five months that Zedekiah, also a son of Josiah, was king of Judah. In the fifth month of Zedekiah's eleventh year as king, the people who lived in Jerusalem were taken away into exile.*

God Calls Jeremiah

⁴The Lord's message came to me:

⁵"Before I made you in your mother's
     womb,
  I knew you.
Before you were born,
  I chose you for a special work.
  I chose you to be a prophet* to the
     nations."

⁶Then I said, "But, Lord God, I don't know how to speak. I am only a boy."
⁷But the Lord said to me,

"Don't say, 'I am only a boy.'
  You must go everywhere I send you
  and say everything I tell you to say.
⁸ Don't be afraid of anyone.
  I am with you, and I will protect you."
  This message is from the Lord.

⁹Then the Lord reached out with his hand and touched my mouth. He said to me,

"Jeremiah, I am putting my words in your
     mouth.
¹⁰ Today I have put you in charge of nations
     and kingdoms.
  You will pull up and tear down.

You will destroy and overthrow.
You will build up and plant."

Two Visions

¹¹The Lord's message came to me: "Jeremiah, what do you see?"
I answered, "I see a stick made from almond wood."
¹²The Lord said to me, "You have seen very well, and I am watchingᶜ to make sure that my message to you comes true."
¹³The Lord's message came to me again: "Jeremiah, what do you see?"
I answered, "I see a pot of boiling water. That pot is tipping over from the north."

¹⁴ The Lord said to me, "Something terrible
     will come from the north.
  It will happen to all the people who live
     in this country.
¹⁵ In a short time I will call all the people in
     the northern kingdoms."
  This is what the Lord said.

"The kings of those countries will come
     and set up their thrones near the gates
     of Jerusalem.
  They will attack the city walls of
     Jerusalem.
  They will attack all the cities in Judah.
¹⁶ And I will announce judgment against my
     people,
  because they are evil and have turned
     away from me.
  They offered sacrifices to other gods
  and worshiped idols* they made with
     their own hands.

¹⁷"As for you, Jeremiah, get ready.
  Stand up and speak to the people.
  Tell them everything that I tell you to say.
  Don't be afraid of the people.
  If you are afraid of them,
  I will give you good reason to be afraid
     of them.
¹⁸ As for me, today I will make you
  like a strong city,
  an iron column,
  a bronze wall.
  You will be able to stand

ᵃ**1:1** *priests ... of Anathoth* These priests probably belonged to the family of the priest Abiathar. Abiathar was a high priest in Jerusalem during the time David was king. He was sent away to Anathoth by King Solomon. See 1 Kings 2:26.
ᵇ**1:2** *the 13th year ... Josiah* That is, 627 B.C.

ᶜ**1:12** *watching* This is a wordplay. *Shaqed* is the Hebrew word for "almond wood," and *shoqed* means "watching."

against everyone in the land,
against the kings of the land of Judah,
the leaders of Judah,
the priests of Judah,
and against the people of the land of
Judah.
19 All those people will fight against you,
but they will not defeat you,
because I am with you,
and I will save you."
This message is from the LORD.

Judah Was Not Faithful

2 ¹The LORD's message came to me: ²"Jeremiah, go and speak to the people of Jerusalem. Say to them:

"'At the time you were a young nation, you
were faithful to me.
You followed me like a young bride.
You followed me through the desert,
through a land that had never been used
for farmland.
3 The people of Israel* were a holy gift to
the LORD.
They were the first fruit to be gathered
by the Lord.
Any people who tried to hurt them were
judged guilty.
Bad things happened to those wicked
people.'"
This message is from the LORD.

4 Family of Jacob,* hear the LORD's message.
Tribes of Israel, listen.

5 This is what the LORD says:
"Do you think that I was not fair to your
ancestors*?
Is that why they turned away from me?
Your ancestors worshiped worthless
idols,*
and they became worthless themselves.
6 Your ancestors did not say,
'The LORD brought us out of Egypt.
He led us through the desert,
through a dry and rocky land.
He led us through a dark and dangerous
land.
No one lives there;
people don't even travel through that
land.
But the Lord led us through that land.
So where is he now?'

7 "I brought you into a good land,
a land filled with many good things.
I did this so that you could eat the fruit
and crops that grow there.
But you only made my land 'dirty.'
I gave that land to you,
but you made it a bad place.

8 "The priests did not ask,
'Where is the LORD?'

The people who know the law did not
want to know me.
The leaders of the people of Israel
turned against me.
The prophets spoke*ᵃ* in the name of the
false god Baal.*
They worshiped worthless idols."

9 The LORD says, "So now I will accuse you
again,
and I will also accuse your
grandchildren.
10 Go across the sea to the Islands of
Kittim.*ᵇ*
Send someone to the land of Kedar.*
Look very carefully.
See if anyone has ever done anything
like this.
11 Has any nation ever stopped worshiping
their old gods
so that they could worship new gods?
No! And their gods are not really gods at
all!
But my people stopped worshiping their
glorious God
and started worshiping idols that are
worth nothing.

12 "Skies, be shocked at what happened!
Shake with great fear!"
This message is from the LORD.
13 "My people have done two evil things.
They turned away from me,
and they dug their own water cisterns.*ᶜ*
I am the source of living water;
those cisterns are broken and cannot
hold water.

14 "Israel is not a slave, is he?
He was not born a slave, was he?
Then why did the enemy carry him away
as a captive?
15 Like a lion the enemy has roared at Israel.
They have destroyed your*ᵈ* land.
Your cities have been burned,
and no one is left in them.
16 People from Memphis and Tahpanhes*ᵉ*
have smashed the top of your head.
17 This trouble is your own fault.
The LORD your God was leading you the
right way,*ᶠ*
but you turned away from him.

---

*ᵃ*2:8 *spoke* Or "prophesied."
*ᵇ*2:10 *Islands of Kittim* The name means the Island
of Cyprus. But the name was often used for the
other islands and coastlands of the Mediterranean
Sea.
*ᶜ*2:13 *they dug ... cisterns* That is, they made false
gods.
*ᵈ*2:15 *your* Hebrew, "his," referring to "Israel," which
here means his people, as in verse 16.
*ᵉ*2:16 *Memphis and Tahpanhes* Two cities in Egypt.
*ᶠ*2:17 *was leading ... way* This is not in the ancient
Greek version.

18 People of Judah,* think about this:
   How did it help you to go to Egypt and
      drink from the Nile River?
   How did it help you to go to Assyria and
      drink from the Euphrates River?
19 You have done wrong,
   and that will only bring punishment to
      you.
   Trouble will come to you,
      and it will teach you a lesson.
   Think about it and understand how bad it
      is to turn away from your God.
   It is wrong not to fear and respect me."
   This message is from Lord GOD
      All-Powerful.
20 "Judah, long ago you broke free from me,
   like an ox that breaks its yoke and the
      ropes that held it.
   You said to me, 'I will not serve you!'
   On every high hill and under every green
      tree,
   you acted like a prostitute.ᵃ
21 Judah, I planted you like a special vine.
   You were all from good seed.
   How did you turn into a different vine
      that grows bad fruit?
22 Even if you wash yourself with lye,
   even if you use much soap,
   I can still see your guilt."
   This message is from the LORD God.
23 "Judah, how can you say to me,
   'I am not guilty because I have not
      worshiped the Baal idols'?
   Think about what you did in the valley.
   Think about what you have done.
   You are like a fast she-camel
      that runs from place to place.
24 You are like a wild donkey that lives in
      the desert.
   At mating time, she sniffs the wind.
   No one can control her when she is in
      heat.
   At mating time, every male that wants
      her will get her.
   She is easy to find.
25 Judah, stop chasing after idols!
   Stop wanting those other gods.
   But you say, 'It is no use! I cannot stop!
   I love those other gods.
   I can't stop chasing them.'

26 "A thief is ashamed
   when people catch him stealing.
   The people of Israel should be ashamed
      too
   and so should their kings and leaders,
      priests and prophets.
27 They say to pieces of wood,
   'You are my father.'
   They say to a rock,
   'You gave birth to me.'
   All these people will be ashamed.

ᵃ2:20 On every ... prostitute This means the people
worshiped their false gods in these places.

They don't look to me for help.
   They have turned their backs to me.
But when the people of Judah get into
   trouble, they say to me,
   'Come and save us!'
28 But where are the idols you made for
      yourselves?
   Let's see if they come and save you
      when you are in trouble!
   People of Judah, you have as many idols
      as you have cities!
29 "Why do you argue with me?
   You have all turned against me."
   This message is from the LORD.
30 "I punished you people of Judah,
   but it did not help.
   You did not come back
      when you were punished.
   With your swords you killed the prophets
      who came to you.
   Like a dangerous lion, you killed the
      prophets."
31 People of this generation, pay attention to
      the LORD's message!

   "Have I been like a desert to the people of
      Israel?
   Have I been like a dark and dangerous
      land to them?
   My people say, 'We are free to go our own
      way.
   We will not come back to you!'
   Why do they say these things?
32 A young woman does not forget her
      jewelry.
   A bride does not forget to wear her
      wedding dress.
   But my people have forgotten me too
      many times to count.

33 "Judah, you have become so good at
      finding lovers.
   Even the worst women could learn
      some evil ways from you.
34 You have blood on your hands!
   It is the blood of poor, innocent people.
   You did not catch them breaking into your
      house.
   You killed them for no reason!
35 But still, you say, 'I am innocent.
   God is not angry with me.'
   So I will also judge you guilty of lying,
      because you say,
   'I have done nothing wrong.'
36 You go from one place to another looking
      for help,
   always changing your mind.
   But Egypt will also disappoint you,
      just as Assyria did.
37 So you will eventually leave Egypt too,
   and you will hide your face in shame.
   You trusted these countries,
      but the LORD rejected them, so they
      cannot help you win.

3

¹"If a man divorces his wife and she goes
and marries someone else,
the first husband cannot take her back.
If he did,ᵃ it would make the land
unclean.*
Judah,* you and all your false gods are like
a prostitute with many lovers!
So why do you think you can come back
to me?"
This message is from the LORD.
²"Look up to the bare hilltops, Judah.
Is there any place where you have not
had sex with your lovers?
You sat by the road waiting for lovers,
like an Arab in the desert.
You made the land 'dirty'
with all the evil sins you did
when you were unfaithful to me.
³ You sinned, so the rain has not come.
There has not been any springtime
rains.
But still you refuse to be ashamed.
The look on your face is like that of a
prostitute who refuses to be ashamed.
⁴ But didn't you just call me 'Father?'
Didn't you say,
'You have been my friend since I was a
child?'
⁵ You also said,
'God will not always be angry with me.
His anger will not continue forever.'

"Judah, you say that,
but you do as much evil as you can."

The Two Bad Sisters: Israel and Judah

⁶The LORD spoke to me during the time
King Josiah was ruling the nation of Judah.*
He said, "Jeremiah, you saw the bad things
Israelᵇ did! You saw how she was unfaithful to
me. She was unfaithful to me with every idol*
on every hill and under every green tree. ⁷I
said to myself, 'Israel will come back to me
after she has finished doing these evil things.'
But she did not come back to me. And Israel's
unfaithful sister, Judah, saw what she did.
⁸Israel was unfaithful, and she knew why I
sent her away. Israel knew that I divorced her
because she committed the sin of adultery.
But that did not make her unfaithful sister
afraid. Judah was not afraid. She also went out
and acted like a prostitute. ⁹Judah did not care
that she was acting like a prostitute. So she
made her country 'dirty.' She committed the
sin of adultery by worshiping idols made out
of stone and wood. ¹⁰Israel's unfaithful sister did not come back to me with her whole

heart. She only pretended that she came back
to me." This message is from the LORD.
¹¹The LORD said to me, "Israel was not faithful to me, but she had a better excuse than
unfaithful Judah. ¹²Jeremiah, look toward the
north and speak this message:

'Come back, you faithless people of Israel.'
This message is from the LORD.
'I will stop frowning at you.
I am full of mercy.'
The LORD says,
'I will not be angry with you forever.
¹³ But you must recognize your sin.
You turned against the LORD your God.
That is your sin.
You worshiped the idols of other nations.
You worshiped them under every green
tree.
You did not obey me.'"
This message is from the LORD.

¹⁴ The LORD says, "You people are unfaithful, but come back to me because I am your
master. I will take one person from every city
and two people from every family and bring
you to Zion.* ¹⁵Then I will give you new rulers who will be faithful to me. They will lead
you with knowledge and understanding. ¹⁶In
those days there will be many of you in the
land." This message is from the LORD.
"At that time people will never again say, 'I
remember the days when we had the Box of
the LORD's Agreement.*' They will not even
think about the Holy Box anymore. They
will not even remember or miss it. They will
never make another Holy Box. ¹⁷At that time
the city of Jerusalem will be called the 'LORD's
Throne.' All nations will come together in the
city of Jerusalem to give honor to the name of
the LORD. They will not follow their stubborn,
evil hearts anymore. ¹⁸In those days the family of Judah will join the family of Israel. They
will come together from a land in the north to
the land I gave to their ancestors.*

¹⁹"I, the LORD, said,
'I want to treat you like my own
children.
I want to give you a pleasant land, a
land more beautiful than any other
nation.'
I thought that you would call me 'Father.'
I thought that you would always follow
me.
²⁰ But you have been like a woman
who is unfaithful to her husband.
Family of Israel, you have been unfaithful
to me!"
This message is from the LORD.
²¹ You can hear crying on the bare hills.
The people of Israel are crying and
praying for mercy.
They became very evil.
They forgot the LORD their God.

ᵃ3:1 *If he did* It was against the Law of Moses for
a man to marry a woman he had divorced if that
woman had become another man's wife. See Deut.
24:1–4.
ᵇ3:6 *Israel* Here, the name Israel means the northern kingdom of Israel. Israel was destroyed by the
Assyrians about 100 years before Jeremiah's time.

22"People of Israel, you are unfaithful to me,
   but come back to me.
Come back and I will forgive[a] you
   for being unfaithful.

"Just say, 'Yes, we will come back,
   because you are the LORD our God.
23 It was foolish to worship idols on the
   hills.
All the loud parties on the mountains
   were wrong.
Surely the salvation of Israel
   comes from the LORD our God.
24 That terrible false god Baal* has eaten
   everything our fathers owned.
This has happened since we were
   children.
That terrible false god took
   our fathers' sheep and cattle
   and their sons and daughters.
25 Let us lie down in our shame.
   Let our shame cover us like a blanket.
We have sinned against the LORD our God.
   We and our fathers have sinned.
We have not obeyed the LORD our God
   from the time we were children.'"

4 ¹This message is from the LORD.
"Israel, if you want to come back,
   then come back to me.
Throw away your idols.*
   Don't wander farther away from me.
2 If you do these things,
   then you will be able to use my name to
   make a promise.
You will be able to say,
   'As the LORD lives.'
You will be able to use these words
   in a truthful, honest, and right way.
If you do these things,
   the nations will be blessed by the Lord.
They will brag about what
   the Lord has done."

³This is what the LORD says to the people of
Judah and to Jerusalem:

"Your fields have not been plowed.
   Plow those fields!
   Don't plant seeds among the thorns.
4 Become the LORD's people.
   Change your hearts.[b]
Men of Judah and people of Jerusalem, if
   you don't change,
   then I will become very angry.
My anger will spread fast like a fire,
   and it will burn you up.
No one will be able to put out that fire
   because of the evil you have done."

Disaster From the North

5"Give this message to the people of Judah:

Tell everyone in the city of Jerusalem:
   'Blow the trumpet all over the country.'
Shout out loud and say,
   'Come together!
Let us all escape to the strong cities for
   protection.'
6 Raise the signal flag toward Zion.*
   Run for your lives! Don't wait!
Do this because I am bringing disaster
   from the north.[c]
I am bringing terrible destruction."
7 A lion has come out of his cave.
   A destroyer of nations has begun to
   march.
He has left his home to destroy your land.
   Your towns will be destroyed.
   There will be no one left to live in them.
8 The LORD is angry with us,
   so put on sackcloth* and cry out loud!
9 The LORD says, "When this happens,
   the king and his officers will lose their
   courage.
The priests will be filled with fear,
   and the prophets will be shocked."

¹⁰Then I, Jeremiah, said, "Lord GOD, you
have tricked the people of Judah and Jerusalem. You said to them, 'You will have
peace.' But now the sword is pointing at their
throats!"

11 At that time this message will be given
   to the people of Judah and Jerusalem:
"A hot wind blows from the bare hills.
   It comes from the desert to my people.
It is not like the gentle wind that is used
   to separate the grain from the chaff.*
12 It is a stronger wind than that,
   and it comes from me.
Now I will announce my judgment against
   the people of Judah."
13 Look! The enemy rises up like a cloud.
   His chariots* look like a windstorm.
His horses are faster than eagles.
It will be very bad for us!
   We are ruined!

14 People of Jerusalem, wash the evil from
   your hearts.
Make your hearts pure so that you can be
   saved.
   Don't continue making evil plans.
15 Listen! The voice of a messenger
   from the land of Dan[d] is speaking.

---

[a]3:22 *forgive* Literally, "heal."
[b]4:4 *Change your hearts* Literally, "Be circumcised
to the LORD. Cut away the foreskin of your hearts."
See "circumcise" in the Word List. Jeremiah is saying that real circumcision must be from inside a
person's heart (mind).
[c]4:6 *north* The Babylonian army came from this
direction to attack Judah. Armies from countries
north and east of Israel often came this way to
attack Judah and Israel.
[d]4:15 *land of Dan* The people from the tribe of Dan
lived near the border in the northern part of Israel.
They would be the first to be attacked by an enemy
from the north.

Someone is bringing bad news
   from the hill country of Ephraim[a]:
16"Report it to this nation.[b]
   Spread the news to the people in
      Jerusalem.
   Enemies are coming from a faraway
      country.
   They are shouting words of war
      against the cities of Judah.
17 The enemy has surrounded Jerusalem
      like men guarding a field.
   Judah, you turned against me,
      so the enemy is coming against you."
   This message is from the LORD.

18"The way you lived and the things you did
      brought this trouble to you.
   It is your evil that made your life so hard.
   Your evil life brought the pain
      that hurts deep in your heart."

Jeremiah's Cry

19 My sadness and worry is making my
      stomach hurt.
   I am bent over in pain.
   I am so afraid.
   My heart is pounding inside me.
   I cannot keep quiet, because I have heard
      the trumpet blow.
   The trumpet is calling the army to war.
20 Disaster follows disaster.
   The whole country is destroyed!
   Suddenly my tents are destroyed.
   My curtains are torn down.
21 LORD, how long must I see the war flags?
   How long must I hear the war trumpets?

22 The Lord said, "My people are foolish.
   They don't know me.
   They are stupid children.
   They don't understand.
   They are skillful at doing evil,
      but they don't know how to do good."

Disaster Is Coming

23 I looked at the earth.
   It was empty;
      there was nothing on it.
   I looked at the sky,
      and its light was gone.[c]
24 I looked at the mountains,
      and they were shaking.
   All the hills were trembling.
25 I looked, but there were no people.
   All the birds of the sky had flown away.
26 I looked, and the good land had become a
      desert.

All the cities in that land were
      destroyed by the LORD and his great
      anger.

27 This is what the LORD says:
   "The whole country will be ruined,
      but I will not completely destroy the
      land.
28 So the people in the land will cry for the
      dead.
   The sky will grow dark.
   I have spoken and will not change.
   I have made a decision, and I will not
      change my mind."

29 The people of Judah* will hear the sound
      of the horse soldiers and the archers,*
      and the people will run away!
   Some of them will hide in caves;[d]
      some will hide in the bushes;
      some will climb up into the rocks.
   All the cities of Judah will be empty.
   No one will live in them.

30 Judah, you have been destroyed.
   So what are you doing now?
   Why are you putting on your best red
      dress?
   Why are you putting on your gold
      jewelry?
   Why are you putting on your eye makeup?
   You make yourself beautiful,
      but it is a waste of time.
   Your lovers hate you.
   They are trying to kill you.
31 I hear a cry like a woman in labor,
      a scream like a woman giving birth to
      her first baby.
   It is the cry of daughter Zion.[e]
   She is lifting her hands in prayer, saying,
   "Oh! I am about to faint!
   Murderers are all around me!"

The Evil of the People of Judah

5 ¹The Lord says, "Walk the streets of Jerusalem. Look around and think about these
things. Search the public squares of the city.
See if you can find one good person, one who
does honest things and who searches for the
truth. If you find one good person, I will forgive Jerusalem. ²The people make promises
and say, 'As the LORD lives.' But they don't
really mean it!"

3 LORD, I know that you want people
      to be loyal to you.
   You hit the people of Judah,*
      but they did not feel any pain.
   You destroyed them,
      but they refused to learn their lesson.
   They became very stubborn.

---

[a]4:15 *hill country of Ephraim* This was the central
part of the land that had been the northern kingdom of Israel.
[b]4:16 *"Report ... nation"* The Hebrew text here is
hard to understand.
[c]4:23 *the earth ... gone* Jeremiah is comparing his
country to the time before people were put on the
earth. See Gen. 1:1.

[d]4:29 *hide in caves* This is from the ancient Greek
version.
[e]4:31 *daughter Zion* Another name for Jerusalem.
See "Zion" in the Word List.

They refused to be sorry for the bad
   things they did.

4 But I said to myself,
"It must be only the poor who are so
   foolish.
They have not learned the way of the
   LORD.
They don't know the teachings of their
   God.
5 So I will go to the leaders of Judah.
   I will talk to them.
Surely the leaders know the way of the
   LORD,
   Surely they know the law of their God."
But the leaders had all joined together
   to break away from serving the LORD.
6 They turned against God,
   so a lion from the forest will attack
      them.
   A wolf from the desert will kill them.
A leopard is hiding near their cities.
   It will tear to pieces anyone who comes
      out of the city.
That's because the people of Judah have
   sinned again and again.
They have wandered away from the
   LORD many times.

7 The Lord said, "Judah, give me one good
   reason why I should forgive you.
   Your children have abandoned me.
   They made promises to idols* that are
      not really gods!
I gave your children everything they
   needed,
   but they were still unfaithful to me!
   They spent their time with prostitutes.
8 They are like horses that have had plenty
   to eat and are ready to mate.
   They are like a horse that is calling its
      neighbor's wife.
9 Should I punish the people of Judah for
   doing these things?"
   This message is from the LORD.
"You know I should punish a nation such
   as this.
   I should give it the punishment it
      deserves.

10 "Go along the rows of Judah's grapevines.
   Cut down the vines. (But don't
      completely destroy them.)
   Cut off all their branches, because they
      don't belong to the LORD.
11 The family of Israel and the family of
      Judah
   have been unfaithful to me in every
      way."
   This message is from the LORD.

12 "Those people lied about the LORD.
   They said, 'He will not do anything to us.
   Nothing bad will happen to us.
   We will never see an army attack us.

We will never starve.'
13 The prophets* are only empty wind.^{a}
   The word of God is not in them.^{b}
   Bad things will happen to them."

14 The LORD God All-Powerful said these
      things:
"The people said I would not punish them.
   So, Jeremiah, the words I give you will be
      like fire,
   and these people will be like wood.
   That fire will burn them up completely."
15 Family of Israel, this message is from the
      LORD.
"I will soon bring a nation from far away to
      attack you.
   It is an old nation;
      it is an ancient nation.
   The people of that nation speak a
      language that you do not know.
   You cannot understand what they say.
16 Their arrow bags are like open graves.
   All their men are strong soldiers.
17 They will eat all the crops that you
      gathered.
   They will eat all your food.
   They will destroy your sons and
      daughters.
   They will eat your flocks and your herds.
      They will eat your grapes and your figs.
   They will destroy your strong cities with
      their swords.
   They will destroy the strong cities that
      you trust in.

18 This message is from the LORD:
"But, Judah, when these terrible days
      come,
   I will not fully destroy you.
19 The people of Judah will ask you,
   'Jeremiah, why has the LORD our God
      done this bad thing to us?'
   Give them this answer:
   'You people of Judah have left the LORD,
      and you have served foreign idols in
         your own land.
   You did these things,
      so now you will serve foreigners in a
         land that does not belong to you.'

20 "Tell this message to the family of Jacob,
      and tell it in the nation of Judah.
21 Hear this message,
      you foolish people who have no sense.
   You have eyes, but you don't see!
   You have ears, but you don't listen!
22 Surely you are afraid of me."
   This message is from the LORD.
"You should shake with fear in front of me.
   I am the one who made the sandy
      shores to hold back the sea.

---

^{a}5:13 *wind* This is a wordplay. The Hebrew word for
wind is like the word for spirit.
^{b}5:13 *The word ... them* Literally, "And the 'He said'
is not in them."

I made it that way to keep the water in
its place forever.
The waves may pound the beach, but
they will not destroy it.
The waves may roar as they come in,
but they cannot go beyond the beach.
23 But the people of Judah are stubborn.
They are always planning ways to turn
against me.
They turned away from me and left me.
24 The people of Judah never say to
themselves,
'Let's fear and respect the LORD our God.
He gives us autumn and spring rains at
just the right time.
He makes sure that we have the harvest
at just the right time.'
25 People of Judah, you have done wrong.
So the rains and the harvest have not
come.
Your sins have kept you from enjoying
the good things from the LORD.
26 There are evil men among my people.
They are like men who make nets for
catching birds.*a*
They set their traps,
but they catch people instead of birds.
27 Their houses are full of lies,
like a cage full of birds.
Their lies made them rich and powerful.
28 They have grown big and fat ₁from the
evil they have done₁.
There is no end to the evil they do.
They will not plead the case of children
who have no parents.
They will not help these orphans.
They will not let the poor be judged
fairly.
29 Should I punish the people of Judah for
doing these things?"
This message is from the LORD.
"You know I should punish a nation such
as this.
I should give it the punishment it
deserves.

30 "A terrible and shocking thing
has happened in the land of Judah.
31 The prophets tell lies.
The priests will not do what they were
chosen to do,*b*
and my people love it this way!
But what will you people do
when your punishment comes?

The Enemy Surrounds Jerusalem

6 ¹ "Run for your lives, people of Benjamin!
Run away from the city of Jerusalem!
Blow the war trumpet in the city of
Tekoa!

Put up the warning flag in the city of
Beth Hakkerem!
Do these things because disaster is
coming from the north.*c*
Terrible destruction is coming to you.
2 Jerusalem,*d* you are like a beautiful
meadow.*e*
But I will destroy you!
3 Enemy shepherds will surround you
with all their flocks.
They will set up their tents all around
you,
and each one will let his sheep eat the
grass.

4 "Get ready to fight against Jerusalem.
Get up! We will attack the city at noon.
But it is already getting late.
The evening shadows are growing long.
5 So get up! We will attack the city at night!
Let's destroy the strong walls that are
around Jerusalem."

6 This is what the LORD All-Powerful says:
"Cut down the trees around Jerusalem,
and build a siege mound*f* against it.
This city should be punished
because inside there is no justice—only
slavery.
7 As a well keeps its water fresh,
so Jerusalem keeps its wickedness fresh.
I hear about the robbing and violence in
this city all the time.
I see nothing but pain and sickness
there all the time.
8 Listen to this warning, Jerusalem,
or I will turn my back on you.
I will make your land an empty desert.
No one will be able to live there."

9 This is what the LORD All-Powerful says:
"Gather*g* the people of Israel* who
were left on their land.
Gather them the way you would gather
the last grapes on a grapevine.
Check each vine, like the workers check
each vine when they pick the grapes."
10 Who can I speak to?
Who can I warn?
Who will listen to me?

c **6:1** *north* The Babylonian army came from this
direction to attack Judah. Armies from countries
north and east of Israel often came this way to
attack Judah and Israel.
d **6:2** *Jerusalem* Literally, "daughter Zion." See "Zion"
in the Word List.
e **6:2** *you are like a beautiful meadow* The Hebrew
text here is hard to understand.
f **6:6** *siege mound* A large pile of dirt and rock that
an army put against the wall of a city they were
attacking. This made it easier for the enemy soldiers
to climb over the wall into the city.
g **6:9** *Gather* Or "glean." There was a law that a farmer
must leave some grain in his field during harvest,
so that poor people and travelers could find something to eat. See Lev. 19:9; 23:22.

a **5:26** *men … birds* The Hebrew text here is hard to
understand.
b **5:31** *priests … were chosen to do* The Hebrew text
here is hard to understand.

The people of Israel have closed their
  ears,
    so they cannot hear my warnings.
  They don't like the LORD's teachings.
    They don't want to hear his message.
¹¹ But I am full of the LORD's anger,
    and I am tired of holding it in!
  The Lord said, "Pour out my anger on the
    children playing in the streets
    and on the young soldiers gathered
      there as well.
  A man and his wife will both be captured
    as well as all the old people.
¹² Their houses will be given to others.
    Their fields and their wives will be
      given to other people.
  I will raise my hand and punish the
    people of Judah.*"
  This message is from the LORD.

¹³"All the people of Israel want more and
    more money.
    All of them, from the least important to
      the most important, are like that.
    Even the prophets* and priests tell lies.
¹⁴ They should bandage the wounds my
    people have suffered,
    but they treat their wounds like small
      scratches.
  They say, 'It's all right, everything is all
    right.'
    But it is not all right!
¹⁵ They should be ashamed of the evil things
    they do,
    but they are not ashamed at all.
  They don't know enough to be
    embarrassed by their sins.
  So they will be punished with everyone
    else.
  They will be thrown to the ground
    when I punish the people."
  This is what the LORD said.

¹⁶ This is what the LORD says:
  "Stand at the crossroads and look.
    Ask where the old road is.
    Ask where the good road is, and walk
      on that road.
  If you do, you will find rest for yourselves.
    But you people have said, 'We will not
      walk on the good road.'
¹⁷ I chose watchmen to watch over you.
    I told them, 'Listen for the sound of the
      war trumpet.'
    But they said, 'We will not listen!'
¹⁸ So listen, all you nations,
    and pay attention, you people in those
      countries.ᵃ
¹⁹ Hear this, people of the earth:
  I am going to bring disaster to the
    people of Judah
    because of all the evil they planned,

and because they ignored my messages.
    They refused to obey my law.

²⁰"Why do you bring me incense* from the
    country of Shebaᵇ?
  Why do you bring me sweet-smelling
    cane from a faraway country?
  Your burnt offerings* don't make me
    happy.
    Your sacrifices don't please me."

²¹ So this is what the LORD says:
  "I will give the people of Judah problems.
    They will be like stones that make
      people fall.
  Fathers and sons will stumble over them.
    Friends and neighbors will die."

²² This is what the LORD says:
  "An army is coming from the north.ᶜ
    A great nation is coming from faraway
      places on earth.
²³ The soldiers carry bows and spears.
    They are cruel; they have no mercy.
  They are so powerful.
    They sound like the roaring ocean as
      they ride their horses.
  That army is coming, ready for battle.
    It is coming to attack you, Jerusalem.ᵈ"
²⁴ We have heard the news about that army,
    and we are paralyzed with fear.
  We feel trapped by our troubles,
    in pain like a woman giving birth.
²⁵ Don't go out into the fields.
    Don't go on the roads
  because the enemy has swords,
    and there is danger everywhere.
²⁶ My people, put on sackcloth*
    and roll in the ashes.ᵉ
  Cry loudly for the dead.
    Cry as if you lost an only son.
  Do this because the destroyer
    will come against us very quickly.

²⁷"Jeremiah, I want you to be
    like a worker who tests metals.
  You will test my people
    and watch how they live.
²⁸ My people have turned against me,
    and they are very stubborn.
  They say bad things about people.
    They are like bronze and iron
      that are covered with rust and tarnish.

ᵇ**6:20** *Sheba* A land south of Israel, located where
part of Saudi Arabia is today. Sheba controlled the
spice trade in the time of Jeremiah.
ᶜ**6:22** *north* The Babylonian army came from this
direction to attack Judah. Armies from countries
north and east of Israel often came this way to
attack Judah and Israel.
ᵈ**6:23** *Jerusalem* Literally, "daughter Zion." See "Zion"
in the Word List.
ᵉ**6:26** *roll in the ashes* This is one way people
showed that they were sad or crying for a dead
person.

ᵃ**6:18** *pay … countries* The Hebrew text here is hard
to understand.

29 ⌜They are like a worker who tried to make
        silver pure.⌟
   The bellows*a* blew strongly, and the fire
        became hotter,
      but only lead came from the fire.*b*
   The worker wasted his time
        trying to make that silver pure.
   In the same way the evil was not removed
        from my people.
30 My people will be called 'Rejected Silver.'
   They will be given that name
      because the LORD did not accept them."

Jeremiah's Temple Sermon

7 ¹This is the LORD's message to Jeremiah:
²"Jeremiah, stand at the gate of the LORD's
house. Teach this message at the gate:

"'Hear the message from the LORD, all you
people of the nation of Judah.* All you who
come through these gates to worship the
LORD, hear this message. ³The LORD is the
God of the people of Israel.* This is what the
LORD All-Powerful says: Change your lives
and do good things. If you do this, I will let
you live in this place.*c* ⁴Don't trust the lies
that some people say. They say, "This is the
Temple* of the LORD, the Temple of the LORD,
the Temple of the LORD!*d*" ⁵If you change your
lives and do good things, I will let you live in
this place. You must be fair to each other. ⁶You
must be fair to strangers. You must help widows and orphans. Don't kill innocent people!
And don't follow other gods, because they
will only ruin your lives. ⁷If you obey me, I
will let you live in this place. I gave this land
to your ancestors* for them to keep forever.

⁸"'But you are trusting lies that are worthless. ⁹Will you steal and murder? Will you
commit adultery*? Will you falsely accuse
other people? Will you worship the false god
Baal* and follow other gods that you have not
known? ¹⁰If you commit these sins, do you
think that you can stand before me in this
house that is called by my name? Do you
think you can stand before me and say, "We
are safe," just so you can do all these terrible
things? ¹¹This Temple is called by my name.
Is this Temple nothing more to you than a
hideout for robbers? I have been watching
you.'" This message is from the LORD.

¹²"'You people of Judah, go now to the
town of Shiloh. Go to the place where I first

---

*a*6:29 **bellows** A tool for blowing air on a fire to
make the fire hotter.

*b*6:29 **lead came from the fire** Workers melted metals like silver to make the metals pure. Lead was the
first metal to melt, so the workers poured the lead
out, leaving the other metal pure. Here, Jeremiah is
saying the people are all bad—they are all lead and
no silver!

*c*7:3 **I will ... place** This can also mean "I will live
with you."

*d*7:4 **This is ... LORD** Many people in Jerusalem
thought the Lord would always protect the city
where his Temple was, so it didn't matter how evil
they were.

---

made a house for my name. The people of
Israel also did evil things. Go and see what I
did to that place because of the evil they did.*e*
¹³You people of Israel were doing all these
evil things. This message is from the LORD! I
spoke to you again and again, but you refused
to listen to me. I called to you, but you did not
answer. ¹⁴So I will destroy the house called
by my name in Jerusalem. I will destroy that
Temple as I destroyed Shiloh. And that house
in Jerusalem that is called by my name is the
Temple you trust in. I gave that place to you
and to your ancestors. ¹⁵I will throw you away
from me just as I threw away all your brothers
from Ephraim.*'

¹⁶"As for you, Jeremiah, don't pray for
these people of Judah. Don't beg for them or
pray for them. Don't beg me to help them.
I will not listen to your prayer for them. ¹⁷I
know you see what they are doing in the
towns of Judah. You can see what they are
doing in the streets of the city of Jerusalem.
¹⁸This is what the people of Judah are doing:
The children gather wood. The fathers use
the wood to make a fire. The women make
the dough and then make cakes of bread to
offer to the Queen of Heaven.* The people
of Judah pour out drink offerings to worship
other gods. They do this to make me angry.
¹⁹But I am not the one they are really hurting." This message is from the LORD. "They
are only hurting themselves. They are bringing shame on themselves."

²⁰So this is what the LORD says: "I will
show my anger against this place. I will punish people and animals. I will punish the trees
in the field and the crops that grow in the
ground. My anger will be like a hot fire—no
one will be able to stop it."

Obedience Is Better Than Sacrifice

²¹This is what the LORD All-Powerful, the
God of Israel,* says: "Go and offer as many
burnt offerings* and sacrifices as you want.
Eat the meat of those sacrifices yourselves. ²²I
brought your ancestors* out of Egypt. I spoke
to them, but I did not give them any commands about burnt offerings and sacrifices. ²³I
only gave them this command: 'Obey me and
I will be your God, and you will be my people.
Do all that I command, and good things will
happen to you.'

²⁴"But your ancestors did not listen to me.
They did not pay attention to me. They were
stubborn and did what they wanted to do.
They did not become good. They became even
more evil—they went backward, not forward.
²⁵From the day that your ancestors left Egypt
to this day, I have sent my servants to you.
My servants are the prophets.* I sent them to
you again and again. ²⁶But your ancestors did

---

*e*7:12 **Go ... they did** Shiloh was probably destroyed
by the Philistines in the time of Eli and Samuel. See
1 Sam. 4.

not listen to me. They did not pay attention to me. They were very stubborn and did evil even worse than their fathers did.

27"Jeremiah, you will tell these things to the people of Judah.* But they will not listen to you. You will call to them, but they will not answer you. 28So you must tell them these things: 'This is the nation that did not obey the LORD its God. These people did not listen to God's teachings. They don't know the true teachings.'

· The Valley of Slaughter

29"Jeremiah, cut off your hair and throw it away.a Go up to the bare hilltop and cry, because the LORD has rejected this generation of people. He has turned his back on these people. And in anger he will punish them. 30Do this because I have seen the people of Judah* doing evil things." This message is from the LORD. "They have set up their idols,* and I hate those idols. They have set up idols in the Temple* that is called by my name. They have made my house 'dirty'! 31The people of Judah built the high places* of Topheth in the Valley of Ben Hinnom where they killed their own sons and daughters and burned them as sacrifices. This is something I never commanded. Something like this never even entered my mind! 32So I warn you. The days are coming," says the LORD, "when people will not call this place Topheth or the Valley of Ben Hinnom anymore. No, they will call it the Valley of Slaughter. They will give it this name because they will bury the dead people in Topheth until there is no more room to bury anyone else. 33Then the bodies of the dead people will become food for the birds of the sky. Wild animals will eat the bodies of those people. There will be no one left alive to chase the birds or animals away. 34I will bring an end to the sounds of joy and happiness in the towns of Judah and in the streets of Jerusalem. There will be no more sounds of the bride and bridegroom in Judah or Jerusalem. The land will become an empty desert."

8 1This message is from the LORD: "At that time men will take the bones of the kings and important rulers of Judah from their tombs.* They will take the bones of the priests and prophets* from their tombs. They will take the bones of all the people of Jerusalem from their tombs. 2They will spread the bones on the ground under the sun, the moon, and the stars. The people of Jerusalem love to worship the sun, the moon, and the stars. No one will gather the bones and bury them again. So the bones of those people will be like dung thrown on the ground.

3"I will force the people of Judah to leave their homes and their land. They will be taken away to foreign lands. Some of the people of Judah who were not killed in the war will wish that they had been killed." This message is from the LORD.

Sin and Punishment

4"Jeremiah, say this to the people of Judah*:

'This is what the LORD says:
You know if a man falls down,
    he gets up again.
And if a man goes the wrong way,
    he turns around and comes back.
5   The people of Judah went the wrong way.
    But why do the people of Jerusalem
        continue going the wrong way?
    They believe their own lies.
    They refuse to turn around and come
        back.
6   I have listened to them very carefully,
        but they don't say what is right.
    They are not sorry for their sins.
    They don't think about the evil they
        have done.
    They do things without thinking.
    They are like horses running into a
        battle.
7   Even the birds in the sky
        know the right time to do things.
    The storks, doves, swifts, and thrushes
        know when it is time to fly to a new
        home.
    But my people don't know what the LORD
        wants them to do.

8   "'You keep saying, "We have the LORD's
        teachings. So we are wise!"
    But this is not true, because the scribes*
        have lied with their pens.
9   These "wise people" refused to listen to
        the LORD's teachings.
    So they are not really wise at all.
    These "wise people" were trapped.
    They became shocked and ashamed.
10 So I will give their wives to other men.
    I will give their fields to new owners.
    All the people of Israel* want more and
        more money.
    All of them, from the least important to
        the most important, are like that.
    Even the prophets* and priests tell lies.
11 They should bandage the wounds my
        people have suffered,
    but they treat their wounds like small
        scratches.
    They say, "It's all right, everything is all
        right."
    But it is not all right!
12 They should be ashamed of the evil things
        they do,
    but they are not ashamed at all.
    They don't know enough to be
        embarrassed by their sins.
    So they will be punished with everyone
        else.

---

a7:29 cut ... away This showed that Jeremiah was sad.

They will be thrown to the ground
　　when I punish the people."
This is what the LORD said.

13"'I will take away their fruit and crops
　　so that there will be no harvest, says the
　　LORD.
There will be no grapes on the vine and
　　no figs on the fig tree.
Even the leaves will become dry and
　　die.
I will take away the things I gave
　　them.'"[a]

14"They will say, 'Why are we just sitting
　　here?
Come, let's run to the strong cities.
If the LORD our God is going to make us
　　die, then let's die there.
We have sinned against the LORD,
　　so God gave us poisoned water to drink.
15 We hoped to have peace,
　　but nothing good has come.
We hoped that he would forgive us,
　　but only disaster has come.
16 From the land of the tribe of Dan,
　　we hear the snorting[b] of the enemy's
　　horses.
The ground shakes from the pounding
　　of their hooves.
They have come to destroy the land
　　and everything in it.
They have come to destroy the city
　　and all the people who live there.'"

17"People of Judah, I am sending poisonous
　　snakes[c] to attack you.
These snakes cannot be controlled.
They will bite you."
This message is from the LORD.

18 God, I am very sad and afraid.
19 Listen to my people.
　　Everywhere in this country, people are
　　crying for help.
They say, "Is the LORD still at Zion*?
　　Is Zion's King still there?"

But God says, "The people of Judah
　　worshiped their worthless foreign
　　idols.*
That made me very angry!
　　Why did they do that?"
20 And the people say,
　　"Harvest time is over.
Summer is gone, and still we have not
　　been saved."

21 My people are hurt, so I am hurt.
　　I am too sad to speak.
22 Surely there is some medicine in Gilead.
　　Surely there is a doctor in Gilead.
So why are the wounds of my people not
　　healed?

9 1If my head were filled with water,
　　and if my eyes were a fountain of
　　tears,
I would cry day and night for my people
　　who have been destroyed.

2 If only I had a place in the desert—
　　a house where travelers spend the
　　night—
so I could leave my people.
I could go away from them,
　　because they are all unfaithful to God.
They have all turned against him.

3"They use their tongues like a bow;
　　lies fly from their mouths like arrows.
Lies, not truth, have grown strong in this
　　land.
They go from one sin to another.
　　They don't know me."
This is what the LORD said.

4"Watch your neighbors!
　　Don't trust your own brothers,
because every brother is a cheat.
　　Every neighbor talks behind your back.
5 Everyone lies to their neighbor.
　　No one speaks the truth.
The people of Judah* have taught
　　their tongues to lie.
They sinned until they were too tired
　　to come back.
6 One bad thing followed another,
　　and lies followed lies.
The people refused to know me."
This is what the LORD said.

7 So the LORD All-Powerful says,
"A worker heats metal in a fire to test it
　　and see if it is pure.
I will test the people of Judah like that.
　　I have no other choice.
My people have sinned.
8 The people of Judah have tongues as
　　sharp as arrows.
Their mouths speak lies.
They all speak kindly to their neighbors,
　　but they are secretly planning ways to
　　attack them.
9 Should I punish the people of Judah for
　　doing these things?"
This message is from the LORD.
"You know I should punish a nation such
　　as this.
I should give it the punishment it
　　deserves."

10 I, Jeremiah, will cry for the mountains.
　　I will sing a funeral song for the empty

---

[a]8:13 *I will take away ... gave them* The Hebrew
text here is hard to understand.
[b]8:16 *snorting* The sound caused by forcing breath
very hard through the nose.
[c]8:17 *poisonous snakes* This probably means one of
Judah's enemies.

fields,
because all the animals were taken
away.
No one travels there now.
The sounds of cattle cannot be heard.
The birds have flown away,
and the animals are gone.

11 The Lord says,[a] "I will make the city of
Jerusalem a pile of garbage.
It will be a home for jackals.*
I will destroy the cities in the land of
Judah,
so no one will live there."

12 Is there a man who is wise enough to
understand these things?
Is there someone who has been taught
by the LORD?
Can anyone explain his message?
Why was the land ruined?
Why was it made like an empty desert
where no one goes?

13 The LORD answered,
"It is because the people of Judah stopped
following my teachings.
I gave them my teachings,
but they refused to listen to me.
They did not follow my teachings.
14 The people of Judah lived their own way.
They were stubborn.
They followed the false god Baal.*
Their fathers taught them to follow
those false gods."

15 So the LORD All-Powerful, the God of
Israel, says,
"I will soon make the people of Judah
eat bitter food and drink poisoned
water.
16 I will scatter the people of Judah
throughout other nations.
They will live in strange nations
that they and their fathers never knew
about.
I will send men with swords.
They will kill the people of Judah.
They will kill them until all the people
are gone."

17 This is what the LORD All-Powerful says:
"Now think about these things!
Call for the women who get paid to cry
at funerals.
Send for the people who are good at
that job.
18 The people say,
'Let those women come quickly and cry
for us.
Then our eyes will fill with tears

that flow over our eyelids like streams of
water.'

19"The sound of loud crying is heard from
Zion:
'We are really ruined!
We are so ashamed!
We must leave our land, because our
houses have been destroyed.
Now our houses are only piles of
rock.'"

20 Now, women of Judah, listen to the
message from the LORD.
Listen to the words from his mouth.
Teach your daughters how to cry loudly.
Each of them must learn to sing this
funeral song:
21"Death has climbed in through our
windows
and has come into our palaces.
Death has come to our children who play
in the streets
and to the young men who meet in the
public places."

22 This is what you should say:
"The LORD says, 'Dead bodies will lie in
the fields like dung.
Their bodies will lie on the ground like
grain a farmer has cut.
But there will be no one to gather
them.'"

23 This is what the LORD says:
"The wise must not brag
about their wisdom.
The strong men must not brag
about their strength.
The rich must not brag
about their money.
24 But if someone wants to brag, then let
them brag about this:
Let them brag that they learned to know
me.
Let them brag that they understand that I
am the LORD,
that I am kind and fair,
and that I do good things on earth.
I love this kind of bragging."
This message is from the LORD.

25This is what the LORD says: "The time is
coming when I will punish all those who are
circumcised* only in the body. 26I am talking
about the people of the nations of Egypt, Judah,
Edom, Ammon, Moab, and all those who live
in the desert. The circumcision they do is not
the kind the Lord wants. But the people of
Israel are not really circumcised either. They
are not circumcised in their hearts."

The Lord and the Idols

10 1Family of Israel,* listen to the LORD!
2This is what he says:

"Don't live like people from other nations.
Don't be afraid of special signs in the
sky.*a*
The other nations are afraid of what they
see in the sky.
But you must not be afraid of them.
3 The customs of other people are worth
nothing.
Their idols* are nothing but wood from
the forest.
Their idols are made by workers with
their chisels.*b*
4 They make their idols beautiful with
silver and gold.
They use hammers and nails to fasten
their idols down
so that they will not fall over.
5 The idols of the other nations are like
a scarecrow in a cucumber field.
They cannot walk.
They cannot talk, and the people must
carry them.
So don't be afraid of their idols.
They cannot hurt you.
And they cannot help you either."

6 Lord, there is no one like you.
You are great!
Your name is great and powerful!
7 Everyone should respect you, King of all
the nations.
You deserve their respect.
There are many wise men among the
nations,
but not one of them is as wise as you.

8 All the people of the other nations are
stupid and foolish.
Their teachings come from worthless
wooden statues.
9 They use silver from the city of Tarshish
and gold from the city of Uphaz and
make their statues.
Carpenters and metalworkers make the
idols.
They put blue and purple clothes on
them.
"Wise men" make these "gods."
10 But the Lord is the only true God.
He is the only God who is alive.
He is the King who rules forever.
The earth shakes when he is angry.
The people of the nations cannot stop
his anger.

11 The Lord says, "Tell them this message:
'These false gods did not make heaven
and earth.

They will be destroyed and disappear
from heaven and earth.'"*c*

12 God is the one who used his power and
made the earth.
He used his wisdom and built the
world.
With his understanding
he stretched the sky over the earth.
13 God causes the loud thunder,
and he causes great floods of water to
fall from the sky.
He makes clouds rise in the sky every
place on earth.
He sends lightning with the rain.
He brings out the wind from his
storehouses.

14 People are so stupid!
Metalworkers are fooled by the idols
that they themselves made.
These statues are nothing but lies.
They are stupid.*d*
15 These idols are worth nothing.
They are something to make fun of.
In the time of judgment
they will be destroyed.
16 But Jacob's God*e* is not like the idols.
He made everything,
and Israel is the family that God chose
to be his own people.
His name is Lord All-Powerful.

Destruction Is Coming

17 Get everything you own and prepare to
leave.
People of Judah,* you are trapped in the
city,
and the enemy is all around it.
18 This is what the Lord says:
"This time, I will throw the people of
Judah out of this country.
I will bring pain and trouble to them.
I will do this so that they will learn their
lesson."*f*

19 I am hurt badly.
I am injured and I cannot be healed.
But I told myself, "This is my sickness;
I must suffer through it."
20 My tent is ruined.
All its ropes are broken.

*c*10:11 *Tell this message ... earth* This part was written in Aramaic, not Hebrew. This was the language
people used often when writing to people in
other countries. It was also the language spoken in
Babylon.
*d*10:14 *They are stupid* Literally, "They have no
spirit." This might also mean "They are not alive."
*e*10:16 *Jacob's God* Literally, "Jacob's share." This
means that God and Jacob (the people of Israel) had
a special relationship—God belonged to Israel, and
Israel belonged to God."
*f*10:18 *they will learn their lesson* The Hebrew text
here is hard to understand.

*a*10:2 *special signs in the sky* People believed that
such things as comets, meteors, or eclipses of the
sun and moon could be used to learn what was
going to happen in the future.
*b*10:3 *chisels* Sharp tools used to carve wood or
stone.

My children left me.
They are gone.
No one is left to put up my tent.
No one is left to fix a shelter for me.
²¹ The shepherds are stupid.
They don't try to find the LORD.
They are not wise,
so their flocks are scattered and lost.
²² Listen! A loud noise!
The noise is coming from the north.^a
It will destroy the cities of Judah.
Judah will become an empty desert.
It will be a home for jackals.*

²³ LORD, I know people don't really know
how to live right.
²⁴ LORD, correct us!
But be fair!
Don't punish us in anger!
²⁵ If you are angry,
then punish the other nations.
They don't know or respect you.
They don't worship you.
Those nations destroyed Jacob's family.
They destroyed Israel completely.
They destroyed Israel's homeland.

The Agreement Is Broken

11 ¹This is the message from the LORD:
²"Jeremiah, listen to the words of this
agreement and tell them to the people living
in Jerusalem and the rest of Judah.* ³Tell them
that this is what the LORD, the God of Israel,*
says: 'Bad things will happen to anyone who
does not obey this agreement. ⁴I am talking
about the agreement I made with your ancestors* when I brought them out of that furnace^b
called Egypt.' At that time I told them, 'Listen
to me and obey all the commands I give you.
Then you will be my people and I will be your
God.'

⁵"I did this to keep the promise that I had
made to your ancestors. I promised to give
them a very fertile land—a land flowing with
milk and honey. And you are living in that
country today."

I answered, "Amen,* LORD."

⁶The LORD said to me, "Jeremiah, tell this
message in the towns of Judah and in the
streets of Jerusalem: 'Listen to the words of
this agreement, and then obey these laws. ⁷I
gave a warning to your ancestors at the time I
brought them out of the land of Egypt. I have
warned them again and again to this day. I
told them to obey me. ⁸But your ancestors
did not listen to me. They were stubborn and
did what their own evil hearts wanted. The
agreement says that bad things will happen to

them if they don't obey. So I made all the bad
things happen to them. I commanded them to
obey the agreement, but they did not.'"

⁹The LORD said to me, "Jeremiah, I know
that the people of Judah and the people living
in Jerusalem have made secret plans. ¹⁰They
are committing the same sins that their ancestors did. Their ancestors refused to listen to
my message. They followed and worshiped
other gods. The family of Israel and the family
of Judah have broken the agreement I made
with their ancestors."

¹¹So this is what the LORD says: "I will soon
make something terrible happen to the peo-
ple of Judah. They will not be able to escape.
They will be sorry and cry to me for help, but
I will not listen to them. ¹²The people in the
towns of Judah and in the city of Jerusalem
will go and pray to their idols* for help. They
burn incense* to those idols. But their idols
will not be able to help the people of Judah
when that terrible disaster comes.

¹³"People of Judah, you have many idols—
there are as many idols as there are towns in
Judah. You have built many altars for worshiping that disgusting god Baal*—there are as
many altars as there are streets in Jerusalem.

¹⁴"As for you, Jeremiah, don't pray for
these people of Judah. Don't beg for them.
Don't say prayers for them. I will not listen.
They will suffer and then call to me for help,
but I will not listen.

¹⁵"Judah is the one I love, but why is she in
my temple?
She has done too many evil things.
Judah, do you think vows* and sacrifices
will keep you from being destroyed?
Will I then allow you to enjoy your evil
ways?"

¹⁶ The LORD gave you a name.
He called you, "A green olive tree,
beautiful to look at."
But with a powerful storm, the LORD will
set that tree on fire,
and its branches will be burned up.^c
¹⁷ The LORD All-Powerful planted you,
and he said that disaster will come to
you.
That is because the family of Israel
and the family of Judah have done evil
things.
They offered sacrifices to Baal,
and that made him angry!

Evil Plans Against Jeremiah

¹⁸The LORD showed me that the men of
Anathoth^d were making plans against me.

---

^a**10:22** *north* The Babylonian army came from this
direction to attack Judah. Armies from countries
north and east of Israel often came this way to
attack Judah and Israel.
^b**11:4** *furnace* Literally, "iron furnace." That is, an
oven hot enough to soften iron so that it can be
hammered into something useful.

^c**11:15–16** The meaning of these verses is
uncertain.
^d**11:18** *men of Anathoth* Anathoth was Jeremiah's
hometown. The people who were plotting against
him there included his own relatives. See Jer. 12:6.

The Lord showed me what they were doing, so I knew they were against me. ¹⁹Before the Lord showed me that the people were against me, I was like a gentle lamb waiting to be butchered. I did not understand that they were against me. They were saying this about me: "Let us destroy the tree and its fruit! Let us kill him! Then people will forget him." ²⁰But, Lord, you are a fair judge. You know how to test people's hearts and minds. I will tell you my arguments, and I will let you give them the punishment they deserve.

²¹The men from Anathoth were planning to kill Jeremiah. They said to him, "Don't prophesy* in the name of the Lord, or we will kill you." The Lord made a decision about the men from Anathoth. ²²The Lord All-Powerful said, "I will soon punish these men from Anathoth. Their young men will die in war. Their sons and daughters will die from hunger. ²³No one from the city of Anathoth will be left. No one will survive. I will punish them and cause something bad to happen to them."

Jeremiah Complains to God

12 ¹Lord, if I argue with you,
you are always right.
But I want to ask you about some things
  that don't seem right.
  Why are wicked people successful?
  Why do people you cannot trust have
    such easy lives?
² You have put these wicked people here
    like plants with strong roots.
  They grow and produce fruit.
  With their mouths they say that you are
    near and dear to them,
  but in their hearts they are really far
    away from you.
³ But you know my heart, Lord.
  You see me and test my mind.
  Drag the evil people away like sheep to be
    killed.
  Choose them for the day of slaughter.
⁴ How much longer will the land be dry?
  How long will the grass be dry and
    dead?
  The birds and the animals of this land
    have all died,
  and it is the fault of the wicked.
  But they are saying,
  "Jeremiah will not live long enough
    to see what happens to us."

God's Answer to Jeremiah

⁵"Jeremiah, if running in a race against men
    makes you tired,
  how will you race against horses?
  If you trip and fall in a safe place,
    what will you do in a dangerous place?
  What will you do in the thornbushes
    that grow along the Jordan River?
⁶ These men are your own brothers.
  Members of your own family are making
    plans against you.

People from your own family are
    shouting at you.
Don't trust them,
  even when they speak to you like
    friends.

The Lord Rejects Judah

⁷"I have abandoned my house.
  I have left my own property.ᵃ
I have given Judah,* the one I love, to her
    enemies.
⁸ My own people turned against me like a
    wild lion.
  They roared at me,
    so I turned away from them.
⁹ My own people have become like
    a dying animal surrounded by vultures.
  These birds are circling around her.
  Come on, wild animals.
  Come get something to eat.
¹⁰ Many shepherds have ruined my
    vineyard.*
  They have trampled the plants in my
    field.
  They have made my beautiful field a
    desert.
¹¹ They have turned it into an empty desert.
  It is dry and dead.
  The whole land has been ruined,
    and no one is left to care for it.
¹² The empty hills are covered with soldiers
    who have come to destroy everything.
  The Lord is using them to punish that
    land from one end to the other.
  No one is safe.
¹³ The people will plant wheat,
    but they will harvest only thorns.
  They will work hard until they are very
    tired,
    but they will get nothing for all their
    work.
  They will be ashamed of their crop.
  The Lord's anger caused this."

The Lord's Promise to Israel's Neighbors

¹⁴This is what the Lord says: "I will tell you what I will do for all those who live around the land of Israel.* They are very wicked. They have destroyed the land I gave to the people of Israel. I will pull the evil people up and throw them out of their land, and I will pull the people of Judah up with them. ¹⁵But after I pull them up out of their land, I will feel sorry for them. I will bring each family back to its own property and to its own land. ¹⁶I want these people to learn their lessons well. In the past they taught my people to use Baal's* name to make promises. Now, I want them to learn to use my name. I want them to say, 'As the Lord lives ....' If they do that, I will allow them to be successful, and I will let them live among my people. ¹⁷But if a nation

---

ᵃ**12:7** *house ... my own property* That is, the people of Judah.

does not listen to my message, I will completely destroy it. I will pull it up like a dead plant." This message is from the LORD.

The Sign of the Loincloth

13 ¹This is what the LORD said to me: "Jeremiah, go and buy a linen loincloth.ᵃ Then put it around your waist. Don't let it get wet."

²So I bought a linen loincloth, just as the LORD told me to do, and I put it around my waist. ³Then the message from the LORD came to me a second time. ⁴This was the message: "Jeremiah, take the loincloth you bought and are wearing, and go to Perath.ᵇ Hide the loincloth there in a crack in the rocks."

⁵So I went to Perath and hid the loincloth there, just as the LORD told me to do. ⁶Many days later the LORD said to me, "Now, Jeremiah, go to Perath. Get the loincloth that I told you to hide there."

⁷So I went to Perath and dug the loincloth out of the crack in the rocks where I had hidden it. But now I could not wear the loincloth, because it was ruined. It was not good for anything.

⁸Then the message from the LORD came to me. ⁹This is what the LORD said: "The loincloth is ruined and not good for anything. In the same way, I will ruin the proud people of Judah* and Jerusalem. ¹⁰I will ruin them because they refuse to listen to my messages. They are stubborn and do only what they want to do. They follow and worship other gods. They will be like this linen loincloth. They will be ruined and not good for anything. ¹¹A loincloth is wrapped tightly around a man's waist. In the same way, I wrapped the family of Israel* and the family of Judah around me." This message is from the LORD. "I did that so that they would be my people and bring me fame, praise, and honor. But my people did not listen to me."

Warnings to Judah

¹²"Jeremiah, say to the people of Judah,* 'This is what the LORD, the God of Israel,* says: Every wineskin* should be filled with wine.' They will laugh and say to you, 'Of course, we know that every wineskin should be filled with wine.' ¹³Then you will say to them, 'This is what the LORD says: I will make everyone who lives in this land helpless, like a drunken man. I am talking about the kings who sit on David's* throne. I am also talking about the priests, the prophets,* and all the people who live in Jerusalem. ¹⁴I will make them stumble

and fall against each another, even the fathers and sons.' This message is from the LORD. 'I will not feel sorry or have pity for them. I will not allow compassion to stop me from destroying the people of Judah.'"

¹⁵ Listen and pay attention.
　　The LORD has spoken to you.
　　Do not be proud.
¹⁶ Honor the LORD your God.
　　Praise him or he will bring darkness.
　　Praise him before you fall on the dark
　　　hills.
　　You people of Judah are hoping for light,
　　　but the Lord will turn the light into
　　　thick darkness.
　　He will change it into the deepest
　　　gloom.
¹⁷ If you people of Judah don't listen to him,
　　I will hide and cry.
　　Your pride will cause me to cry.
　　I will cry very hard.
　　My eyes will overflow with tears,
　　　because the LORD's flockᶜ will be
　　　captured.
¹⁸ Tell these things to the king and his wife,
　　"Come down from your thrones.
　　Your beautiful crowns have fallen from
　　　your heads."
¹⁹ The cities in the Negev* are locked.
　　No one can open them.
　　All the people of Judah have been taken
　　　away as captives.
　　They were carried away as prisoners.

²⁰ Jerusalem, look!
　　The enemy is coming from the northᵈ!
　　Where is your flockᵉ?
　　God gave that beautiful flock to you.
²¹ What will you say when the LORD asks
　　　you to account for that flock?
　　You were supposed to teach the people.
　　Your leaders were supposed to lead
　　　them.
　　So you will suffer pain and trouble,
　　　like a woman giving birth.
²² You might ask yourself,
　　"Why has this bad thing happened to
　　　me?"
　　It happened because of your many sins.
　　Because of your sins, your skirt was torn
　　　off,
　　and your sandals were taken away.
　　They did this to embarrass you.

ᵃ**13:1** *loincloth* A common undergarment in ancient Judah. It was a short skirt that was wrapped around the hips. It reached about halfway down the thighs.
ᵇ**13:4** *Perath* Probably a village near Jerusalem. This town is called Parah in the list of the cities of the land of Benjamin in Josh. 18:23. But this name also means the Euphrates River.

ᶜ**13:17** *LORD's flock* This is a figurative name for the people of Judah. The Lord is thought of as a shepherd, while his people are seen as his flock of sheep.
ᵈ**13:20** *north* The Babylonian army came from this direction to attack Judah. Armies from countries north and east of Israel often came this way to attack Judah and Israel.
ᵉ**13:20** *flock* Here, the word "flock" refers to all the towns around Jerusalem, as if Jerusalem were the shepherd and the towns of Judah were her flock.

²³ A black man cannot change the color of
     his skin,
    and a leopard cannot change its spots.
In the same way, Jerusalem, you cannot
    change and do good.
You always do bad things.

²⁴"I will force you to leave your homes.
    You will run in all directions.
    You will be like chaff* blown away by
     the desert wind.
²⁵ This is what will happen to you.
    This is your part in my plans."
This message is from the LORD.
  "Why will this happen?
    Because you forgot me.
    You trusted false gods.
²⁶ Jerusalem, I will pull your skirt up over
     your face.
Everyone will see you,
    and you will be ashamed.
²⁷ I saw the terrible things you did.ᵃ
    I saw you laughing and having sex with
     your lovers.
    I know about your plans to be like a
     prostitute.
    I have seen you on the hills and in the
     fields.
    It will be very bad for you, Jerusalem.
    How long will you continue doing your
     dirty sins?"

Drought and False Prophets

14 ¹This is the LORD's message to Jeremiah about the droughtᵇ:

²"The nation of Judah* cries for people who
     have died.
    The people in the cities of Judah grow
     weaker and weaker.
    They lie on the ground.
People in Jerusalem, cry to God for help.
³ The leaders of the people send their
     servants to get water.
    The servants go to the water storage
     places,
    but they don't find any water.
    The servants come back with empty jars,
    so they are ashamed and embarrassed.
    They cover their heads from shame.
⁴ No one prepares the ground for crops.ᶜ
    No rain falls on the land.
    The farmers are depressed.
    So they cover their heads from shame.
⁵ Even the mother deer in the field leaves
    her newborn baby alone,

because there is no grass.
⁶ Wild donkeys stand on the bare hills.
    They sniff the wind like jackals.*
But their eyes cannot find any food,
    because there are no plants to eat.

⁷"We know that this is our fault.
    We are now suffering because of our
     sins.
    LORD, do something to help us for the
     good of your name.
We admit that we have left you many
     times.
We have sinned against you.
⁸ God, you are the hope of Israel*!
    You save Israel in times of trouble.
But now it seems like you are a stranger
     in the land,
    like a traveler who only stays one night.
⁹ You seem like a man who has been
     attacked by surprise,
    like a soldier who does not have the
     power to save anyone.
But, LORD, you are with us.
    We are called by your name, so don't
     leave us without help!"

¹⁰This is what the LORD says about the
people of Judah: "The people of Judah really
love to leave me. They don't stop themselves
from leaving me. So now the LORD will not
accept them. Now he will remember the
evil they do. He will punish them for their
sins."

¹¹Then the LORD said to me, "Jeremiah,
don't pray for good things to happen to the
people of Judah. ¹²They might begin to fast*
and pray to me, but I will not listen to their
prayers. Even if they offer burnt offerings*
and grain offerings to me, I will not accept
them. I will destroy the people of Judah with
war. I will take away their food, and they will
starve. And I will destroy them with terrible
diseases."

¹³But I said, "Lord GOD, the prophets were
telling the people something different. They
were telling the people of Judah, 'You will not
suffer from war or from hunger. The Lord will
give you peace in this land.'"

¹⁴Then the LORD said to me, "Jeremiah,
those prophets are telling lies in my name.
I did not send them or command them or
speak to them. Their prophecies came from
false visions, worthless magic, and their own
wishful thinking. ¹⁵So this is what I say about
the prophets who are speaking in my name.
I did not send them. They said, 'No enemy
with swords will ever attack this country.
There will never be hunger in this land.' So
those prophets will die from hunger or by an
enemy's sword. ¹⁶And the people they spoke
to will be thrown into the streets. The people
will die from hunger and war. I will punish
them, and no one will be there to bury them,
their wives, their sons, or their daughters.

ᵃ**13:27 I saw ... you did** This is probably talking
about worshiping false gods. But part of that worship was having sex with temple prostitutes.
ᵇ**14:1 drought** A time when no rain falls, and the
crops become dry and die.
ᶜ**14:4 No one ... crops** This follows the ancient
Greek version. The Hebrew text here is hard to
understand.

17"Jeremiah, speak this message
    to the people of Judah:
'My eyes fill with tears night and day
    without stopping.
I cry for my virgin daughter,*a* my dear
    people,
    because someone hit them and crushed
        them.
They have been hurt very badly.
18 If I go into the country,
    I see the bodies of those killed in war.
If I go into the city,
    I see people sick from hunger.
The priests and prophets continue their
        work,
    but they don't understand what is
        happening.'"

19 LORD, have you completely rejected the
        nation of Judah?
    Do you hate Zion*?
You hurt us so badly that we cannot be
    made well again.
    Why did you do that?
We were hoping for peace,
    but nothing good has come.
We were hoping for a time of healing,
    but only terror came.
20 LORD, we know that we are wicked.
    We know that our ancestors* did evil
        things.
    Yes, we sinned against you.
21 LORD, for the good of your name, don't
        push us away.
    Don't take away the honor from your
        glorious throne.
Remember your agreement with us
    and do not break it.
22 Foreign idols* don't have the power to
        bring rain.
    The sky does not have the power to
        send down showers of rain.
You are our only hope.
    You are the one who made all these
        things.

15 ¹The LORD said to me, "Jeremiah,
        even if Moses and Samuel were here
to pray for the people of Judah, I would not
feel sorry for them. Send the people of Judah
away from me! Tell them to go! ²They might
ask you, 'Where will we go?' Tell them this is
what the LORD says:

"'I have chosen some people to die.
    They will die.
I have chosen some to be killed with
        swords.
    They will be killed with swords.
I have chosen some to die from hunger.
    They will die from hunger.

I have chosen some to be taken away to a
        foreign country.
    They will be prisoners there.
³ I will send four kinds of destroyers against
        them.'
    This message is from the LORD.
'I will send the enemy with a sword to
        kill.
I will send the dogs to drag their bodies
        away.
I will send birds of the air and wild
        animals
    to eat and destroy their bodies.
⁴ I will make the people of Judah
    an example of something terrible for all
        the people on earth.
I will do this to the people of Judah
    because of what Manasseh*b* did in
        Jerusalem.
    Manasseh was the son of King
        Hezekiah.
    Manasseh was a king of Judah.'

⁵"No one will feel sorry for you, city of
        Jerusalem.
    No one will be sad and cry for you.
    No one will go out of their way to even
        ask how you are.
⁶ Jerusalem, you left me."
    This message is from the LORD.
"Again and again you left me!
    So I will punish and destroy you.
    I am tired of holding back your
        punishment.
⁷ I will separate the people of Judah with
        my pitchfork.*c*
    I will scatter them at the city gates of
        the land.
My people have not changed,
    so I will destroy them.
    I will take away their children.
⁸ Many women will lose their husbands.
    There will be more widows than there
        is sand in the sea.
I will bring a destroyer at noontime.
    The destroyer will attack the mothers of
        the young men of Judah.
I will bring pain and fear on the people of
        Judah.
    I will make this happen very quickly.
⁹ The enemy will attack with swords and
        kill the people.
    They will kill the survivors* from Judah.
A woman with seven children will lose
        them.
    She will cry until she becomes weak
        and struggles to breathe.
    She will be upset and confused,
        because her bright day has become
        dark."

---

*a*14:17 *virgin daughter* Another name for
Jerusalem.

*b*15:4 *Manasseh* Manasseh was the most evil king
of Judah according to 2 Kings 21:1–16. He worshiped many gods.

*c*15:7 *pitchfork* A tool with sharp points for throwing hay from one place to another.

Jeremiah Complains to God Again

10 Mother, I am sorry
that you gave birth to me.
I am the one who must accuse
and criticize the whole land.
I have not loaned or borrowed anything,
but everyone curses me.

11 Surely, LORD, I have served you well.
In times of disaster and trouble, I prayed
to you about my enemies.

God Answers Jeremiah

12 "Jeremiah, you know that no one
can shatter a piece of iron.
I mean the kind of iron that is from the
north.ᵃ
And no one can shatter a piece of
bronze either.

13 The people of Judah* have many treasures.
I will give these riches to other people.
They will not have to buy them,
because Judah has many sins.
The people sinned in every part of
Judah.

14 People of Judah, I will make you slaves of
your enemies.
You will be slaves in a land that you
never knew.
I am very angry.
My anger is like a hot fire,
and you will be burned."

15 LORD, you understand me.
Remember me and take care of me.
People are hurting me.
Give them the punishment they
deserve.
You are being patient with them.
But don't destroy me while you remain
patient with them.
Think about me.
Think about the pain I suffer for you.

16 Your words came to me, and I ate them
up.
They made me very happy.
I was glad to be called by your name,
LORD All-Powerful.

17 I never sat with the crowd
as they laughed and had fun.
I sat by myself because of your influence
on me.
You filled me with anger at the evil
around me.

18 I don't understand why I still hurt.
I don't understand why my wound is
not cured and cannot be healed.
I think you have changed.
You are like a spring of water that
became dry.
You are like a spring whose water has
stopped flowing.

19 Then the LORD said, "Jeremiah, if you
change and come back to me,
I will not punish you.
If you change and come back to me,
then you may serve me.
If you speak important things, not
worthless words,
then you may speak for me.
The people of Judah should change
and come back to you.
But don't you change and be like them.

20 I will make you strong.
The people will think you are strong,
like a wall made of bronze.
The people of Judah will fight against you,
but they will not defeat you.
They will not defeat you,
because I am with you.
I will help you, and I will save you."

This message is from the LORD.
21 "I will save you from these evil people.
They frighten you, but I will save you
from them."

The Day of Disaster

16 ¹The LORD's message came to me:
²"Jeremiah, you must not get married.
You must not have sons or daughters in this
place."

³This is what the LORD says about the sons
and daughters who are born in the land of
Judah* and about their mothers and fathers:
⁴"They will die from terrible diseases. And
no one will cry for them or bury them. Their
bodies will lie on the ground like dung. Or
they will die in war or starve to death. Their
dead bodies will be food for the birds of the
sky and the wild animals of the earth."

⁵So the LORD says, "Jeremiah, don't go into
a house where people are eating a funeral
meal. Don't go there to cry for the dead or
to show your sorrow. Don't do these things,
because I have taken back my blessing. I will
not be kind to the people of Judah. I will not
feel sorry for them." This message is from the
LORD.

⁶"Important people and common people
will die in the land of Judah. No one will bury
them or cry for them. No one will cut himself
or shave his head to show sorrow for them.
⁷No one will bring food to those who are crying for the dead. No one will comfort those
whose mother or father has died. No one will
offer a drink to comfort those who are crying
for the dead.

⁸"Jeremiah, don't go into a house where
the people are having a party. Don't go into
that house and sit down to eat and drink.
⁹This is what the LORD All-Powerful, the God
of Israel* says: I will soon stop the sounds
of people having fun. I will stop the happy
sounds of people enjoying a wedding party.
This will happen during your lifetime. I will
do these things very soon.

ᵃ**15:12** *north* The Babylonian army came from this
direction to attack Judah. Armies from countries
north and east of Israel often came this way to
attack Judah and Israel.

¹⁰"Jeremiah, you will tell the people of Judah these things, and the people will ask you, 'Why has the LORD said these terrible things to us? What have we done wrong? What sin have we done against the LORD our God?' ¹¹You must tell them: 'Terrible things will happen to you because your ancestors* stopped following me.' This message is from the LORD. 'They stopped following me and began to follow and serve other gods. They worshiped those other gods. Your ancestors left me and stopped obeying my law. ¹²But you people have sinned more than your ancestors. You are very stubborn, and you are doing only what you want to do. You are not obeying me. Because you do only what you want to do, ¹³I will throw you out of this country. I will force you to go to a foreign land. You will go to a land that you and your ancestors never knew. There you can serve false gods all you want to. I will not help you or show you any favors.'

¹⁴"People make promises and say, 'As surely as the LORD lives—the Lord who brought the Israelites out of the land of Egypt ....' But the time is coming," says the LORD, "when people will not say that. ¹⁵They will say something new. They will say, 'As surely as the LORD lives—the Lord who brought the Israelites out of the northern land, who brought them out of all the countries where he had sent them ....' Why will they say that? Because I will bring the Israelites back to the land that I gave to their ancestors.

¹⁶"I will soon send for many fishermen to come to this land." This message is from the LORD. "They will catch the people of Judah. After that happens, I will send for many hunters*ᵃ* to come to this land. They will hunt the people of Judah on every mountain and hill and in the cracks of the rocks. ¹⁷I see everything they do. The people of Judah cannot hide the things they do. Their sin is not hidden from me. ¹⁸I will pay the people of Judah back for the evil things they did—I will punish them two times for every sin. I will do this because they have made my land 'dirty.' They made my land 'dirty' with their terrible idols.* I hate those idols, but they have filled my country with their idols."

¹⁹ LORD, you are my strength and my
        protection.
    You are a safe place to run to in time of
        trouble.
    The nations will come to you from all
        around the world.
    They will say, "Our fathers had false
        gods.
    They worshiped those worthless idols,
        but the idols did not help them.

²⁰ Can people make real gods for
        themselves?
    No, they can only make statues that are
        not really gods."

²¹ The Lord says, "I will teach those who
        make idols.
    Right now I will teach them about my
        power and my strength.
    Then they will know that I am God.
    They will know that I am the LORD.

Guilt Written on the Heart

17 ¹"The sins of Judah* are written
    where they cannot be erased—
    cut into stone with an iron pen,
        cut deep with a hard tip into the stone
        that is the hearts of the people.
    Their sins are carved into the horns of
        their altars.ᵇ
² Their children remember the altars
        that were dedicated to false gods.
    They remember the wooden poles
        that were dedicated to Asherah.*
    They remember those things
        under the green trees and on the hills.
³ They remember those things
        on the mountains in the open country.
    The people of Judah have many treasures.
        I will give those things to other people.
    People will destroy all the high places* in
        your country.
    You worshiped there,
        and that was a sin.
⁴ You will lose the land I gave you.
    I will let your enemies take you to be
        their slaves.
    That is because I am very angry.
    My anger is like a hot fire, and you will
        be burned forever."

Trusting in People and Trusting in God

⁵ This is what the LORD says:
    "Bad things will happen to those
        who put their trust in people.
    Bad things will happen to those
        who depend on human strength.
    That is because they have stopped
        trusting the LORD.
⁶ They are like a bush in a desert where no
        one lives.
    It is in a hot and dry land.
    It is in bad soil.
    That bush does not know
        about the good things that God can give.
⁷ But those who trust in the LORD will be
        blessed.
    They know that the LORD will do what
        he says.

ᵇ**17:1 horns of their altars** The corners of altars were shaped like horns, and the blood of sacrifices was smeared on them. So Jeremiah may mean that the people's sins have made their altars unfit for sacrifices.

ᵃ**16:16 fishermen ... hunters** This means the enemy soldiers from Babylon.

8 They will be strong like trees planted near
   a stream
   that send out roots to the water.
   They have nothing to fear when the days
   get hot.
   Their leaves are always green.
   They never worry, even in a year that has
   no rain.
   They always produce fruit.

9 "Nothing can hide its evil as well as the
   human mind.
   It can be very sick,
   and no one really understands it.
10 But I am the LORD,
   and I can look into a person's heart.
   I can test a person's mind and decide
   what each one should have.
   I can give each person the right
   payment for what they do.
11 Sometimes a bird will hatch an egg
   that it did not lay.
   Those who cheat to get money
   are like that bird.
   But when their lives are half finished,
   they will lose the money.
   At the end of their lives, it will be clear
   that they were fools."

12 From the very beginning, our Temple*
   has been a glorious throne for God.
   It is a very important place.
13 LORD, you are the hope of Israel.*
   You are like a spring of living water.
   Those who stop following the LORD
   will have a very short life.*ᵃ

Jeremiah's Third Complaint

14 LORD, if you heal me,
   I surely will be healed.
   Save me,
   and I surely will be saved.
   Lord, I praise you!
15 The people of Judah* continue to ask me
   questions.
   They say, "Jeremiah, what about the
   message from the LORD?
   Let's see that message come true."

16 LORD, I did not run away from you.
   I followed you.
   I became the shepherdᵇ you wanted.
   I did not want the terrible day to come.
   LORD, you know what I said.
   You see all that is happening.
17 LORD, don't ruin me.
   I depend on you in times of trouble.

18 People are hurting me.
   Make them ashamed,
   but don't disappoint me.
   Let them be filled with fear,
   but don't give me any reason to fear.
   Bring the terrible day of disaster to my
   enemies.
   Break them, and break them again.

Keeping the Sabbath Day Holy

19 This is what the LORD said to me: "Jeremiah, go and stand at the People's Gate,ᶜ where the kings of Judah* go in and out. Tell the people my message, and then go to all the other gates of Jerusalem and do the same." 20 Say to the people, "Listen to this message from the LORD. Listen, kings of Judah. Listen, all you people of Judah. All you who come through these gates into Jerusalem, listen to me! 21 This is what the LORD says: 'Be careful that you don't carry a load on the Sabbath* day. And don't bring a load through the gates of Jerusalem on the Sabbath day. 22 Don't bring a load out of your houses on the Sabbath day. Don't do any work on that day. You must make the Sabbath day a holy day. I gave this same command to your ancestors,* 23 but they did not obey me. They did not pay attention to me. Your ancestors were very stubborn. I punished them, but it did not do any good. They did not listen to me. 24 But you must be careful to obey me, says the LORD. You must not bring a load through the gates of Jerusalem on the Sabbath. You must make the Sabbath day a holy day. You will do this by not doing any work on that day.

25 "'If you obey this command, the kings and leaders will be from David's* family. It will be the kings who sit on David's throne and the leaders from Judah and Jerusalem who come through the gates of Jerusalem riding on chariots* and on horses. And Jerusalem will have people living in it forever. 26 People will come to Jerusalem from the towns and villages of Judah, from the land where the tribe of Benjamin lives,ᵈ from the western foothills, from the hill country, and from the Negev.* All these people will bring burnt offerings,* sacrifices, grain offerings, incense,* and thank offerings to the Temple* of the LORD in Jerusalem.

27 "'But if you don't listen to me and obey me, bad things will happen. If you carry loads into Jerusalem on the Sabbath day, you are not keeping it as a holy day. So I will start a fire that cannot be put out. That fire will start at the gates of Jerusalem, and it will burn until it burns even the palaces.'"

ᵃ**17:13 will have a very short life** Literally, "he will be written in the dirt." This might mean that a person's name was written on a list of people who would soon die, or that a person's life will soon be gone—like a name written in the sand.
ᵇ**17:16 shepherd** God's people are sometimes called his "sheep," and the person who takes care of them is called the "shepherd."

ᶜ**17:19 People's Gate** This might be one of the gates into Jerusalem or perhaps one of the southern gates into the Temple area used by those who were not priests.
ᵈ**17:26 the land where … Benjamin lives** The land of Benjamin was just north of the land of Judah.

The Potter and the Clay

18 ¹This is the message that came to Jeremiah from the LORD: ²"Jeremiah, go down to the potter's* house. I will give you my message there."

³So I went down to the potter's house. I saw the potter working with clay at the wheel. ⁴He was making a pot from clay. But there was something wrong with the pot. So the potter used that clay again, and he made another pot. He used his hands to shape the pot the way he wanted it to be.

⁵Then this message from the LORD came to me: ⁶"Family of Israel,* you know that I can do the same thing with you. You are like the clay in the potter's hands, and I am like the potter. ⁷There may come a time when I will speak about a nation or a kingdom that I will pull up by its roots. Or maybe I will say that I will pull that nation or kingdom down and destroy it. ⁸But if the people of that nation change their hearts and lives and stop doing evil things, I will change my mind and not follow my plans to bring disaster to them. ⁹There may come another time when I speak about a nation that I will build up or plant. ¹⁰But if I see that nation doing evil things and not obeying me, I will think again about the good I had planned to do for that nation.

¹¹"So, Jeremiah, say to the people of Judah and those who live in Jerusalem, 'This is what the LORD says: I am preparing troubles for you right now. I am making plans against you. So stop doing the evil things you are doing. Each person must change and start doing good things.' ¹²But the people of Judah will answer, 'It will not do any good to try. We will continue to do what we want. We will do what our stubborn, evil hearts want.'"

¹³ Listen to what the LORD says:
"Ask the other nations this question:
'Have you ever heard of anyone doing
the evil things that Israel has done?'
And Israel is special to God.
Israel is like God's bride!
¹⁴ You know that rocks never leave the fields
by themselves.ᵃ
You know that the snow on the
mountains of Lebanon never melts.
You know that cool, flowing streams don't
become dry.
¹⁵ But my people have forgotten about me.
They make offerings to worthless idols.*
My people stumble in the things they do.
They stumble around in the old paths of
their ancestors.*

My people would rather walk along back
roads and poor highways
than to follow me on the good roads.
¹⁶ So Judah's country will become an empty
desert.
People will whistle and shake their heads
every time they pass by.
They will be shocked at how the country
was destroyed.
¹⁷ I will scatter the people of Judah.*
They will run from their enemies.
I will scatter the people of Judah like an
east wind that blows things away.
I will destroy them.
They will not see me coming to help
them.
No, they will see me leaving."

Jeremiah's Fourth Complaint

¹⁸Then the enemies of Jeremiah said, "Come, let us make plans against Jeremiah. Surely the teaching of the law by the priest will not be lost, and the advice from the wise men will still be with us. We will still have the words of the prophets.* So let us tell lies about him. That will ruin him. We will not pay attention to anything he says."

¹⁹ LORD, listen to me!
Listen to my arguments and decide who
is right.
²⁰ I have been good to the people of Judah,*
but now they are paying me back with
evil.
They are trying to trap me and kill me.
²¹ So make their children starve in a famine.*
Let their enemies defeat them with
swords.
Let their wives be without children.
Turn their wives into widows.
Let the men from Judah be put to death.
Let the young men be killed in battle.
²² Let there be crying in their houses.
Make them cry when you suddenly
bring an enemy against them.
Let all this happen because my enemies
tried to trap me.
They hid traps for me to step in.
²³ LORD, you know about their plans to kill
me.
Don't forgive their crimes.
Don't erase their sins.
Destroy my enemies!
Punish them while you are angry!

The Broken Jar

19 ¹The LORD said to me, "Jeremiah, go and buy a clay jar from a potter.* ²Go out to the Valley of Ben Hinnom, near the front of the Potsherd Gate.ᵇ Take some of the elders* of the people and some priests with

---

ᵃ**18:14** *You know ... themselves* In Hebrew this sounds like, "Would anyone leave the Rock, Shaddai?" Rock and Shaddai are two names for God, but this could also be translated, "Does Lebanon's snow ever melt from Shaddai's mountain?" Here, this is probably Mount Hermon.

ᵇ**19:2** *Potsherd Gate* The exact location of this gate is not known, though it was probably at the southwestern part of the city.

you. Tell them what I tell you. ³Say to those who are with you, 'King of Judah* and people of Jerusalem, listen to this message from the Lord! This is what the Lord All-Powerful, the God of the people of Israel,* says: I will soon make a terrible thing happen to this place! Everyone who hears about it will be amazed and full of fear. ⁴I will do these things because the people of Judah have stopped following me. They have made this a place for foreign gods. The people of Judah have burned sacrifices in this place to other gods. The people long ago did not worship those gods. Their ancestors* did not worship them. These are new gods from other countries. The kings of Judah filled this place with the blood of innocent children. ⁵The kings of Judah built high places* for the god Baal.* They use those places to burn their sons in the fire. They burned their sons as burnt offerings to the god Baal. I did not tell them to do that. I did not ask them to offer their sons as sacrifices. I never even thought of such a thing. ⁶Now people call this place Topheth and the Valley of Hinnom. But I give you this warning. This message is from the Lord: The days are coming, when people will call this place the Valley of Slaughter. ⁷At this place, I will ruin the plans of the people of Judah and Jerusalem. The enemy will chase them, and I will let the people of Judah be killed with swords in this place. I will make their dead bodies food for the birds and wild animals. ⁸I will completely destroy this city. People will whistle and shake their heads when they pass by Jerusalem. They will be shocked when they see how the city was destroyed. ⁹The enemy will bring its army around the city. That army will not let people go out to get food, so the people in the city will begin to starve. They will become so hungry that they will eat the bodies of their own sons and daughters, and then they will begin to eat each other.'

¹⁰"Jeremiah, tell this to the people, and while they are watching, break the jar. ¹¹Then say this: 'The Lord All-Powerful says, I will break the nation of Judah and the city of Jerusalem, just as someone breaks a clay jar! And like a broken jar, the nation of Judah cannot be put together again. The dead people will be buried here in Topheth until there is no more room. ¹²I will do this to these people and to this place. I will make this city like Topheth.' This message is from the Lord. ¹³'The houses in Jerusalem will become as "dirty" as this place, Topheth. The kings' palaces will be ruined like this place, Topheth, because the people worshiped false gods on the roofs of their houses.ᵃ They worshiped the stars and burned sacrifices to honor them. They gave drink offerings to false gods.'"

ᵃ19:13 *roofs of their houses* People built their houses with flat roofs that were used as an extra room.

¹⁴Then Jeremiah left Topheth where the Lord had told him to speak. Jeremiah went to the Lord's Temple* and stood in the courtyard* of the Temple. Jeremiah said to all the people: ¹⁵"This is what the Lord All-Powerful, the God of Israel says: 'I said I would bring many disasters to Jerusalem and the villages around it. I will soon make this happen because the people are very stubborn. They refuse to listen and obey me.'"

Jeremiah and Pashhur

20 ¹Pashhur son of Immer was a priest. He was the highest officer in the Temple* of the Lord. When he heard Jeremiah say those things in the Temple yard, ²he had Jeremiah the prophet* beaten. And he had Jeremiah's hands and feet locked between large blocks of wood. This was at the Upper Gate of Benjamin of the Temple. ³The next day Pashhur took Jeremiah out from between the blocks of wood. Then Jeremiah said to him, "The Lord's name for you is not Pashhur. Now his name for you is, 'Surrounded by Terror.' ⁴That is your name because of what the Lord says: 'I will soon make you a terror to yourself and to all your friends. You will watch enemies killing your friends with swords. I will give all the people of Judah* to the king of Babylon. He will take them away to the country of Babylon, and his army will kill the people of Judah with their swords. ⁵The people of Jerusalem worked hard to build things and become wealthy, but I will give all these things to their enemies. The king in Jerusalem has many treasures, but I will give all the treasures to the enemy. The enemy will take them and carry them away to the country of Babylon. ⁶And, Pashhur, you and all the people living in your house will be taken away. You will be forced to go and live in the country of Babylon. You will die in Babylon, and you will be buried in that foreign country. You told lies to your friends. You said these things would not happen. But all your friends will also die and be buried in Babylon.'"

Jeremiah's Fifth Complaint

7 Lord, you tricked me, and I certainly was fooled.
  You are stronger than I am, so you won.
  I have become a joke.
  People laugh at me and make fun of me all day long.
8 Every time I speak, I shout.
  I am always shouting about violence and destruction.
  I tell the people about the message that I received from the Lord.
  But they only insult me
  and make fun of me.
9 Sometimes I say to myself,
  "I will forget about him.
  I will not speak anymore in his name."

But when I say that, his message is like a
fire burning inside me!
It feels like it is burning deep in my
bones!
I get tired of trying to hold his message
inside.
And finally, I am not able to hold it in.
10 I hear people whispering against me.
Everywhere, I hear things that frighten
me.
Even my friends are speaking against
me.
People are just waiting for me to make a
mistake.
They are saying,
"Let us lie and say that he did something
bad.
Maybe we can trick Jeremiah.
Then we will have him.
We will finally be rid of him.
Then we will grab him and take our
revenge on him."
11 But the LORD is with me.
He is like a strong soldier.
So those who are chasing me will fall.
They will not defeat me.
They will fail.
They will be disappointed.
They will be ashamed,
and they will never forget that shame.

12 LORD All-Powerful, you test good people.
You look deeply into a person's mind.
I told you my arguments against these
people.
So let me see you give them the
punishment they deserve.
13 Sing to the LORD! Praise the LORD!
He saves the lives of the poor!
He saves them from the wicked!

Jeremiah's Sixth Complaint

14 Curse the day that I was born!
Don't bless the day my mother had me.
15 Curse the man who told my father the
news that I was born.
"It's a boy!" he said.
"You have a son."
He made my father very happy
when he told him the news.
16 Let that man be like the cities the LORD
destroyed.[a]
He had no pity on them.
Let him hear shouts of war in the
morning;
let him hear battle cries at noontime,
17 because he did not kill me
while I was in my mother's womb.
If he had killed me then,
my mother would have been my grave,
and I would not have been born.

18 Why did I have to come out of her body?
All I have seen is trouble and sorrow,
and my life will end in shame.

God Rejects King Zedekiah's Request

21 ¹This is the message that came to Jeremiah from the LORD. This was when King Zedekiah of Judah sent Pashhur[b] son of Malkijah and the priest Zephaniah son of Maaseiah to Jeremiah. They brought a message for Jeremiah. ²They said to Jeremiah, "Pray to the LORD for us. Ask him what will happen. We want to know, because King Nebuchadnezzar of Babylon is attacking us. Maybe the LORD will do great things for us, as he did in the past. Maybe he will make Nebuchadnezzar stop attacking us and leave."

³Then Jeremiah answered Pashhur and Zephaniah. He said, "Tell King Zedekiah, ⁴'This is what the LORD, the God of Israel, says: You have weapons of war in your hands that you are using to defend yourselves from the Babylonians and their king. But I will make those weapons worthless.

"'The army from Babylon is outside the wall all around the city. Soon I will bring that army into Jerusalem. ⁵I myself will fight against you people of Judah. I will fight against you with my own powerful hand. I am very angry with you, so I will fight against you with my own powerful arm. I will fight very hard against you and show how angry I am. ⁶I will kill everything living in Jerusalem, both people and animals. They will die from a terrible disease that will spread all through the city. ⁷After that happens,'" says the LORD, "'I will give King Zedekiah of Judah and all his officials to King Nebuchadnezzar of Babylon. And I will give to Nebuchadnezzar the people who remain alive in Jerusalem—those who did not die from the terrible disease and the people who did not die in war or from hunger. I will give them all to King Nebuchadnezzar. The people of Judah will be captured by their enemies who want to kill them. Nebuchadnezzar's army will use their swords to kill the people of Judah and Jerusalem. Nebuchadnezzar will not show any mercy. He will not feel sorry for them.'

⁸"Also tell the people of Jerusalem, 'This is what the LORD says: Understand that I will let you choose to live or die. ⁹Anyone who stays in Jerusalem will die in war or from hunger or disease. But anyone who goes out of Jerusalem and surrenders to the Babylonians attacking you will live. Only those who leave the city will win anything in this war—their lives! ¹⁰I have decided to make trouble for the city of Jerusalem. I will not help this city!'" This message is from the LORD. "'I will give the city of Jerusalem to the king of Babylon. He will burn it with fire.'

---

[a] **20:16** *cities the LORD destroyed* That is, Sodom and Gomorrah. See Gen. 19.

[b] **21:1** *Pashhur* This is not the same Pashhur as the man in Jer. 20:1.

11"Say this to Judah's royal family:
'Listen to the message from the LORD.
12 Family of David,* this is what the LORD says:
You must judge people fairly every day.
    Protect the victims from the criminals.
If you don't do that,
    then I will become very angry.
My anger will be like a fire
    that no one will be able to put out.
This will happen because you
    have done evil things.'
13"Jerusalem, I am against you.
    You sit on top of the mountain.
    You sit like a queen over this valley.
You people of Jerusalem say,
    'No one can attack us.
    No one can come into our strong city.'
But listen to this message from the LORD:
14 'You will get the punishment you deserve.
    I will start a fire in your forests
    that will completely burn everything
        around you.'"

Judgment Against Evil Kings

22 ¹The LORD said, "Jeremiah, go down to the king's palace. Go to the king of Judah* and tell this message there: ²'Listen to this message from the LORD, King of Judah. You rule from David's* throne, so listen. King, you and your officials must listen well. All of your people who come through the gates of Jerusalem must listen to the message from the Lord. ³This is what the LORD says: Do what is right and fair. Protect those who have been robbed from the ones who robbed them. Don't hurt or do anything wrong to orphans or widows. Don't kill innocent people. ⁴If you obey these commands, kings who sit on David's throne will continue to come through the gates into the city of Jerusalem. They will come through the gates with their officials. The kings, their officials, and their people will come riding in chariots* and on horses. ⁵But if you don't obey these commands, this is what the LORD says: I, the LORD, promise that this king's palace will be destroyed—it will become a pile of rocks.'"

⁶This is what the LORD says about the palace where the king of Judah lives:

"The palace is tall like the forests of Gilead,
    like the mountains of Lebanon.
But I will make it like a desert,
    as empty as a city where no one lives.
⁷ I will send men to destroy the palace,
    each armed with weapons.
They will cut up your strong, beautiful
        cedar beams
    and throw them into the fire.

⁸"People from many nations will pass by this city. They will ask one another, 'Why has the LORD done such a terrible thing to Jerusalem? Jerusalem was such a great city.'

⁹This will be the answer to that question: 'God destroyed Jerusalem because the people of Judah stopped following the agreement of the LORD their God. They worshiped and served other gods.'"

Judgment Against King Jehoahaz

¹⁰ Don't cry for the king who has died.ᵃ
    Don't cry for him.
But cry very hard for the king
    who must leave this place.ᵇ
Cry for him because he will never return
    or see his homeland again.

¹¹This is what the LORD says about Jehoahazᶜ son of Josiah, who became king of Judah after his father Josiah died: "Jehoahaz has gone away from Jerusalem. He will never return. ¹²Jehoahaz will die in the place where the Egyptians have taken him, and he will not see this land again."

Judgment Against King Jehoiakim

¹³"It will be very bad for King Jehoiakim.
    He is doing wrong so that he can build
        his palace.
    He is cheating people so that he can
        build rooms upstairs.
    He is not paying his own people.
    He is making them work for nothing.

¹⁴"Jehoiakim says,
    'I will build myself a great palace, with
        huge rooms upstairs.'
So he built it with large windows.
    He used cedar wood for paneling, and
        he painted it red.

¹⁵"Jehoiakim, having a lot of cedar in your
        house
    does not make you a great king.
Your father Josiah was satisfied to have
        food and drink.
    He did what was right and fair,
        so everything went well for him.
¹⁶ Josiah helped poor and needy people,
        so everything went well for him.
    Jehoiakim, what does it mean "to know
        God"?
    It means living right and being fair.
    That is what it means to know me.
    This message is from the LORD.

ᵃ**22:10** *the king who has died* That is, King Josiah who was killed in battle against the Egyptians in 609 B.C.
ᵇ**22:10** *the king ... place* This means Josiah's son, Jehoahaz. He became king after Josiah died. He is also called Shallum. King Neco of Egypt defeated Josiah. And Neco took Jehoahaz off the throne of Judah and made him a prisoner in Egypt.
ᶜ**22:11** *Jehoahaz* The Hebrew text has "Shallum," another name for Jehoahaz.

¹⁷"Jehoiakim, your eyes look only for what
benefits yourself.
  You are always thinking about getting
    more for yourself.
  You are willing to kill innocent people.
  You are willing to steal things from
    other people."

¹⁸ So this is what the LORD says to King
  Jehoiakim son of Josiah:
  "The people of Judah* will not cry for
    Jehoiakim.
  They will not say to each another,
    'Brother, I am so sad!
    Sister, I am so sad!'
  They will not cry for Jehoiakim.
  They will not say about him,
    'Master, I am so sad!
    King, I am so sad!'
¹⁹ The people of Jerusalem will bury
    Jehoiakim like a donkey.
  They will drag his body away and
    throw it outside the gates of
    Jerusalem.

²⁰"Judah, go up to the mountains of Lebanon
    and cry out.
  Let your voice be heard in the
    mountains of Bashan.
  Cry out in the mountains of Abarim,
    because all your 'lovers' will be
    destroyed.

²¹"Judah, you felt safe,
    but I warned you.
  I warned you,
    but you refused to listen.
  You have lived like this from the time you
    were young.
  And from the time you were young,
    you have not obeyed me, Judah.
²² Judah, the punishment I give will come
    like a storm,
  and it will blow all your shepherds
    away.
  You thought some of the other nations
    would help you.
  But these nations will also be defeated.
    Then you will really be disappointed.
  You will be ashamed of all the evil things
    you did.

²³"King, you seem so safe in your palace of
    cedar.
  It's as if you live in Lebanon!ᵃ
  But when your punishment comes, you
    will groan.
  You will be in pain like a woman giving
    birth!"

Judgment Against King Jehoiachin

²⁴"As surely as I live," says the LORD, "I
will do this to you, Jehoiachin son of Jehoiakim, king of Judah: Even if you were a signet ring* on my right hand, I would still pull
you off. ²⁵Jehoiachin, I will give you to King
Nebuchadnezzar of Babylon and the Babylonians. Those are the people you are afraid of.
They want to kill you. ²⁶I will throw you and
your mother into another country where neither of you was born. You and your mother
will die in that country. ²⁷Jehoiachin, you will
want to come back to your land, but you will
never be allowed to come back."

²⁸ Jehoiachin is like a broken pot that
    someone threw away.
  He is like a pot that no one wants.
  Why will Jehoiachin and his children be
    thrown out
    and sent away into a foreign land?
²⁹ Land, land, land of Judah!
    Listen to this message from the LORD!
³⁰ The LORD says, "Write this down about
    Jehoiachin:
  'He does not have children anymore!
  Jehoiachin will not be successful
    because none of his children will sit on
      the throne of David.*
  None of his children will rule in Judah.'"

23 ¹"It will be very bad for the shepherds of the people of Judah. They are
destroying the sheep. They are making the
sheep run from my pasture in all directions."
This message is from the LORD. ²They are responsible for my people. And
this is what the LORD, the God of Israel, says
to them: "You shepherds have made my sheep
run away in all directions. You have forced
them to go away, and you have not taken care
of them. But I will take care of you—I will
punish you for the evil things you did." This
message is from the LORD: ³"I sent my sheep
to other countries. But I will gather together
my sheep that are left, and I will bring them
back to their pasture. When my sheep are
back in their pasture, they will have many
children and grow in number. ⁴I will place
new shepherds over my sheep. They will take
care of my sheep, and my sheep will never
again feel afraid. None of my sheep will be
lost." This message is from the LORD.

The Good "Branch"
⁵ This message is from the LORD:
  "The time is coming,
    when I will raise up a good 'branch'
      from David's family.
  He will be a king who will rule in a wise
    way.
  He will do what is fair and right in the
    land.
⁶ When he rules, Judah* will be saved,
    and Israel* will live in safety.

ᵃ**22:23** *It's as if ... Lebanon* The king's palace in
Jerusalem was built with wood from the mountains
of Lebanon, which was famous for its cedar trees.

This will be his name:
The Lord Makes Things Right for Us.*a*

7"So the time is coming," says the Lord, "when people will not make a promise by saying, 'As surely as the Lord lives, the one who brought the Israelites out of the land of Egypt ....' 8But people will say something new: 'As surely as the Lord lives, the one who brought the Israelites out of the land of the north and out of all the countries where he had sent them ....' Then the people of Israel will live in their own land."

Judgments Against False Prophets

9 A message to the prophets:
I am very sad—my heart is broken.
All my bones are shaking.
Because of the Lord and his holy words,
I am like a man who is drunk.
10 The land of Judah* is full of people who commit adultery.*
They are unfaithful in many ways.
The Lord cursed the land,
and it became very dry.
The plants are dried and dying in the pastures.
The fields have become like the desert.
The prophets are evil.
They use their influence and power in the wrong way.
11"The prophets and even the priests are evil.
I have seen them doing evil things in my own Temple.*"
This message is from the Lord.
12"I will stop giving my messages to them.
They will walk in darkness.
The road will be slippery for those prophets and priests,
and they will fall in that darkness.
I will bring disaster on them;
I will punish them."
This message is from the Lord.
13"I saw the prophets of Samaria* doing wrong things.
I saw them prophesy* in the name of the false god Baal.*
They led the people of Israel away from the Lord.
14 I have even seen the prophets of Jerusalem doing sinful things.
They are committing adultery*
and living a life of lies.
They support their fellow prophets
and never stop doing evil.
They have become like Sodom*;
they are all like Gomorrah.*"
15 So this is what the Lord All-Powerful says about those Jerusalem prophets:

"I will make them suffer.
Their food will be bitter, their water like poison.
I will punish them because they started a spiritual sickness
that spread through the whole country.

16 This is what the Lord All-Powerful says:
"Don't pay attention to what those prophets are saying to you.
They are trying to fool you.
They talk about visions,*
but they did not get their visions from me.
Their visions come from their own minds.
17 Some of the people hate the real messages from the Lord,
so the prophets give them a different message.
They say, 'You will have peace.'
Some of the people are very stubborn.
They do only what they want to do.
So the prophets say,
'Nothing bad will happen to you!'
18 But none of these prophets has stood in the heavenly council.*b
None of them has seen or heard the message from the Lord.
None of them has paid close attention to his message.
19 Now the punishment from the Lord will come like a storm.
His anger will be like a tornado.
It will come crashing down on the heads of those wicked people.
20 The Lord's anger will not stop until he finishes what he plans to do.
When that day is over,
you will understand this clearly.
21 I did not send those prophets,
but they ran to tell their messages.
I did not speak to them,
but they spoke in my name.
22 If they had stood in my heavenly council,
then they would have told my messages to the people of Judah.
They would have stopped the people from doing bad things.
They would have stopped them from doing evil."

23 This message is from the Lord.
"I am God, and I am always near.
I am not far away.
24 Someone might try to hide from me in some hiding place.
But it is easy for me to see that person,
because I am everywhere in heaven and earth."
This is what the Lord said.

---

*a*23:6 *The Lord Makes Things Right for Us* This is a wordplay. In Hebrew this is like the name Zedekiah, the king of Judah at the time this prophecy was probably given. But Jeremiah is talking about another king.

*b*23:18 *heavenly council* The people in the Old Testament often talk about God as the leader of a council of heavenly beings (angels). Compare 1 Kings 22:19–23; Isa. 6:1–8 and Job 1 and 2.

25"There are prophets who tell lies in my name. They say, 'I have had a dream! I have had a dream!' I heard them say those things. 26How long will this continue? They think up lies and then they teach them to the people. 27They are trying to make the people of Judah forget my name by telling each other these false dreams. They are trying to make my people forget me, just as their ancestors* forgot me and worshiped the false god Baal.* 28Straw is not the same as wheat! In the same way, the dreams of those prophets are not messages from me. If people want to tell about their dreams, let them. But those who hear my message must speak it truthfully. 29You must treat my message carefully, like a fire or like a hammer that can smash a rock." This message is from the LORD.

30This message is from the LORD. "So I am against the false prophets.* They keep stealing my words from one another. 31I am against the false prophets." This message is from the LORD. "They use their own words and pretend that it is a message from me. 32I am against the false prophets who tell false dreams." This message is from the LORD. "They mislead my people with their lies and false teachings. I did not send them to teach the people. I never commanded them to do anything for me. They cannot help the people of Judah at all." This message is from the LORD.

The Sad Message From the Lord

33"The people of Judah,* or a prophet,* or a priest may ask you, 'Jeremiah, what is the announcement of the LORD?' You will answer them and say, 'You are a heavy load*a* to the LORD, and I will throw down this heavy load.' This message is from the LORD.

34"A prophet, or a priest, or maybe one of the people might say, 'This is an announcement from the LORD ....' Because of that lie, I will punish that person and their whole family. 35This is what you will say to one another: 'What did the LORD answer?' or 'What did the LORD say?' 36But you will never again use the expression, 'The announcement of the LORD.' That is because his message should not be a heavy load for anyone. But you changed the words of our God. He is the living God, the LORD All-Powerful!

37"If you want to learn about God's message, ask a prophet, 'What answer did the LORD give you?' or 'What did the LORD say?' 38But don't say, 'What was the announcement from the LORD?' If you use these words, the LORD will say this to you: 'You should not have called my message an 'announcement from the LORD.' I told you not to use those words. 39But you called my message a heavy load, so I will pick you up like a heavy load

and throw you away from me. I gave the city of Jerusalem to your ancestors.* But I will throw you and that city away from me, 40and I will make you a disgrace forever. You will never forget your shame.'"

The Good Figs and the Bad Figs

24 1The LORD showed me these things: I saw two baskets of figs arranged in front of the Temple* of the LORD. (I saw this vision after King Nebuchadnezzar of Babylon took Jehoiachin*b* as a prisoner. Jehoiachin, the son of King Jehoiakim, and all his important officials were taken away from Jerusalem. They were taken to Babylon. Nebuchadnezzar also took away all the carpenters and metalworkers of Judah.*) 2One basket had very good figs in it, the kind that ripen early in the season. But the other basket had rotten figs. They were too rotten to eat.

3The LORD said to me, "What do you see, Jeremiah?"

I answered, "I see figs. The good figs are very good, and the rotten figs are very rotten. They are too rotten to eat."

4Then the message from the LORD came to me. 5The LORD, the God of Israel, said, "The people of Judah were taken from their country. Their enemy brought them to Babylon. Those people will be like these good figs. I will be kind to them. 6I will protect them. I will bring them back to the land of Judah. I will not tear them down—I will build them up. I will not pull them up—I will plant them so that they can grow. 7I will make them want to know me. They will know that I am the LORD. They will be my people, and I will be their God. I will do this because the prisoners in Babylon will turn to me with their whole hearts.

8"But King Zedekiah of Judah will be like those figs that are too rotten to eat. Zedekiah, his high officials, all those who are left in Jerusalem, and those people of Judah who are living in Egypt will be like the rotten figs. 9"I will punish them. Their punishment will shock all the people on earth. People will make fun of those people from Judah. People will tell jokes about them and curse them in all the places where I scatter them. 10I will bring war, famine,* and disease against them. I will attack them until they have all been killed. Then they will no longer be on the land that I gave to them and to their ancestors.*"

A Summary of Jeremiah's Message

25 1This is the message that came to Jeremiah concerning all the people of Judah.* This message came in the fourth year that Jehoiakim*c* son of Josiah was king of Judah. The fourth year of his time as king

---

*a***23:33** *heavy load* This is a wordplay. The Hebrew word for "announcement" is like the word translated "heavy load."
*b***24:1** *Jehoiachin* The Hebrew text has "Jeconiah," another name for King Jehoiachin, who was taken prisoner in the year 597 B.C.
*c***25:1** *the fourth year ... Jehoiakim* This was about 605 B.C.

was the first year that Nebuchadnezzar was king of Babylon. [2]This is the message that Jeremiah the prophet* spoke to all the people of Judah and all the people of Jerusalem:

[3]I have given you messages from the LORD again and again for these past 23 years. I have been a prophet since the 13th year that Josiah son of Amon was the king of Judah. I have spoken messages from the LORD to you from that time until today. But you have not listened. [4]The LORD has sent his servants, the prophets, to you over and over again. But you have not listened to them. You have not paid any attention to them.

[5]Those prophets said, "Change your lives and stop doing evil! If you change, you can return to the land that the LORD gave you and your ancestors* long ago. He gave you this land to live in forever. [6]Don't follow other gods. Don't serve or worship them. Don't worship idols* that someone has made. That only makes me angry with you. By doing this you only hurt yourselves."[a]

[7]"But you did not listen to me." This message is from the LORD. "You worshiped idols that someone made, and that made me angry. And it only hurt you."

[8]So this is what the LORD All-Powerful says, "You have not listened to my messages. [9]I will soon send for all the tribes of the north.[b] This message is from the LORD. "I will soon send for King Nebuchadnezzar of Babylon. He is my servant. I will bring those people against the land of Judah and against the people of Judah. I will bring them against all the nations around you too. I will destroy all those countries. I will make those lands like an empty desert forever. People will see those countries, and whistle at how badly they were destroyed. [10]I will bring an end to the sounds of joy and happiness in those places. There will be no more happy sounds of the brides and bridegrooms. I will take away the sound of people grinding meal. I will take away the light of the lamp. [11]That whole area will be an empty desert. All these people will be slaves of the king of Babylon for 70 years.

[12]"But when the 70 years have passed, I will punish the king of Babylon. I will punish the nation of Babylon." This message is from the LORD. "I will punish the land of the Babylonians for their sins. I will make that land a desert forever. [13]I said many bad things will happen to Babylon, and all of them will happen. Jeremiah spoke about those foreign nations. And all the warnings are written in this book. [14]Yes, the people of Babylon will

have to serve many nations and many great kings. I will give them the punishment they deserve for all the things they have done."

Judgment on the Nations of the World

[15]The LORD, the God of Israel, said this to me: "Jeremiah, take this cup of wine from my hand. It is the wine of my anger. I am sending you to different nations. Make all the nations drink from this cup. [16]They will drink this wine. Then they will vomit and act like crazy people. They will do this because of the war that I will soon bring against them."

[17]So I took the cup of wine from the LORD's hand. I went to those nations and I made them drink from the cup. [18]I poured this wine for the people of Jerusalem and Judah.* I made the kings and leaders of Judah drink from the cup. I did this so that they would become an empty desert. I did this so that place would be destroyed so badly that people would whistle and say curses about it. And it happened—Judah is like that now.

[19]I also made Pharaoh, the king of Egypt, drink from the cup. I made his officials, his important leaders, and all his people drink from the cup of the LORD's anger.

[20]I also made all the Arabs and all the kings of the land of Uz drink from the cup.

I made all the kings of the land of the Philistines* drink from the cup. These were the kings of the cities of Ashkelon, Gaza, Ekron, and what remains of the city Ashdod.

[21]Then I made the people of Edom, Moab, and Ammon drink from the cup.

[22]I made all the kings of Tyre and Sidon drink from the cup.

I also made all the kings of the faraway countries drink from that cup. [23]I made the people of Dedan, Tema, and Buz drink from the cup. I made all those who cut their hair at their temples drink from the cup. [24]I made all the kings of Arabia drink from the cup. These kings live in the desert. [25]I made all the kings from Zimri, Elam, and Media drink from the cup. [26]I made all the kings of the north, those who were near and far, drink from the cup. I made them drink one after the other. I made all the kingdoms that are on earth drink from the cup of the anger of the LORD. But the king of Babylon will drink from this cup after all these other nations.

[27]"Jeremiah, say to those nations, this is what the LORD All-Powerful, the God of the people of Israel, says: 'Drink this cup of my anger. Get drunk from it and vomit. Fall down and don't get up. Don't get up because I am bringing wars against you.'

[28]"They will refuse to take the cup from your hand. They will refuse to drink it, but you will tell them, 'This is what the LORD All-Powerful says: You will surely drink from this cup! [29]I am already making these bad things happen to Jerusalem, the city that is called by my name. Maybe you people think that you

---

[a]25:6 By doing this you only hurt yourselves This is from the ancient Greek version. The standard Hebrew text has "Then I will not hurt you."

[b]25:9 north The Babylonian army came from this direction to attack Judah. Armies from countries north and east of Israel often came this way to attack Judah and Israel.

will not be punished, but you are wrong. You will be punished! I am giving the command for war to come against all the people of the earth.'" This message is from the LORD.

30"Jeremiah, you will give them this
    message:
    'The LORD shouts from above.
    He shouts from his holy Temple.*
    He shouts against his people.
        His shouts are loud like the songs of
            people walking on grapes to make
            wine.
31 The noise spreads to all the people on
        earth.
    What is all the noise about?
    The LORD tells why he is punishing all
        the nations.
    He has given his arguments against
        them.
    He has judged them,
        and now he is killing the wicked with
            his sword.'"
    This message is from the LORD.

32 This is what the LORD All-Powerful says:
    "Disasters will soon spread
        from country to country.
    They will come like a powerful storm
        to all the faraway places on earth!"

33The dead bodies of those people will reach from one end of the country to the other. No one will cry for them. No one will gather up their bodies and bury them. They will be left lying on the ground like dung.

34 Shepherds, you should be leading the
        sheep.
    Start crying, you great leaders!
        Roll around on the ground in pain, you
            leaders of the sheep.
    It is now time for your slaughter.
        You will be scattered everywhere, like
            pieces flying from a broken jar.
35 There will be no place for the shepherds
        to hide.
    They will not escape.
36 I hear the shepherds shouting.
    I hear the leaders of the sheep crying,
        because the LORD is destroying their
            pastures.
37 Those peaceful pastures will be ruined
        because of the LORD's anger.
38 He is like an angry lion that has left his
        cave.
    And because of his terrible anger
    and by the attacks of the enemy army,
        their land will become an empty desert.

Jeremiah's Lesson at the Temple

26 ¹This message came from the LORD during the first year that Jehoiakim[a]

son of Josiah was king of Judah.* ²The LORD said, "Jeremiah, stand in the Temple* yard of the LORD. Give this message to all the people of Judah who are coming to worship at the Temple of the LORD. Tell them everything that I tell you to speak. Don't leave out any part of my message. ³Maybe they will listen and obey my message. Maybe they will stop living such evil lives. If they change, I will change my mind about my plans to punish them. I am planning this punishment because of the many evil things they have done. ⁴You will say to them, 'This is what the LORD says: I gave my teachings to you. You must obey me and follow my teachings. ⁵You must listen to what my servants say to you. The prophets* are my servants. I have sent my prophets to you again and again, but you did not listen to them. ⁶If you don't obey me, I will make my Temple in Jerusalem just like my Holy Tent at Shiloh.[b] People all over the world will think of Jerusalem when they ask for bad things to happen to other cities.'"

⁷The priests, the prophets, and all the people heard Jeremiah say all these words at the LORD's Temple. ⁸Jeremiah finished speaking everything the LORD had commanded him to say to the people. Then the priests, the prophets, and all the people grabbed Jeremiah. They said, "You will die for saying such terrible things! ⁹How dare you say such a thing in the name of the LORD! How dare you say that this Temple will be destroyed like the one at Shiloh! How dare you say that Jerusalem will become a desert with no one living in it!" All the people gathered around Jeremiah in the Temple of the LORD.

¹⁰Now the rulers of Judah heard about everything that was happening. So they came out of the king's palace. They went up to the LORD's Temple. They took their places at the entrance of the New Gate. The New Gate is a gate leading to the LORD's Temple. ¹¹Then the priests and the prophets spoke to the rulers and all the other people. They said, "Jeremiah should be killed. He said bad things about Jerusalem. You heard him say those things."

¹²Then Jeremiah spoke to all the rulers of Judah and all the other people. He said, "The LORD sent me to say these things about this Temple and this city. Everything that you have heard is from the Lord. ¹³You people, change your lives! You must start doing good! You must obey the LORD your God. If you do that, he will change his mind. He will not do the bad things he told you about. ¹⁴As for me, I am in your power. Do to me what you think is good and right. ¹⁵But if you kill me, be sure of one thing. You will be guilty of killing an innocent person. You will make this city and everyone living in it guilty too. The LORD

---

[a]**26:1** *the first year ... Jehoiakim* This was 609 B.C.

[b]**26:6** *my Holy Tent at Shiloh* The Holy Place at Shiloh was probably destroyed during the time of Samuel. See Jer. 7 and 1 Sam. 4.

really did send me to you. The message you heard really is from the Lord."

16Then the rulers and all the people spoke. They said to the priests and the prophets, "Jeremiah must not be killed. What he told us comes from the LORD our God."

17Then some of the elders* stood up and spoke to all the people. 18They said, "Micah the prophet was from the city of Moresheth. He was a prophet during the time that Hezekiah was king of Judah. Micah said this to all the people of Judah:

'This is what the LORD All-Powerful says:
Zion* will be destroyed.
  It will become a plowed field.
Jerusalem will become a pile of rocks.
Temple Mount will be an empty hill*
  overgrown with bushes.'   *Micah 3:12*

19"King Hezekiah of Judah and the people of Judah did not kill Micah. You know that Hezekiah respected the LORD and wanted to please him. So the LORD changed his mind and didn't do the bad things to Judah that he said he would do. If we hurt Jeremiah, we will bring many troubles on ourselves. And those troubles will be our own fault."

20In the past there was another man who spoke the LORD's message. His name was Uriah son of Shemaiah from the city of Kiriath Jearim. Uriah said the same things against this city and this land that Jeremiah did. 21King Jehoiakim, his army officers, and the leaders of Judah heard Uriah and became angry. King Jehoiakim wanted to kill Uriah, but Uriah heard about it. Uriah was afraid, so he escaped to the land of Egypt. 22But King Jehoiakim sent Elnathan son of Acbor and some other men to Egypt. 23They brought Uriah from Egypt and took him to King Jehoiakim. Jehoiakim ordered Uriah to be killed with a sword. Uriah's body was thrown into the burial place where the poor are buried.

24There was an important man named Ahikam son of Shaphan who supported Jeremiah. He kept Jeremiah from being killed by the priests and prophets.

The Lord Made Nebuchadnezzar Ruler

27 1A message from the LORD came to Jeremiah. It came during the fourth year that Zedekiah*b* son of Josiah was king of Judah.* 2This is what the LORD said to me: "Jeremiah, make a yoke* out of straps and poles. Put that yoke on the back of your neck. 3Then send a message to the kings of Edom, Moab, Ammon, Tyre, and Sidon. Send the message with the messengers of these kings who have come to Jerusalem to see King Zedekiah of Judah. 4Tell them to give the message to their masters. Tell them that this is what the LORD All-Powerful, the God of Israel, says: 'Tell your masters that 5I made the earth and all the people on it. I made all the animals on the earth. I did this with my great power and my strong arm. I can give the earth to anyone I want. 6Now I have given all your countries to King Nebuchadnezzar of Babylon. He is my servant. I will make even the wild animals obey him. 7All nations will serve Nebuchadnezzar and his son and his grandson. Then the time will come for Babylon to be defeated. Many nations and great kings will make Babylon their servant.

8"'But if some nations or kingdoms refuse to serve King Nebuchadnezzar of Babylon and refuse to be put under his control, I will punish them, says the LORD. I will destroy them with war, hunger, and disease. I will use Nebuchadnezzar to destroy any nation that fights against him. 9So don't listen to your prophets. Don't listen to those who use magic to tell what will happen in the future. Don't listen to those who say they can interpret dreams. Don't listen to those who talk to the dead or to people who practice magic. All of them tell you, "You will not be slaves to the king of Babylon." 10But they are telling you lies. They will only cause you to be taken far from your homeland. I will force you to leave your homes, and you will die in another land.

11"'But the nations that put their necks under the yoke of the king of Babylon and obey him will live. I will let them stay in their own country and serve the king of Babylon,' says the LORD. 'The people from those nations will live in their own land and farm it.'"

12I gave the same message to King Zedekiah of Judah. I said, "Zedekiah, you must place your neck under the yoke of the king of Babylon and obey him. If you serve the king of Babylon and his people, you will live. 13If you don't agree to serve the king of Babylon, you and your people will die from war, hunger, and disease. This is what the LORD said would happen. 14But the false prophets* are saying, 'You will never be slaves to the king of Babylon.'

"Don't listen to those prophets, because they are telling you lies. 15'I didn't send them,' says the LORD. 'They are telling lies and saying that the message is from me. So I will send you people of Judah away. You will die, and the prophets who spoke to you will die also.'"

16Then I told the priests and all the people that this is what the LORD says: "Those false prophets are saying, 'The Babylonians took many things from the LORD's Temple.* These things will be brought back soon.' Don't

---

*a***26:18** *empty hill* Or "high place," a term usually used for local shrines (places for worship) where people often worshiped idols.
*b***27:1** *the fourth year … Zedekiah* The standard Hebrew text has "At the beginning of the kingship of Jehoiakim." This is probably a scribal error. Verse 3 talks about Zedekiah, and 28:1 says "that same year" was the fourth year of Zedekiah's reign (594–593 B.C.).

listen to them because they are telling you lies. ¹⁷Don't listen to those prophets. Serve the king of Babylon. Accept your punishment, and you will live. There is no reason for you to cause this city of Jerusalem to be destroyed. ¹⁸If they are prophets and their message is from the Lord, let them pray. Let them pray about the things that are still in the Lord's Temple. Let them pray about the things that are still in the king's palace. And let them pray about the things that are still in Jerusalem. Let them pray that all those things will not be taken away to Babylon.

¹⁹"This is what the Lord All-Powerful says about the things that are still left in Jerusalem. In the Temple, there are the pillars, the bronze sea, the moveable stands, and other things.ᵃ King Nebuchadnezzar of Babylon left those things in Jerusalem. ²⁰He didn't take them away when he took Jehoiachin son of Jehoiakim king of Judah away as a prisoner. Nebuchadnezzar also took other important people away from Judah and Jerusalem. ²¹This is what the Lord All-Powerful, the God of the people of Israel, says about the things still left in the Lord's Temple and in the king's palace and in Jerusalem: ²²'All those things will also be taken to Babylon. They will be brought to Babylon until the day comes when I go to get them,' says the Lord. 'Then I will bring those things back. I will put them back in this place.'"

The False Prophet Hananiah

28 ¹In the fifth month of the fourth year that Zedekiahᵇ was king of Judah,* the prophet* Hananiah son of Azzur spoke to me. Hananiah was from the town of Gibeon. Hananiah was in the Lord's Temple* when he spoke to me. The priests and all the people were there also. This is what Hananiah said: ²"The Lord All-Powerful, the God of the people of Israel, says: 'I will break the yoke* that the king of Babylon has put on the people of Judah. ³Before two years are over, I will bring back all the things that King Nebuchadnezzar of Babylon took from the Lord's Temple. Nebuchadnezzar has carried those things to Babylon. But I will bring them back here to Jerusalem. ⁴I will also bring the king of Judah, Jehoiachin son of Jehoiakim, back to this place. And I will bring back all the people of Judah that Nebuchadnezzar forced to leave their homes and go to Babylon,' says the Lord. 'So I will break the yoke that the king of Babylon put on the people of Judah.'"

⁵Then the prophet Jeremiah answered the prophet Hananiah. They were standing in the Temple of the Lord. The priests and all the people there could hear Jeremiah's answer.

⁶Jeremiah said to Hananiah, "Amen*! May the Lord do that. May the Lord make the message you say come true. May he bring the things of the Lord's Temple back to this place from Babylon. And may he bring all those who were forced to leave their homes back to this place.

⁷"But listen to what I have to say to you and to all the people. ⁸There were prophets long before you and I became prophets, Hananiah. They spoke against many countries and great kingdoms and always warned that war, hunger, and disease would come to them. ⁹So the prophet who says that we will have peace must be tested. People can know that he really was sent by the Lord only if his message comes true."

¹⁰Jeremiah was wearing a yoke around his neck. The prophet Hananiah took the yoke from Jeremiah's neck and broke it. ¹¹Then Hananiah spoke loudly so that all the people could hear him. He said, "This is what the Lord says: 'In the same way, I will break the yoke of King Nebuchadnezzar of Babylon. He put that yoke on all the nations of the world, but I will break it before two years are over.'"

After Hananiah said that, Jeremiah left the Temple.

¹²Then the message from the Lord came to Jeremiah. This happened after Hananiah had taken the yoke off Jeremiah's neck and had broken it. ¹³The Lord said to Jeremiah, "Go and tell Hananiah that this is what the Lord says: 'You have broken a wooden yoke, but I will make a yoke of iron in the place of the wooden yoke. ¹⁴The Lord All-Powerful, the God of Israel, is the one saying this. I will put a yoke of iron on the necks of all these nations. I will do that to make them serve King Nebuchadnezzar of Babylon, and they will be slaves to him. I will even give Nebuchadnezzar control over the wild animals.'"

¹⁵Then the prophet Jeremiah said to the prophet Hananiah, "Listen, Hananiah! The Lord did not send you. But you have made the people of Judah trust in lies. ¹⁶So this is what the Lord says: 'Soon I will take you from this world, Hananiah. You will die this year, because you taught the people to turn against the Lord.'"

¹⁷Hananiah died in the seventh month of that same year.

A Letter to the Captives in Babylon

29 ¹Jeremiah sent a letter to the captives* in Babylon. He sent it to the elders,* the priests, the prophets,* and all the other people Nebuchadnezzar had taken from Jerusalem to Babylon. ²(This letter was sent after King Jehoiachin, the queen mother, the officials and the leaders of Judah* and Jerusalem, the carpenters, and the metalworkers had been taken from Jerusalem.) ³King Zedekiah of Judah sent Elasah son of Shaphan and Gemariah son of

ᵃ27:19 pillars ... other things For a description of these things, see 1 Kings 7:23–37.
ᵇ28:1 the fourth year ... Zedekiah This was about 594–593 B.C.

Hilkiah to King Nebuchadnezzar. Jeremiah gave them the letter to take to Babylon. This is what the letter said:

⁴This is what the LORD All-Powerful, the God of the people of Israel,* says to all the people he sent into captivity from Jerusalem to Babylon: ⁵"Build houses and live in them. Settle in the land. Plant gardens and eat the food you grow. ⁶Get married and have sons and daughters. Find wives for your sons, and let your daughters be married. Do this so that they also may have sons and daughters. Have many children and grow in number in Babylon. Don't become fewer in number. ⁷Also, do good things for the city I sent you to. Pray to the LORD for the city you are living in, because if there is peace in that city, you will have peace also." ⁸The LORD All-Powerful, the God of the people of Israel, says, "Don't let your prophets and those who practice magic fool you. Don't listen to the dreams they have. ⁹They are telling lies, and they are saying that their message is from me. But I didn't send it." This message is from the LORD.

¹⁰This is what the LORD says: "Babylon will be powerful for 70 years. After that time, I will come to you people who are living in Babylon. I will keep my good promise to bring you back to Jerusalem. ¹¹I say this because I know the plans that I have for you." This message is from the LORD. "I have good plans for you. I don't plan to hurt you. I plan to give you hope and a good future. ¹²Then you will call my name. You will come to me and pray to me, and I will listen to you. ¹³You will search for me, and when you search for me with all your heart, you will find me. ¹⁴I will let you find me." This message is from the LORD. "And I will bring you back from your captivity. I forced you to leave this place. But I will gather you from all the nations and places where I have sent you," says the LORD, "and I will bring you back to this place."

¹⁵You people might say, "But the LORD has given us prophets here in Babylon." ¹⁶But this is what the LORD says about your relatives who were not carried away to Babylon. I am talking about the king who is sitting on David's* throne now and all the other people who are still in the city of Jerusalem. ¹⁷The LORD All-Powerful says, "I will soon bring war, hunger, and disease against those who are still in Jerusalem. And I will make them the same as bad figs that are too rotten to eat. ¹⁸I will attack those who are still in Jerusalem with war, hunger, and disease. I will cause such pain that all the kingdoms of the earth will be

frightened at what has happened to those people. They will be destroyed. People will whistle with amazement when they hear what happened. And people will use them as an example when they ask for bad things to happen to people. People will insult them wherever I force them to go. ¹⁹I will make all these things happen because the people of Jerusalem have not listened to my message." This message is from the LORD. "I sent my message to them again and again. I used my servants, the prophets, to give my messages to them, but they didn't listen." This message is from the LORD. ²⁰"You people are captives. I forced you to leave Jerusalem and go to Babylon. So listen to the message from the LORD."

²¹This is what the LORD All-Powerful says about Ahab son of Kolaiah and Zedekiah son of Maaseiah: "These two men have been telling you lies. They have said that their message is from me. I will give these two prophets to King Nebuchadnezzar of Babylon. And he will kill these prophets in front of all you people who are captives in Babylon. ²²All the Jewish captives will use these men as examples when they ask for bad things to happen to other people. The captives will say: 'May the LORD treat you like Zedekiah and Ahab. The king of Babylon burned those two in the fire!' ²³They did very bad things among the people of Israel. They committed the sin of adultery* with their neighbors' wives. They also spoke lies and said those lies were a message from me, the LORD. I did not tell them to do that. I know what they have done. I am a witness." This message is from the LORD.

God's Message to Shemaiah

²⁴Also give a message to Shemaiah from the Nehelam family. ²⁵This is what the LORD All-Powerful, the God of Israel, says: "Shemaiah, you sent letters to all the people in Jerusalem and to the priest Zephaniah son of Maaseiah. You also sent letters to all the priests. You sent those letters in your own name and not by the authority of the LORD. ²⁶Shemaiah, this is what you said in your letter to Zephaniah: 'Zephaniah, the LORD has made you priest in place of Jehoiada. You are to be in charge of the LORD's Temple.* You should arrest anyone who acts like a crazy personᵃ and acts like a prophet.* You should put that person's feet between large blocks of wood and put neck ironsᵇ on him. ²⁷Now Jeremiah

---

ᵃ29:26 crazy person Here, Shemaiah is referring to Jeremiah. See verses 27–28.
ᵇ29:26 neck irons A ring made from iron. People put the rings around prisoners, necks. They often fastened a chain to the ring to control the prisoners.

is acting like a prophet. So why didn't you arrest him? [28]Jeremiah has sent this message to us in Babylon: You people in Babylon will be there for a long time, so build houses and settle down. Plant gardens and eat what you grow.'"

[29]Zephaniah the priest read the letter to Jeremiah the prophet. [30]Then this message from the Lord came to Jeremiah: [31]"Jeremiah, send this message to all the captives* in Babylon: 'This is what the Lord says about Shemaiah, the man from the Nehelam family: Shemaiah has spoken to you, but I didn't send him. He has made you believe a lie. [32]Because Shemaiah has done that, this is what the Lord says: I will soon punish Shemaiah, the man from the Nehelam family. I will completely destroy his family, and he will not share in the good things I will do for my people.'" This message is from the Lord. "'I will punish Shemaiah because he has taught the people to turn against the Lord.'"

Promises of Hope

30 [1]This is the message that came to Jeremiah from the Lord. [2]The Lord, the God of the people of Israel,* said, "Jeremiah, write in a book the words I have spoken to you. Write this book for yourself. [3]Do this because the days will come"—this message is from the Lord—"when I will bring my people, Israel and Judah,* back from exile.*" This message is from the Lord. "I will put the people back in the land that I gave to their ancestors.* Then my people will own that land again."

[4]The Lord spoke this message about the people of Israel and Judah. [5]This is what the Lord said:

"We hear people crying from fear.
  There is fear, not peace.

[6]"Ask this question and consider it:
  Can a man have a baby? Of course not!
Then why do I see every strong man
  holding his stomach
  like a woman having labor pains?
Why is everyone's face turning white
  like a dead man?

[7]"This is a very important time for Jacob.*
  This is a time of great trouble.
There will never be another time like
  this,
  but Jacob will be saved.

[8]"At that time," says the Lord All-Powerful, "I will break the yoke* from the necks of the people of Israel and Judah, and I will break the ropes holding you. People from foreign countries will never again force my people to be slaves. [9]The people of Israel and Judah will not serve foreign countries. No, they will serve the Lord their God. I will send them

David* their king,[a] and they will serve him.

[10]"So Jacob, my servant, don't be afraid!"
  This message is from the Lord.
  "Israel, don't be afraid.
  I will save you from that faraway place.
You are captives[b] in that faraway land,
  but I will save your descendants.
I will bring them back from that land.
Jacob will have peace again.
  People will not bother Jacob.
There will be no enemy to frighten my
  people.
[11] People of Israel and Judah, I am with
  you."
  This message is from the Lord.
  "I will save you.
I sent you to those nations,
  but I will completely destroy all of them.
It is true; I will destroy those nations,
  but I will not destroy you.
You must be punished for the bad things
  you did,
  but I will discipline you fairly."

[12] This is what the Lord says:
  "You people of Israel and Judah have a
  wound that cannot be cured.
  You have an injury that will not heal.
[13] There is no one to care for your sores,
  so you will not be healed.
[14] You became friends with many nations,
  but those nations don't care about you.
  Your 'friends' have forgotten you.
I hurt you like an enemy.
  I punished you very hard.
I did this because of your great guilt.
  I did this because of your many sins.
[15] Israel and Judah, why are you still crying
  about your wound?
  There is no cure for it.
I, the Lord, did this to you
  because of your great guilt.
  I did this because of your many sins.
[16] Those nations destroyed you,
  but now they have been destroyed.
Israel and Judah, your enemies will
  become captives.*
They stole things from you,
  but others will steal from them.
They took things from you in war,
  but others will take things from them in
  war.
[17] And I will bring your health back
  and heal your wounds," says the Lord,
  "because other people said you were
  outcasts.[c]
  They said, 'No one cares about Zion.*'"

---

[a]**30:9 David their king** This means another king of Israel who will be great like King David.
[b]**30:10 captives** People taken away as prisoners. Here, it means the Jewish people who were taken to Babylon.
[c]**30:17 outcasts** People who are thrown out of a group by others who don't like or respect them.

18 This is what the Lord says:
"Jacob's people are now in captivity,
  but they will come back.
And I will have pity on Jacob's houses.
The city*a* is now only an empty hill
  covered with ruined buildings,
  but the city will be rebuilt on its hill.
And the king's palace will be rebuilt
  where it should be.
19 People in those places will sing songs of
    praise,
  and there will be the sound of laughter.
I will give them many children.
  Israel and Judah will not be small.
I will bring honor to them.
  No one will look down on them.
20 Jacob's family will be like the family of
    Israel long ago.
I will make Israel and Judah strong,
  and I will punish those who hurt them.
21 One of their own people will lead them.
  That ruler will come from my people.
People can come close to me only if I ask
    them to.
So I will ask that leader to come to me,
  and he will be close to me.
22 You will be my people,
  and I will be your God."

23 The Lord was very angry!
  He punished the people.
The punishment came like a storm.
  It came like a tornado against those
    wicked people.
24 The Lord will be angry
  until he is through punishing them.
He will be angry until he finishes
  the punishment he planned.
When that day comes,
  you people of Judah will understand.

The New Israel

31 ¹This is what the Lord said, "At that time I will be the God of all the tribes of Israel.* And they will be my people."

2 This is what the Lord says:
"The people who escaped the enemy's
    sword will find comfort in the desert.
  Israel will go there looking for rest."
3 From far away, the Lord
  will appear to his people.

The Lord says, "I love you people with a
    love that continues forever.
That is why I have continued
  showing you kindness.
4 Israel, my bride, I will rebuild you.
  You will be a country again.
You will pick up your tambourines again.
  You will dance with all the other people
    who are having fun.

5 You farmers of Israel will plant vineyards*
    again.
You will plant the vineyards on the hills
  around the city of Samaria.
The farmers will enjoy the fruit
  from the vineyards.
6 There will be a time when watchmen*b*
  shout this message:
'Come, let's go up to Zion*
  to worship the Lord our God!'
Even the watchmen in the hill country of
  Ephraim*c* will shout that message."

7 This is what the Lord says:
"Be happy and sing for Jacob*!
  Shout for Israel, the greatest of the
    nations!
Sing your praises and shout:
  'The Lord has saved his people!*d*
He has saved those who are left alive
  from the nation of Israel.'
8 Remember, I will bring Israel
  from that country in the north.
I will gather the people of Israel
  from the faraway places on earth.
Some of the people will be blind and
    crippled.
Some of the women will be pregnant
    and ready to give birth.
But many people will come back.
9 They will come back crying,
  but I will lead them and comfort them.
I will lead them by streams of water.
I will lead them on an easy road,
  where they will not stumble.
I will lead them in that way
  because I am Israel's father.
And Ephraim* is my firstborn* son.

10 "Nations, listen to this message from the
    Lord!
Tell this message in the faraway lands by
    the sea:
'God scattered the people of Israel,
  but he will bring them back together.
And he will watch over his flock
  like a shepherd.'
11 The Lord will bring Jacob back.
  He will save his people from those who
    are stronger.
12 The people of Israel will come to the top
    of Zion,
  and they will shout with joy.
Their faces will shine with happiness
  about the good things the Lord gives
    them.

---

*b***31:6 watchmen** This usually means a guard who stands on the city walls watching for people coming to the city. Here, it probably means the prophets.
*c***31:6 hill country of Ephraim** This was the central part of the land that had been the northern kingdom of Israel.
*d***31:7 The Lord has saved his people** Or "Lord, save your people!" This is often a shout of victory.

*a***30:18 city** This probably refers to Jerusalem. But it might also mean all the cities of Israel and Judah.

He will give them grain, new wine,
    olive oil, young sheep and cattle.
They will be like a garden
    that has plenty of water.
And the people of Israel will not
    be troubled anymore.
13 Then the young women of Israel
    will be happy and dance.
And the men, young and old,
    will join in the dancing.
I will change their sadness into happiness.
I will comfort my people, making them
    happy instead of sad.
14 I will give the priests plenty of food.
    And my people will be filled and satisfied
        with the good things I give them."
This message is from the LORD.

15 This is what the LORD says:
"A sound is heard in Ramah—
    bitter crying and great sadness.
Rachel[a] cries for her children,
    and she refuses to be comforted,
    because her children are gone."

16 But the LORD says, "Stop crying.
    Don't fill your eyes with tears.
You will be rewarded for your work."
    This message is from the LORD.
"The people of Israel will come back from
    their enemy's land.
17 Israel, there is hope for you."
    This message is from the LORD.
"Your children will come back to their
    own land.
18 I have heard Ephraim crying.
    I heard Ephraim say this:
'LORD, you punished me, and I learned my
    lesson.
I was like a calf that was never trained.
Please stop punishing me,
    and I will come back to you.
You really are the LORD my God.
19 LORD, I wandered away from you.
    But I learned about the bad things I did.
So I changed my heart and life.
I am ashamed and embarrassed about
    the foolish things I did when I was
    young.'
20 You know that Ephraim is my dear son.
    I love that child.
Yes, I often criticized Ephraim,
    but I still think about him.
I love him very much,
    and I really do want to comfort him."
This message is from the LORD.

21 "People of Israel, repair the road signs.
    Put up signs that show the way home.
Watch the road.

Remember the road you are leaving on.
Israel, my bride, come home.
    Come back to your towns.
22 Unfaithful daughter,
    how long will you wander around?"

"The LORD has created something new in
    the land:
    A woman surrounding a man.[b]"

23This is what the LORD All-Powerful, the God of Israel, says: "I will again do good things for the people of Judah.* I will bring back those who were taken away as prisoners. At that time the people in the land of Judah and in its towns will once again use these words: 'May the LORD bless you, good home and holy mountain[c]!' 24"People in all the towns of Judah will live together in peace. Farmers and those who move around with their flocks will live peacefully together in Judah. 25I will give rest and strength to those who are weak and tired."

26After hearing that, I, Jeremiah, woke up and looked around. My sleep was very pleasant.

27"The days are coming," says the LORD, "when I will help the family of Israel and Judah to grow. I will help their children and animals to grow too. It will be like planting and caring for a plant. 28In the past I watched over Israel and Judah, but I watched for the time to pull them up. I tore them down. I destroyed them. I gave many troubles to them. But now I will watch over them to build them up and make them strong." This message is from the LORD.

29"People will not use this saying anymore:

'The parents ate the sour grapes,
    but the children got the sour taste.'[d]

30No, people will die for their own sins. Those who eat sour grapes will get the sour taste."

The New Agreement

31This is what the LORD said, "The time is coming when I will make a new agreement with the family of Israel* and with the family of Judah.* 32It will not be like the agreement* I made with their ancestors.* I made that agreement when I took them by the hand and brought them out of Egypt. I was their master, but they broke that agreement." This message is from the LORD.

---

[b]31:22 *A woman surrounding a man* The Hebrew text here is hard to understand. It might be part of some saying that was familiar to the people in Jeremiah's time.
[c]31:23 *good home and holy mountain* This was a blessing for the Temple and for Mount Zion, the mountain the Temple was built on.
[d]31:29 *The parents ... sour taste* This means the children were suffering for things their parents did.

[a]31:15 *Rachel* Jacob's wife. Here, this means all the women who are crying for their husbands and children who have died in the war with Babylon.

³³"In the future I will make this agreement with the people of Israel." This message is from the LORD. "I will put my teachings in their minds, and I will write them on their hearts. I will be their God, and they will be my people. ³⁴People will not have to teach their neighbors and relatives to know the LORD, because all people, from the least important to the most important, will know me." This message is from the LORD. "I will forgive them for the evil things they did. I will not remember their sins."

The Lord Will Never Leave Israel

35 The LORD makes the sun shine in the day,
   and he makes the moon and the stars
      shine at night.
He stirs up the sea so that its waves crash
      on the shore.
The LORD All-Powerful is his name.

This is what the LORD says:
³⁶"The descendants of Israel* will never stop
      being a nation.
That would happen only if I lost control
   of the sun, moon, stars, and sea."

37 The LORD says, "I will never reject the
      descendants of Israel.
That would happen only if people could
      measure the sky above,
   and learn all the secrets of the earth
      below.
Only then would I reject them for the bad
      things they have done."
This message is from the LORD.

The New Jerusalem

³⁸This message is from the LORD, "The days are coming when the city of Jerusalem will be rebuilt for the LORD. The whole city will be rebuilt—from the Tower of Hananel to the Corner Gate. ³⁹The measuring line* will stretch from the Corner Gate straight to the hill of Gareb and then turn to the place named Gorah. ⁴⁰The whole valley where dead bodies and ashes are thrown and all the terraces down to the bottom of Kidron Valley all the way to the corner of Horse Gate will be holy to the LORD. The city of Jerusalem will never again be torn down or destroyed."

Jeremiah Buys a Field

32 ¹This is the message from the LORD that came to Jeremiah during the tenth year that Zedekiah was king of Judah.*ᵇ The tenth year of Zedekiah was the 18th year of Nebuchadnezzar. ²At that time the army of the king of Babylon was surrounding the city of Jerusalem, and Jeremiah was under arrest in the courtyard of the guard. This courtyard was at the palace of the king of Judah. ³King Zedekiah of Judah had put Jeremiah in prison in that place. Zedekiah didn't like the things Jeremiah prophesied.* Jeremiah had said, "This is what the LORD says: 'I will soon give the city of Jerusalem to the king of Babylon. Nebuchadnezzar will capture this city. ⁴King Zedekiah of Judah will not escape from the army of the Babylonians. But he will surely be given to the king of Babylon. And Zedekiah will speak to the king of Babylon face to face. He will see him with his own eyes. ⁵The king of Babylon will take Zedekiah to Babylon. Zedekiah will stay there until I have punished him.' This message is from the LORD. 'If you fight against the army of the Babylonians, you will not succeed.'"

⁶While Jeremiah was a prisoner, he said, "This message from the LORD came to me. This was the message: ⁷'Jeremiah, your cousin, Hanamel, will come to you soon. He is the son of your uncle Shallum. Hanamel will say to you, "Jeremiah, buy my field near the town of Anathoth. Buy it because you are my nearest relative. It is your right and your responsibility to buy that field."'

⁸"Then it happened just as the LORD said. My cousin Hanamel came to me in the courtyard of the guard. Hanamel said to me, 'Jeremiah, buy my field near the town of Anathoth, in the land of the tribe of Benjamin. Buy that land for yourself because it is your right to buy it and own it.'"

So I knew that this was a message from the LORD. ⁹I bought the field at Anathoth from my cousin Hanamel. I weighed out 17 shekelsᶜ of silver for him. ¹⁰I signed the deed* and had a copy of the deed sealed up.ᵈ I got some men to witness what I had done, and I weighed out the silver on the scales. ¹¹Then I took the sealed copy of the deed, which contained the demands and limits of my purchase, and the copy that was not sealed. ¹²I gave the deed to Baruch son of Neriah, the son of Mahseiah. I did this while my cousin Hanamel and the other witnesses were there. They also signed the deed. There were also many people of Judah sitting in the courtyard who saw me give the deed to Baruch.

¹³With all the people watching, I said to Baruch, ¹⁴"This is what the LORD All-Powerful, the God of Israel, says: 'Take both copies of the deed—the sealed copy and the copy that was not sealed—and put them in a clay jar. Do this so that these deeds will last a long time.' ¹⁵The LORD All-Powerful, the God of Israel, says, 'In the future my people will once again buy houses, fields, and vineyards* in the land of Israel.'"

ᶜ**32:9 shekel** 2/5 of an ounce (11.5 g).
ᵈ**32:10 sealed up** Important documents were rolled up and tied with a string. Then a piece of clay or wax was put on the string. Then a person's mark was put in that clay or wax. This way, people could prove nothing in the document was changed.

ᵃ**31:39 measuring line** A rope or chain for measuring property lines.
ᵇ**32:1 the tenth year ... Judah** This was 588-587 B.C. This was the year Jerusalem was destroyed by Nebuchadnezzar.

16After I gave the deed to Baruch son of Neriah, I prayed to the LORD:

17"LORD God, with your great power you made the earth and the sky. There is nothing too hard for you to do. 18LORD, you are loyal and kind to thousands of people, but you also bring punishment to children for their fathers' sins. Great and powerful God, your name is the LORD All-Powerful. 19You plan and do great things, LORD. You see everything that people do. You give a reward to those who do good things, and you punish those who do bad things—you give them what they deserve. 20LORD, you have been doing powerful miracles in the land of Egypt until now, in Israel and elsewhere. You are the one who made yourself as famous as you are today. 21LORD, you used powerful miracles and brought your people Israel out of Egypt. You used your own powerful hand to do this. Your power was amazing!

22"LORD, you gave the Israelites this land that you promised to give to their ancestors* long ago. It is a very good land filled with many good things. 23They came into this land and took it for their own. But they didn't obey you. They didn't follow your teachings or do what you commanded. So you made all these terrible things happen to them.

24"And now the enemy has surrounded the city. They are building ramps so that they can get over the walls of Jerusalem and capture it. Because of war, hunger, and disease, the city of Jerusalem will fall to the Babylonian army. The Babylonians are attacking the city now. LORD, you said this would happen, and now you see it is happening.

25"Lord GOD, all those bad things are happening. But now you are telling me, 'Jeremiah, buy the field with silver and choose some men to witness the purchase.' You are telling me this while the Babylonian army is ready to capture the city. Why should I waste my money like that?"

26Then this message from the LORD came to Jeremiah: 27"Jeremiah, I am the LORD. I am the God of every person on the earth. You know that nothing is impossible for me." 28The LORD also said, "I will soon give the city of Jerusalem to the Babylonian army and to King Nebuchadnezzar of Babylon. The army will capture the city. 29The Babylonian army is already attacking the city of Jerusalem. They will soon enter the city and start a fire. They will burn down this city. There are houses in this city where the people of Jerusalem made me angry by offering sacrifices to the false god Baal* on the housetops. And they poured out drink offerings to other idol gods. The Babylonian army will burn down those houses. 30I have watched the people of Israel and the people of Judah. Everything they do is evil. They have done evil things since they were young. The people of Israel have made me very angry because they worship idols* that they made with their own hands." This message is from the LORD. 31"From the time that Jerusalem was built until now, the people of this city have made me angry. This city has made me very angry, so I must remove it from my sight. 32I will destroy Jerusalem because of all the evil things the people of Israel and Judah have done. The people, their kings, leaders, their priests and prophets, the people of Judah, and the people of Jerusalem have all made me angry.

33"They should have come to me for help, but they turned their backs to me. I tried to teach them again and again, but they would not listen to me. I tried to correct them, but they would not listen. 34They have made their idols, and I hate those idols. They put their idols in the Temple* that is called by my name, so they made my Temple 'dirty.'

35"In the Valley of Ben Hinnom,a they built high places* to the false god Baal. They built those worship places so that they could burn their sons and daughters as sacrifices. I never commanded them to do such a terrible thing. I never even thought the people of Judah would do such a terrible thing.

36"You people are saying, 'The king of Babylon will capture Jerusalem. He will use war, hunger, and disease to defeat this city.' But this is what the LORD, the God of the people of Israel, says: 37'I have forced the people of Israel and Judah to leave their land. I was very angry with them, but I will bring them back to this place. I will gather them from the land where I forced them to go. I will bring them back to this place. I will let them live in peace and safety. 38The people of Israel and Judah will be my people, and I will be their God. 39I will give them the desire to be one, united people. They will have one goal—to worship me all their lives. They and their children will want to do this.

40"'I will make an agreement with the people of Israel and Judah that will last forever. In this agreement I will never turn away from them. I will always be good to them. I will make them want to respect me. Then they will never turn away from me. 41They will make me happy. I will enjoy doing good to them. And I will surely plant them in this land and make them grow. I will do this with all my heart and soul.'"

a32:35 Valley of Ben Hinnom This valley is also called "Gehenna." This name comes from the Hebrew name "Ge Hinnom—Hinnom's Valley." This place became an example of how God punishes wicked people.

⁴²This is what the LORD says: "I have brought this great disaster to the people of Israel and Judah. In the same way I will bring good things to them. I promise to do good things for them. ⁴³You people are saying, 'This land is an empty desert. There are no people or animals here. The Babylonian army defeated this country.' But in the future people will once again buy fields in this land. ⁴⁴They will use their money and buy fields. They will sign and seal their agreements. They will witness the people signing their deeds. They will again buy fields in the land where the tribe of Benjamin lives, in the area around Jerusalem, in the towns of the land of Judah, in the hill country, in the western foothills, and in the area of the southern desert. This will happen because I will bring them back home." This message is from the LORD.

The Promise of God

33 ¹While Jeremiah was still locked up in the courtyard* of the guards, the message from the LORD came to him a second time: ²"The LORD made the earth, and he keeps it safe. The LORD is his name. He says, ³'Judah, pray to me, and I will answer you. I will tell you important secrets. You have never heard these things before.' ⁴The LORD is the God of Israel. This is what he says about the houses in Jerusalem and about the palaces of the kings of Judah: 'The enemy will pull these houses down. They will build ramps up to the top of the city walls. They will use swords and fight the people in these cities.

⁵"'The people in Jerusalem have done many bad things. I am angry with them. I have turned against them, so I will kill many people there. The Babylonian army will come to fight against Jerusalem. There will be many dead bodies in the houses in Jerusalem.

⁶"'But then I will heal the people in that city. I will let them enjoy peace and safety. ⁷I will make good things happen to Judah and Israel again and make them strong as in the past. ⁸They sinned against me, but I will wash away that sin. They fought against me, but I will forgive them. ⁹Then Jerusalem will be a wonderful place. The people will be happy. People from other nations will praise it when they hear about the good things happening there. They will hear about the good things I am doing for Jerusalem.'

¹⁰"You people are saying, 'Our country is an empty desert. There are no people or animals living there.' It is now quiet in the streets of Jerusalem and in the towns of Judah. But it will be noisy there soon. ¹¹There will be sounds of joy and happiness. There will be the happy sounds of a bride and groom. There will be the sounds of people bringing their gifts to the LORD's Temple.* They will say, 'Praise the LORD All-Powerful! The LORD is good! His faithful love will last forever!' They will say this because I will again do good things to Judah. It will be as it was in the beginning." This is what the LORD said.

¹²The LORD All-Powerful says, "This place is empty now. There are no people or animals living here. But there will be people in all the towns of Judah. There will be shepherds, and there will be pastures where they will let their flocks rest. ¹³Shepherds will count their sheep as the sheep walk in front of them. They will be counting their sheep all around the country—in the hill country, in the western foothills, in the Negev,* and in all the other towns of Judah."

The Good Branch

¹⁴This message is from the LORD: "I made a special promise to the people of Israel and Judah. The time is coming when I will do what I promised. ¹⁵At that time I will make a good 'branch' grow from David's* family. That branch will do what is good and right for the country. ¹⁶When he rules, Judah will be saved. The people of Jerusalem will live in safety. This will be his name: 'The LORD Makes Things Right For Us.'"

¹⁷The LORD says, "Someone from David's family will always sit on the throne and rule the family of Israel. ¹⁸And there will always be priests from the family of Levi. They will always stand before me and offer burnt offerings* and sacrifice grain offerings and give sacrifices to me."

¹⁹This message from the LORD came to Jeremiah. ²⁰The LORD says, "I have an agreement with day and night. I agreed that they will continue forever. You cannot change that agreement. Day and night will always come at the right time. If you could change that agreement, ²¹then you could change my agreement* with David and Levi. Then descendants from David would not be the kings, and the family of Levi would not be priests. ²²But I will give many descendants to my servant David and to the tribe of Levi. They will be as many as the stars in the sky—no one can count all the stars. And they will be as many as the grains of sand on the seashore—no one can count the grains of sand."

²³Jeremiah received this message from the LORD: ²⁴"Jeremiah, have you heard what the people are saying? They are saying, 'The LORD turned away from the two families of Israel and Judah. He chose those people, but now he does not even accept them as a nation.'"

²⁵The LORD says, "If my agreement with day and night does not continue, and if I had not made the laws for the sky and earth, maybe I would leave those people. ²⁶Then maybe I would turn away from Jacob's* descendants. And then maybe I would not let David's descendants rule over the descendants of Abraham,* Isaac,* and Jacob. But David is my servant, and I will be kind to those people. I will again cause good things to happen to them."

A Warning to Zedekiah

34 ¹The message from the LORD came to Jeremiah. The message came at the time when King Nebuchadnezzar of Babylon was fighting against Jerusalem and all the towns around it. Nebuchadnezzar had with him all his army and the armies of all the kingdoms and peoples in the empire he ruled.

²This was the message: "This is what the LORD, the God of the people of Israel, says: Jeremiah, go to King Zedekiah of Judah and give him this message: 'Zedekiah, this is what the LORD says: I will give the city of Jerusalem to the king of Babylon very soon, and he will burn it down. ³Zedekiah, you will not escape from the king of Babylon. You will surely be caught and given to him. You will see the king of Babylon with your own eyes. He will talk to you face to face, and you will go to Babylon. ⁴But listen to the promise of the LORD, King Zedekiah of Judah. This is what the LORD says about you: You will not be killed with a sword. ⁵You will die in a peaceful way. People made funeral fires to honor your ancestors,* the kings who ruled before you became king. In the same way people will make a funeral fire to honor you. They will cry for you and sadly say, "Oh, my master!" I myself make this promise to you.'" This message is from the LORD.

⁶So Jeremiah gave the message from the LORD to Zedekiah in Jerusalem. ⁷This was while the army of the king of Babylon was fighting against Jerusalem. The army of Babylon was also fighting against the cities of Judah that had not been captured. These cities were Lachish and Azekah. These were the only fortified cities left in the land of Judah.

The People Break an Agreement

⁸King Zedekiah had made an agreement with all the people in Jerusalem to give freedom to all the Hebrew slaves. A message from the LORD came to Jeremiah after Zedekiah had made that agreement. ⁹Everyone was supposed to free their Hebrew slaves. All male and female Hebrew slaves were to be set free. No one was supposed to keep another person from the tribe of Judah in slavery. ¹⁰So all the leaders of Judah and all the people accepted this agreement. They would free their male and female slaves so that they would no longer serve them. Everyone agreed, and so all the slaves were set free. ¹¹But after that,ᵃ the people who had slaves changed their minds.

So they took the people they had set free and made them slaves again.

¹²Then this message from the LORD came to Jeremiah: ¹³"This is what the LORD, the God of the people of Israel, says: 'I brought your ancestors* out of the land of Egypt, where they were slaves. When I did that, I made an agreement* with them. ¹⁴I said to your ancestors, "At the end of every seven years, everyone must set their Hebrew slaves free. If you have fellow Hebrews who have sold themselves to you, you must let them go free after they have served you for six years." But your ancestors did not listen to me or pay attention to me. ¹⁵A short time ago you changed your hearts to do what is right. Everyone set free their fellow Hebrews who were slaves. And you even made an agreement before me in the Temple* that is called by my name. ¹⁶But now you have changed your minds. You have shown that you do not honor my name, because each of you has taken back the male and female slaves that you had set free. You have forced them to become slaves again.'

¹⁷"So this is what the LORD says: 'You people have not obeyed me. You have not given freedom to your fellow Hebrews. So, because you have not given them freedom, I will give a special kind of freedom—freedom to die in war or by disease or by hunger! This message is from the LORD. When the other nations see what I have done to you, they will all be shocked. ¹⁸I will hand over those who broke my agreement and have not kept the promises they made before me. They cut a calf into two pieces before me and walked between the two pieces.ᵇ ¹⁹These are the people who walked between the two pieces of the calf when they made the agreement before me: the leaders of Judah and Jerusalem, the important officials of the court, the priests, and the people of the land. ²⁰So I will give them to their enemies and to everyone who wants to kill them. Their bodies will become food for the birds of the air and for the wild animals of the earth. ²¹I will give King Zedekiah of Judah and his leaders to their enemies and to everyone who wants to kill them. I will give Zedekiah and his people to the army of the king of Babylon, even though that army has left Jerusalem.ᶜ ²²But I will give the order,' says the LORD, 'to bring the Babylonian army back to Jerusalem. That

---

ᵃ**34:11** *after that* In the summer of 588 B.C., the Egyptian army came to help the people of Jerusalem. So the Babylonian army had to leave Jerusalem for a short time to fight the Egyptians. The people of Jerusalem thought God had helped them, and things were back to normal, so they didn't keep their promise. They took the slaves they had set free back into slavery.

ᵇ**34:18** *They … two pieces* This is part of a ceremony people used when they made an important agreement. An animal was cut into two pieces. Those who were making the agreement would walk between the pieces. Then they would say something like, "May this same thing happen to me if I don't keep the agreement." See Gen. 15.

ᶜ**34:21** *left Jerusalem* In the summer of 588 B.C., the Egyptian army came to help the people of Jerusalem. So the Babylonian army had to leave Jerusalem for a short time to fight the Egyptians. See Jer. 37:5. See also the footnote to Jer. 34:11.

army will fight against Jerusalem. They will capture it, set it on fire, and burn it down. And I will destroy the towns in the land of Judah. They will become empty deserts. No one will live there.'"

The Recabite Family's Good Example

35 ¹During the time when Jehoiakim was king of Judah, the message from the LORD came to Jeremiah. Jehoiakim was the son of King Josiah. This was the message from the LORD: ²"Jeremiah, go to the Recabite family.ᵃ Invite them to come to one of the side rooms of the Temple* of the LORD. Offer them wine to drink."

³So I went to get Jaazaniahᵇ son of Jeremiah,ᶜ who was the son of Habazziniah. And I got all of Jaazaniah's brothers and sons and the whole family of the Recabites together. ⁴Then I brought them into the Temple of the LORD. We went into the room of the sons of Hanan, the son of Igdaliah. Hanan was a man of God.ᵈ The room was next to the room where the princes of Judah stay. It was over the room of Maaseiah son of Shallum. Maaseiah was the doorkeeper in the Temple. ⁵Then I put some bowls full of wine and some cups in front of the Recabite family. And I said to them, "Drink some wine."

⁶But the Recabite family answered, "We never drink wine. We never drink it because our ancestor* Jonadab son of Recab gave us this command: 'You and your descendants must never drink wine. ⁷Also you must never build houses, plant seeds, or plant vineyards.* You must never do any of those things. You must live only in tents. If you do that, you will live a long time in the land where you move from place to place.' ⁸So we have obeyed everything our ancestor Jonadab commanded us. None of us ever drinks wine, and neither do our wives, sons, or daughters. ⁹We never build houses to live in, we never own vineyards or fields, and we never plant crops. ¹⁰We have lived in tents and have obeyed everything our ancestor Jonadab commanded us. ¹¹But when King Nebuchadnezzar of Babylon attacked the country of Judah, we did go into Jerusalem. We said to each other, 'Come, we must enter the city of Jerusalem so that we can escape the Babylonian army and the Aramean army.' So we have stayed in Jerusalem."

¹²Then this message from the LORD came to Jeremiah: ¹³"The LORD All-Powerful, the God of Israel, says to go and tell this message to the people of Judah and to the people of Jerusalem: 'You should learn a lesson and obey my message.' This message is from the LORD. ¹⁴'Jonadab son of Recab ordered his sons not to drink wine, and that command has been obeyed. To this day the descendants of Jonadab have obeyed their ancestor's command. They do not drink wine. But I am the LORD, and I have given you people of Judah messages again and again. But you did not obey me. ¹⁵I sent my servants the prophets to you people of Israel and Judah. I sent them to you again and again. They said, "You must each stop doing evil things and do what is right. Don't follow other gods. Don't worship or serve them. If you obey me, you will live in the land I have given to you and your ancestors." But you have not paid attention to my message. ¹⁶The descendants of Jonadab obeyed the commands that their ancestor gave them, but the people of Judah have not obeyed me.'

¹⁷"So this is what the LORD God All-Powerful, the God of Israel, says: 'I said that many bad things would happen to Judah and Jerusalem. I will soon make all those bad things happen. I spoke to the people, but they refused to listen. I called out to them, but they didn't answer me.'"

¹⁸Then Jeremiah said to the Recabite family, "This is what the LORD All-Powerful, the God of Israel, says: 'You have obeyed the commands of your ancestor Jonadab. You have followed all of his teachings. You have done everything he commanded.' ¹⁹So the LORD All-Powerful, the God of Israel, says: 'There will always be a descendant of Jonadab son of Recab to serve me.'"

King Jehoiakim Burns Jeremiah's Scroll

36 ¹The message from the LORD came to Jeremiah. This was during the fourth year that Jehoiakimᵉ son of Josiah was king of Judah. This was the message from the Lord: ²"Jeremiah, get a scroll* and write on it all the messages I have spoken to you. I have spoken to you about the nations of Israel and Judah and all the other nations. Write all the words that I have spoken to you from the time that Josiah was king, until now. ³Maybe the people of Judah will hear what I am planning to do to them and will stop doing bad things. If they will do that, I will forgive them for the terrible sins they have committed."

⁴So Jeremiah called a man named Baruch son of Neriah. Jeremiah spoke the messages the LORD had given him. While he spoke, Baruch wrote the messages on the scroll. ⁵Then Jeremiah said to Baruch, "I cannot go to the LORD's Temple.* I am not allowed to go there. ⁶So I want you to go to the Temple of

---

ᵃ**35:2** *Recabite family* A group of people descended from Jonadab son of Recab. The family was very loyal to the Lord. See 2 Kings 10:15–28 for the story of Jonadab. Also in verses 6, 18.

ᵇ**35:3** *Jaazaniah* He was the head of the Recabite family at that time.

ᶜ**35:3** *Jeremiah* This is not the prophet Jeremiah, but a different man with the same name.

ᵈ**35:4** *man of God* This is usually an honorable title for a prophet. We know nothing else about Hanan.

ᵉ**36:1** *the fourth year ... Jehoiakim* This was about 605 B.C.

the Lord. Go there on a day of fasting* and read to the people the messages from the scroll. Read to the people the messages from the Lord that you wrote on the scroll as I spoke them to you. Read them to all the people of Judah who come into Jerusalem from the towns where they live. ⁷Perhaps they will ask the Lord to help them. Perhaps each person will stop doing bad things. The Lord has announced that he is very angry with them." ⁸So Baruch son of Neriah did everything Jeremiah the prophet* told him to do. Baruch read aloud the scroll that had the Lord's messages written on it. He read it in the Lord's Temple.

⁹In the ninth month of the fifth year that Jehoiakim was king, a fast was announced. All those who lived in the city of Jerusalem and everyone who had come into Jerusalem from the towns of Judah were supposed to fast before the Lord. ¹⁰At that time Baruch read the scroll that contained Jeremiah's words. He read the scroll in the Temple of the Lord to all the people who were there. Baruch was in the room of Gemariah in the upper courtyard when he read from the scroll. That room was located at the entrance of the New Gate of the Temple. Gemariah was the son of Shaphan. Gemariah was a scribe* in the Temple.

¹¹A man named Micaiah heard all the messages from the Lord that Baruch read from the scroll. Micaiah was the son of Gemariah, the son of Shaphan. ¹²When Micaiah heard the messages from the scroll, he went down to the secretary's room in the king's palace. All the royal officials were sitting there in the king's palace. These are the names of the officials: Elishama the secretary, Delaiah son of Shemaiah, Elnathan son of Acbor, Gemariah son of Shaphan, Zedekiah son of Hananiah; all the other royal officials were there too. ¹³Micaiah told them everything he had heard Baruch read from the scroll.

¹⁴Then all the officials sent a man named Jehudi to Baruch. (Jehudi was the son of Nethaniah, son of Shelemiah. Shelemiah was the son of Cushi.) Jehudi said to Baruch, "Bring the scroll that you read from and come with me."

Baruch son of Neriah took the scroll and went with Jehudi to the officials.

¹⁵Then the officials said to Baruch, "Sit down and read the scroll to us."

So Baruch read the scroll to them.

¹⁶When the royal officials heard all the messages from the scroll, they were afraid and looked at one another. They said to Baruch, "We must tell King Jehoiakim about these messages on the scroll." ¹⁷Then the officials asked Baruch, "Tell us, Baruch, where did you get these messages that you wrote on the scroll? Did you write down what Jeremiah said to you?"

¹⁸"Yes," Baruch answered. "Jeremiah spoke, and I wrote down all the messages with ink on this scroll."

¹⁹Then the royal officials said to Baruch, "You and Jeremiah must go and hide. Don't tell anyone where you are hiding."

²⁰Then the royal officials put the scroll in the room of Elishama the scribe. They went to King Jehoiakim and told him all about the scroll.

²¹So King Jehoiakim sent Jehudi to get the scroll. Jehudi brought the scroll from the room of Elishama the scribe. Then Jehudi read the scroll to the king and all the servants who stood around the king. ²²The time this happened was in the ninth month,ᵃ so King Jehoiakim was sitting in the part of the palace used for winter. There was a fire burning in a small fireplace in front of the king. ²³Jehudi began to read from the scroll. But after he would read two or three columns, King Jehoiakim would grab the scroll. Then he would cut those columns off the scroll with a small knife and throw them into the fireplace. Finally, the whole scroll was burned in the fire. ²⁴And, when King Jehoiakim and his servants heard the message from the scroll, they were not afraid. They did not tear their clothes to show sorrow for doing wrong.

²⁵Elnathan, Delaiah, and Gemariah tried to talk King Jehoiakim out of burning the scroll, but he would not listen to them. ²⁶Instead King Jehoiakim commanded some men to arrest Baruch the scribe and Jeremiah the prophet. These men were Jerahmeel, a son of the king, Seraiah son of Azriel, and Shelemiah son of Abdeel. But they could not find Baruch and Jeremiah, because the Lord had hidden them.

²⁷King Jehoiakim burned the scroll on which Baruch had written all the words that Jeremiah had spoken to him. Then this message from the Lord came to Jeremiah:

²⁸"Get another scroll. Write all the messages on it that were on the first scroll that King Jehoiakim of Judah burned. ²⁹Also tell King Jehoiakim of Judah that this is what the Lord says: 'Jehoiakim, you burned that scroll. You said, "Why did Jeremiah write that the king of Babylon will surely come and destroy this land and kill all the people and animals in it?" ³⁰So this is what the Lord says about King Jehoiakim of Judah: Jehoiakim's descendants will not sit on David's* throne. When Jehoiakim dies, he will not get a king's funeral, but his body will be thrown out on the ground. His body will be left out in the heat of the day and the cold frost of the night. ³¹I, the Lord, will punish Jehoiakim and his children, and I will punish his officials. I will do this because they are wicked. I have promised to bring terrible disasters on them and on all those who live in Jerusalem and on the people from Judah. I will bring all the bad things on them,

---

ᵃ**36:22** *ninth month* That is, November–December.

just as I promised, because they have not listened to me.'"

³²Then Jeremiah took another scroll and
gave it to Baruch son of Neriah, the scribe. As
Jeremiah spoke, Baruch wrote on the scroll
the same messages that were on the scroll
that King Jehoiakim had burned in the fire.
And many other words like those messages
were added to the second scroll.

Jeremiah Is Put Into Prison

37 ¹Nebuchadnezzar was the king of
Babylon. He appointed Zedekiah son
of Josiah to be the king of Judah in the place of
Jehoiachin son of Jehoiakim. ²But Zedekiah,
his servants, and the people of Judah did not
pay attention to the messages the LORD had
given to Jeremiah the prophet.*

³King Zedekiah sent Jehucal son of Shelemiah and the priest Zephaniah son of
Maaseiah to Jeremiah the prophet with a
message. This was the message they brought
to Jeremiah: "Jeremiah, pray to the LORD our
God for us."

⁴At that time Jeremiah had not yet been put
into prison, so he was free to go anywhere
he wanted. ⁵Also at that time Pharaoh's army
had marched from Egypt toward Judah. The
Babylonian army had surrounded the city of
Jerusalem in order to defeat it. Then they had
heard about the army from Egypt marching
toward them. So the army from Babylon left
Jerusalem to fight with the army from Egypt.

⁶This message from the LORD came to Jeremiah the prophet: ⁷"This is what the LORD,
the God of the people of Israel, says: 'Jehucal
and Zephaniah, I know that King Zedekiah of
Judah sent you to me to ask questions. Tell
King Zedekiah this: Pharaoh's army marched
out of Egypt to come here to help you against
the army of Babylon. But Pharaoh's army
will go back to Egypt. ⁸After that, the army
from Babylon will come back here and attack
Jerusalem. Then they will capture and burn
it.' ⁹This is what the LORD says: 'People of
Jerusalem, don't fool yourselves. Don't say to
yourselves, "The army of Babylon will surely
leave us alone." They will not. ¹⁰People of
Jerusalem, even if you could defeat all the
Babylonian army that is attacking you, there
would still be a few wounded men left in their
tents. Even those few wounded men would
come out of their tents and burn Jerusalem
down.'"

¹¹When the Babylonian army left Jerusalem to fight the army of the Pharaoh of Egypt,
¹²Jeremiah wanted to travel from Jerusalem
to the land of Benjamin.ᵃ He wanted to be
there for a division of some property that
belonged to his family. ¹³But when Jeremiah

got to the Benjamin Gate of Jerusalem,ᵇ the
captain in charge of the guards arrested him.
The captain's name was Irijah son of Shelemiah. Shelemiah was the son of Hananiah.
So Irijah the captain arrested Jeremiah and
said, "Jeremiah, you are leaving us to join the
Babylonian side."

¹⁴Jeremiah said to Irijah, "That is not true!
I am not leaving to join the Babylonians." But
Irijah refused to listen to Jeremiah. And Irijah
arrested Jeremiah and took him to the royal
officials of Jerusalem. ¹⁵Those officials were
very angry with Jeremiah. They gave an order
for Jeremiah to be beaten. Then they put him
in a prison. The prison was in the house of
Jonathan, a scribe* for the king of Judah. His
house had been made into a prison. ¹⁶They
put Jeremiah into a cell under the house of
Jonathan. The cell was in a dungeon* under
the ground. Jeremiah was there for a long
time.

¹⁷Then King Zedekiah sent for Jeremiah
and had him brought to the palace. Zedekiah
talked to Jeremiah in private. He asked Jeremiah, "Is there any message from the LORD?"

Jeremiah answered, "Yes, there is a message
from the LORD. Zedekiah, you will be given to
the king of Babylon." ¹⁸Then Jeremiah said
to King Zedekiah, "What have I done wrong?
What crime have I done against you or your
officials or the people of Jerusalem? Why have
you thrown me into prison? ¹⁹King Zedekiah,
where are your prophets now? They told you
a false message. They said, 'The king of Babylon will not attack you or this land of Judah.'
²⁰But now, my lord, king of Judah, please listen to me. Please let me bring my request to
you. This is what I ask: Don't send me back to
the house of Jonathan the scribe. If you send
me back, I will die there."

²¹So King Zedekiah gave orders for Jeremiah to be put under guard in the courtyard.
And he ordered that Jeremiah should be given
bread from the street bakers. He was given
bread until there was no more bread in the
city. So Jeremiah stayed under guard in the
courtyard.

Jeremiah Is Thrown Into a Cistern

38 ¹Some of the royal officials heard
what Jeremiah was saying. They were
Shephatiah son of Mattan, Gedaliah son of
Pashhur, Jehucal son of Shelemiah, and Pashhur son of Malkijah. Jeremiah was telling all
the people this message: ²"This is what the
LORD says: 'Everyone who stays in Jerusalem will die from war, hunger, or disease.
But everyone who surrenders to the army of
Babylon will live and escape with their lives.'
³And this is what the LORD says: 'This city
of Jerusalem will surely be given to the army

ᵃ37:12 *the land of Benjamin* Jeremiah was going
to his hometown, Anathoth, which was in the land
of Benjamin.

ᵇ37:13 *Benjamin Gate of Jerusalem* This gate led
out of Jerusalem to the road which went north to
the land of Benjamin.

of the king of Babylon. He will capture this city.'"

⁴Then the royal officials who heard what Jeremiah was telling the people went to King Zedekiah. They said to the king, "Jeremiah should be put to death. He is discouraging the soldiers who are still in the city and everyone else by what he is saying. He is not looking for peace; he is just trying to cause trouble."

⁵So King Zedekiah said to the officials, "Jeremiah is in your control. I cannot do anything to stop you."

⁶So the officials took Jeremiah and put him into Malkijah's cistern. Malkijah was the king's son. The cistern was in the Temple* yard where the king's guard stayed. They used ropes to lower Jeremiah into the cistern. The cistern didn't have any water in it, only mud. And Jeremiah sank down into the mud.

⁷But a man named Ebed Melech heard that the officials had put Jeremiah into the cistern. Ebed Melech was from Ethiopia, and he was a eunuch* in the king's palace. King Zedekiah was sitting at the Benjamin Gate, so Ebed Melech left the king's palace and went to talk to the king at the gate. ⁸⁻⁹Ebed Melech said, "My lord and king, these officials have done evil. They have treated Jeremiah the prophet* badly. They have thrown him into a cistern and left him there to die."ᵃ

¹⁰Then King Zedekiah gave a command to Ebed Melech, the Ethiopian. This was the command: "Ebed Melech, take threeᵇ men from the palace with you, and go get Jeremiah out of the cistern before he dies."

¹¹So Ebed Melech took the men with him. But first he went to a room under the storeroom in the king's palace. He took some old rags and worn-out clothes from that room. Then he let the rags down with some ropes to Jeremiah in the cistern. ¹²Ebed Melech, the Ethiopian, said to Jeremiah, "Put these old rags and worn-out clothes under your arms. When we pull you out, these rags will pad your underarms. Then the ropes will not hurt you." So Jeremiah did as Ebed Melech said. ¹³The men pulled Jeremiah up with the ropes and lifted him out of the cistern. And Jeremiah stayed under guard in the Temple yard.

Zedekiah Asks Jeremiah Some Questions

¹⁴Then King Zedekiah sent someone to get Jeremiah the prophet.* He had Jeremiah brought to the third entrance to the Temple* of the LORD. Then the king said, "Jeremiah, I am going to ask you something. Don't hide anything from me, but tell me everything honestly."

¹⁵Jeremiah said to Zedekiah, "If I give you an answer, you will probably kill me. And even if I give you advice, you will not listen to me."

¹⁶But King Zedekiah secretly swore an oath* to Jeremiah. Zedekiah said, "As surely as the LORD lives, who gives us breath and life, I will not kill you, Jeremiah. And I promise not to give you to the officials who want to kill you."

¹⁷Then Jeremiah said to King Zedekiah, "The LORD God All-Powerful is the God of Israel. This is what he says, 'If you surrender to the officials of the king of Babylon, your life will be saved, and Jerusalem will not be burned down. And you and your family will live. ¹⁸But if you refuse to surrender, Jerusalem will be given to the Babylonian army. They will burn Jerusalem down, and you will not escape from them.'"

¹⁹But King Zedekiah said to Jeremiah, "But I am afraid of the men of Judah who have already gone over to the side of the Babylonian army. I am afraid that the soldiers will give me to those men, and they will treat me badly and hurt me."

²⁰But Jeremiah answered, "The soldiers will not give you to the men of Judah. King Zedekiah, obey the LORD by doing what I tell you. Then things will go well for you, and your life will be saved. ²¹But if you refuse to surrender to the army of Babylon, the LORD has shown me what will happen. This is what he has told me: ²²All the women who are left in the house of the king of Judah will be brought out. They will be brought to the important officials of the king of Babylon. Your women will make fun of you with a song. This is what they will say:

'Your friends were stronger than you,
    and they led you the wrong way.
You trusted them,
    but now your feet are stuck in the mud,
    and your friends have left you.'

²³"All your wives and children will be brought out. They will be given to the Babylonian army. You yourself will not escape from the army of Babylon. You will be captured by the king of Babylon, and Jerusalem will be burned down."

²⁴Then Zedekiah said to Jeremiah, "Don't tell anyone that I have been talking to you. If you do, you might die. ²⁵If the officials find out that I talked to you, they will come to you and say, 'Jeremiah, tell us what you said to King Zedekiah and what he said to you. Be honest with us, and tell us everything, or we will kill you.' ²⁶If they say this to you, tell them, 'I was begging the king not to send me back to the cell in the dungeon* under Jonathan's house. If I were to go back there, I would die.'"

²⁷It happened that the royal officials of the king did come to Jeremiah to question him.

ᵃ**38:8-9** *left him there to die* Literally, "he will starve to death because there is no more bread in the city."
ᵇ**38:10** *three* This is found in one ancient Hebrew copy. Most Hebrew copies have "30."

So Jeremiah told them everything the king had ordered him to say. Then they left Jeremiah alone. No one had heard what Jeremiah and the king had talked about.

²⁸So Jeremiah stayed under guard in the Temple yard until the day Jerusalem was captured.

The Fall of Jerusalem

39 ¹This is how Jerusalem was captured: During the tenth month of the ninth year that Zedekiah was king of Judah, King Nebuchadnezzar of Babylon marched against Jerusalem with his whole army. He surrounded the city to defeat it. ²And on the ninth day of the fourth month in Zedekiah's eleventh year, the wall of Jerusalem was broken through. ³Then all the royal officials of the king of Babylon came into the city of Jerusalem. They came in and sat down at the Middle Gate. These are the names of the officials: Nergal-Sharezer, the governor of the district of Samgar, a very high official; Nebo Sarsekim, another very high official; and various other important officials were there also.

⁴King Zedekiah of Judah saw the officials from Babylon, so he and the soldiers with him ran away. They left Jerusalem at night. They went out through the king's garden and out through the gate that was between the two walls. Then they went toward the desert. ⁵The Babylonian army chased Zedekiah and the soldiers with him. They caught up with Zedekiah in the plains of Jericho. They captured Zedekiah and took him to King Nebuchadnezzar of Babylon. Nebuchadnezzar was at the town of Riblah in the land of Hamath. At that place, Nebuchadnezzar decided what to do to Zedekiah. ⁶There at the town of Riblah, the king of Babylon killed Zedekiah's sons and he killed all the royal officials of Judah while Zedekiah watched. ⁷Then Nebuchadnezzar tore out Zedekiah's eyes. He put bronze chains on Zedekiah and took him to Babylon.

⁸The army of Babylon set fire to the king's palace and the houses of the people of Jerusalem. And they broke down the walls of Jerusalem. ⁹Nebuzaradan was the commander of the king of Babylon's special guards. He took all the people who had surrendered to him and all the people still in Jerusalem and made them captives.* He carried them away to Babylon. ¹⁰But commander Nebuzaradan left behind some of the poor people of Judah who owned nothing. Nebuzaradan gave them vineyards* and farmland in Judah.

¹¹Nebuchadnezzar also gave an order about Jeremiah to commander Nebuzaradan: ¹²"Find Jeremiah and take care of him. Don't hurt him. Give him whatever he asks for."

¹³So Nebuzaradan, the commander of the king's special guards, Nebushazban, a chief officer in the army of Babylon, Nergal-Sharezer, a high official, and all the other officers of the army of Babylon sent for Jeremiah. ¹⁴They had Jeremiah taken out of the Temple* yard where he had been under the guard of the king of Judah. They turned Jeremiah over to Gedaliah^a son of Ahikam, the son of Shaphan. Gedaliah had orders to take Jeremiah back home. So Jeremiah was taken home, and he stayed among his own people.

The Lord's Message to Ebed Melech

¹⁵While the guards were watching Jeremiah in the Temple* yard, a message from the LORD came to him. This was the message: ¹⁶"Jeremiah, go and tell Ebed Melech^b the Ethiopian this message: 'This is what the LORD All-Powerful, the God of the people of Israel, says: Very soon I will make my messages about this city of Jerusalem come true. My messages will come true through disaster, not through something good. You will see everything come true with your own eyes. ¹⁷But I will save you on that day, Ebed Melech.' This is the message from the LORD. 'You will not be given to the people you are afraid of. ¹⁸I will save you, Ebed Melech. You will not die from a sword, but you will escape and live. That will happen because you have trusted in me.'" This message is from the LORD.

Jeremiah Is Set Free

40 ¹The message from the LORD came to Jeremiah after he was set free at the city of Ramah. Nebuzaradan, the commander of the king of Babylon's special guards, found Jeremiah in Ramah. Jeremiah was bound with chains. He was with all the captives* from Jerusalem and Judah. They were being taken away in captivity to Babylon. ²When commander Nebuzaradan found Jeremiah, he spoke to him. He said, "Jeremiah, the LORD, your God, announced that this disaster would come to this place. ³And now the LORD has done everything just as he said he would do. This disaster happened because you people of Judah sinned against the LORD. You didn't obey the LORD. ⁴But now, Jeremiah, I will set you free. I am taking the chains off your wrists. If you want to, come with me to Babylon, and I will take good care of you. But if you don't want to come with me, then don't come. Look, the whole country is open to you. Go anywhere you want. ⁵Or go back to Gedaliah^c son of Ahikam, the son of Shaphan. The king of Babylon has chosen Gedaliah to be governor over the towns of Judah. Go and live with Gedaliah among the people. Or you can go anywhere you want."

Then Nebuzaradan gave Jeremiah some food and a present and let him go. ⁶So Jeremiah

---

^a**39:14 Gedaliah** Gedaliah was the man who Nebuchadnezzar appointed as his governor for the land of Judah.
^b**39:16 Ebed Melech** See Jer. 38:7-13.
^c**40:5 Or … Gedaliah** Or "Before Gedaliah goes back, return to him …."

went to Gedaliah son of Ahikam at Mizpah. He stayed with Gedaliah among those who were left behind in the land of Judah.

The Short Rule of Gedaliah

⁷There were some soldiers from the army of Judah, officers and their men, still out in the open country when Jerusalem was destroyed. They heard that the king of Babylon had put Gedaliah son of Ahikam in charge of those who were left in the land. Those who were left were men, women, and children who were very poor. They were not carried off to Babylon as captives.* ⁸So the soldiers came to Gedaliah at Mizpah. They were Ishmael son of Nethaniah, Johanan and his brother Jonathan, sons of Kareah, Seraiah son of Tanhumeth, sons of Ephai from Netophah, and Jaazaniah son of the Maacathite, and the men who were with them.

⁹Gedaliah son of Ahikam, son of Shaphan, made an oath* to make the soldiers and their men feel more secure. This is what he said: "You soldiers, don't be afraid to serve the Babylonian people. Settle down in the land and serve the king of Babylon. If you do this, things will go well for you. ¹⁰I myself will live in Mizpah. I will speak for you before the Chaldeans* who come here. You leave that work to me. You should harvest the wine, the summer fruit, and the oil. Put what you harvest in your storage jars. Live in the towns that you control."

¹¹All the people of Judah who were in the countries of Moab, Ammon, Edom, and all the other countries heard that the king of Babylon had left some people of Judah in the land. And they heard that the king of Babylon had chosen Gedaliah son of Ahikam, son of Shaphan, to be governor over them. ¹²When the people of Judah heard this news, they came back to the land of Judah. They came back to Gedaliah at Mizpah from all the countries where they had been scattered. So they came back and gathered a large harvest of wine and summer fruit.

¹³Johanan son of Kareah and all the officers of the army of Judah who were still in the open country came to Gedaliah. Gedaliah was at the town of Mizpah. ¹⁴Johanan and the officers with him said to Gedaliah, "Do you know that Baalis, the king of the Ammonites, wants to kill you? He has sent Ishmael son of Nethaniah to kill you." But Gedaliah son of Ahikam didn't believe them.

¹⁵Then Johanan son of Kareah spoke to Gedaliah in private at Mizpah. Johanan said to Gedaliah, "Let me go and kill Ishmael son of Nethaniah. No one will know anything about it. We should not let Ishmael kill you. That would cause all the people of Judah who are gathered around you to be scattered to different countries again. And that would mean that the few survivors* of Judah would be lost."

¹⁶But Gedaliah son of Ahikam said to Johanan son of Kareah, "Don't kill Ishmael. The things you are saying about Ishmael are not true."

41

¹In the seventh month, Ishmael son of Nethaniah (the son of Elishama) came to Gedaliah son of Ahikam. Ishmael came with ten of his men. They came to the town of Mizpah. Ishmael was a member of the king's family. He had been one of the officers of the king of Judah. Ishmael and his men ate a meal with Gedaliah. ²While they were eating together, Ishmael and his ten men got up and killed Gedaliah son of Ahikam with a sword. Gedaliah was the man the king of Babylon had chosen to be governor of Judah. ³Ishmael also killed all the men of Judah who were with Gedaliah at the town of Mizpah. He also killed the Babylonian soldiers who were there with Gedaliah.

⁴⁻⁵The day after Gedaliah was murdered, 80 men came to Mizpah. They were bringing grain offerings and incense* to the LORD's Temple.* They had shaved off their beards, torn their clothes, and cut themselves.ᵃ They came from Shechem, Shiloh, and Samaria. None of these men knew that Gedaliah had been murdered. ⁶Ishmael left Mizpah and went to meet the 80 men. He criedᵇ while he walked out to meet them. Ishmael met them and said, "Come with me to meet with Gedaliah son of Ahikam." ⁷⁻⁸As soon as they were in the city, Ishmael and the men with him began to kill the 80 men and throw them into a deep cistern! But ten of the men said to Ishmael, "Don't kill us! We have hidden some things in a field. We have wheat and barley and oil and honey." So Ishmael stopped and didn't kill them with the others. ⁹(Ishmael threw the dead bodies into the cistern until it was full, and that cistern was very big! It had been built by a king of Judah named Asa. King Asa had made the cistern so that during war there would be water in the city.ᶜ Asa did this to protect his city from King Baasha of Israel.)

¹⁰Ishmael captured all the other people in the town of Mizpah and started to cross over to the country of the Ammonites. They included the king's daughters, and all those who were left there. Nebuzaradan, the commander of the king of Babylon's special guards, had chosen Gedaliah to watch over those people.

¹¹Johanan son of Kareah and all the army officers who were with him heard about

---

ᵃ**41:4–5** *shaved … cut themselves* The men did this to show that they were sad about the destruction of the Lord's Temple in Jerusalem.
ᵇ**41:6** *He cried* Ishmael was acting like he was sad about the destruction of the Temple.
ᶜ**41:9** *King Asa … city* King Asa lived about 300 years before the time of Gedaliah. See 1 Kings 15:22 for the story about Asa building defenses for Mizpah.

all the evil things Ishmael had done. ¹²So Johanan and the army officers with him took their men and went to fight Ishmael son of Nethaniah. They caught Ishmael near the big pool of water that is at the town of Gibeon. ¹³When the captives that Ishmael had taken saw Johanan and the army officers, they were very happy. ¹⁴Then all the captives who Ishmael had taken from the town of Mizpah ran to Johanan son of Kareah. ¹⁵But Ishmael and eight of his men escaped from Johanan and ran away to the Ammonites.

¹⁶So Johanan son of Kareah and all his army officers rescued the captives. Ishmael had murdered Gedaliah and then he had taken those people from Mizpah. Among the survivors were soldiers, women, children, and court officials. Johanan brought them back from the town of Gibeon.

The Escape to Egypt

¹⁷⁻¹⁸Johanan and the other army officers were afraid of the Chaldeans.* The king of Babylon had chosen Gedaliah to be governor of Judah. But Ishmael murdered Gedaliah, and Johanan was afraid that the Chaldeans would be angry. So they decided to run away to Egypt. On the way to Egypt, they stayed at Geruth Kimham, near the town of Bethlehem.

42 ¹While they were at Geruth Kimham, Johanan son of Kareah and Jezaniah son of Hoshaiah went to Jeremiah the prophet.* All the army officers went with Johanan and Jezaniah. All the people, from the least important to the most important, went to Jeremiah. ²They said to him, "Jeremiah, please listen to what we ask. Pray to the LORD your God for all those who are survivors* from the family of Judah. Jeremiah, you can see that there are not many of us left. At one time there were many of us. ³Jeremiah, pray that the LORD your God will tell us where we should go and what we should do."

⁴Then Jeremiah the prophet answered, "I understand what you want me to do. I will pray to the LORD your God, as you asked me to do. I will tell you everything he says. I will not hide anything from you."

⁵Then the people said to Jeremiah, "If we don't do everything the LORD your God tells us, then we hope the LORD will be a true and faithful witness against us. We know he will send you to tell us what to do. ⁶It doesn't matter if we like the message or if we don't like the message. We will obey the LORD our God. We are sending you to the Lord for a message from him. We will obey what he says. Then good things will happen to us. Yes, we will obey the LORD our God."

⁷At the end of ten days, the message from the LORD came to Jeremiah. ⁸Then Jeremiah called together Johanan son of Kareah and the army officers who were with him. He also called all the other people together, from the least important to the most important. ⁹Then Jeremiah said to them, "This is what the LORD, the God of the people of Israel, says. You sent me to him. I asked the LORD what you wanted me to ask. This is what he says: ¹⁰'If you will stay in Judah, I will make you strong—I will not destroy you. I will plant you, and I will not pull you up. I will do this because I am sad about the terrible things that I made happen to you. ¹¹Now you are afraid of the king of Babylon. But don't be afraid of him. Don't be afraid of the king of Babylon,' says the LORD, 'because I am with you. I will save you. I will rescue you. He will not get his hands on you. ¹²I will be kind to you, and the king of Babylon will also treat you with mercy. He will bring you back to your land.' ¹³But you might say, 'We will not stay in Judah.' If you say that, you will disobey the LORD your God. ¹⁴And you might say, 'No, we will go and live in Egypt. We will not be bothered with war there. We will not hear the trumpets of war, and in Egypt we will not be hungry.' ¹⁵If you say that, listen to this message from the LORD, you survivors from Judah. This is what the LORD All-Powerful, the God of the people of Israel, says: 'If you decide to go and live in Egypt, this will happen: ¹⁶You are afraid of the sword of war, but it will defeat you there. And you are worried about hunger, but you will be hungry in Egypt. You will die there. ¹⁷Everyone who decides to go live in Egypt will die by war, hunger, or disease. Not one person who goes to Egypt will survive. Not one of them will escape the terrible things that I will bring to them.'

¹⁸"This is what the LORD All-Powerful, the God of the people of Israel, says: 'I showed my anger against Jerusalem. I punished the people who lived there. In the same way I will show my anger against everyone who goes to Egypt. People will use you as an example when they ask for bad things to happen to other people. You will become like a curse word. People will be ashamed of you, and they will insult you. And you will never see Judah again.'

¹⁹"Survivors of Judah, the LORD told you: 'Don't go to Egypt.' I warn you right now, ²⁰you are making a mistake that will cause your deaths. You sent me to the LORD your God. You said to me, 'Pray to the LORD our God for us. Tell us everything the LORD our God says to do. We will obey him.' ²¹So today, I have told you the message from the Lord. But you have not obeyed the LORD your God. You have not done all that he sent me to tell you to do. ²²So now be sure you understand this: You want to go live in Egypt. But these things will happen to you in Egypt: You will die by a sword, or hunger, or terrible sickness."

43 ¹So Jeremiah finished telling the people the message from the LORD their God. He told them everything that the LORD their God had sent him to tell them.

²Azariah son of Hoshaiah, Johanan son of Kareah, and some other men were proud and stubborn. They became angry with Jeremiah. They said to him, "Jeremiah, you are lying! The LORD our God didn't send you to say to us, 'You must not go to Egypt to live there.' ³Jeremiah, we think that Baruch son of Neriah is encouraging you to be against us. He wants you to give us to the Babylonians. He wants you to do this so they can kill us. Or he wants you to do this so that they can make us captives* and take us to Babylon."

⁴So Johanan, the army officers, and all the people disobeyed the LORD's command. The Lord had commanded them to stay in Judah. ⁵But instead of obeying the LORD, Johanan and the army officers took the survivors from Judah to Egypt. In the past the enemy had taken the survivors to other countries, but they had come back to Judah. ⁶Now Johanan and all the army officers took all the men, women, and children and led them to Egypt. Among those people were the king's daughters. (Nebuzaradan had put Gedaliah in charge of those people. Nebuzaradan was the commander of the king of Babylon's special guards.) Johanan also took Jeremiah the prophet and Baruch son of Neriah. ⁷These people didn't listen to the LORD. So they all went to Egypt to the town of Tahpanhes.ᵃ

⁸In the town of Tahpanhes, Jeremiah received this message from the LORD: ⁹"Jeremiah, get some large stones. Take them and bury them in the clay and brick sidewalk in front of Pharaoh's official building in Tahpanhes. Do this while the people of Judah are watching you. ¹⁰Then say to those who are watching you: 'This is what the LORD All-Powerful, the God of Israel, says: I will send for King Nebuchadnezzar of Babylon to come here. He is my servant, and I will set his throne over these stones I have buried here. Nebuchadnezzar will spread his canopyᵇ above these stones. ¹¹He will come here and attack Egypt. He will bring death to those who are to die. He will bring captivity to those who are to be taken captive. And he will bring the sword to those who are to be killed with a sword. ¹²Nebuchadnezzar will start a fire in the temples of the false gods of Egypt. He will burn the temples and he will take the idols* away. Shepherds pick the bugs and thorns off their clothes to make them clean. In the same way Nebuchadnezzar will pick Egypt clean. Then he will safely leave Egypt. ¹³He will destroy the memorial stones* that are in the temple of the Sun Godᶜ in Egypt, and he will burn down the temples of the false gods of Egypt.'"

ᵃ**43:7 Tahpanhes** A town in northeastern Egypt.
ᵇ**43:10 canopy** A temporary covering used for shade. It is like a tent without sides.
ᶜ**43:13 Sun God** This was the most important god in Egypt.

The Lord Warns the People of Judah

44 ¹Jeremiah received a message from the LORD for all the people of Judah living in Egypt. The message was for the people of Judah living in the towns of Migdol, Tahpanhes, Memphis, and southern Egypt. This was the message: ²"This is what the LORD All-Powerful, the God of Israel, says: 'You people saw the disasters that I brought on the city of Jerusalem and on all the towns of Judah. The towns are empty piles of stones today. ³They were destroyed because the people living in them did evil. They gave sacrifices to other gods, and that made me angry! Your people and your ancestors* did not worship those gods in the past. ⁴I sent my servants, the prophets, to those people again and again. They spoke my message and said to the people, "Don't do this terrible thing. I hate for you to worship idols.*" ⁵But they didn't listen to the prophets or pay attention to them. They didn't stop doing wicked things. They didn't stop making sacrifices to other gods. ⁶So I showed my anger against them. I punished the towns of Judah and the streets of Jerusalem. My anger made Jerusalem and the towns of Judah the empty piles of stone they are today.'

⁷"So this is what the LORD God All-Powerful, the God of Israel, says: 'Why are you hurting yourselves by continuing to worship idols? You are separating the men and women, the children and babies from the family of Judah. And so you leave yourselves without anyone left from the family of Judah. ⁸Why do you people want to make me angry by making idols? Now you are living in Egypt. And now you are making me angry by offering sacrifices to the false gods of Egypt. You will destroy yourselves, and it will be your own fault. The people of all the other nations on the earth will say bad things about you and make fun of you. ⁹Have you forgotten about the wicked things your ancestors did? And have you forgotten about the wicked things the kings and queens of Judah did? Have you forgotten about the wicked things you and your wives did in Judah and in the streets of Jerusalem? ¹⁰Even to this day the people of Judah have not made themselves humble. They have not shown any respect for me, and they have not followed my teachings. They have not obeyed the laws I gave you and your ancestors.'

¹¹"So this is what the LORD All-Powerful, the God of Israel, says: 'I have decided to make terrible things happen to you. I will destroy the whole family of Judah. ¹²There were a few survivors from Judah. They came here to Egypt. But I will destroy the few survivors from the family of Judah. They will be killed with swords or die from hunger. The people of other nations will point at them and wish evil for them. People will be shocked and frightened by what has happened to them. The name Judah will become a curse word and an insult. ¹³I will punish

those who have gone to live in Egypt. I will use war, hunger, and disease to punish them. I will punish them just as I punished the city of Jerusalem. [14]Not one of the few survivors of Judah who have gone to live in Egypt will escape my punishment. None of them will survive to come back to Judah. They want to come back to Judah and live there. But not one of them will go back to Judah, except a few people who escape.'"

[15]There were many people from Judah living in southern Egypt. Many of the women from Judah were meeting together in a large group and making sacrifices to other gods, and their husbands knew what they were doing. Those men said to Jeremiah, [16]"We will not listen to the message from the LORD that you spoke to us. [17]We promised to make sacrifices to the Queen of Heaven,* and we will do everything we promised. We will offer sacrifices and pour out drink offerings in worship to her. We did that in the past. Our ancestors, our kings, and our officials did that in the past. All of us did those things in the towns of Judah and in the streets of Jerusalem. When we worshiped the Queen of Heaven, we had plenty of food. We were successful. Nothing bad happened to us. [18]But then we stopped making sacrifices to the Queen of Heaven, and we stopped pouring out drink offerings to her. And we have had problems ever since we stopped worshiping her. Our people have been killed by war and hunger."

[19]Then the women spoke up[a] and said to Jeremiah, "Our husbands knew what we were doing. We had their permission to make sacrifices to the Queen of Heaven. We had their permission to pour out drink offerings to her. Our husbands also knew that we were making cakes that looked like her."

[20]Then Jeremiah spoke to all the men and women who told him these things. [21]He said, "The LORD remembered that you made sacrifices in the towns of Judah and in the streets of Jerusalem. You and your ancestors, your kings, your officials, and the people of the land did that. He remembered what you had done and thought about it. [22]The LORD hated the terrible things you did, and he could not be patient with you any longer. So he made your country an empty desert. No one lives there now. Other people say bad things about that country. [23]The reason all those bad things happened to you is because you made sacrifices to other gods. You sinned against the LORD. You didn't obey him or follow his teachings or the laws he gave you. You didn't keep your part of the agreement.[b]"

[24]Then Jeremiah spoke to all the men and women. He said, "All you people of Judah who are now in Egypt, listen to this message from the LORD. [25]This is what the LORD All-Powerful, the God of the people of Israel, says: 'You women did what you said you would do. You said, "We will keep the promises we made. We promised to make sacrifices and pour out drink offerings to the Queen of Heaven." So go ahead. Do what you promised you would do. Keep your promises.' [26]But listen to this message from the LORD, all you people of Judah who are living in Egypt: 'I use my own great name to make this promise: None of the people of Judah who are now living in Egypt will ever again use my name to make promises. They will never again say, "As surely as the Lord GOD lives ...." [27]I am watching over the people of Judah, but I am not watching over them to take care of them. I am watching over them to bring them harm. The people of Judah who live in Egypt will die from hunger or be killed in war until they are completely destroyed. [28]Some people of Judah will escape being killed by the sword. They will come back to Judah from Egypt. But only a few people of Judah will escape. Then the survivors* of Judah who came to live in Egypt will know whose word proves to be true. They will know whether it was my word or their word that came true. [29]I will give you people proof,' says the LORD, 'that I will punish you here in Egypt. Then you will know for sure that my promises to harm you will really happen. [30]This will be your proof that I will do what I say.' This is what the LORD says: 'Pharaoh Hophra is the king of Egypt. His enemies want to kill him. I will give Pharaoh Hophra to his enemies. Just as I gave Zedekiah king of Judah to his enemy Nebuchadnezzar, in the same way I will give Pharaoh Hophra to his enemies.'"

A Message to Baruch

45 [1]In the fourth year that Jehoiakim[c] son of Josiah was king of Judah, Jeremiah the prophet* spoke these things to Baruch son of Neriah. Baruch wrote them on a scroll.* This is what Jeremiah said to Baruch: [2]"This is what the LORD, the God of Israel, says to you: [3]'Baruch, you have said, "It is very bad for me. The LORD has given me sorrow along with my pain. I am very tired. I am worn out because of my suffering. I cannot find rest." [4]Jeremiah, tell Baruch that this is what the LORD says: I will tear down what I have built, and I will pull up what I have planted. I will do that everywhere in Judah. [5]Baruch, you are looking for great things for yourself. Don't look for them, because I will make terrible things happen to all the people.' This is what the LORD said. 'You will have to

---

[a]44:19 Then the women spoke up This is from the ancient Greek version.

[b]44:23 agreement This probably means the Law of Moses, the commands and agreement God made with the Israelites.

[c]45:1 the fourth year ... Jehoiakim This was about 605 B.C.

go many places. But I will let you escape alive wherever you go.'"

The Lord's Messages About the Nations

46 ¹These messages about different nations came to Jeremiah the prophet.*

Messages About Egypt

²This message is about the nation of Egypt. It is about the army of Pharaoh Neco king of Egypt. His army was defeated at the town of Carchemish. Carchemish is on the Euphrates River. King Nebuchadnezzar of Babylon defeated the army of Pharaoh Neco at Carchemish in the fourth year that Jehoia-kimᵃ son of Josiah was king of Judah. This is the LORD's message to Egypt:

³"Get your large and small shields ready.
　　March out for battle.
⁴ Get the horses ready.
　　Soldiers, get on your horses.
　Go to your places for battle.
　　Put your helmets on.
　Sharpen your spears.
　　Put your armor* on.
⁵ What do I see?
　　That army is afraid.
　The soldiers are running away.
　　Their brave soldiers are defeated.
　They run away in a hurry.
　　They don't look back.
　　There is danger all around."
　This is what the LORD said.

⁶"Fast men cannot run away.
　Strong soldiers cannot escape.
　They will all stumble and fall.
　　This will happen in the north, by the
　　　Euphrates River.
⁷ Who is coming like the Nile River?
　　Who is coming like that strong, fast
　　　river?
⁸ It is Egypt that comes
　　like the rising Nile River.
　It is Egypt that comes
　　like that strong, fast river.
　Egypt says, 'I will come and cover the
　　earth.
　I will destroy the cities and the people
　　in them.'
⁹ Horse soldiers, charge into battle.
　　Chariot drivers, drive fast.
　March on, brave soldiers.
　　Soldiers from Cush and Put, carry your
　　　shields.
　Soldiers from Lydia, use your bows.

¹⁰"But on that day, the Lord GOD All-Powerful
　　will win.
　He will give his enemies the
　　punishment they deserve.

His sword will kill until it is finished,
　until it has satisfied its thirst for blood.
Yes, the Lord GOD All-Powerful will kill
　them as a sacrifice
　in the land of the north by the
　　Euphrates River.

¹¹"Egypt, go to Gilead and get some
　medicine.
　You will make up many medicines, but
　　they will not help.
　You will not be healed.
¹² The nations will hear you crying.
　Your cries will be heard all over the
　　earth.
　One 'brave soldier' will run into another
　　'brave soldier.'
　And both 'brave soldiers' will fall down
　　together."

¹³This is the message the LORD spoke to Jeremiah the prophet about Nebuchadnezzar coming to attack Egypt.

¹⁴"Announce this message in Egypt.
　　Tell it in the city of Migdol.
　　Tell it in Memphis and Tahpanhes.
　'Get ready for war,
　　because people all around you are being
　　　killed with swords.'
¹⁵ Egypt, your strong soldiers will be killed.
　　They will not be able to stand
　　because the LORD will push them down.
¹⁶ They will stumble again and again.
　　They will fall over each other.
　They will say, 'Get up, let's go back to our
　　own people.
　Let us go back to our homeland.
　Our enemy is defeating us.
　We must get away.'
¹⁷ In their homelands, those soldiers will
　　say,
　'Pharaoh, the king of Egypt, is only a lot
　　of noise.
　His time of glory is over.'"
¹⁸ This message is from the King.
　　The King is the LORD All-Powerful.
　"I promise, as surely as I live,
　　a powerful leader will come.
　He will be like Mount Tabor or Mount
　　Carmel among smaller mountains.
¹⁹ People of Egypt, pack your things.
　Get ready for captivity,
　　because Memphis will be a ruined,
　　　empty land.
　Those cities will be destroyed,
　　and no one will live there.

²⁰"Egypt is like a beautiful cow.
　　But a horseflyᵇ is coming from the

ᵃ**46:2** *the fourth year ... Jehoiakim* This was about 605 B.C.

ᵇ**46:20** *horsefly* A large insect that often flies around cows and horses and bites them.

north[a] to attack her.

21 The hired soldiers in Egypt's army are like
fat calves.
They will all turn and run away.
They will not stand strong against the
attack.
Their time of destruction is coming.
They will soon be punished.

22 Egypt is like a snake hissing
and trying to escape.
The enemy comes closer and closer,
and the Egyptian army is trying to
slither away.
The enemy will attack Egypt with axes,
like men cutting down trees."

23 This is what the LORD says:
"They will chop down Egypt's forest.
There are many trees in that forest,
but they will all be cut down.
There are more enemy soldiers than
locusts.*
There are so many soldiers that no one
can count them.

24 Egypt will be ashamed.
The enemy from the north will defeat
her."

25 The LORD All-Powerful, the God of Israel,
says, "Very soon I will punish Amon,[b] the god
of Thebes, and I will punish Pharaoh, Egypt,
and her gods. I will punish the kings of Egypt,
and I will punish the people who depend on
Pharaoh. 26 I will let all of them be defeated
by their enemies—their enemies want to kill
them. I will give the people to King Nebuchadnezzar of Babylon and his servants.

"Long ago, Egypt lived in peace. And after
all these times of trouble, Egypt will live in
peace again." This is what the LORD said.

A Message for Northern Israel

27 "Jacob,* my servant, do not be afraid.
Do not be frightened, Israel.
I will save you from those faraway places.
I will save your children from the
countries where they are captives.*
Jacob will have peace and safety again,
and no one will make him afraid."

28 This is what the LORD says.
"Jacob, my servant, do not be afraid.
I am with you.
I sent you away to many different places.
But I will not destroy you completely.
But I will destroy all those nations.

You must be punished for the bad things
you did.
So I will not let you escape your
punishment.
I will discipline you, but I will be fair."

A Message About the Philistine People

47 1 This is the message from the LORD
that came to Jeremiah the prophet*
about the Philistines.* This message came
before Pharaoh attacked the city of Gaza.

2 This is what the LORD says:
"Look, the enemy is gathering in the
north[c] like rising water.
They will come like a river spilling over
its banks.
They will cover the whole country like a
flood.
They will cover the towns and the
people living in them.
Everyone in the country will cry for help.
Everyone will cry out in pain.

3 They will hear the sound of running
horses,
the noisy chariots,* the rumbling
wheels.
Fathers will not be able to protect their
children.
They will be too weak to help,

4 because the time has come
to destroy all the Philistines.
The time has come to destroy
Tyre and Sidon's remaining helpers.
The LORD will destroy the Philistines,
the survivors from the Island of Crete.[d]

5 The people from Gaza will be sad and
shave their heads.
The people from Ashkelon will be
silenced.
Survivors from the valley, how long will
you cut yourselves?[e]

6 "Sword of the LORD, you have not stopped.
How long will you keep fighting?
Go back into your scabbard[f]!
Stop! Be still!

7 But how can the sword of the Lord rest?
The LORD gave it a command.
He commanded it to attack
the city of Ashkelon and the seacoast."

---

[a]46:20 north The Babylonian army came from this
direction to attack Judah. Armies from countries
north and east of Israel often came this way to
attack Judah and Israel.
[b]46:25 Amon For many centuries Amon was
the most important god of Egypt. At the time of
this prophecy, he was not worshiped as much in
northern Egypt. But he was still the most important
god in southern Egypt, especially around the old
Egyptian capital city of Thebes.

[c]47:2 north The Babylonian army came from this
direction to attack Judah. Armies from countries
north and east of Israel often came this way to
attack Judah and Israel.
[d]47:4 Island of Crete Literally, "Island of Caphtor."
Sometimes this means Crete, and sometimes it
means Cyprus. The Bible says the Philistines originally came from Caphtor.
[e]47:5 sad ... cut yourselves The people did these
things to show their sadness.
[f]47:6 scabbard A holder for a sword.

A Message About Moab

48 ¹This message is about the country of Moab. This is what the LORD All-Powerful, the God of the people of Israel, says:[a]

"It will be bad for Mount Nebo.[b]
  Mount Nebo will be ruined.
The town of Kiriathaim will be humbled.
  It will be captured.
The strong place will be humbled.
  It will be shattered.
² Moab will not be praised again.
  Men in Heshbon will plan Moab's defeat.
They will say, 'Come, let us put an end to that nation.'
Madmenah, you will also be silenced.
  The sword will chase you.
³ Listen to the cries from Horonaim.
  They are cries of much confusion and destruction.
⁴ Moab will be destroyed.
  Her little children will cry for help.
⁵ Moab's people go up the path to Luhith.
  They are crying bitterly as they go.
On the road down to the town of Horonaim,
  cries of pain and suffering can be heard.
⁶ Run away! Run for your lives!
  Run away like a weed[c] blowing through the desert.

⁷"You trust in the things you made and in your wealth,
  so you will be captured.
The god Chemosh* will be taken into captivity,
  and his priests and officials will be taken with him.
⁸ The Destroyer will come against every town.
  Not one town will escape.
The valley will be ruined.
  The high plain will be destroyed.
The LORD said this would happen,
  so it will happen.
⁹ Spread salt over the fields in Moab.
  The country will be an empty desert.[d]
Moab's towns will become empty.
  No one will live in them.
¹⁰ Bad things will happen to those who don't obey the LORD and don't use their swords to kill those people.

¹¹"Moab has never known trouble.
  Moab is like wine left to settle.
Moab has never been poured from one jar to another.

He has not been taken into captivity.
So he tastes as he did before,
  and his smell has not changed."
¹² This is what the LORD says:
  "But I will soon send men
    to pour you from your jars.[e]
  Then they will empty the jars
    and smash them to pieces."

¹³Then the people of Moab will be ashamed of their false god, Chemosh. They will be like the people of Israel who trusted that god in Bethel[f] but were ashamed when he did not help them.

¹⁴"You cannot say, 'We are good soldiers.
  We are brave men in battle.'
¹⁵ The enemy will attack Moab.
  The enemy will enter its towns and destroy them.
  Its best young men will be killed in the slaughter."
This message is from the King.
  The King's name is the LORD All-Powerful.
¹⁶"The end of Moab is near.
  Moab will soon be destroyed.
¹⁷ All you who live around Moab should cry for that country.
  You know how famous Moab is.
  So cry for it.
Say, 'The ruler's power is broken.
  Moab's power and glory is gone.'

¹⁸"You people living in Dibon,[g]
  come down from your place of honor.
Sit on the ground in the dust,
  because the Destroyer is coming.
And he will destroy your strong cities.

¹⁹"You people living in Aroer,
  stand next to the road and watch.
See the man running away.
  See that woman running away.
  Ask them what happened.

²⁰"Moab will be ruined and filled with shame.
  Moab will cry and cry.
Announce at the Arnon River[h]
  that Moab is destroyed.
²¹ People on the high plain have been punished.
  Judgment has come to the towns
    of Holon, Jahzah, and Mephaath.

---

[a]**48:1** *This message ... says* See Isa. 15 for a similar message.
[b]**48:1** *Mount Nebo* A mountain in Moab, a country east of Israel.
[c]**48:6** *weed* In Hebrew this word is like the name "Aroer," an important city in Moab.
[d]**48:9** The Hebrew text here is hard to understand.
[e]**48:12** *jars* This probably means the cities in Moab.
[f]**48:13** *in Bethel* This means the temple that King Jeroboam built in the town of Bethel (see 1 Kings 12:28–33). It is not clear if this means the people still worshiped the Lord there, but in a wrong way, or if they worshiped a false god, perhaps the Canaanite god El or Baal.
[g]**48:18** *Dibon* A city in the country of Moab.
[h]**48:20** *Arnon River* An important river in Moab.

²² Judgment has come to the towns
        of Dibon, Nebo, and Beth Diblathaim.
²³ Judgment has come to the towns
        of Kiriathaim, Beth Gamul, and Beth
        Meon.
²⁴ Judgment has come to the towns
        of Kerioth and Bozrah.
    Judgment has come to all the towns
        of Moab, far and near.
²⁵ Moab's strength has been cut off.
    Its arm has been broken."
    This is what the LORD said.

²⁶"The people of Moab thought they were
        greater than the LORD.
    So punish them until they act like a
        drunk,
        falling and rolling around in his vomit.
    Then people will make fun of them.

²⁷"Moab, you made fun of Israel.
    Israel was caught by a gang of thieves.
    Every time you spoke about Israel,
        you shook your head and acted as if you
        were better than Israel.
²⁸ People in Moab, leave your towns.
    Go live among the rocks;
    be like a dove that makes its nest
        at the opening of a cave."

²⁹"We have heard about Moab's pride.
    He was very proud.
    He thought he was important.
    He was always bragging.
    He was very, very proud."

³⁰ The LORD says, "I know Moab gets angry
        quickly and brags about himself,
    but his boasts are lies.
    He cannot do what he says.
³¹ So I cry for Moab.
    I cry for everyone in Moab.
    I cry for the men from Kir Hareseth.
³² I cry with the people of Jazer for Jazer.
    Sibmah, in the past your vines spread all
        the way to the sea.
    They reached as far as the town of Jazer.
    But the Destroyer has taken your fruit and
        grapes.
³³ Joy and happiness are gone from the large
        vineyards* of Moab.
    I stopped the flow of wine from the
        winepresses.*
    There is no singing and dancing from
        people walking on the grapes to make
        wine.
    There are no shouts of joy.

³⁴"The people of the towns of Heshbon and
Elealeh are crying. Their cry is heard even as
far away as the town of Jahaz. Their cry is
heard from the town of Zoar, as far away as
the towns of Horonaim and Eglath Shelishiyah. Even the waters of Nimrim are dried
up. ³⁵I will stop Moab from making burnt

offerings on the high places.* I will stop them
from making sacrifices to their gods." This is
what the LORD said.

³⁶"I am very sad for Moab. My heart cries
like the sad sound of a flute playing a funeral
song. I am sad for the people from Kir Hareseth. Their money and riches have all been
taken away. ³⁷Everyone has a shaved head.
Everyone's beard is cut off. Everyone's hands
are cut and bleeding.ᵃ Everyone is wearing
sackcloth* around their waists. ³⁸People are
crying for the dead everywhere in Moab—on
every housetop and in every public square.
There is sadness because I have broken Moab
like an empty jar." This is what the LORD
said.

³⁹"Moab is shattered. The people are
crying. Moab surrendered. Now Moab is
ashamed. People make fun of Moab, but what
happened fills them with fear."

⁴⁰ The LORD says, "Look! An eagle is diving
        down from the sky.
    It is spreading its wings over Moab.
⁴¹ The towns of Moab will be captured.
    The strong hiding places will be
        defeated.
    At that time Moab's soldiers will be filled
        with fear, like a woman giving birth.
⁴² The nation of Moab will be destroyed,
        because they thought that they were
        more important than the LORD."

⁴³ This is what the LORD says:
    "People of Moab, fear, deep holes, and
        trapsᵇ wait for you.
⁴⁴ People will be afraid and run away,
        and they will fall into the deep holes.
    Anyone who climbs out of the deep holes
        will be caught in the traps.
    I will bring the year of punishment to
        Moab."
    This is what the LORD said.

⁴⁵"People have run from the powerful
        enemy.
    They ran to safety in the town of
        Heshbon.
    But a fire started in Heshbon.
    That fire started in Sihon's town,ᶜ
        and it is destroying the leaders of Moab.
    It is destroying those proud people.
⁴⁶ It will be bad for you, Moab.
    Chemosh's people are being destroyed.
    Your sons and daughters are being taken
        away as prisoners and captives.*

ᵃ**48:37** *Everyone ... cut and bleeding* The people
did these things to show their sadness for people
who had died.
ᵇ**48:43** *fear, deep holes, and traps* This is a wordplay
in Hebrew. The Hebrew words are "Pahad, Pahat,
and Pah."
ᶜ**48:45** *Sihon's town* This was Heshbon. See Num.
21:25–30.

⁴⁷"Moab's people will be taken away as captives. But in days to come, I will bring them back." This message is from the Lord.

This ends the judgment on Moab.

A Message About Ammon

49 ¹This message is about the Ammonites. This is what the Lord says:

"Ammonites, do you think that
the people of Israel don't have children?
Do you think there are no children
to take the land when the parents die?
Maybe that is why Milcom* took Gad's^a
land?"

² The Lord says, "The time will come in
Rabbah of Ammon^b
when people hear the sounds of battle.
Rabbah of Ammon will be destroyed.
It will be an empty hill covered with
ruined buildings,
and the towns around it will be burned.
Those people forced the people of Israel
to leave their own land.
But later, Israel will force them to
leave."
This is what the Lord said.

³"People in Heshbon, cry because the town
of Ai is destroyed!
Women in Rabbah of Ammon, cry!
Put on sackcloth* and cry.
Run to the city for safety,
because the enemy will take away the god
Milcom,
with his priests and officials.
⁴ You brag about your strength,
but you are losing your strength.
You trust in your wealth to save you.
You think no one would even think of
attacking you."
⁵ But this is what the Lord All-Powerful
says:
"I will bring troubles to you from every
side.
You will all run away,
and no one will be able to bring you
together again."

⁶"The Ammonites will be taken away as captives.* But the time will come when I will bring the Ammonites back." This message is from the Lord.

A Message About Edom

⁷This message is about Edom. This is what the Lord All-Powerful says:

"Is there no more wisdom in Teman*?
Are the wise men of Edom not able to
give good advice?
Have they lost their wisdom?
⁸ You people living in Dedan, run away and
hide,
because I will punish Esau* for the bad
things he did.

⁹"Workers pick grapes from grapevines,
but they leave a few grapes on the
plants.
If thieves come at night,
they don't take everything.
¹⁰ But I will take everything from Esau.
I will find all his hiding places.
He will not be able to hide from me.
His children, relatives, and neighbors will
all die.
¹¹ No one will be left to care for his
children.
His wives will have no one to depend
on."

¹²This is what the Lord says: "Some people don't deserve to be punished, but they suffer. But, Edom, you deserve to be punished, so you will really be punished. You will not escape the punishment you deserve. You will be punished." ¹³The Lord says, "By my own power, I make this promise: I promise that the city of Bozrah will be destroyed. It will become a ruined pile of rocks. People will use it as an example when they ask for bad things to happen to other cities. People will insult that city, and all the towns around Bozrah will become ruins forever."

¹⁴ I heard a message from the Lord:
He sent this messenger to the nations.
This is the message:
"Gather your armies together!
Get ready for battle!
March against the nation of Edom!
¹⁵ Edom, I will make you become
unimportant.
Everyone will hate you.
¹⁶ Edom, you made other nations afraid,
so you thought you were important.
But your pride has fooled you.
You live in caves, high on the cliff.
Your home is high in the hills.
But even if you build your home as high
as an eagle's nest,
I will bring you down from there."
This is what the Lord said.

¹⁷"Edom will be destroyed.
People will be shocked to see the
destroyed cities.
They will whistle from amazement at
the destroyed cities.
¹⁸ Edom will be destroyed like Sodom* and
Gomorrah* and the towns around
them.

^a**49:1** *Gad's* One of the tribes of Israel. Their land was on the east side of the Jordan River, near the country of Ammon.
^b**49:2** *Rabbah of Ammon* The capital city of the Ammonites.

No one will live there."
This is what the LORD said.

19"Sometimes a lion will come from the thick bushes near the Jordan River. And it will go into the fields where people put their sheep and cattle. I am like that lion. I will go to Edom. And I will frighten the people and make them run away. None of their young men will stop me. No one is like me. No one will challenge me. None of their leaders will stand up against me."

20 So listen to what the LORD has planned
   to do to the people of Edom.
Listen to what he has decided
   to do to the people in Teman.
The enemy will drag away the young kids
   of Edom's flock.
Edom's pastures will be empty
   because of what they did.
21 At the sound of Edom's fall,
   the earth will shake.
Their cry will be heard
   all the way to the Red Sea.

22 The LORD will be like an eagle
   flying over the animal it will attack.
He will be like an eagle
   spreading its wings over Bozrah.
At that time Edom's soldiers will be filled
   with fear.
They will cry out like a woman giving
   birth.

A Message About Damascus

23This message is about the city of Damascus:

"The towns of Hamath and Arpad are
   afraid.
They are afraid because they heard the
   bad news.
They are discouraged.
They are worried and afraid.
24 The city of Damascus has become weak.
   The people want to run away.
   They are ready to panic.
They are overcome with fear and pain,
   like a woman giving birth.

25"Damascus is a happy city.
   The people have not left that 'fun city'
   yet.
26 So the young men will die in the public
   squares of that city.
   All her soldiers will be killed at that
   time."
This is what the LORD All-Powerful said.
27"I will set the walls of Damascus on fire.
   The fire will completely burn up the
   strong forts of Ben-Hadad.a"

A Message About Kedar and Hazor

28This message is about the tribe of Kedar* and the rulers of Hazor. King Nebuchadnezzar of Babylon defeated them. This is what the LORD says:

"Go and attack the tribe of Kedar.
   Destroy the people of the East.
29 Their tents and flocks will be taken away.
   Their tents and all their riches will be
   carried off.
   Their enemy will take away the camels.
Men will shout this to them:
   'Terrible things are happening all around
   us.'
30 Run away quickly!
   People in Hazor, find a good place to
   hide."
This message is from the LORD.
"Nebuchadnezzar has made plans against
   you.
He thought of a smart plan to defeat
   you.

31"There is a nation that feels so safe and
   secure
   that it does not have gates or fences to
   protect it.
And no one lives near enough to help
   them.
   So attack that nation!" says the LORD.
32"Their camels are there to be taken in
   battle.
   Their large herds of cattle will be yours.
I will scatter them throughout the
   earth—those people who cut their
   hair short.b
I will bring disaster on them from every
   direction."
This message is from the LORD.
33"Hazor will become a home for wild dogs,
   an empty desert forever.
No one will live there.
   No one will stay in that place."

A Message About Elam

34Early in the time when Zedekiah was king of Judah, Jeremiah the prophet* received a message from the LORD about the nation of Elam.c

35 The LORD All-Powerful says,
"I will break Elam's bow very soon.
   It is Elam's strongest weapon.
36 I will bring the four winds against Elam.
   I will bring them from the four corners
   of the skies.
I will send the people of Elam
   to every place on the earth where the
   four winds blow.

a49:27 Ben-Hadad This was the name of several of the kings of Aram-Damascus.

b49:32 cut their hair short Literally, "cut on the side of their heads," a custom different from that of Israelite men.

c49:34 Elam A nation east of Babylon.

Elam's captives* will be carried away to
every nation.
37 I will break Elam to pieces
while their enemies are watching.
I will break Elam in front of the people
who want to kill them.
I will bring terrible troubles to them.
I will show them how angry I am."
This message is from the LORD.
"I will send a sword to chase Elam.
The sword will chase them until I have
killed them all.
38 I will show Elam that I am in control,
and I will destroy its king and his
officials."
This message is from the LORD.
39"But in the future I will make good things
happen to Elam."
This message is from the LORD.

A Message About Babylon

50 ¹This is the message the LORD spoke
through the prophet* Jeremiah about
Babylon and its people.

2"Announce this to all nations!
Lift up a flag and announce the
message!
Speak the whole message and say,
'The nation of Babylon will be captured.
The god Bel* will be put to shame.
The god Marduk* will be very afraid.
Babylon's idols* will be put to shame.
Her gods will be filled with terror.'
3 A nation from the north will attack
Babylon.
That nation will make Babylon like an
empty desert.
No one will live there.
Both men and animals will run away."
4 The LORD says, "At that time
the people of Israel and the people of
Judah will be together.
They will cry and cry together,
and together, they will go look for the
LORD their God.
5 They will ask how to go to Zion.*
They will start to go in that direction.
They will say, 'Come, let us join ourselves
to the LORD.
Let's make an agreement that will last
forever.
Let's make an agreement that we will
never forget.'

6"My people have been like lost sheep.
Their shepherds led them the wrong
way
and made them wander around in the
mountains and hills.
They forgot where their resting place
was.
7 Whoever found my people hurt them.
And those enemies said,
'We did nothing wrong.'

Those people sinned against the LORD,
their true resting place.
He was the God who their fathers
trusted in.

8"Run away from Babylon.
Leave the land of the Babylonians.
Be like the goats that lead the flock.
9 I will bring many nations together from
the north.
This group of nations will get ready for
war against Babylon.
Babylon will be captured by people from
the north.
Those nations will shoot many arrows at
Babylon.
Their arrows will be like soldiers
who don't come back from war with
their hands empty.
10 The enemy will take all the wealth from
the Chaldeans.
The soldiers will take all they want."
This is what the LORD said.

11"Babylon, you are excited and happy.
You took my land.
You dance around like a young cow
that got into the grain.
Your laughter is like the happy sounds
that horses make.
12 Now your mother will be very ashamed.
The woman who gave you birth will be
embarrassed.
Babylon will be the least important of all
the nations.
She will be an empty, dry desert.
13 The LORD will show his anger,
so no one will live there.
Babylon will be completely empty.
Everyone who passes by Babylon will be
afraid.
They will shake their heads when they
see how badly it has been destroyed.

14"Prepare for war against Babylon.
All you soldiers with bows, shoot your
arrows at Babylon.
Don't save any of your arrows.
Babylon has sinned against the LORD.
15 Soldiers around Babylon,
shout the cry of victory!
Babylon has surrendered!
Her walls and towers have been pulled
down!
The LORD is giving her people
the punishment they deserve.
You nations should give Babylon
the punishment she deserves.
Do to her what she has done to other
nations.
16 Don't let the people from Babylon plant
their crops.
Don't let them gather the harvest.
The soldiers of Babylon brought many
prisoners to their city.

Now the enemy soldiers have come,
   so the prisoners are going back home.
They are running back to their own
   countries.

17 "Israel is like a flock of sheep
   that was scattered all over the country.
Israel is like sheep that were chased away
   by lions.
The first lion to attack
   was the king of Assyria.
The last lion to crush Israel's bones
   was King Nebuchadnezzar of Babylon.

18 So this is what the LORD All-Powerful, the
   God of Israel, says:
  'I will soon punish the king of Babylon and
    his country
   as I punished the king of Assyria.

19 "'I will bring Israel back to his own fields.
   He will eat food that grows on Mount
    Carmel and in the land of Bashan.
   He will eat and be full.
   He will eat on the hills in the lands of
    Ephraim* and Gilead.'"

20 The LORD says, "At that time people will
   try hard to find Israel's guilt,
   but there will be no guilt.
People will try to find Judah's sins,
   but no sins will be found.
That is because I am saving a few
   survivors* from Israel and Judah.
And I am forgiving them for all their sins."

21 The LORD says, "Attack the country of
   Merathaim!
   Attack the people living in Pekod!
   Attack them!
   Kill them and destroy them completely!
   Do everything I commanded you!

22 "The noise of battle can be heard all over
   the country.
   It is the noise of much destruction.

23 Babylon was called
   'The Hammer of the Whole Earth.'
But now the 'Hammer' is shattered.
   Babylon is the most ruined of the
    nations.

24 Babylon, I set a trap for you,
   and you were caught before you knew
    it.
You fought against the LORD,
   so you were found and captured.

25 The LORD has opened up his storeroom
   and brought out the weapons of his
    anger.
The LORD God All-Powerful brought out
   those weapons,
   because he has work to do in the land of
    the Chaldeans.*

26 "Come against Babylon from far away.
   Break open the storehouses where she
    keeps her grain.

Destroy Babylon completely.
   Don't leave anyone alive.
Pile up her dead bodies like big piles of
   grain.

27 Kill all the young men in Babylon.
   Let them be slaughtered like bulls.
How terrible for them that their day of
   defeat has come!
   It is time for them to be punished.

28 People are running out of Babylon.
   They are escaping from that country and
    coming to Zion.
They are telling everyone the good news
   about what the Lord is doing.
The LORD our God is giving Babylon the
   punishment it deserves.
The Lord is destroying Babylon, because
   it destroyed his Temple*!

29 "Call for the archers.*
   Tell them to attack Babylon.
Tell them to surround the city.
   Don't let anyone escape.
Pay her back for the bad things she has
   done.
   Do to her what she has done to other
    nations.
Babylon did not respect the LORD.
   Babylon was very rude to the Holy One
    of Israel.
   So punish Babylon.

30 Babylon's young men will be killed in the
   streets.
   All her soldiers will die on that day."
This is what the LORD says.

31 "Babylon, you are too proud,
   and I am against you,"
   says the Lord GOD All-Powerful.
"I am against you,
   and the time has come for you to be
    punished.

32 Proud Babylon will stumble and fall,
   and no one will help her get up.
I will start a fire in her towns.
   That fire will completely burn up
    everyone around her."

33 This is what the LORD All-Powerful says:
"The people of Israel and Judah are slaves.
   The enemy took them, and the enemy
    will not let Israel go.

34 But God will get them back.
   His name is the LORD God All-Powerful.
He will defend them very strongly.
   He will argue their case so that he can
    let their land rest.
But there will be no rest for those living
   in Babylon."

35 The LORD says,
"Sword, kill the people living in Babylon.
   Sword, kill the king's officials
   and the wise men of Babylon.

36 Sword, kill the priests of Babylon.

They will be like fools.
Sword, kill the soldiers of Babylon.
They will be full of fear.
37 Sword, kill the horses and chariots* of
    Babylon.
Sword, kill all the soldiers hired from
    other countries.
They will be like frightened women.
Sword, destroy the treasures of Babylon.
    Those treasures will be taken away.
38 Sword, strike the waters of Babylon.
    Those waters will be dried up.
Babylon has many, many idols.
    These idols show that the people of
        Babylon are foolish.
So bad things will happen to them.
39 Babylon will never again be filled with
    people.
Wild dogs, ostriches,* and other desert
    animals will live there.
But no one will live there ever again.
40 God completely destroyed Sodom* and
    Gomorrah*
    and the towns around them.
In the same way no one will live in
    Babylon,
    and no one will ever go to live there.

41 "Look! There are people coming from the
    north.
They come from a powerful nation.
Many kings are coming together from all
    around the world.
42 Their armies have bows and spears.
    The soldiers are cruel.
    They have no mercy.
The soldiers come riding on their horses;
    the sound is as loud as the roaring sea.
They stand in their places, ready for
    battle.
They are ready to attack you, city of
    Babylon.
43 The king of Babylon heard about those
    armies,
    and he is paralyzed with fear.
He is overcome with fear and pain,
    like a woman giving birth.

44 "Sometimes a lion will come
    from the thick bushes near the Jordan
        River.
It will walk into the fields
    where people have their animals.
I will be like that lion;
    I will chase Babylon from its land.
Who should I choose to do this?
    There is no one like me.
    There is no one who can challenge me.
No shepherd will come to chase me away.
    I will chase away the Babylonians."

45 Listen to what the LORD has planned
    to do to Babylon.
Listen to what he has decided
    to do to the Babylonians.

"I promise that an enemy will drag away
    the young kids of Babylon's flock,
    and Babylon will become an empty
        pasture.
46 Babylon will fall,
    and that fall will shake the earth.
People in all nations will hear about
    the destruction of Babylon."

51

1 The LORD says,
"I will cause a powerful, destructive
    wind to blow against Babylon and the
    Babylonians.*a*
2 I will send foreigners to winnow*b*
    Babylon,
    and they will take everything from the
        city.
Armies will surround the city,
    and there will be terrible destruction.
3 The Babylonian soldiers will not get to
    use their bows and arrows.
They will not even put on their armor.*
Don't feel sorry for the soldiers of
    Babylon.
    Destroy her army completely!
4 Babylon's soldiers will be killed in the
    land of the Chaldeans.
They will be badly wounded in the
    streets of Babylon."

5 The LORD All-Powerful
    did not leave Israel and Judah alone, like
        a widow.
No, they are guilty
    of leaving the Holy One of Israel.
They left him,
    but he has not left them.

6 Run away from Babylon.
    Run to save your lives!
    Don't stay and be killed because of
        Babylon's sins!
It is time for the LORD to punish the
    Babylonians for the bad things they
    have done.
Babylon will get the punishment that
    she should have.
7 Babylon was like a golden cup in the
    LORD's hand.
Babylon made the whole world drunk.
The nations drank Babylon's wine,
    so they went crazy.
8 But Babylon will suddenly fall and be
    broken.
    Cry for her!
Get medicine for her pain,
    and maybe she can be healed.

*a***51:1** *Babylonians* Literally, "Leb Kammai." In
Hebrew this was a secret way of writing "Chaldeans."
*b***51:2** *winnow* To separate grain from the hulls
around it. Farmers threw the grain with the hulls
into the air. The wind blew the hulls away and left
the good grain.

9 We tried to heal Babylon,
  but she cannot be healed.
So let us leave her,
  and let each of us go to our own
    country.
God in heaven will decide Babylon's
  punishment.
He will decide what will happen to
  Babylon.
10 The LORD got even for us.
  Come, let's tell about that in Zion.*
Let's tell what the LORD our God has done.

11 Sharpen the arrows!
  Get your shields!
The LORD has stirred up the kings of the
    Medes*
because he wants to destroy Babylon.
The army from Babylon destroyed his
    Temple in Jerusalem,
so he will give them the punishment
  they deserve.
12 Lift up a flag against the walls of Babylon.
  Bring more guards.
Put the watchmen in their places.
  Get ready for a secret attack.
The LORD will do what he has planned.
  He will do what he said he would do
    against the people of Babylon.
13 Babylon, you live near much water.
  You are rich with treasures, but your
    end as a nation has come.
It is time for you to be destroyed.
14 The LORD All-Powerful used his name to
    make this promise:
"Babylon, I will fill you with so many
    enemy soldiers they will be like a
    cloud of locusts.*
They will win their war against you.
They will stand over you shouting their
    victory cry."

15 The LORD used his great power and made
    the earth.
He used his wisdom to build the world
  and his understanding to stretch out the
    skies.
16 When he thunders, the waters in the
    skies roar.
He sends clouds all over the earth.
He sends lightning with the rain.
He brings out the wind from his
    storehouses.
17 But people are so stupid.
  They don't understand what God has
    done.
Skilled workers make statues of false gods.
  Those statues are only false gods.
They show how foolish those workers
    are.
Those statues are not alive.
18 Those idols* are worthless.
  People made them, and they are
    nothing but a joke.
Their time of judgment will come,

and those idols will be destroyed.
19 But God, who is Jacob's* Portion, is not
    like those worthless statues.
People didn't make God;
  God made his people.
He made everything.
His name is the LORD All-Powerful.

20 The Lord says, "Babylon, you are my club.
  I used you to smash nations.
  I used you to destroy kingdoms.
21 I used you to smash horse and rider.
  I used you to smash chariot and driver.
22 I used you to smash men and women.
  I used you to smash men, old and
    young.
  I used you to smash young men and
    young women.
23 I used you to smash shepherds and flocks.
  I used you to smash farmers and oxen.
  I used you to smash governors and
    important officials.
24 But I will repay Babylonia and all the
    Babylonians for all the evil things they
    did to Zion.
  I will pay them back so that you can see
    it, Judah."
This is what the LORD said.

25 The LORD says,
"Babylon, you are like a volcano
  that destroys the whole country.
But I have turned against you,
  and I will turn you into a burned-out
    mountain.
26 People will not take stones from Babylon
    to use as the foundation of a building.
  That is because they will not find any
    stones big enough for cornerstones.
Your city will be a pile of broken rocks
    forever."
This is what the LORD said.

27 "Lift up the war flag in the land!
  Blow the trumpet in all the nations!
Prepare the nations for war against
    Babylon.
Call these kingdoms to come fight against
    Babylon:
  Ararat, Minni, and Ashkenaz.
Choose a commander to lead the army
    against her.
Send so many horses that they are like a
    swarm of locusts.
28 Get the nations ready for battle against
    her.
  Get the kings of the Medes ready.
Get their governors and all their
    important officials ready.
  Get all the countries they rule ready for
    battle against Babylon.
29 The land shakes and moves like it is in
    pain.
  It will shake when the LORD does what
    he planned to Babylon.

The LORD's plan is to make the land of
    Babylon into an empty desert.
No one will live there.
30 Babylon's soldiers have stopped fighting.
    They stay in their forts.
Their strength is gone.
    They have become like frightened
        women.
Babylon's houses are burning.
    The bars of her gates are broken.
31 One messenger follows another.
    Messenger follows messenger.
They announce to the king of Babylon
    that his whole city has been captured.
32 The places where people cross the rivers
        have been captured.
The swamplands are burning.
    All of Babylon's soldiers are afraid."

33 This is what the LORD All-Powerful, the
        God of the people of Israel, says:
"Babylon is like a threshing* floor,
    where people beat the grain at harvest
        time.
    And the time to beat Babylon is coming
        soon.

34 "King Nebuchadnezzar of Babylon
        destroyed us in the past.
    In the past he hurt us.
In the past he took our people away,
    and we became like an empty jar.
He took the best we had.
    He was like a giant monster that ate
        everything until it was full.
He took the best we had
    and then threw us away.
35 Babylon did terrible things to hurt us.
    Now I want those things to happen to
        Babylon."

The people living in Zion said,
"The people of Babylon are guilty of killing
        our people.
    Now they are being punished for the
        bad things they did."
The city of Jerusalem said those things.
36 So this is what the LORD says:
"I will defend you, Judah.
    I will make sure that Babylon is
        punished.
I will dry up Babylon's sea.
    And I will make her water springs
        become dry.
37 Babylon will become a pile of ruined
        buildings,
    a place fit only for wild dogs.
People will be shocked and shake their
        heads at what is left there.
    It will be a place where no one lives.

38 "The people of Babylon are like roaring
        young lions.
    They growl like baby lions.
39 They are acting like powerful lions.

I will give a party for them.
    I will make them drunk.
They will laugh and have a good time,
    and then they will sleep forever.
    They will never wake up."

This is what the LORD said.
40 "Babylon will be like sheep, rams, and
        goats waiting to be killed.
    I will lead them to the slaughter.

41 "Sheshach[a] will be defeated.
    The best and proudest country
        of the whole earth will be taken captive.
    People from other nations will look at
        Babylon,
    and what they see will make them
        afraid.
42 The sea will rise over Babylon.
    Its roaring waves will cover her.
43 Babylon will be like a dry, desert land.
    Its cities will be empty ruins.
    No one will live in those cities.
    No one will even travel through them.
44 I will punish the false god Bel in Babylon.
    I will make him vomit out the people he
        swallowed.
The wall around Babylon will fall,
    and other nations will stop coming to
        Babylon.
45 Come out of the city of Babylon, my
        people.
    Run to save your lives.
    Run from the LORD's great anger.

46 "Don't be sad, my people.
    Rumors will spread, but don't be afraid.
One rumor comes this year.
    Another rumor will come next year.
There will be rumors about terrible
        fighting in the country.
There will be rumors about rulers fighting
        against other rulers.
47 The time will surely come
    when I will punish the false gods of
        Babylon,
    and the whole land of Babylon will be put
        to shame.
There will be many dead people,
    lying in the streets of that city.
48 Then heaven and earth and all that is in
        them
    will shout with joy about Babylon.
They will shout because an army came
        from the north
    and fought against Babylon."
This is what the LORD said.

49 "Babylon killed people from Israel.
    Babylon killed people from every place
        on earth.
    So Babylon must fall!

[a] 51:41 *Sheshach* Jeremiah used a special code to
create this secret name for Babylon.

50 You people escaped the swords.
    You must hurry and leave Babylon.
    Don't wait!
You are in a faraway land,
    but remember the Lord where you are
    and remember Jerusalem."

51"We people of Judah are ashamed.
    We have been insulted,
because strangers have gone into
    the holy places of the Lord's Temple."

52 The Lord says, "The time is coming,
    when I will punish the idols of Babylon.
At that time wounded people will cry
    with pain everywhere in that country.
53 Babylon might grow until she touches the
    sky.
Babylon might make her forts strong,
    but I will send people to fight against
    that city.
And they will destroy her."
This is what the Lord said.

54"We can hear people crying in Babylon.
    We hear the sound of people destroying
    things in the land of Babylon.
55 The Lord will destroy Babylon very soon.
    He will stop the loud noises in that city.
Enemies will come roaring in like ocean
    waves.
People all around will hear that roar.
56 The army will come and destroy Babylon.
    Its soldiers will be captured, and their
    bows will be broken,
This will happen because
    the Lord punishes people for the bad
    things they do.
He gives them the full punishment
    they deserve.
57 I will make Babylon's wise men
    and important officials drunk.
I will make the governors, officers,
    and soldiers drunk too.
Then they will sleep forever.
    They will never wake up."
This is what the King said.
    His name is the Lord All-Powerful.

58 This is what the Lord All-Powerful says:
    "Babylon's thick, strong wall will be pulled
    down.
    Her high gates will be burned.
The people of Babylon will work hard,
    but it will not help.
They will get very tired
    trying to save the city.
But they will only be fuel for the flames."

Jeremiah Sends a Message to Babylon

59This is the message that Jeremiah gave to
the officer Seraiah[a] son of Neriah. Neriah was

the son of Mahseiah. Seraiah went to Babylon
with King Zedekiah of Judah. This happened
in the fourth year that Zedekiah[b] was king of
Judah. At that time Jeremiah gave this message to Seraiah, the officer. 60Jeremiah had
written on a scroll* all the terrible things that
would happen to Babylon. He had written all
these things about Babylon.

61Jeremiah said to Seraiah, "Seraiah, go to
Babylon. Be sure to read this message so that
all the people can hear you. 62Then say, 'Lord,
you have said that you will destroy this place,
Babylon. You will destroy it so that no people
or animals will live in it. This place will be an
empty ruin forever.' 63After you finish reading this scroll, tie a stone to it and throw it
into the Euphrates River. 64Then say, 'In the
same way Babylon will sink. Babylon will rise
no more. It will sink because of the terrible
things that I will make happen here.'"

The words of Jeremiah end here.

The Fall of Jerusalem

52 1Zedekiah was 21 years old when
he became king of Judah. He ruled
in Jerusalem for eleven years. His mother's
name was Hamutal daughter of Jeremiah.[c]
Hamutal's family was from the town of Libnah. 2Zedekiah did evil things, just as King
Jehoiakim had done. The Lord did not like
Zedekiah doing those evil things. 3Terrible
things happened to the people of Jerusalem and Judah because the Lord was angry
with them. Finally, he threw them out of his
presence.

Zedekiah rebelled against the king of Babylon. 4So in the ninth year of Zedekiah's rule,
on the tenth day of the tenth month,[d] King
Nebuchadnezzar of Babylon marched against
Jerusalem with his whole army. The army of
Babylon set up their camp outside of Jerusalem. Then they built ramps all around the city
walls so that they could get over the walls.
5The city of Jerusalem was surrounded by
the army of Babylon until the eleventh year
that Zedekiah[e] was king. 6By the ninth day
of the fourth month of that year, the hunger
in the city was very bad. There was no food
left for the people in the city to eat. 7On that
day the army of Babylon broke into Jerusalem.
The soldiers of Jerusalem ran away. They left
the city at night. They went through the gate
between the two walls. That gate was near
the king's garden. Even though the army of
Babylon had surrounded the city, the soldiers
of Jerusalem still ran away toward the desert.

a51:59 Seraiah Seraiah was a brother of Baruch,
Jeremiah's secretary.

b51:59 the fourth year … Zedekiah That is,
594–593 B.C.
c52:1 Jeremiah This is not the prophet Jeremiah,
but a different man with the same name.
d52:4 ninth year … tenth month That is, January of
588 B.C.
e52:5 the eleventh year … Zedekiah That is, 587 B.C.

⁸But the Babylonian army chased King Zedekiah and caught him on the plains of Jericho. All of Zedekiah's soldiers ran away. ⁹The army of Babylon captured King Zedekiah and took him to the king of Babylon who was at the city of Riblah, in the land of Hamath. At Riblah the king of Babylon announced his judgment on King Zedekiah. ¹⁰There at the town of Riblah, the king of Babylon killed Zedekiah's sons while Zedekiah watched. The king of Babylon also killed all the royal officials of Judah. ¹¹Then the king of Babylon tore out Zedekiah's eyes. He put bronze chains on him and took him to Babylon. In Babylon he put Zedekiah into prison. He stayed in prison until the day he died.

¹²Nebuzaradan was the commander of the king of Babylon's special guard. He was one of the king's most important officials while at Jerusalem. He came to Jerusalem on the tenth day of the fifth month, in the 19th year that Nebuchadnezzar*a* was king. ¹³Nebuzaradan burned the LORD's Temple,* the king's palace, and every important building in Jerusalem, as well as all the houses. ¹⁴All the Babylonian soldiers that were with the commander broke down the walls around Jerusalem. ¹⁵Commander Nebuzaradan took the people who were still in Jerusalem*b* and those who had surrendered earlier and made them captives. He took them and the skilled craftsmen who were left in Jerusalem as captives to Babylon. ¹⁶But Nebuzaradan left some of the poorest people behind in the land. He left them to work in the vineyards* and the fields.

¹⁷The Babylonian army broke up the bronze columns of the LORD's Temple. They also broke up the stands and the bronze tank*c* that were in the LORD's Temple. They carried all that bronze to Babylon. ¹⁸The army of Babylon also took these things from the Temple: pots, shovels, lamp snuffers,* large bowls, pans, and all the bronze things that were used in the Temple service. ¹⁹The commander of the king's special guards took these things away: basins, firepans,* large bowls, pots, lampstands, pans, and bowls used for drink offerings. He took everything that was made of gold or silver. ²⁰The two pillars, the Sea and the twelve bronze bulls under it, and the moveable stands were very heavy. King Solomon had made those things for the LORD's Temple. The bronze that those things

were made of was so heavy it could not be weighed.

²¹Each of the bronze pillars was 31 feet*d* tall. Each pillar was almost 21 feet*e* around. Each pillar was hollow. The wall of each pillar was 3 inches*f* thick. ²²The bronze capital* on top of the first pillar was over 5 feet*g* tall. It was decorated with a net design and bronze pomegranates* all around it. The other pillar had pomegranates too. It was like the first pillar. ²³There were 96 pomegranates on the sides of the pillars. All together, there were 100 pomegranates above the net design that went around the pillars.

²⁴The commander of the king's special guards took Seraiah the high priest and Zephaniah the next highest priest as prisoners. The three doorkeepers were also taken as prisoners. ²⁵The commander of the king's special guards also took the officer in charge of the fighting men. He also took seven of the king's advisors as prisoners. They were still there in Jerusalem. He also took the scribe* who was in charge of putting people in the army. And he took 60 of the ordinary people who were there in the city. ²⁶-²⁷Nebuzaradan, the commander, took all these officials and brought them to the king of Babylon. The king of Babylon was at the city of Riblah. Riblah is in the country of Hamath. There at the city of Riblah, the king ordered all of them to be killed.

So the people of Judah were taken from their country. ²⁸This is how many people Nebuchadnezzar carried into captivity:

In Nebuchadnezzar's 7th year*h* as king of Babylon, 3023 people were taken from Judah.

²⁹ In Nebuchadnezzar's 18th year*i* as king of Babylon, 832 people were taken from Jerusalem.

³⁰ In Nebuchadnezzar's 23rd year*j* as king, Nebuzaradan took 745 people of Judah into captivity. Nebuzaradan was the commander of the king's special guards.

In all, 4600 people were taken captive.

Jehoiachin Is Set Free

³¹King Jehoiachin of Judah was in prison in Babylon for 37 years. In the 37th year of his imprisonment,*k* King Evil Merodach of Babylon was very kind to Jehoiachin. He let

---

*a*52:12 *the 19th year ... Nebuchadnezzar* That is, 587 B.C.

*b*52:15 *the people ... Jerusalem* This is from the ancient Greek version. The phrase, "some of the poorest people," which appears in the standard Hebrew text, seems to have been accidentally copied from the next verse.

*c*52:17 *bronze columns ... tank* These verses list the things that the Babylonian army took away from the Lord's Temple. For a description of the Temple furniture, see 1 Kings 7:13–26.

*d*52:21 *31 feet* Literally, "18 cubits" (9.33 m).

*e*52:21 *21 feet* Literally, "12 cubits" (6.22 m).

*f*52:21 *3 inches* Literally, "4 fingers" (7.4 cm).

*g*52:22 *5 feet* Or "1.63 m." Literally, "5 cubits" which would be 8' 6" (2.6 m), but see 2 Kings 25:17.

*h*52:28 *Nebuchadnezzar's 7th year* That is, from the middle of 598 B.C. to the middle of 597 B.C.

*i*52:29 *Nebuchadnezzar's 18th year* That is, from the middle of 588 B.C. to the middle of 587 B.C.

*j*52:30 *Nebuchadnezzar's 23rd year* That is, from the middle of 582 B.C. to the middle of 581 B.C.

*k*52:31 *37th year of his imprisonment* That is, 561 B.C.

Jehoiachin out of prison in that year. This was the same year that Evil Merodach became king of Babylon. He set Jehoiachin free from prison on the 25th day of the 12th month. [32]Evil Merodach spoke kindly to Jehoiachin. He gave Jehoiachin a place of honor higher than the other kings who were with him in Babylon. [33]So Jehoiachin took his prison clothes off. For the rest of his life, he ate regularly at the king's table. [34]Every day the king of Babylon paid Jehoiachin enough to take care of his needs until the day Jehoiachin died.

Lamentations

Jerusalem Cries Over Her Destruction

1 [1]Jerusalem once was a city full of people,
  but now the city is so empty.
Jerusalem was one of the greatest cities in
    the world,
  but now she[a] has become like a widow.
She was once a princess among cities,
  but now she has been made a slave.
[2] She cries bitterly in the night.
  Her tears are on her cheeks.
She has no one to comfort her.
Many nations were friendly to her,
  but not one of them comforts her now.
All her friends have turned their backs on
    her
  and have become her enemies.
[3] Judah suffered very much,
  and then she was taken into captivity.
She lives among other nations
  but has found no rest.
The people who chased her caught her
  where there was no way out.[b]
[4] The roads to Zion* are very sad,
  because no one comes to Zion for the
    festivals anymore.
All of Zion's gates have been destroyed;
  all her priests groan in sorrow.
Zion's young women have been taken
    away,[c]
  and all this made Zion sad.
[5] Jerusalem's enemies have won.
  Her enemies have been successful.
This happened because the LORD
    punished her.
He punished Jerusalem for her many
    sins.
Her children have gone away.
  Their enemies captured them and took
    them away.
[6] The beauty of Daughter Zion[d]

has gone away.
Her princes were like deer
  that cannot find a meadow to feed in.
They walk away without strength
  from those who chased them.
[7] Jerusalem thinks back.
She remembers the time when she was
    hurt
  and when she lost her home.
She remembers all the nice things
  that she had in the past.
She remembers those nice things
  that she had in the old days.
She remembers when her people
  were captured by the enemy.
She remembers when there was no one
  to help her.
When her enemies saw her, they laughed,
  because she was destroyed.
[8] Jerusalem sinned very badly.
Because Jerusalem sinned,
  she became a ruined city that people
    shake their heads about.
In the past people respected her.
But now they hate her,
  because they abused her.
Jerusalem groaned and turned away.
[9] Jerusalem's skirts were dirty.
  She gave no thought to what would
    become of her.
Her fall was amazing.
  She had no one to comfort her.
She says, "LORD, see how I am hurt!
  See how my enemy thinks he is so
    great!"

[10] The enemy stretched out his hand.
  He took all her nice things.
In fact, she saw the foreign nations go
    inside her Temple.*
And, LORD, you said those people could
    not join in our assembly!
[11] All the people of Jerusalem are groaning.
  All of her people are looking for food.
They are giving away all their nice
    things for food to stay alive.
Jerusalem says, "Look, LORD. Look at me!
  See how people hate me.

---

[a]1:1 *she* Throughout this poem, the city of Jerusalem is represented as a woman.
[b]1:3 *where ... way out* Or "in the narrow valleys."
[c]1:4 *have been taken away* This is from the ancient Greek version. The standard Hebrew text has "are upset."
[d]1:6 *Daughter Zion* Another name for Jerusalem. Also in 2:1, 8, 13, 18.

12 All you who pass by on the road,
    you don't seem to care.
  But look at me and see.
    Is there any pain like my pain?
    Is there any pain like the pain that has
      come to me?
    Is there any pain like the pain that the
      Lord has punished me with?
  He has punished me on the day
    of his great anger.
13 The Lord sent fire from above
    that went down into my bones.
  He stretched out a net for my feet.
    He turned me all the way around.
  He made me into a wasteland.
    I am sick all day.

14 "My sins were tied up like a yoke.*
    My sins were tied up in the Lord's
      hands.
  His yoke is on my neck.
    He has made me weak.
  He has given me to those
    who I cannot stand up against.
15 "The Lord rejected all my powerful men
    who were inside the city.
  Then he brought a group of people against
    me.
    He brought them to kill my young
      soldiers.
  The Lord has trampled his dearest city*
    like grapes in a winepress.

16 "I cry about all these things.
    Tears are flowing down my cheeks.
  There is no one near to comfort me.
    There is no one who can make me feel
      better.
  My children are like a wasteland,
    because the enemy won."

17 Zion spread out her hands.
    There was no one to comfort her.
  The Lord had given orders to Jacob's*
    enemies.
    He ordered them to surround the city.
  Jerusalem has become a dirty rag
    that her enemies threw away.

18 Now Jerusalem says, "I refused to listen
    to the Lord,
    so he is right for doing these things.
  So listen, all you people!
    Look at my pain!
  My young women and men
    have gone into captivity.
19 I called out to my lovers,
    but they tricked me.
  My priests and my elders
    have died in the city.
  They were looking for food for themselves.
    They wanted to keep themselves alive.

20 "Look at me, Lord. I am in distress!
    I am upset, as if my heart turned upside
      down inside of me.
  I feel this way because
    I have been so stubborn.
  Out in the streets,
    I lost my children to the swords.
  Inside, it is like death.

21 "Listen to me, I am groaning.
    I have no one to comfort me.
  All my enemies have heard of my trouble.
    They are happy that you did this to me.
  You said there would be a time of
    punishment.
    You said you would punish my enemies.
  Now do what you said.
    Let my enemies be like I am now.

22 "Look how evil my enemies are!
    Then you can treat them
      the same way you treated me because of
        all my sins.
  Do this because I am groaning again and
    again.
  Do this because my heart is sick."

The Lord Destroyed Jerusalem

2 ¹Look how the Lord has covered
    daughter Zion* with the cloud of his
      anger.
  He has thrown her, the glory of Israel,*
    from the sky to the ground.
  In his anger he showed no care even for
    the Temple where he rests his feet.*
2 The Lord destroyed the houses of Jacob.*
    He destroyed them without mercy.
  In his anger he destroyed
    the fortresses of Daughter Judah.
  He threw the kingdom of Judah
    and its rulers to the ground.
  He ruined the kingdom of Judah.
3 He was angry, and he destroyed
    all the strength of Israel.
  He took away his right hand from Israel.
    He did this when the enemy came.
  He burned like a flaming fire in Jacob.
    He was like a fire that burns all around.
4 He bent his bow like an enemy.
    He held his sword in his right hand.
  He killed all the good-looking men of
    Judah.
    He killed them as if they were the
      enemy.
  He poured out his anger
    like a fire on the tents of Zion.

5 The Lord has become like an enemy.
    He has swallowed up Israel.

*2:1 daughter Zion The city of Jerusalem pictured as a young woman. Similar language is used in verses 8, 13, 15, and 18. See "Zion" in the Word List. *2:1 Temple ... feet Literally, "the footstool of his feet," meaning the place God lived among his people.

*1:15 dearest city Literally, "virgin daughter Judah," a name for the city of Jerusalem.

He has swallowed up all her palaces
and all her fortresses.
He has made much sadness and crying
for the dead in Daughter Judah.

6 He pulled up his own tent[a]
as if it were a garden.
He has ruined the place where the people
came together to worship him.
The LORD has made people forget
the special assemblies and special days
of rest[b] in Zion.
He rejected the king and the priests.
He was angry and rejected them.

7 He rejected his altar,
and he left his holy place of worship.
He let the enemy pull down the walls
of the palaces of Jerusalem.
The enemy shouted with joy in the LORD's
Temple.*
They made noise as though it were a
festival.

8 The LORD planned to destroy
the wall of Daughter Zion.
He marked the wall with a measuring
line.
He didn't stop himself from destroying
it.
He made all the walls cry out in sadness.
Together they wasted away.

9 Jerusalem's gates have sunk into the
ground.
The bars on her gates are completely
destroyed.
Her king and princes have been taken to
other nations.
The teaching of the law has stopped.
And her prophets no longer receive
visions* from the LORD.

10 The elders of Zion* sit on the ground.
They sit on the ground and are quiet.
They pour dust on their heads.
They put on sackcloth.*
The young women of Jerusalem
bow their heads to the ground in
sorrow.

11 My eyes are worn out with tears,
and my insides are upset.
My heart feels like it has been poured on
the ground;
I feel this way because of the destruction
of my people.
Children and babies are fainting
in the public squares of the city.

12 They ask their mothers,
"Where is the bread and wine?"

as they pour out their life in their
mother's laps.

13 My dear Jerusalem, what can I say about
you?
What can I compare you to?
What can I say you are like?
How can I comfort you, city of Zion?
You have been hurt much too badly for
anyone to heal.

14 Your prophets saw visions for you,
but their visions were only worthless
lies.
They didn't speak against your sins.
They didn't try to make things better.
They spoke messages for you,
but they were false messages that fooled
you.

15 Those who pass by on the road
clap their hands and laugh at you.
They make fun of Jerusalem,
shaking their heads at the sight of her.
They ask, "Is this the city that people
called
'The Most Beautiful City'
and 'The Joy of all the Earth'?"

16 All your enemies laugh at you.
They whistle and grind their teeth at
you.
They say, "We have swallowed them up!
This is the day we were hoping for.
We have finally seen this happen!"

17 The LORD did what he planned to do.
He did what he said he would do.
He did what he commanded a long time
ago.
He destroyed, and he had no pity.
He made your enemies happy because
of what happened to you.
He made your enemies strong.

18 Cry out with all your heart[c] to the Lord!
Jerusalem, let tears roll down your walls.
Let your tears flow like a stream day and
night.
Don't stop crying
or let your eyes dry.

19 Get up and cry throughout the night.
Pour out your heart as if it were water.
Pour out your heart before the Lord.
Lift up your hands in prayer to the Lord.
Ask him to let your starving children
live.
They are fainting with hunger in all the
streets of the city.

20 Look at us, LORD!
Have you ever treated anyone else so
badly?

---

a 2:6 *his own tent* This is a reference to the Lord's
Temple in Jerusalem.
b 2:6 *special days of rest* Or "Sabbaths." This might
mean Saturday, or it might mean all the special days
when the people were not supposed to work.
c 2:18 *Cry out … heart* Or "Their hearts cried out."

Is it right for women to eat their own
babies, the children they have cared
for?
Should priests and prophets be killed in
the Temple of the Lord?

21 Young men and old men
lie on the ground in the streets of the
city.
My young women and young men
have been killed by the sword.
You killed them on the day of your anger.
You killed them without mercy!

22 You invited terror to come to me
from all around.
You invited terror as though you were
inviting it to a festival.
No one escaped
on the day of the Lord's anger.
My enemy killed the people
who I raised and brought up.

The Meaning of Suffering

3 ¹I am a man who has seen much trouble.
The Lord beat us with a stick,
and I saw it happen.

2 He led and brought me
into darkness, not light.

3 He turned his hand against me.
He did this again and again, all day.

4 He wore out my flesh and skin.
He broke my bones.

5 He built up bitterness and trouble against
me.
He surrounded me with bitterness and
trouble.

6 He put me in the dark,
like someone who died long ago.

7 He shut me in, so I could not get out.
He put heavy chains on me.

8 Even when I cry out and ask for help,
he does not listen to my prayer.

9 He has blocked up my path with stones.
He has made my path crooked.

10 He is like a bear about to attack me,
like a lion that is in a hiding place.

11 He led me off my path.
He tore me to pieces and ruined me.

12 He made his bow ready.
He made me the target for his arrows.

13 He shot me in the stomach
with his arrows.

14 I have become a joke to all my people.
All day long they sing songs about me
and make fun of me.

15 The Lord gave me this poison to drink.
He filled me with this bitter drink.

16 He pushed my teeth into rocky ground.
He pushed me into the dirt.

17 I thought I would never have peace
again.
I forgot about good things.

18 I said to myself,
"I no longer have any hope
that the Lord will help me."

19 Lord, remember, I am very sad,
and I have no home.
Remember the bitter poison that you gave
me.

20 I remember well all my troubles,
and I am very sad.

21 But then I think about this,
and I have hope:

22 We are still alive because
the Lord's faithful love never ends.

23 Every morning he shows it in new ways!
Lord, you are so very true and loyal!

24 I say to myself, "The Lord is my God,
and I trust him."ᵃ

25 The Lord is good to those who wait for
him.
He is good to those who look for him.

26 It is good to wait quietly
for the Lord to save them.

27 It is good for a man to wear his yoke*
from the time he is young.

28 He should sit alone and be quiet
when the Lord puts his yoke on him.

29 He should bow down to the Lord.
Maybe there is still hope.

30 He should turn his cheek to the one who
hits him
and let people insult him.

31 He should remember that
the Lord does not reject people forever.

32 When he punishes,
he also has mercy.
He has mercy because of his great love
and kindness.

33 He does not enjoy causing people pain.
He does not like to make anyone
unhappy.

34 He does not like any prisoner on earth to
be trampled down.

35 He does not like anyone to be unfair to
another person.
Some people will do such things right in
front of God Most High.

36 He does not like anyone to cheat another
person.
He does not like any of these things.

37 No one can say something and make it
happen,
unless the Lord orders it.

38 God Most High commands
both good and bad things to happen.

39 No one alive can complain
when he punishes them for their sins.

40 Let us check and see what we have done.
Then let us turn back to the Lord.

41 Let us lift up our hearts and our hands
to the God of heaven.

ᵃ**3:24** *The Lord ... him* Or "The Lord is my portion
and I trust him.

⁴² Let us say to him, "We have sinned and
have been stubborn.
    Because of this, you have not forgiven
    us.
⁴³ You wrapped yourself with anger.
    You chased us.
    You killed us without mercy!
⁴⁴ You wrapped yourself in a cloud
    so that no prayer could get through.
⁴⁵ You made us like garbage and dirt
    to the other nations.
⁴⁶ All of our enemies
    speak angrily against us.
⁴⁷ We have been frightened.
    We have fallen into a pit.
    We have been badly hurt.
    We have been broken."
⁴⁸ My eyes flow with streams of tears.
    I cry because of the destruction of my
    people.
⁴⁹ My eyes will flow without stopping.
    I will keep on crying.
⁵⁰ I will continue to cry
    until you look down and see us, Lord!
    I will continue to cry
    until you see us from heaven.
⁵¹ My eyes make me sad, when I see
    what happened to the young women in
    my city.
⁵² For no reason, my enemies hunted me
    like a bird.
⁵³ They threw me alive into a pit
    and then threw stones at me.
⁵⁴ Water came up over my head.
    I said to myself, "I am finished."
⁵⁵ Lord, I called your name
    from the bottom of the pit.
⁵⁶ You heard my voice.
    You didn't close your ears.
    You didn't refuse to rescue me.
⁵⁷ You came to me on the day that I called
    out to you.
    You said to me, "Don't be afraid."
⁵⁸ You defended me
    and bought me back to life.
⁵⁹ Lord, you have seen my trouble.
    Now judge my case for me.
⁶⁰ You have seen how my enemies
    have hurt me.
    You have seen all the evil plans
    that they made against me.
⁶¹ You heard them insult me, Lord.
    You have heard all the evil plans that
    they made against me.
⁶² The words and the thoughts of my
    enemies
    are against me all the time—
⁶³ when they sit down and when they
    stand up.
    Look how they make fun of me!
⁶⁴ Give them back what they deserve, Lord.
    Pay them back for what they have
    done.
⁶⁵ Make them stubborn
    and then curse them.

⁶⁶ Chase them in anger and destroy them.
    Wipe them off the face of the earth,
    Lord!

The Horrors of the Attack on Jerusalem

4 ¹See how the gold has grown dark,
    how the pure gold has changed.
    There are jewelsᵃ scattered all around
    at every street corner.
² The people of Zion* were worth a lot.
    They were worth their weight in gold.
    But now the enemy treats them
    like old clay jars.
    The enemy treats them
    like clay jars made by a potter.
³ Even a wild dog feeds her babies.
    Even the jackal lets her pups suck at her
    breast.
    But the daughter of my peopleᵇ is cruel.
    She is like the ostrich* in the desert that
    forgets its eggs in the sand.
⁴ Babies are so thirsty
    their tongues stick to the roof of their
    mouths.
    Young children ask for bread,
    but no one gives them any.
⁵ Those who ate rich food
    are now dying in the streets.
    Those who grew up wearing nice red
    clothes
    now pick through garbage piles.
⁶ The sin of the daughter of my people
    was very great.
    Their sin was greater than the sins
    of Sodom* and Gomorrah.*
    Sodom and Gomorrah were destroyed
    suddenly.
    No human hand caused their
    destruction.ᶜ
⁷ Some of the men of Judah
    were dedicated* to God in a special
    way.
    They were very pure.
    They were whiter than snow,
    and whiter than milk.
    Their bodies were red like coral
    and their beards like sapphire stones.
⁸ But now their faces are blacker than soot.
    No one even recognizes them in the
    streets.
    Their skin is wrinkled over their bones.
    Their skin is like wood.
⁹ It was better for those who were killed by
    the sword
    than for those who died of hunger.
    Those starving people were sad and hurt.
    They died because they got no food
    from the field.

ᵃ**4:1** *jewels* The meaning of the Hebrew word here
is uncertain.
ᵇ**4:3** *daughter of my people* Another name for
Jerusalem. Also in verse 6.
ᶜ**4:6** *No human hand … destruction* The Hebrew
text here is hard to understand.

10 Then even nice women
    cooked their own children.
The children were food
    for their mothers.
This happened when my people
    were destroyed.

11 The LORD used all of his anger.
    He poured out all his anger.
He made a fire in Zion
    that burned it down to the foundations.

12 The kings of the earth could not believe
    what had happened.
The people of the world could not believe
    what had happened.
They could not believe
    that enemies would be able to come
        through the city gates of Jerusalem.

13 This happened because the prophets
    of Jerusalem sinned.
This happened because the priests
    of Jerusalem did evil things.
They were shedding the blood of good
    people
    in the city of Jerusalem.

14 The prophets and priests walked around
    like blind men in the streets.
They had become dirty with blood.
    No one could even touch their clothes
        because they were dirty.

15 People shouted, "Go away!
    Go away! Don't touch us."
They wandered around and had no home.
People in other nations said,
    "We don't want them to live with us."

16 The LORD himself destroyed them.
    He didn't look after them anymore.
He didn't respect the priests.
    He was not friendly to the elders* of
        Judah.

17 We have worn out our eyes looking for
    help,
    but no help comes.
We kept on looking for a nation to save
    us.
We kept watch from our watchtower,
    but no nation came to us.

18 Our enemies hunted us all the time.
    We could not even go out into the
        streets.
Our end came near. Our time was up.
    Our end came!

19 The men who chased us
    were faster than eagles in the sky.
They chased us into the mountains.
    They hid in the desert to catch us.

20 The king was very important to us.
    He was like the breath we breathe,
        but he was trapped by them.
The LORD himself chose the king, and we
    said this about the king,
    "We will live in his shadow.
    He protects us from the nations."

21 Be happy, people of Edom.
    Be happy, you who live in the land of
        Uz.

But remember, the cup of the Lord's anger
    will come around to you too.
When you drink from that cup,
    you will get drunk and strip off all your
        clothes.

22 Your punishment is complete, Zion.
    You will not go into captivity again.
But the LORD will punish your sins,
    people of Edom.
He will uncover your sins.

A Prayer to the Lord

5 1Remember, LORD, what happened to us.
    Look and see our shame.

2 Our land has been turned over to
    strangers.
Our houses have been given to
    foreigners.

3 We have become orphans.
    We have no father.
Our mothers have become like widows.

4 We have to buy the water that we drink.
    We have to pay for the wood that we
        use.

5 We are forced to wear a yoke* on our
    necks.
We get tired, and we have no rest.

6 We made an agreement with Egypt.
    We also made an agreement with
        Assyria* to get enough bread.

7 Our ancestors sinned against you, and
    now they are dead.
And we are suffering because of their
    sins.

8 Slaves have become our rulers.
    No one can save us from them.

9 We risk our lives to get food.
    There are men in the desert with
        swords.

10 Our skin is hot like an oven.
    We have a high fever because of our
        hunger.

11 The enemy raped the women of Zion.*
    They raped the women in the cities of
        Judah.

12 The enemy hanged our princes.
    They didn't honor our elders.

13 The enemy made our young men
    grind grain at the mill.
Our young men stumbled
    under loads of wood.

14 The elders no longer sit at the gates of the
    city.
The young men no longer make music.

15 We have no more joy in our hearts.
    Our dancing has changed to crying for
        the dead.

16 The crown has fallen from our head.
    Things have gone bad for us because we
        sinned.

17 For this reason our hearts have become
    sick,
    and our eyes cannot see clearly.

18 Mount Zion is a wasteland.
    Foxes run around on Mount Zion.

¹⁹ But you rule forever, LORD.
    Your kingly chair lasts forever and ever.
²⁰ You seem to have forgotten us forever.
    You seem to have left us alone for such
        a long time.

²¹ Bring us back to you, LORD.
    We will gladly come back to you.
    Make our lives as they were before.
²² You were very angry with us.
    Have you completely rejected us?

Ezekiel

Introduction

1 ¹⁻³I am the priest, Ezekiel son of Buzzi. I was in exile* by the Kebar Canal in Babylonia when the skies opened up, and I saw visions* of God. This was on the fifth day of the fourth month of the thirtieth year.ᵃ (This was the fifth year of King Jehoiachin's exile. The word of the LORD came to Ezekiel. The power of the LORD came over him at that place.)

The Chariot of the Lord—God's Throne

⁴I was watching a big storm come in from the north. It was a big cloud with a strong wind, and there was fire flashing from it. Light was shining out all around it. It looked like hot metalᵇ glowing in a fire. ⁵Inside the cloud, there were four living beings that looked like people. ⁶But each one of them had four faces and four wings. ⁷Their legs were straight. Their feet looked like calves' feet, and they sparkled like polished brass. ⁸Under their wings were human arms. There were four living beings. Each living being had four faces and four wings. ⁹The wings touched each other. The living beings did not turn when they moved. They went in the direction they were looking.

¹⁰Each living being had four faces. In the front they each had a man's face. There was a lion's face on the right side and a bull's face on the left side. There was an eagle's face on the back. ¹¹Their wings were spread out over them. With two of the wings each living being reached out to touch the one near it, and with the other two wings it covered its body. ¹²Each living being went in the direction it was looking. They went wherever the spiritᶜ caused them to go, but they did not turn when they moved. ¹³That is what the living beings looked like.

Inside the area between the living beings, there was something that looked like burning coals of fire. This fire was like small torches that kept moving around among the living beings. The fire glowed brightly and lightning flashed from it. ¹⁴The living beings ran back and forth—as fast as lightning.ᵈ

¹⁵⁻¹⁶I was looking at the living beings when I noticed four wheels that touched the ground. There was one wheel by each living being. All the wheels looked the same. The wheels looked as if they were made from a clear, yellow jewel. They looked like there was a wheel inside a wheel. ¹⁷They could turn to move in any direction. ⌊But the living beings⌋ did not turn when they moved.ᵉ

¹⁸The rims of the wheels were tall and frightening. There were eyes all over the rims of all four wheels.

¹⁹The wheels always moved with the living beings. If the living beings went up into the air, the wheels went with them. ²⁰They went wherever the spirit wanted them to go, and the wheels went with them, because the power that moved the living being was in the wheels. ²¹So if the living beings moved, the wheels moved. If the living beings stopped, the wheels stopped. If the wheels went into the air, the living beings went with them, because the spirit was in the wheels.

²²There was an amazing thing over the heads of the living beings. It was like a bowlᶠ turned upside down, and the bowl was clear like crystal. ²³Under this bowl, each living being had wings reaching out to the one next to it. Two wings spread out one way and two wings spread out the other way, covering its body.

²⁴Then I heard the wings. Every time the living beings moved, their wings made a very loud noise like a lot of water rushing by. They were loud like ⌊the Lord⌋ All-Powerful. They were as loud as an army or a crowd of people.

ᵃ**1:1–3 fifth day ... year** If the year refers to Ezekiel's age, this is the same as the fifth year of exile, that is, July 31, 593 B.C.
ᵇ**1:4 hot metal** The Hebrew word might mean "melted copper," "an alloy of gold and silver," or "amber." Also in verse 27.
ᶜ**1:12 spirit** Or "wind." Also in verse 20.

ᵈ**1:14** Or "And there was something like lighting shooting back and forth among the living beings."
ᵉ**1:17 The wheels ... moved** Or "The wheels could move in any four directions, but they did not turn when they moved."
ᶠ**1:22 bowl** This Hebrew word is the same word used in Gen. 1:6–7 to describe the dome of the sky.

When the living beings stopped moving, they put their wings down by their side.

²⁵The living beings stopped moving and lowered their wings. Then there was another loud sound that came from above the bowl over their heads. ²⁶There was something that looked like a throne on top of the bowl. It was blue like sapphire. There was also something that looked like a man sitting on the throne. ²⁷I looked at him from his waist up. He looked like hot metal with fire all around him. I looked at him from his waist down. It looked like fire with a glow that was shining all around him. ²⁸The light shining around him was like a rainbow in a cloud. It was the Glory of the Lord.* As soon as I saw that, I fell to the ground. I bowed with my face to the ground, and then I heard a voice speaking to me.

The Lord Speaks to Ezekiel

2 ¹The voice said, "Son of man,ᵃ stand up and I will speak with you."

²Then the Spirit came into meᵇ and lifted me up on my feet, and I listened to the one who spoke to me. ³He said, "Son of man, I am sending you to speak to the family of Israel. Those people and their ancestors turned against me many times. They have sinned against me many times—and they are still sinning against me today. ⁴I am sending you to speak to them, but they are very stubborn. They are very hardheaded, but you must speak to them. You must say, 'This is what the Lord God says.' ⁵They are a rebellious people, so they may not listen to you and stop sinning, but at least they will know that there is a prophet* living among them.

⁶"Son of man, don't be afraid of the people or what they say. It is true: they will turn against you and try to hurt you. Their words will be sharp like thorns and will sting like scorpions. But don't be afraid of what they say. They are a rebellious people, but don't be afraid of them. ⁷You must tell them what I say whether they listen and stop sinning or not. They are a rebellious people!

⁸"Son of man, you must listen to what I say to you. Don't turn against me like those rebellious people. Open your mouth and ₗaccept the words I give you and then speak them to the peopleₗ. Eat these words."

⁹Then I saw an arm reach out toward me. It was holding a scroll* with words written on it. ¹⁰It rolled the scroll open in front of me. Words were on the front and on the back of the scroll. There were all kinds of sad songs, sad stories, and warnings.

3 ¹God said to me, "Son of man,ᶜ eat what you see. Eat this scroll, and then go tell these things to the family of Israel."

²So I opened my mouth and he put the scroll into my mouth. ³Then God said, "Son of man, I am giving you this scroll. Swallow it! Let that scroll fill your body."

So I ate the scroll. It was as sweet as honey in my mouth.

⁴Then God said to me, "Son of man, go to the family of Israel. Speak my words to them. ⁵I am not sending you to some foreigners you cannot understand. You don't have to learn another language. I am sending you to the family of Israel. ⁶I am not sending you to many different countries where people speak languages you cannot understand. If you went to those people and spoke to them, they would listen to you. But you will not have to learn those hard languages. ⁷No, I am sending you to the family of Israel. Only, these people have hard heads—they are very stubborn! And the people of Israel will refuse to listen to you. They don't want to listen to me. ⁸But I will make you just as stubborn as they are, and your head just as hard. ⁹A diamond is harder than flint rock. In the same way you will be more stubborn than they are, and your head will be harder. Then you will not be afraid of them or those who always turn against me."

¹⁰Then God said to me, "Son of man, listen to every word I say to you and remember them. ¹¹Then go to all of your people in exile* and tell them, 'This is what the Lord God says ....' They will not listen, and they will not stop sinning, but you must still tell them my message."

¹²Then the Spiritᵈ lifted me up, and I heard a voice behind me. It was very loud, like thunder. It said, "Blessed is the Glory of the Lord*!" ¹³Then the wings of the living beings began moving. The wings made a very loud noise as they touched each other, and the wheels in front of them began making a noise as loud as thunder. ¹⁴The Spirit lifted me and took me away. I was very sad and upset in my spirit, but I felt the Lord's power in me. ¹⁵I went to the people of Israel who were forced to live in Tel Avivᵉ by the Kebar Canal. I sat there among them for seven days, shocked and silent.

The Watchman of Israel

¹⁶After seven days, the word of the Lord came to me. He said, ¹⁷"Son of man, I am making you a watchman* for Israel. I will tell you about bad things that will happen to them, and you must warn Israel. ¹⁸If I say, 'These evil people will die!' Then you must

---

ᵃ**2:1** *Son of man* This was usually just a way of saying "a person" or "a human being." Here, it is a way of addressing Ezekiel, as one the Lord chose to be his prophet. It is used in this sense throughout this book.
ᵇ**2:2** *the Spirit came into me* Or "a wind came."

ᶜ**3:1** *Son of man* This was usually just a way of saying "a person" or "a human being." Here, it is a way of addressing Ezekiel. Also in verses 3, 4, 10, 17, 25.
ᵈ**3:12** *Spirit* Or "wind." Also in verse 24.
ᵉ**3:15** *Tel Aviv* This was a place outside of Israel. The name means "Spring Hill."

warn them. You must tell them to change their lives and stop doing evil. If you don't warn them, they will die because they sinned. But I will also make you responsible for their death, because you did not go to them and save their lives.

¹⁹"If you warn them and tell them to change their lives and stop doing evil, but they refuse to listen, they will die because they sinned. But since you warned them, you will have saved your own life.

²⁰"If good people stop being good and begin to do evil, and I send something that makes them stumble and sin, they will die because they sinned. But since you did not warn them and remind them of the good things they had done, I will make you responsible for their death.

²¹"But if you warn good people and tell them to stop sinning, and they listen to your warning and stop sinning, they will not die. In that way you will have saved your own life."

²²The Lord's power came to me. He said to me, "Get up and go to the valley.ᵃ I will speak to you in that place."

²³So I got up and went out to the valley. The Glory of the Lord* was there—as I had seen it by the Kebar Canal. So I bowed with my face to the ground. ²⁴But the Spirit came into me and lifted me up on my feet. He said to me, "Go home and lock yourself in your house. ²⁵Son of man, people will come with ropes and tie you up. They will not let you go out among the people. ²⁶I will make your tongue stick to the roof of your mouth—you will not be able to talk. So they will not have anyone to teach them that they are doing wrong, because they are always turning against me. ²⁷But I will talk to you, and then I will allow you to speak. But you must say to them, 'This is what the Lord God says.' If a person wants to listen, fine. If a person refuses to listen, fine. But those people always turn against me.

Warnings About the Attack of Jerusalem

4 ¹"Son of man,ᵇ take a brick and scratch a picture on it. Draw a picture of a city—the city of Jerusalem. ²And then pretend you are an army surrounding the city. Build a dirt wall around the city to help you attack it. Build a dirt road leading up to the city wall. Bring battering ramsᶜ and set up army camps around the city. ³And then take an iron pan and put it between you and the city. It will be like an iron wall separating you and the city.

In this way you will show that you are against it. You will surround the city and attack it. This is an example for the family of Israel to show that I will destroy Jerusalem.

⁴"Then you must lie down on your left side. You must do this thing that shows that you are taking the sins of the people of Israel on yourself. You will carry the guilt for as many days as you lie on your left side. ⁵You must bear the guilt of Israel for 390 days.ᵈ In this way I am telling you how long Israel will be punished; one day equals one year.

⁶"After that time, you will lie on your right side for 40 days. This time you will bear the guilt of Judah for 40 days. One day equals one year. I am telling you how long Judah must be punished.

⁷"Now, roll up your sleeve and raise your arm over the brick. Act like you are attacking the city of Jerusalem. Do this to show that you are speaking as my messenger to the people. ⁸Now look, I am tying ropes on you. You will not be able to roll over from one side to the other until your attack against the cityᵉ is finished.

⁹"You must get some grain to make bread. Get some wheat, barley, beans, lentils, millet, and spelt.* Mix all these things together in one bowl and grind them to make flour. You will use this flour to make bread. You will eat only this bread during the 390 days that you lie on your side. ¹⁰You will be allowed to use only 1 cupᶠ of that flour each day to make bread. You will eat that bread from time to time throughout the day. ¹¹You can drink only 3 cupsᵍ of water each day. You can drink it from time to time throughout the day. ¹²You must make your bread each day. You must get dry human dung and burn it. Then you must cook the bread over this burning dung. You must eat this bread in front of the people."

¹³Then the Lord said, "This will show that the family of Israel will eat unclean* bread in foreign countries and that I am the one who forced them to leave Israel and go to those countries!"

¹⁴Then I said, "Oh, but Lord God, I have never eaten any unclean food. I have never eaten meat from an animal that died from a disease or from an animal that was killed by a wild animal. I have never eaten unclean meat—not from the time that I was a little baby until now. None of that bad meat ever entered my mouth."

¹⁵Then God said to me, "Very well, I will let you use dry cow dung to cook your bread. You don't have to use dry human dung."

ᵃ3:22 the valley Possibly, Jezreel Valley, a fertile area where many battles were fought. It is often called simply "The Valley."
ᵇ4:1 Son of man This was usually just a way of saying "a person" or "a human being." Here, it is a way of addressing Ezekiel. Also in verse 16.
ᶜ4:2 battering rams Heavy logs that soldiers used to break holes into the gates or walls around a city.

ᵈ4:5 390 days The ancient Greek version has "190 days."
ᵉ4:8 your attack against the city This is a wordplay. The Hebrew word can mean "famine," "time of trouble," or "attack against a city."
ᶠ4:10 1 cup Literally, "20 shekels" (230 g).
ᵍ4:11 3 cups Literally, "1/6 hin" (.5 l).

¹⁶Then God said to me, "Son of man, I am destroying Jerusalem's supply of bread. People will have only a little bread to eat. They will be very worried about their food supply, and they will have only a little water to drink. Every time they take a drink, they will feel more afraid. ¹⁷That is because there will not be enough food and water for everyone. They will be terrified as they watch each other wasting away because of their sins.

People of Jerusalem Scattered

5 ¹⁻²"Son of man,ᵃ after your famineᵇ you must do this: Take a sharp sword and use it like a barber's razor. Shave off your hair and beard. Put the hair on a scale and weigh it. Separate it into three equal parts. Put a third of your hair on the brick that has the picture of the city on it. Burn that hair in that 'city.' Then use the sword and cut a third of your hair into small pieces all around the outside of the 'city.' Next, throw a third of your hair into the air and let the wind blow it away. This will show that I will pull out my sword and chase some of the people into faraway countries. ³But then you must get a few of those hairs and wrap them up in your robe. ⁴Take some of those hairs and throw them into the fire. This will show that a fire will start there and burn throughout the whole house of Israel.ᶜ"

⁵Then the Lord GOD said to me, "The brick is a picture of Jerusalem. I put Jerusalem in the middle of other nations with countries all around her. ⁶The people rebelled against my commands. They were worse than any of the other nations! They broke more of my laws than any of the people in the countries around them. They refused to listen to my commands. They did not obey my laws."

⁷So the Lord GOD says, "I will do this because you did not obey my laws and commands. You broke more of my laws than the people who lived around you, and you did what even they know is wrong!" ⁸So the Lord GOD says, "So now, even I am against you! I will punish you while those other people watch. ⁹I will do things to you that I have never done before. And I will never do those terrible things again, because you did so many terrible things. ¹⁰People in Jerusalem will be so hungry that parents will eat their own children, and children will eat their own parents. I will punish you in many ways, and those who are left alive, I will scatter to the winds."

¹¹The Lord GOD says, "Jerusalem, I promise by my life that I will punish you! I promise that I will punish you, because you did terrible things to my Holy Place. You did horrible things that made it dirty. I will punish you. I will not show any mercy or feel sorry for you. ¹²A third of your people will die inside the city from diseases and hunger. Another third will die in battle outside the city. And then I will pull out my sword and chase the last third of your people into faraway countries. ¹³Only then will I stop being angry with your people. I will know that they have been punished for the bad things they did to me. They will know that I am the LORD and that I spoke to them because of my strong loveᵈ for them!"

¹⁴God said, "Jerusalem, I will destroy you—you will be nothing but a pile of rocks. The people around you will make fun of you. Everyone who walks by will make fun of you. ¹⁵People around you will make fun of you, but you will also be a lesson for them. They will see that I was angry and punished you. I was very angry and I warned you. I, the LORD, told you what I would do. ¹⁶I told you I would send you terrible times of hunger. I told you I would send you things that would destroy you. I told you that I would take away your supply of food and that those times of hunger would come again and again. ¹⁷I told you I would send hunger and wild animals against you that would kill your children. I told you there would be disease and death everywhere in the city. I told you I would bring enemy soldiers to fight against you. I, the LORD, told you all these things would happen!"

Prophecies Against Israel

6 ¹Then the word of the LORD came to me again. ²He said, "Son of man,ᵉ turn toward the mountains of Israel. Speak against them for me. ³Tell the mountains this: "'Mountains of Israel, listen to this message from the Lord GOD! The Lord GOD says these things to the hills and mountains and to the ravines and valleys. Look! I am bringing the enemy to fight against you. I will destroy your high places.* ⁴Your altars* will be broken into pieces. Your incense* altars will be smashed, and I will throw down your dead bodies in front of your filthy idols.* ⁵I will put the dead bodies of the people of Israel in front of their filthy idols. I will scatter your bones around your altars. ⁶Bad things will happen wherever your people live. Their cities will become piles of rock. Their high places will be destroyed so that those places of worship will never be used again. The altars will all be destroyed. People will never worship those filthy idols again. The incense altars will be smashed. Everything you made will be destroyed completely. ⁷Your people will be killed, and then you will know that I am the LORD!'"

ᵃ**5:1–2** *Son of man* This was usually just a way of saying "a person" or "a human being." Here, it is a way of addressing Ezekiel.

ᵇ**5:1–2** *your famine* Or "your attack on the city." See Ezek. 4:8.

ᶜ**5:4** *house of Israel* This probably means the people of the northern ten tribes of Israel.

ᵈ**5:13** *strong love* The Hebrew word means strong feelings like love, hate, anger, zeal, or jealousy.

ᵉ**6:2** *Son of man* This was usually just a way of saying "a person" or "a human being." Here, it is a way of addressing Ezekiel. Also in 7:2.

⁸God said, "But I will let a few of your people escape. They will live in other countries for a short time. I will scatter them and force them to live in other countries. ⁹Then the survivors* will be taken as prisoners. They will be forced to live in other countries, but they will remember me. I broke their spirit.ᵃ They will hate themselves for the evil things they did. In the past, they turned away from me and left me. They chased after their filthy idols. They were like a woman leaving her husband and running off with another man. They did many terrible things, ¹⁰but they will learn that I am the Lord. Then they will know that if I say that I will do something, I will do it! They will know that I caused all the troubles that happened to them."

¹¹Then the Lord God said to me, "Clap your hands and stamp your feet. Speak against all the terrible things that the people of Israel have done. Warn them that they will be killed by disease and hunger. Tell them they will be killed in war. ¹²People far away will die from disease. People near this place will be killed with swords, and those who are left in the city will starve to death. Only then will I stop being angry. ¹³Only then will you know that I am the Lord. You will know this when you see your dead bodies in front of your filthy idols and around their altars. Those bodies will be near every one of your places for worship,ᵇ on every high hill and mountain, under every green tree and every oak tree with leaves. You offered your sacrifices everywhere. They were a sweet smell for your filthy idols. ¹⁴But I will raise my arm over you and punish you and your people, wherever they live! I will destroy your country! It will be emptier than Diblah Desert.ᶜ Then they will know that I am the Lord!"

Disaster Is Coming to Jerusalem

7 ¹Then the word of the Lord came to me. ²He said, "Now, son of man, here is a message from the Lord God. This message is for the land of Israel:

"The end!
   The end is coming.
   The whole country will be destroyed.
³ Your end is coming now!
   I will show how angry I am with you.
   I will punish you for the evil things you did.
   I will make you pay for all the terrible things you did.
⁴ I will not show you any mercy
   or feel sorry for you.
   I am punishing you
   for the evil things you did.

You have done such terrible things.
   Now, you will know that I am the Lord."

⁵This is what the Lord God said: "There will be one disaster after another! ⁶The end is coming, and it will come quickly! ⁷You people living in Israel, do you hear the whistle? The enemy is coming. That time of punishment is coming very soon. The noise of the enemy is getting louder and louder on the mountains. ⁸Very soon now, I will show you how angry I am. I will show all of my anger against you. I will punish you for the evil things you did. I will make you pay for all the terrible things you did. ⁹I will not show you any mercy or feel sorry for you. I am punishing you for the evil things you did. You have done such terrible things. Now, you will know that I am the Lord.

¹⁰"That time of punishment has come like a plant sprouting, budding, and flowering. God has given the signal, the enemy is prepared, and the proud king *(Nebuchadnezzar)* is ready. ¹¹This violent man is ready to punish the evil people. There are many people in Israel—but he is not one of them. He is not a person in that crowd. He is not some important leader from them.

¹²"The time of punishment has come. The day is here. Those who buy things will not be happy, and those who sell things will not feel bad about selling them because that terrible punishment will happen to everyone. ¹³The people who sold their propertyᵈ will never go back to it. Even if some people escape alive, they will never go back to their property, because this vision* is for the whole crowd. So even if some people escape alive, it will not make everyone feel better.

¹⁴"They will blow the trumpet to warn the people. The people will get ready for battle, but they will not go out to fight because I will show the whole crowd how angry I am. ¹⁵The enemy with his sword is outside the city. Disease and hunger is inside the city. If some people go out into the fields, enemy soldiers will kill them. If they stay in the city, hunger and disease will destroy them.

¹⁶"But some people will escape. The survivors will run to the mountains, but they will not be happy. They will be sad for all their sins. They will cry and make sad noises like doves. ¹⁷They will be too tired and sad to raise their arms. Their legs will be like water. ¹⁸They will wear sackcloth* and be covered with fear. You will see the shame on every face. They will shave their heads to show their sadness. ¹⁹They will throw their silver

---

ᵈ**7:13** *sold their property* In ancient Israel property did not belong to a person, it belonged to a family. People might sell their property, but at the time of Jubilee their family would get the land back. Here, Ezekiel says the people will never get their property again.

ᵃ**6:9** *spirit* Literally, "heart."
ᵇ**6:13** *places for worship* Or "high places." See "high place" in the Word List.
ᶜ**6:14** *Diblah Desert* This is probably "Riblah Desert."

idols* into the streets. They will treat their gold statues like dirty rags, because those things will not be able to save them when the LORD shows his anger. Those things were nothing but a trap that caused the people to fall. They will not give food to the people or put food in their bellies.

20"They used their beautiful jewelry and made an idol. They were proud of that statue. They made their terrible statues. They made those filthy things, so I will throw them away like a dirty rag. 21I will let strangers take them. Those strangers will make fun of them. They will kill some of the people and take others away as prisoners. 22I will turn my head away from them—I will not look at them. The strangers will ruin my Temple—they will go into the secret parts of that holy building and make it unfit for worship.

23"Make chains for the prisoners, because many people will be punished for killing other people. There will be violence every place in the city. 24I will bring evil people from other nations, and they will get all the houses of the people of Israel. I will stop all you powerful people from being so proud. Those people from other nations will get all your places of worship.

25"You will shake with fear. You will look for peace, but there will be none. 26You will hear one sad story after another. You will hear nothing but bad news. You will look for a prophet and ask him for a vision. The priests will have nothing to teach you, and the elders* will not have any good advice to give you. 27Your king will be crying for the people who died. The leaders will wear sackcloth. The common people will be very afraid, because I will pay them back for what they did. I will decide their punishment, and I will punish them. Then they will know that I am the LORD."

Sinful Things Done at the Temple

8 ¹One day I, Ezekiel, was sitting in my house, and the elders of Judah were sitting there in front of me. This was on the fifth day of the sixth month of the sixth year of exile.a Suddenly, the power of the Lord GOD came on me. ²I saw something that looked like fire, like a man's body. From the waist down, he was like fire. From the waist up, he was bright and shining like hot metalb in a fire. ³Then I saw something that looked like an arm. The arm reached out and grabbed me by the hair on my head. Then the Spiritc lifted me into the air, and in God's vision, he took me to Jerusalem. He took me to the inner gate—the gate that is on the north side. The

statue that makes God jealous is by that gate. ⁴But the Glory of the God of Israel was there. The Glory looked just like the vision I saw in the valley ⌊by the Kebar Canal⌋.

⁵God spoke to me. He said, "Son of man,d look toward the north." So I looked, and there, north of the Altar Gate by the entrance, was that statue that made God jealous.

⁶Then God said to me, "Son of man, do you see what terrible things the people of Israel are doing? They built that thing here, right next to my Temple! And if you come with me, you will see even more terrible things!"

⁷So I went to the entrance to the courtyard, and I saw a hole in the wall. ⁸God said to me, "Son of man, make a hole in the wall." So I made a hole in the wall, and there I saw a door.

⁹Then God said to me, "Go in and look at the terrible, evil things that the people are doing here." ¹⁰So I went in and looked. I saw statues of all kinds of reptilese and animals that you hate to think about. The statues were the filthy idols* that the people of Israel worshiped. There were pictures of those animals carved all around on every wall!

¹¹Then I noticed that Jaazaniah son of Shapham and the 70 elders* of Israel were there with the people worshiping in that place. There they were, right at the front of the people, and each leader had his own incense dish in his hand. The smoke from the burning incense was rising into the air. ¹²Then God said to me, "Son of man, do you see what the elders of Israel do in the dark? Each man has a special room for his own false god. They say to themselves, 'The LORD cannot see us. The LORD left this country.'" ¹³Then he said to me, "If you come with me, you will see these men doing even more terrible things!"

¹⁴Then God led me to the entrance to the LORD's Temple. This gate was on the north side. I saw women sitting there and crying. They were sad about the false god Tammuzf!

¹⁵God said to me, "Son of man, do you see these terrible things? Come with me and you will see things that are even worse than this!" ¹⁶Then he led me to the inner courtyard of the LORD's Temple. There I saw 25 men bowing down and worshiping. They were between the porch and the altar—but they were facing the wrong way. Their backs were to the Holy Place. They were bowing down to worship the sun!

---

a8:1 *sixth year of exile* This is the fall of 592 B.C.
b8:2 *hot metal* The Hebrew word might mean "melted copper," "an alloy of gold and silver," or "amber."
c8:3 *Spirit* Or "wind."

d8:5 *Son of man* This was usually just a way of saying "a person" or "a human being." Here, it is a way of addressing Ezekiel. Also in verses 6, 7, 12, 15, 17.
e8:10 *reptiles* The Hebrew word can mean "lizards," "snakes," and "all kinds of bugs and insects."
f8:14 *Tammuz* People thought this false god died and his wife Ishtar asked everyone to be sad and cry with her. Ishtar hoped this would bring him back to life. This ceremony was on the 2nd day of the fourth month (June/July). This month was named Tammuz because of this ceremony.

¹⁷Then God said, "Son of man, do you see this? The people of Judah think my Temple is so unimportant that they will do these terrible things here in my Temple! This country is filled with violence, and they constantly do things to make me angry. Look, they are wearing rings in their noses to honor the moon like a false god!ᵃ ¹⁸I will show them my anger! I will not show them any mercy or feel sorry for them! They will shout to me—but I refuse to listen to them!"

God's Messengers Punish Jerusalem

9 ¹Then God shouted to the leaders in charge of punishing the city. Each leader had his own destructive weapon in his hand.ᵇ ²Then I saw six men walking on the road from the upper gate. This gate is on the north side. Each man had his own deadly weapon in his hand. One of the men wore linen clothes.ᶜ He wore a scribe's pen and ink setᵈ at his waist. Those men went to the bronze altar in the Temple and stood there. ³Then the Glory of the God of Israel rose from above the Cherub angels* where he had been. Then the Glory went to the door of the Temple and stopped when he was over the threshold. Then he called to the man wearing the linen clothes and the scribe's pen and ink set.

⁴Then the LORD (Glory) said to him, "Go through the city of Jerusalem. Put a mark on the forehead of everyone who feels sad and upset about all the terrible things people are doing in this city."

⁵⁻⁶Then I heard God say to the other men, "I want you to follow the first man. You must kill all those who do not have the mark on their foreheads. It doesn't matter if they are elders,* young men or young women, children or mothers—you must use your weapon and kill everyone who does not have the mark on their forehead. Don't show any mercy. Don't feel sorry for anyone. Start here at my Temple." So they started with the elders in front of the Temple.

⁷He said to them, "Make this Temple unclean*—fill this courtyard with dead bodies! Now go!" So they went and killed the people in the city.

⁸I stayed there while the men went to kill the people. I bowed with my face to the ground and said, "Oh, Lord GOD, in showing your anger against Jerusalem, are you killing all the survivors in Israel?"

⁹He said, "The family of Israel and Judah has committed many terrible sins! People are being murdered everywhere in this country, and the city is filled with crime. That is because the people say to themselves, 'The LORD left this country. He cannot see what we are doing.' ¹⁰So I will not show any mercy or feel sorry for them. They brought it on themselves. I am only giving them the punishment they deserve!"

¹¹Then the man wearing linen clothes and a scribe's pen and ink set spoke up. He said, "I have done what you commanded."

The Glory of the Lord Leaves the Temple

10 ¹Then I looked up at the bowlᵉ over the heads of the Cherub angels. The bowl looked clear blue like sapphire, and there was something that looked like a throne over it. ²Then the one sitting on the throne said to the man dressed in linen clothes,ᶠ "Step into the area between the wheelsᵍ under the Cherub angels. Take a handful of the burning coals from between the Cherub angels and go throw them over the city of Jerusalem."

The man walked past me. ³The Cherub angels were standing in the area southʰ of the Temple as the man walked to them. The cloud filled the inner courtyard. ⁴Then the Glory of the LORD rose up off the Cherub angels near the threshold of the door of the Temple. Then the cloud filled the Temple, and the bright light from the Glory of the LORD filled the whole courtyard. ⁵The noise from the wings of the Cherub angels could be heard all the way out into the outer courtyard. The sound was very loud—like the thundering voice when God All-Powerful speaks.

⁶God had given the man dressed in linen clothes a command. He had told him to go into the area between the wheels among the Cherub angels and get some hot coals. So the man went there and stood by the wheel. ⁷One of the Cherub angels reached out his hand and took some of the hot coals from the area between the Cherub angels. He poured the coals into the man's hands, and the man left. ⁸(The Cherub angels had what looked like human arms under their wings.)

⁹Then I noticed that there were four wheels. There was one wheel by each Cherub angel, and the wheels looked like a clear yellow jewel. ¹⁰There were four wheels, and they all looked the same. They looked like there was a wheel in a wheel. ¹¹They could go in any direction when they moved, but ₗthe Cherub angels₎ did not turn around when they moved. They went in the direction that the

---

ᵃ**8:17 Look ... god** Or "Look at them putting that cut branch in their noses."
ᵇ**9:1 Each ... hand** In Hebrew this is like Ezek. 8:11.
ᶜ**9:2 linen clothes** Priests usually wore these clothes.
ᵈ**9:2 scribe's pen and ink set** A scribe was a person who copied official documents and counted supplies and things. Scribes often carried a small board with dry ink in it and a pen. They could put water on the ink and then write with it. Also in verse 11.

ᵉ**10:1 bowl** This Hebrew word is the same word used in Gen. 1:6–7 to describe the dome of the sky.
ᶠ**10:2 linen clothes** Priests usually wore these clothes.
ᵍ**10:2 area between the wheels** The Hebrew word can mean "chariot wheel," "whirling (spinning) wheel," or "tumbling weed." See chapter 1 for Ezekiel's full description. Also in verse 6.
ʰ**10:3 south** Literally, "right."

head was looking. They did not turn around when they moved. [12]There were eyes all over their bodies. There were eyes on their backs, on their arms, on their wings, and on their wheels—on all four wheels! [13]These wheels were what I heard called, "the area between the wheels."

[14-15]Each Cherub angel had four faces. The first was the face of a Cherub,[a] the second was the face of a man, the third was a lion's face, and the fourth was an eagle's face. (These Cherub angels were the living beings I saw in the vision by the Kebar Canal.[b])

Then the Cherub angels rose into the air, [16]and the wheels rose with them. When the Cherub angels raised their wings and flew into the air, not even the wheels turned around. [17]If they flew into the air, the wheels went with them. If they stood still, so did the wheels, because the spirit[c] of the living being was in them.

[18]Then the Glory of the LORD rose from the threshold of the Temple, moved to the place over the Cherub angels, and stopped there. [19]Then the Cherub angels raised their wings and flew into the air. I saw them leave. The wheels went with them. Then they stopped at the East Gate of the LORD's Temple. The Glory of the God of Israel was in the air above them.

[20]These were the living beings under the Glory of the God of Israel in the vision at the Kebar Canal, and now I realized they were Cherub angels. [21]Each living being had four faces, four wings, and something that looked like human arms under their wings. [22]The faces of the Cherub angels were the same as the four faces on the living beings in the vision by the Kebar Canal. They all looked straight ahead in the direction they were going.

Prophecies Against the Leaders

11 [1]Then the Spirit[d] carried me to the East Gate of the LORD's Temple. This gate faces the east, ₍where the sun comes up₎. I saw 25 men there at the entrance of this gate. Some of the leaders were among them, including Jaazaniah son of Azzur and Pelatiah son of Benaiah.

[2]Then God spoke to me and said, "Son of man,[e] these are the men who make evil plans for this city. They always tell the people to do evil things. [3]These men say, 'We will be building our houses again very soon. We are as safe in this city as meat in a pot!' [4]So you must speak to the people for me. Son of man, prophesy against the people."

[5]Then the Spirit of the LORD came on me. He said to me, "Tell them that this is what the LORD said: House of Israel, you are planning big things. But I know what you are thinking. [6]You have killed many people in this city. You have filled the streets with dead bodies. [7]Now, the Lord GOD says this, 'The dead bodies are the meat, and the city is the pot. But he (Nebuchadnezzar) will come and take you out of this safe pot. [8]You are afraid of the sword, but I am bringing the sword against you!'" This is what the Lord GOD said.

[9]He also said, "I will take you out of this city and give you to strangers. I will punish you. [10]You will die by the sword. I will punish you here in Israel, so you will know that I am the LORD. [11]Yes, this place will be the cooking pot, and you will be the meat cooking in it. I will punish you here in Israel. [12]Then you will know that I am the LORD. It was my law that you broke. You did not obey my commands. You decided to live like the nations around you."

[13]As soon as I finished speaking for God, Pelatiah son of Benaiah died! I fell to the ground. I bowed with my face touching the ground and said, "Oh, Lord GOD, you are going to completely destroy all the survivors of Israel!"

Prophecies Against Survivors in Jerusalem

[14]But then the word of the LORD came to me. He said, [15]"Son of man, remember your brothers, the family of Israel. They were forced to leave their country, but I will bring them back.[f] But now, the people living in Jerusalem are saying, 'Stay far away from the LORD. This land was given to us—it is ours!'

[16]"So tell them this: The Lord GOD says, 'It is true, I forced my people to go far away to other nations. I did scatter them among many countries. But I will be their temple for a short time while they are in those other countries. [17]But you must tell those people that the Lord GOD will bring them back. I have scattered you among many nations, but I will gather you together and bring you back from those nations. I will give the land of Israel back to you. [18]When my people come back, they will destroy all the terrible, filthy idols* that are here now. [19]I will bring them together and make them like one person. I will put a new spirit[g] in them. I will take away that heart of stone, and I will put a real heart in its place. [20]Then they will obey my laws and my commands. They will do the things I tell them. They will be my people, and I will be their God.'"

---

[a]**10:14–15** *face of a Cherub* This is the bull's face mentioned in Ezek. 1:10. See Ezek. 10:22.
[b]**10:14–15** *vision by the Kebar Canal* See Ezek. 1.
[c]**10:17** *spirit* Or "wind."
[d]**11:1** *Spirit* Or "wind."
[e]**11:2** *Son of man* This was usually just a way of saying "a person" or "a human being." Here, it is a way of addressing Ezekiel. Also in verses 4, 15.

[f]**11:15** *They were … back* This is a wordplay. The word meaning "redeemed" sounds like the word meaning "exiled."
[g]**11:19** *Spirit* Or "wind."

The Glory of the Lord Leaves Jerusalem

²¹Then God said, "But now, their hearts belong to those terrible, filthy idols,* and I must punish those people for the bad things they have done." This is what the Lord God said. ²²Then the Cherub angels raised their wings and flew into the air. The wheels went with them. The Glory of the God of Israel was above them. ²³The Glory of the Lord rose into the air and left the city and stopped on the hill east of Jerusalem.ᵃ ²⁴Then the Spiritᵇ lifted me into the air and brought me back to Babylonia. It brought me back to the people who were forced to leave Israel. I saw all this in the vision of God. Then the one I saw in the vision rose into the air and left me. ²⁵Then I spoke to the people in exile.* I told them about everything the Lord showed me.

Ezekiel Leaves Like a Captive

12 ¹Then the word of the Lord came to me. He said, ²"Son of man,ᶜ you live among rebellious people who always turn against me. They have eyes to see what I have done for them, but they don't see those things. They have ears to hear what I told them to do, but they don't hear my commands, because they are a rebellious people. ³So, son of man, pack your bags. Act like you are going to a faraway country. Do this so that the people can see you. Maybe they will see you—but they are a very rebellious people.

⁴"During the day, take your bags outside so that the people can see you. Then in the evening, pretend you are going away. Act as if you are a prisoner going to a faraway country. ⁵While the people are watching, make a hole in the wall and go out through that hole in the wall. ⁶At night, put your bag on your shoulder and leave. Cover your face so that you cannot see where you are going. You must do these things so that the people can see you, because I am using you as an example to the family of Israel."

⁷So I did as I was commanded. During the day, I took my bags and acted as if I were going to a faraway country. That evening, I used my hands and made a hole in the wall. During the night, I put my bag on my shoulder and left. I did this so that all the people could see me.

⁸The next morning, the word of the Lord came to me. He said, ⁹"Son of man, did the rebellious people of Israel ask you what you were doing? ¹⁰Tell them that this is what the Lord God said. This sad message is about the leader of Jerusalem and all the people of Israel who live there. ¹¹Tell them, 'I am an example for all of you. What I have done will happen to you.' You will be forced to go to a faraway

country as prisoners. ¹²And your leader will make a hole in the wall and sneak out at night. He will cover his face so that people will not recognize him. His eyes will not be able to see where he is going. ¹³He will try to escape, but I will catch him! He will be caught in my trap. Then I will bring him to Babylonia—the land of the Chaldeans. But he will not be able to see where he is going.ᵈ ¹⁴I will force the king's people to live in the foreign countries around Israel, and I will scatter his army to the winds. The enemy soldiers will chase after them. ¹⁵Then they will know that I am the Lord. They will know that I scattered them among the nations. They will know that I forced them to go to other countries.

¹⁶"But I will let a few of the people live. They will not die from the disease, hunger, and war. I will let them live so that they can tell other people about the terrible things they did against me. Then they will know that I am the Lord."

Shake With Fear

¹⁷Then the word of the Lord came to me. He said, ¹⁸"Son of man, you must act as if you are very frightened. You must shake when you eat your food. You must act worried and afraid when you drink your water. ¹⁹You must say this to the common people: 'This is what the Lord God says to the people living in Jerusalem and in the other parts of Israel. You will be very worried while you eat your food. You will be terrified while you drink your water, because everything in your country will be destroyed! This will happen because the people living there are so violent. ²⁰Many people live in your cities now, but those cities will be ruined. Your whole country will be destroyed! Then you will know that I am the Lord.'"

Disaster Will Come

²¹Then the word of the Lord came to me. He said, ²²"Son of man, why do people quote this saying about the land of Israel:

'Trouble will not come soon;
    what is seen in visions will not come'?

²³"Tell the people that the Lord God will end that saying. They will not say that about Israel anymore. Now they will quote this saying:

'Trouble will come soon;
    what is seen in visions will happen.'

²⁴"There will not be any more false visions in Israel. There will not be any more magicians telling things that don't come true. ²⁵That's because I am the Lord, and whatever I command to happen will happen! I will not let the

---

ᵃ**11:23 hill east of Jerusalem** This is the Mount of Olives.

ᵇ**11:24 spirit** Or "wind."

ᶜ**12:2 Son of man** This was usually just a way of saying "a person" or "a human being." Here, it is a way of addressing Ezekiel. Also in verses 3, 9, 18, 22, 27.

ᵈ**12:13 But he … is going** The enemy will poke out his eyes and make him blind.

time stretch out. Those troubles are coming soon—in your own lifetime. You rebellious people, when I say something, I make it happen." This is what the Lord God said.

26Then the word of the Lord came to me. He said, 27"Son of man, the people of Israel think that the visions I give you are for a time far in the future. They think you are talking about things that will happen many years from now. 28So you must tell them this: 'The Lord God says, I will not delay any longer. If I say something will happen, it will happen!'" This is what the Lord God said.

Warnings Against False Prophets

13 1Then the word of the Lord came to me. He said, 2"Son of man,*a* you must speak to the prophets of Israel for me. They are only saying what they want to say. You must speak to them. Tell them this: 'Listen to this message from the Lord! 3This is what the Lord God says. Bad things will happen to you foolish prophets. You are following your own spirits. You are not telling people what you really see in visions.

4"'Israel, your prophets will be like foxes running through empty, destroyed buildings. 5You have not put soldiers near the broken walls of the city. You have not built walls to protect the family of Israel. So when the day comes for the Lord to punish you, you will lose the war!

6"'False prophets* said they saw visions. They did their magic and said things would happen—but they lied. They said the Lord sent them—but they lied. They are still waiting for their lies to come true.

7"'False prophets, the visions you saw were not true. You did your magic and said things would happen, but you lied! You said that the Lord said those things, but I did not speak to you!'"

8So now, the Lord God really will speak. He says, "You told lies. You saw visions that were not true. So now I am against you!" This is what the Lord God said. 9"I will punish the prophets who saw false visions and told lies. I will remove them from my people. Their names will not be in the list of the family of Israel. They will never again come to the land of Israel. Then you will know that I am the Lord God!

10"Again and again those false prophets* lied to my people. They said there would be peace, but there is no peace. The people need to fix the walls and prepare for war. But they only slap a thin coat of plaster*b* over the broken walls. 11Tell them that I will send hail

and a strong rain. The wind will blow hard, and a tornado will come. Then the wall will fall down. 12When the wall falls down, the people will ask the prophets, 'What happened to the plaster you put on the wall?'" 13The Lord God says, "I am angry and I will send a storm against you. I am angry and I will send a strong rain. I am angry and I will make hail fall from the sky and completely destroy you! 14You put plaster on the wall, but I will destroy the whole wall. I will pull it to the ground. The wall will fall on you, and then you will know that I am the Lord. 15I will finish showing my anger against the wall and those who put plaster on it. Then I will say, 'There is no wall, and there are no workers to put plaster on it.'

16"All these things will happen to the false prophets of Israel. They speak to the people of Jerusalem and say there will be peace, but there is no peace." This is what the Lord God said.

17God said, "Son of man, look at the women prophets in Israel. They say the things they want to say, so you must speak against them for me. You must say this to them: 18'This is what the Lord God says: Bad things will happen to you women. You sew cloth bracelets for people to wear on their arms. You make special scarves for people to wear on their heads. ⌊You say those things have magic powers⌋ to control people's lives. You trap the people only to keep yourselves alive! 19You make them think I am not important. You turn them against me for a few handfuls of barley and a few scraps of bread. You tell lies to my people. They love to listen to lies. You kill those who should live, and you let people live who should die. 20So this is what the Lord God says to you: You make those cloth bracelets to trap people, but I will set them free. I will tear those bracelets off your arms, and the people will be free from you. They will be like birds flying from a trap. 21And I will tear up those scarves and save my people from your power. They will escape from your trap, and you will know that I am the Lord.

22"'You prophets tell lies. Your lies hurt good people—I did not want to hurt them! You support the wicked and encourage them. You don't tell them to change their lives. You don't try to save their lives! 23So you will not see any more useless visions or do any more magic. I will save my people from your power, and you will know that I am the Lord.'"

Warnings Against Idol Worship

14 1Some of the elders* of Israel came to me. They sat down to talk with me. 2The word of the Lord came to me. He said, 3"Son of man,*c* these men came to talk to you.

---

*a*13:2 *Son of man* This was usually just a way of saying "a person" or "a human being." Here, it is a way of addressing Ezekiel. Also in verse 17.

*b*13:10 *plaster* A type of mud or cement that people used to cover a wall and make it smooth. This is also a wordplay. The Hebrew word is like the word meaning "It will fall." Also in verse 14.

*c*14:3 *Son of man* This was usually just a way of saying "a person" or "a human being." Here, it is a way of addressing Ezekiel. Also in verse 13.

But they still have their filthy idols.* They kept the things that made them sin. They still worship those statues, so why do they come to me for advice? Should I answer their questions? ⁴But I will give them an answer. You must tell them this: 'This is what the Lord God says: If any Israelites come to a prophet and ask me for advice, I myself will answer their questions. I will answer them even if they still have their filthy idols, even if they kept the things that made them sin, and even if they still worship those statues. I will speak to them in spite of all their filthy idols. ⁵This is because I want to touch their hearts. I want to show them that I love them, even though they left me for their filthy idols.'

⁶"So tell the family of Israel, 'This is what the Lord God says: Come back to me and leave your filthy idols. Turn away from those terrible, false gods. ⁷If any Israelites or foreigners who live in Israel come to me for advice, I will give them an answer. I will answer them even if they still have their filthy idols, even if they kept the things that made them sin, and even if they worship those statues. This is the answer I will give them: ⁸I will turn against them and destroy them. They will be an example to others. People will laugh at them. I will remove them from my people. Then you will know that I am the Lord! ⁹And if a prophet is foolish enough to give his own answer, I will show him how foolish he is! I will use my power against him. I will destroy him and remove him from among my people, Israel. ¹⁰So both the one who came for advice and the prophet who gave an answer will get the same punishment. ¹¹Why? So that those prophets will stop leading my people away from me, and my people will stop being filthy with sin. Then they will be my special people, and I will be their God.'" This is what the Lord God said.

Jerusalem Will Be Punished

¹²Then the word of the Lord came to me. He said, ¹³"Son of man, any nation that leaves me and sins against me. I will punish I will stop their food supply. I might cause a famine* and remove the people and animals from that country. ¹⁴I would punish that country even if Noah, Daniel, and Jobᵃ lived there. They could save their own lives by their goodness, ⌊but they could not save the whole country⌋." This is what the Lord God said.

¹⁵"Or I might send wild animals through that country to kill all the people. Then no one would travel through that country because of the wild animals. ¹⁶If Noah, Daniel, and Job lived there, those three men could save their own lives. But I promise by my own

life that they could not save the lives of other people—not even their own sons and daughters! That evil country would be destroyed." This is what the Lord God said.

¹⁷"Or I might send an enemy army to fight against that country. The soldiers would destroy that country—I would remove all the people and animals from that country. ¹⁸If Noah, Daniel, and Job lived there, those three men could save their own lives. But I promise by my own life that they could not save the lives of other people—not even their own sons and daughters! That evil country would be destroyed." This is what the Lord God said.

¹⁹"Or I might send a disease against that country. I will pour my anger down on the people. I will remove all the people and animals from that country. ²⁰If Noah, Daniel, and Job lived there, those three men could save their own lives because they are good men. But I promise by my own life that they could not save the lives of other people—not even their own sons and daughters!" This is what the Lord God said.

²¹Then the Lord God said, "So think how bad it will be for Jerusalem. I will send all four of those punishments against that city! I will send enemy soldiers, hunger, disease, and wild animals against that city. I will remove all the people and animals from that country. ²²Some of the people will escape from that country. They will bring their sons and daughters and come to you for help. Then you will see how bad those people really are, and you will feel better about all the troubles that I am bringing to Jerusalem. ²³You will see how they live and all the bad things they do. Then you will know that I had a good reason for punishing them." This is what the Lord God said.

Jerusalem, the Vine, Will Be Burned

15 ¹Then the word of the Lord came to me. He said, ²"Son of man,ᵇ are the pieces of wood from a grapevineᶜ any better than the little branches cut from trees in the forest? ³Can you use that wood from a grapevine to make anything? Can you use that wood to make pegs to hang dishes on? ⁴People throw that wood into the fire. The ends burn, and the middle is scorched. ⁵If you cannot make anything from that wood before it is burned, you surely cannot make anything from that wood after it is burned! ⁶So people throw the pieces of wood from a grapevine into the fire just like wood from any other tree in the forest. In the same way I will throw the people living in Jerusalem into the fire!" This is what the Lord God said. ⁷"I

ᵃ**14:14 Noah, Daniel, and Job** Three men from ancient times. They were famous for being very good and wise men. Here, Daniel might be the Danel in the writings from Ras Shamra. Also in verses 16, 18, 20.

ᵇ**15:2 Son of man** This was usually just a way of saying "a person" or "a human being." Here, it is a way of addressing Ezekiel.

ᶜ**15:2 grapevine** The prophets often spoke of Israel as God's vineyard or grapevine. Also in 16:2, 3, 6.

will punish those people. But some of them will be like the sticks that don't burn completely. They will be punished, but they will not be destroyed completely. You will see that I punished them, and you will know that I am the LORD! [8]I will destroy that country because the people left me ₁to worship false gods₁." This is what the Lord GOD said.

God's Love for Jerusalem

16 [1]Then the word of the LORD came to me. He said, [2]"Son of man, tell the people of Jerusalem about the terrible things they have done. [3]You must say, 'This is what the Lord GOD says to Jerusalem: Look at your history. You were born in Canaan.* Your father was an Amorite. Your mother was a Hittite. [4]Jerusalem, on the day you were born, there was no one to cut your navel cord. No one put salt on you and washed you to make you clean. No one wrapped you in cloth. [5]No one felt sorry for you or took care of you. On the day you were born, your parents threw you out into the field, because no one wanted you.

[6]"'Then I passed by. I saw you lying there, kicking in the blood. You were covered with blood, but I said, "Please live!" Yes, you were covered with blood, but I said, "Please live!" [7]I helped you grow like a plant in the field. You grew and grew. You became a young woman: your periods began, your breasts grew, and your hair began to grow. But you were still bare and naked. [8]I looked you over. I saw you were ready for love, so I spread my clothes over you[a] and covered your nakedness. I promised to marry you. I made the agreement[b] with you, and you became mine.'" This is what the Lord GOD said. [9]"'I washed you in water. I poured water over you to wash away the blood that was on you, and then I put oil on your skin. [10c] I gave you a nice dress and soft leather sandals, a linen headband, and a silk scarf. [11]I also gave you some jewelry. I put bracelets on your arms and a necklace around your neck. [12]I gave you a nose ring, earrings, and a beautiful crown to wear. [13]You were beautiful in your gold and silver jewelry, your linen, silk, and embroidered material. You ate the best foods. You were very, very beautiful, and you became the queen! [14]You became famous for your beauty, all because I made you so lovely!'" This is what the Lord GOD said.

Jerusalem, the Unfaithful Bride

[15]"But you began to trust in your beauty. You used the good name you had and became unfaithful to me. You acted like a prostitute with every man who passed by. You gave yourself to them all! [16]You took your beautiful clothes and used them to decorate your places for worship.[d] And you acted like a prostitute there. You gave yourself to every man who came by! [17]Then you took your beautiful jewelry that I gave you, and you used the gold and silver to make statues of men, and you had sex with them too! [18]Then you took the beautiful cloth and made clothes for those statues. You took the perfume and incense I gave you and put it in front of those idols.* [19]I gave you bread, honey, and oil, but you gave that food to your idols. You offered them as a sweet smell to please your false gods. You acted like a prostitute with those false gods!" This is what the Lord GOD said.

[20]"You and I had children together, but you took our children. You killed them and gave them to those false gods! But that is only some of the evil things you did when you were unfaithful to me and went to those false gods. [21]You slaughtered[e] my sons and then passed them through the fire to those false gods. [22]You left me and did all those terrible things. You never remembered what happened when you were young. You did not remember that you were naked and kicking in blood when I found you.

[23]"After all these evil things, ... it will be very bad for you!" The Lord GOD said all these things. [24]"After all those things, you made a mound for worshiping that false god. You built those places for worshiping false gods on every street corner. [25]You built your mounds at the head of every road. Then you degraded your beauty. You used it to catch every man who walked by. You raised your skirt so that they could see your legs, and you acted like a prostitute with those men. [26]Then you went to Egypt, your neighbor that is always ready for sex. With more and more sexual sin, you made me angry. [27]So I punished you! I took away part of your land. I let your enemies, the daughters of the Philistines,* do what they wanted to you. Even they were shocked at the evil things you did. [28]Then you went to have sex with Assyria.* You could not get enough. You were never satisfied. [29]So you turned to Canaan,* and then to Babylonia, and still you were not satisfied. [30]You are so weak. You let all those men cause you to sin. You acted just like a prostitute who wants to be the one in control." This is what the Lord GOD said.

[31]God said, "But you were not exactly like a prostitute. You built your mounds at the head

---

[a]**16:8** *spread my clothes over you* This showed that he was agreeing to protect and care for her. See Ruth 3:1–15.

[b]**16:8** *agreement* Here, this means the marriage agreement. But it also refers to the agreement God made with the people of Israel. See "agreement" in the Word List.

[c]**16:10** *Verses 10–13* All the materials in this list are the things used in building the Holy Tent. See Ex. 25–40.

[d]**16:16** *places for worship* Or "high places." See "high place" in the Word List. Also in verses 31, 39.

[e]**16:21** *slaughter* This usually means to kill an animal and cut it into pieces for meat, but it often means to kill people as if they were animals.

of every road, and you built your places for worship at every street corner. You had sex with all those men, but you did not ask them to pay you like a prostitute does. ³²You are a woman guilty of adultery. You would rather have sex with strangers than with your own husband. ³³Most prostitutes force men to pay them for sex, but you gave money to your many lovers. You paid all the men around to come in to have sex with you. ³⁴You are just the opposite of most prostitutes who force men to pay them, because you pay the men to have sex with you."

³⁵Prostitute, listen to the message from the Lord. ³⁶This is what the Lord God says: "You have spent your money*a* and let your lovers and filthy gods see your naked body and have sex with you. You have killed your children and poured out their blood. This was your gift to those false gods. ³⁷So I am bringing all of your lovers together. I will bring all the men you loved and all the men you hated. I will bring them all together and let them see you naked.*b* They will see you completely naked. ³⁸Then I will punish you. I will punish you as a murderer and a woman who committed the sin of adultery. You will be punished as if by an angry and jealous husband. ³⁹I will let those lovers have you. They will destroy your mounds. They will burn your places for worship. They will tear off your clothes and take your beautiful jewelry. They will leave you bare and naked ₍as you were when I found you₎. ⁴⁰They will bring a crowd of people and throw rocks at you to kill you. Then they will cut you into pieces with their swords. ⁴¹They will burn your house. They will punish you so that all the other women can see. I will stop you from living like a prostitute. I will stop you from paying money to your lovers. ⁴²Then I will stop being angry and jealous. I will calm down. I will not be angry anymore. ⁴³Why will all these things happen? Because you did not remember what happened when you were young. You did all those bad things and made me angry. So I had to punish you for doing them, but you planned even more terrible things." This is what the Lord God said.

⁴⁴"All the people who talk about you will now have one more thing to say. They will say, 'Like mother, like daughter.' ⁴⁵You are your mother's daughter. You don't care about your husband or your children. You are like your sister. Both of you hated your husband and your children. ₍You are like your parents.₎ Your mother was a Hittite and your father was an Amorite. ⁴⁶Your older sister was Samaria. She lived to the north of you with her daughters.

Your younger sister was Sodom.*c* She lived to the south of you with her daughters. ⁴⁷You did all the terrible things they did, but you also did much worse! ⁴⁸I am the Lord God. As I live, I swear that your sister Sodom and her daughters never did as many bad things as you and your daughters.

⁴⁹"Your sister Sodom and her daughters were proud. They had too much to eat and too much time on their hands, and they did not help poor, helpless people. ⁵⁰Sodom and her daughters became too proud and began to do terrible things in front of me. So I punished them!

⁵¹"And Samaria did only half as many bad things as you did. You did many more terrible things than Samaria! You have done so many more terrible things than your sisters have done. Sodom and Samaria seem good compared to you. ⁵²So you must bear your shame. You have made your sisters look good compared to you. You have done terrible things, so you should be ashamed.

⁵³"I destroyed Sodom and the towns around it, and I destroyed Samaria and the towns around it. And I will destroy you too, Jerusalem. But I will build those cities again, and I will rebuild you too. ⁵⁴I will comfort you. Then you will remember the terrible things you did, and you will be ashamed. ⁵⁵So you and your sisters will be rebuilt. Sodom and the towns around her, Samaria and the towns around her, and you and the towns around you will all be rebuilt.

⁵⁶"In the past, you were proud and made fun of your sister Sodom. But you will not do that again. ⁵⁷You did that before you were punished, before your neighbors started making fun of you. The daughters of Edom*d* and Philistia are making fun of you now. ⁵⁸Now you must suffer for the terrible things you did." This is what the Lord said.

God Remains Faithful

⁵⁹This is what the Lord God said: "I will treat you like you treated me! You broke your marriage promise. You did not respect our agreement. ⁶⁰But I will remember the agreement we made when you were young. I made an agreement with you that will continue forever! ⁶¹I will bring your sisters to you, and I will make them your daughters. That was not in our agreement, but I will do that for you. Then you will remember the terrible things you did, and you will be ashamed. ⁶²So I will make my agreement with you, and you will know that I am the Lord. ⁶³You will remember me, and you will be so ashamed of the evil things you did that you will not be able to say

---

*a*16:36 *spent your money* Literally, "poured out your copper." This might also mean "you have done the things that stain you with sin."

*b*16:37 *let them see you naked* The Hebrew words are like the words meaning "to be carried away as a prisoner to a foreign country."

*c*16:46 *Samaria ... Sodom* Ezekiel is saying the people in Judah are just as evil as the people who lived in Samaria and Sodom—and those people were so evil that God completely destroyed those cities.

*d*16:57 *Edom* Or "Aram."

anything. But I will make you pure, and you will never be ashamed again!" This is what the Lord God said.

The Eagle and the Vine

17 ¹Then the word of the Lord came to me. He said, ²"Son of man,ᵃ tell this story to the family of Israel. Ask them what it means. ³Say to them:

"'A large eagle with big wings came to
  Lebanon.
He had feathers covered with spots.
⁴ He broke the top out of the big cedar tree
  (Lebanon)
  and brought it to Canaan.*
He set the branch down in a city of
  merchants.*
⁵ Then the eagle took some of the seeds
  from Canaan.
He planted them in good soil by a good
  river.
⁶ The seeds grew and became a grapevine.
  It was a good vine.
The vine was not tall,
  but it spread to cover a large area.
The vine grew stems,
  and smaller vines grew very long.
⁷ Then another eagle with big wings saw
  the grapevine.
The eagle had many feathers.
The grapevine wanted this new eagle
  to care for it.
So it stretched its roots and branches
  toward the eagle.
Its branches stretched toward this eagle.
The branches grew away from the field
  where it was planted.
The grapevine wanted the new eagle to
  water it.
⁸ The grapevine was planted in a good field
  near plenty of water.
It could have grown branches and fruit.
It could have become a very good
  grapevine.'"

⁹ This is what the Lord God says:
"Do you think that plant will succeed?
No, the new eagle will pull the plant from
  the ground,
  and the bird will break the plant's roots.
It will eat up all the grapes.
Then the new leaves will wilt.
  That plant will be very weak.
It will not take strong arms
  or a powerful nation to pull that plant
  up by the roots.
¹⁰ Will the plant grow where it is planted?
No, the hot east wind will blow, and the
  plant will become dry and die.
It will die there where it was planted."

King Zedekiah Punished

¹¹The word of the Lord came to me. He said, ¹²"Explain this story to the people of Israel who always turn against me. Tell them this: The first eagle is the king of Babylonia. He came to Jerusalem and took away the king and other leaders. He brought them to Babylonia. ¹³Then Nebuchadnezzar made an agreement with a man from the king's family. Nebuchadnezzar forced that man to make a promise. So this man promised to be loyal to Nebuchadnezzar. Nebuchadnezzar made this man the new king of Judah. Then he took all the powerful men away from Judah. ¹⁴So Judah became a weak kingdom that could not turn against King Nebuchadnezzar. The people were forced to keep the agreement Nebuchadnezzar made with the new king of Judah. ¹⁵But this new king tried to rebel against Nebuchadnezzar anyway! He sent messengers to Egypt to ask for help. The new king asked for many horses and soldiers. Now, do you think the new king of Judah will succeed? Do you think the new king will have enough power to break the agreement and escape punishment?"

¹⁶The Lord God says, "By my life, I swear that this new king will die in Babylonia! Nebuchadnezzar made this man the new king of Judah, but he broke his promise with Nebuchadnezzar. This new king ignored that agreement. ¹⁷The king of Egypt will not be able to save the king of Judah. He might send many soldiers, but Egypt's great power will not save Judah. Nebuchadnezzar's army will build dirt roads and dirt walls to capture the city. Many people will die. ¹⁸But the king of Judah will not escape, because he ignored his agreement. He broke his promise to Nebuchadnezzar." ¹⁹The Lord God makes this promise: "By my life, I swear that I will punish the king of Judah, because he ignored my warnings and broke our agreement. ²⁰I will set my trap, and he will be caught in it. Then I will bring him to Babylon, and I will punish him there. I will punish him because he turned against me, ²¹and I will destroy his army. I will destroy his best soldiers and scatter them to the wind. Then you will know that I am the Lord and that I told you these things."

²²This is what the Lord God says:

"I will take a branch from a tall cedar tree.
  I will take a small branch from the top
  of the tree,
  and I myself will plant it on a very high
  mountain.
²³ I myself will plant it on a high mountain
  in Israel.
  That branch will grow into a tree.
It will grow branches and make fruit
  and become a beautiful cedar tree.
Many birds will sit on its branches
  and live in the shadows under its
  branches.

ᵃ**17:2 Son of man** This was usually just a way of saying "a person" or "a human being." Here, it is a way of addressing Ezekiel.

²⁴"Then the other trees will know that
    I make tall trees fall to the ground,
       and I make small trees grow tall.
    I make green trees become dry,
       and I make dry trees become green.
    I am the LORD.
    If I say that I will do something, then I
      will do it!"

True Justice

18 ¹The word of the LORD came to me. He said, ²"Why do you people say this proverb:

'The parents ate the sour grapes,
    but the children got the sour taste'ᵃ?"

³But the Lord GOD says, "By my life, I swear that people in Israel will not think this proverb is true anymore! ⁴I will treat everyone, child and parent, just the same. The one who sins is the one who will die!

⁵"A person who is good will live! He is fair and does what is right. ⁶He doesn't go to the mountains to share food offered to idols.* He doesn't pray to those filthy idols in Israel. He doesn't commit adultery* with his neighbor's wife or with a woman during her period. ⁷He doesn't take advantage of others. If someone borrows money from him, he might take something of value before he gives the money. But when that person pays him back, he returns what he took. He gives food to the hungry and clothes to people who need them. ⁸If someone wants to borrow money from him, he lends the money and doesn't charge interest on the loan. He refuses to be crooked. He is always fair with everyone. People can trust him. ⁹He obeys my laws and studies my rules so that he can learn to be fair and dependable. He is good, so he will live.

¹⁰"But someone like that might have a son who does not do any of these good things. The son steals things and kills people. ¹¹He does things his father never did. He goes to the mountains and eats foods offered to false gods. He commits the sin of adultery with his neighbor's wife. ¹²He mistreats poor, helpless people. He takes advantage of them. When a debt is paid,ᵇ he does not give back what he took from them. He prays to filthy idols and does other terrible things. ¹³He lends money to people who need it, but he forces them to pay interest on the loan. The evil son will not be allowed to live. He will be put to death because he did such terrible things, and he will be responsible for his own death.

¹⁴"Now, that evil son might also have a son. But this son sees the bad things his father did, and he refuses to live as his father did. He treats people fairly. ¹⁵He does not go to the mountains and eat foods offered to false gods. He does not pray to filthy idols in Israel. He does not commit the sin of adultery with his neighbor's wife. ¹⁶He does not take advantage of people. If someone borrows money from him, the good son takes something of value and then gives the other person the money. When that person pays him back, the good son gives back what he took. The good son gives food to hungry people, and he gives clothes to those who need them. ¹⁷He helps the poor. If people want to borrow money, the good son lends them the money, and he does not charge interest on the loan. He obeys my laws and follows them. He will not be put to death for his father's sins. The good son will live. ¹⁸The father hurts people and steals things. He never does anything good for my people! He will die because of his own sins.

¹⁹"You might ask, 'Why will the son not be punished for his father's sins?' The reason is that the son was fair and did good things. He very carefully obeyed my laws, so he will live. ²⁰The one who sins is the one who will be put to death. A son will not be punished for his father's sins, and a father will not be punished for his son's sins. A good man's goodness belongs to him alone, and a bad man's evil belongs to him alone.

²¹"Now, if evil people change their lives, they will live and not die. They might stop doing all the bad things they did and begin to carefully obey all my laws. They might become fair and good. ²²God will not remember all the bad things they did. He will remember only their goodness, so they will live!"

²³The Lord GOD says, "I don't want evil people to die. I want them to change their lives so that they can live!

²⁴"Now, maybe good people might stop being good. They might change their lives and begin to do all the terrible things that evil people have done in the past. (The evil people changed, so they can live.) So if those good people change and become bad, God will not remember all the good things they did. He will remember that they turned against him and began to sin. So they will die because of their sin.

²⁵"You people might say, 'The Lord isn't fair!' But listen, family of Israel. I am fair. You are the ones who are not fair! ²⁶If good people change and become evil, they must die for the bad things they do. ²⁷And if evil people change and become good and fair, they will save their lives. They will live! ²⁸They saw how wicked they were and came back to me. They stopped doing the evil things they did in the past. So they will live! They will not die!"

²⁹The people of Israel said, "That's not fair! The Lord isn't fair!"

"I am fair! You are the ones who are not fair! ³⁰Why? Because, family of Israel, I will judge each of you only for what you do!" This

---

ᵃ**18:2** *The parents ... sour taste* This means the children were suffering for things their parents did.
ᵇ**18:12** *When a debt is paid* See Deut. 24:12–13 for the rules about making loans to the poor.

is what the Lord God said. "So come back to me! Stop committing those crimes and do away with those things that cause you to sin! ³¹Throw away all the terrible idols with which you committed your crimes! Change your heart and spirit. People of Israel, why should you do things that will cost you your life? ³²I don't want to kill you! Please come back and live!" This is what the Lord God said.

A Sad Song About Israel

19 ¹The Lord said to me, "You must sing this sad song about the leaders of Israel:

²"'Your mother is like a female lion,
    lying there with the male lions.
She went to lie down with the young
        male lions
    and had many babies.
³ One of her cubs gets up.
    He has grown to be a strong young lion.
    He has learned to catch his food.
    He killed and ate a man.

⁴"'The people heard him roar,
    and they caught him in their trap.
They put hooks in his mouth
    and carried the young lion to Egypt.

⁵"'The mother lion had hoped that cub
        would become the leader,
    but now she has lost all hope.
So she took another of her cubs
    and trained him to be a lion.
⁶ He hunted with the adult lions
    and became a strong young lion.
He learned to catch his food.
    He killed and ate a man.
⁷ He attacked the palaces and destroyed the
        cities.
    Everyone in that country was too afraid
        to speak when hearing his growl.
⁸ Then the people who lived around him
        set a trap for him,
    and they caught him in their trap.
⁹ They put hooks on him and locked him
        up.
They had him in their trap,
    so they took him to the king of Babylon.
And now, you cannot hear his roar
    on the mountains of Israel.

¹⁰"'Your mother is like a grapevine
        planted near the water.
She had plenty of water,
    so she grew many strong vines.
¹¹ Then she grew large branches.
    They were like a strong walking stick.
    They were like a king's scepter.*
The vine grew taller and taller.
    It had many branches and reached to
        the clouds.
¹² But the vine was pulled up by the roots,
    and thrown down to the ground.

The hot east wind blew and dried its fruit.
    The strong branches broke, and they
        were thrown into the fire.

¹³"'Now that grapevine is planted in the
        desert.
    It is a very dry and thirsty land.
¹⁴ A fire started in the large branch
    and spread to destroy all of its vines and
        fruit.
So there was no strong walking stick.
    There was no king's scepter.'

This was a sad song about death, and it was sung as a sad song about death."

Israel Turned Away From God

20 ¹One day, some of the elders* of Israel came to me to ask the Lord for advice. This was on the tenth day of the fifth month of the seventh year of exile.ᵃ The elders sat down in front of me.

²Then the word of the Lord came to me. He said, ³"Son of man,ᵇ speak to the elders of Israel. Tell them 'This is what the Lord God says: Have you come to ask me advice? If you have, I will not give it to you.' ⁴Should you judge them? Will you judge them, son of man? You must tell them about the terrible things their fathers have done. ⁵You must tell them, 'This is what the Lord God says: On the day I chose Israel, I raised my hand to Jacob's family and made a promise to them in Egypt. When I let them know who I was, I raised my hand and said, "I am the Lord your God." ⁶On that day, I promised to take you out of Egypt and lead you to the land I was giving to you. That was a good land filled with many good things.ᶜ It was the most beautiful of all countries!"

⁷"'I told the family of Israel to throw away their horrible idols.* I told them not to become filthy with those filthy statues from Egypt. I said, "I am the Lord your God." ⁸But they turned against me and refused to listen to me. They did not throw away their horrible idols. They did not leave their filthy statues in Egypt. So I decided to destroy them in Egypt—to let them feel the full force of my anger. ⁹But I did not destroy them. I had already told the Egyptians that I would bring my people out of Egypt. I did not want to ruin my good name, so I did not destroy Israel in front of those other people. ¹⁰I brought the family of Israel out of Egypt. I led them into the desert. ¹¹Then I gave them my laws and told them all my rules. All those who obey

---

ᵃ**20:1** *seventh year of exile* This was the summer of 591 B.C.
ᵇ**20:3** *Son of man* This was usually just a way of saying "a person" or "a human being." Here, it is a way of addressing Ezekiel. Also in verses 4, 27, 46.
ᶜ**20:6** *land … things* Literally, "land flowing with milk and honey." Also in verse 15.

680

them will live. 12I also told them about all the special days of rest, which were a special sign between us. They showed that I am the Lord and that I was making them special to me.

13"But the family of Israel turned against me in the desert. They did not follow my laws. They refused to obey my rules—even though people who obey my laws live because of them. They treated my special days of rest as if they were not important. They worked on those days many times. I decided to destroy them in the desert—to let them feel the full force of my anger. 14But I did not destroy them. The other nations saw me bring Israel out of Egypt. I did not want to ruin my good name, so I did not destroy Israel in front of those other people. 15I made another promise to those people in the desert. I promised that I would not bring them into the land I was giving them. That was a good land filled with many good things. It was the most beautiful of all countries!

16"The people of Israel refused to obey my rules or to follow my laws. They treated my days of rest as if they were not important. They did all these things because their hearts belonged to their filthy idols. 17But I felt sorry for them, so I did not destroy them. I did not completely destroy them in the desert. 18I spoke to their children and told them, "Don't be like your parents. Don't make yourselves filthy with their filthy idols. Don't follow their laws or obey their commands. 19I am the Lord. I am your God. Obey my laws and keep my commands. Do the things I tell you. 20Show that my days of rest are important to you. Remember, they are a special sign between us. I am the Lord, and these days show you that I am your God."

21"But the children turned against me and did not obey my laws. They did not keep my commands—even though people who obey my laws live because of them. They treated my special days of rest as though they were not important. So I decided to destroy them completely in the desert—to let them feel the full force of my anger. 22But I stopped myself. The other nations saw me bring Israel out of Egypt. I did not want to ruin my good name, so I did not destroy Israel in front of those other people. 23So I made another promise to those people in the desert. I promised to scatter them among the nations, to send them to many different countries.

24"The people of Israel did not obey my commands. They refused to obey my laws. They treated my special days of rest as though they were not important, and they worshiped the filthy idols of their fathers. 25So I gave them laws that were not good. I gave them commands that would not bring life. 26I let them make themselves filthy with their gifts. They even began to sacrifice their own first-born children. In this way I would destroy them. Then they would know that I am the

Lord.' 27So now, son of man, speak to the family of Israel. Tell them, 'This is what the Lord God says: The people of Israel said bad things about me and made evil plans against me. 28But I still brought them to the land I promised to give them. They saw all the hills and green trees, so they went to all those places to worship. They took their sacrifices and anger offerings*a* to all those places. They offered their sacrifices that made a sweet smell, and they offered their drink offerings at those places. 29I asked the people of Israel why they were going to the high places. But that high place is still there today.*b*'

30"Since Israel did those things, speak to them and tell them, 'This is what the Lord God says: You people have made yourselves filthy by doing the things your ancestors* did. You have acted like a prostitute. You have left me to be with the horrible gods your ancestors worshiped. 31You are giving the same kind of gifts. You are putting your children in the fire as a gift to your false gods. You are still making yourself filthy with these filthy idols today! Do you really think that I should let you come to me and ask me for advice? I am the Lord God. By my life, I swear that I will not answer your questions or give you advice! 32You keep saying you want to be like the other nations. You live like the people in other nations. You serve pieces of wood and stone idols!'"

33The Lord God says, "By my life, I swear that I will rule over you as king. But I will raise my powerful arm and punish you. I will show my anger against you! 34I will bring you out of these other nations. I scattered you among these nations, but I will gather you together and bring you back from these countries. But I will raise my powerful arm and punish you. I will show my anger against you! 35I will lead you into a desert as I did before, but this will be a place where other nations live. We will stand face to face, and I will judge you. 36I will judge you as I judged your ancestors in the desert near Egypt." This is what the Lord God said.

37"I will judge you guilty and punish you according to the agreement.* 38I will remove all those who turned against me and sinned against me. I will remove them from your homeland. They will never again come to the land of Israel. Then you will know that I am the Lord."

39Now, family of Israel, this is what the Lord God says: "Whoever wants to worship their filthy idols, let them go and worship them. But later, don't think you will get any advice from me. You will not ruin my name

---

*a*20:28 *anger offerings* The people called these meals "fellowship offerings," but Ezekiel is making fun of them and saying that those meals only made God angry.

*b*20:29 *But that ... today* Literally, "And its name is still called Bamah (high place) to this day."

anymore—not when you continue to give your gifts to your filthy idols!"

⁴⁰The Lord GOD says, "People must come to my holy mountain—the high mountain in Israel—to serve me! The whole family of Israel will be on their land; they will be there in their country. There you can come to ask me for advice, and you must come there to bring me your offerings. You must bring the first part of your crops to me there. You must bring all your holy gifts to me in that place. ⁴¹Then I will be pleased with the sweet smell of your sacrifices. That will happen when I bring you back. I scattered you among many nations, but I will gather you together and make you my special people again. And all the nations will see it. ⁴²Then you will know that I am the LORD. You will know this when I bring you back to the land of Israel, the land I promised to give to your ancestors. ⁴³In that country you will remember all the evil things you did that made you filthy, and you will be ashamed. ⁴⁴Family of Israel, you did many evil things, and you should be destroyed because of them. But to protect my good name, I will not give you the punishment you really deserve. Then you will know that I am the LORD." This is what the Lord GOD said.

⁴⁵Then the word of the LORD came to me. He said, ⁴⁶"Son of man, look toward the Negev, the southern part of Judah. Speak against the Negev Forest.ᵃ ⁴⁷Say to the Negev Forest, 'Listen to the word of the LORD. This is what the Lord GOD said: Look, I am ready to start a fire in your forest. The fire will destroy every green tree and every dry tree. The flame that burns will not be put out. All the land from south to north will be burned by the fire. ⁴⁸Then all people will see that I, the LORD, have started the fire. The fire will not be put out!'"

⁴⁹Then I said, "Oh, Lord GOD! If I say this, the people will say that I am only telling them stories."

Babylon, the Sword

21 ¹So the word of the LORD came to me again. He said, ²"Son of man,ᵇ look toward Jerusalem and speak against their holy places. Speak against the land of Israel for me. ³Say to the land of Israel, 'This is what the LORD said: I am against you! I will pull my sword from its sheath.* I will remove all people from you—the good and the evil. ⁴I will cut off both good people and evil people from you. I will pull my sword from its sheath and use it against all people from south to north. ⁵Then everyone will know that I am the LORD. They will know that I have pulled my sword from its sheath. My sword will not go back

---

ᵃ**20:46** *Negev Forest* God is probably making fun of the people. The Negev is a desert area. There are no forests in the Negev.
ᵇ**21:2** *Son of man* This was usually just a way of saying "a person" or "a human being." Here, it is a way of addressing Ezekiel. Also in verses 6, 9, 12, 14, 19, 28.

---

into its sheath again until it is finished.'

⁶"Son of man, make sad sounds like a sad person with a broken heart. Make these sad sounds in front of the people. ⁷Then they will ask you, 'Why are you making these sad sounds?' Then you must say, 'Because of the sad news that is coming. Every heart will melt with fear. All hands will become weak. Every spirit will become weak. All knees will be like water.' Look, that bad news is coming. These things will happen!" This is what the Lord GOD said.

The Sword Is Ready

⁸The word of the LORD came to me. He said, ⁹"Son of man, speak to the people for me. Say this, 'This is what the Lord GOD says:

"'Look, a sword, a sharp sword,
        and it has been polished.
¹⁰ The sword was made sharp for killing.
        It was polished to flash like lightning.
    My son, you ran away from the stick I
        used to punish you.
        You refused to be punished with that
        wooden stick.
¹¹ So the sword has been polished.
        Now it can be used.
    The sword was sharpened and polished.
        Now it can be put in the hand of the
        killer.

¹²"'Son of man, shout out and scream because the sword will be used against my people and all the rulers of Israel. They wanted war—so they will be with my people when the sword comes. So slap your thigh to show your sadness, ¹³because it is not just a test. You refused to be punished with the wooden stick, so what else should I use to punish you? ⌊A sword?⌋'" This is what the Lord GOD said.

¹⁴"Son of man, clap your hands to show your sadness, and speak to the people for me.

"Let the sword come down twice,
        no, three times!
This sword is for killing the people.
    This is the sword for the great killing.
    This sword will cut into them.
¹⁵ Their hearts will melt with fear,
        and many people will fall.
    The sword will kill many people
        by the city gates.
    Yes, the sword will flash like lightning.
        It was polished to kill the people!
¹⁶ Sword, be sharp!
    Cut on the right side.
    Cut straight ahead.
    Cut on the left side.
    Go wherever your edge was chosen to go.

¹⁷"Then I, too, will clap my hands
        and stop showing my anger.
    I, the LORD, have spoken!"

Jerusalem Punished

18The word of the LORD came to me. He said, 19"Son of man, draw two roads that the sword of the king of Babylon can use to come to Israel. Both roads will come from the same country. Then draw a sign at the head of the road to the city. 20Use the sign to show which road the sword will use. One road leads to the Ammonite city of Rabbah. The other road leads to Judah, to the protected city, Jerusalem. 21The king of Babylon has come to where the two roads separate. He uses magic to learn which way to go: He shakes his arrows, he asks his family idols,* and he looks at the liver*a* from an animal he has killed.

22"The signs tell him to take the road on his right, the road leading to Jerusalem! He plans to bring the battering rams.*b* He will give the command, and his soldiers will begin the killing. They will shout the battle cry. Then they will build a wall of dirt around the city. They will build a dirt road leading up to the walls. They will build wooden towers to attack the city. 23Those magic signs mean nothing to the people of Israel. They have the promises they made. But ⌊the Lord⌋ will remember their sin, so the Israelites will be captured."

24This is what the Lord GOD says: "You have done many evil things. Your sins are very clear. You forced me to remember that you are guilty, so the enemy will catch you in his hand. 25And you, evil leader of Israel, you will be killed. Your time of punishment has come! The end is here!"

26This is what the Lord GOD says: "Take off the turban*! Take off the crown! The time has come to change. The important leaders will be brought low, and those who are not important now will become important leaders. 27I will completely destroy that city! But this will not happen until the right man becomes the new king. Then I will let him have this city."

The Ammonites Punished

28"Son of man, speak to the people for me. Say this, 'This is what the Lord GOD says to the people of Ammon and their shameful god:

"'Look, a sword!
    The sword is out of its sheath.*
    It has been polished.
The sword is ready to kill.
    It was polished to flash like lightning!

29"'Your visions* are useless.
    Your magic will not help you.
    It is only a bunch of lies.
The sword is now at the throats of evil
    men.

They will soon be only dead bodies.
    Their time has come.
The time has come for their evil to end.

Prophecy Against Babylon

30"'Put the sword back in its sheath.* Babylon, I will judge you in the place where you were created, in the land where you were born. 31I will pour out my anger against you. My anger will burn you like a hot wind. I will hand you over to cruel men.*c* Those men are skilled at killing people. 32You will be like fuel for the fire. Your blood will flow deep into the earth—people will never remember you again. I, the LORD, have spoken!'"

Ezekiel Speaks Against Jerusalem

22 1The word of the LORD came to me. He said, 2"Son of man,*d* will you judge the city of murderers? Will you tell her about all the terrible things she has done? 3You must say, 'This is what the Lord GOD says: The city is full of murderers, so her time of punishment will come. She made filthy idols* for herself, and those idols made her filthy!

4"'People of Jerusalem, you killed many people. You made filthy idols. You are guilty, and the time has come to punish you. Your end has come. Other nations will make fun of you and laugh at you. 5People far and near will make fun of you. You have ruined your name. You are filled with confusion.

6"'Look, all the leaders in Israel are using their strength just to kill other people. 7And the people in Jerusalem don't respect their parents. There in the city, they abuse the foreigners. They cheat orphans and widows in that place. 8You hate all that I consider holy. You treat my special days of rest as if they are not important. 9In Jerusalem, people tell lies in order to kill innocent people. They go to the mountains to worship false gods and then come back to Jerusalem to eat their fellowship meals.

"'In Jerusalem, people commit many sexual sins. 10There men commit sexual sins with their father's wife. There the men rape women—even during their monthly time of bleeding. 11One man commits a terrible sin against his own neighbor's wife. Another man has sex with his daughter-in-law and makes her unclean.* Another man rapes his father's daughter—his very own sister. 12There men accept bribes to kill people. You lend money and charge interest on the loans. You cheat your neighbors just to make a little money. You have even forgotten me.' This is what the Lord GOD said.

13"'Now look! I will slam my hand down and stop you! I will punish you for cheating

---

*a*21:21 *arrows, idols, liver* People who believed in false gods used these things to try to learn the future.
*b*21:22 *battering rams* Heavy logs that soldiers used to break holes into the gates or walls around a city.

*c*21:31 *cruel men* This is a wordplay. The Hebrew word is like the word meaning "to burn."
*d*22:2 *Son of man* This was usually just a way of saying "a person" or "a human being." Here, it is a way of addressing Ezekiel. Also in verses 18, 24.

and killing people. ¹⁴Will you be brave then? Will you be strong at the time I come to punish you? I am the Lord. I have spoken, and I will do what I said! ¹⁵I will scatter you among the nations. I will force you to go to many countries. I will completely destroy the filthy things in this city. ¹⁶But Jerusalem, you will become unclean. And the other nations will see all these things happen. Then you will know that I am the Lord.'"

Israel Is Like Worthless Waste

¹⁷The word of the Lord came to me. He said, ¹⁸"Son of man, bronze, iron, lead, and tin are important metals, but when a worker melts silver to make it pure, those metals are poured off as waste. Israel has become like that waste to me. ¹⁹So this is what the Lord God says: 'All of you have become like worthless waste. So I will gather you into Jerusalem. ²⁰Workers put silver, bronze, iron, lead, and tin into a fire. They blow on the fire to make it hotter. Then the metals begin to melt. In the same way I will put you in my fire and melt you. That fire is my hot anger. ²¹I will put you in my fire of anger and blow on it, and you will begin to melt. ²²In that city, you will be like silver melting in a fire. Then you will know that I am the Lord, and that I poured out my anger on you.'"

Ezekiel Speaks Against Jerusalem

²³The word of the Lord came to me. He said, ²⁴"Son of man, speak to Israel. Tell her that she is not pure.ᵃ I am angry at that country, so that country has not received its rain. ²⁵The prophets in Jerusalem are making evil plans. They are like a lion—it roars when it begins to eat the animal it caught. They have destroyed many lives. They have taken many valuable things and made widows of many of the women in Jerusalem.

²⁶"The priests have really hurt my teachings. They don't treat my holy* things right—they don't show they are important. They treat holy things the same as things that are not holy. They treat clean* things like things that are unclean. They don't teach the people about these things. They refuse to respect my special days of rest. They treat me as though I am not important.

²⁷"The leaders in Jerusalem are like a wolf eating the animal it has caught. They attack people and kill them just to get rich.

²⁸"The prophets don't warn the people—they cover up the truth. They are like workers who don't really repair a wall—they only put plaster over the holes. They only see lies. They do their magic to learn the future, but they only tell lies. They say, 'This is what the Lord God said.' But they are only lying—the Lord did not speak to them!

²⁹"The common people take advantage of each other. They cheat and steal from each other. They get rich by taking advantage of poor, helpless beggars, and they really cheat the foreigners. They are not fair to them at all!

³⁰"I asked the people to ₗchange their lives and₎ protect their country. I asked people to fix the walls. I wanted them to stand by those holes in the wall and fight to protect their city. But no one came to help! ³¹So I will show them my anger—I will completely destroy them. I will punish them for the evil things they have done. It is all their fault." This is what the Lord God said.

23

¹The word of the Lord came to me. He said, ²"Son of man,ᵇ listen to this story about Samaria and Jerusalem. There were two sisters, daughters of the same mother. ³They became prostitutes in Egypt while they were still young girls. That's where they first let men touch and handle their young breasts. ⁴The older daughter was named Oholah,ᶜ and her sister was named Oholibah.ᵈ They became my wives, and we had children. I am using the name Oholah to mean Samaria and the name Oholibah to mean Jerusalem.

⁵"Then Oholah became unfaithful ⬛⬛—she began to live like a prostitute. She h⬛⬛o want her lovers. She saw the Assyrian ⬛⬛ ⁶in their blue uniforms. They were a⬛ some young men riding horses. The⬛⬛re leaders and officers, ⁷and Oholah gave herself to all those men. All of them were handpicked soldiers in the Assyrian army, and she wanted them all! She became filthy with their filthy idols.* ⁸Besides that, she never stopped her love affair with Egypt. Egypt made love to her when she was a young girl. Egypt was the first lover to touch her young breasts. Egypt poured his untrue love on her. ⁹So I let her lovers have her. She wanted Assyria, so I gave her to them! ¹⁰They rapedᵉ her. They took her children and killed her. They punished her, and women still talk about her.

¹¹"Her younger sister Oholibah saw all these things happen. But Oholibah sinned more than her sister did! She was more unfaithful than Oholah. ¹²She wanted the Assyrian leaders and officers. She wanted those soldiers in blue uniforms riding their horses. They were all handsome young men.

ᵃ22:24 not pure This is a wordplay. The Hebrew word also means "not rained on."

ᵇ23:2 Son of man This was usually just a way of saying "a person" or "a human being." Here, it is a way of addressing Ezekiel. Also in verse 36.
ᶜ23:4 Oholah This name means "Tent." It probably refers to the Holy Tent where the people of Israel went to worship God.
ᵈ23:4 Oholibah This name means "My Tent is in her ₗcountry,₎" Also in verses 18, 21.
ᵉ23:10 raped Literally, "revealed her nakedness." The Hebrew word meaning "revealed" is like the word meaning "carried away as a prisoner to a faraway country."

13I saw that both women were going to ruin their lives with the same mistakes.

14"Oholibah continued to be unfaithful to me. In Babylon, she saw pictures of men carved on the walls. These were pictures of Chaldean* men wearing their red uniforms. 15They wore belts around their waists and long turbans* on their heads. All those men looked like chariot* officers. They all looked like native-born Babylonian men, 16and Oholibah wanted them. 17So the Babylonian men came to her bed to have sex with her. They used her and made her so filthy that she became disgusted with them.

18"Oholibah let everyone see that she was unfaithful. She let so many men enjoy her naked body that I became disgusted with her—just as I had become disgusted with her sister. 19But Oholibah thought about her time as a prostitute in Egypt when she was young, and she turned to even more prostitution. 20She remembered the lovers who excited her there, who were like animals in their sexual desires and abilities.

21"Oholibah, you dreamed of those times when you were young, when your lovers touched and handled your young breasts. 22So Oholibah, this is what the Lord God says: 'You became disgusted with your lovers, but I will bring them here, and they will surround you. 23I will bring all the men from Babylon, especially the Chaldeans. I will bring the men from Pekod, Shoa, and Koa, and all the men from Assyria. I will bring all the leaders and officers, all those desirable young men, chariot officers, and handpicked soldiers riding their horses. 24That crowd of men will come to you in large groups, riding on their horses and in their chariots. They will have their spears, shields, and helmets. They will gather around you, and I will tell them what you have done to me. Then they will punish you their own way. 25I will show you how jealous I am. They will become angry and hurt you. They will cut off your nose and ears. They will kill you with a sword. Then they will take your children and burn whatever is left of you. 26They will take your nice clothes and jewelry. 27So I will stop your dreams about your love affair with Egypt. You will never again look for them. You will never remember Egypt again!'"

28This is what the Lord God says: "I am giving you to the men you hate. I am giving you to the men you became disgusted with. 29And they will show how much they hate you! They will take everything you worked for, and they will leave you bare and naked! People will clearly see your sins. They will see that you acted like a prostitute and dreamed wicked dreams. 30You did those bad things when you left me to chase after the other nations. You did those bad things when you began to worship their filthy idols. 31You followed your sister and lived as she did. You, yourself, took her cup of poison and held it in your hands.ᵃ" 32This is what the Lord God says:

> "You will drink your sister's cup of poison.
> It is a tall, wide cup of poison.
> It holds much poison.
> People will laugh at you and make fun of you.
> 33 You will stagger like a drunk.
> You will become very dizzy.
> That is the cup of destruction and devastation.
> It is like the cup of punishment that your sister drank.
> 34 You will drink the poison in that cup.
> You will drink it to the last drop.
> You will throw down the glass and break it to pieces.
> You will tear at your breasts from the pain.
> This will happen because I am the Lord God,
> and this is what I said."

35"So this is what the Lord God said: 'Jerusalem, you forgot me. You threw me away and left me behind. So now you must suffer for leaving me and living like a prostitute. You must suffer for your wicked dreams.'"

Judgment Against Oholah and Oholibah

36The Lord God said to me, "Son of man, will you judge Oholah and Oholibah? Then tell them about the terrible things they have done. 37They committed the sin of adultery.* They are guilty of murder. They acted like prostitutes—they left me to be with their filthy idols.* They had my children, but they forced them to pass through fire. They did this to give food to their filthy idols. 38They also treated my special days of rest and my holy place as though they were not important. 39They killed their children for their idols, and then they went into my holy place and made it filthy too! They did this inside my Temple*! 40"They have sent for men from faraway places. You sent a messenger to these men, and they came to see you. You bathed for them, painted your eyes, and put on your jewelry. 41You sat on a fine bed with a table set before it. You put my incenseᵇ and my oilᶜ on this table.

42"The noise in Jerusalem sounded like a

ᵇ23:41 my incense A special blend of spices that were burned as a gift to God. This special incense was to be burned only in the Temple. See Ex. 30:34–38.
ᶜ23:41 my oil The special oil that was used for anointing priests and things in the Temple to make them holy (special). See Ex. 30:22–33.

crowd of people having a party.*a* Many people came to the party. People were already drinking as they came in from the desert. They gave bracelets and beautiful crowns to the women. [43]Then I spoke to one of the women who was worn out from her sexual sins. I asked her, 'Will they continue to do sexual sins with her, and she with them?' [44]But they kept going to her as they would go to a prostitute. Yes, they went again and again to Oholah and Oholibah, those wicked women.

[45]"But good men will judge them guilty of adultery and murder, because Oholah and Oholibah committed adultery and their hands are covered with blood!"

[46]This is what the Lord God said: "Gather the people together to punish and terrorize Oholah and Oholibah. [47]They will throw stones at these women and kill them. They will cut the women to pieces with their swords. They will kill their children and burn their houses. [48]In this way I will remove that shame from this country, and all the other women will be warned not to do the shameful things you have done. [49]They will punish you for the wicked things you did. You will be punished for worshiping your filthy idols. Then you will know that I am the Lord God."

The Pot and the Meat

24 [1]The word of the Lord God came to me. This was on the tenth day of the tenth month in the ninth year of exile.*b* He said, [2]"Son of man,*c* write today's date and this note: 'On this date the army of the king of Babylon surrounded Jerusalem.' [3]Tell this story to the family who refuses to obey *(Israel)*. Tell them, 'This is what the Lord God says:

"'Put the pot on the fire.
    Put on the pot and pour in the water.
[4] Put in the pieces of meat.
    Put in every good piece, the thighs and
        the shoulders.
Fill the pot with the best bones.
[5] Use the best animals in the flock.
Pile the wood under the pot,
    and boil the pieces of meat.
Boil the soup until even the bones
    are cooked.

[6]"'So this is what the Lord God says:
It will be bad for Jerusalem.

It will be bad for that city of murderers.
Jerusalem is like a pot with rust on it,
    and those spots of rust cannot be
        removed!
That pot is not clean, and the rust
    cannot be removed,
so the meat must be thrown out and not
    divided among the priests.
[7] Jerusalem is like a pot with rust on it.
    This is because the blood from the
        murders is still there!
She put the blood on the bare rock.
    She did not pour the blood on the
        ground and cover it with dirt.*d*
[8] I put her blood on the bare rock
    so that it would not be covered.
I did this so that people would become
    angry and punish her for killing
        innocent people.

[9]"'So this is what the Lord God says:
It will be bad for that city of murderers!
    I will pile up plenty of wood for the fire.
[10] Put plenty of wood under the pot.
    Light the fire.
Cook the meat until it is well done.
    Mix in the spices,*e*
    and let the bones be burned up.
[11] Then let the pot stand empty on the coals.
    Let it become so hot that its stains*f*
        begin to glow.
Those stains will be melted away.
    The rust will be destroyed.

[12]"'Jerusalem might work hard
    to scrub away her stains.
But that 'rust' will not go away!
    Only the fire of punishment will remove
        it.

[13]"'You sinned against me
    and became stained with sin.
I wanted to wash you and make you
    clean,
    but the stains would not come out.
I will not try washing you again
    until my hot anger is finished with you!

[14]"'I am the Lord. I said your punishment would come, and I will make it happen. I will not hold back the punishment or feel sorry for you. I will punish you for the evil things you did. This is what the Lord God said.'"

---

*a*23:42 *party* The Hebrew word is like the word for a fellowship offering, a time when people came to share a meal and enjoy themselves together with the Lord. Here, it seems this time of worship turned into a wild party. See Deut 14:22–29; 26:1–15.
*b*24:1 *ninth year of exile* This was Jan. 15, 588 B.C., the date that Nebuchadnezzar began his attack on Jerusalem.
*c*24:2 *Son of man* This was usually just a way of saying "a person" or "a human being." Here, it is a way of addressing Ezekiel. Also in verses 16, 25.

*d*24:7 *blood … dirt* The Law of Moses teaches that whoever killed an animal for food must pour the blood on the ground and cover it with dirt. This showed that they were giving the life of that animal back to God. See Lev. 17:1–16 and Deut. 12:1–25. If the blood was not covered with dirt, it was a witness against the killer. See Gen. 4:10, Job 15:18, and Isa. 26:21.
*e*24:10 *Mix in the spices* The meaning of this sentence is uncertain.
*f*24:11 *stains* Or "bronze."

The Death of Ezekiel's Wife

¹⁵Then the word of the Lord came to me. He said, ¹⁶"Son of man, you love your wife very much, but I am going to take her away from you. Your wife will die suddenly, but you must not show your sadness. You must not cry loudly. You will cry and your tears will fall, ¹⁷but you must mourn* quietly. Dress as you normally do; wear your turban* and sandals; don't cover your mustache, and don't eat the food people normally eat when someone dies."

¹⁸The next morning I told the people what God had said. That evening, my wife died. The next morning I did what God commanded. ¹⁹Then the people said to me, "Why are you doing this? What does it mean?"

²⁰Then I said to them, "The word of the Lord came to me. He told me ²¹to speak to the family of Israel. The Lord God said, 'Look, I will destroy my holy place. You are proud of that place and sing songs of praise about it. You love to see it. You really love that place. But I will destroy it, and your children that you left behind will be killed in battle. ²²But you will do the same things that I have done about my dead wife. You will not cover your mustache or eat the food people normally eat when someone dies. ²³You will wear your turbans and your sandals. You will not show your sadness publicly or cry publicly, but you will waste away with guilt and talk to each other quietly about your grief. ²⁴So Ezekiel is an example for you. You will do all the same things he did. That time of punishment will come, and then you will know that I am the Lord.'"

²⁵⁻²⁶The Lord said, "Son of man, I will take away the place that makes the people feel safe—Jerusalem, that beautiful city that makes them so happy. They really love that place. They love to look at it. But I will take it away from them, and I will also take their children. On that day one of the survivors will come to you with the bad news about Jerusalem. ²⁷That same day you will be able to talk to the messenger. You will not be silent anymore. This will be a sign to the people, and they will know that I am the Lord."

Prophecy Against Ammon

25 ¹The word of the Lord came to me. He said, ²"Son of man,ᵃ look toward the people of Ammon and speak against them for me. ³Say to them: 'Listen to the word of the Lord God! This is what the Lord God says: You were happy when my holy place was destroyed. You were against the land of Israel when it was polluted. You were against the family of Judah when the people were carried away as prisoners. ⁴So I will give you

to the people from the east. They will get your land. Their armies will set up their camps in your country. They will live among you and eat your fruit and drink your milk.

⁵"'I will make the city Rabbah a pasture for camels and the country of Ammon a sheep pen. Then you will know that I am the Lord. ⁶This is what the Lord says: You were happy that Jerusalem was destroyed. You clapped your hands and stamped your feet. You had fun insulting the land of Israel, ⁷so I will punish you. You will be like the valuable things soldiers take in war. You will lose your inheritance and die in faraway lands. I will destroy your country! Then you will know that I am the Lord.'"

Prophecy Against Moab and Seir

⁸This is what the Lord God says: "Moab and Seirᵇ say, 'The family of Judah is just like any other nation.' ⁹I will cut into Moab's shoulder—I will take away the cities that are on its borders—the glory of the land, Beth Jeshimoth, Baal Meon, and Kiriathaim. ¹⁰Then I will give these cities to the people of the east. They will get your land. I will also let those people from the east destroy the Ammonites, and people will forget they were ever a nation. ¹¹So I will punish Moab, and then they will know that I am the Lord."

Prophecy Against Edom

¹²This is what the Lord God says: "The people of Edom turned against the family of Judah and tried to get even. The people of Edom are guilty." ¹³So the Lord God says: "I will punish Edom. I will destroy the people and the animals in Edom. I will destroy the whole country of Edom, all the way from Teman to Dedan. The Edomites will be killed in battle. ¹⁴I will use my people Israel and get even against Edom. In this way the people of Israel will show my anger against Edom. Then the people of Edom will know that I punished them." This is what the Lord God said.

Prophecy Against the Philistines

¹⁵This is what the Lord God says: "The Philistines* tried to get even. They were very cruel. They let their anger burn inside them too long." ¹⁶So the Lord God said, "I will punish the Philistines. Yes, I will destroy those people from Crete. I will completely destroy those people who live on the seacoast. ¹⁷I will punish them—I will get even. I will let my anger teach them a lesson. Then they will know that I am the Lord!"

The Sad Message About Tyre

26 ¹In the eleventh year of exile,ᶜ on the first day of the month, the word

---

ᵃ**25:2 Son of man** This was usually just a way of saying "a person" or "a human being." Here, it is a way of addressing Ezekiel.

ᵇ**25:8 Seir** Or "Edom."

ᶜ**26:1 eleventh year of exile** This was probably the summer of 587 B.C. See 2 Kings 25:3.

of the LORD came to me. He said, ²"Son of man,ᵃ Tyre said bad things about Jerusalem: 'Hurray! The city gate protecting the people is destroyed! The city gate is open for me. The city of Jerusalem is ruined, so I can get plenty of valuable things out of it!'"

³So the Lord GOD says: "I am against you, Tyre! I will bring many nations to fight against you. They will come again and again, like waves on the beach.

⁴"The enemy soldiers will destroy the walls of Tyre and pull down her towers. I will also scrape the topsoil from her land. I will make Tyre a bare rock. ⁵Tyre will become a place by the sea for spreading fishing nets. I have spoken!" The Lord GOD says, "Tyre will be like the valuable things soldiers take in war. ⁶Her daughters on the mainland will be killed in battle. Then they will know that I am the LORD."

Nebuchadnezzar Will Attack Tyre

⁷This is what the Lord GOD says: "I will bring an enemy from the north against Tyre. That enemy is Nebuchadnezzar, the great king of Babylon! He will bring a very large army. There will be horses, chariots,* horse soldiers and many other soldiers. They will be from many different nations. ⁸Nebuchadnezzar will kill your daughters on the mainland. He will build towers to attack your city. He will build a dirt road around your city and a dirt road leading up to the walls. ⁹He will bring the logs to break down your walls. He will use picks and break down your towers. ¹⁰There will be so many of his horses that the dust from them will cover you. Your walls will shake at the noise of horse soldiers, wagons, and chariots when the king of Babylon enters the city through your city gates. Yes, they will come into your city because its walls will be pulled down. ¹¹The king of Babylon will come riding through your city. His horses' hoofsᵇ will come pounding over your streets. He will kill your people with swords. The strong columns in your city will fall to the ground. ¹²Nebuchadnezzar's men will take away your riches. They will take the things you wanted to sell. They will break down your walls and destroy your pleasant houses. They will throw the wood and stones into the sea like garbage. ¹³So I will stop the sound of your happy songs. People will not hear your harps anymore. ¹⁴I will make you a bare rock. You will be a place by the sea for spreading fishing nets! You will not be rebuilt, because I, the LORD, have spoken!" This is what the Lord GOD said.

Other Nations Will Cry for Tyre

¹⁵This is what the Lord GOD says to Tyre: "The countries along the Mediterranean coast will shake at the sound of your fall. That will happen when your people are hurt and killed. ¹⁶Then all the leaders of the countries by the sea will step down from their thrones and show their sadness. They will take off their special robes and their beautiful clothes. Then they will put on their 'clothes of shaking.' They will sit on the ground and shake with fear. They will be shocked at how quickly you were destroyed. ¹⁷They will sing this sad song about you:

"'Tyre, you were a famous city.ᶜ
    People came from across the sea to live
        in you.ᵈ
You were famous,
    but now you are gone!
You were strong on the sea,
    and so were the people who lived in
        you.
You made all who live on the mainland
    afraid of you.
¹⁸ Now, on the day you fall,
    the countries along the coast will shake
        with fear.
You started many colonies along the coast.
    Now those people will be afraid when
        you are gone!'"

¹⁹This is what the Lord GOD says: "Tyre, you will become an old, empty city. No one will live there. I will cause the sea to flow over you. The great sea will cover you. ²⁰I will send you down into that deep hole—to the place of death. You will join those who died long ago. I will send you to the world below, like all the other old, empty cities. You will be with all the others who go down to the grave. No one will live in you then. You will never again be in the land of the living! ²¹Other people will be afraid about what happened to you. You will be finished. People will look for you, but they will never find you again." That is what the Lord GOD says.

Tyre, the Door to the Seas

27 ¹The word of the LORD came to me again. He said, ²"Son of man,ᵉ sing this sad song about Tyre: ³Say this about Tyre:

"'Tyre, you are the door to the seas.
    You are the merchant* for many nations.
    You travel to many countries along the
        coast.
    This is what the Lord GOD says:
    Tyre, you think that you are so beautiful.
    You think you are perfectly beautiful!

ᶜ**26:17 you were a famous city** This can also mean "People have cried for you."

ᵈ**26:17 People … you** This can also mean "People have lived in you for a long time."

ᵉ**27:2 Son of man** This was usually just a way of saying "a person" or "a human being." Here, it is a way of addressing Ezekiel.

ᵃ**26:2 Son of man** This was usually just a way of saying "a person" or "a human being." Here, it is a way of addressing Ezekiel.

ᵇ**26:11 hoofs** The hard part of a horse's foot.

4 The Mediterranean Sea is the border
    around your city.
  Your builders made you perfectly
    beautiful,
  like the ships that sail from you.
5 Your builders used cypress trees
    from the mountains of Senir to make
      your planks.
  They used cedar trees from Lebanon
    to make your mast.
6 They used oak trees from Bashan
    to make your oars.
  They used pine trees from Cyprus
    to make the cabin on your deck.*a*
  They decorated that shelter with ivory.
7 For your sail,
    they used colorful linen made in Egypt.
  That sail was your flag.
  The coverings over your cabin were blue
    and purple.
  They came from the coast of Cyprus.*b*
8 Men from Sidon and Arvad rowed your
    boats for you.
  Tyre, your wise men were the pilots on
    your ships.
9 The elders and wise men from Byblos*c*
    were on board to help put caulking*d*
      between the boards on your ship.
  All the ships of the sea and their sailors
    came to trade and do business with you.

10 "'Men from Persia, Lud, and Put were in
your army. They were your men of war who
hung their shields and helmets on your walls.
They brought honor and glory to your city.
11 Men from Arvad and Cilicia were guards
standing on the wall around your city. Men
from Gammad were in your towers. They
hung their shields on the walls around your
city and made your beauty complete.

12 "'Tarshish* was one of your best custom-
ers. They traded silver, iron, tin, and lead for
all the wonderful things you sold. 13 People
in Greece, Turkey, and the area around the
Black Sea traded with you. They traded slaves
and bronze for the things you sold. 14 People
from the nation*e* of Togarmah traded horses,
war horses, and mules for the things you sold.
15 The people of Rhodes*f* traded with you.
You sold your things in many places. People
brought ivory tusks and ebony wood to pay
you. 16 Aram traded with you because you had
so many good things. They traded emeralds,
purple cloth, fine needlework, fine linen,

coral,* and rubies for the things you sold.
17 "'The people in Judah and Israel traded
with you. They paid for the things you sold
with the wheat, olives, early figs, honey, oil,
and balm.*g* 18 Damascus was a good customer.
They traded with you for the many wonderful
things you had. They traded wine from Helbon
and white wool for those things. 19 Damascus
traded wine from Uzal for the things you sold.
They paid with wrought iron, cassia,* and
sugar cane. 20 Dedan provided good business
and traded with you for saddle blankets and
riding horses. 21 Kedar* and all the leaders
of Kedar* traded lambs, rams, and goats for
your goods. 22 The merchants* of Sheba and
Raamah traded with you. They traded all the
best spices and every kind of precious stone
and gold for your goods. 23 Haran, Canneh,
Eden, the merchants of Sheba, Asshur, and
Kilmad traded with you. 24 They paid with
the finest clothing, blue cloth, cloth with fine
needlework, rugs of many colors, and the
strongest ropes. These were the things they
traded with you. 25 The ships from Tarshish
carried the things you sold.*j*

"'Tyre, you are like one of those cargo
    ships.
  You are on the sea, loaded with many
    riches.
26 Your oarsmen rowed you far out to sea.
  But a powerful east wind will destroy
    your ship at sea.
27 All your wealth will spill into the sea.
  Your wealth—the things you buy and
    sell—will spill into the sea.
  Your whole crew—sailors, pilots, and the
    men who put caulking between the
      boards on your ship—
  will spill into the sea.
  The merchants* and soldiers in your city
    will all sink into the sea.
  That will happen on the day
    that you are destroyed!

28 "'You send your merchants to faraway
    places.
  Those places will shake with fear when
    they hear your pilots' cry!
29 Your whole crew will jump ship.
  The sailors and pilots will jump ship and
    swim to the shore.
30 They will be very sad about you.
  They will cry, throw dust on their
    heads, and roll in ashes.
31 They will shave their heads for you.
  They will put on sackcloth.*
  They will cry for you like someone crying
    for someone who died.

32 "'And in their loud crying they will sing
this sad song about you:

*a*27:6 *deck* The floor of a ship.
*b*27:7 *Cyprus* Literally, "Elishah." This might be the
area near Enkomi, Cyprus, or it might be the Greek
islands.
*c*27:9 *Byblos* Literally, "Gebal."
*d*27:9 *caulking* Often a mixture of tar and rope that
was put between the boards to make a ship water-
tight so that it would not leak. Also in verse 27.
*e*27:14 *nation* Literally, "house." This might mean
the royal family of that country.
*f*27:15 *Rhodes* Or "Dedan." See verse 20.

*g*27:17 *balm* An ointment from some kinds of trees
and plants. It is used as medicine.

"'No one is like Tyre!
  Tyre is destroyed, in the middle of the
    sea!
33 Your merchants sailed across the seas.
  You satisfied many people with your great
    wealth and the things you sold.
  You made the kings of the earth rich!
34 But now you are broken by the seas
  and by the deep waters.
  All the things you sell
  and all your people have fallen.
35 All the people living on the coast
  are shocked about you.
  Their kings are terrified.
  Their faces show their shock.
36 The merchants in other nations
  whistle about you.
  What happened to you will frighten
    people,
  because you were destroyed.
  You are gone forever.'"

Tyre Thinks It Is Like a God

28 ¹The word of the LORD came to me. He
said, ²"Son of man,ᵃ say to the ruler of
Tyre, 'This is what the Lord GOD says:

"'You are very proud!
  And you say, "I am a god!
  I sit on the seat of gods
  in the middle of the seas."

"'But you are a man and not God!
  You only think you are a god.
3 You think you are wiser than Danielᵇ
  and no secret is hidden from you.
4 Through your wisdom and understanding
    you have gotten riches for yourself.
  And you put gold and silver in your
    treasuries.
5 Through your great wisdom and trade,
    you have made your riches grow.
  And now you are proud because of those
    riches.

6"'So this is what the Lord GOD says:
  Tyre, you thought you were like a god.
7 I will bring strangers to fight against you.
  They are most terrible among the
    nations!
  They will pull out their swords
    and use them against the beautiful
      things your wisdom brought you.
  They will ruin your glory.
8 They will bring you down to the grave.
  You will be like a sailor who died at sea.
9 That person will kill you.
  Will you still say, "I am a god"?
  No, he will have you in his power!

You will see that you are a man, not
    God!
10 Strangers will treat you like a foreignerᶜ
  and kill you,
  because I gave the command!'"
This is what the Lord GOD said.

¹¹The word of the LORD came to me. He
said, ¹²"Son of man, sing this sad song about
the king of Tyre. Say to him, 'This is what the
Lord GOD says:

"'You were the perfect man—
  so full of wisdom and perfectly
    handsome.
13 You were in Eden, the garden of God.
  You had every precious stone—
  rubies, topaz, and diamonds,
  beryls, onyx, and jasper,
  sapphires, turquoise, and emeralds.
  And each of these stones was set in gold.
  You were given this beauty on the day
    you were created.
  God made you strong.
14 You were one of the chosen Cherubs*
    who spread your wings over my throne.
  I put you on the holy mountain of God.
  You walked among the jewels that
    sparkled like fire.
15 You were good and honest when I created
    you,
  but then you became evil.
16 Your business brought you many riches.
  But they also put cruelty inside you, and
    you sinned.
  So I treated you like something unclean
    and threw you off the mountain of God.
  You were one of the chosen Cherubs
    who spread your wings over my throne.
  But I forced you to leave the jewels
    that sparkled like fire.
17 Your beauty made you proud.
  Your glory ruined your wisdom.
  So I threw you down to the ground,
    and now other kings stare at you.
18 You did many wrong things.
  You were a very crooked merchant.*
  In this way, you made the holy places
    unclean.
  So I brought fire from inside you.
  It burned you!
  You burned to ashes on the ground.
  Now everyone can see your shame.

19"'All the people in other nations
    were shocked about what happened to
      you.
  What happened to you will make people
    very afraid.
  You are finished!'"

ᵃ**28:2** *Son of man* This was usually just a way of saying "a person" or "a human being." Here, it is a way of
addressing Ezekiel. Also in verses 12, 21.
ᵇ**28:3** *Daniel* A wise man from ancient times. This
might be Daniel from the Bible, or the Danel mentioned in the writings from Ras Shamra.

ᶜ**28:10** *foreigner* Literally, "uncircumcised." This
means a person who did not share in the agreement God made with Israel. See "circumcise, circumcision" in the Word List.

The Message Against Sidon

²⁰The word of the LORD came to me. He said, ²¹"Son of man, look toward Sidon and speak for me against that place. ²²Say, 'This is what the Lord GOD says:

"'I am against you, Sidon!
  Your people will learn to respect me.
I will punish Sidon.
  Then people will know that I am the
    LORD.
Then they will learn that I am holy, and
    they will treat me that way.
²³ I will send disease and death to Sidon,
  and many people inside the city will
    die.
Soldiers outside the city will kill many
    people.
Then people will know that I am the
    LORD!'"

The Nations Will Stop Laughing at Israel

²⁴"'Then the surrounding nations that hate Israel will no longer be like stinging nettles*a* and painful thorns. And they will know that I am the Lord GOD.'"

²⁵This is what the Lord GOD said: "I scattered the people of Israel among other nations, but I will gather the family of Israel together again. Then the nations will know that I am holy, and they will treat me that way. At that time the people of Israel will live in their land—I gave that land to my servant Jacob.* ²⁶They will live safely in the land. They will build houses and plant vineyards. I will punish the nations around them that hated them. Then the people of Israel will live in safety, and they will know that I am the LORD their God."

The Message Against Egypt

29 ¹On the twelfth day of the tenth month of the tenth year of exile,*b* the word of the Lord GOD came to me. He said, ²"Son of man,*c* look toward Pharaoh, king of Egypt. Speak for me against him and Egypt. ³Say, 'This is what the Lord GOD says:

"'I am against you, Pharaoh, king of Egypt.
  You are the great monster*d* lying beside
    the Nile River.
  You say, "This is my river!
    I made this river!"

⁴⁻⁵"'But I will put hooks in your jaws.
  The fish in the Nile River will stick to
    your scales.
I will pull you and your fish up
  out of your rivers and onto the dry land.
You will fall on the ground,
  and no one will pick you up or bury
    you.
I will give you to the wild animals and
    birds.
  You will be their food.
⁶ Then all the people living in Egypt
  will know that I am the LORD!

"'Why will I do these things?
  Because the people of Israel leaned on
    Egypt for support,
  but Egypt was only a weak blade of
    grass.
⁷ The people of Israel leaned on Egypt for
    support,
  but Egypt only pierced their hands and
    shoulder.
They leaned on you for support,
  but you broke and twisted their back.'"

⁸ So this is what the Lord GOD says:
"I will bring a sword against you.
  I will destroy all your people and
    animals.
⁹ Egypt will be empty and destroyed.
  Then they will know that I am the
    LORD."

God said, "Why will I do these things? Because you said, 'This is my river. I made this river.' ¹⁰So I am against you. I am against the many branches of your Nile River. I will destroy Egypt completely. The cities will be empty from Migdol to Aswan and as far as the border of Ethiopia. ¹¹No person or animal will pass through Egypt. Nothing will pass through or settle there for 40 years. ¹²I will destroy Egypt. The cities will be in ruins for 40 years! I will scatter the Egyptians among the nations. I will make them strangers*e* in foreign lands."

¹³This is what the Lord GOD says: "I will scatter the people of Egypt among many nations. But at the end of 40 years, I will gather those people together again. ¹⁴I will bring back the Egyptian captives. I will bring back the Egyptians to the land of Pathros, to the land where they were born. But their kingdom will not be important. ¹⁵It will be the least important kingdom. It will never again lift itself above the other nations. I will make them so small that they will not rule over the nations. ¹⁶And the family of Israel will never again depend on Egypt. The Israelites will remember their sin—they will remember that they turned to Egypt for help and not to God, and they will know that I am the Lord GOD."

---

*a***28:24** *nettles* Plants covered with stinging hairs.
*b***29:1** *tenth year of exile* This was the winter of 587 B.C.
*c***29:2** *Son of man* This was usually just a way of saying "a person" or "a human being." Here, it is a way of addressing Ezekiel. Also in verse 18.
*d***29:3** *great monster* There were ancient stories about a sea monster that fought against God. The prophets called Egypt that sea monster many times. But here, this might mean the crocodiles that rest on the banks of the Nile River.

*e***29:12** *I will ... strangers* Or "I will scatter them ...."

Babylon Will Get Egypt

¹⁷On the first day of the first month in the twenty-seventh year of exile,ᵃ the word of the LORD came to me. He said, ¹⁸"Son of man, King Nebuchadnezzar of Babylon made his army fight hard against Tyre. They shaved every soldier's head. Every shoulder was rubbed bare from carrying heavy loads. Nebuchadnezzar and his army worked hard to defeat Tyre, but they got nothing from all that hard work." ¹⁹So this is what the Lord GOD says: "I will give Egypt to King Nebuchadnezzar of Babylon, and he will carry away the people. He will take the many valuable things in Egypt to pay his army. ²⁰I will give Egypt to Nebuchadnezzar as a reward for the hard work he did for me." This is what the Lord GOD said!

²¹"On that day I will make the family of Israel strong. So Ezekiel, I will let you speak to them. Then they will know that I am the LORD."

The Army of Babylon Will Attack Egypt

30 ¹The word of the LORD came to me again. He said, ²"Son of man,ᵇ speak for me. Say, 'This is what the Lord GOD says:

"'Cry and say,
    "A terrible day is coming."
³ That day is near!
    Yes, the LORD's day for judging is near.
    It will be a cloudy day,
        the time for judging the nations.
⁴ A sword will come against Egypt!
    People in Ethiopia will shake with fear,
        when Egypt falls.
    The army of Babylon will take the
        Egyptians as prisoners.
    Egypt's foundations will be torn down.

⁵"'Many people made peace agreements with Egypt. But all those people from Ethiopia, Put, Lud, all Arabia, Libya, and the people of Israelᶜ will be destroyed!

⁶"'This is what the Lord GOD says:
    Those who support Egypt will fall!
        The pride in her power will end.
    The people in Egypt will be killed in battle,
        all the way from Migdol to Aswan.
    This is what the Lord GOD said!
⁷ Egypt will join the other countries
        that were destroyed.
    Its cities will be among those
        that are in ruins.

---

⁸ I will start a fire in Egypt,
    and all her helpers will be destroyed.
    Then they will know that I am the LORD!

⁹"'At that time I will send out messengers. They will go in ships to carry the bad news to Ethiopia. Ethiopia now feels safe, but the people of Ethiopia will shake with fear when Egypt is punished. That time is coming!'"

¹⁰ This is what the Lord GOD says:
    "I will use the king of Babylon.
    I will use Nebuchadnezzar to destroy
        the people of Egypt.
¹¹ Nebuchadnezzar and his people
        are the most terrible of the nations,
    and I will bring them to destroy Egypt.
    They will pull out their swords against
        Egypt.
    They will fill the land with dead bodies.
¹² I will make the Nile River become dry
        land.
    Then I will sell the dry land to evil
        people.
    I will use strangers to make that land
        empty.
    I, the LORD, have spoken!"

The Idols of Egypt Will Be Destroyed

¹³ This is what the Lord GOD says:
    "I will also destroy the idols* in Egypt.
    I will take the statues away from
        Memphis.
    There will no longer be a leader in the
        land of Egypt.
    I will put fear there instead.
¹⁴ I will make Pathros empty.
    I will start a fire in Zoan.
    I will punish Thebes.
¹⁵ I will pour out my anger against Pelusium,
        the fortress* of Egypt!
    I will destroy the people of Thebes.
¹⁶ I will start a fire in Egypt;
        the city of Pelusium will ache with fear.
    The soldiers will break into the city of
        Thebes,
    and Memphis will have new troubles
        every day.
¹⁷ The young men of Heliopolis and
        Bubastisᵈ will die in battle,
    and the women will be taken away as
        prisoners.
¹⁸ It will be a dark day in Tahpanhes when I
        break Egypt's control.ᵉ
    Her proud power will be finished!
    A cloud will cover Egypt,
    and her daughters will be taken away as
        prisoners.
¹⁹ So I will punish Egypt.
    Then they will know that I am the
        LORD!"

ᵃ**29:17** *twenty-seventh year of exile* This was in the spring of 571 B.C.
ᵇ**30:2** *Son of man* This was usually just a way of saying "a person" or "a human being." Here, it is a way of addressing Ezekiel. Also in verse 21.
ᶜ**30:5** *people of Israel* Literally, "sons of the agreement." This might mean "all the people who made peace agreements with Egypt," or it might mean "Israel, the people who made the agreement with God."

ᵈ**30:17** *Heliopolis and Bubastis* Hebrew, "On and Pi Beseth," cities in Egypt.
ᵉ**30:18** *control* Literally, "yoke."

Egypt Will Become Weak Forever

²⁰On the seventh day of the first month of the eleventh year of exile,ᵃ the word of the LORD came to me. He said, ²¹"Son of man, I have broken the arm of Pharaoh, king of Egypt. No one will wrap his arm with a bandage. It will not heal, so his arm will not be strong enough to hold a sword."

²²This is what the Lord GOD says: "I am against Pharaoh, king of Egypt. I will break both his arms, the strong arm and the arm that is already broken. I will make the sword fall from his hand. ²³I will scatter the Egyptians among the nations. ²⁴I will make the arms of the king of Babylon strong. I will put my sword in his hand, but I will break the arms of Pharaoh. Then Pharaoh will cry out in pain, the kind of cry that a dying man makes. ²⁵So I will make the arms of the king of Babylon strong, but the arms of Pharaoh will fall. Then they will know that I am the LORD.

"I will put my sword in the hand of the king of Babylon. Then he will stretch the sword out against the land of Egypt. ²⁶I will scatter the Egyptians among the nations. Then they will know that I am the LORD!"

Assyria Is Like a Cedar Tree

31 ¹On the first day of the third month in the eleventh year of exile, the word of the LORD came to me. He said, ²"Son of man,ᵇ say this to Pharaoh, king of Egypt, and to his people:

"'You are so great!
　　Who can I compare you to?
³ Assyria was a cedar tree in Lebanon
　　with beautiful branches,
　　with forest shade,
　　and very tall.
　　Its top was among the clouds!
⁴ The water made the tree grow.
　　The deep river made the tree tall.
　　Rivers flowed around the place
　　　where the tree was planted.
　　Only small streams flowed from that tree
　　　to all the other trees of the field.
⁵ So that tree was taller than all the other
　　　trees of the field,
　　and it grew many branches.
　　There was plenty of water,
　　　so the tree branches spread out.
⁶ All the birds of the sky made their nests
　　　in the branches of that tree,
　　and all the animals of the field gave birth
　　　under the branches of that tree.
　　All the great nations lived
　　　under the shade of that tree.
⁷ The tree was very beautiful.
　　It was so large!

It had such long branches.
　　Its roots had plenty of water.
⁸ Even the cedar trees in God's garden
　　were not as big as this tree.
　　Cypress trees did not have as many
　　　branches.
　　Plane trees did not have such branches.
　　No tree in God's garden
　　　was as beautiful as this tree.
⁹ I gave it many branches
　　and made it beautiful.
　　And all the trees in Eden, God's garden,
　　　were jealous!'"

¹⁰So this is what the Lord GOD says: "That tree grew tall. Its top reached up to the clouds. It grew so big that it became proud! ¹¹So I let a powerful king have that tree. That ruler punished the tree for the bad things it did. I took that tree out of my garden. ¹²Strangers—the most terrible people in the world—cut it down and scattered its branches on the mountains and in the valleys. Its broken limbs drifted down the rivers flowing through that land. There was no more shadow under that tree, so all the people left. ¹³Now birds live in that fallen tree. Wild animals walk over its fallen branches.

¹⁴"Now, none of the trees by that water will be proud. They will not try to reach the clouds. None of the strong trees that drink that water will brag about being tall, because all of them must die. They will all go down into the world below, to Sheol,* the place of death. They will join the other people who died and went down into that deep hole."

¹⁵This is what the Lord GOD says: "I made the people cry on the day that tree went down to Sheol. I covered him with the deep ocean. I stopped its rivers and all the water stopped flowing. I made Lebanon mourn* for it. All the trees of the field became sick with sadness for that big tree. ¹⁶I made the tree fall—and the nations shook with fear at the sound of the falling tree. I sent the tree down to the place of death to join the other people who had gone down into that deep hole. In the past, all the trees of Eden, the best of Lebanon, drank that water. The trees were comforted in the world below. ¹⁷Yes, those trees also went down with the big tree to the place of death. They joined the people who were killed in battle. That big tree made the other trees strong. Those trees had lived under the big tree's shadow among the nations.

¹⁸"Egypt, there were many big and powerful trees in Eden. Which of those trees should I compare you to? They all went down into the world below! And you, too, will join those foreignersᶜ in that place of death. You will lie there among the people killed in battle.

ᵃ**30:20** *eleventh year of exile* This was the summer of 587 B.C. Also in 31:1.
ᵇ**31:2** *Son of man* This was usually just a way of saying "a person" or "a human being." Here, it is a way of addressing Ezekiel.

ᶜ**31:18** *foreigners* Literally, "uncircumcised." This means people who did not share in the agreement God made with Israel. See "circumcise, circumcision" in the Word List.

"Yes, that will happen to Pharaoh and to the crowds of people with him!" This is what the Lord God said.

Pharaoh: a Lion or a Dragon?

32 ¹On the first day of the twelfth month in the twelfth year of exile,ᵃ the word of the Lord came to me. He said, ²"Son of man,ᵇ sing this sad song about Pharaoh, king of Egypt. Say to him:

"'You thought you were like a powerful
　　young lion walking proud among the
　　nations.
But really, you are like a dragonᶜ in the
　　lakes.
You push your way through the streams.
You make the water muddy with your
　　feet
and stir up the rivers of Egypt.'"

³This is what the Lord God says:

"I have gathered many people together.
　　Now I will throw my net over you.
　　Then those people will pull you in.
⁴ Then I will drop you on the dry ground.
　　I will throw you down in the field.
I will let all the birds come and eat you.
I will let wild animals from every place
　　come and eat you until they are full.
⁵ I will scatter your body on the mountains.
　　I will fill the valleys with your dead
　　body.
⁶ I will pour your blood on the mountains,
　　and it will soak down into the ground.
　　The rivers will be full of you.
⁷ I will make you disappear.
I will cover the sky and make the stars
　　dark.
I will cover the sun with a cloud, and
　　the moon will not shine.
⁸ I will darken the lights in the sky over
　　you.
I will make your whole country dark."
This is what the Lord God said.

⁹"I will make many people sad and upset when I bring an enemy to destroy you. Nations you don't even know will be upset. ¹⁰I will make many people shocked about you. Their kings will be terrified of you, when I swing my sword before them. They will shake with fear on the day you fall. Each king will be afraid for his own life."

¹¹That will happen because of what the Lord God said: "The sword of the king of Babylon will come to fight against you. ¹²I will use those soldiers to kill your people in battle. They come from the most terrible of the nations. They will destroy the things Egypt is proud of. The people of Egypt will be destroyed. ¹³There are many animals by the rivers in Egypt. I will also destroy all those animals. People will not make the waters muddy with their feet anymore. The hoofs of cattle will not make the water muddy anymore. ¹⁴So I will make the water in Egypt calm. I will cause their rivers to run slowly—they will be slick like oil." This is what the Lord God said. ¹⁵"I will make the land of Egypt empty. That land will lose everything. I will punish all the people living in Egypt. Then they will know that I am the Lord God!

¹⁶"This is a sad song that people will sing for Egypt. The daughters in other nations will sing this sad song. They will sing it as a sad song about Egypt and all its people." This is what the Lord God said.

Egypt to Be Destroyed

¹⁷On the fifteenth day of that month in the twelfth year of exile, the word of the Lord came to me. He said, ¹⁸"Son of man, cry for the people of Egypt. Lead Egypt and the daughters from powerful nations to the grave. Lead them to the world below where they will be with the other people who went down into that deep hole. ¹⁹"Egypt, you are no better than anyone else! Go down to the place of death. Go lie down with those foreigners.ᵈ

²⁰"Egypt will go to be with all the other men who were killed in battle. The enemy has pulled her and all her people away. ²¹"Strong and powerful men were killed in battle. Those foreigners went down to the place of death. And from that place, those who were killed will speak to Egypt and his helpers.

²²⁻²³"Assyria* and all its army are there in the place of death. Their graves are deep down in that deep hole. All the Assyrian soldiers were killed in battle, and their graves are all around his grave. When they were alive, they made people afraid, but they were all killed in battle.

²⁴"Elam is there and all its army is around her grave. All of them were killed in battle. Those foreigners went deep down into the ground. When they were alive, they made people afraid. But they carried their shame with them down to that deep hole. ²⁵They have made a bed for Elam and all its soldiers who were killed in battle. Elam's army is all around its grave. All those foreigners were

ᵃ**32:1** *twelfth year of exile* This was early spring, 585 B.C. Also in verse 17.
ᵇ**32:2** *Son of man* This was usually just a way of saying "a person" or "a human being." Here, it is a way of addressing Ezekiel. Also in verse 18.
ᶜ**32:2** *dragon* This might be a crocodile or a giant sea creature. The giant sea creature represented the power of the sea, and the Nile River made Egypt a powerful nation.
ᵈ**32:19** *foreigners* Literally, "uncircumcised." This means people who did not share in the agreement God made with Israel. See "circumcise, circumcision" in the Word List.

killed in battle. When they were alive, they scared people. But they carried their shame with them down into that deep hole. They were put with all the other people who were killed.

²⁶"Meshech, Tubal, and all their armies are there. Their graves are around it. All those foreigners were killed in battle. When they were alive, they made people afraid. ²⁷But now they are lying down by the powerful men who died long, long ago! They were buried with their weapons of war. Their swords will be laid under their heads. But their sins are on their bones, because when they were alive, they scared people.

²⁸"Egypt, you also will be destroyed, and you will lie down by those foreigners. You will lie with the other soldiers who were killed in battle.

²⁹"Edom is there also. His kings and other leaders are there with him. They were powerful soldiers, but now they lie with the other men who were killed in battle. They are lying there with those foreigners. They are there with the other people who went down into that deep hole.

³⁰"The rulers from the north are there, all of them, and there are all the soldiers from Sidon. Their strength scared people, but they are embarrassed. Those foreigners lie there with the other men who were killed in battle. They carried their shame with them down into that deep hole.

³¹"Yes, Pharaoh and all his army will be killed in battle. Pharaoh will be comforted when he sees his many men and all the others who went down into the place of death." This is what the Lord GOD said.

³²"People were afraid of Pharaoh when he was alive, but he will lie down next to those foreigners. Pharaoh and his army will lie down with all the other soldiers who were killed in battle." This is what the Lord GOD said.

God Chooses Ezekiel to Be a Watchman

33 ¹The word of the LORD came to me. He said, ²"Son of man,ᵃ speak to your people. Say to them, 'Whenever I bring enemy soldiers to fight against a country, the people choose someone to be a watchman.* ³If this guard sees enemy soldiers coming, he blows the trumpet and warns the people. ⁴If people hear the warning but ignore it, the enemy will capture them and take them away as prisoners. They will be responsible for their own death. ⁵They heard the trumpet, but they ignored the warning. So they are responsible for their own deaths. If they had paid attention to the warning, they could have saved their own lives.

⁶"'But what if the guard sees the enemy soldiers coming, but does not blow the trumpet? Since he doesn't warn the people, the enemy will capture them and take them away as prisoners. They will be taken away because they sinned, but the guard will also be responsible for their deaths.'

⁷"Now, son of man, I am choosing you to be a watchman for the family of Israel. If you hear a message from my mouth, you must warn the people for me. ⁸I might say to you, 'These evil people will die.' Then you must go warn them for me. If you don't warn them and tell them to change their lives, those evil people will die because they sinned. But I will make you responsible for their deaths. ⁹But if you do warn the evil people to change their lives and stop sinning, and if they refuse to stop, they will die because they sinned. But you have saved your life.

God Does Not Want to Destroy People

¹⁰"So, son of man, speak to the family of Israel for me. They might say, 'We have sinned and broken the law. Our sins are too heavy to bear. We rot away because of them. What can we do to live?'

¹¹"You must say to them, 'The Lord GOD says: By my life, I swear that I don't enjoy seeing people die—not even evil people! I don't want them to die. I want them to come back to me. I want them to change their lives so that they can really live. So come back to me! Stop doing bad things! Why must you die, family of Israel?'

¹²"Son of man, tell your people: 'The good things people did in the past will not save them if they become bad and begin to sin. In the same way the bad things people did in the past will not destroy them if they turn from their evil. So remember, the good things people did in the past will not save them if they begin to sin.'

¹³"Maybe I will tell good people that they will live. But maybe those good people will begin to think that the good things they did in the past will save them. So they might begin to do bad things, but I will not remember the good things they did in the past! No, they will die because of the bad things they begin to do.

¹⁴"Or maybe I will tell some evil people that they will die. But they might change their lives, stop sinning, and begin to live right. They might become good and fair. ¹⁵They might give back the things they took when they loaned money. They might pay for the things they stole. They might begin to follow the laws that give life and stop doing bad things. Then they will surely live. They will not die. ¹⁶I will not remember the bad things they did in the past, because now they live right and are fair. So they will live!

¹⁷"But your people say, 'That's not fair! The Lord cannot be like that!'

ᵃ**33:2 Son of man** This was usually just a way of saying "a person" or "a human being." Here, it is a way of addressing Ezekiel. Also in verses 7, 10, 12, 24, 30.

"But they are the people who are not fair! They are the people who must change! [18]If good people stop doing good and begin to sin, they will die because of their sins. [19]And if evil people stop doing wrong and start living right and being fair, they will live. [20]You still say that I am not fair, but I am telling you the truth. Family of Israel, everyone will be judged for what they do!"

Jerusalem Has Been Taken

[21]On the fifth day of the tenth month in the twelfth year of exile,[a] a person who had escaped from the battle in Jerusalem came to me and said, "The city has been taken!" [22]The power of the Lord GOD had come on me the evening before that person came to me so that I could speak. But when that person came to me, the LORD opened my mouth and let me speak again. [23]Then the word of the LORD came to me. He said, [24]"Son of man, there are Israelites who live in the ruined cities in Israel. They are saying, 'Abraham was only one man, and God gave him all this land. Now, we are many people, so surely this land belongs to us! It is our land!' [25]"You must tell them that this is what the Lord GOD says: 'You eat meat with the blood still in it. You look to your idols* for help. You murder people, so why should I give you this land? [26]You depend on your own sword. Each of you does terrible things. Each of you commits sexual sins with his neighbor's wife, so you cannot have the land!' [27]"You must tell them that this is what the Lord GOD says: "By my life, I promise that the people living in the ruined cities will be killed with a sword! If any people are out in the country, I will let animals kill and eat them. If people are hiding in the fortresses* and the caves, they will die from disease. [28]I will make that place an empty wasteland. That country will lose all the things it was proud of. The mountains of Israel will become empty. No one will pass through that place. [29]The people have done many terrible things, so I will make that place an empty wasteland. Then they will know that I am the LORD." [30]"'And now about you, son of man. Your people lean against the walls and stand in their doorways talking about you. They tell each other, "Come on, let's go hear what the LORD says." [31]So they come to you as if they were my people. They sit in front of you as if they were my people. They hear your words, but they will not do the things you say. They only want to do what feels good. They only want to cheat people and make more money. [32]"'You are nothing to these people but a singer singing love songs. You have a good voice. You play your instrument well. They listen to your words, but they will not do

what you say. [33]But the things you sing about really will happen, and then the people will know that there was a prophet living among them.'"

Israel Is Like a Flock of Sheep

34 [1]The word of the LORD came to me. He said, [2]"Son of man,[b] speak against the shepherds of Israel for me. Speak to them for me. Tell them that this is what the Lord GOD says: 'You shepherds of Israel have only been feeding yourselves. It will be very bad for you! Why don't you shepherds feed the flock? [3]You eat the fat sheep and use their wool to make clothes for yourselves. You kill the fat sheep, but you don't feed the flock. [4]You have not made the weak strong. You have not cared for the sick sheep. You have not put bandages on the sheep that were hurt. Some of the sheep wandered away, and you did not go get them and bring them back. You did not go to look for the lost sheep. No, you were cruel and severe—that's the way you tried to lead the sheep!

[5]"'And now the sheep are scattered because there was no shepherd. They became food for every wild animal, so they were scattered. [6]My flock wandered over all the mountains and on every high hill. My flock was scattered over all the face of the earth. There was no one to search or to look for them.'"

[7]So, you shepherds, listen to the word of the LORD. The Lord GOD says, [8]"I swear that wild animals will catch my sheep and my people will become food for all those animals, because they did not have any real shepherds. My shepherds did not look out for my flock. They did not feed my flock. No, they only killed the sheep and fed themselves!"

[9]So, you shepherds, listen to the word of the LORD! [10]The LORD says, "I am against the shepherds. I will demand my sheep from them. I will fire them. They will not be my shepherds anymore. Then the shepherds will not be able to feed themselves, and I will save my flock from their mouths. Then my sheep will not be food for them."

[11]The Lord GOD says, "I myself will be their Shepherd. I will search for my sheep and take care of them. [12]If a shepherd is with his sheep when they begin to wander away, he will go searching for them. In the same way I will search for my sheep. I will save them and bring them back from all the places where they were scattered on that dark and cloudy day. [13]I will bring them back from those nations. I will gather them from those countries and bring them back to their own land. I will feed them on the mountains of Israel, by the streams, and in all the places where people live. [14]I will lead them to grassy fields.

---

[a]**33:21** *twelfth year of exile* This was the winter of 586 B.C.

[b]**34:2** *Son of man* This was usually just a way of saying "a person" or "a human being." Here, it is a way of addressing Ezekiel.

They will go to the place high on the mountains of Israel and lie down on good ground and eat the grass. They will eat in rich grassland on the mountains of Israel. 15Yes, I will feed my flock, and I will lead them to a place of rest." This is what the Lord God said.

16"I will search for the lost sheep. I will bring back the sheep that were scattered and put bandages on the sheep that were hurt. I will make the weak sheep strong, but I will destroy the fat and powerful shepherds. I will feed them the punishment they deserve."

17This is what the Lord God says: "And you, my flock, I will judge between one sheep and another. I will judge between the male sheep and the male goats. 18You can eat the grass growing on the good land. So why do you also crush the grass that other sheep want to eat? You can drink plenty of clear water. So why do you also stir the water that other sheep want to drink? 19My flock must eat the grass you crushed with your feet, and they must drink the water you stir with your feet!"

20So the Lord God says to them: "I myself will judge between the fat sheep and the thin sheep! 21You push with your side and shoulder. You knock down all the weak sheep with your horns. You push until you have forced them away, 22so I will save my flock. They will not be caught by wild animals anymore. I will judge between one sheep and another. 23Then I will put one shepherd over them, my servant David. He will feed them and be their shepherd. 24Then I, the Lord God, will be their God, and my servant David will be the ruler living among them. I, the Lord, have spoken.

25"And I will make a peace agreement with my sheep. I will take harmful animals away from the land. Then the sheep can be safe in the desert and sleep in the woods. 26I will bless the sheep and the places around my hill. I will cause the rains to fall at the right time and will shower them with blessings. 27And the trees growing in the field will produce their fruit. The earth will give its harvest, so the sheep will be safe on their land. I will break the yokes* on them and save them from the power of the people who made them slaves. Then they will know that I am the Lord. 28They will not be caught like an animal by the nations anymore. Those animals will not eat them anymore. No, they will live safely. No one will make them afraid. 29I will give them some land that will make a good garden. Then they will not suffer from hunger in that land or suffer the insults from the nations anymore. 30Then they will know that I am the Lord their God. The family of Israel will know that I am with them and that they are my people." This is what the Lord God said!

31"You are my sheep, the sheep of my grassland. You are only human beings, and I am your God." This is what the Lord God said.

The Message Against Edom

35 1The word of the Lord came to me. He said, 2"Son of man,*a* look toward Mount Seir and speak against it for me. 3Say to it, 'This is what the Lord God says:

"'I am against you, Mount Seir!
  I will punish you and make you an
    empty wasteland.
4 I will destroy your cities,
  and you will become empty.
  Then you will know that I am the Lord.
5 Why? Because you have always been
    against my people.
  You used your sword against Israel
    at the time of their trouble,
    at the time of their final punishment.'"

6So the Lord God says, "But I promise by my own life that I will let death have you. Death will chase you. You did not hate killing people, so death will chase you. 7I will make Mount Seir an empty ruin. I will kill everyone who enters or leaves that city. 8I will cover its mountains with those who are killed. There will be dead bodies all over your hills, in your valleys, and in all your ravines. 9I will make you empty forever. No one will live in your cities. Then you will know that I am the Lord."

10You said, "These two nations and countries, Israel and Judah, will be mine. We will take them for our own."

But the Lord is there! 11And the Lord God says, "You were jealous of my people. You were angry and hateful to them. So by my life, I swear that I will punish you the same way you hurt them! I will punish you and let my people know that I am with them. 12And then you, too, will know that I have heard all your insults. You said many bad things against the mountain of Israel. You said, 'Israel has been destroyed! We will chew them up like food!' 13And you were proud and said things against me. You spoke too many times, and I have heard every word you said. Yes, I heard you."

14This is what the Lord God says: "All the earth will be happy when I destroy you. 15You were happy when the country of Israel was destroyed. I will treat you the same way. Mount Seir and the whole country of Edom will be destroyed. Then you will know that I am the Lord."

The Land of Israel Will Be Rebuilt

36 1"Son of man,*b* speak to the mountains of Israel for me. Tell them to listen to the word of the Lord! 2Tell them that this is

a35:2 Son of man This was usually just a way of saying "a person" or "a human being." Here, it is a way of addressing Ezekiel.
b36:1 Son of man This was usually just a way of saying "a person" or "a human being." Here, it is a way of addressing Ezekiel. Also in verse 17.

what the Lord God says: 'The enemy said bad things against you. They said, Hurray! Now the ancient mountains[a] will be ours!'

3"So speak to the mountains of Israel for me. Tell them that this is what the Lord God says: 'The enemy destroyed your cities and attacked you from every direction. They did this so that you would belong to the other nations. Then people talked and whispered about you.'"

4So, mountains of Israel, listen to the word of the Lord God! This is what the Lord God says to the mountains, hills, streams, valleys, empty ruins, and abandoned cities that have been looted and laughed at by the other nations around them. 5The Lord God says, "I swear, I will let my strong feelings speak for me! I will let Edom and the other nations feel my anger. They took my land for themselves. They really had a good time when they showed how much they hated this land. They took the land for themselves, just so they could destroy it."

6"So say these things about the land of Israel. Speak to the mountains and to the hills, to the streams, and to the valleys. Tell them that this is what the Lord God says: 'I will let my strong feelings and anger speak for me, because you had to suffer the insults from those nations.'"

7So this is what the Lord God says: "I am the one making this promise! I swear that the nations around you will have to suffer for those insults.

8"But mountains of Israel, you will grow new trees and produce fruit for my people Israel. My people will soon come back. 9I am with you, and I will help you. People will till your soil and plant seeds in you. 10There will be many people living on you. The whole family of Israel—all of them—will live there. The cities will have people living in them. The destroyed places will be rebuilt. 11I will give you many people and animals, and they will grow and have many children. I will bring people to live on you as in the past. I will make it better for you than before. Then you will know that I am the Lord. 12Yes, I will lead many people—my people, Israel—to your land. You will be their property, and you will not take away their children again."

13This is what the Lord God says: "Land of Israel, people say bad things to you. They say you destroyed your people. They say you took the children away from your people. 14But you will not destroy people anymore or take away their children again." This is what the Lord God said. 15"I will not let those other nations insult you anymore. You will not be hurt by them anymore. You will not take the children away from your people again." This is what the Lord God said.

The Lord Will Protect His Name

16Then the word of the Lord came to me. He said, 17"Son of man, the family of Israel lived in their own country, but they made that land filthy by the bad things they did. To me, they were like a woman who becomes unclean* because of her monthly time of bleeding. 18They spilled blood on the ground when they murdered people in the land. They made the land filthy with their idols,* so I showed them how angry I was. 19I scattered them among the nations and spread them through all the lands. I gave them the punishment they deserved for the bad things they did. 20But even in those other nations, they ruined my good name. How? Those nations said, 'These are the Lord's people, but they left his land.'

21"The people of Israel ruined my holy name wherever they went, and I felt sorry for my name. 22So tell the family of Israel that this is what the Lord God says: 'Family of Israel, you ruined my holy name in the places where you went. I am going to do something to stop this. I will not do it for your sake, Israel. I will do it for my holy name. 23I will show the nations how holy my great name really is. You ruined my good name in those nations! But I will show you that I am holy. I will make you respect my name, and then those nations will know that I am the Lord.'" This is what the Lord God said.

24"I will take you out of those nations, gather you together, and bring you back to your own land. 25Then I will sprinkle pure water on you and make you pure. I will wash away all your filth, the filth from those nasty idols, and I will make you pure. 26I will also put a new spirit in you to change your way of thinking. I will take out the heart of stone from your body and give you a tender, human heart. 27I will put my Spirit inside you[b] and change you so that you will obey my laws. You will carefully obey my commands. 28Then you will live in the land that I gave to your ancestors.* You will be my people, and I will be your God. 29Also, I will save you and keep you from becoming unclean. I will command the grain to grow. I will not bring a famine* against you. 30I will give you large crops of fruit from your trees and the harvest from your fields so that you will never again feel the shame of being hungry in a foreign country. 31You will remember the bad things you did. You will remember that those things were not good. Then you will hate yourselves because of your sins and the terrible things you did."

32The Lord God says, "I want you to remember this: I am not doing these things for your

---

[a]36:2 mountains Literally, "high places," usually a reference to places of worship. See "high place" in the Word List.

[b]36:27 I will put my Spirit inside you Or "I will make my Spirit live among you."

good! ⌐I am doing them for my good name.⌐ Family of Israel, you should be ashamed and embarrassed about the way you lived!"

³³This is what the Lord God says: "On the day that I wash away your sins, I will bring people back to your cities. The ruined cities will be rebuilt. ³⁴People will begin again to work the land so when other people pass by they will not see ruins anymore. ³⁵They will say, 'In the past, this land was ruined, but now it is like the Garden of Eden. The cities were destroyed. They were ruined and empty, but now they are protected, and there are people living in them.'

³⁶"Then the nations that are still around you will know I am the Lord and that I rebuilt those places. I planted things in this land that was empty. I am the Lord. I said this, and I will make it happen!"

³⁷This is what the Lord God says: "I will also let the family of Israel come to me and ask me to do these things for them. I will make them grow and become many people. They will be like flocks of sheep. ³⁸During the special festivals, Jerusalem was filled with flocks of sheep and goats that had been made holy. In the same way the cities and ruined places will be filled with flocks of people. Then they will know that I am the Lord."

The Vision of the Dry Bones

37 ¹The Lord's power came on me. The Spirit*ᵃ* of the Lord carried me out of the city and put me down in the middle of the valley.*ᵇ* The valley was full of dead men's bones. ²There were many bones lying on the ground in the valley. The Lord made me walk all around among the bones. I saw the bones were very dry.

³Then the Lord God said to me, "Son of man,*ᶜ* can these bones come to life?"

I answered, "Lord God, only you know the answer to that question."

⁴The Lord God said to me, "Speak to these bones for me. Tell them, 'Dry bones, listen to the word of the Lord! ⁵This is what the Lord God says to you: I will cause breath*ᵈ* to come into you, and you will come to life! ⁶I will put sinew and muscles on you, and I will cover you with skin. Then I will put breath in you, and you will come back to life! Then you will know that I am the Lord God.'"

⁷So I spoke to the bones for the Lord, as he said. I was still speaking, when I heard the loud noise. The bones began to rattle, and bone joined together with bone! ⁸There before my eyes, I saw sinew and muscles

begin to cover the bones. Skin began to cover them, but there was no breath in them.

⁹Then the Lord God said to me, "Speak to the wind*ᵉ* for me. Son of man, speak to the wind for me. Tell the wind that this is what the Lord God says: 'Wind, come from every direction and breathe air into these dead bodies! Breathe into them and they will come to life again!'"

¹⁰So I spoke to the wind for the Lord, as he said, and the breath came into the dead bodies. They came to life and stood up. There were many men—a very large army!

¹¹Then the Lord God said to me, "Son of man, these bones are like the whole family of Israel. The people of Israel say, 'Our bones have dried up;*ᶠ* our hope is gone. We have been completely destroyed!' ¹²So speak to them for me. Tell them this is what the Lord God says: 'My people, I will open your graves and bring you up out of them! Then I will bring you to the land of Israel. ¹³My people, I will open your graves and bring you up out of your graves, and then you will know that I am the Lord. ¹⁴I will put my Spirit*ᵍ* in you, and you will come to life again. Then I will lead you back to your own land. Then you will know that I am the Lord. You will know that I said this and that I made it happen.'" This is what the Lord said.

Judah and Israel to Become One Again

¹⁵The word of the Lord came to me again. He said, ¹⁶"Son of man, get one stick and write this message on it: 'This stick belongs to Judah and his friends,*ʰ* the people of Israel.' Then take another stick and write on it, 'This stick of Ephraim belongs to Joseph and his friends, the people of Israel.' ¹⁷Then join the two sticks together. In your hand, they will be one stick.

¹⁸"Your people will ask you to explain what that means. ¹⁹Tell them that this is what the Lord God says: 'I will take the stick of Joseph, which is in the hand of Ephraim and his friends, the people of Israel. Then I will put that stick with the stick of Judah, and make them one stick. In my hand, they will become one stick!'

²⁰"Take the sticks that you wrote on and hold them in front of you. ²¹Tell the people that this is what the Lord God says: 'I will gather the people of Israel from among the nations. I will gather them from all around and bring them back to their own land. ²²I will make them one nation in their land among the mountains of Israel. There will be one king over them all. They will no longer be two nations. They will not be split into two

---

*ᵃ***37:1** *Spirit* Or "wind."
*ᵇ***37:1** *the valley* Possibly, Jezreel Valley, a fertile area where many battles were fought. It is often called simply "The Valley."
*ᶜ***37:3** *Son of man* This was usually just a way of saying "a person" or "a human being." Here, it is a way of addressing Ezekiel. Also in verses 9, 11, 16.
*ᵈ***37:5** *breath* Or "wind" or "a spirit."
*ᵉ***37:9** *wind* Or "breath" or "spirit." Also in verse 10.
*ᶠ***37:11** *bones … dried up* This is a way of saying, "We have lost our strength."
*ᵍ***37:14** *Spirit* Or "spirit" or "wind."
*ʰ***37:16** *friends* This is a wordplay. The Hebrew word is like the word meaning "joined together."

kingdoms anymore. 23And they will no longer continue to make themselves filthy with their idols* and horrible statues or with any of their other crimes. Instead, I will save them from all the places where they have sinned, and I will wash them and make them pure. They will be my people, and I will be their God.

24"'And my servant David will be the king over them. There will be only one shepherd over all of them. They will live by my rules and obey my laws. They will do the things I tell them. 25They will live on the land that I gave to my servant Jacob. Your ancestors* lived in that place, and my people will live there. They and their children and their grandchildren will live there forever. My servant David will be their leader forever. 26And I will make a peace agreement with them. This agreement will continue forever. I agree to give them their land. I agree to make them numerous and to put my holy place among them forever. 27My Holy Tent will be with them. Yes, I will be their God and they will be my people. 28The other nations will know that I am the LORD, and they will know that I make Israel my special people by putting my holy place there among them forever.'"

The Message Against Gog

38 1The word of the LORD came to me. He said, 2"Son of man,a look toward Gog in the land of Magog. He is the most important leader of the nations of Meshech and Tubal. Speak for me against Gog. 3Tell him that this is what the Lord GOD says: 'Gog, you are the most important leader of the nations of Meshech and Tubal, but I am against you. 4I will capture you and bring you back. I will bring back all the men in your army, all the horses, and horse soldiers. I will put hooks in your mouths, and I will bring all of you back. All the soldiers will be wearing their uniforms with all their shields and swords. 5Soldiers from Persia, Ethiopia, and Put will be with them. They will all be wearing their shields and helmets. 6There will also be Gomer with all its groups of soldiers, and there will be the nation of Togarmahb from the far north with all its groups of soldiers. There will be many people in that parade of prisoners.

7"'Be prepared. Yes, prepare yourself and the armies that have joined with you. You must watch and be ready. 8After a long time you will be called for duty. In the later years you will come into the land that has been healed from war. The people in that land were gathered from many nations and brought back to the mountains of Israel. In the past, the mountains of Israel had been destroyed again and again. But these people will have come back from those other nations. They all will have lived in safety. 9But you will come to attack them. You will come like a storm. You will come like a thundercloud covering the land. You and all your groups of soldiers from many nations will come to attack them.'"

10This is what the Lord GOD says: "At that time an idea will come into your mind. You will begin to make an evil plan. 11You will say, 'I will go attack the country that has towns without walls (Israel). The people there live in peace and think they are safe. There are no walls around the cities to protect them. They don't have any locks on their gates—they don't even have gates! 12I will defeat them and take all their valuable things away from them. I will fight against the places that were destroyed but now have people living in them. I will fight against the people who were gathered from the nations. Now they have cattle and property. They live at the crossroads of the world.c'

13"Sheba, Dedan, and merchants* of Tarshish and all the cities they trade with will ask you, 'Did you come to capture valuable things? Did you bring your groups of soldiers together to grab the good things and to carry away silver, gold, cattle, and property? Did you come to take all those valuable things?'

14"Son of man, speak to Gog for me. Tell him that this is what the Lord GOD says: 'You will come to attack my people while they are living in peace and safety. 15You will come from your place out of the far north, and you will bring many people with you. All of them will ride on horses. You will be a large and a powerful army. 16You will come to fight against my people Israel. You will be like a thundercloud covering the land. When that time comes, I will bring you to fight against my land. Then, Gog, the nations will learn how powerful I am! They will learn to respect me and know that I am holy. They will see what I will do to you!'"

17This is what the Lord GOD says: "At that time people will remember that I spoke about you in the past. They will remember that I used my servants, the prophets of Israel. They will remember that the prophets of Israel spoke for me in the past and said that I would bring you to fight against them."

18The Lord GOD said, "At that time Gog will come to fight against the land of Israel. I will show my anger. 19In my anger and strong emotions, I make this promise: I promise that there will be a strong earthquake in the land of Israel. 20At that time all living things will shake with fear. The fish in the sea, the birds in the air, the wild animals in the fields, and all the little creatures crawling on the ground will shake with fear. The mountains will fall

---

a**38:2 Son of man** This was usually just a way of saying "a person" or "a human being." Here, it is a way of addressing Ezekiel. Also in verse 14.
b**38:6 nation of Togarmah** Or "Beth Togarmah."

c**38:12 They live ... the world** The powerful countries must travel through there to get to all the other powerful countries.

down and the cliffs will break apart. Every wall will fall to the ground!"

21The Lord GOD says, "On the mountains of Israel, I will call for every kind of terror against[a] Gog. His soldiers will be so afraid that they will attack each other and kill each other with their swords. 22I will punish Gog with diseases and death. I will cause hailstones, fire, and sulfur to rain down on Gog and his groups of soldiers from many nations. 23Then I will show how great I am. I will prove that I am holy. Many nations will see me do these things, and they will learn who I am. Then they will know that I am the LORD.

The Death of Gog and His Army

39 1"Son of man,[b] speak against Gog for me. Tell him that this is what the Lord GOD says: 'Gog, you are the most important leader of the countries Meshech and Tubal, but I am against you. 2I will capture you and bring you back. I will bring you from the far north. I will bring you to fight against the mountains of Israel. 3But I will knock your bow from your left hand and your arrows from your right hand. 4You will be killed on the mountains of Israel. You, your groups of soldiers, and all the other nations with you will be killed in the battle. I will give you as food to every kind of bird that eats meat and to all the wild animals. 5You will not enter the city. You will be killed out in the open fields. I have spoken!'" This is what the Lord GOD said.

6"I will send fire against Magog and those people living along the coast. They think they are safe, but they will know that I am the LORD. 7And I will make my holy name known among my people Israel. I will not let people ruin my holy name anymore. The nations will know that I am the LORD. They will know that I am the Holy One in Israel. 8That time is coming! It will happen!" This is what the LORD said. "That is the day I am talking about.

9"At that time people living in the cities of Israel will go out to the fields. They will collect the enemy's weapons and burn them. They will burn all the shields, bows and arrows, clubs and spears. They will use the weapons as firewood for seven years. 10They will not have to gather wood from the fields or chop firewood from the forests because they will use the weapons as firewood. They will take the valuable things from the soldiers who wanted to steal from them. They will take the good things from the soldiers who took good things from them." This is what the Lord GOD said.

11"At that time I will choose a place in Israel to bury Gog. He will be buried in the Valley of the Travelers,[c] east of the Dead Sea. It will block the road for travelers, because Gog and all his army will be buried in that place. People will call it 'The Valley of Gog's Army.' 12It will take seven months for the family of Israel to bury them. They must do this to make the land pure. 13The common people will bury the enemy soldiers, and the people will become famous on the day that I bring honor to myself." The Lord GOD said those things.

14"Workers will be given a full-time job burying the dead soldiers to make the land pure. The workers will work for seven months. They will go around looking for dead bodies. 15They will go around looking, and if anyone sees a bone, a marker will be put up by it. The sign will stay there until the grave-diggers come and bury the bone in the Valley of Gog's Army. 16The city of the dead will be named Hamonah.[d] In this way they will make the country pure."

17This is what the Lord GOD said: "Son of man, speak to all the birds and wild animals for me. Tell them, 'Come here! Come here! Gather around. Come eat this sacrifice I am preparing for you. There will be a very big sacrifice on the mountains of Israel. Come, eat the meat and drink the blood. 18You will eat the meat from the bodies of powerful soldiers and drink the blood from world leaders. They will be like rams, lambs, goats, and fat bulls from Bashan. 19You can eat all the fat you want and drink blood until you are full. You will eat and drink from my sacrifice, which I will kill for you. 20You will have plenty of meat to eat at my table. There will be horses and chariot drivers, powerful soldiers, and all the other fighting men.'" This is what the Lord GOD said.

21"I will let the other nations see what I have done, and they will begin to respect me! They will see my power that I used against the enemy. 22Then from that day on, the family of Israel will know that I am the LORD their God. 23And the nations will know why the family of Israel was carried away as prisoners to other countries. They will learn that my people turned against me, so I turned away from them. I let their enemies defeat them, so my people were killed in battle. 24They sinned and made themselves filthy, so I punished them for the things they did. I turned away from them and refused to help them."

25So this is what the Lord GOD says: "Now I will bring the family of Jacob back from captivity. I will have mercy on the whole family of Israel. I will show my strong feelings for my holy name. 26The people will forget their

---

[a]38:21 *every kind of terror against* This is from the ancient Greek version. The standard Hebrew text has "a sword against."

[b]39:1 *Son of man* This was usually just a way of saying "a person" or "a human being." Here, it is a way of addressing Ezekiel. Also in verse 17.

[c]39:11 *Valley of the Travelers* This is a wordplay on the name Arabah Valley.

[d]39:16 *Hamonah* This Hebrew word means "crowd."

shame and all the times they turned against
me. They will live in safety on their own land.
No one will make them afraid. 27I will bring
my people back from other countries. I will
gather them from the lands of their enemies.
Then many nations will see how holy I am.
28They will know that I am the LORD their
God. That is because I made them leave their
homes and go as prisoners to other countries.
But then I gathered them together again and
brought them back to their own land. 29I will
pour out my Spirit on the family of Israel, and
I will never turn away from my people again."
This is what the Lord GOD said.

The New Temple

40 1In the twenty-fifth year after we
were taken away into captivity, at the
beginning of the year, on the tenth day of the
month,[a] the LORD's power came on me. This
was fourteen years after the Babylonians took
Jerusalem. On that day, the LORD took me
there in a vision.*
2In a vision, God carried me to the land
of Israel. He put me down near a very high
mountain. On the mountain in front of me
was a building that looked like a city.[b] 3The
LORD took me to that place. There was a man
there who looked like polished bronze. He
had a cloth tape measure and a measuring
rod in his hand. He was standing by the gate.
4The man said to me, "Son of man,[c] use your
eyes and ears. Look at these things and listen
to me. Pay attention to everything that I show
you, because you have been brought here so
that I can show you these things. You must
tell the family of Israel all that you see."
5I saw a wall that went all the way around
the outside of the Temple.* In the man's hand
there was a ruler for measuring things. It was
6 cubits[d] long using the long measurement,[e]
so the man measured the thickness of the
wall. It was one ruler[f] thick. He measured the
height of the wall. It was one ruler tall.
6Then the man went to the east gate. He
walked up its steps and measured the opening for the gate. It was one ruler wide. 7The
guardrooms were one ruler long and one ruler
wide. The walls between the rooms were 5
cubits[g] thick. The opening by the porch at the
end of the gateway that faced the Temple was
also one ruler wide. 8Then he measured the
porch. 9It was 8 cubits[h] long. He measured
the walls on either side of the gate. Each side
wall was 2 cubits[i] wide. The porch was at
the end of the gateway that faced the Temple.
10There were three little guardrooms on each
side of the gateway. All these rooms and their
side walls measured the same. 11The man
measured the entrance to the gateway. It was
10 cubits[j] wide and 13 cubits[k] long. 12There
was a low wall in front of each room. That
wall was 1 cubit[l] tall and 1 cubit thick. The
rooms were square. Each wall was 6 cubits
long.
13The man measured the gateway from the
outside edge of the roof of one room to the
outside edge of the roof of the opposite room.
It was 25 cubits.[m] Each door was directly
opposite the other door. 14[n] He measured the
faces of all the side walls, including the side
walls on either side of the porch at the courtyard. The total was 60 cubits.[o] 15From the
inside edge of the outer gate to the far end of
the porch was 50 cubits.[p] 16There were small
windows[q] above all the guardrooms, the side
walls, and the porch. The wide part of the
windows faced into the gateway. There were
carvings of palm trees on the walls that were
on either side of the gateway.

The Outer Courtyard

17Then the man led me into the outer
courtyard. I saw thirty rooms and a pavement
that went all the way around the courtyard.
The rooms were along the wall and faced in
toward the pavement. 18The pavement was as
wide as the gates were long. The pavement
reached to the inside end of the gateway.
This was the lower pavement. 19The man
measured the distance from the inside of the
lower gateway to the outside of the ⌊inner⌋
courtyard. It was 100 cubits[r] on the east side
as well as on the north side.
20Then the man measured the length and
width of the north gate that was in the wall
surrounding the outer courtyard. 21This gateway, its three rooms on each side, and its
porch all measured the same as the first gate.
The gateway was 50 cubits long and 25 cubits

[a]**40:1** *tenth day of the month* This was the Day of Atonement, 573 B.C. See Lev. 23:26; 25:9.
[b]**40:2** *On the mountain ... city* Or "On the mountain, there was a building that looked like a city with a city south of it."
[c]**40:4** *Son of man* This was usually just a way of saying "a person" or "a human being." Here, it is a way of addressing Ezekiel.
[d]**40:5** *6 cubits* 10' 2 7/16" (3.11 m). Also in verse 12.
[e]**40:5** *long measurement* Literally, "a cubit and a handbreadth." This cubit equals 20 5/8" (51.83 cm).
[f]**40:5** *one ruler* That is, 6 cubits (10' 2 7/16" or 3.11 m). Also in verses 6, 7.
[g]**40:7** *5 cubits* 8' 6" (2.6 m). Also in verses 30, 48.
[h]**40:9** *8 cubits* 13' 7 1/4" (4.2 m).
[i]**40:9** *2 cubits* 3' 4 13/16" (104 cm).
[j]**40:11** *10 cubits* 17' 1/16" (5.18 m).
[k]**40:11** *13 cubits* 22' 1 1/4" (6.74 m).
[l]**40:12** *1 cubit* 20 3/8" (51.83 cm). Also in verse 42.
[m]**40:13** *25 cubits* 42' 6 1/8" (12.96 m). Also in verses 21, 25, 29, 33, 36.
[n]**40:14** The meaning of this verse in the Hebrew text is uncertain.
[o]**40:14** *60 cubits* 102' 3/8" (31.1 m).
[p]**40:15** *50 cubits* 85' 5/16" (25.92 m). Also in verses 21, 25, 29. 33, 36.
[q]**40:16** *small windows* These let the soldiers defending the city shoot arrows out at the enemy. The narrow part of the window was on the enemy's side of the wall to give the smallest target.
[r]**40:19** *100 cubits* 170' 5/8" (51.83 m). Also in verse 23, 27, 47.

wide. 22Its windows, its porch, and its carvings of palm trees measured the same as the east gate. ⌊On the outside,⌋ there were seven steps leading up to the gate. Its porch was at the inside end of the gateway. 23Across the courtyard from the north gate, there was a gate to the inner courtyard. It was like the gate on the east. The man measured from the gate ⌊on the inner wall⌋ to the gate ⌊on the outer wall⌋. It was 100 cubits from gate to gate.

24Then the man led me to the south wall. I saw a gate in the south wall. He measured its side walls and its porch. They measured the same as the other gates. 25The gateway and its porch had windows all around like the other gates. The gateway was 50 cubits long and 25 cubits wide. 26There were seven steps going up to this gate. Its porch was at the inside end of the gateway. It had carvings of palm trees on the walls that were on either side of the gateway. 27A gate was on the south side of the inner courtyard. The man measured from the gate ⌊on the inner wall⌋ to the gate ⌊on the outer wall⌋. It was 100 cubits from gate to gate.

The Inner Courtyard

28Then the man led me through the south gate into the inner courtyard. He measured this gate. This gateway measured the same as the other gates to the inner courtyard. 29Its rooms, side walls, and porch also measured the same as the other gates. There were windows all around the gateway and its porch. The gateway was 50 cubits long and 25 cubits wide. 30The porch was 25 cubits wide and 5 cubits long. 31And its porch was at the end of the gateway next to the outer courtyard. Carvings of palm trees were on the walls ⌊on either side of the gateway⌋. There were eight steps leading up to the gate.

32Then the man led me into the inner courtyard on the east side. He measured the gate. It measured the same as the other gates. 33Its rooms, side walls, and porch also measured the same as the other gates. There were windows all around the gateway and its porch. The gateway was 50 cubits long and 25 cubits wide. 34And its porch was at the end of the gateway next to the outer courtyard. Carvings of palm trees were on the walls on either side of the gateway. There were eight steps leading up to the gate.

35Then the man led me to the north gate. He measured it, and it measured the same as the other gates. 36Its rooms, side walls, and porch also measured the same as the other gates. There were windows all around the gateway and its porch. The gateway was 50 cubits long and 25 cubits wide. 37And its porcha was at the end of the gateway next to the outer courtyard. Carvings of palm trees were on the walls on either side of the

gateway. There were eight steps leading up to the gate.

The Rooms for Preparing Sacrifices

38There was also a doorway in the side walls of the gates. That doorway led into a room where the priests washed the sacrifices. 39There were two tables on each side of the door of this porch. The animals for the burnt offerings,* the sin offerings,* and the guilt offerings were killed on these tables. 40There were also two tables on each side of the door on the outside wall of this porch. 41So there were four tables on the inside wall and four tables on the outside wall—eight tables that the priests used when they killed the animals for sacrifices. 42There were also four tables made from cut stone for the burnt offerings. These tables were 1 1/2 cubitsb long, 1 1/2 cubits wide, and 1 cubit high. On these tables, the priests put their tools that they used to kill the animals for the burnt offerings and other sacrifices. 43There were meat hooks three inches longc on all the walls in this area. The meat of the offerings was put on the tables.

The Priests' Rooms

44There were two roomsd in the inner courtyard. One was by the north gate facing south. The other room was by the southe gate facing north. 45The man said to me, "The room that looks to the south is for the priests who are on duty and serving in the Temple area. 46But the room that looks to the north is for the priests who are on duty and serving at the altar.* The priests are from the tribe of Levi. But the priests in this second group are the descendants of Zadok. They are the only people who can carry the sacrifices to the altar to serve the Lord.f"

47The man measured the ⌊inner⌋ courtyard. The courtyard was a perfect square. It was 100 cubits long and 100 cubits wide. The altar was in front of the Temple.

The Porch of the Temple

48Then the man led me to the porch of the Temple and measured the walls on either side of the porch. Each side wall was 5 cubits thick and 3 cubitsg wide. The opening between them was 14 cubits.h 49The porch was 20 cubitsi wide and 12 cubitsj long.k

b40:42 1 1/2 cubits 30 5/8" (77.75 cm).
c40:43 meat hooks ... long Or "Double shelves three inches wide ...."
d40:44 two rooms Or "rooms for the singers."
e40:44 south This is from the ancient Greek version. The Hebrew text has "east."
f40:46 carry the sacrifices ... the Lord Literally, "approach the Lord to serve him."
g40:48 3 cubits 5' 1 3/16" (1.55 m).
h40:48 14 cubits 23' 9 11/16" (7.26 m).
i40:49 20 cubits 34' 1/8" (10.37 m). Also in 41:2, 4.
j40:49 12 cubits 20' 4 7/8" (6.22 m).
k40:49 20 ... long Literally, "20 cubits long ... 12 cubits wide."

a40:37 porch The Hebrew text has "side walls."

Ten steps went up to the porch. There were two columns for the walls on either side of the porch—one at each wall.

The Holy Place of the Temple

41 [1]Then the man led me into the Holy Place. He measured the walls on either side of the room. The side walls were 6 cubits[a] thick on each side. [2]The door was 10 cubits[b] wide. The sides of the doorway were 5 cubits[c] on each side. He measured that room. It was 40 cubits[d] long and 20 cubits wide.

The Most Holy Place in the Temple

[3]Then the man went into the last room. He measured the walls on either side of the doorway. Each side wall was 2 cubits[e] thick and 7 cubits[f] wide. The doorway was 6 cubits wide. [4]Then he measured the length of the room. It was 20 cubits long and 20 cubits wide. He said to me, "This is the Most Holy Place."

Other Rooms Around the Temple

[5]Then the man measured the wall of the Temple. It was 6 cubits thick. There were side rooms all around the Temple. They were 4 cubits[g] wide. [6]The side rooms were on three different floors, one above the other. There were 30 rooms on each floor. The wall of the Temple was built with ledges. The side rooms rested on these ledges but were not connected to the Temple wall itself. [7]Each floor of the side rooms around the Temple was wider than the floor below. The walls of the rooms around the Temple became narrower the higher they went so that the rooms on the top floors were wider. A stairway went up from the lowest floor to the highest floor through the middle floor.

[8]I also saw that the Temple had a raised base all the way around it. It was the foundation for the side rooms, and it was a full ruler[h] high. [9]The outer wall of the side rooms was 5 cubits thick. There was an open area between the side rooms of the Temple [10]and the priests' rooms. It was 20 cubits[i] wide and went all the way around the Temple. [11]The doors of the side rooms opened onto the raised base. There was one entrance on the north side and one entrance on the south side. The raised base was 5 cubits wide all around.

[12]There was a building in this restricted area west of the Temple. The building was 70 cubits[j] wide and 90 cubits[k] long. The wall

of the building was 5 cubits thick all around. [13]Then the man measured the Temple. The Temple was 100 cubits[l] long. The restricted area, including the building and its walls, was also 100 cubits long. [14]The restricted area on the east side, in front of the Temple, was 100 cubits long.

[15]The man measured the length of the building in the restricted area at the rear of the Temple. It was 100 cubits from one wall to the other wall.

The Most Holy Place, the Holy Place, and the Porch ₁that looked out onto the inner₁ courtyard [16]had wood paneling on all the walls. All the windows and doors had wood trim around them. By the doorway, the Temple had wood paneling from the floor up to the windows and up to the part of the wall [17]over the doorway.

On all the walls in the inner room and the outer room of the Temple were carvings [18]of Cherub angels and palm trees. A palm tree was between each Cherub angel. Every Cherub angel had two faces. [19]One face was a man's face looking toward the palm tree on one side. The other face was a lion's face looking toward the palm tree on the other side. They were carved all around on the Temple. [20]From the floor to the area above the door, Cherub angels and palm trees were carved on all walls of the Holy Place.

[21]The walls on either side of the Holy Place were square. In front of the Most Holy Place, there was something that looked like [22]an altar* made from wood. It was 3 cubits[m] high and 2 cubits long. Its corners, its base, and its sides were wood. The man said to me, "This is the table that is before the LORD."

[23]Both the Holy Place and the Most Holy Place had a double door. [24]Each of the doors was made from two smaller doors. Each door was really two swinging doors. [25]Also Cherub angels and palm trees were carved on the doors of the Holy Place. They were like those carved on the walls. There was a wood roof over the front of the porch. [26]There were windows with frames around them and palm trees on the walls on both sides of the porch, on the roof over the porch, and on the rooms around the Temple.

The Priests' Room

42 [1]Then the man led me through the north gate out into the outer courtyard. He led me to a building with many rooms that was west of the restricted area and the building on the north side. [2]This building was 100 cubits[n] long and 50 cubits[o] wide. People entered it from the courtyard on the north side. [3]The building was three stories tall

---

a**41:1** *6 cubits* 10' 2 7/16" (3.11 m). Also in verses 3, 5.
b**41:2** *10 cubits* 17' 1/16" (5.18 m).
c**41:2** *5 cubits* 8' 6" (2.6 m). Also in verses 9, 12.
d**41:2** *40 cubits* 68' 1/4" (20.73 m).
e**41:3** *2 cubits* 3' 4 13/16" (104 cm). Also in verse 22.
f**41:3** *7 cubits* 11' 10 13/16" (3.63 m).
g**41:5** *4 cubits* 6' 9 5/8" (2.1 m).
h**41:8** *full ruler* That is, 6 cubits (10' 2 7/16" or 3.11 m).
i**41:10** *20 cubits* 34' 1/8" (10.37 m).
j**41:12** *70 cubits* 119' 7/16" (36.28 m).
k**41:12** *90 cubits* 153' 9/16" (46.65 m).

l**41:13** *100 cubits* 170' 5/8" (51.83 m). Also in verse 15.
m**41:22** *3 cubits* 5' 1 3/16" (1.55 m).
n**42:2** *100 cubits* 170' 5/8" (51.83 m).
o**42:2** *50 cubits* 85' 5/16" (25.92 m).

and had balconies. The 20-cubit[a] inner courtyard was between the building and the Temple. On the other side, the rooms faced the
pavement of the outer courtyard. [4]There was a
path 10 cubits[b] wide and 100 cubits long running along the south side of the building, even
though the entrance was on the north side.
[5-6]Since this building was three stories tall
and did not have columns like those columns
of the outer courtyards, the top rooms were
farther back than the rooms on the middle
and bottom floors. The top floor was narrower
than the middle floor, which was narrower
than the bottom floor because the balconies
used this space. [7]There was a wall outside that
was parallel to the rooms and ran along the
outer courtyard. It ran in front of the rooms
for 50 cubits. [8]The row of rooms that ran
along the outer courtyard was 50 cubits long,
although the total length of the building, as on
the Temple side, was 100 cubits long. [9]The
entrance was below these rooms at the east
end of the building so that people could enter
from the outer courtyard. [10]The entrance was
at the start of the wall beside the courtyard.

There were rooms on the south side, by the
restricted area and the other building. These
rooms had a [11]path in front of them. They
were like the rooms on the north side. They
had the same length and width and the same
kind of doors. [12]The entrance to the lower
rooms was at the east end of the building so
that people could enter from the open end of
the path by the wall.

[13]The man said to me, "The north rooms
and south rooms across from the restricted
area are holy. These rooms are for the priests
who offer the sacrifices to the LORD. That is
where the priests will put the most holy offerings and eat them. That is because that place
is holy. The most holy offerings are the grain
offerings, the sin offerings,* and the guilt
offerings. [14]The priests who enter the holy
area must leave their serving clothes in that
holy place before they go out into the outer
courtyard, because these clothes are holy. If
a priest wants to go to the part of the Temple
where the other people are, he must go to
those rooms and put on other clothes."

The Outer Courtyard

[15]The man had finished measuring inside
the Temple area. Then he brought me out
through the east gate and measured all
around that area. [16]He measured the east side
with the ruler. It was 500 cubits[c] long. [17]He
measured the north side. It was 500 cubits
long. [18]He measured the south side. It was
500 cubits long. [19]He went around to the
west side and measured it. It was 500 cubits
long. [20]He measured the four walls that went

all the way around the Temple. The wall was
500 cubits long and 500 cubits wide. It separated the holy area from the area that is not
holy.*

The Lord Will Live Among His People

43 [1]The man led me to the east gate.
[2]There the Glory of the God of Israel
came from the east. God's voice was loud like
the sound of the sea. The ground was bright
with the light from the Glory of God. [3]The
vision* that I saw was like the vision I saw by
the Kebar Canal. I bowed with my face to the
ground. [4]The Glory of the LORD* came into
the Temple through the east gate.

[5]Then the Spirit[d] picked me up and brought
me into the inner courtyard. The Glory of
the LORD filled the Temple. [6]I heard someone
speaking to me from inside the Temple. The
man was still standing beside me. [7]The voice
from the Temple said to me, "Son of man,[e]
this is the place with my throne and footstool.
I will live in this place among the people of
Israel forever. The family of Israel will not
ruin my holy name again. The kings and their
people will not bring shame to my name by
committing sexual sins[f] or by burying the
dead bodies of their kings in this place. [8]They
will not bring shame to my name by putting
their threshold next to my threshold, and
their doorposts next to my doorposts. In the
past, only a wall separated them from me. So
they brought shame to my name every time
they sinned and did those terrible things. That
is why I became angry and destroyed them.
[9]Now let them take their sexual sins and the
dead bodies of their kings far away from me.
Then I will live among them forever.

[10]"Now, son of man, tell the family of Israel
about the Temple. Then, when they learn
about the plans for the Temple, they will be
ashamed of their sins. [11]And they will be
ashamed of all the bad things they have done.
Let them know the design of the Temple. Let
them know how it should be built, where the
entrances and exits are, and all the designs
on it. Teach them about all its rules and all its
laws. Write these things for everyone to see
so that they can obey all the laws and rules for
the Temple. [12]This is the law of the Temple:
The whole area surrounding it on the top of
the mountain is most holy. This is the law of
the Temple.

The Altar

[13]"These are the measurements of the altar*
in cubits using the long measurement[g]: There

---

[a]**42:3 20-cubits** 34' 1/8" (10.37 m).
[b]**42:4 10 cubits** 17' 1/16" (5.18 m).
[c]**42:16 500 cubits** 850' 3 1/16" (259.16 m).

[d]**43:5 Spirit** Or "spirit" or "wind."
[e]**43:7 Son of man** This was usually just a way of saying "a person" or "a human being." Here, it is a way of
addressing Ezekiel. Also in verses 10, 18.
[f]**43:7 sexual sins** This might also mean "turning
away from God and being unfaithful to him."
[g]**43:13 long measurement** Literally, "a cubit and a
handbreadth." This cubit equals 20 5/8" (51.83 cm).

was a gutter all the way around the base of the altar. It was 1 cubit[a] deep, and each side was 1 cubit wide. There was a rim around the edge 1 span[b] high. This is how tall the altar was: [14]From the ground to the lower ledge, the base measured 2 cubits.[c] It was 1 cubit wide. It measured 4 cubits[d] from the smaller ledge to the larger ledge. It was 2 cubits wide. [15]The place for the fire on the altar was 4 cubits high. The four corners were shaped like horns. [16]The place for the fire on the altar was 12 cubits[e] long by 12 cubits wide. It was perfectly square. [17]The ledge was also square, 14 cubits[f] long by 14 cubits wide. The border around it was 1/2 cubit[g] wide. (The gutter around the base was 1 cubit wide.) The steps going up to the altar were on the east side."

[18]Then the man said to me, "Son of man, this is what the Lord GOD says: 'These are the rules for the altar: At the time you build the altar, use these rules to offer burnt offerings* and to sprinkle blood on it. [19]You will give a young bull as a sin offering* to the men from Zadok's family. These men are the priests from the tribe of Levi. They are the men who serve me by bringing the offerings to me.'" This is what the Lord GOD said. [20]"You will take some of the bull's blood and put it on the altar's four horns, on the four corners of the ledge, and on the rim around it. In this way you will make the altar pure. [21]Then take the bull for the sin offering and burn it in the proper place in the Temple area, outside the Temple building.

[22]"On the second day you will offer a male goat that has nothing wrong with it. It will be for a sin offering. The priests will make the altar pure the same way they made it pure with the bull. [23]When you have finished making the altar pure, you will offer a young bull that has nothing wrong with it and a ram from the flock that has nothing wrong with it. [24]Then you will offer them before the LORD. The priests will sprinkle salt on them. Then they will offer the bull and ram up as a burnt offering to the LORD. [25]You will prepare a goat every day for seven days for a sin offering. Also, you will prepare a young bull and a ram from the flock. These animals must have nothing wrong with them. [26]For seven days the priests will make the altar pure and ready for use in worshiping God. [27]On the eighth day, and every day after that, the priests must offer your burnt offerings and fellowship offerings* on the altar. Then I will accept you." This is what the Lord GOD said.

The Outer Gate

44 [1]Then the man brought me back to the east gate of the Temple area. We were outside the gate and the gate was shut. [2]The LORD said to me, "This gate will stay shut. It will not be opened. No one will enter through it, because the LORD of Israel has entered through it. So it must stay shut. [3]Only the ruler of the people may sit at this gate when he eats a meal with the LORD. He must enter through the porch of the gateway and go out the same way."

The Holiness of the Temple

[4]Then the man led me through the north gate to the front of the Temple. I looked and saw the Glory of the LORD* filling the LORD's Temple. I bowed with my face touching the ground. [5]The LORD said to me, "Son of man,[h] look very carefully! Use your eyes and ears. Look at these things, and listen very carefully to everything that I tell you about all the rules and laws about the LORD's Temple. Look carefully at the entrances to the Temple and at all the exits from the holy place. [6]Then give this message to all the people of Israel who refused to obey me. Tell them, 'This is what the Lord GOD said: Family of Israel, I have had enough of the terrible things you have done! [7]You brought foreigners into my Temple who are not circumcised and have not given themselves to me.[i] In this way you made my Temple unclean. You broke our agreement and did terrible things, and then you gave me the offerings of bread, the fat, and the blood. But this only made my Temple unclean. [8]You did not take care of my holy things. No, you let foreigners have responsibility of my holy place!'"

[9]This is what the Lord GOD says: "A foreigner who is not truly circumcised must not come into my Temple—not even a foreigner living permanently among the people of Israel. He must be circumcised, and he must give himself completely to me before he can come into my Temple. [10]In the past, the Levites left me when Israel turned away from me. Israel left me to follow their idols.* The Levites will be punished for their sin. [11]The Levites were chosen to serve in my holy place. They guarded the gates of the Temple. They served in the Temple. They killed the animals for the sacrifices and burnt offerings for the people. They were chosen to help the people and to serve them. [12]But the Levites helped the people sin against me! They helped the people worship their idols! So I am making this promise against them: 'They will be punished for their sin.'" This is what the Lord GOD said.

---

[a]**43:13** *1 cubit* 20 3/8" (51.83 cm).
[b]**43:13** *1 span* The distance from the tip of the thumb to the tip of the little finger, about 9" (23 cm).
[c]**43:14** *2 cubits* 3' 4 13/16" (104 cm). Also in verse 17.
[d]**43:14** *4 cubits* 6' 9 5/8" (2.1 m).
[e]**43:16** *12 cubits* 20' 4 7/8" (6.22 m).
[f]**43:17** *14 cubits* 23' 9 11/16" (7.26 m).
[g]**43:17** *1/2 cubit* 10 3/16" (25.92 cm).

[h]**44:5** *Son of man* This was usually just a way of saying "a person" or "a human being." Here, it is a way of addressing Ezekiel.
[i]**44:7** *not circumcised ... to me* Literally, "not circumcised in their heart or in their body." See "circumcise" in the Word List. Also in verse 9.

¹³"So the Levites will not bring offerings to me like the priests. They will not come near any of my holy things or the things that are most holy. They must carry their shame because of the terrible things that they did. ¹⁴But I will let them take care of the Temple. They will work in the Temple and do the things that must be done in it.

¹⁵"The priests are all from the tribe of Levi. But only priests from Zadok's family took care of my holy place when the people of Israel turned away from me. So only Zadok's descendants will bring offerings to me. They will stand before me to offer me the fat and the blood from the animals they sacrifice." This is what the Lord God said! ¹⁶"They will enter my holy place and come near my table to serve me. They will take care of the things I gave them. ¹⁷When they enter the gates of the inner courtyard, they will wear linen clothes. They will not wear wool while they serve at the gates of the inner courtyard and in the Temple. ¹⁸They will wear linen turbans* on their heads, and they will wear linen underwear. They will not wear anything that makes them sweat. ¹⁹Before they go out into the outer courtyard to the people, they will take off the clothes they wear while serving me. They will put these clothes away in the holy rooms. Then they will put on other clothes. In this way they will not let people touch those holy clothes.

²⁰"These priests will not shave their heads or let their hair grow long.ᵃ The priests may only trim the hair of their heads. ²¹None of the priests may drink wine when they go into the inner courtyard. ²²The priests must not marry a widow or a divorced woman. No, they must only marry a virgin* from the family of Israel or a woman whose dead husband was a priest.

²³"Also, the priests must teach my people the difference between things that are holy* and things that are not holy. They must help my people know what is clean and what is unclean. ²⁴The priests will be the judges in court. They will follow my laws when they judge people. They will obey my laws and my rules at all my special feasts. They will respect my special days of rest and keep them holy. ²⁵They will not go near a dead person to make themselves unclean. But they may make themselves unclean if the dead person is their father, mother, son, daughter, brother, or a sister who is not married. ²⁶After the priest has been made clean, he must wait seven days. ²⁷Then he can go back into the holy place. But on the day he goes into the inner courtyard to serve in the holy place, he must offer a sin offering for himself." This is what the Lord God said.

²⁸"About the land that will belong to the Levites: I am their property. You will not give the Levites any land in Israel. I am their share in Israel. ²⁹They will get to eat the grain offerings, the sin offerings, and the guilt offerings. Everything the people in Israel give to the Lord will be theirs. ³⁰And the first part of the harvest from every kind of crop will be for the priests. You will also give the priests the first part of your flour. This will bring blessings to your house. ³¹The priests must not eat any bird or animal that has died a natural death or has been torn to pieces by a wild animal.

The Division of the Land for Holy Use

45 ¹"You will divide the land for the Israelite tribes by throwing lots.* At that time you will separate out a part of the land. It will be a holy part for the Lord. The land will be 25,000 cubitsᵇ long and 20,000 cubitsᶜ wide.ᵈ All this land will be holy. ²A square area that is 500 cubitsᵉ long on each side will be for the Temple. There will be an open space around the Temple that is 50 cubitsᶠ wide. ³In the holy area you will measure 25,000 cubits long and 10,000 cubitsᵍ wide. The Temple will be in this area. The Temple area will be the Most Holy Place.

⁴"This holy part of the land will be for the priests, the servants of the Temple. This is where they approach the Lord to serve him. It will be a place for the priests' houses and a place for the Temple. ⁵Another area, 25,000 cubits long and 10,000 cubits wide, will be for the Levites who serve in the Temple. This land will also become cities for the Levites.

⁶"And you will give the city an area that is 5000 cubitsʰ wide and 25,000 cubits long. It will be along the side of the holy area. It will be for all the family of Israel. ⁷The ruler will have land on both sides of the holy area and the land belonging to the city. It will be next to the holy area and the area belonging to the city. It will be the same width as the land that belongs to a tribe. It will go all the way from the west border to the east border. ⁸This land will be the ruler's property in Israel. So he will not need to make life hard for my people anymore. But they will give the land to the Israelites for their tribes."

⁹This is what the Lord God said: "Enough, you rulers of Israel! Stop being cruel and stealing things from people! Be fair and do what is right! Stop forcing my people out

---

ᵃ**44:20 These priests … grow long** This would show that they are sad, and the priests must be happy about serving the Lord.

ᵇ**45:1 25,000 cubits** 8.05 miles (12.96 km). Also in verses 4, 6.

ᶜ**45:1 20,000 cubits** 6.44 miles (10.37 km).

ᵈ**45:1 20,000 cubits wide** This is from the ancient Greek version. The standard Hebrew text has 10,000 cubits (3.22 miles or 5.18 km) wide.

ᵉ**45:2 500 cubits** 850' 3 1/16" (259.16 m).

ᶠ**45:2 50 cubits** 85' 5/16" (25.92 m).

ᵍ**45:3 10,000 cubits** 3.22 miles (5.18 km). Also in verse 5.

ʰ**45:6 5000 cubits** 1.61 miles (2.6 km).

from their homes!" This is what the Lord
GOD said.

10"Stop cheating people. Use accurate
scales and measures! 11The ephah and the
bath must be the same size: A bath and an
ephah must both equal 1/10 homer.*a* Those
measures will be based on the homer. 12A
shekel*b* must equal 20 gerahs. A mina must
equal 60 shekels. It must be equal to 20 shekels plus 25 shekels plus 15 shekels.

13"This is a special offering that you must
give:

1/6 ephah*c* of wheat for every homer of
    wheat;
1/6 ephah of barley for every homer of
    barley;
14 1/10 bath*d* of olive oil for every cor*e* of
    olive oil;
    (Remember: Ten baths make a homer,
    and ten baths make a cor.)
15 and one sheep for every 200 sheep from
    every watering hole in Israel.

"Those special offerings are for the grain
offerings, for the burnt offerings,* and for the
fellowship offerings.* These offerings are to
remove the sins of the people." This is what
the Lord GOD said.

16"Everyone in the country will give to this
offering for the ruler of Israel. 17But the ruler
must give the things needed for the special
holy days. The ruler must provide the burnt
offerings, the grain offerings, and the drink
offerings for the feast days, for the New
Moon,* for the Sabbaths,* and for all the other
special meeting days of the family of Israel.
He must give all the sin offerings,* grain offerings, burnt offerings, and fellowship offerings
that are used to make the family of Israel
pure."

18This is what the Lord GOD says: "In the
first month, on the first day of the month, you
will take a young bull that has nothing wrong
with it. You must use that bull to make the
Temple pure. 19The priest will take some of
the blood from the sin offering and put it on
the doorposts of the Temple and on the four
corners of the ledge of the altar* and on the
posts of the gate to the inner courtyard. 20You
will do the same thing on the seventh day of
that month for anyone who has sinned by
mistake or without knowing it. So you will
make the Temple pure.

Offerings During the Passover

21"On the 14th day of the first month you
must celebrate the Passover.* The Festival

of Unleavened Bread* begins at this time. It
continues for seven days. 22At that time the
ruler will offer a bull for himself and for all
the people of Israel. The bull will be for a sin
offering.* 23During the seven days of the festival, the ruler will offer seven bulls and seven
rams that have nothing wrong with them.
They will be burnt offerings* to the LORD. The
ruler will offer one bull on every day of the
seven days of the festival, and he will offer a
male goat every day for a sin offering. 24The
ruler will give an ephah*f* of barley as a grain
offering with each bull, and an ephah of barley
with each ram. He must give a hin*g* of oil for
each ephah of grain. 25He must do the same
thing for the seven days of the Festival of
Shelters,. This festival begins on the 15th day
of the seventh month. These offerings will be
the sin offering, the burnt offering, the grain
offering, and the oil offering."

The Ruler and the Festivals

46 1This is what the Lord GOD says: "The
east gate of the inner courtyard will
be closed on the six working days. But it will
be opened on the Sabbath* day and on the day
of the New Moon.* 2The ruler will go into the
porch of that gate and stand by the gatepost.
Then the priests will offer the ruler's burnt
offering* and fellowship offerings.* The ruler
will worship at the opening of that gate and
then go out. But the gate will not be shut until
evening. 3On the Sabbath day and on the day
of the New Moon, the common people will
also worship the LORD at that gate.

4"The ruler will offer burnt offerings to the
LORD on the Sabbath. He must provide six
lambs that have nothing wrong with them
and a ram that has nothing wrong with it.
5He must give an ephah of grain as an offering
with the ram. As for the grain offering with
the lambs, the ruler can give as much as he
wants. But he must give 1 hin of olive oil for
each ephah of grain.

6"On the day of the New Moon he must
offer a young bull that has nothing wrong
with it. He will also offer six lambs and a
ram that have nothing wrong with them.
7The ruler must give an ephah of grain as an
offering with the bull and an ephah of grain
as an offering with the ram. As for the grain
offering with the lambs, he can give as much
as he wants. But he must give 1 hin of olive oil
for each ephah of grain.

8"When the ruler goes in, he must enter at
the porch of the east gate—and he must leave
that same way.

9"When the common people come to meet
with the LORD at the special festivals, whoever
enters through the north gate to worship will

---

*a*45:11 *homer* A measure equal to about 7 bushels
or about 60 gallons (220 l). Also in verse 13.

*b*45:12 *shekel* A weight equal to 2/5 of an ounce or
11.5 grams. This also became an amount of money.

*c*45:13 *1/6 ephah* 14 cups (3.67 l).

*d*45:14 *1/10 bath* 1/2 gallon (2.2 l).

*e*45:14 *cor* 55 gallons (220 l).

*f*45:24 *ephah* A dry measure (3/5 bushel or 22 l).
Also in 46:5, 7, 11.

*g*45:24 *hin* A liquid measure (1 gallon or 3.2 l). Also
in 46:5, 7, 11.

go out through the south gate, and whoever enters through the south gate will go out through the north gate. People must not return the same way they entered. Each person must go out straight ahead. [10]The ruler should be there among the people. When the people go in, the ruler will go in with them, and when they go out, the ruler will too.

[11]"At the festivals and other special meetings, an ephah of grain as an offering must be offered with each young bull, and an ephah of grain as an offering must be offered with each ram. As for the grain offering with the lambs, the ruler can give as much as he wants. But he must give 1 hin of olive oil for each ephah of grain.

[12]"When the ruler gives a freewill offering to the LORD—it might be a burnt offering, a fellowship offering, or a freewill offering—the east gate will be opened for him. Then he will offer his burnt offering and his fellowship offerings as he does on the Sabbath day. After he leaves, the gate will be shut.

The Daily Offering

[13]"Every day you will provide a year-old lamb that has nothing wrong with it. It will be for a burnt offering* to the LORD. You will provide it every morning. [14]Also, you will offer a grain offering with the lamb every morning. You will give ⅙ ephah[d] of flour and ⅓ hin[b] of oil to make the fine flour moist. It will be the daily grain offering to the LORD. [15]So they will give the lamb, the grain offering, and the oil every morning for a burnt offering forever."

Laws of Inheritance for the Ruler

[16]This is what the Lord GOD says: "If the ruler gives a gift from part of his land to any of his sons, it will belong to his sons. It is their property. [17]But if the ruler gives a gift from part of his land to one of his slaves, the gift will belong to the slave only until the year of freedom.[c] Then the gift will go back to the ruler. Only the ruler's sons will keep a gift of land from the ruler. [18]And the ruler will not take any of the people's land or force them to leave their land. He must give some of his own land to his sons. In that way my people will not be forced to lose their land."

The Special Kitchens

[19]The man led me through the entrance at the side of the gate. He led me to the holy rooms for the priests on the north side. There I saw a place at the west end of the path. [20]The man said to me, "This is where the priests will boil the guilt offering and the sin offering* and will bake the grain offering. Why? So they will not need to bring these offerings out into the outer courtyard. So they will not bring those holy things out where the common people are."

[21]Then the man led me out to the outer courtyard. He led me to the four corners of the courtyard. I saw smaller courtyards in each corner of the large courtyard. [22]There was a small, enclosed area in each of the four corners of the courtyard. Each small courtyard was 40 cubits[d] long and 30 cubits[e] wide. The four areas measured the same. [23]There was a brick wall around each of the four small courtyards, and there were places built into the brick walls for cooking. [24]The man said to me, "These are the kitchens where those who serve at the Temple cook the sacrifices for the people."

The Water Flowing From the Temple

47 [1]The man led me back to the entrance of the Temple. I saw water coming out from under the east gate of the Temple. (The front of the Temple is on the east side.) The water flowed down from under the south end of the Temple and ran south of the altar.* [2]The man led me out through the north gate and then around the outside to the outer gate on the east side. The water was flowing out on the south side of the gate.

[3]The man walked east with a tape measure in his hand. He measured 1000 cubits.[f] Then he told me to walk through the water at that place. The water was only ankle deep. [4]He measured another 1000 cubits. Then he told me to walk through the water at that place. There the water came up to my knees. Then he measured another 1000 cubits and told me to walk through the water at that place. There the water was waist deep. [5]He measured another 1000 cubits, but there the water was too deep to cross. It had become a river. The water was deep enough to swim in. It was a river that was too deep to cross. [6]Then the man said to me, "Son of man,[g] did you pay close attention to the things you saw?"

Then the man led me back along the side of the river. [7]As I walked back along the side of the river, I saw many trees on both sides of the water. [8]He said to me, "This water flows east, down to the Arabah Valley. [9]This water flows into the Dead Sea so that the water in that sea becomes fresh and clean. There are many fish in this water, and all kinds of animals live where this river goes. [10]You can see fishermen standing by the river all the way from En Gedi to En Eglaim. You can see them throwing their fishing nets and catching many kinds of fish. There are as many kinds of fish

---

[a]**46:14** *1/6 ephah* 14 cups (3.67 l).
[b]**46:14** *1/3 hin* A liquid measure (1/3 gallon or 1 l).
[c]**46:17** *year of freedom* Or "Jubilee." See "Jubilee" in the Word List.

[d]**46:22** *40 cubits* 68' 1/4" (20.73 m).
[e]**46:22** *30 cubits* 51' 3/16" (15.55 m).
[f]**47:3** *1000 cubits* 1/3 mile (518.32 m).
[g]**47:6** *Son of man* This was usually just a way of saying "a person" or "a human being." Here, it is a way of addressing Ezekiel.

in the Dead Sea as there are in the Mediterranean Sea. [11]But the swamps and small marshes will not become fresh. They will be left for salt. [12]All kinds of fruit trees will grow on both sides of the river. Their leaves never will become dry and fall. The fruit will never stop growing on those trees. The trees will produce fruit every month, because the water for the trees comes from the Temple. The fruit from the trees will be for food, and their leaves will be for healing."

Division of the Land for the Tribes

[13]This is what the Lord GOD says: "These are the borders for dividing the land among the twelve tribes of Israel. Joseph will have two parts. [14]You will divide the land equally. I promised to give this land to your ancestors,* so I am giving this land to you.

[15]"Here are the borders of the land: On the north side, it goes from the Mediterranean Sea by way of Hethlon where the road turns toward Hamath and on to Zedad, [16]Berothah, Sibraim (which is on the border between Damascus and Hamath) and Hazer Hatticon, which is on the border of Hauran. [17]So the border will go from the sea to Hazar Enan on the northern border of Damascus and Hamath. This will be on the north side.

[18]"On the east side, the border will go from Hazar Enan between Hauran and Damascus and continue along the Jordan River between Gilead and the land of Israel to the eastern sea and all the way to Tamar. This will be the eastern border.

[19]"On the south side, the border will go from Tamar all the way to the oasis at Meribah-kadesh. Then it will go along the Brook of Egypt to the Mediterranean Sea. This will be the southern border.

[20]"On the west side, the Mediterranean Sea will be the border all the way to the area in front of Lebo Hamath. This will be your western border.

[21]"So you will divide this land among you for the tribes of Israel. [22]You will divide it as a property for yourselves and for the foreigners who live among you and who have had children among you. These foreigners will be residents—they will be like natural born Israelites. You will divide some land for them among the tribes of Israel. [23]The tribe where that resident lives must give him some land." This is what the Lord GOD said!

The Land for the Tribes of Israel

48 [1-7]"The northern border goes east from the Mediterranean Sea to Hethlon to Hamath Pass and then all the way to Hazar Enan. This is on the border between Damascus and Hamath. The land for the tribes in this group will go from the east of these borders to the west. From north to south, the tribes in this area are Dan, Asher, Naphtali, Manasseh, Ephraim, Reuben, and Judah.

The Special Section of Land

[8]"The next area of land will be for a special use. This land is south of Judah's land. This area is 25,000 cubits[a] long from north to south. From east to west, it will be as wide as the land that belongs to the other tribes. The Temple will be in the middle of this section of land. [9]You will dedicate* this land to the LORD. It will be 25,000 cubits long and 20,000 cubits[b] wide. [10]This special area of land will be divided among the priests and Levites.

"The priests will get one part of this area. The land will be 25,000 cubits long on the north side, 10,000 cubits[c] wide on the west side, 10,000 cubits wide on the east side, and 25,000 cubits long on the south side. The LORD's Temple will be in the middle of this area of land. [11]This land is for Zadok's descendants. These men were chosen to be my holy priests, because they continued to serve me when the other people of Israel left me. Zadok's family did not leave me like the other people from the tribe of Levi. [12]This share from this holy part of the land will be especially for these priests. It will be next to the land of the Levites.

[13]"Next to the land for the priests, the Levites will have a share of the land. It will be 25,000 cubits long and 10,000 cubits wide. They will get the full length and width of this land—25,000 cubits long and 20,000 cubits wide. [14]The Levites will not sell or trade any of this land. They will not be able to sell any of it. They must not cut up this part of the country, because this land belongs to the LORD—it is very special. It is the best part of the land.

The Shares for the City Property

[15]"There will be an area of land 5000 cubits[d] wide by 25,000 cubits long that is left over from the land given to the priests and Levites. This land can be for the city, for grasslands for animals, and for building houses. The common people may use this land. The city will be in the middle of it. [16]These are the city's measurements: The north side will be 4500 cubits.[e] The south side will be 4500 cubits. The east side will be 4500 cubits. The west side will be 4500 cubits. [17]The city will have grasslands. These grasslands will be 250 cubits[f] on the north and 250 cubits on the

[a]**48:8 25,000 cubits** 8.05 miles (12.96 km). Also in verses 9, 13, 15, 20, 21–22.
[b]**48:9 20,000 cubits** 6.44 miles (10.37 km). Most Greek copies have 25,000 cubits, and the standard Hebrew text has 10,000 cubits, but see Ezek. 45:1. Also in verse 13.
[c]**48:10 10,000 cubits** 3.22 miles (5.18 km). Also in verses 13, 18.
[d]**48:15 5000 cubits** 1.61 miles (2.6 km).
[e]**48:16 4500 cubits** 1.45 miles (2.33 km). Also in verses 30, 32–34.
[f]**48:17 250 cubits** 425' 1 1/2" (129.58 m).

south. They will be 250 cubits on the east and 250 cubits on the west. ¹⁸What is left of the length along the side of the holy area will be 10,000 cubits on the east and 10,000 cubits on the west. This land will be along the side of the holy area. This land will grow food for the city workers. ¹⁹The city workers from all the tribes of Israel will farm this land.

²⁰"This special area of land will be square. It will be 25,000 cubits long by 25,000 cubits wide. You must set apart this area for its special purposes. One part is for the priests, one part is for the Levites, and one part is for the city.

²¹⁻²²"Part of that special land will be for the ruler of the country. That special area of land is square. It is 25,000 cubits long by 25,000 cubits wide. Part of this special land is for the priests, part of it is for the Levites, and part of it is for the Temple. The Temple is in the middle of this area of land. The rest of the land belongs to the ruler of the country. The ruler will get the area between the land of Benjamin and the land of Judah.

²³⁻²⁷"South of this special area will be the land for the tribes that lived east of the Jordan River. Each tribe will get a section of land that goes from the eastern border to the Mediterranean Sea. From north to south, these tribes are Benjamin, Simeon, Issachar, Zebulun, and Gad.

²⁸"The southern border of Gad's land will go from Tamar to the oasis at Meribah-kadesh, then along the Brook of Egypt to the Mediterranean Sea. ²⁹This is the land that you will divide among the tribes of Israel. This is what each group will get." This is what the Lord God said!

The Gates of the City

³⁰"These are the gates of the city. The gates will be named for the tribes of Israel.

"The north side of the city will be 4500 cubits long. ³¹There will be three gates: Reuben's Gate, Judah's Gate, and Levi's Gate.

³²"The east side of the city will be 4500 cubits long. There will be three gates: Joseph's Gate, Benjamin's Gate, and Dan's Gate.

³³"The south side of the city will be 4500 cubits long. There will be three gates: Simeon's Gate, Issachar's Gate, and Zebulun's Gate.

³⁴"The west side of the city will be 4500 cubits long. There will be three gates: Gad's Gate, Asher's Gate, and Naphtali's Gate.

³⁵"The distance around the city will be 18,000 cubits.ᵃ From now on, the name of the city will be THE LORD IS THERE.ᵇ"

ᵃ**48:35** *18,000 cubits* 5.8 miles (9.33 km).
ᵇ**48:35** THE LORD IS THERE In Hebrew this name sounds like Jerusalem.

Daniel

Daniel Taken to Babylon

1 ¹Nebuchadnezzar king of Babylon came to Jerusalem and surrounded it with his army. This happened during the third year that Jehoiakimᶜ was king of Judah. ²The Lord allowed Nebuchadnezzar to defeat Jehoiakim king of Judah. Nebuchadnezzar took all the dishes and other things from God's Temple* and carried them to Babylon. He put those things in the temple of his gods.

³Then King Nebuchadnezzar ordered Ashpenaz, the man in charge of his officials,* to bring some of the boys into the palace to train them. He was to include boys from among the Israelites,ᵈ from important Judean families, and from the royal family of Judah. ⁴King Nebuchadnezzar wanted only healthy boys who did not have any bruises, scars, or

ᶜ**1:1** *the third year … Jehoiakim* This was about 605 B.C.
ᵈ**1:3** *Israelites* Here, this probably means "ordinary citizens of Judah and Israel." But it could mean "people from the northern tribes of Israel."

anything wrong with their bodies. He wanted handsome, smart young men who were able to learn things quickly and easily to serve in his palace. He told Ashpenaz to teach these young men the language and writings of the Chaldeans.*

⁵King Nebuchadnezzar gave the young men a certain amount of food and wine every day. This was the same kind of food that he ate. He wanted them to be trained for three years. After that, they would become servants of the king of Babylon. ⁶Among those young men were Daniel, Hananiah, Mishael, and Azariah from the tribe of Judah. ⁷Ashpenaz gave them Babylonian names. Daniel's new name was Belteshazzar, Hananiah's was Shadrach, Mishael's was Meshach, and Azariah's was Abednego.

⁸Daniel did not want to eat the king's rich food and wine because it would make him unclean.* So he asked Ashpenaz for permission not to make himself unclean in this way. ⁹God caused Ashpenaz, the man in charge

of the officials, to be kind and loyal to Daniel. [10]But Ashpenaz told Daniel, "I am afraid of my master, the king. He ordered me to give you this food and drink. If you don't eat this food, you will begin to look weak and sick. You will look worse than other young men your age. The king will see this, and he will become angry with me. He might cut off my head. And it would be your fault."

[11]Then Daniel talked to the guard who had been put in charge of Daniel, Hananiah, Mishael, and Azariah by Ashpenaz. [12]He said, "Please give us this test for ten days: Don't give us anything but vegetables to eat and water to drink. [13]Then after ten days, compare us with the other young men who eat the king's food. See for yourself who looks healthier, and then decide how you want to treat us, your servants."

[14]So the guard agreed to test Daniel, Hananiah, Mishael, and Azariah for ten days. [15]After ten days, Daniel and his friends looked healthier than all the young men who ate the king's food. [16]So the guard continued to take away the king's special food and wine and to give only vegetables to Daniel, Hananiah, Mishael, and Azariah.

[17]God gave these four young men the wisdom and ability to learn many different kinds of writing and science. Daniel could also understand all kinds of visions* and dreams.

[18]At the end of the three years of training, Ashpenaz brought all the young men to King Nebuchadnezzar. [19]The king talked to them and found that none of the young men were as good as Daniel, Hananiah, Mishael, and Azariah. So these four young men became the king's servants. [20]Every time the king asked them about something important, they showed great wisdom and understanding. The king found they were ten times better than all the magicians and wise men in his kingdom. [21]So Daniel served the king until the first year that Cyrus[a] was king.

Nebuchadnezzar's Dream

2 [1]During Nebuchadnezzar's second year as king, he had dreams. They bothered him, and he could not sleep. [2]So the king called his wise men to come to him. They used magic and watched the stars. They did this to try to interpret dreams and to learn what would happen in the future. The king wanted them to tell him what he had dreamed, so they came in and stood in front of him. [3]Then the king said to them, "I had a dream that bothers me. I want to know what it means."

[4]Then the Chaldeans* answered the king. They spoke Aramaic[b] and said, "King, live forever! Please tell your dream to us, your servants, and then we will tell you what it means."

[5]Then King Nebuchadnezzar said to them, "No, you must tell me the dream, and then you must tell me what it means. If you don't, I will give an order for you to be cut into pieces. And I will order your houses to be destroyed until they are nothing but piles of dust and ashes. [6]But if you tell me my dream and explain its meaning, I will give you gifts, rewards, and great honor. So tell me about my dream and what it means."

[7]Again the wise men said to the king, "Please, Sir, tell us about the dream, and we will tell you what it means."

[8]Then King Nebuchadnezzar answered, "I know that you are trying to get more time. You know that I meant what I said. [9]You know that you will be punished if you don't tell me about my dream. So you have all agreed to lie to me. You are hoping for more time so that I will forget what I want you to do. Now tell me the dream. If you can tell me the dream, I will know that you can tell me what it really means."

[10]The Chaldeans answered the king. They said, "There is not a man on earth who can do what the king is asking! No king has ever asked the wise men, the men who do magic, or the Chaldeans to do something like this. Not even the greatest and most powerful king has ever asked his wise men to do such a thing. [11]The king is asking something that is too hard to do. Only the gods could tell the king his dream and what it means. But the gods don't live with people."

[12]When the king heard that, he became very angry. So he gave an order for all the wise men of Babylon to be killed. [13]King Nebuchadnezzar's order to kill all the wise men was announced. The king's men were sent to look for Daniel and his friends to kill them.

[14]Arioch was the commander of the king's guards. He was going to kill the wise men of Babylon, but Daniel talked to him. Daniel spoke politely to Arioch [15]and said, "Why did the king order such a severe punishment?"

Then Arioch explained the whole story about the king's dreams, and Daniel understood. [16]When Daniel heard the story, he went to King Nebuchadnezzar. Daniel asked the king to give him some more time. Then he would tell the king what the dream meant.

[17]So Daniel went to his house. He explained the whole story to his friends Hananiah, Mishael, and Azariah. [18]Daniel asked his friends to pray to the God of heaven that God would be kind to them and help them understand this secret. Then Daniel and his friends would not be killed with the other wise men of Babylon.

[19]During the night, God explained the secret to Daniel in a vision.* Then Daniel praised the God of heaven. [20]He said,

[a]1:21 the first year ... Cyrus This was about 539–538 B.C.

[b]2:4 Aramaic The text of Daniel from here to 7:28 is written in Aramaic. See "Aramaic" in the Word List.

"Praise God's name forever and ever!
  Power and wisdom belong to him.
21 He changes the times and seasons.
  He gives power to kings,
  and he takes their power away.
  He gives wisdom to people, so they
    become wise.
  He lets people learn things and become
    wise.
22 He knows hidden secrets that are hard to
    understand.
  Light lives with him,
  so he knows what is in the dark and
    secret places.
23 God of my ancestors,* I thank you and
    praise you.
  You gave me wisdom and power.
  You told us what we asked for.
  You told us about the king's dream."

Daniel Tells What the Dream Means

24Then Daniel went to Arioch, the man who King Nebuchadnezzar had chosen to kill the wise men of Babylon. Daniel said to Arioch, "Don't kill the wise men of Babylon. Take me to the king. I will tell him what his dream means."

25So very quickly, Arioch took Daniel to the king. Arioch said to the king, "I have found a man among the captives[a] from Judah who can tell the king what his dream means."

26The king asked Daniel (Belteshazzar) a question. He said, "Are you able to tell me about my dream, and what it means?"

27Daniel answered, "King Nebuchadnezzar, no wise man, no man who does magic, and no Chaldean could tell the king the secret things he has asked about. 28But there is a God in heaven who tells secret things. God has given King Nebuchadnezzar dreams to show him what will happen later. This was your dream, and this is what you saw while lying on your bed: 29King, as you were lying there on your bed, you began thinking about what might happen in the future. God can tell people about secret things—he has shown you what will happen in the future. 30God also told this secret to me, not because I have greater wisdom than other men, but so that you, king, may know what it means. In that way you will understand what went through your mind.

31"King, in your dream you saw a large statue in front of you that was very large and shiny. It was very impressive. 32The head of the statue was made from pure gold. Its chest and the arms were made from silver. The belly and upper part of the legs were made from bronze. 33The lower part of the legs was made from iron. Its feet were made partly of iron and partly of clay. 34While you were looking at the statue, you saw a rock that was cut loose, but not by human hands. Then the rock hit the statue on its feet of iron and clay and smashed them. 35Then the iron, the clay, the bronze, the silver, and the gold broke to pieces all at the same time. And all the pieces became like chaff* on a threshing* floor in the summertime. The wind blew them away, and there was nothing left. No one could tell that a statue had ever been there. Then the rock that hit the statue became a very large mountain and filled up the whole earth.

36"That was your dream. Now we will tell the king what it means. 37King, you are the most important king. The God of heaven has given you a kingdom, power, strength, and glory. 38He has given you control, and you rule over people and the wild animals and the birds. Wherever they live, God has made you ruler over them all. King Nebuchadnezzar, you are that head of gold on the statue.

39"Another kingdom will come after you, but it will not be as great as your kingdom. Next, a third kingdom will rule over the earth—that is the bronze part. 40Then there will be a fourth kingdom. That kingdom will be strong like iron. Just as iron breaks things and smashes them to pieces, that fourth kingdom will break all the other kingdoms and smash them to pieces.

41"You saw that the feet and toes of the statue were partly clay and partly iron. That means the fourth kingdom will be a divided kingdom. It will have some of the strength of iron in it just as you saw the iron mixed with clay. 42The toes of the statue were partly iron and partly clay. So the fourth kingdom will be partly strong like iron and partly weak like clay. 43You saw the iron mixed with clay, but iron and clay don't completely mix together. In the same way the people of the fourth kingdom will be a mixture. They will not be united as one people.

44"During the time of the kings of the fourth kingdom, the God of heaven will set up another kingdom that will continue forever. It will never be destroyed. And it will be the kind of kingdom that cannot be passed on to another group of people. This kingdom will crush all the other kingdoms. It will bring them to an end, but that kingdom itself will continue forever.

45"King Nebuchadnezzar, you saw a rock cut from a mountain, but no one cut that rock. The rock broke the iron, the bronze, the clay, the silver, and the gold to pieces. In this way God showed you what will happen in the future. The dream is true, and you can trust that this is what it means."

46Then King Nebuchadnezzar bowed down in front of Daniel to honor him. The king praised him. He gave an order that an offering and incense be given to honor Daniel. 47Then the king said to Daniel, "I know for sure your God is the God over all gods and the Lord over all kings. He tells people about

a2:25 captives People taken away as prisoners. Here, it means the Jewish people who were taken to Babylon.

things they cannot know. I know this is true because you were able to tell these secret things to me."

⁴⁸Then the king gave Daniel a very important job in his kingdom and gave him many expensive gifts. Nebuchadnezzar made Daniel ruler over the whole province of Babylon and put him in charge of all the wise men of Babylon. ⁴⁹Daniel asked the king to make Shadrach, Meshach, and Abednego important officials over the province of Babylon. The king did as Daniel asked. Daniel himself became one of the important officials who was always near the king.

The Idol of Gold and the Hot Furnace

3 ¹King Nebuchadnezzar had a gold idol* made that was 60 cubitsᵃ high and 6 cubitsᵇ wide. Then he set the idol up on the plain of Dura in the province of Babylon. ²Then he called the satraps,* prefects,* governors, advisors, treasurers, judges, rulers, and all the other officials in his kingdom to come together. He wanted all of them to come to the dedication* ceremony for the idol.

³So all the men came and stood in front of the idol that King Nebuchadnezzar had set up. ⁴Then the man who makes announcements for the king spoke in a loud voice, "All you people from many nations and language groups, listen to me. This is what you are commanded to do: ⁵You must bow down as soon as you hear the sound of all the musical instruments. When you hear the horns, flutes, lyres,* sambucas,ᶜ harps, bagpipes,ᵈ and all the other musical instruments, you must bow down the gold idol. King Nebuchadnezzar has set this idol up. ⁶Whoever does not bow down and worship this gold idol will immediately be thrown into a very hot furnace.*"

⁷So as soon as they heard the sound of the horns, flutes, lyres, sambucas, bagpipes, and all the other musical instruments, they bowed down and worshiped the gold idol. All the peoples, nations, and different language groups there worshiped the gold idol that King Nebuchadnezzar had set up.

⁸Then some of the Chaldeans* came up to the king and began speaking against the people from Judah. ⁹They said, "King, may you live forever! ¹⁰King, you gave a command.

ᵃ**3:1** *60 cubits* About 87' 4" (27 m) using the short cubit.
ᵇ**3:1** *6 cubits* About 8' 9" (2.7 m) using the short cubit.
ᶜ**3:5** *sambucas* A musical instrument, possibly a seven stringed instrument like a harp. The name in Hebrew comes from some other language, possibly Greek.
ᵈ**3:5** *bagpipes* A musical instrument with a bag and several horns or pipes. The name in Hebrew comes from some other language, possibly from the Greek word "symphony."

You said that everyone who hears the sound of the horns, flutes, lyres, sambucas, harps, bagpipes, and all the other musical instruments must bow down and worship the gold idol. ¹¹And you also said that whoever does not bow down and worship the gold idol will be thrown into a very hot furnace. ¹²There are some Judeans who you made important officials in the province of Babylon that ignored your order, King. Their names are Shadrach, Meshach, and Abednego. They don't worship your gods, and they didn't bow down to worship the gold idol you set up."

¹³Nebuchadnezzar became very angry. He called for Shadrach, Meshach, and Abednego. So they were brought to him. ¹⁴And Nebuchadnezzar said to them, "Shadrach, Meshach, and Abednego, is it true that you don't worship my gods? And is it true that you didn't bow down and worship the gold idol I have set up? ¹⁵Now when you hear the sound of the horns, flutes, lyres, sambucas, harps, bagpipes, and all the other musical instruments, you must bow down and worship the gold idol. If you are ready to worship the idol I have made, that is good. But if you don't worship it, you will be thrown very quickly into the hot furnace. Then no god will be able to save you from my power!"

¹⁶Shadrach, Meshach, and Abednego answered the king, "Nebuchadnezzar, we don't need to explain these things to you. ¹⁷If you throw us into the hot furnace, the God we serve can save us. And if he wants to, he can save us from your power. ¹⁸But even if God does not save us, we want you to know, King, that we refuse to serve your gods. We will not worship the gold idol you have set up."

¹⁹Then Nebuchadnezzar became very angry with Shadrach, Meshach, and Abednego. He gave an order for the oven to be heated seven times hotter than it usually was. ²⁰Then he commanded some of the strongest soldiers in his army to tie up Shadrach, Meshach, and Abednego. He told the soldiers to throw them into the hot furnace.

²¹So Shadrach, Meshach, and Abednego were tied up and thrown into the hot furnace. They were wearing their robes, pants, cloth caps, and other clothes. ²²The king was very angry when he gave the command, so the soldiers quickly made the furnace very hot. The fire was so hot that the flames killed the strong soldiers. They were killed when they went close to the fire to throw in Shadrach, Meshach, and Abednego. ²³Shadrach, Meshach, and Abednego fell into the fire. They were tied up very tightly.

²⁴Then King Nebuchadnezzar jumped to his feet. He was very surprised and he asked his advisors, "We tied only three men, and we threw only three men into the fire. Is that right?"

His advisors said, "Yes, King."

²⁵The king said, "Look! I see four men walking around in the fire. They are not tied up and they are not burned. The fourth man looks like an angel.ᵃ"

²⁶Then Nebuchadnezzar went to the opening of the hot furnace. He shouted, "Shadrach, Meshach, and Abednego, come out! Servants of the Most High God, come here!"

So Shadrach, Meshach, and Abednego came out of the fire. ²⁷When they came out, the satraps, prefects, governors, and royal advisors crowded around them. They could see that the fire had not burned Shadrach, Meshach, and Abednego. Their bodies were not burned at all. Their hair was not burned, and their robes were not burned. They didn't even smell as if they had been near fire.

²⁸Then Nebuchadnezzar said, "Praise the God of Shadrach, Meshach, and Abednego. Their God has sent his angel and saved his servants from the fire! These three men trusted their God and refused to obey my command. They were willing to die instead of serving or worshiping any other god. ²⁹So I now make this law: Anyone from any nation or language group who says anything against the God of Shadrach, Meshach, and Abednego will be cut into pieces, and their house will be destroyed until it is a pile of dirt and ashes. No other god can save his people like this."

³⁰Then the king gave Shadrach, Meshach, and Abednego more important jobs in the province of Babylon.

Nebuchadnezzar's Dream About a Tree

4 ¹King Nebuchadnezzar sent this letter to the many nations and language groups living around the world.

Greetings:

²I am very happy to tell you about the miracles and wonderful things that the Most High God did for me.

³ God has done amazing miracles!
　He has done powerful miracles!
His kingdom continues forever;
　his rule will continue for all generations.

⁴I, Nebuchadnezzar, was at my palace. I was happy and successful. ⁵I had a dream that made me afraid. I was lying on my bed, and I saw pictures and visions* in my mind. These things made me very afraid. ⁶So I gave an order that all the wise men of Babylon be brought to me to tell me what my dream meant. ⁷When the men of magic and the Chaldeans* came, I told them about the dream, but they could not tell me what it meant. ⁸Finally, Daniel came to me. (I gave Daniel the name, Belteshazzar, to honor my god. The spirit of the holy gods is in him.) I told him about my dream.

⁹I said, "Belteshazzar, you are the most important of all the men of magic. I know that the spirit of the holy gods is in you. I know there is no secret that is too hard for you to understand. This was what I dreamed. Tell me what it means. ¹⁰These are the visions I saw while I was lying in my bed: I looked, and there in front of me was a tree standing in the middle of the earth. The tree was very tall. ¹¹The tree grew large and strong. The top of the tree touched the sky.ᵇ It could be seen from anywhere on earth. ¹²The leaves of the tree were beautiful. It had much good fruit on it. And on the tree was plenty of food for everyone. The wild animals found shelter under the tree, and the birds lived in its branches. Every animal ate from the tree.

¹³"I was looking at those things in the vision while lying on my bed. And then I saw a holy angel coming down from heaven. ¹⁴He spoke very loud and said, 'Cut down the tree, and cut off its branches. Strip off its leaves. Scatter its fruit around. The animals that are under the tree will run away. The birds that are in its branches will fly away. ¹⁵But let the stump and roots stay in the ground. Put a band of iron and bronze around it. The stump and roots will stay in the field with the grass all around it. It will live among the wild animals and plants in the fields. It will become wet with dew. ¹⁶He will not think like a man any longer. He will have the mind of an animal. Seven seasons will pass while he is like this.'

¹⁷"Holy angels announced this punishment so that all the people on earth may know that God Most High rules over human kingdoms. God gives those kingdoms to whoever he wants, and he chooses humble people to rule them.

¹⁸"That is what I, King Nebuchadnezzar, dreamed. Now, Belteshazzar,ᶜ tell me what it means. None of the wise men in my kingdom can tell me what that dream means. But Belteshazzar, you can interpret the dream because the spirit of the holy gods is in you."

¹⁹Then Daniel (also called Belteshazzar) became very quiet for a while. What he was thinking bothered him. So the king said, "Belteshazzar, don't let the dream or its meaning make you afraid."

Then Belteshazzar answered the king, "My lord, I wish the dream were about your

---

ᵃ**3:25** *angel* Literally, "son of the god."

ᵇ**4:10–11** *middle of the earth … sky* The Babylonians thought the earth was flat and round like a plate or a wheel. And they thought the sky was like a glass bowl turned upside down on the earth.
ᶜ**4:18** *Belteshazzar* Another name for Daniel.

enemies, and I wish the meaning of the dream were about those against you. ²⁰⁻²¹You saw a tree in your dream. The tree grew large and strong. Its top touched the sky, and it could be seen from all over the earth. Its leaves were beautiful, and it had plenty of fruit. The fruit gave plenty of food for everyone. It was a home for the wild animals, and its branches were nesting places for the birds. You saw that tree. ²²King, you are that tree! You have become great and powerful. You are like the tall tree that touched the sky—your power reaches to the far parts of the earth.

²³"King, you saw a holy angel coming down from heaven. He said, 'Cut the tree down and destroy it. Put a band of iron and bronze around the stump and leave the stump and its roots in the ground. Leave it in the grass in the field. It will become wet with dew. He will live like a wild animal. Seven seasons will pass while he is like this.'

²⁴"King, this is the meaning of the dream. God Most High has commanded these things to happen to my lord the king: ²⁵King Nebuchadnezzar, you will be forced to go away from people. You will live among the wild animals. You will eat grass like cattle, and you will become wet with dew. Seven seasons will pass, and then you will learn this lesson. You will learn God Most High rules over human kingdoms and gives them to whoever he wants.

²⁶"The command to leave the stump of the tree and its roots in the ground means this: Your kingdom will be given back to you. This will happen when you learn that Most High God rules your kingdom. ²⁷So, King, please accept my advice. Stop sinning and do what is right. Stop doing bad things and be kind to poor people. Then you might continue to be successful."

²⁸All these things happened to King Nebuchadnezzar. ²⁹⁻³⁰Twelve months after the dream, King Nebuchadnezzar was walking on the roof*ᵃ* of his palace in Babylon. While on the roof, the king said, "Look at Babylon! I built this great city. It is my palace. I built this great place by my power. I built this place to show how great I am."

³¹The words were still in his mouth when a voice came from heaven. The voice said, "King Nebuchadnezzar, these things will happen to you: Your power as king has been taken away from you. ³²You will be forced to go away from people. You will live with the wild animals and eat grass like an ox. Seven seasons will pass before you learn your lesson. Then you will learn that God Most High rules over human kingdoms and gives them to whoever he wants."

³³These things happened immediately. Nebuchadnezzar was forced to go away from

people. He began eating grass like an ox. He became wet from dew. His hair grew long like the feathers of an eagle, and his nails grew long like the claws of a bird.

³⁴Then at the end of that time, I, Nebuchadnezzar, looked up toward heaven, and I was in my right mind again. Then I gave praise to God Most High. I gave honor and glory to him who lives forever.

> God rules forever!
> His kingdom continues for all
>   generations.
> ³⁵ People on earth are not really important.
> God does what he wants
>   with the powers of heaven
>   and the people on earth.
> No one can stop his powerful hand
>   or question what he does.

³⁶At that time God gave me my right mind again, and he gave back my great honor and power as king. My advisors and the royal people began to ask my advice again. I became the king again—even greater and more powerful than before. ³⁷Now I, Nebuchadnezzar, give praise, honor, and glory to the King of Heaven. Everything he does is right. He is always fair, and he is able to make proud people humble!

The Writing on the Wall

5 ¹King Belshazzar gave a big party for 1000 of his officials. The king was drinking wine with them. ²As Belshazzar was drinking his wine, he ordered his servants to bring the gold and silver cups. His grandfather*ᵇ* Nebuchadnezzar had taken these cups from the Temple* in Jerusalem. King Belshazzar wanted his royal people, his wives, and his slave women* to drink from those cups. ³So they brought the gold cups that had been taken from the Temple of God in Jerusalem, and the king and his officials, his wives, and his women slaves drank from them. ⁴As they were drinking, they gave praise to their idol gods, which were only statues made from gold, silver, bronze, iron, wood, and stone.

⁵Suddenly, a person's hand appeared and began writing on the wall. The fingers scratched words into the plaster on the wall, near the lampstand in the king's palace. The king was watching the hand as it wrote.

⁶King Belshazzar was very afraid. His face became white from fear, and his knees were shaking and knocking together. He could not stand up because his legs were too weak. ⁷The king called for the men of magic and the Chaldeans* to be brought to him. He said to these wise men, "I will give a reward to anyone

---

*ᵃ*4:29–30 **roof** In ancient Israel, houses had flat roofs that were used as an extra room.

*ᵇ*5:2 **grandfather** Or "father." It is uncertain that Belshazzar was really Nebuchadnezzar's grandson. Here, the word "father" might only mean "the previous king." Also in verses 11, 18.

who can read this writing and explain to me what it means. I will give him purple robes[a] to wear and will put a gold chain around his neck. I will make him the third highest ruler in the kingdom."

8So all the king's wise men came in, but they could not read the writing or understand what it meant. 9King Belshazzar's officials were confused, and the king became even more afraid and worried. His face was white from fear.

10Then the king's mother came into the place where the party was. She had heard the voices of the king and his royal officials. She said, "King, may you live forever! Don't be afraid! Don't let your face be so white with fear! 11There is a man in your kingdom who has the spirit of the holy gods in him. In the days of your father, this man showed that he could understand secrets. He showed that he was very smart and very wise. He showed that he was like the gods in these things. Your grandfather, King Nebuchadnezzar, put this man in charge of all the wise men. He ruled over all the men of magic and the Chaldeans. 12The man I am talking about is named Daniel. The king gave him the name Belteshazzar. He is very smart and he knows many things. He could interpret dreams, explain secrets, and find the answer to very hard problems. Call for Daniel, he will tell you what the writing on the wall means."

13So they brought Daniel to the king and he asked, "Is your name Daniel, one of the captives my father the king brought here from Judah? 14I have heard that the spirit of the gods is in you and that you understand secrets and are very smart and very wise. 15The wise men and the men of magic were brought to me to read this writing on the wall. I wanted them to explain to me what it means, but they could not explain it. 16I have heard that you are able to explain what things mean, and that you can find the answer to very hard problems. If you can read this writing on the wall and explain to me what it means, this is what I will do for you: I will give you purple robes to wear and will put a gold chain around your neck. Then you will become the third highest ruler in the kingdom."

17Then Daniel answered the king, "King Belshazzar, you can keep your gifts for yourself, or you can give them to someone else. But I will still read the writing on the wall for you and explain what it means.

18"King, God Most High made your grandfather Nebuchadnezzar a very great and powerful king and gave him great wealth. 19People from many nations and language groups were very afraid of Nebuchadnezzar because God made him a very powerful king. Nebuchadnezzar killed whoever he wanted and let those who pleased him live. If he wanted to make people important, he made them important. If he wanted to bring them down, he brought them down.

20"But Nebuchadnezzar became proud and stubborn, so his power was taken away from him. He was taken off his royal throne and stripped of his glory. 21Then Nebuchadnezzar was forced to go away from people. His mind became like the mind of an animal. He lived with the wild donkeys and ate grass like an ox. He became wet with dew. These things happened to him until he learned his lesson. He learned that God Most High rules over human kingdoms, and he gives them to whoever he wants.

22"But Belshazzar, you already knew this. You are Nebuchadnezzar's grandson,[b] but still you have not made yourself humble. 23No, you did not become humble. Instead, you have turned against the Lord of heaven. You ordered the drinking cups from his Temple to be brought to you. Then you and your royal officials, your wives, and your slave women* drank wine from those cups. You gave praise to the gods of silver and gold, of bronze, iron, wood, and stone. They are not really gods; they cannot see or hear or understand anything. But you did not give honor to the God who has the power over your life and everything you do. 24So because of that, God sent the hand that wrote on the wall. 25These are the words that were written on the wall:

MENE, MENE, TEKEL, UPARSIN.

26"This is what these words mean:

MENE[c]:
    God has counted the days until your
        kingdom will end.
27 TEKEL[d]:
    You have been weighed on the scales
        and found not good enough.
28 UPARSIN[e]:
    Your kingdom is being taken from you.
        It will be divided among the Medes and
        Persians.*"

29Then Belshazzar gave an order for Daniel to be dressed in purple clothes. A gold chain was put around his neck, and he was

---

[a]5:7 purple robes These clothes showed that a person was rich and powerful, like a king. Also in verses 16, 29.

[b]5:22 grandson Or "son." This does not necessarily mean they were from the same family. It might only mean that Belshazzar was one of the kings of Babylon after Nebuchadnezzar was king.
[c]5:26 MENE A weight, like the Hebrew word "mina." This is like the word "to count."
[d]5:27 TEKEL A weight, like the Hebrew word "shekel." This word is like the word meaning "to weigh."
[e]5:28 UPARSIN Literally, "peres," a weight. This word is like the word meaning "to divide" or "to split." It is also like the name of the country of Persia.

appointed the third highest ruler in the kingdom. [30]That very same night, Belshazzar, king of the Babylonians, was killed. [31]A man named Darius the Mede became the new king. Darius was about 62 years old.

Daniel and the Lions

6 [1]Darius thought it would be a good idea to choose 120 satraps* to rule throughout his kingdom. [2]He chose three men to rule over the 120 satraps. Daniel was one of the three supervisors. The king put these men in this position to keep anyone from cheating him. [3]Daniel proved himself to be a better supervisor than any of the others. He did this by his good character and great ability. The king was so impressed with Daniel that he planned to make him ruler over the whole kingdom. [4]But when the other supervisors and the satraps heard about this, they were very jealous. They tried to find reasons to accuse Daniel. So they watched what Daniel did as he went about doing the business of the government. But they could not find anything wrong with him, so they could not accuse him of doing anything wrong. Daniel was a man people could trust. He did not cheat the king, and he worked very hard.

[5]Finally they said, "We will never find any reason to accuse Daniel of doing something wrong. So we must find something to complain about that is connected to the law of his God."

[6]So the two supervisors and the satraps went as a group to the king. They said, "King Darius, live forever! [7]The supervisors, prefects,* satraps, advisors, and governors have all agreed on something. We think that the king should make this law and that everyone must obey it: For the next 30 days, whoever prays to any god or man except you, King, will be thrown into the lions' den. [8]Now, King, make the law and sign the paper it is written on so that it cannot be changed, because the laws of the Medes and Persians* cannot be canceled or changed." [9]So King Darius made the law and signed it.

[10]Daniel always prayed to God three times every day. Three times every day, he bowed down on his knees to pray and praise God. Even though Daniel heard about the new law, he still went to his house to pray. He went up to the upper room of his house and opened the windows that faced toward Jerusalem. Then Daniel bowed down on his knees and prayed just as he always had done.

[11]Then the supervisors and satraps went as a group and found Daniel praying and asking God for help. [12]So they went to the king and talked to him about the law he had made. They said, "King Darius, you signed a law that says, for the next 30 days anyone who prays to any god or man except you, the king, would be thrown into the lions' den. You did sign that law, didn't you?"

The king answered, "Yes, I signed that law, and the laws of the Medes and Persians cannot be canceled or changed."

[13]Then they said to the king, "That man Daniel is not paying any attention to you. He is one of the captives[a] from Judah, and he is not paying attention to the law you signed. Daniel still prays to his God three times every day."

[14]The king became very sad and upset when he heard this. He decided to save Daniel. He worked until sunset trying to think of a way to save him. [15]Then the men went as a group to the king and said to him, "Remember, King, that the law of the Medes and Persians says that no law or command signed by the king can ever be canceled or changed."

[16]So King Darius gave the order. They brought Daniel and threw him into the lions' den. The king said to Daniel, "May the God you serve save you!" [17]A big rock was brought and put over the opening of the lions' den. Then the king used his ring and put his seal* on the rock. He also used the rings of his officials and put their seals on the rock. This showed that no one could move that rock and bring Daniel out of the lion's den. [18]Then King Darius went back to his house. He did not eat that night. He did not want anyone to come and entertain him. He could not sleep all night.

[19]The next morning, King Darius got up just as it was getting light and ran to the lions' den. [20]He was very worried. When he got to the lions' den, he called to Daniel. He said, "Daniel, servant of the living God, has your God been able to save you from the lions? You always serve your God."

[21]Daniel answered, "King, live forever! [22]My God sent his angel to save me. The angel closed the lions' mouths. The lions have not hurt me because my God knows I am innocent. I never did anything wrong to you, King."

[23]King Darius was very happy. He told his servants to lift Daniel out of the lions' den. And when Daniel was lifted out of the den, they did not find any injury on his body. The lions did not hurt Daniel because he trusted in his God.

[24]Then the king gave a command to bring the men who had accused Daniel to the lions' den. The men and their wives and children were thrown into the lion's den. The lions grabbed them before they hit the floor. The lions ate their bodies and then chewed on their bones.

[25]Then King Darius wrote this letter to all the people from other nations and language groups all around the world:

---

[a]**6:13** *captives* People taken away as prisoners. Here, it means the Jewish people who were taken to Babylon.

Greetings:

26I am making a new law. This law is for people in every part of my kingdom. All of you must fear and respect the God of Daniel.

Daniel's God is the living God;
   he lives forever.
His kingdom will never be destroyed.
   His rule will never end.
27 God helps and saves people.
   He does amazing miracles in heaven
      and on earth.
   He saved Daniel from the lions.

28So Daniel was successful during the time Darius was king and when Cyrus the Persian was king.

Daniel's Dream About Four Animals

7 1During the first year that Belshazzar*a* was king of Babylon, Daniel had a dream. He saw these visions* while he was lying on his bed, and he wrote what he had dreamed. 2Daniel said, "I saw my vision at night. In the vision the wind was blowing from all four directions. These winds made the sea rough. 3I saw four big animals and each one was different from the others. These four animals came up out of the sea.

4"The first animal looked like a lion, but it had wings like an eagle. As I watched, its wings were torn off. It was helped up from the ground, and it stood up on two feet like a human. Then it was given a human mind.

5"Then I saw another animal there in front of me that looked like a bear. It was raised up on one of its sides, and it had three ribs in its mouth between its teeth. It was told, 'Get up and eat all the meat you want!'

6"After that, I noticed another animal in front of me. It looked like a leopard, but it had four wings on its back. This animal had four heads. It was given authority to rule.

7"After that, in my vision at night I looked, and there in front of me was a fourth animal. It looked very cruel and terrifying. It looked very strong, with large iron teeth. This animal crushed and ate its victims and walked on whatever was left of them. This fourth animal was different from all the animals I saw before it. This animal had ten horns.

8"While I was looking at the horns and thinking about them, another horn grew up among them. This was a little horn with eyes like a human. It also had a mouth that was bragging. Then the little horn pulled out three of the other horns.

Judgment of the Fourth Animal

9"As I was looking, thrones were put in their places,

and the Ancient King*b* sat on his throne.
   His clothes were as white as snow.
   His hair was as white as wool.
His throne was made from fire,*c*
   and its wheels were made from flames.
10 A river of fire flowed out from in front of
      the Ancient King.
   Millions of people were serving him.
   Hundreds of millions of people stood in
      front of him.
   Court was ready to begin,
      and the books were opened.

11"I kept on looking because the little horn was bragging. I kept watching until finally the fourth animal was killed. Its body was destroyed, and it was thrown into the burning fire. 12The authority and rule of the other animals had been taken from them. But they were permitted to live for a certain period of time.

13"In my vision at night I looked, and there in front of me was someone who looked like a human being.*d* He was coming on the clouds in the sky. He came up to the Ancient King, and the King's servants brought him before the King.

14"The one who looked like a human being was given authority, glory, and complete ruling power. People from every nation and language group will serve him. His rule will last forever. His kingdom will continue forever. It will never be destroyed.

The Meaning of Daniel's Dream

15"I, Daniel, was confused and worried. The visions* that went through my mind bothered me. 16I went to someone who was standing there and asked him what all this meant. So he explained it to me. 17He said, 'The four great animals are four kingdoms that will come from the earth. 18But God's holy* people will receive the kingdom, and they will have the kingdom forever and ever.'

19"Then I wanted to know what the fourth animal was and what it meant. The fourth animal was different from all the other animals. It was very terrible and had iron teeth and bronze claws. It was the animal that crushed and ate its victims and walked on whatever was left. 20I wanted to know about the ten horns that were on the fourth animal's head and about the little horn that grew there. That little horn pulled out three of the other ten horns. That little horn had eyes and a mouth that kept on bragging, and it looked bigger than the other horns. 21As I was watching, this little horn

---

*a*7:1 *the first year ... Belshazzar* This was about 553 B.C.

*b*7:9 *Ancient King* Literally, "Ancient of Days." This name pictures God as a great king who has ruled since ancient times. Also in verses 10, 13, 22.
*c*7:9 *fire* Or "light."
*d*7:13 *someone ... human being* Or "a person, a real human being." Literally, "like a son of man." This means he looked like a normal person, not an angel or an animal.

began attacking and making war against God's holy people and killing them. ²²The little horn kept killing God's holy people until the Ancient King came and judged him. The Ancient King announced his decision about the little horn. This judgment helped God's holy people, and they received the kingdom.

²³"And he explained this to me: 'The fourth animal is a fourth kingdom that will come on the earth. It will be different from all the other kingdoms. That fourth kingdom will destroy people all around the world. It will walk on and crush nations all around the world. ²⁴The ten horns are ten kings that will come from this fourth kingdom. After those ten kings are gone, another king will come. He will be different from the kings who ruled before him. He will defeat three of the other kings. ²⁵This special king will say things against God Most High, and he will hurt and kill God's special people. That king will try to change the times and laws that have already been set. God's holy people will be under that king's power for three and one-half years.ᵃ

²⁶"But the court will decide what should happen, and that king's power will be taken away. His kingdom will end completely. ²⁷Then God's holy people will rule over the kingdom and all the people from all the kingdoms of earth.ᵇ This kingdom will last forever, and people from all the other kingdoms will respect and serve them.'

²⁸"And that was the end of the dream. I, Daniel, was very afraid. My face became very white from fear, and I did not tell the other people what I saw and heard."

Daniel's Vision of a Ram and a Goat

8 ¹After that vision,ᶜ I, Daniel, saw another vision* during the third year that Belshazzarᵈ was king. ²In the vision I saw that I was in the city of Susa.ᵉ Susa was the capital city in the province of Elam. I was standing by the Ulai River. ³I looked up and saw a ram standing at the side of the river. The ram had two long horns. The horns were both long, but one horn was longer than the other horn. The long horn was farther back than the other horn. ⁴I watched the ram run into things with its horns. I watched the ram run to the west, to the north, and to the south. No animal could stop the ram, and no one could save the other animals. That ram did whatever it wanted, and it became very powerful.

⁵I thought about the ram. While I was watching, I saw a male goat come from the west. It had one large horn that was easy to see. It ran so fast its feet barely touched the ground.

⁶The goat came to the ram with the two horns. (This was the ram I had seen standing by the Ulai River.) The goat was very angry and ran at the ram. ⁷As I watched, the goat ran at the ram and broke both of the ram's horns. The ram could not stop the goat. The goat knocked it to the ground and walked all over it. There was no one to save the ram from the goat.

⁸So the goat became very powerful. But after he became strong, his big horn broke off. Then four horns grew in place of the one big horn. Those four horns were easy to see. They pointed in four different directions.

⁹Then a little horn grew from one of those four horns. It grew and became very big. It grew toward the southeast, toward the Beautiful Land. ¹⁰The little horn became very big. It grew until it reached the sky. It even threw some of heaven's armyᶠ to the ground and trampled them. ¹¹That little horn became very strong, and it turned against God, the Ruler of heaven's army. It stopped the daily sacrifices* that were offered to the Ruler. And the holy place where people worshiped the Ruler was pulled down. ¹²Because of this sin, the daily sacrifices were stopped. Truth was thrown down to the ground. The little horn did these things and was very successful.

¹³Then I heard two holy onesᵍ talking with each other. One of them asked the other one, who had been speaking, "How long will the things in this vision last—the stopping of the daily sacrifices, the sin that destroys, and the trampling down of the holy place and heaven's army?"

¹⁴The other holy one said, "This will last for 2300 days. Then the holy place will be repaired."

The Vision Is Explained to Daniel

¹⁵I, Daniel, saw this vision* and tried to understand what it meant. While I was thinking about the vision, someone who looked like a man suddenly stood in front of me. ¹⁶Then I heard a man's voice. This voice came from above the Ulai River. The voice called out, "Gabriel, explain the vision to this man."

¹⁷So Gabriel, the angel who looked like a man, came to me. I was very afraid and fell down to the ground. But Gabriel said to me, "Human,ʰ understand that this vision is about the time of the end."

¹⁸While Gabriel was speaking, I fell to the ground and went to sleep. It was a very deep sleep. Then Gabriel touched me and lifted me

---

ᵃ**7:25** *three and one-half years* Literally, "time, times and half time."

ᵇ**7:27** *God's holy people ... earth* Literally, "The rule and kingdom and greatness of the kingdoms under heaven will be given to the saints."

ᶜ**8:1** *After that vision* Here, the original language changes from Aramaic (see "Aramaic" in the Word List) back to Hebrew.

ᵈ**8:1** *the third year ... Belshazzar* This was about 551 B.C.

ᵉ**8:2** *Susa* The capital city of Persia.

ᶠ**8:10** *heaven's army* Or "the stars." Also in verses 11 and 13.

ᵍ**8:13** *holy ones* Here, these are probably angels.

ʰ**8:17** *Human* Literally, "Son of man."

to my feet. ¹⁹He said, "Now, I will explain the vision to you. I will tell you what will happen in the future. Your vision was about the end times.

²⁰"You saw a ram with two horns. The horns are the countries of Media and Persia. ²¹The goat is the king of Greece. The big horn between its eyes is the first king. ²²That horn broke off and four horns grew in its place. The four horns are four kingdoms. Those four kingdoms will come from the nation of the first king, but they will not be as strong as the first king.

²³"When the end is near for those kingdoms, there will be a very bold and cruel king who will be very tricky. This will happen when many people have turned against God. ²⁴This king will be very powerful, but his power does not come from himself.ᵃ This king will cause terrible destruction. He will be successful in everything he does. He will destroy powerful people—even God's holy* people.

²⁵"This king will be very smart and tricky. He will use his wisdom and lies to be successful. He will think that he is very important. He will destroy many people, when they least expect it. He will try to fight even the Prince of Princes. But that cruel king's power will be destroyed, and it will not be a human hand that destroys him.

²⁶"What I said and the vision about those times are true. But seal* up the vision, because those things will not happen for a long, long time."

²⁷I, Daniel, became very weak. I was sick for several days after that vision. Then I got up and went back to work for the king, but I was very upset about the vision. I did not understand what it meant.

Daniel's Prayer

9 ¹These things happened during the first year that Darius son of Ahasuerusᵇ was king. Darius was a Mede by birth, but he was appointed to be the king of Babylon. ²During his first year as king, I was studying the Scripturesᶜ and noticed in the LORD's message to Jeremiah that 70 years would pass before Jerusalem would be rebuilt.

³Then I turned to the Lord God. I prayed to him and asked him for help. I did not eat any food. I put ashes on my head and put on the clothes that showed I was sad. ⁴I prayed to the LORD my God and told him about all my sins. I said, "Lord, you are a great and awesome God. You keep your agreement of love and kindness with people who love you. You keep your agreement with the people who obey your commands.

⁵"But we have sinned. We have done wrong. We have done evil things. We turned against you. We turned away from your commands and good decisions. ⁶The prophets were your servants. They spoke for you to our kings, to our leaders, to our fathers, and to the common people in our country. But we did not listen to them.

⁷"Lord, you are innocent, and the shame belongs to us, even now. Shame belongs to the people from Judah and Jerusalem, and to all the people of Israel, to those who are near and to those you scattered among many nations. They should be ashamed of all the evil things they did against you.

⁸"LORD, we should all be ashamed. All our kings and leaders should be ashamed. Our ancestors* should be ashamed, because we sinned against you.

⁹"But, Lord our God, you are kind and forgiving, even though we rebelled against you. ¹⁰We have not obeyed the LORD our God. He used his servants, the prophets, and gave us laws, but we have not obeyed his laws. ¹¹All the people of Israel disobeyed your teachings and turned away from you. They did not listen to you. We sinned, so you did what you promised to do. All the curses and promisesᵈ in the Law of Moses, your servant, happened to us.

¹²"God said those things would happen to us and our leaders, and he made them happen. He made terrible things happen to us. No other city suffered the way Jerusalem suffered. ¹³All those terrible things happened to us. This happened just as it is written in the Law of Moses, but we still have not asked the LORD our God for help. We still have not stopped sinning. We still do not pay attention to your truth, Lord. ¹⁴The LORD kept the terrible things ready for us—he made them happen to us. The LORD our God did this because he is fair in everything he does. But we still have not listened to him.

¹⁵"Lord our God, you used your power and brought us out of Egypt. We are your people. You are famous because of that, even today. We have sinned and done terrible things. ¹⁶Lord, we and our ancestors sinned against you, so your people and your city became a disgrace to everyone around us. You do so many good things, so stop being angry at Jerusalem, your city, your holy mountain.

¹⁷"Now, our God, hear your servant's prayer. Listen to my prayer for mercy. For your own sake, do good things for your holy place.ᵉ ¹⁸My God, listen to me! Open your eyes and see all the terrible things that have happened to us. See what has happened to the city that is called by your name. I am not

---

ᵃ8:24 *but his power ... himself* Some ancient versions don't have these words, so they may have been accidentally copied from verse 22.
ᵇ9:1 *Ahasuerus* Or "Xerxes."
ᶜ9:2 *Scriptures* Literally, "scrolls."

ᵈ9:11 *curses and promises* Part of the agreement that God made with the people of Israel. See, for example, Deuteronomy 27–30.
ᵉ9:17 *do ... holy place* Literally, "let your face shine on your holy place."

saying we are good people. That is not why I am asking these things. I am asking these things because I know you are kind. ¹⁹Lord, listen to me! Forgive us! Lord, pay attention, and then do something! Don't wait! Do something now! Do it for your own good! My God, do something now, for your city and your people who are called by your name."

The Vision About the 70 Weeks

²⁰I was praying to the Lord my God about his holy mountain and telling about my sins and the sins of the people of Israel. ²¹That was the time of the evening sacrifices. While I was still praying, Gabriel, the one I saw in the first vision,* flew quickly to me and touched me. He came at the time of the evening sacrifice.* ²²Gabriel helped me understand the things I wanted to know. He said, "Daniel, I have come to give you wisdom and to help you understand. ²³When you first started praying, the command was given to come speak to you. God loves you very much! You will understand this command, and you will understand the vision.

²⁴"God has allowed 70 weeks^a for your people and your holy city, Daniel. The 70 weeks are ordered for these reasons: to stop doing bad things, to stop sinning, to make people pure, to bring the goodness that continues forever, to put a seal* on visions and prophets, and to dedicate a very holy place.

²⁵"Learn and understand these things, Daniel. From the time that the message went out to go back and rebuild Jerusalem until the time for the chosen king^b to come will be seven weeks. Then Jerusalem will be rebuilt. There will again be places for people to meet together in Jerusalem, and there will be a ditch around the city to protect it. Jerusalem will be built for 62 weeks, but there will be many troubles during that time. ²⁶After the 62 weeks, the chosen one will be killed.^{c} He will be gone.^{d} Then the people of the future leader will destroy the city and the holy place. That end will come like a flood. War will continue until the end. God has ordered that place to be completely destroyed.

²⁷"Then the future ruler will make an agreement with many people. That agreement will continue for one week. The offerings and sacrifices will stop for a half of a week. And a destroyer will come. He will do terrible, destructive things,^{e} but God has ordered that destroyer to be completely destroyed."

Daniel's Vision by the Tigris River

10 ¹During the third year that Cyrus was the king of Persia, these things were shown to Daniel. (Daniel's other name is Belteshazzar.) They are true, but very hard to understand. Daniel understood them because they were explained to him in a vision.*

²At that time I, Daniel, was very sad for three weeks. ³During those three weeks, I didn't eat any fancy food; I didn't eat any meat or drink any wine. I didn't put any oil on my head. I didn't do any of these things for three weeks.

⁴On the 24th day of the first month of the year, I was standing beside the great Tigris River. ⁵While I was standing there, I looked up and I saw a man standing in front of me. He was wearing linen* clothes. He wore a belt made of pure gold^f around his waist. ⁶His body was like a smooth, shiny stone. His face was bright like lightning. His eyes were like flames of fire. His arms and feet were shiny like polished brass. His voice was loud like a crowd of people.

⁷I, Daniel, was the only one who saw the vision. The men with me didn't see the vision, but they were still afraid. They were so afraid that they ran away and hid. ⁸So I was left alone. I was watching this vision, and it made me afraid. I lost my strength. My face turned white like a dead person's face, and I was helpless. ⁹Then I heard the man in the vision talking. As I listened to his voice, I fell into a deep sleep, with my face on the ground.

¹⁰Then a hand touched me. When that happened, I got on my hands and knees. I was so afraid that I was shaking. ¹¹The man in the vision said to me, "Daniel, God loves you very much. Think very carefully about the words I will speak to you. Stand up; I have been sent to you." And when he said this, I stood up. I was still shaking because I was afraid. ¹²Then the man in the vision started talking again. He said, "Daniel, do not be afraid. From the very first day you decided to get wisdom and to be humble in front of God, he has been listening to your prayers. I came to you because you have been praying. ¹³But the prince (angel) of Persia has been fighting against me for 21 days. Then Michael, one of the most important princes (angels), came to help me because I was stuck there with the king of Persia. ¹⁴Now I have come to you, Daniel, to explain to you what will happen to your people in the future. The vision is about a time in the future."

¹⁵While the man was talking to me, I bowed low with my face toward the ground. I could not speak. ¹⁶Then the one who looked like a man touched my lips. I opened my mouth and started to speak. I said to the one standing in front of me, "Sir, I am upset and afraid because of what I saw in the vision. I

---

^{a}**9:24 week** Or "unit of seven." The Hebrew word could mean "week" or "a period of seven years." Also in verses 25, 27.
^{b}**9:25 chosen king** Literally, "anointed one."
^{c}**9:26 killed** Literally, "cut off."
^{d}**9:26 He will be gone** Or "He will have nothing."
^{e}**9:27 He will do … things** Or "He will come on the wings of terrible destruction."
^{f}**10:5 pure gold** Literally, "gold from Uphaz."

feel helpless. 17Sir, I am Daniel your servant. How can I talk with you? My strength is gone and it is hard for me to breathe."

18The one who looked like a man touched me again. When he touched me, I felt better. 19Then he said, "Daniel, don't be afraid. God loves you very much. Peace be with you. Be strong now, be strong."

When he spoke to me, I became stronger. Then I said, "Sir, you have given me strength. Now you can speak."

20So then he said, "Daniel, do you know why I have come to you? Soon I must go back to fight against the prince *(angel)* of Persia. When I go, the prince *(angel)* of Greece will come. 21But Daniel, before I go, I must first tell you what is written in the *Book of Truth*. No one stands with me against those evil angels except Michael, the prince *(angel)* over your people.

11 1"During the first year that Darius the Mede*a* was king, I stood up to support Michael*b* in his fight against the prince *(angel)* of Persia.

2"Now then, Daniel, I tell you the truth: Three more kings will rule in Persia. Then a fourth king will come who will be much richer than all the other kings of Persia before him. He will use his riches to get power and turn everyone against the kingdom of Greece. 3Then a very strong and powerful king will come who will rule with much power. He will do anything he wants. 4Just as he comes to power, his kingdom will be broken up and scattered in all directions. It will not be divided among his descendants. And it will not be ruled in the same way because that kingdom will be pulled up and given to other people.

5"The southern king will become strong, but then one of his commanders will defeat him. The commander will begin to rule, and he will be very powerful.

6"Then after a few years, the southern king and that commander will make an agreement. The daughter of the southern king will marry the northern king. She will do this to bring peace, but she and the southern king will not be strong enough. People will turn against her and against the one who brought her to that country. And they will turn against her child and against the one who helped her.

7"But someone from her family will come to take the southern king's place. He will attack the armies of the northern king. He will go into that king's strong fort. He will fight and win. 8He will take their gods and their metal idols* and their expensive things made from silver and gold. He will take those things away to Egypt. Then he will not bother the northern king for a few years. 9The northern king will attack the southern kingdom.

But he will lose, and then he will go back to his own country.

10"The northern king's sons will prepare for war. They will get a large army together. It will move through the land very quickly, like a powerful flood. That army will fight all the way to the strong fort of the southern king. 11Then the southern king will become very angry and march out to fight against the northern king. The northern king will have a large army, but he will lose the war. 12The northern army will be defeated, and those soldiers will be carried away. The southern king will be very proud, and he will kill thousands of soldiers from the northern army. But he will not continue to be successful. 13The northern king will get another army that will be larger than the first one. After several years he will attack. His army will be ready for war. It will be very large and it will have many weapons.

14"In those times many people will be against the southern king. Some of your own people who love to fight will rebel against the southern king. They will not win, but they will make the vision come true. 15Then the northern king will come. He will build ramps against the walls and will capture a strong city. The southern army will not have the power to fight back. Even the best soldiers from the southern army will not be strong enough to stop the northern army.

16"The northern king will do whatever he wants. No one will be able to stop him. He will gain power and control in the Beautiful Land, and he will have the power to destroy it. 17The northern king will decide to use all his power to fight against the southern king, and he will make an agreement with the southern king. The king of the north will let one of his daughters marry the southern king so that he can defeat the southern king. But those plans will not succeed. His plans will not help him.

18"Then the northern king will turn his attention to the countries along the coast of the Mediterranean Sea. He will defeat many of those cities, but then a commander will put an end to the pride and rebellion of that northern king. The commander will make the northern king ashamed.

19"After that happens, the northern king will go back to the strong forts of his own country. But he will be weak and will fall. He will be finished.

20"After the northern king, there will be a new ruler who sends out tax collectors so that he can live like a king. But after a few years, he will be destroyed, although he will not die in battle.

21"That ruler will be followed by a very cruel and hated man, who will not have the honor of being from a king's family.*c* He will

---

become a ruler by being tricky. He will attack the kingdom when the people feel safe. ²²He will defeat large and powerful armies. He will even defeat the leader with the agreement. ²³Many nations will make agreements with that cruel and hated ruler, but he will lie and trick them. He will gain much power, but only a few people will support him.

²⁴"When the richest countries feel safe, that cruel and hated ruler will attack them. He will attack at just the right time and will be successful where his ancestors* were not successful. He will take things from the countries he defeated, and he will give them to his followers. He will plan to defeat and destroy strong cities. He will be successful—but only for a short time.

²⁵"That very cruel and hated ruler will have a very large army. He will use that army to show his strength and courage and attack the southern king. The southern king will get a very large and powerful army and go to war. But the people who are against him will make secret plans, and the southern king will be defeated. ²⁶People who were supposed to be good friends of the southern king will try to destroy him. His army will be defeated. Many of his soldiers will be killed in battle. ²⁷Those two kings will want to make trouble. They will sit around the table planning their lies, but it will not do either one of them any good because God has set a time for their end to come.

²⁸"The northern king will go back to his own country with much wealth. Then he will decide to do bad things against the holy agreement.ᵃ He will do the things he planned, and then he will go back to his own country.

²⁹"At the right time, the northern king will attack the southern king again. But this time he will not be successful as he was before. ³⁰Ships from Cyprus will come and fight against the northern king. He will see those ships coming and be afraid. Then he will turn back and take out his anger on the holy agreement. He will turn back and help those who stopped following the holy agreement. ³¹The northern king will send his army to do terrible things to the Temple* in Jerusalem. They will stop the people from offering the daily sacrifice.* Then they will do something really terrible. They will set up that terrible thing that causes destruction.

³²"The northern king will use lies and smooth talking to trick those who quit following the holy agreement, so they will sin even worse. But those who know God and obey him will be strong. They will fight back.

³³"Those wise teachers will help the other people understand what is happening. But even they will have to suffer persecution. Some of them will be killed with swords.

Some of them will be burned or taken prisoner. Some of them will have their homes and things taken away. ³⁴When those wise people are punished, they will receive some help, but many people who join them will be hypocrites.* ³⁵Some of the wise people will stumble and make mistakes. But the persecution must come so that they can be made stronger and purer until the time of the end. Then, at the right time, that time of the end will come.

The King Who Praises Himself

³⁶"The northern king will do whatever he wants. He will brag about himself. He will praise himself and think that he is even better than a god. He will say things that no one has ever heard. He will say those things against the God of gods. He will be successful until all the evil things have happened. Then what God has planned to happen will happen. ³⁷"That northern king will not care about the gods his ancestors* worshiped. He will not care about the gods women worship. He will not care about any god. Instead, he will praise himself and make himself more important than any god. ³⁸The northern king will not worship any god, but he will worship power. Power and strength will be his god. His ancestors didn't love power as he does. He will honor the god of power with gold and silver, expensive jewels, and gifts. ³⁹"That northern king will attack strong fortresses* with the help of this foreign god. He will give much honor to the foreign rulers who join him. He will put many people under their rule. He will make the rulers pay him for the land they rule over.

⁴⁰"At the time of the end, the southern king will fight a battle against the northern king. The northern king will attack him with chariots* and soldiers on horses and many large ships. The northern king will rush through the land like a flood. ⁴¹The northern king will attack the Beautiful Land. He will defeat many countries. But Edom, Moab, and the leaders of Ammon will be saved from him. ⁴²The northern king will show his power in many countries. Egypt will also learn how powerful he is. ⁴³He will get treasures of gold and silver and all the riches of Egypt. The Libyans and Ethiopians will obey him. ⁴⁴But that northern king will hear news from the east and the north that will make him afraid and angry. He will go to completely destroy many nations. ⁴⁵He will set up his king's tents between the sea and the beautiful holy mountain.ᵇ But finally, that bad king will die. There will be no one to help him when his end comes.

12 ¹"Daniel, at that time the great prince (angel) Michael will stand up. Michael is in charge of your people. There will be a

---

ᵃ**11:28** *holy agreement* This probably means the Jewish people.

ᵇ**11:45** *holy mountain* The mountain Jerusalem is built on.

time of much trouble, the worst time since nations have been on earth. But Daniel, at that time every one of your people whose name is found written in the book ˻of life˼ will be saved. ²There are many who are dead and buried.ᵃ Some of them will wake up and live forever, but others will wake up to shame and disgrace forever. ³The wise people will shine as bright as the sky. Those who teach others to live right will shine like stars forever and ever.ᵇ

⁴"But you, Daniel, keep this message a secret. You must close the book and keep this secret until the time of the end. Many people will go here and there looking for true knowledge, and the true knowledge will increase."

⁵Then I, Daniel, noticed two other men. One man was standing on my side of the river, and the other was standing on the other side. ⁶The man who was dressed in linen* was standing over the water in the river. One of the two men said to him, "How long will it be before these amazing things come true?"

⁷The man dressed in linen and standing over the water lifted his right and left hands toward heaven. And I heard him make a promise using the name of God who lives forever. He said, "It will be for three and one-half years.ᶜ The power of the holy people will be broken, and then all these things will finally come true."

⁸I heard the answer, but I really didn't understand. So I asked, "Sir, what will happen after all this comes true?"

⁹He answered, "Go on about your life Daniel. The message is hidden. It will be a secret until the time of the end. ¹⁰Many people will be made pure—they will make themselves clean.* But evil people will continue to be evil. And those wicked people will not understand these things, but the wise people will understand them.

¹¹"The daily sacrifice* will be stopped. There will be 1290 days from that time until the time that the terrible thing that destroys is set up. ¹²The one who waits for and comes to the end of the 1335 days will be very happy.

¹³"As for you, Daniel, go and live your life until the end. You will get your rest. At the end you will rise from death and receive your share of the promise."

ᵃ**12:2** *are dead and buried* Literally, "sleep in the dust."
ᵇ**12:3** Or "The wise and successful teachers will shine like the sun rays in the sky. Those who make others innocent will shine like the stars forever." In Hebrew this is like Isa. 52:13 and Isa. 53:11.

ᶜ**12:7** *three and one-half years* Literally, "a time, times, and half a time."

Hosea

The Lord God's Message Through Hosea

1 ¹This is the LORD's message that came to Hosea son of Beeri during the time that Uzziah, Jotham, Ahaz, and Hezekiah were kings of Judah, and Jeroboam son of Joash was king of Israel.

²This was the LORD's first message to Hosea. The LORD said, "Go, marry a prostitute who has had children as a result of her prostitution. Do this because the people in this country have acted like prostitutes—they have been unfaithful to the LORD."

The Birth of Jezreel

³So Hosea married Gomer daughter of Diblaim. She became pregnant and gave birth to a son for Hosea. ⁴The LORD said to Hosea, "Name him Jezreel,ᵈ because soon I will punish the family of Jehu for the people he killed at Jezreel Valley.ᵉ Then I will put an end to the kingdom of the nationᶠ of Israel. ⁵And at that time I will break Israel's bow at Jezreel Valley."

The Birth of Lo-Ruhamah

⁶Then Gomer became pregnant again and gave birth to a daughter. The LORD said to Hosea, "Name her Lo-Ruhamah,ᵍ because I will not show mercy to the nation of Israel anymore, nor will I forgive them. ⁷But I will show mercy to the nation of Judah. I will save them, but I will not use bows or swords or war horses and soldiers to save them. I will save them by my own power.ʰ

ᵈ**1:4** *Jezreel* This name in Hebrew means "God will plant seeds."

ᵉ**1:4** *people ... at Jezreel Valley* See 2 Kings 9–10 for the story of Jehu's revolt at Jezreel Valley.
ᶠ**1:4** *nation* Literally, "house." This might mean the royal family of that country. Also in verse 6.
ᵍ**1:6** *Lo-Ruhamah* This name in Hebrew means "She receives no mercy." Also in verse 8.
ʰ**1:7** *by my own power* Literally, "by the LORD their God."

The Birth of Lo-Ammi

[8]After Gomer had finished nursing Lo-Ruhamah, she became pregnant again and gave birth to a son. [9]Then the Lord said, "Name him Lo-Ammi,[a] because you are not my people, and I am not your God."

The Lord Speaks to the Nation of Israel

[10]"In the future the number of the people of Israel will be like the sand of the sea, which you cannot measure or count. In the same place that God told them, 'You are not my people,' he will call them 'children of the Living God.'

[11]"Then the people of Judah and the people of Israel will be gathered together. They will choose a ruler for themselves, and their nation will be too large for the land.[b] Jezreel's day will be great!"

2 [1]"Then you will say to your brothers, 'You are my people,' and you will say to your sisters, 'He has shown mercy to you.'"[c]

[2]"Argue with your mother.[d] Argue with her because she is no longer my wife, and I am no longer her husband! Tell her to stop being like a prostitute. Tell her to take away her lovers[e] from between her breasts. [3]If she refuses to stop her adultery, I will strip her naked and leave her like the day she was born. I will take away her people, and she will be like an empty, dry desert. I will kill her with thirst. [4]I will have no pity on her children because they are the children of prostitution. [5]Their mother has acted like a prostitute. She should be ashamed of what she did. She said, 'I will go to my lovers,[f] who give me food and water, wool and linen, wine and olive oil.'

[6]"So I, the Lord, will block Israel's road with thorns, and I will build a wall. Then she will not be able to find her path. [7]She will run after her lovers, but she will not be able to catch up with them. She will look for her lovers, but she will not be able to find them. Then she will say, 'I will go back to my first husband (the Lord). Life was better for me when I was with him. Life was better then than it is now.'

[8]"Israel didn't know that I, the Lord, was the one who gave her grain, wine, and oil. I kept giving her more and more silver and gold, but she used this silver and gold to make statues of Baal.* [9]So I will return and take back my grain at the time it is ready to be harvested. I will take back my wine at the time the grapes are ready. I will take back my wool and linen. I gave those things to her so that she could cover her naked body. [10]Now I will strip her. She will be naked, so all her lovers can see her. No one will be able to save her from my power.[g] [11]I will take away all her fun. I will stop her festivals, her New Moon* celebrations, and her days of rest. I will stop all her special feasts. [12]I will destroy her vines and fig trees. She said, 'My lovers gave these things to me.' But I will change her gardens—they will become like a wild forest. Wild animals will come and eat from those plants.

[13]"Israel served false gods,[h] so I will punish her. She burned incense* to those false gods. She dressed up—she put on her jewelry and nose ring. Then she went to her lovers and forgot me." This is what the Lord has said.

[14]"So I, the Lord, will speak romantic words to her. I will lead her into the desert and speak tender words. [15]There I will give her vineyards.* I will give her Achor Valley as a doorway of hope. Then she will answer as she did when she came out of the land of Egypt." [16]This is what the Lord says.

"At that time you will call me 'My husband.' You will not call me 'My Baal.'[i] [17]I will take the names of those false gods out of her mouth. Then people will not use those names again.

[18]"At that time I will make an agreement for the Israelites with the animals of the field, the birds of the sky, and the crawling things on the ground. I will break the bow, the sword, and the weapons of war in that land. I will make the land safe, so the people of Israel can lie down in peace. [19]And I will make you my bride forever. I will make you my bride with goodness and justice and with love and mercy. [20]I will make you my faithful bride. Then you will really know the Lord. [21]And at that time I will answer." This is what the Lord says.

"I will speak to the skies,
    and they will give rain to the earth.
[22] The earth will produce grain, wine, and oil,
    and they will meet Jezreel's needs.
[23] I will sow her many seeds[j] on her land.
    To Lo-Ruhamah,[k] I will show mercy.

[a]**1:9 Lo-Ammi** This name in Hebrew means "not my people."

[b]**1:11 their nation … land** Literally, "they will go up from the land."

[c]**2:1** Or "Then say to your brothers, 'My people,' and to your sisters, 'You have been shown mercy.'"

[d]**2:2 mother** This means the nation of Israel.

[e]**2:2 her lovers** Or "adulteries." Adultery means breaking a marriage promise by sexual sin. God was like a husband to Israel. But Israel was worshiping false gods—this was spiritual adultery against God.

[f]**2:5 lovers** This means Israel's false gods. Also in verses 7, 10, 13.

[g]**2:10 power** Literally, "hand."

[h]**2:13 false gods** Literally, "Baals."

[i]**2:16 My Baal** This is a wordplay. Baal was a Canaanite god, but the name also means "lord or husband."

[j]**2:23 I will sow her many seeds** Jezreel, Lo-Ruhamah, and Lo-Ammi are Hosea's children. But the names also have special meanings. The name Jezreel means "God will plant seeds." But Jezreel is also the name of a large valley in Israel. This probably shows that God will bring his people back to Israel.

[k]**2:23 Lo-Ruhamah** This name in Hebrew means "She receives no mercy."

To Lo-Ammi,*a* I will say, 'You are my
people.'
And they will say to me,
  'You are our God.'"

Hosea Buys Gomer Back From Slavery

3 ¹Then the LORD said to me again, "Gomer*b* has many lovers, but you must continue loving her. Do this because it is an example of the LORD's love for Israel. He continues to love them, but they continue to turn to other gods, and they love to eat those raisin cakes.*c*"

²So I bought Gomer back for 6 ounces*d* of silver and 9 bushels*e* of barley. ³Then I told her, "You must stay at home with me for many days. You will not be like a prostitute. You will not have sexual relations with another man. I will be your husband."

⁴In the same way the people of Israel will continue many days without a king or a leader. They will be without a sacrifice or a memorial stone.* They will be without an ephod* or a household god. ⁵After this, the people of Israel will come back and look for the LORD their God and for David their king. In the last days they will come to honor the LORD and his goodness.

The Lord Is Angry Against Israel

4 ¹People of Israel, listen to the LORD's message. The LORD will tell his argument against those who live in this country. "The people in this country don't really know God. They are not true and loyal to him. ²They swear, lie, kill, and steal. They commit the sin of adultery* and have their babies. They murder one person after another.*f* ³So the country is like someone crying for the dead, and all of its people are weak. Even the animals of the field, the birds of the sky, and the fish in the sea are dying.*g* ⁴No one should argue or blame another person. Priests, my argument is with you!*h* ⁵You priests will fall in the daytime. And at night the prophet will also fall with you. I will also destroy your mother.

⁶"My people are destroyed because they have no knowledge. You priests have refused to learn, so I will refuse to let you be priests for me. You have forgotten the law of your God, so I will forget your children. ⁷They became proud. They sinned more and more against

me, so I will change their honor to shame."

⁸The priests fed on the people's sins. They wanted more and more of their sin offerings.*i* ⁹So the priests are no different from the people. I will punish them for the things they did. I will pay them back for the wrong things they did. ¹⁰They will eat, but they will not be satisfied. They will commit sexual sins, but they will not have babies.*j* This is because they left the LORD and became like prostitutes.

¹¹"Sexual sins, strong drink, and new wine ruin a person's ability to think straight. ¹²My people are asking pieces of wood for advice. They think those sticks will answer them! They have chased after those false gods like prostitutes and have left their own God. ¹³They make sacrifices on the tops of the mountains and burn incense* on the hills under oak trees, poplar trees, and elm trees.*k* The shade under those trees looks nice. So your daughters lie under those trees like prostitutes, and your daughters-in-law commit sexual sins.

¹⁴"I cannot blame*l* your daughters for being prostitutes or your daughters-in-law for committing sexual sins, because the men go and have sex with prostitutes and offer sacrifices with the temple prostitutes.*m* So these fools are destroying themselves.

The Shameful Sins of Israel

¹⁵"Israel, just because you act like a prostitute doesn't mean that Judah should feel guilty too. People, don't go to Gilgal* or Beth Aven.*n* Don't use the LORD's name to make promises. Don't say, 'As the LORD lives ...!' ¹⁶The LORD has given many things to Israel. He is like a shepherd who takes his sheep to a large field with plenty of grass. But Israel is stubborn like a young cow that runs away again and again.

¹⁷"Ephraim* has joined his idols,* so leave him alone. ¹⁸Ephraim has joined their drunkenness. Let them continue to be prostitutes. Let them be with their lovers.*o* ¹⁹They went to those gods for safety, and they have lost

---

*i***4:8** This is a wordplay. The word "sins" also means "sin offerings." So instead of eating sacrifices, the priests became hungry for sin itself.

*j***4:10** *They ... babies* A part of worshiping the false gods was having sexual relations with temple prostitutes. The people thought this would make the gods happy. And then the gods would give the people large families and good crops.

*k***4:13** *under ... trees* Trees and groves were an important part of worshiping false gods.

*l***4:14** *blame* This word can mean "visit," "put in charge of," "take account of," or "to hold responsible for."

*m***4:14** *temple prostitutes* Women who were prostitutes at the temples of the false gods. Their sexual sins were part of worshiping those false gods.

*n***4:15** *Beth Aven* A name meaning "House of Evil." It is a wordplay on the name "Bethel," a name meaning "House of God." There was a temple in this town. Also in 5:8.

*o***4:18** *lovers* This means Israel's false gods.

---

*a***2:23** *Lo-Ammi* This name in Hebrew means "not my people."

*b***3:1** *Gomer* Literally, "a woman."

*c***3:1** *raisin cakes* This food was used in the feasts that honored false gods such as the "Queen of Heaven."

*d***3:2** *6 ounces* Literally, "15 ₍shekels₎" (172.5 g).

*e***3:2** *9 bushels* Literally, "1 homer and 1 *letek*" (231 l).

*f***4:2** *and have ... another* Literally, "they break out, and blood touches blood."

*g***4:3** *dying* Literally, "being taken away."

*h***4:4** Or "The people cannot complain or blame someone else. The people are helpless, like arguing with a priest." Many times the priests and Levites served as judges, and their decisions were final.

their ability to think.[a] Their altars will bring them shame.

The Leaders Cause Israel and Judah to Sin

5 [1] "Priests, nation[b] of Israel, and people in the king's family, listen to me. You have been judged guilty!

"You were like a trap at Mizpah[c] and like a net spread on the ground at Tabor.[d] [2] You have done many evil things,[e] so I will punish you all. [3] I know Ephraim.* I know what Israel has done. Ephraim, right now you act like a prostitute. Israel is dirty with sin. [4] The people of Israel have done many evil things, and these evil things keep them from coming back to their God. They are always thinking of ways to chase after other gods. They don't know the LORD. [5] Israel's pride is a witness against them,[f] so Israel and Ephraim will stumble in their sin. But Judah will also stumble with them.

[6] "The leaders of the people went to look for the LORD. They took their sheep and cattle with them, but they did not find the LORD because he refused to accept them. [7] They have not been faithful to the LORD. Their children are from some stranger. And now, he will destroy them and their land again.[g]

A Prophecy of Israel's Destruction

[8] "Blow the horn in Gibeah.
    Blow the trumpet in Ramah.[h]
Give the warning at Beth Aven.
    The enemy is behind you, Benjamin.
[9] Ephraim* will become empty
    at the time of punishment.
I, God, warn the families of Israel
    that this really will happen.
[10] The leaders of Judah are like thieves
    trying to steal someone's property,
so I will pour out my anger
    on them like water.
[11] Ephraim will be punished.
He will be crushed and pressed like
    grapes,
    because he decided to follow filth.
[12] I will destroy Ephraim
    as a moth eats a piece of cloth.

I will ruin Judah,
    like rot on a piece of wood.
[13] Ephraim saw his sickness, and Judah saw
    his wound,
    so they went to Assyria for help.
They told their problems to the great king,
    but he cannot heal you or cure your
    wound.
[14] I will be like a lion to Ephraim,
    like a young lion to the nation of Judah.
I—yes, I myself—will rip them to pieces.
I will carry them away,
    and no one can save them.
[15] I will go back to my place,
    until the people admit they are guilty,
    until they come looking for me.
Yes, in their trouble they will try very
    hard to find me."

The Rewards of Coming Back to the Lord

6 [1] "Come, let's go back to the LORD.
    He hurt us, but he will heal us.
He wounded us, but he will put
    bandages on us.
[2] After two days he will bring us back to
    life.
He will raise us up on the third day.
    Then we can live near him.
[3] Let's learn about the LORD.
    Let's try very hard to know him.
We know he is coming,
    like we know the dawn is coming.
He will come to us like the rain,
    like the spring rain that waters the
    ground."

The People Are Not Faithful

[4] "Ephraim,* what should I do with you?
    Judah, what should I do with you?
Your faithfulness is like a morning mist.
    Your faithfulness is like the dew that
    goes away early in the morning.
[5] I used the prophets
    and made laws for the people.
The people were killed at my command,
    but good things will come from those
    decisions.[i]
[6] This is because I want faithful love,
    not sacrifice.
I want people to know God,
    not to bring burnt offerings.*
[7] But the people broke the agreement as
    Adam did.[j]
    They were unfaithful to me in their
    country.
[8] Gilead is a city of people who do evil—
    people who have tricked and killed
    others.
[9] The priests are like gangs of robbers
    hiding and waiting on the road to attack
    someone.

---

[a] **4:19 They ... think** Or "The wind has carried them away on its wings" or "The spirit held them tight in its wings." The Hebrew text here is hard to understand.

[b] **5:1 nation** Literally, "house." This might mean the royal family of that country. Also in verse 14.

[c] **5:1 Mizpah** A mountain in Israel. The people worshiped the false gods on many of the hills and mountains.

[d] **5:1 Tabor** A mountain in Israel.

[e] **5:2 You ... evil things** The Hebrew text here is hard to understand. It seems to be a wordplay of some kind.

[f] **5:5 them** Literally, "his face."

[g] **5:7 And now ... again** The Hebrew text here is hard to understand.

[h] **5:8 Gibeah, Ramah** Cities on Judah's border with Israel.

[i] **6:5 but good things ... decisions** Or "I cut them with the prophets. I killed them with the words from my mouth. Light will come from your decisions."

[j] **6:7 as Adam did** See Gen. 3.

They murder people before they reach
  safety in Shechem.
They do such evil things.
10 I have seen a terrible thing in the nation[a]
  of Israel.
Ephraim was unfaithful to God.
  Israel is dirty with sin.
11 Judah, there is also a time of harvest for
  you.
It will happen when I bring my people
  back from captivity.[b]

7

1 "I will heal Israel!
  Then people will know that Ephraim
  sinned.
They will know about Samaria's[c] lies.
They will know about the thieves who
  come and go in that town.
2 They don't believe that I will remember
  their crimes.
The bad things they did are all around.
  I can see their sins clearly.
3 Their evil makes their king happy.
  Their false gods please their leaders.
4 A baker presses dough to make bread.
  He puts the bread in the oven.
He does not make the fire hotter
  while the bread is rising.
But the people of Israel are not like that.
  They are always making their fire
  hotter.
5 On Our King's Day, the leaders get so
  drunk that they get sick.
They become crazy with wine
  and make agreements with people who
  laugh at God.
6 The people make their secret plans.
  Their hearts burn with excitement like
  an oven.
Their excitement burns all night,
  and in the morning it is like a hot fire."
7 They are all like hot ovens.
  They destroyed their rulers.
All their kings fell.
  Not one of them called to me for help.

Israel and the Nations

8 "Ephraim* mixes with the nations.
  Ephraim is like a cake that was not
  cooked on both sides.
9 Strangers destroy Ephraim's strength,
  but Ephraim does not know it.
Gray hairs[d] are also sprinkled on Ephraim,
  but Ephraim does not know it.
10 Ephraim's pride speaks against him.
  The people had many troubles,

but they still didn't go back to the Lord
  their God.
They didn't look to him for help.
11 So Ephraim has become like a silly dove
  without understanding.
The people called to Egypt for help.
  They went to Assyria for help.
12 They go to those countries for help,
  but I will trap them.
I will throw my net over them,
  and I will bring them down like the
  birds of the sky.
I will punish them for their agreements.[e]
13 It will be very bad for those who left me.
  They refused to obey me, so they will
  be destroyed.
I saved them,
  but they speak lies against me.
14 They never call to me from their hearts.
  Yes, they cry on their beds.
And they cut themselves when they ask
  for grain and new wine.
But in their hearts, they have turned
  away from me.
15 I trained them and made their arms
  strong,
but they made evil plans against me.
16 But they were like a boomerang.*
  They changed directions,
  but they did not come back to me.[f]
Their leaders bragged about their
  strength,
but they will be killed with swords.
And the people in Egypt will laugh at
  them.

Idol Worship Leads to Destruction

8

1 "Put the trumpet to your lips and give
the warning. Be like an eagle over the
Lord's house.[g] The Israelites have broken
my agreement.* They have not obeyed my
law. 2 They yell out at me, 'My God, we in
Israel know you!' 3 But Israel refused the good
things, so the enemy chases him. 4 The Israelites chose their kings, but they didn't come to
me for advice. They chose leaders, but they
didn't choose men I knew. The Israelites used
their silver and gold to make idols* for themselves, so they will be destroyed. 5-6 He has
refused your calf, Samaria.[h] God says, 'I am
very angry with the Israelites.' The people
of Israel will be punished for their sin. Some
worker made those statues. They are not God.

Samaria's calf will be broken into pieces. [7]The Israelites did a foolish thing—it was like trying to plant the wind. But they will get only troubles—they will harvest a whirlwind. The grain in the fields will grow, but it will give no food. Even if it grew something, strangers would eat it.

[8]"Israel was destroyed;
　　its people are scattered among the
　　　nations,
　　like some dish that was thrown away
　　　because no one wanted it.
[9] Ephraim* went to his 'lovers.'[a]
　　Like a stubborn donkey, they led him off
　　　to Assyria.
[10] Yes, Israel was taken to the nations,
　　but I will bring them back.
　　But first, they must suffer a little
　　　by carrying the burden of that mighty
　　　　king.

Israel Forgets God and Worships Idols

[11]"Ephraim* built more and more altars,*
　　and that was a sin.
　　They have been altars of sin for Ephraim.
[12] Even if I wrote 10,000 laws for Ephraim,
　　he would treat them as if they were for
　　　some stranger.
[13] The Israelites love sacrifices.[b]
　　They offer the meat and eat it.
　　The Lord does not accept their sacrifices.
　　He remembers their sins,
　　　and he will punish them.
　　They will be carried away as prisoners to
　　　Egypt.
[14] Israel has built palaces for their kings,
　　and now Judah builds fortresses.*
　　But they have forgotten their Maker!
　　So I will send a fire to destroy their
　　　cities and fortresses!"

The Sadness of Exile

9 [1]Israel, don't celebrate like the nations do. Don't be happy. You acted like a prostitute and left your God. You committed your sexual sin[c] on every threshing* floor. [2]But the grain from those threshing floors will not provide enough food for Israel. There will not be enough wine for Israel.

[3]The Israelites will not stay in the Lord's land. Ephraim* will return to Egypt. In Assyria they will eat food that they should not eat. [4]They will not be able to give offerings of wine to the Lord. None of their sacrifices will please him. What they offer will be like food eaten at a funeral—whoever eats it will

become unclean. They can eat that food for their own hunger, but it cannot be taken into the Lord's Temple.* [5]They will not be able to celebrate the Lord's feasts or festivals.[d]

[6]The people of Israel left because the enemy took everything from them. But Egypt will take the people themselves. Memphis[e] will bury them. Weeds will grow over their silver treasures, and thorns will grow where the Israelites lived.

Israel Rejected the True Prophets

[7]The prophet says, "Israel, learn this: The time of punishment has come. The time has come for you to pay for the evil things you did." But the people of Israel say, "The prophet is a fool. This man with ₁God's₁ Spirit is crazy." The prophet says, "You will be punished for your terrible sins. You will be punished for your hate." [8]God and the prophet are like guards watching over Ephraim,* but there are many traps along his way. And people hate the prophet, even in the house of his God.

[9]The Israelites have gone deep into ruin as in the time of Gibeah.* The Lord will remember the Israelites' sins, and he will punish their sins.

Israel Is Ruined by Its Worship of Idols

[10]"At the time I *(the Lord)* found Israel, they were like fresh grapes in the desert. They were like the first figs on a fig tree at the beginning of the season. But when they came to Baal Peor,[f] they changed. So I had to cut them off like rotten fruit.[g] They became like the terrible things that they loved.

The Israelites Will Have No Children

[11]"Like a bird, Ephraim's* glory will fly away. There will be no more pregnancies, no more births, and no more babies. [12]But even if the Israelites do raise their children, it will not help, because I will take the children away from them. I will leave them, and they will have nothing but troubles."

[13]I can see that Ephraim is leading his children into a trap. Ephraim will lead his children out to the killer. [14]Lord, give them what you will. Give them a womb that loses babies and breasts that cannot give milk.

[15] All their evil is in Gilgal*;
　　I began hating them there.
　　I will force them to leave my house
　　　because of the evil things they do.
　　I will not love them anymore.

---

[a]**8:9 lovers** This means Israel's false gods.
[b]**8:13 The Israelites love sacrifices** The meaning of the Hebrew text here is uncertain.
[c]**9:1 You committed your sexual sin** This means the people were not faithful to God. But it also means the people had sexual relations with temple prostitutes. They believed their false gods would give them many children and good crops.

[d]**9:5** Literally, "What will you do for a day of solemn assembly, for the Lord's festival day?"
[e]**9:6 Memphis** An important city in Egypt.
[f]**9:10 Baal Peor** This happened when Moses was still leading the Israelites in the desert. Read Num. 25:1–5.
[g]**9:10 they changed … rotten fruit** This is a wordplay that can also mean "they dedicated themselves to a shameful idol."

Their leaders are rebels who turned
   against me.
16 Ephraim will be punished.
   Their root is dying.
   They will not have any more babies.
   They might give birth to babies,
      but I will kill the precious babies who
         come from their bodies.
17 Those people will not listen to my God,
   so he will refuse to listen to them.
   And they will wander among the nations
      without a home.

Israel's Riches Led to Its Worship of Idols

10 ¹Israel is like a vine that grows plenty
   of fruit.
   But as Israel got more and more things,
      he built more and more altars* to honor
         false gods.
   His land became better and better,
      so he put up better and better stones to
         honor false gods.
2 The people of Israel tried to trick God,
   but now they must accept their guilt.
   The LORD will break down their altars
      and destroy their memorial stones.*

The Evil Decisions of the Israelites

³Now the Israelites say, "We have no king.
We don't honor the LORD. And his king cannot do anything to us."

⁴They make promises, but they are only
telling lies. They don't keep their promises.
They make agreements ₗwith other countries.
God does not like those agreements₎. The
judges are like poisonous weeds growing in
a plowed field.

⁵The people from Samaria* worship the
calves at Beth Aven.ᵃ They will cry. The
priests will cry, because their beautiful idol
is gone. It was carried away. ⁶It was carried
away as a gift to the great king of Assyria. He
will keep Ephraim's* shameful idol. Israel will
be ashamed of its idol.ᵇ ⁷Samaria's false godᶜ
will be destroyed. It will be like a piece of
wood floating away on the water's surface.

⁸Israel sinned and built many high places.*
The high places of Avenᵈ will be destroyed.
Thorns and weeds will grow on their altars.*
Then they will say to the mountains, "Cover
us!" and to the hills, "Fall on us!"

Israel Will Pay for Sin

⁹"Israel, you have sinned since the time of
Gibeah.* (And the people have continued to
sin there.) Those evil people at Gibeah will be
trapped by war. ¹⁰I will come to punish them.

Armies will come together against them and
punish the Israelites for both of their sins.ᵉ

¹¹"Ephraim* is like a trained young cow
that loves to walk on grain on the threshing*
floor. I will put a good yoke* on her neck. I
will put the ropes on Ephraim. Then Judah
will begin plowing. Jacob* will break the
ground himself."

¹²If you plant goodness, you will harvest
faithful love. Plow your ground, and you will
harvest with the LORD. He will come, and he
will make goodness fall on you like rain.

¹³But you planted evil, and you harvested
trouble. You ate the fruit of your lies, because
you had trusted in your power and your soldiers. ¹⁴So your armies will hear the noise of
battle, and all your fortresses* will be destroyed.
It will be like the time Shalmanᶠ destroyed
Beth Arbel. At that time of war mothers were
killed with their children. ¹⁵And this will happen to you at Bethel, because you did so many
evil things. When that day begins, the king of
Israel will be fully destroyed.

Israel Has Forgotten the Lord

11 ¹The Lord said, "I loved Israel when
   he was a child,
   and I called my son out of Egypt.
2 But the more Iᵍ called the Israelites,
   the more they left me.
   The Israelites gave sacrifices to the false
      godsʰ
   and burned incense* to the idols.*

³"But I was the one who taught Ephraim* to
   walk.
   I took the Israelites in my arms.
   I healed them,
      but they don't know that.
4 I led them with ropes,ⁱ
      but they were ropes of love.
   I was like a person who set them free.ʲ
   I bent down and fed them.

⁵"The Israelites will not go back to Egypt.
The king of Assyria will become their king,
because they refused to turn back to God.
⁶The sword will swing against their cities
and kill their strong men. It will destroy their
leaders.

⁷"My people expect me to come back. They
will call to God above, but he will not help
them."ᵏ

ᵉ**10:10** This probably refers to worship at Gibeah
and Beth Aven.
ᶠ**10:14** *Shalman* This is probably Shalmaneser, king
of Assyria.
ᵍ**11:2** *I* This is from the ancient Greek version. The
standard Hebrew text has "they."
ʰ**11:2** *false gods* Literally, "Baals."
ⁱ**11:4** *ropes* The Hebrew says, "ropes of a man."
ʲ**11:4** *set them free* Literally, "lifted the yoke from
their jaws."
ᵏ**11:7** Or "My people are hanging ₗon poles₎ around
my dwelling place. They called up to him, but he
didn't lift them up."

ᵃ**10:5** *Beth Aven* A name meaning "House of Evil." It
is a wordplay on the name "Bethel," a name meaning
"House of God." There was a temple in this town.
ᵇ**10:6** *idol* Or "advice."
ᶜ**10:7** *false god* Or "king."
ᵈ**10:8** *high places of Aven* Aven means "evil" or
"wickedness." This probably means the temple and
other places of worship at Bethel.

The Lord Will Not Destroy Israel

8"Ephraim,* I don't want to give you up.
    Israel, I want to protect you.
I don't want to make you like Admah.
    I don't want to make you like Zeboiim.*
I am changing my mind.
    My love for you is too strong.
9 I will not let my terrible anger win.
    I will not destroy Ephraim again.
I am God and not a human.
    I am the Holy One.
I am with you.
    I will not show my anger.
10 I will roar like a lion.
    I will roar, and my children will come
        and follow me.
My children will come from the west,
    shaking with fear.
11 They will come from Egypt,
    shaking like birds.
They will come shaking like doves from
    the land of Assyria,
and I will take them back home."
    This is what the Lord said.

12"Ephraim surrounded me with false gods.
    The people of Israel turned against me.*
But Judah still walks with God*
    and is true to the Holy One.*"

The Lord Is Against Israel

12 ¹Ephraim* is wasting its time; Israel
"chases the wind" all day long. The
people tell more and more lies and steal more
and more. They have made agreements with
Assyria, and they are carrying their olive oil
to Egypt.

²The Lord says, "I have a complaint against
Israel.* Jacob* must be punished for the bad
things he did. ³While Jacob was still in his
mother's womb, he began to trick his brother.*
Jacob was a strong young man, and at that
time he fought with God. ⁴Jacob wrestled with
God's angel and won.* He cried and asked for
a favor. That happened at Bethel. There he
spoke to us. ⁵Yes, Yahweh* is the God of the

armies.* His name is Yahweh. ⁶So come back
to your God. Be loyal to him. Do the right
thing, and always trust in your God!

⁷"Jacob is a tricky merchant.* He even
cheats his friend! Even his scales* lie.
⁸Ephraim said, 'I am rich! I have found true
riches! No one will learn about my crimes. No
one will learn about my sins.'

⁹"But I am still the Lord your God, as I was
when you left the land of Egypt. I will make
you live in tents, as you do during the Festival
of Shelters.* ¹⁰I spoke to the prophets and
gave them many visions.* I gave the prophets
many ways to teach my lessons to you. ¹¹But
the people in Gilead* have sinned. There are
many terrible idols in that place. They offer
sacrifices to bulls at Gilgal.* They have many
altars.* There are rows and rows of altars—
like the rows of dirt in a plowed field.

¹²"Jacob ran away to the land of Aram.
There Israel* worked for a wife. He kept sheep
to get another wife. ¹³But the Lord used a
prophet and brought Israel out of Egypt. He
used a prophet and kept Israel safe. ¹⁴But
Ephraim made the Lord very angry. Ephraim
killed many people, so he will be punished
for his crimes. His Lord will make him bear
his shame."

Israel Has Ruined Itself

13 ¹"The tribe of Ephraim* made itself
very important in Israel. Ephraim
spoke and people shook with fear. But
Ephraim sinned by worshiping Baal.* ²Now
the Israelites sin more and more. They make
idols* for themselves. Workers make those
fancy statues from silver, and then they talk
to their statues. They offer sacrifices to them,
and they kiss those calf idols. ³That is why
those people will soon disappear. They will be
like a fog that comes early in the morning and
then quickly disappears. The Israelites will be
like chaff* that is blown from the threshing*
floor. The Israelites will be like smoke that
goes out a window and disappears.

⁴"I have been the Lord your God since the
time you were in the land of Egypt. You did not
know any other god except me. I am the one
who saved you. ⁵I knew you in the desert—I
knew you in that dry land. ⁶I gave food to the
Israelites, and they ate it. They became full
and satisfied. They became proud, and then
they forgot me.

⁷"That is why I will be like a lion to them.
I will be like a leopard waiting by the road. ⁸I

---

a **11:8 Admah, Zeboiim** Two cities that were
destroyed when God destroyed Sodom and Gomorrah. See Gen. 19; Deut. 29:23.

b **11:12 Ephraim … me** Or "Ephraim surrounded me
with lies. The house of Israel surrounded me with
deception."

c **11:12 God** Literally, "El." This might be one of the
names of God, or it might be El, the most important
god of the Canaanites. It is not clear if this means
Judah was being faithful to God or if Judah was
worshiping the false gods.

d **11:12 Holy One** This is a plural form in the Hebrew
text and may refer to God or to Canaanite false
gods.

e **12:2 Israel** Literally, "Judah."

f **12:3 he … his brother** Or "he grabbed his brother's
heel." This is a wordplay. The Hebrew word is like the
name "Jacob." Read Gen. 25:26.

g **12:4 Jacob wrestled … and won** Read Gen.
32:22–28.

h **12:5 Yahweh is the God of the armies** This is like one
of the names for God. It is usually translated "Lord
All-Powerful."

i **12:7 Jacob … merchant** Literally, "Cannan."

j **12:7 scales** Or "balances," a tool for weighing
things.

k **12:9 as … Shelters** Literally, "as in the days of meeting." This might also refer to the meeting of God
with his people in the Holy Tent (see "Holy Tent" in
the Word List) during their wandering in the desert.

will attack them like a bear whose cubs were robbed from her. I will attack them and rip open their chests. I will be like a lion or other wild animal tearing and eating its prey.

Israel Cannot Be Saved From God's Anger

9"Israel, I helped you, but you turned against me. So now I will destroy you. 10Where is your king? Can he save you in any of your cities? Where are your judges? You asked for them, saying, 'Give me a king and leaders.'*a* 11I was angry, and I gave you a king. And when I became very angry, I took him away.

12"Ephraim* tried to hide his guilt.
　He thought his sins were a secret,
　　but he will be punished.
13 His punishment will be like the pain of a
　　woman giving birth.
　He will not be a wise son.
　The time will come for his birth,
　　and he will not survive.

14"I will save them from the grave.
　I will rescue them from death.
　Death, where are your diseases?
　Grave, where is your power?
　I am not looking for revenge.
15 Israel grows among his brothers,
　　but a powerful east wind will come—
　　　the LORD's wind will blow from the
　　　desert.
　Then his well will dry up.
　His spring of water will be dry.
　The wind will take away anything of
　　value.
16 Samaria must be punished
　　because she turned against her God.
　The Israelites will be killed with swords.
　Their children will be torn to pieces,
　　and their pregnant women will be
　　　ripped open."

Return to the Lord

14 1Israel, you fell and sinned against God. So come back to the LORD your God. 2Think about what you will say, and come back to the LORD. Say to him,

　"Take away our sin,
　　and accept these words as our sacrifice.
　We offer you the praise from our lips.*b*

3"Assyria will not save us.
　We will not ride on war horses.
　We will never again say, 'Our God'
　　to something we made with our hands.
　This is because you are the one who
　　shows mercy to orphans."

The Lord Will Forgive Israel

4 The Lord says,
　"I will forgive them for leaving me.
　I will show them my love without limits,
　　because I have stopped being angry.
5 I will be like the dew to Israel.
　Israel will blossom like the lily.*
　He will grow like the cedar trees of
　　Lebanon.
6 His branches will grow,
　　and he will be like a beautiful olive tree.
　He will be like the sweet smell
　　from the cedar trees of Lebanon.
7 The people of Israel will again live under
　　my protection.
　They will grow like grain.
　They will bloom like a vine.
　They will be like the wine of Lebanon.

The Lord Warns Israel About Idols

8"Ephraim,* I will have nothing more to do
　　with idols.*
　I am the one who answers your prayers
　　and watches over you.*c*
　I am like a fir tree that is always green.
　Your fruit comes from me."

Final Advice

9 A wise person understands these things,
　　and a smart person should learn them.
　The LORD's ways are right.
　Good people will live by them.
　Sinners will die by them.*d*

---

*b***14:2** *praise from our lips* Literally, "the fruit of our lips."
*c***14:8** *and watches over you* This is a wordplay. The Hebrew word is like the name "Assyria." God is saying that he, not some foreign country, protects Israel.
*d***14:9** *Good ... die by them* Literally, "Good people will walk on them. Sinners will stumble on them."

Joel

Locusts Will Destroy the Crops

1 ¹Joel son of Pethuel received this message from the LORD:

² Leaders, listen to this message!
  Listen to me, all you people who live in the land.
  Has anything like this ever happened in your life?
  Did anything like this happen during your fathers' lifetime?
³ You will tell these things to your children,
  and your children will tell their children,
  and your grandchildren will tell the people of the next generation.
⁴ What the cutting locust*a* has left,
  the swarming locust has eaten.
  And what the swarming locust has left,
  the hopping locust has eaten.
  And what the hopping locust has left,
  the destroying locust has eaten!

The Locusts—A Powerful Army

⁵ Drunks, wake up and cry!
  All of you who drink wine, cry
  because your sweet wine is finished.
  You will not taste it again.
⁶ A powerful nation came to attack my land.
  Its soldiers were too many to count.
  Its weapons were as sharp as a lion's teeth
  and as powerful as a lion's jaw.

⁷ It destroyed my grapevine.
  Its good vines withered and died.
  It destroyed my fig tree,
  stripped off the bark and threw it away.

The People Cry

⁸ Cry like a young woman crying
  because the man she was ready to marry has died.
⁹ Priests, servants of the LORD, cry
  because there will be no more grain and drink offerings in the LORD's Temple.*
¹⁰ The fields are ruined.
  Even the ground is crying
  because the grain is destroyed;
  the new wine is dried up,
  and the olive oil is gone.

¹¹ Be sad, farmers!
  Cry loudly for the grapes,
  for the wheat, and for the barley,
  because the harvest in the field is ruined.
¹² The vines have become dry,
  and the fig tree is dying.
  All the trees in the field—
  the pomegranate, the palm, and the apple—have withered.
  And happiness among the people has died.
¹³ Priests, put on sackcloth* and cry loudly.
  Servants of the altar,* cry loudly.
  Servants of my God, you will sleep in sackcloth,
  because there will be no more grain and drink offerings in God's Temple.

The Terrible Destruction of the Locusts

¹⁴Tell the people that there will be a special time of fasting. Call them together for a special meeting. Bring the leaders and everyone living in the land together at the Temple* of the LORD your God, and pray to the LORD.

¹⁵Be sad because the LORD's special day is near. At that time punishment will come like an attack from God All-Powerful. ¹⁶Our food is gone. Joy and happiness are gone from the Temple of our God. ¹⁷We planted seeds, but the seeds became dry and dead lying in the soil. Our plants are dry and dead. Our barns are empty and falling down.

¹⁸The animals are hungry and groaning. The herds of cattle wander around confused because they have no grass to eat. The sheep are dying.*b* ¹⁹LORD, I am calling to you for help. Fire has changed our green fields into a desert. Flames have burned all the trees in the field. ²⁰Wild animals also need your help. The streams are dry—there is no water! Fire has changed our green fields into a desert.

The Coming Day of the Lord

2 ¹Blow the trumpet on Zion.*
  Shout a warning on my holy mountain.
  Let all the people who live in the land shake with fear.
  The LORD's special day is coming;
  it is near.
² It will be a dark, gloomy day.
  It will be a dark and cloudy day.

---

*a***1:4** *locust* See "locust" in the Word List. Here, Joel might be talking about an enemy army.

*b***1:18** *dying* Literally, "being punished."

At sunrise you will see the army spread
    over the mountains.
  It will be a great and powerful army.
There has never been anything like it
    before,
  and there will never be anything like it
    again.

3 The army will destroy the land
    like a burning fire.
In front of them the land will be
    like the Garden of Eden.
Behind them the land will be
    like an empty desert.
Nothing will escape them.
4 They look like horses.
  They run like war horses.
5 Listen to them.
It is like the noise of chariots*
    riding over the mountains.
It is like the noise of flames
    burning the chaff.*
They are a powerful people,
  who are ready for war.
6 Before this army, people shake with fear.
  Their faces become pale from fear.

7 The soldiers run fast.
  They climb over the walls.
Each soldier marches straight ahead.
  They don't move from their path.
8 They don't trip each other.
  Each soldier walks in his own path.
If one of the soldiers is hit and falls down,
  the others keep right on marching.
9 They run to the city.
  They quickly climb over the wall.
They climb into the houses.
  They climb through the windows like
    thieves.
10 Before them, earth and sky shake.
  The sun and the moon become dark,
    and the stars stop shining.
11 The Lord calls loudly to his army.
  His camp is very large.
The army obeys his commands.
  His army is very powerful.
The Lord's special day is a great and
    terrible day.
  No one can stop it.

The Lord Tells the People to Change

12 This is the Lord's message:
"Now come back to me with all your heart.
  Cry and mourn,* and don't eat anything!
  Show that you are sad for doing wrong.
13 Tear your hearts, not your clothes.*"
Come back to the Lord your God.
  He is kind and merciful.
  He does not become angry quickly.
  He has great love.
Maybe he will change his mind

about the bad punishment he planned.
14 Who knows, maybe he will change his
    mind
  and leave behind a blessing for you.
Then you can give grain and drink
    offerings
  to the Lord your God.

Pray to the Lord

15 Blow the trumpet at Zion.*
  Call for a special meeting.
  Call for a special time of fasting.
16 Bring the people together.
  Call for a special meeting.
Bring together the old men,
  the children, and the small babies still
    at their mother's breasts.
Let the bride and her new husband
  come from their bedroom.
17 Let the priests, the Lord's servants,
  cry between the porch[b] and the altar.*
All of them should say this:
"Lord, have mercy on your people.
  Don't let your people be put to shame.
  Don't let other people tell jokes about
    your people.
Don't let the other nations laugh at us and
    say,
  'Where is their God?'"

The Lord Will Restore the Land

18 Then the Lord cared very much about his
    land.
  He felt sorry for his people.
19 The Lord spoke to his people.
He said, "I will send you grain, wine, and
    oil.
  You will have plenty.
I will not shame you among the nations
    anymore.
20 No, I will force the people from the
    north[c] to leave your land
  and make them go into a dry, empty
    land.
Some of them will go to the eastern sea
  and some to the western sea.
They did such terrible things,
  but they will be like a dead and rotting
    body.
  There will be such a terrible smell!"

The Land Will Be Made New Again

21 Land, don't be afraid.
  Be happy and full of joy.
  The Lord will do great things.
22 Animals of the field, don't be afraid.
  The desert pastures will grow grass.
The trees will grow fruit.
  The fig trees and the vines will grow
    plenty of fruit.

---

a 2:13 *Tear your hearts, not your clothes* People tore
their clothes to show sadness. Here, God wants the
people to feel sad for the bad things they had done.

b 2:17 *porch* An open area in front of the Temple.
c 2:20 *north* The Babylonian army came from this
direction to attack Judah. Armies from countries
north and east of Israel often came this way to
attack Judah and Israel.

23 So be happy, people of Zion.*
  Be joyful in the LORD your God.
  He will be good and give you rain.
  He will send you the early rains
    and the late rains like before.
24 The threshing* floors will be filled with
    wheat,
    and the barrels will overflow with wine
      and olive oil.
25 "I, the LORD, sent my army against you.
    The swarming locusts
    and the hopping locusts
    and the destroying locusts
    and the cutting locusts*a* ate everything
      you had.
  But I, the LORD, will pay you back
    for those years of trouble.
26 Then you will have plenty to eat.
    You will be full.
  You will praise the name of the LORD your
    God.
  He has done wonderful things for you.
  My people will never again be ashamed.
27 You will know that I am with Israel.
  You will know that I am the LORD your
    God.
    There is no other God.
  My people will never be ashamed again."

God Will Give His Spirit to All People

28 "After this, I will pour out my Spirit on all
    kinds of people.
  Your sons and daughters will prophesy,
    your old men will have dreams,
    and your young men will see visions.*
29 In those days I will pour out my Spirit
    even on servants, both men and
      women.
30 I will work wonders* in the sky and on
    the earth.
    There will be blood, fire, and thick
      smoke.
31 The sun will be changed into darkness,
    and the moon will be as red as blood.
  Then the great and fearful day of the LORD
    will come!
32 And everyone who trusts in the LORD*b*
    will be saved.
  There will be survivors on Mount Zion*
    and in Jerusalem,
    just as the LORD said.
  Yes, those left alive will be the ones the
    LORD has called.

Judah's Enemies Will Be Punished

3 1 "Yes, at that time I will bring back the
    people of Judah and Jerusalem from
captivity. 2 I will also gather all the nations
together. I will bring all these nations down
into Jehoshaphat Valley.*c* There I will judge
them. Those nations scattered my people,
Israel. They forced them to live in other
nations, so I will punish those nations. They
divided up my land. 3 They threw lots* for my
people. They sold boys to buy a prostitute,
and they sold girls to buy wine to drink.

4 "Tyre! Sidon! All of you areas of Philistia! You are not important to me!*d* Are you
punishing me for something I did? You might
think that you are punishing me, but I will
soon punish you. 5 You took my silver and
gold. You took my precious treasures and put
them in your temples.*e*

6 "You sold the people of Judah and Jerusalem to the Greeks. That way you could take
them far from their land. 7 You sent my people
to that faraway place, but I will bring them
back. And I will punish you for what you did.
8 I will sell your sons and daughters to the
people of Judah. Then they will sell them to
the faraway Sabeans.*f*" This is what the LORD
said.

Prepare for War

9 Announce this among the nations:
  Prepare for war!
    Wake up the strong men!
  Let all the men of war come near.
    Let them come up!
10 Beat your plows into swords.
  Make spears from your pruning hooks.*g*
  Let the weak man say,
    "I am a strong soldier."
11 All you nations, hurry!
  Come together in that place.
  LORD, bring your strong soldiers.
12 Wake up, nations!
  Come to Jehoshaphat Valley.
  There I will sit to judge
    all the surrounding nations.
13 Bring the sickle,*
    because the harvest is ripe.*h*
  Come, walk on the grapes,
    because the winepress is full.
  The barrels will be full and spilling over,
    because their evil is great.

14 There are many, many people
    in the Valley of Decision.*i*
  The LORD's special day is near
    in the Valley of Decision.

---

*c***3:2 Jehoshaphat Valley** This name means "The
LORD judges."
*d***3:4 You are not important to me** Literally, "What
are you to me?"
*e***3:5 temples** Here, the temples were used to worship idols.
*f***3:8 Sabeans** A group of people from the Arabian
Desert.
*g***3:10 pruning hooks** These tools were used to
prune (cut) branches of trees. Read Isa. 2:4.
*h***3:13 harvest is ripe** This time of judgment is compared to harvest time.
*i***3:14 Valley of Decision** This is like the name
"Jehoshaphat Valley."

---

*a***2:25 swarming locusts ... cutting locusts** See
Joel 1:4.
*b***2:32 who trusts in the Lord** Literally, "who calls on
the name of the LORD," meaning to show faith in him
by worshiping him or praying to him for help.

15 The sun and the moon will become dark.
The stars will stop shining.
16 The LORD God will shout from Zion.*
He will shout from Jerusalem,
and the sky and the earth will shake.
But the LORD God will be a safe place
for his people.
He will be a place of safety
for the people of Israel.
17"Then you will know
that I am the LORD your God.
I live on Zion, my holy mountain.
Jerusalem will become holy.
Strangers will never pass through
that city again.

A New Life for Judah Promised

18"On that day, the mountains will drip
with sweet wine.
The hills will flow with milk,
and water will flow through all the
empty rivers of Judah.
A fountain will come from the LORD's
Temple.*
It will give water to Acacia Valley.
19 Egypt will be empty.
Edom will be an empty wilderness,
because they were cruel to the people of
Judah.
They killed innocent people[a]
in their country.
20 But there will always be people
living in Judah.
People will live in Jerusalem
through many generations.
21 Those people killed my people,
so I really will punish them!"
The LORD God will live in Zion*!

[a] **3:19 killed innocent people** Literally, "shed innocent blood."

Amos

Introduction

1 ¹This is the message of Amos, one of the shepherds from the city Tekoa. He saw visions* about Israel during the time that Uzziah was king of Judah and Jeroboam son of Joash was king of Israel. This was two years before the earthquake.

Punishment for Aram

2 Amos said,
"The LORD will shout like a lion in Zion.*
His loud voice will roar from Jerusalem.
The green pastures of the shepherds will
turn brown and die.
Even Mount Carmel[b] will become dry."

³This is what the LORD says: "I will definitely punish the people of Damascus for the many crimes they did.[c] They crushed the people of Gilead* with iron threshing* tools. ⁴So I will start a fire at Hazael's[d] house that will destroy the great palaces of Ben-Hadad.[e]

⁵"I will also break open the gates of Damascus[f] and remove the one who sits on the throne in the Valley of Aven.[g] I will remove the symbol of power from Beth Eden,[h] and the Arameans will be defeated and taken back to Kir.[i]" This is what the LORD said.

Punishment for the Philistines

⁶This is what the LORD says: "I will definitely punish the people of Gaza[j] for the many crimes they did. They took an entire nation of people and sent them as slaves to Edom.* ⁷So I will start a fire at the wall of Gaza that will destroy the high towers in Gaza. ⁸And I will destroy the one who sits on the throne in Ashdod. I will destroy the king who holds the scepter in Ashkelon. I will punish the people of Ekron.[k] Then the Philistines who are still left alive will die." This is what the LORD God said.

[b] **1:2 Mount Carmel** A mountain in northern Israel. The name means "God's vineyard." This shows that it was a very fertile hill.
[c] **1:3 for the many crimes they did** Literally, "for three crimes ... and for four ...." This shows that these people were very sinful—and it was time to punish them. Also in verses 6, 9, 11, 13; 2:1, 4, 6.
[d] **1:4 Hazael** Hazael was the king of Aram (Syria). He murdered Ben-Hadad I so that he could become king. See 2 Kings 8:7.
[e] **1:4 Ben-Hadad** Ben-Hadad II, the son of Hazael,
king of Aram (Syria). See 2 Kings 13:3.
[f] **1:5 Damascus** The capital city of Aram (Syria).
[g] **1:5 the Valley of Aven** A name that can mean "Restful Valley" or "Empty Valley of Misfortune."
[h] **1:5 Beth Eden** The royal city of Aram (Syria) on Mount Lebanon. This name means "House of Pleasure" or "Paradise."
[i] **1:5 Kir** Or "Kur," an area controlled by the Assyrians. See Amos 9:7.
[j] **1:6 Gaza** An important city of the Philistines.
[k] **1:8 Ashdod, Ashkelon, Ekron** Important cities of the Philistines.

Punishment for Phoenicia

⁹This is what the Lord says: "I will definitely punish the people of Tyre*a* for the many crimes they did. They took an entire nation and sent them as slaves to Edom.* They did not remember the agreement they had made with their brothers *(Israel)*. ¹⁰So I will start a fire at the walls of Tyre that will destroy the high towers in Tyre."

Punishment for the Edomites

¹¹This is what the Lord says: "I will definitely punish the people of Edom* for the many crimes they did. Edom chased his brother *(Israel)* with the sword. Edom showed no mercy. Edom's anger continued forever—he kept tearing and tearing at Israel like a wild animal. ¹²So I will start a fire at Teman*b* that will destroy the high towers of Bozrah.*c*"

Punishment for the Ammonites

¹³This is what the Lord says: "I will definitely punish the Ammonites*d* for the many crimes they did. They killed the pregnant women in Gilead.* The Ammonites did this so that they could take that land and make their country larger. ¹⁴So I will start a fire at the wall of Rabbah*e* that will destroy the high towers of Rabbah. Troubles will come to them like a whirlwind*f* into their country. ¹⁵Then their kings and leaders will be captured. They will all be taken together." This is what the Lord said.

Punishment for Moab

2 ¹This is what the Lord says: "I will definitely punish the people of Moab* for the many crimes they did. Moab burned the bones of the king of Edom* into lime. ²So I will start a fire in Moab that will destroy the high towers of Kerioth.*g* There will be terrible shouting and the sounds of a trumpet, and Moab will die. ³So I will bring an end to the kings*h* of Moab, and I will kill all the leaders of Moab." This is what the Lord said.

Punishment for Judah

⁴This is what the Lord says: "I will definitely punish Judah for the many crimes they did. They refused to obey the Lord's teachings and they did not keep his commands. Their ancestors* believed lies, and those same lies caused the people of Judah to stop following God. ⁵So I will start a fire in Judah that will destroy the high towers of Jerusalem."

Punishment for Israel

⁶This is what the Lord says: "I will definitely punish Israel for the many crimes they have done. They sold honest people for a little silver. They sold the poor for the price of a pair of sandals.⁷They pushed their faces into the ground and walked on them. They stopped listening to suffering people. Fathers and sons had sexual relations with the same woman. They ruined my holy name. ⁸They took clothes from the poor, and then they sat on those clothes while worshiping at their altars.* They loaned money to the poor, and then they took their clothes as a promise for payment.*i* They made people pay fines and used the money to buy wine for themselves to drink in the temple of their god.

⁹"But it was I who destroyed the Amorites*j* before them. They were as tall as cedar trees and as strong as oaks, but I destroyed their fruit above and their roots below.*k*

¹⁰"I was the one who brought you from the land of Egypt. For 40 years I led you through the desert. I helped you take the Amorites' land. ¹¹I made some of your sons to be prophets* and some of your young men to be Nazirites.* People of Israel, it is true." This is what the Lord said. ¹²"But you made the Nazirites drink wine. You told the prophets not to prophesy.* ¹³You are like a heavy weight to me. I am bent low like a wagon loaded with too much straw. ¹⁴No one will escape, not even the fastest runner. Strong men will not be strong enough. Soldiers will not be able to save themselves. ¹⁵People with bows and arrows will not survive. Fast runners will not escape. People on horses will not escape alive. ¹⁶At that time even very brave soldiers will run away. They will not take the time to put their clothes on." This is what the Lord said.

Warning to Israel

3 ¹People of Israel, listen to this message! This is what the Lord said about you, Israel. This message is about all the families that I brought from the land of Egypt. ²"There are many families on earth, but you are the only family I chose to know in a special way. And you turned against me, so I will punish you for all your sins."

---

*a*1:9 *Tyre* The capital city of Phoenicia.
*b*1:12 *Teman* A city at the northern part of the country of Edom.
*c*1:12 *Bozrah* A city in the southern part of Edom.
*d*1:13 *Ammonites* The Ammonites were the descendants of Ben-Ammi, son of Lot. Read Gen. 19:38.
*e*1:14 *Rabbah* The capital city of the Ammonites.
*f*1:14 *whirlwind* A strong wind that blows in a circle.
*g*2:2 *Kerioth* A city in Moab. This might be Ar, the capital city of Moab.
*h*2:3 *kings* Literally, "judges."

*i*2:8 *as a promise for payment.* See Deut. 24:12–13 for the rules about making loans to the poor.
*j*2:9 *Amorites* One of the nations who lived in Canaan before the Israelites came. They were the people who scared the Israelites while Moses was leading them in the desert. See Num. 13:33.
*k*2:9 *fruit above ... below* This means the parents and their children.

The Cause of Israel's Punishment

³ Two people will not walk together
    unless they have agreed to do so.
⁴ A lion will roar in the forest
    only if it catches its prey.
  A young lion roaring in his cave
    means he has caught something to eat.
⁵ A bird doesn't fly into a trap
    unless there is food in it.
  If a trap closes,
    it will catch the bird.
⁶ If people hear the warning blast of a
    trumpet,
  they shake with fear.
  If trouble comes to a city,
    the Lord caused it to happen.

⁷When the Lord God decides to do something, he will first tell his servants, the prophets.* ⁸When a lion roars, people are frightened. When the Lord speaks, prophets prophesy.*

⁹⁻¹⁰Go to the high towers in Ashdod*ᵃ* and Egypt and announce this message: "Come to the mountains of Samaria. There you will see great confusion, because the people don't know how to live right. They were cruel to other people. They took things from other people and hid those things in their high towers. Their treasuries are filled with things they took in war."

¹¹So the Lord says, "An enemy will come to that land and take away your strength. He will take the things you hid in your high towers."

¹²The Lord says,

"A lion might attack a lamb,
  and a shepherd might try to save the
    lamb.
But the shepherd will save
  only a part of that lamb.
He might pull two legs
  or a part of an ear from the lion's
    mouth.
In the same way, most of the people of
  Israel will not be saved.
Those who live in Samaria
  will save only a corner from a bed, or a
    piece of cloth from a couch."

¹³This is what the Lord God All-Powerful says: "Warn the family of Jacob* about these things. ¹⁴Israel sinned, and I will punish them for their sins. And when I do, I will also destroy the altars* at Bethel.*ᵇ* The horns of the altar* will be cut off and fall to the ground. ¹⁵I will destroy the winter house with the summer house. The houses of ivory will be destroyed. Many houses will be destroyed." This is what the Lord said.

The Women Who Love Pleasure

4 ¹Listen to me, you cows of Bashan*ᶜ* on Samaria's mountain. You hurt the poor and crush those in need. You tell your husbands,*ᵈ* "Bring us something to drink!"

²The Lord God made a promise. He promised by his holiness, that troubles will come to you. People will use hooks and take you away as prisoners. They will use fishhooks to take away your children. ³Your city will be destroyed. The women will rush out through cracks in the wall and throw themselves onto the pile of dead bodies.*ᵉ*

This is what the Lord says: ⁴"Go to Bethel and sin. Go to Gilgal*ᶠ* and sin even more. Offer your sacrifices in the morning. Bring a tenth of your crops for the three-day festival. ⁵And offer a thank offering made with yeast. Tell everyone about the freewill offerings.*ᵍ* Israel, you love to do those things. So go and do them." This is what the Lord said.

⁶"I didn't give you any food to eat.*ʰ* There was no food in any of your cities, but you didn't come back to me." This is what the Lord said.

⁷"I also stopped the rain, and it was three months before harvest time. So no crops grew. Then I let it rain on one city, but not on another. Rain fell on one part of the country, but on the other part of the country, the land became very dry. ⁸So the people from two or three cities staggered to another city to get water, but there was not enough water for everyone. Still you didn't come to me for help." This is what the Lord said.

⁹"I made your crops die from heat and disease. I destroyed your gardens and your vineyards.* Locusts* ate your fig trees and olive trees. But you still didn't come to me for help." This is what the Lord said.

¹⁰"I sent diseases against you, as I did to Egypt. I killed your young men with swords. I took away your horses. I made your camp smell very bad from all the dead bodies, but still you didn't come back to me for help." This is what the Lord said.

---

*ᶜ***4:1** *cows of Bashan* This means the wealthy women in Samaria. Bashan, an area east of the Jordan River, was famous for its big bulls and cows.
*ᵈ***4:1** *your husbands* Literally, "their masters."
*ᵉ***4:3** *throw ... dead bodies* Or "You will be thrown away. People will take you to Mount Hermon." The Hebrew text here is hard to understand. It is not clear if the women will be "thrown away" or if the women will be "throwing something away."
*ᶠ***4:4** *Bethel ... Gilgal* Places of worship for the people of Israel. God wanted the people of Israel and the people of Judah to worship him only in the Temple at Jerusalem.
*ᵍ***4:4–5** *Offer your sacrifices ... freewill offerings* All these things were against the Law of Moses. The leaders and false priests started these new festivals and different ways of worshiping God.
*ʰ***4:6** *I didn't give you any food to eat* Literally, "I gave you clean teeth."

*ᵃ***3:9–10** *Ashdod* An important city of the Philistines.
*ᵇ***3:14** *Bethel* A town in Israel. This name means "God's house."

¹¹"I destroyed you as I destroyed Sodom* and Gomorrah.* And those cities were completely destroyed. You were like a burned stick pulled from a fire, but still you didn't come back to me for help." This is what the LORD says.

¹²"So, Israel, this is what I will do to you. You people of Israel, prepare to meet your God."

13 He is the one who made the mountains.
   He created the wind.*ᵃ*
   He lets people know his thoughts.
He changes the darkness into dawn.
   He walks over the mountains of the earth.
   His name is YAHWEH,* LORD God All-Powerful.

A Sad Song for Israel

5 ¹People of Israel, listen to this song. This funeral song is about you.

2 The virginᵇ of Israel has fallen.
   She will not get up anymore.
   She was left alone, lying in the dirt.
   There is no one to lift her up.

³This is what the Lord GOD says:

"Officers leaving the city with 1000 men
   will return with only 100 men.
Officers leaving the city with 100 men
   will return with only ten men."

The Lord Encourages Israel to Come Back

4 The LORD says this to the nationᶜ of Israel:
   "Come looking for me and live.
5   But don't look in Bethel.
   Don't go to Gilgal.
   Don't cross the border and go down to Beersheba.*ᵈ*
   The people of Gilgal will be taken away as prisoners,*ᵉ*
   and Bethel will be destroyed.*ᶠ*
6   Come to the LORD and live.
   If you don't go to him, a fire will start at Joseph's house,*ᵍ*

and no one in Bethelʰ can stop it.
⁷⁻⁹You should go to the Lord for help.
   He is the one who made the Pleiades and Orion.*ⁱ*
He changes darkness into the morning light.
He changes the day into the dark night.
He calls for the waters of the sea and
   pours them out on the earth.
   His name is YAHWEH*!
He keeps one strong city safe,
   and he lets another strong city be destroyed."

The Evil Things That the Israelites Did

You change goodness to poison.*ʲ*
You killed justice,
   and let it fall to the ground.
10 You hate those prophets, who go to public places and speak against evil,
   even though they teach good, simple truths.
11 You take unfair taxesᵏ from the poor.
   You take loads of wheat from them.
You build fancy houses with cut stone,
   but you will not live in them.
You plant beautiful vineyards,*
   but you will not drink the wine from them.
12 This is because I know about your many sins.
   You have done some very bad things:
   You hurt people who do right,
   you accept money to do wrong,
   and you keep the poor from receiving justice in court.
13 At that time wise teachers will be quiet,
   because it is a bad time.
14 You say that God is with you,
   so you should do good things, not evil.
Then you will live,
   and the LORD God All-Powerful will be with you.
15 Hate evil and love goodness.
   Bring justice back into the courts.
Maybe then the LORD God All-Powerful
   will be kind to the survivors* from Joseph's family.

A Time of Great Sadness Is Coming

16 The Lord GOD All-Powerful says,
   "People will be crying in the public places.
   They will be crying in the streets.

---

*ᵃ***4:13** *the wind* Or "your minds."
*ᵇ***5:2** *virgin* The Hebrew word can mean "a woman who has not had sexual relations with anyone," but here, it means the city of Samaria.
*ᶜ***5:4** *nation* Literally, "house." This might mean the royal family of that country.
*ᵈ***5:5** *Bethel, Gilgal, Beersheba* Ancient places of worship. Abraham and Jacob built altars in these places, but God had told the Israelites that they should go to the Temple in Jerusalem to worship him.
*ᵉ***5:5** *taken away as prisoners* In Hebrew this sounds like the name "Gilgal."
*ᶠ***5:5** *destroyed* The Hebrew word is like the name "Beth Aven." This name means "House of Wickedness." The prophets often used this name for Bethel.
*ᵍ***5:6** *Joseph's house* Here, this means the ten-tribe nation of Israel. Joseph was the ancestor of the tribes of Ephraim and Manasseh in Israel.

*ʰ***5:6** *Bethel* This name means "El's house" or "the house of God." There was a temple here where the people from the northern tribes worshiped.
*ⁱ***5:7–9** *Pleiades and Orion* Two well-known groups of stars (constellations).
*ʲ***5:7–9** *poison* Literally, "wormwood," a type of plant with bitter leaves. It could be used as a medicine, or if strong enough, as a poison.
*ᵏ***5:11** *take unfair taxes* The meaning of the Hebrew word here is uncertain.

They will hire the professional criers.[a]

17 People will be crying in the vineyards,*
    because I will pass through and punish
    you."
  This is what the LORD said.

18 Some of you want to see
    the LORD's special day of judgment.
  Why do you want to see that day?
    His special day will bring darkness, not
    light.

19 You will be like someone who escapes
    from a lion
  only to be attacked by a bear,
  or like someone who goes into the safety
    of his house,
  leans against the wall,
  and is bitten by a snake.

20 The LORD's special day will be
    a day of darkness, not light—a day of
    gloom, without a ray of light.

The Lord Rejects Israel's Worship

21 "I hate your festivals;
    I will not accept them.
  I don't enjoy your religious meetings.

22 Even if you offer me burnt offerings* and
    grain offerings,
  I will not accept them.
  I will not even look at the fat animals
    you give as fellowship offerings.*

23 Take your noisy songs away from here.
    I will not listen to the music from your
    harps.

24 But let justice flow like a river,
    and let goodness flow like a stream that
    never becomes dry.

25 Israel, you offered me sacrifices
    and offerings in the desert for 40 years.[b]

26 But you also carried statues
    of Sakkuth, your king, and Kaiwan.[c]
  There was also that star god[d]
    that you made for yourselves.

27 So I will send you as captives,
    far beyond Damascus."
  This is what the LORD says.
    His name is God All-Powerful.

Israel's Good Times Will Be Taken Away

6 ¹Oh, look at the people enjoying life in
    Zion,*

and those on Mount Samaria who feel
    so safe.
They are such important leaders of a most
    important nation.
The "House of Israel" comes to you for
    advice.

2 Go look at Calneh.
  From there, go to the large city Hamath.
  Go to the Philistine city of Gath.[e]
  Are you better than these kingdoms?
    Their countries are larger than yours.

3 You people are rushing toward the day of
    punishment.
  You bring near the rule of violence.

4 But now you lie on ivory beds
    and stretch out on your couches.
  You eat tender young lambs from the flock
    and young calves from the stable.

5 You play your harps,
    and like David, you practice on[f] your
    musical instruments.

6 You drink wine in fancy cups.[g]
  You use the best perfumes.
  And it doesn't even bother you
    that Joseph's family is being destroyed.

7You people are stretched out on your
couches now, but your good times will end.
You will be taken away as prisoners to a foreign country, and you will be some of the first
people taken. 8The Lord GOD used his own
name and made an oath.* The LORD God All-
Powerful said,

"I hate what Jacob* is proud of.
  I hate his strong towers.
  So I will let an enemy take the city
    and everything in it."

There Will Be Few Israelites Left Alive

9At that time ten people in one house might
survive, but they too will die. 10And when
someone dies, a relative will come to get the
body so that it can be taken out and burned.[h]
Relatives will come to take away the bones.
They will call to anyone who might be hiding
back in the house, "Are there any other dead
bodies in there with you?"
  That person will answer, "No, ..."[i]
  But the relative will interrupt and say,
"Hush! We must not mention the name of the
LORD."

[a]5:16 *professional criers* People who went to
funerals and cried loudly for the dead. Families
and friends of the dead person often gave food or
money to these people.
[b]5:25 Or "Israel, did you offer me sacrifices and
offerings in the desert for 40 years?"
[c]5:26 *Sakkuth, your king, and Kaiwan* Or "Sakkuth,
Moloch, and Kaiwan," names of Assyrian gods.
[d]5:26 *star god* This might be to honor a special god
or all the stars in the sky. Many people thought the
sun, moon, stars, and planets were gods or angels.
This verse might also be translated, "You carried
the shelter for your king and the footstool for your
idols."The star of your gods that you made for yourselves." The ancient Greek version adds the names of
these gods: Moloch and Raphan.

[e]6:2 *Calneh, Hamath, Gath* Powerful Babylonian,
Syrian, and Philistine cities that were all captured by
the Assyrians.
[f]6:5 *practice on* Or "invent." The Hebrew word
means to "think," "become skilled," or "design."
[g]6:6 *fancy cups* Very large bowls used in worship
rituals.
[h]6:10 *And when ... burned* The meaning of the
Hebrew text here is uncertain.
[i]6:10 *No, ...* The full answer might have been, "No,
praise the LORD," but the person was interrupted.

11 Look, the Lord God will give the
     command,
   and the large houses will be broken to
     pieces,
   and the small houses will be broken to
     small pieces.
12 Do horses run over loose rocks?
   No, and people don't use cows for
     plowing.
   But you turned everything upside down.
   You changed justice and goodness to
     bitter poison.
13 You are so excited about defeating Lo
     Debar.*a*
   And you boast, "We have taken
     Karnaim*b* by our own strength."

14"But Israel, I will bring a nation against
you that will bring troubles to your whole
country from Lebo Hamath to Arabah Brook."
This is what the Lord God All-Powerful said.

The Vision of the Locusts

7 ¹This is what the Lord showed me: He
     was making locusts.* This was at the
time the second crop began to grow, after the
king's people had cut the first crop. ²Before
the locusts could eat all the grass in the country, I said, "Lord God, I beg you, forgive us!
Jacob* cannot survive! He is too small!"
³Then the Lord changed his mind about
this. The Lord said, "It will not happen."

The Vision of the Fire

⁴This is what the Lord God showed me: I
saw the Lord God calling for judgment by fire.
The fire destroyed the ocean and was beginning to eat up the land. ⁵But I said, "Lord
God, stop, I beg you! Jacob* cannot survive!
He is too small!"
⁶Then the Lord changed his mind about
this. The Lord God said, "It will not happen
either."

The Vision of the Plumb Line

⁷This is what the Lord showed me: He
stood by a wall with a plumb line*c* in his
hand. (The wall had been marked with a
plumb line.) ⁸The Lord said to me, "Amos,
what do you see?"
I said, "A plumb line."
Then the Lord said to me, "See, I will put a
plumb line among my people Israel. I will not
let their 'crooked ways' pass inspection anymore. ⁹Isaac's high places* will be destroyed.
Israel's holy places will be made into a pile of
rocks. I will attack and kill Jeroboam's*d* family
with swords."

Amaziah Tries to Stop Amos

¹⁰Amaziah, a priest at Bethel,*e* sent this
message to Jeroboam, the king of Israel:
"Amos is making plans against you. He is trying to make the people of Israel fight against
you. He has been speaking so much that this
country cannot hold all his words. ¹¹Amos has
said, 'Jeroboam will die by the sword, and the
people of Israel will be taken as prisoners out
of their country.'"
¹²Amaziah also said to Amos, "You seer,* go
down to Judah and eat there.*f* Do your prophesying* there. ¹³But don't prophesy anymore
here at Bethel. This is Jeroboam's holy place.
This is Israel's temple."
¹⁴Then Amos answered Amaziah, "I am
not a professional prophet, and I am not from
a prophet's family. I raise cattle and take care
of sycamore trees. ¹⁵I was a shepherd and the
Lord took me from following the sheep. The
Lord said to me, 'Go, prophesy to my people
Israel.' ¹⁶So listen to the Lord's message. You
tell me, 'Don't prophesy against Israel. Don't
speak against Isaac's family.' ¹⁷But the Lord
says, 'Your wife will become a prostitute in
the city. Your sons and daughters will be killed
with swords. Other people will take your land
and divide it among themselves, and you will
die in a foreign*g* country. The people of Israel
will definitely be taken from this country as
prisoners.'"

The Vision of the Ripe Fruit

8 ¹This is what the Lord showed me: I saw
     a basket of summer fruit. ²He said to me,
"Amos, what do you see?"
I said, "A basket of summer fruit."
Then the Lord said to me, "The end*h* has
come to my people Israel. I will not ignore
their sins anymore. ³Their temple songs will
become funeral songs." This is what the Lord
God said. "There will be dead bodies everywhere. In silence, people will take out the
dead bodies and throw them onto the pile.*i*"

Merchants Only Want to Make Money

4 Listen to me, you who trample on
     helpless people.
   You are trying to destroy the poor of this
     country.

---

*a*6:13 *Lo Debar* This name means "nothing."
*b*6:13 *Karnaim* This name means "horns." Horns
were a symbol of strength.
*c*7:7 *plumb line* A string with a weight on one end
used to show how straight the walls of a building
were. Sometimes the line was coated with paint or
chalk to mark a straight line.
*d*7:9 *Jeroboam* The king of Israel. See verse 10.
*e*7:10 *Bethel* A town in Israel. This name means
"God's house."
*f*7:12 *eat there* This shows that Amaziah thought
that Amos was a professional prophet who prophesied to receive food or money.
*g*7:17 *foreign* Literally, "unclean." See "unclean" in
the Word List.
*h*8:2 *end* This Hebrew word sounds like the word for
"summer fruit."
*i*8:3 *In silence ... the pile* Or "People will be saying,
'Hush!'" See Amos 6:10.

5 You merchants* say,
  "When will the New Moon* be over so
      that we can sell grain?
  When will the Sabbath be over
    so that we can bring out more wheat to
      sell?
  We can raise the price
    and make the measure smaller.ᵃ
  We can fix the scales
    and cheat the people.ᵇ
6 The poor cannot pay their loans,
    so we will buy them as slaves.
  We will buy those helpless people
    for the price of a pair of sandals.
  Oh, and we can sell the wheat
    that was spilled on the floor."

⁷The LORD made a promise. He used his name, "Pride of Jacob," and made this promise:

  "I will never forget what those people did.
8 There will be an earthquake
    that will shake the whole land because
      of what they did.
  Everyone living there will cry for those
      who died.
  The land will be tossed around.
  The whole land will rise and fall like the
      Nile River in Egypt."

9 The LORD also said, "At that time
    I will make the sun set at noon
    and make the land dark on a clear day.
10 I will change your festivals into days of
      crying for the dead.
  All your songs will be songs of sadness
      for those who are dead.
  I will put mourning* clothes on every
      body
    and baldness on every head.ᶜ
  I will cause mourning everywhere,
    like that for an only son who has died.
  It will be a very bitter end."

A Famine of God's Word

¹¹The Lord GOD says:

  "Look, the days are coming
    when I will cause a famine* in the land.
  The people will not be hungry for bread.
  They will not be thirsty for water.
  No, they will be hungry for words from
      the LORD.
12 The people will wander around the
      country,
    from the Dead Sea to the Mediterranean
      Sea,

and from the north part of the country
    to the east.
They will go back and forth looking for a
    message from the LORD,
  but they will not find it.
13 At that time the beautiful young men and
      women
    will become weak from thirst.
14 They made promises by the sin of
      Samaria,ᵈ
  They said,
    'Dan,ᵉ as surely as your god lives, we
      promise ....'
  And they said,
    'As surely as the god of Beershebaᶠ lives,
      we promise ....'
  But they will fall
    and never get up again."

Vision of the Lord Standing by the Altar

9 ¹I saw the Lord standing by the altar,* and
  he said,

  "Hit the top of the columns,
    and shake them to the ground.
  Push them and they will fall
    on everyone's head.
  As for those who survive,
    I will kill them with a sword.
  None of them will run away.
  None of them will escape.
2 If they dig deep into the ground,ᵍ
    I will pull them from there.
  If they go up into the skies,ʰ
    I will bring them down from there.
3 If they hide at the top of Mount Carmel,ⁱ
    I will find them there and take them
      from that place.
  If they try to hide from me at the bottom
      of the sea,
    I will command the snake, and it will
      bite them.
4 If they are captured and taken away by
      their enemies,
    I will command the sword,
    and it will kill them there.
  Yes, I will watch over them,
    but I will watch for ways to give them
      troubles,
    not for ways to do good things."

Punishment Will Destroy the People
5 The Lord GOD All-Powerful will touch the
      land,
    and the land will melt.

ᵃ8:5 *We ... smaller* Literally, "We will make the ephah small and the shekel large."
ᵇ8:5 *We ... people* Literally, "Cheat with lying balances."
ᶜ8:10 *baldness ... head* People shaved their heads to show that they were very sad or upset.

ᵈ8:14 *sin of Samaria* The calf god in Samaria.
ᵉ8:14 *Dan* One of Israel's holy places was in this city.
ᶠ8:14 *Beersheba* A town in Judah. This name means "well of the oath *(promise)*."
ᵍ9:2 *ground* Literally, "Sheol, the place of the dead."
ʰ9:2 *skies* Or "heaven."
ⁱ9:3 *Mount Carmel* A mountain in northern Israel. This name means "God's vineyard." This shows that it was a very fertile hill.

Then all the people who live in the land
will cry for the dead.
The land will rise and fall like the Nile
River in Egypt.
6 He built his upper rooms above the skies.
He put his skies[a] over the earth.
He calls for the waters of the sea
and pours them out as rain on the land.
Yᴀʜᴡᴇʜ* is his name.

The Lord Promises Destruction for Israel
7 This is what the Lᴏʀᴅ says:

"Israel, you are like the Ethiopians to me.
I brought Israel out of the land of Egypt,
the Philistines* from Caphtor,[b]
and the Arameans from Kir.[c]"

8 The Lord Gᴏᴅ is watching this sinful
kingdom.
The Lᴏʀᴅ said,
"I will wipe Israel off the face of the earth,
but I will never completely destroy
Jacob's* family.
9 I am giving the command
to scatter the people of Israel among all
nations.
But it will be like someone sifting flour.
A person shakes flour through a sifter.[d]
The good flour falls through, but the bad
lumps are caught.

---

[a]9:6 skies Literally, "dome" or "vault."
[b]9:7 Caphtor An island west of Israel, probably
Crete or Cyprus.
[c]9:7 Kir Where the Arameans came from and where
the Assyrians sent them in exile. There are several
places with this name.
[d]9:9 sifter Something like a cup with a screen on its
bottom. A sifter is used for removing large lumps
from the good flour.

10 "Sinners among my people say,
'Nothing bad will happen to us.'
But all of them will be killed with
swords."

God Promises to Restore the Kingdom
11 "David's tent[e] has fallen,
but at that time I will set it up again.
I will fix its holes and repair its ruined
parts.
I will set it up as it was before.
12 Then the people left alive in Edom,*
and all the people called by my name,
will look to me for help."
This is what the Lᴏʀᴅ said,
and he will make it happen.
13 The Lᴏʀᴅ says, "A time of great blessing
is coming.
Workers will still be harvesting when it
is time to plow the fields again.
They will still be trampling the grapes
when it is time for a new crop.
Sweet wine will drip from the mountains
and pour from the hills.
14 I will bring my people, Israel,
back from captivity.
They will rebuild the ruined cities,
and they will live in them.
They will plant vineyards*
and drink the wine they produce.
They will plant gardens
and eat the crops they produce.
15 I will plant my people on their land,
and never again will they be pulled up
out of the land that I gave them."
This is what the Lᴏʀᴅ your God said.

---

[e]9:11 David's tent This probably means the city of
Jerusalem or the country of Judah.

Obadiah

Edom Will Be Punished
1 This is the vision* of Obadiah. This is what
the Lord Gᴏᴅ says about Edom:*

We heard a report from the Lᴏʀᴅ.
A messenger was sent to the nations.
He said, "Let's go fight against Edom."

The Lord Speaks to Edom
2 "Edom,* I will make you the smallest
nation.
Everyone will hate you very much.
3 Your pride has fooled you.

You live in those caves high on the cliff.
Your home is high in the hills.
So you say to yourself,
'No one can bring me to the ground.'"

Edom Will Be Brought Low
4 This is what the Lᴏʀᴅ says:
"Even though you fly high like the eagle
and put your nest among the stars,
I will bring you down from there.
5 You really will be ruined!
Thieves will come to you.
Robbers will come in the night,

and they will take all they want.
When workers gather grapes in your
vineyards,
they will leave a few grapes behind.

6 But the enemy will search hard for Esau's
hidden treasures,
and they will find them all.

7 All those who are your friends
will force you out of the land.
Those who were at peace with you will
trick you,
and they will defeat you.
The soldiers who fought by your side
are planning a trap for you.
They say, 'He doesn't expect a thing!'"

8 The LORD says, "On that day,
I will destroy the wise people from
Edom.*
I will destroy the intelligent people from
the mountain of Esau.*a*

9 Teman,*b* your brave soldiers will be afraid.
Everyone will be destroyed from the
mountain of Esau.
Many people will be killed.

10 You will be covered with shame
because you were very cruel to your
brother Jacob.*
So you will be destroyed completely.

11 You joined the enemies of Israel.
Strangers carried Israel's treasures away.
Foreigners entered Israel's city gate.
They threw lots* to decide what part of
Jerusalem they would get.
And you were right there with them,
waiting to get your share.

12 You should not have laughed*c*
at your brother's trouble.
You should not have been happy
when they destroyed Judah.
You should not have bragged*d*
at the time of their trouble.

13 You should not have entered the city gate
of my people
and laughed at their problems.
You should not have taken their treasures
in the time of their trouble.

14 You should not have stood where the
roads cross

and destroyed those who were trying to
escape.
You should not have captured those who
escaped alive.

15 The Day of the LORD is coming soon
to all the nations.
And the evil you did to others
will happen to you.
The same bad things
will fall down on your own head.

16 You spilled*e* blood on my holy mountain,*f*
so other nations will spill your blood.*g*
You will be finished.
It will be as if you never existed.

17 But there will be survivors on Mount
Zion.
They will be my special people.
The nation of Jacob*h* will take back
what belongs to it.

18 The family of Jacob will be like a fire.
The nation of Joseph will be like a
flame.
But the nation of Esau*i* will be like ashes.
The people of Judah will burn Edom,
and they will destroy it.
Then there will be no survivors
in the nation of Esau."
This will happen because
the LORD said it would.

19 Then people from the Negev*
will live on the mountain of Esau.
And people from the foothills
will take the Philistine lands.
They will live in the land of Ephraim and
Samaria.
Gilead will belong to Benjamin.

20 People from Israel were forced to leave
their homes,
but they will take back the land of
Canaan,* all the way to Zarephath.
People from Judah were forced to leave
Jerusalem and live in Sepharad.*j*
But they will take back the cities of the
Negev.

21 The winners*k* will go up on Mount Zion
to rule the people who live on Esau's
mountain.
And the kingdom will belong to the
LORD.

---

*e***16** *spilled* Literally, "drank."
*f***16** *holy mountain* One of the mountains Jerusalem
was built on. Sometimes Zion is used to mean
Jerusalem itself. Also in verses 17, 21.
*g***16** *spill your blood* Literally, "drink and swallow."
*h***17** *nation of Jacob* Literally, "the house of Jacob."
This could mean the people of Israel or only its
leaders.
*i***18** *nation of Esau* Literally, "the house of Esau."
*j***20** *Sepharad* This is probably Spain.
*k***21** *winners* Or "saviors." Those who led their people
to victory in war.

*a***8** *mountain of Esau* That is, Mount Seir.
*b***9** *Teman* One of Edom's important cities in the
south, maybe its capital city.
*c***12** *laughed* Literally, "looked." Also in verse 13.
*d***12** *bragged* Literally, "made your mouth big."

Jonah

God Calls and Jonah Runs

1 ¹The Lord spoke to Jonah*a* son of Amittai: ²"Nineveh*b* is a big city. I have heard about the many evil things the people are doing there. So go there and tell them to stop doing such evil things."

³But Jonah tried to run away from the Lord. He went to Joppa*c* and found a boat that was going to the faraway city of Tarshish.* Jonah paid money for the trip and went on the boat. He wanted to travel with the people on this boat to Tarshish and run away from the Lord.

The Great Storm

⁴But the Lord brought a great storm on the sea. The wind made the sea very rough. The storm was very strong, and the boat was ready to break apart. ⁵The men wanted to make the boat lighter to stop it from sinking, so they began throwing the cargo*d* into the sea. The sailors were very afraid. Each man began praying to his god.

Jonah had gone down into the boat to lie down, and he went to sleep. ⁶The captain of the boat saw Jonah and said, "Wake up! Why are you sleeping? Pray to your god! Maybe your god will hear your prayer and save us!"

What Caused This Storm?

⁷Then the men said to each other, "We should throw lots* to find out why this is happening to us."

So the men threw lots. The lots showed that the troubles came to them because of Jonah. ⁸Then the men said to Jonah, "It is your fault that this terrible thing is happening to us. Tell us, what have you done? What is your job? Where do you come from? What is your country? Who are your people?"

⁹Jonah said to them, "I am a Hebrew. I worship the Lord, the God of heaven, who made the land and the sea."

¹⁰Jonah told the men he was running away from the Lord. The men became very afraid when they learned this. They asked Jonah,

"What terrible thing did you do against your God?"

¹¹The wind and the waves of the sea were becoming stronger and stronger. So the men said to Jonah, "What should we do to save ourselves? What should we do to you to make the sea calm?"

¹²Jonah said to the men, "I know I did wrong—that is why the storm came on the sea. So throw me into the sea, and the sea will become calm."

¹³Instead, the men tried to row the ship back to the shore, but they couldn't do it. The wind and the waves of the sea were too strong—and they were becoming stronger and stronger.

Jonah's Punishment

¹⁴So the men cried to the Lord, "Lord, please don't say we are guilty of killing an innocent man. Please don't make us die for killing him. We know you are the Lord, and you will do whatever you want."

¹⁵So the men threw Jonah into the sea. The storm stopped, and the sea became calm. ¹⁶When the men saw this, they began to fear and respect the Lord. They offered a sacrifice* and made special promises to the Lord.

¹⁷When Jonah fell into the sea, the Lord chose a very big fish to swallow Jonah. He was in the stomach of the fish for three days and three nights.

Jonah's Prayer

2 ¹While Jonah was in the stomach of the fish, he prayed to the Lord his God. He said,

²"I was in very bad trouble.
  I called to the Lord for help,
  and he answered me.
I was deep in the grave.*
  I cried to you, Lord,
  and you heard my voice.

³"You threw me into the sea.
  Your powerful waves splashed over me.
I went down, down into the deep sea.
  The water was all around me.
⁴ Then I thought,
  'Now I must go where you cannot see me,'
  but I continued looking to your holy
    Temple* for help.

⁵"The seawater closed over me.

*a*1:1 *Jonah* This is probably the same prophet mentioned in 2 Kings 14:25.
*b*1:2 *Nineveh* The capital city of the country of Assyria. Assyria destroyed Israel in 722–721 B.C.
*c*1:3 *Joppa* A town on the coast of Israel by the Mediterranean Sea.
*d*1:5 *cargo* The Hebrew word can mean "dishes," "jars," or "tools." Here, this could mean all the jars and boxes the boat carried on its way to Tarshish or the rigging and other heavy tools on the boat.

The water covered my mouth,
and I could not breathe.[a]
I went down, down into the deep sea.
Seaweed wrapped around my head.
6 I was at the bottom of the sea,
the place where the mountains begin.
I thought I was locked in this prison
forever,
but the Lord my God took me out of my
grave.
God, you gave me life again!

7"My soul gave up all hope,
but then I remembered the Lord.
I prayed to you,
and you heard my prayers in your holy
Temple.

8"Some people worship useless idols,*
but those statues never help them.[b]
9 I will give sacrifices to you,
and I will praise and thank you.
I will make special promises to you,
and I will do what I promise."
Salvation only comes from the Lord!

10Then the Lord spoke to the fish, and it
vomited Jonah out of its stomach onto the dry
land.

God Calls and Jonah Obeys

3 1Then the Lord spoke to Jonah again and
said, 2"Go to that big city Nineveh, and
say what I tell you."

3So Jonah obeyed the Lord and went to
Nineveh. It was a very large city. A person had
to walk for three days to travel through it.

4Jonah went to the center of the city and
began speaking to the people. He said, "After
40 days, Nineveh will be destroyed!"

5The people of Nineveh believed God.
They decided to stop eating for a time to think
about their sins. They put on special clothes
to show they were sorry. All the people in the
city did this, from the most important to the
least important.

6When the king of Nineveh heard about
this, he left his throne, removed his robe, put
on special clothes to show that he was sorry,
and sat in ashes.[c] 7The king wrote a special
message and sent it throughout the city:

A command from the king and his great
rulers:
For a short time no person or animal
should eat anything. No herd or flock will
be allowed in the fields. Nothing living
in Nineveh will eat or drink water. 8But

every person and every animal must be
covered with a special cloth to show they
are sad. People must cry loudly to God.
Everyone must change their life and stop
doing bad things. 9Who knows? Maybe
God will stop being angry and change his
mind, and we will not be punished.

10God saw what the people did. He saw
that they stopped doing evil. So God changed
his mind and did not do what he planned. He
did not punish the people.

God's Mercy Makes Jonah Angry

4 1Jonah was not happy that God saved the
city. Jonah became angry. 2He complained
to the Lord and said, "I knew this would happen! I was in my own country, and you told
me to come here. At that time I knew that
you would forgive the people of this evil city,
so I decided to run away to Tarshish.* I knew
that you are a kind God. I knew that you
show mercy and don't want to punish people.
I knew that you are kind, and if these people
stopped sinning, you would change your plans
to destroy them. 3So now, Lord, just kill me.
It is better for me to die than to live."

4Then the Lord said, "Do you think it is
right for you to be angry just because I did
not destroy those people?"

5Jonah went out of the city to a place near
the city on the east side. He made a shelter
for himself and sat there in the shade, waiting
to see what would happen to the city.

The Gourd Plant and the Worm

6The Lord made a gourd plant grow quickly
over Jonah. This made a cool place for Jonah
to sit and helped him to be more comfortable.
He was very happy because of this plant.

7The next morning, God sent a worm to eat
part of the plant. The worm began eating the
plant, and the plant died.

8After the sun was high in the sky, God
caused a hot east wind to blow. The sun became
very hot on Jonah's head, and he became very
weak. He asked God to let him die. He said, "It
is better for me to die than to live."

9But God said to Jonah, "Do you think it
is right for you to be angry just because this
plant died?"

Jonah answered, "Yes, it is right for me to
be angry! I am angry enough to die!"

10And the Lord said, "You did nothing for
that plant. You did not make it grow. It grew
up in the night, and the next day it died. And
now you are sad about it. 11If you can get
upset over a plant, surely I can feel sorry for a
big city like Nineveh. There are many people
and animals in that city. There are more than
120,000 people there who did not know they
were doing wrong."[d]

[a]2:5 mouth, and I could not breathe Or "The water
surrounded me to my soul." The Hebrew word for
soul also means "life," "self," or "appetite," and "throat"
or "mouth."
[b]2:8 Or "People who worship useless things have
left the one who is kind to them."
[c]3:6 sat in ashes People did this to show that they
were sad.

[d]4:11 people ... wrong Literally, "people who do not
know their right from their left." This might mean
"innocent children."

Micah

Samaria and Israel to Be Punished

1 ¹During the time that Jotham, Ahaz, and Hezekiah were kings of Judah, the word of the LORD came to Micah. Micah was from Moresheth. He saw these visions about Samaria and Jerusalem.

2 Listen, all you people!
    Earth and everyone on it,ᵃ listen!
The Lord GOD will come from his holy
    temple.
The Lord will come as a witness* against
    you.
3 See, the LORD is coming out of his place.
    He is coming down to walk on the high
    placesᵇ of the earth.
4 The mountains will melt under him
    like wax before a fire.
The valleys will split open
    and flow like water down a steep hill.
5 This will happen because of Jacob's* sin,
    because of the sins of the nationᶜ of
    Israel.

Samaria, the Cause of Sin

What caused Jacob to sin?
    It was Samaria.
Where is the high place in Judah?
    It is Jerusalem.
6 So I will change Samaria into a pile of
    rocks in the field,
    a place ready for planting grapes.
I will push Samaria's stones down into the
    valley,
    leaving nothing but the foundations.
7 All her idols*
    will be broken into pieces.
Her prostitute's wages (idols)
    will be burned in fire.
I will destroy all her statues of false gods,
    because Samaria got her riches by being
        unfaithful to me.ᵈ
So those things will be taken by people
    who are not faithful to me.ᵉ

Micah's Great Sadness

8 I will be very sad about what will happen.
    I will go without sandals and clothes.
I will cry like a dog.ᶠ
    I will mourn* like a bird.ᵍ
9 Samaria'sʰ wound cannot be healed.
    Her disease has spread to Judah.
It has reached the city gate of my people;
    it has spread all the way to Jerusalem.
10 Don't tell it in Gath.ⁱ
    Don't cry in Acco.ʲ
Roll yourself in the dust at Beth Ophrah.ᵏ
11 You people living in Shaphir,ˡ
    pass on your way, naked and ashamed.
The people living in Zaananᵐ will not
    come out.
The people in Beth Ezelⁿ will cry
    and take their support from you.
12 The people living in Marothᵒ
    wait for something good to happen,
even though trouble has come down from
    the LORD
    and has reached the city gate of
        Jerusalem.
13 You people living in Lachish,ᵖ
    get the horses ready for your chariots.*
You are guilty of the same sins Israelᵠ
    committed,
    and you brought those sins to
        Jerusalem.ʳ
14 So you must give goodbye gifts
    to Moreshethˢ in Gath.

ᵃ**1:2 everyone on it** Literally, "its fullness."
ᵇ**1:3 high places** Here, this might mean simply "hills," or it might be the places for worshiping God or false gods. These places were often on the hills and mountains.
ᶜ**1:5 nation** Literally, "house." This might mean the royal family of that country.
ᵈ**1:7 her riches ... me** Literally, "her wages were a prostitute's wages."
ᵉ**1:7 will be ... to me** Literally, "will return to prostitute's wages."
ᶠ**1:8 dog** Literally, "jackal," a kind of wild dog.
ᵍ**1:8 bird** Literally, "ostrich," a large bird.
ʰ**1:9 Samaria** The capital city of the northern kingdom of Israel.
ⁱ**1:10 Gath** This is a wordplay. This name means "tell."
ʲ**1:10 Acco** This name means "cry."
ᵏ**1:10 Beth Ophrah** This name means "house of dust."
ˡ**1:11 Shaphir** This name means "beautiful."
ᵐ**1:11 Zaanan** This name means "come out."
ⁿ**1:11 Beth Ezel** This name means "house of support."
ᵒ**1:12 Maroth** This name means "bitter," "angry," or "sad."
ᵖ**1:13 Lachish** This name is like the Hebrew word meaning "horse."
ᵠ**1:13 Israel** Here, probably the northern kingdom of Israel centered in Samaria.
ʳ**1:13 Jerusalem** Literally, "Daughter Zion." See "Zion" in the Word List.
ˢ**1:14 Moresheth** Micah's hometown.

The houses in Aczib*a* will trick
  the kings of Israel.
15 You people who live in Mareshah,*b*
  I will bring someone against you who
    will take the things you own.
The Glory* of Israel
  will come into Adullam.*c*
16 So cut off your hair, make yourself bald,*d*
  because you will cry for the children
    you love.
Make yourself bald like an eagle*e* and
  show your sadness,
  because your children will be taken
    away from you.

The Evil Plans of People

2 ¹Trouble will come to those who
    make plans to sin.
They lie on their beds making their evil
  plans.
Then when the morning light comes, they
  do what they planned,
  because they have the power to do what
    they want.
2 They want fields,
  so they take them.
They want houses,
  so they take them.
They cheat a man
  and take his house and his land.

The Lord's Plans to Punish the People

3 That is why the LORD says:
"Look, I am planning trouble against this
  family.
You will not be able to save yourselves.*f*
You will stop being proud,
  because bad times are coming.
4 Then people will sing songs about you.
  They will sing this sad song:
'We are ruined!
  The LORD took away our land and gave
    it to other people.
Yes, he took my land away from me.
  He has divided our fields ⌊among our
    enemies⌋.
5 So we will not be able to measure
  the land
  and divide it among the LORD's people.'"

Micah Is Asked Not to Prophesy

6 The people say, "Don't prophesy* to us.
Don't say those bad things about us.
Nothing bad will happen to us."

7 But people of Jacob,*
  I must say these things.
The LORD is losing his patience
  because of the bad things you did.
If you lived right,
  I could say nice words to you.
8 But you attack my people like enemies.
  You steal the clothes off the backs of
    people walking by.
They think they are safe,
  but you are there to treat them like
    prisoners of war.*g*
9 You have taken nice houses
  away from the women of my people.
You have taken my wealth
  away from their small children forever.
10 Get up and leave!
  This will not be your place of rest,
    because you ruined it.
You made it unclean, so it will be
  destroyed!
  It will be a terrible destruction!

11 These people don't want to listen to me.
  But if a man comes telling lies,
    they will accept him.
They would accept a false prophet* if he
  comes and says,
  "There will be good times in the future,
    with plenty of wine and beer."

The Lord Will Bring His People Together

12 Yes, people of Jacob,*
  I will bring all of you together.
I will bring together all those in Israel*
  who are still living.
I will put them together
  like sheep in the sheep pen,
  like a flock in its pasture.
Then the place will be filled
  with the noise of many people.
13 The "One Who Breaks Through Walls"
  will push through and walk to the front
    of his people.
They will break through the gates and
  leave that city.
They will leave with their king marching
  before them—
  with the LORD at the front of his people.

The Leaders of Israel Are Guilty of Evil

3 ¹Then I said, "Listen, leaders of Jacob*
    and officers of the nation*h* of Israel*!
You should know what justice is.
2 But you hate good and love evil.
  You tear the skin off the people
  and tear the flesh off their bones.
3 You are destroying my people.*i*

---

*a*1:14 *Aczib* This name means "lie" or "trick."
*b*1:15 *Mareshah* The name means "a person who takes things."
*c*1:15 *Adullam* A cave that David hid in when he ran away from Saul. See 1 Sam. 22:1.
*d*1:16 *cut ... bald* This showed that a person made a special agreement with God or that a person was very sad.
*e*1:16 *eagle* Or "vulture." See "vulture" in the Word List.
*f*2:3 *save yourselves* Literally, "take your necks off it."

*g*2:8 *They think ... war* Or "Returning from war, they think they are safe."
*h*3:1 *nation* Literally, "house." This might mean the royal family of that country.
*i*3:3 *You are destroying my people* Literally, "⌊You⌋ who eat the flesh of my people."

You take their skin off them and break
their bones.
You chop their bones up like meat to put
in the pot!
4 Then you will pray to the Lord,
but he will not answer you.
No, he will hide his face from you,
because what you do is evil."

False Prophets

5 Some false prophets* are telling lies to
the Lord's people. This is what the Lord says
about them:

"These prophets are led by their stomachs.
They promise peace for those who give
them food,
but they promise war to those who do
not give them food.

6 "This is why it is like night for you
and you don't have visions.*
You cannot see what will happen in the
future,
so it is like darkness to you.
The sun has gone down on the prophets.
They cannot see what will happen in the
future,
so it is like darkness to them.
7 The seers* are ashamed.
The fortunetellers* are embarrassed.
None of them will say anything,
because God will not speak to them."

Micah Is an Honest Prophet of God

8 But the Lord's Spirit has filled me
with power, goodness, and strength.
So I can tell Jacob* about his crimes,
and so I can tell Israel* about his sins!

The Leaders of Israel Are to Blame

9 Leaders of Jacob* and rulers of Israel,
listen to me!
You hate the right way of living!
If something is straight,
then you make it crooked!
10 You build Zion* by murdering people.ᵃ
You build Jerusalem by cheating people!
11 The judges in Jerusalem accept bribes
to help them decide who wins in court.
The priests in Jerusalem must be paid
before they will teach the people.
People must pay the prophets
before they will look into the future.
Then those leaders expect the Lord to
help them.
They say, "The Lord lives here with us,
so nothing bad will happen to us."

12 Leaders, because of you, Zion will be
destroyed.
It will become a plowed field.
Jerusalem will become a pile of rocks.

Temple Mount will be an empty hillᵇ
overgrown with bushes.

The Law Will Come From Jerusalem

4 ¹In the last days the mountain of the
Lord's Temple* will be on the highest
of all mountains.
It will be raised higher than the hills.
There will be a steady stream of people
going there.
2 People from many nations will go there
and say,
"Come, let's go up to the mountain of the
Lord,
to the Temple of the God of Jacob.*
Then God will teach us his way of living,
and we will follow him."

His teaching, the Lord's message, will
begin in Jerusalem on Mount Zion*
and will go out to all the world.
3 Then God will act as judge to end
arguments between people in many
places.
He will decide what is right for great
nations far and near.
They will stop using their weapons for
war.
They will hammer their swords into
plows
and use their spears to make tools for
harvesting.
All fighting between nations will end.
They will never again train for war.
4 They will sit under their own
grapevine and fig tree.
No one will make them afraid.
That is because the Lord All-Powerful
said it would happen like that.

5 All the people from other nations follow
their own gods,
but we will follow the Lord our God
forever and ever!ᶜ

The Kingdom to Be Brought Back

6 The Lord says,
"Jerusalem was hurt and crippled.
She was thrown away.
She was hurt and punished,
but I will bring her back to me.

7 "The people of that 'crippled' city
will be the only ones left alive.
They were forced to leave,
but I will make them into a strong
nation."
The Lord will be their king.
He will rule from Mount Zion* forever.

ᵇ**3:12 empty hill** Or "high place," a term usually used
for local shrines (places for worship) where people
often worshiped idols.
ᶜ**4:5** Or "All the nations will walk in the name of
their gods, but we will walk in the name of the Lord
our God, forever and ever!"

ᵃ**3:10 murdering people** Literally, "bloodshed."

8 And you, Tower of Flocks,*a*
    your time will come.
Ophel, hill of Zion,
    you will again be the seat of
      government.
Yes, the kingdom will be in Jerusalem
    like it was in the past.

Why Must the Israelites Go to Babylon?

9 Now, why are you crying so loudly?
    Is your king gone?
Have you lost your wise leader?
    Is that why you are suffering like a
      woman in labor?
10 Cry out, you people of Jerusalem,*b* and
    feel the pain,
    as if you were giving birth.
You must go out of the city
    and live in the fields.
You will go away to Babylon,
    but you will also be saved from that
      place.
The Lord will come and rescue you there.
    He will take you away from your
      enemies.

The Lord Will Destroy the Other Nations

11 Many nations have come to fight against
    you.
They say, "Look, there is Zion*!
    Let's attack her!"

12 They have their plans,
    but they don't know what the Lord is
      planning.
He brought them here
    for a special purpose.
They will be crushed
    like grain on a threshing* floor.

Israel Will Defeat Its Enemies

13"People of Jerusalem, get up and crush
    them!
I will make you very strong.
    It will be as if you have horns of iron
      and hooves of bronze.
You will beat many people into small
    pieces.
You will give their wealth to the Lord.
You will give their treasure to the Lord
    of all the earth."

5 ¹Now strong city,*c* gather your soldiers!
    They are surrounding us for the
      attack!
They will hit the Judge of Israel
    on the cheek with a stick.

The Messiah to Be Born in Bethlehem

2 But you, Bethlehem Ephrathah,
    are the smallest town in Judah.
Your family is almost too small to count,
    but the "Ruler of Israel" will come from
      you to rule for me.
His beginnings*d* are from ancient times,
    from long, long ago.
3 The Lord*e* will give up his people
    until the woman gives birth to her
      child, the promised king.
Then the rest of his brothers
    will come back to the people of Israel.
4 Then the Ruler of Israel will stand
    in the power of the Lord and
    in the wonderful name of the Lord his
      God
and care for his people.
They will live in peace
    because at that time his greatness will
      reach to the ends of the earth.*f*
5 There will be peace.
Yes, the Assyrian army will come into our
    country
    and trample our large buildings.
But the Ruler of Israel*g* will choose
    seven shepherds and eight leaders.*h*
6 They will use their swords
    and rule the Assyrians.
They will rule the land of Nimrod*i*
    with their swords in hand.
They will use their swords
    to rule those people.
But then the Ruler of Israel will save us
    from the Assyrians
    when they come into our land and walk
      on our territory.
7 But those from Jacob* who are still living
    and scattered among the nations
    will be like dew from the Lord that
      does not depend on anyone.
They will be like rain on the grass
    that does not wait for anyone.
8 Those from Jacob who are still living
    are scattered among the nations.
But they will be like a lion
    among the animals in the forest.
They will be like a young lion
    among flocks of sheep.
If the lion passes through,
    he goes where he wants to go.
If he attacks an animal,
    no one can save it.
The survivors will be like that.

*d*5:2 *beginnings* Or "family origins."
*e*5:3 *The Lord* Or "the Ruler of Israel."
*f*5:4 *They ... the earth* Or "They will settle here because at that time his kingdom will extend to the ends of the earth."
*g*5:5 *the Ruler of Israel* Or "we."
*h*5:5 *seven shepherds and eight leaders* Or "seven shepherds, no eight leaders."
*i*5:6 *land of Nimrod* Another name for Assyria.

*a*4:8 *Tower of Flocks* Or "Migdal Eder." This probably means a part of Jerusalem. The leaders would be like shepherds in a tower watching their sheep.
*b*4:10 *people of Jerusalem* Literally, "daughter Zion," a name for Jerusalem. Also in verse 13. See "Zion" in the Word List.
*c*5:1 *strong city* Literally, "daughter of troops."

9 You will lift your hand against your
    enemies,
    and you will destroy them.

People Will Depend on God

10 The Lord says,
"At that time I will take away your horses,
    and I will destroy your chariots.*
11 I will destroy the cities in your country.
    I will pull down all your fortresses.*
12 You will no longer try to do magic.
    You will have no more fortunetellers.*
13 I will destroy your statues of false gods.
    I will pull down your memorial stones.*
    You will not worship what your hands
    have made.
14 I will destroy the Asherah poles*
    and your false gods.ᵃ
15 Some nations will not listen to me,
    but I will show my anger and get my
    revenge."

The Lord's Complaint

6 ¹Now hear what the Lord says:
"Present your argument to the
    mountains.
    Let the hills hear your story.ᵇ
2 The Lord has a complaint against his
    people.
    Mountains,
    listen to the Lord's complaint.
    Foundations of the earth,
    hear the Lord.
    He will prove that Israel is wrong!"

3 He says, "My people, tell me what I did!
    Did I do something wrong against you?
    Did I make life too hard for you?
4 I will tell you what I did.
    I sent Moses, Aaron, and Miriam to you.
    I brought you from the land of Egypt.
    I freed you from slavery.
5 My people, remember the evil plans
    of Balak king of Moab.
    Remember what Balaam son of Beor said
    to Balak.
    Remember what happened from Acacia to
    Gilgal,ᶜ
    and you will know the Lord is right!"

What Does God Want From Us?

6 What must I bring when I come to meet
    with the Lord?
    What must I do when I bow down to
    God above?
    Should I come to him with burnt
    offerings* and a year-old calf?
7 Will the Lord be pleased with a thousand
    rams
    or with ten thousand rivers of oil?

Should I offer him my first child to pay for
    my wrongs?
    Should I sacrifice my very own child for
    my sins?

8 Human, the Lord has told you what
    goodness is.
    This is what he wants from you:
    Be fair to other people.
    Love kindness and loyalty,
    and humbly obey your God.

What Were the Israelites Doing?

9 The Lord shouts to the city:
"A wise person respects the Lord's name.ᵈ
    So pay attention to the punishing rod
    and to the one who uses it!ᵉ
10 Do the wicked still hide treasures
    that they have stolen?
    Do they still cheat people
    with baskets that are too small?ᶠ
    Yes, all of this is still happening!
11 Some people carry special weights
    that they use to cheat people when they
    weigh their goods.
    Should I pardon them?
12 The rich in that city are still cruel.
    The people there still tell lies.
    Yes, they tell their lies.
13 So I have begun to punish you.
    I will destroy you because of your sins.
14 You will eat, but you will not become full.
    You will still be hungry and empty.ᵍ
    You will try to bring people to safety,
    but people with swords will kill the
    people you rescued.
15 You will plant your seeds,
    but you will not gather food.
    You will try to squeeze oil from your
    olives,
    but you will not get any oil.
    You will crush your grapes,
    but you will not get enough juice to
    have wine to drink.
16 This is because you obey the laws of
    Omri.ʰ
    You do all the evil things that Ahab's
    family does.
    You follow their teachings,
    so I will let you be destroyed.
    People will whistle in amazement
    when they see your destroyed city.
    Then you will bear the shame
    that the other nations bring to you."ⁱ

ᵃ5:14 *false gods* Or "cities."
ᵇ6:1 This is like a court case. The mountains and hills
are the judge and jury.
ᶜ6:5 *Acacia to Gilgal* This story is found in Num.
22–25.

ᵈ6:9 *the Lord's name* Literally, "your name."
ᵉ6:9 *So pay attention … uses it* The Hebrew text
here is hard to understand.
ᶠ6:10 *baskets … too small* Literally, "short ephahs."
An ephah is about 1/2 bushel.
ᵍ6:14 *You … empty* The Hebrew text here is unclear.
ʰ6:16 *Omri* A king of Israel who led his nation to
worship false gods. See 1 Kings 16:21–26.
ⁱ6:16 *Then … you* Or "My people's shame will be
taken away."

Micah Is Upset at the Evil People Do

7 ¹I am upset because I am
like fruit that has been gathered,
like grapes that have already been
picked.

There are no grapes left to eat.
There are none of the early figs that I
love.

² By this I mean that all the faithful people
are gone.

There are no good people left.
Everyone is planning to kill someone.
Everyone is trying to trap their brother.

³ People are good at doing bad things with
both hands.

Officials ask for bribes.
Judges take money to change their
decisions in court.

"Important leaders" do whatever they
want to do.

⁴ Even the best of them is as crooked
as a tangled thornbush.

The Day of Punishment Is Coming

Your prophets said this day would come,
and the day of your watchmen*a* has
come.

Now you will be punished.
Now you will be confused!

⁵ Don't trust your neighbor
or trust a friend!

Don't even speak freely with your wife.

⁶ Your enemies will be the people in your
own house.

A son will not honor his father.
A daughter will turn against her mother.
A daughter-in-law will turn against her
mother-in-law.

The Lord Is the Savior

⁷ So I will look to the LORD for help.
I will wait for God to save me.
My God will hear me.

⁸ I have fallen, but enemy, don't laugh at
me!

I will get up again.
I sit in darkness now,
but the LORD will be a light for me.

The Lord Forgives

⁹ I sinned against the LORD,
so he was angry with me.

But he will argue my case for me in court.
He will do what is right for me.

Then he will bring me out into the light,
and I will see that he is right.

¹⁰ My enemy said to me,
"Where is the LORD your God?"

But my enemy will see this,
and she will be ashamed.

At that time I will laugh at her.*b*
People will walk over her,*c* like mud in
the streets.

The Jews to Return

¹¹ The time will come when your walls will
be rebuilt.

At that time the country will grow.

¹² Your people will come back to your land.
They will come back from Assyria and
from the cities of Egypt.

They will come from Egypt
and from the other side of the Euphrates
River.

They will come from the sea in the west
and from the mountains in the east.

¹³ The land was ruined by the people
who lived there and by what they did.

¹⁴ So rule your people with your rod.
Rule the flock of people who belong to
you.

That flock lives alone in the woods
and up on Mount Carmel.

That flock lives in Bashan and Gilead
as they did in the past.

Israel Will Defeat Its Enemies

¹⁵ I did many miracles when I took you out
of Egypt.

I will let you see more miracles like that.

¹⁶ The nations will see those miracles,
and they will be ashamed.

They will see that their "power"
is nothing compared to mine.

They will be amazed
and put their hands over their mouths.

They will cover their ears
and refuse to listen.

¹⁷ They will crawl in the dust like a snake.
They will shake with fear.

They will be like insects crawling
from their holes in the ground
and coming to the LORD our God.

God, they will fear and respect you!

Praise for the Lord

¹⁸ There is no God like you.
You take away people's guilt.

God will forgive his people who survive.
He will not stay angry with them forever,
because he enjoys being kind.

¹⁹ He will come back and comfort us again.
He will throw all our sins into the deep
sea.

²⁰ God, please be true to Jacob.*
Be kind and loyal to Abraham,*d* as you
promised our ancestors* long ago.

---

*b***7:10** *laugh at her* Literally, "my eyes will stare at
her."

*c***7:8–10** *enemy, don't laugh … walk over her* This
probably refers to an enemy city, such as the capital
of Edom.

*d***7:20** *Abraham* Here, Abraham is used to mean all
the people of Israel. See "Abraham" in the Word List.

---

*a***7:4** *watchmen* Another name for prophets. This
shows that the prophets were like guards who
stood on a city's wall and watched for trouble coming from far away.

Nahum

1 ¹This book is the vision* of Nahum from Elkosh. This is the sad message about the city of Nineveh.ᵃ

The Lord Is Angry at Nineveh

² The Lᴏʀᴅ is a jealous God.
   The Lᴏʀᴅ punishes the guilty,
   and he is very angry.
   The Lᴏʀᴅ punishes his enemies,
   and he stays angry with them.
³ The Lᴏʀᴅ is patient,
   but he is also very powerful!
   The Lᴏʀᴅ will punish the guilty;
   he will not let them go free.
   He will use whirlwinds and storms to
      show his power.
   People walk on the dusty ground,
   but he walks on the clouds.
⁴ He will speak harshly to the sea,
   and it will become dry.
   He will dry up all the rivers.
   The rich lands of Bashan and Carmel
      become dry and dead.
   The flowers in Lebanon fade away.
⁵ The Lord will come,
   and the mountains will shake
   and the hills will melt away.
   He will come,
   and the earth will shake with fear.
   The earth and everyone on it
   will shake with fear.
⁶ No one can stand against his great anger.
   No one can endure his terrible anger.
   His anger will burn like fire.
   The rocks will shatter when he comes.
⁷ The Lᴏʀᴅ is good.
   He is a safe place to go to in times of
      trouble.
   He takes care of those who trust him.
⁸ But he will completely destroy his
      enemies.
   He will wash them away like a flood
   and chase them into the darkness.
⁹ Why are you making plans against the
      Lᴏʀᴅ?
   He will bring complete destruction,
   so you will not cause trouble again.
¹⁰ You will be destroyed completely
   like thornbushes burning under a pot.
   You will be destroyed
   like dry weeds that burn quickly.

¹¹ Someone from Nineveh is making evil
      plans against the Lᴏʀᴅ.
   That advisor is a worthless
      troublemaker.
¹² This is what the Lᴏʀᴅ said:
   "The people of Assyria are at full strength.
   They have many soldiers,
   but they will all be cut down.
   They will all be finished.
   My people, I made you suffer,
   but I will make you suffer no more.
¹³ Now I will set you free from the power of
      Assyria.
   I will take the yoke* off your neck
   and tear away the chains holding you."

¹⁴ King of Assyria, the Lᴏʀᴅ gave this
      command about you:
   "You will not have any descendants to
      wear your name.
   I will destroy your carved idols*
   and metal statues that are in the temple
      of your gods.
   I am preparing your grave,
   because your end is coming soon!ᵇ"

¹⁵ Judah, look!
   There, coming over the mountains, is a
      messenger bringing good news!
   He says there is peace.
   Judah, celebrate your special festivals
   and do what you promised.
   Those worthless troublemakers will not
      come through and attack you again.
   They have all been destroyed.

Nineveh Will Be Destroyed

2 ¹An enemy is coming to attack you,
   so guard the strong places of your city.
   Watch the road.
   Get ready for war.
   Prepare for battle!
² Yes, the Lᴏʀᴅ changed Jacob's* pride.
   He made it like Israel's pride.
   The enemy destroyed them
   and ruined their grapevines.

³ The shields of his soldiers are red.
   Their uniforms are bright red.
   Their chariots* are shining like flames of
      fire

ᵃ1:1 *Nineveh* The capital city of the country of Assyria. Assyria destroyed Israel in 722–721 ʙ.ᴄ.

ᵇ1:14 *because your end is coming soon* Or "you are not important" or "you are so hated."

and are lined up for battle.
Their horses are ready to go.

4 The chariots race wildly through the
    streets
    and rush back and forth through the
    square.
  They look like burning torches,
    like lightning flashing from place to
    place!

5 The enemy calls for his best soldiers.
    They stumble as they rush ahead.
  They run to the wall
    and set up their shield over the
    battering ram.

6 But the gates by the rivers are open,
    and the enemy comes flooding in and
    destroys the king's palace.

7 The enemy takes away the queen,
    and her slave girls moan sadly like
    doves.
  They beat their breasts to show their
    sadness.

8 Nineveh is like a pool whose water
    is draining away.
  People yell, "Stop! Stop running away!"
    But it does not do any good.

9 Take the silver!
    Take the gold!
  There are many things to take.
    There are many treasures.

10 Now Nineveh is empty.
    Everything is stolen.
    The city is ruined.
  People have lost their courage,
    their hearts are melting with fear,
    their knees are knocking together,
    their bodies are shaking,
    and their faces are pale from fear.

11 Where is the lion's cave (Nineveh) now?
    The male and female lions lived there.
    Their babies were not afraid.

12 The lion (king of Nineveh) killed people
    to feed his cubs and lionesses.
  He filled his cave with men's bodies.
  He filled his cave with women he had
    killed.

13 The LORD All-Powerful says,
  "I am against you, Nineveh.
  I will burn your chariots
    and kill your 'young lions' in battle.
    You will not hunt anyone on earth again.
  People will never again hear bad news
    from your messengers."

Bad News for Nineveh

3 1It will be very bad for that city of
    murderers.
  Nineveh is a city full of lies.
  It is filled with things taken from other
    countries.

It is filled with plenty of people
    that it hunted and killed.

2 You can hear the sounds of whips
    and the noise of wheels.
  You can hear horses galloping
    and chariots* bouncing along!

3 Soldiers on horses are attacking,
    their swords are shining,
    their spears are gleaming!
  There are many dead people.
    Dead bodies are piled up—too many
      bodies to count.
  People are tripping over the dead
    bodies.

4 All this happened because of Nineveh.
    Nineveh is like a prostitute who could
      never get enough.
  She wanted more and more.
  She sold herself to many nations,
    and she used her magic to make them
      her slaves.

5 The LORD All-Powerful says,
  "I am against you, Nineveh.
    I will pull your dress^a up over your face.
    I will let the nations see your naked body.
    The kingdoms will see your shame.

6 I will throw dirty things on you
    and treat you in a hateful way.
    People will look at you and laugh.

7 Everyone who sees you will be shocked.
    They will say, 'Nineveh is destroyed.
    Who will cry for her?'
  I know I cannot find anyone
    to comfort you, Nineveh."

8Nineveh, are you better than Thebes^b
on the Nile River? Thebes also had water all
around her to protect herself from enemies.
She used that water like a wall too. 9Ethio-
pia and Egypt made Thebes strong. Libya and
the Sudan supported her, 10but Thebes was
defeated. Her people were taken away as prisoners to a foreign country. Soldiers beat her
small children to death at every street corner.
They threw lots* to see who got to keep the
important people as slaves. They put chains
on all the important men of Thebes.

11So, Nineveh, you will also fall like a
drunk. You will try to hide. You will look
for a safe place away from the enemy. 12But
Nineveh, all your strong places will be like
fig trees. When new figs become ripe, people
come and shake the tree. The figs fall into
their mouths. They eat them, and the figs are
gone.

13Nineveh, your people are all like
women—and the enemy soldiers are ready to
take them. The gates of your land are open

---

^{a}**3:5 pull your dress** This is a wordplay in Hebrew.
The Hebrew word also means "to destroy a country
and take its people away as prisoners to other
nations."
^{b}**3:8 Thebes** A great city in Egypt. It was destroyed
in 663 B.C. by the Assyrian army.

wide for your enemies to come in. Fire has destroyed the wooden bars across the gates.

¹⁴Get water and store it inside your city, because the enemy soldiers will surround your city. Make your defenses strong! Get clay to make more bricks and mix the mortar. Get the molds for making bricks. ¹⁵You can do all these things, but the fire will still destroy you completely. And the sword will kill you. Your land will look like a swarm of grasshoppers came and ate everything.

Nineveh, you grew and grew. You became like a swarm of grasshoppers. You were like a swarm of locusts. ¹⁶You have many traders who go places and buy things. They are as many as the stars in the sky. They are like locusts that come and eat until everything is gone and then leave. ¹⁷And your government officials are also like locusts that settle on a stone wall on a cold day. But when the sun comes up, the rocks become warm, and the locusts all fly away. And no one knows where.

¹⁸King of Assyria, your shepherds fell asleep. These powerful men are sleeping. And now your sheep have wandered away on the mountains. There is no one to bring them back. ¹⁹Nineveh, you have been hurt badly, and nothing can heal your wound. Everyone who hears the news of your destruction claps their hands. They are all happy, because they all felt the pain you caused again and again.

Habakkuk

Habakkuk Complains to God

1 ¹This is the message that was given to Habakkuk the prophet.*

²Lord, I continue to ask for help. When will you listen to me? I cried to you about the violence, but you did nothing! ³People are stealing things and hurting others. They are arguing and fighting. Why do you make me look at these terrible things? ⁴The law is weak and not fair to people. Evil people win their fights against good people. So the law is no longer fair, and justice does not win anymore.

The Lord Answers Habakkuk

⁵"Look at the other nations! Watch them, and you will be amazed. I will do something in your lifetime that will amaze you. You would not believe it even if you were told about it. ⁶I will make the Babylonians*ᵃ* a strong nation. They are cruel and powerful fighters. They will march across the earth. They will take houses and cities that don't belong to them. ⁷The Babylonians will scare the other people. They will do what they want to do and go where they want to go. ⁸Their horses will be faster than leopards and more dangerous than wolves at sunset. Their horse soldiers will come from faraway places. They will attack their enemies quickly, like a hungry eagle swooping down from the sky. ⁹The one thing they all want to do is fight. Their armies will march fast like the wind in the desert. And the Babylonian soldiers will take many prisoners—as many as the grains of sand.

¹⁰"The Babylonian soldiers will laugh at the kings of other nations. Foreign rulers will be like jokes to them. The Babylonian soldiers will laugh at the cities with tall, strong walls. They will simply build dirt roads up to the top of the walls and easily defeat the cities. ¹¹Then they will leave like the wind and go on to fight against other places. The only thing the Babylonians worship is their own strength."

Habakkuk's Second Complaint

¹² Lord, you are the one who lives forever!
   You are my holy God who never dies!ᵇ
Lord, you created the Babylonians to do
   what must be done.
   Our Rock,* you created them to punish
   people.

¹³ Your eyes are too good to look at evil.
   You cannot stand to see people doing
   wrong.
So why do you permit such evil?
   How can you watch while the wicked
   destroy people who are so much
   better?

¹⁴ You made people like fish in the sea.
   They are like little sea animals without
   a leader.

¹⁵ The enemy catches all of them with hooks
   and nets.
   The enemy catches them in his net and
   drags them in,
   and the enemy is very happy with what
   he caught.

ᵃ**1:6** *Babylonians* Literally, "Chaldeans," a tribe of Arameans who gained control in Babylon. King Nebuchadnezzar was from this tribe.

ᵇ**1:12** *Lord, you are ... never dies* Or "Lord, you have been my holy God forever! Surely we will not die."

¹⁶ His net helps him live like the rich
    and enjoy the best food.
  So the enemy worships his net.
    He makes sacrifices* and burns incense*
      to honor his net.
¹⁷ Will he continue to take riches with his
      net?
  Will he continue destroying people
      without showing mercy?

2 ¹I will stand like a guard and watch.
    I will wait to see what the LORD will
      say to me.
  I will wait and learn how he answers my
      questions.

God Answers Habakkuk

²The LORD answered me, "Write down
what I show you. Write it clearly on a sign
so that the message will be easy to read.ᵃ
³This message is about a special time in the
future. This message is about the end, and it
will come true. Just be patient and wait for
it. That time will come; it will not be late.
⁴This message cannot help those who refuse
to listen to it, but those who are good will live
because they believe it.

⁵"Wine can trick a person. In the same way
a strong man's pride can fool him, but he will
not find peace. He is like death—he always
wants more and more. And, like death, he
will never be satisfied. He will continue to
defeat other nations and to make those people his prisoners. ⁶But soon enough, all those
people will laugh at him and tell stories about
his defeat. They will laugh and say, 'It's too
bad that the man who took so many things
will not get to keep them! He made himself
rich by collecting debts.'

⁷"Strong man, you have taken money from
people. One day they will wake up and realize what is happening, and they will stand
against you. Then they will take things from
you, and you will be very afraid. ⁸You have
stolen things from many nations, so they will
take much from you. You have killed many
people and destroyed lands and cities. You
have killed all the people there.

⁹"Look at you people! You get rich by cheating people, and it hurts your own family! You
build your houses high on the cliffs to protect
yourself from danger. ¹⁰You planned shameful
things, and that will bring shame to your own
family. You have done wrong, and it will cost
you your life. ¹¹The stones of the walls will
cry out against you. Even the wooden raftersᵇ
in your own house will prove that you are
wrong.

¹²"Look at them! They kill people to build
their city and do wicked things to make their
walled city strong. ¹³But the LORD All-Powerful

has decided that a fire will destroy everything
that those people worked to build. All their
work will be for nothing. ¹⁴Then people
everywhere will know about the Glory of the
LORD.* This news will spread just as water
spreads out into the sea. ¹⁵It will be very
bad for those who become angry and make
other people suffer. Like an angry drunk, they
knock others to the ground and strip them
naked, just to see their naked bodies.ᶜ

¹⁶"But they will know the Lord's anger. It
will be like a cup of poison in the LORD's right
hand. They will taste that anger, and then
they will fall to the ground like drunks.

"Evil ruler, you will drink from that cup.
You will get shame, not honor. ¹⁷You hurt
many people in Lebanon and stole many animals there. So you will be afraid because of
the people who died and because of the bad
things you did to that country. You will be
afraid because of what you did to those cities
and to the people who lived there."

The Message About Idols

¹⁸Their false god will not help them, because
it is only a statue that someone covered with
metal. It is only a statue, so whoever made it
cannot expect it to help. That statue cannot
even speak! ¹⁹Look at them! They speak to
a wooden statue and tell it, "Get up! Rescue
me." They talk to a stone that cannot speak
and say, "Wake up!" Don't you know those
things cannot help you? That statue may be
covered with gold and silver, but there is no
life in it.

²⁰But the LORD is in his holy temple, so the
whole earth should be silent in his presence
and show him respect.

Habakkuk's Prayer

3 ¹The Shiggayon prayer of Habakkuk the
prophet.ᵈ

² LORD, I have heard the news about you.
    I am amazed, LORD, at the powerful
        things you did in the past.
  Now I pray that you will do great things
        in our time.
    Please make these things happen in our
        own days.
  But in your anger, remember to show
        mercy to us.   *Selah**

³ God is coming from Teman.*
    The Holy One is coming from Mount
        Paran.*   *Selah*

  The Glory of the LORD* covers the
        heavens,
    and his praise fills the earth!

ᶜ**2:15** *Like an angry drunk ... bodies* The Hebrew
text here is hard to understand.
ᵈ**3:1** Or "The prayer of Habakkuk on the Shiggayon."
The meaning of the Hebrew word "Shiggayon" is
not known.

ᵃ**2:2** *Write down ... easy to read* Or "Write the vision
clearly on tablets so that the person who reads it
can run and tell other people."
ᵇ**2:11** *rafters* Boards that support the roof.

4 Rays of light shine from his hand, a
    bright, shining light.
  There is such power hiding in that
    hand.
5 The sickness went before him,
  and the destroyer followed behind him.*a*
6 The LORD stood and judged the earth.
  He looked at the people of all the
    nations,
  and they shook with fear.
  For many years the mountains stood
    strong,
  but those mountains fell to pieces.
  Those old, old hills fell down.
  God has always been able to do that.

7 I saw that the cities of Cushan were in
    trouble
  and that the houses of Midian trembled
    with fear.
8 LORD, were you angry at the rivers?
  Were you angry at the streams?
  Were you angry at the sea?
  Were you angry when you rode your
    horses and chariots to victory?

9 Even then you showed your rainbow.
  It was proof of your agreement with the
    families of the earth.*b*   Selah

  And the dry land split the rivers.
10 The mountains saw you and shook.
  The water flowed off the land.
  The water from the sea made a loud
    noise
  as it lost its power over the land.
11 The sun and the moon lost their
    brightness.
  They stopped shining when they saw
    your bright flashes of lightning.
  That lightning was like spears and
    arrows shooting through the air.

a3:5 This probably refers to the diseases and the
Angel of Death that God sent against the Egyptians
when God freed Israel from slavery.
b3:9 rainbow … earth See Gen. 9.

12 In anger you walked on the earth
  and punished the nations.
13 You came to save your people
  and to lead your chosen king*c* to victory.
  You killed the leader in every evil family,
  from the least important person
  to the most important in the land.*d* Selah

14 You used Moses' walking stick
  to stop the enemy soldiers.
  Those soldiers came
  like a powerful storm to fight against us.
  They thought they could defeat us easily,
  as robbing the poor in secret.
15 But you marched your horses
  through the deep water, stirring up the
    mud.
16 My whole body shook when I heard the
    story.
  My lips trembled.
  I felt weak deep down in my bones
  and stood there shaking.
  But I will wait patiently for destruction to
  come to those who attack us.

Always Rejoice in the Lord
17 Figs might not grow on the fig trees,
  and grapes might not grow on the vines.
  Olives might not grow on the olive trees,
  and food might not grow in the fields.
  There might not be any sheep in the pens
  or cattle in the barns.
18 But I will still be glad in the LORD
  and rejoice in God my savior.

19 The Lord GOD gives me my strength.
  He helps me run fast like a deer.
  He leads me safely on the mountains.

  To the music director. On my stringed
instruments.

c3:13 chosen king Literally, "anointed one."
d3:13 You killed … in the land Literally, "You struck
the head from the wicked house. From the foundation to the neck they were laid bare."

Zephaniah

1 ¹This is the message that the LORD gave
to Zephaniah. He received this message
during the time that Josiah son of Amon was
king of Judah. Zephaniah was the son of Cush,
who was the son of Gedaliah. Gedaliah was
the son of Amariah, who was the son of
Hezekiah.

The Lord's Day for Judging the People
²The Lord says, "I will destroy everything
on earth.*e* ³I will destroy all the people and all
the animals. I will destroy the birds in the air

e1:2 earth Or "the land" or "the country." Also in
verse 18.

and the fish in the sea. I will destroy the evil people and everything that makes them sin. I will remove all people from the earth." This is what the LORD said.

4"I will punish Judah and the people living in Jerusalem. I will remove from this place the last signs of Baal* worship, the priests, and all the people who ⁵go up on their roofs to worship the stars.ᵃ People will forget about those false priests. Some people say they worship me. They promised to worship me, but now they worship the false god Milcom.* So I will remove them from that place. ⁶Some people turned away from the LORD and stopped following me. They stopped asking the LORD for help, so I will remove them from that place."

⁷Be silent before the Lord GOD, because the LORD's day for judging the people is coming soon. The LORD has prepared his sacrifice, and he has told his invited guests to get ready.ᵇ

⁸The Lord said, "On the LORD's day of sacrifice, I will punish the king's sons and other leaders. I will punish all the people wearing clothes from other countries. ⁹At that time I will punish all the people who jump over the thresholdᶜ and those who fill their master's houseᵈ with lies and violence."

¹⁰The LORD also said, "At that time people will be calling for help at Fish Gate in Jerusalem and mourning* in the new part of town. They will hear the sound of destruction in the hills around the city. ¹¹You people living in the lower part of town will cry, because all the traders and rich merchants* will be destroyed.

¹²"At that time I will take a lamp and search through Jerusalem. I will find all those who are satisfied to live their own way. They say, 'The LORD does nothing. He does not help, and he does not hurt!' I will find them, and I will punish them. ¹³Then others will take their wealth and destroy their houses. Those who built houses will not live in them, and those who planted vineyards will not drink the wine from the grapes."

¹⁴The LORD's special day for judging is coming soon! It is near and coming fast. People will hear very sad sounds on the LORD's special day of judgment. Even strong soldiers will cry. ¹⁵The Lord will show his anger at that time. It will be a time of terrible troubles and a time of destruction. It will be a time of darkness—a black, cloudy, and stormy day. ¹⁶It will be like wartime when people hear horns and trumpets in the defense towers and protected cities.

¹⁷The Lord said, "I will make life very hard on the people. They will walk around like the blind who don't know where they are going. That will happen because they sinned against the LORD. Their blood will be spilled on the ground. Their dead bodies will lie like dung on the ground. ¹⁸Their gold and silver will not help them! At that time the Lord will become very upset and angry. The LORD will destroy the whole worldᵉ! He will completely destroy everyone on earth!"

God Asks People to Change Their Lives

2 ¹Shameless people, change your lives ²before you become like a dry and dying flower. In the heat of day, a flower will wilt and die. You will be like that when the LORD shows his terrible anger. So change your lives before the LORD shows his anger against you! ³All you humble people, come to the LORD! Obey his laws. Learn to do good things. Learn to be humble. Maybe then you will be safe when the LORD shows his anger.

The Lord Will Punish Israel's Neighbors

⁴No one will be left in Gaza. Ashkelon will be destroyed. By noon, the people will be forced to leave Ashdod. Ekronᶠ will be empty.ᵍ ⁵You Cretansʰ living by the sea, this message from the LORD is about you. Canaan,* land of the Philistines, you will be destroyed—no one will live there! ⁶Your land by the sea will become empty fields for shepherds and their sheep. ⁷Then the land will belong to the survivors* from Judah. The LORD their God will remember the people from Judah and restore their fortunes. Then they will let their sheep eat the grass in those fields. In the evenings they will lie down in the empty houses of Ashkelon.

⁸The LORD says, "I know what the people of Moab and Ammon did. They embarrassed my people. They took their land to make their own countries larger. ⁹So, as surely as I am alive, Moab and the people of Ammon will be destroyed like Sodom* and Gomorrah.* I am the LORD All-Powerful, the God of Israel, and I promise those countries will be destroyed completely forever. Their land will be overgrown with weeds. It will be like the land covered with salt by the Dead Sea. The survivors of my people will take that land and everything left in it."

ᵃ1:5 stars Literally, "army of heaven." This might mean the stars and planets or the angels.

ᵇ1:7 prepared ... get ready Literally, "prepared his sacrifice. He has made his called ones holy." Here, this time of judgment is compared to a fellowship meal when priests offered a sacrifice to God and had the guests get ready for this special meal with God.

ᶜ1:9 people wearing ... threshold This probably means the priests and people who worshiped foreign gods, such as Dagon, or people who copied their ways of worshiping. See 1 Sam. 5:5.

ᵈ1:9 master's house This means the temple where the people worshiped God or their false gods.

ᵉ1:18 world Or "land" or "country."

ᶠ2:4 Gaza, Ashkelon, Ashdod, Ekron Philistine cities. In Hebrew, Zephaniah is making wordplays on the names of these cities.

ᵍ2:4 empty In Hebrew this word is like the word meaning "Philistines." Also in verse 6.

ʰ2:5 Cretans People from Crete. The Philistines came from that island.

¹⁰This will happen to the people of Moab and Ammon because they were so proud and cruel and humiliated the people of the LORD All-Powerful. ¹¹They will be afraid of the LORD, because he will destroy their gods. Then everyone in all the faraway lands will worship the LORD. ¹²People of Ethiopia, this even means you! The Lord's sword will kill your people. ¹³Then the Lord will turn north and punish Assyria. He will destroy Nineveh—that city will be like an empty, dry desert. ¹⁴Only sheep and wild animals will live in those ruins. Owls and crows will sit on the columns that are left standing. Their calls will be heard coming through the windows. Crows will sit on the doorsteps. Black birds*a* will make their homes in those empty houses. ¹⁵Nineveh is so proud now. It is such a happy city. The people think they are safe. They think Nineveh is the greatest place in the world, but it will be destroyed! It will be an empty place where only wild animals go to rest. People who pass by will whistle and shake their heads when they see how badly the city was destroyed.

The Future of Jerusalem

3 ¹Jerusalem, your people fought against God. They hurt other people, and you have been stained with sin. ²They didn't listen to me or accept my teachings. Jerusalem didn't trust the LORD. Jerusalem didn't go to her God. ³Jerusalem's leaders are like roaring lions. Her judges* are like hungry wolves that come in the evening to attack the sheep— and in the morning nothing is left. ⁴Her prophets* are always making secret plans to get more and more. Her priests have treated holy* things as if they were not holy. They have done bad things to God's teachings. ⁵But God is still in that city, and he continues to be good. He does not do anything wrong. He continues to help his people. Morning after morning he makes good decisions for them. Not a day passes without his justice. He never gives a decision that is crooked or is something to be ashamed of.

⁶The Lord says, "I have destroyed whole nations and their defense towers. I destroyed their streets and now no one goes there anymore. Their cities are empty—no one lives there anymore. ⁷I tell you this so that you will learn a lesson. I want you to fear and respect me. If you do this, your home will not be destroyed, and I will not have to punish you the way I planned." But those evil people only wanted to do more of the same evil things they had already done!

⁸The LORD said, "So just wait! Wait for me to stand and judge you. I have the right to bring people from many nations and use them to punish you. I will use them to show my anger against you. I will use them to show how upset I am—and the whole country will be destroyed. ⁹Then I will change people from other nations so that they can speak the language clearly and call out the name of the LORD. They will all worship me together, shoulder to shoulder, as one people. ¹⁰People will come all the way from the other side of the river in Ethiopia. My scattered people will come to me. My worshipers will come and bring their gifts to me.

¹¹"Then, Jerusalem, you will no longer be ashamed of the wrong things your people do against me. That is because I will remove all the bad people from Jerusalem. I will take away all the proud people. There will not be any of them on my holy mountain.*b* ¹²I will let only meek and humble people stay in my city, and they will trust the LORD's name. ¹³The survivors* of Israel will not do bad things or tell lies. They will not try to trick people with lies. They will be like sheep that eat and lie down in peace—and no one will bother them."

A Happy Song

¹⁴ Jerusalem, sing and be happy!
    Israel, shout for joy!
Jerusalem, be happy and have fun!
¹⁵ The LORD stopped your punishment.
    He destroyed your enemies' strong
      towers.
    King of Israel, the LORD is with you.
    You don't need to worry about anything
      bad happening.
¹⁶ At that time Jerusalem will be told,
    "Be strong, don't be afraid!
¹⁷ The LORD your God is with you.
    He is like a powerful soldier.
    He will save you.
    He will show how much he loves you
      and how happy he is with you.
    He will laugh and be happy about you,
¹⁸   like people at a party.
    I will take away your shame.
    I will make them stop hurting you.*c*
¹⁹ At that time I will punish those who hurt
      you.
    I will save my hurt people
      and bring back those who were forced
        to leave.
    I will give them praise and honor
      everywhere,
    even in places where they suffered
      shame.
²⁰ At that time I will lead you back home.
    I will bring your people back together.
    I will cause people everywhere to honor
      and praise you.
    You will see me bring back all the
      blessings you once had."
    This is what the LORD said.

---

a **2:14 Black birds** Or "cedar beams."

b **3:11 holy mountain** Mount Zion, one of the mountains Jerusalem was built on.

c **3:18** The Hebrew text here is hard to understand.

Haggai

It Is Time to Build the Temple

1 ¹On the first day of the sixth month of the second year that Darius was king of Persia, Haggai received a message from the LORD. This message was for Zerubbabel son of Shealtiel and Joshua son of Jehozadak. Zerubbabel was the governor of Judah and Joshua was the high priest. This is the message: ²This is what the LORD All-Powerful said, "The people say it is not yet the right time to build the LORD's Temple.*"

³Again Haggai received a message from the LORD. Haggai spoke this message: ⁴"You people think the right time has come for you to live in nice houses. You live in houses with beautiful wooden paneling on the walls, but the LORD's house is still in ruins. ⁵Now the LORD All-Powerful says, 'Think about what is happening. ⁶You have planted many seeds, but you have gathered only a few crops. You have food to eat, but not enough to get full. You have something to drink, but not enough to get drunk. You have some clothes to wear, but not enough to keep warm. You earn a little money, but you don't know where it all goes. It's as though there is a hole in your pocket!'*"

⁷The LORD All-Powerful said, "Think about what you are doing. ⁸Go up to the mountains, get the wood, and build the Temple. Then I will be pleased with the Temple, and I will be honored." This is what the LORD said.

⁹The LORD All-Powerful said, "You people look for a big harvest, but when you go to gather the crop, there is only a little grain. So you bring that grain home, and then I send a wind that blows it all away. Why is this happening? Because my house is still in ruins while each of you runs home to take care of your own house. ¹⁰That is why the sky holds back its dew and why the earth holds back its crops.

¹¹"I gave the command for the land and the mountains to be dry. The grain, the new wine, the olive oil, and everything the earth produces will be ruined.* All the people and all the animals will become weak."

Work Begins on the New Temple

¹²The LORD God had sent Haggai to speak to Zerubbabel son of Shealtiel and to the high priest, Joshua son of Jehozadak. So these men and all the people listened to the voice of the LORD their God and to the words of Haggai the prophet. And the people showed their fear and respect for the LORD their God.

¹³Then Haggai, the LORD's messenger, delivered this message to the people: "The LORD says, 'I am with you!'"

¹⁴Zerubbabel son of Shealtiel was the governor of Judah. Joshua son of Jehozadak was the high priest. The LORD made them and the rest of the people excited about working on the Temple* of their God, the LORD All-Powerful. ¹⁵So they began this work on the 24th day of the sixth month in the second year Darius was the king.

The Lord Encourages the People

2 ¹On the 21st day of the seventh month, this message from the LORD came to Haggai: ²"Speak to Zerubbabel son of Shealtiel, the governor of Judah, and to Joshua son of Jehozadak, the high priest, and to all the people. Say this: ³'How many of you people look at this Temple* and try to compare it to the beautiful Temple that was destroyed? What do you think? Does this Temple seem like nothing when you compare it with the first Temple? ⁴But the LORD says, "Zerubbabel, don't be discouraged!" And the LORD says, "Joshua son of Jehozadak, you are the high priest. Don't be discouraged! And all you people who live in the land, don't be discouraged! Continue this work, because I am with you." This is what the LORD All-Powerful said.

⁵"'I made an agreement with you when you left Egypt, and I have kept my promise. My Spirit is with you, so don't be afraid!' ⁶This is what the LORD All-Powerful said, 'In just a little while, I will once again shake things up. I will shake heaven and earth, and I will shake the sea and the dry land. ⁷I will shake up the nations, and they will come to you with wealth from every nation. And then I will fill this Temple with glory.*' That is what the LORD All-Powerful said! ⁸'All their silver really belongs to me! And all the gold is mine!' This is what the LORD All-Powerful said. ⁹And the LORD All-Powerful said 'This last Temple will be more beautiful than the first one, and I will

---

*a*1:6 *You ... pocket* Or "The one who saves money is putting it into a purse full of holes."

*b*1:11 *dry ... ruined* The Hebrew word "dry" is like the Hebrew word "ruined."

bring peace to this place.' Remember, this is what the LORD All-Powerful said."

Today Begins a Time of Blessing

¹⁰On the 24th day of the ninth month in the second year Darius was king of Persia, this message from the LORD came to Haggai the prophet: ¹¹"The LORD All-Powerful commands you to ask the priests what the law says about these things: ¹²'Suppose a man carries some meat in the fold of his clothes. This meat is part of a sacrifice, so it is holy.* If his clothes touch some bread, cooked food, wine, oil, or some other food, will the thing the clothes touch become holy?'"

The priests answered, "No."

¹³Then Haggai said, "Whoever touches a dead body will become unclean.* Now if they touch anything else, will it also become unclean?"

The priests answered, "Yes, it will become unclean."

¹⁴Then Haggai said, "This is what the LORD God said: 'This is also true for the people of this nation. They were not pure and holy before me. So anything they did with their hands and anything they offered at the altar became unclean.

¹⁵"'Think about what has happened to you. Think about how things were before you began working on the LORD's Temple.* ¹⁶People wanted 20 measures of grain, but there were only 10 measures in the pile. People wanted

to get 50 jars of wine from the wine vat, but there were only 20. ¹⁷That was because I punished you. I sent the diseases that killed your plants and the hail that destroyed the things you made with your hands. I did this, but still you did not come to me.' This is what the LORD said.

¹⁸"⌊The Lord said,⌋ 'Today is the 24th day of the ninth month. You have finished laying the foundation of the LORD's Temple. So notice what happens from this day forward: ¹⁹Your seed for planting is still in the barn. And look at the vines, the fig trees, and the pomegranate* and olive trees. They have not yet produced any fruit. But beginning today, I will bless you.'"

²⁰Another message from the LORD came to Haggai on the 24th day of the month. This is the message: ²¹"Go to Zerubbabel, the governor of Judah and tell him that I will shake heaven and earth. ²²And I will overthrow many kings and kingdoms and destroy the power of the kingdoms of those other people. I will destroy their chariots* and their riders. I will defeat their war horses and riders. These armies are friends now, but they will turn against each other and kill each other with swords." ²³This is what the LORD All-Powerful said. "Zerubbabel son of Shealtiel, my servant, I have chosen you. At that time I will use you like a signet ring* to prove that I have done these things!"

This is what the LORD All-Powerful said.

Zechariah

The Lord Wants His People to Return

1 ¹Zechariah son of Berekiah received a message from the LORD. This was in the eighth month of the second year that Darius*ᵃ* was king in Persia. (Zechariah was the son of Berekiah, who was the son of Iddo the prophet.) This is that message:

²The LORD became very angry with your ancestors.* ³So you must tell the people what he says, "Come back to me, and I will come back to you." This is what the LORD All-Powerful said.

⁴"Don't be like your ancestors. In the past the prophets spoke to them and said, 'The LORD All-Powerful wants you to change your evil way of living. Stop doing evil things!' But your ancestors did not listen to me." This is what the LORD said.

⁵"Your ancestors are gone, and those prophets did not live forever. ⁶The prophets were my servants. I used them to tell your ancestors about my laws and teachings. Your ancestors finally learned their lesson and said, 'The LORD All-Powerful did what he said he would do. He punished us for the way we lived and for all the evil things we did.' So they came back to God."

The Four Horses

⁷On the 24th day of the eleventh month (Shebat) of the second year that Darius was king of Persia, Zechariah received another message from the LORD. (This was Zechariah son of Berekiah, son of Iddo.) This is the message:

⁸At night I saw a man riding a red horse. He was standing among some myrtle bushes in the valley. Behind him, there were red, brown, and white horses. ⁹I said, "Sir, what are these horses for?"

---

*ᵃ*1:1 *the second year ... Darius* That is, about 520 B.C. Also in verse 7.

Then the angel speaking to me said, "I will show you what these horses are for."

¹⁰Then the man standing among the myrtle bushes said, "The Lord sent these horses to go here and there on earth."

¹¹Then the horses spoke to the Lord's angel standing among the myrtle bushes and said, "We have walked here and there on the earth, and everything is calm and quiet."

¹²Then the Lord's angel said, "Lord All-Powerful, how long before you comfort Jerusalem and the cities of Judah? You have shown your anger at these cities for 70 years now."

¹³Then the Lord answered the angel who was talking with me. He spoke good, comforting words. ¹⁴Then the angel told me to tell the people this:

The Lord All-Powerful says:
"I have a strong love for Jerusalem and
　　Zion.*
¹⁵ And I am very angry at the nations that
　　feel so safe.
　I was only a little angry,
　　and I used them to punish my people.
　But they caused too much damage."
¹⁶ So the Lord says,
"I will come back to Jerusalem and comfort
　　her."
The Lord All-Powerful says,
"Jerusalem will be rebuilt,
　　and my house will be built there."

¹⁷ The angel also said,
"The Lord All-Powerful says,
　'My towns will be rich again.
　I will comfort Zion.
　　I will again choose Jerusalem to be my
　　　special city.'"

The Four Horns and Four Workers

¹⁸Then I looked up and I saw four horns. ¹⁹So I asked the angel who was talking with me, "What do these horns mean?"

He said, "These are the horns that forced the people of Israel, Judah, and Jerusalem to go to foreign countries."

²⁰The Lord showed me four workers. ²¹I asked him, "What are these four workers coming to do?"

He said, "The horns represent the nations that attacked the people of Judah and forced them to go to foreign countries. The horns 'threw' the people of Judah to the foreign countries. The horns didn't show mercy to anyone. But these four workers have come to frighten the horns and throw them away."

Measuring Jerusalem

2 ¹Then I looked up and saw a man holding a rope for measuring things. ²I asked him, "Where are you going?"

He said to me, "I am going to measure Jerusalem, to see how wide and how long it is."

³Then the angel who was speaking to

me left, and another angel went out to talk to him. ⁴He said to him, "Run and tell that young man this:

'Jerusalem will be a city without walls,
　　because there will be too many people
　　and animals living there.'
⁵ The Lord says,
'I will be a wall of fire around her, to
　　protect her,
　and to bring glory to that city, I will live
　　there.'"

God Calls His People Home

The Lord says,
⁶"Hurry! Leave the land in the North
　in a hurry.
Yes, it is true that I scattered your people
　in every direction.
⁷ You people from Zion now live in Babylon.
　Escape! Run away from that city!"
⁸ The Lord sent me to the nations that took
　　away your wealth.
　He sent me to bring you honor.
　And this is what the Lord All-Powerful
　　said:
"If anyone even touches you, it is as if they
　　did it to the pupil of my eye.
⁹ I will punish them,
　and you, their slaves, will take all their
　　wealth."
　When this happens, then you will know
　　that the Lord All-Powerful sent me.

¹⁰ The Lord says,
"Zion, be happy, because I am coming,
　and I will live in your city.
¹¹ At that time people from many nations
　　will come to me.
They will become my people,
　and I will live in your city."
Then you will know
　that the Lord All-Powerful sent me.

¹² The Lord will again choose Jerusalem to
　　be his special city.
　Judah will be his share of the holy land.
¹³ Everyone, be quiet!
　The Lord is coming out of his holy
　　house.

The High Priest

3 ¹The angel showed me Joshua the high priest, standing in front of the angel of the Lord and Satan was standing by Joshua's right side. Satan was there to accuse Joshua of doing wrong. ²Then ₗthe angel of₎ the Lord said, "The Lord says that you are wrong, and he will continue to correct you! The Lord has chosen Jerusalem to be his special city. He saved that city—it was like a burning stick pulled from the fire."

³Joshua was wearing a dirty robe as he stood in front of the angel. ⁴Then the angel said to the other angels standing near him,

"Take those dirty clothes off Joshua." Then the angel spoke to Joshua. He said, "Now, I have taken away your guilt, and I am giving you a new change of clothes."

⁵Then I said, "Put a clean turban* on his head." So they put the clean turban on him and also put clean clothes on him while the LORD's angel stood there. ⁶Then the LORD's angel said this to Joshua:

⁷ This is what the LORD All-Powerful said:
"Live the way I tell you,
    and do everything I say.
And you will be in charge of my Temple.
    You will take care of its courtyard.
You will be free to go anywhere in my
        Temple,
    just as these angels standing here.
⁸ Listen, Joshua, you who are the high
        priest,
    and listen, you fellow priests seated
        before him.
You are all examples to show what will
        happen when I bring my special
        servant.
    He is called, THE BRANCH.
⁹ Look, I put a special stone in front of
        Joshua.
    There are seven sidesᵃ on that stone.
I will carve a special message on it.
    This will show that in one day, I will
        remove the guilt from this land."

¹⁰ The LORD All-Powerful says,
"At that time people will sit and talk
    with their friends and neighbors.
They will invite each other to sit under
    the fig trees and grapevines."

The Lampstand and the Two Olive Trees

4 ¹Then the angel who was talking to me returned and woke me up. I was like a person waking up from sleep. ²Then the angel asked me, "What do you see?"

I said, "I see a solid gold lampstand. There are seven lampsᵇ on the lampstand, and there is a bowl on top of it. There are seven tubes coming from the bowl. One tube goes to each lamp. ⌊The tubes bring the oil in the bowl to each of the lamps.⌋ ³There are two olive trees by the bowl, one on the right side and one on the left side. ⌊These trees produce the oil for the lamps.⌋" ⁴Then I asked the angel who was speaking with me, "Sir, what do these things mean?"

⁵The angel speaking with me said, "Don't you know what these things are?"

"No sir," I said.

⁶He said, "This is the message from the LORD to Zerubbabel: 'Your help will not come from your own strength and power. No, your help will come from my Spirit.' This is what the LORD All-Powerful says. ⁷That tall mountain will be like a flat place for Zerubbabel. He will build the Temple, and when the most important stone is put in place, the people will shout, 'Beautiful! Beautiful!'"

⁸The LORD's message to me also said, ⁹"Zerubbabel will lay the foundations for my Temple, and he will finish building it. Then you will know that the LORD All-Powerful sent me to you people. ¹⁰People will not be ashamed of the small beginnings, and they will be very happy when they see Zerubbabel with the plumb line,ᶜ measuring and checking the finished building. Now the seven sidesᵈ of the stone you saw represent the eyes of the LORD looking in every direction. They see everything on earth."

¹¹Then I said to him, "I saw one olive tree on the right side of the lampstand and one on the left side. What do those two olive trees mean?" ¹²I also said to him, "I saw two olive branches by the gold tubes with gold colored oil flowing from them. What do these things mean?"

¹³Then the angel said to me, "Don't you know what these things mean?"

I said, "No, sir."

¹⁴So he said, "They represent the two men chosenᵉ to serve the LORD of the whole world."

The Flying Scroll

5 ¹I looked up again, and I saw a flying scroll.* ²The angel asked me, "What do you see?"

I said, "I see a flying scroll that is 30 feetᶠ long and 15 feetᵍ wide."

³Then the angel told me, "There is a curse written on that scroll. On one side of the scroll, there is a curse against thieves and on the other side is a curse against people who lie when they make promises. ⁴The LORD All-Powerful says, 'I will send that scroll to the houses of thieves and people who lie when they use my name to make promises. That scroll will settle there and destroy even the stones and wooden posts of their houses.'"

The Woman and the Bucket

⁵The angel who was talking to me went outside and said, "Look! What do you see coming?"

ᶜ**4:10** *plumb line* A string with a weight on one end used to show how straight the walls of a building were. Sometimes the line was coated with paint or chalk to mark a straight line.
ᵈ**4:10** *sides* This is a wordplay. The Hebrew word also means "eyes."
ᵉ**4:14** *men chosen* Literally, "sons of extra pure olive oil." Often a special oil was poured over new kings, priests, and prophets. This showed that these people were chosen by God.
ᶠ**5:2** *30 feet* Literally, "20 cubits" (8.88 m).
ᵍ**5:2** *15 feet* Literally, "10 cubits" (4.44 m).

ᵃ**3:9** *sides* Literally, "eyes."
ᵇ**4:2** *lamps* These lamps made light by burning olive oil.

⁶I said, "I don't know. What is it?"

He said, "That is a measuring bucket." He also said, "That bucket is for measuring the sins[a] of the people in this country."

⁷A lid made of lead was lifted off the bucket, and there was a woman in the bucket. ⁸The angel said, "The woman represents evil." Then the angel pushed the woman down into the bucket and put the lead lid back on it. ⁹Then I looked up and saw two women with wings like a stork. They flew out, and with the wind in their wings, they picked up the bucket. They flew through the air carrying the bucket. ¹⁰Then I asked the angel who was speaking with me, "Where are they carrying the bucket?"

¹¹The angel told me, "They are going to build a house for it in Shinar.[b] After they build that house, they will put the bucket there."

The Four Chariots

6 ¹Then I turned around. I looked up and saw four chariots* going between two bronze mountains. ²Red horses were pulling the first chariot. Black horses were pulling the second chariot. ³White horses were pulling the third chariot, and horses with red spots were pulling the fourth chariot. ⁴I asked the angel who was talking with me, "Sir, what does this mean?"

⁵The angel said, "These are the four winds.[c] They have just come from the Lord of the whole world. ⁶The black horses will go north, the red horses will go east, the white horses will go west, and the horses with red spots will go south."

⁷The red spotted horses were anxious to go look at their part of the earth, so the angel told them, "Go walk through the earth." So they went walking through their part of the earth.

⁸Then he shouted at me and said, "Look, those horses that were going north finished their job ⌊in Babylon⌋. They have calmed my spirit; I am not angry now!"

Joshua the Priest Gets a Crown

⁹Then I received another message from the Lord. He said, ¹⁰"Heldai, Tobijah, and Jedaiah have come from the captives[d] in Babylon. Get silver and gold from these men and then go to the house of Josiah son of Zephaniah. ¹¹Use the silver and gold to make a crown. Put it on the head of the high priest, Joshua son of Jehozadak. ¹²Then tell him this is what the Lord All-Powerful says:

'There is a man called The Branch.
  He will grow strong,
  and he will build the Lord's Temple.
¹³ He will build the Lord's Temple,
  and he will receive the honor.
He will sit on his throne and be the ruler,
  and a priest will stand by his throne.
These two men will work together in
  peace.'

¹⁴"They will put the crown in the Temple to be a reminder for Heldai, Tobijah, Jedaiah, and Zephaniah's son, Josiah. It will help them remember ⌊that the king's power comes from God⌋. ¹⁵People living far away will come and build the Lord's Temple." Then you will know for sure that the Lord All-Powerful sent me to you people. All these things will happen if you do what the Lord your God says.

The Lord Wants Kindness and Mercy

7 ¹Zechariah received a message from the Lord in the fourth year that Darius[e] was the king of Persia. This was on the fourth day of the ninth month (Kislev). ²The people of Bethel sent Sharezer, Regem-Melech, and his men to ask the Lord a question. ³They went to the prophets and to the priests at the Temple of the Lord All-Powerful. They asked them this question: "For many years we have shown our sadness for the destruction of the Temple. In the fifth month of each year we have had a special time of crying and fasting.* Should we continue to do this?"

⁴I received this message from the Lord All-Powerful: ⁵"Tell the priests and the other people in this country this: 'For seventy years you fasted and showed your sadness in the fifth month and in the seventh month. But was that fasting really for me? ⁶And when you ate and drank, was that for me? No, it was for your own good. ⁷The Lord used the earlier prophets to say the same thing long ago. That was when Jerusalem was still a rich city filled with people and there were still people living in the surrounding towns, in the Negev, and in the western foothills.'"

⁸ This is the Lord's message to Zechariah:
⁹"This is what the Lord All-Powerful said:
'You must do what is right and fair.
You must be kind and
  show mercy to each other.
¹⁰ Don't hurt widows and orphans,
  strangers, or poor people.
Don't even think of doing bad things to
  each other!'"

---

[a]**5:6 sins** The Hebrew text has "their eye," but with a minor change of one character it becomes "their guilt."

[b]**5:11 Shinar** The flat land that the tower of Babel and the city of Babylon were built on. Read Gen. 11:2.

[c]**6:5 four winds** Or "four spirits." Four winds often means "winds that blow from every direction: north, south, east, and west."

[d]**6:10 captives** People taken away as prisoners. Here, it means the Jewish people who were taken to Babylon.

[e]**7:1 the fourth year … Darius** This was about 518 B.C.

11 But they refused to listen
and refused to do what he wanted.
They closed their ears so that they
could not hear what God said.
12 They were very stubborn
and would not obey the law.
The LORD All-Powerful used his Spirit
and sent messages to his people through
the prophets.
But the people would not listen,
so the LORD All-Powerful became very
angry.
13 So the LORD All-Powerful said,
"I called to them,
and they did not answer.
So now, if they call to me,
I will not answer.
14 I will bring the other nations against them
like a storm.
They didn't know those nations,
but the country will be destroyed
after those nations pass through.
This pleasant country will be destroyed."

The Lord Promises to Bless Jerusalem

8 ¹This is a message from the LORD All-Powerful. ²The LORD All-Powerful says, "I have a very strong love for Mount Zion. I love her so much that I became angry when she was not faithful to me." ³The LORD says, "I have come back to Zion, and I am living in Jerusalem. Jerusalem will be called FAITHFUL CITY. The mountain of the LORD All-Powerful will be called HOLY MOUNTAIN."

⁴The LORD All-Powerful says, "Old men and women will again be seen in the public places in Jerusalem. People will live so long that they will need their walking sticks. ⁵And the city will be filled with children playing in the streets. ⁶The survivors* will think it is wonderful, and so will I!"

⁷The LORD All-Powerful says, "Look, I am rescuing my people from countries in the east and west. ⁸I will bring them back here, and they will live in Jerusalem. They will be my people, and I will be their good and faithful God."

⁹The LORD All-Powerful says, "Be strong! You people are hearing the same message today that the prophets gave when the LORD All-Powerful first laid the foundations to rebuild his Temple. ¹⁰Before that time, people didn't have the money to hire workers or to rent animals. And it was not safe for people to come and go. There was no relief from all the troubles. I had turned everyone against their neighbor. ¹¹But it is not like that now. It will not be like that for the survivors." This is what the LORD All-Powerful said.

¹²"These people will plant in peace. Their grapevines will produce grapes. The land will give good crops, and the skies will give rain. I will give all these things to my people. ¹³People began using the names Israel and Judah in their curses. But I will save Israel and Judah, and their names will become a blessing. So don't be afraid. Be strong!"

¹⁴The LORD All-Powerful says, "Your ancestors made me angry, so I decided to destroy them. I decided not to change my mind." This is what the LORD All-Powerful said. ¹⁵"But now I have changed my mind. And in the same way I have decided to be good to Jerusalem and to the people of Judah. So don't be afraid! ¹⁶But you must do this: Tell the truth to your neighbors. When you make decisions in your cities, be fair and do what is right. Do what brings peace. ¹⁷Don't make secret plans to hurt your neighbors. Don't make false promises. You must not enjoy doing these things, because I hate them!" This is what the LORD said.

¹⁸I received this message from the LORD All-Powerful. ¹⁹The LORD All-Powerful says, "You have special days of sadness and fasting* in the fourth month, the fifth month, the seventh month, and the tenth month.ᵃ These days of sadness must be changed into days of happiness. They will be good and happy festivals. And you must love truth and peace."

20 The LORD All-Powerful says,
"In the future, people from many cities
will come to Jerusalem.
21 People from different cities will greet
each other and say,
'We are going to worship the LORD
All-Powerful.'
ₗAnd the other person will say,ⱼ
'I would like to go with you!'"

²²Many people and many powerful nations will come to Jerusalem to find the LORD All-Powerful and to worship him. ²³The LORD All-Powerful says, "At that time many foreigners speaking different languages will come to a Jewish man, take hold of the hem of his robe, and ask, 'We heard that God is with you. Can we come with you to worship him?'"

Judgment Against Other Nations

9 ¹This is the LORD's message against the land of Hadrach and against the city of Damascus. The tribes of Israel are not the only people who know about God. Everyone looks to him for help.ᵇ ²This message is also against the city of Hamath near Damascus. And this message is against Tyre and Sidon, even though those people have been so wise and skillful. ³Tyre is built like a fort. The people there have collected so much silver that it is like dust, and gold is as common as clay. ⁴But the Lord will take it all. He will destroy her powerful navy and that city will be destroyed by fire!

ᵃ8:19 *days ... month* These were days when the people remembered the destruction of Jerusalem and the Temple. See 2 Kings 25:1-25 and Jer. 41:1-17; 52:1-12.
ᵇ9:1 The Hebrew text here is hard to understand.

⁵The people in Ashkelon will see this and they will be afraid. The people of Gaza will shake with fear, and the people of Ekron will lose all hope when they see this happen. There will be no king left in Gaza. No one will live in Ashkelon anymore. ⁶The people in Ashdod will not even know who their real fathers are. The Lord says, "I will completely destroy the proud Philistines.* ⁷They will no longer eat meat with the blood still in it or any other forbidden food. Any Philistine left alive will become a part of my people; they will be just one more tribe in Judah. The people of Ekron will become a part of my people, as the Jebusites did. ⁸I will protect my country. I will not let enemy armies pass through it. I will not let them hurt my people anymore. With my own eyes I have seen how much my people have suffered."

The Future King

⁹ People of Zion,ᵃ rejoice!
    People of Jerusalem, shout with joy!
Look, your king is coming to you!
    He is the good king who won the
        victory, but he is humble.
    He is riding on a donkey, on a young
        donkey born from a work animal.
¹⁰ I will take the war chariots* away from
        Ephraim*
    and the horse soldiers from Jerusalem.
    I will destroy the bows used in war.

    Your king will bring news of peace to the
        nations.
    He will rule from sea to sea,
    from the Euphrates River to the ends of
        the earth.

The Lord Will Save His People

¹¹ Jerusalem, we used blood to seal your
        agreement,*
    so I am setting your people free from
        that empty hole in the ground.ᵇ
¹² Prisoners, go home!
    Now you have something to hope for.
I am telling you now,
    I am coming back to you.
¹³ Judah,* I will use you like a bow.
    Ephraim,* I will use you like arrows.
Israel,* I will use you like a sword
    to fight against the men of Greece.
¹⁴ The Lord will appear to them,
    and he will shoot his arrows like
        lightning.
The Lord God will blow the trumpet,
    and the army will rush forward like a
        desert dust storm.
¹⁵ The Lord All-Powerful will protect them.
    The soldiers will use rocks and slings* to
        defeat the enemy.

ᵃ9:9 Literally, "Daughter of Zion," meaning the city of Jerusalem. See "Zion" in the Word List.
ᵇ9:11 empty hole in the ground People stored water in large holes in the ground. People sometimes used those holes as prisons.

They will spill the blood of their enemies.
    It will flow like wine.
    It will be like the blood that is thrown
        on the corners of the altar!
¹⁶ At that time the Lord their God
    will save his people
    like a shepherd saves his sheep.
They will be very precious to him.
    They will be like sparkling jewels in his
        land.
¹⁷ Everything will be good and beautiful!
    There will be a wonderful crop,
    but it will not be just the food and wine.
    It will be all the young men and
        women!

The Lord's Promises

10 ¹Pray to the Lord for rain in the spring-time. The Lord will send the lightning and the rain will fall, and he will make the plants grow in each person's field.

²People use their little statues and magic to learn what will happen in the future, but that is useless. They see visions and tell about their dreams, but it is nothing but worthless lies. So the people are like sheep wandering here and there crying for help, but there is no shepherd to lead them.

³The Lord says, "I am very angry with the shepherds. I made them responsible for what happens to my sheep." (The people of Judah are his flock, and the Lord All-Powerful really does take care of his flock. He cares for them as a soldier cares for his beautiful war horse.)

⁴"The cornerstone, the tent peg, the war bow, and the advancing soldiers will all come ⌊from Judah⌋ together. ⁵They will defeat their enemy,—it will be like soldiers marching through mud in the streets. They will fight, and since the Lord is with them, they will defeat even the enemy soldiers riding horses. ⁶I will make Judah's family strong. I will help Joseph's family win the war. I will bring them back safely and comfort them. It will be as if I never left them. I am the Lord their God, and I will help them. ⁷The people of Ephraim* will be as happy as soldiers who have too much to drink. Their children will be rejoicing and they, too, will be happy. They will all have a happy time together with the Lord.

⁸"I will whistle for them and call them all together. I really will save them. There will be many people. ⁹Yes, I have been scattering my people throughout the nations. But in those faraway places, they will remember me. They and their children will survive, and they will come back. ¹⁰I will bring them back from Egypt and Assyria. I will bring them to the area of Gilead. And since there will not be enough room, I will also let them live in nearby Lebanon." ¹¹As beforeᶜ, the Lord will strike the waves, and the people will walk across their sea of troubles. He will make the waters of the Nile

ᶜ10:11 As before Read Ex. 19:14–31.

River dry up. He will destroy Assyria's pride and Egypt's power. ¹²The Lord will make his people strong, and they will live for him and his name. This is what the Lord said.

God Will Punish the Other Nations

11 ¹Lebanon, open your gates so that the fire will come
and burn your cedar trees.ᵃ
² The cypress trees will cry because the
cedar trees have fallen.
Those powerful trees will be taken
away.
Oak trees in Bashan will cry
for the forest that was cut down.
³ Listen to the crying shepherds.
Their powerful leaders were taken
away.
Listen to the roaring of the young lions.
Their thick bushes near the Jordan
River have all been taken away.

⁴The Lord my God says, "Care for the sheep that have been raised to be killed. ⁵Buyers kill their sheep and are not punished. Those who sell the sheep and say, 'Praise the Lord, I am rich!' The shepherds don't feel sorry for their sheep. ⁶And I don't feel sorry for the people who live in this country." This is what the Lord said: "Look, I will let everyone be under the control of their neighbor and king. I will let them destroy the country—I will not stop them!"

⁷So I took care of the sheep that had been raised to be killed—those poor sheep. I found two sticks. I called one stick Favor, and I called the other stick Union. Then I began caring for the sheep. ⁸I fired the three shepherds all in one month. I got angry at the sheep, and they began to hate me. ⁹Then I said, "I quit! I will not take care of you! I will let those who want to die, die. I will let those who want to be destroyed, be destroyed, and those who are left will destroy each other." ¹⁰Then I took the stick named Favor, and I broke it. I did this to show that God's agreement with his people was broken. ¹¹So that day the agreement was finished, and those poor sheep watching me knew that this message was from the Lord.

¹²Then I said, "If you want to pay me, pay me. If not, don't!" So they paid me 30 pieces of silver. ¹³Then the Lord told me, "So that's how much they think I'm worth. Throw that large amount of moneyᵇ into the Temple treasury." So I took the 30 pieces of silver and threw them into the treasury at the Lord's Temple. ¹⁴Then I cut the stick named Union into two pieces. I did this to show that the union between Judah and Israel had been broken.

ᵃ**11:1 cedar trees** In this poem, the trees, bushes, and animals are symbols for the leaders of the countries around Judah.
ᵇ**11:13 large amount of money** The Lord was making fun of the people. This was only the amount of money a person paid for a slave.

¹⁵Then the Lord said to me, "Now, get the things a foolish shepherd might use. ¹⁶This will show that I will get a new shepherd for this country. But this young man will not be able to take care of the sheep that are being destroyed. He will not be able to heal the hurt sheep or feed those that are left alive. And the healthy ones will be eaten completely—only their hoofs will be left."

¹⁷ Too bad for you, you worthless shepherd!
You abandoned my sheep.
Punish him!
Strike his arm and right eye with a
sword.
His arm will be useless.
His right eye will be blind.

Visions About the Nations Around Judah

12 ¹This is a message from the Lord about Israel. The Lord is the one who made the earth and the sky, and he put the human spirit in people. And this is what the Lord said: ²"Look, I will make Jerusalem like a cup of poison to the nations around her. The nations will come and attack that city, and all of Judah will be caught in the trap. ³But I will make Jerusalem like a heavy rock—those who try to take it will hurt themselves. They will be cut and scratched. All the nations on earth will come together to fight against Jerusalem. ⁴But at that time I will scare the horse, and the soldier riding it will panic. I will make all the enemy horses blind, but my eyes will be open—and I will be watching over Judah's family. ⁵The leaders of Judah will encourage the people and say, 'The Lord All-Powerful is your God. He makes us strong.' ⁶At that time I will make the leaders of Judah like a fire burning in a forest. They will destroy their enemies like fire burning straw. They will destroy the enemy all around them, and the people in Jerusalem will again be able to sit back and relax."

⁷The Lord will save the people of Judah first, so the people in Jerusalem will not be able to brag too much. David's family and the other people who live in Jerusalem will not be able to brag that they are better than the other people in Judah. ⁸But the Lord will protect the people in Jerusalem. Even the man who trips and falls will become a great soldier like David. And the men from David's family will be like gods—like the Lord's own angel leading the people.

⁹The Lord says, "At that time I will destroy the nations that came to fight against Jerusalem. ¹⁰I will fill David's family and the people living in Jerusalem with a spirit of kindness and mercy. They will look to me, the one they stabbed, and they will be very sad. They will be as sad as someone crying over the death of their only son, as sad as someone crying over the death of their firstborn* son. ¹¹There will be a time of great sadness and crying in

Jerusalem. It will be like the time people cry over the death of Hadad Rimmon[a] in Megiddo Valley. [12]Each and every family will cry by itself. The men in David's family will cry by themselves, and their wives will cry by themselves. The men in Nathan's family will cry by themselves, and their wives will cry by themselves. [13]The men in Levi's family will cry by themselves, and their wives will cry by themselves. The men in Simeon's family will cry by themselves, and their wives will cry by themselves. [14]And the same thing will happen in all the other tribes. The men and women will cry by themselves."

13 [1]But at that time a new spring of water will be opened for David's family and for the other people living in Jerusalem. That fountain will be to wash away their sins and to make the people pure.

No More False Prophets

[2]The LORD All-Powerful says, "At that time I will remove all the idols* from the earth. People will not even remember their names, and I will remove the false prophets and unclean* spirits from the earth. [3]Whoever continues to prophesy* will be punished. Even their parents, their own mother and father, will say to them, 'You have spoken lies in the name of the LORD, so you must die!' Their own mother and father will stab them for prophesying. [4]At that time the prophets will be ashamed of their visions and prophecies. They will not wear the rough cloth that shows a person is a prophet. They will not wear those clothes to trick people with the lies they call prophecies. [5]They will say, 'I am not a prophet. I am a farmer. I have worked as a farmer since I was a little child.' [6]But other people will say, 'Then what are these wounds in your hands?' He will say, 'I was beaten in the house of my friends.'"

[7]The LORD All-Powerful says, "Sword, hit the shepherd! Hit my friend! Hit the shepherd, and the sheep will run away. And I will punish those little ones. [8]Two-thirds of the people in the land will be hurt and die, but one-third will survive. [9]Then I will test those survivors by giving them many troubles. The troubles will be like the fire a person uses to prove silver is pure. I will test them the way a person tests gold. Then they will call to me for help, and I will answer them. I will say, 'You are my people.' And they will say, 'The LORD is my God.'"

The Day of Judgment

14 [1]Look, the LORD has a special day of judgment coming, when the riches you have taken will be divided in your city. [2]I will bring all the nations together to fight against Jerusalem. They will capture the city

and destroy the houses. The women will be raped, and half of the people will be taken away as prisoners. But the rest of the people will not be taken from the city. [3]Then the LORD will go to war with those nations. It will be a real battle. [4]At that time he will stand on the Mount of Olives, the hill east of Jerusalem. The Mount of Olives will split in half. Part of the mountain will move to the north, and part to the south. A deep valley will open up, from the east to the west. [5]You will try to run away as that mountain valley comes closer and closer to you. You will run away like the time you ran from the earthquake during the time of King Uzziah of Judah. But the LORD my God will come, and all his holy ones[b] will be with him.

[6-7]That will be a very special day. There will not be any light, cold, or frost. Only the LORD knows how, but there will not be any day or night. Then, when darkness usually comes, there will still be light. [8]At that time water will flow continually from Jerusalem.[c] That stream will split and part of it will flow east, and part of it will flow west to the Mediterranean Sea. And it will flow all year long, in the summer as well as in the winter. [9]And the LORD will be the King of the whole world at that time. The LORD is One. His name is One. [10]At that time the whole area around Jerusalem will become empty as the Arabah desert. The country will be like a desert from Geba to Rimmon in the Negev. But the whole city of Jerusalem will be rebuilt—from Benjamin Gate to the First Gate (that is, the Corner Gate) and from the Tower of Hananel to the king's winepresses.* [11]People will move there to live. No enemy will come to destroy them anymore. Jerusalem will be safe.

[12]But the LORD will punish the nations that fought against Jerusalem. He will send a terrible disease against them. Their skin will begin to rot while the people are still alive. Their eyes will rot in their sockets, and their tongues will rot in their mouths. [13-15]That terrible disease will be in the enemy camp, and all their horses, mules, camels, and donkeys will catch that terrible disease.

At that time they will be afraid of the LORD. Each man will grab his neighbor's hand, and they will fight each other. Even Judah will fight against Jerusalem. This will happen even while armies from all the nations are surrounding the city. There will much gold, silver, and clothing. [16]Some of the people who came to fight Jerusalem will survive. And every year they will come to worship the king, the LORD All-Powerful. They will come to celebrate the Festival of Shelters.* [17]And if people from any of the families on earth don't go to Jerusalem to worship the King, the LORD

---

[b]**14:5** *holy ones* Here, this probably means angels.
[c]**14:8** *water ... Jerusalem* Literally, "living water will flow from Jerusalem." Jerusalem's main water supply, the Gihon spring, did not flow continuously.

[a]**12:11** *Hadad Rimmon* Possibly a name for the Syrian fertility god.

All-Powerful, no rain will fall on their land. [18]If any of the families in Egypt don't come to celebrate the Festival of Shelters, they will get that terrible disease that the LORD caused the enemy nations to get. [19]That will be the punishment for Egypt, and for any other nation that does not come to celebrate the Festival of Shelters.

[20]At that time even the harnesses on the horses will have the label, HOLY TO THE LORD.[a]

[a]14:20 *HOLY TO THE LORD* These words were written on everything that was used in the Temple. This showed that these things belonged to the Lord, and that they could be used only for special purposes. Dishes with this labels could be used only by the priests in a holy place.

And all the pots used in the LORD's Temple will be just as important as the bowls used at the altar. [21]In fact, every dish in Jerusalem and Judah will have the label, HOLY TO THE LORD ALL-POWERFUL. All the people offering sacrifices will come, take those dishes, and cook their special meals in them.

At that time there will not be any merchants* buying and selling things[b] in the Temple of the LORD All-Powerful.

[b]14:21 *merchants … selling things* Literally, "Canaanites."

Malachi

1 ¹This is a message from the LORD to Israel. God used Malachi to tell this message to the people.

God Loves Israel

²The LORD said, "I love you people."

But you said, "What shows you love us?"

The LORD said, "Esau was Jacob's brother, but I chose[c] Jacob. ³And I did not accept[d] Esau. I destroyed his hill country.[e] His country was destroyed, and now only wild dogs[f] live there."

⁴The people of Edom might say, "We were destroyed, but we will go back and rebuild our cities."

But the LORD All-Powerful says, "If they rebuild their cities, I will destroy them again." That is why people say Edom is an evil country—a nation the LORD hates forever.

⁵You people saw these things, and you said, "The LORD is great, even outside of Israel!"

The People Don't Respect God

⁶The LORD All-Powerful said, "Children honor their fathers. Servants honor their masters. I am your Father, so why don't you honor me? I am your master, so why don't you respect me? You priests don't respect my name.

"But you say, 'What have we done that shows we don't respect your name?'

⁷"You bring unclean* bread to my altar.

[c]1:2 *chose* Or "loved."
[d]1:3 *did not accept* Or "hated."
[e]1:3 *his hill country* This means the country of Edom. Edom was another name for Esau.
[f]1:3 *wild dogs* Literally, "jackals."

"But you ask, 'What makes that bread unclean?'

"It is unclean because you show no respect for my altar. ⁸You bring blind animals as sacrifices,* and that is wrong. You bring sick and crippled animals for sacrifices, and that is wrong. Try giving those sick animals as a gift to your governor. Would he accept those sick animals? No, he would not accept them." This is what the LORD All-Powerful said.

⁹"Now try asking God to be good to you. But he will not listen to you, and it is all your fault." This is what the LORD All-Powerful said.

¹⁰"I wish one of you would close the Temple* doors to stop the lighting of useless fires on my altar. I am not pleased with you. I will not accept your gifts." This is what the LORD All-Powerful said.

¹¹"People all around the world respect my name. All around the world they bring good gifts to me and burn good incense* as a gift to me, because my name is important to all of them." This is what the LORD All-Powerful said.

¹²"But you people show that you don't respect my name. You say that the LORD's altar is unclean. And you don't like the food from that altar. ¹³You smell the food and refuse to eat it. You say it is bad. Then you bring sick, crippled, and hurt animals to me. You try to give sick animals to me as sacrifices, but I will not accept them. ¹⁴Some people have good, male animals that they could give as sacrifices, but don't. Some people bring good animals and promise to give those healthy animals to me. But then they secretly exchange those good animals and

give me sick animals instead. Bad things will happen to those people. I am the Great King and people all around the world respect me!" This is what the LORD All-Powerful said.

Rules for Priests

2 ¹"Priests, this rule is for you. ²Listen to me! Pay attention to what I say. Show honor to my name. If you don't respect my name, bad things will happen to you. You will say blessings,ᵃ but they will become curses.* I will make bad things happen because you don't show respect for my name." This is what the LORD All-Powerful said.

³"Look, I will punish your descendants. During the festivals, you priests offer sacrifices* to me. You take the dung and inside parts from the dead animals and throw them away. But I will smear the dung on your faces, and you will be thrown away with it! ⁴Then you will learn why I am giving you this command. I am telling you these things so that my agreement with Levi* will continue." This is what the LORD All-Powerful said.

⁵The Lord said,₁ "I made that agreement with Levi. I promised to give him life and peace—and I gave him those things. Levi respected me and showed honor to my name. ⁶He taught the true teachings and didn't teach lies. Levi was honest, and he loved peace. He followed me and saved many people from being punished for the evil things they did. ⁷A priest should know God's teachings. People should be able to go to a priest and learn God's teachings. A priest should be God's messenger to the people.

⁸"But you priests stopped following me! You used the teachings to make people do wrong. You ruined the agreement* with Levi." This is what the LORD All-Powerful said. ⁹"You don't live the way I told you. You have not accepted my teachings. So I will cause people to hate you and think you are worth nothing."

Judah Was Not True to God

¹⁰We all have the same father. The same God made every one of us. So why do people cheat one another? They show that they don't respect the agreement. They don't respect the agreement that our ancestors made with God. ¹¹The people of Judah cheated other people. People in Jerusalem and Israel did terrible things. God loves the Temple,* but the people in Judah didn't respect the LORD's holy Temple. The people of Judah began to worship a foreign goddess. ¹²The LORD will remove them from Judah's family. They might bring gifts to the LORD All-Powerful—but it will not help. ¹³You can cry and cover the LORD's altar with tears, but the Lord will not accept your gifts. He will not be pleased with the things you bring to him.

¹⁴You ask, "Why are our gifts not accepted?" It is because the LORD saw the evil things you did—he is a witness* against you. He saw you cheat on your wife. You have been married to her since you were young. She was your girlfriend. Then you made your vows* to each other—and she became your wife. ¹⁵God wants husbands and wives to become one body and one spirit. Why? So that they would have holy children and protect that spiritual unity. Don't cheat on your wife. She has been your wife from the time you were young.

¹⁶The LORD, the God of Israel, says, "I hate divorce, and I hate the cruel things that men do. So protect your spiritual unity. Don't cheat on your wife."

The Special Time of Judgment

¹⁷You have taught wrong things, and it makes the LORD very sad. People were doing evil things, but you said that this pleased the LORD and that he accepted those things. And you taught that God does not punish people for the evil they do.

3 ¹The LORD All-Powerful says, "I am sending my messenger to prepare the way for me. Then suddenly, the Lord you are looking for will come to his temple.ᵇ Yes, the messenger you are waiting for, the one who will tell about my agreement,* is really coming!

²"No one can prepare for that time or stand against him when he comes. He will be like a burning fire. He will be like the strong soap people use to make things clean. ³He will make the Levites* clean.* He will make them pure, like silver is made pure with fire! He will make them pure like gold and silver. Then they will bring gifts to the LORD, and they will do things the right way. ⁴Then the LORD will accept the gifts from Judah and Jerusalem. It will be as it was in the past—as the time long ago. ⁵Then I will bring you to justice. I will be an expert witness and testify about the evil things people do. I will speak out against those who do evil magic or commit adultery.* I will speak out against those who make false promises and cheat their workers and don't pay them the money they promised. I will testify against those who don't help strangers, or widows and orphans. And I will testify against those who don't respect me." This is what the LORD All-Powerful said.

Stealing From God

⁶"I am the LORD, and I don't change. You are Jacob's children, and you have not been completely destroyed. ⁷But you never obeyed my laws. Even your ancestors stopped following me. Come back to me, and I will come back to you." This is what the LORD All-Powerful said.

"You say, 'How can we come back?'

ᵃ**2:2 blessings** Words asking for good things to happen to a person who tries to obey God's law.

ᵇ**3:1 temple** Or "palace."

8"People should not steal things from God, but you stole things from me.

"You say, 'What did we steal from you?'

"You should have given me one-tenth of your things. You should have given me special gifts. 9In this way your whole nation has stolen things from me, so bad things are happening to you." This is what the LORD All-Powerful said.

10The LORD All-Powerful says, "Try this test. Bring one-tenth of your things to me. Put them in the treasury. Bring food to my house. Test me! If you do these things, I will surely bless you. Good things will come to you like rain falling from the sky. You will have more than enough of everything. 11I will not let pests destroy your crops. All your grapevines will produce grapes." This is what the LORD All-Powerful said.

12"People from other nations will be good to you. You will have a wonderful country." This is what the LORD All-Powerful said.

The Special Time of Judgment

13The LORD says, "You said cruel things to me."

But you ask, "What did we say about you?"

14You said, "It is useless to worship God. We did what the LORD All-Powerful told us, but we didn't gain anything. We cried like people at a funeral to show we were sorry for our sins, but it didn't help. 15We think proud people are happy. Evil people succeed. They do evil things to test God's patience, and God does not punish them."

16Then the LORD's followers spoke with each other, and the LORD listened to them. There is a book in front of him. In that book are the names of his followers. They are the people who honor the LORD's name.

17The LORD said, "They belong to me. I will be kind to them. Parents are very kind to their children who obey them. In the same way I will be kind to my followers. 18You people will come back to me, and you will learn the difference between good and evil. You will learn the difference between someone who follows God and someone who does not.

4 1"That time of judgment is coming. It will be like a hot furnace. All the proud people will be punished. All the evil people will burn like straw. At that time they will be like a bush burning in the fire, and there will not be a branch or root left." This is what the LORD All-Powerful said.

2"But, for my followers, goodness will shine on you like the rising sun. And it will bring healing power like the sun's rays. You will be free and happy, like calves freed from their stalls.a 3Then you will walk on the evil people—they will be like ashes under your feet. I will make this happen at the time of judgment." This is what the LORD All-Powerful said.

4"Remember and obey the law of my servant Moses. I gave those laws and rules to him at Mount Horeb.* They are for all the people of Israel.

5"Look, I will send Elijah the prophet to you. He will come before that great and terrible time of judgment from the LORD. 6Elijah will help the parents become close to their children, and he will help the children become close to their parents. This must happen, or I will come and completely destroy your country."

---

a4:2 *stalls* Small rooms or areas surrounded by a fence where people keep their animals.

The
New
Testament

Matthew

The Family History of Jesus
(Lk. 3:23b–38)

1 ¹This is the family history of Jesus Christ. He came from the family of David* and from the family of Abraham.*

² Abraham was the father of Isaac.
Isaac was the father of Jacob.*
Jacob was the father of Judah and his brothers.

³ Judah was the father of Perez and Zerah. (Their mother was Tamar.)
Perez was the father of Hezron.
Hezron was the father of Ram.

⁴ Ram was the father of Amminadab.
Amminadab was the father of Nahshon.
Nahshon was the father of Salmon.

⁵ Salmon was the father of Boaz. (His mother was Rahab.)
Boaz was the father of Obed. (His mother was Ruth.)
Obed was the father of Jesse.

⁶ Jesse was the father of King David.
David was the father of Solomon. (His mother had been Uriah's wife.)

⁷ Solomon was the father of Rehoboam.
Rehoboam was the father of Abijah.
Abijah was the father of Asa.

⁸ Asa was the father of Jehoshaphat.
Jehoshaphat was the father of Jehoram.
Jehoram was the father of Uzziah.

⁹ Uzziah was the father of Jotham.
Jotham was the father of Ahaz.
Ahaz was the father of Hezekiah.

¹⁰ Hezekiah was the father of Manasseh.
Manasseh was the father of Amon.
Amon was the father of Josiah.

¹¹ Josiah was the grandfather of Jehoiachinᵃ and his brothers, who lived during the time that the people were taken away to Babylon.

¹² After they were taken to Babylon:
Jehoiachin was the father of Shealtiel.
Shealtiel was the grandfather of Zerubbabel.

¹³ Zerubbabel was the father of Abiud.
Abiud was the father of Eliakim.
Eliakim was the father of Azor.

¹⁴ Azor was the father of Zadok.

Zadok was the father of Achim.
Achim was the father of Eliud.

¹⁵ Eliud was the father of Eleazar.
Eleazar was the father of Matthan.
Matthan was the father of Jacob.

¹⁶ Jacob was the father of Joseph.
Joseph was the husband of Mary, and Mary was the mother of Jesus, who is called the Christ.*

¹⁷So there were fourteen generations from Abraham to David. There were also fourteen generations from David until the people were taken away to Babylon. And there were fourteen more from the time the people were taken to Babylon until Christ was born.

The Birth of Jesus Christ
(Lk. 2:1–7)

¹⁸This is how the birth of Jesus Christ happened. His mother Mary was engaged to marry Joseph. But before they married, he learned that she was expecting a baby. (She was pregnant by the power of the Holy Spirit.*) ¹⁹Mary's husband, Joseph, was a good man. He did not want to cause her public disgrace, so he planned to divorce her secretly.

²⁰But after Joseph thought about this, an angel from the Lord came to him in a dream. The angel said, "Joseph, son of David,* don't be afraid to accept Mary to be your wife. The baby inside her is from the Holy Spirit. ²¹She will give birth to a son. You will name him Jesus.ᵇ Give him that name because he will save his people from their sins."

²²All this happened to make clear the full meaning of what the Lord said through the prophet*: ²³"The virgin* will be pregnant and will give birth to a son. They will name him Immanuel."ᶜ (Immanuel means "God with us.")

²⁴When Joseph woke up, he did what the Lord's angel told him to do. He married Mary. ²⁵But Joseph did not have sexual relations with her until her son was born. And he named him Jesus.

Wise Men Come to Visit Jesus

2 ¹Jesus was born in the town of Bethlehem in Judea during the time when Herod*

ᵃ**1:11** *Jehoiachin* Literally, "Jechoniah," another name for Jehoiachin.

ᵇ**1:21** *Jesus* The name Jesus means "the Lᴏʀᴅ (Yᴀʜᴡᴇʜ) saves."

ᶜ**1:23** Quote from Isa. 7:14.

was king. After Jesus was born, some wise men* from the east came to Jerusalem. ²They asked people, "Where is the child who has been born to be the king of the Jews? We saw the star that shows he was born. We saw it rise in the sky in the east and have come to worship him."

³When King Herod heard about this, it upset him as well as everyone else in Jerusalem. ⁴Herod called a meeting of all the leading Jewish priests and teachers of the law. He asked them where the Christ* would be born. ⁵They answered, "In the town of Bethlehem in Judea, just as the prophet* wrote:

6 'Bethlehem, in the land of Judah,
    you are important among the rulers of
    Judah.
  Yes, a ruler will come from you,
    and that ruler will lead Israel, my
    people.'"   *Micah 5:2*

⁷Then Herod had a private meeting with the wise men from the east. He learned from them the exact time they first saw the star. ⁸Then he sent them to Bethlehem. He said, "Go and look carefully for the child. When you find him, come tell me. Then I can go worship him too."

⁹After the wise men heard the king, they left. They saw the same star they had seen in the east, and they followed it. The star went before them until it stopped above the place where the child was. ¹⁰They were very happy and excited to see the star.

¹¹The wise men came to the house where the child was with his mother Mary. They bowed down and worshiped him. Then they opened the boxes of gifts they had brought for him. They gave him treasures of gold, frankincense,* and myrrh.* ¹²But God warned the wise men in a dream not to go back to Herod. So they went home to their own country a different way.

Jesus' Parents Take Him to Egypt

¹³After the wise men* left, an angel from the Lord came to Joseph in a dream. The angel said, "Get up! Take the child with his mother and escape to Egypt. Herod* wants to kill the child and will soon start looking for him. Stay in Egypt until I tell you to come back." ¹⁴So Joseph got ready and left for Egypt with the child and the mother. They left during the night. ¹⁵Joseph stayed in Egypt until Herod died. This gave full meaning to what the Lord said through the prophet*: "I called my son to come out of Egypt."ᵃ

Herod Kills the Baby Boys in Bethlehem

¹⁶Herod* saw that the wise men* had fooled him, and he was very angry. So he gave an order to kill all the baby boys in Bethlehem

and the whole area around Bethlehem. Herod had learned from the wise men the time the baby was born. It was now two years from that time. So he said to kill all the boys who were two years old and younger. ¹⁷This gave full meaning to what God said through the prophet* Jeremiah:

¹⁸"A sound was heard in Ramah—
    bitter crying and great sadness.
  Rachel cries for her children,
    and she cannot be comforted, because
      her children are gone." *Jeremiah 31:15*

Joseph and Mary Return From Egypt

¹⁹While Joseph was in Egypt, Herod* died. An angel from the Lord came to Joseph in a dream ²⁰and said, "Get up! Take the child with his mother and go to Israel. Those who were trying to kill the child are now dead."

²¹So Joseph took the child and the mother and went to Israel. ²²But he heard that Archelaus was now king in Judea. Archelaus became king when his father Herod died. So Joseph was afraid to go there. Then, after being warned in a dream, he went away to the area of Galilee. ²³He went to a town called Nazareth and lived there. This gave full meaning to what God said through the prophets.* God said the Christᵇ would be called a Nazarene.ᶜ

John Prepares the Way for Jesus
(Mk. 1:1–8; Lk. 3:1–9, 15–17; Jn. 1:19–28)

3 ¹When it was the right time, John the Baptizer* began telling people a message from God. This was out in the desert area of Judea. ²John said, "Change your hearts and lives, because God's kingdom* is coming soon." ³John is the one Isaiah the prophet* was talking about when he said,

"There is someone shouting in the desert:
  'Prepare the way for the Lord.
    Make the road straight for him.'"
                                    Isaiah 40:3

⁴John's clothes were made from camel's hair, and he had a leather belt around his waist. For food, he ate locusts* and wild honey. ⁵People came to John from Jerusalem and the rest of Judea and from all the areas along the Jordan River. ⁶They confessed the bad things they had done, and John baptized* them in the Jordan.

⁷Many Pharisees* and Sadducees* came to where John was baptizing people. When John saw them, he said, "You are all snakes! Who warned you to run from God's judgment that

---

ᵃ**2:15** Quote from Hos. 11:1.

ᵇ**2:23 the Christ** Literally, "he." See "Christ" in the Word List.
ᶜ**2:23 Nazarene** A person from the city of Nazareth. This name sounds like the Hebrew word for "branch." So Matthew may be referring to the promise of a "branch" of David's family. See Isa. 11:1.

is coming? ⁸Change your hearts! And show by the way you live that you have changed. ⁹I know what you are thinking. You want to say, 'but Abraham* is our father!' That means nothing. I tell you, God could make children for Abraham from these rocks. ¹⁰The ax is now ready to cut down the trees.ᵃ Every tree that does not produce good fruit will be cut down and thrown into the fire.

¹¹"I baptize you with water to show that you have changed your hearts and lives. But there is someone coming later who is able to do more than I can. I am not good enough to be the slave who takes off his sandals. He will baptize you with the Holy Spirit* and with fire. ¹²He will come ready to clean the grain.ᵇ He will separate the good grain from the straw, and he will put the good part into his barn. Then he will burn the useless part with a fire that cannot be stopped."

Jesus Is Baptized by John
(Mk. 1:9–11; Lk. 3:21–22)

¹³Then Jesus came from Galilee to the Jordan River. He came to John, wanting John to baptize* him. ¹⁴But John tried to stop him. John said, "Why do you come to me to be baptized? I should be baptized by you!"

¹⁵Jesus answered, "Let it be this way for now. We should do whatever God says is right." Then John agreed.

¹⁶So Jesus was baptized. As soon as he came up ,out of the water, the sky opened, and he saw God's Spirit coming down on him like a dove. ¹⁷A voice from heaven said, "This is my Son, the one I love. I am very pleased with him."

The Temptation of Jesus
(Mk. 1:12–13; Lk. 4:1–13)

4 ¹Then the Spirit* led Jesus into the desert. He was taken there to be tempted by the devil. ²Jesus ate nothing for 40 days and nights. After this, he was very hungry. ³The devilᶜ came to tempt him and said, "If you are the Son of God, tell these rocks to become bread."

⁴Jesus answered him, "The Scriptures* say,

'It is not just bread that keeps people alive. Their lives depend on what God says.'"
Deuteronomy 8:3

⁵Then the devil led Jesus to the holy* city of Jerusalem and put him on a high place at the edge of the Temple* area. ⁶He said to Jesus, "If you are the Son of God, jump off, because the Scriptures say,

'God will command his angels to help you,
    and their hands will catch you,
so that you will not hit your foot on a
    rock.'"   *Psalm 91:11–12*

⁷Jesus answered, "The Scriptures also say,

'You must not test the Lord your God.'"
Deuteronomy 6:16

⁸Then the devil led Jesus to the top of a very high mountain and showed him all the kingdoms of the world and all the wonderful things in them. ⁹The devil said, "If you will bow down and worship me, I will give you all these things."

¹⁰Jesus said to him, "Get away from me, Satan*! The Scriptures say,

'You must worship the Lord your God.
    Serve only him!'"   *Deuteronomy 6:13*

¹¹So the devil left him. Then some angels came to Jesus and helped him.

Jesus Begins His Work in Galilee
(Mk. 1:14–15; Lk. 4:14–15)

¹²Jesus heard that John was put in prison, so he went back to Galilee. ¹³But he did not stay in Nazareth. He went to live in Capernaum, a town near Lake Galilee in the area near Zebulun and Naphtali. ¹⁴He did this to give full meaning to what the prophet* Isaiah said:

¹⁵"Listen, land of Zebulun and land of
        Naphtali,
    lands by the road that goes to the sea,
        the area past the Jordan River—
    Galilee, where those from other nations
        live.
¹⁶ The people who live in spiritual darkness
    have seen a great light.
The light has shined for those
    who live in the land that is as dark as a
        grave."   *Isaiah 9:1–2*

¹⁷From that time Jesus began to tell people his message: "Change your hearts and lives, because God's kingdom* is coming soon."

Jesus Chooses Some Followers
(Mk. 1:16–20; Lk. 5:1–11)

¹⁸As Jesus was walking by Lake Galilee, he saw two brothers, Simon (called Peter) and Simon's brother Andrew. These brothers were fishermen, and they were fishing in the lake with a net. ¹⁹Jesus said to them, "Come, follow me, and I will make you a different kind of fishermen. You will bring in people, not fish." ²⁰Simon and Andrew immediately left their nets and followed him.

²¹Jesus continued walking by Lake Galilee. He saw two other brothers, James and John, the sons of Zebedee. They were in a boat with

---

ᵃ**3:10 trees** The people who don't obey God. They are like "trees" that will be cut down.
ᵇ**3:12 clean the grain** Meaning that Jesus will separate the good people from those who are bad.
ᶜ**4:3 The devil** Literally, "The tempter."

their father Zebedee. They were preparing their nets to catch fish. Jesus told the brothers to come with him. 22So they immediately left the boat and their father, and they followed Jesus.

Jesus Teaches and Heals the People
(Lk. 6:17–19)

23Jesus went everywhere in the country of Galilee. He taught in the synagogues* and told the Good News about God's kingdom.* And he healed all the people's diseases and sicknesses. 24The news about Jesus spread all over Syria, and people brought to him all those who were sick. They were suffering from different kinds of diseases and pain. Some had demons* inside them, some suffered from seizures, and some were paralyzed. Jesus healed them all. 25Large crowds followed him—people from Galilee, the Ten Towns,* Jerusalem, Judea, and the area across the Jordan River.

Jesus Teaches the People
(Lk. 6:20–23)

5 1When Jesus saw the crowds of people there, he went up on a hill and sat down. His followers came and sat next to him. 2Then Jesus began teaching the people. He said,

3"Great blessings belong to those who know
    they are spiritually in need.*a*
God's kingdom* belongs to them.

4 Great blessings belong to those who are
    sad now.
God will comfort them.

5 Great blessings belong to those who are
    humble.
They will be given the land God
    promised.*b*

6 Great blessings belong to those who want
    to do right more than anything else.*c*
God will fully satisfy them.

7 Great blessings belong to those who show
    mercy to others.
Mercy will be given to them.

8 Great blessings belong to those whose
    thoughts are pure.
They will be with God.

9 Great blessings belong to those who work
    to bring peace.
God will call them his sons and
    daughters.

10 Great blessings belong to those who suffer
    persecution for doing what is right.
God's kingdom belongs to them.

11"People will insult you and hurt you. They will lie and say all kinds of evil things about you because you follow me. But when they do that, know that great blessings belong to you. 12Be happy about it. Be very glad because you have a great reward waiting for you in heaven. People did these same bad things to the prophets* who lived before you.

You Are Like Salt and Light
(Mk. 9:50; 4:21; Lk. 14:34–35; 8:16)

13"You are the salt of the earth. But if the salt loses its taste, it cannot be made salty again. Salt is useless if it loses its salty taste. It will be thrown out where people will just walk on it.

14"You are the light that shines for the world to see. You are like a city built on a hill that cannot be hidden. 15People don't hide a lamp under a bowl. They put it on a lampstand. Then the light shines for everyone in the house. 16In the same way, you should be a light for other people. Live so that they will see the good things you do and praise your Father in heaven.

Jesus and the Old Testament Writings

17"Don't think that I have come to destroy the Law of Moses* or the teaching of the prophets.* I have come not to destroy their teachings but to give full meaning to them. 18I assure you that nothing will disappear from the law until heaven and earth are gone. The law will not lose even the smallest letter or the smallest part of a letter until it has all been done.

19"A person should obey every command in the law, even one that does not seem important. Whoever refuses to obey any command and teaches others not to obey it will be the least important in God's kingdom.* But whoever obeys the law and teaches others to obey it will be great in God's kingdom. 20I tell you that you must do better than the teachers of the law and the Pharisees.* If you are not more pleasing to God than they are, you will never enter God's kingdom.

Jesus Teaches About Anger

21"You have heard that it was said to our people long ago, 'You must not murder anyone.*d* Any person who commits murder will be judged.' 22But I tell you, don't be angry with anyone. If you are angry with others, you will be judged. And if you insult someone, you will be judged by the high court. And if you call someone a fool, you will be in danger of the fire of hell.

23"So, what if you are offering your gift at the altar* and remember that someone has something against you? 24Leave your gift there and go make peace with that person. Then come and offer your gift.

---

*a*5:3 *those ... in need* Literally, "the poor in spirit."
*b*5:5 *They will ... promised* This is the meaning of these words in Ps. 37:11. Here, they probably refer to a spiritual "promised land," but they can also mean "The earth will belong to them."
*c*5:6 *want ... more than anything else* Literally, "hunger and thirst for righteousness."

*d*5:21 Quote from Ex. 20:13; Deut. 5:17.

25"If anyone wants to take you to court, make friends with them quickly. Try to do that before you get to the court. If you don't, they might hand you over to the judge. And the judge will hand you over to a guard, who will throw you into jail. 26I assure you that you will not leave there until you have paid everything you owe.

Jesus Teaches About Sexual Sin

27"You have heard that it was said, 'You must not commit adultery.'*'a 28But I tell you that if a man looks at a woman and wants to sin sexually with her, he has already committed that sin with her in his mind. 29If your right eye makes you sin, take it out and throw it away. It is better to lose one part of your body than to have your whole body thrown into hell. 30If your right hand makes you sin, cut it off and throw it away. It is better to lose one part of your body than for your whole body to go into hell.

Jesus Teaches About Divorce
(Mt. 19:9; Mk. 10:11–12; Lk. 16:18)

31"It was also said, 'Any man who divorces his wife must give her a written notice of divorce.'b 32But I tell you that any man who divorces his wife, except for the problem of sexual sin, is causing his wife to be guilty of adultery.* And whoever marries a divorced woman is guilty of adultery.

Jesus Teaches About Making Promises

33"You have heard that it was said to our people long ago, 'When you make a vow,* you must not break your promise. Keep the vows that you make to the Lord.'c 34But I tell you, when you make a promise, don't try to make it stronger with a vow. Don't make a vow using the name of heaven, because heaven is God's throne. 35Don't make a vow using the name of the earth, because the earth belongs to him.d Don't make a vow using the name of Jerusalem, because it also belongs to him, the great King. 36And don't even say that your own head is proof that you will keep your promise. You cannot make one hair on your head white or black. 37Say only 'yes' if you mean 'yes,' and say only 'no' if you mean 'no.' If you say more than that, it is from the Evil One.*

Jesus Teaches About Fighting Back
(Lk. 6:29–30)

38"You have heard that it was said, 'An eye for an eye, and a tooth for a tooth.'e 39But I tell you, don't fight back against someone who wants to do harm to you. If they hit you on the right cheek, let them hit the other cheek too. 40If anyone wants to sue you in court and take your shirt, let them have your coat too. 41If a soldier forces you to walk with him one mile,f go with him two. 42Give to anyone who asks you for something. Don't refuse to give to anyone who wants to borrow from you.

Love Your Enemies
(Lk. 6:27–28, 32–36)

43"You have heard that it was said, 'Love your neighborg and hate your enemy.' 44But I tell you, love your enemies. Pray for those who treat you badly. 45If you do this, you will be children who are truly like your Father in heaven. He lets the sun rise for all people, whether they are good or bad. He sends rain to those who do right and to those who do wrong. 46If you love only those who love you, why should you get a reward for that? Even the tax collectors* do that. 47And if you are nice only to your friends, you are no better than anyone else. Even the people who don't know God are nice to their friends. 48What I am saying is that you must be perfect, just as your Father in heaven is perfect.

Jesus Teaches About Giving

6 1"Be careful! When you do something good, don't do it in front of others so that they will see you. If you do that, you will have no reward from your Father in heaven.

2"When you give to those who are poor, don't announce that you are giving. Don't be like the hypocrites.* When they are in the synagogues* and on the streets, they blow trumpets before they give so that people will see them. They want everyone to praise them. The truth is, that's all the reward they will get. 3So when you give to the poor, don't let anyone know what you are doing.h 4Your giving should be done in private. Your Father can see what is done in private, and he will reward you.

Jesus Teaches About Prayer
(Lk. 11:2–4)

5"When you pray, don't be like the hypocrites.* They love to stand in the synagogues* and on the street corners and pray loudly. They want people to see them. The truth is, that's all the reward they will get. 6But when you pray, you should go into your room and close the door. Then pray to your Father. He is there in that private place. He can see what is done in private, and he will reward you.

7"And when you pray, don't be like the people who don't know God. They say the

---

a**5:27** Quote from Ex. 20:14; Deut. 5:18.
b**5:31** Quote from Deut. 24:1.
c**5:33** See Lev. 19:12; Num. 30:2; Deut. 23:21.
d**5:35** *the earth … him* Literally, "it is the footstool of his feet."
e**5:38** Quote from Ex. 21:24; Lev. 24:20.

f**5:41** *one mile* Literally, "one *milion*," about 1.5 km.
g**5:43** Quote from Lev. 19:18.
h**6:3** *don't … doing* Literally, "don't let your left hand know what your right hand is doing."

same things again and again. They think that if they say it enough, their god will hear them. [8]Don't be like them. Your Father knows what you need before you ask him. [9]So this is how you should pray:

'Our Father in heaven,
    we pray that your name will always be
      kept holy.*
[10] We pray that your kingdom* will come—
    that what you want will be done here
      on earth, the same as in heaven.
[11] Give us the food we need for today.
[12] Forgive our sins,
    just as we have forgiven those who did
      wrong to us.
[13] Don't let us be tempted,
    but save us from the Evil One.*'[a]

[14]Yes, if you forgive others for the wrongs they do to you, then your Father in heaven will also forgive your wrongs. [15]But if you don't forgive others, then your Father in heaven will not forgive the wrongs you do.

Jesus Teaches About Fasting

[16]"When you fast,* don't make yourselves look sad like the hypocrites.* They put a look of suffering on their faces so that people will see they are fasting. The truth is, that's all the reward they will get. [17]So when you fast, wash your face and make yourself look nice. [18]Then no one will know you are fasting, except your Father, who is with you even in private. He can see what is done in private, and he will reward you.

You Cannot Serve Two Masters
(Lk. 12:33–34; 11:34–36; 16:13)

[19]"Don't save treasures for yourselves here on earth. Moths and rust will destroy them. And thieves can break into your house and steal them. [20]Instead, save your treasures in heaven, where they cannot be destroyed by moths or rust and where thieves cannot break in and steal them. [21]Your heart will be where your treasure is.

[22]"The only source of light for the body is the eye. If you look at people and want to help them, you will be full of light.* [23]But if you look at people in a selfish way, you will be full of darkness.* And if the only light you have is really darkness, you have the worst kind of darkness.[b]

[24]"You cannot serve two masters at the same time. You will hate one and love the other, or you will be loyal to one and not care about the other. You cannot serve God and Money[c] at the same time.

Put God's Kingdom First
(Lk. 12:22–34)

[25]"So I tell you, don't worry about the things you need to live—what you will eat, drink, or wear. Life is more important than food, and the body is more important than what you put on it. [26]Look at the birds. They don't plant, harvest, or save food in barns, but your heavenly Father feeds them. Don't you know you are worth much more than they are? [27]You cannot add any time to your life by worrying about it.

[28]"And why do you worry about clothes? Look at the wildflowers in the field. See how they grow. They don't work or make clothes for themselves. [29]But I tell you that even Solomon, the great and rich king, was not dressed as beautifully as one of these flowers. [30]If God makes what grows in the field so beautiful, what do you think he will do for you? It's just grass—one day it's alive, and the next day someone throws it into a fire. But God cares enough to make it beautiful. Surely he will do much more for you. Your faith is so small! [31]"Don't worry and say, 'What will we eat?' or 'What will we drink?' or 'What will we wear?' [32]That's what those people who don't know God are always thinking about. Don't worry, because your Father in heaven knows that you need all these things. [33]What you should want most is God's kingdom* and doing what he wants you to do. Then he will give you all these other things you need. [34]So don't worry about tomorrow. Each day has enough trouble of its own. Tomorrow will have its own worries.

Be Careful About Criticizing Others
(Lk. 6:37–38, 41–42)

7 [1]"Don't judge others, and God will not judge you. [2]If you judge others, you will be judged the same way you judge them. God will treat you the same way you treat others.

[3]"Why do you notice the small piece of dust that is in your friend's eye, but you don't notice the big piece of wood that is in your own? [4]Why do you say to your friend, 'Let me take that piece of dust out of your eye'? Look at yourself first! You still have that big piece of wood in your own eye. [5]You are a hypocrite*! First, take the wood out of your own eye. Then you will see clearly to get the dust out of your friend's eye.

[6]"Don't give something that is holy* to dogs. They will only turn and hurt you. And don't throw your pearls to pigs. They will only step on them.

---

[a]**6:13** Some Greek copies add: "For the kingdom and the power and the glory belong to you forever and ever. Amen."
[b]**6:23** Literally, "[22]The lamp of the body is the eye. So, if your eye is pure, your whole body will be full of light. [23]But if your eye is evil, your whole body will be dark. So, if the light in you is darkness, how much is the darkness."

[c]**6:24** *Money* Or "*mamona*," an Aramaic word meaning "wealth."

Ask God for What You Need
(Lk. 11:9–13)

7"Continue to ask, and God will give to you. Continue to search, and you will find. Continue to knock, and the door will open for you. 8Yes, whoever continues to ask will receive. Whoever continues to look will find. And whoever continues to knock will have the door opened for them.

9"Do any of you have a son? If he asked for bread, would you give him a rock? 10Or if he asked for a fish, would you give him a snake? Of course not! 11You people are so bad, but you still know how to give good things to your children. So surely your heavenly Father will give good things to those who ask him.

A Very Important Rule

12"Do for others what you would want them to do for you. This is the meaning of the Law of Moses* and the teaching of the prophets.*

The Way to Heaven and the Way to Hell
(Lk. 13:24)

13"You can enter true life only through the narrow gate. The gate to hell is very wide, and there is plenty of room on the road that leads there. Many people go that way. 14But the gate that opens the way to true life is narrow. And the road that leads there is hard to follow. Only a few people find it.

What People Do Shows What They Are
(Lk. 6:43–44; 13:25–27)

15"Be careful of false prophets.* They come to you and look gentle like sheep. But they are really dangerous like wolves. 16You will know these people because of what they do. Good things don't come from people who are bad, just as grapes don't come from thornbushes, and figs don't come from thorny weeds. 17In the same way, every good tree produces good fruit, and bad trees produce bad fruit. 18A good tree cannot produce bad fruit, and a bad tree cannot produce good fruit. 19Every tree that does not produce good fruit is cut down and thrown into the fire. 20You will know these false people by what they do.*a*

21"Not everyone who calls me Lord will enter God's kingdom.* The only people who will enter are those who do what my Father in heaven wants. 22On that last Day* many will call me Lord. They will say, 'Lord, Lord, by the power of your name we spoke for God. And by your name we forced out demons* and did many miracles.*' 23Then I will tell those people clearly, 'Get away from me, you people who do wrong. I never knew you.'

Two Kinds of People
(Lk. 6:47–49)

24"Whoever hears these teachings of mine and obeys them is like a wise man who built his house on rock. 25It rained hard, the floods came, and the winds blew and beat against that house. But it did not fall because it was built on rock.

26"Whoever hears these teachings of mine and does not obey them is like a foolish man who built his house on sand. 27It rained hard, the floods came, and the winds blew and beat against that house. And it fell with a loud crash."

28When Jesus finished speaking, the people were amazed at his teaching. 29He did not teach like their teachers of the law. He taught like someone who has authority.

Jesus Heals a Sick Man
(Mk. 1:40–45; Lk. 5:12–16)

8 1Jesus came down from the hill, and a large crowd followed him. 2Then a man sick with leprosy* came to him. The man bowed down before Jesus and said, "Lord, you have the power to heal me if you want."

3Jesus touched the man. He said, "I want to heal you. Be healed!" Immediately the man was healed from his leprosy. 4Then Jesus said to him, "Don't tell anyone about what happened. But go and let the priest look at you.*b* And offer the gift that Moses* commanded for people who are made well. This will show everyone that you are healed."

Jesus Heals an Officer's Servant
(Lk. 7:1–10; Jn. 4:43–54)

5Jesus went to the city of Capernaum.* When he entered the city, an army officer* came to him and begged for help. 6The officer said, "Lord, my servant is very sick at home in bed. He can't move his body and has much pain."

7Jesus said to the officer, "I will go and heal him."

8The officer answered, "Lord, I am not good enough for you to come into my house. You need only to give the order, and my servant will be healed. 9I know this, because I understand authority. There are people who have authority over me, and I have soldiers under my authority. I tell one soldier, 'Go,' and he goes. I tell another soldier, 'Come,' and he comes. I say to my servant, 'Do this,' and my servant obeys me."

10When Jesus heard this, he was amazed. He said to those who were with him, "The truth is, this man has more faith than anyone I have found, even in Israel.* 11Many people will come from the east and from the west. These people will sit and eat with Abraham,* Isaac,* and Jacob* in God's kingdom.* 12And those who should have the kingdom will be thrown out. They will be thrown outside into

---

a7:20 by what they do Literally, "by their fruits."

b8:4 let the priest look at you The Law of Moses said a priest must decide when a person with leprosy was well.

the darkness, where people will cry and grind their teeth with pain."

13Then Jesus said to the officer, "Go home. Your servant will be healed the way you believed he would." Right then his servant was healed.

Jesus Heals Many People
(Mk. 1:29–34; Lk. 4:38–41)

14Jesus went to Peter's house. He saw that Peter's mother-in-law was in bed with a high fever. 15He touched her hand, and the fever left her. Then she stood up and began to serve him.

16That evening people brought to Jesus many people who had demons* inside them. He spoke and the demons left the people. He healed all those who were sick. 17So Jesus made clear the full meaning of what Isaiah the prophet* said:

"He took away our diseases and carried
    away our sicknesses."   *Isaiah 53:4*

Following Jesus
(Lk. 9:57–62)

18When Jesus saw the crowd around him, he told his followers to go to the other side of the lake. 19Then a teacher of the law came to him and said, "Teacher, I will follow you any place you go."

20Jesus said to him, "The foxes have holes to live in. The birds have nests. But the Son of Man* has no place to rest."

21Another of Jesus' followers said to him, "Lord, I will follow you too, but let me go and bury my father first."

22But Jesus said to him, "Follow me, and let those who are dead bury their own dead."

Jesus' Followers See His Power
(Mk. 4:35–41; Lk. 8:22–25)

23Jesus got into a boat, and his followers went with him. 24After the boat left the shore, a very bad storm began on the lake. The waves covered the boat. But Jesus was sleeping. 25The followers went to him and woke him. They said, "Lord, save us! We will drown!"

26Jesus answered, "Why are you afraid? You don't have enough faith." Then he stood up and gave a command to the wind and the water. The wind stopped, and the lake became very calm.

27The men were amazed. They said, "What kind of man is this? Even the wind and the water obey him!"

Jesus Sends Demons Out of Two Men
(Mk. 5:1–20; Lk. 8:26–39)

28Jesus arrived at the other side of the lake in the country of the Gadarene*a* people. There, two men who had demons* inside them came

to him. They lived in the burial caves and were so dangerous that no one could use the road by those caves. 29They came to Jesus and shouted, "What do you want with us, Son of God? Did you come here to punish us before the right time?"

30Near that place there was a large herd of pigs feeding. 31The demons begged Jesus, "If you make us leave these men, please send us into that herd of pigs."

32Jesus said to them, "Go!" So the demons left the men and went into the pigs. Then the whole herd of pigs ran down the hill into the lake, and all were drowned. 33The men who had the work of caring for the pigs ran away. They went into town and told the people everything that happened, especially about the men who had the demons. 34Then the whole town went out to see Jesus. When the people saw him, they begged him to leave their area.

Jesus Heals a Crippled Man
(Mk. 2:1–12; Lk. 5:17–26)

9 1Jesus got into a boat and went back across the lake to his own town. 2Some people brought to him a man who was paralyzed and was lying on a mat. Jesus saw that these people had much faith. So he said to the paralyzed man, "Young man, you will be glad to hear this. Your sins are forgiven."

3Some of the teachers of the law heard what Jesus said. They said to themselves, "What an insult to God for this man to say that!"

4Jesus knew what they were thinking. So he said, "Why are you thinking such evil thoughts? 5–6The Son of Man* has power on earth to forgive sins. But how can I prove this to you? Maybe you are thinking it was easy for me to say, 'Your sins are forgiven.' There's no proof that it really happened. But what if I say to the man, 'Stand up and walk'? Then you will be able to see that I really have this power." So Jesus said to the paralyzed man, "Stand up. Take your mat and go home."

7The man stood up and went home. 8The people saw this and they were amazed. They praised God for letting someone have such power.

Matthew (Levi) Follows Jesus
(Mk. 2:13–17; Lk. 5:27–32)

9When Jesus was leaving, he saw a man named Matthew sitting at the place for collecting taxes. Jesus said to him, "Follow me." So he got up and followed Jesus.

10Jesus ate dinner at Matthew's house. Many tax collectors* and others with bad reputations came and ate with him and his followers. 11The Pharisees* saw that Jesus was eating with these people. They asked his followers, "Why does your teacher eat with tax collectors and other sinners?"

12Jesus heard them say this. So he said to them, "It is the sick people who need a doctor,

---

*a***8:28** *Gadarene* From Gadara, an area southeast of Lake Galilee.

not those who are healthy. 13You need to go and learn what this Scripture means: 'I don't want animal sacrifices; I want you to show kindness to people.'*a I did not come to invite good people. I came to invite sinners."

Jesus Is Not Like Other Religious Leaders
(Mk. 2:18–22; Lk. 5:33–39)

14Then the followers of John* came to Jesus and said, "We and the Pharisees* fast* often, but your followers don't ever fast. Why?"

15Jesus answered, "At a wedding the friends of the bridegroom* are not sad while he is with them. They cannot fast then. But the time will come when the bridegroom will be taken from them. Then they will fast.

16"When someone sews a patch over a hole in an old coat, they never use a piece of cloth that has not already been shrunk. If they do, the patch will shrink and pull away from the coat. Then the hole will be worse. 17Also, people never pour new wine into old wineskins.* They would break, the wine would spill out, and the wineskins would be ruined. People always put new wine into new wineskins, which won't break, and the wine stays good."

Jesus Gives Life to a Dead Girl and Heals a Sick Woman
(Mk. 5:21–43; Lk. 8:40–56)

18While Jesus was still talking, a leader of the synagogue* came to him. The leader bowed down before him and said, "My daughter has just died. But if you will come and touch her with your hand, she will live again."

19So Jesus and his followers went with the man.

20On the way, there was a woman who had been bleeding for twelve years. She came close behind Jesus and touched the bottom of his coat. 21She was thinking, "If I can touch his coat, I will be healed."

22Jesus turned and saw the woman. He said, "Be happy, dear woman. You are made well because you believed." Then the woman was healed.

23Jesus continued going with the Jewish leader and went into the leader's house. He saw people there who make music for funerals. And he saw a crowd of people crying loudly. 24Jesus said, "Go away. The girl is not dead. She is only sleeping." But the people laughed at him. 25After the people were put out of the house, Jesus went into the girl's room. He held the girl's hand, and the girl stood up. 26The news about this spread all around the area.

Jesus Heals More People

27As Jesus was going away from there, two blind men followed him. They said loudly,

"Show kindness to us, Son of David.*"

28Jesus went inside, and the blind men went with him. He asked them, "Do you believe that I am able to make you see again?" They answered, "Yes, Lord, we believe."

29Then Jesus touched their eyes and said, "You believe that I can make you see again, so it will happen." 30Then the men were able to see. Jesus gave them a strong warning. He said, "Don't tell anyone about this." 31But they left and spread the news about Jesus all around that area.

32As these two men were leaving, some people brought another man to Jesus. This man could not talk because he had a demon* inside him. 33Jesus forced the demon out, and the man was able to talk. The people were amazed and said, "We have never seen anything like this in Israel.*"

34But the Pharisees* said, "The ruler of demons is the one that gives him power to force demons out."

Jesus Feels Sorry for the People

35Jesus traveled through all the towns and villages. He taught in their synagogues* and told people the Good News about God's kingdom.* He healed all kinds of diseases and sicknesses. 36Jesus saw the many people and felt sorry for them because they were worried and helpless—like sheep without a shepherd to lead them. 37Jesus said to his followers, "There is such a big harvest of people to bring in. But there are only a few workers to help harvest them. 38God owns the harvest. Ask him to send more workers to help gather his harvest."

Jesus Sends His Apostles on a Mission
(Mk. 3:13–19; 6:7–13; Lk. 6:12–16; 9:1–6)

10 1Jesus called his twelve followers together. He gave them power over evil spirits and power to heal every kind of disease and sickness. 2These are the names of the twelve apostles*:

Simon (also called Peter),
Andrew, the brother of Peter,
James, the son of Zebedee,
John, the brother of James,
3 Philip,
Bartholomew,
Thomas,
Matthew, the tax collector,*
James, the son of Alphaeus,
Thaddaeus,
4 Simon, the Zealot,*
Judas Iscariot (the one who handed Jesus over to his enemies).

5Jesus sent the twelve men out with these instructions: "Don't go to the non-Jewish people. And don't go into any town where the Samaritans* live. 6But go to the people of Israel.* They are like sheep that are lost.

---

a9:13 Quote from Hos. 6:6.

7When you go, tell them this: 'God's kingdom* is coming soon.' 8Heal the sick. Bring the dead back to life. Heal the people who have leprosy.* And force demons* out of people. I give you these powers freely, so help others freely. 9Don't carry any money with you—gold or silver or copper. 10Don't carry a bag. Take only the clothes and sandals you are wearing. And don't take a walking stick. A worker should be given what he needs.

11"When you enter a city or town, find some worthy person there and stay in his home until you leave. 12When you enter that home, say, 'Peace be with you.' 13If the people in that home welcome you, they are worthy of your peace. May they have the peace you wished for them. But if they don't welcome you, they are not worthy of your peace. Take back the peace you wished for them. 14And if the people in a home or a town refuse to welcome you or listen to you, then leave that place and shake the dust off your feet.a 15I can assure you that on the judgment day it will be worse for that town than for the people of Sodom* and Gomorrah.*

Jesus Warns About Troubles
(Mk. 13:9–13; Lk. 21:12–17)

16"Listen! I am sending you, and you will be like sheep among wolves. So be smart like snakes. But also be like doves and don't hurt anyone. 17Be careful! There are people who will arrest you and take you to be judged. They will whip you in their synagogues.* 18You will be taken to stand before governors and kings. People will do this to you because you follow me. You will tell about me to those kings and governors and to the non-Jewish people. 19When you are arrested, don't worry about what to say or how you should say it. At that time you will be given the words to say. 20It will not really be you speaking; the Spirit of your Father will be speaking through you.

21"Brothers will turn against their own brothers and hand them over to be killed. Fathers will hand over their own children to be killed. Children will fight against their own parents and will have them killed. 22Everyone will hate you because you follow me. But the one who remains faithful to the end will be saved. 23When you are treated badly in one city, go to another city. I promise you that you will not finish going to all the cities of Israel before the Son of Man* comes again.

24"Students are not better than their teacher. Servants are not better than their master. 25Students should be happy to be treated the same as their teacher. And servants should be happy to be treated the same

as their master. If those people call me 'the ruler of demons,' and I am the head of the family,b then it is even more certain that they will insult you, the members of the family!

Fear God, Not People
(Lk. 12:2–7)

26"So don't be afraid of those people. Everything that is hidden will be shown. Everything that is secret will be made known. 27I tell you all this secretly,c but I want you to tell it publicly.d Whatever I tell you privately,e you should shout for everyone to hear.f

28"Don't be afraid of people. They can kill the body, but they cannot kill the soul. The only one you should fear is God, the one who can send the body and the soul to be destroyed in hell. 29When birds are sold, two small birds cost only a penny. But not even one of those little birds can die without your Father knowing it. 30God even knows how many hairs are on your head. 31So don't be afraid. You are worth more than a whole flock of birds.

Don't Be Ashamed of Your Faith
(Lk. 12:8–9)

32"If you stand before others and are willing to say you believe in me, then I will tell my Father in heaven that you belong to me. 33But if you stand before others and say you do not believe in me, then I will tell my Father in heaven that you do not belong to me.

Following Jesus May Bring You Trouble
(Lk. 12:51–53; 14:26–27)

34"Do not think that I have come to bring peace to the earth. I did not come to bring peace. I came to bring trouble.g 35I have come to make this happen:

'A son will turn against his father.
A daughter will turn against her mother.
A daughter-in-law will turn against her
    mother-in-law.
36 Even members of your own family will be
    your enemies.'   *Micah 7:6*

37"Those who love their father or mother more than they love me are not worthy of me. And those who love their son or daughter more than they love me are not worthy of me. 38Those who will not accept the cross* that is given to them when they follow me are not worthy of me. 39Those who try to keep the life they have will lose it. But those who give up their life for me will find true life.

---

a10:14 *shake the dust off your feet* A warning. It would show that they were finished talking to these people.

b10:25 *call me … family* Literally, "call the head of the household Beelzebul." See verse 9:34.
c10:27 *secretly* Literally, "in the dark."
d10:27 *publicly* Literally, "in the light."
e10:27 *privately* Literally, "in the ear."
f10:27 *for everyone to hear* Literally, "on the housetops."
g10:34 *trouble* Literally, "a sword."

God Will Bless Those Who Welcome You
(Mk. 9:41)

40"Whoever accepts you also accepts me. And whoever accepts me accepts the one who sent me. 41Whoever accepts a prophet* because he is a prophet will get the same reward a prophet gets. And whoever accepts a godly person just because that person is godly will get the same reward a godly person gets. 42Whoever helps any of these little ones because they are my followers will definitely get a reward, even if they only give them a cup of cold water."

John Sends Men to Ask Jesus a Question
(Lk. 7:18–35)

11 ¹When Jesus finished these instructions for his twelve followers, he left there. He went to the towns in Galilee to teach the people and tell them God's message.

2When John was in prison, he heard about the things that were happening—things the Christ* would do. So he sent some of his followers to Jesus. 3They asked him, "Are you the one we have been expecting, or should we wait for someone else?"

4Jesus answered, "Go tell John what you have heard and seen: 5The blind can see. The crippled can walk. People with leprosy* are healed. The deaf can hear. The dead are brought back to life. And the Good News* is being told to the poor. 6Great blessings belong to those who don't have a problem accepting me."

7When John's followers left, Jesus began talking to the people about John. He said, "What did you people go out to the desert to see? Someone who is weak, like a stem of grass[a] blowing in the wind? 8Really, what did you expect to see? Someone dressed in fine clothes? Of course not. People who wear fine clothes are all in kings' palaces. 9So what did you go out to see? A prophet*? Yes, John is a prophet. But I tell you, he is more than that. 10This Scripture* was written about him:

'Listen! I will send my messenger ahead of
    you.
He will prepare the way for you.'
                                    Malachi 3:1

11"The truth is that John the Baptizer* is greater than anyone who has ever come into this world. But even the least important person in God's kingdom* is greater than John. 12Since the time John the Baptizer came until now, God's kingdom has been going forward strongly.[b] And people have been trying to take control of it by force. 13Before John came, the Law of Moses* and all the prophets told about

the things that would happen. 14And if you believe what they said, then John is Elijah.[c] He is the one they said would come. 15You people who hear me, listen!

16"What can I say about the people who live today? What are they like? The people today are like children sitting in the marketplace. One group of children calls to the other group,

17 'We played flute music for you,
        but you did not dance;
    we sang a funeral song,
        but you were not sad.'

18Why do I say people are like that? Because John came, not eating like other people or drinking wine, and people say, 'He has a demon* inside him.' 19The Son of Man* came eating and drinking, and people say, 'Look at him! He eats too much and drinks too much wine. He's a friend of tax collectors* and other sinners.' But wisdom is shown to be right by what it does."

Jesus Warns People Who Refuse to Believe
(Lk. 10:13–15)

20Then Jesus criticized the cities where he did most of his miracles.* He criticized these cities because the people there did not change their lives and stop sinning. 21Jesus said, "It will be bad for you Chorazin*! It will be bad for you Bethsaida*! I did many miracles in you. If these same miracles had happened in Tyre* and Sidon,* the people there would have changed their lives a long time ago. They would have worn sackcloth* and put ashes on themselves to show that they were sorry for their sins. 22But I tell you, on the day of judgment it will be worse for you than for Tyre and Sidon.

23"And you, Capernaum,* will you be lifted up to heaven? No! You will be thrown down to the place of death. I did many miracles in you. If these same miracles had happened in Sodom,* the people there would have stopped sinning, and it would still be a city today. 24But I tell you, it will be worse for you in the day of judgment than for Sodom."

Jesus Offers Rest to His People
(Lk. 10:21–22)

25Then Jesus said, "I praise you, Father, Lord of heaven and earth. I am thankful that you have hidden these things from those who are so wise and so smart. But you have shown them to people who are like little children. 26Yes, Father, you did this because it's what you really wanted to do.

27"My Father has given me everything. No one knows the Son—only the Father knows the Son. And no one knows the Father—only

---

[a]11:7 *stem of grass* Literally, "reed."
[b]11:12 *has been … strongly* Or "has suffered violence."
[c]11:14 *Elijah* See Mal. 4:5–6.

the Son knows the Father. And the only people who will know about the Father are those the Son chooses to tell.

28"Come to me all of you who are tired from the heavy burden you have been forced to carry. I will give you rest. 29Accept my teaching.[a] Learn from me. I am gentle and humble in spirit. And you will be able to get some rest. 30Yes, the teaching that I ask you to accept is easy. The load I give you to carry is light."

Jesus Is Lord Over the Sabbath Day
(Mk. 2:23–28; Lk. 6:1–5)

12 1About that same time, Jesus was walking through the fields of grain on a Sabbath* day. His followers were with him, and they were hungry. So they began to pick the grain and eat it. 2The Pharisees* saw this. They said to Jesus, "Look! Your followers are doing something that is against the law to do on the Sabbath day."

3Jesus said to them, "You have read what David* did when he and those with him were hungry. 4David went into God's house. He and those with him ate the bread that was offered to God. It was against the law for David or those with him to eat that bread. Only the priests were allowed to eat it. 5And you have read in the Law of Moses* that on every Sabbath day the priests at the Temple* break the law about the Sabbath day. But they are not wrong for doing that. 6I tell you that there is something here that is greater than the Temple. 7The Scriptures* say, 'I don't want animal sacrifices; I want you to show kindness to people.'[b] You don't really know what that means. If you understood it, you would not judge those who have done nothing wrong.

8"The Son of Man* is Lord over the Sabbath day."

Jesus Heals a Man on the Sabbath Day
(Mk. 3:1–6; Lk. 6:6–11)

9Jesus went from there to their synagogue.* 10In the synagogue there was a man with a crippled hand. Some Jews there were looking for a reason to accuse Jesus of doing wrong. So they asked him, "Is it right to heal on the Sabbath* day?"[c]

11Jesus answered, "If any of you has a sheep and it falls into a ditch on the Sabbath day, you will take the sheep and help it out of the ditch. 12Surely a man is more important than a sheep. So it is right to do good on the Sabbath day."

13Then Jesus said to the man with the crippled hand, "Hold out your hand." The man held out his hand, and it became well again, the same as the other hand. 14But the Pharisees* left and made plans to kill Jesus.

Jesus Is God's Chosen Servant

15Jesus knew what the Pharisees* were planning. So he left that place, and many people followed him. He healed all who were sick, 16but he warned them not to tell others who he was. 17This was to give full meaning to what Isaiah the prophet* said when he spoke for God:

18"Here is my servant,
　the one I have chosen.
He is the one I love,
　and I am very pleased with him.
I will fill him with my Spirit,*
　and he will bring justice to the nations.
19 He will not argue or shout;
　no one will hear his voice in the streets.
20 He will not break off even a bent stem of
　grass.[d]
He will not put out even the weakest
　flame.
He will not give up until he has made
　justice victorious.
21 All people will hope in him." *Isaiah 42:1–4*

Jesus' Power Is From God
(Mk. 3:20–30; Lk. 11:14–23; 12:10)

22Then some people brought a man to Jesus. This man was blind and could not talk, because he had a demon* inside him. Jesus healed the man, and he could talk and see. 23All the people were amazed at what Jesus did. They said, "Maybe he is the promised Son of David*!"

24When the Pharisees* heard this, they said, "This man uses the power of Satan[e] to force demons out of people. Satan is the ruler of demons."

25Jesus knew what the Pharisees were thinking. So he said to them, "Every kingdom that fights against itself will be destroyed. And every city or family that is divided against itself will not survive. 26So if Satan* forces out his own demons,[f] then he is fighting against himself, and his kingdom will not survive. 27You say that I use the power of Satan to force out demons. If that is true, then what power do your people use when they force out demons? So your own people will prove that you are wrong. 28But I use the power of God's Spirit to force out demons, and this shows that God's kingdom* has come to you. 29Whoever wants to enter a strong man's house and steal his things must first tie him up. Then they can steal the things from his

---

[a]11:29 *Accept my teaching* Literally, "Take my yoke upon you." A yoke was put on the neck of a work animal for pulling a load. It was a Jewish symbol for the law. See Acts 15:10; Gal. 5:1.
[b]12:7 Quote from Hos. 6:6.
[c]12:10 *"Is it right ... day"* It was against Jewish law to work on the Sabbath day.

[d]12:20 *stem of grass* Literally, "reed."
[e]12:24 *Satan* Literally, "Beelzebul" (the devil). Also in verse 27.
[f]12:26 *if Satan ... demons* Literally, "if Satan forces out Satan."

house. ³⁰Whoever is not with me is against me. And anyone who does not work with me is working against me.

³¹"So I tell you, people can be forgiven for every sinful thing they do and for every bad thing they say against God. But anyone who speaks against the Holy Spirit* will not be forgiven. ³²You can even speak against the Son of Man* and be forgiven. But anyone who speaks against the Holy Spirit will never be forgiven—not now or in the future.

What You Do Shows What You Are
(Lk. 6:43–45)

³³"If you want good fruit, you must make the tree good. If your tree is not good, it will have bad fruit. A tree is known by the kind of fruit it produces. ³⁴You snakes! You are so evil. How can you say anything good? What people say with their mouths comes from what fills their hearts. ³⁵Those who are good have good things saved in their hearts. That's why they say good things. But those who are evil have hearts full of evil, and that's why they say things that are evil. ³⁶I tell you that everyone will have to answer for all the careless things they have said. This will happen on the day of judgment. ³⁷Your words will be used to judge you. What you have said will show whether you are right or whether you are guilty."

Some People Doubt Jesus' Authority
(Mk. 8:11–12; Lk. 11:29–32)

³⁸Then some of the Pharisees* and teachers of the law answered Jesus. They said, "Teacher, we want to see you do a miracle* as a sign from God."

³⁹Jesus answered, "Evil and sinful people are the ones who want to see a miracle as a sign. But no miracle will be done to prove anything to them. The only sign will be the miracle that happened to the prophet* Jonah.ᵃ ⁴⁰Jonah was in the stomach of the big fish for three days and three nights. In the same way, the Son of Man* will be in the grave three days and three nights. ⁴¹On the judgment day, you people who live now will be compared with the people from Nineveh,ᵇ and they will be witnesses who show how guilty you are. Why do I say this? Because when Jonah preached to those people, they changed their lives. And you are listening to someone greater than Jonah, but you refuse to change!

⁴²"On the judgment day, you people who live now will also be compared with the Queen of the South,ᶜ and she will be a witness who shows how guilty you are. I say this because she traveled from far, far away to listen to Solomon's wise teaching. And I tell you that someone greater than Solomon is right here, but you won't listen!

The Danger of Emptiness
(Lk. 11:24–26)

⁴³"When an evil spirit comes out of a person, it travels through dry places looking for a place to rest, but it finds none. ⁴⁴So it says, 'I will go back to the home I left.' When it comes back, it finds that home still empty. It is all neat and clean. ⁴⁵Then the evil spirit goes out and brings seven other spirits more evil than itself. They all go and live there, and that person has even more trouble than before. It is the same way with the evil people who live today."

Jesus' Followers Are His True Family
(Mk. 3:31–35; Lk. 8:19–21)

⁴⁶While Jesus was talking to the people, his mother and brothers stood outside. They wanted to talk to him. ⁴⁷Someone told him, "Your mother and brothers are waiting for you outside. They want to talk to you."

⁴⁸Jesus answered, "Who is my mother? Who are my brothers?" ⁴⁹Then he pointed to his followers and said, "See! These people are my mother and my brothers. ⁵⁰My true brother and sister and mother is anyone who does what my Father in heaven wants."

A Story About a Farmer Sowing Seed
(Mk. 4:1–9; Lk. 8:4–8)

13 ¹That same day Jesus went out of the house and sat by the lake. ²A large crowd gathered around him. So he got into a boat and sat down. All the people stayed on the shore. ³Then Jesus used stories to teach them many things. He told them this story:

"A farmer went out to sow seed. ⁴While he was scattering the seed, some of it fell by the road. The birds came and ate all that seed. ⁵Other seed fell on rocky ground, where there was not enough dirt. It grew very fast there, because the soil was not deep. ⁶But when the sun rose, it burned the plants. The plants died because they did not have deep roots. ⁷Some other seed fell among thorny weeds. The weeds grew and stopped the good plants from growing. ⁸But some of the seed fell on good ground. There it grew and made grain. Some plants made 100 times more grain, some 60 times more, and some 30 times more. ⁹You people who hear me, listen!"

Why Jesus Used Stories to Teach
(Mk. 4:10–12; Lk. 8:9–10)

¹⁰The followers came to Jesus and asked, "Why do you use these stories to teach the people?"

¹¹Jesus answered, "Only you can know the secret truths about God's kingdom.* Those

---

ᵃ**12:39 Jonah** The story of Jonah is found in the Old Testament book of Jonah.
ᵇ**12:41 Nineveh** City where Jonah preached. See Jonah 3.
ᶜ**12:42 Queen of the South** Or "Queen of Sheba." She traveled about 1000 miles (1600 km) to learn God's wisdom from Solomon. See 1 Kings 10:1–13.

other people cannot know these secret truths. 12The people who have some understanding will be given more. And they will have even more than they need. But those who do not have much understanding will lose even the little understanding that they have. 13This is why I use these stories to teach the people: They see, but they don't really see. They hear, but they don't really hear or understand. 14So they show that what Isaiah said about them is true:

'You people will listen and listen,
    but you will not understand.
You will look and look,
    but you will not really see.
15 Yes, the minds of these people are now
    closed.
    They have ears, but they don't listen.
    They have eyes, but they refuse to see.
If their minds were not closed,
    they might see with their eyes;
    they might hear with their ears;
    they might understand with their minds.
Then they might turn back to me and be
    healed.'   Isaiah 6:9–10

16But God has blessed you. You understand what you see with your eyes. And you understand what you hear with your ears. 17I can assure you, many prophets* and godly people wanted to see what you now see. But they did not see it. And many prophets and godly people wanted to hear what you now hear. But they did not hear it.

Jesus Explains the Story About Seed
(Mk. 4:13–20; Lk. 8:11–15)

18"So listen to the meaning of that story about the farmer:

19"What about the seed that fell by the path? That is like the people who hear the teaching about God's kingdom* but do not understand it. The Evil One* comes and takes away what was planted in their hearts.

20"And what about the seed that fell on rocky ground? That is like the people who hear the teaching and quickly and gladly accept it. 21But they do not let the teaching go deep into their lives. They keep it only a short time. As soon as trouble or persecution* comes because of the teaching they accepted, they give up.

22"And what about the seed that fell among the thorny weeds? That is like the people who hear the teaching but let worries about this life and love for money stop it from growing. So it does not produce a crop in their lives.

23"But what about the seed that fell on the good ground? That is like the people who hear the teaching and understand it. They grow and produce a good crop, sometimes 100 times more, sometimes 60 times more, and sometimes 30 times more."

A Story About Wheat and Weeds

24Then Jesus used another story to teach them. Jesus said, "God's kingdom* is like a man who planted good seed in his field. 25That night, while everyone was asleep, the man's enemy came and planted weeds among the wheat and then left. 26Later, the wheat grew, and heads of grain grew on the plants. But at the same time the weeds also grew. 27Then the man's servants came to him and said, 'You planted good seed in your field. Where did the weeds come from?'

28"The man answered, 'An enemy planted weeds.'

"The servants asked, 'Do you want us to go and pull up the weeds?'

29"He answered, 'No, because when you pull up the weeds, you might also pull up the wheat. 30Let the weeds and the wheat grow together until the harvest time. At the harvest time I will tell the workers this: First, gather the weeds and tie them together to be burned. Then gather the wheat and bring it to my barn.'"

What Is God's Kingdom Like?
(Mk. 4:30–34; Lk. 13:18–21)

31Then Jesus told the people another story: "God's kingdom* is like a mustard seed that a man plants in his field. 32It is the smallest of all seeds. But when it grows, it is the largest of all garden plants. It becomes a tree big enough for the birds to come and make nests in its branches."

33Then Jesus told them another story: "God's kingdom is like yeast that a woman mixes into a big bowl of flour to make bread. The yeast makes all the dough rise."

34Jesus used stories to tell all these things to the people. He always used stories to teach them. 35This was to make clear the full meaning of what the prophet* said:

"I will speak using stories;
    I will tell things that have been secrets
    since the world was made."   Psalm 78:2

Jesus Explains a Hard Story

36Then Jesus left the people and went into the house. His followers came to him and said, "Explain to us the meaning of the story about the weeds in the field."

37He answered, "The man who planted the good seed in the field is the Son of Man.* 38The field is the world. The good seed are the people in God's kingdom.* The weeds are the people who belong to the Evil One.* 39And the enemy who planted the bad seed is the devil. The harvest is the end of time. And the workers who gather are God's angels.

40"The weeds are pulled up and burned in the fire. It will be the same at the end of time. 41The Son of Man will send his angels, and they will find the people who cause sin and all those who do evil. The angels will take those people out of his kingdom.* 42They will throw them into the place of fire. There the people will be crying and grinding their teeth with pain. 43Then the godly people will shine like the sun. They will be in the kingdom of their Father. You people who hear me, listen!

Stories About a Treasure and a Pearl

44"God's kingdom* is like a treasure hidden in a field. One day a man found the treasure. He hid it again and was so happy that he went and sold everything he owned and bought the field.

45"Also, God's kingdom is like a merchant* looking for fine pearls. 46One day he found a very fine pearl. He went and sold everything he had to buy it.

A Story About a Fishing Net

47"Also, God's kingdom* is like a net that was put into the lake. The net caught many different kinds of fish. 48It was full, so the fishermen pulled it to the shore. They sat down and put all the good fish in baskets. Then they threw away the bad fish. 49It will be the same at the end of time. The angels will come and separate the evil people from the godly people. 50They will throw the evil people into the place of fire. There the people will cry and grind their teeth with pain."

51Then Jesus asked his followers, "Do you understand all these things?"

They said, "Yes, we understand."

52Then Jesus said to the followers, "So every teacher of the law who has learned about God's kingdom has some new things to teach. He is like the owner of a house. He has new things and old things saved in that house. And he brings out the new with the old."

Jesus Goes to His Hometown
(Mk. 6:1–6; Lk. 4:16–30)

53When Jesus finished teaching with these stories, he left there. 54He went to the town where he grew up. He taught the people in the synagogue,* and they were amazed. They said, "Where did this man get such wisdom and this power to do miracles*? 55Isn't he just the son of the carpenter we know? Isn't his mother's name Mary, and aren't his brothers James, Joseph, Simon, and Judas? 56And don't all his sisters still live here in town? How is he able to do these things?" 57So they had a problem accepting him.

But Jesus said to them, "People everywhere give honor to a prophet,* but in his own town or in his own home a prophet does not get any honor." 58Jesus did not do many miracles there, because the people did not believe in him.

Herod Thinks Jesus Is John the Baptizer
(Mk. 6:14–29; Lk. 9:7–9)

14 1About that time, Herod,* the ruler of Galilee, heard what the people were saying about Jesus. 2So he said to his servants,

"This man is really John the Baptizer.* He must have risen from death, and that is why he can do these miracles.*"

How John the Baptizer Was Killed

3Before this time, Herod* had arrested John.* He had him chained and put in prison. He arrested John because of Herodias, the wife of Philip, Herod's brother. 4John had told him, "It is not right for you to be married to Herodias." 5Herod wanted to kill him, but he was afraid of the people. They believed that John was a prophet.*

6On Herod's birthday, the daughter of Herodias danced for him and his group. Herod was very pleased with her. 7So he promised that he would give her anything she wanted. 8Herodias told her daughter what to ask for. So she said to Herod, "Give me the head of John the Baptizer* here on this plate."

9King Herod was very sad. But he had promised to give the daughter anything she wanted. And the people eating with Herod had heard his promise. So he ordered what she asked to be done. 10He sent men to the prison, where they cut off John's head. 11And the men brought John's head on a plate and gave it to the girl. Then she took the head to her mother, Herodias. 12John's followers came and got his body and buried it. Then they went and told Jesus what happened.

Jesus Feeds More Than 5000
(Mk. 6:30–44; Lk. 9:10–17; Jn. 6:1–14)

13When Jesus heard what happened to John,* he left in a boat. He went alone to a place where no one lived. But the people heard that Jesus had left. So they left their towns and followed him. They went by land to the same place he went. 14When Jesus got out of the boat, he saw a large crowd of people. He felt sorry for them, and he healed the ones who were sick.

15Late that afternoon, the followers came to Jesus and said, "No one lives in this place. And it is already late. Send the people away so they can go to the towns and buy food for themselves."

16Jesus said, "The people don't need to go away. You give them some food to eat."

17The followers answered, "But we have only five loaves of bread and two fish."

18Jesus said, "Bring the bread and the fish to me." 19Then he told the people to sit down on the grass. He took the five loaves of bread and the two fish. He looked into the sky and thanked God for the food. Then he broke the bread into pieces, which he gave to the followers, and they gave the food to the people. 20Everyone ate until they were full. When they finished eating, the followers filled twelve baskets with the pieces of food that were not eaten. 21There were about 5000 men there who ate. There were also women and children who ate.

Jesus Walks on Water
(Mk. 6:45–52; Jn. 6:16–21)

22Then Jesus made the followers get into the boat. He told them to go to the other side of the lake. He said he would come later. He stayed there to tell everyone they could go home. 23After Jesus said goodbye to the people, he went up into the hills by himself to pray. It was late, and he was there alone. 24By this time the boat was already a long way from shore. Since the wind was blowing against it, the boat was having trouble because of the waves.

25Between three and six o'clock in the morning, Jesus' followers were still in the boat. Jesus came to them. He was walking on the water. 26When they saw him walking on the water, it scared them. "It's a ghost!" they said, screaming in fear.

27But Jesus quickly spoke to them. He said, "Don't worry! It's me! Don't be afraid."

28Peter said, "Lord, if that is really you, tell me to come to you on the water."

29Jesus said, "Come, Peter."

Then Peter left the boat and walked on the water to Jesus. 30But while Peter was walking on the water, he saw the wind and the waves. He was afraid and began sinking into the water. He shouted, "Lord, save me!"

31Then Jesus caught Peter with his hand. He said, "Your faith is small. Why did you doubt?"

32After Peter and Jesus were in the boat, the wind stopped. 33Then the followers in the boat worshiped Jesus and said, "You really are the Son of God."

Jesus Heals Many Sick People
(Mk. 6:53–56)

34After they crossed the lake, they came to the shore at Gennesaret. 35Some men there saw Jesus and knew who he was. So they sent word to the other people throughout that area that Jesus had come. The people brought all their sick people to him. 36They begged Jesus to let them only touch the edge of his coat to be healed. And all the sick people who touched his coat were healed.

God's Law and Human Traditions
(Mk. 7:1–23)

15 1Then some Pharisees* and teachers of the law came to Jesus. They came from Jerusalem and asked him, 2"Why do your followers not obey the traditions we have from our great leaders who lived long ago? Your followers don't wash their hands before they eat!"

3Jesus answered, "And why do you refuse to obey God's command so that you can follow those traditions you have? 4God said, 'You must respect your father and mother.'*a And God also said, 'Whoever says anything bad to

their father or mother must be killed.'*b 5But you teach that a person can say to their father or mother, 'I have something I could use to help you. But I will not use it for you. I will give it to God.' 6You are teaching them not to respect their father. So you are teaching that it is not important to do what God said. You think it is more important to follow those traditions you have. 7You are hypocrites*! Isaiah was right when he spoke for God about you:

8 'These people honor me with their words,
    but I am not really important to them.
9 Their worship of me is worthless.
   ' The things they teach are only human
    rules.'"   *Isaiah 29:13*

10Jesus called the people to him. He said, "Listen and understand what I am saying. 11It is not what people put in their mouth that makes them wrong.*c It is what comes out of their mouth that makes them wrong."

12Then the followers came to Jesus and asked, "Do you know that the Pharisees are upset about what you said?"

13Jesus answered, "Every plant that my Father in heaven has not planted will be pulled up by the roots. 14Stay away from the Pharisees. They lead the people, but they are like blind men leading other blind men. And if a blind man leads another blind man, both of them will fall into a ditch."

15Peter said, "Explain to us what you said earlier to the people."

16Jesus said, "Do you still have trouble understanding? 17Surely you know that all the food that enters the mouth goes into the stomach. Then it goes out of the body. 18But the bad things people say with their mouth come from the way they think. And that's what can make people wrong. 19All these bad things begin in the mind: evil thoughts, murder, adultery,* sexual sins, stealing, lying, and insulting people. 20These are the things that make people wrong. Eating without washing their hands will never make people unacceptable to God."

Jesus Helps a Non-Jewish Woman
(Mk. 7:24–30)

21Jesus went from there to the area of Tyre and Sidon. 22A Canaanite woman from that area came out and began shouting, "Lord, Son of David,* please help me! My daughter has a demon* inside her, and she is suffering very much."

23But Jesus did not answer her. So the followers came to him and said, "Tell her to go away. She keeps crying out and will not leave us alone."

24Jesus answered, "God sent me only to the lost people*d of Israel.*"

---

*a15:4 Quote from Ex. 20:12; Deut. 5:16.
*b15:4 Quote from Ex. 21:17.
*c15:11 *wrong* Literally, "unclean" or "not pure," meaning unacceptable to God. Also in verse 18.
*d15:24 *people* Literally, "sheep."

²⁵Then the woman came over to Jesus and bowed before him. She said, "Lord, help me!"

²⁶He answered her with this saying: "It is not right to take the children's bread and give it to the dogs."

²⁷The woman said, "Yes, Lord, but even the dogs eat the pieces of food that fall from their master's table."

²⁸Then Jesus answered, "Woman, you have great faith! You will get what you asked for." And right then the woman's daughter was healed.

Jesus Heals Many People

²⁹Then Jesus went from there to the shore of Lake Galilee. He went up on a hill and sat down.

³⁰A large crowd of people came to him. They brought many other sick people and put them before him. There were people who could not walk, people who were blind, crippled, or deaf, and many others. Jesus healed them all. ³¹People were amazed when they saw that those who could not speak were now able to speak. Crippled people were made strong. Those who could not walk were now able to walk. The blind were able to see. Everyone thanked the God of Israel* for this.

Jesus Feeds More Than 4000
(Mk. 8:1–10)

³²Jesus called his followers to him and said, "I feel sorry for these people. They have been with me three days, and now they have nothing to eat. I don't want to send them away hungry. They might faint while going home."

³³The followers asked Jesus, "Where can we get enough bread to feed all these people? We are a long way from any town."

³⁴Jesus asked, "How many loaves of bread do you have?"

They answered, "We have seven loaves of bread and a few small fish."

³⁵Jesus told the people to sit on the ground. ³⁶He took the seven loaves of bread and the fish. Then he gave thanks to God for the food. He broke the bread into pieces, which he gave to the followers, and they gave the food to the people. ³⁷All the people ate until they were full. After this, the followers filled seven baskets with the pieces of food that were not eaten. ³⁸There were about 4000 men there who ate. There were also some women and children. ³⁹After they all ate, Jesus told the people they could go home. He got into the boat and went to the area of Magadan.

Some People Doubt Jesus' Authority
(Mk. 8:11–13; Lk. 12:54–56)

16 ¹The Pharisees* and Sadducees* came to Jesus. They wanted to test him. So they asked him to show him a miracle* as a sign from God.

²Jesus answered, "When you people see the sunset, you know what the weather will be. If the sky is red, you say we will have good weather. ³And in the morning, if the sky is dark and red, you say that it will be a rainy day. These are signs of the weather. You see these signs in the sky and know what they mean. In the same way, you see the things that are happening now. These are also signs, but you don't know their meaning. ⁴It is the evil and sinful people who want to see a miracle as a sign from God. But no miracle will be done to prove anything to them. The only sign will be the miracle that happened to Jonah.ᵃ" Then Jesus went away from there.

Jesus' Followers Misunderstand Him
(Mk. 8:14–21)

⁵Jesus and his followers went across the lake. But the followers forgot to bring bread. ⁶Jesus said to the followers, "Be careful! Guard against the yeast* of the Pharisees* and the Sadducees.*"

⁷The followers discussed the meaning of this. They said, "Did Jesus say this because we forgot to bring bread?"

⁸Jesus knew that they were talking about this. So he asked them, "Why are you talking about not having bread? Your faith is small. ⁹Do you still not understand? Remember the five loaves of bread that fed the 5000 people and the many baskets you filled with the bread that was left? ¹⁰And remember the seven loaves of bread that fed the 4000 people and the many baskets you filled that time? ¹¹So how could you think that I am concerned about bread? I am telling you to be careful and guard against the yeast of the Pharisees and the Sadducees."

¹²Then the followers understood what Jesus meant. He was not telling them to guard against the yeast used in bread. He was telling them to guard against the teaching of the Pharisees and the Sadducees.

Peter Says Jesus Is the Christ
(Mk. 8:27–30; Lk. 9:18–21)

¹³Jesus went to the area of Caesarea Philippi. He said to his followers, "Who do people say I amᵇ?"

¹⁴They answered, "Some people say you are John the Baptizer.* Others say you are Elijah.* And some say you are Jeremiah* or one of the prophets.*"

¹⁵Then Jesus said to his followers, "And who do you say I am?"

¹⁶Simon Peter answered, "You are the Christ,* the Son of the living God."

¹⁷Jesus answered, "You are blessed, Simon son of Jonah. No one taught you that. My Father in heaven showed you who I am. ¹⁸So

---

ᵃ**16:4 Jonah** A prophet in the Old Testament. After three days in a big fish he came out alive, just as Jesus would come out from the tomb on the third day.

ᵇ**16:13 I am** Literally, "the Son of Man is."

I tell you, you are Peter.*a* And I will build my church* on this rock. The power of death*b* will not be able to defeat my church. ¹⁹I will give you the keys to God's kingdom.* When you speak judgment here on earth, that judgment will be God's judgment. When you promise forgiveness here on earth, that forgiveness will be God's forgiveness."*c*

²⁰Then Jesus warned his followers not to tell anyone he was the Christ.

Jesus Says He Must Die
(Mk. 8:31–9:1; Lk. 9:22–27)

²¹From that time Jesus began telling his followers that he must go to Jerusalem. He explained that the older Jewish leaders, the leading priests, and the teachers of the law would make him suffer many things. And he told his followers that he must be killed. Then, on the third day, he would be raised from death.

²²Peter took Jesus away from the other followers to talk to him alone. He began to criticize him. He said, "God save you from those sufferings, Lord! That will never happen to you!"

²³Then Jesus said to Peter, "Get away from me, Satan*d*! You are not helping me! You don't care about the same things God does. You care only about things that people think are important."

²⁴Then Jesus said to his followers, "If any of you want to be my follower, you must stop thinking about yourself and what you want. You must be willing to carry the cross* that is given to you for following me. ²⁵Any of you who try to save the life you have will lose it. But you who give up your life for me will find true life. ²⁶It is worth nothing for you to have the whole world if you yourself are lost. You could never pay enough to buy back your life. ²⁷The Son of Man* will come again with his Father's glory* and with his angels. And he will reward everyone for what they have done. ²⁸Believe me when I say that there are some people standing here who will see the Son of Man coming with his kingdom before they die."

Jesus Is Seen With Moses and Elijah
(Mk. 9:2–13; Lk. 9:28–36)

17 ¹Six days later, Jesus took Peter, James, and John the brother of James and went up on a high mountain. They were all alone there. ²While these followers watched him,

---

*a***16:18** *Peter* The Greek name "Peter," like the Aramaic name "Cephas," means "rock."

*b***16:18** *power of death* Literally, "gates of Hades."

*c***16:19** *When you speak … God's forgiveness* Literally, "Whatever you bind on earth will have been bound in heaven, and whatever you loose on earth will have been loosed in heaven."

*d***16:23** *Satan* Name for the devil meaning "the enemy." Jesus means that Peter was talking like Satan.

Jesus was changed. His face became bright like the sun, and his clothes became white as light. ³Then two men were there, talking with him. They were Moses* and Elijah.*

⁴Peter said to Jesus, "Lord, it is good that we are here. If you want, I will put three tents here—one for you, one for Moses, and one for Elijah."

⁵While Peter was talking, a bright cloud came over them. A voice came from the cloud and said, "This is my Son, the one I love. I am very pleased with him. Obey him!"

⁶The followers with Jesus heard this voice. They were very afraid, so they fell to the ground. ⁷But Jesus came to them and touched them. He said, "Stand up. Don't be afraid." ⁸The followers looked up, and they saw that Jesus was now alone.

⁹As Jesus and the followers were coming down the mountain, he gave them this command: "Don't tell anyone about what you saw on the mountain. Wait until the Son of Man* has been raised from death. Then you can tell people about what you saw."

¹⁰The followers asked Jesus, "Why do the teachers of the law say that Elijah must come*e* before the Christ* comes?"

¹¹Jesus answered, "They are right to say Elijah is coming. And it is true that Elijah will make all things the way they should be. ¹²But I tell you, Elijah has already come. People did not know who he was, and they treated him badly, doing whatever they wanted to do. It is the same with the Son of Man. Those same people will make the Son of Man suffer." ¹³Then the followers understood that when Jesus said Elijah, he was really talking about John the Baptizer.*

Jesus Frees a Boy From an Evil Spirit
(Mk. 9:14–29; Lk. 9:37–43a)

¹⁴Jesus and the followers went back to the people. A man came to Jesus and bowed before him. ¹⁵The man said, "Lord, be kind to my son. He suffers so much from the seizures he has. He often falls into the fire or into the water. ¹⁶I brought him to your followers, but they could not heal him."

¹⁷Jesus answered, "You people today have no faith. Your lives are so wrong! How long must I stay with you? How long must I continue to be patient with you? Bring the boy here." ¹⁸Jesus gave a strong command to the demon* inside the boy. The demon came out of the boy, and the boy was healed.

¹⁹Then the followers came to Jesus alone. They said, "We tried to force the demon out of the boy, but we could not. Why were we not able to make the demon go out?"

²⁰Jesus answered, "You were not able to make the demon go out, because your faith is too small. Believe me when I tell you, if your faith is only as big as a mustard* seed you

---

*e***17:10** *Elijah must come* See Mal. 4:5–6.

can say to this mountain, 'Move from here to there,' and it will move. You will be able to do anything." 21 *a*

Jesus Talks About His Death
(Mk. 9:30–32; Lk. 9:43b–45)

22Later, the followers met together in Galilee. Jesus said to them, "The Son of Man* will be handed over to the control of other men, 23who will kill him. But on the third day he will be raised from death." The followers were very sad to hear that Jesus would be killed.

Jesus Teaches About Paying Taxes

24Jesus and his followers went to Capernaum.* There the men who collect the two-drachma Temple* tax came to Peter and asked, "Does your teacher pay the Temple tax?"

25Peter answered, "Yes, he does."

Peter went into the house where Jesus was. Before Peter could speak, Jesus said to him, "The kings on the earth get different kinds of taxes from people. But who are those who pay the taxes? Are they the king's children? Or do other people pay the taxes? What do you think?"

26Peter answered, "The other people pay the taxes."

Jesus said, "Then the children of the king don't have to pay taxes. 27But we don't want to upset these tax collectors.* So do this: Go to the lake and fish. After you catch the first fish, open its mouth. Inside its mouth you will find a four-drachma coin. Take that coin and give it to the tax collectors. That will pay the tax for you and me."

Who Is the Greatest?
(Mk. 9:33–37; Lk. 9:46–48)

18 1About that time the followers came to Jesus and asked, "Who is the greatest in God's kingdom*?"

2Jesus called a little child to come to him. He stood the child in front of the followers. 3Then he said, "The truth is, you must change your thinking and become like little children. If you don't do this, you will never enter God's kingdom. 4The greatest person in God's kingdom is the one who makes himself humble like this child.

5"Whoever accepts a little child like this in my name is accepting me.

Jesus Warns About Causes of Sin
(Mk. 9:42–48; Lk. 17:1–2)

6"If one of these little children believes in me, and someone causes that child to sin, it will be very bad for that person. It would be better for them to have a millstone* tied around their neck and be drowned in the deep sea. 7I feel sorry for the people in the

world because of the things that make people sin. These things must happen, but it will be very bad for anyone who causes them to happen.

8"If your hand or your foot makes you sin, cut it off and throw it away. It is better for you to lose part of your body and have eternal life than to have two hands and two feet and be thrown into the fire that burns forever. 9If your eye makes you sin, take it out and throw it away. It is better for you to have only one eye and have eternal life than to have two eyes and be thrown into the fire of hell.

Jesus Uses a Story About a Lost Sheep
(Lk. 15:3–7)

10"Be careful. Don't think these little children are not important. I tell you that these children have angels in heaven. And those angels are always with my Father in heaven. 11 *b*

12"If a man has 100 sheep, but one of the sheep is lost, what will he do? He will leave the other 99 sheep on the hill and go look for the lost sheep. Right? 13And if he finds the lost sheep, he is happier about that one sheep than about the 99 sheep that were never lost. I can assure you, 14in the same way your Father in heaven does not want any of these little children to be lost.

When Someone Hurts You
(Lk. 17:3)

15"If your brother or sister in God's family does something wrong, go and tell them what they did wrong. Do this when you are alone with them. If they listen to you, then you have helped them to be your brother or sister again. 16But if they refuse to listen, go to them again and take one or two people with you. Then there will be two or three people who will be able to tell all that happened.*c* 17If they refuse to listen to them, then tell the church.* And if they refuse to listen to the church, treat them as you would treat someone who does not know God or who is a tax collector.*

18"I can assure you that when you speak judgment here on earth, it will be God's judgment. And when you promise forgiveness here on earth, it will be God's forgiveness.*d* 19To say it another way, if two of you on earth agree on anything you pray for, my Father in heaven will do what you ask. 20Yes, if two or three people are together believing in me, I am there with them."

---

*b*18:11 Some Greek copies add verse 11: "The Son of Man came to save lost people." See Lk. 19:10.
*c*18:16 *Then … happened* See Deut. 19:15.
*d*18:18 *when you speak … God's forgiveness* Literally, "whatever you bind on earth will have been bound in heaven, and whatever you loose on earth will have been loosed in heaven."

---

*a*17:21 Some Greek copies add verse 21: "But that kind of spirit comes out only with prayer and fasting."

A Story About Forgiveness

²¹Then Peter came to Jesus and asked, "Lord, when someone*ᵃ* won't stop doing wrong to me, how many times must I forgive them? Seven times?"

²²Jesus answered, "I tell you, you must forgive them more than seven times. You must continue to forgive them even if they do wrong to you seventy-seven times.*ᵇ*"

²³"So God's kingdom* is like a king who decided to collect the money his servants owed him. ²⁴The king began to collect his money. One servant owed him several thousand pounds*ᶜ* of silver. ²⁵He was not able to pay the money to his master, the king. So the master ordered that he and everything he owned be sold, even his wife and children. The money would be used to pay the king what the servant owed.

²⁶"But the servant fell on his knees and begged, 'Be patient with me. I will pay you everything I owe.' ²⁷The master felt sorry for him. So he told the servant he did not have to pay. He let him go free.

²⁸"Later, that same servant found another servant who owed him a hundred silver coins.* He grabbed him around the neck and said, 'Pay me the money you owe me!'

²⁹"The other servant fell on his knees and begged him, 'Be patient with me. I will pay you everything I owe.'

³⁰"But the first servant refused to be patient. He told the judge that the other servant owed him money, and that servant was put in jail until he could pay everything he owed. ³¹All the other servants saw what happened. They felt very sorry for the man. So they went and told their master everything that happened.

³²"Then the master called his servant in and said, 'You evil servant. You begged me to forgive your debt, and I said you did not have to pay anything! ³³So you should have given that other man who serves with you the same mercy I gave you.' ³⁴The master was very angry, so he put the servant in jail to be punished. And he had to stay in jail until he could pay everything he owed.

³⁵"This king did the same as my heavenly Father will do to you. You must forgive your brother or sister with all your heart, or my heavenly Father will not forgive you."

Jesus Teaches About Divorce
(Mk. 10:1–12)

19 ¹After Jesus said all these things, he left Galilee. He went into the area of Judea on the other side of the Jordan River. ²Many people followed him. Jesus healed the sick people there.

³Some Pharisees* came to Jesus. They tried to make him say something wrong. They asked him, "Is it right for a man to divorce his wife for any reason he chooses?"

⁴Jesus answered, "Surely you have read this in the Scriptures*: When God made the world, 'he made people male and female.'*ᵈ* ⁵And God said, 'That is why a man will leave his father and mother and be joined to his wife. And the two people will become one.'*ᵉ* ⁶So they are no longer two, but one. God has joined them together, so no one should separate them."

⁷The Pharisees asked, "Then why did Moses* give a command allowing a man to divorce his wife by writing a certificate of divorce*ᶠ*?"

⁸Jesus answered, "Moses allowed you to divorce your wives because you refused to accept God's teaching. But divorce was not allowed in the beginning. ⁹I tell you that whoever divorces his wife, except for the problem of sexual sin, and marries another woman is guilty of adultery.*"

¹⁰The followers said to Jesus, "If that is the only reason a man can divorce his wife, it is better not to marry."

¹¹He answered, "This statement is true for some, but not for everyone—only for those who have been given this gift. ¹²There are different reasons why some men don't marry.*ᵍ* Some were born without the ability to produce children. Others were made that way later in life. And others have given up marriage because of God's kingdom.* This is for anyone who is able to accept it."

Jesus Welcomes Children
(Mk. 10:13–16; Lk. 18:15–17)

¹³Then the people brought their little children to Jesus so that he could lay his hands on* them to bless them and pray for them. When the followers saw this, they told the people to stop bringing their children to him. ¹⁴But Jesus said, "Let the little children come to me. Don't stop them, because God's kingdom* belongs to people who are like these children." ¹⁵After Jesus blessed the children, he left there.

A Rich Man Refuses to Follow Jesus
(Mk. 10:17–31; Lk. 18:18–30)

¹⁶A man came to Jesus and asked, "Teacher, what good thing must I do to have eternal life?"

¹⁷Jesus answered, "Why do you ask me about what is good? Only God is good. But if

---

*ᵃ***18:21** *someone* Literally, "my brother."

*ᵇ***18:22** *seventy-seven times* Or "seventy times seven," a very large number, meaning there should be no limit to forgiveness.

*ᶜ***18:24** *several thousand pounds* Literally, "10,000 *talanta*" or "talents." A talent was about 27 to 36 kg (60 to 80 pounds) of gold, silver, or copper coins.

*ᵈ***19:4** Quote from Gen. 1:27; 5:2.

*ᵉ***19:5** Quote from Gen. 2:24.

*ᶠ***19:7** *a command ... certificate of divorce* See Deut. 24:1.

*ᵍ***19:12** *some men don't marry* Literally, "there are eunuchs."

you want to have eternal life, obey the law's commands."

[18]The man asked, "Which ones?"

Jesus answered, "'You must not murder anyone, you must not commit adultery,* you must not steal, you must not tell lies about others, [19]you must respect your father and mother,'[a] and 'love your neighbor[b] the same as you love yourself.'[c]"

[20]The young man said, "I have obeyed all these commands. What else do I need?"

[21]Jesus answered, "If you want to be perfect, then go and sell all that you own. Give the money to the poor, and you will have riches in heaven. Then come and follow me!"

[22]But when the young man heard Jesus tell him to give away his money, he was sad. He didn't want to do this, because he was very rich. So he left.

[23]Then Jesus said to his followers, "The truth is, it will be very hard for a rich person to enter God's kingdom.* [24]Yes, I tell you, it is easier for a camel to go through the eye of a needle than for a rich person to enter God's kingdom."

[25]The followers were amazed to hear this. They asked, "Then who can be saved?"

[26]Jesus looked at them and said, "This is something that people cannot do. But God can do anything."

[27]Peter said to him, "We left everything we had and followed you. So what will we have?"

[28]Jesus said to them, "When the time of the new world comes, the Son of Man* will sit on his great and glorious throne. And I can promise that you who followed me will sit on twelve thrones, and you will judge the twelve tribes of Israel.* [29]Everyone who has left houses, brothers, sisters, father, mother, children, or farms to follow me will get much more than they left. And they will have eternal life. [30]Many people who are first now will be last in the future. And many who are last now will be first in the future.

Jesus Uses a Story About Farm Workers

20 [1]"God's kingdom* is like a man who owned some land. One morning, the man went out very early to hire some people to work in his vineyard.* [2]He agreed to pay the workers one silver coin* for working that day. Then he sent them into the vineyard to work.

[3]"About nine o'clock the man went to the marketplace and saw some other people standing there. They were doing nothing. [4]So he said to them, 'If you go and work in my field, I will pay you what your work is worth.'

[a]**19:19** Quote from Ex. 20:12–16; Deut. 5:16–20.
[b]**19:19** *your neighbor* Or "others." Jesus' teaching in Lk. 10:25–37 makes clear that this includes anyone in need.
[c]**19:19** Quote from Lev. 19:18.

[5]So they went to work in the vineyard.

"The man went out again about twelve o'clock and again at three o'clock. Both times he hired some others to work in his vineyard. [6]About five o'clock the man went to the marketplace again. He saw some other people standing there. He asked them, 'Why did you stand here all day doing nothing?'

[7]"They said, 'No one gave us a job.'

"The man said to them, 'Then you can go and work in my vineyard.'

[8]"At the end of the day, the owner of the field said to the boss of all the workers, 'Call the workers and pay them all. Start by paying the last people I hired. Then pay all of them, ending with the ones I hired first.'

[9]"The workers who were hired at five o'clock came to get their pay. Each worker got one silver coin. [10]Then the workers who were hired first came to get their pay. They thought they would be paid more than the others. But each one of them also received one silver coin. [11]When they got their silver coin, they complained to the man who owned the land. [12]They said, 'Those people were hired last and worked only one hour. But you paid them the same as us. And we worked hard all day in the hot sun.'

[13]"But the man who owned the field said to one of them, 'Friend, I am being fair with you. You agreed to work for one silver coin. Right? [14]So take your pay and go. I want to give the man who was hired last the same pay I gave you. [15]I can do what I want with my own money. Why would you be jealous because I am generous?'

[16]"So those who are last now will be first in the future. And those who are first now will be last in the future."

Jesus Talks Again About His Death
(Mk. 10:32–34; Lk. 18:31–34)

[17]Jesus was going to Jerusalem. His twelve followers were with him. While they were walking, he gathered the followers together and spoke to them privately. He said to them, [18]"We are going to Jerusalem. The Son of Man* will be handed over to the leading priests and the teachers of the law, and they will say he must die. [19]They will hand him over to the foreigners, who will laugh at him and beat him with whips, and then they will kill him on a cross. But on the third day after his death, he will be raised to life again."

A Mother Asks a Special Favor
(Mk. 10:35–45)

[20]Then Zebedee's wife came to Jesus and brought her sons. She bowed before Jesus and asked him to do something for her.

[21]Jesus said, "What do you want?"

She said, "Promise that one of my sons will sit at your right side in your kingdom and the other at your left."

[22]So Jesus said to the sons, "You don't

understand what you are asking. Can you drink from the cup[a] that I must drink from?"

The sons answered, "Yes, we can!"

²³Jesus said to them, "It is true that you will drink from the cup that I drink from. But it is not for me to say who will sit at my right or my left. My Father has decided who will do that. He has prepared those places for them."

²⁴The other ten followers heard this and were angry with the two brothers. ²⁵So Jesus called the followers together. He said, "You know that the rulers of the non-Jewish people love to show their power over the people. And their important leaders love to use all their authority over the people. ²⁶But it should not be that way with you. Whoever wants to be your leader must be your servant. ²⁷Whoever wants to be first must serve the rest of you like a slave. ²⁸Do as I did: The Son of Man* did not come for people to serve him. He came to serve others and to give his life to save many people."

Jesus Heals Two Blind Men
(Mk. 10:46–52; Lk. 18:35–43)

²⁹When Jesus and his followers were leaving Jericho, a large crowd followed him. ³⁰There were two blind men sitting by the road. They heard that Jesus was coming by. So they shouted, "Lord, Son of David,* please help us!"

³¹The people there criticized the blind men and told them to be quiet. But they shouted more and more, "Lord, Son of David, please help us!"

³²Jesus stopped and said to them, "What do you want me to do for you?"

³³They answered, "Lord, we want to be able to see."

³⁴Jesus felt sorry for the blind men. He touched their eyes, and immediately they were able to see. Then they became followers of Jesus.

Jesus Enters Jerusalem Like a King
(Mk. 11:1–11; Lk. 19:28–38; Jn. 12:12–19)

21 ¹Jesus and his followers were coming closer to Jerusalem. But first they stopped at Bethphage at the hill called the Mount of Olives.* From there Jesus sent two of his followers into town. ²He said to them, "Go to the town you can see there. When you enter it, you will find a donkey with her colt. Untie them both, and bring them to me. ³If anyone asks you why you are taking the donkeys, tell them, 'The Master needs them. He will send them back soon.'"

⁴This showed the full meaning of what the prophet* said:

⁵"Tell the people of Zion,[b]
'Now your king is coming to you.
He is humble and riding on a donkey.
He is riding on a young donkey, born
　from a work animal.'"　　*Zechariah 9:9*

⁶The followers went and did what Jesus told them to do. ⁷They brought the mother donkey and the young donkey to him. They covered the donkeys with their coats, and Jesus sat on them. ⁸On the way to Jerusalem many people spread their coats on the road for Jesus. Others cut branches from the trees and spread them on the road. ⁹Some of the people were walking ahead of Jesus. Others were walking behind him. They all shouted,

"Praise[c] to the Son of David*!
'Welcome! God bless the one who
　comes in the name of the Lord!'
　　　　　　　　Psalm 118:25–26

Praise to God in heaven!"

¹⁰Then Jesus went into Jerusalem. All the people in the city were confused. They asked, "Who is this man?"

¹¹The crowds following Jesus answered, "This is Jesus. He is the prophet from the town of Nazareth in Galilee."

Jesus Goes to the Temple
(Mk. 11:15–19; Lk. 19:45–48; Jn. 2:13–22)

¹²Jesus went into the Temple* area. He threw out all those who were selling and buying things there. He turned over the tables that belonged to those who were exchanging different kinds of money. And he turned over the benches of those who were selling doves. ¹³Jesus said to them, "The Scriptures* say, 'My Temple will be called a house of prayer.'[d] But you are changing it into a 'hiding place for thieves.'[e]"

¹⁴Some blind people and some who were crippled came to Jesus in the Temple area. Jesus healed them. ¹⁵The leading priests and the teachers of the law saw the wonderful things he was doing. And they saw the children praising him in the Temple area. The children were shouting, "Praise to the Son of David.*" All this made the priests and the teachers of the law angry.

¹⁶They asked Jesus, "Do you hear what these children are saying?"

He answered, "Yes. The Scriptures say, 'You have taught children and babies to give

---

[a]**20:22** *cup* A symbol of suffering. Jesus used the idea of drinking from a cup to mean accepting the suffering he would face in the terrible events that were soon to come. Also in verse 23.

[b]**21:5** *people of Zion* Literally, "daughter of Zion," meaning the city of Jerusalem.

[c]**21:9** *Praise* Literally, "Hosanna," a Hebrew word used in praying to God for help. Here, it was probably a shout of celebration used in praising God or his Messiah. Also in the last line of this verse and in verse 15.

[d]**21:13** Quote from Isa. 56:7.

[e]**21:13** Quote from Jer. 7:11.

praise.'ᵃ Have you not read that Scripture?"

¹⁷Then Jesus left them and went out of the city to Bethany, where he spent the night.

Jesus Shows the Power of Faith
(Mk. 11:12–14, 20–24)

¹⁸Early the next morning, Jesus was going back to the city. He was very hungry. ¹⁹He saw a fig tree beside the road and went to get a fig from it. But there were no figs on the tree. There were only leaves. So Jesus said to the tree, "You will never again produce fruit!" The tree immediately dried up and died.

²⁰When the followers saw this, they were very surprised. They asked, "How did the fig tree dry up and die so quickly?"

²¹Jesus answered, "The truth is, if you have faith and no doubts, you will be able to do the same as I did to this tree. And you will be able to do more. You will be able to say to this mountain, 'Go, mountain, fall into the sea.' And if you have faith, it will happen. ²²If you believe, you will get anything you ask for in prayer."

Jewish Leaders Doubt Jesus' Authority
(Mk. 11:27–33; Lk. 20:1–8)

²³Jesus went into the Temple* area. While Jesus was teaching there, the leading priests and the older leaders of the people came to him. They said, "Tell us! What authority do you have to do these things you are doing? Who gave you this authority?"

²⁴Jesus answered, "I will ask you a question too. If you answer me, then I will tell you what authority I have to do these things. ²⁵Tell me: When John baptized* people, did his authority come from God, or was it only from other people?"

The priests and the Jewish leaders talked about Jesus' question. They said to each other, "If we answer, 'John's baptism was from God,' then he will say, 'Then why didn't you believe John?' ²⁶But we can't say John's baptism was from someone else. We are afraid of the people, because they all believe John was a prophet.*"

²⁷So they told Jesus, "We don't know the answer."

Jesus said, "Then I will not tell you who gave me the authority to do these things.

Jesus Uses a Story About Two Sons

²⁸"Tell me what you think about this: There was a man who had two sons. He went to the first son and said, 'Son, go and work today in the vineyard.*'

²⁹"The son answered, 'I will not go.' But later he decided he should go, and he went.

³⁰"Then the father went to the other son and said, 'Son, go and work today in the vineyard.' He answered, 'Yes, sir, I will go and work.' But he did not go.

³¹"Which of the two sons obeyed his father?"

The Jewish leaders answered, "The first son."

Jesus said to them, "The truth is, you are worse than the tax collectors* and the prostitutes. In fact, they will enter God's kingdom* before you enter. ³²John came showing you the right way to live, and you did not believe him. But the tax collectors and prostitutes believed John. You saw that happening, but you would not change. You still refused to believe him.

God Sends His Son
(Mk. 12:1–12; Lk. 20:9–19)

³³"Listen to this story: There was a man who owned a vineyard.* He put a wall around the field and dug a hole for a winepress.* Then he built a tower. He leased the land to some farmers and then left on a trip. ³⁴Later, it was time for the grapes to be picked. So the man sent his servants to the farmers to get his share of the grapes.

³⁵"But the farmers grabbed the servants and beat one. They killed another one and then stoned to death a third servant. ³⁶So the man sent some other servants to the farmers. He sent more servants than he sent the first time. But the farmers did the same thing to them that they did the first time. ³⁷So the man decided to send his son to the farmers. He said, 'The farmers will respect my son.'

³⁸"But when the farmers saw the son, they said to each other, 'This is the owner's son. This vineyard will be his. If we kill him, it will be ours.' ³⁹So the farmers took the son, threw him out of the vineyard, and killed him.

⁴⁰"So what will the owner of the vineyard do to these farmers when he comes?"

⁴¹The Jewish priests and leaders said, "He will surely kill those evil men. Then he will lease the land to other farmers, who will give him his share of the crop at harvest time."

⁴²Jesus said to them, "Surely you have read this in the Scriptures*:

'The stone that the builders refused to
    accept became the cornerstone.*
The Lord did this, and it is wonderful to
    us.'   *Psalm 118:22-23*

⁴³"So I tell you that God's kingdom* will be taken away from you. It will be given to people who do what God wants in his kingdom. ⁴⁴Whoever falls on this stone will be broken. And it will crush anyone it falls on."ᵇ

⁴⁵When the leading priests and the Pharisees* heard these stories, they knew that Jesus was talking about them. ⁴⁶They wanted to find a way to arrest Jesus. But they were afraid to do anything, because the people believed that Jesus was a prophet.*

ᵃ21:16 Quote from Ps. 8:2 (Greek version).   ᵇ21:44 Some Greek copies do not have verse 44.

A Story About People Invited to a Dinner
(Lk. 14:15–24)

22 [1]Jesus used some more stories to teach the people. He said, [2]"God's kingdom* is like a king who prepared a wedding feast for his son. [3]He invited some people to the feast. When it was ready, the king sent his servants to tell the people to come. But they refused to come to the king's feast.

[4]"Then the king sent some more servants. He said to them, 'I have already invited the people. So tell them that my feast is ready. I have killed my best bulls and calves to be eaten. Everything is ready. Come to the wedding feast.'

[5]"But when the servants told the people to come, they refused to listen. They all went to do other things. One went to work in his field, and another went to his business. [6]Some of the other people grabbed the servants, beat them, and killed them. [7]The king was very angry. He sent his army to kill those who murdered his servants. And the army burned their city.

[8]"After that, the king said to his servants, 'The wedding feast is ready. I invited those people, but they were not good enough to come to my feast. [9]So go to the street corners and invite everyone you see. Tell them to come to my feast.' [10]So the servants went into the streets. They gathered all the people they could find, good and bad alike, and brought them to where the wedding feast was ready. And the place was filled with guests.

[11]"When the king came in to meet the guests, he saw a man there who was not dressed in the right clothes for a wedding. [12]The king said, 'Friend, how were you allowed to come in here? You are not wearing the right clothes.' But the man said nothing. [13]So the king told some servants, 'Tie this man's hands and feet. Throw him out into the darkness, where people are crying and grinding their teeth with pain.'

[14]"Yes, many people are invited. But only a few are chosen."

The Jewish Leaders Try to Trick Jesus
(Mk. 12:13–17; Lk. 20:20–26)

[15]Then the Pharisees* left the place where Jesus was teaching. They made plans to catch him saying something wrong. [16]They sent some men to Jesus. They were some of their own followers and some from the group called Herodians.* They said, "Teacher, we know you are an honest man. We know you teach the truth about God's way. You are not afraid of what others think about you. All people are the same to you. [17]So tell us what you think. Is it right to pay taxes to Caesar* or not?"

[18]But Jesus knew that these men were trying to trick him. So he said, "You hypocrites*! Why are you trying to catch me saying something wrong? [19]Show me a coin used for paying the tax." They showed Jesus a silver coin.* [20]Then he asked, "Whose picture is on the coin? And whose name is written on the coin?"

[21]They answered, "It is Caesar's picture and Caesar's name."

Then Jesus said to them, "Give to Caesar what belongs to Caesar, and give to God what belongs to God."

[22]When they heard what Jesus said, they were amazed. They left him and went away.

Some Sadducees Try to Trick Jesus
(Mk. 12:18–27; Lk. 20:27–40)

[23]That same day some Sadducees* came to Jesus. (Sadducees believe that no one will rise from death.) The Sadducees asked Jesus a question. [24]They said, "Teacher, Moses* told us that if a married man dies and had no children, his brother must marry the woman. Then they will have children for the dead brother.[a] [25]There were seven brothers among us. The first brother married but died. He had no children. So his brother married the woman. [26]Then the second brother also died. The same thing happened to the third brother and all the other brothers. [27]The woman was the last to die. [28]But all seven men had married her. So when people rise from death, whose wife will she be?"

[29]Jesus answered, "You are so wrong! You don't know what the Scriptures* say. And you don't know anything about God's power. [30]At the time when people rise from death, there will be no marriage. People will not be married to each other. Everyone will be like the angels in heaven. [31]Surely you have read what God said to you about people rising from death. [32]God said, 'I am the God of Abraham,* the God of Isaac,* and the God of Jacob.'*[b] So they were not still dead, because he is the God only of living people."

[33]When the people heard this, they were amazed at Jesus' teaching.

Which Command Is the Most Important?
(Mk. 12:28–34; Lk. 10:25–28)

[34]The Pharisees* learned that Jesus had made the Sadducees* look so foolish that they stopped trying to argue with him. So the Pharisees had a meeting. [35]Then one of them, an expert in the Law of Moses,* asked Jesus a question to test him. [36]He said, "Teacher, which command in the law is the most important?"

[37]Jesus answered, "'Love the Lord your God with all your heart, all your soul, and all your mind.'[c] [38]This is the first and most important command. [39]And the second command is like the first: 'Love your neighbor[d]

---

[a]**22:24 if … dead brother** See Deut. 25:5, 6.
[b]**22:32** Quote from Ex. 3:6.
[c]**22:37** Quote from Deut. 6:5.
[d]**22:39 your neighbor** Or "others." Jesus' teaching in Lk. 10:25–37 makes clear that this includes anyone in need.

the same as you love yourself.'[a] [40]All the law and the writings of the prophets* take their meaning from these two commands."

Is the Christ David's Son or David's Lord?
(Mk. 12:35–37; Lk. 20:41–44)

[41]So while the Pharisees* were together, Jesus asked them a question. [42]He said, "What do you think about the Christ*? Whose son is he?"

The Pharisees answered, "The Christ is the Son of David.*"

[43]Jesus said to them, "Then why did David call him 'Lord'? David was speaking by the power of the Spirit.* He said,

[44] 'The Lord God said to my Lord:
  Sit by me at my right side,
    and I will put your enemies under your
      control.[b]'   Psalm 110:1

[45]David calls the Christ 'Lord.' So how can he be David's son?" [46]None of the Pharisees could answer Jesus' question. And after that day, no one was brave enough to ask him any more questions.

Jesus Criticizes the Religious Leaders
(Mk. 12:38–40; Lk. 11:37–52; 20:45–47)

23 [1]Then Jesus spoke to the people and to his followers. He said, [2]"The teachers of the law and the Pharisees* have the authority to tell you what the Law of Moses* says. [3]So you should obey them. Do everything they tell you to do. But their lives are not good examples for you to follow. They tell you to do things, but they don't do those things themselves. [4]They make strict rules that are hard for people to obey. They try to force others to obey all their rules. But they themselves will not try to follow any of those rules.

[5]"The only reason they do what they do is for other people to see them. They make the little Scripture* boxes[c] they wear bigger and bigger. And they make the tassels[d] on their prayer clothes long enough for people to notice them. [6]These men love to have the places of honor at banquets and the most important seats in the synagogues.* [7]They love for people to show respect to them in the marketplaces and to call them 'Teacher.'

[8]"But you must not be called 'Teacher.' You are all equal as brothers and sisters. You

have only one Teacher. [9]And don't call anyone on earth 'Father.' You have one Father. He is in heaven. [10]And you should not be called 'Master.' You have only one Master, the Christ.* [11]Whoever serves you like a servant is the greatest among you. [12]People who think they are better than others will be made humble. But people who humble themselves will be made great.

[13]"It will be bad for you teachers of the law and you Pharisees! You are hypocrites*! You close the way for people to enter God's kingdom.* You yourselves don't enter, and you stop those who are trying to enter. [14] [e]

[15]"It will be bad for you teachers of the law and you Pharisees! You are hypocrites. You travel across the seas and across different countries to find one person who will follow your ways. When you find that person, you make him worse than you are. And you are so bad that you belong in hell!

[16]"It will be bad for you teachers of the law and you Pharisees! You guide the people, but you are blind. You say, 'If anyone uses the name of the Temple* to make a promise, that means nothing. But anyone who uses the gold that is in the Temple to make a promise must keep that promise.' [17]You are blind fools! Can't you see that the Temple is greater than the gold on it? It's the Temple that makes the gold holy*!

[18]"And you say, 'If anyone uses the altar* to make a promise, that means nothing. But anyone who uses the gift on the altar to make a promise must keep that promise.' [19]You are blind! Can't you see that the altar is greater than any gift on it? It's the altar that makes the gift holy! [20]Whoever uses the altar to make a promise is really using the altar and everything on the altar. [21]And anyone who uses the Temple to make a promise is really using the Temple and God, who lives in it. [22]Whoever uses heaven to make a promise is using God's throne and the one who is seated on it.

[23]"It will be bad for you teachers of the law and you Pharisees! You are hypocrites! You give God a tenth of the food you get, even your mint, dill, and cumin.[f] But you don't obey the really important teachings of the law—being fair, showing mercy, and being faithful. These are the things you should do. And you should also continue to do those

---

[a]**22:39** Quote from Lev. 19:18.
[b]**22:44** *control* Literally, "feet."
[c]**23:5** *Scripture boxes* Small leather boxes containing four important Scriptures. Some Jews tied these to the forehead and left arm to show their devotion to God and his word. Many Pharisees made these bigger to show that they were more religious than others.
[d]**23:5** *tassels* Decorations made from wool threads that hung down from the four corners of the clothing or prayer shawls worn by Jews. They were supposed to be reminders of God's commands (see Num. 15:38–41).

[e]**23:14** Some Greek copies add verse 14: "It will be bad for you, teachers of the law and you Pharisees. You are hypocrites. You cheat widows and take their homes. Then you make long prayers so that people can see you. So you will have a worse punishment." See Mk. 12:40; Lk. 20:47.
[f]**23:23** *You give … cumin* Literally, "You tithe mint, dill, and cumin." The Law of Moses required Israelites to share their food supply by dedicating a tenth of their field crops and livestock to God (see Lev. 27:30–32; Deut. 26:12). This did not include such small garden plants as those mentioned here. So these Pharisees were giving more than required to be sure they were not breaking the Law.

other things. 24You guide the people, but you are blind! Think about a man picking a little fly out of his drink and then swallowing a camel! You are like that.*

25"It will be bad for you teachers of the law and you Pharisees! You are hypocrites! You wash clean the outside of your cups and dishes. But inside they are full of what you got by cheating others and pleasing yourselves. 26Pharisees, you are blind! First make the inside of the cup clean and good. Then the outside of the cup will also be clean.

27"It will be bad for you teachers of the law and you Pharisees! You are hypocrites! You are like tombs* that are painted white. Outside they look fine, but inside they are full of dead people's bones and all kinds of filth. 28It is the same with you. People look at you and think you are godly. But on the inside you are full of hypocrisy* and evil.

29"It will be bad for you teachers of the law and you Pharisees! You are hypocrites! You build tombs for the prophets.* And you show honor to the graves of the godly people who were killed. 30And you say, 'If we had lived during the time of our ancestors,* we would not have helped them kill these prophets.' 31So you give proof that you are descendants of those who killed the prophets. 32And you will finish the sin that your ancestors started!

33"You are snakes! You are from a family of poisonous snakes! You will not escape God. You will all be judged guilty and go to hell! 34So I tell you this: I send to you prophets and teachers who are wise and know the Scriptures. You will kill some of them. You will hang some of them on crosses. You will beat some of them in your synagogues. You will chase them from town to town.

35"So you will be guilty for the death of all the good people who have been killed on earth. You will be guilty for the killing of that godly man Abel. And you will be guilty for the killing of Zechariah*b son of Berachiah. He was killed between the Temple and the altar. You will be guilty for the killing of all the good people who lived between the time of Abel and the time of Zechariah. 36Believe me when I say that all these things will happen to you people who are living now.

Jesus Warns the People of Jerusalem
(Lk. 13:34–35)

37"O Jerusalem, Jerusalem! You kill the prophets.* You stone to death those that God has sent to you. Many, many times I wanted to help your people. I wanted to gather them together as a hen gathers her chicks under her wings. But you did not let me. 38Now your house will be left completely empty. 39I tell you, you will not see me again until

that time when you will say, 'Welcome! God bless the one who comes in the name of the Lord.'*c"

Jesus Warns About the Future
(Mk. 13:1–31; Lk. 21:5–33)

24 1Jesus left the Temple* area and was walking away. But his followers came to him to show him the Temple's buildings. 2He asked them, "Are you looking at these buildings? The fact is, they will be destroyed. Every stone will be thrown down to the ground. Not one stone will be left on another."

3Later, Jesus was sitting at a place on the Mount of Olives.* The followers came to be alone with him. They said, "Tell us when these things will happen. And what will happen to prepare us for your coming and the end of time?"

4Jesus answered, "Be careful! Don't let anyone fool you. 5Many people will come and use my name. They will say, 'I am the Christ.*' And they will fool many people. 6You will hear about wars that are being fought. And you will hear stories about other wars beginning. But don't be afraid. These things must happen before the end comes. 7Nations will fight against other nations. Kingdoms will fight against other kingdoms. There will be times when there is no food for people to eat. And there will be earthquakes in different places. 8These things are only the beginning of troubles, like the first pains of a woman giving birth.

9"Then you will be arrested and handed over to be punished and killed. People all over the world will hate you because you believe in me. 10During that time many believers will lose their faith. They will turn against each other and hate each other. 11Many false prophets* will come and cause many people to believe things that are wrong. 12There will so much more evil in the world that the love of most believers will grow cold. 13But the one who remains faithful to the end will be saved. 14And the Good News I have shared about God's kingdom* will be told throughout the world. It will be spread to every nation. Then the end will come.

15"Daniel the prophet* spoke about 'the terrible thing that causes destruction.'*d You will see this terrible thing standing in the holy place." (You who read this should understand what it means.) 16"The people in Judea at that time should run away to the mountains. 17They should run away without wasting time to stop for anything. If they are on the roof of their house, they must not go down to get anything out of the house. 18If they are in the field, they must not go back to get a coat.

---

*a***23:24 You are like that** Meaning "You worry about the smallest mistakes but commit the biggest sin."
*b***23:35 Abel, Zechariah** In the Hebrew Old Testament, these are the first and last persons murdered.

*c***23:39** Quote from Ps. 118:26. •
*d***24:15 'the terrible thing … destruction'** See Dan. 9:27; 12:11 (also Dan. 11:31).

¹⁹"During that time it will be hard for women who are pregnant or have small babies! ²⁰Pray that it will not be winter or a Sabbath* day when these things happen and you have to run away, ²¹because it will be a time of great trouble. There will be more trouble than has ever happened since the beginning of the world. And nothing as bad as that will ever happen again.

²²"But God has decided to make that terrible time short. If it were not made short, no one would continue living. But God will make that time short to help the people he has chosen.

²³"Someone might say to you at that time, 'Look, there is the Christ!' Or someone else might say, 'There he is!' But don't believe them. ²⁴False Christs and false prophets will come and do great miracles and wonders,ᵃ trying to fool the people God has chosen, if that is possible. ²⁵Now I have warned you about this before it happens.

²⁶"Someone might tell you, 'The Christ is there in the desert!' But don't go into the desert to look for him. Someone else might say, 'There is the Christ in that room!' But don't believe it. ²⁷When the Son of Man* comes, everyone will see him. It will be like lightning flashing in the sky that can be seen everywhere. ²⁸It's like looking for a dead body: You will find it where the vultures* are gathering above.

²⁹"Right after the trouble of those days, this will happen:

'The sun will become dark,
   and the moon will not give light.
The stars will fall from the sky,
   and everything in the sky will be
      changed.'ᵇ

³⁰"Then there will be something in the sky that shows the Son of Man is coming. All the people of the world will cry. Everyone will see the Son of Man coming on the clouds in the sky. He will come with power and great glory.* ³¹He will use a loud trumpet to send his angels all around the earth. They will gather his chosen people from every part of the earth.

³²"The fig tree teaches us a lesson: When its branches become green and soft, and new leaves begin to grow, then you know that summer is near. ³³In the same way, when you see all these things happening, you will know that the timeᶜ is near, ready to come. ³⁴I assure you that all these things will happen while some of the people of this time are still

living. ³⁵The whole world, earth and sky, will be destroyed, but my words will last forever.

Only God Knows When the Time Will Be
(Mk. 13:32–37; Lk. 17:26–30, 34–36)

³⁶"No one knows when that day or time will be. The Son and the angels in heaven don't know when it will be. Only the Father knows.

³⁷"When the Son of Man* comes, it will be the same as what happened during Noah's time. ³⁸In those days before the flood, people were eating and drinking, marrying and giving their children to be married right up to the day Noah entered the boat. ³⁹They knew nothing about what was happening until the flood came and destroyed them all.

"It will be the same when the Son of Man comes. ⁴⁰Two men will be working together in the field. One will be taken and the other will be left. ⁴¹Two women will be grinding grain with a mill.* One will be taken and the other will be left.

⁴²"So always be ready. You don't know the day your Lord will come. ⁴³Obviously, a homeowner who knew what time a thief was planning to come would be ready and not let the thief break in. ⁴⁴So you also must be ready. The Son of Man will come at a time when you don't expect him.

Good Servants and Bad Servants
(Lk. 12:41–48)

⁴⁵"Who is the wise and trusted servant? The master trusts one servant to give the other servants their food at the right time. Who is the one the master trusts to do that work? ⁴⁶When the master comes and finds that servant doing the work he gave him, it will be a day of blessing for that servant. ⁴⁷I can tell you without a doubt, the master will choose that servant to take care of everything he owns.

⁴⁸But what will happen if that servant is evil and thinks his master will not come back soon? ⁴⁹He will begin to beat the other servants. He will eat and drink with others who are drunk. ⁵⁰Then the master will come when the servant is not ready, at a time when the servant is not expecting him. ⁵¹Then the master will punish that servant. He will send him away to be with the hypocrites,* where people will cry and grind their teeth with pain.

A Story About Ten Girls

25 ¹"At that time God's kingdom* will be like ten girls who went to wait for the bridegroom.* They took their lamps with them. ²Five of the girls were foolish, and five were wise. ³The foolish girls took their lamps with them, but they did not take extra oil for the lamps. ⁴The wise girls took their lamps and more oil in jars. ⁵When the bridegroom was very late, the girls could not keep their eyes open, and they all fell asleep.

ᵃ24:24 *miracles and wonders* Here, amazing acts done by Satan's power.
ᵇ24:29 See Isa. 13:10, 34:4.
ᶜ24:33 *time* The time Jesus has been talking about when something important will happen. See Lk. 21:31, where Jesus says that this is the time for God's kingdom to come.

6"At midnight someone announced, 'The bridegroom is coming! Come and meet him!'

7"Then all the girls woke up. They made their lamps ready. 8But the foolish girls said to the wise girls, 'Give us some of your oil. The oil in our lamps is all gone.'

9"The wise girls answered, 'No! The oil we have might not be enough for all of us. But go to those who sell oil and buy some for yourselves.'

10"So the foolish girls went to buy oil. While they were gone, the bridegroom came. The girls who were ready went in with the bridegroom to the wedding feast. Then the door was closed and locked.

11"Later, the other girls came. They said, 'Sir, sir! Open the door to let us in.'

12"But the bridegroom answered, 'Certainly not! I don't even know you.'

13"So always be ready. You don't know the day or the time when the Son of Man* will come.

A Story About Three Servants
(Lk. 19:11-27)

14"At that time God's kingdom* will also be like a man leaving home to travel to another place for a visit. Before he left, he talked with his servants. He told his servants to take care of his things while he was gone. 15He decided how much each servant would be able to care for. The man gave one servant five bags of money.a He gave another servant two bags. And he gave a third servant one bag. Then he left. 16The servant who got five bags went quickly to invest the money. Those five bags of money earned five more. 17It was the same with the servant who had two bags. That servant invested the money and earned two more. 18But the servant who got one bag of money went away and dug a hole in the ground. Then he hid his master's money in the hole.

19"After a long time the master came home. He asked the servants what they did with his money. 20The servant who got five bags brought that amount and five more bags of money to the master. The servant said, 'Master, you trusted me to care for five bags of money. So I used them to earn five more.'

21"The master answered, 'You did right. You are a good servant who can be trusted. You did well with that small amount of money. So I will let you care for much greater things. Come and share my happiness with me.'

22"Then the servant who got two bags of money came to the master. The servant said, 'Master, you gave me two bags of money to care for. So I used your two bags to earn two more.'

23"The master answered, 'You did right. You are a good servant who can be trusted. You did well with a small amount of money. So I will let you care for much greater things. Come and share my happiness with me.'

24"Then the servant who got one bag of money came to the master. The servant said, 'Master, I knew you were a very hard man. You harvest what you did not plant. You gather crops where you did not put any seed. 25So I was afraid. I went and hid your money in the ground. Here is the one bag of money you gave me.'

26"The master answered, 'You are a bad and lazy servant! You say you knew that I harvest what I did not plant and that I gather crops where I did not put any seed. 27So you should have put my money in the bank. Then, when I came home, I would get my money back. And I would also get the interest that my money earned.'

28"So the master told his other servants, 'Take the one bag of money from that servant and give it to the servant who has ten bags. 29Everyone who uses what they have will get more. They will have much more than they need. But people who do not use what they have will have everything taken away from them.' 30Then the master said, 'Throw that useless servant outside into the darkness, where people will cry and grind their teeth with pain.'

The Son of Man Will Judge All People

31"The Son of Man* will come again with divine greatness,* and all his angels will come with him. He will sit as king on his great and glorious throne. 32All the people of the world will be gathered before him. Then he will separate everyone into two groups. It will be like a shepherd separating his sheep from his goats. 33He will put the sheep on his right and the goats on his left.

34"Then the king will say to the godly people on his right, 'Come, my Father has great blessings for you. The kingdom* he promised is now yours. It has been prepared for you since the world was made. 35It is yours because when I was hungry, you gave me food to eat. When I was thirsty, you gave me something to drink. When I had no place to stay, you welcomed me into your home. 36When I was without clothes, you gave me something to wear. When I was sick, you cared for me. When I was in prison, you came to visit me.'

37"Then the godly people will answer, 'Lord, when did we see you hungry and give you food? When did we see you thirsty and give you something to drink? 38When did we see you with no place to stay and welcome you into our home? When did we see you without clothes and give you something to wear? 39When did we see you sick or in prison and care for you?'

40"Then the king will answer, 'The truth is,

a25:15 bags of money Literally, "talanta" or "talents." A talent was about 27 to 36 kg (60 to 80 pounds) of gold, silver, or copper coins. Also in verses 20, 22, 24, 28.

anything you did for any of my people here,[a] you also did for me.'

41"Then the king will say to the evil people on his left, 'Get away from me. God has already decided that you will be punished. Go into the fire that burns forever—the fire that was prepared for the devil and his angels. 42You must go away because when I was hungry, you gave me nothing to eat. When I was thirsty, you gave me nothing to drink. 43When I had no place to stay, you did not welcome me into your home. When I was without clothes, you gave me nothing to wear. When I was sick and in prison, you did not care for me.'

44"Then those people will answer, 'Lord, when did we see you hungry or thirsty? When did we see you without a place to stay? Or when did we see you without clothes or sick or in prison? When did we see any of this and not help you?'

45"The king will answer, 'The truth is, anything you refused to do for any of my people here, you refused to do for me.'

46"Then these evil people will go away to be punished forever. But the godly people will go and enjoy eternal life."

The Jewish Leaders Plan to Kill Jesus
(Mk. 14:1–2; Lk. 22:1–2; Jn. 11:45–53)

26 1After Jesus finished saying all these things, he said to his followers, 2"You know that the day after tomorrow is Passover.* On that day the Son of Man* will be handed over to his enemies to be killed on a cross."

3Then the leading priests and the older Jewish leaders had a meeting at the palace where the high priest* lived. The high priest's name was Caiaphas. 4In the meeting they tried to find a way to arrest and kill Jesus without anyone knowing what they were doing. They planned to arrest Jesus and kill him. 5They said, "We cannot arrest Jesus during Passover. We don't want the people to become angry and cause a riot."

A Woman Does Something Special
(Mk. 14:3–9; Jn. 12:1–8)

6Jesus was in Bethany at the house of Simon the leper.* 7While he was there, a woman came to him. She had an alabaster* jar filled with expensive perfume. She poured the perfume on Jesus' head while he was eating.

8The followers saw the woman do this and were upset at her. They said, "Why waste that perfume? 9It could be sold for a lot of money, and the money could be given to those who are poor."

10But Jesus knew what happened. He said, "Why are you bothering this woman? She did a very good thing for me. 11You will always

have the poor with you.[b] But you will not always have me. 12This woman poured perfume on my body. She did this to prepare me for burial after I die. 13The Good News* will be told to people all over the world. And I can assure you that everywhere the Good News is told, the story of what this woman did will also be told, and people will remember her."

Judas Agrees to Help Jesus' Enemies
(Mk. 14:10–11; Lk. 22:3–6)

14Then one of the twelve followers went to talk to the leading priests. This was the follower named Judas Iscariot. 15He said, "I will hand Jesus over to you. What will you pay me for doing this?" The priests gave him 30 silver coins. 16After that, Judas waited for the best time to hand Jesus over to them.

The Passover Meal
(Mk. 14:12–21; Lk. 22:7–14, 21–23; Jn. 13:21–30)

17On the first day of the Festival of Unleavened Bread,* the followers came to Jesus. They said, "We will prepare everything for you to eat the Passover* meal. Where do you want us to have the meal?"

18Jesus answered, "Go into the city. Go to a man I know. Tell him that the Teacher says, 'The chosen time is near. I will have the Passover meal with my followers at your house.'" 19They obeyed and did what Jesus told them to do. They prepared the Passover meal.

20In the evening Jesus was at the table with the twelve followers. 21They were all eating. Then Jesus said, "Believe me when I say that one of you twelve here will hand me over to my enemies."

22The followers were very sad to hear this. Each one said, "Lord, surely I am not the one!"

23Jesus answered, "One who has dipped his bread in the same bowl with me will be the one to hand me over. 24The Son of Man* will suffer what the Scriptures* say will happen to him. But it will be very bad for the one who hands over the Son of Man to be killed. It would be better for him if he had never been born."

25Then Judas, the very one who would hand him over, said to Jesus, "Teacher, surely I am not the one you are talking about, am I?"

Jesus answered, "Yes, it is you."

The Lord's Supper
(Mk. 14:22–26; Lk. 22:15–20; 1 Cor. 11:23–25)

26While they were eating, Jesus took some bread and thanked God for it. He broke off some pieces, gave them to his followers and said, "Take this bread and eat it. It is my body."

27Then he took a cup of wine, thanked God for it, and gave it to them. He said, "Each one of you drink some of it. 28This wine is my

---

[a]25:40 *any of my people here* Literally, "one of the least of these brothers of mine." Also in verse 45.

[b]26:11 *You will ... with you* See Deut. 15:11.

blood, which will be poured out to forgive the sins of many and begin the new agreement* from God to his people. ²⁹I want you to know, I will not drink this wine again until that day when we are together in my Father's kingdom* and the wine is new. Then I will drink it again with you."

³⁰They all sang a song and then went out to the Mount of Olives.*

Jesus Says His Followers Will Leave Him
(Mk. 14:27–31; Lk. 22:31–34; Jn. 13:36–38)

³¹Jesus told the followers, "Tonight you will all lose your faith in me. The Scriptures* say,

'I will kill the shepherd,
    and the sheep will run away.'
                                    Zechariah 13:7

³²But after I am killed, I will rise from death. Then I will go into Galilee. I will be there before you go there."

³³Peter answered, "All the other followers may lose their faith in you. But my faith will never be shaken."

³⁴Jesus answered, "The truth is, tonight you will say you don't know me. You will deny me three times before the rooster crows."

³⁵But Peter answered, "I will never say I don't know you! I will even die with you!" And all the other followers said the same thing.

Jesus Prays Alone
(Mk. 14:32–42; Lk. 22:39–46)

³⁶Then Jesus went with his followers to a place called Gethsemane. He said to them, "Sit here while I go there and pray." ³⁷He told Peter and the two sons of Zebedee to come with him. Then he began to be very sad and troubled. ³⁸Jesus said to Peter and the two sons of Zebedee, "My heart is so heavy with grief, I feel as if I am dying. Wait here and stay awake with me."

³⁹Then Jesus went on a little farther away from them. He fell to the ground and prayed, "My Father, if it is possible, don't make me drink from this cup.ᵃ But do what you want, not what I want." ⁴⁰Then he went back to his followers and found them sleeping. He said to Peter, "Could you men not stay awake with me for one hour? ⁴¹Stay awake and pray for strength against temptation. Your spirit wants to do what is right, but your body is weak."

⁴²Then Jesus went away a second time and prayed, "My Father, if I must do thisᵇ and it is not possible for me to escape it, then I pray that what you want will be done."

⁴³Then he went back to the followers. Again he found them sleeping. They could not stay awake. ⁴⁴So he left them and went away one more time and prayed. This third time he prayed, he said the same thing.

⁴⁵Then Jesus went back to the followers and said, "Are you still sleeping and resting? The time has come for the Son of Man* to be handed over to the control of sinful men. ⁴⁶Stand up! We must go. Here comes the one who will hand me over."

Jesus Is Arrested
(Mk. 14:43–50; Lk. 22:47–53; Jn. 18:3–12)

⁴⁷While Jesus was still speaking, Judas, one of the twelve apostles* came there. He had a big crowd of people with him, all carrying swords and clubs. They had been sent from the leading priests and the older leaders of the people. ⁴⁸Judasᶜ planned to do something to show them which one was Jesus. He said, "The one I kiss will be Jesus. Arrest him." ⁴⁹He went to Jesus and said, "Hello, Teacher!" Then Judas kissed him.

⁵⁰Jesus answered, "Friend, do the thing you came to do."

Then the men came and grabbed Jesus and arrested him. ⁵¹When that happened, one of the followers with Jesus grabbed his sword and pulled it out. He swung it at the servant of the high priest* and cut off his ear.

⁵²Jesus said to the man, "Put your sword back in its place. People who use swords will be killed with swords. ⁵³Surely you know I could ask my Father and he would give me more than twelve armies of angels. ⁵⁴But it must happen this way to show the truth of what the Scriptures* said."

⁵⁵Then Jesus said to the crowd, "Why do you come to get me with swords and clubs as if I were a criminal. Every day I sat in the Temple* area teaching. You did not arrest me there. ⁵⁶But all these things have happened to show the full meaning of what the prophets* wrote." Then all of Jesus' followers left him and ran away.

Jesus Before the Jewish Leaders
(Mk. 14:53–65; Lk. 22:54–55, 63–71;
Jn. 18:13–14, 19–24)

⁵⁷The men who arrested Jesus led him to the house of Caiaphas the high priest.* The teachers of the law and the older Jewish leaders were gathered there. ⁵⁸Peter followed Jesus but stayed back at a distance. He followed him to the yard of the high priest's house. Peter went in and sat with the guards. He wanted to see what would happen to Jesus.

⁵⁹The leading priests and the high council tried to find something against Jesus so that they could kill him. They tried to find people

---

ᵃ**26:39 cup** A symbol of suffering. Jesus used the idea of drinking from a cup to mean accepting the suffering he would face in the terrible events that were soon to come.
ᵇ**26:42 do this** Literally, "drink this," referring to the "cup," the symbol of suffering in verse 39.

ᶜ**26:48 Judas** Literally, "the one who handed him over."

to lie and say that Jesus had done wrong. [60]Many people came and told lies about him. But the council could find no real reason to kill him. Then two people came [61]and said, "This man[a] said, 'I can destroy the Temple* of God and build it again in three days.'"

[62]Then the high priest stood up and said to Jesus, "Don't you have anything to say about these charges against you? Are they telling the truth?" [63]But Jesus said nothing.

Again the high priest said to Jesus, "You are now under oath.* I command you by the power of the living God to tell us the truth. Tell us, are you the Christ,* the Son of God?"

[64]Jesus answered, "Yes, that's right. But I tell you, in the future you will see the Son of Man* sitting at the right side of God. And you will see the Son of Man coming on the clouds of heaven."

[65]When the high priest heard this, he tore his clothes in anger. He said, "This man has said things that insult God! We don't need any more witnesses. You all heard his insulting words. [66]What do you think?"

The Jewish leaders answered, "He is guilty, and he must die."

[67]Then some there spit in Jesus' face, and they hit him with their fists. Others slapped him. [68]They said, "Show us that you are a prophet,[b] Christ! Tell us who hit you!"

Peter Is Afraid to Say He Knows Jesus
(Mk. 14:66–72; Lk. 22:56–62; Jn. 18:15–18, 25–27)

[69]While Peter was sitting outside in the yard, a servant girl came up to him. She said, "You were with Jesus, that man from Galilee."

[70]But Peter told everyone there that this was not true. "I don't know what you are talking about," he said.

[71]Then he left the yard. At the gate another girl saw him and said to the people there, "This man was with Jesus of Nazareth."

[72]Again, Peter said he was never with Jesus. He said, "I swear to God I don't know the man!"

[73]A short time later those standing there went to Peter and said, "We know you are one of them. It's clear from the way you talk."

[74]Then Peter began to curse. He said, "I swear to God, I don't know the man!" As soon as he said this, a rooster crowed. [75]Then he remembered what Jesus had told him: "Before the rooster crows, you will say three times that you don't know me." Then Peter went outside and cried bitterly.

Jesus Is Taken to Governor Pilate
(Mk. 15:1; Lk. 23:1–2; Jn. 18:28–32)

27 [1]Early the next morning, all the leading priests and older leaders of the people met and decided to kill Jesus. [2]They tied him, led him away, and handed him over to Pilate,* the governor.

Judas Kills Himself
(Acts 1:18–19)

[3]Judas saw that they had decided to kill Jesus. He was the one who had handed him over. When he saw what happened, he was very sorry for what he had done. So he took the 30 silver coins back to the priests and the older leaders. [4]Judas said, "I sinned. I handed over to you an innocent man to be killed."

The Jewish leaders answered, "We don't care! That's a problem for you, not us."

[5]So Judas threw the money into the Temple.* Then he went out from there and hanged himself.

[6]The leading priests picked up the silver coins in the Temple. They said, "Our law does not allow us to keep this money with the Temple money, because this money has paid for a man's death." [7]So they decided to use the money to buy a field called Potter's Field. This field would be a place to bury people who died while visiting in Jerusalem. [8]That is why that field is still called the Field of Blood. [9]This showed the full meaning of what Jeremiah the prophet* said:

> "They took 30 silver coins. That was
> how much the people of Israel* decided
> to pay for his life. [10]They used those 30
> silver coins to buy the potter's field, as
> the Lord commanded me."[c]

Governor Pilate Questions Jesus
(Mk. 15:2–5; Lk. 23:3–5; Jn. 18:33–38)

[11]Jesus stood before Pilate,* the governor, who asked him, "Are you the king of the Jews?"

Jesus answered, "Yes, that's right."

[12]Then, when the leading priests and the older Jewish leaders made their accusations against Jesus, he said nothing.

[13]So Pilate said to him, "Don't you hear all these charges they are making against you? Why don't you answer?"

[14]But Jesus did not say anything, and this really surprised the governor.

Pilate Tries but Fails to Free Jesus
(Mk. 15:6–15; Lk. 23:13–25; Jn. 18:39–19:16)

[15]Every year at Passover* time the governor would free one prisoner—whichever one the people wanted him to free. [16]At that time there was a man in prison who was known to be very bad. His name was Barabbas.[d] [17]When a crowd gathered, Pilate* said to them, "I will free one man for you. Which one do you want me to free: Barabbas or Jesus

---

[a]**26:61 This man** That is, Jesus. His enemies avoided saying his name.

[b]**26:68 prophet** A prophet often knows things that are hidden to other people.

[c]**27:10 "They took ... me"** See Zech. 11:12–13; Jer. 32:6–9.

[d]**27:16 Barabbas** In some Greek copies the name is Jesus Barabbas.

who is called the Christ*?" ¹⁸Pilate knew that they had handed Jesus over to him because they were jealous of him.

¹⁹While Pilate was sitting there in the place for judging, his wife sent a message to him. It said, "Don't do anything with that man. He is not guilty. Last night I had a dream about him, and it troubled me very much."

²⁰But the leading priests and older Jewish leaders told the people to ask for Barabbas to be set free and for Jesus to be killed.

²¹Pilate said, "I have Barabbas and Jesus. Which one do you want me to set free for you?"

The people answered, "Barabbas!"

²²Pilate asked, "So what should I do with Jesus, the one called the Christ?"

All the people said, "Kill him on a cross!"

²³Pilate asked, "Why do you want me to kill him? What wrong has he done?"

But they shouted louder, "Kill him on a cross!"

²⁴Pilate saw that there was nothing he could do to make the people change. In fact, it looked as if there would be a riot. So he took some water and washed his hands[a] in front of them all. He said, "I am not guilty of this man's death. You are the ones who are doing it!"

²⁵The people answered, "We will take full responsibility for his death. You can blame us and even our children!"

²⁶Then Pilate set Barabbas free. And he told some soldiers to beat Jesus with whips. Then he handed him over to the soldiers to be killed on a cross.

Pilate's Soldiers Make Fun of Jesus
(Mk. 15:16–20; Jn. 19:2–3)

²⁷Then Pilate's* soldiers took Jesus into the governor's palace. All the soldiers gathered around him. ²⁸They took off Jesus' clothes and put a red robe on him. ²⁹Then they made a crown from thorny branches and put it on his head, and they put a stick in his right hand. Then they bowed before him, making fun of him. They said, "We salute you, king of the Jews!" ³⁰They spit on him. Then they took his stick and kept hitting him on the head with it. ³¹After they finished making fun of him, the soldiers took off the robe and put his own clothes on him again. Then they led him away to be killed on a cross.

Jesus Is Nailed to a Cross
(Mk. 15:21–32; Lk. 23:26–39; Jn. 19:17–19)

³²The soldiers were going out of the city with Jesus. They saw a man from Cyrene named Simon, and they forced him to carry Jesus' cross. ³³They came to the place called Golgotha. (Golgotha means "The Place of the Skull.") ³⁴There the soldiers gave Jesus some wine mixed with gall.[b] But when he tasted it, he refused to drink it.

³⁵The soldiers nailed Jesus to a cross. Then they threw dice to divide his clothes between them. ³⁶The soldiers stayed there to guard him. ³⁷They put a sign above his head with the charge against him written on it: "THIS IS JESUS, THE KING OF THE JEWS."

³⁸Two criminals were nailed to crosses beside Jesus—one on the right and the other on the left. ³⁹People walked by and shouted insults at Jesus. They shook their heads ⁴⁰and said, "You said you could destroy the Temple* and build it again in three days. So save yourself! Come down from that cross if you really are the Son of God!"

⁴¹The leading priests, the teachers of the law, and the older Jewish leaders were also there. They made fun of Jesus the same as the other people did. ⁴²They said, "He saved others, but he can't save himself! People say he is the king of Israel.* If he is the king, he should come down now from the cross. Then we will believe in him. ⁴³He trusted God. So let God save him now, if God really wants him. He himself said, 'I am the Son of God.'" ⁴⁴And in the same way, the criminals on the crosses beside Jesus also insulted him.

Jesus Dies
(Mk. 15:33–41; Lk. 23:44–49; Jn. 19:28–30)

⁴⁵At noon the whole country became dark. The darkness continued for three hours. ⁴⁶About three o'clock Jesus cried out loudly, "Eli, Eli, lema sabachthani?" This means "My God, my God, why have you left me alone?"[c]

⁴⁷Some of the people standing there heard this. They said, "He is calling Elijah."[d]

⁴⁸Quickly, one of them ran and got a sponge. He filled the sponge with sour wine and tied the sponge to a stick. Then he used the stick to give the sponge to Jesus to get a drink from it. ⁴⁹But the others said, "Don't bother him. We want to see if Elijah will come to save him."

⁵⁰Again Jesus cried out loudly and then died.[e]

⁵¹When Jesus died, the curtain* in the Temple* was torn into two pieces. The tear started at the top and tore all the way to the bottom. Also, the earth shook and rocks were broken. ⁵²The graves opened, and many of God's people who had died were raised from death. ⁵³They came out of the graves. And after Jesus was raised from death, they went into the holy city, and many people saw them.

[b]27:34 *gall* Probably used as a drug to relieve pain.
[c]27:46 Quote from Ps. 22:1.
[d]27:47 *"He is calling Elijah"* The word for "My God" (*Eli* in Hebrew or *Eloi* in Aramaic) sounded to the people like the name of Elijah, a famous man who spoke for God about 850 B.C.
[e]27:50 *died* Literally, "let his spirit leave."

[a]27:24 *washed his hands* Pilate did this as a sign to show that he wanted no part in what the people did.

54The army officer* and the soldiers guarding Jesus saw this earthquake and everything that happened. They were very afraid and said, "He really was the Son of God!"

55Many women were standing away from the cross, watching. These were the women who had followed Jesus from Galilee to care for him. 56Mary Magdalene, Mary the mother of James and Joseph, and the mother of James and John*a* were there.

Jesus Is Buried
(Mk. 15:42–47; Lk. 23:50–56; Jn. 19:38–42)

57That evening a rich man named Joseph came to Jerusalem. He was a follower of Jesus from the town of Arimathea. 58He went to Pilate* and asked to have Jesus' body. Pilate gave orders for the soldiers to give Jesus' body to him. 59Then Joseph took the body and wrapped it in a new linen cloth. 60He put Jesus' body in a new tomb* that he had dug in a wall of rock. Then he closed the tomb by rolling a very large stone to cover the entrance. After he did this, he went away. 61Mary Magdalene and the other woman named Mary were sitting near the tomb.

The Tomb of Jesus Is Guarded

62That day was the day called Preparation day.* The next day, the leading priests and the Pharisees* went to Pilate.* 63They said, "Sir, we remember that while that liar was still alive he said, 'I will rise from death in three days.' 64So give the order for the tomb* to be guarded well for three days. His followers might come and try to steal the body. Then they could tell everyone that he has risen from death. That lie will be even worse than what they said about him before."

65Pilate said, "Take some soldiers and go guard the tomb the best way you know." 66So they all went to the tomb and made it safe from thieves. They did this by sealing the stone in the entrance and putting soldiers there to guard it.

News That Jesus Has Risen From Death
(Mk. 16:1–8; Lk. 24:1–12; Jn. 20:1–10)

28 1The day after the Sabbath* day was the first day of the week. That day at dawn Mary Magdalene and the other woman named Mary went to look at the tomb.* 2Suddenly an angel of the Lord came from the sky, and there was a huge earthquake. The angel went to the tomb and rolled the stone away from the entrance. Then he sat on top of the stone. 3The angel was shining as bright as lightning. His clothes were as white as snow. 4The soldiers guarding the tomb were very afraid of the angel. They shook with fear and then became like dead men.

5The angel said to the women, "Don't be afraid. I know you are looking for Jesus, the one who was killed on the cross. 6But he is not here. He has risen from death, as he said he would. Come and see the place where his body was. 7And go quickly and tell his followers, 'Jesus has risen from death. He is going into Galilee and will be there before you. You will see him there.'" Then the angel said, "Now I have told you."

8So the women left the tomb quickly. They were afraid, but they were also very happy. They ran to tell his followers what happened. 9Suddenly, Jesus was there in front of them. He said, "Hello!" The women went to him and, holding on to his feet, worshiped him. 10Then Jesus said to them, "Don't be afraid. Go tell my followers*b* to go to Galilee. They will see me there."

Report to the Jewish Leaders

11The women went to tell the followers. At the same time, some of the soldiers who were guarding the tomb* went into the city. They went to tell the leading priests everything that happened. 12Then the priests met with the older Jewish leaders and made a plan. They paid the soldiers a lot of money 13and said to them, "Tell the people that Jesus' followers came during the night and stole the body while you were sleeping. 14If the governor hears about this, we will talk to him and keep you out of trouble." 15So the soldiers kept the money and obeyed the priests. And that story is still spread among the Jews even today.

Jesus Talks to His Followers
(Mk. 16:14–18; Lk. 24:36–49; Jn. 20:19–23; Acts 1:6–8)

16The eleven followers went to Galilee, to the mountain where Jesus told them to go. 17On the mountain the followers saw Jesus. They worshiped him. But some of the followers did not believe that it was really Jesus. 18So he came to them and said, "All authority in heaven and on earth is given to me. 19So go and make followers of all people in the world. Baptize* them in the name of the Father and the Son and the Holy Spirit.* 20Teach them to obey everything that I have told you to do. You can be sure that I will be with you always. I will continue with you until the end of time."

---

*a***27:56** *James and John* Literally, "the sons of Zebedee."

*b***28:10** *followers* Literally, "brothers."

Mark

John Prepares the Way for Jesus
(Mt. 3:1–12; Lk. 3:1–9, 15–17; Jn. 1:19–28)

1 ¹The Good News* about Jesus Christ, the Son of God,ᵃ begins ²with what the prophet* Isaiah said would happen. He wrote:

"Listen! I will send my messenger ahead of you.
He will prepare the way for you."
Malachi 3:1

³"There is someone shouting in the desert:
'Prepare the way for the Lord.
Make the road straight for him.'"
Isaiah 40:3

⁴So John the Baptizer* came and was baptizing* people in the desert area. He told them to be baptized to show that they wanted to change their lives, and then their sins would be forgiven. ⁵All the people from Judea, including everyone from Jerusalem, came out to John. They confessed the bad things they had done, and he baptized them in the Jordan River.

⁶John wore clothes made from camel's hair and a leather belt around his waist. He ate locusts* and wild honey. ⁷This is what John told the people: "There is someone coming later who is able to do more than I can. I am not good enough to be the slave who stoops down to untie his sandals. ⁸I baptize you with water, but the one who is coming will baptize you with the Holy Spirit.*"

Jesus Is Baptized by John
(Mt. 3:13–17; Lk. 3:21–22)

⁹About that time Jesus came from the town of Nazareth in Galilee to the place where John was. John baptized* Jesus in the Jordan River. ¹⁰As Jesus was coming up out of the water, he saw the sky torn open, The Spirit* came down on him like a dove. ¹¹A voice came from heaven and said, "You are my Son, the one I love. I am very pleased with you."

Jesus Goes Away to Be Tempted
(Mt. 4:1–11; Lk. 4:1–13)

¹²Then the Spirit* sent Jesus into the desert alone. ¹³He was there for 40 days, being tempted by Satan.* During this time he was out among the wild animals. Then angels came and helped him.

Jesus Begins His Work in Galilee
(Mt. 4:12–17; Lk. 4:14–15)

¹⁴After John was put in prison, Jesus went into Galilee and told people the Good News* from God. ¹⁵He said, "The right time is now here. God's kingdom* is near. Change your hearts and lives, and believe the Good News!"

Jesus Chooses Some Followers
(Mt. 4:18–22; Lk. 5:1–11)

¹⁶Jesus was walking by Lake Galilee. He saw Simonᵇ and his brother, Andrew. These two men were fishermen, and they were throwing a net into the lake to catch fish. ¹⁷Jesus said to them, "Come, follow me, and I will make you a different kind of fishermen. You will bring in people, not fish." ¹⁸So they immediately left their nets and followed Jesus.

¹⁹Jesus continued walking by Lake Galilee. He saw two more brothers, James and John, the sons of Zebedee. They were in their boat, preparing their nets to catch fish. ²⁰Their father Zebedee and the men who worked for him were in the boat with the brothers. When Jesus saw the brothers, he told them to come. They left their father and followed Jesus.

Jesus Frees a Man From an Evil Spirit
(Lk. 4:31–37)

²¹Jesus and his followers went to Capernaum.* On the Sabbath* day, Jesus went into the synagogue* and taught the people. ²²They were amazed at his teaching. He did not teach like their teachers of the law. He taught like someone with authority. ²³While Jesus was in the synagogue, a man was there who had an evil spirit inside him. The man shouted, ²⁴"Jesus of Nazareth! What do you want with us? Did you come to destroy us? I know who you are—God's Holy One!"

²⁵Jesus, his voice full of warning, said, "Be quiet, and come out of him!" ²⁶The evil spirit made the man shake. Then the spirit made a loud noise and came out of him.

²⁷The people were amazed. They asked each other, "What is happening here? This man is teaching something new, and he

ᵃ**1:1** *the Son of God* Some Greek copies do not have these words.

ᵇ**1:16** *Simon* Simon's other name was Peter. Also in verses 29, 36.

teaches with authority! He even commands evil spirits, and they obey him." 28So the news about Jesus spread quickly everywhere in the area of Galilee.

Jesus Heals Many People
(Mt. 8:14–17; Lk. 4:38–41)

29Jesus and the followers left the synagogue.* They all went with James and John to the home of Simon and Andrew. 30Simon's mother-in-law was very sick. She was in bed and had a fever. The people there told Jesus about her. 31So he went to her bed. Jesus held her hand and helped her stand up. The fever left her, and she was healed. Then she began serving them.

32That night, after the sun went down, the people brought to Jesus many who were sick. They also brought those who had demons* inside them. 33Everyone in the town gathered at the door of that house. 34Jesus healed many of those who had different kinds of sicknesses. He also forced many demons out of people. But he would not allow the demons to speak, because they knew who he was.a

Jesus Goes to Other Towns
(Lk. 4:42–44)

35The next morning Jesus woke up very early. He left the house while it was still dark and went to a place where he could be alone and pray. 36Later, Simon and his friends went to look for Jesus. 37They found him and said, "Everyone is looking for you!"

38Jesus answered, "We should go to another place. We can go to other towns around here, and I can tell God's message to those people too. That is why I came." 39So Jesus traveled everywhere in Galilee. He spoke in the synagogues,* and he forced demons* out of people.

Jesus Heals a Sick Man
(Mt. 8:1–4; Lk. 5:12–16)

40A man who had leprosy* came to Jesus. The man bowed on his knees and begged him, "You have the power to heal me if you want."

41Jesus felt sorry for the man. So he touched him and said, "I want to heal you. Be healed!" 42Immediately the leprosy disappeared, and the man was healed.

43Jesus told the man to go, but he gave him a strong warning: 44"Don't tell anyone about what I did for you. But go and let the priest look at you.b And offer a gift to God because you have been healed. Offer the gift that Moses* commanded.c This will show everyone that you are healed." 45The man left there and told everyone he saw that Jesus had

healed him. So the news about Jesus spread. And that is why he could not enter a town if people saw him. He stayed in places where people did not live. But people came from all the towns to the places where he was.

Jesus Heals a Crippled Man
(Mt. 9:1–8; Lk. 5:17–26)

2 1A few days later, Jesus came back to Capernaum.* The news spread that he was back home. 2A large crowd gathered to hear him speak. The house was so full that there was no place to stand, not even outside the door. While Jesus was teaching, 3some people brought a paralyzed man to see him. He was being carried by four of them. 4But they could not get the man inside to Jesus because the house was so full of people. So they went to the roof above Jesus and made a hole in it. Then they lowered the mat with the paralyzed man on it. 5When Jesus saw how much faith they had, he said to the paralyzed man, "Young man, your sins are forgiven."

6Some of the teachers of the law were sitting there. They saw what Jesus did, and they said to themselves, 7"Why does this man say things like that? What an insult to God! No one but God can forgive sins."

8Jesus knew immediately what these teachers of the law were thinking. So he said to them, "Why do you have these questions in your minds? 9–10The Son of Man* has power on earth to forgive sins. But how can I prove this to you? Maybe you are thinking it was easy for me to say to the crippled man, 'Your sins are forgiven.' There's no proof it really happened. But what if I say to the man, 'Stand up. Take your mat and walk'? Then you will be able to see if I really have this power or not." So Jesus said to the paralyzed man, 11"I tell you, stand up. Take your mat and go home."

12Immediately the paralyzed man stood up. He picked up his mat and walked out of the room. Everyone could see him. They were amazed and praised God. They said, "This is the most amazing thing we have ever seen!"

Levi (Matthew) Follows Jesus
(Mt. 9:9–13; Lk. 5:27–32)

13Jesus went to the lake again, and many people followed him there. So Jesus taught them. 14He was walking beside the lake, and he saw a man named Levi, son of Alphaeus. Levi was sitting at his place for collecting taxes. Jesus said to him, "Follow me." Then Levi stood up and followed Jesus.

15Later that day, Jesus and his followers ate at Levi's house. There were also many tax collectors* and others with bad reputations eating with them. (There were many of these people who followed Jesus.) 16When some teachers of the law who were Pharisees* saw Jesus eating with such bad people, they asked his followers, "Why does he eat with tax collectors and sinners?"

---

a1:34 *who he was* Meaning that the demons knew that Jesus was the Christ, the Son of God.
b1:44 *let the priest look at you* The Law of Moses said a priest must decide when a person with leprosy was well.
c1:44 *Moses commanded* See Lev. 14:1–32.

[17]When Jesus heard this, he said to them, "It is the sick people who need a doctor, not those who are healthy. I did not come to invite good people. I came to invite sinners."

Jesus Is Not Like Other Religious Leaders
(Mt. 9:14–17; Lk. 5:33–39)

[18]The followers of John* and the Pharisees* were fasting.* Some people came to Jesus and said, "John's followers fast, and the followers of the Pharisees fast. But your followers don't fast. Why?"

[19]Jesus answered, "At a wedding the friends of the bridegroom* are not sad while he is with them. They cannot fast while the bridegroom is still there. [20]But the time will come when the bridegroom will be taken from them. Then they will fast.

[21]"When someone sews a patch over a hole in an old coat, they never use a piece of cloth that is not yet shrunk. If they do, the patch will shrink and pull away from the coat. Then the hole will be worse. [22]Also, no one ever pours new wine into old wineskins.* The wine would break them, and the wine would be ruined along with the wineskins. You always put new wine into new wineskins."

Jesus Is Lord Over the Sabbath Day
(Mt. 12:1–8; Lk. 6:1–5)

[23]On the Sabbath* day, Jesus and his followers were walking through some grain fields. The followers picked some grain to eat. [24]Some Pharisees* said to Jesus, "Why are your followers doing this? It is against the law to pick grain on the Sabbath."

[25]Jesus answered, "You have read what David* did when he and the people with him were hungry and needed food. [26]It was during the time of Abiathar the high priest.* David went into God's house and ate the bread that was offered to God. And the Law of Moses* says that only priests can eat that bread. David also gave some of the bread to the people with him."

[27]Then Jesus said to the Pharisees, "The Sabbath day was made to help people. People were not made to be ruled by the Sabbath. [28]So the Son of Man* is Lord of every day, even the Sabbath."

Jesus Heals a Man on the Sabbath Day
(Mt. 12:9–14; Lk. 6:6–11)

3 [1]Another time Jesus went into the synagogue.* In the synagogue there was a man with a crippled hand. [2]Some Jews there were watching Jesus closely. They were waiting to see if he would heal the man on a Sabbath* day. They wanted to see Jesus do something wrong so that they could accuse him. [3]Jesus said to the man with the crippled hand, "Stand up here so that everyone can see you."

[4]Then Jesus asked the people, "Which is the right thing to do on the Sabbath day: to do good or to do evil? Is it right to save a life or to destroy one?" The people said nothing to answer him.

[5]Jesus looked at the people. He was angry, but he felt very sad because they were so stubborn. He said to the man, "Hold out your hand." The man held out his hand, and it was healed. [6]Then the Pharisees* left and made plans with the Herodians* about a way to kill Jesus.

Many Follow Jesus

[7]Jesus went away with his followers to the lake. A large crowd of people from Galilee followed them. [8]Many also came from Judea, from Jerusalem, from Idumea, from the area across the Jordan River, and from the area around Tyre and Sidon. These people came because they heard about all that Jesus was doing.

[9]Jesus saw how many people there were, so he told his followers to get a small boat and make it ready for him. He wanted the boat so that the crowds of people could not push against him. [10]He had healed many of them, so all the sick people were pushing toward him to touch him. [11]Some people had evil spirits inside them. When the evil spirits saw Jesus, they bowed before him and shouted, "You are the Son of God!" [12]But Jesus gave the spirits a strong warning not to tell anyone who he was.

Jesus Chooses His Twelve Apostles
(Mt. 10:1–4; Lk. 6:12–16)

[13]Then Jesus went up on a hill and invited those he wanted to go with him. So they joined him there. [14]And he chose twelve men and called them apostles.* He wanted these twelve men to be with him, and he wanted to send them to other places to tell people God's message. [15]He also wanted them to have the power to force demons* out of people. [16]These are the names of the twelve men Jesus chose:

Simon (the one Jesus named Peter),
[17] James and his brother John, the sons of Zebedee (the ones Jesus named Boanerges, which means "Sons of Thunder"),
[18] Andrew,
   Philip,
   Bartholomew,
   Matthew,
   Thomas,
   James, the son of Alphaeus,
   Thaddaeus,
   Simon, the Zealot,*
[19] Judas Iscariot (the one who handed Jesus over to his enemies).

Jesus' Power Is From God
(Mt. 12:22–32; Lk. 11:14–23; 12:10)

[20]Then Jesus went home, but again a large crowd gathered there. There were so many

people that he and his followers could not eat. [21]His family heard about all these things. They went to get him because people said he was crazy.

[22]And the teachers of the law from Jerusalem said, "Satan[a] is living inside him! He uses power from the ruler of demons* to force demons out of people."

[23]So Jesus called them together and talked to them using some stories. He said, "Satan* will not force his own demons out of people. [24]A kingdom that fights against itself will not survive. [25]And a family that is divided will not survive. [26]If Satan is against himself and is fighting against his own people, he will not survive. That would be the end of Satan. [27]"Whoever wants to enter a strong man's house and steal his things must first tie him up. Then they can steal the things from his house.

[28]"I want you to know that people can be forgiven for all the sinful things they do. They can even be forgiven for the bad things they say against God. [29]But anyone who speaks against the Holy Spirit* will never be forgiven. They will always be guilty of that sin."

[30]Jesus said this because the teachers of the law had accused him of having an evil spirit inside him.

Jesus' Followers Are His True Family
(Mt. 12:46–50; Lk. 8:19–21)

[31]Then Jesus' mother and brothers came. They stood outside and sent someone in to tell him to come out. [32]Many people were sitting around Jesus. They said to him, "Your mother and brothers are waiting for you outside."

[33]Jesus asked, "Who is my mother? Who are my brothers?" [34]Then he looked at the people sitting around him and said, "These people are my mother and my brothers! [35]My true brother and sister and mother are those who do what God wants."

A Story About a Farmer Sowing Seed
(Mt. 13:1–9; Lk. 8:4–8)

4 [1]Another time Jesus began teaching by the lake, and a large crowd gathered around him. He got into a boat so that he could sit and teach from the lake. All the people stayed on the shore near the water. [2]Jesus used stories to teach them many things. One of his lessons included this story:

[3]"Listen! A farmer went out to sow seed. [4]While he was scattering the seed, some of it fell by the road. The birds came and ate all that seed. [5]Other seed fell on rocky ground, where there was not enough dirt. It grew quickly there because the soil was not deep. [6]But then the sun rose and the plants were burned. They died because they did not have deep roots. [7]Some other seed fell among thorny weeds. The weeds grew and stopped the good plants

from growing. So they did not make grain. [8]But some of the seed fell on good ground. There it began to grow, and it made grain. Some plants made 30 times more grain, some 60 times more, and some 100 times more."

[9]Then Jesus said, "You people who hear me, listen!"

Why Jesus Used Stories to Teach
(Mt. 13:10–17; Lk. 8:9–10)

[10]Later, Jesus was away from the people. The twelve apostles* and his other followers asked him about the stories.

[11]Jesus said, "Only you can know the secret truth about God's kingdom.* But to those other people I tell everything by using stories. [12]I do this so that,

'They will look and look but never really see;
  they will listen and listen but never understand.
If they saw and understood, they might change and be forgiven.'"   *Isaiah 6:9–10*

Jesus Explains the Story About Seed
(Mt. 13:18–23; Lk. 8:11–15)

[13]Then Jesus said to the followers, "Do you understand this story? If you don't, how will you understand any story? [14]The farmer is like someone who plants God's teaching in people. [15]Sometimes the teaching falls on the path. That is like some people who hear the teaching of God. As soon as they hear it, Satan* comes and takes away the teaching that was planted in them.

[16]"Other people are like the seed planted on rocky ground. They hear the teaching, and they quickly and gladly accept it. [17]But they don't allow it to go deep into their lives. They keep it only a short time. As soon as trouble or persecution* comes because of the teaching they accepted, they give up.

[18]"Others are like the seed planted among the thorny weeds. They hear the teaching, [19]but their lives become full of other things: the worries of this life, the love of money, and everything else they want. This keeps the teaching from growing, and it does not produce a crop[b] in their lives.

[20]"And others are like the seed planted on the good ground. They hear the teaching and accept it. Then they grow and produce a good crop—sometimes 30 times more, sometimes 60 times more, and sometimes 100 times more."

Use the Understanding You Have
(Lk. 8:16–18)

[21]Then Jesus said to them, "You don't take a lamp and hide it under a bowl or a bed, do you? Of course not. You put it on a lampstand.

---

*b*4:19 *produce a crop* Meaning to do the good things God wants his people to do.

22Everything that is hidden will be made clear. Every secret thing will be made known. 23You people who hear me, listen! 24Think carefully about what you are hearing. God will know how much to give you by how much you understand now. But he will give you more than you deserve. 25The people who have some understanding will receive more. But those who do not have much will lose even the small amount they have."

Jesus Uses a Story About Seed

26Then Jesus said, "God's kingdom* is like a man who plants seed in the ground. 27The seed begins to grow. It grows night and day. It doesn't matter whether the man is sleeping or awake, the seed still grows. He doesn't know how it happens. 28Without any help the ground produces grain. First the plant grows, then the head, and then all the grain in the head. 29When the grain is ready, the man cuts it. This is the harvest time."

What Is God's Kingdom Like?
(Mt. 13:31–32, 34–35; Lk. 13:18–19)

30Then Jesus said, "What can I use to show you what God's kingdom* is like? What story can I use to explain it? 31God's kingdom is like a mustard seed, which is smaller than any other seed on earth that you can plant. 32But when you plant it, it grows and becomes the largest of all the plants in your garden. It has branches that are very big. The wild birds can come and make nests there and be protected from the sun."

33Jesus used many stories like these to teach the people. He taught them all they could understand. 34He always used stories to teach them. But when he was alone with his followers, Jesus explained everything to them.

Jesus' Followers See His Power
(Mt. 8:23–27; Lk. 8:22–25)

35That day, at evening, Jesus said to his followers, "Come with me across the lake." 36So they left the crowd behind and went with Jesus in the boat he was already in. There were also other boats that went with them. 37A very bad wind came up on the lake. The waves were coming over the sides and into the boat, and it was almost full of water. 38Jesus was inside the boat, sleeping with his head on a pillow. The followers went and woke him. They said, "Teacher, don't you care about us? We are going to drown!"

39Jesus stood up and gave a command to the wind and the water. He said, "Quiet! Be still!" Then the wind stopped, and the lake became calm.

40He said to his followers, "Why are you afraid? Do you still have no faith?"

41They were very afraid and asked each other, "What kind of man is this? Even the wind and the water obey him!"

Jesus Frees a Man From Evil Spirits
(Mt. 8:28–34; Lk. 8:26–39)

5 1Jesus and his followers went across the lake to the area where the Gerasene people lived. 2When Jesus got out of the boat, a man came to him from the caves where the dead are buried. This man had an evil spirit living inside him. 3He lived in the burial caves. No one could keep him tied up, even with chains. 4Many times people had put chains on his hands and feet, but he broke the chains. No one was strong enough to control him. 5Day and night he stayed around the burial caves and on the hills. He would scream and cut himself with rocks.

6While Jesus was still far away, the man saw him. He ran to Jesus and bowed down before him. 7-8As Jesus was saying, "You evil spirit, come out of this man," the man shouted loudly, "What do you want with me, Jesus, Son of the Most High God? I beg you in God's name not to punish me!"

9Then Jesus asked the man, "What is your name?"

The man answered, "My name is Legion,ᵃ because there are many spirits inside me." 10The spirits inside the man begged Jesus again and again not to send them out of that area.

11A large herd of pigs was eating on a hill near there. 12The evil spirits begged Jesus, "Send us to the pigs. Let us go into them." 13So Jesus allowed them to do this. The evil spirits left the man and went into the pigs. Then the herd of pigs ran down the hill and into the lake. They were all drowned. There were about 2000 pigs in that herd.

14The men who had the work of caring for the pigs ran away. They ran to the town and to the farms and told everyone what happened. The people went out to see. 15They came to Jesus, and they saw the man who had the many evil spirits. He was sitting down and was wearing clothes. He was in his right mind again. When they saw this, they were afraid. 16Those who had seen what Jesus did told the others what happened to the man who had the demons* living in him. And they also told about the pigs. 17Then the people began to beg Jesus to leave their area.

18Jesus was preparing to leave in the boat. The man who was now free from the demons begged to go with him. 19But Jesus did not allow the man to go. He said, "Go home to your family and friends. Tell them about all that the Lord did for you. Tell them how the Lord was good to you."

20So the man left and told the people in the Ten Towns* about the great things Jesus did for him. Everyone was amazed.

ᵃ5:9 Legion This name means very many. A legion was about 6000 men in the Roman army.

Jesus Gives Life to a Dead Girl and Heals a Sick Woman
(Mt. 9:18–26; Lk. 8:40–56)

21Jesus went back to the other side of the lake in the boat. There, a large crowd of people gathered around him on the shore. 22A leader of the synagogue* came. His name was Jairus. He saw Jesus and bowed down before him. 23He begged Jesus again and again, saying, "My little daughter is dying. Please come and lay your hands on* her. Then she will be healed and will live."

24So Jesus went with Jairus. Many people followed Jesus. They were pushing very close around him.

25There among the people was a woman who had been bleeding for the past twelve years. 26She had suffered very much. Many doctors had tried to help her, and all the money she had was spent, but she was not improving. In fact, her sickness was getting worse.

27The woman heard about Jesus, so she followed him with the other people and touched his coat. 28She thought, "If I can just touch his clothes, that will be enough to heal me." 29As soon as she touched his coat, her bleeding stopped. She felt that her body was healed from all the suffering. 30Jesus immediately felt power go out from him, so he stopped and turned around. "Who touched my clothes?" he asked.

31The followers said to Jesus, "There are so many people pushing against you. But you ask, 'Who touched me?'"

32But Jesus continued looking for the one who touched him. 33The woman knew that she was healed, so she came and bowed at Jesus' feet. She was shaking with fear. She told Jesus the whole story. 34He said to her, "Dear woman, you are made well because you believed. Go in peace. You will not suffer anymore."

35While Jesus was still there speaking, some men came from the house of Jairus, the synagogue leader. They said, "Your daughter is dead. There is no need to bother the Teacher."

36But Jesus did not care what the men said. He said to the synagogue leader, "Don't be afraid; just believe."

37Jesus let only Peter, James, and John the brother of James go with him. 38They went to the synagogue leader's house, where Jesus saw many people crying loudly. There was a lot of confusion. 39He entered the house and said, "Why are you people crying and making so much noise? This child is not dead. She is only sleeping." 40But everyone laughed at him.

Jesus told the people to leave the house. Then he went into the room where the child was. He brought the child's father and mother and his three followers into the room with him. 41Then Jesus held the girl's hand and said

to her, "*Talitha, koum!*" (This means "Little girl, I tell you to stand up!") 42The girl immediately stood up and began walking. (She was twelve years old.) The father and mother and the followers were amazed. 43Jesus gave the father and mother very strict orders not to tell people about this. Then he told them to give the girl some food to eat.

Jesus Goes to His Hometown
(Mt. 13:53–58; Lk. 4:16–30)

6 1Jesus left and went back to his hometown. His followers went with him. 2On the Sabbath* day Jesus taught in the synagogue,* and many people heard him. They were amazed and said, "Where did this man get this teaching? How did he get such wisdom? Who gave it to him? And where did he get the power to do miracles*? 3Isn't he just the carpenter we know—Mary's son, the brother of James, Joses, Judas, and Simon? And don't his sisters still live here in town?" So they had a problem accepting him.

4Then Jesus said to them, "People everywhere give honor to a prophet,* except in his own town, with his own people, or in his home." 5Jesus was not able to do any miracles there except the healing of some sick people by laying his hands on* them. 6He was surprised that the people there had no faith. Then he went to other villages in that area and taught.

Jesus Sends His Apostles on a Mission
(Mt. 10:1, 5–15; Lk. 9:1–6)

7Jesus called his twelve apostles* together. He sent them out in groups of two and gave them power over evil spirits. 8This is what he told them: "Take nothing for your trip except a stick for walking. Take no bread, no bag, and no money. 9You can wear sandals, but don't take extra clothes. 10When you enter a house, stay there until you leave that town. 11If any town refuses to accept you or refuses to listen to you, then leave that town and shake the dust off your feet[a] as a warning to them."

12The apostles left and went to other places. They talked to the people and told them to change their hearts and lives. 13They forced many demons* out of people and put olive oil on[b] many who were sick and healed them.

Herod Thinks Jesus Is John the Baptizer
(Mt. 14:1–12; Lk. 9:7–9)

14King Herod* heard about Jesus, because Jesus was now famous. Some people said, "He is John the Baptizer.* He must have risen from death, and that is why he can do these miracles.*" 15Other people said, "He is Elijah.*"

---

[a]**6:11 shake the dust off your feet** A warning. It would show that they were finished talking to these people.

[b]**6:13 put olive oil on** Olive oil was used like a medicine.

And others said, "He is a prophet.* He is like the prophets who lived long ago."

¹⁶Herod heard these things about Jesus. He said, "I killed John by cutting off his head. Now he has been raised from death!"

How John the Baptizer Was Killed

¹⁷Herod* himself had ordered his soldiers to arrest John and put him in prison. Herod did this to please his wife Herodias. She had been married to Herod's brother Philip, but then Herod married her. ¹⁸John told Herod, "It is not right for you to be married to your brother's wife." ¹⁹So Herodias hated John. She wanted him dead, but she was not able to persuade Herod to kill him. ²⁰Herod was afraid to kill John, because he knew that he was a good and holy* man. So he protected him. He liked listening to John, although what John said left him with so many questions.

²¹Then the right time came for Herodias to cause John's death. It happened on Herod's birthday. Herod gave a dinner party for the most important government leaders, the commanders of his army, and the most important people in Galilee. ²²The daughter of Herodias came to the party and danced. When she danced, Herod and the people eating with him were very pleased.

So King Herod said to the girl, "I will give you anything you want." ²³He promised her, "Anything you ask for I will give to you—even half of my kingdom."

²⁴The girl went to her mother and asked, "What should I ask King Herod to give me?"

Her mother answered, "Ask for the head of John the Baptizer.*"

²⁵So right then the girl went back in to the king. She said to him, "Please give me the head of John the Baptizer. Bring it to me now on a plate."

²⁶King Herod was very sad, but he didn't want to break the promise he had made to her in front of his guests. ²⁷So he sent a soldier to cut off John's head and bring it to him. The soldier went and cut off John's head in the prison. ²⁸He brought the head back on a plate and gave it to the girl, and the girl gave it to her mother. ²⁹John's followers heard about what happened, so they came and got John's body and put it in a tomb.*

Jesus Feeds More Than 5000
(Mt. 14:13–21; Lk. 9:10–17; Jn. 6:1–14)

³⁰The apostles* Jesus had sent out came back to him. They gathered around him and told him about all they had done and taught. ³¹Jesus and his followers were in a very busy place. There were so many people that he and his followers did not even have time to eat. He said to them, "Come with me. We will go to a quiet place to be alone. There we will get some rest."

³²So Jesus and his followers went away alone. They went in a boat to a place where no one lived. ³³But many people saw them leave and knew who they were. So people from every town ran to the place where they were going and got there before Jesus. ³⁴As Jesus stepped out of the boat, he saw a large crowd waiting. He felt sorry for them, because they were like sheep without a shepherd to care for them. So he taught the people many things.

³⁵It was now very late in the day. Jesus' followers came to him and said, "No one lives around here, and it is already very late. ³⁶So send the people away. They need to go to the farms and towns around here to buy some food to eat."

³⁷But Jesus answered, "You give them some food to eat."

They said to Jesus, "We can't buy enough bread to feed all these people. We would all have to work a month to earn enough to buy that much bread!"

³⁸Jesus asked them, "How many loaves of bread do you have now? Go and see."

They counted their loaves of bread. They came to Jesus and said, "We have five loaves of bread and two fish."

³⁹Then Jesus said to them, "Tell everyone to sit in groups on the green grass." ⁴⁰So all the people sat in groups. There were about 50 or 100 people in each group.

⁴¹Jesus took the five loaves and two fish. He looked up to the sky and thanked God for the food. Then he broke the bread into pieces, which he gave to his followers to distribute to the people. Then he divided the two fish among everyone there.

⁴²They all ate until they were full. ⁴³After they finished eating, the followers filled twelve baskets with the pieces of bread and fish that were left. ⁴⁴There were about 5000 men there who ate.

Jesus Walks on Water
(Mt. 14:22–33; Jn. 6:16–21)

⁴⁵Then Jesus told the followers to get into the boat. He told them to go to the other side of the lake to Bethsaida. He said he would come later. He stayed there to tell everyone they could go home. ⁴⁶After he said goodbye to them, he went up into the hills to pray.

⁴⁷That night, the boat was still in the middle of the lake. Jesus was alone on the land. ⁴⁸He saw the boat far away on the lake. And he saw the followers working hard to row the boat. The wind was blowing against them. Sometime between three and six o'clock in the morning, Jesus went out to the boat, walking on the water. He continued walking until he was almost past the boat. ⁴⁹But the followers saw Jesus walking on the water. They thought he was a ghost, and they started screaming. ⁵⁰It scared them all to see him. But he spoke to them and said, "Don't worry! It's me! Don't be afraid." ⁵¹When he got into the boat with the followers, the wind stopped. The followers were completely amazed. ⁵²They could

not believe what happened. It was like the miracle he did with the bread. They still didn't understand what that meant.

Jesus Heals Many Sick People
(Mt. 14:34–36)

53Jesus and his followers went across the lake and came to shore at Gennesaret. They tied the boat there. 54When they were out of the boat, the people there saw Jesus. They knew who he was, 55so they ran to tell others throughout that area. They brought sick people on mats to every place Jesus went. 56Jesus went into towns, cities, and farms around that area. And every place he went, the people brought sick people to the marketplaces. They begged him to let them touch any part of his coat. And all those who touched him were healed.

God's Law and Human Traditions
(Mt. 15:1–20)

7 1Some Pharisees* and some teachers of the law came from Jerusalem and gathered around Jesus. 2They saw that some of his followers ate food with hands that were not clean, meaning that they did not wash their hands in a special way. 3The Pharisees and all the other Jews never eat before washing their hands in this special way. They do this to follow the traditions they have from their great leaders who lived long ago. 4And when these Jews buy something in the market, they never eat it until they wash it in a special way. They also follow other rules from their people who lived before them. They follow rules like the washing of cups, pitchers, and pots.*a*

5The Pharisees and teachers of the law said to Jesus, "Your followers don't follow the traditions we have from our great leaders who lived long ago. They eat their food with hands that are not clean. Why do they do this?"

6Jesus answered, "You are all hypocrites.* Isaiah was right when he wrote these words from God about you:

'These people honor me with their words,
but I am not really important to them.
7 Their worship of me is worthless.
The things they teach are only human
rules.'   *Isaiah 29:13*

8You have stopped following God's commands, preferring instead the man-made rules you got from others."

9Then he said, "You show great skill in avoiding the commands of God so that you can follow your own teachings! 10Moses* said, 'You must respect your father and mother.'*b* He also said, 'Whoever says anything bad to their father or mother must be killed.'*c* 11But

you teach that people can say to their father or mother, 'I have something I could use to help you, but I will not use it for you. I will give it to God.' 12You are telling people that they do not have to do anything for their father or mother. 13So you are teaching that it is not important to do what God said. You think it is more important to follow those traditions you have, which you pass on to others. And you do many things like that."

14Jesus called the people to him again. He said, "Everyone should listen to me and understand what I am saying. 15There is nothing people can put in their mouth that will make them wrong.*d* People are made wrong by what comes from inside them." 16 *e*

17Then Jesus left the people and went into the house. The followers asked Jesus about what he had told the people. 18He said, "Do you still have trouble understanding? Surely you know that nothing that enters the mouth from the outside can make people unacceptable to God. 19Food does not go into a person's mind. It goes into the stomach. Then it goes out of the body." (When Jesus said this, he meant there is no food that is wrong for people to eat.)

20And Jesus said, "The things that make people wrong are the things that come from the inside. 21All these bad things begin inside a person, in the mind: bad thoughts, sexual sins, stealing, murder, 22adultery,* greed, doing bad things to people, lying, doing things that are morally wrong, jealousy, insulting people, proud talking, and foolish living. 23These evil things come from inside a person. And these are the things that make people unacceptable to God."

Jesus Helps a Non-Jewish Woman
(Mt. 15:21–28)

24Jesus went from there to the area around Tyre. He did not want the people in that area to know he was there, so he went into a house. But he could not stay hidden. 25A woman heard that he was there. Her little daughter had an evil spirit inside her. So the woman came to Jesus and bowed down near his feet. 26She was not a Jew. She was born in Phoenicia, an area in Syria. She begged Jesus to force the demon* out of her daughter.

27Jesus told the woman, "It is not right to take the children's bread and give it to the dogs. First let the children eat all they want."

28She answered, "That is true, Lord. But the dogs under the table can eat the pieces of food that the children don't eat."

29Then he told her, "That is a very good answer. You may go. The demon has left your daughter."

30The woman went home and found her

---

*a***7:4** *pots* Some Greek copies add "and couches."
*b***7:10** Quote from Ex. 20:12; Deut. 5:16.
*c***7:10** Quote from Ex. 21:17.
*d***7:15** *wrong* Literally, "unclean" or "not pure," meaning unacceptable to God. Also in verse 20.
*e***7:16** Some Greek copies add verse 16: "You people who hear me, listen!"

daughter lying on the bed. The demon was gone.

Jesus Heals a Deaf Man

31Then Jesus left the area around Tyre and went through Sidon. On his way to Lake Galilee he went through the area of the Ten Towns.* 32While he was there, some people brought a man to him who was deaf and could not talk clearly. The people begged Jesus to put his hand on the man to heal him.

33Jesus led the man away from the people to be alone with him. He put his fingers in the man's ears. Then he spit on a finger and put it on the man's tongue. 34Jesus looked up to the sky and with a loud sigh he said, "Ephphatha!" (This means "Open!") 35As soon as Jesus did this, the man was able to hear. He was able to use his tongue, and he began to speak clearly.

36Jesus told the people not to tell anyone about this. But the more he told them not to say anything, the more people they told. 37They were all completely amazed. They said, "Look at what he has done. It's all good. He makes deaf people able to hear and gives a new voice to people who could not talk."

Jesus Feeds More Than 4000
(Mt. 15:32–39)

8 1Another time there were many people with Jesus. The people had nothing to eat. So he called his followers to him and said, 2"I feel sorry for these people. They have been with me for three days, and now they have nothing to eat. 3I should not send them home hungry. If they leave without eating, they will faint on the way home. Some of them live a long way from here."

4Jesus' followers answered, "But we are far away from any towns. Where can we get enough bread to feed all these people?"

5Then Jesus asked them, "How many loaves of bread do you have?"

They answered, "We have seven loaves of bread."

6Jesus told the people to sit on the ground. Then he took the seven loaves and gave thanks to God. He broke the bread into pieces and gave them to his followers. He told them to give the bread to the people, and they did as he said. 7The followers also had a few small fish. Jesus gave thanks for the fish and told them to give the fish to the people.

8They all ate until they were full. Then the followers filled seven baskets with the pieces of food that were left. 9There were about 4000 men who ate. After they ate, Jesus told them to go home. 10Then he went in a boat with his followers to the area of Dalmanutha.

Some People Doubt Jesus' Authority
(Mt. 16:1–4; Lk. 11:16, 29)

11The Pharisees* came to Jesus and asked him questions. They wanted to test him. So they asked him to do a miracle* as a sign from God. 12Jesus sighed deeply and said, "Why do you people ask to see a miracle as a sign? I want you to know that no miracle will be done to prove anything to you." 13Then Jesus left them and went in the boat to the other side of the lake.

Jesus' Followers Misunderstand Him
(Mt. 16:5–12)

14The followers had only one loaf of bread with them in the boat. They forgot to bring more bread. 15Jesus warned them, "Be careful! Guard against the yeast* of the Pharisees* and the yeast of Herod.*"

16The followers discussed the meaning of this. They said, "He said this because we have no bread."

17Jesus knew that the followers were talking about this. So he asked them, "Why are you talking about having no bread? Do you still not see or understand? Are you not able to understand? 18Do you have eyes that can't see? Do you have ears that can't hear? Remember what I did before, when we did not have enough bread? 19I divided five loaves of bread for 5000 people. Remember how many baskets you filled with pieces of food that were not eaten?"

The followers answered, "We filled twelve baskets."

20"And when I divided seven loaves of bread for 4000 people, how many baskets did you fill with the leftover pieces?"

They answered, "We filled seven baskets."

21Then he said to them, "You remember these things I did, but you still don't understand?"

Jesus Heals a Blind Man in Bethsaida

22Jesus and his followers came to Bethsaida. Some people brought a blind man to him and begged him to touch the man. 23So Jesus held the blind man's hand and led him out of the village. Then he spit on the man's eyes. He laid his hands on* him and asked, "Can you see now?"

24The man looked up and said, "Yes, I see people. They look like trees walking around."

25Again Jesus laid his hands on the man's eyes, and the man opened them wide. His eyes were healed, and he was able to see everything clearly. 26Jesus told him to go home. He said, "Don't go into the town."

Peter Says Jesus Is the Christ
(Mt. 16:13–20; Lk. 9:18–21)

27Jesus and his followers went to the towns in the area of Caesarea Philippi. While they were traveling, Jesus asked the followers, "Who do people say I am?"

28They answered, "Some people say you are John the Baptizer.* Others say you are Elijah.* And others say you are one of the prophets.*"

²⁹Then Jesus asked, "Who do you say I am?"

Peter answered, "You are the Christ.*"

³⁰Jesus told the followers, "Don't tell anyone who I am."

Jesus Says He Must Die
(Mt. 16:21-28; Lk. 9:22-27)

³¹Then Jesus began to teach his followers that the Son of Man* must suffer many things. He taught that the Son of Man would not be accepted by the older Jewish leaders, the leading priests, and the teachers of the law. He said that the Son of Man must be killed and then rise from death after three days. ³²Jesus told them everything that would happen. He did not keep anything secret.

Peter took Jesus away from the other followers to talk to him alone. Peter criticized him for saying these things. ³³But Jesus turned and looked at his followers. Then he criticized Peter. He said to Peter, "Get away from me, Satan^a! You don't care about the same things God does. You care only about things that people think are important."

³⁴Then Jesus called the crowd and his followers to him. He said, "Any of you who want to be my follower must stop thinking about yourself and what you want. You must be willing to carry the cross* that is given to you for following me. ³⁵Any of you who try to save the life you have will lose it. But you who give up your life for me and for the Good News* will save it. ³⁶It is worth nothing for you to have the whole world if you yourself are lost. ³⁷You could never pay enough to buy back your life. ³⁸People today are so sinful. They have not been faithful to God. As you live among them, don't be ashamed of me and my teaching. If that happens, I^b will be ashamed of you when I come with the glory* of my Father and the holy* angels."

9 ¹Then Jesus said, "Believe me when I say that some of you people standing here will see God's kingdom* come with power before you die."

Jesus Is Seen With Moses and Elijah
(Mt. 17:1-13; Lk. 9:28-36)

²Six days later, Jesus took Peter, James, and John and went up on a high mountain. They were all alone there. While these followers watched him, Jesus was changed. ³His clothes became shining white—whiter than anyone on earth could make them. ⁴Then two men were there talking with Jesus. They were Elijah* and Moses.*

⁵Peter said to Jesus, "Teacher, it is good that we are here. We will put three tents here—one for you, one for Moses, and one for Elijah." ⁶Peter did not know what to say,

because he and the other two followers were so afraid.

⁷Then a cloud came and covered them. A voice came from the cloud and said, "This is my Son, the one I love. Obey him!"

⁸The followers looked, but they saw only Jesus there alone with them.

⁹As Jesus and the followers were walking back down the mountain, he gave them these instructions: "Don't tell anyone about what you saw on the mountain. Wait until after the Son of Man* rises from death. Then you can tell people what you saw."

¹⁰So the followers waited to say anything about what they saw. But they discussed among themselves what Jesus meant about rising from death. ¹¹They asked him, "Why do the teachers of the law say that Elijah must come^c first?"

¹²Jesus answered, "They are right to say that Elijah must come first. Elijah makes all things the way they should be. But why do the Scriptures* say that the Son of Man will suffer much and that people will think he is worth nothing? ¹³I tell you that Elijah has already come. And people did to him all the bad things they wanted to do. The Scriptures said this would happen to him."

Jesus Frees a Boy From an Evil Spirit
(Mt. 17:14-20; Lk. 9:37-43a)

¹⁴Then Jesus, Peter, James, and John went to the other followers. They saw many people around them. The teachers of the law were arguing with the followers. ¹⁵When the people saw Jesus, they were very surprised and ran to welcome him.

¹⁶Jesus asked, "What are you arguing about with the teachers of the law?"

¹⁷A man answered, "Teacher, I brought my son to you. He is controlled by an evil spirit that keeps him from talking. ¹⁸The spirit attacks him and throws him on the ground. He foams at the mouth, grinds his teeth, and becomes very stiff. I asked your followers to force the evil spirit out, but they could not."

¹⁹Jesus answered, "You people today don't believe! How long must I stay with you? How long must I be patient with you? Bring the boy to me!"

²⁰So the followers brought the boy to Jesus. When the evil spirit saw Jesus, it attacked the boy. The boy fell down and rolled on the ground. He was foaming at the mouth.

²¹Jesus asked the boy's father, "How long has this been happening to him?"

The father answered, "Since he was very young. ²²The spirit often throws him into a fire or into water to kill him. If you can do anything, please have pity on us and help us."

²³Jesus said to the father, "Why did you say 'if you can'? All things are possible for the one who believes."

^a**8:33** *Satan* Name for the devil meaning "the enemy." Jesus means that Peter was talking like Satan.

^b**8:38** *I* Literally, "the Son of Man" (Jesus).

^c**9:11** *Elijah must come* See Mal. 4:5-6.

²⁴Immediately the father shouted, "I do believe. Help me to believe more!"

²⁵Jesus saw that all the people were running there to see what was happening. So he spoke to the evil spirit. He said, "You evil spirit that makes this boy deaf and stops him from talking—I command you to come out of him and never enter him again!"

²⁶The evil spirit screamed. It caused the boy to fall on the ground again, and then it came out. The boy looked as if he was dead. Many people said, "He is dead!" ²⁷But Jesus took hold of his hand and helped him stand up.

²⁸Then Jesus went into the house. His followers were alone with him there. They said, "Why weren't we able to force that evil spirit out?"

²⁹Jesus answered, "That kind of spirit can be forced out only with prayer.ᵃ"

Jesus Talks About His Death
(Mt. 17:22–23; Lk. 9:43b–45)

³⁰Then Jesus and his followers left there and went through Galilee. Jesus did not want the people to know where they were. ³¹He wanted to teach his followers alone. He said to them, "The Son of Man* will be handed over to the control of other men, who will kill him. After three days, he will rise from death." ³²But the followers did not understand what he meant, and they were afraid to ask him.

Who Is the Greatest?
(Mt. 18:1–5; Lk. 9:46–48)

³³Jesus and his followers went to Capernaum.* They went into a house, and Jesus said to them, "I heard you arguing on the way here today. What were you arguing about?" ³⁴But the followers did not answer, because their argument on the road was about which one of them was the greatest.

³⁵Jesus sat down and called the twelve apostles* to him. He said, "Whoever wants to be the most important must make others more important than themselves. They must serve everyone else."

³⁶Then Jesus took a small child and stood the child in front of the followers. He held the child in his arms and said, ³⁷"Whoever accepts children like these in my name is accepting me. And anyone who accepts me is also accepting the one who sent me."

Whoever Is Not Against Us Is For Us
(Lk. 9:49–50)

³⁸Then John said, "Teacher, we saw a man using your name to force demons* out of someone. He is not one of us. So we told him to stop, because he does not belong to our group."

³⁹Jesus said, "Don't stop him. Whoever uses my name to do powerful things will not soon say bad things about me. ⁴⁰Whoever is not against us is with us. ⁴¹I can assure you that anyone who helps you by giving you a drink of water because you belong to the Christ* will definitely get a reward.

Jesus Warns About Causes of Sin
(Mt. 18:6–9; Lk. 17:1–2)

⁴²"If one of these little children believes in me, and someone causes that child to sin, it will be very bad for that person. It would be better for them to have a millstone* tied around their neck and be drowned in the sea. ⁴³If your hand makes you sin, cut it off. It is better for you to lose part of your body and have eternal life than to have two hands and go to hell. There the fire never stops. ⁴⁴ ᵇ ⁴⁵If your foot makes you sin, cut it off. It is better for you to lose part of your body and have eternal life than to have two feet and be thrown into hell. ⁴⁶ ᶜ ⁴⁷If your eye makes you sin, take it out. It is better for you to have only one eye and enter God's kingdom* than to have two eyes and be thrown into hell. ⁴⁸The worms that eat the people in hell never die. The fire there is never stopped.

⁴⁹"Everyone will be salted with fire.ᵈ

⁵⁰"Salt is good. But if it loses its salty taste, you can't make it good again. So, don't lose that good quality of salt you have. And live in peace with each other."

Jesus Teaches About Divorce
(Mt. 19:1–12)

10 ¹Then Jesus left there and went into the area of Judea and across the Jordan River. Again, many people came to him, and Jesus taught them as he always did.

²Some Pharisees* came to Jesus and tried to make him say something wrong. They asked him, "Is it right for a man to divorce his wife?"

³Jesus answered, "What did Moses* command you to do?"

⁴The Pharisees said, "Moses allowed a man to divorce his wife by writing a certificate of divorce."ᵉ

⁵Jesus said, "Moses wrote that command for you because you refused to accept God's teaching. ⁶But when God made the world, 'he made people male and female.'ᶠ ⁷'That is why

---

ᵇ**9:44** Some Greek copies add verse 44, which is the same as verse 48.

ᶜ**9:46** Some Greek copies add verse 46, which is the same as verse 48.

ᵈ**9:49** Some Greek copies add, "and every sacrifice will be salted with salt." In the Old Testament salt was put on sacrifices. This verse could mean that Jesus' followers will be tested by suffering and that they must offer themselves to God as sacrifices.

ᵉ**10:4** *"Moses ... certificate of divorce"* See Deut. 24:1.

ᶠ**10:6** Quote from Gen. 1:27; 5:2.

ᵃ**9:29** *prayer* Some Greek copies have "prayer and fasting."

a man will leave his father and mother and be joined to his wife. ⁸And the two people will become one.'ª So they are no longer two, but one. ⁹God has joined them together, so no one should separate them."

¹⁰Later, when the followers and Jesus were in the house, they asked him again about the question of divorce. ¹¹He said, "Whoever divorces his wife and marries another woman has sinned against his wife. He is guilty of adultery.* ¹²And the woman who divorces her husband and marries another man is also guilty of adultery."

Jesus Welcomes Children
(Mt. 19:13–15; Lk. 18:15–17)

¹³People brought their small children to Jesus, so that he could lay his hands on* them to bless them. But the followers told the people to stop bringing their children to him. ¹⁴Jesus saw what happened. He did not like his followers telling the children not to come. So he said to them, "Let the little children come to me. Don't stop them, because God's kingdom* belongs to people who are like these little children. ¹⁵The truth is, you must accept God's kingdom like a little child accepts things, or you will never enter it." ¹⁶Then Jesus held the children in his arms. He laid his hands on them and blessed them.

A Rich Man Refuses to Follow Jesus
(Mt. 19:16–30; Lk. 18:18–30)

¹⁷Jesus started to leave, but a man ran to him and bowed down on his knees before him. The man asked, "Good Teacher, what must I do to get the life that never ends?"

¹⁸Jesus answered, "Why do you call me good? Only God is good. ¹⁹And you know his commands: 'You must not murder anyone, you must not commit adultery,* you must not steal, you must not lie, you must not cheat, you must respect your father and mother ....'ᵇ"

²⁰The man said, "Teacher, I have obeyed all these commands since I was a boy."

²¹Jesus looked at the man in a way that showed how much he cared for him. He said, "There is still one thing you need to do. Go and sell everything you have. Give the money to those who are poor, and you will have riches in heaven. Then come and follow me."

²²The man was upset when Jesus told him to give away his money. He didn't want to do this, because he was very rich. So he went away sad.

²³Then Jesus looked at his followers and said to them, "It will be very hard for a rich person to enter God's kingdom*!"

²⁴The followers were amazed at what Jesus said. But he said again, "My children, it is very hard to enter God's kingdom! ²⁵It is

easier for a camel to go through the eye of a needle than for a rich person to enter God's kingdom!"

²⁶The followers were even more amazed and said to each other, "Then who can be saved?"

²⁷Jesus looked at them and said, "That is something people cannot do, but God can. He can do anything."

²⁸Peter said to Jesus, "We left everything to follow you!"

²⁹Jesus said, "I can promise that everyone who has left their home, brothers, sisters, mother, father, children, or farm for me and for the Good News* about me ³⁰will get a hundred times more than they left. Here in this world they will get more homes, brothers, sisters, mothers, children, and farms. And with these things they will have persecutions.* But in the world that is coming they will also get the reward of eternal life. ³¹Many people who have the highest place now will have the lowest place in the future. And the people who have the lowest place now will have the highest place then."

Jesus Talks Again About His Death
(Mt. 20:17–19; Lk. 18:31–34)

³²Jesus and those with him were on their way to Jerusalem. He was at the front of the group. His followers were wondering what was happening, and the people who followed behind them were feeling afraid. Jesus gathered the twelve apostles* again and talked with them alone. He told them what would happen in Jerusalem. ³³He said, "We are going to Jerusalem. The Son of Man* will be handed over to the leading priests and teachers of the law. They will say that he must die and will hand him over to the foreigners, ³⁴who will laugh at him and spit on him. They will beat him with whips and kill him. But on the third day after his death, he will rise to life again."

James and John Ask for a Favor
(Mt. 20:20–28)

³⁵Then James and John, sons of Zebedee, came to Jesus and said, "Teacher, we want to ask you to do something for us."

³⁶Jesus asked, "What do you want me to do for you?"

³⁷The sons answered, "Let us share the great honor you will have as king. Let one of us sit at your right side and the other at your left."

³⁸Jesus said, "You don't understand what you are asking. Can you drink from the cupᶜ that I must drink from? Can you be baptized

---

ª**10:8** Quote from Gen. 2:24.
ᵇ**10:19** Quote from Ex. 20:12–16; Deut. 5:16–20.

ᶜ**10:38** *cup* A symbol of suffering. Jesus used the idea of drinking from a cup to mean accepting the suffering he would face in the terrible events that were soon to come. Also in verse 39.

with the same baptism*a* that I must go through?"

³⁹The sons answered, "Yes, we can!"

Jesus said to the sons, "It is true that you will drink from the cup that I drink from. And you will be baptized with the same baptism that I must go through. ⁴⁰But it is not for me to say who will sit at my right or my left. God has prepared those places for the ones he chooses."

⁴¹When the other ten followers heard this, they were angry with James and John. ⁴²Jesus called all the followers together. He said, "The non-Jewish people have men they call rulers. You know that those rulers love to show their power over the people. And their important leaders love to use all their authority over the people. ⁴³But it should not be that way with you. Whoever wants to be your leader must be your servant. ⁴⁴Whoever wants to be first must serve the rest of you like a slave. ⁴⁵Follow my example: Even the Son of Man* did not come for people to serve him. He came to serve others and to give his life to save many people."

Jesus Heals a Blind Man
(Mt. 20:29–34; Lk. 18:35–43)

⁴⁶Then they came to the town of Jericho. When Jesus left there with his followers, a large crowd was with them. A blind man named Bartimaeus (meaning "son of Timaeus") was sitting by the road. He was always begging for money. ⁴⁷He heard that Jesus from Nazareth was walking by. So he began shouting, "Jesus, Son of David,* please help me!"

⁴⁸Many people criticized the blind man and told him to be quiet. But he shouted more and more, "Son of David, please help me!"

⁴⁹Jesus stopped and said, "Tell him to come here."

So they called the blind man and said, "You can be happy now. Stand up! Jesus is calling you." ⁵⁰The blind man stood up quickly. He left his coat there and went to Jesus.

⁵¹Jesus asked the man, "What do you want me to do for you?"

He answered, "Teacher, I want to see again."

⁵²Jesus said, "Go. You are healed because you believed." Immediately the man was able to see again. He followed Jesus down the road.

Jesus Enters Jerusalem Like a King
(Mt. 21:1–11; Lk. 19:28–40; Jn. 12:12–19)

11 ¹Jesus and his followers were coming closer to Jerusalem. They came to the towns of Bethphage and Bethany at the Mount of Olives.* There Jesus sent two of his followers to do something. ²He said to them, "Go to the town you can see there. When you enter it, you will find a young donkey that no one has ever ridden. Untie it and bring it here to me. ³If anyone asks you why you are taking the donkey, tell them, 'The Master needs it. He will send it back soon.'"

⁴The followers went into the town. They found a young donkey tied in the street near the door of a house, and they untied it. ⁵Some people were standing there and saw this. They asked, "What are you doing? Why are you untying that donkey?" ⁶The followers answered the way Jesus told them, and the people let them take the donkey.

⁷The followers brought the donkey to Jesus. They put their coats on it, and Jesus sat on it. ⁸Many people spread their coats on the road for Jesus. Others cut branches in the fields and spread the branches on the road. ⁹Some of them were walking ahead of Jesus. Others were walking behind him. Everyone shouted,

"'Praise*b* Him!'
'Welcome! God bless the one who
   comes in the name of the Lord!'
                                    Psalm 118:25–26

¹⁰"God bless the kingdom of our father
      David.*
   That kingdom is coming!
   Praise to God in heaven!"

¹¹Jesus entered Jerusalem and went to the Temple.* He looked at everything in the Temple area, but it was already late. So he went to Bethany with the twelve apostles.*

Jesus Says a Fig Tree Will Die
(Mt. 21:18–19)

¹²The next day, Jesus was leaving Bethany. He was hungry. ¹³He saw a fig tree with leaves. So he went to the tree to see if it had any figs growing on it. But he found no figs on the tree. There were only leaves, because it was not the right time for figs to grow. ¹⁴So Jesus said to the tree, "People will never eat fruit from you again." His followers heard him say this.

Jesus Goes to the Temple
(Mt. 21:12–17; Lk. 19:45–48; Jn. 2:13–22)

¹⁵Jesus went to Jerusalem and entered the Temple* area. He began driving out the people who were buying and selling things there. He turned over the tables that belonged to those who were exchanging different kinds of money. And he turned over the benches of those who were selling doves. ¹⁶He refused to allow anyone to carry things through the

---

*a***10:38** *baptized with the same baptism* Baptism, which usually means to be immersed in water, has a special meaning here—being covered or "buried" in troubles. Also in verse 39.

*b***11:9** *Praise* Literally, "Hosanna," a Hebrew word used in praying to God for help. Here, it was probably a shout of celebration used in praising God or his Messiah. Also in verse 10.

Temple area. ¹⁷Then Jesus began teaching the people and said, "It is written in the Scriptures,* 'My Temple will be called a house of prayer for all nations.'ᵃ But you have changed it into a 'hiding place for thieves.'ᵇ"

¹⁸When the leading priests and the teachers of the law heard what Jesus said, they began trying to find a way to kill him. They were afraid of him because all the people were amazed at his teaching. ¹⁹That night Jesus and his followers left the city.

Jesus Shows the Power of Faith
(Mt. 21:20–22)

²⁰The next morning Jesus was walking with his followers. They saw the fig tree that he spoke to the day before. The tree was dry and dead, even the roots. ²¹Peter remembered the tree and said to Jesus, "Teacher, look! Yesterday, you told that fig tree to die. Now it is dry and dead!"

²²Jesus answered, "Have faith in God. ²³The truth is, you can say to this mountain, 'Go, mountain, fall into the sea.' And if you have no doubts in your mind and believe that what you say will happen, then God will do it for you. ²⁴So I tell you to ask for what you want in prayer. And if you believe that you have received those things, then they will be yours. ²⁵When you are praying, and you remember that you are angry with another person about something, then forgive that person. Forgive them so that your Father in heaven will also forgive your sins." ²⁶ ᶜ

Jewish Leaders Doubt Jesus' Authority
(Mt. 21:23–27; Lk. 20:1–8)

²⁷Jesus and his followers went again to Jerusalem. Jesus was walking in the Temple* area. The leading priests, the teachers of the law, and the older Jewish leaders came to him. ²⁸They said, "Tell us! What authority do you have to do these things? Who gave you this authority?"

²⁹Jesus answered, "I will ask you a question. You answer my question. Then I will tell you whose authority I use to do these things. ³⁰Tell me: When John baptized* people, did his authority come from God or was it only from other people? Answer me."

³¹These Jewish leaders talked about Jesus' question. They said to each other, "If we answer, 'John's baptism was from God,' then he will say, 'Then why didn't you believe John?' ³²But we can't say that John's baptism was from someone else." (These leaders were afraid of the people, because the people believed that John was a prophet.*)

³³So the leaders answered Jesus, "We don't know the answer."

ᵃ11:17 Quote from Isa. 56:7.
ᵇ11:17 Quote from Jer. 7:11.
ᶜ11:26 Some early Greek copies add verse 26: "But if you don't forgive others, then your Father in heaven will not forgive your sins."

Jesus said, "Then I will not tell you who gave me the authority to do these things."

God Sends His Son
(Mt. 21:33–46; Lk. 20:9–19)

12 ¹Jesus used stories to teach the people. He said, "A man planted a vineyard.* He put a wall around the field and dug a hole for a winepress.* Then he built a tower. He leased the land to some farmers and left for a trip.

²"Later, it was time for the grapes to be picked. So the man sent a servant to the farmers to get his share of the grapes. ³But the farmers grabbed the servant and beat him. They sent him away with nothing. ⁴Then the man sent another servant to the farmers. They hit this servant on the head, showing no respect for him. ⁵So the man sent another servant. The farmers killed this servant. The man sent many other servants to the farmers. The farmers beat some of them and killed the others.

⁶"The man had only one person left to send to the farmers. It was his son. He loved his son, but he decided to send him. He said, 'The farmers will respect my son.'

⁷"But the farmers said to each other, 'This is the owner's son, and this vineyard will be his. If we kill him, it will be ours.' ⁸So they took the son, threw him out of the vineyard, and killed him.

⁹"So what will the man who owns the vineyard do? He will go and kill those farmers. Then he will lease the land to others. ¹⁰Surely you have read this in the Scriptures*:

'The stone that the builders refused to
    accept became the cornerstone.*
¹¹ The Lord did this, and it is wonderful to
    us.'"   *Psalm 118:22–23*

¹²When these Jewish leaders heard this story, they knew it was about them. They wanted to find a way to arrest Jesus, but they were afraid of what the crowd would do. So they left him and went away.

The Jewish Leaders Try to Trick Jesus
(Mt. 22:15–22; Lk. 20:20–26)

¹³Later, the Jewish leaders sent some Pharisees* and some men from the group called Herodians* to Jesus. They wanted to catch him saying something wrong. ¹⁴They went to Jesus and said, "Teacher, we know that you are an honest man. You are not afraid of what others think about you. All people are the same to you. And you teach the truth about God's way. Tell us, is it right to pay taxes to Caesar*? Should we pay them or not?"

¹⁵But Jesus knew that these men were really trying to trick him. He said, "Why are you trying to catch me saying something wrong? Bring me a silver coin.* Let me see it." ¹⁶They gave Jesus a coin and he asked,

"Whose picture is on the coin? And whose name is written on it?" They answered, "It is Caesar's picture and Caesar's name."

¹⁷Then Jesus said to them, "Give to Caesar what belongs to Caesar, and give to God what belongs to God." The men were amazed at what Jesus said.

Some Sadducees Try to Trick Jesus
(Mt. 22:23–33; Lk. 20:27–40)

¹⁸Then some Sadducees* came to Jesus. (Sadducees believe that no one will rise from death.) They asked him a question: ¹⁹"Teacher, Moses* wrote that if a married man dies and had no children, his brother must marry the woman. Then they will have children for the dead brother.ᵃ ²⁰There were seven brothers. The first brother married but died. He had no children. ²¹So the second brother married the woman. But he also died and had no children. The same thing happened with the third brother. ²²All seven brothers married the woman and died. None of the brothers had any children with her. And she was the last to die. ²³But all seven brothers had married her. So at the time when people rise from death, whose wife will she be?"

²⁴Jesus answered, "How could you be so wrong? It's because you don't know what the Scriptures* say. And you don't know anything about God's power. ²⁵When people rise from death, there will be no marriage. People will not be married to each other. All people will be like angels in heaven. ²⁶Surely you have read what God said about people rising from death. In the book where Moses wrote about the burning bush,ᵇ it says that God told Moses this: 'I am the God of Abraham,* the God of Isaac,* and the God of Jacob.'*ᶜ ²⁷So they were not still dead, because he is the God only of living people. You Sadducees are so wrong!"

Which Command Is the Most Important?
(Mt. 22:34–40; Lk. 10:25–28)

²⁸One of the teachers of the law came to Jesus. He heard Jesus arguing with the Sadducees* and the Pharisees.* He saw that Jesus gave good answers to their questions. So he asked him, "Which of the commands is the most important?"

²⁹Jesus answered, "The most important command is this: 'People of Israel,* listen! The Lord our God is the only Lord. ³⁰Love the Lord your God with all your heart, all your soul, all your mind, and all your strength.'ᵈ ³¹The second most important command is this: 'Love your neighborᵉ the same as you

love yourself.'ᶠ These two commands are the most important."

³²The man answered, "That was a good answer, Teacher. You are right in saying that God is the only Lord and that there is no other God. ³³And you must love God with all your heart, all your mind, and all your strength. And you must love others the same as you love yourself. These commands are more important than all the animals and sacrifices we offer to God."

³⁴Jesus saw that the man answered him wisely. So he said to him, "You are close to God's kingdom.*" And after that time, no one was brave enough to ask Jesus any more questions.

Is the Christ David's Son or David's Lord?
(Mt. 22:41–46; Lk. 20:41–44)

³⁵Jesus was teaching in the Temple* area. He asked, "Why do the teachers of the law say that the Christ* is the son of David*? ³⁶With the help of the Holy Spirit,* David himself says,

'The Lord God said to my Lord:
　Sit by me at my right side,
　and I will put your enemies under your
　　control.ᵍ'　　　　　　　　　Psalm 110:1

³⁷David himself calls the Christ 'Lord.' So how can the Christ be David's son?" Many people listened to Jesus and were very pleased.

Jesus Criticizes the Teachers of the Law
(Mt. 23:1–36; Lk. 20:45–47)

³⁸Jesus continued teaching. He said, "Be careful of the teachers of the law. They like to walk around wearing clothes that look important. And they love for people to show respect to them in the marketplaces. ³⁹They love to have the most important seats in the synagogues* and the places of honor at banquets. ⁴⁰But they cheat widows and take their homes. Then they try to make themselves look good by saying long prayers. God will punish them very much."

True Giving
(Lk. 21:1–4)

⁴¹Jesus sat near the Temple* collection boxʰ and watched as people put money into it. Many rich people put in a lot of money. ⁴²Then a poor widow came and put in two very small copper coins, worth less than a penny.

⁴³Jesus called his followers to him and said, "This poor widow put in only two small coins. But the truth is, she gave more than all those rich people. ⁴⁴They have plenty, and

---

ᵃ12:19 if … dead brother See Deut. 25:5, 6.
ᵇ12:26 burning bush See Ex. 3:1–12.
ᶜ12:26 Quote from Ex. 3:6.
ᵈ12:29–30 Quote from Deut. 6:4–5.
ᵉ12:31 your neighbor Or "others." Jesus' teaching in Lk. 10:25–37 makes clear that this includes anyone in need.

ᶠ12:31 Quote from Lev. 19:18.
ᵍ12:36 control Literally, "feet."
ʰ12:41 collection box A special box in the Jewish place for worship where people put their gifts to God.

they gave only what they did not need. This woman is very poor, but she gave all she had. It was money she needed to live on."

Jesus Warns About the Future
(Mt. 24:1–44; Lk. 21:5–33)

13 ¹Jesus was leaving the Temple* area. One of his followers said to him, "Teacher, look how big those stones are! What beautiful buildings!"

²Jesus said, "Do you see these great buildings? They will all be destroyed. Every stone will be thrown down to the ground. Not one stone will be left on another."

³Later, Jesus was sitting at a place on the Mount of Olives.* He was alone with Peter, James, John, and Andrew. They could all see the Temple, and they said to Jesus, ⁴"Tell us when these things will happen. And what will show us it is time for them to happen?"

⁵Jesus said to them, "Be careful! Don't let anyone fool you. ⁶Many people will come and use my name. They will say, 'I am the one' and will fool many people. ⁷You will hear about wars that are being fought. And you will hear stories about other wars beginning. But don't be afraid. These things must happen before the end comes. ⁸Nations will fight against other nations. Kingdoms will fight against other kingdoms. There will be times when there is no food for people to eat. And there will be earthquakes in different places. These things are only the beginning of troubles, like the first pains of a woman giving birth.

⁹"You must be careful! There are people who will arrest you and take you to be judged for being my followers. They will beat you in their synagogues.* You will be forced to stand before kings and governors. You will tell them about me. ¹⁰Before the end comes, the Good News* must be told to all nations. ¹¹Even when you are arrested and put on trial, don't worry about what you will say. Say whatever God tells you at the time. It will not really be you speaking. It will be the Holy Spirit.*

¹²"Brothers will turn against their own brothers and hand them over to be killed. Fathers will hand over their own children to be killed. Children will fight against their own parents and have them killed. ¹³All people will hate you because you follow me. But those who remain faithful to the end will be saved.

¹⁴"You will see 'the terrible thing that causes destruction.'ᵃ You will see this thing standing in the place where it should not be." (Reader, I trust you understand what this means.) "Everyone in Judea at that time should run away to the mountains. ¹⁵They should run away without wasting time to stop for anything. If someone is on the roof of their house, they must not go down to take things

out of the house. ¹⁶If someone is in the field, they must not go back to get a coat.

¹⁷"During that time it will be hard for women who are pregnant or have small babies. ¹⁸Pray that these things will not happen in winter, ¹⁹because those days will be full of trouble. There will be more trouble than has ever happened since the beginning, when God made the world. And nothing that bad will ever happen again. ²⁰But the Lord has decided to make that terrible time short. If it were not made short, no one could survive. But the Lord will make that time short to help the special people he has chosen.

²¹"Someone might say to you at that time, 'Look, there is the Christ*!' Or another person might say, 'There he is!' But don't believe them. ²²False Christs and false prophets* will come and do miracles and wonders,ᵇ trying to fool the people God has chosen, if that is possible. ²³So be careful. Now I have warned you about all this before it happens.

²⁴"During the days following that time of trouble,

'The sun will become dark,
    and the moon will not give light.
²⁵ The stars will fall from the sky,
    and everything in the sky will be
        changed.'ᶜ

²⁶"Then people will see the Son of Man* coming in the clouds with great power and glory.* ²⁷He will send his angels all around the earth. They will gather his chosen people from every part of the earth.

²⁸"The fig tree teaches us a lesson: When its branches become green and soft, and new leaves begin to grow, then you know that summer is near. ²⁹In the same way, when you see all these things happening, you will know that the timeᵈ is near, ready to come. ³⁰I assure you that all these things will happen while some of the people of this time are still living. ³¹The whole world, earth and sky, will be destroyed, but my words will last forever.

³²"No one knows when that day or time will be. The Son and the angels in heaven don't know when that day or time will be. Only the Father knows. ³³Be careful! Always be ready. You don't know when that time will be.

³⁴"It's like a man who goes on a trip and leaves his house in the care of his servants. He gives each one a special job to do. He tells the servant guarding the door to always be ready. And this is what I am telling you now. ³⁵You must always be ready. You don't know when the owner of the house will come back.

ᵇ**13:22** *miracles and wonders* Here, amazing acts done by Satan's power.
ᶜ**13:24–25** See Isa. 13:10, 34:4.
ᵈ**13:29** *time* The time Jesus has been talking about when something important will happen. See Lk. 21:31, where Jesus says that this is the time for God's kingdom to come.

ᵃ**13:14** *'the terrible thing ... destruction'* See Dan. 9:27; 12:11 (also Dan. 11:31).

He might come in the afternoon, or at midnight, or in the early morning, or when the sun rises. 36If you are always ready, he will not find you sleeping, even if he comes back earlier than expected. 37I tell you this, and I say it to everyone: 'Be ready!'"

The Jewish Leaders Plan to Kill Jesus
(Mt. 26:1–5; Lk. 22:1–2; Jn. 11:45–53)

14 1It was now only two days before the Passover* and the Festival of Unleavened Bread.* The leading priests and teachers of the law were trying to find a way to arrest Jesus without the people seeing it. Then they could kill him. 2They said, "But we cannot arrest Jesus during the festival. We don't want the people to be angry and cause a riot."

A Woman Does Something Special
(Mt. 26:6–13; Jn. 12:1–8)

3Jesus was in Bethany at the house of Simon the leper.* While he was eating there, a woman came to him. She had an alabaster* jar filled with expensive perfume made of pure nard.* She opened the jar and poured the perfume on Jesus' head.

4Some of the followers there saw this. They were upset and complained to each other. They said, "Why waste that perfume? 5It was worth a full year's pay.a It could have been sold and the money given to those who are poor." And they told the woman what a bad thing she had done.

6Jesus said, "Leave her alone. Why are you giving her such trouble? She did a very good thing for me. 7You will always have the poor with you,b and you can help them any time you want. But you will not always have me. 8This woman did the only thing she could do for me. She poured perfume on my body before I die to prepare it for burial. 9The Good News* will be told to people all over the world. And I can assure you that everywhere the Good News is told, the story of what this woman did will also be told, and people will remember her."

Judas Agrees to Help Jesus' Enemies
(Mt. 26:14–16; Lk. 22:3–6)

10Then Judas Iscariot, one of the twelve apostles,* went to talk to the leading priests about handing Jesus over to them. 11They were very happy about this, and they promised to pay him. So he waited for the best time to hand Jesus over to them.

The Passover Meal
(Mt. 26:17–25; Lk. 22:7–14, 21–23; Jn. 13:21–30)

12It was now the first day of the Festival of Unleavened Bread*—the day the lambs were killed for the Passover.* Jesus' followers came to him and said, "We will go and prepare everything for you to eat the Passover meal. Where do you want us to have the meal?"

13Jesus sent two of his followers into the city. He said to them, "Go into the city. You will see a man carrying a jar of water. He will come to you. Follow him. 14He will go into a house. Tell the owner of the house, 'The Teacher asks that you show us the room where he and his followers can eat the Passover meal.' 15The owner will show you a large room upstairs that is ready for us. Prepare the meal for us there."

16So the followers left and went into the city. Everything happened the way Jesus said. So the followers prepared the Passover meal.

17In the evening, Jesus went to that house with the twelve apostles.* 18While they were all at the table eating, he said, "Believe me when I say that one of you will hand me over to my enemies—one of you eating with me now."

19The followers were very sad to hear this. Each one said to Jesus, "Surely I am not the one!"

20Jesus answered, "It is one of you twelve—the one who is dipping his bread in the same bowl with me. 21The Son of Man* will suffer what the Scriptures* say will happen to him. But it will be very bad for the one who hands over the Son of Man to be killed. It would be better for him if he had never been born."

The Lord's Supper
(Mt. 26:26–30; Lk. 22:15–20; 1 Cor. 11:23–25)

22While they were eating, Jesus took some bread and thanked God for it. He broke off some pieces, gave them to his followers and said, "Take and eat this bread. It is my body."

23Then he took a cup of wine, thanked God for it, and gave it to them. They all drank from the cup. 24Then he said, "This wine is my blood, which will be poured out for many to begin the new agreement* from God to his people. 25I want you to know, I will not drink this wine again until that day when I drink it in God's kingdom* and the wine is new."

26They all sang a song and then went out to the Mount of Olives.*

Jesus Says His Followers Will Leave Him
(Mt. 26:31–35; Lk. 22:31–34; Jn. 13:36–38)

27Then Jesus told the followers, "You will all lose your faith. The Scriptures* say,

'I will kill the shepherd,
    and the sheep will run away.'
                                    Zechariah 13:7

28But after I am killed, I will rise from death. Then I will go to Galilee. I will be there before you come."

29Peter said, "All the other followers may lose their faith. But my faith will never be shaken."

---

a14:5 *a full year's pay* Literally, "300 denarii *(silver coins)*." One coin, a Roman denarius, was the average pay for one day's work.
b14:7 *You will ... with you* See Deut. 15:11.

[30]Jesus answered, "The truth is, tonight you will say you don't know me. You will say it three times before the rooster crows twice."

[31]But Peter strongly protested, "I will never say I don't know you! I will even die with you!" And all the other followers said the same thing.

Jesus Prays Alone
(Mt. 26:36–46; Lk. 22:39–46)

[32]Jesus and his followers went to a place named Gethsemane. He said to them, "Sit here while I pray." [33]But he told Peter, James, and John to come with him. He began to be very distressed and troubled, [34]and he said to them, "My heart is so heavy with grief, I feel as if I am dying. Wait here and stay awake."

[35]Jesus went on a little farther away from them, fell to the ground, and prayed. He asked that, if possible, he would not have this time of suffering. [36]He said, "*Abba,*[a] Father! You can do all things. Don't make me drink from this cup.[b] But do what you want, not what I want."

[37]Then he went back to his followers and found them sleeping. He said to Peter, "Simon, why are you sleeping? Could you not stay awake with me for one hour? [38]Stay awake and pray for strength against temptation. Your spirit wants to do what is right, but your body is weak."

[39]Again Jesus went away and prayed the same thing. [40]Then he went back to the followers and again found them sleeping. They could not stay awake. They did not know what they should say to him.

[41]After Jesus prayed a third time, he went back to his followers. He said to them, "Are you still sleeping and resting? That's enough! The time has come for the Son of Man* to be handed over to the control of sinful men. [42]Stand up! We must go. Here comes the man who is handing me over to them."

Jesus Is Arrested
(Mt. 26:47–56; Lk. 22:47–53; Jn. 18:3–12)

[43]While Jesus was still speaking, Judas, one of the twelve apostles,* came there. He had a big crowd of people with him, all carrying swords and clubs. They had been sent from the leading priests, the teachers of the law, and the older Jewish leaders.

[44]Judas[c] planned to do something to show them which one was Jesus. He said, "The one I kiss will be Jesus. Arrest him and guard him while you lead him away." [45]So Judas went over to Jesus and said, "Teacher!" Then he kissed him. [46]The men grabbed Jesus and arrested him. [47]One of the followers standing near Jesus grabbed his sword and pulled it out. He swung it at the servant of the high priest* and cut off his ear.

[48]Then Jesus said, "Why do you come to get me with swords and clubs as if I were a criminal? [49]Every day I was with you teaching in the Temple* area. You did not arrest me there. But all these things have happened to show the full meaning of what the Scriptures* said." [50]Then all of Jesus' followers left him and ran away.

[51]One of those following Jesus was a young man wearing only a linen cloth. When the people tried to grab him, [52]he left the cloth in their hands and ran away naked.

Jesus Before the Jewish Leaders
(Mt. 26:57–68; Lk. 22:54–55, 63–71;
Jn. 18:13–14, 19–24)

[53]Those who arrested Jesus led him to the house of the high priest.* All the leading priests, the older Jewish leaders, and the teachers of the law were gathered there. [54]Peter followed Jesus but stayed back at a distance. He followed him to the yard of the high priest's house. He went into the yard and sat there with the guards, warming himself by their fire.

[55]The leading priests and the whole high council tried to find something that Jesus had done wrong so they could kill him. But the council could find no proof that would allow them to kill Jesus. [56]Many people came and told lies against Jesus, but they all said different things. None of them agreed.

[57]Then some others stood up and told more lies against Jesus. They said, [58]"We heard this man[d] say, 'I will destroy this Temple* built by human hands. And three days later, I will build another Temple not made by human hands.'" [59]But also what these people said did not agree.

[60]Then the high priest stood up before everyone and said to Jesus, "These people said things against you. Do you have something to say about their charges? Are they telling the truth?" [61]But Jesus said nothing to answer him.

The high priest asked Jesus another question: "Are you the Christ,* the Son of the blessed God?"

[62]Jesus answered, "Yes, I am the Son of God. And in the future you will see the Son of Man* sitting at the right side of God All-Powerful. And you will see the Son of Man coming on the clouds of heaven."

[63]When the high priest heard this, he tore his clothes in anger. He said, "We don't need any more witnesses! [64]You all heard these

---

[a]**14:36 *Abba*** An Aramaic word that was used by Jewish children as a name for their fathers.

[b]**14:36 *cup*** A symbol of suffering. Jesus used the idea of drinking from a cup to mean accepting the suffering he would face in the terrible events that were soon to come.

[c]**14:44 *Judas*** Literally, "the one who handed him over."

[d]**14:58 *this man*** That is, Jesus. His enemies avoided saying his name.

insults to God. What do you think?"

Everyone agreed that Jesus was guilty and must be killed. [65]Some of the people there spit at him. They covered his eyes and hit him with their fists. They said, "Be a prophet[a] and tell us who hit you!" Then the guards led Jesus away and beat him.

Peter Is Afraid to Say He Knows Jesus
(Mt. 26:69–75; Lk. 22:56–62; Jn. 18:15–18, 25–27)

[66]While Peter was still in the yard, a servant girl of the high priest came there. [67]She saw him warming himself by the fire. She looked closely at him and said, "You were with Jesus, that man from Nazareth."

[68]But Peter said this was not true. "That makes no sense," he said. "I don't know what you are talking about!" Then he left and went to the entrance of the yard, and a rooster crowed.[b]

[69]When the servant girl saw him there, she began saying again to the people standing around, "This man is one of them." [70]Again Peter said it was not true.

A short time later, the people standing there said, "We know you are one of them, because you are from Galilee."

[71]Then Peter began to curse. He said, "I swear to God, I don't know this man you are talking about!"

[72]As soon as Peter said this, the rooster crowed the second time. Then he remembered what Jesus had told him: "Before the rooster crows twice, you will say three times that you don't know me." Then Peter began to cry.

Governor Pilate Questions Jesus
(Mt. 27:1–2, 11–14; Lk. 23:1–5; Jn. 18:28–38)

15 [1]Very early in the morning, the leading priests, the older Jewish leaders, the teachers of the law, and the whole high council decided what to do with Jesus. They tied him, led him away, and handed him over to Governor Pilate.

[2]Pilate asked Jesus, "Are you the king of the Jews?"

Jesus answered, "Yes, that is right."

[3]The leading priests accused Jesus of many things. [4]So Pilate asked Jesus another question. He said, "You can see that these people are accusing you of many things. Why don't you answer?"

[5]But Jesus still did not answer, and this really surprised Pilate.

Pilate Tries but Fails to Free Jesus
(Mt. 27:15–31; Lk. 23:13–25; Jn. 18:39–19:16)

[6]Every year at the Passover* time the governor would free one prisoner—whichever one the people wanted. [7]There was a man in prison at that time named Barabbas. He and the rebels with him had been put in prison for committing murder during a riot.

[8]The people came to Pilate* and asked him to free a prisoner as he always did. [9]Pilate asked them, "Do you want me to free the king of the Jews?" [10]Pilate knew that the leading priests had handed Jesus over to him because they were jealous of him. [11]But the leading priests persuaded the people to ask Pilate to free Barabbas, not Jesus.

[12]Pilate asked the people again, "So what should I do with this man you call the king of the Jews?"

[13]The people shouted, "Kill him on a cross!"

[14]Pilate asked, "Why? What wrong has he done?"

But the people shouted louder and louder, "Kill him on a cross!"

[15]Pilate wanted to please the people, so he set Barabbas free for them. And he told the soldiers to beat Jesus with whips. Then he handed him over to the soldiers to be killed on a cross.

[16]Pilate's soldiers took Jesus into the governor's palace (called the Praetorium). They called all the other soldiers together. [17]They put a purple robe on Jesus, made a crown from thorny branches, and put it on his head. [18]Then they began shouting, "Welcome, king of the Jews!" [19]They kept on beating his head with a stick and spitting on him. Then they bowed down on their knees and pretended to honor him as a king. [20]After they finished making fun of him, they took off the purple robe and put his own clothes on him again. Then they led him out of the palace to be killed on a cross.

Jesus Is Nailed to a Cross
(Mt. 27:32–44; Lk. 23:26–39; Jn. 19:17–19)

[21]There was a man from Cyrene named Simon walking into the city from the fields. He was the father of Alexander and Rufus. The soldiers forced him to carry Jesus' cross. [22]They led Jesus to the place called Golgotha. (Golgotha means "The Place of the Skull.") [23]There they gave him some wine mixed with myrrh,* but he refused to drink it. [24]The soldiers nailed Jesus to a cross. Then they divided his clothes among themselves, throwing dice to see who would get what.

[25]It was nine o'clock in the morning when they nailed Jesus to the cross. [26]There was a sign with the charge against him written on it. It said, "THE KING OF THE JEWS." [27]They also nailed two criminals to crosses beside Jesus—one on the right and the other on the left. [28] [c]

---

[a]**14:65** *prophet* A prophet often knows things that are hidden to other people.
[b]**14:68** Some Greek copies do not have "and a rooster crowed."

[c]**15:28** Some Greek copies add verse 28: "And this showed the full meaning of the Scripture that says, 'They put him with criminals.'"

29People walked by and said bad things to Jesus. They shook their heads and said, "You said you could destroy the Temple* and build it again in three days. 30So save yourself! Come down from that cross!"

31The leading priests and the teachers of the law were also there. They made fun of Jesus the same as the other people did. They said to each other, "He saved others, but he can't save himself! 32If he is really the Christ,* the king of Israel,* he should come down from the cross now. When we see this, then we will believe in him." The criminals on the crosses beside Jesus also said bad things to him.

Jesus Dies
(Mt. 27:45–56; Lk. 23:44–49; Jn. 19:28–30)

33At noon the whole country became dark. This darkness continued until three o'clock. 34At three o'clock Jesus cried out loudly, *"Eloi, Eloi, lama sabachthani."* This means "My God, my God, why have you left me alone?"[a]

35Some of the people standing there heard this. They said, "Listen! He is calling Elijah."[b]

36One man there ran and got a sponge. He filled the sponge with sour wine and tied it to a stick. Then he used the stick to give the sponge to Jesus to get a drink from it. The man said, "We should wait now and see if Elijah will come to take him down from the cross."

37Then Jesus cried out loudly and died.

38When Jesus died, the curtain* in the Temple* was torn into two pieces. The tear started at the top and tore all the way to the bottom. 39The army officer* who was standing there in front of the cross saw what happened when Jesus died. The officer said, "This man really was the Son of God!"

40Some women were standing away from the cross, watching. Among these women were Mary Magdalene, Salome, and Mary the mother of James and Joses. (James was her youngest son.) 41These were the women who had followed Jesus in Galilee and cared for him. Many other women who had come with Jesus to Jerusalem were also there.

Jesus Is Buried
(Mt. 27:57–61; Lk. 23:50–56; Jn. 19:38–42)

42This day was called Preparation day. (That means the day before the Sabbath* day.) It was becoming dark. 43A man named Joseph from Arimathea was brave enough to go to Pilate* and ask for Jesus' body. Joseph was an important member of the high council. He was one of the people who wanted God's kingdom* to come.

44Pilate was surprised to hear that Jesus was already dead. So he called for the army officer* in charge and asked him if Jesus was already dead. 45When Pilate heard it from the officer, he told Joseph he could have the body.

46Joseph bought some linen cloth. He took the body from the cross, wrapped it in the linen, and put the body in a tomb* that was dug in a wall of rock. Then he closed the tomb by rolling a large stone to cover the entrance. 47Mary Magdalene and Mary the mother of Joses saw the place where Jesus was put.

News That Jesus Has Risen From Death
(Mt. 28:1–8; Lk. 24:1–12; Jn. 20:1–10)

16 1The next day after the Sabbath* day, Mary Magdalene, Salome, and Mary the mother of James bought some sweet-smelling spices to put on Jesus' body. 2Very early on that day, the first day of the week, the women were going to the tomb.* It was very early after sunrise. 3The women said to each other, "There is a large stone covering the entrance of the tomb. Who will move the stone for us?"

4Then the women looked and saw that the stone was moved. The stone was very large, but it was moved away from the entrance. 5The women walked into the tomb and saw a young man there wearing a white robe. He was sitting on the right side of the tomb. The women were afraid.

6But the man said, "Don't be afraid. You are looking for Jesus from Nazareth, the one who was killed on a cross. He has risen from death! He is not here. Look, here is the place they put him when he was dead. 7Now go and tell his followers. And be sure to tell Peter. Tell them, 'Jesus is going into Galilee and will be there before you come. You will see him there, as he told you before.'"

8The women were very afraid and confused. They left the tomb and ran away. They did not tell about what happened, because they were afraid.[c]

Some Followers See Jesus
(Mt. 28:9–10; Jn. 20:11–18; Lk. 24:13–35)

9Jesus rose from death early on the first day of the week. He appeared first to Mary Magdalene. One time in the past Jesus had forced seven demons* out of Mary. 10After Mary saw Jesus, she went and told his followers. They were very sad and were crying. 11But Mary told them that Jesus was alive. She said that she had seen Jesus, but they did not believe her.

---

[a]15:34 Quote from Ps. 22:1.

[b]15:35 *He is calling Elijah"* The word for "My God" (*Eli* in Hebrew or *Eloi* in Aramaic) sounded to the people like the name of Elijah, a famous man who spoke for God about 850 B.C.

[c]16:8 Some of the oldest Greek copies end the book here. A few later copies have this shorter ending: "But they soon gave all the instructions to Peter and those with him. After that, Jesus himself sent them out from east to west with the holy message that will never change—that people can be saved forever."

¹²Later, Jesus appeared to two followers while they were walking in the country. But Jesus did not look the same as before he was killed. ¹³These followers went back to the other followers and told them what happened. Again, the followers did not believe them.

Jesus Talks to His Followers
(Mt. 28:16–20; Lk. 24:36–49; Jn. 20:19–23; Acts 1:6–8)

¹⁴Later, Jesus appeared to the eleven followers while they were eating. He criticized them because they had so little faith. They were stubborn and refused to believe the people who said Jesus had risen from death.

¹⁵He said to them, "Go everywhere in the world. Tell the Good News* to everyone. ¹⁶Whoever believes and is baptized* will be saved. But those who do not believe will be judged guilty. ¹⁷And the people who believe will be able to do these things as proof: They will use my name to force demons* out of people. They will speak in languages they never learned. ¹⁸If they pick up snakes or drink any poison, they will not be hurt. They will lay their hands on sick people, and they will get well."

Jesus Goes Back to Heaven
(Lk. 24:50–53; Acts 1:9–11)

¹⁹After the Lord Jesus said these things to his followers, he was carried up into heaven. There, Jesus sat at the right side of God. ²⁰The followers went everywhere in the world telling people the Good News,* and the Lord helped them. By giving them power to do miracles* the Lord proved that their message was true.

Luke

Luke Writes About the Life of Jesus

1 ¹Most Honorable Theophilus:

Many others have tried to give a report of the things that happened among us to complete God's plan. ²What they have written agrees with what we learned from the people who saw those events from the beginning. They also served God by telling people his message. ³I studied it all carefully from the beginning. Then I decided to write it down for you in an organized way. ⁴I did this so that you can be sure that what you have been taught is true.

Zechariah and Elizabeth

⁵During the time when Herod* ruled Judea, there was a priest named Zechariah. He belonged to Abijah's group.ᵃ His wife came from the family of Aaron. Her name was Elizabeth. ⁶Zechariah and Elizabeth were both good people who pleased God. They did everything the Lord commanded, always following his instructions completely. ⁷But they had no children. Elizabeth could not have a baby, and both of them were very old.

⁸Zechariah was serving as a priest before God for his group. It was his group's time to serve. ⁹The priests always chose one priest to offer the incense,* and Zechariah was the one chosen this time. So he went into the Temple* of the Lord to offer the incense. ¹⁰There was a large crowd outside praying at the time the incense was offered.

¹¹Then, on the right side of the incense table an angel of the Lord came and stood before Zechariah. ¹²When he saw the angel, Zechariah was upset and very afraid. ¹³But the angel said to him, "Zechariah, don't be afraid. Your prayer has been heard by God. Your wife Elizabeth will give birth to a baby boy, and you will name him John. ¹⁴You will be very happy, and many others will share your joy over his birth. ¹⁵He will be a great man for the Lord. He will never drink wine or beer. Even before he is born, he will be filled with the Holy Spirit.*

¹⁶"John will help many people of Israel* return to the Lord their God. ¹⁷John himself will go ahead of the Lord and make people ready for his coming. He will be powerful like Elijah* and will have the same spirit. He will make peace between fathers and their children. He will cause people who are not obeying God to change and start thinking the way they should."

¹⁸Zechariah said to the angel, "How can I know that what you say is true? I am an old man, and my wife is also old."

¹⁹The angel answered him, "I am Gabriel, the one who always stands ready before God. He sent me to talk to you and to tell you this good news. ²⁰Now, listen! You will not be able to talk until the day when these things happen. You will lose your speech because you did not believe what I told you. But everything I said will really happen."

²¹Outside, the people were still waiting for

ᵃ**1:5** *Abijah's group* Jewish priests were divided into 24 groups. See 1 Chron. 24.

Zechariah. They were surprised that he was staying so long in the Temple. ²²Then Zechariah came outside, but he could not speak to them. So the people knew that he had seen a vision* inside the Temple. He was not able to speak, so he could only make signs to the people. ²³When his time of service was finished, he went home.

²⁴Later, Zechariah's wife Elizabeth became pregnant. So she did not go out of her house for five months. She said, ²⁵"Look what the Lord has done for me! He decided to help me. Now people will stop thinking there is something wrong with me."

The Virgin Mary

²⁶⁻²⁷During Elizabeth's sixth month of pregnancy, God sent the angel Gabriel to a virgin* girl who lived in Nazareth, a town in Galilee. She was engaged to marry a man named Joseph from the family of David.* Her name was Mary. ²⁸The angel came to her and said, "Greetings! The Lord is with you; you are very special to him."

²⁹But Mary was very confused about what the angel said. She wondered, "What does this mean?"

³⁰The angel said to her, "Don't be afraid, Mary, because God is very pleased with you. ³¹Listen! You will become pregnant and have a baby boy. You will name him Jesus. ³²He will be great. People will call him the Son of the Most High God, and the Lord God will make him king like his ancestor David. ³³He will rule over the people of Jacob* forever; his kingdom will never end."

³⁴Mary said to the angel, "How will this happen? I am still a virgin."

³⁵The angel said to Mary, "The Holy Spirit* will come to you, and the power of the Most High God will cover you. The baby will be holy and will be called the Son of God. ³⁶And here's something else: Your relative Elizabeth is pregnant. She is very old, but she is going to have a son. Everyone thought she could not have a baby, but she has been pregnant now for six months. ³⁷God can do anything!"

³⁸Mary said, "I am the servant of the Lord God. Let this thing you have said happen to me!" Then the angel went away.

Mary Visits Zechariah and Elizabeth

³⁹Mary got up and went quickly to a town in the hill country of Judea. ⁴⁰She went into Zechariah's house and greeted Elizabeth. ⁴¹When Elizabeth heard Mary's greeting, the unborn baby inside her jumped, and she was filled with the Holy Spirit.*

⁴²In a loud voice she said to Mary, "God has blessed you more than any other woman. And God has blessed the baby you will have. ⁴³You are the mother of my Lord, and you have come to me! Why has something so good happened to me? ⁴⁴When I heard your voice, the baby inside me jumped with joy. ⁴⁵Great blessings are yours because you believed what the Lord said to you! You believed this would happen."

Mary Praises God

⁴⁶Then Mary said,

⁴⁷"I praise the Lord with all my heart.
　　I am very happy because God is my
　　　Savior.
⁴⁸ I am not important,
　　but he has shown his care for me, his
　　　lowly servant.
　　From now until the end of time,
　　　people will remember how much God
　　　blessed me.
⁴⁹ Yes, the Powerful One has done great
　　　things for me.
　　His name is very holy.
⁵⁰ He always gives mercy to those who
　　　worship him.
⁵¹ He reached out his arm and showed his
　　　power.
　　He scattered those who are proud and
　　　think great things about themselves.
⁵² He brought down rulers from their
　　　thrones
　　and raised up the humble people.
⁵³ He filled the hungry with good things,
　　but he sent the rich away with nothing.
⁵⁴ God has helped Israel—the people he
　　　chose to serve him.
　　He did not forget his promise to give us
　　　his mercy.
⁵⁵ He has done what he promised to our
　　　ancestors,* to Abraham* and his
　　　children forever."

⁵⁶Mary stayed with Elizabeth for about three months and then went home.

The Birth of John

⁵⁷When it was time for Elizabeth to give birth, she had a boy. ⁵⁸Her neighbors and relatives heard that the Lord was very good to her, and they were happy for her.

⁵⁹When the baby was eight days old, they came to circumcise* him. They wanted to name him Zechariah because this was his father's name. ⁶⁰But his mother said, "No, he will be named John."

⁶¹The people said to Elizabeth, "But no one in your family has that name." ⁶²Then they made signs to his father, "What would you like to name him?"

⁶³Zechariah asked for something to write on. Then he wrote, "His name is John." Everyone was surprised. ⁶⁴Then Zechariah could talk again, and he began praising God. ⁶⁵And all their neighbors were afraid. In all the hill country of Judea people continued talking about these things. ⁶⁶Everyone who heard about these things wondered about them. They thought, "What will this child be?" They could see that the Lord was with him.

Zechariah Praises God

⁶⁷Then Zechariah, John's father, was filled with the Holy Spirit* and told the people a message from God:

⁶⁸"Praise to the Lord God of Israel.*
      He has come to help his people and has
         given them freedom.
⁶⁹ He has given us a powerful Savior
         from the family of his servant David.*
⁷⁰ This is what he promised
         through his holy* prophets* long ago.
⁷¹ He will save us from our enemies
         and from the power of all those who
            hate us.
⁷² God said he would show mercy to our
            fathers,*
         and he remembered his holy
            agreement.*
⁷³ This was the promise he made to our
            father Abraham,*
⁷⁴   a promise to free us from the power of
            our enemies,
         so that we could serve him without fear
⁷⁵   in a way that is holy and right for as
            long as we live.

⁷⁶"Now you, little boy, will be called a
            prophet of the Most High God.
      You will go first before the Lord to
            prepare the way for him.
⁷⁷ You will make his people understand that
            they will be saved by having their sins
            forgiven.

⁷⁸"With the loving mercy of our God,
         a new day*ᵃ* from heaven will shine on
            us.
⁷⁹ It will bring light to those who live in
            darkness, in the fear of death.
      It will guide us into the way that brings
            peace."

⁸⁰And so the little boy John grew up and became stronger in spirit. Then he lived in areas away from other people until the time when he came out to tell God's message to the people of Israel.

The Birth of Jesus Christ
(Mt. 1:18–25)

2 ¹It was about that same time that Augustus Caesar* sent out an order to all people in the countries that were under Roman rule. The order said that everyone's name must be put on a list. ²This was the first counting of all the people while Quirinius was governor of Syria. ³Everyone traveled to their own hometowns to have their name put on the list.

⁴So Joseph left Nazareth, a town in Galilee, and went to the town of Bethlehem in Judea. It was known as the town of David.* Joseph went there because he was from the family of David. ⁵Joseph registered with Mary because she was engaged to marry him. (She was now pregnant.) ⁶While Joseph and Mary were in Bethlehem, the time came for her to have the baby. ⁷She gave birth to her first son. She wrapped him up well and laid him in a box where cattle are fed. She put him there because the guest room was full.

Some Shepherds Hear About Jesus

⁸That night, some shepherds were out in the fields near Bethlehem watching their sheep. ⁹An angel of the Lord appeared to them, and the glory* of the Lord was shining around them. The shepherds were very afraid. ¹⁰The angel said to them, "Don't be afraid. I have some very good news for you— news that will make everyone happy. ¹¹Today your Savior was born in David's town. He is Christ,* the Lord. ¹²This is how you will know him: You will find a baby wrapped in pieces of cloth and lying in a feeding box."

¹³Then a huge army of angels from heaven joined the first angel, and they were all praising God, saying,

¹⁴"Praise God in heaven,
         and on earth let there be peace to the
            people who please him."

¹⁵The angels left the shepherds and went back to heaven. The shepherds said to each other, "Let's go to Bethlehem and see this great event the Lord has told us about."

¹⁶So they went running and found Mary and Joseph. And there was the baby, lying in the feeding box. ¹⁷When they saw the baby, they told what the angels said about this child. ¹⁸Everyone was surprised when they heard what the shepherds told them. ¹⁹Mary continued to think about these things, trying to understand them. ²⁰The shepherds went back to their sheep, praising God and thanking him for everything they had seen and heard. It was just as the angel had told them.

²¹When the baby was eight days old, he was circumcised,* and he was named Jesus. This name was given by the angel before the baby began to grow inside Mary.

Jesus Is Presented in the Temple

²²The time came for Mary and Joseph to do the things the Law of Moses* taught about being made pure.*ᵇ* They brought Jesus to Jerusalem so that they could present him to the Lord. ²³It is written in the law of the Lord: "When a mother's first baby is a boy, he shall

---

*ᵇ***2:22 pure** The Law of Moses said that 40 days after a Jewish woman gave birth to a baby, she must be made ritually clean by a ceremony at the Temple. See Lev. 12:2–8.

---

*ᵃ***1:78 new day** Literally, "dawn," used here as a symbol, probably meaning the Lord's Messiah.

be called 'special for the Lord.'"[a] 24The law of the Lord also says that people must give a sacrifice*: "You must sacrifice two doves or two young pigeons."[b] So Joseph and Mary went to Jerusalem to do this.

Simeon Sees Jesus

25A man named Simeon lived in Jerusalem. He was a good man who was devoted to God. He was waiting for the time when God would come to help Israel.* The Holy Spirit* was with him. 26The Holy Spirit told him that he would not die before he saw the Christ* from the Lord. 27The Spirit led Simeon to the Temple.* So he was there when Mary and Joseph brought the baby Jesus to do what the Jewish law said they must do. 28Simeon took the baby in his arms and thanked God:

29"Now, Lord, you can let me, your servant,
    die in peace as you said.
30 I have seen with my own eyes how you
    will save your people.
31   Now all people can see your plan.
32 He is a light to show your way to the
    other nations.
    And he will bring honor to your people
    Israel."

33Jesus' father and mother were amazed at what Simeon said about him. 34Then Simeon blessed them and said to Mary, "Many Jews will fall and many will rise because of this boy. He will be a sign from God that some will not accept. 35So the secret thoughts of many will be made known. And the things that happen will be painful for you—like a sword cutting through your heart."

Anna Sees Jesus

36Anna, a prophetess,* was there at the Temple.* She was from the family of Phanuel in the tribe of Asher. She was now very old. She had lived with her husband seven years 37before he died and left her alone. She was now 84 years old. Anna was always at the Temple; she never left. She worshiped God by fasting* and praying day and night. 38Anna was there when Joseph and Mary came to the Temple. She praised God and talked about Jesus to all those who were waiting for God to free Jerusalem.

Joseph and Mary Return Home

39Joseph and Mary finished doing all the things that the law of the Lord commanded. Then they went home to Nazareth, their own town in Galilee. 40The little boy Jesus was developing into a mature young man, full of wisdom. God was blessing him.

Jesus as a Boy

41Every year Jesus' parents went to Jerusalem for the Passover* festival. 42When Jesus was twelve years old, they went to the festival as usual. 43When the festival was over, they went home, but Jesus stayed in Jerusalem. His parents did not know about it. 44They traveled for a whole day thinking that Jesus was with them in the group. They began looking for him among their family and close friends, 45but they did not find him. So they went back to Jerusalem to look for him there. 46After three days they found him. Jesus was sitting in the Temple* area with the religious teachers, listening and asking them questions. 47Everyone who heard him was amazed at his understanding and wise answers. 48When his parents saw him, they wondered how this was possible. And his mother said, "Son, why did you do this to us? Your father and I were very worried about you. We have been looking for you."

49Jesus said to them, "Why did you have to look for me? You should have known that I must be where my Father's work is.[c]" 50But they did not understand the meaning of what he said to them.

51Jesus went with them to Nazareth and obeyed them. His mother was still thinking about all these things. 52As Jesus grew taller, he continued to grow in wisdom. God was pleased with him and so were the people who knew him.

John Prepares the Way for Jesus
(Mt. 3:1-12; Mk. 1:1-8; Jn. 1:19-28)

3 1It was the 15th year of the rule of Tiberius Caesar.* These men were under Caesar:

Pontius Pilate,* the governor of Judea;
Herod,* the ruler of Galilee;
Philip, Herod's brother, the ruler of Iturea
   and Trachonitis;
Lysanias, the ruler of Abilene.

2Annas and Caiaphas were the high priests.* During this time, John, the son of Zechariah, was living in the desert, and he received a message from God. 3So he went through the whole area around the Jordan River and told the people God's message. He told them to be baptized* to show that they wanted to change their lives, and then their sins would be forgiven. 4This is like the words written in the book of Isaiah the prophet*:

"There is someone shouting in the desert:
'Prepare the way for the Lord.
   Make the road straight for him.
5 Every valley will be filled,
      and every mountain and hill will be
         made flat.

---

[a]2:23 "When ... 'special for the Lord'" See Ex. 13:2, 12.
[b]2:24 Quote from Lev. 12:8.

[c]2:49 where ... work is Or "in my Father's house."

Crooked roads will be made straight,
and rough roads will be made smooth.
6 Then everyone will see how God will
save his people!'"   *Isaiah 40:3-5*

7Crowds of people came to be baptized by John. But he said to them, "You are all snakes! Who warned you to run from God's judgment that is coming? 8Change your hearts! And show by your lives that you have changed. I know what you are about to say—'but Abraham* is our father!' That means nothing. I tell you that God can make children for Abraham from these rocks! 9The ax is now ready to cut down the trees.*a* Every tree that does not produce good fruit will be cut down and thrown into the fire."

10The people asked John, "What should we do?"

11He answered, "If you have two shirts, share with someone who does not have one. If you have food, share that too."

12Even the tax collectors* came to John. They wanted to be baptized. They said to him, "Teacher, what should we do?"

13He told them, "Don't take more taxes from people than you have been ordered to collect."

14The soldiers asked him, "What about us? What should we do?"

He said to them, "Don't use force or lies to make people give you money. Be happy with the pay you get."

15Everyone was hoping for the Christ* to come, and they wondered about John. They thought, "Maybe he is the Christ."

16John's answer to this was, "I baptize you in water, but there is someone coming later who is able to do more than I can. I am not good enough to be the slave who unties his sandals. He will baptize you with the Holy Spirit* and with fire. 17He will come ready to clean the grain.*b* He will separate the good grain from the straw, and he will put the good part into his barn. Then he will burn the useless part with a fire that cannot be stopped." 18John said many other things like this to encourage the people to change, and he told them the Good News.*

How John's Work Later Ended

19John criticized Herod* the ruler for what he had done with Herodias, the wife of Herod's brother, as well as for all the other bad things he had done. 20So Herod added another bad thing to all his other wrongs: He put John in jail.

Jesus Is Baptized by John
(Mt. 3:13–17; Mk. 1:9–11)

21When all the people were being baptized,* Jesus came and was baptized too. And while he was praying, the sky opened, 22and the Holy Spirit* came down on him. The Spirit looked like a real dove. Then a voice came from heaven and said, "You are my Son, the one I love. I am very pleased with you."

The Family History of Joseph
(Mt. 1:1–17)

23When Jesus began to teach, he was about 30 years old. People thought that Jesus was Joseph's son.

Joseph was the son of Eli.
24 Eli was the son of Matthat.
Matthat was the son of Levi.
Levi was the son of Melchi.
Melchi was the son of Jannai.
Jannai was the son of Joseph.
25 Joseph was the son of Mattathias.
Mattathias was the son of Amos.
Amos was the son of Nahum.
Nahum was the son of Esli.
Esli was the son of Naggai.
26 Naggai was the son of Maath.
Maath was the son of Mattathias.
Mattathias was the son of Semein.
Semein was the son of Josech.
Josech was the son of Joda.
27 Joda was the son of Joanan.
Joanan was the son of Rhesa.
Rhesa was the son of Zerubbabel.
Zerubbabel was the son of Shealtiel.
Shealtiel was the son of Neri.
28 Neri was the son of Melchi.
Melchi was the son of Addi.
Addi was the son of Cosam.
Cosam was the son of Elmadam.
Elmadam was the son of Er.
29 Er was the son of Joshua.
Joshua was the son of Eliezer.
Eliezer was the son of Jorim.
Jorim was the son of Matthat.
Matthat was the son of Levi.
30 Levi was the son of Simeon.
Simeon was the son of Judah.
Judah was the son of Joseph.
Joseph was the son of Jonam.
Jonam was the son of Eliakim.
31 Eliakim was the son of Melea.
Melea was the son of Menna.
Menna was the son of Mattatha.
Mattatha was the son of Nathan.
Nathan was the son of David.
32 David was the son of Jesse.
Jesse was the son of Obed.
Obed was the son of Boaz.
Boaz was the son of Salmon.
Salmon was the son of Nahshon.
33 Nahshon was the son of Amminadab.
Amminadab was the son of Admin.
Admin was the son of Arni.
Arni was the son of Hezron.
Hezron was the son of Perez.
Perez was the son of Judah.
34 Judah was the son of Jacob.

*a***3:9** *trees* Meaning the people who don't obey God. They are like "trees" that will be cut down.
*b***3:17** *clean the grain* Meaning that Jesus will separate the good people from those who are bad.

Jacob was the son of Isaac.
Isaac was the son of Abraham.
Abraham was the son of Terah.
Terah was the son of Nahor.
35 Nahor was the son of Serug.
Serug was the son of Reu.
Reu was the son of Peleg.
Peleg was the son of Eber.
Eber was the son of Shelah.
36 Shelah was the son of Cainan.
Cainan was the son of Arphaxad.
Arphaxad was the son of Shem.
Shem was the son of Noah.
Noah was the son of Lamech.
37 Lamech was the son of Methuselah.
Methuselah was the son of Enoch.
Enoch was the son of Jared.
Jared was the son of Mahalaleel.
Mahalaleel was the son of Cainan.
38 Cainan was the son of Enos.
Enos was the son of Seth.
Seth was the son of Adam.
Adam was the son of God.

Jesus Is Tempted by the Devil
(Mt. 4:1–11; Mk. 1:12–13)

4 ¹Now filled with the Holy Spirit* Jesus returned from the Jordan River. And then the Spirit led him into the desert. ²There the devil tempted Jesus for 40 days. Jesus ate nothing during this time, and when it was finished, he was very hungry.

³The devil said to him, "If you are the Son of God, tell this rock to become bread."

⁴Jesus answered, "The Scriptures* say,

'It is not just bread that keeps people
        alive.'"   *Deuteronomy 8:3*

⁵Then the devil took Jesus and in a moment of time showed him all the kingdoms of the world. ⁶The devil said to him, "I will make you king over all these places. You will have power over them, and you will get all the glory.* It has all been given to me. I can give it to anyone I want. ⁷I will give it all to you, if you will only worship me."

⁸Jesus answered, "The Scriptures say,

'You must worship the Lord your God.
    Serve only him.'"   *Deuteronomy 6:13*

⁹Then the devil led Jesus to Jerusalem and put him on a high place at the edge of the Temple* area. He said to him, "If you are the Son of God, jump off! ¹⁰The Scriptures say,

'God will command his angels to take care
        of you.'   *Psalm 91:11*

¹¹It is also written,

'Their hands will catch you
    so that you will not hit your foot on a
        rock.'"   *Psalm 91:12*

¹²Jesus answered, "But the Scriptures also say,

'You must not test the Lord your God.'"
                                    Deuteronomy 6:16

¹³The devil finished tempting Jesus in every way and went away to wait until a better time.

Jesus Begins His Work in Galilee
(Mt. 4:12–17; Mk. 1:14–15)

¹⁴Jesus went back to Galilee with the power of the Spirit.* Stories about him spread all over the area around Galilee. ¹⁵He began to teach in the synagogues,* and everyone praised him.

Jesus Goes to His Hometown
(Mt. 13:53–58; Mk. 6:1–6)

¹⁶Jesus traveled to Nazareth, the town where he grew up. On the Sabbath* day he went to the synagogue* as he always did. He stood up to read. ¹⁷The book of Isaiah the prophet* was given to him. He opened the book and found the place where this is written:

¹⁸"The Spirit of the Lord is on me.
He has chosen me to tell good news to
        the poor.
He sent me to tell prisoners that they are
        free
    and to tell the blind that they can see
        again.
He sent me to free those who have been
        treated badly
19   and to announce that the time has come
        for the Lord to show his kindness."
                                    Isaiah 61:1–2; 58:6

²⁰Jesus closed the book, gave it back to the helper, and sat down. As everyone in the synagogue watched him closely, ²¹he began to speak to them. He said, "While you heard me reading these words just now, they were coming true!"

²²Everyone there said good things about Jesus. They were amazed to hear him speak such wonderful words. They said, "How is this possible? Isn't he Joseph's son?"

²³Jesus said to them, "I know you will tell me the old saying: 'Doctor, heal yourself.' You want to say, 'We heard about the things you did in Capernaum.* Do those same things here in your own hometown!'" ²⁴Then he said, "The truth is, a prophet is not accepted in his own hometown.

²⁵-²⁶"During the time of Elijah* it did not rain in Israel for three and a half years. There was no food anywhere in the whole country. There were many widows in Israel during that time. But the fact is, Elijah was sent to none of those widows in Israel. He was sent only to a widow in Zarephath, a town in Sidon.

27"And there were many people with leprosy* living in Israel during the time of the prophet Elisha.* But none of them were healed; the only one was Naaman. And he was from the country of Syria, not Israel."

28When the people in the synagogue heard this, they were very angry. 29They got up and forced Jesus to go out of town. Their town was built on a hill. They took Jesus to the edge of the hill to throw him off. 30But he walked through the middle of the crowd and went away.

Jesus Frees a Man From an Evil Spirit
(Mk. 1:21–28)

31Jesus went to Capernaum, a city in Galilee. On the Sabbath* day he taught the people. 32They were amazed at his teaching because he spoke with authority.

33In the synagogue* there was a man who had an evil spirit from the devil inside him. The man shouted loudly, 34"Jesus of Nazareth! What do you want with us? Did you come here to destroy us? I know who you are—God's Holy One!" 35But Jesus warned the evil spirit to stop. He said, "Be quiet! Come out of the man!" The evil spirit threw the man down on the ground in front of everyone. Then the evil spirit left the man and did not hurt him.

36The people were amazed. They said to each other, "What does this mean? With authority and power he commands evil spirits and they come out." 37And so the news about Jesus spread to every place in the whole area.

Jesus Heals Peter's Mother-in-Law
(Mt. 8:14–17; Mk. 1:29–34)

38Jesus left the synagogue* and went to Simon's*ª house. Simon's mother-in-law was very sick. She had a high fever. They asked Jesus to do something to help her. 39He stood very close to her and ordered the sickness to go away. The sickness left her, and she got up and began serving them.

Jesus Heals Many Others

40When the sun went down, the people brought their sick friends to Jesus. They had many different kinds of sicknesses. Jesus laid his hands on* each sick person and healed them all. 41Demons* came out of many people. The demons shouted, "You are the Son of God." But Jesus gave a strong command for the demons not to speak, because they knew he was the Christ.*

Jesus Goes to Other Towns
(Mk. 1:35–39)

42The next day Jesus went to a place to be alone. The people looked for him. When they found him, they tried to stop him from leaving. 43But he said to them, "I must tell the Good News* about God's kingdom* to other towns too. This is why I was sent."

44Then Jesus told the Good News in the synagogues* in Judea.

Jesus Chooses Some Followers
(Mt. 4:18–22; Mk. 1:16–20)

5 1As Jesus stood beside Lake Galilee,ᵇ a crowd of people pushed to get closer to him and to hear the teachings of God. 2Jesus saw two boats at the shore of the lake. The fishermen were washing their nets. 3Jesus got into the boat that belonged to Simon. He asked Simon to push off a little from the shore. Then he sat down in the boat and taught the people on the shore.

4When Jesus finished speaking, he said to Simon, "Take the boat into the deep water. If all of you will put your nets into the water, you will catch some fish."

5Simon answered, "Master, we worked hard all night trying to catch fish and caught nothing. But you say I should put the nets into the water, so I will." 6The fishermen put their nets into the water. Their nets were filled with so many fish that they began to break. 7They called to their friends in the other boat to come and help them. The friends came, and both boats were filled so full of fish that they were almost sinking.

8-9The fishermen were all amazed at the many fish they caught. When Simon Peter saw this, he bowed down before Jesus and said, "Go away from me, Lord. I am a sinful man!" 10James and John, the sons of Zebedee, were amazed too. (James and John worked together with Simon.)

Jesus said to Simon, "Don't be afraid. From now on your work will be to bring in people, not fish!"

11The men brought their boats to the shore. They left everything and followed Jesus.

Jesus Heals a Sick Man
(Mt. 8:1–4; Mk. 1:40–45)

12One time Jesus was in a town where a very sick man lived. This man was covered with leprosy.* When the man saw Jesus, he bowed before Jesus and begged him, "Lord, you have the power to heal me if you want."

13Jesus said, "I want to heal you. Be healed!" Then he touched the man, and immediately the leprosy disappeared. 14Then Jesus said, "Don't tell anyone about what happened. But go and let the priest look at you.ᶜ And offer a gift to God for your healing as Moses* commanded. This will show people that you are healed."

15But the news about Jesus spread more and more. Many people came to hear him and to be healed of their sicknesses. 16Jesus often

---

ª**4:38** *Simon* Simon's other name was Peter. Also in 5:3, 4, 5, 10.

ᵇ**5:1** *Galilee* Literally, "Gennesaret."

ᶜ**5:14** *let the priest look at you* The Law of Moses said a priest must decide when a person with leprosy was well.

went away to other places to be alone so that he could pray.

Jesus Heals a Crippled Man
(Mt. 9:1–8; Mk. 2:1–12)

[17]One day Jesus was teaching the people. The Pharisees* and teachers of the law were sitting there too. They had come from every town in Galilee and Judea and from Jerusalem. The Lord was giving Jesus the power to heal people. [18]There was a man who was paralyzed, and some other men were carrying him on a mat. They tried to bring him and put him down before Jesus. [19]But there were so many people that they could not find a way to Jesus. So they went up on the roof and lowered the crippled man down through a hole in the ceiling. They lowered the mat into the room so that the crippled man was lying before Jesus. [20]Jesus saw how much faith they had and said to the sick man, "Friend, your sins are forgiven."

[21]The Jewish teachers of the law and the Pharisees thought to themselves, "Who is this man who dares to say such things? What an insult to God! No one but God can forgive sins."

[22]But Jesus knew what they were thinking and said, "Why do you have these questions in your minds? [23–24]The Son of Man* has power on earth to forgive sins. But how can I prove this to you? Maybe you are thinking it was easy for me to say, 'Your sins are forgiven.' There's no proof that it really happened. But what if I say to the man, 'Stand up and walk'? Then you will be able to see that I really have this power." So Jesus said to the paralyzed man, "I tell you, stand up! Take your mat and go home!"

[25]The man immediately stood up in front of everyone. He picked up his mat and walked home, praising God. [26]Everyone was completely amazed and began to praise God. They were filled with great respect for God's power. They said, "Today we saw amazing things!"

Levi (Matthew) Follows Jesus
(Mt. 9:9–13; Mk. 2:13–17)

[27]After this Jesus went out and saw a tax collector* sitting at his place for collecting taxes. His name was Levi. Jesus said to him, "Follow me!" [28]Levi got up, left everything, and followed Jesus.

[29]Then Levi gave a big dinner at his house for Jesus. At the table there were many tax collectors and some other people too. [30]But the Pharisees* and those who taught the law for the Pharisees began to complain to the followers of Jesus, "Why do you eat and drink with tax collectors and other sinners?"

[31]Jesus answered them, "It is the sick people who need a doctor, not those who are healthy. [32]I have not come to ask good people to change. I have come to ask sinners to change the way they live."

Jesus Is Not Like Other Religious Leaders
(Mt. 9:14–17; Mk. 2:18–22)

[33]They said to Jesus, "John's followers often fast* and pray, the same as the followers of the Pharisees.* But your followers eat and drink all the time."

[34]Jesus said to them, "At a wedding you can't ask the friends of the bridegroom* to be sad and fast while he is still with them. [35]But the time will come when the groom will be taken away from them. Then his friends will fast."

[36]Jesus told them this story: "No one takes cloth off a new coat to cover a hole in an old coat. That would ruin the new coat, and the cloth from the new coat would not be the same as the old cloth. [37]Also, no one ever pours new wine into old wineskins.* The new wine would break them. The wine would spill out, and the wineskins would be ruined. [38]You always put new wine into new wineskins. [39]No one who drinks old wine wants new wine. They say, 'The old wine is just fine.'"

Jesus Is Lord Over the Sabbath Day
(Mt. 12:1–8; Mk. 2:23–28)

6 [1]One time on a Sabbath* day, Jesus was walking through some grain fields. His followers picked the grain, rubbed it in their hands, and ate it. [2]Some Pharisees* said, "Why are you doing that? It is against the Law of Moses* to do that on the Sabbath day."

[3]Jesus answered, "You have read about what David* did when he and the people with him were hungry. [4]David went into God's house. He took the bread that was offered to God and ate it. And he gave some of the bread to the people with him. This was against the Law of Moses, which says that only the priests can eat that bread." [5]Then Jesus said to the Pharisees, "The Son of Man* is Lord over the Sabbath day."

Jesus Heals a Man on the Sabbath Day
(Mt. 12:9–14; Mk. 3:1–6)

[6]On another Sabbath* day Jesus went into the synagogue* and taught the people. A man with a crippled right hand was there. [7]The teachers of the law and the Pharisees* were watching Jesus closely. They were waiting to see if he would heal on the Sabbath day. They wanted to see him do something wrong so that they could accuse him. [8]But Jesus knew what they were thinking. He said to the man with the crippled hand, "Get up and stand here where everyone can see." The man got up and stood there. [9]Then Jesus said to them, "I ask you, which is the right thing to do on the Sabbath day: to do good or to do evil? Is it right to save a life or to destroy one?"

[10]Jesus looked around at all of them, then said to the man, "Hold out your hand." The man held out his hand, and it was healed. [11]The Pharisees and the teachers of the law

got so mad they couldn't think straight. They talked to each other about what they could do to Jesus.

Jesus Chooses His Twelve Apostles
(Mt. 10:1–4; Mk. 3:13–19)

12A few days later, Jesus went out to a mountain to pray. He stayed there all night praying to God. 13The next morning he called his followers. He chose twelve of them and called them apostles.* These are the ones he chose:

14 Simon (Jesus named him Peter),
Andrew, brother of Peter,
James,
John,
Philip,
Bartholomew,
15 Matthew,
Thomas,
James, the son of Alphaeus,
Simon, called the Zealot,*
16 Judas, the son of James,
Judas Iscariot (the one who turned against Jesus).

Jesus Teaches and Heals the People
(Mt. 4:23–25; 5:1–12)

17Jesus and the apostles* came down from the mountain. Jesus stood on a flat place. A large crowd of his followers was there. Also, there were many people from all around Judea, Jerusalem, and the seacoast cities of Tyre* and Sidon.* 18They all came to hear Jesus teach and to be healed of their sicknesses. He healed the people who were troubled by evil spirits. 19Everyone was trying to touch him, because power was coming out from him. Jesus healed them all.

20Jesus looked at his followers and said,

"Great blessings belong to you who are poor.
God's kingdom* belongs to you.
21 Great blessings belong to you who are hungry now.
You will be filled.
Great blessings belong to you who are crying now.
You will be happy and laughing.

22"People will hate you because you belong to the Son of Man.* They will make you leave their group. They will insult you. They will think it is wrong even to say your name. When these things happen, know that great blessings belong to you. 23You can be happy then and jump for joy, because you have a great reward in heaven. The ancestors* of those people did the same things to the prophets.*

24"But how bad it will be for you rich people, because you had your easy life.

25 How bad it will be for you people who are full now,
because you will be hungry.
How bad it will be for you people who are laughing now,
because you will be sad and cry.

26"How bad it is when everyone says nothing but good about you. Just look at the false prophets.* Their ancestors always said good things about them.

Love Your Enemies
(Mt. 5:38–48; 7:12a)

27"But I say to you people who are listening to me, love your enemies. Do good to those who hate you. 28Ask God to bless the people who ask for bad things to happen to you. Pray for the people who are mean to you. 29If someone hits you on the side of your face, let them hit the other side too. If someone takes your coat, don't stop them from taking your shirt too. 30Give to everyone who asks you for something. When someone takes something that is yours, don't ask for it back. 31Do for others what you want them to do for you.

32"If you love only those who love you, should you get any special praise for doing that? No, even sinners love those who love them! 33If you do good only to those who do good to you, should you get any special praise for doing that? No, even sinners do that! 34If you lend things to people, always expecting to get something back, should you get any special praise for that? No, even sinners lend to other sinners so that they can get back the same amount!

35"I'm telling you to love your enemies and do good to them. Lend to people without expecting to get anything back. If you do this, you will have a great reward. You will be children of the Most High God. Yes, because God is good even to the people who are full of sin and not thankful. 36Give love and mercy the same as your Father gives love and mercy.

Be Careful About Criticizing Others
(Mt. 7:1–5)

37"Don't judge others, and God will not judge you. Don't condemn others, and you will not be condemned. Forgive others, and you will be forgiven. 38Give to others, and you will receive. You will be given much. It will be poured into your hands—more than you can hold. You will be given so much that it will spill into your lap. The way you give to others is the way God will give to you."

39Jesus told them this story: "Can a blind man lead another blind man? No. Both of them will fall into a ditch. 40Students are not better than their teacher. But when they have been fully taught, they will be like their teacher.

41"Why do you notice the small piece of dust that is in your friend's eye, but you don't see the big piece of wood that is in your own eye? [42]You say to your friend, 'Let me get that little piece of dust out of your eye.' Why do you say this? Can't you see that big piece of wood in your own eye? You are a hypocrite.* First, take the wood out of your own eye. Then you will see clearly to get the dust out of your friend's eye.

Only Good Trees Produce Good Fruit
(Mt. 7:17–20; 12:34b–35)

[43]"A good tree does not produce bad fruit. And a bad tree does not produce good fruit. [44]Every tree is known by the kind of fruit it produces. You won't find figs on thorny weeds. And you can't pick grapes from thornbushes! [45]Good people have good things saved in their hearts. That's why they say good things. But those who are evil have hearts full of evil, and that's why they say things that are evil. What people say with their mouths comes from what fills their hearts.

Two Kinds of People
(Mt. 7:24–27)

[46]"Why do you call me, 'Lord, Lord,' but you don't do what I say? [47]The people who come to me, who listen to my teachings and obey them—I will show you what they are like: [48]They are like a man building a house. He digs deep and builds his house on rock. The floods come, and the water crashes against the house. But the flood cannot move the house, because it was built well.

[49]"But the people who hear my words and do not obey are like a man who builds a house without preparing a foundation. When the floods come, the house falls down easily and is completely destroyed."

Jesus Heals an Officer's Servant
(Mt. 8:5–13; Jn. 4:43–54)

7 [1]Jesus finished saying all these things to the people. Then he went into Capernaum.* [2]In Capernaum there was an army officer.* He had a servant who was very sick; he was near death. The officer loved the servant very much. [3]When he heard about Jesus, he sent some older Jewish leaders to him. He wanted the men to ask Jesus to come and save the life of his servant. [4]The men went to Jesus. They begged Jesus to help the officer. They said, "This officer is worthy to have your help. [5]He loves our people and he built the synagogue* for us."

[6]So Jesus went with them. He was coming near the officer's house when the officer sent friends to say, "Lord, you don't need to do anything special for me. I am not good enough for you to come into my house. [7]That is why I did not come to you myself. You need only to give the order, and my servant will be healed. [8]I know this because I am a man under the authority of other men. And I have soldiers under my authority. I tell one soldier,

'Go,' and he goes. And I tell another soldier, 'Come,' and he comes. And I say to my servant, 'Do this,' and my servant obeys me."

[9]When Jesus heard this, he was amazed. He turned to the people following him and said, "I tell you, this is the most faith I have seen anywhere, even in Israel.*"

[10]The group that was sent to Jesus went back to the house. There they found that the servant was healed.

Jesus Brings a Woman's Son Back to Life

[11]The next day Jesus and his followers went to a town called Nain. A big crowd was traveling with them. [12]When Jesus came near the town gate, he saw some people carrying a dead body. It was the only son of a woman who was a widow. Walking with her were many other people from the town. [13]When the Lord saw the woman, he felt very sorry for her and said, "Don't cry." [14]He walked to the open coffin and touched it. The men who were carrying the coffin stopped. Jesus spoke to the dead son: "Young man, I tell you, get up!" [15]Then the boy sat up and began to talk, and Jesus gave him back to his mother.

[16]Everyone was filled with fear. They began praising God and said, "A great prophet* is here with us!" and "God is taking care of his people."

[17]This news about Jesus spread all over Judea and to all the other places around there.

John Sends Men to Ask Jesus a Question
(Mt. 11:2–19)

[18]John's followers told him about all these things. John called for two of his followers. [19]He sent them to the Lord to ask, "Are you the one we heard was coming, or should we wait for someone else?"

[20]So the men came to Jesus. They said, "John the Baptizer* sent us to you with this question: 'Are you the one who is coming, or should we wait for someone else?'"

[21]Right then Jesus healed many people of their sicknesses and diseases. He healed those who had evil spirits and made many who were blind able to see again. [22]Then he said to John's followers, "Go tell John what you have seen and heard: The blind can see. The crippled can walk. People with leprosy* are healed. The deaf can hear. The dead are brought back to life. And the Good News* is being told to the poor. [23]Great blessings belong to those who don't have a problem accepting me."

[24]When John's followers left, Jesus began talking to the people about John: "What did you people go out into the desert to see? Someone who is weak, like a stem of grass[a] blowing in the wind? [25]Really, what did you expect to see? Someone dressed in fine

---

[a]**7:24** *stem of grass* Literally, "reed."

clothes? Of course not. People who wear fancy clothes and live in luxury are all in kings' palaces. 26So what did you go out to see? A prophet*? Yes, John is a prophet. But I tell you, he is more than that. 27This Scripture* was written about him:

'Listen! I will send my messenger ahead of
   you.
He will prepare the way for you.'
                                    Malachi 3:1

28I tell you, no one ever born is greater than John. But even the least important person in God's kingdom* is greater than John."

29(When the people heard this, they all agreed that God's teaching was good. Even the tax collectors* agreed. These were the people who were baptized* by John. 30But the Pharisees* and experts in the law refused to accept God's plan for themselves; they did not let John baptize them.)

31"What shall I say about the people of this time? What can I compare them to? What are they like? 32They are like children sitting in the marketplace. One group of children calls to the other children and says,

'We played flute music for you,
   but you did not dance;
we sang a sad song,
   but you did not cry.'

33John the Baptizer came and did not eat the usual food or drink wine. And you say, 'He has a demon* inside him.' 34The Son of Man* came eating and drinking. And you say, 'Look at him! He eats too much and drinks too much wine! He is a friend of tax collectors and other sinners!' 35But wisdom is shown to be right by those who accept it."

Simon the Pharisee

36One of the Pharisees* asked Jesus to eat with him. Jesus went into the Pharisee's house and took a place at the table. 37There was a sinful woman in that town. She knew that Jesus was eating at the Pharisee's house. So the woman brought some expensive perfume in an alabaster* jar. 38She stood at Jesus' feet, crying. Then she began to wash his feet with her tears. She dried his feet with her hair. She kissed his feet many times and rubbed them with the perfume. 39When the Pharisee who asked Jesus to come to his house saw this, he thought to himself, "If this man were a prophet,*a he would know that the woman who is touching him is a sinner!"

40In response, Jesus said to the Pharisee, "Simon, I have something to say to you."

Simon said, "Let me hear it, Teacher."

41Jesus said, "There were two men. Both men owed money to the same banker. One man owed him 500 silver coins.* The other man owed him 50 silver coins. 42The men had no money, so they could not pay their debt. But the banker told the men that they did not have to pay him. Which one of those two men will love him more?"

43Simon answered, "I think it would be the one who owed him the most money."

Jesus said to him, "You are right." 44Then he turned to the woman and said to Simon, "Do you see this woman? When I came into your house, you gave me no water for my feet. But she washed my feet with her tears and dried my feet with her hair. 45You did not greet me with a kiss, but she has been kissing my feet since I came in. 46You did not honor me with oil for my head, but she rubbed my feet with her sweet-smelling oil. 47I tell you that her many sins are forgiven. This is clear, because she showed great love. People who are forgiven only a little will love only a little."

48Then Jesus said to her, "Your sins are forgiven."

49The people sitting at the table began to think to themselves, "Who does this man think he is? How can he forgive sins?"

50Jesus said to the woman, "Because you believed, you are saved from your sins. Go in peace."

The Group With Jesus

8 1The next day, Jesus traveled through some cities and small towns. Jesus told the people a message from God, the Good News about God's kingdom.* The twelve apostles* were with him. 2There were also some women with him. Jesus had healed these women of sicknesses and evil spirits. One of them was Mary, who was called Magdalene. Seven demons had come out of her. 3Also with these women were Joanna, the wife of Chuza (the manager of Herod's* property), Suzanna, and many other women. These women used their own money to help Jesus and his apostles.

A Story About a Farmer Sowing Seed
(Mt. 13:1–17; Mk. 4:1–12)

4A large crowd came together. People came to Jesus from every town, and he told them this story:

5"A farmer went out to sow seed. While he was scattering the seed, some of it fell beside the road. People walked on the seed, and the birds ate it all. 6Other seed fell on rock. It began to grow but then died because it had no water. 7Some other seed fell among thorny weeds. This seed grew, but later the weeds stopped the plants from growing. 8The rest of the seed fell on good ground. This seed grew and made 100 times more grain."

Jesus finished the story. Then he called out, "You people who hear me, listen!"

---

a7:39 prophet A prophet often knows things that are hidden to other people.

[9]Jesus' followers asked him, "What does this story mean?"

[10]He said, "You have been chosen to know the secret truths about God's kingdom.* But I use stories to speak to other people. I do this so that,

'They will look,
  but they will not see,
and they will listen,
  but they will not understand.'   *Isaiah 6:9*

Jesus Explains the Story About Seed
(Mt. 13:18–23; Mk. 4:13–20)

[11]"This is what the story means: The seed is God's teaching. [12]Some people are like the seed that fell beside the path. They hear God's teaching, but then the devil comes and causes them to stop thinking about it. This keeps them from believing it and being saved. [13]Others are like the seed that fell on rock. That is like the people who hear God's teaching and gladly accept it. But they don't have deep roots. They believe for a while. But when trouble comes, they turn away from God.

[14]"What about the seed that fell among the thorny weeds? That is like the people who hear God's teaching, but they let the worries, riches, and pleasures of this life stop them from growing. So they never produce a crop.*a* [15]And what about the seed that fell on the good ground? That is like the people who hear God's teaching with a good, honest heart. They obey it and patiently produce a good crop.

Use the Understanding You Have
(Mk. 4:21–25)

[16]"No one lights a lamp and then covers it with a bowl or hides it under a bed. Instead, they put the lamp on a lampstand so that the people who come in will have enough light to see. [17]Everything that is hidden will become clear. Every secret thing will be made known, and everyone will see it. [18]So think carefully about what you are hearing. The people who have some understanding will receive more. But those who do not have understanding will lose even what they think they have."

Jesus' Followers Are His True Family
(Mt. 12:46–50; Mk. 3:31–35)

[19]Jesus' mother and brothers came to visit him. But they could not get close to him, because there were so many people. [20]Someone said to Jesus, "Your mother and your brothers are standing outside. They want to see you."

[21]Jesus answered them, "My mother and my brothers are those who listen to God's teaching and obey it."

Jesus' Followers See His Power
(Mt. 8:23–27; Mk. 4:35–41)

[22]One day Jesus and his followers got into a boat. He said to them, "Come with me across the lake." And so they started across. [23]While they were sailing, Jesus slept. A big storm blew across the lake, and the boat began to fill with water. They were in danger. [24]The followers went to Jesus and woke him. They said, "Master! Master! We will drown!"

Jesus got up. He gave a command to the wind and the waves. The wind stopped, and the lake became calm. [25]He said to his followers, "Where is your faith?"

They were afraid and amazed. They said to each other, "What kind of man is this? He commands the wind and the water, and they obey him."

Jesus Frees a Man From Evil Spirits
(Mt. 8:28–34; Mk. 5:1–20)

[26]Jesus and his followers sailed on across the lake. They sailed to the area where the Gerasene people live, across from Galilee. [27]When Jesus got out of the boat, a man from that town came to him. This man had demons* inside him. For a long time he had worn no clothes. He did not live in a house but in the caves where the dead are buried. [28–29]The demon inside the man had often seized him, and he had been put in jail with his hands and feet in chains. But he would always break the chains. The demon inside him would force him to go out to the places where no one lived. Jesus commanded the evil spirit to come out of the man. When the man saw Jesus, he fell down before him, shouting loudly, "What do you want with me, Jesus, Son of the Most High God? Please, don't punish me!"

[30]Jesus asked him, "What is your name?"

The man answered, "Legion."*b* (He said his name was "Legion" because many demons had gone into him.) [31]The demons begged Jesus not to send them into the bottomless pit.*c* [32]On that hill there was a big herd of pigs eating. The demons begged Jesus to allow them to go into the pigs. So he allowed them to do this. [33]Then the demons came out of the man and went into the pigs. The herd of pigs ran down the hill into the lake, and all were drowned.

[34]The men who were caring for the pigs ran away and told the story in the fields and in the town. [35]People went out to see what had happened. They came to Jesus and found the man sitting there at the feet of Jesus. The man had clothes on and was in his right mind again; the demons were gone. This made the people afraid. [36]The men who saw these

---

*b*8:30 *"Legion"* This name means very many. A legion was about 6000 men in the Roman army.
*c*8:31 *bottomless pit* Literally, "the abyss," something like a deep hole where evil spirits are kept.

*a*8:14 *produce a crop* Meaning to do the good things God wants his people to do.

things happen told the others all about how Jesus made the man well. 37All those who lived in the area around Gerasa asked Jesus to go away because they were afraid.

So Jesus got into the boat to go back to Galilee. 38The man he had healed begged to go with him. But Jesus sent him away, saying, 39"Go back home and tell people what God did for you."

So the man went all over town telling what Jesus had done for him.

Jesus Gives Life to a Dead Girl and Heals a Sick Woman
(Mt. 9:18–26; Mk. 5:21–43)

40When Jesus went back to Galilee, the people welcomed him. Everyone was waiting for him. 41–42A man named Jairus came to him. He was a leader of the synagogue.* He had only one daughter. She was twelve years old, and she was dying. So Jairus bowed down at the feet of Jesus and begged him to come to his house.

While Jesus was going to Jairus' house, the people crowded all around him. 43A woman was there who had been bleeding for twelve years. She had spent all her money on doctors,a but no doctor was able to heal her. 44The woman came behind Jesus and touched the bottom of his coat. At that moment, her bleeding stopped. 45Then Jesus said, "Who touched me?"

They all said they had not touched him. And Peter said, "Master, people are all around you, pushing against you."

46But Jesus said, "Someone touched me. I felt power go out from me." 47When the woman saw that she could not hide, she came forward, shaking. She bowed down before Jesus. While everyone listened, she told why she touched him. Then she said that she was healed immediately when she touched him. 48Jesus said to her, "My daughter, you are made well because you believed. Go in peace."

49While Jesus was still speaking, someone came from the house of the synagogue leader and said, "Your daughter has died! Don't bother the Teacher anymore."

50Jesus heard this and said to Jairus, "Don't be afraid! Just believe and your daughter will be well."

51Jesus went to the house. He let only Peter, John, James, and the girl's father and mother go inside with him. 52Everyone was crying and feeling sad because the girl was dead. But Jesus said, "Don't cry. She is not dead. She is only sleeping."

53The people laughed at him, because they knew that the girl was dead. 54But Jesus held her hand and called to her, "Little girl, stand up!" 55Her spirit came back into her, and she stood up immediately. Jesus said, "Give her something to eat." 56The girl's parents were amazed. He told them not to tell anyone about what happened.

Jesus Sends His Apostles on a Mission
(Mt. 10:5–15; Mk. 6:7–13)

9 1Jesus called his twelve apostles* together. He gave them power to heal sicknesses and power to force demons* out of people. 2He sent them to tell about God's kingdom* and to heal the sick. 3He said to them, "When you travel, don't take a walking stick. Also, don't carry a bag, food, or money. Take for your trip only the clothes you are wearing. 4When you go into a house, stay there until it is time to leave. 5If the people in the town will not welcome you, go outside the town and shake the dust off your feet as a warning to them."

6So the apostles went out. They traveled through all the towns. They told the Good News* and healed people everywhere.

Herod Is Confused About Jesus
(Mt. 14:1–12; Mk. 6:14–29)

7Herod* the ruler heard about all these things that were happening. He was confused because some people said, "John the Baptizer has risen from death." 8Others said, "Elijah* has come to us." And some others said, "One of the prophets* from long ago has risen from death." 9Herod said, "I cut off John's head. So who is this man I hear these things about?" Herod continued trying to see Jesus.

Jesus Feeds More Than 5000
(Mt. 14:13–21; Mk. 6:30–44; Jn. 6:1–14)

10When the apostles* came back, they told Jesus what they had done on their trip. Then he took them away to a town called Bethsaida. There, he and his apostles could be alone together. 11But the people learned where Jesus went and followed him. He welcomed them and talked with them about God's kingdom.* He healed the people who were sick.

12Late in the afternoon, the twelve apostles came to Jesus and said, "No one lives in this place. Send the people away. They need to find food and places to sleep in the farms and towns around here."

13But Jesus said to the apostles, "You give them something to eat."

They said, "We have only five loaves of bread and two fish. Do you want us to go buy food for all these people?" There are too many! 14(There were about 5000 men there.)

Jesus said to his followers, "Tell the people to sit in groups of about 50 people."

15So the followers did this and everyone sat down. 16Then Jesus took the five loaves of bread and two fish. He looked up into the sky and thanked God for the food. Then he broke

---

a8:43 She had spent … doctors Some Greek copies do not have these words.

it into pieces, which he gave to the followers to give to the people. ¹⁷They all ate until they were full. And there was a lot of food left. Twelve baskets were filled with the pieces of food that were not eaten.

Peter Says Jesus Is the Christ
(Mt. 16:13–19; Mk. 8:27–29)

¹⁸One time Jesus was praying alone. His followers came together there, and he asked them, "Who do the people say I am?"

¹⁹They answered, "Some people say you are John the Baptizer. Others say you are Elijah.* And some people say you are one of the prophets* from long ago that has come back to life."

²⁰Then Jesus said to his followers, "And who do you say I am?"

Peter answered, "You are the Christ* from God."

²¹Jesus warned them not to tell anyone.

Jesus Says He Must Die
(Mt. 16:21–28; Mk. 8:30–9:1)

²²Then Jesus said, "The Son of Man* must suffer many things. He will be rejected by the older Jewish leaders, the leading priests, and teachers of the law. And he will be killed. But after three days he will be raised from death."

²³Jesus continued to say to all of them, "Any of you who want to be my follower must stop thinking about yourself and what you want. You must be willing to carry the cross* that is given to you every day for following me. ²⁴Any of you who try to save the life you have will lose it. But you who give up your life for me will save it. ²⁵It is worth nothing for you to have the whole world if you yourself are destroyed or lost. ²⁶Don't be ashamed of me and my teaching. If that happens, I*ᵃ will be ashamed of you when I come with my divine greatness* and that of the Father and the holy angels. ²⁷Believe me when I say that some of you people standing here will see God's kingdom* before you die."

Jesus Is Seen With Moses and Elijah
(Mt. 17:1–8; Mk. 9:2–8)

²⁸About eight days after Jesus said these things, he took Peter, John, and James and went up on a mountain to pray. ²⁹While Jesus was praying, his face began to change. His clothes became shining white. ³⁰Then two men were there, talking with him. They were Moses* and Elijah.* ³¹They also looked bright and glorious. They were talking with Jesus about his death that would happen in Jerusalem. ³²Peter and the others were asleep. But they woke up and saw the glory* of Jesus. They also saw the two men who were standing with him. ³³When Moses and Elijah were

leaving, Peter said, "Master, it is good that we are here. We will put three tents here—one for you, one for Moses, and one for Elijah." (He did not know what he was saying.)

³⁴While Peter was saying these things, a cloud came all around them. Peter, John, and James were afraid when the cloud covered them. ³⁵A voice came from the cloud and said, "This is my Son. He is the one I have chosen. Obey him."

³⁶When the voice stopped, only Jesus was there. Peter, John, and James said nothing. And for a long time after that, they told no one about what they had seen.

Jesus Frees a Boy From an Evil Spirit
(Mt. 17:14–18; Mk. 9:14–27)

³⁷The next day, Jesus, Peter, John, and James came down from the mountain. A large group of people met Jesus. ³⁸A man in the group shouted to him, "Teacher, please come and look at my son. He is the only child I have. ³⁹An evil spirit comes into him, and then he shouts. He loses control of himself and foams at the mouth. The evil spirit continues to hurt him and almost never leaves him. ⁴⁰I begged your followers to make the evil spirit leave my son, but they could not do it."

⁴¹Jesus answered, "You people today have no faith. Your lives are all wrong. How long must I be with you and be patient with you?" Then Jesus said to the man, "Bring your son here."

⁴²While the boy was coming, the demon* threw the boy to the ground. The boy lost control of himself. But Jesus gave a strong command to the evil spirit. Then the boy was healed, and Jesus gave him back to his father. ⁴³All the people were amazed at the great power of God.

Jesus Talks About His Death
(Mt. 17:22–23; Mk. 9:30–32)

The people were still amazed about all the things Jesus did. He said to his followers, ⁴⁴"Don't forget what I will tell you now: The Son of Man* will soon be handed over to the control of other men." ⁴⁵But the followers did not understand what he meant. The meaning was hidden from them so that they could not understand it. But they were afraid to ask Jesus about what he said.

Who Is the Greatest?
(Mt. 18:1–5; Mk. 9:33–37)

⁴⁶Jesus' followers began to have an argument about which one of them was the greatest. ⁴⁷Jesus knew what they were thinking, so he took a little child and stood the child beside him. ⁴⁸Then he said to the followers, "Whoever accepts a little child like this in my name is accepting me. And anyone who accepts me is also accepting the one who sent me. The one among you who is the most humble—this is the one who is great."

ᵃ**9:26** *I* Literally, "the Son of Man" (Jesus).

Whoever Is Not Against You Is for You
(Mk. 9:38–40)

49John answered, "Master, we saw someone using your name to force demons* out of people. We told him to stop because he does not belong to our group."

50Jesus said to him, "Don't stop him. Whoever is not against you is for you."

A Samaritan Town

51The time was coming near when Jesus would leave and go back to heaven. He decided to go to Jerusalem. 52He sent some men ahead of him. They went into a town in Samaria to make everything ready for him. 53But the people there would not welcome Jesus because he was going toward Jerusalem. 54James and John, the followers of Jesus, saw this. They said, "Lord, do you want us to call fire down from heaven and destroy those people?"a 55But Jesus turned and criticized them for saying this.b 56Then he and his followers went to another town.

Following Jesus
(Mt. 8:19–22)

57They were all traveling along the road. Someone said to Jesus, "I will follow you anywhere you go."

58He answered, "The foxes have holes to live in. The birds have nests. But the Son of Man* has no place where he can rest his head."

59Jesus said to another man, "Follow me!"

But the man said, "Lord, let me go and bury my father first."

60But Jesus said to him, "Let the people who are dead bury their own dead. You must go and tell about God's kingdom.*"

61Another man said, "I will follow you, Lord, but first let me go and say goodbye to my family."

62Jesus said, "Anyone who begins to plow a field but looks back is not prepared for God's kingdom."

Jesus Sends the 72 Men

10 1After this, the Lord chose 72c more followers. He sent them out in groups of two. He sent them ahead of him into every town and place where he planned to go. 2He said to them, "There is such a big harvest of people to bring in. But there are only a few workers to help harvest them. God owns the harvest. Ask him to send more workers to help bring in his harvest.

3"You can go now. But listen! I am sending you, and you will be like sheep among wolves. 4Don't carry any money, a bag, or sandals. Don't stop to talk with people on the road. 5Before you go into a house, say, 'Peace be with this home.' 6If the people living there love peace, your blessing of peace will stay with them. But if not, your blessing of peace will come back to you. 7Stay in the peace-loving house. Eat and drink what the people there give you. A worker should be given his pay. Don't leave that house to stay in another house.

8"If you go into a town and the people welcome you, eat the food they give you. 9Heal the sick people who live there, and tell them, 'God's kingdom* is coming to you soon!'

10"But if you go into a town, and the people don't welcome you, then go out into the streets of that town and say, 11'Even the dirt from your town that sticks to our feet we wipe off against you. But remember that God's kingdom is coming soon.' 12I tell you, on the judgment day it will be worse for the people of that town than for the people of Sodom.*

Jesus Warns People Who Refuse to Believe
(Mt. 11:20–24)

13"It will be bad for you, Chorazin*! It will be bad for you, Bethsaida*! I did many miracles* in you. If those same miracles had happened in Tyre* and Sidon,* then the people in those cities would have changed their lives and stopped sinning a long time ago. They would have worn sackcloth* and sat in ashes to show that they were sorry for their sins. 14But on the judgment day it will be worse for you than for Tyre and Sidon. 15And you, Capernaum,* will you be lifted up to heaven? No, you will be thrown down to the place of death!

16"When anyone listens to you my followers, they are really listening to me. But when anyone refuses to accept you, they are really refusing to accept me. And when anyone refuses to accept me, they are refusing to accept the one who sent me."

Satan Falls

17When the 72 followers came back from their trip, they were very happy. They said, "Lord, even the demons* obeyed us when we used your name!"

18Jesus said to them, "I saw Satan* falling like lightning from the sky. 19He is the enemy, but know that I have given you more power than he has. I have given you power to crush his snakes and scorpions under your feet. Nothing will hurt you. 20Yes, even the spirits obey you. And you can be happy, not because you have this power, but because your names are written in heaven."

Jesus Prays to the Father
(Mt. 11:25–27; 13:16–17)

21Then the Holy Spirit* made Jesus feel very happy. Jesus said, "I praise you, Father,

---

a9:54 Some Greek copies add "as Elijah did?"
b9:55 Some Greek copies add "And he said, 'You don't know what kind of spirit you belong to. 56The Son of Man did not come to destroy people's lives but to save them.'"
c10:1 72 Some Greek copies say 70. Also in verse 17.

Lord of heaven and earth. I am thankful that you have hidden these things from those who are so wise and so smart. But you have shown them to people who are like little children. Yes, Father, you did this because it's what you really wanted to do.

²²"My Father has given me all things. No one knows who the Son is—only the Father knows. And only the Son knows who the Father is. The only people who will know about the Father are those the Son chooses to tell."

²³Then Jesus turned to his followers. They were there alone with him. He said, "It is a great blessing for you to see what you now see! ²⁴I tell you, many prophets* and kings wanted to see what you now see, but they could not. And they wanted to hear what you now hear, but they could not."

A Story About the Good Samaritan

²⁵Then an expert in the law stood up to test Jesus. He said, "Teacher, what must I do to get eternal life?"

²⁶Jesus said to him, "What is written in the law? What do you understand from it?"

²⁷The man answered, "'Love the Lord your God with all your heart, all your soul, all your strength, and all your mind.'ᵃ Also, 'Love your neighbor the same as you love yourself.'ᵇ"

²⁸Jesus said, "Your answer is right. Do this and you will have eternal life."

²⁹But the man wanted to show that the way he was living was right. So he said to Jesus, "But who is my neighbor?"

³⁰To answer this question, Jesus said, "A man was going down the road from Jerusalem to Jericho. Some robbers surrounded him, tore off his clothes, and beat him. Then they left him lying there on the ground almost dead.

³¹"It happened that a Jewish priest was going down that road. When he saw the man, he did not stop to help him. He walked away. ³²Next, a Levite* came near. He saw the hurt man, but he went around him. He would not stop to help him either. He just walked away.

³³"Then a Samaritan* man traveled down that road. He came to the place where the hurt man was lying. He saw the man and felt very sorry for him. ³⁴The Samaritan went to him and poured olive oil and wineᶜ on his wounds. Then he covered the man's wounds with cloth. The Samaritan had a donkey. He put the hurt man on his donkey, and he took him to an inn. There he cared for him. ³⁵The next day, the Samaritan took out two silver coins* and gave them to the man who worked at the inn. He said, 'Take care of this hurt man. If you spend more money on him, I will pay it back to you when I come again.'"

ᵃ10:27 Quote from Deut. 6:5.
ᵇ10:27 Quote from Lev. 19:18.
ᶜ10:34 *olive oil and wine* These were used like medicine to soften and clean wounds.

³⁶Then Jesus said, "Which one of these three men do you think was really a neighbor to the man who was hurt by the robbers?"

³⁷The teacher of the law answered, "The one who helped him."

Jesus said, "Then you go and do the same."

Mary and Martha

³⁸While Jesus and his followers were traveling, he went into a town, and a woman named Martha let him stay at her house. ³⁹She had a sister named Mary. Mary was sitting at Jesus' feet and listening to him teach. ⁴⁰But her sister Martha was busy doing all the work that had to be done. Martha went in and said, "Lord, don't you care that my sister has left me to do all the work by myself? Tell her to help me!"

⁴¹But the Lord answered her, "Martha, Martha, you are getting worried and upset about too many things. ⁴²Only one thing is important. Mary has made the right choice, and it will never be taken away from her."

Jesus Teaches About Prayer
(Mt. 6:9-15)

11 ¹One time Jesus was out praying, and when he finished, one of his followers said to him, "John* taught his followers how to pray. Lord, teach us how to pray too."

²Jesus said to the followers, "This is how you should pray:

'Father, we pray that your name will
     always be kept holy.
We pray that your kingdom* will come.
³ Give us the food we need for each day.
⁴ Forgive our sins,
     just as we forgive everyone who has
          done wrong to us.
And don't let us be tempted.'"

Ask God for What You Need
(Mt. 7:7-11)

⁵⁻⁶Then Jesus said to them, "Suppose one of you went to your friend's house very late at night and said to him, 'A friend of mine has come into town to visit me. But I have nothing for him to eat. Please give me three loaves of bread.' ⁷Your friend inside the house answers, 'Go away! Don't bother me! The door is already locked. My children and I are in bed. I cannot get up and give you the bread now.' ⁸I tell you, maybe friendship is not enough to make him get up to give you the bread. But he will surely get up to give you what you need if you continue to ask. ⁹So I tell you, continue to ask, and God will give to you. Continue to search, and you will find. Continue to knock, and the door will open for you. ¹⁰Yes, whoever continues to ask will receive. Whoever continues to look will find. And whoever continues to knock will have the door opened for them. ¹¹Do any of you have a son? What would you do if your son

asked you for a fish? Would any father give him a snake? ¹²Or, if he asked for an egg, would you give him a scorpion? Of course not! ¹³Even you who are bad know how to give good things to your children. So surely your heavenly Father knows how to give the Holy Spirit* to the people who ask him."

Jesus' Power Is From God
(Mt. 12:22–30; Mk. 3:20–27)

¹⁴One time Jesus was sending a demon* out of a man who could not talk. When the demon came out, the man was able to speak. The crowds were amazed. ¹⁵But some of the people said, "He uses the power of Satan*ᵃ* to force demons out of people. Satan is the ruler of demons."

¹⁶Some others there wanted to test Jesus. They asked him to do a miracle as a sign from God. ¹⁷But he knew what they were thinking. So he said to them, "Every kingdom that fights against itself will be destroyed. And a family that fights against itself will break apart. ¹⁸So if Satan* is fighting against himself, how will his kingdom survive? You say that I use the power of Satan to force out demons. ¹⁹But if I use Satan's power to force out demons, then what power do your people use when they force out demons? So your own people will prove that you are wrong. ²⁰But I use the power of God to force out demons. This shows that God's kingdom* has come to you.

²¹"When a strong man with many weapons guards his own house, the things in his house are safe. ²²But suppose a stronger man comes and defeats him. The stronger man will take away the weapons that the first man trusted to keep his house safe. Then the stronger man will do what he wants with the other man's things.

²³"Whoever is not with me is against me. And anyone who does not work with me is working against me.

The Danger of Emptiness
(Mt. 12:43–45)

²⁴"When an evil spirit comes out of someone, it travels through dry places, looking for a place to rest. But it finds no place to rest. So it says, 'I will go back to the home I left.' ²⁵When it comes back, it finds that home all neat and clean. ²⁶Then the evil spirit goes out and brings back seven other spirits more evil than itself. They all go and live there, and that person has even more trouble than before."

The People God Blesses

²⁷As Jesus was saying these things, a woman with the people there called out to him, "Blessings from God belong to the woman who gave birth to you and fed you!" ²⁸But Jesus said, "The people who hear the

teaching of God and obey it—they are the ones who have God's blessing."

Some People Doubt Jesus' Authority
(Mt. 12:38–42; Mk. 8:12)

²⁹The crowd grew larger and larger. Jesus said, "The people who live today are evil. They ask for a miracle* as a sign from God. But no miracle will be done to prove anything to them. The only sign will be the miracle that happened to Jonah.*ᵇ* ³⁰Jonah was a sign for those who lived in Nineveh.*ᶜ* It is the same with the Son of Man.* He will be a sign for the people of this time.

³¹"On the judgment day, you people who live now will be compared with the Queen of the South,*ᵈ* and she will be a witness who shows how guilty you are. Why do I say this? Because she traveled from far, far away to listen to Solomon's wise teaching. And I tell you that someone*ᵉ* greater than Solomon is right here, but you won't listen!

³²"On the judgment day, you people who live now will also be compared with the people from Nineveh, and they will be witnesses who show how guilty you are. I say this because when Jonah preached to those people, they changed their hearts and lives. And you are listening to someone greater than Jonah, but you refuse to change!

Be a Light for the World
(Mt. 5:15; 6:22–23)

³³"No one takes a light and puts it under a bowl or hides it. Instead, they put it on a lampstand so that the people who come in can see. ³⁴The only source of light for the body is the eye. When you look at people and want to help them, you are full of light. But when you look at people in a selfish way, you are full of darkness.*ᶠ* ³⁵So be careful! Don't let the light in you become darkness. ³⁶If you are full of light, and there is no part of you that is dark, then you will be all bright, as though you have the light of a lamp shining on you."

Jesus Criticizes the Religious Leaders
(Mt. 23:1–36; Mk. 12:38–40; Lk. 20:45–47)

³⁷After Jesus had finished speaking, a Pharisee* asked Jesus to eat with him. So he went and took a place at the table. ³⁸But the

---

*ᵇ***11:29** *Jonah* A prophet in the Old Testament. After three days in a big fish he came out alive, just as Jesus would come out from the tomb on the third day.

*ᶜ***11:30** *Nineveh* City where Jonah preached. See Jonah 3.

*ᵈ***11:31** *Queen of the South* Or "Queen of Sheba." She traveled about 1000 miles (1600 km) to learn God's wisdom from Solomon. See 1 Kings 10:1–13.

*ᵉ***11:31** *someone* Literally, "something." Also in verse 32.

*ᶠ***11:34** Literally, "The lamp of the body is your eye. When your eye is pure, your whole body is full of light. But if it is evil, your body is dark."

---

*ᵃ***11:15** *Satan* Literally, "Beelzebul" (the devil). Also in verses 18 and 19.

Pharisee was surprised when he saw that Jesus did not wash his hands[a] first before the meal. [39]The Lord said to him, "The washing you Pharisees do is like cleaning only the outside of a cup or a dish. But what is inside you? You want only to cheat and hurt people. [40]You are foolish! The same one who made what is outside also made what is inside. [41]So pay attention to what is inside. Give to the people who need help. Then you will be fully clean.

[42]"But it will be bad for you Pharisees! You give God a tenth of the food you get, even your mint, your rue, and every other little plant in your garden.[b] But you forget to be fair to others and to love God. These are the things you should do. And you should also continue to do these other things.

[43]"It will be bad for you Pharisees because you love to have the most important seats in the synagogues.* And you love for people to show respect to you in the marketplaces. [44]It will be bad for you, because you are like hidden graves. People walk on them without knowing it."

[45]One of the experts in the law said to Jesus, "Teacher, when you say these things about the Pharisees, you are criticizing our group too."

[46]Jesus answered, "It will be bad for you, you experts in the law! You make strict rules that are very hard for people to obey.[c] You try to force others to obey your rules. But you yourselves don't even try to follow any of those rules. [47]It will be bad for you, because you build tombs* for the prophets.* But these are the same prophets your ancestors* killed! [48]And now you show all people that you agree with what your ancestors did. They killed the prophets, and you build tombs for the prophets! [49]This is why God in his wisdom said, 'I will send prophets and apostles[d] to them. Some of my prophets and apostles will be killed by evil men. Others will be treated badly.'

[50]"So you people who live now will be punished for the deaths of all the prophets who were killed since the beginning of the world. [51]You will be punished for the killing of Abel.[e] And you will be punished for the

killing of Zechariah,[f] who was killed between the altar* and the Temple.* Yes, I tell you that you people will be punished for them all.

[52]"It will be bad for you, you experts in the law! You have taken away the key to learning about God. You yourselves would not learn, and you stopped others from learning too."

[53]When Jesus went out, the teachers of the law and the Pharisees began to give him much trouble. They tried to make him answer questions about many things. [54]They were trying to find a way to catch Jesus saying something wrong.

Don't Be Like the Pharisees

12 [1]Many thousands of people came together. There were so many people that they were stepping on each other. Before Jesus spoke to the people, he said to his followers, "Be careful of the yeast* of the Pharisees.* I mean that they are hypocrites.* [2]Everything that is hidden will be shown, and everything that is secret will be made known. [3]What you say in the dark will be told in the light. And what you whisper in a private room will be shouted from the top of the house."

Fear Only God
(Mt. 10:28–31)

[4]Then Jesus said to the people, "I tell you, my friends, don't be afraid of people. They can kill the body, but after that they can do nothing more to hurt you. [5]I will show you the one to fear. You should fear God, who has the power to kill you and also to throw you into hell. Yes, he is the one you should fear.

[6]"When birds are sold, five small birds cost only two pennies. But God does not forget any of them. [7]Yes, God even knows how many hairs you have on your head. Don't be afraid. You are worth much more than many birds.

Don't Be Ashamed of Your Faith
(Mt. 10:32–33; 12:32; 10:19–20)

[8]"I tell you, if you stand before others and are willing to say you believe in me, then I[g] will say that you belong to me. I will say this in the presence of God's angels. [9]But if you stand before others and say you do not believe in me, then I will say that you do not belong to me. I will say this in the presence of God's angels.

[10]"Whoever says something against the Son of Man* can be forgiven. But whoever speaks against the Holy Spirit* will not be forgiven.

[11]"When men bring you into the synagogues* before the leaders and other important men, don't worry about what you will say. [12]The Holy Spirit will teach you at that time what you should say."

---

[a]**11:38** *wash his hands* Washing the hands was a Jewish religious custom that the Pharisees thought was very important.

[b]**11:42** *You give ... garden* Literally, "You tithe mint, rue, and every herb." The Law of Moses required Israelites to share their food supply by dedicating a tenth of their field crops and livestock to God (see Lev. 27:30–32; Deut. 26:12). This did not include such small garden plants as those mentioned here. So these Pharisees were giving more than required to be sure they were not breaking the Law.

[c]**11:46** *You make ... obey* Literally, "You put heavy burdens on people that are hard for them to carry."

[d]**11:49** *prophets and apostles* People chosen by God to tell his Good News to the world.

[e]**11:51** *Abel* In the Hebrew Old Testament, the first person to be murdered.

[f]**11:51** *Zechariah* In the Hebrew Old Testament, the last person to be murdered.

[g]**12:8** *I* Literally, "the Son of Man" (Jesus).

Jesus Warns Against Selfishness

13One of the men in the crowd said to Jesus, "Teacher, our father just died and left some things for us. Tell my brother to share them with me."

14But Jesus said to him, "Who said I should be your judge or decide how to divide your father's things between you two?" 15Then Jesus said to them, "Be careful and guard against all kinds of greed. People do not get life from the many things they own."

16Then Jesus used this story: "There was a rich man who had some land. His land grew a very good crop of food. 17He thought to himself, 'What will I do? I have no place to keep all my crops.'

18"Then he said, 'I know what I will do. I will tear down my barns and build bigger barns! I will put all my wheat and good things together in my new barns. 19Then I can say to myself, I have many good things stored. I have saved enough for many years. Rest, eat, drink, and enjoy life!'

20"But God said to that man, 'Foolish man! Tonight you will die. So what about the things you prepared for yourself? Who will get those things now?'

21"This is how it will be for anyone who saves things only for himself. To God that person is not rich."

Put God's Kingdom First
(Mt. 6:25–34; 19–21)

22Jesus said to his followers, "So I tell you, don't worry about the things you need to live—what you will eat or what you will wear. 23Life is more important than food, and the body is more important than what you put on it. 24Look at the birds. They don't plant, harvest, or save food in houses or barns, but God feeds them. And you are worth much more than crows. 25None of you can add any time to your life by worrying about it. 26And if you can't do the little things, why worry about the big things?

27"Think about how the wildflowers grow. They don't work or make clothes for themselves. But I tell you that even Solomon, the great and rich king, was not dressed as beautifully as one of these flowers. 28If God makes what grows in the field so beautiful, what do you think he will do for you? That's just grass—one day it's alive, and the next day someone throws it into a fire. But God cares enough to make it beautiful. Surely he will do much more for you. Your faith is so small!

29"So don't always think about what you will eat or what you will drink. Don't worry about it. 30That's what all those people who don't know God are always thinking about. But your Father knows that you need these things. 31What you should be thinking about is God's kingdom.* Then he will give you all these other things you need.

Don't Trust in Money

32"Don't fear, little flock. Your Father wants to share his kingdom with you. 33Sell the things you have and give that money to those who need it. This is the only way you can keep your riches from being lost. You will be storing treasure in heaven that lasts forever. Thieves can't steal that treasure, and moths can't destroy it. 34Your heart will be where your treasure is.

Always Be Ready
(Mt. 24:42–44)

35"Be ready! Be fully dressed and have your lights shining. 36Be like servants who are waiting for their master to come home from a wedding party. The master comes and knocks, and the servants immediately open the door for him. 37When their master sees that they are ready and waiting for him, it will be a great day for those servants. I can tell you without a doubt, the master will get himself ready to serve a meal and tell the servants to sit down. Then he will serve them. 38Those servants might have to wait until midnight or later for their master. But they will be glad they did when he comes in and finds them still waiting.

39"Remember this: If the owner of the house knew what time a thief was coming, he would not allow the thief to enter his house. 40So you also must be ready, because the Son of Man* will come at a time when you don't expect him!"

Who Is the Trusted Servant?
(Mt. 24:45–51)

41Peter said, "Lord, did you tell this story for us or for all people?"

42The Lord said, "Who is the wise and trusted servant? The master trusts one servant to give the other servants their food at the right time. Who is the servant that the master trusts to do that work? 43When the master comes and finds him doing the work he gave him, it will be a day of blessing for that servant! 44I can tell you without a doubt, the master will choose that servant to take care of everything he owns.

45"But what will happen if that servant is evil and thinks his master will not come back soon? He will begin to beat the other servants, men and women. He will eat and drink until he has had too much. 46Then the master will come when the servant is not ready, at a time when the servant is not expecting him. Then the master will punish that servant and send him away to be with the other people who don't obey.

47"That servant knew what his master wanted him to do. But he did not make himself ready or try to do what his master wanted. So that servant will be punished very much! 48But what about the servant who does not know what his master wants? He also does things that deserve punishment. But he will get less punishment than the servant who knew what he should do. Whoever has been given much will be responsible for much. Much more will be expected from the one who has been given more."

Following Jesus May Bring You Trouble
(Mt. 10:34–36)

49Jesus continued speaking: "I came to bring fire to the world. I wish it were already burning! 50There is a kind of baptism*a* that I must suffer through. I feel very troubled until it is finished. 51Do you think I came to give peace to the world? No, I came to divide the world! 52From now on, a family of five will be divided, three against two, and two against three.

53 A father and son will be divided:
   The son will turn against his father.
   The father will turn against his son.
A mother and her daughter will be
      divided:
   The daughter will turn against her
      mother.
   The mother will turn against her
      daughter.
A mother-in-law and her daughter-in-law
      will be divided:
   The daughter-in-law will turn against
      her mother-in-law.
   The mother-in-law will turn against her
      daughter-in-law."

Understanding the Times
(Mt. 16:2–3)

54Then Jesus said to the people, "When you see clouds growing bigger in the west, you say, 'A rainstorm is coming.' And soon it begins to rain. 55When you feel the wind begin to blow from the south, you say, 'It will be a hot day.' And you are right. 56You hypocrites*! You can understand the weather. Why don't you understand what is happening now?

Settle Your Problems
(Mt. 5:25–26)

57"Why can't you decide for yourselves what is right? 58Suppose someone is suing you, and you are both going to court. Try hard to settle it on the way. If you don't settle it, you may have to go before the judge. And the judge will hand you over to the officer, who will throw you into jail. 59I tell you, you will not get out of there until you have paid every cent you owe."

Change Your Hearts

13 1Some people there with Jesus at that time told him about what had happened to some worshipers from Galilee.

Pilate* had them killed. Their blood was mixed with the blood of the animals they had brought for sacrificing.* 2Jesus answered, "Do you think this happened to those people because they were more sinful than all other people from Galilee? 3No, they were not. But if you don't decide now to change your lives, you will all be destroyed like those people! 4And what about those 18 people who died when the tower of Siloam fell on them? Do you think they were more sinful than everyone else in Jerusalem? 5They were not. But I tell you if you don't decide now to change your lives, you will all be destroyed too!"

The Useless Tree

6Jesus told this story: "A man had a fig tree. He planted it in his garden. He came looking for some fruit on it, but he found none. 7He had a servant who took care of his garden. So he said to his servant, 'I have been looking for fruit on this tree for three years, but I never find any. Cut it down! Why should it waste the ground?' 8But the servant answered, 'Master, let the tree have one more year to produce fruit. Let me dig up the dirt around it and fertilize it. 9Maybe the tree will have fruit on it next year. If it still does not produce, then you can cut it down.'"

Jesus Heals a Woman on the Sabbath

10Jesus taught in one of the synagogues* on the Sabbath* day. 11A woman was there who had an evil spirit inside her. It had made the woman crippled for 18 years. Her back was always bent; she could not stand up straight. 12When Jesus saw her, he called to her, "Woman, you have been made free from your sickness!" 13He laid his hands on* her, and immediately she was able to stand up straight. She began praising God.

14The synagogue leader was angry because Jesus healed on the Sabbath day. He said to the people, "There are six days for work. So come to be healed on one of those days. Don't come for healing on the Sabbath day."

15The Lord answered, "You people are hypocrites*! All of you untie your work animals and lead them to drink water every day—even on the Sabbath day. 16This woman that I healed is a true descendant of Abraham.*b* But Satan* has held her for 18 years. Surely it is not wrong for her to be made free from her sickness on a Sabbath day!" 17When Jesus said this, all those who were criticizing him felt ashamed of themselves. And all the people were happy for the wonderful things he was doing.

What Is God's Kingdom Like?
(Mt. 13:31–33; Mk. 4:30–32)

18Then Jesus said, "What is God's kingdom* like? What can I compare it to? 19God's

---

*a***12:50 baptism** This word, which usually means to be immersed in water, has a special meaning here—being covered or "buried" in troubles.

*b***13:16 true descendant of Abraham** Literally, "daughter of Abraham."

kingdom is like the seed of the mustard* plant. Someone plants this seed in their garden. The seed grows and becomes a tree, and the birds build nests on its branches."

20Jesus said again, "What can I compare God's kingdom with? 21It is like yeast that a woman mixes into a big bowl of flour to make bread. The yeast makes all the dough rise."

The Narrow Door
(Mt. 7:13–14, 21–23)

22Jesus was teaching in every town and village. He continued to travel toward Jerusalem. 23Someone said to him, "Lord, how many people will be saved? Only a few?"

Jesus said, 24"The door to heaven is narrow. Try hard to enter it. Many people will want to enter there, but they will not be able to go in. 25If a man locks the door of his house, you can stand outside and knock on the door, but he won't open it. You can say, 'Sir, open the door for us.' But he will answer, 'I don't know you. Where did you come from?' 26Then you will say, 'We ate and drank with you. You taught in the streets of our town.' 27Then he will say to you, 'I don't know you. Where did you come from? Get away from me! You are all people who do wrong!'

28"You will see Abraham,* Isaac,* Jacob,* and all the prophets* in God's kingdom.* But you will be left outside. There you will cry and grind your teeth with pain. 29People will come from the east, west, north, and south. They will sit down at the table in God's kingdom. 30People who have the lowest place in life now will have the highest place in God's kingdom. And people who have the highest place now will have the lowest place in God's kingdom."

Jesus Will Die in Jerusalem
(Mt. 23:37–39)

31Just then some Pharisees* came to Jesus and said, "Go away from here and hide. Herod* wants to kill you!"

32Jesus said to them, "Go tell that fox,ᵃ 'Today and tomorrow I am forcing demons* out of people and finishing my work of healing. Then, the next day, the work will be finished.' 33After that, I must go, because all prophets* should die in Jerusalem.

34"Jerusalem, Jerusalem! You kill the prophets. You stone to death the people God has sent to you. How many times I wanted to help your people. I wanted to gather them together as a hen gathers her chicks under her wings. But you did not let me. 35Now your home will be left completely empty. I tell you, you will not see me again until that time when you will say, 'Welcome! God bless the one who comes in the name of the Lord.'ᵇ"

Is It Right to Heal on the Sabbath Day?

14 1On a Sabbath* day, Jesus went to the home of a leading Pharisee* to eat with him. The people there were all watching him very closely. 2A man with a bad diseaseᶜ was there in front of him. 3Jesus said to the Pharisees and experts in the law, "Is it right or wrong to heal on the Sabbath day?" 4But they would not answer his question. So he took the man and healed him. Then he sent the man away. 5Jesus said to the Pharisees and teachers of the law, "If your son or work animal falls into a well on the Sabbath day, you know you would pull him out immediately." 6The Pharisees and teachers of the law could say nothing against what he said.

Don't Make Yourself Important

7Then Jesus noticed that some of the guests were choosing the best places to sit. So he told this story: 8"When someone invites you to a wedding, don't sit in the most important seat. They may have invited someone more important than you. 9And if you are sitting in the most important seat, they will come to you and say, 'Give this man your seat!' Then you will have to move down to the last place and be embarrassed. 10So when someone invites you, go sit in the seat that is not important. Then they will come to you and say, 'Friend, move up here to this better place!' What an honor this will be for you in front of all the other guests. 11Everyone who makes themselves important will be made humble. But everyone who makes themselves humble will be made important."

You Will Be Rewarded

12Then Jesus said to the Pharisee* who had invited him, "When you give a lunch or a dinner, don't invite only your friends, brothers, relatives, and rich neighbors. At another time they will pay you back by inviting you to eat with them. 13Instead, when you give a feast, invite the poor, the crippled, and the blind. 14Then you will have great blessings, because these people cannot pay you back. They have nothing. But God will reward you at the time when all godly people rise from death."

A Story About People Invited to a Dinner
(Mt. 22:1–10)

15One of the men sitting at the table with Jesus heard these things. The man said to him, "It will be a great blessing for anyone to eat a meal in God's kingdom*!"

16Jesus said to him, "A man gave a big dinner. He invited many people. 17When it was time to eat, he sent his servant to tell the guests, 'Come. The food is ready.' 18But all the guests said they could not come. Each

---

ᵃ**13:32 fox** Jesus means that Herod is clever and sly like a fox.
ᵇ**13:35** Quote from Ps. 118:26.

ᶜ**14:2 disease** The man had dropsy, a sickness that causes the body to swell larger and larger.

one made an excuse. The first one said, 'I have just bought a field, so I must go look at it. Please excuse me.' 19Another man said, 'I have just bought five pairs of work animals; I must go and try them out. Please excuse me.' 20A third man said, 'I just got married; I can't come.'

21"So the servant returned and told his master what happened. The master was angry. He said, 'Hurry! Go into the streets and alleys of the town. Bring me the poor, the crippled, the blind, and the lame.'

22"Later, the servant said to him, 'Master, I did what you told me to do, but we still have places for more people.' 23The master said to the servant, 'Go out to the highways and country roads. Tell the people there to come. I want my house to be full! 24None of those people I invited first will get to eat any of this food.'"

Decide if You Can Follow Me
(Mt. 10:37–38)

25Many people were traveling with Jesus. He said to them, 26"If you come to me but will not leave your family, you cannot be my follower. You must love me more than your father, mother, wife, children, brothers, and sisters—even more than your own life! 27Whoever will not carry the cross* that is given to them when they follow me cannot be my follower.

28"If you wanted to build a building, you would first sit down and decide how much it would cost. You must see if you have enough money to finish the job. 29If you don't do that, you might begin the work, but you would not be able to finish. And if you could not finish it, everyone would laugh at you. 30They would say, 'This man began to build, but he was not able to finish.'

31"If a king is going to fight against another king, first he will sit down and plan. If he has only 10,000 men, he will try to decide if he is able to defeat the other king who has 20,000 men. 32If he thinks he cannot defeat the other king, he will send some men to ask for peace while that king's army is still far away.

33"It is the same for each of you. You must leave everything you have to follow me. If not, you cannot be my follower.

Don't Lose Your Influence
(Mt. 5:13; Mk. 9:50)

34"Salt is a good thing. But if the salt loses its salty taste, you can't make it salty again. 35It is worth nothing. You can't even use it as dirt or dung. People just throw it away.

"You people who hear me, listen!"

Joy in Heaven
(Mt. 18:12–14)

15 1Many tax collectors* and sinners came to listen to Jesus. 2Then the Pharisees* and the teachers of the law began to complain, "Look, this man*a* welcomes sinners and even eats with them!"

3Then Jesus told them this story: 4"Suppose one of you has 100 sheep, but one of them gets lost. What will you do? You will leave the other 99 sheep there in the field and go out and look for the lost sheep. You will continue to search for it until you find it. 5And when you find it, you will be very happy. You will carry it 6home, go to your friends and neighbors and say to them, 'Be happy with me because I found my lost sheep!' 7In the same way, I tell you, heaven is a happy place when one sinner decides to change. There is more joy for that one sinner than for 99 good people who don't need to change.

8"Suppose a woman has ten silver coins,*b* but she loses one of them. She will take a light and clean the house. She will look carefully for the coin until she finds it. 9And when she finds it, she will call her friends and neighbors and say to them, 'Be happy with me because I have found the coin that I lost!' 10In the same way, it's a happy time for the angels of God when one sinner decides to change."

Story About Two Sons

11Then Jesus said, "There was a man who had two sons. 12The younger son said to his father, 'Give me now the part of your property that I am supposed to receive someday.' So the father divided his wealth between his two sons.

13"A few days later the younger son gathered up all that he had and left. He traveled far away to another country, and there he wasted his money living like a fool. 14After he spent everything he had, there was a terrible famine throughout the country. He was hungry and needed money. 15So he went and got a job with one of the people who lived there. The man sent him into the fields to feed pigs. 16He was so hungry that he wanted to eat the food the pigs were eating. But no one gave him anything.

17"The son realized that he had been very foolish. He thought, 'All my father's hired workers have plenty of food. But here I am, almost dead because I have nothing to eat. 18I will leave and go to my father. I will say to him: Father, I have sinned against God and have done wrong to you. 19I am no longer worthy to be called your son. But let me be like one of your hired workers.' 20So he left and went to his father.

The Younger Son Returns

"While the son was still a long way off, his father saw him coming and felt sorry for him. So he ran to him and hugged and kissed him. 21The son said, 'Father, I have sinned against

*a*15:2 *this man* That is, Jesus. His enemies avoided saying his name.
*b*15:8 *silver coins* Each coin, a Greek drachma, was worth the average pay for one day's work.

God and have done wrong to you. I am no longer worthy to be called your son.'

22"But the father said to his servants, 'Hurry! Bring the best clothes and put them on him. Also, put a ring on his finger and good sandals on his feet. 23And bring our best calf and kill it so that we can celebrate with plenty to eat. 24My son was dead, but now he is alive again! He was lost, but now he is found!' So they began to have a party.

The Older Son Complains

25"The older son had been out in the field. When he came near the house, he heard the sound of music and dancing. 26So he called to one of the servant boys and asked, 'What does all this mean?' 27The boy said, 'Your brother has come back, and your father killed the best calf to eat. He is happy because he has his son back safe and sound.'

28"The older son was angry and would not go in to the party. So his father went out and begged him to come in. 29But he said to his father, 'Look, for all these years I have worked like a slave for you. I have always done what you told me to do, and you never gave me even a young goat for a party with my friends. 30But then this son of yours comes home after wasting your money on prostitutes, and you kill the best calf for him!'

31"His father said to him, 'Oh, my son, you are always with me, and everything I have is yours. 32But this was a day to be happy and celebrate. Your brother was dead, but now he is alive. He was lost, but now he is found.'"

True Wealth

16 1Jesus said to his followers, "Once there was a rich man. He hired a manager to take care of his business. Later, he learned that his manager was cheating him. 2So he called the manager in and said to him, 'I have heard bad things about you. Give me a report of what you have done with my money. You can't be my manager anymore.'

3"So, the manager thought to himself, 'What will I do? My master is taking my job away from me. I am not strong enough to dig ditches. I am too proud to beg. 4I know what I will do! I will do something to make friends, so that when I lose my job, they will welcome me into their homes.'

5"So the manager called in each person who owed the master some money. He asked the first one, 'How much do you owe my master?' 6He answered, 'I owe him 100 jars*a* of olive oil.' The manager said to him, 'Here is your bill. Hurry! Sit down and make the bill less. Write 50 jars.'

7"Then the manager asked another one, 'How much do you owe my master?' He answered, 'I owe him 100 measures*b* of wheat.' Then the manager said to him, 'Here is your bill; you can make it less. Write 80 measures.'

8"Later, the master told the dishonest manager that he had done a smart thing. Yes, worldly people are smarter in their business with each other than spiritual people are.

9"I tell you, use the worldly things you have now to make 'friends' for later. Then, when those things are gone, you will be welcomed into a home that lasts forever. 10Whoever can be trusted with small things can also be trusted with big things. Whoever is dishonest in little things will be dishonest in big things too. 11If you cannot be trusted with worldly riches, you will not be trusted with the true riches. 12And if you cannot be trusted with the things that belong to someone else, you will not be given anything of your own.

13"You cannot serve two masters at the same time. You will hate one master and love the other. Or you will be loyal to one and not care about the other. You cannot serve God and Money*c* at the same time."

God's Law Cannot Be Changed
(Mt. 11:12–13)

14The Pharisees* were listening to all these things. They criticized Jesus because they all loved money. 15Jesus said to them, "You make yourselves look good in front of people. But God knows what is really in your hearts. What people think is important is worth nothing to God.

16"Before John the Baptizer* came, people were taught the Law of Moses* and the writings of the prophets.* But since the time of John, the Good News* about God's kingdom* is being told. And everyone is trying hard to get into it. 17But even the smallest part of a letter in the law cannot be changed. It would be easier for heaven and earth to pass away.

Divorce and Remarriage

18"Any man who divorces his wife and marries another woman is guilty of adultery.* And the man who marries a divorced woman is also guilty of adultery."

The Rich Man and Lazarus

19Jesus said, "There was a rich man who always dressed in the finest clothes. He was so rich that he was able to enjoy all the best things every day. 20There was also a very poor man named Lazarus. Lazarus' body was covered with sores. He was often put by the rich man's gate. 21Lazarus wanted only to eat the scraps of food left on the floor under the rich man's table. And the dogs came and licked his sores.

---

*a***16:6 jars** Greek *batous,* from the Hebrew *bath,* about 20 quarts or 22 liters.

*b***16:7 measures** Greek *korous,* from the Hebrew *cor,* about 200 quarts or 220 liters.

*c***16:13 Money** Or *"mamona,"* an Aramaic word meaning "wealth."

22"Later, Lazarus died. The angels took him and placed him in the arms of Abraham.* The rich man also died and was buried. 23He was sent to the place of death*a* and was in great pain. He saw Abraham far away with Lazarus in his arms. 24He called, 'Father Abraham, have mercy on me! Send Lazarus to me so that he can dip his finger in water and cool my tongue. I am suffering in this fire!'

25"But Abraham said, 'My child, remember when you lived? You had all the good things in life. But Lazarus had nothing but problems. Now he is comforted here, and you are suffering. 26Also, there is a big pit between you and us. No one can cross over to help you, and no one can come here from there.'

27"The rich man said, 'Then please, father Abraham, send Lazarus to my father's house on earth. 28I have five brothers. He could warn my brothers so that they will not come to this place of pain.'

29"But Abraham said, 'They have the Law of Moses* and the writings of the prophets* to read; let them learn from that.'

30"The rich man said, 'No, father Abraham! But if someone came to them from the dead, then they would decide to change their lives.'

31"But Abraham said to him, 'If your brothers won't listen to Moses and the prophets, they won't listen to someone who comes back from the dead.'"

Sin and Forgiveness
(Mt. 18:6-7, 21-22; Mk. 9:42)

17 1Jesus said to his followers, "Things will surely happen that will make people sin. But it will be very bad for anyone who makes this happen. 2It will be very bad for anyone who makes one of these little children sin. It would be better for them to have a millstone* tied around their neck and be drowned in the sea. 3So be careful!

"If your brother or sister in God's family does something wrong, warn them. If they are sorry for what they did, forgive them. 4Even if they do something wrong to you seven times in one day, but they say they are sorry each time, you should forgive them."

How Big Is Your Faith?

5The apostles* said to the Lord, "Give us more faith!"

6The Lord said, "If your faith is as big as a mustard* seed, you can say to this mulberry tree, 'Dig yourself up and plant yourself in the ocean!' And the tree will obey you.

Be Good Servants

7"Suppose one of you has a servant who has been working in the field, plowing or caring for the sheep. When he comes in from work, what would you say to him? Would you say, 'Come in, sit down and eat'? 8Of course not! You would say to your servant, 'Prepare something for me to eat. Then get ready and serve me. When I finish eating and drinking, then you can eat.' 9The servant should not get any special thanks for doing his job. He is only doing what his master told him to do. 10It is the same with you. When you finish doing all that you are told to do, you should say, 'We are not worthy of any special thanks. We have only done the work we should do.'"

Be Thankful

11Jesus was traveling to Jerusalem. He went from Galilee to Samaria. 12He came into a small town, and ten men met him there. They did not come close to him, because they all had leprosy.* 13But the men shouted, "Jesus! Master! Please help us!"

14When Jesus saw the men, he said, "Go and show yourselves to the priests."*b*

While the ten men were going to the priests, they were healed. 15When one of them saw that he was healed, he went back to Jesus. He praised God loudly. 16He bowed down at Jesus' feet and thanked him. (He was a Samaritan.*) 17Jesus said, "Ten men were healed; where are the other nine? 18This man is not even one of our people. Is he the only one who came back to give praise to God?" 19Then Jesus said to the man, "Stand up! You can go. You were healed because you believed."

The Coming of God's Kingdom
(Mt. 24:23-28, 37-41)

20Some of the Pharisees* asked Jesus, "When will God's kingdom* come?"

Jesus answered, "God's kingdom is coming, but not in a way that you can see it. 21People will not say, 'Look, God's kingdom is here!' or 'There it is!' No, God's kingdom is here with you.*c*

22Then Jesus said to his followers, "The time will come when you will want very much to see one of the days of the Son of Man,* but you will not be able to. 23People will say to you, 'Look, there it is!' or 'Look, here it is!' Stay where you are; don't go away and search.

When Jesus Comes Again

24"When the Son of Man* comes again, you will know it. On that day he will shine like lightning flashes across the sky. 25But first, the Son of Man must suffer many things. The people of today will refuse to accept him.

26"When the Son of Man comes again, it will be the same as it was when Noah lived. 27People were eating, drinking, and getting

---

*b***17:14** *show yourselves to the priests* The Law of Moses said a priest must decide when a person with leprosy was well.
*c***17:21** *here with you* Or "inside you."

*a***16:23** *place of death* Literally, "Hades."

married even on the day when Noah entered the boat. Then the flood came and killed them all.

²⁸"It will be the same as during the time of Lot, when God destroyed Sodom.* Those people were eating, drinking, buying, selling, planting, and building houses for themselves. ²⁹They were doing these things even on the day when Lot left town. Then fire and sulfur rained down from the sky and killed them all. ³⁰This is exactly how it will be when the Son of Man comes again.

³¹"On that day if a man is on his roof, he will not have time to go inside and get his things. If a man is in the field, he cannot go back home. ³²Remember what happened to Lot's wife*ᵃ!

³³"Whoever tries to keep the life they have will lose it. But whoever gives up their life will save it. ³⁴That night there may be two people sleeping in one room. One will be taken and the other will be left. ³⁵There may be two women working together. One will be taken and the other will be left." ³⁶ ᵇ

³⁷The followers asked Jesus, "Where will this be, Lord?"

Jesus answered, "It's like looking for a dead body—you will find it where the vultures* are gathering above."

God Will Answer His People

18 ¹Then Jesus taught the followers that they should always pray and never lose hope. He used this story to teach them: ²"Once there was a judge in a town. He did not care about God. He also did not care what people thought about him. ³In that same town there was a woman whose husband had died. She came many times to this judge and said, 'There is a man who is doing bad things to me. Give me my rights!' ⁴But the judge did not want to help the woman. After a long time, the judge thought to himself, 'I don't care about God. And I don't care about what people think. ⁵But this woman is bothering me. If I give her what she wants, then she will leave me alone. But if I don't give her what she wants, she will bother me until I am sick.'"

⁶The Lord said, "Listen, there is meaning in what the bad judge said. ⁷God's people shout to him night and day, and he will always give them what is right. He will not be slow to answer them. ⁸I tell you, God will help his people quickly. But when the Son of Man* comes again, will he find people on earth who believe in him?"

Being Right With God

⁹There were some people who thought they were very good and looked down on everyone else. Jesus used this story to teach them: ¹⁰"One time there was a Pharisee* and a tax collector.* One day they both went to the Temple* to pray. ¹¹The Pharisee stood alone, away from the tax collector. When the Pharisee prayed, he said, 'O God, I thank you that I am not as bad as other people. I am not like men who steal, cheat, or commit adultery.* I thank you that I am better than this tax collector. ¹²I fast* twice a week, and I give a tenth of everything I get!'

¹³"The tax collector stood alone too. But when he prayed, he would not even look up to heaven. He felt very humble before God. He said, 'O God, have mercy on me. I am a sinner!' ¹⁴I tell you, when this man finished his prayer and went home, he was right with God. But the Pharisee, who felt that he was better than others, was not right with God. People who make themselves important will be made humble. But those who make themselves humble will be made important."

Jesus Welcomes Children
(Mt. 19:13–15; Mk. 10:13–16)

¹⁵Some people brought their small children to Jesus so that he could lay his hands on* them to bless them. But when the followers saw this, they told the people not to do this. ¹⁶But Jesus called the little children to him and said to his followers, "Let the little children come to me. Don't stop them, because God's kingdom* belongs to people who are like these little children. ¹⁷The truth is, you must accept God's kingdom like a little child accepts things, or you will never enter it."

A Rich Man Refuses to Follow Jesus
(Mt. 19:16–30; Mk. 10:17–31)

¹⁸A religious leader asked Jesus, "Good Teacher, what must I do to get eternal life?"

¹⁹Jesus said to him, "Why do you call me good? Only God is good. ²⁰And you know his commands: 'You must not commit adultery,* you must not murder anyone, you must not steal, you must not tell lies about others, you must respect your father and mother ....'ᶜ"

²¹But the leader said, "I have obeyed all these commands since I was a boy."

²²When Jesus heard this, he said to the leader, "But there is still one thing you need to do. Sell everything you have and give the money to those who are poor. You will have riches in heaven. Then come and follow me."

²³But when the man heard Jesus tell him to give away his money, he was sad. He didn't want to do this, because he was very rich.

²⁴When Jesus saw that the man was sad, he said, "It will be very hard for rich people to enter God's kingdom.* ²⁵It is easier for a camel to go through the eye of a needle than for a rich person to enter God's kingdom."

ᵃ**17:32** *Lot's wife* The story about Lot's wife is found in Gen. 19:15–17, 26.

ᵇ**17:36** A few Greek copies add verse 36: "Two men will be in the same field. One man will be taken, but the other man will be left behind."

ᶜ**18:20** Quote from Ex. 20:12–16; Deut. 5:16–20.

Who Can Be Saved?

²⁶When the people heard this, they said, "Then who can be saved?"

²⁷Jesus answered, "God can do things that are not possible for people to do."

²⁸Peter said, "Look, we left everything we had and followed you."

²⁹Jesus said, "I can promise that everyone who has left their home, wife, brothers, parents, or children for God's kingdom* ³⁰will get much more than they left. They will get many times more in this life. And in the world that is coming they will get the reward of eternal life."

Jesus Talks Again About His Death
(Mt. 20:17–19; Mk. 10:32–34)

³¹Then Jesus talked to the twelve apostles* alone. He said to them, "Listen, we are going to Jerusalem. Everything that God told the prophets* to write about the Son of Man* will happen. ³²He will be handed over to the foreigners, who will laugh at him, insult him, and spit on him. ³³They will beat him with whips and then kill him. But on the third day after his death, he will rise to life again." ³⁴The apostles tried to understand this, but they could not; the meaning was hidden from them.

Jesus Heals a Blind Man
(Mt. 20:29–34; Mk. 10:46–52)

³⁵Jesus came near the city of Jericho. There was a blind man sitting beside the road. He was begging people for money. ³⁶When he heard the people coming down the road, he asked, "What is happening?"

³⁷They told him, "Jesus, the one from Nazareth, is coming here."

³⁸The blind man was excited and said, "Jesus, Son of David,* please help me!"

³⁹The people who were in front, leading the group, criticized the blind man. They told him to be quiet. But he shouted more and more, "Son of David, please help me!"

⁴⁰Jesus stopped there and said, "Bring that man to me!" When he came close, Jesus asked him, ⁴¹"What do you want me to do for you?"

He said, "Lord, I want to see again."

⁴²Jesus said to him, "You can see now. You are healed because you believed."

⁴³Then the man was able to see. He followed Jesus, thanking God. Everyone who saw this praised God for what happened.

Zacchaeus

19 ¹Jesus was going through the city of Jericho. ²In Jericho there was a man named Zacchaeus. He was a wealthy, very important tax collector.* ³He wanted to see who Jesus was. There were many others who wanted to see Jesus too. Zacchaeus was too short to see above the people. ⁴So he ran to a place where he knew Jesus would come.

Then he climbed a sycamore tree so he could see him.

⁵When Jesus came to where Zacchaeus was, he looked up and saw him in the tree. Jesus said, "Zacchaeus, hurry! Come down! I must stay at your house today."

⁶Zacchaeus hurried and came down. He was happy to have Jesus in his house. ⁷Everyone saw this. They began to complain, "Look at the kind of man Jesus is staying with. Zacchaeus is a sinner!"

⁸Zacchaeus said to the Lord, "I want to do good. I will give half of my money to the poor. If I have cheated anyone, I will pay them back four times more."

⁹Jesus said, "Today is the day for this family to be saved from sin. Yes, even this tax collector is one of God's chosen people.ᵃ ¹⁰The Son of Man* came to find lost people and save them."

Use What God Gives You
(Mt. 25:14–30)

¹¹As the crowd listened to what he was saying, Jesus went on to tell a story. He was now near Jerusalem and knew that the people thought it was almost time for God's kingdom* to come. ¹²So he said, "A very important man was preparing to go to a country far away to be made a king. Then he planned to return home and rule his people. ¹³So he called ten of his servants together. He gave a bag of moneyᵇ to each servant. He said, 'Do business with this money until I come back.' ¹⁴But the people in the kingdom hated the man. They sent a group to follow him to the other country. There they said, 'We don't want this man to be our king.'

¹⁵"But the man was made king. When he came home, he said, 'Call those servants who have my money. I want to know how much more money they earned with it.' ¹⁶The first servant came and said, 'Sir, I earned ten bags of money with the one bag you gave me.' ¹⁷The king said to him, 'That's great! You are a good servant. I see that I can trust you with small things. So now I will let you rule over ten of my cities.'

¹⁸"The second servant said, 'Sir, with your one bag of money I earned five bags.' ¹⁹The king said to this servant, 'You can rule over five cities.'

²⁰"Then another servant came in and said to the king, 'Sir, here is your bag of money. I wrapped it in a piece of cloth and hid it. ²¹I was afraid of you because you are a hard man. You even take money that you didn't earn and gather food that you didn't grow.'

ᵃ**19:9 one of God's chosen people** Literally, "a son of Abraham."

ᵇ**19:13 bag of money** One bag of money was a Greek mina, enough to pay a person for working three months. Also in verses 16, 18, 20, 24, 25.

22"Then the king said to him, 'What a bad servant you are! I will use your own words to condemn you. You said that I am a hard man. You said that I even take money that I didn't earn and gather food that I didn't grow. 23If that is true, you should have put my money in the bank. Then, when I came back, my money would have earned some interest.' 24Then the king said to the men who were watching, 'Take the bag of money away from this servant and give it to the servant who earned ten bags of money.'

25"The men said to the king, 'But sir, that servant already has ten bags of money.'

26"The king said, 'People who use what they have will get more. But those who do not use what they have will have everything taken away from them. 27Now where are my enemies? Where are the people who did not want me to be king? Bring my enemies here and kill them. I will watch them die.'"

Jesus Enters Jerusalem Like a King
(Mt. 21:1–11; Mk. 11:1–11; Jn. 12:12–19)

28After Jesus said these things, he continued traveling toward Jerusalem. 29He came near Bethphage and Bethany, towns near the hill called the Mount of Olives.* He sent out two of his followers. 30He said, "Go into the town you can see there. When you enter the town, you will find a young donkey tied there that no one has ever ridden. Untie it, and bring it here to me. 31If anyone asks you why you are taking the donkey, you should say, 'The Master needs it.'"

32The two followers went into town. They found the donkey exactly like Jesus told them. 33They untied it, but its owners came out. They said to the followers, "Why are you untying our donkey?"

34The followers answered, "The Master needs it." 35So the followers brought the donkey to Jesus. They put their coats on its back. Then they put Jesus on the donkey. 36He rode along the road toward Jerusalem. The followers spread their coats on the road before him.

37Jesus was coming close to Jerusalem. He was already near the bottom of the Mount of Olives. The whole group of followers was happy. They were very excited and praised God. They thanked God for all the powerful things they had seen. 38They said,

"'Welcome! God bless the king who comes
    in the name of the Lord.'   Psalm 118:26

Peace in heaven and glory* to God!"

39Some of the Pharisees* said to Jesus, "Teacher, tell your followers not to say these things."

40But Jesus answered, "I tell you, if my followers didn't say them, these stones would shout them."

Jesus Cries for Jerusalem

41Jesus came near Jerusalem. Looking at the city, he began to cry for it 42and said, "I wish you knew today what would bring you peace. But it is hidden from you now. 43A time is coming when your enemies will build a wall around you and hold you in on all sides. 44They will destroy you and all your people. Not one stone of your buildings will stay on top of another. All this will happen because you did not know the time when God came to save you."

Jesus Goes to the Temple
(Mt. 21:12–17; Mk. 11:15–19; Jn. 2:13–22)

45Jesus went into the Temple* area. He began to throw out the people who were selling things there. 46He said, "The Scriptures* say, 'My Temple will be a house of prayer.'ᵃ But you have changed it into a 'hiding place for thieves.'ᵇ

47Jesus taught the people in the Temple area every day. The leading priests, the teachers of the law, and some of the leaders of the people wanted to kill him. 48But they did not know how they could do it, because everyone was listening to him. The people were very interested in what Jesus said.

Jewish Leaders Doubt Jesus' Authority
(Mt. 21:23–27; Mk. 11:27–33)

20 ¹One day Jesus was in the Temple* area teaching the people. He was telling them the Good News.* The leading priests, teachers of the law, and older Jewish leaders came to talk to Jesus. 2They said, "Tell us what authority you have to do these things. Who gave you this authority?"

3Jesus answered, "I will ask you a question too. Tell me: 4When John* baptized* people, did his authority come from God or was it only from other people?"

5The priests, the teachers of the law, and the Jewish leaders all talked about this. They said to each other, "If we answer, 'John's baptism was from God,' then he will say, 'Then why did you not believe John?' 6But if we say that John's baptism was from someone else, the people will stone us to death. They all believe that John was a prophet.*" 7So they answered, "We don't know the answer."

8So Jesus said to them, "Then I will not tell you who gave me the authority to do these things."

God Sends His Son
(Mt 21:33–46; Mk. 12:1–12)

9Then Jesus told the people this story: "A man planted a vineyard.* He leased the land to some farmers. Then he went away for a long time. 10Later, it was time for the grapes to be picked. So the man sent a servant to

ᵃ**19:46** Quote from Isa. 56:7.
ᵇ**19:46** Quote from Jer. 7:11.

those farmers so that they would give him his share of the grapes. But they beat the servant and sent him away with nothing. [11]So the man sent another servant. They beat this servant too and showed no respect for him. They sent the servant away with nothing. [12]So the man sent a third servant to the farmers. They hurt this servant badly and threw him out.

[13]"The owner of the vineyard said, 'What will I do now? I will send my son. I love my son very much. Maybe the farmers will respect my son.' [14]When the farmers saw the son, they said to each other, 'This is the owner's son. This vineyard will be his. If we kill him, it will be ours.' [15]So the farmers threw the son out of the vineyard and killed him.

"What will the owner of the vineyard do? [16]He will come and kill those farmers. Then he will lease the land to some other farmers."

When the people heard this story, they said, "This should never happen!" [17]But Jesus looked into their eyes and said, "Then what does this verse mean:

'The stone that the builders refused to
    accept became the cornerstone*'?
                                      Psalm 118:22

[18]Everyone who falls on that stone will be broken. If that stone falls on you, it will crush you!"

[19]When the teachers of the law and the leading priests heard this story, they knew it was about them. So they wanted to arrest Jesus right then, but they were afraid of what the people would do.

The Jewish Leaders Try to Trick Jesus
(Mt. 22:15–22; Mk. 12:13–17)

[20]So the Jewish leaders waited for the right time to get Jesus. They sent some men to him, who pretended to be sincere. They wanted to find something wrong with what Jesus said. (If they found something wrong, then they could hand him over to the governor, who had the authority to arrest him.) [21]So the men said to Jesus, "Teacher, we know that what you say and teach is true. It doesn't matter who is listening—you teach the same to all people. You always teach the truth about God's way. [22]Tell us, is it right for us to pay taxes to Caesar* or not?"

[23]But Jesus knew that these men were trying to trick him. He said to them, [24]"Show me a silver coin.* Whose name and picture are on it?"

They said, "Caesar's."

[25]He said to them, "Then give to Caesar what belongs to Caesar, and give to God what belongs to God."

[26]The men were amazed at his wise answer. They could say nothing. They were not able to trick Jesus there in front of the people. He said nothing they could use against him.

Some Sadducees Try to Trick Jesus
(Mt. 22:23–33; Mk. 12:18–27)

[27]Some Sadducees* came to Jesus. (Sadducees believe that people will not rise from death.) They asked him, [28]"Teacher, Moses* wrote that if a married man dies and had no children, his brother must marry his widow. Then they will have children for the dead brother.[a] [29]One time there were seven brothers. The first brother married a woman but died. He had no children. [30]Then the second brother married the woman, and he died. [31]And the third brother married the woman, and he died. The same thing happened with all the other brothers. They all died and had no children. [32]The woman was the last to die. [33]But all seven brothers married her. So when people rise from death, whose wife will this woman be?"

[34]Jesus said to the Sadducees, "On earth, people marry each other. [35]Some people will be worthy to be raised from death and live again after this life. In that life they will not marry. [36]In that life people are like angels and cannot die. They are children of God, because they have been raised from death. [37]Moses clearly showed that people are raised from death. When Moses wrote about the burning bush,[b] he said that the Lord is 'the God of Abraham,* the God of Isaac,* and the God of Jacob.'*[c] [38]So they were not still dead, because he is the God only of living people. Yes, to God they are all still living."

[39]Some of the teachers of the law said, "Teacher, your answer was very good." [40]No one was brave enough to ask him another question.

Is the Christ David's Son or David's Lord?
(Mt. 22:41–46; Mk. 12:35–37)

[41]Then Jesus said, "Why do people say that the Christ* is the Son of David*? [42]In the book of Psalms, David* himself says,

'The Lord God said to my Lord:
    Sit by me at my right side,
[43]   and I will put your enemies under your
        power.[d]   Psalm 110:1

[44]David calls the Christ 'Lord.' So how can the Christ also be David's son?"

Warning Against the Teachers of the Law
(Mt. 23:1–36; Mk. 12:38–40; Lk. 11:37–54)

[45]While all the people were listening to Jesus, he said to his followers, [46]"Be careful of the teachers of the law. They like to walk around wearing clothes that look important.

[a]**20:28 if ... dead brother** See Deut. 25:5, 6.
[b]**20:37 burning bush** See Ex. 3:1–12.
[c]**20:37 'the God of ... Jacob'** Words taken from Ex. 3:6.
[d]**20:43 and I ... power** Literally, "until I make your enemies a footstool for your feet."

And they love for people to show respect to them in the marketplaces. They love to have the most important seats in the synagogues* and the places of honor at banquets. ⁴⁷But they cheat widows and take their homes. Then they try to make themselves look good by saying long prayers. God will punish them very much."

True Giving
(Mk. 12:41–44)

21 ¹Jesus looked up and saw some rich people putting their gifts to God into the Temple* collection box. ²Then he saw a poor widow put two small copper coins into the box. ³He said, "This poor widow gave only two small coins. But the truth is, she gave more than all those rich people. ⁴They have plenty, and they gave only what they did not need. This woman is very poor, but she gave all she had to live on."

Jesus Warns About the Future
(Mt. 24:1–14; Mk. 13:1–13)

⁵Some of the followers were talking about the Temple.* They said, "This is a beautiful Temple, built with the best stones. Look at the many good gifts that have been offered to God."

⁶But Jesus said, "The time will come when all that you see here will be destroyed. Every stone of these buildings will be thrown down to the ground. Not one stone will be left on another."

⁷Some followers asked Jesus, "Teacher, when will these things happen? What will show us that it is time for these things to happen?"

⁸Jesus said, "Be careful! Don't be fooled. Many people will come using my name. They will say, 'I am the Christ*' and 'The right time has come!' But don't follow them. ⁹When you hear about wars and riots, don't be afraid. These things must happen first. Then the end will come later."

¹⁰Then Jesus said to them, "Nations will fight against other nations. Kingdoms will fight against other kingdoms. ¹¹There will be great earthquakes, sicknesses, and other bad things in many places. In some places there will be no food for the people to eat. Terrible things will happen, and amazing things will come from heaven to warn people.

¹²"But before all these things happen, people will arrest you and do bad things to you. They will judge you in their synagogues* and put you in jail. You will be forced to stand before kings and governors. They will do all these things to you because you follow me. ¹³But this will give you an opportunity to tell about me. ¹⁴Decide now not to worry about what you will say. ¹⁵I will give you the wisdom to say things that none of your enemies can answer. ¹⁶Even your parents, brothers, relatives, and friends will turn against you. They

will have some of you killed. ¹⁷Everyone will hate you because you follow me. ¹⁸But none of these things can really harm you. ¹⁹You will save yourselves by continuing strong in your faith through all these things.

The Destruction of Jerusalem
(Mt. 24:15–21; Mk. 13:14–19)

²⁰"You will see armies all around Jerusalem. Then you will know that the time for its destruction has come. ²¹The people in Judea at that time should run away to the mountains. The people in Jerusalem must leave quickly. If you are near the city, don't go in! ²²The prophets* wrote many things about the time when God will punish his people. The time I am talking about is when all these things must happen. ²³During that time, it will be hard for women who are pregnant or have small babies, because very bad times will come to this land. God will be angry with these people. ²⁴Some of the people will be killed by soldiers. Others will be made prisoners and taken to all the different countries. The holy city of Jerusalem will be under the control of foreigners until their time is completed.

Don't Fear
(Mt. 24:29–31; Mk. 13:24–27)

²⁵"Amazing things will happen to the sun, moon, and stars. And people all over the earth will be upset and confused by the noise of the sea and its crashing waves. ²⁶They will be afraid and worried about what will happen to the world. Everything in the sky will be changed. ²⁷Then people will see the Son of Man* coming in a cloud with power and great glory.* ²⁸When these things begin to happen, stand up tall and don't be afraid. Know that it is almost time for God to free you!"

My Words Will Live Forever
(Mt. 24:32–35; Mk. 13:28–31)

²⁹Then Jesus told this story: "Look at all the trees. The fig tree is a good example. ³⁰When it turns green, you know that summer is near. ³¹In the same way, when you see all these things happening, you will know that God's kingdom* is coming very soon.

³²"I assure you that all these things will happen while some of the people of this time are still living. ³³The whole world, earth and sky, will be destroyed, but my words will last forever.

Be Ready All the Time

³⁴"Be careful not to spend your time having parties and getting drunk or worrying about this life. If you do that, you won't be able to think straight, and the end might come when you are not ready. ³⁵It will come as a surprise to everyone on earth. ³⁶So be ready all the time. Pray that you will be able to get through all these things that will happen and stand safe before the Son of Man.*"

[37]During the day Jesus taught the people in the Temple* area. At night he went out of the city and stayed all night on the Mount of Olives.* [38]Every morning all the people got up early to go listen to Jesus at the Temple.

The Jewish Leaders Plan to Kill Jesus
(Mt. 26:1–5, 14–16; Mk. 14:1–2, 10–11; Jn. 11:45–53)

22 [1]It was almost time for the Jewish Festival of Unleavened Bread,* called the Passover.* [2]The leading priests and teachers of the law wanted to kill Jesus. But they were trying to find a quiet way to do it, because they were afraid of what the people would do.

Judas Agrees to Help Jesus' Enemies
(Mt. 26:14–16; Mk. 14:10–11)

[3]One of Jesus' twelve apostles* was named Judas Iscariot. Satan* entered him, [4]and he went and talked with the leading priests and some of the soldiers who guarded the Temple.* He talked to them about a way to hand Jesus over to them. [5]The priests were very happy about this. They promised to give Judas money for doing this. [6]He agreed. Then he waited for the best time to hand him over to them. He wanted to do it when no one was around to see it.

The Passover Meal
(Mt. 26:17–25; Mk. 14:12–21; Jn. 13:21–30)

[7]The Day of Unleavened Bread[a] came. This was the day when the Jews always killed the lambs for the Passover.* [8]Jesus said to Peter and John, "Go and prepare the Passover meal for us to eat."

[9]They said to him, "Where do you want us to prepare the meal?"

He said to them, [10]"When you go into the city, you will see a man carrying a jar of water. Follow him. He will go into a house. [11]Tell the owner of the house, 'The Teacher asks that you please show us the room where he and his followers can eat the Passover meal.' [12]Then the owner will show you a large room upstairs that is ready for us. Prepare the meal there."

[13]So Peter and John left. Everything happened the way Jesus said. So they prepared the Passover meal.

The Lord's Supper
(Mt. 26:26–30; Mk. 14:22–26; 1 Cor. 11:23–25)

[14]The time came for them to eat the Passover* meal. Jesus and the apostles* were together at the table. [15]Jesus said to them, "I wanted very much to eat this Passover meal with you before I die. [16]I will never eat another Passover meal until it is given its full meaning in God's kingdom.*"

[17]Then Jesus took a cup of wine. He gave thanks to God for ſt and said, "Take this cup and give it to everyone here. [18]I will never drink wine again until God's kingdom comes."

[19]Then he took some bread and thanked God for it. He broke off some pieces, gave them to the apostles and said, "This bread is my body that I am giving for you. Eat this to remember me." [20]In the same way, after supper, Jesus took the cup of wine and said, "This wine represents the new agreement* from God to his people. It will begin when my blood is poured out for you."[b]

Who Will Turn Against Jesus?

[21]Jesus said, "But here on this table is the hand of the one who will hand me over to my enemies. [22]The Son of Man* will do what God has planned. But it will be very bad for the one who hands over the Son of Man to be killed."

[23]Then the apostles* asked each other, "Which one of us would do that?"

Be Like a Servant

[24]Later, the apostles* began to argue about which one of them was the most important. [25]But Jesus said to them, "The kings of the world rule over their people, and those who have authority over others want to be called 'the great providers for the people.' [26]But you must not be like that. The one with the most authority among you should act as if he is the least important. The one who leads should be like one who serves. [27]Who is more important: the one serving or the one sitting at the table being served? Everyone thinks it's the one being served, right? But I have been with you as the one who serves.

[28]"You men have stayed with me through many struggles. [29]So I give you authority to rule with me in the kingdom the Father has given me. [30]You will eat and drink at my table in that kingdom. You will sit on thrones and judge the twelve tribes of Israel.*

Peter Will Be Tested and Fail
(Mt. 26:31–35; Mk. 14:27–31; Jn. 13:36–38)

[31]"Satan* has asked to test you men like a farmer tests his wheat. O Simon, Simon,[c] [32]I have prayed that you will not lose your faith! Help your brothers be stronger when you come back to me."

[33]But Peter said to Jesus, "Lord, I am ready to go to jail with you. I will even die with you!"

[34]But Jesus said, "Peter, before the rooster crows tomorrow morning, you will say you don't know me. You will say this three times."

---

[a]**22:7** *Day of Unleavened Bread* Same as Passover.

[b]**22:20** A few Greek copies do not have Jesus' words in the last part of verse 19 and all of verse 20.
[c]**22:31** *Simon* Simon's other name was Peter.

Be Ready for Trouble

35Then Jesus said to the apostles,* "Remember when I sent you out without money, a bag, or sandals? Did you need anything?"

The apostles said, "No."

36Jesus said to them, "But now if you have money or a bag, carry that with you. If you don't have a sword, sell your coat and buy one. 37The Scriptures* say,

'He was considered a criminal.'   Isaiah 53:12

This Scripture must happen. It was written about me, and it is happening now."

38The followers said, "Look, Lord, here are two swords."

Jesus said to them, "That's enough."*a*

Jesus Prays Alone
(Mt. 26:36–46; Mk. 14:32–42)

39–40Jesus left the city and went to the Mount of Olives.* His followers went with him. (He went there often.) He said to his followers, "Pray for strength against temptation."

41Then Jesus went about 50 steps away from them. He knelt down and prayed, 42"Father, if you are willing, please don't make me drink from this cup.*b* But do what you want, not what I want." 43Then an angel from heaven came to help him. 44Jesus was full of pain; he struggled hard in prayer. Sweat dripped from his face like drops of blood falling to the ground.*c* 45When he finished praying, he went to his followers. He found them asleep, worn out from their grieving. 46Jesus said to them, "Why are you sleeping? Get up and pray for strength against temptation."

Jesus Is Arrested
(Mt. 26:47–56; Mk. 14:43–50; Jn. 18:3–11)

47While Jesus was speaking, a crowd came up. It was led by Judas, one of the twelve apostles.* He came over to Jesus to kiss him. 48But Jesus said to him, "Judas, are you using the kiss of friendship to hand over the Son of Man* to his enemies?" 49The followers of Jesus were standing there too. They saw what was happening and said to Jesus, "Lord, should we use our swords?" 50And one of them did use his sword. He cut off the right ear of the servant of the high priest.* 51Jesus said, "Stop!" Then he touched the servant's ear and healed him.

52Jesus spoke to the group that came to arrest him. They were the leading priests, the older Jewish leaders, and the Jewish soldiers. He said to them, "Why did you come out here with swords and clubs? Do you think I am a criminal? 53I was with you every day in the Temple* area. Why didn't you try to arrest me there? But this is your time—the time when darkness rules."

Peter Is Afraid to Say He Knows Jesus
(Mt. 26:57–58, 69–75; Mk. 14:53–54, 66–72; Jn. 18:12–18, 25–27)

54They arrested Jesus and took him away to the house of the high priest.* Peter followed Jesus but stayed back at a distance. 55The soldiers started a fire in the middle of the yard and sat together. Peter sat with them. 56A servant girl saw him sitting there. She could see because of the light from the fire. She looked closely at Peter's face. Then she said, "This man was also with Jesus."

57But Peter said this was not true. He said, "Lady, I don't know him." 58A short time later, someone else saw Peter and said, "You are also one of them."

But Peter said, "Man, I am not!"

59About an hour later, another man said, "It's true. I'm sure this man was with him, because he is from Galilee."

60But Peter said, "Man, I don't know what you are talking about!"

Immediately, while he was still speaking, a rooster crowed. 61Then the Lord turned and looked into Peter's eyes. And Peter remembered what the Lord had said, "Before the rooster crows in the morning, you will say three times that you don't know me." 62Then Peter went outside and cried bitterly.

The Guards Treat Jesus Badly
(Mt. 26:67–68; Mk. 14:65)

63The men guarding Jesus made fun of him and beat him. 64They covered his eyes so that he could not see them. Then they hit him and said, "Be a prophet*d* and tell us who hit you!" 65And they shouted all kinds of insults at him.

Jesus Before the Jewish Leaders
(Mt. 26:59–66; Mk. 14:55–64; Jn. 18:19–24)

66The next morning, the older leaders of the people, the leading priests, and the teachers of the law came together. They led Jesus away to their high council. 67They said, "If you are the Christ,* then tell us that you are."

Jesus said to them, "If I tell you I am the Christ, you will not believe me. 68And if I ask you, you will not answer. 69But beginning now, the Son of Man* will sit at the right side of God All-Powerful."

70They all said, "Then are you the Son of God?" Jesus said to them, "You are right in saying that I am."

71They said, "Why do we need witnesses now? We all heard what he said!"

---

*a*22:38 *"That's enough"* Or "Enough of that!" meaning "Don't talk anymore about such things."

*b*22:42 *cup* A symbol of suffering. Jesus used the idea of drinking from a cup to mean accepting the suffering he would face in the terrible events that were soon to come.

*c*22:44 Some Greek copies do not have verses 43 and 44.

*d*22:64 *prophet* A prophet often knows things that are hidden to other people.

Governor Pilate Questions Jesus
(Mt. 27:1–2, 11–14; Mk. 15:1–5; Jn. 18:28–38)

23 ¹Then the whole group stood up and led Jesus away to Pilate.* ²They began to accuse Jesus and said to Pilate, "We caught this man trying to change the thinking of our people. He says we should not pay taxes to Caesar.* He calls himself the Christ,* a king."

³Pilate asked Jesus, "Are you the king of the Jews?"

Jesus answered, "Yes, what you say is true."

⁴Pilate said to the leading priests and the people, "I find nothing wrong with this man."

⁵But they kept on saying, "His teaching is causing trouble all over Judea. He began in Galilee, and now he is here!"

Pilate Sends Jesus to Herod

⁶Pilate* heard this and asked if Jesus was from Galilee. ⁷He learned that Jesus was under Herod's* authority. Herod was in Jerusalem at that time, so Pilate sent Jesus to him.

⁸When Herod saw Jesus, he was very happy. He had heard all about him and had wanted to meet him for a long time. Herod wanted to see a miracle,* so he was hoping that Jesus would do one. ⁹He asked him many questions, but Jesus said nothing. ¹⁰The leading priests and teachers of the law were standing there shouting things against Jesus. ¹¹Then Herod and his soldiers laughed at him. They made fun of him by dressing him in clothes like kings wear. Then Herod sent him back to Pilate. ¹²In the past Pilate and Herod had always been enemies. But on that day they became friends.

Pilate Tries but Fails to Free Jesus
(Mt. 27:15–26; Mk. 15:6–15; Jn. 18:39–19:16)

¹³Pilate* called all the people together with the leading priests and the Jewish leaders. ¹⁴He said to them, "You brought this man to me. You said he was trying to change the people. But I judged him before you all and have not found him guilty of the things you say he has done. ¹⁵Herod* didn't find him guilty either. He sent him back to us. Look, he has done nothing bad enough for the death penalty. ¹⁶So, after I punish him a little, I will let him go free." ¹⁷ ᵃ

¹⁸But they all shouted, "Kill him! Let Barabbas go free!" ¹⁹(Barabbas was a man who was in jail for starting a riot in the city and for murder.)

²⁰Pilate wanted to let Jesus go free. So again Pilate told them that he would let him go. ²¹But they shouted again, "Kill him! Kill him on a cross!"

²²A third time Pilate said to the people, "Why? What wrong has he done? He is not guilty. I can find no reason to kill him. So I will let him go free after I punish him a little."

²³But the people continued to shout. They demanded that Jesus be killed on a cross. Their shouting got so loud that ²⁴Pilate decided to give them what they wanted. ²⁵They wanted Barabbas to go free—the one who was in jail for starting a riot and for murder. Pilate let Barabbas go free. And he handed Jesus over to be killed. This is what the people wanted.

Jesus Is Nailed to a Cross
(Mt. 27:32–44; Mk. 15:21–32; Jn. 19:17–19)

²⁶The soldiers led Jesus away. At that same time there was a man from Cyrene named Simon coming into the city from the fields. The soldiers forced him to carry Jesus' cross and walk behind him.

²⁷A large crowd followed Jesus. Some of the women were sad and crying. They felt sorry for him. ²⁸But Jesus turned and said to the women, "Women of Jerusalem, don't cry for me. Cry for yourselves and for your children too. ²⁹The time is coming when people will say, 'The women who cannot have babies are the ones God has blessed. It's really a blessing that they have no children to care for.' ³⁰Then the people will say to the mountains, 'Fall on us!' They will say to the hills, 'Cover us!'ᵇ ³¹If this can happen to someone who is good, what will happen to those who are guilty?ᶜ"

³²There were also two criminals led out with Jesus to be killed. ³³They were led to a place called "The Skull." There the soldiers nailed Jesus to the cross. They also nailed the criminals to crosses beside Jesus—one on the right and the other on the left.

³⁴Jesus said, "Father, forgive them. They don't know what they are doing."ᵈ

The soldiers threw dice to divide Jesus' clothes between them. ³⁵The people stood there watching everything. The Jewish leaders laughed at Jesus. They said, "If he is God's Chosen One, the Christ,* then let him save himself. He saved others, didn't he?"

³⁶Even the soldiers laughed at Jesus and made fun of him. They came and offered him some sour wine. ³⁷They said, "If you are the king of the Jews, save yourself!" ³⁸(At the top of the cross these words were written: "THIS IS THE KING OF THE JEWS.")

³⁹One of the criminals hanging there began to shout insults at Jesus: "Aren't you the Christ? Then save yourself, and save us too!"

⁴⁰But the other criminal stopped him. He said, "You should fear God. All of us will die soon. ⁴¹You and I are guilty. We deserve to die because we did wrong. But this man has

ᵃ**23:17** A few Greek copies add verse 17: "Every year at the Passover festival, Pilate had to release one prisoner to the people."
ᵇ**23:30** Quote from Hos. 10:8.
ᶜ**23:31** *If this can happen … guilty* Literally, "If they do these things in the green tree, what will happen in the dry?"
ᵈ**23:34** *Jesus said, "Father … doing"* Some early copies of Luke do not have these words.

done nothing wrong." [42]Then he said, "Jesus, remember me when you begin ruling as king!"

[43]Then Jesus said to him, "I promise you, today you will be with me in paradise.*"

Jesus Dies
(Mt. 27:45–56; Mk. 15:33–41; Jn. 19:28–30)

[44]It was about noon, but it turned dark throughout the land until three o'clock in the afternoon, [45]because the sun stopped shining. The curtain* in the Temple* was torn into two pieces. [46]Jesus shouted, "Father, I put my life in your hands!"[a] After Jesus said this, he died.

[47]The army officer* there saw what happened. He praised God, saying, "I know this man was a good man!"

[48]Many people had come out of the city to see all this. When they saw it, they felt very sorry and left. [49]The people who were close friends of Jesus were there. Also, there were some women who had followed Jesus from Galilee. They all stood far away from the cross and watched these things.

Jesus Is Buried
(Mt. 27:57–61; Mk. 15:42–47; Jn. 19:38–42)

[50-51]A man named Joseph was there from the Jewish town of Arimathea. He was a good man, who lived the way God wanted. He was waiting for God's kingdom* to come. Joseph was a member of the Jewish council. But he did not agree when the other Jewish leaders decided to kill Jesus. [52]He went to Pilate* and asked for the body of Jesus. [53]He took the body down from the cross and wrapped it in cloth. Then he put it in a tomb* that was dug in a wall of rock. This tomb had never been used before. [54]It was late on Preparation day.* When the sun went down, the Sabbath* day would begin.

[55]The women who had come from Galilee with Jesus followed Joseph. They saw the tomb. Inside they saw where he put Jesus' body. [56]Then they left to prepare some sweet-smelling spices to put on the body.

On the Sabbath day they rested, as commanded in the Law of Moses.*

News That Jesus Has Risen From Death
(Mt. 28:1–10; Mk. 16:1–8; Jn. 20:1–10)

24 [1]Very early Sunday morning, the women came to the tomb* where Jesus' body was laid. They brought the sweet-smelling spices they had prepared. [2]They saw that the heavy stone that covered the entrance had been rolled away. [3]They went in, but they did not find the body of the Lord Jesus. [4]They did not understand this. While they were wondering about it, two men in shining clothes stood beside them. [5]The women were very afraid. They bowed down with their faces to the ground. The men said to them, "Why are you looking for a living person here? This is a place for dead people. [6]Jesus is not here. He has risen from death. Do you remember what he said in Galilee? [7]He said the Son of Man* must be handed over to the control of sinful men, be killed on a cross, and rise from death on the third day." [8]Then the women remembered what Jesus had said.

[9]The women left the tomb and went to the eleven apostles* and the other followers. They told them everything that happened at the tomb. [10]These women were Mary Magdalene, Joanna, Mary, the mother of James, and some others. They told the apostles everything that happened. [11]But the apostles did not believe what they said. It sounded like nonsense. [12]But Peter got up and ran to the tomb to see. He looked in, but he saw only the cloth that Jesus' body had been wrapped in. It was just lying there. Peter went away to be alone, wondering what had happened.[b]

On The Road to Emmaus
(Mk. 16:12–13)

[13]That same day two of Jesus' followers were going to a town named Emmaus. It is about seven miles[c] from Jerusalem. [14]They were talking about everything that had happened. [15]While they were talking, discussing these things, Jesus himself came near and walked with them. [16](But the two men were not allowed to recognize Jesus.) [17]He asked them, "What's this I hear you discussing with each other as you walk?"

The two men stopped, their faces looking very sad. [18]The one named Cleopas said, "You must be the only person in Jerusalem who doesn't know what has just happened there."

[19]Jesus said, "What are you talking about?"

They said, "It's about Jesus, the one from Nazareth. To God and to all the people he was a great prophet.* He said and did many powerful things. [20]But our leaders and the leading priests handed him over to be judged and killed. They nailed him to a cross. [21]We were hoping that he would be the one to free Israel.* But then all this happened.

"And now something else: It has been three days since he was killed, [22]but today some of our women told us an amazing thing. Early this morning they went to the tomb* where the body of Jesus was laid. [23]But they did not find his body there. They came and told us they had seen some angels in a vision.* The angels told them Jesus was alive! [24]So some of our group went to the tomb too. It was just as the women said. They saw the tomb, but they did not see Jesus."

---

[a]**23:46** *"I put ... hands"* Literally, "I put my spirit in your hands." Quote from Ps. 31:5.

[b]**24:12** A few Greek copies do not have this verse.

[c]**24:13** *seven miles* Literally, "seven *stadious*," almost 12 km.

²⁵Then Jesus said to the two men, "You are foolish and slow to realize what is true. You should believe everything the prophets said. ²⁶The prophets said the Christ* must suffer these things before he begins his time of glory.*" ²⁷Then he began to explain everything that had been written about himself in the Scriptures.* He started with the books of Moses* and then he talked about what the prophets had said about him.

²⁸They came near the town of Emmaus, and Jesus acted as if he did not plan to stop there. ²⁹But they wanted him to stay. They begged him, "Stay with us. It's almost night. There's hardly any daylight left." So he went in to stay with them.

³⁰Joining them at the supper table, Jesus took some bread and gave thanks. Then he broke some off and gave it to them. ³¹Just then the men were allowed to recognize him. But when they saw who he was, he disappeared. ³²They said to each other, "When he talked to us on the road, it felt like a fire burning in us. How exciting it was when he explained to us the true meaning of the Scriptures!"

³³So the two men got up then and went back to Jerusalem. There they found the followers of Jesus meeting together. The eleven apostles* and the people with them ³⁴said, "The Lord really has risen from death! He appeared to Simon."

³⁵Then the two men told what had happened on the road. They talked about how they recognized Jesus when he shared the bread with them.

Jesus Appears to His Followers
(Mt. 28:16–20; Mk. 16:14–18; Jn. 20:19–23; Acts 1:6–8)

³⁶While the two men were saying these things to the other followers, Jesus himself came and stood among them. He said to them, "Peace be with you."

³⁷This surprised the followers. They were afraid. They thought they were seeing a ghost. ³⁸But Jesus said, "Why are you troubled? Why do you doubt what you see? ³⁹Look at my hands and my feet. It's really me. Touch me. You can see that I have a living body; a ghost does not have a body like this."

⁴⁰After Jesus told them this, he showed them his hands and his feet. ⁴¹The followers were amazed and very, very happy to see that Jesus was alive. They still could not believe what they saw. He said to them, "Do you have any food here?" ⁴²They gave him a piece of cooked fish. ⁴³While the followers watched, he took the fish and ate it.

⁴⁴Jesus said to them, "Remember when I was with you before? I said that everything written about me must happen—everything written in the Law of Moses,* the books of the prophets,* and the Psalms."

⁴⁵Then Jesus helped the followers understand these Scriptures* about him. ⁴⁶Jesus said to them, "It is written that the Christ* would be killed and rise from death on the third day. ⁴⁷⁻⁴⁸You saw these things happen—you are witnesses. You must go and tell people that they must change and turn to God, which will bring them his forgiveness. You must start from Jerusalem and tell this message in my name to the people of all nations. ⁴⁹Remember that I will send you the one my Father promised. Stay in the city until you are given that power from heaven."

Jesus Goes Back to Heaven
(Mk. 16:19–20; Acts 1:9–11)

⁵⁰Jesus led his followers out of Jerusalem almost to Bethany. He raised his hands and blessed his followers. ⁵¹While he was blessing them, he was separated from them and carried into heaven. ⁵²They worshiped him and went back to Jerusalem very happy. ⁵³They stayed at the Temple* all the time, praising God.

John

Christ Comes to the World

1 ¹Before the world began, the Word*ᵃ* was there. The Word was with God, and the Word was God. ²He was there with God in the beginning. ³Everything was made through him, and nothing was made without him. ⁴In him there was life, and that life was a light for the people of the world. ⁵The light*ᵇ* shines in the darkness,* and the darkness has not defeated*ᶜ* it.

⁶There was a man named John,* who was sent by God. ⁷He came to tell people about the light. Through him all people could hear about the light and believe. ⁸John was not the light.

---

*ᵃ***1:1** *Word* The Greek word is "*logos*," meaning any kind of communication. It could be translated "message." Here, it means Christ—the way God told the world about himself. Also in verses 10, 14, 16.

*ᵇ***1:5** *light* Meaning Christ, the Word, who brought to the world understanding about God. Also in verse 7.

*ᶜ***1:5** *defeated* Or "understood."

But he came to tell people about the light. ⁹The true light was coming into the world. This is the true light that gives light to all people.

¹⁰The Word was already in the world. The world was made through him, but the world did not know him. ¹¹He came to the world that was his own. And his own people did not accept him. ¹²But some people did accept him. They believed in him, and he gave them the right to become children of God. ¹³They became God's children, but not in the way babies are usually born. It was not because of any human desire or plan. They were born from God himself.

¹⁴The Word became a man and lived among us. We saw his divine greatness*—the greatness that belongs to the only Son of the Father. The Word was full of grace* and truth. ¹⁵John told people about him. He said loudly, "This is the one I was talking about when I said, 'The one who is coming after me is greater than I am, because he was living before I was even born.'"

¹⁶Yes, the Word was full of grace and truth, and from him we all received one blessing after another.ᵃ ¹⁷That is, the law was given to us through Moses,* but grace and truth came through Jesus Christ. ¹⁸No one has ever seen God. The only Son is the one who has shown us what God is like. He is himself God and is very close to the Father.ᵇ

John Tells About the Christ
(Mt. 3:1–12; Mk. 1:1–8; Lk. 3:1–9, 15–17)

¹⁹The Jewish leaders in Jerusalem sent some priests and Levites* to John* to ask him, "Who are you?" He told them the truth. ²⁰Without any hesitation he said openly and plainly, "I am not the Christ.*"

²¹They asked him, "Then who are you? Are you Elijah*?"

He answered, "No, I am not Elijah."

They asked, "Are you the Prophetᶜ?"

He answered, "No, I am not the Prophet."

²²Then they said, "Who are you? Tell us about yourself. Give us an answer to tell the people who sent us. What do you say about yourself?"

²³John told them the words of the prophet* Isaiah:

"I am the voice of someone shouting in the desert:
 'Make a straight road ready for the Lord.'"   *Isaiah 40:3*

²⁴These Jews were sent from the Pharisees.* ²⁵They said to John, "You say you are not the Christ. You say you are not Elijah or the Prophet. Then why do you baptize* people?"

²⁶John answered, "I baptize people with water. But there is someone here with you that you don't know. ²⁷He is the one who is coming later. I am not good enough to be the slave who unties the strings on his sandals."

²⁸These things all happened at Bethany on the other side of the Jordan River. This is where John was baptizing people.

Jesus, the Lamb of God

²⁹The next day John saw Jesus coming toward him and said, "Look, the Lamb* of God. He takes away the sins of the world! ³⁰This is the one I was talking about when I said, 'There is a man coming after me who is greater than I am, because he was living even before I was born.' ³¹I did not know who he was. But I came baptizing people with water so that Israel* could know that Jesus is the Christ.*"

³²-³³Then John said, "I also did not know who the Christ was. But the one who sent me to baptize* with water told me, 'You will see the Spirit* come down and rest on a man. He is the one who will baptize with the Holy Spirit.' I have seen this happen. I saw the Spirit come down from heaven like a dove and rest on this man. ³⁴So this is what I tell people: 'He is the Son of God.'"

The First Followers of Jesus

³⁵The next day John was there again and had two of his followers with him. ³⁶He saw Jesus walking by and said, "Look, the Lamb* of God!"

³⁷The two followers heard him say this, so they followed Jesus. ³⁸Jesus turned and saw the two men following him. He asked, "What do you want?"

They said, "Rabbi, where are you staying?" ("Rabbi" means "Teacher.")

³⁹He answered, "Come with me and you will see." So the two men went with him. They saw the place where he was staying, and they stayed there with him that day. It was about four o'clock.

⁴⁰These men followed Jesus after they had heard about him from John. One of them was Andrew, the brother of Simon Peter. ⁴¹The first thing Andrew did was to go and find his brother Simon. Andrew said to him, "We have found the Messiah." ("Messiah" means "Christ.*")

⁴²Then Andrew brought Simon to Jesus. Jesus looked at him and said, "You are Simon, the son of John. You will be called Cephas." ("Cephas" means "Peter.ᵈ")

ᵃ**1:16** *one blessing after another* Literally, "grace in place of grace."

ᵇ**1:18** *The only Son ... Father* Or more literally, "The only God, who is very close to the Father, has shown us what he is like." Some other Greek copies say, "The only Son is very close to the Father and has shown us what he is like."

ᶜ**1:21** *Prophet* They probably meant the prophet that God told Moses he would send. See Deut. 18:15–19. Also in verse 24.

ᵈ**1:42** *Peter* The Greek name "Peter," like the Aramaic name "Cephas," means "rock."

43The next day Jesus decided to go to Galilee. He met Philip and said to him, "Follow me." 44Philip was from the town of Bethsaida, the same as Andrew and Peter. 45Philip found Nathanael and told him, "We have found the man that Moses* wrote about in the law. The prophets* wrote about him too. He is Jesus, the son of Joseph. He is from Nazareth."

46But Nathanael said to Philip, "Nazareth! Can anything good come from Nazareth?"

Philip answered, "Come and see."

47Jesus saw Nathanael coming toward him and said, "This man coming is a true Israelite,* one you can trust.*a"

48Nathanael asked, "How do you know me?"

Jesus answered, "I saw you when you were under the fig tree, before Philip told you about me."

49Then Nathanael said, "Teacher, you are the Son of God. You are the King of Israel.*"

50Jesus said to him, "Do you believe this just because I said I saw you under the fig tree? You will see much greater things than that!" 51Then he said, "Believe me when I say that you will all see heaven open. You will see 'angels of God going up and coming down'b on the Son of Man.*"

The Wedding at Cana

2 1Two days later there was a wedding in the town of Cana in Galilee, and Jesus' mother was there. 2Jesus and his followers were also invited. 3At the wedding there was not enough wine, so Jesus' mother said to him, "They have no more wine."

4Jesus answered, "Dear woman, why are you telling me this? It is not yet time for me to begin my work."

5His mother said to the servants, "Do what he tells you."

6There were six large stone waterpots there that were used by the Jews in their washing ceremonies.c Each one held about 20 or 30 gallons.d

7Jesus said to the servants, "Fill the waterpots with water." So they filled them to the top.

8Then he said to them, "Now dip out some water and take it to the man in charge of the feast."

So they did what he said. 9Then the man in charge tasted it, but the water had become wine. He did not know where the wine had come from, but the servants who brought the water knew. He called the bridegroom* 10and said to him, "People always serve the best wine first. Later, when the guests are drunk, they serve the cheaper wine. But you have saved the best wine until now."

11This was the first of all the miraculous signs* Jesus did. He did it in the town of Cana in Galilee. By this he showed his divine greatness,* and his followers believed in him.

12Then Jesus went to the town of Capernaum.* His mother and brothers and his followers went with him. They all stayed there a few days.

Jesus at the Temple
(Mt. 21:12–13; Mk. 11:15–17; Lk. 19:45–46)

13It was almost time for the Jewish Passover,* so Jesus went to Jerusalem. 14There in the Temple* area he saw men selling cattle, sheep, and doves. He saw others sitting at tables, exchanging and trading people's money. 15Jesus made a whip with some pieces of rope. Then he forced all these men and the sheep and cattle to leave the Temple area. He turned over the tables of the money traders and scattered their money. 16Then he said to those who were selling pigeons, "Take these things out of here! Don't make my Father's house a place for buying and selling!"

17When this happened, his followers remembered what was written in the Scriptures*:

"My strong devotion to your Temple will
    destroy me."   Psalm 69:9

18Some Jews said to Jesus, "Show us a miracle* as a sign from God. Prove that you have the right to do these things."

19Jesus answered, "Destroy this temple and I will build it again in three days."

20They answered, "People worked 46 years to build this Temple! Do you really believe you can build it again in three days?"

21But the temple Jesus meant was his own body. 22After he was raised from death, his followers remembered that he had said this. So they believed the Scriptures, and they believed the words Jesus said.

23Jesus was in Jerusalem for the Passover festival. Many people believed in him because they saw the miraculous signs* he did. 24But Jesus did not trust them, because he knew how all people think. 25He did not need anyone to tell him what a person was like. He already knew.

Jesus and Nicodemus

3 1There was a man named Nicodemus, one of the Pharisees.* He was an important Jewish leader. 2One night he came to Jesus and said, "Teacher, we know that you are a teacher sent from God. No one can do these miraculous signs* that you do unless they have God's help."

---

a1:47 you can trust Literally, "in whom is no deceit." In the Old Testament, Israel's other name, Jacob, is explained with words that mean "deceit" or "trickery," for which he was well known. See Gen. 27:35, 36.
b1:51 Quote from Gen. 28:12.
c2:6 washing ceremonies The Jews had religious rules about washing in special ways before eating, before worshiping in the Temple, and at other special times.
d2:6 20 or 30 gallons Literally, "2 or 3 metretas," about 80 to 120 liters.

³Jesus answered, "I assure you, everyone must be born again. Anyone who is not born again cannot be in God's kingdom.*"

⁴Nicodemus said, "How can a man who is already old be born again? Can he go back into his mother's womb and be born a second time?"

⁵Jesus answered, "Believe me when I say that everyone must be born from water and the Spirit.* Anyone who is not born from water and the Spirit cannot enter God's kingdom. ⁶The only life people get from their human parents is physical. But the new life that the Spirit gives a person is spiritual. ⁷Don't be surprised that I told you, 'You must be born again.' ⁸The wind blows wherever it wants to. You hear it, but you don't know where it is coming from or where it is going. It is the same with everyone who is born from the Spirit."

⁹Nicodemus asked, "How is all this possible?"

¹⁰Jesus said, "You are an important teacher of Israel,* and you still don't understand these things? ¹¹The truth is, we talk about what we know. We tell about what we have seen. But you people don't accept what we tell you. ¹²I have told you about things here on earth, but you do not believe me. So I'm sure you will not believe me if I tell you about heavenly things! ¹³The only one who has ever gone up to heaven is the one who came down from heaven—the Son of Man.*

¹⁴"Moses lifted up the snake in the desert.ᵈ It is the same with the Son of Man. He must be lifted up too. ¹⁵Then everyone who believes in him can have eternal life."ᵇ

¹⁶Yes, God loved the world so much that he gave his only Son, so that everyone who believes in him would not be lost but have eternal life. ¹⁷God sent his Son into the world. He did not send him to judge the world guilty, but to save the world through him. ¹⁸People who believe in God's Son are not judged guilty. But people who do not believe are already judged, because they have not believed in God's only Son. ¹⁹They are judged by this fact: The lightᶜ has come into the world. But they did not want light. They wanted darkness,* because they were doing evil things. ²⁰Everyone who does evil hates the light. They will not come to the light, because the light will show all the bad things they have done. ²¹But anyone who follows the true way comes to the light. Then the light will show that whatever they have done was done through God.

Jesus and John the Baptizer

²²After this, Jesus and his followers went into the area of Judea. There he stayed with his followers and baptized* people. ²³John was also baptizing people in Aenon, a place near Salim with plenty of water. People were going there to be baptized. ²⁴This was before John was put in prison.

²⁵Some of John's followers had an argument with another Jew about religious washing.ᵈ ²⁶Then they came to John and said, "Teacher, remember the man who was with you on the other side of the Jordan River? He is the one you were telling everyone about. He is also baptizing people, and many are going to him."

²⁷John answered, "A person can receive only what God gives. ²⁸You yourselves heard me say, 'I am not the Christ.* I am only the one God sent to prepare the way for him.' ²⁹The bride always belongs to the bridegroom.* The friend who helps the bridegroom just waits and listens. He is happy just to hear the bridegroom talk. That's how I feel now. I am so happy that he is here. ³⁰He must become more and more important, and I must become less important.

The One Who Comes From Heaven

³¹"The one who comes from above is greater than all others. The one who is from the earth belongs to the earth. He talks about things that are on the earth. But the one who comes from heaven is greater than all others. ³²He tells what he has seen and heard, but people don't accept what he says. ³³Whoever accepts what he says has given proof that God speaks the truth. ³⁴God sent him, and he tells people what God says. God gives him the Spirit* fully. ³⁵The Father loves the Son and has given him power over everything. ³⁶Whoever believes in the Son has eternal life. But those who do not obey the Son will never have that life. They cannot get away from God's anger."

Jesus Talks to a Woman in Samaria

4 ¹Jesus learned that the Pharisees* had heard the report that he was making and baptizing* more followers than John. ²(But really, Jesus himself did not baptize anyone; his followers baptized people for him.) ³So he left Judea and went back to Galilee. ⁴On the way to Galilee he had to go through the country of Samaria.

⁵In Samaria Jesus came to the town called Sychar, which is near the field that Jacob gave to his son Joseph. ⁶Jacob's well was there. Jesus was tired from his long trip, so he sat down beside the well. It was about noon. ⁷A

ᵈ**3:14 Moses lifted ... desert** When God's people were dying from snake bites, God told Moses to put a brass snake on a pole for them to look at and be healed. See Num. 21:4–9.
ᵇ**3:15** Some scholars think that Jesus' words to Nicodemus continue through verse 21.
ᶜ**3:19 light** This means Christ, the Word, who brought to the world understanding about God.

ᵈ**3:25 religious washing** The Jews had religious rules about washing in special ways before eating, before worshiping in the Temple, and at other special times.

Samaritan* woman came to the well to get some water, and Jesus said to her, "Please give me a drink." 8This happened while his followers were in town buying some food.

9The woman answered, "I am surprised that you ask me for a drink! You are a Jew and I am a Samaritan woman!" (Jews have nothing to do with Samaritans.*a*)

10Jesus answered, "You don't know what God can give you. And you don't know who I am, the one who asked you for a drink. If you knew, you would have asked me, and I would have given you living water."

11The woman said, "Sir, where will you get that living water? The well is very deep, and you have nothing to get water with. 12Are you greater than our ancestor Jacob*? He is the one who gave us this well. He drank from it himself, and his sons and all his animals drank from it too."

13Jesus answered, "Everyone who drinks this water will be thirsty again. 14But anyone who drinks the water I give will never be thirsty again. The water I give people will be like a spring flowing inside them. It will bring them eternal life."

15The woman said to Jesus, "Sir, give me this water. Then I will never be thirsty again and won't have to come back here to get more water."

16Jesus told her, "Go get your husband and come back."

17The woman answered, "But I have no husband."

Jesus said to her, "You are right to say you have no husband. 18That's because, although you have had five husbands, the man you live with now is not your husband. That much was the truth."

19The woman said, "Sir, I can see that you are a prophet.*b* 20Our fathers worshiped on this mountain. But you Jews say that Jerusalem is the place where people must worship."

21Jesus said, "Believe me, woman! The time is coming when you will not have to be in Jerusalem or on this mountain to worship the Father. 22You Samaritans worship something you don't understand. We Jews understand what we worship, since salvation comes from the Jews. 23But the time is coming when the true worshipers will worship the Father in spirit and truth. In fact, that time is now here. And these are the kind of people the Father wants to be his worshipers. 24God is spirit. So the people who worship him must worship in spirit and truth."

25The woman said, "I know that the Messiah is coming." (Messiah is the one called Christ.*) "When he comes, he will explain everything to us."

26Then Jesus said, "He is talking to you now—I am the Messiah."

27Just then Jesus' followers came back from town. They were surprised because they saw Jesus talking with a woman. But none of them asked, "What do you want?" or "Why are you talking with her?"

28Then the woman left her water jar and went back to town. She told the people there, 29"A man told me everything I have ever done. Come see him. Maybe he is the Christ." 30So the people left the town and went to see Jesus.

31While the woman was in town, Jesus' followers were begging him, "Teacher, eat something!"

32But Jesus answered, "I have food to eat that you know nothing about."

33So the followers asked themselves, "Did someone already bring him some food?"

34Jesus said, "My food is to do what the one who sent me wants me to do. My food is to finish the work that he gave me to do. 35When you plant, you always say, 'Four more months to wait before we gather the grain.' But I tell you, open your eyes, and look at the fields. They are ready for harvesting now. 36Even now, the people who harvest the crop are being paid. They are gathering crops for eternal life. So now the people who plant can be happy together with those who harvest. 37It is true when we say, 'One person plants, but another person harvests the crop.' 38I sent you to harvest a crop that you did not work for. Others did the work, and you get the profit from their work."

39Many of the Samaritan people in that town believed in Jesus. They believed because of what the woman had told them about him. She had told them, "He told me everything I have ever done." 40The Samaritans went to Jesus. They begged him to stay with them. So he stayed there two days. 41Many more people became believers because of the things he said.

42The people said to the woman, "First we believed in Jesus because of what you told us. But now we believe because we heard him ourselves. We know now that he really is the one who will save the world."

Jesus Heals an Official's Son
(Mt. 8:5–13; Lk. 7:1–10)

43Two days later Jesus left and went to Galilee. 44(Jesus had said before that a prophet* is not respected in his own country.) 45When he arrived in Galilee, the people there welcomed him. They had been at the Passover* festival in Jerusalem and had seen everything he did there.

46Jesus went to visit Cana in Galilee again. Cana is where he had changed the water into wine. One of the king's important officials lived in the city of Capernaum.* This man's son was sick. 47The man heard that Jesus had

---

*a***4:9** *Jews have nothing to do with Samaritans* Or "Jews don't use things that Samaritans have used."
*b***4:19** *prophet* A prophet often knows things that are hidden to other people.

come from Judea and was now in Galilee. So he went to Jesus and begged him to come to Capernaum and heal his son, who was almost dead. [48]Jesus said to him, "You people must see miraculous signs* and wonders* before you will believe in me."

[49]The king's official said, "Sir, come before my little son dies."

[50]Jesus answered, "Go. Your son will live."

The man believed what Jesus told him and went home. [51]On the way home the man's servants came and met him. They said, "Your son is well."

[52]The man asked, "What time did my son begin to get well?"

They answered, "It was about one o'clock yesterday when the fever left him."

[53]The father knew that one o'clock was the same time that Jesus had said, "Your son will live." So the man and everyone in his house believed in Jesus.

[54]That was the second miraculous sign that Jesus did after coming from Judea to Galilee.

Jesus Heals a Man at a Pool

5 [1]Later, Jesus went to Jerusalem for a special Jewish festival. [2]In Jerusalem there is a pool with five covered porches. In Aramaic* it is called Bethzatha.[a] This pool is near the Sheep Gate. [3]Many sick people were lying on the porches beside the pool. Some of them were blind, some were crippled, and some were paralyzed.[b] [4][c] [5]One of the men lying there had been sick for 38 years. [6]Jesus saw him lying there and knew that he had been sick for a very long time. So he asked him, "Do you want to be well?"

[7]The sick man answered, "Sir, there is no one to help me get into the water when it starts moving. I try to be the first one into the water. But when I try, someone else always goes in before I can."

[8]Then Jesus said, "Stand up! Pick up your mat and walk." [9]Immediately the man was well. He picked up his mat and started walking.

The day all this happened was a Sabbath* day. [10]So some Jews said to the man who had been healed, "Today is the Sabbath. It is against our law for you to carry your mat on the Sabbath day."

[11]But he answered, "The man who made me well told me, 'Pick up your mat and walk.'"

[12]They asked him, "Who is the man who told you to pick up your mat and walk?"

[13]But the man who had been healed did not

*a*5:2 *Bethzatha* Also called Bethsaida or Bethesda, a pool of water north of the Temple in Jerusalem.
*b*5:3 At the end of verse 3 some Greek copies add "and they waited for the water to move."
*c*5:4 A few later copies add verse 4: "Sometimes an angel of the Lord came down to the pool and shook the water. After this, the first person to go into the pool was healed from any sickness he had."

know who it was. There were many people there, and Jesus had left.

[14]Later, Jesus found the man at the Temple* and said to him, "See, you are well now. But stop sinning or something worse may happen to you!"

[15]Then the man left and went back to the Jews who questioned him. He told them that Jesus was the one who made him well.

[16]Jesus was doing all this on the Sabbath day. So these Jews began trying to make him stop. [17]But he said to them, "My Father never stops working, and so I work too."

[18]This made them try harder to kill him. They said, "First this man was breaking the law about the Sabbath day. Then he said that God is his Father! He is making himself equal with God!"

Jesus Has God's Authority

[19]But Jesus answered, "I assure you that the Son can do nothing alone. He does only what he sees his Father doing. The Son does the same things that the Father does. [20]The Father loves the Son and shows him everything he does. This man was healed. But the Father will show the Son greater things than this to do. Then you will all be amazed. [21]The Father raises the dead and gives them life. In the same way, the Son gives life to those he wants to.

[22]"Also, the Father judges no one. He has given the Son power to do all the judging. [23]God did this so that all people will respect the Son the same as they respect the Father. Anyone who does not respect the Son does not respect the Father. He is the one who sent the Son.

[24]"I assure you, anyone who hears what I say and believes in the one who sent me has eternal life. They will not be judged guilty. They have already left death and have entered into life. [25]Believe me, an important time is coming. That time is already here. People who are dead will hear the voice of the Son of God. And those who listen will live. [26]Life comes from the Father himself. So the Father has also allowed the Son to give life. [27]And the Father has given him the power to judge all people because he is the Son of Man.*

[28]"Don't be surprised at this. A time is coming when all people who are dead and in their graves will hear his voice. [29]Then they will come out of their graves. Those who did good in this life will rise and have eternal life. But those who did evil will rise to be judged guilty.

[30]"I can do nothing alone. I judge only the way I am told. And my judgment is right, because I am not trying to please myself. I want only to please the one who sent me.

Jesus Says More to the Jewish Leaders

[31]"If I tell people about myself, they cannot be sure that what I say is true. [32]But there is

someone else who tells people about me, and I know that what he says about me is true.

³³"You sent men to John,* and he told you what is true. ³⁴I don't need anyone to tell people about me, but I remind you of what John said so that you can be saved. ³⁵John was like a lamp that burned and gave light, and you were happy to enjoy his light for a while.

³⁶"But I have a proof about myself that is greater than anything John said. The things I do are my proof. These are what my Father gave me to do. They show that the Father sent me. ³⁷And the Father who sent me has given proof about me himself. But you have never heard his voice. You have never seen what he looks like. ³⁸The Father's teaching does not live in you, because you don't believe in the one the Father sent. ³⁹You carefully study the Scriptures.* You think that they give you eternal life. These same Scriptures tell about me! ⁴⁰But you refuse to come to me to have that life.

⁴¹"I don't want praise from you or any other human. ⁴²But I know you—I know that you have no love for God. ⁴³I have come from my Father and speak for him, but you don't accept me. But when other people come speaking only for themselves, you accept them. ⁴⁴You like to have praise from each other. But you never try to get the praise that comes from the only God. So how can you believe? ⁴⁵Don't think that I will be the one to stand before the Father and accuse you. Moses* is the one to accuse you. And he is the one you hoped would save you. ⁴⁶If you really believed Moses, you would believe me, because he wrote about me. ⁴⁷But you don't believe what he wrote, so you can't believe what I say."

Jesus Feeds More Than 5000
(Mt. 14:13–21; Mk. 6:30–44; Lk. 9:10–17)

6 ¹Later, Jesus went across Lake Galilee (also known as Lake Tiberias). ²A great crowd of people followed him because they saw the miraculous signs* he did in healing the sick. ³Jesus went up on the side of the hill and sat there with his followers. ⁴It was almost the time for the Jewish Passover* festival.

⁵Jesus looked up and saw a crowd of people coming toward him. He said to Philip, "Where can we buy enough bread for all these people to eat?" ⁶He asked Philip this question to test him. Jesus already knew what he planned to do.

⁷Philip answered, "We would all have to work a month to buy enough bread for each person here to have only a little piece!"

⁸Another follower there was Andrew, the brother of Simon Peter. Andrew said, ⁹"Here is a boy with five loaves of barley bread and two little fish. But that is not enough for so many people."

¹⁰Jesus said, "Tell everyone to sit down." This was a place with a lot of grass, and about 5000 men sat down there. ¹¹Jesus took the loaves of bread and gave thanks for them. Then he gave them to the people who were waiting to eat. He did the same with the fish. He gave them as much as they wanted.

¹²They all had plenty to eat. When they finished, Jesus said to his followers, "Gather the pieces of fish and bread that were not eaten. Don't waste anything." ¹³So they gathered up the pieces that were left. The people had started eating with only five loaves of barley bread. But the followers filled twelve large baskets with the pieces of food that were left.

¹⁴The people saw this miraculous sign that Jesus did and said, "He must be the Prophet*[a] who is coming into the world."

¹⁵Jesus knew that the people planned to come get him and make him their king. So he left and went into the hills alone.

Jesus Walks on Water
(Mt. 14:22–27; Mk. 6:45–52)

¹⁶That evening Jesus' followers went down to the lake. ¹⁷It was dark now, and Jesus had not yet come back to them. They got into a boat and started going across the lake to Capernaum.* ¹⁸The wind was blowing very hard. The waves on the lake were becoming bigger. ¹⁹They rowed the boat about three or four miles.[b] Then they saw Jesus. He was walking on the water, coming to the boat. They were afraid. ²⁰But he said to them, "Don't be afraid. It's me." ²¹When he said this, they were glad to take him into the boat. And then the boat reached the shore at the place they wanted to go.

The People Look for Jesus

²²The next day came. Some people had stayed on the other side of the lake. They knew that Jesus did not go with his followers in the boat. They knew that the followers had left in the boat alone. And they knew it was the only boat that was there. ²³But then some boats from Tiberias came and landed near the place where the people had eaten the day before. This was where they had eaten the bread after the Lord gave thanks. ²⁴The people saw that Jesus and his followers were not there now. So they got into the boats and went to Capernaum* to find Jesus.

Jesus, the Bread of Life

²⁵The people found Jesus on the other side of the lake. They asked him, "Teacher, when did you come here?"

²⁶He answered, "Why are you looking for me? Is it because you saw miraculous signs*? The truth is, you are looking for me because you ate the bread and were satisfied. ²⁷But

---

[a]*6:14 Prophet* They probably meant the prophet that God told Moses he would send. See Deut. 18:15–19.

[b]*6:19 three or four miles* Literally, "25 or 30 *stadia*," about 5 or 6 km.

earthly food spoils and ruins. So don't work to get that kind of food. But work to get the food that stays good and gives you eternal life. The Son of Man* will give you that food. He is the only one qualified by God the Father to give it to you."

28The people asked Jesus, "What does God want us to do?"

29Jesus answered, "The work God wants you to do is this: to believe in the one he sent."

30So the people asked, "What miraculous sign will you do for us? If we can see you do a miracle, then we will believe you. What will you do? 31Our ancestors* were given manna* to eat in the desert. As the Scriptures* say, 'He gave them bread from heaven to eat.'ᵃ"

32Jesus said, "I can assure you that Moses* was not the one who gave your people bread from heaven. But my Father gives you the true bread from heaven. 33God's bread is the one who comes down from heaven and gives life to the world."

34The people said, "Sir, from now on give us bread like that."

35Then Jesus said, "I am the bread that gives life. No one who comes to me will ever be hungry. No one who believes in me will ever be thirsty. 36I told you before that you have seen me, and still you don't believe. 37The Father gives me my people. Every one of them will come to me. I will always accept them. 38I came down from heaven to do what God wants, not what I want. 39I must not lose anyone God has given me. But I must raise them up on the last day. This is what the one who sent me wants me to do. 40Everyone who sees the Son and believes in him has eternal life. I will raise them up on the last day. This is what my Father wants."

41Some Jews began to complain about Jesus because he said, "I am the bread that comes down from heaven." 42They said, "This is Jesus. We know his father and mother. He is only Joseph's son. How can he say, 'I came down from heaven'?"

43But Jesus said, "Stop complaining to each other. 44The Father is the one who sent me, and he is the one who brings people to me. I will raise them up on the last day. Anyone the Father does not bring to me cannot come to me. 45It is written in the prophets*: 'God will teach them all.'ᵇ People listen to the Father and learn from him. They are the ones who come to me. 46I don't mean that there is anyone who has seen the Father. The only one who has ever seen the Father is the one who came from God. He has seen the Father.

47"I can assure you that anyone who believes has eternal life. 48I am the bread that gives life. 49Your ancestors ate the manna God gave them in the desert, but it didn't keep them from dying. 50Here is the bread that

comes down from heaven. Whoever eats this bread will never die. 51I am the living bread that came down from heaven. Whoever eats this bread will live forever. This bread is my body. I will give my body so that the people in the world can have life."

52Then the Jews began to argue among themselves. They said, "How can this man give us his body to eat?"

53Jesus said, "Believe me when I say that you must eat the body of the Son of Man, and you must drink his blood. If you don't do this, you have no real life. 54Those who eat my body and drink my blood have eternal life. I will raise them up on the last day. 55My body is true food, and my blood is true drink. 56Those who eat my body and drink my blood live in me, and I live in them. 57"The Father sent me. He lives, and I live because of him. So everyone who eats me will live because of me. 58I am not like the bread that your ancestors ate. They ate that bread, but they still died. I am the bread that came down from heaven. Whoever eats this bread will live forever."

59Jesus said all this while he was teaching in the synagogue* in the city of Capernaum.*

Many Followers Leave Jesus

60When Jesus' followers heard this, many of them said, "This teaching is hard. Who can accept it?"

61Jesus already knew that his followers were complaining about this. So he said, "Is this teaching a problem for you? 62Then what will you think when you see the Son of Man* going up to where he came from? 63It is the Spirit* that gives life. The body is of no value for that. But the things I have told you are from the Spirit, so they give life. 64But some of you don't believe." (Jesus knew the people who did not believe. He knew this from the beginning. And he knew the one who would hand him over to his enemies.) 65Jesus said, "That is why I said, 'Anyone the Father does not help to come to me cannot come.'"

66After Jesus said these things, many of his followers left and stopped following him.

67Jesus asked the twelve apostles,* "Do you want to leave too?"

68Simon Peter answered him, "Lord, where would we go? You have the words that give eternal life. 69We believe in you. We know that you are the Holy One from God."

70Then Jesus answered, "I chose all twelve of you. But one of you is a devil." 71He was talking about Judas, the son of Simon Iscariot. Judas was one of the twelve apostles, but later he would hand Jesus over to his enemies.

Jesus and His Brothers

7 ¹After this, Jesus traveled around the country of Galilee. He did not want to travel in Judea, because the Jewish leaders there wanted to kill him. ²It was time for the

---

ᵃ**6:31** Quote from Ps. 78:24.
ᵇ**6:45** Quote from Isa. 54:13.

Jewish Festival of Shelters.* ³So his brothers said to him, "You should leave here and go to the festival in Judea. Then your followers there can see the miracles* you do. ⁴If you want to be well known, you must not hide what you do. So, if you can do such amazing things, let the whole world see you do them. Let them see these things you do." ⁵Jesus' brothers said this because even they did not believe in him.

⁶Jesus said to them, "The right time for me has not yet come, but any time is right for you to go. ⁷The world cannot hate you. But the world hates me, because I tell the people in the world that they do evil things. ⁸So you go to the festival. I will not go now, because the right time for me has not yet come." ⁹After Jesus said this, he stayed in Galilee.

¹⁰So his brothers left to go to the festival. After they left, Jesus went too, but he did not let people see him. ¹¹At the festival the Jewish leaders were looking for him. They said, "Where is that man?"

¹²There was a large group of people there. Many of them were talking secretly to each other about Jesus. Some people said, "He is a good man." But others said, "No, he fools the people." ¹³But no one was brave enough to talk about him openly. They were afraid of the Jewish leaders.

Jesus Teaches in Jerusalem

¹⁴When the festival was about half finished, Jesus went to the Temple* area and began to teach. ¹⁵The Jewish leaders were amazed and said, "How did this man learn so much? He never had the kind of teaching we had!"

¹⁶Jesus answered, "What I teach is not my own. My teaching comes from the one who sent me. ¹⁷People who really want to do what God wants will know that my teaching comes from God. They will know that this teaching is not my own. ¹⁸If I taught my own ideas, I would just be trying to get honor for myself. But if I am trying to bring honor to the one who sent me, I can be trusted. Anyone doing that is not going to lie. ¹⁹Moses* gave you the law,* right? But you don't obey that law. If you do, then why are you trying to kill me?"

²⁰The people answered, "A demon* is making you crazy! We are not trying to kill you."

²¹Jesus said to them, "I did one miracle* on a Sabbath* day, and you were all surprised. ²²But you obey the law Moses gave you about circumcision*—and sometimes you do it on a Sabbath day. (Really, Moses is not the one who gave you circumcision. It came from our ancestors* who lived before Moses.) Yes, you often circumcise baby boys on a Sabbath day. ²³This shows that someone can be circumcised on a Sabbath day to obey the Law of Moses. So why are you angry with me for healing a person's whole body on the Sabbath day? ²⁴Stop judging by the way things look. Be fair and judge by what is really right."

The People Wonder if Jesus Is the Christ

²⁵Then some of the people who lived in Jerusalem said, "This is the man they are trying to kill. ²⁶But he is teaching where everyone can see and hear him. And no one is trying to stop him from teaching. Maybe the leaders have decided that he really is the Christ.* ²⁷But when the real Christ comes, no one will know where he comes from. And we know where this man's home is."

²⁸Jesus was still teaching in the Temple* area when he said loudly, "Do you really know me and where I am from? I am here, but not by my own decision. I was sent by one who is very real. But you don't know him. ²⁹I know him because I am from him. He is the one who sent me."

³⁰When Jesus said this, the people tried to grab him. But no one was able even to touch him, because the right time for him had not yet come. ³¹But many of the people believed in Jesus. They said, "We are waiting for the Christ to come. When he comes, will he do more miraculous signs* than this man has done?"

The Jewish Leaders Try to Arrest Jesus

³²The Pharisees* heard what the people were saying about Jesus. So the leading priests and the Pharisees sent some Temple* police to arrest him. ³³Then Jesus said, "I will be with you a little while longer. Then I will go back to the one who sent me. ³⁴You will look for me, but you will not find me. And you cannot come where I am."

³⁵These Jews said to each other, "Where will this man go that we cannot find him? Will he go to the Greek cities where our people live? Will he teach the Greek people there? ³⁶He says, 'You will look for me, but you will not find me.' He also says, 'You cannot come where I am.' What does this mean?"

Jesus Talks About the Holy Spirit

³⁷The last day of the festival came. It was the most important day. On that day Jesus stood up and said loudly, "Whoever is thirsty may come to me and drink. ³⁸If anyone believes in me, rivers of living water will flow out from their heart. That is what the Scriptures* say." ³⁹Jesus was talking about the Spirit.* The Spirit had not yet been given to people, because Jesus had not yet been raised to glory.* But later, those who believed in Jesus would receive the Spirit.

The People Argue About Jesus

⁴⁰When the people heard the things that Jesus said, some of them said, "This man really is the Prophet.ᵃ"

⁴¹Other people said, "He is the Christ.*"

ᵃ7:40 Prophet They probably meant the prophet that God told Moses he would send. See Deut. 18:15–19.

And others said, "The Christ will not come from Galilee. 42The Scriptures* say that he will come from the family of David.* And they say that he will come from Bethlehem, the town where David lived." 43So the people did not agree with each other about Jesus. 44Some of the people wanted to arrest him. But no one tried to do it.

The Jewish Leaders Refuse to Believe

45The Temple* police went back to the leading priests and the Pharisees.* The priests and the Pharisees asked, "Why didn't you bring Jesus?"

46The Temple police answered, "We have never heard anyone say such amazing things!"

47The Pharisees answered, "So he has fooled you too! 48You don't see any of the leaders or any of us Pharisees believing in him, do you? 49But those people out there know nothing about the law.* They are under God's curse!"

50But Nicodemus was there in that group. He was the one who had gone to see Jesus before.a He said, 51"Our law will not let us judge anyone without first hearing them and finding out what they have done."

52The Jewish leaders answered, "You must be from Galilee too! Study the Scriptures.* You will find nothing about a prophetb coming from Galilee." 53Then they all left and went home.

The Woman Caught in Adultery

8 1Jesus went to the Mount of Olives.* 2Early in the morning he went back to the Temple* area. The people all came to him, and he sat and taught them.

3The teachers of the law and the Pharisees* brought a woman they had caught in bed with a man who was not her husband. They forced her to stand in front of the people. 4They said to Jesus, "Teacher, this woman was caught in the act of adultery.* 5The Law of Moses* commands us to stone to death any such woman. What do you say we should do?"

6They were saying this to trick Jesus. They wanted to catch him saying something wrong so that they could have a charge against him. But Jesus stooped down and started writing on the ground with his finger. 7The Jewish leaders continued to ask him their question. So he stood up and said, "Anyone here who has never sinned should throw the first stone at her." 8Then Jesus stooped down again and wrote on the ground.

9When they heard this, they began to leave one by one. The older men left first, and then the others. Jesus was left alone with the woman standing there in front of him. 10He looked up again and said to her, "Where did they all go? Did no one judge you guilty?"

11She answered, "No one, sir."

Then Jesus said, "I don't judge you either. You can go now, but don't sin again."c

Jesus Is the Light of the World

12Later, Jesus talked to the people again. He said, "I am the light of the world. Whoever follows me will never live in darkness.* They will have the light that gives life."

13But the Pharisees* said to Jesus, "When you talk about yourself, you are the only one to say that these things are true. So we cannot accept what you say."

14Jesus answered, "Yes, I am saying these things about myself. But people can believe what I say, because I know where I came from. And I know where I am going. But you don't know where I came from or where I am going. 15You judge me the way people judge other people. I don't judge anyone. 16But if I judge, my judging is true, because when I judge I am not alone. The Father who sent me is with me. 17Your own law says that when two witnesses say the same thing, you must accept what they say. 18I am one of the witnesses who speaks about myself. And the Father who sent me is my other witness."

19The people asked, "Where is your father?"

Jesus answered, "You don't know me or my Father. But if you knew me, you would know my Father too." 20Jesus said these things while he was teaching in the Temple* area, near the room where the Temple offerings were kept. But no one arrested him, because the right time for him had not yet come.

Some Jews Don't Understand Jesus

21Again, Jesus said to the people, "I will leave you. You will look for me, but you will die in your sin. You cannot come where I am going."

22So the Jewish leaders asked themselves, "Will he kill himself? Is that why he said, 'You cannot come where I am going'?"

23But Jesus said to them, "You people are from here below, but I am from above. You belong to this world, but I don't belong to this world. 24I told you that you would die in your sins. Yes, if you don't believe that I AM,d you will die in your sins."

25They asked, "Then who are you?"

Jesus answered, "I am what I have told you

a7:50 He was the one ... before The story about Nicodemus going and talking to Jesus is in Jn. 3:1–21.

b7:52 a prophet Two early Greek copies have "the Prophet," which would mean the "prophet like Moses" mentioned in Deut. 18:15. In Acts 3:22 and 7:37 this is understood to be the Messiah, as in verse 40 above.

c8:11 The oldest and best Greek copies do not have verses 7:53–8:11. Other copies have this section in different places.

d8:24 I AM This is like the name of God used in the Old Testament. See Isa. 41:4; 43:10; Ex. 3:14. However, it can also mean "I am he (the Christ)." Also in verses 28 and 58.

from the beginning. 26I have much more I could say to judge you. But I tell people only what I have heard from the one who sent me, and he speaks the truth."

27They did not understand who he was talking about. He was telling them about the Father. 28So he said to them, "You will lift up*a* the Son of Man.* Then you will know that I AM. You will know that whatever I do is not by my own authority. You will know that I say only what the Father has taught me. 29The one who sent me is with me. I always do what pleases him. So he has not left me alone." 30While he was saying these things, many people believed in him.

Jesus Talks About Freedom From Sin

31So Jesus said to the Jews who believed in him, "If you continue to accept and obey my teaching, you are really my followers. 32You will know the truth, and the truth will make you free."

33They answered, "We are Abraham's* descendants. And we have never been slaves. So why do you say that we will be free?"

34Jesus said, "The truth is, everyone who sins is a slave—a slave to sin. 35A slave does not stay with a family forever. But a son belongs to the family forever. 36So if the Son makes you free, you are really free. 37I know you are Abraham's descendants. But you want to kill me, because you don't want to accept my teaching. 38I am telling you what my Father has shown me. But you do what your father has told you."

39They said, "Our father is Abraham."

Jesus said, "If you were really Abraham's descendants, you would do what Abraham did. 40I am someone who has told you the truth I heard from God. But you are trying to kill me. Abraham did nothing like that. 41So you are doing what your own father did."

But they said, "We are not like children who never knew who their father was. God is our Father. He is the only Father we have."

42Jesus said to them, "If God were really your Father, you would love me. I came from God, and now I am here. I did not come by my own authority. God sent me. 43You don't understand the things I say, because you cannot accept my teaching. 44Your father is the devil. You belong to him. You want to do what he wants. He was a murderer from the beginning. He was always against the truth. There is no truth in him. He is like the lies he tells. Yes, the devil is a liar. He is the father of lies. 45"I am telling you the truth, and that's why you don't believe me. 46Can any of you prove that I am guilty of sin? If I tell the truth, why don't you believe me? 47Whoever belongs to God accepts what he says. But you don't

accept what God says, because you don't belong to God."

Jesus Talks About Himself and Abraham

48The Jews there answered, "We say you are a Samaritan.* We say a demon* is making you crazy! Are we not right when we say this?"

49Jesus answered, "I have no demon in me. I give honor to my Father, but you give no honor to me. 50I am not trying to get honor for myself. There is one who wants this honor for me. He is the judge. 51I promise you, whoever continues to obey my teaching will never die."

52The Jews said to Jesus, "Now we know that you have a demon in you! Even Abraham* and the prophets* died. But you say, 'Whoever obeys my teaching will never die.' 53Do you think you are greater than our father Abraham? He died, and so did the prophets. Who do you think you are?"

54Jesus answered, "If I give honor to myself, that honor is worth nothing. The one who gives me honor is my Father. And you say that he is your God. 55But you don't really know him. I know him. If I said I did not know him, I would be a liar like you. But I do know him, and I obey what he says. 56Your father* Abraham was very happy that he would see the day when I came. He saw that day and was happy."

57The Jews said to Jesus, "What? How can you say you have seen Abraham? You are not even 50 years old!"

58Jesus answered, "The fact is, before Abraham was born, I AM." 59When he said this, they picked up stones to throw at him. But Jesus hid, and then he left the Temple* area.

Jesus Heals a Man Born Blind

9 1While Jesus was walking, he saw a man who had been blind since the time he was born. 2Jesus' followers asked him, "Teacher, why was this man born blind? Whose sin made it happen? Was it his own sin or that of his parents?"

3Jesus answered, "It was not any sin of this man or his parents that caused him to be blind. He was born blind so that he could be used to show what great things God can do. 4While it is daytime, we must continue doing the work of the one who sent me. The night is coming, and no one can work at night. 5While I am in the world, I am the light of the world."

6After Jesus said this, he spit on the dirt, made some mud and put it on the man's eyes. 7Jesus told him, "Go and wash in Siloam pool." (Siloam means "Sent.") So the man went to the pool, washed and came back. He was now able to see.

8His neighbors and some others who had seen him begging said, "Look! Is this the same man who always sits and begs?"

---

*a***8:28 lift up** Meaning to be nailed to a cross and "lifted up" on it to die. It may also have a second meaning: to be "lifted up" from death to heaven.

⁹Some people said, "Yes! He is the one." But others said, "No, he can't be the same man. He only looks like him."

So the man himself said, "I am that same man."

¹⁰They asked, "What happened? How did you get your sight?"

¹¹He answered, "The man they call Jesus made some mud and put it on my eyes. Then he told me to go to Siloam and wash. So I went there and washed. And then I could see."

¹²They asked him, "Where is this man?"

He answered, "I don't know."

Some Pharisees Have Questions

¹³Then the people brought the man to the Pharisees.* ¹⁴The day Jesus had made mud and healed the man's eyes was a Sabbath* day. ¹⁵So the Pharisees asked the man, "How did you get your sight?"

He answered, "He put mud on my eyes. I washed, and now I can see."

¹⁶Some of the Pharisees said, "That man does not obey the law about the Sabbath day. So he is not from God."

Others said, "But someone who is a sinner cannot do these miraculous signs.*" So they could not agree with each other.

¹⁷They asked the man again, "Since it was your eyes he healed, what do you say about him?"

He answered, "He is a prophet.*"

¹⁸The Jewish leaders still did not believe that this really happened to the man—that he was blind and was now healed. But later they sent for his parents. ¹⁹They asked them, "Is this your son? You say he was born blind. So how can he see?"

²⁰His parents answered, "We know that this man is our son. And we know that he was born blind. ²¹But we don't know why he can see now. We don't know who healed his eyes. Ask him. He is old enough to answer for himself." ²²They said this because they were afraid of the Jewish leaders. The leaders had already decided that they would punish anyone who said Jesus was the Christ.* They would stop them from coming to the synagogue.* ²³That is why his parents said, "He is old enough. Ask him."

²⁴So the Jewish leaders called the man who had been blind. They told him to come in again. They said, "You should honor God by telling the truth. We know that this man is a sinner."

²⁵The man answered, "I don't know if he is a sinner. But I do know this: I was blind, and now I can see."

²⁶They asked, "What did he do to you? How did he heal your eyes?"

²⁷He answered, "I have already told you that. But you would not listen to me. Why do you want to hear it again? Do you want to be his followers too?"

²⁸At this they shouted insults at him and said, "You are his follower, not us! We are followers of Moses.* ²⁹We know that God spoke to Moses. But we don't even know where this man comes from!"

³⁰The man answered, "This is really strange! You don't know where he comes from, but he healed my eyes. ³¹We all know that God does not listen to sinners, but he will listen to anyone who worships and obeys him. ³²This is the first time we have ever heard of anyone healing the eyes of someone born blind. ³³This man must be from God. If he were not from God, he could not do anything like this."

³⁴The Jewish leaders answered, "You were born full of sin! Are you trying to teach us?" And they told the man to get out of the synagogue and to stay out.

Spiritual Blindness

³⁵When Jesus heard that they had forced the man to leave, he found him and asked him, "Do you believe in the Son of Man*?"

³⁶The man said, "Tell me who he is, sir, so I can believe in him."

³⁷Jesus said to him, "You have already seen him. The Son of Man is the one talking with you now."

³⁸The man answered, "Yes, I believe, Lord!" Then he bowed and worshiped Jesus.

³⁹Jesus said, "I came into this world so that the world could be judged. I came so that people who are blind*ᵃ* could see. And I came so that people who think they see would become blind."

⁴⁰Some of the Pharisees* were near Jesus. They heard him say this. They asked, "What? Are you saying that we are blind too?"

⁴¹Jesus said, "If you were really blind, you would not be guilty of sin. But you say that you see, so you are still guilty."

The Shepherd and His Sheep

10 ¹Jesus said, "It is certainly true that when a man enters the sheep pen, he should use the gate. If he climbs in some other way, he is a robber. He is trying to steal the sheep. ²But the man who takes care of the sheep enters through the gate. He is the shepherd. ³The man who guards the gate opens the gate for the shepherd. And the sheep listen to the voice of the shepherd. He calls his own sheep, using their names, and he leads them out. ⁴He brings all of his sheep out. Then he goes ahead of them and leads them. The sheep follow him, because they know his voice. ⁵But sheep will never follow someone they don't know. They will run away from him, because they don't know his voice."

---

*ᵃ*9:39 *people who are blind* Jesus is talking about people who are spiritually blind (without understanding), not physically blind.

⁶Jesus told the people this story, but they did not understand what it meant.

Jesus Is the Good Shepherd

⁷So Jesus said again, "I assure you, I am the gate for the sheep. ⁸All those who came before me were thieves and robbers. The sheep did not listen to them. ⁹I am the gate. Whoever enters through me will be saved. They will be able to come in and go out. They will find everything they need. ¹⁰A thief comes to steal, kill, and destroy. But I came to give life—life that is full and good.

¹¹"I am the good shepherd, and the good shepherd gives his life for the sheep. ¹²The worker who is paid to keep the sheep is different from the shepherd. The paid worker does not own the sheep. So when he sees a wolf coming, he runs away and leaves the sheep alone. Then the wolf attacks the sheep and scatters them. ¹³The man runs away because he is only a paid worker. He does not really care for the sheep.

¹⁴⁻¹⁵"I am the shepherd who cares for the sheep. I know my sheep just as the Father knows me. And my sheep know me just as I know the Father. I give my life for these sheep. ¹⁶I have other sheep too. They are not in this flock here. I must lead them also. They will listen to my voice. In the future there will be one flock and one shepherd.ᵃ ¹⁷The Father loves me because I give my life. I give my life so that I can get it back again. ¹⁸No one takes my life away from me. I give my own life freely. I have the right to give my life, and I have the right to get it back again. This is what the Father told me."

¹⁹Again the Jews were divided over what Jesus was saying. ²⁰Many of them said, "A demon* has come into him and made him crazy. Why listen to him?"

²¹But others said, "These aren't the words of someone controlled by a demon. A demon cannot heal the eyes of a blind man."

The Jewish Leaders Against Jesus

²²It was winter, and the time came for the Festival of Dedicationᵇ at Jerusalem. ²³Jesus was in the Temple* area at Solomon's Porch.* ²⁴The Jewish leaders gathered around him. They said, "How long will you make us wonder about you? If you are the Christ,* then tell us clearly."

²⁵Jesus answered, "I told you already, but you did not believe. I do miracles* in my Father's name. These miracles show who I am. ²⁶But you do not believe, because you are not my sheep. ²⁷My sheep listen to my voice. I know them, and they follow me. ²⁸I give my

sheep eternal life. They will never die, and no one can take them out of my hand. ²⁹My Father is the one who gave them to me, and he is greater than all.ᶜ No one can steal my sheep out of his hand. ³⁰The Father and I are one."

³¹Again the Jews there picked up stones to kill Jesus. ³²But he said to them, "The many wonderful things you have seen me do are from the Father. Which of these good things are you killing me for?"

³³They answered, "We are not killing you for any good thing you did. But you say things that insult God. You are only a man, but you say you are the same as God! That is why we are trying to kill you!"

³⁴Jesus answered, "It is written in your law that God said, 'I said you are gods.'ᵈ ³⁵This Scripture* called those people gods—the people who received God's message. And Scripture is always true. ³⁶So why do you accuse me of insulting God for saying, 'I am God's Son'? I am the one God chose and sent into the world. ³⁷If I don't do what my Father does, then don't believe what I say. ³⁸But if I do what my Father does, you should believe in what I do. You might not believe in me, but you should believe in the things I do. Then you will know and understand that the Father is in me and I am in the Father."

³⁹They tried to get Jesus again, but he escaped from them.

⁴⁰Then he went back across the Jordan River to the place where John* began his work of baptizing* people. Jesus stayed there, ⁴¹and many people came to him. They said, "John never did any miraculous signs,* but everything John said about this man is true." ⁴²And many people there believed in Jesus.

The Death of Lazarus

11 ¹There was a man named Lazarus who was sick. He lived in the town of Bethany, where Mary and her sister Martha lived. ²(Mary is the same woman who put perfume on the Lord and wiped his feet with her hair.) Mary's brother was Lazarus, the man who was now sick. ³So Mary and Martha sent someone to tell Jesus, "Lord, your dear friend Lazarus is sick."

⁴When Jesus heard this he said, "The end of this sickness will not be death. No, this sickness is for the glory* of God. This has happened to bring glory to the Son of God." ⁵Jesus loved Martha and her sister and Lazarus. ⁶So when he heard that Lazarus was sick, he stayed where he was two more days ⁷and then said to his followers, "We should go back to Judea."

⁸They answered, "But Teacher, those Jews there tried to stone you to death. That was

---

ᵃ**10:16** *I have other sheep … shepherd* Jesus means he has followers who are not Jews. See Jn. 11:52.
ᵇ**10:22** *Festival of Dedication* Hanukkah, a special week in December celebrating the time in 165 B.C. when the Jerusalem Temple was made pure and ready again for Jewish worship.

ᶜ**10:29** *he … than all* Some Greek copies have "they are greater than all."
ᵈ**10:34** Quote from Ps. 82:6.

only a short time ago. Now you want to go back there?"

⁹Jesus answered, "There are twelve hours of light in the day. Whoever walks in the day will not stumble and fall because they can see with the light from the sun.ᵃ ¹⁰But whoever walks at night will stumble because there is no light."

¹¹Then Jesus said, "Our friend Lazarus is now sleeping, but I am going there to wake him."

¹²The followers answered, "But, Lord, if he can sleep, he will get well." ¹³They thought Jesus meant that Lazarus was literally sleeping, but he really meant that Lazarus was dead.

¹⁴So then Jesus said plainly, "Lazarus is dead. ¹⁵And I am glad I was not there. I am happy for you because now you will believe in me. We will go to him now."

¹⁶Then Thomas, the one called "Twin," said to the other followers, "We will go too. We will die there with Jesus."

Jesus in Bethany

¹⁷Jesus arrived in Bethany and found that Lazarus had already been dead and in the tomb* for four days. ¹⁸Bethany was about two milesᵇ from Jerusalem. ¹⁹Many Jews had come to see Martha and Mary. They came to comfort them about their brother Lazarus.

²⁰When Martha heard that Jesus was coming, she went out to greet him. But Mary stayed home. ²¹Martha said to Jesus, "Lord, if you had been here, my brother would not have died. ²²But I know that even now God will give you anything you ask."

²³Jesus said, "Your brother will rise and be alive again."

²⁴Martha answered, "I know that he will rise to live again at the time of the resurrection* on the last day."

²⁵Jesus said to her, "I am the resurrection. I am life. Everyone who believes in me will have life, even if they die. ²⁶And everyone who lives and believes in me will never really die. Martha, do you believe this?"

²⁷Martha answered, "Yes, Lord. I believe that you are the Christ,* the Son of God. You are the one who was coming to the world."

Jesus Cries

²⁸After Martha said these things, she went back to her sister Mary. She talked to Mary alone and said, "The Teacher is here. He is asking for you." ²⁹When Mary heard this, she stood up and went quickly to Jesus. ³⁰He had not yet come into the village. He was still at the place where Martha met him. ³¹The Jews who were in the house comforting Mary saw her get up and leave quickly. They thought she was going to the tomb* to cry there. So they

followed her. ³²Mary went to the place where Jesus was. When she saw him, she bowed at his feet and said, "Lord, if you had been here, my brother would not have died."

³³When Jesus saw Mary crying and the people with her crying too, he was very upset and deeply troubled. ³⁴He asked, "Where did you put him?"

They said, "Lord, come and see."

³⁵Jesus cried.

³⁶And the Jews said, "Look! He loved Lazarus very much!"

³⁷But some of them said, "Jesus healed the eyes of the blind man. Why didn't he help Lazarus and stop him from dying?"

Jesus Raises Lazarus From Death

³⁸Again feeling very upset, Jesus came to the tomb.* It was a cave with a large stone covering the entrance. ³⁹He said, "Move the stone away."

Martha said, "But, Lord, it has been four days since Lazarus died. There will be a bad smell." Martha was the sister of the dead man.

⁴⁰Then Jesus said to her, "Remember what I told you? I said that if you believed, you would see God's divine greatness.*"

⁴¹So they moved the stone away from the entrance. Then Jesus looked up and said, "Father, I thank you that you heard me. ⁴²I know that you always hear me. But I said these things because of the people here around me. I want them to believe that you sent me." ⁴³After Jesus said this he called in a loud voice, "Lazarus, come out!" ⁴⁴The dead man came out. His hands and feet were wrapped with pieces of cloth. He had a handkerchief covering his face.

Jesus said to the people, "Take off the cloth and let him go."

The Jewish Leaders Plan to Kill Jesus
(Mt. 26:1–5; Mk. 14:1–2; Lk. 22:1–2)

⁴⁵There were many Jews who came to visit Mary. When they saw what Jesus did, many of them believed in him. ⁴⁶But some of them went to the Pharisees* and told them what Jesus did. ⁴⁷Then the leading priests and Pharisees called a meeting of the high council. They said, "What should we do? This man is doing many miraculous signs.* ⁴⁸If we let him continue doing these things, everyone will believe in him. Then the Romans will come and take away our Temple* and our nation."

⁴⁹One of the men there was Caiaphas. He was the high priest* that year. He said, "You people know nothing! ⁵⁰It is better for one man to die for the people than for the whole nation to be destroyed. But you don't realize this."

⁵¹Caiaphas did not think of this himself. As that year's high priest, he was really prophesying* that Jesus would die for the Jewish people. ⁵²Yes, he would die for the Jewish people.

ᵃ11:9 from the sun Literally, "of this world."
ᵇ11:18 two miles Literally, "15 stadia," almost 3 km.

But he would also die for God's other children scattered all over the world. He would die to bring them all together and make them one people.

⁵³That day the Jewish leaders began planning to kill Jesus. ⁵⁴So Jesus stopped traveling around openly among the Jews. He went away to a town called Ephraim in an area near the desert. He stayed there with his followers.

⁵⁵It was almost time for the Jewish Passover* festival. Many people from the country went to Jerusalem before the Passover. They went to do the special things to make themselves pure for the festival. ⁵⁶The people looked for Jesus. They stood in the Temple area and asked each other, "Is he coming to the festival? What do you think?" ⁵⁷But the leading priests and the Pharisees had given a special order about Jesus. They said that anyone who knew where he was must tell them so that they could arrest him.

Jesus in Bethany With His Friends
(Mt. 26:6–13; Mk. 14:3–9)

12 ¹Six days before the Passover* festival, Jesus went to Bethany. That is where Lazarus lived, the man Jesus raised from death. ²There they had a dinner for Jesus. Martha served the food, and Lazarus was one of the people eating with Jesus. ³Mary brought in a pintᵃ of expensive perfume made of pure nard.* She poured the perfume on Jesus' feet. Then she wiped his feet with her hair. And the sweet smell from the perfume filled the whole house.

⁴Judas Iscariot, one of Jesus' followers, was there—the one who would later hand Jesus over to his enemies. Judas said, ⁵"That perfume was worth a full year's pay.ᵇ It should have been sold, and the money should have been given to the poor people." ⁶But Judas did not really care about the poor. He said this because he was a thief. He was the one who kept the moneybag for the group of followers. And he often stole money from the bag.

⁷Jesus answered, "Don't stop her. It was right for her to save this perfume for today—the day for me to be prepared for burial. ⁸You will always have those who are poor with you.ᶜ But you will not always have me."

The Plot Against Lazarus
⁹Many of the Jews heard that Jesus was in Bethany, so they went there to see him. They also went there to see Lazarus, the one Jesus raised from death. ¹⁰So the leading priests made plans to kill Lazarus too. ¹¹Because of him, many Jews were leaving them and

believing in Jesus. That is why they wanted to kill Lazarus too.

Jesus Enters Jerusalem Like a King
(Mt. 21:1–11; Mk. 11:1–11; Lk. 19:28–40)

¹²The next day the people in Jerusalem heard that Jesus was coming there. These were the crowds of people who had come to the Passover* festival. ¹³They took branches of palm trees and went out to meet Jesus. They shouted,

"'Praiseᵈ Him!'
'Welcome! God bless the one who comes in the name of the Lord!'
Psalm 118:25–26

God bless the King of Israel!"

¹⁴Jesus found a donkey and rode on it, as the Scriptures* say,

¹⁵"Do not be afraid, people of Zionᵉ!
Look! Your king is coming.
He is riding on a young donkey."
Zechariah 9:9

¹⁶The followers of Jesus did not understand at that time what was happening. But after he was raised to glory,* they understood that this was written about him. Then they remembered that they had done these things for him.

¹⁷There were many people with Jesus when he raised Lazarus from death and told him to come out of the tomb.* Now they were telling others about what Jesus did. ¹⁸That's why so many people went out to meet him—because they had heard about this miraculous sign* he did. ¹⁹So the Pharisees* said to each other, "Look! Our plan is not working. The people are all following him!"

Jesus Talks About Life and Death
²⁰There were some Greeks* there too. These were some of the people who went to Jerusalem to worship at the Passover* festival. ²¹They went to Philip, who was from Bethsaida in Galilee. They said, "Sir, we want to meet Jesus." ²²Philip went and told Andrew. Then Andrew and Philip went and told Jesus.

²³Jesus said to them, "The time has come for the Son of Man* to receive his glory.* ²⁴It is a fact that a grain of wheat must fall to the ground and die before it can grow and produce much more wheat. If it never dies, it will never be more than a single seed. ²⁵Whoever

---

ᵃ**12:3 pint** Literally, "litra," a Roman pound, equal to 327 grams (11.5 ounces).
ᵇ**12:5 a full year's pay** Literally, "300 denarii (silver coins)." One coin, a Roman denarius, was the average pay for one day's work.
ᶜ**12:8 You will … with you** See Deut. 15:11.

ᵈ**12:13 Praise** Literally, "Hosanna," a Hebrew word used in praying to God for help. Here, it was probably a shout of celebration used in praising God or his Messiah.
ᵉ**12:15 people of Zion** Literally, "daughter of Zion," meaning the city of Jerusalem. See "Zion" in the Word List.

loves the life they have now will lose it. But whoever is willing to give up their life in this world will keep it. They will have eternal life. 26Whoever serves me must follow me. My servants must be with me everywhere I am. My Father will give honor to anyone who serves me.

Jesus Talks About His Death

27"Now I am very troubled. What should I say? Should I say, 'Father save me from this time of suffering'? No, I came to this time so that I could suffer. 28Father, do what will bring you glory*!"

Then a voice came from heaven, "I have already brought glory to myself. I will do it again."

29The people standing there heard the voice. They said it was thunder.

But others said, "An angel spoke to him!"

30Jesus said, "That voice was for you and not for me. 31Now is the time for the world to be judged. Now the ruler of this world* will be thrown out. 32I will be lifted up*a* from the earth. When that happens, I will draw all people to myself." 33Jesus said this to show how he would die.

34The people said, "But our law says that the Christ* will live forever. So why do you say, 'The Son of Man* must be lifted up'? Who is this 'Son of Man'?"

35Then Jesus said, "The light*b* will be with you for only a short time more. So walk while you have the light. Then the darkness* will not catch you. People who walk in the darkness don't know where they are going. 36So put your trust in the light while you still have it. Then you will be children of light." When Jesus finished saying these things, he went away to a place where the people could not find him.

Some Jews Refuse to Believe in Jesus

37The people saw all these miraculous signs* Jesus did, but they still did not believe in him. 38This was to give full meaning to what Isaiah the prophet* said:

"Lord, who believed what we told them? Who has seen the Lord's power?"
Isaiah 53:1

39This is why the people could not believe. Because Isaiah also said,

40"God made the people blind. He closed their minds.

He did this so that they would not see with their eyes and understand with their minds.
He did it so that they would not turn and be healed."
Isaiah 6:10

41Isaiah said this because he saw Jesus' divine greatness.* So he spoke about him.

42But many people believed in Jesus. Even many of the Jewish leaders believed in him, but they were afraid of the Pharisees,* so they did not say openly that they believed. They were afraid they would be ordered to stay out of the synagogue.* 43They loved praise from people more than praise from God.

Jesus' Teaching Will Judge People

44Then Jesus said loudly, "Everyone who believes in me is really believing in the one who sent me. 45Everyone who sees me is really seeing the one who sent me. 46I came into this world as a light. I came so that everyone who believes in me will not stay in darkness.

47"I did not come into the world to judge people. I came to save the people in the world. So I am not the one who judges those who hear my teaching and do not obey. 48But there is a judge for all those who refuse to believe in me and do not accept what I say. The message I have spoken will judge them on the last day. 49That is because what I taught was not from myself. The Father who sent me told me what to say and what to teach. 50And I know that whatever he says to do will bring eternal life. So the things I say are exactly what the Father told me to say."

Jesus Washes His Followers' Feet

13 1It was almost time for the Jewish Passover* festival. Jesus knew that the time had come for him to leave this world and go back to the Father. Jesus had always loved the people in the world who were his. Now was the time he showed them his love the most.

2Jesus and his followers were at the evening meal. The devil had already persuaded Judas Iscariot to hand Jesus over to his enemies. (Judas was the son of Simon.) 3The Father had given Jesus power over everything. Jesus knew this. He also knew that he had come from God. And he knew that he was going back to God. 4So while they were eating, Jesus stood up and took off his robe. He got a towel and wrapped it around his waist. 5Then he poured water into a bowl and began to wash the followers' feet.*c* He dried their feet with the towel that was wrapped around his waist.

6He came to Simon Peter. But Peter said to him, "Lord, you should not wash my feet."

---

*a***12:32** *lifted up* Meaning to be nailed to a cross and "lifted up" on it to die. It may also have a second meaning: to be "lifted up" from death to heaven. Also in verse 34.

*b***12:35** *light* This means Christ, as in Jn. 1:5–9. Also, it is a symbol of goodness and truth, qualities associated with Christ and his kingdom.

*c***13:5** *wash ... feet* A social custom of the first century, because people wore open sandals on very dusty roads. It was a humble duty, usually done by a servant. Also in verses 6–14.

⁷Jesus answered, "You don't know what I am doing now. But later you will understand."

⁸Peter said, "No! You will never wash my feet."

Jesus answered, "If I don't wash your feet, you are not one of my people."

⁹Simon Peter said, "Lord, after you wash my feet, wash my hands and my head too!"

¹⁰Jesus said, "After a person has a bath, his whole body is clean. He needs only to wash his feet. And you are clean, but not all of you." ¹¹Jesus knew who would hand him over to his enemies. That is why he said, "Not all of you are clean."

¹²When Jesus finished washing their feet, he put on his clothes and went back to the table. He asked, "Do you understand what I did for you? ¹³You call me 'Teacher.' And you call me 'Lord.' And this is right, because that is what I am. ¹⁴I am your Lord and Teacher. But I washed your feet. So you also should wash each other's feet. ¹⁵I did this as an example for you. So you should serve each other just as I served you. ¹⁶Believe me, servants are not greater than their master. Those who are sent to do something are not greater than the one who sent them. ¹⁷If you know these things, great blessings will be yours if you do them.

¹⁸"I am not talking about all of you. I know the people I have chosen. But what the Scriptures* say must happen: 'The man who shared my food has turned against me.'ᵃ ¹⁹I am telling you this now before it happens. Then when it happens, you will believe that I AM.ᵇ ²⁰I assure you, whoever accepts the person I send also accepts me. And whoever accepts me also accepts the one who sent me."

Jesus Tells Who Will Turn Against Him
(Mt. 26:20–25; Mk. 14:17–21; Lk. 22:21–23)

²¹After Jesus said these things, he felt very troubled. He said openly, "Believe me when I say that one of you will hand me over to my enemies."

²²His followers all looked at each other. They did not understand who Jesus was talking about. ²³One of the followers was next to Jesus and was leaning close to him. This was the one Jesus loved very much. ²⁴Simon Peter made signs to this follower to ask Jesus who he was talking about.

²⁵That follower leaned closer to Jesus and asked, "Lord, who is it?"

²⁶Jesus answered him, "I will dip this bread into the dish. The man I give it to is the one." So Jesus took a piece of bread, dipped it, and gave it to Judas Iscariot, the son of Simon. ²⁷When Judas took the bread, Satan* entered him. Jesus said to Judas, "What you will do—do it quickly!" ²⁸No one at the table understood

why Jesus said this to Judas. ²⁹Since Judas was the one in charge of the money, some of them thought that Jesus meant for him to go and buy some things they needed for the feast. Or they thought that Jesus wanted him to go give something to the poor.

³⁰Judas ate the bread Jesus gave him. Then he immediately went out. It was night.

Jesus Talks About His Death

³¹When Judas was gone, Jesus said, "Now is the time for the Son of Man* to receive his glory.* And God will receive glory through him. ³²If God receives glory through him, he will give glory to the Son through himself. And that will happen very soon."

³³Jesus said, "My children, I will be with you only a short time more. You will look for me, but I tell you now what I told the Jewish leaders: Where I am going you cannot come. ³⁴I give you a new command: Love each other. You must love each other just as I loved you. ³⁵All people will know that you are my followers if you love each other."

Jesus Says Peter Will Deny Him
(Mt. 26:31–35; Mk. 14:27–31; Lk. 22:31–34)

³⁶Simon Peter asked Jesus, "Lord, where are you going?"

Jesus answered, "Where I am going you cannot follow now. But you will follow later."

³⁷Peter asked, "Lord, why can't I follow you now? I am ready to die for you!"

³⁸Jesus answered, "Will you really give your life for me? The truth is, before the rooster crows, you will say three times that you don't know me."

Jesus Comforts His Followers

14 ¹Jesus said, "Don't be troubled. Trust in God, and trust in me. ²There are many rooms in my Father's house. I would not tell you this if it were not true. I am going there to prepare a place for you. ³After I go and prepare a place for you, I will come back. Then I will take you with me, so that you can be where I am. ⁴You know the way to the place where I am going."

⁵Thomas said, "Lord, we don't know where you are going, so how can we know the way?"

⁶Jesus answered, "I am the way, the truth, and the life. The only way to the Father is through me. ⁷If you really knew me, you would know my Father too. But now you know the Father. You have seen him."

⁸Philip said to him, "Lord, show us the Father. That is all we need."

⁹Jesus answered, "Philip, I have been with you for a long time. So you should know me. Anyone who has seen me has seen the Father too. So why do you say, 'Show us the Father'? ¹⁰Don't you believe that I am in the Father and the Father is in me? The things I have told you don't come from me. The Father lives in

ᵃ**13:18 has turned against me** Literally, "has lifted up his heel against me." Quote from Ps. 41:9.
ᵇ**13:19 I AM** This is like the name of God used in the Old Testament. See Isa. 41:4; 43:10; Ex. 3:14. However, it can also mean "I am he (the Christ)."

me, and he is doing his own work. [11]Believe me when I say that I am in the Father and the Father is in me. Or believe because of the miracles* I have done.

[12]"I can assure you that whoever believes in me will do the same things I have done. And they will do even greater things than I have done, because I am going to the Father. [13]And if you ask for anything in my name, I will do it for you. Then the Father's glory* will be shown through the Son. [14]If you ask me for anything in my name, I will do it.

The Promise of the Holy Spirit

[15]"If you love me, you will do what I command. [16]I will ask the Father, and he will give you another Helper[a] to be with you forever. [17]The Helper is the Spirit of truth.[b] The people of the world cannot accept him, because they don't see him or know him. But you know him. He lives with you, and he will be in you.

[18]"I will not leave you all alone like orphans. I will come back to you. [19]In a very short time the people in the world will not see me anymore. But you will see me. You will live because I live. [20]On that day you will know that I am in the Father. You will know that you are in me and I am in you. [21]Those who really love me are the ones who not only know my commands but also obey them. My Father will love such people, and I will love them. I will make myself known to them."

[22]Then Judas (not Judas Iscariot) said, "Lord, how will you make yourself known to us, but not to the world?"

[23]Jesus answered, "All who love me will obey my teaching. My Father will love them. My Father and I will come to them and live with them. [24]But anyone who does not love me does not obey my teaching. This teaching that you hear is not really mine. It is from my Father who sent me.

[25]"I have told you all these things while I am with you. [26]But the Helper will teach you everything and cause you to remember all that I told you. This Helper is the Holy Spirit* that the Father will send in my name. [27]"I leave you peace. It is my own peace I give you. I give you peace in a different way than the world does. So don't be troubled. Don't be afraid. [28]You heard me say to you, 'I am leaving, but I will come back to you.' If you loved me, you would be happy that I am going back to the Father, because the Father is greater than I am. [29]I have told you this now, before it happens. Then when it happens, you will believe.

[30]"I will not talk with you much longer. The ruler of this world* is coming. He has no power over me. [31]But the world must know that I love the Father. So I do exactly what the Father told me to do.

"Come now, let's go."

Jesus Is Like a Vine

15 [1]Jesus said, "I am the true vine, and my Father is the gardener. [2]He cuts off every branch[c] of mine that does not produce fruit.[d] He also trims every branch that produces fruit to prepare it to produce even more. [3]You have already been prepared to produce more fruit by the teaching I have given you. [4]Stay joined to me and I will stay joined to you. No branch can produce fruit alone. It must stay connected to the vine. It is the same with you. You cannot produce fruit alone. You must stay joined to me.

[5]"I am the vine, and you are the branches. If you stay joined to me, and I to you, you will produce plenty of fruit. But separated from me you won't be able to do anything. [6]If you don't stay joined to me, you will be like a branch that has been thrown out and has dried up. All the dead branches like that are gathered up, thrown into the fire and burned. [7]Stay joined together with me, and follow my teachings. If you do this, you can ask for anything you want, and it will be given to you. [8]Show that you are my followers by producing much fruit. This will bring honor[e] to my Father.

[9]"I have loved you as the Father has loved me. Now continue in my love. [10]I have obeyed my Father's commands, and he continues to love me. In the same way, if you obey my commands, I will continue to love you. [11]I have told you these things so that you can have the true happiness that I have. I want you to be completely happy. [12]This is what I command you: Love each other as I have loved you. [13]The greatest love people can show is to die for their friends. [14]You are my friends if you do what I tell you to do. [15]I no longer call you servants, because servants don't know what their master is doing. But now I call you friends, because I have told you everything that my Father told me.

[16]"You did not choose me. I chose you. And I gave you this work: to go and produce fruit—fruit that will last. Then the Father will give you anything you ask for in my name. [17]This is my command: Love each other.

Jesus Warns His Followers

[18]"If the world hates you, remember that they hated me first. [19]If you belonged to the world, the world would love you as it loves its own people. But I have chosen you to be

---

[a]**14:16** *Helper* Or "Comforter," the Holy Spirit (see "Holy Spirit" in the Word List). Also in verse 26.

[b]**14:17** *Spirit of truth* The Holy Spirit (see "Holy Spirit" in the Word List). It was his work to help Jesus' followers understand God's truth. See Jn. 16:13.

[c]**15:2** *branch* The "branches" are Jesus' followers. See verse 5.

[d]**15:2** *produce fruit* Meaning the way Jesus' followers must live to show they belong to him. See verses 7–10.

[e]**15:8** *honor* Or "glory." See "glory" in the Word List.

different from those in the world. So you don't belong to the world, and that is why the world hates you.

20"Remember the lesson I told you: Servants are not greater than their master. If people treated me badly, they will treat you badly too. And if they obeyed my teaching, they will obey yours too. 21They will do to you whatever they did to me, because you belong to me. They don't know the one who sent me. 22If I had not come and spoken to the people of the world, they would not be guilty of sin. But now I have spoken to them. So they have no excuse for their sin.

23"Whoever hates me also hates my Father. 24I did things among the people of the world that no one else has ever done. If I had not done those things, they would not be guilty of sin. But they have seen what I did, and still they hate me and my Father. 25But this happened to make clear the full meaning of what is written in their law: 'They hated me for no reason.'*a*

26"I will send you the Helper*b* from the Father. The Helper is the Spirit of truth*c* who comes from the Father. When he comes, he will tell about me. 27And you will tell people about me too, because you have been with me from the beginning.

16
1"I have told you all this so that you won't lose your faith when you face troubles. 2People will tell you to leave their synagogues* and never come back. In fact, the time will come when they will think that killing you would be doing service for God. 3They will do this because they have not known the Father, and they have not known me. 4I have told you all this now to prepare you. So when the time comes for these things to happen, you will remember that I warned you.

The Work of the Holy Spirit

"I did not tell you these things at the beginning, because I was with you then. 5Now I am going back to the one who sent me. And none of you asks me, 'Where are you going?' 6But you are filled with sadness because I have told you all this. 7Let me assure you, it is better for you that I go away. I say this because when I go away I will send the Helper to you. But if I did not go, the Helper would not come.

8"When the Helper comes, he will show the people of the world how wrong they are about sin, about being right with God, and about judgment. 9He will prove that they are guilty of sin, because they don't believe in me. 10He will show them how wrong they are about how to be right with God. The Helper will do this, because I am going to the Father.

You will not see me then. 11And he will show them how wrong their judgment is, because their leader*d* has already been condemned.

12"I have so much more to tell you, but it is too much for you to accept now. 13But when the Spirit* of truth comes, he will lead you into all truth. He will not speak his own words. He will speak only what he hears and will tell you what will happen in the future. 14The Spirit of truth will bring glory* to me by telling you what he receives from me. 15All that the Father has is mine. That is why I said that the Spirit will tell you what he receives from me.

Sadness Will Turn Into Happiness

16"After a short time you won't see me. Then after another short time you will see me again."

17Some of the followers said to each other, "What does he mean when he says, 'After a short time you won't see me. Then after another short time you will see me again'? And what does he mean when he says, 'Because I am going to the Father'?" 18They also asked, "What does he mean by 'a short time'? We don't understand what he is saying."

19Jesus saw that the followers wanted to ask him about this. So he said to them, "Are you asking each other what I meant when I said, 'After a short time you won't see me. Then after another short time you will see me again'? 20The truth is, you will cry and be sad, but the world will be happy. You will be sad, but then your sadness will change to happiness.

21"When a woman gives birth to a baby, she has pain, because her time has come. But when her baby is born, she forgets the pain. She forgets because she is so happy that a child has been born into the world. 22It is the same with you. Now you are sad, but I will see you again, and you will be happy. You will have a joy that no one can take away. 23In that day you will not have to ask me about anything. And I assure you, my Father will give you anything you ask him for in my name. 24You have never asked for anything in this way before. But ask in my name, and you will receive. And you will have the fullest joy possible.

Victory Over the World

25"I have told you these things, using words that hide the meaning. But the time will come when I will not use words like that to tell you things. I will speak to you in plain words about the Father. 26Then you will be able to ask the Father for things in my name. I'm not saying that I will have to ask the Father for you. 27The Father himself loves you because you have loved me. And he loves you because

---

*a*15:25 *'They hated me for no reason'* These words could be from Ps. 35:19 or Ps. 69:4.
*b*15:26 *Helper* Or "Comforter." Also in 16:7, 8.
*c*15:26 *Spirit of truth* The Holy Spirit (see "Holy Spirit" in the Word List). It was his work to help Jesus' followers understand God's truth. See Jn. 16:13.

*d*16:11 *their leader* Literally, "the ruler of this world," meaning Satan. See "Satan" in the Word List.

you have believed that I came from God. ²⁸I came from the Father into the world. Now I am leaving the world and going back to the Father."

²⁹Then his followers said, "You are already speaking plainly to us. You are not using words that hide the meaning. ³⁰We can see now that you know all things. You answer our questions even before we ask them. This makes us believe that you came from God."

³¹Jesus said, "So now you believe? ³²Listen to me. A time is coming when you will be scattered, each to his own home. In fact, that time is already here. You will leave me, and I will be alone. But I am never really alone, because the Father is with me.

³³"I have told you these things so that you can have peace in me. In this world you will have troubles. But be brave! I have defeated the world!"

Jesus Prays for Himself and His Followers

17 ¹After Jesus said these things, he looked toward heaven and prayed, "Father, the time has come. Give glory* to your Son so that the Son can give glory to you. ²You gave the Son power over all people so that he could give eternal life to all those you have given to him. ³And this is eternal life: that people can know you, the only true God, and that they can know Jesus Christ, the one you sent. ⁴I finished the work you gave me to do. I brought you glory on earth. ⁵And now, Father, give me glory with you. Give me the glory I had with you before the world was made.

⁶"You gave me some people from the world. I have shown them what you are like. They belonged to you, and you gave them to me. They have obeyed your teaching. ⁷Now they know that everything I have came from you. ⁸I told them the words you gave me, and they accepted them. They realized the fact that I came from you and believed that you sent me. ⁹I pray for them now. I am not praying for the people in the world. But I am praying for these people you gave me, because they are yours. ¹⁰All I have is yours, and all you have is mine. And my glory is seen in them.

¹¹"Now I am coming to you. I will not stay in the world, but these followers of mine are still in the world. Holy Father, keep them safe by the power of your name—the name you gave me. Then they will be one, just as you and I are one. ¹²While I was with them, I kept them safe by the power of your name—the name you gave me. I protected them. And only one of them was lost—the one who was sure to be lost. This was to show the truth of what the Scriptures* said would happen.

¹³"I am coming to you now. But I pray these things while I am still in the world. I say all this so that these followers can have the true happiness that I have. I want them to be completely happy. ¹⁴I have given them your teaching. And the world has hated them, because they don't belong to the world, just as I don't belong to the world.

¹⁵"I am not asking you to take them out of the world. But I am asking that you keep them safe from the Evil One.* ¹⁶They don't belong to the world, just as I don't belong to the world. ¹⁷Make them ready for your service through your truth. Your teaching is truth. ¹⁸I have sent them into the world, just as you sent me into the world. ¹⁹I am making myself completely ready to serve you. I do this for them, so that they also might be fully qualified for your service.

²⁰"I pray not only for these followers but also for those who will believe in me because of their teaching. ²¹Father, I pray that all who believe in me can be one. You are in me and I am in you. I pray that they can also be one in us. Then the world will believe that you sent me. ²²I have given them the glory that you gave me. I gave them this glory so that they can be one, just as you and I are one. ²³I will be in them, and you will be in me. So they will be completely one. Then the world will know that you sent me and that you loved them just as you loved me.

²⁴"Father, I want these people you have given me to be with me in every place I am. I want them to see my glory—the glory you gave me because you loved me before the world was made. ²⁵Father, you are the one who always does what is right. The world does not know you, but I know you, and these followers of mine know that you sent me. ²⁶I showed them what you are like, and I will show them again. Then they will have the same love that you have for me, and I will live in them."

Jesus Is Arrested
(Mt. 26:47–56; Mk. 14:43–50; Lk. 22:47–53)

18 ¹When Jesus finished praying, he left with his followers and went across the Kidron Valley. He went into a garden there, his followers still with him.

²Judas, the one responsible for handing Jesus over, knew where this place was. He knew because Jesus often met there with his followers. ³So Judas led a group of soldiers to the garden, along with some guards from the leading priests and the Pharisees.* They were carrying torches, lanterns, and weapons.

⁴Jesus already knew everything that would happen to him. So he went out and asked them, "Who are you looking for?"

⁵They answered, "Jesus from Nazareth."

He said, "I am Jesus."^a (Judas, the one responsible for handing Jesus over, was standing there with them.) ⁶When Jesus said, "I am Jesus," the men moved back and fell to the ground.

---

^a**18:5** *"I am Jesus"* Literally, "I am," which could have the same meaning here that it has in 8:24, 28, 58; 13:19. Also in verse 8.

[7]He asked them again, "Who are you looking for?"

They said, "Jesus from Nazareth."

[8]Jesus said, "I told you that I am Jesus. So if you are looking for me, let these other men go free." [9]This was to show the truth of what Jesus said earlier: "I have not lost anyone you gave me."

[10]Simon Peter had a sword, which he pulled out. He struck the servant of the high priest* and cut off his right ear. (The servant's name was Malchus.) [11]Jesus said to Peter, "Put your sword back in its place! I must drink from the cup[a] the Father has given me."

Jesus Is Brought Before Annas
(Mt. 26:57–58; Mk. 14:53–54; Lk. 22:54)

[12]Then the soldiers with their commander and the Jewish guards arrested Jesus. They tied him [13]and brought him to Annas, the father-in-law of Caiaphas. Caiaphas was the high priest* that year. [14]He was also the one who had told the other Jewish leaders that it would be better if one man died for all the people.

Peter Lies About Knowing Jesus
(Mt. 26:69–70; Mk. 14:66–68; Lk. 22:55–57)

[15]Simon Peter and another one of Jesus' followers went with Jesus. This follower knew the high priest.* So he went with Jesus into the yard of the high priest's house. [16]But Peter waited outside near the door. The follower who knew the high priest came back outside and spoke to the gatekeeper. Then he brought Peter inside. [17]The girl at the gate said to Peter, "Are you also one of the followers of that man?"

Peter answered, "No, I am not!"

[18]It was cold, so the servants and guards had built a fire. They were standing around it, warming themselves, and Peter was standing with them.

The High Priest Questions Jesus
(Mt. 26:59–66; Mk. 14:55–64; Lk. 22:66–71)

[19]The high priest* asked Jesus questions about his followers and what he taught them. [20]Jesus answered, "I have always spoken openly to all people. I always taught in the synagogues* and in the Temple* area. All the Jews come together there. I never said anything in secret. [21]So why do you question me? Ask the people who heard my teaching. They know what I said."

[22]When Jesus said this, one of the guards standing there hit him. The guard said, "You should not talk to the high priest like that!"

[23]Jesus answered, "If I said something wrong, tell everyone here what was wrong. But if what I said is right, then why do you hit me?"

[24]So Annas sent Jesus to Caiaphas the high priest. He was still tied.

Peter Lies Again
(Mt. 26:71–75; Mk. 14:69–72; Lk. 22:58–62)

[25]Simon Peter was standing at the fire, keeping himself warm. The other people said to Peter, "Aren't you one of the followers of that man?"

Peter denied it. He said, "No, I am not."

[26]One of the servants of the high priest* was there. He was a relative of the man whose ear Peter had cut off. The servant said, "I think I saw you with him in the garden!"

[27]But again Peter said, "No, I was not with him!" As soon as he said this, a rooster crowed.

Jesus Is Brought Before Pilate
(Mt. 27:1–2, 11–31; Mk. 15:1–20; Lk. 23:1–25)

[28]Then the guards took Jesus from Caiaphas' house to the Roman governor's palace. It was early in the morning. The Jews there would not go inside the palace. They did not want to make themselves unclean,[b] because they wanted to eat the Passover* meal. [29]So Pilate* went outside to them and asked, "What do you say this man has done wrong?"

[30]They answered, "He is a bad man. That is why we brought him to you."

[31]Pilate said to them, "You take him yourselves and judge him by your own law."

The Jewish leaders answered, "But our law does not allow us to punish anyone by killing them." [32](This was to show the truth of what Jesus said about how he would die.)

[33]Then Pilate went back inside the palace. He called for Jesus and asked him, "Are you the king of the Jews?"

[34]Jesus said, "Is that your own question, or did other people tell you about me?"

[35]Pilate said, "I'm not a Jew! It was your own people and their leading priests who brought you before me. What have you done wrong?"

[36]Jesus said, "My kingdom does not belong to this world. If it did, my servants would fight so that I would not be handed over to the Jewish leaders. No, my kingdom is not an earthly one."

[37]Pilate said, "So you are a king."

Jesus answered, "You are right to say that I am a king. I was born for this: to tell people about the truth. That is why I came into the world. And everyone who belongs to the truth listens to me."

[38]Pilate said, "What is truth?" Then he went out to the Jewish leaders again and said to them, "I can find nothing against this man. [39]But it is one of your customs for me to free one prisoner to you at the time of the

---

[a]**18:11** *cup* A symbol of suffering. Jesus used the idea of drinking from a cup to mean accepting the suffering he would face in the terrible events that were soon to come.

[b]**18:28** *unclean* Going into a non-Jewish place would ruin the special cleansing the Jews did to make themselves fit for worship. See Jn. 11:55.

Passover. Do you want me to free this 'king of the Jews'?"

⁴⁰They shouted back, "No, not him! Let Barabbas go free!" (Barabbas was a rebel.)

19

¹Then Pilate ordered that Jesus be taken away and whipped. ²The soldiers made a crown from thorny branches and put it on his head. Then they put a purple robe around him. ³They kept coming up to him and saying, "Hail to the king of the Jews!" And they hit him in the face.

⁴Again Pilate came out and said to the Jewish leaders, "Look! I am bringing Jesus out to you. I want you to know that I find nothing I can charge him with." ⁵Then Jesus came out wearing the crown of thorns and the purple robe. Pilate said to the Jews, "Here is the man!"

⁶When the leading priests and the Jewish guards saw Jesus they shouted, "Kill him on a cross! Kill him on a cross!"

But Pilate answered, "You take him and nail him to a cross yourselves. I find nothing I can charge him with."

⁷The Jewish leaders answered, "We have a law that says he must die, because he said he is the Son of God."

⁸When Pilate heard this, he was more afraid. ⁹So he went back inside the palace and asked Jesus, "Where are you from?" But Jesus did not answer him. ¹⁰Pilate said, "You refuse to speak to me? Remember, I have the power to make you free or to kill you on a cross."

¹¹Jesus answered, "The only power you have over me is the power given to you by God. So the one who handed me over to you is guilty of a greater sin."

¹²After this, Pilate tried to let Jesus go free. But the Jewish leaders shouted, "Anyone who makes himself a king is against Caesar.* So if you let this man go free, that means you are not Caesar's friend."

¹³When Pilate heard this, he brought Jesus out to the place called "The Stone Pavement." (In Aramaic* the name is *Gabbatha.*) Pilate sat down on the judge's seat there. ¹⁴It was now almost noon on Preparation day* of Passover week. Pilate said to the Jews, "Here is your king!"

¹⁵They shouted, "Take him away! Take him away! Kill him on a cross!"

Pilate asked them, "Do you want me to kill your king on a cross?"

The leading priests answered, "The only king we have is Caesar!"

¹⁶So Pilate handed Jesus over to them to be killed on a cross.

Jesus Is Nailed to a Cross
(Mt. 27:32–44; Mk. 15:21–32; Lk. 23:26–39)

The soldiers took Jesus. ¹⁷He carried his own cross to a place called "The Place of the Skull." (In Aramaic* the name of this place is "Golgotha.") ¹⁸There they nailed Jesus to the cross. They also nailed two other men to

crosses. They put them on each side of Jesus with him in the middle.

¹⁹Pilate* told them to write a sign and put it on the cross. The sign said, "JESUS OF NAZARETH, THE KING OF THE JEWS." ²⁰The sign was written in Aramaic, in Latin, and in Greek. Many of the Jews read this sign, because the place where Jesus was nailed to the cross was near the city.

²¹The leading Jewish priests said to Pilate, "Don't write, 'The King of the Jews.' But write, 'This man said, I am the King of the Jews.'"

²²Pilate answered, "I will not change what I have written."

²³After the soldiers nailed Jesus to the cross, they took his clothes and divided them into four parts. Each soldier got one part. They also took his tunic.* It was all one piece of cloth woven from top to bottom. ²⁴So the soldiers said to each other, "We should not tear this into parts. Let's throw lots* to see who will get it." This happened to make clear the full meaning of what the Scriptures* say:

> "They divided my clothes among them,
>   and they threw lots for what I was
>   wearing."   *Psalm 22:18*

So the soldiers did this.

²⁵Jesus' mother stood near his cross. Her sister was also standing there with Mary the wife of Clopas, and Mary Magdalene. ²⁶Jesus saw his mother. He also saw the follower he loved very much standing there. He said to his mother, "Dear woman, here is your son." ²⁷Then he said to the follower, "Here is your mother." So after that, this follower took Jesus' mother to live in his home.

Jesus Dies
(Mt. 27:45–56; Mk. 15:33–41; Lk. 23:44–49)

²⁸Later, Jesus knew that everything had been done. To make the Scriptures* come true he said, "I am thirsty."ᵃ ²⁹There was a jar full of sour wine there, so the soldiers soaked a sponge in it. They put the sponge on a branch of a hyssop plant and lifted it to Jesus' mouth. ³⁰When he tasted the wine, he said, "It is finished." Then he bowed his head and died.

³¹This day was Preparation day.* The next day was a special Sabbath* day. The Jewish leaders did not want the bodies to stay on the cross on the Sabbath day. So they asked Pilate* to order that the legs of the men be broken. And they asked that the bodies be taken down from the crosses. ³²So the soldiers came and broke the legsᵇ of the two men on the crosses beside Jesus. ³³But when the soldiers came close to Jesus, they saw that he was already dead. So they did not break his legs.

ᵃ19:28 *"I am thirsty"* See Ps. 22:15; 69:21.
ᵇ19:32 *broke the legs* The legs were broken to make those on the crosses die more quickly.

³⁴But one of the soldiers stuck his spear into Jesus' side. Immediately blood and water came out. ³⁵(The one who saw this happen has told about it. He told about it so that you also can believe. The things he says are true. He knows that he tells the truth.) ³⁶These things happened to give full meaning to the Scriptures that said, "None of his bones will be broken"ᵃ ³⁷and "People will look at the one they stabbed."ᵇ

Jesus Is Buried
(Mt. 27:57–61; Mk. 15:42–47; Lk. 23:50–56)

³⁸Later, a man named Joseph from Arimathea asked Pilate* for the body of Jesus. (Joseph was a follower of Jesus, but he did not tell anyone, because he was afraid of the Jewish leaders.) Pilate said Joseph could take Jesus' body, so he came and took it away.

³⁹Nicodemus went with Joseph. He was the man who had come to Jesus before and talked to him at night. He brought about 100 poundsᶜ of spices—a mixture of myrrh* and aloes.* ⁴⁰These two men took Jesus' body and wrapped it in pieces of linen cloth with the spices. (This is how the Jews bury people.) ⁴¹In the place where Jesus was killed on the cross, there was a garden. In the garden there was a new tomb.* No one had ever been buried there before. ⁴²The men put Jesus in that tomb because it was near, and the Jews were preparing to start their Sabbath* day.

News That Jesus Has Risen From Death
(Mt. 28:1–10; Mk. 16:1–8; Lk. 24:1–12)

20 ¹Early on Sunday morning, while it was still dark, Mary Magdalene went to the tomb.* She saw that the large stone was moved away from the entrance. ²So she ran to Simon Peter and the other follower (the one Jesus loved very much). She said, "They have taken the Lord out of the tomb, and we don't know where they put him."

³So Peter and the other follower started going to the tomb. ⁴They were both running, but the other follower ran faster than Peter and reached the tomb first. ⁵He bent down and looked in. He saw the pieces of linen cloth lying there, but he did not go in.

⁶Then Simon Peter finally reached the tomb and went in. He saw the pieces of linen lying there. ⁷He also saw the cloth that had been around Jesus' head. It was folded up and laid in a different place from the pieces of linen. ⁸Then the other follower went in—the one who had reached the tomb first. He saw what had happened and believed. ⁹(These followers did not yet understand from the Scriptures* that Jesus must rise from death.)

Jesus Appears to Mary Magdalene
(Mk. 16:9–11)

¹⁰Then the followers went back home. ¹¹But Mary stood outside the tomb,* crying. While she was crying, she bent down and looked inside the tomb. ¹²She saw two angels dressed in white sitting where Jesus' body had been. One was sitting where the head had been; the other was sitting where the feet had been.

¹³The angels asked Mary, "Woman, why are you crying?"

Mary answered, "They took away the body of my Lord, and I don't know where they put him." ¹⁴When Mary said this, she turned around and saw Jesus standing there. But she did not know that it was Jesus.

¹⁵He asked her, "Woman, why are you crying? Who are you looking for?"

She thought that this was the man who takes care of the garden. So she said to him, "Did you take him away, sir? Tell me where you put him. I will go and get him."

¹⁶Jesus said to her, "Mary."

She turned toward him and said in Aramaic,* "Rabboni," which means "Teacher."

¹⁷Jesus said to her, "You don't need to hold on to me! I have not yet gone back up to the Father. But go to my followersᵈ and tell them this: 'I am going back to my Father and your Father. I am going back to my God and your God.'"

¹⁸Mary Magdalene went to the followers and told them, "I saw the Lord!" And she told them what he had said to her.

Jesus Appears to His Followers
(Mt. 28:16–20; Mk. 16:14–18; Lk. 24:36–49)

¹⁹The day was Sunday, and that same evening the followers were together. They had the doors locked because they were afraid of the Jewish leaders. Suddenly, Jesus was standing there among them. He said, "Peace be with you!" ²⁰As soon as he said this, he showed them his hands and his side. When the followers saw the Lord, they were very happy.

²¹Then Jesus said again, "Peace be with you. It was the Father who sent me, and I am now sending you in the same way." ²²Then he breathed on them and said, "Receive the Holy Spirit.* ²³If you forgive the sins of anyone, their sins are forgiven. If there is anyone whose sins you don't forgive, their sins are not forgiven."

Jesus Appears to Thomas

²⁴Thomas (called Didymus) was one of the twelve, but he was not with the other followers when Jesus came. ²⁵They told him, "We saw the Lord." Thomas said, "That's hard to believe. I will have to see the nail holes in his hands, put my finger where the nails were, and put my hand into his side. Only then will I believe it."

ᵃ**19:36** Quote from Ps. 34:20. The idea is from Ex. 12:46; Num. 9:12.
ᵇ**19:37** Quote from Zech. 12:10.
ᶜ**19:39** *100 pounds* Literally, "100 *litras*" (Roman pounds), equal to 32.7 kg (72 pounds).
ᵈ**20:17** *followers* Literally, "brothers."

26A week later the followers were in the house again, and Thomas was with them. The doors were locked, but Jesus came and stood among them. He said, "Peace be with you!" 27Then he said to Thomas, "Put your finger here. Look at my hands. Put your hand here in my side. Stop doubting and believe."

28Thomas said to Jesus, "My Lord and my God!"

29Jesus said to him, "You believe because you see me. Great blessings belong to the people who believe without seeing me!"

Why John Wrote This Book

30Jesus did many other miraculous signs* that his followers saw, which are not written in this book. 31But these are written so that you can believe that Jesus is the Christ,* the Son of God. Then, by believing, you can have life through his name.

Jesus Appears to Seven Followers

21 1Later, Jesus appeared again to his followers by Lake Galilee.ᵃ This is how it happened: 2Some of the followers were together—Simon Peter, Thomas (called Didymus), Nathanael from Cana in Galilee, the two sons of Zebedee, and two other followers. 3Simon Peter said, "I am going out to fish."

The other followers said, "We will go with you." So all of them went out and got into the boat. They fished that night but caught nothing.

4Early the next morning Jesus stood on the shore. But the followers did not know it was Jesus. 5Then he said to them, "Friends, have you caught any fish?"

They answered, "No."

6He said, "Throw your net into the water on the right side of your boat. You will find some fish there." So they did this. They caught so many fish that they could not pull the net back into the boat.

7The follower Jesus loved very much said to Peter, "That man is the Lord!" When Peter heard him say it was the Lord, he wrapped his coat around himself. (He had taken his clothes off to work.) Then he jumped into the water. 8The other followers went to shore in the boat. They pulled the net full of fish. They were not very far from shore, only about 100 yards. 9When they stepped out of the boat and onto the shore, they saw a fire of hot coals. There were fish on the fire and some bread there too. 10Then Jesus said, "Bring some of the fish that you caught."

11Simon Peter got into the boat and pulled the net to the shore. It was full of big fish—153 of them! But even with that many fish, the net did not tear. 12Jesus said to them, "Come and eat." None of the followers would ask him, "Who are you?" They knew he was the Lord. 13Jesus walked over to get the bread and gave it to them. He also gave them the fish.

14This was now the third time Jesus appeared to his followers after he was raised from death.

Jesus Talks to Peter

15When they finished eating, Jesus said to Simon Peter, "Simon, son of John, do you love me more than these other men love me?"

Peter answered, "Yes, Lord, you know that I love you."

Then Jesus said to him, "Take care of my lambs.ᵇ"

16Again Jesus said to him, "Simon, son of John, do you love me?"

Peter answered, "Yes, Lord, you know that I love you."

Then Jesus said, "Take care of my sheep."

17A third time Jesus said, "Simon, son of John, do you love me?"

Peter was sad because Jesus asked him three times, "Do you love me?" He said, "Lord, you know everything. You know that I love you!"

Jesus said to him, "Take care of my sheep. 18The truth is, when you were young, you tied your own belt and went where you wanted. But when you are old, you will put out your hands, and someone else will tie your belt. They will lead you where you don't want to go." 19(Jesus said this to show how Peter would die to give glory* to God.) Then he said to Peter, "Follow me!"

20Peter turned and saw the follower Jesus loved very much walking behind them. (This was the follower who had leaned against Jesus at the supper and said, "Lord, who is it that will hand you over?") 21When Peter saw him behind them, he asked Jesus, "Lord, what about him?"

22Jesus answered, "Maybe I want him to live until I come. That should not matter to you. You follow me!"

23So a story spread among the followers of Jesus. They were saying that this follower would not die. But Jesus did not say he would not die. He only said, "Maybe I want him to live until I come. That should not matter to you."

24That follower is the one who is telling these things. He is the one who has now written them all down. We know that what he says is true.

25There are many other things that Jesus did. If every one of them were written down, I think the whole world would not be big enough for all the books that would be written.

ᵃ21:1 *Lake Galilee* Literally, "Lake of Tiberias," another name for Lake Galilee. See Jn. 6:1.

ᵇ21:15 *lambs* Jesus uses this word and the word "sheep" in verses 16 and 17 to mean his followers, as in Jn. 10.

Acts

Luke Writes Another Book

1 ¹Dear Theophilus,
The first book I wrote was about everything Jesus did and taught from the beginning ²until the day he was carried up into heaven. Before he went, he talked to the apostles* he had chosen. With the help of the Holy Spirit,* he told them what they should do. ³This was after his death, but he showed them that he was alive, proving it to them in many ways. The apostles saw Jesus many times during the 40 days after he was raised from death. He spoke to them about God's kingdom.* ⁴One time when Jesus was eating with them, he told them not to leave Jerusalem. He said, "Wait here until you receive what the Father promised to send. Remember, I told you about it before. ⁵John baptized* people with water, but in a few days you will be baptized with the Holy Spirit."

Jesus Is Carried Up Into Heaven

⁶The apostles* were all together. They asked Jesus, "Lord, is this the time for you to give the people of Israel* their kingdom again?"

⁷Jesus said to them, "The Father is the only one who has the authority to decide dates and times. They are not for you to know. ⁸But the Holy Spirit* will come on you and give you power. You will be my witnesses. You will tell people everywhere about me—in Jerusalem, in the rest of Judea, in Samaria, and in every part of the world."

⁹After Jesus said this, he was lifted up into the sky. While they were watching, he went into a cloud, and they could not see him. ¹⁰They were staring into the sky where he had gone. Suddenly two men wearing white clothes were standing beside them. ¹¹They said, "Men from Galilee, why are you standing here looking into the sky? You saw Jesus carried away from you into heaven. He will come back in the same way you saw him go."

A New Apostle Is Chosen

¹²Then the apostles* went back to Jerusalem from the Mount of Olives. This mountain is about a half mile from Jerusalem. ¹³When they entered the city, they went to the upstairs room where they were staying. These are the ones who were there:

Peter,
John,
James,
Andrew,
Philip,
Thomas,
Bartholomew,
Matthew,
James (the son of Alphaeus),
Simon, the Zealot,*
and Judas (the son of James).

¹⁴The apostles were all together. They were constantly praying with the same purpose. Some women, Mary the mother of Jesus, and his brothers were there with the apostles.

¹⁵After a few days there was a meeting of the believers.* There were about 120 of them. Peter stood up and said, ¹⁶⁻¹⁷"Brothers and sisters, in the Scriptures* the Holy Spirit* said through David* that something must happen. He was talking about Judas, one of our own group. Judas served together with us. The Spirit said that Judas would lead men to arrest Jesus."

¹⁸(Judas was paid money for doing this. His money was used to buy him a field. But he fell on his head, his body broke open, and all his intestines poured out. ¹⁹And all the people of Jerusalem learned about this. That is why they named that field Akeldama, which in their language means "field of blood.")

²⁰Peter said, "In the book of Psalms, this is written about Judas:

'People should not go near his land;
no one should live there.'   *Psalm 69:25*

And it is also written:

'Let another man have his work.'
     Psalm 109:8

²¹⁻²²"So now another man must join us and be a witness of Jesus' resurrection.* He must be one of those men who were part of our group during all the time the Lord Jesus was with us. He must have been with us from the time John was baptizing* people until the day when Jesus was carried up from us into heaven."

²³They put two men before the group. One was Joseph Barsabbas. He was also called Justus. The other man was Matthias. ²⁴⁻²⁵They

prayed, "Lord, you know the minds of all people. Show us which one of these two men you choose to do this work. Judas turned away from it and went where he belongs. Lord, show us which man should take his place as an apostle!" 26Then they used lots* to choose one of the two men. The lots showed that Matthias was the one the Lord wanted. So he became an apostle with the other eleven.

The Coming of the Holy Spirit

2 1When the day of Pentecost* came, they were all together in one place. 2Suddenly a noise came from heaven. It sounded like a strong wind blowing. This noise filled the whole house where they were sitting. 3They saw something that looked like flames of fire. The flames were separated and stood over each person there. 4They were all filled with the Holy Spirit,* and they began to speak different languages. The Holy Spirit was giving them the power to do this.

5There were some godly Jews in Jerusalem at this time. They were from every country in the world. 6A large crowd came together because they heard the noise. They were surprised because, as the apostles* were speaking, everyone heard in their own language.

7They were all amazed at this. They did not understand how the apostles could do this. They said, "Look! These men we hear speaking are all from Galilee.a 8But we hear them in our own languages. How is this possible? We are from all these different places: 9Parthia, Media, Elam, Mesopotamia, Judea, Cappadocia, Pontus, Asia,* 10Phrygia, Pamphylia, Egypt, the areas of Libya near the city of Cyrene, Rome, 11Crete, and Arabia. Some of us were born Jews, and others have changed their religion to worship God like Jews. We are from these different countries, but we can hear these men in our own languages! We can all understand the great things they are saying about God."

12The people were all amazed and confused. They asked each other, "What is happening?" 13But others were laughing at the apostles, saying they were drunk from too much wine.

Peter Speaks to the People

14Then Peter stood up with the other eleven apostles.* He spoke loudly so that all the people could hear. He said, "My Jewish brothers and all of you who live in Jerusalem, listen to me. I will tell you something you need to know. Listen carefully. 15These men are not drunk as you think; it's only nine o'clock in the morning. 16But Joel the prophet* wrote about what you see happening here today. This is what he wrote:

17 'God says:
  In the last days I will pour out my Spirit*
    on all people.
  Your sons and daughters will prophesy.*
  Your young men will see visions.*
  Your old men will have special dreams.
18 In those days I will pour out my Spirit on
    my servants, men and women,
  and they will prophesy.
19 I will work wonders* in the sky above.
  I will cause miraculous signs* on the
    earth below.
  There will be blood, fire, and thick
    smoke.
20 The sun will be changed into darkness,
  and the moon will be as red as blood.
  Then the great and glorious day of the
    Lord will come.
21 And everyone who trusts in the Lordb will
    be saved.'   Joel 2:28-32

22"My fellow Israelites,* listen to these words: Jesus from Nazareth was a very special man. God clearly showed this to you. He proved it by the miracles,* wonders, and miraculous signs he did through Jesus. You all saw these things, so you know this is true. 23Jesus was handed over to you, and you killed him. With the help of evil men, you nailed him to a cross. But God knew all this would happen. It was his plan—a plan he made long ago. 24Jesus suffered the pain of death, but God made him free. He raised him from death. There was no way for death to hold him. 25David* said this about him:

'I saw the Lord before me always;
  he is at my right side to keep me safe.
26 So my heart is happy,
  and the words I speak are words of joy.
  Yes, even my body will live with hope,
27 because you will not leave me in the
    place of death.c
  You will not let the body of your Holy
    One rot in the grave.
28 You taught me how to live.
  You will come close to me and give me
    great joy.'   Psalm 16:8-11

29"My brothers, I can tell you for sure about David, our great ancestor. He died, was buried, and his tomb* is still here with us today. 30He was a prophet and knew something that God had said. God had promised David that someone from his own family would sit on David's throne as king.d 31David knew this before it happened. That is why he said this about that future king:

b2:21 who trusts in the Lord Literally, "who calls on the name of the Lord," meaning to show faith in him by worshiping him or praying to him for help.
c2:27 place of death Literally, "Hades." Also in verse 31.
a2:7 from Galilee The people thought men from Galilee could speak only their own language.
d2:30 God had promised ... as king See 2 Sam. 7:12, 13 and Ps. 132:11.

'He was not left in the place of death.
 His body did not rot in the grave.'

David was talking about the Christ* rising from death. ³²So Jesus is the one God raised from death. We are all witnesses of this. We saw him. ³³Jesus was lifted up to heaven. Now he is with God, at God's right side. The Father has given the Holy Spirit to him, as he promised. So Jesus has now poured out that Spirit. This is what you see and hear. ³⁴David was not the one who was lifted up to heaven. David himself said,

'The Lord God said to my Lord:
 Sit at my right side,
³⁵   until I put your enemies under your
     power.ᵃ'   *Psalm 110:1*

³⁶"So, all the people of Israel* should know this for certain: God has made Jesus to be Lord and Christ. He is the man you nailed to the cross!"
³⁷When the people heard this, they felt very, very sorry. They asked Peter and the other apostles, "Brothers, what should we do?"
³⁸Peter said to them, "Change your hearts and lives and be baptized,* each one of you, in the name of Jesus Christ. Then God will forgive your sins, and you will receive the gift of the Holy Spirit. ³⁹This promise is for you. It is also for your children and for the people who are far away. It is for everyone the Lord our God calls to himself."
⁴⁰Peter warned them with many other words; he begged them, "Save yourselves from the evil of the people who live now!" ⁴¹Then those who accepted what Peter said were baptized. On that day about 3000 people were added to the group of believers.

The Believers Share

⁴²The believers spent their time listening to the teaching of the apostles.* They shared everything with each other. They ateᵇ together and prayed together. ⁴³Many wonders* and miraculous signs* were happening through the apostles, and everyone felt great respect for God. ⁴⁴All the believers stayed together and shared everything. ⁴⁵They sold their land and the things they owned. Then they divided the money and gave it to those who needed it. ⁴⁶The believers shared a common purpose, and every day they spent much of their time together in the Temple* area. They also ate together in their homes. They were happy to share their food and ate with joyful hearts. ⁴⁷The believers praised God and

were respected by all the people. More and more people were being saved every day, and the Lord was adding them to their group.

Peter Heals a Crippled Man

3 ¹One day Peter and John went to the Temple* area. It was three o'clock in the afternoon, which was the time for the daily Temple prayer service. ²As they were entering the Temple area, a man was there who had been crippled all his life. He was being carried by some friends who brought him to the Temple every day. They put him by one of the gates outside the Temple. It was called Beautiful Gate. There he begged for money from the people going to the Temple. ³That day he saw Peter and John going into the Temple area. He asked them for money.
⁴Peter and John looked at the crippled man and said, "Look at us!" ⁵He looked at them; he thought they would give him some money. ⁶But Peter said, "I don't have any silver or gold, but I do have something else I can give you. By the power of Jesus Christ from Nazareth—stand up and walk!"
⁷Then Peter took the man's right hand and lifted him up. Immediately his feet and legs became strong. ⁸He jumped up, stood on his feet, and began to walk. He went into the Temple area with them. He was walking and jumping and praising God. ⁹⁻¹⁰All the people recognized him. They knew he was the crippled man who always sat by the Beautiful Gate to beg for money. Now they saw this same man walking and praising God. They were amazed. They did not understand how this could happen.

Peter Speaks to the People

¹¹The man was holding on to Peter and John. All the people were amazed. They ran to Peter and John at Solomon's Porch.*
¹²When Peter saw this, he said to the people, "My Jewish brothers, why are you surprised at this? You are looking at us as if it was our power that made this man walk. Do you think this was done because we are good? ¹³No, God did it! He is the God of Abraham,* the God of Isaac,* and the God of Jacob.* He is the God of all our fathers.* He gave glory* to Jesus, his special servant. But you handed him over to be killed. Pilate* decided to let him go free. But you told Pilate you did not want him. ¹⁴Jesus was holy* and good, but you said you did not want him. You told Pilate to give you a murdererᶜ instead of Jesus. ¹⁵And so you killed the one who gives life! But God raised him from death. We are witnesses of this—we saw it with our own eyes.
¹⁶"This crippled man was healed because we trusted in Jesus. It was Jesus' power that made him well. You can see this man, and you know

---

ᵃ**2:35** *until I put ... power* Literally, "until I make your enemies a footstool for your feet."
ᵇ**2:42** *ate* Literally, "broke bread." This may mean a meal or the Lord's Supper, the special meal Jesus told his followers to eat to remember him. Also in verse 46. See Lk. 22:14–20.

ᶜ**3:14** *murderer* Barabbas, the man the Jews chose to let go free instead of Jesus. See Lk. 23:18.

him. He was made completely well because of faith in Jesus. You all saw it happen!

17"My brothers, I know that what you did to Jesus was done because you did not understand what you were doing. And your leaders did not understand any more than you did. 18But God said these things would happen. Through the prophets* he said that his Christ* would suffer and die. I have told you how God made this happen. 19So you must change your hearts and lives. Come back to God, and he will forgive your sins. 20Then the Lord will give you times of spiritual rest. He will send you Jesus, the one he chose to be the Christ.

21"But Jesus must stay in heaven until the time when all things will be made right again. God told about this time when he spoke long ago through his holy prophets. 22Moses* said, 'The Lord your God will give you a prophet. That prophet will come from among your own people. He will be like me. You must obey everything he tells you. 23And anyone who refuses to obey that prophet will die, separated from God's people.'*a*

24"Samuel, and all the other prophets who spoke for God after Samuel, said that this time would come. 25And what those prophets talked about is for you, their descendants. You have received the agreement that God made with your fathers. God said to your father Abraham, 'Every nation on earth will be blessed through your descendants.'*b* 26God has sent his special servant Jesus. He sent him to you first. He sent him to bless you by causing each of you to turn away from your evil ways."

The Apostles and the Jewish High Council

4 1While Peter and John were speaking to the people, some Jewish leaders came up to them. There were some priests, the captain of the soldiers that guarded the Temple,* and some Sadducees.* 2They were upset because of what Peter and John were teaching the people. By telling people about Jesus, the apostles* were teaching that people will rise from death. 3The Jewish leaders arrested Peter and John and put them in jail. It was already night, so they kept them in jail until the next day. 4But many of the people who heard the apostles believed what they said. There were now about 5000 men in the group of believers.

5The next day the Jewish rulers, the older Jewish leaders, and the teachers of the law met in Jerusalem. 6Annas the high priest,* Caiaphas, John, and Alexander were there. Everyone from the high priest's family was there. 7They made Peter and John stand before all the people. They asked them over and over, "How did you make this crippled man well? What power did you use? By whose authority did you do this?"

8Then Peter was filled with the Holy Spirit* and said to them, "Rulers of the people and you older leaders, 9are you questioning us today about what we did to help this crippled man? Are you asking us what made him well? 10We want all of you and all the people of Israel* to know that this man was made well by the power of Jesus Christ from Nazareth. You nailed Jesus to a cross, but God raised him from death. This man was crippled, but he is now well. He is able to stand here before you because of the power of Jesus! 11Jesus is

'the stone*c* that you builders thought was
    not important.
But this stone has become the
    cornerstone.*'   *Psalm 118:22*

12Jesus is the only one who can save people. His name is the only power in the world that has been given to save anyone. We must be saved through him!"

13The Jewish leaders understood that Peter and John had no special training or education. But they also saw that they were not afraid to speak. So the leaders were amazed. They also realized that Peter and John had been with Jesus. 14They saw the crippled man standing there beside the apostles. They saw that he was healed, so they could say nothing against the apostles.

15The Jewish leaders told them to leave the council meeting. Then the leaders talked to each other about what they should do. 16They said, "What shall we do with these men? Everyone in Jerusalem knows about the miracle* they did as a sign from God. It's too obvious. We can't say it didn't happen. 17But we must make them afraid to talk to anyone again about that man. Then this problem will not spread among the people."

18So the Jewish leaders called Peter and John in again. They told the apostles not to say anything or to teach anything in the name of Jesus. 19But Peter and John answered them, "What do you think is right? What would God want? Should we obey you or God? 20We cannot be quiet. We must tell people about what we have seen and heard."

21-22The Jewish leaders could not find a way to punish the apostles, because all the people were praising God for what had been done. This miracle was a sign from God. The man who was healed was more than 40 years old. So the Jewish leaders warned the apostles again and let them go free.

Peter and John Return to the Believers

23Peter and John left the meeting of Jewish leaders and went to their own group. They told the group everything that the leading priests and the older Jewish leaders had said to them. 24When the believers heard this,

---

*a***3:22-23** Quote from Deut. 18:15, 19.
*b***3:25** Quote from Gen. 22:18; 26:24.
*c***4:11** *stone* A picture or symbol meaning Jesus.

they all prayed to God with one purpose. They said, "Master, you are the one who made the sky, the earth, the sea, and everything in the world. 25Our ancestor David* was your servant. With the help of the Holy Spirit* he wrote these words:

'Why are the nations shouting?
Why are the people planning such useless
    things?

26 The kings of the earth prepare themselves
    to fight,
    and the rulers all come together against
    the Lord and against his Christ.*'
                                    Psalm 2:1–2

27That's what actually happened when Herod,* Pontius Pilate,* the other nations, and the people of Israel* all came together against Jesus here in Jerusalem. He is your holy* Servant, the one you made to be the Christ. 28These people who came together against Jesus made your plan happen. It was done because of your power and your will. 29And now, Lord, listen to what they are saying. They are trying to make us afraid. We are your servants. Help us to say what you want us to say without fear. 30Help us to be brave by showing us your power. Make sick people well. Cause miraculous signs* and wonders* to happen by the authority*a* of Jesus, your holy servant."

31After the believers prayed, the place where they were meeting shook. They were all filled with the Holy Spirit, and they continued to speak God's message* without fear.

The Believers Share

32The whole group of believers was united in their thinking and in what they wanted. None of them said that the things they had were their own. Instead, they shared everything. 33With great power the apostles* were making it known to everyone that the Lord Jesus was raised from death. And God blessed all the believers very much. 34None of them could say they needed anything. Everyone who owned fields or houses sold them. They brought the money they got 35and gave it to the apostles. Then everyone was given whatever they needed.

36One of the believers was named Joseph. The apostles called him Barnabas, a name that means "one who encourages others." He was a Levite* born in Cyprus. 37Joseph sold a field he owned. He brought the money and gave it to the apostles.

Ananias and Sapphira

5 1There was a man named Ananias. His wife's name was Sapphira. Ananias sold some land he had, 2but he gave only part of the money to the apostles.* He secretly kept some of the money for himself. His wife knew this, and she agreed with it.

3Peter said, "Ananias, why did you let Satan* fill your mind with such an idea? You kept part of the money for yourself and lied about it to the Holy Spirit*! 4Before you sold the field, it belonged to you, right? And even after you sold it, you could have used the money any way you wanted. How could you even think of doing such a thing? You lied to God, not to us!"

5-6When Ananias heard this, he fell down and died. Some young men came and wrapped his body. They carried it out and buried it. And everyone who heard about this was filled with fear.

7About three hours later his wife came in. Sapphira did not know about what had happened to her husband. 8Peter said to her, "Tell me how much money you got for your field. Was it this much?"

Sapphira answered, "Yes, that was all we got for the field."

9Peter said to her, "Why did you and your husband agree to test the Spirit of the Lord? Listen! Do you hear those footsteps? The men who buried your husband are at the door. They will carry you out in the same way." 10At that moment Sapphira fell down by his feet and died. The young men came in and saw that she was dead. They carried her out and buried her beside her husband. 11The whole group of believers*b* and all the other people who heard about this were filled with fear.

Proofs From God

12The apostles* were given the power to do many miraculous signs* and wonders* among the people. They were together in Solomon's Porch,* and they all had the same purpose. 13None of the other people dared to stand with the apostles, but everyone was saying wonderful things about them. 14More and more people believed in the Lord, and many men and women were added to the group of believers. 15So the people brought those who were sick into the streets and put them on little beds and mats. They were hoping that Peter's shadow might fall on them as he walked by. 16People came from all the towns around Jerusalem. They brought those who were sick or troubled by evil spirits. All of them were healed.

The Apostles Are Arrested

17The high priest* and all his friends, a group called the Sadducees,* became very jealous. 18They grabbed the apostles* and put them in jail. 19But during the night, an angel of the Lord opened the doors of the jail. The angel led the apostles outside and said, 20"Go

---

*a*4:30 *authority* Literally, "name."   *b*5:11 *group of believers* Literally, "church."

and stand in the Temple* area. Tell the people everything about this new life." ²¹When the apostles heard this, they did what they were told. They went into the Temple area about sunrise and began to teach the people.

The high priest and his friends came together and called a meeting of the high council and all the older Jewish leaders. They sent some men to the jail to bring the apostles to them. ²²When the men went to the jail, they could not find the apostles there. So they went back and told the Jewish leaders about this. ²³They said, "The jail was closed and locked. The guards were standing at the doors. But when we opened the doors, the jail was empty!" ²⁴The captain of the Temple guards and the leading priests heard this. They were confused and wondered what it all meant.

²⁵Then another man came and told them, "Listen! The men you put in jail are standing in the Temple area teaching the people." ²⁶The captain and his men went out and brought the apostles back. But the soldiers did not use force, because they were afraid of the people. They were afraid the people would stone them to death.

²⁷The soldiers brought the apostles in and made them stand before the council. The high priest questioned them. ²⁸He said, "We told you never again to teach as followers of that man. But look at what you have done! You have filled Jerusalem with your teaching. And you are trying to blame us for his death."

²⁹Peter and the other apostles answered, "We must obey God, not you! ³⁰You killed Jesus by nailing him to a cross. But God, the same God our fathers* had, raised Jesus up from death. ³¹Jesus is the one God honored by giving him a place at his right side. He made him our Leader and Savior. God did this to give all the people of Israel* the opportunity to change and turn to God to have their sins forgiven. ³²We saw all these things happen, and we can say that they are true. The Holy Spirit* also shows that these things are true. God has given this Spirit to all those who obey him."

³³When the council members heard this, they became very angry. They began to plan a way to kill the apostles. ³⁴But one member of the council, a Pharisee* named Gamaliel, stood up. He was a teacher of the law, and all the people respected him. He told the men to make the apostles leave the meeting for a few minutes. ³⁵Then he said to them, "Men of Israel, be careful of what you are planning to do to these men. ³⁶Remember when Theudas appeared? He said he was an important man, and about 400 men joined him. But he was killed, and all who followed him were scattered and ran away. They were not able to do anything. ³⁷Later, during the time of the census, a man named Judas came from Galilee. Many people joined his group, but

he was also killed, and all his followers were scattered. ³⁸And so now I tell you, stay away from these men. Leave them alone. If their plan is something they thought up, it will fail. ³⁹But if it is from God, you will not be able to stop them. You might even be fighting against God himself!"

The Jewish leaders agreed with what Gamaliel said. ⁴⁰They called the apostles in again. They beat them and told them not to talk to people about Jesus again. Then they let them go free. ⁴¹The apostles left the council meeting. They were happy because they were given the honor of suffering dishonor for Jesus. ⁴²The apostles did not stop teaching the people. They continued to tell the Good News*—that Jesus is the Christ.* They did this every day in the Temple area and in people's homes.

Seven Men Chosen for a Special Work

6 ¹More and more people were becoming followers of Jesus. But during this same time, the Greek-speaking followers began to complain against the other Jewish followers. They said that their widows were not getting their share of what the followers received every day. ²The twelve apostles* called the whole group of followers together.

The apostles said to them, "It would not be right for us to give up our work of teaching God's word in order to be in charge of getting food to people. ³So, brothers and sisters, choose seven of your men who have a good reputation. They must be full of wisdom and the Spirit.* We will give them this work to do. ⁴Then we can use all our time to pray and to teach the word of God."

⁵The whole group liked the idea. So they chose these seven men: Stephen (a man with great faith and full of the Holy Spirit), Philip,ᵃ Prochorus, Nicanor, Timon, Parmenas, and Nicolaus (a man from Antioch who had become a Jew). ⁶Then they put these men before the apostles, who prayed and laid their hands on* them.

⁷The word of God was reaching more and more people. The group of followers in Jerusalem became larger and larger. Even a big group of Jewish priests believed and obeyed.

Some Jews Against Stephen

⁸Stephen received a great blessing. God gave him power to do great wonders* and miraculous signs* among the people. ⁹But some of the Jews there were from the synagogue* of Free Men,* as it was called. The group included Jews from Cyrene, Alexandria, Cilicia, and Asia.* They started arguing with Stephen. ¹⁰But the Spirit* was helping him speak with wisdom. His words were so strong that these Jews could not argue with him.

ᵃ6:5 *Philip* Not the apostle named Philip.

¹¹So they told some men to say, "We heard Stephen say bad things against Moses* and against God!" ¹²By doing this, these Jews upset the people, the older Jewish leaders, and the teachers of the law. They became so angry that they came and grabbed Stephen and took him to a meeting of the high council.

¹³The Jews brought some men into the meeting to tell lies about Stephen. These men said, "This man is always saying things against this holy place and against the Law of Moses. ¹⁴We heard him say that Jesus from Nazareth will destroy this place and change what Moses told us to do." ¹⁵Everyone there in the council meeting was staring at Stephen. They saw that his face looked like the face of an angel.

Stephen's Speech

7 ¹The high priest* said to Stephen, "Is all this true?" ²Stephen answered, "My Jewish fathers and brothers, listen to me. Our great and glorious God appeared to Abraham, our ancestor,* when he was in Mesopotamia. This was before he lived in Haran. ³God said to him, 'Leave your country and your people, and go to the country I will show you.'ᵃ

⁴"So Abraham left the country of Chaldea.ᵇ He went to live in Haran. After his father died, God sent him to this place, where you live now. ⁵But God did not give Abraham any of this land, not even a foot of it. But God promised that in the future he would give Abraham this land for himself and for his children. This was before Abraham had any children.

⁶"This is what God said to him: 'Your descendants will live in another country. They will be strangers. The people there will make them slaves and do bad things to them for 400 years. ⁷But I will punish the nation that made them slaves.'ᶜ And God also said, 'After those things happen, your people will come out of that country. Then they will worship me here in this place.'ᵈ

⁸"God made an agreement with Abraham; the sign for this agreement was circumcision.* And so when Abraham had a son, he circumcised him when he was eight days old. His son's name was Isaac. Isaac also circumcised his son Jacob. And Jacob did the same for his sons who became the twelve great ancestors of our people.

⁹"These ancestors of ours became jealous of their brother Joseph and sold him to be a slave in Egypt. But God was with him ¹⁰and saved him from all his troubles. Pharaoh was the king of Egypt then. He liked Joseph and respected him because of the wisdom God gave him. Pharaoh gave Joseph the job of being a governor of Egypt. He even let him rule over all the people in Pharaoh's house. ¹¹But all the land of Egypt and of Canaan* became dry. It became so dry that food could not grow, and the people suffered very much. Our people could not find anything to eat.

¹²"But Jacob heard that there was food in Egypt. So he sent our people there. This was their first trip to Egypt. ¹³Then they went there a second time. This time Joseph told his brothers who he was. And Pharaoh learned about Joseph's family. ¹⁴Then Joseph sent some men to tell Jacob, his father, to come to Egypt. He also invited all his relatives, a total of 75 people. ¹⁵So Jacob went down to Egypt. He and our other ancestors lived there until they died. ¹⁶Later, their bodies were moved to Shechem, where they were put in a tomb.* It was the same tomb that Abraham had bought in Shechem from the sons of Hamor. He paid them with silver.

¹⁷"The number of our people in Egypt grew. There were more and more of our people there. The promise that God made to Abraham was soon to come true. ¹⁸Then a different king began to rule Egypt, one who knew nothing about Joseph. ¹⁹This king tricked our people. He treated them badly, making them leave their children outside to die.

²⁰"This was the time when Moses* was born. He was a very beautiful child, and for three months his parents took care of him at home. ²¹When they put him outside, Pharaoh's daughter took him. She raised him as her own son. ²²The Egyptians taught Moses everything they knew. He was powerful in all he said and did.

²³"When Moses was about 40 years old, he decided to visit his own people, the people of Israel.* ²⁴He saw one of them being mistreated by an Egyptian, so he defended him. Moses hit the Egyptian to pay him back for hurting the man. He hit him so hard that it killed him. ²⁵Moses thought that his people would understand that God was using him to save them. But they did not understand.

²⁶"The next day, Moses saw two of his own people fighting. He tried to make peace between them. He said, 'Men, you are brothers! Why are you trying to hurt each other?' ²⁷The man who was hurting the other one pushed Moses away and said to him, 'Did anyone say you could be our ruler and judge? ²⁸Will you kill me just as you killed that Egyptian yesterday?'ᵉ ²⁹When Moses heard him say this, he left Egypt. He went to live in the land of Midian, where he was a stranger. During the time he lived there, he had two sons.

³⁰"Forty years later Moses was in the desert near Mount Sinai. An angel appeared to him in the flame of a burning bush. ³¹When Moses saw this, he was amazed. He went near to look closer at it. He heard a voice; it was the Lord's. ³²The Lord said, 'I am the

---

ᵃ**7:3** Quote from Gen. 12:1.
ᵇ**7:4** *Chaldea* Or "Babylonia," a land in the southern part of Mesopotamia. See verse 2.
ᶜ**7:7** Quote from Gen. 15:13–14.
ᵈ**7:7** Quote from Gen. 15:14; Ex. 3:12.

ᵉ**7:28** Quote from Ex. 2:14.

same God your ancestors had—the God of Abraham,* the God of Isaac,* and the God of Jacob.*[a] Moses began to shake with fear. He was afraid to look at the bush.

33"The Lord said to him, 'Take off your sandals, because the place where you are now standing is holy ground. 34I have seen my people suffer much in Egypt. I have heard my people crying and have come down to save them. Come now, Moses, I am sending you back to Egypt.'[b]

35"This Moses was the one his people said they did not want. They said, 'Did anyone say you could be our ruler and judge?'[c] But he is the one God sent to be a ruler and savior. God sent him with the help of an angel, the one Moses saw in the burning bush. 36So Moses led the people out of Egypt. He worked wonders* and miraculous signs* in Egypt, at the Red Sea, and then in the desert for 40 years.

37"This is the same Moses who said these words to the people of Israel: 'God will give you a prophet.* That prophet will come from among your own people. He will be like me.'[d] 38This same Moses was with the gathering of God's people in the desert. He was with the angel who spoke to him at Mount Sinai, and he was with our ancestors. He received life-giving words from God to give to us.

39"But our ancestors did not want to obey Moses. They rejected him. They wanted to go back to Egypt again. 40They said to Aaron, 'Moses led us out of the country of Egypt. But we don't know what has happened to him. So make some gods to go before us and lead us.'[e] 41So the people made an idol that looked like a calf. Then they brought sacrifices to it. They were very happy with what they had made with their own hands. 42But God turned against them and let them continue worshiping the army of false gods in the sky. This is what God says in the book that contains what the prophets wrote:

'People of Israel, you did not bring me
     blood offerings and sacrifices* in the
     desert for 40 years;
43   You carried with you the tent for
          worshiping Moloch
     and the image of the star of your god
          Rephan.
     These were the idols you made to
          worship.
     So I will send you away beyond
          Babylon.'   *Amos 5:25-27*

44"The Holy Tent[f] was with our ancestors in the desert. God told Moses how to make this tent. He made it like the plan that God showed him. 45Later, Joshua led our ancestors to capture the lands of the other nations. Our people went in and God made the other people go out. When our people went into this new land, they took with them this same tent. Our people received this tent from their fathers, and our people kept it until the time of David.* 46God was very pleased with David. He asked God to let him build a Temple* for the people of Jacob.[g] 47But Solomon was the one who built the Temple.

48"But the Most High God does not live in houses built by human hands. This is what the prophet[h] writes:

49 'The Lord says,
     Heaven is my throne,
          and the earth is where I rest my feet.
     So do you think you can build a house for
          me?
     Do I need a place to rest?
50   Remember, I made all these things!'"
                              Isaiah 66:1-2

51Then Stephen said, "You stubborn Jewish leaders! You refuse to give your hearts to God or even listen to him. You are always against what the Holy Spirit* wants you to do. That's how your ancestors were, and you are just like them! 52They persecuted* every prophet who ever lived. They even killed those who long ago said that the Righteous One would come. And now you have turned against that Righteous One and killed him. 53You are the people who received God's law, which he gave you through his angels. But you don't obey it!"

Stephen Is Killed

54When those in the council meeting heard this, they became very angry. They were so mad they were grinding their teeth at him. 55But Stephen was full of the Holy Spirit.* He looked up into heaven and saw the glory* of God. And he saw Jesus standing at God's right side. 56Stephen said, "Look! I see heaven open. And I see the Son of Man* standing at God's right side."

57Everyone there started shouting loudly, covering their ears with their hands. Together they all ran at Stephen. 58They took him out of the city and began throwing stones at him. The men who told lies against Stephen gave their coats to a young man named Saul. 59As they were throwing the stones at him, Stephen was praying. He said, "Lord Jesus, receive my spirit!" 60He fell on his knees and shouted, "Lord, don't blame them for this sin!" These were his last words before he died.

---

*a***7:32** Quote from Ex. 3:6.
*b***7:34** Quote from Ex. 3:5–10.
*c***7:35** Quote from Ex. 2:14.
*d***7:37** Quote from Deut. 18:15.
*e***7:40** Quote from Ex. 32:1.
*f***7:44** *Holy Tent* Literally, "Tent of the Testimony." See "Holy Tent" in the Word List.

*g***7:46** *for the people of Jacob* Some Greek copies have "for the God of Jacob."
*h***7:48** *prophet* Isaiah, who spoke for God about 740–700 B.C.

8 ¹⁻³Saul agreed that the killing of Stephen was a good thing. Some godly men buried Stephen and cried loudly for him.

Trouble for the Believers

On that day the Jews began to persecute* the church* in Jerusalem, making them suffer very much. Saul was also trying to destroy the group. He went into their houses, dragged out men and women, and put them in jail. All the believers left Jerusalem. Only the apostles* stayed. The believers went to different places in Judea and Samaria. ⁴They were scattered everywhere, and in every place they went, they told people the Good News.*

Philip Tells the Good News in Samaria

⁵Philip*ᵃ* went to the city of Samaria and told people about the Christ.* ⁶The people there heard Philip and saw the miraculous signs* he was doing. They all listened carefully to what he said. ⁷Many of these people had evil spirits inside them, but Philip made the evil spirits leave them. The spirits made a lot of noise as they came out. There were also many weak and crippled people there. Philip made these people well too. ⁸What a happy day this was for that city!

⁹Now there was a man named Simon who lived in that city. Before Philip came there, Simon had been doing magic and amazing all the people of Samaria. He bragged and called himself a great man. ¹⁰All the people—the least important and the most important—believed what he said. They said, "This man has the power of God that is called 'the Great Power.'" ¹¹Simon amazed the people with his magic for so long that the people became his followers. ¹²But Philip told the people the Good News* about God's kingdom* and the power of Jesus Christ. Men and women believed Philip and were baptized.* ¹³Simon himself also believed, and after he was baptized, he stayed close to Philip. When he saw the miraculous signs* and powerful things Philip did, he was amazed.

¹⁴The apostles* in Jerusalem heard that the people of Samaria had accepted the word of God. So they sent Peter and John to the people in Samaria. ¹⁵When Peter and John arrived, they prayed for the Samaritan believers to receive the Holy Spirit.* ¹⁶These people had been baptized in the name of the Lord Jesus, but the Holy Spirit had not yet come down on any of them. This is why Peter and John prayed. ¹⁷When the two apostles laid their hands on* the people, they received the Holy Spirit.

¹⁸Simon saw that the Spirit was given to people when the apostles laid their hands on them. So he offered the apostles money. ¹⁹He said, "Give me this power so that when I lay my hands on someone, they will receive the Holy Spirit."

²⁰Peter said to Simon, "You and your money should both be destroyed because you thought you could buy God's gift with money. ²¹You cannot share with us in this work. Your heart is not right before God. ²²Change your heart! Turn away from these evil thoughts and pray to the Lord. Maybe he will forgive you. ²³I see that you are full of bitter jealousy and cannot stop yourself from doing wrong."

²⁴Simon answered, "Both of you pray to the Lord for me, so that what you have said will not happen to me."

²⁵Then the two apostles told the people what they had seen Jesus do. They told them the message* of the Lord. Then they went back to Jerusalem. On the way, they went through many Samaritan towns and told people the Good News.

Philip Teaches a Man From Ethiopia

²⁶An angel of the Lord spoke to Philip. The angel said, "Get ready and go south on the road that leads down to Gaza from Jerusalem—the road that goes through the desert."

²⁷So Philip got ready and went. On the road he saw a man from Ethiopia. He was a eunuch* and an important officer in the service of Candace, the queen of the Ethiopians. He was responsible for taking care of all her money. This man had gone to Jerusalem to worship. ²⁸Now he was on his way home. He was sitting in his chariot* reading from the book of Isaiah the prophet.*

²⁹The Spirit* said to Philip, "Go to that chariot and stay near it." ³⁰So he went toward the chariot, and he heard the man reading from Isaiah the prophet. Philip asked him, "Do you understand what you are reading?"

³¹The man answered, "How can I understand? I need someone to explain it to me." Then he invited Philip to climb in and sit with him. ³²The part of the Scriptures* that he was reading was this:

"He was like a sheep being led to the
　　butcher.
He was like a lamb that makes no sound
　　as its wool is being cut off.
　　He said nothing.
³³ He was shamed, and all his rights were
　　taken away.
His life on earth has ended.
　　So there will be no story about his
　　descendants."   *Isaiah 53:7-8*

³⁴The officer said to Philip, "Please, tell me, who is the prophet talking about? Is he talking about himself or about someone else?" ³⁵Philip began to speak. He started with this same Scripture and told the man the Good News* about Jesus.

³⁶While they were traveling down the road, they came to some water. The officer

---

ᵃ**8:5** *Philip* Not the apostle named Philip.

said, "Look, here is water! What is stopping me from being baptized*?" ³⁷ ᵃ ³⁸Then the officer ordered the chariot to stop. Both Philip and the officer went down into the water, and Philip baptized him. ³⁹When they came up out of the water, the Spirit of the Lord took Philip away; the officer never saw him again. The officer continued on his way home. He was very happy. ⁴⁰But Philip appeared in a city called Azotus. He was going to the city of Caesarea. He told people the Good News in all the towns on the way from Azotus to Caesarea.

Saul Becomes a Follower of Jesus

9 ¹In Jerusalem Saul was still trying to scare the followers of the Lord, even saying he would kill them. He went to the high priest* ²and asked him to write letters to the synagogues* in the city of Damascus. Saul wanted the high priest to give him the authority to find people in Damascus who were followers of the Way.* If he found any believers there, men or women, he would arrest them and bring them back to Jerusalem.

³So Saul went to Damascus. When he came near the city, a very bright light from heaven suddenly shined around him. ⁴He fell to the ground and heard a voice saying to him, "Saul, Saul! Why are you persecuting* me?"

⁵Saul said, "Who are you, Lord?"

The voice answered, "I am Jesus, the one you are persecuting. ⁶Get up now and go into the city. Someone there will tell you what you must do."

⁷The men traveling with Saul just stood there, unable to speak. They heard the voice, but they saw no one. ⁸Saul got up from the ground and opened his eyes, but he could not see. So the men with him held his hand and led him into Damascus. ⁹For three days Saul could not see; he did not eat or drink.

¹⁰There was a follower of Jesus in Damascus named Ananias. In a vision* the Lord said to him, "Ananias!"

Ananias answered, "Here I am, Lord."

¹¹The Lord said to him, "Get up and go to the street called Straight Street. Find the house of Judasᵇ and ask for a man named Saul from the city of Tarsus. He is there now, praying. ¹²He has seen a vision in which a man named Ananias came and laid his hands on* him so that he could see again."

¹³But Ananias answered, "Lord, many people have told me about this man. They told me about the many bad things he did to your holy people* in Jerusalem. ¹⁴Now he has come here to Damascus. The leading priests

have given him the power to arrest all people who trust in you.ᶜ"

¹⁵But the Lord Jesus said to Ananias, "Go! I have chosen Saul for an important work. He must tell about me to other nations and their rulers and to the people of Israel.* ¹⁶I will show him all that he must suffer for me."

¹⁷So Ananias left and went to the house of Judas. He laid his hands on Saul and said, "Saul, my brother, the Lord Jesus sent me. He is the one you saw on the road when you came here. He sent me so that you can see again and also be filled with the Holy Spirit.*" ¹⁸Immediately, something that looked like fish scales fell off Saul's eyes. He was able to see! Then he got up and was baptized.* ¹⁹After he ate, he began to feel strong again.

Saul Begins to Tell About Jesus

Saul stayed with the followers of Jesus in Damascus for a few days. ²⁰Soon he began to go to the synagogues* and tell people about Jesus. He told the people, "Jesus is the Son of God!"

²¹All the people who heard Saul were amazed. They said, "This is the same man who was in Jerusalem trying to destroy the people who trust in Jesusᵈ! And that's why he has come here—to arrest the followers of Jesus and take them back to the leading priests."

²²But Saul became more and more powerful in proving that Jesus is the Christ.* His proofs were so strong that the Jews who lived in Damascus could not argue with him.

Saul Escapes From Some Jews

²³After many days, some Jews made plans to kill Saul. ²⁴They were watching the city gates day and night. They wanted to kill Saul, but he learned about their plan. ²⁵One night some followers that Saul had taught helped him leave the city. They put him in a basket and lowered it down through a hole in the city wall.

Saul in Jerusalem

²⁶Then Saul went to Jerusalem. He tried to join the group of followers, but they were all afraid of him. They did not believe that he was really a follower of Jesus. ²⁷But Barnabas accepted Saul and took him to the apostles.* He told them how Saul had seen the Lord on the road and how the Lord had spoken to Saul. Then he told them how boldly Saul had spoken for the Lord in Damascus.

²⁸And so Saul stayed with the followers and went all around Jerusalem speaking boldly for the Lord. ²⁹He often had arguments with the Greek-speaking Jews, who began

---

ᵃ**8:37** Some late copies of Acts add verse 37: "Philip answered, 'If you believe with all your heart, you can.' The officer said, 'I believe that Jesus Christ is the Son of God.'"
ᵇ**9:11** *Judas* This is not either of the apostles named Judas.

ᶜ**9:14** *who trust in you* Literally, "who call on your name," meaning to show faith in Jesus by worshiping him or praying to him for help.
ᵈ**9:21** *who trust in Jesus* Literally, "who call on this name."

making plans to kill him. ³⁰When the believers* learned about this, they took Saul to Caesarea, and from there they sent him to the city of Tarsus.

³¹The church* in Judea, Galilee, and Samaria had a time of peace. With the help of the Holy Spirit,* the groups of believers became stronger and showed their respect for the Lord by the way they lived. So the church everywhere grew in numbers.

Peter in Lydda and Joppa

³²Peter was traveling through all the areas around Jerusalem, and he stopped to visit the believers*a* who lived in Lydda. ³³There he met a man named Aeneas, who was paralyzed and had not been able to get out of bed for the past eight years. ³⁴Peter said to him, "Aeneas, Jesus Christ heals you. Get up and make your bed!" He stood up immediately. ³⁵All the people living in Lydda and on the plain of Sharon saw him, and they decided to follow the Lord.

³⁶In the city of Joppa there was a follower of Jesus named Tabitha. Her Greek name, Dorcas, means "a deer." She was always doing good things for people and giving money to those in need. ³⁷While Peter was in Lydda, Tabitha became sick and died. They washed her body and put it in an upstairs room. ³⁸The followers in Joppa heard that Peter was in Lydda, which was not far away. So they sent two men, who begged him, "Hurry, please come quickly!"

³⁹Peter got ready and went with them. When he arrived, they took him to the upstairs room. All the widows stood around him. They were crying and showing him the coats and other clothes that Tabitha had made during her time with them. ⁴⁰Peter sent all the people out of the room. He knelt down and prayed. Then he turned to Tabitha's body and said, "Tabitha, stand up!" She opened her eyes. When she saw Peter, she sat up. ⁴¹He gave her his hand and helped her stand up. Then he called the believers and the widows into the room. He showed them Tabitha; she was alive!

⁴²People everywhere in Joppa learned about this, and many believed in the Lord. ⁴³Peter stayed in Joppa for many days at the home of a man named Simon, who was a leatherworker.*

Peter and Cornelius

10 ¹In the city of Caesarea there was a man named Cornelius, a Roman army officer* in what was called the Italian Unit. ²He was a religious man. He and all the others who lived in his house were worshipers of the true God. He gave much of his money to help the poor people and always prayed

to God. ³One afternoon about three o'clock, Cornelius had a vision.* He clearly saw an angel from God coming to him and saying, "Cornelius!"

⁴Staring at the angel and feeling afraid, Cornelius said, "What do you want, sir?"

The angel said to him, "God has heard your prayers and has seen your gifts to the poor. He remembers you and all you have done. ⁵Send some men now to the city of Joppa to get a man named Simon, who is also called Peter. ⁶He is staying with someone also named Simon, a leatherworker* who has a house beside the sea." ⁷The angel who spoke to Cornelius left. Then Cornelius called two of his servants and a soldier. The soldier was a religious man, one of his close helpers. ⁸Cornelius explained everything to these three men and sent them to Joppa.

⁹The next day they were coming near Joppa about noon, when Peter was going up to the roof to pray. ¹⁰He was hungry and wanted to eat. But while they were preparing the food for Peter to eat, he had a vision. ¹¹He saw something coming down through the open sky. It looked like a big sheet being lowered to the ground by its four corners. ¹²In it were all kinds of animals, reptiles, and birds. ¹³Then a voice said to him, "Get up, Peter; kill anything here and eat it."

¹⁴But Peter said, "I can't do that, Lord! I have never eaten anything that is not pure or fit to be used for food."

¹⁵But the voice said to him again, "God has made these things pure. Don't say they are unfit to eat." ¹⁶This happened three times. Then the whole thing was taken back up into heaven. ¹⁷Peter wondered what this vision meant.

The men Cornelius sent had found Simon's house. They were standing at the door. ¹⁸They asked, "Is Simon Peter staying here?"

¹⁹While Peter was still thinking about the vision, the Spirit* said to him, "Listen, three men are looking for you. ²⁰Get up and go downstairs. Go with these men without wondering if it's all right, because I sent them." ²¹So Peter went downstairs and said to them, "I think I'm the man you are looking for. Why did you come here?"

²²The men said, "A holy* angel told Cornelius to invite you to his house. He is an army officer. He is a good man, one who worships God, and all the Jewish people respect him. The angel told him to invite you to his house so that he can listen to what you have to say." ²³Peter asked the men to come in and stay for the night.

The next day Peter got ready and went away with the three men. Some of the believers* from Joppa went with him. ²⁴The next day they came to the city of Caesarea. Cornelius was waiting for them and had already gathered his relatives and close friends at his house.

---

*a*9:32 **believers** Literally, "holy ones," a name for people who believe in Jesus. Also in verse 41.

²⁵When Peter entered the house, Cornelius met him. He fell down at Peter's feet and worshiped him. ²⁶But Peter told him to get up. Peter said, "Stand up! I am only a man like you." ²⁷Peter continued talking with Cornelius. Then Peter went inside and saw a large group of people gathered there.

²⁸Peter said to the people, "You understand that it is against our law for a Jew to associate with or visit anyone who is not a Jew. But God has shown me that I should not consider anyone unfit or say they are not pure. ²⁹That's why I didn't argue when your men asked me to come here. Now, please tell me why you sent for me."

³⁰Cornelius said, "Four days ago, I was praying in my house. It was at this same time—three o'clock in the afternoon. Suddenly there was someone standing before me wearing bright, shiny clothes. ³¹He said, 'Cornelius, God has heard your prayer and has seen your gifts to the poor. He remembers you and all you have done. ³²So send some men to the city of Joppa and tell Simon Peter to come. He is staying with another man named Simon, a leatherworker who has a house beside the sea.' ³³So I sent for you immediately. It was very good of you to come here. Now we are all here before God to hear everything the Lord has commanded you to tell us."

Peter Speaks in the House of Cornelius

³⁴Peter began to speak: "I really understand now that God does not consider some people to be better than others. ³⁵He accepts anyone who worships him and does what is right. It is not important what nation they come from. ³⁶God has spoken to the people of Israel.* He sent them the Good News* that peace has come through Jesus Christ, the Lord of all people.

³⁷"You know what has happened all over Judea. It began in Galilee after John* told the people they needed to be baptized.* ³⁸You know about Jesus from Nazareth. God made him the Christ* by giving him the Holy Spirit* and power. Jesus went everywhere doing good for people. He healed those who were ruled by the devil, showing that God was with him.

³⁹"We saw all that Jesus did in Judea and in Jerusalem. But he was killed. They put him on a cross made of wood. ⁴⁰But on the third day after his death, God raised him to life and let him be seen openly. ⁴¹He was not seen by everyone, but only by us, the ones God had already chosen to be witnesses. We ate and drank with him after he was raised from death.

⁴²"Jesus told us to go and speak to the people. He told us to tell them that he is the one God chose to be the Judge of all who are living and all who have died. ⁴³Everyone who believes in Jesus will have their sins forgiven through his name. All the prophets* agree that this is true."

The Spirit Comes to Non-Jewish People

⁴⁴While Peter was still speaking these words, the Holy Spirit* came down on all those who were listening to his speech. ⁴⁵The Jewish believers who came with Peter were amazed that the Holy Spirit had been poured out as a gift also to people who were not Jews. ⁴⁶They heard them speaking different languages and praising God. Then Peter said, ⁴⁷"How can anyone object to these people being baptized* in water? They have received the Holy Spirit the same as we did!" ⁴⁸So Peter told them to baptize Cornelius and his relatives and friends in the name of Jesus Christ. Then they asked Peter to stay with them for a few days.

Peter Returns to Jerusalem

11 ¹The apostles* and the believers* in Judea heard that non-Jewish people had accepted God's teaching too. ²But when Peter came to Jerusalem, some Jewish believers*ᵃ argued with him. ³They said, "You went into the homes of people who are not Jews and are not circumcised,* and you even ate with them!"

⁴So Peter explained the whole story to them. ⁵He said, "I was in the city of Joppa. While I was praying, I had a vision.* I saw something coming down from heaven. It looked like a big sheet being lowered to the ground by its four corners. It came down close to me, ⁶and I looked inside. I saw all kinds of animals, including wild ones, as well as reptiles and birds. ⁷I heard a voice say to me, 'Get up, Peter. Kill anything here and eat it!'

⁸"But I said, 'I can't do that, Lord! I have never eaten anything that is not pure or fit to be used for food.'

⁹"But the voice from heaven answered again, 'God has made these things pure. Don't say they are unfit to eat!'

¹⁰"This happened three times. Then the whole thing was taken back into heaven. ¹¹Suddenly there were three men standing outside the house where I was staying. They had been sent from Caesarea to get me. ¹²The Spirit* told me to go with them without wondering if it was all right. These six brothers here also went with me, and we went to the house of Cornelius. ¹³He told us about the angel he had seen standing in his house. The angel said, 'Send some men to Joppa to get Simon, the one who is also called Peter. ¹⁴He will speak to you, and what he tells you will save you and everyone living in your house.'

¹⁵"After I began speaking, the Holy Spirit came on them just as he came on us at the beginning.ᵇ ¹⁶Then I remembered the words

---

ᵃ**11:2 Jewish believers** Literally, "those of circumcision." This may mean Jews who thought all followers of Christ must be circumcised and obey the Law of Moses. See Gal. 2:12.

ᵇ**11:15 beginning** The beginning of the church on the day of Pentecost. See Acts 2.

of the Lord Jesus: 'John baptized* people in water, but you will be baptized in the Holy Spirit.' ¹⁷God gave these people the same gift he gave us who believed in the Lord Jesus Christ. So how could I object to what God wanted to do?"

¹⁸When the Jewish believers heard this, they stopped arguing. They praised God and said, "So God is also allowing the non-Jewish people to change their hearts and have the life he gives!"

The Good News Comes to Antioch

¹⁹The believers were scattered by the persecution*ᵃ* that began when Stephen was killed. Some of them went as far as Phoenicia, Cyprus, and Antioch. They told the Good News* in these places, but only to Jews. ²⁰Some of these believers were men from Cyprus and Cyrene. When these men came to Antioch, they began speaking to people who were not Jews.*ᵇ* They told them the Good News about the Lord Jesus. ²¹The Lord was helping these men, and a large number of people believed and decided to follow the Lord.

²²When the church* in Jerusalem heard about this, they sent Barnabas to Antioch. ²³⁻²⁴Barnabas was a good man, full of the Holy Spirit* and faith. When he went to Antioch and saw how God had blessed the believers there, he was very happy. He encouraged them all, saying, "Always be faithful to the Lord. Serve him with all your heart." Many more people became followers of the Lord.

²⁵Then Barnabas went to the city of Tarsus to look for Saul. ²⁶When he found him, he brought him to Antioch. They stayed there a whole year. Every time the church came together, Barnabas and Saul met with them and taught many people. It was in Antioch that the followers were called "Christ-followers" for the first time.

²⁷About that same time some prophets* went from Jerusalem to Antioch. ²⁸One of them, named Agabus, stood up and spoke with the help of the Spirit. He said, "A very bad time is coming to the whole world. There will be no food for people to eat." (This time of famine happened when Claudius was emperor.*) ²⁹The Lord's followers decided that they would each send as much as they could to help their brothers and sisters who lived in Judea. ³⁰They gathered the money and gave it to Barnabas and Saul, who took it to the elders* in Judea.

*ᵃ*11:19 *persecution* A time when the Jewish leaders in Jerusalem were punishing people who believed in Christ. See Acts 8:1–4.

*ᵇ*11:20 *people who were not Jews* Literally, "Hellenists," meaning people who have been influenced by Greek culture. Some Greek copies have "Greeks."

Herod Agrippa Hurts the Church

12 ¹During this same time, King Herod* began to persecute* some of the people who were part of the church.* ²He ordered James, the brother of John, to be killed with a sword. ³Herod saw that many of the Jews liked this, so he decided to arrest Peter too. This happened during the Festival of Unleavened Bread.* ⁴He arrested Peter and put him in jail, where he was guarded by a group of 16 soldiers. Herod planned to bring Peter before the people, but he wanted to wait until after the Passover festival. ⁵So Peter was kept in jail, but the church was constantly praying to God for him.

Peter Leaves the Jail

⁶One night, Peter, bound with two chains, was sleeping between two of the soldiers. More soldiers were guarding the door of the jail. Herod* was planning to bring Peter out before the people the next day. ⁷Suddenly an angel of the Lord was standing there, and the room was filled with light. The angel tapped Peter on the side and woke him up. The angel said, "Hurry, get up!" The chains fell off Peter's hands. ⁸The angel said, "Get dressed and put on your sandals." Peter did as he was told. Then the angel said, "Put on your coat and follow me."

⁹So the angel went out and Peter followed. He did not know if the angel was really doing this. He thought he might be seeing a vision.* ¹⁰Peter and the angel went past the first guard and the second guard. Then they came to the iron gate that separated them from the city. The gate opened for them by itself. After they went through the gate and walked about a block, the angel suddenly left.

¹¹Peter realized then what had happened. He thought, "Now I know that the Lord really sent his angel to me. He rescued me from Herod and from everything those Jews thought would happen to me."

¹²When Peter realized this, he went to the home of Mary, the mother of John, who was also called Mark. Many people were gathered there and were praying. ¹³Peter knocked on the outside door. A servant girl named Rhoda came to answer it. ¹⁴She recognized Peter's voice, and she was very happy. She even forgot to open the door. She ran inside and told the group, "Peter is at the door!" ¹⁵The believers said to her, "You are crazy!" But she continued to say that it was true. So they said, "It must be Peter's angel."

¹⁶But Peter continued to knock. When the believers opened the door, they saw him. They were amazed. ¹⁷Peter made a sign with his hand to tell them to be quiet. He explained to them how the Lord led him out of the jail. He said, "Tell James and the other brothers what happened." Then he left and went to another place.

¹⁸The next day the soldiers were very

upset. They wondered what happened to Peter. [19]Herod looked everywhere for him but could not find him. So he questioned the guards and then ordered that they be killed.

The Death of Herod Agrippa

Later, Herod* moved from Judea. He went to the city of Caesarea and stayed there a while. [20]Herod was very angry with the people from the cities of Tyre and Sidon. But these cities needed food from his country, so a group of them came to ask him for peace. They were able to get Blastus, the king's personal servant, on their side.

[21]Herod decided on a day to meet with them. On that day he was wearing a beautiful royal robe. He sat on his throne and made a speech to the people. [22]The people shouted, "This is the voice of a god, not a man!" [23]Herod did not give the glory* to God. So an angel of the Lord caused him to get sick. He was eaten by worms inside him, and he died.

[24]The message* of God was spreading, reaching more and more people.

[25]After Barnabas and Saul finished their work in Jerusalem, they returned to Antioch, taking John Mark with them.

Barnabas and Saul Given a Special Work

13 [1]In the church* at Antioch there were some prophets* and teachers. They were Barnabas, Simeon (also called Niger), Lucius (from the city of Cyrene), Manaen (who had grown up with King Herod[a]), and Saul. [2]These men were all serving the Lord and fasting* when the Holy Spirit* said to them, "Appoint Barnabas and Saul to do a special work for me. They are the ones I have chosen to do it."

[3]So the church fasted and prayed. They laid their hands on* Barnabas and Saul and sent them out.

Barnabas and Saul in Cyprus

[4]Barnabas and Saul were sent out by the Holy Spirit.* They went to the city of Seleucia. Then they sailed from there to the island of Cyprus. [5]When Barnabas and Saul came to the city of Salamis, they told the message* of God in the Jewish synagogues.* John Mark was with them to help.

[6]They went across the whole island to the city of Paphos. There they met a Jewish man named Barjesus who did magic. He was a false prophet.* [7]He always stayed close to Sergius Paulus, who was the governor and a very smart man. He invited Barnabas and Saul to come visit him, because he wanted to hear the message of God. [8]But the magician Elymas (as Barjesus was called in Greek) spoke against them, trying to stop the governor from believing in Jesus. [9]But Saul (also known as Paul), filled with the Holy Spirit, looked hard at Elymas [10]and said, "You son of the devil, full of lies and all kinds of evil tricks! You are an enemy of everything that is right. Will you never stop trying to change the Lord's truths into lies? [11]Now the Lord will touch you and you will be blind. For a time you will not be able to see anything—not even the light from the sun."

Then everything became dark for Elymas. He walked around lost. He was trying to find someone to lead him by the hand. [12]When the governor saw this, he believed. He was amazed at the teaching about the Lord.

Paul and Barnabas Go to Antioch in Pisidia

[13]Paul and the people with him sailed away from Paphos. They came to Perga, a city in Pamphylia. There John Mark left them and returned to Jerusalem. [14]They continued their trip from Perga and went to Antioch, a city near Pisidia.

On the Sabbath* day they went into the Jewish synagogue* and sat down. [15]The Law of Moses* and the writings of the prophets* were read. Then the leaders of the synagogue sent a message to Paul and Barnabas: "Brothers, if you have something to say that will help the people here, please speak."

[16]Paul stood up, raised his hand to get their attention, and said, "People of Israel* and all you others who worship the true God, please listen to me! [17]The God of Israel chose our ancestors.* And during the time our people lived in Egypt as foreigners, he made them great. Then he brought them out of that country with great power. [18]And he was patient with them for 40 years in the desert. [19]God destroyed seven nations in the land of Canaan* and gave their land to his people. [20]All this happened in about 450 years.

"After this, God gave our people judges until the time of Samuel* the prophet. [21]Then the people asked for a king. God gave them Saul, the son of Kish. Saul was from the tribe of Benjamin. He was king for 40 years. [22]After God took Saul away, God made David* their king. This is what God said about David: 'David, the son of Jesse, is the kind of person who does what pleases me. He will do everything I want him to do.'

[23]"As he promised, God has brought one of David's descendants to Israel to be their Savior. That descendant is Jesus. [24]Before he came, John* told all the people of Israel what they should do. He told them to be baptized* to show they wanted to change their lives. [25]When John was finishing his work, he said, 'Who do you think I am? I am not the Christ. He is coming later, and I am not worthy to be the slave who unties his sandals.'

[26]"My brothers, sons in the family of Abraham,* and you other people who also worship the true God, listen! The news about this salvation has been sent to us. [27]The Jews living in

---

a **13:1 King Herod** Literally, "Herod the tetrarch." See "Herod Agrippa I" in the Word List.

Jerusalem and their leaders did not realize that Jesus was the Savior. The words the prophets wrote about him were read every Sabbath day, but they did not understand. They condemned Jesus. When they did this, they made the words of the prophets come true. 28They could not find any real reason why Jesus should die, but they asked Pilate* to kill him.

29"These Jews did all the bad things that the Scriptures* said would happen to Jesus. Then they took Jesus down from the cross and put him in a tomb.* 30But God raised him up from death! 31After this, for many days, those who had gone with Jesus from Galilee to Jerusalem saw him. They are now his witnesses to our people.

32"We tell you the Good News* about the promise God made to our ancestors. 33We are their descendants, and God has made this promise come true for us. God did this by raising Jesus from death. We also read about this in Psalm 2:

'You are my Son.
    Today I have become your Father.'
                                Psalm 2:7

34God raised Jesus from death. Jesus will never go back to the grave and become dust. So God said,

'I will give you the true and holy promises
    that I made to David.'   Isaiah 55:3

35But in another Psalm it says,

'You will not let your Holy One rot in the
    grave.'   Psalm 16:10

36David did God's will during the time he lived. Then he died and was buried like all his ancestors. And his body did rot in the grave! 37But the one God raised from death did not rot in the grave. 38-39Brothers, understand what we are telling you. You can have forgiveness of your sins through this Jesus. The Law of Moses could not free you from your sins. But you can be made right with God if you believe in Jesus. 40So be careful! Don't let what the prophets said happen to you:

41 'Listen, you people who doubt!
    You can wonder, but then go away and
        die;
    because during your time,
    I will do something that you will not
        believe.
    You will not believe it, even if someone
        explains it to you!'"   Habakkuk 1:5

42As Paul and Barnabas were leaving the synagogue, the people asked them to come again on the next Sabbath day and tell them more about these things. 43After the meeting, many of the people followed Paul and Barnabas, including many Jews and people who had changed their religion to be like Jews and worship the true God. Paul and Barnabas encouraged them to continue trusting in God's grace.*

44On the next Sabbath day, almost all the people in the city came together to hear the word of the Lord. 45When the Jews there saw all these people, they became very jealous. Shouting insults, they argued against everything Paul said. 46But Paul and Barnabas spoke very boldly. They said, "We had to tell God's message* to you Jews first, but you refuse to listen. You have made it clear that you are not worthy of having eternal life. So we will now go to those who are not Jews. 47This is what the Lord told us to do:

'I have made you a light for the other
        nations,
    to show people all over the world the
        way to be saved.'"   Isaiah 49:6

48When the non-Jewish people heard Paul say this, they were happy. They gave honor to the message of the Lord, and many of them believed it. These were the ones chosen to have eternal life.

49And so the message of the Lord was being told throughout the whole country. 50But the Jews there caused some of the important religious women and the leaders of the city to be angry and turn against Paul and Barnabas and throw them out of town. 51So Paul and Barnabas shook the dust off their feet.a Then they went to the city of Iconium. 52But the Lord's followers in Antioch were happy and filled with the Holy Spirit.*

Paul and Barnabas in Iconium

14 1Paul and Barnabas went to the city of Iconium. As they did in Antioch, they entered the Jewish synagogue.* They spoke to the people there. They spoke so well that many Jews and Greeks believed what they said. 2But some of the Jews did not believe. They said things that caused the non-Jewish people to be angry and turn against the Lord's followers.

3So Paul and Barnabas stayed in Iconium a long time, and they spoke bravely for the Lord. They told the people about God's grace.* The Lord proved that what they said was true by causing miraculous signs* and wonders* to be done through them. 4But some of the people in the city agreed with the Jews who did not believe Paul and Barnabas. Others followed the apostles. So the city was divided.

5Some of the Jews there, as well as their leaders and some of the non-Jewish people, were determined to hurt Paul and Barnabas. They wanted to stone them to death. 6When

a13:51 shook the dust off their feet A warning. It showed they were finished talking to these people.

Paul and Barnabas learned about this, they left the city. They went to Lystra and Derbe, cities in Lycaonia, and to the surrounding areas. 7They told the Good News* there too.

Paul in Lystra and Derbe

8In Lystra there was a man who had something wrong with his feet. He had been born crippled and had never walked. 9He was sitting and listening to Paul speak. Paul looked straight at him and saw that the man believed God could heal him. 10So Paul shouted, "Stand up on your feet!" The man jumped up and began walking around.

11When the people saw what Paul did, they shouted in their own Lycaonian language. They said, "The gods have come down to us in the form of humans!" 12The people began to call Barnabas "Zeus,*" and they called Paul "Hermes,*" because he was the main speaker. 13The temple of Zeus was near the city. The priest of this temple brought some bulls and flowers to the city gates. The priest and the people wanted to offer a sacrifice to Paul and Barnabas.

14But when the apostles,* Barnabas and Paul, understood what the people were doing, they tore their own clothes.a Then they ran in among the people and shouted to them: 15"Men, why are you doing this? We are not gods. We are human just like you. We came to tell you the Good News.* We are telling you to turn away from these worthless things. Turn to the true living God, the one who made the sky, the earth, the sea, and everything that is in them.

16"In the past God let all the nations do what they wanted. 17But God was always there doing the good things that prove he is real. He gives you rain from heaven and good harvests at the right times. He gives you plenty of food and fills your hearts with joy."

18Even after saying all this, Paul and Barnabas still could hardly stop the people from offering sacrifices to them.

19Then some Jews came from Antioch and Iconium and persuaded the people to turn against Paul. So they threw stones at him and dragged him out of the town. They thought they had killed him. 20But when the followers of Jesus gathered around him, he got up and went back into the town. The next day he and Barnabas left and went to the city of Derbe.

The Return to Antioch in Syria

21They also told the Good News* in the city of Derbe, and many people became followers of Jesus. Then Paul and Barnabas returned to the cities of Lystra, Iconium, and Antioch. 22In those cities they helped the followers grow stronger in their faith and encouraged them to continue trusting God. They told them, "We must suffer many things on our way into God's kingdom.*" 23They also chose elders* for each church* and stopped eating for a period of time to pray for them. These elders were men who had put their trust in the Lord Jesus, so Paul and Barnabas put them in his care.

24Paul and Barnabas went through the country of Pisidia. Then they came to the country of Pamphylia. 25They told people the message* of God in the city of Perga, and then they went down to the city of Attalia. 26And from there they sailed away to Antioch in Syria. This is the city where the believers had put them into God's care and sent them to do this work. Now they had finished it.

27When they arrived, they gathered the church together and told them about all that God had done with them. They said, "God opened a door so that the non-Jewish people could also believe!" 28And they stayed there a long time with the Lord's followers.

The Meeting at Jerusalem

15 1Then some men came to Antioch from Judea and began teaching the non-Jewish believers: "You cannot be saved if you are not circumcised* as Moses* taught us." 2Paul and Barnabas were against this teaching and argued with these men about it. So the group decided to send Paul, Barnabas, and some others to Jerusalem to talk more about this with the apostles* and elders.*

3The church* helped them get ready to leave on their trip. The men went through the countries of Phoenicia and Samaria, where they told all about how the non-Jewish people had turned to the true God. This made all the believers very happy. 4When the men arrived in Jerusalem, the apostles, the elders, and the whole church welcomed them. Paul, Barnabas, and the others told about all that God had done with them. 5Some of the believers in Jerusalem had belonged to the Pharisees.* They stood up and said, "The non-Jewish believers must be circumcised. We must tell them to obey the Law of Moses!"

6Then the apostles and the elders gathered to study this problem. 7After a long debate, Peter stood up and said to them, "My brothers, I am sure you remember what happened in the early days. God chose me from among you to tell the Good News* to those who are not Jewish. It was from me that they heard the Good News and believed. 8God knows everyone, even their thoughts, and he accepted these non-Jewish people. He showed this to us by giving them the Holy Spirit* the same as he did to us. 9To God, those people are not different from us. When they believed, God made their hearts pure. 10So now, why are you putting a heavy burdenb around

---

a14:14 tore ... clothes This showed they were very upset.

b15:10 burden The Jewish law. Some of the Jews tried to make the non-Jewish believers follow this law.

the necks of the non-Jewish followers? Are you trying to make God angry? We and our fathers* were not able to carry that burden. ¹¹No, we believe that we and these people will be saved the same way—by the grace* of the Lord Jesus."

¹²Then the whole group became quiet. They listened while Paul and Barnabas told about all the miraculous signs* and wonders* that God had done through them among the non-Jewish people. ¹³When they finished speaking, James said, "My brothers, listen to me. ¹⁴Simon Peter has told us how God showed his love for the non-Jewish people. For the first time God accepted them and made them his people. ¹⁵The words of the prophets* agree with this too:

¹⁶ 'I will return after this.
    I will build David's* house again.
    It has fallen down.
 I will build again the parts of his house
        that have been pulled down.
    I will make his house new.
¹⁷ Then the rest of the world will look for
        the Lord God—
    all those of other nations who are my
        people too.
    The Lord said this.
    And he is the one who does all these
        things.'   Amos 9:11–12

¹⁸ 'All this has been known from the
        beginning of time.'ᵃ

¹⁹"So I think we should not make things hard for those who have turned to God from among the non-Jewish people. ²⁰Instead, we should send a letter telling them only the things they should not do:

 Don't eat food that has been given to
    idols.* This makes the food unclean.
 Don't be involved in sexual sin.
 Don't eat meat from animals that have
    been strangled or any meat that still has
    the blood in it.

²¹They should not do any of these things, because there are still men in every city who teach the Law of Moses. The words of Moses have been read in the synagogue* every Sabbath* day for many years."

The Letter to the Non-Jewish Believers
²²The apostles,* the elders,* and the whole church* wanted to send some men with Paul and Barnabas to Antioch. The group decided to choose some of their own men. They chose Judas (also called Barsabbas) and Silas, men who were respected by the believers.* ²³The group sent the letter with these men. The letter said:

From the apostles and elders, your brothers.

To all the non-Jewish brothers in the city of Antioch and in the countries of Syria and Cilicia.

Dear Brothers:

 ²⁴We have heard that some men have come to you from our group. What they said troubled and upset you. But we did not tell them to do this. ²⁵We have all agreed to choose some men and send them to you. They will be with our dear friends, Barnabas and Paul. ²⁶Barnabas and Paul have given their lives to serve our Lord Jesus Christ. ²⁷So we have sent Judas and Silas with them. They will tell you the same things. ²⁸We agree with the Holy Spirit* that you should have no more burdens, except for these necessary things:

²⁹ Don't eat food that has been given to
    idols.*
 Don't eat meat from animals that have
    been strangled or any meat that still has
    the blood in it.
 Don't be involved in sexual sin.

If you stay away from these, you will do well.

We say goodbye now.

³⁰So Paul, Barnabas, Judas, and Silas left Jerusalem and went to Antioch. There they gathered the group of believers together and gave them the letter. ³¹When the believers read it, they were happy. The letter comforted them. ³²Judas and Silas, who were also prophets,* said many things to encourage the believers and make them stronger in their faith. ³³After Judas and Silas stayed there for a while, they left. They received a blessing of peace from the believers. Then they went back to those who had sent them. ³⁴ ᵇ

³⁵But Paul and Barnabas stayed in Antioch. They and many others taught the believers and told other people the Good News* about the Lord.

Paul and Barnabas Separate
³⁶A few days later, Paul said to Barnabas, "We should go back to all the towns where we told people the message* of the Lord. We should visit our brothers and sisters in God's family to see how they are doing." ³⁷Barnabas wanted to bring John Mark with them too. ³⁸But on their first trip John Mark did not continue with them in the work. He had left them at Pamphylia. So Paul did

ᵃ**15:18** See Isa. 45:21.

ᵇ**15:34** Some Greek copies add verse 34: "But Silas decided to remain there."

not think it was a good idea to take him this time. ³⁹Paul and Barnabas had a big argument about this. It was so bad that they separated and went different ways. Barnabas sailed to Cyprus and took Mark with him.

⁴⁰Paul chose Silas to go with him. The believers* in Antioch put Paul into the Lord's care and sent him out. ⁴¹Paul and Silas went through the countries of Syria and Cilicia, helping the churches* grow stronger.

Timothy Goes With Paul and Silas

16 ¹Paul went to the city of Derbe and then to Lystra, where a follower of Jesus named Timothy lived. Timothy's mother was a Jewish believer, but his father was a Greek. ²The believers* in the cities of Lystra and Iconium had only good things to say about him. ³Paul wanted Timothy to travel with him, but all the Jews living in that area knew that his father was a Greek. So Paul circumcised* Timothy to please the Jews.

⁴Then Paul and those with him traveled through other cities. They gave the believers the rules and decisions from the apostles* and elders* in Jerusalem. They told them to obey these rules. ⁵So the churches* were becoming stronger in the faith and were growing bigger every day.

Paul Is Called to Macedonia

⁶Paul and those with him went through the areas of Phrygia and Galatia because the Holy Spirit* did not allow them to tell the Good News* in the province of Asia.* ⁷When they reached the border of Mysia, they tried to go on into Bithynia, but the Spirit of Jesus did not let them go there. ⁸So they passed by Mysia and went to the city of Troas.

⁹That night Paul saw a vision.* In it, a man from Macedonia* came to Paul. The man stood there and begged, "Come across to Macedonia and help us." ¹⁰After Paul had seen the vision, we*ᵃ* immediately prepared to leave for Macedonia. We understood that God had called us to tell the Good News to those people.

The Conversion of Lydia

¹¹We left Troas in a ship and sailed to the island of Samothrace. The next day we sailed to the city of Neapolis. ¹²Then we went to Philippi, a Roman colony and the leading city in that part of Macedonia.* We stayed there for a few days.

¹³On the Sabbath* day we went out the city gate to the river. There we thought we might find a special place for prayer. Some women had gathered there, so we sat down and talked with them. ¹⁴There was a woman there named Lydia from the city of Thyatira.

Her job was selling purple cloth. She was a worshiper of the true God. Lydia was listening to Paul, and the Lord opened her heart to accept what Paul was saying. ¹⁵She and all the people living in her house were baptized.* Then she invited us into her home. She said, "If you think I am a true believer in the Lord Jesus, come stay in my house." She persuaded us to stay with her.

Paul and Silas in Jail

¹⁶One day we were going to the place for prayer, and a servant girl met us. She had a spirit*ᵇ* in her that gave her the power to tell what would happen in the future. By doing this she earned a lot of money for the men who owned her. ¹⁷She started following Paul and the rest of us around. She kept shouting, "These men are servants of the Most High God! They are telling you how you can be saved!" ¹⁸She continued doing this for many days. This bothered Paul, so he turned and said to the spirit, "By the power of Jesus Christ, I command you to come out of her!" Immediately, the spirit came out.

¹⁹When the men who owned the servant girl saw this, they realized that they could no longer use her to make money. So they grabbed Paul and Silas and dragged them to the public square to meet with the authorities. ²⁰They brought Paul and Silas before the Roman officials and said, "These men are Jews, and they are making trouble in our city. ²¹They are telling people to do things that are not right for us as Romans to do."

²²The whole crowd turned against Paul and Silas. The officials tore the clothes off both men and ordered that they be beaten with rods. ²³They were beaten severely and thrown into jail. The officials told the jailer, "Guard them very carefully!" ²⁴When the jailer heard this special order, he put Paul and Silas far inside the jail and bound their feet between large blocks of wood.

²⁵About midnight Paul and Silas were praying and singing songs to God. The other prisoners were listening to them. ²⁶Suddenly there was an earthquake so strong that it shook the foundation of the jail. All the doors of the jail opened, and the chains on all the prisoners fell off. ²⁷The jailer woke up and saw that the jail doors were open. He thought that the prisoners had already escaped, so he got his sword and was ready to kill himself.*ᶜ* ²⁸But Paul shouted, "Don't hurt yourself! We are all here!"

²⁹The jailer told someone to bring a light. Then he ran inside and, shaking with fear, fell down in front of Paul and Silas. ³⁰Then he brought them outside and said, "Men, what must I do to be saved?"

---

*ᵃ***16:10 we** Luke, the writer, apparently went with Paul to Macedonia but did not leave Philippi with him. (See verse 40.) The first person pronoun occurs again in 20:5–21:18 and 27:1–28.

*ᵇ***16:16 spirit** A spirit from the devil that gave special knowledge.

*ᶜ***16:27 kill himself** He thought the leaders would kill him for letting the prisoners escape.

31They said to him, "Believe in the Lord Jesus and you will be saved—you and all who live in your house." 32So Paul and Silas told the message* of the Lord to the jailer and all the people who lived in his house. 33It was late at night, but the jailer took Paul and Silas and washed their wounds. Then the jailer and all his people were baptized.* 34After this the jailer took Paul and Silas home and gave them some food. All the people were very happy because they now believed in God.

35The next morning the Roman officials sent some soldiers to tell the jailer, "Let these men go free."

36The jailer said to Paul, "The officials have sent these soldiers to let you go free. You can leave now. Go in peace."

37But Paul said to the soldiers, "Those officials did not prove that we did anything wrong, but they beat us in public and put us in jail. And we are Roman citizens.a Now they want us to go away quietly. No, they must come here themselves and lead us out!"

38The soldiers told the officials what Paul said. When they heard that Paul and Silas were Roman citizens, they were afraid. 39So they came and told them they were sorry. They led them out of the jail and asked them to leave the city. 40But when Paul and Silas came out of the jail, they went to Lydia's house. They saw some of the believers* there and encouraged them. Then they left.

Paul and Silas in Thessalonica

17 1Paul and Silas traveled through the cities of Amphipolis and Apollonia. They came to the city of Thessalonica, where there was a Jewish synagogue.* 2Paul went into the synagogue to see the Jews as he always did. The next three weeks, on each Sabbath* day, he discussed the Scriptures* with them. 3He explained the Scriptures to show them that the Christ* had to die and then rise from death. He said, "This Jesus that I am telling you about is the Christ." 4Some of the Jews there believed Paul and Silas and decided to join them. Also, a large number of Greeks who were worshipers of the true God and many important women joined them.

5But the Jews who did not believe became jealous, so they got some bad men from around the city center to make trouble. They formed a mob and caused a riot in the city. They went to Jason's house, looking for Paul and Silas. They wanted to bring them out before the people. 6When they did not find them, they dragged Jason and some of the other believers to the city leaders. The people shouted, "These men have made trouble everywhere in the world, and now they have come here too! 7Jason is keeping them in his house. They all do things against the laws of

Caesar.* They say there is another king called Jesus."

8When the city leaders and the other people heard this, they became very upset. 9They made Jason and the other believers deposit money to guarantee that there would be no more trouble. Then they let them go.

Paul and Silas Go to Berea

10That same night the believers* sent Paul and Silas to another city named Berea. When they arrived there, they went to the Jewish synagogue.* 11The people in Berea were more open-minded than those in Thessalonica. They were so glad to hear the message Paul told them. They studied the Scriptures* every day to make sure that what they heard was really true. 12The result was that many of them believed, including many important Greek women and men.

13But when the Jews in Thessalonica learned that Paul was telling people God's message* in Berea, they came there too. They upset the people and made trouble. 14So the believers immediately sent Paul away to the coast, but Silas and Timothy stayed in Berea. 15Those who went with Paul took him to the city of Athens. They returned with a message for Silas and Timothy to come and join him as soon as they could.

Paul in Athens

16While Paul was waiting for Silas and Timothy in Athens, he was upset because he saw that the city was full of idols.* 17In the synagogue* he talked with the Jews and with the Greeks who were worshipers of the true God. He also went to the public square every day and talked with everyone who came by. 18Some of the Epicurean and some of the Stoic philosophers* argued with him.

Some of them said, "This man doesn't really know what he is talking about. What is he trying to say?" Paul was telling them the Good News* about Jesus and the resurrection.* So they said, "He seems to be telling us about some other gods."

19They took Paul to a meeting of the Areopagus council.* They said, "Please explain to us this new idea that you have been teaching. 20The things you are saying are new to us. We have never heard this teaching before, and we want to know what it means." 21(The people of Athens and the foreigners who lived there spent all their time either telling or listening to all the latest ideas.)

22Then Paul stood up before the meeting of the Areopagus council and said, "Men of Athens, everything I see here tells me you are very religious. 23I was going through your city and I saw the things you worship. I found an altar that had these words written on it: 'TO AN UNKNOWN GOD.' You worship a god that you don't know. This is the God I want to tell you about.

a16:37 Roman citizens Roman law said that Roman citizens must not be beaten before their trial.

24"He is the God who made the whole world and everything in it. He is the Lord of the land and the sky. He does not live in temples built by human hands. 25He is the one who gives people life, breath, and everything else they need. He does not need any help from them. He has everything he needs. 26God began by making one man, and from him he made all the different people who live everywhere in the world. He decided exactly when and where they would live.

27"God wanted people to look for him, and perhaps in searching all around for him, they would find him. But he is not far from any of us. 28It is through him that we are able to live, to do what we do, and to be who we are. As your own poets have said, 'We all come from him.'

29"That's right. We all come from God. So you must not think that he is like something people imagine or make. He is not made of gold, silver, or stone. 30In the past people did not understand God, and he overlooked this. But now he is telling everyone in the world to change and turn to him. 31He has decided on a day when he will judge all the people in the world in a way that is fair. To do this he will use a man he chose long ago. And he has proved to everyone that this is the man to do it. He proved it by raising him from death!"

32When the people heard about Jesus being raised from death, some of them laughed. But others said, "We will hear more about this from you later." 33So Paul left the council meeting. 34But some of the people joined with Paul and became believers. Among these were Dionysius, a member of the Areopagus council, a woman named Damaris, and some others.

Paul in Corinth

18 1Later, Paul left Athens and went to the city of Corinth. 2There he met a Jewish man named Aquila, who was born in the country of Pontus. But he and his wife, Priscilla, had recently moved to Corinth from Italy. They left Italy because Claudius* had given an order for all Jews to leave Rome. Paul went to visit Aquila and Priscilla. 3They were tentmakers, the same as Paul, so he stayed with them and worked with them.

4Every Sabbath* day Paul went to the synagogue* and talked with both Jews and Greeks, trying to persuade them to believe in Jesus. 5But after Silas and Timothy came from Macedonia,* Paul spent all his time telling God's message* to the Jews, trying to convince them that Jesus is the Christ.* 6But they disagreed with what Paul was teaching and started insulting him. So Paul shook the dust from his clothes.a He said to them, "If you are not saved, it will be your own fault! I have done all I can do. After this I will go only to the non-Jewish people."

7Paul left the synagogue and moved into the home of Titius Justus, a man who was a worshiper of the true God. His house was next to the synagogue. 8Crispus was the leader of that synagogue. He and all the people living in his house believed in the Lord Jesus. Many other people in Corinth also listened to Paul. They, too, believed and were baptized.*

9During the night, Paul had a vision.* The Lord said to him, "Don't be afraid, and don't stop talking to people. 10I am with you, and no one will be able to hurt you. Many of my people are in this city." 11Paul stayed there for a year and a half teaching God's message to the people.

Paul Is Brought Before Gallio

12During the time that Gallio was the governor of Achaia,* some of the Jews came together against Paul. They took him to court. 13They said to Gallio, "This man is teaching people to worship God in a way that is against our law!"

14Paul was ready to say something, but Gallio spoke to the Jews. He said, "I would listen to you if your complaint was about a crime or other wrong. 15But it is only about words and names—arguments about your own law. So you must solve this problem yourselves. I don't want to be a judge of these matters." 16So Gallio made them leave the court.

17Then they all grabbed Sosthenes, the leader of the synagogue.* They beat him before the court. But this did not bother Gallio.

Paul Returns to Antioch

18Paul stayed with the believers* for many days. Then he left and sailed for Syria. Priscilla and Aquila were also with him. At Cenchrea Paul cut off his hair,b because he had made a promise to God. 19Then they went to the city of Ephesus, where Paul left Priscilla and Aquila. While Paul was in Ephesus, he went into the synagogue* and talked with the Jews. 20They asked him to stay longer, but he refused. 21He left them and said, "I will come back to you again if God wants me to." And so he sailed away from Ephesus.

22When Paul arrived at Caesarea, he went to Jerusalem and visited the church* there. After that, he went to Antioch. 23Paul stayed in Antioch for a while. Then he left there and went through the countries of Galatia and Phrygia. He traveled from town to town in these countries, helping all the followers grow stronger in their faith.

---

a18:6 shook the dust from his clothes A warning. It showed Paul was finished talking to these Jews.

b18:18 cut off his hair This may show that Paul was ending a Nazirite vow, a time of special dedication and service promised to God. See "Nazirite" in the Word List.

Apollos in Ephesus and Corinth

24A Jew named Apollos came to Ephesus. Born in the city of Alexandria, he was an educated man who knew the Scriptures* well. 25He had been taught about the Lord and was always excited*a* to talk to people about Jesus. What he taught was right, but the only baptism* he knew about was the baptism that John* taught. 26Apollos began to speak very boldly in the synagogue.* When Priscilla and Aquila heard him speak, they took him to their home and helped him understand the way of God better.

27Apollos wanted to go to Achaia.* So the believers* in Ephesus helped him. They wrote a letter to the Lord's followers in Achaia and asked them to accept Apollos. When he arrived there, he was a great help to those who had believed in Jesus because of God's grace.* 28He argued very strongly against the Jews before all the people. He clearly proved that the Jews were wrong. He used the Scriptures and showed that Jesus is the Christ.*

Paul in Ephesus

19 1While Apollos was in the city of Corinth, Paul was visiting some places on his way to Ephesus. In Ephesus he found some other followers of the Lord. 2He asked them, "Did you receive the Holy Spirit* when you believed?"

These followers said to him, "We have never even heard of a Holy Spirit!"

3Paul asked them, "So what kind of baptism* did you have?"

They said, "It was the baptism that John* taught."

4Paul said, "John told people to be baptized to show they wanted to change their lives. He told people to believe in the one who would come after him, and that one is Jesus."

5When these followers heard this, they were baptized in the name of the Lord Jesus. 6Then Paul laid his hands on* them, and the Holy Spirit came on them. They began speaking different languages and prophesying.* 7There were about twelve men in this group.

8Paul went into the synagogue* and spoke very boldly. He continued doing this for three months. He talked with the Jews, trying to persuade them to accept what he was telling them about God's kingdom.* 9But some of them became stubborn and refused to believe. In front of everyone, they said bad things about the Way.* So Paul left these Jews and took the Lord's followers with him. He went to a place where a man named Tyrannus had a school. There Paul talked with people every day. 10He did this for two years. Because of this work, everyone in Asia,* Jews and Greeks,* heard the word of the Lord.

The Sons of Sceva

11God used Paul to do some very special miracles.* 12Some people carried away handkerchiefs and clothes that Paul had used and put them on those who were sick. The sick people were healed, and evil spirits left them.

13-14Some Jews also were traveling around forcing evil spirits out of people. The seven sons of Sceva, one of the leading priests, were doing this. These Jews tried to use the name of the Lord Jesus to make the evil spirits go out of people. They all said, "By the same Jesus that Paul talks about, I order you to come out!"

15But one time an evil spirit said to these Jews, "I know Jesus, and I know about Paul, but who are you?"

16Then the man who had the evil spirit inside him jumped on these Jews. He was much stronger than all of them. He beat them up and tore their clothes off. They all ran away from that house.

17All the people in Ephesus, Jews and Greeks,* learned about this. They were all filled with fear and gave great honor to the Lord Jesus. 18Many of the believers began to confess, telling about all the evil things they had done. 19Some of them had used magic. These believers brought their magic books and burned them before everyone. These books were worth about 50,000 silver coins.*b* 20This is how the word of the Lord was spreading in a powerful way, causing more and more people to believe.

Paul Plans a Trip

21After this, Paul made plans to go to Jerusalem. He planned to go through the regions of Macedonia* and Achaia,* and then go to Jerusalem. He thought, "After I visit Jerusalem, I must also visit Rome." 22Timothy and Erastus were two of his helpers. Paul sent them ahead to Macedonia. But he stayed in Asia* for a while.

Trouble in Ephesus

23But during that time there was some trouble in Ephesus about the Way.* This is how it all happened: 24There was a man named Demetrius. He worked with silver. He made little silver models that looked like the temple of the goddess Artemis. The men who did this work made a lot of money. 25Demetrius had a meeting with these men and some others who did the same kind of work. He told them, "Men, you know that we make a lot of money from our business. 26But look at what this man Paul is doing. Listen to what he is saying. He has convinced many people in Ephesus and all over Asia* to change their religion. He says the gods that people make by hand are not real. 27I'm

---

*a***18:25** *excited* Or "on fire with the Spirit."

*b***19:19** *silver coins* Probably Greek drachmas. One coin was worth the average pay for one day's work.

afraid this is going to turn people against our business. But there is also another problem. People will begin to think that the temple of the great goddess Artemis is not important. Her greatness will be destroyed. And Artemis is the goddess that everyone in Asia and the whole world worships."

28When the men heard this, they became very angry. They shouted, "Great is Artemis, the goddess of Ephesus!" 29The whole city was thrown into confusion. The people grabbed Gaius and Aristarchus, men from Macedonia* who were traveling with Paul, and rushed all together into the stadium. 30Paul wanted to go in and talk to the people, but the Lord's followers did not let him go. 31Also, some leaders of the country who were friends of Paul sent him a message telling him not to go into the stadium.

32Some people were shouting one thing and others were shouting something else. The meeting was very confused. Most of the people did not know why they had come there. 33Some Jews made a man named Alexander stand before the crowd, and they told him what to say. Alexander waved his hand, trying to explain things to the people. 34But when the people saw that Alexander was a Jew, they all began shouting the same thing. For two hours they continued shouting, "Great is Artemis of Ephesus! Great is Artemis of Ephesus! Great is Artemis ...!"

35Then the city clerk persuaded the people to be quiet. He said, "Men of Ephesus, everyone knows that Ephesus is the city that keeps the temple of the great goddess Artemis. Everyone knows that we also keep her holy rock.a 36No one can deny this, so you should be quiet. You must stop and think before you do anything else.

37"You brought these menb here, but they have not said anything bad against our goddess. They have not stolen anything from her temple. 38We have courts of law and there are judges. Do Demetrius and those men who work with him have a charge against anyone? They should go to the courts. Let them argue with each other there.

39"Is there something else you want to talk about? Then come to the regular town meeting of the people. It can be decided there. 40I say this because someone might see this trouble today and say we are rioting. We could not explain all this trouble, because there is no real reason for this meeting." 41After the city clerk said this, he told the people to go home.

Paul Goes to Macedonia and Greece

20 1When the trouble stopped, Paul invited the Lord's followers to come visit him. After encouraging them, he told them goodbye and left for Macedonia.* 2On his way through Macedonia he had many words of encouragement for the followers in various places. Then he went to Greece 3and stayed there three months.

Paul was ready to sail for Syria, but some Jews were planning something against him. So he decided to go back through Macedonia to Syria. 4These men were traveling with him: Sopater, the son of Pyrrhus, from the city of Berea; Aristarchus and Secundus, from the city of Thessalonica; Gaius, from the city of Derbe; Timothy; and two men from Asia,* Tychicus and Trophimus. 5These men went first, ahead of Paul. They waited for us in the city of Troas. 6We sailed from the city of Philippi after the Festival of Unleavened Bread.* We met these men in Troas five days later and stayed there seven days.

Paul's Last Visit to Troas

7On Sundayc we all met together to eat the Lord's Supper.d Paul talked to the group. Because he was planning to leave the next day, he continued talking until midnight. 8We were all together in a room upstairs, and there were many lights in the room. 9There was a young man named Eutychus sitting in the window. Paul continued talking, and Eutychus became very, very sleepy. Finally, he went to sleep and fell out of the window. He fell to the ground from the third floor. When the people went down and lifted him up, he was dead.

10Paul went down to where Eutychus was, knelt down beside him, and put his arms around him. He said to the other believers, "Don't worry. He is alive now." 11Then Paul went upstairs again, broke off some pieces of bread and ate. He spoke to them a long time. It was early morning when he finished, and then he left. 12The Lord's followers took Eutychus home alive, and they were all greatly comforted.

The Trip From Troas to Miletus

13We went on ahead of Paul and sailed for the city of Assos, planning to meet him there. This is what he told us to do because he wanted to go by land. 14When he caught up with us at Assos, we took him on board, and we all sailed to Mitylene. 15The next day, we sailed away from there and came to a place near the island of Chios. Then the next day, we sailed to the island of Samos. A day later, we came to the city of Miletus. 16Paul had

---

a19:35 holy rock Probably a meteorite or rock that the people thought looked like Artemis and worshiped.

b19:37 men Gaius and Aristarchus, the men traveling with Paul.

c20:7 Sunday Literally, "first day of the week," which for the Jews began at sunset on Saturday. But if Luke is using Greek time here, then the meeting was Sunday night.

d20:7 to eat the Lord's Supper Literally, "to break bread." This may mean a meal or the Lord's Supper, the special meal Jesus told his followers to eat to remember him. See Lk. 22:14–20.

already decided not to stop at Ephesus. He did not want to stay too long in Asia.* He was hurrying because he wanted to be in Jerusalem on the day of Pentecost* if possible.

Paul Speaks to the Elders From Ephesus

¹⁷In Miletus Paul sent a message back to Ephesus, telling the elders* of the church* in Ephesus to come to him.

¹⁸When they came, Paul said to them, "You know about my life from the first day I came to Asia.* You know the way I lived all the time I was with you. ¹⁹The Jews planned things against me, and this gave me much trouble. But you know that I always served the Lord, sometimes with tears. I never thought about myself first. ²⁰I always did what was best for you. I told you the Good News* about Jesus in public before the people and also taught in your homes. ²¹I told everyone—Jewish and non-Jewish people—to change and turn to God. I told them all to believe in our Lord Jesus.

²²"But now I must obey the Spirit* and go to Jerusalem. I don't know what will happen to me there. ²³I know only that in every city the Holy Spirit tells me that troubles and even jail wait for me. ²⁴I don't care about my own life. The most important thing is that I finish my work. I want to finish the work that the Lord Jesus gave me to do—to tell people the Good News about God's grace.

²⁵"And now listen to me. I know that none of you will ever see me again. All the time I was with you, I told you the Good News about God's kingdom.* ²⁶So today I can tell you one thing that I am sure of: God will not blame me if some of you are not saved. ²⁷I can say this because I know that I told you everything that God wants you to know. ²⁸Be careful for yourselves and for all the people God has given you. The Holy Spirit gave you the work of caring for^a this flock.^b You must be like shepherds to the church of God.^c This is the church that God bought with his own blood.^d ²⁹I know that after I leave, some men will come into your group. They will be like wild wolves and will try to destroy the flock. ³⁰Also, men from your own group will begin to teach things that are wrong. They will lead some of the Lord's followers away from the truth to follow them. ³¹So be careful! And always remember what I did during the three years I was with you. I never stopped reminding each one of you how you should live, counseling you day and night and crying over you.

³²"Now I am putting you in God's care. I am depending on the message* about his grace

to make you strong. That message is able to give you the blessings that God gives to all his holy people.* ³³When I was with you, I never wanted anyone's money or fine clothes. ³⁴You know that I always worked to take care of my own needs and the needs of the people who were with me. ³⁵I always showed you that you should work just as I did and help people who are weak. I taught you to remember the words of the Lord Jesus: 'You will have a greater blessing when you give than when you receive.'"

³⁶When Paul finished speaking, he knelt down, and they all prayed together. ^{37–38}They cried and cried. They were especially sad because Paul had said they would never see him again. They hugged him and kissed him. Then they went with him to the ship to say goodbye.

Paul Goes to Jerusalem

21 ¹After we said goodbye to the elders,* we sailed away straight to Cos island. The next day we went to the island of Rhodes, and from there we went to Patara. ²There we found a ship that was going to the area of Phoenicia. We got on the ship and sailed away.

³We sailed near the island of Cyprus. We could see it on the north side, but we did not stop. We sailed to the country of Syria. We stopped at Tyre because the ship needed to unload its cargo there. ⁴We found the Lord's followers there and stayed with them for seven days. They warned Paul not to go to Jerusalem because of what the Spirit* had told them. ⁵But when our time there was up, we returned to the ship to continue our trip. All the followers, even the women and children, came with us to the seashore. We all knelt down on the beach, prayed, ⁶and said goodbye. Then we got on the ship, and the followers went home.

⁷We continued our trip from Tyre and went to the city of Ptolemais. We greeted our brothers and sisters in God's family there and stayed with them one day. ⁸The next day we left Ptolemais and went to the city of Caesarea. We went into the home of Philip and stayed with him. He had the work of telling the Good News.* He was one of the seven helpers.^e ⁹He had four unmarried daughters who had the gift of prophesying.*

¹⁰After we had been there for several days, a prophet* named Agabus came from Judea. ¹¹He came to us and borrowed Paul's belt. He used it to tie his own hands and feet. He said, "The Holy Spirit tells me, 'This is how the Jews in Jerusalem will tie up the man who wears this belt.^f Then they will hand him over to people who don't know God.'"

---

^a**20:28 gave … caring for** Literally, "made you overseers of."

^b**20:28 flock** A flock is many sheep. Here, it means a group of God's people who follow their leaders (elders) like sheep following a shepherd.

^c**20:28 of God** Some Greek copies say, "of the Lord."

^d**20:28 his own blood** Or "the blood of his own Son."

^e**21:8 seven helpers** Men chosen for a special work. See Acts 6:1–6.

^f**21:11 belt** Paul's belt; so Agabus means that the Jews in Jerusalem will tie Paul up (arrest him).

¹²When we heard this, we and the other followers there begged Paul not to go to Jerusalem. ¹³But he said, "Why are you crying and making me feel so sad? I am willing to be put in jail in Jerusalem. I am even ready to die for the name of the Lord Jesus!"

¹⁴We could not persuade him to stay away from Jerusalem. So we stopped begging him and said, "We pray that what the Lord wants will be done."

¹⁵After this, we got ready and left for Jerusalem. ¹⁶Some of the followers of Jesus from Caesarea went with us. These followers took us to the home of Mnason, a man from Cyprus, who was one of the first people to be a follower of Jesus. They took us to his home so that we could stay with him.

Paul Visits James

¹⁷The brothers and sisters in Jerusalem were very happy to see us. ¹⁸The next day Paul went with us to visit James, and all the elders* were there. ¹⁹After greeting them, Paul told them point by point all that God had used him to do among the non-Jewish people.

²⁰When the leaders heard this, they praised God. Then they said to Paul, "Brother, you can see that thousands of Jews have become believers, but they think it is very important to obey the Law of Moses.* ²¹They have been told that you teach the Jews who live in non-Jewish regions to stop following the Law of Moses. They have heard that you tell them not to circumcise* their sons or follow our other customs.

²²"What should we do? The Jewish believers here will learn that you have come. ²³So we will tell you what to do: Four of our men have made a vowᵃ to God. ²⁴Take these men with you and share in their cleansing ceremony.ᵇ Pay their expenses so that they can shave their heads.ᶜ This will prove to everyone that the things they have heard about you are not true. They will see that you obey the Law of Moses in your own life.

²⁵"In regard to the non-Jewish believers, we have already sent a letter to them saying what we think they should do:

'Don't eat food that has been given to idols.*
Don't eat meat from animals that have been strangled or any meat that still has the blood in it.
Don't be involved in sexual sin.'"

ᵃ**21:23 vow** Probably a Nazirite vow, a time of special dedication and service promised to God. See "Nazirite" in the Word List.
ᵇ**21:24 cleansing ceremony** The special things Jews did to end the Nazirite vow. Also in verse 26.
ᶜ**21:24 shave their heads** To show that their vow was finished.

Paul Is Arrested

²⁶So Paul took the four men with him. The next day he shared in their cleansing ceremony. Then he went to the Temple* area and announced the time when the days of the cleansing ceremony would be finished. On the last day an offering would be given for each of the men.

²⁷When the seven-day period was almost finished, some Jews from Asia* saw Paul in the Temple area. They stirred up everyone into an angry mob. They grabbed Paul ²⁸and shouted, "Men of Israel,* help us! This is the man who is teaching things that are against the Law of Moses,* against our people, and against this Temple of ours. This is what he teaches people everywhere. And now he has brought some Greeks* into the Temple area and has made this holy place unclean!" ²⁹(The Jews said this because they had seen Trophimus with Paul in Jerusalem. Trophimus was a man from Ephesus. The Jews thought that Paul had taken him into the holy area of the Temple.)

³⁰An angry reaction spread throughout the city, and everyone came running to the Temple. They grabbed Paul and dragged him out of the holy area, and the gates were closed immediately. ³¹While they were trying to kill Paul, the commander of the Roman army in Jerusalem got word that the whole city was in a state of riot. ³²Immediately the commander ran to where the crowd had gathered, taking with him some army officers* and soldiers. When the people saw the commander and his soldiers, they stopped beating Paul.

³³The commander went over to Paul and arrested him. He told his soldiers to tie him up with two chains. Then he asked, "Who is this man? What has he done wrong?" ³⁴Some people there were shouting one thing, and others were shouting something else. Because of all this confusion and shouting, the commander could not learn the truth about what had happened. So he told the soldiers to take Paul to the army building. ³⁵⁻³⁶The whole crowd was following them. When the soldiers came to the steps, they had to carry Paul. They did this to protect him, because the people were ready to hurt him. The people were shouting, "Kill him!"

³⁷When the soldiers were ready to take Paul into the army building, he asked the commander, "Can I say something to you?"

The commander said, "Oh, you speak Greek? ³⁸Then you are not the man I thought you were. I thought you were the Egyptian who started some trouble against the government not long ago and led four thousand terrorists out to the desert."

³⁹Paul said, "No, I am a Jew from Tarsus in the country of Cilicia. I am a citizen of that important city. Please, let me speak to the people."

⁴⁰The commander told Paul he could speak.

So he stood on the steps and waved his hand so that the people would be quiet. The people became quiet and Paul spoke to them in Aramaic.*

Paul Speaks to the People

22 ¹Paul said, "My brothers and fathers, listen to me! I will make my defense to you."

²When the Jews heard Paul speaking Aramaic,* they became very quiet. Then Paul said,

³"I am a Jew, born in Tarsus in the country of Cilicia. I grew up in this city. I was a student of Gamaliel,ᵃ who carefully taught me everything about the law of our fathers.* I was very serious about serving God, the same as all of you here today. ⁴I persecuted* the people who followed the Way.* Some of them were killed because of me. I arrested men and women and put them in jail.

⁵"The high priest* and the whole council of older Jewish leaders can tell you that this is true. One time these leaders gave me some letters. The letters were to the Jewish brothers in the city of Damascus. I was going there to arrest the followers of Jesus and bring them back to Jerusalem for punishment.

Paul Tells About His Conversion

⁶"But something happened to me on my way to Damascus. It was about noon when I came close to Damascus. Suddenly a bright light from heaven shined all around me. ⁷I fell to the ground and heard a voice saying to me, 'Saul, Saul, why are you persecuting* me?'

⁸"I asked, 'Who are you, Lord?' The voice said, 'I am Jesus from Nazareth, the one you are persecuting.' ⁹The men who were with me did not understand the voice, but they saw the light.

¹⁰"I said, 'What shall I do, Lord?' The Lord answered, 'Get up and go into Damascus. There you will be told all that I have planned for you to do.' ¹¹I could not see, because the bright light had made me blind. So the men led me into Damascus.

¹²"In Damascus a man named Ananiasᵇ came to me. He was a man who was devoted to God and obeyed the Law of Moses.* All the Jews who lived there respected him. ¹³He came to me and said, 'Saul, my brother, look up and see again!' Immediately I was able to see him.

¹⁴"Ananias told me, 'The God of our fathers* chose you long ago to know his plan. He chose you to see the Righteous One and to hear words from him. ¹⁵You will be his witness to all people. You will tell them what you have seen and heard. ¹⁶Now, don't wait any longer. Get up, be baptized* and wash away

your sins, trusting in Jesus to save you.ᶜ

¹⁷"Later, I came back to Jerusalem. I was praying in the Temple* area, and I saw a vision.* ¹⁸I saw Jesus, and he said to me, 'Hurry and leave Jerusalem now! The people here will not accept the truth you tell them about me.'

¹⁹"I said, 'But, Lord, the people know that I was the one who put the believers in jail and beat them. I went through all the synagogues* to find and arrest the people who believe in you. ²⁰The people also know that I was there when Stephen, your witness, was killed. I stood there and agreed that they should kill him. I even held the coats of the men who were killing him!'

²¹"But Jesus said to me, 'Leave now. I will send you far away to the non-Jewish people.'"

²²The people stopped listening when Paul said this last thing. They all shouted, "Get rid of this man! He doesn't deserve to live." ²³They kept on shouting, ripping off their clothes and throwing dust into the air.ᵈ ²⁴Then the commander told the soldiers to take Paul into the army building and beat him. He wanted to make Paul tell why the people were shouting against him like this. ²⁵So the soldiers were tying Paul, preparing to beat him. But he said to an army officer* there, "Do you have the right to beat a Roman citizenᵉ who has not been proven guilty?"

²⁶When the officer heard this, he went to the commander and told him about it. The officer said, "Do you know what you are doing? This man is a Roman citizen!"

²⁷The commander came to Paul and said, "Tell me, are you really a Roman citizen?"

He answered, "Yes."

²⁸The commander said, "I paid a lot of money to become a Roman citizen."

But Paul said, "I was born a citizen."

²⁹The men who were preparing to question Paul moved away from him immediately. The commander was afraid because he had already put Paul in chains, and he was a Roman citizen.

Paul Speaks to the Jewish Leaders

³⁰The next day the commander decided to learn why the Jews were accusing Paul. So he ordered the leading priests and the whole high council to meet together. He had Paul's chains taken off and had him brought in to face the council.

23 ¹Paul looked at the council members and said, "Brothers, I have lived my

---

ᵃ**22:3 Gamaliel** A very important teacher of the Pharisees, a Jewish religious group. See Acts 5:34.
ᵇ**22:12 Ananias** In Acts there are three men with this name. See Acts 5:1 and 23:2 for the other two.
ᶜ**22:16 trusting in Jesus to save you** Literally, "calling on his name," meaning to show faith in Jesus by worshiping him or praying to him for help.
ᵈ**22:23 ripping … air** These actions were signs of very strong anger.
ᵉ**22:25 Roman citizen** Roman law said that Roman citizens must not be beaten before their trial. Also at 23:27.

life in a good way before God. I have always done what I thought was right." [2]Ananias,[a] the high priest,* was there. When he heard this, he told the men who were standing near Paul to hit him in the mouth. [3]Paul said to Ananias, "God will hit you too! You are like a dirty wall that has been painted white. You sit there and judge me, using the Law of Moses.* But you are telling them to hit me, and that is against the law."

[4]The men standing near Paul said to him, "Are you sure you want to insult God's high priest like that?"

[5]Paul said, "Brothers, I did not know this man was the high priest. The Scriptures* say, 'You must not say bad things about a leader of your people.'[b]"

[6]Paul knew that some of the men in the council meeting were Sadducees* and some were Pharisees.* So he shouted, "My brothers, I am a Pharisee and my father was a Pharisee! I am on trial here because I believe that people will rise from death."

[7]When Paul said this, a big argument started between the Pharisees and the Sadducees. The group was divided. [8](The Sadducees believe that after people die, they will not live again as an angel or as a spirit. But the Pharisees believe in both.) [9]All these Jews began shouting louder and louder. Some of the teachers of the law, who were Pharisees, stood up and argued, "We find nothing wrong with this man. Maybe an angel or a spirit really did speak to him."

[10]The argument turned into a fight, and the commander was afraid that the Jews would tear Paul to pieces. So he told the soldiers to go down and take Paul away from these Jews and put him in the army building.

[11]The next night the Lord Jesus came and stood by Paul. He said, "Be brave! You have told people in Jerusalem about me. You must do the same in Rome."

Some Jews Plan to Kill Paul

[12]The next morning some of the Jews made a plan to kill Paul. They made a promise to themselves that they would not eat or drink anything until they had killed him. [13]There were more than 40 of them who made this plan. [14]They went and talked to the leading priests and the older Jewish leaders. They said, "We have promised ourselves that we will not eat or drink until we have killed Paul. [15]So this is what we want you to do: Send a message to the commander from you and the high council. Tell him you want him to bring Paul out to you. Say that you want to ask him more questions. We will be waiting to kill him while he is on the way here."

[16]But Paul's nephew heard about this plan. He went to the army building and told Paul. [17]Then Paul called one of the army officers* and said to him, "Take this young man to the commander. He has a message for him." [18]So the army officer brought Paul's nephew to the commander. The officer said, "The prisoner Paul asked me to bring this young man to you. He has something to tell you."

[19]The commander led the young man to a place where they could be alone. The commander asked, "What do you want to tell me?"

[20]The young man said, "Some Jews have decided to ask you to bring Paul down to their council meeting tomorrow. They want you to think that they plan to ask Paul more questions. [21]But don't believe them! More than 40 of them are hiding and waiting to kill him. They have all promised not to eat or drink until they have killed him. Now they are waiting for you to say yes."

[22]The commander sent the young man away, telling him, "Don't tell anyone that you have told me about their plan."

Paul Is Sent to Caesarea

[23]Then the commander called two army officers.* He said to them, "I need some men to go to Caesarea. Get 200 soldiers ready. Also, get 70 soldiers on horses and 200 men to carry spears. Be ready to leave at nine o'clock tonight. [24]Get some horses for Paul to ride so that he can be taken to Governor Felix safely." [25]The commander wrote a letter that said:

[26]From Claudius Lysias.

To the Most Honorable Governor Felix.

Greetings:

[27]Some Jews had taken this man and planned to kill him. But I learned that he is a Roman citizen, so I went with my soldiers and saved him. [28]I wanted to know why they were accusing him. So I brought him before their council meeting. [29]This is what I learned: The Jews said this man did some things that were wrong. But these charges were about their own Jewish laws, and there was nothing worthy of jail or death. [30]I was told that some of the Jews were making a plan to kill him. So I decided to send him to you. I also told those Jews to tell you what they have against him.

[31]The soldiers did what they were told. They got Paul and took him to the city of Antipatris that night. [32]The next day the soldiers on horses went with Paul to Caesarea, but the other soldiers and the spearmen went back to the army building in Jerusalem. [33]The soldiers on horses entered Caesarea, gave the

---

[a]23:2 *Ananias* Not the same man named Ananias in Acts 22:12.
[b]23:5 Quote from Ex. 22:28.

letter to Governor Felix, and then turned Paul over to him.

³⁴The governor read the letter and asked Paul, "What country are you from?" The governor learned that Paul was from Cilicia. ³⁵The governor said, "I will hear your case when the Jews who are accusing you come here too." Then the governor gave orders for Paul to be kept in the palace built by Herod.*

Some Jews Accuse Paul

24 ¹Five days later Ananias, the high priest,* went to the city of Caesarea. He brought with him some of the older Jewish leaders and a lawyer named Tertullus. They went to Caesarea to make charges against Paul before the governor. ²⁻³Paul was called into the meeting, and Tertullus began to make his accusations.

Tertullus said, "Most Honorable Felix, our people enjoy much peace because of you, and many wrong things in our country are being made right through your wise help. For this we all continue to be very thankful. ⁴But I don't want to take any more of your time. So I will say only a few words. Please be patient. ⁵This man is a troublemaker. He causes trouble with the Jews everywhere in the world. He is a leader of the Nazarene group. ⁶⁻⁸Also, he was trying to make the Temple* unclean, but we stopped him.ᵃ You can decide if all this is true. Ask him some questions yourself." ⁹The other Jews agreed and said it was all true.

Paul Defends Himself Before Felix

¹⁰The governor made a sign for Paul to speak. So Paul answered, "Governor Felix, I know that you have been a judge over this nation for a long time. So I am happy to defend myself before you. ¹¹I went to worship in Jerusalem only twelve days ago. You can learn for yourself that this is true. ¹²These Jews who are accusing me did not find me arguing with anyone at the Temple* or making trouble with the people. And I was not making trouble or arguing in the synagogues* or any other place in the city. ¹³These men cannot prove the things they are saying against me now.

¹⁴"But I will tell you this: I worship the God of our fathers* as a follower of the Way,* which these Jews say is not the right way, and I believe everything that is taught in the Law of Moses* and all that is written in the books of the prophets.* ¹⁵I have the same hope in God that these Jews have—the hope that all people, good and bad, will be raised from death. ¹⁶This is why I always try to do

what I believe is right before God and before everyone.

¹⁷⁻¹⁸"I was away from Jerusalem for many years. I went back there to take money to help my people. I also had some gifts to offer at the Temple. I was doing this when some Jews saw me there. I had finished the cleansing ceremony.ᵇ I had not made any trouble, and no one was gathering around me. ¹⁹But some Jews from Asia* were there. They should be here, standing before you. If I have really done anything wrong, they are the ones who should accuse me. They were there! ²⁰Ask these men here if they found any wrong in me when I stood before the high council meeting in Jerusalem. ²¹I did say one thing when I stood before them and shouted, 'You are judging me today because I believe that people will rise from death!'"

²²Felix already understood a lot about the Way. He stopped the trial and said, "When commander Lysias comes here, I will decide what to do with you." ²³Felix told the army officer* to keep Paul guarded but to give him some freedom and to let his friends bring whatever he needed.

Paul Speaks to Felix and His Wife

²⁴After a few days Felix came with his wife Drusilla, who was a Jew. Felix asked for Paul to be brought to him. He listened to Paul talk about believing in Christ Jesus. ²⁵But Felix became afraid when Paul spoke about things like doing right, self-control, and the judgment that will come in the future. He said, "Go away now. When I have more time, I will call for you." ²⁶But Felix had another reason for talking with Paul. He hoped Paul would pay him a bribe, so he sent for Paul often and talked with him.

²⁷But after two years, Porcius Festus became governor. So Felix was no longer governor. But he left Paul in prison to please the Jews.

Paul Asks to See Caesar

25 ¹Festus became governor, and three days later he went from Caesarea to Jerusalem. ²The leading priests and the important Jewish leaders made charges against Paul before Festus. ³They asked Festus to do them a favor. They wanted him to send Paul back to Jerusalem because they had a plan to kill Paul on the way. ⁴But Festus answered, "No, Paul will be kept in Caesarea. I will be going there soon myself, ⁵and your leaders can go with me. If this man has really done anything wrong, they can accuse him there."

⁶Festus stayed in Jerusalem another eight or ten days and then went back to Caesarea. The next day Festus told the soldiers to bring

ᵃ24:6–8 Some Greek copies add 6b-8a: "And we wanted to judge him by our own law. ⁷But the officer Lysias came and used great force to take him from us. ⁸And Lysias ordered those who wanted to accuse him to come to you."

ᵇ24:17–18 *cleansing ceremony* The special things Jews did to end the Nazirite vow. See "Nazirite" in the Word List.

Paul before him. Festus was seated on the judgment seat. [7]Paul came into the room, and the Jews who had come from Jerusalem stood around him. They made many serious charges against him, but they could not prove anything. [8]Paul defended himself, saying, "I have done nothing wrong against the Jewish law, against the Temple,* or against Caesar.*"

[9]But Festus wanted to please the Jews. So he asked Paul, "Do you want to go to Jerusalem for me to judge you there on these charges?"

[10]Paul said, "I am standing at Caesar's judgment seat now. This is where I should be judged. I have done nothing wrong to the Jews, and you know it. [11]If I have done something wrong, and the law says I must die, then I agree that I should die. I don't ask to be saved from death. But if these charges are not true, then no one can hand me over to these people. No, I want Caesar to hear my case!"

[12]Festus talked about this with his advisors. Then he said, "You have asked to see Caesar, so you will go to Caesar!"

Festus Asks King Agrippa About Paul

[13]A few days later King Agrippa* and Bernice* came to Caesarea to visit Festus. [14]They stayed there many days, and Festus told the king about Paul's case. Festus said, "There is a man that Felix left in prison. [15]When I went to Jerusalem, the leading priests and the older Jewish leaders there made charges against him. They wanted me to order his death. [16]But I told them, 'When a man is accused of doing something wrong, Romans don't hand him over for others to judge. First, he must face the people accusing him. And then he must be allowed to defend himself against their charges.'

[17]"So when these Jews came here for the trial, I did not waste time. The next day I sat on the judgment seat and ordered Paul to be brought in. [18]The Jews stood up and accused him. But they did not accuse him of the kind of crimes I thought they would. [19]Their charges were all about their own religion and about a man named Jesus. Jesus died, but Paul said that he is still alive. [20]I did not have any idea about how to judge these matters. So I asked Paul, 'Do you want to go to Jerusalem and be judged there?' [21]But Paul asked to be kept in Caesarea. He wants a decision from the emperor.* So I ordered that he be held until I could send him to Caesar* in Rome."

[22]Agrippa said to Festus, "I would like to hear this man too."

Festus said, "Tomorrow you can hear him."

[23]The next day Agrippa and Bernice came to the meeting with great show, acting like very important people. They entered the room with military leaders and important men of the city. Festus ordered the soldiers to bring Paul in.

[24]Festus said, "King Agrippa and all of you gathered here with us, you see this man. All the Jewish people, here and in Jerusalem, have complained to me about him. When they complain about him, they shout that he should be killed. [25]When I judged him, I did not find him guilty of any crime worthy of death. But he asked to be judged by Caesar, so I decided to send him to Rome. [26]However, I don't really know what to tell Caesar that this man has done wrong. So I have brought him before all of you—especially you, King Agrippa. I hope that you can question him and give me something to write to Caesar. [27]I think it is foolish to send a prisoner to Caesar without making some charges against him."

Paul Before King Agrippa

26 [1]Agrippa* said to Paul, "You may now speak to defend yourself." Paul raised his hand to get their attention and began to speak. [2]He said, "King Agrippa, I feel fortunate that I can stand here before you today and answer all the charges these Jews have made against me. [3]I am very happy to talk to you, because you know so much about all the Jewish customs and the things the Jews argue about. Please listen to me patiently.

[4]"All the Jews know about my whole life. They know the way I lived from the beginning in my own country and later in Jerusalem. [5]These Jews have known me for a long time. If they want to, they can tell you that I was a good Pharisee.* And the Pharisees obey the laws of the Jewish religion more carefully than any other group. [6]Now I am on trial because I hope for the promise that God made to our fathers.* [7]This is the promise that all the twelve tribes of our people hope to receive. For this hope the Jews serve God day and night. My king, the Jews have accused me because I hope for this same promise. [8]Why do you people think it is impossible for God to raise people from death?

[9]"I used to think that I should do everything I could against Jesus from Nazareth. [10]And that's what I did, beginning in Jerusalem. The leading priests gave me the authority to put many of God's people in jail. And when they were being killed, I agreed that it was a good thing. [11]I visited all the synagogues* and punished them, trying to make them curse[a] Jesus. My anger against these people was so strong that I went to other cities to find them and punish them.

Paul Tells About Seeing Jesus

[12]"One time the leading priests gave me permission and the authority to go to the city of Damascus. [13]On the way there, at noon, I saw a light from heaven, brighter than the

---

[a]26:11 *curse* Literally, "blaspheme," the same as saying they did not believe in Jesus.

sun. It shined all around me and those traveling with me. ¹⁴We all fell to the ground. Then I heard a voice talking to me in Aramaic.* The voice said, 'Saul, Saul, why are you persecuting* me? You are only hurting yourself by fighting me.'

¹⁵"I said, 'Who are you, Lord?'

"The Lord said, 'I am Jesus. I am the one you are persecuting. ¹⁶Stand up! I have chosen you to be my servant. You will tell people about me—what you have seen today and what I will show you. This is why I have come to you. ¹⁷I will keep you safe from your own people and from the non-Jewish people, the ones I am sending you to. ¹⁸You will make them able to understand the truth. They will turn away from darkness to the light. They will turn away from the power of Satan, and they will turn to God. Then their sins can be forgiven, and they can be given a place among God's people—those who have been made holy* by believing in me.'"

Paul Tells About His Work

¹⁹Paul continued speaking: "King Agrippa,* after I had this vision* from heaven, I obeyed it. ²⁰I began telling people to change their hearts and lives and turn back to God. And I told them to do what would show that they had really changed. I went first to people in Damascus. Then I went to Jerusalem and to every part of Judea and told the people there. I also went to the non-Jewish people.

²¹"This is why the Jews grabbed me and were trying to kill me at the Temple.* ²²But God helped me, and he is still helping me today. With God's help I am standing here today and telling all people what I have seen. But I am saying nothing new. I am saying only what Moses* and the prophets* said would happen. ²³They said that the Christ* would die and be the first to rise from death. They said that he would bring the light of God's saving truth^a to the Jewish people and to the non-Jewish people."

Paul Tries to Persuade Agrippa

²⁴While Paul was still defending himself, Festus shouted, "Paul, you are out of your mind! Too much study has made you crazy."

²⁵Paul said, "Most Honorable Festus, I am not crazy. What I am saying is true. It all makes perfect sense. ²⁶King Agrippa* knows about all this, and I can speak freely to him. I know that he has heard about these things, because they happened where everyone could see them. ²⁷King Agrippa, do you believe what the prophets* wrote? I know you believe!"

²⁸King Agrippa said to Paul, "Do you think you can persuade me to become a 'Christ-follower' so easily?"

²⁹Paul said, "It is not important if it is easy or if it is hard. I pray to God that not only

you but that everyone listening to me today could be saved and be just like me—except for these chains I have!"

³⁰King Agrippa, Governor Festus, Bernice,* and all the people sitting with them stood up ³¹and left the room. They were talking to each other. They said, "This man has done nothing worthy of being put to death or even put in jail." ³²And Agrippa said to Festus, "We could let him go free, but he has asked to see Caesar.*"

Paul Sails for Rome

27 ¹It was decided that we would sail for Italy. An army officer* named Julius, who served in the emperor's* special army, was put in charge of guarding Paul and some other prisoners on the trip. ²We got on a ship from the city of Adramyttium that was ready to sail to different places in Asia.* Aristarchus, a man from Thessalonica in Macedonia,* went with us.

³The next day we came to the city of Sidon. Julius was very good to Paul and gave him freedom to go visit his friends there, who gave him whatever he needed. ⁴We left that city and sailed close to the island of Cyprus because the wind was blowing against us. ⁵We went across the sea by Cilicia and Pamphylia. Then we came to the city of Myra in Lycia. ⁶There the army officer found a ship from the city of Alexandria that was going to Italy. So he put us on it.

⁷We sailed slowly for many days. It was hard for us to reach the city of Cnidus because the wind was blowing against us. We could not go any farther that way, so we sailed by the south side of the island of Crete near Salmone. ⁸We sailed along the coast, but the sailing was hard. Then we came to a place called Safe Harbors, near the city of Lasea.

⁹We had lost much time, and it was now dangerous to sail, because it was already after the Jewish day of fasting.^{b} So Paul warned them, ¹⁰"Men, I can see that there will be a lot of trouble on this trip. The ship, everything in it, and even our lives may be lost!" ¹¹But the captain and the owner of the ship did not agree with Paul. So the army officer accepted what they said instead of believing Paul. ¹²Also, that harbor was not a good place for the ship to stay for the winter, so most of the men decided that we should leave there. They hoped we could reach Phoenix, where the ship could stay for the winter. Phoenix, a city on the island of Crete, had a harbor that faced southwest and northwest.

The Storm

¹³Then a good wind began to blow from the south. The men on the ship thought, "This is

^{a}**26:23** *bring ... truth* Literally, "proclaim light."

^{b}**27:9** *day of fasting* The Day of Atonement, an important Jewish holy day in the fall of the year. This was the time of year that bad storms happened on the sea.

the wind we wanted, and now we have it!" So they pulled up the anchor. We sailed very close to the island of Crete. 14But then a very strong wind called the "Northeaster" came from across the island. 15This wind took the ship and carried it away. The ship could not sail against the wind, so we stopped trying and let the wind blow us.

16We went below a small island named Cauda. With the island protecting us from the wind, we were able to bring in the lifeboat, but it was very hard to do. 17After the men brought the lifeboat in, they tied ropes around the ship to hold it together. The men were afraid that the ship would hit the sandbanks of Syrtis.* So they lowered the sail and let the wind carry the ship.

18The next day the storm was blowing against us so hard that the men threw some things out of the ship.a 19A day later they threw out the ship's equipment. 20For many days we could not see the sun or the stars. The storm was very bad. We lost all hope of staying alive—we thought we would die.

21The men did not eat for a long time. Then one day Paul stood up before them and said, "Men, I told you not to leave Crete. You should have listened to me. Then you would not have all this trouble and loss. 22But now I tell you to be happy. None of you will die, but the ship will be lost. 23Last night an angel came to me from God—the God I worship and belong to. 24The angel said, 'Paul, don't be afraid! You must stand before Caesar.* And God has given you this promise: He will save the lives of all those sailing with you.' 25So men, there is nothing to worry about. I trust God, and I am sure everything will happen just as his angel told me. 26But we will crash on an island."

27On the fourteenth night we were still being blown around in the Adriatic Sea.* The sailors thought we were close to land. 28They threw a rope into the water with a weight on the end of it. They found that the water was 120 feet deep. They went a little farther and threw the rope in again. It was 90 feet deep. 29The sailors were afraid that we would hit the rocks, so they threw four anchors into the water. Then they prayed for daylight to come. 30Some of the sailors wanted to leave the ship, and they lowered the lifeboat to the water. They wanted the other men to think that they were throwing more anchors from the front of the ship. 31But Paul told the army officer* and the other soldiers, "If these men do not stay in the ship, you will lose all hope of survival." 32So the soldiers cut the ropes and let the lifeboat fall into the water.

33Just before dawn Paul began persuading all the people to eat something. He said, "For the past two weeks you have been waiting and watching. You have not eaten for 14 days. 34Now I beg you to eat something. You need it to stay alive. None of you will lose even one hair off your heads." 35After he said this, Paul took some bread and thanked God for it before all of them. He broke off a piece and began eating. 36All the men felt better and started eating too. 37(There were 276 people on the ship.) 38We ate all we wanted. Then we began making the ship lighter by throwing the grain into the sea.

The Ship Is Destroyed

39When daylight came, the sailors saw land, but they did not know what land it was. They saw a bay with a beach and wanted to sail the ship to the beach if they could. 40So they cut the ropes to the anchors and left the anchors in the sea. At the same time, they untied the ropes that were holding the rudders. Then they raised the front sail into the wind and sailed toward the beach. 41But the ship hit a sandbank. The front of the ship stuck there and could not move. Then the big waves began to break the back of the ship to pieces.

42The soldiers decided to kill the prisoners so that none of the prisoners could swim away and escape. 43But Julius the army officer* wanted to let Paul live. So he did not allow the soldiers to kill the prisoners. He told the people who could swim to jump into the water and swim to land. 44The others used wooden boards or pieces of the ship. And this is how all the people went safely to land.

Paul on the Island of Malta

28 1When we were safe on land, we learned that the island was called Malta. 2The people who lived there were very good to us. It was raining and very cold, so they built a fire and welcomed all of us. 3Paul gathered a pile of sticks for the fire. He was putting the sticks on the fire, and a poisonous snake came out because of the heat and bit him on the hand. 4When the people living on the island saw the snake hanging from his hand, they said, "This man must be a murderer! He did not die in the sea, but Justiceb does not want him to live."

5But Paul shook the snake off into the fire and was not hurt. 6The people thought he would swell up or fall down dead. They waited and watched him for a long time, but nothing bad happened to him. So they changed their opinion. They said, "He is a god!"

7There were some fields around that same area. They were owned by a man named Publius, the most important Roman official on the island. He welcomed us into his home and was very good to us. We stayed in his house for three days. 8Publius' father was very sick.

---

a27:18 *threw some things ... ship* The men did this to make the ship lighter so that it would not sink easily.

b28:4 *Justice* The people thought there was a goddess named Justice who would punish bad people.

He had a fever and dysentery,* but Paul went to him and prayed for him. He laid his hands on* the man and healed him. 9After this happened, all the other sick people on the island came to Paul, and he healed them too.

10-11The people on the island gave us many honors. And after we had been there three months and were ready to leave, they provided us everything we needed for our trip.

Paul Goes to Rome

We got on a ship from Alexandria that had stayed on the island of Malta during the winter. On the front of the ship was the sign for the twin gods.[a] 12We stopped at the city of Syracuse. We stayed there three days and then left. 13We came to the city of Rhegium. The next day a wind began to blow from the southwest, so we were able to leave. A day later we came to the city of Puteoli. 14We found some believers* there, who asked us to stay with them a week. Finally, we came to Rome. 15The brothers and sisters in Rome heard about us and came out to meet us at the Market of Appius[b] and at the Three Inns.[c] When Paul saw these believers, he thanked God and felt encouraged.

Paul in Rome

16When we came to Rome, Paul was allowed to live alone. But a soldier stayed with him to guard him.

17Three days later Paul sent for some of the most important Jews. When they came together, he said, "My brothers, I have done nothing against our people or against the customs of our fathers.* But I was arrested in Jerusalem and handed over to the Romans. 18They asked me many questions, but they could not find any reason why I should be put to death. So they wanted to let me go free. 19But the Jews there did not want that. So I had to ask to come to Rome to have my trial before Caesar.* That doesn't mean I am accusing my people of doing anything wrong. 20That is why I wanted to see you and talk with you. I am bound with this chain because I believe in the hope of Israel.*"

21The Jews answered Paul, "We have received no letters from Judea about you. None of our Jewish brothers who have traveled from there brought news about you or told us anything bad about you. 22We want to hear your ideas. We know that people everywhere are speaking against this new group."

23Paul and the Jews chose a day for a meeting. On that day many more of these Jews met with Paul at his house. He spoke to them all day long, explaining God's kingdom* to them. He used the Law of Moses* and the writings of the prophets* to persuade them to believe in Jesus. 24Some of the Jews believed what he said, but others did not believe. 25They had an argument among themselves and were ready to leave. But Paul said one more thing to them: "The Holy Spirit* spoke the truth to your fathers through Isaiah the prophet. He said,

26 'Go to this people and tell them:
    You will listen and you will hear,
      but you will not understand.
    You will look and you will see,
      but you will not understand what you
        see.
27 Yes, the minds of these people are now
        closed.
    They have ears, but they don't listen.
    They have eyes, but they refuse to see.
    If their minds were not closed,
      they might see with their eyes;
      they might hear with their ears;
      they might understand with their
        minds.
    Then they might turn back to me and be
      healed.'   Isaiah 6:9–10

28"I want you Jews to know that God has sent his salvation to the non-Jewish people. They will listen!" 29 d

30Paul stayed two full years in his own rented house. He welcomed all the people who came and visited him. 31He told them about God's kingdom and taught them about the Lord Jesus Christ. He was very bold, and no one tried to stop him from speaking.

---

[a]28:10–11 twin gods Statues of Castor and Pollux, Greek gods.
[b]28:15 Market of Appius A town about 43 miles (69 km) from Rome.
[c]28:15 Three Inns A town about 30 miles (48 km) from Rome.

[d]28:29 Some late copies of Acts add verse 29: "After Paul said this, the Jews left, still having a big argument with each other."

Romans

1 ¹Greetings from Paul, a servant of Christ Jesus.

God chose me to be an apostle* and gave me the work of telling his Good News.* ²God promised long ago through his prophets* in the Holy Scriptures* to give this Good News to his people. ³⁻⁴The Good News is about God's Son, Jesus Christ our Lord. As a human, he was born from the family of David,* but through the Holy Spirit*ᵃ* he was shown to be God's powerful Son when he was raised from death.

⁵Through Christ, God gave me the special work of an apostle—to lead people of all nations to believe and obey him. I do all this to honor Christ. ⁶You are some of those who have been chosen to belong to Jesus Christ.

⁷This letter is to all of you in Rome. God loves you, and he has chosen you to be his holy people.*

Grace* and peace to you from God our Father and from the Lord Jesus Christ.

A Prayer of Thanks

⁸First I want to say that I thank my God through Jesus Christ for all of you. I thank him because people everywhere in the world are talking about your great faith. ⁹⁻¹⁰Every time I pray, I always remember you. God knows this is true. He is the one I serve with all my heart by telling people the Good News* about his Son. I pray that I will be allowed to come to you. It will happen if God wants it. ¹¹I want very much to see you and give you some spiritual gift to make your faith stronger. ¹²I mean that I want us to help each other with the faith that we have. Your faith will help me, and my faith will help you.

¹³Brothers and sisters, I want you to know that I have planned many times to come to you, but something always happens to change my plans. I would like to see the same good result among you that I have had from my work among the other non-Jewish people.

¹⁴I must serve all people—those who share in Greek culture and those who are less civilized,ᵇ the educated as well as the ignorant. ¹⁵That is why I want so much to tell the Good News to you there in Rome.

¹⁶I am proud of the Good News, because it is the power God uses to save everyone who believes—to save the Jews first, and now to save those who are not Jews. ¹⁷The Good News shows how God makes people right with himself. God's way of making people right begins and ends with faith. As the Scriptures* say, "The one who is right with God by faith will live forever."ᶜ

All People Have Done Wrong

¹⁸God shows his anger from heaven against all the evil and wrong things that people do. Their evil lives hide the truth they have. ¹⁹This makes God angry because they have been shown what he is like. Yes, God has made it clear to them.

²⁰There are things about God that people cannot see—his eternal power and all that makes him God. But since the beginning of the world, those things have been easy for people to understand. They are made clear in what God has made. So people have no excuse for the evil they do.

²¹People knew God, but they did not honor him as God, and they did not thank him. Their ideas were all useless. There was not one good thought left in their foolish minds. ²²They said they were wise, but they became fools. ²³Instead of honoring the divine greatness* of God, who lives forever, they traded it for the worship of idols—things made to look like humans, who get sick and die, or like birds, animals, and snakes.

²⁴People wanted only to do evil. So God left them and let them go their sinful way. And so they became completely immoral and used their bodies in shameful ways with each other. ²⁵They traded the truth of God for a lie. They bowed down and worshiped the things God made instead of worshiping the God who made those things. He is the one who should be praised forever. Amen.*

²⁶Because people did those things, God left them and let them do the shameful things they wanted to do. Women stopped having natural sex with men and started having sex with other women. ²⁷In the same way, men stopped having natural sex with women and began wanting each other all the time. Men did shameful things with other men, and in their bodies they received the punishment for those wrongs.

ᵃ**1:3-4** *Holy Spirit* Literally, "spirit of holiness."
ᵇ**1:14** *those who share ... civilized* Literally, "Greeks and barbarians." See "Greek" in the Word List.
ᶜ**1:17** Quote from Hab. 2:4.

²⁸People did not think it was important to have a true knowledge of God. So God left them and allowed them to have their own worthless thinking. And so they do what they should not do. ²⁹They are filled with every kind of sin, evil, greed, and hatred. They are full of jealousy, murder, fighting, lying, and thinking the worst things about each other. They gossip ³⁰and say evil things about each other. They hate God. They are rude, proud, and brag about themselves. They invent ways of doing evil. They don't obey their parents, ³¹they are foolish, they don't keep their promises, and they show no kindness or mercy to others. ³²They know God's law says that anyone who lives like that should die. But they not only continue to do these things themselves, but they also encourage others who do them.

Let God Be the Judge

2 ¹So do you think that you can judge those other people? You are wrong. You too are guilty of sin. You judge them, but you do the same things they do. So when you judge them, you are really condemning yourself. ²God judges all who do such things, and we know his judgment is right. ³And since you do the same things as those people you judge, surely you understand that God will punish you too. How could you think you would be able to escape his judgment? ⁴God has been kind to you. He has been very patient, waiting for you to change. But you think nothing of his kindness. Maybe you don't understand that God is kind to you so that you will decide to change your lives.

⁵But you are so stubborn! You refuse to change. So you are making your own punishment greater and greater. You will be punished on the day when God will show his anger. On that day everyone will see how right God is to judge people. ⁶He will reward or punish everyone for what they have done. ⁷Some people live for God's glory,* for honor, and for life that cannot be destroyed. They live for those things by always continuing to do good. God will give eternal life to them. ⁸But others are selfish and refuse to follow truth. They follow evil. God will show his anger and punish them. ⁹He will give trouble and suffering to everyone who does evil—to the Jews first and also to those who are not Jews. ¹⁰But he will give glory, honor, and peace to everyone who does good—to the Jews first and also to those who are not Jews. ¹¹God judges everyone the same. It doesn't matter who they are.

¹²People who have the law* and those who have never heard of the law are all the same when they sin. People who don't have the law and are sinners will be lost. And, in the same way, those who have the law and are sinners will be judged by the law. ¹³Hearing the law does not make people right with God. They will be right before him only if they always do what the law says.

¹⁴Those who are not Jews don't have the law. But when they naturally do what the law commands without even knowing the law, then they are their own law. This is true even though they don't have the written law. ¹⁵They show that in their hearts they know what is right and wrong, the same as the law commands, and their consciences agree. Sometimes their thoughts tell them that they have done wrong, and this makes them guilty. And sometimes their thoughts tell them that they have done right, and this makes them not guilty.

¹⁶All this will happen on the day when God will judge people's secret thoughts through Jesus Christ. This is part of the Good News* that I tell everyone.

The Jews and the Law

¹⁷What about you? You say you are a Jew. You trust in the law and proudly claim to be close to God. ¹⁸You know what God wants you to do. And you know what is important, because you have learned the law. ¹⁹You think you are a guide for people who don't know the right way, a light for those who are in the dark. ²⁰You think you can show foolish people what is right. And you think you are a teacher for those who are just beginning to learn. You have the law, and so you think you know everything and have all truth. ²¹You teach others, so why don't you teach yourself? You tell them not to steal, but you yourself steal. ²²You say they must not commit adultery,* but you yourself are guilty of that sin. You hate idols,* but you steal them from their temples. ²³You are so proud that you have God's law, but you bring shame to God by breaking his law. ²⁴As the Scriptures* say, "People in other nations insult God because of you."ᵃ

²⁵If you follow the law,* then your circumcision* has meaning. But if you break the law, then it is as if you were never circumcised. ²⁶Those who are not Jews are not circumcised. But if they do what the law says, it is as if they were circumcised. ²⁷You have the written law and circumcision, but you break the law. So those who are not circumcised in their bodies, but still obey the law, will show that you are guilty.

²⁸You are not a true Jew if you are only a Jew in your physical body. True circumcision is not only on the outside of the body. ²⁹A true Jew is one who is a Jew inside. True circumcision is done in the heart. It is done by the Spirit,* not by the written law. And anyone who is circumcised in the heart by the Spirit gets praise from God, not from people.

3 ¹So, do Jews have anything that others don't have? Do they get any benefit from being circumcised? ²Yes, the Jews have many benefits. The most important one is this: God trusted the Jews with his teachings. ³It is true

ᵃ**2:24** Quote from Isa. 52:5. See also Ezek. 36:20–23.

that some Jews were not faithful to God. But will that stop God from doing what he promised? [4]No, even if everyone else is a liar, God will always do what he says. As the Scriptures say about him,

"You will be proved right in what you say,
    and you will win when people accuse
        you."   *Psalm 51:4*

[5]When we do wrong, that shows more clearly that God is right. So can we say that God does wrong when he punishes us? (That's the way some people think.) [6]Of course not. If God could not punish us, how could he judge the world?

[7]Someone might say, "When I lie, it really gives God glory,* because my lie makes his truth easier to see. So why am I judged a sinner?" [8]It would be the same to say, "We should do evil so that good will come." Many people criticize us, saying that's what we teach. They are wrong, and they should be condemned for saying that.

All People Are Guilty

[9]So are we Jews better than other people? No, we have already said that those who are Jews, as well as those who are not Jews, are the same. They are all guilty of sin. [10]As the Scriptures* say,

"There is no one doing what is right, not
    even one.
[11]   There is no one who understands.
    There is no one who is trying to be with
        God.
[12]   They have all turned away from him,
        and now they are of no use to anyone.
    There is no one who does good, not even
        one."   *Psalm 14:1–3*

[13]"Their words come from mouths that are
    like open graves.
    They use their lying tongues to deceive
        others."   *Psalm 5:9*

"Their words are like the poison of
    snakes."   *Psalm 140:3*

[14]"Their mouths are full of cursing and angry
    words."   *Psalm 10:7*

[15]"They are always ready to kill someone.
[16]   Everywhere they go they cause trouble
        and ruin.
[17]   They don't know how to live in peace."
                                   Isaiah 59:7–8

[18]"They have no fear or respect for God."
                                   Psalm 36:1

[19]What the law* says is for those who are under the law. It stops anyone from making excuses. And it brings the whole world

under God's judgment, [20]because no one can be made right with God by following the law. The law only shows us our sin.

How God Makes People Right

[21]But God has a way to make people right, and it has nothing to do with the law. He has now shown us that new way, which the law and the prophets* told us about. [22]God makes people right through their faith in[a] Jesus Christ. He does this for all who believe in Christ. Everyone is the same. [23]All have sinned and are not good enough to share God's divine greatness.* [24]They are made right with God by his grace.* This is a free gift. They are made right with God by being made free from sin through Jesus Christ. [25-26]God gave Jesus as a way to forgive people's sins through their faith in him. God can forgive them because the blood sacrifice of Jesus pays for their sins. God gave Jesus to show that he always does what is right and fair. He was right in the past when he was patient and did not punish people for their sins. And in our own time he still does what is right. God worked all this out in a way that allows him to judge people fairly and still make right any person who has faith in Jesus.

[27]So do we have any reason to boast about ourselves? No reason at all. And why not? Because we are depending on the way of faith, not on what we have done in following the law. [28]I mean we are made right with God through faith, not through what we have done to follow the law. This is what we believe. [29]God is not only the God of the Jews. He is also the God of those who are not Jews. [30]There is only one God. He will make Jews[b] right with him by their faith, and he will also make non-Jews[c] right with him through their faith. [31]So do we destroy the law by following the way of faith? Not at all! In fact, faith causes us to be what the law actually wants.

The Example of Abraham

4 [1]So what can we say about Abraham,* the father of our people? What did he learn about faith? [2]If Abraham was made right by the things he did, he had a reason to boast about himself. But God knew different. [3]That's why the Scriptures* say, "Abraham believed God, and because of this he was accepted as one who is right with God."[d]

[4]When people work, their pay is not given to them as a gift. They earn the pay they get. [5]But people cannot do any work that will make them right with God. So they must trust in him. Then he accepts their faith, and that makes them right with him. He is the one who makes even evil people right. [6]David* said the same thing when he was

[a]**3:22** *their faith in* Or "the faithfulness of."
[b]**3:30** *Jews* Literally, "circumcision."
[c]**3:30** *non-Jews* Literally, "uncircumcision."
[d]**4:3** Quote from Gen. 15:6.

talking about the blessing people have when God accepts them as good without looking at what they have done:

> 7"It is a great blessing
>   when people are forgiven for the
>   wrongs they have done,
>   when their sins are erased!
> 8 It is a great blessing when the Lord
>   accepts people
>   as if they are without sin!"   *Psalm 32:1–2*

9Is this blessing only for those who are circumcised*? Or is it also for those who are not circumcised? We have already said that it was because of Abraham's faith that he was accepted as one who is right with God. 10So how did this happen? Did God accept Abraham before or after he was circumcised? God accepted him before his circumcision. 11Abraham was circumcised later to show that God accepted him. His circumcision was proof that he was right with God through faith before he was circumcised. So Abraham is the father of all those who believe but are not circumcised. They believe and are accepted as people who are right with God. 12And Abraham is also the father of those who have been circumcised. But it is not their circumcision that makes him their father. He is their father only if they live following the faith that our father Abraham had before he was circumcised.

God's Promise Received Through Faith

13Abraham* and his descendants received the promise that they would get the whole world. But Abraham did not receive that promise because he followed the law.* He received that promise because he was right with God through his faith. 14If people could get God's promise by following the law, then faith is worthless. And God's promise to Abraham is worthless, 15because the law can only bring God's anger on those who disobey it. But if there is no law, then there is nothing to disobey.

16So people get what God promised by having faith. This happens so that the promise can be a free gift. And if the promise is a free gift, then all of Abraham's people will get that promise. The promise is not just for those who live under the Law of Moses.* It is for all who live with faith as Abraham did. He is the father of us all. 17As the Scriptures* say, "I have made you a father of many nations."*a This is true before God, the one Abraham believed—the God who gives life to the dead and speaks of things that don't yet exist as if they are real.

18There was no hope that Abraham would have children, but Abraham believed God and continued to hope. And that is why he became the father of many nations. As God told him, "You will have many descendants."*b 19Abraham was almost a hundred years old, so he was past the age for having children. Also, Sarah could not have children. Abraham was well aware of this, but his faith in God never became weak. 20He never doubted that God would do what he promised. He never stopped believing. In fact, he grew stronger in his faith and just praised God. 21Abraham felt sure that God was able to do what he promised. 22So that's why "he was accepted as one who is right with God."*c 23These words ("he was accepted") were written not only for Abraham. 24They were also written for us. God will also accept us because we believe. We believe in the one who raised Jesus our Lord from death. 25Jesus was handed over to die for our sins, and he was raised from death to make us right with God.

Right With God

5 1We have been made right with God because of our faith. So we have peace with God through our Lord Jesus Christ. 2Through our faith, Christ has brought us into that blessing of God's grace* that we now enjoy. And we are very happy because of the hope we have of sharing God's glory.* 3And we are also happy with the troubles we have. Why are we happy with troubles? Because we know that these troubles make us more patient. 4And this patience is proof that we are strong. And this proof gives us hope. 5And this hope will never disappoint us. We know this because God has poured out his love to fill our hearts through the Holy Spirit* he gave us.

6Christ died for us when we were unable to help ourselves. We were living against God, but at just the right time Christ died for us. 7Very few people will die to save the life of someone else, even if it is for a good person. Someone might be willing to die for an especially good person. 8But Christ died for us while we were still sinners, and by this God showed how much he loves us.

9We have been made right with God by the blood sacrifice of Christ. So through Christ we will surely be saved from God's anger. 10I mean that while we were God's enemies, he made friends with us through his Son's death. And the fact that we are now God's friends makes it even more certain that he will save us through his Son's life. 11And not only will we be saved, but we also rejoice right now in what God has done for us through our Lord Jesus Christ. It is because of Jesus that we are now God's friends.

Adam and Christ

12Sin came into the world because of what one man did. And with sin came death. So this is why all people must die—because all

---

a4:17 Quote from Gen. 17:5.

b4:18 Quote from Gen. 15:5.
c4:22 Quote from Gen. 15:6.

people have sinned. [13]Sin was in the world before the Law of Moses.* But God does not consider people guilty of sin if there is no law. [14]But from the time of Adam to the time of Moses, everyone had to die. Adam died because he sinned by not obeying God's command. But even those who did not sin that same way had to die.

That one man, Adam, can be compared to Christ, the one who was coming in the future. [15]But God's free gift is not like Adam's sin. Many people died because of the sin of that one man. But the grace* that people received from God was much greater. Many received God's gift of life by the grace of this other man, Jesus Christ. [16]After Adam sinned once, he was judged guilty. But the gift of God is different. His free gift came after many sins, and it makes people right with him. [17]One man sinned, and so death ruled all people because of that one man. But now some people accept God's full grace and his great gift of being made right. Surely they will have true life and rule through the one man, Jesus Christ.

[18]So that one sin of Adam brought the punishment of death to all people. But in the same way, Christ did something so good that it makes all people right with God. And that brings them true life. [19]One man disobeyed God and many became sinners. But in the same way, one man obeyed God and many will be made right. [20]The law was brought in so that more people would sin the way Adam did. But where sin increased, there was even more of God's grace. [21]Sin once used death to rule us. But God gave us more of his grace so that grace could rule by making us right with him. And this brings us eternal life through Jesus Christ our Lord.

Dead to Sin but Alive in Christ

6 [1]So do you think we should continue sinning so that God will give us more and more grace*? [2]Of course not! Our old sinful life ended. It's dead. So how can we continue living in sin? [3]Did you forget that all of us became part of Christ Jesus when we were baptized*? In our baptism* we shared in his death. [4]So when we were baptized, we were buried with Christ and took part in his death. And just as Christ was raised from death by the wonderful power of the Father, so we can now live a new life.

[5]Christ died, and we have been joined with him by dying too. So we will also be joined with him by rising from death as he did. [6]We know that our old life was put to death on the cross with Christ. This happened so that our sinful selves would have no power over us. Then we would not be slaves to sin. [7]Anyone who has died is made free from sin's control.

[8]If we died with Christ, we know that we will also live with him. [9]Christ was raised from death. And we know that he cannot die again. Death has no power over him now.

[10]Yes, when Christ died, he died to defeat the power of sin one time—enough for all time. He now has a new life, and his new life is with God. [11]In the same way, you should see yourselves as being dead to the power of sin and alive for God through Christ Jesus.

[12]But don't let sin control your life here on earth. You must not be ruled by the things your sinful self makes you want to do. [13]Don't offer the parts of your body to serve sin. Don't use your bodies to do evil, but offer yourselves to God, as people who have died and now live. Offer the parts of your body to God to be used for doing good. [14]Sin will not be your master, because you are not under law. You now live under God's grace.

Slaves of Goodness

[15]So what should we do? Should we sin because we are under grace* and not under law? Certainly not! [16]Surely you know that you become the slaves of whatever you give yourselves to. Anything or anyone you follow will be your master. You can follow sin, or you can obey God. Following sin brings spiritual death, but obeying God makes you right with him. [17]In the past you were slaves to sin—sin controlled you. But thank God, you fully obeyed what you were taught. [18]You were made free from sin, and now you are slaves to what is right. [19]I use this example from everyday life because you need help in understanding spiritual truths. In the past you offered the parts of your body to be slaves to your immoral and sinful thoughts. The result was that you lived only for sin. In the same way, you must now offer yourselves to be slaves to what is right. Then you will live only for God.

[20]In the past you were slaves to sin, and you did not even think about doing right. [21]You did evil things, and now you are ashamed of what you did. Did those things help you? No, they only brought death. [22]But now you are free from sin. You have become slaves of God, and the result is that you live only for God. This will bring you eternal life. [23]When people sin, they earn what sin pays—death. But God gives his people a free gift—eternal life in Christ Jesus our Lord.

An Example From Marriage

7 [1]Brothers and sisters, you all understand the Law of Moses.* So surely you know that the law rules over people only while they are alive. [2]It's like what the law says about marriage: A woman must stay married to her husband as long as he is alive. But if her husband dies, she is made free from the law of marriage. [3]But if she marries another man while her husband is still alive, the law says she is guilty of adultery.* But if her husband dies, she is made free from the law of marriage. So if she marries another man after her husband dies, she is not guilty of adultery.

⁴In the same way, my brothers and sisters, your old selves died and you became free from the law* through the body of Christ. Now you belong to someone else. You belong to the one who was raised from death. We belong to Christ so that we can be used in service to God. ⁵In the past we were ruled by our sinful selves. The law made us want to do sinful things. And those sinful desires controlled our bodies, so that what we did only brought us spiritual death. ⁶In the past the law held us as prisoners, but our old selves died, and we were made free from the law. So now we serve God in a new way, not in the old way, with the written rules. Now we serve God in the new way, with the Spirit.*

Our Fight Against Sin

⁷You might think I am saying that sin and the law* are the same. That is not true. But the law was the only way I could learn what sin means. I would never have known it is wrong to want something that is not mine. But the law said, "You must not want what belongs to someone else."ᵃ ⁸And sin found a way to use that command and make me want all kinds of things that weren't mine. So sin came to me because of the command. But without the law, sin has no power. ⁹Before I knew the law, I was alive. But when I heard the law's command, sin began to live, ¹⁰and I died spiritually. The command was meant to bring life, but for me it brought death. ¹¹Sin found a way to fool me by using the command to make me die.

¹²Now the law is holy,* and the command is holy and right and good. ¹³Does this mean that something that is good brought death to me? No, it was sin that used the good command to bring me death. This shows how terrible sin really is. It can use a good command to produce a result that shows sin at its very worst.

The War Inside Us

¹⁴We know that the law* is spiritual, but I am not. I am so human. Sin rules me as if I were its slave. ¹⁵I don't understand why I act the way I do. I don't do the good I want to do, and I do the evil I hate. ¹⁶And if I don't want to do what I do, that means I agree that the law is good. ¹⁷But I am not really the one doing the evil. It is sin living in me that does it. ¹⁸Yes, I know that nothing good lives in me—I mean nothing good lives in the part of me that is not spiritual. I want to do what is good, but I don't do it. ¹⁹I don't do the good that I want to do. I do the evil that I don't want to do. ²⁰So if I do what I don't want to do, then I am not really the one doing it. It is the sin living in me that does it.

²¹So I have learned this rule: When I want to do good, evil is there with me. ²²In my mind I am happy with God's law. ²³But I see another law working in my body. That law makes war against the law that my mind accepts. That other law working in my body is the law of sin, and that law makes me its prisoner. ²⁴What a miserable person I am! Who will save me from this body that brings me death? ²⁵I thank God for his salvation through Jesus Christ our Lord!

So in my mind I am a slave to God's law, but in my sinful self I am a slave to the law of sin.

Life in the Spirit

8 ¹So now anyone who is in Christ Jesus is not judged guilty. ²That is because in Christ Jesus the law of the Spirit* that brings life made youᵇ free. It made you free from the law that brings sin and death. ³The law* was without power because it was made weak by our sinful selves. But God did what the law could not do: He sent his own Son to earth with the same human life that everyone else uses for sin. God sent him to be an offering to pay for sin. So God used a human life to destroy sin. ⁴He did this so that we could be right just as the law said we must be. Now we don't live following our sinful selves. We live following the Spirit.

⁵People who live following their sinful selves think only about what they want. But those who live following the Spirit are thinking about what the Spirit wants them to do. ⁶If your thinking is controlled by your sinful self, there is spiritual death. But if your thinking is controlled by the Spirit, there is life and peace. ⁷Why is this true? Because anyone whose thinking is controlled by their sinful self is against God. They refuse to obey God's law. And really they are not able to obey it. ⁸Those who are ruled by their sinful selves cannot please God.

⁹But you are not ruled by your sinful selves. You are ruled by the Spirit, if that Spirit of God really lives in you. But whoever does not have the Spirit of Christ does not belong to Christ. ¹⁰Your body will always be dead because of sin. But if Christ is in you, then the Spirit gives you life, because Christ made you right with God. ¹¹God raised Jesus from death. And if God's Spirit lives in you, he will also give life to your bodies that die. Yes, God is the one who raised Christ from death, and he will raise you to life through his Spirit living in you.

¹²So, my brothers and sisters, we must not be ruled by our sinful selves. We must not live the way our sinful selves want. ¹³If you use your lives to do what your sinful selves want, you will die spiritually. But if you use the Spirit's help to stop doing the wrong things you do with your body, you will have true life.

ᵃ**7:7** Quote from Ex. 20:17; Deut. 5:21.

ᵇ**8:2 you** Some Greek copies have "me." Also in the next sentence.

¹⁴The true children of God are those who let God's Spirit lead them. ¹⁵The Spirit that we received is not a spirit that makes us slaves again and causes us to fear. The Spirit that we have makes us God's chosen children. And with that Spirit we cry out, "*Abba,ᵃ* Father." ¹⁶And the Spirit himself speaks to our spirits and makes us sure that we are God's children. ¹⁷If we are God's children, we will get the blessings God has for his people. He will give us all that he has given Christ. But we must suffer like Christ suffered. Then we will be able to share his glory.*

We Will Have Glory in the Future

¹⁸We have sufferings now, but these are nothing compared to the great glory* that will be given to us. ¹⁹Everything that God made is waiting with excitement for the time when he will show the world who his children are. The whole world wants very much for that to happen. ²⁰Everything God made was allowed to become like something that cannot fulfill its purpose. That was not its choice, but God made it happen with this hope in view: ²¹That the creation would be made free from ruin—that everything God made would have the same freedom and glory that belong to God's children.

²²We know that everything God made has been waiting until now in pain like a woman ready to give birth to a child. ²³Not only the world, but we also have been waiting with pain inside us. We have the Spirit* as the first part of God's promise. So we are waiting for God to finish making us his own children. I mean we are waiting for our bodies to be made free. ²⁴We were saved to have this hope. If we can see what we are waiting for, that is not really hope. People don't hope for something they already have. ²⁵But we are hoping for something we don't have yet, and we are waiting for it patiently.

²⁶Also, the Spirit helps us. We are very weak, but the Spirit helps us with our weakness. We don't know how to pray as we should, but the Spirit himself speaks to God for us. He begs God for us, speaking to him with feelings too deep for words. ²⁷God already knows our deepest thoughts. And he understands what the Spirit is saying, because the Spirit speaks for his people in the way that agrees with what God wants.

²⁸We know that in everything God works for the good of those who love him. These are the people God chose, because that was his plan. ²⁹God knew them before he made the world. And he decided that they would be like his Son. Then Jesus would be the firstborn* of many brothers and sisters. ³⁰God planned for them to be like his Son. He chose them and

made them right with him. And after he made them right, he gave them his glory.

God's Love in Christ Jesus

³¹So what should we say about this? If God is for us, no one can stand against us. And God is with us. ³²He even let his own Son suffer for us. God gave his Son for all of us. So now with Jesus, God will surely give us all things. ³³Who can accuse the people God has chosen? No one! God is the one who makes them right. ³⁴Who can say that God's people are guilty? No one! Christ Jesus died for us, but that is not all. He was also raised from death. And now he is at God's right side, speaking to him for us. ³⁵Can anything separate us from Christ's love? Can trouble or problems or persecution* separate us from his love? If we have no food or clothes or face danger or even death, will that separate us from his love? ³⁶As the Scriptures* say,

"For you we are in danger of death all the
　time.
　People think we are worth no more
　　than sheep to be killed."　*Psalm 44:22*

³⁷But in all these troubles we have complete victory through God, who has shown his love for us. ³⁸⁻³⁹Yes, I am sure that nothing can separate us from God's love—not death, life, angels, or ruling spirits. I am sure that nothing now, nothing in the future, no powers, nothing above us or nothing below us—nothing in the whole created world—will ever be able to separate us from the love God has shown us in Christ Jesus our Lord.

God and the Jewish People

9 ¹I am in Christ and I am telling you the truth. I am not lying. And my conscience, ruled by the Holy Spirit,* agrees that what I say now is true. ²I have great sorrow and always feel much sadness ³for my own people. They are my brothers and sisters, my earthly family. I wish I could help them. I would even have a curse on me and cut myself off from Christ if that would help them. ⁴They are the people of Israel,* God's chosen children. They have the glory* of God and the agreements he made between himself and his people. God gave them the Law of Moses,* the Temple* worship, and his promises. ⁵They are the descendants of our great fathers,* and they are the earthly family of Christ. And Christ is God over all things. Praise him foreverᵇ! Amen.*

⁶I don't mean that God failed to keep his promise to the Jewish people. But only some of the people of Israel are really God's people.ᶜ

ᵃ**8:15 Abba** An Aramaic word that was used by Jewish children as a name for their fathers.

ᵇ**9:5 And Christ ... forever** This can also mean "May God, who rules over all things, be praised forever!"
ᶜ**9:6 God's people** Literally, "Israel," the people God chose to bring his blessings to the world.

[7]And only some of Abraham's* descendants are true children of Abraham. This is what God said to Abraham: "Your true descendants will be those who come through Isaac."[a] [8]This means that not all of Abraham's descendants are God's true children. Abraham's true children are those who become God's children because of the promise he made to Abraham. [9]Here is what God said in that promise: "About this time next year I will come back, and Sarah will have a son."[b]

[10]And that is not all. Rebecca also had sons, and they had the same father. He is our father Isaac. [11-12]But before the two sons were born, God told Rebecca, "The older son will serve the younger."[c] This was before the boys had done anything good or bad. God said this before they were born so that the boy he wanted would be chosen because of God's own plan. He was chosen because he was the one God wanted to call, not because of anything the boys did. [13]As the Scriptures* say, "I loved Jacob, but I hated Esau."[d]

[14]So what does this mean? That God is not fair? We cannot say that. [15]God said to Moses, "I will show mercy to anyone I want to show mercy to. I will show pity to anyone I choose."[e] [16]So God will choose anyone he decides to show mercy to, and his choice does not depend on what people want or try to do. [17]In the Scriptures God says to Pharaoh*: "I made you king so that you could do this for me. I wanted to show my power through you. I wanted my name to be announced throughout the world."[f] [18]So God shows mercy to those he wants to show mercy to and makes stubborn those he wants to make stubborn.

[19]So one of you will ask me, "If God controls what we do, why does he blame us for our sins?" [20]Don't ask that. You are only human and have no right to question God. A clay jar does not question the one who made it. It does not say, "Why did you make me like this?" [21]The one who makes the jar can make anything he wants. He uses the same clay to make different things. He might make one thing for special purposes and another for daily use.

[22]It is the same way with what God has done. He wanted to show his anger and to let people see his power. But he patiently endured those he was angry with—people who were ready to be destroyed. [23]He waited with patience so that he could make known the riches of his glory* to the people he has chosen to receive his mercy. God has already prepared them to share his glory. [24]We are those people, the ones God chose not only from the Jews but also from those who are not Jews. [25]As the Scriptures say in the book of Hosea,

"The people who are not mine—
    I will say they are my people.
And the people I did not love—
    I will say they are the people I love."
                                        Hosea 2:23

[26]And,

"Where God said in the past,
    'You are not my people'—
    there they will be called children of the
        living God."   *Hosea 1:10*

[27]And Isaiah cries out about Israel:

"There are so many people of Israel, they
    are like the grains of sand by the sea.
    But only a few of them will be saved.
[28] Yes, the Lord will quickly finish judging
    the people on the earth." *Isaiah 10:22–23*

[29]It is just as Isaiah said:

"The Lord All-Powerful allowed some of
    our people to live.
If he had not done that,
    we would now be like Sodom,*
    and we would be like Gomorrah.*"
                                        Isaiah 1:9

[30]So what does all this mean? It means that people who are not Jews were made right with God because of their faith, even though they were not trying to make themselves right. [31]And the people of Israel, who tried to make themselves right with God by following the law, did not succeed. [32]They failed because they tried to make themselves right by the things they did. They did not trust in God to make them right. They fell over the stone that makes people fall. [33]The Scriptures talk about that stone:

"Look, I put in Zion* a stone that will make
    people stumble.
It is a rock that will make people fall.
But anyone who trusts in him will never
    be disappointed."   *Isaiah 8:14; 28:16*

10

[1]Brothers and sisters, what I want most is for all the people of Israel to be saved. That is my prayer to God. [2]I can say this about them: They really try hard to follow God, but they don't know the right way. [3]They did not know the way that God makes people right with him. And they tried to make themselves right in their own way. So they did not accept God's way of making people right. [4]Christ ended the law so that everyone who believes in him is made right with God.

[5]Moses writes about being made right by following the law. He says, "The person who

---

[a]**9:7** Quote from Gen. 21:12.
[b]**9:9** Quote from Gen. 18:10, 14.
[c]**9:11–12** Quote from Gen. 25:23.
[d]**9:13** Quote from Mal. 1:2–3.
[e]**9:15** Quote from Ex. 33:19.
[f]**9:17** Quote from Ex. 9:16.

obeys these laws is the one who will have life through them."[a] [6]But this is what the Scriptures say about being made right through faith: "Don't say to yourself, 'Who will go up into heaven?'" (This means "Who will go up to heaven to get Christ and bring him down to earth?") [7]"And don't say, 'Who will go down into the world below?'" (This means "Who will go down to get Christ and bring him up from death?")

[8]This is what the Scripture says: "God's teaching is near you; it is in your mouth and in your heart."[b] It is the teaching of faith that we tell people. [9]If you openly say, "Jesus is Lord" and believe in your heart that God raised him from death, you will be saved. [10]Yes, we believe in Jesus deep in our hearts, and so we are made right with God. And we openly say that we believe in him, and so we are saved.

[11]Yes, the Scriptures say, "Anyone who trusts in him will never be disappointed."[c] [12]It says this because there is no difference between those who are Jews and those who are not. The same Lord is the Lord of all people. And he richly blesses everyone who looks to him for help. [13]Yes, "everyone who trusts in the Lord[d] will be saved."[e]

[14]But before people can pray to the Lord for help, they must believe in him. And before they can believe in the Lord, they must hear about him. And for anyone to hear about the Lord, someone must tell them. [15]And before anyone can go and tell them, they must be sent. As the Scriptures say, "How wonderful it is to see someone coming to tell good news!"[f]

[16]But not all the people accepted that good news. Isaiah said, "Lord, who believed what we told them?"[g] [17]So faith comes from hearing the Good News.* And people hear the Good News when someone tells them about Christ.

[18]But I ask, "Did those people not hear the Good News?" Yes, they heard—as the Scriptures say,

"Their voices went out all around the
　　world.
　　Their words went everywhere in the
　　　world."
　　　　　　　　　　　　　　　Psalm 19:4

[19]Again I ask, "Did the people of Israel not understand?" Yes, they did understand. First, Moses says this for God:

"I will use those who are not really a
　　nation to make you jealous.
　I will use a nation that does not
　　understand to make you angry."
　　　　　　　　　　　　Deuteronomy 32:21

[20]Then Isaiah is bold enough to say this for God:

"The people who were not looking for
　　me—
　　they are the ones who found me.
　I made myself known to those who did
　　not ask for me."　　　　　*Isaiah 65:1*

[21]But about the people of Israel God says,

"All day long I stood ready to accept those
　　people,
　　but they are stubborn and refuse to
　　　obey me."　　　　　　　　*Isaiah 65:2*

God Has Not Forgotten His People

11 [1]So I ask, "Did God force his people to leave him?" Of course not. I myself am an Israelite.* I am from the family of Abraham,* from the tribe of Benjamin. [2]God chose the Israelites to be his people before they were born. And he did not force them to leave. Surely you know what the Scriptures* say about Elijah.* The Scriptures tell about Elijah praying to God against the people of Israel.* He said, [3]"Lord, they have killed your prophets* and destroyed your altars.* I am the only prophet still living, and they are trying to kill me now."[h] [4]But what answer did God give to Elijah? God said, "I have kept for myself seven thousand men who have never given worship to Baal.*"[i]

[5]It is the same now. God has chosen a few people by his grace.* [6]And if he chose them by grace, then it is not what they have done that made them his people. If they could be made his people by what they did, his gift of grace would not really be a gift.

[7]So this is what has happened: The people of Israel wanted God's blessing, but they did not all get it. The people he chose did get his blessing, but the others became hard and refused to listen to him. [8]As the Scriptures say,

"God caused the people to fall asleep."
　　　　　　　　　　　　　　　Isaiah 29:10

"God closed their eyes so that they could
　　not see,
　　and he closed their ears so that they
　　　could not hear.
　This continues until now."
　　　　　　　　　　　　Deuteronomy 29:4

a **10:5** Quote from Lev. 18:5.
b **10:6–8** Quotes from Deut. 30:12–14.
c **10:11** Quote from Isa. 28:16.
d **10:13** *who trusts in the Lord* Literally, "who calls on the name of the Lord," meaning to show faith in him by worshiping him or praying to him for help.
e **10:13** Quote from Joel 2:32.
f **10:15** Quote from Isa. 52:7.
g **10:16** Quote from Isa. 53:1.

h **11:3** Quote from 1 Kings 19:10, 14.
i **11:4** Quote from 1 Kings 19:18.

9And David says,

"Let those people be caught and trapped at
their own feasts.
Let them fall and be punished.
10 Let their eyes be closed so that they
cannot see.
And let them be troubled forever."

Psalm 69:22-23

11So I ask: When the Jews fell, did that fall
destroy them? No! But their mistake brought
salvation to those who are not Jews. The purpose of this was to make the Jews jealous.
12Their mistake brought rich blessings to the
world. And what they lost brought rich blessings to the non-Jewish people. So surely the
world will get much richer blessings when
enough Jews become the kind of people God
wants.

13Now I am speaking to you people who
are not Jews. I am an apostle* to the non-Jewish people. So while I have that work, I will
do the best I can. 14I hope I can make my
own people jealous. That way, maybe I can
help some of them to be saved. 15God turned
away from the Jews. When that happened, he
became friends with the other people in the
world. So when he accepts the Jews, it will be
like bringing people to life after death. 16If the
first piece of bread is offered to God, then the
whole loaf is made holy.* If the roots of a tree
are holy, the tree's branches are holy too.

17It is as if some of the branches from an
olive tree have been broken off, and the
branch of a wild olive tree has been joined
to that first tree. If you are not a Jew, you are
the same as that wild branch, and you now
share the strength and life of the first tree.
18But don't act as if you are better than those
branches that were broken off. You have no
reason to be proud of yourself, because you
don't give life to the root. The root gives life
to you. 19You might say, "Branches were broken off so that I could be joined to their tree."
20That is true. But those branches were broken off because they did not believe. And you
continue to be part of the tree only because
you believe. Don't be proud, but be afraid. 21If
God did not let the natural branches of that
tree stay, he will not let you stay if you stop
believing.

22So you see that God is kind, but he can
also be very strict. He punishes those who
stop following him. But he is kind to you, if
you continue trusting in his kindness. If you
don't continue depending on him, you will be
cut off from the tree. 23And if the Jews will
believe in God again, he will accept them
back. He is able to put them back where they
were. 24It is not natural for a wild branch to
become part of a good tree. But you non-Jewish people are like a branch cut from a wild
olive tree. And you were joined to a good
olive tree. But those Jews are like a branch

that grew from the good tree. So surely they
can be joined to their own tree again.

25I want you to understand this secret truth,
brothers and sisters. This truth will help you
understand that you don't know everything.
The truth is this: Part of Israel has been made
stubborn, but that will change when enough
non-Jewish people have come to God. 26And
that is how all Israel will be saved. The Scriptures say,

"The Savior will come from Zion*;
he will take away all evil from the
family of Jacob.*
27 And I will make this agreement with
those people
when I take away their sins."

Isaiah 59:20-21; 27:9

28The Jews refuse to accept the Good
News,* so they are God's enemies. This has
happened to help you who are not Jews. But
they are still God's chosen people, and he
loves them because of the promises he made
to their ancestors.* 29God never changes his
mind about the people he calls. He never
decides to take back the blessings he has
given them. 30At one time you refused to
obey God. But now you have received mercy,
because the Jews refused to obey. 31And now
they are the ones who refuse to obey, because
God showed mercy to you. But this happened
so that they can also receive mercy from him.
32All people have refused to obey God. And
he has put them all together as people who
don't obey him so that he can show mercy
to everyone.

Praise to God

33Yes, God's riches are very great! His wisdom and knowledge have no end! No one can
explain what God decides. No one can understand his ways. 34As the Scriptures* say,

"Who can know what is on the Lord's
mind?
Who is able to give him advice?"

Isaiah 40:13

35"Who has ever given God anything?
God owes nothing to anyone."   *Job 41:11*

36Yes, God made all things. And everything
continues through him and for him. To God
be the glory* forever! Amen.*

Give Your Lives to God

12 1So I beg you, brothers and sisters,
because of the great mercy God has
shown us, offer your lives*a* as a living sacrifice* to him—an offering that is only for God

---

*a***12:1** *lives* Literally, "bodies." Paul is using the language of Old Testament animal sacrifice to express
the idea of a complete giving of oneself to God.

and pleasing to him. Considering what he has done, it is only right that you should worship him in this way. [2]Don't change yourselves to be like the people of this world, but let God change you inside with a new way of thinking. Then you will be able to understand and accept what God wants for you. You will be able to know what is good and pleasing to him and what is perfect.

[3]God has given me a special gift, and that is why I have something to say to each one of you. Don't think that you are better than you really are. You must see yourself just as you are. Decide what you are by the faith God has given each of us. [4]Each one of us has one body, and that body has many parts. These parts don't all do the same thing. [5]In the same way, we are many people, but in Christ we are all one body. We are the parts of that body, and each part belongs to all the others.

[6]We all have different gifts. Each gift came because of the grace* God gave us. Whoever has the gift of prophecy* should use that gift in a way that fits the kind of faith they have. [7]Whoever has the gift of serving should serve. Whoever has the gift of teaching should teach. [8]Whoever has the gift of comforting others should do that. Whoever has the gift of giving to help others should give generously. Whoever has the gift of leading should work hard at it. Whoever has the gift of showing kindness to others should do it gladly.

[9]Your love must be real. Hate what is evil. Do only what is good. [10]Love each other in a way that makes you feel close like brothers and sisters. And give each other more honor than you give yourself. [11]As you serve the Lord, work hard and don't be lazy. Be excited about serving him! [12]Be happy because of the hope you have. Be patient when you have troubles. Pray all the time. [13]Share with God's people who need help. Look for people who need help and welcome them into your homes.

[14]Wish only good for those who treat you badly. Ask God to bless them, not curse them. [15]When others are happy, you should be happy with them. And when others are sad, you should be sad too. [16]Live together in peace with each other. Don't be proud, but be willing to be friends with people who are not important to others. Don't think of yourself as smarter than everyone else.

[17]If someone does you wrong, don't try to pay them back by hurting them. Try to do what everyone thinks is right. [18]Do the best you can to live in peace with everyone. [19]My friends, don't try to punish anyone who does wrong to you. Wait for God to punish them with his anger. It is written: "I am the one who punishes; I will pay people back,"[a] says the Lord. [20]But you should do this:

"If you have enemies who are hungry,
    give them something to eat.
If you have enemies who are thirsty,
    give them something to drink.
In doing this you will make them feel
    ashamed.[b]"   *Proverbs 25:21-22*

[21]Don't let evil defeat you, but defeat evil by doing good.

Obey Your Government Rulers

13 [1]All of you must obey the government rulers. Everyone who rules was given the power to rule by God. And all those who rule now were given that power by God. [2]So anyone who is against the government is really against something God has commanded. Those who are against the government bring punishment on themselves. [3]People who do right don't have to fear the rulers. But those who do wrong must fear them. Do you want to be free from fearing them? Then do only what is right, and they will praise you.

[4]Rulers are God's servants to help you. But if you do wrong, you have reason to be afraid. They have the power to punish, and they will use it. They are God's servants to punish those who do wrong. [5]So you must obey the government, not just because you might be punished, but because you know it is the right thing to do.

[6]And this is why you pay taxes too. Those rulers are working for God, and they give all their time to the work of ruling. [7]Give everyone what you owe them. If you owe them any kind of tax, then pay it. Show respect to those you should respect. And show honor to those you should honor.

Loving Others Is the Only Law

[8]You should owe nothing to anyone, except that you will always owe love to each other. The person who loves others has done all that the law* commands. [9]The law says, "You must not commit adultery,* you must not murder anyone, you must not steal, you must not want what belongs to someone else."[c] All these commands and all other commands are really only one rule: "Love your neighbor[d] the same as you love yourself."[e] [10]Love doesn't hurt others. So loving is the same as obeying all the law.

[11]I say this because you know that we live in an important time. Yes, it is now time for you to wake up from your sleep. Our salvation is nearer now than when we first believed.

---

[a]**12:19** Quote from Deut. 32:35.

[b]**12:20** *you will make them feel ashamed* Literally, "you will pour burning coals on their head." People in Old Testament times often put ashes on their heads to show that they were sad or sorry.

[c]**13:9** Quote from Ex. 20:13–15, 17.

[d]**13:9** *your neighbor* Or "others." Jesus' teaching in Lk. 10:25–37 makes clear that this includes anyone in need.

[e]**13:9** Quote from Lev. 19:18.

[12]The night* is almost finished. The day* is almost here. So we should stop doing whatever belongs to darkness.* We should prepare ourselves to fight evil with the weapons that belong to the light.* [13]We should live in a right way, like people who belong to the day. We should not have wild parties or be drunk. We should not be involved in sexual sin or any kind of immoral behavior. We should not cause arguments and trouble or be jealous. [14]But be like the Lord Jesus Christ, so that when people see what you do, they will see Christ. Don't think about how to satisfy the desires of your sinful self.

Don't Criticize Others

14 [1]Be willing to accept those who still have doubts about what believers can do. And don't argue with them about their different ideas. [2]Some people believe they can eat any kind of food,[a] but those who have doubts eat only vegetables. [3]Those who know they can eat any kind of food must not feel that they are better than those who eat only vegetables. And those who eat only vegetables must not decide that those who eat all foods are wrong. God has accepted them. [4]You cannot judge the servants of someone else. Their own master decides if they are doing right or wrong. And the Lord's servants will be right, because the Lord is able to make them right.

[5]Some people might believe that one day is more important than another. And others might believe that every day is the same. Everyone should be sure about their beliefs in their own mind. [6]Those who think one day is more important than other days are doing that for the Lord. And those who eat all kinds of food are doing that for the Lord. Yes, they give thanks to God for that food. And those who refuse to eat some foods do that for the Lord. They also give thanks to God.

[7]We don't live or die just for ourselves. [8]If we live, we are living for the Lord. And if we die, we are dying for the Lord. So living or dying, we belong to the Lord. [9]That is why Christ died and rose from death to live again—so that he could be Lord over those who have died and those who are living.

[10]So why do you judge your brother or sister in Christ? Or why do you think that you are better than they are? We will all stand before God, and he will judge us all. [11]Yes, the Scriptures* say,

"'As surely as I live,' says the Lord,
    'Everyone will bow before me;
    everyone will say that I am God.'"

Isaiah 45:23

[12]So each of us will have to explain to God about the things we do.

Don't Cause Others to Sin

[13]So we should stop judging each other. Let's decide not to do anything that will cause a problem for a brother or sister or hurt their faith. [14]I know that there is no food that is wrong to eat. The Lord Jesus is the one who convinced me of that. But if someone believes that something is wrong, then it is wrong for that person.

[15]If you hurt the faith of your brother or sister because of something you eat, you are not really following the way of love. Don't destroy anyone's faith by eating something they think is wrong. Christ died for them. [16]Don't allow what is good for you to become something they say is evil. [17]In God's kingdom,* what we eat and drink is not important. Here is what is important: a right way of life, peace, and joy—all from the Holy Spirit.* [18]Whoever serves Christ by living this way is pleasing God, and they will be accepted by others.

[19]So let's try as hard as we can to do what will bring peace. Let's do whatever will help each other grow stronger in faith. [20]Don't let the eating of food destroy the work of God. All food is right to eat, but it is wrong for anyone to eat something that hurts the faith of another person. [21]It is better not to eat meat or drink wine or do anything else that hurts the faith of your brother or sister.

[22]You should keep your beliefs about these things a secret between yourself and God. It is a blessing to be able to do what you think is right without feeling guilty. [23]But anyone who eats something without being sure it is right is doing wrong. That is because they did not believe it was right. And if you do anything that you believe is not right, it is sin.

15 [1]Some of us have no problem with these things. So we should be patient with those who are not so strong and have doubts. We should not do what pleases us [2]but do what pleases them and is for their good. We should do whatever helps everyone grow stronger in faith. [3]Even Christ did not live trying to please himself. As the Scriptures* say about him, "Those people who insulted you have also insulted me."[b] [4]Everything that was written in the past was written to teach us. Those things were written so that we could have hope. That hope comes from the patience and encouragement that the Scriptures give us. [5]All patience and encouragement come from God. And I pray that God will help you all agree with each other, as Christ Jesus wants. [6]Then you will all be joined together. And all together you will give glory* to God the Father of our Lord Jesus Christ. [7]Christ accepted you, so you should

---

[a]**14:2** *any kind of food* The Jewish law said there were some foods that Jews could not eat. When they became followers of Christ, some of them did not understand that they could now eat all foods.

[b]**15:3** Quote from Ps. 69:9.

accept each other. This will bring honor[a] to God. [8]I tell you that Christ became a servant of the Jews to show that God has done what he promised their great ancestors.* [9]Christ also did this so that the non-Jewish people could praise God for the mercy he gives to them. The Scriptures say,

"So I will give thanks to you among the
      people of other nations;
   I will sing praise to your name."
                                      Psalm 18:49

[10]And the Scriptures say,

"You people of other nations should be
      happy together with God's people."
                                   Deuteronomy 32:43

[11]The Scriptures also say,

"Praise the Lord all you people of other
      nations;
   all people should praise the Lord."
                                      Psalm 117:1

[12]And Isaiah says,

"Someone will come from Jesse's family.[b]
   He will come to rule over the nations,
   and they will put their hope in him."
                                      Isaiah 11:10

[13]I pray that the God who gives hope will fill you with much joy and peace as you trust in him. Then you will have more and more hope, and it will flow out of you by the power of the Holy Spirit.

Paul Talks About His Work

[14]My brothers and sisters, I know without a doubt that you are full of goodness and have all the knowledge you need. So you are certainly able to counsel each other. [15]But I have written to you very openly about some things that I wanted you to remember. I did this because God gave me this special gift: [16]to be a servant of Christ Jesus for those who are not Jews. I serve like a priest whose duty it is to tell God's Good News.* He gave me this work so that you non-Jewish people could be an offering that he will accept—an offering made holy* by the Holy Spirit.*

[17]That is why I feel so good about what I have done for God in my service to Christ Jesus. [18]I will not talk about anything I did myself. I will talk only about what Christ has done with me in leading the non-Jewish people to obey God. They have obeyed him because of what I have said and done. [19]And they obeyed him because of the power of the

miraculous signs* and wonders* that happened—all because of the power of God's Spirit. I have told people the Good News about Christ in every place from Jerusalem to Illyricum.* And so I have finished that part of my work. [20]I always want to tell the Good News in places where people have never heard of Christ. I do this because I don't want to build on the work that someone else has already started. [21]But as the Scriptures* say,

"Those who were not told about him will
      see,
   and those who have not heard about
      him will understand."   Isaiah 52:15

Paul's Plan to Visit Rome

[22]That's what has kept me so busy and prevented my coming to see you even though I have wanted to come many times.

[23]Now I have finished my work in these areas. And for many years I have wanted to visit you. [24]So I will visit you when I go to Spain. Yes, I hope to visit you while I am traveling to Spain, and I will stay and enjoy being with you. Then you can help me continue on my trip.

[25]Now I am going to Jerusalem to help God's people there. [26]Some of them are poor, and the believers in Macedonia* and Achaia* wanted to help them. So they gathered some money to send them. [27]They were happy to do this. And it was like paying something they owed them, because as non-Jews they have been blessed spiritually by the Jews. So now they should use the material blessings they have to help the Jews. [28]I am going to Jerusalem to make sure the poor get this money that has been given for them.

After I finish that, I will leave for Spain and stop to visit you on the way. [29]And I know that when I visit you, I will bring you Christ's full blessing.

[30]Brothers and sisters, I beg you to help me in my work by praying to God for me. Do this because of our Lord Jesus and the love that the Spirit* gives us. [31]Pray that I will be saved from those in Judea who refuse to accept our message. And pray that this help I am bringing to Jerusalem will please God's people there. [32]Then, if God wants me to, I will come to you. I will come with joy, and together you and I will have a time of rest. [33]The God who gives peace be with you all. Amen.*

Paul Has Some Final Things to Say

16 [1]I want you to know that you can trust our sister in Christ, Phoebe. She is a special servant* of the church* in Cenchrea. [2]I ask you to accept her in the Lord. Accept her the way God's people should. Help her with anything she needs from you. She has helped me very much, and she has helped many others too.

---

[a] 15:7 *honor* Or "glory." See "glory" in the Word List.
[b] 15:12 *Jesse's family* Jesse was the father of David, king of Israel. Jesus was from their family.

³Give my greetings to Priscilla and Aquila, who have worked together with me for Christ Jesus. ⁴They risked their own lives to save mine. I am thankful to them, and all the non-Jewish churches are thankful to them. ⁵Also, give greetings to the church that meets in their house.

Give greetings to my dear friend Epaenetus. He was the first person to follow Christ in Asia.* ⁶Greetings also to Mary. She worked very hard for you. ⁷And greet Andronicus and Junia. They are my relatives, and they were in prison with me. They were followers of Christ before I was. And they are some of the most important of the ones Christ sent out to do his work.ᵃ

⁸Give my greetings to Ampliatus, my dear friend in the Lord, ⁹and to Urbanus. He has worked together with me for Christ. Give greetings also to my dear friend Stachys ¹⁰and to Apelles, who has proved himself to be a true follower of Christ. Give greetings to everyone in the family of Aristobulus ¹¹and to Herodion, my relative. Greetings to all those in the family of Narcissus who belong to the Lord ¹²and to Tryphaena and Tryphosa, women who work very hard for the Lord. Greetings to my dear friend Persis. She has also worked very hard for the Lord. ¹³Greetings also to Rufus, one of the Lord's chosen people, and to his mother, who has been a mother to me too.

¹⁴Give my greetings to Asyncritus, Phlegon, Hermes, Patrobas, Hermas, and all the brothers in Christ who are with them. ¹⁵Give greetings to Philologus and Julia, to Nereus and his sister, to Olympas, and to all of God's people with them. ¹⁶Give each other the special greeting of God's people.ᵇ All the churches that belong to Christ send their greetings to you.

ᵃ16:7 most important ... work Literally, "important among (or to) the apostles."
ᵇ16:16 the special greeting of God's people Literally, "a holy kiss."

¹⁷Brothers and sisters, I want you to be very careful of those who cause arguments and hurt people's faith by teaching things that are against what you learned. Stay away from them. ¹⁸People like that are not serving our Lord Christ. They are only pleasing themselves. They use fancy talk and say nice things to fool those who don't know about evil. ¹⁹Everyone has heard that you do what you were taught, and I am very happy about that. But I want you to be wise about what is good and to know nothing about what is evil.

²⁰The God who brings peace will soon defeat Satan* and give you power over him.

The grace* of our Lord Jesus be with you.

²¹Timothy, a worker together with me, sends you his greetings. Also Lucius, Jason, and Sosipater (these are my relatives) send their greetings.

²²I am Tertius, the one writing this letter for Paul. I send you my own greetings as one who belongs to the Lord.

²³Gaius is letting me and the whole church here use his home. He sends his greetings to you. Erastus and our brother Quartus also send their greetings. Erastus is the city treasurer here. ²⁴ ᶜ

²⁵Praise God! He is the one who can make you strong in faith. He can use the Good News* that I teach to make you strong. It is the message about Jesus Christ that I tell people. That message is the secret truth that was hidden for ages and ages but has been made known. ²⁶It has now been shown to us. It was made known by what the prophets* wrote, as God commanded. And it has now been made known to all people so that they can believe and obey God, who lives forever. ²⁷Glory* forever to the only wise God through Jesus Christ. Amen.*

ᶜ16:24 Some Greek copies add verse 24: "The grace of our Lord Jesus Christ be with you all. Amen."

1 Corinthians

1 ¹Greetings from Paul. I was chosen to be an apostle* of Christ Jesus. God chose me because that is what he wanted. Greetings also from Sosthenes, our brother in Christ.

²To God's church* in Corinth, you who have been made holy* because you belong to Christ Jesus. You were chosen to be God's holy people* together with all people everywhere who

trust in the Lordᵈ Jesus Christ—their Lord and ours.

³Grace* and peace to you from God our Father and the Lord Jesus Christ.

ᵈ1:2 who trust in the Lord Literally, "who call on the name of the Lord," meaning to show faith in him by worshiping or praying to him for help.

Paul Gives Thanks to God

[4]I always thank my God for you because of the grace* that he has given you through Christ Jesus. [5]In him you have been blessed in every way. You have been blessed in all your speaking and all your knowledge. [6]This proves that what we told you about Christ is true. [7]Now you have every gift from God while you wait for our Lord Jesus Christ to come again. [8]He will keep you strong until the end so that on the day when our Lord Jesus Christ comes, you will be free from all blame. [9]God is faithful. He is the one who has chosen you to share life with his Son, Jesus Christ our Lord.

Problems in the Church at Corinth

[10]Brothers and sisters, by the authority of our Lord Jesus Christ, I beg all of you to agree with each other. You should not be divided into different groups. Be completely joined together again with the same kind of thinking and the same purpose.

[11]My brothers and sisters, some members of Chloe's family told me that there are arguments among you. [12]This is what I mean: One of you says, "I follow Paul," and someone else says, "I follow Apollos." Another says, "I follow Peter,*" and someone else says, "I follow Christ." [13]Christ cannot be divided into different groups. It wasn't Paul who died on the cross for you, was it? Were you baptized* in Paul's name? [14]I am thankful that I did not baptize any of you except Crispus and Gaius. [15]I am thankful because now no one can say that you were baptized in my name. [16](I also baptized the family of Stephanas, but I don't remember that I myself baptized any others.) [17]Christ did not give me the work of baptizing people. He gave me the work of telling the Good News.* But he sent me to tell the Good News without using clever speech, which would take away the power that is in the cross[a] of Christ.

God's Power and Wisdom in Christ

[18]The teaching about the cross seems foolish to those who are lost. But to us who are being saved it is the power of God. [19]As the Scriptures* say,

"I will destroy the wisdom of the wise.
I will confuse the understanding of the
    intelligent."   *Isaiah 29:14*

[20]So what does this say about the philosopher,* the law expert, or anyone in this world who is skilled in making clever arguments? God has made the wisdom of the world look foolish. [21]This is what God in his wisdom decided: Since the world did not find him through its own wisdom, he used the message* that sounds foolish to save those who believe it.

[22]The Jews ask for miraculous signs,* and the Greeks* want wisdom. [23]But this is the message we tell everyone: Christ was killed on a cross. This message is a problem for Jews, and to other people it is nonsense. [24]But Christ is God's power and wisdom to the people God has chosen, both Jews and Greeks. [25]Even the foolishness of God is wiser than human wisdom. Even the weakness of God is stronger than human strength.

[26]Brothers and sisters, God chose you to be his. Think about that! Not many of you were wise in the way the world judges wisdom. Not many of you had great influence, and not many of you came from important families. [27]But God chose the foolish things of the world to shame the wise. He chose the weak things of the world to shame the strong. [28]And God chose what the world thinks is not important—what the world hates and thinks is nothing. He chose these to destroy what the world thinks is important. [29]God did this so that no one can stand before him and boast about anything. [30]It is God who has made you part of Christ Jesus. And Christ has become for us wisdom from God. He is the reason we are right with God and pure enough to be in his presence. Christ is the one who set us free from sin. [31]So, as the Scriptures say, "Whoever boasts should boast only about the Lord."[b]

The Message About Christ on the Cross

2 [1]Dear brothers and sisters, when I came to you, I told you the secret truth of God. But I did not use fancy words or great wisdom. [2]I decided that while I was with you I would forget about everything except Jesus Christ and his death on the cross. [3]When I came to you, I was weak and shook with fear. [4]My teaching and my speaking were not with wise words that persuade people. But the proof of my teaching was the power that the Spirit* gives. [5]I did this so that your faith would be in God's power, not in human wisdom.

God's Wisdom

[6]We teach wisdom to people who are mature, but the wisdom we teach is not from this world. It is not the wisdom of the rulers of this world, who are losing their power. [7]But we speak God's secret wisdom that has been hidden from everyone until now. God planned this wisdom for our glory.* He planned it before the world began. [8]None of the rulers of this world understood this wisdom. If they had understood it, they would not have killed our great and glorious Lord on a cross. [9]But as the Scriptures* say,

---

[a]1:17 *cross* Paul uses the cross as a picture of the Good News, the story of Christ's death to pay for people's sins. The cross (Christ's death) was God's way to save people.

[b]1:31 Quote from Jer. 9:24.

"No one has ever seen,
no one has ever heard,
no one has ever imagined
what God has prepared for those who
love him." *Isaiah 64:4*

[10]But God has shown us these things through the Spirit.*

The Spirit knows all things. The Spirit even knows the deep secrets of God. [11]It is like this: No one knows the thoughts that another person has. Only the person's spirit that lives inside knows those thoughts. It is the same with God. No one knows God's thoughts except God's Spirit. [12]We received the Spirit that is from God, not the spirit of the world. We received God's Spirit so that we can know all that God has given us.

[13]When we say this, we don't use words taught to us by human wisdom. We use words taught to us by the Spirit. We use the Spirit's words to explain spiritual truths. [14]People who do not have God's Spirit do not accept the things that come from his Spirit. They think these things are foolish. They cannot understand them, because they can only be understood with the Spirit's help. [15]We who have the Spirit are able to make judgments about all these things. But anyone without the Spirit is not able to make proper judgments about us. [16]As the Scriptures say,

"Who can know what is on the Lord's mind?
Who is able to give him advice?" *Isaiah 40:13*

But we have been given Christ's way of thinking.

Teachers Are Only God's Servants

3 [1]Brothers and sisters, when I was there, I could not talk to you the way I talk to people who are led by the Spirit. I had to talk to you like ordinary people of the world. You were like babies in Christ. [2]And the teaching I gave you was like milk, not solid food. I did this because you were not ready for solid food. And even now you are not ready. [3]You are still not following the Spirit. You are jealous of each other, and you are always arguing with each other. This shows that you are still following your own selfish desires. You are acting like ordinary people of the world. [4]One of you says, "I follow Paul," and someone else says, "I follow Apollos." When you say things like that, you are acting like people of the world.

[5]Is Apollos so important? Is Paul so important? We are only servants of God who helped you believe. Each one of us did the work God gave us to do. [6]I planted the seed and Apollos watered it. But God is the one who made the seed grow. [7]So the one who plants is not important, and the one who waters is not

important. Only God is important, because he is the one who makes things grow. [8]The one who plants and the one who waters have the same purpose. And each one will be rewarded for his own work. [9]We are workers together for God, and you are like a farm that belongs to God.

And you are a house that belongs to God. [10]Like an expert builder I built the foundation of that house. I used the gift that God gave me to do this. Other people are building on that foundation. But everyone should be careful how they build. [11]The foundation that has already been built is Jesus Christ, and no one can build any other foundation. [12]People can build on that foundation using gold, silver, jewels, wood, grass, or straw. [13]But the work that each person does will be clearly seen, because the Day* will make it plain. That Day will appear with fire, and the fire will test everyone's work. [14]If the building they put on the foundation still stands, they will get their reward. [15]But if their building is burned up, they will suffer loss. They will be saved, but it will be like someone escaping from a fire.

[16]You should know that you yourselves are God's temple.*a* God's Spirit* lives in you. [17]If you destroy God's temple, God will destroy you, because God's temple is holy.* You yourselves are God's temple.

[18]Don't fool yourselves. Whoever thinks they are wise in this world should become a fool. That's the only way they can be wise. [19]I say this because the wisdom of this world is foolishness to God. As the Scriptures* say, "He catches those who think they are wise in their own clever traps."*b* [20]The Scriptures also say, "The Lord knows the thoughts of the wise. He knows that their thoughts are worth nothing."*c* [21]So there is not a person on earth that any of you should be boasting about. Everything is yours: [22]Paul, Apollos, Peter,* the world, life, death, the present, and the future—all these are yours. [23]And you belong to Christ, and Christ belongs to God.

Apostles of Christ

4 [1]You should think of us as servants of Christ, the ones God has trusted to do the work of making known his secret truths. [2]Those who are trusted with such an important work must show that they are worthy of that trust. [3]But I don't consider your judgment on this point to be worth anything. Even an opinion from a court of law would mean nothing. I don't even trust my own judgment. [4]I don't know of any wrong I have done, but that does not make me right. The Lord is the one who must decide if I have done well or not. [5]So don't judge anyone now. The time for

---

*a***3:16** *temple* God's house—the place where God's people worship him. Here, it means that believers are the spiritual temple where God lives.
*b***3:19** Quote from Job 5:13.
*c***3:20** Quote from Ps. 94:11.

judging will be when the Lord comes. He will shine light on everything that is now hidden in darkness. He will make known the secret purposes of our hearts. Then the praise each person should get will come from God.

[6]Brothers and sisters, I have used Apollos and myself as examples for you. I did this so that you could learn from us the meaning of the words, "Follow what the Scriptures* say." Then you will not brag about one person and criticize another. [7]Who do you think you are? Everything you have was given to you. So, if everything you have was given to you, why do you act as if you got it all by your own power?

[8]You think you have everything you need. You think you are rich. You think you have become kings without us. I wish you really were kings. Then we could rule together with you. [9]But it seems to me that God has given me and the other apostles* the last place. We are like prisoners condemned to die, led in a parade for the whole world to see—not just people but angels too. [10]We are fools for Christ, but you think you are so wise in Christ. We are weak, but you think you are so strong. People give you honor, but they don't honor us. [11]Even now we still don't have enough to eat or drink, and we don't have enough clothes. We often get beatings. We have no homes. [12]We work hard with our own hands to feed ourselves. When people insult us, we ask God to bless them. When people treat us badly, we accept it. [13]When people say bad things about us, we try to say something that will help them. But people still treat us like the world's garbage—everyone's trash.

[14]I am not trying to make you feel ashamed, but I am writing this to counsel you as my own dear children. [15]You may have ten thousand teachers in Christ, but you don't have many fathers. Through the Good News* I became your father in Christ Jesus. [16]So I beg you to be like me. [17]That is why I am sending Timothy to you. He is my son in the Lord. I love him and trust him. He will help you remember the way I live in Christ Jesus—a way of life that I teach in all the churches* everywhere.

[18]Some of you are acting so proud, it seems as though you think I won't be coming there again. [19]But I will come to you very soon, the Lord willing. Then I will see if these proud talkers have the power to do anything more than talk. [20]God's kingdom* is not seen in talk but in power. [21]Which do you want: that I come to you with punishment, or that I come to you with love and gentleness?

A Moral Problem in the Church

5 [1]I don't want to believe what I am hearing—that there is sexual sin among you. And it is such a bad kind of sexual sin that even those who have never known God don't allow it. People say that a man there has

his father's wife. [2]And still you are proud of yourselves! You should have been filled with sadness. And the man who committed that sin should be put out of your group. [3]I cannot be there with you in person, but I am with you in spirit. And I have already judged the man who did this. I judged him the same as I would if I were really there. [4]Come together in the name of our Lord Jesus. I will be with you in spirit, and you will have the power of our Lord Jesus with you. [5]Then turn this man over to Satan.* His sinful self[a] has to be destroyed so that his spirit will be saved on the day when the Lord comes again.

[6]Your proud talk is not good. You know the saying, "Just a little yeast* makes the whole batch of dough rise." [7]Take out all the old yeast, so that you will be a new batch of dough. You really are bread without yeast—Passover bread.[b] Yes, Christ our Passover Lamb[c] has already been killed. [8]So let us eat our Passover meal, but not with the bread that has the old yeast, the yeast of sin and wrongdoing. But let us eat the bread that has no yeast. This is the bread of goodness and truth.

[9]I wrote to you in my letter that you should not associate with people who sin sexually. [10]But I did not mean the people of this world. You would have to leave the world to get away from all the people who sin sexually, or who are greedy and cheat each other, or who worship idols. [11]I meant you must not associate with people who claim to be believers* but continue to live in sin. Don't even eat with a brother or sister who sins sexually, is greedy, worships idols, abuses others with insults, gets drunk, or cheats people.

[12-13]It is not my business to judge those who are not part of the group of believers. God will judge them, but you must judge those who are part of your group. The Scriptures* say, "Make the evil person leave your group."[d]

Judging Problems Between Believers

6 [1]When one of you has something against someone else in your group, why do you go to the judges in the law courts? The way they think and live is wrong. So why do you let them decide who is right? Why don't you let God's holy people* decide who is right? [2]Don't you know that God's people will judge the world? So if you will judge the world, then surely you can judge small arguments like this. [3]You know that in the future we will judge angels. So surely we can judge life's

---

[a]**5:5 sinful self** Or "body." Literally, "flesh."

[b]**5:7 Passover bread** The special bread without yeast that the Jews ate at their Passover meal. Paul means that believers are free from sin, just as the Passover bread was free from yeast.

[c]**5:7 Passover Lamb** Jesus was a sacrifice for his people, like a lamb killed for the Jewish Passover Feast.

[d]**5:12–13** Quote from Deut. 22:21, 24.

ordinary problems. 4So if you have such matters to be judged, why do you take them to those who are not part of the church*? They mean nothing to you. 5I say this to shame you. Surely there is someone in your group wise enough to judge a complaint between two believers.* 6But now one believer goes to court against another, and you let people who are not believers judge their case!

7The lawsuits that you have against each other show that you are already defeated. It would be better for you to let someone wrong you. It would be better to let someone cheat you. 8But you are the ones doing wrong and cheating. And you do this to your own brothers and sisters in Christ!

9-10Surely you know that people who do wrong will not get to enjoy God's kingdom.* Don't be fooled. These are the people who will not get to enjoy his kingdom: those who sin sexually, those who worship idols,* those who commit adultery,* men who let other men use them for sex or who have sex with other men, those who steal, those who are greedy, those who drink too much, those who abuse others with insults, and those who cheat. 11In the past some of you were like that. But you were washed clean, you were made holy,* and you were made right with God in the name of the Lord Jesus Christ and by the Spirit of our God.

Use Your Bodies for God's Glory

12"I am allowed to do anything," you say. My answer to this is that not all things are good. Even if it is true that "I am allowed to do anything," I will not let anything control me like a slave. 13Someone else says, "Food is for the stomach, and the stomach for food." Yes, and God will destroy them both. But the body is not for sexual sin. The body is for the Lord, and the Lord is for the body. 14And God will raise our bodies from death with the same power he used to raise the Lord Jesus. 15Surely you know that your bodies are parts of Christ himself. So I must never take what is part of Christ and join it to a prostitute! 16The Scriptures* say, "The two people will become one."a So you should know that anyone who is joined with a prostitute becomes one with her in body. 17But anyone who is joined with the Lord is one with him in spirit.

18So run away from sexual sin. It involves the body in a way that no other sin does. So if you commit sexual sin, you are sinning against your own body. 19You should know that your body is a templeb for the Holy Spirit* that you received from God and that lives in you. You don't own yourselves. 20God paid a very high price to make you his. So honor God with your body.

a6:16 Quote from Gen. 2:24.
b6:19 temple God's house—the place where God's people worship him. Here, it means that believers are the spiritual temple where God lives.

About Marriage

7 1Now I will discuss the things you wrote me about. You asked if it is better for a man not to have any sexual relations at all. 2But sexual sin is a danger, so each man should enjoy his own wife, and each woman should enjoy her own husband. 3The husband should give his wife what she deserves as his wife. And the wife should give her husband what he deserves as her husband. 4The wife does not have power over her own body. Her husband has the power over her body. And the husband does not have power over his own body. His wife has the power over his body. 5Don't refuse to give your bodies to each other. But you might both agree to stay away from sex for a while so that you can give your time to prayer. Then come together again so that Satan* will not be able to tempt you in your weakness. 6I say this only to give you permission to be separated for a time. It is not a rule. 7I wish everyone could be like me. But God has given each person a different ability. He makes some able to live one way, others to live a different way.

8Now for those who are not married and for the widows I say this: It is good for you to stay single like me. 9But if you cannot control your body, then you should marry. It is better to marry than to burn with sexual desire.

10Now, I have a command for those who are married. Actually, it is not from me; it is what the Lord commanded. A wife should not leave her husband. 11But if a wife does leave, she should remain single or get back together with her husband. And a husband should not divorce his wife.

12The advice I have for the others is from me. The Lord did not give us any teaching about this. If you have a wife who is not a believer, you should not divorce her if she will continue to live with you. 13And if you have a husband who is not a believer, you should not divorce him if he will continue to live with you. 14The husband who is not a believer is set apart for God through his believing wife. And the wife who is not a believer is set apart for God through her believing husband. If this were not true, your children would be unfit for God's use. But now they are set apart for him.

15But if the husband or wife who is not a believer decides to leave, let them leave. When this happens, the brother or sister in Christ is free. God chose you to have a life of peace. 16Wives, maybe you will save your husband; and husbands, maybe you will save your wife. You don't know now what will happen later.

Live as God Called You

17But each one of you should continue to live the way the Lord God has given you to live—the way you were when God chose you. This is a rule I make for all the churches.* 18If a man was already circumcised* when he was chosen, he should not change his circumcision. If a man was without circumcision when he was chosen, he should not be circumcised. 19It is not important if anyone is circumcised or not. What is important is obeying God's commands. 20Each one of you should stay the way you were when God chose you. 21If you were a slave when God chose you, don't let that bother you. But if you can be free, then do it. 22If you were a slave when the Lord chose you, you are now free in the Lord. You belong to the Lord. In the same way, if you were free when you were chosen, you are now Christ's slave. 23God paid a high price for you, so don't be slaves to anyone else. 24Brothers and sisters, in your new life with God, each one of you should continue the way you were when God chose you.

Questions About Getting Married

25Now I write about people who are not married.*a* I have no command from the Lord about this, but I give my opinion. And I can be trusted, because the Lord has given me mercy. 26This is a time of trouble. So I think it is good for you to stay the way you are. 27If you have a wife, don't try to get free from her. If you are not married, don't try to find a wife. 28But if you decide to marry, that is not a sin. And it is not a sin for a girl who has never married to get married. But those who marry will have trouble in this life, and I want you to be free from this trouble.

29Brothers and sisters, this is what I mean: We don't have much time left. So starting now, those who have wives should be the same as those who don't. 30It should not be important whether you are sad or whether you are happy. If you buy something, it should not matter to you that you own it. 31You should use the things of the world without letting them become important to you. This is how you should live, because this world, the way it is now, will soon be gone.

32I want you to be free from worry. A man who is not married is busy with the Lord's work. He is trying to please the Lord. 33But a man who is married is busy with things of the world. He is trying to please his wife. 34He must think about two things—pleasing his wife and pleasing the Lord. A woman who is not married or a girl who has never married is busy with the Lord's work. She wants to give herself fully—body and spirit—to the Lord. But a married woman is busy with things of the world. She is trying to please her husband. 35I am saying this to help you. I am not trying to limit you, but I want you to live in the right way. And I want you to give yourselves fully to the Lord without giving your time to other things.

36A man might think that he is not doing the right thing with his fiancée. She might be almost past the best age to marry.*b* So he might feel that he should marry her. He should do what he wants. It is no sin for them to get married. 37But another man might be more sure in his mind. There may be no need for marriage, so he is free to do what he wants. If he has decided in his own heart not to marry his fiancée, he is doing the right thing. 38So the man who marries his fiancée does right, and the man who does not marry does better.

39A woman should stay with her husband as long as he lives. But if the husband dies, the woman is free to marry any man she wants, but he should belong to the Lord. 40The woman is happier if she does not marry again. This is my opinion, and I believe that I have God's Spirit.

About Food Offered to Idols

8 1Now I will write about meat that is sacrificed*c* to idols.* We know that "we all have knowledge," as you say. But this knowledge puffs a person up with pride, while love helps the church grow stronger. 2Whoever thinks they know something does not yet know anything as they should. 3But whoever loves God is known by God.

4So this is what I say about eating meat: We know that an idol is really nothing in the world, and we know that there is only one God. 5It's really not important if there are things called gods in heaven or on earth—and there are many of these "gods" and "lords" out there. 6For us there is only one God, and he is our Father. All things came from him, and we live for him. And there is only one Lord, Jesus Christ. All things were made through him, and we also have life through him.

7But not all people know this. Some have had the habit of worshiping idols. So now when they eat meat, they still feel as if it belongs to an idol. They are not sure that it is right to eat this meat. So when they eat it, they feel guilty. 8But food will not bring us closer to God. Refusing to eat does not make us less pleasing to God, and eating does not make us closer to him.

9But be careful with your freedom. Your freedom to eat anything may make those who have doubts about what they can eat fall into sin. 10You understand that it's all right to eat anything, so you can eat even in an idol's temple. But someone who has doubts might see you eating there, and this might encourage them to eat meat sacrificed to idols too. But they really think it is wrong. 11So this weak brother or sister—someone Christ died for— is lost because of your better understanding.

---

*b***7:36 She ... to marry** Or "He may have trouble controlling his desires."

*c***8:1 sacrificed** Killed and offered as a gift to show worship. Also in verse 10.

*a***7:25 people who are not married** Literally, "virgins."

12When you sin against your brothers and sisters in Christ in this way and you hurt them by causing them to do things they feel are wrong, you are also sinning against Christ. 13So if the food I eat makes another believer fall into sin, I will never eat meat again. I will stop eating meat, so that I will not make my brother or sister sin.

Rights That Paul Has Not Used

9 ¹I am a free man. I am an apostle.* I have seen Jesus our Lord. You people are an example of my work in the Lord. ²Others may not accept me as an apostle, but surely you do. You are proof that I am an apostle in the Lord.

³Some people want to judge me. So this is the answer I give them: ⁴We have the right to eat and drink, don't we? ⁵We have the right to bring a believing wife with us when we travel, don't we? The other apostles and the Lord's brothers and Peter* all do this. ⁶And are Barnabas and I the only ones who must work to earn our living? ⁷No soldier ever serves in the army and pays his own salary. No one ever plants a vineyard* without eating some of the grapes himself. No one takes care of a flock of sheep without drinking some of the milk himself.

⁸These aren't just my own thoughts. God's law says the same thing. ⁹Yes, it is written in the Law of Moses*: "When a work animal is being used to separate grain, don't keep it from eating the grain."ᵃ When God said this, was he thinking only about work animals? No. ¹⁰He was really talking about us. Yes, that was written for us. The one who plows and the one who separates the grain should both expect to get some of the grain for their work. ¹¹We planted spiritual seed among you, so we should be able to harvest from you some things for this life. Surely that is not asking too much. ¹²Others have this right to get things from you. So surely we have this right too. But we don't use this right. No, we endure everything ourselves so that we will not stop anyone from obeying the Good News* of Christ. ¹³Surely you know that those who work at the Temple* get their food from the Temple. And those who serve at the altar* get part of what is offered at the altar. ¹⁴It is the same with those who have the work of telling the Good News. The Lord has commanded that those who tell the Good News should get their living from this work.

¹⁵But I have not used any of these rights, and I am not trying to get anything from you. That is not my purpose for writing this. I would rather die than to have someone take away what for me is a great source of pride. ¹⁶It's not my work of telling the Good News that gives me any reason to boast. That is my duty—something I must do. If I don't tell people the Good News, I am in real trouble. ¹⁷If I

did it because it was my own choice, I would deserve to be paid. But I have no choice. I must tell the Good News. So I am only doing the duty that was given to me. ¹⁸So what do I get for doing it? My reward is that when I tell people the Good News I can offer it to them for free and not use the rights that come with doing this work.

¹⁹I am free. I belong to no other person, but I make myself a slave to everyone. I do this to help save as many people as I can. ²⁰To the Jews I became like a Jew so that I could help save Jews. I myself am not ruled by the law,* but to those who are ruled by the law I became like someone who is ruled by the law. I did this to help save those who are ruled by the law. ²¹To those who are without the law I became like someone who is without the law. I did this to help save those who are without the law. (But really, I am not without God's law—I am ruled by the law of Christ.) ²²To those who are weak, I became weak so that I could help save them. I have become all things to all people. I did this so that I could save people in any way possible. ²³I do all this to make the Good News known. I do it so that I can share in the blessings of the Good News.

²⁴You know that in a race all the runners run, but only one runner gets the prize. So run like that. Run to win! ²⁵All who compete in the games use strict training. They do this so that they can win a prize*—one that doesn't last. But our prize is one that will last forever. ²⁶So I run like someone who has a goal. I fight like a boxer who is hitting something, not just the air. ²⁷It is my own body I fight to make it do what I want. I do this so that I won't miss getting the prize myself after telling others about it.

Warning From History

10 ¹Brothers and sisters, I want you to know what happened to our ancestors* who were with Moses.* They were all under the cloud,ᵇ and they all walked through the sea. ²They were all baptizedᶜ into Moses in the cloud and in the sea. ³They all ate the same spiritual food, ⁴and they all drank the same spiritual drink. They drank from that spiritual rock that was with them, and that rock was Christ. ⁵But God was not pleased with most of those people, so they were killed in the desert.

⁶And these things that happened are examples for us. These examples should stop us from wanting evil things like those people did. ⁷Don't worship idols* as some of them

---

ᵃ9:9 Quote from Deut. 25:4.

ᵇ10:1 *cloud* The cloud that led and protected the people of Israel on their journey out of Egypt, across the Red Sea, and through the wilderness. See Ex. 13:20–22; 14:19, 20.
ᶜ10:2 *baptized* See "baptize" in the Word List. Here, Paul seems to mean that what happened to the Jews with Moses can be compared to the baptism of a believer into Christ.

did. As the Scriptures* say, "The people sat down to eat and drink and then got up to have a wild party."*a* *8*We should not commit sexual sins as some of them did. In one day 23,000 of them died because of their sin. *9*We should not test Christ*b* as some of them did. Because of that, they were killed by snakes. *10*And don't complain as some of them did. Because they complained, they were killed by the angel that destroys.

*11*The things that happened to those people are examples. They were written to be warnings for us. We live in the time that all those past histories were pointing to. *12*So anyone who thinks they are standing strong should be careful that they don't fall. *13*The only temptations that you have are the same temptations that all people have. But you can trust God. He will not let you be tempted more than you can bear. But when you are tempted, God will also give you a way to escape that temptation. Then you will be able to endure it.

*14*So, my dear friends, stay away from worshiping idols. *15*You are intelligent people. Judge for yourselves the truth of what I say now. *16*The cup of blessing*c* that we give thanks for is a sharing in the blood sacrifice of Christ, isn't it? And the bread that we break is a sharing in the body of Christ, isn't it? *17*There is one loaf of bread, so we who are many are one body, because we all share in that one loaf.

*18*And think about what the people of Israel* do. When they eat the sacrifices,*d* they are united by sharing what was offered on the altar.* *19*So, am I saying that sacrifices to idols are the same as those Jewish sacrifices? No, because an idol is nothing, and the things offered to idols are worth nothing. *20*But I am saying that when food is sacrificed to idols, it is an offering to demons,* not to God. And I don't want you to share anything with demons. *21*You cannot drink the cup of the Lord and then go drink a cup that honors demons. You cannot share a meal at the Lord's table and then go share a meal that honors demons. *22*Doing that would make the Lord jealous.*e* Do you really want to do that? Do you think we are stronger than he is?

Use Your Freedom for God's Glory

23"All things are allowed," you say. But not all things are good. "All things are allowed." But some things don't help anyone. *24*Try to do what is good for others, not just what is good for yourselves.

*25*Eat any meat that is sold in the meat market. Don't ask questions about it to see if it is

something you think is wrong to eat. *26*You can eat it, "because the earth and everything in it belong to the Lord."*f*

*27*Someone who is not a believer might invite you to eat with them. If you want to go, then eat anything that is put before you. Don't ask questions to see if it is something you think is wrong to eat. *28*But if someone tells you, "That food was offered to idols,*" then don't eat it. That's because some people think it is wrong, and it might cause a problem for the person who told you that. *29*I don't mean that you think it is wrong. But the other person might think it is wrong. That's the only reason not to eat it. My own freedom should not be judged by what another person thinks. *30*I eat the meal with thankfulness. So I don't want to be criticized because of something I thank God for.

*31*So if you eat, or if you drink, or if you do anything, do it for the glory* of God. *32*Never do anything that might make other people do wrong—Jews, non-Jews, or anyone in God's church.* *33*I do the same thing. I try to please everyone in every way. I am not trying to do what is good for me. I am trying to do what is good for the most people so that they can be saved.

11 *1*Follow my example, just as I follow the example of Christ.

Being Under Authority

*2*I praise you because you remember me in all things. You follow closely the teachings I gave you. *3*But I want you to understand this: The head of every man is Christ. And the head of a woman is the man.*g* And the head of Christ is God.

*4*Every man who prophesies* or prays with his head covered brings shame to his head. *5*But every woman who prays or prophesies should have her head covered. If her head is not covered, she brings shame to her head. Then she is the same as a woman who has her head shaved. *6*If a woman does not cover her head, it is the same as cutting off all her hair. But it is shameful for a woman to cut off her hair or to shave her head. So she should cover her head.

*7*But a man should not cover his head, because he is made like God and is God's glory.* But woman is man's glory. *8*Man did not come from woman. Woman came from man. *9*And man was not made for woman. Woman was made for man. *10*So that is why a woman should have her head covered with something that shows she is under authority.*h* Also, she should do this because of the angels.

---

*a***10:7** Quote from Ex. 32:6.
*b***10:9** *Christ* Some Greek copies say, "the Lord."
*c***10:16** *cup of blessing* The cup of wine that believers in Christ thank God for and drink at the Lord's Supper.
*d***10:18** *sacrifices* Animals killed and offered as gifts to God.
*e***10:22** *make the Lord jealous* See Deut. 32:16, 17.

*f***10:26** Quote from Ps. 24:1; 50:12; 89:11.
*g***11:3** *the man* This could also mean "her husband."
*h***11:10** *have her head ... authority* Literally, "have authority on her head." This could also be translated, "keep control of her head," meaning "do what will keep people from misunderstanding her uncovered head."

[11]But in the Lord the woman needs the man, and the man needs the woman. [12]This is true because woman came from man, but also man is born from woman. Really, everything comes from God.

[13]Decide this for yourselves: Is it right for a woman to pray to God without something on her head? [14]Even nature itself teaches you that wearing long hair is shameful for a man. [15]But wearing long hair is a woman's honor. Long hair is given to the woman to cover her head. [16]Some people may still want to argue about this. But we and the churches* of God don't accept what those people are doing.

The Lord's Supper

[17]In the things I tell you now I don't praise you. Your meetings hurt you more than they help you. [18]First, I hear that when you meet together as a church* you are divided. And this is not hard to believe [19]because of your idea that you must have separate groups to show who the real believers are!

[20]When you all come together, it is not really the Lord's Supper[a] you are eating. [21]I say this because when you eat, each one eats without waiting for the others. Some people don't get enough to eat or drink, while others have too much.[b] [22]You can eat and drink in your own homes. It seems that you think God's church is not important. You embarrass those who are poor. What can I say? Should I praise you? No, I cannot praise you for this.

[23]The teaching I gave you is the same that I received from the Lord: On the night when the Lord Jesus was handed over to be killed, he took bread [24]and gave thanks for it. Then he divided the bread and said, "This is my body; it is for you. Eat this to remember me." [25]In the same way, after they ate, Jesus took the cup of wine. He said, "This cup represents the new agreement* from God, which begins with my blood sacrifice. When you drink this, do it to remember me." [26]This means that every time you eat this bread and drink this cup, you are telling others about the Lord's death until he comes again.

[27]So if you eat the bread or drink the cup of the Lord in a way that does not fit its meaning, you are sinning against the body and the blood of the Lord. [28]Before you eat the bread and drink the cup, you should examine your own attitude. [29]If you eat and drink without paying attention to those who are the Lord's body, your eating and drinking will cause you to be judged guilty. [30]That is why many in your group are sick and weak, and many have died. [31]But if we judged ourselves in the right way, then God would not judge us. [32]But when the Lord judges us, he punishes us to show us the right way. He does this so that we will not be condemned with the world.

[33]So, my brothers and sisters, when you come together to eat, wait for each other. [34]If some are too hungry to wait, they should eat at home. Do this so that your meeting together will not bring God's judgment on you. I will tell you what to do about the other things when I come.

Gifts From the Holy Spirit

12[1]Now, brothers and sisters, I want you to understand about spiritual gifts. [2]You remember the lives you lived before you were believers. You let yourselves be influenced and led away to worship idols*—things that have no life. [3]So I tell you that no one who is speaking with the help of God's Spirit says, "Jesus be cursed." And no one can say, "Jesus is Lord," without the help of the Holy Spirit.*

[4]There are different kinds of spiritual gifts, but they are all from the same Spirit. [5]There are different ways to serve, but we serve the same Lord. [6]And there are different ways that God works in people, but it is the same God who works in all of us to do everything.

[7]Something from the Spirit can be seen in each person. The Spirit gives this to each one to help others. [8]The Spirit gives one person the ability to speak with wisdom. And the same Spirit gives another person the ability to speak with knowledge. [9]The same Spirit gives faith to one person and to another he gives gifts of healing. [10]The Spirit gives to one person the power to do miracles,* to another the ability to prophesy,* and to another the ability to judge what is from the Spirit and what is not. The Spirit gives one person the ability to speak in different kinds of languages, and to another the ability to interpret those languages. [11]One Spirit, the same Spirit, does all these things. The Spirit decides what to give each one.

The Body of Christ

[12]A person has only one body, but it has many parts. Yes, there are many parts, but all those parts are still just one body. Christ is like that too. [13]Some of us are Jews and some of us are not; some of us are slaves and some of us are free. But we were all baptized* to become one body through one Spirit.* And we were all given[c] the one Spirit.

[14]And a person's body has more than one part. It has many parts. [15]The foot might say, "I am not a hand, so I don't belong to the body." But saying this would not stop the foot from being a part of the body. [16]The ear might say, "I am not an eye, so I don't belong to the body." But saying this would not make the ear stop being a part of the body. [17]If the whole body were an eye, it would not be able to hear. If the whole body were an ear, it would

---

[a]**11:20** *Lord's Supper* The special meal Jesus told his followers to eat to remember him. See Lk. 22:14–20.
[b]**11:21** *have too much* Literally, "get drunk."

[c]**12:13** *given* Literally, "given to drink."

not be able to smell anything. 18–19If each part of the body were the same part, there would be no body. But as it is, God put the parts in the body as he wanted them. He made a place for each one. 20So there are many parts, but only one body.

21The eye cannot say to the hand, "I don't need you!" And the head cannot say to the foot, "I don't need you!" 22No, those parts of the body that seem to be weaker are really very important. 23And the parts that we think are not worth very much are the parts we give the most care to. And we give special care to the parts of the body that we don't want to show. 24The more beautiful parts don't need this special care. But God put the body together and gave more honor to the parts that need it. 25God did this so that our body would not be divided. God wanted the different parts to care the same for each other. 26If one part of the body suffers, then all the other parts suffer with it. Or if one part is honored, then all the other parts share its honor.

27All of you together are the body of Christ. Each one of you is a part of that body. 28And in the church* God has given a place first to apostles,* second to prophets,* and third to teachers. Then God has given a place to those who do miracles,* those who have gifts of healing, those who can help others, those who are able to lead, and those who can speak in different kinds of languages. 29Not all are apostles. Not all are prophets. Not all are teachers. Not all do miracles. 30Not all have gifts of healing. Not all speak in different kinds of languages. Not all interpret those languages. 31Continue to give your attention to the spiritual gifts you consider to be the greatest. But now I want to point out a way of life that is even greater.

Let Love Be Your Guide

13 1I may speak in different languages, whether human or even of angels. But if I don't have love, I am only a noisy bell or a ringing cymbal. 2I may have the gift of prophecy,* I may understand all secrets and know everything there is to know, and I may have faith so great that I can move mountains. But even with all this, if I don't have love, I am nothing. 3I may give away everything I have to help others, and I may even give my body as an offering to be burned. But I gain nothing by doing all this if I don't have love.

4Love is patient and kind. Love is not jealous, it does not brag, and it is not proud. 5Love is not rude, it is not selfish, and it cannot be made angry easily. Love does not remember wrongs done against it. 6Love is never happy when others do wrong, but it is always happy with the truth. 7Love never gives up on people. It never stops trusting, never loses hope, and never quits.

8Love will never end. But all those gifts will come to an end—even the gift of prophecy, the gift of speaking in different kinds of languages, and the gift of knowledge. 9These will all end because this knowledge and these prophecies we have are not complete. 10But when perfection comes, the things that are not complete will end.

11When I was a child, I talked like a child, I thought like a child, and I made plans like a child. When I became a man, I stopped those childish ways. 12It is the same with us. Now we see God as if we are looking at a reflection in a mirror. But then, in the future, we will see him right before our eyes. Now I know only a part, but at that time I will know fully, as God has known me. 13So these three things continue: faith, hope, and love. And the greatest of these is love.

Use Spiritual Gifts to Help the Church

14 1Love should be the goal of your life, but you should also want to have the gifts that come from the Spirit.* And the gift you should want most is to be able to prophesy.* 2I will explain why. Those who have the gift of speaking in a different language are not speaking to people. They are speaking to God. No one understands them—they are speaking secret things through the Spirit. 3But those who prophesy are speaking to people. They help people grow stronger in faith, and they give encouragement and comfort. 4Those who speak in a different language are helping only themselves. But those who prophesy are helping the whole church.*

5I would like all of you to have the gift of speaking in different languages. But what I want more is for you to prophesy. Anyone who prophesies is more important than those who can only speak in different languages. However, if they can also interpret those languages, they are as important as the one who prophesies. If they can interpret, then the church can be helped by what they say.

6Brothers and sisters, will it help you if I come to you speaking in different languages? No, it will help you only if I bring you a new truth or some knowledge, prophecy,* or teaching. 7This is true even with lifeless things that make sounds—like a flute or a harp. If the different musical notes are not made clear, you can't understand what song is being played. Each note must be played clearly for you to be able to understand the tune. 8And in a war, if the trumpet does not sound clearly, the soldiers will not know it is time to prepare for fighting.

9It is the same with you. If you don't speak clearly in a language people know, they cannot understand what you are saying. You will be talking to the air! 10It is true that there are many different languages in the world, and they all have meaning. 11But if I don't understand the meaning of what someone is saying, it will just be strange sounds to me, and I will sound just as strange to them. 12That's why you who want spiritual gifts so much should prefer those gifts that help the church grow stronger.

13So those who have the gift of speaking in a different language should pray that they can also interpret what they say. 14If I pray in a different language, my spirit is praying, but my mind does nothing. 15So what should I do? I will pray with my spirit, but I will also pray with my mind. I will sing with my spirit, but I will also sing with my mind. 16You might be praising God with your spirit. But someone there without understanding cannot say "Amen*" to your prayer of thanks, because they don't know what you are saying. 17You may be thanking God in a good way, but others are not helped.

18I thank God that my gift of speaking in different kinds of languages is greater than any of yours. 19But in the church meetings I would rather speak five words that I understand than thousands of words in a different language. I would rather speak with my understanding, so that I can teach others.

20Brothers and sisters, don't think like children. In evil things be like babies, but in your thinking you should be like full-grown adults. 21As the Scriptures*a* say,

> "Using those who speak a different
> language
> and using the lips of foreigners,
> I will speak to these people.
> But even then, they will not obey me."
>
> *Isaiah 28:11–12*

This is what the Lord says.

22And from this we see that the use of different languages shows how God deals with those who don't believe, not with those who believe. And prophecy shows how God works through those who believe, not through unbelievers. 23Suppose the whole church meets together and you all speak in different languages. If some people come in who are without understanding or don't believe, they will say you are crazy. 24But suppose you are all prophesying and someone comes in who does not believe or who is without understanding. Their sin will be shown to them, and they will be judged by everything you say. 25The secret things in their heart will be made known. So they will bow down and worship God. They will say, "Without a doubt, God is here with you."*b*

Your Meetings Should Be Helpful to All

26So, brothers and sisters, what should you do? When you meet together, one person has a song, another has a teaching, and another has a new truth from God. One person speaks

in a different language, and another interprets that language. The purpose of whatever you do should be to help everyone grow stronger in faith. 27When you meet together, if anyone speaks to the group in a different language, it should be only two or no more than three people who do this. And they should speak one after the other. And someone else should interpret what they say. 28But if there is no interpreter, then anyone who speaks in a different language should be quiet in the church meeting. They should speak only to themselves and to God.

29And only two or three prophets* should speak. The others should judge what they say. 30And if a message from God comes to someone who is sitting, the first speaker should be quiet. 31You can all prophesy* one after the other. This way everyone can be taught and encouraged. 32The spirits of prophets are under the control of the prophets themselves. 33God is not a God of confusion but a God of peace. This is the rule for all the meetings of God's people.

34The women should keep quiet in these church* meetings. They are not allowed to speak out but should be under authority, as the Law of Moses says. 35If there is something they want to know, they should ask their own husbands at home. It is shameful for a woman to speak up like that in the church meeting.

36God's teaching did not come from you, and you are not the only ones who have received it. 37If you think you are a prophet or that you have a spiritual gift, you should understand that what I am writing to you is the Lord's command. 38If you do not accept this, you will not be accepted.

39So my brothers and sisters, continue to give your attention to prophesying. And don't stop anyone from using the gift of speaking in different languages. 40But everything should be done in a way that is right and orderly.

The Good News About Christ

15 1Now, brothers and sisters, I want you to remember the Good News* I told you about. You received that Good News message, and you continue to base your life on it. 2It is that Good News that saves you, but you must continue believing the message just as I told it to you. If you don't, then you believed for nothing.

3I gave you the message that I received. I told you the most important truths: that Christ died for our sins, as the Scriptures* say; 4that he was buried and was raised to life on the third day, as the Scriptures say; 5and that he appeared to Peter and then to the twelve apostles.* 6After that, Christ appeared to more than 500 of the brothers and sisters at the same time. Most of them are still living today, but some have died. 7Then he appeared to James and later to all the apostles. 8Last of all, he appeared to me. I was different, like a

---

*a***14:21** *Scriptures* Literally, "law," which sometimes means the Old Testament.
*b***14:25** See Isa. 45:14 and Zech. 8:23.

baby born before the normal time.

⁹All the other apostles are greater than I am. I say this because I persecuted* the church* of God. That is why I am not even good enough to be called an apostle. ¹⁰But, because of God's grace,* that is what I am. And his grace that he gave me was not wasted. I worked harder than all the other apostles. (But I was not really the one working. It was God's grace that was with me.) ¹¹So then it is not important if I told you God's message or if it was the other apostles who told you—we all tell people the same message, and this is what you believed.

We Will Be Raised From Death

¹²We tell everyone that Christ was raised from death. So why do some of you say that people will not be raised from death? ¹³If no one will ever be raised from death, then Christ has never been raised. ¹⁴And if Christ has never been raised, then the message we tell is worth nothing. And your faith is worth nothing. ¹⁵And we will also be guilty of lying about God, because we have told people about him, saying that he raised Christ from death. And if no one is raised from death, then God never raised Christ from death. ¹⁶If those who have died are not raised, then Christ has not been raised either. ¹⁷And if Christ has not been raised from death, then your faith is for nothing; you are still guilty of your sins. ¹⁸And those in Christ who have already died are lost. ¹⁹If our hope in Christ is only for this life here on earth, then people should feel more sorry for us than for anyone else.

²⁰But Christ really has been raised from death—the first one of all those who will be raised. ²¹Death comes to people because of what one man did. But now there is resurrection* from death because of another man. ²²I mean that in Adam all of us die. And in the same way, in Christ all of us will be made alive again. ²³But everyone will be raised to life in the right order. Christ was first to be raised. Then, when Christ comes again, those who belong to him will be raised to life. ²⁴Then the end will come. Christ will destroy all rulers, authorities, and powers. Then he will give the kingdom to God the Father.

²⁵Christ must rule until God puts all enemies under his control.*ᵃ ²⁶The last enemy to be destroyed will be death. ²⁷As the Scriptures* say, "God put everything under his control."ᵇ When it says that "everything" is put under him, it is clear that this does not include God himself. God is the one putting everything under Christ's control. ²⁸After everything has been put under Christ, then the Son himself will be put under God. God is the one who put everything under Christ. And Christ will be put under God so that God

will be the complete ruler over everything.

²⁹If no one will ever be raised from death, then what will the people do who are baptized* for those who have died? If the dead are never raised, then why are people baptized for them?

³⁰And what about us? Why do we put ourselves in danger every hour? ³¹I face death every day. That is true, brothers and sisters, just as it is true that I am proud of what you are because of Christ Jesus our Lord. ³²I fought wild animals in Ephesus. If I did that only for human reasons, then I have gained nothing. If we are not raised from death, "Let us eat and drink, because tomorrow we die."ᶜ

³³Don't be fooled: "Bad friends will ruin good habits." ³⁴Come back to your right way of thinking and stop sinning. Some of you don't know God. I say this to shame you.

What Kind of Body Will We Have?

³⁵But someone may ask, "How are the dead raised? What kind of body will they have?" ³⁶These are stupid questions. When you plant something, it must die in the ground before it can live and grow. ³⁷And when you plant something, what you plant does not have the same "body" that it will have later. What you plant is only a seed, maybe wheat or something else. ³⁸But God gives it the body that he has planned for it, and he gives each kind of seed its own body. ³⁹All things made of flesh are not the same: People have one kind of flesh, animals have another, birds have another, and fish have yet another kind. ⁴⁰Also there are heavenly bodies and earthly bodies. But the beauty of the heavenly bodies is one kind, and the beauty of the earthly bodies is another. ⁴¹The sun has one kind of beauty, the moon has another kind, and the stars have another. And each star is different in its beauty.

⁴²It will be the same when those who have died are raised to life. The body that is "planted" in the grave will ruin and decay, but it will be raised to a life that cannot be destroyed. ⁴³When the body is "planted," it is without honor. But when it is raised, it will be great and glorious. When the body is "planted," it is weak. But when it is raised, it will be full of power. ⁴⁴The body that is "planted" is a physical body. When it is raised, it will be a spiritual body.

There is a physical body. So there is also a spiritual body. ⁴⁵As the Scriptures* say, "The first man, Adam, became a living person.ᵈ"ᵉ But the last Adamᶠ is a life-giving spirit. ⁴⁶The spiritual man did not come first. It was the physical man that came first; then came the spiritual. ⁴⁷The first man came from the dust

---

ᵃ15:25 control Literally, "feet."
ᵇ15:27 Quote from Ps. 8:6.
ᶜ15:32 Quote from Isa. 22:13; 56:12.
ᵈ15:45 person Literally, "soul."
ᵉ15:45 Quote from Gen. 2:7.
ᶠ15:45 Adam The name Adam means "man." Here, "the last Adam" refers to Christ, the "man of heaven."

of the earth. The second man came from heaven. [48]All people belong to the earth. They are like that first man of earth. But those who belong to heaven are like that man of heaven. [49]We were made like that man of earth, so we will also be made like that man of heaven.

[50]I tell you this, brothers and sisters: Our bodies of flesh and blood cannot have a part in God's kingdom.* Something that will ruin cannot have a part in something that never ruins. [51]But listen, I tell you this secret: We will not all die, but we will all be changed. [52]It will only take the time of a second. We will be changed as quickly as an eye blinks. This will happen when the last trumpet blows. The trumpet will blow and those who have died will be raised to live forever. And we will all be changed. [53]This body that ruins must clothe itself with something that will never ruin. And this body that dies must clothe itself with something that will never die. [54]So this body that ruins will clothe itself with that which never ruins. And this body that dies will clothe itself with that which never dies. When this happens, the Scriptures will be made true:

"Death is swallowed in victory." *Isaiah 25:8*

[55]"O death, where is your victory?
Where is your power to hurt?" *Hosea 13:14*

[56]Death's power to hurt is sin, and the power of sin is the law. [57]But we thank God who gives us the victory through our Lord Jesus Christ!

[58]So, my dear brothers and sisters, stand strong. Don't let anything change you. Always give yourselves fully to the work of the Lord. You know that your work in the Lord is never wasted.

The Collection for Believers in Judea

16 [1]Now, about the collection of money for God's people: Do the same as I told the Galatian churches* to do. [2]On the first day of every week, each of you should take some of your money and put it in a special place. Save up as much as you can from what you are blessed with. Then you will not have to gather it all after I come. [3]When I arrive, I will send some men to take your gift to Jerusalem. These will be the ones you all agree should go. I will send them with letters of introduction. [4]If it seems good for me to go too, we can all travel together.

Paul's Plans

[5]I plan to go through Macedonia,* so I will come to you after that. [6]Maybe I will stay with you for a time. I might even stay all winter. Then you can help me on my trip, wherever I go. [7]I don't want to come see you now, because I would have to leave to go to other places. I hope to stay a longer time with you, if the Lord allows it. [8]But I will stay in Ephesus until Pentecost.* [9]I will stay here, because a good opportunity for a great and growing work has been given to me now. And there are many people working against it.

[10]Timothy might come to you. Try to make him feel comfortable with you. He is working for the Lord the same as I am. [11]So none of you should refuse to accept Timothy. Help him continue on his trip in peace so that he can come back to me. I am expecting him to come back with the other brothers.

[12]Now about our brother Apollos: I strongly encouraged him to visit you with the other brothers. He prefers not to come now, but he will come when he has the opportunity.

Paul Ends His Letter

[13]Be careful. Hold firmly to your faith. Have courage and be strong. [14]Do everything in love.

[15]You know that Stephanas and his family were the first believers in Achaia.* They have given themselves to the service of God's people. I ask you, brothers and sisters, [16]to follow the leading of people like these and others who work hard and serve together with them.

[17]I am happy that Stephanas, Fortunatus, and Achaicus have come. You are not here, but they have filled your place. [18]They have been a great encouragement to me and to you as well. You should recognize the value of such people.

[19]The churches* in Asia* send you their greetings. Aquila and Priscilla greet you in the Lord. Also the church that meets in their house sends greetings. [20]All the brothers and sisters send their greetings. Give each other the special greeting of God's people.[a]

[21]Here's my greeting in my own handwriting—PAUL.

[22]If anyone does not love the Lord, let that person be separated from God—lost forever!

Come, O Lord![b]

[23]The grace* of the Lord Jesus be with you.

[24]My love be with all of you in Christ Jesus.

---

[a]**16:20** *the special greeting of God's people* Literally, "a holy kiss."

[b]**16:22** *Come, O Lord* This is a translation of the Aramaic "*marana tha.*"

2 Corinthians

1 ¹Greetings from Paul, an apostle* of Christ Jesus. I am an apostle because that is what God wanted. Greetings also from Timothy our brother in Christ.

To God's church* in Corinth and to all of God's holy people* throughout Achaia.*

²Grace* and peace to you from God our Father and the Lord Jesus Christ.

Paul Gives Thanks to God

³Praise be to the God and Father of our Lord Jesus Christ. He is the Father who is full of mercy, the God of all comfort. ⁴He comforts us every time we have trouble so that when others have trouble, we can comfort them with the same comfort God gives us. ⁵We share in the many sufferings of Christ. In the same way, much comfort comes to us through Christ. ⁶If we have troubles, it is for your comfort and salvation. If we are comforted, it is so that we can comfort you. And this helps you patiently accept the same sufferings we have. ⁷Our hope for you is strong. We know that you share in our sufferings. So we know that you also share in our comfort.

⁸Brothers and sisters, we want you to know about the trouble we suffered in Asia.* We had great burdens there, which were greater than our own strength. We even gave up hope for life. ⁹In fact, it seems like God has been telling us we are going to die. But this is so that we will not trust in ourselves but in God, who raises people from death. ¹⁰He saved us from these great dangers of death, and he will continue to save us. We feel sure he will always save us. ¹¹And you can help us with your prayers. Then many people will give thanks for us—that God blessed us because of their many prayers.

The Change in Paul's Plans

¹²This is what we are proud of, and I can say with a clear conscience that it is true: In everything we have done in the world, we have done it with an honest and pure heart from God. And this is even truer in what we have done with you. We did this by God's grace,* not by the kind of wisdom the world has. ¹³We write to you only what you can read and understand. And I hope you will fully understand, ¹⁴just as you already understand many things about us. I hope you will understand that you can be proud of us, just as we will be proud of you on the day when

our Lord Jesus Christ comes again.

¹⁵I was very sure of all this. That is why I made plans to visit you first. Then you could be blessed twice. ¹⁶I planned to visit you on my way to Macedonia* and again on my way back. I wanted to get help from you for my trip to Judea. ¹⁷Do you think that I made these plans without really thinking? Or maybe you think I make plans as the world does, saying yes and no at the same time.

¹⁸But if you can believe God, then you can believe that what we tell you is never both yes and no. ¹⁹The Son of God, Jesus Christ, the one that Silas, Timothy, and I told you about was not yes and no. In Christ it has always been yes. ²⁰The yes to all of God's promises is in Christ. And that is why we say "Amen*" through Christ to the glory* of God. ²¹And God is the one who makes you and us strong in Christ. God is also the one who chose us for his work.ᵃ ²²He put his mark on us to show that we are his. Yes, he put his Spirit* in our hearts as the first payment that guarantees all that he will give us.

²³I tell you this, and I ask God to be my witness that this is true: The reason I did not come back to Corinth was that I did not want to punish or hurt you. ²⁴I don't mean that we are trying to control your faith. You are strong in faith. But we are workers with you for your own happiness.

2 ¹So I decided that my next visit to you would not be another visit to make you sad. ²If I make you sad, then who will make me happy? Only you can make me happy—you, the ones I made sad. ³I wrote you a letter so that when I came to you I would not be made sad by those who should make me happy. I felt sure that all of you would share my joy. ⁴When I wrote to you before, I was very troubled and my heart was full of sadness. I wrote with many tears. I did not write to make you sad, but to let you know how much I love you.

Forgive the Person Who Did Wrong

⁵Someone in your group has caused sadness—not to me, but to all of you. I mean he has caused sadness to all in some way. (I don't want to make it sound worse than it really

ᵃ**1:21 chose us for his work** Literally, "anointed us." In Greek this word is related to the title "Christ," which means "anointed one." See "anoint" and "Christ" in the Word List.

is.) 6The punishment that most of your group gave him is enough for him. 7But now you should forgive him and encourage him. This will keep him from having too much sadness and giving up completely. 8So I beg you to show him that you love him. 9This is why I wrote to you. I wanted to test you and see if you obey in everything. 10If you forgive someone, then I also forgive them. And what I have forgiven—if I had anything to forgive—I forgave it for you, and Christ was with me. 11I did this so that Satan* would not win anything from us. We know very well what his plans are.

Paul Leaves Troas to Find Titus

12I went to Troas to tell people the Good News* of Christ. The Lord gave me a good opportunity there. 13But I had no peace because I did not find my brother Titus. So I said goodbye and went to Macedonia.*

Victory Through Christ

14But thanks be to God, who always leads us in victory through Christ. God uses us to spread his knowledge everywhere like a sweet-smelling perfume. 15Our offering to God is to be the perfume of Christ that goes out to those who are being saved and to those who are being lost. 16To those who are being lost, this perfume smells like death, and it brings them death. But to those who are being saved, it has the sweet smell of life, and it brings them life. So who is good enough to do this work? 17Certainly not those who are out there selling God's message* for a profit! But we don't do that. With Christ's help we speak God's truth honestly, knowing that we must answer to him.

Servants of God's New Agreement

3 1Why are we beginning again to tell you all these good things about ourselves? Do we need letters of introduction to you or from you, like some other people? 2No, you yourselves are our letter, written on our hearts. It is known and read by all people. 3You show that you are a letter from Christ that he sent through us. This letter is not written with ink but with the Spirit* of the living God. It is not written on stone*a* tablets but on human hearts.

4We can say this, because through Christ we feel sure before God. 5I don't mean that we are able to do anything good ourselves. It is God who makes us able to do all that we do. 6He made us able to be servants of a new agreement* from himself to his people. It is not an agreement of written laws, but it is of the Spirit. The written law brings death, but the Spirit gives life.

An Agreement With Greater Glory

7The old agreement*b* that brought death, written with words on stone, came with God's glory.* In fact, the face of Moses* was so bright with glory (a glory that was ending) that the people of Israel* could not continue looking at his face. 8So surely the new agreement that comes from the life-giving Spirit* has even more glory. 9This is what I mean: That old agreement judged people guilty of sin, but it had glory. So surely the new agreement that makes people right with God has much greater glory. 10That old agreement had glory. But it really loses its glory when it is compared to the much greater glory of the new agreement. 11If the agreement that was brought to an end came with glory, then the agreement that never ends has much greater glory.

12We are so sure of this hope that we can speak very openly. 13We are not like Moses, who put a covering over his face. He covered his face so that the people of Israel would not see it. The glory was disappearing, and Moses did not want them to see it end. 14But their minds were closed. And even today, when those people read the writings of the old agreement,*c* that same covering hides the meaning. That covering has not been removed for them. It is taken away only through Christ. 15Yes, even today, when they read the Law of Moses, there is a covering over their minds. 16But when someone changes and follows the Lord, that covering is taken away. 17The Lord is the Spirit, and where the Spirit of the Lord is, there is freedom. 18And our faces are not covered. We all show the Lord's glory, and we are being changed to be like him. This change in us brings more and more glory, which comes from the Lord, who is the Spirit.

Spiritual Treasure in Clay Jars

4 1God, with his mercy, gave us this work to do, so we don't give up. 2But we have turned away from secret and shameful ways. We don't use trickery, and we don't change the teaching of God. We teach the truth plainly. This is how we show people who we are. And this is how they can know in their hearts what kind of people we are before God. 3The Good News* that we tell people may be hidden, but it is hidden only to those who are lost. 4The ruler*d* of this world* has blinded the minds of those who don't believe. They cannot see the light of the Good News—the message about the divine greatness* of Christ. Christ is the one who is exactly like God. 5We don't tell people about ourselves. But we tell people that Jesus Christ is Lord, and we tell

*b***3:7 agreement** In verses 7–11 literally, "service" or "ministry."
*c***3:14 old agreement** See "agreement" in the Word List. Here, "old agreement" is used to mean the Law of Moses on which that agreement was based.
*d***4:4 The ruler** Literally, "The god."

*a***3:3 stone** Meaning the law that God gave to Moses, which was written on stone tablets. Also in verse 7. See Ex. 24:12; 25:16.

them that we are your servants for Jesus. [6]God once said, "Let light shine out of the darkness!"[a] And this is the same God who made his light shine in our hearts to let us know that his own divine greatness is seen in the face of Christ.

[7]We have this treasure from God, but we are only like clay jars that hold the treasure. This is to show that the amazing power we have is from God, not from us. [8]We have troubles all around us, but we are not defeated. We often don't know what to do, but we don't give up. [9]We are persecuted,* but God does not leave us. We are hurt sometimes, but we are not destroyed. [10]So we constantly experience the death of Jesus in our own bodies, but this is so that the life of Jesus can also be seen in our bodies. [11]We are alive, but for Jesus we are always in danger of death, so that the life of Jesus can be seen in our bodies that die. [12]So death is working in us, but the result is that life is working in you.

[13]The Scriptures* say, "I believed, so I spoke."[b] Our faith is like that too. We believe, and so we speak. [14]God raised the Lord Jesus from death, and we know that he will also raise us with Jesus. God will bring us together with you, and we will stand before him. [15]All these things are for you. And so the grace* of God is being given to more and more people. This will bring more and more thanks to God for his glory.*

Living by Faith

[16]That is why we never give up. Our physical body is becoming older and weaker, but our spirit inside us is made new every day. [17]We have small troubles for a while now, but these troubles are helping us gain an eternal glory.* That eternal glory is much greater than our troubles. [18]So we think about what we cannot see, not what we see. What we see lasts only a short time, and what we cannot see will last forever.

5 [1]We know that our body—the tent we live in here on earth—will be destroyed. But when that happens, God will have a home for us to live in. It will not be the kind of home people build here. It will be a home in heaven that will continue forever. [2]But now we are tired of this body. We want God to give us our heavenly home. [3]It will clothe us and we will not be naked. [4]While we live in this tent, we have burdens and so we complain. I don't mean that we want to remove this tent, but we want to be clothed with our heavenly home. Then this body that dies will be covered with life. [5]This is what God himself made us for. And he has given us the Spirit* as the first payment to guarantee the life to come.

[6]So we always have confidence. We know that while we live in this body, we are away from the Lord. [7]We live by what we believe will happen, not by what we can see. [8]So I say that we have confidence. And we really want to be away from this body and be at home with the Lord. [9]Our only goal is to always please the Lord, whether we are living here in this body or there with him. [10]We must all stand before Christ to be judged. Everyone will get what they should. They will be paid for whatever they did—good or bad—when they lived in this earthly body.

Helping People Become God's Friends

[11]We know what it means to fear the Lord, so we try to help people accept the truth. God knows what we really are, and I hope that in your hearts you know us too. [12]We are not trying to prove ourselves to you again. But we are telling you about ourselves. We are giving you reasons to be proud of us. Then you will have an answer for those who are proud about what can be seen. They don't care about what is in a person's heart. [13]If we are crazy, it is for God. If we have our right mind, it is for you. [14]The love of Christ controls us, because we know that one person died for everyone. So all have died. [15]He died for all so that those who live would not continue to live for themselves. He died for them and was raised from death so that they would live for him.

[16]From this time on we don't think of anyone as the world thinks of people. It is true that in the past we thought of Christ as the world thinks. But we don't think that way now. [17]When anyone is in Christ, it is a whole new world.[c] The old things are gone; suddenly, everything is new! [18]All this is from God. Through Christ, God made peace between himself and us. And God gave us the work of bringing people into peace with him. [19]I mean that God was in Christ, making peace between the world and himself. In Christ, God did not hold people guilty for their sins. And he gave us this message of peace to tell people. [20]So we have been sent to speak for Christ. It is like God is calling to people through us. We speak for Christ when we beg you to be at peace with God. [21]Christ had no sin, but God made him become sin[d] so that in Christ we could be right with God.

6 [1]We are workers together with God. So we beg you: Don't let the grace* that you received from God be for nothing. [2]God says,

"I heard you at the right time,
    and I gave you help on the day of
        salvation."   *Isaiah 49:8*

I tell you that the "right time" is now. The "day of salvation" is now.

---

[a]**4:6 Let ... darkness** See Gen. 1:3
[b]**4:13** Quote from Ps. 116:10.
[c]**5:17 When anyone ... world** Or "Anyone who is in Christ is a new creation."
[d]**5:21 sin** Or "an offering for sin."

³We don't want people to find anything wrong with our work. So we do nothing that will be a problem to others. ⁴But in every way we show that we are servants of God. We never give up, even though we face troubles, difficulties, and problems of every kind. ⁵We are beaten and thrown into prison. People get upset at us and fight against us. We work hard, and sometimes we get no sleep or food. ⁶We show that we are God's servants by our pure lives, by our understanding, by our patience, and by our kindness. We show it by the Holy Spirit,* by genuine love, ⁷by speaking the truth, and by depending on God's power. This right way of living has prepared us to defend ourselves against every kind of attack.

⁸Some people honor us, but others shame us. Some people say good things about us, but others say bad things. Some people say we are liars, but we speak the truth. ⁹To some people we are not known, but we are well known. We seem to be dying, but look! We continue to live. We are punished, but we are not killed. ¹⁰We have much sadness, but we are always rejoicing. We are poor, but we are making many people rich in faith. We have nothing, but really we have everything.

¹¹We have spoken freely to you people in Corinth. We have opened our hearts to you. ¹²Our feelings of love for you have not stopped. It is you who have stopped your feelings of love for us. ¹³I speak to you as if you were my children. Do the same as we have done—open your hearts also.

We Are God's Temple

¹⁴You are not the same as those who don't believe. So don't join yourselves to them. Good and evil don't belong together. Light and darkness cannot share the same room. ¹⁵How can there be any unity between Christ and the devil*ᵃ*? What does a believer have in common with an unbeliever? ¹⁶God's temple*ᵇ* cannot have anything to do with idols,* and we are the temple of the living God. As God said,

"I will live with them and walk with them;
I will be their God, and they will be my
    people."   *Leviticus 26:11–12*

¹⁷"So come away from those people
    and separate yourselves from them, says
    the Lord.
Don't touch anything that is not clean,
    and I will accept you."   *Isaiah 52:11*

---

*ᵃ***6:15 the devil** Literally, "beliar," one form of the Hebrew word "belial," which means "worthlessness" and was used to refer to the devil or the enemy of Christ.
*ᵇ***6:16 God's temple** God's house—the place where God's people worship him. Here, it means that believers are the spiritual temple where God lives.

¹⁸"I will be your father,
    and you will be my sons and daughters,
    says the Lord All-Powerful."
                            2 Samuel 7:8, 14

7 ¹Dear friends, we have these promises from God. So we should make ourselves pure—free from anything that makes our body or our soul unclean. Our respect for God should make us try to be completely holy* in the way we live.

Paul's Joy

²Open your hearts to us. We have not done wrong to anyone or caused harm to anyone. And we have not cheated anyone. ³I do not say this to blame you. I told you before that we love you so much we would live or die with you. ⁴I feel that I can tell you anything. I am very proud of you. Even with all the troubles we have had, I am greatly encouraged and feel very happy.

⁵When we came into Macedonia,* we had no rest. We found trouble all around us. We had fighting on the outside and fear on the inside. ⁶But God encourages those who are troubled, and he certainly encouraged us by bringing Titus to us. ⁷It was so good to see him, but we were encouraged even more to hear about the encouragement you gave him. He told us that you really want to see me and that you are very sorry for what you did. And he told us how ready and willing you are to help me. When I heard this, I was so much happier.

⁸Even if the letter I wrote you made you sad, I am not sorry I wrote it. I know that letter made you sad, and I was sorry for that. But it made you sad only for a short time. ⁹Now I am happy, not because you were made sad, but because your sorrow made you decide to change. That is what God wanted, so you were not hurt by us in any way. ¹⁰The kind of sorrow God wants makes people decide to change their lives. This leads them to salvation, and we cannot be sorry for that. But the kind of sorrow the world has will bring death. ¹¹You had the kind of sorrow God wanted you to have. Now see what that sorrow has brought you: It has made you very serious. It made you want to prove that you were not wrong. It made you angry and afraid. It made you want to see me. It made you care. It made you want the right thing to be done. You proved that you were not guilty in any part of that problem. ¹²The main reason I wrote that letter was not because of the one who did the wrong or the one who was hurt. I wrote so that you would realize, before God, how very much you care for us. ¹³And that is what was so encouraging to us.

We were greatly encouraged, but we were especially pleased to see how happy Titus was. You all made him feel so much better. ¹⁴I had bragged about you to Titus, and you didn't embarrass me. We have always told you the truth, and now what we told Titus about you has been shown to be true. [15]And his love for you is stronger when he remembers that you were all ready to obey. You welcomed him with respect and fear. [16]I am so happy that I can trust you fully.

Help for God's People in Judea

8 [1]And now, brothers and sisters, we want you to know about the grace* that God gave the churches* in Macedonia.* [2]Those believers have been tested by great troubles, and they are very poor. But they gave much because of their great joy. [3]I can tell you that they gave as much as they were able and even more than they could afford. No one told them to do this. It was their idea. [4]But they asked us again and again—they begged us to let them share in this service for God's people. [5]And they gave in a way that we did not expect: They gave themselves to the Lord and to us before they gave their money. This is what God wants.

[6]So we asked Titus to help you finish this special work of giving. He is the one who started this work. [7]You are rich in everything—in faith, in speaking ability, in knowledge, in the willingness to help, and in the love you learned from us. And so we want you to also be rich in this work of giving.

[8]I am not ordering you to give, but I want to see how real your love is by comparing you with others who have been so ready and willing to help. [9]You know the grace of our Lord Jesus Christ. You know that he gave up his heavenly riches for you. He gave up everything so that you could be richly blessed.

[10]This is what I think you should do: Last year you were the first to want to give, and you were the first who gave. [11]So now finish the work you started. Then your "doing" will be equal to your "wanting to do." Give from what you have. [12]If you want to give, your gift will be accepted. Your gift will be judged by what you have, not by what you don't have. [13]We don't want you to have troubles while others are comforted. We want everything to be equal. [14]At this time you have plenty and can provide what they need. Then later, when they have plenty, they can provide what you need. Then everyone will have an equal share. [15]As the Scriptures* say,

"Those who gathered much did not have
          too much,
     and those who gathered little did not have
          too little."   *Exodus 16:18*

Titus and His Companions

[16]I thank God because he gave Titus the same love for you that I have. [17]Titus agreed to do what we asked. In fact, he himself wanted very much to come see you. [18]We are sending with Titus the brother who is praised by all the churches.* He is praised because of his service to the Good News.* [19]Also, he was chosen by the churches to go with us when we carry this gift. We are doing this service to bring honor*a* to the Lord and to show that we really want to help.

[20]We are being careful so that no one will criticize us about the way we are caring for this large gift. [21]We are trying to do what is right. We want to do what the Lord accepts as right and also what people think is right. [22]Also, we are sending with them our brother who is always ready to help. He has proved this to us in many ways. And he wants to help even more now because he has much faith in you. [23]Now about Titus—he is my partner. He is working together with me to help you. And about the other brothers—they are sent from the churches, and they bring honor to Christ. [24]So show these men that you really have love. Show them why we are proud of you. Then all the churches can see it.

Your Giving Is a Blessing

9 [1]I really don't need to write to you about this help for God's people. [2]I know that you want to help. I have been bragging about you to the people in Macedonia.* I told them that you people in Achaia* have been ready to give since last year. And your desire to give has made most of the people here ready to give also. [3]But I am sending the brothers to you. I don't want our bragging about you in this to be for nothing. I want you to be ready just as I said you would be. [4]If any of those from Macedonia come with me, and they find that you are not ready, we will be ashamed. We will be ashamed that we were so sure of you. And you will be ashamed too! [5]So I thought that I should ask these brothers to come there before we do. They will help in getting together the generous gift you promised. Then it will be ready when we come, and it will be seen as a blessing you are giving, not as something you were forced to do.

[6]Remember this: The one who plants few seeds will have a small harvest. But the one who plants a lot will have a big harvest. [7]Each one of you should give what you have decided in your heart to give. You should not give if it makes you unhappy or if you feel forced to give. God loves those who are happy to give. [8]And God can give you more blessings than you need, and you will always have plenty of everything. You will have enough to give to every good work. [9]As the Scriptures* say,

"He gives generously to the poor;
     his goodness will continue forever."
                              Psalm 112:9

a8:19 honor Or "glory." See "glory" in the Word List.

¹⁰God is the one who gives seed to those who plant, and he gives bread for food. And God will give you spiritual seed and make that seed grow. He will produce a great harvest from your goodness. ¹¹God will make you rich in every way so that you can always give freely. And your giving through us will make people give thanks to God.

¹²The service you are offering helps God's people with their needs, but that is not all it does. It is also bringing more and more thanks to God. ¹³This service is a proof of your faith, and people will praise God because of it. They will praise him because you are following the message* about Christ—the message you say you believe. They will praise God because you freely share with them and with all people. ¹⁴And when they pray, they will wish they could be with you. They will feel this way because of the great grace* that God gave you. ¹⁵Thanks be to God for his gift that is too wonderful to describe.

Paul Defends His Ministry

10 ¹I, Paul, am begging you with the gentleness and the kindness of Christ. Some say that I am bold when I am writing you from a distance, but not when I am there with you. ²They think our motives for what we do are like those of the world. I plan to be very bold against those people when I come. I hope I will not need to use that same boldness with you. ³We live in this world, but we don't fight our battles in the same way the world does. ⁴The weapons we use are not human ones. Our weapons have power from God and can destroy the enemy's strong places. We destroy people's arguments, ⁵and we tear down every proud idea that raises itself against the knowledge of God. We also capture every thought and make it give up and obey Christ. ⁶We are ready to punish anyone there who does not obey, but first we want you to be fully obedient.

⁷You must look at the facts before you. If you feel sure you belong to Christ, you must remember that we belong to Christ the same as you do. ⁸It may seem as though we boast too much about the authority the Lord gave us. But he gave us this authority to strengthen you, not to hurt you. So I will not be ashamed of whatever boasting we do. ⁹I don't want you to think that I am trying to scare you with my letters. ¹⁰Some people say, "Paul's letters are powerful and sound important, but when he is with us, he is weak and the worst speaker you have ever heard." ¹¹Those people should know this: When we are there with you, we will show the same power that we show now in our letters.

¹²We don't dare put ourselves in the same class with those who think they are so important. We don't compare ourselves to them. They use themselves to measure themselves, and they judge themselves by what they themselves are. This shows that they know nothing.

¹³But we will not boast about anything outside the work that was given us to do. We will limit our boasting to the work God gave us, but this work includes our work with you. ¹⁴We would be boasting too much only if we had not already come to you. But we have come to you with the Good News* of Christ. ¹⁵We limit our boasting to the work that is ours. We don't boast about the work other people have done. We hope that your faith will continue to grow. We hope that you will help our work to grow much larger. ¹⁶We want to tell the Good News in the areas beyond your city. We don't want to boast about work that has already been done in someone else's area. ¹⁷"Whoever boasts should boast only about the Lord."ᵃ ¹⁸What people say about themselves means nothing. What counts is whether or not the Lord says they have done well.

Paul and the False Apostles

11 ¹I wish you would be patient with me even when I am a little foolish. But you are already patient with me. ²I am jealous for you with a jealousy that comes from God. I promised to give you to Christ. He must be your only husband. I want to give you to Christ to be his pure bride.ᵇ ³But I am afraid that your minds will be led away from your true and pure following of Christ. This could happen just as Eve was tricked by that snake with his clever lies. ⁴You seem to be quite patient with anyone who comes to you and tells you about a Jesus that is different from the Jesus we told you about. You seem very willing to accept a spirit or a message that is different from the Spirit* and message* that you received from us.

⁵I don't think that those "super apostles*" are any better than I am. ⁶It is true that I am not a trained speaker, but I do have knowledge. We have shown this to you clearly in every way.

⁷I did the work of telling God's Good News* to you without pay. I humbled myself to make you important. Do you think that was wrong? ⁸I accepted pay from other churches.* I took their money so that I could serve you. ⁹If I needed something when I was with you, I did not trouble any of you. The brothers who came from Macedonia* gave me all that I needed. I did not allow myself to be a burden to you in any way. And I will never be a burden to you. ¹⁰No one there in Achaia* will stop me from boasting about that. I say this with the truth of Christ in me. ¹¹And why do I not burden you? Do you think it is because I don't love you? God knows that I love you.

ᵃ**10:17** Quote from Jer. 9:24.
ᵇ**11:2 bride** Literally, "virgin."

12And I will continue doing what I am doing now, because I want to stop those people from having a reason to boast. They would like to say that the work they boast about is the same as ours. 13They are false apostles, lying workers. They only pretend to be apostles of Christ. 14That does not surprise us, because even Satan* changes himself to look like an angel of light.*a* 15So it does not surprise us if Satan's servants make themselves look like servants who work for what is right. But in the end those people will get the punishment they deserve.

Paul Tells About His Sufferings

16I tell you again: No one should think that I am a fool. But if you think I am a fool, then accept me as you would accept a fool. Then I can boast a little too. 17But I am not talking the way the Lord would talk. I am boasting like a fool. 18Others are boasting about their lives in the world. So I will boast too. 19You are wise, so you will gladly be patient with fools! 20I say this because you are even patient with someone who forces you to do things and uses you. You are patient with those who trick you, or think they are better than you, or hit you in the face! 21I am ashamed to say it, but we were too "weak" to do such things to you.

But if anyone dares to boast, I will too. (I am talking like a fool.) 22Are those people Hebrews? So am I. Are they Israelites*b*? So am I. Are they from Abraham's* family? So am I. 23Are they serving Christ? I am serving him more. (I am crazy to talk like this.) I have worked much harder than they have. I have been in prison more often. I have been hurt more in beatings. I have been near death many times.

24Five times the Jews have given me their punishment of 39 lashes with a whip. 25Three different times I was beaten with rods. One time I was almost killed with rocks. Three times I was in ships that were wrecked, and one of those times I spent the night and the next day in the sea. 26In my constant traveling I have been in danger from rivers, from thieves, from my own people, and from people who are not Jews. I have been in danger in cities, in places where no one lives, and on the sea. And I have been in danger from people who pretend to be believers* but are not.

27I have done hard and tiring work, and many times I did not sleep. I have been hungry and thirsty. Many times I have been without food. I have been cold and without clothes. 28And there are many other problems. One of these is the care I have for all the churches.* I worry about them every day. 29I feel weak every time another person is

weak. I feel deeply upset every time another person is led into sin.

30If I must boast, I will boast about the things that show I am weak. 31God knows that I am not lying. He is the God and Father of the Lord Jesus, and he is to be praised forever. 32When I was in Damascus, the governor under King Aretas wanted to arrest me, so he put guards around the city. 33But some friends put me in a basket. Then they put the basket through a hole in the wall and lowered me down. So I escaped from the governor.

A Special Blessing in Paul's Life

12 1There is more that I have to say about myself. It won't help, but I will talk now about visions* and revelations from the Lord. 2I know a man*c* in Christ who was taken up to the third heaven. This happened 14 years ago. I don't know if the man was in his body or out of his body, but God knows. 3–4And I know that this man was taken up to paradise.* I don't know if he was in his body or away from his body, but he heard things that he is not able to explain. He heard things that no one is allowed to tell. 5I will boast about a man like that, but I will not boast about myself. I will boast only about my weaknesses.

6But if I wanted to say more about myself, I would not be a fool, because I would be telling the truth. But I won't say any more, because I don't want people to think more of me than what they see me do or hear me say.

7But I must not be too proud of the wonderful things that were shown to me. So a painful problem*d* was given to me—an angel from Satan,* sent to make me suffer, so that I would not think that I am better than anyone else. 8I begged the Lord three times to take this problem away from me. 9But the Lord said, "My grace* is all you need. Only when you are weak can everything be done completely by my power." So I will gladly boast about my weaknesses. Then Christ's power can stay in me. 10Yes, I am glad to have weaknesses if they are for Christ. I am glad to be insulted and have hard times. I am glad when I am persecuted* and have problems, because it is when I am weak that I am really strong.

Paul's Love for the Believers in Corinth

11I have been talking like a fool, but you made me do it. You people are the ones who should say good things about me. I am worth nothing, but those "super apostles*" are not worth any more than I am! 12When I was with you, I patiently did the things that prove I am an apostle—signs,* wonders,* and miracles.* 13So you received everything that the other churches* have received. Only one thing was

---

*a*11:14 *angel of light* Messenger from God. The devil fools people so that they think he is from God.
*b*11:22 *Hebrews ... Israelites* Other names for the Jewish people.

*c*12:2 *a man* In 12:2–5 Paul is probably talking about himself.
*d*12:7 *painful problem* Literally, "thorn in the flesh."

different: I was not a burden to you. Forgive me for this!

¹⁴I am now ready to visit you for the third time, and I will not be a burden to you. I don't want any of the things you own. I only want you. Children should not have to save things to give to their parents. Parents should save to give to their children. ¹⁵So I am happy to give everything I have for you. I will even give myself for you. If I love you more, will you love me less?

¹⁶It is clear that I was not a burden to you, but you think that I was tricky and used lies to catch you. ¹⁷Did I cheat you by using any of the men I sent to you? You know I didn't. ¹⁸I asked Titus to go to you, and I sent our brother with him. Titus did not cheat you, did he? No, you know that his actions and his attitude were the same as ours.

¹⁹Do you think that we have been defending ourselves to you all this time? No, we say these things in Christ and before God. You are our dear friends, and everything we do is to make you stronger. ²⁰I do this because I am afraid that when I come, you will not be what I want you to be. And I am afraid that I will not be what you want me to be. I am afraid that I will find arguing, jealousy, anger, selfish fighting, evil talk, gossip, pride, and confusion there. ²¹I am afraid that when I come to you again, my God will make me humble before you. I may have to cry over the loss of some who sinned before. Many of them have still not changed their hearts to be sorry for their evil lives, their sexual sins, and the shameful things they have done.

Final Warnings and Greetings

13 ¹This will be my third time to visit you. And remember, "For every complaint there must be two or three people to say that they know it is true."ᵃ ²When I was with you the second time, I gave a warning to those who had sinned. I am not there now, but I am giving another warning to them and to

ᵃ**13:1** Quote from Deut. 19:15.

anyone else who has sinned: When I come to you again, I will punish you. ³You want proof that Christ is speaking through me. My proof is that he is not weak in dealing with you but is showing his power among you. ⁴It is true that Christ was weak when he was killed on the cross, but he lives now by God's power. It is also true that we share his weakness, but in dealing with you we will be alive in him by God's power.

⁵Look closely at yourselves. Test yourselves to see if you are living in the faith. Don't you realize that Christ Jesus is in you? Of course, if you fail the test, he is not in you. ⁶But I hope you will see that we have not failed the test. ⁷We pray to God that you will not do anything wrong. Our concern here is not for people to see that we have passed the test in our work with you. Our main concern is that you do what is right, even if it looks as if we have failed the test. ⁸We cannot do anything that is against the truth but only what promotes the truth. ⁹We are happy to be weak if you are strong. And this is what we pray—that your lives will be made completely right again. ¹⁰I'm writing this before I come so that when I am there I will not have to use my authority to punish you. The Lord gave me that authority to make you stronger, not to destroy you.

¹¹Now, brothers and sisters, be filled with joy. Try to make everything right, and do what I have asked you to do. Agree with each other, and live in peace. Then the God of love and peace will be with you.

¹²Give each other the special greeting of God's people.ᵇ All of God's holy people* here send you their greetings.

¹³I pray that you will enjoy the grace* of the Lord Jesus Christ, the love of God, and the fellowshipᶜ of the Holy Spirit.*

ᵇ**13:12** *the special greeting of God's people* Literally, "a holy kiss."
ᶜ**13:13** *fellowship* This can mean a sharing or participation in the Holy Spirit or the loving association and unity among believers that is created by the Spirit.

Galatians

1 ¹Greetings from Paul, an apostle.* I was chosen to be an apostle, but not by any group or person here on earth. My authority came from none other than Jesus Christ and God the Father, who raised Jesus from death. ²Greetings also from all those in God's family who are with me.

To the churches* in Galatiaᵈ:

³I pray that God our Father and the Lord Jesus Christ will be good to you and give you

ᵈ**1:2** *Galatia* Probably the area where Paul began churches on his first missionary trip. Read Acts 13 and 14.

peace. ⁴Jesus gave himself for our sins to free us from this evil world we live in. This is what God our Father wanted. ⁵The glory* belongs to God forever and ever. Amen.*

There Is Only One Good News Message

⁶A short time ago God chose you to follow him. He chose you through his grace* that came through Christ. But now I am amazed that you are already turning away and believing something different from the Good News* we told you. ⁷There is no other message that is the Good News, but some people are confusing you. They want to change the Good News about Christ. ⁸We told you the true Good News message. So anyone who tells you a different message should be condemned—even if it's one of us or even an angel from heaven! ⁹I said this before. Now I say it again: You have already accepted the Good News. Anyone who tells you another way to be saved should be condemned!

¹⁰Now do you think I am trying to make people accept me? No, God is the one I am trying to please. Am I trying to please people? If I wanted to please people, I would not be a servant of Jesus Christ.

Paul's Authority Is From God

¹¹Brothers and sisters, I want you to know that the Good News* message I told you was not made up by anyone. ¹²I did not get my message from any other human. The Good News is not something I learned from other people. Jesus Christ himself gave it to me. He showed me the Good News that I should tell people.

¹³You have heard about my past life in the Jewish religion. I persecuted* the church* of God very much. I tried to destroy his people. ¹⁴I was becoming a leader in the Jewish religion. I did better than most other Jews my own age. I tried harder than anyone else to follow the traditions we got from our ancestors.*

¹⁵But God had special plans for me even before I was born. So he chose me through his grace.* He wanted me ¹⁶to tell the Good News about his Son to the non-Jewish people. So God let me see and learn about his Son. When this happened, I did not get advice or help from anyone. ¹⁷I did not go to Jerusalem to see those who were apostles* before I was. But, without waiting, I went away to Arabia. Later, I went back to the city of Damascus.

¹⁸Three years later I went to Jerusalem to meet Peter.* I stayed with him 15 days. ¹⁹I met no other apostles—only James, the brother of the Lord. ²⁰God knows there is nothing untrue in any of this. ²¹Later, I went to the areas of Syria and Cilicia.

²²The groups of believersᵃ in Judea who belong to Christ had never met me before.

ᵃ**1:22 groups of believers** Literally, "churches" or "assemblies." See "church" in the Word List.

²³They had only heard this about me: "This man was persecuting us. But now he is telling people about the same faith that he once tried to destroy." ²⁴These believers praised God because of me.

The Other Apostles Accepted Paul

2 ¹After 14 years I went back to Jerusalem with Barnabas and took Titus with me. ²I went there because God showed me that I should go. I explained to them the message* that I tell the non-Jewish people. I also met alone with those who were considered to be the leaders. I wanted to be sure we were in agreement so that my past work and the work I do now would not be wasted.

³Titus, who was with me, is a Greek.* But these leaders still did not force him to be circumcised.* ⁴We needed to talk about these problems, because some who pretended to be our brothers had come into our group secretly. They came in like spies to find out about the freedom we have in Christ Jesus. They wanted to make us slaves, ⁵but we did not agree with anything those false brothers wanted. We wanted the truth of the Good News* to continue for you.

⁶Those men who were considered to be important did not change the Good News message I tell people. (It doesn't matter to me if they were "important" or not. To God everyone is the same.) ⁷But these leaders saw that God had given me a special work, the same as Peter. God gave Peter the work of telling the Good News to the Jews. But God gave me the work of telling the Good News to the non-Jewish people. ⁸God gave Peter the power to work as an apostle* for the Jewish people. God gave me the power to work as an apostle too, but for those who are not Jews. ⁹James, Peter, and John seemed to be the leaders. And they saw that God had given me this special gift of ministry, so they accepted Barnabas and me. They said to us, "We agree that you should go to those who are not Jews, and we will go to the Jews." ¹⁰They asked us to do only one thing—to remember to help those who are poor. And this was something that I really wanted to do.

Paul Shows That Peter Was Wrong

¹¹When Peter came to Antioch, he did something that was not right. I stood against him, because he was wrong. ¹²This is what happened: When Peter first came to Antioch, he ate and associated with the non-Jewish people. But when some Jewish men came from James, Peter separated himself from the non-Jews. He stopped eating with them, because he was afraid of the Jews who believe that all non-Jewish people must be circumcised.* ¹³So Peter was a hypocrite.* The other Jewish believers joined with him, so they were hypocrites too. Even Barnabas was influenced by what these Jewish believers

did. ¹⁴They were not following the truth of the Good News.* When I saw this, I spoke to Peter in front of everyone. I said, "Peter, you are a Jew, but you don't live like one. You live like someone who is not a Jew. So why are you trying to force those who are not Jewish to live like Jews?"

¹⁵We are Jews by birth. We were not born "sinners," as we call those who are not Jews. ¹⁶But we know that no one is made right with God by following the law.* It is trusting in*a* Jesus Christ that makes a person right with God. So we have put our faith in Christ Jesus, because we wanted to be made right with God. And we are right with him because we trusted in*b* Christ—not because we followed the law. I can say this because no one can be made right with God by following the law.

¹⁷We Jews came to Christ to be made right with God, so it is clear that we were sinners too. Does this mean that Christ makes us sinners? Of course not. ¹⁸But I would be wrong to begin teaching again those things that I gave up. ¹⁹It was the law itself that caused me to end my life under the law. I died to the law so that I could live for God. I have been nailed to the cross with Christ. ²⁰So I am not the one living now—it is Christ living in me. I still live in my body, but I live by faith in*c* the Son of God. He is the one who loved me and gave himself to save me. ²¹I am not the one destroying the meaning of God's grace.* If following the law is how people are made right with God, then Christ did not have to die.

God's Blessing Comes Through Faith

3 ¹You people in Galatia are so foolish! Why do I say this? Because I told you very clearly about the death of Jesus Christ on the cross. But now it seems as though you have let someone use their magical powers to make you forget. ²Tell me this one thing: How did you receive the Spirit*? Did you receive the Spirit by following the law*? No, you received the Spirit because you heard the message about Jesus and believed it. ³You began your life in Christ with the Spirit. Now do you try to complete it by your own power? That is foolish. ⁴You have experienced many things. Were all those experiences wasted? I hope they were not wasted! ⁵Does God give you the Spirit because you follow the law? Does God work miracles* among you because you follow the law? No, God gives you his Spirit and works miracles among you because you heard the message about Jesus and believed it.

⁶The Scriptures* say the same thing about Abraham.* "Abraham believed God, and because of this faith he was accepted as one who is right with God."*d* ⁷So you should know

that the true children of Abraham are those who have faith. ⁸The Scriptures told what would happen in the future. These writings said that God would make the non-Jewish people right through their faith. God told this Good News* to Abraham before it happened. God said to Abraham, "I will use you to bless all the people on earth."*e* ⁹Abraham believed this, and because he believed, he was blessed. All people who believe are blessed the same as Abraham was.

¹⁰But people who depend on following the law to make them right are under a curse. As the Scriptures say, "They must do everything that is written in the law. If they do not always obey, they are under a curse."*f* ¹¹So it is clear that no one can be made right with God by the law. The Scriptures say, "The one who is right with God by faith will live forever."*g*

¹²The law does not depend on faith. No, it says that the only way a person will find life by the law is to obey its commands.*h* ¹³The law says we are under a curse for not always obeying it. But Christ took away that curse. He changed places with us and put himself under that curse. The Scriptures say, "Anyone who is hung on a tree*i* is under a curse."*j* ¹⁴Because of what Jesus Christ did, the blessing God promised to Abraham was given to all people. Christ died so that by believing in him we could have the Spirit that God promised.

The Law and the Promise

¹⁵Brothers and sisters, let me give you an example from everyday life: Think about an agreement that one person makes with another. After that agreement is made official, no one can stop it or add anything to it, and no one can ignore it. ¹⁶God made promises to Abraham* and his Descendant.*k* The Scripture* does not say, "and to your descendants." That would mean many people. But it says, "and to your Descendant." That means only one, and that one is Christ. ¹⁷This is what I mean: The agreement that God gave to Abraham was made official long before the law* came. The law came 430 years later. So the law could not take away the agreement and change God's promise.

¹⁸Can following the law give us the blessing God promised? If we could receive it by following the law, then it would not be God's promise that brings it to us. But God freely

---

*e***3:8** Quote from Gen. 12:3.
*f***3:10** Quote from Deut. 27:26.
*g***3:11** Quote from Hab. 2:4.
*h***3:12** *the only way … commands* See Lev. 18:5.
*i***3:13** *hung on a tree* Deut. 21:22–23 says that when a person was killed for doing wrong, his body was hung on a tree to show shame. Paul means the cross of Jesus was like that.
*j***3:13** Quote from Deut. 21:23.
*k***3:16** *Descendant* Literally, "seed," which could also mean "family." In that case, it would refer to the one family of God in Christ.

---

*a***2:16** *trusting in* Or "the faithfulness of."
*b***2:16** *because we trusted in* Or "through the faithfulness of."
*c***2:20** *faith in* Or "the faithfulness of."
*d***3:6** Quote from Gen. 15:6.

gave his blessings to Abraham through the promise God made.

¹⁹So what was the law for? The law was given to show the wrong things people do. The law would continue until the special Descendant of Abraham came. This is the Descendant mentioned in the promise, which came directly from God. But the law was given through angels, and the angels used Moses as a mediator* to give the law to the people. ²⁰But when God gave the promise, there was no mediator, because a mediator is not needed when there is only one side, and God is one.ᵃ

The Purpose of the Law of Moses

²¹Does this mean that the law* works against God's promises? Of course not. The law was never God's way of giving new life to people. If it were, then we could be made right with God by following the law. ²²But this is not possible. The Scriptures* put the whole world in prison under the control of sin, so that the only way for people to get what God promised would be through faith inᵇ Jesus Christ. It is given to those who believe in him.

²³Before this faith came, the law held us as prisoners. We had no freedom until God showed us the way of faith that was coming. ²⁴I mean the law was the guardian in charge of us until Christ came. After he came, we could be made right with God through faith. ²⁵Now that the way of faith has come, we no longer need the law to be our guardian.

²⁶⁻²⁷You were all baptized* into Christ, and so you were all clothed with Christ. This shows that you are all children of God through faith in Christ Jesus. ²⁸Now, in Christ, it doesn't matter if you are a Jew or a Greek,* a slave or free, male or female. You are all the same in Christ Jesus. ²⁹You belong to Christ, so you are Abraham's* descendants. You get all of God's blessings because of the promise that God made to Abraham.

4 ¹This is what I am saying: When young children inherit all that their father owned, they are still no different from his slaves. It doesn't matter that they own everything. ²While they are children, they must obey those who are chosen to care for them. But when they reach the age the father set, they are free. ³It is the same for us. We were once like children, slaves to the useless rulesᶜ of this world. ⁴But when the right time came, God sent his Son, who was born from a woman and lived under the law. ⁵God did this so that he could buy the freedom of those who were under the law. God's purpose was to make us his children.

⁶Since you are now God's children, he has sent the Spirit of his Son into your hearts. The Spirit* cries out, "Abba,ᵈ Father." ⁷Now you are not slaves like before. You are God's children, and you will receive everything he promised his children.

Paul's Love for the Galatian Believers

⁸In the past you did not know God. You were slaves to gods that were not real. ⁹But now you know the true God. Really, though, it is God who knows you. So why do you turn back to the same kind of weak and useless rules you followed before? Do you want to be slaves to those things again? ¹⁰⁻¹¹It worries me that you follow teachings about special days, months, seasons, and years. I fear that my work for you has been wasted.

¹²Brothers and sisters, I became like you. So please become like me. You were very good to me before. ¹³You know that I came to you the first time because I was sick. That was when I told the Good News* to you. ¹⁴My sickness was a burden to you, but you did not stop showing me respect or make me leave. Instead, you welcomed me as if I were an angel from God. You accepted me as if I were Jesus Christ himself! ¹⁵You were very happy then. Where is that joy now? I can say without a doubt that you would have done anything to help me. If it had been possible, you would have taken out your own eyes and given them to me. ¹⁶Am I now your enemy because I tell you the truth?

¹⁷Those peopleᵉ are working hard to persuade you, but this is not good for you. They want to persuade you to turn against us and work hard for them. ¹⁸It is good for you to work hard, of course, if it is for something good. That's something you should do whether I am there or not. ¹⁹My little children, I am in pain again over you, like a mother giving birth. I will feel this pain until people can look at you and see Christ. ²⁰I wish I could be with you now. Then maybe I could change the way I am talking to you. Now I don't know what to do about you.

The Example of Hagar and Sarah

²¹Some of you people want to be under the law.* Tell me, do you know what the law says? ²²The Scriptures* say that Abraham* had two sons. The mother of one son was a slave woman, and the mother of the other son was a free woman. ²³Abraham's son from the slave woman was born in the normal human way. But the son from the free woman was born because of the promise God made to Abraham.

²⁴This true story makes a picture for us. The two women are like the two agreements

---

ᵃ**3:20** Literally, "But the mediator is not of one, but God is one."
ᵇ**3:22** *faith in* Or "the faithfulness of."
ᶜ**4:3** *rules* Or "powers." Also in verse 9.

ᵈ**4:6** *Abba* An Aramaic word that was used by Jewish children as a name for their fathers.
ᵉ**4:17** *Those people* The false teachers who were bothering the believers in Galatia. See Gal. 1:7.

between God and his people. One agreement is the law that God made on Mount Sinai.* The people who are under this agreement are like slaves. The mother named Hagar is like that agreement. 25So Hagar is like Mount Sinai in Arabia. She is a picture of the earthly Jewish city of Jerusalem. This city is a slave, and all its people are slaves to the law. 26But the heavenly Jerusalem that is above is like the free woman, who is our mother. 27The Scriptures say,

"Be happy, woman—you who cannot have
    children.
Be glad you never gave birth.
Shout and cry with joy!
    You never felt those labor pains.
The woman who is alone*a* will have more
    children
    than the woman who has a husband."

Isaiah 54:1

28My brothers and sisters, you are children who were born because of God's promise, just as Isaac was. 29But the other son of Abraham, who was born in the normal way, caused trouble for the one who was born by the power of the Spirit.* It is the same today. 30But what do the Scriptures say? "Throw out the slave woman and her son! The son of the free woman will receive everything his father has, but the son of the slave woman will receive nothing."*b* 31So, my brothers and sisters, we are not children of the slave woman. We are children of the free woman.

Keep Your Freedom

5 1We have freedom now, because Christ made us free. So stand strong in that freedom. Don't go back into slavery again. 2Listen! I, Paul, tell you that if you start following the law by being circumcised,* then Christ cannot help you. 3Again, I warn everyone: If you allow yourselves to be circumcised, then you must follow the whole law.* 4If you try to be made right with God through the law, your life with Christ is finished—you have left God's grace.* 5I say this because our hope of being right with God comes through faith. And the Spirit* helps us feel sure as we wait for that hope. 6When someone belongs to Christ Jesus, it is not important if they are circumcised or not. The important thing is faith—the kind of faith that works through love.

7You were doing so well. Who caused you to stop following the truth? 8It certainly wasn't the one who chose you. 9Be careful! "Just a little yeast" makes the whole batch of dough rise."*c* 10I trust in the Lord that you will not believe those different ideas. Someone is trying to confuse you. Whoever it is will be punished.

11My brothers and sisters, I don't teach that a man must be circumcised. If I do teach circumcision, then why am I still being persecuted*? If I still taught circumcision, then my message about the cross would not be a problem. 12I wish those people who are bothering you would add castration*d* to their circumcision.

13My brothers and sisters, God chose you to be free. But don't use your freedom as an excuse to do what pleases your sinful selves. Instead, serve each other with love. 14The whole law is made complete in this one command: "Love your neighbor*e* the same as you love yourself."*f* 15If you continue hurting each other and tearing each other apart, be careful, or you will completely destroy each other.

The Spirit and Human Nature

16So I tell you, live the way the Spirit* leads you. Then you will not do the evil things your sinful self wants. 17The sinful self wants what is against the Spirit, and the Spirit wants what is against the sinful self. They are always fighting against each other, so that you don't do what you really want to do. 18But if you let the Spirit lead you, you are not under law.*g*

19The wrong things the sinful self does are clear: committing sexual sin, being morally bad, doing all kinds of shameful things, 20worshiping false gods, taking part in witchcraft,* hating people, causing trouble, being jealous, angry or selfish, causing people to argue and divide into separate groups, 21being filled with envy, getting drunk, having wild parties, and doing other things like this. I warn you now as I warned you before: The people who do these things will not have a part in God's kingdom.* 22But the fruit that the Spirit produces in a person's life is love, joy, peace, patience, kindness, goodness, faithfulness, 23gentleness, and self-control. There is no law against these kinds of things. 24Those who belong to Christ Jesus have crucified their sinful self. They have given up their old selfish feelings and the evil things they wanted to do. 25We get our new life from the Spirit, so we should follow the Spirit. 26We must not feel proud and boast about ourselves. We must not cause trouble for each other or be jealous of each other.

---

*a***4:27 woman ... alone** This means her husband has left her.

*b***4:30** Quote from Gen. 21:10.

*c***5:9 "Just ... rise"** A proverb meaning that a small thing (like a little wrong teaching) can make a big problem or that just one person can have a bad influence on the whole group.

*d***5:12 castration** Paul uses a word that means "to cut off" in place of "circumcision," which means "to cut around," to show how angry he is at the false teachers for forcing non-Jewish men to be circumcised.

*e***5:14 your neighbor** Or "others." Jesus' teaching in Lk. 10:25–37 makes clear that this includes anyone in need.

*f***5:14** Quote from Lev. 19:18.

*g***5:18 law** Here, a law system, like the Law of Moses,

Help Each Other

6 ¹Brothers and sisters, someone in your group might do something wrong. You who are following the Spirit* should go to the one who is sinning. Help make that person right again, and do it in a gentle way. But be careful, because you might be tempted to sin too. ²Help each other with your troubles. When you do this, you are obeying the law of Christ. ³If you think you are too important to do this, you are only fooling yourself. ⁴Don't compare yourself with others. Just look at your own work to see if you have done anything to be proud of. ⁵You must each accept the responsibilities that are yours.

Never Stop Doing Good

⁶Whoever is being taught God's word should share the good things they have with the one who is teaching them.

⁷If you think you can fool God, you are only fooling yourselves. You will harvest what you plant. ⁸If you live to satisfy your sinful self, the harvest you will get from that will be eternal death. But if you live to please the Spirit,* your harvest from the Spirit will be eternal life. ⁹We must not get tired of doing good. We will receive our harvest of eternal life at the right time. We must not give up. ¹⁰When we have the opportunity to do good to anyone, we should do it. But we should give special attention to those who are in the family of believers.

Paul Ends His Letter

¹¹This is my own handwriting. You can see how big the letters are. ¹²Those men who are trying to force you to be circumcised* are only doing it so that their people will accept them. They are afraid they will be persecuted* if they follow only the cross*a* of Christ. ¹³They are circumcised, but they don't obey the law* themselves. They want you to be circumcised so that they can boast about what they did to you.

¹⁴I hope I will never boast about things like that. The cross of our Lord Jesus Christ is my only reason for boasting. Through Jesus' death on the cross the world is dead*b* to me, and I am dead to the world. ¹⁵It doesn't matter if anyone is circumcised or not. The only thing that matters is this new life we have from God.*c* ¹⁶Peace and mercy to those who follow this rule—to all God's people.*d*

¹⁷So don't give me any more trouble. I have scars on my body that show*e* I belong to Jesus.

¹⁸My brothers and sisters, I pray that the grace* of our Lord Jesus Christ will be with your spirits. Amen.*

---

*a***6:12** *cross* Paul uses the cross as a picture of the Good News, the story of Christ's death to pay for people's sins. The cross (Christ's death) was God's way to save people. Also in verse 14.
*b***6:14** *is dead* Literally, "has been crucified."
*c***6:15** *this new life … God* Or "being the new people God has made."
*d***6:16** *all of God's people* Literally, "the Israel of God."
*e***6:17** *scars … show* Many times Paul was beaten by people who tried to stop him from teaching about Christ. The scars were from these beatings.

Ephesians

1 ¹Greetings from Paul, an apostle* of Christ Jesus. I am an apostle because that is what God wanted.

To God's holy people* living in Ephesus,*f* believers who belong to Christ Jesus.

²Grace* and peace to you from God our Father and the Lord Jesus Christ.

Spiritual Blessings in Christ

³Praise be to the God and Father of our Lord Jesus Christ. In Christ, God has given us every spiritual blessing in heaven. ⁴In Christ, he chose us before the world was made. He chose us in love to be his holy people*—people who could stand before him without any fault. ⁵And before the world was made, God decided to make us his own children through Jesus Christ. This was what God wanted, and it pleased him to do it. ⁶And this brings praise to God because of his wonderful grace.* God gave that grace to us freely. He gave us that grace in Christ, the one he loves.

⁷In Christ we are made free by his blood sacrifice. We have forgiveness of sins because of God's rich grace. ⁸God gave us that grace fully and freely. With full wisdom and understanding ⁹he let us know his secret plan. This was what God wanted, and he planned to do it through Christ. ¹⁰God's goal was to finish his plan when the right time came. He

---

*f***1:1** *in Ephesus* Some Greek copies do not have the words "in Ephesus."

planned that all things in heaven and on earth be joined together with Christ as the head.

¹¹In Christ we were chosen to be God's people. God had already planned for us to be his people, because that is what he wanted. And he is the one who makes everything agree with what he decides and wants. ¹²We Jews were the first to hope in Christ. And we were chosen so that we would bring praise to God in all his glory.* ¹³It is the same with you. You heard the true message, the Good News* about your salvation. When you heard that Good News, you believed in Christ. And in Christ, God put his special mark on you by giving you the Holy Spirit* that he promised. ¹⁴The Spirit is the first payment that guarantees we will get all that God has for us. Then we will enjoy complete freedom as people who belong to him. The goal for all of us is the praise of God in all his glory.

Paul's Prayer

¹⁵⁻¹⁶That is why I always remember you in my prayers and thank God for you. I have done this ever since I heard about your faith in the Lord Jesus and your love for all of God's people. ¹⁷I always pray to the great and glorious Father, the God of our Lord Jesus Christ. I pray that he will give you the Spirit,* who will let you know truths about God and help you understand them, so that you will know him better.

¹⁸I pray that God will open your minds to see his truth. Then you will know the hope that he has chosen us to have. You will know that the blessings God has promised his holy people* are rich and glorious. ¹⁹And you will know that God's power is very great for us who believe. It is the same as the mighty power ²⁰he used to raise Christ from death and put him at his right side in the heavenly places. ²¹He put Christ over all rulers, authorities, powers, and kings. He gave him authority over everything that has power in this world or in the next world. ²²God put everything under Christ's power and made him head over everything for the church.* ²³The church is Christ's body. It is filled with him. He makes everything complete in every way.

From Death to Life

2 ¹In the past you were spiritually dead because of your sins and the things you did against God. ²Yes, in the past your lives were full of those sins. You lived the way the world lives, following the ruler of the evil powers* over the earth. That same spirit is now working in those who refuse to obey God. ³In the past·all of us lived like that, trying to please our sinful selves. We did all the things our bodies and minds wanted. Like everyone else in the world, we deserved to suffer God's anger just because of the way we were.

⁴But God is rich in mercy, and he loved us very much. ⁵We were spiritually dead because of all we had done against him. But he gave us new life together with Christ. (You have been saved by God's grace.*) ⁶Yes, it is because we are a part of Christ Jesus that God raised us from death and seated us together with him in the heavenly places. ⁷God did this so that his kindness to us who belong to Christ Jesus would clearly show for all time to come the amazing richness of his grace.

⁸I mean that you have been saved by grace because you believed. You did not save yourselves; it was a gift from God. ⁹You are not saved by the things you have done, so there is nothing to boast about. ¹⁰God has made us what we are. In Christ Jesus, God made us new people so that we would spend our lives doing the good things he had already planned for us to do.

One in Christ

¹¹You were not born as Jews. You are the people the Jews call "uncircumcised.ᵃ" Those Jews who call you "uncircumcised" call themselves "circumcised." (Their circumcision* is only something they themselves do to their bodies.) ¹²Remember that in the past you were without Christ. You were not citizens of Israel,* and you did not know about the agreementsᵇ with the promises that God made to his people. You had no hope, and you did not know God. ¹³Yes, at one time you were far away from God, but now in Christ Jesus, you are brought near to him. You are brought near to God through the blood sacrifice of Christ.

¹⁴Christ is the reason we are now at peace. He made us Jews and you who are not Jews one people. We were separated by a wall of hate that stood between us, but Christ broke down that wall. By giving his own body, ¹⁵Christ ended the law with its many commands and rules. His purpose was to make the two groups become one in him. By doing this he would make peace. ¹⁶Through the cross Christ ended the hate between the two groups. And after they became one body, he wanted to bring them both back to God. He did this with his death on the cross. ¹⁷Christ came and brought the message of peace to you non-Jews who were far away from God. And he brought that message of peace to those who were near to God. ¹⁸Yes, through Christ we all have the right to come to the Father in one Spirit.*

¹⁹So now you non-Jewish people are not visitors or strangers, but you are citizens together with God's holy people.* You belong to God's family. ²⁰You believers are like a building that God owns. That building was

---

ᵃ2:11 **uncircumcised** People not having the mark of circumcision like the Jews have.

ᵇ2:12 **agreements** The agreements with special promises that God gave at various times to people in the Old Testament. See "agreement" in the Word List.

built on the foundation that the apostles* and prophets* prepared. Christ Jesus himself is the most important stone*a* in that building. 21The whole building is joined together in Christ, and he makes it grow and become a holy temple*b* in the Lord. 22And in Christ you are being built together with his other people. You are being made into a place where God lives through the Spirit.

Paul's Work for the Non-Jewish People

3 1So I, Paul, am a prisoner because I serve Christ Jesus for you who are not Jews. 2Surely you know that God gave me this work through his grace* to help you. 3God let me know his secret plan by showing it to me. I have already written a little about this. 4And if you read what I wrote, you can see that I understand the secret truth about Christ. 5People who lived in other times were not told that secret truth. But now, through the Spirit,* God has made it known to his holy apostles* and prophets.* 6And this is the secret truth: that by hearing the Good News,* those who are not Jews will share with the Jews in the blessings God has for his people. They are part of the same body, and they share in the promise God made through Christ Jesus.

7By God's special gift of grace, I became a servant to tell that Good News. He gave me that grace by using his power. 8I am the least important of all God's people. But he gave me this gift—to tell the non-Jewish people the Good News about the riches Christ has. These riches are too great to understand fully. 9And God gave me the work of telling all people about the plan for his secret truth. That secret truth has been hidden in him since the beginning of time. He is the one who created everything. 10His purpose was that all the rulers and powers in the heavenly places will now know the many different ways he shows his wisdom. They will know this because of the church.* 11This agrees with the plan God had since the beginning of time. He did what he planned, and he did it through Christ Jesus our Lord. 12In Christ we come before God with freedom and without fear. We can do this because of our faith in Christ. 13So I ask you not to be discouraged because of what is happening to me. My sufferings are for your benefit—for your honor and glory.*

The Love of Christ

14So I bow in prayer before the Father. 15Every family in heaven and on earth gets its true name from him. 16I ask the Father with his great glory* to give you the power to be strong in your spirits. He will give you that strength through his Spirit.* 17I pray that

Christ will live in your hearts because of your faith. I pray that your life will be strong in love and be built on love. 18And I pray that you and all God's holy people* will have the power to understand the greatness of Christ's love—how wide, how long, how high, and how deep that love is. 19Christ's love is greater than anyone can ever know, but I pray that you will be able to know that love. Then you can be filled with everything God has for you.

20With God's power working in us, he can do much, much more than anything we can ask or think of. 21To him be glory in the church* and in Christ Jesus for all time, forever and ever. Amen.*

The Unity of the Body

4 1So, as a prisoner for the Lord, I beg you to live the way God's people should live, because he chose you to be his. 2Always be humble and gentle. Be patient and accept each other with love. 3You are joined together with peace through the Spirit.* Do all you can to continue as you are, letting peace hold you together. 4There is one body and one Spirit, and God chose you to have one hope. 5There is one Lord, one faith, and one baptism.* 6There is one God and Father of us all, who rules over everyone. He works through all of us and in all of us.

7Christ gave each one of us a special gift. Everyone received what he wanted to give them. 8That is why the Scriptures* say,

"He went up high into the sky;
    he took prisoners with him, and he gave
        gifts to people."   *Psalm 68:18*

9When it says, "He went up," what does it mean? It means that he first came down low to earth. 10So Christ came down, and he is the same one who went up. He went up above the highest heaven in order to fill everything with himself. 11And that same Christ gave these gifts to people: He made some to be apostles,* some to be prophets,* some to go and tell the Good News,* and some to care for and teach God's people.*c* 12Christ gave these gifts to prepare God's holy people* for the work of serving, to make the body of Christ stronger. 13This work must continue until we are all joined together in what we believe and in what we know about the Son of God. Our goal is to become like a full-grown man—to look just like Christ and have all his perfection.

14Then we will no longer be like babies. We will not be people who are always changing like a ship that the waves carry one way and then another. We will not be influenced by every new teaching we hear from people

*a*2:20 *most important stone* Literally, "cornerstone." The first and most important stone in a building.
*b*2:21 *temple* God's house—the place where God's people worship him. Here, it means that believers are the spiritual temple where God lives.

*c*4:11 *to care for … people* Literally, "to be shepherds and teachers."

who are trying to deceive us—those who make clever plans and use every kind of trick to fool others into following the wrong way. [15]No, we will speak the truth with love. We will grow to be like Christ in every way. He is the head, [16]and the whole body depends on him. All the parts of the body are joined and held together, with each part doing its own work. This causes the whole body to grow and to be stronger in love.

The Way You Should Live

[17]I have something from the Lord to tell you. I warn you: Don't continue living like those who don't believe. Their thoughts are worth nothing. [18]They have no understanding, and they know nothing because they refuse to listen. So they cannot have the life that God gives. [19]They have lost their feeling of shame and use their lives to do what is morally wrong. More and more they want to do all kinds of evil. [20]But that way of life is nothing like what you learned when you came to know Christ. [21]I know that you heard about him, and in him you were taught the truth. Yes, the truth is in Jesus. [22]You were taught to leave your old self. This means that you must stop living the evil way you lived before. That old self gets worse and worse, because people are fooled by the evil they want to do. [23]You must be made new in your hearts and in your thinking. [24]Be that new person who was made to be like God, truly good and pleasing to him.

[25]So you must stop telling lies. "You must always speak the truth to each other,"[a] because we all belong to each other in the same body. [26]"When you are angry, don't let that anger make you sin,"[b] and don't stay angry all day. [27]Don't give the devil a way to defeat you. [28]Whoever has been stealing must stop it and start working. They must use their hands for doing something good. Then they will have something to share with those who are poor.

[29]When you talk, don't say anything bad. But say the good things that people need—whatever will help them grow stronger. Then what you say will be a blessing to those who hear you. [30]And don't make the Holy Spirit* sad. God gave you his Spirit as proof that you belong to him and that he will keep you safe until the day he makes you free. [31]Never be bitter, angry, or mad. Never shout angrily or say things to hurt others. Never do anything evil. [32]Be kind and loving to each other. Forgive each other the same as God forgave you through Christ.

5 [1]You are God's dear children, so try to be like him. [2]Live a life of love. Love others just as Christ loved us. He gave himself for us—a sweet-smelling offering and sacrifice* to God.

[3]But there must be no sexual sin among you. There must not be any kind of evil or selfishly wanting more and more, because such things are not right for God's holy people.* [4]Also, there must be no evil talk among you. Don't say things that are foolish or filthy. These are not for you. But you should be giving thanks to God. [5]You can be sure of this: No one will have a place in the kingdom of Christ and of God if that person commits sexual sins, or does evil things, or is a person who selfishly wants more and more. A greedy person like that is serving a false god.

[6]Don't let anyone fool you with words that are not true. God gets very angry when people who don't obey him talk like that. [7]So don't have anything to do with them. [8]In the past you were full of darkness,* but now you are full of light* in the Lord. So live like children who belong to the light. [9]This light produces every kind of goodness, right living, and truth. [10]Try to learn what pleases the Lord. [11]Have no part in the things that people in darkness do, which produce nothing good. Instead, tell everyone how wrong those things are. [12]It is really very shameful to even talk about the things those people do in secret. [13]But the light makes clear how wrong those things are. [14]Yes, everything is made clear by the light. This is why we say,

"Wake up, you who are sleeping!
	Rise from death,
	and Christ will shine on you."

[15]So be very careful how you live. Live wisely, not like fools. [16]I mean that you should use every opportunity you have for doing good, because these are evil times. [17]So don't be foolish with your lives, but learn what the Lord wants you to do. [18]Don't be drunk with wine, which will ruin your life, but be filled with the Spirit.* [19]Encourage each other with psalms, hymns, and spiritual songs. Sing and make music in your hearts to the Lord. [20]Always give thanks to God the Father for everything in the name of our Lord Jesus Christ.

Wives and Husbands

[21]Be willing to serve each other out of respect for Christ.

[22]Wives, be willing to serve your husbands the same as the Lord. [23]A husband is the head of his wife, just as Christ is the head of the church.* Christ is the Savior of the church, which is his body. [24]The church serves under Christ, so it is the same with you wives. You should be willing to serve your husbands in everything.

[25]Husbands, love your wives the same as Christ loved the church and gave his life for it. [26]He died to make the church holy.* He used the telling of the Good News* to make the church clean by washing it with water. [27]Christ died so that he could give the church

[a]4:25 Quote from Zech. 8:16.
[b]4:26 Quote from Ps. 4:4 (Greek version).

to himself like a bride in all her beauty. He died so that the church could be holy and without fault, with no evil or sin or any other thing wrong in it.

28And husbands should love their wives like that. They should love their wives as they love their own bodies. The man who loves his wife loves himself, 29because no one ever hates his own body, but feeds and takes care of it. And that is what Christ does for the church 30because we are parts of his body. 31The Scriptures* say, "That is why a man will leave his father and mother and join his wife, and the two people will become one."*a 32That secret truth is very important—I am talking about Christ and the church. 33But each one of you must love his wife as he loves himself. And a wife must respect her husband.

Children and Parents

6 1Children, obey your parents the way the Lord wants, because this is the right thing to do. 2The command says, "You must respect your father and mother."*b That is the first command that has a promise with it. 3That promise is: "Then all will go well with you, and you will have a long life on the earth."*c

4Fathers, don't make your children angry, but raise them with the kind of teaching and training you learn from the Lord.

Slaves and Masters

5Slaves, obey your masters here on earth with fear and respect. And do this with a heart that is true, just as you obey Christ. 6You must do this not just to please your masters while they are watching, but all the time. Since you are really slaves of Christ, you must do with all your heart what God wants. 7Do your work, and be happy to do it. Work as though it is the Lord you are serving, not just an earthly master. 8Remember that the Lord will give everyone a reward for doing good. Everyone, slave or free, will get a reward for the good things they do.

9Masters, in the same way, be good to your slaves. Don't say things to scare them. You know that the one who is your Master and their Master is in heaven, and he treats everyone the same.

Wear the Full Armor of God

10To end my letter I tell you, be strong in the Lord and in his great power. 11Wear the full armor of God. Wear God's armor so that you can fight against the devil's clever tricks. 12Our fight is not against people on earth. We are fighting against the rulers and authorities and the powers of this world's darkness. We are fighting against the spiritual powers of evil in the heavenly places. 13That is why you need to get God's full armor. Then on the day of evil you will be able to stand strong. And when you have finished the whole fight, you will still be standing.

14So stand strong with the belt of truth tied around your waist, and on your chest wear the protection of right living. 15On your feet wear the Good News* of peace to help you stand strong. 16And also use the shield of faith with which you can stop all the burning arrows that come from the Evil One.* 17Accept God's salvation as your helmet. And take the sword of the Spirit*—that sword is the teaching of God. 18Pray in the Spirit at all times. Pray with all kinds of prayers, and ask for everything you need. To do this you must always be ready. Never give up. Always pray for all of God's people.

19Also pray for me—that when I speak, God will give me words so that I can tell the secret truth about the Good News without fear. 20I have the work of speaking for that Good News, and that is what I am doing now, here in prison. Pray that when I tell people the Good News, I will speak without fear as I should.

Final Greetings

21I am sending you Tychicus, the brother we love. He is a faithful servant of the Lord's work. He will tell you everything that is happening with me. Then you will know how I am and what I am doing. 22That's why I am sending him—to let you know how we are and to encourage you.

23I pray that God the Father and the Lord Jesus Christ will give peace and love with faith to all the brothers and sisters there. 24God's grace* to all of you who love our Lord Jesus Christ with love that never ends.

*a***5:31** Quote from Gen. 2:24.
*b***6:2** Quote from Ex. 20:12; Deut. 5:16.
*c***6:3** Quote from Ex. 20:12; Deut. 5:16.

Philippians

1

¹Greetings from Paul and Timothy, servants of Jesus Christ.

To all of you in Philippi who are God's holy people* in Christ Jesus, including your elders*ᵃ* and special servants.*

²Grace* and peace to you from God our Father and the Lord Jesus Christ.

Paul's Prayer

³I thank God every time I remember you. ⁴And I always pray for all of you with joy. ⁵I thank God for the help you gave me while I told people the Good News.* You helped from the first day you believed until now. ⁶I am sure that the good work God began in you will continue until he completes it on the day when Jesus Christ comes again.

⁷I know I am right to think like this about all of you because you are so close to my heart. This is because you have all played such an important part in God's grace* to me—now, during this time that I am in prison, and whenever I am defending and proving the truth of the Good News. ⁸God knows that I want very much to see you. I love all of you with the love of Christ Jesus.

⁹This is my prayer for you:

that your love will grow more and more;
that you will have knowledge and
    understanding with your love;
¹⁰ that you will see the difference between
    what is important and what is not and
    choose what is important;
that you will be pure and blameless for
    the coming of Christ;
¹¹ that your life will be full of the many good
    works that are produced by Jesus
    Christ to bring glory* and praise to
    God.

Paul's Troubles Help the Lord's Work

¹²Brothers and sisters, I want you to know that all that has happened to me has helped to spread the Good News.* ¹³All the Roman guards and all the others here know that I am in prison for serving Christ. ¹⁴My being in prison has caused most of the believers* to put their trust in the Lord and to show more courage in telling people God's message.*

¹⁵Some people are telling the message about Christ because they are jealous and bitter. Others do it because they want to help. ¹⁶They are doing it out of love. They know that God gave me the work of defending the Good News. ¹⁷But those others tell about Christ because of their selfish ambition. Their reason for doing it is wrong. They only do it because they think it will make trouble for me in prison. ¹⁸But that doesn't matter. What is important is that they are telling people about Christ, whether they are sincere or not. So I am glad they are doing it.

I will continue to be glad, ¹⁹because I know that your prayers and the help the Spirit* of Jesus Christ gives me will cause this trouble to result in my freedom.*ᵇ* ²⁰I am full of hope and feel sure I will not have any reason to be ashamed. I am certain I will continue to have the same boldness to speak freely that I always have. I will let God use my life to bring more honor to Christ. It doesn't matter whether I live or die. ²¹To me, the only important thing about living is Christ. And even death would be for my benefit.*ᶜ* ²²If I continue living here on earth, I will be able to work for the Lord. But what would I choose—to live or to die? I don't know. ²³It would be a hard choice. Sometimes I want to leave this life and be with Christ. That would be much better for me; ²⁴however, you people need me here alive. ²⁵I am sure of this, so I know that I will stay here and be with you to help you grow and have joy in your faith. ²⁶When I am there with you again, you will be bursting with pride over what Christ Jesus did to help me.

²⁷Just be sure you live as God's people in a way that honors the Good News of Christ. Then if I come and visit you or if I am away from you, I will hear good things about you. I will know that you stand together with the same purpose and that you work together like a team to help others believe the Good News. ²⁸And you will not be afraid of those who are against you. All of this is proof from God that you are being saved and that your enemies will be lost. ²⁹God has blessed you in ways that serve Christ. He allowed you to believe in Christ. But that is not all. He has also given you the honor of suffering for Christ. Both of these bring glory* to Christ. ³⁰You saw the

---

*ᵃ*1:1 *elders* Here, literally, "overseers." See "elders" in the Word List.

*ᵇ*1:19 *freedom* Or "salvation."

*ᶜ*1:21 *death ... benefit* Paul says that death would be better, because death would bring him nearer to Christ.

difficulties I had to face, and you hear that I am still having troubles. Now you must face them too.

Be United and Care for Each Other

2 ¹Think about what we have in Christ: the encouragement he has brought us, the comfort of his love, our sharing in his Spirit,* and the mercy and kindness he has shown us. If you enjoy these blessings, ²then do what will make my joy complete: Agree with each other, and show your love for each other. Be united in your goals and in the way you think. ³In whatever you do, don't let selfishness or pride be your guide. Be humble, and honor others more than yourselves. ⁴Don't be interested only in your own life, but care about the lives of others too.

Learn From Christ to Be Unselfish

⁵In your life together, think the way Christ Jesus thought.

⁶ He was like God in every way,
   but he did not think that his being equal
      with God was something to use for
      his own benefit.
⁷ Instead, he gave up everything, even his
      place with God.
   He accepted the role of a servant,
      appearing in human form.
   During his life as a man,
⁸ he humbled himself by being fully
      obedient to God,
   even when that caused his death—
      death on a cross.
⁹ So God raised him up to the most
      important place
   and gave him the name that is greater
      than any other name.
¹⁰ God did this so that every person will
      bow down to honor the name of
      Jesus.
   Everyone in heaven, on earth, and
      under the earth will bow.
¹¹ They will all confess, "Jesus Christ is
      Lord,"
   and this will bring glory* to God the
      Father.

Be the People God Wants You to Be

¹²My dear friends, you always obeyed what you were taught. Just as you obeyed when I was with you, it is even more important for you to obey now that I am not there. So you must continue to live in a way that gives meaning to your salvation. Do this with fear and respect for God. ¹³Yes, it is God who is working in you. He helps you want to do what pleases him, and he gives you the power to do it.

¹⁴Do everything without complaining or arguing ¹⁵so that you will be blameless and pure, children of God without any fault. But you are living with evil people all around you,

who have lost their sense of what is right. Among those people you shine like lights in a dark world, ¹⁶and you offer them the teaching that gives life. So I can be proud of you when Christ comes again. You will show that my work was not wasted—that I ran in the race and won.

¹⁷Your faith makes you give your lives as a sacrifice* in serving God. Maybe I will have to offer my own life with your sacrifice. But if that happens, I will be glad, and I will share my joy with all of you. ¹⁸You also should be glad and share your joy with me.

News About Timothy and Epaphroditus

¹⁹With the blessing of the Lord Jesus, I hope I will be able to send Timothy to you soon. I will be glad to learn how you are. ²⁰I have no one else like Timothy, who genuinely cares for you. ²¹Others are interested only in their own lives. They don't care about the work of Christ Jesus. ²²You know the kind of person Timothy is. He has served with me in telling the Good News* like a son with his father. ²³I plan to send him to you quickly, as soon as I know what will happen to me. ²⁴I am sure the Lord will help me come to you soon.

²⁵For now, I think I must send Epaphroditus back to you. He is my brother in God's family, who works and serves with me in the Lord's army. When I needed help, you sent him to me, ²⁶but now he wants very much to see all of you again. He is worried because you heard that he was sick. ²⁷He was sick and near death. But God helped him and me too, so that I would not have even more grief. ²⁸So I want very much to send him to you. When you see him, you can be happy. And I can stop worrying about you. ²⁹Welcome him in the Lord with much joy. Give honor to people like Epaphroditus. ³⁰He should be honored because he almost died for the work of Christ. He put his life in danger so that he could help me. This was help that you could not give me.

Christ Is More Important Than Anything

3 ¹And now, my brothers and sisters, be filled with joy in the Lord. It is no trouble for me to write the same things to you again. I want to be sure that you are prepared.

²Be careful of the dogs—those people whose work does no one any good. They want to cut off everyone who isn't circumcised.ᵃ ³But we are the ones who have the true circumcisionᵇ—we who worship God through his Spirit.* We don't trust in ourselves or anything we can do. We take pride only in Christ Jesus. ⁴Even if I am able to trust in myself, still

ᵃ3:2 want to cut off ... circumcised There is a play on words here in Greek. The key word is like "circumcision" (see the Word List), but it means "mutilation" or "cutting to pieces."
ᵇ3:3 we are ... circumcision Literally, "we are the circumcision." See "circumcision" in the Word List.

I don't do it. If anyone else thinks they have a reason to trust in themselves, they should know that I have a greater reason for doing so. [5]I was circumcised on the eighth day after my birth. I am from the people of Israel* and the tribe of Benjamin. I am a true Jew, and so were my parents. The law* was very important to me. That is why I became a Pharisee.* [6]I was such a fanatic that I persecuted* the church.* And no one could find fault with how I always obeyed the law.

[7]At one time all these things were important to me. But because of Christ, I decided that they are worth nothing. [8]Not only these things, but now I think that all things are worth nothing compared with the greatness of knowing Christ Jesus my Lord. Because of Christ, I lost all these things, and now I know that they are all worthless trash. All I want now is Christ. [9]I want to belong to him. In Christ I am right with God, but my being right does not come from following the law. It comes from God through faith. God uses my faith in[a] Christ to make me right with him. [10]All I want is to know Christ and the power that raised him from death. I want to share in his sufferings and be like him even in his death. [11]Then there is hope that I myself will somehow be raised from death.

Trying to Reach the Goal

[12]I don't mean that I am exactly what God wants me to be. I have not yet reached that goal. But I continue trying to reach it and make it mine. That's what Christ Jesus wants me to do. It is the reason he made me his. [13]Brothers and sisters, I know that I still have a long way to go. But there is one thing I do: I forget what is in the past and try as hard as I can to reach the goal before me. [14]I keep running hard toward the finish line to get the prize that is mine because God has called me through Christ Jesus to life up there in heaven.

[15]All of us who have grown to be spiritually mature should think this way too. And if there is any of this that you don't agree with, God will make it clear to you. [16]But we should continue following the truth we already have.

[17]Brothers and sisters, join together in following my example. Also, learn by watching those who are living the way we showed you. [18]There are many who live like enemies of the cross of Christ. I have often told you about them. And it makes me cry to tell you about them now. [19]The way they live is leading them to destruction. They have replaced God with their own desires. They do shameful things, and they are proud of what they do. They think only about earthly things. [20]But the government that rules us is in heaven. We are waiting for our Savior, the Lord Jesus Christ, to come from there. [21]He will change our

humble bodies and make them like his own glorious body. Christ can do this by his power, with which he is able to rule everything.

Some Things to Do

4 [1]My dear brothers and sisters, I love you and want to see you. You bring me joy and make me proud of you. Continue following the Lord as I have told you.

[2]Euodia and Syntyche, you both belong to the Lord, so please agree with each other. [3]For this I make a special request to my friend who has served with me so faithfully: Help these women. They worked hard with me in telling people the Good News,* together with Clement and others who worked with me. Their names are written in the book of life.[b]

[4]Always be filled with joy in the Lord. I will say it again. Be filled with joy.

[5]Let everyone see that you are gentle and kind. The Lord is coming soon. [6]Don't worry about anything, but pray and ask God for everything you need, always giving thanks for what you have. [7]And because you belong to Christ Jesus, God's peace will stand guard over all your thoughts and feelings. His peace can do this far better than our human minds.[c]

[8]Brothers and sisters, continue to think about what is good and worthy of praise. Think about what is true and honorable and right and pure and beautiful and respected. [9]And do what you learned and received from me—what I told you and what you saw me do. And the God who gives peace will be with you.

Paul Thanks the Philippian Believers

[10]I am so happy, and I thank the Lord that you have again shown your care for me. You continued to care about me, but there was no way for you to show it. [11]I am telling you this, but not because I need something. I have learned to be satisfied with what I have and with whatever happens. [12]I know how to live when I am poor and when I have plenty. I have learned the secret of how to live through any kind of situation—when I have enough to eat or when I am hungry, when I have everything I need or when I have nothing. [13]Christ is the one who gives me the strength I need to do whatever I must do.

[14]But it was good that you helped me when I needed help. [15]You people in Philippi remember when I first told the Good News* there. When I left Macedonia,* you were the only church* that gave me help. [16]Several times you sent me things I needed when I was in Thessalonica. [17]Really, it is not that I want to get gifts from you. But I want you to have the benefit that comes from giving. [18]I have everything I need. I have even more

[b]4:3 *book of life* God's book that contains the names of his chosen people. See Rev. 3:5; 21:27.
[c]4:7 *can do ... minds* Literally, "surpasses (is better than) every mind," which could also have the meaning "is beyond all understanding."

[a]3:9 *my faith in* Or "the faithfulness of."

than I need. I have all I need because Epaph-roditus brought your gift to me. Your gift is like a sweet-smelling sacrifice* offered to God. God accepts that sacrifice and it pleases him. ¹⁹My God will use his glorious riches to give you everything you need. He will do this through Christ Jesus. ²⁰Glory* to our God and Father forever and ever. Amen.*

²¹Give our greetings to God's people there—to each one who belongs to Christ Jesus. Those in God's family who are with me send you their greetings. ²²And greetings to you from all of God's people here, especially those who work in the service of the emperor.*

²³The grace* of the Lord Jesus Christ be with you all.

Colossians

1 ¹Greetings from Paul, an apostle* of Christ Jesus. I am an apostle because that is what God wanted. Greetings also from Timothy, our brother in Christ.

²To the holy* and faithful brothers and sisters in Christ who live in Colossae.

Grace* and peace to you from God our Father.

³In our prayers we always thank God for you. He is the Father of our Lord Jesus Christ. ⁴We thank him because we have heard about the faith you have in Christ Jesus and the love you have for all of God's people. ⁵Your faith and love continue because you know what is waiting for you in heaven—the hope you have had since you first heard the true message, the Good News* ⁶that was told to you. Throughout the world, this Good News is bringing blessings and is spreading. And that's what has been happening among you since the first time you heard it and understood the truth about God's grace. ⁷You heard it from Epaphras, our dear friend and co-worker. He is a faithful servant of Christ for us.ᵃ ⁸He also told us about the love you have from the Spirit.*

⁹Since the day we heard these things about you, we have continued praying for you. This is what we pray:

that God will make you completely sure of what he wants by giving you all the wisdom and spiritual understanding you need;
¹⁰ that this will help you live in a way that brings honor to the Lord and pleases him in every way;
that your life will produce good works of every kind and that you will grow in your knowledge of Godᵇ;
¹¹ that God will strengthen you with his own great power, so that you will be patient and not give up when troubles come.

Then you will be happy ¹²and give thanks to the Father. He has made you able to have what he has promised to give all his holy people,* who live in the light.* ¹³God made us free from the power of darkness.* And he brought us into the kingdom of his dear Son. ¹⁴The Son paid the price to make us free. In him we have forgiveness of our sins.

The Son of God Is the Same as God

¹⁵ No one can see God,
but the Son is exactly like God.
He rules over everything that has been made.ᶜ
¹⁶ Through his power all things were made:
things in heaven and on earth, seen and not seen—
all spiritual rulers, lords, powers, and authorities.
Everything was made through him and for him.

¹⁷ The Son was there before anything was made.
And all things continue because of him.
¹⁸ He is the head of the body, which is the church.*
He is the beginning of everything else.
And he is the first among all who will be raised from death.ᵈ
So in everything he is most important.

¹⁹ God was pleased for all of himself to live in the Son.
²⁰ And through him, God was happy to bring all things back to himself again—
things on earth and things in heaven.
God made peace by using the blood sacrifice of his Son on the cross.

²¹At one time you were separated from God. You were his enemies in your minds, because

---

ᵃ**1:7 us** Many ancient Greek copies have "you."
ᵇ**1:10 that your life ... God** Or "that your knowledge of God will produce more and more good works of every kind in your life."

ᶜ**1:15 He ... made** Literally, "⌊He is the⌋ firstborn of all creation." See "firstborn" in the Word List.
ᵈ**1:18 first ... death** Literally, "firstborn from the dead."

the evil you did was against him. ²²But now he has made you his friends again. He did this by the death Christ suffered while he was in his body. He did it so that he could present you to himself as people who are holy,* blameless, and without anything that would make you guilty before him. ²³And that is what will happen if you continue to believe in the Good News* you heard. You must remain strong and sure in your faith. You must not let anything cause you to give up the hope that became yours when you heard the Good News. That same Good News has been told to everyone on earth, and that's the work that I, Paul, was given to do.

Paul's Work for the Church

²⁴I am happy in my sufferings for you. There is much that Christ must still suffer. And I gladly accept my part of those sufferings in my body for the good of his body, the church.* ²⁵I became a servant of the church because God gave me a special work to do. This work helps you. My work is to tell the complete message of God. ²⁶This message is the secret truth that was hidden since the beginning of time. It was hidden from everyone for ages, but now it has been made known to God's holy people.* ²⁷God decided to let his people know just how rich and glorious that truth is. That secret truth, which is for all people, is that Christ lives in you, his people. He is our hope for glory.* ²⁸So we continue to tell people about Christ. We use all wisdom to counsel every person and teach every person. We are trying to bring everyone before God as people who have grown to be spiritually mature in Christ. ²⁹To do this, I work and struggle using the great strength that Christ gives me. That strength is working in my life.

2 ¹I want you to know that I am trying very hard to help you. And I am trying to help those in Laodicea and others who have never seen me. ²I want them to be strengthened and joined together with love and to have the full confidence that comes from understanding. I want them to know completely the secret truth that God has made known. That truth is Christ himself. ³In him all the treasures of wisdom and knowledge are kept safe.

⁴I tell you this so that no one can fool you by telling you ideas that seem good, but are false. ⁵Even though I am far away, my thoughts are always with you. I am happy to see your good lives and your strong faith in Christ.

Continue to Live in Christ

⁶You accepted Christ Jesus as Lord, so continue to live following him. ⁷You must depend on Christ only, drawing life and strength from him. Just as you were taught the truth, continue to grow stronger in your understanding of it. And never stop giving thanks to God.

⁸Be sure you are not led away by the teaching of those who have nothing worth saying

and only plan to deceive you. That teaching is not from Christ. It is only human tradition and comes from the powers that influence*a* this world. ⁹I say this because all of God lives in Christ fully, even in his life on earth. ¹⁰And because you belong to Christ you are complete, having everything you need. Christ is ruler over every other power and authority.

¹¹In Christ you had a different kind of circumcision,* one that was not done by human hands. That is, you were made free from the power of your sinful self. That is the kind of circumcision Christ does. ¹²When you were baptized,* you were buried with Christ, and you were raised up with him because of your faith in God's power. God's power was shown when he raised Christ from death.

¹³You were spiritually dead because of your sins and because you were not free from the power of your sinful self. But God gave you new life together with Christ. He forgave all our sins. ¹⁴Because we broke God's laws, we owed a debt—a debt that listed all the rules we failed to follow. But God forgave us of that debt. He took it away and nailed it to the cross. ¹⁵He defeated the rulers and powers of the spiritual world. With the cross he won the victory over them and led them away as defeated and powerless prisoners for the whole world to see.

Don't Follow Rules That People Make

¹⁶So don't let anyone make rules for you about eating and drinking or about Jewish customs (festivals, New Moon* celebrations, or Sabbath* days). ¹⁷In the past these things were like a shadow that showed what was coming. But the new things that were coming are found in Christ. ¹⁸Some people enjoy acting as if they are humble and love to worship angels.*b* They always talk about the visions* they have seen. Don't listen to them when they say you are wrong because you don't do these things. It is so foolish for them to feel such pride, because it is all based on their own human ideas. ¹⁹They don't keep themselves under the control of the head. Christ is the head, and the whole body depends on him. Because of Christ all the parts of the body care for each other and help each other. So the body is made stronger and held together as God causes it to grow.

²⁰You died with Christ and were made free from the powers that influence this world. So why do you act as if you still belong to the world? I mean, why do you follow rules like these: ²¹"Don't eat this," "Don't taste that," "Don't touch that"? ²²These rules are talking about earthly things that are gone after they are used. They are only human commands

*a*2:8 *powers that influence* Or "elementary rules of." Also in verse 20.
*b*2:18 *worship angels* Or "worship with angels" (that they see in visions).

and teachings. 23These rules may seem to be wise as part of a made-up religion in which people pretend to be humble and punish their bodies. But they don't help people stop doing the evil that the sinful self wants to do.

Your New Life in Christ

3 1You were raised from death with Christ. So live for what is in heaven, where Christ is sitting at the right hand of God. 2Think only about what is up there, not what is here on earth. 3Your old self has died, and your new life is kept with Christ in God. 4Yes, Christ is now your life, and when he comes again, you will share in his glory.*

5So put everything evil out of your life: sexual sin, doing anything immoral, letting sinful thoughts control you, and wanting things that are wrong. And don't keep wanting more and more for yourself, which is the same as worshiping a false god. 6God will show his anger against those who don't obey him,*a* because they do these evil things. 7You also did these things in the past, when you lived like them.

8But now put these things out of your life: anger, losing your temper, doing or saying things to hurt others, and saying shameful things. 9Don't lie to each other. You have taken off those old clothes—the person you once were and the bad things you did then. 10Now you are wearing a new life, a life that is new every day. You are growing in your understanding of the one who made you. You are becoming more and more like him. 11In this new life it doesn't matter if you are a Greek* or a Jew, circumcised* or not. It doesn't matter if you speak a different language or even if you are a Scythian.*b* It doesn't matter if you are a slave or free. Christ is all that matters, and he is in all of you.

Your New Life With Each Other

12God has chosen you and made you his holy people.* He loves you. So your new life should be like this: Show mercy to others. Be kind, humble, gentle, and patient. 13Don't be angry with each other, but forgive each other. If you feel someone has wronged you, forgive them. Forgive others because the Lord forgave you. 14Together with these things, the most important part of your new life is to love each other. Love is what holds everything together in perfect unity. 15Let the peace that Christ gives control your thinking. It is for peace that you were chosen to be together in one body.*c* And always be thankful.

16Let the teaching of Christ live inside you richly. Use all wisdom to teach and counsel each other. Sing psalms, hymns, and spiritual songs with thankfulness in your hearts to God. 17Everything you say and everything you do should be done for Jesus your Lord. And in all you do, give thanks to God the Father through Jesus.

Your New Life at Home

18Wives, be willing to serve your husbands. This is the right thing to do in following the Lord.

19Husbands, love your wives, and be gentle to them.

20Children, obey your parents in everything. This pleases the Lord.

21Fathers, don't upset your children. If you are too hard to please, they might want to stop trying.

22Servants, obey your masters in everything. Obey all the time, even when they can't see you. Don't just pretend to work hard so that they will treat you well. No, you must serve your masters honestly because you respect the Lord. 23In all the work you are given, do the best you can. Work as though you are working for the Lord, not any earthly master. 24Remember that you will receive your reward from the Lord, who will give you what he promised his people. You are serving the Lord Christ. 25Remember that anyone who does wrong will be punished for that wrong. And the Lord treats everyone the same.

4 1Masters, give what is good and fair to your servants. Remember that you have a Master in heaven.

Some Things to Do

2Never stop praying. Be ready for anything by praying and being thankful. 3Also pray for us. Pray that God will give us an opportunity to tell people his message.* I am in prison for doing this. But pray that we can continue to tell people the secret truth that God has made known about Christ. 4Pray that I will say what is necessary to make this truth clear to everyone.

5Be wise in the way you act with those who are not believers. Use your time in the best way you can. 6When you talk, you should always be kind and wise. Then you will be able to answer everyone in the way you should.

News About Those With Paul

7Tychicus is my dear brother in Christ. He is a faithful helper and he serves the Lord with me. He will tell you everything that is happening with me. 8That is why I am sending him. I want you to know how we are, and I am sending him to encourage you. 9I am sending him with Onesimus, the faithful and dear brother from your group. They will tell you everything that has happened here.

---

*a***3:6** *against ... him* Some Greek copies do not have these words.

*b***3:11** *Scythians* Known as wild and uncivilized people.

*c***3:15** *body* Christ's spiritual body, meaning the church—his people.

¹⁰Aristarchus, the one here in prison with me, sends you his greetings. Mark, the cousin of Barnabas, also sends his greetings. (I have already told you what to do about Mark. If he comes, welcome him.) ¹¹And greetings from Jesus, the one who is also called Justus. These are the only Jewish believers who work with me for God's kingdom.* They have been a great comfort to me.

¹²Epaphras, another servant of Jesus Christ from your group, sends his greetings. He constantly struggles for you in prayer. He prays that you will grow to be spiritually mature and have everything that God wants for you.

¹³I know that he has worked hard for you and the people in Laodicea and in Hierapolis. ¹⁴Greetings also from Demas and our dear friend Luke, the doctor.

¹⁵Give our greetings to the brothers and sisters in Laodicea. Greetings also to Nympha and to the church* that meets in her house. ¹⁶After this letter is read to you, be sure it is also read to the church in Laodicea. And you read the letter that I wrote to them. ¹⁷Tell Archippus, "Be sure to do the work the Lord gave you."

¹⁸Here's my greeting in my own handwriting—PAUL. Remember me in prison. God's grace* be with you.

1 Thessalonians

1 ¹Greetings from Paul, Silas, and Timothy. To the church* of those in Thessalonica, who are in God the Father and the Lord Jesus Christ.

Grace* and peace be yours.

The Life and Faith of the Thessalonians

²We always remember you when we pray, and we thank God for all of you. ³Every time we pray to God our Father we thank him for all that you have done because of your faith. And we thank him for the work you have done because of your love. And we thank him that you continue to be strong because of your hope in our Lord Jesus Christ.

⁴Brothers and sisters, God loves you. And we know that he has chosen you to be his people. ⁵When we brought the Good News* to you, we came with more than words. We brought that Good News with power, with the Holy Spirit,* and with the sure knowledge that it was true. Also you know how we lived when we were with you. We lived that way to help you. ⁶And you became like us and like the Lord. You suffered much, but still you accepted the teaching with joy. The Holy Spirit gave you that joy.

⁷You became an example to all the believers in Macedonia* and Achaia.* ⁸The Lord's teaching has spread from you throughout Greece and beyond. In fact, your faith in God has become known everywhere, so we never have to tell anyone about it. ⁹People everywhere are already telling the story about the good way you accepted us when we were there with you. They tell about how you stopped worshiping idols* and changed to serve the living and true God. ¹⁰And you began waiting for God's Son to come from heaven—the Son God raised from death. He

is Jesus, who saves us from God's angry judgment that is coming.

Paul's Work in Thessalonica

2 ¹Brothers and sisters, you know that our visit to you was not a failure. ²Before we came to you, people in Philippi abused us with insults and made us suffer. You know all about that. And then, when we came to you, many people there caused trouble for us. But our God gave us the courage we needed to tell you his Good News.* ³When we encourage people to believe the Good News, it's not out of wrong motives. We are not trying to trick or fool anyone. ⁴No, it was God who gave us this work but only after he tested us and saw that we could be trusted to do it. So when we speak, we are not trying to please people. We are only trying to please God. He is the one who can see what is in our hearts.

⁵You know that we never tried to influence you by saying nice things about you. We were not trying to get your money. We had no greed to hide from you. God knows that this is true. ⁶We were not looking for praise from people—not from you or anyone else.

⁷When we were with you, as apostles* of Christ we could have used our authority to make you help us. But we were very gentle*a* with you. We were like a mother caring for her little children. ⁸We loved you very much, so we were happy to share God's Good News with you. But not only that—we were also happy to share even our own lives with you. ⁹Brothers and sisters, I know that you remember how hard we worked. We worked night and day to support ourselves, so that we would

---

a2:7 But ... gentle Several Greek copies have "But we became babies."

not be a burden to anyone while we did the work of telling you God's Good News.

[10]When we were there with you believers, we were pure, honest, and without fault in the way we lived. You know, just as God does, that this is true. [11]You know that we treated each one of you the way a father treats his own children. [12]We encouraged you, we comforted you, and we told you to live good lives for God. He calls you to be part of his glorious kingdom.

[13]Also, we always thank God because of the way you accepted his message.* You heard it and accepted it as God's message, not our own. And it really is God's message. And it works in you who believe. [14]Brothers and sisters, you are like God's churches* in Christ Jesus that are in Judea.[a] You were treated badly by your own people, just as God's people in Judea were treated badly by the other Jews there. [15]Those Jews killed the Lord Jesus and the prophets.* And they forced us to leave their country. They are not pleasing to God, and they are against everyone else. [16]And they are trying to stop us from teaching those who are not Jews. They don't want them to be saved. But they are just adding more and more sins to the ones they already have. Now the time has come for them to suffer God's anger.

Paul's Desire to Visit Them Again

[17]Brothers and sisters, we were separated from you for a short time. But even though we were not there, our thoughts were still with you. We wanted very much to see you, and we tried very hard to do this. [18]Yes, we wanted to come to you. I, Paul, tried more than once to come, but Satan* stopped us. [19]You are our hope, our joy, and the crown* we will be proud of when our Lord Jesus Christ comes. [20]You bring us honor and joy.

3 [1-2]We could not come to you, but it was very hard to wait any longer. So we decided to send Timothy to you and stay in Athens alone. Timothy is our brother. He works with us for God to tell people the Good News* about Christ. We sent Timothy to strengthen and encourage you in your faith. [3]We sent him so that none of you would be upset by the troubles we have now. You yourselves know that we must have these troubles. [4]Even when we were with you, we told you that we would all have to suffer. And you know that it happened just as we said. [5]This is why I sent Timothy to you, so that I could know about your faith. I sent him when I could not wait anymore. I was afraid that the devil who tempts people might have defeated you with temptations. Then our hard work would have been wasted.

[6]But now Timothy has come back from his visit with you and told us good news about your faith and love. He told us that you always remember us in a good way. He told us that

you want very much to see us again. And it is the same with us—we want very much to see you. [7]So, brothers and sisters, we are encouraged about you because of your faith. We have much trouble and suffering, but still we are encouraged. [8]Our life is really full if you stand strong in the Lord. [9]We have so much joy before our God because of you! So we thank God for you. But we cannot thank him enough for all the joy we feel. [10]Night and day we continue praying with all our heart that we can come there and see you again. We want to give you everything you need to make your faith strong.

[11]We pray that our God and Father and our Lord Jesus will prepare the way for us to come to you. [12]We pray that the Lord will make your love grow. We pray that he will give you more and more love for each other and for all people. We pray that you will love everyone in the same way we love you. [13]This will strengthen your desire to do what is right, and you will be holy* and without fault before our God and Father when our Lord Jesus comes with all his holy people.*

A Life That Pleases God

4 [1]Brothers and sisters, now I have some other things to tell you. We taught you how to live in a way that will please God. And you are living that way. Now we ask and encourage you in the Lord Jesus to live that way more and more. [2]You know all that we told you to do by the authority of the Lord Jesus. [3]God wants you to be holy.* He wants you to stay away from sexual sins. [4]God wants each one of you to learn to control your own body. Use your body in a way that is holy and that gives honor to God.[b] [5]Don't let your sexual desires control you like the people who don't know God. [6]Never wrong any of your fellow believers* or cheat them in this way. The Lord will punish those who do that. We have already told you this and warned you about it. [7]God chose us to be holy. He does not want us to live in sin. [8]So anyone who refuses to obey this teaching is refusing to obey God, not us. And God is the one who gives you his Holy Spirit.*

[9]We don't need to write to you about having love for your brothers and sisters in Christ. God has already taught you to love each other. [10]In fact, you love the brothers and sisters in all of Macedonia.* We encourage you now, brothers and sisters, to show your love more and more.

[11]Do all you can to live a peaceful life. Mind your own business, and earn your own living, as we told you before. [12]If you do these things, then those who are not believers will respect the way you live. And you will not have to depend on others for what you need.

---

[a]2:14 *Judea* The Jewish land where Jesus lived and taught and where the church first began.

[b]4:4 Or "God wants each of you to learn to live with your wife in a way that is holy and that gives honor to God."

The Lord's Coming

13Brothers and sisters, we want you to know about those who have died. We don't want you to be sad like other people—those who have no hope. 14We believe that Jesus died, but we also believe that he rose again. So we believe that God will raise to life through Jesus any who have died and bring them together with him when he comes.

15What we tell you now is the Lord's own message. Those of us who are still living when the Lord comes again will join him, but not before those who have already died. 16The Lord himself will come down from heaven with a loud command, with the voice of the archangel,* and with the trumpet call of God. And the people who have died and were in Christ will rise first. 17After that, we who are still alive at that time will be gathered up with those who have died. We will be taken up in the clouds and meet the Lord in the air. And we will be with the Lord forever. 18So encourage each other with these words.

Be Ready for the Lord's Coming

5 1Now, brothers and sisters, we don't need to write to you about times and dates. 2You know very well that the day when the Lord comes again will be a surprise, like a thief who comes at night. 3People will say, "We have peace and we are safe." At that time destruction will come to them quickly, like the pains of a woman giving birth. And those people will not escape.

4But you, brothers and sisters, are not living in darkness.* And so that day will not surprise you like a thief. 5You are all people who belong to the light.* You belong to the day.* We don't belong to the night* or to darkness. 6So we should not be like other people. We should not be sleeping. We should be awake and have self-control. 7People who sleep, sleep at night. People who drink too much, drink at night. 8But we belong to the day, so we should control ourselves. We should wear faith and love to protect us. And the hope of salvation should be our helmet.

9God did not choose us to suffer his anger. God chose us to have salvation through our Lord Jesus Christ. 10Jesus died for us so that we can live together with him. It is not important if we are alive or dead when Jesus comes. 11So encourage each other and help each other grow stronger in faith, just as you are already doing.

Final Instructions and Greetings

12Now brothers and sisters, we ask you to recognize the value of those who work hard among you—those who, as followers of the Lord, care for you and tell you how to live. 13Show them the highest respect and love because of the work they do.

Live in peace with each other. 14We ask you, brothers and sisters, to warn those who will not work. Encourage those who are afraid. Help those who are weak. Be patient with everyone. 15Be sure that no one pays back wrong for wrong. But always try to do what is good for each other and for all people.

16Always be full of joy. 17Never stop praying. 18Whatever happens, always be thankful. This is how God wants you to live in Christ Jesus.

19Don't stop the work of the Holy Spirit.* 20Don't treat prophecy* like something that is not important. 21But test everything. Keep what is good, 22and stay away from everything that is evil.

23We pray that God himself, the God of peace, will make you pure—belonging only to him. We pray that your whole self—spirit, soul, and body—will be kept safe and be blameless when our Lord Jesus Christ comes. 24The one who chose you will do that for you. You can trust him.

25Brothers and sisters, please pray for us. 26Give all the brothers and sisters the special greeting of God's people.*a* 27I tell you by the authority of the Lord to read this letter to all the brothers and sisters. 28The grace* of our Lord Jesus Christ be with you.

*a*5:26 *the special greeting of God's people* Literally, "a holy kiss."

2 Thessalonians

1 1Greetings from Paul, Silas, and Timothy. To the church* of those in Thessalonica, who are in God our Father and the Lord Jesus Christ.

2Grace* and peace to you from God the Father and the Lord Jesus Christ.

3We thank God for you always. And that's what we should do, because you give us good reason to be thankful: Your faith is growing more and more. And the love that every one of you has for each other is also growing. 4So we tell the other churches of God how proud we are of you. We tell them how you patiently continue to be strong and have faith, even though you are being persecuted* and are suffering many troubles.

Paul Tells About God's Judgment

⁵This is proof that God is right in his judgment. He wants you to be worthy of his kingdom.* Your suffering is for that kingdom. ⁶God will do what is right. He will punish those who are causing you trouble. ⁷And he will bring relief to you who are troubled. He will bring it to you and to us when the Lord Jesus comes from heaven for all to see, together with his powerful angels. ⁸He will come with burning fire to punish those who don't know God—those who refuse to accept the Good News* about our Lord Jesus Christ. ⁹They will be punished with a destruction that never ends. They will not be allowed to be with the Lord but will be kept away from his great power. ¹⁰This will happen on the day when the Lord Jesus comes to receive honor with his holy people.* He will be admired among all who have believed. And this includes you because you believed what we told you.

¹¹That is why we always pray for you. We ask our God to help you live the good way he wanted when he chose you. The goodness you have makes you want to do good. And the faith you have makes you work. We pray that with his power God will help you do these things more and more. ¹²Then the name of our Lord Jesus will be honored because of you, and you will be honored because of him. This can happen only by the grace* of our God and the Lord Jesus Christ.

Evil Things Will Happen

2 ¹Brothers and sisters, we have something to say about the coming of our Lord Jesus Christ. We want to talk to you about that time when we will meet together with him. ²Don't let yourselves be easily upset or worried if you hear that the day of the Lord has already come. Someone might say that this idea came from us—in something the Spirit* told us, or in something we said, or in a letter we wrote. ³Don't be fooled by anything they might say. That day of the Lord will not come until the turning away from God happens. And that day will not come until the Man of Evil appears, the one who belongs to hell.ᵃ ⁴He will stand against and put himself above everything that people worship or think is worthy of worship. He will even go into God's Templeᵇ and sit there, claiming that he is God.

⁵I told you before that all these things would happen. Remember? ⁶And you know

what is stopping that Man of Evil now. He is being stopped now so that he will appear at the right time. ⁷The secret power of evil is already working in the world now. But there is one who is stopping that secret power of evil. And he will continue to stop it until he is taken out of the way. ⁸Then that Man of Evil will appear. But the Lord Jesus will kill him with the breath that comes from his mouth. The Lord will come in a way that everyone will see, and that will be the end of the Man of Evil.

⁹When that Man of Evil comes, it will be the work of Satan.* He will come with great power, and he will do all kinds of false miracles, signs, and wonders. ¹⁰The Man of Evil will use every kind of evil to fool those who are lost. They are lost because they refused to love the truth and be saved. ¹¹So God will send them something powerful that leads them away from the truth and causes them to believe a lie. ¹²They will all be condemned because they did not believe the truth and because they enjoyed doing evil.

You Are Chosen for Salvation

¹³Brothers and sisters, you are people the Lord loves. And we always thank God for you. That's what we should do, because God chose you to be some of the first peopleᶜ to be saved. You are saved by the Spirit* making you holy* and by your faith in the truth. ¹⁴God chose you to have that salvation. He chose you by using the Good News* that we told you. You were chosen so that you can share in the glory* of our Lord Jesus Christ. ¹⁵So, brothers and sisters, stand strong and continue to believe the teachings we gave you when we were there and by letter.

¹⁶⁻¹⁷We pray that the Lord Jesus Christ himself and God our Father will comfort you and strengthen you in every good thing you do and say. God loved us and gave us through his grace* a wonderful hope and comfort that has no end.

Pray for Us

3 ¹And now, brothers and sisters, pray for us. Pray that the Lord's teaching will continue to spread quickly. And pray that people will give honor to that teaching, the same as happened with you. ²And pray that we will be protected from crooked and evil people. Not everyone believes in the Lord, you know.

³But the Lord is faithful. He will give you strength and protect you from the Evil One.* ⁴The Lord gives us confidence that you are doing what we told you and that you will continue to do it. ⁵We pray that the Lord will cause you to feel God's love and remember Christ's patient endurance.

ᵃ2:3 belongs to hell Literally, "is the son of destruction."
ᵇ2:4 Temple Probably the Temple in Jerusalem. See "Temple" in the Word List.
ᶜ2:13 to be … people Some Greek copies say, "from the beginning."

The Obligation to Work

6Brothers and sisters, by the authority of our Lord Jesus Christ we tell you to stay away from any believer who refuses to work. People who refuse to work are not following the teaching that we gave them. 7You yourselves know that you should live like we do. We were not lazy when we were with you. 8We never accepted food from anyone without paying for it. We worked and worked so that we would not be a burden to any of you. We worked night and day. 9We had the right to ask you to help us. But we worked to take care of ourselves so that we would be an example for you to follow. 10When we were with you, we gave you this rule: "Whoever will not work should not be allowed to eat."

11We hear that some people in your group refuse to work. They are doing nothing except being busy in the lives of others. 12Our instruction to them is to stop bothering others, to start working and earn their own food. It is by the authority of the Lord Jesus Christ that we are urging them to do this. 13Brothers and sisters, never get tired of doing good.

14If there are some there who refuse to do what we tell you in this letter, remember who they are. Don't associate with them. Then maybe they will feel ashamed. 15But don't treat them as enemies. Counsel them as fellow believers.*

Final Words

16We pray that the Lord of peace will give you peace at all times and in every way. The Lord be with you all.

17Here's my greeting in my own handwriting—PAUL. I do this in all my letters to show they are from me. This is the way I write.

18The grace* of our Lord Jesus Christ be with you all.

1 Timothy

1

1Greetings from Paul, an apostle* of Christ Jesus. I am an apostle by the command of God our Savior and Christ Jesus our hope.

2To Timothy, a true son to me in the faith we share.

Grace,* mercy, and peace from God the Father and Christ Jesus our Lord.

Warnings Against False Teachings

3When I went to Macedonia,* I asked you to stay in Ephesus. Some people there are teaching things that are not true, and I want you to tell them to stop. 4Tell them not to give their time to meaningless stories and to long lists of names to prove their family histories. Such things only cause arguments. They don't help God's work, which is done only by faith. 5My purpose in telling you to do this is to promote love—the kind of love shown by those whose thoughts are pure, who do what they know is right, and whose faith in God is real. 6But some have missed this key point in their teaching and have gone off in another direction. Now they talk about things that help no one. 7They want to be teachers of the law,a but they don't know what they are talking about. They don't even understand the things they say they are sure of.

8We know that the law is good if someone uses it right. 9We also know that the law is not made for those who do what is right. It is made for those who are against the law and refuse to follow it. The law is for sinners who are against God and all that is pleasing to him. It is for those who have no interest in spiritual things and for those who kill their fathers or mothers or anyone else. 10It is for those who commit sexual sins, homosexuals, those who sell slaves, those who tell lies, those who don't tell the truth under oath, and those who are against the true teaching of God. 11That teaching is part of the Good News* that our blessed God gave me to tell. In it we see his glory.*

Thanks for God's Mercy

12I thank Christ Jesus our Lord because he trusted me and gave me this work of serving him. He gives me strength. 13In the past I insulted Christ. As a proud and violent man, I persecuted his people. But God gave me mercy because I did not know what I was doing. I did that before I became a believer. 14But our Lord gave me a full measure of his grace.* And with that grace came the faith and love that are in Christ Jesus.

15Here is a true statement that should be accepted without question: Christ Jesus came into the world to save sinners, and I am the worst of them. 16But I was given mercy so that in me Christ Jesus could show that he

---

a1:7 law Probably the Jewish law that God gave to Moses on Mount Sinai. See Ex. 19 and 20. Also in verse 8.

has patience without limit. Christ showed his patience with me, the worst of all sinners. He wanted me to be an example for those who would believe in him and have eternal life. [17]Honor and glory* to the King who rules forever. He cannot be destroyed and cannot be seen. Honor and glory forever and ever to the only God. Amen.*

[18]Timothy, you are like a son to me. What I am telling you to do agrees with the prophecies[a] that were told about you in the past. I want you to remember those prophecies and fight the good fight of faith. [19]Continue to trust in God and do what you know is right. Some people have not done this, and their faith is now in ruins. [20]Hymenaeus and Alexander are men like that. I have given them to Satan* so that they will learn not to speak against God.

God Wants Us to Pray for Everyone

2 [1]First of all, I ask that you pray for all people. Ask God to bless them and give them what they need. And give thanks. [2]You should pray for rulers and for all who have authority. Pray for these leaders so that we can live quiet and peaceful lives—lives full of devotion to God and respect for him. [3]This is good and pleases God our Savior.

[4]God wants everyone to be saved and to fully understand the truth. [5]There is only one God, and there is only one way that people can reach God. That way is through Christ Jesus, who as a man [6]gave himself to pay for everyone to be free. This is the message that was given to us at just the right time. [7]And I was chosen as an apostle* to tell people that message. (I am telling the truth. I am not lying.) I was chosen to teach those who are not Jews to believe and understand the truth.

Special Instructions for Men and Women

[8]I want the men everywhere to pray. Men who lift their hands in prayer must be devoted to God and pleasing to him. They must be men who keep themselves from getting angry and having arguments.

[9]And I want the women to make themselves attractive in the right way. Their clothes should be sensible and appropriate. They should not draw attention to themselves with fancy hairstyles or gold jewelry or pearls or expensive clothes. [10]But they should make themselves attractive by the good things they do. That is more appropriate for women who say they are devoted to God.

[11]A woman should learn while listening quietly and being completely willing to obey. [12]I don't allow a woman to teach a man or tell him what to do. She must listen quietly, [13]because Adam was made first. Eve was made later. [14]Also, Adam was not the one who was

tricked.[b] It was the woman who was tricked and became a sinner. [15]But women will be saved in their work of having children. They will be saved if they continue to live in faith, love, and holiness with sensible behavior.

Leaders in the Church

3 [1]It is a true statement that anyone whose goal is to serve as an elder[c] has his heart set on a good work. [2]An elder[d] must be such a good man that no one can rightly criticize him. He must be faithful to his wife.[e] He must have self-control and be wise. He must be respected by others. He must be ready to help people by welcoming them into his home. He must be a good teacher. [3]He must not drink too much, and he must not be someone who likes to fight. He must be gentle and peaceful. He must not be someone who loves money. [4]He must be a good leader of his own family. This means that his children obey him with full respect. [5]If a man does not know how to lead his own family, he will not be able to take care of God's church.*

[6]An elder must not be a new believer. It might make him too proud of himself. Then he would be condemned for his pride the same as the devil was. [7]An elder must also have the respect of people who are not part of the church. Then he will not be criticized by others and be caught in the devil's trap.

Special Servants

[8]In the same way, the men who are chosen to be special servants* must have the respect of others. They must not be men who say things they don't mean or who spend their time drinking too much. They must not be men who will do almost anything for money. [9]They must follow the true faith that God has now made known to us and always do what they know is right. [10]You should test them first. Then, if you find that they have done nothing wrong, they can be special servants.

[11]In the same way, the women[f] must have the respect of others. They must not be women who speak evil about other people. They must have self-control and be women who can be trusted in everything.

[12]The men who are special servants must be faithful in marriage.[g] They must be good

---

[a]*1:18 prophecies* Things that prophets said about Timothy's life before those things happened.

[b]*2:14 Adam was not ... tricked* The devil tricked Eve, and Eve caused Adam to sin. See Gen. 3:1–13.

[c]*3:1 whose ... elder* Literally, "who aspires to supervision."

[d]*3:2 elder* Here, literally, "overseer." See "elders" in the Word List.

[e]*3:2 faithful to his wife* Literally, "a man of one woman."

[f]*3:11 women* Probably the women who serve as special servants (See Rom. 16:1). It could be translated, "their wives," meaning the wives of the special servants, although there is no word for "their" in the Greek text.

[g]*3:12 faithful in marriage* Literally, "a man of one woman."

leaders of children and their own families. [13]Those who do well as special servants are making an honorable place for themselves. And they will feel very sure of their faith in Christ Jesus.

The Secret of Our Life

[14]I hope I can come to you soon. But I am writing this to you now, [15]so that, even if I cannot come soon, you will know how people should live in the family[a] of God. That family is the church* of the living God. And God's church is the support and foundation of the truth. [16]Without a doubt, the secret of our life of worship is great:

Christ[b] was shown to us in human form;
the Spirit* proved that he was right;
he was seen by angels.
The message* about him was told to the nations;
people in the world believed in him;
he was taken up to heaven in glory.*

A Warning About False Teachers

4 [1]The Spirit* clearly says that in the last times some will turn away from what we believe. They will obey spirits that tell lies. And they will follow the teachings of demons.* [2]Those teachings come through people who tell lies and trick others. These evil people cannot see what is right and what is wrong. It is like their conscience has been destroyed with a hot iron. [3]They say that it is wrong to marry. And they say that there are some foods that people must not eat. But God made these foods, and those who believe and who understand the truth can eat them with thanks. [4]Everything that God made is good. Nothing he made should be refused if it is accepted with thanks to him. [5]Everything he created is made holy* by what he has said and by prayer.

Be a Good Servant of Christ Jesus

[6]Tell this to the brothers and sisters there. This will show that you are a good servant of Christ Jesus. You will show that you are made strong by the words of faith and good teaching you have followed. [7]People tell silly stories that don't agree with God's truth. Don't follow what these stories teach. But teach yourself to be devoted to God. [8]Training your body helps you in some ways. But devotion to God helps you in every way. It brings you blessings in this life and in the future life too. [9]Here is a true statement that should be accepted without question: [10]We hope in the living God, the Savior of all people. In particular, he is the Savior of all those who believe in him. This is why we work and struggle.

[11]Command and teach these things. [12]You are young, but don't let anyone treat you as if you are not important. Be an example to show the believers how they should live. Show them by what you say, by the way you live, by your love, by your faith, and by your pure life. [13]Continue to read the Scriptures* to the people, encourage them, and teach them. Do this until I come. [14]Remember to use the gift you have, which was given to you through a prophecy[c] when the group of elders* laid their hands on* you. [15]Continue to do these things. Give your life to doing them. Then everyone can see that your work is progressing. [16]Be careful in your life and in your teaching. Continue to live and teach rightly. Then you will save yourself and those who listen to your teaching.

5 [1]Don't speak angrily to an older man. But talk to him as if he were your father. Treat the younger men like brothers. [2]Treat the older women like mothers. And treat the younger women with respect like sisters.

Taking Care of Widows

[3]Take care of widows who really need help. [4]But if a widow has children or grandchildren, the first thing they need to learn is this: to show their devotion to God by taking care of their own family. They will be repaying their parents, and this pleases God. [5]A widow who really needs help is one who has been left all alone. She trusts God to take care of her. She prays all the time, night and day, and asks God for help. [6]But the widow who uses her life to please herself is really dead while she is still living. [7]Tell the believers there to take care of their family so that no one can say they are doing wrong. [8]Everyone should take care of all their own people. Most important, they should take care of their own family. If they do not do that, then they do not accept what we believe. They are worse than someone who does not even believe in God.

[9]To be added to your list of widows, a woman must be 60 years old or older. She must have been faithful to her husband.[d] [10]She must be known for the good she has done: raising children, welcoming travelers into her home, serving the needs[e] of God's people, helping those in trouble, and using her life to do all kinds of good.

[11]But don't put younger widows on that list. When their strong physical needs pull them away from their commitment to Christ, they will want to marry again. [12]Then they will be guilty of not doing what they first promised to do. [13]Also, these younger widows begin to

[c]**4:14** *prophecy* Something said about Timothy's life before that thing happened.
[d]**5:9** *faithful to her husband* Literally, "a woman of one man."
[e]**5:10** *serving the needs* Literally, "washing the feet," a social custom of the first century, because people wore open sandals on very dusty roads.

[a]**3:15** *family* Literally, "house." This could mean that God's people are like God's temple.
[b]**3:16** *Christ* Literally, "who." Some Greek copies have "God."

waste their time going from house to house. They also begin to gossip and try to run other people's lives. They say things they should not say. ¹⁴So I want the younger widows to marry, have children, and take care of their homes. If they do this, our enemy will not have any reason to criticize them. ¹⁵But some of the younger widows have already turned away to follow Satan.*

¹⁶If any woman who is a believer has widows in her family, she*a* should take care of them herself. Then the church* will not have that burden and will be able to care for the widows who have no one else to help them.

More About Elders and Other Matters

¹⁷The elders* who lead the church in a good way should receive double honor*b*—in particular, those who do the work of counseling and teaching. ¹⁸As the Scriptures* say, "When a work animal is being used to separate grain, don't keep it from eating the grain."*c* And the Scriptures also say, "A worker should be given his pay."*d*

¹⁹Don't listen to someone who accuses an elder. You should listen to them only if there are two or three others who can say what the elder did wrong. ²⁰Tell those who sin that they are wrong. Do this in front of the whole church so that the others will have a warning.

²¹Before God and Jesus Christ and the chosen angels, I tell you to make these judgments without any prejudice. Treat every person the same.

²²Think carefully before you lay your hands on* anyone to make him an elder. Don't share in the sins of others. Keep yourself pure.

²³Timothy, stop drinking only water, and drink a little wine. This will help your stomach, and you will not be sick so often.

²⁴The sins of some people are easy to see. Their sins show that they will be judged. But the sins of some others are seen only later. ²⁵It is the same with the good things people do. Some are easy to see. But even if they are not obvious now, none of them will stay hidden forever.

Special Instructions for Slaves

6 ¹All those who are slaves should show full respect to their masters. Then God's name and our teaching will not be criticized. ²Some slaves have masters who are believers, so they are brothers. Does this mean they should show their masters any less respect? No, they should serve them even better, because they are helping believers, people they should love.

This is what you must teach and tell everyone to do.

False Teaching and True Riches

³Some people will teach what is false and will not agree with the true teaching of our Lord Jesus Christ. They will not accept the teaching that produces a life of devotion to God. ⁴They are proud of what they know, but they understand nothing. They are sick with a love for arguing and fighting about words. And that brings jealousy, quarrels, insults, and evil mistrust. ⁵They are always making trouble, because they are people whose thinking has been confused. They have lost their understanding of the truth. They think that devotion to God is a way to get rich.

⁶Devotion to God is, in fact, a way for people to be very rich, but only if it makes them satisfied with what they have. ⁷When we came into the world, we brought nothing. And when we die, we can take nothing out. ⁸So, if we have food and clothes, we will be satisfied with that. ⁹People who want to be rich bring temptations to themselves. They are caught in a trap. They begin to want many foolish things that will hurt them. These things ruin and destroy people. ¹⁰The love of money causes all kinds of evil. Some people have turned away from what we believe because they want to get more and more money. But they have caused themselves a lot of pain and sorrow.

Some Things to Remember

¹¹But you belong to God. So you should stay away from all those things. Always try to do what is right, to be devoted to God, and to have faith, love, patience, and gentleness. ¹²We have to fight to keep our faith. Try as hard as you can to win that fight. Take hold of eternal life. It is the life you were chosen to have when you confessed your faith in Jesus— that wonderful truth that you spoke so openly and that so many people heard. ¹³Before God and Christ Jesus I give you a command. Jesus is the one who confessed that same wonderful truth when he stood before Pontius Pilate.* And God is the one who gives life to everything. Now I tell you this: ¹⁴Do what you were commanded to do without fault or blame until the time when our Lord Jesus Christ comes again. ¹⁵God will make that happen at the right time. God is the blessed and only Ruler. He is the King of all kings and the Lord of all lords. ¹⁶God is the only one who never dies. He lives in light so bright that people cannot go near it. No one has ever seen him; no one is able to see him. All honor and power belong to him forever. Amen.*

¹⁷Give this command to those who are rich with the things of this world. Tell them not to be proud. Tell them to hope in God, not their money. Money cannot be trusted, but God takes care of us richly. He gives us everything to enjoy. ¹⁸Tell those who are rich to do good—to be rich in good works. And tell them they should be happy to give and

---

*a***5:16** *woman … she* Some Greek copies have "man or woman … he/she."

*b***5:17** *double honor* Or "double pay."

*c***5:18** Quote from Deut. 25:4.

*d***5:18** Quote from Lk. 10:7.

ready to share. [19]By doing this, they will be saving up a treasure for themselves. And that treasure will be a strong foundation on which their future life will be built. They will be able to have the life that is true life.

[20]Timothy, God has trusted you with many things. Keep these things safe. Stay away from people who talk about useless things that are not from God and who argue against you with a "knowledge" that is not knowledge at all. [21]Some people who claim to have that "knowledge" have gone completely away from what we believe.

God's grace* be with you all.

2 Timothy

1 [1]Greetings from Paul, an apostle* of Christ Jesus. I am an apostle because God wanted me to be. God sent me to tell people about the promise of life that is in Christ Jesus.

[2]To Timothy, a dear son to me.

Grace,* mercy, and peace to you from God the Father and from Christ Jesus our Lord.

Thanksgiving and Encouragement

[3]I always remember you in my prayers day and night. And in these prayers I thank God for you. He is the God my ancestors* served, and I have always served him with a clear conscience. [4]I remember that you cried for me. I want very much to see you so that I can be filled with joy. [5]I remember your true faith. That kind of faith first belonged to your grandmother Lois and to your mother Eunice. I know you now have that same faith. [6]That is why I want you to remember the gift God gave you. God gave you that gift when I laid my hands on* you. Now I want you to use that gift and let it grow more and more, like a small flame grows into a fire. [7]The Spirit* God gave us does not make us afraid. His Spirit is a source of power and love and self-control.

[8]So don't be ashamed to tell people about our Lord Jesus. And don't be ashamed of me—I am in prison for the Lord. But suffer with me for the Good News.* God gives us the strength to do that.

[9]God saved us and chose us to be his holy* people, but not because of anything we ourselves did. God saved us and made us his people because that was what he wanted and because of his grace.* That grace was given to us through Christ Jesus before time began. [10]And now it has been shown to us in the coming of our Savior Christ Jesus. He destroyed death and showed us the way to have life. Yes, through the Good News Jesus showed us the way to have life that cannot be destroyed.

[11]I was chosen to tell people that message as an apostle* and teacher. [12]And I suffer now because of that work. But I am not ashamed. I know the one I have believed, and I am sure that he is able to protect what he has trusted me with until that Day.*

[13]What you heard me teach is an example of what you should teach. Follow that model of right teaching with the faith and love we have in Christ Jesus. [14]This teaching is a treasure that you have been trusted with. Protect it with the help of the Holy Spirit, who lives inside us.

[15]You know that everyone in Asia* has left me. Even Phygelus and Hermogenes have left me. [16]I pray that the Lord will show mercy to the family of Onesiphorus. Many times Onesiphorus encouraged me. He was not ashamed that I was in prison. [17]No, he was not ashamed. When he came to Rome, he looked and looked for me until he found me. [18]I pray that the Lord Jesus will make sure Onesiphorus receives mercy from the Lord God on that Day. You know how many ways this brother helped me in Ephesus.

A Loyal Soldier of Christ Jesus

2 [1]Timothy, you are a son to me. Be strong in the grace* that we have because we belong to Christ Jesus. [2]What you have heard me teach publicly you should teach to others. Share these teachings with people you can trust. Then they will be able to teach others these same things. [3]As a good soldier of Christ Jesus, accept your share of the troubles we have. [4]A soldier wants to please his commanding officer, so he does not spend any time on activities that are not a part of his duty. [5]Athletes in a race must obey all the rules to win. [6]The farmer who works hard deserves the first part of the harvest. [7]Think about what I am saying. The Lord will help you understand it all.

[8]Remember Jesus Christ. He is from the family of David.* After Jesus died, he was raised from death. This is the Good News* that I tell people. [9]And because I tell that message, I am suffering. I am even bound with chains like someone who has really done wrong. But God's message is not bound. [10]So I patiently accept all these troubles. I do this to help the

people God has chosen so that they can have the salvation that is in Christ Jesus. With this salvation comes glory* that never ends.

[11]Here is a true statement:

If we died with him, we will also live
    with him.
[12] If we remain faithful even in suffering, we
    will also rule with him.
If we refuse to say we know him, he will
    refuse to say he knows us.
[13] If we are not faithful, he will still be
    faithful,
because he cannot be false to himself.

A Worker Who Pleases God

[14]Keep on telling everyone these truths. And warn them before God not to argue about words. Such arguments don't help anyone, and they ruin those who listen to them. [15]Do your best to be the kind of person God will accept, and give yourself to him. Be a worker who has no reason to be ashamed of his work, one who applies the true teaching in the right way.

[16]Stay away from people who talk about useless things that are not from God. That kind of talk will lead a person more and more against God. [17]Their evil teaching will spread like a sickness inside the body. Hymenaeus and Philetus are men like that. [18]They have left the true teaching. They say that the day when people will be raised from death has already come and gone. And they are destroying the faith of some people.

[19]But God's strong foundation never moves, and these words are written on it: "The Lord knows those who belong to him."[a] Also, these words are written there: "Everyone who says they believe in the Lord must stop doing wrong."

[20]In a large house there are things made of gold and silver. But there are also things made of wood and clay. Some of these are used for special purposes, others for ordinary jobs. [21]The Lord wants to use you for special purposes, so make yourself clean from all evil. Then you will be holy,* and the Master can use you. You will be ready for any good work.

[22]Stay away from the evil things a young person like you typically wants to do. Do your best to live right and to have faith, love, and peace, together with others who trust in the Lord with pure hearts. [23]Stay away from foolish and stupid arguments. You know that these arguments grow into bigger arguments. [24]As a servant of the Lord, you must not argue. You must be kind to everyone. You must be a good teacher, and you must be patient. [25]You must gently teach those who don't agree with you. Maybe God will let them change their hearts so that they can accept the truth. [26]The devil

has trapped them and now makes them do what he wants. But maybe they can wake up to see what is happening and free themselves from the devil's trap.

Many People Will Stop Loving God

3 [1]Remember this: There are some terrible times coming in the last days. [2]People will love only themselves and money. They will be proud and boast about themselves. They will abuse others with insults. They will not obey their parents. They will be ungrateful and against all that is pleasing to God. [3]They will have no love for others and will refuse to forgive anyone. They will talk about others to hurt them and will have no self-control. They will be cruel and hate what is good. [4]People will turn against their friends. They will do foolish things without thinking and will be so proud of themselves. Instead of loving God, they will love pleasure. [5]They will go on pretending to be devoted to God, but they will refuse to let that "devotion" change the way they live. Stay away from these people!

[6]Some of them go into homes and get control over weak women, whose lives are full of sin—women who are led into sin by all the things they want. [7]These women always want to learn something new, but they are never able to fully understand the truth. [8]Just as Jannes and Jambres[b] fought against Moses,* these people fight against the truth. Their thinking has been confused. The faith they have and teach is worthless. [9]But they will not succeed in what they are trying to do. Everyone will see how foolish they are. That is what happened to Jannes and Jambres.

Last Instructions

[10]But you know all about me. You know what I teach and the way I live. You know my goal in life. You know my faith, my patience, and my love. You know that I never stop trying. [11]You know about my persecutions* and my sufferings. You know all the things that happened to me in Antioch, Iconium, and Lystra—the persecution I suffered in those places. But the Lord saved me from all of it. [12]Everyone who wants to live showing true devotion to God in Christ Jesus will be persecuted. [13]People who are evil and cheat others will become worse and worse. They will fool others, but they will also be fooling themselves.

[14]But you should continue following the teaching you learned. You know it is true, because you know you can trust those who taught you. [15]You have known the Holy Scriptures[c] since you were a child. These

---

[a]2:19 Quote from Num. 16:5.

[b]3:8 *Jannes and Jambres* Probably the magicians who opposed Moses in Pharaoh's court. See Ex. 7:11–12, 22.

[c]3:15 *Holy Scriptures* Writings that Jews and followers of Christ accepted to be from God—the Old Testament.

Scriptures are able to make you wise. And that wisdom leads to salvation through faith in Christ Jesus. 16All Scripture is given by God. And all Scripture is useful for teaching and for showing people what is wrong in their lives. It is useful for correcting faults and teaching the right way to live. 17Using the Scriptures, those who serve God will be prepared and will have everything they need to do every good work.

4 1Before God and Jesus Christ I give you a command. Christ Jesus is the one who will judge all people—those who are living and those who have died. He is coming again to rule in his kingdom.* So I give you this command: 2Tell everyone God's message.* Be ready at all times to do whatever is needed. Tell people what they need to do, tell them when they are doing wrong, and encourage them. Do this with great patience and careful teaching.

3The time will come when people will not listen to the true teaching. But people will find more and more teachers who please them. They will find teachers who say what they want to hear. 4People will stop listening to the truth. They will begin to follow the teaching in false stories. 5But you should control yourself at all times. When troubles come, accept them. Do the work of telling the Good News.* Do all the duties of a servant of God.

6My life is being given as an offering for God. The time has come for me to leave this life here. 7I have fought the good fight. I have finished the race. I have served the Lord faithfully. 8Now, a prize is waiting for me—the crown* that will show I am right with God. The Lord, the judge who judges rightly, will give it to me on that Day.* Yes, he will give it to me and to everyone else who is eagerly looking forward to his coming.

Personal Notes

9Do your best to come to me as soon as you can. 10Demas loved this world too much. That is why he left me. He went to Thessalonica. Crescens went to Galatia. And Titus went to Dalmatia. 11Luke is the only one still with me. Get Mark and bring him with you when you come. He can help me in my work here. 12I sent Tychicus to Ephesus.

13When I was in Troas, I left my coat there with Carpus. So when you come, bring it to me. Also, bring my books. The books written on parchment* are the ones I need.

14Alexander the metalworker caused me so much harm. The Lord will punish him for what he did. 15He fought against everything we teach. You should be careful that he doesn't hurt you too.

16The first time I defended myself, no one helped me. Everyone left me. I pray that God will forgive them. 17But the Lord stayed with me. The Lord gave me strength so that I could tell the Good News* everywhere. He wanted all those who are not Jews to hear that Good News. So I was saved from the lion's mouth. 18The Lord will save me when anyone tries to hurt me. He will bring me safely to his heavenly kingdom. Glory* forever and ever be the Lord's. Amen.*

Final Greetings

19Give my greetings to Priscilla and Aquila and to the family of Onesiphorus. 20Erastus stayed in Corinth. And I left Trophimus in Miletus—he was sick. 21Try as hard as you can to come to me before winter.

Greetings to you from Eubulus, Pudens, Linus, Claudia, and all the brothers and sisters here.

22The Lord be with your spirit. Grace* be with you.

Titus

1 1Greetings from Paul, a servant of God and an apostle* of Jesus Christ. I was sent to help God's chosen people have faith and understand the truth that produces a life of devotion to God. 2This faith and knowledge make us sure that we have eternal life. God promised that life to us before time began—and God does not lie. 3At the right time, God let the world know about that life. He did this through the telling of the Good News message,* and he trusted me with that work. I told people that message because God our Savior commanded me to.

4To Titus, a true son to me in the faith we share together.

Grace* and peace to you from God the Father and Christ Jesus our Savior.

Titus' Work in Crete

5I left you in Crete so that you could finish doing what still needed to be done. And I also left you there so that you could choose men to be elders* in every town. 6To be an elder, a man must not be guilty of living in a wrong way. He must be faithful to his wife,[a] and his children must be faithful to God.[b] They must not be known as children who are wild or don't obey. [7]An elder[c] has the job of taking care of God's work. So people should not be able to say that he lives in a wrong way. He must not be someone who is proud and selfish or who gets angry quickly. He must not drink too much, and he must not be someone who likes to fight. He must not be a man who will do almost anything for money. [8]An elder must be ready to help people by welcoming them into his home. He must love what is good. He must be wise. He must live right. He must be devoted to God and pleasing to him. And he must be able to control himself. [9]An elder must be faithful to the same true message we teach. Then he will be able to encourage others with teaching that is true and right. And he will be able to show those who are against this teaching that they are wrong.

[10]This is important, because there are many people who refuse to obey—people who talk about worthless things and mislead others. I am talking especially about those who say that men who are not Jews must be circumcised* to please God. [11]These people must be stopped, because they are destroying whole families by teaching what they should not teach. They teach only to cheat people and make money. [12]Even one of their own prophets said, "Cretans are always liars. They are evil animals and lazy people who do nothing but eat." [13]The words that prophet said are true. So tell those people that they are wrong. You must be strict with them. Then they will become strong in the faith, [14]and then they will stop paying attention to the stories told by these Jews. They will stop following the commands of those who have turned away from the truth.

[15]To people who are pure, everything is pure. But to those who are full of sin and don't believe, nothing is pure. Really, their thinking has become evil and their consciences have been ruined. [16]They say they know God, but the evil things they do show that they don't accept him. They are disgusting. They refuse to obey God and are not capable of doing anything good.

Following the True Teaching

2 [1]You, however, must tell everyone how to live in a way that agrees with the true teaching. [2]Teach the older men to have self-control, to be serious, and to be wise. They must be strong in faith, in love, and in patience.

[3]Also, teach the older women to live the

way those who serve the Lord should live. They should not go around saying bad things about others or be in the habit of drinking too much. They should teach what is good. [4]By doing this they will teach the younger women to love their husbands and children. [5]They will teach them to be wise and pure, to take care of their homes, to be kind, and to be willing to serve their husbands. Then no one will be able to criticize the teaching God gave us.

[6]In the same way, tell the young men to be wise. [7]You should be an example for them in every way by the good things you do. When you teach, be honest and serious. [8]And your teaching should be clearly right so that you cannot be criticized. Then anyone who is against you will be ashamed. There will not be anything bad they can say about us.

[9]And tell this to those who are slaves: They should be willing to serve their masters at all times; they should try to please them, not argue with them; [10]they should not steal from them; and they should show their masters that they can be trusted. Then, in everything they do, they will show that the teaching of God our Savior is good.

[11]That is the way we should live, because God's grace* has come. That grace can save everyone. [12]It teaches us not to live against God and not to do the bad things the world wants to do. It teaches us to live on earth now in a wise and right way—a way that shows true devotion to God. [13]We should live like that while we are waiting for the coming of our great God and Savior Jesus Christ. He is our great hope, and he will come with glory.* [14]He gave himself for us. He died to free us from all evil. He died to make us pure—people who belong only to him and who always want to do good.

[15]These are the things you should tell people. Encourage them, and when they are wrong, correct them. You have full authority to do this, so don't let anyone think they can ignore you.

The Right Way to Live

3 [1]Remind your people that they should always be under the authority of rulers and government leaders. They should obey these leaders and be ready to do good. [2]Tell them not to speak evil of anyone but to live in peace with others. They should be gentle and polite to everyone.

[3]In the past we were foolish too. We did not obey, we were wrong, and we were slaves to the many things our bodies wanted and enjoyed. We lived doing evil and being jealous. People hated us and we hated each other. [4]But then the kindness and love of God our Savior was made known. [5]He saved us because of his mercy, not because of any good things we did. He saved us through the washing that made us new people. He saved us by making us new through the Holy Spirit.* [6]God poured out to

---

[a]1:6 *faithful to his wife* Literally, "a man of one woman."

[b]1:6 *faithful to God* This word can mean "trustworthy" or "believers." Here, both meanings may be included. Compare this verse with 1 Tim. 3:4.

[c]1:7 *elder* Here, literally, "overseer." See "elders" in the Word List.

us that Holy Spirit fully through Jesus Christ our Savior. [7]We were made right with God by his grace.* God saved us so that we could be his children and look forward to receiving life that never ends. [8]This is a true statement.

And I want you to be sure that the people understand these things. Then those who believe in God will be careful to use their lives for doing good. These things are good and will help everyone.

[9]Stay away from those who have foolish arguments, who talk about useless family histories, or who make trouble and fight about what the Law of Moses teaches. These things are useless and will not help anyone. [10]Give a warning to all those who cause arguments. If they continue to cause trouble after a second warning, then don't associate with them.

[11]You know that people like that are evil and sinful. Their sins prove they are wrong.

Final Instructions and Greetings

[12]I will send Artemas and Tychicus to you. When I send them, try hard to come to me at Nicopolis. I have decided to stay there this winter. [13]Zenas the lawyer and Apollos will be traveling from there. Do all that you can to help them prepare for their trip. Be sure that they have everything they need. [14]Our people must learn to use their lives for doing good and helping anyone who has a need. Then they will not have empty lives.

[15]All the people with me here send you their greetings. Give my greetings to those who love us in the faith.

Grace* be with you all.

Philemon

[1]Greetings from Paul, a prisoner for Jesus Christ, and from Timothy, our brother.

To Philemon, our dear friend and worker with us. [2]Also to our sister Apphia, to Archippus, who serves with us in the Lord's army, and to the church* that meets in your home.

[3]Grace* and peace to you from God our Father and the Lord Jesus Christ.

Philemon's Love and Faith

[4]I remember you in my prayers. And I always thank my God for you. [5]I thank God because I hear about the love you have for all of God's holy people* and the faith you have in the Lord Jesus. [6]I pray that the faith you share will make you understand every blessing we have in Christ. [7]My brother, you have shown love to God's people, and your help has greatly encouraged them. What a great joy and encouragement that has been to me.

Accept Onesimus as a Brother

[8]There is something that you should do. And because of the authority I have in Christ, I feel free to command you to do it. [9]But I am not commanding you; I am asking you to do it out of love. I, Paul, am an old man now, and I am a prisoner for Christ Jesus. [10]I am asking you for my son Onesimus. He became my son while I was in prison. [11]In the past he was useless to you. But now he has become useful[a] for both you and me.

[12]I am sending him back to you, but it's as hard as losing part of myself. [13]I would like to keep him here to help me while I am still in prison for telling the Good News.* By helping me here, he would be representing you. [14]But I did not want to do anything without asking you first. Then whatever you do for me will be what you want to do, not what I forced you to do.

[15]Onesimus was separated from you for a short time. Maybe that happened so that you could have him back forever, [16]not to be just a slave, but better than a slave, to be a dear brother. That's what he is to me. And I know he will mean even more to you, both as your slave and as one who shares your faith in the Lord.

[17]If you accept me as your friend, then accept Onesimus back. Welcome him like you would welcome me. [18]If he has done any wrong to you or owes you anything, charge that to me. [19]I, Paul, am writing this in my own handwriting: I will pay back anything Onesimus owes. And I will say nothing about what you owe me for your own life. [20]So, my brother, as a follower of the Lord please do this favor[b] for me. It would be such a great encouragement to me as your brother in Christ. [21]I write this letter knowing that you will do what I ask, and even more than I ask.

[22]Also, please prepare a room for me. I hope that God will answer your prayers and that I will be able to come and see you.

[a]11 useless ... useful Paul here makes a play on words with the name Onesimus, which means "useful."

[b]20 please do this favor Paul here makes another wordplay on the name Onesimus, using a verb related to it.

Final Greetings

23Epaphras is a prisoner with me for Christ Jesus. He sends you his greetings. 24Also Mark, Aristarchus, Demas, and Luke send their greetings. They are workers together with me.

25The grace* of our Lord Jesus Christ be with your spirit.

Hebrews

God Has Spoken Through His Son

1 1In the past God spoke to our people through the prophets.* He spoke to them many times and in many different ways. 2And now in these last days, God has spoken to us again through his Son. He made the whole world through his Son. And he has chosen his Son to have all things. 3The Son shows the glory* of God. He is a perfect copy of God's nature, and he holds everything together by his powerful command. The Son made people clean from their sins. Then he sat down at the right side*a* of God, the Great One in heaven. 4The Son became much greater than the angels, and God gave him a name that is much greater than any of their names.

5God never said this to any of the angels:

"You are my Son.
Today I have become your Father."
Psalm 2:7

God also never said about an angel,

"I will be his Father,
and he will be my son." *2 Samuel 7:14*

6And then, when God sent his firstborn* Son into the world, he said,

"Let all God's angels worship the Son."*b*

7This is what God said about the angels:

"He changes his angels into winds*c*
and his servants into flaming fire."
Psalm 104:4

8But this is what he said about his Son:

"God your kingdom will last forever and ever.
You use your authority for justice.

9 You love what is right and hate what is wrong.
So God, your God, has chosen you,
giving you more honor and joy than anyone like you."
Psalm 45:6-7

10God also said,

"O Lord, in the beginning you made the earth,
and your hands made the sky.
11 These things will disappear, but you will stay.
They will all wear out like old clothes.
12 You will fold them up like a coat,
and they will be changed like clothes.
But you never change,
and your life will never end."
Psalm 102:25-27

13And God never said this to an angel:

"Sit at my right side
until I put your enemies under your power.*d*"
Psalm 110:1

14All the angels are spirits who serve God and are sent to help those who will receive salvation.

Our Salvation Is Greater Than the Law

2 1So we must be more careful to follow what we were taught. We must be careful so that we will not be pulled away from the true way. 2The teaching that God spoke through angels was shown to be true. And every time his people did something against that teaching, they were punished for what they did. They were punished when they did not obey that teaching. 3So surely we also will be punished if we don't pay attention to the salvation we have that is so great. It was the Lord Jesus who first told people about it. And those who heard him proved to us that it is true. 4God also proved it by using miraculous signs,* wonders,* and all kinds of miracles.* And he proved it by giving people various

---

*a*1:3 *right side* The place of honor and authority (power).

*b*1:6 *"Let ... Son"* These words are found in Deut. 32:43 in the ancient Greek version and in a Hebrew scroll from Qumran.

*c*1:7 *winds* This can also mean "spirits."

*d*1:13 *until I put ... power* Literally, "until I make your enemies a footstool for your feet."

gifts through the Holy Spirit* in just the way he wanted.

Christ Became Like People to Save Them

⁵God did not choose angels to be the rulers over the new world that was coming. That future world is the world we have been talking about. ⁶It is written some place in the Scriptures,*

"Why are people so important to you?
    Why do you even think about them?
Why do you care about the son of man*?
    Is he so important?
⁷ For a short time you made him lower
        than the angels.
    You crowned him with glory* and
        honor.
⁸ You put everything under his control.*"
                                    Psalm 8:4-6

If God put everything under his control, then there was nothing left that he did not rule. But we don't yet see him ruling over everything. ⁹For a short time Jesus was made lower than the angels, but now we see him wearing a crown of glory and honor because he suffered and died. Because of God's grace,* Jesus died for everyone.

¹⁰God—the one who made all things and for whose glory all things exist—wanted many people to be his children and share his glory. So he did what he needed to do. He made perfect the one who leads those people to salvation. He made Jesus a perfect Savior through his suffering.

¹¹Jesus, the one who makes people holy,* and those who are made holy are from the same family. So he is not ashamed to call them his brothers and sisters. ¹²He says,

"God, I will tell my brothers and sisters
        about you.
    Before all your people I will sing your
        praises."   *Psalm 22:22*

¹³He also says,

"I will trust in God."   *Isaiah 8:17*

And he says,

"I am here, and with me are the children
        God has given me."   *Isaiah 8:18*

¹⁴These children are people with physical bodies. So Jesus himself became like them and had the same experiences they have. Jesus did this so that, by dying, he could destroy the one who has the power of death—the devil.

¹⁵Jesus became like these people and died so that he could free them. They were like slaves all their lives because of their fear of death. ¹⁶Clearly, it is not angels that Jesus helps. He helps the people who are from Abraham.* ¹⁷For this reason, Jesus had to be made like us, his brothers and sisters, in every way. He became like people so that he could be their merciful and faithful high priest* in service to God. Then he could bring forgiveness for the people's sins. ¹⁸And now he can help those who are tempted. He is able to help because he himself suffered and was tempted.

Jesus Is Greater Than Moses

3 ¹So, my brothers and sisters, those chosen by God to be his holy people,* think about Jesus. He is the one we believe God sent to save us and to be our high priest.* ²God made him our high priest, and he was faithful to God just as Moses* was. He did everything God wanted him to do in God's house. ³When someone builds a house, people will honor the builder more than the house. It is the same with Jesus. He should have more honor than Moses. ⁴Every house is built by someone, but God built everything. ⁵Moses was faithful as a servant in God's whole house. He told people what God would say in the future. ⁶But Christ is faithful in ruling God's house as the Son. And we are God's house, if we remain confident of the great hope we are glad to say we have.

We Must Continue to Follow God

⁷So it is just as the Holy Spirit* says:

"If you hear God's voice today,
⁸   don't be stubborn as you were in the
        past, when you turned against God.
    That was the day you tested God in the
        desert.
⁹ For 40 years in the desert your people
        saw what I did.
    But they tested me and my patience.
¹⁰ So I was angry with them.
    I said, 'Their thoughts are always
        wrong.
    They have never understood my ways.'
¹¹ So I was angry and made a promise:
    'They will never enter my place of rest.'"
                                    Psalm 95:7-11

¹²So, brothers and sisters, be careful that none of you has the evil thoughts that cause so much doubt that you stop following the living God. ¹³But encourage each other every day, while you still have something called "today."* Help each other so that none of you will be fooled by sin and become too hard to change. ¹⁴We have the honor of sharing in all

---

ª2:6 son of man This can mean any human, but the name "Son of Man" (see the Word List) is often used to mean Jesus, who showed what God planned for all people to be.
ᵇ2:8 control Literally, "feet."

ᶜ3:13 today This word is taken from verse 7. It means it is important to do this now, while there is still opportunity.

that Christ has if we continue until the end to have the sure faith we had in the beginning. [15]That's why the Spirit said,

"If you hear God's voice today,
don't be stubborn as in the past when
you turned against God." *Psalm 95:7-8*

[16]Who were those who heard God's voice and turned against him? It was all the people Moses* led out of Egypt. [17]And who was God angry with for 40 years? He was angry with those who sinned. And their dead bodies were left in the desert. [18]And which people was God talking to when he promised that they would never enter his place of rest? He was talking to those who did not obey him. [19]So we see that they were not allowed to enter and have God's rest, because they did not believe.

4 [1]And we still have the promise that God gave those people. That promise is that we can enter his place of rest. So we should be very careful that none of you fails to get that promise. [2]Yes, the good news about it was told to us just as it was to them. But the message they heard did not help them. They heard it but did not accept it with faith. [3]Only we who believe it are able to enter God's place of rest. As God said,

"I was angry and made a promise:
'They will never enter my place of rest.'"
Psalm 95:11

But God's work was finished from the time he made the world. [4]Yes, somewhere in the Scriptures* he talked about the seventh day of the week. He said, "So on the seventh day God rested from all his work."[a] [5]But in the Scripture above God said, "They will never enter my place of rest."

[6]So the opportunity is still there for some to enter and enjoy God's rest. But those who first heard the good news about it did not enter, because they did not obey. [7]So God planned another special day. It is called "today." He spoke about that day through David* a long time later using the words we quoted before:

"If you hear God's voice today,
don't be stubborn." *Psalm 95:7-8*

[8]We know that Joshua* did not lead the people into the place of rest that God promised. We know this because God spoke later about another day for rest. [9]This shows that the seventh-day rest[b] for God's people is still to come. [10]God rested after he finished his work. So everyone who enters God's place of rest

will also have rest from their own work just as God did. [11]So let us try as hard as we can to enter God's place of rest. We must try hard so that none of us will be lost by following the example of those who refused to obey God.

[12]God's word[c] is alive and working. It is sharper than the sharpest sword and cuts all the way into us. It cuts deep to the place where the soul and the spirit are joined. God's word cuts to the center of our joints and our bones. It judges the thoughts and feelings in our hearts. [13]Nothing in all the world can be hidden from God. He can clearly see all things. Everything is open before him. And to him we must explain the way we have lived.

Jesus Is the High Priest Who Helps Us

[14]We have a great high priest* who has gone to live with God in heaven. He is Jesus the Son of God. So let us continue to express our faith in him. [15]Jesus, our high priest, is able to understand our weaknesses. When Jesus lived on earth, he was tempted in every way. He was tempted in the same ways we are tempted, but he never sinned. [16]With Jesus as our high priest, we can feel free to come before God's throne where there is grace.* There we receive mercy and kindness to help us when we need it.

5 [1]Every Jewish high priest is chosen from among men. That priest is given the work of helping people with the things they must do for God. He must offer to God gifts and sacrifices* for sins. [2]The high priest has his own weaknesses. So he is able to be gentle with those who do wrong out of ignorance. [3]He offers sacrifices for their sins, but he must also offer sacrifices for his own sins.

[4]To be a high priest is an honor. But no one chooses himself for this work. That person must be chosen by God just as Aaron* was. [5]It is the same with Christ. He did not choose himself to have the honor of becoming a high priest. But God chose him. God said to Christ,

"You are my Son.
Today I have become your Father."
Psalm 2:7

[6]And in another part of the Scriptures* God says,

"You are a priest forever—
the kind of priest Melchizedek* was."
Psalm 110:4

[7]While Christ lived on earth he prayed to God, asking for help from the one who could save him from death. He prayed to God with loud cries and tears. And his prayers were answered because of his great respect for God. [8]Jesus was the Son of God, but he

---

*a***4:4** Quote from Gen. 2:2.

*b***4:9** *seventh-day rest* Literally, "Sabbath rest," meaning a sharing in the rest God began after he created the world.

*c***4:12** *God's word* God's teachings and commands.

still suffered, and through his sufferings he learned to obey whatever God says. [9]This made him the perfect high priest, who provides the way for everyone who obeys him to be saved forever. [10]God made him high priest, just like Melchizedek.

Warning Against Falling Away

[11]We have many things to tell you about this. But it is hard to explain because you have stopped trying to understand. [12]You have had enough time that by now you should be teachers. But you need someone to teach you again the first lessons of God's teaching. You still need the teaching that is like milk. You are not ready for solid food. [13]Anyone who lives on milk is still a baby and is not able to understand much about living right. [14]But solid food is for people who have grown up. From their experience they have learned to see the difference between good and evil.

6 [1-2]So we should be finished with the beginning lessons about Christ. We should not have to keep going back to where we started. We began our new life by turning away from the evil we did in the past and by believing in God. That's when we were taught about baptisms,[a] laying hands on* people, the resurrection* of those who have died, and the final judgment. Now we need to go forward to more mature teaching. [3]And that's what we will do if God allows.

[4-6]After people have left the way of Christ, can you make them change their lives again? I am talking about people who once learned the truth, received God's gift, and shared in the Holy Spirit.* They were blessed to hear God's good message* and see the great power of his new world. But then they left it all behind, and it is not possible to make them change again. That's because those who leave Christ are nailing him to the cross again, shaming him before everyone.

[7]Some people are like land that gets plenty of rain and produces a good crop for those who farm it. That kind of land has God's blessing. [8]But other people are like land that grows only thorns and weeds. It is worthless and in danger of being cursed by God. It will be destroyed by fire.

[9]Dear friends, I am not saying this because I think it is happening to you. We really expect that you will do better—that you will do the good things that will result in your salvation. [10]God is fair, and he will remember all the work you have done. He will remember that you showed your love to him by helping his people and that you continue to help them. [11]We want each of you to be willing and eager to show your love like that the rest of your life. Then you will be sure to get what

you hope for. [12]We don't want you to be lazy. We want you to be like those who, because of their faith and patience, will get what God has promised.

[13]God made a promise to Abraham.* And there is no one greater than God, so he made the promise with an oath* in his own name—an oath that he would do what he promised. [14]He said, "I will surely bless you. I will give you many descendants."[b] [15]Abraham waited patiently for this to happen, and later he received what God promised.

[16]People always use the name of someone greater than themselves to make a promise with an oath. The oath proves that what they say is true, and there is no more arguing about it. [17]God wanted to prove that his promise was true. He wanted to prove this to those who would get what he promised. He wanted them to understand clearly that his purposes never change. So God said something would happen, and he proved what he said by adding an oath. [18]These two things cannot change: God cannot lie when he says something, and he cannot lie when he makes an oath.

So these two things are a great help to us who have come to God for safety. They encourage us to hold on to the hope that is ours. [19]This hope is like an anchor for us. It is strong and sure and keeps us safe. It goes behind the curtain.[c] [20]Jesus has already entered there and opened the way for us. He has become the high priest* forever, just like Melchizedek.*

The Priest Melchizedek

7 [1]Melchizedek* was the king of Salem and a priest for God the Most High. He met Abraham* when Abraham was coming back after defeating the kings. That day Melchizedek blessed him. [2]Then Abraham gave him a tenth of everything he had.

The name Melchizedek, king of Salem, has two meanings. First, Melchizedek means "king of justice." And "king of Salem" means "king of peace." [3]No one knows who his father or mother was or where he came from.[d] And no one knows when he was born or when he died. Melchizedek is like the Son of God in that he will always be a priest.

[4]You can see that Melchizedek was very great. Abraham, our great ancestor, gave him a tenth of everything he won in battle. [5]Now the law says that those from the tribe of Levi

---

[b]**6:14** Quote from Gen. 22:17.

[c]**6:19** *curtain* The spiritual curtain in the heavenly temple, which was symbolized by the physical one that separated the inner sanctuary (and God's presence) from the other room in the Holy Tent and in the Jerusalem Temple. See "curtain" in the Word List. Also in 10:20.

[d]**7:3** *No one ... came from* Literally, "Melchizedek was without father, without mother, without genealogy."

---

[a]**6:1–2** *baptisms* The word here may mean the baptism (brief 'burial' in water) of believers in Christ, or it may mean Jewish ceremonial washings.

who become priests must get a tenth from their own people, even though they and their people are both from the family of Abraham. [6]Melchizedek was not even from the tribe of Levi, but Abraham gave him a tenth of what he had. And Melchizedek blessed Abraham— the one who had God's promises. [7]And everyone knows that the more important person always blesses the less important person.

[8]Those priests get a tenth, but they are only men who live and then die. But Melchizedek, who got a tenth from Abraham, continues to live, as the Scriptures* say. [9]Now those from the family of Levi are the ones who get a tenth from the people. But we can say that when Abraham paid Melchizedek a tenth, then Levi also paid it. [10]Levi was not yet born, but he already existed in his ancestor Abraham when Melchizedek met him.

[11]The people were given the law* under the system of priests from the tribe of Levi. But no one could be made spiritually perfect through that system of priests. So there was a need for another priest to come. I mean a priest like Melchizedek, not Aaron.* [12]And when a different kind of priest comes, then the law must be changed too. [13-14]We are talking about our Lord Christ, who belonged to a different tribe. No one from that tribe ever served as a priest at the altar.* It is clear that Christ came from the tribe of Judah. And Moses* said nothing about priests belonging to that tribe.

Jesus Is a Priest Like Melchizedek

[15]And these things become even clearer when we see that another priest has come who is like Melchizedek.* [16]He was made a priest, but not because he met the requirement of being born into the right family. He became a priest by the power of a life that will never end. [17]This is what the Scriptures* say about him: "You are a priest forever—the kind of priest Melchizedek was."[a]

[18]The old rule is now ended because it was weak and worthless. [19]The Law of Moses* could not make anything perfect. But now a better hope has been given to us. And with that hope we can come near to God.

[20]Also, it is important that God made a promise with an oath* when he made Jesus high priest.* When those other men became priests, there was no oath. [21]But Christ became a priest with God's oath. God said to him,

> "The Lord has made a promise with an
>   oath
> and will not change his mind:
> 'You are a priest forever.'"   *Psalm 110:4*

[22]So this means that Jesus is the guarantee of a better agreement* from God to his people.

[a]**7:17** Quote from Ps. 110:4.

[23]Also, when one of those other priests died, he could not continue being a priest. So there were many of those priests. [24]But Jesus lives forever. He will never stop serving as a priest. [25]So Christ can save those who come to God through him. Christ can do this forever, because he always lives and is ready to help people when they come before God.

[26]So Jesus is the kind of high priest we need. He is holy. He has no sin in him. He is pure and not influenced by sinners. And he is raised above the heavens. [27]He is not like those other priests. They had to offer sacrifices* every day, first for their own sins, and then for the sins of the people. But Jesus doesn't need to do that. He offered only one sacrifice for all time. He offered himself. [28]The law chooses high priests who are men and have the same weaknesses that all people have. But after the law, God spoke the oath that made his Son high priest. And that Son, made perfect through suffering, will serve forever.

Jesus Our High Priest

8 [1]Here is the point of what we are saying: We have a high priest* like that, who sits on the right side[b] of God's throne in heaven. [2]Our high priest serves in the Most Holy Place.[c] He serves in the true place of worship[d] that was made by God, not by anyone here on earth.

[3]Every high priest has the work of offering gifts and sacrifices* to God. So our high priest must also offer something to God. [4]If our high priest were now living on earth, he would not be a priest. I say this because there are already priests here who follow the law by offering gifts to God. [5]The work that these priests do is really only a copy and a shadow of what is in heaven. That is why God warned Moses* when he was ready to build the Holy Tent*: "Be sure to make everything exactly like the pattern I showed you on the mountain."[e] [6]But the work that has been given to Jesus is much greater than the work that was given to those priests. In the same way, the new agreement* that Jesus brought from God to his people is much greater than the old one. And the new agreement is based on better promises.

[7]If there was nothing wrong with the first agreement,* then there would be no need for a second agreement. [8]But God found something wrong with the people. He said,

> "The time is coming, says the Lord,
>   when I will give a new agreement to
>   the people of Israel* and to the people
>   of Judah.*

[b]**8:1** *right side* The place of honor and authority (power).

[c]**8:2** *Most Holy Place* Literally, "holies" for "holy of holies," the spiritual place where God lives and is worshiped.

[d]**8:2** *place of worship* Literally, "Tabernacle" or "tent."

[e]**8:5** Quote from Ex. 25:40.

9 It will not be like the agreement that I
        gave to their fathers.
    That is the agreement I gave when I
        took them by the hand and led them
        out of Egypt.
    They did not continue following the
        agreement I gave them,
    and I turned away from them, says the
        Lord.
10 This is the new agreement I will give the
        people of Israel.
    I will give this agreement in the future,
        says the Lord:
    I will put my laws in their minds,
    and I will write my laws on their hearts.
    I will be their God,
        and they will be my people.
11 Never again will anyone have to teach
        their neighbors or their family to
        know the Lord.
    All people—the greatest and the least
        important—will know me.
12 And I will forgive the wrongs they have
        done,
    and I will not remember their sins."
                                    Jeremiah 31:31–34

¹³God called this a new agreement, so
he has made the first agreement old. And
anything that is old and useless is ready to
disappear.

Worship Under the Old Agreement

9 ¹The first agreement* had rules for worship and a place for worship here on earth.
²This place was inside a tent. The first area
in the tent was called the Holy Place. In the
Holy Place were the lamp and the table with
the special bread offered to God. ³Behind the
second curtain* was a room called the Most
Holy Place.* ⁴In the Most Holy Place was a
golden altar* for burning incense.* And also
there was the Box of the Agreement.* The
Box was covered with gold. Inside this Box
was a golden jar of manna* and Aaron's rod—
the rod that once grew leaves. Also in the Box
were the flat stones with the Ten Commandments of the old agreement on them. ⁵Above
the Box were the Cherub angels* that showed
God's glory.* These Cherub angels were over
the place of mercy.ᵃ But we cannot say everything about this now.

⁶Everything in the tent was made ready in
the way I have explained. Then the priests
went into the first room every day to do their
worship duties. ⁷But only the high priest*
could go into the second room, and he went
in only once a year. Also, he could never enter
that room without taking blood with him. He
offered that blood to God for himself and for

the sins the people committed without knowing they were sinning.

⁸The Holy Spirit* uses those two separate
rooms to teach us that the way into the Most
Holy Placeᵇ was not open while the first room
was still there. ⁹This is an example for us
today. It shows that the gifts and sacrifices*
the priests offer to God are not able to make
the consciences of the worshipers completely
clear. ¹⁰These gifts and sacrifices are only
about food and drink and special washings.
They are only rules about the body. God gave
them for his people to follow until the time of
his new way.

Worship Under the New Agreement

¹¹But Christ has already come to be the
high priest.* He is the high priest of the good
things we now have. But Christ does not
serve in a place like the tent that those other
priests served in. He serves in a better place.
Unlike that tent, this one is perfect. It was
not made by anyone here on earth. It does
not belong to this world. ¹²Christ entered the
Most Holy Place only one time—enough for
all time. He entered the Most Holy Place by
using his own blood, not the blood of goats or
young bulls. He entered there and made us
free from sin forever.

¹³The blood of goats and bulls and the
ashes of a cow were sprinkled on those who
were no longer pure enough to enter the
place of worship. The blood and ashes made
them pure again—but only their bodies. ¹⁴So
surely the blood sacrifice of Christ can do
much more. Christ offered himself through
the eternal Spiritᶜ as a perfect sacrifice* to
God. His blood will make us completely clean
from the evil we have done. It will give us
clear consciences so that we can worship the
living God.

¹⁵So Christ brings a new agreement* from
God to his people. He brings this agreement so that those who are chosen by God
can have the blessings God promised, blessings that last forever. This can happen only
because Christ died to free people from sins
committed against the commands of the first
agreement.*

¹⁶When someone dies and leaves a will,*
there must be proof that the one who wrote
the will is dead. ¹⁷A will means nothing while
the one who wrote it is still living. It can be
used only after that person's death. ¹⁸That
is why blood was needed to begin the first
agreement between God and his people.
¹⁹First, Moses* told the people every command in the law. Then he took the blood of
young bulls and mixed it with water. He used
red wool and a branch of hyssop* to sprinkle

ᵃ**9:5** *place of mercy* Or "mercy seat," a place on top
of the "Box of the Agreement," where the high priest
put the blood of an animal once a year to pay for
the sins of the people.

ᵇ**9:8** *Most Holy Place* Literally, "holies" for "holy of
holies," the spiritual place where God lives and is
worshiped. Also in verses 12, 24.
ᶜ**9:14** *Spirit* Probably the Holy Spirit. See "Holy
Spirit" in the Word List.

the blood and water on the book of the law and on all the people. ²⁰Then he said, "This is the blood that makes the agreement good—the agreement that God commanded you to follow."ᵃ ²¹In the same way, Moses sprinkled the blood on the Holy Tent.* He sprinkled the blood over everything used in worship. ²²The law* says that almost everything must be made clean by blood. Sins cannot be forgiven without a blood sacrifice.

Christ's Sacrifice Takes Away Sins

²³These things are copies of the real things that are in heaven. These copies had to be made clean by animal sacrifices.* But the real things in heaven must have much better sacrifices. ²⁴Christ went into the Most Holy Place. But it was not the man-made one, which is only a copy of the real one. He went into heaven, and he is there now before God to help us.

²⁵The high priest* enters the Most Holy Place* once every year. He takes with him blood to offer. But he does not offer his own blood like Christ did. Christ went into heaven, but not to offer himself many times like the high priest offers blood again and again. ²⁶If Christ had offered himself many times, he would have needed to suffer many times since the time the world was made. But he came to offer himself only once. And that once is enough for all time. He came at a time when the world is nearing an end. He came to take away all sin by offering himself as a sacrifice.

²⁷Everyone must die once. Then they are judged. ²⁸So Christ was offered as a sacrifice one time to take away the sins of many people. And he will come a second time, but not to offer himself for sin. He will come the second time to bring salvation to those who are waiting for him.

Christ's Sacrifice Makes Us Perfect

10 ¹The law* gave us only an unclear picture of the good things coming in the future. The law is not a perfect picture of the real things. The law tells people to offer the same sacrifices* every year. Those who come to worship God continue to offer those sacrifices. But the law can never make them perfect. ²If the law could make people perfect, those sacrifices would have already stopped. They would already be clean from their sins, and they would not still feel guilty. ³But that's not what happens. Their sacrifices make them remember their sins every year, ⁴because it is not possible for the blood of bulls and goats to take away sins.

⁵So when Christ came into the world he said,

"You don't want sacrifices and offerings,
    but you have prepared a body for me.

ᵃ**9:20** Quote from Ex. 24:8.

⁶ You are not pleased with the sacrifices of
    animals killed and burned
  or with offerings to take away sins.
⁷ Then I said, 'Here I am, God.
    It is written about me in the book of the
      law.
  I have come to do what you want.'"
                                    Psalm 40:6-8

⁸Christ first said, "You don't want sacrifices and offerings. You are not pleased with animals killed and burned or with sacrifices to take away sin." (These are all sacrifices that the law commands.) ⁹Then he said, "Here I am, God. I have come to do what you want." So God ends that first system of sacrifices and starts his new way. ¹⁰Jesus Christ did the things God wanted him to do. And because of that, we are made holy* through the sacrifice of Christ's body. Christ made that sacrifice one time—enough for all time.

¹¹Every day the priests stand and do their religious service. Again and again they offer the same sacrifices, which can never take away sins. ¹²But Christ offered only one sacrifice for sins, and that sacrifice is good for all time. Then he sat down at the right side of God. ¹³And now Christ waits there for his enemies to be put under his power.ᵇ ¹⁴With one sacrifice Christ made his people perfect forever. They are the ones who are being made holy.

¹⁵The Holy Spirit* also tells us about this. First he says,

¹⁶"This is the agreementᶜ I will make with
      my people in the future, says the
      Lord.
  I will put my laws in their hearts.
  I will write my laws in their minds."
                                  Jeremiah 31:33

¹⁷Then he says,

  "I will forget their sins
    and never again remember the evil they
      have done."   *Jeremiah 31:34*

¹⁸And after everything is forgiven, there is no more need for a sacrifice to pay for sins.

Come Near to God

¹⁹And so, brothers and sisters, we are completely free to enter the Most Holy Place.ᵈ We can do this without fear because of the blood sacrifice of Jesus. ²⁰We enter through a new way that Jesus opened for us. It is a living way

ᵇ**10:13** *to be put under his power* Literally, "to be made a footstool for his feet."
ᶜ**10:16** *agreement* The new and better agreement that God has given to his people through Jesus. See "agreement" in the Word List.
ᵈ**10:19** *Most Holy Place* Literally, "holies" for "holy of holies," the spiritual place where God lives and is worshiped.

that leads through the curtain—Christ's body. 21And we have a great priest who rules the house of God. 22Sprinkled with the blood of Christ, our hearts have been made free from a guilty conscience, and our bodies have been washed with pure water. So come near to God with a sincere heart, full of confidence because of our faith in Christ. 23We must hold on to the hope we have, never hesitating to tell people about it. We can trust God to do what he promised.

Help Each Other Be Strong

24We should think about each other to see how we can encourage each other to show love and do good works. 25We must not quit meeting together, as some are doing. No, we need to keep on encouraging each other. This becomes more and more important as you see the Day* getting closer.

Don't Turn Away From Christ

26If we decide to continue sinning after we have learned the truth, then there is no other sacrifice* that will take away sins. 27If we continue sinning, all that is left for us is a fearful time of waiting for the judgment and the angry fire that will destroy those who live against God. 28Whoever refused to obey the Law of Moses* was found guilty from the testimony given by two or three witnesses. Such people were not forgiven. They were killed. 29So think how much more punishment people deserve who show their hate for the Son of God—people who show they have no respect for the blood sacrifice that began the new agreement* and once made them holy or who insult the Spirit* of God's grace.* 30We know that God said, "I will punish people for the wrongs they do; I will repay them."a And he also said, "The Lord will judge his people."b 31It is a terrible thing to face punishment from the living God.

Keep the Courage and Patience You Had

32Remember the days when you first learned the truth. You had a hard struggle with much suffering, but you continued strong. 33Sometimes people said hateful things to you and mistreated you in public. And sometimes you helped others who were being treated that same way. 34Yes, you helped them in prison and shared in their suffering. And you were still happy when everything you owned was taken away from you. You continued to be happy, because you knew that you had something much better—something that would continue forever.

35So don't lose the courage that you had in the past. Your courage will be rewarded richly. 36You must be patient. After you have

done what God wants, you will get what he promised you. 37He says,

"Very soon now, the one who is coming
  will come and will not be late.
38 The person who is right with me
  will live by trusting in me.
But I will not be pleased with the one
  who turns back in fear."

Habakkuk 2:3–4 (Greek version)

39But we are not those who turn back and are lost. No, we are the people who have faith and are saved.

Faith

11 1Faith is what makes real the things we hope for. It is proof of what we cannot see. 2God was pleased with the people who lived a long time ago because they had faith like this.

3Faith helps us understand that God created the whole world by his command. This means that the things we see were made by something that cannot be seen.

4Cain* and Abel* both offered sacrifices* to God. But Abel offered a better sacrifice to God because he had faith. God said he was pleased with what Abel offered. And so God called him a good man because he had faith. Abel died, but through his faith he is still speaking.

5Enoch was carried away from this earth, so he never died. The Scriptures* tell us that before he was carried off, he was a man who pleased God. Later, no one knew where he was, because God had taken Enoch to be with him. This all happened because he had faith. 6Without faith no one can please God. Whoever comes to God must believe that he is real and that he rewards those who sincerely try to find him.

7Noah was warned by God about things that he could not yet see. But he had faith and respect for God, so he built a large boat to save his family. With his faith, Noah showed that the world was wrong. And he became one of those who are made right with God through faith.

8God called Abraham to travel to another place that he promised to give him. Abraham did not know where that other place was. But he obeyed God and started traveling because he had faith. 9Abraham lived in the country that God promised to give him. He lived there like a visitor who did not belong. He did this because he had faith. He lived in tents with Isaac and Jacob, who also received the same promise from God. 10Abraham was waiting for the cityc that has real foundations. He was waiting for the city that is planned and built by God.

a10:30 Quote from Deut. 32:35.
b10:30 Quote from Deut. 32:36.
c11:10 city The spiritual "city" where God's people live with him. Also called "the heavenly Jerusalem." See Heb. 12:22.

¹¹Sarah was not able to have children, and Abraham was too old. But he had faith in God, trusting him to do what he promised. And so God made them able to have children. ¹²Abraham was so old he was almost dead. But from that one man came as many descendants as there are stars in the sky. So many people came from him that they are like grains of sand on the seashore.

¹³All these great people continued living with faith until they died. They did not get the things God promised his people. But they were happy just to see those promises coming far in the future. They accepted the fact that they were like visitors and strangers here on earth. ¹⁴When people accept something like that, they show they are waiting for a country that will be their own. ¹⁵If they were thinking about the country they had left, they could have gone back. ¹⁶But they were waiting for a better country—a heavenly country. So God is not ashamed to be called their God. And he has prepared a city for them.

¹⁷⁻¹⁸God tested Abraham's faith. God told him to offer Isaac as a sacrifice. Abraham obeyed because he had faith. He already had the promises from God. And God had already said to him, "It is through Isaac that your descendants will come."ᵃ But Abraham was ready to offer his only son. He did this because he had faith. ¹⁹He believed that God could raise people from death. And really, when God stopped Abraham from killing Isaac, it was as if he got him back from death.

²⁰Isaac blessed the future of Jacob and Esau. He did that because he had faith. ²¹And Jacob, also because he had faith, blessed each one of Joseph's sons. He did this while he was dying, leaning on his rod and worshiping God.

²²And when Joseph was almost dead, he spoke about the people of Israel* leaving Egypt. And he told them what they should do with his body. He did this because he had faith.

²³And the mother and father of Moses* hid him for three months after he was born. They did this because they had faith. They saw that Moses was a beautiful baby. And they were not afraid to disobey the king's order.

²⁴⁻²⁵Moses grew up and became a man. He refused to be called the son of Pharaoh's daughter. He chose not to enjoy the pleasures of sin that last such a short time. Instead, he chose to suffer with God's people. He did this because he had faith. ²⁶He thought it was better to suffer for the Christ* than to have all the treasures of Egypt. He was waiting for the reward that God would give him.

²⁷Moses left Egypt because he had faith. He was not afraid of the king's anger. He continued strong as if he could see the God no one can see. ²⁸Moses prepared the Passover* and spread the blood on the doorways of the people of Israel, so that the angel of deathᵇ would not kill their firstborn* sons. Moses did this because he had faith.

²⁹And God's people all walked through the Red Sea as if it were dry land. They were able to do this because they had faith. But when the Egyptians tried to follow them, they were drowned.

³⁰And the walls of Jericho fell because of the faith of God's people. They marched around the walls for seven days, and then the walls fell.

³¹And Rahab, the prostitute, welcomed the Israelite* spies like friends. And because of her faith, she was not killed with the ones who refused to obey.

³²Do I need to give you more examples? I don't have enough time to tell you about Gideon, Barak, Samson, Jephthah, David, Samuel, and the prophets.* ³³All of them had great faith. And with that faith they defeated kingdoms. They did what was right, and God helped them in the ways he promised. With their faith some people closed the mouths of lions. ³⁴And some were able to stop blazing fires. Others escaped from being killed with swords. Some who were weak were made strong. They became powerful in battle and defeated other armies. ³⁵There were women who lost loved ones but got them back when they were raised from death. Others were tortured* but refused to accept their freedom. They did this so that they could be raised from death to a better life. ³⁶Some were laughed at and beaten. Others were tied up and put in prison. ³⁷They were killed with stones. They were cut in half. They were killed with swords. The only clothes some of them had were sheepskins or goatskins. They were poor, persecuted,* and treated badly by others. ³⁸The world was not good enough for these great people. They had to wander in deserts and mountains, living in caves and holes in the ground.

³⁹God was pleased with all of them because of their faith. But not one of them received God's great promise. ⁴⁰God planned something better for us. He wanted to make us perfect. Of course, he wanted those great people to be made perfect too, but not before we could all enjoy that blessing together.

We Also Should Follow Jesus' Example

12 ¹We have all these great people around us as examples. Their lives tell us what faith means. So we, too, should run the race that is before us and never quit. We should remove from our lives anything that would slow us down and the sin that so often makes us fall. ²We must never stop looking to Jesus. He is the leader of our faith, and he is the one

---

ᵃ**11:17–18** Quote from Gen. 21:12.

ᵇ**11:28** *angel of death* Literally, "the destroyer." To punish the Egyptians, God sent an angel to kill the oldest son in each home. See Ex. 12:29-32.

who makes our faith complete. He suffered death on a cross. But he accepted the shame of the cross as if it were nothing because of the joy he could see waiting for him. And now he is sitting at the right side of God's throne. [3]Think about Jesus. He patiently endured the angry insults that sinful people were shouting at him. Think about him so that you won't get discouraged and stop trying.

God Is Like a Father

[4]You are struggling against sin, but you have not had to give up your life for the cause. [5]You are children of God, and he speaks words of comfort to you. You have forgotten these words:

> "My child, don't think the Lord's discipline
>   is worth nothing,
>   and don't stop trying when he corrects
>   you.
> [6] The Lord disciplines everyone he loves;
>   and he punishes everyone he accepts as
>   a child."   *Proverbs 3:11–12*

[7]So accept sufferings like a father's discipline. God does these things to you like a father correcting his children. You know that all children are disciplined by their fathers. [8]So, if you never receive the discipline that every child must have, you are not true children and don't really belong to God. [9]We have all had fathers here on earth who corrected us with discipline. And we respected them. So it is even more important that we accept discipline from the Father of our spirits. If we do this, we will have life. [10]Our fathers on earth disciplined us for a short time in the way they thought was best. But God disciplines us to help us so that we can be holy* like him. [11]We don't enjoy discipline when we get it. It is painful. But later, after we have learned our lesson from it, we will enjoy the peace that comes from doing what is right.

Be Careful How You Live

[12]You have become weak, so make yourselves strong again. [13]Live in the right way so that you will be saved and your weakness will not cause you to be lost.

[14]Try to live in peace with everyone. And try to keep your lives free from sin. Anyone whose life is not holy* will never see the Lord. [15]Be careful that no one fails to get God's grace.* Be careful that no one loses their faith and becomes like a bitter weed growing among you. Someone like that can ruin your whole group. [16]Be careful that no one commits sexual sin. And be careful that no one is like Esau and never thinks about God. As the oldest son, Esau would have inherited everything from his father. But he sold all that for a single meal. [17]You remember that after Esau did this, he wanted to get his father's blessing. He wanted that blessing so much that he

cried. But his father refused to give him the blessing, because Esau could find no way to change what he had done.

[18]You have not come to a place that can be seen and touched, like the mountain the people of Israel* saw, which was burning with fire and covered with darkness, gloom, and storms. [19]There is no sound of a trumpet or a voice speaking words like those they heard. When they heard the voice, they begged never to hear another word. [20]They did not want to hear the command: "If anything, even an animal, touches the mountain, it must be killed with stones."*a* [21]What they saw was so terrible that Moses said, "I am shaking with fear."*b c*

[22]But you have come to Mount Zion,* to the city of the living God, the heavenly Jerusalem.*d* You have come to a place where thousands of angels have gathered to celebrate. [23]You have come to the meeting of God's firstborn*e* children. Their names are written in heaven. You have come to God, the judge of all people. And you have come to the spirits of good people who have been made perfect. [24]You have come to Jesus—the one who brought the new agreement* from God to his people. You have come to the sprinkled blood*f* that tells us about better things than the blood of Abel.*

[25]Be careful and don't refuse to listen when God speaks. Those people refused to listen to him when he warned them on earth. And they did not escape. Now God is speaking from heaven. So now it will be worse for those who refuse to listen to him. [26]When he spoke before, his voice shook the earth. But now he has promised, "Once again I will shake the earth, but I will also shake heaven."*g* [27]The words "once again" clearly show us that everything that was created will be destroyed—that is, the things that can be shaken. And only what cannot be shaken will remain.

[28]So we should be thankful because we have a kingdom that cannot be shaken. And because we are thankful, we should worship God in a way that will please him. We should do this with respect and fear, [29]because our God is like a fire that can destroy us.

---

*a*12:20 Quote from Ex. 19:12–13.

*b*12:21 Quote from Deut. 9:19.

*c*12:18–21 These verses refer to things that happened to the people of Israel in the time of Moses as described in Ex. 19.

*d*12:22 *Jerusalem* Here, the spiritual city of God's people.

*e*12:23 *firstborn* The first son born in a Jewish family had the most important place in the family and received special blessings. All of God's children are like that.

*f*12:24 *sprinkled blood* The blood (death) of Jesus.

*g*12:26 Quote from Hag. 2:6.

Worship That Pleases God

13 ¹Continue loving each other as brothers and sisters in Christ. ²Always remember to help people by welcoming them into your home. Some people have done that and have helped angels without knowing it. ³Don't forget those who are in prison. Remember them as though you were in prison with them. And don't forget those who are suffering. Remember them as though you were suffering with them.

⁴Marriage should be honored by everyone. And every marriage should be kept pure between husband and wife. God will judge guilty those who commit sexual sins and adultery.* ⁵Keep your lives free from the love of money. And be satisfied with what you have. God has said,

"I will never leave you;
I will never run away from you."
Deuteronomy 31:6

⁶So we can feel sure and say,

"The Lord is my helper;
I will not be afraid.
People can do nothing to me." *Psalm 118:6*

⁷Remember your leaders. They taught God's message to you. Remember how they lived and died, and copy their faith. ⁸Jesus Christ is the same yesterday, today, and forever. ⁹Don't let all kinds of strange teachings lead you into the wrong way. Depend only on God's grace* for spiritual strength, not on rules about foods. Obeying those rules doesn't help anyone.

¹⁰We have a sacrifice.ᵃ And those priests who serve in the Holy Tent* cannot eat from the sacrifice we have. ¹¹The high priest* carries the blood of animals into the Most Holy Placeᵇ and offers that blood for sins. But the bodies of those animals are burned outside the camp. ¹²So Jesus also suffered outside the city. He died to make his people holy* with his own blood. ¹³So we should go to Jesus outside the camp and accept the same shame that he had. ¹⁴Here on earth we don't have a city that lasts forever. But we are waiting for the city that we will have in the future. ¹⁵So through Jesus we should never stop offering our sacrifice* to God. That sacrifice is our praise, coming from lips that speak his name. ¹⁶And don't forget to do good and to share what you have with others, because sacrifices like these are very pleasing to God.

¹⁷Obey your leaders. Be willing to do what they say. They are responsible for your spiritual welfare, so they are always watching to protect you. Obey them so that their work will give them joy, not grief. It won't help you to make it hard for them.

¹⁸Continue praying for us. We feel right about what we do, because we always try to do what is best. ¹⁹And I beg you to pray that God will send me back to you soon. I want this more than anything else.

²⁰⁻²¹I pray that the God of peace will give you every good thing you need so that you can do what he wants. God is the one who raised from death our Lord Jesus, the Great Shepherd of his sheep. He raised him because Jesus sacrificed his blood to begin the new agreement* that never ends. I pray that God will work through Jesus Christ to do the things in us that please him. To him be glory* forever. Amen.*

²²My brothers and sisters, I beg you to listen patiently to what I have said. I wrote this letter to strengthen you. And it is not very long. ²³I want you to know that our brother Timothy is out of prison. If he comes to me soon, we will both come to see you.

²⁴Give my greetings to all your leaders and to all God's people. All those from Italy send you their greetings.

²⁵God's grace be with you all.

ᵃ**13:10** *sacrifice* Literally, "altar." Here, it means the sacrifice (offering) of Jesus. He gave his life to pay for people's sins.
ᵇ**13:11** *Most Holy Place* Literally, "the holies," the place in the Jewish Tabernacle or Temple where God met the high priest.

James

1

¹Greetings from James, a servant of God and of the Lord Jesus Christ.

To God's people*a* who are scattered all over the world.

Faith and Wisdom

²My brothers and sisters, you will have many kinds of trouble. But this gives you a reason to be very happy. ³You know that when your faith is tested, you learn to be patient in suffering. ⁴If you let that patience work in you, the end result will be good. You will be mature and complete. You will be all that God wants you to be.

⁵Do any of you need wisdom? Ask God for it. He is generous and enjoys giving to everyone. So he will give you wisdom. ⁶But when you ask God, you must believe. Don't doubt him. Whoever doubts is like a wave in the sea that is blown up and down by the wind. ⁷⁻⁸People like that are thinking two different things at the same time. They can never decide what to do. So they should not think they will receive anything from the Lord.

True Riches

⁹Believers who are poor should be glad that God considers them so important. ¹⁰Believers who are rich should be glad when bad things happen them that humble them. Their riches won't keep them from disappearing as quickly as wildflowers. ¹¹As the sun rises and gets hotter, its heat dries up the plants, and the flowers fall off. The flowers that were so beautiful are now dead. That's how it is with the rich. While they are still making plans for their business, they will die.

Temptation Does Not Come From God

¹²Great blessings belong to those who are tempted and remain faithful! After they have proved their faith, God will give them the crown* of eternal life. God promised this to all people who love him. ¹³Whenever you feel tempted to do something bad, you should not say, "God is tempting me." Evil cannot tempt God, and God himself does not tempt anyone. ¹⁴You are tempted by the evil things you want. Your own desire leads you away and traps you. ¹⁵Your desire grows inside you

until it results in sin. Then the sin grows bigger and bigger and finally ends in death.

¹⁶My dear brothers and sisters, don't be fooled about this. ¹⁷Everything good comes from God. Every perfect gift is from him. These good gifts come down from the Father who made all the lights in the sky. But God never changes like the shadows from those lights. He is always the same. ¹⁸God decided to give us life through the true message* he sent to us. He wanted us to be the most important of all that he created.

Listening and Obeying

¹⁹My dear brothers and sisters, always be more willing to listen than to speak. Keep control of your anger. ²⁰Anger does not help you live the way God wants. ²¹So get rid of everything evil in your lives—every kind of wrong you do. Be humble and accept God's teaching that is planted in your hearts. This teaching can save you.

²²Do what God's teaching says; don't just listen and do nothing. When you only sit and listen, you are fooling yourselves. ²³Hearing God's teaching and doing nothing is like looking at your face in the mirror ²⁴and doing nothing about what you saw. You go away and immediately forget how bad you looked. ²⁵But when you look into God's perfect law that sets people free, pay attention to it. If you do what it says, you will have God's blessing. Never just listen to his teaching and forget what you heard.

The True Way to Worship God

²⁶You might think you are a very religious person. But if your tongue is out of control, you are fooling yourself. Your careless talk makes your offerings to God worthless. ²⁷The worship that God wants is this: caring for orphans or widows who need help and keeping yourself free from the world's evil influence. This is the kind of worship that God accepts as pure and good.

Love All People

2

¹My dear brothers and sisters, you are believers in our glorious Lord Jesus Christ. So don't treat some people better than others. ²Suppose someone comes into your meeting wearing very nice clothes and a gold ring. At the same time a poor person comes in wearing old, dirty clothes. ³You show special

---

a 1:1 **God's people** Literally, "the twelve tribes." Believers in Christ are like the tribes of Israel, God's chosen people in the Old Testament.

attention to the person wearing nice clothes. You say, "Sit here in this good seat." But you say to the poor person, "Stand there!" or "Sit on the floor by our feet!" [4]Doesn't this show that you think some people are more important than others? You set yourselves up as judges—judges who make bad decisions.

[5]Listen, my dear brothers and sisters. God chose the poor people in the world to be rich in faith. He chose them to receive the kingdom* God promised to those who love him. [6]But you show no respect to those who are poor. And you know that the rich are the ones who always try to control your lives. And they are the ones who take you to court. [7]And the rich are the ones who insult the wonderful name of Christ, the name by which you are known.

[8]One law rules over all other laws. This royal law is found in the Scriptures*: "Love your neighbor[a] the same as you love yourself."[b] If you obey this law, you are doing right. [9]But if you are treating one person as more important than another, you are sinning. You are guilty of breaking God's law.

[10]You might follow all of God's law. But if you fail to obey only one command, you are guilty of breaking all the commands in that law. [11]God said, "Don't commit adultery.*"[c] The same God also said, "Don't kill."[d] So if you don't commit adultery, but you kill someone, you are guilty of breaking all of God's law.

[12]You will be judged by the law that makes people free. You should remember this in everything you say and do. [13]Yes, you must show mercy to others. If you do not show mercy, then God will not show mercy to you when he judges you. But the one who shows mercy can stand without fear before the Judge.

Faith and Good Works

[14]My brothers and sisters, if a person claims to have faith but does nothing, that faith is worth nothing. Faith like that cannot save anyone. [15]Suppose a brother or sister in Christ comes to you in need of clothes or something to eat. [16]And you say to them, "God be with you! I hope you stay warm and get plenty to eat," but you don't give them the things they need. If you don't help them, your words are worthless. [17]It is the same with faith. If it is just faith and nothing more—if it doesn't do anything—it is dead.

[18]But someone might argue, "Some people have faith, and others have good works." My answer would be that you can't show me your faith if you don't do anything. But I will show

you my faith by the good I do. [19]You believe there is one God. That's good, but even the demons* believe that! And they shake with fear.

[20]You fool! Faith that does nothing is worth nothing. Do you want me to prove this to you? [21]Our father* Abraham* was made right with God by what he did. He offered his son Isaac to God on the altar.* [22]So you see that Abraham's faith and what he did worked together. His faith was made perfect by what he did. [23]This shows the full meaning of the Scriptures* that say, "Abraham believed God, and because of this faith he was accepted as one who is right with God."[e] Abraham was called "God's friend."[f] [24]So you see that people are made right with God by what they do. They cannot be made right by faith alone.

[25]Another example is Rahab. She was a prostitute, but she was made right with God by something she did. She helped those who were spying for God's people. She welcomed them into her home and helped them escape by a different road.[g]

[26]A person's body that does not have a spirit is dead. It is the same with faith—faith that does nothing is dead!

Controlling the Things We Say

3 [1]My brothers and sisters, not many of you should be teachers. I say this because, as you know, we who teach will be judged more strictly than others.

[2]We all make many mistakes. A person who never said anything wrong would be perfect. Someone like that would be able to control their whole body too. [3]We put bits into the mouths of horses to make them obey us. With these bits we can control their whole body. [4]It is the same with ships. A ship is very big, and it is pushed by strong winds. But a very small rudder controls that big ship. And the one who controls the rudder decides where the ship will go. It goes where he wants it to go. [5]It is the same with our tongue. It is a small part of the body, but it can boast about doing great things.

A big forest fire can be started with only a little flame. [6]The tongue is like a fire. It is a world of evil among the parts of our body. It spreads its evil through our whole body and starts a fire that influences all of life. It gets this fire from hell.

[7]Humans have control over every kind of wild animal, bird, reptile, and fish, and they have controlled all these things. [8]But no one can control the tongue. It is wild and evil, full of deadly poison. [9]We use our tongues to praise our Lord and Father, but then we curse people who were created in God's likeness. [10]These praises and curses come from the same mouth.

---

[a]**2:8 your neighbor** Or "others." Jesus' teaching in Lk. 10:25–37 makes clear that this includes anyone in need.
[b]**2:8** Quote from Lev. 19:18.
[c]**2:11** Quote from Ex. 20:14; Deut. 5:18.
[d]**2:11** Quote from Ex. 20:13; Deut. 5:17.

[e]**2:23** Quote from Gen. 15:6.
[f]**2:23** Quote from 2 Chron. 20:7; Isa. 41:8.
[g]**2:25 She helped ... road** The story about Rahab is found in Josh. 2:1–21.

My brothers and sisters, this should not happen. [11]Do good water and bad water flow from the same spring? Of course not. [12]My brothers and sisters, can a fig tree make olives? Or can a grapevine make figs? No, and a well full of salty water cannot give good water.

True Wisdom

[13]Are there any among you who are really wise and understanding? Then you should show your wisdom by living right. You should do what is good with humility. A wise person does not boast. [14]If you are selfish and have bitter jealousy in your hearts, you have no reason to boast. Your boasting is a lie that hides the truth. [15]That kind of "wisdom" does not come from God. That "wisdom" comes from the world. It is not spiritual. It is from the devil. [16]Where there is jealousy and selfishness, there will be confusion and every kind of evil. [17]But the wisdom that comes from God is like this: First, it is pure. It is also peaceful, gentle, and easy to please. This wisdom is always ready to help people who have trouble and to do good for others. This wisdom is always fair and honest. [18]People who work for peace in a peaceful way get the blessings that come from right living.

Give Yourselves to God

4 [1]Do you know where your fights and arguments come from? They come from the selfish desires that make war inside you. [2]You want things, but you don't get them. So you kill and are jealous of others. But you still cannot get what you want. So you argue and fight. You don't get what you want because you don't ask God. [3]Or when you ask, you don't receive anything, because the reason you ask is wrong. You only want to use it for your own pleasure.

[4]You people are not faithful to God! You should know that loving what the world has is the same as hating God. So anyone who wants to be friends with this evil world becomes God's enemy. [5]Do you think the Scriptures* mean nothing? The Scriptures say, "The Spirit* God made to live in us wants us only for himself."[a] [6]But the kindness God shows is greater. As the Scripture says, "God is against the proud, but he is kind to the humble."[b]

[7]So give yourselves to God. Stand against the devil, and he will run away from you. [8]Come near to God and he will come near to you. You are sinners, so clean sin out of your lives.[c] You are trying to follow God and the world at the same time. Make your thinking pure. [9]Be sad, be sorry, and cry! Change your laughter into crying. Change your joy into sadness. [10]Be humble before the Lord, and he will make you great.

You Are Not the Judge

[11]Brothers and sisters, don't say anything against each other. If you criticize your brother or sister in Christ or judge them, you are criticizing and judging the law they follow. And when you are judging the law, you are not a follower of the law. You have become a judge. [12]God is the one who gave us the law, and he is the Judge. He is the only one who can save and destroy. So it is not right for you to judge anyone.

Let God Plan Your Life

[13]Some of you say, "Today or tomorrow we will go to some city. We will stay there a year, do business, and make money." Listen, think about this: [14]You don't know what will happen tomorrow. Your life is like a fog. You can see it for a short time, but then it goes away. [15]So you should say, "If the Lord wants, we will live and do this or that." [16]But now you are proud and boast about yourself. All such boasting is wrong. [17]If you fail to do what you know is right, you are sinning.

A Warning to Rich and Selfish People

5 [1]You rich people, listen! Cry and be very sad because much trouble will come to you. [2]Your riches will rot and be worth nothing. Your clothes will be eaten by moths. [3]Your gold and silver will rust, and that rust will be a proof that you were wrong. That rust will eat your bodies like fire. You saved your treasure in the last days. [4]People worked in your fields, but you did not pay them. They are crying out against you. They harvested your crops. Now the Lord All-Powerful has heard their cries.

[5]Your life on earth was full of rich living. You pleased yourselves with everything you wanted. You made yourselves fat, like an animal ready for the day of slaughter.[d] [6]You showed no mercy to good people. They were not against you, but you killed them.

Be Patient

[7]Brothers and sisters, be patient; the Lord will come. So be patient until that time. Look at the farmers. They have to be patient. They have to wait for their valuable crop to grow and produce a harvest. They wait patiently for the first rain and the last rain.[e] [8]You must be patient too. Never stop hoping. The Lord is coming soon. [9]Brothers and sisters, don't complain against each other. If you don't stop complaining, you will be judged guilty. And the Judge is ready to come!

---

[a]**4:5** *"The Spirit ... himself"* Other possible translations: "God strongly desires the spirit that he made to live in us." Or "The spirit that he made to live in us is full of envious desires." See Ex. 20:5.

[b]**4:6** Quote from Prov. 3:34.

[c]**4:8** *so clean sin out of your lives* Literally, "so wash your hands."

[d]**5:5** *You made yourselves fat ... slaughter* Literally, "You fattened your hearts for the day of slaughter."

[e]**5:7** *first rain ... last rain* The "first rain" came in the fall, and the "last rain" came in the spring.

[10]Brothers and sisters, follow the example of the prophets* who spoke for the Lord. They suffered many bad things, but they were patient. [11]And we say that those who accepted their troubles with patience now have God's blessing. You have heard about Job's patience.[a] You know that after all his troubles, the Lord helped him. This shows that the Lord is full of mercy and is kind.

Be Careful What You Say

[12]My brothers and sisters, it is very important that you not use an oath when you make a promise. Don't use the name of heaven, earth, or anything else to prove what you say. When you mean yes, say only "yes." When you mean no, say only "no." Do this so that you will not be judged guilty.

The Power of Prayer

[13]Are you having troubles? You should pray. Are you happy? You should sing. [14]Are you sick? Ask the elders* of the church* to come and rub oil on you[b] in the name of the Lord and pray for you. [15]If such a prayer is offered in faith, it will heal anyone who is sick. The Lord will heal them. And if they have sinned, he will forgive them.

[16]So always tell each other the wrong things you have done. Then pray for each other. Do this so that God can heal you. Anyone who lives the way God wants can pray, and great things will happen. [17]Elijah* was a person just like us. He prayed that it would not rain. And it did not rain on the land for three and a half years! [18]Then Elijah prayed that it would rain. And the rain came down from the sky, and the land grew crops again.

Helping People When They Sin

[19]My brothers and sisters, if anyone wanders away from the truth and someone helps that person come back, [20]remember this: Anyone who brings a sinner back from the wrong way will save that person from eternal death and cause many sins to be forgiven.

[a]5:11 *Job's patience* See the book of Job in the Old Testament.

[b]5:14 *rub oil on you* Oil was used like medicine.

1 Peter

1 [1]Greetings from Peter, an apostle* of Jesus Christ.

To God's chosen people who are away from their homes—people scattered all over the areas of Pontus, Galatia, Cappadocia, Asia, and Bithynia. [2]God planned long ago to choose you and to make you his holy people,* which is the Spirit's* work. God wanted you to obey him and to be made clean by the blood sacrifice[c] of Jesus Christ.

I pray that you will enjoy more and more of God's grace* and peace.

A Living Hope

[3]Praise be to the God and Father of our Lord Jesus Christ. God has great mercy, and because of his mercy he gave us a new life. This new life brings us a living hope through Jesus Christ's resurrection from death. [4]Now we wait to receive the blessings God has for his children. These blessings are kept for you in heaven. They cannot be ruined or be destroyed or lose their beauty.

[5]God's power protects you through your faith, and it keeps you safe until your salvation comes. That salvation is ready to be given to you at the end of time. [6]I know the thought of that is exciting, even if you must suffer through different kinds of troubles for a short time now. [7]These troubles test your faith and prove that it is pure. And such faith is worth more than gold. Gold can be proved to be pure by fire, but gold will ruin. When your faith is proven to be pure, the result will be praise and glory* and honor when Jesus Christ comes.

[8]You have not seen Christ, but still you love him. You can't see him now, but you believe in him. You are filled with a wonderful and heavenly joy that cannot be explained. [9]Your faith has a goal, and you are reaching that goal—your salvation.

[10]The prophets* studied carefully and tried to learn about this salvation. They spoke about the grace* that was coming to you. [11]The Spirit* of Christ was in those prophets. And the Spirit was telling about the sufferings

[c]1:2 *made clean ... sacrifice* Or "sprinkled with the blood," which probably compares the beginning of the new agreement by the blood sacrifice of Christ (Mk. 14:24) with Moses' sprinkling the blood of animal sacrifices on the people of Israel to seal the agreement God made with them (Ex. 24:3-8). See also Heb. 9:15-26.

that would happen to Christ and about the glory that would come after those sufferings. The prophets tried to learn about what the Spirit was showing them—when it would happen and what the world would be like at that time.

[12]It was made clear to them that their service was not for themselves. They were serving you when they told about the things you have now heard. You heard them from those who told you the Good News* with the help of the Holy Spirit sent from heaven. Even the angels would like very much to know more about these things you were told.

A Call to Holy Living

[13]So prepare your minds for service. With complete self-control put all your hope in the grace* that will be yours when Jesus Christ comes. [14]In the past you did not have the understanding you have now, so you did the evil things you wanted to do. But now you are children of God, so you should obey him and not live the way you did before. [15]Be holy* in everything you do, just as God is holy. He is the one who chose you. [16]In the Scriptures* God says, "Be holy, because I am holy."[a]

[17]You pray to God and call him Father, but he will judge everyone the same way—by what they do. So while you are visiting here on earth, you should live with respect for God. [18]You know that in the past the way you were living was useless. It was a way of life you learned from those who lived before you. But you were saved from that way of living. You were bought, but not with things that ruin like gold or silver. [19]You were bought with the precious blood of Christ's death. He was a pure and perfect sacrificial Lamb.* [20]Christ was chosen before the world was made, but he was shown to the world in these last times for you. [21]You believe in God through Christ. God is the one who raised him from death and gave honor to him. So your faith and your hope are in God.

[22]You have made yourselves pure by obeying the truth. Now you can have true love for your brothers and sisters. So love each other deeply—with all your heart. [23]You have been born again. This new life did not come from something that dies. It came from something that cannot die. You were born again through God's life-giving message* that lasts forever. [24]The Scriptures say,

"Our lives are like the grass of spring,
    and any glory* we enjoy is like the
        beauty of a wildflower.
The grass dries up and dies,
    and the flower falls to the ground.
[25] But the word of the Lord lasts forever."
                        Isaiah 40:6-8

And that word is the Good News* that was told to you.

The Living Stone and the Holy Nation

2 [1]So then, stop doing anything to hurt others. Don't lie anymore, and stop trying to fool people. Don't be jealous or say bad things about others. [2]Like newborn babies hungry for milk, you should want the pure teaching that feeds your spirit. With it you can grow up and be saved. [3]You have already tasted the goodness of the Lord.

[4]The Lord Jesus is the living stone.[b] The people of the world decided that they did not want this stone. But he is the one God chose as one of great value. So come to him. [5]You also are like living stones, and God is using you to build a spiritual house.[c] You are to serve God in this house as holy* priests, offering him spiritual sacrifices* that he will accept because of Jesus Christ. [6]The Scriptures* say,

"Look, I have chosen a cornerstone* of
    great value,
    and I put that stone in Zion.*
Anyone who trusts in him will never be
    disappointed."
                        Isaiah 28:16

[7]So, that stone means honor for you who believe. But for those who don't believe he is

"the stone that the builders refused to
    accept,
    which became the most important
        stone."
                        Psalm 118:22

[8]For them he is also

"a stone that makes people stumble,
    a rock that makes people fall." *Isaiah 8:14*

People stumble because they don't obey what God says. This is what God planned to happen to those people.

[9]But you are his chosen people, the King's priests. You are a holy nation, people who belong to God. He chose you to tell about the wonderful things he has done. He brought you out of the darkness of sin into his wonderful light.

[10] In the past you were not a special people,
    but now you are God's people.
Once you had not received mercy,
    but now God has given you his mercy.[d]

Live for God

[11]Dear friends, you are like visitors and strangers in this world. So I beg you to keep

---

[b]**2:4 stone** The most important stone in God's spiritual temple or house (his people).
[c]**2:5 house** God's house—the place where God's people worship him. Here, it means that believers are the spiritual building where God lives.
[d]**2:10 In the past ... his mercy** See Hos. 2:23.

[a]**1:16** Quote from Lev. 11:44, 45; 19:2; 20:7.

your lives free from the evil things you want to do, those desires that fight against your true selves. ¹²People who don't believe are living all around you. They may say that you are doing wrong. So live such good lives that they will see the good you do, and they will give glory* to God on the day he comes.

Obey Every Human Authority

¹³Be willing to serve the people who have authority*a* in this world. Do this for the Lord. Obey the king, the highest authority. ¹⁴And obey the leaders who are sent by the king. They are sent to punish those who do wrong and to praise those who do good. ¹⁵When you do good, you stop ignorant people from saying foolish things about you. This is what God wants. ¹⁶Live like free people, but don't use your freedom as an excuse to do evil. Live as those who are serving God. ¹⁷Show respect for all people. Love all the brothers and sisters of God's family. Respect God, and honor the king.

The Example of Christ's Suffering

¹⁸Slaves, be willing to serve your masters. Do this with all respect. You should obey the masters who are good and kind, and you should obey the masters who are bad. ¹⁹One of you might have to suffer even when you have done nothing wrong. If you think of God and bear the pain, this pleases God. ²⁰But if you are punished for doing wrong, there is no reason to praise you for bearing that punishment. But if you suffer for doing good and you are patient, this pleases God. ²¹This is what you were chosen to do. Christ gave you an example to follow. He suffered for you. So you should do the same as he did:

²²"He never sinned,
   and he never told a lie."   *Isaiah 53:9*

²³People insulted him, but he did not insult them back. He suffered, but he did not threaten anyone. No, he let God take care of him. God is the one who judges rightly. ²⁴Christ carried our sins in his body on the cross. He did this so that we would stop living for sin and live for what is right. By his wounds you were healed. ²⁵You were like sheep that went the wrong way. But now you have come back to the Shepherd and Protector of your lives.

Wives and Husbands

3 ¹In the same way, you wives should be willing to serve your husbands. Then, even those who have refused to accept God's teaching will be persuaded to believe because of the way you live. You will not need to say

anything. ²Your husbands will see the pure lives that you live with respect for God. ³It is not fancy hair, gold jewelry, or fine clothes that should make you beautiful. ⁴No, your beauty should come from inside you—the beauty of a gentle and quiet spirit. That beauty will never disappear. It is worth very much to God.

⁵It was the same with the holy* women who lived long ago and followed God. They made themselves beautiful in that same way. They were willing to serve their husbands. ⁶I am talking about women like Sarah. She obeyed Abraham,* her husband, and called him her master. And you women are true children of Sarah if you always do what is right and are not afraid.

⁷In the same way, you husbands should live with your wives in an understanding way, since they are weaker than you. You should show them respect, because God gives them the same blessing he gives you—the grace* of true life. Do this so that nothing will stop your prayers from being heard.

Suffering for Doing Right

⁸So all of you should live together in peace. Try to understand each other. Love each other like brothers and sisters. Be kind and humble. ⁹Don't do wrong to anyone to pay them back for doing wrong to you. Or don't insult anyone to pay them back for insulting you. But ask God to bless them. Do this because you yourselves were chosen to receive a blessing. ¹⁰The Scriptures* say,

"If you want to enjoy true life
   and have only good days,
   then avoid saying anything hurtful,
   and never let a lie come out of your
      mouth.
¹¹ Stop doing what is wrong, and do good.
   Look for peace, and do all you can to
      help people live peacefully.
¹² The Lord watches over those who do
      what is right,
   and he listens to their prayers.
   But he is against those who do evil."
                              Psalm 34:12-16

¹³If you are always trying to do good, no one can really harm you. ¹⁴But you may suffer for doing right. If that happens, you have God's blessing. "Don't be afraid of the people who make you suffer; don't be worried."*b* ¹⁵But keep the Lord Christ holy in your hearts. Always be ready to answer everyone who asks you to explain about the hope you have. ¹⁶But answer them in a gentle way with respect. Keep your conscience clear. Then people will see the good way you live as followers of Christ, and those who say bad things about you will be ashamed of what they said. ¹⁷It is better to suffer for doing good than

---

*a*2:13 *people … authority* Literally, "every human creation," meaning rulers, governors, presidents, or other government leaders.

*b*3:14 Quote from Isa. 8:12.

for doing wrong. Yes, it is better if that is what God wants.

18 Christ himself suffered when he died for you,
　and with that one death he paid for your sins.
He was not guilty,
　but he died for people who are guilty.
　He did this to bring all of you to God.
In his physical form he was killed,
　but he was made alive by the Spirit.* *a*

19And by the Spirit he went and preached to the spirits in prison. 20Those were the spirits who refused to obey God long ago in the time of Noah. God was waiting patiently for people while Noah was building the big boat. And only a few—eight in all—were saved in the boat through the floodwater. 21And that water is like baptism,* which now saves you. Baptism is not the washing of dirt from the body. It is asking God for a clean conscience. It saves you because Jesus Christ was raised from death. 22Now he has gone into heaven. He is at God's right side and rules over angels, authorities, and powers.

Changed Lives

4 1Christ suffered while he was in his body. So you should strengthen yourselves with the same kind of thinking Christ had. The one who accepts suffering in this life has clearly decided to stop sinning. 2Strengthen yourselves so that you will live your lives here on earth doing what God wants, not the evil things that people want to do. 3In the past you wasted too much time doing what those who don't know God like to do. You were living immoral lives, doing the evil things you wanted to do. You were always getting drunk, having wild drinking parties, and doing shameful things in your worship of idols.

4Now those "friends" think it is strange that you no longer join them in all the wild and wasteful things they do. And so they say bad things about you. 5But they will have to face God to explain what they have done. He is the one who will soon judge everyone—those who are still living and those who have died. 6Some were told the Good News* before they died. They were criticized by others in their life here on earth. But it was God's plan that they hear the Good News so that they could have a new life through the Spirit.* *b*

Be Good Managers of God's Gifts

7The time is near when all things will end. So keep your minds clear, and control yourselves. This will help you in your prayers. 8Most important of all, love each other deeply, because love makes you willing to forgive many sins. 9Open your homes to each other and share your food without complaining. 10God has shown you his grace* in many different ways. So be good servants and use whatever gift he has given you in a way that will best serve each other. 11If your gift is speaking, your words should be like words from God. If your gift is serving, you should serve with the strength that God gives. Then it is God who will be praised in everything through Jesus Christ. Power and glory* belong to him forever and ever. Amen.*

Suffering as a Follower of Christ

12My friends, don't be surprised at the painful things that you are now suffering, which are testing your faith. Don't think that something strange is happening to you. 13But you should be happy that you are sharing in Christ's sufferings. You will be happy and full of joy when Christ shows his glory.* 14When people say bad things to you because you follow Christ, consider it a blessing. When that happens, it shows that God's Spirit, the Spirit of glory, is with you. 15You may suffer, but don't let it be because you murder, steal, make trouble, or try to control other people's lives. 16But if you suffer because you are a "Christ-follower," don't be ashamed. You should praise God for that name. 17It is time for judging to begin. That judging will begin with God's family. If it begins with us, then what will happen to those who don't accept the Good News* of God?

18"If it is hard for even a good person to be saved,
　what will happen to the one who
　is against God and full of sin?"
Proverbs 11:31 (Greek version)

19So if God wants you to suffer, you should trust your lives to him. He is the one who made you, and you can trust him. So continue to do good.

The Flock of God

5 1Now I have something to say to the elders* in your group. I am also an elder. I myself have seen Christ's sufferings. And I will share in the glory* that will be shown to us. I beg you to 2take care of the group of people you are responsible for. They are God's flock.*c* Watch over that flock because you want to, not because you are forced to do it. That is how God wants it. Do it because you are happy to serve, not because you want money. 3Don't be like a ruler over those you are responsible for. But be good examples to them. 4Then when Christ the Ruling Shepherd comes, you will get a crown*—one that

---

*a*3:18 *by the Spirit* Or "in the spirit." Also in verse 19.
*b*4:6 *through the Spirit* Or "in the spirit," meaning in the spiritual or heavenly realm.

*c*5:2 *God's flock* God's people. They are like a flock of sheep that need to be cared for.

will be glorious and never lose its beauty.

⁵Young people, I have something to say to you too. You should accept the authority of the elders. You should all have a humble attitude in dealing with each other.

> "God is against the proud,
> but he is kind to the humble."
>
> Proverbs 3:34

⁶So be humble under God's powerful hand. Then he will lift you up when the right time comes. ⁷Give all your worries to him, because he cares for you.

⁸Control yourselves and be careful! The devil is your enemy, and he goes around like a roaring lion looking for someone to attack and eat. ⁹Refuse to follow the devil. Stand strong in your faith. You know that your brothers and sisters all over the world are having the same sufferings that you have.

¹⁰Yes, you will suffer for a short time. But after that, God will make everything right.

He will make you strong. He will support you and keep you from falling. He is the God who gives all grace. He chose you to share in his glory in Christ. That glory will continue forever. ¹¹All power is his forever. Amen.*

Final Greetings

¹²Silas will bring this letter to you. I know that he is a faithful brother in Christ. I wrote this short letter to encourage you. I wanted to tell you that this is the true grace* of God. Stand strong in that grace.

¹³The church in Babylonᵃ sends you greetings. They were chosen just as you were. Mark, my son in Christ, also sends his greetings. ¹⁴Give each other a special greetingᵇ of love when you meet.

Peace to all of you who are in Christ.

ᵃ5:13 *The church in Babylon* Literally, "She in Babylon."
ᵇ5:14 *special greeting* Literally, "kiss."

2 Peter

1 ¹Greetings from Simon Peter, a servant and apostle* of Jesus Christ.

To all of you who share in the same valuable faith that we have. This faith was given to us because our God and Savior Jesus Christ always does what is good and right.

²Grace* and peace be given to you more and more, because now you know God and Jesus our Lord.

God Has Given Us Everything We Need

³Jesus has the power of God. And his power has given us everything we need to live a life devoted to God. We have these things because we know him. Jesus chose us by his glory* and goodness, ⁴through which he also gave us the very great and rich gifts that he promised us. With these gifts you can share in being like God. And so you will escape the ruin that comes to people in the world because of the evil things they want.

⁵Because you have these blessings, do all you can to add to your life these things: to your faith add goodness; to your goodness add knowledge; ⁶to your knowledge add self-control; to your self-control add patience; to your patience add devotion to God; ⁷to your devotion add kindness toward your brothers and sisters in Christ, and to this kindness add love. ⁸If all these things are in you and growing, you will never fail to be useful to God.

You will produce the kind of fruit that should come from your knowledge of our Lord Jesus Christ. ⁹But those who don't grow in these blessings are blind. They cannot see clearly what they have. They have forgotten that they were cleansed from their past sins.

¹⁰My brothers and sisters, God called you and chose you to be his. Do your best to live in a way that shows you really are God's called and chosen people. If you do all this, you will never fall. ¹¹And you will be given a very great welcome into the kingdom* of our Lord and Savior Jesus Christ, a kingdom that never ends.

¹²You already know these things. You are very strong in the truth you have. But I am always going to help you remember them. ¹³While I am still living here on earth, I think it is right for me to remind you of them. ¹⁴I know that I must soon leave this body. Our Lord Jesus Christ has shown me that. ¹⁵I will try my best to make sure you remember these things even after I am gone.

We Saw Christ's Glory

¹⁶We told you about the power of our Lord Jesus Christ. We told you about his coming. The things we told you were not just clever stories that people invented. No, we saw the greatness of Jesus with our own eyes. ¹⁷Jesus heard the voice of the great and glorious God.

That was when he received honor and glory* from God the Father. The voice said, "This is my Son, the one I love. I am very pleased with him." [18]And we heard that voice. It came from heaven while we were with Jesus on the holy mountain.[a]

[19]This makes us more sure about what the prophets* said. And it is good for you to follow closely what they said, which is like a light shining in a dark place. You have that light until the day begins and the morning star brings new light to your minds. [20]Most important of all, you must understand this: No prophecy* in the Scriptures* comes from the prophet's own understanding. [21]No prophecy ever came from what some person wanted to say. But people were led by the Holy Spirit* and spoke words from God.

False Teachers

2 [1]In the past there were false prophets* among God's people. It is the same now. You will have some false teachers in your group. They will teach things that are wrong—ideas that will cause people to be lost. And they will teach in a way that will be hard for you to see that they are wrong. They will even refuse to follow the Master who bought their freedom. And so they will quickly destroy themselves. [2]Many people will follow them in the morally wrong things they do. And because of them, others will say bad things about the way of truth we follow. [3]These false teachers only want your money. So they will use you by telling you things that are not true. But the judgment against these false teachers has been ready for a long time. And they will not escape God who will destroy them.

[4]When angels sinned, God did not let them go free without punishment. He sent them to hell. He put those angels in caves of darkness, where they are being held until the time when God will judge them.

[5]And God punished the evil people who lived long ago. He brought a flood to the world that was full of people who were against God. But he saved Noah and seven other people with him. Noah was a man who told people about living right.

[6]God also punished the evil cities of Sodom and Gomorrah. He burned them until there was nothing left but ashes. He used those cities as an example of what will happen to people who are against God. [7]But he saved Lot, a good man who lived there. Lot was greatly troubled by the morally bad lives of those evil people. [8]This good man lived with those evil people every day, and his good heart was hurt by the evil things he saw and heard.

[9]So you see that the Lord God knows how to save those who are devoted to him. He will save them when troubles come. And the Lord will hold evil people to punish them on the day of judgment. [10]That punishment is for those who are always doing the evil that their sinful selves want to do. It is for those who hate the Lord's authority.

These false teachers do whatever they want, and they are so proud of themselves. They are not afraid even to say bad things against the glorious ones.[b] [11]The angels are much stronger and more powerful than these beings. But even the angels don't accuse them and say bad things about them to the Lord.

[12]But these false teachers speak evil against what they don't understand. They are like animals that do things without really thinking—like wild animals that are born to be caught and killed. And, like wild animals, they will be destroyed. [13]They have made many people suffer. So they themselves will suffer. That is their pay for what they have done.

They think it is fun to do evil where everyone can see them. They enjoy the evil things that please them. So they are like dirty spots and stains among you—they bring shame to you in the meals you eat together. [14]Every time they look at a woman, they want her. They are always sinning this way. And they lead weaker people into the trap of sin. They have taught themselves well to be greedy. They are under a curse.[c]

[15]These false teachers left the right way and went the wrong way. They followed the same way that the prophet Balaam* went. He was the son of Beor, who loved being paid for doing wrong. [16]But a donkey told him that he was doing wrong. A donkey cannot talk, of course, but that donkey spoke with a man's voice and stopped the prophet from acting so crazy.

[17]These false teachers are like springs that have no water. They are like clouds that are blown by a storm. A place in the deepest darkness has been kept for them. [18]They boast with words that mean nothing. They lead people into the trap of sin. They find people who have just escaped from a wrong way of life and lead them back into sin. They do this by using the evil things people want to do in their human weakness. [19]These false teachers promise those people freedom, but they themselves are not free. They are slaves to a mind that has been ruined by sin. Yes, people are slaves to anything that controls them.

[20]People can be made free from the evil in the world. They can be made free by knowing our Lord and Savior Jesus Christ. But if they go back into those evil things and are controlled by them, then it is worse for them than it was before. [21]Yes, it would be better for them to have never known the right way. That would be better than to know the right

---

[a]**1:17–18** This event is described in the gospels. See Mt. 17:1–8; Mk. 9:2–8; Lk. 9:28–36.

[b]**2:10** *the glorious ones* Literally, "the glories." These seem to be some kind of angelic beings.

[c]**2:14** *under a curse* Literally, "children of a curse," meaning that God will punish them.

way and then to turn away from the holy* teaching that was given to them. 22What they did is like these true sayings: "A dog vomits and goes back to what it threw up."*a And, "After a pig is washed, it goes back and rolls in the mud again."

Jesus Will Come Again

3 1My friends, this is the second letter I have written to you. I wrote both letters to you to help your honest minds remember something. 2I want you to remember the words that the holy prophets* spoke in the past. And remember the command that our Lord and Savior gave us. He gave us that command through your apostles.*

3It is important for you to understand what will happen in the last days. People will laugh at you. They will live following the evil they want to do. 4They will say, "Jesus promised to come again. Where is he? Our fathers have died, but the world continues the way it has been since it was made."

5But these people don't want to remember what happened long ago. The skies were there, and God made the earth from water and with water. All this happened by God's word. 6Then the world was flooded and destroyed with water. 7And that same word of God is keeping the skies and the earth that we have now. They are being kept to be destroyed by fire. They are kept for the day of judgment and the destruction of all people who are against God.

8But don't forget this one thing, dear friends: To the Lord a day is like a thousand years, and a thousand years is like a day. 9The Lord is not being slow in doing what he promised—the way some people understand slowness. But God is being patient with you. He doesn't want anyone to be lost. He wants everyone to change their ways and stop sinning.

10But the day when the Lord comes again will surprise everyone like the coming of a thief. The sky will disappear with a loud noise. Everything in the sky will be destroyed with fire. And the earth and everything in it will be burned up.b 11Everything will be destroyed in this way. So what kind of people should you be? Your lives should be holy* and devoted to God. 12You should be looking forward to the day of God, wanting more than anything else for it to come soon. When it comes, the sky will be destroyed with fire, and everything in the sky will melt with heat. 13But God made a promise to us. And we are waiting for what he promised—a new sky and a new earth. That will be the place where goodness lives.

14Dear friends, we are waiting for this to happen. So try as hard as you can to be without sin and without fault. Try to be at peace with God. 15Remember that we are saved because our Lord is patient. Our dear brother Paul told you that same thing when he wrote to you with the wisdom that God gave him. 16That's what he says in all his letters when he writes about these things. There are parts of his letters that are hard to understand, and some people give a wrong meaning to them. These people are ignorant and weak in faith. They also give wrong meanings to the other Scriptures.* But they are destroying themselves by doing that.

17Dear friends, you already know about this. So be careful. Don't let these evil people lead you away by the wrong they do. Be careful that you do not fall from your strong faith. 18But grow in the grace* and knowledge of our Lord and Savior Jesus Christ. Glory* be to him, now and forever! Amen.*

a2:22 Quote from Prov. 26:11.

b3:10 *will be burned up* Among the other readings of this text in early Greek copies, many have "will be found," and one has "will disappear."

1 John

1 1We want to tell you about the Wordc that gives life—the one who existed before the world began. This is the one we have heard and have seen with our own eyes. We saw what he did, and our hands touched him. 2Yes, the one who is life was shown to us. We saw him, and so we can tell others about him. We now tell you about him. He is the eternal life that was with God the Father and was shown to us. 3We are telling you about what we have seen and heard because we want you to have fellowshipd with us. The fellowship

c1:1 *Word* The Greek word is *"logos,"* meaning any kind of communication. Here, it means Christ—the way God told people about himself.

d1:3 *fellowship* Associating with people and sharing things together with them. Believers in Christ share love, joy, sorrow, faith, and other things with each other and with God. Also in verse 7.

we share together is with God the Father and his Son Jesus Christ. ⁴We write these things to you so that you can be full of joy with us.

God Forgives Our Sins

⁵We heard the true teaching from God. Now we tell it to you: God is light,* and in him there is no darkness.* ⁶So if we say that we share in life with God, but we continue living in darkness, we are liars, who don't follow the truth. ⁷We should live in the light, where God is. If we live in the light, we have fellowship with each other, and the blood sacrifice of Jesus, God's Son, washes away every sin and makes us clean.

⁸If we say that we have no sin, we are fooling ourselves, and the truth is not in us. ⁹But if we confess our sins, God will forgive us. We can trust God to do this. He always does what is right. He will make us clean from all the wrong things we have done. ¹⁰If we say that we have not sinned, we are saying that God is a liar and that we don't accept his true teaching.

Jesus Is Our Helper

2 ¹My dear children, I write this letter to you so that you will not sin. But if anyone sins, we have Jesus Christ to help us. He always did what was right, so he is able to defend us before God the Father. ²Jesus is the way our sins are taken away. And he is the way all people can have their sins taken away too.

³If we obey what God has told us to do, then we are sure that we know him. ⁴If we say we know God but do not obey his commands, we are lying. The truth is not in us. ⁵But when we obey God's teaching, his love is truly working in us. This is how we know that we are living in him. ⁶If we say we live in God, we must live the way Jesus lived.

Jesus Told Us to Love Others

⁷My dear friends, I am not writing a new command to you. It is the same command you have had since the beginning. This command is the teaching you have already heard. ⁸But what I write is also a new command. It is a true one; you can see its truth in Jesus and in yourselves. The darkness* is passing away, and the true light is already shining.

⁹Someone might say, "I am in the light,*" but if they hate any of their brothers or sisters in God's family, they are still in the darkness. ¹⁰Those who love their brothers and sisters live in the light, and there is nothing in them that will make them do wrong. ¹¹But whoever hates their brother or sister is in darkness. They live in darkness. They don't know where they are going, because the darkness has made them blind.

¹² I write to you, dear children,
    because your sins are forgiven through
        Christ.

¹³ I write to you, fathers,
    because you know the one who existed
        from the beginning.
  I write to you, young people,
    because you have defeated the Evil
        One.*

¹⁴ I write to you, children,
    because you know the Father.
  I write to you, fathers,
    because you know the one who existed
        from the beginning.
  I write to you, young people,
    because you are strong.
  The word of God lives in you,
    and you have defeated the Evil One.

¹⁵Don't love this evil world or the things in it. If you love the world, you do not have the love of the Father in you. ¹⁶This is all there is in the world: wanting to please our sinful selves, wanting the sinful things we see, and being too proud of what we have. But none of these comes from the Father. They come from the world. ¹⁷The world is passing away, and all the things that people want in the world are passing away. But whoever does what God wants will live forever.

Don't Follow the Enemies of Christ

¹⁸My dear children, the end is near! You have heard that the enemy of Christ* is coming. And now many enemies of Christ are already here. So we know that the end is near. ¹⁹These enemies were in our group, but they left us. They did not really belong with us. If they were really part of our group, they would have stayed with us. But they left. This shows that none of them really belonged with us.

²⁰You have the gift[a] that the Holy One[b] gave you. So you all know the truth. ²¹Do you think I am writing this letter because you don't know the truth? No, I am writing because you do know the truth. And you know that no lie comes from the truth.

²²So who is the liar? It is the one who says Jesus is not the Christ. Whoever says that is the enemy of Christ—the one who does not believe in the Father or in his Son. ²³Whoever does not believe in the Son does not have the Father, but whoever accepts the Son has the Father too.

²⁴Be sure that you continue to follow the teaching you heard from the beginning. If you do that, you will always be in the Son and in the Father. ²⁵And this is what the Son promised us—eternal life.

²⁶I am writing this letter about those who are trying to lead you into the wrong way. ²⁷Christ gave you a special gift. You still have this gift in you. So you don't need anyone to

---

[a]**2:20 gift** Literally, "anointing." This might mean the Holy Spirit. Or it might mean teaching or truth as in verse 24. Also in verse 27.
[b]**2:20 Holy One** God or Christ.

teach you. The gift he gave you teaches you about everything. It is a true gift, not a false one. So continue to live in Christ, as his gift taught you.

28Yes, my dear children, live in him. If we do this, we can be without fear on the day when Christ comes again. We will not need to hide and be ashamed when he comes. 29You know that Christ always did what was right. So you know that all those who do what is right are God's children.

We Are God's Children

3 1The Father has loved us so much! This shows how much he loved us: We are called children of God. And we really are his children. But the people in the world don't understand that we are God's children, because they have not known him. 2Dear friends, now we are children of God. We have not yet been shown what we will be in the future. But we know that when Christ comes again, we will be like him. We will see him just as he is. 3He is pure, and everyone who has this hope in him keeps themselves pure like Christ.

4Anyone who sins breaks God's law. Yes, sinning is the same as living against God's law. 5You know that Christ came to take away people's sins. There is no sin in Christ. 6So whoever lives in Christ does not continue to sin. If they continue to sin, they have never really understood Christ and have never known him.

7Dear children, don't let anyone lead you into the wrong way. Christ always did what was right. So to be good like Christ, you must do what is right. 8The devil has been sinning since the beginning. Anyone who continues to sin belongs to the devil. The Son of God came for this: to destroy the devil's work.

9Those who are God's children do not continue to sin, because the new life God gave them*a* stays in them. They cannot keep sinning, because they have become children of God. 10So we can see who God's children are and who the devil's children are. These are the ones who are not God's children: those who don't do what is right and those who do not love their brothers and sisters in God's family.

We Must Love One Another

11This is the teaching you have heard from the beginning: We must love each other. 12Don't be like Cain.* He belonged to the Evil One.* Cain killed his brother. But why did he kill him? Because what Cain did was evil, and what his brother did was good.

13Brothers and sisters, don't be surprised when the people of this world hate you. 14We know that we have left death and have come into life. We know this because we love each other as brothers and sisters. Anyone who does not love is still in death. 15Anyone who hates a fellow believer* is a murderer.*b* And you know that no murderer has eternal life.

16This is how we know what real love is: Jesus gave his life for us. So we should give our lives for each other as brothers and sisters. 17Suppose a believer who is rich enough to have all the necessities of life sees a fellow believer who is poor and does not have even basic needs. What if the rich believer does not help the poor one? Then it is clear that God's love is not in that person's heart. 18My children, our love should not be only words and talk. No, our love must be real. We must show our love by the things we do.

19-20That's how we know we belong to the way of truth. And when our hearts make us feel guilty, we can still have peace before God, because God is greater than our hearts. He knows everything.

21My dear friends, if we don't feel that we are doing wrong, we can be without fear when we come to God. 22And God gives us what we ask for. We receive it because we obey God's commands and do what pleases him. 23This is what God commands: that we believe in his Son Jesus Christ, and that we love each other as he commanded. 24All who obey God's commands live in God. And God lives in them. How do we know that God lives in us? We know because of the Spirit* he gave us.

John Warns Against False Teachers

4 1My dear friends, many false prophets* are in the world now. So don't believe every spirit, but test the spirits to see if they are from God. 2This is how you can recognize God's Spirit. One spirit says, "I believe that Jesus is the Christ* who came to earth and became a man." That Spirit is from God. 3Another spirit refuses to say this about Jesus. That spirit is not from God. This is the spirit of the enemy of Christ. You have heard that the enemy of Christ is coming, and now he is already in the world.

4My dear children, you belong to God, so you have already defeated these false prophets. That's because the one who is in you is greater than the one who is in the world. 5And they belong to the world, so what they say is from the world too. And the world listens to what they say. 6But we are from God. So the people who know God listen to us. But the people who are not from God don't listen to us. That is how we know the Spirit that is true and the spirit that is false.

---

*a*3:9 the new life God gave them Literally, "his seed."

*b*3:15 Anyone ... murderer Those who hate someone have in their mind the same motive that causes murder. So, morally, hating is equal to murder. Jesus taught his followers about this sin. See Mt. 5:21–26.

Love Comes From God

[7]Dear friends, we should love each other, because love comes from God. Everyone who loves has become God's child. And so everyone who loves knows God. [8]Anyone who does not love does not know God, because God is love. [9]This is how God showed his love to us: He sent his only Son into the world to give us life through him. [10]True love is God's love for us, not our love for God. He sent his Son as the way to take away our sins.

[11]That is how much God loved us, dear friends! So we also must love each other. [12]No one has ever seen God. But if we love each other, God lives in us. If we love each other, God's love has reached its goal—it is made perfect in us.

[13]We know that we live in God and God lives in us. We know this because he gave us his Spirit.* [14]We have seen that the Father sent his Son to be the Savior of the world, and this is what we tell people now. [15]Anyone who says, "I believe that Jesus is the Son of God," is a person who lives in God, and God lives in that person. [16]So we know the love that God has for us, and we trust that love.

God is love. Everyone who lives in love lives in God, and God lives in them. [17]If God's love is made perfect in us, we can be without fear on the day when God judges the world. We will be without fear, because in this world we are like Jesus.[a] [18]Where God's love is, there is no fear, because God's perfect love takes away fear. It is his punishment that makes a person fear. So his love is not made perfect in the one who has fear.

[19]We love because God first loved us. [20]If we say we love God but hate any of our brothers or sisters in his family, we are liars. If we don't love someone we have seen, how can we love God? We have never even seen him. [21]God gave us this command: If we love God, we must also love each other as brothers and sisters.

God's Children Win Against the World

5 [1]The people who believe that Jesus is the Christ* are God's children. Anyone who loves the Father also loves the Father's children. [2]How do we know that we love God's children? We know because we love God and we obey his commands. [3]Loving God means obeying his commands. And God's commands are not too hard for us, [4]because everyone who is a child of God has the power to win against the world. [5]It is our faith that has won

the victory against the world. So who wins against the world? Only those who believe that Jesus is the Son of God.

God Told Us About His Son

[6]Jesus Christ is the one who came. He came with water and with blood.[b] He did not come by water only. No, Jesus came by both water and blood. And the Spirit* tells us that this is true. The Spirit is the truth. [7]So there are three witnesses that tell us about Jesus: [8]the Spirit, the water, and the blood. These three witnesses agree.

[9]We believe people when they say something is true. But what God says is more important. And this is what God told us: He told us the truth about his own Son. [10]Whoever believes in the Son of God has the truth that God told us. But people who do not believe God make God a liar, because they do not believe what God told us about his Son. [11]This is what God told us: God has given us eternal life, and this life is in his Son. [12]Whoever has the Son has life, but whoever does not have the Son of God does not have life.

We Have Eternal Life Now

[13]I write this letter to you who believe in the Son of God. I write so that you will know that you have eternal life now. [14]We can come to God with no doubts. This means that when we ask God for things (and those things agree with what God wants for us), God cares about what we say. [15]He listens to us every time we ask him. So we know that he gives us whatever we ask from him.

[16]Suppose you see your fellow believer* sinning (sin that does not lead to eternal death). You should pray for them. Then God will give them life. I am talking about people whose sin does not lead to eternal death. There is sin that leads to death. I don't mean that you should pray about that kind of sin. [17]Doing wrong is always sin. But there is sin that does not lead to eternal death.

[18]We know that those who have been made God's children do not continue to sin. The Son of God keeps them safe.[c] The Evil One* cannot hurt them. [19]We know that we belong to God, but the Evil One controls the whole world. [20]And we know that the Son of God has come and has given us understanding. So now we can know the one who is true, and we live in that true God. We are in his Son, Jesus Christ. He is the true God, and he is eternal life. [21]So, dear children, keep yourselves away from false gods.

---

[b]**5:6 water, blood** Probably meaning the water of Jesus' baptism and the blood he shed on the cross.
[c]**5:18 The Son ... safe** Literally, "The one who was born from God keeps him safe" or "... keeps himself safe."
[a]**4:17 Jesus** Literally, "that one."

2 John

¹Greetings from the Elder.ᵃ

To the ladyᵇ chosen by God and to her children.

I truly love all of you. And I am not the only one. All those who know the truthᶜ love you in the same way. ²We love you because of the truth—the truth that lives in us. That truth will be with us forever.

³Grace,* mercy, and peace will be with us from God the Father and from his Son, Jesus Christ, as we live in truth and love.

⁴I was very happy to learn about some of your children. I am happy that they are following the way of truth, just as the Father commanded us. ⁵And now, dear lady, I tell you: We should all love each other. This is not a new command. It is the same command we had from the beginning. ⁶And loving means living the way he commanded us to live. And

God's command is this: that you live a life of love. You heard this command from the beginning.

⁷Many false teachers are in the world now. They refuse to say that Jesus Christ came to earth and became a man. Anyone who refuses to accept this fact is a false teacher and the enemy of Christ. ⁸Be careful! Don't lose the reward you have worked for. Be careful so that you will receive all of your reward.

⁹Everyone must continue to follow only the teaching about Christ. Whoever changes that teaching does not have God. But whoever continues to follow the teaching about Christ has both the Father and his Son. ¹⁰Don't accept those who come to you but do not bring this teaching. Don't invite them into your house. Don't welcome them in any way. ¹¹If you do, you are helping them with their evil work.

¹²I have much to say to you. But I don't want to use paper and ink. Instead, I hope to come visit you. Then we can be together and talk. That will make us very happy. ¹³The children of your sisterᵈ who was chosen by God send you their love.

ᵃ**1** *Elder* This is probably John the apostle. "Elder" means an older man or a special leader in the church (as in Titus 1:5).
ᵇ**1** *lady* This might mean a woman. Or, in this letter, it might mean a church. If it is a church, then "her children" would be the people of the church. Also in verse 5.
ᶜ**1** *truth* The truth or "Good News" about Jesus Christ that joins all believers together.

ᵈ**13** *sister* Sister of the "lady" in verse 1. This might be another woman or another church.

3 John

¹Greetings from the Elder.ᵉ

To my dear friend Gaius, a person I truly love.

²My dear friend, I know that you are doing well spiritually. So I pray that everything else is going well with you and that you are enjoying good health. ³Some believers* came and told me about the truthᶠ in your life. They told me that you continue to follow the way of truth. This made me very happy. ⁴It always

gives me the greatest joy when I hear that my children are following the way of truth.

⁵My dear friend, it is good that you continue to help the believers. They are people you don't even know. ⁶They told the church* about the love you have. Please help them to continue their trip. Help them in a way that will please God. ⁷They went on their trip to serve Christ. They did not accept any help from people who are not believers. ⁸So we should help them. When we help them, we share with their work for the truth.

⁹I wrote a letter to the church, but Diotrephes will not listen to what we say. He always wants to be the leader. ¹⁰When I

ᵉ**1** *Elder* This is probably John the apostle. "Elder" means an older man or a special leader in the church (as in Titus 1:5).
ᶠ**3** *truth* The truth or "Good News" about Jesus Christ that joins all believers together. Also in verses 8, 12.

come, I will talk with him about what he is doing. He lies and says evil things about us, but that is not all. He refuses to welcome and help the believers who travel there. And he will not let anyone else help them. If they do, he makes them leave the church.

¹¹My dear friend, don't follow what is bad; follow what is good. Whoever does what is good is from God. But whoever does evil has never known God.

¹²Everyone says good things about Demetrius, and the truth agrees with what they say. Also, we say good about him. And you know that what we say is true.

¹³I have many things I want to tell you. But I don't want to use pen and ink. ¹⁴I hope to visit you soon. Then we can be together and talk. ¹⁵Peace to you. The friends here with me send their love. Please give our love to each one of the friends there.

Jude

¹Greetings from Jude, a servant of Jesus Christ and a brother of James.

To those who have been chosen and are loved by God the Father and have been kept safe in Jesus Christ.

²Mercy, peace, and love be yours more and more.

God Will Punish Those Who Do Wrong

³Dear friends, I wanted very much to write to you about the salvation we all share together. But I felt the need to write to you about something else: I want to encourage you to fight hard for the faith that God gave his holy people.* God gave this faith once, and it is good for all time. ⁴Some people have secretly entered your group. These people have already been judged guilty for what they are doing. Long ago the prophets* wrote about them. They are against God. They have used the grace* of our God in the wrong way—to do sinful things. They refuse to follow Jesus Christ, our only Master and Lord.

⁵I want to help you remember some things you already know: Remember that the Lord saved his people by bringing them out of the land of Egypt. But later he destroyed all those who did not believe. ⁶And remember the angels who lost their authority to rule. They left their proper home. So the Lord has kept them in darkness, bound with everlasting chains, to be judged on the great day. ⁷Also, remember the cities of Sodom* and Gomorrah* and the other towns around them. Like those angels they were full of sexual sin and involved themselves in sexual relations that are wrong. And they suffer the punishment of eternal fire, an example for us to see.

⁸It is the same way with these people who have entered your group. They are guided by dreams. They make themselves dirty with sin. They reject God's authority and say bad things against the glorious ones.ᵃ ⁹Not even the archangel* Michael did this. Michael argued with the devil about who would have the body of Moses.* But Michael did not dare to condemn even the devil for his false accusations. Instead, Michael said, "The Lord punish you!"

¹⁰But these people criticize things they don't understand. They do understand some things. But they understand these things not by thinking, but by feeling, the way dumb animals understand things. And these are the things that destroy them. ¹¹It will be bad for them. They have followed the way that Cain* went. To make money, they have given themselves to following the wrong way that Balaam* went. They have fought against God like Korahᵇ did. And like Korah, they will be destroyed.

¹²These people are like dirty spots among you—they bring shame to you in the special meals you share together. They eat with you and have no fear. They take care of only themselves. They are like clouds without rain. The wind blows them around. They are like trees that have no fruit at harvest time and are pulled out of the ground. So they are twice dead. ¹³Like the dirty foam on the wild waves in the sea, everyone can see the shameful things they do. They are like stars that wander in the sky. A place in the blackest darkness has been kept for them forever.

¹⁴Enoch, the seventh descendant from Adam, said this about these people: "Look, the Lord is coming with thousands and thousands of his holy* angels ¹⁵to judge everyone. He will punish all those who are against him for all the evil they have done in their lack of respect for him. Yes, the Lord will punish all

---

ᵃ8 the glorious ones Literally, "the glories." These seem to be some kind of angelic beings.
ᵇ11 Korah He turned against Moses. See Num. 16:1-40.

these sinners who don't honor him. He will punish them for all the evil things they have said against him."

16These people always complain and find wrong in others. They always do the evil things they want to do. They boast about themselves. The only reason they say good things about others is to get what they want.

A Warning and Things to Do

17Dear friends, remember what the apostles* of our Lord Jesus Christ said would happen. 18They told you, "In the last times there will be people who laugh at God and do only what they want to do—things that are against God." 19These are the people who divide you. They are not spiritual, because they don't have the Spirit.*

20But you, dear friends, use your most holy faith to build yourselves up even stronger. Pray with the help of the Holy Spirit. 21Keep yourselves safe in God's love, as you wait for the Lord Jesus Christ in his mercy to give you eternal life.

22Help those who have doubts. 23Rescue those who are living in danger of hell's fire. There are others you should treat with mercy, but be very careful that their filthy lives don't rub off on you.a

Praise God

24God is strong and can keep you from falling. He can bring you before his glory* without any wrong in you and give you great joy. 25He is the only God, the one who saves us. To him be glory, greatness, power, and authority through Jesus Christ our Lord for all time past, now, and forever. Amen.*

a23 that ... on you Literally, "hating even their undershirt that is defiled from the flesh."

Revelation

John Tells About This Book

1 1This is a revelationb from Jesus Christ, which God gave him to show his servants what must happen soon. And Christ sent his angel to show it to his servant John, 2who has told everything he saw. It is the truth that Jesus Christ told him; it is the message from God. 3Great blessings belong to the person who reads the words of this message from God and to those who hear this message and do what is written in it. There is not much time left.

John Writes to the Churches

4From John,
To the seven churches* in the province of Asia*:

Grace* and peace to you from the one who is, who always was, and who is coming; and from the seven spirits before his throne; 5and from Jesus Christ. Jesus is the faithful witness. He is first among all who will be raised from death. He is the ruler of the kings of the earth.

Jesus is the one who loves us and has made us free from our sins with his blood sacrifice. 6He made us his kingdom* and priests who serve God his Father. To Jesus be glory* and power forever and ever! Amen.*

7Look, Jesus is coming with the clouds! Everyone will see him, even those who piercedc him. All peoples of the earth will cry loudly because of him. Yes, this will happen! Amen.

8The Lord God says, "I am the Alpha and the Omega.d I am the one who is, who always was, and who is coming. I am the All-Powerful."

9I am John, your fellow believer.* We are together in Jesus, and we share these things: suffering, the kingdom, and patient endurance. I was on the island of Patmose because I was faithful to God's message* and to the truth of Jesus. 10On the Lord's Day, the Spirit* took control of me. I heard a loud voice behind me that sounded like a trumpet. 11It said, "Write down in a book what you see, and send it to the seven churches: to Ephesus, Smyrna, Pergamum, Thyatira, Sardis, Philadelphia, and Laodicea."

12I turned to see who was talking to me. When I turned, I saw seven golden lampstands. 13I saw someone among the lampstands who looked like the Son of Man.* He was dressed in a long robe, with a golden sash tied around his chest. 14His head and hair

b1:1 revelation An opening up (making known) of truth that was hidden.

c1:7 pierced When Jesus was killed, he was stabbed with a spear in the side. See Jn. 19:34.
d1:8 Alpha ... Omega The first and last letters in the Greek alphabet, meaning the beginning and the end.
e1:9 Patmos A small island in the Aegean Sea, near the coast of modern Turkey.

were white like wool—wool that is white as snow. His eyes were like flames of fire. [15]His feet were like brass that glows hot in a furnace. His voice was like the noise of flooding water. [16]He held seven stars in his right hand. A sharp two-edged sword came out of his mouth. He looked like the sun shining at its brightest time.

[17]When I saw him, I fell down at his feet like a dead man. He put his right hand on me and said, "Don't be afraid! I am the First and the Last. [18]I am the one who lives. I was dead, but look, I am alive forever and ever! And I hold the keys of death and Hades.* [19]So write what you see. Write the things that happen now and the things that will happen later. [20]Here is the hidden meaning of the seven stars that you saw in my right hand and the seven golden lampstands that you saw: The seven lampstands are the seven churches. The seven stars are the angels of the seven churches.

Jesus' Letter to the Church in Ephesus

2 [1]"Write this to the angel of the church* in Ephesus:

"Here is a message from the one who holds the seven stars in his right hand and walks among the seven golden lampstands.

[2]"I know what you do, how hard you work and never give up. I know that you don't accept evil people. You have tested those who say they are apostles* but are not. You found that they are liars. [3]You never stop trying. You have endured troubles for my name and have not given up.

[4]"But I have this against you: You have left the love you had in the beginning. [5]So remember where you were before you fell. Change your hearts and do what you did at first. If you don't change, I will come to you and remove your lampstand from its place. [6]But there is something you do that is right—you hate the things that the Nicolaitans[a] do. I also hate what they do.

[7]"Everyone who hears this should listen to what the Spirit* says to the churches. To those who win the victory I will give the right to eat the fruit from the tree of life,* which is in God's paradise.*

Jesus' Letter to the Church in Smyrna

[8]"Write this to the angel of the church* in Smyrna:

"Here is a message from the one who is the First and the Last, the one who died and came to life again.

[9]"I know your troubles, and I know that you are poor, but really you are rich! I know the insults you have suffered from people who say they are Jews. But they are not true Jews. They are a group[b] that belongs to Satan.* [10]Don't be afraid of what will happen to you. I tell you, the devil will put some of you in prison. He will do this to test you. You will suffer for ten days, but be faithful, even if you have to die. If you continue to be faithful, I will give you the crown* of life.

[11]"Everyone who hears this should listen to what the Spirit* says to the churches. Those who win the victory will not be hurt by the second death.

Jesus' Letter to the Church in Pergamum

[12]"Write this to the angel of the church* in Pergamum:

"Here is a message from the one who has the sharp two-edged sword.

[13]"I know where you live. You live where Satan* has his throne, but you are true to me. You did not refuse to tell about your faith in me even during the time of Antipas. Antipas was my faithful witness[c] who was killed in your city, the city where Satan lives.

[14]"But I have a few things against you. You have people there who follow the teaching of Balaam.* Balaam taught Balak how to make the people of Israel* sin. They sinned by eating food offered to idols* and by committing sexual sins. [15]It is the same in your group. You have people who follow the teaching of the Nicolaitans. [16]So change your hearts! If you don't change, I will come to you quickly and fight against these people with the sword that comes out of my mouth.

[17]"Everyone who hears this should listen to what the Spirit* says to the churches!

"I will give the hidden manna* to everyone who wins the victory. I will also give each one a white stone that has a new name written on it. And no one will know this name except the one who gets the stone.

Jesus' Letter to the Church in Thyatira

[18]"Write this to the angel of the church* in Thyatira:

"Here is a message from the Son of God, the one who has eyes that blaze like fire and feet like shining brass.

[19]"I know what you do. I know about your love, your faith, your service, and your patience. I know that you are doing more now than you did at first. [20]But I have this against you: You let that woman Jezebel do what she wants. She says that she is a prophet,[d] but she is leading my people away with her teaching. Jezebel leads my people to commit sexual sins and to eat food that is offered to idols.* [21]I have given her time to change her heart and

---

[a]**2:6** *Nicolaitans* A religious group that followed wrong ideas. Also in verse 15.

[b]**2:9** *group* Literally, "synagogue."

[c]**2:13** *faithful witness* A person who speaks God's message truthfully, even in times of danger.

[d]**2:20** *prophet* Jezebel was a false prophet. She claimed to speak for God, but she didn't really speak God's truth.

turn away from her sin, but she does not want to change.

²²"So I will throw her on a bed of suffering. And all those who commit adultery* with her will suffer greatly. I will do this now if they don't turn away from the things she does. ²³I will also kill her followers. Then all the churches will see that I am the one who knows what people feel and think. And I will repay each of you for what you have done.

²⁴"But others of you in Thyatira have not followed her teaching. You have not learned the things they call 'Satan's* deep secrets.' This is what I say to you: I will not put any other burden on you. ²⁵Only hold on to the truth you have until I come.

²⁶"I will give power over the nations to all those who win the victory and continue until the end to do what I want. ²⁷They will rule the nations with an iron rod. They will break them to pieces like clay pots.ᵃ ²⁸They will have the same power I received from my Father, and I will give them the morning star. ²⁹Everyone who hears this should listen to what the Spirit* says to the churches.

Jesus' Letter to the Church in Sardis

3 ¹"Write this to the angel of the church* in Sardis:

"Here is a message from the one who has the seven spirits and the seven stars.

"I know what you do. People say that you are alive, but really you are dead. ²Wake up! Make yourselves stronger before what little strength you have left is completely gone. I find that what you do is not good enough for my God. ³So don't forget what you have received and heard. Obey it. Change your hearts and lives! You must wake up, or I will come to you and surprise you like a thief. You will not know when I will come.

⁴"But you have a few people in your group there in Sardis who have kept themselves clean. They will walk with me. They will wear white clothes, because they are worthy. ⁵Everyone who wins the victory will be dressed in white clothes like them. I will not remove their names from the book of life. I will say that they belong to me before my Father and before his angels. ⁶Everyone who hears this should listen to what the Spirit* says to the churches.

Jesus' Letter to the Church in Philadelphia

⁷"Write this to the angel of the church* in Philadelphia:

"Here is a message from the one who is holy and true, the one who holds the key of David.* When he opens something, it cannot be closed. And when he closes something, it cannot be opened.

⁸"I know what you do. I have put before you an open door that no one can close. I know you are weak, but you have followed my teaching. You were not afraid to speak my name. ⁹Listen! There is a groupᵇ that belongs to Satan.* They say they are Jews, but they are liars. They are not true Jews. I will make them come before you and bow at your feet. They will know that you are the people I have loved. ¹⁰You followed my command to endure patiently. So I will keep you from the time of trouble that will come to the world—a time that will test everyone living on earth.

¹¹"I am coming soon. Hold on to the faith you have, so that no one can take away your crown.* ¹²Those who win the victory will be pillars* in the temple of my God. I will make that happen for them. They will never again have to leave God's temple. I will write on them the name of my God and the name of the city of my God. That city is the new Jerusalem.ᶜ It is coming down out of heaven from my God. I will also write my new name on them. ¹³Everyone who hears this should listen to what the Spirit* says to the churches.

Jesus' Letter to the Church in Laodicea

¹⁴"Write this to the angel of the church* in Laodicea:

"Here is a message from the Amen,ᵈ the faithful and true witness, the ruler of all that God has made.

¹⁵"I know what you do. You are not hot or cold. I wish that you were hot or cold! ¹⁶But you are only warm—not hot, not cold. So I am ready to spit you out of my mouth. ¹⁷You say you are rich. You think you have become wealthy and don't need anything. But you don't know that you are really miserable, pitiful, poor, blind, and naked. ¹⁸I advise you to buy gold from me—gold made pure in fire. Then you will be rich. I tell you this: Buy clothes that are white. Then you will be able to cover your shameful nakedness. I also tell you to buy medicine to put on your eyes. Then you will be able to see.

¹⁹"I correct and punish the people I love. So show that nothing is more important to you than living right. Change your hearts and lives. ²⁰Here I am! I stand at the door and knock. If you hear my voice and open the door, I will come in and eat with you. And you will eat with me.

²¹"I will let everyone who wins the victory sit with me on my throne. It was the same with me. I won the victory and sat down with my Father on his throne. ²²Everyone who hears this should listen to what the Spirit* says to the churches."

ᵇ**3:9** *group* Literally, "synagogue."
ᶜ**3:12** *new Jerusalem* The spiritual city where God's people live with him.
ᵈ**3:14** *Amen* Used here, as a name for Jesus, it means to agree strongly that something is true.

ᵃ**2:26–27** These verses are almost the same as Ps. 2:8–9.

John Sees Heaven

4 ¹Then I looked, and there before me was an open door in heaven. And I heard the same voice that spoke to me before. It was the voice that sounded like a trumpet. It said, "Come up here, and I will show you what must happen after this." ²Immediately the Spirit* took control of me, and there in heaven was a throne with someone sitting on it. ³The one sitting there was as beautiful as precious stones, like jasper and carnelian. All around the throne was a rainbow with clear colors like an emerald.

⁴In a circle around the throne were 24 other thrones with 24 elders* sitting on them. The elders were dressed in white, and they had golden crowns on their heads. ⁵Lightning flashes and noises of thunder came from the throne. Before the throne there were seven lamps burning, which are the seven Spirits of God. ⁶Also before the throne there was something that looked like a sea of glass, as clear as crystal.

In front of the throne and on each side of it there were four living beings. They had eyes all over them, in front and in back. ⁷The first living being was like a lion. The second was like a bull. The third had a face like a man. The fourth was like a flying eagle. ⁸Each of these four living beings had six wings. They were covered all over with eyes, inside and out. Day and night they never stopped saying,

"Holy, holy, holy is the Lord God
    All-Powerful.
He always was, he is, and he is coming."

⁹These living beings were giving glory* and honor and thanks to the one who sits on the throne, the one who lives forever and ever. And every time they did this, ¹⁰the 24 elders bowed down before the one who sits on the throne. They worshiped him who lives forever and ever. They put their crowns down before the throne and said,

¹¹"Our Lord and God!
You are worthy to receive glory and honor
    and power.
You made all things.
Everything existed and was made because
    you wanted it."

Who Can Open the Scroll?

5 ¹Then I saw a scroll* in the right hand of the one sitting on the throne. The scroll had writing on both sides and was kept closed with seven seals.* ²And I saw a powerful angel, who called in a loud voice, "Who is worthy to break the seals and open the scroll?" ³But there was no one in heaven or on earth or under the earth who could open the scroll or look inside it. ⁴I cried and cried because there was no one who was worthy to open the scroll or look inside. ⁵But one of the elders* said to me, "Don't cry! The Lion*ª from the tribe of Judah has won the victory. He is David's* descendant. He is able to open the scroll and its seven seals."

⁶Then I saw a Lamb* standing in the center near the throne with the four living beings around it. The elders were also around the Lamb. The Lamb looked as if it had been killed. It had seven horns and seven eyes, which are the seven spirits of God that were sent into all the world. ⁷The Lamb came and took the scroll from the right hand of the one sitting on the throne. ⁸After the Lamb took the scroll, the four living beings and the 24 elders bowed down before the Lamb. Each one of them had a harp. Also, they were holding golden bowls full of incense,* which are the prayers of God's holy people.* ⁹And they all sang a new song to the Lamb:

"You are worthy to take the scroll
    and to open its seals,
because you were killed,
    and with your blood sacrifice you
        bought people for God
    from every tribe, language, race of
        people, and nation.
¹⁰ You made them to be a kingdom and to be
        priests for our God.
    And they will rule on the earth."

¹¹Then I looked, and I heard the voices of many angels. The angels were around the throne, the four living beings, and the elders. There were thousands and thousands of angels—10,000 times 10,000. ¹²The angels said in a loud voice,

"All power, wealth, wisdom, and strength
    belong to the Lamb who was killed.
He is worthy to receive honor, glory,*
    and praise!"

¹³Then I heard every created being that is in heaven and on earth and under the earth and in the sea, everything in all these places, saying,

"All praise and honor and glory and power
    forever and ever
to the one who sits on the throne and to
    the Lamb!"

¹⁴The four living beings said, "Amen*!" And the elders bowed down and worshiped.

The Lamb Opens the Scroll

6 ¹Then I watched as the Lamb* opened the first of the seven seals.* Then I heard one of the four living beings speak with a voice like thunder. It said, "Come!" ²I looked, and there before me was a white horse. The rider on the horse held a bow and was given a

ª**5:5 Lion** Used here to refer to Jesus.

crown.* He rode out to defeat the enemy and win the victory.

³The Lamb opened the second seal. Then I heard the second living being say, "Come!" ⁴Then another horse came out, a red one. The rider on the horse was given power to take away peace from the earth so that people would kill each other. He was given a big sword.

⁵The Lamb opened the third seal. Then I heard the third living being say, "Come!" I looked, and there before me was a black horse. The rider on the horse held a pair of scales in his hand. ⁶Then I heard something that sounded like a voice. The voice came from where the four living beings were. It said, "A quart*ᵃ* of wheat or three quarts of barley will cost a full day's pay. But don't harm the supply of olive oil and wine!"

⁷The Lamb opened the fourth seal. Then I heard the voice of the fourth living being say, "Come!" ⁸I looked, and there before me was a pale-colored horse. The rider on the horse was death, and Hades* was following close behind him. They were given power over a fourth of the earth—power to kill people with the sword, by starving, by disease, and with the wild animals of the earth.

⁹The Lamb opened the fifth seal. Then I saw some souls under the altar.* They were the souls of those who had been killed because they were faithful to God's message* and to the truth they had received. ¹⁰These souls shouted in a loud voice, "Holy and true Lord, how long until you judge the people of the earth and punish them for killing us?" ¹¹Then each one of them was given a white robe. They were told to wait a short time longer. There were still some of their brothers and sisters in the service of Christ who must be killed as they were. These souls were told to wait until all the killing was finished.

¹²Then I watched while the Lamb opened the sixth seal. There was a great earthquake, and the sun became as black as sackcloth.*ᵇ* The full moon became red like blood. ¹³The stars in the sky fell to the earth like a fig tree dropping its figs when the wind blows. ¹⁴The sky was split in the middle and both sides rolled up like a scroll.* And every mountain and island was moved from its place.

¹⁵Then all the people—the kings of the world, the rulers, the army commanders, the rich people, the powerful people, every slave, and every free person—hid themselves in caves and behind the rocks on the mountains. ¹⁶They said to the mountains and the rocks, "Fall on us. Hide us from the face of the one who sits on the throne. Hide us from the anger of the Lamb! ¹⁷The great day for their anger has come. No one can stand against it."

The 144,000 People of Israel

7 ¹After this happened I saw four angels standing at the four corners of the earth. The angels were holding the four winds of the earth. They were stopping the wind from blowing on the land or the sea or on any tree. ²Then I saw another angel coming from the east. This angel had the seal* of the living God. The angel called out in a loud voice to the four angels. These were the four angels that God had given the power to hurt the earth and the sea. The angel said to them, ³"Don't harm the land or the sea or the trees before we mark the foreheads of those who serve our God."

⁴Then I heard how many people had God's mark on their foreheads. There were 144,000. They were from every tribe of the people of Israel*:

⁵	from the tribe of Judah	12,000
	from the tribe of Reuben	12,000
	from the tribe of Gad	12,000
⁶	from the tribe of Asher	12,000
	from the tribe of Naphtali	12,000
	from the tribe of Manasseh	12,000
⁷	from the tribe of Simeon	12,000
	from the tribe of Levi	12,000
	from the tribe of Issachar	12,000
⁸	from the tribe of Zebulun	12,000
	from the tribe of Joseph	12,000
	from the tribe of Benjamin	12,000

The Great Crowd

⁹Then I looked, and there was a large crowd of people. There were so many people that no one could count them all. They were from every nation, tribe, race of people, and language of the earth. They were standing before the throne and before the Lamb.* They all wore white robes and had palm branches in their hands. ¹⁰They shouted loudly, "Victory belongs to our God, who sits on the throne, and to the Lamb."

¹¹The elders* and the four living beings were there. All the angels were standing around them and the throne. The angels bowed down on their faces before the throne and worshiped God. ¹²They said, "Amen*! Praise, glory,* wisdom, thanks, honor, power, and strength belong to our God forever and ever. Amen!"

¹³Then one of the elders asked me, "Who are these people in white robes? Where did they come from?"

¹⁴I answered, "You know who they are, sir."

And the elder said, "These are the ones who have come out of the great suffering. They have washed their robes*ᶜ* with the blood of the Lamb, and they are clean and white. ¹⁵So

---

*ᵃ***6:6** *quart* Literally, "*choinix*," the amount of the daily ration of grain for a soldier. Equals about 1 liter.
*ᵇ***6:12** *sackcloth* Literally, "sackcloth of hair." See "sackcloth" in the Word List.

*ᶜ***7:14** *washed their robes* Meaning that they had believed in Jesus and had been made clean from sin by his blood sacrifice. See Rev. 5:9; Heb. 9:14; 10:14–22; Acts 22:16; 1 Jn. 1:7.

now these people are before the throne of God. They worship God day and night in his temple. And the one who sits on the throne will protect them. [16]They will never be hungry again. They will never be thirsty again. The sun will not hurt them. No heat will burn them. [17]The Lamb in front of the throne will be their shepherd. He will lead them to springs of water that give life. And God will wipe away every tear from their eyes."

The Seventh Seal

8 [1]The Lamb* opened the seventh seal.* Then there was silence in heaven for about half an hour. [2]And I saw the seven angels who stand before God. They were given seven trumpets.

[3]Another angel came and stood at the altar.* This angel had a golden holder for incense.* The angel was given much incense to offer with the prayers of all God's holy people.* The angel put this offering on the golden altar before the throne. [4]The smoke from the incense went up from the angel's hand to God. The smoke went up with the prayers of God's people. [5]Then the angel filled the incense holder with fire from the altar and threw it down on the earth. Then there were flashes of lightning, thunder and other noises, and an earthquake.

The First of Seven Trumpet Blasts

[6]Then the seven angels with the seven trumpets prepared to blow their trumpets.

[7]The first angel blew his trumpet. Then hail and fire mixed with blood was poured down on the earth. And a third of the earth and all the green grass and a third of the trees were burned up.

[8]The second angel blew his trumpet. Then something that looked like a big mountain burning with fire was thrown into the sea. And a third of the sea became blood. [9]And a third of the created beings in the sea died, and a third of the ships were destroyed.

[10]The third angel blew his trumpet. Then a large star, burning like a torch, fell from the sky. It fell on a third of the rivers and on the springs of water. [11]The name of the star was Bitterness.[a] And a third of all the water became bitter. Many people died from drinking this bitter water.

[12]The fourth angel blew his trumpet. Then a third of the sun and a third of the moon and a third of the stars were struck. So a third of them became dark. A third of the day and night was without light.

[13]While I watched, I heard an eagle that was flying high in the air. The eagle said in a loud voice, "Terrible! Terrible! How terrible for those who live on the earth! The terrible trouble will begin after the sounds of the trumpets that the other three angels will blow."

The Fifth Trumpet Begins the First Terror

9 [1]The fifth angel blew his trumpet. Then I saw a star fall from the sky to the earth. The star was given the key to the deep hole that leads down to the bottomless pit. [2]Then the star opened the hole leading to the pit. Smoke came up from the hole like smoke from a big furnace. The sun and sky became dark because of the smoke from the hole.

[3]Then locusts* came out of the smoke and went down to the earth. They were given the power to sting like scorpions. [4]They were told not to damage the fields of grass or any plant or tree. They were to hurt only those who did not have God's mark on their foreheads. [5]They were not given the power to kill them but only to cause them pain for five months—pain like a person feels when stung by a scorpion. [6]During those days people will look for a way to die, but they will not find it. They will want to die, but death will hide from them.

[7]The locusts looked like horses prepared for battle. On their heads they wore something that looked like a gold crown. Their faces looked like human faces. [8]Their hair was like women's hair. Their teeth were like lions' teeth. [9]Their chests looked like iron breastplates. The sound their wings made was like the noise of many horses and chariots hurrying into battle. [10]The locusts had tails with stingers like scorpions. The power they had to give people pain for five months was in their tails. [11]They had a ruler, who was the angel of the bottomless pit. His name in Hebrew is Abaddon.[b] In Greek it is Apollyon.[c]

[12]The first terror is now past. There are still two other terrors to come.

The Sixth Trumpet Blast

[13]The sixth angel blew his trumpet. Then I heard a voice coming from the horns on the four corners of the golden altar* that is before God. [14]It said to the sixth angel who had the trumpet, "Free the four angels who are tied at the great river Euphrates." [15]These four angels had been kept ready for this hour and day and month and year. The angels were set free to kill a third of all the people on the earth. [16]I heard how many troops on horses were in their army. There were 200,000,000.

[17]In my vision,* I saw the horses and the riders on the horses. They looked like this: They had breastplates that were fiery red, dark blue, and yellow like sulfur. The heads of the horses looked like heads of lions. The horses had fire, smoke, and sulfur coming out of their mouths. [18]A third of all the people on

---

[a]**8:11** *Bitterness* Literally, "Wormwood," a very bitter plant; here, it is a symbol of bitter sorrow.

[b]**9:11** *Abaddon* A Hebrew name meaning "death" or "destruction." See Job 26:6 and Ps. 88:11.
[c]**9:11** *Apollyon* A name that means "destroyer."

earth were killed by these three plagues coming out of the horses' mouths: the fire, the smoke, and the sulfur. ¹⁹The horses' power was in their mouths and also in their tails. Their tails were like snakes that have heads to bite and hurt people.

²⁰The other people on earth were not killed by these plagues. But these people still did not change their hearts and turn away from worshiping the things they had made with their own hands. They did not stop worshiping demons* and idols* made of gold, silver, bronze, stone, and wood—things that cannot see or hear or walk. ²¹They did not change their hearts and turn away from killing other people or from their evil magic, their sexual sins, and their stealing.

The Angel and the Little Scroll

10 ¹Then I saw another powerful angel coming down from heaven. The angel was dressed in a cloud. He had a rainbow around his head. The angel's face was like the sun, and his legs were like poles of fire. ²The angel was holding a small scroll.* The scroll was open in his hand. He put his right foot on the sea and his left foot on the land. ³He shouted loudly like the roaring of a lion. After he shouted, the voices of seven thunders spoke.

⁴The seven thunders spoke, and I started to write. But then I heard a voice from heaven that said, "Don't write what the seven thunders said. Keep those things secret."

⁵Then the angel I saw standing on the sea and on the land raised his right hand to heaven. ⁶The angel made a promise by the power of the one who lives forever and ever. He is the one who made the skies and all that is in them. He made the earth and all that is in it, and he made the sea and all that is in it. The angel said, "There will be no more waiting! ⁷In the days when the seventh angel is ready to blow his trumpet, God's secret plan will be completed—the Good News* that God told to his servants, the prophets.*"

⁸Then I heard the same voice from heaven again. It said to me, "Go and take the open scroll that is in the angel's hand. This is the angel who is standing on the sea and on the land."

⁹So I went to the angel and asked him to give me the little scroll. He said to me, "Take the scroll and eat it. It will be sour in your stomach, but in your mouth it will be sweet like honey." ¹⁰So I took the little scroll from the angel's hand and ate it. In my mouth it tasted sweet like honey, but after I ate it, it was sour in my stomach. ¹¹Then I was told, "You must prophesy* again about many races of people, many nations, languages, and rulers."

The Two Witnesses

11 ¹Then I was given a measuring rod as long as a walking stick. I was told, "Go and measure the temple*a* of God and the altar,* and count the people worshiping there. ²But don't measure the yard outside the temple. Leave it alone. It has been given to those who are not God's people. They will show their power over the holy city for 42 months. ³And I will give power to my two witnesses. And they will prophesy* for 1260 days. They will be dressed in sackcloth.*"

⁴These two witnesses are the two olive trees and the two lampstands that stand before the Lord of the earth. ⁵If anyone tries to hurt the witnesses, fire comes from the mouths of the witnesses and kills their enemies. Anyone who tries to hurt them will die like this. ⁶These witnesses have the power to stop the sky from raining during the time they are prophesying. These witnesses have power to make the water become blood. They have power to send every kind of plague to the earth. They can do this as many times as they want.

⁷When the two witnesses have finished telling their message, the beast will fight against them. This is the beast that comes up from the bottomless pit. It will defeat and kill them. ⁸The bodies of the two witnesses will lie in the street of the great city. This city is named Sodom* and Egypt. These names for the city have a special meaning. This is the city where the Lord was killed. ⁹People from every race of people, tribe, language, and nation will look at the bodies of the two witnesses for three and a half days. The people will refuse to bury them. ¹⁰Everyone on the earth will be happy because these two are dead. They will have parties and send each other gifts. They will do this because these two prophets brought much suffering to the people living on earth.

¹¹But after three and a half days, God let life enter the two witnesses again. They stood on their feet. All those who saw them were filled with fear. ¹²Then the two witnesses heard a loud voice from heaven say, "Come up here!" And both of them went up into heaven in a cloud. Their enemies watched them go.

¹³At that same time there was a great earthquake. A tenth of the city was destroyed. And 7000 people were killed in the earthquake. Those who did not die were very afraid. They gave glory* to the God of heaven.

¹⁴The second terror is now past. The third terror is coming soon.

The Seventh Trumpet Blast

¹⁵The seventh angel blew his trumpet. Then there were loud voices in heaven. The voices said,

---

*a*11:1 *temple* God's house—the place where God's people worship and serve him. Here, John sees it pictured as the special building in Jerusalem for Jewish worship. Also in verse 19.

"The kingdom of the world has now
    become the kingdom of our Lord and
    of his Christ.*
And he will rule forever and ever."

16Then the 24 elders* bowed down on
their faces and worshiped God. These are the
elders who sit on their thrones before God.
17The elders said,

"We give thanks to you, Lord God
    All-Powerful.
You are the one who is and who always
    was.
We thank you because you have used
    your great power
    and have begun to rule.
18 The people of the world were angry,
    but now is the time for your anger.
Now is the time for the dead to be judged.
It is time to reward your servants, the
    prophets,*
    and to reward your holy people,*
    the people, great and small, who respect
    you.
It is time to destroy those people who
    destroy the earth!"

19Then God's temple in heaven was
opened. The Box of the Agreement*a* could be
seen in his temple. Then there were flashes
of lightning, noises, thunder, an earthquake,
and a great hailstorm.

The Woman Giving Birth and the Dragon

12 1And then a great wonder appeared in
heaven: There was a woman who was
clothed with the sun, and the moon was under
her feet. She had a crown of twelve stars on her
head. 2She was pregnant and cried out with
pain because she was about to give birth.

3Then another wonder appeared in heaven:
There was a giant red dragon there. The
dragon had seven heads with a crown on each
head. It also had ten horns. 4Its tail swept a
third of the stars out of the sky and threw
them down to the earth. It stood in front of
the woman who was ready to give birth to
the baby. It wanted to eat the woman's baby
as soon as it was born.

5The woman gave birth to a son, who would
rule all the nations with an iron rod. And her
child was taken up to God and to his throne.
6The woman ran away into the desert to a
place that God had prepared for her. There
she would be taken care of for 1260 days.

7Then there was a war in heaven. Michael*b*

*a***11:19 Box of the Agreement** This is like the special
box kept in the Most Holy Place of the Israelite
Holy Tent and, later, the Jerusalem Temple, which
contained "proof" of the agreement between God
and his people. See "Box of the Agreement" in the
Word List.

*b***12:7 Michael** The archangel—leader of God's
angels. See Jude 9.

and his angels fought against the dragon.
The dragon and its angels fought back, 8but
they were not strong enough. The dragon
and its angels lost their place in heaven. 9It
was thrown down out of heaven. (This giant
dragon is that old snake, the one called the
devil or Satan, who leads the whole world
into the wrong way.) The dragon and its
angels were thrown to the earth.

10Then I heard a loud voice in heaven say,
"The victory and the power and the kingdom
of our God and the authority of his Christ*
have now come. These things have come,
because the accuser of our brothers and sisters has been thrown out. He is the one who
accused them day and night before our God.
11They defeated him by the blood sacrifice of
the Lamb* and by the message of God that
they told people. They did not love their lives
too much. They were not afraid of death. 12So
rejoice, you heavens and all who live there!
But it will be terrible for the earth and sea,
because the devil has gone down to you. He
is filled with anger. He knows he doesn't have
much time."

13The dragon saw that he had been thrown
down to the earth. So he chased the woman
who had given birth to the child. 14But the
woman was given the two wings of a great
eagle. Then she could fly to the place that
was prepared for her in the desert. There
she would be taken care of for three and a
half years. There she would be away from the
dragon.*c* 15Then the dragon poured water out
of its mouth like a river. It poured the water
toward the woman so that the flood would
carry her away. 16But the earth helped the
woman. The earth opened its mouth and
swallowed the river that came from the
mouth of the dragon. 17Then the dragon was
very angry with the woman. It went away to
make war against all her other children. Her
children are those who obey God's commands
and have the truth that Jesus taught.

18The dragon stood on the seashore.

The Beast From the Sea

13 1Then I saw a beast coming up out of
the sea. It had ten horns and seven
heads. There was a crown on each of its
horns. It had an evil name written on each
head. 2This beast looked like a leopard, with
feet like a bear's feet. It had a mouth like a
lion's mouth. The dragon gave the beast all of
its power and its throne and great authority.

3One of the heads of the beast looked as if
it had been wounded and killed, but the death
wound was healed. All the people in the
world were amazed, and they all followed the
beast. 4People worshiped the dragon because
it had given its power to the beast, and they
also worshiped the beast. They asked, "Who

*c***12:14 dragon** Here and in verse 15 literally, "snake."
See verse 9 above.

is as powerful as the beast? Who can make war against it?"

⁵The beast was allowed to boast and speak insults against God. It was allowed to use its power for 42 months. ⁶The beast opened its mouth to insult God—to insult his name, the place where he lives, and all those who live in heaven. ⁷It was given power to make war against God's holy people* and to defeat them. It was given power over every tribe, race of people, language, and nation. ⁸Everyone living on earth would worship the beast. These are all the people since the beginning of the world whose names are not written in the Lamb's* book of life. The Lamb is the one who was killed.

⁹Anyone who hears these things should listen to this:

¹⁰ Whoever is to be a prisoner,
   will be a prisoner.
  Whoever is to be killed with a sword,
   will be killed with a sword.

This means that God's holy people must have patience and faith.

The Beast From the Earth

¹¹Then I saw another beast coming up out of the earth. He had two horns like a lamb, but he talked like a dragon. ¹²This beast stood before the first beast and used the same power the first beast had. He used this power to make everyone living on the earth worship the first beast. The first beast was the one that had the death wound that was healed. ¹³The second beast did great miracles.ᵃ He even made fire come down from heaven to earth while people were watching.

¹⁴This second beast fooled the people living on earth by using the miracles that he had been given the power to do for the first beast. He ordered people to make an idol* to honor the first beast, the one that was wounded by the sword but did not die. ¹⁵The second beast was given power to give life to the idol of the first beast. Then the idol could speak and order all those who did not worship it to be killed. ¹⁶The second beast also forced all people, small and great, rich and poor, free and slave, to have a mark put on their right hand or on their forehead. ¹⁷No one could buy or sell without this mark. (This mark is the name of the beast or the number of its name.)

¹⁸Anyone who has understanding can find the meaning of the beast's number. This requires wisdom. This number is the number of a man. It is 666.

God's People Sing a New Song

14 ¹Then I looked, and there before me was the Lamb,* who was standing on Mount Zion.ᵇ There were 144,000 people with him. They all had his name and his Father's name written on their foreheads.

²And I heard a sound from heaven as loud as the crashing of floodwaters or claps of thunder. But it sounded like harpists playing their harps. ³The people sang a new song before the throne and before the four living beings and the elders.* The only ones who could learn the new song were the 144,000 who had been bought from the earth. No one else could learn it.

⁴These are the ones who did not do sinful things with women. They kept themselves pure. Now they follow the Lamb wherever he goes. They were bought from among the people of the earth as the first to be offered to God and the Lamb. ⁵They are not guilty of telling lies; they are without fault.

The Three Angels

⁶Then I saw another angel flying high in the air. The angel had the eternal Good News* to announce to the people living on earth—to every nation, tribe, language, and race of people. ⁷The angel said in a loud voice, "Fear God and give him praise. The time has come for God to judge all people. Worship God. He made the heavens, the earth, the sea, and the springs of water."

⁸Then the second angel followed the first angel and said, "She is destroyed! The great city of Babylon is destroyed! She made all the nations drink the wine of her sexual sin and of God's anger."

⁹A third angel followed the first two angels. This third angel said in a loud voice, "God will punish all those who worship the beast and the beast's idol* and agree to have the beast's mark on their forehead or on their hand. ¹⁰They will drink the wine of God's anger. This wine is prepared with all its strength in the cup of God's anger. They will be tortured* with burning sulfur before the holy angels and the Lamb.* ¹¹And the smoke from their burning pain will rise forever and ever. There will be no rest, day or night, for those who worship the beast and its idol or who wear the mark of its name." ¹²This means that God's holy people* must be patient. They must obey God's commands and keep their faith in Jesus.

¹³Then I heard a voice from heaven. It said, "Write this: From now on there are great blessings for those who belong to the Lord when they die."

The Spirit* says, "Yes, that is true. They will rest from their hard work. What they have done will stay with them."

ᵃ13:13 *miracles* False miracles—amazing acts done by the power of the devil.

ᵇ14:1 *Mount Zion* Another name for Jerusalem, here meaning the spiritual city where God's people live with him.

The Earth Is Harvested

¹⁴I looked and there before me, sitting on a white cloud, was one who looked like the Son of Man.* He had a gold crown on his head and a sharp sickle* in his hand. ¹⁵Then another angel came out of the temple. This angel called to the one who was sitting on the cloud, "Take your sickle and gather from the earth. The time to harvest has come, and the fruit on the earth is ripe." ¹⁶So the one who was sitting on the cloud swung his sickle over the earth. And the earth was harvested.

¹⁷Then another angel came out of the temple in heaven. This angel also had a sharp sickle. ¹⁸And then another angel, one with power over the fire, came from the altar.* He called to the angel with the sharp sickle and said, "Take your sharp sickle and gather the bunches of grapes from the earth's vine. The earth's grapes are ripe." ¹⁹The angel swung his sickle over the earth. He gathered the earth's grapes and threw them into the great winepress of God's anger. ²⁰The grapes were squeezed in the winepress outside the city. Blood flowed out of the winepress. It rose as high as the heads of the horses for a distance of 200 miles.ᵃ

The Angels With the Last Plagues

15 ¹Then I saw another wonder in heaven. It was great and amazing. There were seven angels bringing seven plagues. These are the last plagues, because after these, God's anger is finished.

²I saw what looked like a sea of glass mixed with fire. All those who had won the victory over the beast and his idol* and over the number of its name were standing by the sea. These people had harps that God had given them. ³They sang the song of Moses,* the servant of God, and the song of the Lamb*:

"Great and wonderful are the things you do,
   Lord God All-Powerful.
Right and true are your ways,
   Ruler of the nations.
⁴ All people will fear you, O Lord.
All people will praise your name.
   Only you are holy.
All people will come and worship before
   you,
because it is clear that you do what is
   right."

⁵After this I saw the temple, the holy place of God's presence,ᵇ in heaven. It was opened, ⁶and the seven angels bringing the seven plagues came out. They were dressed in clean, shining linen cloth. They wore golden bands tied around their chests. ⁷Then one of the

ᵃ**14:20** *200 miles* Literally, "1600 *stadia,*" a little less than 300 km.
ᵇ**15:5** *holy place of God's presence* Literally, "tent of the testimony." See "Holy Tent" in the Word List. Read Ex. 25:8–22.

four living beings gave seven golden bowls to the seven angels. The bowls were filled with the anger of God, who lives forever and ever. ⁸The temple was filled with smoke from the glory* and the power of God. No one could enter the temple until the seven plagues of the seven angels were finished.

The Bowls Filled With God's Anger

16 ¹Then I heard a loud voice from the temple. It said to the seven angels, "Go and pour out the seven bowls of God's anger on the earth."

²The first angel left. He poured out his bowl on the land. Then all those who had the mark of the beast and who worshiped its idol* got sores that were ugly and painful.

³The second angel poured out his bowl on the sea. Then the sea became blood like a dead man's blood. And everything living in the sea died.

⁴The third angel poured out his bowl on the rivers and the springs of water. The rivers and the springs of water became blood. ⁵Then I heard the angel of the waters say to God,

"You are the one who is and who always
   was.
You are the Holy One.
You are right in these judgments you have
   made.
⁶ The people have spilled the blood of your
   holy people* and your prophets.*
Now you have given those people blood
   to drink.
   This is what they deserve."

⁷And I heard the altar* say,

"Yes, Lord God All-Powerful,
   your judgments are true and right."

⁸The fourth angel poured out his bowl on the sun. The sun was given power to burn the people with fire. ⁹The people were burned by the great heat. They cursed the name of God, who had control over these plagues. But they refused to change their hearts and lives and give glory* to God.

¹⁰The fifth angel poured out his bowl on the throne of the beast. And darkness covered the beast's kingdom. People bit their tongues because of the pain. ¹¹They cursed the God of heaven because of their pain and the sores they had. But they refused to change their hearts and turn away from the evil things they did.

¹²The sixth angel poured out his bowl on the great river Euphrates. The water in the river was dried up. This prepared the way for the rulers from the east to come. ¹³Then I saw three evil spirits that looked like frogs. They came out of the mouth of the dragon, out of the mouth of the beast, and out of the mouth of the false prophet.* ¹⁴These evil spirits are the spirits of demons.* They have power to

do miracles.ᵃ They go out to the rulers of the whole world to gather them for battle on the great day of God All-Powerful.

¹⁵"Listen! I will come at a time you don't expect, like a thief. Great blessings belong to those who stay awake and keep their clothes with them. They will not have to go without clothes and be ashamed for people to see them."

¹⁶Then the evil spirits gathered the rulers together to the place that in Hebrew is called Armageddon.

¹⁷The seventh angel poured out his bowl into the air. Then a loud voice came out of the temple from the throne. It said, "It is finished!" ¹⁸Then there were flashes of lightning, noises, thunder, and a big earthquake. This was the worst earthquake that has ever happened since people have been on earth. ¹⁹The great city split into three parts. The cities of the nations were destroyed. And God did not forget to punish Babylon the Great. He gave that city the cup filled with the wine of his terrible anger. ²⁰Every island disappeared and there were no more mountains. ²¹Giant hailstones fell on the people from the sky. These hailstones weighed almost 100 poundsᵇ each. People cursed God because of this plague of the hail. It was terrible.

The Woman on the Red Beast

17 ¹One of the seven angels came and spoke to me. This was one of the angels that had the seven bowls. The angel said, "Come, and I will show you the punishment that will be given to the famous prostitute. She is the one sitting over many waters. ²The rulers of the earth sinned sexually with her. The people of the earth became drunk from the wine of her sexual sin."

³Then the angel carried me away by the Spirit* to the desert. There I saw a woman sitting on a red beast. The beast was covered with evil names. It had seven heads and ten horns. ⁴The woman was dressed in purple and red. She was shining with the gold, jewels, and pearls that she was wearing. She had a golden cup in her hand. This cup was filled with terribly evil things and the filth of her sexual sin. ⁵She had a title written on her forehead. This title has a hidden meaning. This is what was written:

THE GREAT BABYLON
MOTHER OF PROSTITUTES
AND THE EVIL THINGS OF THE EARTH

⁶I saw that the woman was drunk. She was drunk with the blood of God's holy people.* She was drunk with the blood of those who told about their faith in Jesus.

ᵃ16:14 *miracles* False miracles—amazing acts done by the power of the devil.
ᵇ16:21 *100 pounds* Literally, *"talanton"* or "talent." A talent was about 27 to 36 kg (60 to 80 pounds).

When I saw the woman, I was fully amazed. ⁷Then the angel said to me, "Why are you amazed? I will tell you the hidden meaning of this woman and the beast she rides—the beast with seven heads and ten horns. ⁸The beast you saw was once alive, but now it is not. However, it will come up out of the bottomless pit and go away to be destroyed. The people who live on the earth will be amazed when they see the beast, because it was once alive, is no longer living, but will come again. These are the people whose names have never been written in the book of life since the beginning of the world.

⁹"You need wisdom to understand this. The seven heads on the beast are the seven hills where the woman sits. They are also seven rulers. ¹⁰Five of the rulers have already died. One of the rulers lives now, and the last ruler is coming. When he comes, he will stay only a short time. ¹¹The beast that was once alive but is no longer living is an eighth ruler. This eighth ruler also belongs to the first seven rulers. And he will go away to be destroyed.

¹²"The ten horns you saw are ten rulers. These ten rulers have not yet received their kingdom, but they will receive power to rule with the beast for one hour. ¹³All ten of these rulers have the same purpose. And they will give their power and authority to the beast. ¹⁴They will make war against the Lamb.* But the Lamb will defeat them, because he is Lord of lords and King of kings. And with him will be his chosen and faithful followers—the people he has called to be his."

¹⁵Then the angel said to me, "You saw the waters where the prostitute sits. These waters are the many peoples, the different races, nations, and languages in the world. ¹⁶The beast and the ten horns you saw will hate the prostitute. They will take everything she has and leave her naked. They will eat her flesh and destroy her with fire. ¹⁷God put the idea in their minds to do what would complete his purpose. They agreed to give the beast their power to rule until what God has said is completed. ¹⁸The woman you saw is the great city that rules over the kings of the earth."

Babylon Is Destroyed

18 ¹Then I saw another angel coming down from heaven. This angel had great power. The angel's glory* made the earth bright. ²The angel shouted with a powerful voice,

"She is destroyed!
    The great city of Babylon is destroyed!
She has become a home for demons.*
    That city has become a place for every
        unclean spirit to live.
She is a city filled with all kinds of
        unclean birds.
She is a place where every unclean and
        hated animal lives.

3 All the peoples of the earth have drunk
the wine of her sexual sin and of
God's anger.
The rulers of the earth sinned sexually
with her,
and the merchants* of the world grew
rich from the great wealth of her
luxury."

4Then I heard another voice from heaven
say,

"Come out of that city, my people,
so that you will not share in her sins.
Then you will not suffer any of the
terrible punishment she will get.
5 That city's sins are piled up as high as
heaven.
God has not forgotten the wrongs she
has done.
6 Give that city the same as she gave to
others.
Pay her back twice as much as she did.
Prepare wine for her that is twice as strong
as the wine she prepared for others.
7 She gave herself much glory and rich
living.
Give her that much suffering and
sadness.
She says to herself, 'I am a queen sitting
on my throne.
I am not a widow;
I will never be sad.'
8 So in one day she will suffer
great hunger, mourning,* and death.
She will be destroyed by fire,
because the Lord God who judges her is
powerful.

9"The rulers of the earth who sinned sexually with her and shared her wealth will see
the smoke from her burning. Then they will
cry and be sad because of her death. 10The
rulers will be afraid of her suffering and stand
far away. They will say,

'Terrible! How terrible, O great city,
O powerful city of Babylon!
Your punishment came in one hour!'

11"And the merchants of the earth will cry
and be sad for her. They will be sad because
now there is no one to buy the things they
sell—12gold, silver, jewels, pearls, fine linen
cloth, purple cloth, silk, and scarlet cloth, all
kinds of citron wood, and all kinds of things
made from ivory, expensive wood, bronze,
iron, and marble. 13They also sell cinnamon,
spice, incense,* frankincense,* myrrh,* wine,
olive oil, fine flour, wheat, cattle, sheep,
horses, carriages, and slaves—yes, even
human lives. The merchants will cry and say,

14 'O Babylon, the good things you wanted
have left you.

All your rich and fancy things have
disappeared.
You will never have them again.'

15"The merchants will be afraid of her suffering and will stand far away from her. They
are the ones who became rich from selling
those things to her. They will cry and be sad.
16They will say,

'Terrible! How terrible for the great city!
She was dressed in fine linen;
she wore purple and scarlet cloth.
She was shining with gold, jewels, and
pearls!
17 All these riches have been destroyed in
one hour!'

"Every sea captain, all those who travel
on ships, the sailors, and all those who earn
money from the sea stood far away from Babylon. 18They saw the smoke from her burning.
They cried out, 'There was never a city like
this great city!' 19They threw dust on their
heads and cried loudly to show the deep sorrow they felt. They said,

'Terrible! How terrible for the great city!
All those who had ships on the sea
became rich because of her wealth!
But she has been destroyed in one hour!
20 Be happy because of this, O heaven!
Be happy, God's holy people* and
apostles* and prophets*!
God has punished her because of what
she did to you.'"

21Then a powerful angel picked up a large
rock. This rock was as big as a large millstone.* The angel threw the rock into the sea
and said,

"That is how the great city of Babylon will
be thrown down.
It will never be found again.
22 O Babylon, the music of people playing
harps and other instruments, flutes
and trumpets, will never be heard in
you again.
No worker doing any job will ever be
found in you again.
The sound of a millstone will never be
heard in you again.
23 The light of a lamp will never shine in
you again.
The voices of a bridegroom* and bride
will never be heard in you again.
Your merchants were the world's great
people.
All the nations were tricked by your
magic.
24 You are guilty of the death of the
prophets, of God's holy people,
and of all those who have been killed on
earth."

People in Heaven Praise God

19 ¹After this I heard what sounded like a large crowd of people in heaven. The people were saying,

"Hallelujah*ᵃ*!
  Victory, glory,* and power belong to our
    God.
² His judgments are true and right.
  Our God has punished the prostitute.
    She is the one who ruined the earth
      with her sexual sin.
  God has punished the prostitute to
    pay her back for the death of his
    servants."

³These people also said,

"Hallelujah!
  She is burning and her smoke will rise
    forever and ever."

⁴Then the 24 elders* and the four living beings bowed down. They worshiped God, who sits on the throne. They said,

"Amen*! Hallelujah!"

⁵Then a voice came from the throne and said,

"Praise our God, all you who serve him!
  Praise our God, all you small and great
    who honor him!"

⁶Then I heard something that sounded like a large crowd of people. It was as loud as crashing waves or claps of thunder. The people were saying,

"Hallelujah!
  Our Lord God rules.
  He is the All-Powerful.
⁷ Let us rejoice and be happy and give God
    glory!
  Give God glory, because the wedding of
    the Lamb* has come.
  And the Lamb's bride has made herself
    ready.
⁸ Fine linen was given to the bride for her
    to wear.
  The linen was bright and clean."

(The fine linen means the good things that God's holy people* did.)

⁹Then the angel said to me, "Write this: Great blessings belong to those who are invited to the wedding meal of the Lamb!" Then the angel said, "These are the true words of God."

¹⁰Then I bowed down before the angel's feet to worship him. But the angel said to me,

"Don't worship me! I am a servant like you and your brothers and sisters who have the truth of Jesus. So worship God! Because the truth of Jesus is the spirit of prophecy.*"

The Rider on the White Horse

¹¹Then I saw heaven open. There before me was a white horse. The rider on the horse was called Faithful and True, because he is right in his judging and in making war. ¹²His eyes were like burning fire. He had many crowns on his head. A name was written on him, but he was the only one who knew its meaning. ¹³He was dressed in a robe dipped in blood, and he was called the Word of God. ¹⁴The armies of heaven were following the rider on the white horse. They were also riding white horses. They were dressed in fine linen, white and clean. ¹⁵A sharp sword came out of the rider's mouth, a sword that he would use to defeat the nations. And he will rule the nations with a rod of iron. He will crush the grapes in the winepress of the terrible anger of God All-Powerful. ¹⁶On his robe and on his leg was written this name:

KING OF KINGS AND LORD OF LORDS

¹⁷Then I saw an angel standing in the sun. In a loud voice the angel said to all the birds flying in the sky, "Come together for the great supper of God. ¹⁸Come together so that you can eat the bodies of rulers and army commanders and famous men. Come to eat the bodies of the horses and their riders and the bodies of all people—free, slave, small, and great."

¹⁹Then I saw the beast and the rulers of the earth. Their armies were gathered together to make war against the rider on the horse and his army. ²⁰But the beast was captured, and the false prophet* was also captured. He was the one who did the miraclesᵇ for the beast. He had used these miracles to trick those who had the mark of the beast and worshiped its idol.* The false prophet and the beast were thrown alive into the lake of fire that burns with sulfur. ²¹Their armies were killed with the sword that came out of the mouth of the rider on the horse. All the birds ate these bodies until they were full.

The 1000 Years

20 ¹I saw an angel coming down out of heaven. The angel had the key to the bottomless pit. The angel also held a large chain in his hand. ²The angel grabbed the dragon, that old snake, also known as the devil or Satan. The angel tied the dragon with the chain for 1000 years. ³Then the angel threw the dragon into the bottomless pit and closed it. The angel locked it over the dragon.

---

*ᵃ***19:1** *Hallelujah* This means "Praise God!" Also in verses 3, 4, 6.

*ᵇ***19:20** *miracles* False miracles—amazing acts done by the power of the devil.

The angel did this so that the dragon could not trick the people of the earth until the 1000 years were ended. After 1000 years the dragon must be made free for a short time.

⁴Then I saw some thrones and people sitting on them. These were the ones who had been given the power to judge. And I saw the souls of those who had been killed because they were faithful to the truth of Jesus and the message* from God. They did not worship the beast or its idol.* They did not receive the mark of the beast on their foreheads or on their hands. They came back to life and ruled with Christ for 1000 years. ⁵(The rest of the dead did not live again until the 1000 years were ended.)

This is the first resurrection.* ⁶Great blessings belong to those who share in this first resurrection. They are God's holy people.* The second death has no power over them. They will be priests for God and for Christ. They will rule with him for 1000 years.

The Defeat of Satan

⁷When the 1000 years are ended, Satan* will be made free from his prison. ⁸He will go out to trick the nations in all the earth, the nations known as Gog and Magog. Satan will gather the people for battle. There will be more people than anyone can count, like sand on the seashore.

⁹I saw Satan's army march across the earth and gather around the camp of God's people and the city that God loves. But fire came down from heaven and destroyed Satan's army. ¹⁰And he (the one who tricked these people) was thrown into the lake of burning sulfur with the beast and the false prophet.* There they would be tortured* day and night forever and ever.

People of the World Are Judged

¹¹Then I saw a large white throne. I saw the one who was sitting on the throne. Earth and sky ran away from him and disappeared. ¹²And I saw those who had died, great and small, standing before the throne. Some books were opened. And another book was opened—the book of life. The people were judged by what they had done, which is written in the books.

¹³The sea gave up the dead who were in it. Death and Hades* gave up the dead who were in them. All these people were judged by what they had done. ¹⁴And Death and Hades were thrown into the lake of fire. This lake of fire is the second death. ¹⁵And anyone whose name was not found written in the book of life was thrown into the lake of fire.

The New Jerusalem

21 ¹Then I saw a new heaven and a new earth. The first heaven and the first earth had disappeared. Now there was no sea. ²And I saw the holy city, the new Jerusalem,ᵃ coming down out of heaven from God. It was prepared like a bride dressed for her husband.

³I heard a loud voice from the throne. It said, "Now God's home is with people. He will live with them. They will be his people. God himself will be with them and will be their God. ⁴He will wipe away every tear from their eyes. There will be no more death, sadness, crying, or pain. All the old ways are gone."

⁵The one who was sitting on the throne said, "Look, I am making everything new!" Then he said, "Write this, because these words are true and can be trusted."

⁶The one on the throne said to me, "It is finished! I am the Alpha and the Omega,ᵇ the Beginning and the End. I will give free water from the spring of the water of life to anyone who is thirsty. ⁷All those who win the victory will receive all this. And I will be their God, and they will be my children. ⁸But those who are cowards, those who refuse to believe, those who do terrible things, those who kill, those who sin sexually, those who do evil magic, those who worship idols,* and those who tell lies—they will all have a place in the lake of burning sulfur. This is the second death."

⁹One of the seven angels came to me. This was one of the angels who had the seven bowls full of the seven last plagues. The angel said, "Come with me. I will show you the bride, the wife of the Lamb.*" ¹⁰The angel carried me away by the Spirit* to a very large and high mountain. The angel showed me the holy city, Jerusalem. The city was coming down out of heaven from God.

¹¹The city was shining with the glory* of God. It was shining bright like a very expensive jewel, like a jasper. It was clear as crystal. ¹²The city had a large, high wall with twelve gates. There were twelve angels at the gates. On each gate was written the name of one of the twelve tribes of Israel.* ¹³There were three gates on the east, three gates on the north, three gates on the south, and three gates on the west. ¹⁴The walls of the city were built on twelve foundation stones. On the stones were written the names of the twelve apostles* of the Lamb.

¹⁵The angel who talked with me had a measuring rod made of gold. The angel had this rod to measure the city, its gates, and its wall. ¹⁶The city was built in a square. Its length was equal to its width. The angel measured the city with the rod. The city was 12,000 *stadia*ᶜ long, 12,000 *stadia* wide, and 12,000 *stadia*

ᵃ**21:2 new Jerusalem** The spiritual city where God's people live with him.

ᵇ**21:6 Alpha ... Omega** The first and last letters in the Greek alphabet, meaning the beginning and the end.

ᶜ**21:16 stadia** One Greek *stadion* was 600 feet, about 185 meters.

high. [17]The angel also measured the wall. It was 144 cubits[a] high. (The angel was using the same measurement that people use.) [18]The wall was made of jasper. The city was made of pure gold, as pure as glass.

[19]The foundation stones of the city walls had every kind of expensive jewels in them. The first foundation stone was jasper, the second was sapphire, the third was chalcedony, the fourth was emerald, [20]the fifth was onyx, the sixth was carnelian, the seventh was yellow quartz, the eighth was beryl, the ninth was topaz, the tenth was chrysoprase, the eleventh was jacinth, and the twelfth was amethyst. [21]The twelve gates were twelve pearls. Each gate was made from one pearl. The street of the city was made of pure gold, as clear as glass.

[22]I did not see a temple in the city. The Lord God All-Powerful and the Lamb were the city's temple. [23]The city did not need the sun or the moon to shine on it. The glory of God gave the city light. The Lamb was the city's lamp.

[24]The peoples of the world will walk by the light given by the Lamb. The rulers of the earth will bring their glory into the city. [25]The city's gates will never close on any day, because there is no night there. [26]The greatness and the honor of the nations will be brought into the city. [27]Nothing unclean will ever enter the city. No one who does shameful things or tells lies will ever enter the city. Only those whose names are written in the Lamb's book of life will enter the city.

22 [1]The angel showed me the river of the water of life, clear as crystal. The river flows from the throne of God and the Lamb. [2]It flows down the middle of the street of the city. The tree of life* is on each side of the river, and it produces fruit every month, twelve times a year. The leaves of the tree are for healing the nations.

[3]Nothing that God judges guilty will be there in that city. The throne of God and the Lamb will be in the city. God's servants will worship him. [4]They will see his face. God's name will be written on their foreheads. [5]There will never be night again. People will not need the light of a lamp or the light of the sun. The Lord God will give them light. And they will rule like kings forever and ever.

[6]Then the angel said to me, "These words are true and can be trusted. The Lord, the God of the spirits of the prophets,* has sent his angel to show his servants what must happen soon: [7]'Listen, I am coming soon! Great blessings belong to the one who obeys the words of prophecy* in this book.'"

[8]I am John. I am the one who heard and saw these things. After I heard and saw them, I bowed down to worship at the feet of the angel who showed them to me. [9]But the angel said to me, "Don't worship me! I am a servant like you and your brothers the prophets. I am a servant like all those who obey the words in this book. You should worship God!"

[10]Then the angel told me, "Don't keep secret the words of prophecy in this book. The time is near for these things to happen. [11]Let anyone who is doing wrong continue to do wrong. Let anyone who is unclean continue to be unclean. Let anyone who is doing right continue to do right. Let anyone who is holy* continue to be holy."

[12]"Listen, I am coming soon! I will bring rewards with me. I will repay everyone for what they have done. [13]I am the Alpha and the Omega,[b] the First and the Last, the Beginning and the End.

[14]"Great blessings belong to those who have washed their robes.[c] They will have the right to eat the food from the tree of life. They can go through the gates into the city. [15]Outside the city are all those who live like dogs—those who do evil magic, those who sin sexually, those who murder, those who worship idols, and those who love to lie and pretend to be good.

[16]"I, Jesus, have sent my angel to tell you these things for the churches.* I am the descendant from the family of David.* I am the bright morning star."

[17]The Spirit and the bride say, "Come!" Everyone who hears this should also say, "Come!" All who are thirsty may come; they can have the water of life as a free gift if they want it.

[18]I warn everyone who hears the words of prophecy in this book: If anyone adds anything to these, God will give that person the plagues written about in this book. [19]And if anyone takes away from the words of this book of prophecy, God will take away that person's share of the tree of life and of the holy city, which are written about in this book.

[20]Jesus is the one who says that all of this is true. Now he says, "Yes, I am coming soon."

Amen*! Come, Lord Jesus!

[21]The grace* of the Lord Jesus be with all people.

---

[b]**22:13** *Alpha ... Omega* The first and last letters in the Greek alphabet, meaning the beginning and the end.

[c]**22:14** *washed their robes* Meaning that they had believed in Jesus and had been made clean from sin by his blood sacrifice. See Rev. 5:9; 7:14; Heb. 9:14; 10:14–22; Acts 22:16; 1 Jn. 1:7.

[a]**21:17** *cubits* A cubit is the length of a man's arm from the elbow to the tip of the little finger, about half a meter.

Word List

A Aaron Moses' brother, who was chosen as the first high priest of Israel.

Abel The son of Adam and Eve who was killed by his brother Cain. Read Gen. 4:1–16.

Abib Or "Nisan," the first month of the ancient Hebrew calendar. The name means "young heads of grain." It was the beginning of spring, about mid-March to mid-April.

Abraham The most respected ancestor of the Jewish people. Through him God promised to make a great nation and bless all the people of the earth. Read Gen. 12:1–3.

Achaia The region in the southern part of Greece where the ancient cities of Athens and Corinth were located.

Adriatic Sea The sea between Greece and Italy, including the central part of the Mediterranean Sea.

adultery Breaking a marriage promise by committing sexual sin.

agreement A contract or agreement from God to his people. The agreement that God gave his people at Mount Sinai, based on the Law of Moses, became the most important for the Israelites or Jews. It replaced or renewed all other agreements, such as that given earlier to Abraham. In the New Testament it is referred to as the "old" or "first" agreement. After Jesus Christ came and offered his life as payment for the sins of all people, God was able to offer a "new" and "better" agreement based on Christ's sacrifice.

Agreement Where this is marked, it is literally "Testimony," a word that usually refers to the flat stones with the Ten Commandments written on them, which were evidence or "proof" of the agreement between God and Israel.

Agrippa Herod Agrippa II, great-grandson of Herod the Great.

Ahaz A king of Judah who ruled with his father Jotham from 735 to 732 B.C., and then alone from 732 to 715 B.C.

alabaster A beautiful kind of stone that can be carved.

aloes The oil from a sweet-smelling wood that was used to make perfume (Ps. 45:8; Prov. 7:17) or the bitter juice from a cactus-like plant that was used to prepare bodies for burial (Jn. 19:39).

altar A raised area, pile of stones, or table where sacrifices were offered as gifts to God. An important altar was the one in front of the Temple in Jerusalem. See also "golden altar."

Amen A Hebrew word meaning "That's right," "True," or "Yes." It is used to express strong agreement with what has been said.

Anakites Descendants of Anak. They were a family famous for tall and powerful fighting men. See Num. 13:33.

ancestors Literally, "fathers," meaning a person's parents, grandparents, and all the other people that person is descended from. In the New Testament it usually refers to people who lived during Old Testament times.

anoint To pour a special oil on people or things to show that they have been chosen by God and set apart for a special work or purpose.

apostle A follower of Jesus chosen to represent him in a special way. During his earthly ministry, Jesus named twelve men as apostles. They had the specific responsibility and authority to represent him and proclaim his message throughout the world. Later, he appeared to Paul and gave him a similar commission, especially to non-Jewish people. Barnabas, Paul's missionary companion, and James, the brother of Jesus, are also called apostles, as well as several others in the New Testament. Some of these occurrences of the word, however, have the more general sense of "messenger" or "representative."

aqueduct A ditch or pipe that carries water from one place to another.

Aram A country north of Israel that included much of modern-day Syria. See Isa. 7:1; 17:3.

Aramaic The language of the Arameans, which became the main language of trade and diplomacy in the ancient near east during the Assyrian, the Neo-Babylonian, and Persian empires. Throughout this period of the first century B.C. it was common for official letters to be written in Aramaic. Similar to Hebrew, it later became the common language of many Jews and is the spoken "Hebrew" referred to in the New Testament.

Ararat The ancient country of Urartu, an area in eastern Turkey.

archangel The leader among God's angels.

archer A person skilled in using a bow to shoot arrows.

Areopagus council A group of important leaders in Athens who served like judges.

armor bearer A young man who carried a soldier's weapons.

armor The special clothes soldiers wore to protect themselves in war.

army officer A centurion, a Roman army officer who had authority over 100 soldiers.

Artaxerxes The king of Persia about 465–424 B.C. He was the son of Xerxes. See Ezra 4:7; 7:1.

Asherah pole A wooden pole (originally, perhaps, a tree trunk) that was set up to honor the goddess Asherah.

Asherah An important Canaanite goddess, the wife of the Canaanite god El and possibly Baal. People thought she could help them have children.

Ashtoreth Or "Astarte," an important Canaanite goddess, the wife of the Canaanite god Baal and possibly El. Called the "Queen of Heaven," she was the goddess of love and war.

Asia The geographical area, sometimes called Asia Minor, that is now the western part of modern Turkey.

Assyria A powerful nation northeast of Israel.

Baal A false god worshiped by the Canaanites. They believed he brought rain and storms and made the land produce good crops.

Balaam A non-Israelite prophet in the Old Testament who was hired by Balak, king of Moab, to curse his enemy Israel. Read Num. 22–24.

baptism A Greek word usually referring to the act of dipping or "burying" a person briefly in water, connected with their decision to change their life and turn to God, trusting him to forgive their sins. For people coming to faith in Jesus Christ it was an expression of their trust in his death as the sacrifice God accepted to pay for their sins. Described as a sharing in the death, burial, and resurrection of Christ, it marked the beginning of their new life in Christ as part of God's people. See Acts 2:38; Rom. 6:3, 4; Gal. 3:26–28; Col. 2:12, 13.

baptize To perform the act of baptism. See "baptism."

Bashan The northern part of Israel east of the Jordan River.

Bel One of the names of the god Marduk, the most important god of the Babylonians.

believer Where this word is marked, it is literally "brother," a term used by followers of Jesus Christ to refer to fellow members of God's family.

Bernice King Agrippa's sister, the oldest daughter of Herod Agrippa I.

Bethsaida A town by Lake Galilee that Jesus visited during his teaching ministry and where he performed many miracles.

blacksmith A person who makes weapons, tools or other things from iron.

boomerang A curved stick used in hunting birds. When thrown properly, it flies low to the ground and suddenly curves upward, often returning to the thrower. Literally, "a bow of throwing" or "a bow of deception."

Box of God's Agreement See "Box of the Agreement."

Box of the Agreement Or traditionally, "Ark of the Covenant." The special box kept in the Most Holy Place of the Israelite Holy Tent and, later, the Jerusalem Temple. It contained the stone tablets with the Ten Commandments written on them, which were evidence or "proof" of the agreement between God and his people. In some passages it is literally, "Box of the Testimony" or simply, "Testimony" (see "Agreement"). See Ex. 25:10–22; 1 Kings 8:1–9.

Box of the LORD's Agreement See "Box of the Agreement."

bridegroom A man who is getting married.

bronze A type of metal made from copper mixed with tin. The Hebrew word can mean "copper," "brass," or "bronze."

burnt offering A gift to God. Usually these were animals that were killed and completely burned on the altar.

C Caesar The name or title given to the emperor (ruler) of Rome.

Cain The son of Adam and Eve who killed his brother Abel. Read Gen. 4:1–16.

Canaan The land where the Canaanites lived. In the time of Joshua the Israelites fought for this land and eventually controlled most of it. It was generally the same area that was later called Palestine and included what are now Israel and Lebanon.

Capernaum A town on the northern shore of Lake Galilee where Jesus often spent time and taught.

capital A decorated cap made of stone or wood and placed on top of each of the columns that support the roof of a building.

captive One of those who have been defeated in battle and are taken away as prisoners.

caravan A group of traders with their animals that carried products from one place to another.

Carmel A famous mountain (or high hill) in northern Israel that had good soil and plenty of rain. The name means "God's vineyard." See Isa. 33:9; 35:2.

cassia The fragrant dried flowers of the ancient cinnamon tree that were used in anointing oil and as perfume.

chaff The seed coverings and stems separated from the seeds of plants like wheat or barley. Farmers saved the seeds but let the wind blow the useless chaff away.

Chaldeans An important tribe in Babylon. Sometimes this name means simply "people from Babylonia." King Nebuchadnezzar was from this tribe, as were other kings of Babylon. Well educated people, they studied science, history, languages, and astronomy, but they also believed they could do magic and look at the stars to learn what would happen in the future.

chariot A small, two-wheeled cart pulled by horses and used in war.

Chemosh The national god of the country of Moab.

Cherub angels Winged beings like angels that serve God, usually as guards around his throne or other holy places. Two statues of these beings were on the cover of the Box of the Agreement that represented God's presence. See Ex. 25:10–22.

Cherub See Cherub angels.

Chorazin A town by Lake Galilee that Jesus visited during his teaching ministry and where he performed many miracles.

Christ Literally, "Anointed," a title that comes from the Old Testament ceremony in which perfumed oil was poured or rubbed on someone being appointed to a high office, especially that of prophet, priest, or king, to show that this person was chosen by God for that role. The Hebrew word is "Messiah," a title used for Old Testament kings and for the one God would send as prophet, priest, and king to bring people back to a good relationship with him.

church Literally, "assembly" or "community," the people who have been brought together as God's family through their common faith in Jesus Christ. The word often refers to a group of believers who meet together or who live in the same area, but it is also used to mean the worldwide community of all believers in Christ.

circumcise, circumcision Cutting off the foreskin of the male sex organ. This was done to every Jewish baby boy as a mark of the agreement God made with Abraham. Read Gen. 17:9–14. Sometimes "circumcision" is used with "heart" in the figurative sense of true devotion to God. (See Jer. 9:26; Rom. 2:28.) In the New Testament "circumcision" is also used in a spiritual sense to refer to the changed life of believers who have come to share in the new agreement God gave his people through Jesus. (See Php. 3:3; Col. 2:11.)

City of David Jerusalem, especially the southeastern and oldest part of the city.

Claudius The emperor (ruler) of Rome, 41–54 A.D.

clean Pure or acceptable. When it refers to animals, it means fit to be eaten. When it refers to things, it means fit to be used. When it refers to people, it means fit to participate in the worship of God at the Holy Tent (Tabernacle) or Temple. See Lev. 11–15 for the Old Testament rules about clean and unclean things.

coral A hard, stone-like substance, usually pink, red, or black, that is formed from the skeletons of tiny sea animals and covers the ocean floor in certain areas.

cornerstone The first and most important stone of a building.

courtyard The large open area around a king's palace or outside the Temple.

cross The wooden post that Romans used to execute criminals. It is a symbol of shame, suffering and death. Just as Jesus was willing to suffer death on a cross for all people, so he asks his followers to be willing to give up their lives for him.

crown Literally, "wreath," a ring of leaves or branches that was placed on the head of the winners of athletic contests to honor them. It is a symbol of victory and reward.

cud The food that is brought up from the stomach of some animals (like cattle) and chewed again. See Lev. 11.

curse To ask for bad things to happen to a person or thing. As a noun it is a request for or warning about bad things to come.

curtain The curtain that separated the inner sanctuary (Most Holy Place) from the front room in the Tabernacle (see "Holy Tent") and in the Jerusalem Temple. It represented the spiritual barrier that kept people from entering God's presence. When Jesus died, the curtain was torn open (Mt. 27:51), which was a symbol to show that in the heavenly temple the way into God's presence had been opened. See Heb. 10:19, 20.

cymbals A pair of circular metal plates that are hit against each other to make a loud sound.

Cyprus Literally, "the land of Kittim." This could be either Cyprus or Crete.

Cyrus A king of Persia who ruled about 550–530 B.C.

D Dagon A false god worshiped by the Canaanites in the hope that he would give them a good harvest of grain. When the Philistines settled in Canaan, they adopted Dagon as their most important god.

darkness A symbol for the kinds of things

that describe Satan's kingdom, such as sin and evil.

David Israel's greatest king, who ruled about 1000 years before Christ. Besides being a great military and political leader, he was a deeply spiritual man and a gifted musician, who wrote many of the Psalms. He made plans and arrangements for the building of the first Temple in Jerusalem ("the city of David"), which was actually completed by his son Solomon. The Scriptures said that a descendant of David would be God's chosen messiah (king), who would establish an eternal kingdom. For that reason, Jesus is sometimes called "the Son of David."

Day of Atonement Also called "Yom Kippur," a very important holy day for the people of Israel. On this day the high priest went into the Most Holy Place and performed the ceremony that made it pure and atoned for (covered or erased) the sins of the people. See Lev. 16:1–34; 23:26–32.

day A symbol for the kinds of things that describe God's kingdom, such as goodness and truth.

Day The day Christ will come to judge everyone and take his people to live with him.

dedicate To offer something to God with a promise that it will be used only for him, or to set apart something for a special purpose, which means it can then be used only for that purpose.

dedication The act of dedicating something to God. See "dedicate."

deed A written record that proves who owns a certain piece of property. See Jer. 32.

demon An evil spirit from the devil.

director This title is part of a phrase found at the beginning of many of the Psalms. It could also mean "performer."

discharge Fluid from a person's body, including pus from sores, a man's semen, or a woman's period flow.

divine greatness Literally, "glory," a word that refers to the special qualities of God. See "glory."

dungeon A deep pit in the ground, like a cave, used as a prison.

dysentery A very bad intestinal sickness that causes pain and diarrhea.

Edom A country southeast of Judah. It is also known as Seir after the mountain range by that name in Edom. The Edomites are descendants of Esau, Jacob's twin brother. At times, they were enemies of the Israelites.

elders (in Revelation) The 24 elders in Revelation could be the great leaders of God's people under both the Old Testament and New Testament periods, combining the leaders of the twelve tribes of Israel and Jesus' twelve apostles. Or they could be angels as leaders of heavenly worship, corresponding to the 24 groups of priests in charge of worship in the Old Testament.

elders (New Testament) A group of men chosen to lead a church. Also called "overseers" and "pastors" (shepherds), they have the work of caring for God's people. See Acts 14:23; 20:17, 28; Eph. 4:11; Php. 1:1; 1 Tim. 3:1–7; Tit. 1:5–9; 1 Pet. 5:1–3.

elders (Old Testament) Older men who were city leaders and helped make decisions for the people.

Elijah A very important Israelite leader and prophet who spoke for God during a 25-year period ending about 850 B.C. In the time of Jesus, the Jews were expecting Elijah to come again before the Messiah. See Mal. 4:5–6.

Elisha A prophet who served as an assistant to the prophet Elijah and carried on Elijah's ministry after about 850 B.C.

emperor Caesar, the ruler (leader) of the Roman empire.

ephod A special vest (coat) worn by the Israelite high priest. See Ex. 28:6–14.

Ephraim The second son of Joseph and the name of one of the tribes of Israel. Sometimes it is used as the name for the northern kingdom of Israel, since Ephraim was most often the leading tribe.

Esau Jacob's twin brother. Also, another name for Edom. The Edomites were descendants of Esau.

Ethiopia Or "Cush," a country in Africa by the Red Sea.

eunuch A public official or a servant in charge of the women in a ruler's household. Originally, a man who had been castrated so that he could not have sex.

Euphrates One of the two large rivers flowing through the countries of Babylonia and Assyria.

Evil One The devil or Satan, the ruler of demons and enemy of God.

exile Living away from one's home country, usually by force.

false prophet A person who claims to speak for God but does not really speak God's truth.

famine A time when there is not enough rain for crops to grow, causing people and animals to die without enough food or water.

fast To live without food for a time of prayer or mourning.

fathers Important ancestors of the Jewish people, especially the leaders of the tribes of Israel.

fawn A baby deer.

fellowship offering An offering to God that was also eaten by the person giving the sacrifice and shared with others, especially during New Moon celebrations.

Festival of Harvest A one-day celebration of the wheat harvest in the spring, fifty days after Passover, during which the first part of the new crop was offered to God. Often called "Festival of Weeks," it was later known as "Pentecost" (from the Greek word meaning "fifty").

Festival of Shelters A special week each year when the Israelites, and later the Jews, lived in tents to remember God's protection during the time their people wandered in the desert for 40 years with Moses. Also called "Festival of Ingathering" (Ex. 23:16; 34:22). Read Lev. 23:33–36, 39–43.

Festival of Unleavened Bread An important and holy week for the people of Israel and their descendants. In the time of the Old Testament it began the day after Passover, but by New Testament times the two festivals had become one. To prepare for it, the people threw out all their yeast and ate only bread without yeast for seven days."

firepan A small shovel used for removing ashes from an altar.

first agreement The contract God gave to the Israelites when he gave them the Law of Moses. See "agreement."

firstborn The first child born into a family. The first son was very important in ancient times and became the head of the family at the father's death. From this idea the word developed the meaning of a person who has a place of honor, a high position, or special importance. This is the sense of the word when it is used in the New Testament to refer to Jesus Christ. (It had already been used in the Old Testament to describe the Messiah. See Ps. 89:27.)

fortress A building or city with tall, strong walls for protection.

fortuneteller A person who tries to use magic to learn what will happen in the future.

frankincense Special dried tree sap that was burned to make a sweet-smelling smoke and offered as a gift to God. See "incense."

Free Men Jews who had been slaves or whose fathers had been slaves, but were now free.

furnace Or "kiln," an oven for baking bricks to make them hard.

G gazelle A small, fast kind of antelope, an animal like a deer.

Gibeah A place where some men from the tribe of Benjamin committed a terrible sin. See Judges 19 and 20.

Gilead The area east of the Jordan River where the tribes of Reuben, Gad, and half the tribe of Manasseh lived. See Num. 26:29.

Gilgal A city in Israel where people had worshiped God but later became known as a place where people worshiped false gods.

gittith This might be a type of instrument, a tune, a music style, or a performer in the Temple orchestra such as Obed Edom from Gath (the Gittite). See I Chron. 15:21; 16:4–7.

Glory of the LORD One of the forms God used when he appeared to people. It was like a bright, shining light. In the book of Numbers it might have been a bright light or a tall cloud.

glory A word that refers to the special qualities of God. Often it means brightness, referring to the way he appears to people. Sometimes it means majesty or power, referring to a kind of greatness that cannot be compared to anything in human experience. It can also include the ideas of wealth, honor, fame, or respect, especially in expressions of praise.

Glory See "Glory of the LORD."

goad A sharp stick that a person used to make animals go the right way.

God's kingdom The "reign" or "rule" of God over all people who submit to him by accepting Jesus as the Christ (the appointed king), who represents God's kingdom on earth. Jesus was the perfect example of submission to the will of God. When people give control of their lives to Jesus, they become part of God's kingdom and begin to enjoy the blessings he has promised his people from the beginning. (Note that in Matthew this term also translates the Greek word "kingdom" by itself or the phrase, "the kingdom of the heavens," which was used by Jews as a way to avoid saying the divine name.)

golden altar The table made from acacia wood and covered with gold that was used in the Holy Tent for burning incense as a gift to God.

goldsmith A person who makes things from gold.

Gomorrah A city that God destroyed, together with the city of Sodom, because the people living there were so evil. See Gen. 19.

Good News In the Gospels this is usually the news about the coming of God's kingdom (see above) or its representative Jesus Christ. In other places it is, more specifically, the news or message of God's grace—that he has made a way through Jesus Christ for people to be made right with him and enjoy his blessings now and forever.

grace The love and kindness that God shows in his complete willingness to give people favors he does not owe them and blessings they don't deserve.

grave Or "Sheol," the home of the dead. This word is often used as a metaphor for death.

Greek A non-Jewish person anywhere throughout the first century world who was influenced by Greek language and culture.

H Hades The Greek word for "Sheol," the home of the dead. It is often used as a metaphor for death.

hands on See "lay hands on."

Hermes A Greek god. The Greeks believed he was a messenger for the other gods.

Herod (1) Herod I (the Great), king of Judea and all of Palestine (40–4 B.C.), Mt. 2:1–22; Lk. 1:5; Acts 23:35. (2) Herod Antipas, son of Herod the Great, tetrarch (ruler) of Galilee and Perea (4 B.C.–39 A.D.), Mt. 14:1–6; Mk. 6:14–22; 8:15; Lk. 3:1, 19; 8:3; 9:7, 9; 13:31; 23:7–15; Acts 4:27; 13:1. (3) Herod Agrippa I, grandson of Herod the Great, king of Palestine (37–44 A.D.), Acts 12:1, 6–21.

Herodians Members of a Jewish political group who were supporters of Herod and cooperated with the Pharisees in finding a way to stop Jesus from teaching.

Hezekiah A king of Judah who ruled about 715–686 B.C.

high place A place of worship usually on top of a hill, a mountain, or a man-made platform. Although high places were sometimes used for the worship of God, they are most often associated with pagan worship of false gods.

high priest The most important priest and leader of the Israelites or the Jews, God's people under the "old agreement." Under the "new agreement" the high priest for God's people is Jesus Christ. Read Heb. 7:11–8:13.

Holy Box See "Box of the Agreement."

holy bread This was the special bread that was set out on a table in the Holy Tent as an offering to God. It is also called "show-bread" or "bread of the Presence." Normally, only the priests were allowed to eat this bread. See Lev. 24:5–9.

holy people Literally, "saints" or "holy ones," a term used in the New Testament to describe followers of Jesus Christ as God's special people. They are holy because they have been made pure through Christ and belong only to God. See "holy."

Holy Place The room in the Holy Tent (Tabernacle) and in the Temple that was used by the Israelite priests to do their daily service for God.

Holy Spirit Also called the Spirit of God, the Spirit of Christ, and the Comforter. In union with God and Christ, he does God's work among people in the world.

Holy Tent Or "Tabernacle," the special tent described in the Law of Moses, where God lived among his people and where the Israelite priests performed their worship duties. It was often called the "Meeting Tent" because it was where the Israelites went to meet with God. It was used until Solomon built the Temple in Jerusalem.

holy When referring to people or things, holy means set apart or chosen for a special use; especially, belonging to God or used only for him. It can also mean pure or perfect, worthy of God and fit for his service. When God is called holy, in addition to the idea of pure and perfect, it often means he is completely separate or different from and above everything else that exists. In the New Testament God's people are holy because they have been made perfect and pure through Christ and, with the help of the Holy Spirit, keep themselves away from sin and live only for God.

horns of the altar The horn-shaped corners of the altar (see "altar") used for burning sacrifices that was in the courtyard of the Holy Tent (see "Holy Tent") and Temple (see "Temple"). See Ex. 27:2; 38:2. The incense altar inside the Holy Tent also had corners shaped like horns. See Ex. 30:2; 37:25. The law said that a person accused of killing someone (except willful murder) could run into the Holy Place (see "Holy Place"), take hold of these horns, and not be punished. See Ex. 21:12–14.

hypocrisy Pretending to be good while hiding wrong motives.

hypocrite A person with wrong motives who pretends to be good.

hyssop A plant with fine branches and leaves used for sprinkling blood or water in cleansing ceremonies.

idol A statue of a false god that people worship. It can also mean anything that is more important to a person than God.

Illyricum A Roman province north and west of Greece.

incense Special dried tree sap that was burned to make a sweet-smelling smoke and offered as a gift to God.

Isaac The son of Abraham and one of the most important ancestors of the Israelites or Jews.

Israel Another name for Jacob (see Gen. 32:24–28) and for the nation God chose to accomplish his plan of blessing the world through the Messiah (see "Christ"). The people of Israel were the descendants of Jacob's twelve sons. In the New Testament this name is sometimes used in a broader sense to mean all of God's people.

Israelite Belonging to the nation of Israel (see "Israel").

J jackal A kind of wild dog that stays where there are no people. Jackals usually hunt together in a pack.

Jacob Or "Israel," ancestor of the people of Israel (also called Israelites and, later, Jews). See Gen. 32:24–28 for the story of how Jacob was given the name Israel. He was the father of twelve sons from whom the twelve tribes of Israel descended, and the name Jacob continued to be used for the nation or people of Israel.

Jeremiah A man who spoke for God about 600 B.C.

John the Baptizer The man God chose to tell people about Christ's coming and to prepare them by warning them to change their lives and by baptizing them (see "baptize") as a sign of their decision to change. Read Mt. 3; Mk. 1:1–11; Lk. 1:5–25, 57–80; 3:1–18.

John See "John the Baptizer."

Joshua The Israelite military captain who, after Moses died, took his place as the leader of the Israelites and led them into the land that God had promised them.

Jotham A king of Judah who ruled with his father Uzziah from 750 to 740 B.C., and then alone from 740 to 732 B.C.

Jubilee A special horn and the festival marked by the blowing of it to announce that the time had come for slaves to be set free and land returned to the original owners. See Lev. 25:9.

Judah One of the 12 sons of Jacob (Israel); also the tribe and, later, the nation named after him. Described as the "southern kingdom," it was made up of the Israelite tribes that occupied the southern part of Palestine, while the northern tribes were united into a "northern kingdom" known as Israel.

judge One of the civic leaders who judged, led, and protected the people of Israel before their first king was appointed.

judgment pouch A piece of clothing like a bib or an apron that covered the high priest's chest. See Ex. 28:15–30.

K Kedar An Arabian tribe that lived in the desert southeast of the land of Judah.

kingdom See "God's kingdom."

L Lamb A symbolic name for Jesus Christ. It means that he was an offering for sin like the lambs that were offered as a sacrifice to God in the Old Testament.

law This usually refers to God's law as it is represented in the Mosaic Law, the rules he gave to the Israelites through Moses (See Ex. 34:29–32). Sometimes it may mean the principle of law rather than a specific law or set of laws.

lay hands on This act was a way of asking God to bless people in a special way—to heal them, to cause the Holy Spirit to come into them, or to give them power for a special work.

leatherworker Or "tanner," a person who makes leather from animal skins.

Lebanon A country north of Israel, famous for its great cedar and pine trees.

leper A person who has leprosy. See "leprosy."

leprosy A very bad skin disease. The word in the text has a broad sense, which may include many different types of skin disease.

Levi The tribe of Israel from which the priests (descendants of Aaron) and the priests' helpers were chosen.

Levite Any of the men from the tribe of Levi, who helped the Israelite priests in the Holy Tent (Tabernacle) and Temple. In later periods some Levites worked for the civil government.

light A symbol for the kinds of things that describe God or his kingdom, such as goodness and truth.

lily A kind of flower. In the Song of Solomon, it is probably a red flower.

linen Thread or cloth made from the fibers of the flax plant.

locusts Insects like grasshoppers that could destroy a large crop very quickly. See Ex. 10. The Law of Moses said that locusts could be eaten. See Lev. 11:21–22.

loom A machine used for making cloth.

lots Stones, sticks, or bones used like dice for making decisions. See Prov. 16:33.

lyre A musical instrument with strings, like a harp.

M Macedonia The northern part of Greece, where Thessalonica and Philippi were.

make ... pure Or "make atonement for ...." The Hebrew word means "to cover," or "to erase" a person's sins.

man of God Another title for a prophet. See "prophet."

manna The special food provided by God that the Israelites gathered daily from the ground during the 40 years they wandered through the desert. See Ex. 16:4–36.

Marduk The most important god of the Babylonian people.

maskil The meaning of this word is uncertain. It might mean "a poem of meditation," "a poem of instruction," or "a skillfully written poem."

mast The tall pole to which the sail is tied on a sailboat.

Medes and Persians See "Medes."

Medes People of the Medo-Persian Empire (also called Media), which defeated the Neo-Babylonian Empire in 539 B.C. See Isa. 13:17.

mediator A person who helps one person talk to or give something to another person.

medium A person who tries to talk with the spirits of people who have died.

Meeting Tent See "Holy Tent."

Melchizedek A priest and king who lived in the time of Abraham. See Gen. 14:17–24.

memorial stone A stone that was set up to help people remember something special. In ancient Israel, people often set up stones at places where they worshiped false gods.

merchant A person who earns a living by buying and selling things.

mercy-cover The top part of the Box of the Agreement. The Hebrew word can mean "lid," "cover," or "the place where sins are atoned (covered, erased, or forgiven)."

message See "Good News."

miktam The meaning of this word is uncertain. It might mean "a well-arranged song."

Milcom A god worshiped by the Ammonites,

probably the same as the god Molech. See 1 Kings 11:5, 7.

mildew A kind of fungus that often grows on cloth, leather, or wood that is in a warm, damp place. The Hebrew word also means "leprosy" or "skin disease."

mill Two large, flat rocks used for grinding grain to make flour.

Millo Probably the stone foundation walls that were built on the steep slopes southeast of the Temple area in Jerusalem.

millstone A large, round stone used for grinding grain.

miracle An amazing act done by the power of God.

miraculous sign An amazing act that demonstrates the power of God.

Moab A country east of the Dead Sea, named after one of Lot's sons. See Gen. 19:37.

Molech A false god. This name is like the Hebrew word meaning "king."

Moses One of the most important leaders of the Israelites during the time of the Old Testament. God used him to give the people his law, which is often called "the Law of Moses."

Most Holy Place Literally, "holy of holies," the most important room in the Holy Tent or the Temple, where the Box of the Agreement was kept. It was like a throne room where God sat as king of Israel and where the high priest entered into his presence on the Day of Atonement.

Mount Horeb Another name for Mount Sinai.

Mount of Olives A hill east of the city of Jerusalem from which a person could see the Temple area.

Mount Paran This is probably an important mountain west of the Gulf of Aqaba and north of Mount Sinai.

Mount Sinai The mountain located somewhere on the Sinai Peninsula (the eastern part of modern-day Egypt) where God gave his laws to Moses and the Israelites. Also called Mount Horeb. See Ex. 19 and 20.

Mount Zion See "Zion."

mourn, mourners To express sorrow for someone who has died or for something lost. In ancient Israel people often put on special clothes, cried very loudly, and put ashes on their head to show their sadness. Professional "mourners" were sometimes paid to do this at a funeral.

mustard A plant that has a very small seed but grows taller than a man.

myrrh Sweet-smelling sap from the bark of trees or other plants that was used for perfume and also to prepare bodies for burial. Mixed with wine, it was probably used to relieve pain (Mk. 15:23).

N **nard** Very expensive oil from the root of the nard plant. It was used as a perfume.

Nazirite A person who has made a special vow of dedication to God. This name is from the Hebrew word meaning "to separate" or "to consecrate" and refers to the promise Nazirites made to separate themselves from others and dedicate themselves to God by following certain requirements. See Num. 6:1–21.

Negev The desert area in the southern part of Judah.

Nephilim A kind of superhuman race that appeared before the flood. Sometimes translated "giants," the name might come from a Hebrew word meaning "people who have fallen." Later, the Nephilim were a famous family whose men were tall and powerful fighters. See Gen. 6:2–4; Num. 13:32–33.

new agreement The "better agreement" that God has given to his people through Jesus Christ. See "agreement."

New Moon The first day of the month for Israelites or Jews, which they celebrated as a special day of rest and worship. The people met together and shared in the fellowship offerings like those described in Lev. 7:16–21.

night A symbol for the kinds of things that describe Satan's kingdom, such as sin and evil.

Nisan See "Abib."

O **oath** A strong declaration that one will tell the truth or keep a promise, often using the name of God or something else known to be real or important. It may include a wish to be punished if the promise is not kept.

official measure Literally, "shekel of the

Holy Place," the standard measure of weight used in the Tabernacle and the Temple.

official Where this is marked the word in the text is "eunuch," a man in an important government position or a servant in charge of a ruler's household. See "eunuch."

onyx A precious stone with layers of blue or gray.

ostrich A fast-running bird with very long legs and neck. The largest and most powerful of all birds, it commonly lives in the desert.

P **papyrus** A reed-like plant used to make a type of paper used for writing. It was also used to make many other things, such as baskets, rope, sandals, roofing material, and even boats.

paradise A wonderful place of blessing, where God's people go when they die.

parchment Something like paper made from the skins of sheep and used for writing on.

Passover A very important holy day for the people of Israel and their descendants. They ate a special meal on this day every year to remember that God made them free from slavery in Egypt in the time of Moses. The name may come from the word in Ex. 12:13, 23, 27 that means "to pass over" or "to protect."

Pentecost An Israelite or Jewish festival celebrating the wheat harvest fifty days after Passover. See "Festival of Harvest."

persecute To hurt, cause trouble for, or do bad things to someone, especially because of their beliefs.

persecution The act of persecuting or being persecuted. See "persecute."

Persians See "Medes."

Peter Where this is marked, the Greek text has "Cephas," the Aramaic name for Peter, one of Jesus' twelve apostles. Both names mean "rock."

Pharaoh A title for the king of Egypt.

Pharisee A person who belonged to a Jewish religious group that claimed to follow carefully all Jewish laws and customs.

Philistines The people who lived in an area along the coast of Palestine. They occupied the land of Canaan (see "Canaan") before the Israelites entered it and were their strongest enemy.

philosopher A person who spends much time studying, thinking, talking, or writing about different ideas and trying to gain wisdom.

Pilate, Pontius The Roman governor of Judea, 26–36 A.D. Read Lk. 23:1–3.

pillar One of the tall, carved stones used to hold up the roof of a building.

pomegranate A red fruit filled with tiny seeds, each covered with a sweet, juicy part of the fruit.

potter Someone who makes pottery (jars, bowls, etc.) from clay. The Hebrew word also means "creator" or "a person who makes new things."

prefect An important government official.

Preparation day Friday, the day before the Sabbath day.

prize See "crown."

prophecy A message or teaching from God. Also, the ability and authority from God to speak for him.

prophesy To speak or teach things from God.

prophet A person who speaks a message from God. Many of the books in the Old Testament are messages spoken or written by "the prophets," who were some of those God chose to speak for him. God often used dreams or visions to tell or show his prophets what they should say.

prophetess A woman prophet.

proverb A wise saying or short story that teaches a lesson.

pure See "make … pure."

Q Queen of Heaven Probably the false goddess Astarte. She was the goddess of sex and war, worshiped by the people of Mesopotamia. They thought she was the planet Venus, which looks like a star in the sky.

quiver A bag or container for carrying arrows.

R Rahab A dragon or sea monster that people thought controlled the sea. Rahab

is often a symbol for God's enemies or for anything evil.

resurrection Being raised from death to live again.

Rezin A king of Aram who ruled about 740–731 B.C.

Rock A name for God that means he is a place where people can find safety, like a high mountain or the strong wall of a fortress.

ruler of the evil powers See "Satan."

ruler of this world See "Satan."

S Sabbath Saturday, the seventh day of the week and a special day for Israelites or Jews. By God's command it was set aside as a time for the people to rest and honor God.

sackcloth A rough cloth made from animal hair that people sometimes wore to show sadness.

sacrifice To offer a gift to God as an expression of worship, thanksgiving, or payment for sin. Also, the gift that is offered. In the Old Testament it was usually a special animal that was killed and burned on an altar. The Old Testament sacrifices offered for sins were symbolic of the perfect sacrifice that God himself would provide through Jesus Christ. Jesus gave his own life as a sacrifice to pay for the sins of all people. See Heb. 10:1–14.

Sadducees A leading Jewish religious group. They accepted only the first five books of the Old Testament and believed that people will not live again after death.

Samaria During Old Testament times, the capital city of Israel, the northern Israelite kingdom. In New Testament times, the name refers to the central hill country, the general area that had been occupied by the northern kingdom.

Samaritans During New Testament times, the people who lived in Samaria, the region north of Judea. They were part Jewish and followed the Law of Moses, but the Jews of Judea did not accept them as pure descendants of Israel.

Samuel The last judge (leader) and first prophet of Israel.

sapphire A rare and valuable blue stone.

Satan A name for the devil meaning "the enemy," or "the accuser."

satrap An official who ruled over a Persian province.

scepter A special stick carried by kings to show their authority.

scribe Originally, an educated man who was skilled in reading and writing. By New Testament times scribes had become a distinct social and political group. Because of their work in copying the Scriptures and writing down explanations of the Law of Moses, many became experts in the law and were respected as teachers, lawyers, or judges.

Scripture Part of the Scriptures or "Holy Writings"—the Old Testament.

scroll A long roll of paper or leather used for writing on.

seal A small stone or ring with a picture carved in it that was pressed into wet clay or hot wax to hold down the loose end of a scroll. It left a special mark, also called a seal, that was like a signature to keep anyone from opening the scroll except the right person.

seer A kind of prophet (see "prophet") who received messages from God in visions.

Selah A word appearing in Psalms and Habakkuk that was apparently an instruction for the singers or musicians, perhaps meaning to pause or to get louder.

Sennacherib A king of Assyria who ruled about 706–681 B.C.

Seraph angels Special angels that God used as messengers. The name might mean that they were bright like fire.

Sharon Valley The lowlands along the coast of Palestine.

sheath A leather or metal case for carrying a sword or knife.

sheminith The meaning of this word is uncertain, but it may refer to a type of instrument, a special way of tuning an instrument, or one of the groups that played harps in the Temple orchestra. See 1 Chron. 15:21.

Sheol The place where people go when they die. This usually means the grave, but it can mean the place where spirits go.

Sheshbazzar A governor of Judah mentioned several times in the book of Ezra. He is possibly the same person as the one named Zerubbabel, mentioned in Ezra 2:2 and elsewhere. If they are not the same man,

then Sheshbazzar was the first governor of Judah, and Zerubbabel was the second.

sickle A tool with a curved blade for harvesting grain and other crops.

Sidon A non-Jewish city on the coast of Phoenicia (modern Lebanon).

sign See "miraculous sign."

signet ring A type of seal that was worn on the finger. See "seal."

silver coin Or "denarius," a Roman coin that was worth the average pay for one day's work.

sin offering Or "purification offering," a sacrifice that was offered to God to remove impurities from sin and make a person fit to worship God.

skin disease Traditionally translated "leprosy," the Hebrew word means any of several diseases that cause rashes or sores on the skin.

slave woman Or "concubine," a woman who was owned by a man and treated like a wife.

sling A strip of leather used for throwing rocks.

snuffers Tools used to put out the flame on lamps.

Sodom A city that God destroyed, together with the city of Gomorrah, because the people living there were so evil. See Gen. 19.

Solomon's Porch An area on the east side of the Temple, covered by a roof.

Son of David A name for the Christ (Messiah) because it was prophesied that he would come from the family of David. See "David."

son of David Any person from the family of David. See "David."

Son of Man The name that Jesus most often used for himself. The phrase in Hebrew or Aramaic means "human being" or "mankind," but in Dan. 7:13–14 it is used of a future savior and king, and this was later understood to be the Messiah, the one God would send to save his people.

song of David This phrase (or a variation of it) is found at the beginning of many of the Psalms. It could also mean "a song dedicated to David."

sorcery When a person tries to use the power of demons and evil spirits to do magic.

special servant The Greek word is *diakonos*, which is usually translated "servant." However, in three places (Rom. 16:1; Php. 1:2; 1 Tim. 3:8–13) the service of those so described is associated with a local church, indicating that they were chosen to serve in some special way. Compare Acts 6:1–6.

spelt A kind of grain like wheat.

Spirit See "Holy Spirit."

survivors People who have escaped a disaster. Where this is marked, it means the Jewish people who survived the destruction of Judah and Israel by its enemies.

synagogue A place in many cities where Jews gathered for prayer, study of the Scriptures, and other public meetings.

Syrtis A shallow area in the sea near the Libyan coast.

Ttar Or "pitch," a thick oil that must be heated to become liquid and that is used to seal the boards with which ships are built.

Tarshish A city far away from Israel, probably in Spain, famous for its large ships that sailed the Mediterranean Sea.

tax collector A Jew hired by the Romans to collect taxes. Tax collectors often cheated, and the other Jews hated them.

Teman An area in the northern part of Edom, although the name means "South."

Temple The permanent building in Jerusalem that replaced the portable "Holy Tent" that was used by the Israelites from the time of their wandering in the desert to the reign of King Solomon, when the first Temple was built. Like the Holy Tent, the Temple was the center of Israelite worship, although provision was made for it to be "a house of prayer for all nations" (Isa. 56:7).

Ten Towns Greek, "Decapolis," an area on the east side of Lake Galilee that once had ten main towns.

Tent of the Agreement Literally, "Tent of the Testimony," the tent where the Box of the Agreement was kept. See "Holy Tent."

Tent, Holy See "Holy Tent."

thank offering A special fellowship offering that people gave to praise God and thank

him for doing good things for them. A part of the animal being offered was burned on the altar, but the people ate most of it in a fellowship meal at the Temple. See Lev. 7:11–26.

the Way A symbolic name used by followers of Jesus Christ to describe their faith as "the way" to God through Jesus.

threshing Putting newly harvested wheat or other grain on a hard floor and walking on it or beating it with special tools to separate the hulls (see "chaff") from the grain.

Thummim See "Urim."

Tigris One of the two large rivers that flow through the countries of Babylonia and Assyria.

tomb A grave dug in a wall of rock or a building where a dead body is buried. It can also be a small building made to show respect for important people who had died.

torture To hurt or cause someone pain, often to force them to say something against their will.

traitor A person who turns against his or her own country, friends, or family and does anything to help their enemy.

tree of life The tree whose fruit gives people the power to live forever. See Gen. 2:9; 3:22 and Rev. 22:1–2.

tribute Money paid to a foreign king or nation for protection.

tunic A piece of clothing like a long undershirt.

turban A head covering made by wrapping a long piece of cloth around the top part of the head or around a cap worn on the head.

Tyre A non-Jewish city on the coast of Phoenicia (modern Lebanon).

Unclean Impure or unacceptable. When it refers to animals, it means not fit to be eaten. When it refers to things, it means not pure or fit to be used, especially in the worship of God. When it refers to people, it means not fit to be in the area of the Holy Tent (Tabernacle) or Temple or to participate in the worship of God there. See Lev. 11–15 for the Old Testament rules about what was clean and unclean.

unleavened Referring to bread that is made without yeast or anything else to make it rise.

Urim The Urim and Thummim were probably small stone, metal, or wooden pieces that the high priest kept in the judgment pouch he wore. They were used, perhaps like dice, to get answers from God. See Ex. 28:30.

Uzziah A king of Judah who ruled with his father Amaziah from 792 to 767 B.C., and then alone from 767 to 740 B.C.

V

vineyard A garden or farm where grapes are grown.

virgin A woman, especially a young woman, who is not married and has never had sexual relations.

vision Something like a dream used by God to speak to people.

vow A very strong promise that a person makes, sometimes to God and often using the name of God or something else known to be real or important. It may include a wish to be punished if the promise is not kept.

vulture Or "eagle," a bird of prey that eats dead animals.

W

wafer A thin bread, like a cracker, made without yeast.

watchman A guard who stood on the city wall, looked for enemy soldiers, and warned the people of the city if he saw trouble coming.

will The legal paper that people sign to give instructions about what should be done with their possessions after they die.

winepress A place dug in rock used to mash grapes and collect the juice for making wine.

wineskin A bag made from the skin of an animal and used for storing wine.

wise men Literally, "magi," probably meaning pagan religious scholars who studied the stars to predict future events.

witchcraft Using magic or the power of Satan.

witness Anyone who tells what they have seen or heard.

wizard A person who uses the power of Satan or evil spirits to do magic.

wonders Miracles that cause people to react with amazement and fear of God.

Y

YAHWEH A Hebrew name for God that is usually translated LORD. It is like the Hebrew word meaning "He is" or "He makes things exist."

yeast The part of bread dough that makes it rise. Sometimes it is used as a symbol of bad influence.

yoke A pole that was put across the shoulders of men, usually slaves, or animals and used in pulling or carrying heavy loads.

Z

Zealot A term used to describe Jews who had an enthusiastic desire or "zeal" to maintain the purity of Judaism—the land, the Temple, observance of the law and the traditions. This desire included a willingness to do whatever necessary to protect this purity against any outside threat, such as Roman control. This kind of spirit eventually brought about the formation of a group of Jewish patriots known as the Zealots. (Note that in Mt. 10:4 and Mk. 3:18 "Zealot" is used to translate the Aramaic term, "Cananaean," which had the same meaning.)

Zeus The most important of the gods in which the ancient Greeks believed.

Zion The southeastern part of the mountain that Jerusalem is built on. Sometimes it means the city of Jerusalem, the people of God living there, or the Temple.

Map 1 1034

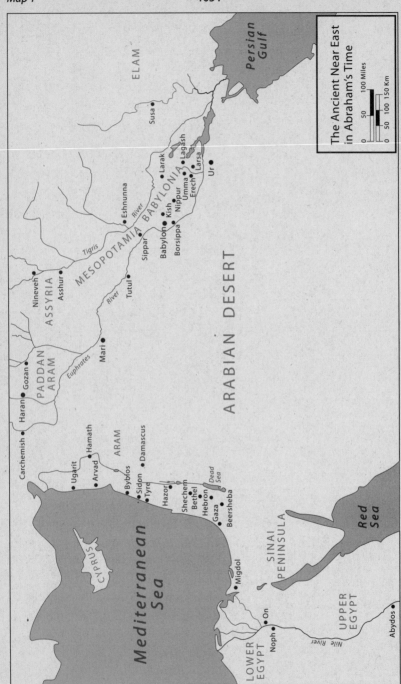

The Ancient Near East in Abraham's Time

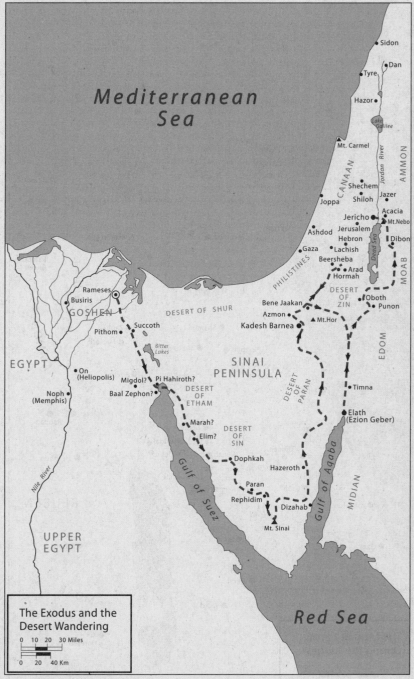

Mediterranean
Sea

Sidon
Dan
Tyre
Hazor
Lake Galilee
Mt. Carmel
Jordan River
AMMON
CANAAN
Shechem
Shiloh
Jazer
Joppa
Jericho
Acacia
Jerusalem
Mt.Nebo
Ashdod
Hebron
Dibon
Gaza
Lachish
Dead Sea
Beersheba
MOAB
Arad
Hormah
PHILISTINES
DESERT
OF
ZIN
Oboth
Rameses
Busiris
Bene Jaakan
Punon
GOSHEN
DESERT OF SHUR
Azmon
Mt.Hor
Succoth
Kadesh Barnea
EDOM
Pithom
Bitter Lakes
SINAI
PENINSULA
EGYPT
On
(Heliopolis)
Migdol?
Pi Hahiroth?
DESERT
OF
PARAN
Noph
(Memphis)
Baal Zephon?
DESERT
OF
ETHAM
Timna
Marah?
Elim?
DESERT
OF
SIN
Nile River
Dophkah
Hazeroth
Elath
(Ezion Geber)
Gulf of Suez
Paran
Rephidim
Dizahab
Gulf of Aqaba
MIDIAN
UPPER
EGYPT
Mt. Sinai
Red Sea

The Exodus and the
Desert Wandering

0   10   20   30 Miles
0   20   40 Km

Map 3   1036

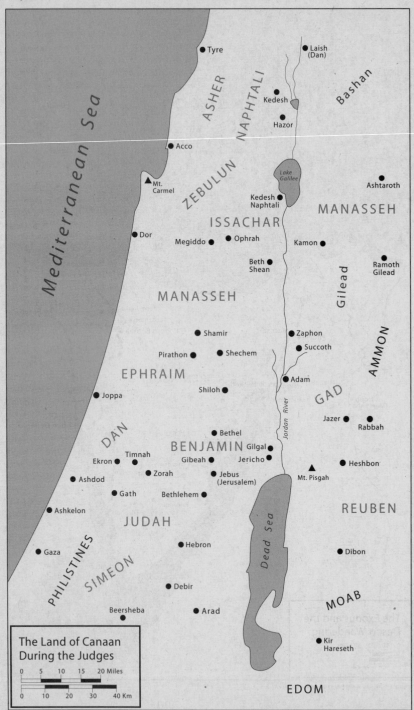

The Land of Canaan
During the Judges

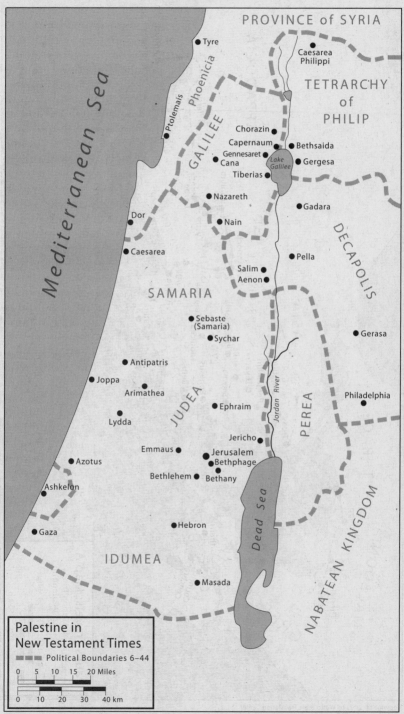

PROVINCE of SYRIA

Mediterranean Sea

Tyre

Caesarea Philippi

TETRARCHY of PHILIP

Phoenicia

Ptolemais

GALILEE

Chorazin

Capernaum · Bethsaida
Gennesaret
Cana   Lake Galilee · Gergesa
Tiberias

Dor

Nazareth

Gadara

Caesarea

Nain

DECAPOLIS

Salim
Aenon

Pella

SAMARIA

Sebaste
(Samaria)
Sychar

Gerasa

Antipatris

Joppa

Arimathea

JUDEA

Ephraim

Jordan River

PEREA

Philadelphia

Lydda

Jericho

Emmaus

Jerusalem
Bethphage
Bethlehem   Bethany

Azotus

Ashkelon

Hebron

Dead Sea

Gaza

IDUMEA

NABATEAN KINGDOM

Masada

Palestine in
New Testament Times
- - - Political Boundaries 6–44

0   5   10   15   20 Miles

0   10   20   30   40 km

Map 5   1038

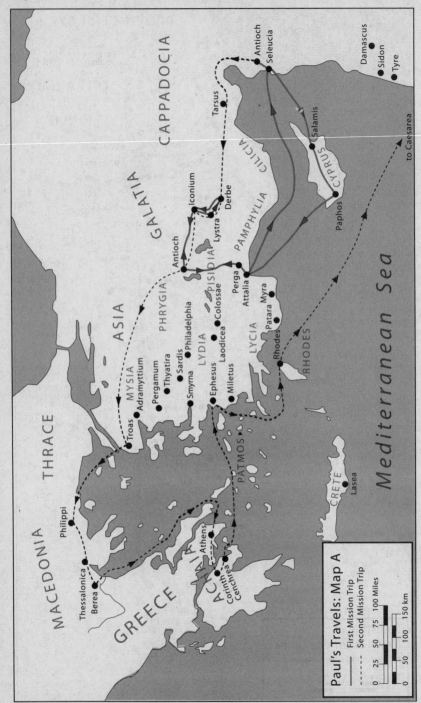

Paul's Travels: Map A

First Mission Trip
Second Mission Trip

0 25 50 75 100 Miles
0 50 100 150 km

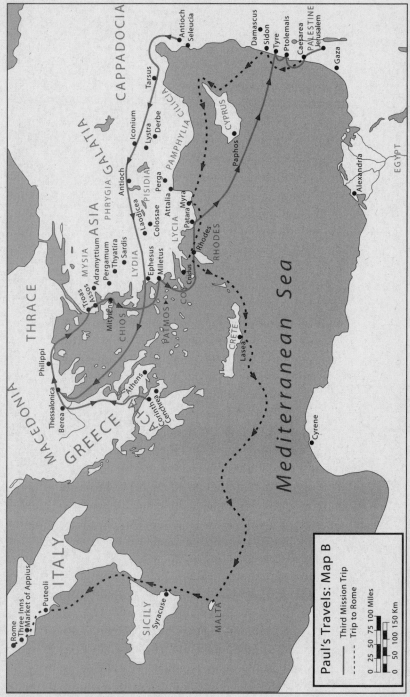

Paul's Travels: Map B

Third Mission Trip

Trip to Rome

0 25 50 75 100 Miles

0 50 100 150 Km